P9-DED-580

WORLD AUTHORS
1990-1995

EDITOR
Clifford Thompson

STAFF CONTRIBUTORS
Denise Bonilla
Christopher Mari
Edward Moran
Janet Pech
Brian Solomon
Selma Yampolsky

THE H. W. WILSON COMPANY
NEW YORK   DUBLIN

Library of Congress Cataloging-in-Publication Data
World Authors 1990–1995 / edited by Clifford Thompson.
   p. cm.
  Includes bibliographical references.
  ISBN 0-8242-0956-7 (alk. paper)
  1. Authors—20th Century—Biography—Dictionaries. 2.
I. Thompson, Clifford.
PN771.W675   1999
809'.04—dc21
 [B]   CIP
          99-048161

Acknowledgments for the use of copyrighted materials appear at the end of the volume.

Table of Contents

Preface v

List of Authors vii

Biographical Sketches 1

Acknowledgments 863

PREFACE

Not taking into account the four-volume *World Authors 1900–1950*, published in 1997, *World Authors 1990–1995* is the 14th installment of the Wilson Authors Series, begun in 1942. *World Authors 1990–1995* comprises biographical articles on 320 novelists, poets, dramatists, essayists, social scientists, biographers, and other authors who have published significant work within the period indicated. While critical attention and acclaim continue to be criteria for inclusion in the Wilson Authors Series, we have made every effort to represent the diversity of voices and ethnicity of authors both within the United States and elsewhere.

Unlike those in previous books in the series, each article in *World Authors 1990–1995* begins with an introductory paragraph, summarizing the author's contribution to his or her genre.

More than 130 authors have contributed autobiographical essays, solely for use in this book. Separately, these documents make fascinating reading; taken together, they reveal the wide variety of experiences, influences, opinions, and approaches to the creative process that shape contemporary literature. "The challenge for any writer is to be faithful at once to your vision and your place, to the truth you have laboriously found and the people whom this truth might serve," Scott Russell Sanders writes here. Alicia Ostriker explains, "I tell my students that they must write what they are afraid to write; and I attempt to do so myself." Pico Iyer reveals that he has found his "greatest fictional inspiration in the books of Graham Greene. In him, as in the finest prose writers from Melville to Wilde, wisdom is always chastened—made human—by compassion." Each article in *World Authors 1990–1995* provides a starting point for understanding the writer's unique contribution to the world of books.

The opportunity to share one's enthusiasm for a particular subject, and the chance to learn a great deal oneself, are among the pleasures of editing a volume such as this. I am grateful for the opportunity to edit *World Authors 1990–1995*, and I am equally grateful to the following people for their assistance: H. W. Wilson's staff of in-house writers, listed on the title page; Miriam Helbok and the rest of the staff of *Current Biography*; Hilary D. Claggett, senior editor, for her invaluable editorial and organizational support; Gray Young, Beth Levy, and Jacquelene Latif, of the production staff; Sabra Moore, photo researcher; and Michael Schulze, H. W. Wilson's vice president for General Reference.

Clifford Thompson

November 1999

World Authors

Virginia Hamilton Adair 1

Douglas Adams 2

Ama Ata Aidoo 6

Elizabeth Alexander 8

Meena Alexander 9

Julia Alvarez 12

Stephen E. Ambrose 15

Robert Antoni 18

Terri Apter 21

Deirdre Bair 23

Houston A. Baker 26

Nicholson Baker 28

Pat Barker 32

Robert Barnard 34

Andrea Barrett 37

Gregory Bateson 41

Charles Baxter 44

Louis Begley 47

Thomas Berry 52

Sven Birkerts 54

Julia Blackburn 57

Lawrence Block 59

Roy Blount 63

Alain Bosquet 65

Karl Dietrich Bracher 69

John Gregory Brown 72

Larry Brown 73

Anatole Broyard 76

James Buchan 79

Christopher Buckley 80

Lois McMaster Bujold 83

Melvin Jules Bukiet 86

James Lee Burke 88

Octavia Butler 91

Robert Olen Butler 95

Fox Butterfield 98

Michael Cadnum 100

Peter Cameron 102

Fritjof Capra 104

Orson Scott Card 106

Jacqueline Carey 108

Jim Carroll 109

Justin Cartwright 113

Ana Castillo 116

Rosa Chacel 118

Vikram Chandra 122

Frank Chin 123

Paulo Coelho 127

Thomas H. Cook 130

Bernard Cooper 132

Dennis Cooper 134

J. California Cooper 136

Jennifer C. Cornell 138

Ellis Cose 140

Douglas Coupland 143

Stanley Crouch 145

Fred D'Aguiar 150

Edwidge Danticat 154

Thulani Davis 156

Richard Dawkins 158

Louis De Bernières 162

Jonathan Dee 164

Rick DeMarinis 167

David Denby 169

Colin Dexter 170

Charles Dickinson 173

Ghislain de Diesbach 175

Deborah Digges 177

John Dizikes 180

Mark Doty 181

Ann Douglas 183

Roddy Doyle 187

Martin Duberman 190

Rikki Ducornet 194

Carol Ann Duffy 196

Duong Thu Huong 198

Andrea Dworkin 200

Michael Eric Dyson 205

Gerald Early 208

David Eddings 212

Bret Easton Ellis 215

Trey Ellis 219

Laura Esquivel 221

Susan Faludi 223

Tibor Fischer 227

Leon Forrest 228

Connie May Fowler 230

Jonathan Franzen 232

Ian Frazier 234

Esther Freud 237

Carl Friedman 239

David Galef 241

Stephen Gallagher 243

Amy Gerstler 245

Reginald Gibbons 247

Dagoberto Gilb 249

Dana Gioia 251

Marita Golden 253

Rebecca Goldstein 257

Lyndall Gordon 259

Neil Gordon 263

Vivian Gornick 264

Barbara Gowdy 268

Bob Greene 271

Eamon Grennan 275

John Grisham 278

Winston Groom 282

Güneli Gün 285

Batya Gur 287

Jessica Tarahata Hagedorn 289

Brian Hall 291

Pete Hamill 294

Sam Hamill 298

Ron Hansen 300

James Earl Hardy 303

E. Lynn Harris 306

Eddy L. Harris 309

Robert Harris 311

John (Hooper) Harvey 313

John (Robert) Harvey 316

Jon Hassler 318

Ehud Havazelet 322

David Haynes 324

William Least Heat-Moon 326

Ursula Hegi 328

Juan Felipe Herrera 330

Everett Hoagland 332

Janet Hobhouse 334

Adam Hochschild 336

Eva Hoffman 339

bell hooks 342

Janette Turner Hospital 346

Siri Hustvedt 349

Lewis Hyde 351

Daikichi Irokawa 353

Alan Isler 355

Pico Iyer 356

Jabra Ibrahim Jabra 360

Kelvin Christopher James 363

Sébastien Japrisot 364

Christopher Jencks 366

Gish Jen 370

Jia Pingwa 373

Ha Jin 375

Gayl Jones 378

Gwyneth A. Jones 381

Rodney Jones 384

Cynthia Kadohata 386

Donald Keene 388

James Kelman 391

Randall Kenan 394

Philip Kerr 396

August Kleinzahler 398

Bernard Knox 399

Dean Koontz 402

William Kotzwinkle 405

Jonathan Kozol 409

Eric Kraft 413

Gary Krist 416

Hanif Kureishi 418

Jonathan Kwitny 424

Simon Lane 426

Lawrence L. Langer 428

Joe R. Lansdale 432

Jeanne Larsen 435

Jonathan Larson 437

Caroline Leavitt 440

Tom LeClair 441

Li-Young Lee 442

Jonathan Lethem 445

Anthony Lewis 448

Alan Lightman 451

Seymour Martin Lipset 453

Timothy Liu 458

Margot Livesey 462

Bette Bao Lord 464

James Lord 467

Bret Lott 469

Glenn C. Loury 472

Thomas Lux 476

Amin Maalouf 478

Denis MacEoin 480

Bernard MacLaverty 483

Dale Maharidge 485

Andrei Makine 488

Thomas Mallon 489

Tatyana Mamonova 492

Alberto Manguel 495

Hilary Mantel 497

Manning Marable 500

David Margolis 502

Seth Jacob Margolis 505

Javier Marías 507

David Markson 509

Greg Matthews 511

Armistead Maupin 514

Nathan McCall 519

J. D. McClatchy 520

Elizabeth McCracken 523

Alice McDermott 525

Eugene McEldowney 529

William McIlvanney 530

Jay McInerney 533

Vonda N. McIntyre 536

Bill McKibben 538

Reginald McKnight 542

Terry McMillan 544

Brad Meltzer 548

Daniel Menaker 549

Barbara Mertz 551

Paul Metcalf 556

Steven Millhauser 560

Anna Mitgutsch 563

Mo Yan 565

Bill Moody 566

Rick Moody 568

Lorrie Moore 571

Jan Morris 574

Walter Mosley 578

David Mura 583

Albert Murray 587

Gloria Nagy 591

Lawrence Naumoff 593

Jay Neugeboren 596

Geoff Nicholson 600

Stewart O'Nan 602

Alicia Ostriker 605

Camille Paglia 608

Charles Palliser 613

Tim Parks 615

Jill Paton Walsh 618

James Patterson 622

Tim Pears 624

Dale Peck 626

Victor Pelevin 628

Arturo Pérez-Reverte 630

Graham Petrie 632

Henry Petroski 634

Nicholas Pileggi 636

Belva Plain 638

Gerald Posner 641

Padgett Powell 643

Richard Powers 645

E. Annie Proulx 647

David Quammen 651

Jonathan Raban 654

Marie Redonnet 657

Adolph L. Reed 661

Donald Revell 663

Alberto Rios 664

Julián Ríos 665

Paul Roazen 668

Graham Robb 672

Tom Robbins 675

Michèle Roberts 679

Kim Stanley Robinson 681

Roxana Robinson 685

Mark Rudman 687

Norman Rush 690

James Sallis 692

Mark Salzman 695

Scott R. Sanders 698

Luc Sante 701

Sapphire 704

Ken Saro-Wiwa 707

Valerie Sayers 710

Grace Schulman 712

Sandra Jean Scofield 716

Elizabeth Searle 718

Carolyn See 720

Lisa See 723

Bob Shacochis 726

Neil Sheehan 728

Dan Simmons 732

Mona Simpson 735

James Park Sloan 738

Hedrick Smtih 740

Art Spiegelman 744

John Shelby Spong 748

Ilan Stavans 752

Shelby Steele 754

Peter Steinhart 758

Bruce Sterling 760

Gerald Stern 764

Virgil Suarez 767

Su Tong 770

Terese Svoboda 772

Marly Swick 774

Arthur Sze 776

Luci Tapahonso 778

Studs Terkel 779

Alexander Theroux 784

Uwe Timm 787

Frederic Tuten 789

Douglas Unger 791

Gerald Vizenor 795

William T. Vollman 800

Anne Waldman 803

David Foster Wallace 807

Michele Wallace 809

Robert James Waller 811

Geoffrey C. Ward 815

Irvine Welsh 817

Lawrence Weschler 821

Cornel West 823

Dorothy West 827

Kate Wilhelm 830

Joy Williams 834

Patricia J. Williams 836

Terry Tempest Williams 838

William Julius Wilson 840

David Wiltse 845

Tim Winton 846

Tobias Wolff 849

Bob Woodward 852

Shay Youngblood 857

Eric Zencey 859

WORLD AUTHORS
1990-1995

WORLD AUTHORS
1990-1995

Adair, Virginia Hamilton

1913– Poet

"I've always written poems," Virginia Hamilton Adair said in an interview with the *New Yorker* (December 25, 1995/January 1, 1996). "I never stopped. I never know what I think until I read it in one of my poems." Something of an anomaly among modern poets, Adair was 83 years old when she published her first collection, *Ants on the Melon* (1996). Her works, which were described in *Time* (May 27, 1996) as having "the elegant fizz of brut champagne," have, in her ninth decade, earned her numerous accolades and suddenly pushed her to the forefront of American poetry. Her follow-up collection is *Beliefs and Blasphemies* (1998).

Virginia Hamilton Adair was born in New York City in 1913. As a child growing up in New Jersey, Adair was constantly exposed to literature. Indeed, Adair's longtime friend, the poet Robert Mezey, in a brief biography of Adair included in the afterword of *Ants on the Melon*, wrote that Adair's upbringing had taught her that poetry "was an intimate and essential part of life and had nothing to do with worldly ambition or celebrity." Adair's father, Robert Browning Hamilton, an insurance executive, was an amateur poet whose poem "Along the Road" was quite popular in his time. According to the *New York Review of Books* (May 23, 1996), Mezey recalls Adair saying that one of her earliest memories is of her father reading to her from Homer's *Iliad* as she looked at him through the bars of her crib.

Educated at Mount Holyoke College, Adair was twice awarded the school's Glascock Prize for poetry. After graduating from Mount Holyoke, she attended graduate school at Harvard/Radcliffe, where she began publishing her poems in magazines and journals such as the *Atlantic Monthly* and the *New Republic*. It was at a Harvard law school dance that Adair met the dark-haired, southern-accented Douglass Adair Jr., her future husband. After receiving her master's degree from Harvard/Radcliffe, Adair began working toward her Ph.D. at the University of Wisconsin at Madison. Her studies were cut short, however, when, in 1937, she moved back east to marry Adair.

The young couple's lives were, judging from Adair's poems, very happy. Douglass's career as an historian (he had long since abandoned his interest in law) necessitated that the couple make numerous moves to cities up and down the East Coast, including New Haven, Connecticut; Princeton,

New Jersey; and Williamsburg, Virginia. Though she worked in a state mental hospital during World War II, most of Adair's time during this period was spent raising her family, which had grown to include three children. She also continued to publish her poems sporadically, earning some acclaim.

After Douglass was offered a position at the Claremont Graduate School, the family packed up and moved to California. There, Adair began teaching at local colleges and eventually became a full professor at California Polytechnic University in Pomona. "She was really a cultural missionary," Ruth Harmer-Carew, Adair's colleague, told the *New Yorker* (December 25, 1995/January 1, 1996). "She was going to bring Donne and Herbert and Blake and ballad makers and Romantic poets, along with Dylan Thomas and Robert Frost, to the darker shores of Pomona from Claremont." By this time, Adair, despite her earlier success, had abandoned any desire she may have had for literary fame. "To be acclaimed young is heady, / later on a drag," she wrote in her poem "Red Camelias." Though she has offered many reasons for deciding to stop publishing her work, one very important factor was her children's response: "They didn't like me for writing," she said in the *New Yorker* interview. "It took time from them. Sometimes, I'd think, if I don't get half an hour to myself, I'm going to go crazy. I could hear Douglass sort of shooing and shushing the children: 'Now don't disturb Ginny. She's writing.' And I knew at that moment that they hated me for wanting to write, and I even hated Douglass for shooing them." Equally, if not more, important was the fact that she learned from her husband that sometimes too much ambition is accompanied by devastating effects. By all accounts a charismatic overachiever, Douglass Adair coauthored (with Walton Hamilton) *The Power to Govern*, a book that influenced political policy throughout the Roosevelt administration, when he was only 25. Well-liked and extremely respected among his colleagues, Douglass nonetheless was tormented by a desire for recognition and perfection in all his pursuits. This desire, Adair has said, ultimately contributed to his suicide in 1968.

Adair's quest for solace after Douglass's death led not only to a slew of highly emotional poems (some of which are included in *Ants on the Melon*), but also to her discovery of Zen Buddhism. "I submitted, and it was strange and wonderful," she said in the *New Yorker* interview. "And it stayed strange and wonderful. A whole section of my beliefs and blasphemies are Zen." Eventually she even helped found a Zen center atop California's Mount Baldy.

In the mid-1980s, however, Adair again received bad news—that she was suffering from glaucoma, a disease that, over the next decade, would slowly rob her of her sight. Despite her blindness, she continued to write, albeit in a very different manner. "I used to revise and revise and revise," she said in the *New Yorker* interview. "I'd rake over this midden and piles of trash, poems I hadn't finished or wasn't satisfied with, and I'd type things out with arrows and notes—'Move this down here,' 'Bring this up here,'; they were full of interlardings. Now I can't even do that. Now what I do is full of typos that make me sound even more of a fool than I am." Since her loss of sight she has relied heavily on friends like Mezey to assist her by reading her poems aloud and making the revisions she dictates.

In the late 1980s, at Mezey's request, the two poets began sifting through Adair's thousands of poems to create a small collection of her works. "I really didn't get into the game," Adair told the *New York Times* (August 7, 1996) about her decision to collect these poems. "I did a book. I felt very good about having a collection of my poems in one place. And then what Bob did is to send some manuscripts around. I didn't even know he had done it." At first, Mezey's surreptitious actions were to no avail. Dozens of rejection slips poured in from various publishers. Mezey then decided to send a few of the poems to Alice Quinn, the poetry editor of the *New Yorker*. After deciding to publish the poems, Quinn sent them on to five book editors, among them Daniel Menaker, a former *New Yorker* colleague who had become a senior editor at Random House. Menaker liked what he read and quickly agreed to publish Adair's poems.

The collection, *Ants on the Melon*, was published in 1996. Containing 87 poems, the book quickly made Adair and her poetry the objects of a generous amount of praise. After being shown some of her works, fellow poet Galway Kinnell announced that Adair had "arrived into our world like a comet," as she told the *New Yorker* (December 25, 1995/January 1, 1996). *Time* (May 27, 1996) hailed *Ants on the Melon* as "something of a miracle." Further praise was offered by A. Alvarez in the *New York Review of Books* (May 23, 1996): "Virginia Adair may be very old, but at least her wonderful first book has appeared while she is still with us." *Ants on the Melon* was successful not only with critics but with the general public as well. To date, it is in its fourth printing, with almost 19,000 copies published. According to the *New York Times* (August 7, 1996), this is highly "unusual for first books by poets, who are considered fortunate if 1,000 copies are sold."

Adair's acclaim, however, was not universal. Among certain poets, there have been some grumblings that Adair's success has more to do with her age and sorrow-filled life story than with the merits of her work. "I share the opinion of most of the poets that I've talked to in being distinctly underwhelmed," the poet J. D. McClatchy said in an interview with the *New York Times* (August 7, 1996). "Her story seems to be the story, not the work. She seems to me to be a curiosity rather than a genuine discovery. The work has its pleasures and surprises, but it seems to me to be pretty loosely put together and not compelling at all."

Of Adair's follow-up collection of poetry, *Beliefs and Blasphemies*, Ray Olson in *Booklist* (July 19, 1998) commented that its poems, on religious themes, were "confidently crafted and very readable," as those in *Ants on the Melon* had been. "Some of Adair's scenarios surprise," Olson wrote. "[S]everal of these poems may become pulpit and church program favorites, as their witty and intelligent meditativeness well suits them to be."

Adair's own opinion of her unusual success lies somewhere between the views of those who hail her as a great artist and those who attribute her popularity to shrewd marketing of her life's story. "It's hard for me to say what I think about it because it's kind of embarrassing," she told the *New York Times* (August 7, 1996). "I think the stuff is very good—technically very good. And I think it's interesting to a lot of people. I am surprised at the chain of events, but I think it's the fact that I'm 83 and living here in one room and that I'm blind and I'm also kind of gamy. I think they gambled on this book, and I think part of it is this old nut, a character."

—J. P.

SUGGESTED READING: *New Yorker* p132+ Dec. 25, 1995/Jan. 1, 1996; *New York Review of Books* p4+ May 23, 1996; *New York Times* p11 Aug. 7, 1996; *New York Times Book Review* p9 June 23, 1996; *Time* p80 May 27, 1996

SELECTED BOOKS: *Ants on the Melon*, 1996; *Beliefs and Blasphemies*, 1998

Adams, Douglas

Mar. 11, 1952– Novelist

"Douglas Adams is a . . . NUT," Sue Martin declared in the *Los Angeles Times Book Review* (February 3, 1985). "And not of the macadamia variety." Best known for his five-book *Hitchhiker's Guide to the Galaxy* series, an outrageous and satiric science fiction epic that offers a gleefully pessimistic view of modern society, the novelist Douglas Adams has delighted fans of the genre with, in the words of Eric Zorn of the *Chicago Tribune* (October 28, 1982), his "intelligent parodies of [its] hallowed conventions." Adams's infectious, surreal wit quickly caught on with college audiences as well, boosting him to a level of fame matched by few, if any, contemporary British humorists. In addition to the five books that make up the *Hitchhiker* "trilogy," which have sold more than 14 million copies worldwide, the *Hitchhiker's Guide* has appeared in the form of a radio series, stage adaptations, a BBC television program, a record album, and a computer game. "Well, we don't have a braille version, and we don't have *Hitchhiker's Guide* dental floss," Adams joked in an interview with Desson Howe for the *Washington Post* (November 23, 1984). He is also the author of the highly successful Dirk Gently detective novel series, as well as *Last Chance to See* (1990), a nonfiction book about endangered animals that was written in collaboration with Mark Carwardine.

Adams has tried to avoid being pigeonholed as a science fiction writer; instead, he has categorized himself as a comedy writer who happens to borrow from the literary devices of science fiction to lampoon contemporary culture. "Why bother writing a send-up of science fiction?" Adams asked Jennifer Crichton during an interview for *Publishers Weekly* (January 14, 1983). "It may give you a 10-minute sketch, but that's about all. I'd rather use the devices of science fiction to send up everything else." The whimsical, stream of consciousness style and the allegorical nature of Adams's works have led critics to compare him to Lewis Carroll, Jonathan Swift, Laurence Sterne, and Kurt Vonnegut Jr. In the words of Bruce Harris of Harmony Books, one of Adams's American publishers, as quoted by Crichton, "Adams has that same kind of eye [as Vonnegut], using aliens and spaceships as a new metaphor to write about human emotions and behavior, to make the people on Earth more ridiculous, lovable, and interesting."

Douglas Noël Adams was born on March 11, 1952, in Cambridge, England, to Janet (Donovan) Adams, a nurse, and Christopher Douglas Adams, a management consultant. After attending Brentwood School, in Essex, Adams entered St. John's College at Cambridge University, where he earned B.A. and M.A. degrees in English literature. While he was at Cambridge, Adams first tried his hand at writing comedy sketches as a member of the Footlights Revue Club, the university's performing arts society, which at one time included several members of the wildly irreverent Monty Python comedy troupe.

After graduating from Cambridge in 1974, Adams earned a meager existence as a free-lance comedy scriptwriter for BBC Radio. To make ends meet, he took on a series of odd jobs, including a stint as a bodyguard for Qatar's royal al-Thani family. His duties in that capacity included "standing up and sitting down, opening and shutting doors, and running away if anyone turned up with a gun or a hand grenade," as he recalled to Jennifer Crichton. By the age of 24 Adams was so frustrated by his failure to achieve success as a writer that he nearly left London to pursue another career. "I was all washed up, and I'd barely started," he told Eric Zorn. "I kept thinking of how far the Beatles had come by the time they were 24, and there I was, a failure." Near the end of his rope financially and emotionally, Adams submitted an outline for a sto-

ry to a BBC producer that involved the destruction of Earth. The plot was partly based on an idea that had come to him when he was 19 years old, flat broke, and traveling around the Continent with a copy of the *Hitchhiker's Guide to Europe*. "I was lying drunk in a field in Innsbruck [Austria] and gazing at the stars," Adams told Crichton. "It occurred to me that somebody ought to write a hitchhiker's guide to the galaxy." The BBC not only accepted Adams's "Hitchhiker" prototype but also hired him as a script editor for the popular science fiction television program *Doctor Who*.

Presented as a 12-part radio series, *The Hitchhiker's Guide to the Galaxy* was first broadcast in March 1978 with a "huge blaze of no publicity at all," in Adams's words. Although the first few episodes were greeted with what its creator has described as a "thudding silence," the biting cosmic humor of the series eventually won *Hitchhiker's Guide* such a large and loyal following that Adams was approached by Pan Books to write a novel based on his radio scripts. While he was in the process of writing the book, his editor, eager to capitalize on the popularity of the radio series, told him to stop at the page he was on so that they could rush the book to print.

A year after the radio series hit the airwaves, *The Hitchhiker's Guide to the Galaxy* (1979) was published in Britain; it immediately jumped to the top of the *London Times*'s best-seller list. Described by Peter Kemp of the *Listener* (December 18 & 25, 1980) as "a sardonically funny exercise in galactic globe-trotting," *The Hitchhiker's Guide to the Galaxy* depicts the adventures of Arthur Dent, an amiably dull Englishman who wakes up one Thursday to find that the entire planet is about to be destroyed to make way for an intergalactic expressway. Dent's friend, Ford Prefect, a stranded interstellar hitchhiker, saves their lives by thumbing a ride on a passing spaceship that is manned by the life-form with the third worst poetry in the universe. The two are then propelled through a series of chaotic interplanetary adventures with the aid of an electronic travel guide, "The Hitchhiker's Guide to the Galaxy," to which Prefect is a contributor. On their improbable travels, Dent and Prefect meet up with a bizarre cast of characters that includes Zaphod Beeblebrox, the two-headed, three-armed president of the galaxy, who is on the run in a stolen spaceship; Marvin, a chronically depressed robot; and the planet designer Slartibartfast, who is working on Earth Mark Two.

Although some critics faulted *The Hitchhiker's Guide to the Galaxy* for its clipped pace and "sometimes damagingly sophomoric" tone, most had only praise for the twisted comic genius of Adams's first novel. In her review for the *Washington Post Book World* (November 23, 1980), Lisa Tuttle called *The Hitchhiker's Guide* "extremely funny" and added, "There's nothing dull about the *Guide*, which is inspired lunacy that leaves hardly a science fictional cliché alive." Gerald Jonas of the *New York Times Book Review* (January 25, 1981) found the book to be "a delightful exception" to the rule that most "humorous science fiction novels have notoriously limited audiences."

Adams's next novel, *The Restaurant at the End of the Universe* (1980), picks up the action where the first book left off, with the central figures careening through time and space on their way to Milliways, a hip restaurant/nightclub where the featured nightly entertainment is the apocalypse. Catapulted through a frenetic series of near-disasters and silly predicaments, the group encounters, among other things, the leader of the galaxy's loudest rock band, who is spending a year dead for tax reasons, and an eccentric old hermit who is believed to be the ruler of the universe. Dent and Prefect eventually join up with a ship full of "useless" professionals (among them advertising executives, hairdressers, and management consultants) who are on a mission to populate a primitive planet that turns out to be prehistoric Earth. The wildly popular sequel was applauded by most critics, among them Peter Kemp, who declared that Adams's "surreal, comic creativity" made the book "almost unputdownable." "If [*Restaurant*] does not make you laugh . . . ," Philip Howard proclaimed in the *London Times* (February 7, 1981), "you guys are so unhip, it's a wonder your bums don't fall off."

With *Life, the Universe and Everything* (1982), the third installment in the *Hitchhiker's* series, the now familiar story, like some critics' patience, began to wear thin. The first of Adams's novels not derived from his radio scripts, *Life, the Universe and Everything* continues the misadventures of Arthur Dent and Ford Prefect as they cope with life on both prehistoric and modern-day Earth before once again traveling through time and space, this time to save the galaxy from annihilation by the murderous Krikkit robots. Sally Emerson of the *Illustrated London News* (September 1982) found "much of the writing [to be] dazzling," with some "episodes of comic genius," but most reviewers echoed the assessment of Richard Brown of the *London Times Literary Supplement* (September 24, 1982), who lamented that the third installment highlighted "the extent to which the humor depends on a limited repertoire of gimmicks." "Though by no means lacking in enthusiastic drive," Brown added, "[*Life, the Universe and Everything*] does little to suggest that the idea could or should be taken much further."

Despite its tepid critical reception in Britain, *Life, the Universe, and Everything* solidified Adams's popularity in the United States, where it remained on the *New York Times* best-seller list for 15 weeks. The combination of the third book and PBS broadcasts of the BBC television version of *The Hitchhiker's Guide to the Galaxy* helped elevate Adams to cult-hero status, and his speaking engagements on college campuses and appearances at science fiction conventions drew thousands of fans. For the most part, Adams found his legion of American fans to be "really strange, really weird," as he told Eric Zorn, noting that "most of them are sort of sallow and overweight." "There was a phase when people were phoning me up all the time," Adams recalled to Desson Howe, "one guy actually claiming to be Zaphod Beeblebrox. That got very wearying."

In 1983 Adams was at the peak of his popularity on both sides of the Atlantic, but his stardom had put him at an artistic crossroads. Although he admittedly enjoyed the fame and fortune the *Hitchhiker* books brought him, he was resisting the temptation to write another installment. Tired of the continual requests from his publisher and fans for more books and seeking a break from the grueling round of promotional tours, Adams moved to Los Angeles to work on a film version of the *Hitchhiker* story with the producer and director Ivan Reitman. The venture backfired, however, with Adams getting "completely screwed by the Hollywood system," as he complained to Michele Field for a *Publishers Weekly* (February 1, 1991) interview, and the movie was never made. "It was a terrible experience," Adams explained to Marc Conly in an interview for the *Bloomsbury Review* (May/June 1989). "At the end of it, I felt I'd hit my first major failure of my career. I felt very disoriented by it. I went back to England because people were constantly asking me to write another *Hitchhiker* book. . . . I was running for shelter a bit, agreeing to do another book while I wanted to write something else."

So Long, and Thanks for All the Fish (1984), the fourth book in the Hitchhiker "trilogy," finds Arthur Dent back on a mysteriously restored, modern-day Earth, where he falls in love, learns how to fly (without the aid of an airplane), and sets off on another romp through the galaxy—his mission now being to read God's last message. The novel scored a major commercial success despite the fact that it was nearly universally panned by the critics as an unnecessary extension of the series. In his evaluation for *Fantasy Review* (April 1985), Paul M. Lloyd predicted that *So Long, and Thanks for All the Fish* was "likely to provoke more yawns than smiles," adding that "Adams would have done well to stop while he was ahead." Reviewing the novel in *Science Fiction Review* (May 1986), Allen Varney agreed, noting that Adams "basically treads water for 150 pages." "There are two or three good lines," he continued, "but the inventiveness is gone." "That book was a mistake . . . ," Adams admitted to Marc Conly. "I was writing it on the one hand resenting the fact that I was doing another *Hitchhiker* book, and trying to do something else, and falling between the two stools. [It is] not a book I'm happy with, and it certainly was a very miserable experience writing it."

Adams made a clean break from the *Hitchhiker* format with his next novel, *Dirk Gently's Holistic Detective Agency* (1987). Borrowing from old, unaired *Doctor Who* material, the comic mystery features Dirk Gently, a psychic private investigator who solves cases by examining, in his own words, "the fundamental interconnectedness of all things," and Richard MacDuff, a computer software designer who enlists Gently to solve the murder of his boss, who has become a somewhat bewildered ghost. Through the familiar devices of time travel and comic bungling, the main characters find themselves in a race to save humanity from extinction. The novel's outrageous plot and ridiculous parodies of the modern world made it a hit with Adams's fans. Even though some critics continued to find Adams's overbearing wit annoying, if not offensive, many considered it his best novel up to that time. "Following a tradition which stretches from [Laurence] Sterne to [P. G.] Wodehouse," John Nicholson wrote for the *London Times* (June 18, 1987), "what signifies most here is the quality of the writing, the asides and allusions, and—above all—the jokes. Mr. Adams scores very high on all counts." Although Mat Coward conceded in the *Listener* (June 25, 1987) that *Dirk Gently* was "a hugely entertaining novel," he also suggested that "Adams may have suffered the worst possible fate for a writer who doesn't die before 30: that he wrote his best book first."

Dirk Gently was also featured in Adams's next novel, *The Long Dark Tea-Time of the Soul* (1988). Once again taking a satiric look at modern society, Adams poked fun at everything from the hypocrisy in religion to the "smug self-satisfaction of the modern sellout," as Marc Conly put it. Described by Cathleen Schine of the *New York Times Book Review* (March 12, 1989) as "a clever and funny novel about an English detective, an American girl in a bad mood, and a Norse god who sells his soul to an advertising executive," *The Long Dark Tea-Time* was another commercial success. "Adams [expands] disgruntled comic bungling to cosmic proportions," Schine wrote. "He is *The Whole Earth Catalog*'s Kingsley Amis." Despite finding the novel "a pleasure to read," Schine ultimately concluded that "in spite of all the nimble plots, the skillful writing, and the underlying wit of his work, Mr. Adams is a bit banal." That sentiment was shared by other critics, who faulted Adams for his tendency to resort to formula to accommodate his manic concepts and self-righteous parodies of the human condition, but Marc Conly felt that Adams's "social awareness and the accuracy of his barbs keep the narrative . . . from becoming too frothy."

In 1988 Adams, who was in the midst of an early midlife crisis, took a sabbatical from writing novels to embark on a yearlong journey with the zoologist Mark Carwardine in search of some of the world's endangered species. The two parlayed the expedition into a BBC Radio series and a book entitled *Last Chance to See* (1990), a poignant, often amusing travelogue that calls attention to the plight of several animal species facing imminent extinction. The book, which received high praise in England and the United States, revealed Adams's more serious side and helped shed his reputation for frivolity. The experience did wonders for his writer's

block as well. "Three or four years ago I was just wallowing," Adams admitted in the interview with Michele Field. "I'd had years of output and very little input. . . . Going off and doing *Last Chance to See* was very much like cleaning off my desk: clearing space so that I could work again."

With renewed confidence, Adams returned to the *Hitchhiker* saga, penning a fifth installment, *Mostly Harmless* (1992). The book revives many of the characters and much of the deranged wit and inventiveness of the earlier books in the series, with the action whipping back and forth between parallel universes—one in which the Earth still exists, another in which it does not. Bill Sharp of the *New York Times Book Review* (November 1, 1992) described it as "more of the same zany, nonsensical, mostly plotless and pointless mayhem" that Adams fans have come to revere.

In addition to books, Adams has written an array of sophisticated computer games, including an interactive novel based on the *Hitchhiker* books and another called *Bureaucracy*, an "'Indiana Jones' type of adventure" in which the "object is to get your bank to acknowledge a change-of-address card," as he explained to Michele Field. Adams has also created a CD-ROM version of *Last Chance to See*.

Since the publication of *Mostly Harmless* in 1992, Adams has not published any novels. He abandoned plans for a third installment of the *Dirk Gently* series after he had worked on the book for months. "Books had turned into a monster for me," he told *Newsweek* (April 13, 1998). "I thought, I'm spending my entire life sitting in a dark room and writing." Needing "a bit of mental crop rotation," he started his London-based production company, the Digital Village, with a founder of *Wired* magazine and three former television executives. In 1998 Digital Village produced the CD-ROM *Starship Titanic*, a project that involved two years of work by more than three dozen people. The new game, according to *Newsweek*, "revives the intimacy of the old text-only computer games that let players talk to characters and combines it with top-of-the-line graphics and game design." Noting that the CD-ROM utilizes a language parser with more than 30,000 words and 16 hours of recorded dialogue by various actors (including John Cleese as the voice of the parrot), J. C. Herz of the *New York Times* (April 9, 1998) remarked that "the language interface, which seems like an intuitive interface for any sort of virtual world, is fairly sophisticated and flexible."

In 1983 Douglas Adams collaborated with the comedian John Lloyd on *The Meaning of Liff*, a mock dictionary of British place names, such as "Papple: what a baby does to soup with his spoon" and "Ulingswick: a grossly overdeveloped epiglottis." The two followed up on the book's success with a sequel, *The Deeper Meaning of Liff* (1990). At present he is about to begin work on a new novel, tentatively titled *The Chaos Engineer*. Adams has saved the failed Dirk Gently material for possible use in a sixth *Hitchhiker* novel. —C.M.

SUGGESTED READING: *Bloomsbury Review* May/June 1989; *Chicago Tribune* I p14+ Oct. 28, 1982; *Fantasy Review* Apr. 1985; *Guardian* p33 July 23, 1992; *Illustrated London News* Sep. 1982; *Listener* Dec. 18 & 25, 1980, June 25, 1987; *London Times* June 18, 1987; *London Times Literary Supplement* Sep. 24, 1982; *Los Angeles Times Book Review* Feb. 3, 1985; *Newsweek* Apr. 13, 1998; *New York Times* Apr. 9, 1998; *New York Times Book Review* Jan. 25, 1981, Mar. 13, 1989, Nov. 1, 1992; *People* p79+ May 20, 1991; *Publisher's Weekly* p47+ Jan. 14 1983, p62+ Feb. 1, 1991; *Washington Post Book Review* C p1+ Nov. 23, 1984; *Contemporary Authors* vol. 106, 1982, *Contemporary Authors New Revision Series* vol. 34, 1991; *Contemporary Literary Criticism* vol. 27, 1984, vol. 60, 1990; *Who's Who*, 1993

SELECTED BOOKS: *The Hitchhiker's Guide to the Galaxy*, 1979; *The Restaurant at the End of the Universe*, 1980; *Life, the Universe and Everything*, 1982; *So Long, and Thanks for All the Fish*, 1984; *The Original Hitchhiker Radio Scripts*, 1985; *Dirk Gently's Holistic Detective Agency*, 1987; *The Long Dark Tea-Time of the Soul*, 1988; *Mostly Harmless*, 1992; with John Lloyd—*The Meaning of Liff*, 1983; *The Deeper Meaning of Liff*, 1990; with Mark Carwardine—*Last Chance to See*, 1990

Aidoo, Ama Ata

Mar. 23, 1942– Novelist; short-story writer; playwright; poet

Ama Ata Aidoo, the Ghanaian playwright, short-story writer, novelist, and poet, believes in breaking with tradition. In her work, she criticizes the ancient custom of polygamy and the traditional place of women in African culture. At the same time, she believes in a distinct African identity and, more specifically, in an African female identity, one that is based not in servitude but in independence and a sense of self-worth. This individuality fuels her exploration of colonialism and slavery and of how they still have significance for Africans today. Aidoo believes that one should question all traditions and, through that questioning, allow all people—regardless of race, nationality, gender, or religion—to be considered equals in the eyes of all humanity.

Born just before many African nations freed themselves from the chains of colonialism, Aidoo has watched the continent grow in its self-determination, but, in her opinion, it has not evolved nearly enough. In many cases, colonial leaders have been replaced by Africans who use the idea of nationalism as a self-serving tool to bolster their own power bases and keep their people oppressed. In a *Massachusetts Review* (Spring 1995) interview with Anuradha Dingwaney Needham, Aidoo noted that some types of nationalism are not healthy, especially those that border on fascism as well as those that are "evident in the posturings of Africans in the diaspora; [that form] becomes an excuse, a kind of smokescreen behind which these people lead their lives uninterrupted and still manage to convince themselves that they are still very much in tune with what's going on at home." Nonetheless, Aidoo does see a positive role for pan-Africanism, as she told Needham: "I still think we need an African identification, for there surely are an African people." Aidoo feels that Africans need to see themselves as a whole community before taking on other, more specific identities.

These themes figure very prominently in two of Aidoo's major works, *No Sweetness Here* (1970), a short-story collection, and *Our Sister Killjoy* (1977), an experimental novel that blends prose, poetry, and the epistolary form. Her third major work and most recently published book, *Changes* (1991), explores the life of a divorced, career-minded African woman who becomes the wife of an already married man, so that she can avoid the responsibilities that being a first wife entails in many African cultures.

Christina Ama Ata Aidoo was born on March 23, 1942, in the Fanti town of Abeadzi Kyiakor, in central Ghana. She is the daughter of Nana Yaw Fama, a chief of the town, and his wife Maame Abba Abasema. Because of her father's position, she was raised in a royal household, which greatly enhanced her creativity, as she was exposed to traditions, folklore, and ritual. From 1961 to 1964 she attended Wesley Girls' High School. She then moved on to the University of Ghana, Legon, where she immersed herself in a writers' workshop and the school of drama. Her first published work, the play *The Dilemma of a Ghost*, was completed in 1964, the year she graduated, and was performed for three nights in March at the university theater.

In *The Dilemma of a Ghost*, Ato Yawson, a young man from Ghana who was educated in the United States, returns home with his African-American wife, Eulalie Rush. The couple has married without alerting Ato's family in Ghana. The focus of the play is the conflict between traditional African communal values and American values of independence. This conflict is compounded by Eulalie's own ignorance and immaturity and by Ato himself, who is unable to help his wife become accustomed to a foreign way of life and cannot conciliate his two worlds. In the end Ato's mother helps to save the family from falling apart by, according to the *Dictionary of Literary Biography* (1992), "asserting the integrative nature of traditional African norms and values over the disruptive Western ones." In this work, Aidoo, through her characterizations, displayed her concerns about the African social convention of perceiving women as second-class citizens. The play also highlighted the difference in ideologies between black people in the West and those in Africa—a legacy of the slave trade. The critic Dapo Adelugba, writing for *African Literature Today* (1976), found that Aidoo's chief strength as a writer was her dialogue: "Her success in creating levels of language, in matching literary grace with veracity of characterization, in suiting . . . the action to the word, the word to the action, is commendable in such a young dramatist."

With *Anowa* (1970), her second play, Aidoo continued to develop the themes of her debut work, especially the role of women in society. Set during the colonial period of the Gold Coast, the play focuses on Anowa's development as a woman and her understanding of how society can prevent a woman from reaching her full potential. Anowa rejects all of the men her parents have found suitable for her to marry, deciding instead to marry her great love, Kofi Ako. Ako later turns against her and tries to divorce her, but Anowa refuses, repudiating the charges that are brought against her by her husband, who insists that she is infertile. Anowa, in a remarkable act of defiance, turns the blame on Ako. Ako, in turn, commits suicide because of this challenge to his manhood. Anowa also takes her own life, frustrated by her inability to find meaning in living. Though Aidoo based this play on a famous folk tale, Eldred Jones, writing for *African Literature Today* (1976), believed that *Anowa* "takes on the dimension of myth without losing its social relevance."

No Sweetness Here (1970) is a collection of short stories that still hold many inflections of the oral tradition. Written over a four- or five-year period, the collection contains 11 tales depicting women who reveal their full intellectual and physical capabilities. The author explored many issues in the book—from childhood in a sexist environment to the effects of modernization on women.

In 1970 Aidoo became a lecturer at the University of Ghana, Cape Coast, where she would later become a professor of English. Her daughter was also born around this time. For a year (1974–75) she worked at the Washington bureau of the Phelps-Stokes Fund's Ethnic Studies Program as a professor. Because her time was so divided, she did not publish any new work until *Our Sister Killjoy*, her first novel, appeared in 1977. Aidoo explained in her interview with Needham for the *Massachusetts Review* that she had started working on the book in 1972 but that the demands of motherhood and teaching proved too much for her to continue writing it—until she went to Washington, where she had time to work on it properly. By the time she returned to Ghana, she had sent the book to the publisher.

According to the *Dictionary of Literary Biography*, however, there were other reasons for Aidoo's literary silence, which was "probably aggravated by the political climate in Ghana at the time: a long, orchestrated display of military brutality and blatant corruption, climaxing in indiscriminate incarceration, especially of Ghana's intelligentsia and students." *My Sister Killjoy*, in its innovative form and aggressive tone, reflects Aidoo's politics of the time and represents her disgust with the corruption and abuses that were occurring in her own country. The novel, which is composed of a prologue and three parts, is about a young woman, Sissie, who travels first to Germany and later to England. At the heart of the novel are Sissie's impressions of oppression and bondage—from the plight of a young German housewife, Marija, to that of the African students who dwell in England in horrific conditions due to the psychological bondage of colonialism. The novel is part political tirade, part travelogue. Its last section, "A Love Letter," is a general epistle, ostensibly directed at Sissie's ex-boyfriend but, in actuality, directed at all African men who have gone to the West and have not returned home, as Sissie does. Most critics applauded Aidoo's social commentary, but some felt uneasy about her criticisms of Western culture.

Aidoo's next work, *Someone Talking to Sometime* (1985), was her first volume of poetry. It collected some of her older poems, which had first been published in anthologies as early as the 1960s, along with new poems—totaling 44 in all. Though the poems differ from one another in form, the recurring themes of Aidoo's previous work are continually present in this book as well: her criticism of society is mixed with her belief in the self, and her view of the problems of human existence is tempered with humor. Her two following works were *The Eagle and the Chickens and Other Stories* (1986) and *Birds and Other Poems* (1987), both written for children—another departure for the ever-experimental Aidoo.

In 1991 Aidoo published a second novel, *Changes*, a story about lovers, a subject the author once said she would never tackle—her argument being that there were more important issues to address. The main character is a woman named Esi, a career-minded Ghanaian, and through her character Aidoo explored the issues facing contemporary African women who are married: marital rape, careers and their effect on relationships, and the consequences of compromise. In the novel, Esi is raped by her first husband and decides to leave him, telling no one the reason for the divorce. She has an affair with a married man and feels a relief from the burdens of marriage and motherhood, and her happiness is reflected in her work. When her new love, Ali Kondey, asks her to marry him, she agrees to become his second wife. (In African cultures it is not uncommon for a man to have more than one wife.) Because she is a second wife, there are fewer demands put on her, but Esi comes to resent the fact that her husband is unable to give her

the attention and commitment she needs. The critics applauded Aidoo's return to adult fiction. The *Black Scholar* (Winter 1995) critic found that Aidoo "continues to explore the cultural and psychic tensions of a society caught between two worlds and two histories. At a very human level, Aidoo seems to suggest that only responsible individual engagement can assure the possibility of partial triumph." A writer for the *Journal of Modern African Studies* (March 1996) compared this work to *Our Sister Killjoy* and found that it "is in fact a much more balanced and even-tempered work, handling gravely serious material with an autumnal humor and a breezy lightness of touch which are refreshing after the polemical solemnities of her male compatriot novelists."
—C.M.

SUGGESTED READING: *African Literature Today* p72+ 1976; *Black Scholar* p55+ Winter 1995; *Essence* p76+ Feb. 1994; *Guardian* p17 Apr. 2, 1991; *Journal of Modern African Studies* p179+ Mar. 1996; *Literary Review* p464 + Summer 1991; *Massachusetts Review* p123+ Spring 1995; *Ms.* p96 Jan. 1991, p52+ July 1993; *Studies in Short Fiction* p161+ Spring 1995; *Contemporary Authors* nrs vol. 101, 1981; *Dictionary of Literary Biography* vol. 117, 1992

SELECTED WORKS: Fiction—*No Sweetness Here*, 1970; *Our Sister Killjoy*, 1977; *Changes*, 1991; Poetry—*Someone Talking to Sometime*, 1985; Drama—*The Dilemma of a Ghost*, 1964; *Anowa*, 1970; Juvenile—*The Eagle and the Chickens and Other Stories*, 1986; *Birds and Other Poems*, 1987

Barbara Kigozi/Courtesy of Elizabeth Alexander

Alexander, Elizabeth

May 30, 1962– Poet and dramatist

Elizabeth Alexander, a greatly respected poet and playwright, received high marks from critics across the United States for her first collection of poetry, *The Venus Hottentot* (1990). The collection's title poem takes its name from the Hottentot Venus, a 19th-century African woman who was exhibited across Europe a physical curiosity. A large part of the collection focuses on some of the more personal elements of Alexander's life, including reflections on her family, her first lover, and her first time away from home. Her second collection of po-

ems, *Body of Life* (1996), developed these themes and added new ones to the author's repertoire. Alexander is also the author of a play in verse, *Diva Studies* (1996), which premiered at the Yale School of Drama.

Elizabeth Alexander was born on May 30, 1962, in New York City. She is the daughter of Clifford Leopold Alexander, a leading business consultant who had been a special counsel to U.S. president Lyndon Johnson. He later became the chairman of the United States Equal Employment Opportunity Commission under President Jimmy Carter. Her mother, Adele (Logan) Alexander, is a historian and writer who also lectures on African-American and women's history at the University of Maryland.

In 1984 Elizabeth Alexander received her bachelor's degree from Yale University. Three years later she graduated with an M.A. from Boston University, before going on to her doctoral studies at the University of Pennsylvania. In 1991 she became an assistant professor of English at the University of Chicago.

Saartjie Baartman, the real-life "Hottentot Venus" for which Alexander's 1990 poetry collection was named, was one of the 19th century's most exploited women. Baartman, a tiny woman, was taken from Africa and exhibited in Europe because of her unusually large buttocks. A French scientist, Baron Georges Léopold Chrétien Frédéric Dagobert Cuvier, offered her half the profits of a tour of Europe, if she would accompany him to Europe. She left her menial job in Cape Town and for 18 months traveled between Paris and London as a sideshow novelty, accompanied by an animal trainer. She was forced to emerge from a cage completely nude and was subsequently prodded by members of the scientific community and anyone else who had paid the price of admission. In 1815, at the age of 25, Baartman died, but she remained a showpiece even after her death: Cuvier dissected her, and put her genitalia in a bell jar on display in the Muse de l'Homme in Paris.

The first of the four parts of Alexander's collection deals with Baartman, providing her with a first-person, posthumous response to her captor. Part Two contains a popular history of the Western world, delivered by voices of the author's family from Harlem, Jamaica, and Washington, D.C. This section discusses her grandparents, the poet's first summer away from her home, and a first love. Parts three and four look at Alexander's African ancestry and praise the noted figures Paul Robeson, Duke Ellington, John Coltrane, and Romare Bearden. Alexander received high praise for this slim but moving volume. In the *New York Times Book Review* (September 30, 1990), Doris Jean Austin acclaimed the collection as "a historical mosaic with profound cultural integrity. The title work exhumes the previous century's mutilated victim of science and history and sets her amid today's heroic voices. The current proliferation of benign, yet soothing works of poetry gives *The Venus Hottentot* a particularly exhilarating quality. Readers owe themselves the many pleasures to be found in this book; Elizabeth Alexander creates intellectual magic in poem after poem." Lenard D. Moore of *Library Journal* (May 1, 1990) wrote that "It is evident that Alexander has an eye for accuracy in describing the past as well as the present, but this work is more than reportage; it is a very imaginative collection of poems that should appeal to many readers." Particularly impressed with the title poem, Stephen Yenser of *Poetry* (July 1991) proclaimed, "I am not sure that [the title poem] will prove to be this book's most important poem to Elizabeth Alexander herself, but I am sure, or as sure as I can be, that it will be a landmark in American poetry, and that *The Venus Hottentot* is a superb first book, and that Elizabeth Alexander can be about as good a poet as she cares to be."

With Patricia Redmond, Alexander co-authored the phototext for Houston A. Baker's *Workings of the Spirit: The Poetics of Afro-American Women's Writing* (1990). Her next project was a play, *Diva Studies*, produced at Yale School of Drama at the University Theater in 1996. In the play Alexander attempted to redefine the word "diva," an opera term that has become a label for any popular female singer. For her new definition, Alexander told Alvin Klein of the *New York Times* (April 28, 1996), she had particular attributes in mind: "The diva certainly is and looks fabulous, but it's not only a presentational fabulousness. It's survival. Fortitude is the word I keep coming back to. And passion, stamina, and strength. The power from within radiates outward. It's about being a tough cookie. And it's about generosity. Her glory is not something she hoards. If you are magnificent, you have enough to spare." While the author claimed that many great divas inspired her play, including Patti LaBelle, Eartha Kitt, Dorothy Dandridge, and Leontyne Price, she noted that her greatest influence was her maternal grandmother, Wononah

Bond Logan, a social worker in New York City who retired in the 1970s. "She knew how to read the world around her," Alexander told Alvin Klein, "how to navigate narrow straits—and come up with a withering remark at any given moment. She was competent and glamorous in a world that said black women are not supposed to be."

Alexander wrote the introduction to Melvin Dixon's *Love Instruments* in 1995. She released her second volume of poetry, *Body of Life*, in 1996. A critic for the *Washington Post Book World* (February 16, 1997) wrote that she "continues to fashion crisp, clean, occasionally elliptical poems that demand intelligent input from readers. In a notable departure from the earlier work, Alexander at times inserts a coarse word or two to make her point. Graceful elegance and easy musicality still prevail, however, amid poems of personal experience that manage to avoid being nauseatingly insular, and poems about historical events that reveal a judicious use of detail."

On September 18, 1993, Elizabeth Alexander married Adolfo Parades, a salesman. The couple lives in Chicago. Alexander continues to teach at the University of Chicago and contributes to a variety of periodicals. She is also a member of the Modern Language Association of America. —C.M.

SELECTED WORKS: Poetry—*The Venus Hottentot*, 1990; *Body of Life*, 1996; Drama—*Diva Studies*, 1996

SUGGESTED READING: *Library Journal* p90 May 1, 1990; *New York Times* p14 Sep. 19, 1993, Apr. 28, 1996; XIIICN p17 Apr. 28, 1996; *New York Times Book Review* p20 Sep. 30, 1990; *Poetry* p233 July 1991; *Washington Post Book World* p12 Feb. 16, 1997; *Weekly Mail and Guardian* Dec. 15, 1995; *Contemporary Authors* vol. 135, 1992

Alexander, Meena

Feb. 17, 1951– Poet; novelist

Born in India, educated in Sudan and Britain, and now a resident of the United States, Meena Alexander is a writer defined by migrancy. She considers herself "a poet who also writes prose," and her work has been influenced by the many places she has lived. She often writes about an individual's quest for identity—a quest that has engaged Alexander since her childhood. "Her work offers a deeply honest insight into the mind of a woman trying to balance the disparate halves of her existence," Hema N. Nair wrote in *Ms.* (January/February 1994). She frequently tackles political as well as personal themes, and often expresses them through the eyes of the "other," a term she uses for individuals who perceive themselves as

Ram Rahman

Meena Alexander

"What does it mean to have a place to go to? To have a home? I think these questions haunt me and structure my writing. At times I think I make up a home in words, words that slip and slide and sometimes perish on the tongue. Yet the task of poetry is to touch that living flesh, work a joy through its rhythms, ride a sense to the edge of self. And though a self can only exist in place, place is so often a palimpsest, etching out the ways in which our being in the physical world clarifies quite precisely at the edges of the invisible.

"As a child I traveled a great deal between continents and had to learn to absorb those great shifts into my psyche. There were times in class in the British school to which I went when I would not open my mouth, times when I felt I was lost between languages, when I felt my flesh bruised by the incipient violence of English, which still felt like a colonial language. I am speaking now of the school I went to as a child in Khartoum. My father, a meteorologist, was seconded by the Indian government to Sudan, at the time of Sudanese independence and part of each year I spent in Khartoum, a dry desert city I grew to love; the other part of the year was spent in Kerala, enjoying the green glory of the monsoon season. So back and forth I traveled as a child, my many worlds bound together by voices that well out of my imagination.

"Indeed I am haunted by thresholds, zones of movement and change, fluid borders where rivers meet, traffic islands in the midst of city blocks, transit lounges in great international airports. And I see this haunting as part of what it means to live at the tail end of the century. Yet this is only part of my story, the migratory bit, moving as a child between Kerala and Khartoum. The other part comes from rootedness, great houses slipping into dirt, paddy fields where water rises covering up the traces of tiny children, wells into which women have jumped and vanished. Indeed these fissured geographies make up an irreducible truth for one, one I struggle to translate into words. And between the body which I am and the language which comes to me, falls the shadow, the shadow I call myself.

"I think of myself as a poet who also writes prose. I do not think there is any real distinction to be made between the highly charged language of poetry and that of prose. To use a Sanskrit word, both exist as kavya.

"I have been described as a 'self-made' writer. Obviously at some level, each and every writer is self-made. I do come out of a rich and complex heritage, of that I have no doubt. At the same time as an immigrant in America I had to invent myself, and for me this invention is part and parcel of the task of writing myself into being, part of a migratory process which has been there for me since childhood. I wrote my memoir *Fault Lines* because I felt I was living in a place where I had no history, that I had to use words to make up a past. But the invention of a past is always also part of the project of living, part of combing out, braiding together the fragile, tangled strands of memory.

outsiders or observers, as somehow different or separated from those around them.

In a personal statement submitted to *World Authors 1990–1995* describing her background and influences, Alexander writes: "My parents, who had an arranged marriage, grew up in villages just 12 miles apart from each other in the green coastal state of Kerala in South India. Yet they witnessed the fierce turbulence of the Nationalist era in India and Gandhi's nonviolent movement made a great impression on both of them. My grandparents on my mother's side were Gandhians and I was raised on tales of the Vaikom satyagraha, the Salt March, and the ceaseless spinning of khadi. Yet I was born after independence and never witnessed these events, they come as memories to me, through a generation that has passed on. So I am haunted by what it means to remember, what one needs to forget in order to continue. I think my writing comes from a historical moment, haunted in some sense by a feeling of belatedness.

"The landscape of Kerala where I spent much of my childhood has marked my work, there are wells and rivers and old teak houses in my writing. In my poem 'House of a Thousand Doors' I imagine a grandmother figure perpetually excluded from the ancestral house. Why? Because she is a woman, because she carries a debt, just by being female. So this burden is part of her flesh, part of her being. And another poem I wrote at about the same time, after I came to America where I now live, is called 'Hotel Alexandria' and in it I see an old woman rocking at the threshold of the apartment building she has been cast out of. The building is to be gentrified and she has nowhere to go.

"It's as if a girlchild stood at the brink of a river. Her hair all wet, tossed in sunlight and her grandmother bent over and took a comb made of bone and combed out the child's tangled hair, patiently working out the knots from the roots out, drying the hair, braiding it in sunlight. As a writer I have to be both the child with the wet tangled hair, taking pleasure in her bath, the scents of hibiscus lotion on her skin, in her hair, then with bent head enduring the comb. And I have to be the old grandmother in her white cotton sari, standing feet bare at the water's edge, stooping over the child, taking shining black hair in her gnarled hands, combing it through. And this doubleness becomes part of making sense, making up a lost history.

"What do you want to write about next, people sometimes ask. I want very simply to write about being human, above love, loss, loneliness, about touching mortality and enduring. And these simple themes, small human stories come to me across many borders, in many migrant voices."

Meena Alexander was born Mary Elizabeth Alexander on February 17, 1951, in Allahabad, India. Her parents, George and Mary Alexander, had given her anglicized versions of her grandmothers' names, Mariamma and Eli. Mary Elizabeth, however, changed her name to Meena at the age of 15 to distance herself from the influences of British imperialism. A precocious child, she had begun writing poetry at the age of 10. "I found that I could escape to another world through words," she recalled to Hema N. Nair. "Writing freed me from the constraints that would otherwise bind me." Among these constraints were contradictory feelings, both of strength and of shame, which she perceived as inherent to womanhood. Much of her early writing dealt with social injustice, particularly as it pertained to the condition of women.

While living in Sudan, Alexander attended Khartoum University, where she also tutored in English, and received a B.A. in 1969. She later moved with her family to England and earned a Ph.D. from the University of Nottingham in 1973.

Alexander briefly lectured at the University of Stirling before returning to India, in 1974, to lecture in English at the University of Delhi. The following year she taught French and English at Jawaharlal Nehru University, also in Delhi, and from 1975 to 1977, she taught English at the Central Institute of English and Foreign Language in Hyderabad, India. Her last academic position in India was at the University of Hyderabad, where she was a lecturer for two years beginning in 1977, and a reader in English in 1979. She also briefly lectured at Osmania University in 1978 and was a visiting fellow at the Sorbonne in 1979.

In 1976 she published her first work, a collection of poems entitled *The Bird's Bright Ring*, which she followed in 1977 with two other poetry collections, *Without Place* and *I Root My Name*, and a one-act play, *In the Middle Earth*. She pub-

lished *The Poetic Self: Towards a Phenomenology of Romanticism*, a work of literary criticism, in 1979.

Meena Alexander married David Lelyveld on May 1, 1979. The couple moved to the United States soon afterward and settled in New York City. "I was so struck by that moment," she told Jeffrey R. Young of *The Chronicle of Higher Education* (March 14, 1997). "The moment of arriving in the United States. . . . I thought, what does this mean to be naturalized? What does it mean to be natured? What is that transformation?"

In 1980 Alexander published her fourth book of poetry, *Stone Roots*. She also began teaching at Fordham University as an assistant professor of English. After seven years she left Fordham and joined the faculty of the City University of New York (CUNY) as an assistant professor of English at Hunter College, a division of CUNY. Two years later she moved to the CUNY Graduate Center, where she was an associate professor until 1992, when she became a full professor of English and Women's Studies at both the Graduate Center and Hunter College—positions she retains. She also lectures in the writing program of Columbia University, which she has done since 1990.

After an eight-year hiatus, Alexander began publishing again in 1988 with *House of a Thousand Doors*, a work of both poetry and prose. The following year she published *The Storm: A Poem in Five Parts*, a book-length poem, and *Women in Romanticism: Mary Wollstonecraft, Dorothy Wordsworth, and Mary Shelley*, her second work of literary criticism. She published her first novel, *Nampally Road*, in 1991.

Alexander published the memoir *Fault Lines* in 1993. The title refers to her concept of herself as "a woman cracked by multiple migrations," and the book represents the efforts of "a woman with no fixed place, a creature struggling to make herself up in a new world." Alexander discusses her experiences moving back and forth between India, Sudan, and New York and the effects these experiences have had on her memory and her writing. One of the major figures in the book is her Grandmother Kunju, an activist in early 20th-century India. Alexander never knew her but reconstructs her based on family accounts. *Publishers Weekly* chose *Fault Lines* as one of the best books of 1993.

In the Fall 1996 issue of *Amerasia Journal*, Helena Grice of the University of Wales compared *Fault Lines* to Maxine Hong Kingston's *The Woman Warrior*, another memoir of immigrant life in America from a female perspective. "Alexander treats her writings as a search for a homeland . . . ," Grice wrote. "[She] is engaged in a quest for her own autobiographical truth, from diverse sources of meaning. . . . Alexander's voice joins a growing choir of multiethnic female voices singing the diaspora story."

River and Bridge, Alexander's most recent book comprised exclusively of poetry, was first published in 1995 and was reissued in an expanded edition the following year. In a review that appeared in the Fall 1997 issue of *World Literature Today*, John Oliver Perry commented that "generally the poems remain at least elusive, unparaphrasable, yet a few social protests are relatively direct." The inspirations for many of the poems in this collection range from current events in such places as Iraq, India, and New York, to personal occurrences such as the births of her children and her own childhood memories. "Although it is often clearly feminine/female and occasionally hits a distinctively postcolonial/racial note, Meena Alexander's poetry as well as her prose predicates a distinctly nondualistic sense of herself as sheer energy," Perry wrote. "Many almost overt clues bring out of seclusion the still shy sexuality that she recognizes as empowering her creativity." *Sandhya Rosenblum*, her second novel, and *The Shock of Arrival: Post-Colonial Reflections*, a collection of poetry and prose, were also published in 1996.

Her latest work of fiction, the novel *Manhattan Music*, was published in 1997. In it she compares the plight of immigrants to that of Frankenstein's monster—in that immigrants lead patchwork existences and contain bits and pieces of different cultures. They need their memories to survive, in the same way the monster required electricity for life. The novel helped Alexander reach an understanding of her own identity, she told Jeffrey R. Young, "an acceptance that this is where I am and that it makes sense to be an American. It's almost like a second birth."

"Alexander's writing is imbued with a poetic grace shot through with an inner violence, like a shimmering piece of two-toned silk," Nair wrote. "With her gift of heightened sensibility, she can take a tragic, violent situation and juxtapose it with a description of terrible beauty." Others, like Young, have also commented on Alexander's gift for expression. "'Isms' spring to mind when discussing her work—feminism, multiculturalism, and postcolonialism," he wrote, "but these are cold, technical terms to describe writing that is so lyrical, so personal."

To some extent, Alexander cannot help but personalize issues of racism, colonialism, and sexism—her writings about "the other" are most often about herself and her life in America. Many of her works are closely linked, representing her ongoing effort to understand the cultural shifts she has gone through and her struggle to come to terms with an American identity for herself. Her earlier poems were written in French, and while her later poems are usually in English, they often contain references to Hindi and Malayalam, the languages of her childhood. "She uses her observations of the world around her, her memory and experience, to trigger self-exploration," Young wrote. Alexander still visits India almost every year and often documents these journeys and the memories they revive in her writing.

Meena Alexander has written poetry and prose for numerous publications, including the *New York Times Magazine* and *Poetry Review* and the anthologies *Contemporary Indian Poetry* (1990), *Modern Indian Poetry in English* (1991), *Charlie Chan Is Dead: Contemporary Asian-American Fiction* (1995), *Sister to Sister* (1996), and the CD–ROM series *American Journey* (1996). Her poems have been translated into Hindi, Malayalam, French, Arabic, Spanish, Italian, and German. She was the recipient of the Altrusa International Award in 1973 and a MacDowell Fellowship in 1993. She has one son, Adam Kuruvilla, and one daughter, Svati Mariam.—B.S.

SUGGESTED READING: *Amerasia Journal* p164+ Fall 1996; *The Chronicle of Higher Education* B p8+ Mar. 14, 1997, with photo; *Ms.* p71 Jan./Feb. 1994, with photo; *World Literature Today* p867 Fall 1997; *International Authors and Writers Who's Who* 15th ed., 1997/1998

SELECTED WORKS: Poetry—*The Bird's Bright Ring*, 1976; *Without Place*, 1977; *I Root My Name*, 1977; *Stone Roots*, 1980; *The Storm: A Poem in Five Parts*, 1989; *Night Scene: The Garden*, 1992; *River and Bridge*, 1995; Fiction—*Nampally Road*, 1991; *Sandhya Rosenblum*, 1996; *Manhattan Music*, 1997; Poetry and fiction—*House of a Thousand Doors*, 1988; *The Shock of Arrival: Post-Colonial Reflections*, 1996; Nonfiction—*The Poetic Self: Towards a Phenomenology of Romanticism*, 1979; *Women in Romanticism: Mary Wollstonecraft, Dorothy Wordsworth, and Mary Shelley*, 1989; *Fault Lines*, 1993; Drama—*In the Middle Earth*, 1977

Alvarez, Julia

Mar. 27, 1950– Novelist; poet

The novelist, essayist, and poet Julia Alvarez has played a major role in bringing the realities of life as a Dominican-American to literary light. Alvarez became famous for the autobiographical *How the Garcia Girls Lost Their Accents* (1991), the intertwined stories of the four Garcia sisters making their way as Dominican refugees in New York. With her next novel, *In the Time of the Butterflies* (1994), she turned to the gory last days of the Trujillo regime in the Dominican Republic. This novel is also the story of four sisters, three of whom were murdered by Trujillo's henchmen for their political activism. Their story contains "a forceful political undercurrent," as do all of Alvarez's novels, according to Jonathan Bing in *Publishers Weekly* (December 16, 1996), dealing as they do with four-daughter families in a culture of machismo. In *¡Yo!*, her 1996 novel, Alvarez returned to the lives of the Garcia sisters, exploring the impact—

revealed through various voices—of having a famous writer in the family. Alvarez is also the author of the nonfiction work *Something to Declare* (1998).

In her autobiographical statement for *World Authors 1990–1995*, Julia Alvarez, born on March 27, 1950, writes: "I grew up in the Dominican Republic in Spanish, learning English in the local American school my parents had decided to send me to. I was not a born writer. No one could sit me down to solitude and a book when there was adventure in the backyard and a tribe of women who cooked and cleaned in the complex of family houses I lived in. They were my first muses, Gladys, Rosario, Altagracia, the maids and criadas, living together at the back of the property, wearing their spirit kerchiefs, smoking their cachimbos, always good for a neat story for a curious girl who much preferred 'true' stories to my American Dick and Jane books.

"Those first ten years on the island, we were living in a bloody dictatorship; my father, already exiled once, was now back and had again become involved in the underground. We were under suspicion and living under siege. But in the way of children, I didn't think anything adults did could go wrong. All I knew was that suddenly one day we were on a plane to New York because the SIM (the Secret Police) were after my father. I was beside myself with my luckiness. I had heard from the maids that Nueva York was a magic city. I would get to see the miracle of the snow, buildings that pricked the sky with their tops, and a host of other things which heretofore had only been the province of stories.

"We arrived in New York City that August, and nothing I had been told had prepared me for the shock of America: I was silenced with astonishment. Huge buildings, doors that opened when you approached them, staircases with moving steps that did your climbing for you! All around me people were speaking in English, but not the slow, carefully enunciated English of my Dominican classroom, but gibberish, the kind of talk that I always had to strain to understand. It was like finding myself at the foot of the tower of Babel, people saying incomprehensible things all around me. What was most frightening to me, particularly as the months went by, was that I found myself losing my Spanish without yet a foothold in English. I found myself without language, without any ground to stand on at all.

"Especially once I started school, I was thrust into an unfriendly world. As the first Hispanic kid in my class, I was the Other, the kids threw stones at me, telling me to go back to where I came from; they called me names whose exact meaning I couldn't understand but whose implications were all too clear to me.

"I couldn't defend myself. I didn't know their language well enough to talk back. Their language. I determined that I would learn it to save myself. I began writing. As I sat down in the quiet solitude of the blank sheet of paper, I began to make sense

of my new life in this country. I grew older and made my life here—not here, in the United States, but here in the language; it gave me ground to stand on as I pushed away from my family and the old culture with its repressive ideas of what my role as a female should be. Words gave me a kind of psychic freedom and a tool. I could remake myself with them and create the self I was moving towards. I did not have to accept the old world mold for what my life should be as a Hispanic female. I did not have to accept the new world mold of what my life should be as an assimilated American-Hispanic minority female. I was in a sense in no man's land, no woman's land. But that no man's land is any writer's blank page. 'Language is the only homeland,' Milosz, the Czech poet and immigrant, once said. Or as Derek Walcott, also from the islands, once said in a poem about a narrator wanderer much like himself: 'I have no homeland now but imagination.'

"This duality of cultures, languages, frames of reference which at first seemed the source of so much tension was in fact the foundation of my vocation as a writer. Through the bridge of words, I connected both worlds. In fact, on paper, I created a new culture that dips into the island or the states for material and inspiration; that brings Latino characters or Latin American history into the English language; a new language that uses phrases from Spanish in my English, that applies the rhythm of my Romance native language to my adopted second language. These new kinds of combinations and possibilities are what excite me as a writer. Though I call myself a Latina writer, I think of myself more and more as a writer of the planet. Globally, we are a population on the move, subject to vast migrations due to political, economic, geographical forces. Down the road lives a family from Bosnia with children born here in Weybridge. The Palestinian family in town goes to a Mosque in Montreal and to field days in Addison. It's this richness of background and influence, this connection to more than one frame of reference, this multiculturalism—if you will—that enriches our literature and creates a new kind of humane race out of us fractious and self-promoting humans. And the stories and poems we create are what give meaning and glue to our common humanity."

Julia Alvarez attended Connecticut College and graduated from Middlebury College in 1971. She received a Master of Fine Arts degree from Syracuse University in 1975.

How the Garcia Girls Lost Their Accents, termed by some a novel and by others a collection of interwoven stories, was highly praised. Obviously autobiographical, it details the arrival in New York of the Garcia family and their four daughters. Back home in the Dominican Republic, they had been part of the oligarchy, the girls living sheltered, pampered lives until their father engaged in attempts to overthrow the dictator Rafael Trujillo. The Garcia girls, thus, are not merely immigrant children but refugees, whose experiences are different from those of people who struggled to come to America for economic reasons but similar in the sense that assimilation into American culture is a hard-won achievement for all. Donna Rifkind, in the *New York Times Book Review* (October 6, 1991), commented that Alvarez "has . . . beautifully captured the threshold experience of the new immigrant, where the past is not yet a memory and the future remains an anxious dream."

In the Time of the Butterflies is based on the true story of the Mirabal sisters of the Dominican Republic. Three of the four sisters, murdered by Trujillo's henchmen on their way back from a visit to their husbands, political prisoners of the dictator's regime, are known as *las mariposas*—the butterflies. As Roberto Gonzalez Echevarria noted in the *New York Times Book Review* (December 18, 1994), "The Mirabel sisters, already admired for their resistance to the Trujillo regime before they were murdered, became part of Dominicans' struggle for social and political justice, and the day of their death is observed in many parts of Latin America today." Gonzalez Echevarria saw *In the Time of the Butterflies* as an attempt by Alvarez to teach her American self about her roots. The events in the novel are framed by a Dominican-American's visits to the surviving sister, the keeper of the shrine. Gonzalez Echevarria pointed out that "the most convincing parts of *In the Time of the Butterflies* have to do with Dede, the survivor, and her anguished role as memorialist, which in turn becomes . . . Alvarez's role. It is here that we best understand the depths of . . . Alvarez's despair and the authenticity of her effort to represent the inner drama of her conversion to an American self."

Ilan Stavans, in the *Nation* (November 7, 1994), described the novel as "full of pathos and passion, with beautifully crafted anecdotes interstitched to create a patchwork quilt of memory and ideology. . . . Alvarez takes a decidedly unique approach: She examines the martyrdom of these three Dominican women as a gender battlefield— three brave, subversive wives crushed by a phallocentric regime." He viewed Alvarez's achievement as a linking of the old and the new, which "calls attention to the Latin American foundations of Hispanic fiction in English and dares . . . to turn the novel into a political artifact." Katherine Powers in the *Christian Science Monitor* (October 17, 1994) concurred, noting that *In the Time of the Butterflies* "succeeds magnificently. . . . It does not pretend to be a record of events, but a rendition of reality. . . . Alvarez's translation of historical events into fiction achieves . . . the nuance and irony of truth."

Alvarez continued the story of "the Garcia girls" in *¡Yo!*, another loosely structured but complex collection of narratives, this time centered on Yolanda, who has become a famous writer. Yolanda's own voice is not heard; instead she is the focus of tales told by her cousin, her husband, her landlady, her parents, servants, and other characters. "These memorable, deeply interrelated short pieces," according to Janet Ingraham in *Library Journal* (October 1, 1996), combine to "introduce many alluring vignettes for the one story they combine—uneasily and ingeniously—to complete"—the story of "the feistiest and most perplexing of the Garcia sisters." "*Yo*, of course, means 'I' in Spanish, but Alvarez has shrewdly left the self at the center of the novel absent," Jonathan Bing noted. "Yolanda isn't granted a voice in the novel. Instead, Alvarez builds the book around the memories of those who have suffered the manipulations of the budding author. The liberty a writer takes with her family and background is a subject of increasing importance to Alvarez." The writer told Bing that the invented stories in *Garcia Girls* have actually become catalysts of retrieved memories for her sisters.

Also autobiographical in part is Alvarez's collection of poems, *Homecoming: New and Collected Poems* (1996), an expanded version of an earlier volume, *Homecoming*, published in 1984. Reviewers praised the new collection, singling out in particular the section called "Housekeeping," which evokes her childhood. The *Publishers Weekly* (March 18, 1996) reviewer praised the section's "thoughtful, accessible poems." Christine Stenstrom in *Library Journal* (April 1, 1996) noted that "the daily activities of cleaning, washing, and ironing are transformed into metaphors for the female experience: domesticity as both nourishing and stifling." Alvarez compares her mother's mastery of the "high art" of "woman's work" to her own career as a writer:

> I did not want to be her counterpart!
> I struck out . . . but became my
> mother's child: a woman working at
> home on her art, housekeeping paper
> as if it were her heart.

Alvarez published her second book of poetry, *The Other Side*: *El Otro Lado*, in 1995. The title poem, in 21 cantos, is a narrative of the time Alvarez spent in a Dominican artists' colony. Feeling too cosseted in the colony, she goes off to a fishing village, where the local folk priest tells her to "Come home / to serve your santo and your own people." But instead of returning either to the village or the artists' colony, she returns to her real home and life, "a life of choice, a life of words." Philip Gambone in the *New York Times Book Review* (July 16, 1995) characterized the themes embraced in the poems as similar to those in *How the Garcia Girls Lost Their Accents*: "the 'seeing double' of biculturalism and the power of language" to draw one into the deepest recesses of consciousness.

Ilan Stavans summed up Alvarez's artistic progress: "[H]er haunting second novel easily surpasses her earlier achievement. . . . [I]t exhibits quick, solid maturing as an artist."

Alvarez's *Something to Declare*, published in 1998, is a collection of previously published essays. The book is divided into two sections—the first exploring Alvarez's experiences as a woman straddling two cultures, the second offering her feminist views. Alvarez's "warm personality shines through and keeps one reading," wrote a critic for *Kirkus Reviews* (June 15, 1998), who called the collection "a pleasing but not probing foray by the author into herself and others."

Julia Alvarez told Jonathan Bing that for 10 years, including two as a poet-in-residence for the Kentucky Arts Commission, she had been "a migrant poet" who "would go anywhere" in the country. She returned to teach English at Middlebury College, in Vermont, where she has lived since 1988. She married Bill Eichner, a surgeon, there, but spends part of every year in the Dominican Republic. She turned increasingly to the writing of fiction, rather than poetry, because, she told Bing, "I think that what's hard for me about writing poetry is that it is so naked." In 1998 Alvarez contributed a piece to *Half and Half: Writers on Growing Up Biracial and Bicultural*, a collection that also features work by Lisa See and Indira Ganesan, among others.

—S. Y.

SUGGESTED READING: *Library Journal* p102 May 1, 1991, p84 Apr. 1, 1996, p124 Oct. 1, 1996; *Nation* p552+ Nov. 7, 1994; *New York Times Book Review* p14 Oct. 6, 1991, p28 Dec. 18, 1994, p20 July 16, 1995, p19 Feb. 9, 1997; *New York Times Magazine* p 67 Mar. 23, 1997; *Publishers Weekly* p67 Mar. 18, 1996, p39 Dec. 16, 1996

SELECTED BOOKS: Fiction—*How the Garcia Girls Lost Their Accents*, 1991; *In the Time of the Butterflies*, 1994; *¡Yo!*, 1996; Poetry—*Homecoming*, 1984; *The Other Side: El Otro Lado*, 1995; *Homecoming: New and Collected Poems*, 1996; Nonfiction—*Half and Half: Writers on Growing Up Biracial and Bicultural* (with others), 1998; *Something to Declare*, 1998

George Durean/Courtesy of Simon and Schuster

Ambrose, Stephen E.

1936– Biographer; historian

The American biographer and historian Stephen E. Ambrose believes in the power of chance events to change history—and he has personal experience with this phenomenon. In 1962 Louisiana State University Press published his first book, a biography of President Abraham Lincoln's wartime chief of staff, the army general Henry W. Halleck. Ambrose recalled in a 1996 interview for *Publishers Weekly*: "I doubt they ran off a thousand copies, but one of them found its way to Dwight Eisenhower." Eisenhower, impressed with the work, called Ambrose and invited the author to visit him on his farm in Gettysburg. After an extensive conversation Eisenhower asked Ambrose—then only 28 years old and an assistant professor at the University of New Orleans—to aid in the editing of his papers and to write his authorized biography. Ambrose was shocked: "I asked Ike, 'Why me?' and he said, 'I read your book on Halleck.' He really could have knocked me over with that." Since that meeting more than 30 years ago, Ambrose has written 21 books, mostly on 20th-century American events and personalities, including multivolume works on the lives of Eisenhower and President Richard Nixon and several books on World War II. The work of a self-described hero worshiper, Ambrose's 1996 volume *Undaunted Courage* takes the reader back to the early 19th century for an account of one of the greatest adventures in American history: the exploration of the Louisiana Purchase by Meriwether Lewis and William Clark at the behest of President Thomas Jefferson. This book, like many of his others, has received generous praise since its publication. The *New York Review of Books* (April 4, 1996) article about *Undaunted Courage* read: "Ambrose has written a very readable narrative. . . . [His] judgements are shrewd and balanced. . . . If a reader knows little of the expedition and wants a solid readable account of it, then this book is a good place to begin." Ambrose's recent works include *Citizen Soldiers: The U.S. Army from the Norman-*

dy Beaches to the Bulge to the Surrender of Germany, June 7, 1944–May 7, 1945 and *Americans at War*, both published in the fall of 1997; and *Lewis & Clark: Voyage of Discovery* (1998).

Ambrose, in an autobiography written for *World Authors 1990–1995*, discusses his life and the influences on his work: "I was born in 1936 and grew up in Whitewater, Wisconsin, a small town where my father was the M.D. My high school had only 300 students but was good enough to offer two years of Latin, which taught me the centrality of verbs—placement, form, tense.

"At the University of Wisconsin, I started as a pre-med, but after a course on American history with William B. Hesseltine I switched my major. He was a great teacher of writing, with firm rules such as: abandon chronology at your peril; use the active voice; avoid adverbs whenever possible; be frugal with adjectives, as they are but the salt and pepper for the meat (nouns).

"On to LSU, where I studied for my M.A. under T. Harry Williams, another fine historian who stressed the importance of writing well. After getting my M.A. degree in 1958, I returned to Wisconsin to do my Ph.D. work under Hesseltine.

"Funny thing, Harry Williams was a much better writer than Hesseltine, but Hesseltine was the better teacher of writing. We graduate students once asked him: 'How can you demand so much from us when your own books are not all that well written?' as we confronted him with a review of one of his books that praised his research and historical understanding but deplored his writing. Hesseltine laughed and replied, 'My dear boys, you have a better teacher than I did.'

"From 1960 to 1995 [I was] a full-time teacher (University of New Orleans, Rutgers, Kansas State, Naval War College, UC Berkeley, a number of European schools, among others), something that has been invaluable to my writing. There is nothing like standing before 50 students at 8 A.M. to start talking about an event that occurred 100 years ago, because the look on their faces is a challenge—'Let's see you keep me awake.' You learn what works and what doesn't in a hurry.

"Teaching and writing are one to me: in each case I am telling a story. As I sit at my computer or stand at the podium, I think of myself as sitting around the campfire after a day on the trail, telling stories that I hope will have the members of the audience, or the readers, leaning forward just a bit, wanting to know what happens next.

"Some of the rules of writing I've developed on my own include: never try to write about a battle until you have walked the ground; when you write about politicians, keep in mind that somebody has to do it; you are a storyteller, not God, so your job is not to pass judgments but to explain, illustrate, inform, and entertain.

"The idea for a book comes in a variety of ways. I started as a Civil War historian because Hesseltine taught the Civil War. I wrote about Eisenhower because he asked me to become his biographer, on

the basis of a book I had done on Henry Halleck, Lincoln's chief of staff. I never wanted to write about Nixon, but my editor (Alice Mayhew at Simon & Schuster) made me do it by saying, 'Where else can you find a greater challenge?' I did Crazy Horse and Custer because I took my family camping in the Black Hills of South Dakota and got hooked on the country, and the topic brought me back to the Black Hills many times. I did Meriwether Lewis to have an excuse to keep returning to Montana, thus covering even more of the American West.

"My World War II books flowed out of the association with Eisenhower, along with my feelings toward the GIs. I was 10 years old when the war ended. I thought the returning veterans were giants who had saved the world from barbarism. I still think so. I remain a hero worshiper. Over the decades I've interviewed thousands of the veterans. It is a privilege to hear their stories, then write them up.

"What drives me is curiosity. I want to know how this or that was done—Lewis and Clark getting to the Pacific; the GIs on D-Day; Crazy Horse's victory over George Custer at the Little Big Horn; the making of an elite company in the 101st Airborne, and so on. And I've found that if I want to know, I've got to do the research and then write it up myself. For me, the act of writing is the act of learning.

"I'm blessed to have Moira Buckley Ambrose as my wife. She was an English Lit major and school teacher; she is an avid reader; she has a great ear. At the end of each writing day, she sits with me, and I read aloud what I've done. After more than three decades of this, I still can't dispense with requiring her first of all to say, 'That's good, that's great, way to go.' But then we get to work. We make many changes. This reading-aloud business is critical to me—I've developed an ear of my own, so I can hear myself read—as it reveals awkward passages better than anything else. If I can't read it smoothly it needs fixing.

"Hesseltine used to tell his students that the art of writing is the art of applying the seat of the pants to the seat of a chair. It is a monk's existence, the loneliest job in the world. As Moira and I have five kids (at one time all teens together; the phone in the evenings can be imagined) I started going to bed at eight to get up at four and have three quiet hours for writing before the teaching day began. The kids grew up and moved out, and I retired in May 1995, but I keep to the habit.

"I'm sometimes asked which of my books is my own favorite. My answer is whatever one I'm working on. Right now (early 1996) it is the American army in the campaign of northwest Europe, June 7, 1944 to May 7, 1945. I think the greatest achievement of the American republic in the 18th century was the army at Valley Forge; in the 19th century it was the Army of the Potomac; in the 20th century it was the U.S. Army in northwest Europe. I want to know how it was done and how that army outfought the Germans. To do a book of this scope is daunting but rewarding. I get paid for interviewing the old soldiers and reading their private memoirs. My job is to pick out the best one of every 50 or so stories and pass it along to readers, along with commentary on what it illustrates and teaches. It is a wonderful way to make a living."

In 1970, after Doubleday published his first volume on Eisenhower—*The Supreme Commander: The War Years of General Dwight D. Eisenhower*—Ambrose became full professor at the University of New Orleans. He subsequently published two more volumes on Eisenhower before his editor at Doubleday, John Ware, left to form his own literary agency. Ambrose went with Ware, who immediately set up an auction for his next book—the winner being the vice president and editorial director of Simon & Schuster, Alice E. Mayhew. Ambrose has had a good working relationship with Mayhew for many years and has long since dismissed his literary agent in favor of negotiating his contracts personally.

Mayhew was the inspiration behind what Ambrose called "the biggest surprise of [his] whole writing career." As he states in his autobiography, she asked him to consider writing a definitive biography of Richard Nixon, which had never been attempted. Ambrose had never been an admirer of Nixon. In fact, in 1969, when the Vietnam War was at its peak and the author was teaching at Kansas State, Nixon—then president—went to speak at the university; Ambrose was asked to leave after he and his wife heckled Nixon with shouts of "Napalm!" In Mayhew's opinion, Ambrose's animosity toward Nixon made him the perfect person to undertake the biography.

Ambrose, who first told Mayhew, "I don't want to spend five years with that son of a bitch," was finally persuaded by his editor to do the Nixon biography. The result was a three-volume, critically acclaimed work comprising *Nixon: The Education of a Politician 1913–1962* (1987), *Nixon: The Triumph of a Politician 1962–1972* (1989), and *Nixon: The Ruin and Recovery of a Politician 1973–1990* (1991). Ambrose has said that while he still has a low opinion of Nixon, whom he met only after the three books were written, he has developed a respect for some of Nixon's accomplishments. Owing to both this newfound respect and his role as a historian, he has expressed his objections to recent indictments of Nixon, including the director Oliver Stone's 1995 film version of the politician's life. "If Stone wants to say this [movie] is history," Ambrose has said, "then damn it, he has an obligation to honor the integrity of the past."

An unabashed admirer of great figures in American history, Ambrose also supports those he believes will be great figures in the future—including the former Joint Chiefs of Staff chairman Colin Powell. Ambrose, according to the *New Yorker* (October 9, 1995), first heard of Powell in the late 1970s, when the latter was one of a group of army officers trying to boost the morale of the Unite States Army after the Vietnam War. The biographer's first personal contact with the general came in 1992, when Powell sent him a letter expressing how much he had enjoyed Ambrose's book *Band of Brothers*—the story of an elite parachute unit in World War II. That letter began a correspondence between the two men that intensified in 1995, when Ambrose began sending Powell weekly letters urging him to run for the presidency in 1996. Ambrose explained in his interview with the *New Yorker*: "I told him I wouldn't stop until he told me no. And he hasn't told me no." Though Powell did not then seek the presidency, Ambrose maintains his admiration for the general, likening him in many ways to Eisenhower.

Ambrose continues to write about history, publishing *D-Day: June 6, 1944: The Climactic Battle of World War II* (1994) to coincide with the 50th anniversary of the invasion. *Publishers Weekly* (November 7, 1994) stated that Ambrose's account of those events was "unsurpassed in detail, emotion, and suspense." The *Library Journal* (May 1, 1994) reviewer found that "Ambrose has updated the familiar story of the massive amphibious landings with new information, deft historical perspective, and a gripping narrative."

In 1996, after 20 years of retracing the Lewis and Clark trail across the country with his family, Ambrose published his account of those explorers' journey in his best-selling, well-received biography of Meriwether Lewis, *Undaunted Courage: Meriwether Lewis, Thomas Jefferson and the Opening of the American West*. In his introduction, he wrote: "This book has been a labor of love. . . . The Lewis and Clark experience has brought us together so many times in so many places that we cannot measure or express what it has meant to our marriage and our family." Ambrose interwove his family's reactions to retracing the adventurers' steps in a shorter narrative written for *Lewis & Clark: Voyage of Discovery* (1998), a coffee-table book featuring the work of *National Geographic* photographer Sam Abell. Evaluating the work for *Booklist* (September 15, 1998), Gilbert Taylor wrote, "Ambrose, drawing on his hikes and canoe trips to all the monuments between St. Louis and Fort Clatsop associated with the explorers, melds his memories and own journal entries with a new Lewis and Clark narrative spiced by entries from their journals. Akin to religious pilgrims, Ambrose and companions (including Dayton Duncan and film producer Ken Burns) often re-read passages from those journals at the locale an entry was written, allowing Ambrose to comment on the place's contemporary appearance, whether pristine (Gates of the Rocky Mountains), or altered (the dammed-up Missouri River). . . . Ambrose remarks that his obsession changed his life, and surely his travelogue/tribute will change the vacation plans of some readers as well."

The focus of *Citizen Soldiers: The U.S. Army from the Normandy Beaches to the Bulge to the Surrender of Germany, June 7, 1944–May 7, 1945* is the experience of ordinary enlisted men in the U.S. Army in World War II. As a press release from the book's publisher, Simon & Schuster, read: "The campaign in northwest Europe, 1944–45, was . . . a critical test of many things, including tactics and weapons, supply lines, the skill of generals, and the proper deployment of air power. Yet above all else, Ambrose contends, it was a test of how well America had succeeded in creating an army of citizen soldiers from scratch." The novelist Joseph Heller, in one of several glowing prepublication blurbs for the book, called *Citizen Soldiers* "just about the most gripping account of the Second World War that I have ever read."

As part of what *Publishers Weekly* (September 8, 1997) termed "an outpouring of Ambrosia" in the fall of 1997, the University Press of Mississippi published *Americans at War*, a collection of 15 essays that span Ambrose's career. The subjects of these pieces range from a discussion of the atomic bomb to profiles of army generals Custer, Mac-Arthur, and Patton to speculation about the future of war. The *Publishers Weekly* critic termed the book "a précis of a brilliant career." In the fall of 1997 Ambrose also unveiled *The American Heritage New History of World War II*, his revised and updated version of C. L. Sulzberger's 1966 work.

Stephen E. Ambrose and his wife, Moira, have five children: Stephanie, Barry, Andy, Grace, and Hugh. He divides his time between Bay St. Louis, Mississippi, and Helena, Montana. He is the founder of the Eisenhower Center and president of the National D-Day Museum in New Orleans.
—C.M.

SUGGESTED READING: *Booklist* Sep. 15, 1998; *Publishers Weekly* p41 Nov. 7, 1994, p50+ Jan. 22, 1996, Sep. 8, 1997; *Library Journal* p119 May 1, 1994; *Newsweek* p34 Sep. 11, 1995; *New Yorker* p31 Oct. 9, 1995; *New York Review of Books* p18+ Apr. 4, 1996; *New York Times Book Review* p9+ Mar. 10, 1996

SELECTED BOOKS: *Halleck: Lincoln's Chief of Staff*, 1962; *The Supreme Commander: The War Years of General Dwight D. Eisenhower*, 1970; *Nixon: The Education of a Politician 1913–1962*, 1987; *Nixon: The Triumph of a Politician 1962–1972*, 1989; *Nixon: Ruin and Recovery 1973–1990*, 1991; *D-Day: June 6, 1994: The Climactic Battle of World War II*, 1994; *Undaunted Courage: Meriwether Lewis, Thomas Jefferson and the Opening of the American West*, 1996; *Citizen Soldiers: The U.S. Army from the Normandy Beaches to the Bulge to the Surrender of Germany, June 7, 1944–May 7, 1945*, 1997; *Americans at War*, 1997; *The American Heritage New History of World War II*, 1997; *Lewis & Clark: Voyage of Discovery*, 1998

Antoni, Robert

May 7, 1958– Novelist

More than 200 years ago, Robert Antoni's ancestors settled in the British colony that is now the island nation of Trinidad and Tobago. In his novels *Divina Trace* (1992) and *Blessed Is the Fruit* (1997), Antoni has created a cosmogony for the postcolonial West Indies that embraces multicultural myths, religion, political and economic history, and social analysis, all filtered through the colorful dialect of his characters. Pregnancy and birth are recurring themes—an implication, perhaps, that his Caribbean world is in the process of rebirth.

Robert Antoni submitted the following autobiographical statement to *World Authors 1990–1995*: "I was born in the United States while my father attended medical school, but my parents come from the West Indian island of Trinidad, where our family history goes back over two hundred years. When I was two we moved to Freeport, Bahamas, where I grew up. I carry three passports: US, Trinidad and Tobago, and the Bahamas. I come from a family of artists: my brother Brian is also an author, and my sister Janine is a conceptual artist and sculptor.

"Believing that it was my fate to follow in my father's footsteps, I completed all of the science courses required for medical school at Duke University. But when I returned home to the Bahamas in the summer following my junior year, I had a critical water-skiing accident; I skied into a boulder wall, suffering a profound concussion, which left me unconscious for a week and hospitalized in intensive care for a month. I have no memory recall of that month, but when I 'woke up' I said that I wanted to become a writer. I was 21 years of age, and I had scarcely read a novel; my interests had always been the sciences. When I returned to Duke I switched to an English major (I remained an extra year in order to complete it), and I began reading and writing for the first time. I have never looked back.

"After Duke I went to the Writing Seminars at Johns Hopkins for an MA degree, then to the Writers' Workshop at the University of Iowa, where I completed an M.F.A. and a Ph.D. I have attended more creative writing workshops than probably anybody, and I am now a professor at the University of Miami where I teach my own writing workshops to graduates and undergraduates, in addition to literature classes.

"From my very first attempts to write I discovered that despite any lack of a literary background, I was privileged to have a rich oral tradition of storytelling upon which to draw. Growing up in the Bahamas, I lived in the same home with a grandmother from one side and a grandfather from the other. In those days there was no television or movie theater, no library or bookstore; our evening's entertainment was listening to stories, primarily my grandparents' and parents' stories of settling in

Trinidad. All of those oral tales continue to provide the inspiration and the subject matter for my own stories.

"My fictional world is the island of Corpus Christi, which in some ways resembles Trinidad, but could be any West Indian island. I consider myself profoundly Caribbean, and all of my writing belongs profoundly to the region. This in no way excludes my alliance to the United States; for me, to be Caribbean is to embrace my hybrid self, my multiple ethnicities and languages. I can trace my heritage to America, Europe (England, Spain, France, Italy, Germany), to Africa and Asia. They all flow in my veins, and I claim them all—fiercely. My on-going project as a prose writer is to discover hybrid literary forms which live up to my hybrid Caribbean reality.

"In *Divina Trace* (winner of the 1992 Commonwealth Prize for Best First Book) there are seven narrators, each speaking a distinct Caribbean dialect, each representing a different ethnic group. They are all telling the story of Magdalena Divina, represented later in the novel by a mysterious black Madonna (based on La Divina Pastora, a black Madonna kept in the Catholic Church in Siparia, an East Indian village in southern Trinidad). What becomes clear is that in addition to Magdalena's story, each of the narrators is telling their individual story, as well as the saga of the Domingo family to which they belong.

"But near the middle of the book the black Madonna comes to life, and she tells the reader her own version. Magdalena, however, represents the East Indian element in the novel, and she tells her story as a retelling of the *Ramayana* (the love story of Rama and Sita, oldest and most popular of the Hindu myths). Then, in the very center of the novel, I (as author) take over from Magdalena in the voice of Hanuman, the monkey god, who tells his tale of the monkey tribes (in the *Ramayana* it is the counter-plot and a retelling of the main story). I tell Hanuman's tale in my own invented monkey language, consisting of hundreds of species of monkeys and prehistoric apes, all the proponents and detractors of evolutionary theory—as well as references to the Bible, Freud, Joyce, Faulkner, García Márquez, and everything else I could manage to throw into it. It only goes on for a dozen pages, and I like to warn [prospective] readers that it is meant to be played with, not puzzled over. Of course, the final version of Magdalena's story, this story of the Caribbean, belongs to the reader.

"My second novel, *Blessed Is the Fruit*, is told in the voices of two 33-year-old West Indian women: Lilla, mistress of a once grand Colonial mansion which is rotting and falling down around her, and her black servant Vel, who has come to live with her, seeking refuge from her poor village. These two women have been abandoned by their husbands and the rest of the world. They have been living together for 10 years when (due to a series of incidents outside of her control) Vel finds herself pregnant. Fearing that should Lilla discover the pregnancy she will send her home, back to the poverty from which she came, Vel 'binds her belly' and makes several attempts to abort the child—from the pharmacist's drugs, to bush medicine and obeah magic. After one last fierce and brutal attempt, Lilla discovers her wounded; she carries her upstairs to her own room, lays Vel in her own bed, and ministers to her.

"From this quiet place the novel begins and ends as Lilla and Vel tell their stories to this unborn child. They call the child Bolom, a character from Caribbean folklore: the mythical unborn child struggling for life, destined to die before its birth. This Bolom, however, will live. And it is through the course of the novel that both women discover how much they need and love one another, and they come to accept responsibility for this child of the Caribbean as their own. It is through the course of the novel that the reader integrates these two parallel stories that history and prejudice and privilege have kept carefully separate, shattering the metaphorical pane of glass that prevents Lilla and Vel from embracing each other.

"In addition to my novels, I have published short stories in the *Paris Review*, *Ploughshares*, *Missouri Review* and other periodicals. I am a frequent contributor and a senior editor to the literary journal *Conjunctions*. Together with Bradford Morrow I edited a special issue of *Conjunctions* titled *Archipelago*, the first anthology to collect three generations of Caribbean writers from the regions' three major languages. My travel stories appear regularly in *Outside* magazine. I have recently been included in Faber and Faber' s Caribbean Series (London, England), with editions of *Blessed Is the Fruit* and *Divina Grace* forthcoming, as well as a new novel, *My Grandmother's Erotic Folktales and Stories of Adventure with Occasional Orgies in Her Boardinghouse for American Soldiers During the War, Including Her Confrontations with the Kentucky Colonel, the Tanzanian Devil and the King of Chacachacari* (the title, I believe, is self-explanatory).

"Together with Miami and the Caribbean, I spend several months a year in Barcelona, Spain, my wife's home, writing in the shadow of Christopher Columbus at the end of the Ramblas. We have a two-year-old son, Gabriel, named after the angel."

In *Divina Trace*, Antoni sought to create a multicultural cosmogony for the small island of Corpus Christi, which, because of the harmony in which its people live, is a kind of earthly paradise. The tale of the eerie appearance of Magdalena Divina, in some narratives a 15-year-old and in others a 13-year-old, has elements of African-derived Obeah, Roman Catholicism, and Hinduism, depending on who among the novel's characters is telling it. Sometimes Magdalena becomes a walking statue; sometimes she is a kind of rag doll; and sometimes her story is an explanation for a statue of a "Black Madonna" brought from Europe hundreds of years before.

The story's main narrator is Johnny Domingo, now 90 years old. Magdalena eventually appears to Johnny and tells him the story herself. Up to now the reader has been carried along in a more or less recognizably Caribbean fashion, by characters who speak in dialects of varying thickness. Suddenly the reader is dropped into a quite different perspective, which, although narrated in the thickest of Caribbean dialect, is presented in verse and reflects an East Indian worldview. It is, in a way, a parody of the *Ramayana* mixed with elements of Catholicism and some of the legends of the Warrahoon, indigenous people who have migrated to the island from the South American mainland. In the middle of this passage comes a narrative from Hanuman, the monkey god, in which Antoni satirizes postmodernism, structuralism, feminism, and deconstructionism:

> Is now Sugriva vervet, is now he cromagnum, redhowler you hot: "Boy, you ga chisel fa dis de whole of you strife and breath! Aye commission you pietà, a great stonestatue, michelangelo fa me potto mausoleum. Monument it proboscis, lemurlike, poststructural. Monument it of feminist francosimarbre. Monument it of Luce, Kristeva, Cixous—Beauvoir as me potto black mummy!"

Gustavo Pérez-Firmat, reviewing the novel in the *Washington Post* (February 2, 1992), felt that although "this is the kind of writing that sends graduate students into fits of ecstasy (intertextuality! polyphony! heteroglossia!), it's difficult to say how many others will be willing to plow through the novel's 'mudthick-mudswamp of monkeylanguage.'" One of the dominant images in the novel is that of the callaloo, a West Indian melange of diverse ingredients. "Since the Caribbean is itself a callaloo of races and cultures, the archipelago may indeed require a similarly heterogenous rendering. But the ingredients do need to be compatible," Pérez-Firmat added. He concluded that the "fundamental problem may be that *Divina Trace* proceeds from the conviction . . . that the Caribbean is an exceptional space, the theater for the unfolding of what Alejo Carpentier termed 'marvelous American reality.' But the Caribbean is not out of this world."

The *Kirkus* (December 1, 1991) reviewer had much the same attitude, commenting that "a reader . . . eventually just feels buried" in the language that delineates "the swollen diameter of Antoni's mythic purpose, when in fact all he has to tell is a small story."

Blessed Is the Fruit (1997), Antoni's second novel, also takes place in Corpus Christi. It differs from *Divina Trace* chiefly in its more realistic approach, but both novels center on a theme of pregnancy and childbirth. In *Blessed Is the Fruit*, Vel's attempt to abort her fetus leads Lilla to nurse her back to health and draws the two women closer, as they await the birth of "Bolom," to whom they address their stories. Lilla has been living a life of despair and loneliness since she was abandoned by her husband, but the act of saving the child's life gives her renewed hope. Vel, who had tried to abort the child because she feared it would die like all her previous babies or have nothing to look forward to but starvation, is also given new hope. Assured that she and the child will live, she finds she is able to face the future, which she imagines thus:

> Convert this big old house in a boarding-home for women. Women, or women with children that ain't got no father, no husband. And we could serve the meals in the dining room at the big dining table, cause that table plenty big enough, and we already got all the silvers and all the chinas that we could need. Tea could serve afternoons in the parlour-room. And Bolom, we could *dance* too! Oh, yes! We could host the dances pon evenings for we guests in the boarding-home.

The two women's lives interweave more tightly as the barriers of race and class that might have separated them evaporate. Critical responses to *Blessed Is the Fruit* were generally favorable. "Antoni attempts to give life to the historical forces that mold the soul of a nation—in this case the postcolonial West Indies," June Vigor wrote in *Booklist* (March 15, 1997). "Antoni hits all his notes with lyrical precision," she concluded. "The lilting patois of the islands, both Lilla's white colonial and Vel's 'local,' offers the reader not a language barrier, but a bridge; it's a language of the heart that's as direct and infectious as a calypso beat."

Justine Elias in the *New York Times Book Review* (July 20, 1997) termed the novel's two voices "a fugue of overlapping memories. . . . Vel's acute observations of island life are filtered through Lilla's hazy comprehension of the world around her. But even when the tale becomes wildly overcooked, Antoni's lyrical, incantatory prose vividly evokes a world of soul-crippling repression and forbidden desires."

In *Divina Trace*, when Johnny Domingo asks his grandfather, Papee Vince, why their home had no books of stories, only books of facts, Papee Vince answers, "I suppose we have so many of we own stories to tell, so many of we own stories to hear out, we never found the time to look fa no others." Johnny protests, "But what about *our* books? *Our* Literature?" Papee Vince points out that no one would want to "read out a story dead, that they could hear in a hundred different *living* versions," and he adds, "you have to know youself pretty good before you can write out any storybooks, and that is something we are only now beginning to learn." He concludes that "you never truly grow up until the death of you second parent. Whether that death is natural, psychological, or the result of bloody murder. Only then can you come to know youself. And in fact, we only just finish matriciding we mummy-England the other day." Antoni's self-appointed task seems to be to catch up with the storytelling that needs to be done since "the other day."

—S. Y.

SUGGESTED READING: *Booklist* p1226 Mar. 15, 1997; *New York Times Book Review* p20 July 20, 1997; *Washington Post Book World* p9 Feb. 2, 1992

SELECTED BOOKS: *Divina Trace*, 1992; *Blessed Is the Fruit*, 1997

Mark Gerson

Apter, Terri

1950(?)– Nonfiction writer; social psychologist

Terri Apter, a social psychologist affiliated with Cambridge University, has spent much of her life (and all of her life as a published author) attempting to debunk the societal myths associated with women, particularly those regarding the bonds between mother and daughter, successful women in the workplace, and aging. Each of her books has challenged long-held misconceptions about women and has received very good reviews in American newspapers and periodicals. As a psychologist, Apter conducts interviews with scores of women to support her theories. She has studied the psychological stages of women's lives as well as their biological phases, and the results have been surprising—for example, many more women are comfortable with their identities after midlife than was previously supposed. Many of her books—which include *Altered Loves: Mothers and Daughters During Adolescence* (1991), *Working

Women Don't Have Wives: Professional Success in the 1990s (1994), *Secret Paths: Women in the New Midlife* (1995), and *Best Friends: The Pleasures and Perils of Girls' and Women's Friendships* (1998)—paint a much more optimistic picture of female development than has been generally accepted. Apter is a fellow of Clare Hall at Cambridge University, from which she received her Ph.D. and where she writes and lectures about various topics in social psychology. She is also a regular guest on BBC radio as Radio Cambridgeshire's "resident psychologist."

In her autobiography for *World Authors 1990–1995*, Terri Apter, born in about 1950, writes: "I was born in Chicago, the daughter of two physicians: my father was a psychoanalyst and my mother was an ophthalmologist. I enjoyed, in many ways, a stable upbringing in a caring and educated family. For a variety of reasons, however, I was engaged in debilitating psychological dramas which drained me emotionally and intellectually. As a result, I had odd and unsatisfactory relationships with friends, who rapidly realized that other children were more interesting, and with teachers, who were bemused both by the high expectations they (baselessly) had of me and by my persistence in achieving something well below average. I was also bewildered by racial and religious divisions so clearly marked in that city: lacking the courage to explore and understand my urban surroundings, I became a homebody, however constricting I found that home.

"What I lacked and what I craved was a psychological privacy, or an intimacy devoid of analysis and criticism. I felt cramped by the prevailing assumption that my mental processes were the narrative property of an expert. I also felt hedged in by the fact that I was held morally responsible not only for my voluntary behavior, but also for those unconscious motives revealed by accidents and mistakes. Who I was and what I was, seemed determinable by psychoanalytic theory, rather than discoverable through my own experience.

"Throughout my childhood, I had enormous support from my sister, from whom I learned the power of a child's humor and resistance. Together we developed a counter-narrative to our parents' expert analyses of us and the people we knew. In adolescence I discovered the great English and Russian novelists and learned that there was a way out of the psychoanalytic narrative—that great writers could portray a highly specific story that had warmth and generosity, as well as acuity. While other critics were excited by the ways in which psychoanalytic theory could be rediscovered within fictional texts, I found them a refuge from dogma. I was also enchanted by the critical tone of the English novelists and found their astute social criticism and amusement at others' certainties a liberation. The layered, multifaceted, and flexible intelligence of writers such as Jane Austen, Emily Brontë, and George Eliot was, for me, like a magical cure for asthma: it provided a clean-air verbal space, in contrast to the rigid principles of the human mind I (undoubtedly wrongly) interpreted as the prevailing assumptions of the adults closest to me. I hoped to join their ranks and published two novels in my early adulthood, but the dense social and psychological texture which so enchanted me in others' fiction, eluded my own. I turned to literary criticism, which gave me the opportunity to explore the techniques of those soul-saving writers.

"Any early awareness of the women's movement was numbed by my misguided assumption that I had already marched through it. My mother, who came of age in the 1940s, was a firm resister of the feminine mystique: she was a career woman, forever active, forever setting herself new goals in what was then masculine terrain. She was far ahead of her time in her awareness that women had a variety of needs, that the role of housewife and mother was unlikely to fulfill these needs, and that they were impeded from taking equal place alongside men partly because men feared their sexuality. As a result of this maternally generated head start in feminism, I thought I had little in common with women who were still fighting feminine stereotypes. When I had children of my own, however, the conflicting structures in my domestic life and the working world turned what had once been a simple trajectory into a maze. *Working Women Don't Have Wives* explores the continuing contradictions of professional women's efforts to mother children in an employment structure that has developed when workers have been serviced by wives. The experience of motherhood also pushed me to reconsider the mother-daughter relationship: no longer was rampant criticism of the mother quite so comforting. This powerful relationship also focused my growing sense of community with other women, and I hoped to see a variety of family interactions, especially during that complex time of adolescence. *Altered Loves: Mothers and Daughters During Adolescence* brought the subjectivity of both parent and child into focus, and brought me back to a previous enemy—psychology. Though I now write as a psychologist, I have retained an aversion to theories which so often silence the individual's own story of her experience, and I retain the conviction that the expert is the interviewee, not the interviewer. *Secret Paths: Women in the New Midlife* is an attempt to bring to life the experience of women's maturity and their resistance to stereotypes and stagnation. My aim is to highlight people's psychological efforts and catch their creativity and courage in action."

In *Altered Loves* Apter expressed the view that mothers and daughters have a much more intimate relationship than had previously been theorized. (The original psychological theory was that mothers and daughters were jealous and resentful of each other.) Apter described the mother-daughter relationship in more of an optimistic light, stating:

"It is a two-way umbilical cord through life." She believes that in the daughter there is a basic identification with the mother—and that there is a common bond of femininity between them that distinguishes the mother-daughter relationship from all other familial ones. One of the great fears among daughters, she concluded, is that they are "preprogramed" to be just like their mothers. Apter, however, sees this usually negative aspect of mother-daughter relationships much more positively: "Here is someone [the mother] who is always there for you, supportive and all loving." During her study of mothers and daughters, Apter discovered that even women in their 30s and 40s felt orphaned after the deaths of their mothers.

Apter's next book, *Working Women Don't Have Wives*, published in 1994, confronts the issue of women in the workplace. As she had in writing her previous work, Apter interviewed a large number of women, this time about their professions and their families. Most of the women Apter interviewed had been educated in the 1970s or afterward and had assumed that they could balance high-powered careers and families—only to discover that they could not. According to a review of Apter's book in the *New York Times Book Review* (January 30, 1994), "Most [of the women interviewed] discovered that they did not want those careers after all, or that they could not have them if they wanted families as well. With money and education no object, many simply quit." Apter believes that most women want and need economic stability and independence in order to feel like adults, yet also wish they had the time to be good mothers to their children. Though the pursuit of both goals is reasonable, only men are usually able to achieve both, more than likely, Apter concluded, because they have wives to "take responsibility for family maintenance" while women do not.

For *Secret Paths* (1995), Apter interviewed a group of women entering middle age and presented the thesis that women come into a renewed sense of self in the second half of their lives, instead of entering a period of despair, an idea that had previously been promulgated. According to the *Washington Post Book World* (August 13, 1995), "Apter engagingly outlines the steps these women went through as they disentangled themselves from previous lives and set new goals, often making tradeoffs that led them away from a comfortable lifestyle or long-held career plans." Susan Dundon wrote in the *New York Times Book Review* (June 25, 1995) that Apter, in *Secret Paths,* was able to produce "insightful passages on the balance of power as it shifts in midlife marriages; on love and disengagement in the relationship between midlife women and their mothers; and on the nature of love and experience as they apply to women at this time of their lives." Apter sees the woman in midlife as someone who is maturing psychologically. Once a woman gets past the series of compromises she may have had to negotiate during the first half of her life, she enters the second with a sense of her own determination, power, and independence.

In *The Confident Child: Raising a Child to Try, Learn, and Care* (1997), Apter outlines parental strategies for instilling confidence in their children by building self-esteem, reinforcing problem-solving abilities, and teaching their children how to interact with and understand others. Drawing on Daniel Goleman's concept of "emotional intelligence" as well as on her own five-year study of children between the ages of five and 15, Apter explains how parents, through a technique she calls "emotional coaching," can nurture children's self-esteem by responding appropriately to their emotions. In addition, Apter maintains, it is important for parents to help children learn to manage their own emotions in appropriate ways. The paperback edition, published in 1998, is entitled *The Confident Child: Raising Children to Believe in Themselves: A Practical, Compassionate Guide.*

Apter's most recent work weds her experience with women's development to her research on the inner lives of children. In *Best Friends: The Pleasures and Perils of Girls' and Women's Friendships,* she and coauthor Ruthellen Josselson, a practicing psychotherapist, seek to restore the central role of same-sex friendships in understanding not only women's development during adolescence but also their lifelong efforts to build, maintain, or restore self-esteem, their shifting approaches to confrontation and intimacy, and their changing definitions of self. Through numerous anecdotes the authors address the enduring impact on girls' self-images of their early experiences of betrayal and deceit, loyalty and intimacy, jealousy and envy, and admiration and empathy. How a girl negotiates the path between the extremes of cruelty and loving support that female friendships can provide during adolescence often plays a role in determining the habits and patterns she may fall prey to in later life, the authors suggest; therefore, understanding these issues is crucial to healthy development because it gives women the opportunity to change, grow, and enhance their current and future friendships.

Terri Apter lives in Cambridge, England, with her husband and two daughters.
—C.M.

SUGGESTED READING: *New York Times Book Review* p9 July 1, 1990, p14 Jan. 30, 1994, p16 June 25, 1995; *Washington Post Book World* p6 Aug. 13, 1995

SELECTED BOOKS: *Altered Loves: Mothers and Daughters During Adolescence*, 1991; *Working Women Don't Have Wives: Professional Success in the 1990s*, 1994; *Secret Paths: Women in the New Midlife*, 1995; *The Confident Child: Raising a Child to Try, Learn, and Care,* 1997; with Ruthellen Josselson—*Best Friends: The Pleasures and Perils of Girls' and Women's Friendships,* 1990

Miriam Berkley

Bair, Deirdre

1935– Biographer

Deirdre Bair is a biographer who delves deeply into the lives of her subjects. Having started out as a cultural journalist, she returned to school after she had become a wife and a mother, completing her Ph.D. degree at Columbia University and converting her doctoral thesis into a full-fledged biography of Samuel Beckett, which was published in 1978. While working on the book, she began teaching at the University of Pennsylvania in Philadelphia. Since leaving the university, she has published two more biographies—on Simone de Beauvoir and Anaïs Nin, published in 1990 and 1995, respectively. Each of these works is an exhaustively detailed study of its subject's family life, sexuality, and literary legacy. Bair provides "warts and all" portraits of her subjects that occasionally deflate their legends, and she reveals autobiographical elements in their work; most of all, however, she humanizes her subjects. Whether tackling the effects of the political situation in Ireland on Beckett's writing, Beauvoir's feminism and her relationship with Jean-Paul Sartre, or Nin's contributions to literature, Bair links these authors' lives to their work with intelligence and skill.

In her autobiography for *World Authors 1990–1995*, Bair, born in 1935, writes: "I grew up in a household of readers, the oldest of three children, in a small town just outside Pittsburgh, Pennsylvania. My parents tell me that at the age of four I announced that I would become Brenda Starr and therefore needed a typewriter to start my own newspaper. I began my professional writing life as a journalist during my last two years of high school and throughout my undergraduate study at the University of Pennsylvania. I worked for a succession of newspapers doing everything from proofreading, to writing exposes of local school and zoning boards, and (my favorite) interviewing visiting writers. Literary journalism soon became my chosen profession, but in those days (1960s) when women were on staff at all, they were usually relegated to the beats none of the men wanted.

"As I had married young (21) and had my first child a year later (a son, followed shortly by a daughter), I soon realized that a workday starting with the police blotter at 6 a.m. and finishing with the Zoning Board of Appeals at midnight was incompatible with a happy family life. At the age of 30, suffering from severe burnout, I changed careers.

"I was selected for the first class at Columbia University's School of the Arts, a two-year program in nonfiction leading to a Master of Fine Arts degree. This was the autumn before the 1968 upheavals that rocked the campus, and as I was commuting to New York from my home in Connecticut, I decided that the most expedient course of action would be to transfer to the Graduate Faculties, get a one-year Master of Arts degree, and then return to some form of literary journalism. However, I found myself entranced by the luxury of time to read, think, and talk about literature, and I knew I had to find a way to continue on to the Ph.D. This was made possible when I was selected for the Danforth Foundation's innovative program of Graduate Fellowships for Women, which give us necessary support to pursue advanced degrees as swiftly as possible so that we might become a scholarly presence on college and university campuses throughout the country.

"I received a Ph.D. in English and Comparative Literature from Columbia in 1972, but I made the conscious decision not to seek a teaching position because I knew that I wanted to expand my doctoral dissertation into a full-scale biography of Samuel Beckett. I also knew that in the waning days of New Criticism and the waxing years of the supremacy of abstract literary theory, biography was anathema: when I announced to a prospective department that I was writing one, I probably wouldn't be hired anyway.

"For the next six years, I worked at part-time teaching and freelance writing to support the research for the book that became the first biography of Samuel Beckett. Only then did I become a university professor, a tenured position that I held from 1976–88. I resigned when I realized that dedicated good teaching was, for me at least, incompatible with the swift completion of scholarship.

"I am primarily interested in our contemporary culture. I'm curious about who we are and how we got to be this way, and so I have focused on biography. In particular, I wanted to write about people whose lives and work contributed to changes in our culture and society. Beckett's plays revolutionized theater; Simone de Beauvoir's *The Second Sex* changed the lives of half the human race throughout the world; Anaïs Nin's views of woman's erotic life had a major impact on the burgeoning woman's movement in the 1970s; and C. G. Jung (the subject of my present research) is certainly one of the most influential figures of our time.

"I don't write fiction because quite frankly, I don't really like to write about myself, my family, and friends, and that's what it usually becomes. I do, however, write about a great variety of subjects, everything from travel to baseball, my minor passions.

"I have been told that I am a curious anomaly: the biographer who studies the lives of others but does not want very much to be known about herself. So I will end this essay with a formal statement about myself from a book jacket, which I think is quite enough: 'Deirdre Bair is the author of the biographies *Samuel Beckett*, winner of the National Book Award; *Simone de Beauvoir*, a *New York Times* "Best Book of the Year" and a finalist for the *Los Angeles Times* Book Prize; *Anaïs Nin*, a *New York Times* "Notable Book of the Year"; and the forthcoming *C. G. Jung*. She has been a literary journalist and tenured university professor with a specialty in contemporary comparative literature and culture, and has held fellowships from (among others) the John Simon Guggenheim Foundation, the Rockefeller Foundation, and the Mary Ingraham Bunting Institute of Radcliffe College. She has participated in international scholarly congresses and writers' institutes in the United States, Europe, and Australia. She writes and lectures on a wide variety of subjects ranging from literary biography to intellectual history, popular culture and feminist studies.'"

Deirdre Bair was married and a mother in the 1950s, in an era when fewer women worked outside the home. She told *Publishers Weekly* (April 13, 1990) that her involvement in journalism began out of necessity: "My husband [Lavon H. Bair] was in the navy and never home, so I was both mother and father to our children [Von Scott and Katherine Tracy]. I worked as a journalist, because a navy salary simply wasn't enough to live on. Then my husband went to graduate school, and I worked full-time to support us." This early experience of self-determination paved the way for her return to school at the then-advanced age of 30. When it came time for her to develop her doctoral thesis into *Samuel Beckett: A Biography* (1978), Bair's boldness helped her gain access to the standoffish Beckett, who had guarded the details of his life obsessively. She wrote him a letter stating that she would like to meet him, and when she finally did, she bluntly told him that she needed access to all his personal effects. As she explained to Wendy Smith of *Publishers Weekly*: "I think he may have been so stunned by the request that he said, 'All right!' I didn't have the problems so many biographers do; everything was available to me, and the permission to use it was there from the beginning."

While many critics applauded *Samuel Beckett: A Biography*, there was a vocal minority who complained that Bair had strained too much to find autobiographical details in Beckett's work. Benjamin DeMott, for example, wrote in the *Atlantic* (July 1978), "It's better to have been over-humanized, if you're an abstractionist, than never have been humanized at all." Most assessments were quite favorable, however. A reviewer for *Newsweek* (June 5, 1978) marveled: "So out of nowhere, this unknown English teacher at the University of Pennsylvania has produced what has to be the one indispensable book on Beckett." The *Library Journal* (June 15, 1978) reviewer was amazed at the extent to which the biographer had fleshed out Beckett's character, remarking: "Bair makes us marvel at the creative process and have compassion for the maker."

During a conversation over lunch in Boston with her friend Richard McDonough, Bair remarked that she would like to write about an independent woman for her next biography. Considering the number of women Bair knew in the 1960s and 1970s who were being told they could "have it all"—careers and romance—but were finding that they couldn't, she asked McDonough if there had ever been a woman who had "had it all." As they threw out names, one of them mentioned Simone de Beauvoir, the great French feminist philosopher and intellectual, who had spent 50 years in an open relationship with the French existentialist Jean-Paul Sartre. Bair knew in an instant that Beauvoir was the perfect subject.

When in 1981 Bair talked to Simone de Beauvoir about writing her biography, she found that Beauvoir raised many more stipulations than had Beckett. Bair stated simply that she had not worked with Beckett that way and was not prepared to make concessions to Beauvoir; Beauvoir then agreed to give Bair all the information she needed. Bair, who understands the many problems in attempting to write a biography about a living subject, still believes that there are also many advantages. As she told Smith of *Publishers Weekly*: "For example, if Beauvoir said something in her memoirs, and someone I interviewed had a contradictory view, I'd just go over there and ask her about it. It was the same with Beckett."

Though that aspect of the biographer's relationship with her subjects was familiar, there were other aspects that were considerably different. Bair maintained a very formal relationship with Beckett until the day he died; with Beauvoir things were considerably more at ease, as Bair told Smith: "With Beauvoir from the very beginning, it was, 'Ah, Deirdre, sit down. Ah, Deirdre, we're going to have drinks with these feminists, we're going to do this, we're going to do that.' I was the one holding back, because I realized how marvelous this distance that Beckett had given me was, and how necessary."

Regardless of the differences in her relationships with her two subjects, *Simone de Beauvoir: A Biography* (1990) received mostly high marks, just as *Beckett* had received 12 years before. A writer for *Library Journal* (March 1, 1990) found the book to be "an interesting, thought-provoking work that should dispel many myths" but felt that Bair "might well have given us a greater feel for the woman and emphasized her feminist stance." The *New Republic* (June 11, 1990) contradicted this statement, arguing that Bair "is perpetually discovering this remarkable woman and explaining her to us, responding throughout to Beauvoir's behavior and feelings." Diane Johnson, in the *New York Times Book Review* (April 15, 1990), wrote that the emphasis on Beauvoir as a writer was the most significant contribution of Bair's biography, noting that Beauvoir, a great writer and philosopher in her own right, chose to submit to Sartre's enormous ego and become, in effect, his other self, supporting him in his every endeavor: "It is the writer that comes across most clearly in Deirdre Bair's book. . . . Beauvoir lived the often solitary, roistering, egotistical, hardworking, promiscuous, slightly alcoholic, affirmative life of a writer—but it was the life of a prototypical 20th-century male writer that she had the will to choose."

Bair's next project was a biography of someone who was no longer living—the controversial erotic writer and diarist Anaïs Nin. Considered even by her biographer a "major minor character" in the history of literature, Nin was nonetheless a notable figure, according to Bair. When critics accused Nin of embellishing or lying about her life in her diaries, the reading public turned against her, accusing her of being a fraud. Bair thinks that is an unfair assessment, suggesting in her biography that Nin's diaries are themselves an artistic achievement. She also points out how trends in literary criticism have led to the conclusion that many authors are "liars" because critics hold them to their word much more scrupulously than ordinary people do with one another. Bair, in the biography, highlighted Nin's contributions to the feminist movement, claiming that she helped free women from long-held misconceptions about their sexuality.

Reviews of *Anaïs Nin: A Biography* were mixed, some of them tending, or at least seeming, to correlate with the reviewers' appraisals of Nin herself. The *Financial Times* (April 22–23, 1995) was scathingly critical of both the tone of Bair's biography and Nin's status as a literary figure: "It's time to blow the whistle on Anaïs Nin. This massive, adoring biography . . . encourages the myth that Nin is a significant 20th-century writer and feminist thinker. She is neither." The *Chicago Tribune* (March 19, 1995) criticized the core of Bair's book: "In focusing relentlessly on Nin's sexual relationships, Bair does not remind us enough that Nin lived in one of the great ages of artistic exploration. . . . Another factor largely missing here is the fun Nin was having." In a more balanced evaluation of the book for the *Washington Post Book*

World (April 16, 1995), Marie Arana-Ward wrote: "Deirdre Bair delivers this sometimes unbearably operatic story with not an ounce of sentimentality or censure. It is no mean achievement." Among the more admiring critics was Aurelie Sheehan, who contended in the *Review of Contemporary Fiction* (Fall 1995) that "Bair's biography makes it clear that Nin is a significant figure in our cultural and literary history. She lived through the beginnings of psychoanalysis and was deeply affected by the work of Freud and Jung. Influenced by surrealism, Nin exalted the imagination and used it in a unique way. . . . A stake supporting an unruly vine, this biography is the requisite companion to strengthen the study of Nin's life and work and deepen our immersion in questions of truthtelling and image-making, the creation of the story and the self."

Deirdre Bair lives in Easton, Connecticut.
—C.M.

SUGGESTED READING: *Atlantic* p85 July 1978; *Chicago Tribune* XIV p5 Mar. 19, 1995; *Financial Times* p23 Apr. 22+ 1995; *Library Journal* p1271 July 15, 1978, p93 Mar. 1, 1990; *New Republic* p27 June 11, 1990; *Newsweek* p96 June 5, 1978; *New York Observer* p63 June 3, 1990; *New York Times Book Review* Apr. 15, 1990, p7 Mar. 5, 1995; *Publishers Weekly* p47+ Apr. 13, 1990; *Review of Contemporary Fiction* Fall 1995; *Washington Post Book World* p3+ Apr. 16, 1995; *Contemporary Authors* vol. 81–84, 1979

SELECTED WORKS: *Samuel Beckett: A Biography*, 1978; *Simone de Beauvoir: A Biography*, 1990; *Anaïs Nin: A Biography*, 1995

Baker, Houston A., Jr.

Mar. 22, 1943– Literary critic; professor

One of America's most prolific literary theorists, Houston A. Baker Jr. has helped define the genre of African-American literary criticism, which has developed since the late 1960s. Named the president of the Modern Language Association in 1992, Baker has been a professor at the University of Pennsylvania since 1974. He is known for his eclecticism, and has attracted attention for his controversial theories regarding the relevance of rap and hip-hop culture to education and to the study of literature in particular. Among his published works of criticism are *Blues, Ideology and Afro-American Literature* (1984), *Modernism and the Harlem Renaissance* (1987), *Workings of the Spirit: The Poetics of Afro-American Women's Writing* (1990), and *Black Studies, Rap and the Academy* (1993).

Houston Alfred Baker Jr. was born on March 22, 1943, in Louisville, Kentucky. He attended Howard University, in Washington, D.C., in the early 1960s, and graduated magna cum laude with a bachelor's degree in 1965. He received his master's degree and his Ph.D. from the University of Califor-

Tommy Leonardi/Courtesy of the Center for the Study of Black Literature and Culture, University of Pennsylvania

nia in Los Angeles (UCLA) in 1966 and 1968, respectively. Concurrently, he also pursued graduate studies at the University of Edinburgh from 1967 to 1968.

In the summer of 1966, Baker took his first teaching position, as an instructor at Howard. He left to be an instructor at Yale University, in New Haven, Connecticut, in 1968, and a year later he was an assistant professor of English literature, specializing in the Victorian/Pre-Raphaelite period. Baker's academic pursuits rarely had much to do with the emerging field of African-American studies until he was asked by members of Yale's Drama School to help organize a black drama workshop.

Baker's next academic position, which he began in 1970, was that of professor at the University of Virginia, in Charlottesville. He began making a conscious effort to read and comprehend African-American literature, taking as his inspiration such theorists as Addison Gayle, Larry Neal, and Stephen Henderson. One of the fruits of his labor was the anthology *Black Literature in America* (1971) which he edited. In 1972 he published a collection of his own essays, *Long Black Song: Essays in Black American Literature and Culture.*

Baker became a full professor at Yale in 1973 but left the following year for the University of Pennsylvania, in Philadelphia, where he was made director of Afro-American Studies. He continued his work in African-American writing in 1974, with the publication of *Singers of Daybreak: Studies in Black American Literature.* In 1977 he stepped down as director of Afro-American Studies, but remained a professor of English.

In the late 1970s, Baker edited various of works of African-American literary criticism, including *Reading Black: Essays in the Criticism of African, Caribbean, and Black American Literature* (1976), and he published a third book of his own essays, *The Journey Back: Issues in Black Literature and Criticism* in 1980. He also published *No Matter Where You Travel, You Still Be Black* (1979), a collection of his poems.

The University of Pennsylvania named Baker the Albert M. Greenfield Professor of Human Relations in 1982, and he continues to hold that position. In 1984 he published one of his most important critical volumes, *Blues, Ideology, and Afro-American Literature*, which Michael Bérubé of the *Voice Literary Supplement* (October 1992) described as a work that "should be on every literary critic's shelf." In it Baker analyzed the philosophy and terminology of country blues music and applied them to the study of African-American literature. Some felt that the two subjects were too incongruous, while other critics remarked that Baker was damaging the blues tradition by trying to marry it to French poststructuralism and other schools of critical thought. In response, Baker commented in *African American Review* (Winter 1992) that "the project here is to try . . . to present a statement that has the freshness about it of a language reworked, a terminology-that-is-in-every-way-familiar *de*familiarized in a way that will provide openings for scholars and undergraduates and so forth—and, quite frankly, a way of unifying what was already a quite substantial body of material that had come before the notion of 'booking it.'"

Baker was influential in the establishment of the Center for the Study of Black Literature and Culture in 1987; the Center's opening conference was turned into the book *Afro-American Literary Study in the 1990s* (1989), which Baker co-edited with Patricia Redmond. Among Baker's other works during the 1980s were two more books of poetry, *Spirit Run* (1981) and *Blues Journeys Home* (1985), and the critical study *Modernism and the Harlem Renaissance* (1987), which F. Elaine DeLancey called, in the *Journal of Modern Literature* (Fall 1989), a "critical triumph." DeLancey praised Baker's fresh analysis of the crucial period in African American literature and also wrote that the study forced the reader to re-evaluate the Harlem Renaissance in completely different terms.

In 1990, Baker published *Workings of the Spirit: The Poetics of Afro-American Women's Writing*. "It began to dawn on me that I had no choice, either as a man or as an expressive culture-critic, reader, of Afro-American culture, but to take up the texts of Afro-American women—to sort of put my ear to that sounding-post," Baker told *African American Review*.

In the 1990s, the very concept of African-American studies has come under attack by conservatives throughout the nation. Baker himself has been criticized for his views, which have often been at odds with academic "traditionalists." An-

other of Baker's recent books, *Black Studies, Rap, and the Academy* (1993), did not help in this respect; many academicians were incensed at Baker's suggestions that literary critics should take a serious look at rap music and that educators should, in turn, use it to teach literature to their students. "Most of the young people I've bumped into these days, at one place or another, understand rap music," Baker told Clarence Waldron for *Jet* (January 29, 1990). "They understand MTV; they understand the film culture represented by a person like Spike Lee. They spend a lot of time talking to one another about these things." Baker went on to comment that "any English teacher who has not attended a popular music concert or sat in front of MTV for a couple of hours isn't fit to teach. . . . You have to start where [the students] are."

Houston Baker was a visiting professor at Cornell University in 1977 and at Haverford College from 1983 to 1985. He was a member of the Fulbright-Hays literature screening committee from 1973 to 1974 and has been a member of Howard University's committee on scholarly worth since 1973. In 1992 he was named president of the Modern Language Association. Among his many accolades are the Alfred Longueil Poetry Award from UCLA (1966), and fellowships from the Center for Advanced Study of the Behavioral Sciences, the National Humanities Center, and the Rockefeller Minority Group. In addition to his books, Baker has written articles and reviews for such periodicals as *Victorian Poetry*, *Poetics Today*, *Yale Review*, and the *Journal of African–Afro-American Affairs*, and he was an advisory editor for the *Columbia Literary History of the United States*. He and his wife, Charlotte Pierce, have one son, Mark Frederick. —B.S.

SUGGESTED READING: *African American Review* p547+ Winter 1992; *Jet* p16+ Jan. 29, 1990, with photo; *Journal of Modern Literature* p225+ Fall 1989; *Voice Literary Supplement* p15+ Oct. 1992, with photo; *International Authors and Writers Who's Who 1997/98*; *Who's Who Among African Americans 1998*

SELECTED WORKS: As editor—*Black Literature in America*, 1971; *Twentieth-Century Interpretations of Native Son*, 1972; *Reading Black: Essays in the Criticism of African, Caribbean, and Black American Literature*, 1976; *Renewal: A Volume of Black Poems* (with Charlotte Pierce-Baker), 1977; *A Dark and Sudden Beauty: Two Essays in Black American Poetry by George Kent and Stephen Henderson*, 1977; *English Literature: Opening up the Canon, Selected Papers from the English Institute, 1979* (with Leslie Fiedler), 1981; *Three American Literatures: Essays in Chicano, Native American, and Asian-American Literature for Teachers of "American" Literature*, 1982; *Narrative of the Life of Fredrick Douglass, An American Slave, Written by Himself*, 1982; *Belief versus Theory in*

Black American Literary Criticism (with Joe Weixlmann), 1985; *Afro-American Literary Study in the 1990s* (with Patricia Redmond), 1989; *Black British Cultural Studies: A Reader* (with Manthia Diawara and Ruth H. Lindborg), 1996; Nonfiction—*Long Black Song: Essays in Black American Literature and Culture*, 1972; *Singers of Daybreak: Studies in Black American Literature*, 1974; *A Many-Colored Coat of Dreams: The Poetry of Countee Cullen*, 1974; *The Journey Back: Issues in Black Literature and Criticism*, 1980; *Blues, Ideology, and Afro-American Literature*, 1984; *Reading Black: Essays in the Criticism of African Caribbean and Black American Literature*, 1976; *Modernism and the Harlem Renaissance*, 1987; *Afro-American Poetics: Revisions of Harlem & the Black Aesthetic*, 1988; *Workings of the Spirit: The Poetics of Afro-American Women's Writing*, 1990; *Black Studies, Rap, and the Academy*, 1993; Poetry—*No Matter Where You Travel, You Still Be Black*, 1979; *Spirit Run*, 1981; *Blues Journeys Home*, 1985

Katherine Cumming / Courtesy of Vintage Contemporaries

Baker, Nicholson

Jan. 7, 1957– Novelist; nonfiction writer

Nicholson Baker has been described by Robert Mc-Crum for the *New York Times Book Review* (May 17, 1998) as "an exquisite literary anatomist, a writer who cares obsessively about the devilish detail of everyday existence." Baker's first two novels, *The Mezzanine* (1988) and *Room Temperature* (1990), are distinguished by a near-absence of plot

and by Baker's gift for elevating mundane human activities to the level of high comedy. In his works, Baker has dissected such subjects as tying one's shoes, riding escalators, and using rest-room paper-towel dispensers, describing them in ways that simultaneously produce recognition in the reader and reveal variously the social, historical, and technological significance of acts that are generally considered to be unworthy of scrutiny. With two more of his novels, *Vox* (1991), a pastiche of phone-sex conversations, and *The Fermata* (1994), Baker applied his fascination with detail to the subject of sex. In his most recent novel, *The Everlasting Story of Nory* (1998), Baker assumes the persona of a nine-year-old girl. "Every book I've written I've tried to make very different from the one before," he told the *New York Times* (June 8, 1998). "I'd like to have all my books make the same point . . . that a single human being can think about a lot of different things. There can be nerdy parts and sordid parts and, with some luck, noble parts and morally nuanced parts." Baker has also stirred controversy in library circles with his impassioned essays that decry the practices of disposing of infrequently used books and removing card catalogs in favor of electronic databases.

Nicholson Baker was born on January 7, 1957 in Rochester, New York, the son of Douglas Baker, an advertising executive, and Ann (Nicholson) Baker. He has one sister. Baker's interest in gadgetry, evident in *The Mezzanine* and other works, seems to have developed when he was very young; in the *Washington Post* (January 16, 1992), Martha Sherrill reported that as a child Baker wanted to be an inventor. "Then I gradually realized the arts were easier," Baker told Sherrill. The first area of the arts to capture his fancy was music. He took up the bassoon when he was in the fourth grade, and by his graduation from high school, in 1974, he had developed sufficient skill with the instrument to enroll at the Eastman School of Music, in Rochester, with the aim of one day becoming a composer. Baker even performed briefly, as a substitute bassoonist, with the Rochester Philharmonic Orchestra.

In *U and I: A True Story* (1991), Baker's first nonfiction book, he described the event that led to his giving up music in favor of writing. One Sunday during the time he was a student at Eastman, he saw his mother laughing uncontrollably at a *New York Times Book Review* essay on golf by the writer John Updike. In contrast to her laughter at her family's antics and anecdotes, Baker wrote, his mother's "delight that Sunday had no charity or encouragement in it: it was miraculous, sourced in the nowhere of print, unaided by ham mannerisms. . . . Nothing is more impressive than the sight of a complex person suddenly ripping out a laugh over some words in a serious book or periodical. . . . I began increasingly to want to be a part of the prosperous-seeming world of books (prosperous in contrast, that is, to the grant-dependent and sparsely attended concerts for living composers, whose ranks I had up until then wanted to join), where there was money for screaming full-page ads and where success was quantified as it was on the *Billboard* charts." Baker left Eastman after one year and entered Haverford College, in Haverford, Pennsylvania, from which he received his B.A. degree in English in 1980.

After Baker's graduation from college, his career path appeared to take still another hairpin turn when he went to work in New York City as a Wall Street oil analyst. Explaining that decision to William Grimes for the *New York Times* (January 30, 1992), Baker recalled, "I got very excited about the idea of financial markets. It seemed alien and interesting that there would be a price for a given piece of information and that you could trace the percolation of an idea through a community by seeing the fluctuation of its price." Baker spent about a year and a half working on Wall Street, first as an oil analyst and then as a stockbroker, an occupation he gave up "after two weeks and a series of psychosomatic illnesses," as Grimes phrased it. Baker then moved to Berkeley, California, where he lived with his future wife, Margaret Brentano, and her parents, and where he turned his attention to writing. In Berkeley, he honed his skills in a two-week writing workshop with the avant-garde short-story writer Donald Barthelme, and before long some of his short fiction pieces were published in the *New Yorker* and the *Atlantic*.

Those successes were followed by what James Kaplan, in an article for *Vanity Fair* (January 1992), called "a long fallow period" during which Baker "couldn't find the voice he wanted to speak in." Moving to Boston, Baker supported himself for the next several years by working variously as a word processor, an office temp, and a technical writer while he further developed his literary voice. In his early writing he made a conscious effort to follow a plot outline, but as he explained to one interviewer, he found that conventional technique frustrating. "So I got rid of the plot," he said, as quoted in *Contemporary Authors* in 1992. "I felt enormous relief that I didn't have to pretend to do something that didn't interest me."

One product of Baker's new approach to fiction writing was *The Mezzanine*, his first novel. Its narrator is Howie, a young man working in a large office complex. While tying his shoes, Howie breaks a shoelace; on his lunch hour, he walks to a nearby store to buy a new pair of laces, stops to enjoy a cookie and a carton of milk, then returns to work. Howie examines the smallest details of each of these actions, engaging in a great deal of free association (his digressions frequently take the form of footnotes, which range in length from a few lines to several pages). In contrast to his myriad comical observations about everyday occurrences, Howie's disclosures about his personal life are few, with the result that the occasional revelation—such as the lone reference to his having been mugged and the fear he has subsequently felt—becomes almost startling.

The Mezzanine was enthusiastically received by the critics. In the *New York Times Book Review* (February 5, 1989), for example, Robert Plunket pronounced it "a very funny book about the human mind, in particular that part of the mind that processes the triviality of daily events that seem to have no importance but end up occupying so much of our existence. . . . There is a first-rate comic mind at work here." David Gates, writing in *Newsweek* (January 2, 1989), was equally impressed: "(*The Mezzanine*) never switches on the rhetoric to bathe details in fake luminosity; it peddles no unifying vision. Some readers may have a problem with that: Art, they'll say, must do more. More than show us our lives afresh? Maybe in Baker's next book. But most writers never get *this* far."

The narrator of *Room Temperature*, Baker's second novel, is a young man—Mike—who, like Howie, delights in making observations about everyday life and recalling outwardly unremarkable events. Mike's ruminations occur during a twenty-minute period in which he bottle-feeds his infant daughter, whom he refers to affectionately as "the Bug." Unlike *The Mezzanine*, however, *Room Temperature* contains no footnotes and includes glimpses into the narrator's personal life, such as details about his relationship with his wife. At one point Mike notes, "She had begun writing in a spiral notebook every night, but I gathered that it was mostly observations about the newborn Bug. I would bring her her glass of water and get in bed while she sat against her pillow with her knees up, and I would stare from inches away at the lamplit overlapping-squares pattern of her flannel pajama bottoms (why didn't the ink with which the pattern was printed ruin the fluffiness of the flannel's nap?) and try to 'read' by ear what Bug-events she had found noteworthy that day. I wanted, as a first step, to isolate some simple word, like 'sleep' or 'milk,' from the complicated sequences of felt-tipped sniffing sounds her pen made."

The critical response to *Room Temperature* was largely positive. Julian Loose, evaluating the book for the *New Statesman & Society* (April 6, 1990), found that its "fascinating reveries on material objects . . . add up to an entrancing evocation of a common man's uncommon inner life." Similarly, Lawrence Norfolk announced in the *Times Literary Supplement* (April 27, 1990) that with *Room Temperature* Baker had made "a rapid transition from experimental writer to writer of successful experiments." Among the few dissenters was Wendy Lesser, who wrote in the *New York Times Book Review* (April 15, 1990), "Where *The Mezzanine* was filled with breathtaking similes, . . . this book . . . tends toward the labored discussion of similes . . . The endearing virtues of Mr. Baker's earlier narrator . . . have here become irritating characteristics."

The "U" of *U and I: A True Story*, Baker's third book, is his literary hero John Updike. An unusual blend of memoir and criticism, *U and I* reveals Baker's idolization of—and relentless self-comparison with—the older writer, whom he has met only in passing. The book was published to considerable acclaim. Some critics praised it in spite of, and others because of, Baker's obsessive admiration for Updike and his even more obsessive desire to reveal every quirky, embarrassing aspect of that admiration. In a representative assessment, Joseph Coates observed in the *Chicago Tribune* (April 28, 1991) that the book was a "hyperaware, brilliant, but sometimes maddeningly self-absorbed" work in which Baker had "the courage to make extreme demands on his readers and the talent to reward them handsomely if they can stay with him."

Baker's reputation grew considerably with the appearance of his fourth book, undoubtedly because of the titillating nature of his subject and the growing popularity of telephone sex lines. *Vox* (1992) consists almost entirely of an extended dialogue between the characters Jim and Abby, who converse via one such phone line, at a cost of $1.90 per minute. Disclosing little about themselves beyond their first names and general geographical regions (Jim lives on the West Coast, Abby on the East Coast), the two strangers spend hours describing to each other, in provocative detail, their sexual fantasies. Banking on *Vox*'s broad appeal, its publisher, Random House, ordered a relatively large first printing of 50 thousand copies and devised a promotional campaign that featured such gimmicks as wrapping review galleys in brown paper, choosing Valentine's Day as the book's publication date, and setting up a toll-free telephone number, so that, as Lynn Darling put it in *Esquire* (February 1994), "a prospective reader could listen to a breathy voice deliver a hint of the pleasures within [the book's] pages."

The promotional blitz paid off, for despite decidedly mixed notices, *Vox* was the first of Baker's works to become a best-seller. Many critics suggested that the book's long-distance telephone encounter and its characters' unwillingness to divulge personal information could be seen as representing the wariness and fear of intimacy that exist between people in the age of AIDS, and that Jim and Abby's conversation might be said to symbolize the struggle to achieve closeness in spite of those obstacles. There was some disagreement, however, over how well Baker had tackled those subjects. More than one reviewer complained that, because Jim and Abby talk in a similar manner, it is sometimes difficult to tell who is speaking, with the result that neither emerges as a distinct, emotionally involving character. Others ranked the book among the author's most successful efforts. "*Vox* isn't just Baker's hottest book; it's also his warmest," David Gates wrote in *Newsweek* (January 27, 1992). "We know little about Jim and Abby beyond how they talk and what gets them wild; still we genuinely get to like them." Randall Short, who evaluated the novel for the *New York Times Book Review* (February 16, 1992), applauded Baker for having "produced a compelling and irresistible

tale, a tour de force illustration of the fantasy inherent in eroticism."

Lee Lescaze observed in the *Wall Street Journal* (January 31, 1992) that as a writer Baker often plays "the smart aleck, the youngster seeing how far he can go and get away with it," in defying conventional structure and traditional bounds of good taste. He went too far, in the opinion of many critics, with *The Fermata* (1994). The book's protagonist is the self-centered, 35-year-old Arno Strine, who since childhood has had the ability to freeze time at will, putting the world in a kind of suspended animation that leaves him as its only conscious, autonomous human being. Arno uses his unique talent to stare at, undress, and fondle the women whose actions he has frozen. (The novel's title refers to the symbol used in musical scores to signify a pause of indefinite length.)

Perhaps the harshest criticism of *Fermata* came from Michiko Kakutani of the *New York Times* (February 8, 1994): "None of Mr. Baker's talents as a writer, his ability to reinvent the mundane rituals of daily life or limn the inner lives of his characters, are on display in this volume. . . . Instead, the reader is treated to the spectacle of a talented writer trying to lower himself to the level of those sophomoric scribes who write letters to *Penthouse* and *Hustler*. At one point, Arno refers to his own pornographic jottings as 'rot.' It's a term that applies perfectly to *The Fermata*." A number of other critics were similarly unimpressed. But in a dissenting opinion, Joanne Trestrail contended in the *Chicago Tribune* (February 6, 1994), "Baker, like Arno, knows he's on thin ice here. He sets out to explore an unattractive impulse in himself and follow where it leads. And he comes through all right: he stays true to his odd vision."

Explaining to Lynn Darling for the *Esquire* article his aim in writing *The Fermata*, Baker said, "I just felt, having written *Vox*, that there were other, more uncomfortable things that were also true about the way that men thought about sex that *Vox* hadn't captured. I just felt that I'd left things out that were maybe more objectionable. . . . I wanted to pose a number of questions. Are there degrees of violation? [Are Arno Strine's actions] worse because he's smarter and should know better, or [are they] a little more okay? I just want to have written a book that provokes thought on this topic, because it's very tricky. I mean, men really have amoral kinds of urges and things, I think. We might as well tell the truth about it."

The publication of *Vox* and *The Fermata* led at least one of his peers to question Baker's literary status. The novelist Elizabeth Hand, author of *Waking the Moon*, wrote in the *Washington Post* (May 5, 1996), "Before he became the best-selling author of those works of sex populi . . . Nicholson Baker was a Serious Writer. That is, critically acclaimed, his books savored by the cognoscenti but sadly ignored by the masses (too many odd words, not enough sex). The above-named novels fixed that (fewer words, odd sex), but left some readers scratching their heads: What happened to the man who wrote *The Mezzanine* and *Room Temperature* and *U and I*, this last a droll meditation upon John Updike (another Serious Writer who found that nothing succeeds like slick sex)?"

In addition to short stories and book-length works, Baker has published a number of essays in such periodicals as the *New Yorker*, *Atlantic Monthly*, and *Utne Reader*. Most prominent among these has been "Discards," which appeared in the *New Yorker* on April 4, 1994 and which lamented the nationwide trend among libraries toward destroying traditional card catalogs ("a monument of intergenerational intellect") and replacing them with electronic databases. Decrying the practice as a "national paroxysm of shortsightedness and anti-intellectualism," Baker argued that electronic databases are less efficient for cross-referencing and for finding entries with variant spellings, for example. He also pointed out that items are often entered into the databases by unqualified data-entry clerks, which increases the chance of errors. Baker maintained that the idiosyncratic card catalogs, with their distinct typographical style and handwritten notations, provide an important record of the history of ideas and of library usage that is being wiped out as data is converted to computerized formats. Baker's campaign has won him support from some prominent librarians, and he told D. T. Max for the *New York Observer* (May 9, 1994), "I've gotten more mail for that than for anything else I've written, and it's mostly, 'Go, man, go.'" Baker also harshly criticized the decision by the San Francisco Public Library to weed some 200,000 books from its shelves to make room for computer terminals. Quoted by the *New York Times* (January 26, 1997), Baker said, "My real gripe about the San Francisco Public Library is that they were, without any permission from the people, transforming a great research institution into a mediocre public library, and doing that by throwing books in a landfill."

In 1996 Random House published Baker's next book, *The Size of Thoughts: Essays and Other Lumber*, a collection of essays he had written for the *New Yorker* and the *Atlantic Monthly*. In one piece, Baker focused his attention on minute details in the everyday objects he had observed, ranging from unassembled model airplanes ("basilica of the unbuilt") to a counter display of "ninety-nine cent Trim-brand diapers sitting near the drugstore's cash register like a bucket of fleshly netted minnows." In other essays, he offered a paean to eccentric and endangered marks of punctuation, such as the "colash" (:—), the "semi-colash" (;—), and the "commash" (,—), and offered his ruminations on the art of writing on rubber with ballpoint pens. Also included in *The Size of Thoughts* is one of Baker's essays on the vanishing library card-catalogs. In the *Washington Post*, Hand suggested that "Readers and writers, serious and otherwise, will find much delight here." She continued, "The clarity of Baker's writing sometimes betrays a cer-

tain icy chill, as of standing at the edge of some remote alpine lake and peering down through vast crystalline depths to the very bottom—nothing left to the imagination, no murky nutrient-rich sludge. Still, *The Size of Thoughts* is replete with charm and wit and literary bravura. Anyone who can hone his prodigious intellect on Pottery Barn advertisements deserves Nicholson Baker's success, and more." Michiko Kakutani began her *New York Times* (April 2, 1996) review of the book with these words: "If writers had bumper stickers, Nicholson Baker's would read: 'God dwells in the details.'" The review concludes: "Give Mr. Baker a tiny, concrete subject like model airplanes or the history of the semicolon . . . and he can dazzle, proving indisputably that he is the master of the miniature, the lord of the Lilliputian, the bard of the small."

After the publication of *The Size of Thoughts*, in 1996, Baker and his family took up residence for one year in Ely, England, where he began work on his fifth novel. Published in 1998 and entitled *The Everlasting Story of Nory*, the novel is told from the point of view of its nine-year-old heroine, Eleanor Winslow, an American student at a school in the fictional city of Threll, England. According to Baker, the character of Eleanor is based on his own daughter, Alice, who was nine when he began writing the book. An often playful comic pastiche of fantasies, dreams, and private musings, cast at times in a child's secret language of made-up words and malapropisms, the novel focuses on Eleanor's inner life, and it marked a forceful departure from Baker's earlier novels, which were all written from the viewpoint of adult males. It prompted some critics to make allusions to the work of Lewis Carroll, as did Robert McCrum, whose review, entitled "Through the Looking Glass," appeared in the *New York Times Book Review* (May 17, 1998). McCrum wrote that "this latest novel represents a huge, and risky, departure in [Baker's] choice of fictional viewpoint," and that *The Everlasting Story of Nory* "may prove to be a bridge to a greater maturity" for its author.

Nicholson Baker, who stands about six feet, four inches tall, sports wire-frame glasses and a thick beard. "He is often described, by himself and by others, as awkward and bumbling and shy," Lynn Darling commented, noting that Baker's resulting persona "offers a friendly counterweight to his towering self-confidence." Darling observed further that Baker's voice has "a softly reassuring quality." Baker married Margaret Brentano in 1985; the couple have a daughter and a son. In about 1992 the Baker family moved from Mount Morris, New York, where they had lived since 1988, to Berkeley, California.

—C.T./E.M.

SUGGESTED READING: *Advocate* p102+ Aug. 22, 1995; *Esquire* p76+ Feb. 1994, with photo; *Library Journal* p104+ July 1995; *New Statesman & Society* p38 Apr. 6, 1990, p44 Feb. 10, 1995; *New York Times* C p15+ Jan. 30, 1992, with photo, C p15 Apr. 2, 1996, with photo, B p4 Aug. 30, 1996, I p10 Jan. 26, 1997; *New York Times Book Review* p20 July 16, 1995, p12 Apr. 14, 1996, p32 Apr. 20, 1997, p14+ May 14, 1998; *New York Times Magazine* p38 Aug. 18, 1996, with photo; *New Yorker* p64+ Apr. 4, 1994, p92+ June 26, 1995; *Spectator* p41 June 24, 1995; *Times Literary Supplement* Apr. 27, 1990; *Utne Reader* p30+ May 1995, with photo; *Vanity Fair* p199+ June 1992, with photo; *Washington Post* C p1+ Jan. 16, 1992, with photos, B p1 June 9, 1995, C p7 July 7, 1996; *Washington Post Book Review* X p15 Feb. 12, 1995, X p4 May 5, 1996, with photo

SELECTED BOOKS: Fiction—*The Mezzanine*, 1988; *Room Temperature*, 1990; *Vox*, 1992; *The Fermata*, 1994; *The Everlasting Story of Nory*, 1998; Nonfiction—*U and I: A True Story*, 1991; *The Size of Thoughts: Essays and Other Lumber*, 1996

Pat Barker

Barker, Pat

May 8, 1943– Novelist

The English novelist Pat Barker looks to her working-class roots—especially the stories of her grandparents—for the inspiration for her celebrated fiction. Her first novel, *Union Street* (1982), the story of a group of working-class women, drew heavily on her experiences growing up in industrial Thornaby-on-Tees, even though she does not consider it an autobiographical work. Since that book's publication, Barker has written seven more novels, four of which explore further the lives of working-class people and three of which make up a trilogy about World War I. *The Ghost Road* (1995), the last book of this trilogy, which also includes *Regeneration* (1991) and *The Eye in the Door* (1993), won England's highest literary award, the Booker Prize.

Pat Barker was born on May 8, 1943, in Thornaby-on-Tees, in northern industrial England. At the time of her birth her parents were unmarried; they married when she was seven, in 1950, after having had another child. The family soon grew too large for the back room of the pub where they were living, and young Pat was sent to live with her grandparents. Though she felt unwanted initially, she now considers the move to have been good fortune. As she told the *Guardian* (September 11, 1993): "With my parents, A-levels would have been out of the question. . . . Being brought up by talkative grandparents is very good if you're going to write about the past because you get the bits that don't get into the history books." Not long into her stay with her grandparents, her father injured his back and was no longer able to work; soon after that her grandfather's fish-and-chips shop failed, and both households were forced to go on national assistance. Through all of this, Barker's home was filled with stories about the history of her family.

Barker attended the London School of Economics and Political Science, from which she graduated with a bachelor of science degree in 1965. After graduation she taught at the university level until 1970, when she left to care for her sickly grandmother. At the age of 26, after the birth of the first of her two children, John and Annabel, she began writing fiction, but she failed to publish any of the three books she penned during that period. She told the *New York Times* (December 6, 1995): "I was writing things that I shouldn't have been trying to write. I was writing sensitive middle-class lady novels, and it's not what I am."

She then met the English novelist Angela Carter, who was helping to teach a writing course in which Barker was enrolled. Carter encouraged Barker to delve into her past more, to use her working-class origins as the basis for her fiction. Barker followed Carter's advice, and it paid off in the publication of her first novel, *Union Street*. This novel, about the lives of several women in an unnamed northern England industrial town, was heralded as a stunningly realistic portrait of a darker side of England. Meredith Tax, writing the review for the *Village Voice* (December 6, 1983), stated: "One mark of a fine realistic novel is that for all the blood, the word sensationalism never ever enters your mind because you care about the people. . . . Life is full of illness and terror and death, all mixed together with love and birth and children's games, and [Barker] wants to write about life." At the age of 39, Barker became an author of recognized significance, earning a place on the 1983 Best of Young British Novelists list and winning the Fawcett Prize. *Union Street* was adapted to the big screen as *Stanley and Iris,* a film starring Robert De Niro and Jane Fonda.

Her next novel, the 1984 volume *Blow Your House Down*, embraced a similar theme and received equally good reviews. The story concerns a group of poor prostitutes who attempt to make a living while a Jack the Ripper–type stalker is on the loose. As in her earlier novel, Barker gave the reader not stereotypes but complex characters who reveal a great deal about the human condition. Carola Dibbell, in her review for the *Village Voice* (September 11, 1984), noted that the women's motives were economic. "They sell—actually rent out—their bodies as a last resort. None of them is on drugs and only one's a drunk. Only one has a pimp, and that in the loosest sense. Two are lesbians. Most are mothers." These women's customers are also well-developed characters. As Dibbell observed: "Most of the customers are married and . . . they want to complain about their problems at home more than they want sex. But what they're paying for is to not be criticized." The men do not seek to escape to other women, but merely seek compassion from other human beings who are sympathetic to their shared problems of poverty and lack of respect—who are, like the husbands, at the bottom of the social pecking order.

This Century's Daughter (1986), Barker's third novel, is the story of a woman, Liza Jarrett Wright, who recounts to a homosexual social worker named Steven her life of poverty, the loss of her son in World War II, and the story of her wild daughter, whose own daughter ends up being raised by Liza. Norman Shrapnel wrote in the *Guardian* that *This Century's Daughter* maintained the "vigor, concern, and power of observation" of Barker's earlier novels. Anne Boston, in *New Society*, wrote: "Pat Barker gives an authentic voice to the lives of the poor and dispossessed as few other English contemporary novels have managed to do." Barker's fourth novel, *The Man Who Wasn't There*, published in 1989, was not praised as highly as her previous books; Samuel Hynes, writing for the *New York Times Book Review* (March 29, 1992), believed the book to be simply "less successful."

As a new decade dawned, Barker refocused her energy toward a consideration of World War I. As a girl Barker had been fascinated by her grandfather's stories of the war and by the scars he had received from a bayonet; her first attempt at creative writing, a poem she composed when she was 11, was about the war. As a student in London she had studied the exchange of telegrams that had preceded the outbreak of the fighting.

The eventual result of her fascination was a war trilogy, starting in 1991 with the publication of *Regeneration*, a novel in which the author wrote about real places and people and fictionalized conversations and events. She chose as her characters some of the greatest of the English wartime writers, including Robert Graves, Wilfred Owen, and Siegfried Sassoon. The focus of the novel is the relationship between Sassoon and Dr. William Rivers, a leading expert of the era on post-traumatic stress syndrome. Sassoon met Rivers at the psychiatric military hospital in Craiglockhart, as did Owen, who was killed when he returned to the front only a short time before the Armistice. The reason that these men, decorated war heroes (especially Sassoon), went to Craiglockhart was not that they were suffering from shell-shock but that they wished to protest England's involvement in the war.

Herbert Mitgang, reviewing the book for the *New York Times* (April 15, 1992), wrote: "Ms. Barker makes the conversations between her poets and the doctors at the hospital sound absolutely authentic. We are aware that she is inventing dialogue for her characters, but it is informed invention." The *Washington Post* (April 3, 1992) reviewer wrote, "Barker has broken into new territory with *Regeneration*. The book's concerns are historical and primarily masculine. But the novel also echoes the feminism of Barker's earlier work." Barker also filled her version of Craiglockhart with a score of shell-shock patients: from Anderson, a war-weary doctor who cannot stand the sight of a single drop of blood, to Burns, who has been unable to eat since he fell face-first into the stomach of a dead German, to Billy Prior, who hasn't spoken since he picked up an eyeball of a fellow soldier. A film version of *Regeneration,* starring Jonathan Pryce and James Wilby, was released in 1997.

Billy Prior is the focus of the novel *The Eye in the Door*, published in 1993. This novel shifts the action to London, a few months later. Prior is a bisexual working-class officer who experiences "fugue states"—periods in which he cannot recall his actions. England's public, influenced by a manipulative press, has grown tired of blaming the Germans for the war and is instead focusing on its own citizenry: "a rag tag collection of Quakers, socialists, suffragettes, syndicalists, Seventh Day Adventists and God knows what else." Included in this group are homosexuals. As the *Guardian* (September 21, 1993) stated in its review: "By highlighting the war's persecuted sexual and political dissenters, *The Eye in the Door* . . . shows [Barker's] commitment to the process of reclaiming silenced voices." *New York Newsday* (May 15, 1994) cheered: "This brave novel attempts, and succeeds at, much more than most of what's being published. There's nothing sanitized or prettified here, and that too is encouraging." *The Eye in the Door* earned for Barker the *Guardian* Fiction Prize.

Though critics disagreed about whether or not *The Ghost Road* can stand apart from the previous two volumes, most agreed that it is an ambitious book. It further explores such issues as Prior's sexuality while also including gripping accounts of frontline action, which prompted many critics to applaud Barker's ability to portray men's perspectives. Since Barker had made a name for herself as a chronicler of lower-class women's lives, many critics had patronizingly suggested that she could not write about anything else. As the author has said, many asked in effect, "But uh, can she do men?—as though that were some sort of Everest." Claudia Roth Pierpont, reviewing *The Ghost Road* for the *New York Times Book Review* (December 31, 1995), wrote: "The author has certainly proved that she can 'do men,' but her real tour de force may lie in having reinvented herself while retaining all the vigor of her old unrespectable themes."

Barker's most recent work, *Another World* (1999), was described by Ruth Rendell in London's *Sunday Times* as an "old-fashioned novel in a modern idiom [that] remains one of the best things she has ever done, [and is] surely the most moving." Powerfully evoking the stranglehold of the past upon the present, both in the form of an elderly grandfather's reliving of the battlefield death of his brother during World War I and in the main character's dawning recognition that a murder may have been committed in his house during its previous ownership, Barker sorts through the "intricate particulars with commendable economy while simultaneously constructing a rich narrative that's as attentive to the kitchen-sink minutiae of domestic frustration . . . as to her story's more immediately dramatic matters," according to a writer for *Kirkus Reviews* (February 15, 1999). The reviewer concluded: "Of such imaginative complexity and generosity are first-rate fiction made, and Barker keeps on making it about as well as anybody now writing."

Pat Barker lives in Durham, England.
—C.M.

SUGGESTED READING: *Chicago Tribune* XIV p3 Dec. 24, 1995; *Guardian* p28 Sep. 11, 1993, p11 Sep. 21, 1993; Kirkus Reviews Feb. 15, 1999; *Library Journal* p108 Apr. 15, 1994; *New York Newsday* p37 Apr. 12, 1992, p31 May 15, 1994; *New York Times* C p21 Apr. 15, 1992, C p17 Dec. 6, 1995; *New York Times Book Review* p1+ Mar. 29, 1992, p9 May 15, 1994, p5 Dec. 31, 1995; *New York Review of Books* p19+ Feb. 15, 1996; *Publishers Weekly* p63 Mar. 14, 1994; *Times Literary Supplement* p12+ Mar. 22, 1996; *Village Voice* p51 Dec. 6, 1983, p15 Sep. 11, 1984; *Washington Post* D p1+ Apr. 3, 1992, *Washington Post Book World* p1+ Dec. 17, 1995; *Contemporary Authors* vol. 122, 1988; *Contemporary Literary Criticism* vol. 32, 1985

SELECTED BOOKS: *Union Street*, 1982; *Blow Your House Down*, 1984; *This Century's Daughter*, 1986; *The Man Who Wasn't There*, 1989; *Regeneration*, 1991; *The Eye in the Door*, 1993; *The Ghost Road*, 1995; *Another World*, 1999

Barnard, Robert

Nov. 23, 1936– Novelist; short-story writer; critic

Whether writing under his real name or under his recently adopted pseudonym, Bernard Bastable, veteran British novelist Robert Barnard understands well the process of intertwining satire, wit, and suspense. The author of more than two dozen mystery novels, as well as several critical works on English literature, Barnard is celebrated for his acid humor and intricate plotting. "He plots a mystery as well as any other writer alive," a *Time* reviewer wrote in 1985, "and he never takes the easy path of repeating a winning formula." Ever present in his books is a healthy dose of scathing satire that is equally critical of all levels of British society—from the working class to the middle classes to the aristocracy. As Maude McDaniel wrote in the *Washington Post*, Barnard's "gift for satire is so biting that, except for protagonists, he has trouble turning out really likable characters." "All my characters are pretty awful in one way or another," Barnard conceded in one interview, "partly because they are suspects in a murder investigation and I don't really believe that nice people are potential committers of murders."

Critics have noted that it is difficult to characterize a "typical" Robert Barnard mystery. "Barnard, currently one of the most prolific of British mystery writers," wrote a *Washington Post Book World*

Robert Barnard

(September 20, 1992) reviewer, "is also one of the most varied—with settings ranging from Australia to Norway and all over the English class map. What remains consistent is his wit, sharp eye for social and individual nuances, and clean prose." Indeed, his books have examined an extremely broad range of subjects, including the opera world, in *Death on the High C's* (1978); World War II England, in *Out of the Blackout* (1985), Australian academia, in *Death of an Old Goat* (1974); and Wolfgang Amadeus Mozart, in *Dead, Mr. Mozart* (1994) and *Too Many Notes, Mr. Mozart* (1995).

In an autobiographical statement for *World Authors 1990-1995*, Robert Barnard writes: "I was born in a small fishing and yachting town in Essex, Burnham-on-Crouch, on the 23rd November 1936, but within months we had moved to a similar small town, also in Essex, called Brightlingsea, and it was there that I grew up. My early memories are often of war: of my father prophesying around the kitchen table at the time of the Battle of Britain that 'the Germans will be here within a week' (he was not naturally optimistic by nature, I think); of us children parading in nasty, hairy khaki uniforms up and down our little street; of the whine of doodlebugs in the later months of the war. But there was fellowship in the dugout shelters during air-raids, and the privations and the meagre food were at least shared by all.

"I went to Colchester Royal Grammar School (1948–56), where I was a totally inconspicuous boy, bad at games and not notably good at school work. I turned out, however, to be the sort of child who does much better at exams than he deserves: I still remember the condescension with which my brighter contemporaries enquired how I had got on in the GCE and Advanced GCE exams and their frank amazement when I told them. It was no doubt this ability which enabled me to get an Exhibition to Balliol College, Oxford. I don't think I then knew it was Lord Peter Wimsey's college, but I wouldn't have cared: Sayers seemed to me intolerably dated. I was a Christie man, and have remained one.

"Oxford was immensely liberating. I began to lose the shyness which was my main characteristic as a child, and I became much more involved in politics—for me, as for many others, the disgraceful invasion of Suez was the catalyst that changed a vague support for the Labour Party into something more active. There was opera, too: the Operatic Club put on sturdy performances, with professional and amateur singers mixing and piano accompaniment, of justly and unjustly neglected works, and London was less than an hour away. After hearing Joan Sutherland as Gilda (more wonderful than either of her recorded performances) friends and I campaigned to persuade Covent Garden to put on *Lucia di Lammermoor* for her. I don't imagine ours was any sort of decisive influence on the decision, however.

"After working for the Fabian Society for a year, and deciding that active politics were not for me, I went to Australia to teach English Literature at the University of New England. My five years there (dust, rolling vistas and gallons of beer and cheap sherry) were notable for my getting married, learning my trade as an academic, and perhaps for planting some seeds which later became my first crime novel, *Death of an Old Goat*. After five years I got a lectureship at the University of Bergen, Norway, and transferred from an area that had not seen rain in three years to one that saw nothing but for about 320 days a year.

"Norway is, for me, a *locus mirabilis*, a Nirvanah, a rainbow's end place. It is very easy to sneer: there is a certain complacency about some of the people (Ibsen satirized it), an insularity too, a lack of daring in their politics and their artistic life. But the experience of living for 17 years in the world's most beautiful and spectacular landscapes has an effect that is almost impossible to describe. The cliche 'breathtaking' to describe a view can be used for no other landscape, and only begins to describe the effect the Norwegian mountains and fjords have on the traveller or the resident.

"And I began writing there (occasionally, or, the rare sunny days, sitting outside looking over the fjord in Bergen or Tromsø, where I became Professor of English in 1976). *Old Goat* was published in 1974, and from then on there followed a steady stream of crime novels of a faintly old-fashioned kind. Crucial to my career in America was my being taken up by Scribner's, who liked my fifth novel, *Unruly Son*, which they gave the leaden title *Death of a Mystery Writer*. It was a minor success because they believed in it, and my popularity in the States has since then been greater than that in Britain, and is the basis of my income, my ability to live off my writing. I remain happily with them, and with the same editor, Susanne Kirk.

"I went full-time as a writer in 1983, and moved reluctantly back to England. Why? I found that the Britain I was writing about was Britain of the Fifties when I was growing up—Harold Macmillan's Britain, and not Margaret Thatcher's. I felt if I went on like that my books would become more and more period pieces. Since returning my books have gradually stopped being the comic, stylised entertainments they were, and have become darker: it is a sad, unsatisfactory, un-confident place, the Britain of today, and unlovely to boot, with its history shunned and neglected, and its green places desecrated to make palaces for shopping in. The long grind of a decade and a half of mass unemployment has destroyed the spirit of its people. This may be a passing phase, but it seems to be passing very slowly.

"Perhaps as a relief from the darker colour of most of my books these days, I have started recently writing historical crime novels under the pseudonym Bernard Bastable. Especially enjoyable have been the two Mr. Mozart books (this is an alternative Mozart, who stayed on in England after his 1764 visit, and spends his time bemoaning the climate and people and fantasizing how honoured and rich he would have been if he had stayed on in his musical and civilized homeland). They have been sheer pleasure to write.

"My favourite book in my earlier vein is *Sheer Torture*. Of the more serious ones I particularly like *Masters of the House* and *A Scandal in Belgravia*.

Will my books live? I have no idea. But I have been able to live off them, and that is still, when I stop to contemplate, a matter for wonder and gratitude."

Representative of Barnard's many novels, in terms of its warm critical reception, is *Out of the Blackout* (1985), a mystery with a decidedly historical bent. In it, Barnard wrote of a trainful of children arriving in a small town after fleeing the 1941 London blitz. On the train is an unknown child who is able to divulge few details about his life and his family. The child, eventually adopted by a local family, is haunted by his memories. As an adult, he becomes obsessed with his past and sets out to unravel the mystery of his life in wartime London. Barnard's treatment of an historical setting in *Out of the Blackout* was commended by many critics. "[Barnard] shows himself adept at capturing the flavor of a period (without recourse to obvious props) as he is at evoking the feel of a neighborhood or pinning down a social type," John Gross wrote in the *New York Times* (July 12, 1985). Carolyn See wrote in the *Los Angeles Times* (July 25, 1985) that she "learned a lot about the political climate of the prewar British underclass [and] gained the satisfaction of learning once again that right (often) triumphs over wrong, and intelligence is better than ignorance and stupid cruelty." Derrick Murdock of the Toronto *Globe and Mail* (April 6, 1985) was even more complimentary in his review of *Out of the Blackout*. "Barnard is an inventive, witty writer and skillful satirist, but without question this is the most original novel he has yet written, with an ending as totally satisfying as it is unexpected," Murdock wrote.

In 1992 Barnard published *A Fatal Attachment*, a psychological mystery involving a woman, Lydia Perceval, who systematically destroys the egos of teenage boys in her Yorkshire village through seduction and manipulation. When Lydia is found dead, two police detectives step in to handle the investigation and discover which of her numerous conquests is the killer. Throughout the investigation the secrets of Lydia's lethal charm are slowly revealed. The book's extremely intricate plot led Marilyn Stasio to comment in the *New York Times Book Review* (August 23, 1992) that "Robert Barnard could teach spiders a trick or two about spinning webs."

In 1995, writing under the name Bernard Bastable, Robert Barnard released the second in a series of "alternative history" books that examine the life that Wolfgang Amadeus Mozart might have led had he lived to old age. This book, *Too Many Notes, Mr. Mozart*, offers a widowed Mozart reduced to giving piano lessons to Princess Victoria, heir apparent to the throne of England. Through a series of unusual developments, Mozart becomes a confidant and protector of the young princess. When Victoria is nearly poisoned during a visit to Windsor Castle, her uncle, the newly crowned King William IV, calls upon Mozart to make discreet inquiries as to who may have been behind the act. Though the book is one of Barnard's personal favorites, it received only tepid reviews. "Bastable imagines his characters and their setting so fully and seamlessly and offers such appealing possibilities that readers will wish this slight piece offered Mozart and Victoria more range," read a review of the book in *Publishers Weekly* (April 29, 1996).

Once again writing under his given name, Robert Barnard followed *Too Many Notes, Mr. Mozart* with *The Habit of Widowhood*, a collection of 17 short stories. Designated "page-turner of the week" by *People* for the week of October 10, 1996, the book offers an array of narrators including Albert Edward, Prince of Wales ("Balmorality"), a dog who offers his own account of a murder ("Dog Television"), and even Jane Eyre ("Reader, I Strangled Him"). Critics wrote glowingly of *The Habit of Widowhood*. "The wealth of ideas and inventions here might well be hoarded by other authors for a series of novels," wrote a reviewer for *Publishers Weekly* (July 29, 1996), "but Barnard has such profligate wit and imagination that he can afford to deliver this abundance in a single volume."

The Corpse at the Haworth Tandoori, Barnard's 1999 novel, finds detective Charlie Peace in the town of Haworth, in northern England, to investigate the murder of a young man whose body is found outside an Indian restaurant. The trail of clues leads Peace to suspect a young Irish handyman, Declan O'Hearn. "The characters are intriguingly off-beat and the scenario is beyond bizarre, yet never quite beyond belief," according to the *Kirkus Reviews* (February 1, 1999) critic. "Suspense seldom flags in a steadily absorbing story." —J. P.

SUGGESTED READING: *Library Journal* p118 Aug. 1996; *New York Times Book Review* p17 Aug. 23, 1992; *Publishers Weekly* p55 Apr. 29, 1996, p74 July 29, 1996; *Washington Post Book World* p12 Sep. 20, 1992; *Contemporary Authors* nrs vol. 20, 1987

SELECTED BOOKS: Fiction—*Death of an Old Goat*, 1974; *A Little Local Murder*, 1976; *Blood Brotherhood*, 1977; *Death on the High C's*, 1978; *Death of a Mystery Writer*, 1979; *Death of a Literary Widow*, 1980; *Death in a Cold Climate*, 1981; *Death of a Perfect Mother*, 1981; *Death by Sheer Torture*, 1982; *Death and the Princess*, 1982; *The Case of the Missing Brontë*, 1983; *School for Murder*, 1984; *Corpse in a Gilded Cage*, 1984; *Out of the Blackout*, 1985; *Fete Fatale*, 1985; *Political Suicide*, 1986; *Bodies*, 1986; *The Cherry Blossom Corpse*, 1987; *A City of Strangers*, 1990; *A Fatal Attachment*, 1992; *A Scandal in Belgravia*, 1992; *A Hovering of Vultures*, 1993; *The Masters of the House*, 1994; *The Bad Samaritan*, 1995; *The Habit of Widowhood*, 1996; *The Corpse at the Haworth Tandoori*, 1999; Nonfiction—*Imagery and Theme in the novels of Dickens*, 1974; *A Short History of English Literature*, 1984; as Bernard Bastable: Fiction—*To Die Like a Gentleman*, 1993; *Dead, Mr. Mozart*, 1994; *Too Many Notes, Mr. Mozart*, 1995

Barry Goldstein/Courtesy of W. W. Norton

Barrett, Andrea

Nov. 16, 1954– Novelist; professor

"It's hard to explain how much one can love writing," author Andrea Barrett once told the *Baltimore Sun* (March 9, 1997). "If people knew how happy it can make you, we would all be writing all the time. It's the greatest secret of the world." Despite her taking such pleasure in the writing process, producing a successful book was not easy for Barrett; for more than a decade she composed stories and novels that never made their way into print. When she finally realized her dream of getting published, with *Lucid Stars* (1988), the reception was one of high acclaim. She then reached further into her literary arsenal and began creating stories that interwove historical occurrences and characters with fictionalized plots. With four successful books under her belt, Barrett published *Ship Fever* (1996), a collection of short stories that earned her international recognition as well as the National Book Award.

Andrea Barrett was born in Boston, Massachusetts, on November 16, 1954, to Walter Barrett and Jacquelyn Knifong. The future author grew up largely on Cape Cod, where she developed a deep passion for the ocean as well as for the history surrounding it. "We didn't live right on the water, but I could walk to it and did every day," Barrett recalled in an interview with *Salon Magazine* (December 2, 1998). "And that must have got this started in me somewhere. I was always within sniffing range of the ocean and usually within sight of it. I think the landscape you grow up in probably does mark you in ways you don't even understand."

The author took an unconventional route to her literary education, applying to colleges before she was even a senior and then dropping out of high school after her junior year. She went immediately to Union College in Schenectady, New York, where she began her college education despite never receiving a high school diploma. She initially did not pursue a career in literature, instead training to become a biologist. She received her bachelor's degree in biology from Union College in 1974 and then briefly studied zoology in graduate school at the University of Massachusetts in Amherst. Abandoning this subject, she left the university but then came back for a second turn, this time studying medieval and Reformation theological history. It was during this second trip back to graduate school that Barrett came to realize the nature of her true interest. "Writing papers about the Inquisition or the early days of the Franciscan order, I was going through exactly the same process I use now to make my fiction," she told *Publishers Weekly* (August 10, 1998).

During this time, Barrett moved to Rochester, New York, where her husband was in the midst of completing an M.D./Ph.D. program. She took secretarial jobs and would write stories on the side, going to the library in search of books on the craft of writing. Unfortunately, her work went nowhere, and Barrett became increasingly discouraged. Then, in 1984, she attended the Bread Loaf Writers Conference in Vermont, where she was able to get a critique of a novel she had written. The author told her she was a promising, talented writer—who needed to throw her current novel in the garbage. Although initially upset at this piece of advice, the next day Barrett did just that and begin writing a new novel, one that would eventually become *Lucid Stars*.

That novel tells the classic tale of boy-meets-girl, in this case with numerous twists and turns. It begins in 1955, when 19-year-old Penny falls in love with Benjamin and the two begin a life together. As the years progress, Benjamin's infidelities wear on Penny's patience, and the two, whose marriage produces two children, divorce. As the core of this union slowly unravels over a 25-year period, it becomes a new constellation in the sky, "joined for a few minutes by the wandering moon."

Reaction to Barrett's debut novel was largely mixed. The *New York Times* (January 29, 1989) reviewer wrote that "Initially the prose in this sidereal drama suffers from a certain slackness, but as the novel gains momentum it deepens, and Ms. Barrett's language adeptly rises, or falls, to portray occasions of considerable unhappiness." The reviewer went on to note that Barrett "also possesses the gift of forgiving her characters more readily than they do one another—which is neither more nor less than they deserve. In doing so, she has made a spacious and sympathetic debut." Offering an opposing view of the novel was the *Spectator* (March 11, 1989), which commented that Barrett "finds the fixed, arbitrary patterns stars make (hence the book's title) more interesting than the historical resonances her narrative achieves, so the point here is like, really, you know how everything changes and yet, er, everything stays the same, you know?" However, the reviewer concluded by writing, "My point is that *Lucid Stars* wouldn't be worth mentioning if it did not also contain beautifully recorded dialogue and enough nice touches to prove that, despite the sloppy thought behind the very idea of the book, the author does know what makes her characters tick."

Barrett's next novel, *Secret Harmonies* (1989), again delves into the subject of family relationships, with the focus this time on a character named Reba Dwyer. Reba attempts to flee her restrictive family life, which includes her timid brother and handicapped sister, and enters a conservatory. After failing to fit in there, she returns home and ultimately marries an old friend, though the marriage is not a happy one for her. As things get progressively worse for her, Reba eventually tries to find inner happiness and to come to terms with herself. Although this literary offering did not receive the level of attention of her debut novel, *Publishers Weekly* (August 11, 1989) called the novel "[p]oignant and atmospheric" and applauded Barrett's "[e]legant, accessible writing."

For her third novel, *The Middle Kingdom* (1991), Barrett again wrote of a female character who is unhappy with her life and who attempts to overcome that unhappiness. Here, 30-year-old Grace, after accompanying her husband on a business trip to China, realizes that she no longer loves him and decides to begin an adventure of her own. She decides to stay in Beijing while her husband continues to tour with a mistress, and Grace soon befriends a female scientist. While taking in her new culture and surroundings, she also takes on lovers and is soon pregnant. She also finds a fulfilling job and comes to accept her situation without regret or worry about her future.

Reaction to *The Middle Kingdom* was tepid, with many reviewers praising Barrett's writing but not her tale. The *New York Times Book Review* (June 23, 1991) wrote "Ms. Barrett is a solid writer, and *The Middle Kingdom* is a thoughtfully plotted book. Yet Grace is a troublesome character. . . . Though I understood her, I found it difficult to care for her. And Ms. Barrett never does manage to communicate just what it is about China that attracts her heroine—or, for that matter, how the experience of living in that country changes her." Similarly, the *Washington Post* (May 5, 1991) lamented, "In *The Middle Kingdom* Andrea Barrett does not perhaps cross new thresholds into the soul of women or the heart of China, but her novel is en-

gaging. She writes with felicity, intelligence, and humor."

Barrett's next novel was titled *The Forms of Water* (1993), and it examines the many generations of the Auberon family living in upstate New York. In a quest to see his own homestead (a 200-acre plot of undeveloped woodland at the edge of a manmade lake in Massachusetts), the eldest family member, Brendan, persuades his nephew Henry to steal a nursing home vehicle and take him there. What ensues is a trip that highlights the two men's vastly different personalities, as well as the history of the family, revealed through concerned relatives' recollections. All through the novel, however, a tragedy lurks.

The *New York Times Book Review* (June 13, 1993) called the Auberon clan an "appealingly wretched family," adding that ". . . Ms. Barrett nicely details the quiet agonies of people who have fallen from grace through bad luck and worse judgment and suggests that if you can't regain paradise, you can at least make peace with its loss." The *Washington Post* (June 7, 1993) called the novel "intelligent and elegiac" and praised Barrett as a "skillful writer" who "moves smoothly among the many consciousness that inhabit her book, giving us the clearly defined and differentiated personalities . . ."

The author's fifth literary work was a stylistic departure from her past novels and her most successful endeavor to date. Published in 1996, *Ship Fever and Other Stories* combines fiction with historical narrative. The title story, which many critics singled out as exceptional, takes the reader back in time to Ireland's Great Famine, during which thousands of Irish immigrants make the harrowing journey across the Atlantic to Canada. Instead of finding salvation there, however, they were subjected to the horrors of a typhus epidemic. Barrett places the character of Dr. Lauchlin Grant in the midst of this 19th-century scourge, as he leaves Montreal to work at a quarantine station where the immigrants are being held. Here he discovers the horrors of the "ship fever" he had heard about and finds sick, dying, and dead immigrants all thrown together in a floating house of filth.

Barrett received the highest amount of praise for this ghastly tale of disease, but other stories in the collection were also selected as outstanding, including "The Littoral Zone," which tells of a romance between a botanist and a zoologist in the midst of performing marine biology research. Another story that received high marks was "The Marburg Sisters," about a pair of siblings who, named after fairy tale characters, pursue vastly different lifestyles as they grow and, though rivals, maintain intimacy. Also included in the collection is "The English Pupil," which imagines the last year in the life of the Swedish naturalist Linnaeus, as he struggles with his memory and with entrusting his vast knowledge to others before he dies. "The Rare Bird" is another tale that garnered attention; it focuses on a strong-minded ornithologist in England who challenges Linnaeus's theory on the hibernation of doves.

A reviewer for the *San Francisco Chronicle* (February 4, 1996) wrote that the tales are "eloquently told and rich with contrast as Barrett pursues science as a metaphor for longing." Similarly, a *Booklist* (January 1, 1996) critic commended Barrett for stories that are "precise and concentrated, containing a truly remarkable wealth of psychology and social commentary." In the *New York Times Book Review* (January 28, 1996), Thomas Mallon noted that "Even when she leaves historical fiction for contemporary settings, Ms. Barrett hardly abandons taxonomy" and that throughout the book "she maps her characters' origins, differentiates their inherited and acquired characteristics, and especially, evaluates their attempts (usually failures) at transplantation and hybridization." Mallon examined the intricate relationships and turns of fate that Barrett imagines and concedes that "on occasion a reader will be tempted to say she's worked too hard at establishing such connections" between characters, fictional and real. However, Mallon quickly noted, "the arbitrariness of Ms. Barrett's inventions is the arbitrariness of the experimenter who deliberately puts one elements in contact with another in order to see what results. There is an artificiality to some of this maneuvering, and a tendency to spell out connections the way one was taught to write 'Conclusion' before the last step of a lab report—and yet Ms. Barrett's scientific bent is sufficiently rare among fiction writers, and her concoctions so cunningly mixed, that dissatisfaction seems out of place." The reviewer concludes by writing, "Ms. Barrett's narrative laboratory is stocked with a handsome array of equipment. . . . Seen against a larger fictional landscape overpopulated with the sensational and affectless, her work stands out for its sheer intelligence, its painstaking attempt to discern and describe the world's configuration. The overall effect is quietly dazzling, like looking at handmade paper under a microscope."

In the *Washington Post* (February 11, 1996) Nathalie op de Beeck commented in her review that in the story "Rare Bird," the "wordplay on the female protagonist and the swallows strikes a sour note, but Barrett chooses a unique means of portraying a well-read woman circa 1762." She notes that "Ship Fever" represents "an imaginative departure for the author. Even when these new tales follow the dysfunctional-family formula, they have an experimental edge." According to the critic, Barrett's "The Marburg Sisters" is not as successful as her other stories, and "labors to marry the analytical and magical, but bogs down in descriptions of the women's dying father and classically wicked stepmother. Barrett has greater success with her historical fiction, which plucks notable scientists from textbooks and powerfully links immortal names to mortal bodies." Although she notes that "The English Pupil" "begins and ends on the same plateau, without a shocking conclusion"

the reviewer explains that Barrett "prefers to make her point with little ado, then support it with evidence, not unlike a scientist compiling data to establish a proof. Yet this doesn't diminish her tales' lyricism." The review ends with the comment that as a whole, the collection of stories "memorably places geniuses on a human level in an effort to explore universal passions."

Ship Fever and Other Stories earned Barrett a great deal of attention and numerous honors, including the National Book Award. Most common among the many compliments about her book was the acknowledgment that Barrett was able to successfully merge historical scientific fact with engaging fiction. It is a style that Barrett would continue to utilize in her work, although the author has stated she never intended to specifically incorporate science into her stories. "I love short stories, and I had started to teach around the time of my fourth novel and was not only reading more stories but looking at them more intently and watching my students write them. I wanted to learn how to write them, and that's really how that book started," she told *Salon* about *Ship Fever and Other Stories*. "I never had in mind, 'Oh, I'm going to make a book of stories about scientists.' I just wrote some stories trying to teach myself to do certain things."

The author has continued to apply the research techniques she learned as a graduate student to her work, and spends countless hours poring over documents and books she surrounds herself with at home. Barrett's most recent novel, *The Voyage of the Narwhal* (1998), utilized this method, with the real-life details of arctic expeditions as background for a story of family and the boundless ambition of scientists. Her tale concerns a fabled ship called the Narwhal that is attempting to locate the remnants of a previously failed expedition by Sir John Franklin, an actual British explorer who was on a voyage to discover the Northwest Passage but disappeared, along with his entire crew. Sailing on the Narwhal are Erasmus Wells, a middle-aged naturalist who is attempting to redeem himself for past failures in love and career, while simultaneously trying to please his younger sister, Lavinia, by protecting her fiancé, Zeke Voorhees, who is serving as commander of the ship. Erasmus, with his reserved demeanor, stands in contrast to Zeke, a pompous, manipulative man who fails to tell his crew of a secret plan to continue the voyage in search of a new pathway to a polar sea. While Lavinia waits in fear for the return of her fiancé, things onboard the ship go horribly wrong, and the crew is forced to spend the winter locked in by ice. As the book progresses, the narrative shifts back and forth from the expedition and cast of characters aboard the Narwhal to Philadelphia, where Lavinia waits with her friend Alexandra, an independent woman who strains against the period's restrictions on women. The drama that emerges as Zeke leaves the Narwhal to find fame and glory on his own, while Alexandra fights social repression, highlights a powerful look at human relationships and the costs of both subservience and ego.

The Voyage of the Narwhal won a positive reception from the nation's book critics, all of whom continued to praise Barrett's prose style. *Salon Magazine* (September 8, 1998) exclaimed, "It's been a long time since an American novel appeared that's as stately and composed as Andrea Barrett's *The Voyage of the Narwhal*," adding that Barrett "has shaped a compelling narrative" that is "solid, unhurried, reflective, and totally wedded to plot." The reviewer concluded by praising the book as Barrett's "own creation, marvelously imagined and beautifully told. A first-rate novel and a welcome, old-fashioned read." The *New York Times Book Review* (September 13, 1998) notice read, "Although I sometimes wanted Barrett's emotional reserve toward the characters to break, so that we could feel the highs and lows more, in the end perhaps this too is part of the fabric of the story." The review went on to state that "Barrett's marvelous achievement is to have reimagined so graphically that cusp of time when Victorian certainty began to question whether it could encompass the world with its outward-bound enthusiasm alone—when it started to glimpse the dark ballast beneath the iceberg's dazzling tip."

The *Denver Post* (September 20, 1998) called *The Voyage of the Narwhal* "a luminous work of historical fiction that explores the far reaches of the Arctic and of men's souls," adding that the novel "is an excellent demonstration of Barrett's exceedingly fine and thorough hand at blending historical and natural detail with life-shaping conflict." *San Francisco Chronicle* (October 4, 1998) writer Michael Upchurch commented that the novel ". . . is so skillfully researched that an unalerted reader would be sorely pressed to determine the line between fiction and fact." The reviewer exalted the novel's "masterful evocation of the arctic, its supple rendering of power struggles in the claustrophobic confines of the Narwhal, and its seamless blend of action and thought" and wrote that Barrett brings "curiosity, passion, and intelligence to her task—qualities to be prized in any fiction."

A more mixed commentary could be found in the pages of the *New York Times* (September 4, 1998), where critic Michiko Kakutani applauded Barrett for giving readers "an old-fashioned 19th-century novel that brings together the two abiding concerns in her work to date: the mysterious allure of science and the equally mysterious bonds of familial love and resentment." *The Voyage of the Narwhal*, wrote Kakutani, "showcases Ms. Barrett's gifts for extracting high drama from the complex world of science and natural history and for placing her characters in situations that reveal their fundamental natures." The reviewer noted that on another level, the novel "is a story of scientific hubris and sheer pig-headed ambition, a story meant, in some ways, to recall such disparate works as Mary Shelley's *Frankenstein* and Melville's *Moby Dick*." The question Kakutani posed was whether Barrett achieved her large ambitions with *Narwhal*; her answer was, up to a point. "For three-quarters of her tale, she does a masterful job of weaving her philosophical subtext into a glistening narrative, crammed full of rich, pictoral description and tingling suspense," the critic remarked. "Only in the novel's final pages does drama give way to melodramatic contrivance and genuine moral dilemmas to easy, sentimental resolutions." Kakutani explained her opinion by writing that "Ms. Barrett does a superb job of conjuring up the hermetic life on board a ship, and the magic and terror of the arctic north. Combining a naturalist's eye with a novelist's imagination. . . . At the same time, Ms. Barrett nimbly sketches in the personalities of the Narwhal's crew." However, she later noted, "In the last few sections of Narwhal, Ms. Barrett's fluent plotting gives way to a flurry of increasingly contrived events that seem to belong more to a big Hollywood movie than to the foregoing portions of the novel. Although these developments make *Narwhal* feel like a slighter, slicker work than it means to be, they do not tarnish Ms. Barrett's very real achievements: her ability to convey to the reader her psychological insights into her characters, her understanding of the fickle role that chance and luck play in people's lives, and her appreciation of the raw, unaccommodated power of nature." Kakutani concluded her review by writing that Barrett has written "a powerful and gripping—if finally flawed—novel."

Andrea Barrett has received numerous awards for both her short stories and her novels, including the Peden Prize (1992) for best short fiction for *Missouri Review*, the *Southern Review* Fiction Prize (1996), for "Ship Fever," the Pushcart Prize (1997) for "The Forest," and the *Salon Magazine* Book Award (1998) for The *Voyage of the Narwhal*. Despite such acclaim, Barrett remains surprised at the interest that her books and their subject matter have generated. As she told *Salon*, "Maybe it's still true that if you write what really interests you, other people will be interested in it too, no matter how seemingly obscure or arcane it is. If you can make a narrative out of it."

Barrett has been described by *Publishers Weekly* as a "lanky" woman with an "animated face" that lies under "a crown of long tresses." She continues to make her home in Rochester, New York, with her husband and is currently at work on a new novel. —D.B.

SUGGESTED READING: *Amazon Books* (online); *Baltimore Sun* (online) Mar. 9, 1997; *Booklist* (online) Jan.1, 1996; *Denver Post* (online) Sep. 20, 1998; *Nation* p32+ Jan 29, 1996; *New York Times* p30 Jan. 29, 1989, p24 June 23, 1991, p20 June 13, 1993, Jan. 28, 1996, Sep. 4, 1998, Sep. 13, 1998; *Publishers Weekly* p443 Aug. 11, 1989, p363+ Aug. 10, 1998; *Salon Magazine* (online) Sep. 8, 1998, Dec. 2, 1998; *San Francisco Chronicle* (online) Feb. 4, 1996, Oct. 4, 1998; *Spectator* p42+ Mar. 11, 1989; *Washington Post* p11 May 5, 1991, D p2 June 7, 1993; *Contemporary Authors*, 1997

SELECTED WORKS: *Lucid Stars*, 1988; *Secret Harmonies*, 1989; *The Middle Kingdom*, 1991; *The Forms of Water*, 1993; *Ship Fever and Other Stories*, 1996; *The Voyage of the Narwhal*, 1998

Bateson, Gregory

May 9, 1904– July 4, 1980 Scientist; essayist

The English-born social theorist Gregory Bateson trained as a zoologist and anthropologist, but his investigations included cybernetics and psychiatry. Works published in his lifetime include *Naven* (1936), his first book, in which he combined ethnographic reporting with a theory of behavior involving a feedback mechanism he termed "schismogenesi"s; *Balinese Character* (1942), the product of investigations conducted in Bali with Margaret Mead; *Communication, the Social Matrix of Psychiatry* (1951), a study of the role of communication between patients and psychiatrists, written with Jurgen Ruesch; and the collections *Steps to an Ecology of Mind: Collected Essays in Anthropology, Psychiatry, Evolution, and Epistemology* (1972) and *A Sacred Unity: Further Steps to an Ecology of Mind* (1991). Bateson's last work, which was completed by his daughter Mary Catherine Bateson, was *Angels Fear: Towards an Epistemology of the Sacred*, a sequel to *Mind and Nature: A Necessary Unity* (1979), in which he had tried to discern the interconnectedness of consciousness and the universe. In all his work, Bateson was more concerned with asking useful questions than with positing definitive answers, and he often sought to demonstrate the oneness of the universe.

Gregory Bateson was born on May 9, 1904 in England, the son and grandson of eminent Cambridge University scientists. His father, William Bateson, a fellow of St. John's College, was the first British professor of genetics, and named Gregory, his third son, in honor of Gregor Mendel, the nineteenth-century scientist known as the "father of genetics." His mother, Caroline Beatrice Durham, was the daughter of a well-known surgeon.

Gregory grew up in Grantchester, a town just outside Cambridge, and frequently accompanied his older brothers on their "beetling" expeditions to study and collect nature specimens. In 1913 he was sent to a preparatory school in Kent, and in 1917 he entered Charterhouse School. Following the untimely deaths of both his brothers (one a casualty of World War I, the other a suicide), he felt obliged to follow them in studying natural sciences at St. John's. Accordingly, he entered Cambridge in 1922 to read zoology. In 1925 he received his B.A. with first-class honors, then left on a trip to the Galapagos Islands, after which he joined William Beebe on a New York Zoological Society oceanographic expedition.

Upon his return to England, Bateson made the difficult decision to leave zoology to find a field of his own. An initial investigation into psychology left him unimpressed, but a meeting in 1925 with the Cambridge ethnologist A. C. Haddon was decisive: Haddon persuaded Bateson to study anthropology, and the following year urged him to do field work in Melanesia. Propelled by a desire to escape Caroline Bateson's possessiveness—"I fled from my mother," he later recalled, according to David Lipset in *Gregory Bateson: The Legacy of a Scientist* (1980)—he obtained a student grant in 1927, and spent 10 months with the Baining people of New Britain. Ultimately he found them poor subjects for study because they were secretive and difficult to talk with, and his research foundered. In 1929 he started over again in New Guinea, with the Iatmul, a Sepik River group which both fascinated and perplexed him. The following year he returned home to develop his field notes, and went on to receive his M.A. for a thesis on "Social Structures of the Iatmul People of the Sepik River," published in 1932. A work of descriptive rather than theoretical anthropology, it is interspersed with self-critical comments on the inadequacy of his research, and is a commentary on, as much as a record of, the process of anthropological investigation. The thesis was written as a series of imaginary dialogues that he termed "metalogues," a form characteristic of his later writing.

In 1931, as a fellow of St. John's and a recipient of a Royal Society grant, Bateson returned to New Guinea to work with the Iatmul and collect data for his first book, *Naven* (1936). In the course of his expedition he met the anthropologists Margaret Mead and Reo Fortune, who were married to each other at the time. The three camped and worked together for a time, exchanging methodologies and ideas. Together they also read a draft copy of Ruth Benedict's *Patterns of Culture*, a book that influenced Bateson to attempt to distinguish societies by their dominant psychological patterns, as Benedict had done. Back in Cambridge, between 1933 and 1936, Bateson finished *Naven*, which takes its title from the name of an Iatmul ceremony that marks a child's first performance of an adult task. The rites involve dramatized role reversals, transvestism, and simulated homosexual intercourse. In *Naven*, Bateson first identified types of reciprocal behavior that he termed "schismogenesis." In "symmetrical schismogenesis," one person's boasting, for example, triggers boasting in return. In "complementary schismogenesis," one action elicits the opposite, as where assertive behavior begets submissiveness. These observations anticipated the principle of feedback in the cybernetic theory that would later fascinate Bateson. He wrote in the epilogue to *Naven* that he "was trying not only to explain by fitting data together but also to use the explanatory process as an example within which the principles of explanation could be seen and studied." Throughout the book, he mentions possible shortcomings in his methodology and suggests modifications that might be made to his explanations. Most commentators agreed that while Bateson's ethnographical descriptions were intriguing, his exposition was labored. A. R. Radcliffe-Brown concluded in a review in the *American Journal of Sociology* (Vol. 43, 1937) that the book was "to be recommended to thoughtful people [but] not likely to have wide circulation." (Nevertheless, *Naven* was reissued by Stanford University Press in 1958.)

In 1936, despite the misgivings of his mother, Bateson married Margaret Mead in Singapore, and they spent the next two years working together in Bali. There Bateson shot films of Balinese life, which Mead annotated. The resulting documents are considered the earliest use of film as a primary tool in ethnographic research. In her memoir, *Blackberry Winter*, Mead referred to their collaboration as "the perfect intellectual and emotional partnership in which there was no pulling and hauling resulting from competing temperamental views of the world." The film record, which was the basis of their book *Balinese Character: A Photographic Analysis* (1942), includes a sequence showing the way a Balinese mother arouses her child's expectations of feeding or affection, but then withdraws her attention, leaving the child frustrated and, ultimately, more passive.

Bateson and Mead had a daughter, the anthropologist Mary Catherine Bateson, who was born in 1939, the year after their return to New York. Her candid, affectionate double portrait of her parents, *With a Daughter's Eye* (1984), describes the few years the three spent together as a family unit, and elucidates not only her father's parental concerns but his role as her mentor and working colleague. During World War II, from 1942 to 1945, Gregory Bateson was usually away on assignment with the United States Office of Strategic Services (OSS), even though he did not become an American citizen until 1956. Based in southeast Asia, he worked as a "psychological planner," broadcasting misleading information designed to lower Japanese morale. A year after coming home, depressed by the OSS work (which he felt was a violation of the purposes of human communication), and his faltering marriage, Bateson left his family and went into therapy. He and Mead divorced in 1950 but maintained a collegial friendship until her death.

In 1942 Bateson and Mead had taken part in interdisciplinary conferences on the new field of cybernetics, sponsored by the Josiah Macy, Jr., Foundation. Bateson called his participation in these discussions, as quoted in *About Bateson: Essays on Gregory Bateson* (1977), "one of the great events of my life." In 1947 he received a Guggenheim Fellowship to research the application of cybernetic theory to anthropological data. Concurrently, he taught anthropology as a visiting professor at the New School for Social Research and at Harvard University between 1946 and 1948. For the rest of his life, his financial support came from such temporary lectureships and a succession of institution-

al grants. Both Mead and David Lipset, his future biographer, suggested that Bateson's difficulty in finding a permanent teaching post stemmed from his insistence on an interdisciplinary approach and his suspicion of textbooks that presented information as incontrovertible fact. A lover of abstract thought, Bateson pursued investigation for its own sake, and enjoyed raising questions that led to further questions, without coming to conclusions.

In 1948 Bateson began a new chapter in his intellectual development when he joined the psychiatrist Jurgen Ruesch on a research project at the Langley Porter Clinic of the University of California Medical School in San Francisco. The results of their study of the role of patient-psychiatrist communication in psychotherapy were published jointly as *Communication, the Social Matrix of Psychiatry* (1951). By 1949 Bateson had moved to Palo Alto, where he lectured to medical students as an ethnologist attached to the Veterans Administration Hospital. There he began new research on alcoholism and schizophrenia. Working with his concept of schismogenesis, and ideas from cybernetics, which can be considered a form of communications theory, he saw alcohol addiction as a form of feedback, a self-regenerating pathological process. Later, out of this Palo Alto work, he developed one of his major papers, "The Cybernetics of Self: A Theory of Alcoholism," published in *Psychiatry* in 1971. His other line of investigation, which involved informal talks with schizophrenic patients, led him to the belief that communication was the key to the disease. Accordingly, he worked from 1954 to 1959, on a grant from the Josiah Macy Foundation, to determine if children can be "trained" to become schizophrenic. Studying mother-and-child relations, he developed the famous double bind theory, presented in his classic paper, "Toward a Theory of Schizophrenia" (1956), which strongly influenced the Scottish psychiatrist R. D. Laing. The theory proposes that a child may become schizophrenic as a result of conflicting messages, generally the mixing of affection and rejection, from a parent, usually a mother (a bias, his daughter suggested, that reflected his own difficult relationship with his mother). He found corroboration of his theory partly in an account written by a 19th-century Englishman, John Perceval, describing his own psychosis and treatment. As editor of Perceval's narrative, Bateson was struck by the patient's statement that he had wanted to talk, but that neither his family nor his physicians would listen to him.

In 1951 Bateson married Betty Sumner, the secretary on the project he had done with Ruesch. The marriage yielded a son, John, but ended in divorce in 1958. Three years later Bateson married Lois Cammack, a psychiatric social worker. They had one daughter, Nora. In 1961 he received the Frieda Fromm-Reichman Award of the American Academy of Psychoanalysis, but soon thereafter left the field. Always skeptical of applied social science (including psychotherapy) for what he deemed its meddling interventions in people's lives, he was moved to assert, according to Lipset, in 1962 that "while I have cared for several schizophrenic patients, I have never been intellectually interested in them. . . . Always my intellectual focus has been on general principles."

Turning to more purely theoretical investigations, between 1963 and 1972, Bateson studied the communication of dolphins, first in the Virgin Islands, then at the Oceanic Institute in Hawaii, while also lecturing in anthropology at the University of Hawaii. In 1968 he chaired a conference of the Wenner-Gren Foundation for Anthropological Research at Burg Wartenstein, Austria. His role in guiding the thinking of the assembled scholars is documented in *Our Own Metaphor* (1972), a book by Mary Catherine Bateson, who acted as rapporteur of the proceedings.

In 1971 and 1972, despite the onset of emphysema, Bateson led a group of undergraduates to Asia to investigate parallels between cybernetic theory and Buddhism. The group then continued on to Africa. Among the students was David Lipset, who began interviewing Bateson in anticipation of writing his biography. In addition to interviews with Bateson, Lipset's book, *Gregory Bateson: The Legacy of a Scientist*, published in 1980, made use of previously unavailable documents and discussions with Bateson's contemporaries.

When Bateson returned to California, he began lecturing at Kresge College of the University of California at Santa Cruz. There he conducted challenging—but well-attended—seminars; one, for example, on "The Ecology of the Mind," was devoted to the epistemological premises in behavior and perception as found in human cultures, plant morphology, and animal behavior. At around the same time, *Steps to an Ecology of Mind* (1972) appeared. The volume is a collection of Bateson's previously published articles and lectures from 1935 to 1970, chosen by Mark Engel, one of his former students, as examples of "better thinking" than that of most American academics. This thinking and Bateson's views on education attracted the attention of California's erudite governor, Jerry Brown, and in 1976 he appointed Bateson a member of the state Board of Regents, to stir things up a bit.

In 1978 (the year Margaret Mead died), Bateson developed lung cancer. During a temporary remission he worked with Mary Catherine Bateson on a manuscript he had begun some time earlier. An account of Bateson's attempts to discern the "meta-pattern" that connects all things, it was published the year before his death as *Mind and Nature: A Necessary Unity*. As D. W. Harding put it in "Single Mind, Double Bind," his *New York Review of Books* (October 19, 1972) tribute to Bateson's work, Bateson was concerned with the nature of the human mind as "a network of interactions relating the individual with . . . society . . . species and . . . the universe at large." John Pfeiffer, in a review of *Mind and Nature* in the *New York Times* (April 29,

1979) found it "an extraordinary testament . . . by one of the most creative investigators of our times." Stephen J. Gould, admitted that the book was very difficult, but his review in the *Christian Science Monitor* (July 9, 1979) concluded that "if I revel in the world's complexity, why insist that an honest attempt to deal with it be unambiguous and, therefore, unoriginal."

In 1979 Bateson and his family went to live in Big Sur, California, at the Esalen Institute, a center of thought for the counterculture since the 1960s. Although he rejected almost everything the institute stood for, he found it easier to live with that skepticism than with the "disgust . . . that conventional occidental ways of . . . life inspire in me," as he wrote in *Angels Fear*. He was especially horrified by problems with the environment and the way human beings, in his opinion, seem bent on destroying a planet they do not comprehend.

Up until his death on July 4, 1980, at the Zen Center in San Francisco, Gregory Bateson worked on a book that he intended to write with Mary Catherine Bateson. For seven years afterward she worked to organize and complete her father's draft manuscript; in 1987 it was published as *Angels Fear: Towards an Epistemology of the Sacred*, and, to some extent, continues the exploration of the ideas in *Mind and Nature*. Chapters by Bateson alternate in *Angels Fear* with his daughter's "metalogues": chapters in the form of imaginary conversations with her father that attempt to explain the points he has made and to indicate the shape the book might have taken had he lived. It is, in Lipset's words, an explanation of "the way in which, in a nondualistic [i.e., without distinction between mind and matter] view of the world, a new concept of the sacred emerges."

Bateson was "granite-faced," according to his *New York Times* (July 7, 1980) obituary, a rumpled, slouching figure who had, according to Mary Catherine Bateson, "more limbs and height than he knew what to do with." Generally gregarious and the center of any group, he could frequently be peevish and opinionated. Bateson probably best summed up his own career as a search for "the wider knowing" that is "the glue holding together the starfishes and sea anemones and redwood forests and human committees." John Brockman, editor of *About Bateson*, acknowledged that Bateson's presentation of his ideas could be very challenging for the average reader, as Bateson was known for his involutions and repetitions of the same theme in different terms, as well as his neologisms and idiosyncratic use of familiar words. Bateson himself acknowledged (in *About Bateson*) that "very few people have any idea of what I am talking about." Nevertheless, Brockman felt that he was "the most underrated writer of the century." To Mary Catherine Bateson, her father's "richest legacy lay in his questions and in his way of formulating questions," she wrote in *Angels Fear*. And as Lipset concluded in his biography, if his much-admired mentor's "questions and ideals sometimes exceed

him, they do so from a tantalizing distance rather than from an impossible one. It remains to be seen what the future will make of them and of him." Gregory Bateson was a fellow of the American Academy for the Advancement of Science and held an honorary D.Sci. from Northwestern University (1972). The library of the University of California at Santa Cruz maintains a Bateson Archive.
—E. M.

SUGGESTED READING: *American Journal of Sociology* 1937; *Christian Science Monitor* July 9, 1979; *New York Review of Books* Oct. 19, 1972; *New York Times* Apr. 29, 1979, July 7, 1980; *New Yorker* May 27, 1974; (London) *Times* July 7, 1980; Bateson, M. C. *Our Own Metaphor: A Personal Account of a Conference on the Effects of Conscious Purpose on Human Adaptation*, 1972; Bateson, M. C. *With a Daughter's Eye: A Memoir of Margaret Mead and Gregory Bateson*, 1984; Brockman, John, ed. *About Bateson: Essays on Gregory Bateson*, 1977; Lipset, D. *Gregory Bateson: The Legacy of a Scientist*, 1980; Mead, Margaret. *Blackberry Winter: My Earlier Years*, 1972; Rieber, Robert W., ed. *The Individual, Communication, and Society: Essays in Memory of Gregory Bateson*, 1989; *Dictionary of American Biography* Suppl. 10, 1976-1980, 1995

SELECTED BOOKS: *Naven, a Survey of the Problems Suggested by a Composite Picture of the Culture of a New Guinea Tribe Drawn from Three Points of View*, 1936, 2d rev. ed. 1958; *Mind and Nature: A Necessary Unity*, 1979; with Margaret Mead—*Balinese Character: A Photographic Analysis*, 1942, 1962; with J. Ruesch—*Communication, the Social Matrix of Psychiatry*, 1951, 2d ed. 1968; with Mary Catherine Bateson—*Angels Fear: Towards an Epistemology of the Sacred*, 1987; as editor: *Perceval's Narrative: A Patient's Account of His Psychosis, 1830-1832*, 1961

Charles Baxter

Baxter, Charles

May 13, 1947– Novelist; short-story writer; poet; essayist

The American novelist, short-story writer, and essayist Charles Baxter has made the dusty territory of a small town in Michigan his literary turf. *First Light* (1987), his first novel, spirals back in time to show the early stages of the relationship between a brother and a sister, and *Shadow Play* (1993) examines the relationship between two foster broth-

ers. Baxter's real theme, according to Lorrie Moore, is how the good Midwestern values of niceness and passivity "contribute to the rot and demise of a community." He sets his stories in those "shadowy corners of civilization in which barbarity manages to nestle and thrive." Francine Prose in the *New York Times Book Review* (April 6, 1997) remarked that what "gives the work its density is not *event* so much as psychological depth, the intricate renderings of characters' habits and longings, and of the exterior world that impinges on their private hopes and fears." She concluded that Baxter's real concerns are religious: "Baxter convinces us of the soul's existence by precisely representing his characters' inner lives, their imaginative sensibilities and acutely detailed perceptions." Baxter's collections of short stories, *Harmony of the World* (1984), *Through the Safety Net* (1985), *A Relative Stranger* (1990), and *Believers* (1997), touching on the same themes, have been termed "brilliant" by Moore and other critics. Chuck Wachtel in the *Nation* (April 7, 1997) called Baxter "a master craftsman" who "knows that craft is more than something to be good at."

For *World Authors 1990–1995*, Charles Baxter, born on May 13, 1947, writes: "I was born in Minneapolis, Minnesota. I have two older brothers. My father, John T. Baxter, sold insurance; for a time, my mother worked in radio, writing commercials. They were both friends of musicians and writers in Minneapolis-Saint Paul. They befriended Sinclair Lewis, who lived nearby, and my mother corresponded with him for several years. My aunt Helen, who had been trained in Paris, was a portrait artist of children, and her work was very much in the style of Mary Cassatt.

"My father died of a heart attack a few months after I was born, in 1948. My mother remarried in 1950, and we all moved out to my stepfather's estate, a place called 'World's End,' on Lake Minnetonka, about an hour west of Minneapolis. It had been my stepfather's idea to have an estate in the English style, complete with horses and grazing sheep. The place was said to be haunted, and both my brothers and I suspected that, indeed, it was. A large library with leather bound books and uncut pages was in the north end of the house.

"I attended Macalester College and the State University of New York at Buffalo, taught public school in Pinconning, Michigan, a town located in the Saginaw valley near Lake Huron. I then taught at Wayne State University for several years before coming to the University of Michigan. During my graduate school years in Buffalo, I began to write long fiction, the first of three failed novels, fortunately never published. During this time, I was also writing poetry. I had been very much under the influence of postmodernist writers such as Donald Barthelme and other abstractionist modernist writers, but by the end of the 1970's, I came to feel that I had reached a dead end. I had mastered neither the form nor the content of fiction in any apparent way.

"As a result, I turned to short fiction, to short stories, and to the people among whom I had lived in the Midwest. This change produced the stories in my first book of fiction (there had been two small-press books of poetry before that), *Harmony of the World*. These stories are set in the Midwest and are about a certain kind of life: the stories deal with people whose achievements have somehow not met their expectations, and many of them are doing their best to adjust to that diminution. This theme is extended in the next book of stories, *Through the Safety Net*, where the 'downsizing' of American expectations produces more anxious and even violent results. I felt that Americans in the 1980's were beginning to lose some faith in the future and in their own security, and the stories are often about the eruptions of the unexpected in their midst.

"Since then, there have been two novels, *First Light*, a family novel written in reverse chronology, and *Shadow Play*, a book that combines certain features of the Faust story and the Don Quixote story in a Midwestern small city, Five Oaks, where I have set many of my narratives. I have written many more stories, collected in *A Relative Stranger* and in a new book, *Believers*. *A Relative Stranger* is very much about the possibilities inherent in situations where strangers—who may have something in common—happen to meet. *Believers* is more about the small and large articles of faith and belief that people cling to in order to get from day to day, with a concluding novella about a trio of Americans travelling to Nazi Germany in 1938.

"I have a particular love for the short story form, which as a rule is sympathetic to characters who indulge their impulses and who, perhaps because of that, are usually unofficial in the culture at large, and therefore almost invisible. Although my stories are often set in the Midwest, I don't necessarily think of myself as a regionalist. William Carlos Williams wrote that 'anywhere is everywhere,' and I have always felt the truth of that statement: everything in the world eventually arrives on your doorstep, if only you are alert enough to see it. My fiction is more about impulses than about great plans and schemes. It seeks to make unfamiliar what might have seemed, at first glance, quite ordinary and banal. It seeks to bring a sense of sometimes terrible strangeness back to daily life."

In an essay, "Dysfunctional Narratives; Or 'Mistakes Were Made,'" published in *Ploughshares* (Fall 1994), Charles Baxter posited the "singularly unhappy idea" that the greatest influence on American fiction over the last few decades may have been Richard Nixon, "the inventor . . . for our time, of the concept of *deniability*." Baxter wrote not only of the shoddy politics of the times but also of "dysfunctional narrative as literary art." He took for an example the "brilliantly observant and relentless" novel *A Thousand Acres* by Jane Smiley, in which, he claimed, "the characters . . . are not acting upon events in present narrative time but are reacting obscurely to harms done to them in the psychic past, from unthinkable impulses that will go forever unexplained." In the dysfunctional narrative, characters are not permitted to make mistakes and then to acknowledge them. The end result is that in "the absence of any clear moral vision, we get moralizing. . . . I am nostalgic—as a writer, of course—for stories with mindful villainy, villainy with clear motives that any adult would understand, bad behavior with a sense of *scale*, that would give back to us our imaginative grip on the despicable and the admirable and our capacity to have some opinions about the two." It has been Baxter's literary goal to "balance issues . . . of concern . . . socially with matters of the soul and the heart—to make them reflect each other," he told Jon Elsen in an interview in the *New York Times Book Review* (February 14, 1993).

In Baxter's story "Super Night" from *Believers*, first published in *TriQuarterly* (Fall 1994), a working-class wife immediately realizes her husband has made a terrible mistake when, after a night of drinking with their unprepossessing upstairs neighbor, he repeats the neighbor's story of having murdered a child. The husband, a skilled automobile mechanic, is haunted by the idea that the neighbor has gone unpunished for his evil deed. The wife believes the neighbor has actually been narrating the plot of a movie he saw on television: "A harmless and ugly man, she decided, who worked upholstering furniture and who, after hours, imagined himself as a dangerous character in the movies. The movies were getting into everything now. They could spread over everyone, like the flu." Her husband, however, acts out his impulse to avenge the child's death by tampering with the man's car. This act "wasn't meant to kill him, exactly . . . ," he tells his wife. "Paralyze him, maybe." As a result of the tampering, the neighbor suffers broken bones. When the wife brings the neighbor some food after his release from the hospital, he tells her that Jesus has a plan for him: "He told me I should despair." The woman can do nothing to alter what has happened in reality, so she retreats into her own imagination and warns the imaginary boy of the neighbor's story to run away before he gets killed.

The story encapsulates Baxter's concerns: marginalized people living lives of quiet despair, the internalization of machismo by men, moral decisions, mistaken actions taken to right wrongs, the pervasiveness of television values, and acceptance of responsibility by the characters for their actions. Various critics have ranked Baxter with the best contemporary American short-story writers. William Ferguson, reviewing *A Relative Stranger* in the *New York Times* (October 21, 1990), noted that Baxter's leading characters have an "abiding failure . . . to imagine what is most real." "By contrast," he concluded, "Charles Baxter's chronicling of such human debilities represents a continuing triumph of the imaginative will."

First Light, Baxter's first published novel, is narrated in reverse chronological order. The chief character, an astrophysicist, is reunited with her brother, a car salesman who has remained in the town where they were born. The novel explores their relationship, returning them to the past, until at the end the brother first meets his newborn sister. Michiko Kakutani, reviewing the novel in the *New York Times*, declared *First Light* a novel that "gleams with the smoky chiaroscuro of familial love recalled through time."

Shadow Play, Baxter's second novel, is set in the same small town, "a town of 'prideful' lies, 'sun-smelted' ponds, and 'apples dry-rotting in the hot dust of the driveway,'" according to Lorrie Moore in the *New York Times Book Review* (February 14,1993). *Shadow Play* begins in a rainstorm, with the eight-year old Wyatt planning to run away from home: "Wyatt was packing. He had had enough. It was time to leave, to move on." By the end of the novel, he is a man who has seen his cousin and "sort of brother," Cyril, contract lung cancer from working in a plant that Wyatt, a bureaucrat, has permitted to violate the occupational safety laws. He has rowed Cyril out on a lake, given him the blessing that he has asked for, and handed him the weight that enables Cyril to drown himself. He has attempted to take vengeance by burning the factory owner's house down. Later, forced to play golf with the factory owner to preserve appearances, he has learned that he has destroyed nothing but the neighborhood stray dog. Having "had enough" Wyatt then flees to Brooklyn with his wife and children and his insane mother, seeing New York as "a place that they couldn't spoil anymore, because it had already been spoiled a century ago." There, according to Lorrie Moore, Wyatt "can attempt something un-Midwestern, something unthwarted, adventurous, something like a coda, a twilight sequel; in unecological times, an ecology of hope and loss." Moore concluded that Baxter "has steadily taken beautiful and precise language and gone into the ordinary and secret places of people—their moral and emotional quandaries, their typically American circumstances, their burning intelligence, their negotiations with what is trapped, stunted, violent, sustaining, decent, or miraculous in their lives. In writing about ordinary people he derives narrative authority from having imagined farther and more profoundly than we have."

The *Publishers Weekly* (February 24, 1997) reviewer found a division between the short stories and the title novella of *Believers* (1997). "Ambitious and accomplished, the shorter works here tackle slippery themes and subjects—fleeting moments of truth; the ambiguities of daily life and the defenses through which ordinary men and women attempt to clarify them." Of the title novella, however, in which a priest traveling with a corrupt couple to Nazi Germany loses his faith, the reviewer said that "the suppleness of the author's observations coarsens into heavy ironies and almost melodramatic revelations," as when the narrator announces, "This is a story . . . about fascism, and believers, a story of the American Midwest, and of how I came to be conceived and brought into the world by a priest. I suppose that announcing all this information ahead of time is poor form. I don't care. My existence is not the point of this story, in any case."

Chuck Wachtel, reviewing *Believers* in the *Nation* (April 7, 1997), found all of Baxter's techniques viable: "Charles Baxter is a remarkable storyteller." Wachtel pronounced Baxter's narratives "as plausible as they are utterly amazing. Things often arise suddenly: a wind-borne piece of paper delivers an ominous message, a husband comes home with surprising and improbable news. . . . The conflict doesn't so much reside in the sudden arrival of the unexpected—a dramatic element that goes back to the first storytellers—but in the manner in which this new component penetrates and uneasily fits itself into a character's fate. The stories proceed from an idea of experience that feels new, yet mysteriously familiar."

Francine Prose, reviewing *Believers* in the *New York Times Book Review* (April 6, 1997), found that "the eloquence of the language—the quirky intelligence, the humor, the lively rhythmic assurance of sentences and paragraphs"—makes the stories pleasurable to read. But she also discovered a deeper meaning, in that nearly all "the narratives concern a Manichaean struggle between the powers of love and the forces of violence." Many of the stories end "on a note of acceptance, with a character resolving to live bravely amid the contradictions of a painful, frightening, deeply flawed—and ineffably beautiful—world."

Also published in 1997 was Baxter's *Burning Down the House: Essays on Fiction*. The collection deals with what Baxter sees as the shortcomings of contemporary fiction. It received a stamp of approval in the *New York Times Book Review* (May 4, 1997) from Emily Barton, who pronounced it to be "not a rigorous work of literary criticism, but . . . a pleasure to read," in part for its frequent comic undertones. As the editor of the 1999 volume *The Business of Memory: The Art of Remembering in an Age of Forgetting*, Baxter recruited 12 writers—among them Bernard Cooper, Margot Livesey, and James Alan McPherson—to address various subjects related to memory in contemporary life. The topics include the recent popularity of memoirs and the recovered-memory phenomenon.

Charles Baxter lives in Ann Arbor and teaches at the University of Michigan. He has received grants from the National Endowment for the Arts, the Guggenheim Foundation, and the Michigan Arts Council, and, in 1991, a Lila Wallace-Reader's Digest Foundation Award for Writers.
—S. Y.

SUGGESTED READING: *Nation* p 33+ Apr. 7, 1997; *New York Times Book Review* p7 Feb. 14, 1993, p7 Apr. 6, 1997; *Ploughshares* p 67+ Fall 1994; *Publishers Weekly* p65 Feb. 24, 1997; *Contemporary Authors* nrs vol. 40, 1993

SELECTED BOOKS: Fiction—*Harmony of the World*, 1984; *Through the Safety Net*, 1985; *First Light*, 1987; *A Relative Stranger*, 1990; *Shadow Play*, 1993; *Believers*, 1997; Nonfiction—*Burning Down the House: Essays on Fiction*, 1997; Poetry—*Chameleon*, 1970; *Imaginary Paintings and Other Poems*, 1990; As editor—*The Business of Memory: The Art of Remembering in an Age of Forgetting*, 1999

Jessica White

Begley, Louis

Oct. 6, 1933– Novelist; lawyer

"When one thinks about something one is going to write, one operates on a fairly elevated plane of existence; one is concerned with characters, narrative, words . . ." author Louis Begley once told *Vanity Fair* (February 1993). "It's a magical, elevated activity which calls things forth from inside one that other forms of intellectual activity don't." Despite such passionate feelings toward the art, Louis Begley's writing career did not begin until late in his life. Although he earned his undergraduate degree in English literature, for more than 30 years, Begley worked as a contract lawyer for a prestigious firm in New York. Having abandoned his earlier predilection for writing fiction, Begley did not begin to consider producing a book of his own until he was 57. Drawing on his dramatic childhood as a young Jewish boy escaping Nazi Poland, Begley then wrote *Wartime Lies*, a harrowing tale of a man who assumes various identities to avoid capture by the Nazis in war-torn Europe. The novel was a phenomenal success. Begley has competed four additional books, all of which feature complex male characters who struggle to uncover their true selves. These novels have earned Begley a reputation as a craftsman of fiction that is multifarious and engaging.

Louis Begley was born Ludwik Begleiter in Stryj, Poland, on October 6, 1933. His father, born Dawid Begleiter, worked as a physician in the Polish army while his mother, Franciszka, was a homemaker. Growing up comfortably in a wealthy household, young Ludwik and his family were thrown into a state of bitter turmoil when they, along with millions of other Jews, were forced to leave their home and flee the Nazi occupation of Poland during World War II. While his father was forced by the Soviets to spend the war years in Samarkand, Begley and his mother moved from one boardinghouse to another across Poland. They managed to survive the Nazi reign of terror, though Ludwik lost all of his grandparents, his aunt, and his cousins to the war. After reuniting with Dawid, the family stayed briefly in Paris after the war, before immigrating to the U.S. in 1947, where they became Edward, Frances, and Louis Begley. Settling first in Manhattan and then Brooklyn, Louis struggled to fit in with his new classmates and often found himself picked on because of his European clothes and Polish accent. He quickly improved his English and was able to distinguish himself among the students at Erasmus High School, where he excelled in his literature classes. He was unable to forget his past experiences in Poland, however, and he found himself not only struggling with his own identity in this new world, but also coping with his parents' forlornness. In an interview with *Vanity Fair*'s Joan Juliet Buck, Begley commented on this time in his life, "Everybody seemed to be moving so much faster than I was, they knew about things I didn't know, they were playing sports I didn't know how to play. . . . My father got his medical license very quickly, and it all started up again—but I could see them as lost in this meaningless borough and lost in this meaningless world . . . it was all so forlorn, and it felt so hopeless . . . this sense of being lost in a sea of strangeness and difference, the absence of real affective links to anybody except me."

After high school, Begley was able to obtain a scholarship to Harvard University, and while there he published several short stories in the *Harvard Advocate*. By the time he was a sophomore, however, he had decided that he was not going to aim his career toward writing. "I read a story in class and quit," he told Buck. "I came to the conclusion that I had nothing to say. I felt I didn't know anything beyond my Polish experience well enough to write about it. I didn't know what a family was in this country, or about how they lived, or anything about the New World . . . I felt there was nothing that came before that was useful."

Begley still lived with the horrors of war that he had witnessed as a child and struggled to reconcile his past as a Jewish exile with his largely Gentile, affluent surroundings at Harvard. In addition to the survivor's guilt that many victims of extreme devastation such as the Holocaust experience, Begley wrestled with an all-consuming self-consciousness about his environs. To cope, the college student gave up writing and instead focused his attention toward activities that would not require him to spend hours reflecting on his life in Poland. As he told Buck, "I thought if I could just soak up enough experiences, if I could spend enough long nights doing this or that, enough time with the people I most wanted to resemble, somehow whatever was in me that was immutably wrong, wrong and disgraceful, would be changed into this happier, more sunlit, more acceptable material."

Begley graduated summa cum laude from Harvard, one of two English students (the other being renowned author John Updike) to achieve that honor at the institution in 1954. Begley had wanted to pursue the study of literature, but when he failed to get a Rhodes scholarship, he decided to volunteer for the U.S. Army instead. Stationed in Germany, Begley put forth a great deal of effort in his duties, even hiring a tutor to learn German. While he was there, he took a visit to Paris, where he met up with a young American, Sally Higginson, with whom he had attended Harvard. The pair married in February 1956, and although he had entertained thoughts of becoming a professor of comparative literature, he abandoned the idea in the face of her disapproval and instead attended Harvard Law School.

After graduating law school, in 1959, Begley joined the law firm of Debevoise & Plimpton and after several years was sent to represent the firm in Paris. He remained there for three years, during which time he and his wife, who had had two children, separated (they divorced in 1970) and he built a solid reputation in corporate law. In 1974, he married Anne Muhlstein Dujarric dela Riviere, who had two children from a previous marriage. Together, the couple had three children. Begley continued to practice law with his firm (of which he became a partner in 1968) but started to ponder a philosophical question that had been raised in his reading of the work of the ancient Roman poet Catullus. "It was a question of good deeds," he told the *Chicago Tribune*'s Lisa Anderson (November 19, 1991). "What is the reward for good deeds? What happens if you have no good deeds and no expectations?" These questions led Begley to explore further issues of why a person survives horrors and a question Begley said he asked himself after the war: "Is life worth living after I have seen it for what it is?" With all of these philosophical ideas occupying his mind, the lawyer began to wonder if he should begin writing again and whether he should use his writing to expound on his experiences in the war. He took a three-month leave of absence from his firm and completed *Wartime Lies* in 1991. That book tells the story of Maciek, a young Jewish boy who travels with his aunt around Poland during World War II, trying to escape Nazi persecution. As told through the hardened eyes of his grown-up self, the novel tracks Maciek's journey through an elaborate network of lies he must maintain in order to avoid detection. He must pretend to be his aunt's son (as was common in those times, his mother and other relatives split up in order to lessen the chances of being observed), as well as an Aryan, Catholic Pole. He and his aunt move from one rural town to another, seeking shelter with Polish families who blackmail them for their silence. Along the way Maciek struggles to come to terms with his controlling guardian, a life of lies, and the guilt-laden knowledge that while his life is spared, millions of his fellow Jews are tortured and killed. As Begley explained in an interview with the *London Observer* (November 3, 1991) "He has so acquired the skill of lying that he has become disconnected. There is a distance between the thing that is inside him and the figure he presents to the world." The man Maciek becomes in the ensuing years in America is merely a shadow of his former identity, a man who has had to lie about who he is and who cannot bear to remember his own childhood. "No matter how long or gaily the music plays, Maciek will not rise to dance again," Begley concludes. In short, Maciek has done no good deeds to look back upon in his adulthood—a circumstance that hearkens back to Begley's original premise about the nature of the good deed.

Wartime Lies proved to be a resoundingly successful debut novel. Although it was published with nary a stir, it soon gained momentum in critics' circles and ultimately became the winner of Ireland's top literary award, the *Irish Times*—Aer Lingus International Fiction Prize, as well as being nominated for the National Book Award. *Time* (May 27, 1991) called the book a "remarkable, elegiac novel," and the *New York Review of Books* (June 15, 1991) proclaimed that Begley had created an "austere moral and psychological fable of survival" written with "a kind of muted and stunned air, as if the words are sticking in his throat." The *London Review of Books* (November 19, 1992) labeled it a "stylish and gripping account," adding that "Between moments of speeded-up heart-rate there are miniature scenes and ironies of great depth and reach." The reviewer gave Begley's style a mixed response, however. "It is Begley's achievement to have made his story manageable, orderly and limited," he wrote, "but contrarily and contrariwise, I wish it could have been vaster, confused, and opaque." The *Times Literary Supplement* (August 16, 1991) had a similarly mixed review, writing that *Wartime Lies* "is an extremely polished book, and this is both its strength and its undoubted weakness . . . . Begley assumes that the smooth, moralistic retelling of his story can, somehow, do justice to it." The critic concluded by writing, "I hope Begley will now go on to tell his own wartime story directly."

In fact, Begley's novel proved to be so captivating and true-to-life that many readers assumed it was a thinly disguised autobiography and wondered how many of the book's events were culled from Begley's own wartime experiences. Begley himself has continued to assert that *Wartime Lies* is not a memoir and told the *Washington Post's* Charles Trueheart (November 4, 1991) that readers should not try to figure out which parts of the book are true, that to make such an attempt is like trying to unscramble eggs. "I think it's a disservice to the book and a disservice to the reader. If the book is worth reading at all, it's worth reading because of what it says precisely and not because it's a guide to my life."

With the tremendous success of his first novel, Begley decided to continue with his writing, and over the course of a year's worth of weekends, he finished *The Man Who Was Late* (1992), a book many consider a type of sequel to *Wartime Lies*. The novel tells the life story of a troubled man named Ben through the eyes of his closest friend, Jack. Through private letters and journal entries, Jack reflects on the deceased Ben, a divorced, wealthy international investment banker who has spent his life hiding from his identity: a European Jew who escaped the Nazis during World War II. In place of his true self, he has fabricated a network

of lies and invented a person whom he doesn't even know, joking to Jack that a life of self-deception meant that he "was never really certain how he felt about anything or anybody." Ben does manage to fall in love with a woman in Paris; however, when she offers to leave her abusive husband for him, he cannot bear the weight of another's love for him and flees to Brazil, where he takes up with a prostitute. His wartime past and failure at love haunt him leading him to take drastic measures and leaving Jack to try and make sense of his friend's life.

Reviews for *The Man Who Was Late* were more mixed than those for Begley's previous book. The *New York Review of Books* (January 28, 1993) critic wrote, "With *The Man Who Was Late*, the organization is as sophisticated as the content. It is a very clever, elegant, and readable novel; and very serious as well." Similarly, *New York Newsday* (January 18, 1993) offered a glowing review that called Begley's work "a second transformation of the dross of experience into sublime art." Reviewer Dan Cryer wrote, "Jack's narrative frames Ben's spectacular rise and fall in an elegiac, Gatsby-like glow. If what drove Fitzgerald's doomed self-made hero was a yearning for acceptance among the rich and famous, what propels Begley's contemporary lost soul is a fantasy of global elegance and mastery." The critic concluded by stating, "Begley's prose is an elegant, perfectly pitched vehicle for this dark tale. It sings, but the song is infinitely sad . . ." The *Financial Times* (January 31, 1993) reviewer wrote, "Begley is a novelist of extraordinary sophistication and sensitivity, with ambitions that seem to bypass much recent writing and head straight for Proust territory." The critic added that the character Ben is a "scarily precious creature, a man who has enveloped a troubled soul with epicurianism and eroticism, thereby refining himself to the point of nonexistence. Indeed, some readers may find themselves a bit worn by Begley's occasionally cloying irony and detail." However, the *Financial Times* concluded that the novel "remains a compelling examination of the dangers of denying a damaged self."

The *Wall Street Journal* (February 8, 1993) was slightly more mixed in its critique of the book: "Although there is some fluid and admirable writing throughout the book, the overall tone is oddly smug." The reviewer, Joseph Olshan, noted that Begley "seems compelled to write a novel that is keen on behavioral nuance and shrewd social commentary, yet both aspects are curiously missing from *The Man Who Was Late*." It is later stated that ". . . one grows aware of a certain lack of incisive attention paid to the kinds of character-building particulars that would deepen our sense of Ben as well as Jack, the narrator." However, Olshan was not without praise for Begley's literary style, writing, " . . . yet Mr. Begley is clearly a very gifted writer who has a sharp eye for cultural details, a keen, sensual feeling for the refinements that privileged life has to offer. One only hopes that his next subject will be more carefully chosen, something to which he will be able to successfully graft his considerable talent so that the resulting fiction will truly flower." In similar fashion, *People* (March 29, 1993) was of two minds on the book, stating that Begley's writing "fully captures Ben's torment and the slow, exacting toll it takes on his soul," but adding, "At its best Begley's powerful style is lyrical, and at its worst it is self-consciously ornate, with such phrases as 'irremediable existential tardiness.' Nonetheless this oddly sensual novel does not disappoint." In perhaps the most ambivalent review of the book, Michiko Kakutani of the *New York Times* (January 15, 1993) wrote that the book's "melodramatic events and Ben's boisterous sexual liaisons are recounted in decorous, Jamesian prose whose very understatement and subtlety somehow work to heighten the story's emotional impact. Mr. Begley writes with marvelous authority about the world of high finance and the world of the leisured rich, and his eye for detail and social ritual imbues this book with a rich patina of verisimilitude." However, the reviewer went on to point out that "while these qualities make *The Man Who Was Late* a delight to read, one finishes the novel vaguely unsatisfied and unmoved." Of the character Ben, Kakutani wrote, "His repudiation of his past, his failure to acknowledge the proddings of his own heart, his reluctance to try to change his life—all serve to make him a static and strangely opaque character." The review concluded, "Because we are never granted admittance to his heart, because his emotional reserve is never really penetrated by Jack (or Mr. Begley), he ultimately remains an emotional cipher about whom it's impossible to care."

In 1994 Begley published another novel, *As Max Saw It*, which tells the story of a successful Harvard professor named Max who struggles with his sexual relationships amid the changing sexual norms of the 1970s and '80s. Like the central characters in Begley's other books, Max is accepted among the upper crust of society but never feels comfortable there, deeming himself an "imposter" among his friends. When he repeatedly meets up with an old college buddy, Charlie, he finds himself intrigued by Charlie's gay lover, Toby. Slowly, Max is drawn into Charlie and Toby's life, his sexuality now in question, and when Toby contracts a deadly disease (it is assumed to be AIDS, though it is never labeled as such in the book), Max becomes deeply entangled in the unfolding drama. Spanning the 15 years (the novel begins with Nixon's resignation in 1974 and ends with the Tiananmen Square uprising in 1989), *As Max Saw It* records how Max goes from being an outside observer of, to a participant in, life.

In one of the most overwhelmingly favorable reviews of the novel, the *New York Times* (April 24, 1994) critic wrote that "Among the many inspired touches here are the omission of quotation marks . . . also effective is Mr. Begley's judicious use of classical allusions and symbolism." Critic Bruce

Bawer added that "While capturing the day-to-day sense that life consists simply of one thing after another, the novel races inexorably toward an ending that genuinely stuns even as it reveals the underlying pattern, the figure in the carpet of Max's life." Bawer concluded by writing, "*As Max Saw It* points up the brutal consequences of dishonesty and self-deception in supposedly private matters. It is a consummately beautiful—and major—work of literary art." The *Chicago Tribune* (May 23, 1994) offered a less glowing review, classifying Begley's writing as "prose that frequently seems quaintly out of date" though elegant at times. The reviewer was also not impressed with Begley's punctuation style, noting, "The total absence of quotation marks seems to serve no purpose other than to compel the reader to re-read passages that may be either narrative or dialogue." The review ends, however, with the assertion that "for the most part, the text flows free of such oddities, a sinewy, urbane vernacular that serves the narrative and the characterization beautifully," making it "an entertaining novel of manners" and "a tragedy of the starkest order." In similar fashion, *Time* (April 18, 1994) was full of praise for Begley's writing, but more restrained when it came to evaluating the book itself. "Containing nary an ill-chosen word, [this] may turn out to be the most perfectly constructed novel of 1994 . . . the joy of reading Begley lies in his beautiful, economical virtuosity; characters are etched in three lines; epigram and description are effortlessly paired. . . . But for all of Begley's talent and painstaking technique, the novel never transcends artifice." Likewise, the *Library Journal* (April 1, 1994) wrote, "Begley's writing is as readable and fluid as ever, but the story goes by so quickly that we barely have time to get a feeling for the characters before it is all over."

Even more harsh was *New York Newsday*'s Joyce Johnson (April 17, 1994), who wrote, "Begley's view of life—acerbic, ironic, detached—seems quintessentially European. When he confers it upon a contemporary American character like Max, the fit is imperfect and so is the voice that comes with it, too often redolent of the discreet hesitations and Byzantine locutions of the later Henry James." One of the novel's central flaws, Johnson maintained, is that the reader is never given any inside look at the characters of Toby and Charlie. "What we do not know unfortunately, and what Begley never manages to convey to us, is how much love Toby and Charlie felt for each other. . . . ," she wrote in her review, adding that Begley seems to be "in pursuit of a grand metaphor for his central preoccupation, and that overrode his interest in his characters." This lack of character depth is also a point of criticism from *Kirkus Reviews* (March 1, 1994), which stated that "In a novel seemingly about a man's coming to terms with his own humanity and the depth of feeling within his heart, Begley is unlikely here to evoke any depth of feeling in the reader's heart. He's too busy flaunting his considerable knowledge about the pretensions of the rich and the portentousness of the gifted. The problem is, although Max is supposed to become a more sympathetic character as the book progresses, Begley never really lets us inside the heart of his protagonist." *Kirkus* did relent in its criticism to offer the conclusion that despite these problems, "*As Max Saw It* is an enjoyable read, most notably for the magnificent character of Charlie Swan, a man so outsized in his feelings and appetites that he dwarfs everyone else in the novel."

The title character of Begley's next book, *About Schmidt* (1996), is a retired lawyer who mourns his wife, who has recently died of cancer. Schmidt also struggles with the impending marriage of his daughter, Charlotte, to an ambitious Jewish lawyer. Although he refuses to admit it, Schmidt is plagued by anti-Semitic feelings, and he cannot connect emotionally with his yuppie daughter or her newfound family. Feeling that his loneliness is only emphasized by his large home in the Hamptons, Schmidt decides to give the house to Charlotte as a wedding present. She refuses it, however, a move that accents her distance from him. He then begins an affair with a Puerto Rican waitress, who manages to get him to support her artist/drug dealer boyfriend. This leads to further complications and to introspection on the part of Schmidt.

Critics were overwhelmingly pleased with this literary offering from Begley. Although *New York Newsday* (September 3, 1996) declared that a more vivid picture of Schmidt's diseased wife was needed, the reviewer applauded the author's achievement in making the reader "truly care about Schmidt, despite his anti-Semitism and lack of self-knowledge. " The review added, "By blinding his flawed hero, Begley has painted an indelible portrait of a man with a hole where his soul should be." *Time* (September 16, 1996) offered this critique of the novel: "In what could be called a novel of bad manners, Begley again demonstrates that he can reveal the complexities of society and personality with a clear eye and graceful style." In another rave review, *Publishers Weekly* (June 17, 1996) praised Begley's use of "sublime, delicious irony" to show Schmidt's metamorphosis. "Begley guides the narrative with smooth aplomb and dry humor, providing a wealth of acutely observed social detail and a clear depiction of emotional dysfunction," the review stated. "Though his classic Holocaust novel, *Wartime Lies*, is a standard Begley can't improve upon, this elegant, sophisticated novel is another study in self-deception that confirms his reputation as a masterful literary novelist."

The *New York Review of Books* (October 31, 1996) went a step further, proclaiming ". . . this is Begley's best book by far, one informed by a relaxed and genial wisdom that, after the social and intellectual flamboyance of its predecessors, seems all the more unexpected and impressive." Perhaps the most enthusiastic critic was Phyllis Rose in the *New York Times Book Review* (September 22,

1996), who called the book "subtle and intelligent" and characterized it by stating: "It resolutely refuses transcendence. The temperature never goes up. The pitch never varies. You never feel you are being manipulated into a falsely emotional response. . . . It never tries to mean more than it says—in fact, tries strenuously not to. This, to me, is the great pleasure of reading Louis Begley. His exceptional literary intelligence is always in control, making me wonder if more novelists shouldn't develop the virtues of lawyers as writers; accuracy, economy, abjuring the language of emotion."

Begley's most recent literary offering is 1998's *Mistler's Exit*, a book that again features an older man attempting to sort out his life. This time, the central character is Thomas Mistler, a wealthy and distinguished advertising executive who learns that he has liver cancer and will soon die. But instead of feeling sorrow, Mistler is practically joyful at the news, and instead of telling his wife and family the diagnosis, he immediately sets off for Venice, where he takes faith in the "lingering taste of sweet" his favorite city has to offer. Once there he begins to ponder his past and doomed future but is soon distracted by a young photographer with whom he begins an affair. When that liaison ends, Mistler runs into Bella, a woman he was in love with at Harvard. Although one could assume he is tormented with desire and despair, Mistler is really detached and indifferent to everything in his life, including his affairs. He runs into various friends from his past, and they all confirm that he acted like a pompous fool when he was around them. He ultimately leaves Venice to make a last-ditch effort to connect with his family.

Reviewers were less impressed with this novel than with Begley's previous works. The *Columbus Dispatch* (November 29, 1998) printed one of the more negative reviews, with critic Laura Beckwith calling the character of Mistler "not only unlikeable, but unremarkable" and "not only mean and shallow" but "unforgivingly boring" as well. She also remarked that "Certainly, plenty of good books have been written with nasty protagonists. *Mistler's Exit*, however, is not one of them." Calling the novel both "predictable and unbelievable," Beckwith wrote that the book's brevity (running only 206 pages) was "perhaps both its salvation and its weakness. The reader's boredom with Mistler is short-lived. But perhaps because it is so sketchy, the book doesn't give us anything but a surface understanding of him." The *San Francisco Chronicle* (September 6, 1998) was more enthusiastic about the book, calling Begley's design "nothing less than magnificent" and "grand" in its conception. In its execution, however, according to the reviewer, "the writing goes oddly slack, and *Mistler's Exit* ends in a fascinating disappointment after the Alhambra-like subtlety with which Begley built the best of his prior novels." Still, the critic contended that Mistler emerges as one of Begley's most approachable characters, a figure Begley "plainly cares about." But in the end, the review concludes, "the novel's tremendous opportunity slips away" and what emerges is a "good book that could have been better."

The *New York Times* took the opposite view, calling *Mistler's Exit* a "brilliantly, brutally countercathartic" novel that brings "an estimable set of novels to a new pinnacle of darkness." The *Denver Post* (September 13, 1998) was equally generous in its review, calling the book as "engaging" as Begley's previous novels due to the author's honesty. "Begley's protagonist is neither a hero nor a villain; instead, Mistler has that rare literary attribute, humanity," the reviewer wrote. The critique goes on to note that Begley "retains a playful, confident control over the movement of his story. . . . He is a novelist's novelist, a virtuoso, but not a show-off or a snob." Because Begley can write with equal aplomb about high society or the darker obsessions in life, the reviewer described the author's style by writing, "Begley stands with one foot in the busy street, and the other in the shadowed temple of art."

Begley's novel *About Schmidt* was a National Book Critics' Circle Award and *Los Angeles Times* Book Award finalist. He has also received the American Academy of Letters prize for literature.

Louis Begley remains a senior partner in his law firm while continuing to write fiction. As he told *Vanity Fair*, "[Writing] is the least sordid occupation in the world, more pleasant than any I have ever encountered." He and his wife have homes in Manhattan, Long Island, and Paris.

—D.B.

SUGGESTED READING: *Amazon Books* (online); *Chicago Tribune* p1 Nov. 19, 1991, p3 May 23, 1994; *Columbus Dispatch* (on-line) Nov. 29, 1998; *Denver Post* (on-line) Sep. 13, 1998; *Financial Times* p27 Jan. 31, 1993; *Kirkus Reviews* (on-line) Nov. 1, 1992, Mar. 1, 1994; *Library Journal* p128 Apr. 1, 1994; *London Observer* p68 Nov. 3, 1991; *London Review of Books* p15+ Nov. 19, 1992; *Newsweek* p51 July 29, 1991; *New Statesman and Society* p39 Jan. 15, 1993; *New York Newsday* p44 Jan. 18, 1993, p38 Apr. 17, 1994, pB2 Sep. 3, 1996; *New York Review of Books* p38 June 15, 1991, p16+ Jan. 28, 1993, p63 Oct. 31, 1996; *New York Times* p7 May 5, 1991, pC25 Jan. 15, 1993, p3 Jan. 31, 1993, pC1 Apr. 14, 1993, p13 Apr. 24, 1994, p13 Sep. 22, 1996; *People* p30 Mar. 29, 1993; *Publishers Weekly* p44 June 17, 1996; *San Francisco Chronicle* (on-line) Sep. 6, 1998; *Time* p69 May 27, 1991, p30 Feb 1, 1993, p 79 Apr. 18, 1994, p80 Sep. 16, 1996; *Times Literary Supplement* p23 Aug. 16, 1991; *Vanity Fair* p72+ Feb. 1993; *Wall Street Journal* pA10 Feb. 8, 1993; *Washington Post* pD1 Nov. 4, 1991; *Contemporary Authors*, 1994

SELECTED BOOKS: *Wartime Lies*, 1991; *The Man Who Was Late*, 1992; *As Max Saw It*, 1994; *About Schmidt*, 1996; *Mistler's Exit,* 1998

Courtesy of Thomas Berry

Berry, Thomas

1914– Nonfiction writer; theologian; environmentalist

Thomas Berry, the American theologian and environmentalist, is a man not easily classified. A concerned and passionate intellectual, Father Berry spent the majority of his career studying world religions and philosophies before turning, two decades ago, to the environment, which he has since made his chief subject. He has concluded that Confucianism and the religions of American Indians have had much more respect for nature than Western religions in the Judeo-Christian tradition, which tend to look to the next world for perfection, leaving this one to its corruption—a bold stance for a Catholic priest to take. Father Berry is remarkably complex—a man who loves humanity yet does not perceive mankind to be the center of the universe, a professor who believes that universities do not educate their students enough with regard to the ecosystem, a priest who contends that the destruction of the earth's natural resources has to do in part with humanity's belief that this mortal life is not as important as the afterlife. He has advocated the teaching of a "new story" of the universe, one in which Darwinism is taught along with spirituality, and in which the earth and all its components are seen as part of a continuing transformation.

In his third-person autobiography, written for *World Authors 1990–1995*, Father Berry discusses his life's experiences and the influences they have had on his work: "Thomas Berry is a historian of cultures and a writer with special concern for a renewal of the integral functioning of the planet Earth after the devastation of the planet that has taken place in this late 20th century. He considers that this is the terminal period of the Cenozoic Era (the technological period). He proposes we move into a future Ecozoic Era (the ecological period), a period when humans would be present to the planet in a mutually enhancing manner.

"He comes from the hill country of the southern Appalachians in North Carolina, was born in 1914, entered a monastery [Saint Michael's Monastery in Union City, New Jersey] in 1934. During his years of study in a monastic setting he became profoundly influenced by the writings of Aristotle and by his medieval commentator, Saint Thomas Aquinas. This discipline of thought he considers among the most important aspects of his intellectual training. In these years he was also influenced by his studies of Augustine of Hippo and by Dante Alighieri."

Father Berry was ordained a Roman Catholic priest of the Passionist Congregation in 1942. "His doctoral degree in history is from the Catholic University of America [1949]. His mentor was Professor Frederich Engel de Janosi who introduced him to the work of the Italian philosopher of history, Giambattista Vico. From this 18th-century scholar and his outstanding work, *The New Science of the Nature of the Nations*, [Berry] learned to think of human history in a comprehensive context, both in its continuity through the centuries and its extent throughout the continents." Father Berry's doctoral thesis on the Italian philosopher, *The Historical Theory of Giambattista Vico*, was published by the Catholic University Press.

"In 1948 he went to China to teach Western history at Fujen University in Beijing. This provided his immediate experience of the northern Chinese world of the pre-Mao period. At this time he began his acquaintance also with the Chinese language which he continued to study throughout the following years after his return to America in 1949. [He was forced out of China that year due to the Communist takeover.] The Chinese in their classical period, in his estimation, had one of the best understandings of any of the classical civilizations for what a human being is and how this role is fulfilled in relation to the natural world." From 1951 to 1954, during the Korean War, Father Berry served in the United States Army, becoming a first lieutenant.

"In the late 1950s and early 1960s his thought was powerfully influenced by Pierre Teilhard de Chardin, especially by three of his teachings; that the universe from the beginning had a psychic-spiritual as well as a physical material aspect, that the human story and the universe story are integral with each other, that Western Christian peoples should give greater emphasis to the evolutionary model of creation and diminish their excessive emphasis on redemption-salvation. It was in this period also he did extensive readings in Rachel Carson and the naturalist writers; Henry Thoreau, John Muir, Aldo Leopold, and Loren Eiseley.

"Professor Berry began his teaching career at Seton Hall University in New Jersey in 1956 with the courses that he gave in Chinese and Japanese history and culture. Later after his study of the Sanskrit language he began courses in the cultural history of India. For several years in the early 1960s he taught in the Institute of Asian Studies at Saint John's University in New York. Afterwards, from 1966 until 1979 he directed the doctoral program in the History of Religions at Fordham University in New York.

"His principal concern after 1975 has been with environmental and ecological issues. He has been especially concerned with the order of magnitude of what is happening. He considers that the greatest single need of the human community is to accept our new story of the universe, the story of the evolutionary sequence of transformations through which the planet has come to be what it is; to accept this story as our sacred story along with all the other sacred stories of the universe that are possessed by the human community. Only in this manner, he proposes, can we obtain a realistic understanding of just where the human venture is in this late 20th century and how to deal with this situation. We need to understand that the human venture is integral with the Earth venture. The Earth is the base system. The human is a subsystem of the Earth system. What happens to the Earth happens inevitably to the human. What happens outside of the human affects the inner faculties of the human, our imagination, sensitivities, and understanding.

"Among the more important aspects of his life has been his association with the educational program of the indigenous T'Boli people in the South Cotabato region of Mindanao. It was for these peoples that he wrote his outline of twelve principles for understanding the universe and the role of the human in the universe. This outline became the basis for *The Universe Story* as written later in collaboration with Brian Swimme.

"Founder of the Riverdale Center of Religions Research in Riverdale, New York, he was its director from its beginning in 1970 until its termination in 1995. There he had collected a library with selected texts in Sanskrit and Chinese languages from the Hindu, Buddhist and Confucian-Taoist traditions. There he also had a special room for study of the indigenous peoples of the North American continent. Professor Berry was also president of the American Teilhard Association from 1975 until 1987. The meetings took place at the Research Center. During this time the Association published a series of papers entitled *Teilhard Studies*.

"His book entitled *Buddhism* was published in 1968. *The Religions of India* in 1972. Later his basic book on ecology, entitled *The Dream of the Earth*, was published in October 1988, by Sierra Club Books. *Befriending the Earth, A Theology of Reconciliation Between Humans and the Earth*, was published by Twenty Third Publications in

1991. A book written with the cosmologist Brian Swimme, *The Universe Story: From the Primordial Flaring Forth to the Ecozoic Era, A Celebration of the Unfolding of the Cosmos*, was published by Harper San Francisco in the fall of 1992. The story of the Universe presented there is proposed as the context for an educational program from the earliest years through university and professional training, an education suited to the needs of the emerging twenty-first century.

"In 1995 he retired back to the hill country of North Carolina. There he is collecting his essays written over these past years for publication. He also hopes to do a book containing his observations on the twentieth century and some of his thoughts on the twenty-first century with the hope that it might provide for the oncoming generations some sense of where they are in the ongoing movement of history."

In her paper "Thomas Berry and the New Story," Professor Mary Evelyn Tucker of Bucknell University described how Berry has evolved from a cultural historian to a historian of the earth. "Berry sees himself . . . not as a theologian but as a geologian." Examining Berry's idea that "there can be no peace among humans without peace on the planet," Tucker gave an introduction to Berry's work, outlining his various phases and concisely explaining his observations and conclusions. Berry believes that humanity's inclination toward selfishness and planetary abuse necessitates a call to reflect on a "new story" of the universe, one in which we move away from our various cultural identifications and toward our original pattern of relating to the earth. Tucker wrote: "By articulating a new mythic consciousness of our profound connectedness to the earth, we may be able to reverse the self-destructive cultural tendencies we have put in motion with regard to the planet." As Berry's knowledge of various cultures grew, he understood the need to do away with petty differences and in many ways became a harbinger of the multiculturalism movement of the 1990s. Yet no philosophies affected his thinking more than the those of the American Indians and Confucianists, who believed in the spirituality of all things—from people and animals to the sea and earth. These people have not been perfect ecologists according to the 20th-century ideal; in fact, in China, the birthplace of Confucianism, many abuses—including deforestation—have occurred. Still, Berry maintains that their traditions are fundamental to the creation of a new type of spirituality of nature in our era. As Tucker wrote in her paper, these people's "way of life may have much to teach us as we are learning, rather painfully, the limits of natural resources and the consequences of mindless growth."
—C.M.

SUGGESTED READING: Tucker, M. E. *Thomas Berry and the New Story*, 1997; *Contemporary Authors* vol. 23–24, 1970

SELECTED BOOKS: *Buddhism*, 1968; *The Religions of India*, 1972; *The Dream of the Earth*, 1988; *Befriending the Earth: A Theology of Reconciliation Between Humans and the Earth*, 1991; *The Universe Story: From the Primordial Flaring Forth to the Ecozoic Era, A Celebration of the Unfolding of the Cosmos* (with B. Swimme), 1992

Susan Lippman

Birkerts, Sven

1951– Nonfiction writer; critic

The American literary and social critic Sven Birkerts has moved from the realm of pure literary criticism to a Marshall McLuhan–like focus on the implications of the media message for life in the postmodern world—with a particular concentration on the philosophy of reading. He has continued, however, to be one of the most important American literary critics, with reviews frequently appearing in the *New York Times Book Review* and the *New Republic*. His articles in such mainstream publications as the *Atlantic*, *Harper's*, and the *American Scholar* and scholarly journals like the *Georgia Review* dissect the impact of new-media technologies on contemporary American life. The half-dozen collections of his essays have ranged from the literary pieces in *An Artificial Wilderness* (1987) and *Readings* (1998) to the social criticism in *The Gutenberg Elegies* (1995).

For *World Authors 1990-1995*, Sven Birkerts writes: "I was born in Pontiac, Michigan in 1951 into a Latvian-speaking household. Though we were not exceedingly bookish (my father read only news magazines and architectural journals, my mother was an avid reader of novels), my childhood was charged by various significant encounters with books, and by the early years of high school I was already convinced that one could do nothing more exalted than write novels. That notion persisted for the next two decades, ambitiousness combining with intense frustration, as my attempts to write fiction seemed to come to nought. My protagonists were forever sitting in front of windows or in diners reflecting on the larger questions of existence.

"In retrospect, I see it as a critical life-choice that I did not go on in college after taking a B.A. degree (University of Michigan). I drifted, instead, into the world of bookselling and supported myself for many years at a modest level by buying and selling books. What I did not consider, really, until I was in my late twenties, was that all of my reading outside the university had given me a peculiar sort of literary education. It was then, at a complete dead-end with my fictional projects, that I decided to write an essay about the underappreciated Austrian writer Robert Musil. I discovered (and I have written about this) an immediate sense of liberation. The ease of critical composition was, I felt, the very inverse of the difficulty of creating fiction. My path was made easier by the fact that after I had written that first essay, I was invited to do others, and that after I had a handful of pieces in my dossier it was easy to find work writing for magazines.

"At first the central interest was in writing about lesser-known European authors in translation, authors like Max Frisch, Blaise Cendrars, Michel Tournier, and others. But in what seemed at the time an unrelated development, I also discovered an interest in thinking about television and its place in our cultural life. That interest soon widened, embracing what I thought of as our postmodern media age. In each of my books leading up to *The Gutenberg Elegies* I included essays that reflected on these subjects.

"I had written a great many of these essays, reviews on various authors and trends, before I decided to enter the National Book Critics Circle competition for its annual reviewing citation. In 1985 I won the award and was thereupon contacted by several agents who wanted to know if I had a book underway. I organized the various essays I had written and with what I now recognize as enormous luck, found a publisher. William Morrow & Co. published my first collection, *An Artificial Wilderness: Essays on 20th Century Literature*, and in later years also published *The Electric Life: Essays on Poetry* and *American Energies: Essays on Fiction*.

"During the years I was writing the essays for these books, I was gripped by an increasing sense of crisis. I had begun to recognize, with growing clarity, that there were new forces in the culture that were changing everything about the way we read, write, and carry on our intellectual business. At first, fearing that this was too great a subject to handle in essay format, I steered away, tried instead to write about what might be called the phenomenology of reading. But the more I burrowed into this topic, the more I recognized that reading could no longer be discussed without a simultaneous investigation of computers and electronic communications. Without meaning to, then, I wrote myself into what has become in the past few years a controversy of sorts—a public debate about the various pros and cons of computer technology.

"This past decade, then, has had me moving from the world of bookselling into writing and teaching. I have taught writing and literature courses at Boston University, Harvard University, Emerson College, and am presently a member of the core faculty at the Bennington Writing Seminars, a low-residency MFA program. I have also joined Donald Hall as coauthor of the writing textbook *Writing Well*, and have written and edited, for Allyn & Bacon, *The Evolving Canon*, a literature textbook. These recent years have also seen the birth of two children, Mara and Liam.

"My most recent project, since the publication in 1994 of *The Gutenberg Elegies*, has been editing *Tolstoy's Dictaphone: Technology,* and *The Muse,* the first Graywolf Forum."

As might be expected, given the skepticism with which he views new technology, Sven Birkerts sent the above autobiography to *World Authors 1990-1995* on pages that appear to have passed through a manual typewriter. Having unsuccessfully set out to become a novelist, Birkerts became, instead, a passionate apologist for the written word—for the book, especially the novel—which in his opinion serves "as a kind of fertile unconscious out of which can be distilled the patterns and meanings we cannot live without," as he remarked in "Second Thoughts," first published in the *Review of Contemporary Fiction.*

Birkerts's first book of collected essays, *An Artificial Wilderness: Essays on 20th Century Literature,* is a broad-based appreciation of great modern writing. Essays on German-language fiction and Russian literature discuss such writers as Robert Musil and Osip Mandelstam. Malcolm Lowry, Derek Walcott, Jorge Luis Borges, and V. S. Naipaul are also given consideration. "His awareness of the 'brutalities of history,' especially as observed by European writers, removes any suggestion of cozy connoisseurship," Donald Hall wrote in the *New York Times Book Review* (November 8, 1987). Hall was impressed by Birkerts's "love for literature and concern over the condition of our culture."

In *The Electric Life: Essays on Modern Poetry* (1989), Birkerts attempted to ponder "language," "the nature of creativity," and "the place of poetry in a world riven by political and social unrest," as he wrote in the preface. He also gave close readings of poems in the modern canon—and some not so canonical. Helen Benedict in the *New York Times Book Review* (April 16, 1989) termed *The Electric Life* "a book for poetry readers who wish to be awakened by fresh arguments—intelligent enough to challenge yet provocative enough to be open to question and debate." Her cavil was that Birkerts "[tends] to be annoyingly, though wittily, snide."

American Energies: Essays on Fiction (1992) takes on "the present state and direction of American fiction." The section titled "Backgrounds" deals with the new nostalgia, on the one hand, and the influence of electronic media on readers and writers on the other. In "American Writers" Birkerts reviewed important works, expressing his view that American fiction is generally in a state of decline. "It's the lack of depth and resonance in novels that worries him," David Holmstrom observed in the *Christian Science Monitor* (August 17, 1992). Holmstrom pointed out that Birkerts sees "American culture spun into confection by technology," and this is reflected, Birkerts feels, in fiction.

It was with *The Gutenberg Elegies: The Fate of Reading in an Electronic Age*, an attempt on Birkerts's part to take up the mantle of Marshall McLuhan, that Birkerts made a splash on the contemporary scene. A collection of essays dealing with the way "the screen" has changed our perceptions of ourselves and the world and why these changes are not to the advantage of humanity, *The Gutenberg Elegies* contains a section, "The Reading Self," describing the genesis of Birkerts's own passion for reading, which reviewers generally found moving and interesting. The other two sections, "The Electronic Millennium," devoted to textual reinterpretation through electronic media, and "Critical Mass: Three Meditations," in which Birkerts examined the impact of electronic media on human cultures, aroused a great deal of controversy.

Many reviewers praised the book, among them Steven Kellman in the *Georgia Review* (Fall 1995). Kellman cited Birkerts's essay in *The Artificial Wilderness* in praise of Derek Walcott and then quoted from Walcott's poem "Volcano" in *Sea Grapes*, in which Walcott declared that to be a reader instead of a writer, "making the love of masterpieces / superior to attempting / to repeat or outdo them. . . . requires awe, / which has been lost to our time." "Birkerts," Kellman noted, "is just such an ideal reader, and the anguish of it all is that he must practice his demanding antique art during the protoelectronic era, when texts are scrolled and scanned, and the solid verities of print are melting into the inexorable flow of digitized data." He agreed with Birkerts's argument that "the electronic hive is fostering a collectivization that is antithetical to inwardness, imagination, and individuality."

David Simpson, however, writing in *The American Scholar* (Winter 1996), took such pronouncements with a grain of salt: "Technical breakthroughs . . . tend to trigger extreme emotional reactions, particularly among intellectuals. This is something that both Webheads and neo-Luddites alike might ponder as computer technology moves beyond the high-tech era into the *ultra-* or *meta*-tech stage. It is also something to bear in mind when assessing works such as Sven Birkerts's *Gutenberg Elegies*, yet another somber meditation on the demise of literary culture and the death of the book." Simpson thought that while Birkerts's thesis that the death of the book will result in the death of individuality and the death of the "soul" does have a certain validity, on the one hand, the book is not dead, and on the other, "it is not any particular medium but symbolic communication in general and in whatever form that makes us human and develops our inner selves."

In his well-reviewed 1998 essay collection, *Readings*, Birkerts took on topics ranging from the negative aspects of the information age to American nostalgia to the work of such writers and poets as Robert Lowell, Don DeLillo, and Anne Tyler.

Birkerts has shown himself to be rather intractable in his view of the negative effects of computer technology on society. He has sometimes tried to present the other side of the case, but his alarm at the tendencies he sees in modern society has tended to dominate his arguments. "Though I class myself as one of the resisters," he wrote in "The Fate of the Book," "I think I can see how certain tendencies that I deplore might seem seductive to others. . . . Have we not made too great a fetish of the book, and too large a cult of the author?" Birkerts, in part, answers that loaded question by observing that he is "preoccupied with the shifting of the ground of value." He believes that "we are certainly tipping the sacred ontological scales. . . . Meaning what? Meaning that our living has gradually less to do with things, places, and human presence, and more to do with messages, mediated exchanges, ersatz environments, and virtual engagements of all descriptions." No one who has played telephone tag with another's voice mail or answering machine could quarrel with that. But what is Birkerts's prescription for what he sees as the disease of modern civilization? He calls on us "to stall somehow the rush to interconnectivity, that comes—as all interconnectivity must—at the expense of the here and now. Certainly the survival of that archaic entity called the soul depends on resistance."

— S. Y.

SUGGESTED READING: *American Scholar* p138+ Winter 1996; *Christian Science Monitor* p14 Aug. 17, 1992; *Georgia Review* p740+ Fall 1995; *New York Times Book Review* p16 Nov. 8, 1987, p21 Apr. 16, 1989, p14 Dec. 18, 1994

SELECTED BOOKS: Nonfiction—*An Artificial Wilderness: Essays on 20th Century Literature*, 1987; *The Electric Life: Essays on Modern Poetry*, 1989; *The Longwood Introduction to Fiction*, 1992; *American Energies: Essays on Fiction*, 1992; *Literature: The Evolving Canon*, 1993; *The Gutenberg Elegies: The Fate of Reading in an Electronic Age*, 1995; *Readings*, 1998; As editor—*Writing Well* (with D. Hall), 1994

Blackburn, Julia

Aug. 12, 1948– Novelist; biographer; essayist

The English writer Julia Blackburn has ranged far from her native London in her writing, having attempted to capture the exotic worlds of travelers to and exiles in primitive deserts and jungles. Daisy Bates, who left Great Britain to live in the Australian desert, and Napoleon, dying on St. Helena, far from the courts, wars, and intrigues of Europe, are among her subjects. She has been concerned as well with the extraordinary lives of missionaries and colonists, some of whom were her own ancestors. Reviewers have responded to *The Emperor's Last Island* (1991), *Daisy Bates in the Desert* (1994), and the novels *The Book of Color* (1995) and *The Leper's Companions* (1999) with universal acclaim. Jean Nathan, reviewing *The Emperor's Last Island* in the *New York Times Book Review* (November 1, 1992), summed up most reviewers' responses to Blackburn's work: "a dazzling collage of geography, biography, and autobiography, displaying a spontaneity and breadth not usually encountered in conventional histories or biographies."

For *World Authors 1990–1995*, Julia Blackburn writes: "I was born on August 12, 1948, in London. For the first seven years of my life we lived on the top floor of a tall house with a flat roof instead of a garden. I was very short-sighted but no one knew that as yet and I used to watch the rotating covers of the chimney pots and wonder why they didn't flap their wings and fly away.

"My father was the poet Thomas Blackburn (1916–1977), my mother is a painter. I was brought up in a world in which the daily experiences of life were continually being reflected back into art. My father wrote poems about his own alcoholism, about family upheavals, about chaos, while my mother was producing very surreal figurative paintings. I remember walking down the stairs and looking at a painting of a child standing on a table in the desert and realising it was a portrait of me. I remember being shocked by poems that made aspects of private family life into such public property.

"My father was an English teacher, first at a school and later at a college. He taught me a huge love of words and their power. He could recite endlessly from Shakespeare, Yeats, Wordsworth, and Blake, as well as from less likely authors such as Kipling and Vachel Lindsay. I inherited this ability to memorise, my mind full of speeches, verses and songs.

"I studied English Literature at York University and then lived rather haphazardly in Spain, Amsterdam, Wales, and London. I ghostwrote a book on conjuring, compiled the H and L for a dictionary of English usage and had numerous jobs as an editor, proofreader, researcher, and anything else to do with words that came along. I wanted to write but I was afraid of writing, or at least I was afraid of fiction, which seemed to me to be such a wide and dangerous sea. I once had six quiet months in Spain with a typewriter and produced nothing but nonsense poems and little line drawings of people and fish.

"While living in Spain I learnt about the possibilities of research. I worked with a friend on a huge and unwieldy tome which was to be a study of world creation myths. The U.S. agent who rejected the outline and a few chapters said quite kindly that it was the sort of thing someone might attempt as the summation of a long life's work in this field. But this research led to my first book *The White Men* (1978), an anthology of stories about the first response of aboriginal peoples to the arrival of the white settlers, missionaries and colonists. I tried to allow the stories to speak for themselves, so that the logic of the cargo cults, the ghost dances, and many other back-against-the-wall responses would be obvious.

"My next book was a quite formal biography of the Victorian traveler, naturalist and conservationist *Charles Waterton* (1989). During the four years that I worked on it I learnt how one can seem to get to know a person in spite of the fact that they are long since dead.

"*The Emperor's Last Island* (1991) marked a movement away from the objectivity of research. The underlying theme of the book is based on a quote from Hamlet, ' I could be bounded in a nutshell and count myself a king / of infinite space, were it not that I have bad dreams.' This was how I saw Napoleon during his final years as a prisoner on the island of St. Helena. Here was a man who had been a king of 'infinite space' but was now bounded and plagued by his own bad dreams. In trying to see Napoleon more clearly, I made use of my own thoughts about fame and power, my own memories and the experience of the long journey to St. Helena that I made with my husband and our two young children. It was a strange liberation in my writing to dare to say, 'I remember . . . I wonder . . . I once walked down a road . . .'

"I had carried the story of *Daisy Bates in the Desert* (1994) in my mind ever since I first heard of this complicated and contradictory lady some 30 years ago. I had no clear idea of how to structure the book but I started with an attempt to disentangle the truth of Daisy's life from the web of fantasies she had spun around herself. I wrote fragments about my own childhood in trying to understand hers and in that way I allowed our two lives to run on parallel lines. After I had seen the deserts of southern Australia where she had lived and had met several people who could remember her, I found I could move into a first person narrative. I combined my memories of the landscape and the people with hers, so that in a curious way our experiences could be allowed to fuse.

"My most recent book is *The Book of Colour* (1995). This was I suppose an act of exorcism. I wrote it at a great speed (for me at least), never knowing where it was going to lead me next and I was very glad when it was finished. It is a book about the childhood of my father and my grandfather and the idea that we inherit from our families, not only the colour of skin, the shape of lip or nostrils, but also the fears, rages, and confusions that are passed down from one generation to the next. I was trying to look at the fear I knew when I was a child, and the fear I saw in my father which had in turn come from his childhood. I called the book a fiction as an act of defiance when I had reached the last page, but really apart from the presence of a talking pig and a few invented details the book holds very closely to family history.

"I am now at a curious borderline between fact and fiction and not sure where my writing will lead me. At the moment I am working on something set in the 15th century in which all the people who come and go are products of my own invention. It is a new territory which pleases me greatly."

Julia Blackburn's "new territory" has been the one that she herself has inhabited all along, according to the majority of critics. *The Emperor's Last Island* is the story of Napoleon's exile, "helplessly suspended out of time and history," on St. Helena, a small tropical island in the south Atlantic. Jean Nathan, who noted in the *New York Times Book Review* piece that the book combined elements of geography, biography, and autobiography, went on to observe that *The Emperor's Last Island* "is experienced as an elegy not just to 'an emperor and an island in a distant time that has been and gone long ago,' but to the fragility of man, nature, and creative pursuit." Michiko Kakutani, writing in the *New York Times* (July 31, 1992), found *The Emperor's Last Island* to be "the sort of book Bruce Chatwin might have written: it draws on a wealth of historical research . . . but imparts its erudition with insouciant charm." Blackburn, according to Kakutani, "has found a lucid, intimate voice, capable of accommodating everything from her own childhood memories to obscure historical footnotes."

With *Daisy Bates in the Desert*, Blackburn deepened her biographical style. Daisy Bates was born in Ireland in the 1860s. She was given to lying about her origins, describing herself as coming from an upper-class family rather than from the orphanage where she had grown up in poverty. In middle age, she began to study the Aborigines of Australia. In 1913 she returned to live with them in the wilderness, emerging in 1934 and again spending time in the outback in her old age. Blackburn's theory of why Daisy Bates regarded the Aborigines as her people, choosing to ignore her son, for example, is that she wanted to recreate her past and reinvent her life. Blackburn joined her on that journey, both physically and imaginatively:

> She leaves Australia and after five years she comes back to Australia. She watches the coastline slip away until it is lost within the horizon and five years later she watches as it surfaces again out of the far distance. She packs her bags to go and she packs her bags to return.
>
> As I write this I can see myself standing on the deck of a ship, staring at the sea, the sky, the land; the wind cold on my face and all three elements seeming to be made out of the same translucent grey mist; layers of mist shifting and moving. I am no longer sure what year it was or where I was going but I can remember the intensity of my exhilaration because as I stood there I really felt for a brief moment that it was possible to become another person just by the fact of departure. It was as if the person I had been was left behind on the shore; a tiny figure standing there all alone and waving a white handkerchief at the vast silhouette of the ship as it churned out across the water.

Blackburn told Margalit Fox for the *New York Times Book Review* (August 14, 1994) that she "got so used to [Bates's] life from her diaries and letters that I used it as if it were my own life." Fox pointed out that although Daisy Bates was not always truthful, the archival materials she left behind enabled Blackburn "to convey a sense of what the desert must have been like: the chronic hardship, the rootlessness, the sea of blowing sand." Blackburn told Fox that when she visited the Great Victoria Desert at Ooldea, where Bates lived among the Aborigines for nearly two decades, "I was in tears with it. Even the bleakness of it was somehow as it should be."

Michiko Kakutani noted in the *New York Times* (September 2, 1994) that Blackburn's immersion in Bates's life "is a lot like a gifted actress impersonating a famous person, inhabiting the subject's life while filling out the imaginative crevices with memories and associations of her own." The result, Kakutani observed, is a book "filled with wonderfully sharp, poetic images that give the reader a vivid, pictorial sense of Bates's day-to-day existence in the red hills of the desert: . . . caring for three old people deserted by their kin, 'scrabbling like a terrier dog in the sand, digging out rabbits and lizards' for their dinner, cutting wood and lighting fires; . . . homesick for the landscape of

Ireland, propping a stalk of cabbage against an acacia tree near her tent so her eyes could rest on something green. . . ." Linda Simon in the *New York Times Book Review* (August 14, 1994) remarked on Blackburn's "special affinity for exploring the congruence between emotional and physical landscapes." She concluded, "Julia Blackburn suggests new possibilities for the relationship between biographer and subject. Hers is a bold literary experiment; it results in an eloquent and illuminating portrait."

Metaphysical memory; "remanance," the exploration of vanished traces of memory; metamorphosis; and the sharing of dreams and curses by generations are the themes of *The Book of Color*. Blackburn's first novel begins in the past, with the story of a fanatical British missionary on one of the Seychelles Islands in the Indian Ocean, who elicits a curse that pursues his wife and his grandson. The present-day, female narrator asks whether it is "possible to inherit memories just as well as the color of eyes and hair, the shape of the lip or nostril? Is it possible that I can seem to remember my father's childhood as if it was something I had experienced myself, and could this process be allowed to move back through the generations as far as a person wished to take it?" The book ends with the narrator's conclusion that she has completed her exploration of inherited memory:

> So that's it. All over and done with.
> The house has been walked through.
> I have entered as many rooms as I could find and I have tried to describe what I saw there. I have come back outside now and I have just heard the door click shut behind me.
> The pig is walking off into the distance unconcerned.

Michiko Kakutani, in the *New York Times* (September 19, 1995), praised Blackburn's "rich, highly patterned prose that uses repeated motifs, images, and phrases to create a narrative that is less literary than musical and visual in effect." Blackburn discarded what Kakutani regarded as "conventional Freudian" backgrounds for her characters' distorted psyches, instead providing "more primitive mythic explanations: magic and curses and spells, contagious emotions and prophetic visions. As a consequence, her narrative vibrates with symbolism and portent. Every event, every encounter, every object shimmers with talismanic power: the landscape becomes a mirror of the characters' emotions, even as the characters' actions turn into emblematic gestures for generations to come." Kakutani, however, found *The Book of Color* less than fully realized: "Not only do the main characters blur together before the reader can really care about them as individuals, but their experiences tend to be translated into metaphors before they're even rudimentarily established as compelling concerns."

James Saynor, in the *New York Times Book Review* (October 1, 1995), disagreed: "Blackburn's tropical cocktail of themes relating to race, dementia, sorcery, and Victorian venery—along with her mellow writing style—puts one in mind of Jean Rhys's *Wide Sargasso Sea*. . . . She offers a swirl of exotic imagery, from zombies and werewolves to giant tortoises and talking pigs. But the surrealism is cleverly integrated into a pithy moral package. Her fantasy world is like a dream tableau by Henri Rousseau: wild yet punctilious."

In Blackburn's second novel, *The Leper's Companions* (1999), a woman recovering from the loss of a loved one retreats from the contemporary world into a 15th-century English village. "Blackburn's fantasy is a bit dull because of flat prose and thin characterization, yet exerts a certain hypnotic fascination," the *Booklist* (April 1, 1999) reviewer wrote.

Julia Blackburn, whether the rest of her career is spent writing fiction or not, seems likely to continue exploring "the invented life." Believing that all experience has a mythical quality, she crafts her prose to blur the lines between poetry and prose, reality and imagination, and dreams and memory. —S. Y.

SUGGESTED READING: *New York Times* C p25 July 31, 1992, C p26 Sep. 2, 1994, C p17 Sep. 19, 1995; *New York Times Book Review* p3 Nov. 1, 1992, p1 Aug. 14, 1994, p27 Oct. 1, 1995; *Times Literary Supplement* p28 Jan. 31, 1992

SELECTED BOOKS: Fiction—*The Book of Color*, 1995; *The Leper's Companions*, 1999; Nonfiction—*Charles Waterton*, 1989; *The Emperor's Last Island*, 1991; *Daisy Bates in the Desert*, 1994; As editor—*The White Men*, 1978

Block, Lawrence

June 24, 1938– Novelist; short-story writer

"I don't rewrite much," American author Lawrence Block said in an interview with *Publishers Weekly* (April 25, 1986). "I write books in quite a short time, usually no more than two months, with long periods in between when I just think." Block's speed and efficiency have resulted in an the production of an extensive oeuvre. The author of more than 50 fiction and nonfiction books, countless articles and short stories for publications like *Writer's Digest* and *Alfred Hitchcock Mystery Magazine*, and a plethora of pseudonymous works from early in his career, he has proven himself to be one of the most prolific writers of the late 20th century.

Best known as a mystery and suspense writer, Block is the creator of four separate detective series—those featuring, respectively, Evan Tanner, Chip Harrison, Bernie Rhodenbarr, and Matthew

Penguin USA

Lawrence Block

Scudder. By his own estimation, he is particularly well suited for the mystery genre. "[Mystery fans are] the most loyal, discriminating, and intelligent of readers, and I always feel I can write just what I want to write without feeling they won't understand what I'm getting at," he told the *Publishers Weekly* reporter.

Born on June 24, 1938 in Buffalo, New York, the son of Arthur Jerome and Lenore (Nathan) Block, Lawrence Block has said that he has long known that he would eventually become a writer. Even in high school, "I could write smoothly and well, long before I had anything to say," he told *Publishers Weekly*.

In a statement submitted to *World Authors 1990–1995* describing his life and career thus far, Block writes: "I was fifteen years old and a junior at Bennett High School in Buffalo, New York, when I decided (or discovered, or realized) that I was going to become a writer. Before then it had never occurred to me; afterward, it never occurred to me to do anything else.

"I wrote poems at first. Because they were short, I suppose, and because I had a facility with rhyme and meter that made verse come easily. The stuff sounded good, even though it didn't amount to anything. I wrote little sketches and worked my way up to short stories, and I sent everything off to magazines, and everything came back. That can be devastating, I guess, but it wasn't, because it was what I expected. I displayed the rejection slips on the wall over my desk. I saw them, not as evidence of failure, but as badges of my membership in the profession.

"This would very likely have changed, but it wasn't very long before I'd sold a story. It was a crime story, although I didn't realize that until it was finished and I was trying to think of someplace to send it. I sent it to *Manhunt*, revised it at the editor's suggestion, and had it accepted for publication.

"That was during my sophomore year at Antioch College. The following summer I got a job as an assistant editor at a literary agency, and I dropped out to keep the job, because it seemed to be providing more of an education than I could ever get in a classroom. After a year I decided to go back to school, but it was down on the farm and I'd already seen Paree—I'd sold a dozen stories and a few articles and a couple of paperback novels, and what did I care about Tobias Smollett and Milton's *Lycidas*?

"I dropped out again, this time at the college's suggestion. I moved to New York and wrote a book or two, moved back to Buffalo and bought a half-interest in a doomed jazz club, met and married an otherwise blameless young woman, moved to New York, wrote more books, fathered a child, moved back to Buffalo yet again, fathered a second child, moved to Racine, Wisconsin, to edit a numismatic magazine, moved back east to New Jersey, fathered a third child, bought an old farm near the Delaware River, got divorced, and moved back to New York.

"And so on.

"The early work consisted largely of crime fiction, along with a slew of paperback novels euphemistically called adult fiction. (I've long wondered why; they are, in point of fact, just the sort of childish thing one puts away upon becoming an adult.) I also wrote a lot of sexually-oriented nonfiction, some but not all under a doctor's by-line. (This last might more accurately be described as fiction in the guise of nonfiction, consisting largely of case histories that were in fact fabrications.)

"In the late sixties I found my own voice as a writer and produced seven books about a character named Evan Tanner. In the middle seventies I quit writing under pen names, and created the two series characters with whom I'm most commonly associated, an alcoholic ex-cop named Matthew Scudder and a lighthearted burglar named Bernie Rhodenbarr. Twenty-plus years later, I'm still writing about these guys. Scudder's changed a lot over the years. Bernie's stayed pretty much the same.

"In 1977 I stopped drinking. In 1983 I got married a second time. In 1985 we moved to Florida, for reasons I have long since ceased to recall. In 1987 we closed the Florida house and spent a couple of years without a fixed address, driving to and fro across America. In 1990 we moved back to New York.

"I've occasionally remarked that I can't imagine living anywhere other than New York, or doing anything other than writing. But how could that be true? Imagination is a writer's stock in trade. If I can imagine myself as a book-selling burglar or a dogged detective or an insomniac spy, it shouldn't be hard to envision myself in other settings, doing other things.

"And there are other occupations I might have turned my hand to, and it's possible I could have prospered in them, and even enjoyed them. But I'm glad to leave those several roads untaken. If anything's truly meant in this world, then I was meant to be a writer, and I feel supremely fortunate to have found out so early."

On the subject of his earliest works, Block is reluctant to divulge many details. "For several years now I've declined to identify my pseudonymous early work," he said in one interview. "They are inferior work, categorically inferior, and I'd rather not be specifically linked to any of them, although I'm not reluctant to discuss that apprenticeship in general." It was not until Block wrote the initial book of his Evan Tanner series, *The Thief Who Couldn't Sleep* (1966), that he found his voice as a writer and produced a work that he considered truly original. In addition to *The Thief Who Couldn't Sleep*, Block penned seven more books in this series that offers an unusual blend of insomnia and international intrigue: *The Canceled Czech* (1967), *Tanner's Twelve Swingers* (1967), *Two for Tanner* (1967), *Tanner's Tiger* (1968), *Here Comes a Hero* (1968), *Me Tanner, You Jane* (1970), and *Tanner on Ice* (1998). For the last-named book, the first Evan Tanner novel in nearly three decades, Block circumvented the aging process by explaining that Tanner has been in cryonic hybernation—from which he has now been revived, for an adventure in Burma.

By the time he published the final Evan Tanner book, Block was already working on two other series, writing each under the pseudonym of the series' protagonist. His Paul Kavanagh series yielded three books: *Such Men are Dangerous: A Novel of Violence* (1969), *The Triumph of Evil* (1971), and *Not Comin' Home to You* (1974). Block's Chip Harrison novels, a series about a chess enthusiast, included five books: *No Score* (1970), *Chip Harrison Scores Again* (1971), *Make Out with Murder* (1974, published in the United Kingdom as *Five Little Rich Girls*, 1985), and *The Topless Tulip Caper* (1975). Some of these stories were later packaged together in *A.K.A. Chip Harrison* (1983), which includes *Make Out with Murder* and *The Topless Tulip Caper*, and *Introducing Chip Harrison* (1984), which includes *No Score* and *Chip Harrison Scores Again*. Both of these compilations were published under the name Lawrence Block.

In 1976 Block began work on his Matthew Scudder series, one of two (the other comprising the Bernie Rhodenbarr novels) that remain active. The books revolve around the various exploits of Matthew Scudder, an ex–New York City police officer turned unlicensed private investigator. The books trace not only Scudder's adventures through the seedy underbelly of New York, but also his personal battle with alcoholism and his eventual partici-

pation in the 12-step Alcoholics Anonymous program. "Matt Scudder . . . has been hailed as a fresh character and a welcome inductee into the pantheon of desultory, boozed-up P.I.'s of contemporary fiction," Teresa Carpenter wrote in the *New York Times Book Review* (October 20, 1991). "Scudder doesn't look down on degenerates and occasionally participates in their depravity, a conceit that has kept readers off balance through . . . speculating whether Scudder will fall off the wagon or otherwise succumb to the siren's call of vice."

In 1994 Block published *A Long Line of Dead Men* (1994), the 12th installment in the Matthew Scudder series. The book involves a private club, purported to have originated during Babylonian times, which meets once a year for dinner and—infinitely more importantly—to read aloud the names of the club members who have died over the past year. The club is eventually left with only one surviving member, who must then choose another 30 members to begin the cycle again. The problem is that the new members are suddenly dying at a rate that is "way over the probabilities." The club's remaining members hire Matt Scudder to investigate the strange happenings, which in the past year have included an S&M sex killing, three—possibly four—suicides that could have been faked, several suspicious traffic accidents, a mugging, and a cab driver shot while on duty. The novel received reviews typical of those inspired by Block's Matthew Scudder novels. "[Block's] portrait of a man who has reached the age when he turns first to the obituary page and becomes depressed over his own life choices is letter-perfect," David Willis McCullough wrote in the *New York Times Book Review* (October 2, 1994). "His decidedly dark sense of humor has never been more in focus." Further praise was offered by Christopher Lehmann-Haupt in the *New York Times* (October 20, 1994): "What is most impressive here, as usual in this series, is how far the plot can stray from suspensefulness without losing the reader's interest as Scudder attends his A.A. meetings, dallies with his various women, and absorbs a New York City bar life so atmospheric that you can almost smell the beer in the woodwork." The other titles in the Matthew Scudder series include *Sins of the Fathers* (1976), *In the Midst of Death* (1976), *Time to Murder and Create* (1977), *A Stab in the Dark* (1981), *Eight Million Ways to Die* (1982), *When the Sacred Ginmill Closes* (1986), *Out on the Cutting Edge* (1989), *A Ticket to the Boneyard* (1990), *A Dance at the Slaughterhouse* (1991), *A Walk Among the Tombstones* (1992), and *The Devil Knows You're Dead* (1993).

Block's other active series is that about Bernard "Bernie" Grimes Rhodenbarr, a Greenwich Village bookseller by day and burglar by night. "Bernie's world abounds with New Yorky things—addresses, restaurants, behaviors—and is peopled by low-lifes and the wine-and-cheese crowd," a critic wrote in a *Chicago Tribune* (March 4, 1981) review of *The Burglar Who Studied Spinoza*. Beginning in 1977 with *Burglars Can't Be Choosers*, the series now includes seven other Bernie novels: *The Burglar in the Closet* (1978), *The Burglar Who Liked to Quote Kipling* (1979), *The Burglar Who Studied Spinoza* (1981), *The Burglar Who Painted Like Mondrian* (1983), *The Burglar Who Traded Ted Williams* (1994), *The Burglar Who Thought He Was Bogart* (1995), and *The Burglar in the Library* (1997).

The Burglar Who Traded Ted Williams was described by Michael Dirda in the *Washington Post Book World* (April 25, 1994) as " a cool summer-drink of a book—light, fizzy, a bit tart, and exceptionally refreshing, especially to any reader who's spent the winter slogging through tax forms, law briefs, or school texts." Such a comment is typical of critics' reaction to novels in the Bernie series, which, while set in the same city as the Matthew Scudder novels, tend to be much lighter and more humorous. In this particular novel, Bernie, who has resisted the lure of burglary for nearly a year, learns that the rent on his bookstore is about to be raised by several hundred percent. After commiserating with his longtime friend, Carolyn Kaiser, a lesbian who works as a dog groomer, Bernie decides—out of desperation—that the time is right to reenter the criminal world. After breaking into an apartment, Bernie finds a dead body locked in the bathroom. He immediately replaces all the items he was about to steal and quickly leaves the scene. The next morning, however, he finds himself charged with an entirely different robbery—one of an extremely valuable baseball card collection. Stuck without a decent alibi, Bernie sets out to clear his name, a process that includes more break-ins and a love affair. "Anyone requiring escapist reading will find [the novel] a real steal," Dirda wrote.

Bernie made his most recent appearance in *The Burglar Who Thought He Was Bogart* (1995). In it, Bernie, who has been partaking in a heavy Bogart-movie-watching binge (accompanied by a beautiful foreign woman, he has just sat through some 28 films in 14 nights), accepts a seemingly simple burglary job. Things quickly go awry, however, and Bernie finds himself in the middle of a complex scheme to loot the treasury of a foreign nation. Interwoven throughout this plot of foreign intrigue are multiple references to characters, dialogue, and scenes from a slew of vintage films. The book's retro theme is taken to such an extent that Bernie, who, as the title suggests, sees himself in the "quintessential Bogart role" of "the beautiful loser cooly victorious in defeat," winds up acting out the farewell scene from "Casablanca" with his mysterious movie-watching companion.

Block's most recent Matthew Scudder novel, *Even the Wicked* (1997), involves a serial killer who calls himself "the Will of the People" and whose targets include the requisite list of mobsters, child molesters, and other assorted lowlifes—and, oddly, a drama critic.

Published in 1998, Block's *Hit Man* is a collection of stories featuring a professional assassin named Keller. In an advance review, a writer for *Publishers Weekly* (November 10, 1997) called the book a "smoothly integrated collection" in which "Block's narrative skills, and his matchless ease with off-center conversation, are on display." In the 1999 Bernie Rhodenbarr novel, *The Burglar in the Rye*, Bernie has the job of stealing the letters of a J. D. Salinger–like writer before they can be published by the writer's ex-agent.

In addition to his fiction writing, Block has also written numerous nonfiction books. The subject matter he is willing to tackle is seemingly endless. Among these books are: *A Guide Book of Australian Coins* (1965), *Swiss Shooting Talers and Medals* (1965), *Writing the Novel: From Plot to Print* (1979), *Real Food Places: A Guide to Restaurants That Serve Fresh, Wholesome Food* (with Cheryl Morrison, 1981), *Telling Lies for Fun and Profit: A Manual for Fiction Writers, Write for Your Life* (1986), and *Spider, Spin Me a Web: Lawrence Block on Writing Fiction* (1988).

Lawrence Block has been the recipient of numerous awards, including the 1979 Nero Wolfe Award for Best Mystery for *The Burglar Who Liked to Quote Kipling*, the Private Eye Writers of America's Shamus Award (1983 and 1985), and the Japanese Maltese Falcon Award for *When the Sacred Ginmill Closes*. Additionally, in 1994, the Mystery Writers of America named him a Grand Master, an award given to writers who have made significant and lasting contributions to the mystery genre. —J. P.

SUGGESTED READING: *Booklist* p1282 Mar. 15, 1995; *Entertainment Weekly* p54+ Nov. 12, 1993; *New York Times* p46 Oct. 15, 1989, C p19 Oct. 20, 1994; *New York Times Book Review* p32 Oct. 20, 1991, p34 Oct. 2, 1994, p18 Dec. 24, 1995, p26 Apr. 10, 1994; *People* p29 July 3, 1995; *Publishers Weekly* p56+ Apr. 25, 1986, p68 May 27, 1996, p64 Nov. 18, 1996; *Times Literary Supplement* p21 Mar. 3, 1995; *Washington Post Book World* B p2 Apr. 25, 1994; *Contemporary Authors* vol. 45, 1995

SELECTED BOOKS: Fiction—*The Girl With the Long Green Heart*, 1965; *The Thief Who Couldn't Sleep*, 1966; *Deadly Honeymoon*, 1967; *The Canceled Czech*, 1967; *Tanner's Twelve Swingers*, 1967; *Two for Tanner*, 1967; *Tanner's Tiger*, 1968; *Here Comes a Hero*, 1968; *After the First Death*, 1968; *The Specialists*, 1969; *Me Tanner, You Jane*, 1970; *Ronald Rabbit Is a Dirty Old Man*, 1971; *Sins of the Fathers*, 1976; *In the Midst of Death*, 1976; *Time to Murder and Create*, 1977; *Burglars Can't Be Choosers*, 1977; *The Burglar in the Closet*, 1978; *The Burglar Who Liked to Quote Kipling*, 1979; *Ariel*, 1980; *Code of Arms* (with H. King), 1981; *The Burglar Who Studied Spinoza*, 1981; *Eight Million Ways to Die*, 1982; *The Burglar Who Painted Like

Mondrian, 1983; *Sometimes They Bite*, 1983; *Like a Lamb to the Slaughter*, 1984; *Such Men Are Dangerous: A Novel of Violence*, 1985; *Not Comin' Home to You*, 1986; *The Triumph of Evil*, 1986; *Sweet Slow Death*, 1986; *When the Sacred Ginmill Closes*, 1986; *Coward's Kiss*, 1987; *You Could Call It Murder*, 1987; *Random Walk: A Novel for a New Age*, 1988; *Out on the Cutting Edge*, 1989; *A Ticket to the Boneyard*, 1990; *A Dance at the Slaughterhouse*, 1991; *A Walk Among the Tombstones*, 1992; *The Devil Knows You're Dead*, 1993; *Some Days You Get the Bear*, 1993; *The Burglar Who Traded Ted Williams*, 1994; *A Long Line of Dead Men*, 1994; *The*

Burglar Who Thought He Was Bogart, 1995; *Even the Wicked*, 1997; *The Burglar in the Library*, 1997; *Hit Man*, 1998; *Tanner on Ice*, 1998; *The Burglar in the Rye*, 1999; As Chip Harrison— *No Score*, 1970; *Chip Harrison Scores Again*, 1971; *Make Out with Murder*, 1974; *The Topless Tulip Caper*, 1975; Nonfiction—*A Guide Book of Australian Coins*, 1965; *Swiss Shooting Talers and Medals* (with D. R. Krause), 1965; *Writing the Novel: From Plot to Print*, 1979; *Real Food Places: A Guide to Restaurants That Serve Fresh, Wholesome Food* (with C. Morrison), 1981; *Write for Your Life*, 1986; *Spider, Spin Me a Web: Lawrence Block on Writing Fiction*, 1988

Slick Lawson/Courtesy of Ballantine Books

Blount, Roy

Oct. 4, 1941– Humorist; nonfiction writer; screenwriter

One of the most noted humorists of the past three decades, Roy Blount Jr. has an undeniable talent for delivering biting commentary about the events of everyday life. Drawing heavily on his southern upbringing, he has written about a myriad of subjects, ranging from politics and sports to "down home" cuisine. His long list of works also includes humorous dips into verse and song. An accomplished performer as well, he has produced a comedic off-Broadway stage act. Blount has also written a memoir, applying his southern brand of humor to such personal topics as marriage and his relationship with his parents. With more than 14 published books, numerous articles and essays,

and even television and film scripts to his credit, Roy Blount Jr. has built a reputation as one of America's premier humor writers.

In a statement submitted to *World Authors 1990–1995*, Blount writes: "I was born October 4, 1941, in Indianapolis, Indiana. The date makes me neither a child of the Depression nor a Baby Boomer—I have no generation—and the place indicates that I am a Hoosier, when in fact I am a Southerner, who, however, has lived for the last 30 years in western Massachusetts and New York City. Whenever I try to define myself, I am reminded of a man whose name, Bossom, irritated Winston Churchill. 'It is neither one thing nor the other,' Churchill complained.

"I was reared by Southern parents in Decatur, Georgia, which was sort of its own small town and sort of a suburb of Atlanta. My grandfathers were a Mississippi railroad worker who died insane and a north Florida carpenter-contractor stricken by the Depression. My parents followed my father's work to Indiana and Ohio before putting down roots in Decatur when I was 18 months old. My father was a zone manager for two dying automobiles, Packard and Edsel, then became a successful savings-and-loan executive who died before that homey industry turned fast-and-loose and collapsed in scandal. My mother was a gravely overqualified, though not highly educated, housewife. My father was a staunch Methodist, my mother a Dionysian one. I am a secular humanist, I guess, with a warm spot in my heart for the old hymns.

"My mother taught me to read phonetically, with a Southern accent; language is primarily oral to me, but that doesn't mean I grew up among storytellers—my parents were more given to expectations, hurt looks, and cryptic remarks. I went to a Southern university, Vanderbilt, on a scholarship given to potential sportswriters, but my heroes were *New Yorker* humorists (Benchley, Thurber, Perelman, White) and for the college paper I wrote not about sports but in favor of racial integration, in the early days of the Civil Rights Movement. After a year of graduate school at Harvard, where I earned a master's degree and lost interest in becoming an academic, I served two years in New York City as a disaffected Army lieutenant fecklessly opposed to the Vietnam buildup.

"After the Army I got a job as a reporter for the *Atlanta Journal*, became a liberal op-ed columnist, then reverted to sportswriting when a job opened up at *Sports Illustrated*. Finally in 1975—after writing my first book, about Pittsburgh's National Football League team—I abandoned regular employment to become a free-lance magazine writer.

"For a while I concentrated on *New Yorker* humor pieces, but I found that tradition to be confining and that market insufficient to support my family. As of this writing I have contributed to 116 different publications—profiles, essays, sketches, verse, short stories, reviews, and accounts of adventures both outdoor (down Amazon headwaters on a raft) and indoor (modeling, after a fashion, for *Gentleman's Quarterly*). And indoor-outdoor (touring as a member of an authors' rock and roll band). I have written about politics, sports, music, food, drink, gender issues, books, comedians, language, travel, science, animals, economics, anatomy, and family life. Preferably, about all of those things together. My 14 books to date include a novel set in the White House, a slim double-volume of verse (from one end, it's *Soupsongs* [1989], about food, then you flip it over and from the other end, it's *Webster's Ark*, about the odd animals whose habitat is the dictionary), a consideration of myself in light of the Carter Administration and vice-versa (*Crackers* [1980]), a disquisition on hair, an anthology of Southern humor, a memoir, another volume of verse accompanying photographs of dogs, and several collections of disparate essays, sketches, and so on. I have had two one-act plays and one screenplay produced, I've created and performed (to a considerable extent simultaneously) a one-man show off-Broadway, and I've appeared on the radio, on television and in movies. I've written introductions to books by Mark Twain, Erskine Caldwell, A. J. Liebling, Ernie Bushmiller, Jr., and Phil Rizzuto, and to a lexicographical work entitled *The F Word* [1995]. I have worked with and learned from just about all the comic writers of my time, from Dan Jenkins to Garrison Keillor, and many of the comic performers, from Minnie Pearl to Bill Murray. The ones I haven't worked with—Richard Pryor, Donald Barthelme—I have savored and studied.

"All very miscellaneous, but all to various extents humorous and first-personal. For as long as I can remember, it has been my strenuous pleasure to mess around with the sounds and roots and interconnections of words; the themes I dwell on, whatever the nominal subject at hand, are the mysteries of race, sex, utterance, identity, and intimate relations that have bothered me since I was a child. Language seems to me intrinsically comic—noises of the tongue, lips, larynx, and palate rendered in ink on paper with the deepest and airiest thoughts in mind and the harshest and tenderest feelings at heart. Life, however, is not comic, and writing that

scants this consideration is just silly. My most recent book, the memoir (*Be Sweet* [1998]), attempts to bring all these concerns to a head by dwelling on such sore points as family secrets and what makes a person vocationally funny.

"I would like to think that I have carried on the tradition of Mark Twain as filtered through the old *New Yorker* and have pushed the envelope as regards ribaldry, catholicity, outspokenness on public issues, conjunctions of dark and light, literariness, vernacularity, synesthesia, negative capability, and personal frankness. I still haven't figured out how I can be so ill-defined."

In 1974 Blount wrote his first book, *About Three Bricks Shy of a Load*, which detailed the story of the Pittsburgh Steelers football team. The book received glowing reviews, including one in the *New York Times Book Review* (December 1, 1974), in which Robert W. Creamer called it a "terrific book" and added, "I have never read anything else on pro football, fiction or nonfiction, as good as this." In a piece on Blount written many years later, *Time* reporter Donald Morrison commented that *About Three Bricks Shy of a Load* "did for the Pittsburgh Steelers roughly what Sherman did for the South." *Washington Post* writer Larry L. King has deemed the book "the most comic treatise on professional football extinct or extant."

Blount's next book, *Crackers: This Whole Many-Sided Thing of Jimmy, More Carters, Ominous Little Animals, Sad-Singing Women, My Daddy, and Me*, was published in 1980. The book, which was a resounding success, examined the Carter administration and concluded that it would have been more effective had the president utilized more of a "redneck" approach to government. Critic Harry Crews, in his review for the *Washington Post* (November 2, 1980), wrote that the book is "a triumph over subject, proving—if it needed proving again—that there are no dull subjects, only dull writers." Crews concluded that the book was "the funniest book I've read in a decade."

Two years later Blount published a collection of his magazine articles titled *One Fell Soup; or I'm Just a Bug on the Windshield of Life*. Culled from a variety of sources, including *Esquire* and the *New Yorker*, the pieces address a wide range of topics. He followed *One Fell Soup* with two additional collections of articles and essays: *What Men Don't Tell Women* (1984) and *Not Exactly What I Had in Mind* (1985).

Soon afterward, he published *It Grows on You: A Hair-Raising Survey of Human Plumage* (1986) and *Now, Where Were We?* (1989), two more additions to his series of essay and article collections. *Now, Where Were We?* drew mixed reviews. In the *New York Times Book Review* (April 2, 1989), Deborah Mason wrote that Blount is "a self-styled rube with an agile intellect and a scatty imagination" and that his book is "brilliantly loopy and reassuringly subversive," and placed him "in serious contention for the title of America's most cherished humorist." Ralph Novak of *People* (April 23, 1989) spoke in less glowing terms about the book. According to Novak, Blount devoted too much of the book to his "good-'ol-boy image." Additionally, he found many of the articles to be annoyingly verbose; citing a particular passage from "Where I Get My Ideas" that goes on for seven-and-a-half pages, Novak wondered, "Get paid by the word for that one, did we, Roy?"

Indeed, while Blount's collections of essays have been critical successes overall, critics besides Novak have taken exception to Blount's style of writing and have considered his articles excessive in length or simply unfunny. Taffy Cannon of the *Los Angeles Times* (December 13, 1985) wrote that Blount's stories are "considerably funnier in a bar at midnight than spread at meandering and pointless length across the printed page." Other critics, including *Washington Post Book World* (January 23, 1983) writer Larry L. King, have praised Blount as one of the funniest writers in modern times. After reading *One Fell Soup*, King announced: "It gives me great pleasure to here officially designate [Blount] . . . a semi-genius at the very least. I have been reading his stuff for years, and he seldom fails to break me up." King has also called Blount "Andy Rooney with a Georgia accent, only funnier."

Blount next published the comic novel *First Hubby* (1990), a touching look at the life of Guy Fox, husband to the first woman president of the United States. Full of Blount's down-home humor, *First Hubby* received good reviews. In the *New York Times Book Review* (June 10, 1990), Christopher Buckley called it "clever" and added that "in places, it's downright dazzling." *Time* (June 25, 1990) writer John Skow acclaimed Blount as "good company whatever he's writing."

The following year, Blount published another collection of articles, called *Camels Are Easy, Comedy's Hard*, followed three years later by *Roy Blount's Book of Southern Humor*, a compilation of humorous stories from such noted southerners as Alice Walker and Louis Armstrong. During his more than 20-year writing career, Blount has also produced a book of verse, *Soupsongs/Webster's Ark* (1987) and a one-man show, *Roy Blount's Happy Hour and a Half*. *Soupsongs/Webster's Ark* was not as well received as some of Blount's essay collections; *New York Times Book Review* (February 7, 1988) writer Daniel Pinkwater called its onslaught of food rhymes a "dish only some can tackle." Blount's one-man show, however, which ran Off-Broadway in January and February 1986, was hailed by the *New Yorker* as "the most humorous and engaging 50 minutes in town."

In May 1998 Blount published his memoir, *Be Sweet: A Conditional Love Story*, which delves into the author's relationships with his parents, children, and friends, as well as his many adventures as a writer. Blount continues to work as a free-lance writer for a wide variety of publications

and has also written for television shows and movies. He has appeared as a guest on many programs, including *The Tonight Show, Good Morning America*, and *Politically Incorrect*.

Roy Blount Jr., who has two children and two grandchildren, divides his time between homes in New York City and western Massachusetts.—D.B.

SUGGESTED READING: *Los Angeles Times* Dec. 13,1985; *New York Times Book Review* Dec. 1, 1974, p20 Feb. 7, 1988, p9 Apr. 2, 1989, p7 June 10, 1990, with photo; *People Weekly* p33 Apr. 23, 1989, with photo; *Time* p72 June 25, 1990; *Washington Post* Nov. 2, 1980; *Washington Post Book World* Jan. 23, 1983; *Contemporary Authors*, 1996

SELECTED WORKS: Nonfiction—*About Three Bricks Shy of a Load*, 1974; *Crackers: This Whole Many-Sided Thing About Jimmy, More Carters, Ominous Little Animals, Sad-Singing Women, My Daddy, and Me*, 1980; *One Fell Soup; or I'm Just a Bug on the Windshield of Life*, 1982; *What Men Don't Tell Women*, 1984; *Not Exactly What I Had in Mind*, 1985; *It Grows on You: A Hair-Raising Survey of Human Plumage*, 1986; *Soupsongs/Webster's Ark*, 1987; *Now, Where Were We?*, 1989; *Camels Are Easy, Comedy's Hard*, 1991; *Be Sweet: A Conditional Love Story*, 1998; Fiction—*First Hubby*, 1990; As editor—*Roy Blount's Book of Southern Humor*, 1994

Bosquet, Alain

1919– Mar. 17, 1998 Novelist; poet

The French poet and novelist Alain Bosquet was born in Odessa, then part of the Soviet Union and now in Ukraine. Originally named Anatole Bisk, he was educated in Belgium and France. His was a life of displacement, soldiering, and adventure, followed by the contemplative peace of a writer's study. He wrote more than 50 books, but only one of his autobiographical novels has been printed in English: *Une Mère russe*, translated as *A Russian Mother* and published to critical acclaim. Bosquet's poetry has been published in seven bilingual editions, including two volumes titled *Selected Poems* in 1963 and 1973, respectively, and *God's Torment* (1994), with English translations by such distinguished writers as Samuel Beckett, Edouard Roditi, Lawrence Durrell, and Denise Levertov. Brian Swann in *Library Journal* (October 1, 1973) pointed out "the hardness and shape of much discipline" in Bosquet's poetry. The *Petit Robert* dictionary of names (1989) entry for Bosquet, in the poet's own translation from French, notes: "As journalist, essayist, translator, polemicist and novelist . . . , he has never ceased being faithful to poetry. From Surrealism, he has kept a

Alain Bosquet

F. Ferramh

taste for verbal violence and lucidity, but not that of a language liberated from the discipline of traditional writing."

Alain Bosquet, who was born in 1919 and died of cancer on March 17, 1998, wrote the following autobiographical statement for *World Authors 1990–1995*: "To be born in Russia, to grow up in Belgium, to flee to the United States, to see peace again in Germany, to live in France: that doesn't look serious. That is my destiny. At times I have been embarrassed by it, and then tell myself this is of as much importance as a comma in a poem, not more. I have no memory of Russia; I was less than six months old when my parents took me to Varna, in Bulgaria. My grandfather was rich: he had hidden more than a million rubles worth of jewelry in a wall, at the time of the civil war. Disappeared! The year of my birth, my father, sentenced to death—too much to the Left for the 'Whites,' too much to the Right for the others— owed his liberty to the publication of a book of his poems, because his jailer of the 'Cheka' was also a poet. The symbol is flattering; but all symbols are suspect.

"I still carry with me two images from when I was four: I saw a saxophone for the first time, a sublime serpent; and I spoke to a legless cripple. He filled me with disgust, not pity.

"At age five I was taken to live in Belgium, to which I owe a great deal. First of all, to have been a good student. I loved geography, history and glamorous films. I was very much in love with Greta Garbo, Marlene Dietrich, Ginger Rogers and Marcelle Chantal. Just an ordinary and acceptable boy. One day, at the zoo in Antwerp, I pinched the ankle of a giraffe; she drowned me in her saliva.

"After the skirmishes of 1940—for me, that's what they were—I dreamed of a Europe, united and glorious. To have to endure a Nazi Europe didn't bother me all that much. I changed my mind quickly upon my arrival in the United States at the end of 1941, already a veteran of two armies at age 21. I became the managing editor of the Gaullist paper in N.Y., called *The Voice of France*. There I came in contact with all the great writers and artists who had fled Europe and the war, like Mondrian, Breton, Chagall, Dali, Jules Romains, Thomas Mann, Saint-John Perse, etc. My first book of poems was published in Manhattan: *L'image impardonable*, with the encouragement of Breton. In September of 1942 I volunteered for the American Army and ended up the year after with Supreme Headquarters in London, as a participant in the preparation of D-Day.

"My only baptism was, intellectually, that of Hiroshima, preceded by the opening of Auschwitz in 1945. I had the 'opportunity' to visit Ravensbruck, among other concentration camps, the day after it was freed; the impact of those images has never left me and became the source of themes in some of my work.

"In 1948 I co-founded, with Edouard Roditi, an international literary review in Berlin, *Das Lot*, which introduced to the Germans some of the finest writers of the world who had been forbidden during the Nazi era. After five years of being a high functionary and a professional victor, I prepared my retreat from active history and opted for literature. I finished my studies at the Sorbonne in Paris and published my first semi-autobiographical novel, *La Grande Eclipse*, a derisive view of the war and its aftermath. My second volume of poems, *La vie est clandestine*, had already appeared in France after the war, and was very warmly received by those who counted at the time. There followed in the next 50 years a multitude of literary activities, including about 20 volumes of poetry and as many novels and short stories. Two of the novels received important literary prizes and became best sellers: *La Confession Mexicaine*, 1965, the story of an abstract French painter visiting Mexico, whose life and art were transformed by the revelation of the pre-Columbian civilization; *A Russian Mother* (recently published in the U.S.), 1978, the fictionalized story of my mother as seen through the upheavals of our century. As for my main occupation as a poet, practically every poetry prize available came my way, beginning with *Premier Testament*, 1957, and ending with *Je ne suis pas un poete d'eau douce*, 1996, my collected poems in one volume. A poet crosses a century; a century crosses a poet: without this osmosis, one's work would hardly be credible. The poem must write its poet. There have also been several volumes of aphorisms, the whole now in one volume, *La fable et le fouet*, 1995. The aphorism is naked, without the assistance of a character, of music, of any kind of apparatus. One accepts it or refuses it, period. Those published in this volume represent about a quarter of those written. One can read therein realistic or delirious definitions, fables, happenings, proverbs, maxims, sayings, but also projects for stories and light comedy scenes.

"There have been numerous translations in the world of my poetry. Those most recently translated into English are *God's Torment*, 1987, and *No More Me*, 1995. Artists who have illustrated some of these poems are Andre Masson, Fernand Leger, Max Ernst, Wilfredo Lam, Matta, Dorothea Tanning, etc...

"As a translator, I have introduced to the French reader the first complete anthology of American poetry, in 1956, followed by translations of Emily Dickinson, Walt Whitman, Carl Sandburg, Conrad Aiken, James Laughlin, and many others. Throughout these past fifty years I have published numerous literary reviews, as well as anthologies of several foreign poets.

"My gods are Van Eyck, Velasquez, Seurat, Mondrian. Painting is like a drug for me, an art I admire deeply and which I am incapable of harming, since I am no painter. There are poets, too, who are my gods, but they are my competitors.

"Who influenced me? Gottfried Benn who, in 1949, taught me to see man with the eyes of a physician: putrid flesh, chemical errors, defective secretions. I open one of his letters: 'Neither hope nor hate: that is my equilibrium.' Later, Saint-John Perse: 'Celebration of light and shadows, impenitent celebration.' I remember a line he wrote me during the war in Korea: 'One must walk through any form of life, even literary, as an animal of Luxury.' Beckett: 'Expression, any expression, is torture.' Cioran: 'Nothingness becomes amusing; therefore, let it be impeccably arranged.'

"My ideas are not particularly original. I know the planet is shrinking. Death will come this evening; mine in three minutes, and yours, dear reader, a quarter of an hour later. Ravaillac or Booth or Himmler will return and drop an atomic bomb. This attitude is quite healthy: it allows me to write only what is not minor: I mean, according to my own narrow criteria.

"Finally, what is it I say in my poems? Always the same thing: I am dying, I am dying, I am astonished not to be dead as yet. The rest is verbal fantasy: iguanas who become prophets, islands one marries, rocks that open a parliament to discuss the future of the human race. My profound truths are to be found in my words: I should say that I, a tiny spot of flesh, have settled inside of the realm of language. What I am all day long is of no use to what I write. The poem invents its poet. This misunderstanding is prolific. I should be capable of repudiating myself."

Alain Bosquet arrived in New York in late 1941. He became a U.S. citizen—and a soldier— preparing for the Allied armies' landing in Normandy in 1944. After the war and his postwar experiences of Germany, Bosquet chose to settle in Paris. The im-

mediate postwar literary scene was not a welcoming one. As Germaine Bree observed in an afterword to *A Russian Mother* (1996), the intellectual climate was dominated by the existentialists Jean-Paul Sartre and Simone de Beauvoir. "But," Bree added, "they were far from reflecting fully the mood of the hour. There was room for other, new voices. Bosquet's was one of these." Bosquet joined the critical staffs of *Combat*, *Le Monde*, and *Le Figaro* and quickly made a name for himself in the Parisian literary world. He left that world only temporarily to teach and lecture at universities in the United States, including Brandeis in Massachusetts and the University of Wisconsin in Madison. He was married in 1954.

Alain Bosquet's first bilingual book was *Selected Poems* of 1963. The volume contains translations by Samuel Beckett, Charles Gunther, Edouard Roditi, and Ruth Whitman. The collaboration *Conversations with Dali*, translated by Joachim Neugroschel, followed in 1969. Bosquet and Salvador Dali, "the bad boy of surrealism," as the *Choice* (March 1970) reviewer called him, were friends. Bosquet, on whom the influence of other surrealists was not minimal, directed "rapid fire questions" at Dali, which sparked "immediate responses of sense and nonsense in odd proportions, and in often witty and sharply barbed perceptions," the *Choice* critic said. "Dali's exhibitionist conversations with Bosquet . . . add up to the funniest art book in some time," W. O. Dane wrote in *Library Journal* (September 15, 1969).

The bilingual volume *Selected Poems* of 1973 contains selections from *Quatre testaments et autres poèmes* (1967) and *100 notes pour une solitude* (1970), translated by Samuel Beckett, Lawrence Durrell, Wallace Fowlie, and Jean Paul and Elizabeth Malaquais. Filled with the strange juxtapositions of surrealism, these poems have a light tone. Nevertheless, in the words of the *Choice* reviewer, Bosquet, seeing "death at work everywhere . . . portrays his tragic vision of a world on the road to Nothingness." He couches the tragic vision, however, sometimes in images that provoke a smile, as in "Deuxieme Testament / Second Testament." "En moi, c'est la guerre civile. / Mon oranger n'aime pas mes genoux. . . ." becomes, in Samuel Beckett's translation, "In me civil war. / My orange tree my knees displease. . ." While clearly a vision of decay, both of the body and the world around it, this has a somewhat comic tone. One stanza begins, "Fresh sighs for sale! / Prime doubts a penny!" and ends "Fresh hopes for sale! Prime sooth a penny!" The *Choice* reviewer commented on the "imaginative expertise of the translators," which "successfully rendered" the "mood and prosody of many of Bosquet's poems."

Melvin B. Yoken and Juliet G. Lapointe translated *100 notes pour une solitude* as *Speech Is Plurality* (1978). Further poems from *100 notes pour une solitude* were joined with poems from *Notes pour un amour* (1972) in *Instead of Music* (1980), translated by William Frawley. The third volume of the

Notes trilogy, *Notes pour un pluriel*, has not been translated. The *Choice* (November 1980) critic pointed out that the first volume is written in the third person, the second in the second person familiar, and the third in the first person plural, which joins the writer to the "diversity of the real world." M. B. Markus in *Library Journal* (March 1, 1980), terming Bosquet's poems "limpid," observed that "often they elude thought and call upon the imagination. Familiar objects—trees, sea, sun, moon, animals—become animated, take on human characteristics, and communicate with the poet. . . . Startling . . . images are the basis for his exploration of the power . . . of words, his relationship with the world, and death."

No Matter No Fact, published in 1988, is another bilingual compendium of Bosquet's poems. The translators for this volume, published by New Directions, James Laughlin's press, were Samuel Beckett, Denise Levertov, and Edouard Roditi. *God's Torment* (1994), a monograph, translated by Edouard Roditi, was Bosquet's next publication in English. In the foreword, Bosquet declared himself an atheist, but one tempted by God. He asks himself, "Can someone who eschews prayer and dogma call himself an intermittent believer?" The question is answered by the poems in the book. Bosquet's reply in the foreword is, "But if I know my limits, my poems do not. They feed upon God as they might upon a plane tree or a stork. I'm an atheist hassled by belief."

As he explained, one of Bosquet's major themes is death. In 1994 he published *Demain sans moi* (Tomorrow without me, tr. *No More Me*, 1995) with translations by Samuel Beckett, Lawrence Durrell, James Laughlin, Roger Little, and William Jay Smith. In one of the poems, "A Film," translated by William Jay Smith and published in the *New Yorker*, he thinks about his life "coming to an end" and turned into a film by a director: "Would I agree to play myself, / exaggerating my nervous tics / and suffering in some aesthetic fashion?" He had his cavils: "I insist: / no profiles, please, no flattering grins. / As for my books, whose fidelity I now find questionable, / they'd better be signed by some other poet." Adele O. Sullivan, reviewing the volume in *French Review* (April 1996), wrote, "The poet is often unpityingly candid about the physical details of his impending demise," but he is "often refreshingly witty." She noted that Bosquet informs us that the book is "the swan song to his career as a published poet," but she observed that this "collection bears witness to a poet's tenacity." In the poems Bosquet expressed gratitude: "He acknowledges the potential of the poetic words to renew his perception through the mediation of various objects of his affection, human or inanimate." He referred to "le plaisir du mot" ("the pleasure of the word") and "la volupté du verbe" ("the voluptuousness of the verb"). Sullivan concluded that through "his persistent collaboration with the lingua franca and its potential for variation in tone and cadence, Bosquet has sustained a voice at once concise and nuanced."

Bosquet sometimes displayed an ironic playfulness, which could easily be misread. In the brief opening section of *A Russian Mother*, an autobiographical novel translated by Barbara Bray, he depicted the narrator, who is both himself and a fictional character, as going about Paris buttonholing various people and repeating, "You're my mother, you're dead; all I feel is relief." It becomes clear from the ensuing narrative that all he feels is, indeed, not at all relief. His mother is not dead; she is about to die. Bosquet looks back at their relationship. He addresses his mother, as he does throughout the book: "For more than thirty years you yourself had tried to make your son happy whether he liked it or not, but now you were facing the facts: your version of happiness didn't appeal to him. And his aims—fame; power; originality at any price; an intellectual victory every day and a new enemy every week to minister to his own self-respect; outshining and despising other poets; attaining the invulnerable heights of civilized cynicism—all these were irksome to you." Bosquet's clear-eyed look at himself was interpreted by Michele Wolf in the *New York Times Book Review* (April 28, 1996) as meaning that he "cares more about writing than people." Yet, Wolf continued, "for the purposes of his book that is enough, yielding an eloquent exploration of the mutual appreciations and frustrations of his relationship with his mother." F. C. St. Aubyn in *Choice* (May 1996) termed *A Russian Mother* a "powerful stirring novel in a splendid translation."

Bosquet's attachment to his mother is demonstrated in his telling of an anecdote at the end of the novel: the Russian police, newly installed after the revolution, famous for their revolutionary zeal and brutality, held Alexander Bisk, Bosquet's father, in a prison where all the inmates were eventually executed. Bisk was in the hands of one Kostia Chervenko, a dangerous man who fancied himself a poet, "at once ardent and confused, realistic and mystical." Berthe Turiansky Bisk, Bosquet's mother-to-be, saved her husband by having copies of a book of his poems printed overnight with a dedication to Chervenko and presenting one to him. Chervenko let her husband go. "That was your finest hour," Bosquet concluded the book. He received the Grand Prix of the Académie Française for *Une Mère russe* when it was published in France in 1978.

Georges et Arnold, Arnold et Georges (1995) was another of Bosquet's autobiographical novels, this one more fictional than faithful to reality. Georges, the young son of a rich French family, and Arnold, a tormented son of Russian refugees, study botany together and become friends in the novel, which starts in the 1960s. Arnold is based on Bosquet himself, who chose to have that character's life end in suicide. Georges, however, also represents aspects of Bosquet. John L. Brown, reviewing the novel in *World Literature Today* (September 1996), observed that "many of the long exchanges between Georges and Arnold seem like a dialogue between the author and himself. . . . Speaking as 'Georges,' Bosquet evokes his experiences as a control officer in Germany and expresses deep anguish as he observes the suffering, the corruption, the traffic in refugee children sold as prostitutes." Simultaneously published with *Georges et Arnold, Arnold et Georges* was *La fable et le fouet* (The fable and the whip), "a collection of aphorisms . . . which echo many of the philosophical exchanges between Georges and Arnold," according to Brown.

Not only have Bosquet's books not been "signed by some other poet," but his poetry has been collected in one volume: *Je ne suis pas un poète d'eau douce: Poésies complètes 1945–1994* (I am not a softwater poet: Complete poetry 1945–1944), published in 1996. Also published in 1996 was *Les fruits de l'an dernier* (Last year's fruits).
—S. Y.

SUGGESTED READING: *Choice* p57 Mar. 1970, p401 Nov. 1980, p 1484 May 1996; *French Review* p845+ Apr. 1996; *Library Journal* p3041 Sep. 15, 1969, p2864 Oct. 1, 1973, p618 Mar. 1, 1980; *New York Times* B p11 Apr. 8, 1998; *New York Times Book Review* p23 Apr. 28, 1996; *World Literature Today* p 348+ Sep. 1996

SELECTED BOOKS IN ENGLISH TRANSLATION: Fiction—*A Russian Mother* (tr. B. Bray), 1996; Nonfiction— *Conversations with Dali*, (tr. J. Neugroschel), 1969; Poetry—*Selected Poems*, (tr. S. Beckett, C. Gunther, E. Roditi, R. Whitman), 1963; *Selected Poems* (tr. S. Beckett, L. Durrell, W. Fowlie, E. & J. Malaquais), 1973; *Speech Is Plurality* (tr. M. B. Yoken, J. G. Lapointe), 1978; *Instead of Music* (tr. W. Frawley), 1980; *No Matter No Fact* (tr. S. Beckett, D. Levertov, E. Roditi), 1988; *God's Torment* (tr. E. Roditi), 1994; *No More Me* (tr. R. Little, J. Laughlin, W. J. Smith, L. Durrell, S. Beckett), 1995

Courtesy of Karl Dietrich Bracher

Bracher, Karl Dietrich

Mar. 13, 1922– Historian; editor

Noted German political scientist and historian Karl Dietrich Bracher is one of the world's foremost authorities on the collapse of the German Weimar Republic (1919–1933) and the rise of Adolf Hitler and the Third Reich. A product of this volatile era of German history, Bracher couples his firsthand knowledge of these events with his background in

classical studies and philosophy to create a balanced perspective on both historical and current events in Germany. His books' subjects have ranged from fundamental studies on the rise of totalitarian states to philosophical discussions on the need for a better understanding of the importance of civil liberties. Although he has written prolifically in German and other languages, only four major works have been translated into English: *The German Dictatorship* (1970), *The German Dilemma* (1974), *The Age of Ideologies* (1984), and *Turning Points in Modern Times* (1995).

In an autobiographical essay for *World Authors 1990–1995*, Karl Dietrich Bracher writes: "I was born in Stuttgart in 1922 and grew up during the years of political crisis in Europe which led Germany into totalitarian dictatorship (1933) and finally into war (1939). First I underwent the broad classical education (with Latin and Greek) of the humanistic gymnasium in Stuttgart and, among others, learned to play the piano and contrabass. But from 1940 on I had to stay in military service and take part in the North African war, until I was taken prisoner and in 1943 came to the United States of America, fortunately. Life in the P.O.W. Camp Concordia (Kansas) until 1945 offered opportunities to begin with the study of history by reading, and to turn the experience of political crisis, of Nazi politics and destructive war, into learning by trying to analyze and understand its lessons for postwar politics in Germany and Europe.

"My background in classical studies, literature, and philosophy; the gymnasium, my parents' liberal home (both teachers); had worked as an antidote to the totalitarian spirit of the time and remained an intellectual reference point during my war service and the years as prisoner of war in America.

My encounter with and experience of a previously unknown, optimistic conception of history in America's democracy subsequently formed a strong contrast to the German dictatorship and the European catastrophe with its underlying sense of pessimism.

"Thus already during my studies in the P.O.W. camp in Kansas, and then even more so during my studies at Tübingen after the war, my love for classical history became a bridge across which my gaze fell upon history as a whole, coming to rest finally on the deeply distressing and controversial recent past, which I knew from bitter personal experience. My dissertation in ancient history—which did not appear in print in the turbulent year 1948 due to a shortage of paper (but was recently published by Böhlau, in Wien, 1987)—already took aim rather boldly at a fundamental problem in the history of political ideas in times of crisis: namely the question of decline and progress in the thought of the early Roman Empire. In recalling the classical discussion about the transformation of the Roman Empire, I was, at the same time, dealing with the then-topical theme of the crisis of progress, which is in many ways reminiscent of the discussion about crisis and decline that is going on today. To pursue this problem in a comparative and contrasting fashion also for the modern period, I next shifted my focus—more keenly on the contrasting image of America's 'new world' since the 17th century and on the recent history of Germany and Europe. The Salzburg seminar for American Studies in 1948, and a year of research at Harvard, allowed me to link up with the political sciences. Thereafter my wife, who comes from a family of the German resistance, also contributed her critical experiences to my efforts to frame the problem in a topical and concrete way.

"Now I definitively turned to contemporary history and political science. In the newly founded Institute of Political Science at Berlin I began (1950) work on my book *Die Auflösung* (dissolution) *der Weimarer Republik.*

"Weimar was still close. Few wished a return to the agitated atmosphere of the First Republic, which I had experienced at its unfortunate end. To be sure, during the early postwar years there were many discussions about that first democracy and its failure. In particular, people were seeking an explanation for the incomprehensible—the eruption of barbarism, the seductive power of totalitarian dictatorship. The Weimar discussion became an important reference point as the Federal Republic was being built. But the issue of concern to me in my study of ancient history, on the one hand, and in my encounters with dozens of the political and social-scientists (like James Bryce, Max Weber, Guglielmo Ferrero) and in conversations with Arnold Brecht, Sigmund Neumann, and Ernst Fraenkel, on the other, went straight beyond Ranke's dictum of history 'as it actually happened,' and was later indicated in the subtitle of my book on Weimar (1955): the problem of power and the decline of power in democracies.

"This approach to a complex theme contained three focal points and directions for research. First, my studies had made one thing clear to me: in contrast to the prevailing notions of a more or less sudden process of the 'destruction' or 'failure' of the Weimar Republic, what we were actually dealing with was a multi-causal and progressive process of 'dissolution,' which I had already sketched out in a preliminary study in 1952. Second, in contrast to mere description, but also to the terse explanatory models of Marxist or liberal, conservative, or nationalist bent, all of which in some way contain apologetic elements, I was concerned with analyzing the structure of power. This meant that an accurate description of the events had to be preceded by a systematic part: the 'problems of the structure of power.' Third, based on this approach I also tried to structure the narrative of the process of dissolution itself. I did this by drawing a distinction between different phases in the 'loss of power' by the democratic forces, the 'power vacuum' in the political sphere, and finally the gradual 'seizure of power' by a dictatorial movement. That movement took decisive advantage of the paralysis, indeed partial self-paralysis, of parliamentary democracy—it assumed the reins of government in what appeared to be a democratic and legal way, but subsequently it became impossible to dislodge.

"After my book on Weimar had appeared in 1955, the general discussion centered largely on the question if and to what degree the fate of that democracy was fatally preconditioned by structural defects of state and society reaching back to 1918 and even further into 19th-century German history. Since then the comprehensive work of Juan Linz and Alfred Stepan (eds.) on *The Breakdown of Democratic Regimes* (1978) has confirmed, on a worldwide basis, the usefulness of my 'model' of power decay, power vacuum, power seizure. In that longdrawn controversy on structural history, my analysis, quite different from Marxist interpretations, was based on a multi-causal approach; indeed the crucial role of groups and persons acting in decisive situations came out particularly with respect to the events of 1932–1933. Hitler achieved power not because of irresistible structural processes, but because of decisions or nondecisions of persons brought to the fore through the crisis of democracy, and because of the pseudo-legal revolutionary tactics of its enemies to the right—while its enemies to the left also followed a destructive course, unwittingly supporting the success of National Socialism.

"With two associates, Gerhard Schulz and Wolfgang Sauer, in an ensuing volume on *Die Nationalsozialistische Machtergreifung* (Power Seizure) (1960) I attempted to bring out the reverse side of the power vacuum: namely the complex, violent, and often seemingly even anarchic nature, yet at the same time the overriding totalitarian character of the process leading to the Hitler regime. The controversies around this process have since become intensified. During the 1950s it seemed evident that the technique of totalitarian power seizure was a new phenomenon of the 20th century, differing from classical dictatorships and typically with ideological one-party movements of the Right as of the Left. Whatever the different origins and appearances, the aims and promises of Fascism or National Socialism, of Leninism or Stalinism, of Communist or nationalist-racist 'revolutions,' the overriding experience was that of monopolist regimes claiming, with plebiscitarian acclamation, the total identity of the government with the governed, of the party with the state, of chiliastic ideas with the needs of the citizen, and the complete abolition of civil liberties.

"Yet the 1960s marked a new attitude toward ideologies, especially among the young. This became evident with the rise of the New Left and the renaissance of quasi-Marxist orientations in social and political studies. Thus while I worked on my following books *The German Dictatorship* (1969) and *The German Dilemma* (1971), also new theories of Fascism became fashionable; they served as a generalizing instrument of ideological warfare against all non-socialist political systems. At the same time, I was engaged in defense of the concept of totalitarianism that was strongly denounced from left-wing, pro-Communist views. In order to stem the trends towards political radicalisms, I became convinced that one of the foremost tasks of democratic scholars should be to correct the ideological confusion in political terminology; this was the purpose of two booklets *Controversies in Contemporary History* (1976) and *Key Words in History* (1978).

"How our generation has lived since the First World War through the extreme experiences of decaying democracies and of mass murdering dictatorships, but also with the unexpected chance of democratic revival I have then analyzed in the broad comparative study *Die Krise Europas* (1976); a new edition (1993) leads from 1917 to 1992. Moreover, in my following book *The Age of Ideologies* (1982), to delineate the impact of ideologies in our century, while in two further collections of essays (*History and Violence*, 1981, and *The Totalitarian Experience*, 1987), I stressed the importance of comparative studies on democracy versus dictatorship, old and new.

"The engagement with these themes, as dominant in our century as controversial, has been given new weight by the largely unexpected events of 1989 and their world historical consequences. The collapse of Communism and its ideology in Europe, and more still the shocking full realization of the totalitarian reality of both forms of rule, the Communist and the Nazi version, signal a new epoch of history. They bring full circle a development which leads from World War I into the totalitarian revolutions, left and right, of 1917 and 1922, 1933 and 1948, ending finally, after the defeat of National Socialism, in more than 40 years of confrontation between Communist dictatorship and Western democracy. Thus my latest book, *Wendezeiten der Geschichte* (1992) or *Turning Points in Modern Times* (1995) deals with the heavy legacies, problems, and chances at the turn of the century."

In addition to penning his own historical and political books and essays, Karl Dietrich Bracher has been a member of the editorial boards of a variety of periodicals, including *Politische Vierteljahresschrift* (until 1970), *Neue Politische Literatur*, *Bonner Historische Forschungen*, *Journal of Contemporary History*, *Government and Opposition*, *Societas*, *Zeitschrift für Politik*, *Tempo Presente*, *Risorgimento*, *European Journal of International Affairs*, *History of the Twentieth Century*, *Bonner Schriften zur Politik und Zeitgeschichte*, and *Quellen zur Geschichte des Parliamentarismus*. He was also a joint editor of *Modern Constitutionalism and Democracy* (2 vols. 1966) and *Bibliographie zur Politik* (1970, 1976, 1982) and the editor of *Nach 25 Jahren* (1970).

Among his many accolades, Bracher has received fellowships from Stanford's Center for Advanced Study in the Behavioral Sciences, the British Academy, and the American Philosophical Society. A former member of the Institute for Advanced Study at Princeton (1967–1968, 1974–1975) and the Wilson Center in Washington, D.C. (1980–1981), he served as chairman of the board of the Institute for Zeitgeschichte in Munich (1980–1988) and chairman of the German Association of Political Science (1965–1967). Bracher was a visiting professor at Oxford University in 1971 and at Tel Aviv University in 1974. He is an honorary member of the American Academy of Arts and Sciences.

For a number of years Bracher worked in Berlin, first as a research assistant and the head of the department at the Institute of Political Science (1950–1958), then as a lecturer at the German Hochschule for Politik and a professor at Free University (1955–1958). Since 1959 he has been a professor of Political Science and Contemporary History at the University of Bonn.

Karl Dietrich Bracher is the son of Theodor Bracher and Gertrud Zimmermann. In 1951 he married Dorothee Schleicher; they have one son and one daughter. He currently resides in Bonn, Germany. —C.M.

SUGGESTED READING: *German Tribune* p8 May 2, 1982; *Scala* 1979, p4 Sep.–Oct. 1987; *International Who's Who, 1998*

SELECTED BOOKS IN ENGLISH TRANSLATION: *The German Dictatorship*, 1970; *The German Dilemma*, 1974; *The Age of Ideologies*, 1984; *Turning Points in Modern Times*, 1995

J. M. Eddins Jr.

Brown, John Gregory

1960– Novelist; journalist; short-story writer

The New Orleans–born novelist and short-story writer John Gregory Brown, who is white, might be said to have produced fiction that falls outside the realm of his personal experience; his two novels feature characters who are black or female. The first, *Decorations in a Ruined Cemetery* (1994), is told through the use of multiple narrators—a daunting approach even for more seasoned writers. *Library Journal* (December 1993) described *Decorations* as being "studded with Gothic details . . . Heavy with family intrigue . . . a small gem." Brown's second novel—set, like his first, in New Orleans—is *The Wrecked, Blessed Body of Shelton Lafleur* (1996).

In his autobiography written for *World Authors 1990–1995*, Brown, born in 1960, describes his upbringing and his early need for a creative expenditure: "I have not wandered very far in my work from New Orleans, the city where I was born, the fifth of eight children in a Catholic family. I began to write at a very young age as a response, I think, to the sheer cacophony of such a large household, as a way of making my voice heard—even if I was, for so many years, the only audience to that voice." He received his bachelor's degree in English from Tulane University in 1982 and graduated Phi Beta Kappa. He moved on to Louisiana State University for his master's degree in English, which he received in 1984. In the next year he won first place in the 1985 short fiction contest held by the *Village Advocate* with "The Mower." He soon became a lecturer in English literature at North Carolina State University, a position he held until 1987.

In that year Brown moved on to Johns Hopkins University to work on a second master's degree in the Writing Seminars. At Johns Hopkins he won a place as a teaching fellow and later, after receiving his degree, taught seminars in writing. He left teaching in 1989, opting to become a staff writer and news editor for the *Columbia Flier/Howard County Times*. During this time he also submitted a collection of short stories, entitled "Degas' House," to the Associated Writing Programs' Fiction Contest, winning honorable mention. He returned to teaching and to Johns Hopkins in 1993—the same year that the Durham (North Carolina) *Sun* published his short story "This Summer." After a year he left Johns Hopkins for Sweet Briar College and an associate professorship in English. He also became the director of creative writing at the school.

In his autobiography for *World Authors 1990–1995*, he tells of his experiences writing his first two novels and his hopes for his third: "I liked to say about my first novel, *Decorations in a Ruined Cemetery*, that I was the only novelist who had managed to set a book in New Orleans and not mention Mardi Gras. In fact, though, what I did attempt to present in *Decorations* and in my second novel, *The Wrecked, Blessed Body of Shelton Lafleur,* was a portrait of the city that emphasized not the familiar seedy Bourbon Street settings or the aristocratic social circles of so many other New Orleans novels, but the places that had fascinated me as a child: the manmade Monkey Hill, the oak trees of Audubon Park, the Lake Pontchartrain Causeway, the shops on Magazine Street, the ramshackle neighborhoods of shotgun houses, the Mississippi River levee, and of course the city's gloriously Gothic cemeteries.

"I have been surprised—though perhaps I should not have been—by the thematic focus of my work, particularly its emphasis on race. I was born in 1960, and by the time I was aware of the world around me, all of the overt signs of segregation had been eliminated. There were no longer 'colored' water fountains or 'colored' restrooms. Integration of the schools had, at least nominally, been accomplished. But there were, of course, more subtle indications of racism and racial division in the city, and when I set out to write *Decorations*, where the central action of the novel occurs during the 1960s, I soon realized that I could not write the book without addressing the issue of race.

"Other issues in my work—my concern with religious faith, the difficult and often tragic bonds of the family, and the redemptive power of attempting to tell the story of one's life—are not so surprising to me and continue to occupy my thoughts as I work on my third novel, *Audubon's Watch*, which recounts a single night in the life of the ornithologist and artist John James Audubon.

"In this novel, Audubon is a young man—only thirty-six—and he has just begun to set about accomplishing all he hopes to accomplish. I am aware, as I write this novel, that I am exploring a particularly challenging period in the artist's development—he has painted a few accomplished works; his gifts, though not fully developed, have been recognized. What, then, will he do now? What will he make not simply of his art but of his life?"

Decorations in a Ruined Cemetery received, for the most part, very favorable reviews. The novel tells of the events of one day in 1965, when Dr. Thomas Eagen, a general practitioner in the black sections of New Orleans, leaves his second wife, Catherine, taking with him their two daughters, Meredith and Lowell. Through a car accident the family is reacquainted with Murphy Warrington, a former assistant of Thomas's father in the statuary and gravestone business. Murphy reveals to Thomas a family secret, which, even 25 years later, has ramifications for Thomas and his family. The story has several narrators, including Meredith, Murphy, and, through letters, Catherine. A writer for the *Southern Review* (Spring 1994) declared that "for a novelist who is young, white, and male to attempt such a narrative division of labor takes daring (or 'nerve,' depending on one's sympathies), and the stratagem doesn't pay off ." Other critics were far more admiring; a piece in the *Hudson Review* (Autumn 1994) read: "Faulkner invented a dozen ways of [merging voices], dissolving them into multiple and competing voices. Now John Gregory Brown has found a fresh way to do it too, in what may be the best first novel of the year." A writer for the *New York Times Book Review* (January 30, 1994) was even more enthusiastic about Brown's abilities: "For a book to be like [this], the label 'first novel' seems grudging and dismissive. Artistry like this is unclassifiable."

Brown's second novel, *The Wrecked, Blessed Body of Shelton Lafleur*, used devices similar to those in his first: it is set in the New Orleans of the past (in this case in the 1930s) and features an unusual narrative arrangement, in which the older Shelton serves as a guardian angel of sorts to his younger self. Shelton is injured in a fall as a child and is crippled for life. Struck dumb by fear of the authorities who take care of him after his fall, he never finds his way back to his foster mother and is instead sent to an orphanage for black boys. After spending several years in the orphanage he runs away to search for his lost past.

According to Nina Auerbach, writing in the *New York Times Book Review* (August 18, 1996), "because of [Brown's] sentimental glorification, Shelton's story is absorbing but rarely moving." Auerbach found this second novel to be a "vivid" one, "but also a self-conscious and derivative one." A writer for *Library Journal* (April 1, 1996) found the book's style "sometimes beautiful, sometimes grandiose" and "the imagery and symmetry . . . often heavy-handed—all of which can waylay the story before the concluding payoffs."

John Gregory Brown has received several awards for his work, including the Lyndhurst Prize in 1993, which brought in a three-year, $120,000 stipend. He won the Lillian Smith Book Award for his first novel, which was named by the Southern Regional Council as the year's greatest achievement in fiction pertaining to the South. He was also presented with the prestigious Steinbeck Award, which carried a stipend of £10,000, for his first novel. Additionally, he was a regional winner for *Granta*'s Best Young American Novelists competition. A versatile writer, he wrote a script for the CBS television program *The Road Home* in 1994, and numerous columns, essays, articles, and book reviews have appeared in the *Los Angeles Times*, the *Columbia Flier/Howard County Times*, *Laurel Leader*, the *Raleigh News & Observer*, *Southern Changes*, and *Spectator Magazine*. His third novel, *Audubon's Watch*, is to be published by Houghton Mifflin.

—C.M.

SUGGESTED READING: *Hudson Review* p499+ Autumn 1994; *Library Journal* p168+ Dec. 1993, p114 Apr. 1, 1996; *New York Times Book Review* p17 Jan. 30, 1994, p17 Aug. 18, 1996; Southern Review Spring 1994

SELECTED BOOKS: *Decorations in a Ruined Cemetery*, 1994; *The Wrecked, Blessed Body of Shelton Lafleur*, 1996

Brown, Larry

July 9, 1951– Novelist; short-story writer

Larry Brown, a highly regarded author of novels and short stories, first gained notice in 1988, when he published his well-received short story collection *Facing the Music*. Since that time he has continued to focus on average working-class people in the rural South who suffer from disease, alcoholism, haunting memories of war, and more. Brown's style is raw and realistic, reflecting the characters' resignation about their lives as well as the occasional glimmers of hope that things might get better. In his first, sparse novel, *Dirty Work* (1989), Brown used a conversation between two disabled Vietnam veterans to make a moving antiwar statement. His next collection of stories, *Big Bad Love* (1990), focused on love lost in the course of marriage. His critically lauded second novel, *Joe* (1991), painted a portrait of a tough, decent man who performs shady acts for a local timber company. Brown's most recent works are *On Fire* (1994), a memoir of his days with the fire department, and *Father and Son* (1996), a novel about a disabled World War II veteran and his angry, law-breaking son.

Miriam Berkley

Larry Brown

William Larry Brown was born in Oxford, Mississippi, on July 9, 1951. His parents—Knox Brown, a farmer, and Leona Barlow Brown, a postmaster and later a store owner—both significantly influenced their son's writing. Knox Brown, a World War II veteran, was a sharecropper who frequently moved from place to place in order to find work; he also drank often to escape the difficulties of his life. His experiences in the war later popped up in some of the veterans' stories in Larry Brown's *Dirty Work* as well as in the past of Virgil Davis, the crippled veteran in *Father and Son*. Leona Brown was an avid reader and passed the trait down to her son. "I've always liked to read; I got that from my mother," Brown told Bob Summer in an interview for *Publishers Weekly* (October 11, 1991). "When I was a kid I had my school books, which I didn't care much for, and my library books—hunting stories, fishing stories, cowboy stories, Zane Grey— nothing you would call literature. It took me a long time to even learn what literature was."

After graduating from high school in 1969, Brown enlisted in the United States Marine Corps and was stationed at a barracks in Philadelphia, where he spent a good deal of time listening to the stories of disabled veterans who had just come back from the Vietnam War. Brown saved these memories and later used them to shape the characters in *Dirty Work*. When he left the Marine Corps in 1972, he returned to Mississippi, where he worked at the family's grocery store and at a variety of odd jobs—which included cleaning carpets, cutting wood, hauling hay, and installing fences— before joining the Oxford Fire Department in 1973. A year later he married Mary Annie Coleman; the couple had three children, Billy Rae, Shane, and LeAnne.

In 1980, when Brown was 29, he decided to try his hand at writing. As he told Bob Summer in *Publishers Weekly*: "I had been wondering how books get written and if someone could teach himself how to write. And I thought I could make some money off of it. Of course, I didn't know what I was doing. I didn't even know about double spacing. I typed the whole novel single spaced, 327 pages. I worked on it every spare moment I could find for about seven months." The novel he wrote reflected what he was reading in those days—mostly block-buster novels by such authors as Stephen King, Louis L'Amour, and Harold Robbins. It was about a man-eating bear terrorizing Yellowstone National Park—a place Brown had never visited. He sent the manuscript to various publishing houses and received rejection after rejection. After some time he put the novel away and continued to work on stories, churning out one after another for two years until he had amassed nearly 100. Finally, the biking magazine *Easyrider* published one of his stories after rejecting a few earlier submissions. Two years later *Fiction International* accepted a narrative poem, which was later included in *Facing the Music*.

Even with these early successes, Brown had yet to find his literary voice—and had come to feel he wouldn't find it in a how-to book on writing. In 1982 he decided to enroll in a short story writing course at the University of Mississippi, in Oxford, taught by the noted author Ellen Douglas. Brown, who had not previously attended college, has since stated in interviews that Douglas had a major effect on both his writing and his understanding of literature. Since taking her class he has intensely studied the work of Raymond Carver, Flannery O'Connor, and William Faulkner, another native of Oxford, Mississippi. Douglas helped Brown find appropriate subject matter for his raw style— specifically, the lives of rural people who are often living in desperate economic conditions.

Around that time, Brown began going to Square Books, Oxford's major bookstore and literary hangout. The store's owner, Richard Howorth, introduced him to still more serious fiction by contemporary writers, such as Richard Ford, Pete Dexter, Clyde Edgerton, and Harry Crews.

In 1987 Brown published "Facing the Music," his second story, in the *Mississippi Review*. The story intrigued Shannon Ravenel, an editor at Algonquin Books, a publishing house in Chapel Hill, North Carolina. "He handled that story with the most incredible directness and courage," she later told Peter Applebome of the *New York Times* (March 5, 1990). "It was one where the writer's eye stayed wide open and never blinked and never compromised." Within a year, Ravenel and Algonquin Books published *Facing the Music* (1988), Brown's collection of stories about lower-middle-class characters. The book received glowing reviews.

A year later, Algonquin Books published Brown's first novel, *Dirty Work* (1989). The story of two disabled Vietnam veterans—one black, without arms or legs; the other white, hideously disfigured and prone to madness and seizures—the story takes place in a veterans' hospital where the two men, in very distinct voices, share their war stories, squashed dreams, and fears. The book was widely cheered in the critical press. In the *New York Times* (September 23, 1989), Herbert Mitgang wrote that "There has been no antiwar novel—certainly no first novel—quite like Larry Brown's *Dirty Work* since Dalton Trumbo's *Johnny Got His Gun*. . . . It is a powerful and original work all his own that moves along in short, staccato chapters with indisputably authentic language. At times, the reader feels he is eavesdropping on a conversation between foreigners, not Americans. For these two men inhabit the alien world of the unseen, half-dead hospitalized wounded." In his review of the book for *Newsweek* (November 20, 1989), Peter S. Prescott had one minor criticism of the novel. "At the very end, Brown succumbs to the Southern writer's disease: with block and tackle he drags in some superfluous melodrama," Prescott wrote. "But by then it hardly matters. A man who can write this kind of story with such understatement, and who can infuse it with a lightly comic tone, can be forgiven a climactic excess."

In 1990 Brown published another collection of short fiction, *Big Bad Love*. The stories focus on marriage after love has left the relationship; most of the characters are poor, boozing southern men and their sometimes malicious, sometimes domineering wives. In the *Washington Post Book World* (December 23, 1990), Clancy Siegel wrote that "Almost all the stories point to or spring from the author's angry despair at love gone wrong as irretrievably as seasons advance. . . . There is a bitterness so acrid it comes out the other end as purgation, even laughter."

A year later Brown published his next novel, *Joe* (1991). The title character, Joe Ransom, is a good man, even if he has a somewhat shady agreement with the local lumber company—to help poison scrub timber. To complicate Joe's life, he has an ex-wife who is often on his mind, a pregnant 19-year-old daughter, a wild younger son who never appears in the novel, and an on-again, off-again girlfriend the same age as his daughter. Over the years each of them has had a lot of trouble with Joe, partially because of his drinking. While nearly everyone in his private life considers Joe to be bad news, at work he has attracted a scrappy 15-year-old shadow named Gary Jones. Gary works to keep his own family together—which is difficult when his father has only one concern: to wring as much alcohol as he can from each dollar.

Joe received sterling reviews. In the *New York Times Book Review* (November 10, 1991), Leon Rooke remarked that "The novel, written in a luminescent prose tempered by wit, moves gracefully forward by tracking the independent movements of its three artfully conceived and skillfully balanced principals. As their lives mesh, the novel's momentum, and its rewards, build." A *Time* (October 28, 1991) critic felt that "The new novel is clear, simple and powerful, and it is great, rowdy fun to read."

For his next work, Brown tried his hand at nonfiction and produced a memoir of his days as a fireman. Published in 1994, *On Fire* received mixed reviews. While some readers were fascinated with the lives of firemen, David Nicholson of the *Washington Post* (March 1, 1994) complained that the book reads like "a series of journal entries. Some chapters are less than 10 lines long and, while we encounter and re-encounter the people who appear here—Brown's wife and children, his fellow firefighters—the lack of a sustained narrative means we don't get to know them the way we do the characters in his novels and stories." Madison Smartt Bell, writing for the *New York Times* (February 6, 1994), disagreed and suggested that "in this book, Mr. Brown goes through his life with the same meticulous attention with which Thoreau circled the woods around Walden Pond."

Two years later, Brown published his third novel, *Father and Son* (1996). As its title suggests, the book looks at a father and son—Virgil and Glen—over a period of five days in 1968. Virgil, a disabled World War II veteran, has made his family miserable with his alcoholism. Glen has recently been released from prison, after serving three years for vehicular manslaughter following the death of a small child. He went to jail bitter and came out worse—a hardened criminal who kills an old enemy and rapes a woman as soon as he is free. His hatred of his father causes him to lash out at everything and everyone, especially Bobby Blanchard, the county sheriff who is also Virgil's illegitimate son. Adding to the confusion, Blanchard has fallen in love with Jewel, Glen's girlfriend, with whom Glen has a child. The book received high praise. Anthony Quinn, a freelance writer reviewing the novel for the *New York Times* (September 22, 1996), felt that "*Father and Son* is about the violence in men's hearts and the accidents of birth that may have hatched it there. For the most part it is an engrossing tale, and nicely detailed: the torpid rhythms of life in the small-town South are wonderfully caught. If the book has a flaw, it is that it feels overschematized. The symmetries Mr. Brown establishes occasionally look too neat." James Hynes of the *Washington Post* (September 26, 1996) disagreed, asserting that "this is a powerful, suspenseful, and moving literary entertainment, the work of an enormously gifted natural writer. *Father and Son* unfolds with biblical simplicity and the slow inexorability of a classical tragedy." —C.M.

SUGGESTED READING: *Chicago Tribune* V p1+ June 19, 1990; *New York Times* p13 Sep. 23, 1989, C p11 Mar. 5, 1990, Feb.6, 1994, Sep. 22, 1996; *New York Times Book Review* p25 Nov.

10, l991, Feb. 6, 1994; *Newsweek* p81 Nov. 20, 1989; *Publishers Weekly* p46+ Oct. 11, 1991; *Time* p96 Oct. 28, 1991; *Washington Post* C p2 Mar. 1, 1994, Sep. 26, 1996; *Washington Post Book World* Dec. 23, 1990; *Contemporary Authors* vol. 134 1992

SELECTED WORKS: Fiction—*Facing The Music*, 1988; *Dirty Work*, 1989; *Big Bad Love*, 1990; *Joe*, 1991; *Father and Son*, 1996; Memoir—*On Fire*, 1994

Broyard, Anatole

July 16, 1920– Oct. 11, 1990 Book critic; essayist; short-story writer

After publishing several acclaimed short stories in the 1950s, Anatole Broyard inspired predictions that he would become a great novelist; instead, he embarked on a career as a book critic at the *New York Times*, through which he became one of the most influential voices in American literature. *Intoxicated by My Illness*, published in 1992—two years after his death—is a compilation of essays on death and dying that Broyard wrote during his ultimately unsuccessful battle with prostate cancer. The following year saw the publication of *Kafka Was the Rage*, an unfinished memoir of Broyard's exploits among the intellectual elite of New York City's Greenwich Village during the 1950s.

Anatole Paul Broyard was born on July 16, 1920, in the French Quarter of New Orleans, Louisiana, to Paul Broyard and Edna (Miller) Broyard. When Anatole was six years old, he moved with his parents and siblings to the Bedford-Stuyvesant section of Brooklyn, New York, where he grew up in a working-class environment in a family that was never intellectually inclined. "My parents had no idea even what the *New York Times* was, let alone being able to imagine that Anatole might write for it," Broyard's sister Shirley recalled to Henry Louis Gates, Jr. for the *New Yorker* (June 17, 1996).

Anatole attended Boys High School in Bedford-Stuyvesant. After graduating in the late 1930s, he entered Brooklyn College but did not graduate. To a certain degree, he was self-educated.

Broyard served in World War II as a member of the United States Army and eventually attained the rank of captain. He coped with the rigors of army life through constant consultation of a volume of the poetry of Wallace Stevens. Just after the start of the war, Broyard married his first wife, Aida. They soon had a daughter, whom Anatole named Gala, after the wife of Spanish surrealist painter Salvador Dalí. While Broyard was in the Army, Aida and Gala stayed with his family in Brooklyn. He decided he wanted to open a second-hand book store in New York when he came home and started sending his wife money to save for him for this purpose.

After Anatole's return from the war in 1945, the Broyards moved to Manhattan's Greenwich Village and took up a "bohemian" lifestyle. He quickly drifted away from Aida, and they divorced; she took their daughter Gala with her to California, where she later remarried. Meanwhile, Broyard opened his bookstore and began attending night classes at the New School for Social Research, courtesy of the G.I. Bill. His bookstore brought him into contact with the intellectual luminaries of Greenwich Village at the time, including the poets W. H. Auden and Dylan Thomas.

In the late 1940s and early 1950s, Broyard gained a reputation as a budding literary mind, due to a series of short stories and essays in such journals as *Partisan Review* and *Commentary*. Chief among these early pieces were an essay on the so-called "hipster" generation, of which he was a part in his Village days, and the short story "What the Cystoscope Said" (1954). A fictionalized account of his father's terminal illness, "What the Cystoscope Said" ran in the literary magazine *Discovery*. Among those impressed by the story was the Atlantic Monthly Press, which offered Broyard a $20,000 advance to expand it into a novel. Broyard was thus touted as a hot new novelist, without having written one book. *Advertisements for Myself* (1959), Norman Mailer's skewering of his literary contemporaries, reserves a rare bit of praise for Broyard, about whom Mailer declared, "I would buy a novel by him the day it appeared." However, for reasons that have been a subject of debate among those who expected great things from him, Broyard never wrote a single novel.

In 1958 Broyard began working at the New School for Social Research as a lecturer in sociology and literature. He also taught at New York University's Division of General Education. As a writing teacher he enjoyed a reputation for being demanding yet knowledgeable. He met Alexandra "Sandy" Nelson in January of 1961, and in less than a year they were married. "Anatole was very hip," she told Gates. "It wasn't a pose—it was in his sinew, in his bones. And, when he was talking to you, you just felt that you were receiving all this radiance from him." Anatole and Alexandra moved to Connecticut in 1963. Later that year they had a son, Todd, and in 1966 a daughter, Bliss. After Todd's birth, Broyard felt it was at last time to settle down professionally, and he took a full-time copywriter position at Wunderman Ricotta & Kline, a Manhattan advertising agency.

Still lecturing at the New School, Broyard left advertising in 1971 and began a professional association with the *New York Times* that would continue for the rest of his life. He started as a writer of features, then became a book critic, which was perhaps his true calling. In 1974 he published a collection of those pieces under the title *Aroused by Books*. The volume contained 107 of his pieces published between 1971 and 1973, the majority of which were book reviews. He left the New School in 1979, and lectured in creative writing at Columbia University from 1978 to 1980, after which he devoted himself completely to his duties at the *New York Times*.

In 1980 he published an anthology of 50 personal essays he had written for the *Times* between 1977 and 1979 entitled *Men, Women, and Other Anticlimaxes*. The essays generally deal with a former New Yorker's thoughts on living in Connecticut. Henry Gates described the essays as "brief impromptus, tonally flawless. To read them is to feel that you are in the company of someone who is thinking things through. The essays are often urbane and sophisticated, but not unbearably so, and they can be unexpectedly moving."

Broyard met with great success in his years as a literary critic. His book reviews were known for their enthusiasm and reflected his genuine love of books. As fellow critic Alfred Kazin remarked at his memorial service, in a speech reprinted in the *New York Times* (November 25, 1990), Broyard possessed "an addiction to literature by no means common among literary journalists." In fact, Kazin went on to say that Broyard possessed a deep literary passion "against which, as measure and representation of human existence, the life around him often seemed hollow and mean to the point of being disgraceful." Broyard's opinionated style did not always endear him to editors and readers, however; he was considered a "neoconservative" by some and had no love for the growing genre of feminist literature.

Broyard's inability to complete a novel remained for him a source of great regret and frustration. His success at the *New York Times* had brought him prosperity and fame but was for him a meager consolation.

In 1984 he transferred from the daily *Times* to work exclusively on the *New York Times Book Review*, published with the Sunday edition. He continued writing book reviews for the *Times* until 1986, and the following year he was appointed editor of the *Book Review*. In 1989, with both of their children grown, Broyard and his wife moved to Cambridge, Massachusetts. A friend of Broyard's, who was a senior editor at the publishing company Harcourt Brace Jovanovich, encouraged him to write his autobiography, and he began work on a memoir, but his progress came to a halt in August 1989, when he was diagnosed with inoperable cancer of the prostate. He shortly thereafter ended his 18-year employment at the *New York Times*.

The disease quickly spread to his lymph nodes and lower spine, and it was clear that there was not much that could be done. Rejecting radical surgery, Broyard opted for what is known as "hormonal manipulation," a treatment that relies a great deal on the patient's emotional strength and willpower.

Broyard abandoned his memoir and devoted himself to compiling a series of his essays on coping with death and dying, some new and some previously published in the *Times*. Facing his own imminent death, Broyard worked vigorously in his final months to put the volume together. "When you learn that your life is threatened," Broyard wrote in one of the essays, "you can turn toward this knowledge or away from it. I turned toward it." In another section, he observed, "my sickness has purified me, weakening my worst parts and strengthening the best." Doctors felt that Broyard might live for several more years, but he died on October 11, 1990, in Boston, Massachusetts, less than 14 months after being diagnosed with cancer. He was 70 years old.

The collection of essays Broyard had been working on was published posthumously in 1992, under the name *Intoxicated by My Illness*. The title is a reference to what Broyard described as his initial reaction to learning of his disease: a burst of imaginative energy that shook him out of his longstanding writer's block. Three of the essays included in the collection were written by Broyard in 1989 and 1990, while he was dying of prostate cancer. The collection is divided into three sections: the first chronicles Broyard's own battle with cancer, the second consists of Broyard's analysis of works written on the subjects of death and illness, and the third section includes "What the Cystoscope Said."

Steven Baugh, who reviewed the book in the *Journal of the American Medical Association* (February 2, 1994), called it "an absorbing introspection on living with a terminal illness." Baugh admired Broyard's unflinching courage in the face of his terminal condition and the way in which he managed to inject humor into some of the essays. He also specifically pointed to the essay "The Patient Examines His Doctor" as particularly valuable to people in the medical profession seeking to understand the needs of the patient. "Through his examination of the process of death, Broyard discovers himself," Baugh wrote, "His insights lead us to reflect on ourselves and, as future physicians, to understand patients' struggles as well."

Broyard's final efforts did not ring so true to Madeline Marget of *Commonweal* (January 15, 1993), who wrote that "In *Intoxicated by My Illness*, Anatole Broyard, instead of confronting the reality of illness, tried to rise above it." Marget believed that Broyard's attempt at transcendence fell flat and resulted in a "wrongheaded and offensive" book. She found Broyard's essays to be superficial and self-absorbed and felt that *Intoxicated by My Illness* could be damaging to someone actually going through a terminal illness. "For blaming the victim, I've never seen the equal of this," she proclaimed. The expression of pain and grief is invalidated by Broyard, according to Marget, who maintained that the author had written a "denial and falsification of suffering." Marget also drew attention to the possibility that Broyard's celebrity influenced the quality of his care.

The review in the *New York Times*, Broyard's old professional home, was much kinder. "Many other people have chronicled their last months . . .," Eugene Kennedy wrote (May 10, 1992),

"Few are as vivid as Broyard, who brilliantly surveys a variety of books on illness and death along the way as he draws us into his writer's imagination, set free now by what he describes with a sense of relief as the deadline of life." Kennedy also pointed to "The Patient Examines the Doctor" as the centerpiece of the collection and described the entire volume as "a virtuoso performance in which [Broyard] plays and revels in his writer's art."

Broyard's unfinished memoir was finally assembled and published by his widow in 1993. Entitled *Kafka Was the Rage: A Greenwich Village Memoir*, the book is a collection of sketches detailing Broyard's life in Greenwich Village in the years following World War II. Much of the material focuses on the two major preoccupations of Broyard's life—writing and women. A great portion is devoted to Broyard's tempestuous relationship with the avant-garde painter Sheri Donatti, a disciple of Anaïs Nin. Among the sketches is a touching piece about Broyard's close friend and fellow book reviewer Saul Silverman, who died of leukemia.

In the *Chicago Tribune* (November 14, 1993), Robert Olen Butler described *Kafka Was the Rage* as "a remarkable and deeply personal book." He praised the way in which Broyard captured the spirit of Greenwich Village in the late 1940s and the sensuality of his experiences: "The book is full of Anatole Broyard's remarkable spirit and sensibilities and power of the word."

Kafka Was the Rage reminded Joyce Johnson of Ernest Hemingway's unfinished memoir about Paris, *A Movable Feast*. In her *Washington Post* (December 26, 1993) review, she remarked that each book is the product of an elderly man reflecting on his bygone bohemian youth. Johnson questioned Broyard's treatment of Sheri Donatti, who she felt was never sufficiently fleshed out as a character, and also criticized what she felt were Broyard's antifeminist sentiments, despite her admission that the book "also made me feel deeply nostalgic when I wasn't wincing." Broyard, she wrote, re-created a "Golden Age" of Greenwich Village with what she described as "historical poignancy."

Morris Dickstein of the *New York Times* (October 31, 1993) saw a bizarre dichotomy in Broyard's memoir: as he put it, "an odd mix of nostalgia and disdain." Dickstein maintained that Broyard's superior attitude distanced him from his memories and made his characters seem somehow alien. Because of Broyard's frustrated literary ambitions, Dickstein felt, the author infused *Kafka Was the Rage* with a great deal of bitterness, often expressed as misogynistic and anti-intellectual attitudes. The juxtaposition of affection and derision, Dickstein admitted, does at times yield humorous passages, and the prose, according to Dickstein, possessed a "chiseled brilliance."

In an obituary in the *National Review* (November 5, 1990), Ernest van den Haag wrote that Broyard "commanded language and it obeyed him." Gates described Broyard's columns as "suffused with both worldliness and high culture. Wry, mandarin, even self-amused at times, he wrote like a man about town, but one who just happened to have all of Western literature at his fingertips." However, Broyard's writing was sometimes deemed offensive by critics and readers. Among other things, he was accused of anti-Semitism and a low regard for women.

Another sticky area of Broyard's life and work was his racial identity: he was an African-American who successfully "passed" for white throughout most of his professional life. Both Paul and Edna Broyard were light-skinned blacks, and Anatole's complexion was even lighter. Paul Broyard made the professional decison to "pass" when he learned he would have trouble getting into the carpenter's union in Brooklyn as a black man. Anatole Broyard kept his race secret, even from his own children; only a select few knew the truth while he was alive. He even served in the army as a white man.

Broyard's main motivation for hiding his race was that he did not wish to be pigeonholed as a "Negro writer," which he feared would limit his audience. He wanted his writing to be judged on the basis of his talent rather than his race, and he sought to deal with universal concepts rather than specifically "black" issues. Nevertheless, some who knew of Broyard's true racial identity resented him: Gates recounted an incident in which Broyard was spotted in New York's Washington Square Park by the jazz legend Charlie Parker, who remarked to a companion, "He's one of us, but he doesn't want to admit he's one of us." It was not until Broyard was literally on his deathbed that Todd and Bliss learned—from their mother—of their father's racial heritage.—B.S.

SUGGESTED READING: *Chicago Tribune* p5+ Nov. 14, 1993, with photo; *Commonweal* p22+ Jan. 15, 1993; *Journal of the American Medical Association* p402 Feb. 2, 1994; *National Review* p24 Nov. 5, 1990; *New Leader* p2 Dec. 27, 1993; *New York Times* VII p15 Nov. 25, 1990, with photo, VII p7 May 10, 1992, VII p12 Oct. 31, 1993; *New Yorker* p66+ June 17, 1996, with drawing; *Time* p57 Oct. 22, 1990, with photo; *Washington Post* X p2 Dec. 26, 1993

SELECTED WORKS: *Aroused by Books*, 1974; *Men, Women, and Other Anticlimaxes*, 1980; *Intoxicated by My Illness: And Other Writings on Life and Death*, 1992; *Kafka Was the Rage*, 1993

Jerry Bauer/Courtesy of Farrar, Straus and Giroux

Buchan, James

1954– Nonfiction writer; novelist

One of Great Britain's most respected and versatile writers, James Buchan has garnered the praise of critics for both his fiction and nonfiction works. He is the author of *A Parish of Rich Women* (1984), his first novel, as well as the 1995 spy epic *Heart's Journey in Winter*. More recently, he published *Frozen Desire: The Meaning of Money* (1997), an analytical study that gained him a great deal of international attention. His most significant work aside from his books was the 10 years he spent as a foreign correspondent for the *Financial Times*.

James Buchan was born in 1954 in the United Kingdom. He is the grandson of Scottish novelist John Buchan. James Buchan's schooling included the study of Persian and Arabic. He worked for 10 years as a correspondent for the *Financial Times*, stationed for the majority of his time in Bonn, Germany.

In 1984 James Buchan published *A Parish of Rich Women*. The plot deals in part with young people in the Chelsea section of London who are slowly succumbing to the perils of heroin addiction. Buchan gives his protagonist, Adam, an impressive knowledge of Middle Eastern politics, which Buchan himself possesses due to time he spent there during his correspondent years. In the course of the novel, Adam finds himself in Beirut, whose war-ravaged citizens are compared by Buchan to the heroin addicts in Chelsea's upper-class. The book won the UK's Whitbread Award for Best First Novel.

Buchan's second novel, *Davey Chadwick*, was published in 1987. The story revolves around a man who leaves his London home to live with his wife in an Italian house that has fallen into decay. To pay for the upkeep of her home, he must engage in a number of shady business dealings. Four years after *Davey Chadwick*, Buchan followed up with his third novel, *Slide*. The central character, Richard Verey, spends great amounts of time traveling throughout the world in a vain attempt to run away from who he is. Some of the stops along the way include stints in the foreign service and on Wall Street.

Drawing on his experience in Germany, Buchan next wrote *Heart's Journey in Winter* (1995). It is set in Bonn in 1983, with the Cold War still in full swing. Two of the book's main characters are British spy Richard Fisher and American spy Polina Mertz. They find themselves caught up in a complex plot involving a critical arms control agreement code-named "the Golden Plough." Several important figures of the period, such as then-Prime Minister Margaret Thatcher, are characters in the novel.

Booklist (July 19, 1995) reviewer Alice Joyce described the work as a "provocative thriller" and "an uncompromisingly literate spy novel." Joyce also praised Buchan's strong development of several of the key characters and commented that "Buchan's riveting tale should prove . . . mesmerizing to fans of the [spy] genre." *Heart's Journey in Winter* was given the *Manchester Guardian* Fiction Award for 1995. Shortly after its original publication, the book was re-released under title *The Golden Plough*.

Instead of waiting several years between books, as he had done in the past, Buchan published his fifth novel, *High Latitudes*, just one year after *Heart's Journey in Winter*. The book tells the story of a doomed romance involving one Jane Haddon, the wealthy managing director of a lucrative textile company. Buchan gives her history through a series of interspersed flashback sequences. The novel contains numerous references to the history of money, a subject that first attracted the author's interest during his years with the *Financial Times*. "To be sure," read a critique of the novel in *Kirkus Reviews* (October 1, 1996), "the sordid details of late-'80s convulsive capitalism are used here to form a precise, withering critique of Thatcher's England." However, the review also mentioned that the novel did not have enough of a human element and that it often seemed cold.

The fascination with the history of money Buchan picked up during his years with the *Financial Times* and hinted at in *High Latitudes* became the topic of the author's next book, a nonfiction work entitled *Frozen Desire: The Meaning of Money* (1997). From the earliest days of barter to the present world of computerized banking, Buchan traces the history of the human race's all-encompassing invention. The overall conclusion he comes to is that money has had a negative effect on humanity and can be blamed for many of its ills. He deplores the acquisition of money as an end in itself.

Buchan's incisive knowledge of his subject was praised by such reviewers as Frank Kermode of the *London Review of Books* (September 18, 1997), who also pointed out the author's ability to communicate his knowledge of an often difficult topic to the reader. In another analysis of *Frozen Desire*, the *Kirkus Reviews* (August 15, 1997) disagreed with Kermode, stating that "these often murky essays will add precious little to anyone's understanding of what makes the world go around." *Frozen Desires* was, according to the *New Statesman* (December 5, 1997), the most widely reviewed economics book of 1997. In its own review, the magazine described the book as "an original and elegant work." Buchan's novel *A Good Place to Die* was published in the U.K. in 1999.

"I don't believe this country [the UK] has a better writer to offer than James Buchan," opined critic Michael Hofmann in the *London Review of Books* (April 20, 1995). "I see no particular limitation to his scope or style: his stunningly curt dialogues and ravishing recitatives are equally persuasive." Hofmann strongly praised Buchan through the course of his commentary, noting his strengths as a writer in understanding "the factual world," as well as his engaging eloquence: "compared to his, how unthinking, unsupple, and uninteresting most prose is." An Amazon.com profile of James Buchan agreed with much of Hofmann's assessment, asking, "Is there another writer in the English-speaking world more distinctive and adventurous than [James] Buchan?"—B.S.

SUGGESTED READING: Amazon.com; *Booklist* July 19, 1995; *Kirkus Reviews* Oct. 1, 1996, Aug. 15, 1997; *London Review of Books* p3+ Apr. 20, 1995; p3+ Sep. 18, 1997; *New Statesman* p50 Dec. 5, 1997

SELECTED BOOKS: Fiction—*A Parish of Rich Women*, 1984; *Davey Chadwick*, 1987; *Slide*, 1991; *Heart's Journey in Winter*, 1995; *High Latitudes*, 1996; *A Good Place to Die*, 1999; Nonfiction—*Frozen Desire: The Meaning of Money,* 1997

Barrie Barnett/Courtesy of Random House

Buckley, Christopher

1952– Novelist; humorist; editor

Christopher Buckley is best known for his ability to pen wickedly funny satire. The Washington, D.C.–based author has written novels and satirical essays and is a regular contributor to the *New Yorker*, among other magazines. "Chris's humor is based on observation and appreciation of the absurd," John Tierney, the *New York Times Magazine* columnist, has said.

Buckley began his career as a novelist with *Steaming to Bamboola: The World of a Tramp Freighter* (1982), which was based on his experiences as a deckhand aboard a Norwegian ship. A stint in the early 1980s as a speechwriter for then–vice president George Bush produced the fodder for Buckley's second novel, *The White House Mess* (1986), a best-seller, which was acclaimed for its uproarious humor. Buckley has also authored the satirical thriller *Wet Work* (1991), and *Wry Martinis* (1997), a collection of his essays. Buckley's third novel, *Thank You for Smoking* (1994), which features a politically incorrect tobacco-industry spokesman as the protagonist, takes aim at the hypocritical workings in the nation's capital. In 1998 he published a satire, co-written with John Tierney, entitled *God Is My Broker: A Monk-Tycoon Reveals the 7½ Laws of Spiritual and Financial Growth* (1998). His most recent novel is *Little Green Men* (1999). In addition to writing, Buckley has served since 1990 as the editor of *Forbes FYI*, which is often spiced with his deadpan wit.

Born in New York City in 1952, Christopher Taylor Buckley grew up in Stamford, Connecticut, "the only child of parents who were very busy becoming famous," as he once put it. His father, William F. Buckley Jr., is the founder of the conservative magazine *National Review* and the host of the weekly television show *Firing Line* as well as a syndicated columnist and a prolific novelist. His mother, Patricia (Taylor) Buckley, is a prominent New York socialite. While growing up, Buckley rarely ate dinner with his parents on weekdays; he spent time with them on weekends. "We had what people today call 'quality time,'" he remarked to Leslie Kaufman, who profiled him for the *Washington Post* (June 10, 1994). His first memories of his father are of seeing him work on an old Royal typewriter. "I'd sit on his lap and watch," he told Marie Arana-Ward for the *Washington Post* (July 14, 1996). "I was sitting there one night, when he put aside his work and taught me how to touch type. I was only six, but I took to it immediately and performed for him from time to time."

After attending several Catholic elementary schools, the 13-year-old Buckley was sent to high school at Portsmouth Abbey, an elite New England boarding school run by Benedictine monks. He has described the instruction there as first-rate, but has said that he felt isolated from modern society. With mock bitterness Buckley told Leslie Kaufman, "From 66 to 1970—Woodstock, the 68 convention, the assassinations, the Summer of Love, Haight-Ashbury, the Beatles, the Rolling Stones, all the concentrated gorgeousness that the 20th century was heaving up—I was in study halls with monks." Buckley did, however, go through a rebellious phase in his late teens, during which he grew his hair long and experimented with drugs.

After completing high school Buckley longed for an adventure before starting college. "I had grown up on yachts, but I didn't *want* yachts," he recalled to John Lombardi during a conversation for the New York *Daily News* (May 11, 1986). "I wanted to ship out." With the help of his father, in 1970 he secured a job as a deckhand on a Norwegian freighter that traveled around the world. After spending six months at sea performing menial labor, Buckley came home with two tattoos, one of which he subsequently had surgically removed because it featured an expletive. In 1971 he enrolled at Yale University, in New Haven, Connecticut, from which he graduated cum laude, with a B.A. degree in English. Soon after leaving college, he was hired by Clay Felker, the editor of *Esquire*, to fill an entry-level editorial job. By the age of 25, he had worked his way up to the position of managing editor.

In 1979 Buckley decided to get out from behind his desk and become a deckhand aboard a tramp freighter once again. During the 78-day voyage he took across the Atlantic Ocean and back, he kept notes for what would become his first book, *Steaming to Bamboola* (the name comes from a Chinese steward's mispronunciation of Bermuda). Because Buckley was often seen writing, a few members of the crew suspected that he was either an undercover police officer or a spy. "There was a guy who threatened to throw me over the side," Buckley was quoted in *Contemporary Authors* (1993) as saying. The novel was enthusiastically received by reviewers, among them P. L. Adams of the *Atlantic Monthly* (May 1982), who wrote, "Most people go to sea because they have nowhere else to go, a revelation that gives an undertone of melancholy to Mr.

Buckley's sympathetic account of his shipmates on a tramp steamer. Character sketches, marine reminiscences, and events of the voyage are neatly mingled. The ship did indeed carry her fair share of drunks, drug addicts, feuding officers, and plain maniacs, without whom life aboard would have been safer for the author but far less entertaining for the reader."

After returning to New York in 1980, Buckley resumed working at *Esquire*. Shortly thereafter he was offered a position as a speechwriter for George Bush, who had recently been elected vice president. Though Buckley had never written speeches before, he accepted the position. "I was his only speechwriter, so I got to know him," he told Marie Arana-Ward. "The man has impeccable instincts, great 'gentillesse.'" Despite his respect for Bush, Buckley resigned after only 18 months. "I found out to my chagrin that all my hard work on speeches didn't matter because nobody cares what a vice president says," he remarked to John Blades, during an interview for the *Chicago Tribune* (June 27, 1994). "But it was a great adventure—the motorcades, the flashing lights, the flying around on Air Force 2."

Upon taking the job Buckley had promised Bush that he would not write an account of his experiences. "I'd read about 10 or 12 White House memoirs, and I was somewhat appalled . . . ," he told Edwin McDowell for the *New York Times* (April 16, 1986). "Then one day, bingo, one of those light bulbs just went off. I said, 'Let's write a fake memoir.'" The result, which took Buckley three years to write, is *The White House Mess*, a satire about Washington politics. John Tierney observed, "Washington is a perfect town for someone with [Buckley's] eye. Washington is the perfect setup line, a great straight man, because it takes itself so seriously." The book's narrator, Herbert Wadlough, is an unassuming accountant who has been vaulted into an important White House position because his friend Thomas Nelson Tucker was elected to succeed Ronald Reagan as president. As the story begins, on January 20, 1989, the president-elect and Mrs. Tucker are waiting for Reagan to join them in their limousine to proceed to inaugural ceremonies on Capitol Hill. Reagan refuses to budge, however, saying that he has a sore back and, besides, the weather is too cold. When Tucker asks him when he might be ready to move, Reagan replies, "Spring." After an elaborate ruse is orchestrated to get Reagan out of the White House, the novel then goes on to "deface the Tucker presidency," Christopher Lehmann-Haupt wrote in the *New York Times* (March 10, 1986), "and make it the worst (and funniest) in American history."

Lehmann-Haupt was only one of many reviewers to laud Buckley's book; another, David Brooks of *Insight* (March 31, 1986), declared the work to be "the rarest of creatures, a truly irreverent piece of political humor. It renews hope that political humor is not extinct." In mid-April 1986 the book appeared at number 14 on the *New York Times*'s fiction best-seller list; the number 10 selection at the same time was *High Jinx*, by William F. Buckley Jr. The elder Buckley told Edwin McDowell that he "couldn't be more pleased" by his son's literary success and would never have predicted it, considering the young man's seeming aversion to reading books as a boy.

In addition to his work as a novelist, Buckley had pursued a career as a freelance magazine writer. In 1986 he was given an assignment by *Condé Nast Traveler* to take a trip on the yacht of Malcolm Forbes, the wealthy publisher. Buckley soon learned that Forbes and the business tycoon John Kluge were planning a trip to Peru and Brazil, and he was invited to join them. "I was casting around for a book idea," Buckley recalled to Andrew L. Yarrow for the *New York Times Book Review* (February 24, 1991), "and thought, 'There's one—a comedy of manners about two billionaires going up the Amazon to the heart of darkness.'" The novel he ended up crafting, *Wet Work*, is a satirical thriller about Charley Becker, a wealthy American businessman who seeks to avenge the death of his granddaughter from a cocaine overdose by hunting the Peruvian drug lord he feels is responsible—and methodically killing a host of street pushers, middlemen, and importers along the way. Working on the novel, Buckley told Yarrow, was "the worst writing experience of my life." "The words flowed like glue," he added. "I rewrote it five times. I don't know why it was so hard—maybe because I don't read thrillers."

In his assessment of the bloody—but funny—novel for the *New York Times Book Review* (February 24, 1991), Robert Stuart Nathan wrote, "The real joy of *Wet Work* lies in the abandon with which Mr. Buckley scatters his epigrammatic wit, letting hardly a paragraph pass without hilarious decoration. . . . If the novel fails on any level, it is the absence of moral weight at the story's heart. Despite the passion of Charley Becker's mission, one nearly forgets the cause of his righteousness. . . . In the end, however, *Wet Work* survives its central conceit and triumphs with the sheer bounty of its laughter." Unlike Buckley's previous novel, *Wet Work* did not sell well, and for a time his financial situation was insecure. Fortunately, he was able to land a well-paying job in 1990 as the editor of *Forbes FYI*, a quarterly lifestyle supplement to *Forbes* magazine.

Buckley brought his penchant for humor to *FYI*, and in the fall of 1991, he crafted a story, as a hoax, about the financially strapped Soviet Union's plan to auction off the embalmed corpse of its communist founder, V. I. Lenin, as a way to raise money. "A $15 million floor was set," Buckley wrote, "as well as conditions (to be enforced by the International Court of Justice at the Hague), that the corpse not be used for any 'commercial or improper' purpose. (Estimated annual upkeep: $10,000-$15,000, varies with climate)." With the approval of Steve Forbes, the magazine's editor-in-chief, Buckley faxed copies of the article to about 70 news organi-

zations, including ABC News. On November 5, 1991, Peter Jennings reported the story on *World News Tonight*, naming as its source a "*Forbes* business publication." *USA Today* published the item in the following day's edition, citing the ABC story. The Soviet government was not amused; Internal Affairs Minister Victor Barannikov called the report a "brazen lie" and a "serious provocation." Buckley, delighted by the fuss he had caused, immediately owned up to his authorship. "Some days it is good to be alive," he remarked to Charles Trueheart of the *Washington Post* (November 7, 1991). "This is one of them." Jennings, though angry, eventually took the joke with reasonably good humor. "Given the chaos in the Soviet Union, even this was believable," he told Trueheart. "But we were had." The anchorman said that he and the ABC editors had trusted that the account was credible because *Forbes* was "widely regarded in America, until now, as a responsible news organization."

Continuing his work as a novelist, Buckley penned *Thank You for Smoking*, a satire on the tobacco industry. The timing of the book's publication, in the spring of 1994, seemed fortuitous because at that time, the House of Representatives was holding hearings on the health risks of smoking. During those proceedings, several tobacco-company executives testified that there was no proof of a link between cigarette smoking and certain diseases, only to find themselves accused, by Congress and by the media, of brazenly lying. "I watched [the hearings] with a sinking feeling," Buckley remarked to Alex Witchel, during a conversation for the *New York Times* (June 30, 1994). "All these executives holding up their hands saying, 'We don't think cigarettes are addictive.' I got depressed. It was so much better than satire, how could I compete?"

The protagonist in *Thank You for Smoking*, Nick Naylor, is very good at his job of defending tobacco interests. In one particularly amusing chapter, Naylor is confronted during an appearance on *Nightline* by a senator from Vermont, who plans to introduce legislation in Congress requiring that skull-and-crossbones labels be placed on cigarette packages. Naylor counters with a suggestion that the same labels be slapped onto "those deadly chunks of solid, low-density lipoprotein that go by the name of Vermont cheddar cheese." In his admiring assessment of the book for the *New York Times* (June 23, 1994), Christopher Lehmann-Haupt noted, "Superficially, *Thank You for Smoking* may seem even handed by ridiculing both the tobacco industry and the so-called neo-Puritans and fascists who want smoking banned. But to read the two positions as balanced is to accept the tobacco lobby's outlook. . . . The true target of Mr. Buckley's Swiftian barbs is the attitude that perfect liberty constitutes the right to make a profit no matter who pays for it, even at the cost of life itself." Other reviewers expressed enthusiasm for *Thank You for Smoking*, among them R. Z. Sheppard of

Time (July 18, 1994), who wrote, "The superior goofball plot, raffish cast, and zany sex scenes (a critical test for a humorist) make this the funniest of Buckley's books. The style alternates between *Saturday Night Live* and Raymond Chandler." The actor and director Mel Gibson has purchased the film rights to the book.

Buckley collaborated with Tierney to produce the novel *God Is My Broker: A Monk-Tycoon Reveals the 7½ Laws of Spiritual and Financial Growth* (1998). The simple plot, in which a failed Wall Street trader escapes to a financially troubled monastery where the monks make undrinkable and unsalable wine, is a satire of self-help gurus and their best-selling books. The trader (whom the monks dub Brother Ty, short for "Tycoon") is soon culling investment tips from the scriptures, but in matters of finance the abbot prefers the advice of Deepak Chopra to that of God. Eventually certain monks become followers of popular authors such as Stephen R. Covey and Anthony Robbins, which causes the monks to divide into warring factions. Deborah Stead, writing in the *New York Times* (May 3, 1998), called the novel a "hilarious book—sly, smart and deeply satisfying." In the *New York Times Book Review* (March 29, 1998), Dwight Garner observed that "Buckley and Tierney deserved credit for good timing as well as for their generally tart prose." Garner was referring to the spate of get-rich-quick advice and spiritual self-help books that were published around the same time as *God Is My Broker*. In 1999 Buckley published *Little Green Men*, a comic novel about a Washington, D.C.–based talk-show host who is abducted by aliens.

Christopher Buckley lives in Washington, D.C., with his wife, the former Lucy Gregg, and their children, Caitlin and Conor. A smoker since his early teens, Buckley quit the habit on September 14, 1988, after having spent the previous 72 hours with a friend who was dying of lung cancer. A regular contributor to the *New Yorker*, Buckley has also published his work in the *New York Times*, the *Washington Post*, *USA Today*, *Architectural Digest*, *National Review*, *Vogue*, *Vanity Fair*, and the *Washington Monthly*. His essays typically offer amusing observations on American life and culture; a collection of them, *Wry Martinis* (1997), generated admiring reviews. "His pieces on women and fashion, in particular, have a winningly un-PC, only partially reconstructed male chauvinist pig quality. And his political satires . . . suggest that Buckley not only knows where the bodies are buried, but that he can wisely autopsy them," Sara Nelson wrote in *The Book Report*.

During his conversation with Kaufman, Buckley said he had never been pressured by his father, whom he closely resembles, to continue the family tradition of conservative commentary: "I think he knew I would be an incompetent editor of *National Review*. Maybe in his heart of hearts nothing would have pleased him more than to hand down the reins. But he graciously never said so. My goal is more modest, to make the world laugh at its conceits. And, so far, it's working."

—S. Y.

SUGGESTED READING: *The Book Report*, (on-line); *New York Daily News Magazine* p14+ May 11, 1986; *New York Times* C p19 Apr. 16, 1986, C p1+ June 30, 1994; *New York Times Book Review* p20 Mar. 29, 1998, III p13 May 3, 1998; *People* p121+ May 17, 1982; *Publishers Weekly* p38+ Jan. 25, 1991; *Contemporary Authors* vol. 139, 1993

SELECTED BOOKS: *Steaming to Bamboola: The World of a Tramp Freighter*, 1982; *The White House Mess*, 1986; *Wet Work*, 1991; *Thank You for Smoking*, 1994; *Wry Martinis*, 1997; *Little Green Men*, 1999; with J. Tierney—*God Is My Broker: A Monk-Tycoon Reveals the 7½ Laws of Spiritual and Financial Growth*, 1998; *Little Green Men*, 1999

Miriam Berkley

Bujold, Lois McMaster

Nov. 2, 1949– Science fiction writer

Lois McMaster Bujold is one of the most critically acclaimed and commercially successful science fiction authors of recent years. She is most known for her series of books, set one thousand years in the future, chronicling the adventures of Miles Vorkosigan, a soldier with a physical handicap. The series has included such books as *The Warrior's Apprentice* (1986), *The Vor Game* (1990), *Mirror Dance* (1994), and *Komarr* (1998). Her books have earned her multiple Hugo and Nebula Awards, and she is the only author other than Robert A. Heinlein to win three Hugos for best novel.

The author was born Lois Joy McMaster on November 2, 1949, in Columbus, Ohio. Her mother, Laura Elizabeth (Gerould) McMaster, was a homemaker, and her father, Robert Charles McMaster was a professor of engineering. Her interest in science fiction dates back to her childhood, when her father introduced her to the sci-fi pulp magazines of which he was an avid reader. She made her first writing attempts in junior high school, composing fragmented pieces in which she would try to imitate the prose styles of her favorite authors.

Lois McMaster attended Upper Arlington High School, obtaining her diploma in 1967. In 1968, she enrolled in Ohio State University. She was initially interested in majoring in English but gave it up: "My heart was in the creative, not the critical end of things," she commented in an autobiographical press release. Instead of English, she developed a fascination with wildlife and photography; combining the two, she engaged in a six-week biology study tour of East Africa. The landscape she observed would later inspire the background for her first novel, *Shards of Honor* (1986).

On October 9, 1971, while still attending Ohio State, she married John Frederic Bujold. She then dropped out and began working the same year at the Ohio State University Hospital as a pharmacy technician. With the exception of a short Sherlock Holmes vignette, Bujold wrote nothing during this period. She did, however, read a great deal, as she had access to Ohio State's vast library. She continued to work at Ohio State for six years, but when her daughter, Anne Elizabeth, was born in 1979, she stopped working professionally to become a homemaker, a role she has continued to fill throughout her career as a published author. The Bujolds moved to Marion, Ohio, in 1980; their second child, Paul Andre, was born the following year.

By 1982 she had begun to seriously take up writing at home in her spare time, after a friend, Lillian Stewart Carl, started selling some of her own writing. "It occurred to me that if she could do it, I could do it too," Bujold said in her autobiography. She first tried her hand at writing a novella, then a full-scale novel, receiving encouragement from Carl as well as from fantasy writer Patricia C. Wrede, with whom she was also acquainted. "I quickly discovered that writing was far too demanding and draining to justify as a hobby and that only serious professional recognition would satisfy me," she wrote.

Between 1983 and 1985, Bujold wrote three novels, *Shards of Honor*, *The Warrior's Apprentice*, and *Ethan of Athos*, but she still had no publisher. Her first success actually came with a short story entitled "Barter." At the end of 1984, the piece was accepted for publication by *Twilight Zone* magazine (this story would eventually be adapted as an episode of the horror/fantasy television series *Tales from the Darkside* in 1986.) One year later, all three of Bujold's unpublished novels were bought by New York publishing house Baen Books.

Bujold's first novel, the sci-fi romance *Shards of Honor*, was published in June 1986. The novel's plot takes place approximately one thousand years in the future, when the civilization of Earth has spread out across the stars. Its two main characters are Cordelia Naismith and Aral Vorkosigan, a scientist and military commander, respectively. Although they are on opposite sides of a violent conflict, unexpected circumstances force the two to work together in order to survive, and they eventually fall in love. "It's a bit of a Romeo and Juliet in space tale, if those two protagonists had been middle-aged, sensible, and responsible," Bujold suggested in an interview conducted by the Internet Book Information Center (IBIC). "I recommend it . . . if you are not allergic to a love story in your SF."

Ethan of Athos appeared just two months after *Shards of Honor*. The protagonist is Dr. Ethan Urquhart, an obstetrician on an all-male planet on which the population is continued using a preserved stock of ovarian cultures. When this stock runs out, Ethan is forced to leave his sheltered world in search of new samples.

With her third published novel, *The Warrior's Apprentice* (released by Baen in December 1986), Bujold returned to the characters she introduced in *Shards of Honor*. This is the first of the long line of books recounting the adventures of Bujold's most enduring character, Miles Vorkosigan, who is the son of Cordelia and Aral. Deformed at birth, Miles is unable to continue his father's legacy by joining the military academy, and *The Warrior's Apprentice* details his struggle to overcame his handicap and find his own way in life. In her IBIC interview, Bujold described the novel as "the keystone book" in her Miles Vorkosigan series. The novel has been optioned by Warner Brothers for a possible motion picture adaptation.

In 1987 the science fiction digest magazine *Analog* (which had been her father's favorite) began publishing Bujold's fourth novel, *Falling Free*, in serialized form. The serial continued into early 1988, and that same year Baen Books released the novel in a single volume. Although it takes place in the same fictional universe as Bujold's previous novels, the events of *Falling Free* occur before the time of Miles Vorkosigan. The story concerns a race of legless, four-handed people genetically created by a corporation to work easily in a low-gravity environment. Human engineer Leo Graf engages in an effort to free this race from being exploited by the company that made them. Bujold intended the novel to be an homage to magazines such as *Analog*, which had nurtured her love for science fiction during childhood. The character Leo Graf was inspired by her late engineer father.

A significant critical as well as commercial success, *Falling Free* gained the attention of the Science Fiction Writers of America (SFWA), the organization that yearly bestows the prestigious Nebula Awards, one of science fiction literature's two main accolades. In 1988 *Falling Free* earned Bujold the Nebula for best novel.

For her next novel, Bujold returned to Miles Vorkosigan, the character introduced in *The Warrior's Apprentice*. The result was *Brothers in Arms* (1989), the success of which proved that the character was popular enough to sustain a full-fledged series. The tale is set entirely in London, making it unusual among science fiction novels. "It's very much a tale of what happens in between the sorts of missions that are more usual space-opera fodder," the author said to the IBIC.

Bujold's work once again appeared in *Analog* in 1989 with the publication of the novella "The Mountains of Mourning," a sci-fi murder mystery. The piece garnered both the Nebula as well as science fiction's other major award, the Hugo, both in the category of best novella. Another of Bujold's stories published in *Analog* that year, "Labyrinth," won the readers' poll conducted by the science fiction magazine.

Bujold's final project of 1989 was *Borders of Infinity*, her first short story anthology. It contained both "Mountains of Mourning" and "Labyrinth," as well as a new title story and a framing narrative. All three stories featured Miles Vorkosigan, the character who had been gaining in popularity after appearing in two previous Bujold novels. In the title story, Miles finds himself in a P.O.W. camp, where he has been sent on a rescue mission.

The now-popular Miles Vorkosigan saga was continued in 1990 with *The Vor Game*. Several plot strings in this novel were continuations of elements begun in *The Warrior's Apprentice*, such as the reappearance of the Dendarii Mercenaries, a fighting force previously created by Miles. The opening section was published in *Analog* under the title "The Weatherman," and won the magazine's readers' poll for best novella of 1990. For the novel itself, Bujold gained a Hugo Award.

Throughout the summer and fall of 1991, *Analog* serialized the second of Bujold's novels to appear in their pages, *Barrayar*. Baen published it in book form later in the year, resulting in Bujold winning a second consecutive best novel Hugo. Taking place before the Vorkosigan chronicles, Barrayar is actually a direct sequel to *Shards of Honor*, Bujold's first novel. This journey into the past of her created universe allowed Bujold to further explore the relationship between Cordelia and Aral, the parents of Miles Vorkosigan. "It's really a book about the price of becoming a parent," the author said in her IBIC interview, "and a deeper commentary on the romance in the previous book, being about how hopes are betrayed by realities, but also about how such betrayals are survived."

Bujold made a temporary departure from the Vorkosigan series in 1992, when she published *The Spirit Ring*, which remains as of this writing her only historical fantasy novel. The novel's plot, set in a magical pseudo-Renaissance, was actually adapted from the folk tale "The Grateful Dead," which the author discovered as the subject of her great-uncle's Ph.D. thesis. It did not succeed commercially to the degree that many of her science

fiction novels have. "I'd call *The Spirit Ring* artistically successful," the author stated in her IBIC interview, "in that I met some of the challenges I set for myself . . . in writing my first quasi-historical novel." In addressing the commercial shortcomings of the book, Bujold suggested, "I need to do several more fantasy novels to build up that audience. I'd like to do more fantasy, as time permits, though not necessarily sequels to that book."

The author returned to the adventures of Miles Vorkosigan in 1994 with *Mirror Dance*. The book was intended as a direct sequel to *Brothers in Arms* and features Mark, Miles's clone brother who was introduced in that earlier novel. The novel opens with the murder of Miles Vorkosigan, whose body is stored in a cryogenic chamber that is then promptly lost. The Dendarii Mercenaries as well as the government of Miles's home planet of Barrayar must then locate the body so that Miles can be brought back to life. "It's a book about identity," commented Bujold to the IBIC, "how you get it, how you lose it, how you win it back." The book earned Bujold her third Hugo Award, a feat equaled only by science fiction luminary Robert A. Heinlein.

Analog printed Bujold's Vorkosigan novel *Cetaganda* in chapter form in late 1995, with the official hardcover release taking place in June of 1996. The story features Miles and his cousin Ivan attending the funeral of the empress of an enemy government on the planet after which the novel is named.

The author took another break from her familiar imaginary universe when she signed on as an editor for the anthology *Women at War* (1995). The collection, which she co-edited with Roland Green, consists of science fiction tales featuring women in military roles.

Bujold produced her second anthology in 1996. Originally printed as a science fiction convention souvenir, *The Dreamweaver's Dilemma* was soon published commercially. It contains many early stories and essays that had never before been in print. "The title story," Bujold explained to the IBIC, "was my first serious effort at a professional tale and was the seed from which Miles's more elaborate universe later grew." In addition to its previously unpublished material, *The Dreamweaver's Dilemma* contained "The Mountains of Mourning," the Hugo and Nebula Award–winning novella of seven years prior.

Memory (1996) marked Bujold's sixth Vorkosigan novel. In Bujold's interview with the Internet Book Information Center, she described *Memory* as "a culmination of the Miles series toward which I had been obliquely working since the beginning."

Bujold's most recent foray into the universe of Miles Vorkosigan was the novel *Komarr*, published in 1998. The novel takes its name from the planet on which it takes place, where Miles is assigned on his first mission as Imperial Auditor. This mission involves investigating an "accident" that has curtailed the important terraforming project that can transform Komarr into a completely habitable world. *A Civil Campaign*, the eighth novel in the Miles Vorkosigan series, was published in September 1999.

Due to her successful and ongoing series, Bujold has become mostly associated with the character Miles Vorkosigan. Among science fiction fans, she is known for her sharp wit and the believable manner in which she portrays military life (some of her books have, in fact, been included on the reading lists of military ethics courses). Many have assumed that the author must have some military experience, yet in fact the closest she ever came to the military was the stories told to her by her Vietnam-veteran husband, John. "I start with the assumption that soldiering is a job, and a person is always larger than a job," she stated in *Writer's Digest* (July 1994). "I think myself into their situation." She has also expressed an interest in history, which she believes has influenced her writing.

Although her books are often marketed under the genre of "military sci-fi," in her interview with the Internet Book Information Center, Bujold described her work as "character-centered action-adventure." In tying together science fiction and character-oriented elements, Bujold employs what she has described as her "diskworld theory" (*Writer's Digest*, July 1994). This theory involves finding a common ground between universal themes, such as love, and more bizarre, esoteric concerns of the kind often found in sci-fi tales.

Bujold is a member of the professional organizations Science Fiction Writers of America and Novelists Inc. She instructed at summer writing workshops at her alma mater of Ohio State University from 1990 to 1992. In addition to *Twilight Zone* and *Analog*, she has also published fiction in such periodicals as *American Fantasy*, *Far Frontiers*, and *New Destinies*, as well as nonfiction pieces in such publications as *The Bulletin of the SFWA*, and *Ohio Writer* Magazine.

Lois McMaster Bujold and John Frederic Bujold are now divorced. The author has resided in Minneapolis, Minnesota, since 1995. —B.S.

SUGGESTED READING: "An IBIC Interview with Lois McMaster Bujold," *IBIC.Journal* (Jan. 20, 1999, on-line); *Writer's Digest* p6+ July 1994

SELECTED WORKS: *Shards of Honor*, 1986; *Ethan of Athos*, 1986; *The Warrior's Apprentice*, 1986; *Falling Free*, 1988; *Brothers in Arms*, 1989; *Borders of Infinity*, 1989; *The Vor Game*, 1990; *Barrayar*, 1991; *The Spirit Ring*, 1992; *Mirror Dance*, 1994; *Cetaganda*, 1996; *The Dreamweaver's Dilemma*, 1996; *Memory*, 1996; *Komarr*, 1998; As editor, with Roland J. Green, *Women at War*, 1995

Bukiet, Melvin Jules

1953– Novelist; short-story writer

The American short-story writer and novelist Melvin Jules Bukiet has, to some extent, stepped into the shoes left by Bernard Malamud in chronicling Jewish life. Unlike Malamud, Bukiet is concerned not with the capacity of Jews to endure, even to embrace, suffering, but with the specifics of the 20th-century Jewish experience in Europe—specifically, the Holocaust. Bukiet, a "crackpot realist" by his own definition, has written about the unimaginably tragic and gruesome in comic terms. Reviewing *While the Messiah Tarries* (1995), a collection of short stories, in *Library Journal* (April 1, 1995), Molly Abramowitz compared Bukiet's insights into human character to those of Isaac Bashevis Singer and noted that Bukiet "adds freshness and depth to Jewish storytelling." Bukiet's 1996 novel *After* drew the remark from *Publishers Weekly* (July 8, 1996) that "Bukiet's mordant humor and insight into human character are matched by his audacity and hyperbolic imagination" in an "incandescent mix." Bukiet's novel *Signs and Wonders*, about a latter-day Messiah, was published to acclaim in 1999.

For *World Authors 1990–1995*, Melvin Jules Bukiet writes: "I never talk about my work and my life doesn't interest me.

"Where does that leave a presumptive 800-word autobiographer? In this case, the answer may be a meandering amalgam of a few stories and a lot of half-baked literary and theological theory. But if a life is what an individual makes of it, and thoughts and stories are the center of my existence, they ought to reflect the time I've had so far, and so be it.

"I was born in 1953 in New York City, but my wife claims that I was really born in a shtetl, because almost everyone I knew came from Proszowice, Poland. Despite the skyline in the distance, the customs, language and culture of pre-War Jewish Poland surrounded me. Could it be the discontinuity between the dense isolation of my family and the expansiveness of the city that shaped my self and my work?

"I was the first child not merely of my father, Joseph, and my mother, Rose, but of an entire unrelated clan of men who survived the Holocaust. Their families had been murdered, but they were tough, smart, lucky, and had a fierce determination to make lives in the New World. My first memory is of several unmarried 'uncles' staying up all night to build a life size—for me— fire engine for my second birthday. I was the hope for the future, in the flesh.

"Jumping decades, I am entirely pro-natal (which by no means means anti-choice) and have three children of my own. Between myself and my younger sister and six younger cousins, we have given our parents twenty-three grandchildren. Maybe this reflects a crazed desire to repopulate the world that was destroyed in Europe in the 1940s.

"I was a smart child. I received A's in elementary school and skipped grades, and, above all, read. I read at my desk and on the subways and by flashlight in my bed. I read *Three Billy Goats Gruff* and *Gone with the Wind* and *Crime and Punishment* and then, in the late 1960s, I read Jack Kerouac and Norman Mailer.

"So enthralled was I by the concept of documenting the world on paper that I decided to echo Mr. Mailer and produce the *Armies of the Night* of the May Day demonstrations of 1971. ('If the government doesn't stop the war, we'll stop the government!') The result was 17 pages long and examined in full the American involvement in Vietnam, the youth culture, love, sex, etc., and a few other subjects. But something was missing, and I started a story, 'Peanuts, Popcorn, and Crackerjacks.' This line from a baseball song was a terrible title for a circus story. A sad clown killed himself. Teen angst.

"Three times, at Sarah Lawrence College and then in the MFA program at Columbia University, I tried to turn that story into a novel, and each time it collapsed of its own weight after about a hundred pages. Still, I pursued the idea that I could sit on the other side of the library desk and make black marks on white paper make a universe. Sometimes when people ask about my 'motivation,' I answer, 'I don't know how to do anything else.'

"At about the point where the circus story, sans clown, began to grow into *Sandman's Dust* (Arbor House, 1986) I started another story, very metafictional, about a young poet (mis)translating for an older, foreign poet on the stage of the 92nd Street Y. Somehow, it never jelled, and I'm not sure why, but I placed it back in a place I had never been, Proszowice, the town of my father's childhood. Suddenly, the story, 'New Words for Old,' worked. I had another idea, and set it, too, in Proszowice.

"Although I usually eschew first person narrators as too simple, too narcissistic, and incapable of accomplishing what the godly, omniscient 19th-century third person can, these stories were both related by an unnamed 12-year-old boy. Eventually I sought stories for my hero. Some came easily; others—there *had* to be a violin story—by sheer willpower. The result was *Stories of an Imaginary Childhood* (Northwestern University Press, 1992, winner of the Edward Lewis Wallant Award for the best Jewish/American fiction of the year).

"This book was loved by an audience that yearned for a sentimental 'Fiddler on the Roof' Yiddishkeit and never saw the essential weirdness of the author imagining himself growing up in that dead world. So-called 'second generation' writers are darker than the first, for if Elie Wiesel and Primo Levi had a life to recall on the distant shore of the chasm that split their universe, for us there was no Before. If not for the War, my father would never have come to the United States and met my mother (whose family fled the Tzar a generation earlier). In the beginning was Auschwitz.

"Teaching nowadays, I urge my students to abandon the traditional writing workshop dictum of writing what one knows, because I prefer more imaginative and flamboyant, in both style and content, fiction. Yet for the last decade I have been unable to escape the shackles of 20th-century Jewish experience. I never write about the War itself, because the notion of turning atrocity into art appalls me, but I have pushed the boundaries of this forbidden domain chronologically. 'Imaginary Childhood' takes place in 1928 while my subsequent collection, *While the Messiah Tarries* (Harcourt Brace, 1995), and a novel, *After* (St. Martin's Press, 1996), occur post-1945. Together these books act as bookends to the inner text.

"And behind the blunt evil of history, what First Cause do we find, what eternal ongoing power, but a deity. I believe in God, but I don't like Him, for the simple reason that I don't think He likes me or the rest of the Jews. Chosen people, indeed, chosen to be flayed, flogged and burnt through the millennia. If we know and judge our peers by their actions, the deity likewise bears responsibility for the cruel mortal world we inhabit. In religious faith lies the freedom to kill, so I'd rather adhere to a radical humanism that says that We may be better than God, because We have made the twin qualities of morality and beauty."

In an essay entitled "Crackpot Realism: Fiction for the Forthcoming Millennium" in the *Review of Contemporary Fiction* (Spring 1996, reprinted from *Tikkun*), Melvin Jules Bukiet declared that "two kinds of literature . . . endure: that which utterly transcends its era, and that which perfectly reflects it." The first kind, according to Bukiet, deals with the eternal verities and is the kind most "mainstream" writers wish to produce. The second, in our time, echoes the widespread fascination with coincidence and conspiracy. To Bukiet, Thomas Pynchon is among the "chief lights" of the writers who work in this second form and whom Bukiet has deemed "crackpot realists"; Salman Rushdie, a "writer compelled to live an existence of intrigue by virtue of the *fatwah* of a dead cleric," is a real-life example who makes the genre "frighteningly less crackpot and considerably more real." According to Bukiet, "The technological wheels of modern life that throw the crackpots are particularly American."

The Holocaust, which informs Bukiet's sensibility, is, in his terms, not directly portrayable. Nevertheless, it has forced him into "crackpot realism," the "weirdness" of "imagining himself in that dead world," as he does in *Stories of an Imaginary Childhood*. Bukiet has reacted to the "boom industry" in Holocaust studies in an op-ed piece in the *New York Times* (May 3, 1995) by maintaining,

"It's not memory that is being served, but politics—or worse yet, fashion." He believes that although, inevitably, memory will fade, it is necessary to carry on the message of the Partisan Hymn *Mir Zaynen Do* ("We Are Here") even when there are few to listen. "Once memory fades, the only way history endures is through art, myth or liturgy, and that's being shaped ad hoc. I have more faith in the power of Art Spiegelman's *Maus* to convey the terror than all the guided tours in the world."

While the Messiah Tarries is a group of stories of Jews living in America and awaiting the Messiah. Compared by reviewers to Isaac Bashevis Singer, Bukiet "adds freshness and depth to Jewish storytelling," according to Molly Abramowitz. The Jews in these stories go about their daily lives while also seeking answers to the age-old questions. Answers tarry, along with the Messiah.

In *After*, Bukiet portrayed the aftermath of the Holocaust. The story of three Jews liberated from the concentration camps in 1945, *After* was described by Steve Stern, in a prepublication blurb, as "a Baedeker of hell, compiled through a collaboration of Jerzy Kosinski and Joseph Heller"—the latter novelist being an "older second cousin to the crackpots," in Bukiet's estimation. The three survivors deal with "crackpot American GIs, a sleazy, makeshift-cabaret impresario, and a demented German aristocrat" in a black market rendered with black humor—a not un-Hellerian cast of characters and situation. Neil Gordon called *After* "an act of Jewish testimony of the first order" and "an unforgettable contribution . . . to American and world literature." The *Publishers Weekly* (July 8, 1996) reviewer found the plan of Isaac, the ringleader of the motley crew of black marketeers, to acquire a treasure of gold taken from the teeth of murdered Jews, to be "the culmination of a series of dangerous adventures involving comic pratfalls, miraculous reunions, sudden betrayals, and lightning changes of fortune." The reviewer added, "Bukiet's mordant humor and insight into human character are matched by his audacity and hyperbolic imagination."

Bukiet's 1999 novel, *Signs and Wonders*, is set late in the 20th century and written from the point of view of one Snakes Hammurabi, who has been sentenced to a term on a barge-like German prison for the crime of relieving himself on a church altar. After a storm sets the prison adrift, Snakes and his 12 fellow prisoners survive, thanks to the actions of one of them—the theretofore silent Ben Alef. The seeming miracles brought about by Alef lead the other men to believe that he is the Messiah. The novel contains many 20th-century parallels to biblical characters and events, such as a latter-day Mary Magdalene and hell in the form of Disneyland. In a representative review of the book, Elizabeth Hand wrote in the *Washington Post Book World* that *Signs and Wonders* is "a daringly original millennial novel, horrific and hilarious by turns, brilliant, black, bitterly funny. . . . the Real Thing, a book that goes off like a bomb in the reader's head and echoes there long after."

Bukiet, who lives in New York City, teaches at Sarah Lawrence College. He was appointed fiction editor of *Tikkun* in 1992.
—S. Y.

SUGGESTED READING: *Booklist* p1478 Apr. 1, 1995; *Library Journal* p127 Apr. 1, 1995; *New York Times* I p19 May 15, 1993, A p23 May 3, 1995; *Paris Review* p223 Fall 1995; *Publishers Weekly* p72 July 8, 1996; *Review of Contemporary Fiction* p13 Spring 1996

SELECTED BOOKS: *Sandman's Dust*, 1986; *Stories of an Imaginary Childhood*, 1992; *While the Messiah Tarries*, 1995; *After*, 1996; *Signs and Wonders*, 1999

Miriam Berkley

Burke, James Lee

Dec. 5, 1936– Mystery writer

After publishing three books before the age of 35, James Lee Burke disappeared from the literary landscape for over a decade. Although his first two works were critically acclaimed novels—*Half of Paradise* (1965) and *To the Bright and Shining Sun* (1970)—he was unable to sell another novel after the disappointing reception of *Lay Down My Sword and Shield* (1971). This is not to say that Burke had given up writing—in fact he was writing prolifically during this period—it was simply that no publishing house saw fit to take on another one of his books. He made a modest comeback with his novel *Two for Texas* (1983), published in a paperback edition, but he didn't expect to ever see his work in hardcover again. After publishing a collection of acclaimed short stories, he returned to notice with *The Lost Get-Back Boogie* (1986), a novel that had received nearly 100 rejection slips but was nominated for a Pulitzer Prize after its publication. Since that time he has become the author of the Dave Robicheaux crime series, which began with *The Neon Rain* (1987). The Robicheaux mysteries have been praised for their detail, particularly for their realistic depiction of a recovering alcoholic detective. Additionally, critics have lauded Burke's lyrical descriptions of Louisiana. Burke's latest releases are *Cimarron Rose* (1997), the first novel in a new detective series featuring country lawyer Billy Bob Holland, a figure who, like Robicheaux, fights for the weak and oppressed while battling his personal demons, and *Heartwood* (1999), which also features Holland.

James Lee Burke, Jr. was born on December 5, 1936 in Houston, Texas, the son of James Lee Burke, a natural gas engineer, and the former Frances Benbow. In an interview with *Publisher's Weekly* (April 20, 1992), Burke said, "I wanted to be a writer since I was a little boy. In the fourth grade my cousin Lynn and I started writing stories for the *Saturday Evening Post* in Big Chief notebooks." He continued his writing in college, publishing his first story at age 19 in the college literary magazine at the University of Southwest Louisiana. After receiving honorable mention in a story contest, Burke transferred to the University of Missouri in 1957, received his bachelor's degree in 1959, and obtained his master's degree in teaching in 1960. After his graduate work, Burke took a position with the Sinclair Oil Company but later returned to the university to teach. He subsequently worked in various positions as a surveyor and a social worker in Los Angeles, California, between 1962 and 1964.

During this period Burke completed his first novel *Half of Paradise*. The story focuses on three men who are imprisoned—two literally, one by addiction—and the attempts of each to free himself from the shackles of his past. Four years after its completion, the novel was published in 1965 to generally good, albeit reserved reviews. The *New York Times Book Review* (March 16, 1965) noted that "the romantic dialogue is a passionate and finely pitched one, and I have never read better prison scenes. On the debit side: although the language of the book is compact, it is not truly sharp-edged until the latter stages, when it acquires perceptibly greater sensitivity. . . . No reservations alter the important things about the book: it is an exciting piece of writing and a solid debut for a writer to be taken absolutely seriously." R. F. Cayton of *Library Journal* (March 1, 1965) wrote, "While this work reads well—and at times excitingly so—the lack of empathy on the author's part for his characters—and I think life in general—disturbs me."

Following the release of his debut novel, Burke relocated several times, at one point becoming an instructor for the United States Forest Service Job Corps Conservation Center in Frenchburg, Kentucky. "I guess it happens to a lot of guys who go from grad school into university teaching," the author told *Writer's Digest* (January 1993). "You feel you're missing something. So I went from job to job. We bounced all over the country, literally." While settling in at the University of Montana as a teacher, he composed his next novel, *To the Bright and Shining Sun* (1970).

Set in a Kentucky mining town, the story focuses on teenager Perry James, a third-generation miner. *To the Bright and Shining Sun* opens during a lockout of the United Mine Workers and continues through the union's victory, which oddly leaves conditions in the mine worse than ever. Perry, who knows little of the world outside his mining town, is given the chance to learn a trade and even drives a bootlegger's truck to make ends meet. All his hopes for the future, however, are destroyed when his father is killed in a blast set by nonunion workers. According to the *New York Times Book Review* (August 9, 1970), the author "takes the harsh facts [of life in the Kentucky Hills] and brings them to life in a surging, bitter novel as authentic as moonshine. . . . [There] emerges a picture not merely of social inequity, but of character and atavistic pride—for Perry James is at all times his own man in an unjust world." Sister Melinda Keane, in *Best Sellers* (September 1, 1970), echoed the thoughts of other critics when she noted that "the novel presents an interesting and sometimes competently handled story of the life of Kentucky miners. What it has not managed to do is capture that life itself."

After falling out with the agent who aided in the sales of his first two novels, Burke switched to the William Morris Agency, which negotiated the sale of his third book, *Lay Down My Sword and Shield* (1971), to T. Y. Crowell. The book received unfavorable reviews. Though he remained with the William Morris Agency for the next six years, he decided to take the manuscript of his new novel, *The Lost Get-Back Boogie*, to a new publisher. Much to his surprise, Burke was unable to sell the novel. "I thought the early success was there to stay. But that was a vanity. It was 13 years before I was in hardback again," he said during the *Publisher's Weekly* interview.

Despite the difficulties he experienced while searching for a publisher for *The Lost Get-Back Boogie*, Burke did not stop producing new material. In fact he had a number of unpublished short stories and novels in manuscript form that he continued to circulate to various agents and publishers. He returned to his teaching career, still confident that he could get published again. "I thought that my talent was there for a reason and honestly believed that these guys were all wet. . . ," he explained to *Publisher's Weekly*, adding, "To me those editors were just dumbheads." An unfortunate side effect of his inability to be published was that he began drinking heavily. With the help of Alcoholics Anonymous, however, Burke, who has said he was once a "white-knuckle alcoholic," has been able to regain his sobriety.

In 1978 Andren Dubus, Burke's cousin, introduced him to the agent Phillip Spitzer. Spitzer sold Burke's *Two for Texas* in 1983 as a paperback original. Despite this success, Burke began to believe that his work would never be put in hardcover again; *The Lost Get-Back Boogie* had now received more than 90 rejection slips. Just as the situation began to look hopeless, he received word that the Louisiana State University Press was going to publish *The Convict and Other Stories* (1985), a collection of his short fiction. A year later they published a revised version of *The Lost Get-Back Boogie*, which was nominated for a Pulitzer Prize. "I owe those people at LSU Press a lot," Burke told *Writer's Digest* (January 1993). "They resurrected my whole career. Suddenly I was back in business."

The author also owes something to his friend and fellow writer Rick DeMarinis, who helped inspire Burke's Dave Robicheaux crime series. As Burke has described it, the pair were fishing one day during his long publishing drought, when DeMarinis suggested that Burke write a crime novel since he had already tackled almost every other genre. Burke soon began work on this new project and sent two chapters of his first Robicheaux novel, *The Neon Rain*, to Charles Willeford, the author of the Hoke Mosley series (*Miami Blues*, *New Hope for the Dead*). Willeford, who saw plenty of potential in the character Dave Robicheaux, encouraged Burke to continue working on the book. After Burke sent the book to Spitzer, he was stunned to discover that three publishing houses were taking bids on the novel. Ultimately Rob Cowley, an editor at Henry Holt, bought both *The Neon Rain* (1987) and its sequel, *Heaven's Prisoners* (1988).

Burke's detective Dave Robicheaux is a Vietnam veteran tortured by flashbacks and dreams. While extremely moral, he inevitably resorts to extreme violence in situations that warrant such behavior. Once a Louisiana police officer, he retires later in the series and opens a tackle and bait shop. Like Burke, Robicheaux is a recovering alcoholic. In *Library Journal* (August 1989), Beth Ann Mills wrote, "Robicheaux is a complex and very believable character, battling alcoholism, haunted by his wife's death, struggling to hold onto his Catholic faith. Surrounded by violence, he is a man of integrity trying to find an honorable way out."

In 1989 Burke published *Black Cherry Blues*, his third Robicheaux mystery. As the novel opens, Robicheaux is attempting to come to terms with the violent death of his wife (an event described in *Heaven's Prisoners*) while running his bait store and raising his adopted six-year-old daughter, Alafair. Robicheaux soon runs into an old friend who leads him through a series of events that result in the detective's being framed for murder. In his review of the novel, Peter S. Prescott of *Newsweek*

(October 2, 1989) wrote, "Burke writes well, with a strong sense of place. He's able to provide three psychopathic murders, each different from the others. The plot takes a few implausible turns . . . but this is a strong performance." Other critics, however, did not enjoy this mystery as much as the earlier books in the series. Writing for the *New York Times Book Review* (October 8, 1989), Marilyn Stasio complained about how "the thin story that emerges between nature studies and character portraits deals implausibly with a Mafia takeover of Indian lands." She added, "With so little action to occupy him, the soulful hero falls on his old, self-indulgent habits of analyzing his dreams and examining his conscience for existential guilt."

In the next few years, Burke produced several more books, including *Ohio's Heritage* (1989), co-written with Kenneth E. Davison; *Texas City, Nineteen Forty-Seven* (1992); and the Robicheaux novels *A Morning for Flamingos* (1990) and *A Stained White Radiance* (1992). In 1993 he released another Robicheaux novel, *In the Electric Mist with Confederate Dead*, which received high praise from critics. This mystery involves a 1957 lynching victim whose body has resurfaced in the bayou, the New Orleans mob, and mutilated female bodies that turn up all over Louisiana. Gene Lyons of *Entertainment Weekly* (April 30, 1993), who called this book "as satisfying as any novel Burke has written," wrote, "It's hard to imagine readers not bolting it down like a steaming platter of crawfish étouffée." Summing up his love of the series, D. T. Max of *New York Newsday* (May 12, 1993) confessed, "The Robicheaux mysteries, albeit predictable, are great for a number of reasons. There's the writing, which is probably the best going among mystery authors. The weather, all those hurricanes and eight-color sunsets, is almost a character in itself. And there are the Cajun accents, culture and food. . . . But my own reason for loving these books is that Robicheaux is crazier and possibly more dangerous than the people he pursues, and he knows it. . . . So the fight here is no good guys against bad but Robicheaux sane versus Robicheaux crazy."

Dixie City Jam (1994), Burke's next installment in the series, received mixed reviews. In this episode Robicheaux attempts to outsmart neo-Nazis, Mafia henchmen, and a fake nun, as everyone races to raise a German submarine that sank off the coast of New Orleans during World War II. *Booklist* (July 1994) critic Bill Ott wrote, "Burke keeps it all fresh by never losing sight of the soft edges around his hard characters and by somehow being able to crank out a little extra lyricism at just the right moment." On the other hand *Time* (September 5, 1994) complained that "the series shows signs of wear. Other Burke plots have been fanciful, but this one is too big and operatic for anything but a James Bond thunderation." Burke's two most recent Robicheaux novels, *Burning Angel* (1995) and *Cadillac Jukebox* (1996), received mostly favorable reviews.

In recent years Burke has developed a new series of detective adventures featuring a Texas country lawyer named Billy Bob Holland. Holland is a complex character with a variety of torments: a twisted family background, his father's death, and his great-grandfather's affair with Jennie, the Rose of Cimarron. Most importantly, he is haunted by his time spent as a Texas Ranger, during which he accidentally killed his own partner. On top of this is a plot in which Holland must defend his unrecognized illegitimate son, Lucas Smothers, who has been accused of raping and murdering his girlfriend, Roseanne Hazlitt. The first release of this series, Cimarron Rose (1997), deftly cements Holland's character while at the same time developing a complex mystery. Most reviewers praised the book. In the New York Times Book Review (August 10, 1997), Marilyn Stasio wrote, "Burke weaves in family history and regional legends and gives voice to a parade of local sadists and psychopaths, some of them in so-called law enforcement. But the story is a simple one about the cruelty of youth—how it's taught, how it's learned and what it does to both teacher and pupil." Kirkus Reviews (July 1, 1997) noted: "[Cimarron Rose has] all the roiling intensity of the Robicheaux stories. Even the ragged ends make other mystery novels look anemic."

Heartwood, the second Holland novel, was published in 1999. It received a mixed review from Bill Ott in Booklist (Apr. 15, 1999), who praised the novel's "lyrical prose . . . elegiac tone, and . . . complex, tormented hero," but criticized its overabundance of echoes to previous books. Among the book's characters are what Ott terms as "A classic Burke villain: the rich guy whose polished veneer masks a lifetime of brutality. . . , Mexican American gang members, and the dissolute sons of the town's wealthy class." Overall, Ott calls Heartwood "a strong novel on its own terms, if a mild disappointment to longtime Burke fans."

James Lee Burke has been married to Pearl Pai since January 22, 1960. They have four children: James, Andree, Pamela, and Alafair. He has received numerous awards, including a Breadloaf Fellowship (1970), a Southern Federation of State Arts Agencies grant (1977), a Pulitzer Prize nomination in 1987 for The Lost Get-Back Boogie, the Edgar Allan Poe Award from the Mystery Writers of America for Black Cherry Blues (1989), and a 1989 Guggenheim Fellowship.

In 1996 Heaven's Prisoners was released as a film starring Alec Baldwin.

—C.M.

SUGGESTED READING: Best Sellers Sep. 1, 1970; Booklist p1893 July 1994, Apr. 15, 1999; Chicago Tribune V p2 Aug. 1, 1994; Entertainment Weekly Apr. 30, 1993; Publishers Weekly p33+ Apr. 20, 1992; Kirkus Reviews p967 July 1, 1997; Library Journal p90 Mar. 1, 1965, p95 July 1970, p114 Aug. 1989; Newsweek Oct. 2, 1989; New York Newsday p48 May 12, 1993; New York Times VII p14 Apr. 5, 1992; New York Times Book Review p46 Mar. 16, 1965, p333 Aug. 9, 1970, p20 Oct. 8, 1989, p18 Aug. 10, 1997; Newsweek p76 Oct. 2, 1989; Publisher's Weekly Apr. 20, 1992; Time p73 Sep. 5, 1994; Writer's Digest Jan.1993; Contemporary Authors New Revised Series Vol. 41, 1994

SELECTED WORKS: Fiction—Half of Paradise, 1965; To the Bright and Shining Sun, 1970; Lay Down My Sword and Shield, 1971; Two For Texas, 1983; The Convict and Other Stories, 1985; The Lost Get-Back Boogie, 1986; The Neon Rain, 1987; Heaven's Prisoners, 1988; Black Cherry Blues, 1989; A Morning for Flamingos, 1990; A Stained White Radiance, 1992; Texas City, Nineteen Forty- Seven, 1992; In the Electric Mist with Confederate Dead, 1993; Dixie City Jam, 1994; Burning Angel, 1995; Cadillac Jukebox, 1996; Cimarron Rose, 1997; Heartwood, 1999; Nonfiction (with Kenneth E. Davidson)— Ohio's Heritage, 1989

Miriam Berkley

Butler, Octavia

June 22, 1947– Science fiction writer

"Cautionary tales," Octavia Butler told Frances D. Louis for Emerge (June 1994), "That is what I hope I am writing." For more than 20 years, Octavia Butler has been producing some of the most original sci-fi/fantasy novels the genre has ever seen, combining elements of mysticism, African-American history, and science in post-apocalyptic tales. In her stories she comments on topics of morality, family, and sex roles in society through the resilient female characters who emerge from her graceful prose. The only major black female author of science fiction today, Octavia Butler has helped open new doors for female novelists and the genre itself.

Octavia Estelle Butler was born on June 22, 1947, in Pasadena, California, to Laurice and Octavia M. (Guy) Butler. Her father died when she was still a baby, and as a result, she was raised by her mother, grandmother, and other relatives, all of whom were strict Baptists. Butler developed a love of fiction at an early age, and, preferring the company of books, found herself alienated from her peers. With an active mind that constantly concocted stories out of daydreams, she quickly outgrew children's books and made a brave attempt to procure books from the adult section of her local library. When the librarian refused to allow her entrance, she bided her time in the magazine section and soon found herself drawn to the science fiction periodicals. By the age of 12, Butler's vivid imagination began to flow out onto the pages of her notebook, and soon she began to write science fiction stories that reflected a wisdom and creativity well beyond her years. The young girl was also inspired by the sci-fi movies of her generation, particularly one titled *Devil Girl from Mars*, which so disgusted her that she set out to write a better storyline. That story later served as her frame of reference for her *Patternmaster* series.

As a teenager, Butler took solace in her writing and had already submitted stories to magazines by the time she entered Pasadena City College. During her first semester there she won a short-story contest, but she made no other significant advancements in her writing career during college, choosing instead to focus on her English, history, and anthropology classes. She received her A.A. degree in 1968 and moved on to California State University in Los Angeles, where, as she told Lisa See for *Publishers Weekly* (December 13, 1993), she took "everything but nursing classes. I'm a little dyslexic and worried about killing people." (For the same reason, Butler has never learned to drive.)

She next began classes at the University of California at Los Angeles and simultaneously won admission into the Open Door Program of the Screenwriters Guild, in which she had the opportunity to take a class taught by Harlan Ellison. He suggested that Butler enroll in the Clarion Science Fiction Writer's Workshop (a six-week "science fiction writing boot camp," according to Butler) held in Pennsylvania. Butler jumped at the chance and traveled across the country in 1970 to attend the workshop, where she promptly sold two of her stories. The experience also served as an important boost to Butler's self-image, when, surrounded by fellow science fiction writers from all walks of life, she realized that she was not alone in her aspirations. "To write science fiction you have to be kind of a loner, live in your head, and, at the same time, have a love for talking," she told See. "Clarion was a good place for that."

Although she drew strength from her experience at Clarion, Butler faced a turbulent period in the ensuing five years, during which she did not sell any of her writing. Instead, she rose at 2 or 3 o'clock every morning to write her stories, then worked at blue-collar jobs—washing dishes, sweeping floors, and sorting potato chips—during the day. A turning point in this routine came when she was unexpectedly laid off from a telephone solicitation job right before Christmas 1974. Deciding it was time to sink or swim, Butler jumped from writing short stories to composing a novel. The author had been intimidated by the thought of writing a full-length work, but she began to focus on the notion of each chapter as a short story. As a result she managed to complete *Patternmaster* in only a few months. Based on the short stories she had written as a child, *Patternmaster* was picked up by Doubleday. The publishing house also offered to buy what would be Butler's next two books, *Mind of My Mind* and *Survivor*. The remaining books in Butler's *Patternmaster* series include *Wild Seed* and *Clay's Ark*.

In *Patternmaster*, Butler depicted an agrarian society ruled by a specially bred group of telepathic people controlled by the Patternmaster, Doro. Mentally linked in a hierarchical "pattern," the telepaths, or Patternists, plan to create a superhuman race, but their communities are threatened by attack from other humans, called Clayarks, who have been horribly mutated through a genetic disease. The Patternists and Clayarks are the focus of a story that delves into the struggles between classes, as well as the conflict between the identity of the group and the needs of the individual. *Mind of My Mind* (1977) and *Survivor* (1978) continue the storyline. The successful series not only won Butler a reputation as an oddity in her field (there were few black science fiction writers at the time and of those, all were male), but also established her as a premier science fiction writer. The books treated topics that Butler would explore again and again in her career, namely sexism and racism.

Published in 1980, *Wild Seed* takes place on Earth in the period between 1690 and 1840 and serves as the "prequel" to the first three books in the *Patternmaster* series. More than her previous books, *Wild Seed* consistently crosses the line between historical fact and science fiction: in this case, by examining Doro's past as well as the history of American slavery up until the eve of the Civil War. In this book, as in its predecessors, a black woman, Anyanwu, emerges as a strong central character. Anyanwu challenges Doro's attempts to control her, and stands apart in the novel as a voice of reason and logic. Doro roams the earth in the form of many vastly different bodies. He seeks to dominate the "Wild Seed," a group of witches and seers. But Doro meets his match in Anyanwu; they engage in a battle of wills that takes them over land and time.

Butler's independent black female characters, such as Anyanwu, are realistically drawn women with difficult choices to make, but above all they are survivors. Such characters are as rare in science fiction as Butler herself. "The fact that they're black is not the most important thing on my mind," she told See. "I'm just interested in telling a story, hopefully a good one." Butler, however, is well aware of her status. "I'm the only black woman writing science fiction today *because* I'm the only black woman writing science fiction," she remarked. "I don't mean to be facetious, but it's true." Perhaps the paucity of strong feminist voices in science fiction has caused Butler to explore the theme of gender-bending as well. In *Wild Seed*, her characters can change from male to female and vice versa. Critics have noted that, by blurring the lines of gender in her novels, Butler creates strong, multi-dimensional characters who evolve with their adapted roles.

The events of the final novel in the series, *Clay's Ark* (1984), occur after the action of *Wild Seed* but before that of the original *Patternmaster* trilogy. In the not-so-distant future of America, this time in the California desert, a father and his two daughters are kidnapped. The Earth, the family soon discovers, has been invaded by a deadly microorganism that attacks in the same manner as a virus—only this disease allows its survivors to bond with it. The survivors develop enormous powers—and an all-consuming need to spread the disease and colonize the newly transformed. The central character in the novel is Asa Elias (Eli) Doyle, an American space traveler who is responsible for bringing the Clayark disease to Earth. When he realizes what he has done, he and other survivors of the disease go into hiding, hoping to halt the contagion's spread.

Critics once again praised Butler for her lucid prose and storytelling prowess. Algis Budrys wrote in the *Magazine of Fantasy and Science Fiction* (August 1984) that "Butler creates this tale with verve, originality, and an apparent gift for the circumstantial detail, circumstantially told." Gerald Jonas wrote in the *New York Times Book Review* (December 29, 1996) that Butler was "evenhanded in her characterizations" as well as "accomplished in her action scenes." "In exquisitely measured doses of revelation, Ms. Butler lets us enter the minds of victims and perpetrators alike," Jonas stated in his review. "She moves with ease between past and present, always telling us just what we need to know in order to follow the next stage of the swiftly paced narrative."

In the midst of writing her *Patternist* series, Butler felt the urge to take her craft in a different direction, so she wrote the novel *Kindred* (1979). Marketed as mainstream fiction, *Kindred* tells the story of Dana, a black woman transported back in time to the antebellum South and the plantation of her ancestors. Dana must try to save her white, slave-owning ancestor so as to ensure her own birth a century later.

Butler was moved to write the story because of what she saw as a "generation gap" between herself and her mother. As she explained to See, "She was a maid and I wished she wasn't. I didn't like seeing her go through back doors. . . . I also had this friend who could recite history but didn't feel it. . . . He hadn't sorted out yet what the older generation had gone through." Butler wanted to create a book that would involve a modern-day black woman with the events of the past, capturing a history that readers could empathize with and learn from. "If my mother hadn't put up with those humiliations, I wouldn't have eaten very well or lived very comfortably," she told See. "So I wanted to write a novel that would make others feel the history: the pain and fear that black people had to live through in order to endure."

Kindred was a crossover success for Butler, who, since the beginning of her career, had been consistently and strictly billed as a science fiction writer. The novel became a popular supplement to African-American studies programs in classrooms around the country. Joanna Russ described *Kindred* for the *Magazine of Fantasy and Science Fiction* (February 1980) as "exciting and fast-moving, and the past occurs without a break in style—a technique that makes it more real—even down to characters' speech."

The success of *Kindred* landed Butler another book deal, which she took advantage of to create the *Xenogenesis* series. The books deal with apocalyptic themes and were largely inspired by the politics of the Cold War and concern about nuclear weapons. Butler told See that her intense interest in current events led her to incorporate Reagan-era politics into her work. "I started the series at a time when Reagan was saying we could have winnable nuclear wars and how we'd all be safer if we had nuclear weapons," she said. "I thought if people believed this, then there must be something wrong with us as human beings."

This revelation, as well as her research into captive breeding, led Butler to construct a scenario in which "human behavior is put at the service of hierarchal behavior." The story that emerged was a tale of extraterrestrials who provide relief to suffering post-nuclear survivors by changing their genetic structure through interbreeding. Throughout the *Xenogenesis* series, these aliens, the Oankali, travel and interbreed with other species in an attempt to improve their own gene pool, while simultaneously offering a chance of hope for nuclear war survivors by combining the best qualities of each species through the services of a third sex called ooloi, who manipulate the genes into a new species. During the course of this intergalactic experiment, it becomes evident that the humans are hierarchical in nature, which causes their prejudices and class divisions. Without the extraterrestrials' intervention, Butler implied, these hierarchical characteristics would cause mankind's eventual self-destruction.

Dawn (1987), the first book in the *Xenogenesis* trilogy, features yet another strong black female character, Lilith, at its core. Writing for the *Christian Science Monitor* (August 7, 1987), Frances Deutsch Louis did not find the novel impressive in comparison to Butler's past work, particularly her short story "Bloodchild." Louis wrote that *Dawn* is merely "a shadow" of the earlier piece, and that "The power of Butler's astonishing imagination is vitiated by a slow-motion flatness that may result from the strain of serial novelization, a condition readers must come to expect as long as publishers pay more for quantity than quality."

The next novel in the series, *Adulthood Rites* (1988), focused on Lilith's son Akin, a product of the aliens' genetic experiments who possesses the intellect of an adult. Akin is kidnapped by resentful humans who cannot bear children of their own and so resist the Oankali movement by abducting hybrid children for their cause. The novel leads to the rebels' ultimate realization (in part brought by Akin) that humankind as they know it will never be the same. In the *St. Louis Post-Dispatch* (October 22, 1988), Jim Creighton gave an unenthusiastic review; although he found the series itself to be "ambitious" and "well-constructed," the second novel seemed "less compelling than the first, perhaps because it lacks the suspense generated in *Dawn* by Lilith's slowly diminishing fear and growing understanding of the Oankali." Creighton went on to say that while *Adulthood Rites* "never creates quite the same tension," it is nevertheless a "well-written, thoughtful novel."

The third novel, *Imago* (1989), centers around Jodahs, who, as the first ooloi born to a human mother, faces an uncertain future. Jodahs will not become an adult with a permanent gender until he/she is 30 years old. Jodahs is capable of the extremes of good and bad—from curing cancer to creating plague—and the future of the Oankali aliens as well as humans depends on how he/she moves into adulthood. This final book in the trilogy did not fare well critically either: Ted White for the *Washington Post* (June 25, 1989) declared, "It's all so sweet and nice, and everybody lives happily ever after. If only everyone didn't have to talk about it so much! Most of the wordage in this book is taken up with one character explaining to another the properties of the Oankali and the benefits to be found in the merger of races." White also took exception to the numerous holes he found in the plot, the lack of a substantial subplot, and omission of physical description: "It is a little surprising that a first-person narration by someone with what is described as multiple and sophisticated sensory organs has so little description or evocation of sights, smells, etc., and virtually no insight into what this sensory input must feel like." The reviewer concluded that "all in all, this is an anticlimactic book with which to conclude a trilogy."

After finishing the series, Butler entered a period of writer's block, which she referred to as "literary metamorphosis" on good days and "literary menopause" on bad ones. The problem, she told See, was that she was bored with what she had been doing and knew she wanted her next book to be about a woman who starts her own religion, but the words were not forthcoming. Butler broke the block when she began to explore poetry. "I'm the kind of person who looks for a complex way to say something," she told See. "Poetry simplifies it. When I started to write poetry, I was forced to pay attention word by word, line by line." Some of this poetry eventually made its way into her book, titled *Parable of the Sower* (1993).

Parable of the Sower takes place in a devastated not-so-distant future and tells the story of Lauren, a black teenager who suffers from "hyperempathy," a condition (caused by drugs her mother took when pregnant with her) that makes her take on the pain of those around her. Living in an enclosed suburban community of 11 extended families, Lauren spends her time observing and writing down her thoughts and poetry as the world outside collapses in a haze of robbery, rape, and murder. When her father is killed and her community is invaded by bandits, Lauren is forced to flee, joining a handful of other survivors who journey to a safer location. As they travel west on deserted highways, Lauren begins to read to them some of her writings and poetry, and they come to regard her as a prophet. A new religion, Earthseed, is born, which is based on Lauren's motto of "God Is Change" and which promotes a faith of adaptability in the face of their declining civilization.

Butler's disturbing fantasy novel drew praise from critics. Writing for *Library Journal* (October 15, 1993), Jackie Cassada called *Parable of the Sower* "simple, direct, and deeply felt" and lauded its allegorical quality. Gerald Jonas offered an enthusiastic assessment in the *New York Times Book Review* (January 2, 1994): "As a novel, *Parable of the Sower* . . . succeeds on multiple levels. A gripping tale of survival and a poignant account of growing up sane in a disintegrating world, it is at bottom a subtle and disturbing exposition of the gospel according to Lauren." Julie Phillips of the *Village Voice* (February 15, 1994) was slightly less impressed with the dialogue and communication between characters, which she called the "most static" element of the novel. According to Phillips, "The tension comes less from the interplay of [Butler's] people than from the delicate erosion of their world." While commenting that the character Lauren grows "less dynamic" as her status rises within her group of survivors, Phillips could not help but conclude about the novel, "Yet what's touching about it—and what it shares with the best future-world novels—is how inadequate the solutions are. Religion, Butler acknowledges, is unlikely to foster the permanent revolution, and real community is a utopian ideal. Still, there's a sneaky millenarianism to her vision as well." Michael T. Berger in *Black Scholar* (Fall 1994) also offered a mixed review of *Parable of the Sower*, noting that, while the character Lauren is "believable," the other characters that Butler creates are not drawn as vividly. Furthermore, "The repetitiveness and boredom in the community which is waiting for something to happen are conveyed realistically almost to the point of losing the reader." Berger admitted that "at times throughout the novel, one wishes that Butler would have filled in more details about exactly how things have declined in America. Many structural aspects of the novel are taken for granted. Furthermore, the language is often lackluster and the plot development slow." Berger put aside these problems with the book to conclude that Butler "has created a story that raises questions for our own time, and has created in Lauren a way to reflect on our own ability to understand and truly feel for others."

Like *Kindred*, *Parable of the Sower* was marketed as a mainstream fiction novel. The following year, she decided to release a collection of stories and essays she had written in the past, many of which had earned her awards and other accolades. The book was titled *Bloodchild and Other Stories*; the most celebrated piece in the volume was the title novella, which Butler had written in 1985. In this work, which Butler calls her "pregnant-man" story, humans, living on another planet, are valued for their reproductive abilities, and males give birth in order to expand an alien race. The tale highlighted issues of power and gender prevalent in our own society, and in 1985 it won her the Nebula Award, the Hugo Award, and the Locus Award, three of the genre's top honors. In addition, her short story "Speech Sounds" (also included in the volume) won her a Hugo Award.

Bloodchild and Other Stories was welcomed by critics, who applauded its diversity of story content and Butler's graceful prose. Gerald Jonas of the *New York Times* (October 15, 1995) wrote that Butler "excels in the calm straightforward presentation of characters and societies in extremis" and that the book serves as a "fine example of how science fiction . . . can jar us into a new appreciation of familiar truths." The *Washington Post* (October 29, 1995) offered a lukewarm review, calling her tale of incest, "Next of Kin," a "slight if uplifting piece" and "Speech Sounds," the award-winning story set aboard a bus bound for Pasadena, California, a "short and heart-breaking near-future tale." In *Booklist* (September 1, 1995), meanwhile, Janet St. John enthusiastically commented that in *Bloodchild* "Butler graces new mansions of thought with her eloquent, distinguished, and poignant prose." St. John went on to note that "Butler's imagination is strong—and so is her awareness of how to work real issues subtly into the text of her fiction." The reviewer concluded that "Although this book is little in size, its ideas and aims are splendidly large."

In 1995 Octavia Butler was awarded a $295,000 MacArthur Grant, an honor known as the "genius" grant, which is given to creative individuals who "push the boundaries of their fields." Butler was the first science fiction writer ever to win this prestigious award. In November 1998, Butler published

a sequel to *Parable of the Sower* entitled *Parable of the Talents: A Novel*. Butler spends her spare time researching developments in biology and genetics. She makes her home in Pasadena, California, where she has lived all of her life. —D.B.

SUGGESTED READING: *Amazon.com* Aug. 31, 1998; *The Black Scholar* p52+ Fall 1994; *Booklist* Sep. 1, 1995; *Christian Science Monitor* B p6 Aug. 7, 1987; *Emerge* p65+ June 1994; *Library Journal* Oct. 15, 1993; *Magazine of Fantasy and Science Fiction* Feb. 1980, Aug. 1984; *New York Times* p16 Jan. 2, 1994, Oct. 15, 1995, Dec. 29, 1996; *Publishers Weekly* p50+ Dec. 13, 1993; *St. Louis Post-Dispatch* D p4 Oct. 22, 1988; *Village Voice* p67+ Dec. 9, 1989, p91 Feb. 15, 1994; *Voices from the Gaps* (on-line) Sep. 1, 1998; *Warner Books* (on-line); *Washington Post* p8 June 25, 1989, p8 Oct. 29, 1995; *Book Review Digest* 1995, 1996; *Contemporary Authors*, 1993; *Something About the Author*, 1996

SELECTED WORKS: *Patternmaster*, 1976; *Mind of My Mind*, 1977; *Survivor*, 1978; *Kindred*, 1979; *Wild Seed*, 1980; *Clay's Ark*, 1984; *Dawn: Xenogenesis*, 1987; *Adulthood Rites*, 1988; *Imago*, 1989; *Parable of the Sower*, 1993; *Bloodchild and Other Stories*, 1995; *Parable of Talents: A Novel*, 1998

Butler, Robert Olen

Jan. 20, 1945– Novelist; short-story writer

The American novelist and short-story writer Robert Olen Butler has had a very diverse career: he has been a steel-mill worker, a cab driver, an editor, and a teacher of both high school and college students. These experiences, he has suggested, have had a very healthy effect on his fiction, which is characterized by a variety of subject matter and by an unflinching honesty. For years he wrote in relative obscurity—a situation that changed in 1993, when he was awarded the Pulitzer Prize in short fiction for his collection *A Good Scent from a Strange Mountain*, in which he used the first-person voice to tell the tales of Vietnamese characters living in America. Although many critics have branded him a "Vietnam writer" based on that work, Butler has rejected the label as inaccurate. Much of his recent work has borne this out: his follow-up book, the novel *They Whisper* (1994), concerns the nature of sexual relationships. His most recent short-story collection, *Tabloid Dreams* (1996), is a complete departure from his earlier work—each story is based on a front-page headline of a supermarket tabloid and written as if the event described had really happened. One story, for example, has a 79-year-old former president John F. Kennedy going to Sotheby's to retrieve a memento

Miriam Berkley

Robert Olen Butler

tered through the media. In an interview with the *New York Times* (April 20, 1997), Butler noted: "The Vietnamese people were the warmest, most open and welcoming people I've ever met, and they just invited me into their homes and into their culture and into their lives." Butler did not find himself in a combat situation in Vietnam but was instead assigned to be the administrative assistant to the foreign service officer who advised the mayor of Saigon. Butler lived in an old French hotel and would frequently go out in the middle of the night to sit and talk with the people of Saigon in alleys and doorways. While in Vietnam he also found time to write a play.

When he returned to the United States in 1972, he began working on prose fiction in order to capture, in his words, "the ravishing sensuality" of Vietnam. That same year he also married Marylin Geller, a poet, with whom he has a son, Joshua Robert. (Butler's first, brief marriage had been to Carol Supplee.) In 1972 he also became an editor and reporter for *Electronic News* in New York City. Commuting to and from his home in Sea Cliff on the Long Island Rail Road, using a lapboard, he wrote his first novels. Though he moved around for the next couple of years—first returning home to Granite City to become a high school teacher (1973–1974) and then going to Chicago to work as a reporter (1974–1975)—Butler continued to hone his craft by reworking his novels. By 1975 he had settled in New York again, this time as editor-in-chief of *Energy User News,* a position he held for the next 10 years.

Butler's first novel, *The Alleys of Eden,* was published in 1981, after 21 publishers had turned it down. The book, the first of a Vietnam trilogy, helped to categorically redefine the general perception of the Vietnam novel. The story of an American GI's love affair with a Vietnamese prostitute, it is a far cry from the battle-heavy works of fiction that have been produced by many writers on Vietnam. In one of the many impressive reviews that the novel received, the critic Anatole Broyard wrote in the *New York Times* (November 11, 1982): "Mr. Butler seems to have studied and learned from the best masters: his time shifts are reminiscent of Ford Maddox Ford." A reviewer for the *Los Angeles Times* (February 11, 1982) noted: "Butler has an ability to catch tiny shifts of feeling, momentary estrangements, sudden dislocations of mood—a tool as valuable to the novelist as a scalpel to the surgeon." While the book garnered these and other glowing reviews, it sold only a few thousand copies.

Undaunted, Butler published the sequel *Sun Dogs* in the following year. The novel focuses on a secondary character introduced in his previous book—Wilson Hand, a former prisoner of war turned private eye—and on how he must come to grips with his ex-wife's suicide and his own haunting memories of the war. A writer for the *Fort Worth Star-Telegram* (November 14, 1982) commented: "Butler is showing himself to be a master

from among his late wife's possessions. In *The Deep Green Sea* (1998), his latest novel, Butler does, however, address the war in Vietnam once again, this time focusing on a veteran's return to the former Saigon.

Robert Olen Butler Jr. was born in Granite City, Illinois, on January 20, 1945 to Robert Butler Sr. and Lucille Francis (Hall) Butler. His father was a college theater professor at the nearby University of St. Louis; his mother was an executive secretary. Robert Jr. shared his father's interest in the stage, at least initially, and enrolled in Northwestern University as a theater major, wanting to become an actor. According to one interview, sometime before graduating in 1967 he decided that he would "rather write the words than mouth them" and began to turn his attention to playwriting. In the same interview he noted that he began writing on his 21st birthday: "For a time I had been thinking of writing, and I thought, well if I'm going to write, I'd better do something. So I sat down and wrote my first full-length play in the following couple of months, and from then on I've tried to be very productive, never having a period of more than a few weeks go by when I was not either planning or executing a major project."

By the time he enrolled in the master's program at the University of Iowa, he was working on playwriting full-time. After receiving his M.A. in playwriting in 1969, the future novelist was on the verge of being drafted for service in the Vietnam War, so he enlisted in the army. He was assigned to army intelligence and spent a year learning Vietnamese. When he was sent overseas in 1971, he discovered a Vietnam that was far different from the one the American public generally encoun-

stylist. He moves from the most feverish of prose to a flatness and sparseness that is reminiscent of the best of [Raymond] Chandler and [Dashiell] Hammett. And most importantly, he has something to say."

Butler's next novel was not the book that would complete his Vietnam trilogy. Instead, he published *Countrymen of Bones* (1983), a fictional account of the incidents surrounding the detonation of the first atomic bomb at Los Alamos. The story centers on an archeologist named Darrell, who discovers in the desert, 10 miles from where the army is going to detonate the bomb, the burial site of an Aztec sun king, along with the remains of three women buried at his feet with their necks broken. As Darrell is surveying the site, the army tells him he must finish his work in 10 weeks—or the site will be destroyed. Anatole Broyard, writing for the *New York Times* (October 12, 1983) found the work to be "a brilliant novel of ideas . . . never pretentious or didactic."

On Distant Ground (1985) completed Butler's Vietnam trilogy. This installment focused on another veteran, David Fleming, an army intelligence officer who is brought home in disgrace to face court-martial for freeing an important Vietcong prisoner. The book's reviews were mixed, with some critics echoing Clancy Sigal, who wrote in the *Chicago Tribune* (March 31, 1985): "If only the author had drastically reduced David's reflections and had concentrated more on sheer action, even adventure, leaving the literary 'sensitivity' to one side, *On Distant Ground* could have been in the same league as *Dog Soldiers* and *A Rumor of War*."

Butler's next two novels are strikingly different in their subject matter: *Wabash* (1987) is the story of one family's struggles in a fictional Depression-era steel town, and *The Deuce* (1989) is the tale of a young, half-Vietnamese, half-American street hustler getting by in New York City. Typically, the books received mostly good reviews but sold few copies. The *New York Times Book Review* (September 3, 1989) noted that *The Deuce* "is most haunting in its sensuous memories of Saigon, in its fleeting evocations of the prostitute bars and what it's like to be a child sleeping in the next room while your mother makes love with a stranger."

Even with six published novels, Butler had yet to find a wide audience. Though he had been well regarded in serious literary circles as a Vietnam writer (a label he disdains), commercial success continued to elude him. It was not until 1992, when he published his short-story collection *A Good Scent from a Strange Mountain,* that he found a large readership—and then only because he was awarded the Pulitzer Prize. Butler first got the idea for writing *A Good Scent from a Strange Mountain* while he was working on *The Deuce*. He then set about developing a story to be read on National Public Radio: "Crickets," about a Vietnamese father trying to interest his Americanized son interested in cricket fighting. As Butler told the *New York Times* interviewer Peter Applebome:

"Seven hours later I had a short story. Twenty-four hours after that I had ideas for two dozen more stories. The first-person voice and being compelled to write that little story somehow unhooked something, and I suddenly had access to all these voices. . . . I told Allen Peacock, my editor, about it, and he said: 'Great. Let's do a book.'"

The collection is unusual, perhaps even unique, in its content, tracing the Vietnamese experience in America—particularly Louisiana, where the author currently resides. Writing in the first person and in a way that lent a great deal of both humor and empathy to the Vietnamese plight, Butler captured an experience not his own as if it were. George Packer, reviewing the book for the *New York Times Book Review* (June 7, 1992), remarked on how the stories "are the work of a writer who is intoxicated by Vietnam and the Vietnamese, who loves what has alienated so many other Americans, including novelists: the strange lingual tones, the ambiguity of relations in an ancient and complex society, the teeming nightmare streets of Saigon." A writer for the *Times Literary Supplement* (December 10, 1993) marveled: "All these stories are written in the first person, but instead of inhabiting the 'I' as the actor does a role, Butler has grasped the essence of his characters, and all the details and particulars that make them individuals."

The *New York Times* (April 20, 1993) reported that Butler was completely taken aback by the announcement that he had won the Pulitzer Prize for *A Good Scent from a Strange Mountain*. "I had no warning, zero," he told the *Times*. "It came as a total surprise, something remarkable and wonderful that hit with the abruptness of a bolt of bayou lightning." The collection also won the Rosenthal Foundation Award as well as a nomination for the PEN/Faulkner Award, and on the strength of the book Butler won a Guggenheim Fellowship.

Yet Butler was not satisfied to bask in past successes and was not interested in remaining a "Vietnam writer" in the public's eye. He soon produced a new novel, *They Whisper,* a story of sex and relationships, narrated by Ira Holloway, a public-relations man. The book explores Ira's relationship with his wife, Fiona, and also focuses on the many women he has loved, from childhood sweethearts to Vietnamese prostitutes. Many critics were impressed with Butler's sudden shift in subject matter, and most had favorable opinions of the novel. *Library Journal* (December 1993) noted how the author "explores the contrast between Fiona's austere, guilt-based faith and Ira's search for spiritual meaning through the physical. This lyrical, erotically charged novel will remind many readers of D. H. Lawrence." The novelist Jane Smiley, reviewing the novel for the *New York Times Book Review* (February 13, 1994), was more ambivalent. "The nature of Mr. Butler's rhetorical task makes me back off from judging whether *They Whisper* is a great book, or even a good one, but it is a many-faceted and fascinating one. And it taught me that it has been the fate of many men of the Vietnam generation to live the realities of imperialism, both abroad and in the home, without conviction, but with seething self-doubt and longing."

The author's most recent short-story collection is *Tabloid Dreams* (1996). The inspiration for these stories comes from the lowest rank of the supermarket tabloids, the ones that frequently find Bigfoot, Elvis, or aliens lurking in someone's backyard. According to *Library Journal* (September 1, 1996): "Butler's wicked humor is tempered by genuine compassion for the characters' indelible misfortunes." The *New York Times Book Review* (November 3, 1996) suggested, "If you're frustrated by the way nothing much seems to happen in modern short fiction, you'll find *Tabloid Dreams* a whole different story."

Butler's latest novel *The Deep Green Sea* (1998) centers on a 44-year-old American veteran of the Vietnam War who returns to Ho Chi Minh City (Saigon) to rediscover Vietnam.

Robert Olen Butler lives in Louisiana with his fourth wife, the novelist Elizabeth Dewberry, whom he married in 1995. He has been a professor of fiction writing at McNeese State University since 1985 and continues to publish stories and articles in various journals throughout the country. —C.M.

SUGGESTED READING: *Chicago Tribune* XIV p31 Mar. 31, 1985, XIV p1 Mar. 8, 1987; *Fort Worth Star-Telegram* Nov.14, 1982; *Guardian* p4 June 9, 1993; *Library Journal* p121 Mar. 1, 1992, p169 Dec. 1993, p212 Sep. 1, 1996; *New York Review of Books* p41+ Aug. 12, 1993; *New York Times* Nov. 11, 1982, C p2 Oct. 12, 1983, B p1+ Apr. 20, 1993, C p18 Jan. 27, 1994, Apr. 20, 1997; *New York Times Book Review* p10 Sep. 3, 1989, p 24 June 7, 1992, p12 Feb. 13, 1994, Nov. 3, 1996; *Times Literary Supplement* p19 Dec. 10, 1993; *Contemporary Authors* vol. 112, 1985; *Who's Who in America 1997*

SELECTED BOOKS: *The Alleys of Eden*, 1981; *Sun Dogs*, 1982; *Countrymen of Bones*, 1983; *On Distant Ground*, 1985; *Wabash*, 1987; *The Deuce*, 1989; *A Good Scent from a Strange Mountain*, 1992; *They Whisper*, 1994; *Tabloid Dreams*, 1996; *The Deep Green Sea*, 1998

Butterfield, Fox

July 8, 1939– Journalist

For nearly three decades, the American journalist Fox Butterfield, through his numerous articles for the *New York Times* and several books, has brought forward shocking political exposés, documented the social structures of faraway lands, and explored the roots of violence in America. The author of *China: Alive in the Bitter Sea* (1982), a firsthand account of life in contemporary China, and *All God's Children: The Bosket Family and the American Tradition of Violence* (1995), an examination of American violence from the pre–Civil War era to the present, and a contributing writer for *American Missionaries in China* (1963) and the *Pentagon Papers* (1971), he has devoted his life to the dissemination of knowledge.

Born in Lancaster, Pennsylvania, on July 8, 1939, Fox Butterfield is the son of Lyman H. Butterfield, a historian, and Elizabeth Eaton Butterfield, a college administrator. He was educated at Harvard University, where he received his A.B. (summa cum laude) in 1962 and his M.A. in 1964 and conducted further graduate study from 1964 to 1969.

While a student, Butterfield didn't know exactly what career path he would like to follow. "To the extent that I had thought it out, I was interested in American history," Butterfield said in one interview. "I thought of being a professor, a historian. That was my original inclination. But once I started the courses on China, I was immediately drawn to

Jerry Bauer/Courtesy of Alfred A. Knopf

that, and I don't think I ever really looked back." Indeed, Butterfield became fluent in Mandarin Chinese and had his senior thesis included as a chapter in the 1963 book *American Missionaries in China*.

In 1969 Butterfield began writing for the *New York Times*. During the next 14 years, he worked as a correspondent for the paper in a variety of locales, including Vietnam, Japan, and China. In 1984 he became the *Times*'s Boston bureau chief, a position he continues to hold.

Very early in his career with the *New York Times*, Butterfield was involved in a highly controversial journalistic endeavor. In 1971 he was among the members of the paper's staff who wrote a series of articles—later compiled into a book, *The Pentagon Papers*—based on the 47-volume history of the United States' involvement in the Vietnam War commissioned by former secretary of defense Robert S. McNamara. The articles, which included the full text of numerous government documents, set off a furor that resulted in a temporary restraining order, which interrupted the *Times*'s serialization until a Supreme Court decision allowed the paper to continue publishing the series. "The [Pentagon Papers] do present an accurate account of how policy was made over nearly a quarter of a century—lethal, self-reinforcing clichés neatly organized in numberless, often indistinguishable cables, position papers, and 'action memoranda' flowing endlessly through the typewriters and mimeograph machines," Gaddis Smith wrote in the *New York Times Book Review* (November 28, 1971) upon the publication of *The Pentagon Papers*. "There are no villains for historians to identify or politicians to crucify, for here is an entire generation of foreign-policy leaders—the self-styled best that American society could produce—sharing the madness." For his work on *The Pentagon Papers*, Butterfield and the other 35 contributing authors shared the 1972 Pulitzer Prize for meritorious public service.

More than a decade after *The Pentagon Papers*, Butterfield published *China: Alive in the Bitter Sea*, a book based on his two-year (1979–81) experience as the first Peking-based *New York Times* reporter in 30 years. The book is divided into five sections. The first, "Connections," is an examination of the ways in which the Chinese relate to one another and to foreigners. "Passages," the second section, deals with the various stages of life as it is experienced in China. "Systems," the portion of the book critics found to be the most substantial, is a discussion of contemporary Chinese bureaucratic structure, industry, and agriculture. The book's final sections, "Persuasions" and "Messages," discuss the extremely pervasive Chinese system of social control and the relatively few avenues open to individuals who desire to challenge this system. *China: Alive in the Bitter Sea* received mostly favorable reviews, though some critics added that, as a foreign journalist whose movements were constantly monitored by the Chinese government, Butterfield may have produced a skewed account of the state of the nation. "Destined for a wide audience, this book will undoubtedly influence American perceptions of China," B. M. Frolic wrote in the *New York Times Book Review* (May 30, 1982). "It is informative, disturbing, poignant and absorbing. . . . It is a testament to Mr. Butterfield's skill in reporting, his training in Chinese

studies, and his personal commitment to China. However, in looking to him for the final word about China, we should proceed with caution. As a foreigner and a journalist his experiences were extremely limited. The bulk of his reporting was confined to a few Chinese cities." Butterfield has said that while his book is primarily about urban—rather than rural—China, the writing was informed by his having spoken with people who had lived in both settings. He has also that said that in many respects, urban and rural China resemble one another closely.

All God's Children: The Bosket Family and the American Tradition of Violence, Butterfield's most recent book, was published in 1995. The book focuses on Willie Bosket, a double-murderer by the age of 13, once reputed to be the most dangerous man being held in the New York State prison system. In *All God's Children* Butterfield traced Bosket's family tree—one including criminals of every description—back to the pre–Civil War South, where several of Bosket's ancestors were slaves. "What emerged was not just a portrait of the Boskets, but a new account of the origin and growth of violence in the United States," Butterfield wrote in the book's prologue. He added that violence in this country "grew out of the old white Southern code of honor, an extreme sensitivity to insult and the opinion of others." In the post–Civil War years, Butterfield explained, the almost exclusively white-run legal system prejudged nearly every black defendant as guilty. This caused some blacks to view a reputation for disregarding the law as a badge of honor. "Don't step on my reputation," Pud Bosket, a notorious lawbreaker and Willie's great-grandfather, allegedly said. "My name is all I got." Such a mentality, Butterfield argued, was passed from generation to generation: "The old code has been transmuted into the strictures of the street." Following in Pud's outlaw footsteps were his son, James, and his grandson, Butch, who had a criminal record by age nine. By age 22, Butch was serving a life term for a double homicide in Milwaukee. Shortly after his sentencing, his wife gave birth to Willie, who at age 13 went on a shooting rampage on a Manhattan subway train that culminated in the deaths of two passengers. Young Willie soon received even more notoriety when New York State passed the "Willie Bosket law," which allows juveniles as young as 13 to be tried for murder in adult criminal courts. Reviews of *All God's Children* were tepid at best, with several critics charging that there were numerous holes in Butterfield's basic theory. "This old code of honor, unlike current notions of respect or 'dissing,' was bound up with relationships that held a thick social web intact," Jean Bethke Elshtain wrote in *Commonweal* (April 19, 1996). "That the 18th-century South Carolina back country might have been unusually contentious and violent is certainly plausible. But 10-year-olds didn't roam around killing other 10-year-olds or stabbing sleeping men." Elshtain added, "'There is no doubt—none whatsoever—that children, especially young men, from homes without fathers, are more at risk for every possible harm, both as sufferers and perpetrators. Recognizing that reality would take us a lot further toward understanding Willie Bosket than does the etiquette of 18th-century duels."—J. P.

SUGGESTED READING: *BusinessWeek* p23+ Nov. 20, 1995; *Commonweal* p22+ Apr. 19, 1996; *Newsweek* p90+ Oct. 2, 1995; *New York Times Book Review* p3 Nov. 28, 1971, p1 May 30, 1982; *Contemporary Authors* vol. 119, 1987

SELECTED BOOKS: *The Pentagon Papers* (with others), 1971; *China: Alive in the Bitter Sea*, 1982; *All God's Children: The Bosket Family and the American Tradition of Violence*, 1995

Dave Thomas

Cadnum, Michael

May 3, 1949– Mystery writer; poet

Michael Cadnum, the American author of many horror and mystery novels, considers himself to be primarily a poet. He has published eight volumes of poetry since 1982, as well as individual poems in many literary journals, including *America*, *Commonweal*, and the *Midwest Quarterly*, and critics have seen evidence of Cadnum's poetic tendencies even in his prose, since the publication of his first novel, *Nightlight*, in 1990. A recent poem entitled "The Centrifugal Force Ride," published in *Commonweal* (June 14, 1996), gives the reader an accurate sense of Cadnum's sensibilities. Its last stanza reads: "Some people say we are in love/with

death. But we are in love/with life the way we find it./All the way home we hear the screams." Thought-provoking, lyrical, and touching, Cadnum's work echoes through readers' minds long after it is put down. While some critics have faulted his young-adult horror novels for focusing on adolescents with very depressing lives, Cadnum believes not in giving easy solutions to complex plot lines but in giving his young-adult fiction the same type of edge that his adult fiction maintains. "The edge is made sharper," according to Patrick Jones in *Horn Book* (March/April 1994), "with the introduction of themes not often discussed in YA [young adult] books: shame, guilt, and failure." Regardless of how critics feel about the appropriateness of Cadnum's subject matter, few deny the lyricism of his work, which adds to his fiction a dimension rarely seen in horror novels and lends his poetry what the critics find to be a startling originality.

Michael Cadnum, in an autobiography written expressly for *World Authors 1990–1995*, describes his childhood, the influences on his writing, and his view of his own work: "I grew up in Southern California, where there were very few trees and very few wild creatures. On a summer day I would try to catch an alligator lizard, and sometimes a tail would break off. The tail would dance and jitter long after the animal itself had run away. I came to understand that this was a survival technique. It gave the hunting cat or boy a tantalizing remnant to cling to, while the fundamentally entire living creature escaped.

"My friends and I would find trapdoor spider nests, hollow spools of clay, soft and feathery inside. Sometimes we found horned toads, spiky, angry-looking beasts, not toads at all—a variety of reptile. We called them 'horny toads,' but this name always embarrassed me. When the late winter rains were heavy, the landscape would be enriched by a heavy population of the other kind of toad, real toads, the ones that hop through grass. Toads of all sizes, thick on the ground, so many of them that cars could not back down driveways without leaving a path of amphibians flattened like gloves.

"I was born on May 3, 1949, in St. Joseph's Hospital in Orange, California. Before I could write I drew story pictures on a chalk board that stood on a moveable easel. Well before I could read or write I was drawing stories. My first pencil and paper novel filled about half the pages of a spiral notebook. It was written when I was about twelve years old. It was about a dinosaur who lived in a volcano. When the volcano erupted the dinosaur descended on a nearby village and did great harm.

"In my early teens I began to write poetry. I did not write particularly well, and when I did write a poem that I liked, it was very difficult to get it published. After a period of some years, and hundreds or even thousands of rejection slips, I began publishing fairly regularly in quarterlies. I have published several collections of poems, and in

1984 I was awarded a National Endowment for the Arts Creative Writing Fellowship for my poetry.

"Poetry remains the focus of my efforts, although I have descended to the enduring and perhaps childish habit of writing novels. My first novel was published in the spring of 1990, and I have published some ten novels since then. Some of my novels deal with some element of the supernatural, and this had led some readers to consider me a horror writer. This is a misrepresentation, in a way. I am interested in transformation as a subject, and what I think of as the resurrection of the living. A popular supernatural myth such as a vampire, as in *The Judas Glass*, or a werewolf, as in *Saint Peter's Wolf*, can be the best way to illuminate this theme. While I am interested in telling a strong story, I have no interest in frightening a reader.

"Some of my books have been considered young-adult novels, and I think this is likewise a mistake. While my shorter novels have young adult protagonists, my intention is to be honest about the possibilities and hardships of possessing our own lives. No one can see what the future will bring. In the face of the unknowable we are all young, we are all children.

"I have lived in the San Francisco Bay Area throughout my adult years. I have worked as a crisis counselor at Suicide Prevention, a substitute teacher in Oakland, and have held a number of part-time jobs which gave me the hours and energy to write.

"While I now live where I can see San Francisco and the Golden Gate from my living room window, the emptiness and bare freedom of Southern California must have helped shaped the way I think and feel.

"After a winter rain in Southern California sometimes we can see Catalina Island off in the distance, some twenty or thirty miles across the Pacific Ocean to the west. And sometimes we can see Mount Baldy and Mount Cucamonga to the east, dusted with snow. Perhaps I learned from this that some of the enduring outlines of even our mental landscapes are hard to see. And as I have written and revised so much, nearly every day of my adult life, I have come to wonder at how much emptiness fills each written page, how much of language is pure space. Sometimes the best writing is, like a whisper, very close to silence."

Cadnum's first two novels were adult-oriented and featured time-tested horror themes. *Nightlight* is filled with characters who are tortured by madness, recurring nightmares, and ghosts. *Sleepwalker* (1991) narrowed the focus a bit in reviving the legend of the mummy. An archeologist named Davis Lowry, who is tormented by fits of sleepwalking in which he sees images of his dead wife, finds that his excavation site in England is in chaos—there have been so many accidents that workers are beginning to believe the spot is haunted.

Saint Peter's Wolf (1991), the author's first work to be reviewed for young adults, focuses on supernatural occurrences in the life of a psychologist. In the same year Cadnum published another young-adult novel, *Calling Home*, a dark story concerning an alcoholic teenager who accidentally kills his best friend and soon feels that he is possessed by his friend's spirit.

In 1992 Cadnum returned to adult fiction with the publication of the novel *Ghostwright*, the story of a successful playwright named Speke, who is haunted by the man from whom he stole all of his early play ideas. Marylaine Block, writing for *Library Journal* in July 1992, remarked on how the elliptical style of the novel "keeps readers as uncertain as Speke about what is real, what is only imagined." The young-adult work that Cadnum published that year was *Breaking the Fall*. The novel's main character, Stanley, exhibits antisocial behavior that is caused by a terrible home life. Stanley finds relief by breaking into houses with a friend. Susan L. Rogers, reviewing the book for *School Library Journal* (September 1992), praised Cadnum's prose and characterization: "Mature teens may find a more realistic reflection of a troubled world, in the manner of Robert Cormier, S. E. Hinton, and many adult writers."

Since that time Cadnum has published two more adult novels: *The Horses of the Night* (1993), which is a retelling of the story of Faust, Goethe's tale of the man who sold his soul to the devil for earthy pleasures, and *Skyscape* (1994), about a successful artist who is taken to the desert by a famous psychologist who attempts to restore his creative powers. The reviews for *Skyscape* are typical of the mixed criticisms that Cadnum's other books have inspired. The *Library Journal* critic (September 1, 1994) remarked: "As a study of characters in the cultural spotlight, *Skyscape* is intriguing." Yet William Griffin, in *America* (October 28, 1995), did not believe in the validity of Cadnum's characters, stating: "Whether the characters have an emblematic value beyond their individual identities and occupations remains to be seen." Cadnum also published another young-adult novel, entitled *Taking It*, in 1995.

Cadnum's more recent young adult books include *In a Dark Wood* (1998), *Heat* (1998), and *Rundown* (1999). *In a Dark Wood* is a departure from his contemporary novels in that he retells the legend of Robin Hood from the viewpoint of the sherrif of Nottingham. *Heat* is the story of a young competitive high diver who, in addition to dealing with the physical and psychological recovery from diving accident, must cope with her father's legal troubles. In *Rundown*, a teenage girl fakes an attempted rape and becomes the center of attention, but the police soon suspect that she has not told the truth. *Kirkus Reviews* (January 1, 1998) called it "deep, dark, and moving." *Booklist* (June 1, 1999) was less pleased with it, but noted that Cadnum "demonstrates his usual mastery of mood and characterization in this acutely observed portrait."

Cadnum's volumes of poetry include *The Morning of the Massacre* (1982), *Invisible Mirror* (1986), *By Evening* (1992), *The Cities We Will Never See* (1993), and *Zero at the Bone* (1996). The dark sensibility Cadnum exhibits in his fiction can also be found in his poetry, as in the poem "Brueghel's Hunters," originally published in *America* (March 19–26, 1994): "The hunters have been away / a long time. . . . They do not / see where they are going, / but where they are, / silent, empty of hope / and hate, the snow numbing / their steps as they breathe / the scent of smoke in the cold / that never ends." A mood even more bleak is set in "Rescue," which first appeared in the *Midwest Quarterly* (Spring 1995): "They are coming to save you / and they are far from that hour when they see / they will never hear your voice again."

Michael Cadnum lives with his wife, Sherina, in Albany, California where he is currently working on two new novels as well as his poetry. In addition to his creative writing fellowship from the National Endowment of the Arts, he has won the Helen Bullis Prize from *Poetry Northwest* and the Owl Creek Book Award. —C.M.

SUGGESTED READING: *America* Mar. 19–26, 1994, p27 Oct. 28, 1995; *Booklist* June 1, 1999; *Commonweal* p14 June 14, 1996; *Horn Book* p177+ Mar./Apr. 1994; irkus Review Jan 1. 1998; *Library Journal* p119+ July 1992, p213 Sep. 1, 1994; *Midwest Quarterly* p291 Spring 1995; *New York Times Book Review* p16 Mar. 31, 1991; *School Library Journal* p121 Sep. 1992; *Contemporary Authors* vol. 151, 1996

SELECTED BOOKS: Fiction—*Nightlight*, 1990; *Sleepwalker*, 1991; *Saint Peter's Wolf*, 1991; *Calling Home*, 1991; *Ghostwright*, 1992; *Breaking the Fall*, 1992; *The Horses of the Night*, 1993; *Skyscape*, 1994; *Taking It*, 1995; Poetry—*The Morning of the Massacre*, 1982; *Wrecking the Cactus*, 1985; *Invisible Mirror*, 1986; *Foreign Springs*, 1987; *By Evening*, 1992; *The Cities We Will Never See*, 1993; *The Judas Glass*, 1996; *Zero at the Bone*, 1996; Juvenile—*The Lost and Found House* (ill. S. Johnson and L. Fancher), 1997; *In a Dark Wood*, 1998; *Heat*, 1998; *Rundown*, 1999.

Miriam Berkley

Cameron, Peter

Nov. 29, 1959– Novelist; short-story writer

A novelist and author of short stories, Peter Cameron writes about ordinary people and what is important to them. His stories are often characterized as sensitive, with great attention paid to character interaction. Compared by critics to such authors as Raymond Carver and Ann Beattie, Cameron often employs a minimalist style to evoke universal emotional struggles, in such works as *Leap Year* (1990), *The Weekend* (1994), and *Andorra* (1996).

Born in Pompton Plains, New Jersey on November 29, 1959, Peter Cameron is the son of economist Donald O. Cameron and homemaker Sally (Shaw) Cameron. He attended Hamilton College, where he received a Bachelor's degree in 1982.

Cameron came to New York City after graduating and began working as a subsidiary rights assistant for the publishing company St. Martin's Press. In 1983 he left St. Martin's and became a word processor for the Trust for Public Land, an organization he was still working for as of 1996. Cameron also worked as an assistant professor at Oberlin College, in Ohio, for a brief period in 1987.

His first short story collection, *One Way or Another*, was published in 1986. Its contents set the stage for the type of material Cameron would write in the years to follow. The collection, which focuses on ordinary characters dealing with life's everyday crises, brought Cameron a great deal of critical attention. Reviewers praised his well-crafted stories and sensitive portrayals of characters cut off from such sources of emotional support as close relationships with friends and family. Some critics, however, such as Dan Cryer of *Newsday* (May 26, 1986), found that Cameron's focus on emotionally detached characters resulted in a flat, emotionless style of writing. Cryer, who referred to Cameron as "a member of the literary world's Brat Pack," wrote: "Cameron's characters . . . are painted an obligatory blue: alienated, aimless types afraid of lasting relationships, afraid to believe in anything.

From story to story, they seem entirely interchangeable, untouched by any distinctive tics." Cryer was not impressed by what he perceived as the "business-school efficiency" with which Cameron imbued his characters in their relationships— "If they are not manageable, they are easily disposable." Cameron's narrative voice, according to Cryer, lacked drama and originality. The one story he praised as an exception to this problem was "Archaeology," a young woman's recollection of a failed love affair. Rich in feeling and imagery, "Archaeology," Cryer explained, does not rely on the minimalist style that makes many of the other stories somewhat dull.

Leap Year, Cameron's first novel, was published in 1990. The often satirical story spans 10 months in the lives of a group of New Yorkers involved in troubled romantic relationships. In the *New York Times Book Review* (February 25, 1990), Ellen Pall wrote: "It is suffused with the gentle, decent, and quite individual spirit of its author." Pall compared the novel to well-written television sitcom/drama, referring to it as somewhat of a cross between *Mary Hartman, Mary Hartman* and *Thirtysomething*. She also labeled Cameron's characters "yuppies." "Mr. Cameron can be very funny about the social absurdities of upscale Manhattan life in the late 1980s," she wrote. Pall's assessment of the book was not entirely positive, however. She dismissed a series of catastrophic events, including an earthquake and a kidnapping, as entertaining filler devoid of any substantial meaning or connection to the book's outcome. She also criticized the book's character development: "At the end of *Leap Year*, Mr. Cameron drops the satire and more or less tucks each of his fictional offspring tenderly into bed. They have had many adventures, but it would be difficult to say how any of these experiences have changed them. In fact, since none of these characters was ever more to us than a name and job . . . the question of change hardly arises." Cameron, according to Pall, not only seemed to be too affectionate toward his yuppie characters, but he also failed to capitalize on prime opportunities to satirize their self-centered, materialistic lifestyles. "Focused on surfaces, filled with references to cultural artifacts, the book itself finally becomes an artifact, a souvenir of a very particular slice of Manhattan, circa 1988."

In 1991 Cameron published his second collection of short stories, *Far-Flung*. Most of the pieces center on lives in flux, presenting the reader with characters paralyzed by their changing circumstances. Among the stories contained in the collection are the quirky and humorous "Just Relax," which centers on a former Peace Corps volunteer who works in a theme park while being hounded by her eccentric mother; the more sober "The Half You Don't Know," a tale of an old woman ousted from her home; and "The Winter Bazaar," which details a love affair taking place in a house for sale. One of the best, according to Roxana Robertson (*New York Times* September 21, 1991), is "Not the

Point," about a family trying to move. "This is a bleak vision," Robertson wrote of *Far-Flung*, "a place where emotion is denied and love lacks redemptive power. The writing . . . is often fine, however, and in the best of them Mr. Cameron achieves an elegant poignancy."

Cameron returned to the novel in 1994 with *The Weekend*. Continuing the theme of emotional repression presented in his previous efforts, *The Weekend* focuses on a wealthy couple, John and Marian, who must cope with a visit from Lyle, the former lover of John's brother, Tony, who recently died from an AIDS-related illness. The situation is made even more uncomfortable by the presence of Lyle's new partner, Robert. Cameron explored the feelings of tension, loneliness, and grief that arise under these circumstances. He also looked at the vulnerability and pain that lurk beneath the cosmopolitan veneer of the privileged life. "Peter Cameron fuses two familiar formulas: the comedy of the comfortable class . . . and the drama of the ruminations-on-AIDS novel," Kevin Allman wrote in the *Washington Post* (June 26, 1994). While the situation Cameron presents may be an emotional powderkeg, Allman was disappointed to find that the conflicts ultimately "go off with a pop instead of a bang." "While there's nothing wrong with *The Weekend*," wrote Allman, "there's nothing terribly compelling about it, either. . . . It's neither disagreeable nor poorly written, but at 241 pages, *The Weekend* feels like a short story that's overflowed its banks."

By contrast, in her *New York Times* (May 29, 1994) review of *The Weekend*, Joyce Reiser Kornblatt compared Cameron to the likes of Virginia Woolf, E. M. Forster, F. Scott Fitzgerald, and D. H. Lawrence, all critics of material culture. Kornblatt wrote: "If Mr. Cameron's novel does not always reach that level of artistry, it is still a pleasure to encounter the work of a contemporary American novelist who aspires to such complexity, precision, lyricism, and compassion."

Andorra, Cameron's latest novel, was published in 1996. The book features Alex, a wealthy American, who attempts to get away from the entanglements of his life by going to the small European country from which the book takes its name. Before long, however, he finds himself facing all new complications. "The world of *Andorra* is largely naturalistic," Margot Livesey commented in the *New York Times* (December 29, 1996). Events and relationships develop swiftly, and Cameron injects them with the same type of satirical humor found in his previous works. Livesey noted, however, that "in spite of many humorous touches . . . that [comic] verve is now unmistakably harnessed to a darker purpose." Alex finds that the people who populate his Andorran getaway are consumed with the same grief and sorrow from which he is trying to escape. Livesey praised Cameron's "carefully calibrated prose," and declared that "the beauty of [his] voice, combined with its modulation, goes a long way to make credible Alex's repression and, as we discover, his capacity for violence."

Cameron has had two of his short stories published in the prestigious O. Henry Awards collection: "Homework" (1985) and "Excerpts from Swan Lake" (1986). In 1987 he was the recipient of a National Endowment for the Arts fellowship and won honorable mention for the PEN-Hemingway Award. Cameron is also a member of the Authors Guild.—B.S.

SUGGESTED READING: *New York Times* X p10 Feb. 25, 1990, VII p19 Sep. 29, 1991, VII p16 May 29, 1994, VII p8 Dec. 29, 1996; *Newsday* II p10 May 26, 1986; *Washington Post* X p4 June 26, 1994

SELECTED WORKS: *One Way or Another*, 1986; *Leap Year*, 1990; *Far-Flung*, 1991; *The Weekend*, 1994; *Andorra*, 1996

Dharma World

Capra, Fritjof

Feb. 1, 1939– Scientist; philosopher; nonfiction writer

The author of three international best-sellers, *The Tao of Physics* (1976), *The Turning Point* (1982), and *Uncommon Wisdom* (1988), Fritjof Capra has become a celebrated thinker of the late 20th century and founder of a novel approach to physics—one that blends aspects of that branch of science with mysticism. With the publication of his most recent work, *The Web of Life* (1996), he has solidified his theories. He told Kenneth Woodward

in a *Newsweek* (July 23, 1979) interview: "The new physics proves that what we call objects and events are really patterns in a cosmic process. The Eastern mystics knew that. They called the separation of objects *maya*, an illusion that comes from our categorizing intellect." As Woodward noted, this school of thought has appealed more to mystics than to scientists, who have heaped scorn upon it. In an interview with *ReVISION* (Spring 1981), Capra replied to this criticism: "People who have really studied mysticism, who practice it, and also who write about it know very well that mystical experience has nothing to do with nebulous and unclear thinking. . . . It can be very clear, very precise, and very reliable."

The physicist, systems theorist, and author Fritjof Capra was born in Vienna, Austria, on February 1, 1939. His parents were Heinz Capra, a lawyer, and the former Ingeborg Teuffenbach, a poet. He was educated at the University of Vienna, where he received his Ph.D. in physics in 1966. On July 6 of the previous year, he had married a photographer, Jacqueline Ethore, with whom he now has a daughter. Capra began his career as a research assistant in particle physics at the University of Vienna. After interning there for two years (1966–1968), he took a position as an instructor at the University of California, Santa Cruz, where he taught for two years. In 1970 he worked briefly at the Stanford Linear Accelerator Center before moving on to Imperial College at the University of London, where he held the title of visiting scientist until 1974.

When he returned to California in 1975, he began teaching at the Lawrence Berkeley Laboratory at the University of California and did research there. He soon published his first book, *The Tao of Physics*, a work that served as the foundation for the school of thought that combines mysticism and physics. In the book, in essence, Capra asserted his belief that both quantum and relativity theory, two foundations of 20th-century physics, make us see the universe in much the same way that a Hindu, Buddhist, or Taoist might perceive it. Controversial at the time, *The Tao of Physics* received mixed reviews. The *Choice* (June 1976) critic believed that Capra's thesis was somewhat "simplistic" and commented: "The trouble is that ancient mystical worldviews are far more permanent than scientific theories, and the upholder of such a thesis would be embarrassed when newer theories emerge to replace relativity and quantum mechanics. Even with this limitation, this book would be a rewarding reading experience for physicists as well as the educated layman." Edward Russell, reviewing the book for *Library Journal* (October 15, 1975), felt that the author did not address a central problem—"the Eastern orientation to the inner object, as opposed to the materialistic outer-orientated attitude of Western physics"—but believed that his "synopsis of Eastern thought is noteworthy, and his presentation of modern physics for the layman among the clearest and the most thorough I have seen."

The focus of Capra's next book, *The Turning Point*, was on a holistic approach to the world, our lives, and institutions, a world view that Capra saw as an extension of quantum physics and that comprised, according to David Kolb in *Commonweal* (June 18, 1992), "ideas . . . concerned with bodily, psychic, and economic health." Kolb went on to remark: "Capra contends that the new world is already coalescing. There is danger of political naivete here. . . . It remains to be seen whether the new view and culture will come together and whether they will resist being captured and turned into yet one more 'lifestyle' option for the consumer society." Most reviewers, however, praised Capra's book; *Library Journal* (March 1, 1982) stated: "This work will be welcomed by Capra's followers in undergraduate and larger general collections." The *Choice* (October 1982) review read: "This volume is another classic; it provides enlightenment in these very dark days."

Capra next coauthored a book with Charlene Spretnak, entitled *Green Politics* (1984). That work was about the development and guiding principles of the Greens, a grassroots political party that originated in West Germany in the late 1970s. The book shed light on the organization's beliefs and on the struggle between its fundamentalist Marxist wing and its more pragmatic, ecological wing. The Greens gained their greatest prominence for their opposition to the stationing of rockets in West Germany. The book received mixed reviews. After *Green Politics*, Capra went on to coauthor two more books: *Belonging to the Universe* (1991), written with Brother David Steindl-Rast, investigates the resemblances between new paradigm thinking in science and religion, and *EcoManagement* (1993), written with Ernest Callenbach and colleagues from the Elmwood Institute, which supported ecologically conscious management in business. (Capra also coedited a book with Gunter Pauli—*Steering Business Toward Sustainability* (1995), a collection of essays written by businessmen, economists, ecologists, and other thinkers.)

Capra's book *Uncommon Wisdom* is a collection of conversations between the author and various thinkers, including Werner Heisenberg, R. D. Laing, Alan Watts, Margaret Lock, and Indira Gandhi, aimed at tracing the evolution of Capra's ideas. The reviews of the book ranged widely. On the one hand George Johnson, writing for the *New York Times Book Review* (March 20, 1988), believed that this autobiographical book proves that Capra "was never so much a scientist as a devotee of that grab bag of counterculture magic that has come to be called New Age philosophy. . . . It is not clear who would want to read this book. . . . Mr. Capra's ideas are more cogently expressed in *The Tao of Physics*." On the other hand, R. M. Baird in *Choice* (June 1988) wrote: "In readable prose, Capra brings into focus an emerging cultural paradigm comparable at least to that of the Age of Enlightenment."

With *The Web of Life* Capra attempted to develop further the outline presented in *The Turning Point*, in which he had charted a change from a mechanistic to an ecological worldview. With this latest volume, the author announced a comprehensive theory of living systems, pertinent to everything from individual cells to human beings. The reviews for this book were overwhelmingly positive, even though many critics wondered about the political equations into which such a philosophy might emerge and about how such a theory might gain complete consensus. *Publishers Weekly* (August 12, 1996) found the book to be "a rewarding synthesis that will challenge serious readers." The *Library Journal* (October 15, 1996) critic wrote, "This book is breathtakingly ambitious and certain to generate response. Public and academic libraries will need it."

Fritjof Capra's work has been featured in major American, European, and Asian newspapers and magazines, and he has been the focus of more than 50 interviews and documentaries all over the world. He also co-wrote the screenplay for *Mindwalk*, a 1991 film starring Liv Ullman, Sam Waterston, and John Heard. The film was based on his best-selling *The Turning Point* and was directed by his brother, Bernt Capra. Since leaving the University of California in 1988, he has become the cofounder and director of the Center for Ecoliteracy, based in Berkeley, California, where he lives with his wife and daughter. —C.M.

SUGGESTED READING: *Choice* p 541 June 1976, p305 Oct. 1982, p1541 June 1988; *Commonweal* p378 June 18, 1982; *Library Journal* p1933 Oct. 15, 1975, p557 Mar. 1, 1982, p1231 June 15, 1984, p87 Oct. 15, 1996; *Nation* p775 June 23, 1984; *New Statesman & Society* p29 Feb. 1, 1985; *Newsweek* July 23, 1979; *New York Times Book Review* p27 Mar. 20, 1988; *Publishers Weekly* p69 Aug. 12, 1996; *ReVISION* Spring 1981; *Washington Post* N p47 Nov. 15, 1991; *Contemporary Authors* vol. 107, 1983

SELECTED WORKS: *The Tao of Physics*, 1976; *The Turning Point*, 1982; *Green Politics* (with C. Spretnak), 1984, *Uncommon Wisdom*, 1988; *Belonging to the Universe* (with D. Steindl-Rast), 1991; *EcoManagement* (with E. Callenbach et al), 1993; *The Web of Life*, 1996; As editor—*Steering Business Toward Sustainability* (with G. Pauli), 1995

Card, Orson Scott

Aug. 24, 1951– Novelist; short-story writer

Orson Scott Card, a prolific author who has mastered several genres, is best known as a writer of science-fiction and speculative books—and as the only author to have won science fiction's top awards in two consecutive years, for *Ender's Game* (the 1985 Nebula and the 1986 Hugo) and for *Speaker for the Dead* (the 1986 Nebula and the 1987 Hugo). Several of his novels have been designed to be part of ongoing series, such as "The Tales of Alvin Maker," an imaginative-history epic, set in a version of 19th-century America in which folk magic plays a significant part, and "The Homecoming Saga." Card, who has brought his Mormon sensibility to his speculative fiction as well as to historical dramas, video plays, and advice books, was described as a "literary maverick" by Steven Argyle, writing for *Main Street Journal* (December 1988). Argyle called Card "one of those rare individuals that has the nerve to love what he does and to do what he loves."

Orson Scott Card was born in Richland, Washington, on August 24, 1951. His family was Mormon, a fact that continues to have a strong impact on his writing. "The *Book of Mormon* was probably the first adult book I read all the way through," he told Stephen Argyle. "Much of my writing still reflects the cadence of the language in the scriptures. A lot of my sentences begin with conjunctions the way Joseph Smith's sentences did." It was when his sister introduced him (he was 10) to William L. Shirer's *The Rise and Fall of the Third Reich* that Card had his first profound experience with the power of evil. "I was deeply disturbed by the notion that men could create rational motivations for doing such things," he told Argyle. Card's two-year stint as a Mormon missionary took him to Brazil in 1971, allusions to which can be found in *Speaker for the Dead*. During his college years at Brigham Young University, from which he graduated in 1975 with a major in theater studies, Card adapted many stories for the stage and began writing original play scripts. While still a student, he founded his own repertory theater company, but it was a financial failure despite his efforts to subsidize it through his "pathetic" salary as copy editor of Brigham Young University Press. As he told *Publishers Weekly* (November 30, 1990), "[By] the spring of 1975, I knew that there was no hope of paying off my debts through my salary, so I made a serious effort to write fiction as a career." He left his copy-editing job in 1976 and served for two years as assistant editor of the *Ensign*, a magazine of the Church of Jesus Christ Latter-Day Saints. Card also wrote dramatizations of scripture and church history for Living Scriptures Inc. in Ogden, Utah, while earning his master's degree in English at the University of Utah in 1981.

Immediately after his theatrical debacle, Card had started to send science-fiction stories to *Analog* magazine, which, after some revision, published his "Ender's Game," the story that won him the Campbell Award for best new science-fiction writer. (The story was later expanded to a novel by the same name, published in 1985 by Tor.) Soon, Card's stories began appearing with regularity in major science-fiction journals and in books put out by Dell, Signature, Berkley, and other publishers of that genre. In a 1998 on-line interview with *barnesandnoble.com*, Card called the publication of *Ender's Game* "the foundation of my career—before it, I lived from advance to advance; after it, all my books earned out their advances and I started getting royalties for the first time." Interested in speculative fiction, from 1979 to 1986 he wrote a column for *Science Fiction Review* entitled "You Got No Friends in This World." From 1987 to 1993 he wrote the "Book to Look For" column for *Fantasy and Science Fiction*. In 1983 he moved to North Carolina to became senior editor with *Compute!* Publications, but he left after nine months.

Card's Mormonism, a religious tradition that offers its own interpretation of American history, parallels themes he explores in his speculative fiction. In an interview with Harold Mittelmark for *Inside Books* (January 1989), Card said, "The fantasy that I like best is the fantasy that creates fully developed communities with real characters in them, and the science fiction I like best does that, and, in fact, the mainstream fiction I like best does that." Likewise, his religious worldview and his moral viewpoints are linked, a phenomenon that might be deemed unusual for a science-fiction writer, except perhaps by revisionist critics who see sci-fi elements in the Old Testament Books of Ezekiel and Daniel and the New Testament Book of Revelation. Indeed, Card's official Web site (*Hatrack River*) includes a statement of beliefs, something rarely found in such an environment. The Cardian credo opens with these words: "I believe that human beings exist on earth in order to achieve the purposes of a benevolent God, who cares what we do and wants us to become the best and happiest people our abilities and desires allow us to be." He further affirms his desire to help create a "merciful society" where "no one, regardless of merit, is undeserving of the basic necessities of life" and a "just society" where "no one should have the power to withhold from others those same necessities."

Some of these aspirations form important subtexts to Card's fiction, notably in his series "The Tales of Alvin Maker," which offers an alternative reading of American history organized around less materialistic, exploitative principles. Card describes the Maker books as his "American fantasy" series, which, from its inception in 1987, has grown to include five volumes: *Seventh Son* (1987); *Red Prophet* (1988), *Prentice* (1989); *Alvin Journeyman* (1995), and *Heartfire* (1998). Although not technically part of this series, a later book, *Pastwatch: The Redemption of Christopher*

Columbus (1996), advances a similar "alternative-history" view of the United States by imaging a truly "New World" in which indigenous Maya and Taino cultures have survived the coming of Columbus.

The Alvin Maker books have been welcomed by both critics and readers. Reviewing the state of science-fiction and fantasy books, Martin Morse Wooster, writing in the *Washington Post* (September 24, 1995), declared that Card's "strong story-telling ability" contributed to this "important fantasy series," which Wooster capsulized as follows: "The Alvin Maker series is set in an 'America' of 1815. Spells and hexes are everywhere, as natural a part of life as the wind and the rain. But though many Americans in Card's world possess magical powers, Alvin Smith, seventh son of a seventh son, is a Maker, able to produce work that transcends magical tinkering." In one volume, Alvin protects an African-American child from slave traders; in another, his brother Calvin journeys to Europe to learn wisdom from the likes of Napoleon and Balzac.

"Everything in my life shows up in my fiction, one way or another," Card told an on-line audience for *barnesandnoble.com* (March 20, 1998). Card has used the World Wide Web to his advantage, having created one of the most comprehensive Web sites of any living author. But as for style, "I have no patience with writers who even think about it," he said. "A narrative voice matters; a writer's style matters only insofar as it interferes with his ability to communicate with his audience. . . . My style consists of annoying habits, which I get rid of or control the best I can. So does every writer's style. After we have eliminated all the annoying habits we are conscious of, only the unconscious ones remain; that is our style." He also discussed the publishing world's unwillingness to publish mainstream "out-of-genre" work. "Even at that," he said rather ruefully, "they won't touch anything without some supernatural element. . . . I can't afford to write what won't get published. So . . . I tell ghost stories. I tell stories I care about and believe in—but some stories I would love to tell I can't afford to write and publish."

Card has also served as an editor of two highly acclaimed science-fiction anthologies, both published by Tor: *Future on Fire* (1991) and *Future on Ice* (1998). In the latter volume, Card included 18 stories, all early works from writers who had established themselves as major sci-fi authors by the 1990s. They were selected because, as he wrote, "all have the power to change the soul of the open-minded reader." *Future on Ice* was acclaimed by a reviewer for *Publishers Weekly* (September 28, 1998), who wrote that "Card acquits himself as well as the other authors with one of his own stories, plus a sobering and intelligent opening essay on the religious roots and impact of the genre." Although Card reported on his official Web site that he had compiled a table of contents for a collection

of humorous or satirical science fiction called *Future on Hold*, he acknowledges that that book is "unlikely to be published." When asked in an on-line interview (March 20, 1998) to name the favorite among his books, he replied "the one I'm writing right now"—in this case, a novel of the waking of Sleeping Beauty in 1990 in western Ukraine, called *Enchantment*, published in April 1999. He admitted in the same interview, "I enjoy writing the Alvin books more than anything, though *Homebody* and *Treasure Box* were lots of fun, too."

This versatile author has also continued to write books and plays targeted especially for a Mormon audience. His 1998 musical *Barefoot to Zion* was written, as he put it, "at the behest of the Mormon Church." With his brother Arlen Card as composer, Card built upon a story, initially developed by Kevin and Kahliel Kelly, that described the vicissitudes of pioneering Mormons during the 19th century. *Barefoot to Zion* played to sell-out crowds in Utah that summer. The summer of 1998 was also marked by the publication of *Heartfire*, another volume in his popular "Tales of Alvin Maker" series.

In 1977 Orson Scott Card married Kristine Allen. Their five children, Geoffrey, Emily, Charles, Zina Margaret, and Erin Louisa, have been named in honor of five authors: Chaucer, Dickinson, Dickens, Mitchell, and Alcott, respectively.
—E. M.

SUGGESTED READING: *barnesandnoble.com* (on-line) March 20, 1998; *Inside Books* Jan. 1989; *Main Street Journal* December 1988; *Publishers Weekly* Nov. 30, 1990, p77+ Sep. 28, 1998; *Washington Post Book World* X p8 Sep. 29, 1991, with photo, X p8 Mar. 29, 1992, X p14 Sep. 25, 1994, X p8 Sep. 24, 1995, with photo; *Who's Who in America, 1998*

SELECTED WORKS: Fiction—*Capitol*, 1978; *Hot Sleep*, 1978; *Capitol*, 1978; *A Planet Called Treason*, 1979 (revised as *Treason*, 1988); *Songmaster*, 1979, 1987; *Unaccompanied Sonata and Other Stories*, 1980; *Hart's Hope*, 1983, 1988; *The Worthing Chronicle*, 1983; *Woman of Destiny*, 1984 (published as *Saints*, 1988); *Ender's Game*, 1985; *Speaker for the Dead*, 1986; *Seventh Son* (vol. 1 in Tales of Alvin Maker series), 1987; *Wyrms*, 1987; *Red Prophet* (vol. 2 in "Tales of Alvin Maker" series), 1988; *Treason*, 1988 (rev. ed. of *A Planet Called Treason*); *Prentice* (vol. 3 in "Tales of Alvin Maker" series), 1989; *The Abyss*, 1989; *The Folk of the Fringe*, 1989; *Eye for Eye*, 1990; *Maps in a Mirror: The Short Fiction of Orson Scott Card*, 1990; *The Worthing Saga*, 1990; *Xenocide*, 1991; *The Memory of Earth* (vol. 1 of "Homecoming" series), 1992; *Lost Boys*, 1992; *The Call of Earth* (vol. 2 of "Homecoming" series), 1992; *The Ships of Earth* (vol. 3 of "Homecoming" series), 1994; (with K. H. Kidd) *Lovelock* (vol. 1 in "Mayflower" series), 1994; *Earthfall* (vol. 4 in

"Homecoming" series, 1995; *Earthborn* (vol. 5 in "Homecoming" series), 1995; *Alvin Journeyman* (vol. 4 in "Tales of Alvin Maker" series), 1995; *Pastwatch: The Redemption of Christopher Columbus*, 1996; *Children of the Mind*, 1996; *Treasure Box*, 1996; *Stone Tables*, 1997; *Homebody*, 1998; *Heartfire* (vol. 5 in "Tales of Alvin Maker" series), 1998; *Enchantment*, 1999; Humor—*Saintspeak*, 1982; Nonfiction—*Listen, Mom and Dad*, 1978; *Ainge*, 1982; *Character and Viewpoint*, 1988; *How to Write Science Fiction and Fantasy*, 1990; *A Storyteller in Zion*, 1993; Drama—*The Apostate*, 1970; *In Flight*, 1970; *Across Five Summers*, 1971; *Of Gideon*, 1971; *Stone Tables*, 1973; *A Christmas Carol*, 1974 (revised as *A Dixie Christmas Carol*), 1989;

Father, Mother, Mother, and Mom, 1974; *Liberty Jail*, 1975; *Fresh Courage Take*, 1978; *Elders and Sisters*, 1979; *Wings*, 1982; *Barefoot to Zion*, 1997; Animated Video plays—*Nephi and the Brass Plates*, 1987; *The Nativity*, 1987; *He Is Risen*, 1988; *Journey to the Promised Land*, 1988; *The Prodigal Son*, 1988; *The Good Samaritan*, 1988; *The Joseph Smith Story*, 1988; *Noah and Abinadi*, 1988; Audio plays—*LDS Church History*, 1978-80; *New Testament*, 1980-81; *American History*, 1981-83; *Great Mormon Women*, 1983-84; *Old Testament*, 1984-87; As editor—*Dragons of Light*, 1980, 1988; *Dragons of Darkness*, 1981, 1988; *Future on Fire*, 1991; *Turning Hearts: Stories of Family Life*, 1994; *Future on Ice*, 1998

Carey, Jacqueline

1955(?)– Novelist; short-story writer

Jacqueline Carey is known for her wry wit and her tales of middle-class urban life. Her first collection of short stories, *Good Gossip* (1992), focuses on a group of friends in New York City who are about to enter a more responsible era of their lives but still cling to their gossipy ways and their manic existence. The author's next effort, a novel titled *The Other Family* (1996), is the coming-of-age tale of a 14-year-old girl and her relationships with her bohemian mother and middle-class aunt. Carey's most recent work of fiction, *Wedding Pictures* (1997), a collaborative effort with the illustrator Kathy Osborn, is written completely in dialogue and follows the various mishaps of a young upper-middle-class couple as they prepare for marriage.

Jacqueline Carey was born in about 1955. In 1985, while living three miles up the side of a mountain in Bigfork, Montana, she received a phone call from a friend in New York, which brought back memories of the time Carey had spent in that city. When not staying with friends or in illegal sublets, she had lived in a building on East 6th Street which was so dilapidated that former president Jimmy Carter and his Habitat for Humanity group came one day to repair it. In New York, Carey had worked at a variety of odd jobs: at a law firm as a paralegal, at the *New Yorker* as a receptionist, and at the Rosedale Fish Market. The phone call from New York—to which she returned in the late 1980s—inspired her to write the first of her stories for *Good Gossip*.

A collection of 11 interlocking tales, *Good Gossip* is narrated by Rosemary, a character enthralled by stories of the strange lives of her 30-ish friends. Rosemary describes the activities of a group of New York yuppies, among them Susannah, the girl who came to New York to become an actress and who is now marrying rich, boring Harry Tierney; Dee Kilmartin, who throws wild parties and has had an affair with a 17-year-old boy; and Eileen Filley, a dramatist who takes a job in a card store as her play goes up on Broadway. A *Kirkus Reviews* critic (November 15, 1991) wrote that the characters are filled with "urban fears—including dreams of being found dead in one's apartment . . . and fantasies of escape via professional success, marriage and/or children, or a permanent apartment—[which] distract from dreaded moments of calm reflection." The reviewer went on to call the work "an accurate chronicle, wittily rendered." Stephen McCauley, in the *New York Times Book Review* (March 8, 1992), wrote that the theme of the stories is the friends' inability to stop talking about one another and settle down. He also noted that what makes the stories "so powerfully charming is Ms. Carey's unsentimental affection for her characters and her lively, shrewd observations on numerous apsects of contemporary life. . . . Ms. Carey has a light, exacting touch in her descriptions of people. . . . Gossip, at its best, is a pleasure as irresistible as air-conditioning. Like all good gossip, Jacqueline Carey's stories leave you feeling energized and a bit unsatisfied, if only because you're dying to hear more."

Carey's second book was the novel *The Other Family*, published in 1996. It begins in 1968 and is narrated by Joan Toolan, a 14-year-old hippie-in-training and fledgling political activist who, with her younger brother Hugh, is visiting the mother who abandoned them two years earlier for a more bohemian lifestyle in New York's Greenwich Village. Joan's mother—who remains nameless throughout the novel—left her eccentric pot-smoking musician husband in order to "find" herself, ultimately becoming a hippie with all the trappings of dress and drug use—including a lecherous boyfriend who attempts to seduce Joan in the name of "free love." Joan's mother seems more involved in the life of her sister Iris, who lives across the river in Brooklyn, than in her own.

Iris is married to the successful but overbearing psychiatrist Charles Eberlander. They seem to be an American ideal: They have two well-bred, seemingly perfect daughters, Budge and Polly; a townhouse in Brooklyn Heights; and a summer home in Cold Springs. However, the family has secrets that fascinate young Joan, who weighs her parents' lives against those of the aunt she admires and the uncle she despises. Reviewing *The Other Family* for the *New York Times Book Review* (September 8, 1996), the novelist Karen Karbo remarked that "What makes this novel so wise and so accurate is Ms. Carey's understanding that the Eberlanders' marriage, and that of Joan's parents, would have faltered in any era: the Eberlanders' because Charles fell in love with a younger, less remote version of Iris, and Joan's mother because of her basic inability to be the center of her own life, much less the lives of her children. It wasn't the fault of the Black Panthers, Joan Baez or *Jesus Christ Superstar*. As much as baby boomers would like to believe that the time they lived through changed society—even the way human beings are hard-wired—Ms. Carey, an observer and writer of depth and promise, knows better." A *Publishers Weekly* (July 8, 1996) reviewer wrote that "Carey's wry, taut prose is seamless, her characterization is emphatic and sharp, and her evocation of the new personal freedoms wrought by the '60s—and their resulting broken bonds—is subtle and memorable." Merle Rubin of the *Christian Science Monitor* (September 9, 1996) called the book "compelling . . . bracingly satiric, often funny, yet ultimately rather tragic."

Carey's next creative outing, *Wedding Pictures* (1997), was a collaboration with the illustrator Kathy Osborn, who is known for her work in the *New Yorker*. Though billed as a novel, the book features many full page illustrations and a text written solely in dialogue, similar to a play's script. The book is about the wedding of Kip and Bonnie and the chaotic months of preparation that lead up to it. Many problems surface almost immediately: Kip lives in New York, and Bonnie in Washington, D.C.; they get engaged over the phone but soon realize that one will have to give up his or her job in order to be with the other. An argument ensues, and both Kip and Bonnie quit their jobs the day after the fight. Now out of work, the couple begins to question the validity of the institution of marriage when they discover that Kip's brother George, who has been married four times, is having an affair with Fay, one of Bonnie's bridesmaids. The book received mixed reviews. A reviewer for *Publishers Weekly* (May 5, 1997) called it "Part grown-up comic book, part wry nuptial guide, . . . not a gimmick item, however, but a solid piece of work from two young artists who enhance their already fine reputations . . . with a playful collaboration that perfectly captures how simultaneously vexing and beguiling the months leading up to big events can be." In the *New York Times* (August 10, 1997), Sarah Ferguson wrote that "Carey's witty story sprints along with plenty of unexpected twists and turns, a deftly traced map of preconjugal pitfalls." The reviewer for *Kirkus Reviews* (May 1, 1997), however, warned that "Those expecting a *Serial*-style flash of humor will be disappointed by this rather mundane tale of reluctant newlyweds surrounded by their adulterous siblings, lecherous friends, and insufferable parents. Not engaging enough to stage as a play, these snippets of upper-middle-class banter might make a good half hour on TV."

Carey lives in Montana with her husband, the essayist Ian Frazier, and their children.
—C.M.

SUGGESTED READING: *Christian Science Monitor* p14 Sep. 9, 1996; *Kirkus Reviews* Nov. 15, 1991, p617 May 1, 1997; *Library Journal* p154 July 1996; *New York Times Book Review* p10 Mar. 8, 1992, p8 Sep. 8, 1996, p16 Aug. 10, 1997; *Publishers Weekly* p74 July 8, 1996, p196 May 5, 1997

SELECTED WORKS: *Good Gossip*, 1992; *The Other Family*, 1996; *Wedding Pictures* (with Kathy Osborn), 1997

Carroll, Jim

Aug. 1, 1951– Poet; singer; lyricist

As a poet and rock lyricist, Jim Carroll has translated New York City's rhythms and nuances into various mediums and has attracted comparison to the poetic songwriters Lou Reed and Bob Dylan as well as to the French symbolist poet Arthur Rimbaud. Carroll's oeuvre, which includes prose and spoken-word recordings, has inspired several generations of young artists. At the age of 12, when he and his friends spent most of their time playing basketball and wandering the streets, Carroll began chronicling his experiences in a journal that was published in 1978 as *The Basketball Diaries*. Jack Kerouac, who read some of the diary excerpts in the late 1960s, described Carroll's vigorous language as "better prose than 89 percent of the novelists working today" were capable of producing. In 1995 *The Basketball Diaries* was made into a movie starring Leonardo DiCaprio. In his attempts to mirror New York City's harsh social conditions while revealing his own survivalist and escapist lifestyle, Carroll has suffused his "punk prose" and rock lyrics with images of death, leading Roy Trakin to postulate in the *New York Daily News* (November 23, 1980) that the poet's debut album, *Catholic Boy*, "could do for dying young what the Beach Boys did for surfing."

James Dennis ("from Dionysus," he has explained) Carroll was born on August 1, 1951, in New York City, the son of Thomas Joseph Carroll,

Tamela Glenn/Courtesy of Penguin Books

Jim Carroll

a bartender and World War II veteran, and Agnes (Coyle) Carroll. He and his older brother, Thomas Joseph Carroll, Jr., grew up in an Irish-Catholic household, first in the New York City borough of Manhattan on the East Side, then in the borough's northern section of Inwood, where Carroll's talent as a basketball player—and precocity as a writer—became apparent to his basketball coach, who arranged his admission to Trinity High School on an academic/athletic scholarship. While attending Trinity, an affluent prep school on the Upper West Side, Carroll honed his writing skills as the school newspaper's sports editor and began attending poetry readings at St. Mark's Church in the East Village area of Manhattan, where, at the age of 15, he first became acquainted with the works of such Beat writers as Allen Ginsberg, Frank O'Hara, and Jack Kerouac.

In 1967, at the age of 16, Carroll published his first book of poetry, a limited edition, 17-page collection entitled *Organic Trains*, which prompted the poet Ted Berrigan to declare him "the first truly new American poet" in a 1969 article for *Culture Hero*. With Berrigan's help, Carroll gained entrée into the circle of poets who were involved with what had become known as the St. Mark's Project, including those he had previously known only by their work, such as Ginsberg, Anne Waldman, and John Ashbery. Meanwhile, excerpts of his prose had begun appearing in various small publications, including *Adventures in Poetry*, *Little Caesar*, and *Ant's Forefoot*. The source of these pieces was a journal that Carroll had begun conscientiously keeping at the age of 12 and that would eventually be edited and published in toto as *The Basketball Diaries* (1978). In his journals, Carroll's

profound transformation from disaffected child into prematurely world-weary, heroin-addicted adolescent is traced in the uncompromising (although sometimes fictionally enhanced) detail that characterizes his mature art. Divided into broad sections, beginning with "Fall 63" and ending with "Summer 66," the journals, which quickly gained the author an underground following, would later be referred to by Steve Simels in *Stereo Review* (February 1981) as a "scary, mordantly funny odyssey along the dark underbelly of the 60s."

The first diary entry begins, "Today was my first Biddy League game and my first day in any organized basketball league. I'm enthused about life due to this exciting event." The last passage ends with the words, "I got to go in and puke. I just want to be pure." In an entry dated "Winter 64," he described his first encounter with heroin: "It was about two months back. The funny part is that I thought heroin was the NON-addictive stuff and marijuana was addictive. I only found out later what a dumb ass move it was. Funny, I can remember what vows I'd made never to touch any of that stuff when I was five or six. Now with all my friends doing it, all kinds of vows drop out from under me every day." Recalling that period of his life in an interview with Alex Williams for *New York* (April 24, 1995), Carroll mused, "I think the main reason I started using heroin was that everyone else was always going out drinking, and I hated drinking." Remarkably, Carroll was able to maintain his dual identity as street tough and standout athlete for at least a portion of high school, earning All-City honors in basketball.

By 1970, when a selection of entries from what would become *The Basketball Diaries* appeared in George Plimpton's *Paris Review*, Carroll had become a celebrity in the underground New York literary scene. The excerpts earned him a Random House Young Writer's Award in 1970. After graduating from Trinity High School, Carroll briefly attended Wagner College in Staten Island "for a year, as far as the draft was concerned," he told Williams, but actually for only a few weeks. He then went to Columbia University for an even shorter period and dropped out to continue writing. He was soon hired as an assistant to New York artist Larry Rivers, for whom he stretched canvases and sharpened pencils. Occasionally, he even baby-sat the artist's children, even though he was still shooting heroin. "I was only getting off three or four times a day . . . ," he told Chet Flippo in an interview for *New York* (January 26, 1981), "just to write and to nod. At night, I'd go out and hustle, make some money." ("Nodding" refers to the dreamlike state achieved through the use of heroin.) He became further immersed in the city's art scene through Andy Warhol's Factory, a loose-knit gathering of artists, writers, and onlookers that had collected around Warhol's Union Square warehouse loft. In an article for the *Atlanta Journal* (March 13, 1981), Scott Cain indicated that Carroll even appeared in two Warhol-directed movies, though there is no other record of this.

In 1973 Carroll published *Living at the Movies*, his first full-length book of poetry, to critical acclaim. Five of the book's poems had previously been published in 1970 as *4 Ups and 1 Down*, a limited-edition (300 copies), eight-page pamphlet. In these poems, the writer's language began to move beyond the street slang that permeated his journal entries into a more structured, deliberate style. In the book's title poem, dedicated to Ted Berrigan, Carroll wrote: "So months of cool flowers close in these arms: / decay with their green obscenity. denial of everything / in an instant! / (how strange to be gone) (to be sure) / like Rene Magritte devouring an apple / (or two) / that's my language, divisions of words I know: / 'love:sky.'" "Carroll fully understands the nature of poetry because he perceives and follows the nature of his own life," Gerald Malanga wrote in his review of *Living at the Movies* for *Poetry* (December 1974). "He is original without being unique," Malanga continued. "His technique, however, is in advance of his maturity. At times he is capable of spoiling a good poem by a precious or very sentimental line or phrase."

A persistent myth associated with Jim Carroll is that *Living at the Movies* was nominated for a Pulitzer Prize. Chet Flippo, who recounted to Carroll that his own contact with the Pulitzer Prize committee revealed that no such nomination had been made, reported that Carroll responded that he had been informed that the book's publisher had intended to enter the book for competition. According to Flippo, nothing came of this. What was not a myth, however, was Carroll's escalating addiction to heroin. Like his artistic contemporaries Lou Reed and Iggy Pop, Carroll had allowed his life to become completely dominated by the drug. "I knew I was gonna kill myself if I stayed in New York," he told Flippo. In an interview with Bob Pfeiffer for the *Washington Post* (September 13, 1987), Carroll explained, "I was a total freak for being pulled in every different direction, wanting to take in every scene, . . . and I had to get rid of that ludicrous, vacuous obsession; I had to break away from that as much as being around drugs, because that's a drug too."

In an effort to simplify his life, Carroll left New York in 1973 for San Francisco. Shortly thereafter he made his way up the coast to the art colony of Bolinas, where a number of St. Mark's Project veterans had previously moved, and enrolled at a Marin County methadone clinic. Although he told Flippo that he had "kicked junk cold 15 times," he found it infinitely harder to withdraw from methadone, saying that the symptoms of quitting heroin last about eight days whereas methadone withdrawal leads to a "month of physical torment, at the very least." "You can't get any sleep to escape it," he told Flippo. "I hate even thinking about it. But at any rate, I came out of it. And then I just became a recluse," he added, taking long walks and getting into a writer's routine of work and solitude. "In California," he told Bob Pfeiffer, "I learned how to be myself, and I lost completely that need to make the scene."

In Bolinas Carroll met Rosemary Klemfuss, whom he married in 1978 and who around the same time introduced him to the Bay Area nightclubs, which showcased a number of rock groups from New York City's burgeoning punk/new wave movement, including Television, Blondie, and Talking Heads. Carroll also reconnected with the New York poet and songwriter Patti Smith, whom he had dated and who had been collaborating in poetry readings with guitarist Lenny Kaye. During a 1978 performance in San Diego as an opening act for Smith, in which her band played behind him, Carroll "talked-sang" his latest poetry/lyrics and immediately became fixed upon his career's new direction. "When I'd do readings, people would say, 'Mick Jagger reading poetry—you should do rock'n'roll,'" he recalled to Chet Flippo, citing Henry Miller as an additional influence on his thinking at the time. "Henry Miller's study of Rimbaud, which is really a study of Henry Miller, was the big factor for me going into rock—that was *it*. That whole thing about getting a heart quality out of work rather than just the intellectual quality."

Carroll's entry into rock music coincided with the 1980 mass-market publication of *The Basketball Diaries*, which had been released by a smaller publisher in 1978. The book's sudden availability garnered mainstream critical acclaim for Carroll and made the poet an instant favorite on college campuses throughout the country. In his evaluation for the *American Book Review* (February 1980), Jamie James wrote that the book "is a literary miracle; a description of the formation of an artistic sensibility written by the artist, not in retrospect, but in the process. . . . Despite the adolescent egoism and occasional tendency towards smart-aleckiness, the theme that reverberates through the whole, like the recurring melody of a jazz improv, is the struggle of a boy to hold on to his sense of himself." The book sold about 500,000 copies, in the estimation of its author, and Alex Williams asserted in his *New York* profile of Carroll that a study conducted by the publisher of *The Basketball Diaries* indicated that there were six readers of the book for each purchaser.

Later that year, after being signed to Rolling Stone Records by Mick Jagger, the Jim Carroll Band released *Catholic Boy*, produced by Earl McGrath and featuring, in addition to lyricist Carroll on vocals, Brian Linsley and Terrell Winn on guitar, Steve Linsley on bass, and Wayne Woods on drums. *Catholic Boy* yielded a nationwide college radio hit with the song "People Who Died," a nihilistic rock anthem with snarled, spoken lyrics against a chorus repeating the refrain "Those are people who died, died": "Teddy, sniffing glue, he was 12 years old. / He fell from the roof on East Two-Nine. / Cathy was 11 when she pulled the plug / On 26 reds and a bottle of wine. / Bobby got leukemia, 14 years old. / He looked like 65 when he died. / He was a friend of mine." "People have been puttin' down the song for glorifyin' death," Carroll told Matt Damsker in an interview for the

Philadelphia *Evening Bulletin* (December 17, 1980), "but it really celebrates lives. It's about people who got cut off without fulfillin' their potential." In a conversation with Barbara Graustark of *Newsweek* (September 8, 1980), Carroll clarified his intentions: "I don't want to glorify junk. Susan Sontag once told me that a junkie has a unique chance to rise up and start life over. But I want kids to know it's not hip to indulge yourself at the bottom unless you're planning on one helluva resurrection." Steve Simels called *Catholic Boy* "an extremely impressive debut album, flawed and pretentious at times, but also genuinely ambitious, gripping, and believable." Graustark remarked that although Carroll "isn't much of a singer," not since Lou Reed had "a rock singer so vividly evoked the casual brutality of New York City."

The Jim Carroll Band followed *Catholic Boy* with two more albums, *Dry Dreams* (1982) and *I Write Your Name* (1984), both of which were also produced by Earl McGrath and which featured guest appearances by Lenny Kaye of Patti Smith's band, among others. Comparing *Dry Dreams* to Carroll's debut effort in a review for the *New York Times* (June 20, 1982), Robert Palmer wrote that the second album was an "improvement in several respects, . . .with some new songs that convey the sharpened perceptions and the sense of guilt and dread that are his principal subjects without sounding as pretentious as some of the more ambitious pieces on the earlier album." The notices that greeted *I Write Your Name* were generally more equivocal, with several writers commenting on Carroll's failure to develop a singing voice, an aspect of his music that was beginning to wear against the lyrical appeal of his albums. "The musical voice in which his rocklike poem-songs are presented is far less interesting . . . than his material demands," Bruce Pollock, an editor of *Guitar* magazine, wrote in the *Wilson Library Bulletin* (June 1984). "Though possibly necessary for the adequate performance of these works in concert, the typical rock scores provided for Carroll's lyrics lack the subtlety and power of his best material."

Resuming his literary efforts, Carroll next wrote *The Book of Nods* (1986), a collection of verse and prose poems. Some of the prose poems projected such diverse and hallucinatory imagery as an encounter with the painter Vincent Van Gogh ("With Van Gogh"), the death of a poet ("A Poet Dies"), and religious epiphany ("The Lakes of Sligo"), while other poems took on more personal themes, about his youth in New York City and his development as a writer in California. Noting in his review of the book for *Publishers Weekly* (April 4, 1986) that "Carroll would like to be poetry's renegade stepchild, an avant-gardist," John Mutter concluded, "This is a bad example of serious talent destroyed over the years by negligence and disregard for self-discipline." On a more positive note, Daniel L. Guillory wrote in his review for *Library Journal* (April 15, 1986) that "*The Book of Nods* is always interesting if sometimes uneven."

The next year saw, in addition to a reissue of *The Basketball Diaries*, the publication of a new batch of journals by Carroll entitled *Forced Entries: The Downtown Diaries, 1971–1973*, in which he chronicled his involvement with the Warhol Factory, his encounters with such Greenwich Village art community luminaries as Bob Dylan, Allen Ginsberg, W. H. Auden, and Terry Southern, his move to California, and his victory over heroin. "Carroll's peculiar aura of choirboy innocence transforms even the most decadent happenings into a good-natured romp," John Mutter wrote in *Publishers Weekly* (June 5, 1987), concluding that "his somewhat contrived verse works here to utterly charming effect." In his evaluation of both books for the *New York Times* (July 9, 1987), Christopher Lehmann-Haupt observed that "whether or not one believes Jim Carroll's redemption, his two diaries constitute a remarkable account of New York City's lower depths. At the very least, they should serve further to demystify the usefulness of drugs to writers."

In the late 1980s Carroll focused primarily upon writing and what had become known as the "spoken-word" movement, which refers to the stylized, emotive recitation of one's writing. A contributor to a variety of spoken-word projects, Carroll has also worked in video and film. His work has been included on the extensive Giorno Poetry Systems albums (apparently named for the poet John Giorno), which combine spoken word, straight reading, and music. The series began in 1972 with the double album *The Dial-a-Poem Poets* and culminated in 1984 with *Better an Old Demon than a New God*. The Jim Carroll Band contributed music to the soundtrack of Fritz Kiersch's *Tuff Turf* (1985), in which the poet made a brief appearance as himself. Carroll also appeared in Ron Mann's 1984 movie *Listen to the City*. He has read from his work in the 1983 Giorno Poetry Systems video *Poetry in Motion*, which also contains performances and commentary by Charles Bukowski, Amiri Baraka, and Ntozake Shange, among others. MTV's *Cutting Edge* spoken-word video series also featured readings by Carroll.

More recently, Carroll released the album *Praying Mantis* (1991), his first solo full-length spoken-word effort, which contains selections from his diaries and poetry books as well as some unpublished poems. *Fear of Dreaming: The Selected Poems of Jim Carroll* (1993), contains the complete *Living at the Movies* volume, much of *The Book of Nods*, and poems from the *Praying Mantis* album. *A World Without Gravity: The Best of the Jim Carroll Band* was released in 1993 by Rhino Records. New interest in Carroll was sparked by Scott Kalvert's cinematic adaptation of *The Basketball Diaries*, which premiered at the Sundance Festival in January 1995. Carroll's only comment on the movie, which starred Leonardo DiCaprio as the youthful Jim Carroll, was that "it moves well." He told Alex Williams, "It's hard for me to really register on it because of the personal attachment." Many critics felt that the movie did not do justice to Carroll's original text, and with a time frame unanchored to any specific era, left his prose dangling. Joe Brown from the *Washington Post* wrote that Kalvert's use of the voice-over in the film "betrays Carroll's potent writing; the excerpts sound like self-conscious, sub-Beat babble." Edward Guthmann of the *San Francisco Chronicle* noted somberly that *Diaries* "had the potential to be a great film," but that the director "treats the material with a literalness that flattens it and saps its wild, insolent poetry. Kalvert never finds a visual style, which would have been one way of translating Carroll's point of view into visual terms . . ." Guthmann went on to criticize that "instead of finding a cinematic equivalent for the tough, tortured voice that Carroll brought to his book, Kalvert arranges a series of anecdotal scenes . . . in the end, *Basketball Diaries* is an earnest, botched effort to do justice to Carroll's book."

Looking much the same as he did in his youth, according to interviewers, the six-foot two-inch former basketball star has thin red hair almost as pale as his smooth complexion. Some observers have compared his androgynous appearance to that of David Bowie. Amicably divorced from Rosemary Klemfuss, who remains his friend and lawyer, Jim Carroll has lived in the Inwood section of New York City for the past decade. He still performs with Lenny Kaye and delivers readings and spoken-word performances on college campuses. In the summers he often teaches at the Naropa Institute, the Buddhist university in Colorado where Allen Ginsberg helped found the Jack Kerouac School of Disembodied Poetics. Carroll is currently working on two novels, one about the spiritual crisis of a young painter who abandons art and the other about a Vatican investigation of a miracle. "These are straight, linear novels in the third person," Carroll explained to Williams. "My editor was shocked. He was like, 'Jim! These are money books.' But if I don't get to work on these things, boy, I am betraying a gift; I mean, that's what I would define as a sin." Rising daily at 4:30 a.m. to write, he has kicked a television habit along with his addiction to drugs, although he told Williams that he doesn't "go for that complete abstinence thing" and that he indulges in an occasional margarita.

In 1998 Carroll released an album of songs and spoken-word pieces, *Pools of Mercury*, and published a book of new poetry, *Void of Course.*—D.B.

SUGGESTED READING: *American Book Review* Feb. 1980; *Atlanta Journal* Mar. 13, 1981; *Bulletin of Bibliography* p81+ June 1990; *Evening Bulletin* Dec. 17, 1980; *Library Journal* Apr. 15, 1986; *Newsweek* p80 Sep. 8, 1980, with photo; *New York* p32+ Jan. 26, 1981, with photos, p64+ Apr. 24, 1995, with photos; *New York Daily News* Nov. 23, 1980; *New York Times* June 20, 1982, July 9, 1987; *Publisher's Weekly* Apr. 4, 1986, June 15, 1987; *San Francisco Chronicle* Apr. 21, 1995; *Stereo Review* Feb. 1981; *Washington Post* G p1+ Sep. 13, 1987, with photos, Apr. 21, 1995; *Wilson Library Bulletin* June 1984; *Contemporary Authors New Revision Series* vol 42 1994; *Contemporary Literary Criticism* vol 35 1985

SELECTED WORKS: Poetry—*Organic Trains*, 1967; *4 Ups and 1 Down*, 1970; *Living at the Movies*, 1973; *The Book of Nods*, 1986; *Fear of Dreaming: The Selected Poems of Jim Carroll*, 1993; *Void of Course*, 1998; Nonfiction—*The Basketball Diaries*, 1978; *Forced Entries: The Downtown Diaries, 1971-1973*, 1987; Musical recordings—*Catholic Boy* (with the Jim Carroll Band), 1980; *Dry Dreams* (with the Jim Carroll Band), 1982; *I Write Your Name* (with the Jim Carroll Band), 1984; *A World Without Gravity: The Best of the Jim Carroll Band*, 1993; *Pools of Mercury*, 1998; Spoken-word albums—*The Dial-a-Poem Poets, Giorno Poetry Systems*, 1972; *Disconnected, Giorno Poetry Systems*, 1974; *Life Is a Killer, Giorno Poetry Systems*, 1982; *You're a Hook: The 15 Year Anniversary of Dial-a-Poem, Giorno Poetry Systems*, 1983; *Better an Old Demon than a New God, Giorno Poetry Systems*, 1984; *Praying Mantis*, 1991

Cartwright, Justin

1933– Novelist; film director

The expatriate white South African Justin Cartwright, a novelist and film director, has lived in London nearly all his adult life, a fact that helps explains why both Africa and Britain loom large as settings in his novels of contemporary manners and morals. Such works as *Look At It This Way* (1990) and *In Every Face I Meet* (1995) were shortlisted for the prestigious Booker Prize, and *Masai Dreaming* (1993) was critically acclaimed for the adroit way it explored violence in both Africa and Nazi Germany. In his 1996 book *Not Yet Home: A South African Journey*, Cartwright wrote of three years he spent in his native land as a journalist and film researcher, interspersing this with memoirs of his boyhood around Johannesburg and Pretoria. An autobiographical passage from this book explains Cartwright's deeply felt sense of place: "I have lived in England since I was twenty, longer than I have lived in South Africa, yet I have always felt the pull of the landscape and the people of South Africa. Living in London is for me a continuing pleasure, and I have written novels about London and Londoners twice now with affection and some intimacy, but I have always felt this sense that home was elsewhere, although not necessarily in South Africa. I was also all too aware that my own, bittersweet alienation was not a matter of great significance; after all, I had chosen to leave as

Miriam Berkley

Justin Cartwright

soon as I decently could, and the reasons were not simply and nakedly 'political.'"

Justin Cartwright was born in Cape Town, South Africa, in 1933 and grew up in that country; since completing his studies at Oxford University, he has lived mostly in London. His father, a journalist, was editor of the *Rand Daily Mail*, and his mother's family came from the town of Potchefstroom, in the Transvaal. In *Not Yet Home: A South African Journey*, an essay-cum-memoir, Cartwright discussed the complex post-apartheid culture he observed during the three years he revisited his homeland on assignment, filming documentaries for the BBC and writing for other British media; he interspersed these observations with idyllic flashbacks of childhood in the days when apartheid was taken for granted and when blacks were relegated to living in townships that were "invisible to white South Africans." Recalling how black migrant workers were forced to travel by an old steam train called the *Istimela*, he wrote: "As a schoolboy at Bishops in Cape Town, I had travelled eight times a year the thousand miles by steam train, for nine years. . . . I could remember jumping off at Kimberley for fish and chips and I could remember the tedium of the Karoo, dotted with inquisitive *meerkats*, and the breakfasts at 1 / 6d which sustained us on the thirty-six hour journey." He recalled pony rides on dirt roads near Sandton, where the family had lived when his father was at the newspaper; and the endless veld where "we used to ride and chase guinea-fowl and commune with nature." In revisiting his mother's family, in a farmhouse without electricity, he recalled the "Raymond Carver–like quality" of their lives, "of insecurity and minor triumph immediately fol-

lowed by disaster." These journeys in the mid-1990s led him to conclude that "the very things I had been trying to get away from thirty years ago now seemed to me to be rich and interesting."

At the age of 19, he spent a year as an exchange student in Michigan before taking up studies at Oxford University. He also studied for a time at a university in Johannesburg, a city that has always had a "magic for me." Leaving Oxford, he worked for three years as an advertising copywriter, then made a number of commercials and wildlife films. His early career includes credentials as a film director, including one he made in the late 1970s about King Sobhuza of Swaziland, so it is not surprising that filmic imagery and story lines are often found in his prose writings, such as in *Masai Dreaming*, his 1993 novel. Its plot revolves around the meanderings of Tim Curtiz, who goes to Africa to write a screenplay about a French anthropologist who, around 1940, falls in love with a Masai warrior during her research, only to return to Paris during the Nazi occupation, and thence to Auschwitz.

Cartwright's first two novels, each with a late–Cold War ambience, involved political assassination and international intrigue: *The Revenge* (1978), which had a character supposedly modeled after Richard Nixon, and *The Horse of Darius* (1980), a fictionalized account of the last days of the Shah of Iran. For his next novels, he turned to his native continent as a setting. In these novels set in Africa, such as *Freedom for the Wolves* (1983) *Interior* (1988), and *Masai Dreaming*, Cartwright revisited territory originally blazed by such authors as Joseph Conrad and Graham Greene, both of whom described Africa through the eyes of a dominant European culture. The names of some of Cartwright's characters—James Curtiz and Tim Curtiz, for example—recall the name of Kurtz, the central character in Conrad's *Heart of Darkness*.

His novel *Look At It This Way* is set in the London advertising and media culture of the 1980s. In her assessment for the *New York Times Book Review* (August 1, 1993), Carol Kino noted that the novel has been described as a "trans-Atlantic competitor" of Tom Wolfe's *Bonfire of the Vanities*. The book's narrator, Tim Curtiz, an expatriate American journalist, writes a column from London for a New York magazine, describing, for example, visits to the London Zoo or penning portraits of colorful Londoners he meets. Kino noted that the novel's "true glory lies in its deftly delineated London nouveau riche milieu—one that, although the 80s boom has passed, still looks fresh because it's been so rarely depicted. . . . Throughout, Mr. Cartwright's prose is pleasurably precise and his scenic descriptions unfailing stunners." Kino concluded that "in the end, Mr. Cartwright's novel looks less like a gleefully unflinching vision of Sodom than a mannerly, elegiac, mildly macho tale that seems to lament the loss of a day when Englishmen had the right stuff to conquer the jungle, urban or otherwise." Short-story writer Robert

Carver, writing in the *Spectator* (December 7, 1990), called *Look At It This Way* "the funniest satire of London life I've read in a decade. If you like your humour pitch black, your characters piquant, your narrative subtle and fast, here's your man."

Published in 1993, *Masai Dreaming* is set among the African *moran* warriors who see themselves as the keepers of all the world's cattle. Richard Dooling, writing in the *Washington Post* (January 6, 1996), offered a succinct plot summary of what he called "this gorgeous, terrifying montage of a novel," writing: "Tim Curtiz, a screenwriter, travels to Kenya and finds the place haunted by Masai ghosts, European ghosts, and the Hollywood versions of both." Hoping to make a film about a French anthropologist named Claudia Cohn-Casson, who, half a century earlier, had fallen in love with a warrior in Africa before meeting her doom in Auschwitz, Curtiz interviews tribal elders and casting-couch directors alike. The result, according to Dooling, is "an intensely absorbing narrative about human betrayal and the fall of man," told through "layers of ancient and modern images, of speculations about what really happened, of proposed, romanticized cinematic versions and of the sexual upheavals occurring in Curtiz's own life." By invoking images on different levels—"real," "filmic," "hyperreal"—and by examining violence in Africa together with that of Nazi Germany, Cartwright explored the potential for human violence—and transcendence—everywhere. In *Not Yet Home*, Cartwright describes the evolution of *Masai Dreaming* by declaring, "I had come to the conclusion that part of being human is the acceptance of ethical obligation. Even acceptance is too equivocal a word: inevitability is closer to the truth. If this is so, the arguments about ethics proceeding from a religious belief are simply an inversion of the facts." As Dooling pointed out, "It often seems to the modern traveler that the most redeeming qualities of the human race appear among 'primitive' peoples, but one wonders if this is because their violent impulses are transmitted using only relatively small-scale materials—a spear through the chest of one pompous European, instead of cattle cars and ovens designed to kill 6 million. . . . In the end, the frightening insight here—which would be much more palatable if the writing were bad (instead of painfully excellent) or the perception far fetched—is: 'We are all Jews, all Nazis, all Masai, all humans capable of anything.'"

From 1994 to 1996 Cartwright traveled widely in South Africa as a reporter for two London newspapers—the *Times* and the *Financial Times*—and to help the BBC make a documentary about the post-apartheid era. In the latter capacity, he filmed many events—adaptations of Shakespeare with interracial casts, like Welcome Msomi's *Zulu Macbeth*, of which he wrote: "It seemed to me, if proof were needed, that Shakespeare was instantly recognizable. These were not events taking place a long time ago in Scotland, but Zulu dynastic struggles which were very immediate. And as I write

this, I think of the Venda and their fondness for poisoning and witchcraft." He also covered the World Cup rugby events in South Africa and interviewed such important figures as Bishop Desmond Tutu and author Nadine Gordimer. He documented these years in his 1996 account *Not Yet Home: A South African Journey*, in which he also reminisced about his growing-up years there. In the foreword to this book, he wrote, "Being accredited to some prestigious institution helps the inquisitive traveller pursue his interests under the cover of respectability. I am grateful for the camouflage provided."

A major concern of Cartwright's in *Not Yet Home* is cultural, not political; he sought to determine whether South African can survive as a pluralistic society, whether it can live up to its new motto, "Many cultures, one nation." He wrote: "In South Africa today, I realised, the only common identity is of having suffered apartheid. Apartheid is the defining principle of South Africans in the way that the Holocaust is now the defining principle of Jews. . . . The only possible logical way out of this dilemma is for white South Africans to claim that they, too, were victims of apartheid, that they were brutalized, duped, and perverted." Cartwright's interview with Archbishop Desmond Tutu is recorded in the final chapter of *Not Yet Home*, in which he concluded that "Tutu's role, I saw, was to insist on the innate goodness of the South African people and to insist on their redemption, whatever the evidence to the contrary."

The book is also a meditation on the meaning of culture itself. "Western culture, in its ideal form, strives for truth and perfection," he wrote. "Once you begin to suggest that it is easily adapted to social ends, you have denied its whole purpose. And it is pointless to complain that Western culture is Eurocentric: Western culture is not tied to place or to a specific morality; its contribution to understanding is in its ability to stand outside of religion or ideology or place. So the idea that Western culture is of itself oppressive and exclusive is absurd." Cartwright feels that, with the end of apartheid, the drama has moved from the grand arena of human rights to a meaner one of everyday politics. "My own decision to leave was because of a reluctance to live in the contorted way faced on white South Africans," he concluded.

In *Not Yet Home*, Cartwright speculated as to the nature of the myth that might be found to unite all the diverse groups in South Africa. "Take Blake and Albion, or Wagner and the Teutonic gods, or Thoreau and Walden Pond. The Afrikaner and the Covenant, the Zulu and Isandhlwana, the Indians and Gandhi. There is no end to the competing myths and antipathetic symbols." He devotes much time in the book to his conversations with Nadine Gordimer, who, like him, came to realize over the years that South Africa was more of a home to her than Europe. He found in her works a "strong thread of rationalism. . . . Her prose never soars away, because it is attached by a thin filament of rationality which runs through everything she does and says, so that almost every character and situation has a relevance, sometimes a surfeit of relevance."

In his fifth novel, *Leading the Cheers* (1998), Cartwright explored the notion of America through the tale of Dan Silas, a middle-aged, newly "downsized" Britisher who returns for his high-school reunion in Hollybush, Michigan, where he had briefly lived as a teenager. (Cartwright himself had been an exchange student in Michigan.) With his unemployment and midlife crisis throwing him suddenly open to new prospects, he balances the incredible demands of two high-school friends, Gloria, with whom he had sex on Thomas Jefferson's bed during a class trip, and Gary, who claims to be the reincarnation of a Shawnee Indian. Reviewing the book in the *Times Literary Supplement* (September 11, 1998), Julian Ferraro wrote: "Cartwright skillfully presents Dan's account as an attempt to shake off the cynicism that has made him a successful advertising man, and in some sense to redeem the events of his life. While none of his observations is particularly complex or original, it is the very commonplaceness of his insights that is engaging and often comforting. Like [his] earlier books, *Leading the Cheers* represents an accomplished, and often entertaining, engagement with the paradoxical nature of the relationship between individuality and community."
—E. M.

SUGGESTED READING: *New York Times Book Review* p35 Nov. 26, 1995; *Spectator* p36 Oct. 27, 1990, p40 Sep. 16, 1995, p47 Nov. 25, 1995; *Times Literary Supplement* Oct. 11, 1996, Sep. 11, 1998; *Washington Post* C p2 June 6, 1995

SELECTED BOOKS: Fiction—*Fighting Men*, 1977; *The Revenge*, 1978; *The Horse of Darius*, 1980; *Freedom for the Wolves*, 1983; *Interior*, 1988; *Look At It This Way*, 1990; *Masai Dreaming*, 1993; *In Every Face I Meet*, 1995; *Leading the Cheers*, 1998; Nonfiction—*Not Yet Home: A South African Journey*, 1996

Castillo, Ana

June 15, 1953– Novelist; poet; essayist

Ana Castillo is a Mexican-American author whose voice can be said to speak to all women who have felt at one time or another that the world was made primarily for men. Originally a poet, Castillo was recognized as a rising literary star with the publication of her first novel, *The Mixquiahuala Letters* (1986), and her popularity has increased with the publication of succeeding novels, *Sapogonia* (1990) and *So Far from God* (1993), and the appearance of the short-story collection *Loverboys* (1996). Castillo deftly blends realism with lyrical mysticism and attacks, directly or with humor, the problems of minorities and women in what she sees as a white patriarchal society. "The kind of literature I write is not directed for the mainstream . . . " she told *Publishers Weekly* (August 12, 1996), "and I'm hoping that we're entering a new era now where it will be more and more the case that writers from the fringes occupy the mainstream."

The poet, essayist, short-story writer, and novelist Ana Hernandez Del Castillo was born in Chicago on June 15, 1953, to Mexican parents, Raymond and Raquel Rocha Castillo. She attended public schools in Chicago. The family was poor but shared a wealth of stories from Castillo's grandmother, referred to affectionately in Spanish as Abuelita. When she was around six years of age, young Ana became very sickly; a woman from the local social services department, after coming to Ana's home and examining her, announced that the girl should be hospitalized. Having already lost a great-grandchild who died after being taken away by social services, Abuelita was determined that young Ana would not suffer the same fate. As Castillo recalled in "A Healing Legacy," an article printed in *Ms.* (September/October 1996): "My grandmother, illiterate, wise, healing woman, was going to cure me, not with miracle-cure injections or nutritious food, but with magic. Some people call it faith. Others think of it as procuring the wisdom of ancestors. But here, without going into complicated speculations, we'll call it magic." Castillo was cured. When she was almost 10 years old, her grandmother died; she began writing poetry after her death-a creative outlet she credits to her Abuelita's gift for storytelling.

In 1975 Castillo received a B.A. degree in liberal arts from Northern Illinois University. While still a student she published her first chapbooks of poetry, *Zero Makes Me Hungry* (1975) and *I close my eyes (to see)* (1976). While studying Latin American and Caribbean Studies at the University of Chicago, she published two more books of poetry, *Otro Canto* (1977) and the privately printed volume *The Invitation* (1979). These two volumes were collected and printed along with 16 new poems in the collection *Women Are Not Roses* (1984). In her poetry, Castillo examines female experience and deals with sadness and isolation on a very personal level. She has also written protest poetry. As she explained in an interview with *Publishers Weekly* (August 12, 1996): "Being of Mexican background, being Indian-looking, being a female, coming from a working-class background, and then becoming politicized in high school, that was my direction. I was going to be an artist, a poet. . . . I was a Hispanic protest poet, a complete renegade—and I continue to write that way."

In September 1983 Castillo gave birth to a son, Marcel Ramón Herrera. In 1985 she and her son moved to California. The next year her first novel, *The Mixquiahuala Letters*, was published by Bilingual Press to glowing reviews and steady sales; it went on to receive an American Book Award from the Before Columbus Foundation. The novel concerns a series of letters written by the main character, Theresa, to her friend Alicia. The letters examine relationships between the sexes, societal and cultural impediments to sexual freedom, and Hispanic attitudes concerning gender. In 1988 West End Press published another volume of Castillo's poetry, *My Father Was a Toltec*, whose title refers to the fact that Castillo's father was a member of the Toltec gang in Chicago.

Her next novel, *Sapogonia*, was published by Bilingual Press in 1990, the same year the author and her son moved to Albuquerque, New Mexico. The novel's tale is told by a male narrator, Máximo Madrigal, and is about his obsession with the one woman he cannot seduce. The book deals with the destructive powers of the male-female relationship, and—set in Sapogonia, a fictional country in which Spanish culture and American Indian culture battle for predominance—it takes on the theme of clashing values as well. Castillo underscored the view that the survival of the native culture depends on women carrying on its traditions, and symbolically represented this view with Mamá Grande's devotion to the Virgin. (The book received fine reviews, but there was still trouble surrounding it for Castillo. Without consulting her, Bilingual Press sold the rights to both her novels to Doubleday/Anchor, which published them in paperback in 1992 and 1994, respectively. Castillo, who wanted considerably more involvement with the publication of her own novels, was angered by her publisher's actions. (She now warns young writers to read their contracts thoroughly.)

With the success of her novels, Castillo was able to hire an agent, Susan Bergholz, whom the author acknowledges as playing an important role in the creation of her next novel, *So Far from God* (1993). Initially, Castillo wrote a story involving a little girl named La Loca (the Crazy One), who dies but cannot rise up to heaven; she can rise only to the top of the church. (The author credits *The Lives of the Saints* with giving her the inspiration for the story.) After reading the story, Bergholz believed that it was good enough to expand into a novel. The original story was thus broadened to include La Loca's mother and three sisters. After La Loca's death, she is endowed with clairvoyant powers and helps to rescue members of the family on more than one occasion. La Loca especially helps her sisters—Fe, who goes insane when her finance leaves her; Caridad, who is mutilated by an evil spirit only to be cured and become an apprentice to the old *curandera* (healer woman); and Esperanza, the social conscience of the family and also a television news anchor, who consults her family even after she is killed in the Persian Gulf War. The reviews of the novel were mostly favorable. *Choice* (September 1993) marveled: "With tact, humor, and extraordinary literary prowess, [Castillo] brilliantly exposes the socio-politico-economic concerns of a caring Mexican-American woman. It is an outstanding work of art by a first-rate novelist, writing in a genuine spirit of multiculturalism." Sherri Cutler, writing for *Library Journal* (July 1993), remarked: "Each chapter stands on its own as a complete story, but readers won't be satisfied until they've finished the entire skillfully constructed book." *So Far from God* won the Sandburg Award for fiction in 1993.

In 1994 Castillo published a book of feminist essays, *Massacre of the Dreamers: Essays on Xicanisma*. In the volume's 10 essays, Castillo discusses the roles of women in various aspects of Hispanic society, from political activism to spirituality; she defines the term "Xicanisma" as a new awareness among Hispanic women that all things female must be respected. Castillo's blunt approach to women's issues resulted in divergent reviews. The review in *Ms.* (September/October 1994) stated: "These essays are complex, highly intellectual, and beautifully written. They will be read, understood, and welcomed by her sister Xicanistas (and other feminists). Most importantly, these essays are testimony and proof of an alive mestiza, brown woman, revolutionary consciousness signaling change and real hope." The reviewer in *Choice* (March 1995) disagreed: "Only occasionally does one perceive through this jumble the creative writer capable of communicating a reality and a belief system without hitting one on the head with a sledgehammer." This collection of essays earned Castillo a Ph.D. from the University of Bremen.

In 1996 Castillo published her first collection of stories, *Loverboys*. As the title suggests, the book is about love and relationships, though not all of the "loverboys" are boys. Some of the narrators of the stories are men, some are women; some are heterosexual, while others are homosexual or bisexual. The reviews of the collection were mixed. The *Los Angeles Times* (August 25, 1996) reviewer believed that *Loverboys* "is an uneven, often self-indulgent collection, with its lusty touches and its good moments of insight and humor. It's short on character and story." The *New York Times Book Review* (September 8, 1996) critic enjoyed the collection a bit more, but suggested that "Ms. Castillo's discursive, conversational style seems simply that, as if she'd grown a little too enamored by the sound of her own voice. At its best, though, this voice has a vibrancy that compels attention, jamming ribald humor up against pathos and melancholy desire."

In October 1996, Riverhead Press released an essay collection entitled *Goddess of the Americas*, edited by Castillo and including pieces by such writers as Sandra Cisneros, Elena Poniatowska, and Luis Rodriguez. The essays are thematically linked by the Virgin of Guadeloupe, the blessed patron of the poor people of Latin America. When Julie Grau, an editor at Riverhead, suggested to Castillo that she edit the book, the author felt she could not turn down the opportunity. Though she is not a practicing Catholic, Castillo believes that the worship of the Virgin Mary has important significance for Latin American society as a whole. As she told Samuel Baker for *Publishers Weekly*: "I don't particularly care if people want to worship the Virgin of Guadeloupe, if they get the message that we need to respect the things that we call female, which we don't."

In 1997 Castillo returned to Chicago with her son, settling in the very same apartment where years earlier she had worked on *The Mixquiahuala Letters*. Her new novel, *Peel My Love Like an Onion*, which is due to be published in 1999, focuses on the Gypsy culture in Chicago and is narrated by a Hispanic woman.

Ana Castillo has an eclectic knowledge of a variety of subjects other than creative writing. Over the years she has taught American and Mexican history, the history of pre-Columbian civilizations, and women's studies at a number of universities. She has lectured at the Sorbonne in Paris and at universities in Germany. In 1988 she was honored by the Women's Foundation of San Francisco for her "pioneering excellence in literature." Castillo was a dissertation fellow in the Department of Chicano Studies at the University of California, Santa Barbara in 1989 and 1990. In those years she also won a California Arts Council Fellowship for fiction and a National Endowment for the Arts Fellowship for poetry. —C.M.

SUGGESTED READING: *Chicago Tribune* I p28, Oct. 8, 1993; *Choice* p112 Sep. 1993, p1124 Mar. 1995; *Commonweal* p37 Jan. 14, 1994; *Library Journal* p118 July 1993; *Los Angeles Times* p8 Aug. 25, 1996; *Ms.* p80 Sep./Oct. 1994, p92+ Sep./Oct. 1996; *New York Times Book Review* p22 Oct. 3, 1993, p20 Sep. 8, 1996; *Publishers Weekly* p59+ Aug. 12, 1996; *USA Today* p16 June 16, 1996; *Contemporary Authors* vol. 131, 1991; *Dictionary of Literary Biography* vol. 122, 1992

SELECTED WORKS: Fiction—*The Mixquiahuala Letters*, 1986; *Sapogonia*, 1990; *So Far from God*, 1993; *Loverboys*, 1996; *Peel My Love Like an Onion*, 1999; Nonfiction—*Massacre of the Dreamers: Essays on Xicanisma*, 1994; Poetry— *Zero Makes Me Hungry*, 1975; *I close my eyes (to see)*, 1976; *Otro Canto*, 1977; *The Invitation*, 1979; *Women Are Not Roses*, 1984; *My Father Was a Toltec*, 1988; As editor—*Goddess of the Americas*, 1996

Chacel, Rosa

June 3, 1898– July 27, 1994 Novelist; short-story writer; essayist

The prolific Spanish author Rosa Chacel wrote novels, poetry, essays, short stories, nonfiction, and autobiography over the course of a long life. Her first two novels were written under the influence of her mentor, the philosopher José Ortega y Gasset, but, as a philosophical feminist, she broke from that influence. The University of Nebraska Press commissioned English translations of two of her novels for its European Women Writers series; the first, *The Maravillas District* (1992), a translation of Chacel's 1976 novel *Barrio de Maravillas*, was termed "a seminal work" by *Library Journal* (December 1992). Next came *Memoirs of Leticia Valle* (1994), a translation of *Memorias de Leticia Valle* (1945), also highly praised.

Rosa Chacel was born in Valladolid, Spain, in what was considered Old Castile, on June 3, 1898—the year that Spain was defeated in the Spanish-American War. When she was 10 years old, Chacel and her family moved to Madrid. Both her parents had artistic and literary interests and talents. As a girl Chacel studied art and practiced writing—her intention was to be a sculptor. At age 17 she enrolled at the School of Fine Arts of San Fernando, in Madrid, where she met the painter Timoteo Pérez Rubio, whom she married in 1922.

Courtesy of Agencia Leteraria Carmen Balcells

Her delicate health forced her to halt her studies, however, as the school building was unheated. She then became a member of the Madrid Ateneo, a private library, where she made significant literary contacts.

Rosa Chacel "belongs to the brilliant generation of Spanish artists that were born at the beginning of the 20th century and moved into the cultural vanguard in the 20s and 30s," according to the translator and literary critic Susan Kirkpatrick, who wrote the preface to *The Maravillas District.* Chacel and Pérez Rubio lived in Rome from 1922 to 1927. They then returned to Spain, and in 1930 their son Carlos was born. During those years Chacel took part in the cultural and political life of Madrid as a young sculptor and writer. Soon after the outbreak of the Spanish Civil War, Chacel, as well as most of the generation of artists and intellectuals to which she belonged, went into exile. Chacel and Carlos left Spain for Paris, later living in Athens and Geneva; Pérez Rubio joined them in 1939, after the defeat of the Spanish Republic. From 1940 the family lived in Rio de Janeiro, Brazil, where they remained, except for periodic trips to New York and Buenos Aires, until 1972. From 1959 to 1961 Chacel lived in New York as the recipient of a Guggenheim Fellowship. She returned to Spain in 1972. The fact that Chacel spent some 40 years living outside Spain, combined with censorship under Franco and the difficulty of being taken seriously as a woman in Spain, all contributed to the lack of recognition that she endured in her own country for most of her career.

Rosa Chacel was influenced by the thinking and writing of the philosopher José Ortega y Gasset, an important literary figure during the time when she was coming of age. His influence can be seen particularly in her first two novels: *Estación, ida y vuelta* (1930, Station, Round Trip) and *Teresa* (1941).

Estación, ida y vuelta was written in 1925-26 while Chacel was living in Italy with her husband. Before writing this novel, Chacel had read works by Joyce, Proust, Freud, and Dostoyevsky, as well as essays by Ortega. The book traces the formation of a young novelist, focusing on his interior thought processes. The protagonist minutely analyzes his love affairs, travels, and then returns home to his first love on being informed she is pregnant with their child. There is minimal plot and little action or dialogue. Chacel explained that she was trying "to make the reader understand what I do not even mention," according to Carol Maier, the translator. Chacel called this book the "key that governs all my prose," Janet Pérez noted in *Contemporary Women Writers of Spain.* Pérez observed that Chacel was so influenced by Ortega's writings about the novel that in this work she "set out to apply quite literally Ortega's notions on heightened psychological realism in keeping with his perspectivist vision and contemporary psychological theory." Pérez described Chacel's prose in *Estación, ida y vuelta* as "lively, with vivacious imagery and occasional Proustian touches in the mechanisms of involuntary memory and frequent self-analysis." Chacel acknowledged that she was influenced by Marcel Proust in the conception of this novel.

Chacel met Ortega in person upon her return to Spain in 1930. He proposed the idea of a series of biographies of famous 19th-century Spaniards, a literary endeavor that combined his project of renewing the Spanish novel with the demand at that time for biographies. She wrote her second novel, *Teresa,* at Ortega's explicit suggestion. The book is a novelized biography of the life of Teresa Mancha, who was the mistress of Romantic poet José de Espronceda. Chacel presented the story from Mancha's point of view, describing her experiences, from her abandonment of her husband for the poet to her own loneliness at the time of her death. Although finished in 1933, the novel was not published until 1941. The subgenre of fictional biography was a new one at that time. In writing this book, Chacel had to write about the Romantic era for a contemporary audience. Elizabeth Scarlett, in *Under Construction: The Body in Spanish Novels,* described Chacel's technique as a "free indirect style in narration, which was ostensibly anachronistic in the avant-garde context," and she observed that Chacel's "efforts, while compelling, sometimes result in melodrama and pathos." Unlike Espronceda's depiction of Teresa as deceptive and disillusioning (the view of much scholarship since then), in Chacel's work "it is Espronceda who disillusions Teresa, for his seeming rejection of social norms is only superficial, and his hypocrisy harms only Teresa, who bears the stigma of being his illicit lover." According to Scarlett this representation of events "points out the continuity of patriarchy," an observation "as relevant for the avant-garde literary politics of Chacel's time as it was for the disapproving society in which Teresa found herself adrift."

Chacel's third novel, *Memorias de Leticia Valle* (1945, tr. *Memoirs of Leticia Valle*), has been described as being, among other things, a rebellion against her mentor. *Memoirs of Leticia Valle* is an invented diary of a young girl, 11-year-old Leticia Valle, who has been sent to her uncle's house in Switzerland in the aftermath of a scandal. The tale begins with Leticia living in Valladolid, motherless, in the care of an aunt. When her father—embittered and alcoholic—returns from fighting in Morocco, the three of them move to the village of Simancas, the location of a famous archive. A precocious child, Leticia has received little formal schooling and winds up being taught by the local archivist Don Daniel, whose wife, Doña Luisa, is her piano teacher. Leticia develops intense relationships with both Don Daniel and Doña Luisa, creating a complex triangle in which the adults seem to compete over her. While the novel never states directly who seduced whom or even whether there was actually a seduction, there are allusions to such an incident between Leticia and Don Daniel, and Leticia feels the guilt for it. When her father confronts Don Daniel about this "inconceivable" situation, Daniel kills himself. Immediately afterward, Luisa is taken out of the country by her uncle. From Switzerland Leticia writes of events that she can not bear to describe outright: "I'm afraid that telling about this other thing is more than I have strength for; I'm afraid that it's too hard for me, that I won't be able to make it perfectly clear what impossible things are like, or to show how a person can live in such an environment, knowing those things are about to explode at any minute, when everything will be shattered." Leticia writes her introspective account of the events that lead to her exile in an apparent attempt to understand what has happened to her as well as to affirm herself.

Chacel began writing *Memoirs of Leticia Valle* in France and finished it in Argentina, where it was published in 1945. She has indicated that her idea for the story came from a Dostoyevsky novel, in which a middle-aged man seduces a young girl who then commits suicide, and from her own childhood memory of a similar seduction involving a schoolmaster in Valladolid. She decided to write a version of this story in which the girl is the seducer and it is the older man who must kill himself. The question of whether or not the work is autobiographical comes up due to certain similarities it has to the autobiography of her first 10 years, *Desde el amanecer* (Since the Dawn). According to Maier, the translator of *Memoirs of Leticia Valle*, Chacel explained that the book is not autobiographical even though it is a portrait of herself. Maier noted that Chacel told an interviewer that "she was Leticia, although Leticia's story had never happened to her." Chacel also said that this book was the first one that she worked on independently from Ortega and that it is her "own, it is memories."

In spite of Chacel's desired independence from Ortega, Maier noted that "his aesthetics were crucial in the formulation of Leticia's struggle to understand what has happened to her and the extent of her complicity in it" and also that in "the conceptualization of the novel, in the structure of its incidents, and in Leticia's own raw 'brute force' (*la fuerza bruta*), there are more than hints of both the energy Chacel admired in Ortega and the abrasion between them she has recalled in several of her essays." In spite of Ortega's influence, Elizabeth Scarlett, in *Under Construction: The Body in Spanish Novels*, represents this "novelized (auto)biography" as Chacel's triumph over Ortega: "This time she freely chooses her subject: a girl with no name for herself in society at large who reinvents herself in mind and body and brings about the destruction of her male mentor in the process."

The *Publishers Weekly* (February 7, 1994) reviewer called the book a "dynamic work" and "a powerful and disturbing portrait of a precocious girl's coming-of-age." Scarlett claimed that the work could be read as "a fable of subversion through seduction" and added that in this work Chacel "found the novelistic voice that will be heard again in the more extensive *La sinrazón*."

La sinrazón (Unreason), first published in Argentina in 1960 and winner of the Premio de la Crítica (the Critics' Prize, one of Spain's most prestigious awards) upon its publication in Spain in 1977, has been called Chacel's masterpiece. Chacel herself has called it her favorite of her works. In it, Chacel traced the life and analyzed the character of her protagonist, Santiago Hernández, using the same first-person diary format of *Memoirs of Leticia Valle*. Santiago is an Argentine, raised and educated in Europe. In 1930 he returns to Argentina and marries, has children, and establishes himself in a career. He then has an affair with a woman from his past, which causes him to lose his wife and children. These circumstances propel him toward prolonged soul-searching and possibly his own death. Santiago believes he had certain telekinetic powers, which he apparently has lost, to his great distress. The text of the novel is formed by what Pérez termed his "confessional effort at understanding his life, his loss of innocence and of his hold on life." He eventually realizes his own need for God, faith, something transcendent. Pérez noted the influence of the writer Unamuno on Chacel: "*La sinrazón* is one of Unamuno's terms for faith (since acceptance of the tenets of faith goes against scientific reason), and it is in part through this irrationality that Santiago comes to have some comprehension of his own loss of innocence."

Barrio de Maravillas (*The Maravillas District*), published in 1976, received the Premio de la Crítica that year. In 1992 an English edition, translated by D. A. Demers, was published. It is the first part of trilogy, presented largely in dialogue form, that documents the lives of two female protagonists, Isabel and Elena. *The Maravillas District* begins in 1912, when Isabel and Elena are girls living in Madrid and probing questions of philosophical and aesthetic importance. Thirteen-year-old Elena, the daughter of a singing teacher and the granddaughter of on opera composer, and 11-year-old Isabel, the daughter of an unmarried seamstress, live in the same building and share an unused room as their studio-retreat. The novel explores their growing consciousness of themselves, artistically and intellectually, and their mutual support. Attuned to the lives of their neighbors, together they begin the transition from childhood to adulthood, analyzing issues of existence, identity, and sexuality. This novel ends in 1914, with both girls about to enroll in the Academy of San Fernando, Madrid's most prestigious academy of fine arts.

In her preface to *The Maravillas District*, Susan Kirkpatrick observed, "It would be tempting to say that Chacel rewrites Joyce by offering a portrait of the artist as a young woman, except that the latter term would have to be plural, since Chacel focuses not on the alienated individual but on dialogue, on interactive discovery." Art is a central theme in the novel, as is the erotic origin of aesthetic impulse: Elena and Isabel awaken to their artistic vocation at almost the same time as they do to their sexuality.

Pérez pointed out that while the "aesthetic significance" of the work "is primarily as a view of the arts in Spain before 1914, Chacel also presents a profound and important study of female adolescence." The question of art in relation to history is explored, as is the relationship of art to gender. The prevailing social belief that femininity is not compatible with artistic achievement or political activity is expressed by the girls' friend Ramón when he jokes that to play a part in art and history they would have to cut off their breasts like Amazons. The book ends with the girls puzzling over this issue—exploring their feelings about how Ramón thinks of them and about how they think of themselves. "It seems to me that we have to settle down and think about their theory that we're going to have to cut off quite a few things. . . . That was what he meant when he told us. As they say about slander: 'Slander, there must be something to it.' Because slander passes from one person to the next and you never know to what extent it's true. With this famous theory of theirs we're left with the same question: how much of it is true? That's it—that's what we've got to figure out."

The narrative of *The Maravillas District* is made up of many voices—dramatic dialogue, interior first-person monologue, third-person narration, and a distinct narrator's voice. Kirkpatrick maintained that Chacel's "project—recreating through memory the quality of earlier experience and at the same time subjecting the remembered experience to scrupulous analysis—can best be compared to that of Proust; yet Chacel's style, her theory of memory and of the word, are uniquely her own." She praised the novel's "seductive power" and stated, "Chacel's writing is dense and labyrinthine, but at the same time it is open-ended and dynamic, shaping a narrative design that ends with a query instead of a conclusion." Mary Ellen Beck in *Library Journal* (December 1992) observed that *The Maravillas District* was the work with which Chacel attempted "to retrieve her rightful place in the Spanish literary world." The second two novels in the trilogy are *Acrópolis* (1984) and *Ciencias naturales* (1988, Natural Sciences). Like *The Maravillas District*, both are self-contained narrative units. As in most of Chacel's work, the plot is close to nonexistent. *Acrópolis* follows Elena and Isabel from 1914 to 1931, the years before the Republic. *Ciencias naturales* follows the two women into the postwar period.

In addition to novels, Chacel wrote in many other formats. She contributed to the Spanish literary journal *Revista de Occidente*, founded by Ortega, and to the Argentine journal *Sur*. She published a biography of her husband, an autobiography of her first 10 years, and multiple volumes of her diary. Additionally, she wrote volumes of critical articles, short stories, poems, and essays. Her 1981 *Novelas antes de tiempo* (Novels Ahead of Time), published when she was 82, is a collection of four unfinished novels. Chacel summarized each of these projects, fearing that she might not have time to finish them. Her two major works of nonfiction, *La confesión* (The Confession) and *Saturnal* (The Feast of Saturn), are essay volumes. *La confesión* is Chacel's study of confession as a genre. The confessional works of the writers Galdós, Unamuno, and Cervantes are the ones she considered most important in terms of Spanish literature. In *Saturnal*, drafted for the most part during her stay in New York as a Guggenheim grantee (although it was nearly four decades in gestation), she probed the problems of love, holding sexual equality as a basic postulate.

Chacel's work was almost unknown in Spain for many years. She began to receive serious critical attention in the early 1960s. Not until she returned to live in Spain, in 1972, did she became known as a major Spanish writer. According to Maier, what Chacel referred to as her project remained the same after the 1920s (and the publication of her first novel): "The renovation of Spanish prose, an undertaking begun in a spirit of collaboration with the ideas of Ortega and her colleagues from that period."

Rosa Chacel died at the age of 96 in Madrid. Weeks before her death, while she was in the hospital, King Juan Carlos awarded her Spain's gold medal for fine arts. In 1978, when the Royal Spanish Academy first opened its doors to women, Chacel was a nominee. She was also a contender for the 1985 Cervantes Prize, given for the totality of a writer's production. Chacel twice received the Premio de la Crítica (1976 and 1977), and in 1987 she was given the National Award for Spanish Letters. Julián Marías, the noted Spanish intellectual and critic, said, according to Pérez, that Rosa Chacel "can't be exchanged for anyone else, which means that without her, our literature—that of the Spanish language—would be incomplete."

—Leah Diskin

SUGGESTED READING: *Library Journal* p185 Dec. 1992; *New York Times Book Review* p8 Mar. 13, 1994; *Publisher's Weekly* p78 Feb. 7, 1994; Pérez, J. *Contemporary Women Writers of Spain*, 1988; Scarlett, E. A. *Under Construction: The Body in Spanish Novels*, 1994

SELECTED BOOKS IN ENGLISH TRANSLATION: *The Maravillas District*, 1992; *Memoirs of Leticia Valle*, 1994

Pam Francis Photography

Chandra, Vikram

1961– Novelist; short-story writer

Likened to the work of Salman Rushdie, *Red Earth and Pouring Rain* (1995), the first novel by the Indian writer Vikram Chandra, was praised worldwide by critics for its originality and daring, as it challenged the beliefs and imaginations of readers. Outwardly the story of a monkey who recalls his earlier life as a man, the novel questions the very limits of human perception; the author took pains to suggest that stories have more than one side, that nothing is what it seems on the surface. According to the *London Review of Books* (August 3, 1995), "Indians are certainly not safe from Chandra's irony, but it's more affectionate than his contempt for the British and his dismay at America." Set in India, the novel is relentless in the pace of its storytelling and broad in scope, as it explores in more than 500 pages a seemingly endless mystical city. There has also been great praise for Chandra's most recent volume, *Love and Longing in Bombay* (1997), five stories connected by a single narrator who answers the direct, probing questions of his young friend by spinning tales.

In a sketch written for *World Authors 1990-1995*, Vikram Chandra discusses some of the influences on his work, which stemmed from his childhood in India: "I was born in New Delhi in 1961. My father is a business executive and my mother is a writer of fiction and screenplays. I grew up listening to stories, tales that were told to me by my mother and my aunts. The first story I remember listening to is the *Mahabharata*, which I demanded more of every afternoon after school. 'What happened then?' I would say to my mother. 'What hap-

pened then?' I felt dwarfed by the size of the *Mahabharata*, by its sweep, and loved the men and women in it, and their huge passions.

"I was soon what my friends called a bookworm, and I read fast, and precociously, and promiscuously. I read comic books and thrillers and the classics and what was forbidden. I liked to read until I was dizzy, and after I had read and read I liked nothing better than to watch a film. As a family we saw a lot of movies together. I grew up in a world drenched with stories.

"I began making up my own stories as a child, and then telling them to my friends. I found that I liked telling stories. I finally wrote one down when I was eleven, and I was published a little later, in a school magazine. I knew then that this is what I was, a storyteller, but in India at the time it was very hard to say, 'I want to be a writer when I grow up.' Nobody that I knew of made a living as a writer. I was passionate about movies and thought I might be able to find a job in the film industry.

"I was attending film school at Columbia University in New York when I found, by chance, the translated autobiography of Colonel James Skinner in the library. James 'Sikander' Skinner was the son of a British officer and a Rajput lady, and he became a legendary cavalry officer in the early part of the nineteenth century in India. As I read the story of his amazing and turbulent and tragic life, I grew obsessed with the man, his family, and his time. I dropped out of film school to write what I thought would be a quick novel, but as I wrote the story grew until it became many stories, and a story about many different kinds of stories, and what happens when alien narratives meet each other. This spiraling tale, told by a monkey at a typewriter, took me six years to write, and finally became *Red Earth and Pouring Rain*.

"A journalist in Delhi asked me, 'Is this a novel?' I'm not sure it is. It's an Indian story in English. It is being translated into nine other languages, and won the David Higham Prize for Fiction. I've just finished a collection of short stories [*Love and Longing in Bombay*], which will be published in 1997. These are stories about Bombay, or Mumbai, and again, there is a storyteller telling stories, this time a wily old retiree telling tales to his friends in a waterfront bar.

"I'm interested, as always, in the shape of narratives, the manner in which people construct the world they live in. I worked for a long while as a computer programmer and consultant, and I'm fascinated by the new technology, and think and worry about how it will change the stories we tell, how we tell them. I'm fascinated by the relationship between storyteller and audience, and the engagement between them, which is conducted always through beauty and pleasure.

"I divide my time between Bombay and Washington, D.C. I teach creative writing at George Washington University, where my students keep me on my toes. When I am in Bombay, I work sometimes in the film industry."

Vikram Chandra's *Red Earth and Pouring Rain*, published in 1995 by Little, Brown and Company received very favorable reviews because of its intricacy and originality. Chandra was also complimented on his characterizations and his narration. The *London Review of Books* critic wrote: "Chandra's own best trait is his way with characters. He barely needs to describe them; they materialize delightfully from the way he makes them speak." The *Globe and Mail* (December 30, 1995) gave Chandra high marks as well: "What he tells simply springs into existence, becomes part of the solid world from which new stories emerge, endlessly." Since the novel's story is circular, it is difficult to say where it begins, but within the first few pages the reader is introduced to a young Indian student, Abhay, who has returned to his parents' house in India after studying in the United States. A frisky monkey steals his $40 jeans and Abhay, irritable since his American girlfriend, Amanda, left India after a brief and unendurable stay, pulls out an old toy rifle and shoots him. But this is no ordinary monkey, and Abhay's parents, fearing the wrath of the gods, take it into their home to nurse it back to health. While the monkey lies unconscious, he experiences flashes of confused memories of his previous life as a man, eventually recalling that in his former life he was a poet named Sanjay. He also learns that he can communicate with the human world by using a typewriter. Eventually three gods show up to decide the monkey's fate: Yama, the god of death; Hanuman, a benevolent god who offers to defend Sanjay; and the elephant god Ganesha. The gods finally agree that the monkey will live so long as he can hold an audience for two hours each day by telling them stories. Abhay and a nine-year-old neighbor named Saira gather an audience every day to which they read the monkey's text from the balcony. From this point onward the novel is, according to the *New York Times Book Review* (September 10, 1995), "an assemblage of long stories tracing the lineage of Sanjay, interwoven with sections written by Abhay about his American days, and there are even a few short synopses and revisions offered by Abhay's parents." In the end, the novel is a treatise on how there can be no single version of a story, and how no point of view is at any time absolutely correct. As the reviewer wrote: "What can save and sustain us, as it does Sanjay, is a story, and that story is a big one—one without end, in fact, in a mansion with rooms and rooms and rooms."

Chandra's second book, *Love and Longing in Bombay*, is—at 272 pages—considerably shorter than his first novel, but no less intricate. Its five interconnecting stories, set in modern Bombay, are told by the old, wise retired civil servant Shiv Subramaniam, who responds to all the pointed questions of his young friend, Ranjit Sharma, through storytelling. The stories—some of which were published previously in such periodicals as the *New Yorker* and the *Paris Review*—take on a variety of subjects: a military man who amputates his own

leg without anesthesia; the uneasy friendship between two ambitious society women; an account of two people robbed of illusions by their experiences during World War II. "Shakti," about the two society women, is representative of Chandra's work in its simple and beautiful details and observations: "Dolly was not perfect, she was long everywhere, she was sallow, she wore old jewelry sometimes missing a link here or there, today she wore a tatty green scarf over her shirt, and that was just it. Sheila was perfect, and she knew that however hard she tried she could never achieve the level of careless imperfection that Dolly flaunted." According to *Publishers Weekly* (January 20, 1997), which released its advance review in January 1997, the stories "encompass many levels of human experience and subtly reveal the social and cultural levels of teeming Bombay. . . . Impeccably controlled, intelligent, sensuous and sometimes grim, Chandra's timeless and timely book is remarkably life-affirming, considering the dark areas of the heart he explores." —CM

SUGGESTED READING: *Globe and Mail* C p9 Dec. 30, 1995; *London Review of Books* p16 Aug. 3, 1995; *New York Times Book Review* p38 Sep. 10, 1995; *Publishers Weekly* p392 Jan. 20, 1997

SELECTED BOOKS: *Red Earth and Pouring Rain*, 1995; *Love and Longing in Bombay*, 1997

Chin, Frank

Feb. 25, 1940– Novelist; short-story writer; playwright

Designated by a *Village Voice* reviewer as the "loudmouth godfather to the 1970s Asian American literary movement" and as a "cranky Chinatown Cowboy," Frank Chin at 59 remains one of multicultural America's most provocative and opinionated authors. A novelist, essayist, dramatist, and cultural critic, Chin vents his spleen with equal vigor against "righteous whites" and pusillanimous, politically correct Asian-Americans at risk of bargaining away their birthrights for a mess of melting-pottage. As a self-avowing "Chinaman," Frank Chin helped galvanize a generation of colleagues with Asian roots as they were negotiating a perilous course through the American cultural landscape just after the Vietnam War. Hollywood's stereotypical portrayal of Asians as either sinister or passive has always been an object of Chin's ire. In his essay "The Three-Legged Toad," published in *Bulletproof Buddhists* (1998), he wrote, "Several generations of American-born Chinese Americans huffing hyphens sponged up Charlie Chan–Fu Manchu at the Bijou, never heard of the mandate of heaven, and don't want to now because it's Chinese and sounds

Corky Lee / Courtesy of Coffee House Press

Frank Chin

icky. I belong to one of those generations of the American Cultural Revolution born and raised in the United States between 1925 and 1966."

Among Chin's first literary projects was his co-editorship of *Aiiieeeee!* (1974), a landmark anthology of works by American authors of Asian heritage; its original editors revised it in 1991, to mark the emergence of a younger generation of writers. Chin also claims to be "the first Chinese-American to have a play produced on a New York stage"— *The Chickencoop Chinaman* and *The Year of the Dragon* were first performed at the American Place Theatre in New York during the early 1970s. A number of short stories Chin published over the years were included in the Coffee House Press collection *The Chinaman Pacific & Frisco R.R. Co.* (1988). In his novels Chin routinely makes use of epic Chinese mythology and imagery, as in *Donald Duk* (1991), about a Chinese-American youngster in San Francisco coming to terms with his ancestral heritage, and *Gunga Din Highway* (1994), a satirical critique of how Asians are imagined in Hollywood films. His most recent book, *Bulletproof Buddhists*, includes several first-person essays written over a quarter-century, including an account of a visit to Cuba just after Fidel Castro took power, a commentary on a visit to contemporary Singapore, and reflections on Asian gangs in multicultural Los Angeles in the wake of the 1992 riots.

Chin is especially disdainful of the "model minority" status of Asian-Americans, by which members of that group are elevated to a pinnacle against which other people of color can be invidiously compared by the majority culture. As he wrote in one of the essays in *Bulletproof Buddhists*, "White America is as securely indifferent about us as men

as plantation owners were about their loyal house niggers. House niggers is what America has made of us, admiring us for being patient, submissive, aesthetic, passive, accommodating, essentially feminine in character—what whites call 'Confuciusist,' dreaming us up a goofy version of Chinese culture to preserve in becoming the white man's dream minority." But Chin remains a person of nuance and tries not to be guilty of the monoculturalism he inveighs against; for example, he told an interviewer for the *New York Times* (March 31, 1991) that he had firmly established a practice of reading Shakespeare to his son, then six years old.

Frank Chew Chin Jr. was born in Berkeley, California, on February 25, 1940, the son of Frank Chew Chin and Lile Bowe Yoke (Quan) Chin. As a youngster he attended "American school"; in addition, for two hours every afternoon, he studied Chinese and participated in athletics at the Wah Kue Chinese School in a building the school shared with the Chinese Nationalist Party headquarters in Oakland. Chin credits a teacher at Wah Kue school, an idealistic college professor he knew as Mr. Mah, with awakening his sense of pride in his heritage by challenging the "myth of timid, meek, passive Chinamen."

Chin attended the University of California at Berkeley from 1958 to 1961. In 1961, in the early days of the Castro regime, Chin visited Cuba for two weeks, staying at the American mobster Meyer Lansky's old Riviera Hotel, which had been appropriated in the cause of the revolution. In Cuba, which then had the second-largest Chinatown outside of Asia and San Francisco, Chin was frequently mistaken for an intellectual from mainland China or even for an "existentialist," though he claims the trip's primary purpose was to enable him to go to flamenco clubs and buy a decent guitar or two. A narrative of this trip, interspersed with anecdotes about forays to New Orleans and Iowa City, is included in Chin's essay "I Am Talking to the Strategist Sun Tzu About Life When the Subject of War Comes Up," published in *Amerasia Journal* in 1991 and reprinted in *Bulletproof Buddhas and Other Essays.*

Chin spent two years at the University of Iowa before receiving his bachelor's degree from the State University of California at Santa Barbara, in 1965. (Some published sources differ on the details regarding his undergraduate education.) In California he helped pay his way through college by working as a clerk and brakeman for two railroad companies, the Western Pacific and the Southern Pacific. That experience inspired the settings for a number of short stories he later wrote for small literary magazines; eight of them were reprinted in *The Chinaman Pacific & Frisco R.R. Co.*

Chin's first writing positions, in the late 1960s, were with King Broadcasting in Seattle, where he worked as a story editor and writer. In 1969 he became a part-time lecturer in Asian-American studies at the University of California at Davis and at San Francisco State College, then a hotbed of radical student activity on the West Coast. In 1971 he married Kathleen Chang, the daughter of a prominent family of Chinese emigré intellectuals in the United States. The marriage ended after five years. Beset by messianic visions involving her role in a utopian world order, Chang died by self-immolation in 1996, on the campus of the University of Pennsylvania.

It was in the early 1970s that Chin came to prominence as an interpreter of the Asian-American experience in contemporary culture, as an editor and as a playwright. He was a founder of the Asian American Theater Workshop in 1972; over the next several years, two of his plays, *The Chickencoop Chinaman* and *The Year of the Dragon*, would be produced at the American Place Theatre, in New York. In 1974 he received a Rockefeller Playwrights grant and a National Endowment for the Arts creative writing grant; in the same year he served as an editor, with Jeffrey Chan, Lawson Inada, and Shawn Wong, of the groundbreaking book *Aiiieeeee! An Anthology of Asian American Writers*, published by Howard University Press.

In their introduction to *Aiiieeeee!*, Chin and his colleagues wrote, "Before we can talk about our literature, we have to explain the sensibility. Before we can explain our sensibility we have to outline our histories. Before we can outline our history, we have to dispel the stereotypes." The editors based the book's title on the fact that its contributors were "American born and raised" and "got their China and Japan from the radio, off the silver screen, from television, out of comic books, from the pushers of white American culture that pictured the yellow man as something that when wounded, sad, or angry, or swearing, or wondering whined, shouted, or screamed 'aiiieeeee!'"

A sequel to this book, *The Big Aiiieeeee! An Anthology of Chinese-American and Japanese-American Literature*, edited by the same team, was published in 1991. In this work Chin and his colleagues criticized an American monocultural educational system that demeaned as primitive and alien any who deviated from the majoritarian norm, as when immigrants were told that "to be foreign was to be stupid, backward, sexually unattractive, impotent in modern society."

Published in 1988, *The Chinaman Pacific & Frisco R.R. Co.* includes eight of Chin's short stories that had appeared in various forms in literary magazines during the 1970s. The first of them, the autobiographical "Railroad Standard Time," originally published in *City Lights Journal* in 1978, describes the meditations of a Chinese-American writer-cum-railroad brakeman who, as a "twelve, maybe fourteen" year old, was initiated into his family heritage when he received his grandfather's railroad watch as a gift. Chin, as narrator, makes use of the story to reminisce about his early identity struggles, such as his frustrating quest to find himself in a "MOVIE ABOUT ME" by going to Peter Lorre films at "a matinee in a white neighborhood . . . the only Chinaman in the house," or,

"full of ghostpiss," driving "right past what's left of Oakland's dark wooden Chinatown and dark streets full of dead lettuce and trampled carrot tops, parallel all the time in line with the tracks of the Western Pacific and Southern Pacific railroads." Most of the stories in this collection, such as "The Chinatown Kid" and "The Sons of Chan," alternate between acerbity and nostalgia in describing the psychic landscape of the Chinatowns remembered by their author. In his afterword to *The Chinaman Pacific & Frisco R.R. Co.*, however, Chin launched a no-holds-barred volley against Western hegemony in a magical-realist fairy tale that imagines the psychic fate of an alien French girl in Canton dreaming about an ancestral past in which a gender-bent Joan of Arc is burned by her barbaric ancestors only to reemerge as a Nazi despot in a Christian Dark Age armageddon of militant lesbians and debauched ecclesiastics. A quote from Jack Kroll of *Newsweek* on the book's jacket reads, "A gifted writer and electric sensibility, Frank Chin is part Chinese Lenny Bruce, spritzing a comedy of bitter alienation, and part Number One Son, drawn to the traditional Chinese values—family, duty—which have been diluted by American culture."

In 1991 Coffee House Press published Chin's novel *Donald Duk*, a broadly satirical look at life on the periphery of both China and America as seen through the eyes of the precocious 12-year-old title character. The son of a restaurant owner named King Duk, the boy is forced to straddle the two cultures in San Francisco's Chinatown. Chin's choice of his hero's name, an ancestral moniker that sounds like that of a comic-book character, accentuates the identity conflicts of young Donald, who revolts against his parents' traditional Chinese New Year celebrations. The novel is structured as a series of dreams the boy has during the 15-day celebration. In the dreams young Donald is transported back to the 1860s, when his Chinese ancestors worked as coolie labor on the Central Pacific Railroad. The dream sequences allow Chin, qua Duk, to explore issues of ethnic identity and self-consciousness. The sequences are sometimes related in a dizzying cascade of surrealistic images, as in this passage from the beginning of Chapter 14: "Donald Duk dreams he's sleeping at night and wakes up dreaming, and wakes up from that dream into another, and wakes up into the real." Or: "The dream comes in like a movie all over his eyes." Chin uses the dream sequences as a vehicle for Donald Duk to discover that his ancestors were not the passive, nonassertive characters he sees in American portrayals, but a hard-working group of people who demanded fair treatment from their employers. Duk tells his father: "Everything I dream is true, and nobody knows what we did. Nobody, just me. And I don't want to be the only one who knows, and it makes me mad to be the only one who knows, and everything I dream makes me mad at white people and hate them." Thus is born a sense of community solidarity, in which Duk claims his mission in life is to set the record straight in his junior-high-school history class.

In 1992, along with five other emerging writers "of distinctive literary merit who demonstrate potential for outstanding future work," Chin was awarded a Lannan Fellowship. Two years later Coffee House Press published his *Gunga Din Highway*, a satirical novel lampooning the stereotyped images of Asians in Hollywood films, while also exposing a serious generation gap between older and younger Chinese Americans, a point made by the Tokyo-born author Kenneth LaMott and expanded upon by Chin in "Confessions of a Chinatown Cowboy." The novel's title is derived from the low-caste Hindu water-boy character in Rudyard Kipling's century-old poem "Gunga Din," now widely regarded as a symbol of Asian colonial subservience. *Gunga Din Highway* tells the story of members of two generations of the Kwan family: the elder, Longman, described as "The Chinaman Who Dies" in minor screen epics, and his son, Ulysses, who believes that his father's dream of playing Charlie Chan is a sellout to contemporary identity politics. Although the name Ulysses alludes to Homeric legend, Chin, in an author's note, took pains to explain that his book is divided into four parts (The Creation, The World, The Underworld, and Home) according to "the world of Chinese myth." In this worldview, "the world, the giant, and the Mother of Humanity create a world where every hero is an orphan, a failed scholar, an outlaw, an outcast, an exile on the road of life through danger, ignorance, deception, and enlightenment." The novel consists of alternating first-person passages in which Longman and his son Ulysses unburden their memories. Longman talks about long-ago struggles for a foothold in a recalcitrant white America. Ulysses represents Frank Chin himself, with his narratives of 1960s protest movements and of working on the railroad. The two worlds collide time and time again as young Ulysses seeks to find his own way in life.

In 1998 the University of Hawai'i Press published Chin's *Bulletproof Buddhists and Other Essays*, a collection of six pieces that had earlier appeared in several Asian-American and West Coast publications. The name of the title essay, about Asian-immigrant gang members in Los Angeles, is a reference to their belief that they are protected from violence by Buddha and martial-arts traditions. Most of the selections date from the 1990s; the earliest, "Confessions of a Chinaman Cowboy," was published in the *Bulletin of Concerned Asian Scholars* in 1972. It is primarily in this essay that Chin set forth his critique of identity politics, as when he declared, "America doesn't want [Asians] as a visible native minority. They want us to keep our place as Americanized foreigners ruled by immigrant loyalty. But never having been anything else but born here, I've never been foreign and resent having foreigners telling me my place in America and America telling me I'm foreign." The opening essay, "I Am Talking to the Strategist Sun

Tzu about Life When the Subject of War Comes Up," an account of Chin's 1961 trip to Cuba, was published in *Amerasia Journal* in 1991. In the final essay, "A Chinaman in Singapore," the only one that had not previously appeared in a periodical, Chin recounted his brief visit to Singapore, where he had been invited by the National Arts Council to give a reading of his work. In addition to describing his experiences there, Chin digressed to express his rage at the political stance of some other prominent Asian-American authors, further underscoring his reputation for outspokenness in his own community. "The proof that Chinese are despised," he writes, "is the popularity of the patently white racist rabidly Christian writing of Maxine Hong Kingston, David Henry Hwang, Amy Tan, which are taught in the public schools as the real thing while the Chinese fairy tales they fake are banned. Not one of the champions of Kingston and Tan have done step one of literary criticism."

Mainstream reviewers were not kind to *Bulletproof Buddhists*. Kitty Chen Dean warned in *Library Journal* (June 1, 1998) about "rantings . . . [that] often seem mean-spirited and incomplete," while a reviewer for *Publishers Weekly* (June 13, 1998) found fault with Chin's "emotional . . . bitterly accusatory" tone. A somewhat more positive view was published in the *Village Voice* (September 8, 1998), where Vince Shettweiler pointed out that "Chin's famous faults remain on display—his martial philosophy idealizes a hetero-macho 'manliness,' and his grouchy defense of cultural authenticity is too tactless for current intellectual debates"; but, he concluded, these "famous faults" are redeemed by the book's "streetwise sensibility that, Chin reminds us, is the only hope for our cultural survival."

In the world outside his novels, Chin has been a vocal social critic of the media, which, he believes, portray Asian images in stereotypical fashion. He was quoted in a profile of him in the *New York Times* (March 31, 1991) as saying, "The Jeffersonian ideal that public education would create generations of informed, morally conscious citizens has failed." As a result, children like his fictional Donald Duk struggle to resolve their ethnic self-images within the larger American environment. Particularly incensed at Wayne Wang's film adaptation of Amy Tan's novel *The Joy Luck Club*, he once said, as reported in the *Washington Post* (September 27, 1993), that the film was "not Chinese but white racist." But he reserved his bitterest venom for Miramax's plans to revive the old Charlie Chan series, even though this time the character was to be portrayed by Russell Wong, a Chinese-American, not a Caucasian actor in yellowface, as in the classic films of the 1930s and 1940s. Chin has pointed out, as quoted in the *New York Times* (January 5, 1997), that "Charlie Chan will always be a symbol of white racism, no matter who plays him. If you put a black man in a hood, does that make the Ku Klux Klan a civil rights organization?"

Chin has also been a harsh critic of the "model minority" paradigm by which white Americans are prompted to express their admiration of Asians for maintaining a standard of excellence against which other races are negatively compared. He wrote in "Confessions of a Chinatown Cowboy," "The myth of the Chinese Sojourner, the stereotype of the gutless, passive, effeminate Chinaman has become too precious a part of the American white male legend for America to give it up easily. Virtually everything being written about us today reveals our true racist value to America as a race of white right hands to hit the blacks and 'less assimilated' races in the head with. We're numerous enough to showcase as a minority but don't count enough to take up America's media time and space speaking for ourselves."
—E.M.

SUGGESTED READING: *Amerasia Journal* p175+ 1993, p158+ 1996, p85+ 1997; *Booklist* p111 Sep. 15, 1994; *Library Journal* p220 Feb. 15, 1991, p111+ Oct. 1, 1994; *New York Times* C p17 Oct.

14, 1992, D p7 Oct. 14, 1996, B p1 Nov. 27, 1996, II p20 Jan. 5, 1997; *New York Times Book Review* p22 Jan. 15, 1989, p9 Mar. 31, 1991, p16 Jan. 29, 1995; *Parnassus: Poetry in Review* p88+ 1992; *Publishers Weekly* p99 Sep. 2, 1988, p25+ Feb. 8, 1991, p52 and p67 May 31, 1991, p41+ Aug. 22, 1994; *Village Voice Literary Supplement* pSS23+ Feb. 8, 1994, pSS26+ Mar. 7, 1995; *Washington Post* B p1 Sep. 27, 1993; *Washington Post Book World* R p13 Apr. 7, 1991, p4 Jan. 30, 1994; *World Literature Today* p487+ Summer 1989, p715 Autumn 1991, p360+ Spring 1995

SELECTED WORKS: Fiction—*The Chinaman Pacific & Frisco RR Co.*, 1988; *Donald Duk*, 1991; *Gunga Din Highway*, 1994; Nonfiction—*Bulletproof Buddhists and Other Essays*, 1998; Drama—*The Chickencoop Chinaman*, 1972; *The Year of the Dragon*, 1974; As editor (with others)—*Aiiieeeee!: An Anthology of Asian-American Writers*, 1974; *The Big Aiiieeeee!: An Anthology of Chinese-American and Japanese-American Literature*, 1991

Coelho, Paulo

Aug. 24, 1947– Novelist

One of Brazil's most popular authors, Paulo Coelho has seen his mystical novels sell more than 15 million copies worldwide. Borrowing from ancient tales and using his characters' voices as his own, Coelho has produced stories of physical and philosophical journeys in which an individual's inner conflicts are addressed and resolved through

spiritual re-examination. His books have been translated into more than 30 languages, but, until recently, had barely penetrated the United States market. Thus far Coelho's acceptance has been slow in the United States, in part because reviewers tend to dismiss his work as New Age fiction with overtones of self-help. Coelho, a law school dropout and self-described former hippie, once responded to his critics in a U.S. radio interview by saying, "I try to share with my readers my inner quest; that's basically my spiritual quest. I don't have anything to teach . . . but actually I do have something to share."

Paulo Coelho was born on August 24, 1947, in Rio de Janeiro, Brazil. He briefly attended law school, but dropped out in 1970 in order to travel throughout South America, Mexico, North Africa, and Europe. Two years later he returned home to Brazil and began working as a songwriter, composing pop music lyrics for popular Brazilian singers such as Raul Seixas, Elis Regina, and Maria Bethania. In 1974 Coelho, who had immersed himself in the counterculture lifestyle, was briefly imprisoned for alleged subversive activities against the Brazilian government. After his release he worked for Polygram and CBS Records as an art director. He also worked as a journalist for Brazil's *O Globo* and as a television playwright for *TV O Globo* until 1980, when he once again left South America to travel. During this excursion Coelho explored Europe and Africa and walked the 830–kilometer Road of Santiago, an ancient path used by pilgrims traveling from France to Spain. This 1986 experience inspired Coelho's 1987 book *O Diario de um Mago*, published in English as *The Diary of a Magus* (some sources give the title as *The Diary of*

Omedga) in 1992, and reissued in 1995 as *The Pilgrimage: A Contemporary Quest for Ancient Wisdom.*

The Pilgrimage told the tale of one man's physical and spiritual journey across the ancient Road of Santiago. Although widely read, the book was not as well received as some of Coelho's later works (particularly in the United States), but it placed Coelho on the international literary map. *The Pilgrimage* has been translated into 15 languages and has been a bestseller in Australia, Belgium, Brazil, Canada, Portugal, Switzerland, and France, where it remained at number one for six weeks. In addition, a European multimedia company released a CD-ROM game titled *The Pilgrim* based on the novel.

Coelho's next literary effort was his 1988 breakthrough novel, *O Alquimista* (titled *The Alchemist: A Fable about Following Your Dream* in its 1993 English release). *The Alchemist* tells the story of an Andalusian shepherd boy's journey across North Africa in search of treasure. As in Coelho's previous book, the protagonist is on a road to self-discovery. According to Coelho, the story is derived from a tale in the *Thousand and One Nights* ("Arabian Nights") in which a man searches for hidden treasure only to eventually find it within himself. In an interview with the *UNESCO Courier* (March 1998), Coelho said, "I took four guiding ideas from [the source story]: the personal legend, the language of the signs, the soul of the world, and the need to listen to one's heart. I started the novel with this very short tale as my guide. The rest was vague, like being in a fog. The only thing I knew was that the boy would eventually return to his starting point."

The novel, which had been dropped by its first publisher, became hugely successful first in Brazil (where it has sold more than two million copies), and then around the globe. It reached number one on the best-seller lists of more than 25 countries, including the United States, which, for the first time, was widely introduced to Coelho's work. To date the novel has sold nine million copies and has been translated into 34 languages. *The Alchemist* was also a critical success. Book reviewers around the world labeled Coelho's second literary offering "powerful" and "inspirational." According to press material provided by Coelho's agent, the Yugoslavian publication *Politika* (1997) recommended that "Coelho's *The Alchemist* should be read as a medicine." A reviewer from Finland's *Keskisnomalainen* (1997) newspaper wrote: "*The Alchemist* is a book you don't forget. It is touching and gives [advice] for living." Even the American singing sensation Madonna, in an interview with Germany's *Sonntag-Aktuell*, called *The Alchemist* "a beautiful book about magic, dreams and the treasures we seek elsewhere and then find at our doorstep."

American critics, however, were not so quick to applaud Coelho's novel. *Library Journal* (June 15, 1993) accused the author of using a "familiar theme in a New Age package." *Kirkus Reviews* (May 1, 1993) called the book "an interdenominational, transcendental, inspirational fable—in other words, a bag of wind." On the positive side, *School Library Journal* (July 1993) contributor Sabrina Fraunfelter wrote that "this simple, yet eloquent parable celebrates the richness of the human spirit," and Brad Hooper of *Booklist* (May 1, 1993) also contributed a positive review, noting, "Beneath this novel's compelling story and the shimmering elegance with which it's told, lies a bedrock of wisdom about following one's heart."

In further tribute to Coelho's novel, the composer Walter Taieb recorded a symphony inspired by *The Alchemist.* During 1997, the novel was adapted for the stage in Japan, Turkey, and Yugoslavia, and in 1998, an adaptation was produced for the Phoenix Theater in the United States. When discussing the novel's worldwide success with the *UNESCO Courier*, Coelho stated, "When I wrote *The Alchemist*, I obviously did not know that it was going to be such a success. I only wanted to write about what I believe, which is that everybody needs to live out their personal legend."

Coelho's next writing adventures were the 1990 novel *Brida* and his 1992 work, *As Valkyrias*, or *The Valkyries: An Encounter With Angels.* The latter book, which is presented as an autobiographical quest to speak with his "personal angel," received mixed reviews. Even in the author's country, critiques were not altogether favorable. In the Brazilian publication *BRAZZIL* (May 1996) reviewer Bondo Wyszpolski wrote that *The Valkyries* "lacks the fabulist magic and storytelling charisma of *The Alchemist*, and by its simplicity even makes us feel that we're being talked down to." Wyszpolski went on to dismiss the other characters framing the novel—such as the leather-clad women who ride around on motorcycles in the desert and converse in a "kind of spiritual talk no one understands"—as "too contrived, too derivative." The reviewer did give Coelho some praise for his book, admitting "the confessional tone of *The Valkyries* earns the author some credit for his frankness." He added, however, that "ultimately, the message is too simplistic and the picture too rosy."

While continuing to write for a wide variety of magazines, in 1994 Coelho published *Maktub*, a compilation of his daily columns (also called "Maktub") from the three most widely read newspapers in Brazil, *Folha de Sao Paulo*, *O Dia* and *Journal de Bahia*. That same year he also published the novel *Na Margem do Rio Piedra Eu Senti e Chorei*, or *By The River Piedra I Sat Down and Wept.* The book is narrated by Pilar, a female student in Zaragoza, Spain, who travels to Madrid in order to hear an old childhood friend (referred to only as "he"), who is now a reputed miracle worker, lecture on his beliefs. The friend tries to show Pilar the spirituality he feels he has learned (among other things, he explains how he has seen the feminine side of God), and also confesses that he has been in love with her for many years. Pilar must then decide between continuing her studies or beginning a romance with her old friend.

Wyszpolski was also critical of this novel, likening it to *The Valkyries* and deeming both books "awkward and simplistic." The reviewer also wrote that *By The River Piedra* is "not a particularly memorable tale nor is it particularly well written." *Publishers Weekly* (April 22, 1996) agreed with this assessment, criticizing Coolho for "sacrificing dramatic integrity to polemic, and for insisting on cloaking sermons in fictional trappings." The magazine also called Coelho's characters "stilted," but acknowledged that the author's message "is invariably heartfelt and challenging, emphasizing the feminine aspects of the divine and the charismatic aspects of worship."

By The River Piedra I Sat Down and Wept sold well around the world (it was a best-seller in 15 countries and was translated into 23 languages), but it still did not equal the critical or financial achievements of *The Alchemist*.

Coelho's latest literary offering in translation is *The Fifth Mountain*, published as *O Monte Cinco* in 1996 and made available in the U.S. in early 1998. The novel tells the story of the biblical prophet Elijah, and how, after being identified as a "man of the spirit," he is urged by an angel to leave his homeland of Israel and the seductive charms of Queen Jezebel. After Elijah falls in love with a widow in Zarephath, however, he is forced to confront the physical and religious conflicts within himself.

In *The Fifth Mountain*, Coelho's characters undertake journeys similar to those detailed in his other books, and, like his other novels, it garnered largely mixed reviews in the United States. *Publishers Weekly* (January 26, 1998) was unimpressed with Coelho's retelling of the classic story, calling it "muted" in comparison to the Bible's version. *Library Journal* (February 1, 1998), however, lauded the novel as "fascinating," and added that it is "neither dull nor preachy and should find a niche among readers of popular fiction."

Despite his worldwide popularity and success, Coelho's work has been the subject of heated debate in the United States. While readers abroad have seemingly relished the spiritual advice handed down by Coelho, skeptics in the United States have been slow to accept the New Age sensibility of his writing. This phenomenon has perhaps prevented Coelho from enjoying large-scale American success. As cited in *Contemporary Authors* (1996), a writer for the *Economist* (March 11, 1995) explained that North American book reviewers "denounce [Coelho] as a charlatan, a bore, a seller of snake oil." In interviews, Coelho has defended the spiritual message of his books. "I think my books speak for everyone. There is a necessity to go forward, to follow our *destino* no matter where it takes us," he told *Hispanic* magazine (December 1995)

Paulo Coelho recently completed *O Manual do Guerreiro da Luz* (1997), which is not yet available in English. In the *Times Literary Supplement* (October 8, 1999), Molly McGrann pronounced *Veronika Decides to Die*, translated into English by Margaret Jull Costa for publication in 1999, Coelho's "most literary work so far." The suicide attempt by the title character lands her in a mental hospital, where she finds love and where each of the other patients "suffers from a condition which is the manifestation of a social ill," in McGrann's words. "In Margaret Jull Costa's translation, Coelho's prose is sensibly simple, stark at times with spirituality, but not overtly sentimental as other books," McGrann concluded.

Coelho has received several awards for his writing, including the Chevalier des Arts et des Lettres (France, 1996), the Flaiano International Award (Italy, 1996), the Prix Lectrices d'Elle (France, 1995), and the Golden Book Award (Yugoslavia, 1995 and 1996). He continues to write his daily column, "Maktub," for Brazilian newspapers, and lives in Rio de Janeiro.—D.B.

SUGGESTED READING: *Booklist* May 1, 1993; *BRAZZIL* (on-line) May 1996, Aug. 1996, *Britannica Online* May 18, 1998; *Economist* Mar. 11, 1995; *Hispanic* p12 Dec. 1995, with photo; *Keskisnomalainen* 1997; *Kirkus Reviews* May 1, 1993; *Library Journal* June 15, 1993, p110 Feb. 1, 1998; *Publishers Weekly* p28 Apr. 15, 1996, with photo, p58 Apr. 22, 1996, p70 Jan. 26, 1998; *School Library Journal* July 1993; *UNESCO Courier* p34+ Mar. 1998, with photos; *Contemporary Authors* vol 152, 1996; *Politika* 1997

SELECTED WORKS: Fiction—*O Diário de um Mago*, 1987 (*Diary of a Magus*, 1992 *The Pilgrimage: A Contemporary Quest for Ancient Wisdom*, 1995); *O Alquemista*, 1988 (*The Alchemist: A Fable about Following Your Dream*, 1993); *Brida*, 1990; *As Valkyrias* (*The Valkyries: An Encounter with Angels*), 1992; *Na Margem do Rio Piedra Eu Senti e Chorei* (*By The River Piedra I Sat Down and Wept*), 1994; *O Monte Cinco*, 1996 (*The Fifth Mountain*, 1998); *O Manual de Guerreiro da Luz*, 1997; *Veronika Decides to Die*, 1999 Nonfiction—*Maktub*, 1994

Miriam Berkley

Cook, Thomas H.

Sep. 19, 1947– Mystery writer; nonfiction writer

Although the crime novel is often marked by heavy-handed narrative and hackneyed plot devices, Thomas H. Cook has been held up as one of its finest craftsmen since he began writing in 1980. His many works of murder and mystery, such as *Sacrificial Ground* (1988), *The City When It Rains* (1991), and *The Chatham School Affair* (1996), possess a literary style which many critics cite as a breath of fresh air. In addition to his fictional crime stories, Cook has also ventured into the genre of true crime, chronicling real-life murder mysteries in *Early Graves* (1990) and *Blood Echoes* (1992). Although he has received much praise for his genre works, in his early career Cook occasionally dabbled in mainstream fiction, producing such literary novels as *The Orchids* (1982) and *Elena* (1986).

In an autobiographical statement submitted to *World Authors 1990-1995*, Thomas H. Cook writes, "I was born into a household without books, and did not begin to read with any regularity until I attended college. At that point, two books utterly overwhelmed me, [Melville's] *Moby Dick* and [Faulkner's] *Light in August*. I can no longer recall . . . the qualities I found in these particular books that so altered my own perception of what a book could be. I think it was the sheer density of the voices, their authenticity, that fact that nothing rang false or seemed in the least disingenuous. I could not imagine that these authors wrote for any [other] reason than a passionate need to communicate their visions of the world.

"But it is a far leap from appreciating the writing of others to believing that you can be a writer as well. I certainly entertained no such hope. I had the desire [to] write, but little else, nor did I expect ever to be published. I stayed in college, went to graduate school, and only while working on my Ph.D. dissertation, actually finished a novel. To my great surprise, it was published. I have been writing ever since.

"I suppose I will be known primarily as a mystery writer. I have written quite a few mysteries, although several of my books, *The Orchids*, *Elena*, and *The City When It Rains*, are not mysteries. I tried to write a series character in the mystery genre, but grew bored by the time the third book was published, and thus gave up that particular effort. Since then, my mysteries have concentrated on character, atmosphere, and the internal psychological dynamics of the characters.

"I am told, often by readers, that I write 'sad' books, 'dark' books, and I suppose that is true. These books reflect my vision of human existence, which, I admit, is indeed rather sad, but they do not reflect my personal condition, which is, and always has been, extraordinarily fortunate.

"Perhaps, more than anything, the sadness in my work is a reflection of what I prefer in the works of others, which is a deeply serious, even somber, understanding of our life on earth. I am a great admirer of Melville and Faulkner, as I said, but also of Joseph Conrad, Thomas Hardy and Edith Wharton, writers who are very different, of course, but whose attention to the human fate has always struck me as essentially solemn. My favorite poets are William Butler Yeats and Matthew Arnold for the same reason, that they never seem frivolous to me, never merely pursuing the game of writing, but are truly writers who have a deep commitment to the seriousness of their own observations. Sincerity has always seemed to me the mark of all great writing. It can shine through almost any style, no matter how florid or how minimalist. To be regarded as a 'sincere' writer would surely be enough for me."

Thomas H. Cook was born September 19, 1947, in Fort Payne, Alabama, the son of Virgil Richard Cook and Myrick (Harper) Cook. He attended Georgia State College, where he earned his Bachelor of Arts degree in 1969.

After graduation, Cook relocated to New York City, where he took a job as an advertising executive with U.S. Industrial Chemicals and began doing graduate work at Hunter College. He earned a Master of Arts degree from Hunter in 1972. The following year, he left U.S. Industrial Chemicals and started working as a clerk and typist at the Association for the Help of Retarded Adults. In 1975, he took some time off from working and dedicated himself to further graduate study, this time at Columbia University. In 1976, he was awarded a Master of Philosophy (M.Phil.) degree.

Cook soon moved to Georgia, where beginning in 1978 he taught English and history at Dekalb Community College in Clarkston. His first foray into the world of publishing also came in 1978, when he began serving as a contributing editor to *Atlanta* magazine. On March 17, 1978, he married Susan Terner, a radio writer.

Cook's first published novel, *Blood Innocents*, was issued in 1980. He had worked on it steadily since the 1970s. The novel takes place in New York City and is a crime story of the "police procedural" subgenre. A success in the mystery genre from the start, with his first novel Cook earned a nomination for the Edgar Allan Poe Award, presented by the Mystery Writers of America. Although *Blood Innocents* did not win the award, it paved the way for a successful career in mystery and true-crime writing which continues through the 1990s. Cook left his teaching position in 1981 and his editing job in 1982 in order to devote himself fully to writing.

His next offering, published two years after *Blood Innocents*, was *The Orchids*, a work of literary fiction which brought critical acclaim. This was followed by *Tabernacle* (1983) and, after a three-year break, *Elena* (1986), also a non-mystery work. His 1988 novel *Sacrificial Ground* introduced the character of Atlanta detective Frank Clemons. The novel garnered Cook his second Edgar Allan Poe Award nomination.

Frank Clemons, the detective in *Sacrificial Ground*, appears again in *Flesh and Blood* (1989). In this novel, Clemons switches his base of operations from Atlanta to New York, where he becomes obsessed with solving the murder of a union organizer, which leads him into the underworld of modern-day sweatshops. "Thomas H. Cook triumphs at teaching an old dog new tricks," wrote Marilyn Stasio of the *New York Times* (February 19, 1989), in reference to the author's rejuvenation of a sometimes-tired genre.

Streets of Fire, the second of two Cook novels published in 1989, is set in Birmingham, Alabama in the early 1960s, against the backdrop of the civil rights marches. Troubled by his own conflicting attitudes toward race, a white police detective dedicates himself to solving the murder of a young black girl. The case turns out to have far-reaching political as well as racial ramifications. In a review for the *New York Times* (September 24, 1989), Marilyn Stasio praised the "powerful poignancy" with which Cook portrays the novel's protagonist. "It is only when he reaches for epochal significance that the author overburdens his story with its historical context," Stasio wrote. "Characters become sentimentalized; all events turn portentous; actions lose their ambiguity of motive; and a tone of overwrought lyricism drenches the narrative in melodrama."

Cook's first published novel of the 1990s was *Night Secrets* (1990). The book marked the third appearance of detective Frank Clemons. *Night Secrets* finds Clemons caught up in a murder case that involves a mysterious, alluring gypsy woman who has been arrested for a crime she may not have committed. In a mixed review which appeared in the *New York Times*, Marilyn Stasio wrote that Cook's characterization of the gypsy, a crucial element of the novel, is somewhat lacking. "As always," Stasio added, "the author's gritty cityscape maintains its melancholy charm; but he has written elsewhere with truer feeling about the inhabitants of these lonely streets." Lorenzo Carcaterra, writing in *People* (August 20, 1990), found the novel's characterizations to be so strong that they were actually more engaging than the mystery itself.

Also in 1990, Cook made his first attempt at the nonfiction genre of true crime, publishing *Early Graves: The Shocking True-Crime Story of the Youngest Woman Ever Sentenced to Death Row*. The well-reviewed book details the case of a young woman and her husband, who kidnap, torture, and murder two young girls.

Cook published *The City When It Rains* at the beginning of 1991. The novel's main character is a freelance photographer who works at night in Manhattan. His work draws him into the puzzling suicide of a woman in the Hell's Kitchen section of the city, which inspires him to compile a book-length photo essay. Echoing the opinion of many critics, Marilyn Stasio of the *New York Times* (January 20, 1991) praised the author's avoidance of typical crime novel clichés in *The City When It Rains*. She also cited his excellent pacing as one of the novel's narrative strengths.

Cook's second novel published in 1991 was *Evidence of Blood*. The novel tells the story of a man who finds himself driven to solve a 30-year-old murder case after attending the funeral of a friend, a town sheriff who had been tracking the case before his death. Steven Slosberg of the *New York Times* (October 20, 1991) described *Evidence of Blood* as "a highly satisfying story, strong in color and atmosphere, intelligent and exacting." A *Kirkus Reviews* (August 15, 1991) assessment of the book emphasized its riveting drama and rated it as one of Cook's finest works.

In 1992, Thomas Cook produced his second true crime volume, *Blood Echoes: The Infamous Alday Mass Murder and Its Aftermath*, in which he recounts the true story of two escaped prisoners who broke into a private home and murdered the residents.

With *Mortal Memory* (1993), Cook returned to the theme of the long-term ramifications of murder, which he first explored in *Evidence of Blood*. The book's protagonist is the sole survivor of a killing spree in which a father murdered his entire family and then disappeared. When the young man is contacted by a writer who is compiling a study on fathers who kill their families, the painful memories return to the surface. The *Kirkus Reviews* (February 15, 1993) praised Cook's "impressive narrative simplicity" and keen insightfulness, and declared the novel "finely crafted psychological crime-fare."

Cook extended the theme of murder's ongoing repercussions for the living in his next offering, *Breakheart Hill* (1995). The novel concerns a high school girl's murder and its impact, decades later, on those who knew her. Critic George Needham of *Booklist* (July 19, 1995) found the book to be an immensely powerful work; he particularly marveled at the unexpected climax. The International Association of Crime Writers apparently shared Needham's enthusiasm for the novel, as it awarded Cook their Hammett Prize.

In discussing the initial spark which led to *Breakheart Hill*, Cook told *Publishers Weekly* (October 19, 1998), "My wife and I were driving into New York when we stopped for a hamburger. She noticed a street sign for Breakheart Hill, and that pushed a button for me. By the time we reached the city, I pretty much had the basic sense of a story."

The Chatham School Affair, perhaps Cook's most critically acclaimed novel, was published in 1996. The elderly narrator spins a tale from his youth about a young art teacher who committed a bizarre murder in which he himself may or may not have had a part. Through the course of the book, the narrator tries to sort out exactly what happened all those years ago. Marilyn Stasio, longtime reviewer of Cook's work, noted the novel's Gothic feel as being particularly engaging (*New York Times* September 29, 1996). *The Chatham School Affair* earned Cook both the Edgar Allan Poe Award, for which he had been nominated several times before, as well as the Bram Stoker Award.

The author's most recent work to date is the mystery novel *Instruments of Night*, released in the fall of 1998. In an autobiographical twist, the novel's protagonist is a mystery writer, except in this case he writes grisly tales of murder that reflect his own tortured memories of the murder of his sister, which he witnessed as a child. The plot thickens when the writer is contacted by a wealthy woman who is so taken by his mystery stories that she believes he can solve the half century-old mystery of her best friend's murder. In her latest review, Marilyn Stasio lauds Cook's "appreciation for the nuances of terror," including his intense imagery (*New York Times* November 29, 1998).

Thomas Cook has become known to critics and readers as a mystery writer with an uncanny flair for character development and atmosphere. His descriptions of southern rural life in particular have garnered him great critical praise. He has often been lauded for incorporating grand themes typically ignored in the detective fiction genre. A minority, however, criticize what they see as his penchant for overwrought story elements and plotlines.

Among his own influences and literary interests, Cook cites a fascination with 19th-century fiction. "It's very atmospheric," he said in *Publishers Weekly* (October 19, 1998). "I myself don't write in a minimalist style. For me, the most important thing is the physical atmosphere of a place, but it's also a joy to create new characters."

Cook discussed his philosophy of writing for publication in a recent *Publishers Weekly* (October 19, 1998) interview. "You give a publisher the best book you can," he told interviewer Robert Dahlin, "and at that point, it's out of your hands to a large degree . . . what happens next is out of the publishers hands as well. They don't go out intending to fail with a book."

The author currently resides in New York with his wife, Susan, and their daughter, Justine Ariel. —B.S.

SUGGESTED READING: *Amazon.com*; *Booklist* July 19, 1996; *Kirkus Reviews* Aug. 15, 1991; Feb. 15, 1993; *New York Times* 7 p23 Feb. 19, 1989; p29 Sep. 24, 1989; p22 June 24, 1990; p27 Jan. 20, 1991; p47 Oct. 20, 1991; p28 Sep. 29, 1996, Nov. 29, 1998; *People* p29+ Aug. 20, 1990, with photo; *Publishers Weekly* p43 Oct. 19, 1998, with photo

SELECTED WORKS: Fiction—*Blood Innocents*, 1980; *The Orchids*, 1982; *Tabernacle*, 1983; *Elena*, 1986; *Sacrificial Ground*, 1988; *Streets of Fire*, 1989; *Flesh and Blood*, 1989; *Night Secrets*, 1990; *The City When It Rains*, 1991; *Evidence of Blood*, 1991; *Mortal Memory*, 1993; *Breakheart Hill*, 1995; *The Chatham School Affair*, 1996; *Instruments of Night*, 1998; Nonfiction—*Early Graves: A Shocking True-Crime Story of the Youngest Woman Ever Sentenced to Death Row*, 1990; *Blood Echoes: The Infamous Alday Mass Murder and Its Aftermath*, 1992

Cooper, Bernard

Oct. 3, 1951– Novelist; memoirist

The American author Bernard Cooper is a well-regarded essayist, novelist, and memoirist whose work is strikingly autobiographical. His first book, *Maps to Anywhere* (1990), gathered essays that deal with various aspects of the author's life—including his sentiments toward his aging father and his feelings about the death of his brother. *A Year of Rhymes*, which followed in 1993, was Cooper's fictional account of his struggle to cope with his adored older brother's slow death from leukemia. Cooper's most recent work, the memoir *Truth Serum* (1996), focused on his maturing to adulthood, his gradual acceptance of his homosexuality, and his feelings on watching many of his friends die from AIDS.

Bernard Cooper was born in Los Angeles, California, on October 3, 1951, the son of Edward S. Cooper, an attorney. He received a bachelor's degree in fine arts from the California Institute of the Arts in 1973. Two years later he received his M.F.A. degree.

Miriam Berkley

Bernard Cooper

In 1978 Cooper became an instructor of creative writing at the Otis/Parsons Institute of Art and Design. Starting in 1987, he also began to teach a similar course at the Southern California Institute of Architecture in Los Angeles. While teaching, he also contributed to many periodicals, including the *Georgia Review*, *Grand Street*, the *Yale Review*, *Harper's*, and the *Kenyon Review*. Some of his early work was represented in *The Best American Essays, 1988*.

Cooper's first book, *Maps to Anywhere*, was a collection of about 30 autobiographical essays— some as short as a paragraph—that touch on a variety of topics, including the death of his older brother from leukemia, his father's old age, and his slow acceptance of his own homosexuality. Critical reaction to the book was generally positive. Jonathan Kirsch of the *Los Angeles Times* (October 10, 1990) called Cooper's first book "a curious, luminous and ultimately mysterious book," and commented that the author "has given us a patchwork of prose that achieves the stature of a novel." Similar praise came from Douglas Seibold of the *Chicago Tribune* (May 25, 1990): "Each of these pieces is fully inhabited by lively thought, which in turn endows Cooper's prose with the rigorous precision of poetry."

Cooper's first novel, *A Year in Rhymes*, was a foray into autobiographical fiction. Set in early 1960s Los Angeles, it tells the coming-of-age story of Burt Zerkin, the narrator and younger son of a prosperous Jewish lawyer who provides, comfortably, for his wife and two sons by working on high-profile divorce cases. Burt's older brother, Bob, works for their father as a detective, serving divorce papers and investigating misbehaving

spouses. About halfway through the novel, Bob develops leukemia. As the family faces Bob's imminent death, Burt slowly uncovers his own sexual feelings towards men. Cooper's first novel received mixed reviews. In his review of *A Year in Rhymes* for *New York Newsday* (August 18, 1993), Jonathan Dee complained that the secrecy surrounding Burt's homosexuality never causes any controversy in the book. "Not only is Burt's secret never discovered," Dee wrote, "but the novel seems content to forget the whole matter for very long stretches— which, in the late chapters, puts the narrator in the odd position of paying a kind of lip service to his own sexuality. Nothing comes of it. One might feel for young Burt and thus be glad that he's not made to shoulder any more trouble than his brother's illness has already dealt him; but the novel is weaker for it." Later in his review, Dee commented that the author "gives the impression that he loves all his characters too much to let any ungenerous or unlikeable side of them show through. . . . In his zeal to do right by its characters [this book] becomes the one thing a good novel can never afford to be: unsurprising." Jim Marks of the *Washington Post* (September 16, 1993) disagreed with Dee's assessment: "Although little more than 200 pages, *A Year in Rhymes* has a leisurely feel, apparently loosely structured, anecdotal, packed with incident. Yet the book's casualness is only apparent. Cooper is a master of detail." A writer for *Kirkus Reviews* (June 1, 1993) took the middle road, finding the book "beautifully written and memorable— if not as riveting or as powerful as one might hope."

Cooper's next book, the memoir *Truth Serum*, was published in 1996. The work made no mention of Cooper's brother who died of leukemia, nor of his other brothers, but focused instead on his own life from adolescence to adulthood and his gradual understanding of his homosexuality. He also wrote straightforwardly about his early experiences with the threat of AIDS—a feat lauded by many critics. Craig Seligman, reviewing the memoir for the *New York Times Book Review* (May 5, 1996), wrote, "In *Truth Serum*, Mr. Cooper has figured out how to harness his verbal cleverness, and—more impressively and originally—he's found a way to write about anguish without sacrificing his wit and without stumbling into either reverence or irreverence." The critic for the *Washington Post Book World* (June 9, 1996) praised, "Each of Cooper's 13 essays is as finely crafted and polished as the best fiction; images and metaphors and ideas return and illuminate his characters and episodes." However, the reviewer for *Booklist* (May 1, 1996) was slightly more critical, claiming that while the author's descriptions of his childhood were vivid and powerful, "scenes of Cooper's adult life don't come across with the same intensity, although some of his AIDS memories are quite wrenching and may prove cathartic for many readers. Paul Monette's National Book Award–winning *Becoming A Man* (1992) and Marlene and Christopher Shyer's *Not Like Other Boys* cover similar ground and are more compelling."

Bernard Cooper currently lives in Los Angeles, where he continues to teach creative writing. —C.M.

SUGGESTED READING: *Booklist* May 1, 1996; *Chicago Tribune* May 25, 1990; *Harper's Magazine* p34+ July 1989; *Kirkus Reviews* June 1, 1993; *Los Angeles Times* Oct. 10, 1990; *New York Newsday* Aug. 18, 1993; *New York Times Book Review* p15 May 5, 1996; *Washington Post* C p2 Sep. 16, 1993; *Washington Post Book World* p4+ June 9, 1996; *Contemporary Authors, vol. 134*, 1992

SELECTED WORKS: Fiction—*A Year of Rhymes*, 1993; Nonfiction—*Maps to Anywhere*, 1990; *Truth Serum*, 1996

Michael Matson/Courtesy of Grove Press

Cooper, Dennis

Jan. 10, 1953– Novelist; poet; short-story writer

Dennis Cooper's transgressive and dystopian fiction has been described as "the very stuff of Jesse Helms' worst nightmares" by the author and critic Edmund White, who found elements of French decadent poetry, glam-rock fantasy, and porn-epic imagery in Cooper's work. Once a chapbook cult favorite, Cooper has published several poetry collections and novels and has edited an anthology of contemporary writers, making him an important figure in America's "radical-queer" literary scene. As Jonathan Bing commented in *Publishers Weekly* (March 21, 1994), "Cooper's voyeuristic fascination with adolescent runaways, punks, and social castoffs has led some to view him as the Jean Genet of the American suburbs." Cooper's muse, as Bing points out, has been the "ephemeral, awkward beauty of teenage boys" and the "cadences of adolescent slang and the linguistic turmoil of teenagers attempting to give weight to authentic emotions without sounding clichéd." Cooper's first significant poetry collection, *Idols*, published in 1978, was also one of his last; he has since devoted himself to writing prose fiction, including the novels *Closer* (1989), *Wrong* (1992), *Try* (1994), and *Guide* (1998). In 1992 he edited the anthology *Discontents: New Queer Writers*, published by Amethyst.

Dennis Cooper was born in Pasadena, California, on January 10, 1953, the son of Clifford Cooper, a businessman, and Ann King Cooper. At the age of 14, Dennis began writing poetry after reading the works of such French decadents as Rimbaud and Lautréamont, and the Marquis de Sade. From his earliest years, Cooper experimented with writing that explored the realm of alienation with an uninhibited on-the-edge sensibility. His first attempt at fiction—written when he was an adolescent—was a porn epic influenced by his reading *120 Days of Sodom*, but he burned the manuscript for fear that his mother would find it. Years later, he told the *Voice Literary Supplement* (May 1989) how he was still haunted by that early experience: "That book really did something to me. It just seemed to key into something and open something up. I was so astonished by my reaction to it. It seemed to be so profound about relationships, ideas. I still think it's the greatest book and it's been really in my mind all the time."

Cooper admits he was not a model student. "I was raised very badly," he remembers. "I was a mess and miserable and did a lot of drugs." He was expelled from private school a year before graduating, but he continued to mine his imagination for "weird parodies" and other fantasies in the decadent genre. High school, with its sexual and identity-crisis traumas, has always been a prominent psychic landscape in Cooper's fiction, but there are no Archies or Veronicas in his surreal, erotic-tinged blackboard id-jungle of estrangement and obsession. In the *Publishers Weekly* interview, Cooper described adolescence as "a point at which your childhood's eating at you and adulthood's eating at you and you're just in chaos. I feel like that's the *truth* or something. People in that state are in touch with what the world's really about."

Cooper spent a year at Pitzer College in Claremont, California, but dropped out at the urging of his poetry professor. After a brief stint as a disc jockey, he published his first chapbook, *The Terror of Earrings*, in 1973. Three years later, he founded a small literary magazine, *Little Caesar*, and the Little Caesar Press, serving as editor-in-chief of both until 1982. During these years, he also organized the acclaimed Beyond Baroque reading and performance series in Venice, California, and published several collections of poetry, including *Tiger Beat*

(1978), *Idols* (1979), and *The Tenderness of Wolves* (1981). It was the appearance of *Idols* that first garnered him widespread notice as a writer who discovered sublimity in experiences of disaffection and alienation. Fragments from the biographical note in *Idols* can serve as a window into Cooper's disjointed life: "President of his local chapter of The Dave Clark Five Fan Club. Edited a satirical magazine, *Flunker*, at twelve. Cub Scout. Most unpopular kid in school, Fifth through Eighth grades. Accidentally hit on the head with an axe, barely survives, 1964. Boy Scout, kicked out for long hair. . . . First and last girlfriend, Susie, 1966. . . . Transferred to private boys' school. . . . Vice President of his class, Ninth and Tenth grades. Formed shock-rock band *Coney Island*, lasted six months. Expelled from private school in 11th grade, for insubordination. . . . Hung around Glitter Rock clubs, had sex with the famous. First boyfriend, Julian."

Many of the poems in *Idols* are incantations of obsessive longing for connection with the various young men in whom Cooper sought solace: his classmates, punk idols, hitchhikers and hustlers, literary mentors such as Rimbaud and Verlaine, and pop celebrities including David Bowie, Peter Frampton, and Shawn Cassidy, all of them idolized within the sanctuary of Cooper's confessional verse. Even the offspring of a politician is fair game for his meditations, as in the 13-part "Some Adventures of John F. Kennedy, Jr.," in which he contemplates the private thoughts of a peer forced to grow up in the shadow of a very public trauma: "He remembers / putting a hand to his head, / the squiggle of his thoughts; remembers his mother / was wasted, being bored, a million tears. . ." and, "He knows / there is greatness inside him / and he expects the Bee Gees, / like three wise men / to bring it to him through / the haze of a beer bout, / away on a dance floor / all snug in his wealth."

In 1984, the year after he moved to New York City, Cooper's first prose fiction work, the novella *Safe*, was published by Grove Press. Soon thereafter, he moved for a while to Amsterdam to work on a new novel, *Closer*, confident that the succès d'estime of *Safe* had made him known among mainstream editors eager to discover new authors of the gay-themed fiction. Still, he was unable to persuade any of them to publish *Closer*, with its controversial theme and situations, though Grove finally published it in 1989. In *Closer*, Cooper probed the troubled psyche of George Miles, a tormented adolescent who, with his punk-driven peers and two 40-something men, inhabit a web of anomie and passion in which each of the younger men is at once victim, seducer, and fetish-object. With Cooper's characteristic graphicness, the novel traces their actions with an equally characteristic dispassionate numbness. Cooper later admitted to Vince Aletti (*Voice Literary Supplement*, May 1989) that the character of George Miles was based on a "long lost" real person he had known in high school, one who looked like "everybody I've ever

written about. He had untidy dark hair, large eyes, big lips, smooth, pale skin, thin, tall. I always write about that." Reviewing *Closer* for the *New York Review of Books* (August 17, 1989), Thomas R. Edwards acknowledged that some readers might be squeamish about Cooper's "sensual utopia where effort or regret is quite unknown," but he credited the author's intentions as being both "interesting and honorable." Edwards concluded: "*Closer* is a noncommittal, rigorously descriptive, unmoralizing book, painful or even emetic in effect. But it seems an attempt to face squarely what Cooper sees as the implactions of homosexuality's darket corners. If this is so, it is a work of considerable courage." Cooper later told Jonathan Bing that the "pitiless, uninflected" style of *Closer* was inspired by the work of French filmmaker Robert Bresson. A quotation from Bresson served as the epigraph for Cooper's 1994 novel *Try*, also published by Grove Press: "The thing that matters is not what they show me but what they hide from me and, above all, *what they do not suspect is in them.*" *Try* narrates the convoluted tale of Ziggy, an abused teenager marooned in a dysfunctional sexual netherworld occupied by his two adoptive and predatory fathers, his pornography-dealing uncle, and the one person he can trust, a junkie. The novel is semiautobiographical; Cooper told Bing that the period during which he wrote it was "a really deep [expletive] period in my life. The book was kind of to ground myself in the real world. . . . Ziggy's the first character I've ever done who is trying to understand what's happening to him. And he hasn't gotten very far, but he's trying, and that's like a big step."

Wrong, a collection of stories Cooper wrote over the years, appeared in a Grove Weidenfeld edition in 1992. Heavy with nihilism and drugged-out despair, the stories explore the world of serial killers, revenge, and torment. In the title story, Mike, a drifter, murders another man in the heat of passion. The text reads: "He walked home. He thought of offing himself. 'After death, what's left?' he mumbled. He meant 'to do.' Once you've killed someone, life's [expletive]. It's a few rules and you've already broken the best. He had a beer at the Ninth Circle." *Guide*, Cooper's 1998 novel, deals—as do many of his other works—with characters whose obsessions with sex and violence are more important to them than their lives or those of other people. Critical reaction to the novel was sharply divided.

Cooper has also been a contributing editor to *Artforum* and the organizer of several queer-themed exhibits in New York City galleries. In 1991 *The Undead*, an AIDS-inspired performance piece he conceived with choreographer Ishmael Houston-Jones (a frequent collaborator) and Peter Brosius, was staged at The Kitchen, an experimental venue in lower Manhattan. Robert Massa described it in the *Village Voice* (December 17, 1991) as "a nightmarish collage of obsessive monologues, stilted dialogue, and jerky, brutal dance set against blurry homoerotic projections and blaring music under dim, yellowish light. It's hard to imagine a more honest, bleak portrait of gay desire and alienation in the age of AIDS."

The Undead was created during a period when the American sexual counterculture was bifurcating into a more radical stream, with more radical avant-gardists, Cooper among them, preferring to be labeled as "queer" rather than seek widespread assimilation in the American mainstream. Although Cooper had come of age in the wake of the Stonewall movement, a defining moment for American gay sensibility, he was now emerging as an avatar for the more radical wing of the gay-literature movement. He compiled and edited the groundbreaking *Discontents: New Queer Writers*, a book published in 1992 by Amethyst Press that placed Cooper solidly in the camp of the younger, more radical litterateurs. This book critiqued the Stonewall mindset for validating only the white middle-class male experience as the "official" gay world view—this at a time when Act-Up and Queer Nation were challenging the hegemonies of the older liberal gay establishment, which regarded coming-out and identity as primary, a stance that has been described as "apologetic stateliness" by critic David Van Leer. Reviewing *Discontents* along with Edmund White's *Faber Book of Gay Short Fiction* and Essex Hemphill's *Brother to Brother: New Writings by Black Gay Men* in the *New Republic* (October 12, 1992), Van Leer wrote: "A more confrontational sense of the relation between sexuality and literature is offered in Dennis Cooper's [book]. For Cooper, both sex and fiction are sites of political struggle. . . . It is in the general context of this furious debate between older liberal gays and younger radical queers that Cooper locates his authors. His collection stands as a 'wake-up call' to traditional gay anthologies, with Cooper playing rebel leader to White's role of elder statesman."

Cooper presented his thoughts on such pop-culture figures as Courtney Love and Leonardo Di Caprio in *All Ears: Cultural Criticism, Essays, and Obituaries*, published in 1999. His novel *Period* is scheduled to appear in 2000.
—E. M.

SUGGESTED READING: *Artforum* p8 Oct. 1992, p102 Summer 1993, p62+ Mar. 1995, p26 Summer 1996; *Arts Magazine* p83 Summer 1989; *Critical Quarterly* p105+ Spring 1994, p103+ Autumn 1995; *Journal of American Studies* p365+ Dec. 1996; *Library Journal* p122 May 15 1992, p114 Feb. 1 1993, p158 Jan. 1994; *Nation* p21+ July 1 1991; *National Review* p54+ June 17 1996; *New Republic* p50+ Oct. 12 1992; *New Statesman & Society* p56 Sept. 30 1994; *New York Review of Books* p52+ Aug. 17 1989; *New Yorker* p109 May 16 1994; *OUT-LOOK* p82+ Fall 1989, with photo; *Publishers Weekly*, p60 Dec. 13 1993, p48+ Mar. 21 1994, with photo, p71+ Sept. 23 1996, p37 Nov. 4 1996; *Village Voice* p121 Dec. 17 1991, pSS19 Apr. 11 1995, with photo; *Voice Literary Supplement* p28+ May 1989

SELECTED WORKS: Fiction—*Safe*, 1984; *Closer*, 1989; *Try*, 1994; *Wrong*, 1992; *Guide*, 1998; Nonfiction— *All Ears: Cultural Criticism, Essays, and Obituaries*, 1999; Drama—*The Undead*, 1989; *Knife/Tape/Rope*, 1989; Poetry—*The Terror of Earrings* (chapbook), 1973; *Tiger Beat*, 1978; *Antoine Monnier*, 1978; *Idols*, 1979; *The Tenderness of Wolves*, 1981; as editor— *Discontents: New Queer Writers*, 1992

Cooper, J. California

Novelist; short-story writer

J. California Cooper's vivid and stirring portrayals of African-American women who overcome adversity to lead positive lives have garnered her a large following—even if critics are divided over her merits as a novelist. Originally a playwright, Cooper turned to fiction in the early 1980s at the suggestion of novelist Alice Walker. Cooper's first collection of short stories, *A Piece of Mine* (1984), received high praise in the press for its straightforward language and for its realistic portrayal of ordinary people in everyday situations. Cooper followed that collection with two others: *Homemade Love* (1986) and *Some Soul to Keep* (1987). In 1991 she produced her first novel—*Family*—a multi-generational tale narrated by the dead matriarch of the family. Since that time Cooper has produced two more novels—*In Search of Satisfaction* (1994) and *The Wake of the Wind* (1998)—both of which detail the lives of several generations of African-Americans in the post–Civil War South. Cooper is also the author of two critically acclaimed short-story collections: *The Matter Is Life* (1991) and *Some Pain, Some Love, Sometime* (1995).

Joan California Cooper was born in Berkeley, California, the daughter of Maxine Rosemary Cooper and Joseph C. Cooper. She attended technical high school before enrolling in a series of colleges. Beginning her writing career as a playwright, she has written at least 17 plays. In 1978 she was named Black Playwright of the Year. During her time in the theater, Cooper met the novelist and poet Alice Walker, who admired Cooper's work. Walker suggested to Cooper that she turn her writing skills toward fiction; Cooper agreed to the idea and soon produced her first collection of short stories, *A Piece of Mine*, in 1984.

A Piece of Mine collected 12 short stories, most of which focused on the relationships between men and women. In many of the stories, Cooper installed in her female characters a sense of dignity that grows stronger as the women deal with the abuse inflicted upon them by men. In one of the tales, "Color Me Real," the love of a decent man enables a biracial woman to leave behind the pain inflicted on her by the prejudice of both whites and blacks; in "Sins Leave Scars" the main female character comes to terms with the abuse she suffered as a child.

Homemade Love, Cooper's 1986 short-story collection, received an American Book Award for its portrayal of the lives of ordinary people. In most of the 13 stories in this collection, Cooper's characters discover that true happiness has been in their lives all along. For example, in "Happiness Does Not Come in Colors," three women put aside their criticism of the men whom they hadn't previously considered seriously as marriage partners and find themselves better for it; in "Living" a man trades in his small town life with his wife for a more impressive big city life, only to discover after three days that he truly belongs to a quieter country existence.

In *Some Soul To Keep* (1987), Cooper collected five of her longer stories, which cover ground similar to her earlier two collections. "Sisters of the Rain," for example, tells the story of a hard-working woman who is rewarded with a happier life than that of her wilder, fun-loving friend. In "Red-Winged Blackbirds," a woman survives a near-rape by a racist, sees her parents murdered by a mob, and keeps her virginity while living in the company of prostitutes. Critical reaction to *Some Soul to Keep* was mixed. While many critics praised Cooper's deceptively simple, folksy style, others criticized her stories as monotonous and suggested that the author moralized too often in her fiction.

In 1991 Cooper produced her first novel, *Family*, a complex tale told by a plantation slave named Clora both during her life and after. Clora speaks to the reader directly and colloquially, and begins her family's tale with a Greco-Egyptian ancestor who traveled deep into Africa and married a local woman. From there, Clora takes the reader on a faster-than-light trip through the centuries, explaining how her family was divided by slave traders and taken to different countries. Clora also shows the bizarre entangling of slave bloodlines: an attendant to a plantation mistress who is the mistress's half-sister, and a slave who is whipped by his father—the plantation owner. Clora also tells us about Always, Clora's eldest daughter, who switches her child with that of the plantation mistress's in the hopes that her son will be raised free. (The father of both children is her master, Doak Butler.) Always eventually tries to tell her grown son—now Doak Jr.—the truth, but he responds only with hatred.

The book received somewhat mixed reviews. Writing for the *New York Times Book Review* (December 30, 1990), Roy Hoffman suggested that the novel, "while lingering expressively on the hard details of plantation life, moves too quickly over some of that life's most turbulent occurrences." However, he later added, "In the end though, while this book may be filled with tragedies, it is also about survival. And the lone woman talking to us, recounting the lives of both the oppressors and the oppressed, is as resilient at the end of her story as she was when it began." Thulani Davis's assessment for the *Washington Post* (February 7, 1991) was somewhat harsher, arguing that "the book suffers from a flat first-person narrative that does not allow the characters to take life, a serious lack of information about slavery, and a tendency to cliché: 'But life and time just kept moving on, like it always does.'"

In that same year, Cooper produced another collection of short fiction, *The Matter Is Life* (1991), which contained a novella, entitled "The Doras," and seven short stories. The novella examines the lives of a woman named Dora and her five daughters—Endora, Lovedora, Windora, Splendora, and Andora. Splendora is the least selfish and as such becomes the most likely to find happiness in love and life. The short stories in this collection emphasize the importance of trying to lead a good, honest life and the lack of fulfillment in wealth. But the stories also discuss the dangers apparent in everyday life: "Vanity" looks at how a girl turns to drugs once she becomes involved with a junkie, and "I Told Him!" tells the story of a woman who divorces her cheating husband after many years and remarries successfully. Critics were generally pleased with this collection, albeit with some reservations. *Kirkus Reviews* (May 1, 1991) called the collection "quirky tales in the tradition of Langston Hughes. Though Cooper occasionally leans too heavily on exclamation marks to indicate exuberance, mainly she brings home simple truths in tones that vary from wildly humorous to poignant." Reviewing the book for the *Washington Post* (August 23, 1991), Elizabeth Ferber wrote, "The stories are most successful when imparting a message and a moral, as a modern-day folk tale should. A few begin to fall apart when their 'statements' are made too obviously. Cooper's style is distinct and her craft well-honed. Her power comes from sticking to her instincts, which are to tell a story, plain and simple."

The Search of Satisfaction, Cooper's second novel, was released in 1994. It tells the story of the struggle of two families from the years right after the Civil War through the first few decades of the 20th century. One family's tale begins with Josephus Josephus, a freed slave who took the name his mother had given him as a surname rather than the name of his cruel former masters. Josephus has two daughters—one with another freed slave named Bessel and the other with his alcoholic white mistress. His legitimate daughter, Ruth Mae, remains in the little town of Yoville, while Yinyang, his illegitimate daughter, leaves town and heads to New Orleans, where she supports herself as a masseuse and a lesbian concubine. Ruth Mae struggles to survive but maintains a decent, happy life; Yinyang is obsessed with a materialistic lifestyle, but no matter how many belongings she owns, she is left empty and unsatisfied.

The other family at the center of *In Search of Satisfaction* is the Befoes, the town's wealthy industrial barons. Carl Befoe, the founder of the town munitions plant, is a well-meaning man who is easily manipulated by his daughter Carlene, who embroils the family in one scandal after another. Carlene is engaged to be married to her first cousin, Richard, but soon becomes pregnant by Richard's father. The resulting slow-witted daughter, Richlele, is in turn raped by her own alleged father, Richard. The novel received mixed reviews. Mary Carroll of *Booklist* (August 19, 1994) claimed, "After a slow start, Cooper's latest inexorably involves the reader in the moral dilemmas and decisions of its well-developed characters." The reviewer for *Kirkus Reviews* (July 15, 1994), disagreed, believing that "Cooper . . . relates this meandering tale of two half-sisters in a folksy, dialect-strewn voice that is moralistic—and also pretty dull," and added that the book was "imitative of but in no way equal to Zora Neale Hurston." Valerie Smith of the *Washington Post* (October 11, 1994) agreed with this latter assessment: "Readers will no doubt be entertained by the panoply of plot lines and switches and gratified by the way in which the author distributes rewards and punishments in the novel. But the limitations of style and characterization threaten to leave us, regrettably, in search of satisfaction."

In the next year Cooper brought forth another collection of short stories, *Some Love, Some Pain, Sometime* (1995), which explores many of Cooper's favorite themes. The stories center on black women who want to improve their lives and find great loves but often are required to sacrifice too much in order to get the things they desire most. *Booklist* (October 1, 1995) found the collection to be full of "involving, intimate stories." The *Publishers Weekly* (July 31, 1995) reviewer felt that "Cooper's spirited use of the first person makes every tale . . . engaging."

Most recently Cooper has produced *The Wake of the Wind* (1998), her third novel, and another family saga. In it the reader can find many of the author's familiar themes: family, struggles against prejudice, the power of kindness bringing about redemption. The novel spans almost a century and follows the lives of several black families, starting in the 1760s with Kola and Suwaibu, two young men in Africa who are captured by slave traders and brought to America. One hundred years later Mordecai, a descendant of Suwaibu, and Lifee, a descendant of Kola, meet on a Southern plantation. Lifee is doomed to become the master's mistress but has an overwhelming desire to be free, a desire also shared by Mordecai. At the end of the Civil War, the pair trek across the country to find land upon which to settle. This novel has received some of the best praise of any of Cooper's works. *Kirkus Reviews* (September 1, 1998) proclaimed Cooper's descriptions of the hard years after the war and the couple's skill at outwitting racist whites as "vivid, detailed, and stirring," later calling it "a moving story that combines period detail, terse, flavorful language, and a swift plot to create a portrait of a redoubtable family over time."

J. California Cooper has received the American Library Association Literary Lion Award, the James Baldwin Award, and the Notable Book Award. She has one child, Paris A. Williams. —C.M.

SUGGESTED READING: *Booklist* Aug. 19, 1994, Oct. 1, 1995; *Chicago Tribune* XIV p5 Nov. 6, 1994; *Kirkus Reviews* May 1, 1991, July 15, 1994, Sep. 1, 1998; *New York Times* II p38 July 2, 1989; *New York Times Book Review* p12 Dec. 30, 1990; *Publisher's Weekly* July 31, 1995; *Washington Post* B p3 Feb. 7, 1991, C p4 Aug. 23, 1991, E p3 Oct. 11, 1994; *Contemporary Authors New Revision Series*, vol. 55, 1997; *Who's Who Among African Americans 1998-1999*

SELECTED WORKS: *A Piece of Mine*, 1984; *Homemade Love*, 1986; *Some Soul To Keep*, 1987; *Family*, 1991; *The Matter Is Life*, 1991; *In Search of Satisfaction*, 1994; *Some Love Some Pain, Sometime*, 1995; *The Wake of the Wind*, 1998

Cornell, Jennifer C.

Short-story writer

Jennifer C. Cornell is an author who believes in having a story tell itself. Her first collection of stories, *Departures* (1995), about the daily life of ordinary people in Belfast, received widespread critical acclaim. Alice McDermott, who selected *Departures* for the 1994 Drue Heinz Literature Prize, wrote of the book: "These are stories that succeed without last-minute revelations or authorial summing up, that seem to contain the heart of each story not in some single line or climactic scene, but in every careful sentence along the way, so that the final image always appears to be both inevitable and inspired." In *Departures* Cornell created characters who are not defined primarily by their political beliefs or more than peripherally involved in any of the violence in Northern Ireland; instead, she captured the essence of life in a war-torn country without making the war the central issue. Rather, the main concerns are the relationships between parents and children, Catholics and Protestants, men and women.

For *World Authors 1990–1995*, she writes: "The aspects of my early life which seem important now are these: that I was an only child; that for much of my childhood I accompanied my parents when work or interest took them to Africa, Europe, South America, or Asia, though I can recall strangely little of the experience now; that despite those many months spent traveling, my parents have always lived in the same rented apartment; that I was very young when I went to college, and perhaps for that reason my politics and identity began as an affectation, though I have retained them in spite of their origins and believe I am growing worthy of their claims.

"Though I did write stories as a child I did not set out to be a writer. Even now it's not an occupation I have fully embraced. Hoping to enter a more practical field, I initially earned a degree in biology, specifically, behavioral entomology: I wrote my undergraduate thesis on the behaviour of the buckmoth, *Hemileuca lucina*; somewhere there are two papers in scientific journals which describe the gregarity and defensive responses of the insect in its larval form. After college I worked for a year at various jobs, chiefly scientific illustration of insect parts and the sorting, identification, and preparation of specimens, though I also cleaned cages at an animal facility, served food, cut hair, and briefly tried to arouse the revolutionary spirit of a small group of students at East Boston High.

"During college I'd spent a summer observing red deer on the Isle of Rhum, one of the Inner Hebrides islands off the coast of Scotland; the work was part of an ongoing study conducted by Cambridge University. The experience was disillusioning. What I'd liked about ethology was the field and lab work, the chance to be alone, outside for hours at a time (on Rhum we observed our subjects in twelve-hour shifts), but statistical analysis seemed to alter the facts, the research itself began to seem less necessary than almost any other pursuit, and it troubled me that our results were largely unintelligible to those outside the field. Besides, though I enjoyed collecting and interpreting data, I'd barely passed Physics, Chemistry, Calculus, or any other subject in my major. After twelve months of deliberation following graduation, I decided not to pursue a career in zoology, and instead to go back to Northern Ireland.

"In Belfast I worked for a community centre, helping out in the drop-in cafe (making sandwiches, pouring tea) and with the youth club, and reviving a programme through which Catholic and Protestant children of all ages came together to talk and play. Because of refurbishments in the neighbourhood the old centre was eventually torn down (though I tried to preserve it in the short story, 'Inheritance'). The project was relocated, but by then I had begun a degree in Peace Studies in Derry, during which I developed a thesis regarding the representation of Northern Ireland in British television drama, which I have been developing ever since. A good friend and several colleagues have pointed out that at some point a researcher in the humanities must stop trying to be all-inclusive and accept the fact that whatever one publishes it will not be up to date, but my scientific training, with its strict insistence on topicality, has made that a difficult reality to accept. Hopefully the book will be finished within the next year.

"The Peace Studies degree completed, I was desperate for money so I applied for an M.F.A. back in the States. I brought six rough drafts of stories I'd begun in Belfast with me to Cornell, wrote six more while there, and *Departures* is the result. The book has at its thematic core several stories told by the same narrative voice, though the speaker herself could not be the same person, for her circumstances alter from one story to the next: most significantly, in some she is Catholic, in others Protestant, though she is in each case the young daughter of a man who has recently been bereaved. I had hoped the device would suggest an interconnection of individuals and, through them, the communities from which they are drawn. I hoped too to suggest an equivalence between those communities, a commonality forged if from nothing else from the shared experience of grief. At the same time I did not wish to downplay the reality of the divisions between them, and so several of the stories speak to the difficulty of communication (e.g., 'Outtake'), of connection (e.g., 'Stigmata'), and of the imagination to transcend ('Undertow').

"The collection I am working on now (in addition to the nonfiction book; I am easily bored, disheartened, or distracted when I write and have found it easier to work on several projects at once) is concerned with preventable loss—loss for which we can be held responsible. In this way I hope to reflect on the new social and political realities spawned by the IRA cease-fire of 1994 and the consequences of that brief taste of peace. Again I am drawn to the connective possibilities of the narrative voice, in part because I would like to suggest links not only between the stories in the second collection, but between that collection and the first. What I am interested in is the metaphor implicit in the phrase, 'a body of work,' which one begins to develop, inescapably, as soon as one sets out to write more that one piece. I have recently come to imagine my artistic project not as the product of a sequential equation, but as a living organism whose features may lengthen, even change colour, but will always retain their essential shape. Consequently, like Vladimir Nabokov (if I may make such a big-headed comparison), who frequently revisited themes, images, and even narrative lines familiar from his earlier fiction, the stories in my second collection seek to recast the ideas, and in some case the structure, of those which compose my previous book."

Cornell's *Departures* was published in 1995 to universal praise. Most of the stories concern the ordinary lives of people in and around Belfast, people who are not political in outlook but are still affected by the religious conflict between the Catholics and the Protestants in Northern Ireland; the conflict itself is not the focus of the collection but is merely reflected in the characters' sense of loss and grief. The stories usually focus on relationships, whether between men and women, parents and children, or people and animals. Most of the fathers are unemployed but are lovers of nature and capable storytellers; most of the mothers are portrayed as women whose lives are filled with roads never traveled, untapped energies, and feelings of entrapment. Yet they all endure, because that is the only response they know. As Lisa Nussbaum wrote in *Library Journal* (February 15, 1995): "Some of the protagonists escape into drinking or indifference, while others . . . walk away from responsibility. But most of the characters keep moving forward through a mixture of stubbornness, habit, and quiet courage."

The majority of the dozen stories in this collection focus on Protestants in Northern Ireland, though there are pieces about Catholics. In the "Outtake," a shy young Protestant man manages to strike up a conversation with a woman in a Belfast pub. She forgives his racist remarks regarding the Chinese people she works for in a restaurant, and things between them seem to be progressing smoothly until he makes an off-color comment regarding "rosemary beads," or rosary beads. He soon discovers that she is Catholic, and their flirtation ends. Drunkenly making his way home, he takes a cab to the wrong side of town and sobers up only when he realizes that he may have made a fatal mistake.

Not all of Cornell's plot lines are even this complex; most are deceptively simple in their pretext. "Heat" is about a girl watching her father force a rabbit into a brutal mating so that the daughter can see "wee babies being born." "Rise" concerns a boy who silently starves, surrounded by his mangled butterfly collection. "Inheritance" centers on a group of children so forbidding that they do not allow their own mother to give them birthday parties. An article in the *New York Times Book Review* (April 16, 1995) stated that Cornell "writes model short stories: lucid, inventive, and teeming with overlapping memories, like creamier versions of William Trevor's wry fables of unfulfillment." The *Booklist* (March 1, 1995) reviewer Janet St. John wrote, "The stories offer naturally maturing plots and characters as well as emotional and psychological responses to a life laden with war-zone ethics, unemployment, poverty, and the challenge of daily survival. . . . Cornell's narrators, usually daughters, speak as awakened children, realistic and without romantic ideas."

Jennifer C. Cornell is the recipient of the 1994 Drue Heinz Literature Prize. She is an assistant professor in the English department at Oregon State University, in Corvallis.—CM

SUGGESTED READING: *Booklist* Mar. 1, 1995; *Chicago Review* p42 no. 2, 1996; *Library Journal* Feb. 15, 1995; *New England Review* p14+ Spring 1994; *New York Times Book Review* p21 Apr. 16, 1995; *TriQuarterly* p220+ Spring/Summer 1994

SELECTED BOOKS: *Departures*, 1995

Sigrid Estrada

Cose, Ellis

Feb. 20, 1951– Journalist; nonfiction writer; fiction writer

Ellis Cose is a noted commentator on major issues facing the United States. He has covered such varied topics as energy conservation, the role of the press, immigration, and race and prejudice in a manner that defies conventional ideas of specialization, and his ability to blend hope for the future with hard facts about the present state of the nation is one that few commentators can claim. With his first three books, on the energy crisis, as well as his more recent volumes—among them *The Press* (1988), *The Rage of a Privileged Class* (1993), and *Color-Blind: Seeing Beyond Race in a Race-Obsessed World* (1997)—it has been said that Cose has presented detailed blueprints for helping Americans to better their lives and their relationships with others. While discussing his book *A Man's World: How Real Is Male Privilege-and How High Is Its Price?* (1995) with the *Chicago Tribune* (September 24, 1995), Cose summed up his belief that many of the problems facing his country are oversimplified through categories of "us" and "them": "There are a lot of women, blacks, Latinos, and others who believe there is an Anglo, male-class way of doing things. I think this is far too simplistic. And if we try to do this, we end up with silliness."

The son of Roney and Jetta (Cameron) Cose, Ellis Jonathan Cose was born on February 20, 1951, in Chicago. He was raised in that city's Henry Horner Homes-high-rise projects that were the turf of criminals and brutal police officers. Growing up during the turbulent 1960s and learning about the work of

Martin Luther King Jr. and other civil rights leaders, he felt that he was a part of something greater, and wanted to contribute to the efforts of those he admired. He wanted to be a writer. "In the midst of everything blowing up, the big riots and King getting killed, I got this notion that I had something worthwhile to say," he told Will Nixon for *Publishers Weekly* (March 23, 1992).

He followed a circuitous path to writing, however. His first interests in high school, where he was a self-confessed rebel, were math and physics. He was bored by his English classes, and when he was in danger of failing, his teachers would give him special assignments to enable him to pass. This situation changed during his senior year, when he came under the influence of a teacher named Mrs. Klinger. As Cose told Will Nixon: "Mrs. Klinger said, 'Ellis, what do you propose to do if you don't want to work?' Nobody had ever asked me that before. I told her that if she wanted to judge my ability to use the language, I would write her something."

Cose turned in a series of essays on social issues, particularly race, which eventually amounted to a 200-page manuscript. Mrs. Klinger read the entire work over one weekend; when she returned to school the following Monday, she told young Ellis that she was going to give him an "A" in the course but that she believed she was not really qualified to evaluate the work. She suggested that he send it to a professional. Cose himself had few connections, but Mrs. Klinger happened be taking a course with Gwendolyn Brooks, then the poet laureate of Illinois, and sent the manuscript to her. Brooks soon contacted Cose, told him he was a good writer, and asked him to join her writing group. He joined briefly but quit after a few months. (He was 17 at the time, while most of the other writers in the group were in their 30s and 40s.) He began working on a novel, which was accepted by a faltering publishing house that folded before it could publish the book.

Despite this setback, Cose persisted in building a literary career. While attending the University of Illinois, where he had enrolled in the fall of 1968, he collected his clips from the student newspaper and eventually sent them to Ralph Otwell, the managing editor of the *Chicago Sun-Times*, who was sufficiently impressed to hire the young writer. Still a freshman, Cose started writing a column for the newspaper's special school edition; at the end of the year Otwell called him into a meeting with editor Jim Hoge, and both editors praised his work and offered him a position as a columnist for the regular edition of the paper. At the age of 19 Cose became the youngest columnist ever at a Chicago newspaper. He graduated from the University of Illinois in 1972 and stayed with the *Sun-Times* until 1977, when he went on to earn his master's degree in public policy at George Washington University, in Washington, D.C. For two years in Washington he served as senior fellow and director of energy policy at the Joint Center for Political

Studies. His first books grew from this work: *Energy and the Urban Crisis* (1978) and *Energy and Equity: Some Social Concerns* (1979), the latter of which he edited.

In 1979 he returned to the Midwest and to the world of big-city newspapers, when he joined the *Detroit Free Press* as a columnist. He later served on its editorial board. In 1982 Cose moved to *USA Today* as a special writer covering management and worker issues. Still, he did not leave the energy issue completely behind, and in 1983 he published a third book, *Decentralizing Energy Decisions: The Rebirth of Community Power*. In that same year he began a three-year stint as president of the Institute for Journalism Education and then served during 1987 as the president of the Gannett Center of Media Studies at Columbia University, in New York City. Again immersed in journalism, he began to question the mechanisms of the press and its powers. This pondering inspired another book, and he spent the next year writing one of his more successful works, *The Press*, which examined five journalistic empires-the *New York Times*, the *Washington Post*, the *Los Angeles Times*, and the Gannett and Knight-Ridder chains-that were family-owned and whose CEOs came to power and shaped the industry between 1963 and 1988. The *Chicago Tribune* (April 9, 1989), in its review of Cose's book, stated: "This anecdotal work, heavily larded with the results of extensive interviewing, is a valuable addition to the lore of newspapering and a credible look at the enormous change that has occurred in the field." The *New York Times Book Review* (April 9, 1989) critic Ron Rosenbaum found Cose's book derivative of other works but noted that Cose had broken new ground in one specific subject: "His stories of the struggles of black reporters and editors for a place in these institutions go deeper than statistics and polemics. There are dramatic firsthand accounts of black reporters' painful attempts to tell the truth about themselves and their communities to white editors, ranging from heart-to-heart talks to late-night drink-soaked shouting matches."

After the publication of *The Press*, Cose changed jobs again; this time he began working as an essayist and contributing editor for *Time*. He left the magazine in 1990 and began working on another book. Shortly after he had finished writing *The Press*, Cose visited his friend Paul Delaney, the *New York Times* bureau chief in Madrid, where excitement was then mounting for the Columbus quincentennial in 1992. Cose's visit inspired him to write a book about the whole American experience, from Columbus through the history of immigration to America. *A Nation of Strangers: Prejudice, Politics, and the Populating of America* (1992) analyzed the various waves of immigration, and Cose found a deep vein of nativism pervading the politics of various eras—whether the newest arrivals were Jews, Catholics, Irish, Italians, Asians, or Latin Americans—those who preceded them became as fearful of these new arrivals as the

Anglo-Saxons had been of them. The *New York Times Book Review* (August 16, 1992) piece on Cose's book stated: "Mr. Cose . . . has done thorough and competent research, but his writing is flat and often grammatically leaky. The result is a dry history lesson."

After he was finished drafting *A Nation of Strangers*, the *New York Daily News* offered Cose the chairmanship of the editorial board, a position he held from 1991 to 1993. While there he penned another book, *The Rage of a Privileged Class*, which was published in 1993. In this work, Cose focused on the class of successful blacks in America and why their group seemed to be the one most affected by racism. According to the *Christian Science Monitor* (April 18,1994): "The book's strength is in the attention it pays to the frustrations blacks experience in the Byzantine corporate world and in the multiple victimization they experience from society." In its review, *New York Newsday* (February 13, 1994) noted: "Here we learn that the effects of racism are not limited to the back alleys of the underprivileged but instead manifest themselves in such subtle ways that only by experiencing them can you hope to understand them."

In 1995, the year that Cose moved from the *Daily News* to a position as contributing editor for *Newsweek*, he also published another book, *A Man's World: How Real is Male Privilege—And How High Is Its Price?* In this work the author pondered the question of what currently defines—or should define—maleness. The book garnered some impressive reviews, with Jon Katz, in the *Washington Post Book World* (May 28, 1995), stating: "Cose raises all the right issues. . . . *A Man's World* is a valuable, cogent, and well-written contribution to an enormously complex subject, one that leads men and women closer to rational consideration of America's roiling gender changes." Other critics, like Stephen L. Carter in the *New York Times Book Review* (June 25, 1995), were slightly less impressed: "Among the most talented chroniclers of our national gripiness is Ellis Cose . . . [who] is a great one for posing difficult questions; like most observers of the American scene, he is a little bit weaker when it comes to working out answers."

Recently, Cose has concentrated on the issue of race. In 1997 two books bore his name: *The Darden Dilemma: 12 Black Writers on Justice, Race, and Conflicting Loyalties*, which he edited, and *Color-Blind: Seeing Beyond Race in A Race-Obsessed World*, which he wrote. *Color-Blind* brought Cose some of the best reviews of his career. The *New York Times* (February 9, 1997) review read: "The racial conversation is terribly defensive: each side locks itself in, refusing to take a step toward the other for fear of being rebuffed. Ellis Cose has stepped into the breach from the side of black anger. The sooner someone steps in from the side of white resistance, the better." One of Cose's former employers, *Time* (February 17, 1997), printed this comment: "It takes some courage to be a bleeding moderate. The center is the hardest position to defend because it invites attack from all sides. So be it. *Color-Blind* holds its ground because it accurately assesses the contradictory nature of U.S. race relations: they often get better and worse at the same time."

In 1998 Cose tried his hand at fiction with *The Best Defense*, a legal thriller about a murder caused in part by affirmative action and corporate mergers. *The Best Defense* received consistantly positive reviews. A *Booklist* (August 18, 1998) reviewer called it "a fast-paced, fascinating look at law, journalism, and race relations." and *Kirkus Reviews* (August 1, 1998) praised its "evenhanded" characterizations.

Ellis Cose lives in New York City with his wife, Lee Llambelis. Among his many achievements, he has been a fellow of the Ford Foundation and the Andrew Mellon Foundation, a grantee of the Rockefeller Foundation, and a recipient of the Illinois UPI Award, the New York Association of Black Journalists Award, and the Myers Center's Study of Human Rights in North America Award.—C.M.

SUGGESTED READING: *Booklist* Aug. 18, 1998;*Chicago Tribune* XIV p5 Apr. 9, 1989, Sep. 24, 1995; *Christian Science Monitor* Apr. 18, 1994; *Kirkus Reviews* Aug. 1, 1993; *New York Newsday* p35 Feb. 13, 1994; *New York Times Book Review* p9 Apr. 9, 1989, p18 Aug. 16, 1992, p1 June 25, 1995, p11+ Feb. 9, 1997; *Publishers Weekly* p 47+ Mar. 23, 1992; *Time* p84+ Feb. 17, 1997; *Wall Street Journal* A p14 Jan. 18, 1994; *Washington Post Book World* p8 May 28, 1995; *Contemporary Authors* vol. 119, 1987; *Who's Who in America 1997*

SELECTED BOOKS: Nonfiction—*Energy and the Urban Crisis*, 1978; *Decentralizing Energy Decisions: The Rebirth of Community Power*, 1983; *The Press*, 1988; *A Nation of Strangers: Prejudice, Politics, and the Populating of America*, 1992; *The Rage of a Privileged Class*, 1993; *A Man's World: How Real Is Male Privilege-And How High Is Its Price?*, 1995; *Color-Blind: Seeing Beyond Race in a Race-Obsessed World*; 1997; As editor—*Energy and Equity: Some Social Concerns*, 1979; *The Darden Dilemma: 12 Black Writers on Justice, Race, and Conflicting Loyalties*, 1997; Fiction *The Best Defense, 1998*

Coupland, Douglas

Dec. 30, 1961– Essayist; novelist; sculptor; short-story writer

Canadian fiction writer Douglas Coupland has been called the voice of a generation. He broke onto the scene in 1991 with the controversial novel *Generation X: Tales for an Accelerated Culture*, in which he coined a term that was immediately adopted by the media as a label for the then "twentysomething" crowd. His second book, *Shampoo Planet* (1992), targets a younger group, the teenage set. Each of his novels and short-story collections focuses on the struggles of the post-baby-boomer children of the 1960s and 1970s to cope with life in the 1990s and beyond. Rife with pop-culture allusions and neologisms, his prose style is either loved or hated by critics. While some have hailed Coupland as an ambassador of late 20th-century youth culture with keen insight and an eye for detail, others have deplored him as a "trendy" writer with little storytelling ability, whose books may one day be as dated as the references to bygone TV shows with which they are filled.

Douglas Coupland was born on December 30, 1961 on a Canadian military base in Baden-Sölingen, Germany, to Douglas Charles Thomas Coupland (a doctor with the Canadian air force), and C. Janet (Campbell) Coupland. He grew up in Vancouver, in the Canadian province of British Columbia. Although Mrs. Coupland held a degree in comparative theology, she devoted herself exclusively to raising Douglas and his three brothers. Douglas attended the Emily Carr College of Art and Design in Vancouver, where he earned a degree in studio sculpture in 1984. After graduation he traveled to Hawaii to take an extended course in Japanese business science, which he finished in 1986. He returned to art in 1987, exhibiting his fiberglass and wood sculptures at the Vancouver Art Gallery.

In his first few years on his own, Coupland found himself moving from one menial job to another—including attending at a gas station, copying blueprints, and designing baby cribs—in an effort to make ends meet. His writing career began with a stroke of luck, when an editor at *Vancouver Magazine* got hold of a postcard Coupland had written to a mutual friend. The editor was impressed with Coupland's writing skill, and before long, Coupland was writing for the magazine. While working there, Coupland began to recognize the attributes of the age group he would later categorize as "Generation X:" a disinherited underclass culturally and financially at the mercy of their baby-boomer predecessors.

St. Martin's Press approached him in 1989 to write what was supposed to be a nonfiction "manual" for youths coming of age at the end of the 1980s. With the money he received as an advance on the book, he moved to Palm Springs, California, to seriously pursue a writing career. The St. Martin's project eventually transformed into a work of fiction, the novel *Generation X*, which was published in 1991. The book deals with the trials and tribulations of the children of the Johnson/Nixon era and, inadvertently or not, helped shape the popular perception of this age group as directionless, cynical slackers. The story centers on three friends who live in Palm Springs, California, and toil in low-income, low-potential jobs (Coupland calls them "McJobs.") They are alienated people, in dire need of some kind of validation. The three main characters, Andy, Claire, and Dag, entertain each other by telling stories that depict their shiftless lives and predict a bleak future for their generation. The novel also contains a glossary of sorts, in the form of neologisms defined in the margins. Among these terms are "McJob," "Mid-Twenties Breakdown," and "Lessness," which the author describes as "a philosophy whereby one reconciles oneself with diminishing expectations of material wealth." The novel soon became a best-seller, and many claimed that Coupland had written the defining tome of his generation.

Initially, *Generation X* was far from successful. "My distributor in Canada wouldn't even distribute it," Coupland commented in the *Chicago Tribune* (March 14, 1994). "My friends were laughing at me. It was about a year before anything happened." Slowly, however, the book gained attention. Coupland even hosted a PBS documentary called *The Search for Generation X*.

In the Spring 1996 issue of *Essays on Canadian Writing*, G. P. Lainsbury described *Generation X* as "an example of that rarest of literary phenomena—a 'serious' novel that has achieved widespread popular recognition." Lainsbury wrote that the novel tests the boundaries of what fiction is supposed to be, thus challenging the reader. "Coupland creates a number of interlocking narratives in an attempt to confront the largeness and complexity of the postmodern world," he wrote.

Extending his sights beyond the "Brady Bunch" generation, Coupland next focused his attention on adolescents, the younger children of the baby boomers, for his second novel, *Shampoo Planet* (1992). Coupland referred to this age group as "global teens," raised in the age of video and computers. The author described this group in *U.S. News & World Report* (August 17, 1992) as "socially liberal and fiscally ultraconservative." The novel's narrator, Tyler Johnson, is the younger brother of one of *Generation X*'s main characters. He is slightly more optimistic about the future than the characters of Coupland's previous novel, reflecting the author's belief that teenagers are generally more hopeful than their "Gen X" counterparts. Tyler remains optimistic despite the hard facts of his stepfather moving out and the local chemical plants closing. He is also more conservative than his Gen X elders; he is a young Republican majoring in hotel-motel management.

Critical reaction to *Shampoo Planet* was mixed. "This is a hip, sometimes serious, sometimes silly examination of the generation that grew up during the false abundance of the 1980s . . . who are suddenly faced with the difficult economic reality of the 1990s," wrote Katie Gardner of the *Washington Post* (September 11, 1992). Gardner praised Coupland's ability to depict the anxiety experienced by many young adults of the 1990s, but she also maintained that "[although] Coupland's book nods at seriousness with a glimpse at Tyler's angst, it never quite develops enough depth to make it a true coming-of-age novel." Somewhat more negatively, Maura Sheehy of *Details* (September 1992) lamented that "although Coupland's a master at empathizing with and explaining the generational experience, he's not a great fiction writer." As proof, Sheehy pointed to Coupland's reliance on pop-culture references and sarcasm over narrative and characterization. However, she admitted that "[Coupland] really seems motivated by a sincere empathy for being young; at the heart of his work are people struggling to find a self."

Sophronia Scott Gregory, in *Time*, found such characters as Tyler, his pre-"global teen" sister Daisy, and his hippie mother, Jasmine, "delectable." She preferred *Shampoo Planet* to *Generation X*, claiming that in the former "Coupland does a better job of fleshing out these characters because he views them through the prism of conflict: hippie parents of the '60s raising their global teens of the '90s." She was, however, less pleased with the narrative. "This setup is all well and fine," she wrote, "except Coupland doesn't go anywhere with it. The characters never really do anything. . . . Coupland wants very much to be the voice of this generation, but he must understand that its stories are intriguing enough to stand on their own. He does not have to dance around hair gels and alternative music to tell them."

Perhaps as a result of such criticism, Coupland adopted a more serious tone with his 1994 short-story collection, *Life After God*. The collection, which included sketches by the author, began as a series of short stories written for friends, but as they accumulated, Coupland saw the beginnings of a book. Working from the debatable premise that his was the first American generation raised without religion, Coupland presented a series of vignettes in which maturing "Xers", among them an HIV-positive stockbroker, an alcoholic aerobics instructor, and a retired porn star, attempt to develop their own brand of spirituality. He also explored the effects of a technology-drenched society on this search for religious experience. It was perhaps fitting that an aggressive youth-oriented ad campaign featured Coupland reading passages during video spots on MTV.

Despite the hype, *Life After God* met with some of Coupland's most negative reviews to date. "Whatever it is," remarked Carolyn See in the *Washington Post* (April 1, 1994), "it's God awful." See went on to hope that "there's a special circle in Hell for people who have the audacity and chutzpah to name their own generations." The tone of the book's stories, she complained, was reminiscent of the intentionally vacuous "Deep Thoughts" segments from the television show *Saturday Night Live*. She disputed Coupland's assumptions regarding his generation, which are the foundation of the book, and branded the work "disgracefully written and ineptly illustrated."

In a similar review, Brenda Peterson of the *New York Times* (May 8, 1994) complained, "The range of character and emotion is so slight as to be undetectable." Drawing attention to what she perceived as pettiness and a lack of humanity on the author's part, Peterson wrote, "Mr. Coupland's vision is as perishable and trendy as the brand names that pass here for characters and storylines." Peterson did praise one story in the collection, "1,000 Years (Life After God)," for its more personalized touch, and stated her belief that Coupland could improve as a writer if he ceased to depend on the endless cataloging of details.

Following *Life After God*, Coupland began to receive a steady stream of movie offers but turned them all down to continue devoting himself to writing books. Coupland's third novel, *Microserfs* (1995), which began as an article in *Wired* magazine, took aim at the monolithic software company Microsoft, from the point of view of a bunch of lowly programmers who are members of "Generation X." The protagonist, Daniel, lives in an apartment with some of his fellow Microsoft lackeys, and keeps a computer journal in which he details the persistent problems of his life that are not as easy to eliminate as the "bugs" and "glitches" in the programs he creates at work. Coupland told Steve Lohr for the *New York Times* (May 29, 1994) that his goal in writing the novel was the accurate representation of "life within an information-technology monoculture." "It was like 'Gorillas in the Mist' kind of observation," he explained, describing his weeks associating with real Microsoft programmers to research the book. To promote *Microserfs* Coupland produced a half-hour filmed interview entitled "Close Personal Friend." The film, in which Coupland criticizes the technological/commercial society that he sees as epitomized by the industry dominance of Microsoft, was shown at bookstores in conjunction with the novel's release.

Reviewing *Microserfs* for the *London Review of Books* (June 6, 1996), Tom Vanderbilt wrote, "Despite his severe shortcomings as a novelist, Coupland is adept at a minute catch-all style of reporting." Vanderbilt acknowledged Coupland's ability to keep his finger on the pulse of popular culture, but remarked that "the suspicion develops that he is, in fact, incapable of removing it." He expressed disapproval of Coupland's frequent and often obscure references to old TV shows and other pop-culture artifacts, finding them "endlessly repeated, for lack of better metaphors." The novel's characters suffer as a result, Vanderbilt opined, and are reduced to mere commodities with decidedly contrived personalities and behavior.

Carolyn Alessio of the *Chicago Tribune* (June 25, 1995) perceived a higher level of maturity in *Microserfs* than was evident in Coupland's previous novels. She wrote that Coupland seemed to focus more on substance than on style. Coupland is at his most potent, according to Alessio, when focusing tightly on his group of quirky "techno-geek" characters.

Microserf's "vivid fictional landscape" was also praised by Justin Smallbridge in the *New York Times Book Review* (June 11, 1995). Smallbridge attributed Coupland's success with *Microserfs* to his witty criticism of the mundane diversions that prevent the characters from dealing with deeper, more profound issues. "By the conclusion of the novel, Coupland has achieved an emotional depth that, having sprung from deceptively banal ingredients, is both surprising and satisfying," he wrote.

Coupland experimented more with his next book, *Polaroids from the Dead* (1996), compiling a narrative made up of essays and short stories. All of the characters are the adult children of hippies, and have congregated at a Grateful Dead concert. Here, Coupland is interested in the ways in which the characters respond to their upbringing now that they are becoming parents themselves. As the book progresses, the details of the characters' histories slowly come into focus, much like a Polaroid photograph. Part of the book is reminiscent of the travelogue genre in its depiction of characters who are made to understand more about themselves through their journeys.

In the *New York Times* (July 21, 1996), M. G. Lord wrote that Coupland explored human feeling more deeply in this work than in any of his previous books, and that he abandoned hip allusions in favor of more emotionally rich material. Lord compared *Polaroids from the Dead* to Joan Didion's 1968 essay collection *Slouching Towards Bethlehem*, which also deals with the effects of drug-happy counterculture parents on their children.

Coupland's most recent book, *Girlfriend in a Coma*, was published in 1998. Taking its title from a song by the British pop singer Morrissey, the novel stresses the importance of engaging life in earnest instead of getting caught up in the kind of indulgent irony and time-wasting so common to many of Coupland's earlier Generation X characters. The book's prologue is related by the ghost of Jared, a high school jock who died of leukemia in 1979. The story proper begins with the narrative of Jared's best friend, Richard, and details the years following Jared's death, beginning with his girlfriend Karen's slipping into an irreversible coma. The lives of the other characters revolve around her, and the book's final section is narrated by the comatose Karen, who assesses the present day from a 1979 point of view. Coupland ends the story with the end of the world, which takes place on December 28, 1997.

Girlfriend in a Coma was extolled by Paul Di Filippo of the *Washington Post* (April 2, 1998) as "an eccentric jeremiad worthy of Kurt Vonnegut."

He compared the work favorably to *Ubik* by science-fiction writer Philip K. Dick, in which the visions of dreaming corpses are imposed on reality. While Di Filippo hailed *Girlfriend in a Coma* as a "rousingly old-fashioned and genuinely spooky morality play," he expressed unease with Coupland's placement of 1979 as "the Eden from which we were all exiled."

Coupland has often stated that he speaks only for himself in his writing and doesn't want to be considered a spokesman for his generation, despite others labeling him as such. His readership has consisted primarily of people in their 20s and early 30s, many of whom seem able to directly relate to his perspective. "I'm interested in people my age and younger who have no narrative structure to their lives," Coupland told Steve Lohr for the *New York Times* (May 29, 1994). "The big structure used to be the job, the career arc, and that's no longer there. Neither is family or religion. All these narrative templates have eroded." Coupland's novel *Miss Wyoming*, about a beauty pageant contestant, is due out in 2000.—B.S.

SUGGESTED READING: *Chicago Tribune* p1+ Mar. 14, 1994, with photo, p6 June 25, 1995; *Details* p220 Sep. 1992, with photo; *Essays on Canadian Writing* p229+ Spring 1996; *London Review of Books* p26+ June 6, 1996; *New York Times* VII p13 May 8, 1994, IX p2 May 29, 1994, with photo, VII p8 July 21, 1996; *New York Times Book Review* p54 June 11, 1995, with photo; *People* p105+ Oct. 14, 1991, with photos; *Time* p78+ Oct. 19, 1992, with photo; *U.S. News & World Report* p13 Aug. 17, 1992; *Washington Post* B p6 Sep. 11, 1992, D p2 Apr. 1, 1994, B p2 Apr. 2, 1998

SELECTED WORKS: *Generation X: Tales for an Accelerated Culture*, 1991; *Shampoo Planet*, 1992; *Life After God*, 1994; *Microserfs*, 1995; *Polaroids from the Dead*, 1996; *Girlfriend in a Coma*, 1998

Crouch, Stanley

Dec. 14, 1945– Essayist; critic

In the late 1970s and 1980s, Stanley Crouch built a reputation as both a jazz critic and a pundit with his eye on American society in general and African-American culture and politics in particular. A self-proclaimed "hanging judge," he reserves his harshest attacks for the "reverse" racism preached by some black leaders; the tendency of some of his fellow African-Americans to blame all their troubles on white racism; and black nationalism, which, in his opinion, killed the integrity of the civil rights movement. His first book of essays, *Notes of a Hanging Judge*, consisting mainly of pieces he wrote during his nine years on the staff of the *Village Voice*, appeared in 1990, to generally good reviews. Crouch has since published two more collections of essays: *The American Skin Game, or, The Decoy of Race* (1995), and *Always in Pursuit: Fresh American Perspectives* (1998). Many of these essays appeared originally in the New York *Daily News*, for which he writes a regular column, and the *New Republic*, at which he is a contributing editor. Seen by many as a curmudgeon and by some as a traitor, Crouch views himself as simply a truth-teller. "Deep down, most people agree with me," he has said. "They just have been taught they're not supposed to." Author Ralph Ellison said of Crouch, "He's irreverent. He questions the views of both liberals and conservatives, and that's what critics should do."

The oldest of three children, Stanley Crouch was born on December 14, 1945 in Los Angeles, California. His mother, Emma Bea Crouch, was a domestic who worked six days a week and earned 11 dollars a day; his father, James Crouch, a drug addict and petty criminal, was reportedly serving time for drug possession in a San Francisco jail when Stanley was born. According to Robert S. Boynton's profile of Crouch in the *New Yorker* (November 6, 1995), father and son did not meet until 12 years later, and then "saw each other only occasionally." Crouch has credited his mother, who exposed her son to cultural events and taught him to read before he started school, with helping to counter the negative influences of his surroundings. "My mother was Little Miss Perfect Lower Class," he told Boynton. "She was an aristocrat in that strange American way that has nothing to do with money." He has also acknowledged a debt to the teachers in the public schools he attended. Discussing his school days in an interview with Lynda Richardson for the *New York Times* (August 29, 1993), Crouch recalled, "[Those teachers] were on a mission. They had a perfect philosophy: You WILL learn this. If you came in there and said, 'I'm from a dysfunctional family and a single-parent household,' they would say, 'Boy, I'm going to ask you again. What is eight times eight?'"

Crouch's interest in the arts began when he was very young. As Lynda Richardson reported, during his childhood he "had posters of Dizzy Gillespie hanging everywhere," and while he was a student at Thomas Jefferson High School, he formed a jazz club. After his graduation from high school, Crouch attended East Los Angeles Junior College and Southwest Junior College, but, perhaps because he was more interested in the arts than in his studies, he did not receive a degree from either institution. From 1965 to 1967 he was a member of Studio Watts, a repertory theater company, where he worked as an actor and writer, under the tutelage of Jayne Cortez. The company performed in community and college theaters all over California. Boynton quoted the poet Garrett Hongo describing Crouch's declamatory style: "He had these chant-like lines that resembled Whitman, but they were in a black street vernacular that was eloquent and pissed off. He'd run this rap, with quotations from Shakespeare and Melville, riff on Langston Hughes and Cecil Taylor, and then relate it all to that day's news."

During the summer of 1964, Crouch had helped raise money for the Student Nonviolent Coordinating Committee (SNCC), a pillar organization of the civil rights movement. Following the 1965 riots in the Watts area of Los Angeles, however, the 19-year-old Crouch, like many African-Americans of his generation, grew disenchanted with the civil rights movement and became entranced by the militant, separatist rhetoric of the black nationalists. During that period, Crouch immersed himself in the writings of such radical thinkers as LeRoi Jones (now Imamu Amiri Baraka) and began contributing his own essays, reviews, and poetry to *Liberator*, *Black World*, and *The Journal of Black Poetry*.

From 1968 to 1975, Crouch taught at the Claremont Colleges, in California, first as a poet in residence at Pitzer College (where he replaced Bert Meyers, an early mentor of Crouch's who was on sabbatical), and then as the first full-time faculty member of the Claremont Colleges Black Studies Center. In the latter capacity, he eventually secured a joint appointment with the English department at nearby Pomona College. During his association with the Claremont Colleges, Crouch was involved in a number of thought-provoking and technically polished theater productions, as either writer, director, or actor. In one of those productions, *The Fabulous Miss Marie*, he was directed by the playwright and director George C. Wolfe, a student of his at the time, who went on to become the head of the Joseph Papp Public Theatre in New York City. According to Crouch, his own playwriting and directing influenced Wolfe significantly. Crouch also taught himself to play the drums, and during that period he was a mentor to the jazz musicians David Murray, James Newton, Mark Dresser, Arthur Blythe, and Bobby Bradford, all of whom played in bands that Crouch led in a style he has since dismissed as "misguided." One of these groups was called Black Music Infinity.

Eventually, in the same way that he had drifted away from the nonviolent, integrationist philosophy of the civil rights movement, Crouch gradually began to distance himself from the black nationalists. As he explained to Diana West in an interview for *Insight* (June 18, 1990), "I started to feel that I was in a kind of reverse Ku Klux Klan rally, that I was experiencing a reductive vision of human life. I soon began to fall out with the movement and was accused of having standards that were too 'Western.'" His response to his accusers, as he told West, was, "Goodbye." In the wake of his split with the black nationalist movement, Crouch began reading the works of novelists and social critics, particularly Ralph Ellison and Albert Murray, who "had an all-inclusive vision of America rather than one of cultural separatism," as Lynda Richardson phrased it. In *Notes of a Hanging Judge*, Crouch, praising the work of Murray, described the views he himself came to embrace: "[Murray's] work is that of a writer who knows that to be all-American is to be Indian, African, European, and Asian, if only through cuisine. In fact, an American at his or her best can feel the cowboy (who is white, black, and Mexican), the Negro, the Irish, the Jewish, the Italian, the Asian rise up, depending on the stimulus or the image or the reference."

In 1975 Crouch moved to New York City, where he and David Murray shared an East Village loft above the Tin Palace jazz club, where the two started giving concerts and readings. Soon Crouch started a Sunday afternoon jazz series, and in time, he was booking all the acts for the club, occasionally serving as the bouncer. Also at this time, Crouch began contributing articles to the *Village Voice*, the *Soho Weekly News*, and other periodicals. Meanwhile, Crouch's wife, Samerna, a former Pomona College student, moved to New York and gave birth to their daughter, Dawneen, but they split up soon afterwards, and a cash-strapped Crouch was reduced to sleeping on the couches of his friends in the East Village's bohemian community.

In 1980, with the help of Rudy Langlais, a senior editor at the *Village Voice*, Crouch became a staff writer for that liberal weekly newspaper, specializing in jazz criticism but also contributing other kinds of reviews and opinion pieces. During this period he began to distance himself from the strident voice of black nationalism that was popular then, turning instead to the ideas of Albert Murray and Ralph Ellison, with whom he had become friends. As he told Boynton: "Meeting Albert Murray was pivotal for me. I saw how important it is to free yourself from ideology. When you look at things solely in terms of race or class, you miss what is really going on. American intellectuals have difficulty understanding social complexity. They prefer savage purity and are blinded by their contempt for middle-class achievement." In 1979, in the pages of the *Village Voice*, Crouch had repudiated his former idol, Amiri Baraka, criticizing his fixation on the "white man be devil" concept and calling him "one of the greatest disappointments of this era" and "intellectually irresponsible." Crouch told Diana West that in hiring him, "the *Voice* got something different from what they thought they were going to get. See, the *Voice* wanted a conventional, blame-it-on-the-white-people black person, I think. . . . So I became kind of eccentric." Indeed, most of the articles he wrote during the 1980s reflected no trace of his being guided by black/liberal ideology or, for that matter, by any ideology other than his own.

Another example of his continuing independence of thought was Crouch's 1987 review of the Pulitzer Prize–winning novel *Beloved*, by Toni Morrison, the Nobel Prize laureate in literature in 1993: "*Beloved*, above all else, is a blackface Holocaust novel. It seems to have been written in order to enter American slavery into the big-time martyr ratings contest, a contest usually won by references

to, and works about, the experience of Jews at the hands of Nazis. . . . Though secondary characters . . . are superbly drawn, Morrison rarely gives the impression that her people exist for any purpose other than to deliver a message. *Beloved* fails to rise to tragedy because it shows no sense of the timeless and unpredictable manifestations of evil that preceded and followed American slavery, of the gruesome ditches in the human spirit that prefigure all injustice. Instead, the novel is done in the pulp style that has dominated so many renditions of Afro-American life since *Native Son*. As in all protest pulp fiction, everything is locked into its own time, and is ever the result of external social forces. . . . Had Toni Morrison . . . the passion necessary to liberate her work from the failure of feeling that is sentimentality, there is much that she could achieve."

Evidence of Crouch's eclecticism, and further examples of the uniqueness of his vision, include an article defending the black pop singer Michael Jackson, whose extensive plastic surgery has been cited as proof of racial self-hatred (Crouch compared Jackson's reshaping of his facial features to that practiced for centuries by Africans); an in-depth essay for *The New Republic* on the strengths, weaknesses, broad appeal, and vast potential of the Reverend Jesse Jackson; and similarly thoughtful pieces, based on conversations with homosexual writers, on the politics and prejudices of gay culture.

"Body and Soul," a long essay published in the *Village Voice* in December 1983, detailed Crouch's visit to Italy to cover the Umbria Jazz Festival. It also provided a glimpse of vintage Crouch, as he critiqued musical performances and also, in the tradition of his hero Albert Murray, drew parallels between his own culture and another, thereby celebrating both. Crouch's exacting criticism dismissed one musician, who "bluster[ed] through the tunes with the aimless intensity of a fly caught between a closed window and a screen," but praised a group of instrumentalists whose music "tore away everything that stood in the path of celebration." The essay goes on to describe Crouch's visits to the monuments and museums of Italian cities and to reveal the connections he saw between the African-American and Italian cultures. Discussing, for example, the way the Florentine Renaissance artist Giotto broke with tradition by emphasizing, in his paintings, the individual over the setting, Crouch claimed, "In his own way, Louis Armstrong did the same. He discovered that his powers of imagination could stand alone, with the clarinet and the trombone of the conventional New Orleans band silenced, no longer needed to express the intricate and subtle musicality provided by the multilinear antiphonal style." Near the end of the essay, Crouch wrote, "On that last morning in Rome, I stood before the Coliseum [sic], relaxing into the thought of how much of my own experience had been clarified by exposure to foreign forms."

Aside from jazz, Crouch's most frequent topic in the 1980s—and the object of his most scathing attacks—was the antiwhite, anti-Jewish sentiments proffered by such black leaders as Louis Farrakhan and Kwame Touré (né Stokely Carmichael). Those leaders, Crouch contended, stand for the very same racist behavior that the civil rights movement was born to eradicate. "It's not a matter of trying to defend the white man . . . ," Crouch explained to Diana West. "I'm not going to submit to racism, I don't care whose version of it I happen to come in contact with. I'm not going to submit to superficial thinking about people; I'm not going to submit to any ideas that reduce the rich possibility of human life."

Some 37 of Crouch's essays written between 1979 and 1989 were published together as *Notes of a Hanging Judge* (1990). The book received qualified praise from several corners. In his evaluation for *Time* (April 9, 1990), Jack E. White wrote, "When he sticks to the issues, Crouch is a provocative social analyst," but he observed that Crouch "too often allows his insights into the self-victimization that has come to dominate the black, women's, and homosexual liberation movements to degenerate into viperish personal attacks. . . . When he sets out to make his enemies walk the plank, it is Crouch who goes overboard." Similarly, Deirdre English, writing in the *New York Times Book Review* (March 11, 1990), charged that Crouch's "cool courage" was sometimes "replaced by a hot anger that seems to hurtle his words past their destination and on to some unintended and inappropriate place." Still, she felt that Crouch, "for all his lonely disgruntlement, succeed[ed] in sharing much of the richness and intensity of the life of a contemporary black intellectual," and that when he urged blacks to take responsibility for their own lives, "he [came] off less like a hanging judge than a knowing and anxious father figure."

More than one reviewer noted Crouch's musical sensibility, evident not only in his pieces about jazz but in his use of musical metaphors to discuss other subjects. English, for example, remarked that Crouch "demonstrate[d] a jazz critic's appreciation of [Jesse] Jackson's voice as an instrument." (In the *Insight* profile, Leon Wieseltier of *The New Republic* was quoted as saying, "The key to Stanley Crouch is the music. Jazz gave him a standard of excellence by which he measures black culture and black politics.")

Crouch's second book, published in 1995, is *The All-American Skin Game, or, The Decoy of Race.* It included 31 essays written between 1990 and 1994, a turbulent period in American race relations, when public dialogue was dominated by issues brought to the fore by several polarizing events: the beating of Rodney King; the murder trial of O. J. Simpson; and the charges of sexual harassment brought by Anita Hill against Clarence Thomas, then a nominee for U.S. Supreme Court Justice. In an introduction that acknowledged his intellectual debt to Albert Murray and Ralph Elli-

son, Crouch declared himself a "radical pragmatist" exploring "the central issue of our time, which is maintaining democratic morale." To this end, Crouch wrote, "I affirm whatever I think has the best chance of working, of being both inspirational and unsentimental, of resonating across the categories of false division and beyond the decoy of race." Ideological truisms of Afrocentrism mattered little to Crouch, who decried the still-pervasive divisiveness of tribalism on that continent; he credited the demise of South African apartheid, for example, to "the evangelical humanism at the center of modern democracy, which has no precedents in anything of African origin."

Crouch used jazz throughout *The American Skin Game* as a metaphor for American democracy. For example, he wrote in his essay "From Here to the Horizon: How It Goes": "The demands on and the respect for the individual in the jazz band put democracy into aesthetic action. Each performer must bring technical skill, imagination, and the ability to create coherent statements through improvised interplay with the rest of the musicians. . . . The success of jazz is a victory for democracy, and a symbol of the aesthetic dignity, which is finally spiritual, that performers can achieve and express as they go about inventing music and meeting the challenge of the moment." Other essays in this collection include "Another Long Drink of the Blues: The Race Card in the [O. J.] Simpson Case," and "Doing the Afrocentric Hustle." Crouch saw the Simpson case as "further proof of the fact that black Americans are at the center of our national tale, functioning both as flesh and blood movers and metaphors in [our] ongoing democratic debate."

Also in 1995, Crouch participated, with Shelby Steele, Senator Daniel Patrick Moynihan, and others, in a PBS television special entitled "On Values," which explored issues of "faith, family, and our freedoms." Television critic Walter Goodman wrote in the *New York Times* (February 9, 1995) that Steele and Crouch provided the program's "zestiest moments." Goodman continued: "Speaking of what now passes in some circles as black expression, Mr. Crouch does some rapping of his own: 'If those rap videos and those lyrics were written by a group of white guys who were constantly depicting young black teen-agers as sluts and hostile, murdering trivial brutes who'd shoot people for bumping into them, stepping on their feet, and do nothing but smoke fat reefers and drink 40-ounce bottles of beer and walk around looking like clowns, the civil rights organizations would have been lined up outside the studios years ago." The following year, Crouch, along with Molly Ivins and P. J. O'Rourke, were hired to appear as guest "dueling" columnists on the CBS-TV show *60 Minutes*, but the segment was dropped after eight weeks due to low viewer interest.

In March of 1996, Crouch participated with other writers in a debate, "Presuming the Universality of the Black Experience," at Medgar Evers College, a community college in Brooklyn, New York, that is named after a slain civil-rights worker of the 1960s and has a large African-American enrollment. He used the forum to criticize the victim psychology that he felt characterized much of African-American discourse in recent decades. That fall, he wrote a major piece for the *New York Times Magazine* (September 29, 1996) in which he predicted that, despite human "error, chance, and ambition," race would "cease to mean as much 100 years from today." He envisioned a future in which people would see themselves and others in terms of "perceived identity as defined by your class, livelihood, and cultural preferences," instead of the familiar categories of race, ethnicity, and sexuality. He also expressed his belief that intermarriage among various racial and ethnic groups will produce a more "mixed" America in the future, and asserted that "the current paranoia over mixed marriages should by then be largely a superstition of the past." In 1997, after the beating of Abner Louima, a Haitian man, by Brooklyn police, Crouch was appointed by New York City mayor Rudolph Giuliani to a task force on police and community relations. That panel later came under strong criticism by the mayor's opponents for what they perceived to be its favorable bias toward the city administration and the police force. Although the mayor responded brusquely to unfavorable sections of the panel's report, he also told Crouch that he was impressed by the "quality and clarity of the work" and that he did take the report's findings seriously.

Crouch's third book of essays, *Always in Pursuit: Fresh American Perspectives*, was released in 1998. It included a long piece on his "intellectual hero" Albert Murray. As had his earlier collections, it also included commentaries on jazz and literature, as well as scathing appraisals of cultural figures such as Louis Farrakhan ("our most highly respected racist and all-purpose lunatic") and Leonard Jeffries ("City College buffoon"). "I feel right in the middle of our time, our era, our age," he wrote in the book's preface. Relying on a central motif of "tragic optimism," and disdaining "the Negro militant and the race hustler," whom he described as in thrall to "Massa Karl Marx" and "Mama Africa," Crouch expressed his admiration for African-Americans such as Ronald H. Brown and Johnnie L. Cochran, whom he feels have achieved success in a world not of their making. This evaluation did not sit well with Walter Goodman, who wrote in his commentary "The One-Man March" for the *New York Times Book Review* (February 8, 1998) of "Crouch's oddly dreamy perspective" in which "achievers like Johnnie Cochran and Ron Brown are transformed into classy exemplars of good black power, which to this reader looks a lot like lowdown white power. . . . With all the jazz riffs, Stanley Crouch is an old-fashioned booster at heart, a man of another political time, era, age." In a letter to the editor of that publication (May 15, 1998), Crouch criticized

Goodman's "attempt to narrow my concerns and distort my meanings" and accused his critic of attempting to reduce the complexity of Crouch's views to a "talk-show level of revelation."

A stocky, balding man, Stanley Crouch was described by Diana West as having " an easygoing nature" that "belies his harsh words." He has, however, admitted to having a "wild side": "I can get lower than a snake in wagon tracks," he has said. It was, perhaps, that aspect of his personality that manifested itself in 1988, during an argument over rap music (which he despises) with another *Village Voice* writer, Harry Allen. The argument ended with Crouch punching Allen, and the management at the *Voice* responded by firing Crouch. He was later rehired on a freelance basis.

Crouch is one of the founders of Jazz at Lincoln Center, in New York City, where, as artistic consultant, he works closely with the program's director, trumpeter Wynton Marsalis. Crouch met Marsalis after giving him a favorable review in the early 1980s, when Marsalis was 19. Crouch became Marsalis's mentor, and they have been friends ever since. (In 1988 Crouch wrote a sermon that can be heard on Marsalis's album *The Majesty of the Blues*.) Although some critics have faulted Crouch for what they perceive as a loss of interest in the avant-garde style of jazz he had once championed, others give him credit for valorizing jazz before a new audience at Lincoln Center. Crouch is at work on both a novel with the working title *First Snow in Kokomo*, the story of an African-American expatriate writer who returns home after having lived in Paris since the 1960s, and a biography of the saxophonist and bebop pioneer Charlie Parker. In 1991 Crouch was one of 10 writers to receive the Whiting Writers Award, an honor that carried with it a prize of $30,000. Two years later, he won a grant from the John D. and Catherine T. MacArthur Foundation, known popularly as the "genius grant," in the amount of $290,000. On December 31, 1994 Crouch married the sculptor Gloria Nixon; they live in the Greenwich Village neighborhood of New York City.

—C.T./E.M.

SUGGESTED READING: *America* p471 May 30, 1992; *Booklist* p370, p391 Oct. 15, 1995, with photo, p732 Jan. 1, 1996; *Insight* p46+ June 18, 1990, with photos, p13+ Aug. 15, 1994, with photo; *Library Journal* p82 Nov. 1, 1995; *Nation* p710+ May 21, 1990; *New Republic* p30+ Feb. 12, 1990, p42 Dec. 25, 1995; *New York* p96+ Dec. 23-30, 1996, with photo; *New York Times* p1 July 13, 1991, C p11 Aug. 6, 1991, C p29 Oct. 25, 1991, D p17 May 3, 1992, p47 Aug. 29, 1993, with photo, D p3 Nov. 28, 1993, D p9 Jan. 2, 1994, M p7 Mar. 6, 1994, B p8 May 27, 1994, C p18 Feb. 9, 1995, C p15 Dec. 11, 1995, C p11 Mar. 25, 1996, with photo, D p19 May 24, 1996, C p16 June 19, 1996, B p3 Aug. 22, 1997, E p8 Feb. 5, 1998, with photo, B p5 Apr. 2, 1998, E p1 May 11, 1998; *New York Times Book Review* p9

Mar. 11, 1990, with photo, p7 Nov. 12, 1995, p12 Feb. 8, 1998, p4 May 15, 1998; *New York Times Magazine* p12 Mar. 13, 1994, p170+ Sep. 29, 1996; *New Yorker* p95+ Nov. 6, 1995, with photo; *Salmagundi* p8+ Fall 1996, with photo; *Time* p92 Apr. 9, 1990; *Village Voice* p72+ Sep. 4, 1990, p83+ Mar. 13, 1990, p84+ Mar. 20, 1990, p22+ May 26, 1992, pS18+ Oct. 13, 1992, p10 Dec. 12, 1995, with photo; *Virginia Quarterly Review* p547+ Summer 1996; *Washington Post* B p2 June 15, 1993

SELECTED WORKS: *Notes of a Hanging Judge*, 1990; *The All-American Skin Game, or, The Decoy of Race*, 1995; *Always in Pursuit: Fresh American Perspectives*, 1998

Debbie Dalton/Courtesy of Fred D'Aguiar

D'Aguiar, Fred

Feb. 2, 1960– Novelist; poet

Although Fred D'Aguiar, the British-Guyanese poet and novelist, can claim several races and nationalities (African, Portuguese, British) as his own, he has chosen a Caribbean literary voice. D'Aguiar's penchant for psychology has led him in poetry and fiction to express the mind of his people in the form of what he terms "psychohistory." His first book of poems, *Mama Dot* (1985), published when he was 25, is partly a tribute to his grandmother, who raised him and came to represent for him the enduring and nurturing qualities of women. He went on to publish *Airy Hall* (1989), a book of poems named for the town in Guyana where he and his grandmother lived. D'Aguiar

then turned to his experiences in England for *British Subjects* (1993), his third collection of poetry. As he says, he then felt the need for "a longer and wider canvas." The result was *The Longest Memory* (1994), a powerful historical novel set on a plantation in pre–Civil War Virginia. D'Aguiar's second novel, *Dear Future* (1996), is laid in modern Guyana. A story of a brain-injured boy, told partly from his viewpoint, it has a fragmentary construction faulted by several critics, who, nevertheless, agreed with Sean O'Brien in the *London Review of Books* (June 6, 1996) that it is a "bold, funny, and sensuous book." For the novel *Feeding the Ghosts* (1997), D'Aguiar again turned to slavery, this time taking on the horrors of the slave trade. He has also written *1492*, a dramatic narrative poem, which was broadcast on BBC radio in 1992 and published in various literary journals. D'Aguiar's play, *A Jamaican Airman Foresees His Death*, was produced in 1991 and published in 1995. In that play, a Jamaican who volunteers in the British air force during World War II comes to a tragic end, which has nothing to do with the war and everything to do with British racism. *Sweet Thames*, a poem for film, about the African diaspora, is narrated by Olaudah Esquiano, an actual slave who lived in 18th-century London but who appears in the present as well to contribute the narration. *Sweet Thames* was produced for BBC television in 1992.

For *World Authors 1990–1995*, Fred D'Aguiar writes: "My parents are from Guyana. They emigrated to London, England, where I was born in 1960. Between 1962-72 I lived in Guyana. The rest of my teenage years, adolescence, and young adulthood zoomed by in South London with only a short period away to attend the University of Kent for an undergraduate degree in English with African and Caribbean literature. After completing Secondary School (England's equivalent of High School) I resisted the idea of going to university for three years by training and then working as a psychiatric nurse. My first book of poems, *Mama Dot* (1985) is named after my paternal grandmother, Dorothy, but the book is only obliquely, tangentially about her. She cared for upwards of twenty grandchildren in a large house forty miles from Georgetown. Her huge presence, her selfless and abiding spirit, for want of a better term, inspired a dozen poems about my time in Guyana during its independence from British colonial rule.

"My second book, *Airy Hall* (1989), again, poems, shifts the focus from person to place. Airy Hall is the village in Guyana where I grew up. Here, as in *Mama Dot*, I explore themes of home, memory, and belonging, of absence and the impossibility of return in a series of linked poems.

"*British Subjects* (1993) looks at what it means to be black in '80s and early '90s England and at notions of Englishness, given the presence in the British Isles of a large number of peoples from the former British colonies and their significant contributions to British cultural and economic life.

"All three collections are preoccupied with poetry as song and storytelling (two staples in my childhood), with the primacy of language *in* life and *as* life and with politics. Twin landscapes (England and Guyana) are celebrated along with a twin cultural and racial heritage (African from my grandmothers, European, specifically Portuguese, from my grandfathers), that has morphed into multiple racial and cultural loyalties, since Airy Hall was largely made up of Hindus and Muslims from India alongside other Guyanese of African and Portuguese descent, not to forget the indigenous or native, so-called Amerindian presence.

"My fiction continues obsessions begun in my poems. *The Longest Memory* (1994) arose from a two-year stint as visiting writer at Amherst College. I had always written poems about slavery but felt that I needed a longer and wider canvas on which to explore relationships between fathers and sons, masters and slaves. This came out of a recognition that certain historical hurts afflicted contemporary British, Caribbean, and American societies. The book is set in Virginia and not London because, while the British administered slavery at their Parliament at Westminster, they never allowed it to take root in English soil, except in adjunct trades. Plantations were American and Caribbean realities. Virginia is the genesis of modern constitutional America so I felt it qualified for 'most favored location' status for my ruminations on slavery. Instead of the single omniscient viewpoint I opted for polyphony. Rather than present a conventional historical novel I chose a more nonlinear, psychological approach, a kind of psychohistory.

"I taught for a year at Bates College during a severe winter in Maine and decided that my childhood in Guyana needed to work itself out on the wider, more inclusive playing fields of fiction. The beautiful compression of poetry excluded too much reality as it sought the telling detail, a distillation of metaphor and motif that must represent a host of stimuli, experiences, and ideas. The expansiveness of the prose story as a vehicle for curing the hurts of history and memory suddenly seemed more apposite, since it did not mean that I had to relinquish certain key notions of craft gained from my poetry writing (and perpetual) apprenticeship: a character driven narrative had always been the heart and soul of my poems, a lonely consciousness with a dilemma providing an engine of sorts for the story. Hence my second novel, *Dear Future* (1996), about a child robbed of his future by the politicians of a former, unnamed British colony. Not a trace of autobiography detectable there!

"I teach in the MFA program at the University of Miami, Florida. A third novel, *Feeding the Ghosts* (1997), confirms that teaching and writing are for me symbiotic forces. As I teach transferable skills to do with storytelling and writing as an art and craft, the process clarifies for me what it is that I am trying to say, even as I continue in my novels and poems to say it. Is this clear?: that I understand what I write when I try to articulate the processes of writing to a novice; that talking about the processes of the story and poem generates further explorations in the shapes of the things themselves. I love it. I hope readers and the students I teach do too. I won't stop. I can't stop."

Fred D'Aguiar's father, Malcolm, and his mother, Kathleen Messiah, worked as bus driver and bus conductor, respectively, in London. They divorced before Fred returned from Guyana at the age of 12. Fred lived with his mother, and because she had converted to Islam, he became a Muslim as well, although he was not enthusiastic about it and did not continue the practice for long. While he was still a student at Charlton Boys Secondary School, D'Aguiar displayed an interest in poetry, originally inspired by Papa T, his grandfather in Guyana, who recited English poetry aloud. Before he attended the University of Kent, from which he received his bachelor's degree, D'Aguiar worked as a psychiatric nurse, and during this time he also joined writing workshops at Goldsmith's College of the University of London. He wrote poems in imitation of great English poetry but was not able to reproduce the Jamaican dialect that he admired. Later, but still in his early 20s, he attended a black writers' workshop, Black Ink. In that group, he began to write in "nation language," the name Edward Kamau Brathwaite gave to Caribbean English. By 1984 he had written a group of poems, largely using "nation language," which became the basis of the volume *Mama Dot*.

The poems in the first of the three sections of *Mama Dot* are set in Guyana, and those of the second section deal with the West Indian experience in England, particularly of young men in a psychiatric hospital, where their alienation is only increased by their drug treatment and their conditions tend to deteriorate. The third section is a long poem entitled "Guyanese Days," acknowledging Guyana as the source from which D'Aguiar's creativity springs. "The striking contrast in *Mama Dot* is between the anguished self-awareness that characterizes the poems set in Britain and the peace and wholeness of those that contemplate the poet's Caribbean identity," Robert Stewart wrote in the *Dictionary of Literary Biography* (1996).

Airy Hall (1989), D'Aguiar's second collection of poetry, parallels his first in its structure. The first section expresses his love for Airy Hall, the village of his Guyanese childhood. The second part deals with the formation of Guyanese identity, particularly the political, and the third part is one long poem, in this case, "The Kitchen Bitch." A kitchen bitch is a kind of lamp that casts a small pool of intense light, which, by contrast, also makes the surrounding darkness seem more intense. In this poem, the kitchen bitch is the mental light of a paranoid sensibility. As recounted in the poem, D'Aguiar goes on a hike every year at Hebden

Bridge, where Sylvia Plath is buried. The poem supposes that the leader of the hike is the only one left after everyone else has been killed off, "for the persona of the poem is insane. . . . The landscape of the English countryside thus becomes the setting for a terrifying psychodrama, through which the lone leader outruns the limits of his personal light," Robert Stewart observed.

British Subjects, D'Aguiar's third book, is a collection of poems that "grow from British soil, upon which he as a man of color may feel at home but is viewed as alien, 'one of the throwaway people, the problem who won't go away,'" Whitney Scott wrote in *Booklist* (March 15, 1992). Scott characterized D'Aguiar's poems in *British Subjects* as having for their subject the "search for belonging." The poems, according to Scott, reflect "a nostalgia for a past [D'Aguiar] may never be able to claim." The volume drew praise from Andrew Salkey in *World Literature Today* (August 1994): "The primary thematic thrusts of Fred D'Aguiar's spirited verse support subjects that readily yield themselves up to satire and irony. . . . [H]e achieves peaks of exuberant phrase-making, punning humor, paraphrase, and fancy. . . . Quiet wordplay, fused with accurately patterned, figurative phrasing, resulted in this piquant panoramic vista as seen at night three thousand feet above the lights of London: 'The pearl necklaces of traffic / break, trying to get round / my neck of the woods.'" He compared D'Aguiar to W. H. Auden and Philip Larkin. British reviewers were less favorable to the volume, and although James Wood in the *London Review of Books* (March 24, 1994) also compared D'Aguiar with Larkin, the comparison was unfavorable: "His nine-sonnet sequence, 'Sonnets from Whitley Bay', is full of glum sub-Larkinian accuracy ('a town with five-minute jams and one of most things'), but it never really flowers. One longs for eccentricity, some crease of detail or fold of radiance." Ian Sansom wrote in the *Times Literary Supplement* (January 7, 1994) that D'Aguiar had replaced "his usual gusto" with a "laboured sincerity." Sansom felt that although D'Aguiar "once drew widely on effects of repetition and dialect to produce his linguistic melodies, his tunes are now cheap and cheerless."

Although he gives the desire to narrate a "psychohistory" as the reason for using different voices in his novel, *The Longest Memory*, it is also possible that Fred D'Aguiar refrained from filtering through only one consciousness the events of the novel because the horror of the story, so concentrated, might have proven unendurable to the reader. In the novel a slave, a young man who is the product of the rape of a slave by an overseer, is raised by the woman's husband as his child. The master's daughter has fallen in love with him and secretly taught him to read and write. The slave's adoptive father, who says, "Don't make me remember . . . Rest these eyes, tired of trying not to see. Rest this mouth. Stop tasting the sourness there. Forget. Memory is pain trying to resurrect itself,"

has accommodated himself to the experience of being a slave, but the young man cannot and runs away. The old man betrays him for fear of the terrible punishment his son would undergo at the hands of unfamiliar slave catchers. The father expects that because of his long own history on that plantation and the fact that he played with the master as a child, the son will not receive the punishment that he does, in fact, receive: the son is whipped to death.

"The skill of the poet D'Aguiar is evident in the brevity of language, cryptic phrases, and powerful images which are at once poetic and painful, heighten the drama as each character reflects on their shared histories of slavery and plantation life," Brooke Stephens wrote in the *Quarterly Black Review* (October 1, 1995). Stephens deemed *The Longest Memory* "a remarkable effort by a provocative new voice lending a contemporary perspective to a perplexing and disturbing history," but observed, "Craft and technique overwhelm the story when D'Aguiar strays away from the intense personal narratives and takes on the larger philosophical and moral questions surrounding slavery." Michael Ross, on the other hand, writing in the *New York Times Book Review* (May 7, 1995), thought that D'Aguiar's collage method was a positive contribution to the story. As D'Aguiar "introduces . . . characters, the story gains in complexity. Deftly shuttling between viewpoints and voices, he gives us the testimony of slaves and their masters, chained to a doomed tradition. And yet, despite the broad range of his narrative—now interior monologue, now newspaper editorial, now personal diary—he exhibits an impressive economy of style, allowing his novel to gain in power through its emotional restraint." Angelyn Mitchell, writing in the *Washington Post Book World* (August 13, 1995), admired D'Aguiar's perspective, noting that the "novel's strengths are in its illumination of slavery's devastating psychological effects on all of its participants, black and white, and of the often unexamined psychology of the slave community." Paula Burnett, in the *New Statesman & Society* (September 2, 1994), also was impressed by D'Aguiar's techniques: "The apartheid of the fragmented narrations is cunningly transcended by [the] common idiom. The separate testimonies unravel, in all its tragic poignancy, a story of interracial rape in one generation balanced by doomed interracial love in the next. The black father's misplaced faith in liberalism is inverted in his son's resistance. . . . D'Aguiar brings off the difficult feat of embracing, sincerely, both black militancy and a forgiving pluralism."

For D'Aguiar's second novel, *Dear Future* (1996), he returned to the Caribbean for his setting. An unnamed country very much like Guyana is exposed in its destructive political corruption, which has led to social and family dissolution. The character Red Head is a child abandoned by his parents to the dubious care of his uncles, and the time is just before a presidential election. The novel begins: "Red Head got his name and visionary capacity at age nine when he ran behind an uncle chopping wood and caught the back of the axe on his forehead. His uncle, Beanstalk, feeling the reverberations of a soft wood as it yielded to the blade he'd swung back, looked over his shoulder and saw his favorite nephew half-run, half-walk in a wobbly line, do an about-turn, then flop to the ground in a heap." The national wrestling champion, sponsored by the president, comes to town and loses a wrestling match to Red Head's uncle Bounce. Angry government supporters then march on the town to torch Bounce's home, where Red Head lives. The sections of the novel are "Dreams from the Republic of Nightmares," which encompasses the visions Red Head sees as a result of his injuries; "Nightmares from the Republic of Dreams," in which the wicked but clownlike toadies of the president campaigning for reelection have their adventures; "Homing," set in London, where a poor working mother—actually Red Head's—becomes a "campaign secretary" to fabricate absentee ballots for the president; and "Dear Future," letters from Red Head to the future, in which he writes, "You don't know me. We won't meet."

In a laudatory review in the *Nation* (January 13–20, 1997), Cary Amdahl explained how D'Aguiar's transitions between narrative modes and plot threads fuel the book's emotional power: "If the play of D'Aguiar's prose in these first three sections, and the reach between subtext and text, has made for a refreshing unpredictability, it fails to prepare the reader for the sorrow and the power of 'Dear Future.'" Amdahl concluded that "the images that have been gone over lightly . . . the children huddled in a room making dolls and a toy car from a matchbox and matches while in another room a door is being battered down—these images all flash again in a much harsher light, and D'Aguiar's novel emerges as . . . a much angrier and despairing novel than the light hand has let on, warmhearted but disturbing, straightforward but off-center, all the happiness on a slight incline that has not seemed steep until the attempt to climb back up to it is attempted." The *Publishers Weekly* (July 15, 1996) reviewer judged that D'Aguiar had succeeded "in capturing the cultural stresses that rend the social fabric of an unstable Caribbean nation." Christopher Atamian, writing in the *New York Times Book Review* (November 10, 1996), felt that while "D'Aguiar's prose is . . . witty and rich, he never lets us penetrate deeply enough into his characters' motivations and desires."

D'Aguiar returned to the tragedy of slavery for his third novel, *Feeding the Ghosts*. The protagonist, Mintah, thrown overboard with 131 ailing slaves on the voyage from Africa, is the only one to survive. Bharat Tandon in the *Times Literary Supplement* (August 22, 1997) termed the novel "an extended meditation—often harrowing, sometimes a little self-regarding—on the persistence, necessity, and attendant costs of remembering." Tandon concluded that *Feeding the Ghosts* "is

clearly a poet's novella, less interested in the sheer number of incidents than in the weight they carry; consequently, the most satisfying aspects of the story are D'Aguiar's precise observations of the resonances of language, and its capacity to transform what it describes."

D'Aguiar lives in Miami, where he teaches in the graduate writing program at the University of Miami. He told David Streitfeld in an interview in the *Washington Post Book World* (December 29, 1996) that it was easier for him to live in Miami than in London or in Guyana, because in both of the latter he "was seen as an outsider." D'Aguiar observed, "In London, the duplicity is complicated, a true hydra. Here you have only one thing, the dollar, which rules all. So the aim of every writer in Miami is to give the dollar a conscience." He felt that *Dear Future* had been somewhat overlooked in the United States, as opposed to in Britain, where it got "huge praise." He also noted on that occasion that the Caribbean is really one big place. "Guyana, Venezuela, Suriname—it's best to see it as one mind, spread over a thousand miles. Kamau Brathwaite has a line about a stone that skids, and it arcs and blooms into islands. What he's doing is linking all those places, making the ocean manageable, and doable, and quantifiable."

D'Aguiar's own efforts to make "the ocean manageable" have garnered for him Britain's Whitbread Prize for best first novel. *The Longest Memory* also won the Higham Prize.

—S. Y.

SUGGESTED READING: *Booklist* p1322 Mar. 15, 1992; *London Review of Books* p22 Mar. 24, 1994, p26 June 6, 1996; *Nation* p33 Jan. 13–20, 1997; *New Statesman & Society* p36 Sept. 2, 1994; *New York Times Book Review* p26 May 7, 1995, p56 Nov. 10, 1996; *Publishers Weekly* p56 July 15, 1996; *Times Literary Supplement* p18 Jan. 7, 1994, p22 Aug. 22, 1997; *Washington Post Book World* p8 Aug. 13, 1995, p15 Dec. 29, 1996; *World Literature Today* p864 Aug. 1994; *Dictionary of Literary Biography* 1996

SELECTED BOOKS: Fiction—*The Longest Memory* (1994); *Dear Future*, 1996; *Feeding the Ghosts*, 1997; Poetry—*Mama Dot*, 1985; *Airy Hall*, 1989; *British Subjects*, 1993; Drama—*A Jamaican Airman Foresees His Death*, 1995

Danticat, Edwidge

1969– Novelist; short-story writer

Respect for ancestral lineage, as well as the resilience of mothers and other women cast in the midst of poverty, violence, and unrelenting tradition, are pervasive themes in the work of young Edwidge Danticat. In her mid-20s, this Haitian-born writer began captivating readers with lyrical, almost elegiac, fiction portraying life in contemporary Haiti and in the Haitian diaspora in Brooklyn, which she now calls home. Her first novel, *Breath, Eyes, Memory* (1994), about the coming-of-age of the young Sophie Caco, is loosely based on her own experiences as a child raised by relatives in Duvalier's Haiti before rejoining her refugee parents at the age of 12. Like all of Danticat's writings, this book pays homage above all to the supportive matriarchate that has nurtured her from birth, enduring in the midst of personal and political misery. These experiences also informed her second book, *Krik? Krak!* (1995), a collection of nine short stories of resistance and survival, which was a National Book Award finalist that year. Her second novel, *The Farming of Bones* (1998), is the story of the personal crises of a Haitian housemaid, set against the backdrop of the tensions between Haiti and the Dominican Republic in the 1930s. Danticat is also the recipient of a James Michener Fellowship, a 1995 Pushcart Short Story Prize, and writing awards from *The Caribbean Writer*, *Essence*, and *Seventeen* magazines. In 1996 the British periodical *Granta* placed her on a list of the 20 best young American novelists.

"While I was growing up, most of the writers I knew were either in hiding, missing, or dead," wrote Edwidge Danticat in an autobiographical essay in *Essence* (May 1996). She was describing her childhood during the brutal dictatorship of "Papa Doc" Duvalier in Haiti, where "silence was the law of the land" and "writing was a dangerous activity." It was in 1969, in the waning days of this regime, that Edwidge Danticat was born in Port-au-Prince, the only daughter of André, a cabdriver, and Rose, a textile worker. Both her parents came to the United States in the early 1970s, leaving Edwidge and one of her three brothers in the care of an uncle and aunt in the teeming slum of Bel Air in the Haitian capital. It was not until 1981, when she was 12, that Edwidge finally rejoined her parents in the huge Haitian community in Brooklyn, New York. Confronted with an alien culture and language, she began writing partly as solace from peers who taunted her for her "old country" ways. (During the early 1980s, Haitians in the United States were especially stigmatized for being "boat people" and a high-risk group for AIDS.)

"It was very hard," she told Garry Pierre-Pierre for the *New York Times* (January 26, 1995). "'Haitian' was like a curse. People were calling you, 'Frenchy, go back to the banana boat,' and a lot of the kids would lie about where they came from."

But she and her family were sustained by the mutually supportive living arrangements that fellow immigrants had designed in the East Flatbush section of Brooklyn, an almost communal situation that provided a "shelter in a storm" for the newly dispossessed. Danticat later recalled that she wrote her first short story when she was nine years old, about a little girl who was visited every night "by a clan of women just like the overburdened and underappreciated creatures who were part of my own lineage."

But the "writing demon" could be a "dangerous activity" even for a young woman like Edwidge. In "Women Like Us," the epilogue of *Krik? Krak!*, she recalled her mother's two tradition-bound rules for a woman's life: "always use your 10 fingers" (be the best cook and housekeeper who ever lived), and "never have sex before marriage." Literary pursuits were to be discouraged: "And writing? Writing was forbidden as dark rouge on the cheeks or a first date before 18. It was an act of indolence, something to be done in a corner when you could have been learning to cook."

In Brooklyn Danticat attended Intermediate School 320 in the Crown Heights section, where an influential teacher, Raymond Dussek, took her under his wing. When she was 14, she published her first essay, in *New Youth Connections*, a newspaper written and edited by New York City teenagers for their peers. She first thought about being a nurse but changed her mind after graduating from Clara Barton High School in Brooklyn, which offered specialized health-career courses. Setting her sights on a career in international business, she matriculated at Barnard College, but she took her degree in French literature there before going to Brown University for a master of fine arts degree in writing.

Danticat has since expressed deep concern over the fate of immigrant and minority youngsters like her in New York's public schools, many of whom she fears are falling between the cracks in an increasingly underfunded system. "It's harder just to be thrown in today," she told Joyce Purnick in an interview for the *New York Times* (October 23, 1995). "It's a different school system. I know something about it because my brother is a teacher. Classes are much bigger, schools are crowded, you don't get much attention."

It was while at Brown that Danticat completed work on her first novel, *Breath, Eyes, Memory*, begun as a master's thesis. The successful publication of this work allowed her, at the age of 24, to quit her job working with the filmmaker Jonathan Demme's production company and write on a full-time basis. It also immediately anointed her as the leading spokesperson for a new generation of Haitian Americans, centered in Brooklyn and in Miami. It is a role she accepts with some hesitation. "I think I have been assigned that role," she told Pierre-Pierre in her *New York Times* interview, "but I don't really see myself as the voice for the Haitian-American experience. There are many. I'm just one."

Breath, Eyes, Memory is an account of several generations of women whose spiritual energies converge around the book's central character, 12-year-old Sophie Caco, who, like Edwidge Danticat herself, is summoned from Haiti to a new life as an immigrant child in the United States. It is a novel teeming with tensions revolving around sexual awakening and sexual abuse, generational clashes over the weight of tradition in a new culture, the brutality of the Tonton Macoutes (Duvalier's personal police force), the oppressiveness of secrets, and resistance to spiritual bondage. But the novel is not a polemic: Danticat's realm is almost always encompassed within the domestic sphere of hearth, home, and motherhood. It opens as Sophie prepares a Mother's Day tribute to her guardian, Aunt Tatie, in Croix-aux-Rosets, Haiti, and closes with a grown-up Sophie having to deal with her pregnant mother's suicide in Brooklyn. Sophie, like other Haitian girls, had not escaped the traditional practice of "testing," by which a mother inserts one or more fingers into a daughter's vagina to verify her virginity. Back in Haiti for the burial, Sophie's inner voice cries, "I come from a place where breath, eyes, and memory are one, a place from which you carry your past like the hair on your head . . ." Finally achieving connectedness and continuity with her grandmother, Sophie narrates the older woman's words: "There is a place where women are buried in clothes the color of flames, where we drop coffee on the ground for those who went ahead, where the daughter is never fully a woman until her mother has passed on before her. There is always a place where, if you listen closely in the night, you will hear your mother telling a story and at the end of the tale, she will ask you this question: '*Ou libéré?*' Are you free, my daughter?"

It is this grandmother who acts as a kind of literary mentor to Sophie, telling stories in Haiti's oral *Krik? Krak!* tradition, prefacing them with "let the words bring wings to our feet." But for Sophie, torn between old and new ways, stories such as that of a goddess changing women into butterflies have significance only when Sophie can, with like-minded women, confront the shadowy demons of genital mutilation and sexual abuse that haunt them. Sophie joins a sexual phobia group that uses psychiatry and African spirituality to help women exorcize these psychic scars. She recounts a letter written by an African group member to the absent grandmother who had assisted in her labial excision: "Because of you, I feel like a helpless cripple. I sometimes want to kill myself. All of because what you did to me, a child who could not say no, a child who could not defend herself. It would be easy to hate you, but I can't because you are part of me. You are me."

Reviewers were unanimous in their praise for this prentice novel. Author Bob Shacochis wrote in the *Washington Post Book World* (April 3, 1994) that *Breath, Eyes, Memory* "rewards a reader again and again with small but exquisite and unforgetta-

ble epiphanies. You can actually see Danticat grow and mature, come into her own strength as a writer, throughout the course of this quiet, soul-penetrating story about four generations of women trying to hold on to one another in the Haitian diaspora." Marie F. Jones wrote in *Library Journal* (March 15, 1994): "The book's strength lies in the rarity of its Haitian viewpoint, a voice seldom heard in American literature." And Jim Gladstone wrote in the *New York Times Book Review* (July 10, 1994): "Ms. Danticat's calm clarity of vision takes on the resonance of folk art. In the end, her book achieves an emotional complexity that lifts it out of the realm of the potboiler and into that of poetry."

Danticat's second book, *Krik? Krak!*, is a collection of nine short stories, some sad and tragic, others bittersweet and humorous, that attempt to encompass the Haitian and Haitian-American experience. In Haiti a storyteller begins by saying "Krik?"and the listener answers "Krak!"—words that constitute the markers of storytelling there, much as "Once upon a time" does in other cultures. Danticat sets the tone for this book by quoting from Sal Scalora's "White Darkness/Black Dreamings"; "Krik! Krak! Somewhere by the seacoast, I feel a breath of warm sea air and hear the laughter of children. An old granny smokes her pipe, surrounded by the village children. . . . We tell the stories so that the young ones will know what came before them. They ask Krik? We say Krak! Our stories are kept in our hearts.'"

The opening story, "Children of the Sea," describes a scenario familiar to many Haitian refugees and boat people who fled the Duvalier dictatorship in the 1980s. An anonymous refugee, one of 36 on a little boat, writes lyrical love letters to his beloved while she, still at home on the island, pens somber and graphic epistles about the brutality being experienced there. Their letters, of course, are never exchanged, but are juxtaposed in vivid counterpoint in the narrative. "We spent most of yesterday telling stories," he writes. "Someone says, Krik? You answer, Krak! And they say, I have many stories I could tell you." But the ship is wrecked, and he is forced to throw his notebook overboard before drowning. As this happens, his beloved writes: "last night on the radio, I heard that another boat sank off the coast of the bahamas. I can't think about you being in there in the waves. my hair shivers, from here, I cannot even see the sea. behind these mountains are more mountains and more black butterflies still and a sea that is endless like my love for you." While this is a story of transition, others in the collection concentrate on life at home in Haiti or on the aftermath of the diaspora to the north. In "The Missing Peace," a young girl helps a woman search for her missing mother, a victim of political violence. "New York Day Women," a delicate account of an older Haitian woman making her way through midtown Manhattan, is poignantly narrated by her "American" daughter, who accidentally spies her on a street not far from the advertising agency where she works.

Response to this collection was generally favorable. Robert Houston wrote in the *New York Times Book Review* (April 23, 1995), "The best of these stories humanize, particularize, give poignancy to the lives of people we may have come to think of as faceless emblems of misery, poverty, and brutality." But Houston cautioned that the book is "quite uneven" as a collection, for which he blamed the publisher's poor judgment.

When she learned that *Krik? Krak!* had been nominated for a National Book Award, Danticat observed a moment to pay silent tribute to her spiritual forebears, "all those writers in Haiti who had written out of conviction and then were tortured and killed for their words. Their blood on the walls of prison cells was perhaps the only ink they had."

The Farming of Bones, Danticat's third book and second novel, was published in 1998. Its protagonist is Amabelle Desir, a Haitian domestic in the service of Senora Valencia; Senora has just lost one of her newborn twins to crib death, and her husband, a soldier, is the culprit in a hit-and-run accident that Amabelle and her lover consider avenging. All of this takes place as violence is about to erupt between Haiti and the Dominican Republic. Michael Upchurch, writing in the *New York Times Book Review* (September 27, 1998), felt that the Haitian characters in the novel are "too uniformly noble to be entirely convincing," but he also maintained that *The Farming of Bones* contains powerfully descriptive passages that offer "ample confirmation of Edwidge Danticat's considerable talents."

Danticat makes it clear that her motivations are not only to entertain and uplift but to create a mood of spiritual connectedness with her lineage: "I write to communicate with my ancestors," she wrote in *Essence* (May 1996). "To explore the truth of their lives and to link it to my own. When I write, I think of my foremothers, who, as Zora Neale Hurston once observed, were considered 'the mules of the earth.'" Issues of psychic and physical survival are crucial in her sensibility. She continued: "I write to unearth all those things that scare me, to reach those places in my soul that may seem remote and dark to others. I write to preserve my sanity and to honor the sacrifices made by all those who came before me. The way I figure, it's a privilege just to be given a voice to speak and to be heard. God and the universe will take care of the rest."

—E. M.

SUGGESTED READING: *Essence* p48+ Nov. 1993, with photo, p56 Apr. 1995, with photo, p101+ May 1996, with photo; *Library Journal* p100 Mar. 15. 1994, p67 Nov. 1, 1996; *New York* p50+ Nov. 20, 1995, with photo; *New York Times* C p1 Jan. 26, 1995, with photo, B p3 Oct. 23, 1995, with photo; *New York Times Book Review* p23 July 10, 1994, p22 Apr. 23, 1995; *Washington Post Book World* p6 Apr. 3, 1994, p4 May 14, 1995; Naylor, G., ed. *Children of the Night: The Best Short Stories by Black Writers, 1967 to the Present*, 1996

SUGGESTED BOOKS: *Breath, Eyes, Memory*, 1994; *Krik? Krak!*, 1995; *The Farming of Bones*, 1998

Davis, Thulani

1949(?)– Poet; playwright; novelist

Thulani Davis is a multi-talented writer whose works have appeared in books, magazines, newspapers, and on the stage. In 1985 she joined the ranks of noted artists with the publication of a collection of poetry, *Playing the Changes*, the performance of the opera *X: The Life and Times of Malcolm X*, for which she wrote the libretto, and the start of her regular column in the *Village Voice*, in which she wrote on such issues as race relations and art. In 1992 she published her first novel, *1959*, which was about a young black girl's coming-of-age, set against the backdrop of the growing civil rights movement. Four years later she produced another novel, *Maker of Saints* (1996), an urban mystery involving a pair of young female artists. Davis is also the author of the text for *Malcolm X: The Great Photographs* (1993), as well as the librettos for the operas *The E. & O. Line* (1993) and *Amistad* (1997).

Thulani Davis was born in Virginia about 1949. In October 1962, at the age of 13, she attended an integrated school for the first time. The hostility shown her by her new, white principal and her math teacher, who called her "a little hoodlum," prompted her to rebel. She began sneaking out of her house and getting into fights, once even breaking a girl's arm. According to an article she wrote for the *New York Times* (November 15, 1992), Davis was also influenced by someone she saw on television around the same time: Malcolm X, who was giving speeches around the country and had gained a reputation as a voice of black people's anger. In her words: "Malcolm shocked and fascinated me. I loved his boldness. He made me understand rage, how easily it is used against us and how easily we dupe ourselves. Some would call this delusion; he called it tricknology. He opened my mind, moved it away from provincial, frightened thinking. And he saved me a lot of time because tricknology is time-consuming."

Inspired by Malcolm X's words, Davis began writing poems in the style of revolutionary black poets. Although she now dismisses her early work as "bad," she continued to improve on her writing, particularly her poetry, which culminated years later in the publication of *Playing the Changes* (1985), a collection of poems published by Wesleyan University Press. In the 1970s and 1980s, she worked on her writing with other respected writers such as Ntozake Shange and Jessica Hagedorn. She started writing for the *Village Voice* in 1985, and contributed articles on everything from race relations to black cinema to the state of art in America. She occasionally reviewed films and books for the *New York Times* and *American Film*.

Few authors contribute to operas in the late 20th century, but in October 1985 Davis penned her first libretto, for *X: The Life and Times of Malcolm X*. *X* was a family affair: the storyline was created by Thulani's cousin Christopher Davis, and the jazz-inflected music was composed by his brother, Anthony Davis. The opera was revised for its New York premiere in 1986. Based on the life of the black radical, it stresses the epic qualities of Malcolm X's life, from his youth as a petty criminal, to his heyday as a vocal proponent of the Nation of Islam, to his journey to Mecca, the holy city of Islam, and suggests that he would likely have become a strong conciliatory force had he not been killed shortly after his return to the United States. Although many in the opera community dismissed the Davises' work as too modern, and admirers of jazz spurned it because it was an opera, it generally received high marks for its uniqueness, its narrative power, and its energy.

While working at the *Village Voice*, Davis began writing the novel *1959*, which was published in 1992. In the titular year, a 12-year-old girl named Willie Tarrant, who lives in the town of Turner, Virginia, spends her summer listening to Billie Holiday and thinking about cute boys and new haircuts, and shows little interest in the civil rights movement then in its infancy. But because she is the daughter of a professor at the local black college, Willie is elected to give the young Dr. Martin Luther King Jr. a tour of the facilities. She is subsequently one of six children chosen to desegregate the local white elementary school. Willie, soon enmeshed in the growing struggle for civil rights, watches as adults she has known all her life become passionate about the cause. Most reviews of the novel were mixed. Melissa Fay Greene, writing for the *Washington Post* (January 30, 1992), noted: "The selection of Willie to desegregate the white school raises hope in the reader . . . and Willie would be just the sharp-eyed honest witness one would like to follow through the angry mobs, behind the police escort, through the doors of the hostile white school. But the much-vaunted desegregation does not occur within the novel's time limit, and it feels like a strong plot line inexplicably abandoned." David Gates of *Newsweek* (March 9, 1992) suggested that the author's "account of how a black community discovers its own power— and that power's limits—is persuasive. But she seems to lose interest in the story of her narrator. . . . Selflessness may work in a demonstration; it doesn't play in fiction. . . . As the community comes together, the characters are having the time of their lives—or so we're told. . . . We're

happy for them. But not with them." In the *Women's Review of Books* (May 1992), Gloria T. Hull complained that "*1959* strives toward encyclopedic fullness. . . . This urge to be compendious brings much appreciated documentation of the oral and the otherwise forgotten, but its flip side is a construct that sometimes seems too conscious of itself, the seams and the motivations showing." But the reviewer went on to add that the book was still "an excellent first novel—good, interesting, full of life and talent."

In 1993 Davis wrote the text to accompany photos collected and edited by Howard Chapnick and published as *Malcolm X: The Great Photographs*. The pictures cover the entirety of Malcolm's lifetime, from the marriage of his parents in 1919 to the sentencing of the men who murdered him in 1965. Reviewing the work for *Library Journal* (January 1993), Corinne Nelson wrote, "In the text, novelist Davis . . . doesn't merely retell the story of Malcolm X but tries to describe how phenomenal the man was. A picture speaks a thousand words, and this compilation . . . speaks volumes about this man whose 'face has become an omnipresent icon, a silent image attracting people.'"

Later the same year Davis completed a libretto for the composer Anne LeBaron's *The E. & O. Line* (1993). Based on the ancient myth in which Orpheus tries, but fails, to save his wife Eurydice from Hades, *The E. & O. Line* follows Eurydice on her journey of self-discovery, to an establishment called the Dreamtime Cafe (which represents Hades) in a small southern town.

In 1996 Davis published her second novel, *Maker of Saints*, a literary thriller in which Cynthia "Bird" Kincaid, a young black artist, sets out to investigate the death of her neighbor and close friend, Alex Decatur, a beautiful, talented woman. The police decide that Alex committed suicide, but Bird, unconvinced that her friend killed herself, investigates on her own, and as she is going through Alex's things, she uncovers a collection of videocassettes on which Alex kept her diary. From them Bird learns things about her friend she had never known—secrets about her life, her art, and her relationship with her art-critic boyfriend, Frank Burton. In her search for Alex's killer, Bird comes to some resolutions about her own life and art. This novel, like Davis's previous one, received mixed reviews. Some critics, like Paula L. Woods of the *Washington Post* (December 30, 1996), complained that the novel lacked real focus. "Despite a slam-bang finish," Woods wrote, "Davis's over-reliance on the literary metaphor and well-crafted prose to get the reader there without the equally important engine of plot and pacing results in a book that has a lot of tasty ingredients, generates a lot of intellectual heat, but ultimately delivers too late in terms of old-fashioned, lip-smacking, page-turning storytelling." In the *New York Times Book Review* (November 17, 1996), Lise Funderburg concurred that "Bird's melancholy musings contain some of Ms. Davis's best writing. . . . But these rich pulses are too far apart to build a rhythm, and while Bird is ever drawn to her friend's flame—searching for evidence of murder in a hapless investigation that is more tedious than suspenseful—readers may lose interest in whether she'll finally get burned."

Davis once again collaborated with her cousin Anthony Davis when she wrote the libretto for *Amistad* (1997). The opera was based on an 1839 incident in which the Africans aboard the slave ship Amistad took control of the ship and killed the crew. They landed in New England, where they were imprisoned and placed on trial, and defended by former president John Quincy Adams and future Connecticut governor Roger Baldwin. Eventually, the United States Supreme Court ruled that the Africans were free men and women and thus could go back to Africa or stay in the United States if they wished. Tim Page, a *Washington Post* staff writer, complained in his December 1, 1997, review that "*Amistad* proved pretty much a cardboard-cutout morality sermon—slavery was/is terrible; black people are noble, stoical, and close to God; most white people are brutal, lustful, avaricious slimeballs; and so on." He also admitted that "Thulani Davis has written a fitfully elegant and el-oquent libretto. She has a terrific ear and an innate majesty of expression. Several of the arias and ensembles could easily stand on their own as choice, stark poetry. I hope her next libretto is more scrupulous; she is a writer of great gifts." —C.M.

SUGGESTED READING: *Atlantic* p92+ Sep. 1986; *Booklist* p219 Sep. 15, 1996; *Kirkus Reviews* Nov. 1, 1991, Aug. 15, 1996; *Library Journal* p108 Jan. 1993, p208 Sep. 1, 1996; *New York Times* II p27 Nov. 8, 1992, II p22 Nov. 15, 1992; *New York Times Book Review* p18 Mar. 15, 1992, p25 Nov. 17, 1996, E p2 Feb. 18, 1998; *New Yorker* p118+ Oct. 27, 1986; *Newsweek* p60 Mar. 9, 1992; *Village Voice* p84 Nov. 12, 1996; *Washington Post* C p2 Jan. 30, 1992, B p2 Nov. 1, 1993, G p3 May 1, 1994, D p3, Dec. 30, 1996, Dec. 1, 1997, C p1 Dec. 1, 1997; *Women's Review of Books* p6 May 1992

SELECTED WORKS: Fiction—*1959*, 1992; *Maker of Saints*, 1996; Nonfiction—*Malcolm X: The Great Photographs*, 1993; Poetry—*Playing the Changes*, 1985; Librettos—*X: The Life and Times of Malcom X*, 1985; *The E. & O. Line*, 1993; *Armistad*, 1997

Dawkins, Richard

Mar. 26, 1941– Zoologist; writer; educator

The science fiction writer Douglas Adams once wrote in jest that the answer to "life, the universe, and everything" is 42. Richard Dawkins, a British zoologist and evolutionary biologist who is a friend of Adams's, has a much more specific answer than that, at least regarding questions about life, and it lies in the theories of the great 19th-century British naturalist Charles Darwin. "I want to persuade the reader, not just that the Darwinian world-view happens to be true, but that it is the only known theory that could, in principle, solve the mystery of our existence . . . ," Dawkins wrote. "A good case can be made that Darwinism is true, not just on this planet but all over the universe wherever life may be found."

Dawkins first read Darwin when he was 16 years old, and when he understood Darwin's theories, he stopped believing in God. Since the mid-1970s, he has been one of Darwin's most impassioned supporters, and he has achieved the status of celebrity scientist. A best-selling author, he has published six books—*The Selfish Gene, The Extended Phenotype, The Blind Watchmaker, River Out of Eden, Climbing Mount Improbable,* and *Unweaving the Rainbow*—in each of which he explains in laymen's terms how Darwin's theory of natural selection accounts for the intricacy of everything from spiders' webs to human vision. Dawkins's explanations have become exceedingly popular, especially

Ruth Killick/Courtesy of Penguin Press

in England; as Ravi Mirchandani, who was then with the British division of the publisher Viking, told Ian Parker for the *New Yorker* (September 9, 1996), "If you're an intelligent reader, and you read certain literary novels that everybody has to read, along with seeing [Quentin] Tarantino movies, then reading Richard Dawkins has become part of your cultural baggage."

Richard Dawkins was born on March 26, 1941, in Nairobi, Kenya, to Clinton and Jean (Vyvyan) Dawkins. Discussing with Kam Patel the genesis of his interest in biological evolution, he said, "My father read botany at Oxford and perhaps this has influenced me. My mother has a great love of animals and is passionately concerned about animal welfare—I have certainly been influenced by her in that direction."

Dawkins spent the first eight years of his life in Africa. His father worked for the British colonial administration in Nyasaland, now known as Malawi. During World War II, the family moved to Kenya to be under the protection of the Allied forces. In 1949, the family moved again, this time to England, where Dawkins's father inherited a farm near Chipping Norton, in Oxfordshire. Clinton Dawkins took to his new profession of dairy farmer with entrepreneurial vigor. "He was very enterprising, always devising new schemes and technical inventions. . . . My fascination with computers probably stems from my father's interest in designing cream pasteurizers and other ingenious devices," Richard Dawkins told Thomas Bass. The young Dawkins was not as enthralled as his father was with bucolic life. "While I worked on the farm in the school holidays, I never took to it terribly well," he recalled in the same interview.

Dawkins attended Oxford University for both his undergraduate and graduate education. He studied zoology, partially because he liked the fact that one didn't need a lot of technical knowledge to be able to discuss some of the bigger, speculative questions in the field. "In animal behavior, you can jump straight into controversy and argument," he told Ian Parker. His mentor was Niko Tinbergen, a Dutch animal behaviorist who later won a Nobel Prize. Dawkins received his bachelor's degree in 1962 and his doctoral degree in 1966; for his dissertation, he used mathematical models to simulate decision-making in animals. After a two-year appointment in the zoology department at the University of California at Berkeley, from 1967 to 1969, he returned to Oxford, where he has remained ever since.

Dawkins has been an Oxford University don for the past 27 years, and currently, he is Oxford's first Charles Simonyi Professor of Public Understanding of Science, an unusual position that has freed him from teaching and research duties so that he can devote himself to popularizing Darwin's theories. Though he has not done much original research in evolutionary biology, he has played an important role in his field, because, unlike most scientists, who are notoriously bad at explaining their findings to the public, he is skilled at describing discoveries and hypotheses in language that non-scientists can understand. "Explaining is a difficult art," he wrote in his book *The Blind Watchmaker*. "You can explain something so that your reader understands the words; and you can

explain something so that the reader feels it in the marrow of his bones."

Many readers have not only felt Dawkins's neo-Darwinian message; they have perhaps also been chilled by it. "What are all of us but self-reproducing robots?" he was quoted by Nigel Hawkes as saying in the *London Times* (April 26, 1996). "We have been put together by our genes, and what we do is roam the world looking for a way to sustain ourselves and ultimately produce another robot-a child." Those who resist this interpretation of the natural world have often been the target of Dawkins's considerable rhetorical firepower. He has suggested that astrologers be jailed, and he has likened the Catholic religion to a virus. "I think a case can be made that faith is one of the world's great evils, comparable to the smallpox virus but harder to eradicate," he said in a speech, printed in the *Humanist* (January 1997), to members of the American Humanist Association, which honored him as the 1996 Humanist of the Year.

Dawkins's career as a celebrity scientist began with his first book, the provocatively titled *The Selfish Gene* (1976). Douglas Adams told Ian Parker that for him, reading the book was "one of those absolutely shocking moments of revelation when you understand that the world is fundamentally different from what you thought it was." Many readers confessed in letters to Dawkins that his book had led them to lose their religious faith. Helena Cronin, a philosopher of science, told Parker that the book had a dramatic impact within the scientific community, too. "Very often in science one finds that there are ideas in the air, and lots of people hold them, but they don't even realize they hold them," she said. "The person who can crystallize them, and lay out not only the central idea but its implications for future scientific research can often make a tremendous contribution. And I think that's what *The Selfish Gene* did."

The concept that so many readers of *The Selfish Gene* found revolutionary was Dawkins's contention that behavior and physiology can be explained by the tactics genes use to perpetuate themselves. It was in *The Selfish Gene* that he first proposed his widely known idea that humans are simply robots, "temporary survival machines" that are programmed by "selfish" genes to further replicate their genes. Dawkins explained that even seemingly altruistic acts fit within his model. For example, children share 50 percent of their genes with their mothers, so if a mother were to sacrifice her life to protect her young, her genes would continue to survive. Thus her apparent act of altruism is really a strategy by which her genes ensure their own survival.

Dawkins's starkly Darwinian views have often led scientists to accuse him of being a genetic determinist—that is, someone who believes that all behavior, even that of humans, is determined by genes. But Dawkins is not a strict genetic determinist, because he believes that the evolution of the human brain has allowed humans to bypass their genes. For instance, people have learned that, by using contraception, they can have sex without reproducing, and can thus thwart the process by which their genes reproduce themselves. The idea of using contraception is one of the many notions that have affected human behavior. Dawkins calls such ideas "memes"; he introduced his influential ideas about memes in the last chapter of *The Selfish Gene*. Like genes, memes can replicate, by passing from person to person, and they can also mutate, or change.

Dawkins scoffs at the attempts of others to use Darwinism as a model for constructing human society, because they ignore the influence of memes. In a perversion of Dawkins's ideas, members of the National Front, a neo-Nazi organization in England, argued that racism and nationalism are really means by which certain genes propagate themselves. Dismissing their reasoning, Dawkins told Kam Patel for *THES* (April 28, 1995), "It is almost like saying that because animals do not wear clothes, that is an advocacy of nudism."

In the more than 20 years since the publication of *The Selfish Gene*, Dawkins has spent much of his working life elaborating on the ideas he sketched in that book and addressing the continuing controversy that surrounds theories of evolution. In his second book, *The Extended Phenotype* (1982), in which he expanded his "gene's-eye" view of the world, he discussed the effects genes have on organisms other than their host organisms. "Genes have greater power than they're normally credited with," he explained to Thomas Bass for *Omni* (January 1990). "But that's in the sense of reaching outside the body and manipulating other individuals, even the world at large. That's not a new theory; it's just an upside-down way of expressing what's already known." He cited as examples certain parasites that use other organisms to propagate their DNA.

Dawkins's third book, *The Blind Watchmaker* (1986), addresses one of the arguments repeatedly raised by critics of Dawkins's theories: that is, that the complexity of biological organisms cannot possibly have come about by evolution alone. This view was first advanced approximately 200 years ago by the 18th-century British theologian William Paley, who argued that if you discovered a watch in the countryside, the complexity of its design would lead you to assume that it was created by a watchmaker; similarly, complex biological organisms must have been designed by a "divine watchmaker." In the 20th century, some physicists have used statistical calculations to advance an updated version of Paley's thesis.

In *The Blind Watchmaker*, which is subtitled *Why the Evidence of Evolution Reveals a Universe Without Design,* Dawkins set out to disprove Paley's thesis by showing how simple features can evolve into more complex organs through the accumulation of small changes. To illustrate how this might be possible, Dawkins described innovative experiments in which he used a computer program

to mimic the process of evolution. In 1984, he reported, he wrote a program on his Apple II to generate digital creatures he called "biomorphs." The biomorphs started out as tree-like forms. By introducing random mutations into the form, the computer program produced several biomorph "progeny." Mimicking natural selection, Dawkins then selected one of these offspring and bred it. As he continued to breed more biomorphs in this fashion, he produced biomorphs that looked like insects. "Nothing in my biologist's intuition, nothing in my 20 years' experience of programming computers, and nothing in my wildest dreams prepared me for what actually emerged on screen," he wrote in *The Blind Watchmaker*. "I still cannot conceal from you my feeling of exultation as I first watched these exquisite creatures emerging before my eyes. I distinctly heard the triumphal opening chords of [the German composer Richard Strauss's] *Also Sprach Zarathustra* in my mind. I couldn't eat, and that night 'my' insects swarmed behind my eyelids as I tried to sleep." Later experiments indicated that Dawkins could create a nearly endless variety of quasi-biological forms, including bird-like and frog-like creatures and what looked like human faces.

Dawkins's next book, *River Out of Eden* (1995), provided additional detailed evidence to prove the validity of evolutionary theories. It also offered succinct evolutionary metaphors. "The river of my title is a river of DNA, and it flows through time, not space. It is a river of information, not a river of bones and tissues; a river of abstract instructions for building bodies," he wrote. "Each generation is a filter, a sieve; good genes tend to fall through the sieve into the next generation; bad genes tend to end up in bodies that die young or without reproducing." He explained, among other things, why myopia, cancer, heart disease, and other afflictions common in old age have never been eliminated by natural selection. Because most people have produced children and thus reproduced their genes by the time they reach old age, from a gene's standpoint, there is no great selective pressure to eliminate those afflictions.

Dawkins's 1996 book *Climbing Mount Improbable*, grew out of a series of television lectures. The title refers to a parable that Dawkins made up to show how complexity in biological organisms is possible. "The main lesson of this book is that the evolutionary high ground cannot be approached hastily," he wrote. "Even the most difficult problems can be solved, and even the most precipitous heights can be scaled, if only a slow, gradual, step-by-step pathway can be found. Mount Improbable cannot be assaulted. Gradually, if not always slowly, it must be climbed."

Many reviewers who pointed out that the book examines topics covered in Dawkins's other books still felt that the mass of detail in *Climbing Mount Improbable* made the book an enjoyable read. "There are many intriguing evolutionary tales told here—about the beauties of spiders' webs, about the 40-fold origins of the eye, about the origins of flight," Jon Turney wrote in *New Statesman and Society* (April 26, 1996). In the *National Review* (October 14, 1996), Michael J. Behe expressed a different opinion. Echoing some other critics of Dawkins's work, he wrote that even Dawkins's "lively prose can't disguise the fact that science hasn't a clue as to what might explain the development of life. . . . The problem with all of Dawkins's evolutionary stories is that they speak of changes in whole animals or whole organs at once, ignoring the fundamental insight of modern biology that life is based on highly specific, complex interactions of molecules. A serious study of the possible Darwinian evolution of biology novelty would have to begin with molecules." Behe also expressed skepticism as to whether Dawkins's various computer simulations captured the biochemical reality of evolution.

In his next book, *Unweaving the Rainbow* (1998), Dawkins offered "an extended rebuttal," in the words of a *Wall Street Journal* reviewer, "of perennial anti-science convictions." Melvin Konner of *Scientific American* noted that, in light of Dawkins's earlier publications, "some ideas [are] repeated, but reviewers were generally laudatory: Timothy Ferris, writing in the *New York Times Book Review* (January 10, 1999), praised the author as "one of the most incisive science writers alive."

By his own account, Dawkins has written extensively on the subject of evolution because of his love of the natural world and scientific truth. He has been especially fierce in his criticism of religion, which he considers an archaic meme—a holdover from unenlightened times that ignores scientific truths. "Suppose that, at the moment of Christ's death, the news of it had started traveling at the maximum possible speed around the universe outwards from the earth," he wrote in the *Humanist* (January 1997). "How far would the terrible tidings have traveled by now? Following the theory of special relativity, the answer is that the news could not, under any circumstances whatever, have reached more than one-50th of the way across one galaxy—not one-thousandth of the way to our nearest neighboring galaxy in the 100-million-galaxy-strong universe. The universe at large couldn't possibly be anything other than indifferent to Christ, his birth, his passion, and his death." Dawkins does not believe that without concepts such as God and soul, life is any less worth living. "Think of the composers greater than Beethoven, the scientists greater than Newton, and the poets greater than Donne who were never lucky enough to be born," he told Nigel Hawkes. Pointing out that the vast majority of eggs and sperm never develop into human beings, Dawkins added, "In the face of these stupendous odds, it is we who are here and we should be glad."

In 1995, Dawkins became Oxford's first Charles Simonyi Professor of Public Understanding of Science, a position funded by Charles Simonyi, a wealthy former employee of Microsoft. In his new position, Dawkins has been relieved of his teaching and research duties, which leaves him free to write books and make television appearances, in the hope of dispelling stereotypes of scientists and increasing public knowledge of science. Dawkins recently collaborated with software programmers to create a CD-ROM entitled *The Evolution of Life*, in which he guides users through interactive lessons that explain evolutionary processes. The CD-ROM also contains the program "Cybertation," with which one can breed and animate one's own life forms.

Though he misses the hands-on experience of conducting research, Dawkins does not consider his new position as chief Darwinian pundit insignificant. "I'd rather go to my grave having been [James] Watson or [Francis] Crick [who discovered that DNA has a double helical form] than having discovered a wonderful way of explaining things to people," he told Ian Parker. "But if the discovery you're talking about is an ordinary, run-of-the-mill discovery of the sort being made in laboratories around the world every day, you feel: Well, if I hadn't done this, somebody else would have, pretty soon. So if you have a gift for reaching hundreds of thousands—millions—of people and enlightening them, I think doing that runs a close second to making a really great discovery like Watson and Crick." According to some sources, Dawkins has been very successful as a proselytizer of evolutionary science. "The world must be full of people who are biologists today, rather than physicists, because of Dawkins," the British biologist John Maynard Smith told Parker.

Dawkins is a voracious reader of both fiction and nonfiction. His favorite novelists include P. G. Wodehouse and Evelyn Waugh. Those who think of him as merely a cold scientist may be surprised to learn that he enjoys listening to his current wife, Lalla Ward, read him sonnets. "She is a brilliant reader. I can be moved to tears quite easily by her reading. I try to suppress it, though, because it embarrasses me," he admitted to Kam Patel. Ward, his third wife, is an actor who played the assistant, Romana, on the popular science-fiction TV show *Doctor Who*. Ward has taken an active interest in Dawkins's work. She illustrated his books *River Out of Eden* and *The Blind Watchmaker* and has embroidered seat cushions in their home with colorful biomorph images. Dawkins has one child, a daughter, from a previous marriage. —C.M.

SUGGESTED READING: *Eastsideweek* (on-line) Dec. 11, 1996; *Guardian* (on-line) July 17, 1996, June 11, 1997; *Humanist* p26+ Jan. 1997, with photo; *London Times* Apr. 26, 1996; *National Review* Oct. 14, 1996; *New Statesman and Society* Apr. 26, 1996; *New Yorker* p41+ Sep. 9, 1996, with photo; *New York Times Book Review* Jan. 10, 1999; *Omni* p58+ Jan. 1990, with photo; *People* p64 Apr. 4, 1977, with photo; *Skeptic* p80+ vol. 3, no. 4, 1996, with photo; *THES* (on-line) Apr. 28, 1995; Horgan, John. *The End of Science*, 1996; *Who's Who 1997*

SELECTED BOOKS: *The Selfish Gene*, 1976; *The Extended Phenotype*, 1982; *The Blind Watchmaker*, 1986; *River Out of Eden*, 1995; *Climbing Mount Improbable*, 1996; *Unweaving the Rainbow*, 1998

De Bernières, Louis

Dec. 8, 1954– Novelist

The British novelist Louis de Bernières created a sensation with his first novel, *The War of Don Emmanuel's Nether Parts* (1990), reminiscent of *One Hundred Years of Solitude* by Gabriel García Márquez and, like that celebrated work, set in a fictional Latin American country not unlike Colombia. Susan Lowell in the *New York Times Book Review* (March 1, 1992) observed that "this book . . . is really a romance" in the satirical tradition of *Don Quixote* and that De Bernières had "discovered marvelous new possibilities in this venerable genre." De Bernières set two additional novels— *Señor Vivo and the Coca Lord* (1991) and *The Troublesome Offspring of Cardinal Guzman* (1994)—in the same imaginary Latin American country with its lost, and then found, city of Cochadebajo de los Gatos. De Bernières's 1994 novel, *Corelli's Mandolin*, takes place on the Greek island of Cephallonia over a long period that encompasses the Italian occupation during World War II and the subsequent Greek civil war; like the three novels before it, *Corelli's Mandolin* meanders and digresses through comic and tragic episodes involving numerous characters—some of whom, in this instance, are cats and other animals. In *Corelli's Mandolin* De Bernières "tried to be as true to history as possible," as he wrote in an author's note at the end of the novel. Most critics have agreed with David Horspool, who wrote in the *Times Literary Supplement* (April 8, 1994) that De Bernières's mimetic fiction is filled with humor and humanity, "harmonious to the ear."

Louis de Bernières was born in London on December 8, 1954 to Jean Ashton and Reginald de Bernières-Smart. He spent part of his infancy in the Middle East, according to his publisher, but was educated in England. He received his B.A. degree from Victoria University, Manchester, in 1977; a certificate in education from Leicester Polytechnic in 1981; and his M.A. from the University of London in 1985. He was also briefly an officer cadet at Sandhurst, the British military academy, but left to teach in Colombia, South America, where he also wrangled cattle. When he returned to England, before becoming a full-time writer, he worked as a landscape gardener, a groundskeeper at a mental hospital, a mechanic, and a teacher at a school for delinquents in London—soaking up the varied experiences that would prepare him for a literary career.

The War of Don Emmanuel's Nether Parts (1990) is a prodigious work of the imagination that might have come from the pen of Rabelais. In the author's note, De Bernières explained that in his "imaginary Latin American country," not only had he "jumbled up and adapted incidents from many different countries at different times in their history," but he had "borrowed words and phrases from Brazilian Portuguese and its regional variants, Latin American Spanish and its regional variants, and from many Indian languages and their dialects." All facets of Latin American society, particularly its more coarse and brutal aspects, are held up to ridicule, especially the right-wing repressiveness and the equally inept and destructive leftist armed struggle against it. At the same time, a pervasive good humor and sweetness lend a lighter tone to *The War of Don Emmanuel's Nether Parts*. The "war" begins when one Doña Costanza decides to divert the river that crosses her vast estates so that her swimming pool will not dry up between rainy seasons—not caring that the local *campesinos* will be deprived of their main source of water. The locals turn for protection to Don Emmanuel, an Englishman, who also owns vast estates but who has become part of the surroundings and uses the river for bathing his "nether parts." Meanwhile, government soldiers are inexpertly, and with maximum carnage and torture, battling Communist guerrillas. "The twists and turns of the novel's convoluted plot finally bring the assorted *campesinos*, rebels, soldiers, torturers, aristocrats, apparitions, and Indians together into the same story," James Polk wrote in the *Washington Post Book World* (February 2, 1992). He added that De Bernières "intertwines them in ways that never fail to dazzle."

De Bernières almost always sees both sides, the angelic and the satanic, in every character and class of people, except for those who use the right-wing political miasma as a cloak for their psychopathic desire to torture and mutilate. Most people, in De Bernières's view, have some good in them. Doña Costanza, for instance, not really true to the oligarchy, is kidnapped by the guerrilla band led by a woman, falls in love with one of the men, and joins the group. Only as a hardworking member of the guerrilla band does she achieve happiness. Ultimately, she and Don Emmanuel and the other characters join in an exodus from their home, finding a lost city called Cochadebajo de los Gatos; in this rediscovered place, the characters begin life anew. "The novel's pace is brisk, its prose epigrammatic," Susan Lowell wrote in the *New York Times Book Review* (March 1, 1992). "Farcical incidents alternate with graphic descriptions of torture, ribald sex scenes with tender love stories, political satire with supernatural events." Phoebe-Lou Adams in the *Atlantic* (March 1992) declared that the novel's going from "realistic and blood-chilling brutality to sexual burlesque to political comedy to practical social analysis to helpful ghosts and an army of supernatural cats" led to a "scattershot effect," but she found the book's individual elements to be well-handled and interesting.

While *The War of Don Emmanuel's Nether Parts* is concerned with the oppression of the Latin American people by dictators, oligarchs, and the military and the almost equal toll exacted by those who try to liberate them, in *Señor Vivo and the Coca Lord* De Bernières took a look at the drug wars. The villain, Pablo Escobandodo, known as El Jerarca, is a thinly disguised version of Pablo Escobar, the late drug lord of Medellín in Colombia. According to James Polk in the *Washington Post* (August 17, 1992), De Bernières created in *The War of Don Emmanuel's Nether Parts* "a lighthearted allegory where death and torture played against ribald excess and a profound sense of the absurd." *Señor Vivo and the Coca Lord* "is cut from an identical pattern," Polk declared. Many of the same inhabitants of Cochadebajo de los Gatos appear again, with the addition of El Jerarca, who, fortunately, does not survive, and Dionisio Vivo, who, fortunately, does. Dionisio Vivo is a philosophy professor at Ipasueño University who writes letters to the newspaper about the cocaine trade, to the displeasure of El Jerarca. Very damaged bodies begin to appear outside Dionisio's house. How they became damaged is told in "Another Statistic," termed by John Lennard in the *Times Literary Supplement* (June 21, 1991) a "blankly factual chapter of mutilation." James Polk in the *Washington Post* (August 17, 1992), although he noted the "arguably excessive, ongoing tribute to García Márquez," called *Señor Vivo and the Coca Lord* a "memorable series of bizarre encounters and characters that build a world that is by turns wacky, mystical, and altogether compelling" and in which the "realism is truly magical." Anne Whitehouse in the *New York Times Book Review* (September 13, 1992) deemed the novel, in spite of the pervasive influence of García Márquez, "a wholly original book, with a richly developed narrative, eccentric characters, and vivid descriptions spiked with thought-provoking epigrams."

In the next book in the trilogy, *The Troublesome Offspring of Cardinal Guzman*, the group of characters from *The War of Don Emmanuel's Nether Parts* are living in their isolated semiparadise. Cochadebajo de los Gatos has been a place where "Christianity [was] liberally crossed with pre-Conquest animism, where conquistadors frozen in the mountain snows are brought back to life and form friendships with local Communists . . . and friendly jaguars roam the streets," according to John Sutherland in the *London Review of Books* (September 24, 1992).The only cloud on the characters' horizon is in the form of religious interference from a mad cardinal. The cardinal's "offspring" are a band of demons: the "Contending Heads," the "Hinderer," the "Concealer," and other such monsters, who torment Cardinal Guzman by reminding him of his sins—which include the fathering of real offspring and the arranging of a murder.

John Sutherland commented on De Bernières's ability to mix broad comedy, "visionary flights of great beauty, and graphic descriptions of the most nauseating torture and rape." The novel, he observed, "expresses the author's . . . fascination with the region and his keen political sense that—like the rain forests—it is on the edge of final destruction." Michael Kerrigan in the *Times Literary Supplement* (August 21, 1992) also noted De Bernières's "kaleidoscopic range." The influence of Jorge Amado is stronger here than that of Gabriel García Márquez, Kerrigan wrote, because magic is "just one among many sources of imaginative energy, delightful and disturbing." For James Polk in the *New York Times Book Review* (May 8, 1994), the "wildly comic inventions" in *The Troublesome Offspring of Cardinal Guzman* teach us "that there is simply no institution we can trust. The message of this wondrous novel is: Leave us alone and we'll manage."

De Bernières continued his "assault of an irreverent sense of humor" in *Corelli's Mandolin*, but more restrainedly. On the island of Cephallonia in Greece live a widowed doctor and his beautiful daughter. At the start of the novel, theirs is an almost idyllic life. De Bernières lingers for most of the novel, even after describing the Italian occupation of Greece, on the beauty of the various characters' lives.

Pelagia, the doctor's daughter, falls in love with an Italian officer, Corelli, a musician. By the time Corelli enters the story, the disruptions of war have begun. Pelagia's fiancé, an island fisherman, becomes a warrior, joining the Communists, who, while fighting as partisans against the occupying Italians and later the Germans, betray signs of becoming corrupt slaughterers of their own people. Corelli hides his mandolin with Pelagia when he has to leave to escape the Germans. He promises to return, and the reader understands that this love is a true one and that the lovers will not betray each other. Ultimately, because this is essentially a comedy, they are reunited, but only in old age. Pelagia survives the Italians, the Germans, the earthquake that kills her father, and the Greek civil war, but she is not granted the blessings of a happy life.

Corelli's Mandolin is a story of the way in which people are betrayed by their own human natures into waging war, brutalizing each other, and, finally, foolishly failing to find love until it is almost too late. W. S. Di Piero in the *New York Times Book Review* (November 13, 1994) elaborated on De Bernières's interweaving of treasons: "Italy's Nazi allies become its enemies. The British deceive the partisan forces they are presumably supporting, and vice versa. Pelagia, loving Corelli, violates customary loyalties to her betrothed, and Corelli himself must negotiate conflicting allegiances to his men, his nation, his lover, and his beloved mandolin."

Terming *Corelli's Mandolin* "a high-spirited historical romance," Di Piero observed that De Bernières "wants us to experience not only the apparent facts of his story but also the way in which those little scripts of consciousness critically shape our feeling for facts. He himself says . . . that history is 'hearsay tempered with myth and hazy memory.' That uncertainty and the nervous vitality it induces give this novel its momentum and elasticity." Di Piero's cavils are that De Bernières "sometimes lurches from one dramatic set piece to the next" and that his "instinct for operatic tones leads him into some maudlin writing, like the scene in which Pelagia's betrothed returns to the sea to die, tended by his faithful dolphins." He praised the novel highly, however, for having "at times the rangy, expansive feeling of legend or saga, at other times the cozy intensities of chamber drama."

Roz Kaveney, writing in *New Statesman & Society* (April 22, 1994), felt that De Bernières made a mistake in creating too much of "a fantasy of tourist Greece before tourism" and by sentimentalizing poverty. She called *Corelli's Mandolin* "a generally excellent novel," but thought De Bernières's "tough-minded perception no longer needed all the apparatus of coincidence and omens and comic strong men. At times the magic gets in the way of realism." David Horspool in the *Times Literary Supplement* (April 8, 1994) disagreed. Horspool enjoyed the lighter effects: "De Bernières sees that war can either degrade or elevate human beings, but it is humanity itself, rather than war's effects, which interests him. The lightness of the early chapter, when Iannis cures a long-deaf patient by removing a dried pea from his ear or when Father Arsenios collapses drunk behind a holy screen which only he is allowed to pass, never completely disappears."

Louis de Bernières was awarded the 1991 Commonwealth Writers Prize for the best first novel for *The War of Don Emmanuel's Nether Parts* and the 1992 Commonwealth Writers Prize for *Señor Vivo and the Coca Lord*. *The War of Don Emmanuel's Nether Parts* was named one of the best books of the year 1992 by the *New York Times Book Review*. *Publishers Weekly* similarly selected *Corelli's Mandolin* in 1994.

—S. Y.

SUGGESTED READING: *Atlantic* p125 Mar. 1992; *London Review of Books* p18 Sep. 24, 1992; *New Statesman & Society* p45 Apr. 22, 1994; *New York Times Book Review* p11 Mar. 1, 1992, p24 Sep. 13, 1992, p6 May 8, 1994, p7 Nov. 13, 1994; *Publishers Weekly* p39 Nov. 7, 1994; *Times Literary Supplement* p21 June 21, 1991, p18 Aug. 21, 1992, p21 Apr. 8, 1994; *Washington Post Book World* p1 Feb. 2, 1992, D p2 Aug. 17, 1992

SELECTED BOOKS: *The War of Don Emmanuel's Nether Parts*, 1990; *Señor Vivo and the Coca Lord*, 1991; *The Troublesome Offspring of Cardinal Guzman*, 1994; *Corelli's Mandolin*, 1994

Jennifer Hill / Courtesy of Ticknor & Fields

Dee, Jonathan

1962– Novelist; short-story writer

The American short-story writer and novelist Jonathan Dee has created a quiet critique of American civilization in three novels, *The Lover of History* (1990), *The Liberty Campaign* (1993), and *St. Famous* (1995), which deal, respectively, with modern warfare, the bad seeds planted by past war and American imperialism, and the urban situation, including race relations. Reviewers have tended to agree with Walter Goodman, who in the *New York Times Book Review* (December 24, 1995) observed of the author of the book-within-a-book in *St. Famous*— and, by implication, of Jonathan Dee—that "he can turn out a book on a selling subject that is not at all disgraceful."

For *World Authors 1990–1995*, Jonathan Dee writes: "As a novelist, I sometimes feel my imagination is weakened by a lack of any impulse toward autobiography. I was born in New York City in 1962, the younger of two children; my parents met some ten years earlier, when they both worked in the marketing department of Time-Life. When I was five, the family moved full-time to what had been a vacation house in rural northwestern Connecticut. I attended school there through the eighth grade. I would be remiss if I failed to mention my first success as a writer: at age nine, I won the grand prize in an essay contest on the subject, 'Why I Like to Sell American Seeds' ('American' being a brand name in this case). This led to my picture being run in advertisements on the back of comic books nationwide for the following year. The prize was a thousand dollars—more money than I was to earn from writing for the next seventeen years.

"I went to Phillips Academy in Andover, Massachusetts, and to Yale University, where I majored in American Studies. My last semester in college coincided with the final semester in the academic career of John Hersey, who in addition to his fame as a novelist and reporter was also a revered teacher of writing. From him I have taken not only personal inspiration but also just about every method I employ as a writing teacher myself.

"A few months after graduation I went to work at the *Paris Review* in New York. I stayed for five and a half years; for the first three, I doubled as an associate editor of the magazine and as personal assistant to its founding editor, George Plimpton. I left in the winter of 1990 to write full-time. I am married to Denise Shannon, a literary agent; as I write this, we are expecting the birth of our first child, a girl. We divide our time between an apartment in Manhattan and a house in upstate New York.

"Though I am wary of trying to explain my own novels, I suppose it's safe to say that all three of them have in common a kind of metaphorical setting at the intersection of the private and public spheres, and that they try to weigh some of the incursions made, in our age, on the former by the latter. *The Lover of History* concerns the reactions (or lack thereof) of three young New Yorkers to a quick, remote, thoroughly modern type of war, which America briefly wages in a fictional country called Mazatlan. The fact that the Gulf War broke out in the months just before the book's publication turned out to be both a blessing and a curse in terms of the quality of the critical attention the novel received.

"*The Liberty Campaign* is the story of a retiring advertising executive named Gene Trowbridge, who discovers that a longtime neighbor of his—a man he's never come to know very well—is suspected of a past as a war criminal, a notion which Gene, a man of limited experience, finds scarcely credible. The novel's speculative origins might be found in the case of John Demjanjuk, the Cleveland auto worker who was ultimately deported to Israel to stand trial for murders committed at Treblinka during World War II.

"*St. Famous* records the ordeal of Paul Soloway, a painfully earnest young writer who lives on the Upper West Side of Manhattan. Paul has been working on the same long, ambitious, autobiographical first novel for ten years, and dreams of a prospective but outdated kind of fame (the fame of the intellectual). Instead, he becomes the random victim of a riot, in the aftermath of an unpopular trial verdict; his beating is captured by an anonymous citizen with a video camera. His name becomes a household word, at least for a while, and upon his release from the hospital he is besieged with offers to write a nonfiction book about what's happened to him.

"*St. Famous* was treated by most reviewers, favorably or not, as a piece of social satire—a scolding look at the fetishization of celebrity and victim-

hood. For what it's worth, I had always conceived of it as something quite different: specifically as a kind of broad, unsentimental parable about the state of the novel in our time, its displacement from the center of American culture in favor of a more modern, less intimate sort of art. Milan Kundera once wrote, in answer to the frequently-reported Death of the Novel, that the novel shall not die; rather, it will continue to thrive, in a world that grows increasingly alien to it. It's true that a serious young novelist consigns himself to a life on the cultural margin. On the bright side, this also means that the best motivations to go on writing novels are private ones: as an act arising from a protective impulse toward language, and as a kind of quiet (yet still public) 'Non Serviam' in a society inclined toward the erosion of what we think of as identity. And anyway, in a generation which has brought new work by Ivan Klima, J. M. Coetzee, Danilo Kis, David Grossman, Max Frisch, the case for the novel's exhaustion—which is really the case for the death of the notion of art as a product of an individual consciousness—is still difficult to make."

Jonathan Dee's three novels have generated considerable critical praise. *The Lover of History*, his first novel, the story of three alienated people forced to confront a threat of war, drew the comment from Vince Passaro in the *Voice Literary Supplement* (February 1991) that Dee "is concerned with the clarifications that history brings, whether and how it penetrates the numbed minds of its participants. . . . [T]he radical idea—that you don't get to invent yourself—is the fate that catches up with Dee's . . . characters, and their futile struggle against it raises their drama to the level of tragedy." He concluded that Dee's canvas is not politics but morality and that "his ability to fill that canvas . . . gives *The Lover of History* . . . vitality, daring, and weight."

In *The Liberty Campaign* Gene Trowbridge, a 65-year-old advertising executive about to retire, encounters a mysterious neighbor, Albert Ferdinand. Trowbridge enters a relationship with this neighbor and contemporary after a reporter asks Trowbridge questions leading to the realization that Ferdinand is really a Brazilian officer who was, during a period of military dictatorship, in charge of torturing captives and whose death is desired by the survivors of the regime. Eventually Trowbridge persuades Ferdinand to admit that he is really Captain da Silva. Trowbridge wants to know the facts because, as he tells Ferdinand, "'There was never anything more for me to work for, to worry about, than comfort, and now, maybe as a result, I find I have no anchor, do you see? If I have to find that anchor in the knowledge of evil, so be it. I have to know what you know.'" After one of their later conversations, Trowbridge, who has not grown much out of his self-absorption, asks himself what he would have done in the other man's position:

Would I choose anything if the only other choice available to me was to give up my own life, or even just the things that made up what I knew as normal life? It was hard not to come back to these questions—even though I knew that they, too, were self-serving in their own way, a kind of moral parlor game, a false substitute for experience and truth.

Phoebe-Lou Adams, in the *Atlantic Monthly* (September 1993), observed that as "Trowbridge worries the question of how a civilized man can commit uncivilized horrors, so, nervously, does the reader. Understated in style, unpretentiously commonplace in setting, this is a thoroughly disturbing novel." Fernanda Eberstadt, in the *New York Times Book Review* (August 15, 1993), termed *The Liberty Campaign* "a cogent and provocative novel, in which each event and anecdote serves to illuminate or to amplify . . . Dee's theme of the absence of moral high stakes in American life."

Another iconic American character, who is also an aspect of Dee himself, like the teacher in *The Lover of History* and the advertising executive in *The Liberty Campaign*, is Paul Soloway, the novelist-protagonist of *St. Famous*. Soloway, like Dee's other central male figures, is somewhat baffled by his wife's emotional needs. He is absorbed in his role as a novelist, regarding himself as an "observer" with a "twin consciousness." Fate has handed him another role, however. He has accidentally involved himself in a minor riot while driving through an area where people are protesting the acquittal of a white police officer who has shot a young black man in the back. In the heat of the moment, a group of men, acquaintances of the hardworking and self-sacrificing young Victor Hartley, drag Soloway to Hartley's apartment. At the end of the episode, which is told in flashbacks throughout the book, the other men desert Hartley, who loses his head and beats Soloway severely. Soloway's abduction becomes the news of the day. From a greedy publishing industry, eager to capitalize on that news, he receives offers of the kind of money he would never be paid for his novel to write a book about his experiences. Walter Goodman, in his *New York Times Book Review* article, termed Dee's protagonist "an extravagantly high-minded hero . . . deep into his image of himself as a lone artist resisting the lures of a corrupt society." Goodman held it to Dee's credit, however, that "he makes as strong a case against his hero-artist as against the ostensible tempters. Are these marketeers really so wrong in getting Paul to write a book—their kind of book—about his experiences? What principles is he really upholding by resisting, and at what cost to the people who love him?"

Even Soloway's friend Martin, a rather stereotypical bohemian poet, urges him to take the money—arguing that, rather than representing corruption,

"The money represents popular taste. In a kind of convoluted, corporate way, all that money is a kind of offering to you, from your own people, a bounty offered in exchange for your story. It's all very tribal. It's beautiful in its way. And I don't think that, for a true storyteller, that kind of public need can be so lightly regarded. It's a burden, and you treat it like a nuisance."

Paul does write the book (his manuscript constitutes the flashbacks in which the reader sees his abduction). He has wanted only to work on his novel, but when he goes to an artists' colony resembling Yaddo, he is forced by deadlines to work on the abduction story. The final irony is that Victor Hartley, out on bail, has seen the manuscript and resents the intellectualized, self-centered approach Soloway has taken to his subject, as does Soloway's publisher. Hartley goes to the colony and attempts to seize the manuscript. What follows, told in an epilogue, is what often happens to the Pauls and Victors of this world. One gets rich; the other, separated from the family he has struggled to protect, goes to prison.

A recurrent concern for Dee is the impossibility in America of leading a natural life, a life of instinct, one in which choices really matter. In one scene in *The Liberty Campaign*, Gene Trowbridge, reflecting on his career in advertising, remembers when he was asked to look over a group of models, one of whom was to be chosen for a campaign. Trowbridge muses on the fact that he finds it impossible to distinguish any characteristics that make one model better than another. He finds them to be "like animals whose habitat has been destroyed." Dee finds the model to be a particularly good symbol of the state of bafflement in which most Americans find themselves. In "Venus," a story published in *Gentlemen's Quarterly* (March 1994), a model is hired to represent the Velázquez *Venus* for a party. After grueling hours of holding the same position, she begins to fear that she may become separated from the value of her own beauty.

Beauty was something within her, but not of her; it was something to which she had unusual access and the unusual opportunity to serve. . . . She would do anything, she said to herself, to keep that position. . . . But what should she do? In the world that made her compete, that made her sacrifice, what should she do?

To her distress, the only answer that came back to her was, *Not this. Not this. Not this.*

In Dee's view, the model has no real choice: to the world she is merely an icon. Gene Trowbridge of *The Liberty Campaign* counsels his son, a star baseball player, to retreat for a while after a bad season. The young man looks at him and asks,

"Don't you believe in me?" The father realizes that his son's career is based only on a dream shared by his son and his fans. Having become a star in the eyes of others and himself, he has no choice but to continue his career.

Dee told Ivana Edwards in an interview for the *New York Times* (August 8, 1993) that he refuses to claim that "writing about politics is a political act." It is clear, however, that he does infuse his work with meaning that transcends his characters' dilemmas and universalizes them. Considering himself one of life's observers, he told Edwards that "part of what makes a person an observer is also what leads someone to take up a career like writing." But Dee concluded that the observer posture can give one "the kind of feeling that you're at a little bit of a remove from even sometimes your own life. That's the feeling that sometimes enables you to be a good writer."

—S. Y.

SUGGESTED READING: *Atlantic* p116 Sep. 1993; *New York Times* 13LI p17 Aug. 8, 1993; *New York Times Book Review* p24 Nov. 4, 1990, p10 Aug. 15, 1993, p6 Dec. 24, 1995; *Voice Literary Supplement* p5 Feb. 1991

SELECTED BOOKS: Fiction—*The Lover of History*, 1990; *The Liberty Campaign*, 1993; *St. Famous*, 1995; Nonfiction—*Chronicles of Ancient Egypt*, 1999

DeMarinis, Rick

May 3, 1934– Novelist; short-story writer

The American novelist and short-story writer Rick DeMarinis has become known for lending a comic voice to what are essentially tragic or deeply saddening circumstances, such as children looking for a place in a world that is at best indifferent and at worst brutal. He is the author of such novels as *The Burning Women of Far Cry* (1986), *The Year of the Zinc Penny* (1989), and *The Mortician's Apprentice* (1994) and the short-story collections *Under the Wheat* (1986), *The Coming Triumph of the Free World* (1988), *The Voice of America* (1991), and *Borrowed Hearts* (1999). In those works he has depicted, in the words of a character in "The Swimmer in Hard Light" (one of the stories in *The Coming Triumph of the Free World*), "a new age of innocence" in which we "are naked again, reborn in a high-tech Eden, watched over by disinterested electronic gods." Russell Banks, writing in the *New York Times Book Review* (October 30, 1988), observed that "this nakedness, this innocence . . . is . . . DeMarinis's subject, and he regards it with a protectiveness that is never sentimental and always fierce. His art, then, is comedy of a very high order, the comedy of a decent heart enraged."

The son of Ruth Siik and Alphonse DeMarinis, Rick DeMarinis was born on May 3, 1934 in New York City and raised in California. He attended San Diego State College from 1952 to 1954; his education was interrupted by a stint in the Air Force, in which he served until 1958. He then attended the University of Montana in Missoula, where he received his B.A. in 1961 and his M.A. in 1967. Although he initially intended to study poetry at the University of Montana, "I found I was not a poet, and at any rate I had more fun writing fiction," DeMarinis told Barth Healey for an interview in the *New York Times Book Review* (October 30, 1988).

DeMarinis taught English at the University of Montana from 1967 to 1969 and at San Diego State University until 1976. In 1988 he was appointed professor of English at the University of Texas, El Paso. He has been writer-in-residence at Wichita State University and Arizona State University.

DeMarinis's first book, the novel *A Lovely Monster: The Adventures of Claude Rains and Dr. Tellenbeck*, was published in 1976. A modernized version of the Frankenstein story told by the monster, a high-tech artificial man, it combines fantasy with a hard look at contemporary reality. The monster, like Mary Shelley's, is unable to make the essential human connection—to love. DeMarinis continued to write in a fantastical vein in his next novels, *Scimitar* (1977) and *Cinders* (1978), and in *Jack and Jill: Two Novellas and a Short Story* (1979).

After the warm critical but cool public response to his first efforts, DeMarinis let his talents lie fallow until the publication of his next book, *Under the Wheat* (1986), a short-story collection, which won him the Drue Heinz prize for short fiction. The book's protagonists are bizarre misfits, described by Janet Shaw in the *New York Times Book Review* (December 14, 1986) as "characters who embody on a grand scale the psychological and spiritual deformities of our culture." One character describes his and others' foibles as "entertaining as hell," demonstrating DeMarinis's somewhat Boschian vision.

A character from *Under the Wheat*, an apprentice salesman named Jack, reappears as the narrator of the novel *The Burning Women of Far Cry*. In the latter book Jack is a young teenager observing his mother's third marriage—to Gent Mundy, a gentle giant. Janet Shaw in the *New York Times Book Review* (December 14, 1986) observed that "everyone, except Gent, is obsessed with sex. . . . he's obsessed with love, and in the grim world depicted in Far Cry, that's suicide." Noting the book's farcical beginning, Shaw wrote that by "Part Three, the tone of the novel is as aggressive as a mean drunk. The deft and ironic touch of the opening has become a fist."

DeMarinis's 1988 collection, *The Coming Triumph of the Free World*, was lauded by the novelist Russell Banks in the *New York Times Book Review* (October 30, 1998). Banks called the collection "consistent, original, seductive, and delightfully sad." In particular he praised the story "Medicine Man" as "a vision of the wise man's wisdom. That is, the story intends to convey wisdom itself. And it succeeds." "Medicine Man" is the tale of a miracle healer who is captured by the authorities as he is about to remove a cancerous tumor from the stomach of a hospitalized man. Once he is out of jail, he holes up in an abandoned mine shaft and then returns to the world, taking "the narrator, and the reader, on a metaphysical journey that would make Carlos Castaneda quake," Banks wrote. "One has to go back almost to Flannery O'Connor to find a story that so deliberately, methodically and with such brave comedy transforms ordinary life into the sublime." Banks also compared DeMarinis to Richard Ford and Raymond Carver. "But while their stories, like Hemingway's, so often leave one face to face with the everyday and loving it mainly for its esthetic possibilities, Mr. DeMarinis leaves one facing that same humdrum reality filled with belief in one's ability to transcend it."

The novel *The Year of the Zinc Penny* is a set in 1943, when pennies were made of zinc to save copper for the war effort. Trygve Napoli, the young male protagonist, is left by his cold, selfish mother with her family for four years and then retrieved to live in a Los Angeles household consisting of his mother, her sister, their husbands, and his uncle's teenage son. In his imagination, however, Tryg is a World War II fighter pilot who engages in heroic combat and dies in the arms of a beautiful girl. Michiko Kakutani observed in the *New York Times* (October 3, 1989) that DeMarinis "gives us both a picture of the eternal realities of childhood . . . and a tactile portrait of life in the wartime 40's." She termed DeMarinis "deft . . . in portraying Tryg's mixed feelings . . . of love and resentment, sympathy and irritation. . . . and we see him attempt to use the clear-sighted logic of childhood to solve the mysteries of love and death." Tryg learns that he must be "capable of mustering any necessary lie at will" in order to survive.

Mary-Ann Tirone Smith, reviewing the novel in the *New York Times Book Review* (September 24, 1989), found that the characters were fully drawn and that "their trials evoke laughter and pain as they search for love." "Looking for love," Smith wrote, "was also the theme of Mr. DeMarinis's 1986 novel, *The Burning Women of Far Cry*, but at the core of that book was the bleak message that love can't be found because it doesn't exist. . . . But that dark view is redeemed, at least in part, in *The Year of the Zinc Penny* by Trygve, a small light shining weakly but optimistically through the mayhem that is his love-starved family."

A good example of DeMarinis's themes is the story "Insulation," which appeared in his 1991 collection *The Voice of America*. "Insulation" is a portrait of a distorted and tormented soul, a man who believes he is both hereditarily subject to being struck by lightning and "attractive," drawing monstrous electrical phenomena toward him. A metaphor for the human condition at its extremes, the narrator is fearful lest he be destroyed and, at the same time, awed by his own destructive capacity, which, in the end, kills his wife. Another of the stories in *The Voice of America*, "God Bless America," provides a hilarious glimpse into the lives of two bizarre characters—a "serious" writer and a commercial writer, who are friends despite their antithetical approaches to their craft.

"These are stories of love and hate, rage and jealousy, hard reality and disillusionment, invented by a writer with a wild and unbounded imagination, with characters as real as the people in your life," Larry Brown concluded, reviewing the volume in the *Washington Post Book World* (May 12, 1991). "A good short story can . . . when the writer is as talented as Rick DeMarinis, break the reader's heart."

DeMarinis's next book, *The Mortician's Apprentice*, is a coming-of-age novel that has been compared by some to the book and movie *The Graduate* and by others to *The Catcher in the Rye*. The story is that of Ozzie Santee's adventures in 1950s California, as he graduates from high school, takes a menial job, tries college, and goes on to another job, selling coffins—a position from which he will presumably rise to become the apprentice of his prospective father-in-law, a mortician. For Vince Passaro, writing in *New York Newsday* (August 4, 1994), DeMarinis ranks "among the premier writers at work in the United States," one who "has never been as widely read as his funny, intelligent, beautifully evocative books deserve." This is partly, Passaro felt, because *The Mortician's Apprentice*, among other of DeMarinis's works, offers the unexpected, having "something gentle and thoughtful and quiet about it"—unusual for a book by a male writer and thus confusing to some readers who "want never to be confused about whose world they are visiting." For Robert Plunket, the *New York Times Book Review* (August 14, 1994) critic, *The Mortician's Apprentice* is an inferior version of *The Catcher in the Rye*; although "Ozzie is not really much like Holden Caulfield . . . his problem is the same: how on earth does he fit into the adult world he is about to enter?" Plunket predicted a lack of empathy on the part of the average person with Ozzie, but he found that "in general, *The Mortician's Apprentice* is first-rate comedy writing."

Eleven of the tales in *Borrowed Hearts: New and Selected Stories* (1999) are new, while the remaining 21 are pulled from previous collections. "Here and there," wrote the *Kirkus Reviews* (May 7, 1999) critic, "we catch echoes of T. C. Boyle . . . or Stanley Elkin . . . . Then again, who but DeMarinis could concoct such beguiling horrors as a serial killer in a pawnshop trying to trade a necklace made of human kneecaps for a machete or a toddler traumatized by science-fiction movies who mutilated his new teddy bear with a steak knife? There are few stories here that don't raise the pulse rate."

Russell Banks perhaps summed up DeMarinis's work when he commented that DeMarinis may be "a contemporary avatar of that tradition in American . . . writing that, by way of Hawthorne, Melville, Faulkner, O'Connor, Welty, and Cheever, is essentially religious and, because rooted in the everyday, comic. . . . Most of his characters . . . are lower middle class, out of work and marginal, which he regards not as merely amusing or as a sad sign of the times but as a personally felt affliction, a significantly crippling form of alienation that, faced with humor, patience and mother-wit, makes his characters as close to heroic as we are likely to find these days."

—S. Y.

SUGGESTED READING: *New York Newsday* Aug. 4, 1994; *New York Times* C p21 Oct. 3, 1989, C p17 May 7, 1991; *New York Times Book Review* p26 Dec. 14, 1986, p7 Oct. 30, 1988, p12 Sep. 24, 1989, p14 June 30, 1991, p10 Aug. 14, 1994; *Washington Post* C p2 Sep. 7, 1994

SELECTED BOOKS: *A Lovely Monster: The Adventures of Claude Rains and Dr. Tellenbeck*, 1976; *Scimitar*, 1977; *Cinders*, 1978; *Jack and Jill: Two Novellas and a Short Story*, 1979; *Under the Wheat*, 1986; *The Burning Women of Far Cry*, 1986; *The Coming Triumph of the Free World*, 1988; *The Year of the Zinc Penny*, 1989; *The Voice of America*, 1991; *The Mortician's Apprentice*, 1994; *Borrowed Hearts: New and Selected Stories*, 1999

Denby, David

1943(?)– Film critic; memoirist

For years a film critic for *New York* magazine, now on the staff of the *New Yorker*, David Denby has spent the bulk of his career reviewing movies. He has also edited several film-related books, notably *Awake in the Dark* (1977), an anthology of 20th-century film criticism. In addition to his film criticism, he is known as the author of *Great Books* (1996). Subtitled *My Adventures with Homer, Rousseau, Woolf, and Other Indestructible Writers of the Western World*, the book grew out of his decision to enroll, in 1991, in two of the literature courses he had taken at Columbia University as an undergraduate, in the 1960s. Denby is also the author of *Sentimental Narrative and Social Order in France, 1760–1820* (1994), and his articles have appeared in such periodicals as *Premiere* and the *New Republic*.

David Denby was born in or around 1943. He attended Columbia University, in New York City, and graduated in 1965. In 1969 he edited a book based on the François Truffaut movie *The 400 Blows*. He was appointed the editor of *Film Seventy-Two to Seventy-Three*, a critical anthology compiled by the National Association of Film Critics, in 1973.

By then reviewing movies himself, Denby undertook for his next editorial project a compilation of film criticism in the United States. The result was *Awake in the Dark: An Anthology of American Film Criticism, 1915 to the Present*, published in 1977. Denby chose 44 reviews and essays written over a span of about six decades; the essayists, among them Andrew Sarris, Manny Farber, Pauline Kael, and James Agee, are prominent writers who, as D. A. Green wrote for *Library Journal* (June

1, 1977), had "made their marks." The book contains sections on specific directors and performers, discussion of critical methods, and analyses of various cinematic genres.

A review of *Awake in the Dark* in *Choice* (December 1977) praised Denby's selection, noting that many of the pieces would have been hard to find, and commended the thoughtful arrangement of the essays. D. A. Green noted that Denby had "present[ed] articles and reviews that not only show the evolution of film criticism but also the evolution of film as art." In the *New York Times* (October 16, 1977), Janet Maslin commented favorably that the way that Denby had juxtaposed the articles had brought new life to them.

In 1991, when he was 48, Denby began to go through what he himself described as a midlife crisis. Thinking that one way to cope with this development would be to present himself with new challenges, he decided to retake the two "Great Books" courses Columbia University has offered generations of students. He was curious to see how the courses and students had changed since his years at Columbia, and he wondered how he would react to certain works of literature after so many years. Perhaps most important, he looked forward to enjoying a role other than that of spectator—the role he had played for so many years as a reviewer. Also, Denby was very much interested in the so-called "culture wars," an ongoing conflict among academics about whether the canon of Western literature should remain a required subject or should be scrapped in favor of a more "multicultural" body of texts.

While continuing to write his *New York* movie reviews, the critic immersed himself in the Great Books coursework for two semesters. He even completed all the writing assignments and took the three-hour final examinations. "What struck me most forcefully," James Shapiro, one of the course instructors, was quoted as saying in the *Chronicle of Higher Education* (September 13, 1996), "was that he didn't want to observe the class; he actually wanted to *take* it." "Sizing him up," at the beginning of the semester, Shapiro admitted, "I doubted whether Mr. Denby had the physical stamina for the two-semester course." Denby went on to prove Shapiro wrong, and by the professor's own account, the critic fit in well with the class, and added to discussions without letting his presence become a distraction.

In *Great Books: My Adventures with Homer, Rousseau, Woolf, and Other Indestructible Writers of the Western World*, published in 1996 by Simon and Schuster, Denby described in detail the two courses he took, Literature Humanities and Contemporary Civilization, and discussed the many texts he had studied, among them writings of such authors as Homer, Plato, Thucydides, Virgil, Dante, Shakespeare, Hegel, Austen, Woolf, Marx, and Machiavelli. The book contains chapters dealing with particular writers, thoughts on many of the books Denby had read, and descriptions of his professors, some of the students, and classroom discussions. As a returning student, Denby overcame the intimidation he initially felt at the thought of the "Great Books," and he developed a real fondness for some of them.

According to Kathleen Burke in *Smithsonian* (June 1997), *Great Books* was "highly entertaining and instructive." She praised Denby's ability to "connect" with many of the books that he encountered and to relate them to his life.

Some other reviewers were not impressed. Indeed, Denby's volume became a target of scorn for many academics and academically inclined critics. In the *American Scholar* (Spring 1997), Alan Rutenberg, for one, described Denby as "a poorly-defined, 48-year-old liberal," and charged that he was too influenced by movies and television to seriously assess literary works. Denby produced "precisely what one would expect of a liberal film critic . . . ," Rutenberg wrote, "a lucid journalistic account with a considerable emphasis on personalities, a studied, ironic presentation of autobiography, and a sophisticated liberal politics that maintains a tacit distance from the academic left." The reviewer criticized Denby for portraying himself as a "courageous moderate" instead of taking a clear stand in the culture wars. "With . . . modest criticisms of the academic left, Denby maintains at least the appearance and the sentiments of a liberal position," Rutenberg wrote. "In fact . . . he reacts to . . . the academic left with a rather firm, unfashionable resistance . . . [yet] he also acknowledges the force of the new dispensation—not actually capitulating to the academic left, but often acceding to its terms of reference and debate." Rutenberg did find merit in certain aspects of Denby's book, however, including the author's vivid depiction of his instructors and their respective teaching styles.

In the periodical *Current* (December 1996), the prominent academic Helen Vendler mercilessly labeled *Great Books* "naive, amateurish, and a folly." She accused Denby of letting his preconceptions direct the course of his literary "adventures" and criticized what she perceived as Denby's "muddled thinking," which, she maintained, manifested itself in historically inaccurate appraisals of the Western canon. Denby, according to the reviewer, was unwilling to discuss exactly why these "great" works of literature are considered "great"; instead, his opinions sprang from an unarticulated set of aesthetic assumptions. "Why do I find the spectacle of *New York*'s movie critic 'grieving over' or 'deploring' Virgil's damaged art so irresistibly comic?" Vendler mused.

Despite many mixed reviews, Denby's *Great Books* was named a finalist for the National Book Critics Circle Award in 1997.

Denby married the writer Cathleen Schine in 1981. The couple has two sons, Max and Thomas.—B.S.

SUGGESTED READING: *American Scholar* p290+ Spring 1997; *Choice* p1370 Dec. 1977; *Chronicle of Higher Education* A p64 Sep. 13, 1996; *Current* p34+ Dec. 1996; *Library Journal* p1300 June 1, 1977; *New York Times* p26 Oct. 16, 1977; *Smithsonian* p156+ June 1997; Bogdanovich, Peter, ed. *The Best American Movie Writing 1999*

SELECTED WORKS: *Sentimental Narrative and the Social Order in France, 1760–1820*, 1994; *Great Books: My Adventures with Homer, Rousseau, Woolf, and Other Indestructible Writers of the Western World*, 1996; As editor— *The 400 Blows: A Film by Francois Truffaut from a Filmscript by Francois Truffaut and Marcel Moussy*, 1969; *Film Seventy-Two and Seventy-Three: An Anthology by the National Association of Film Critics*, 1973; *Awake in the Dark: An Anthology of American Film Criticism, 1915 to the Present*, 1977

Dexter, Colin

1930– Mystery writer; novelist

The English mystery writer Colin Dexter shares many of the tastes of his Inspector Morse character. Both love crossword puzzles and beer, the opera, and 19th-century English literature. Dexter views the Morse series, which originated with the publication of *Last Bus to Woodstock* in 1975 and includes a dozen other titles, as having always been semi-autobiographical. Morse was not created entirely with the author in mind, however. Dexter believed that Morse should have a few bad qualities, too; the inspector is therefore stingy, ungrateful,

Miriam Berkley

Colin Dexter

rude to his associates, and, as Dexter told the *Chicago Tribune* (April 6, 1993), "only slightly less miserable with himself than he is with other people." Regardless of these attributes, Inspector Morse and his sidekick, Sergeant Lewis, have thrilled readers on both sides of the Atlantic with their exploits for over two decades. Dexter himself has also become something of a celebrity; a winner of the British Silver Dagger Award from the Crime Writers Association, he has also written the scripts for and has been a consultant on the installments of the PBS series *Mystery!* that feature Morse. Dexter has also made cameos on the show.

In the autobiography he wrote for *World Authors 1990–1995*, Dexter discusses his life and interests and how he became a mystery writer: "I was born in Stamford, Lincolnshire, in 1930, the son of a taxi driver. My father [Alfred Dexter] and my mother [Dorothy Towns] had both left school at the age of 12, and were anxious that their children should grasp the opportunities they themselves had been forced to forgo.

"I was therefore exhorted to work with appropriate diligence, and my schooldays were largely conditioned by a kind of benign emotional blackmail. I was never expected to make beds, wash up dishes, clean shoes, empty chamber pots, or perform any of the other household duties which have so often been the cause of family strife. My job was with the books.

"At the age of 11, I won a scholarship (as in fact my mother had done) to a Grammar School, where I was considered a clever lad, where I won a good many prizes, and where I spent most of my time happily with the Greek and Latin authors. In 1948 I gained a place at Cambridge University.

"At a fairly early stage in my schooling I thought that I could write English reasonably well. And from the age of 12 or so I began to realize that I was perhaps unusually sensitive to the sound, the meaning, and the rhythm of words; particularly to the words of the poets; and particularly at that time to Thomas Gray and John Keats—several of whose works I already had by heart.

"Before going to Cambridge, I was conscripted into the army, where for 18 months in the Royal Corps of Signals I spent my time, mostly in Germany, receiving high-speed Morse code messages from Russian and Eastern European transmission stations. I was informed, quite unreliably, that such work was of vital importance to the defense of the Western democracies. The army failed to discern in me any latent qualities of leadership, most probably because there were none to be discerned.

"Thereafter I spent four enjoyable years at Cambridge. I did well enough there, both academically and on the games field; and I am still a little snootily proud of having studied at one of the world's great universities." (Dexter graduated from Cambridge with a B.A. degree in 1953 and an M.A. degree in 1958.)

"From 1953 to 1966 I taught Greek and Latin to pupils in the 11-18 year range. The ideas of neither Plato nor Locke played much part in my own pedagogic creed which held that the primary purpose of a schoolmaster was to get comparatively stupid pupils through their examinations. For me, such a purpose was quite easily fulfilled, since a good many of the boys and girls I taught were already brighter than I was.

"Deafness, always a family weakness, began to overtake me from my mid-20s. After a series of operations I lost the hearing in my left ear completely; and from my mid-30s I have been able to hear in the right ear only with a hearing aid.

"Because of my deafness, I left teaching in 1966 and took up a post with Oxford University looking after school examinations in English, Latin, Greek, and Ancient History. And licking envelopes. I retired in 1988, after a period of poorish health.

"In short, I spent my working life in education. If I return to the human scene in some future reincarnation, I shall become a Quaker, and take up bird watching.

"As a schoolteacher, I had been coauthor of three sixth-form textbooks, and therefore had some small experience of putting words into print. I wrote no fiction, however, until 1973, when one dank and drizzly Saturday afternoon on holiday with my family in North Wales I covered one page of an exercise book with the first few paragraphs of *Last Bus to Woodstock*, a whodunit featuring two policemen called Inspector Morse and Sergeant Lewis.

"In the longstanding characterization-versus-plot controversy, I am first and foremost concerned with plot. Yet there is no real clash: characterization and plot are subsumed by 'story,' and I am a storyteller. I consider that the central purpose of art is to delight. It has other purposes—to explain, to instruct, to persuade, to disturb—but all I ask of my own readers is that they keep turning the pages with enjoyment.

"Influences on my writing of detective stories? Not many really. Certainly Agatha Christie though, and John Dickson Carr (Carter Dickson)—with Raymond Chandler the writer I'd rather reread than any of them. But I'm not a great reader of crime stories myself; and not even *The Long Goodbye* would find its way into my desert island ration.

"Which authors would I take? Homer, Horace, Gibbon, Dickens, Hardy, Wipling, Housman—the latter, a poet-scholar and a miserable sod, the greatest hero of my life.

"Music has always been important to me, but less so as my deafness has increased. Of all the great composers, Wagner has moved me the most deeply, and (apart from Mozart in his clarinet works) is the only one who can still reduce me to tears. *The Ring* I regard as one of the supreme achievements of the human spirit.

"I can no longer believe in the existence of the Almighty. Politically I have always been a left-winger with an implacable hatred for the British Tory party. Obscene litter disturbs me far more than obscene literature. I am pessimistic about the future of the human race, although a regular diet of beer, whisky, and crossword puzzles keeps me comparatively cheerful.

"It is my belief that luck plays a far bigger part in the scheme of things than is generally conceded; and my own life has been beset by good fortune, particularly my meeting with Dorothy, to whom I have been married for 40 years."

Dexter has said that he has improved with age as a writer and that the Morse books written after his retirement, in 1988, are his favorites. Each of these has received praise in both the United Kingdom and the United States. The *Publishers Weekly* (March 23, 1990) review of *The Wench Is Dead* (1990) describes how Morse investigates a 100-year-old murder on the Oxford canal—a case that Morse has happened upon while in the hospital recovering from his ulcer problems: "A surprising and inspired solution concludes a jolly good read that juxtaposes past and present Oxford with imagination and finesse." The marvelous descriptions of Oxford in all of Dexter's novels were noted by a reviewer for the *Washington Post Book World* (August 2, 1992), who wrote: "How . . . can one improve on Colin Dexter's Oxford, whether in the splendid grounds of an ancient college or the clamor of an authentic pub that meets Inspector Morse's demands for real ale?"

Dexter's next novel, *The Jewel That Was Ours* (1992), developed by Dexter from a story line in the television program, was also hailed as a mystery masterpiece. That book finds Morse searching for clues to the murders of a woman who owned a rare artifact and of a museum curator. The *New York Times Book Review* and *Publishers Weekly* praised the novel, with the latter periodical calling it "a story packed with nuance, wayward angles, and bewildering layers of coincidence, all explicated in masterful style."

The Way Through the Woods, Dexter's 1993 mystery, was yet another of Dexter's works that was critically acclaimed. This novel has Morse and Lewis investigating the disappearance of a young Swedish woman who had been vacationing in England. As the *New York Times* (April 4, 1993) reviewer wrote: "To say that the investigation is tricky is only to hint at the technical density of the plot, which, once all the tantalizing enigmas have been packed up, hinges on the most basic human frailties."

Dexter's equally well praised *The Daughters of Cain* (1995) concerns the murder of a retired Oxford don—a case whose solution at first seems obvious but is later found to involve one ruse after another. In this book Dexter explored Morse's character in greater depth and allowed Sergeant Lewis a moment of glory, having him outwit the ever-vigilant Morse. The *Wall Street Journal* (April 27, 1995) called *The Daughters of Cain* "audacious and amusing" and "the best book yet in this deservedly celebrated series."

Dexter's most recent novel, *Death Is Now My Neighbor*, was released in 1997. In this work, Morse tries to shed light on the shooting death of a woman outside her North Oxford home. His investigation soon takes him to Lonsdale College, where the master is retiring and two senior dons are vying to succeed him. Fans of the series will also be interested to know that Morse's first name—never mentioned in any of the previous novels or on the television series—is finally revealed here. —C.M.

SUGGESTED READING: *Chicago Tribune* V p1+ Apr. 6, 1993; *New York Times Book Review* p17 Apr. 19, 1992, p17 Apr. 4, 1993, p29 Apr. 16, 1995; *Publishers Weekly* p68 Mar. 23, 1990, p71 Mar. 8, 1993; *Wall Street Journal* A p14 May 17, 1993, A p12 Apr. 27, 1995; *Washington Post* C p1 June 21, 1993; *Washington Post Book World* p8 Aug. 2, 1992; *Contemporary Authors* nrs vol. 25, 1989

SELECTED BOOKS: *Last Bus to Woodstock*, 1975; *Last Seen Wearing*, 1976; *The Silent World of Nicholas Quinn*, 1977; *Service of All the Dead*, 1979; *The Dead of Jericho*, 1981; *The Riddle of the Third Mile*, 1983; *The Secret of Annexe 3*, 1986; *The Wench Is Dead*, 1990; *The Jewel That Was Ours*, 1992; *The Way Through the Woods*, 1993; *The Daughters of Cain*, 1995; *Morse's Greatest Mystery and Other Stories*, 1995; *Death Is Now My Neighbor*, 1997

Miriam Berkley

Dickinson, Charles

1951– Writer

The American novelist, short-story writer, and editor Charles Dickinson has helped to bring back to life a type of Midwestern realism that saw its greatest popularity in the days of Sherwood Anderson and Sinclair Lewis. His novels, which have enjoyed critical praise if not overwhelming commercial success, include *Waltz in Marathon* (1983), *Crows* (1985), *With or Without* (1987), and *The Widows' Adventures* (1989). Dickinson has worked in newspapers for nearly 15 years, serving as a copy editor at the *Chicago Sun-Times* from 1983 to 1989 and currently working for the *Chicago Tribune* as an assistant metropolitan editor. His most recent novel, the acclaimed *Rumor Has It* (1991), is a fictionalized treatment of his days on the staff of the *Sun-Times*. That novel, he has said, combines elements from the "two dying industries" in which he is involved—his "livelihood" (newspaper work) and his "life" (fiction writing). As a child growing up in various cities across the Midwest, before he learned to read and write, he carried on imaginary conversations in his head—fascinated with what he called "pretending to write—with the look of it, and the feel of it. I always like dotting my I's. I still do."

For *World Authors 1990-1995*, Charles Dickinson writes: "I was born in Detroit in 1951, and moved almost immediately to a suburb of Milwaukee, then to Indianapolis, and finally to a suburb near Chicago, following my father as he was transferred in his job." (Dickinson's father, Thomas, was in sales, while his mother, the former Barbara Forrester, was an ambulance driver.)

"My parents were not unsupportive of the artistic tendencies of their children—my three sisters and me—but neither were they enthusiastic. They did not disparage, nor did they encourage. I don't know what assessment they made of my talent. It was not discussed.

"I had friends in each of the places where we lived, but my most vivid, fulfilling times were spent alone. I wrote sporadically through those years, but much more of my time was spent playing and illustrating fantasy dice games, living out impossibly successful sports accomplishments hour after hour in my imagination. I filled journals with game summaries, superhuman statistical accomplishments, entire careers. In a way, I was creating characters, but I was too immature to imagine lives beyond the games I placed them within. They were all about statistics and results, with salaries, contracts, and honors, but not families." In eighth grade, according to an interview he gave to *Publishers Weekly* (February 8, 1991), Dickinson began moving away from this type of writing, when he wrote a book about the navy. He continued to write fiction sporadically during his high school and college years.

"It wasn't until I met my wife, Donna [Gawron], in 1976, that I found someone I would rather be with more than I wanted to be by myself. We moved in together three days after meeting and have been together ever since." The couple married in September 1978 and have two children, Louis and Casey. "[Donna] is enthusiasm personified. I mark my commitment to writing to her entrance into my life. She read a bagful of my early stories (a majority of which lacked an ending) and wanted to know how they turned out. She was the first person to truly encourage what I had been doing, to believe in me. She is an artist herself, first a figure skater, then a choreographer and dancer, and a born teacher. Although I don't think American society values its artists, I am proudest of the fact our children have shown artistic inclinations, our son, Louis, in drawing and writing, our daughter, Casey, as a dancer and actress.

"After meeting Donna, I began to write every day. Over the last nearly 20 years writing has defined who I am. I can feel my sense of self-worth, my high spirits, begin to erode when I am away from it for too long. I need that project, that sense of moving forward. When I am in the middle of a novel or story and look around at my journalism colleagues (since 1975 I have held newspaper jobs, currently at the *Chicago Tribune*) I feel fortunate for the balance writing brings to my life." Dickinson's wife also encouraged him to write a novel. One result of that advice was "A Dollar a Mouse," a book the author has described as "kind of quirky and 'different.'" Its main character, Frank Nicer, is in the business of renting out cats to hunt mice. The novel was never published in book form but was serialized in the *Chicago Reader*.

In what Dickinson views as his big break, *Esquire* published his short story "My Livelihood" in May 1982. He then began publishing fiction for various other well-known periodicals, including the *New Yorker* and the *Atlantic*. In 1983 Knopf published his novel *Waltz in Marathon*, making him, as he stated in his interview for *Publishers Weekly*, "the happiest man in the world." This novel is about the exploits of a gentlemanly small-town loan shark named Harry Waltz. Waltz never hires goons to break the arms of people who are indebted to him; instead, he simply attempts to get his money by suggesting that the debtors' good names might be ruined if they do not pay him. This strategy pays off less and less as the changing values of America in the late 1960s produce debtors who scoff at his kind reminders. Christopher Lehmann-Haupt, reviewing the book for the *New York Times* (November 8, 1983), stated: "The very idea of his being a principled usurer is precisely what makes Harry Waltz so interesting, just as it is their self-contradictory behavior that makes all of Mr. Dickinson's characters unusual. It isn't so much villainy they represent as a monumental ordinariness that is fascinating." In *Best Sellers* (January 1984), L. Scott Tomchak wrote, "Charles Dickinson looks deep into the soul of a man whose life is barren and monotonous and draws from it an amazing and beautiful new birth."

Dickinson's novel *Crows*, also published by Knopf, received more mixed reviews. The novel's title alludes to the legends about crows created by a small-town biology professor named Ben Ladysmith, who drowns in a boating accident and whose body cannot be found. His legends are retold by his young sportswriter friend, Robert Cigar, who moves in with Ladysmith's family (much to their chagrin) as part of an effort to find the professor's body. Slowly, as Robert Cigar begins to uncover the man behind the myth, the focus of the novel is also revealed. As Alice Becker, writing about the novel for the *Detroit News* (April 21, 1985), stated: "Robert's exploration of love and commitment, of the way memories can bind and release, and of a person's need to carve out his own private domain" are at the heart of the story.

Some critics did not find Dickinson's novel sufficiently focused. The *New York Times Book Review* (June 30, 1985) notice read: "The trouble with the novel is that the themes never effectively meet. The crow tales are presumably meant to give meaning to the story but in fact rarely do. . . . [Robert Cigar's] desire to remain [in the Midwest] has the potential for emotional richness, but it lies buried in uneven fables and an unconvincing story." A reviewer for the *New Statesman* (August 23, 1985) found that the "landscape and weather are more appealing than the people" and that the book as a whole "seems more symptom than explanation." Still, the *Times Literary Supplement* (November 22, 1985) found qualities in Dickinson's second novel that were similar to those in his first. "The wry and unsentimental appreciation of small-town life in a hard climate, likable characters endowed with pluck and common sense, a quiet charge of suspense, and a resolution at once happy and convincing, make *Crows* and its author a welcome find."

In 1987 Dickinson published a collection of stories, *With or Without*, some of which had previously appeared in periodicals. Most of the stories feature middle- or working-class characters who live ordinary lives. Critics for the most part liked the volume; a writer for *Kirkus Reviews* (March 1, 1987) believed that "at their best, Dickinson's simple stories are as charming as his warmhearted novels *Waltz in Marathon* and *Crows*." Alan Cheuse of the *Chicago Tribune* (April 19, 1987) remarked that Dickinson has "an uncanny eye" and found that "this is the type of collection that you'll read all the way through as soon as you find the time. Buying it will be like giving yourself a box of chocolates in which every piece is a coveted nut."

Two years later the author published *The Widows' Adventures*, a novel he claims to have conceived in its totality from the start. He has said that the novel is based on a story his mother told him about a road trip planned by his grandmother, who did not know how to drive, and his aunt, who was legally blind. Eva Hoffman, reviewing the novel for the *New York Times* (September 13, 1989), called the book "a picaresque tale . . . an affectionate rendition of a relationship, a page-by-page demonstration of what it is like to be inside a longstanding, familial, ordinary, and always complicated intimacy."

Dickinson's most recent novel, *Rumor Has It*, is a tribute to the glory days of the newspaper industry, even though the events of the novel occur during the last day of publication of a fictional tabloid called the *Chicago Bugle*. Dickinson filled his novel with characters who enjoy putting out a newspaper and recounted newsrooms, as the *New York Times* noted, "filled with men and women who signed on despite bad hours and worse pay, benefit packages out of Scrooge & Marley, maniacal editors, bubble-headed publishers, bean-counting financial officers, and union chieftains who couldn't see beyond the ends of their noses." The book received good reviews from many newspapers across the United States, even from real-life Chicago journalists. Media critic Michael Miner of the *Chicago Reader* (who was once an employee of the *Sun-Times*, like Dickinson) said: "People are bemused by the book. They're playing the game of 'who's who?' One reporter felt like she'd been taken advantage of. But the book is literature and that justifies everything—every betrayal of trust."

Dickinson writes for *World Authors 1990-1995*, "Accounts I hear of writers who hate to write or find it painful to write strike no chords with me. It is just the opposite; writing is therapy for me, almost a drug of self-esteem. And then I wonder if perhaps I am not tapping deeply enough, that the pain other writers probe is still inside of me, untouched. For all the positive reviews my books have received and the outward signs of working in the top levels of the art (i.e. publication in the *New Yorker*, *Esquire*, the *Atlantic*, appearances in the O. Henry Awards collection), my writing hasn't appeared to touch many people (if sales and fan mail are any indication) and I think there is an emotional coolness, a distance, to my work.

"I had the disconcerting experience recently of being bored by my own work when I read to an audience from one of my novels. And I think that is because I sense there isn't much of myself in those early books.

"For that reason, I feel I have entered a second stage of my career. I mark the end of the first stage with the publication of *Rumor Has It* in 1991. That novel, and the books and stories that came before it, seem to me now to be the extent of what I could skim from the surface of my life to that point. I had a definite sense of having run out of things to write about when *Rumor Has It* was finished.

"I immediately began another novel that was nothing but a painful false start. In February of 1994 I began writing *20 Years Running*, which I have just completed. It's personal. I am at present stuck in that waiting time when my belief in the book diminishes, the longer it is out of my sight and at the mercy of publishers' assessments.

"For me, writing is easy; being a writer is quite a bit harder."

Charles Dickinson has received many awards for his work, including an Illinois Art Council grant (1982) and a Great Lakes Colleges Association new writers award for fiction (1984). He was twice selected for *O. Henry* collections, for his stories "Risk" and "Child in the Leaves," in 1984 and 1989, respectively. He received the Friends of American Writers top prize for *Crows* in 1986.
—C.M.

SUGGESTED READING: *Best Sellers* Jan. 1984; *Chicago Tribune* XIV p21 Dec.18, 1983; Apr. 19, 1987; *Detroit News* Apr. 21, 1985; *Kirkus Reviews* Mar. 1, 1987; *New York Times* C p21 Sep. 13, 1989, C p22 Jan. 31, 1991; *New York Times Book Review* Nov. 8, 1983, p9 June 30, 1985, p14 Sep. 24, 1989, p12 Jan. 20, 1991; *New Statesman* p28 Aug. 23, 1985; *Publishers Weekly* p40+ Feb. 8, 1991; *Times Literary Supplement* p1310 Nov. 22, 1985; *Contemporary Authors* vol. 128, 1990; *Contemporary Literary Criticism* vol. 49, 1988

SELECTED WORKS: *Waltz in Marathon*, 1983; *Crows*, 1985; *With or Without*, 1987; *The Widows' Adventures*, 1989; *Rumor Has It*, 1991

Diesbach, Ghislain de

Aug. 6, 1931– Novelist; biographer

The French historian, biographer, and novelist Ghislain de Diesbach, as he admits, prefers the aristocratic past to the present as a subject. Poet Richard Howard, who translated his first book, *Iphigénie en Thuringe* (1960, tr. *The Toys of Princes*), remarked in his notes to the book's second edition that the "capital charm" of these tales resides in "their period flavor, an exact administration of the tonalities of the 19th century, that age which so preternaturally dilated from 1789 to Sarajevo." Diesbach went on to write only a few more works of fiction: *Un joli train de vie* (1962, tr. *Happy Families*), which won the Prix Cazes, *Le Grand Mourzouk* (1969), and *Au bon patriote* (1996, To the Good Patriot)—all collections of tales.

He has also written numerous works of history and biography, several of which have won French literary prizes: *Les Secrets du Gotha* (1964, tr. *Secrets of the Gotha*); *George III* (1966); *Service de France* (1972, The Service of France); *Histoire de l'emigration* (1975, History of the Emigration), which was a "Couronné" of the Academie Francais and received the Prix du Nouveau Cercle; *Necker, ou la faillite de la vertu* (1978, Necker, or The Failure of Virtue), recipient of the Prix du Cercle de l'Union; *Madame de Staël* (1983), recipient of a Goncourt Award for biography and the Grand Prize

Ghislain de Diesbach

of *Elle* magazine readers; *La princesse Bibesco* (1986), winner of the Prix des Cent Libraires de Normandie; *La Double vie de la duchesse Colonna* (1988, The Double Life of Duchess Colonna); *Proust* (1991), which won the Prix Marcel Proust, the Prix du Printemps, and the Grand Prix de la Biographie of the Académie Français; *Philippe Jullian, un esthete aux Enfers* (1993, Philippe Jullian, an Aesthete in the Inferno), awarded the Prix Oscar Wilde; and *Chateaubriand* (1995), which won the prize of the French PEN club and the ANF prize. Diesbach's books of essays, *La Tour de Jules Verne en 80 livres* (1969, Jules Verne's Tour in 80 Books), winner of the Prize of the British Academy, and *Le Gentilhomme de notre temps* (1972, The Gentleman of Our Times), were also widely praised.

For *World Authors 1990–1995*, Ghislain de Diesbach, born on August 6, 1931 in Le Havre, France, writes: "Born with the knowledge of revolutions supported by interspersed cries of agony, the recitals of which were piously transmitted from grandparent to grandchild, I early developed a taste for history. I was encouraged in that propensity by World War II, of which certain scenes, from the refugees fleeing in 1940 to the liberation in 1944, taught me more than my textbooks. Accustomed to note what I heard or saw that was picturesque, I continued, the war now over, to go to see old men laden with memories, which I took over to some degree, living by taking on the life of others and returning thus over the course of Time. Ordered by my parents to think more about my future and my choice of career, I answered: 'For me, the only future is the past. . . .' I had as a mentor a greatnephew of Napoleon I who recounted his own memories of many artists and writers of the 19th century and made me into his follower—a school of one—calling me his Eckermann.

"Prepared with a simple diploma, torn away painfully from the law school of Aix-en-Provence, and armed with a good address book, I left in 1958 to conquer Paris. Knowing that literature paid badly and repelled by hard beginnings in an attic, living on dry crusts, I entered an insurance company. Thus, there was nothing to do but to stay there forty years in order to write as I please and avoid writing out of necessity.

"I started with a collection of stories, *Iphigénie en Thuringe* (1960), an evocation of the little German courts of the past. This book, at once frivolous and cynical, was taken more seriously by critics than I had meant it to be and gave me a reputation as a Germanist, as well as a command of the history of the European royal dynasties set forth in *Les Secrets du Gotha* (1964). Between the two I had published a novel, *Un joli train de vie* (1962), the story of a childhood in Le Havre, where I was born, issue of a Swiss family established in France where there were a multitude of Diesbachs, in the service of the monarchy until 1792. Through my greatgrandmother Diesbach, I am a descendant of the emperor Montezuma, roasted by Cortez on a grill in order to relieve him of his treasure, and, through my maternal great-grandmother, a chemist, who, during the naval blockade imposed by Napoleon, discovered the method of making sugar from beets.

"Despite several excursions into the domain of fiction with *Le Grand Mourzouk* (1969), that of sociology with *La Tour de Jules Verne en 80 livres* (1969), and verily that of the good life with *Le Gentilhomme de notre temps* (1992), I have been drawn more and more toward history. In *George III* (1966), I have traced a portrait of the only king Napoleon could not vanquish and discovered the England of the 18th century where so many French people who fled the Revolution found asylum. All of that gave me the idea of undertaking, for the country of welcome, a *Histoire de l'emigration* (1975) during the Revolution. From that troubled period emerged Necker, first adored, then hated, by the public. It interested me to study him as an example of the fickleness of the masses and the ingratitude of governments. *Necker, ou la faillite de la vertu* (1978) led me naturally to his daughter, the stormy and genial *Madame de Staël* (1983) the celebrated 'midwife of the spirit' and inspiration of the liberal thought of the 19th century. Happening on entirely unpublished documents inspired me next to write the lives of two not less remarkable women: *La princesse Bibesco* (1986), the international secret counselor, and *La Double vie de la duchesse Colonna* (1988), a beauty in the court of the Second Empire and talented, but only belatedly recognized, sculptor.

"With a good understanding of society at the beginning of this century through the witnesses I had interviewed earlier, I turned out a biography of Proust (1991) that had some success, like that of *Chateaubriand* (1995), which gained for me the hostility of those who make gods of certain authors without having read them. Telling the truth is not always an easy task; I also tried to do it in writing the life of *Philippe Jullian* (1993), essayist and novelist, moralist and illustrator of *A la recherche du temps perdu*.

"After all those biographies, I returned with pleasure to my beginnings in publishing another collection of stories, *Au bon patriote* (1996), and in creating portraits of personalities encountered during my life, paying thus my debt of honor to the memoirists, my predecessors, in continuing that chain of solidarity over the centuries, thanks to which there will be material from the past for the historians of the future."

—tr. S. Y.

———

Ghislain de Diesbach left Le Havre for Paris as a young man. In Paris he inhabited an apartment in rue vieille de la Temple, according to Richard Howard, the translator of his first book, *Iphigénie en Thuringe*, called in English *The Toys of Princes*. Diesbach lived surrounded by characters like those in an operetta—the counts and countesses, marquesses, barons, and princelings of old German principalities, Swiss cantons, and the Austro-Hungarian empire. That these characters were in his imagination did not stop him from decorating his apartment with a plethora of old hussars' uniforms and antique weapons. Amid these surroundings Diesbach penned insouciant tales of a benevolent princeling and his wife, who turn into monsters when they become besotted by automatons, replicas of their lost loves; a count and a British lady, in love, rich, and beautiful but cursed by the "force of destiny"; a baroness maddened to the point of sexual frenzy by the enchanting melodies of *Die Fledermaus*; and other members of a decadent upper class in the twilight of imperial Europe. The themes that run through these stories are the perilousness of fleshly love, the distortions that art can work upon life, the disasters attendant on creativity, and the mutability of virtue—themes that Diesbach was later to explore in his biographies of Necker, Madame de Staël, and Proust.

In "On the Thunersee," one Baron de La Poyaz loses in an accident on a lake the Barzoi, a diamond that was his prized possession. After a period of madness, he finds the lost treasure in the possession of a peasant girl. He murders her to retrieve the diamond but is forced to keep his find a secret lest the insurance company demand restitution. Finally, to alleviate his feelings of guilt, he goes on a boating excursion, intending to throw the stone back into the lake where it had been lost:

> He pulled it feverishly from his pocket, and at that moment, a sunbeam caused it to sparkle with a thousand yellow fires, like a second sun. The stranger uttered an exclamation of astonishment. The Baron, bewildered, made a mistake. Instead of hurling the Barzoi overboard, he let it drop upon the deck, at the feet of the elegant lady, and threw himself into the lake.

The tone of these stories, which concern monstrosities of human conduct, is always lighthearted. In his Translator's Notes, Howard pronounced the stories to be filled with "pervasive vivacities," and he wrote that he found "the abiding fascination" of "Diesbach's anecdotes of high life and loose living" to be in "their entanglement with *difference*, which we know to be the source of every narrative impulse. Differences of gender, differences of milieu, and differences of generation: the scandal that our desires are not the same, the outrage that our upbringings have alienated us from each other as well as from ourselves. . . ."

The *Times Literary Supplement* (May 25, 1962) reviewer found Diesbach to have "a pretty wit, unaffectedly Englished by . . . Howard," and added, "This book should afford a few hours' amusement to anyone not so solemn as to be outraged by his brand of malicious frivolity." The *Virginia Quarterly Review* (Winter 1963) critic's opinion was that instead "of searching for an author, these characters, eccentrics to the end, seem to have run away with theirs."

Secrets of the Gotha was translated by Margaret Crosland and appeared in the United States in 1968. "The Gotha" is the *Almanach de Gotha*, a compendium of information about the royal houses and upper nobility of Europe that was published from 1764 until 1944. *Secrets of the Gotha* "retails, with verve and conciseness, all the royal scandals which rocked Europe during the 18th and 19th centuries and which now seem so faded and quaint," according to Richard Freedman, writing in *Book World* (June 23, 1968). He deemed Diesbach to have "cast his golden net" over "Ludwig I's involvement with Lola Montez and Ludwig II's with Wagner; Maximilian's Mexican *debacle* at the hands of Juarez; Archduke Rudolph's suicide pact at Mayerling. . . . stories . . . familiar to the most casual reader of European history, but . . . not the less worth retelling for that fact." As G. F. Dole observed in *Library Journal* (September 15, 1968), "no personage is spared the searching and occasionally lighthearted bite of . . . Diesbach's pen." Maurice Richardson in the *New Statesman* (September 8, 1967) called *Secrets of the Gotha* "enchanting, witty, and clearly written," remarking that the book "gives you a marvelous gossipy round-up of crowned heads and consorts and backstairs with Clio pattering up and down taking notes. Open it anywhere and you're almost certain to find a plum."

Diesbach continues to live in Paris, on the Left Bank, in the quarter near Les Invalides. He told *World Authors* that his 1996 volume, *Au bon patriote* (To the Good Patriot), a collection of tales, received the Rotary Club of Paris 1996 prize.

SUGGESTED READING: *Book World* p4 June 23, 1968; *Library Journal* p3124 Sep. 15, 1968; *New Statesman* p292 Sep. 8, 1967; *Times Literary Supplement* p377 May 25, 1962; *Virginia Quarterly Review* p39 Winter 1963

SELECTED BOOKS IN ENGLISH TRANSLATION: *The Toys of Princes*, 1992; *Happy Families*, 1962; Nonfiction—*Secrets of the Gotha*, 1967

Digges, Deborah

Feb. 6, 1950– Poet; memoirist

The American poet Deborah Digges has drawn on her experiences as a youth growing up in the Midwest in the 1950s and 1960s; as a young married woman living in Texas, California, and Massachusetts; and as a mother, for her poetry collections *Vesper Sparrows* (1986), *Late in the Millennium* (1989), and *Rough Music* (1995). Her work has been lauded for celebrating "the primal energy that keeps us fighting against the odds and snatching at pleasures even in our bleakest moments," as Phoebe Pettingell wrote, reviewing *Rough Music* in the *New Leader* (October 9, 1995). Digges's memoir, *Fugitive Spring* (1992), described how she became a poet, using the rich materials of her childhood.

Deborah Digges was born in Jefferson, Missouri, on February 6, 1950, the sixth of the 10 children of Geneva and Everett Sugarbaker Her father was a doctor who established his own cancer clinic, in which the young Deborah helped out, along with her brothers and sisters. The family also had a 16-acre apple orchard in which she worked.

Digges was a rather wild teenager, taking paregoric and occasionally phenobarbitol to calm herself. Her father wanted her to become a medical illustrator, but she preferred to paint surreal canvases. An indifferent student, she left Hope College, in Holland, Michigan, her parents' choice, because of homesickness. She then attended William Jewell College, but did not graduate. She married Charles Digges, the father of her two sons, in 1969. They were divorced in 1980. A second marriage also ended in divorce. Digges described her formative experiences in *Fugitive Spring: Coming of Age in the 50s and 60s* (1992).

Digges had begun to write poetry in Lubbock, Texas, when her first child was an infant and her husband was training to be an air force pilot. "Nothing in my background said I could, or even should, attempt this thing so foreign to me, the poem. I had never formally studied writing of any kind," she wrote in *Fugitive Spring*. Her grammar and spelling were poor. "But over the next weeks and months in Texas, as I wrote down lines on a legal pad, wrote sometimes under the croup tent, the humidifier whirring, the paper, pen, my hair, everything slowly soaking through until the ink began to bleed, the issues of proper syntax and grammar seemed, for the moment, unimportant; as unimportant, for instance, as the fact that year after year, unable to find a screwdriver, my father had secured the fifty or more storm windows on the house in Missouri with a kitchen knife. . . .*workmen, work, and tools, words and things, birth and death . . .The poet . . .gives them a power which makes their old use forgotten . . .*," Digges wrote, quoting from an essay by Ralph Waldo Emerson. "Maybe I began to write poetry in answer to the confused politics of that time," Digges wrote. "We were nobody—Charlie, the baby, and me—to the huge military construct that had brought us to Texas. We had been spun out, like so many others, onto the American landscape, as if by some great destiny machine."

Not long after she had begun writing, Digges started to submit her poetry to small and large journals. She accumulated a large number of rejection slips, which, paradoxically, gave her satisfaction: "'Too elliptical,' said one. I laughed out loud in my happiness. Such a comment implied that someone had actually read the work. He hadn't questioned whether it was poetry. He'd assumed it was and had an opinion on it *as* poetry." She persisted, learning from the early rejections; although she didn't know what "elliptical" meant, she revised her style. Later, she enrolled at the University of California, Riverside, and earned an M.A. at the University of Missouri. She obtained a master of

fine arts degree from the University of Iowa Writers Workshop and later, in 1986, joined the English faculty of Tufts University in Medford, Massachusetts.

Digges's first collection, *Vesper Sparrows*, appeared in 1986. In its 34 poems, "five with birds at their centers, the ordinary and banal become the subjects of 'actual' poetry and music," Rosaly De-Maios Roffman observed in *Library Journal* (May 15, 1986). Bruce Weigl, the poet, remarked in *Choice* (November 1986) that Digges had achieved something uncommon among young poets: "[I]t is abundantly clear that Digges is a poet thoroughly in control of her craft and passionately charged with a genuine love of words." He deemed Digges's form worthy of its content: "a taut narrative line wisely disrupted by lyrical complications of syntax and by strikingly original metaphors." The speaker of the poems, in his opinion, was poised "between intimacy and a reticence that allows the poems their own quiet insistence." He judged them "fresh and worthwhile."

Another poet, Jorie Graham, who reviewed *Vesper Sparrows* for the *New York Times Book Review* (September 28, 1986), found that Digges "traces parentage and asks of nature that it sing along and provide, at every turn, proof of our rightful place among things. Whether she writes about gulls caught inland or a battered child seen at a carnival or childhood memories of her father, a doctor, making his rounds among the dying, life seems to offer itself up for conversion into poetry. . . ." Graham caviled only at what she found to be Digges's habit of "looking for things to feel." She concluded that "Digges is at her strongest where her original and passionate intuition is used to record her emotions rather than generalizing them into vagueness."

Digges's "philosophical insight" was lauded by Doris Lynch, who reviewed her collection *Late in the Millennium* in *Library Journal* (November 1, 1989). Lynch found that in "their grasping for an understanding of life," Digges's portrayals of a friend dying of AIDS, a forest fire, televangelists, and a psychic, the poetry was able to become, as Digges wrote, "like a fist of fire opening/ mid-air plummeting."

Fugitive Spring, Digges's memoir, is the story of the making of a poet. "I think I write to be saved; from what, I'm not sure, since salvation comes always with the next poem, the one I'm about to write," she declared. Although Digges gave up the formal practice of religion, "I would always be religious," she avowed. "Writing became my religion. Images from the Scriptures, the settings and details from the many Bible stories I knew, scientific data, memories of the orchard, the lab, the pond, along with all those years of looking, painting what I saw, began a strange metamorphosis—*On the brink of the waters of life and truth, we are miserably dying*—because I was alone for the first time."

Fugitive Spring received mixed notices. Christopher Lehmann-Haupt, in the *New York Times* (January 6, 1992) termed it "haunting," and evinced understanding of Digges's plight as one of 10 siblings. He found the portrait of Digges's mother, in the chapter entitled "Fugitive Spring," the "most vivid of any that appear in the book." The *Women's Review of Books* (July 1992) critic, Jeanne Schinto, found the volume laden with "images of incarceration," but concluded, "Digges, in the end, manages to loosen her bonds and re-ink the outline of the erased 'particularly she.' She does it with a poet's pen. As Digges so powerfully, movingly—and modestly—tells it she was aided by the times." The *Library Journal* (January 1992) reviewer, however, although noting that Digges's prose "has a poet's grace and vision," found *Fugitive Spring* "disappointingly vague."

Rough Music, Digges's 1995 collection of poetry, was judged by critics to have all the emotional clarity and accurate imagery that they had come to expect from her poems. The poet Mark Doty, according to the publisher, found it "so exhilarating that even its darkest notes shine with a strange joy." Jack Miles, the director of the Claremont Graduate Humanities Center in California, observed on presenting her with the Kingsley Tufts Poetry Award that if "she has been regarded from the beginning as a writer of great promise, in this book she has kept this promise." According to a news release from the Claremont Graduate School, *Rough Music* is "a bold, passionate, and sometimes bitter work that gathers disparate images and details to reveal rich insights into being human."

Digges explained in *Fugitive Spring* that during her childhood she found it difficult to face the idea of becoming a woman. "I have always read myself relentlessly and with reproach into the masculine. . . .That I became a woman seemed simply an imposition of the body onto the mind, and in the end I celebrated the complication," she wrote. "It made for the continuous cultivation of a secret life and a sense of a peculiar anonymity which, in the long run, I have come to understand as the source of my writing." In "Akhmatova," the opening poem of *Rough Music*, drawing on the bitter experience of the Russian poet Anna Akhmatova, Digges wrote that "women are the most dispensable to tyrants."

> . . . .Women are nothing.
> They create the beast to know the depth of
> their desire.
> They are like sparrows,
> the battered coming closest for the grain,
> or the part in the song where the oboe
> breaks your heart like time itself,
> then sneers to laughing.

Digges was able to empathize with a poet like Akhmatova, who lost her husband, had her son imprisoned, and had to destroy her own poetry under Stalin's persecution and re-create it from memory:

> If poetry is fire, it can't be written in the fire,
> but sometime after, written in ashes
> along the frozen road
> if it be written down at all.

Phoebe Pettingell, reviewing *Rough Music* for the *New Leader* (October 9, 1995), explained that its title derives from a medieval custom of drumming outlaws out of town by banging on pots or whatever else made a lot of noise. Although Digges "acknowledges the depression, bitterness, and guilt that accompany the loss of people or things we love . . . her focus is on catharsis and purging, and she finds strength in startling places," Pettingell wrote. "Her rough music is seductively memorable; it should not go unheard." Willard Spiegelman commented in the *Yale Review* (April 1996) that Digges works by "loading every rift of the subject with ore and challenging us to dig it out." He concluded, "Thinking through images, Digges wends her insistent, surprising way down a path alternately straight and curving, placid and perilous."

While teaching at Tufts, Digges lives in faraway Amherst, Massachusetts, where she has been given to keeping numerous cats and several dogs, as well as sheltering other stray or wounded animals. She has also served as a foster mother, and she told Jessie Campbell of the *Observer* (September 18, 1997) that she was writing a book dealing with her experiences as a single mother.

Digges has received many honors, including an Ingram-Merrill Award in 1985, a National Endowment for the Arts grant in 1987, and a Guggenheim Award in 1988.

—S. Y.

SUGGESTED READING: *Atlantic Monthly* p62 Apr. 1998; *American Poetry Review* p26 Apr. 1997; *Choice* p472 Nov. 1986; *Kenyon Review* p84+ Spring 1998; *Kirkus Reviews* Nov. 15, 1991; *Library Journal* p70 May 15, 1986, p91 Nov. 1, 1989, p142 Jan. 1992; *New Leader* p14 Oct. 9, 1995; *New York Times* C p14 Jan. 6,1992; *New York Times Book Review* p32 Sep. 28, 1986; *Women's Review of Books* p23 July 1992; *Yale Review* p160 Apr.1996

SELECTED BOOKS: Poetry—*Vesper Sparrows*, 1986; *Late in the Millennium*, 1989; *Rough Music*, 1995; Memoir—*Fugitive Spring*, 1992

Dizikes, John

Nov. 8, 1932– Nonfiction writer

The American academic John Dizikes is the author of *Opera in America* (1993), the 1994 National Book Critics Award winner for criticism. *Opera in America* has been called the exhaustive and definitive history of opera in the United States and has been praised for its skillful blend of facts and events with fascinating anecdotes. A professor of American studies, Dizikes is the author of two additional scholarly works: *Britain, Roosevelt, and the New Deal* and *Sportsmen and Gamesmen*, the latter a history of sports in the United States since the mid-19th century.

John Dizikes was born on November 8, 1932. In 1950 he began attending Pasadena City College, where he earned his associate of arts degree in 1953. Between 1954 and 1955 he served in the United States Army as a member of a field artillery unit. After leaving the army he resumed his education at the University of California, Los Angeles. There he earned his bachelor of arts degree in 1957, but continued on at the university for two more years as a teaching assistant. In 1959 he joined the doctoral program at Harvard University and earned his Ph.D. by 1964. For one school year (1963–1964), Dizikes worked as a teaching fellow at Harvard; he then joined the staff at the University of Connecticut as an assistant professor for a year. In 1965 Dizikes returned to California, this time joining the staff at the University of California, Santa Cruz, where he continues to teach.

Dizikes followed up his first book, *Britain, Roosevelt, and the New Deal: British Opinion, 1932–1938* (1979), with *Sportsmen and Gamesmen: American Sporting Life in the Age of Jackson* (1981). In the second volume, the author argued that the sporting age in America began in the Jacksonian era of the 19th century and, in substance, was in direct opposition to the types of aristocratic sport which existed in England during the same era—yachting, racing and polo. Dizikes also defines sportsmen and gamesmen differently. He suggests that sportsmen are those who operate within the rules of the particular sport, while gamesmen are those who look to win by breaking the rules. For this work, Dizikes received excellent reviews. A reviewer for *Choice* (June 1981) praised: "The author relies in the main on published papers, diaries, and the like, as well as some newspapers, and his annotated notes are useful. The history of American sport needs many more monographs, and the author's contribution is a notable one." "[This is an] absorbing history of what might be called the American style of play," cheered Peter Schrag of the *Nation* (January 31, 1981). "In general the [book's] argument is sound enough, both in what it explains about the integration of the sports ethic with the capitalist ethic and in its persuasive description of their shared corporate abhorrence of chance."

In 1993 Dizikes published *Opera in America: A Cultural History*, a book that many critics have called the definitive study of opera in the United States. The volume's more than 600 pages describe the evolution of opera in America, starting in the early 18th century and continuing to the present day. In this overview Dizikes focused on the influences of politics, immigration, and war on Americans' appreciation for this predominantly European art form—and on the way Americans' tastes have changed with regard to opera. The book was very favorably reviewed. Admitting some minor criticism, Gary Schmidgall, writing for the *New York Times Book Review* (October 31, 1993), noted: "As with most breakneck tours, the reader is regularly tempted to lag behind and ponder the often curious and delightful material Mr. Dizikes has unearthed (and want more). But he succeeds in disguising a necessarily brusque efficiency with an amiable, unpretentious, occasional wry narrative style and 47 short, artfully contrasting chapters." In a review written for *Booklist* (September 1, 1993), Brad Cooper remarked: "Despite its goodly length and scholarly publisher, this historical narrative is for the general reader—of course, one with an abiding penchant for opera." Cooper added that while reading *Opera in America*, he felt that the author's "enthusiasm [for his subject was] fairly jumping off each page."

In 1994 the National Book Critics Circle presented Dizikes with the criticism prize for *Opera in America*. The judges called the book "definitive" and added that Dizikes's "mastery of a subject that won't sit still—that flourishes in a magnificent opera houses as well as ramshackle town halls—speaks to nothing less than a nation coming of age."

In addition to his three books, Dizikes is a noted contributor to periodicals, including the *Washington Post*, the *New York Times*, the *San Francisco Chronicle*, and the *Times Literary Supplement*. He has also written articles for a number of professional journals, including the *Encyclopedia of American National Biography*, *Sulfur*, the *Yale Review*, and the *Journal of Sport Literature*.

John Dizikes is a professor of American Studies at the University of California, Santa Cruz, where he teaches history of the arts, popular culture and American biography. He has been the recipient of a Fulbright Fellowship to the United Kingdom (1961–63), a gold medal from the Commonwealth Culb of California (1994), and the National Book Critics Circle Award for Criticism (1994). He lives in Santa Cruz with his wife, Ann Dizikes.—C. M.

SUGGESTED READING: *Booklist* Sep. 1, 1993; *Choice* p 18 +, June 1981; *Nation* p119, Jan. 31, 1981; *New York Times* C p 18, Jan. 14, 1994; C p 18, Feb. 14, 1994; *New York Times Book Review* p47+ Oct. 31, 1993; *Washington Post* D p4 Feb. 14, 1994

SELECTED WORKS: *Britain, Roosevelt, and the New Deal: British Opinion, 1932–1938*, 1979; *Sportsmen and Gamesmen: American Sporting Life in the Age of Jackson*, 1981; *Opera in America: A Cultural History*, 1993

Miriam Berkley

Doty, Mark

1953– Poet; essayist

The American Mark Doty had already earned a solid reputation among poets when the 1996 publication of *Heaven's Coast*, his memoir of the final illness of his lover, Wally Roberts, won him popular recognition as well. Doty is known as an "elegiac" poet whose emotional tone and images have, in his more recent volumes of poetry as well as in *Heaven's Coast*, evoked the atmosphere of the time of the AIDS epidemic while always being enmeshed in his evocations of the natural world. His poetry collections *My Alexandria* (1993), *Atlantis* (1995), and *Sweet Machine* (1998), while dealing—as Sean O'Brien remarked in the *Times Literary Supplement* (November 29, 1996)—with "how to live with the knowledge of death," have also as a primary subject "the romantic sea change."

For *World Authors 1990–1995*, Mark Doty writes: "I was born in Maryville, Tennessee, in 1953. Because my father worked for the U.S. Army Corps of Engineers, we moved frequently, living in a number of Tennessee towns. When I was seven we moved to Arizona, and from then on out I attended at least eight schools—in Arizona, California, and Florida—between first grade and my last year of high school. I think that this dislocation

was an important influence in my life as a writer, in two ways. First, books provided me with steady, familiar company, friends you could always have access to; I loved to read, and to lose myself in a story with the kind of wholeheartedness that children bring to reading. Second, my family's constant travel gave me a sense of being an outsider, an observer, which is a feeling that has stayed with me, in one form or another, to this day.

"I was always writing something, but in high school I began to write poetry, out of a sense of wanting to give form to the pressures of feeling within me. The little ballads in Tolkien's *The Lord of the Rings* were the first poems that I can remember really getting under my skin; then I stumbled across Federico Garcia-Lorca's dreamy lyrics, and the strangely luminous songs of Blake. Poetry seemed a gateway, a door into the inner life. My family life was tumultuous and difficult, but I began to see that creative work can be a kind of life-raft, that what we make can help to sustain us through the hardest things. The idea that poetry's a way to keep our spirits going in the face of difficulty has remained central to me.

"I left high school early, studied at the University of Arizona for a year and a half, then dropped out and worked as a janitor and preschool teacher. I continued to write, returned to finish my undergraduate work at Drake University, and then did graduate study in poetry at Goddard College. The process of becoming myself as a poet was allied with becoming myself in other ways, too, with examining my own life and moving towards understanding. My first book, *Turtle Swan*, is mainly concerned with memory and with the process of coming to see myself in the light of my family—explaining the present, in other words, in light of the past. *Bethlehem in Broad Daylight* furthers that process, and begins to look as well at more adult concerns of desire and relationship; it includes, as well, elegies for friends lost to AIDS, which became an increasingly important presence in my life and work.

"In 1989, my partner Wally Roberts and I discovered that he was HIV-positive; grappling with this diagnosis, as well as with his eventual illness and death from complications related to AIDS, has been the central struggle of my work in two books of poems, *My Alexandria* and *Atlantis*. I felt my writing was newly, intensely pressurized by the struggle to understand what was happening to us, by fear and uncertainty, by the weight which the awareness of mortality places upon us. The perennial questions of poetry—how do we love a world that is transient, what does it mean to live in a vanishing present—suddenly were far less abstract to me; they were the questions of every day. The poems in these collections attempt to look closely at the present, and thus they are more lyrical than the poems which came before them; these are poems which want to sing about the beauty and terror of the present.

"To some degree these books represent an attempt to accommodate the fact of impending loss, to try on various stances toward death in order to find some way to make death bearable. Such strategies are doomed to fail, since nothing can stay the plain fact of mortality—but they also seem to me to be human necessities, these attempt to make sense, to talk one's way toward understanding, even if such understandings are always provisional, limited ones.

"After Wally's death in 1994, I turned to an unfamiliar form in order to try to find shape in an unfamiliar experience. *Heaven's Coast* is a memoir which focuses on the first year of grief, examining the waves of feeling which occur in that heightened state of loss and narrating the story of a 12-year relationship. The book's concerned with coastlines—both the geographical kind, where elements meet, and the borderlines between living and dying, the past and the present, presence and absence. The expansiveness of prose was a welcome departure, and I imagine that I will return to the essay as a means of exploring experience. But I am at work now, in 1996, on new poems. Poetry is, for me, my chief means of knowing what I feel and think, a way of sifting through my experience to find the shape or pattern inherent within it. I'm less interested in what we know than in *how*, the process by which we come to knowledge, and I hope that my poems can sing about that process, and involve the reader in these acts of seeking understanding."

———————

Some critics, while praising Doty's lyrical gifts and emotional tenderness, have caviled about Doty's poetics, particularly his use of language. For example, Miriam Levine, reviewing *Bethlehem in Broad Daylight* (1991) in *American Book Review* (February/March 1992), observed that "Doty's poems work best when he finds his way back and forth between the vernacular and the elegant music of desire and loss." She found his language at its most literary, however, somewhat pedestrian, "flat and explanatory." David Baker, reviewing the same volume in *Poetry* (February 1992), also found it to be overly didactic. He complained that Doty's poetry, although it often connects and juxtaposes anecdotal episodes well, sometimes does not "manage enough stylistic rigor to convert anecdote into poetry." He mentioned often getting the feeling of "reading lined prose" and pointed out a "detachment from its own story" in Doty's poetry, noting that Doty does not "seem possessed by his content but, rather, a distant and privileged observer and commentator on it."

My Alexandria, Doty's next volume, won the National Book Critics Circle poetry prize in 1994. As a "series of luminous studies of urban and natural flux, it highlighted the influence on Doty of the poet C. P. Cavafy (to whose eroticized, native cityscape the title pays homage) and pondered, in tender, orderly stanzas, the metaphysical meaning of such evanescent things as a building being demolished; a jellyfish; a drag performance; a dog left to die by the side of the highway; an HIV-positive blood test," according to Jonathan Bing, writing in *Publishers Weekly* (April 15, 1996). In *Library Journal* (April 15, 1993), Frank Lepkowski praised *My Alexandria* in Doty's own words: "Whether finding in singers' voices 'the secret advocates of our hearts' or hearing in a violinist 'the sound that movement / through experience would make, / if we could stand far enough away/ to hear it: lovely and inconsoling,' Doty brings to his work a perfection out of 'hunger, / fused layer upon layer,' creating himself an art . . . of 'how soft things are, / how good, before they disappear.'" Carol Muske wrote in the *New York Times Book Review* (November 5, 1995) of Doty's "lyrical clarity" and of "the kind of unstoppable passionate rightness that enters a poet's voice when he or she has found it: the house, the street, the city, home, even if the windows and doors are draped in black."

In an essay entitled "Horsehair Sofas of the Antarctic: Diane Ackerman's Natural Histories," published in *Parnassus: Poetry in Review* (1995), Doty described how his own perceptions of nature are fused into the epiphanies that make an "occasion . . . for poetry." Contemplation of the mating patterns of turtles and of the disappearance of the resulting eggs into the maw of a fox or raccoon or other predator leads Doty to

> . . . consider the ways in which poets make use of their encounters "in nature." How can we help, now, but consider nature a separate place, as we live in an increasingly developed, built environment? To enter into "nature" is thus to step out of the ordinary, a way of inviting otherness, experience, revelation. Our experiences with the wild are no longer givens, their meanings not self-evident; these encounters must be translated and provided with context, our relation to the world negotiated in words. What are the ways in which experiences of wildness are "read" and rendered? Our first tradition of response is a moral one; it comes to us through very old roots, through spiritual and philosophical teachings that regard animals and plants as metaphors for our conditions, behaviors, and needs. . . . Whatever we see is metaphor for ourselves, and our poetry is full of instances of landscape and animal life as instructive apparition.

Discussing *My Alexandria*, Carol Muske termed Doty's a "transcendent voice." Writing about *Atlantis*, she deemed the poet immanent in his own creation: "Doty is disappearing before our eyes. He writes from the center of that disappearing—a state of profound animation, heightened awareness, subversion of surface. Like the vanished continent of Atlantis, the present he occupies is submerged in loss. But it is luminous, a land bridge between the world of life and death."

In "Nocturne in Black and Gold," Doty contemplates a harbor at night and sees in the fog and lights a vision of endless music. ". . . Haven't we wanted / all along, to try on boundlessness / like mutable, starry clothes?" he asks.

> Doesn't everything rush
> to be something else?
> Won't it be like this,
> where you're going: shore and bay,
> harbor and heaven one continuum
> *sans* coast or margins?

Doty concludes this poem ". . . Go./Don't go. Go." Muske observed that Doty's "elegiac drift" is "stripped of total license . . . what exists is to be contemplated in its constant flux, not possessed, ordered. The mind's natural state is stop-and-flow, even as attention divides to admit bright horror. . . ." She concluded that Doty "has his kingdom—sublime, immediate, disappearing—and his crown: the poems of *Atlantis*."

Helen Vendler, on the other hand, had cavils about *Atlantis* and about Doty's tone as a whole, which she conveyed in the *New Yorker* (April 8, 1996). Like Muske, Vendler noted Doty's stylistic similarities to Elizabeth Bishop. Vendler, however, made the comparison invidious and referred to "Doty's plaintive didacticism."

Heaven's Coast, Doty's memoir of the time of his lover's dying, garnered universal praise. Moving back and forth in time, he detailed both the anguish and the beauty of being with his lover throughout the ordeal. Before his description of the death comes his description of the mourning:

> What my soul requires is this going down into darkness, into the bitterness of salt and chewing at old roots. In my heart I make myself ugly and bitter; I say cruel and harsh things, I spit on hope, I mock the bit of life which is tender beginnings, which is promise, which is hope. I will let myself be ugly, I will have a mouth full of darkness, a heart full of bile, I will be sour and hateful and old. I see the future burning, the oily rags of love going up in the black smoke of the torched body. . . . Much as I want to hold on, want to cling to any perception which might be redemptive, any solid point, what is required of me is what I fear the most: relinquishment, free fall, the fluid pour into absolute emptiness. There is no way around the emptiness, the bitter fact, no way to go but *through*.

David Kirby in the *New York Times Book Review* called *Heaven's Coast* "a terrifying and elegant book, one in which the central character seems to die again and again. Yet each death is seen from a different emotional angle—full of wrath,

sorrow, yearning—until the composition is complete."

Of Doty's collection *Sweet Machine*, published in 1998, a reviewer for *Booklist* (February 1, 1998) wrote, "Doty has proved himself capable of lavish vocabulary and technical mastery, but one has a stronger sense in *Sweet Machine* of his absorption of life's dark, unredeemable underside. Even beauty, Doty's ceaseless redeemer, seems unable, at times, to grace the darkness here, to offer hope, potential, future: 'I am forty-one years old / and ready to get down / on my knees to a kitchen bowl / full of live green. . . .' It is this quality that makes the work more real than any of Doty's previous collections." Doty's memoir, *Firebird*, was scheduled for publication in late 1999.

Doty continued to live in Provincetown after the death of his lover. He also spends three days a week living in New York City, teaching at Columbia University and Sarah Lawrence College. In addition to winning the National Book Critics Circle poetry prize, he was the first American recipient of the T. S. Eliot Prize and a winner of the National Poetry Series contest. For *Atlantis*, he won the *Boston Book Review* Poetry Prize in 1996.

—S. Y.

SUGGESTED READING: *American Book Review* p20 Feb./Mar. 1992; *Library Journal* p94 Apr. 15, 1993; *Nation* p33+ July 15-22, 1996; *New Yorker* p100+ Apr. 8, 1996; *New York Times Book Review* p25 Nov. 5, 1995, p10 Mar. 10, 1996; *Parnassus: Poetry in Review* p143+ vol. 19 no. 2, 1994, p264+ vol. 20 no.1-2, 1995; *Poetry* p282 Feb. 1992; *Publishers Weekly* p44+ Apr. 15, 1996

SELECTED BOOKS: Nonfiction—*Heaven's Coast*, 1996; Poetry—*Turtle Swan*, 1987; *Bethlehem in Broad Daylight*, 1991; *My Alexandria*, 1993; *Atlantis*, 1995; *Sweet Machine*, 1998

Douglas, Ann

Apr. 13, 1942– Historian; nonfiction writer; critic

Ann Douglas, an American social historian, critic, and university professor, is the author of two richly annotated books and a sheaf of scholarly articles that demonstrate her fluency in interpreting both popular and elitist culture in the United States since the Civil War. Writing about topics as diverse as feminine hegemony and the waning of Calvinist theology in the Victorian era, or the ascendancy of the Freudian worldview amidst the vibrant racial dynamics of the 1920s, Douglas has established herself as a forceful though controversial analyst of "Americanist" issues. Published nearly two decades apart, *The Feminization of American Culture* (1977) and *Terrible Honesty. Mongrel Manhattan in the 1920s* (1995) are essentially twin volumes re-

Elizabeth Kendell/Courtesy of Farrar, Straus and Giroux

Ann Douglas

flecting Douglas's ongoing intellectual engagement with gender and racial subtexts in American life. The former book traces the rise of a sentimental matriarchate in the Victorian era, while the latter chronicles its decline under the modernist "culture of momentum" that, to the syncopated beat of psychoanalysis and jazz, shifted America's center of gravity from Brahmin Boston to "mongrel" New York City. Beyond the lecture hall, Douglas has become a kind of role model for a new, hip breed of scholar who does not shrink from being "terribly honest" about personal addictions, whether of sex or of substance, in her case "a little dabbling with drugs" and experiences that ranged from "creative sexual experimentation to promiscuity." In 1987 she told an interviewer for the Columbia American Studies Center's newsletter that she was "one of the few people I know who read Calvin and Jonathan Edwards for pleasure and, on the other hand, I'm also one of the few people I know who at age 45 is still devotedly listening to rock, is keeping up with it, who is teaching and following American film."

"I am by trade and calling an Americanist," she wrote in her introduction to *Terrible Honesty*, "and I believe, contrary to much current academic opinion, that America is a special case in the development of the West. . . . From the start the nation has had a tangible and unique mission concocted of unlimited natural resources, theological obsessions, a multiracial and polyglot population, and unparalleled incentives and opportunities for democratization and pluralism that culminated in the early modern era in the development of the media, all based in New York." When the book was published, she told Tobin Harshaw of the *New York Times Book Review* (December 12, 1995): "I have the unfashionable posture of loving my country. I don't mean in the sense of the Pledge of Allegiance, but in that I believe America was founded on complex social, religious, and political ideas and feelings, and that it is still the most exciting culture, the one where there is the most hope for the most people."

Ann Watson Douglas was born on April 13, 1942 into a comfortable white Anglo-Saxon Protestant family in Morristown, New Jersey, about an hour's drive to the west of Manhattan. Her father died of leukemia when she was eight, and her mother married a "fabulously wealthy" man who introduced his stepdaughter to an even more luxurious lifestyle. But the world she viewed from her limousine window, she told Julie Salamon in *The New York Times* (May 17, 1995), presented a contradiction that she felt compelled to explore in her later books. "You could see that people were mixed," she recalled, "and that mattered to me. I wasn't some budding little civil rights person. It was just that the white world I was in, in which everyone looked a great deal alike—I knew all that hadn't added up to a happy life for me."

A sometimes rebellious teenager, Douglas was once suspended from the elite Milton Academy and, at 17, ran away to New York for several days, registering in a Manhattan YWCA under the pseudonym "Anna Watsonska" in the hope of being identified as a Russian Jew. In 1964 she received her B.A. from Harvard with a concentration in medieval studies. She received an M.Phil in Victorian literature from Oxford and hoped to pursue further studies in that field until driven from it by the "extraordinary dullness" of a Harvard professor. Her deep interest in theology—the ministry was the only other career she seriously considered—led her to explore instead the "sentimental" women's literature of the 19th century and "the meeting ground between popular art . . . and the governing intellectual principles of the time." Her time at Harvard coincided with a profound reevaluation of the role of women in American society—in an era when that role was still fraught with contradictions: though she was the first woman offered a job with the Harvard English faculty, she was prohibited from being a Rhodes Scholar because of her sex. "You were both pushed and dropped; flattered too much, then judged too harshly," she recalled. Contradiction prevailed in her domestic sphere as well, with the collapse of her decade-long marriage and her subsequent involvement with a "brilliant, brilliant, gorgeous human being" who, like Douglas, was a heavy drinker. He died of alcohol poisoning after Douglas had left him in order to deal with her own addiction. Speaking years later of the genesis of *Terrible Honesty*, she said, "In a strange way his death made me know how to do the book. I came to believe that what was important was the impulse towards getting past the thing that leads you to the morass. I realized it was perfectly appropriate to focus on the impulse to create, not the tragic end."

Douglas taught at Princeton before joining the Columbia faculty in 1974. The first of Douglas's books, *The Feminization of American Culture*, offered a thesis that, in the late 19th century, an alliance developed between male clergy and women that eventually imbued society with a sentimental outlook receptive to maintaining a peculiarly female "domestic sphere" apart from the masculine domain of commerce and scholarship. The phenomenon was a function of the dwindling status these two disestablished groups experienced in an expanding industrial society, but it had theological overtones as well. By the late 1800s, Douglas claimed, American Protestant ministers had refined their image of God away from the old Calvinist patriarchal judge and toward one of a more maternal, healing deity, shaped by the theology of Horace Bushnell and others. In her book, Douglas analyzed the writings of 30 clergymen, including Henry Ward Beecher, William Ellery Channing, and Theodore Ledyard Cuyler; and 30 women writers, including Louisa May Alcott, Margaret Fuller, and Harriet Beecher Stowe. By the 1920s the alliance described by Douglas had forged its own powerful matriarchy, only to fall victim in turn to the "matricidal" challenge of Freud and his followers. (This became one of the theses of Douglas's second book, *Terrible Honesty*.)

The Feminization of American Culture was generally well received. It was described as a "responsible and passionate act of scholarship" by the *Atlantic* (May 1977). Gerda Lerner wrote in the *New York Times Book Review* (June 26, 1977) that Douglas "shows that it was the marginal status of clergymen and women that drove them into the pursuit of the audience and led them to debase the culture by sentimentalizing it . . . the textual richness and methodological sophistication of this intellectual and literary history compensate for its overstatement, its lack of historical perspective and its excessive display of erudition. It is a challenging book."

Douglas, however, came under fire from some critics who thought that she had devalued the literary merit of the women writers she studied. The most forceful of these critics, Jane Tompkins, wrote in her book *Sensational Designs: The Cultural Work of American Fiction 1790–1860* (1985) that she was "diametrically opposed" to the way Douglas held such writing in contempt, an attitude "that the male-dominated tradition has always expressed." Tompkins, however, acknowledged that *The Feminization of American Culture* "is nevertheless extremely important because of its powerful and sustained consideration of this long-neglected body of work. Because Douglas successfully focused critical attention on the cultural centrality of sentimental fiction, forcing the realization that it can no longer be ignored, it is now possible for other critics to put forward a new characterization of these novels and not be dismissed." Ann Douglas responded to this judgment in a new preface to a 1988 edition of her book. "The most

controversial aspect of *The Feminization of American Culture* is the relatively low critical esteem in which I held the work of the feminine authors (with the exceptions of Harriet Beecher Stowe and Margaret Fuller) I considered. While respecting the very different evaluation of this material by other scholars, even believing that they may have access to valid criteria I am temperamentally unable to appreciate, I stand by my original assessment."

By 1988, "with the easy advantage of hindsight," Douglas had concluded that she had really "misconceived and misannounced [the book's] underlying purpose. I thought I was addressing the issue of male versus female literary production and self-definition as much as, or more than, I was attending to the problem of a nascent mass print medium . . . and 'elite' art and thinking. . . . My sense of the pressing nature of the second issue, mass-versus-elite art, came late in the book's decade of development, and was written in, often crudely, in the later stages of its progress." She added, "I am now completing a book-length study of the evolution and definition of what are still, with increasing dis-ease, called mass, middle-brow, and high literary art in New York in the 1920s."

In 1995, this, her second book—"a sequel of sorts to my earlier study of Victorian culture"— was published under the title *Terrible Honesty: Mongrel Manhattan in the 1920s* (its original subtitle had been "Studies in Secular Urban Culture 1919–1935"). For its title, Douglas appropriated Raymond Chandler's phrase "terrible honesty" to describe a new "egalitarian popular and mass culture aggressively appropriating forms and ideas across race, class, and gender lines. This culture billed itself as irreverent if not irreligious, the first such in American annals, alert to questions of honesty but hostile to all moralizing. . . . The primary ethos of all the urban moderns was accuracy, precision, and perfect pitch and timing. It was an ethos the white moderns labeled 'terrible honesty.'" The book instantly catapulted Douglas to the status of prominent commentator on the urban cultural scene.

Terrible Honesty is a lengthy and exuberant overview of the frenetic culture that characterized the Manhattan of the Jazz Age, a period when a combination of "skyscraper consciousness" and an flowering of both white and black culture (hence the "mongrel Manhattan" epithet) produced a brilliant amalgam of modernist poetry, jazz, blues, and serious drama. In her view, it was the "collaborative energy" of blacks and whites—a newly liberated downtown intelligentsia and a renascent Harlem—that produced an era with a "unique aura, its sense of having been a specially privileged and charged site of American experience," an era in which this interracial synergy "reached a peak of intensity . . . never seen in American history before or since." And it was also an era that formed "the genres that still dominate mass culture today: the *New Yorker* 'casual,' the syndicated editorial page, the gossip column, the smart urban comedy for stage and screen, the gangster movie, the talk show, the ad layout, the continuity comic strip, the hit-single record, the sexually explicit novel, and the packaged public persona of mass celebrities whether sports heroes, actors, literary stars, or politicians."

Yet, on a more subliminal level, the 1920s was also a decade of "masculinization," when this new mass culture, galvanized in part by Freud, strove to act out the "dark legend" of matricide by casting off the sentimentalized matriarchs of the past, satirized as "Titanesses" in Thomas Beer's 1926 monograph *The Mauve Decade*. "Open disillusion was the sharpest weapon they had in waging the real war," Douglas wrote, "the war against Mother." The foot soldiers in this matricide were the hundreds of "protagonists" who populated mongrel Manhattan (people as diverse as Dorothy Parker, James Thurber, Langston Hughes, Edna St. Vincent Millay, Bessie Smith, and Damon Runyon) or gazed on it from afar (like Freud, Gertrude Stein, Ernest Hemingway, and T. S. Eliot).

An irony of the Prohibition era was, as Douglas points out, that: "almost one-third of my protagonists were alcoholics or problem drinkers. . . . This was the generation that made the terms 'alcoholic' and 'writer' synonymous." Alluding to her own abuse of alcohol, Douglas told Adam Begley in a *Mirabella* (February 1995) interview: "I know that I will spend the rest of my life writing about people who are both self-destructive and creative. I am working with the pathologies of culture and the ways in which they are tied to the most joyous expression."

Arnold Rampersad was one of the reviewers who paid glowing tribute to the book, in a *New York Times Book Review* (February 12, 1995) article entitled "Psychomanhattanalysis." "In its sheer ambition, in the utter comprehensiveness of its determination to probe the lived realities of the age, *Terrible Honesty* stands apart. Ms. Douglas acknowledges having worked 15 years on this book. I am tempted to marvel that a book of such enormous scope and complexity could have been finished so soon. *Terrible Honesty* is a dauntingly long book [606 pages, including a heavily detailed 91-page 'bibliographic essay'], but its pace seldom drops below a sprint. It sparkles with something like that same vital essence that its author locates at the core of the [1920s] in the United States, and astonishes with the multiplicity and astuteness of its insights and associations."

But some critics wondered, for example, whether the 'matriarch/Titanesses' theme had equal validity when applied to the experience of African-Americans. Others faulted her thesis on more general grounds, charging that she oversimplified things too much. Richard Bernstein wrote in the *New York Times* (March 22, 1995): "Ms. Douglas's effort to explain so much with a single metaphor is fascinating, as are most such efforts, and she defends it with numerous elements of proof. And yet

one could also argue that there is a certain glibness in arguments along these lines, a selectivity in the evidence presented, and a reliance on what some scholars call essentialism, the belief that men and women have certain essential characteristics independent of the forces of society. What, after all, is feminization, and why should it be contrary to the impulse toward 'terrible honesty'?" Adam Kirsch, writing in the *Boston Book Review* (June 1995) expressed discomfort about the way in which Douglas based her conclusions on "an uneasy combination of feminism and Freud." Though "intriguing at first sight," the idea that "terrible honesty" was an eruption of the male principle against the Victorian matriarch is oversimplified, in the view of Kirsch, who found that "the book's lack of principles and method is painful to witness. . . . *Terrible Honesty* becomes a series of casual judgments on people and ideas according to Douglas's confused moral code." He concluded: "*Terrible Honesty* is interesting insofar as it treats a decade that marked a tremendous and enduring shift in American culture. But beyond the simple framework of feminine and masculine, optimist and pessimist, Douglas provides nothing but a jumble of half-hearted theories, thumbnail biographies, and lists of dates, people, and things. True to her avowed principles, she does not explain history, she plays with it."

Criticism notwithstanding, the publication of *Terrible Honesty* placed Douglas in the front ranks of scholars of American popular culture. The book won the 1995 Albert J. Beveridge award of the American Historical Association and was designated one of the best books of the year by the American Literature Association, the New York Public Library, and the *New York Times*. "Ann Douglas isn't quite a provocateur in the Camille Paglia mold," wrote Dan Cryer in *Newsday* (February 13, 1995), "though part of her seems determined to try. . . . This willingness to stick her neck out, though, makes her as engaging and as high-spirited as the age she so ably chronicles."

After *Terrible Honesty* was published, Douglas announced that she was working on a new book about her own era, in which she would examine America of the 1940s and 1950s through a prism of terror. But the terror of which she speaks deals more with public pathologies than with sensationalized events. Interviewed for the Columbia [University] American Culture Studies Center, she said: "Terror had an enormous resurgence in popularity beginning in the late [1960s] and lasting through the early [1980s]. Obviously, a lot of this had to do with nuclearism and the fear that the world will end—the extreme situation of terror—and I think this has to do with a sense of who is persecuting whom, which is the big question in American politics during this extended Cold War period. . . . Someone like Nixon in the Watergate crisis was clearly living out a kind of scenario of paranoia that Michael Cimino, Bob Dylan, and a lot of other people were living out in their own ways at the same time." She told Begley, "Start with the term *brinkmanship*. You have to be ready for annihilation at any moment so that you can avoid annihilation. You have to be on the brink so you won't fall off. Mainly you do nothing but look into the abyss."

Douglas's own transgressive personality was capsulized by Adam Begley: "As vibrant in person as she is on paper," he wrote, " Douglas has blond hair with a hint of red, clipped short on the sides, longer on top—a cut that makes her look young, plugged into student styles. . . . She is a marathon talker, endlessly digressive, always deviously circling her subject, piling on anecdotal evidence until she achieves at last a jumble that resembles—amazingly coherent thinking. She slips into free association, startles with random bursts of bold confession."

If Douglas has anything approaching a poetic credo, it is perhaps found in this comment, made to an interviewer: "To believe in [terrible honesty] you have to think there is a truth that can be found, and that's not a post-modernist position. You have to be closer to religious origins—the generation of the [1920s] was truly secular in that it still knew its theology and its varieties of religious experience. We are post-secular, inventing new faiths, without any sense of organizing truths. The truths we accept are so multiple that honesty becomes little more than a stratagem by which you manage your tendencies toward duplicity."
—E. M.

SUGGESTED *READING: Columbia American Studies* Center (newsletter) p26+ Spring 1987, with photo; *New York Review of Books* p50+ Apr. 20, 1995; *New York Times* C p1+ May 17, 1995, with photo; *New York Times Book Review* p13 June 26, 1977, p1+ Feb. 12, 1995; *Times Literary Supplement* p7+ Dec. 15, 1995; Tompkins, J. *Sensational Designs*, 1985

SELECTED BOOKS: *The Feminization of American Culture*, 1977; *Terrible Honesty: Mongrel Manhattan in the 1920s*, 1995

Courtesy of Penguin Publishing

Doyle, Roddy

1958– Novelist; playwright; screenwriter

"Perhaps no one has done so much to create a new set of images for the Ireland of the late 20th century as Roddy Doyle . . . ," the novelist Mary Gordon wrote in the *New York Times Book Review* (April 28, 1996). "Doyle has made his own the gritty world of modern Dublin, violent and generous-hearted, mean-spirited and fed by dreams." In his novels, plays, and screenplays, Doyle has illuminated the frailties and strengths of working-class men, women, and children in his native land, and has revealed with both comedy and pathos a very human side of Ireland, one quite unlike the widely held picture of Ireland as a shamrock-strewn rural paradise. "Ireland has changed drastically in 20 years," Doyle observed to Mary Jordan of the *Washington Post* (February 4, 1994). "It is not the simple place where people are dancing in country crossroads."

Perhaps because he has dealt so forthrightly with the problems of modern Irish society, Doyle has been subjected to strong, and sometimes personal, criticism in his native land. Nevertheless, his novels—*The Commitments, The Snapper,* and *The Van*, which are known collectively as the Barrytown trilogy, and the darker and more complex *Paddy Clarke Ha Ha Ha* and *The Woman Who Walked into Doors*—have been best-sellers in Ireland, as they have in Great Britain, where he first gained popularity, and, more recently, in the United States. *Paddy Clarke Ha Ha Ha* won the Booker Prize, Great Britain's most prestigious literary award, in 1993. It is the first book by an Irish writer to earn the prize. Doyle's novel *A Star Called Henry*, the first installment of a planned trilogy, appeared in 1999.

One of the four children of a printing instructor and a homemaker, Roddy Doyle was born in May 1958 in Dublin, and he grew up in the northern Dublin suburb of Kilbarrack, which became the model for Barrytown, the fictional Dublin suburb where four of his novels are set. Because some aspects of the life of the character Paddy Clarke—

who was born in 1958 and lives in Barrytown and whose parents' marriage is disintegrating—resemble those of Doyle's early years, some observers have speculated that the author based his novel about Paddy on his own childhood. "The place is mine; the time is mine," Doyle admitted to John Rockwell of the *New York Times* (December 20, 1993). "There are memories of my own, running through a field and seeing pheasants fly up, balls of dust under the kitchen table. But the story isn't mine, I'm glad to say. My parents are still happily married." He told another interviewer, "My memories of childhood are overwhelmingly happy."

After graduating from St. Fintan's Christian Brothers School, Doyle attended University College Dublin, from which he received a B.A. degree in English and geography. He then undertook teacher training at Greendale Community School, in Kilbarrack, and after getting certified, he became a member of its faculty. He taught for 14 years at Greendale, where he was known to his students as "Punk" Doyle, because of the earring and Dr. Marten's boots he wore.

In the early 1980s, Doyle began work on his first novel, a gargantuan satire called "Your Granny's a Hunger Striker." "It had a brilliant title, then went seriously downhill," he has said of the tome, which was never published. He wrote his next novel, *The Commitments*, late at night ("because I thought that was what you were supposed to do,") over a six-month period, while living in a one-room apartment. The book failed to spark the interest of any of the publishers to which he sent it, so in 1986, in collaboration with a friend, he had 1,000 copies of the book printed privately, under the "King Farouk" imprint, and sold them himself. One copy landed at William Heinemann, a London-based publishing house. Heinemann published *The Commitments* in 1987; two years later, Random House published it in the United States.

The Commitments tells the story of an assortment of young people who form a band dedicated to covering the great American soul recordings of the 1960s. As runaway egos, divergent musical tastes, and personal entanglements threaten the stability of the band, its charismatic manager, Jimmy Rabbitte Jr., struggles to keep it from self-destructing. Among those who enjoyed the novel was the novelist Kinky Friedman, who, in the *New York Times Book Review* (July 23, 1989), reported that the book offers "a rather graphic spiritual blueprint of what it's like to become a star and how it feels to fall from the sky." Doyle co-wrote the screenplay for the film version of *The Commitments* (1991), which was directed by Alan Parker. Janet Maslin of the *New York Times* (August 14, 1991), one of many critics who praised the movie, described it as "an exuberant valentine to American soul music and the impoverished Dublin teenagers who think of it as magic."

Jimmy Rabbitte Jr. and his parents and siblings are the main characters in the other installments of the Barrytown trilogy, *The Snapper* and *The Van*,

which were published in Ireland in 1990 and 1991, respectively, and simultaneously in the United States in 1992. *The Snapper* (the term is Irish slang for "baby") revolves around the pregnancy of Jimmy Rabbitte's unmarried 20-year-old sister Sharon, which resulted from a drunken encounter, verging on rape, in a nightclub parking lot. Unwilling to name the baby's father, a rather pathetic acquaintance of Jimmy Sr.'s, Sharon pretends to have had a short-lived romance with a Spanish sailor. As her pregnancy progresses and the father's true identity comes to light, neighbors begin to ostracize her. She endures their treatment with the help of her family, especially her father, who reads up on pregnancy and childbirth and becomes her most outspoken ally. Writing in the *New York Times* (October 11, 1992), Bruce Allen declared that Jimmy Sr. is "a wonderful mixture of obscene bluster and boozy sentimentality . . . a self-indulgent buffoon and braggart who cherishes, abuses, and whines for respect from a houseful of rude brawlers exactly like himself. He's intensely real, and [*The Snapper*] comes vividly alive as he begins to understand that he can't control the feisty Sharon, and that there is 'more to life than drinking pints with your mates.'"

The Rabbittes became the Curleys in Doyle's screenplay for *The Snapper*, which Stephen Frears directed. The film was shown on British television in 1993 and released theatrically later that year. Described by Diane Turbide in *Maclean's* (January 31, 1994) as "a hilarious, touching film that in its way endorses family values" and by Joan Juliet Buck in *Vogue* (October 1993) as a "rowdy, humanistic fairy tale," it presented a "truly funny" characterization of everyday life, according to Richard Alleva, who added, in his review for *Commonweal* (March 25, 1994), that the Curley family "is lovingly portrayed."

The absence of narrative in Doyle's first two novels and the reliance on dialogue, particularly of a profane nature, to move the stories along were sore points with some reviewers. As Paul Majendie reported in the *Toronto Globe and Mail* (June 15, 1993), "Some critics complained that if you deleted the expletives from Doyle's novels, the books would virtually vanish. With their flow of dialogue and lack of narrative, the slim novels are no more than draft screenplays, they say." In his defense, Doyle told Eileen Battersby for the *Guardian* (May 17, 1993), "The best way to reveal a character is to get them to open their mouths." Plays, of course, rely almost solely on dialogue to reveal character, and although, by his own account, he is "not a natural playwright," Doyle wrote two plays—*Brownbread* and *War*—in the late 1980s.

The third book in the Barrytown trilogy, *The Van*, includes more narrative than do its predecessors, and critics responded favorably to the change. Anthony Lane of the *New Yorker* (May 26, 1997), for instance, called it "probably Roddy Doyle's best book." "*The Van* is not just a very funny book, it is also faultless comic writing," Guy Mannes-

Abbott declared in the *New Statesman & Society* (August 23, 1991), and in *Library Journal* (July 1992), Brian Kenney wrote that the novel "makes you laugh for pages yet keeps you aware that you could, instead, be crying."

A finalist for the 1991 Booker Prize, *The Van* focuses on the midlife crisis experienced by Jimmy Rabbitte Sr. Laid off from his job as a plasterer, Jimmy invests in a decrepit fish-and-chips van in partnership with his best pal, Bimbo, who is also newly unemployed. As business picks up, their friendship deteriorates, and questions arise about who is the boss. Doyle wrote the screenplay for the movie version of the novel, which Stephen Frears directed and which was released in the United States in 1997. According to Stephen Holden of the *New York Times* (May 16, 1997), the film "unabashedly celebrates a working-class world that other British movies have tended to cast in a bleaker light." By his own account, Doyle "enjoys the social aspects of filmmaking." "I have thought of directing, but I abandoned it," he told Rockwell. "I don't have the visual sense. And working with actors is a mystery to me."

The world of the title character of *Paddy Clarke Ha Ha Ha* is truly bleak in many ways, but his story is far from unrelievedly grim. As Tom Shone put it in a highly laudatory review for the *Spectator* (June 12, 1993), it is "by turns truthful, hilarious, painfully sad and frequently all three at once." An acutely observant 10-year-old, Paddy, who is the narrator of the novel, records with telling details the petty cruelties and everyday wonders that fill the life of a lower-middle-class boy in a town undergoing profound social and physical changes. "We explore Paddy's world as he does, seeing everything through his eyes," Eamonn Wall, a professor of Irish literature, wrote in the *Chicago Tribune* (December 12, 1993). "Concerned with investigating from inside the boy's being, Doyle recalls another great investigator of Dublin and Dubliners, James Joyce, as he adopts an archaeologist's approach and includes a wealth of seemingly random details that eventually form a brilliant collage of a short period—less than a school year—in Paddy Clarke's life." During that year, Paddy's parents separate, and the boy, as Carolyn See wrote in the *Washington Post* (December 17, 1993), "turns from a savage into a sentient being most movingly."

Doyle has traced his interest in writing from a child's point of view to the birth of his first son. "At first it was difficult," he explained to Kim Campbell of the *Christian Science Monitor* (February 2, 1994), "because I had only a vague notion of what Paddy was like. I wasn't sure of his interests. But once I wrote a few scenes and chapters, and once I knew what his interests were, then it became easier, and it was quite enjoyable." He also told Campbell, "I decided to write [*Paddy Clarke*] in the first person, which I hadn't done before, because I thought it would force me to think and write differently."

Almost without exception, critics hailed *Paddy Clarke* as a brilliantly realized work of fiction. Eamonn Wall called it "profound, disturbing, and beautifully crafted." Carolyn See wrote, "It may be one of the great modern Irish novels." "Barrytown is a cuteness-free zone with not a scrap of sentimentality or condescension to be found . . . ," Mary Flanagan wrote in the *New York Times* (January 2, 1994). "There is no resolution here and precious little redemption. But there is luminous writing. And there is Paddy himself, quite unforgettable, especially in those present-tense games and races in which he seems the personification of the life force." On announcing that *Paddy Clarke* had won the Booker Prize as the best British novel of 1993, the chairman of the judging committee called the novel "funny, humane, and sad." "In *Paddy Clarke* there's a lot of humor, and I think it's there so I can kick the legs out from under the reader later on in the book," Doyle told Kim Campbell.

Doyle's next project was *Family*, a four-part miniseries for Irish and British television. Like *Paddy Clarke*, *Family* is the story of a disintegrating marriage, but it contains much more violence and despair than the novel. Set in Ballymun, a dreadful high-rise public housing project, the series focuses on both the relationship between a married couple, Charlo and Paula Spencer, and the social ills that are epidemic in Ballymun. Charlo is a petty crook, wife beater, and possible molester of his own daughter; Paula has turned to alcohol to cope with her husband, whom she still loves in spite of his violence and numerous affairs. Each installment of the series focuses on a different member of the Spencer family, which includes two children.

Family caused a furor in Ireland, especially in Ballymun itself. The unemployment rate among occupants of the housing complex is currently about 60 percent, and many residents condemned the series for unfairly tarnishing the image of people, like themselves, who must struggle mightily to carry on in the face of overwhelming poverty. Others thought that the program accurately depicted the desolation of many tenants' lives. For his part, Doyle said, "The Barrytown trilogy of books was a celebration of poor, often inadequate people, about their struggle to keep heads above water. It was a celebration of their lives, their warmth. This is the flip side, darker, bleak."

Paula Spencer is both the title character and narrator of Doyle's fifth novel, *The Woman Who Walked into Doors* (1996), the title of which alludes to the excuse some battered women use to explain their injuries. Paula relates her story mostly through flashbacks. After she receives word that Charlo, whom she divorced, has been killed by police during a failed robbery attempt, Paula recalls their courtship and marriage, the brief happy period after their wedding, the first time he beat her (when she was pregnant with their first child), and the day she finally threw him out of the house. "One of the reasons the book became engrossing," Doyle told Elizabeth Mitchell of *Eye Magazine*

(May 16, 1996), "was the fact that it allowed me to answer many questions about Paula's life. I didn't want to write a novelization of the series." Members of the domestic-violence organization Women's Aid whom Doyle asked to review the manuscript gave a favorable evaluation of his treatment of the subject of domestic violence, which he has called Ireland's "dirty little secret."

Like the Women's Aid members, literary critics approved of *The Woman Who Walked into Doors*. Writing in the *New York Times Book Review*, Mary Gordon called the book "a small jewel." "It extends [Doyle's] range and adds new and subtle colors to his already impressive palette. . . . [The book] honors not the female experience in the abstract, but the experience of this one woman, Paula Spencer; it examines it with tenderness, but with fearless clearsightedness." James Hynes of the *Washington Post* (April 7, 1996) wrote that Paula "may be Doyle's most successful literary creation yet, a tour de force of literary ventriloquism that gives the lie to the writing-workshop canard that a man can't write from the point of view of a woman, let alone in her voice."

"Doyle just gets better and better"—so stated the author of *Publishers Weekly*'s (July 12, 1999) starred review of *A Star Called Henry*, Doyle's 1999 novel. The first book in a projected trilogy, it traces the inauspicious birth and early manhood of the "handsome, healthy, fearless" Henry Smart, who joins the Irish Republican Army in its early years. "This is history evoked on an intimate and yet earth-shaking scale, with a huge dash of the blarney, some mythical embellishments and a driving narrative that never falters," wrote the *Publishers Weekly* reviewer. "Maybe the Great American novel remains to be written, but on the evidence of its first installment, this is the epic Irish one, created at a high pitch of eloquence."

A self-described soccer fanatic, Roddy Doyle is said to be studious-looking and down-to-earth. "He still acts rather like a teacher," John Rockwell observed. According to Mary Jordan, "His favorite authors are American: Raymond Carver, Flannery O'Connor, Anne Tyler," writers who, in Doyle's words, are "more interested in the characters than their own cleverness."

Doyle lives in a middle-class suburb north of Dublin with his wife, Belinda, a former publicist whom he has known at least since the first printing of *The Commitments*, and their two young sons, Rory and Jack. Doyle, who gave up teaching when *Paddy Clarke* was published, is currently working on a screenplay based on Liam O'Flaherty's 1937 novel, *Famine*.

SUGGESTED READING: *New York Times* C p11+ Dec. 20, 1993, with photo; *Toronto Globe and Mail* A p11 June 15, 1993, with photo; *Washington Post* C p1+ Feb. 4, 1994, with photos; *Contemporary Authors* vol. 143, 1994

SELECTED WORKS: Fiction—*The Commitments*, 1987; *The Snapper*, 1989; *The Van*, 1991; *Paddy Clarke Ha Ha Ha*, 1993; *The Woman Who Walked into Doors*, 1996; *A Star Called Henry*, 1999; Drama—*Brownbread*, 1987; *War*, 1989; Screenplays—*The Commitments*, 1991; *The Snapper*, 1993; *The Van*, 1996; Television—*Family*, 1994

Gene Bagnuto

Duberman, Martin

Aug. 6, 1930– Biographer; memoirist

Martin Duberman's analysis of contemporary American history—particularly as it pertains to race relations and homosexuality—has met with both cheers and criticism for its radical assessments. His opinions and convictions have been as varied as the genres in which he has written—plays, biographies, essays, and memoirs. He first gained notice as a historian when he wrote the scholarly biographies *Charles Frances Adams* (1961) and *James Russell Lowell* (1966). He also caused a minor uproar as a playwright by challenging American ideas about race relations, in the play *In White America* (1963), and about homosexuality, in such later plays as *The Recorder* (1970) and *The Electric Map* (1970). His collection of essays, *The Uncompleted Past* (1969), traces the development of his thinking in the 1960s, and caused a great stir when he claimed, as a historian, that history was both subjective and incapable of teaching people about the workings of modern society. His biography of the entertainer, activist, and athlete Paul Robeson, published in 1989, is generally regarded as the definitive book on Robeson's life. Duberman has continued to explore the theme of homosexuality, in such works as *Stonewall* (1993), which chronicles the rise of the gay movement in America, and his memoirs, *Cures: A Gay Man's Odyssey* (1991) and *Midlife Queer: An Autobiography of a Decade* (1996).

Martin Bauml Duberman was born in New York City on August 6, 1930, the son of Joseph M. Duberman, a Ukrainian immigrant and dress manufacturer, and the former Josephine Bauml, a second-generation Austrian American. Duberman has recalled that as a youth he did not acknowlege or act on his physical attraction to other boys. Instead, he channeled his sexual energy into overachieving in school.

Having become interested early on in acting, at the age of 17 Duberman became seriously involved with the theater, after playing the part of George in Thornton Wilder's play *Our Town* in summer stock in Vermont and New Hampshire. In an interview for the *New York Times* (October 28, 1969), he recalled, "I came home and told my parents I wanted to be an actor. I thought of going to Carnegie Tech. I wish I knew what dissuaded me—perhaps wise parents who said nothing. At any rate, I wound up at Yale, where I did some acting and directing and where I also became fascinated by American history." While at Yale, he also began writing some drama criticism as well as pieces for the stage. He graduated from Yale in 1952, then continued his education at Harvard University, from which he received his master's degree in history in 1953 and his Ph.D. in 1957.

While working on his doctoral thesis, Duberman served as a tutor at Harvard between 1955 and 1957. After receiving his degree, he began teaching at Yale in the fall of 1957. Duberman felt pressure to lead what was considered a "normal" lifestyle in the conservative 1950s—i.e., that of a heterosexual with a thriving career—but just as he was starting his teaching career, he had an affair with a man. Societal restraints, coupled with his own mixed feelings about his sexuality, caused him to end the relationship, and he sought professional help because he felt that he was, in his words, a "sickie." He has said that he was extremely eager to change his sexual orientation, and in the mid-1960s he went through periods of sexual abstinence and therapy with a doctor who subjected him to humiliation and cruelty. At one point in a group session, he recalls, the doctor had Duberman beaten by a fellow group member. During the early 1960s, Duberman kept up the appearance of a heterosexual bachelor.

Duberman first received public notice for his intriguing biography *Charles Francis Adams*, in 1961. The grandson of John Adams and the son of John Quincy Adams, Charles Francis Adams is remembered mainly as the United States minister to England during the American Civil War. His diplomatic skill enabled the United States to continue fighting the Confederacy without interference of the major European powers, particularly England, which seemed on the verge of recognizing the South as a separate nation. He also stalled British construction of warships for use in the South's navy and held off post-war arbitration claims inspired by the damage wrought by the southern warship *Alabama*. The *New York Herald-Tribune* (March 27, 1961) proclaimed that "Mr. Duberman, in telling it again and telling it well, lets us see more clearly than others have done how and why it was Adams' least winning characteristics that made him so effective in London. The chilliest of his tribe fulfilled himself at last, and scored his own kind of triumph." Duberman followed this successful scholarly biography with another, *James Russell Lowell*, about the 19th-century poet, in 1966.

The 1960s were an era of radical politics and Duberman was very much a man of his time. He took a vital interest in the civil rights movement in the early 1960s, partially because of his own liberal thoughts on race, and partially because of his own experience as a marginalized person due to his homosexuality. His radicalism found release in several forms: as an author of articles and books, as a playwright, and in the 1970s, as a gay activist and member of such groups as the Gay Academic Union and the Gay Task Force.

As a playwright, Duberman caused a minor rumble in Off-Broadway theater with the production of his first play, *In White America*, in 1963. In it, the author combined original dialogue with actual letters and stories of the "lost" history of America. Among other documents, he included the journal of a British doctor traveling on a slave ship in the 18th century, a northern reporter's interview with a slave on a New Orleans plantation in the 1800s, and a letter from Thomas Jefferson in which he discussed the superiority of the white race. The cast, which was racially mixed, read exerpts of these documents and others, in the playwright's attempt to show the spectrum of America's opinions on race, right up to Martin Luther King Jr.'s March on Washington, which had taken place in August of that year. "We're going to step on toes," producer Judy Rutherford Marechal told the *New York Herald-Tribune* (October 22, 1963) shortly before the play opened at New York's Sheridan Square Playhouse. "We're going to be in for a lot of controversy."

All of Duberman's subsequent theatrical pieces were marked by some amount of controversy. He followed *In White America* with a series of bold Off-Broadway plays, including *Metaphors* (1968), *Groups* (1968), and *The Colonial Dudes* (1969). In 1970 *The Memory Bank*, a pair of one-act plays, premiered at the Gate Theatre in New York City. The first segment, "The Recorder," is a conversation between a young historian and an older, more distinguished colleague, in which each details how his subjectivity causes him to distort historical facts. The second, "The Electric Map," is about two brothers: Ted, who has a job running an elaborate machine that retells the story of the Civil War battle of Gettysburg, and Jim, who is trying to get Ted to leave town because of a local scandal involving homosexuals. "What I want to show," Duberman told the *New York Times* (June 1, 1969) before the premiere, "is how we, as human beings, use our pasts, create myths, permit distortions to enter into our thinking. What I'm trying to indicate is that both in our private lives as well as in our view of our national history this sort of editing leads to difficulties. It's important that we see the past as a whole, the good and the evil interwoven."

Duberman developed this philosophy in his next book, *The Uncollected Past* (1969.) A collection of his essays written in the 1960s, *The Uncollected Past* details the change in Duberman's intellectual concerns, his embracing of and ultimate dissatisfaction with the study of history, and his feelings on the radicalism of the era. The collection starts with his historical articles written in the early 1960s; these are followed by accounts of his involvement with radical politics and his feelings on educational reform. Unlike some of his contemporaries, Duberman does not call for a more culturally relevant look at history, since he does not believe that history has relevance to the present. Instead, he sees each historical event as unique. Reviews of *The Uncollected Past* were mixed. In the *New York Times Book Review* (January 4, 1970) Eric Foner wrote of Duberman's final essay, "On Becoming A Historian," that "one is left with the strong impression that Duberman did not enter history with any deep commitment—he fell into it, and was never really happy." Christopher Lehmann-Haupt of the *New York Times* (December 15, 1969), however, felt that "Like so many products of the fifties, [Duberman] remains, by his own admission, hung up between the ideas of the forties and the action of the sixties. . . . But all the same, without dwelling on himself, he has produced an impressive odyssey of a mind that went from there to here."

In *Black Mountain: An Exploration in Community* (1972), Duberman pushed his ideas on the relevance of history even further. The subject of *Black Mountain* is the experimental school of the same name that was started in North Carolina in 1933 by former teachers from Rollins College, the faculty of which included many celebrities of art and literature. Plagued by problems, the Black Mountain School closed in 1956. In addition to a history of the institution, the author depicted the daily life of Black Mountain and how its founders attempted to define it as a creative environment. Christopher Lehmann-Haupt of the *New York Times* (November 7, 1972) felt the book was "deeply divided . . . on the one hand a commitment to the past and an attempt to write conventional history; on the other hand a denial of the 'pastness' of the past and an attempt to merge it with the present. And despite all of Duberman's labors to heal the division—by alternately making the present past and the past present—the division is really a harmful one.

Black Mountain is really two books—one reasonably satisfying, the other faintly embarrassing." Duberman defended his work in the *New York Post* (December 4, 1972). "No two historians describing the same event would describe it in the same way," he wrote. "Their fantasies are always projected on—and combined with—the data and I think the whole process should become more overt."

In *Black Mountain*, Duberman publicly admitted his homosexuality for the first time. He had become more comfortable with his sexual orientation in the early 1970s, as the gay rights movement began to take shape. He began to address gay themes in his fictional work as well, as in his play *Payments*, written in 1969 and performed in 1970, in which the main character, a married blue-collar worker from New Jersey, becomes a male prostitute in Manhattan. Duberman also began studying the secret collections of sexually explicit materials in public libraries—the books and magazines librarians never catalog. He made this study a scholarly effort, in part because he felt that gay history up to this point had been neglected. "There's lots of speculation about Walt Whitman," he noted in an interview for the *Washington Post* (April 1, 1976), "and some about Henry James, but we don't know anything about the whole gay subculture." He collected the results of his findings in *About Time: Exploring the Gay Past* (1986). This book was divided into two parts: the first half collected the historical documents on homosexuality Duberman had found in public libraries, and the second collected essays and articles the author had written for various gay periodicals between 1972 and 1982.

Duberman took on his next project, a biography on the performer, activist, athlete, and lawyer Paul Robeson (1898-1976), almost by accident. Paul Robeson Jr. had been considering several people for the job of writing his father's biography, and as luck would have it, the younger Robeson's agent, Frances Goldin, was also Duberman's agent. One day in 1981 Robeson was looking at some of the books in Goldin's living room and came across titles by Duberman. He borrowed them from Goldin and later announced to her that he had found his father's biographer. Duberman himself, while an admirer of Paul Robeson, was not altogether optimistic about the daunting task. In his first meeting with Robeson Jr., Duberman recalled to Sam Staggs of *Publishers Weekly* (January 13, 1989), "I told him he would get in trouble for choosing me, first of all because I'm white, and also because I'm gay and have been politically active for years in the gay movement. He said he had had me thoroughly checked out, and knew all about me."

After getting a written agreement from Robeson Jr. relinquishing the son's editorial authority over the finished manuscript, Duberman was given access to the family archives. It was composed of some 50,000 items, including the diary of Robeson's widow Eslanda (Essie) Goode, who had given up a medical career to become her husband's manager. In 1989 Duberman published *Paul Robeson*, an intimate look at an extremely complex man.

Reviews for the biography were mixed. A reviewer for the *Christian Science Monitor* (March 31, 1989) wrote that "This biography is for everyone, regardless of color—or politics." In *New York* magazine (January 30, 1989), Rhoda Koenig cheered that "Martin Bauml Duberman has given Robeson the chronicle he deserves. Though overlong and, at times, a bit remote, *Paul Robeson* is a serious examination of that towering and mysterious figure, rescuing him from the perils of too little and too much respect." In the *New York Times Book Review* (February 1, 1989), John Patrick Diggins proclaimed, "With consummate narrative talent Mr. Duberman has written a superb biography of a great man who started out with the right moral convictions only to reach the wrong political conclusions." Other critics felt that Duberman was too inclined to agree with Robeson's politics and that he had thus rendered a biased view of his subject. Eric Breindl of the *Wall Street Journal* (April 6, 1989) grumbled, "in the end, Mr. Duberman's political biases keep him from facing the full implications of the new material he has so skillfully unearthed."

In 1991 Duberman produced the first volume of his autobiography, *Cures: A Gay Man's Odyssey*. In it he detailed his prepubescent discovery of his sexual preference, his various attempts to repress his feelings, and his attempts to find a "cure" through psychotherapy and group sessions. He described the underground gay community of the 1950s, a time when secret bars were frequently raided by the police, and when men risked beatings, robbery, or murder to have liaisons with hustlers. He went on to relate how, once he freed himself of his doctor's powerful influence, he became more comfortable with the idea of his own sexuality. *Publishers Weekly* (February 15, 1991) called the memoir an "intense confessional full of witty self-deflation." Andrew Kopkind in the *Nation* (June 10, 1991) wrote that "Duberman . . . has given his spiritual descendants a volume about gay life that will tell them a lot about themselves, as well as about him. It's a life worth knowing."

In the 1990s Duberman continued to focus his literary efforts on descriptions of gay life and history. In 1992 Chelsea House Publishers began planning a series, intended for a teenage audience, about major homosexual figures and topics. As editorial consultant, Duberman was in charge of signing up writers for the 40 planned titles, the first of which was a biography of James Baldwin by Randall Kenan.

In 1993 Duberman published *Stonewall*, a study of the gay rights movement, which started in the summer of 1969 when a group of homosexuals, tired of being harassed by the police on vice violations, fought back. The ensuing riot, which took place in Greenwich Village at a gay bar called the Stonewall Inn, resulted in five days of public demonstrations by supporters of the people who had fought the police. The anniversary of the event is now commemorated by gay activists. In his book,

Duberman followed the lives of six people, beginning with their participation in the spontaneous events at Stonewall and tracing their paths to the formation of a bona fide gay rights movement. Reviews varied greatly; Marvin Liebman of the *Washington Post* (May 24, 1993), praised the author's "attention to detail . . . especially keen on issues of race, gender, and class and on the various meanings of gay identity." Herb Moses of *New York Newsday* (June 27, 1993) claimed that Duberman's book "makes it frighteningly apparent" just how far gays and lesbians have come in the last 30 years, but quibbled that the author "perhaps provides too much information on the squabbling between the various gay organizations involved in Stonewall." Sara M. Evans complained in the *New York Times Book Review* (June 27, 1993) that "The story of Stonewall narrated as a series of coming-out stories may well be a political gesture that seeks to naturalize what society has labeled as deviant. But the effort to dissolve politics and history into personal stories has limits. Coming out, as important as it is, is no longer enough." Such criticism notwithstanding, the director Nigel Finch found enough to admire in Duberman's book to turn it into a movie in 1996.

In that year Duberman's book *Midlife Queer: Autobiography of a Decade 1971–1981*, was published. That volume looks at the first decade of gay liberation, the freedom that gay men and lesbians experienced for the first time, and its sudden end with the onset of the AIDS virus. During the decade, the author had begun to involve himself in a variety of gay organizations, including the Gay Academic Union, the Gay Activists Alliance, and the National Gay Task Force. In anecdotes about his own involvement, Duberman offered the reader a firsthand look at gay life in America, just as homosexuals were "coming out of the closet." As in *Cures*, Duberman also detailed his own public awakening as a gay man and discussed how he ultimately rejected the idea of trying to "cure" his sexual preferences. Walter Kendrick remarked in his review for the *New York Times Book Review* (May 19, 1996) that "Future historians will find a valuable source in Mr. Duberman's eyewitness accounts as well as his acute insider's assessments. But despite the internecine passions Mr. Duberman describes, his prose remains clinically detached and dry. Others might have yelled and screamed, but Mr. Duberman went home to write in his diary." Kendrick later added that the book became "somewhat livelier" in the middle and last sections, which cover the failure to Duberman's plays, due to what he saw as the theater-going public's inability to accept homosexual themes; his approach to maintaining his sanity in the midst of personal conflicts; and the heart attack he suffered in late 1979.

Martin Duberman is also author of the plays *Dudes* (1972), *Inner Limits* (1972), *Elagabalus* (1973), and *Visions of Kerouac* (1977). He has served as editor of *The Antislavery Vanguard: New*

Essays on the Abolitionists (1965) and, with Martha Vicinus and George Chauncey, *Hidden from History: Reclaiming the Gay and Lesbian Past* (1989).

Duberman has received numerous honors, including the Bancroft Prize of 1963, for *Charles Francis Adams*, the Vernon Rice Drama Desk Award of 1963–64, for *In White America*, a National Book Award nomination in 1966, for *James Russell Lowell*, the National Academy of Arts and Letters Award in 1971, for his contribution to literature, the Manhattan Borough President's gold medal in 1988, and the Lambda Book Award and the Myer Award, both in 1990.

In 1999, 35 years' worth of Duberman's essays, articles, and reviews were collected in *Left Out: A Political Journey.*—C.M.

SUGGESTED READING: *Christian Science Monitor* p13 Mar. 31, 1989; *London Review of Books* p16+ Dec. 7, 1989; *Nation* p775 June 10, 1991; *New York* p56 Feb. 2, 1970, p56 Jan. 30, 1989; *New York Herald-Tribune* p27 Mar. 27, 1961, p15 Oct. 22, 1963; *New York Newsday* June 27, 1993; *New York Post* p31 Dec. 4, 1972; *New York Times* II p1+ June 1, 1969, p40 Oct. 28, 1969, p45 Dec. 15, 1969, II p1+ Feb. 22, 1970, p37 Nov. 7, 1972, p23 Feb. 18, 1978, B p4 Nov. 24, 1992, C p8 July 26, 1996, *New York Times Book Review* p6+ Jan. 4, 1970, p1+ Feb. 13, 1989, p9 Apr. 21, 1991, p15 June 27, 1993, p15 May 19, 1996; *Publishers Weekly* p72+ Jan. 13, 1989, p79 Feb. 15, 1991; *Village Voice* p19+ Mar. 7, 1989, p39 June 27, 1993; *Wall Street Journal* A p16 Apr. 6, 1989; *Washington Post* C p13 Apr. 1, 1976, D p2 May 24, 1993; *Contemporary Authors New Revision Series* vol. 63, 1998

SELECTED WORKS: Nonfiction—*Charles Francis Adams*, 1961; *James Russell Lowell*, 1966; *The Uncollected Past*, 1969; *Black Mountain: An Exploration in Community*, 1972; *About Time: Exploring the Gay Past*, 1986; *Paul Robeson*, 1989; *Cures: A Gay Man's Odyssey*, 1991; *Stonewall*, 1993; *Midlife Queer: Autobiography of a Decade 1971–1981*, 1996; *Left Out: A Political Journey*, 1999; Drama—*In White America*, 1963; *Metaphors*, 1968; *Groups*, 1968; *The Colonial Dudes*, 1969; *The Memory Bank*, 1970; *Payments*, 1970; *Dudes*, 1972; *Inner Limits*, 1972; *Elagabalus*, 1973; *Visions of Kerouac*, 1977; *Mother Earth: An Epic of Emma Goldman's Life*, 1991; As editor—*The Antislavery Vanguard: New Essays on the Abolitionists*, 1965; with Marth Vicinus and George Chauncey—*Hidden from History: Reclaiming the Gay and Lesbian Past*, 1989

Ducornet, Rikki

Apr. 19, 1943– Novelist; short-story writer; poet

Rikki Ducornet, the American poet, novelist, short-story writer, and artist, uses the magic of surrealism to transmogrify the harsh realities of the world because she believes in the power of imaginative works to transform evil into good. In the four novels of the "Tetralogy of Elements," as Charlotte Innes observed in the *Nation* (June 6, 1994), Ducornet explores the different forms that the yearning for power—whether for good or evil—takes, combining deep seriousness with an "inspired silliness." In *Phosphor in Dreamland* (1995), Ducornet's fifth novel, she combined "the magic of García Márquez with the eroticism of Henry Miller," according to a *Library Journal* reviewer. Her short-story collection *The Word 'Desire'* was published in 1997; her novel *The Fan-Maker's Inquisition*, scheduled for publication in November 1999, concerns the Marquis de Sade.

Ducornet, born on April 19, 1943, considers the following excerpts from the afterword of her 1993 novel *The Jade Cabinet*, the last book of her tetralogy, to be the story of her apprenticeship as a writer: "I was infected with the venom of language in early childhood when, sitting in a room flooded with sunlight, I opened an alphabet book. B was a Brobdingnagian tiger-striped bumblebee, hovering over a crimson blossom, its stinger distinct. This image was of such potency that my entire face—eyes, nose and lips—was seized by a phantom stinging, and my ears by a hallucinatory buzzing. In this way, and in an instant, I was simultaneously initiated into the alphabet and awakened to Eden.

"In Eden, to see a thing Yahweh had dreamed and to say its name aloud was to bring it surging into the real. The letter B, so solid and threatening, was the embodiment of all its potencies. Looking at that letter, that blossom and that bee was like looking into a mirror from which the skin had been peeled away. The page afforded a passage—transcendental and yet altogether tangible.

"Much later I learned that for the Kabbalist, Beth is female and passive—a little house waiting to be prodded by the thrusting dart of letter A. Aleph, knowing that Beth will always be there, her door open in expectancy, boldly confronts the universe: O vigorous, confident, thrusting Aleph! (Now I know, too, just how erotic the image was—those engorged petals about to be ravished! Perhaps my sensuous life is here somehow reduced to its essential honey!)

"Just as once Persian wizards read a sacred text on the bodies of tigers, I had, from that morning, entered into an exulted state from which I was never to entirely recover, expecting, no, *demanding* enchantment each time I opened a book. That letter

B convinced me of what I think I already knew—that the world is a ceremonial dialogue to be actively engaged, and life's intention the searching out of the fertile passages and places, a fearless looking for the thorny A and B in everything.

"A wood stretched behind the house; it was a place of wild hives, seed rattles, lost feathers, quartz fragments (and occasional arrowheads), and the gods themselves materializing in variable forms: horned beetle, red deer, fox, owl, snake (this was copperhead country), death-head moth, hawk, hummingbird; stinkweed also, and a treacherous mud with a will of its own whose depth, in certain seasons, could not be determined. So many of the games I played there read now like rites of passage. I was very aware of danger—supernatural and actual; every time I penetrated into the wood I crossed a threshold from one cosmic dimension into another. . . .

"It was here that I confronted death for the first time—in the shape of a fox, its inert body animated by a swarm of bees. I stood transfixed beside that vortex and knew *transformation* defines and rules the world. And because I had in a room which now seemed worlds away, been myself changed forever by a letter in a book, I crouched and left a votive gift sublimely *transitional*, before moving on deeper into the world's wood—those gorgeous and terrifying images—like a necromantic alphabet of molten glass—pulsing behind my eyes. . . .

"Language is magic—transforming dead snakes into animate nature. When language fails, as when memory fails, all we can hope for is an airless cabinet reeking of badly preserved specimens!

". . . My childhood heroes were Leeuwenhoek and Lewis Carroll; my ambition, never realized, to paint the museum scenery behind walruses and saber-toothed tigers. Even now I long for my own poetic territory which would include a keeping garden for insects, an extensive zoological library (color plates intact!), a wonder room and a jade cabinet which would, ideally, contain a chimera of mutton-fat jade."

Rikki Ducornet was born in Canton, New York, to Gerard De Gre, a social philosopher who taught at Bard College, and Muriel De Gre, who ran an "enlightened" (her daughter's description) women's program on local radio and, later, television. Ducornet was raised at Bard College, which she also attended, majoring in fine arts with a minor in medieval studies. She told Maria Simson in an interview in *Publishers Weekly* (October 9, 1995) that although she had considered becoming a writer early on, she was discouraged by an encounter with a misguided and hypercritical teacher of creative writing and gave up writing for 10 years. She met Guy Ducornet, a French Fulbright scholar, at Bard. They were married (later divorced) and, during Rikki Ducornet's hiatus from college, moved to Algeria in a Peace Corps–like effort to redress the ravages France had inflicted on the country during

the war for independence. She turned her energies to drawing and printmaking, achieving success as an illustrator of her own, her husband's, her mother's, and others' books and exhibiting her work around the world in such places as the Museum of Fine Arts in Berlin and the National Museum of Fine Art in Mexico. She had an affinity for surrealism and was connected to a surrealist group called Phases.

After graduating from college in 1962, Ducornet spent most of the next 20 years living in France, with sojourns in Canada, South America, and North Africa. Her first book was *From the Star Chamber* (1974), a collection of poems. She told Simson that the book was "rooted in politics" and that it had grown out of her shock at reading about a woman who had been tortured in prison in Greece after a coup d'etat.

She was living in a village in France when she began *The Stain* (1974), the first novel in the Tetralogy of Elements and the one corresponding to Earth. Charlotte Innes, reviewing the tetralogy in the *Nation* (June 6, 1994), called *The Stain* "often brutal, heavy, earthbound," a book that "focuses on the human urge toward spirituality, from organized religion to superstition and black magic." The story, in part, centers on a young girl who is born after her mother is raped in a butcher's shop. She bears a birthmark, a stain in the shape of a hare, on her cheek. This character ultimately finds a kind of redemption in living in the woods and painting scenes of nature. Innes commented that *The Stain*, like all of Ducornet's work, is utterly serious but "sustained by an unlikely partner, inspired silliness—political activism hand in hand with a Disney-run-amok sensibility."

The other books in the tetralogy— *Entering Fire* (Fire; 1986), *The Fountains of Neptune* (Water; 1992), *The Jade Cabinet* (Air; 1993)— have different settings and characters. As Charlotte Innes noted, however, Ducornet's basic premise remains the same: "Each of her books can be read separately, but they also mirror and enrich one another, offering different aspects of the same overarching age-old theme—the capacity to do both good and evil. . . . For Ducornet, 'good' is a life-loving instinct and 'evil' is the destruction or abuse of all that lives or is created, be it a child, a race of people, a garden, or a book. To aim for power is human, she says, whether for 'good,' creative uses or 'evil,' greedy ends. We all contain the capacity, the yearning for both." Innes concluded that each volume in the tetralogy "explores the different forms this yearning takes."

The Complete Butcher's Tales (1994), containing previously published short stories and new tales, appeared after the tetralogy. The *American Book Review* (August/September 1994) critic termed the book "surrealism with a heart—tales that incorporate surrealistic imagery as a part of the emotional context of their characters as opposed to images that are gratuitously bizarre." The reviewer added, "One almost always feels an affinity with narrator or author, even when 'understanding' remains productively just out of reach."

James Sallis in the *New York Times Book Review* (October 29, 1995) termed *Phosphor in Dreamland*, Ducornet's fifth novel, a "work of distorting mirrors and trapdoors, some real, others apparent. . . . Neither floor nor ceiling, nor even sky, is constant. Over and over, the reader falls through one narrative surface onto another." The novel is partly an epistolary description of the imaginary island of Birdland, with a recounting of how its 17th-century poet Phosphor invents the "ocularscope," which like a camera captures images. The images are more verbal than visual and tend to shift kaleidoscopically. Referring also, perhaps, to her own intentions for her work, Ducornet wrote of Phosphor's attempt to capture his island, "His endeavor was greater than epic: It was encyclopedic!" He intends to "chronicle the premonitory signs of earthquakes, the force of waves, the height of tides, the soul of winds, the smell of medicinal springs" and "evoke caverns lucent of carbonate of lime, whirlpools and waterspouts, rainbows, meteors, mirages, and will-o'-the-wisps." Ever concerned with alchemy—transmutation—Ducornet has one character "cured" after a certain encounter with poetry: "Fogginius tottered and lurched about in the morning dew, arousing the many green apes drowsing in the treetops. Hurled into consciousness they responded by screeching, precipitating a million birds into the scarlet sky—those birds that in distant days before pesticides filled the woods with their hot, palpitating bodies, their voices like bells, the philosophical stones of their eggs."

Among the dozen tales in *The Word 'Desire'* are "The Foxed Mirror," about a priest in early 20th-century Mexico, who falls in love with an artist, and the title story, in which the central character has an unexpected reaction to her lover's desire for another woman. Discussing the latter story, Craig Seligman wrote in the *New York Times Book Review* (November 2, 1997) that the "high-toned archaism of [the story's] language suggests a translation that hasn't quite caught the life of the original. And this problem pervades the collection: for all their intelligence and daring, these tales of the erotic betray suspiciously respectable intentions." Seligman declared nevertheless that "the best [stories in the book] build to a moment of simple shock."

Ducornet has been politically active and concerned for the oppressed of the world all her life. A trip to Chiapas, Mexico after an uprising led by the man who called himself Subcomandante Marcos resulted in "On Returning from Chiapas: A Revery in Many Voices," published in the *Review of Contemporary Fiction* (Sprint 1996). Here she tried to evoke Eduardo Galeano, writing in short sections and using the example of Bishop Samel Ruíz García, who preaches liberation more than theology. Sprinkled with citations from Kafka, Noam Chomsky, Elena Poniatowska, Antonio Benitez-Rojo, Bartolomé de Las Casas, Ambar Past, Monica Mansour, the *Popul Vuh*, Kyra Galván, Galeano, Elsa Cross, and Elena Milán, Ducornet wove a tapestry of the pain and hope of the Mexican poor that might be considered a leftist echo of the T. S. Eliot poem *The Waste Land*.

Strange juxtapositions and startling images are not merely Ducornet's artistic stock-in-trade. She told Simson, "I have a visceral belief in the power of the imagination for aesthetic, political, and psychological change." She believes, she told Simson, that evil arises from inability to accept the "uncontrollable chaotic universe. . . . the incapacity to accept . . . that everything is in constant mutation, wanting to freeze it once and for all." For that reason, she never "freezes" her writing, constantly shifting the ground under the readers' feet and making it plain in her prose that she is a poet.

Rikki Ducornet received a Lannan Literary Fellowship for fiction in 1993. *The Jade Cabinet* was shortlisted for the National Book Critics Circle Award for 1994. She lives in Denver, Colorado, and teaches creative writing at the University of Denver.

—S. Y.

SUGGESTED READING: *American Book Review* p27 Aug./Sep. 1994; *Library Journal* p86 Aug. 1996; *Nation* p809 June 6, 1994; *New York Times Book Review* p30 Oct. 29, 1995; *Publishers Weekly* p66+ Oct. 9, 1995, with photo

SELECTED BOOKS: Fiction—*The Stain*, 1974; *The Butcher's Tales*, 1980; *Entering Fire*, 1986; *Haddock's Eyes*, 1987; *The Volatilized Ceiling of Baron Munodi*, 1991; *The Fountains of Neptune*, 1992; *Saida*, 1993; *The Jade Cabinet*, 1993; *The Complete Butcher's Tales*, 1994; *Phosphor in Dreamland*, 1995; *The World 'Desire'*, 1997; Poetry— *From the Star Chamber*, 1974; *Wild Geraniums*, 1975; *Weird Sisters*, 1976; *Knife's Notebook*, 1977; Juvenile—*The Blue Bird*, 1970; *Shazira Shazam and the Devil*, 1972

Duffy, Carol Ann

Dec. 23, 1955– Poet; playwright

The Scottish poet and playwright Carol Ann Duffy is the most renowned of the "New Generation" poets who have emerged in Britain in the last decade. Young, sardonic, and scathingly honest in their work, the New Generation has helped to spur a rise in the sale of poetry collections in Britain, where volumes of poetry have sold better on average in recent years than hardback novels. The BBC and Radio One have begun to carry live poetry readings, and poems appear on billboards and in advertisements all over Britain. Discussing the poet's role in society, Duffy said in an interview with *Bête Noire* (Winter 1988): "Poets don't have solutions, poets are recording human experience. If I'm moved by something, or intrigued, or interested, that's what I am going to write about. But don't ask me what to do."

Carol Ann Duffy was born in Glasgow, Scotland, on December 23, 1955, the daughter of Francis Duffy, an engineer, and the former Mary Black. Shortly after Duffy's birth, the family moved to Stafford, where she was raised. She grew up with four brothers in what she described in *Writers' Monthly* (October 1993) as a "left-wing, Catholic, working-class family." Both her father and her grandfather were extremely political men, Socialists by nature and Labour Party members by affiliation. Her father, in fact, ran—unsuccessfully—as the Labour Party parliamentary candidate in the 1983 general election. Though Duffy considers herself a Socialist, she stated in an interview with *Bête Noire*: "I'm not a member of a political party—I don't like joining things—I like being an outsider." She did, however, publish a poem, "Politico," in *Selling Manhattan* (1987), about her grandfather's imprisonment for political action during the Depression; in it she referred to socialism as "the tree that never grew" and "the bird that never flew."

Duffy was also deeply immersed in Catholicism as a child. In the *Bête Noire* interview, she described her family as "very Catholic: church every Sunday, Communion every week. I could have gone to mass every day at school"—St. Joseph's Convent, which was run by Irish nuns. There was little teaching in the convent past the basics of English, French, Latin, religion, and music. Little importance was placed on subjects such as physics, chemistry, and mathematics. Duffy revealed in her interview: "We had elocution lessons. . . . It was a very old-fashioned school: I think they wanted to turn us into gentlewomen."

Duffy was anything but an old-fashioned gentlewoman. At 16, while she was attending Stafford Girls' High School, she began a 10-year live-in relationship with a man. At about that same time, she decided what she wanted to do with her life: she wanted to become a poet. Two years later she enrolled at Liverpool University to study philosophy and graduated with honors in 1977. While at Liverpool, she was encouraged by an English teacher to publish her poems. Her book *Fleshweathercock* (1974) was published by Outposts, an established publisher of new poets. She has since declined to discuss that work publicly.

After graduation she made her living as a playwright, although she had no particular passion for theater. As she explained to Andrew McAllister of *Bête Noire*: "I have no interest in plays. . . . I mean that was fun, and it was money." She stayed in Liverpool to write her first two plays: *Take My Husband*, a two-act work first performed at the Liverpool Playhouse on December 4, 1982, and *Cavern of Dreams*, also in two acts, staged at the Liverpool Playhouse on August 3, 1984. She also produced revue sketches for her friend, the actor Margi Clark.

Her association with Clark enabled her to get freelance work as a scriptwriter for Granada Television. The television work was steady and helped to pay her bills while she worked on her poetry. She produced two more plays in 1986—*Loss*, a one-act work written for BBC Radio, and *Little Women, Big Boys*, first produced at the Almeida Theatre in London. Meanwhile, attempting to make a name for herself as a poet, she attended workshops, entered competitions, submitted work to literary magazines, and gave readings. Only when she had a full collection of poems with a unifying theme did she go to publishers, using a friend as an agent.

Her poetry collection *Fifth Last Song* (1982) appeared around the time her first play was produced at the Liverpool Playhouse. *Standing Female Nude* (1985) was her first poetry collection put out by Anvil Press, her longtime publisher. She explained to *Writers' Monthly* her reasons for staying with Anvil: "They've got qualities you perhaps don't get in the big publishers. They're personal and consult you about the typeface, the paper, and the cover. I have a very good relationship with the editor there." *Standing Female Nude* was praised by critics for its uncompromising honesty. A writer for *Poetry Review* (March 1986) remarked: "Unconsolatory, tough-minded, and bleak, these poems of Carol Ann Duffy's offer nothing to flatter or to charm the reader—especially the male reader."

Though she realizes that most critics label her as a feminist poet, Duffy dislikes the division between male and female poets. She also disagrees with the notion that her poetry consists chiefly of "male bashing." As the poet, who is a lesbian, told *Writers' Monthly*: "I love men—I've four brothers—but just because individual men are very important in my life, it doesn't mean that I can't see the kind of violence that goes on every day."

Duffy's collection *Selling Manhattan*, published in 1987, is widely thought to contain some of her best work and characterizations. David Tresilian, writing for *Isis* (February 7, 1988), noted that the poet "takes the world outside as her subject, and thinks her way into it. Her poems record fragments of speech: 'Girls Talking,' 'The Brink of Shrieks,' but are not simply reportage. Her figures live because their language does, and in her hands the dramatic monologue takes on the role of reporter and interpreter of living society."

The Other Country, her next volume of poetry, was published in 1990. A critic for *Poetry Review* (Volume 80, Number 3, 1990), Dennis O'Driscoll, noted: "What [Duffy] has done is to delve deeper—out of earshot of both criticism and praise—into the rich seams which she has worked from the start and which are far from exhausted: home, love, money, time, and especially, language." Later in his article he remarked: "Duffy's recent work instills . . . faith and enthusiasm in her readers—a faith that contains the hope of even better things to come." Duffy's next project was the editing of a book of poetry for young feminists, *I Wouldn't*

Thank You for a Valentine (1993). The collection contains the work of such authors as Felice Holman, Nikki Giovanni, Alice Walker, and others from diverse backgrounds and cultures. The anthology's intended readership is girls in grades six through 12, though the poems can also be enjoyed by women of all ages. Critics singled out both Duffy and the anthology for praise.

Mean Time, her next volume of poems, was also published in 1993. The collection's theme took Duffy back to the 1960s, and her school days in Stafford. The *Guardian* (July 27, 1993), in its review, noted: "Duffy has resisted the temptations: *Mean Time*, her latest volume of poems, demonstrates that maturity in a successful writer means having the patience to work on strengths, the character to excise what seems factitious, and the nerve to be true to instinct. *Mean Time* is Duffy's best book yet: beautifully written, adult in its attitudes, no-nonsense yet sensitive." In discussing what inspired the collection, Duffy told *Writers' Monthly*: "I don't think children are nice at all. I don't remember being nice and I don't remember other children being nice. I want to write more about childhood because I haven't gone into it deeply enough. The kind of otherness and callousness of childhood, I'd like to explore."

For her next project, Duffy wrote *Grimm Tales*, stage adaptations of *Grimms' Fairy Tales*, with all their gruesome violence left intact. The work was staged in 1994 under the direction of Tim Supple. The author and director, according to the *Times Literary Supplement* (January 6, 1995) "made a virtue of the Grimms' particular flavor, going for the gore in robust comic defiance of grown-up pieties and current panic about the effects of representing violence."

Even as she returned to the stage, Duffy has continued to work in her first calling, poetry. In 1994 Penguin released her *Selected Poems*. Most recently she edited a poetry anthology called, *Stopping for Death* (1996). The title, an allusion to a poem by Emily Dickinson, suggests the book's theme of meditations on death. *School Library Journal* (August 1996) noted: "Duffy's anthology addresses an often-avoided subject in a conscientious way, and readers will gain from it a healthy understanding of the ways to deal with and move on from loss."

Carol Ann Duffy has received numerous honors for her work, including: First Prize in the National Poetry Competition in 1983, the 1985 and 1990 Scottish Arts Council Book Awards of Merit for *Standing Female Nude* and *The Other Country*, respectively, the 1988 Somerset Maugham Award, the 1989 Dylan Thomas Award, the 1993 Whitbread and Forward Prizes for *Mean Time*, and the 1995 Lannan Literary Award for poetry.

Carol Ann Duffy resides in Manchester with her daughter. *The Pamphlet*, her latest book, is due to be published in 1999.—C.M.

SUGGESTED READING: *Bête Noire* p69+ Winter 1988; *Guardian* p9 July 27, 1993; *Isis* p21 Feb. 7, 1988; *Poetry Review* p58 Mar. 1986, p65 vol. 80 no. 3 1990; *School Library Journal* p168 Aug. 1996; *Times Literary Supplement* p17 Jan. 6, 1995; *Writers' Monthly* p4+ Oct. 1993; *Who's Who 1997*

SELECTED BOOKS: Poetry—*Fleshweathercock*, 1974; *Fifth Last Song*, 1982; *Standing Female Nude*, 1985; *Thrown Voices*, 1986; *Selling Manhattan*, 1987; *The Other Country*, 1990; *Mean Time*, 1993; *Selected Poems*, 1994, *The Pamphlet*, 1999; Drama—*Take My Husband*, 1982; *Cavern of Dreams*, 1984; *Loss*, 1986; *Little Women, Big Boys*, 1986; *Grimm Tales*, 1994; As editor—*I Wouldn't Thank You for a Valentine*, 1993; *Stopping for Death*, 1996

Duong Thu Huong

1947(?)– Novelist

Although the works of dissident Vietnamese author Duong Thu Huong must circulate surreptitiously in her native country—its government sanctions neither the publication of her new works nor the reprinting of old ones—she exerts a significant influence over opinion there, where her books are considered "among the most beloved works in modern Vietnamese literature," according to the *New York Times* (April 12, 1994). She had come from a family of staunch supporters of Ho Chi Minh's revolutionary movements and spent years during the Vietnam War as a volunteer in a morale-building theatrical troupe, but she and the Communist Party came to a parting of the ways in 1989, and she was jailed for seven months for attempting to smuggle her writings out of the country. Two of her five novels have been translated into English and published in the United States: *Paradise of the Blind* (U.S., 1993) and *Novel Without A Name* (U.S., 1995), giving American readers a look at the Vietnam War and its aftermath from the "other side's" point of view. Her work also appears in the short-story anthology by Seven Stories Press, *Night, Again: Contemporary Fiction from Vietnam* (1996).

Duong Thu Huong was born in about 1947 in the People's Democratic Republic of Vietnam (then also known as North Vietnam), the daughter of one of Ho Chi Minh's guerrilla disciples. At the age of 20, during the "War Against the Americans," she saw combat as a member of a volunteer theatrical troupe, emerging at war's end as one of only three survivors in her group of 40. "We were responsible for arranging performances to entertain the soldiers and the people who lived in bombed-out areas—to enhance morale," she told Philip Shenon of the *New York Times* (April 12, 1994). "Our job was to make our voices loud enough to drown out the sound of the bombs." During the 1980s she wrote several novels, which helped establish Huong as one of the most prominent literary voices in postwar Vietnam. (Following correct and polite Vietnamese usage, this biographical sketch refers to the author as "Huong" even though the article is alphabetized under "D" for Duong, her family name.)

In 1990 Huong left the Communist Party. Author and authorities still dispute the facts surrounding this breach: Huong claims she was expelled from the party while officials reportedly have said that she left voluntarily. In April 1991, she was arrested and put in a windowless cell for seven months for trying to smuggle "reactionary documents"—her own writings—out of the country. Three years later, she told Shenon, who interviewed her in Hanoi: "I was taken outside of Hanoi to a compound where I was held in a tiny room. They wanted to know if I had communications with anybody who was dangerous—foreigners or overseas Vietnamese. It is all a pretext to harass me, to frighten me." Huong says she was not mistreated but that she lost 35 pounds during the ordeal. She believes that far-away geopolitical events had a meliorative impact on her prison stay by dissuading her captors from taking a hard, dogmatic line while the Soviet empire was unraveling thousands of miles away. Although her novels have a strong following in Vietnam, her works must circulate clandestinely: state publishing houses there will not publish any new works or reprint her old ones. Shenon reported visiting a frightened bookseller along Trang Tien Street in Hanoi who whispered to him, "We all love her novels. But we cannot have them on our shelves." Her novels *Paradise of the Blind* and *Novel Without a Name* expand the experience of the war beyond partisan prisms, showing American readers in particular that disillusion and dashed idealism were rampant on both sides of the conflict.

In all of Huong's works, she says, "my writing is based on what I see in life. I sometimes see terrible things." This is a reference to the corruption and violence of Communist Party functionaries in Vietnam. These issues dominated her first novel, *Paradise of the Blind*, which Huong wrote in response to a government call to bolster traditional values by encouraging new authors. The book went into several printings and reportedly sold 40,000 copies before it was banned. Published in English by William Morrow in 1993 and billed as "the first Vietnamese novel ever published in the United States," *Paradise of the Blind* was set in the Vietnam and Russia of the 1980s, with little mention of the war that had ravaged Vietnam some two decades earlier. The novel focuses on the experiences of a young woman named Hang, who, with her mother and aunt, struggle to rebuild their lives in a Hanoi slum after their lives have been disrupted by land-reform policies implemented by her uncle Chinh, a Communist bureaucrat unmoved by even

the suffering of his own family. Hang, caught between her mother's subservience and her aunt's bitterness, is eventually forced to support her disabled mother by working in a Russian factory, where she eventually comes into her own, declaring, "I can't squander my life tending these faded flowers, the legacy of past crimes." The novel is unsparing in its negative portrayal of venal party officials, notably Chinh, whose character is based on a prominent real-life union official in Hanoi. As Huong explained: "When I wrote this book, I knew it would cause me trouble. I didn't care about the trouble because I knew I was telling the truth." Shenon added that the novel "offers a vision of Vietnam years after the guns have fallen silent—a nation of haunting beauty, still cursed by poverty but proud of its hard-won independence and rich culture. In this Vietnam, the enemy is not the American military. Miss [H]uong's villains are the Government factotums who betray the revolution that put them in place." Reviewing *Paradise of the Blind* for the *New York Times* (May 19, 1993), Herbert Mitgang wrote that the book provides a "special experience for American readers in that it humanizes a Vietnamese family and turns its members into individuals instead of lumping them together as the once faceless enemy." A writer for *Kirkus Reviews* (January 1, 1993) concluded that the book was "slight, but enriched by vivid characters and telling descriptions of life as it really was in a place of mythic resonances in our own history. A welcome debut."

Set in the 1980s, *Novel Without a Name* has for its narrator a 28-year-old war veteran named Quan, who some 10 years earlier had gone into battle with idealism, only to become disillusioned, as had many of his American counterparts. "Vietnam had been chosen by History," he had once chortled. "After the war, our country would become humanity's paradise." By shifting the narrative back and forth among the contemporary present, the war years, and Quan's childhood, Huong reveals the way in which the optimism of the early revolution and anti-imperialist struggle decayed into combat and corruption. She records, for example, a conversation Quan overhears, in which two Communist officials offer a cynical reappraisal of their society. Describing Marx as the "debauched little dwarf" who had once commanded their allegiance, they grumble: "We demolished the temples and emptied the pagodas so we could hang up portraits of Marx, a new divinity for the masses." And another official admits the hollowness of the ideology that resulted in so many casualties by remarking: "Words are like everything else in life. They're born, they live, they age, they die."

Michiko Kakutani of the *New York Times* (May 30, 1995) faulted the novel for Huong's one-dimensional portraits of minor characters, writing that the book thus "verges on stereotype or caricature, a problem that is not helped by the fact that the language, at least as translated by Phan Huy Duong and Nina McPherson, often feels stilted and cliché." To Katherine Harrison, reviewing the book for the on-line publication *The Reader* (Spring 1995), the language was hardly stilted, but full of "baroque descriptions of rotting flesh and bad food, layering image upon image and interspersing dreams and memory amidst the relentless action of the war. . ." Despite her reservations, Kakutani compared the book's theme to those of other fictional works on the inevitable disillusionment of war, writing: "Not only does *Novel Without a Name* turn the conventional Bildungsroman into a tale of disillusionment, like such American works as Rob Riggan's *Free Fire Zone* and Stephen Wright's *Meditations in Green*, but it also uses a disjointed time sequence, reminiscent of works like Nicholas Proffitt's *Gardens of Stone*, to try to convey the war's disorienting, surreal effect." And Lawrence Klepp wrote in *Newsday* (April 9, 1995) that, along with Bao Ninh's *The Sorrow of War*, Huong's *Novel Without a Name*, by "giving us the battles from the perspective of participants rather than historians . . . help[s] to undermine the politicians' ideological rhetoric that justified the war, and that is a small victory in what otherwise was a defeat for both sides." Even the landscapes Huong evoked have an instructional value, as Nicci Gerrard pointed out in the British newspaper the *Observer* (January 21, 1996): "This is not the Americanised version of Vietnam with poisonous green jungles and skies full of bombs: it is also a country of green fields, pale moons, tea gardens, mist on bright water."

In 1994 Huong was awarded the Order of Arts and Letters by the French government; Culture Minister Jacques Toubon told her at the ceremony: "You are both a dissident and a first-class writer, and you have managed to embody the extraordinary role of Vietnamese women in their fight for liberty and independence." In response, the Vietnamese newspaper *Quan Doi Nhan Dan* (*People's Army*) quoted Vu Tu Nam, secretary-general of the government-backed Vietnamese Writers Association, as saying that the award was a "deplorable action" and "a political move the culture minister of a nation like France should not have made. The fact that he praised her courage is nothing other than to hail her political dissent." Phan Huy Duong, Huong's Vietnamese-to-French translator, commented in the on-line magazine *Eurasie* (September 14, 1998) that Huong is the only Vietnamese writer who has seen her body of work translated into French. He added that Duong Thu Huong's reputation rests on her having been an advocate of democracy and liberty while maintaining her "extraordinary talent as a story-teller." With her novel *Paradise of the Blind* (translated into French as *Les paradis aveugles*) she became, in his words, "the first writer to have the courage to treat the themes of agrarian reform and the demotion of the status of the intellectual under the constraints of Communist power."

Duong Thu Huong lives in Hanoi with her two sons.
—E. M.

SUGGESTED READING: *Eurasie* (on-line) Sep. 14, 1998; *Newsday* p37 Apr. 9, 1995, with photo; *New York Times* C p19 May 19, 1993, A p4 Apr. 12, 1994, with photo, C p15 May 30, 1995, with photo; *Observer* p15 Jan. 21, 1996; *Reader* (on-line) Spring 1995; *Wall Street Journal* A p12 Mar. 22, 1993

SELECTED BOOKS IN ENGLISH TRANSLATION: *Paradise of the Blind*, 1987, 1993; *Novel Without a Name*, 1989, 1995

Dworkin, Andrea

Sep. 26, 1946– Nonfiction writer; political activist

"I have never wanted to be less than a great writer," the feminist Andrea Dworkin has declared, "and I have never been afraid of failing, the reason being that I would rather fail at that than succeed at anything else." Dworkin is the author of eight nonfiction books, two novels, and a collection of short stories, as well as numerous essays on the history, causes, methods, and sexual nature of female subordination. She became widely known in feminist circles when her first book, *Woman Hating*, was published in 1974. Her views on the intractability of male dominance have often met with vehement resistance but have prompted vigorous and thoughtful debate as well. Perhaps her most controversial stance has been that pornography hurts women—a conviction that has led to her crusading work with the lawyer Catharine A. MacKinnon to have pornography classified as a form of sex discrimination. Dismissed as "MacDworkinites' pornocentrism" by Nadine Strossen of the American Civil Liberties Union (ACLU), their philosophy has caused yet another fissure in the increasingly splintered women's movement, creating odd alliances between anticensorship feminists and pornographers, on the one hand, and between antipornography feminists and religious moralists, on the other. Derided as a diversion of energy to a marginal cause by such feminist leaders as Betty Friedan, the antipornography activity attracted young women to a movement that had been prematurely declared dead; in so doing, the issue seemed to indicate that grass-roots feminism and its take-to-the-streets anger was still alive.

Dworkin's political activism has incurred the wrath of publishers, some of whom, she has claimed, were already reluctant to publish her works due to their content alone. After *Woman Hating*, her major nonfiction works have included *Pornography: Men Possessing Women* (1981), *Right-Wing Women* (1983), *Intercourse* (1987), *Letters from a War Zone* (1988), (with C. MacKinnon) *Pornography and Civil Rights: A New Day for Women's Equality* (1988), and *Life After Death:*

Unapologetic Writings on the Continuing War Against Women (1996). A rousing public speaker, Dworkin is "a political firebrand, . . . a street fighter and an unswervingly radical feminist," in the opinion of Lore Dickstein, who wrote of her in the *New York Times* (October 29, 1989), "Revolutions need people like her, women willing to draw fire on the front lines and the barricades." The Andrea Dworkin Web Site prominently features a quote from the renowned feminist Gloria Steinem: "In every century, there are a handful of writers who help the human race to evolve. Andrea is one of them."

Andrea Dworkin was born on September 26, 1946 in Camden, New Jersey, the daughter of Harry Dworkin, a guidance counselor, and Sylvia (Spiegel) Dworkin, a secretary, both of whom were left-leaning activists on behalf of civil rights and workers' struggles, as well as women's issues. In *Letters from a War Zone: Writings 1976–1987* (1988), Dworkin revealed how her views about gender relations were shaped in part by her Jewish heritage: "Being a Jew, one learns to believe in the reality of cruelty and one learns to recognize indifference to human suffering as a fact." Describing close relatives who were Holocaust survivors, Dworkin told Michael Moorcock in an interview for *New Statesman & Society* (April 21, 1995): "I grew up taking hate and extermination seriously. I read all the time, as much as I could," including Che Guevara's *Guerilla Warfare*, which had somehow escaped a censorship purge at her high-school library. "I read it a million times," she said. "I'd plan attacks on the local shopping mall. I got a lot of practice for strategizing real rebellion. It may be why I refuse to think that the rebellion against the oppressors of women should be less real, less material, less serious."

Dworkin became politically active at an early age. She refused to sing Christmas carols in elementary school, bearing the brunt of official punishment as well as anti-Semitic graffiti by her classmates. By the time she was in the sixth grade, she had already decided to be either a writer or a lawyer, with a goal of changing restrictive abortion laws. At the age of eighteen, Dworkin was arrested at an antiwar demonstration in New York City. While incarcerated for four days at the Women's House of Detention, she was subjected to a body-cavity search that left her bleeding for two weeks. Her indignant protests against the humiliating treatment she received in prison were covered by New York newspapers and television crews, as Carole Rosenthal recalled in *Ms.* (February 1977): "Dworkin's public inquiry, her outrage, shocked me. It called attention to something secret and squeamish, but something . . . so obvious I wondered why I'd never thought of it before." As Dworkin told Moorcock, "I understood apartheid. I knew prisons were bad and cruel, but I didn't understand why the male doctors in the Women's House of Detention essentially sexually assaulted me, or even that they did. I knew they ripped up

my vagina with a steel instrument and told dirty jokes about women while they did it. I knew they enjoyed causing me purposeful pain. But there was no public, political conception of rape or sexual assault. Rape rose to being a political issue only when it involved false accusations made by white women against black men."

While attending Bennington College, in Vermont, from which she received a B.A. degree in 1968, Dworkin took a leave of absence to spend some time in Greece. Following her college graduation, she lived for five years in the Netherlands, where she survived an abusive marriage to a Dutch man who battered her even after she'd left him, around 1971. "I was battered—genuinely tortured—when I was married," she later recalled to Moorcock, "but I thought I was the only woman in the world this had ever happened to. I had no political understanding that I was being beaten because I was a woman, or that this man thought I belonged to him, inside out." It was in Europe that her talent for writing blossomed. In an interview with the writer Erica Jong for *Ms.* (June 1988), Dworkin said that she began writing in Europe because she felt Americans do not respect writers or activists the way Europeans do. "For me also, though, it was that I was enraged with this country's policies on Vietnam," she added, "[and] the racism here was deeply distressing to me."

Upon her return to the United States in the early 1970s, Dworkin tried to make a living as a writer but refused to take public-relations or other mundane yet well-paying freelance assignments. "I was too naïve to know that hack writing is the only paying game in town," she wrote in 1981. "I prostituted on the streets for several years," she told Moorcock in 1993. "I had no political understanding of that, nor even of my own homelessness or poverty." Supporting herself as a waitress, teacher, receptionist, salesperson, and factory worker, among other occupations, she eventually landed a position as an assistant to the poet Muriel Rukeyser. "I was the worst assistant in the history of the world," Dworkin recalled in *Letters from a War Zone*. "But Muriel kept me on because she believed in me as a writer . . . She had made great sacrifices in her life for both politics and writing, but none, I suspect, had quite the comic quality of her insistent support for me. Out of mercy (and guilt), I eventually quit."

While she was still working for Rukeyser, Dworkin's first book, *Woman Hating*, was published, in 1974. "I thought that was it," Dworkin wrote in *Letters*. "I was a writer (sort of like being an archangel) forever. . . . I had been through a lot in life, but in writing I was an innocent, a kind of ecstatic idiot. For me, writing was pure, magic, the essence of integrity and power, uncorrupted by anything mean or mundane." In *Woman Hating*, whose stated purpose was "to destroy patriarchal power at its source, the family, [and] in its most hideous form, the nation-state, . . . to destroy the structure of culture as we know it," Dworkin demonstrated the ways in which men have subjugated women through such practices as foot-binding in China, witch-hunting in Europe and colonial America, and the propagation of sex-role mythology both in fairy tales and in pornography. In fairy tales, for instance, female passivity is routinely rewarded while female assertiveness is seen as evil and punishable. Arguing that not only sex roles but gender identity must be eradicated before true sexual equality can be achieved, Dworkin struck a raw nerve with many critics. Reviewing the book for *Library Journal* (June 1, 1974), Ellen Gay Detlefsen declared, "It's harsh, it's argumentative . . . and it's not for the uninitiated." Jeanne Kinney, who called the book "an energetic effort to find out the truth about women's sexuality," wrote in her review for *Best Sellers* (July 1, 1974), "While much of the material repulsed me, it also awakened me to Woman as Victim in ways I never knew existed."

Dworkin's debut as a major figure in the women's movement was marked not only by the publication of her first book but by her first major speech, also in 1974, to more than one thousand women at the National Organization for Women Conference on Sexuality, in New York City. She received a standing ovation. "Women were crying and shaking and shouting," she recalled in *Letters*. "It was one of the most astonishing experiences of my life." To Dworkin's intense annoyance, however, the scant media attention accorded her speech singled out for criticism the one statement she had made that specifically focused on men.

In 1976 Dworkin published a collection of her essays and speeches entitled *Our Blood: Prophecies and Discourses on Sexual Politics*. Heralding Dworkin as "one of the most compelling voices in the women's movement," Carole Rosenthal asserted in her *Ms.* (February 1977) review, "Her gift to readers of *Our Blood* . . . is to make radical ideas seem clear and obvious again. . . . However strongly a reader agrees or takes issue with the essays in this book, Dworkin will never be found dull or dishonest or glib. She is a genuine visionary—bold, thoughtful, willing to take risks." Carol Rumens, writing in the *London Observer* (May 16, 1982), found the essays to be well-written, and noted that "controlled anger does wonders for the prose-style, as many a great speech or sermon can testify." Deploring Dworkin's advocacy of censorship, however, Rumens accused her of possessing "an appalling historical naïveté."

Dworkin's next major work, *Pornography: Men Possessing Women*, was published in 1981, following by a year the appearance of the anthology *Take Back the Night: Women on Pornography*, to which Dworkin contributed, and her own short-story collection, *The New Woman's Broken Heart*. The result of extensive research, including an eight-month stint immersed in the works of the Marquis de Sade—an endeavor that gave her nightmares and nausea and made her feel intensely isolated—*Pornography* seemed to drain Dworkin of any residual optimism she may have had about relations between the sexes. In a speech (included in *Letters*) for a Take Back the Night rally (so-called after women's determination to reclaim the night from rapists), Dworkin maintained, "The fact is that the process of killing . . . is the prime sexual act for men in reality and/or in imagination. . . . Pornography exists because men despise women, and men despise women in part because pornography exists." Elaborating on those ideas in *Pornography*, Dworkin argued that the eroticization of violence in much of pornography incites men to violence against women in real life.

After being out of print for several years, *Pornography* was reissued in 1989 with a new introduction by the author. "Dworkin's style is intense, vivid, and eloquent, infused with a sense of urgency," a reviewer noted in *Publishers Weekly* (September 22, 1989). In his assessment of the first edition for the British periodical *Punch* (February 10, 1982), Stanley Reynolds compared Dworkin to "a Leon Trotsky of the sex war. . . . She is full of power and energy. She writes—dare I say it?—with an aggressive manner, like a man. Except that no men write with such utter conviction these days." In contrast, Sally O'Driscoll, writing in the *Village Voice* (July 15–21, 1981), called Dworkin's rhetoric "simple-minded." "Antipornographers like Dworkin are exploiting women's sexual guilt," O'Driscoll wrote, "not for the purpose of liberating them but to proselytize for their own idea of the 'right' view of female sexuality." Countering that view in an interview with Lynn Rosen for *New Directions for Women* (July/August 1987), Dworkin said, "I don't think commitment [to feminism] means you are accountable in your private life to the women's movement. I think it does mean a recognition that what happens to you in private doesn't just happen to you, that it happens probably to vast numbers of women, that it happens to you because you're a woman, and that what feminism requires from every individual involved is a commitment to be willing to ask the painful questions. I don't think it means adherence to a set of answers."

Since the early 1980s Dworkin has worked closely with Catharine A. MacKinnon, a lawyer and a law professor at the University of Michigan, in campaigning for and drafting legislation that categorizes pornography as a form of sex discrimination, thus allowing civil suits against those who make, sell, or exhibit it. The bill defines pornography as "the graphic, sexually explicit subordination of women through pictures or words." A plaintiff can sue not only for injury from a specific piece of pornography but for injury caused by the atmosphere of discrimination and abuse engendered by pornography. The issue has polarized feminists, many of whom are concerned that the bill threatens free speech and/or, as the group Feminists for Free Expression has argued, "reinforces the 'porn made me do it' excuse for rapists and batterers." Ordinances based on the bill were adopted in Indianapolis, Minneapolis, Los Angeles, and

Bellingham, Washington, but all were either vetoed or defeated in the courts. As co-authors of *Pornography and Civil Rights: A New Day for Women's Equality* (1988), Dworkin and MacKinnon teamed up with advocates of restrictions on "hate speech" in an attempt to broaden their base. Dworkin and MacKinnon's crusade brought a sharp rebuke from Nadine Strossen, president of the ACLU, in her own book *Defending Pornography: Free Speech, Sex, and the Fight for Women's Rights* (1995). Railing against what she called the intimidatory style of "the MacDworkinites' pornocentrism," Strossen argued in favor of free expression and against the distrust of sexuality that she saw as a common denominator of both religious fundamentalism and the ideas of Dworkin and MacKinnon. When asked by Moorcock about her own position on "free speech," Dworkin countered that "women and people of color, especially African-Americans, have been excluded from any rights of speech for most of our history. In the U.S. it costs money to have access to the means of speech. The First Amendment was designed to protect white, land-owning men from the power of the state. This was followed by the Second Amendment, which says, 'and we have guns.' Women and most blacks were chattel, without any speech rights of any kind. So the First Amendment protects the speech rights of Thomas Jefferson, but has Sally Hemmings ever said a word anybody knows about? My own experience is that speech is not free; it costs a lot."

The antipornography movement's sole legal victory has been judicial rather than legislative and, ironically, proved to be a source of disagreement between Dworkin and MacKinnon. In 1992 the Supreme Court of Canada—a nation that did not even have a counterpart to the American Bill of Rights until 1982—altered its obscenity law in *R. v. Butler* to reflect the idea that pornography harms women. "If true equality between male and female persons is to be achieved, we cannot ignore the threat to equality resulting from exposure to audiences of certain types of violent and degrading material," Justice John Sopinka wrote in his decision. "Materials portraying women as a class as objects for sexual exploitation and abuse have a negative impact on the 'individuals' sense of self-worth and acceptance.'" Although the Court's opinion was based on a brief filed by the Women's Legal Education and Action Fund and drafted with MacKinnon's help, Dworkin asked Canadian feminists not to support the new law. "We agree on a lot of things," Dworkin said of herself and MacKinnon in an interview with Jeffrey Toobin for the *New Yorker* (October 3, 1994), "but not this time. My position on obscenity law is unequivocal. Obscenity law is a total dead end in dealing with the pornography industry. . . . [*Butler*] will be used to create a formula for a kind of pornography that the police will accept. I don't think it's going to help deal with the rights of women."

Other books by Dworkin critiqued the economic and cultural constraints that she felt came along with being a woman in contemporary America. In *Right-Wing Women* (1983), which was expanded from an article she had written for *Ms.* in 1979, Dworkin tried to answer one of the most perplexing questions of the Ronald Reagan era: why were women flocking to the Republican party, which was explicitly opposed to the Equal Rights Amendment, equal pay for comparable work, family leave, day care, and other issues that would purportedly enhance women's civil status and economic equality with men. The right wing, according to Dworkin, promised to protect women from male violence, through "form, shelter, safety, rules, and love," if women are obedient and subservient. The left wing, Dworkin asserted, had nothing better to offer women; its leadership, too, was male-dominated and had consistently ignored or worked against equal rights for women. Reviewing *Right-Wing Women* for the *New Republic* (February 21, 1983), the novelist Anne Tyler wrote, "Its language is florid—often beautiful, as a matter of fact, very like a sort of martial poetry, but it's far too emotionally charged for a political analysis." Tyler conceded, however, that "there is plenty to think about in this book. Much of it is intelligent, original, deeply felt."

Whereas *Right-Wing Women* proved to be one of Dworkin's least controversial works, her next book, *Intercourse* (1987), went beyond anything she had yet written in the depth of its analysis of the roots of misogyny. Consequently, it was reviled by some and greeted with enthusiasm by others. Describing intercourse as "the pure, sterile, formal expression of men's contempt for women," Dworkin wrote that "the woman in intercourse is a space inhabited, a literal territory occupied literally; occupied even if there has been no resistance, no force." Erica Jong found the book "thrilling in a way [she] had not found a book about men and women thrilling since *The Second Sex* by Simone de Beauvoir or *The Female Eunuch* by Germaine Greer." For her part, Greer called *Intercourse* "the most shocking book any feminist has yet written." Joanne Glasgow, in a review for *New Directions for Women* (September/October 1987), wrote that *Intercourse* was "a work of imaginative power" and "the most important critique of male/female bonds since Adrienne Rich's *Of Woman Born* [in 1976]."

Many critics assailed the theories in *Intercourse* unsparingly, often employing ad hominem attacks in their scathing assessments. Roy Porter, writing in the *London Review of Books* (June 25, 1987), dismissed the work as a "torrent of filthy abuse . . . against sex and men." "To present women as nothing other than powerless victims," he said, "is a historico-sociological nonsense which profoundly degrades women." Carol Sternhell noted angrily in the *New York Times* (May 3, 1987), "I'm a feminist too—that's why this nonsense disturbs me so much. It's easy to mock a book like *Intercourse*, but I take Ms. Dworkin seriously. In some of her earlier work, . . . she brilliantly deconstructed the culture of misogyny." Sara Maitland wrote in *New Statesman* (June 26, 1987), "Sucked into a prose style which has itself many of the rhythms, surgings and poundings of the literature of sex, it is hard to surface long enough to focus on what this book is trying to say." Many critics, for instance, wondered how Dworkin could reconcile the role of pleasure and desire to a purportedly ideal sexuality in which intercourse would no longer be paramount. "I haven't questioned that intercourse is pleasurable," Dworkin explained in her interview with Lynn Rosen. "What I have questioned is that intercourse is freedom. The conclusion that I came to is that pleasure and freedom are not synonyms."

Dworkin has written two semiautobiographical novels—*Ice and Fire*, which was published in Britain in 1986 and in the United States a year later, and *Mercy* (1990; 1991). Although the female protagonists in both novels are struggling writers who suffer violent sexual abuse, Dworkin has insisted she is not the person in her novels. "If I were writing about myself," she told Rosen, "I wouldn't want you to see all the things that I showed you about this character that I've created. Some things are not so wonderful about her—failures of loyalty and courage, tremendous selfishness and greed. I wouldn't write about myself that way even if it were all true." Indeed, her protagonists often say things that are at odds with Dworkin's politics. The narrator in *Mercy*, for example, asserts that "prostitution is only an apparent oppression that permits some women to be sexually active without bourgeois restraints."

The recurring theme in *Ice and Fire* is "coitus is the punishment for being a woman." Dworkin intended to "create a frame in which people can see exactly what sexual exploitation is and what it costs," as she told an interviewer for *Publishers Weekly* (September 26, 1986). Carol Sternhell found the novel to be "unremittingly depressing," and Maureen Freely, writing in the London *Observer* (April 27, 1986), called the book an effort "to elevate the temper tantrum to an art form." Others charged Dworkin with creating the pornography she deplores. "The reason [*Ice and Fire*] isn't pornographic simply has to do with my skill as a writer," Dworkin told an interviewer for the *Women's Review of Books* (May 1986). "Pure and simple. It has to do with the fact that the kind of prose that I've written has so much control and is, I hope, so masterful in what it shows that what you come away with understanding is the reality of the degradation and what it means. It doesn't do it to you; it allows you to understand something that maybe you have never understood before."

Mercy begins with the protagonist, named Andrea, being sexually molested as a child; by the novel's end, she is a homeless alcoholic who murders men sleeping on the streets of New York City and fire-bombs pornography shops. Wendy Steiner, in an evaluation for the *New York Times* (September 15, 1991), wrote that the book's "language

is lyrical and passionate—a cross between the repetition of the early Gertrude Stein and, ironically, the unfettered flights of Henry Miller. . . . The ambition, the verbal brilliance, in this 'shocking aesthetic' are profoundly affecting." Steiner noted, however, that Dworkin's argument "is also intolerant, simplistic and often just as brutal as what it protests. Ms. Dworkin advocates nothing short of killing men. . . . She is completely ruthless with women who do not share her point of view."

Published in 1996 by The Free Press, Dworkin's *Life and Death: Unapologetic Writings on the Continuing War Against Women* is a collection of her articles and speeches that frame male violence in the context of the oppression of women by various cultures, including commentaries on topical issues such as the O. J. Simpson trial, the war-crime rapes in the Balkans, and the marginalization of women by male rabbis in what she sees as an emergent Orthodox Jewish theocracy in modern Israel, which Dworkin had recently visited. A review of the book in *Publishers Weekly* (December 30, 1996) called it "a revealing personal history" in which Dworkin, "a former battered wife and sex abuse victim, declares autobiography to be the unseen foundation of her nonfiction, and indeed many of these pieces forcefully link the personal to the political."

Dworkin's ideas have become staples of feminist discourse in the 1990s and have turned up in many important works, including Adele M. Stan's *Debating Sexual Correctness* (1995), Laura Kipnis's *Bound And Gagged: Pornography and the Politics of Fantasy in America* (1996), Nadine Strossen's *Defending Pornography* (1995), and even David Shaw's subversive *The Pleasure Police: How Bluenose Busybodies and Lily-Livered Alarmists Are Taking All the Fun Out of Life* (1996). Rene Denfeld's *The New Victorians: A Young Woman's Challenge to the Old Feminist Order* (1995) urged women and their supporters to "take back feminism" from the likes of Dworkin, MacKinnon, Susan Faludi, and others who campaign against pornography and the "freer" expression of sexuality. After *The New Victorians* was reviewed in the *New York Times* (March 19, 1995), Dworkin and MacKinnon wrote a letter to the editor (May 7, 1995) that began: "We would appreciate it if you would not uncritically recycle total lies about our work." The two were protesting Denfeld's imputation that their work claims "that men are ruled by uncontrollable sexual urges, intercourse is rape, and members of the fair sex are superior to their testosterone crazed counterparts," as they quoted from the review. The letter continued, "We have each explicitly and repeatedly denounced systems of inferiority and superiority based on biology. Neither of us has ever said or thought that intercourse is synonymous with rape." Several weeks later, Dworkin again published an impassioned letter in the *New York Times* (July 23, 1995) in protest of an article by Stephen L. Carter that had appeared in the *Times* on June 25. Dworkin defended herself against Carter's charge that she was "well known" for exaggerating the statistics on violence against women. "I believe that systematic violence is one way of keeping women second-class citizens," she wrote. "Nothing in my writing depends on statistics for either its truth or its effect."

Nikki Craft, a colleague of Dworkin's, maintains an extensive Web site dedicated to Dworkin's work. The Web site includes the Andrea Dworkin Online Library and reprints of many of her texts. One of those postings, originally published in the London *Guardian* (January 29, 1998), is an open letter to President Bill Clinton and his family, entitled "Dear Bill and Hillary." In it, Dworkin expresses her disgust at the scandal that ensued after President Clinton engaged in a sexual affair with Monica Lewinsky, a White House intern. Dworkin viewed the incident as one involving "abuse-of-power," and in which a privileged male predator (President Clinton) oppressed a submissive woman (Monica Lewinsky) with the implicit collusion of an equally submissive spouse (Hillary Clinton), accompanied by the "deafening" silence of feminists. Dworkin's "modest proposal" solution: "It will probably bring the FBI to my door, but I think that Hillary should shoot Bill and then President Gore should pardon her."

A self-styled radical, Dworkin has deplored the enervation of the liberal wing of the women's movement that came with the defeat of the ERA in the early 1980s. "For a movement to be effective, it has to have all these different political parts working," she explained to Jean W. Ross. "Radical feminists can do certain things and not other things. Liberal feminists can do certain things and not other things. And they're not the same things. So that's bad. I think our worst problem is that feminism has become a lifestyle word rather than a word that deals with real politics."

Andrea Dworkin has a tousled appearance, with long, curly hair, and she is most often photographed wearing overalls and sneakers. She is consistently close-mouthed about her personal life. *Letters from a War Zone* includes a somewhat tongue-in-cheek interview with herself, in which she stated, "A personal life can only be had in privacy. Once strangers intrude into it, it isn't personal anymore." She has declared herself a lesbian, and she told Erica Jong that she regards lesbianism "exactly as [she] regard[s] being Jewish: as a badge of pride." Since 1974, Dworkin has been living, now in the Park Slope section of Brooklyn, with John Stoltenberg, her "life partner" and the author of *Refusing to Be a Man* (1990) and *The End of Manhood* (1993).

In an often-rhapsodic essay-length memoir entitled "Living with Andrea Dworkin," published in the *Lambda Book Report* (May/June 1994), Stoltenberg related how the two had met after they both walked out of a Greenwich Village poetry reading "because it had turned hateful toward women." In his essay, he defends his companion's intellectual life against detractors and offers a detailed profile of Dworkin's work habits. "Who can explain how

anyone recognizes that they have fallen in love and that life apart is simply unthinkable? All I know is that's what happened to me," he concluded. And, he continued, "living with Andrea has taught me most of all that the world I grew up in and live in as a man is a world that most women can only dream of. And so home has to be the place where that dream is true." Or, as Dworkin herself told Michael Moorcock: "I've always considered writing sacred. I've come to consider the rights of women, including a right to dignity, sacred. This is what I care about. I don't want to give up what I care about."

—E. M.

SUGGESTED READING: *Advocate* p62 Nov. 14, 1995; *Guardian* Jan. 29, 1998; *Lambda Book Report* p9+ May/June 1994, with photo; *Modern Maturity* p22 Sep. 1996, with photos; *Ms.* p60+ June 1988, with photo, p32+ Jan./Feb. 1994; *New Statesman & Society* p16+ Apr. 21, 1995; *New York Times* C p14 July 31, 1996; *New York Times Book Review* p20 Apr. 9, 1995, p47 May 7, 1995, p23 July 23, 1995, p35 Aug. 6, 1995, p4 Oct. 1, 1995; *New York Times Magazine* p8 Apr. 3, 1994; *Publishers Weekly* p46 Dec. 30, 1996; *St. Louis Journalism Review* p11 Nov. 1995; *Washington Post* X p3 Feb. 19, 1995, X p2 Apr. 2, 1995, X p3 June 9, 1996; *Women & Therapy* p171+ 1995

SELECTED BOOKS: Fiction—*The New Woman's Broken Heart*, 1980; *Ice and Fire*, 1986; *Mercy*, 1990; Nonfiction—*Woman Hating*, 1974; *Our Blood: Prophecies and Discourses in Sexual Politics*, 1976; *Pornography: Men Possessing Women*, 1981 (republished with new introduction, 1989); *Right-Wing Women*, 1983; *Intercourse*, 1987; *Letters from a War Zone*, 1988; (with C. MacKinnon) *Pornography and Civil Rights: A New Day for Women's Equality*, 1988; *Life After Death: Unapologetic Writings on the Continuing War Against Women*, 1996

Dyson, Michael Eric

Oct. 23, 1958– Educator; writer; minister.

In one of his raps, the late emcee Notorious B.I.G. declared, "If I wasn't in the rap game / I'd probably have a key knee deep in the crack game / 'Cause the streets is a short stop / Either ya' slangin' crack rock or you got a wicked jump shot." Michael Eric Dyson, who is an educator, ordained minister, public speaker, writer, and influential observer on the subject of gangsta rap, believes that the options open to inner-city African-American youth extend far beyond such limits. "I want to make the intellectual pursuit as sexy, as seductive for young people as Michael Jordan spinning a spherical object

Michael Eric Dyson

through some nets," he told the *Chicago Tribune* (April 29, 1997).

Raised in a ghetto in Detroit, Michigan, Dyson was once a welfare father. He overcame poverty to become one of those few African-American academics deemed "public intellectuals"—people consulted regularly by the media establishment for their insights into racial issues. Dyson has also been called a "hip-hop intellectual," because of his penchant for drawing from sources as diverse as the German philosopher Theodor Adorno and the rapper Snoop Doggy Dogg. A prolific and sometimes controversial writer, he has since the late 1980s produced dozens of magazine, newspaper, and journal articles, and written four books: *Reflecting Black: African-American Cultural Criticism* (1993), *Making Malcolm: The Myth and Meaning of Malcolm X* (1995), *Between God and Gangsta Rap: Bearing Witness to Black Culture* (1996), and *Race Rules: Navigating the Color Line* (1996). "I think of myself as a Trojan horse," he told the *Philadelphia Inquirer* (April 12, 1995). "I don't have an earring in my nose or ear. I don't have my hair combed back in a ponytail, or rough-hewn. I look like an insider. But there's a whole lot of Negroes inside of me. There's a whole lot of black men inside of me. And when I get in somewhere, I let them out."

Michael Eric Dyson was born in Detroit on October 23, 1958 to Addie Mae Leonard, who worked as a teacher's aide in the Detroit public school system. When Michael was two years old, his mother married Everett Dyson, who worked at the Kelsey-Hayes Wheelbrake and Drum Company for 33 years. Everett Dyson, who had four children from a previous marriage, adopted Michael and his older brother; he also fathered three sons with Addie Mae.

Growing up in Detroit, which for many years was referred to as the "murder capital of the world," Dyson became familiar early on with the sights and sounds of violence. Many of his neighbors were either the victims or perpetrators of crime, and he remembers having nightmares about getting shot or robbed at gunpoint. Yet despite the harsh environment, he did not lack spiritual and moral support. His parents, for example, instilled in him their strong work ethic. His black teachers encouraged him to read and learn about African-American history. They also urged him to succeed, not only for his own good, but so as "to extend the long trajectory of African-American progress," as he told *Current Biography* in August 1997.

During his formative years, the church was one of the most important influences on Dyson. Raised a Baptist, he was introduced to the world of "black narrativity" through the powerful sermonizing of black ministers and through poems, plays, and set pieces that were performed during Sunday school. Frederick Sampson and other ministers, who were "erudite and eloquent and also in touch with common people," as Dyson told *Current Biography*, were the first "public intellectuals" he encountered.

Dyson's teachers, ministers, and others recognized his gifts and talents, and their encouragement helped guide him toward college. But Dyson is convinced that he could just as easily have taken the same path that one his brothers, Everett Dyson, followed. According to Dyson, that brother became involved in petty criminal activity. Accused of killing someone he knew, he was convicted of second-degree murder by an all-black jury, which based its decision on eyewitness reports that, with his dying breaths, the victim had uttered a name that sounded something like "Everett." No murder weapon was ever found and no motive ever established, and Dyson believes that his brother was wrongfully convicted. Everett Dyson-Bey, as his brother is now known, is serving a life sentence.

As a youth, Dyson became interested in the "power of words to shape people's behavior . . . and to inspire them," as he told *Current Biography*. He demonstrated his oratorical skills when, at the age of 12, he won a speech contest sponsored by the Optimist Club of Central Detroit. Within a year or two, the intellectually curious Dyson began reading works by such philosophers as Blaise Pascal and Jean-Paul Sartre; at age 14, he began reading the *Harvard Classics*, a set of which he had received as a gift from a neighbor. An autodidact, he read dictionaries to increase his vocabulary—an activity he still engages in—and while at Northwestern High School, he sometimes skipped school and went to the local library, because he didn't think he was getting a good education. "Instead of playing hooky, like any sensible young person would have done, to have fun, my fun was going to the library and reading books," he told *Current Biography*.

Books and learning served as an escape route for Dyson—one that not only would eventually lead him out of the ghetto, but one that also, more immediately, removed him from household responsibilities. When he had speeches to perform, for example, he did not have to pitch in with the cleaning. Sometimes, his father called him a sissy for being more interested in reading philosophy and reciting poetry than in learning about cars with his brothers. Dyson has attributed his father's attitude to the homophobia present in the black community and to the commonly held idea that a male who liked books might be or become gay. His father's attitudes also sprang from his long residence in a tough neighborhood. A big man who sometimes went by the nickname "Muscles," his father knew that reading books did not necessarily help one in a fight. Physical scuffles were common in Michael's neighborhood, and he got into some scuffles himself. When he was 12, he briefly joined some gangs as a way of protecting himself from other neighborhood gangs.

When Dyson attended Detroit public schools, they were still segregated; all his classmates were African-Americans. Then, when he was 17 and in the 11th grade, he won a scholarship to Cranbrook, a nearly all-white prep school located in Bloomfield Hills, a rich suburb of Detroit. At Cranbrook, where he repeated the 11th grade, he was one of only 10 blacks in a student body that numbered about a thousand, and for the first time, he was directly exposed to racism. "This was right when Alex Haley's *Roots* was televised, and among many harsher incidents, a note appeared on my door, 'Nigger go home," he wrote in *Between God and Gangsta Rap*. When he reported such incidents, the headmaster merely shrugged them off as childish pranks. Feeling isolated and alone—and unable to study much on weekends, when he worked in Detroit—he did not do well academically, and Cranbrook officials kicked him out at the beginning of his second year there.

Humiliated, Dyson moved back to Detroit, where he earned his high school diploma after attending night classes at Northwestern High School. Shortly afterward, he met a 26-year-old dancer, actor, and model who had just returned to Detroit after working in New York City. "I fell under her spell through exotic stories she told me about life in the Big Apple, a city I longed to visit," he wrote in his third book. She became pregnant with his child, and the couple married two months later. His wife quit her job as a waitress, and Dyson juggled several jobs in fast food, maintenance, sales, and construction. During a stretch of unemployment, he and his wife had to rely on welfare to get by. Very quickly, the shotgun marriage soured. "My first wife told me she didn't love me two months after we married," he wrote in *Between God and Gangsta Rap*. The couple divorced shortly after the birth of their son, Michael, in 1978.

For the next few years, Dyson hustled various jobs, among them the same factory job his father had held. Despite the hardships he endured, he retained his religious faith and continued to read; he often carried a suitcase full of books with him. In 1979, determined to be a responsible father and ensure a better future for his son, the 21-year-old Dyson moved to Tennessee and enrolled at the all-black Knoxville College. "One of the advantages of going to school when you're older is that you're more serious about it," he told *Current Biography*.

After a couple of years at Knoxville, Dyson transferred to Carson-Newman College, a Southern Baptist institution in Jefferson City, Tennessee. Meanwhile, he had begun preaching at various churches. He had become a licensed Baptist preacher in 1979, and two years later, he was ordained as a minister. Outspoken and fast-talking, he often protested what he perceived as injustice at both school and church. At Carson-Newman, he registered his unhappiness about the lack of black ministers on campus by refusing to fulfill the school's chapel requirement, an omission that led to his expulsion for a year. During that year, he served as a pastor at Thankful Baptist Church, where he petitioned the church to allow women to become deacons. The local Baptist Association objected to his proposal and helped engineer his dismissal from the church.

Dyson graduated magna cum laude from Carson-Newman, with a B.A. degree in philosophy, in 1985. Then, having won a fellowship, he studied religion at Princeton University, in New Jersey, where he received a master's degree in 1991, and a Ph.D. in 1993. While working toward his graduate degrees, Dyson published articles and held various academic positions. From 1988 to 1989, he served as the assistant director of a poverty project at the Hartford Seminary, in Connecticut, from 1988 to 1989. For the next three years, he taught ethics and cultural criticism at Chicago Theological Seminary, and then, for two years, taught courses in American civilization and Afro-American studies at Brown University, in Providence, Rhode Island. Dyson then served as a professor of communication studies at the University of North Carolina at Chapel Hill, and simultaneously directed the school's Institute of African-American Research for two years. In 1997, he joined the faculty of Columbia University, in New York City, as a visiting distinguished professor of African-American studies. He has also continued his pastoral work, as a guest preacher at various churches.

Dyson has written four books, three of which are collections of essays: *Reflecting Black*, *Between God and Gangsta Rap*, and *Race Rules*. In those books, he addressed a wide variety of topics ranging from religion to politics to such well-known black figures as Michael Jordan, O. J. Simpson, and Michael Jackson. He has been especially forceful in his critiques of racial essentialism (the belief that there is a single authentic black being) and of the demonization of young people as nihilistic and violent. Another of his favorite subjects is music (he is an aficionado of hip-hop, opera, jazz, classical, rhythm-and-blues, and country); he has written extensively on rap, which he began listening to right after its birth, in the late 1970s. Although he has criticized the misogyny of some gangsta rap, he has defended the music as a legitimate art form and a means of social protest.

Dyson's longest work on a single topic is *Making Malcolm: The Myth and Meaning of Malcolm X*, in which he attempted to reconcile different intellectual and cultural interpretations of Malcolm X's ideas and legacy. In the first part of the book, Dyson examined the literature on Malcolm X, noting the various and often contrasting ways his persona has been appropriated, so that he is depicted as, for example, a hero, a black nationalist, or a socialist. The second half examines Malcolm X's place in contemporary black nationalist thought—in particular, the ways in which rappers and filmmakers have incorporated his image, experiences, and ideas in their own works.

The author of many articles that have appeared in such publications as the *New York Times*, the *Nation*, the *Chicago Tribune*, *Vibe*, and *Rolling Stone*, and a frequent guest on such television programs as the *Oprah Winfrey Show*, *Good Morning America*, and *Nightline*, and on broadcasts of National Public Radio, Dyson has been called a "black public intellectual." That designation has occasionally subjected him to criticism. Some think that because of the energy he puts into his public intellectual role, his academic writings are intellectually thin; one writer has even labeled him a snake-oil salesman. Dyson has called such attacks "drive-by gangsta-style criticism," and he has speculated that they are motivated in part by professional jealousy.

Like many other "black public intellectuals," in his writings Dyson has often combined analyses of social phenomena with accounts of his personal experiences. *Between God and Gangsta Rap*, for instance, begins with a letter to his brother Everett and ends with a letter to his third wife. Explaining his use of personal anecdote, Dyson told *Current Biography*, "We certainly want people to know that we are human beings after all. We're not writing from an Archimedean point of objectivity outside of human experience. We're writing from within communities. . . . I want to give people a peek into my intellectual workshop. I want to give people a peek into my own soul."

In his books, Dyson has been uncommonly candid about his relations with women. His second marriage, in 1982, was to a nurse, Brenda Joyce Dyson, who, like his first wife, was older than he; they divorced during the time he taught in Chicago. His third wife, Marcia Louise Dyson, who is seven years his senior, is a public relations specialist, marketing consultant, and author of articles on women's issues. Married in 1992, the couple are raising three children. "I believe that the erotic reverence of black women—body, mind, and soul—is a spiritual undertaking for black men . . . ," Dyson wrote in *Essence* (November 1996). "The presence of such love in my life has been one of the clearest signs of the Spirit's bountiful blessing."

Dyson's *I May Not Get There With You: The True Martin Luther King, Jr.* is scheduled for publication in 2000.
—Willie Gin

SUGGESTED READING: *Chicago Tribune* Apr. 29, 1997; *Chronicle of Higher Education* A p6+ Jan. 26, 1996, with photo; *Current Biography* Aug. 1997, with photo; *Herald-Sun, Durham, North Carolina* G p3 May 18, 1997, with photo; *Philadelphia Inquirer* F p1+ Apr. 12, 1995, with photo; *U.S. News & World Report* p48+ Nov. 4, 1996, with photo; *Contemporary Authors* vol. 154, 1997; *Essence* Nov. 1996

SELECTED BOOKS: *Reflecting Black: African-American Cultural Criticism*, 1993; *Making Malcolm: The Myth and Meaning of Malcolm X*, 1995; *Between God and Gangsta Rap: Bearing Witness to Black Culture*, 1996; *Race Rules: Navigating the Color Line*, 1996

Early, Gerald

Apr. 21, 1952– Essayist; poet; educator

"Gerald Early is one of the most exciting and provocative writers of his generation," the novelist, short-story writer, and critic Joyce Carol Oates has said, "and his prose is a continual delight." Under the umbrella of his principal subject—the relationship between black culture and the larger American society—Early has produced books and essays as accomplished and insightful as they are eclectic. *Tuxedo Junction: Essays on American Culture* (1990) and *The Culture of Bruising: Essays on Prizefighting, Literature, and Modern American Culture* (1994), both collections of his own nonfiction pieces, reveal his impressive knowledge of, and unique viewpoints on, such subjects as literature, jazz, and boxing. Among the books he has edited is the two-volume *Speech and Power: The African-American Essay and Its Cultural Content from Polemics to Pulpit* (1992), which contains articles by black writers ranging from Zora Neale Hurston and James Weldon Johnson to Charles Johnson and Henry Louis Gates. Early is a professor of English and director of African and Afro-American studies at Washington University, in St. Louis, Missouri. In addition to prose, he has written a book of poetry, *How the War in the Streets Is Won*, which was published in 1995, as was his most recent nonfiction work, *One Nation Under a Groove*.

Courtesy of Washington University Photographic Services
Gerald Early

Gerald Lyn Early was born on April 21, 1952, in Philadelphia, Pennsylvania, the youngest of the three children (and the only son) of Henry Early, a baker, and Florence Fernandez (Oglesby) Early, a preschool teacher. Henry Early died when his son was nine months old, and thereafter Florence Early reared her children in relative poverty in South Philadelphia. In his book *Daughters: On Family and Fatherhood* (1994), Early characterized his mother as a proud, stoic, and unsentimental woman who was "neither sympathetic nor affectionate" to him while he was growing up. "Whenever I would cry," he wrote, "she would always tell me to hush, that crying never solved anything." He also revealed, "When I was a boy, my mother never told me a single story about her childhood . . .There was a great air of seriousness and purpose about my mother, and I think she thought that to indulge in such memory recitation was sentimental and childish. There was only the immediate concern of survival, of keeping her family together and out of trouble." Recalling his mother's "great skepticism, utter disdain, about the idea of needing other people, of having other people, whether black or white, think that they ever had done or ever could do anything for her," Early observed that he himself had "inherited something of that pride."

Although he has recalled being a "bookish" boy who displayed no particular athletic or fighting ability, Early befriended members of the Fifth and South Streets gang, one of many gangs in the city, and he witnessed many fistfights, one of which he described vividly in an essay in *Tuxedo Junction*. The environment in which he grew up, together with the fact that, as he has written, the South Phil-

adelphia gangs of his generation produced such first-rate prizefighters as Jeff Chandler, Tyrone Everett, and Matthew Saad Muhammad, undoubtedly contributed to Early's fascination with boxing.

In *Daughters*, Early recounted how he described to one of his children the moment he discovered that he wanted to be a writer. The revelation occurred one New Year's Day when he was a boy, while he watched a Mummers' parade with his mother. Periodically, as the costumed men proceeded down Broad Street, Florence Early took her son from their curbside street corner perch to a nearby jazz club so that he could get warm. Early was enchanted by the musicians. "I remember that I was amazed by this tenor saxophone," he wrote. "It was so shiny, golden, and it seemed monstrously big. I thought the thing was made out of pure gold. I thought it was something Arabian, something straight out of a fairy tale . . . It seemed like the coolest thing on Earth." Asked by his daughter if he had wanted to play the instrument, Early responded, "No . . . I wanted to describe it."

Early enrolled at the University of Pennsylvania, in Philadelphia, in the early 1970s. At some point during those years he read the book *Home: Social Essays*, by the poet and playwright Imamu Amiri Baraka, and he has credited that work with inspiring him to write essays, as it "stressed the doctrine of cultural nationalism, which enormously appealed to [his] puritan instincts of renovating the world through a covenant with one's own strength of character and one's sense of election." Early served his apprenticeship as a weekly columnist for his college newspaper, *The Daily Philadelphian*, beginning with a piece on the gang-related murder of his cousin. He received his B.A. degree in English literature, cum laude, in 1974.

During the mid-1970s Early worked for the Philadelphia city government. His job as a member of the Release on Own Recognizance Program, which he has described as "a monumental waste of [his] time and the taxpayers' money," was to interview people who had been arrested to determine whether they were eligible to be released without bail while they awaited trial. He also served a six-month stint as a communications supervisor with the Crisis Intervention Network, whose purpose was to monitor gang activity and control gang-related violence. Early eventually enrolled in the graduate program at Cornell University, in Ithaca, New York, where he earned his M.A. degree in English literature in 1980 and his doctorate in 1982. In the same year, Early, by then married and the father of two young daughters, became an assistant professor of Black Studies at Washington University, in St. Louis. In the summer of 1990, he was promoted to full professor of English and African and Afro-American Studies, and in 1992 he became director of the African and Afro-American Studies program. In the meantime, he had begun publishing articles in *Antaeus*, *Callaloo*, *The Hudson Review*, and several other periodicals.

Twenty-one of those pieces were collected in Early's first book, *Tuxedo Junction*, which was published in 1990. The book's title, as Early explained in the introduction, is the name of a song that was recorded in 1939 by the black musician Erskine Hawkins and that became a "crossover" hit when the white bandleader Glenn Miller released a version of it in the following year. For Early, the song and its history are metaphors for "the doubleness of our American culture, the sense of something being there and being here, of being for 'them' and for 'us' and for all," the phenomenon that "generates the vital syncretism that makes [American culture] function."

Correspondingly, many of the subjects covered in *Tuxedo Junction* are those whose histories are inextricably intertwined with that of the African-American community but whose significance extends beyond it. In an essay about Vanessa Williams, the first black to win the Miss America pageant, Early acknowledged the positive effect of Williams's achievement on the morale of black women while declaring that "the very purpose and motivation of the Miss America contest [was] being called into question, and rightly so, by feminists of every stripe." Early stated in another piece, dedicated to the jazz pianists Thelonious Monk and Earl ("Fatha") Hines: "Hines is the forgotten great man of jazz, and his being forgotten is symbolic of the haphazard way that cultural tradition, black or white, gets passed along to another generation. Tradition in America is characterized by the most intense sort of alienation and by the most intense sense of longing; in the end, we are either hopelessly sentimental or crudely cynical."

The seriousness with which Early views boxing was demonstrated by the number of essays and articles devoted to it in *Tuxedo Junction* as well as by his declaration that "the three most important blacks of the twentieth century" are the heavyweight champions Jack Johnson, the first black to hold the title; Joe Louis, whose 1938 defeat of the German fighter Max Schmeling symbolized, for many, American fortitude in the face of the Depression and growing international tensions; and Muhammad Ali, who represented black defiance by joining the Nation of Islam and by deciding to relinquish his world championship title and serve a prison term rather than fight in the Vietnam War.

In defense of boxing, a sport many have denounced as inhuman and have sought to ban, Early wrote in a piece reprinted in *Tuxedo Junction*, "This moralistic rage of the righteous misses a few major points. First, to ban boxing would not prevent the creation of boxers since *that* process, *that* world would remain intact. And what are we supposed to do with these men who know how to do nothing but fight? I suppose we can continue to lock them in our jails and in our ghettos, out of our sight and untouched by our regard. That, in the end, is precisely what those who wish to ban boxing really want to do: not to safeguard the lives of the men who must do this work but simply to sweep one excessively distasteful and inexplicable sin of bourgeois culture under the rug. Second, those who wish to ban boxing know that they will simply condemn those men to surer deaths by not legally recognizing the sport. Boxing banned will simply become . . . a very popular underground, *totally* unregulated sport. Finally, I think it is fitting to have professional boxing in America as a moral eyesore: the sport and symbol of human waste in a culture that worships its ability to squander."

Tuxedo Junction received very positive reviews. "[Early's] writing challenges, jokes, explains, and sympathizes, and he has a lucid, informal style," a writer for the *New Yorker* (May 21, 1990) observed. "The reader is frequently stimulated to argument and just as frequently excited by Mr. Early's originality." Gene Seymour, evaluating the book for the *Nation* (May 21, 1990), wrote: "The images [in Early's writing] come at you in a thick and heavy rush. At times, the sheer weight of his intelligence and virtuosity can wear you out. After moving from the myth of St. Nicholas and Black Peter to William Godwin's *Caleb Williams* in discussing [Herman Melville's] 'Benito Cereno,' you sense that it even wears Early out sometimes. But you're better off for the workout."

Early's next books, *My Soul's High Song: The Collected Writings of Countee Cullen* (1991), the two volumes of *Speech and Power*, and *Lure and Loathing: Essays on Race, Identity, and the Ambivalence of Assimilation* (1993), were collections that he edited and for which he wrote the introductions. The scholarship that Early brought to his treatment of Cullen, one of the leading poets of the Harlem Renaissance, was widely praised. Writing in *Library Journal* (January 1991), Ellen Kaufman called the introduction to *My Soul's High Song* "a moving portrait of a man whose biography has proven elusive," and in the *New Republic* (April 8, 1991), Jervis Anderson contended that the book "may be the best study of Cullen and his work that has yet appeared."

Citing such nonfiction works as James Baldwin's *The Fire Next Time* (1963), Eldridge Cleaver's *Soul on Ice* (1968), and Albert Murray's *The Omni-Americans* (1970), Early wrote in the introduction to the anthology *Speech and Power*: "Although there have been several outstanding black novels written in the twentieth century, black essays or essay collections have had generally as large, and in some cases an even larger impact on American life and letters than the most successful black novels . . . We cannot fully understand black American literature, the black writer, or the course of black culture as an intellectual construct during the twentieth century without coming to grips with the meaning and function of the essay in the hands of the black American. It is on this simple yet vital premise that this collection is built."

The more than 100 works that make up *Speech and Power* date from the early part of the 20th century to the 1990s. In order to make the collection comprehensive yet wieldy, it was published in two volumes (the second appeared in 1993), each divided into several headings. The section labeled "On Being Black" includes pieces by the black activist and scholar W. E. B. Du Bois and the essayist Shelby Steele; "Boxing" contains essays by the novelist Richard Wright, the former heavyweight champion Floyd Patterson, and Early himself; and the poets Gwendolyn Brooks and Audre Lorde and the novelist Terry McMillan are among the contributors to the section, in the second volume, titled "Autobiography." A writer for the *Antioch Review* (Winter 1994) called *Speech and Power* "an important new collection."

In compiling *Lure and Loathing*, Early used as a "point of departure" the famous assertion made in *The Souls of Black Folk* (1903) by W. E. B. Du Bois: that every African-American feels his or her "twoness" as a result of being "an American, a Negro" with "two souls, two thoughts, two unreconciled strivings; two warring ideals in one dark body, whose dogged strength alone keeps it from being torn asunder," and that that "double consciousness" forces each black person to "see himself through the revelation of the other world." In *Lure and Loathing*, a wide array of contemporary black writers, including Toni Cade Bambara, Stephen Carter, Stanley Crouch, and Nikki Giovanni, addressed Du Bois's statement. A reviewer for *New York Newsday* (July 21, 1993) called the collection "engrossing" and "timely," and in the *Wall Street Journal* (May 20, 1993), Linda Chavez praised Early for assembling in one book such divergent points of view and thereby "demonstrat[ing] that diversity within groups can be as wide as it sometimes is between them." Chavez pronounced *Lure and Loathing* "an especially impressive feat."

Daughters, Early's next book, was written in a comparatively simple, straightforward style. In this brief work he offered a candid description of his relationship with his daughters, Linnet and Rosalind, and he discussed his coming to terms with the learning disability of Linnet, his older daughter; his and his wife's ambivalence over rearing their children in a predominantly white community; and his slow realization that his daughters, growing up in comfort and without the strict emphasis on emotional self-reliance that characterized his upbringing, are "as different from [him] as [he] was from [his] mother." The book's chapters are interspersed with poems that Early wrote for Linnet and Rosalind and with entries from the two girls' diaries. "Mr. Early has the benefit of modern American self-awareness, but . . . his gifts sometimes war with one another," Margo Jefferson wrote in the *New York Times* (December 2, 1994). "How well he describes lives and thoughts in progress. How jarring it is when he interrupts that progress with an elaborate poem or rhetorical flourish. But in the end, how satisfying it is to be in the company of a thoughtful writer and an honest father."

The Culture of Bruising, like *Tuxedo Junction*, is a collection of Early's own essays. As is true of the earlier book, *The Culture of Bruising* is concerned with the boxer as a symbol ("the individual in mass society: marginalized, alone, and consumed by the very demands and acts of his consumption") and with specific boxers, among them the fighters Sonny Liston, Floyd Patterson, Jake LaMotta, and Rocky Graziano. The book also includes an article titled "The Black Intellectual and the Sport of Prizefighting," and other chapters focus on literature, jazz, multiculturalism, baseball, and Malcolm X. The last section, composed of two essays, is titled "Life with Daughters." Reviewing *The Culture of Bruising* for the *Chicago Tribune* (October 9, 1994), Chris Petrakos wrote, "Perhaps what's most compelling about Early's writing is his dazzling flexibility of thought. There's no dogma, no rigidity of purpose other than the intellectual rigor of carefully examining whatever life in America throws into his path. That he shares his observations in such abundance is a gift that can be repaid by letting his words sink into our consciousness . . ." *The Culture of Bruising* won the 1995 National Book Critics Circle Award.

The verses in *How the War in the Streets Is Won: Poems on the Quest of Love and Faith*, Early's first book of poetry, concern subjects—such as jazz and boxing—familiar to readers of his prose. The volume received mixed reviews. A representative assessment was that of a writer for *Library Journal* (June 1, 1995): "At his best, Early catches some hidden corner of an untold story. 'Cock-fight' and 'The Kings of Dead Box' rival the finest poems by many contemporary poets. Unfortunately, such gems are few. At his worst, he juggles adjectives, avoiding clichés by inches." Better received was *One Nation Under a Groove*, Early's brief book on Motown, the record company founded by Berry Gordy Jr. that specialized in "crossover" music by black artists and thus came to symbolize the interrelatedness of black and white cultures. "Because he states straightaway that he comes not to theorize about Motown but simply to think about it, suggesting in his introduction that the book is a 'prelude and fugue to some deeper studies,' Early may be forgiven for certain historical omissions," Mary Elizabeth Williams wrote in the *Nation* (July 3, 1995). "The all-too-short *One Nation* skims the surface of Gerald Early's insights. If this is the prelude, the song is going to be something else."

Gerald Early has been the recipient of several honors, including the 1988 Whiting Writers' Award, which brought with it a cash prize of twenty-five thousand dollars, and the CCLM/General Electric Foundation Award for Younger Writers, also given to him in 1988. His writing was included in the 1991 and 1993 editions of *Best American Essays*. Among many other projects, Early served as a consultant for, and appeared in, Ken Burns's *Baseball*, the nine-part documentary that aired on PBS in 1994, and he was a contributor to Burns's book *Baseball: An Illustrated History*. He is cur-

EDDINGS

rently completing a work on Fisk University. Early is an Episcopalian. Since August 27, 1977, he has been married to Ida Haynes Early, a college administrator. He and his family live in Webster Groves, Missouri.—C. T.

SELECTED WORKS: Nonfiction—*Tuxedo Junction: Essays on American Culture*, 1990; *The Culture of Bruising: Essays on Prizefighting, Literature, and Modern American Culture*, 1991; *One Nation Under a Groove*, 1995; *Daughters: On Family and Fatherhood*, 1994; *Ain't But a Place: An Anthology of African American Writings About St. Louis*, 1998; Poetry—*How the War in the Streets is Won: Poems on the Quest of Love and Faith*, 1995; As editor—*Culture,*

Speech and Power: The African-American Essay and Its Cultural Content from Polemics to Pulpit, 1992; *Power and Lure and Loathing: Essays on Race, Identity, and the Ambivalence of Assimilation*, 1993

SUGGESTED READING: *Antioch Review* Winter 1994; *Chicago Tribune* Oct.9, 1994; *Library Journal* Jan. 1991, June 1, 1995; *Nation* May 21, 1990, July 3, 1995; *New Republic* Apr. 8, 1991; *New York Newsday* July 21, 1993; *New York Times* Dec. 2, 1994; *New Yorker* May 21, 1990; *Wall Street Journal* May 20, 1993; *Contemporary Authors* vol 133 (1991); *Tuxedo Junction: Essays on American Culture* (1990); *Who's Who Among Black Americans 1994–95*

Courtesy of David Eddings

Eddings, David

July 7, 1931– Fantasy novelist

Although his work has received mixed reviews, David Eddings has nonetheless gained one of the largest followings in the fantasy genre. His sword-and-sorcery novels, which consist of two five-part series, the "Belgariad" and the "Malloreon", and two trilogies, the "Elenium" and the "Tamuli," have been best-sellers for over 15 years. He has also written several prequels and supplements to his fantasy epics, including his most recent publication, *The Rivan Codex* (1998), which is a compendium of all the background information pertaining to the world of his novels. In addition to his fantasy works, Eddings is also the author of two "main-

stream" novels, *High Hunt* (1973) and *The Losers* (1992). Many of his books were written with the assistance of his wife, Leigh Eddings.

David Carroll Eddings was born July 7, 1931, in Spokane, Washington, the son of George Wayne Eddings and Theone (Berge) Eddings. He was raised in the Puget Sound area of Washington, just north of Seattle. He first became interested in fantasy and science fiction at the age of 13. By 17, he had begun writing, although not in either the fantasy or SF genres. In his mid-20s, he tried his hand at science fiction, but found that a lack of scientific knowledge prohibited him from writing it convincingly.

Eddings attended Everett Junior College from 1950 to 1952 before enrolling at Reed College, in Portland, Oregon, where he received his B.A. degree in English in 1954. As part of the college's rigorous bachelor's program, Eddings was required to write a novel. "I'm very happy I didn't submit that to a publisher," the author stated in the science fiction/fantasy magazine *Starlog* (January 1995). "I sympathize with my professor, who had to read it."

After graduation, Eddings enlisted in the United States Army. He had been contacted several times by the draft board during the Korean War, but received a deferment each time due to his student status. Once out of college, he decided to volunteer: "I thought, 'Well, they're not really shooting at each other that seriously in Korea right now; let's get this over with.'" (*Starlog* January 1995). As it turned out, with the conflict in Korea over, Eddings was sent instead to Germany, where his college study of the German language served him well. With youthful exuberance, the 23-year-old Eddings falsely claimed he had National Guard experience, and was shocked when the Army put him in charge of his own platoon. "That was one of the most harrowing experiences of my life," he told *Starlog*.

After leaving the service, Eddings enrolled in the University of Washington in Seattle, and earned his master's degree in 1961. On October 27,

1962, he married (Judith) Leigh Schall. He then took on a series of disparate jobs. He started working in the grocery business as a clerk, and eventually worked his way up to store manager. "I've fallen back on this periodically," he told *Starlog*, "although I must say that getting out of the grocery business ranked right up there with getting out of the Army as one of the happier experiences of my life." Next, he entered the aerospace industry, taking a position as a buyer with the Boeing Corporation. "I spent more taxpayer's money than I'll ever be able to replace," Eddings told *Starlog*. When his wife's asthma forced them to move to a dry Midwestern climate, Eddings departed Boeing and taught English at several colleges. Disgruntled at watching administrators' salaries rise while those of the faculty remained static, Eddings abandoned tenure and decided to devote himself to writing professionally.

Living off savings, Eddings wrote a novel he called *High Hunt*, which focused on the tensions that arise among a group of urban businessmen on a deerhunt in the mountains of Washington. To the author's surprise, Putnam accepted the manuscript, and published it in 1973. The novel was a success, and a film adaptation was even considered; however, due to its similarity to the film *Deliverance*, which had been released around the same time, this idea never came to fruition.

After *High Hunt*, Eddings wrote a few more novels during the 1970s, but they went unpublished. (Only one of them, *The Losers*, eventually made it to bookstores, but not until 1992.) He kept trying for success as a mainstream novelist, but it wasn't until he rediscovered the fantasy genre that his writing career took off.

This rediscovery occurred while he was browsing in a bookshop. He spotted a copy of *The Two Towers*, the second book in J. R. R. Tolkien's fantasy trilogy *The Lord of the Rings*, which established the genre in its modern sense. Noticing that the book was in its 73d printing in less than 25 years, Eddings began to wonder if he might finally achieve success writing in this niche, which appeared to have a dedicated audience. The first thing he did toward that end was to construct a detailed map of an imaginary land where his fantasy tales might take place, much like Tolkien's Middle-Earth. This started him thinking about a "back-history" for his world, including religion, culture, kingdoms, and so forth; soon characters embodying good and evil began to crystallize. This preliminary background study took Eddings one year and encompassed 230 pages of material. The world he created was based on the Middle Ages, but included elements from ancient cultures as well as magic and supernatural creatures.

His imaginary world complete, Eddings set about devising an epic story to take place in it. Inspired by Tolkien, he came up with the idea of a trilogy, and proposed it to Ballantine Books, which had been Tolkien's paperback publisher. His letter was apparently lost in the mail, and after failing to receive a response, Eddings wrote a letter of complaint to Ballantine. This strongly worded letter probably did more good for Eddings than the original letter would have done, because he soon got a personal response from Lester Del Rey, president of the Del Rey division of Ballantine Books, who accepted the manuscript. Because booksellers are often hesitant to accept extremely long books from unknown authors, Del Rey later suggested breaking the story up into five books instead of three. "I wasn't very happy about that," Eddings confessed in his *Starlog* interview. "I had absolutely perfect climaxes for each of the three volumes all laid out. . . . But since I had already signed a contract, I didn't have too much choice and had to go along with them. . . . I still think it might have been better presented in three books as opposed to five."

In 1982 Del Rey Books published *Pawn of Prophecy*, the first volume in the five-book series that Eddings named the "Belgariad." This book begins the saga of Garion, a young man whose destiny is connected with an ancient prophecy regarding the fate of the world. The next book in the series was *Queen of Sorcery*, published the same year. In it, Garion begins to learn more about his important role in saving the world from the evil and demented god Torak. *Magician's Gambit* (1984) details Garion's encounter with the legendary wizard Belgarath and his continuing quest to understand his own nature and purpose. In the fourth book, *Castle of Wizardry* (1984), Garion achieves the mystical title of "Belgarion," at the same time that Torak fights for possession of a magical orb that will help him gain dominion over the world. The series was concluded in 1984 with *Enchanter's Endgame*, in which Garion confronts and slays his archenemy, Torak.

The adventures of Garion were continued in Eddings's second five-book saga, the "Malloreon." The first of the series was *Guardians of the West* (1987). Garion, Overlord of the West and husband of Queen Ce'Nedra, must now face the threat of the sorceress Zandramas, who hopes to resurrect the evil Torak. When Zandramas kidnaps Garion's young son for use in her arcane rituals, the Overlord embarks on a rescue mission. The following year, *Guardians of the West* was succeeded by *King of the Murgos*, in which Garion pursues Zandramas toward the mystical realm known only as the Place Which Is No More. The third volume, the *Demon Lord of Keranda*, also published in 1988, follows Garion's struggles against captivity, plague, and other dangers as he approaches a climactic battle with Zandramas. In 1989 Eddings published the fourth volume of the series, *The Sorceress of Darshiva*, which has Zandramas and Garion in a heated race to the Place Which Is No More.

Eddings also began an all-new fantasy series in 1989, set in a completely different world from the Belgariad and the Malloreon. The "Elenium" was set up as a trilogy. Its first installment, *The Diamond Throne* (1989), introduces Sparhawk, a knight who must retrieve the magic Bhelliom gem to save the life of the ailing Queen Ehlana. The middle episode, *The Ruby Knight*, was published the following year, chronicling Sparhawk's search for the Bhelliom through numerous perils. The Elenium concluded in 1991 with *The Sapphire Rose*, in which Sparhawk finds the Bhelliom and discovers its true nature.

It was also in 1991 that Eddings finally unveiled the final chapter of the Malloreon, entitled *The Seeress of Kell*, depicting the titanic collision of Garion and Zandramas in a battle of good and evil, with the fate of Garion's son and of the entire universe hanging in the balance. In a critique of *The Seeress of Kell* from the *Kirkus Reviews* (April 15, 1991), the reviewer complimented Eddings on the "jolly banter" that characterized the book's dialogue. However, the reviewer also found the book anticlimactic, and declared that "fans and nonfans alike will rejoice that the [Malloreon] series is concluded at last."

With both the Elenium and the Malloreon concluded, Eddings made his second foray into mainstream "realistic" fiction with *The Losers* (1992). Written more than 15 years earlier, the book had originally been intended as a follow-up to the successful *High Hunt*. The protagonist of *The Losers* is Raphael Taylor, a promising student drawn into a world of alcoholism and illicit sex through the influence of Damon Flood, a manipulator whom he mistakenly believes is his friend. Driving while drunk, Taylor crashes his car and loses a leg. He drops out of school and moves to Spokane, Washington (the author's hometown), where he is exposed to the problems of the homeless and the otherwise disenfranchised. He soon comes into contact again with Damon Flood, but is now wiser and able to avoid his destructive influence.

The Losers received a dismal critical reception, and Eddings returned to writing fantasy. He began a new trilogy, the "Tamuli," once again chronicling the world of Sparhawk he had introduced in the Elenium. The trilogy's opening book, *Domes of Fire*, was published in 1993. Sir Sparhawk and Queen Ehlana are now married, and must respond to a call for aid from the faraway Tamul Empire. A writer for *Kirkus Reviews* (November 1, 1992) criticized the book for being "uneventful." *Domes of Fire* was followed that same year by *The Shining Ones*, in which Sparhawk encounters the title characters, a mysterious race whose allegiance is hidden. A reviewer for the *Kirkus Reviews* (July 15, 1993) found this volume to be somewhat heavy in dialogue and lacking in action, filled with "lots of pointless embroidery." *The Hidden City* (1994) concluded the trilogy, with Sparhawk rescuing Ehlana from the disciples of the evil god Cyrgon. "Eddings continues to reward lovers of great, sweeping fantasies with creative ingenuity in characterization, world building, and magical effects," *Booklist* reviewer Roland Green declared with regard to *The Hidden City*. "As always, an Eddings tome is a must in fantasy collections of all sizes."

Wishing to return to the realm of the Belgariad and the Malloreon, but not wishing to embark on another series, Eddings settled on the idea of two independent volumes which would serve as prequels to his two first "quintologies." The first of these was *Belgarath the Sorcerer* (1995), and the second *Polgara the Sorceress* (1996). *Belgarath* consists of the memoirs of its fictional title character, an ancient wizard who has witnessed all the events over the millennia which led up to the Belgariad and the Malloreon. The second book is told from the perspective of Belgarath's daughter Polgara, and reveals even more imaginary historical information. The author's wife, Leigh Eddings, was credited with co-authorship on these two books, and Eddings has claimed in recent interviews that his wife has been helping him since the beginning of the Belgariad in 1982, but his publisher, Ballantine Books, preferred not to credit two authors.

In 1998, David and Leigh Eddings sought to completely sum up the world of the Belgariad and the Malloreon with the publication of *The Rivan Codex*, a fully illustrated volume that details the entire background history and material that the Eddingses used as the basis for their 12-book series. Included in the book are 16 maps and numerous drawings by renowned fantasy artist Geoff Taylor. The Eddingses published the book in part as a response to the many questions from fans that they had received over the years regarding their imaginary world. Karen Simonetti of *Booklist* (October 15, 1998) called the work "spellbinding," but a write-up in the *Kirkus Reviews* (September 1, 1998) termed it "a wretched jumble of unreconstructed notes," and classified it for "fanatics only."

Eddings has stated that he is finished writing about the two fantasy realms he explored in his previous epics. However, he intends to continue writing in the fantasy genre. "Building worlds is my hobby," he stated in an interview conducted on America Online's *The Book Report*. "I want to build another one to see if I still know how."

"The technical term for what I'm writing is romance," Eddings said in his *Starlog* interview. "My work is a direct outgrowth of medieval romance." Although he admires the works of J. R. R. Tolkien, Eddings feels that Tolkien was somewhat prudish when it came to depictions of women, and tries in his own writing to push the boundaries of the fantasy genre by including erotic elements.

"I always start with an outline, which is flexible but very, very detailed," Eddings told *Starlog* in describing his writing process. "I'm dealing in a world that never was . . . I have to know where I'm going. I wouldn't want to say I'm outline-bound . . . but I do have it laid out. I may stray once in a while, but I stay pretty close to the road map." Eddings rises each morning at 2:00 and begins writing; he is usually done by sunrise.—B.S.

SUGGESTED READING: *Amazon.com* (on-line); *Booklist* Oct. 15, 1998; "Eddings Interviews," *The World of Eddings* (on-line); *Kirkus Reviews*

Apr. 15, 1991, July 15, 1993, Sep. 1, 1998; *Starlog* (on-line) Jan. 1995; *International Authors and Writers Who's Who 1997/98*

SELECTED WORKS: *High Hunt*, 1973; *Pawn of Prophecy*, 1982; *Queen of Sorcery*, 1982; *Magician's Gambit*, 1984; *Castle of Wizardry*, 1984; *Enchanter's Endgame*, 1984; *Guardians of the West*, 1987; *King of the Murgos*, 1988; *Demon Lord of Keranda*, 1988; *Sorceress of Darshiva*, 1989; *The Diamond Throne*, 1989; *The Ruby Knight*, 1990; *The Sapphire Rose*, 1991; *The Seeress of Kell*, 1991; *The Losers*, 1992; *Domes of Fire*, 1993; *The Shining Ones*, 1993; *The Hidden City*, 1994; *Belgarath the Sorcerer*, 1995; *Polgara the Sorceress*, 1996; *The Rivan Codex*, 1998

Ian Gittler/
Courtesy of Alfred A. Knopf Publishing

Ellis, Bret Easton

Mar. 7, 1964– Novelist

"What I've always been interested in as a writer," Bret Easton Ellis told an interviewer in 1994, "is this idea of a group of people who seem to have everything going for them on the outside. Because of that, they have a lot of freedom. The theme of my fiction is the abuse of that freedom." To date, Ellis has explored that theme in five works of fiction, beginning with the best-seller *Less Than Zero* (1985), a novel about the nihilistic behavior of wealthy, troubled young adults that was published when Ellis was 21 years old. The book established its author as a member of the so-called literary brat pack of the 1980s, a group of highly successful young

writers that also included Jay McInerney, David Leavitt, and Tama Janowitz. Although Ellis is usually seen as a highly visible and controversial pop-culture author, interest in his work has been growing in serious literary circles, and several theoreticians of the novel in the United States and Europe have published scholarly analyses of his work.

One of the publishing industry's most heated controversies in recent years surrounded the publication of Ellis's third novel, *American Psycho* (1991), the narrator of which is a Wall Street investment banker and serial killer. Just before the book's scheduled publication date, Simon & Schuster canceled it, citing its numerous scenes of horrific violence, often involving the sexual abuse and mutilation of women. Some, applauding the decision, labeled Ellis a misogynist; others accused the publisher of censorship or cowardice. Among the latter was the *New York Times* columnist Anna Quindlen, who put her reputation for embracing feminist causes on the line when she defended Ellis's novel thus: "As an epitaph for the [1980s, the book] has a repellent reality. . . . The eternal question about violence in art is whether it simply reflects our worst behavior or inspires it. We are so terrified of inspiration that sometimes we are moved to suppression. But reflection is essential because it often leads to thought, and occasionally to understanding. That is why we publish troubling books." Ellis's most recent novels are *The Informers* (1994) and *Glamorama* (1999).

Bret Easton Ellis was born on March 7, 1964 in Los Angeles, California, the oldest of the three children—and the only son—of Robert Martin Ellis, a real-estate analyst, and Dale (Dennis) Ellis, a homemaker. His maternal grandmother was a writer of children's books. Encouraged by his mother, Ellis himself began writing at a very young age, penning "mini-novels" that he gave as Christmas presents. Ellis received his secondary education at the Buckley School, a private school in Sherman Oaks, California. He told Anka Radakovich of the New York *Daily News* (November 8, 1987) that he was a "Valley boy"—a variation on "Valley girl," a term evoking the speech and consumer sensibility of young, affluent Southern Californians. "I even roamed the malls and said 'Hey, dude,'" Ellis added. From an early age he saw himself as somehow different from his peers, presaging the alienated, anomic characters often found in his adult fiction. Interviewed by Chris Heath for *Rolling Stone* (December 24, 1998–January 7, 1999), he said: "I just couldn't take a lot of pleasure in the things that my classmates would take pleasure in: jungle gyms, merry-go-rounds, sand pits, buckets, and pails, sing-alongs . . . holding hands and dancing in a circle around some kind of plant, pulling toys out of bags and putting the toys back into bags, queuing up for chocolate milk . . . it all seemed hopeless to me."

Against the wishes of his father, who had wanted him to major in business at the University of Southern California, in 1982 Ellis enrolled at Bennington College, in Bennington, Vermont, where he took a creative-writing workshop taught by the writer Joe McGinniss and where he quickly got a reputation for alienating other students by exposing their shadowy secrets in his "fictional" assignments. Impressed by his pupil, McGinniss showed some of Ellis's short fiction to Morgan Entrekin, an editor at Simon & Schuster, and sent some of his essays to Robert Asahina, an editor at *Harper's* magazine. Recognizing Ellis's promise, Entrekin advised him to write a novel. By the time Ellis completed *Less Than Zero*, Asahina had joined Simon & Schuster as an editor, and he and Entrekin bought the book. (Heath claims that Ellis wrote the rough draft of this "beautifully jaded" first novel during an eight-week drug binge in Los Angeles.)

The narrator of *Less Than Zero* is Clay, a freshman at a New England college who has come home to Los Angeles for Christmas break. Over the course of his vacation, Clay offers a deadpan account of the joyless narcotic and sexual escapades of his social circle—members of a generation made cynical and amoral by having experienced too much, too fast. The characters' apathy leads to self-debasement and to one act of shocking cruelty. Some critics hailed Ellis as a distinctive new literary voice, a writer chronicling the previously unexplored troubles of his age group; in a *New Yorker* (July 29, 1985) review, for example, the book was described as "an extraordinarily accomplished first novel whose substance, if true, is simply sickening." Others deplored what they saw as the book's overdependence on sensationalism and its lack of character development. In the *Saturday Review* (July/August, 1985), Larry McCarthy gave voice to both viewpoints: "*Less Than Zero* is not perfect—depravity can only carry a book so far. . . . But [this] is a book you simply don't forget." *Less Than Zero* created a stir in the publishing world, due in part to its fresh subject matter and in part to the fact that its author was still in college. Ellis found himself compared in the print media to such literary giants as F. Scott Fitzgerald, and he quickly became one of the more prominent members of the younger generation of writers, then mostly in their 20s, whose novels were the talk of the literary community. A film adaptation of *Less Than Zero*, directed by Marek Kanievska, was released in 1987.

Ellis graduated from Bennington in 1986. A year later his senior thesis was published as his second novel. The events described in *The Rules of Attraction* take place in New Hampshire at the fictional Camden College (where Clay, the protagonist of *Less Than Zero*, is a student). The main characters are Paul, a drama major; Lauren, an art student; and Sean, a nominal literature major who is having simultaneous affairs with Paul and Lauren. The book's first-person narration rotates among the characters, and it is only through Paul's passages that his trysts with Sean are revealed. As is true with all of Ellis's fiction, the people in *The Rules of Attraction* are, without exception, wealthy; possess an encyclopedic knowledge of designer clothing and brand names of other products; use sex, drugs, and alcohol as means of distracting themselves from the emptiness of their lives; and relate their day-to-day activities in a flat, matter-of-fact manner.

The Rules of Attraction was less successful, both critically and financially, than its predecessor. "It remains ambiguous where Mr. Ellis locates his own intelligence in this book," Scott Spencer wrote in the *New York Times Book Review* (September 13, 1987). "There are flashes of wit that can lead you to suspect he sees and even recoils from the hollowness of the young lives he writes about. . . . Yet these moments of humor are infrequent. Mr. Ellis has it within his grasp to become a satirist, but for now his method of aping the attitudes of the burnt-out works against him. He seems . . . passive in his regard of social rot." In *Newsweek* (September 7, 1987), David Lehman pronounced the novel "more effective as a sociological exhibit than as a work of literary art." Offering qualified praise for the book, Susan Avallone observed in *Library Journal* (September 15, 1987): "Ellis has his pretensions (the book starts and finishes in the middle of a sentence, and one diary entry is in easy French), but he successfully fleshes out his characters and creates involving situations."

In April 1990 Robert Asahina, Ellis's editor at Simon & Schuster, accepted *American Psycho* for publication and set its release date for early in the following year. During the summer of 1990, there were reports in the press that some Simon & Schuster employees, having read portions of the manuscript, objected to its graphic descriptions of sadism, torture, and murder and refused to work on the book. In the fall, *Time* and *Spy* each published passages from *American Psycho* alongside a scathing commentary, which brought the novel to the attention of Richard Snyder, the chairman of Simon & Schuster. After reading the manuscript, Snyder announced in mid-November, one month before the book was due to be shipped to bookstores, that its publication had been canceled. (Ellis would keep his advance, which was widely reported to be $300,000.) Responding to speculation that the decision to scrap the novel had been made by Martin Davis, the chairman of Simon & Schuster's parent company, Paramount Communications, Snyder told David Streitfeld of the *Washington Post* (November 15, 1990) that while Davis had supported the move, "It was I who decided we should not put our name on this book. It's a matter of taste."

The reports about *American Psycho*'s contents, and news of its cancellation, aroused considerable controversy. Speaking in his own defense, Ellis told David Streitfeld, "The book is 400 pages long, and there are less than 40 pages with the type of mayhem [the *Time* and *Spy* articles] quote." Amanda Urban, Ellis's agent, was quoted as saying that the sudden decision not to publish the novel "seems to me to raise the question of whether there is a form of censorship going on." Roger Rosenblatt dismissed that charge in his much-discussed condemnation of *American Psycho* in the *New York Times Book Review* (December 16, 1990): "Censorship is when a government burns your manuscript, smashes your presses, and throws you in jail. . . . If a publishing house is not entitled to withdraw its own book, who is? As for the timing of Simon & Schuster's decision, better late than never." After *American Psycho* was picked up by Vintage Books, Tammy Bruce, the president of the Los Angeles chapter of the National Organization for Women, called for a boycott of the book, referring to it as "a how-to novel on the torture and dismemberment of women."

American Psycho's central character is a self-absorbed 26-year-old investment banker named Patrick Bateman, who provides an exhaustively detailed, present-tense narrative about his social engagements with colleagues; his workouts in a $5,000-a-year health club; his dates; and the homicidal impulses he continually feels and upon which he frequently acts. Patrick (whose younger brother is revealed to be Sean, from *The Rules of Attraction*) symbolizes soullessness—specifically, the worship of material possessions and social standing, the greed, and the lack of compassion often associated with the 1980s and the presidency of Ronald Reagan, during which the book is set. So skewed is Patrick's perception of the world that he often mistakes one acquaintance for another even though he unfailingly identifies the designers of everyone's clothing (most characters are described primarily by their attire); so unvaried are his reactions that he relates his morning grooming routine, complete with the brand names of the numerous products he uses, in the same tone with which he discusses the mutilation of his victims, who include men, children, and animals as well as women. Ellis has admitted that *American Psycho* is autobiographical in some respects, and that he had based the character Patrick Bateman partly on his own father, who had left the Ellis household when Bret was a teenager. He told Chris Heath for *Rolling Stone*, "In many ways I was writing about myself and the life I was living. . . . It is an accurate reflection of who I was at the time of writing it and the kind of life I was living. It was a detailed manifesto of what I would experience on a daily basis, and it was also a very harsh criticism of the way I was living at the time. There was a major dose of self-loathing surrounding that book."

Published in early 1991, *American Psycho* received myriad negative reviews. Some outraged critics protested the book's carnage on moral grounds; others, including the novelist Norman Mailer, considered the work to be an artistic failure because, in their views, Ellis had not done justice to his weighty theme and had given no real insights into his main character's motivations. Among the reviewers in the latter camp was Mim Udovitch, who wrote in the *Village Voice* (February 25, 1991), "Its high-blown aims aside, the book is unbearably bad, more to be pitied than censored," and Jonathan Yardley, who complained in the *Washington Post* (February 27, 1991), "Since [Ellis] has nothing to say, he fills his pages with familiar brand names and inane chatter. . . . What [he] fails to understand is that the book is every bit as empty and infantile as [its characters] are."

Yet *American Psycho* had its defenders. "The miracle of Bret Easton Ellis is that without a plot, without much in the way of characters, and with a throwaway nonstyle that renders the luxurious, the erotic, and the grotesque in the same uninflected drone, . . . he nevertheless makes it virtually impossible to stop reading," Henry Bean declared in the *Los Angeles Times Book Review* (March 17, 1991). "Ellis is, first and last, a moralist. Under cover of his laconic voice, every word in his three novels to date springs from grieving outrage at our spiritual condition. . . . Prudes, squares, and feminist commissars aside, the rest of us should applaud Bret Easton Ellis for setting out in this noble and dangerous direction; his only fault is that he did not go far enough." Catherine Texier referred to *American Psycho* in *New York Newsday* (August 21, 1994) as "an ambitious, nearly brilliant book that nailed the consumer frenzy and greed of the [1980s] and America's obsession with violence."

The publication of *American Psycho* provoked, in addition to hostile reviews and charges of misogyny, more than a dozen anonymous death threats against Ellis. In an interview with Robert Love for *Rolling Stone* (April 4, 1991), Ellis responded to his detractors, admitting that he had been "confused" by the uproar surrounding his novel and saying, "To put it as simply as possible: The acts described in the book are truly, indisputably vile. The book itself is not. Patrick Bateman is a monster. I am not." In fact, he said, the book's violent scenes were "upsetting to write because I had to keep writing *I* all the time. . . . That does a number on you psychologically that I can't quite describe. . . . I cried a few times." He denied that he had purposely written a controversial novel in order to revive his reputation after the disappointing reception accorded *The Rules of Attraction*, but he added, "I'm not going to sit at my typewriter and compose something only so it will not offend a woman's sensibility, and any writer who does that is a wimp." A movie version of *American Psycho* has been planned.

In 1983 Ellis had begun writing sketches in notebooks; 13 of those pieces were eventually published in 1994 as the novel *The Informers*. Set in the 1980s in and around Los Angeles, the loosely connected stories that comprise *The Informers* feature aimless characters unable to form emotional bonds with the people in their lives. In "The Up Escalator," for example, an unhappily married, middle-aged woman carries on a loveless affair with a man approximately the age of her son; "In the Islands" is narrated by a man vacationing in Hawaii with his son, to whom he has nothing to say. A minor character from one story in *The Informers* often turns up as the narrator of another, and the book has some characters in common with Ellis's previous works. Moreover, several stories contain scenes of violence reminiscent of those in *American Psycho*.

The Informers received mixed reviews. Of those who found fault with the book, none was more condemnatory than Michiko Kakutani, who wrote in the *New York Times* (August 2, 1994): "If it's satire that Mr. Ellis is after . . . it is a mission in which he utterly fails; his book completely lacks the social detail and wit upon which satire depends. In fact, the animating emotion of *The Informers* seems to be contempt: the author's contempt for his characters and for his readers. The result is a novel that is as cynical, shallow, and stupid as the people it depicts." The opposite view was expressed by George Stade in the *New York Times Book Review* (September 18, 1994): "For all of his studied neutrality, Mr. Ellis provides his readers with grounds for judgment. . . . A case could be made for Mr. Ellis as a covert moralist and closet sentimentalist, the best kind, the kind who leaves you space in which to respond as your predispositions nudge you, whether as a commissar or hand-wringer or, like me, as an admirer of his intelligence and craft."

Especially after the publication of *The Informers*, scholars in the U.S. and abroad have begun to probe the literary influences of Ellis's work, and some have offered analyses that locate Ellis within the spectrum of late-20th century criticism. In an article he wrote for the *Southern Humanities Review* (Fall 1998), David W. Price discussed *American Psycho* in the context of Mikhail Bakhtin's theories of the novel, specifically his Rabelaisian-influenced theory of grotesque realism. Polish scholar Marek Jedlinski presented a paper on Ellis at the Polish Association for American Studies conference in Poznan in 1995 and later published it in *Tygiel kultury* (February 1996). Jedlinski wrote that his main objective was to "propose an alternative reading of the novel as a *valid work of art* . . .," not merely as a critique of Reaganomics and yuppiedom. Ellis's text, he wrote in his abstract, "usually dubbed hyperrealistic by reviewers, is in fact a massive tangle of factual errors, inconsistencies, mystifications and contradictions, not all of which can be attributed to the main character's dementia." Jedlinski concluded that *American Psycho* was "an assault on Postmodernism, a furious reaction against recent trends in popular and intellectual spheres of culture, rather than an extension thereof." Earlier, American critic Terry Teachout had taken a hatchet swipe at contemporary academic theory while reviewing the novel for *National Review* (June 24, 1991). In an article entitled "Applied Deconstruction," Teachout criticized Ellis's lack of moral compass by writing: "No doubt Ellis spent his undergraduate years steeped in the modish brand of academic nihilism that goes by the name of 'deconstruction,' a school of criticism in which works of art are verbally hacked to pieces in order to prove that nothing means anything. He seems to have learned his lessons well, if a bit too literally."

Interviewed for the *Hotwired* Web site (September 29, 1995), Ellis answered questions about his literary muses by debunking the notion that he had been influenced by William S. Burroughs and acknowledging that the contemporary writers who most interested him included Don Delillo, Robert Stone, Dennis Cooper, James Ellroy, Joan Didion, "some William Vollman [and] among young writers, Pinckney Benedict." When asked whether he thought there was "any writer of literary merit who's been able to be as harsh and violent *and* of serious consideration," he replied: "Yes, Dennis Cooper." Among classical authors, Ellis admitted that "Flaubert is one of my all time favorite writers. . . . Zola, so-so, Balzac, OK, but Flaubert, pretty major."

Glamorama, Ellis's fifth novel, was published by Knopf in 1999. For its setting, Ellis mined the glitzy universe of high fashion in New York, London, and Paris, which he portrayed as a grim global netherworld of drugs, sexual escapades, supermodels, and terrorists. Ellis, reported his friend Julie Grau, "conducted a considerable amount of personal research" for the book, including cruising to Europe on the QE2 and "haunting the fashion shows of Paris." Of all his novels, this one was the most conventionally structured. *Glamorama* is narrated by Victor Ward, a character who had debuted in *The Rules of Attraction* a dozen years earlier, and also includes Sean and Patrick Bateman, who had appeared in several of the earlier novels. Ellis told Chris Heath in the *Rolling Stone* interview that he felt comfortable with these characters because they remind him that "the books are basically concerned about the same things, and I'm basically writing about the same world," a world that includes "a kind of shallowness, vanity, narcissism, an obsession with surfaces, finding the truth in surfaces." James Wolcott, in *Vanity Fair* (October 1998), was not enthusiastic about the novel, writing that *Glamorama* "betrays the strain of a young writer trying to recoup former glory and stay current."

In addition to his fiction, Bret Easton Ellis has written numerous essays about the attitudes of his generation, contributing articles to a variety of publications, including *Rolling Stone*, the *Wall Street Journal*, and the *New York Times*. In his interview with Anka Radakovich for the New York *Daily News* article, he drew a distinction between himself and his characters. "I don't think my behavior patterns mirror the characters. . . . ," he said. "If they did, I'd be in a morgue somewhere. . . . I'm not promiscuous or into drugs. I'm sort of 'Southern California Victorian.' I'm even a little shy." In a similar vein, he told H. J. Kirchhoff in an interview for the Toronto *Globe and Mail* (October 17, 1995), "If you write about a serial killer, there are going to be killings. They cannot just

hang out with their grannies and drink tea. . . . It doesn't seem shocking to me that if I write about contemporary America violence makes its way into my work." Since 1987 Ellis has made his home in New York City, in a large studio apartment that for 10 years had "no furniture to speak of," in the words of Chris Heath, who wrote in his *Rolling Stone* feature that Ellis "slept on a mattress, surrounded by stacks of books, and worked at a small desk just inside the door. The floors were soiled with the trampled-in reminders of too many good parties." Ellis is reportedly working on a memoir about his college years, which he has tentatively titled "Where I Went I Would Not Go Back."
C. T. / E. M.

SUGGESTED READING: *Entertainment Weekly* p54 Aug. 19 1994, p95 Jan. 22 1999; *General Frenetics Homepage* (on-line) June 20, 1998; *Globe and Mail* A p14 Oct. 17 1995, with photo; *Guardian* p23 Apr. 18 1991; *Hotwired* (on-line) Sep. 29, 1995; *New York Daily News* p6 Nov 8 1987, with photo; *New York Observer* p19 Nov. 26 1990; *New York Times* C p17 Dec. 6 1990, IX p1 July 12, 1998, C p7 Dec. 21, 1998; *New York Times Book Review* p14 Sep. 18 1994; *New York* p34 Sep. 9 1985, p32+ Dec. 17 1990; *Rolling Stone* p114+ Dec. 24, 1998–Jan. 7, 1999, with photo; *Southern Humanities Review* p321+ Fall 1998; *Time* p15 July 30 1990; *Vanity Fair* p150+ Oct. 1998, with photo; *Variety* p3 June 13 1984; *Who's Who in America, 1994*

SELECTED BOOKS: *Less Than Zero*, 1985; *The Rules of Attraction*, 1987; *American Psycho*, 1991; *The Informers*, 1994; *Glamorama*, 1999

Miriam Berkley

Ellis, Trey

1962– Novelist; screenwriter

By employing biting satire in his novels and screenplays, the American author Trey Ellis seeks to dispel the many myths surrounding black males. In his first novel, *Platitudes* (1988), Ellis confronted the growing rift between male and female African-American authors by pitting two black writers against each other as they attempt to complete their individual novels. His second book, *Home Repairs* (1993), follows the developing sexual identity and exploits of a black teen who is trans-formed from a nerd into the handyman star of a cable TV show called *Home Repairs. Right Here, Right Now*, his 1999 novel, concerns a self-help maven on a religious quest. Ellis has also penned original screenplays, such as *The Inkwell* (1994), which he intended as a tender coming-of-age story but which, in the hands of director Matty Rich, became a brash discussion of racial and economic problems. Ellis's most recent screen work, *The Tuskegee Airmen* (1995), depicts the struggles of the first all-black fighter squadron and its battles against both American racism and the Nazis during World War II. In an interview for *Entertainment Weekly* (April 29, 1994), Ellis summed up what he believed to be the types of stories black Americans wanted to see in print and on film: "We black people want to see ourselves going to school, going to work, kissing each other. The black middle class are not very different from the white, meaning that they try to send their kids to school and make their house payments. They're still as black as any gangbanger or welfare mother."

In his autobiographical statement for *World Authors 1990–1995*, Trey Ellis wrote: "I was born in Washington, D.C., in 1962. My father was finishing Howard University medical school while my mother supported us by working in the U.S. patent office. They'd met at Howard as undergrads where she graduated magna cum laude.

"We soon moved to the Midwest where I lived until the fifth grade. We spent a year in Dayton, a few more in Detroit and the rest in the wonderfully-named Ypsilanti, Michigan. I am sure that moving so frequently made it easier for me to travel farther and farther from home for the rest of my life.

"My mother went back to school for her master's degree in psychology at the University of Michigan while my father completed his residency in psychiatry there. Then we moved to Hamden, Connecticut, when my father transferred to Yale.

"It was in Hamden, in the fifth grade, that I decided I would become a writer. All I knew about them was that they lived on boats off Nantucket and had skinny wives who wore bikinis all day long. I began writing plays and stories with friends and continued to focus on writing from then on.

"In the eleventh grade, at the boarding school (Phillips Academy, Andover), I was lucky enough to have Alexander Theroux as a writing teacher. He was wonderfully encouraging so by the time I left for Stanford, I was confident on at least trying to become a professional writer.

"Something else that made it much easier for me to gamble on a writing career was my mother's suicide when I was 16. Suddenly I realized that my cautious plans of becoming an engineer first then writing when I retired did not fit into the unpredictable nature of the universe. My father cautioned me to find a more stable career but I purposefully decided to burn all the bridges behind me so I'd have no choice but to make my living with a pen.

"At Stanford I majored in creative writing and studied with Gilbert Sorrentino. *Platitudes*, my first novel, was begun in his introductory creative-writing class in the fall of 1983.

"I'd studied in Florence, Italy, as a sophomore, and returned upon graduation. There I worked four hours every day on *Platitudes* then rushed off on my moped to teach English or work in a nearby gym and sporting-goods store.

"I finished the novel in the spring of 1985, wrapped the hand-written notepads up in duct tape, and entrusted them to one of [my] oldest friends, Danny Workman, who was visiting me. Then I traveled through east, central, west, and north Africa for four months.

"I returned from the amazing journey and met up with my father in Paris. It was there that he told me [he] had AIDS. At first he was in wonderful shape but I left Europe to be near him and ending up nursing him till his death in January 1986. While nursing him I was rewriting and retyping *Platitudes*. It took me a year to find my agent, Eric Ashworth, and it took him several more months to sell the book.

"Soon after the publication of my first novel I had an idea for the new book. I'd been keeping a diary of my romances for several years and thought [that], if fictionalized, it might show the world a glimpse of the inner workings of the adolescent male. *Home Repairs* was published in 1993.

"Here near Los Angeles I am as known for my fiction as for my screenwriting. I have written dozens of scripts for several movie studios including *The Inkwell* and *The Tuskegee Airmen*. I'm often asked which I like better and I usually say whatever I'm not working on at the time. But writing fiction is immensely more satisfying since it is purely mine. Collaborative arts are fine but the quality of the end product seems so much less in your control.

"My wife Erika Ellis is the author of *Good Fences* (Random House)."

In *Platitudes* Trey Ellis attacked the black literary establishment by setting at odds two talented black writers—Isshee Ayam, a successful feminist novelist, and Dewayne Wellington, a toiling postmodernist. When Wellington is unsure of what to do with Earle—the young, overweight protagonist of his novel whose greatest ambitions are to have sex and to attend Cal Tech and M.I.T.—he prints an open letter asking the public for help. He receives a critical barrage from Ayam, who suggests that Wellington move his story to the South where Earle would live with a group of poor but proud black women. Reviewing the book for the *Village Voice* (November 29, 1988), Marcellus Blount remarked, "*Platitudes* is serious fun. Ellis remembers the social antics of teenagers: the sex and romance, anxiety and confusion, trials and frequent tribulations. He manages to insulate himself from thematic censure by manipulating his point of view to make his characters bear the brunt of his criticisms, instead of the real contemporary black writers and white audiences whom they represent." The *New Yorker* (February 13, 1989) praised: "The reader never stops marveling at Mr. Ellis's ear for contemporary language, or rooting for Earle, who emerges from the fray as a full-fledged, loveable character."

Ellis's second novel, *Home Repairs* (1993), was written in the form of a diary. Austin McMillan, the main character, is an upper-class black adolescent who begins his diary in order to keep track of his misadventures with the opposite sex in the hope that he won't repeat the same mistakes. The book chronicles Austin's life from age 16 to his early 30s, and follows his progress from awkward teen to handsome adult, while documenting his relationships with a score of women along the way. *People* (August 2, 1993) noted that "the fun is sharing in Austin's steamy accounts of his insecurities, obsessions, and heartbreaks." Vince Passaro of *New York Newsday* (July 8, 1993), however, complained that "nothing changes Austin, a simple but dense fact that sinks what might have otherwise been a sprightly, witty novel."

Ellis's next project was the screenplay for *The Inkwell* (1994), a semi-autobiographical coming-of-age story set in Inkwell Beach, a vacation spot on Martha's Vineyard that has long been popular with African-Americans. He worked on the screenplay for two years and had hoped to direct the film. Disney's Touchstone Pictures purchased the screenplay in 1992, but nothing else connected with the project turned out as Ellis had expected. Company executives gave the film to director Matty Rich, whose debut movie, *Straight Out of Brooklyn* (1991), was a harrowing story of drugs and family violence set in the Red Hook public housing project of Brooklyn, New York. Rich initially said that he liked the script he had received from Ellis, but he soon began to suggest rewrites. In an interview with Maria Ricapito of *Entertainment Weekly* (April 29, 1994), Ellis recalled that Rich "said my script wasn't black enough. I think it wasn't stereotypically black enough." In the end Ellis distanced himself from the project, even going so far as to attack it in the press and use a pseudonym (Tom Ricostranza) for his screenwriting credit.

Most recently, Ellis completed work on the screenplay for *The Tuskegee Airmen*, the story of an elite group of black World War II fighter pilots who battled against discrimination at home in order to take on the Nazis in Europe. In just over two years of combat, the group received 850 medals and never lost a single bomber in all the escort missions they flew over Italy. The film, released as an HBO original movie in August 1995, was praised by Robert Goldberg of the *Wall Street Journal* (August 28, 1995) for its "crisp" dialogue. Goldberg also remarked that "the story of the Fighting 99th succeeds as an old-time adventure—guns blazing, planes wheeling, bandits closing at three o'clock. It is the type of movie you don't see these days, except in black-and-white reruns, a feel-good tale of champions and obstacles overcome."

In *Right Here, Right Now*, Ellis's 1999 novel, the self-help guru/hustler Ashton Robinson—after smoking marijuana and ingesting a particularly potent cough medicine—is visited by a shape-shifting Brazilian midget, who seduces him before informing him that he is the one chosen by God to "bring the world to the future." "Many amusing scenes for Ellis's faithful, but no match for Sinclair Lewis," was the *Kirkus Reviews* (November 15, 1998) assessment of the book.

In addition to his fiction and film projects, Trey Ellis has also been a contributor to such periodicals as *Playboy* and *Interview*.—C.M.

SUGGESTED READING: *Entertainment Weekly* p19 Apr. 29, 1994; *Nation* p691+ Dec. 19, 1988; *New York Newsday* p56 July 9, 1993; *New York Times* C p11 Aug. 21, 1995; *New Yorker* p93 Feb. 13, 1989; *People* p26+ Aug. 2, 1993; *Variety* p7+ January 24–30, 1994; *Village Voice* p66 Nov. 29, 1988; *Wall Street Journal* A p11 Aug. 28, 1995; *Contemporary Authors, vol. 146*, 1995

SELECTED WORKS: Fiction—*Platitudes*, 1988; *Home Repairs*, 1993; *Right Here, Right Now*, 1999; Film—*The Inkwell*, 1994; *The Tuskegee Airmen*, 1995

Laura Esquivel

Esquivel, Laura

1950– Novelist; screenwriter

"I spent the first years of my life in front of the fire in my mother's and grandmother's kitchen, watching how, when they entered those hallowed precincts, these two wise women turned into priestesses, noble alchemists playing with the four elements of water, air, fire, and earth that compose the universe," the Mexican novelist and screenwriter Laura Esquivel said in her acceptance speech for Mexico's 1992 Woman of the Year Award. "What is most surprising is that they did so with total humility, as if what they were doing was not important at all, as if they were not transforming the world through the purifying power of the fire, as if they didn't know that the food they were preparing, and we were eating, remained in our bodies for many hours, chemically altering our organism, nurturing soul and spirit, giving us identity, language, motherland."

Deeply embedded in Laura Esquivel's writing, particularly in her debut novel *Like Water For Chocolate* (1989) and her screenplay based on that work, is a fervent interest in cooking and eating and the psychological ramifications of those two processes. Part love story, part cookbook, *Like Water for Chocolate* is "a novel in monthly installments with recipes, romances, and home remedies," as the cover to the English translation describes it. Indeed, throughout the book, the reader encounters recipes for dishes—including turkey mole with almonds and sesame seeds, three kings' bread, and quail in rose petal sauce—central to the plot of the story. Esquivel came up with the idea for her novel while cooking. "When I cook certain dishes, I smell my grandmother's kitchen, my grandmother's smells," Esquivel said in an interview with the *New York Times* (February 17, 1993). "I thought: what a wonderful way to tell a story."

Both critics and the general public agreed. Since its publication, *Like Water for Chocolate* has been translated into 26 foreign languages. In 1990 it was the best-selling book in Mexico, and in 1994 the American Booksellers Association awarded Esquivel the ABBY, the American Booksellers Book of the Year, marking the first time this recognition was bestowed upon a foreign author. In that same year, she received recognition at the Sao Paulo Bienal in Brazil for the Portuguese translation of the book and received the Spanish Gastronomy Academy and the Good Table Union's "Count of the Andes" award for the best writer interested in gastronomy.

The film version of *Like Water for Chocolate*, released in 1992, was similarly praised. "Food and passion create a sublime alchemy in *Like Water for Chocolate*, a Mexican film whose characters experience life so intensely that they sometimes smolder," Janet Maslin wrote in the *New York Times* (February 17, 1993). With nearly $20 million in receipts, the movie went on to become the biggest-grossing foreign language film ever in the United States. Esquivel's second novel is *The Law of Love* (1995).

Laura Esquivel was born in 1950 in Mexico City, the third of four children of Julio Caesar Esquivel, a telegraph operator, and his wife, Josefina. She was educated at the Escuela Normal de Maestros, the national teacher's college of Mexico, where she specialized in elementary education. After teaching for eight years, she returned to school to specialize in theater for children. In 1977 Esquivel, along with a group of colleagues, founded Theater and Literature Workshop for Children of SEP. By 1979, she was writing for the Channel 11 children's program *Tiliches, Trebejos y Cachivaces*. Four years later she founded and became director of the Centre of Permanent Invention, where she gave artistic workshops for children.

In 1983 Esquivel met and married Alfonso Arau, a Mexican film director best known in the United States for *Mojado Power*, Mexico's nominee for the 1982 Academy Award for best foreign-language film. After taking a screenwriting course with Arau, she produced her first screenplay, *Chido One, el Tacos de Oro*. The movie, directed by Arau, tells the story of a soccer player who, after becoming famous, suffers a change of values. "We know that the hardest work is to keep yourself open to the world that technology hasn't tamed," Esquivel said in an interview with the *New York Times* (March 3, 1993). "My soccer player eventually returned to his past." *Chido One*, a huge hit in Mexico, was nominated by the Sciences and Cinematographic Arts Academy for the Ariel—the Mexican equivalent of an Oscar—for best script.

In her 1992 Woman of the Year acceptance speech, Esquivel explained that writing *Like Water for Chocolate* was her way of sharing "with all the world my doubts and my experiences in the culinary, amatory, and cosmic spheres." She described the tale as "quite simply the reflection of everything I am as a woman, wife, mother, daughter."

Set during the Mexican Revolution, *Like Water for Chocolate* focuses on the ill-fated love between Tita and her handsome neighbor, Pedro. As the youngest of three daughters living on the de la Garza ranch, Tita must—according to tradition—forgo marriage to care for and cook for her mother until the old woman's death. When Pedro asks Tita's mother for permission to marry Tita, the mother refuses—but suggests that he marry her eldest daughter, Rosaura, instead. Pedro, wanting to be close to Tita, agrees. In the end, after multiple tribulations, the lovers are united—but only after an incendiary finale culminating in the deaths of both.

Throughout the story, elements of magic and surrealism are portrayed as being ordinary. When Tita, forced to bake the cake for her sister's wedding, cries into the batter, wedding guests who eat the cake are suddenly overcome with sadness and longing for their own lost loves. Later in the story, rose petals used to perfume a quail dish arouse such desire in one of the sisters that she literally sets the bathhouse on fire.

Esquivel's follow-up to *Like Water for Chocolate*, *The Law of Love*, was published in 1995. Billed as "the first multimedia novel," the book includes segments that are told through comic-strip panels, a compact disc for the reader to play during critical moments in the story, and pre-Columbian poetry scattered throughout the text. In the story, something of a foray into New Age science fiction, Esquivel wrote of Azucena, an "astroanalyst" living in 23rd-century Mexico City and trying desperately to get in touch with her "twin soul," Rodrigo. Complicating this quest is the fact that the evil Isabel, a candidate for planetary president, is bent on destroying Azucena. In her search for Rodrigo, Azucena travels to the planet Korma, visits several of her past lives, has a computer chip implanted in her brain, and survives several harrowing encounters with Isabel.

The Law of Love, quite unlike *Like Water for Chocolate*, was not generally well-received by critics. What he viewed as a lack of character development led Robert Houston, in the *New York Times Book Review* (November 17, 1996), to dismiss the story's principals as "the cardboard characters of farce or of Saturday morning cartoons." Further, *Publishers Weekly* (July 22, 1996) criticized the book's "fantastical setting and long-winded metaphysical discourse" for "repeatedly upstaging" the love affair between Rodrigo and Azucena. "It is, one hopes, only a brief detour for Ms. Esquivel," wrote Houston. "What was humor and charm in *Like Water for Chocolate* has become in this book simply silliness."

Recent criticisms aside, Esquivel cherishes her success and goes to extensive lengths to thank others for their contributions to it. "In my life, the intense, amorous, passionate union between male and female bore fruit as a book and a film that encompass my family past, my national consciousness, my obsessions, fears, hopes, and, more than anything, my belief in love between woman and man. Love that now is public and circulating among movie theaters and book stores around the world, love that has brought me public acclaim," she said in her Woman of the Year speech. "I am obligated to share that acclaim with my mother, my daughter, my grandmother, my sisters, with Sato, and Tita, and all the women who came before and after them, and who, day after day and year after year, have put us in touch with our true origins. That acclaim must also be shared with all women who have not forgotten that stones do speak and that the earth is a living creature, and who make ordinary acts a ceremony of union with the universe, all through the 12 intense and masculine solar months and the 13 magic and female moons of ev-

ery year of their lives without ever receiving a moment's recognition."
—J. P.

SUGGESTED READING: *Library Journal* p156 July 1996; *New York Times* C p1 Feb. 17, 1993, C p1 Mar. 31, 1993, with photo; *New York Times Book Review*, Nov. 17, 1996; *Publishers Weekly* p225 July 22, 1996; *Washington Post* B p3 Mar. 6, 1993, with photos, D p7 Nov. 26, 1993, with photo

SELECTED WORKS: Fiction—*Like Water for Chocolate*, 1989; *The Law of Love*, 1995; Screenplays—*Chido One, el Tacos de Oro*, 1985; *Like Water for Chocolate*, 1992

Courtesy of William Morrow & Company

Faludi, Susan

Apr. 18, 1959– Nonfiction writer

In her best-selling book, *Backlash: The Undeclared War Against American Women* (1991), Susan Faludi argued that during the 1980s there was a concerted "backlash" against the advances women had made in all spheres of life in the previous decade. The backlash tried to instill in women three ideas that Faludi exposed as myths: first, that feminism was no longer necessary because women had already achieved their goals; second, that women's expanded roles had made them miserable; and finally, that feminism had caused women's predicament by daring to claim that women can and should "have it all"—a fulfilling personal life,

which may or may not include a family, as well as a successful career. The forces behind the backlash, Faludi has contended, were aided by trend-mongers in the media who invented a host of new problems that were supposedly besetting contemporary middle-class women, among them a "man shortage," an "infertility epidemic," a surge in the number of cases of child abuse in day care centers, and a higher incidence of neurosis and depression among single, childless, or career-minded women. One by one, Faludi debunked those stories by revealing the flawed research, skewed statistics, and conservative ideology behind them.

Hailed as "feminism's new manifesto" by Eleanor Smeal, the former president of the National Organization for Women, *Backlash* propelled its author to the status of "feminist du jour," as Faludi once referred to herself with self-deprecating humor. Her highly praised book won the National Book Critics Circle Award for general nonfiction and elicited more attention, including a healthy dose of criticism, than any feminist work since 1963, when Betty Friedan published *The Feminine Mystique*.

In 1999 Faludi surprised many by turning from the problems facing women to the themes tackled in *Stiffed: The Betrayal of the American Man*. Before the publication of her books, Faludi, a respected reporter who won a Pulitzer Prize for explanatory journalism in 1991, had already distinguished herself for 10 years as a thorough, detail-oriented writer with a flair for presenting the human consequences of business decisions and legislation.

Susan Faludi was born on April 18, 1959, in New York City, the only daughter of Steven Faludi, a Hungarian-born Jewish photographer who had spent part of his childhood hiding from the Nazis, and Marilyn Faludi, a writer and editor who had been a homemaker until her divorce in 1976. Susan and her younger brother, Rob, grew up in a conservative Irish and Italian neighborhood in Yorktown Heights, New York, where on one occasion a petitioner who objected to a black family's moving into the area was castigated by an outraged Marilyn Faludi. "We were the neighborhood weirdos," Susan Faludi revealed in a wide-ranging, in-depth interview with Carol Pogash for *Working Woman* (April 1992).

The changes in what were considered acceptable roles for women in the 1960s and 1970s created conflicting ambitions among girls growing up in that era, as Faludi recalled in her interview with Pogash: "I would look at the women in my neighborhood, and they were all mothers, Cub Scout leaders, and cooking chocolate-chip cookies, and part of me wanted to grow up and have a station wagon. But the other part of me wanted to be mayor of New York City." Faludi's mother became frustrated with her circumscribed existence, as she admitted to Pogash: "I could no longer play this role of submissive wife." Pogash quoted an angry Susan Faludi as saying, "My mother has been cheated, and the world's been cheated of her talents."

Determined to make an impact on society in a way denied her mother, Faludi was exhibiting reporter's instincts as early as the fifth grade, when she polled her classmates about their views on such controversial issues as the Equal Rights Amendment, abortion rights, and the Vietnam War. When the results of her poll showed that the students were pro-choice, supported the ERA, and opposed the war, she was attacked by a member of the local chapter of the John Birch Society for inciting Communism with her findings. A similar outcry met her valedictory speech at Yorktown High School, in which she spoke of the need for energy conservation and the social consequences of allowing the creation of test-tube babies.

Faludi began preparing for a career in journalism in high school, where she edited the student newspaper. Something of a crusader even then, she succeeded in putting a halt to student-teacher meetings of born-again Christians by writing articles in which she argued that the meetings violated the principle of the separation of church and state. Following her graduation from high school, Faludi enrolled at Harvard University, in Cambridge, Massachusetts, which she attended on an Elks scholarship. There, she continued to work for social change as the managing editor of the *Harvard Crimson*, for which she wrote about sexual harassment on campus over the objections of both the dean and a professor who had been accused of the crime; the professor was asked to take a leave of absence after Faludi's story was published.

A history and literature major, Faludi earned membership in Phi Beta Kappa in 1980 and graduated, summa cum laude, in 1981, having won an Oliver Dabney History Award for her senior thesis. She spent the summer before her senior year working as an intern reporter for the daily *Staten Island Advance,* and in 1981 she was a stringer for the *Boston Globe.* Upon leaving Harvard Faludi joined the *New York Times* as a news and copy clerk. In her spare time, she wrote freelance stories for the national, metro, living, and business sections of the newspaper until she left the staff in December 1982. During her stint at the paper, she also served as an intern reporter for the business news section. In one of the many instances of sexism in Faludi's life that she recounted to Carol Pogash, a male journalist at the *New York Times* told her that because women were able to carry a baby for nine months they were "biologically more patient than men," as Pogash put it, and that therefore Faludi was "well suited to be an assistant."

In 1983 Faludi accepted a job with the *Miami Herald,* which assigned her to its suburban bureau. The following year she moved on to a general-reporting position at the *Atlanta Journal-Constitution,* where she eventually became a staff writer for the Sunday magazine section. In 1985 she won first prize for news reporting and feature reporting from the Georgia Associated Press. After moving to the West Coast, from 1985 to 1989 she contributed articles to *Mother Jones, Ms.,* and *California Business* while serving as a staff writer for *West,* the Sunday magazine of the *San Jose Mercury News.* During that period she won awards or citations from such professional organizations as Women in Communications, the *Columbia Journalism Review,* the California Newspaper Publishers Association, and the Associated Press of California and Nevada. She also won a Robert F. Kennedy Memorial Journalism Award citation.

From January 1990 to February 1992, Faludi was a staff writer for the San Francisco bureau of the *Wall Street Journal.* In 1991 she won a John Hancock Award for Excellence in Business and Financial Journalism and, in April of that year, a Pulitzer Prize for "The Reckoning," an investigative piece on the human costs of the $5.65 billion leveraged buyout in 1986 of Safeway Stores, Inc., by Kohlberg, Kravis, Roberts & Company that appeared on the front page of the *Wall Street Journal* on May 16, 1990. Going behind the headlines, Faludi revealed that the layoffs, lower wages, and demands for increased productivity had driven one former employee to suicide and that others had suffered heart attacks. "The great success for investors of the Safeway leveraged buyout," Norman Pearlstine, the managing editor of the *Wall Street Journal,* was quoted as saying in the April 10, 1991, edition of that paper, "made it important that business readers understand the deal's human side as well. Susan Faludi provided that understanding through brilliant reporting and penetrating analysis. We're very proud of her work."

"The Reckoning," which was based on more than 100 interviews, generated an almost unprecedented response from the *Wall Street Journal*'s readers, who flooded the newspaper's offices with letters, most of them favorable. Among those who found fault with the piece were the conservative monitoring group Accuracy in Media and Peter A. Magowan, the chairman and chief executive officer of Safeway, who charged Faludi with distortion and selective quotation. James B. Stewart, the front-page editor of the *Wall Street Journal,* told

Carol Pogash that the controversy "only underscored the power of her story and how much people had been affected by it." Faludi, he declared, was a more thorough researcher "than almost any other reporter here."

Backlash grew out of Faludi's curiosity about the background of a 1986 *Newsweek* cover story proclaiming that a college-educated single woman over the age of 40 had a greater chance of being shot by a terrorist than of finding a husband. The article was based on an unpublished and incomplete study (which was first mentioned in a Valentine's Day article in the Stamford, Connecticut, *Advocate*) of women's marriage patterns by a team of sociologists from Harvard and Yale Universities. When she took a closer look at the study, Faludi discovered that the research was flawed and the statistics—that women over 20 had a 20 percent chance of marrying, which dwindled to 5 percent at 35 and to 1.3 percent at 40—were groundless. "What was remarkable to me was that there was so little interest in finding out whether the study was true or false," she said in an interview with Kim Hubbard for *People* (November 11, 1991). "The story simply fit the notion of where women were at that point in history."

Even though Faludi and others wrote articles that exposed the marriage study as invalid, the mainstream media, she has contended, continued to perpetuate the trendy myth of a shortage of men. "No one suggested that women were taking their time because there was no compelling reason to marry," she stated in an interview with Jane Ayres for the *Chicago Tribune* (September 29, 1991). "Women are not economically motivated to marry now, and that's why they don't marry quickly in desperation. But this deliberation is threatening to men. After the *Newsweek* article, I began to see the same theme of women who asked for equality being punished. It appeared in popular novels, movies."

Taking an 18-month leave of absence from *West* magazine, Faludi resolved to publicize the extent of the backlash in a book. "I myself and many women like me were voiceless," she explained in her conversation with Carol Pogash. "Here I was, running around playing social worker, holding up the microphone to all these other sectors of the population who were being shoved off the public stage, and finally I woke up and realized that this was happening much closer to home." Unearthing evidence of backlash in virtually every industry, from the rewriting of the script of Adrian Lyne's 1987 blockbuster movie *Fatal Attraction* to the budget cuts instituted by President Ronald Reagan to the balloon dresses created by the fashion designer Christian Lacroix, Faludi took four years to research and write her book, which was originally scheduled to be published in 1988. She completed work on the book while serving a two-year appointment, beginning in 1989, as an affiliated scholar with Stanford University's Institute for Research on Women and Gender, and in October

1991 Crown Publishers rushed thousands of copies of *Backlash* to bookstores, "just when women were ready to wake up," Faludi acknowledged to Pogash. "Abortion rights were threatened, women were upset by the Clarence Thomas hearings and by the William Kennedy Smith rape case."

Backlash immediately began climbing the *New York Times* best-seller list, and it was quickly taken up by leading feminists as their "clarion call," in Eleanor Smeal's words, to action in the 1990s. Among those who offered early endorsements of the book were the Harvard economist Robert B. Reich, who called it "spellbinding and frightening," and the social critic Barbara Ehrenreich, who found it to be "a rich and juicy read, informed by powerful logic and moral clarity." Published in Great Britain by Chatto & Windus in March 1992, *Backlash* was expected to have the same far-reaching effect overseas as it had had in the United States. Jane Hill, writing in the *Guardian* (March 24, 1992), concluded that "the backlash, clearly, is not just an American phenomenon. . . . Susan Faludi analyzes brilliantly the cultural and political messages with which women are bombarded and reminds us that it is more critical than ever to reject the lie of 'postfeminism.' The truth about women's lives is all the ammunition we need."

The truth, as Faludi discovered, was far different from the version disseminated by the mass media. The "infertility epidemic" among women over the age of 30, who were explicitly admonished for having pursued careers instead of listening to the ticking of their biological clocks, turned out to have been erroneously extrapolated from a French study of women who were trying to get pregnant via artificial insemination because their husbands were sterile. The only real increase in infertility that Faludi found was among younger women—and it was due not to careerism but to chlamydia. Among the dozens of other examples of media distortion that have contributed to the backlash, Faludi cited the difficulties in persuading male programming executives to broadcast television shows with feminist themes; the eager embrace of breast-implant surgery by doctors (and patients) before all the facts about the dangers of silicone were known (or made available); and the promotion of the idea that women were leaving the fast track at work for the "mommy track," a term coined by a *New York Times* reporter in reference to the ideas of Felice N. Schwartz, the founder of Catalyst, a consulting organization that advises corporations on how to deal with women's career advancement.

Some reviewers of *Backlash* criticized Faludi for "massaging reality" by omitting statistics or examples that did not support her thesis that women have been victimized by misogynistic forces, such as her neglecting to mention that the character Hope, the stay-at-home wife and mother on the popular television series *thirtysomething*, finally strikes out in independence in the last episode. "What is also missing," Ellen Goodman wrote in the *New York Times Book Review* (October 27, 1991), "is recognition of the difference among hostility, hypocrisy, and plain old ambivalence. The backlash told women they couldn't have it all and shouldn't even try. But no one invented the ambivalence that many working mothers feel. Ms. Faludi's dark portrait of the new men's movement could also be many shades grayer, tinged with some acknowledgment of mixed male feelings. She is too dismissive of the new school of 'relational' feminists and blames researchers like Judith Wallerstein [the author of *Second Chances: Men, Women and Children a Decade After Divorce*] and theorists like Carol Gilligan [the author of *In a Different Voice*] for the misuse of their ideas." Despite such reservations, Ellen Goodman praised Faludi's "breezy, sharp style" and commended her for not perpetuating a conspiracy theory, concluding that *Backlash* "is an invigorating and thorough report."

Other reviewers, such as Karen Lehrman, who evaluated the book in an article for the *New Republic* (March 16, 1992), were less charitable. "Though her account is full of qualifiers, it is basically a conspiracy theory," Lehrman wrote. "Faludi essentially implies that a cabal of villains has been at work successfully intimidating a large class of victims: women." Gretchen Morgenson concurred in a scathing critique that appeared on the same date in *Forbes*: "[*Backlash*] is badly written, shoddily reported, and insulting to intelligent women. . . . In encouraging women to think of themselves as victims, Faludi discourages them from making the efforts required to succeed in a murderously competitive society; people who feel sorry for themselves don't usually put forth maximum effort. . . . In the opinion of this career woman, *Backlash* is a last gasp of seventies feminism, a final attempt to rally women to a shrill, antimale cause that has been comatose for years."

In her discussion with Jane Ayres, Faludi conceded that "any time women speak up, it will be seen as antimale," but she added that throughout the writing process she had shown the book to a male friend, implying that she had wanted to avoid sounding gratuitously opposed to men. According to more than one reviewer, she was successful. Lauren Green's assessment for the *Chicago Tribune* (December 29, 1991) represents a commonly held view: "*Backlash* is guaranteed to make some readers furious, but it would be wrong to dismiss it is a man-hating screed. . . . Her mountain of evidence and example is thorough, carefully documented, and persuasive." Jane O'Reilly was even more enthusiastic in her review for *New York Newsday* (November 17, 1991): "*Backlash* is more than an important and readable book. It is a gift. Every page provides a click! of recognition, of clarity and consciousness raising." In her interview with Carol Pogash, Faludi expressed her hope that the book would influence women to take action: "To the extent that *Backlash* arms women with information and a good dose of cynicism, I think it will have served its purpose. It's also very large, so it can be thrown at misogynists."

Faludi shifted her focus with her 1999 volume, the 662-page *Stiffed: The Betrayal of the American Man*. This book is built on the thesis that males in the U.S. have been robbed—through the devaluation of skilled manual labor, among other factors—of the opportunity to demonstrate genuine manliness, which the author associates with a sense of being a useful member of society. The media and consumerism, Faludi asserted, are also to blame for the "betrayal" of the subtitle, having marketed a harmful image of manliness and having replaced concern for ordinary men with an emphasis on celebrity culture.

Judith Shulevitz, writing in the *New York Times Book Review* (October 3, 1999), found *Stiffed* to be dangerously retrograde in its assertions. "The real solution" to the problem Faludi addresses, according to Shulevitz, "is to demand that America give [the male blue-collar worker] the education he needs to succeed, not to dismiss the opportunities available to him as meaningless or sinister. Faludi's palpable hunger to return to the working-class values of a half century ago does the men (and women) of the coming century no favors." By contrast, in her review of *Stiffed* for the *Times* (September 28, 1999), Michiko Kakutani—faulting Faludi's earlier book for what she called its "didactic and highly simplistic analysis"—lauded the "far more nuanced and sympathetic assessment" presented in *Stiffed*.

Susan Faludi lives in San Francisco's Haight-Ashbury district. As shy in person as she is bold in her hard-hitting reportage, she intensely dislikes public speaking, bemoaning the disparity between her public and private personas. "It's not intentional, and it bothers me," she admitted to Pogash.—C.T./D.B.

SUGGESTED READING: *Chicago Tribune* VI p3 Sep. 29, 1991, with photo, Dec. 29, 1991; *Cosmopolitan* p207 May 1994, with photo; *Details* p74+ Feb. 1992, with photo; *Forbes* Mar. 16, 1992; *Guardian* p21 Mar. 24 1992, with photo; *New Republic* Mar. 16, 1992; *New York Newsday* Nov. 17, 1991; *New York Times Book Review* Oct. 27, 1991, Oct. 3, 1999; *People* p138+ Nov. 11 1991, with photos; *Working Woman* p64+ Apr. 1992, with photos

SELECTED WORKS: *Backlash: The Undeclared War Against American Women*, 1991; *Stiffed: The Betrayal of the American Man*, 1999

Miriam Berkley

Fischer, Tibor

1959– Writer

In a rare interview, published in *Spike* (March 1996), Tibor Fischer half-jokingly stated that the purpose of his writing was "to give people a few mental lozenges to suck on." His debut novel, *Under the Frog* (1993), a black comedy about an over-sexed basketball team touring Hungary after the 1956 uprising, did just that. Highly regarded among critics, Fischer's novel was nominated for the Booker Prize in the U.K. and also put its author on *Granta*'s Best of Young British Novelists list. Since his debut, Fischer has published two more novels: *The Thought Gang* (1995), about a pair of philosophical bank robbers, and *The Collector Collector* (1997), a tale of love and art, narrated by an antique bowl.

Very little about Fischer's life has been made public. He was born in Stockport, England, in 1959, the son of Hungarian parents who emigrated to the U.K. after the failed 1956 uprising against the government. His mother was captain of the Hungarian women's basketball team—a probable inspiration for his novel *Under the Frog*.

The title of that novel comes from a Hungarian proverb which states that the worst place in the world to be is "under the frog's arse down a coal mine"—an off-color reference to the Soviet Union during the Cold War. The novel is riddled with black humor about Communist oppression since the hero, Gyuri, grows up in the shadow of the Soviet Union under Stalin. During the 1956 revolution, Gyuri's gesture of defiance is his use of the selected speeches of Matyas Rakosi—the Hungarian Communist Party secretary—as toilet paper. A pas-sage from the book reads: "Gyuri was trying to enjoy his sojourn at the hindquarters' headquarters with extracts from these books, but although the idea had been highly pleasing, the reality wasn't as satisfactory. The Communists couldn't even hack it as toilet paper." The novel contains other, similar antics, as when a Hungarian men's basketball team travels naked to a game, looking for sex wherever they can find it. Their mischief is a response to what they are really trying to escape from—life under communism: "So where were the American Imperialists? The British Imperialists? Or even the German ones? They had been promised Imperialists for years on end, Gyuri thought angrily. . . . He had carefully rehearsed the phrase with which he would greet the American invaders: What kept you? Let me take you to many interesting Communists I am sure you will be eager to shoot."

A writer for the *New York Times Book Review* (August 28, 1994) noted that the author, who was born after these events of 1956, was able to capture perfectly they mood of the era in his work: "*Under the Frog* is fully a work of dynamic historical imagination." A reviewer for the *Guardian* (September 23, 1993) called the novel "a hilarious account of life in postwar Hungary."

The central character of Fischer's second novel, *The Thought Gang*, is Edward Coffin, referred to in the novel as Eddie—a bald, disheveled, over-weight, alcoholic professor of philosophy at Cambridge University. Eddie's canon consists of one published book, which his editor has to write for him after Eddie spends his advance on liquor; a couple of other books he has never finished; and one lecture, which he delivers, unchanged, year in and year out. "People who don't like me very much," Eddie explains in the novel, "and who have assessed my progress uncharitably have said: lush, compulsive gambler, zero, drug-dealer, fraud, disaster, slob. People who like me have said much the same."

Eddie leaves England for France with a suitcase of embezzled money, which is destroyed along with his forged identity papers when his rented car overturns in a near-fatal accident. With only four francs and change in the pockets of his tattered clothes, he hitchhikes to Montpelier. In a cheap hotel there he meets Hubert, an ex-con who enjoyed his 10-year sentence, believing that in jail, at least, "no one pretended you were free." Hubert—who has a glass eye, one arm, and one leg—attempts to rob Eddie, but the philosopher has no money, and, as it turns out, Hubert has no bullets. (He could afford only the gun.) Perplexed, Hubert asks his would-be victim: "So how do you like France?"

From this strange first encounter, the professional criminal and professional philosopher decide that they can learn from each other and thus become the Thought Gang, bank robbers who specialize in robberies with philosophical themes. A vampish teller named Jocelyne slips her telephone number in with the loot from the first robbery and eventually becomes Eddie's girlfriend. On the same job, Eddie and Hubert duck into a fancy restaurant to eat fish in order to avoid the police and hence create the "getaway lunch." With each succeeding job the mischief continues. As described by a reviewer for the *New York Times Book Review* (June 25, 1995): "[Eddie and Hubert] give away Thought Gang T-shirts; they rob banks while wearing masks of Nietzsche; they offer to spare any bank whose tellers can quote them a line of philosophy; they rob five banks in one day, fending off a rival gang in the process; they trash the apartment of the special agent brought in to nab them. Finally . . . the Thought Gang achieves its Platonic ideal, a bank robbery announced in advance." Eddie, especially, has fun provoking the special agent—a Corsican antigang expert. According to a book critic at the *Nation* (July 10, 1995), "Some of the funniest writing in *The Thought Gang* involves Eddie and Hubert's dealings with the Corsican."

Reviews of the novel were mixed. John Updike, writing about the book for the *New Yorker* (August 21 & 28, 1995): stated, "Fischer has gifts. His tweaked sentences, which often need rereading, hold angles that make us laugh with recognition." Later in the review, however, Updike commented on such features of the book as Fischer's use of a noticeably high number of words beginning with the letter "z," describing the effect as "a buzz of distraction that makes it . . . hard to take this book seriously." Ron Loewinsohn, in the *New York Times Book Review* (June 25, 1995), however, wrote that Fischer's novel was "an intelligent, thoughtful black comedy by a writer who deserves to be taken seriously." The *Nation* (July 10, 1995) reviewer David L. Ulin praised Fischer as being able captivate the reader "by the sheer force of Eddie's personality and the qualities of thought he brings on his own befuddled movement through the world, daring by magic to turn philosophy into the substance of art." Nicci Gerrard, writing for the *Observer* (December 4, 1994), praised Fischer's *Under the Frog* as going down "as easily as a pint," but criticized *The Thought Gang*, remarking that it goes down "as easily as a mouthful of sawdust and pins." Gerrard believed that Fischer's extensive use of wordplay made the book "very nearly unreadable."

The Collector Collector, Fischer's third novel, was published in London in March 1997. The narrator of the novel is a bowl, thousands of years old, that is able to change its shape at will. Except for a millennium spent sealed in an Egyptian tomb, it has passed through appreciative hands throughout its existence and has observed a good deal of world history. It speaks 5,000 languages and tells stories of its adventures quite readily.

The novel begins when a London auctioneer takes the bowl to the home of an expert to have it authenticated. Rosa, the expert, is also a diviner who can lay hands on an object and pick up its vibes. The bowl shares a psychic relationship with Rosa and, through it, can relate all the stories of its own long existence, some of which were as described by a writer for the *Times Literary Supplement* (March 14, 1997): "A man called Wondernose, in ancient Egypt, has a nose so large that it needs a special rest, and he stores fruit in it. Another man copulates with buildings, and has developed a passion for the Kremlin. A whole village is put to death, horribly, just by using a spoon." The bowl also tells of a 19th-century woman who wrote *Oliver Twist*, *Madame Bovary*, and other great works, only to be beaten to the publisher by a week or two each time.

As much as storytelling is a driving force in *The Collector Collector*, Fischer's penchant for wordplay is equally important. Many critics found this to be off-putting. The *Sunday Times* (March 9, 1997) reviewer Hugo Barnacle wrote, "The bowl's persistent use of rhyming words—despair is 'pain for the brain,' clouds are 'bunched like fuds above the suds,' whatever fuds are—is meant to be clever-clever in the style of Martin Amis or Salman Rushdie, but is equally reminiscent of the signs in public car parks: 'Have You Payed and Displayed?'" Phil Baker, reviewing the novel for the *Times Literary Supplement* (March 14, 1997), believed that the book "shows flashes of brilliance and underdeveloped nods at serious themes, but . . . more often irritates." The *London Times* (March 6, 1997) reviewer wrote that Fischer "is a satirist whose Babelesque brilliance sometimes eclipses sense" but believed that the book's strength "resides in a simple theme [friendship between women] working in counterpoint with complex language."

C.M.

SUGGESTED READING: *Guardian* p9 Sep. 23, 1993, p9 Dec. 6, 1994, p 24 Nov. 10, 1995; *London Times* Mar. 6, 1997; *Nation* p 66+ July 10, 1995; *New Yorker* p106+ Aug. 21&28, 1995; *New York Times Book Review* p10 Aug. 28, 1994, p11 June 25, 1995; *Observer* p19 Dec. 4, 1994; *Spike* Mar. 1996; *Sunday Times* Mar. 9, 1997; *Times Literary Supplement* p22 Mar. 14, 1997; *Washington Post* D p3 Sep. 23, 1993, X p12 Apr. 30, 1995

SELECTED BOOKS: *Under the Frog*, 1993; *The Thought Gang*, 1995; *The Collector Collector*, 1997

Forrest, Leon

Jan. 8, 1937– Nov. 6, 1997 Novelist

Born and bred on Chicago's South Side, Forrest took the ingredients of his upbringing—storytelling, religion, literature, and music—and combined them to produce a series of novels that capture the essence of African-American culture. Writing in a stream-of-consciousness style, Forrest drew characters directly from life and placed them in compelling stories that in many ways echo traditional folktales. Although Forrest, during his lifetime, never received and public accolades given to many writers of similar stature, his novels—*There is a Tree More Ancient Than Eden* (1973), *The Bloodworth Orphans* (1977), *Two Wings to Veil My Face* (1983) and *Divine Days* (1992)—feature what have since been labeled some of the most entertaining and insightful characters in modern literature.

Leon Forrest was born on January 8, 1937, in Chicago, Illinois. He grew up on Chicago's South Side, where his father, described by Forrest as a "self-made man, hypersensitive and high-strung," worked as a railroad bartender. As a writer Forrest drew heavily on the culture that had surrounded him in his childhood: the trappings of both the Catholic and Baptist churches, and the blues and jazz that have played integral roles in the South Side's culture since before Forrest was born. He credits his family with introducing him early on to oral storytelling, which he cites as a vital component of African-American culture, and which would inevitably weave its way into his fiction. Often, returning home from work, his father would relate stories of jazz musicians and others he had encountered on the train.

After high school Forrest attended Wilson Junior College, from 1955 to 1956, then Roosevelt University, from 1957 to 1958. He entered the University of Chicago in 1958, spending two years there before enlisting in the United States Army, in which he served until 1962. Upon his return Forrest reenrolled at the University of Chicago as a student-at-large, thereby fulfilling no degree requirements before leaving the university in 1964.

Forrest's first professional job was as the managing editor of the *Woodlawn Observer*, a local newspaper, where he stayed until 1969. He left that year to become associate editor, and then managing editor, of *Mohammed Speaks,* the publication of the Nation of Islam. He would be the newspaper's last non-Muslim managing editor. In 1973 he left this position to join the faculty at Northwestern University, where he became professor of African-American studies and, later, chair of the department (1985–94). From 1974 to 1979 Forrest also lecturered at Yale University, Rochester Institute of Technology, and Wesleyan University.

Forrest's first novel was *There is a Tree More Ancient Than Eden* (1973), which included an introduction by the famed African-American author Ralph Ellison. The story centers on the complicated relationships among the children of a family that once owned slaves. The novel received good reviews from a variety of sources, particularly *Black World* (January 1974), in which Houston A. Baker compared Forrest's novel to Ellison's *Invisible Man.* Baker wrote that the book "represents an awe-inspiring fusion of American cultural myth, Black American history, Black fundamentalist religion, the doctrine and dogma of Catholicism . . . and an autobiographical recall of days of anxiety and confusion in the city." Zack Gilbert, also in *Black World* (January 1974), deemed the book

"moving and forceful in its poetic flow" and wrote, "Forrest has woven an hypnotic fabric with words that are part jazz, part blues, part gospel."

In other critiques Forrest's first novel was compared to the work of William Faulkner. Joel Motley of the *Harvard Advocate* (Vol. CVII, 1974) called *There is a Tree More Ancient Than Eden* a "powerful work of literature" and stated that while Forrest's stream-of-consciousness writing is reminiscent of Faulkner, Forrest possesses the ability to make this style his own in order to accurately portray the life of urban blacks. In his review for the *New York Times Book Review* (October 21, 1973), L. J. Davis was not as taken with Forrest's style. "[Stream of consciousness] is just fine, but only if we know from whom it is streaming and why it is streaming that way and not another," Davis wrote. "And a pervading sense of doom is certainly a nasty thing to have." In a final jab, Davis wrote that Forrest is "one of those black writers who appear to suffer from the unhappy delusion that they are really William Faulkner."

Forrest's next novel, *The Bloodworth Orphans* (1977), tells the story of the orphaned children, both black and white, of a family of former slave owners. This book yielded mixed reviews. A reviewer for *Publishers Weekly* (March 21, 1977) called the storyline "tiresomely complex," but also wrote of the novel's "torrential eloquence, vivid characterization, and occasional infectious humor." A reviewer for " *Booklist* (May 15, 1977) strongly admired the book's "intense, breathless stream of prose."

Forrest's third novel was *Two Wings to Veil My Face* (1984), in which Nathaniel Witherspoon, a character from *There is a Tree More Ancient Than Eden,* records the life story of a former slave, Momma Sweetie Reed. "As she tells her story," Bernard Rodgers of the *Chicago Tribune Book World* (February 5, 1984) pointed out, "Nathaniel is forced to redefine his own identity, to translate as well as transcribe the meaning of her memories . . . In the end, the secrets Great-Momma Sweetie reveals to Nathaniel . . . radically alter both their lives." In this book Forrest once again presented a seemingly structureless story, to the irritation of some critics. Still, Rodgers concluded, "It is a novel . . . that's not for everyone. Just for those who love the excitement of watching a truly unique writer practice his art; for those who can recognize the magic beneath the mundane, as Forrest does; for those who are willing to accept the challenge of a novel that really is extraordinary and unforgettable."

The year 1992 saw the publication of what many consider to be Forrest's finest work, *Divine Days.* The 1,138-page novel reproduces the journal of Joubert Jones, an aspiring playwright living in Chicago's South Side. The events in *Divine Days* take place over the course of a week in February 1966. Supporting himself as a bartender and reporter, Jones becomes interested in writing his next play about a man named Sugar Groove, a local legend and ladies' man who has mysteriously disappeared. As he tries to find out what happened to Sugar Groove, the reader is introduced to various characters from all walks of life, all interwoven into the magical and turbulent tapestry of 1960s Chicago. *Divine Days* was praised by Stanley Crouch, who wrote in the *New York Times Book Review* (July 25, 1993), "this epic detective story pulls in elements of the Gothic, the tall tale, the parable, the philosophical argument, the novel of ideas, the history lesson, the novel of manners, and the sort of close observation Balzac, Mann, and Hemingway would have admired."

As Jones searches for Sugar Groove, who is, in effect, a surrogate parental figure, he ultimately reaches a new level of self-realization. This process, as documented by Jones's journal, mixes Forrest's stream-of-consciousness style with his knowledge of and admiration for the South Side's musical history. As Crouch noted in his review, "[Forrest] develops his tale through literary 'chorus structures' in which the 'melody' might be metamorphosis and the "chords" motifs—phrases, archetypes, colors, natural elements. . . . The orchestral control from the first chapter to the last is apt to make our most serious novelists both grateful and envious."

Divine Days was given high marks by other critics as well. In his review of the novel for *New Republic* (May 31, 1993), Sven Birkerts called Forrest the "invisible man of contemporary African-American letters." Birkerts offered nothing but praise for the writer's work, claiming that Forrest captures "the soul of a community, and to a degree of a whole culture, exposed by way of speech." In conclusion, Birkerts deemed *Divine Days* a "rare" piece of fiction as well as a "full-out serious work of art."

Forrest published a collection of essays titled *Relocations of the Spirit* in 1994. This compilation consists largely of articles, speeches, and reviews that Forrest had published in a variety of publications. Many contain his personal thoughts on prominent African-American figures, from writers such as Ralph Ellison and Toni Morrison to singing legend Billy Holiday and sports hero Michael Jordan. The central theme that holds all of these articles and essays together, as Forrest was quoted as saying in *African American Review* (Spring 1995), is the African-American propensity for "taking something that is available or, maybe conversely, denied to Blacks and making it into something else for survival and then adding a kind of stamp and style and elegance."

Although *Relocations of the Spirit* was not widely reviewed, the notices that appeared were highly favorable.

Leon Forrest succumbed to cancer on November 6, 1997, at the age of 60. He is survived by his wife, Marianne; a stepson, James Claude Holt; a stepdaughter, Peggie Holt Price; and two grandsons. According to his agent, Faith Childs, before his death Forrest completed a collection of novellas that will be published in the future. Forrest's awards include the Sandburg Medallion from the Chicago Public Library (1978), the Chicago Book of the Year Award (for *Divine Days,* 1992), and the *New York Times* Notable Book of the Year (for *Divine Days,* 1993).—D.B.

SUGGESTED READING: *African American Review* p160+ Spring 1995; *Black World* Jan. 1974; *Booklist* May 15, 1977; жicago Tribune Book World Feb. 5, 1984; *Harvard Advocate* Vol. CVII, 1974; *New Republic* p42+ May 31, 1993; *New York Times* B p8 Nov. 10, 1997; *New York Times Book Review* Oct. 21, 1973, p14 July 25, 1993, p14 May 29, 1994; *Publisher's Weekly* Mar. 21, 1977; *Contemporary Authors,* 1996; *Who's Who Among Black Americans,* 1994–1995

SELECTED BOOKS: *There is a Tree More Ancient Than Eden,* 1973; *The Bloodworth Orphans,* 1977; *Two Wings to Veil My Face,* 1983; *Divine Days,* 1992; *Relocations of the Spirit,* 1994

Mika Fowler

Fowler, Connie May

Jan. 3, 1958– Novelist

The author of three novels, *Sugar Cage,* (1992), *River of Hidden Dreams* (1994), and *Before Women Had Wings* (1996), and numerous essays and short stories, American writer Connie May Fowler is known for mixing elements of history, magic, and folklore into stories set amid the lush topography of her home state of Florida. Her books, particularly *Before Women Had Wings,* in which the protagonist, Bird, is a young girl from an abusive home, tend to have a decidedly autobiographical bent. Though this is a practice that Fowler says allows her to turn her own painful experiences into something valuable, writing such extremely personal material carries its own set of drawbacks. "I couldn't talk about *Sugar Cage* at all, and with *Before Women Had Wings*, I'm walking on eggshells," she said in an interview with *Publishers Weekly* (May 13, 1996). "There are sections I know I can't read in public. . . . I'm very private. A lot of writers are. That's what's so ironic about what we do. On the page, we take off our clothes."

Born on January 3, 1958 in Raleigh, North Carolina, Connie May Fowler is the daughter of Henry Jefferson May, a half-Cherokee and half-Irish country-western singer/songwriter and former police officer and salesman, and Lenore Monita Looney May, a nurse, bookkeeper and homemaker. Within days of her birth, the May family returned to their home in St. Augustine, Florida, where Connie May Fowler spent the first years of her life amid a stifling atmosphere of poverty and domestic violence.

When Fowler was seven her father died. His death, she has said, marked the beginning of an even more turbulent period. "When he was alive, my family's life was completely chaotic, because my parents had a volatile relationship and there was a great deal of violence in the home," Fowler said in an interview with *Kalliope* (Volume 26, Number 2, 1994). "Yet, even given that, when he died, we were all so lost. At least when he was alive, we had a family unit. But once he was gone, the family completely split apart. My sister and mother and I stayed together, but we went from being a self-sufficient—albeit dysfunctional—family to a grieving widow and two children living off welfare. So the years he was alive, in retrospect, seemed like Camelot to me." After her father's death, the remaining family members relocated to Tampa, where her mother worked as a bookkeeper and maid in exchange for room and board in local motels. Until the age of nine or 10, Fowler suffered from a severe speech impediment that made much of what she said incomprehensible. Now completely recovered, Fowler says she believes the speech problem was a direct result of her unstable home life. "I've thought a lot about it," she said in the *Kalliope* interview. "I think I was so frightened that my words would provoke more violence in my life that I just became silent." Fowler sought refuge in reading and writing—pastimes in which neither her speech impediment nor her chaotic surroundings were of any consequence. "I could be transported from the awful circumstances of my life simply by opening a book," she said in a statement issued by her paperback publisher, Ballantine Books. "And writing went hand in hand with reading. I found it difficult to express myself verbally. I was always frightened. . . . But I was able to write my feelings down. Often, when I was having trouble communicating with my mother, I would sit down and write to her. Writing for me was kind of a salvation."

After graduating from high school, Fowler went to the University of Tampa on a full scholarship. There, she began to publish her poetry in various literary magazines, and her work was featured in *Up and Coming Poets of America*, a photographic travel essay by Wendy Grad. At about this time, Fowler's mother, who had long before turned to alcohol to ease the pain of losing her husband, died of cirrhosis of the liver. Following her mother's death Fowler withdrew from school and spent two years traveling throughout the United States and Mexico. Once she was back in Tampa, the university provost spotted her waiting tables at a local restaurant and persuaded her to return to school. In 1985 she graduated with a bachelor's degree, summa cum laude, in English and began working as a freelance writer.

Two years later she married Mike Fowler and moved to Kansas, where she began graduate studies at the University of Kansas. She intended at first to concentrate on poetry, and she now says that it was only under duress ("I was dragged kicking and screaming," she said in the *Kalliope* interview) that she agreed to take a fiction course—a move that would forever change her life. "The fiction professor treated me for the first time in my life as if I was truly a writer," Fowler said in the statement from her publisher. "With her, everything coalesced. Fiction suddenly made sense to me." With the encouragement and mentorship of her professor, Carolyn Doty, Fowler's first short-story assignment evolved into her graduate thesis and eventually into her highly regarded debut novel, *Sugar Cage* (1992). With no previous experience in writing fiction, penning *Sugar Cage* was no easy task. "At first I had no idea what I was doing," she said in her interview with *Kalliope*. "I heard the voices of the characters, and I had the stories, but the form of the novel was so intimidating. I said, 'How in the world am I going to do this?' The novel seemed like a vast, monstrous blob lurking on the horizon. I had no idea how to tackle it. So I started reading. And reading. And reading. I started at the beginning of the 20th century and read up through Toni Morrison. Almost anything I could get. My goal was to internalize the form and the reading really, really helped me do that."

Her efforts were rewarded almost instantly. After receiving a list of agents from her professor, Fowler sent her manuscript to the first person on the list. Days later she and her husband packed their things and began the drive back to Florida. They arrived to find a postcard saying that the agent loved the book and was desperately trying to contact Fowler. Fowler's immediate reaction, she said in the *Kalliope* interview, was, "She's probably a crackpot. I've had nothing but blues my entire life and there's no way this is working out." The interest, however, was genuine, and less than a week later Fowler received an offer for the novel.

Published in 1992, *Sugar Cage* interweaves the stories of nine disparate souls living in Tiama, a small central Florida town dubbed the "prison capital of the world." Touching upon a vast number of subjects, including, "body snatching, a hurricane, a baseball game between prisoners and free men, deaths by cancer and heart attack, unquiet spirits, a pro-segregation rally in 1960s Florida, black women's and white men's magics, and the Vietnam War," as Donald McCaig wrote in the *Washington Post* (January 10, 1992), the novel was an immediate hit with critics. "The book is a cool look at a hot world until it reaches its startling and beautiful conclusion," McCaig concluded.

Fowler followed *Sugar Cage* with *River of Hidden Dreams*, a novel centering on Sadie Hunter, a woman involved in a tempestuous love affair with a Cuban refugee, and the stories she tells of her family's history. Critical reactions to *River of Hidden Dreams* were generally tepid. Most often criticized was the character Sadie, described by Judith Patterson in the *New York Times Book Review* (July 3, 1994) as a "middle-aged, self-alienated, self-analyzing, cliché-spouting post-hippie." "Sadie's commitment phobias trivialize her foremothers' losses, and her transformation by storytelling into a kind and loving woman comes across as no more than conceit," a reviewer wrote in the *Washington Post* (July 31, 1994). Critics, however, also had some kind words about the book. "There is no denying the depth of Connie May Fowler's talent and the breadth of her imagination," Patterson wrote in the *New York Times Book Review* article. "Her vision of an America enriched in the spirit by the mingling of cultures runs deep and true."

In 1996 Fowler published her most recent novel, *Before Women Had Wings*. Narrated by nine-year-old Avocet "Bird" Jackson, a young girl whose family is forced to relocate to Tampa after her alcoholic father commits suicide, the books tells of her life in an abusive home and the salvation she finds in a friendship with Miss Zora, a kind-hearted, mysterious woman from the Everglades. Awarded the 1996 Southern Critics Circle Award for fiction, *Before Women Had Wings* was lauded by critics. "Fowler brilliantly conveys a child's bewilderment when the sources that should provide succor—parents and religion—instead inspire fear: Her depictions of physical violence . . . spare no harrowing details," a reviewer wrote in *Publishers Weekly* (March 11, 1996). Further praise was offered by Nancy Pate in the *Chicago Tribune* (May 28, 1996). "Fowler rises to new storytelling heights," she wrote. "Bird's tale of her troubled family is a thing of heart rending beauty, a moving exploration of love and loss, violence and grief, forgiveness and redemption." *Before Women Had Wings* was made into a television movie (with a screenplay written by Fowler) that starred Oprah Winfrey, Ellen Barkin, and Tina Majorino and aired in the fall of 1997.

In addition to her writing, Fowler is actively involved in several environmental causes. When the National and Oceanic Atmospheric Commission targeted St. Augustine's river as a potential location for its newest national Estuarine Research Reserve, Fowler formed the River to Sea Civic Organization and successfully lobbied state and federal officials to ensure that St. Augustine would be selected. For her efforts, she was later elected the charter president of For Our Reserve, an organization dedicated to supporting the activities of the reserve. Additionally, Fowler, under the auspices of the Florida Humanities Council, tours the state speaking on such topics as wetland preservation and growth management.
—J. P.

SUGGESTED READING: *Chicago Tribune* p3 May 28, 1996; *Kalliope* vol. 26 no. 2, 1994; *New York Times* p16 Feb. 9, 1992; *New York Times Book Review* p22 July 3, 1994; *Publishers Weekly* p41 Mar. 11, 1996, p50+ May 13, 1996; *Washington Post* p3 Jan. 10, 1992, p6 July 31, 1994

SELECTED BOOKS: *Sugar Cage*, 1992; *River of Hidden Dreams*, 1994; *Before Women Had Wings*, 1996

Franzen, Jonathan

Aug. 17, 1959– Novelist

One of the most widely acclaimed authors to enter the literary arena in recent years, Jonathan Franzen produced his first novel before the age of 30. *The Twenty-seventh City* (1988) uses complex subplots and diverse characters to explore a modern, Orwellian version of St. Louis that exists under the heavy-handed regime of a scheming police commissioner. That book received high accolades and paved the way for Franzen's second novel, *Strong Motion* (1992), which examines the issues of environmental abuse and abortion. Part thriller, part social commentary, *Strong Motion* confirmed Franzen's place among the nation's most talented new fiction writers.

Jonathan Franzen was born on August 17, 1959, in Western Springs, Illinois, to Earl T. and Irene (Super) Franzen. He grew up in Saint Louis, where his father worked as a civil engineer and his mother as a homemaker. Franzen majored in German at Swarthmore College, from which he graduated in 1981 with a bachelor of arts degree. He worked part-time as an earthquake analyst for the Department of Earth and Planetary Sciences at Harvard University from 1983 to 1987.

He began writing his first novel at the age of 22, dreaming, as he stated in a *Harper's* (April 1996) essay, of "changing the world." Writing the novel became an all-consuming passion and an arduous six-year process that resulted in *The Twenty-seventh City*. The story is set in a fictionalized, alternate version of St. Louis. The city appoints S. Jammu, an Indian woman related to Indira Gandhi, to the position of police chief—and at first Jammu seems to have brought with her a fresh approach to law enforcement. Soon, however, it becomes apparent that Jammu and her cohorts have a secret agenda and are planning to alter the social, economic, and moral order of the city. What follows is a series of attempts by Jammu to elongate her reign of terror over St. Louis by any means necessary—usually with quiet yet highly effective threats. When Martin Probst, a man with high morals who built the St. Louis Gateway Arch, fails to give in to Jammu's persuasion, she steps up her efforts to include outright terrorism. The book offers a biting commentary on urban decline in the United States.

His debut effort was widely acclaimed by critics across the United States, with Saul Bellow proclaiming *The Twenty-seventh City* an "artful, thoughtful, social, capacious book that bridges the gap between a popular thriller and a literary masterwork," in a review for *Commonweal* (December 4, 1992). Other reviews praised Franzen for producing such an engaging novel at such a young age. *New York Times Book Review* (October 9, 1988) critic Peter Andrews wrote in his review that Franzen's novel is an "impressive debut by a gifted young writer," and R. Z. Sheppard of *Time* (April 14, 1997) wrote that Franzen "displays a striking talent for turning an implausible plot into a convincing omen." Perhaps Franzen received the most acclaim for his often unflattering but realistic look at the American mentality, particularly regarding politics and media. Jeff Jarvis wrote in *People* (October 17, 1988) that "Franzen's voice and his ear for speech are solid. He is a master at capturing the essence of things American . . . [he] draws a sad picture of a decaying America, but he does it with such talent and honesty that reading his book becomes at least as exciting as it is depressing."

In his attempt to cross-breed a suspenseful thriller with a developed literary novel, Franzen created rather complex characters and situations, leading Andrews to admit that "In mixing genres . . . Mr. Franzen runs into some difficult technical problems. . . . [He] is successful partly because he is in such control of his story that he makes you believe things are happening the way he says they are. As the good ones do, he makes you accept his vision." In his review Andrews also made a prediction about the book's audience—one that seemed to come true in the years following *The Twenty-seventh City*'s publication. "I fear Mr. Franzen may pay a price in popular success for the uncompromising way he tells his story," Andrews wrote. "Many of us who love thrillers have become a lazy lot, content with letting the author bring horror to us for our amusement."

In his 1996 *Harper's* essay, Franzen discussed his feelings about his status as a critics' darling. "The media's obsessive interest in my youthfulness surprised me . . . " he wrote. "But the biggest surprise—the true measure of how little I'd heeded my own warning in *The Twenty-seventh City*—was the failure of my culturally engaged novel to engage with the culture I'd intended to provoke." Franzen had hoped to create more than a novelty pop-culture novel; disappointed by the media's lethargic response, he wrote the autobiographical essay to discuss the precarious state of literature in today's society.

The commercial success of *The Twenty-seventh City* enabled Franzen to continue writing full-time. His second novel, *Strong Motion,* met with a mixed critical reaction upon its publication, in 1992. Another effort to combine suspense with social commentary, the novel teems with multifarious characters and subplots. In *Strong Motion*, 30-year-old Harvard seismologist Renee Seitchek works to uncover the cause of a series of earthquakes in the Boston area. As she begins to suspect that the quakes are the result of secret drilling being performed by Sweeting-Aldren, a chemical company trying to bury toxic waste, she also begins to fall in love with 23-year-old Louis Holland, a recent college graduate whose mother has inherited $22 million in Sweeting-Aldren stock. As Seitchek's investigation becomes more intense, her romance with Holland sours. Soon Seitchek discovers she is pregnant, a situation that leads to a confrontation with a staunch antiabortion activist, Reverend Philip Stites, in front of an abortion clinic. As the novel builds to its climax, Franzen successfully connects the running themes of his story—the seismic "strong motion" (a term used for the shaking of the ground near the epicenter of an earthquake) and Renee and Louis's romance. Also compared are the ecological destruction by the chemical company and Seitchek's battle over reproductive rights, and Franzen suggests similarities between the corporate desecration of the environment and anti-abortion activists' interference with women's abortion rights.

Franzen drew some criticism from reviewers for creating "contrivances." Josh Rubins wrote in the *New York Times Book Review* (February 16, 1992) that "Despite the brilliance of individual set pieces and the intelligence and keen observation on almost every page, *Strong Motion* loses momentum and conviction as it expands to meet Mr. Franzen's ambitious specifications." Rubins also took issue with the plot itself, which, "though sporadically fascinating," he felt "soon settles into a conventional potboiler pattern, complete with climactic violence." "The issues that Mr. Franzen wants to take on—the environment, abortion rights, gender roles, materialism, religious fanaticism—seem provocative at first but end up a blur," Rubins added.

Despite finding these flaws in *Strong Motion,* Rubins admitted that Franzen is a gifted writer willing to take risks. Rubins concluded his review by commenting that *Strong Motion,* even though "uneven," is still "less a disappointment than an affirmation of Mr. Franzen's fierce imagination and distinctive seriocomic voice." This type of mixed review was common for *Strong Motion,* with writers praising Franzen ambitiousness but ultimately criticizing him for a plot deemed uncentered and unnecessarily complex.

Jonathan Franzen is Guggenheim Fellow who received the 1988 Whiting Writer's Award for *The Twenty-seventh City.* He is a regular contributor to a wide variety of publications, including the *New Yorker,* and is currently at work on another novel. He married Valerie Cornell, a fiction writer, on October 2, 1982, and the couple reside in New York City.

SUGGESTED READING: *Commonweal* p26 Dec. 4, 1992; *Harper's* p35+ Apr. 1996; *Kirkus Reviews* Oct. 1, 1991, May 22, 1998; *New York Times Book Review* p22 Oct. 9, 1988, p13 Feb. 16, 1992; *People* p39+ Oct. 17, 1988, with photo; *Time* p42+ Apr. 14, 1997, with photo; *Contemporary Authors,* 1991

SELECTED WORKS: *The Twenty-seventh City,* 1988; *Strong Motion,* 1992

Sigrid Estrada

Frazier, Ian

1951– Humorist; nonfiction writer

"Ian Frazier's byline is one of the most reassuring sights in all journalism," Laura Shapiro declared in *Newsweek* (June 12, 1989). As a contributor to the *New Yorker* for two decades, beginning in the mid-1970s, Frazier gained a reputation for writing essays of gentle but pointed satire, and reviewers of his first two essay collections, *Dating Your Mom* (1986) and *Nobody Better, Better than Nobody* (1987), frequently cited his irreverent wit and powers of observation. He became a best-selling author in 1989, with the publication of his third book, *Great Plains.* In the best tradition of such *New Yorker* nonfiction writers as Joseph Mitchell, Frazier had produced a work that defied easy categorization: part travelogue, part history lesson, *Great*

Plains was sprinkled with geographical asides and personal commentary. That volume was followed in 1994 by the even more personal *Family,* Frazier's account of his family's place and participation in American history. He described to Lynn Karpen for the *New York Times Book Review* (November 6, 1994) the experience of writing *Great Plains* and *Family*: "A novelist can say he made things up, and there are all of these veils that exist between him and the reader. But this is me. It was extremely difficult and sometimes I felt quite blatant—like someone going on *Donahue.* I've written a lot of humor in the past, and I wanted to see what it was like not to be ironic at all. Without irony, you can find yourself really mushy, very undefended." His most recent book is the humor collection *Coyote v. Acme* (1996), which won the first Thurber Prize for American Humor in 1997.

Ian Frazier was born in 1951 in Cleveland, the oldest of the five children of David Frazier, a research chemist who spent his entire 37-year career at Standard Oil of Ohio, and Margaret Kathryn (Hursh) Frazier, a high school English teacher. In about 1957 the family moved to Hudson, a once-rural town between Cleveland and Akron that commuters were then transforming into a suburb of Cleveland. In *Family,* Frazier wrote about growing up in the midst of rapid development: "The smells of my childhood are the smells of cut lumber and wet mud and drying cement, and the sounds are hammering, chain saws, and bulldozers." Margaret Frazier had appeared in many amateur theatrical productions before her marriage, and in Hudson she directed plays, some of which featured Frazier, his brother Dave, and his sister Maggie.

Frazier attended Harvard University, in Cambridge, Massachusetts, where he was on the staff of the famous student humor magazine the *Harvard Lampoon* and where, he has said, he ran from police during the riots that broke out in Cambridge in 1970, after National Guard troops killed four students at Kent State University. He was not drafted during the Vietnam War and did not enlist, for, as he admitted in *Family,* "The idea of serving my country had not crossed my mind." During Frazier's junior year his youngest brother, Fritz, died of leukemia, at the age of 15. In *Family*, Frazier referred to his brother's death as "the worst thing that ever happened to me."

As a youngster Frazier had at different times dreamed of becoming a professional actor and a cartoonist (he drew some cartoons for the *Lampoon*). By the time he graduated from Harvard in 1973, with a degree in general studies, however, his experiences in turning out prose for the *Lampoon* had apparently strengthened a desire to write. He applied for work at the *New Yorker* but was turned down because they had "too many Harvard graduates already." He then found a job writing cartoon captions for *Oui*, a sex magazine based in Chicago, but a year later he was back in New York, having been hired by the *New Yorker*'s editor, William Shawn, to write unsigned "Talk of the Town" articles for a weekly salary of $200.

Soon Frazier began contributing longer, attributed pieces—many of them parodies—on a wide range of subjects. "The Bloomsbury Group Live at the Apollo" purports to be liner notes from an album recorded by members of the British literary circle that included Lytton Strachey and Leonard Woolf. Reminiscing about the group's beginnings, the narrator brags, "Now, of course, everybody talks about Virginia Woolf, author of *To the Lighthouse*, and so on. When I first knew her, she was just little Ginny Stephen. But *man*, that chick could *whale*." In another spoof, the writer Samuel Beckett is an airline pilot on "Flyways flight 185 from nothingness to New York's LaGuardia." A style of literary biography is satirized in "Igor Stravinsky: The Selected Phone Calls," in which the composer's telephone bill is deconstructed.

In 1986 those and 22 other pieces that Frazier wrote for the *New Yorker* between 1975 and 1985 were published in book form by Farrar, Straus & Giroux. The title essay, *Dating Your Mom*, encourages men who are looking for committed relationships to start romances with their mothers: "Here is a grown, experienced, loving woman—one you do not have to go to a party or a singles bar to meet." A reviewer for *Newsweek* (February 3, 1986) called Frazier "one of the best of the *New Yorker* humorists." While Edward B. St. John of *Library Journal* (January 1986) was less complimentary, saying of the writer's humor, "It's intellectual, but it's also pretty dumb," the majority of critics agreed with Mordecai Richler, who wrote in the *New York Times Book Review* (January 5, 1986) that the book was "deft, original, and funny," that Frazier "is an elegant miniaturist, a much-needed mockingbird with a fine eye for the absurd," and that "his collection is a pleasure to read."

By the mid-1980s Frazier's writing had taken the form of long "fact pieces," which were often seen in the *New Yorker* under William Shawn. The magazine was becoming famous for this particular brand of journalistic essay, in which the writer examined in detail whatever struck his or her fancy.

Frazier's essay topics demonstrated the interests and themes that would inform his next three books: the history and landscape of the American Midwest, the stranger aspects of very mundane things, and the links between the past and the present. Humor was still an important ingredient in his writing, but he was much more likely to mock himself than others. Five of these pieces became his next published collection, *Nobody Better, Better than Nobody*.

As a number of reviewers pointed out, the essays in Frazier's second book contain information about people and things that initially seem unimportant: a museum in Kansas called the Last Indian Raid, a fishing-tackle store in Manhattan, and bear sightings in Montana, among other subjects. The title piece is about someone famous—Poncé Cruse Evans, who writes the column of household hints under the name Heloise—but Frazier concentrated less on Evans's work than on the details of the columnist's personal life, including her belief that "there's nobody better than me, I'm no better than anybody else." For this book, Frazier was a journalist whose beat was the lives of ordinary people; his mission was to make readers believe that his subjects were worth knowing about. His methods were admired by Christopher Lehmann-Haupt in the *New York Times* (April 16, 1987): "He has a way of sympathizing with his subjects at the same time he's showing how funny they can be. . . . And there is his documentation of the multitude of wacky ways that people act out their passions. . . . Still, it's the rare combination of humor and empathy that gives these casual pieces their special appeal." Paul Gray of *Time* (May 25, 1987) agreed, saying, "The reader winds up laughing and knowing a great deal about subjects . . . that most people can live without. The author's loopy laziness is a pose; he works carefully and hard to make everything look like fun."

During his early years as a *New Yorker* staff writer, Frazier lived in a loft on Canal Street in the New York City borough of Manhattan, in a building that had previously been the Knickerbocker Candy factory. When he moved in, he reported, the loft had no bathroom or kitchen but did have "hundred-pound sacks of imitation coconut flakes lying around." (His mother gave him $800 to have a bathroom installed.) Frazier described his surroundings in "Canal Street," a long piece in the *New Yorker* (April 30, 1990) that managed to combine a funny, endearing portrait of his Romanian landlord with a discourse on modern-day Canal Street and a moving account of the construction, over half a century earlier, of the adjoining Holland Tunnel.

In 1982, feeling a need to be away from William Shawn's "strong gravitational pull," as he put it in an interview with Michael Coffey for *Publishers Weekly* (November 14, 1994), Frazier left the *New Yorker*, sublet his loft to his sister, and rented a house in Kalispell, Montana, with plans to write a novel. After his friend and fellow *New Yorker* contributor, the fiction writer Jamaica Kincaid, told him that his fiction was not "true" and urged him to keep writing nonfiction, he turned his attention to the vastness of the nearby plains. He spent the next three years driving around the Great Plains (logging a total of 25,000 miles) and an additional two years doing research at the New York Public Library. In 1989 *Great Plains* was published by Farrar, Straus & Giroux, the contents having previously appeared in the *New Yorker*.

Packed with stories about the past and present of America's vast prairie lands, the book represented new territory for Frazier in terms of length, style, and content. The writer's enthusiasm as well as his ever-present sense of irony can be seen from the opening lines: "Away to the Great Plains of America, to that immense Western short-grass prairie now mostly plowed under! Away to the still-empty land beyond newsstands and malls and velvet restaurant ropes! . . . Away to the land where TV used to set its most popular dramas, but not anymore!" Frazier wrote of what he saw—the endless sky, tiny local museums, abandoned forts, the birthplace of the bandleader Lawrence Welk— and what his research taught him about such mythic American figures as the Oglala Sioux chief Crazy Horse, General George Armstrong Custer, and the outlaws Bonnie and Clyde. In *Great Plains*, Frazier explored the past to discover what America had been. At a Founders' Day parade in Nicodemus, Kansas, a town founded by blacks in 1877, Frazier imagined that he could see his country the way immigrants and homesteaders had. "Suddenly I felt a joy so strong it almost knocked me down. . . . And I thought, *It could have worked!* This democracy, this land of freedom and equality and the pursuit of happiness—it could have worked! . . . For a moment I could imagine the past rewritten, wars unfought, the buffalo and the Indians undestroyed, the prairie unplundered."

Frazier's search for the meaning behind the complex history of the Plains touched a chord, and the book won immediate approbation, bestsellerdom, and, for its author, a $25,000 Whiting Writers' Award. Many reviewers admired Frazier's descriptive powers and the depth of his research. Laura Shapiro, in *Newsweek* (June 12, 1989), called *Great Plains* "history with a human face" and Frazier "a great storyteller." In the *New York Times Book Review* (June 18, 1989), Sue Hubbell proclaimed, "This is a terrific book," and she wrote of its author, "Frazier is a skilled writer, and he succeeds in interesting us in what interests him. His enthusiasms become ours." Ron Hansen, in the *Washington Post Book World* (May 28, 1989), observed that "there is no mistaking Ian Frazier's respect for the integrity and majesty of the neglected worlds of the plains, nor of his tone of tender elegy for the lore and ways of living that soon may disappear. *Great Plains* is a great book."

During the period that Frazier spent researching and writing *Great Plains*, his father, who was suffering from Alzheimer's disease, contracted pneumonia and died, in 1987. His mother died of liver cancer a year later. Sorting through his parents' belongings, including letters and photographs, he felt compelled to begin another exploration of the past. The resulting book, *Family*, filtered American history through the life stories of Frazier's ancestors. In a typically blunt passage in *Family*, he discussed his reason for writing the book: "I wanted my parents' lives to have meant something. I hunted all over for meanings of any kind—not, I think, simply out of grief or anger at their deaths, but also because the stuff they saved implied that there must have been a reason for saving it. . . . I didn't care if the meanings were far-flung or vague or even trivial. I wanted to pursue them. I hoped maybe I could find a meaning that would defeat death."

Frazier used the research techniques that had worked for him before. He rented a car and followed various trails that led from his parents' apartment—attending a service at the Disciples of Christ church in New Washington, Indiana, which one of his great-great-grandfathers had joined in 1846; going to West Virginia and following the route that another great-great-grandfather had taken as part of the 55th Ohio Volunteer Infantry in the Civil War; and revisiting Hudson, his hometown, where he drove past the cemetery in which his brother, father, and mother lay buried. Each of these places was a point from which Frazier jumped back in time, and as he did in *Great Plains*, he used a combination of observation and research to study events and people from the past—chiefly his own forefathers.

Family contains mini-theses on western migration, the proliferation of religious sects, the death of the Confederate general Stonewall Jackson, and the polluting of Lake Erie. These are all variations on Frazier's theme: that a group of people once had a vision of a Promised Land that was strong enough to carry them overseas to America and spur their journey into the West—but is now a fading memory. Frazier contended that Stonewall Jackson's dying words, "Let us cross over the river and rest under the shade of the trees," referred to the same imaginary landscape that the civil-rights leader Martin Luther King Jr. evoked in his "I Have a Dream" speech, despite the very different causes of those two men. In *Family*, he wrote of King's famous address that it is "a compendium of American places, each lifted from the map and polished with the glow of justice, of freedom, each restored to the best dream of America; and to me, every place in the speech, every site in this coast-to-coast and Southern travelogue, is an America across the river and under the trees. Martin Luther King remembered that America had once been thought of as a promised land. He had the generosity to believe that it actually could be, that somehow it still was."

Family ends, in terms of chronology, with the death of Frazier's mother. The book, which tells of his search for the meaning of her life and death, is intended to be "a long streamer attached to her ankle to mark for a moment the spot where she had disappeared." As a result of writing it, he told *Publishers Weekly*, "I have a much better understanding of what happened to my parents and my grandparents, and why I am like I am. It all pointed to me, saying here's your job, your job is to write." On the whole, critics responded positively to *Family*, while acknowledging their difficulty in classifying the book, which Malcolm Jones Jr., in *Newsweek* (November 7, 1994), called "the weirdest, tastiest, most wondrous fruit on the Frazier family tree." Jones did warn that while "reading about the Fraziers and the families from whom they were descended . . . a reader's eyes can glaze over mighty quick," but most reviewers agreed with David Willis McCullough's assessment in the *New York Times* (November 6, 1994) that in this "book of a lifetime" Frazier had "concocted that rarest of events, a family reunion worth inviting strangers to attend." Frazier himself, aware of the risk he was running in focusing on his own forebears, confessed in his *Publishers Weekly* interview with Michael Coffey, "Basically the difficulty is this: 'Who cares?' As I was working on it people would say, 'Did you have any bank robbers in your family? Was anyone famous?' There's an idea in the society that if you are not a celebrity then you are nobody."

The title piece of Frazier's most recent book, *Coyote v. Acme*, concerns a lawsuit that Wile E. Coyote (the Warner Brothers cartoon character who is continually in pursuit of the Road Runner) brings against the Acme company, manufacturers of the elaborate, dangerously defective gadgets with which the Coyote attempts to snare his prey. "This latest collection . . . harks back to [*Dating Your Mom*]—short, arch, cynical takes on some of the idiocies of American life," a reviewer for *Publishers Weekly* (March 25, 1996) observed. "As usual, Frazier is awfully good, smart and wicked at the same time. . . . Although this book is not Frazier at full-bore, readers of his generation will find an occasional cultural reference long thought lost and find themselves oddly beholden to a fellow who can resurrect Billy Joe McCallister from beneath the Tallahatchie Bridge."

Ian Frazier has light blue eyes, and his long, reddish-blond hair is the basis of his nickname, Sandy. Discussing the length of his hair in *Great Plains*, he told the story of meeting a Sioux Indian at a New York City intersection: "His hair was straight and black with streaks of gray, and it hung to his waist in back. After I saw him, I never cut my hair again." In 1994 the Lila Wallace–Reader's Digest Fund awarded Frazier their $105,000 Writer's Award. His short pieces continue to appear from time to time in *Atlantic Monthly*, and his *New Yorker* piece "Take the F" can be found in *Best American Essays 1996*. Frazier reportedly resigned from his staff position at the *New Yorker* after the magazine used the television comedian Roseanne as a consultant on an issue. He was the editor of *The Best American Essays 1997*. He recently moved from the New York City borough of Brook-

lyn back to Montana, where he lives with his wife, the writer Jacqueline Carey, and their two children.

—Amy Peck

SUGGESTED READING: *Atlantic* p96+, Oct. '94, p 48+ Mar. '96; ibrary Journal Jan. 1986; *Newsweek* p70, Feb. 3, 1986; *New Yorker* June 12, 1989, Apr. 30, 1990, Nov. 7, 1994, Feb. 12, 1996; *New York Times Book Review* Jan. 5, 1986, Apr. 16, 1987, Nov. 6, 1994; *Publishers Weekly* p49+, Nov. 14, 1994, Mar. 25, 1996; *Time* May 25, 1987; *Washington Post Book World* May 28, 1989

SELECTED WORKS: *Dating Your Mom*, 1986; *Nobody Better, Better than Nobody*, 1987; *Great Plains*, 1989; *Family*, 1994; *Coyote v. Acme*, 1996; As editor *The Best American Essays: 1997*, 1997

Christopher Bains

Freud, Esther

1963– Novelist

The British novelist Esther Freud was born in London but was taken at a young age to Morocco, where she lived for two years. Freud used this experience as the basis for her 1991 semi-autobiographical novel *Hideous Kinky*, narrated from the point of view of a five-year-old child. Her next novel, *Peerless Flats* (1993), is a portrait of 1970s London as seen through the eyes of a young teenager who lives with her mother and younger brother in temporary housing for the homeless. In

Summer at Gaglow (1998), first published in England in 1997 as *Gaglow*, Freud drew on her heritage as the great-granddaughter of Sigmund Freud and the daughter of the painter Lucian Freud to depict a Jewish family in Germany during and after World War I and the remnants of that family at the end of the 20th century in London. Although Sigmund Freud himself is not the basis of a character in the novel, the atmosphere of his times is captured, and critics have seen in Michael, the father, aspects of Lucian Freud and in Sarah, the aspiring actress, aspects of Esther Freud herself. Deborah Mason declared in the *New York Times* (May 17,1998) that *Summer at Gaglow* is "a shrewd and absorbing novel, a near-seamless meshing of family feeling, history and imagination,"—components present in all of Freud's work.

In an autobiographical statement submitted to *World Authors 1990–1995*, Freud writes: "I was born in London in 1963, the second of two sisters. My father, the painter Lucian Freud, and my mother were not married and never shared a conventional family home. My mother was extremely young and idealistic and claimed it wasn't what she wanted, to be a housewife, but all the same, life as a single parent with very little money was hard. We moved, first to the country and then, when I was four, to Morocco. Mostly we lived in Marrakech, where my mother's allowance stretched much further than it did at home, and during our two-year stay we travelled over most of the country and, at our most adventurous, into Algeria where my mother enrolled herself in a Sufi college. I was hugely affected by these early travels, and for years afterwards my head was full of stories. I wanted people to know when they looked at me, a small pale child who couldn't read or write, that I'd ridden down a mountain in the saddle bag of a donkey and knew what an oasis was.

"Years later I used the memory of this time to write my first novel, *Hideous Kinky*, which I have now had the strange experience of watching as a film. The whole episode is now more real than it ever in fact was.

"Back in England my sister and I started at Michael Hall, a Rudolf Steiner School in Sussex. I stayed there for the next 10 years, gaining confidence from the stability of the place, much needed, as my mother was endlessly at a loss to find us anywhere permanent to live. We moved 11 times in our first two years. Home, houses, gates, doors, gardens—they were the stuff of my dreams, and in each of my novels the search for a home, the perfect home, or any home, is right there at the heart. But despite this longing for security I decided to become an actress, and at 16 I moved to London.

"Almost as soon as I started acting I began to write. I wrote on busses and during breaks in rehearsal, and once in my dressing room I was so busy scribbling that I forgot to go on for my scene. I enrolled in a weekly creative writing class run by Michelle Roberts. The class was titled "Finding Your Voice" and slowly over that year, that is ex-actly what happened. It took some years more before I found the discipline you need to write a novel, but once I did find it, my need to go off and tour around the country faded, and I realised I'd found something I could do at home."

––––––––––

Although she is the great-granddaughter of Sigmund Freud, Esther's works are known for a lack of the kind of introspection that characterized his writings and philosophy. In the *Boston Phoenix* (May 14, 1998), Megan Harlan observed that Esther's "arch wit, smartly twisting plots, and empathetic grasp of human nature, recalls Jane Austen more than she does the father of modern psychology." Freud told Esther B. Fein during an interview for the *New York Times* (April 29, 1992) that she had no idea what her great-grandfather would think of her first novel, *Hideous Kinky* (1992). "I don't really know what he'd make of it since I've never read any of his works," she said. "I always felt I would read his books when I wanted to, and I just haven't wanted to yet."

The nameless narrator of the semiautobiographical *Hideous Kinky* is a five-year-old girl at the time the action takes place. With her mother, her older sister, her mother's boyfriend, and the boyfriend's wife, the narrator travels to Marrakesh, meeting an assortment of eccentric characters along the way. The novel won praise for its "matter-of-factly whimsical tone" from Sarah Ferguson, writing in the *New York Times Book Review* (May 31, 1992). Gabriele Annan of the *Times Literary Supplement* found in *Hideous Kinky* "a delightful lightness of being" that "springs from the child's acceptance of whatever comes. . . . There is no hanging about . . . no set-pieces, no travel writing; but the landscape sparkles with allure and minor characters stand out vividly against it."

Freud's next novel, *Peerless Flats* (1993), continues in an autobiographical vein. The protagonist, Lisa, is 16 years old and lives with her mother and her five-year-old half-brother, Max, in "Peerless Flats," a housing project set up to provide temporary lodging for the homeless in London. Lisa suffers from problems with drugs, eating disorders, and alcohol. Reviewing the novel for *New Statesman & Society* (March 5, 1993), Melanie McFadyean found it flawed, possessing "a loosely connected set of meanderings" in lieu of a plot, and lacking a sense of history. Nevertheless, she found its strength to be in "characters who live and breathe and have a distinct being, and who are memorable, even if they are neither likeable nor impressive." The *London Review of Books* (March 25, 1993) critic Penelope Fitzgerald agreed that the characters were "wonderfully drawn" and described Lisa as "a heroine who makes *Peerless Flats* a novel of forceful readability and indisputable charm." Shena Mackay observed in the *Times Literary Supplement* (February 19, 1993) that the prose style of *Peerless Flats* matches Lisa's personality: "Sometimes naïve with a jerky lack of continuity, it blossoms into beautiful imagery and sudden stabs of psychological perception."

In *Summer at Gaglow*, Freud expanded her ambitions. The novel spans almost the entire 20th century, beginning with a lavish house party in 1914 at an estate in Germany called Gaglow that is home to a Jewish family, the Belgards. World War I soon puts an end to the Belgards' way of life. Eva, the family member through whose eyes the novel's earliest action is seen, is 11 years old; the protagonist of the events that take place at the end of the 20th century is Eva's granddaughter, Sarah. For Megan Harlan, reviewing *Summer at Gaglow* for the *Boston Phoenix* (May 14, 1998), the novel is not merely a family saga. "Freud places the Holocaust at the invisible heart of this novel, with the two domestic dramas of a Jewish family present and past balanced on either side," she wrote.

Still, in her notice in the *New York Times Book Review* (May 17, 1998), Deborah Mason emphasized Freud's sense of family, and praised the "interplay between generations . . . rendered in haunting dimensions—mysteries of appearance and reality, familiarity and distance, dissolution, and renewal—that make *Summer at Gaglow* a startlingly original novel." Mason compared the novel to an album filled with "stark, unsentimental snapshots of feeling" that stem from "the yearning for home; the deep fear of losing it and oneself along with it; the sweetly mixed blessings of homecoming." Freud, she wrote, "turns our most cherished conceits of family inside out, toppling the tidy flow chart of kinship and offering anarchic new forms of togetherness."
—S.Y.

SUGGESTED READING: *Boston Phoenix* May 14, 1998; *London Review of Books* p22 Mar. 25, 1993; *New Statesman & Society* p41 Mar. 5, 1993; *New York Times Book Review* p30 May 31, 1992, p16 June 20, 1993, p9 May 17, 1998; *Times Literary Supplement* p22 Jan. 31, 1992, p22 Feb. 19, 1993, p24 May 2, 1997

SELECTED BOOKS: *Hideous Kinky*, 1992; *Peerless Flats*, 1993; *Summer at Gaglow*, 1998

Friedman, Carl

1952– Novelist; poet; journalist

The Dutch writer Carl Friedman contributes to a genre that has been called "the literature of trauma, the story of wounds and aftershocks" by Margot Jefferson of the *New York Times* (October 5, 1994). Friedman, the daughter of an Auschwitz survivor, is the author of a novel and a short-story collection that offer a view of the Holocaust from the perspective of a younger generation that knows the horror of that period only second-hand. Her first novel, *Tralievader* (1991, tr. *Nightfather*), published in English in 1994, is narrated by seven-year-old Bette, who mixes the serious with the comic in her depiction of her father's world, a world whose every detail is nuanced by his nightmarish experience of the death camps. Friedman's second novel, *Twee koffers vol* (1993, tr. *The Shovel and the Loom*), set in Amsterdam in 1970, carries this theme forward in a narrative about Chaya, a 20-year-old philosophy student who is confronted with her father's declaration that he, also a camp survivor, is planning to dig up suitcases full of family momentoes buried before the war. The shovel thus becomes a symbol for Chaya's father as the loom represents her mother, a weaver.

Carl Friedman was born in Eindhoven, the Netherlands, in 1952. After living for many years in Antwerp, Belgium, she returned to her native land in 1977 and worked as a translator, journalist, and poet. Friedman's first works were published in a number of important Dutch literary periodicals. Her first novel, *Tralievader*, was published in 1991 and appeared in English as *Nightfather* in 1994; it has also been translated into German. Her second novel, *Twee koffers vol*, appeared in the Netherlands in 1993 and in the United States in 1996 as *The Shovel and the Loom*.

Nightfather is a slim volume, just 130 pages, containing 40 brief vignettes with simple and purposefully banal titles such as "Camp," "Roll Call," "The SS," "Eichmann," "Underpants," and "Heaven." The vignettes are narrated in the voice of a girl named Bette, the seven-year-old daughter of a man, Ephraim, who spent several years in Auschwitz during the war. The brevity of these discourses is perhaps determined by the amount of information that a child of that age can conveniently handle. Through the sparse language of childhood, Bette describes how she and her brothers, Max and Simon, come to an awareness of their father's suffering as well as of the anguish of his enslaved generation. In Bette's understanding, "camp is not so much a place as a condition" that her father "has," much as she and her sibling have "had" German measles or chicken pox. Neither polemical nor self-pitying, the tone of *Nightfather* is rather one of uncritical innocence, an "out-of-the-mouth-of babes" account by children trying to make sense out of the confusions and contradictions of an adult world they cannot fathom.

The vignettes in *Nightfather* are always poignant and telling, never sentimental or moralistic. They are often sardonically humorous, as in "Underpants," the tale of a pair of talking shorts named Heinrich. Once in camp, the father explains to his daughter, he had been issued a pair of blue velvet underpants with ivory buttons in the shape of German eagles, while the other prisoners had gotten only cheap brown-paper bags to wear. Blue-velvet

"Heinrich," it turned out, were shorts that had belonged to Hitler himself before being "arrested and sent to the camp because they knew too much"; or, as Ephraim explains: "They'd been looking up Adolf's asshole for years and had learned the most confidential state secrets that way."

In "Eichmann," Bette is confronted with Nellie, one of her peers, who angrily denounces the monstrous Adolf Eichmann, whose trial she had been watching on television. Nellie is capable of denouncing him only in the most conventional terminology ("The man's an animal! They were right to put him in a glass cage. I'd like to kick him to death, that dirty bastard!"). In stark contrast to these fulminations, the knowing Bette and her father paint a far more benign—and thus more terrifying—picture of Eichmann, who, says Bette, "doesn't look horrible at all, he looks like Mr. Klerk from our school." Her father likewise sees Eichmann as a man whose job was to send throngs to the gas chamber, just as a mailman delivers letters or a baker makes bread. As for Nellie's threats to "kick him to death," Ephraim can only reply: "With those worn-out slippers of hers?"

Although Bette and her father are able to discuss the Holocaust so dispassionately in *Nightfather*, one theme recurs with depressing frequency: the sense of impending doom that has forever shattered the surety of home and village as a sanctuary. For its survivors and the survivors' children, the Holocaust has rendered the world an eternally uncertain place, pervaded with an "anything-might-happen" terror. In "Popolski," Ephraim tells Bette and Simon how he and other prisoners would assuage their thirst by squeezing tiny bits of toothpaste onto their fingers and licking them "when no one was looking." Bette concludes this story with a vignette of her own that indicates how the children of the Holocaust have ingested its lessons:

When Simon and I are brushing our teeth, he slips the toothpaste into the pocket of his pajama jacket.
"We'll take it along to school tomorrow," he whispers.
"What for? We aren't going on a death march, are we?" I say.
"You never know," Simon replies. "Anything might happen."

Reviewers praised *Nightfather* for the lyrical "offstage" voice its narrator employed in describing scenes of such unmitigated horror, much as the bloodiest scenes in Greek tragedy were not portrayed graphically on stage. Carolyn Cohen wrote in the *Boston Book Review*: "In a quiet, lyrical voice [Friedman] preserves the character of her relationship to her father. . . . The most striking feature of the book is its deceptively simple language, and particularly the understated conversations between the narrator, her brother, and her father. . . . Coming of age means knowing the difference between the symbols of the father's experience that imprison and those that liberate." Richard Burgin wrote in the *New York Times Book Review* (December 11, 1994): "Lucidly, concisely, almost lightly at times, Carl Friedman writes about the worst of human abominations without ever compromising her compassion or extinguishing her sense of hope." Describing Friedman's "aesthetic restraint" as "especially impressive," Burgin added: "By telling her story as a series of short vignettes appropriate to how much of each incident a child would remember, she is able to make the precisely edited scenes an effective antidote to the horror and chaos of the subject matter."

For *The Shovel and the Loom*, Friedman used a more mature, philosophical tone. The narrator this time is not a seven-year-old child but a 20-year-old philosophy student, Chaya, who tries to make sense of the Holocaust through her obsessive reading of Nietzsche, Schopenhauer, and other philosophers. Confused by her parents' conflicting evaluation of the genocide—her mother remains in denial and resorts to weaving (the "loom") while her father becomes obsessed with digging up family heirlooms buried in suitcases (the "shovel")—Chaya tries to reclaim her identity, serving as a nanny for an Orthodox Jewish family in Antwerp. By committing herself to caring for the three-year-old Simcha Kalman and by studying the Jewish mysticism advanced by an elderly neighbor, Chaya is able to have her faith in humanity restored. Katherine Alberg, in the *New York Times Book Review* (June 20, 1996), wrote of this turn: "Indeed, this devotion presents itself as a vital part of her search for meaning. Yet in the end, the author gives even this small redemption a tragic twist, as if to acknowledge the ultimate inexplicability of life."

Some critics place Friedman in the tradition of other contemporary Jewish fiction writers who seek to be both "shovel and loom" in digging up past secrets and weaving disparate elements into new patterns. Judith Bolton-Fasman, the book editor for the *Baltimore Jewish Times*, wrote in an article for the *Washington Post Book World* (January 2, 1997): "She keeps company with novelists such as Cynthia Ozick and Rebecca Goldstein, who have energized the Jewish American novel by combining such learning with literary acumen. So Chaya gleans insights about Judaism by immersing herself in physics, the philosophy of Nietzsche and Torah, and concludes that Judaism 'will continue to exist because it's the only religion that promises redemption in exchange for critical thinking. In Judaism, belief always quarrels with logic. That tension is not fought but encouraged.'"

—E. M.

SUGGESTED *READING: Chicago Tribune Books* p5 Sep. 8, 1996; *Library Journal* p130 May 1, 1996; *New York Times* C p17 Oct. 5, 1994; *New York Times Book Review* p14 Dec. 11, 1994, p20 June 30, 1996; *Washington Post Book World* C p2 Jan. 2, 1997

SELECTED BOOKS IN ENGLISH TRANSLATION: *Nightfather*, 1994; *The Shovel and the Loom*, 1996

Courtesy of David Galef

Galef, David

Mar. 27, 1959– Novelist; critic; poet

David Galef is a noted academic and writer whose versatility enables him to contribute to many different genres. For his first book, *Even Monkeys Fall From Trees* (1988), Galef translated and collected Japanese proverbs. His next, *The Little Red Bicycle* (1988), was a children's book. For his subsequent published work, the author went in a completely different direction. *The Supporting Cast: A Study of Flat and Minor Characters* (1993) reevaluates the way readers look at a novel or story's secondary characters and discusses how these characters add to the overall message of the work. He followed this with a novel, *Flesh* (1995), about one man's obsession with his next-door neighbor's infatuation with obese women. A year later he produced another children's book, *Tracks* (1996). Most recently, Galef has been the editor of and a contributor to *Second Thoughts: A Focus on Rereading* (1998) and has written a second novel, *Turning Japanese* (1998), which follows the adventures of an American expatriate in Japan. In addition to these works, he has published a large number of short stories, articles, and poems in many periodicals.

In an autobiographical sketch written for *World Authors 1990-1995*, David Galef discusses his life and work: "I was born in New York and spent my first two years in the Bronx, after which my family moved to Scarsdale. The suburbs of Westchester offered a secure and privileged domain, though that didn't stop me from getting into a lot of arguments and more than a few fights for being a 'smart' kid. My father, a psychoanalyst preoccupied with his work, rarely intervened. My mother, who worked as a teacher for learning-disadvantaged children, died of lymphoma when I was ten. A succession of housekeepers were hired to take care of me and my sister, who was three years older.

"Even before my mother's death, I found life rather lonely and sought solace in fiction. I read anything and everything, especially fantasy like C.S. Lewis's tales of Narnia. Books were my friends, and I would often carry on long conversations with the characters, especially when I didn't want the story to end. As a boy reading boyish books, I fit perfectly on our old blue sofa until I started reading longer volumes and grew too long for the confines of the sofa. (A short story published in 1989, Portrait of a Portrayal,' recounts this type of readerly upbringing.) Like so many others, I read as an escape, appreciating the trick of the thing, the aesthetics of the operation, only after many thousands of books had been consumed.

"In fact, most of my early fiction follows the theme of escape. I started out reading science fiction and fantasy (and one hot summer served as an assistant editor for the now-defunct pulp SF magazine *Galaxy*). I sold my first short story to a computer magazine when just 17 and was elated—then spent the next two years trying to repeat the event. I'd always written creatively from elementary school on, but now I was writing outside the bounds of any coursework. In college, I took a lot of literature classes and worked on my fiction in a few workshops. I submitted stories to magazines partly because I thought they were good enough to be published, but also because I was disenchanted with what I saw out there. My high school and college years coincided with the era of minimalist fiction, which has never satisfied me.

"Still, through an unfashionable literary polish and sheer determination, I slowly amassed a body of work, including fiction taken by Alan Coren at *Punch* magazine in England before I was 20, and later anthologized. I was and still am a ferocious mimic, with a chameleon style that I like to play around with. But a standard voice slowly emerged, polysyllabic and precise, my common theme that of a precocious child, misunderstood but gamely trying to come to terms with life. The tone tends to vary from manic intensity to torporous depression, mirroring the mood swings of such a type. I've published over 60 short stories in periodicals ranging from the Czech *Prague Review* to the *Canadian Prism International* and the *American Shenandoah*, *Confrontation*, and the *Gettysburg Review*. My non-fiction's appeared in the *New York Times*, *Newsday*, the *Village Voice*, *Spy*, and elsewhere.

"After graduating from Princeton in 1981, I taught English in Japan for over a year, learning the language and culture. My first book was an illustrated translation of Japanese proverbs. My second book was a children's book for Random House, and both helped me get through graduate studies in English at Columbia. It was there that I became a critic, and I remain to this day most interested in the mechanics of a work, with style as a function of technique.

"After securing a teaching job at the University of Mississippi, I began work on what would turn out to be my first novel, *Flesh*. It's a Conradian tale in an academic setting: one man's obsession with another man's obsession, a sexual preoccupation in a small Southern town that gets wildly out of hand. Included in the plot are a Faulkner expert who hates the South, a lay preacher who predicts the future, a football player paralyzed from the neck down, and an ever-expanding cast of women.

"My second novel, *Turning Japanese*, is about the drifting existence of an American expatriate in the Japan of late 1970s. The episodic plot follows the struggles of the protagonist Cricket Collins as he fumblingly files by the nets of nationality, language, and family.

"I also write criticism with a writerly focus. For instance, what's behind those brief depictions that somehow manage to fix themselves in the mind of the reader? My pursuit of that question led to *The Supporting Cast: A Study of Flat and Minor Characters*, published by Penn State University Press in 1993. And my interest in how writing is put together parallels a similar interest in the effects of reading, specifically what changes the second time around, when anticipation replaces suspense. This question led to an anthology of essays that I edited and contributed to, *Second Thoughts: A Focus on Rereading*.

"In between books, I've published on Joyce, Woolf, Forster, Ford, T.S. Eliot, Wallace Stevens, and others in *Twentieth Century Literature*, the *Journal of Modern Literature*, *American Literature*, *Scribner's Modern British Writers*, and elsewhere. I also publish a variety of verse in periodicals such as *The Formalist* and *Light*. I've received grants and awards from the Henfield Foundation, *Poets & Writers*, Yaddo Artists' Colony, and the Mississippi Arts Council, among other places.

"I'm now an associate professor of English at the University of Mississippi, specializing in modern British literature and creative writing. In 1992, I married the journalist and magazine editor Beth Weinhouse, and we have a son named Daniel."

Galef's fiction has been widely reviewed. In the novel *Flesh*, the protagonist's sexual peculiarities are observed by his next-door neighbor, who cuts a peephole in the wall between their apartments to watch him seduce women. Writing about the novel for the *New York Times Book Review* (May 21, 1995), Valerie Sayers commented: "David Galef's first novel is a sometimes erotic, always academic comedy. . . . The narrative is silly, clever, amusing and unsettling when it strikes too close to the bone (or the flesh)." David A. Berona, in *Library Journal* (March 15, 1995), called the book "an accomplished debut worth noting," and added: "Although the plot sometimes stretches into the absurd, Galef's story raises serious questions about our culture's obsession with bodies."

Tracks, written for children ages four to seven and illustrated by Tedd Arnold, tells the story of Albert, whose job is to direct the workers laying track for his town's new railroad. During the course of his work, Albert breaks his glasses but has no time to go home and retrieve his spare pair. So with blurry vision, he directs his workers to put track around boulders (cows) and over mountains (pine trees). The next day Albert and his men join the mayor on the train's inaugural ride. Albert realizes his mistake and worries the mayor will be angry with the crazy track work, but is gladdened when he discovers that everyone loves the wild ride.

Galef's work on *Tracks* received mixed reviews. "Arnold's hilarious cartoons, rendered in watercolor and given interesting texture with colored pencils, enhance the light, slapstick mood of the text. This is rollicking good fun that will make for a lively story time," Lauren Peterson cheered in *Booklist* (May 1, 1996). A critic for *Kirkus Reviews* (February 1, 1996) disagreed with this assessment, noting: "This starts with a funny premise, but because the readers see, every step of the way, the truth behind Albert's mistakes, the second trip over the track (with the mayor) is a letdown. Arnold uses a looser style than usual, but the broad humor of the illustrations can't carry the piece." The book nonetheless went into several editions, including an audio-tape version.

In 1998 Galef published *Turning Japanese*. Cricket Collins, the novel's main character, plans to spend a year in Japan after graduating from Cornell in the late 1970s. However, one year turns to five after he realizes how easy it is for him to live in Japan. He makes a good deal of money teaching conversational English to the Japanese, enjoys their culture and society, and has more than enough time to do as he wants. But Collins, as the product of a dysfunctional family, begins to break under the strain of being isolated in a foreign land: he starts to steal, curse his students, and hear voices in his head. Michele Leber, writing in *Booklist* (August 19, 1998), called the novel "interesting from a cross-cultural standpoint but ultimately lacking uplift."

In addition to writing, David Galef has taught a variety of subjects for nearly two decades. He first began teaching English in Japan from 1981 to 1982. After returning to the U.S., he worked as a mathematics and English instructor at the Stanley H. Kaplan Education Centers in Boston and New York between 1983 and 1985. For the next year he taught English at Japanese business seminars in the New York City area. In 1986 he joined the staff at Columbia University, first teaching logic and rhetoric (1986-88) and then Literature Humanities (1988-89). Since 1989 he has been a professor of English at the University of Mississippi. —C.M.

SUGGESTED READING: *Booklist* p 1479 Apr. 15, 1995, May 1, 1996, Aug. 19, 1998; *Journal of Modern Literature* Spring 1990; *Kirkus Reviews* Feb. 1, 1996; *Library Journal* p 98 Mar. 15, 1995; *New York Times Book Review* p 35 May 21, 1995

SELECTED WORKS: Fiction—*Flesh*, 1995; *Turning Japanese*, 1998; Nonfiction—*Even Monkeys Fall from Trees, and Other Japanese Proverbs* (ill. Jun Hashimoto), 1988; *The Supporting Cast: A Study of Flat and Minor Characters*, 1993; As editor—*Second Thoughts: A Focus on Rereading*, 1998; Juvenile—*The Little Red Bicycle* (ill. Carol Nicklaus), 1988; *Tracks* (ill. Tedd Arnold), 1996

Stephen Gallagher

Gallagher, Stephen

Oct. 13, 1954– Novelist; short-story writer; television writer

The British suspense novelist and short-story writer Stephen Gallagher, who has worked as a scriptwriter for radio, television, and film, stated in one interview: "I'm one of those writers with a dimly glimpsed vision of a perfect book in him, and every story that I write is a miserably imperfect attempt to realize it in one form or another." These "imperfect" books have brought him renown as one of the top British writers of his genre and have made him a growing literary star internationally. The author of nine books, among them *Chimera* (1982), *Oktober* (1988), *Down River* (1989), and *Red, Red Robin* (1995), he is swamped with offers to convert his thrillers into films, for both movies and television. On adapting his own work, he told *Interzone* (September/October 1989): "Writing screenplays is a dream, really, because you've spent a year on the book, and the screenplay you can write in three or four weeks." Still, writing complex psychological thrillers and supernatural fiction has remained his first love.

In his autobiography for *World Authors 1990-1995*, Gallagher writes: "I was born in Salford, a once-busy industrial town in the northwest of England, on October 13, 1954. I grew up in the suburbs. My playgrounds were the usual fascinating, off-limits places; the town dump, abandoned railway sidings, the sunken barges and derelict warehouses by the Bridgewater Canal. Anything to which my imagination could fasten itself. I never lacked friends, but as an only child I found I could only stand so much company and actually needed solitude. I had a rich inner fantasy life and, like a yuppie itching for his mobile phone, I didn't like to be out of touch with it for too long.

"My background was working class. My parents were neither pushy nor over-ambitious, but it's clear looking back that they didn't want anything to hold me down. I was lucky that this was the sixties, in which the British class system received a kicking from which—thank God—it has never recovered. I attended the junior school at the end of my street, where the headmaster saw some potential in me and jumped me forward a year. While everyone else had to write a little story every week, he gave me a separate exercise book and told me to work on a long one. And when it was time for me to leave, he pushed to get me into the local grammar school.

"My childhood reading was voracious, wide-ranging, and was fuelled from the twin sources of the Eccles Public Library and the Saturday bookstall on the market close by. The stuff on the bookstall was wonderful and cheap, and was laid out in battered suitcases under a canvas awning. I don't know where it all came from. Rare Victoriana lay side-by-side with gorgeously painted Pan paperbacks, and everything sold for pennies. I never paused to think about what I was buying. Edgar Allan Poe, John Milton, Edgar Rice Burroughs. Ian Fleming. Conan Doyle. H. G. Wells. Tennyson. Steinbeck. Leslie Charteris. And Shakespeare. I was a sucker for a Complete Works in a nice binding. I still have three of them.

"Only now do I realise that there was an underlying structure to what I was doing. I seem to have had an unfailing instinct for sensationalists who caught the popular imagination, from Homer onwards. High art, low culture . . . in my innocence, I was aware of neither.

"My degree was in Drama and English, at Hull University. I didn't have a lot of self-confidence but I had self-belief, which can look like the same thing. If success in school plays had given me an inflated opinion of my acting abilities, being in the company of more talented performers brought it down again. Fortunately, acting was a minor element of the drama course, which covered everything from theatre history to film. I got to write scripts and mess with a TV studio. I programmed for a film club, started an SF [science fiction] society. In August of 1974 two friends and I got together and raised the money to make a documentary on the ancient theatre buildings of Europe. I shot it, cut it, fixed the camera when it broke. I was inexperienced, the movie was sub-competent, but the process of setting it up and making it was the foundation for what would later become my research method.

"When I left Hull, I worked in television for five years. During that time I sold my first radio plays and a couple of paperback spinoffs that were my first break into print." *The Last Rose of Summer*, an adaptation of a radio serial, was published in 1978 and was reprinted under the title *Dying of Paradise* and under the pseudonym Stephen Couper in 1982. Also in 1982, Gallagher published an adaptation of a *Doctor Who* television series script, *Warrior's Gate*, and the sequel to *Dying of Paradise*, *The Ice Belt*, a book that Gallagher—as he has said—is "not burning to see . . . back in print or anything.

"I was married in 1977, and the sale of *Chimera* gave us enough short-term security for me to throw over the job in August 1980 in order to write full-time. We bought open-ended tickets to the U.S., and toured until the money ran out. I came back with a stack of material that I couldn't get into shape straight away, but which would eventually yield the book that would turn my career around.

"Everything looked great from there, but that didn't last. After putting out *Chimera* and *Follower* (1984), my publisher dropped me by turning down *Oktober* on quality grounds. The taint spread and *Oktober* went on to be rejected by every other publisher in town; and they wouldn't even look at *The Boat House* (1991), the novel which followed it. For that part of the eighties we depended on my wife's income and whatever I could make from residuals and short-story sales. My career seemed to be dead in the water, just at the point at which I'd found my voice and a sense of my personal themes.

"It was then that I turned to my notebooks for the background detail in *Valley of Lights* (1987), which was supposed to be a magazine story but which, quite literally, grew to novel length without conscious control. If I could have exerted conscious control it would have stayed within a word-age at which I'd have a more certain chance of selling it. It was a modest little shocker, very firmly within genre, but it sold to the reviving New English Library imprint and was received well enough for them to put out *Oktober* while I worked on the next. The 'unpublishable' *Oktober*, with barely a word altered, outsold *Valley of Lights* and became my first legitimate entry in the bestseller charts.

"It was with the next book, *Down River*, that I think I consolidated a style. Character-driven suspense stories, a naturalistic surface, a sense of much larger myth driving away beneath. My earliest work had largely reflected the genre fiction that I'd loved while I was growing up. Now I started to look through it, for the deeper forms on which the genres fed."

Down River was also the first novel in which Gallagher did not use traditional science fiction or horror themes. A psychological thriller, it is the story of Johnny Mays, an English detective whose time in the police department has driven him insane. Now seeing himself as a sort of avenging angel, he preys vigilante-style on the undesirables of England.

Since the publication of that book, Gallagher has produced four more novels and has achieved fame in the United States as well as the United Kingdom as Britain's top writer of suspense. His next book, *Rain* (1990), was the story of a 17-year-old English girl named Lucy, who runs away from home upon hearing that her sister Christine was killed by a hit-and-run driver. As she is retracing her sister's footsteps though the shadier parts of downtown London, trying to find the killer, a police officer named Joe, a friend of Lucy's father, sets out to bring the girl back home. Anne Billson, writing for *Time Out*, declared: "I'd be very surprised if a better London novel hits the bookshops this year."

In the next two years, Gallagher published two more novels: *The Boat House* (1991), in which he returned to supernatural themes, and *Nightmare, with Angel* (1992). He has spent much of his time since then working on screenplay adaptations of his books; since his increase in popularity, he has received many offers to write television and movie scripts. Yet as he told *Interzone* in 1989, this does not mean he is going to stop writing novels: "I feel that you have to have the prose writing as the spine of a career, and then screen work is something that you can venture out and do to get wider recognition, to find yourself working as a writer but in an interacting social context." Gallagher was as good as his word, publishing *Red, Red Robin*, the story of a woman named Ruth, who hires an escort to accompany her to an office party so that she can hide the affair she is having with a married coworker. After becoming involved with the escort, who turns out to have a pattern of killing his lovers, she is kidnapped by him, escapes, and then attempts to bring him to justice. A review of the novel in the *New York Times Book Review* (November 19, 1995) read: "Ruth's obsession never seems particularly persuasive, nor does the faintly ludicrous showdown at the end. And while the crazed villain does it all . . . he is surprisingly uninteresting." The *Chicago Tribune* (January 26, 1996) reviewer disagreed, believing: "*Red, Red Robin* is not just another tale about a serial killer, and Ruth Lasseter is a unique heroine."

Stephen Gallagher is the author of many works for the BBC and on Yorkshire TV, including "Warrior's Gate" (1981), "Terminus" (1984), "Moving Targets" (1988), and "Chimera" (1991), based on his novel. He also has numerous radio writing credits dating back to 1977, his most recent being "Life Line" in 1993. He has published a great number of short stories in many magazines and has written reviews and other critical pieces for the *Sunday Express* and *Skeleton Crew* magazine.

Among other projects, he is working on a novel for Bantam to be titled *The Painted Bridge* and on a British film version of *The Boat House* as well as on the miniseries adaptation of *Oktober*.

Stephen Gallagher is the son of Albert Gallagher, an engineering worker, and the former Gladys Couper, a hospital switchboard operator. He married Marilyn Ann Evans, a retail manager, in 1977. They have a daughter Ellen Miranada.
—C.M.

SUGGESTED READING: *Chicago Tribune* V p3 Jan. 26, 1995; *Interzone* p47+ Sep.//Oct. 1989; *New York Times Book Review* p26 Nov. 19, 1995; *Time Out* p45 Apr. 4–11, 1990; *Contemporary Authors* vol. 138, 1993

SELECTED BOOKS: *Chimera*, 1982; *Follower*, 1984; *Valley of Lights*, 1987; *Oktober*, 1988; *Down River*, 1989; *Rain*, 1990; *The Boat House*, 1991; *Nightmare, with Angel*, 1992; *Red, Red Robin*, 1995

Miriam Berkley

Gerstler, Amy

Oct. 24, 1956– Poet; professor

Amy Gerstler has emerged as one of the most respected of contemporary poets. Her work, spanning the better part of the past two decades, has been lauded for its unique and diverse voices as well as its spectrum of subject matter. She is a poet who manages to lighten even the gravest issues with humor and can introduce some of the most extraordinary events calmly into the setting of the ordinary. Gerstler has also written fiction, often injecting her work with an ironic tone; in both forms, she has had particular success in exploring issues of sexuality, spirituality, suffering, and death. In 1991 Gerstler's efforts earned her the National Book Critics Circle Award for her breakthrough, highly acclaimed collection of poems, *Bitter Angel*. Since then, she has completed two more compilations, both of which have garnered highly favorable reviews from around the country.

Amy Gerstler was born on October 24, 1956 in San Diego, California, and attended Pitzer College, from which she received her B.A degree. A prolific writer early on, she was 25 when she published her first book of poems, *Yonder*. She followed this up with *Christ's Alpine Inn* (1982), and then published two more books of poetry in 1984, *White Marriage/Recovery* and *Early Heaven*. *White Marriage/Recovery* in particular received significant critical acclaim, and was praised by a reviewer at the *Los Angeles Times Book Review* (April 8, 1984) as an "odd by utterly beguiling bit of small-press ephemera" which was "spare, almost encoded, but richly evocative." The following year Gerstler produced a work of fiction, *Martine's Mouth*, but then returned to poetry and to complete *The True Bride* in 1986. In the next year, Gerstler produced another work of fiction, *Primitive Man*, and was also awarded second place in *Mademoiselle* magazine's fiction contest.

That same year, Gerstler published *Bitter Angel*, her most critically acclaimed work thus far. Characterized as a "cornucopia of innovative forms and ideas" by a reviewer at the *Independent Presses Editor*, *Bitter Angel* is a collection of poems and prose representing a wide array of narrators, including a ghost, a mermaid, and a saint. As is common in her work, Gerstler's poems in this collection probe an assortment of serious, difficult issues, but she often manages to offset these weighty topics with humor. There are also elements of the supernatural and the surreal in her work. In addition, one of the most pervasive themes in Gerstler's poetry is that of sexuality, often juxtaposed with topics of death and suffering. "Before Sex" for instance, contains the verses "The writhing and thrusting's designed to distract us/ from brooding about death," while "Shrine," with a saint-like figure at its center, offers, "Kiss the dust / of the vacant lot. Reunite with it /Preserve your solitude, the only holy / thing about you!" But even as she tackles such weighty concepts, Gerstler can also provide a pop context as frame for her poems, such as in the lighter "Della's Modesty." This piece takes a fictional character—the quietly strong sectretary Della Street from the TV series *Perry Mason*—and intersperses her story with snippets from textbooks on sex, as well as other information on female sexuality.

Bitter Angel's diversity of content and strong lyrical style earned Gerstler the 1991 National Book Critics Circle Award. *Publishers Weekly*'s (December 22, 1989) review read that "Gerstler balances classical allusion with bold experimentation in voice, form and content, creating a tension that gives her work an urgent, honest edge." Similarly, Michael Dirda, writing in the *Washington Post Book World* (March 3, 1991), praised Gerstler for her "sheer acrobatic brilliance" and commented that Gerstler's book "serves up fast talk and jokey lines about weighty matters like the division between soul and body, the yearning for transcendence, the natures of love and suffering." The reviewer added that "By keeping things breezy, Gestler is able to circle around some hard questions without getting bathetic or corny. Perhaps her most memorable pieces are the harrowing prose poem 'Lucky You' and 'Della's Modesty.'"

American Book Review (January/March 1991) critic Sarah Gorham warned potential readers that in *Bitter Angel*, "[Gerstler's] language is hardly prettified. A baby is described as a 'cutlet carved from our larger carcasses' in 'A Father at His Son's Baptism.' Gorham added that within such a style "lies the strength of these poems: the are heavily laden with vernacular speech and with images of viscious irony." She went on to explain, "They strip down all basic assumptions about beauty and truth and holiness, and begin a struggle for redemption from the gutter, the very worst and lowest of all possible starting points. Because of this, the drive for ascension in Gerstler's work becomes that much more valiant, and comic . . . Ultimately, the exuberance and humor of Gerstler's protest becomes itself a form of salvation." Gorham concluded her assessment of the collection with the endorsement, "I am one of those undying romantics, and I adored this book."

In 1993 Gerstler published the poetry collection *Nerve Storm*, which again took on subjects that include death and sexuality. While the reviews were generally positive, the book did not fare as well critically as had her previous collection. With *Nerve Storm* however, reviewers again praised Gerstler for her ability to display the unordinary within the context of common circumstances. A *Library Journal* (September 15, 1993) reviewer commented that "Gerstler . . . suceeds best when her metaphors surprise" and that even within her darker poetry, "Humor and a wry self-knowledge surface often." The review concluded by noting that "Still, the poems that remain with the reader aren't the clever ones but those where the emotion runs deep, particularly 'The Stretcher-Bearers,' where the poet compares a field of boys' corpses to a string of pearls become unstrung. What one longs for is more music."

Gerstler's next book was *Crown of Weeds* (1997) a collection of 41 poems dedicated to her brother, who had died of a brain tumor. Here the poet's tone again fluctuates among the serious, the melancholy, and the lighthearted. In this collection, however, perhaps more so than in her previous books, Gerstler took a deep and often ironic look at the nature of faith, her poems often describing a type of mantra for life and yearning for immortali-

ty. Some of this translated, in critics' eyes, into an abundance of sentimentality, and as a result, reviews of *Crown of Weeds* were mixed. A writer for the *Hudson Review* (Autumn 1997) cheered, "Gerstler is a poet of abundance who keenly observes a world teeming with people of all ages, temperaments, and social classes and sets down her observations in concise, zesty language. Each of the poems she serves up is an entree sufficient for an evening's cogitation." The *Georgia Review*'s (Spring 1998) critic, Fred Muratori, however, was less enthusiastic, offering the assessment that "Gestler is a highly visual poet with both surrealist leanings and connections to the art world. Although she follows her instincts well, she does so within structures that are too easily defined." Muratori concluded that Gerstler's poems "betray the formulas that conceived them, demanding less afterthought once the initial experience of reading them ends."

Amy Gerstler's writing has appeared in numerous publications as well as in catalogs for exhibitions at the Santa Monica Art Museum, the Long Beach Museum of Art, The Whitney Museum of American Art, the Museum of Contemporary Art in Los Angeles, and the Fort Wayne Museum of Art, among others. When she is not composing poetry and prose, she has worked as an English/creative writing teacher at the Art Center College of Design at the University of Southern California and UCLA, and in the graduate writing program at the University of California, Irvine campus. Gerstler makes her home in Los Angeles.

—D.B.

SELECTED WORKS: *Yonder*, 1981; *Christy's Alpine Inn*, 1982; *White Marriage/Recovery*, 1984; *Early Heaven*, 1984; *Martine's Mouth*, 1985; *The True Bride*, 1986; *Primitive Man*, 1987; *Past Lives* (with Alexis Smith), 1989; *Bitter Angel*, 1990; *Nerve Storm*, 1993; *Crown of Weeds*, 1997

SUGGESTED READING: *American Book Review* Jan./Mar. 1991; *American Poetry Review* Jan.–Feb. 1991; *Booklist* Oct. 1, 1993; *Georgia Review* Spring 1998; *Hudson Review* Autumn 1997; *Library Journal* Sep.15, 1993; *Los Angeles Times Book Review* Apr. 8, 1984; *Poetry Previews* (online); *Publishers Weekly* Dec. 22, 1989; *Voice Literary Supplement* Feb. 1990; *Washington Post Book World* Mar. 3, 1991; *Book Review Digest*, 1991, 1994; *Contemporary Authors*, 1993; *Contemporary Literary Criticism*, 1991

Miriam Berkley

Gibbons, Reginald

Jan. 7, 1947– Poet; novelist; editor

As editor since 1981 of *TriQuarterly*, a literary journal that showcases an eclectic array of new talent for an international audience, Reginald Gibbons has devoted a large portion of his career to helping new writers get their start. In addition, Gibbons himself is a gifted poet and fiction writer whose first novel, *Sweetbitter* (1994), received critical acclaim.

In an autobiographical statement submitted to *World Authors 1990–1995*, Gibbons writes: "I was born at St. Joseph's Hospital in Houston, Texas, on Jan. 7, 1947. When I was five, my family moved to an area being developed on the northwest side, beyond the Houston city limit, called Spring Branch (well inside the city limits of present-day Houston). This semi-rural area allowed my father to own two acres of land, on which to keep a horse for his children, some years a large garden (he plowed it, I remember, at least once, with a mule), a calf he'd raise for slaughter, and chickens. I was educated in the public schools in the Spring Branch Independent School District. I studied piano privately, and played the clarinet in school bands and, when I was in my last two years of high school, in the high-school Houston All-City Symphony Orchestra.

"My father sold products to independent grocery stores during the week, out of his car, and worked as a salesman at a new-house lot on the Gulf Freeway, on weekends for many years. My mother worked as a secretary after her four children were all in school.

"I left Texas in 1965 to attend Princeton University, where I was offered a scholarship. At Princeton, I founded a literary magazine, with friends, called *Upstart*; I sang in the Glee Club; I majored in Spanish. I married Virginia Margaret Harris in 1968, whom I had met when she was studying Turkish at Princeton; I graduated in 1969; and then went to Stanford University, where I took an MA in English and Creative Writing in 1971, and a Ph.D. in Comparative Literature in 1974. For my Ph.D., I studied modern poetry (1850+) in English and Romance Languages. At Princeton, I had studied poetry writing with Theodore Weiss, and at Stanford, I studied poetry writing, the translation of poetry, and poetry and criticism, with Donald Davie—these two teachers, although my work turned out to be very different from theirs, were wonderfully generous, supremely intelligent, and immensely helpful to me in my study of how to write poems.

"On the way to Stanford in the summer of 1969, I was summoned to my local draft board in Houston, which heard my case for conscientious objector status, which I was granted. Eventually I was ordered by the U.S. government to report for a physical exam, which I took in Oakland, California, but I also drew a high number in the 'draft lottery' and was not called up for 'alternative service.'

"I published a few poems while an undergraduate and a few more while a graduate student. Early in 1971, I won a Fullbright grant to study in Spain; Virginia and I left Stanford in May of 1971, drove to Texas, brought a VW there, and drove to the east coast, where we boarded a freighter to Europe, taking our VW with us, and spent a month in Turkey, visiting friends and seeing ruins of Ionian Greece, traveling down the coast and then along it some distance eastward; then we returned to Izmir and crossed by ferry to Venice, and drove from there to Spain. After nine months there, we drove to Switzerland to see friends, then to Rotterdam, where we caught another ferry, which also carried our VW, and disembarked in Montreal. We then drove back across the U.S. to California.

"When I left Stanford with my degree in hand in 1974, it was to return to Princeton, New Jersey, where Virginia had been offered a position in the Middle Eastern collections of the Princeton University Library. I taught freshman composition and literature sections at Trenton State College and Princeton University, in 1974–75, then was a Lecturer in Spanish at Livingston College, Rutgers, in 1975–76. From 1976–77 through 1979–80, I was a part-time Lecturer in creative writing at Princeton. In 1980–81 I was a part-time Lecturer, also in creative writing, at Columbia University in Manhattan. In 1981 I was offered the position of editor of *TriQuarterly* magazine at Northwestern University, and moved to Evanston, Illinois. Virginia and I were divorced in 1983; that year I married Cornelia Maude Spelman.

"By the time I moved to Evanston, Illinois, I had published two books of poems, and other works, including translations of poems of two Spanish poets, Luis Cernuda and Jorge Guill.

"I was appointed to a joint staff-faculty position, and taught part-time in the English department at Northwestern during my entire term as editor (1981–1997). For a sense of what my project was at *TriQuarterly* magazine, I refer the reader to the editorials in issues no. 54 and 100, and to the retrospective anthologies *TQ20*, a twentieth-anniversary issue, and *Fiction of the Eighties*, another retrospective of a different kind. I was assisted in editorial duties by Susan Hahn; as editor and thus also as executive director, I planned and published many special issues, including Chicago, Prose from Spain, A Window on Poland, The Writer in Our World, Writing and Well-Being, From South Africa: New Writing, Photographs and Art, New Writing from Mexico, and others. Given the perennial insufficiencies of funding in the U.S. for literary endeavors, I was required to begin raising funds for *TriQuarterly* in 1984, and eventually raised over $1 million for the magazine during my term as editor. With Susan Hahn I also began a book series of new contemporary fiction and poetry, TriQuarterly Books. In 1993 this series became a part of Northwestern University Press, where it continues, for the most part (as of 1998), under my direction.

"Three friendships were of special importance to me in helping me to develop my own thinking about writing and editing—Terrence Des Pres, with whom I edited a special issue of *TriQuarterly* on the great American poet Thomas McGrath; McGrath himself; and William Goyen, whose work I also published in the magazine, and which I have brought back into print through TriQuarterly Books. The work and the conversation of these three writers gave me standards—of artistry, intensity and honesty of feeling, and engagement with the lives of others—that I have sought to live up to as editor and writer.

"Also extraordinarily important in my life has been raising two stepchildren, Sam and Kate Chaltain.

"I published more books of poems, a novel (*Sweetbitter*) and other works, while I was editor of *TriQuarterly*. These are a few of the bare facts of my personal history. More meditative consideration of my own life can be found in two essays, 'American Dreams: 1950s and 1960s,' published in *Shenandoah* magazine (Summer 1997) and 'The Good-Enough Mother-Tongue,' published in *The Southern Review* (Fall 1996)."

In 1985 Gibbons helped edit *TQ 20: Twenty Years of the Best Contemporary Writing and Graphics from TriQuarterly Magazine*. The critic for *Choice* (December 1985) offered a glowing review of the collection, stating that "if there has been a consistently better American literary magazine than *TriQuarterly*, now in its 21st year, that conclusion would be hard to establish." A *Library Journal* (September 1, 1985) reviewer concurred, writing, "It would be presumptuous to say that a single anthology, especially one drawn from work which originally appeared in a single small-press magazine, could encompass the whole of mid–20th-century literature, but *TQ* comes very close." The reviewer concluded by recommending *TQ 20* as "A great value, and a beautifully illustrated one at that, and a worthy continuation of a welcome 'celebratory series.'"

The following year Gibbons and Gerald Graff edited *Criticism in the University*, which examined literary criticism and the role of literary theory in the university setting. The book, as part of the *TriQuarterly* series on criticism and culture, was heartily welcomed by the university community. A reviewer for *World Literature Today* (Spring 1986) wrote of *Criticism in the University*, "its contributors are mainly academics who convey their knowledge and insights clearly and effectively with obvious commitment and a concern for returning literary criticism to a larger cultural context."

In 1992 Gibbons helped to edit a collection of Mexican literature titled *New Writing From Mexico*. Labeled an "exciting" anthology by the *Library Journal* (December 1992), *New Writing From Mexico* covers a wide range of subjects, including feminism, politics, and city life. The review of the collection for *Small Press* (Spring 1993) was positive: "Unlike the too-often superficial characters and solipsistic vision of contemporary U.S. writing, Gibbons's collection gives us people worth caring about and writing not afraid to be at once serious and joyful."

Gibbons's debut novel, *Sweetbitter* (1994), is a story of outcasts—Reuben Sweetbitter, a half-white, half-Choctaw young man who hails from East Texas, and Martha Clarke, a white, upper-class girl who dreams of leaving her small Texas town. The two become an unlikely couple, carrying on their affair in secret for fear of retribution from a color- and class-conscious town. When their tryst is discovered, they flee East Texas in the hopes of deserting both their small town life and the prejudice that surrounds their relationship. Even though they are able to find a degree of happiness with each other and with a new friend they make along the way, they also realize that they can never truly escape from the nature of their relationship.

The novel proved to be a great success. Liz Rosenberg described it for the *Chicago Tribune* (December 18, 1994) as "surprising in every way." She went on to write that *Sweetbitter* is a "rough, bulky work, almost raw in places, with nothing conventional about the prose or the plot. Not an 'easy' or 'pleasant' book, it possesses its own gritty integrity and native genius . . . the promise is rough but real." Rosenberg noted that Gibbons's style was similar to that of many of the young writers whom he had introduced (and continues to introduce) to the world through *TriQuarterly*, and that he adopted a number of different techniques and points of view. "Yet the more difficult the challenge, the more he seems to rise to it," she wrote. Rosenberg also acknowledged *Sweetbitter*'s "share of failures," noting that it is not convincing to her that Martha, with her upbringing, could conceivably have fallen in love with someone as loathed as Reuben. However, this was a small imperfection for Rosenberg, who concluded that "the novel's ending is as strong as its beginning—terrifying and beautiful, a true tour de force . . . It's to the writer's credit that when all is said and done, we still want one page more."

Jennifer Howard of the *Washington Post* (October 16, 1994) was also impressed with Gibbons's debut novel, observing that Gibbons "writes with a poet's graceful attention to language, limning and then blending lovely details of the East Texas landscape, its denizens, its woods, seasons, and storms, with Reuben's half-remembered, bastardized versions of Choctaw myth and Martha's dreamy, at-arm's length relationship to the white world she can't live in yet can't do without."

Michael Duff, writing in the *Small Press* (Spring 1995) had a different opinion of *Sweetbitter*. Duff chastised Gibbons for ignoring several dramatic aspects of Texas history, such as rampant population growth, lynchings, and Native American marginalization. "Against this charged, rich background, Gibbons has fashioned, astonishingly, a thoroughly trite and boring novel. . . . Gibbons has hopelessly trivialized the worthy theme of interracial love and marriage in *Sweetbitter* with his stick figure characters, ponderous plotting, and stultifying prose." Duff admitted to finding the Choctaw Indian lore interesting, but he complained that those stories alone are "not nearly enough to save this sorry tale from drowning in its own bathos."

In 1996 Gibbons published the *TriQuarterly New Writers,* a collection of writings from a diverse sampling of *TriQuarterly* contributors whom Gibbons and his fellow editors sought to expose to a wider audience. It was not well-received by the reviewer for *Publishers Weekly* (May 13, 1996), who criticized the 33 poems and stories in the compilation as lightweight material, the kind which "might be read in the park or on the subway without too much time or strain." The reviewer went on to note that "most of the stories and poems presented are of the slice-of-life variety, and simply because an experience is written down, it does not necessarily make for a moving tale. Despite all attempts to present this compilation as otherwise, it is extremely reductive."

The following year Gibbons published *Sparrow: New and Selected Poems,* a collection of more than 30 years of his own poetry. Reflecting a vast number of literary influences, ranging from Ezra Pound to ancient Chinese poets to contemporary writers, Gibbons's collection concerns the events of his personaal life as well as social issues. As Fred

Muratori wrote for the *Library Journal* (December 1997), the poems "map the shifting interactions of lyric and narrative modes," and Gibbons "combines an imagist's visual acuity . . . with a therapist's attention to gesture." Muratori went on to add that while Gibbons "sometimes finds himself 'getting lost in the pity of it' and allows for some windy passages, [his] honesty of expression and involvement in his subjects prove that at least someone hears the difficult, almost inexpressible stories that would otherwise dissolve in silence."

Reginald Gibbons has received fellowships from the Guggenheim Foundation and the National Endowment for the Arts. He has also won the Carl Sandburg Award (1992), the Anisfield-Wolf Book Award (1995), the Balcones Poetry Prize (1998), and various other awards for his poetry, fiction, and essays. In addition, his work has been included in the *Best American Poetry* and *Pushcart Prize* anthologies. Gibbons published a new book of his poetry, titled *Homage to Longshot O'Leary*, in 1999. —D.B.

SUGGESTED READING: *Chicago Tribune* p4 Dec. 18, 1994, with photo; *Choice* Dec. 1985; *Library Journal* Sep. 1, 1985, p110 Dec. 1997; *Publishers Weekly* p72 May 13, 1996; *Small Press* Spring 1993, Spring 1995; *Washington Post* p8 Oct. 16, 1994; *World Literature Today* Spring 1986;*Book Review Digest* 1986, 1987, 1994, 1995, 1996; *Contemporary Authors*, 1986

SELECTED WORKS: Fiction—*Sweetbitter*, 1994; Poetry—*Roofs Voices Roads*, 1979; *The Ruined Motel*, 1981; *Saints*, 1986; *Sparrow: New and Selected Poems,* 1997; *Homage to Longshot O'Leary*, 1999; As editor—*The Poet's Work*, 1979; *TQ 20: Twenty Years of the Best Contemporary Writing and Art from "TriQuarterly" Magazine,* 1985; *Criticism in the University*, 1986; *The Writer in Our World*, 1986; *New Writing From Mexico*, 1993; *TriQuarterly New Writers*, 1996;

Gilb, Dagoberto

1950– Novelist; short-story writer

Dagoberto Gilb is a critically acclaimed short-story writer and novelist who depicts the lives of working-class Mexican-Americans. His breakthrough collection of stories, *The Magic of the Blood*, appeared in 1993; in the following year he published his first novel, *The Last Known Residence of Mickey Acuna*, the story of one man's life in an El Paso YMCA. The book was noted for its strong evocation of life in a border town. Gilb has received numerous awards for his fiction, including a National Endowment for the Arts fellowship and a Guggenheim fellowship. Still, he is reluctant to become overly comfortable in the literary establishment.

Miriam Berkley

Dagoberto Gilb

As he noted in a *Los Angeles Times* (November 12, 1995) interview: "Art is about being a little wild, taking risks, not necessarily getting approval from somebody; it's the disapproval."

Dagoberto Gilb was born in Los Angeles in 1950, the son of a Mexican mother and an American father. His father, a former Marine of German descent, left his mother early in his son's life. His mother raised him in a tough neighborhood near Watts. According to an interview with Lisa Broadwater of the *Los Angeles Times Magazine* (November 12, 1995), the author claims that he was wild during his youth and that he is thus "the least likely writer."

After completing high school, Gilb enrolled at the University of California. By 1976 he had earned a bachelor's degree and a master's degree in philosophy and religious studies. Though he had completed his degrees, he did not pursue a career in those fields. Instead he became a journeyman carpenter, which allowed him the time to write. "For me, a guy that likes to write, it was great," he told Broadwater during their interview. "I could work for six months and then take off for three and write some stories."

For nearly a decade, Gilb submitted stories to various literary magazines only to be rejected time and again, usually because his writing was considered "too colloquial." Still, he kept at it, slowly developing his craft and fashioning characters who spoke a realistic mix of Spanish and English.

His first collection of stories, *Winners on the Pass Line and Other Stories*, appeared in 1985. While this collection was not widely reviewed, it did enable the author to begin publishing large quantities of short stories and articles in various

magazines and periodicals. In 1987 he became a Dobie–Paisano fellow at the Texas Institute of Letters at the University of Texas and subsequently became a visiting fiction writer at the university for the 1987–1988 school year.

Though Gilb was receiving a greater recognition, he was still unable to support himself as a writer and continued to work as a carpenter. This changed in 1992, when he received a National Endowment for the Arts fellowship, which enabled him to complete his short-story collection *The Magic of the Blood* (1993). Composed of 26 stories (eight of which were published in his previous collection), *The Magic of the Blood* looks at the lives of Mexican-Americans living in the Los Angeles area and parts of the southwestern section of the United States. In an article for *Mellus* (Spring 1997), Barbara J. Sáez of the University of Rhode Island noted: "Gilb's men live a marginal existence, always teetering on the edge of an economic abyss, always in the borderland of culture. For Gilb's characters, the stark reality of 'border' life becomes the new site of struggle, a struggle over economic and cultural survival; it is a much more difficult place for a man to win against the odds."

Many of the stories are striking in the way they deal with the everyday harshness of life. "Al, in Phoenix" imagines an encounter between a skilled mechanic and a fussy car-owner; in "Look on the Bright Side" a working man fights his landlady in court after she has raised his rent illegally. The collection was widely hailed in literary circles; the members of the committee for the Whitling Writers' Awards presented Gilb with a $30,000 check for his work. Gilb was also the recipient of the 1993 Jesse Jones/Texas Institute of Letters Award for best book of fiction and the 1994 PEN/Hemingway Foundation Award for First Fiction, and he was a finalist in the 1994 PEN/Faulkner Award for Fiction.

In 1994 Gilb released his first novel, *The Last Known Residence of Mickey Acuna*. This book focused on the life of a working-class Mexican-American, Mickey Acuna, who has checked into the local YMCA in El Paso, Texas, to await a check from the West Coast. The reader is unsure of Mickey's age or previous occupation. Instead the narrative follows Mickey's daily life at the YMCA and the people he encounters there, including Blind Jimmy, a street musician who wants to be an eight-year-old girl; Sarge, who is obsessed with pornography and fast food; and Omar, who drinks tequila and torments himself by dwelling on a lost love. Critics had mixed feelings about the book. In the *New York Times Book Review* (October 2, 1994) Robert Cohen complained: "It is difficult to know what to make of this ending, given the integrity of the author's approach—or, to put it another way, how sketchy and noncommittal he is on the big questions. . . . And the lack of plot, though it underscores a certain truth about Mickey's plotless life, becomes a bit wearying." But Cohen went on to note that Gilb "writes in a deft, ironic style that is all his own." A critic for *Kirkus Reviews* (June 15, 1994) called the work "a slight first novel," adding: "Towards the end Gilb works up some plot tension concerning the whereabouts of the mysterious check, but it's too little, too late, drowned in a sea of Bukowskian, nothing-matters existentialism."

Dagoberto Gilb lives in El Paso, Texas, with his wife, Rebeca, and their two sons, Antonio and Ricardo. He continues to contribute articles and short stories to magazines and journals. In 1994 he was a visiting writer of the University of Wyoming in Laramie. In 1995 he was the recipient of a Guggenheim fellowship.

—CM

SUGGESTED READING: *Kirkus Reviews* Aug. 1, 1993; June 15, 1994; *Los Angeles Times Magazine* Nov. 12, 1995; *Mellus* p 159-162, Spring 1997; *New York Times* C p 28, Oct. 2, 1993; *New York Times Book Review* p 15, Oct. 2, 1994; *New Yorker* p 74-77, Sep. 29, 1997; *Washington Post* B p 1, May 23, 1994; *Who's Who in America*, 1998

SELECTED WORKS: *Winners on the Pass Line and Other Stories*, 1985; *The Magic of the Blood*, 1993; *The Last Known Residence of Mickey Acuna*, 1994

Star Black

Gioia, Dana

Dec. 24, 1950– Poet; business executive

Dana Gioia is a critic, editor, translator, and leading neoformalist poet who has stirred up controversy with his opinions regarding contemporary American poetry. Gioia has two major critiques of the state of modern-day poetry—that it has strayed too far from its traditional forms and that universities have slowly lessened the general public's appreciation of it by treating it as the exclusive property of academia. Gioia points out how only 50 years ago, American newspapers and popular magazines were liberally sprinkled with poems and poetry reviews. Though he believes that this more general audience may still exist, he sees it as being isolated from modern poetry because literary journals (usually published by universities) have been

the major publishers of poetry in the latter half of the 20th century. As Gioia stated in an interview with Gloria G. Brame for *Eclectic Literary Forum* (Spring 1995): "The voluntary audience of serious contemporary poetry consists mainly of poets, would-be poets, and a few critics. Additionally, there is a slightly larger involuntary and ephemeral audience consisting of students who read contemporary poetry as assigned course work. In sociological terms, it is surely significant that most members of the poetry subculture are literally paid to read poetry: most established poets and critics now work for large educational institutions. Over the last half-century, literary bohemia had been replaced by an academic bureaucracy." Gioia's 1992 critical volume, *Can Poetry Matter?*, a collection of articles on these issues, caused heated debate between academics and poets.

Writing specifically for *World Authors 1990-1995*, the poet, born Michael Dana Gioia on December 24, 1950, discusses his life, his influences, and his hopes for the future of American poetry: "I was born in Hawthorne, California, an industrial town in southwest Los Angeles. My father was then a cab driver. My mother worked as a telephone operator. I was the oldest of four children from what would now be called a cross-cultural marriage. My father was the son of Sicilian immigrants. My mother a Hawthorne-born mixture mostly of Mexican and Native-American. The clash of cultures was not an abstraction in my childhood. My father was the only person in his huge extended family who had not married a Sicilian. We lived next door to my grandparents as well as an aunt, uncle, and three generations of assorted cousins. The adults spoke a Sicilian dialect among themselves.

"I was raised Roman Catholic and attended 12 years of Catholic schools. At parochial school we attended Latin Mass every morning. I also studied Latin through high school. Like millions of other Americans, therefore, I had a trilingual childhood surrounded by the language of the Old World at home, the New World at school, and the Next World in church. Although I was raised in a tough, working-class neighborhood without many of the conventional cultural advantages, I can't imagine a richer background for a poet.

"My parents, who had never attended college, were very serious about our schooling. They made such obvious sacrifices to give us the best education possible that I felt an obligation to do well. I was usually first in my class, though I often got into trouble for violating school rules. In high school I became deeply interested in both music and literature. I had always been a voracious reader—mainly of history and science fiction—but now, at the prompting of my best friend, I independently read two or three novels every week. My early passions included Nabokov, Pynchon, Barth, Borges, and Huxley. I also fell permanently in love with Auden's poetry. I also learned to play several wind instruments in addition to the piano, which I had begun studying in childhood. I lived and breathed 20th-century music, especially Stravinsky, Britten, Tippett, Walton, and Barber. I even began to compose—without instruction or guidance.

"In 1969 I entered Stanford as a freshman of considerable intellectual sophistication and nearly infinite social naivete. I had hardly met the middle class before college, and the elite classes from which Stanford drew most of its students seemed an utter enigma. At first I intended to be a composer, but midway through my sophomore year, which I spent in Vienna studying music and German, I suddenly knew I wanted to be a poet. I was greatly influenced by Ezra Pound's *ABC's of Reading*, which insisted that anyone committed to writing good poetry in English must also study poetry in foreign languages. Upon returning to America, I spent much of the next two years learning French as well as studying poetry in German and Latin. I also became editor of *Sequoia*, Stanford's literary magazine, which was the first of many subsequent editorial involvements.

"In 1973 I went to Harvard graduate school in comparative literature for two years where I studied with Elizabeth Bishop and Robert Fitzgerald. At Harvard I realized that I wanted to be a writer and not a professor, so I decided to pursue a practical career that would allow me to write at night. I returned West to enter Stanford Business School in 1975, where I not only received an M.B.A. but—more important by far—I met my future wife. Upon graduating, we decided to move to New York where it seemed possible to mix a career in business with a passion for literature and the arts.

"Over the next 15 years I worked for General Foods where I eventually became a vice-president. I wrote at night usually after working 10 or 11 hours in the office. For years I was able to keep my writing secret from my colleagues, but eventually I became so well-known that people read about me in the general press. Even then, I resolutely kept the two sides of my life entirely separate.

"Working in business has obvious drawbacks for a poet, but it also offered me some genuine advantages. It gave me freedom to write exactly as I wished. Since my personal notion of poetry was deeply at odds with the indulgent fashions of the 1970s and 1980s, I was able to follow a radically independent course without seeking outside approval. I would write and rewrite a poem through a hundred drafts over several years without worrying about publication, tenure, or the rent. I consider these lonely, exhausting, but productive years my defining period as writer. I also learned a great deal about America by traveling across the country on business visiting factories, warehouses, and sales offices that took me far beyond the narrow academic confines of my school years.

"I probably would have stayed in business until retirement had it not been for the sudden death of our first son a few days before Christmas, 1987. I stopped writing for a year while my wife and I slowly put our lives back together. Although we eventually had two more sons, I had been so deeply transformed by the loss that I eventually resolved to base my life entirely on my writing. In January, 1992 I left business and became a full-time writer.

"The transition from a highly organized business life to the freedom of writing was outwardly successful but inwardly confusing. The success of *Can Poetry Matter?* put me in great demand, and I traveled through England and America giving readings, broadcasts, and lectures. Editors constantly asked me for poems, essays, interviews, and reviews. Having asked that poetry have a more visible place in American public culture, I now found myself drafted into becoming one of its public spokespersons. Although I enjoyed this public role, I gradually found that its constant demands took too much time and energy from my writing. In January, 1996 I fled the metropolitan enchantments of New York for the welcome isolation of rural northern California."

———

In addition to being an editor and a translator, Dana Gioia has published two volumes of poetry, *Daily Horoscope* (1986) and *The Gods of Winter* (1991), the latter about the death of his son Michael Jasper. Gioia has been classified as a leading member of the neoformalist school of poetry by his publishers, Graywolf Press, and by critics because of his carefully structured, frequently narrative poems. Still, according to the review of *The Gods of Winter* in *Library Journal* (May 1, 1991), "It is not the formalism that is of chief interest here . . . but the way some of these poems break out of bland formula into beauty." Gioia is a great believer in the traditions of poetry—rhyme and meter, narrative drive, and other various forms of structure—contending that poetry lost much of its audience with the advent of symbolism and modernism. Gioia, through his poetry, wishes to experiment further with traditional devices, thinking that within them are rich untapped veins of originality. Gioia stated in one interview, "The Beat and Confessional poets were the strongest influences on me. Their unfailing verbosity and heroic self-absorption proved a constant inspiration—showing me everything I didn't want to do. One cannot overestimate the importance of negative examples at certain points in literary history when sensibilities shift." Partially because of experimental writers, Gioia argues, poetry has lost its once great prominence in American letters—where it once had been the source of Henry Wadsworth Longfellow's international fame and had been the means by which John Greenleaf Whittier helped to inspire the abolitionist movement, it is now, according to Gioia, the private playing ground of an exclusive group: poets, would-be poets, and academic critics. The members of this group, most of whom teach in universities, look to these same institutions to maintain their reputations and seal their economic stability, thereby creating a self-perpetuating cycle of insular poetry.

Gioia's most significant contribution as a critic to this discussion is the 1992 book *Can Poetry Matter?* This book of critical essays has caused a great deal of controversy in the poetic and academic communities, which Gioia perceives as being, in many ways, the same group. Gioia pointed out that poets were once people who lived in the "real" world and not in the comfortable confines of tenured professorships. He listed several important examples among the modernists alone: Robert Frost was a farmer, T. S. Eliot a banker and a publisher, and Wallace Stevens a corporate insurance lawyer. Many others became bohemians—Ezra Pound and e.e. cummings, among others. Gioia believes that the problems with modern American poetry began when the academics began hiring bohemian poets to teach creative writing in universities—even when the bohemians had little or no college education. Slowly the universities began to take more and more poets out of society. As Gioia wrote in *Can Poetry Matter?*: "Based mostly in universities, these groups have gradually become the primary audience for contemporary poetry. Consequently, the energy of American poetry, which was once directed outward, is now increasingly focused inward. Reputations are made and rewards distributed within the poetry subculture." This in turn leaves the average reader continually less interested in poetry.

As Gioia has observed, most of the criticism of his work has come from the ranks of the academics. The *North American Review* (November/December 1994) critic found the collection of essays to be chaotic and stated that "other serious problems with this book include, on the one hand, Gioia's constant carping about the academy, the 'university' and the 'creative writing programs'; and on the other hand a kind of poetic Babbittry . . . often betraying his literary intelligence into banality." Yet a reviewer for the *Journal of American Studies* (April 1994) wrote: "This collection of most various essays makes for a somewhat untidy, haphazard book; but it also makes one that is deeply impressive and reassuring: reassuring not because it comforts but because it discomforts."

While serving as a vice-president for General Foods Corporation, Dana Gioia was the literary editor for *Inquiry* magazine from 1977 to 1979 and the poetry editor there from 1979 to 1983. Since 1985 he has been a member of the board of directors of the Wesleyan University Writers Conference, and he has been the president of the board of directors for Story Line Press since 1992. In 1986 he was awarded the Frederick Bock Poetry Prize. He had been a contributor to such magazines as the *New Yorker*, the *Atlantic*, *Kenyon Review*, the *Hudson Review*, and *Poetry*. He lives in Santa Rosa, California with his wife, the former Mary Hiecke, whom he married in 1980, and their two sons, Theodore and Michael Frederick.
—C.M.

SUGGESTED READING: *Eclectic Literary Forum* Spring 1995; *Hudson Review* p429+ Autumn 1996; *Journal of American Studies* p128 Apr. 1994; *Library Journal* p79 May 1, 1991; *New York Times* 13WC p21 Aug. 16, 1992; *North American Review* p44+ Nov./Dec. 1994; *Southern Humanities Review* p199+ Spring 1994; *Contemporary Authors* vol. 130, 1990; *Who's Who in America 1997*

SELECTED BOOKS: Poetry—*Daily Horoscope*, 1986; *The Gods of Winter*, 1991; An Introduction to Poetry, 1993; The Hand of the Poet: Poems and Papers in Mabuscript, 1997; Nonfiction—*Can Poetry Matter?*, 1992; As editor—*The Ceremony and Other Stories*, 1984; *Poems from Italy*, 1985; *The Printed Poem: The Poem as Print*, 1985; *New Italian Poets* (with M. Palma), 1990; *Literature: An Introduction to Fiction, Poetry, and Drama*, 1998; Certain Solitudes:On the Poetry of Donald Justice, 1998; As translator—*Eugenio Montale's Mottetti: Poems of Love*, 1990

Golden, Marita

Apr. 28, 1950– Novelist; memoirist; essayist

The novelist, memoirist, and essayist Marita Golden is a cultural spokesperson whose writing voices many of the concerns and experiences of African-American women. Summing up her reasons for writing, Golden writes in an autobiographical statement for *World Authors 1990–1995*, "As an African-American woman, writing has been my way into a conversation with a revision of the world and its definition with me. Writing has been the way in which I honor who I am and point the way to who I can become." *Migrations of the Heart* (1983) is an account of her experiment as the American wife of a Nigerian in her husband's native land, where her independence and career-mindedness clashed with her husband's traditional expectations. Golden edited the anthology *Wild Women Don't Wear No Blues: Black Women Writers on Love, Men, and Sex* (1993) and went on to write *Saving Our Sons: Raising Black Children in a Turbulent World* (1995), in which she set forth a model for child rearing, and *A Miracle Every Day: Triumph and Transformation in the Lives of Single Mothers* (1999). In addition to her nonfiction works, Golden has authored several novels. Her first, *A Woman's Place*, came out in 1986 and was followed by *Long Distance Life* (1989), *And Do Remember Me* (1992), and *The Edge of Heaven* (1998), all of which deal with history as it relates to the lives of African-American women. The novelist Alice Walker, as quoted by *Poetry and Prose* (on-line), called *Migrations of the Heart* "a book all women will find useful and compelling and all men who love women will find disturbing, painful, and instructive"—a description that might be applied to many of Golden's works.

Marita Golden was born on April 28, 1950 in Washington, D.C., the daughter of Francis Sherman, a taxi driver, and Beatrice (Reid) Sherman, a landlord. During Golden's childhood and adolescence she lived in several of the boarding houses owned by her mother. These houses, she wrote in her autobiographical statement for *World Authors*, were "filled with people whose lives I watched unfold like a thrilling, irresistible narrative." Even more than the circumstances of her upbringing, Golden credits her parents with fostering her creativity. She has described her father as a "talented storyteller," whose tales drew on his own family history as well as the stories of influential African-Americans. "My bedtime stories had nothing to do with Cinderella or Snow White and everything to do with Sojourner Truth and Frederick Douglass. . . . My father told me stories constantly, endlessly, and indirectly taught me what a story was," Golden wrote for *World Authors*. By the time she reached her early teens, Golden showed signs of literary interests and talents, which her mother strongly encouraged in her. "My mother simply told me one day when I was 14 that one day I was going to be a writer," Golden wrote in her statement for *World Authors*. "She had proudly shown off my poems to friends, watched me skip dinner to read, seen my letters to the editor of *The Washington Post* get published, and she anointed me, gave me her blessing, launched me into a world of power and magic." In summary, Golden wrote, "My mother's faith in me and my father's stories are the two most important characteristics of my childhood that groomed me to become a writer."

Golden remained in Washington, D.C., through college; in 1972 she acquired a B.A. degree from American University, where she majored in American Studies and English. She later described college to Maria Koklanaris for the *Washington Post* (May 9, 1991) as "that golden period in your life dedicated to intellectual growth in a very systematic way . . . At [American University] for the first two years I had one really brilliant teacher af-ter another who encouraged me, who built on the confidence that my parents gave me, who made me feel that what I had to say was important." After college, Golden moved first to Baltimore, Maryland, where she worked at a newspaper, and then to New York City, where she earned a master's degree from Columbia University's school of journalism, in 1973. During graduate school, Golden wrote in her statement for *World Authors*, "I realized that while journalism appealed to me, it would not allow me the individual, unique voice that I felt was necessary to writing. . . . So I began to write fiction while maintaining an interest in nonfiction." After finishing her master's degree, Golden worked for the next two years as an associate producer at WNET, Channel 13, New York's public broadcasting affiliate. In 1975 she began teaching at the University of Lagos, in Lagos, Nigeria, where she worked until 1979. Also in about 1975 she married a Nigerian architecture student, whom she had met while in graduate school; she subsequently moved with him to his native country.

Golden's first book, *Migrations of the Heart* (1983), is a memoir of her marriage and life in Nigeria. Once the couple moved, her husband remained unemployed for a long time, in part because his tribal affiliation engendered prejudice against him in his native country, and in part because of Nigeria's poor economy. Golden, in contrast, got prestigious and well-paying jobs. Her husband demanded that she give birth to a son, but when she did, as Diane McWhorter put it in the *New York Times Book Review* (May 1, 1983), Golden had to face "the sad paradox of her African life: Free for once from racial prejudice in the workplace, she was hit with sexual oppression at home." Although McWhorter found *Migrations of the Heart* to be an interesting story that captures "the bunker mentality of the American wives in Lagos," she criticized Golden's writing and found her lacking in understanding of her new culture: "[Golden] seems insulated from the African experience that is supposedly changing her life, and her overwrought self-scrutiny sometimes has the odor of adolescent self-regard." Christine M. Hill, who reviewed the book for *Library Journal* (February 1, 1983), found Golden's African sojourn an "engrossing, fiercely written story," but agreed with McWhorter that "Golden's recollections of her childhood are marred by poetic modifiers and truly gauche mixed metaphors."

The title of Golden's next book, *A Woman's Place* (1986), is perhaps an indirect reference to her experience in Africa of living in a culture where women are restricted and oppressed. The novel, however, deals not with Africa but with a new generation of African-American women for whom peer support and friendship are the primary sources of strength. *Long Distance Life* (1989) tells the story of three generations of one family based in Washington, D.C. The family has traveled a long distance—both geographically and in the degree to which their values and mind-sets have changed—from the North Carolina farm origins of Naomi, the matriarch, to the civil rights struggle that engages her daughter, to the aspirations of one of her grandsons, who becomes a doctor, to the very different life of his brother, who becomes involved with drugs. Laura Shapiro, who reviewed the book for *Newsweek* (November 20, 1989), observed that despite Golden's tendency to use clichés, "these vivid characters have substance, and her tale has the power to move us." Thulani Davis, writing in the *Village Voice Literary Supplement* (May 1990), felt that Golden avoided the emotional heart of her story. "*Long Distance Life* is hemmed in for want of one strong idea to drive the narrative forward," Davis wrote. "Golden doesn't take the naturalistic line that the family is being unraveled by a destructive society; nor does she make her characters responsible. Each of these passive souls has been emotionally abandoned somewhere down the line; still, they hardly seem meant to be emblematic of anything uniquely African-American." *Long Distance Life* was popular with readers and became a best-seller, earning Golden considerable attention.

After returning to the United States, Golden held a series of teaching positions; from 1979 to 1981 she was an assistant professor of English at Roxbury Community College, in Roxbury, Massachusetts, and from 1981 to 1983 she was an assistant professor of journalism at Emerson College, in Boston. By 1991 Golden was teaching in the writing program at George Mason University, in Virginia. She began to realize that there was a dearth of African-American students in the program. "We encourage our kids to play basketball, but we don't encourage them to write," she told Maria Koklanaris. In order to help motivate budding young writers, Golden established the Zora Neale Hurston/Richard Wright Award for the best previously unpublished short story or novel excerpt written by a black college student. Although during their lives Hurston and Wright were "bitter enemies," according to Golden, she "wanted to symbolically bring this man and this woman together as they had not been in life." The award itself was conceived as "another institution for young black writers to gain mentors, make contacts and form relationships, as well as earn recognition for their work," she told Koklanaris. Judges for the award came from Golden's contacts on the board of the PEN/Faulkner Awards and from the Afro-American Writers Guild, which she had founded the year before.

In her next novel, *And Do Remember Me* (1992), Golden again used the civil rights movement as a backdrop, showing how it shaped the lives of the African-American women in her story. Jessie, one of the novel's two protagonists, rises from poverty and abuse in Mississippi to become an acclaimed actress. Macon, the other, is a middle-class academic who, after the black student union is vandalized, must make her students understand that the roots of hate lie just beneath the surface and that

the battle for racial tolerance can never be completely won, or even partially won, without constant vigilance. "This is a bitter truth that Americans have now, in the 90s, to face," Ellen Douglas wrote in her review of the novel for the *Washington Post* (June 21, 1992). "The dangers braved in the 60s, the young heroism, the lives lost, seem almost forgotten; the battles fought 30 years ago seem ominously close to being re-enacted." While Douglas felt there was a serious purpose behind *And Do Remember Me*, she concluded that "Seriousness is not enough to make a novel good, or to give it staying power. *And Do Remember Me* is marred by arbitrary shifts in point of view and by scenes too scantily set. There is a regrettable tendency to overwrite and to write carelessly or stiffly."

In 1992 the Washington, D.C., Commission on the Arts presented Golden with the Mayor's Arts Award for Excellence in Artistic Discipline. Also in that year *An Intimation of Things Distant: The Collected Fiction of Nella Larsen* was published, with a foreword by Golden. Nella Larsen was a writer of the Harlem Renaissance who has been neglected; Golden wrote in her foreword that she identified with Helga Crane, the main character of *Quicksand*, one of Larsen's novels. "Any woman who has searched for a metaphorical place in the sun, a job where she could be paid what she deserved (despite her ovaries), or sought to fashion a love, an affair, or a marriage based on respect and honor for self and partner, has been Helga Crane too. The angst, the tension that rivets the lives of Larsen's heroines makes their dilemmas completely contemporary and timeless."

Golden continued to shed light on women's issues with *Wild Women Don't Wear No Blues: Black Women Writers on Love, Men, and Sex*, a collection of essays that she edited. In her introduction to the book, Golden described growing up in Washington: "As a Black girl, no matter what your class or your complexion . . . you knew there were no Prince Charmings in your neighborhood. . . . And, you like to think that if you'd been Cinderella, you'd have hightailed it away from that positively weird step-mutha before the shoe business. You'd like to think that. But would you?" Carolyn See, reviewing the book for the *Washington Post* (August 20, 1993), observed, "Given that fairy tales don't apply to hard-working black women, how should they think about love, men, sex? This is a handbook of reality. No rescues coming, ladies! No eternal love! No pedestals to put you on. Just a lot of confused human beings, feeling black and blue. And, of course, all this, twisted very slightly, applies to the white population." See encouraged her readers to buy the book, "because if we can 'connect' with this stuff, we might get a handle on understanding all of America. These essays are amazing." Golden also co-edited with Susan Richards Shreve *Skin Deep: Black Women and White Women Write About Race* (1995). In a review for the *Washington Post* (July 16, 1995), Jabari Asim commented that the essays point to Americans' preoccupation with racial difference and noted that, as Golden wrote in the book's introduction, "obsession ain't solution." Asim asserted that "throughout our centuries-long coexistence in this country, blacks and whites alike have come away full of opinions about each other but distressingly devoid of real knowledge." Golden and Shreve's book, Asim continued, aims "to provide a bit of illumination in this regard," and the editors "have assembled a roster of heavy hitters to assist them." Among the book's contributors are Toni Morrison, Alice Walker, and Eudora Welty, as well as bell hooks and Naomi Wolf.

Golden's 1995 book *Saving Our Sons: Raising Black Children in a Turbulent World* deals with Golden's rearing of her son, Michael. Opal J. Moore, who reviewed the book for the *Washington Post* (January 15, 1995), described it as Golden's examination of "the pain and doubt that beleaguers even the most well-prepared, well-educated black women as they face a seemingly insurmountable task—raising their sons in a society that despises them, that has little use or regard for children of any description." Golden herself had, in the *Washington Post Magazine* (October 13, 1991), expressed her pride upon realizing that "not only could I give my son food and shelter but vacations on Puerto Rican beaches too. Despite the doubts and difficulties of single parenthood," she wrote, "I came to believe and know. . . that I was doing the right thing with the life I was chiseling for myself and my child." Nevertheless, in *Saving Our Sons*, Golden recalls the deaths of the college basketball star Len Bias and his brother, and the story of Terrence Brown, whose college plans were derailed when he was accused and convicted of killing a police officer. She expressed fear that her son might come to "inhabit that narrow, corrupt crawl space in the minds of whites and some black people too, a space reserved for criminals, outcasts, misfits, and black men. Soon he would become a permanent suspect." For Golden, Moore wrote, "the black mother must function as a kind of goddess with the power to quilt the world that her sons need to live in." Moore felt *Saving Our Sons* had the positive qualities of a how-to manual; in the end, however, she found it "insistent yet too bland in style to be thoroughly compelling."

Despite Golden's affirmation of herself as a black writer, obliged to speak for her community and also to it in the voice of leadership, she has cautioned other writers not to assume their work speaks only to a narrow audience. As William Grimes reported in the *New York Times* (March 25, 1996), Golden's address at a black writers' conference held at Medgar Evers College in Brooklyn, New York, in 1996 stressed "the necessity and even the duty" of black writers to assume that their experience speaks to everyone in the world. "We are indeed the world. The world is in us, and to say that does not diminish the uniqueness of our triumphs and our journeys and our travails," Golden told the audience.

Golden's next exploration of African-American family relations took the form of a novel. *The Edge of Heaven* (1998) is told from the point of view of a 20-year-old college student whose family is riven when the mother is imprisoned after the death of a daughter. The father, an artist, flees to avoid the violence between himself and his wife and believes his "crime was abandonment, dereliction of duty." Janet Kaye, in her review of the novel in the *New York Times Book Review* (April 5, 1998), called *The Edge of Heaven* "an often affecting story of dashed hopes and domestic discord," but thought that Golden was still in her apprenticeship as a novelist. Kaye observed that "confusion rather than mystery results from [Golden's] decision to withhold key information. . . . Had readers known these facts from the beginning, *The Edge of Heaven* might have been a more cohesive—and an even more absorbing—novel."

Golden's 1999 nonfiction work, *A Miracle Every Day: Triumph and Transformation in the Lives of Single Mothers*, seeks to refute the notion that children of single mothers are destined for unhappiness and lack of success. The book profiles the nurturing relationships between a number of single mothers and their children, who appear to be happy and well-adjusted.
—S. Y.

SUGGESTED READING: *Library Journal* p202 Feb. 1, 1983; *Newsweek* p79 Nov. 20, 1989; *New York Times* C p11 Mar. 25, 1996, with photo; *New York Times Book Review* p16 May 1, 1983, p24 Apr. 5, 1998; *Village Voice Literary Supplement* p26 May 1990; *Washington Post* J p1 May 9, 1991, C p2 Oct. 27, 1992, A p19 Mar. 25, 1995, C p5 May 9, 1995; *Washington Post Book World* p15 Mar. 29, 1992, p12 May 24, 1992, p3 June 21, 1992, p2 Aug. 20, 1993, p5 Jan. 15, 1995, p1 July 16, 1995; *Washington Post Magazine* p26 Oct. 13, 1991; *Politics and Prose* (on-line); *Contemporary Authors* new revision series, vol. 42, 1994

SELECTED BOOKS: Nonfiction—*Migrations of the Heart*, 1983; *Saving Our Sons: Raising Black Children in a Turbulent World*, 1995; *A Miracle Every Day: Triumph and Transformation in the Lives of Single Mothers*, 1999; Fiction—*A Woman's Place*, 1985; *Long Distance Life*, 1989; *And Do Remember Me*, 1992; *The Edge of Heaven*, 1998; As editor—*Wild Women Don't Wear No Blues: Black Women Writers on Love, Men and Sex*, 1993; As co-editor with S. R. Shreve—*Skin Deep: Black Women and White Women Write About Race*, 1993

Miriam Berkley

Goldstein, Rebecca

Feb. 23, 1950– Novelist; short-story writer

Rebecca Goldstein, American novelist and writer of short stories, chose to regard her leaving the world of philosophy (of which she has been a professor) to become a novelist as a divergence, but many reviewers have commented on the philosophical cast of her novels. Her characters, particularly the females who are aspects of Goldstein herself, collide with each other and with aspects of their pasts. Facets of masculinity and femininity, of old-world customs and modern suburban life, of classical studies and physics, of feminist diatribe and Jamesian subtleties, of psychology and fate intertwine in her novels *The Mind-Body Problem* (1983), *The Late-Summer Passion of a Woman of Mind* (1989), *The Dark Sister* (1993), and *Mazel* (1995) and in the short stories included in *Strange Attractors* (1993). Reviewers have disagreed as to whether Goldstein has been completely successful in evoking these different worlds, but all agree that, in the words of Maureen Howard in the *Yale Review* (April 1993), she is unashamed "of clarity and intelligence."

For *World Authors 1990–1995*, Rebecca Goldstein, born on February 23, 1950, writes: "I was born in White Plains, New York. . . . My family was (and is) Orthodox Jewish, and did not exactly fit into White Plains, at least as it was back then, which was fairly homogeneous. We were living in that affluent suburb because my father, who had been born in Poland, was the cantor at the Hebrew Institute of White Plains, a position that brought his family of six to live, in limited circumstances, in a place of much material comfort. This meant

that not only was I often the only Jewish kid in my class and certainly the only Orthodox kid; I was also usually the only one who wasn't in the slightest bit well-off. I got used to being different early on, knowing from the very first day of kindergarten that I couldn't eat the graham crackers that were given out at snack time and being asked by one sweetly sympathetic little girl whether I was 'lergic.

"Looking back, I've always been grateful for being compelled into nonconformity from an early age. I could either have lived in a state of permanent embarrassment over all the aspects of myself and my family that made us so unlike my friends and their families: or, alternatively, just have learned to live with not fitting in. I chose the latter and I tend to think it has helped me all along the way.

"Saturdays, which were, of course, a day of much organized activities for my school friends, was the Sabbath day for my family, and we were restricted from doing much of anything. But we weren't restricted from reading, and that is basically what I did. I wasn't allowed to bring books home from the public library, since carrying is prohibited on the Sabbath. So I would just sit there in the library until dark, Saturday after Saturday, working my way steadily through the stacks. I was very strict with myself. For every storybook I read, I required a 'serious' book, a book of science or history or, at the least, biography. I remember making this rule for myself in the first grade (and that first serious book was on atoms). Looking back now, my childhood assumption that fiction is a frivolous delight both amuses and amazes me, for it, too, determined much about my future life.

"I graduated *summa cum laude* from Barnard College, where I majored in philosophy, having taken a lot of math and science as well, and not a single literature course. Education was a very serious business for me, a privilege that, in my circumstances, I was very far from taking for granted; since reading novels was what I did for *fun*, I didn't see that it could have any part in what college had to teach me.

"And I did truly love studying philosophy, not only for the big questions that it tackled but for the discipline of its method, the elegant formality of its arguments. (This, too, was why I loved math.)

"After Barnard, I went on to get a Ph.D. from Princeton University in philosophy, concentrating on the philosophy of science, and then went back to Barnard College as a tenure-tracked assistant professor in the philosophy department. Graduate study had left me little time to indulge in my passion for novels. I remember having to forego them altogether in the period of intense concentration during which I wrote my dissertation, (which happened to be on a technical aspect of the famous 'mind-body problem'). The very day that I finished my dissertation I went out and splurged on a bunch of yummy novels—great big, sprawling nineteenth-century works (always my favorite)— and I gorged and gorged myself.

"If my days as a graduate student had left me little time for reading fiction, my life as a young professor (and young mother) left me no time at all. How then did I come not to read, but actually to *write* a novel, the summer of 1980? To me the process is still mysterious. I had been through an emotional time, unlike anything I'd ever been through before, the last two years, having not only become a mother but having also lost my father, whom I adored, to a long and terrible illness. In the course of grieving for my father and glorying in my daughter, I found that the very formal, very precise questions I had been trained to analyze weren't gripping me the way they once had. Suddenly, I was asking myself the most 'unprofessional' sorts of questions (I would have snickered at them as a graduate student), such as how does all this philosophy I've studied help me to deal with the brute contingencies of life? How does it relate to life as it's really lived? I wanted to confront such questions in my writing, and I wanted to confront them in a nonacademic mode, in a way that would intimately insert 'real life' into the intellectual struggle. In short, I wanted to write a novel, a philosophically motivated novel.

"Most mysteriously of all, a first line of a novel simply came to me early one morning, as I was dressing for work: 'I'm often asked what it is like to be married to a genius.' I immediately knew, somehow or other, that it was the first line of a novel and not a novel that I had ever read, but one whose content I was going to have to discover for myself.

"That summer, after having finished writing a 'serious' article and sending it off to an academic journal, (by then I found such writing so noncompelling that I didn't even have the patience to proofread my own piece!) I sat down and wrote a novel called *The Mind-Body Problem*, taking off from the gift of that first line and seeing where it led me.

"I've been asked how I even knew how to write a novel, and I suppose that the answer must somehow lie in all the reading I had done, in the passion I had always brought to that reading. My most overwhelming sensation during the writing was exhilaration. The most liberating aspect of all, for me, was that in fiction I was permitted to write with a distinctive, a highly personal, voice. I came to see that, for me, the impersonal voice of traditional academic philosophy (there are many exceptions), which is so much a part of its traditional claim to objectivity, was stifling and unsatisfactory. The possibilities of 'voice' in fiction has yielded me my deepest pleasures in writing. I never tire of experimenting with these possibilities, never cease to be amazed at the voices, so different from my own, that get themselves written by me.

"In any case, the novel was published, my career as a professional philosopher pretty much left smashed on the rocks of that publication, but my new career as a novelist launched.

"Since then I've published three other novels, *The Late Summer Passion of a Woman of Mind*, *The Dark Sister*, (which won a Whiting Writer's Award) and *Mazel*, which won the National Jewish Book Award for 1995 and the Edward Lewis Wallant Award for 1995). I've also published a collection of short stories, *Strange Attractors*, which also won a National Jewish Book Award."

Goldstein wrote her first novel, *The Mind-Body Problem*, when she realized that the philosophical article she was attempting to write was "reproducible," as she told Sandee Brawarsky in a *Publishers Weekly* (October 23, 1995) interview. "I wanted to write something that was distinctly mine." The novel, the story of a graduate student in philosophy who, lacking complete satisfaction in her work, marries a certified genius, was widely praised. Frances Taliaferro in *Harper's* (December 1983) observed that she knew no other "novel of the feminist era that not only anatomizes the dilemma of the intellectual woman in an anti-intellectual society, but also leads the reader into the experience of an intellectual woman's thinking." She lauded Goldstein's "pellucid clarity," which "makes sense of the history of philosophy and makes possible a number of delightfully donnish jokes."

Diane Cole in *Ms.* (January 1994), terming *The Mind-Body Problem* "a confectionery of delight," remarked that "Goldstein succeed[ed] brilliantly in smuggling into her novel short courses on everything from the history of mathematics to the trouble with Talmudic logic." She had cavils, however, about the way in which Goldstein presented her protagonist, finding her "a sad figure who remains all too familiar in real life—a woman who has the spunk to rebel against the tradition-bound mother and her genius mathematician husband, but not enough confidence to define her own character in her own terms, on her own ground."

The Late-Summer Passion of a Woman of Mind is the story of a middle-aged professor whose armor against emotion is penetrated by one of her students. In Goldstein's third novel, *The Dark Sister*, she embarked on a further exploration of the mind-body problem as exemplified by two sisters, in one of whom the distinction between art and life has begun to blur. Hedda, the novelist sister, has been "possessed," and instead of continuing her course of writing strident "JAWs" (Jewish Angry Women) novels, she has begun to write one that appropriates characters and even sentences from Henry James. The other sister, Stella, is narcissistically preoccupied with herself. Hedda, the novelist, with a tenuous grip on her own ego, writes about two sisters, reflecting not only her own and her sister's lives, but the divided self of Alice James, Henry and William's sister.

Angeline Goreau, reviewing the novel in the *New York Times Book Review* (August 11, 1991), observed that Hedda "is increasingly in danger of becoming someone else. Henry? William? No one?" Although praising the novel's advance in complexity over *The Mind-Body Problem*, in that Goldstein used "borrowings and mirrors, parallel plots and 'possession,'" Goreau found that "the characters of Hedda and Stella are not evoked strongly enough to bear the weight of the structure of symbols and references constructed around them." Goreau was more engaged by the 19th-century characters in Hedda's parallel universe.

On the other hand, Michiko Kakutani, in the *New York Times* (August 6, 1991), declared the writing in *The Dark Sister* "clever, observant and nimble." She remarked that Goldstein had demonstrated that fictional characters take on a life of their own, "eluding the control of their creator even as they lay bare the workings of the unconscious." Kakutani observed that Goldstein created "a wicked satire on feminist fiction" while also demonstrating "an uncanny ability to impersonate Henry James, and to work witty variations on the Master's characters and ideas."

A book of short stories, *Strange Attractors*, followed *The Dark Sister*. The stories have a variety of settings and protagonists, but all show that Goldstein, in Brawarsky's words, "is a master at mining intellectual dilemmas." The opening piece, "The Editor's Story," is a narration in the voice of an 88-year-old man who, years ago, read a brilliant novel with shocking sexual passages. He decided to ask the author for additions and was shocked to discover that the novel's creator was a woman—and that he was not able to handle the implications of additional erotic passages she inserted. Richard Burgin in the *New York Times Book Review* (August 8, 1993) called the story "a masterly evocation of how the sexes are socialized and a searing revelation of a guilty, ego-driven soul."

Another story in *Strange Attractors*, "From Dreams of the Dangerous Duke," is set in 19th-century England and told in "a convincingly antiquated prose style," according to Burgin. He found "intellectual rigor" in Goldstein's use of Locke's philosophy. Danielle Crittenden, writing in the *National Review* (June 21, 1993) felt the same story, however, to be a failure of an "ambitious ventriloquist" eager "to adopt trickier, more unfamiliar voices."

It was in *Strange Attractors* that Sacha, Chloe, and Phoebe (in two stories) made their first appearance. Representing three generations of Jewish women, these characters—an actress from the Yiddish stage of Poland, her daughter, a classicist, and her granddaughter, a physicist—assumed possession of Goldstein until she wrote a novel about them entitled *Mazel*. *Mazel*, the Yiddish word for luck, has a somewhat different connotation in the original language; Goldstein has called *mazel* "the imp of metaphysics." Sacha's *mazel* carries her from a shtetl, a small village in Poland, to the Warsaw Yiddish art theater to Palestine and then as a refugee to New York. In America, her daughter, Chloe, has a tenuous connection to traditional Jew-

ish culture and beliefs, which are nonetheless embraced by Sacha's granddaughter, Phoebe. At the end of the novel, as Phoebe is about to give birth, Sacha remembers Phoebe's wedding, when, despite herself, she was drawn into a wild dance—along with Chloe and Phoebe— by a stranger, a "short little lady." The stranger symbolizes *mazel*, that which draws one, willy-nilly, into the wild dance of life.

Lore Dickstein, writing in the *New York Times Book Review* (October 29, 1995), declared the "sendup of suburban Jewish life" in *Mazel* to be "hilarious." She did not give the same approbation to the parts set in earlier times, when "the novel abruptly adopts the tone and style of Yiddish fabulist folk tale. Narrated in a tedious singsong cadence and dosed with saccharine nostalgia, this section . . . wallows in the mud of quaint rural poverty and subjects the reader to didactic lessons in ritual Judaism." But Donna Seaman in *Booklist* (September 15, 1995) offered less qualified praise, calling *Mazel* a heartbreakingly tender and devilishly funny drama, an ebullient, folktale-like novel."

—S. Y.

SUGGESTED READING: *Booklist* p141 Sep. 15, 1995; *Harpers* p74 Dec. 1983; *Library Journal* p191 June 1, 1991; *Ms.* p12 Jan. 1984; *National Review* p81 June 21, 1993; *New York Times* C p16 Aug. 6, 1991; *New York Times Book Review* p29 Aug. 11, 1991, p23 Aug. 8, 1993, p54 Oct. 29, 1995; *Publishers Weekly* p48+ Oct. 23, 1995

SELECTED BOOKS: *The Mind-Body Problem*, 1983; *The Late-Summer Passion of a Woman of Mind*, 1989; *The Dark Sister*, 1993; *Strange Attractors*, 1993; *Mazel*, 1995

Gordon, Lyndall

Nov. 4, 1941– Biographer; memoirist

Born into the small Jewish community of Cape Town, South Africa, in the early 1940s, Lyndall Gordon left her homeland in the late 1960s to study literature at Columbia University and to devote herself to biographies of prominent authors. She has since published two literary biographies of T. S. Eliot, *Eliot's Early Years* (1977) and *Eliot's New Life* (1988), as well as studies on literary women, *Virginia Woolf: A Writer's Life* (1985) and *Charlotte Brontë: A Passionate Life* (1994). Her memoir of growing up Jewish in apartheid South Africa and of her ongoing interaction with several close women friends was published as *Shared Lives* (1992) and cited by the *New York Times* as one of the best books of the year. In *A Private Life of Henry James: Two Women and His Art* (1999), she examines how the artist's life and writings were dramatically in-

Jerry Bauer/Courtesy of W. W. Norton

Lyndall Gordon

fluenced by two women. She teaches literature at St. Hilda's College, Oxford University.

Lyndall Gordon was born on November 4, 1941, "in the circumscribed milieu of Jewish Cape Town," in Cape Town, South Africa, as the daughter of Harry Louis Getz, a lawyer, and Rhoda Press Getz, a teacher who wrote poems that, like Emily Dickinson's, were kept tied up in a drawer. "An old uncle of my father's, an immigrant to South Africa from Russia, had told me that the letters of my family name stood for the Hebrew words, *ger tsadick*, meaning 'good stranger,' which, he said, was the phrase for convert," she wrote in her autobiographical memoir, *Shared Lives*. In this self-reflective work, fed by diary entries and reconstructed dialogue, Gordon described herself and her peers as the "last virgins, growing up in an increasingly fantastic colonial tribe" that was "hopelessly distanced, at the bottom of Africa, from the great world, six thousand miles away, from thoughts that mattered, from cogent opinion, political and otherwise." Even as a young woman, Gordon had premonitions of the fragility and imminent demise of the unequitable regime in her homeland—the Sharpeville massacre and the early activism of Nelson Mandela occurred during the period when she was a student at the University of Cape Town. Her memoir is thus an "attempt to recover what Henry James called 'the visitable past'. . . a doomed way of life, like that of the American South." She later described how the apartheid system fostered a "ghetto mentality" among all groups: the blacks in their segregated townships, the Afrikaners on their "Great Trek" to a Promised Land, and her fellow Jews. She wrote, "The ghetto mentality of eastern Europe fitted rather well in the remoter rural areas

of southern Africa." The overriding theme of *Shared Lives*, though, is "the silence of women's lives in the outback of history, biography, and memoir," which she explores by recounting her staying in touch with four of her girlhood friends, who were "forced into exile and scattered widely" in the larger world beyond South Africa. She decided to write the book when one of the women died in her 30s, "marking the imminence of the moment when our generation will move into the past."

Gordon's early education was in the protective cocoon of the Good Hope Seminary, a girls' school that was just beginning to reel not only with the growing political ferment but with incursions of rock-'n'-roll, as in her description of friends moving to the "intoxicating rhythm" of Elvis Presley impersonations at a school dance. After leaving Good Hope, where she participated in the Habomin Jewish Youth Movement, she took her first trip abroad. "It was part of Movement education to spend a post-matric year in Israel, a lot of it on kibbutz, reading Karl Marx, A. D. Gordon, Berl Katznelson, and other theorists of labour and communal living," she wrote. But she and her friend Jasmine decided to be independent of the Movement and go directly to the Hebrew University in Jerusalem. Disillusioned with the militarism she found in Israel and with the "boorishness of Israeli men," she concluded that "in theory we were valuable additions to the State; in practice we were fodder in her famed enterprise in integration." During this period she reserved special scorn for the weepy female American tourists who carried copies of *Exodus* under their arms and got "ecstatic every time they [saw] a Jewish beggar."

In January 1960, Gordon returned to South Africa "a more subdued character" and began devoting her energies to "the competition of the marriage market and the demands of awakening passions" while continuing to anticipate "the winds of change in Africa." In 1963, the same year that she received her bachelor's degree from the University of Cape Town, she married Siamon Gordon, a professor, whom she had earlier met in the Movement. It was he who encouraged Gordon to write biography, since it would enable her to combine her love for literature and history. Meanwhile, she continued to follow with interest the romantic entanglements of the female friends that would be the premise of *Shared Lives*. "In 1965–6 it was still the norm in all societies for a woman to follow her husband and contrive to be content," she wrote, looking back with disdain at the antiseptic world that was vanishing before her eyes, the apartheid state of mind that was "peculiarly warping for white women, who were left with nothing at all to do but lie in the sun, arrange flowers, and offer each other dainty gifts at morning parties. These small rituals—which defined womanhood in those days—assumed an inordinate importance in the triviality of workless days." Later in the decade, Gordon pursued graduate studies at Columbia University, where she received her Ph.D. in English amidst student takeovers, the Vietnam War, and the discussions over a new, emergent feminism. Gordon wrote acidly and entertainingly of the misogyny she encountered at Columbia, the imperiousness of Lionel Trilling, and her shock at finding that student loans were not available for "mothers."

In her review of *Shared Lives* for the *Washington Post* (October 18, 1992), Judith Chettle wrote: "Gordon wants to 'record the end of a way of life, and, more elusive, the truncated lives of women . . . who were shaped by a warped society yet who were, all the same, portents of the future." And Nora Sayre wrote in the *New York Times Book Review* (October 4, 1992): "Ms. Gordon's narrative centers on friendship, rebellion and death; its circumference is apartheid. . . .We can be grateful that she wrote this rich, moving, and witty book; her excavations of the past in *Shared Lives* really do enlighten us about the present." The book is as much a commentary on political and cultural issues as a deeply felt memoir of her and her friends' web of connectedness. (Three of Gordon's close friends profiled in this book died prematurely, in their 30s and 40s.) In the book's epilogue, entitled "Words," Gordon speculated on the future of the "new" South Africa after the accession to power of Nelson Mandela. Declaring that black women continue to suffer most, she warned against the patriarchal attitudes of the black male ascendancy in her homeland, ending her memoir with the words, "Voices rise, words come, from the country of the past."

While at Columbia, Lyndall Gordon had become interested in the works of T. S. Eliot, particularly the development of his religious ideals. Her first biography was *Eliot's Early Years*, a study of the spiritual and psychological dimensions of the first 40 years of T. S. Eliot's life, up to his climactic 1927 conversion to Anglo-Catholicism. Some 11 years later, Gordon followed this up with *Eliot's New Life*, a study of the poet's mature years, published around the centenary of his birth. In the foreword to this latter book, she wrote: "From 1970 to 1971, I wrote an account of Eliot's earlier life based on unpublished papers (his Notebook and early poems), his letters, his mother's poems, and his wife's diaries. *Eliot's Early Years* brought out the ties between his life and work. At the time, it went against the grain of Eliot studies, which had always stressed his impersonality. The idea that Eliot's poetry was rooted in private aspects of his life has now been accepted, and this has encouraged me to attempt a sequel on the years of Eliot's maturity and great fame."

The former book was not an attempt at "official" biography; Gordon herself described it as a book that "showed the work and the life as complementary parts of one design, an insistent search for salvation," an obvious reference to the spiritual crises that permeated Eliot's identity, as expressed in such poems as "The Wasteland" and "The Love Song of J. Alfred Prufrock." While *Eliot's Early*

Years focuses on Eliot against the backdrop of the Calvinist ethos of his homeland and the Anglo-Catholic aesthetic of his adopted country, *Eliot's New Life*, its sequel, focuses on the four women who dominated Eliot's final decades: Vivienne Haigh-Wood, his first wife, and Valerie Fletcher, his second; Emily Hale, his close American friend; and Mary Trevelyan, his British companion in the 1940s and 1950s. This book concentrates on the "unhappy fact of his marriage, his private penitence, and his public mission" in its quest for an Eliot who was "tracing the conflict between a capacity for love and a more compelling sense of sin." This book considers the mature Eliot, the author of such works as "Four Quartets," "Murder in the Cathedral," and "The Cocktail Party."

Upon the book's publication, Gordon wrote an essay for the *New York Times Book Review* (August 21, 1988) in which she commented that Eliot's "own relations with women were absorbed into what seems an almost predetermined pattern of salvation. Vivienne provided the prolonged sense of sin, Emily the few but radiant moments of sublimity." But his redemptive marriage to Valerie Fletcher, Gordon claimed, rejuvenated the somber Eliot in uncharacteristic ways, causing "his face [to] split into unaccustomed smiles" for photographers upon their 1958 visit to the United States and allowing him to joke with reporters over Prufrock's lack of a love life and even exchange playful repartee with Groucho Marx, with whom he struck up a quick friendship.

This essay claims that another woman had also allowed Eliot to "unbend unexpectedly": Virginia Woolf, who in the early 1920s "had dared to laugh in his white marble face." Gordon's interest in Woolf as a vocalizer of women's suppressed passion led to the publication of her second biography, *Virginia Woolf: A Writer's Life*. Acknowledging her "dependence on Anne Olivier Bell's impeccable edition of *The Diary of Virginia Woolf* and on Quentin Bell, whose biography of his aunt must remain the authoritative account," Gordon affirms that "this life will draw more on her works and use different sources: the unfinished memoirs, the drafts of novels, and some less-known or unpublished pieces like the early 'Memoirs of a Novelist,' which lays the course of her career and her last, unfinished book, *Anon*."

Virginia Woolf: A Writer's Life distinguishes three phases of Woolf's life for study: her early family life with Julia and Leslie Stephen, up to the publication of *To the Lighthouse*; next, "the underground phase of her development when she begins to see herself as an explorer of the deep, as sunken sea- monster or gallant voyager"; finally, the most mature phase, in which she abandons respectable Kensington to search for new freedom in Bloomsbury. Gordon was unequivocal in describing her aim: "This book will rock back and forth between the life and the work," she wrote early on, "coming to rest always on the work." In conclusion, she wrote that the biography "followed the 'dark' side of Virginia Woolf, her exploratory plunges into strange pools," while appropriating its subject's fascination with the image of waves and of submergence, which ironically foreshadowed Woolf's suicide. For Woolf, wrote Gordon, "submergence" was an "image for the hidden act of imaginative daring," and thus she divided this biography into the various "waves" or stages in her subject's life, the various "turning-points that do not coincide with external events." The novelist and poet May Sarton wrote, "We can only be grateful" for *Virginia Woolf: A Writer's Life*, which she admired for its "sensitive, probing restraint as well as percipience all the way through."

The year 1994 saw the publication of Gordon's *Charlotte Brontë: A Passionate Life*, which explored the "fiery, truth- telling, articulate" side of a writer often misread because of the facade she presented as the dutiful but "invisible" Victorian woman. By drawing on unpublished letters and unfinished manuscripts, Gordon constructed a portrait of Charlotte ("the only Brontë to die with human love on her lips") as an advocate of women having a "public voice" and as an inspiration for such writers as Emily Dickinson and Virginia Woolf. The biography did not, as Michiko Kakutani observed in the *New York Times* (December 23, 1994), "aspire to add to the factual record; rather, [Gordon] chooses to use her imaginative sympathies . . . to delineate her subject's rich interior life." And *Publishers Weekly* (November 21, 1994) credited "this eloquent revisionist biography" with revealing "an ambitious writer with tart humor who raged against the constraints society placed on her sex." Gordon wrote: "Against her sisters' unresisting deaths, Charlotte shaped herself as survivor, and so, too, her survivors in fiction. All live by the Christian ideal of humility, but refuse to surrender control of their destinies to fallible figures of authority . . . Charlotte was as strenuous, in her way, as the school . . . she did not deny women their initiative; her novels showed them a difficult but stimulating pilgrimage that would be determined by clear judgment of the ideals about them."

It is not insignificant that the final chapter of *Charlotte Brontë: A Passionate Life* should be entitled "Surviving." Here, Gordon posed the question "Who owned Charlotte's memory?" in reflecting on how Brontë's various publics have defined her legacy over time. She asserted, for example, that while Brontë's husband Arthur Bell Nichols burned many of her letters, "the Brontë legend— the doomed family in Romantic solitude— grew and flourished," attracting pilgrims to Haworth, which fast became a literary shrine. Gordon also examined Brontë's influence on other women writers, such as Emily Dickinson, who read "everything the Brontës published," and Woolf, who also wrote of "society women in compliant artifice." To Gordon, a symbolic link with the strictures of gender is to be found in the 1840s ballet *Giselle*, whose Willis characters ("buried women whose passions

have been denied") vividly "demonstrate the terrible obverse of passion, which was Charlotte Brontë's long fear: the freezing effect of wilful purity, the chilling ideology of automatised lives."

Writing in the *Boston Book Review*, Edwin Frank credited Gordon with writing "an often persuasive, admirably generous account of Charlotte Brontë's life" treated as "a precursor of and continuing inspiration to modern feminism" arguably because "Charlotte's very intimacy with abasement and even degradation sharpened her imagination."

Gordon's sixth book, *A Private Life of Henry James: Two Women and His Art* (1999), focuses both on James's writings and on his relationship with the two women who greatly influenced him. The first is his cousin, Minny Temple, who was diagnosed with tuberculosis at the age of 22 and died two years later. Eventually, James would model such characters as Daisy Miller and Isabel Archer after her. The second woman was Constance Fenimore Woolson, a fellow novelist. Eventually, following a 14- year relationship that ended on bad terms, she would fall to her death from her bedroom window in Venice.

A Private Life of Henry James received varied reviews. Brooke Allen of *The New York Times Book Review (on-line)* wrote that Gordon provides "a remarkably entertaining and informative study" that is "full of fresh material and provocative assertions." The *Kirkus Review* (on-line), being more critical, remarked that "despite the focus on these two relationships, this Jamesian portrait is otherwise little different from other biographers. Although Gordon works hard to detach Minny and [Woolson] from James's shadow, she can't quite unravel his strategies to keep his private life private."

Lyndall Gordon is now on the faculty at St. Hilda's College of Oxford University.
—E.M.

SUGGESTED READING: *New York Times*, C p36, Dec. 23, 1994, with photo, C p1, Mar. 8, 1996, with photo; *New York Times Book Review*, p1, Aug. 21, 1988, p16, Oct. 4, 1992, with photo, p9, Jan. 22, 1995, on-line; *Publishers Weekly*, p60, Nov. 21, 1994; *Washington Post Book World*, p3, Oct. 18, 1992, p4, Jan. 29, 1995, with photo; *Kirkus Review* (on-line)

SELECTED BOOKS: *Eliot's Early Years*, 1977; *Virginia Woolf: A Writer's Life*, 1985; *Eliot's New Life*, 1988; *Shared Lives*, 1992; *Charlotte Brontë: A Passionate Life*, 1994; *A Private Life of Henry James: Two Women and His Art*, 1999

Gordon, Neil

1958– Novelist

Born of Jewish ancestry in South Africa, after his family had been forced to flee Lithuania because of the Nazis, the American novelist Neil Gordon has been exposed, in one way or another, to political repression during much of his life. His first novel, the critically acclaimed *Sacrifice of Isaac* (1995), is more than a political thriller, traveling the gray areas between ideological extremes and producing unexpected answers regarding the quest for universal peace and understanding. The author, who is not a Zionist, does not believe in easy or extremist solutions to difficult political problems—especially the Israeli-Palestinian conflict. Knowing from personal experience that one generation's victims can become the next generation's oppressors, his main character, Luke, sums up the message in *Isaac*: "I just don't believe that the Holocaust was ever about 'them and us,' you know? It was about us, all of us." Gordon has also dismissed Steven Spielberg's film about the Holocaust, *Schindler's List*, as having a "terrible moral simplicity." As a writer, Gordon seeks "a more profound lesson" in the Holocaust. In *Sacrifice of Isaac*, according to *Tikkun* (March/April 1996), Gordon "crafts a fascinating night journey that takes issue with zealots who would use this most heinous of horrors to justify man's ways to God. . . . *Sacrifice of Isaac* is a controversial book, an intensely felt first novel with a passion for peace and coexistence that will surely offend many on the religious and political right." Gordon's second novel, *The Gun Runner's Daughter*, was published in 1998.

Writing for *World Authors 1990-1995*, Neil Gordon discusses his family's history and his own: "I was born in South Africa in 1958. My parents were first-generation South Africans, my grandparents Lithuanians [who] had fled anti-Semitism to become, so ironically, perpetrators rather than victims of racism in Southern Africa. Those of my Lithuanian family who came to South Africa—and a few who went to Israel or America—were the only survivors of the Holocaust, save a single cousin who escaped deportation to Auschwitz and made his way to Palestine.

"My parents, active in the fight against apartheid, had previously emigrated to England, but been forced to return to South Africa for personal reasons. Our final departure to America, following the Sharpeville massacres, was in 1961, the year Nelson Mandela went to prison. I was naturalized at 11 years old, with the rest of my family. Last spring, after 33 years in America, my family went together to the United Nations polling station and, under the necessarily liberal definition of eligibility to vote in the country's first democratic election ever—so much of the country is in exile—cast five votes for the ANC with Mandela at its head.

"I grew up in Massapequa, Long Island until [I was] 11 years old, then in New York, and then in Ann Arbor, Michigan, where I went to college. After my freshman year at the University of Michigan I left college and went to Israel. During my two years there, the turn of Israeli politics—Menachem Begin's election—was deeply disturbing to me, as was my increasing familiarity with Israel increasingly stifling. With a growing feeling of political estrangement from an increasingly hawkish country, and very little attachment to it either personally or as a Jew, I decided to return to Michigan after two years.

"An unexpected effect of my time in Israel was that I had learned some French; on my return to college, having exhausted my allowable number of credits in English literature, I began studying French literature, and, after graduation in 1980, moved to Paris where I spent a year at the Sorbonne. By the end of that year I had been offered a fellowship at Yale University French department, which I accepted. I spent two years in New Haven, and returned to Paris for a year to prepare my oral examinations and perfect my French. During this year, a small cinema close to my house in an obscure corner of Paris screened, over two five-hour evenings, a new film about the Holocaust. The film was called *Shoah*, and I saw it three times.

"When I returned to New Haven to fulfill my obligation to teach, I became increasingly involved with the Yale University Holocaust Video Archive, and worked closely as a teaching assistant with a maverick and radical Israeli professor of French, Shoshana Felman, in courses in Biblical and Holocaust studies. My teaching obligations finished, feeling quite clear that I did not want to remain in academics, I moved to New York, where my college friend Esin Goknar, a painter and photo editor, lived and worked. I worked as the assistant to the editor at the *New York Review of Books* while I wrote my dissertation, 'Stranger than Fiction,' on the short stories of Hawthorne and Balzac. During the writing of the dissertation I began also to publish reviews and journalism. Esin and I were married, and I received my Ph.D. a couple days after the birth of our daughter. Days later, during my paternity leave, I began to write my first novel. *Sacrifice of Isaac* was written, over three years, nearly exclusively between the hours of 9 p.m. and 2 a.m. Shortly after the book was finished and sold, my son was born.

"Patricia Highsmith wrote about her work that she was interested 'in the effect of guilt on her characters' (a forever interesting statement, considering her main criminal characters feel no guilt). My interest is identical, save that the guilt Highsmith so brilliantly explored was that pursuant to crime, whereas what I hope to write about is the effect of political guilt: the guilt of the profiteers, the ideologues, the perpetrators who live in the world of political compromises and ideological choices. More precisely, I find myself interested in the children of the guilty: in my first book I wrote about the son of a compromised Israeli general and the daughter of a Nazi; in my second I am writing about the daughter of an arms trader, implicated in Iran Contra, and the son of a screenwriter who named names for McCarthy. Why this should be so is a mystery to me, as for my own parents, who have remained involved radicals in America as they were in South Africa, I have only the highest admiration. But as the poet Diane Wakoski says, a writer works not from a real but a 'mythologized' past, and perhaps it is not up to them too deeply to understand the sources of their stories."

Sacrifice of Isaac was published by Random House in 1995 to generally favorable reviews. It is the story of two estranged Israeli brothers—Luke and his older brother Danni—who are to meet again after many years. Their father, Yosef Benami, has recently died, and the two brothers are to inherit their father's $10 million art collection. Yosef has left his sons more than a monetary legacy. A statesman, general, author, professor, and war hero, Yosef was also the man who devised the still-secret Italian Passage, though which hundreds of Jews escaped from Vienna to Palestine in 1942. The father's death is only the latest in a string of family tragedies: their mother, Judi, a Holocaust survivor and a noted psychoanalyst, committed suicide after learning that Danni had deserted the army during the 1973 war. (Judi by this time had also left her husband for a number of reasons—Yosef was involved with another woman and Judi herself continually disagreed with her husband's assumption that God asks men to sacrifice their sons in war.)

Danni requests his half of his father's estate in cash—a second act of betrayal, in the opinion of the outraged Luke. Luke flies to Paris in search of his brother but instead meets Danni's lover, Nicole, a violinist with the Paris Opera. Nicole informs Luke that his brother has been missing for months, and soon Luke suspects that Danni has been involved with art smuggling. Luke and Nicole soon fall in love, feeling that Danni at this point may never return. Danni has a partner in Florence named Peter Chevejon—but even he has not seen Danni. The only person who has seen him in recent months is a young Austrian woman named Natalie Hoestermann, the daughter of a mid-ranking Nazi official who had collaborated with Yosef Benami on the Italian Passage. As it turns out, Danni is interested in more than just smuggling art—he wants to uncover the truth about his father's past. From this point, the book becomes a race to uncover the truth about their father, about the Italian Passage, and about duty to the Israeli state.

Some critics have argued that the only fault with this fast-paced and emotionally gripping novel is Gordon's notion of making Natalie, a minor character, the narrator, and having the story line related to her through Luke and Peter Chevejon. As William Boyd wrote in the *New York Times Book Re-*

view: "Could Natalie really know all that was going on in another character's head?" Though many reviewers leveled this criticism, the book still received a great deal of praise. Dan Cryer of *New York Newsday* (July 3, 1995) wrote: "This novel brilliantly dramatizes the tangled skein of family, religion, and nationality. . . . The geographical sweep is international, the pace breakneck, the plot engrossing, the moral perspective penetrating and wise." And *Tikkun*'s reviewer completely disagreed with the criticism of Natalie as narrator, stating: "Natalie may be peripheral to the main action but she is hardly insignificant. . . . Discounting her role is somewhat akin to bypassing Marlowe in *Heart of Darkness*, Ishmael in *Moby-Dick*, or the 'I' in Shelley's sonnet, 'Ozymandias'. . . . It is precisely the 'bystander'—the person who stands outside time or place—who is critical to the record—and the redemption—of history." Regardless of the diverging opinions on this literary technique, critics agree that *Sacrifice of Isaac* has heralded Neil Gordon's entry into the ranks of John Le Carré and Graham Greene.

In 1998 Gordon released his second novel *The Gun Runner's Daughter*. A tale of suspense with moral and psychological overtones, *The Gun Runner's Daughter* focuses on Allison Rosenthal, a 27-year-old lawyer who finds herself defending her father against an arms dealing charge, which is being prosecuted by her former lover. Donna Seaman, reviewing the novel for *Booklist* (August 19, 1998), wrote: "Gordon, the next link in the chain of Graham Greene, John Le Carré, and Joan Didion, brings a subtle but potent poetic energy and distinctive Jewish sensibility to his ingenuous and riveting drama as he explores the moral dilemmas of those who inherit a world shaped by insidious lies and extravagant violence."—C.M.

SUGGESTED READING: *Booklist* Aug. 19, 1998; *New York Newsday* B p4 July 3, 1995; *New York Times* C p16 July 20, 1995; *New York Times Book Review* p12 July 16, 1995; *Tikkun* p69+ Mar./Apr. 1995

SELECTED BOOKS: *Sacrifice of Isaac*, 1995; *The Gun Runner's Daughter*, 1998

Gornick, Vivian

June 14, 1935– Essayist; memoirist

Vivian Gornick is a dedicated feminist with a bold, no-nonsense approach to writing. She perhaps attracted the most attention for her memoir *Fierce Attachments* (1987), a look at the relationship between the independent-minded writer and her overly dramatic mother. A highly meticulous writer, Gornick did not finish her next book until almost 10 years later, but when she did, it was an in-

Sigrid Estrada

Vivian Gornick

stant success. *Approaching Eye Level* (1996) is a collection of essays about various kinds of solitude, from the chosen isolation of a writer to the involuntary loneliness of a single woman. The following year Gornick published *The End of the Novel of Love*, an examination of how the idealistic expectation of love has become an outdated device in the modern novel.

Vivian Gornick was born on June 14, 1935 in New York City to Louis and Bess Gornick, whom she has described as "peasant, immigrant" parents, and she grew up in the borough of the Bronx. She enrolled in the City College of the City University of New York and received her B.A. in 1957. For Gornick, going to college was an escape from the insular urban community of tenement houses where she was raised. "There was no choice but to go away," she told Eleanor J. Bader of *New Directions for Women* (July/August 1987). "There was nothing to stay for. Anyone with ambitions for a largeness in the world had to get out."

Nonetheless, as she told Bader, her politically active parents had instilled in the young Vivian a sense of the importance of the larger community beyond the Bronx. "There was a value in my home on the life of the mind," she told Bader. "Everything was endowed with spiritual meaning. That was my mother's gift to me."

In 1960 Gornick finished her requirements for graduate school and was awarded an M.A. from New York University. She began her professional life as an instructor of English at the State University of New York at Stonybrook from 1966 to 1967, and in 1968 took a similar position at Hunter College of the City University of New York. In 1969 she began her eight-year stint with the downtown weekly the *Village Voice* as a staff writer.

In 1972 Gornick coedited *Woman in Sexist Society: Studies in Power and Powerlessness* with Barbara K. Moran. The book, a collection of 30 essays, discusses the role of women in the modern world. It received favorable recognition in both the mainstream and academic press. Margaret Lichtenberg commented in the *Nation*, as quoted in *Contemporary Authors* (1979), that the book was a "particularly impressive addition to the writings from the women's liberation movement."

The following year, Gornick wrote *In Search of Ali Mahmoud: An American Woman in Egypt*, which documents her attempt to learn more about Arab culture. She had flown to Egypt and stayed with a friend's family. Their hospitality prompted Gornick to investigate their system of values, which prizes close relationships over material possessions. As she recalled, "Tenderness is what you feel in the streets, in the offices, in the conversations."

The book received fairly positive reviews, many of which focused on Gornick's detailed portrayal of the sexism firmly entrenched in Egyptian society. In an article for *Ms.* cited by *Contemporary Authors*, Sara Blackburn commented that "the narrative of [Gornick's] journey is . . . a diary of her relationships with Egyptian men [whom she] manages to portray . . . with a dimension, power, and an understanding that I missed in her depiction of the book's women, who are far more fleeting and remote within the society and to her." Blackburn was also put off by the book's length: "I ended up feeling that I'd been exposed to too much of a good thing, surfeited instead of wanting."

In 1978 Gornick wrote *The Romance of American Communism*, which combines memoir with cultural exploration to give the stories behind the faces of the Communist movement in America. Gornick used interviews with former and present members of the Communist party, along with her own insight as a child of 1950s socialism, to provide a new, inside look at Communist party life. Reviews of the book were largely favorable. A *Choice* (June 1978) critic wrote that, although the book does not contain detailed information on Communist policies, ideologies, and the like, "there is no better place than [this work] to find out what actual day-to-day party life was like, why people joined, why they left, and how Communism touched them spiritually." In *Harper's* (March 1978), Michael Malone lauded Gornick for "contribut[ing] understanding and charity to a part of our citizenry that has been persistently denied both," but did find a flaw in Gornick's writing style, which he called "intense, emotional and occasionally so highly pitched that what should be moving veers into the maudlin." Michael Harrington, writing in the *New York Times Book Review*, agreed, calling the writer's tone "a bit too breathless." Harrington took pains, however, to assert that despite this minor blemish, the book "describes a moral and human complexity that shatters some of our cherished national stereotypes and is therefore extremely valuable."

Gornick's next book, *Essays in Feminism* (1979), was a collection of work written mostly during her *Village Voice* days. The essays look at various issues within the women's movement from the 1960s through the late 1970s, and chronicle feminism's evolution. Esther Stineman of *Library Journal* (December 1, 1978) called the essays "consistently interesting and well written," and F. D. Gray of the *New York Times* called the book "disastrously unhoned" but "potentially elegant" and wrote that "there is much courage, humanity and intelligence in Miss Gornick's brand of feminism." Ellen Posnick of the *New Republic* complained that certain issues, such as birth control and child rearing, were not mentioned in any of the articles, but concluded that "Vivian Gornick seems to have served, really, as a cultural critic, and as such she provides an interesting and useful record of contemporary thought. She writes intelligent prose, full of human awareness and political conscience."

In 1984 Gornick published *Women in Science: Portraits from a World in Transition*. It consists of more than 100 interviews in which women who work in various scientific fields told Gornick about their careers and their lives in relation to those of their male counterparts. "[Gornick's] women all begin to sound alike," the reviewer for *Choice* (February 1984) complained, "with those having 'wrong' views shunted aside as 'old-fashioned.' The results seem highly biased and the portrait does not seem accurate to this reviewer. The subject of women in science is very important; Gornick's contribution is not." Anna Fels of the *Nation* criticized Gornick for her subjectivity, her choice in women participants, and an underlying simplistic equation of art and science. "Gornick's *Lust for Life* vision of scientists (and artists) moving from epiphany to thrilling epiphany rings false," Fels wrote. She also took issue with Gornick's subliminal stereotyping of "the woman who has it all," adding that "one wishes Gornick would permit her women those unconventional, lopsided lives that men have always enjoyed with impunity." The reviewer for the *New York Times Book Review*, however, admitted that the subjects represent a "small thoughtful majority," and added that the book "opens the discussion about women's diverse problems and ambitions in science."

Gornick did not write another book for three years; when she completed *Fierce Attachments: A Memoir* in 1987, she called it her "first book." *Fierce Attachments* compelled critics to take notice of the universal themes contained in the highly personal book—those of mother–daughter relationships and the lives of immigrants in postwar New York.

In the *New York Times Book Review* (April 26, 1987), Mona Simpson called *Fierce Attachments* a "fine, unflinchingly honest book," and added that Gornick "writes directly and cleverly about the fate of women in her generation." Wendy Gimbel wrote in the *Nation* (April 25, 1987), "Re-creating her mother sitting in a Bronx kitchen, she is a distinctive and startling artist—the true subject of this brilliant book," Gimbel noted.

Other reviews were equally enthusiastic. Annette Kolodny wrote for the *Women's Review of Books* (June 1987) that *Fierce Attachments* "reads with the seamlessness of a novel." Gornick, she wrote, was "unsparing in her portraits of others, . . . [but] no less so in rendering up herself." In all, Kolodny found the book to be "a work of deeply honest self-examination, powerfully written and impossible to put down."

Ruth Pavey of the *New Statesman & Society* (July 22, 1988) wrote that while the subject matter—the relationship between an overbearing Jewish mother and contentious daughter—was hardly virgin territory, "this account is very fresh" written with "a painterly feeling for light." Pavey concluded that the book is "gutsy" in its intentions. Enid Dame of *Belles Lettres* (January/February 1988) took exception to the positioning of work and intellect in opposition to the ideals of love and emotion, a conflict that Gornick seemed to dwell on throughout the memoir. Dame wrote, "Personally . . . I found this love versus work dichotomy a bit too schematic." However, the reviewer admitted that "one reads this book not to agree with specific insights but to experience the mother-daughter bond as the author has lived it, in all its furious complications," and added that the book is a "brilliant memoir."

Almost 10 years passed before Gornick published another book, this time a collection, titled *Approaching Eye Level* (1996), of seven essays on the topic of the loneliness and isolation she has felt as a single female writer living in New York City. In exploring the process of growing self-awareness, she discusses a variety of personal experiences, including an early waitressing job (which taught her lessons about the caste system and humiliation), her disappointing marriage, and her disillusionment with regard to the academic arena. Kate Tuttle, a contributing editor at the *Boston Book Review* (on-line) described the essays as "linked not only by taut, precise language but also by the absolute honesty that, perhaps, only comes with experience." In addition, Tuttle wrote, "As expansive in conception as they are terse in language, Gornick's forays into difficult subjects alternately anger, charm, and provoke. But they always engage." *Kirkus Reviews* (July 15, 1996) agreed, and called Gornick "courageous in these pieces, both in what she will say and in what she is willing to see."

Practically all reviews of *Approaching Eye Level* were highly favorable, and many focused on Gornick's honesty and on-the-mark observations on the nature of loneliness. *Booklist* (September 15, 1996) praised Gornick for writing "compellingly about her loneliness, making it another character in her life, as real as any of the people she encounters. . . . her intensity shines a bright light on the reader's own dance with the joys of being alone and the fear of loneliness. A book that lulls, then pounces." Similarly, the *Women's Review of Books*

(October 1996) described the essays as "admirable for their clarity, their honesty and their directness as they plunge headlong down for a good view of the entrails of ordinary life." *Library Journal* (September 1, 1996) called the book "gripping" and concluded that "Gornick's clear writing and honest expression of her own need for personal connections, independence, and meaningful work make the reader feel like a participant observer in all her experiences and personal encounters." The *Nation* (October 21, 1996) echoed these sentiments with the concluding analogy that Gornick, "Like a blues singer who leaves her audience peculiarly uplifted. . . . delivers the gritty truth about human longing in rich metaphor and vivid detail."

Mary Hawthorne of the *New York Times Book Review* (October 12, 1996), however, while admitting the resonance of Gornick's meditations on living alone, criticized the essay on the author's brief foray into the academic life for its "haughty New York provincialism" and "defensive self-righteousness."

The following year Gornick produced another book, *The End of the Novel of Love* (1997), a collection of essays on the themes of love and marriage in 20th-century literature. In particular, Gornick explored the role that the "idea of love" now plays in our lives, asserting that this notion "as a means of illumination—in literature as in life—now comes as something of an anticlimax." In her essays, Gornick reviewed classics of literature and well-known feminist novels alike, and asked whether the days of believing that love can transform an individual are over. For today's novel, Gornick concluded, "I think, love as a metaphor is an act of nostalgia, not of discovery."

Response to *The End of the Novel of Love* was much more divided than reactions to her previous work. *Kirkus Reviews* (August 1, 1997) noted that Gornick wrote in a "pithy, intensely concentrated literary style that is individual, uncannily precise, and a pleasure to read." The reviewer later added that Gornick can "cut to the bone of our common experience with just a few, well-chosen words. What makes her work unusual for a book of this sort is that she persuades by the power of her language—gracefully poised between objective knowledge and subjective experience—more than by discursive argument." In conclusion, *Kirkus* called the book "an exceptionally well-written, original, and thought-provoking set of essays."

Amy Boaz, writing for *Library Journal* (September 1, 1997), agreed for the most part, commenting that "Gornick's critical incisions are swift and certain, and in this latest collection she performs her literary surgery on writers who pursued in their work or represented personally a fatal flaw of self-knowledge." Boaz conceded that Gornick's "hyperbolic pronouncements lose their umph after a while" but quickly added that the author's writing is "so clean and precise that the reader gasps for more. Highly recommended."

In her review for the on-line magazine *Salon* (October 27, 1997), Laura Miller was less impressed with the book, commenting that "this collection of essays doesn't really develop Gornick's argument. It's more as if, having assembled these essays, Gornick and her editors recognized a recurring note, and dubbed the book accordingly. In an omission that seems too glaring to be missed by its perceptive author, *The End of the Novel of Love* never ventures to ask whether other kinds of love—generative, familial, social or even spiritual—might not suit where romance has failed." By contrast, Elizabeth Frank of the *New York Times* (October 19, 1997) felt that Gornick's essays displayed an author grounded in "the moral breadth, psychological acuity, esthetic sophistication and infinite sense of life we expect from good novels and good readers alike" and commended Gornick's ability to "fault literature when it fails."

Vivian Gornick continues to live in New York City, where she works as a freelance writer.—D.B.

SUGGESTED READING: *Amazon.com* Oct. 29, 1998; *Belles Lettres* p9 Jan./Feb. 1988; *Booklist* Sep. 15, 1996; *Boston Book Review* Oct. 26, 1998; *Choice* June 1978, Feb. 1984; *Harper's* Mar. 1978; *Library Journal* Dec. 1, 1978, p177 Sep. 1, 1996, p182 Sep. 1, 1997; *Kirkus Reviews* July 15, 1996, Aug. 1, 1997; *Los Angeles Times* Jan. 8, 1998; *Nation* Apr. 25, 1987, p92 July 15–22, 1991, p29+ Oct. 21, 1996; *New Directions for Women* p13 July/Aug. 1987; *New Stateman & Society* p44 July 22, 1988; *New York Newsday* p14 Apr. 19, 1987; *New York Times* p18 Mar. 14, 1991, p12 Oct. 12, 1996, p32 Oct. 19, 1997; *New York Times Book Review* Apr. 26, 1987; *Publishers Weekly* p64 July 8, 1996, p66 Sep. 8, 1997; *Salon* Oct 27, 1997; *Women's Review of Books* p4+ June 1987, Oct. 1996; *Book Review Digest* 1978, 1979, 1984, 1987, 1997; *Contemporary Authors*, 1979

SELECTED WORKS: *Woman in Sexist Society: Studies in Power and Powerlessness* (editor), 1972; *In Search of Ali Mahmoud: An American Woman in Egypt*, 1973; *The Romance of American Communism*, 1978; *Essays in Feminism*, 1979; *Women in Science: Portraits From a World in Transition*, 1984; *Fierce Attachments: A Memoir*, 1987; *Approaching Eye Level*, 1996; *The End of the Novel of Love*, 1997

Miriam Berkley

Gowdy, Barbara

June 25, 1950– Novelist

The world of the Canadian writer Barbara Gowdy is, in the words of a reviewer for *Maclean's* (November 9, 1992), "a strangely lit place where the human body and human desire often take on unusual forms: one of her characters has two heads, while another enjoys making love to corpses." Since coming to prominence in the late 1980s, Gowdy has published four novels (*Through the Green Valley*, 1988; *Falling Angels*, 1990; *Mister Sandman*, 1995; and *The White Bone*, 1999) and a collection of short stories (*We So Seldom Look on Love*, 1992). While her characters often inhabit an unconventional netherworld that borders on the grotesque, Gowdy is decidedly not a scribe of the macabre or the supernatural. If there is horror in her work, it derives from the disturbed but ultimately commonplace lives that she describes in her narratives. But, as Christopher Lehmann-Haupt observed in the *New York Times* (July 9, 1990), in his review of *Falling Angels* "Despite the extreme oddness of such scenes and characters, Ms. Gowdy manages to convey in her terms the familiar paradoxes of family love."

In a statement for *World Authors 1990–1995*, Barbara Gowdy writes: "I have a brother two years older than I am, a sister one year older and a sister seven years younger. When I was born, on June 25, 1950, my family lived in Windsor, Ontario and my father sold insurance, work he hated. In 1954 he was offered a job at a design company in Toronto and we moved to the suburbs of Don Mills, which was Canada's and maybe even North America's first planned community: an arrangement of pret-

ty—and pretty similar—bungalows on streets with names like Moccasin Trail and Deep Woods Crescent. In the summer we kids went to a day camp called Mildalaca, where we sang what we thought were authentic Indian songs ('Indians are high-minded/Bless my soul, they're double-jointed/They climb hills and don't mind it/All day long'). All day long, as I remember Mildalaca, we sweltered beside a river too polluted to swim in let alone drink from and sang our songs and had our 'pow-wows' and traded 'wampum' (sandwiches). Innocent little racists, we were, dying of thirst.

"In 1963 we moved to another new frontier suburb called Bridlewood. By now I was in high school. I was thin, small and looked about eight at a time when Marilyn Monroe was the ideal woman. In my novel *Falling Angels* there is a character named Lou Field who is thin, angry, ambitious and wears padded bras. I've always denied it, but I'll say here that she and the 13 year-old I was bear a passing resemblance.

"Upon graduation, applauded by all the grown women I knew, I made the dainty leap from 'A' student to a secretary. I lasted a year, and what disheartened me wasn't so much the typing as the making coffee and running errands for the boss's wife. My savings I blew on tuition to York University, where I majored in film and theater arts. I say 'blew' because, like my father selling insurance, I hated it. I hated the laid-back sixties climate, the holding hands and singing 'Should the Circle Be Unbroken?' in Humanities class, and at the end of the first year I dropped out to become a stockbroker. The plan was to make money during the day and live the high life at night. A bad plan, as it turned out (I didn't attract a single client) and so in the summer of 1972 I quit to marry my high-school sweetheart and become a concert pianist. Another bad plan. After three years the marriage fell apart because I spent all my time practicing, and the concert pianist dream fell apart because I wasn't talented enough.

"Back to the office, a publishing house this time, and a job I liked. Editor. Operating on whim (that's what I thought editors did) I peppered memoirs with characters of my own devising, I banned semi-colons and words I despised: mellifluous, serendipity. Somehow I lasted five years, and during those years I remarried and began to write fiction. My first novel was an historical [novel set in Ireland]. It came out in 1988 under the dreadful title: *Through the Green Valley*, which was chosen by my British editor to suggest, I suspect, a cross between *How Green Was My Valley* and *Through a Glass Darkly*.

"In my second novel, *Falling Angels*, I abandoned the past and the pretty prose and wrote about a place and time I knew. But not about people I knew. The temperamental and physical resemblance between me and Lou Field is, as I said, a passing one, and the other characters are pure invention. I consider myself to be a 'leap of imagination' writer, and in *Falling Angels* I was imagining not just a nuclear family but a nuclear-shelter family. What would happen, I wondered, if a father decided to put the backyard bomb shelter to the test, if he and his wife and kids hunkered underground for the two weeks that the government defense pamphlets of the time said were sufficient following a nuclear strike? In answering that question I came up with a short story called 'Disneyland' and it became the pivotal chapter around which the rest of *Falling Angels* grew.

"In 1989, shortly after *Falling Angels* was published, my second marriage ended. Once more in the city (having returned from the farm outside of Toronto where my husband and I had been living) I wrote the stories that became the collection *We So Seldom Look on Love.* The question that sparked every one of those stories as well as my 1995 novel *Mister Sandman* was 'What if?' What if I was a necrophile? What if I was physically deformed? What if I was a transsexual? What if I was a dimwit? I wanted to imagine the unimaginable lives of decent 'abnormal' people whom 'normal' people flinch from and in so doing investigate the pernicious idea of normalcy.

"Two years ago I asked myself: what if I was an elephant? I was reading about how members of the scientific community had finally come around to acknowledging that animals are conscious, emotional creatures who feel pain. Who have stories, it occurred to me . . . who no doubt *tell* stories if, like the elephant, they are endowed with a huge brain, a phenomenal memory and a language system that appears to use not just words but syntax. As I write this, I have just finished the first draft of a novel called *The White Bone,* in which the central characters are African elephants. Also, I'm moving house for something like the 20th time in 25 years."

With the publication, in 1990, of her second novel, *Falling Angels,* Barbara Gowdy began to establish herself as a writer who is consumed with exploring the uncomfortable and unfamiliar territory on the margins of domestic life and telling stories of distressed people who are doomed to be outsiders because of their anatomy or their attitude. No topics and types have been too unsavory for her unromantic pen: she writes with equanimity of necrophiliacs, of the obese and the obtuse and the freakish, of sexual dysfunctionaries and of the emotionally challenged—all of them needy souls striving to communicate in a world that has lost its ability or its grace to deal with them. A version of its fourth chapter was included in *The Best American Short Stories 1989* as "Disneyland," the narrative of a family forced to spend several weeks in an underground fallout shelter by a man who insists on imposing a spartan regime on his wife and three daughters as an ordeal to be endured before a Christmas trip to Disneyland. Using this metaphor of a "nuclear family" in confinement, Gowdy explores what Christopher Lehmann-Haupt, in the

New York Times (July 9, 1990) described as a "malign and grotesque world" whose hell is relieved only by "the author's zany sense of humor." Gowdy paints her "nuclear victims" with compassion and respect, prompting Lehmann-Haupt to conclude that "the novel is as much about transcendence as it is about falling." Gowdy chronicles in respectful narrative the odd machinations of a family striving to communicate with and support each other in the face of a dystopian saga that had begun years earlier when the family's newborn dropped from its mother's arms, perhaps intentionally, into Niagara Falls. The saga ends with the survivors—father and daughters—gathering at the falls to scatter the mother's ashes at the scene of their earlier trauma, a soaring seagull convinces them of a sublimity that transcends their tragedy. *Falling Angels* became a best-seller in Germany, where film director Michael Verhoeven has expressed interest in adapting it for the screen.

In 1992, Gowdy published a collection of eight short stories, *We So Seldom Look on Love,* a title inspired by a line from Frank O'Hara's "Ode to Necrophilia," quoted in the front matter of the Gowdy book: "Well, / it is better / that / O M E O N / S love them E / and we / so seldom look on love / that it seems heinous." The title story is a haunting tale about a young woman and her obsessive love of dead bodies, both animal and human. Though its subject matter might be discomforting to some, this is not a gory tale from the far side; instead, it reads as a sensitive demystification of an often-taboo subject told from the perspective of a woman viscerally obsessed with death and its manifestations. The opening paragraph is evocative of the story's high-mindedness: "When you die, and your earthly self begins turning into your disintegrated self, you radiate an intense current of energy. There is always energy given off when a thing turns into its opposite, when love, for instance, turns into hate. There are always sparks at those extreme points. But life turning into death is the most extreme of extreme points. So just after you die, the sparks are really stupendous. Really magical and explosive."

The unnamed narrator of this story describes herself as having grown up in a "nice, normal, happy family outside a small town in New Jersey." Her early fascination with death begins in this pedestrian setting when, as a child, she conducted elaborate funeral rituals for the bodies of household pets and rodents found in nearby woodlands. As she matures, these activities become imbued with her growing sexual awareness, and she graduates to driving a hearse for a local undertaker, then to engaging in sexual play with Matt, a medical student who shares her interest in autopsies. She is finally drawn to intimacies with the corpses themselves—including that of Matt, after she has assisted him in his suicide-by-hanging. "I really had no idea that I was jumping across a vast behavioral gulf . . . ," she confesses. "Carol said I should have been put away, but I'm not bad-looking, so if offering my body to dead men is a crime, I'd like to know who the victim is." Continuing in a vein of self-affirmation, she adds, "I had discovered myself to be irredeemably abnormal . . . obsession began to storm through me, as if I were a tunnel. I became the medium of obsession as well as both ends of it." She concludes, "I am still a necrophile, occasionally and recklessly. I have found no replacement for the torrid serenity of a cadaver." *Kissed* (1997), a film based on this story, was directed by Lynne Stopkewich, who wrote the screenplay with Angus Fraser. It starred Molly Parker as the narrator, here named Sandra Larson, and Peter Outerbridge as Matt.

Other stories in *We So Seldom Look on Love* include "Body and Soul," about a nine-year-old girl who, born blind and disfigured, was abandoned after birth by her mother, an "eighteen-year-old migrant corn detassler who left the abortion too late"; "Sylvie," about the struggles of a young girl who carries on her torso the atrophied body of her dead Siamese twin; and "The Two-Headed Man," in which a study of a man with a skewed self-image is intertwined with the Christian myth of fall and redemption. This story is of a first-person narration by a malformed man struggling under the burden of two identities: that of Samuel (the name is that of an Old Testament prophet), and that of Simon (who, in the New Testament, helped Christ bear the cross on the way to Calvary). Another character mentioned in the story as one of Samuel/Simon's fantasies, involves the actress Jill St. John, whose family name is also associated with the Passion narrative. But Gowdy paints the religious imagery with a light brush, and it is clear that the author's vision remains primarily that of an artist and humanist. In these and the other stories in the collection, Gowdy makes it clear that her intent is to probe the spiritual dimensions of her characters without resorting to cant or preachiness.

We So Seldom Look on Love was favorably received by readers and reviewers, who agreed that Gowdy was emerging as a leading figure in a new generation of Canada's fiction writers. In a review published in the Canadian periodical *Saturday Night* (September 1992), Gowdy's work was compared with that of other important short-story writers: "In examining these characters—they eat, drink, screw, sin, die, and fall in love just like so-called normal people—Gowdy probes a seminal human condition: How can we feel good about ourselves when the container we are given is so obviously flawed? Instead of treating small, inconsequential events as though they resonate with comic significance—á la Raymond Carver or Alice Munro—Gowdy scrutinizes extraordinary situations until they seem commonplace, until her freaks reenter the terrain of normality. Consequently, *We So Seldom Look on Love* is not just a book about freaks, it is a book about coping mechanisms, about the process of learning to live with oneself." The review judged the book to be "wonderful and unsettling."

In her third novel, *Mister Sandman* (1995), Gowdy continued her sensitive examination of people caught on the edge of unconventional behaviors. Recounting the saga of the Canarys, a family of notorious dissemblers, she again invites the reader to enter a dystopian world of dysfunction in stark contrast to a nostalgic image of the 1950s as a period of innocence and candor. *Mister Sandman* is the story of Gordon Canary, a closeted homosexual ashamed of his "sexual disorder," and his wife Doris, who indulges her own bisexuality in an affair with a Vancouver nurse. There are three children in the household: their daughters Sonja and Marcy, and Joan, Sonja's daughter by a rapist. All three girls exhibit emotional infirmity: Sonja is obese and unmotivated, Marcia is sexually promiscuous, and Joan is autistic. Joan serves as a kind of *tabula rasa*, a mute confessor to which the other family members repair for absolution and the familiar Gowdy transcendence—"pouring their secrets into her gorgeous silence," in the words of novelist Katherine Dunn in her *Washington Post* (March 30, 1997) review. To this strange and searing admixture, Gowdy brings much of the same sensitivity and affirmation that has marked her earlier work. Reviewing *Mister Sandman* for *Maclean's* (November 6, 1995), John Bemrose wrote: "This is a long way from *Father Knows Best*. Indeed, taken together, the Canarys sound like a recipe for the final, catastrophic detonation of the nuclear family. But oddly, nothing of the kind happens. Although burdened by problems, the Canarys live in an atmosphere remarkably free of recrimination and judgment. Their astonishing (and moving) tolerance of each other is really a form of love. It creates a kind of visionary calm at the center of the novel, an abiding sense that all, ultimately, is well—even though, at the time, all hell may be breaking loose. . . . *Mister Sandman* is one of those rare novels that gives sex its true, prominent place in life, without either sensationalism or romantic (or anti-romantic) posing." Katherine Dunn (the author of *Geek Love*) wrote that "*Mister Sandman* . . . cocks a snoot at conventions, both moral and literary, and is so brilliantly crafted and flat-out fun to read that Gowdy makes jubilant sinners of us all. . . . Her luminous, deceptively conversational style shuffles time frames and points of view so smoothly that her intricate narrative flows in molten simplicity. The deliberately mundane takes on magical qualities." *Mister Sandman* was nominated for the Giller Prize and a Governor General's literary award in Canada.

Gowdy's *The White Bone* was published in 1999. That novel, which featured elephants as protagonists, was the subject of something of a controversy that played itself out on the pages of the *New York Times Book Review*. Sarah Boxer, in her review of the novel for the May 16 issue, complained about the difficulty of deciphering the elephants' language. In a letter to the publication printed on June 13, the novelist John Irving praised the novel while taking Boxer to task. He quoted from the let-

ter he had sent to Gowdy's publisher upon reading the novel: "I didn't want to let it pass how much I admired *The White Bone*. Nor was I predisposed to like it. On the contrary, a book about elephants? And the glossary irked me on principle (until I read it). I suspect a lot of readers—no, I mean reviewers—may be 'irked on principle,' but they'll be wrong. These elephants are more distinct and moving as characters than most characters in novels who are humans. . . . Barbara Gowdy's original, ambitious novel deserved a more rigorous reading than Boxer gave it."
—E. M.

SUGGESTED READING: *Belles Lettres: A Review of Books by Women* p4+ Spring 1994, with photo; *Chatelaine* p107+ Oct. 1994, with photos,

p12 Dec. 1995, with photo; *Library Journal* p116 Mar. 1, 1990; *Maclean's* p119+ Nov. 9, 1992, with photo, p81+ Nov. 6, 1995; *New Statesman & Society* p40 Aug. 6, 1993; *New York Times* C p18 Apr. 18, 1997; *New York Times Book Review* p14 May 27, 1990, p28 Aug. 11, 1991, p20 May 11, 1997; *Publishers Weekly* p59 June 17, 1988, p45 Feb. 9, 1990, p61 June 14, 1993; *Saturday Night* p14+ Sep. 1992, with photo; *Times Literary Supplement* p12 Dec. 1, 1995, p23 June 21, 1996; *Village Voice* p74 Aug. 14, 1990; *Washington Post Book World* X p3 Mar. 30, 1997

SELECTED BOOKS: *Through the Green Valley*, 1988; *Falling Angels*, 1990; *We So Seldom Look on Love*, 1992; *Mister Sandman*, 1995; *The White Bone*, 1999

Janet Heintz

Greene, Bob

Mar. 10, 1947– Journalist

"Water covers two-thirds of the earth," a writer for *Playboy* once observed, "and Bob Greene covers the rest." With his column in the *Chicago Tribune*, which is syndicated to more than 200 newspapers nationwide, Greene has earned a reputation for exploring the human side of a dizzying array of subjects, from presidential politics to homelessness to the indecipherable and often-debated lyrics of the rock-'n'-roll classic "Louie Louie." His numerous books include several collections of his columns as well as such full-length works as *Good Morning, Merry Sunshine* (1984), a best-selling account of

the first year in the life of his daughter; *Hang Time: Days and Dreams with Michael Jordan* (1992), a chronicle of two years spent off-court with the legendary athlete; and *Rebound: The Odyssey of Michael Jordan* (1995). Recently Greene has also completed his first novel, *All Summer Long* (1993); a nonfiction book about his generation entitled *The 50 Year Dash: The Feelings, Foibles, and Fears of Being Half-A-Century Old* (1997); and *Chevrolet Summers, Dairy Queen Nights* (1997), a collection of stories about "average" Americans. "One thing that sets Greene apart from other well-known syndicated columnists," Daniel B. Wood wrote in the *Christian Science Monitor* (December 17, 1985), "is that his topics cut a swath across politics, sports, family life, education, and pop culture. In doing so they explore that gap behind the headlines and in front of the statistics and demographic shifts where the true humaneness, irony, and humor of America reside."

Robert Bernard Greene Jr. was born on March 10, 1947 in Columbus, Ohio, the son of Robert Bernard Greene Sr., a business executive, and Phyllis Ann (Harmon) Greene. He has recalled having a happy childhood in which, early on, he demonstrated an interest in newspapers and other news media. At the age of 12, he worked as a "staff boy" on local radio broadcasts of basketball games—an experience he has called one of his most treasured memories—and beginning in the seventh grade, Bob wrote for the Bexley Junior High School *Beacon*. As he recounted in an interview with Jean W. Ross for *Contemporary Authors* (1988), he and a friend managed to get an interview with a star basketball player for Ohio State University whom professional journalists had been unable to reach. "Here two 12-year-old kids had a national exclusive," Greene told Ross. When he was 16, he landed a job as a copy boy at a daily paper in Columbus. He received local attention during his senior year of high school when his essay on the first anniversary of the assassination of President John F. Kennedy appeared in a magazine for teenagers and then in the Columbus *Citizen-Journal.*

In 1965 Greene entered Northwestern University, in Evanston, Illinois, as a journalism major. During college he was an editor of the *Daily Northwestern*, the campus paper, and worked part-time as a stringer for the *Chicago Tribune.* That experience led to his being hired, immediately after he received his bachelor's degree, in 1969, by the *Chicago Sun-Times*, the city's morning tabloid. Assigned to the usual stories on a cub reporter's beat, Greene covered sports, city news, and politics. His editors soon noticed the distinctive style that he brought to even the most mundane news stories and also became aware of the attention that readers accorded Greene's byline. After two years, an unusually short apprenticeship by newspaper standards, the *Sun-Times* gave Greene his own column. "I didn't feel I was so young; it just seemed to me I was doing what I ought to be doing," Greene told Peter Benjaminson in an interview for *Contemporary Authors* (1981). "I always wanted to be, and I basically consider myself to be, a storyteller. I always wanted to tell stories, whatever format they were in. So it was natural that when I was working for newspapers I should be writing a column." He also began contributing pieces to various magazines, including *Harper's* and *Rolling Stone.*

Greene's first book, *We Didn't Have None of Them Fat Funky Angels on the Wall of Heartbreak Hotel, and Other Reports from America* (1971), contained 15 of his daily columns, as well as articles for the *Sun-Times* Sunday magazine, *Midwest.* The title piece was a sketch of the rock-'n'-roll legend Elvis Presley on the occasion of his first personal appearance in Las Vegas in 13 years. The book also included accounts of the 1969 inauguration of President Richard Nixon, a revealing interview with the comedian Jack E. Leonard, and "I Don't Know How You'd Make a Horse Back Up," a deft portrait of the newscaster David Brinkley.

In 1972, acting on an idea that came to him while he was interviewing the rock star Rod Stewart, Greene signed on with the press corps covering that year's presidential campaign. "Stewart and I were talking about the world of a touring band," Greene has recalled. "I had always wanted to do a long, extended tour; not just five or six days, but a whole exhausting, killing thing to see what it does to a person, what it's like to live on a constant edge of fatigue for months on end while the country flashes past you, and you see more crowds, more adulation every day." Although he decided to trail politicians rather than musicians, Greene was less concerned with the candidates' political positions than with covering the campaign as "a massive unique road show."

Written in journal form, *Running: A Nixon–McGovern Campaign Journal* (1973) chronicled Greene's travels with the entourage of press and politicos that followed George McGovern as he made his doomed 1972 run for the presidency against the incumbent, Richard Nixon. Greene captured the disorder of McGovern's campaign, the posturing of Vice-President Spiro T. Agnew, and the atmosphere of the Nixon White House. *Running* won acclaim from such veteran journalists as Joe McGinnis, Pete Hamill, and David Broder, and high marks from critics. "The detail is rich and the observations sharp, albeit without more than casual political insights," L. C. Lewin wrote in the *New York Times Book Review* (May 20, 1973). "As you follow even the most superficial moves of the players, you will not fail to get a solid sense, from their behavior and style in playing out the game, of their real political sensibilities and why they do what they do."

For his next book, *Billion Dollar Baby* (1975), Greene abandoned the stance of outside observer for that of participant when he took a leave of absence from the *Sun-Times*, in 1973, to accompany the enormously popular and self-consciously outrageous Alice Cooper Band on the road. He told Peter Benjaminson, "It seemed to me that the American Dream for kids growing up in the 1940s and 1950s was to become a baseball star, to be Joe DiMaggio or Mickey Mantle. By the 1970s, the dream had turned into the rock'n'-roll dream, and the greatest fantasy a young male could have was to be a rock-'n'-roll star. . . . I'd been on rock tours before as a reporter, but I always thought it would be fascinating to step across the footlights and see what it would be like on the other side." He performed as a back-up singer on one of the group's albums and also appeared on stage, playing the part of Santa Claus and receiving a mock beating from the band at the end of each performance.

In *Billion Dollar Baby*, Greene recounted his experiences as a performer, but showed the negative side of the "dream" as well—the boredom of the superstar's lifestyle, made evident as Alice Cooper (the stage name of lead singer Vincent Furnier) and company passed their days watching television in hotel rooms. "I've never seen so many desperately unhappy young millionaires," Greene said later. "The book was a story about the American Dream and what happens when you achieve it." *Billion Dollar Baby* received extensive praise in the press; Maureen Orth commended Greene in *Newsweek* (January 13, 1975) for "stripping away the glamour surrounding the big-name rock band and exposing it for what it is—a carefully promoted . . . group of young millionaires of questionable talent whom he genuinely likes."

The title of the 400-page collection of some of Greene's most memorable pieces, *Johnny Deadline, Reporter* (1976), was the nickname given to him by his coworkers at the *Sun-Times.* In 1978 Greene left that newspaper for the *Chicago Tribune*, which he felt had become one of the country's best dailies. At the *Tribune* he began his current practice of writing four weekday columns, dropping his Sunday piece in the belief that his readers incorporated his column into their workaday routines. In addition, in 1980 Greene began writing a monthly feature, "American Beat," for *Es-*

quire, and he broke into television as a correspondent for ABC's *Nightline* in 1981, covering as wide a variety of stories on the air as he did in print.

Another compilation of Greene's columns, *American Beat*, appeared in 1983. A particularly intriguing—and to some, disconcerting—piece in the collection was Greene's interview with the convicted mass murderer Richard Speck. Although Speck usually shunned the press, he agreed to meet with Greene because, he told the columnist, "I read your column, man." In "Reflections in a Wary Eye," Greene recounted his interview with Richard Nixon after the latter had resigned the presidency. For the purpose of encouraging would-be authors, Greene also passed on the story of Chuck Ross, who had retyped Jerzy Kozinski's popular novel *Steps* and submitted the manuscript under his own name to some 13 publishers and the same number of literary agents—all of whom rejected it as unpublishable or unworthy of representation.

For years Greene restricted the journalistic use of his own experiences to brief asides in stories on other subjects. He changed this practice with the birth of his daughter, Amanda, when he started a journal in which he chronicled in intimate detail the first year of her life and the effect of her presence on himself and his wife. The idea for the journal, which was excerpted in *Esquire* and *Redbook* and later published as *Good Morning, Merry Sunshine*, came to Greene when, as a father-to-be, he was searching for literature that "could tell him what might lie ahead" but failing to find "anything that dealt on a human level with what happens when a man and a woman bring a new baby home—when a house that held two people suddenly holds three."

Good Morning, Merry Sunshine was generally well received; Larry L. King wrote in the *Chicago Tribune* (May 6, 1984) that Greene had produced "an honest and valuable book, one dealing with new career conflicts, the changing relationships with Greene's own parents, the complex and painful evolutions between married lovers when a strong new force intervenes." Some reviewers were less enthusiastic, and complained that Greene had failed to examine his feelings about fatherhood in an engaging way. David Owen of the *New Republic* (October 1, 1984) called *Good Morning, Merry Sunshine* "a book about Susan Greene's second baby written by her first." He added, "The really annoying thing about the book is that both Greene and his publisher present it as a manifesto of sensitive fatherhood. . . . But Bob Greene's vision of manly child-rearing is quite reactionary. He ducks all the major chores and responsibilities in order to savor his daughter from afar."

The high points of *Cheeseburgers: The Best of Bob Greene* (1985) include a humorous tour of the Playboy Mansion in Chicago, soon after it was permanently vacated by the publisher Hugh Hefner and donated to a local university, and a more in-depth account of Greene's meeting with Richard

Nixon, during which the ex-president, "as the hours went by . . . loosened up . . . and began to talk freely, about his days in the White House, about his relations with the news media, about his views on television, about his new life in New York." In the *Christian Science Monitor* (December 17, 1985), Daniel B. Wood complimented Greene's "uncanny way of writing about personal things— his mother, his diary, his father's baby-shoe-bronzing business—without exuding ego" and his ability to "touch the human element in a story without waxing sentimental . . . in ways that derive universal import from the particular incident."

By 1986 Bob Greene had written, by his own count, some 3,000 columns, exclusive of magazine articles. The effect of such a prolificacy of articles on his personal world-view was substantial. "What has happened," he wrote in an article for *Esquire* (December 1986), "is that I have become virtually incapable of experiencing things in life and then keeping them inside myself. My life runs in 24-hour cycles: I go out and live the day, talking with people and noticing things, and then the next morning I am back in front of a word processor, turning those things into a column for public consumption. . . . I think I have lost the ability to live my life if it's not going to end up on paper." Greene had by that time reduced the number of his appearances on ABC's *Nightline* because "things were finally threatening to get out of hand." "I wasn't even able to sleep anymore," he has said.

Perhaps in an effort to reclaim a time when he had put his thoughts on paper for purposes other than public consumption, Greene published *Be True to Your School: A Diary of 1964* (1987). The book was a partially rewritten version of the diary he kept during his junior and senior years of high school, when he was taught that the practice was a good one for an aspiring journalist. Writing about his everyday life, he had sketched a teenager's world that he felt was universal in many respects since, as he has put it, "everyone falls in love and has his first beer and a best friend and cruises his town in a car and maybe gets into a fight." Greene took some flak for this effort at reconstructing the past. A reviewer for the *Christian Science Monitor* (March 23, 1987) called the book "slow and overlong" and "not quite journalistic Muzak, but close." In the *New York Times Book Review* (June 7, 1987), Joanne Kaufman found Greene "not nearly as compelling here as he thinks he is." Still, the book found a wide readership, including a large number of teenagers, and it became a best-seller. Lou Orfanella, a teacher at Webutuck Junior/Senior High School in Amenia, New York, reviewed *Be True to Your School* for *English Journal* (November 1993) and revealed that he had assigned the book to his senior students to use as a model for their own journals.

Greene's next book, *Homecoming: When the Soldiers Returned from Vietnam* (1989), examined the spiritual wounds left by the Vietnam War. In his column Greene had requested veterans to write to him concerning the reception accorded them on their return from the Vietnam War. He received more than 1,000 responses, mostly from men who had been literally spat upon by antiwar protestors or who had been "made to feel small and unwanted in so many other ways that it felt like being spat upon." Instead of interpreting the letters he received, Greene merely collected and edited the first-hand accounts. In the *New York Times Book Review* (January 22, 1989), Doug Anderson wrote, "Underneath the anger in *Homecoming* is a desire for what the veterans suffered to have meaning in the larger scheme of things. . . . If you have a taste for historical irony, you will like *Homecoming.*"

He Was a Midwestern Boy on His Own (1991), Greene's fifth compilation of columns, took its title from a song by Bob Seger. The book featured an account of Greene's high-school class reunion; an interview with Sean Connery titled "So . . . We Meet At Last, Mr. Bond"; and the story of Elvis Presley's offer, made to President Nixon in 1970, to become a federal agent to help in the fight against, in Presley's words, "drug abuse and Communist brainwashing techniques." Regardless of its subject, each piece was undergirded by Greene's particular vision of the world. "I have gone out to see some things, but part of me is still on Main Street," he has explained. "It's as if the kid on Main Street is always waiting for me to come back and tell him what I have found."

Greene's book *Hang Time: Days and Dreams with Michael Jordan* came about as an indirect result of what he has described as a midlife crisis. On top of the stress of dealing with middle age, Greene was fighting despair brought on by his coverage of a story of shocking child abuse. During this period, in 1990, Greene befriended the Chicago Bulls basketball superstar Michael Jordan. *Hang Time* is at once a portrait of the athlete, a recounting of two of the basketball seasons in which Jordan led the Bulls to the NBA championship, and a reflection on the solace that Greene drew from his friendship with Jordan.

"What makes *Hang Time* absorbing is not so much Jordan as Greene," Armen Keteyian declared in the *Chicago Tribune* (November 8, 1992). "When he is clear-eyed and committed, he remains one of the most penetrating and evocative voices in print. And here he is very good, offering a vivid, enlightening portrait of the world's ultimate sports star. . . . The book does have drawbacks. One is Greene's tendency to gloss over or quickly dismiss the self-absorbed side of Jordan. . . . Then, at times, there is the syrupy tenor of the storytelling. . . . Green also has a tendency to stretch his journalistic eye a bit far, trying to find deep meaning in the bounce of a basketball. . . . But it is Greene's ability to stretch and see beyond basketball that has allowed him and Jordan to connect. And because he does, we do too." Greene's second book about the basketball hero, *Rebound: The Odyssey of Michael Jordan*, was published in the fall of 1995.

In the meantime, Bob Greene had published his first novel in 1993. The semi-autobiographical *All Summer Long* tells the story of three middle-aged friends who briefly leave their families and careers behind and set out on a trip across the United States in an attempt to recover some of the glory of their youth. The novel impressed a writer for *People* (June 14, 1993), who described it as "a testament to the homespun values of family and friendship that endure no matter how far you roam from Small Town, U.S.A." The reviewer judged *All Summer Long*, "despite [its] tendency to be a bit too sweet," to be "as refreshing as a tall glass of iced tea on a July afternoon."

In 1997 Greene released two new books, *The 50 Year Dash: The Feelings, Foibles and Fears of Being Half-A-Century Old* and *Chevrolet Summers, Dairy Queen Nights*. In the first, the author reflected not only on his own 50th birthday, but the collective aging of his generation. He covered a wide variety of topics—everything from his family, to the early 1960s British Invasion bands, to money, to mortality, to the loss of Main Street, America. Many critics felt it was one of his more superficial collections; a reviewer for *Kirkus Reviews* (December 15, 1996) noted that "In a text shamelessly aimed at the blip in birth stats known as the baby boom, the author waxes, in turn, philosophical and nostalgic. . . . Replete with memories of cheeseburgers, the Beach Boys, and innocent childhood, the whimsy is good-natured, homely, and gentle. But it's better taken in column-size doses." Bill Ott of *Booklist* (December 15, 1996) remarked: "As with much of Greene's material, he occasionally hits on an amusing-enough conceit—like the melancholy realization that James Bond's pleasures are all bad for you—but it's rarely enough to sustain an entire . . . well, newspaper column."

Chevrolet Summers, Dairy Queen Nights brought together a number of short columns that looked at American stories that don't make the nightly news, heartwarming and melancholy tales of everyday human experience. As ever, Greene covered a wide variety of subjects: baseball legend Stan Musial reflecting on the game, an elderly mother and daughter sharing a room in a nursing home, an elderly father taking care of his severely retarded adult son, a teenage boy so often teased that he ends up committing suicide. In a review for the *New York Times Book Review* (August 3, 1997), Carol Peace Robins wrote, "It's a hard heart that won't be touched by the stories about everyday life in the United States told by Bob Greene in this collection of columns from the *Chicago Tribune*. . . . There is something for everyone in this variety pack of American life." The reviewer for the *San Antonio Express-News* (August 18, 1997, on-line) proclaimed, "*Chevrolet Summers* is the kind of book you can read piecemeal; it's 104 short stories that only take a few minutes to read. But do yourself a favor and devote a few hours to reading it; you won't want to put it down."

On February 13, 1971, Bob Greene married Susan Bonnet Koebel, a paralegal. Their daughter, Amanda, was born on June 11, 1983. Greene has won a number of awards and honors, including the National Headliner's Award for the best American newspaper column in 1977, and the Peter Lisagor Award in 1981.—C.M.

SELECTED WORKS: Nonfiction—*We Didn't Have None of Them Fat Funky Angels on the Wall of Heartbreak Hotel and Other Reports from America*, 1971; *Running: A Nixon-McGovern Campaign Journal*, 1973; *Billion Dollar Baby*, 1974; *Johnny Deadline, Reporter*, 1976; *American Beat*, 1983; *Good Morning, Merry Sunshine*, 1984; *Cheeseburgers: The Best of Bob Greene*, 1985; *Be True to Your School*: A Diary of 1964, 1987; *Homecoming: When the Soldiers Returned from Vietnam*, 1989; *He Was a Midwestern Boy on His Own*, 1991; *Hang Time: Days and Dreams with Michael Jordan*, 1992; *Rebound: The Odyssey of Michael Jordan*, 1995; *Chevrolet Summers, Dairy Queen Nights*, 1997; *The 50 Year Dash: The Feelings, Foibles, and Fears of Being Half-A-Century Old*, 1997; Fiction—*All Summer Long*, 1993

SUGGESTED READING: *Booklist* Dec. 15, 1996; *Chicago Tribune* May 6, 1984, Nov. 8, 1992; *Christian Science Monitor* Dec. 17, 1985, Mar. 23, 1987; *English Journal* Nov. 1993; *Esquire* p54+ Dec. 1986, with photo; *Kirkus Reviews* Dec. 15, 1996; *New Republic* Oct. 1984; *Newsweek* Jan. 13, 1975; *New York Times Book Review* May 20, 1973, June 7, 1987, Jan. 22, 1989, p20 Mar. 16, 1997, p17 Aug. 3, 1997; *People* June 14, 1993; *Publishers Weekly* p60+ May 4, 1984; *San Antonio Express-News* (on-line) Aug. 18, 1997; *Contemporary Authors* 1981, vol. 107, 1983, 1988; *Contemporary Authors New Revision Series* vol. 27, 1989; *Who's Who in America*, 1998

Eamon Grennan

Grennan, Eamon

Nov. 13, 1941– Poet

The Irish poet, essayist, and scholar Eamon Grennan has dedicated himself, like Chaucer's clerk, to gladly learning and teaching. The trajectory of his life has carried him from Ireland to America, from being a student to being a teacher, but Grennan has always lived the contemplative life of a poet. His images are formed from Irish soil, concerned as he is with domesticity, gardens, and weather. The weather is sometimes a matter of outdoor, sometimes one of emotional climate. His poetry has been collected in *Wildly for Days* (1983), *Twelve Poems* (1988), *What Light There Is* (1989), *As If It Matters* (1991), *So It Goes* (1995), and *Relations* (1998). Grennan joined the English Department at Vassar College in 1974.

For *World Authors 1990–1995*, Eamon Grennan writes: "Sometimes I think of my life as variations on the notion of 'home and away.' The first home was Dublin, where I was born on the thirteenth of November, 1941. From my childhood I mostly remember summers, being wheeled in a pram or walking beside my mother or playing in suburban parks. Long bright days, trips to the seacoast at Blackrock or Seapoint: swimming, lolling on the rocks, picnics of tomatoes and hardboiled eggs, bread and butter, milk and lemonade, my mother in her swimming togs sunbathing, lathering on Nivea Cream, eager for us all to be 'brown as berries.' Summer holidays, too, brought the first real experience of 'away.' First in the sandy seaside village of Bettystown to the north of Dublin, and later in the West of Ireland—where my father was a school inspector—staying in Carraroe, a village in the Gaeltacht (Irish-speaking) area beyond Galway, a day's drive from Dublin to the heart of Connemara, bleak and rocky and beautiful. The freedom of bare feet all day, a coral strand, going into the cowfields and trying not to step on thistles or cowpats, climbing loose stone walls, walking among nettles and brambles, blackberry hedges and fuchsia bushes. Even going to the local school, where the children were all dressed in bawneen tweed or flannel frocks, where the boys had knee britches and shaved heads, and where both girls and boys spoke a pattering musical speedy Irish which left myself and my younger sister and two brothers gaping, at a loss for words, and left my mother—who understood even less than we did—in helpless laughter.

"School was another 'away.' My elementary school was run by nuns, and the primary school by the Christian Brothers. We were taught a lot by rote—especially an abbreviated and nationalistic account of Irish history, to which I think I must owe a lifelong difficulty with the notion of 'history' itself, and with dogmatic nationalism. Still, we learned—maths and geography and Christian Doctrine (at school and at home everything was imbued with Catholic teaching, which we took in with our mothers' milk), and Irish and English. I don't remember what we read in English, although I remember doing the weekly compositions, both in English and Irish, on subjects such as 'An Old Bicycle Tells Its Own Story' or 'An Old Boot Tells the Story of Its Life,' compositions which taught one to have an interest in the minute, to be sympathetically engaged with everyday objects. Sheer, and very localised, imagining. Little tutorials, I guess, in 'negative capability.'

"When I was thirteen I went away to boarding school. Mount Saint Joseph's College, Roscrea, where I remained for five years, was (and is) set in County Tipperary, in the middle of Ireland, and run by the Cistercian monks who lived and prayed and worked in the monastery next door and in the surrounding fields. It taught me about solitude as well as loneliness (and about the difference between the two) as well as some of the joys and virtues of community. It coaxed us to be good in studies as well as good at games, and fostered in me, for whatever reason, a growing love for English literature. (The few times we put on Shakespeare plays were also important, nurturing a love for Shakespeare and theatre which has stayed with me through university and into my life as a teacher.) Beyond classroom and sportsfield Roscrea also had an effect on the spirit. Proximity to the monastery, to the example of the monks in the field, in the cloister, in the classroom, or as disciplinarian deans of the school—monks as curious men, as tyrants, as people—all this expanded an awareness of 'the spiritual life'—as did the weekly High Mass in the monastery, not to mention daily Mass in the chapel at seven each morning, the evening rosary and hymns (impossible to forget the sweet melody and gorgeous Latin of St. Bernard's Salve Regina being belted out by two hundred or so boy voices), and the dazzling, hypnotic ritual of Benediction. What Roscrea left me with was a sense of the proximity of the ordinary world we kids mostly lived in to something else, something for which a number of names might be found.

"When I went to University College, Dublin, I lived at home again. But the life of the university itself—lectures and tutorials, library, pubs, friends, infatuations, literary societies, the novel range of freedoms—was very much an 'away,' its ethos distinct from that of home, and my life was shaped by the need to keep moving between the two. At graduation, then, with a degree in English

and Italian, I put more distance than ever between home and away, first by spending a year in Rome, and then by leaving Ireland for graduate school in the States, where I ended up with a Harvard doctorate in English, a dissertation on Shakespeare's History Plays, and the memory of a student year in Florence—which not only opened my astonished, hungry eyes to art, but led to marriage after graduate school, a teaching job in New York, and an eventual job at Vassar.

"Throughout my years as a graduate student, I didn't write poems, although as an undergraduate I had made a start at it. Then, in 1977, I took an unpaid leave from Vassar and returned to Ireland with Joan and our two children (Kate, who was four, and Conor, who was three), in an attempt to take up again the writing of poems, as well as to involve myself again in the daily (and literary) life of 'home.' To complicate the equation a bit, my literary companions on this pilgrimage were modern American poets such as Bishop, Wright, Williams, Stevens, Snyder, as well as Irish poets such as Patrick Kavanagh and Padraic Fallon, John Montague and Thomas Kinsella, and the work of Irish and American poets of my own generation. I was trying, I suppose, to bring 'away' and 'home' into intimate contact, in the process of becoming—or this would be one way of putting it—an Irish poet who wrote American poems. My subject was whatever our daily life offered—with its surfaces of domesticity, its walks (with binoculars) through the natural landscape (the coast of County Wexford), and its hidden corners of desire. Poetry was becoming my way of paying attention. And while writing of much value may not have come out of that year, the year itself was crucial for me in the way it moved the practise of poetry from the margin to the center of my life.

"Between then and now, nearly twenty years later, the pattern of the life I've led—which has been marked by separation and divorce, and by putting down more roots with Rachel and our daughter, Kira (born in 1986)—has taken some of its main features from the migrant rhythm of living here in America and returning in summers (or for longer periods if possible) to Ireland, either to Dublin or to a cottage in Connemara, as well as from the fact that I divide my working life between teaching, writing poems, and writing criticism—mostly on modern Irish poetry since Yeats. During these years, too, other pivotal facts were the death of my father in 1981 and the death of my mother in 1990. Both died in Dublin, creating a palpable absence in that 'home' part of my life, an absence my poems have visited, as they have visited various moments of my life with my children, those enlivening and bewildering presences (and, of course, absences).

"What shape does it all really make, I wonder? Or what shape do my poems really make of it? Hard to say. I would say, however, that any good poem comes from keeping one ear on the subject and one (in a critical and loving way) on the language itself, and that the language I seek—as a kind of witness to the facts of life—tries to keep in touch both with ordinary speech and with some idea of rhetorical grace: 'normality' with a little bit of 'eloquence' and metrical muscle. If poetry can combine this grace with this ordinariness, then it is—for me at least—at once 'home' and 'away,' both anchoring the self in the known world, and reaching a little bit beyond it."

Reviewing *What Light There Is & Other Poems* (which contains the poems from *Wildly For Days* and later works), Alfred Corn noted in *Poetry* (January 1990), "Dublin, with its back-gardens, parks, and indigenous volubility can be made to yield some of the pleasures of pastoral. . . . [Grennan] has a knack for sensing glimmers of Nature's mysteries in an urban setting." Corn, as an American poet, expressed a wish that Grennan's poetry had improved with his move to America, but observed that "the poems in the first section," written mostly in Ireland, "are better, especially the Dublin poems." Fred Muratori, writing for *Library Journal* (June 15, 1989) found that Grennan's poetry "illuminates. . . 'this stillness in which we go on happening.'" Another American poet, Edward Hirsch, observed in the *New Republic* (June 11, 1990), "The dramatic tension in his work comes from the perceptible gap between his longing for solidity and his sense of the true precariousness of things as they are." He termed "the light that radiates" from Grennan's work "understated, intricate, luminous, consoling."

By the time of the publication of *As If It Matters*, in 1991, Grennan had achieved greater stature as a poet (he had also, perhaps not coincidentally, become a full professor at Vassar College). M. P. White noted in *Choice* (October 1992), "In his celebration of the 'limited / worldly' self, [Grennan] creates stunning metaphors. . . . Like Elizabeth Bishop, he speaks the 'double tongue of detail and the world at large.'" Laurel Blossom in *Small Press* (Summer 1992) claimed for Grennan "a painterly eye." "Like Vermeer, Grennan aims 'To love the scrubbed exactitudes / and the dimmer thing / that shivers at the brink.' He does not focus on the shadows as many poets do, but he acknowledges their power."

With *So It Goes*, in the opinion of most reviewers, Grennan had come to the full realization of his poetic powers. Patricia Monaghan in *Booklist* (November 1, 1995) mentioned Grennan's "fierce sensuality and his narrative ease." She termed the volume "mature poetry, both in subject and in language." Louis McKee in *Library Journal* (November 15, 1995) concurred: "His hard-won maturity and insight enable him to cast light on the shadows and reveal the everyday wonders hidden there. With logic, plain, honest language, precision, and clarity, the author presents a world that has always been but we have rarely noticed. His appreciation of the small things makes these poems memorable."

Grennan's *Relations: New and Selected Poems* was published to acclaim in 1998. "In Grennan's best poems, and there are many in this collection," a writer announced in *Publishers Weekly* (July 27, 1998), "the precision of his observations renders the embodied lives of others with gripping lucidity." The poet's volume *Facing the Music: Irish Poetry in the Twentieth Century* appeared in 1999.

In "Shapes," a narrative poem published in the Summer 1994 issue of the *Gettysburg Review*, Grennan described his finding the body of a friend and the subsequent obsequies, including the cremation in Poughkeepsie, where Vassar College is located, and the scattering of those ashes on the Isis, the portion of the Thames near Oxford, in England. He described the friend's having copied a sentence into a commonplace book, ". . .leaving me something / to make sense of your own going— / the way we are always shaping a little / saving structure for our lives." In "Faith, Hope, and Danger," published in the *Michigan Quarterly Review* of (Winter 1997), Grennan observed a moth circling a light and afterward remembered " . . . a kind / of famished dazzle / and then blackout." He added the image of the "desert fathers . . . scouring / in the Egyptian Sun, / how it singed them / to the bone as they bent—light-headed from hunger, hope and faith—over / the empty page, each / grain of sand a burning word they sensed but / couldn't touch / with their tongues, each / insect noise or watery birdcall / or the ghostly / whisper of mothwings / in the eyeblink of dusk / a soul-dementing / dear distraction / from the main business." The "main business" for Grennan, the "saving structure," is the truth that lives only when it is expressed in poetry.

Grennan has made an effort throughout his life, by teaching first at University College in Dublin, then at Lehman College of City University of New York, and finally at Vassar College, to encourage young poets. He has spent several summers teaching at the International Yeats Summer School in Sligo, where he has delivered such lectures as "Mastery and Beyond: Speech and Silence in *The Tower*" and "A Living Thing: Responding to *Responsibilities*." He has offered numerous poetry readings and workshops and been the recipient of grants from the National Endowment for the Humanities (1986) and the National Endowment for the Arts (1991). He was awarded a Guggenheim Fellowship in 1995. He has published his poems in magazines and journals such as the *New Yorker*, *Grand Street*, the *Irish Times*, the *Kenyon Review*, and many others, and has been included in various anthologies. His literary criticism has appeared in *Shakespeare Quarterly*, *Shakespeare Studies*, and *Modern Language Quarterly*, among other journals.

—S. Y.

SUGGESTED READING: *Booklist* p450 Nov. 1, 1995; *Choice* p298 Oct. 1992; *Library Journal* p61 June 15, 1989, p79 Nov. 15, 1995; *New Republic* p39 June 11, 1990; *Poetry* p287 Jan. 1990; *Small Press* p52 Summer 1992

SELECTED BOOKS: Poetry—*Wildly for Days*, 1983; *Twelve Poems*, 1988, *What Light There Is and Other Poems*, 1989; *As If It Matters*, 1991; *So It Goes*, 1995; *Relations: New and Selected Poems*, 1998; As translator—*Selected Poems of Giacomo Leopardi*, 1995

Anthony Loew/Courtesy of Doubleday

Grisham, John

Feb. 8, 1955– Novelist; former lawyer

When John Grisham's fourth courtroom thriller, *The Client* (1993), landed on the *New York Times* hardcover best-seller list in the top position in March 1993, his three other novels—*The Pelican Brief* (1992), *The Firm* (1991), and *A Time to Kill* (1989), all of which he had completed within the previous four years—were among the top five on the *New York Times* paperback best-seller list. With millions of copies of his books in print and millions of dollars from the sale of movie rights in his pockets, Grisham, a former lawyer and state legislator, had accomplished a rare feat in publishing—one that prompted industry analysts to rank him with such perennial best-selling authors as Stephen King, Danielle Steele, and Michael Crichton. Grisham has said that his fiction adheres to a surefire formula in which "you take some horrible, mean, vicious, nasty conspiracy over here, you put a very sympathetic hero or heroine in the middle of it, you reach a point where their lives are at stake—and you get them out of it." The filmmaker

Sydney Pollack, who directed the film version of *The Firm*, has attributed the writer's phenomenal success to the "suspicious, cynical decade" of the 1990s, in which "all bureaucratic authorities are suspect." Grisham's more recent novels are *The Chamber* (1994), *The Rainmaker* (1995), *The Runaway Jury* (1996), *The Partner* (1997), *The Street Lawyer* (1998), and *The Testament* (1999).

John Grisham was born on February 8, 1955, in Arkansas, the son of a migrant construction worker and a homemaker. He and his four siblings traveled throughout the southern United States, settling briefly wherever their father found work. "We'd move into a small town," Grisham recalled in an interview with Tom Mathews of *Newsweek* (March 15, 1993), "and the first thing we'd do is join a local Baptist church, the second was go to the library and get our library cards and check out all the books we were allowed." In about 1967 the family took up permanent residence in Southaven, Mississippi, a suburb of Memphis, Tennessee. "We didn't have a lot of money," Grisham told a reporter for *People* (March 16, 1992), "but we didn't know it. We were well-fed and loved and scrubbed."

An extraordinarily self-assured teenager, Grisham applied his energies to baseball in high school. "I've always been real confident," he said in the *People* interview, "even in sports, where I had nothing to be confident about." Except for an affinity for the novels of John Steinbeck, he expressed little interest in serious literature. At Mississippi State University he experienced what he has termed "one of those awakenings" and decided to become a tax lawyer. After obtaining a bachelor's degree in accounting from Mississippi State, he enrolled at the University of Mississippi Law School. Because his first course in tax law effectively quashed his interest in the subject, he focused on criminal-defense law instead and discovered, in moot court, that he had a flair for thinking on his feet. In 1981 he graduated from the University of Mississippi Law School with a J.D. degree; he was admitted to the Mississippi bar in the same year.

Almost from the moment Grisham opened his one-man private practice in Southaven, he was dissatisfied with his chosen field. He won his first jury trial—a "gruesome case," as he later described it, in which he defended a man who had shot his wife's lover six times in the head at point-blank range—by arguing that his client had acted in self-defense, because the lover had fired a shot from a .22 caliber pistol that had glanced off the defendant's chest. When Grisham discovered that "it's impossible to feed your family if you are representing garden-variety criminals," as he explained to Tom Mathews, he switched to civil law. Despite winning one of the largest damage settlements ever recorded in De Soto County, on behalf of a boy who had sustained burns covering 92 percent of his body when a water heater exploded, Grisham found the practice of civil law equally frustrating.

Hoping to make an impact on the state's educational system, he won election as a Democrat to the Mississippi state legislature in 1983. He was reelected four years later, but shortly before his second term was up, Grisham resigned his seat. "I realized it was impossible to make changes," he told the reporter for *People*.

Meanwhile, in 1984, Grisham had embarked on a new career course. Inspired by a trial he had observed at the De Soto County courthouse, he decided to try his hand as a writer. "This 10-year-old girl was testifying against a man who had raped her and left her for dead," he recalled in his interview for *People* magazine. "I never felt such emotion and human drama in my life. I became obsessed wondering what it would be like if the girl's father killed that rapist and was put on trial. I had to write it down." For three years Grisham arrived at his office at 5:00 A.M. six days a week, so that he could spend the early morning hours writing—in longhand, in the kind of notebooks used by court reporters—what would become his first novel. He didn't worry about publishing the book, as he explained to Michelle Bearden in an interview for *Publishers Weekly* (February 22, 1993): "Because I have this problem of starting projects and not completing them, my goal for this book was simply to finish it."

Disclaiming "any inspiration from Scott Turow," the lawyer and novelist to whom he is often compared, Grisham has said that he finished the first draft of *A Time to Kill* a month before Turow's first novel, *Presumed Innocent*, was published, in 1987. Grisham mailed his manuscript to 16 literary agents, one of whom, Jay Garon, "smelled a winner right off the bat," as Garon put it. After accumulating more than two dozen rejections over the course of a year, Garon finally sold *A Time to Kill* to Wynwood Press (which has since gone out of business) for $15,000. Five thousand copies of Grisham's novel were printed in June 1989. "I bought 1,000, and another 1,000 were sitting in a warehouse, so you know not many were out there," the author informed Michelle Bearden. Even the book party that was arranged for Grisham by his friend Richard Howorth, the owner of Square Books in Oxford, Mississippi, failed to boost sales, as Howorth had correctly predicted: "Look, if we invite your mama and your wife," Howorth told Grisham, as quoted by Tom Mathews, "your friends and all your relatives, we will do well to sell 50 copies."

A Time to Kill is set in Ford County, a fictional Mississippi community that brings to mind the Yoknapatawpha County of William Faulkner's novels. Its central character is a small-town lawyer, Jake Brigance, who defends, before an all-white jury, a black Vietnam veteran charged with the murders of two white men who raped his 10-year-old daughter. "My motives were pure when I wrote *A Time to Kill*," Grisham told Tom Mathews. "It's better [than my subsequent books] because you can almost smell the biscuits and the eggs and the grits and hear the chatter in the coffee shop; the people

are better, the setting is better; you can feel the sweat sticking to their shirts in the July heat around the courthouse." Grisham's assessment has since been seconded by a number of reviewers, but in its initial release the novel sold so poorly that Grisham resolved to make his next effort "a naked stab at commercial fiction," as he admitted to Mathews.

After mastering the rules of suspense, which he found enumerated in an article in *Writer's Digest*, Grisham devoted two years to writing *The Firm*. A bootleg copy of the manuscript somehow ended up in the hands of a movie scout in New York City, who then sent it to Hollywood, where Paramount bought the film rights for $600,000. Grisham recounted for *People* that the day after the motion picture deal was concluded, in January 1990, "Eighteen publishers begged for the chance to publish it. It was a hoot." Doubleday won the bidding frenzy, purchasing *The Firm* for $200,000. The publishing house also signed the author to a three-book contract, which enabled him to give up his law practice in 1990. "It was fairly easy to close the office down and run all the clients away," he was quoted as saying in *Time* (April 1, 1991).

In *The Firm* (1991), Mitchell McDeere, a student at Harvard Law School, is seduced by an $80,000 salary, a low-interest mortgage, a new BMW, and two country-club memberships into joining the Memphis law firm of Bendini, Lambert & Locke, which turns out to be a front for a Mafia money-laundering operation. No one has ever left the firm alive, and those who have tried to free themselves from its clutches have died mysteriously. Caught in what seems to be a no-win situation—he can either cooperate with an FBI investigation at grave risk to his life or go to prison along with the other members of the firm—McDeere plays each side off against the other until he manages to escape with money from both and abandons his profession.

The critical reception accorded *The Firm* was generally favorable, although some reviewers expressed reservations about Grisham's underdeveloped characters. "*The Firm* is a thriller of the first order, powered to pulse-racing perfection by the realism of its malevolent barristers," Susan Toepfer wrote in *People* (April 8, 1991). "Improbabilities abound, the characters are ciphers—and yet the story has significant strengths, . . . [including] an irresistible plot," Peter S. Prescott declared in *Newsweek* (February 25, 1991). Apparently Grisham had intended to write no less and no more than a gripping story in which a fast pace and unexpected plot twists take precedence over character development, nuance, and depth. "I was determined to write clearly, without all the crap," he told Lois Romano of the *Washington Post* (October 21, 1992). "When you write suspense, you want it lean, fast. There's a conscious effort to keep people up all night." To the reporter for *People* he added, "I write to grab readers. This isn't serious literature."

Within weeks of its publication, *The Firm* appeared on the *New York Times* best-seller list, where it remained for nearly a year. The paperback version of the novel, which was published in February 1992, remained at or near the top of *Publishers Weekly's* mass-market best-seller list for eighteen months. As of March 1993, 600,000 hardcover copies and 6.5 million paperback copies of the book were in print. Translated into 27 languages, *The Firm* also became a best-seller in the Netherlands, Germany, Great Britain, and Italy. In June 1993 a film adaptation of *The Firm* was released to movie theatres in the United States. Directed by Sydney Pollack, the director of Grisham's favorite movie, the 1975 political thriller *Three Days of the Condor*, *The Firm* starred Tom Cruise, Gene Hackman, and Jeanne Tripplehorn. In its first two weeks of release, *The Firm* took in almost $74 million at the box office.

The Firm propelled Grisham into the rarified realm of best-selling novelists. "Having a best-seller is so much fun," he exclaimed to Kelli Pryor for *Entertainment Weekly* (August 2, 1991). "I don't think anybody's having any more fun than I am." More than a year later he was still somewhat awed by his own success. "A lot of times I feel like it's happening to somebody else," Grisham told Michael Lollar of the *Chicago Tribune* (January 8, 1993). "But I'm philosophical about all this, in that five years from now or 10 years from now things are not going to be as hot as they are now. Everything has X number of years to it, and I know that."

Exactly one year after *The Firm* was published, Grisham's next novel, *The Pelican Brief* (1992), which he completed in only 100 days, was shipped to book stores. When the first printing of 425,000 copies sold out, Doubleday ordered several additional press runs. By March 1993 there were 1.35 million hardcover copies and 4.5 million softcover copies of *The Pelican Brief* in print. The title refers to a memo that Darby Shaw, a Tulane University law student, prepares in the course of an investigation into a suspected conspiracy behind the assassinations of two Supreme Court justices. Like McDeere in *The Firm*, Shaw finds herself hunted and nearly trapped by the forces of evil, which are again represented by various bureaucratic agencies, including the FBI and the CIA, as well as by the White House and an independent tycoon. Shaw triumphs in the end, but only by giving up her law career, as McDeere had done. As John Skow noted in his review of the novel for *Time* (March 9, 1992), *The Pelican Brief* "is as close to its predecessor as you can get without running *The Firm* through the office copier. . . . In the finest tradition of 19th-century fiction, [Shaw] is saved from a life of litigation when she drops out of law school perilously close to the bar exam. Honor almost stained is surefire."

The Pelican Brief received mostly mixed reviews. In a typical reaction to the story, one critic objected to the "universal loathsomeness" of the one-dimensional characters and the abundance of implausibilities while lauding the novel's "narrative drive." Christopher Lehmann-Haupt, writing in the *New York Times* (February 27, 1992), called the book an "intriguing but ultimately specious new thriller." "Though *The Pelican Brief* is diverting it is rarely disturbing," he wrote. "The story keeps throwing away its opportunities. The main problem is that the characters are about as complex as so many lengths of lead pipe. . . . Nor is *The Pelican Brief* about anything in particular. If it takes as its premise that people in power are brutally cynical and manipulative and will do just about anything to get a leg up, it never questions that view or explores it even shallowly. . . . All the novel really wants is to be exciting and violent." Other critics were more charitable in their assessments. Despite some "improbabilities," Grisham "has written a genuine page-turner," Frank J. Prial contended in an assessment for the *New York Times Book Review* (March 15, 1992). "He has an ear for dialogue and is a skillful craftsman. Like a composer, he brings all his themes together at the crucial moment for a gripping, and logical, finale." Movie rights to *The Pelican Brief* were sold for a reported $1.28 million. The film version starred Denzel Washington and Julia Roberts.

While *The Pelican Brief* was riding high on the best-seller lists, *A Time to Kill* was reissued as a Dell paperback, in July 1992; by September there were 3.27 million copies of the book in print. In the summer of the same year, all three books were released on audiocassettes, and they quickly claimed the top three slots on *Publishers Weekly's* list of best-selling audio fiction. As of August 1993 the three titles continued to rank among the 10 top-selling audiocassettes, behind, in the number-one spot, Grisham's next effort, *The Client* (1993). Within three months of its publication, there were 2.64 million hardcover copies of *The Client* in print, and rights to a film version had been sold for $2.5 million.

Perhaps more than any of Grisham's previous books, *The Client* seemed tailor-made for the screen, as more than one reviewer pointed out. "*The Client* is a postmodern masterpiece, perfect for turning Grisham's readers into consumers of high-tech literary theory," Adam Begley wrote in *New York Newsday* (March 7, 1993). "This is the self-erasing novel. As you read it, it renders itself obsolete, pointing to its own inadequacy with such ruthless conviction that you know you are plugged into the wrong medium. . . . Mark is a character in a novel who knows that he's really a hammy child actor spending time in textual purgatory before he's translated back into celluloid heaven."

In *The Client's* opening passage, which one reviewer called "irresistible," 11-year-old Mark Sway tries desperately to dissuade a lawyer from committing suicide. During their conversation Mark learns that the lawyer's client, a mobster named Barry ("the Blade") Muldanno, has murdered a United States senator and buried the body under the lawyer's garage. After the lawyer's suicide, Mark—the only living soul, other than the killer himself, to know the truth about the senator's death—is pursued by various groups. To help him elude the FBI, the mob, and child-welfare authorities, Mark hires Reggie Love, a tough, 52-year-old lawyer and divorced grandmother, and outwits his enemies with street smarts he has picked up from watching television.

Several reviewers were admittedly disappointed by *The Client*, one of them going so far as to castigate Grisham for "enraptur[ing] us with a story that has hardly any point." On the other hand, another critic found the book to be "amiable enough entertainment," and a third congratulated the author on his "marketing acumen." Susan Toepfer commented in *People* (March 15, 1993) that "though *The Client* lacks the page-turning drama of *The Firm* and *The Pelican Brief*, it more than compensates with a newfound Grisham humor and slapstick energy." In an interview with Toepfer, Grisham conceded that he had sacrificed a measure of suspense for character development in *The Client*, partly in response to the adverse critical reaction to his earlier efforts. "When reviews are negative but fair, I pay attention," he remarked. "Some said my characters were shallow—and they were. *The Firm* and *The Pelican Brief* are very fast, plot-driven books. I deliberately slowed it down in *The Client*. My wife edits my books as I write them. She's really good with the women characters. We have some spirited discussions, but she's almost always right. That's the frustrating part."

In keeping with his tradition of releasing a book every spring or summer, Grisham's next novel, *The Chamber*, debuted in June 1994. It departed from his formula in that it focused more on the relationship between two of the main characters rather than on thrills. The two main characters in question are Sam Cayhall, a former member of the Ku Klux Klan about to be executed for assisting in the bombing of a liberal Jewish lawyer's office, and his idealistic grandson and personal defense attorney, Adam Hall. While Hall attempts to get his grandfather a stay of execution, he is forced to come to terms with the fact that he loathes Cayhill and his racist and anti-Semitic views. The book sold extremely well, but critics found Grisham's attempt to tackle serious issues to be somewhat unsatisfactory. Tom Nolan of the *Wall Street Journal* (June 13, 1994) remarked: "The story veers away from its expected payoff, turning into something more like a mainstream novel, but without the more fully formed characters such fiction demands. Cayhall seems especially unconvincing, first as an articulate bigot and then as an enlightened penitent. So *The Chamber*, neither true thriller nor real novel, is doubly unsatisfying." Walter Goodman, in his review for the *New York Times* (July 29, 1994), noted that the novel's main function "is to deliver information, and you don't have to read absolutely every word, because all significant facts are repeated, usually more than once. Everything is made explicit; one's imagination is never imposed on."

In April 1995 Grisham published *The Rainmaker*, which sold more than 300,000 copies in its first week and had an initial printing of 2.8 million copies. In the novel, Rudy Baylor, a young lawyer fresh from law school, represents a family whose son is dying of leukemia because the health insurance company refused to pay for a bone marrow transplant. The result, according to Tom Nolan of the *Wall Street Journal* (April 27, 1995), "is Mr. Grisham's most sympathetic hero and most engrossing premise since his first runaway success, *The Firm*." Michiko Kakutani of the *New York Times* (April 28, 1995), however, was unimpressed. In her review she cited "the leadenness of Mr. Grisham's prose, the banality of his characters, and the shocking predictability of his story" as offenses likely to prevent readers from finishing the book.

Grisham's next work, *The Runaway Jury* (1996), took its theme from current headlines, focusing on a woman who seeks compensation from the tobacco industry for the death of her husband from cancer. Grisham received mostly positive critical reviews for the book. Christopher Lehmann-Haupt remarked in the *New York Times* (May 23, 1996) that "the plot's eventual outcome is far more entertainingly unpredictable than anything Mr. Grisham has done before." Tom Nolan wrote in the *Wall Street Journal* (May 29, 1996) that "Mr. Grisham maintains the suspense for a goodly number of pages in this, his seventh and perhaps most exciting book. The formidable court case against the tobacco companies is ably presented, and a host of minor characters are nicely drawn. As in earlier works by Mr. Grisham, though, the plot is advanced at the cost of a certain amount of credibility."

Two of Grisham's more recent works—*The Partner* (1997), about a lawyer who embezzles $90 million from his firm and fakes his own death, and *The Street Lawyer* (1998), the tale of a yuppie lawyer who leaves his high-paying job to work in a street law clinic—have both soared to the top of the best-seller lists. His latest work, *The Testament* (1999), which concerns an aging billionaire who makes last-minute changes to his will in order to prevent his greedy relatives from getting his estate, appears to be poised to do the same.

Grisham has become something of a fixture in the film industry. As soon as he finishes a new novel—sometimes even before he completes it—the movie rights are snapped up by a major Hollywood studio, and the story is turned into a film featuring A-list actors. Since the release of the film adaptation of *The Firm*, there have been screen versions of *The Pelican Brief* (1994), starring Julia Roberts and Denzel Washington; *The Client* (1994), featuring Susan Sarandon and Tommy Lee Jones; *A Time To Kill* (1996), with Sandra Bullock and Matthew McConaughey; *The Chamber* (1996), starring Chris O'Donnell and Gene Hackman; and *The Rainmaker* (1997), starring Danny DeVito and Matt Damon and directed by Francis Ford Coppola. He has also written the original screenplay for British author J. P. Donleavy's *The Ginger Man.*

Despite being derided by most reviewers as formulaic and lacking in character development, Grisham's books are also (as even his most merciless critics have conceded) gripping page-turners. *The Rainmaker* alone sold 300,000 copies in its first week in bookstores, making it "the fastest-selling hardcover book ever, as far as we know," a Doubleday spokesperson told the *New York Times* (April 19, 1995). According to *Harper's Bazaar* (March 1996), as of early 1996 (before the release of *The Runaway Jury*), 50 million copies of his books had been sold, and *Time* (May 27, 1996) reported that the film versions of the first three of his novels to be adapted for the big screen had grossed nearly $600 million worldwide.

John Grisham typically starts working on a book with a chapter-by-chapter outline, although he often does not know the ending when he begins writing. A book takes him only about six months to write, and he hires assistants to do his legal homework for him. In recent years this has given him a great amount of time to enjoy his two children, coach little league baseball, and even build his own ballpark near his home. The Grisham family moved from their farm in Charlottesville, Virginia to Oxford, Mississippi, when they discovered that their farm had become a popular tourist attraction.—C.M.

SUGGESTED READING: *Business Week* p52+ Aug. 19, 1993; *Chicago Tribune* Jan. 8, 1993; *Entertainment Weekly* p24+ Aug. 2, 1991; *Harper's Bazaar* Mar. 1996, *National Review* p51 Apr. 6, 1998; *New York Newsday* Mar. 7, 1993; *New York Times* Feb. 27, 1992, C p11 July 20, 1994, C p27 July 29, 1994, C p11 Apr. 19, 1995, C p33 Apr. 28, 1995, C p20 May 23, 1996, C p11 Mar. 31, 1997, E p18 Nov. 21, 1997; *New York Times Book Review* Mar. 15, 1992, p33+ Oct. 18, 1992; *Newsweek* Feb. 25, 1991, p78+ Mar. 15, 1993; *People* Apr. 8, 1991, p43+ Mar. 16, 1992, Mar. 15, 1993; *Publishers Weekly* p70+ Feb. 22, 1993; *Time* Apr. 1, 1991, Mar. 9, 1992; *Wall Street Journal* A p15 June 13, 1994, A p12 Apr. 27, 1995; *Washington Post* Oct. 21, 1992, D p1 June 10, 1994, A p16 May 29, 1996; *Contemporary Authors* vol. 138, 1992

SELECTED WORKS: *A Time to Kill*, 1989; *The Firm*, 1991; *The Pelican Brief*, 1992; *The Client*, 1993; *The Chamber*, 1994; *The Rainmaker*, 1995; *The Runaway Jury*, 1996; *The Partner*, 1997; *The Street Lawyer*, 1998; *The Testament*, 1999

Groom, Winston

1943– Novelist; nonfiction writer

Winston Groom is not bothered by the fact that he doesn't have name recognition. As the author of *Forrest Gump*—the 1986 novel adapted to the screen in 1994 by the director Robert Zemickis, with Tom Hanks in the title role of an idiot savant—he is pleased with the mark he has made: the film went on to win six Academy Awards, including those for best picture, best actor, and best director. Though the novel received mostly good reviews when it was first published, it has received a much greater boost from the movie, selling copies in the millions and moving to the top of the best-seller list. "It takes something to make a book a best-seller, and just being good doesn't always guarantee it," Groom admitted to Michelle Bearden in an interview for *Publishers Weekly* (April 17, 1995). "*Forrest Gump* is the same damn book I wrote years ago, only it took a movie to get it discovered. And that's okay with me."

While he remains less well-known than the character he created, Groom has gotten his fair share of accolades from the press and fellow writers, starting with the praise he received for his 1978 debut novel *Better Times Than These*, a story of the Vietnam War seen through the eyes of a rifle company. (Groom himself served in a rifle company in Vietnam during the early part of the war.) He

Tom Corcoran/Courtesy of Winston Groom

had been encouraged to write the book by the novelists Willie Morris and James Jones, the latter advising him not to pattern a character too much after himself. As Groom told *Publishers Weekly* (August 12, 1988): "Jim told me that any book that I might write about the war would be autobiographical, so he suggested that I make the main character as different from myself as possible; his reasoning being that if you don't make that separation you are liable to lose control of the character." Groom took that advice and has had a remarkably diverse publishing career because of it, producing works that have ranged from novels about Vietnam, the small-town mentality in the South, and idiots who change the course of history to nonfiction accounts of the last great campaign of the Civil War and the plight of a POW who returned to the United States after 14 years in Vietnam only to be brought up on charges of treason. As Groom has told many people, including Bearden of *Publishers Weekly*: "I'm going to write what I damn well please."

Winston Groom was born in 1943 in Washington, D.C., the son of Winston Francis Groom and the former Ruth Knudsen, a well-off couple from Mobile, Alabama. Groom assumed up until the time he enrolled in the University of Alabama that he would follow in his father's footsteps and become a lawyer. At Alabama, he began writing for the university's humor magazine and eventually began to edit it. Instead of going to law school after graduating in 1965 with a degree in English, Groom found himself in Vietnam as a second lieutenant in the infantry, eventually becoming a captain. Having attended a military prep school and having had relations serve in the armed forces as far back as the French and Indian War, Groom initially had few reservations about serving. While at first wanting to stop "the Commies" from "knocking on the doors of San Francisco," as Groom told Louise Lague of *People* (September 18, 1978), he returned from Vietnam disillusioned by his 13-month experience. "It was a stupid, no-win war where the enemy scared you to death. They'd mine you during lunch."

He came home in 1967 with 20 notebooks on his experience, which he intended to convert into a novel. That novel never came together, and Groom began working at the (now defunct) *Washington Star*. At that paper he made contact with Adam Shaw, a reporter on the rival *Washington Post*, while the two were working the local courts. As it turned out, Shaw was the son of the novelist Irwin Shaw, to whom Groom was soon introduced. From his newspaper work Groom also met Willie Morris, at the time the writer-in-residence for the *Star*. In part because they were both from the South, Morris took a liking to Groom and introduced him to Theron Raines, who would eventually become Groom's agent and friend, and to James Jones, who, along with Morris, advised Groom on his first novel. This group split their time between New York City and the Hamptons, debating issues related to writing and bouncing ideas off one another.

At first Groom said nothing about his idea for a novel. As he told Louise Lague of *People*: "I wasn't going to say to all these famous writers: 'Hey, I want to write a novel too.'" Over breakfast one morning in 1976, Groom talked to Morris about *Better Times Than These*, his novel on Vietnam. Groom wrote the title on a napkin and Morris approved, signing and dating it. From that point Groom had enough confidence to send an outline of the novel to a publisher he knew, who promptly turned it down. Frustrated, Groom quit his job on the paper, moved to New York to write the book, and hired an agent. The novel was soon sold to Summit Books and was published in 1978 to mostly favorable reviews. *Better Times Than These*, according to *Publishers Weekly* (April 17, 1995), sold 60,000 copies in hardcover alone—an impressive outing even for an established novelist.

With a solid debut, Groom settled into the Manhattan-Hamptons literary set and began to write his next novel, *As Summers Die* (1980). The novel's setting is Mobile, Alabama, and the main character, Willie Croft, is a white small-town lawyer who is confronted with the quagmire of southern politics in the 1950s—a poor black family is struggling to keep their oil-rich land from a powerful white family. Croft defends the black family in the midst of controversy. Christopher Lehmann-Haupt, writing for the *New York Times* (October 6, 1980), criticized some of Groom's occasional "failures of syntax, diction, and tone" but overall gave the book a favorable review. "Mr. Groom has invented any number of lively touches. . . . But more than these touches, it is Mr. Groom's endorsement of the American Dream that is so appealing."

In 1983 Groom switched subjects again and co-authored a nonfiction work with Duncan Spencer—*Conversations with the Enemy: The Story of PFC Robert Garwood*. Garwood was a 19-year-old high-school dropout when he was captured by Communist villagers outside Danang in September 1965, just a few days before the end of his tour of duty, and subjected to all sorts of abuse. He learned to do many things in order to survive, including make medicinal teas from herbs, chew the slightly narcotic betel nut, and eat insects, snakes, and rats. Most useful of all he taught himself to speak Vietnamese—a skill that enabled him to communicate with his captors and become an intermediary between the other POWs and the Vietcong. This skill was not strictly beneficial, however, as the other American prisoners came to resent him for it. When he was finally released, in 1979—six years after 591 other POWs had returned home—Garwood was brought up on charges of treason and "having conversations with the enemy." Most of the charges were dropped, but Garwood was court-marshaled and dishonorably discharged. The reviewer for the *Chicago Tribune* (October 16, 1983) believed that "Groom and Spencer deal[t] intelligently with the serious issues of military discipline and of one's obligations to the self and to one's comrades under severe duress." The book was nominated for a Pulitzer Prize.

Groom's next book, *Only*, was published in the following year by Putnam. A memoir about his beloved dog, Fenwick, it was another departure from the types of books he had previously written. *Only* little prepared readers for his next novel, *Forrest Gump*. Groom attributes the idea for the novel to his father, who told him about a mentally impaired boy he knew when he was growing up who could do only one thing well—play the piano. Groom saw in his father's recollection the makings of a fantastic story, about the adventures of a man of subnormal intelligence. As he told the *Globe and Mail* (August 9 1994): "I sat down that same night and began writing *Forrest Gump*. It was the easiest book I've ever written. Basically, it just wrote itself." By the end of the evening he had written the first chapter. In three months he had completed the entire manuscript. The novel sold about 40,000 hardcover and paperback copies in the late 1980s. After the novel's publication, Groom had offers from Hollywood to turn his work into a film. He got as far as writing drafts of screenplays before interest cooled, due to the release of *Rain Man*, a 1988 film starring Dustin Hoffman and Tom Cruise, in which the former plays an idiot savant.

When asked by Lisa Addison of the *Globe and Mail* why the character Forrest Gump appeals to people, Groom explained: "Well, I think a lot of it has to do with the fact that the character has dignity. . . . The book and the movie both show a person who perseveres through all sorts of indignities." The character Gump captured the American imagination with the release of the 1994 film. Sales of the book rose to well over one million, and the buying public was clamoring for more writing about Gump. Groom delivered by publishing the companion volume *Gumpisms: The Wit and Wisdom of Forrest Gump* (1994), which includes such items as "Don't lick nothin' that sticks to your tongue." Groom told Michelle Bearden of *Publishers Weekly* that he was bothered by people's use of Gump's platitudes to make various points. "The funny thing is, I was trying to write a book, not send a message."

In 1988 Groom combined two of his previous themes—the South and Vietnam—in the novel *Gone the Sun*. The story follows the life of Beau Gunn, a failed playwright who has returned from New York City to his small hometown of Beinville, in the South, to take up the editorship of the town's newspaper. A veteran who is tormented by his past, Gunn suddenly finds himself trying to untangle a scandal involving murders, war, and political corruption. The reviews were mixed. The *New York Times* (August 3, 1988) reviewer Michiko Kakutani felt that Groom had unsuccessfully attempted to combine elements of two genres—psychological realism, which suggested higher literary aspirations, and suspense. "Instead of using what happened in Vietnam as a catalyst for examining Beau's psyche, . . . Mr. Groom tends to confine his discussions to problems Beau experiences in incorporating his memory of the war into a new play he's started writing. In fact, Mr. Groom spends very little time on any single aspect of Beau's life—he's too busy pelting the reader with new plot developments and complications."

After spending 1994 promoting the film *Forrest Gump*, Groom published two very different books in 1995. The first, *Shrouds of Glory*, was a nonfiction work focusing on the last great campaign of the Civil War—General Sherman's march to the sea. Groom, as ever, used a very unusual approach, telling the story from the perspective of the southern general Hood, who attempted to divert Sherman's mass destruction. Gary W. Gallagher, writing for the *New York Times Book Review* (April 16, 1995), noted a few historical flaws in *Shrouds of Glory* and had some reservations about the book's general tone. "Obviously captivated by his subject, he has unfortunately produced a superficially researched, error-ridden narrative that contributes little to the literature. The problem lies partly in Mr. Groom's predilection for Lost Cause arguments about outnumbered Confederates steadfastly resisting Yankee hordes."

Still, many reviews of the book were quite favorable. A writer for *New York Newsday* (May 7, 1995) remarked: "On his main subject Groom did serious research, and he has embodied it in an eloquent narrative." Patrick T. Reardon, a reporter for the *Chicago Tribune* (June 25, 1995), found the book to have great merit, partially because of Groom's skill, as a novelist, in infusing dry history with lively narrative. Reardon stated that the author "brings to his task the idiosyncratic sensibility of a fiction writer. Thus he is able, within the conventions of history writing, to infuse his storytelling with energy, surprise, freshness, and power."

Critics were a bit harsher on Groom's second book of 1995, *Gump and Co.*, This awaited sequel follows the adventures of Gump and his very intelligent son as they get involved with all sorts of historic figures and events—from the New Coke recipe to Oliver North and the Iran-Contra affair and even a meeting with Tom Hanks. The reviewer for the *Chicago Tribune* (August 29, 1995) believed that while reading the book, "you could almost hear the theme music playing and the cash registers ringing." Michiko Kakutani, adopting Gump's voice in her scathing review for the *New York Times* (August 15, 1995), wrote, "If I ain't oversteppin' my bounds, I wanna say that this new book *Gump and Co.* is stupid. Well, stupid is as stupid writes. And that's all I have to say about that."

There were favorable reviews, however. The critic for the *Washington Post* (September 5, 1995) found that Gump's adventures through 15 years of American history were as enjoyable as his first romp and called the book "a funny read. I think any people will enjoy and appreciate what it has to say about our times, our world, and ourselves."

In 1999 Groom published *Such a Pretty, Pretty Girl*, his second thriller. Unlike *Gone the Sun*, however, this book is "pleasantly thoughtless, told with wit and without pretense," according to *Kirkus Reviews* (January 15, 1999). *Such a Pretty, Pretty Girl* details the attempts of a Hollywood scriptwriter to discover who is penning threatening letters to his ex-lover Delia, a Los Angeles news anchor. *Booklist* (January 1, 1999) reviewer Donna Seaman was disappointed with the book, noting: "Groom is annoyingly ambivalent about his characters, especially Delia, and there is a sniggering ugliness to the entire tiresome tale."

Winston Groom has won many awards for his work, including the Best Fiction Award from the Southern Library Association for *As Summers Die* in 1980. He, along with his coauthor Duncan Spencer, was nominated for the 1994 Pulitzer Prize for Nonfiction for *Conversations with the Enemy*. In 1969 Groom married Ruth Noble, an importer, whom he divorced in 1974. He has been married to Anne-Clinton Bridges since 1987. They live in Point Clear, Alabama.
—C.M.

SUGGESTED READING: *Booklist* Jan. 1, 1999; *Chicago Tribune* VIII p33 Oct. 16, 1983, XIV p5 June 25, 1995, V p3 Aug. 29, 1995; *Globe and Mail* A p11 Aug. 9, 1994; *Kirkus Reviews* Jan. 15, 1999; *Library Journal* p 92 Sep. 15, 1995; *New York Newsday* p 37 May 7, 1995; *New York Times* Oct. 6, 1980, C p21 Aug. 3, 1988, C p13 Sep. 1, 1994, C p13 Apr. 10, 1995, C p15 Aug. 15, 1995; *New York Times Book Review* Apr. 16, 1995, p15 Sep. 10, 1995; *People* p 95+ Sept. 18, 1978; *Publishers Weekly* p430+ Aug. 12, 1988, p34+ Apr. 17, 1995; *Washington Post* D p1 Sep. 5, 1995; *Contemporary Authors* nrs vol. 50, 1996

SELECTED WORKS: Fiction—*Better Times Than These*, 1978; *As Summers Die*, 1980; *Only*, 1984; *Forrest Gump*, 1986; *Gone the Sun*, 1988; *Gumpisms: The Wit And Wisdom of Forrest Gump*, 1994; *Gump and Co.*, 1995; Nonfiction—*Conversations with the Enemy: The Story of PFC Robert Garwood* (with D. Spencer), 1983; *Shrouds of Glory*, 1995; *Such a Pretty, Pretty Girl*, 1999

Gün, Güneli

May 27, 1939 - Novelist, translator

The Turkish-born novelist Güneli Gün has aimed to express the soul of her people. Gün (her name is a pseudonym) has won praise both for her novels, *Book of Trances* (1979) and *On the Road to Baghdad* (1991), and for her translations of *Night* (1994), by Bilgé Karasu, and *The Black Book* (1995) and *The New Life* (1997), by Orhan Pamuk. In her *New York Times Book Review* (May 22, 1994) assessment of *Night*, Fernanda Eberstadt called Gün "the jauntiest of young Turkish-American novelists" and deemed Karasu's novel "beautifully translated."

In 1998 Güneli Gün composed the following statement (including both third- and first-person sections) for *World Authors 1990–1995*: "Turkish-American fiction writer, translator, and critic Güneli Gün was born on May 27, 1939 in Urfa but grew up in Izmir, where she spent eight years boarding at the American School for Girls, becoming bilingual under the tutelage of fiercely individualistic schoolmarms from New England. Her physician father, Mehmet Hilmi Tamkoç, the son of a wealthy land baron in the heartland, was a Young Turk whose idealism, patriotism, and Kemalism took the family to a number of Anatolian provinces, where he worked to bring hygiene and enlightenment to the obscure corners of the Turkish Republic. Her mother, Şevkiye Alca, was born into the family of the mayor of a sea-resort town of Çeşme on the Aegean.

"Although my mother came from a traditional Ottoman family dead set in its ways, she was also a brave new Turk, whose wit and style put her husband somewhat in the shade, volunteering in province after province for charitable work and to serve as a role model in terms of dress and attitude consistent with Atatürk reforms. It isn't odd that a pair of 'modern' Turkish parents felt, like many in their generation and class, that a second language and culture were essential in rearing their children to become 'Westernized.'"

Gün's natural bent for both art and the theater, along with her passion for literature and philosophy, took her to the United States, where she satisfied her interest in the liberal arts by studying at an American university. She earned her bachelor's degree from Hollies, a women's college in Virginia that is known for its excellence in creative writing. Her professors there included the writer Louis D.

Rubin, the poet John Alexander Allen, the critic John Aldridge, and the novelist William Golding. She earned advanced degrees from the University of Iowa Writers' Workshop and Johns Hopkins University, in Baltimore, where she studied with John Barth, who shared with her a predilection for the fictional material known as the "Thousand and One Nights."

Gün set for herself an exceedingly difficult task: to write in a language she had not heard at her mother's knee. Among writers who have chosen to abandon their mother tongues, only a handful have succeeded in getting their adopted culture to take them seriously as contenders in the literary arena. "But I felt it was something I had to do," Gün has said. "I knew the whole world hated 'the Turk' because the world could not hear what we had to say, projecting on our silence the worst of human faults. I decided I'd have to learn how to make the world listen to us through a language comprehensible to the dominant cultures: English, which I consider the most inclusive and the most playful of all the languages known to man."

Her first novel, *Book of Trances*, was published in London in 1979 and was well received by British critics. This novel's form is allied with the school of magical realism as practiced by South American writers; it was soon translated into Spanish. Gün dedicated her first "trance" to Gabriel García Márquez (whose influence she acknowledges on the very first page), because she felt it was Márquez who taught the Third World writers how to tell their stories to the First World. The second "trance" is dedicated to Idries Shah, the intellectual proponent of Sufism in the West, who led her to her cultural past. In her statement for *World Authors*, she wrote, "Not only have I been severed from my culture, having lived away from my homeland, modern Turkish culture has also been severed from its Ottoman past, both in terms of language and religion. Islam was palatable to me only by virtue of Sufism, which is a form of Gnostic thought and provides food for rebellious minds. I realized this was also true for Islam as understood by Anatolian Turks, as opposed to the Arabs who 'own' the language of the Koran as it was 'inspired' by God.

"Realizing that there are many forms of Islamism, as well as nationalism and feminism, was a truly liberating moment for me. I found my way back to the origins of things through Sufi philosophy, which is so infused into Turkish language and culture that it is hidden only to eyes that cannot perceive it. *Book of Trances* is not only the recital of my entrancement with history but also my entrancement with the English language, through which I retrieved my fictional materials. I had grown up hearing the orally transmitted stories told by the Anatolian folk who had learned to survive, in a country where there is little money and less oil, through their own resourcefulness, industry, and stoicism. I loved and admired our 'iron-belted people' and the folklore that gave them the courage to live their difficult lives. As I too was always in transit like my nomadic ancestors, who survived by opening and transforming their hearts, I identified greatly with the ways of the people of the heartland. It was the impulse to let the world also see, hear and, yes, even love my people that led me to write *Book of Trances.*"

With her picaresque novel *On the Road to Baghdad* came greater visibility, as it was translated into a dozen European languages. Hitting her stride as storyteller who has "begged borrowed and stolen" from the "Thousand and One Nights." Gün traced the life story of Huru, a 16th-century minstrel, who, disguised as a male, journeyed from Istanbul to Baghdad. Huru, John Allen wrote in *World Literature Today* (Winter 1992), "takes us back most appropriately to that fount of the story-teller's art, Scheherazade, in 16th century Baghdad. This legendary figure, who becomes best friends with the heroine, may have been waiting all these years for a worthy disciple to bring her into the present. . . . In giving Scheherazade new presence and reality, Ms. Gün has put together a tour de force of lively and ingenious yarn-spinning, of events that conceal the inevitable as the bizarre. . . . She has captured the message of every authentic teller of tales: that there is order in the world, whether we know it or not, and that miracles are what give life reality." As poet Richard Howard put it in the *Hollies Critic* (April 1992), "Our circumlocutory Circe frames her astonishing tale, in part historical romance, in part a mystical quest, and in part a narrative of personal liberation. . . . [T]his intricate fable manages to confront the nomadic virtues of the Turks with Ottoman imperial culture; the horrors of a particularly violent epoch. . . . [T]he author flings us from Selim the Grim (1512) to Rumi and returns us to the convulsive 'present' of Scheherazade. . . . Trance and transformation are the rule here, not merely for the heroine and her friends, but for the author herself . . . 'despite my longings for fame and fortune, despite my feminist lingo, despite the many forms of chauvinism from which I suffer—I've been taken beyond myself.' It is a religious acknowledgment, one which recurs throughout the text, in various ways, sometimes ruefully, sometimes gingerly, sometimes eagerly, but always with the hope of messages from 'the Invisible Teachers who instruct my heart.'"

On the question of the fundamentalist Islamic ideology of our times, Talat Halman wrote in the book's foreword, "*On the Road to Baghdad* is a more sophisticated alternative to *The Satanic Verses*. Rushdie launches a frontal attack; Gün circumvents, which is a more effective way. Rushdie's is a work of high dudgeon, Gün's of irrepressible high spirits." In the *New Statesman and Society*, (May 31, 1991), Lucasta Miller termed the novel "a worthy feminist tract." "But," Miller added, "this is a novel that kicks against the stereotype.

It's got all the intertextuality and cross-cultural feminism—but it's funny, warm, and whimsical as well . . . a powerful parable about the capacity of the female voice to free itself from the silence imposed by history. . . . Out of the fables of Huru the minstrel and [Scheherazade] the storyteller, Güneli Gün has woven a powerful parable about the capacity of the female voice to free itself from the silence imposed by history." In the *Times Literary Supplement*, Aamer Hussein wrote, "Huru glorifies the Turkish national spirit. . . . That these beliefs are Huru's, conditioned by place and time, rather than the author's, can be assumed by the vociferous presence of Scheherazade, a constant reminder of the continuing influence of the colonized. Gün's reconstruction of a vanished age celebrates cultural distinctions (among Islamic peoples) as well as pluralism, eclecticism and multiple voices." Hussein concluded, "Gün's magical chronicle of 16th-century Baghdad . . . is an intricately woven tapestry, decorated with the spiritual and poetic metaphors of the great civilizations of the Arabs, the Persians and of their conquerors and inheritors, the Turks. . . . It is to Gun's credit that . . . she suggests the sweep of the grand narratives with a plethora of signs and allusions and succeeds in her main task, singing the spirit of an indomitable woman of her people."

In response, Gün has said, "Even the West is beginning to revise its negative view of the Ottoman Empire, the first successful multinational empire whose staying power came from its inclusiveness. Unlike the other great European empires, the Ottomans did not exclude or look down on the nations under their rule. Not only were they tolerant of other cultures and religions, they relished diversity—an extremely contemporary outlook that present-day Turkey could do very well to learn. On the other hand, I too am both fascinated and repelled by the cruel streak that runs through Ottoman history. It's like being in love with a powerful but manipulative man who pushes you away while he pulls you to him, producing in you a terrible obsession. Selim the Grim is a perfect embodiment of this kind of man as well as being the perfect flower of his culture. As a feminist, I know that Selim is a harmful man as a lover. But he can teach a woman a great deal about power and the way the world works. He is a good mentor, but don't ask of him to be a devoted or constant husband."

Gün translated into English the Turkish novelist Orhan Pamuk's *The Black Book* and *The New Life*. She has also translated *Night* by Bilgé Karasu, which won Mobil's 1994 Pegasus literary prize. "I think of myself as a novelist who does translations from time to time," Gün told *World Authors*, "but in fact I've spent the last three years translating three major novels. But I've been reluctant to admit to it. Why? Well, as a writer I'm applauded for being an unruly and disobedient practitioner of literature, but as a translator I'm expected to act the part of a docile handmaiden who obediently renders someone else's 'immortal' words from one language into another for the sheer love of it. The hours are long, the pay is poor, and the praise scanty. To hire out as a contract translator is to agree to become invisible. So, I have opted for becoming visible by annexing the translation to my own literary output by loaning to the translated author my own voice which I've worked out in my own fiction, rendering a translated text that's accurate, yet completely transformed. My conscience is clear about imposing my voice on the original because I consider the translation a 'second original.' Postmodernist critics such as Roland Barthes have taught us that the act of reading is the death of the author and the birth of the critic because, after all, the author is merely the scriptor of a text. Pushing Barthes's notion into the field of translation, one might say that if the author is the scriptor and the translator the trans-scriptor, then the act of translation must be the death of the scriptor and the birth of the transcriptor."

Güneli Gün is married to David Hershiser, a psychologist and associate dean at Oberlin College, in Ohio. Their son, Carl Mehmet Hershiser, is an anthropologist. Gün has taught at Middle East University in Ankara as well as at Oberlin College, giving workshops in creative writing and translation and teaching courses in feminist studies.

SUGGESTED READING: *American Review* July/Aug. 1989; *Guardian* May 23, 1991; *Hollins Critic* Apr. 1992; *Iris* Spring/Summer 1991; *Literary Review* May 1991; *New Statesman & Society* p38 May 31, 1991; *TASG News* Nov. 1991; *Times Literary Supplement* p23 May31, 1991; *World Literature*, Winter 1992; *The World and I* Aug. 1991; "Why I Do What I Do," Güneli Gün, paper given at American Literary Translator's Association Conference, Bloomington, Indiana, 1996

SELECTED WORKS: *Book of Trances*, 1979; *On the Road to Baghdad*, 1991; Translations: Karasu, Bilgé. *Night*, 1994; Pamuk, Orhan. *The Black Book*, 1995, *The New Life*, 1997

Gur, Batya

1947– Mystery writer; professor

Batya Gur's mysteries explore closed, insular societies in Israel—the Jerusalem Psychoanalytic Institute, the literature department at the Hebrew University of Jerusalem, the kibbutz, and most recently, the world of musicians. Her intelligent plotting and vivid descriptions of Jerusalem and its populace have sparked the resurgence of the detective novel in Israeli literature. The translations of her first three Michael Ohayon mysteries—*The Saturday Morning Murder: A Psychoanalytic Case* (1992), *Literary Murder: A Critical Case* (1993), and

Murder on a Kibbutz: A Communal Case (1994)—have made her one of Israel's best-selling authors abroad.

Batya Gur was born in 1947 in Tel Aviv, Israel, the daughter of Holocaust survivors. She studied Hebrew literature and history at the Hebrew University in Jerusalem. After receiving her undergraduate degree, she taught high school literature and lived in the United States for a time. Then, at the age of 39, Gur tired of teaching, and became disenchanted with her master's thesis on the Israeli poet Natan Zack (although she later earned her master's degree). She decided to try writing fiction.

In 1988 Gur published *The Saturday Morning Murder: A Psychoanalytic Case*, in Hebrew. She chose to write a mystery because she felt, as paraphrased by an interviewer for *Panim: Faces of Art and Culture in Israel* (March/April 1996), "it's the least presumptive genre." "If I failed," Gur explained, "no one would notice." The book certainly did not fail, and a version was eventually filmed for television. *The Saturday Morning Murder* introduces Detective Michael Ohayon, a recently divorced 38-year-old born in Morocco. He studied at Cambridge but left before he completed his doctoral thesis, about guilds in the Middle Ages, in order to take care of his family. He is also involved in a doomed affair with a married woman. Ohayon investigates the murder of Eva Neidorf, a noted professor at the Jerusalem Psychoanalytic Institute, who was murdered on a quiet Sabbath morning in Jerusalem. The detective, believing that the professor may have been murdered by one of her colleagues who was jealous of her, must learn about the methods of psychoanalysis and then interrogate every suspect in the hopes of uncovering the true murderer.

The book came out in the U.S. in 1992. American critics were generally pleased by Gur's first novel. Herbert Mitgang of the *New York Times* (August 26, 1992) noted, "In *The Saturday Morning Murder*, the reader encounters independent Jerusalem characters, picks up a smattering of psychoanalysis, finds that the old streets of the city are especially suitable for a mystery, and is left with a wish to meet Chief Inspector Ohayon on his next case." Reviewing the book for *New York Newsday* (July 21, 1992), Shalom Goldman wrote, "When you pick up *The Saturday Morning Murder* and curl up on your own couch, rest assured you are in reliable hands—this is an exciting, instructive, and entertaining novel."

Gur's second mystery, *Literary Murder: A Critical Case*, was published in Israel in 1989 and reached the U.S. in 1993. This installment found Ohayon investigating the link between the murder of Shaul Tirosh, a celebrated Hebrew-language poet who has been bludgeoned, and the death of the poet's protégé, Iddo Dudai, while scuba diving. At first the motive for Tirosh's death seems to be his womanizing: he was involved with two of his colleagues' wives, including Dudai's, and with a graduate student, but Ohayon believes that the answer lies somewhere else. Hebrew University's literary department is rife with jealousies and rivalries. Ohayon decides to learn all he can about the legendary poet, in hopes of discovering who had the most compelling reason to kill him. Like Gur's earlier work, this one reaped much praise in the press. A critic for *Kirkus Reviews* (October 1, 1993) wrote that "the characters' finely detailed moral intrigues pay off in the end." Reviewing the work for *Booklist* (November 15, 1993), Jay Freeman wrote, "Gur . . . knows academia well, and she uses it as a foil to illustrate the social and cultural tensions that permeate Israeli life. At the same time, she tells a fine detective yarn, keeping her cards well hidden until the end, deftly setting up the reader for twists, turns, and surprises." Dan Cryer, a critic for *New York Newsday* (November 22, 1993), noted that "[Gur] knows how various and complicated anyone can be, how the self can be hidden even from its ostensible owner, how the masks we wear display or distort reality. By revealing what's behind self-delusion or role-playing, Gur provides pleasure of a very high order indeed."

Gur's next installment in the series was *Murder on a Kibbutz: A Communal Case* (1991 in Israel, 1994 in the U.S.). Detective Ohayon visits a kibbutz, a close-knit religious community, to investigate the murder of its administrative secretary, who was poisoned in the kibbutz's medical clinic. Ohayon is told time and again by the elders of the community that he could not possibly understand life on a kibbutz, where all 300 members consider one another family. The detective soon realizes, however, that a kibbutz family is the same as any other family, with unsurprising distinctions between the young and old, and with plenty of internal secrets, prejudices, and even enmities. One suspect is Aaron Meroz, a man considered a traitor to the kibbutz, who joined the group as a young man but left a few years later. Meroz, now a lawyer in the government, has recently renewed his acquaintance with many of the people on the kibbutz, including the dead woman. Aside from Meroz, Ohayon must also look for suspects among the kibbutz members, some of whom the victim had alarmed with her reformist ideas about kibbutz life—particularly the proposal that children sleep in their parents' home. Marilyn Stasio of the *New York Times Book Review* (December 11, 1994) wrote that "Ms. Gur . . . can grab readers with dry discussions of 'egalitarian elitism' and fussy deliberations over who picks the peaches and who cuts the dress patterns—seemingly simple housekeeping matters that actually reflect earthshaking political and ideological changes transforming kibbutz society." In the *Chicago Tribune* (December 28, 1994), Nancy Pate proclaimed that "Much of the fascination lies with Gur's knowledge of life on the kibbutz, letting readers view it first through Meroz's eyes and then through Ohayon's. This is a well-written, meaty story, dense with character and plot."

Gur's most recent works are a literary novel, *Lo kach tiarti li*, which has not yet appeared in translation, and her fourth novel in the Ohayon series, *Murder Duet*, which was published in the United States in early 1999 and deals with conflicts among professional classical musicians.—C.M.

SUGGESTED READING: *Booklist* Nov. 15, 1993; *Chicago Tribune* V p6 Dec. 28, 1994; *Kirkus Reviews* Oct. 1, 1993; *New York Newsday* p40+ July 21, 1992, p48 Nov. 22, 1993; *New York Times* C p17 Aug. 26, 1992; *New York Times Book Review* p7 Dec. 26, 1993, p38 Dec. 11, 1994; *Panim: Faces of Art and Culture in Israel* Mar./Apr. 1996

SELECTED WORKS: *The Saturday Morning Murder: A Psychoanalytic Case*, 1992; *Literary Murder: A Critical Case*, 1993; *Murder on a Kibbutz: A Communal Case*, 1994; *Murder Duet*, 1999

Hagedorn, Jessica Tarahata

1949– Novelist; poet; screenwriter

A self-defined "hybrid" Filipino-American, Jessica Tarahata Hagedorn—contemporary novelist, poet, screenwriter, musician, and performance artist—was born in Manila but has lived in the United States since the age of 14, when she came with her siblings and recently divorced mother to live in San Francisco. From her "discovery" as a promising teenage poet by Kenneth Rexroth in the 1960s, to her years as leader and lyricist of the Gangster Choir rock band, to her recent prominence as an exponent of multiculturalism with a hip Asian-American sensibility, Jessica Hagedorn has become, in the words of Ishmael Reed, a "vanguard artist" who writes "the kinds of novels that will be written in the next century." The response to her writing has been mixed, however: some critics see her as an avatar of the new multicultural mosaic that is emerging in end-of-millennium America, while others dismiss her as a polemicist for a bewildering pop-culture cacophony of ethnic, class, and sexual disorientation. There is no escaping these issues in her writings, for they form the substratum of both her novels, *Dogeaters* (1990), a cinematic montage of narrative, dialogue, newspaper clippings, and historical allusions about the underbelly flamboyance of Marcos-era Manila; and *The Gangster of Love* (1996), a transparently autobiographical work about her own coming-of-age as a Filipino immigrant in an American rock band. Jessica Hagedorn has also written several novellas and performance pieces, and her poetry has appeared in numerous anthologies since Rexroth included her youthful verse in *Four Young Women* (1972). The versatile author also edited *Charlie*

Chan Is Dead: An Anthology of Contemporary Asian American Fiction (1993) and, in 1992, wrote the screenplay for Shu Lea Chang's independent feature film *Fresh Kill*. In 1996 she was described as "one of the country's high priestesses of multicultural literature" by Sonemi Sengupta, who interviewed her for the *New York Times* (December 4, 1996).

Although Jessica Hagedorn's move from Manila—where she was born in 1949—to San Francisco was an abrupt one, she counted it fortunate that her mother chose to settle in a cosmopolitan, multiethnic city with a Chinatown that reminded her of home. She told an interviewer: "I realized that one of the positive things about it was that as a female person, I suddenly had a sense of freedom that I never had growing up in Manila in that overprotected colonial environment—the girl with her chaperones and everything that still goes on, that kind of tradition." Hollywood films and comic books also had a major influence in her childhood years; the opening scene of *Dogeaters* recreates the 1956 screening of *All That Heaven Allows*, starring Rock Hudson and Jane Wyman, in a Manila cinema. "I think [film] was a great colonial tool," she said. "Even if it was entertainment, and it was, an industry that was begun out of a desire to entertain and to make money. Somewhat innocent in that way. Crass but innocent. Yet, I think it's a wonderful way to seduce the minds and the hearts of the people. It's a very powerful medium."

Later, she would come under the spell of modern Latin Americans writers, commenting that "They are very close in terms of voice—their humor, their fatalism, their . . . well, that over-used term 'magical realism'. . . . The way they can use language and visions and surrealism without being corny, and the humor that's always there, is very close to a Filipino sensibility." Her response to being "turned on" by Gabriel García Márquez's *One Hundred Years of Solitude*: "It was like holy communion or something."

As a child Jessica liked to write stories for comic books, which she also illustrated, as well as poems. At 14, after her mother had given her a typewriter, a family friend sent some of Jessica's poems to a journalist who in turn sent them on to Kenneth Rexroth, the doyen of the Bay Area's literary scene. Rexroth, who lived in the neighborhood, invited Jessica and her mother for dinner. Hagedorn recalled: "I found out that he was this wonderful poet and semicontroversial, which of course appealed to my rebellious nature and I thought, 'Oh, yummy, you know. It's not some corny old guy.'" Rexroth encouraged her to read other writers and soon convinced her that her vocation was to be an artist. With a "very romantic notion of art, that it was a higher calling," she chose not to pursue a college degree but instead enrolled in a two-year acting and theater-arts program at the American Conservatory Theater.

Hagedorn had always liked contemporary music, and in 1975 she formed her own rock band, Gangster Choir, singing Sly and the Family Stone songs and doing performance pieces with Ntozake Shange. With the help of her friend, the composer Julian Priester, the band soon became a fixture in the Bay Area's poetry and music scene. When asked whether she brought anything of poetry and music into her fiction, she acknowledged it to be "Rhythm. And I think the love of language, the sheer word play. I love words. The sound of words, and puns. It's very Filipino, too. Filipinos love puns and word plays and they love language, the intonations and the nuances." After her move to New York in 1980, she and some colleagues reformed the band to play at CBGB, The Mudd Club, and other new-wave venues. "I just figured, if Sid Vicious can sing, I can sing too," she said. Her experiences as part of the frenetic club scene in downtown Manhattan and elsewhere are fictionally recast in her second novel, *The Gangster of Love.* But it was her first novel, *Dogeaters,* that catapulted her to national attention. Nominated for a National Book Award and drawing its title from a derogatory term for Filipinos, the novel is a transgressive and raucous narrative of "when Hollywood dreams and tropical nightmares violently collide." She began writing the novel when her daughter was born: "Maybe having a child made me realize that I might be old enough to attempt a mature work." *Dogeaters* generously mixes fact and fiction and peppers its nonlinear plot with news clippings, speeches by President McKinley, and military-junta soap-opera scripts. "I play with what is considered fake and made-up and actual facts of history," Hagedorn has admitted. Defending her adventurous methodology in an essay in Philomena Mariani's *Critical Fictions: The Politics of Imaginative Writing*, she wrote: "For us [Filipinos] there is no either/or, for us there is both/and, with many levels happening at the same time." She added: "I wrote *Dogeaters* on my own terms, in the English I reclaim as a Filipino: the English mixed with Spanish and Tagalog. I did not want to use a glossary. I sought to subvert, exorcize, celebrate. Taking on the voices of characters from all levels of society, using fragments of overheard dialogue, newspaper clippings, found historical documents, soap-opera plots, the script for a radio melodrama as foreground for the torture and rape of a young woman. The litany of prayer is both sacred and profane."

Though critics praised *Dogeaters* for its edge, comic energy, and passionate mockery of despotism, many found flaws in the novel's structure and presentation. Blanche d'Alpuget wrote in the *New York Times Book Review* (March 25, 1990) that "Much of the book has the feeling of a roman à clef. . . . The exoticisms become tiresome, more a nervous tic than a desire to make connection across the gulf of culture. That said, *Dogeaters* remains a rich small feast of a book." And John Updike wrote in the *New Yorker* (March 18, 1991): "In general, despite some amusing business with aspects of popular culture, and a few felt characterizations, the disparate materials of *Dogeaters* are not very skillfully handled, certainly not skillfully enough to earn the distinction conferred upon it as an NBA finalist." Others, like Jaimy Gordon in the *American Book Review* (November/December 1990), were annoyed by the untranslated polyglot references, while admitting that they seem "to rise right out of the cacophonous streets" and are a "small price to pay for a splendid ride."

Hagedorn has collaborated on several film and video projects over the years and in 1992 wrote the screenplay for *Fresh Kill*, Shu Lea Chang's eco-apocalyptic film about two lesbian parents trudging through a dystopian, toxic-shock world of environmental terrorism in a punk-surreal, very un-Kansaslike New York. The title, derived from the Dutch word for "fresh stream," is a mock allusion to a notorious floating "ghost-ship" garbage barge that plied East Coast waters in the early 1990s in search of landfill. The following year, Hagedorn edited and wrote the introduction to *Charlie Chan Is Dead: An Anthology of Contemporary Asian American Fiction*, published by Penguin. Despite criticism over her uneven choice of writers to be included, the anthology is considered a good general introduction to its genre.

Her second novel, *Gangster of Love*, a "disappointed immigrant" story, in the words of Maureen Corrigan of the *Nation* (October 28, 1996), follows the exploits of Raquel "Rocky" Rivera, a Filipino emigrée and rock star–wannabe whose life story bears more than a casual resemblance to that of Hagedorn herself. The novel begins as Raquel and her elder brother, Voltaire, are spirited off to America by this mother, Milagros, seeking a new life away from Milagros's unfaithful husband at home. Rocky links up with another rock star, Elvis Chang, and the rest of the book chronicles their discordant romp through the druggy landscape of rock-club gigs on the far side of "Brady Bunch" America ("All camera angles and lighting for these travel pix of America courtesy of Diane Arbus," wrote Corrigan). While reviewers appreciated the novel's subject matter and the milieu it attempted to portray, some expressed discomfort with what they considered to be its structural flaws. *Publishers Weekly* (June 10, 1966) called it "long-awaited but ultimately disappointing," adding, "While Hagedorn's first novel utilized multiple perspectives and collage techniques to great effect, here her occasional shifts in points of view seem motivated mainly by an ability to keep her somewhat meandering novel moving along. . . . Offering little in the way of plot, the book's narcissistic characters and bohemian milieu soon begin to wear thin." But Francine Prose, in the *New York Times Book Review* (September 15, 1996), praised its "racketing, jittery energy" and "the jaunty ease with which it blends ethnic and pop culture, religion and politics, to form a variegated backdrop that impinges, gently but relentlessly, upon her characters' lives," all while asking "serious questions about family, exile, identity, about the problems of learning to operate in another language."

Such questions of identity have engaged Jessica Hagedorn from the start, for she came to America on the first wave of the great immigration surge from Asia and Latin America that began in the mid-1960s—and that changed the complexion of a nation that had heretofore been peopled mostly by the descendants of European immigrants and African slaves. She told Sonemi Sengupta for the *New York Times* (December 4, 1996): "Maybe it's the more positive side of appropriation: you take from many different sources, not to steal, but to pay homage to it, to say those are your influences, to add your own thing. I don't believe in sampling some Tibetan music just to make it sound groovy, but you do your homework, you understand what you're doing with it."

Some of Hagedorn's compatriots have failed to appreciate her bluntness. Once, when accosted by a finger-pointing Filipino heckler shouting "*J'accuse*" for her use of the derogatory term "dogeaters," she replied: "I know, I know. I set the race back 400 years." Recalling this incident for Sengupta, she said, "What is literature for? You don't go to literature and say I need to feel good about my race, so let me read a novel." She added, "If you're too reverent, the art doesn't grow."

When asked by Kay Bonetti to describe her background for an interview with American *Audio Prose Library* (April 1994), Hagedorn replied: "I'm part Spanish. My paternal grandfather came from Spain via Singapore to Manila. On my mother's side, it's more mixture, with a Filipino mother and a father who was Scotch-Irish-French; you know, white American hybrid. And I also have on my father's side a great-great-grandmother who was Chinese. So, I'm a hybrid." In *Danger and Beauty* (1993), a collection of her poetry and prose, Hagedorn described herself in this fashion: "I was born in the Philippines. I am a quintessential bastard. My roots are dubious," and she explained further to Bonetti, "I'm an underdog person, so I align myself with those who seem not to be considered valuable in polite society. I think for a lot of so-called post-colonial peoples, there's a feeling of not being quite legitimate, of not being pure enough. And to me that's the beauty and strength of the culture—it's mixed." As she told Bonetti: "I write because I have to, and if the writing also destroys some of those myths and subverts forms and makes people question the very idea of the writer, the woman, the Filipino-American, the whatever, great!"

—E. M.

SELECTED READING: *American Book Review* p16 Nov./Dec. 1990; *Nation* p64+ Oct. 28, 1996; *New York Times* A p15 Jan. 13, 1992, C p1+ Dec. 4, 1996 with photo; *New York Times Book Review* p1+ Mar. 25, 1990; *New York Times Magazine* p17 May 10, 1992; *New Yorker* p102+ Mar. 18, 1991; *Village Voice* p33+ June 7, 1988, with photos

SELECTED BOOKS: Fiction—*Dogeaters*, 1990; *The Gangster of Love*, 1996; Screenplays—*Fresh Kill*, 1992; As editor—*Charlie Chan Is Dead: An Anthology of Contemporary Asian American Fiction*, 1993

Dede Hatch Photography

Hall, Brian

Aug. 31, 1959– Nonfiction writer; novelist

American travel writer and novelist Brian Hall has often been praised for his eye for detail. He first received notice for his travel book *Stealing from a Deep Place* (1988), in which he vividly recounted his travels through Eastern Europe at the end of the Cold War. Hall followed that work with a novel, *The Dreamers* (1989), which was lauded by critics but failed to find a wide audience. In *The Impossible Country* (1994), another travelogue, he described the disintegration of Yugoslavia. Hall's next book-length work was *The Saskiad* (1997), a coming-of-age novel about an adolescent girl who models her search for her father on Homer's *The Odyssey*. Most recently the author published *Madeleine's World* (1997), a study of his daughter's life from birth to age three.

In an autobiographical statement submitted to *World Authors 1990–1995* in January 1998, Brian Hall writes: "I was born in 1959, and had a placid childhood growing up in Lexington, Massachusetts. My family hardly ever went anywhere— not even the ten miles into Boston—and as the years rolled by, all in the same house, I played in the unchanging yard, advanced with my cohort through the public school, practiced the piano, did my homework, watched megajoules of television, read science fiction, feared bullies, and craved (and won) the approval of my parents and teachers. I was provident, so lacking in desire for anything beyond what I already had that after four years of running a paper route that paid me less than ten dollars a week, I had two thousand dollars in the bank, which I continued to sit on, clueless, until at last I used a small fraction of it to pay for a second month of music camp two summers in a row. (The rest was swallowed by college.) I liked that camp, full of bully-fearing children like me, but at the same time, whenever I was there I would have fierce, longing visions of my yard and my house that left a hollow pain in my chest. Later, in college and on the road, I had a recurrent dream of the distant future, in which, wandering through an alien and ruined landscape, I would come upon that house, still exactly the same, but empty and cobwebbed. I would wander through it, and both an intense nostalgia and an odd relief would permeate me at the thought that that life, my fossilized childhood, was all over now, that I could sift through the remains without anyone bothering me.

"I mention all this because the aching ambivalence about home and belonging—the nostalgia for a nest that can also be a trap, and for an immutability that is also a kind of idiocy and death—is reflected in my writing.

"I never wrote creatively or kept a journal while I was growing up. I knew no one who did anything like that. Through high school I thought I would be a scientist, like my father, but at college—I went to Harvard, partly because it was so close—I switched to English, and spent four years trying to catch up with classmates who'd been reading Dickens back when I was reading Asimov. I loved the literature but disliked the critical papers I had to write, gave up plans for graduate school, and by senior year I was out of ideas for my life. I liked watching other people carve out their lives while I remained uncommitted, but doubted anyone would pay me to do that.

"Perhaps ideas were elsewhere, and I suddenly conceived an urge to run away. Fortuitously, I won a Harvard travel fellowship, then worked three jobs for six months to supplement it and socked away ten thousand dollars. I got on a plane with a bicycle, a tent, and a camping stove and spent the next two years pedaling from England to Greece and from Italy to the top of Norway. I camped in fields and grew so lonely I talked to my stove, but I found something congenial in loneliness, that familiar hollow pain. My greatest pleasure was to meet people who had defined their lives, to spend some time with them, and then to bike away, shedding them.

"Perhaps I was fleeing more than I was seeking, but in that flight lay the idea that had eluded me. In retrospect, it was obvious: I wanted to observe from a safe place, to remain hidden, to dip into lives and leave them. I could become either a sociopath or a writer. If I succeeded as the latter, someone would pay me to do it. I returned to Boston to try.

"Having no experience with creative writing, I started cautiously, writing about my travels in Eastern Europe. This allowed me to practice voice and pacing without having to worry about plot and character motivation. My pacing, in fact, was all wrong, the manuscript was much too long, and no one bought it for two years until a patient editor saw a book buried in there and led me to it, and published it as *Stealing from a Deep Place*. By then I had also written a novel, entitled *The Dreamers*. Still practicing, I had chosen a protagonist somewhat like me: passive, watchful, with fantasies of invulnerability. I gave him a childhood more prisonlike than mine and set him adrift in exile in his 20s. Then I let him drift into a disaster that centered on problems of belonging and commitment.

"By this point, against all my expectations, I had gotten happily married and had settled in Ithaca, New York, where I felt at home. The irony of finding my spiritual home in story-telling and my physical home in the namesake of Odysseus's island, the Ur-home of western narrative, was too much to keep out of a novel, and I wrote *The Saskiad*, about a 12-year-old girl named Saskia who searches for a home partly by constructing around herself an epic into which she fits as the heroine, an epic she models on *The Odyssey*. Unfortunately, I had once again misjudged the pace, and couldn't sell the bloated manuscript. So I turned again to travel writing—my last chance before the planned arrival of children—and chose Yugoslavia. I was drawn to its ethnic tensions because extreme nationalism can be seen as an infantile, sociopathic form of the urge to belong. Yugoslavia disintegrated while I was in it, and my book, *The Impossible Country*, in part describes how various peoples' attempts to define their homes (or homelands) caused them to pull their common house down on their own heads.

"Back at my own home, two daughters came, and my writing slowed. I shortened *The Saskiad* and finally sold it. I had a career and a family, and instead of feeling trapped, I felt enmeshed, a mostly pleasurable sensation made possible by my daily escape into other lives. Approaching middle age, watching my children morph, I now fretted over time rather than place. My most recent book, *Madeleine's World*, is about the growth of consciousness of a baby and toddler (my daughter), culminating in the human awareness of time, change, and death. The book itself, of course, is an effort to thwart time, to create a fossil of a different childhood."

———————————

Brian Hall's debut work, *Stealing from a Deep Place*, was published in 1988. The first section of the book focuses on his bike travels through Romania during the reign of the dictator Nicolae Ceausescu. While never taking his eye from the larger political problems, Hall reported on the lives of individual people. Sad, amusing, and bizarre things occur as Hall's journey takes him to several other nations, including Bulgaria and Hungary. First he is accosted by a Romanian woman who pleads with him to deliver a letter to an Englishman in the West who is the father of her child. Later Hall encounters a Bulgarian con man who actually tries to help him get his bike repaired, and a monk named Yordan whose hospitality may be motivated by amorous intentions. Critics picked up on Hall's deft interpretations of people and events, and praised his work. Many agreed with Walter Goodman, who wrote in the *New York Times* (August 29, 1988) that the travel book "is not orthodox touring stuff, but very enlightening. . . . Here, as elsewhere, Mr. Hall takes notes of some of the sights . . . but keeps his eye mainly on people and politics."

Critics also applauded Hall's first novel, *The Dreamers* (1989). Its main character, Eric, is supposed to be in Vienna studying the Holocaust, but instead he finds himself taking care of a young Austrian woman named Jutta and her son. As life with Jutta becomes more torturous, Eric struggles to keep her small family together, but finds himself slowly sinking into a life of decadence in the seediest parts of Vienna. As the novel ends, both the young man and the reader discover how such situations can suddenly spiral out of control. Lisa Forestier, reviewing the novel for the *New York Times Book Review* (April 23, 1989), noted that "What breaks through the turbid romantic world of *The Dreamers* is the clear and aching truth that all the hero's grand and idealistic ambitions should have coalesced in the power to keep one human soul from sliding through his hands. In this time of minimalist fiction, Mr. Hall's novel is a welcome change." Ursula Hegi of the *Los Angeles Times* (March 19, 1989) called the author "a remarkable young writer" and praised the book as "a brilliant and unsettling first novel."

Although Hall received high praise in the press, his first two books did not sell well. Because of his financial situation, Hall made the difficult decision to shelve the manuscript of his novel *The Saskiad*. "It was clear," he told *Publishers Weekly* (January 13, 1997), "that nonfiction was the way to make money." His next travel book, *The Impossible Country: A Journey through the Last Days of Yugoslavia* (1994), developed out of an article he was commissioned to write for the *New York Times Magazine* in 1989. At the beginning of Hall's book, skirmishes due to ethnic prejudice have brought Yugoslavia to the brink of self-destruction; Hall documented the movement toward civil war on both a national and a human scale. Although Hall acknowledged and emphasized the differences among the three main groups—Muslims, Croats, and Serbs—he also often expressed his own frustration at the factions' unwillingness to get along, and their seeming desire for violence and war. Hall explained in detail the events that led up to the Yugoslavian crisis in a style that is easily accessible to the layperson. Anna Husarska of the *New York Times* (August 21, 1994) deemed *The Impossible Country* "intelligent, witty and full of precious details delivered in a light style," and also noted that it "provides indispensable background for understanding the people who fill the daily reports from the front lines." While most critics were generally pleased with the book, some, like Faye Bowers of the *Christian Science Monitor* (December 7, 1994), remarked that "Hall does not attempt to lay blame or pose solutions. He keeps his opinion almost entirely out of the narrative. With the failure of so many international peace plans, one can understand why. Still, with his experience, knowledge, and familiarity with the people in the region, it would have been nice to hear his views." *Kirkus Reviews* (May 15, 1994, on-line) also took this point of view, but stated that "Hall professes no solutions for the current Balkan trauma. Rather, he offers an elegy of sorts for the promise of humanism and an eyewitness account of the balkanization of mind and action."

After enjoying a good deal of success with nonfiction, Hall returned to writing fiction and began the pruning required to reduce *The Saskiad* to a manageable size. Finally published in early 1997, the book was an immediate success outside of the United States. The story of Saskia, a 12-year-old girl living on a commune near Ithaca, New York, *The Saskiad* was patterned after *The Odyssey*, with Saskia as the female version of Telemachus, Odysseus's son. The book centers on Saskia's search for her father, an environmentalist who left the family years before to do battle with anyone who encroaches on nature. A well-read little girl, she wants to model her life on the travels of mythical heroes like Odysseus and such real-life adventurers as Marco Polo. Saskia attempts to evade her blossoming womanhood by burying herself in books, only to be jolted from her imaginary world when her father returns and seduces her 13-year-old best friend. Hall was inspired to write *The Saskiad* after reading his wife's diaries and listening to stories from her youth. "Girls have the toughest transition [from childhood], so they're the ones who have the most interesting responses. I found high school to be a very unpleasant place, but boys can postpone their sexuality as long as they want if they're uncomfortable with it, whereas girls have it forced upon them," the author explained in a 1997 interview with Mallay Charters of *Publishers Weekly*.

Reviews for *The Saskiad* were overwhelmingly positive. Greg Johnson, in the *New York Times Book Review* (January 19, 1997), cheered: "Brian Hall . . . has given wonderful new dimensions to the traditional coming-of-age story. Deftly employing a classical structure, with nods along the way to modern writers as diverse as Herman Melville, Lewis Carroll, and James Joyce, he has produced a multilayered post-modernist work of exhilarating ambition and inventiveness, an American book of wonders." Stephen Schiff, reviewing the book for the *New Yorker* (March 10, 1997), noted that "this is only his second novel . . . yet he already knows all about harnessing stylistic experimentation to narrative and character. Saskia's voice . . . evolves as she does."

Reviews for Hall's *Madeleine's World*, a nonfiction work published in late 1997, were not as favorable. A "biography" of Hall's daughter from birth to age three, the book struck some critics as little more than the self-indulgence of a doting parent. Randy Cohen, reviewing the work for the *New York Times Book Review* (November 23, 1997), wrote, "One wishes Hall had better used his skill and passion as an observer to link his daughter's story to larger ideas beyond herself. . . . Our language needs a kid version of the word 'uxorious' to convey a man's preoccupation not with his wife but with his baby. Pedomania, perhaps. It is a comic condition of course, and also rather moving, filled with tenderness and affection. But until it passes, those so afflicted should be cautious about the urge toward memoir." *Kirkus Reviews* (September 15, 1997, on-line) countered by applauding "his research on mental and physical development of the infant to the age we now call preschooler," allied with his "close observations," bring about "a

familiarity with myth and the growth of consciousness, and a poetic sensibility that realizes things are not always what they seem."

Brian Hall, the son of Louis Alton Hall, a physicist, and the former Peggy Smith, a librarian, lives in Ithaca, New York, with his wife Pamela Moss, a writer. The couple married on September 27, 1986, and have two daughters, Cora and Madeleine. Hall has contributed articles to *Travel-Holiday*, the *Los Angeles Book Review*, and the *New York Times.*— C.M.

SUGGESTED READING: *Christian Science Monitor* p13, Dec. 7, 1994; *Los Angeles Times Book Review* p3, Mar. 19, 1989; *New Yorker* Mar. 10, 1997; *New York Times* C p18, Aug. 29, 1988; *New York Times Book Review* p23, Apr. 23, 1989, p17, Aug. 21, 1994, p17, Jan. 19, 1997, p13, Nov. 23, 1997; *New Yorker* p92+, Mar. 10, 1997; *Publishers Weekly* p 49+, Jan. 13, 1997; *Contemporary Authors* vol. 137, 1992: *Kirkus Review* (online) May 15, 1994, (on-line) Sep. 15, 1997

SELECTED BOOKS: Nonfiction—*Stealing From a Deep Place*, 1988; *The Impossible Country: A Journey Through the Lasts Days of Yogoslavia*, 1994; *Madeleine's World*, 1997; Fiction—*The Dreamers*, 1989; *The Saskiad*, 1997

Hamill, Pete

June 24, 1935– Newspaper columnist; novelist; memoirist

"To me, news is a verb," the writer Pete Hamill once said. Hamill is an expert on both news and verbs, having built his reputation as one of the finest print journalists in the country on his evocative prose. New Yorkers have been reading Hamill's news stories and columns for over 30 years in such city publications as the *Daily News*, the *New York Post*, and the *Village Voice*, and he has a reputation as the last "romantic" journalist in New York. Outside New York, Hamill is known primarily for his contributions to such magazines as *Esquire*, *Vanity Fair*, *Playboy*, and others, as well as for his novels and books of non-fiction. His novels include *A Killing for Christ* (1968), *The Gift* (1973), *Loving Women* (1990), and *Snow in August* (1997). His nonfiction varies from a study of New York entitled *The Invisible City* (1980), to his memoir *A Drinking Life* (1994), to *Why Sinatra Matters* (1998), a biographical eulogy for legendary entertainer Frank Sinatra.

Pete Hamill was born William Hamill, Jr. on June 24, 1935, in the New York City borough of Brooklyn. His parents, William (Billy) Hamill and the former Anne Devlin, were both Irish immigrants. After breaking his leg in a soccer game, doctors were forced to amputate Billy Hamill's left leg

above the knee to save him from gangrene. He held a few different jobs during Pete's childhood, but also went through periods of unemployment. He was what many people would call an alcoholic— although Hamill might not. As he told Colleen Quinn of *New York* (January 22, 1996), "I don't like the word alcoholic as a noun; I think it's a very useful adjective . . . . We knew all kinds of alcoholics." Anne Hamill sometimes worked as well, as a nurse. Pete was the oldest of their children; he would eventually be joined by five younger brothers and one sister: Tom, Kathleen, Brian, John, Denis, and Joe, in descending order. Due to changes in their income and needs, the family moved several times within the Park Slope neighborhood of Brooklyn.

Pete Hamill attended Catholic school as a boy. He had learned to read early in life, and became a comic book fanatic during World War II, when many of the most popular titles featured a mix of superhero fantasy and wartime reality. From comic books and the newspapers, he gained an interest in both writing and drawing. But not all of his childhood influences were positive. In his 1994 memoir *A Drinking Life*, Hamill recalled that he went to a saloon with his father for the first time at the age of eight. Drinking ginger ale, the young boy watched his father drink beer—and sing, and joke, and laugh with the other men. "From where I was huddled by the wall, he was the star of the place,"

Hamill wrote in his memoir. "Even the portrait of Franklin Delano Roosevelt, hanging in the dim light above the cash register, seemed to approve. This is where men go, I thought; this is what men do."

At the end of World War II an economic recession hit the country. Hamill, in order to help his family, took his first job. He was 10 years old. Although it only lasted for a few months, the job made a strong impression on him: he was in the newspaper business, as a delivery boy for the *Brooklyn Eagle*. The job thrilled him, and though his primary interest had previously been the comics page, he began reading the entire paper, his paper, paying special attention to the sports page, since his father was a Brooklyn Dodgers fan. When Pete was 11, he decided he wanted to be a cartoonist, and even wrote a letter declaring this intention to Milton Caniff, the writer and artist of "Terry and the Pirates" and "Steve Canyon."

In 1949, Pete won a scholarship to Regis High School, a Manhattan college-prep school run by Jesuit priests. He accepted the scholarship, but with mixed feelings—he had already lost his enthusiasm for Catholicism; he mistrusted the elitism inherent in the school's selection process, and perhaps most of all he just wanted to hang out with his neighborhood friends in Brooklyn and drink. He left Regis in the spring of 1951, and finished his sophomore year at a school called St. Agnes. He did not return to high school, taking instead a job in the Brooklyn Navy Yard. Shortly after, at the age of 16, he moved out of his house.

In January 1952 Hamill began taking night classes at the Cartoonists and Illustrators School, in Manhattan. However, the Korean War was still going on, and after his 17th birthday, Hamill joined the Navy. He was stationed in Jacksonville, Florida, and then Pensacola, where he discovered the writers of the Lost Generation. In the stories of Hemingway and Fitzgerald, Hamill saw romantic hard-drinking heroes, and he dreamed of going to Paris, the haven for those expatriates in the 1920s, to study art on the G.I. Bill after the war ended. However, by the mid-1950s, Hamill was back in Brooklyn, drinking and fighting by night, and working by day as an assistant to a graphic designer in an advertising agency. He tried to gain entrance to art schools in Paris, and Columbia University, but was ignored. He received a letter from a Navy buddy who was also interested in art, describing a G.I. Bill–approved program at Mexico City College. "This could be our Paris," the letter suggested. Hamill jumped at the chance.

In the year Hamill spent in Mexico City, he began to write essays and stories. He returned to New York, resigned to a career in graphic design, in 1957, the year Jack Kerouac's Beat novel *On the Road* was published. After reading the book, and then seeing Kerouac read poetry to jazz accompaniment in a club, Hamill wrote some poetry that was published by the literary magazine of the Pratt Institute, where he was studying design. His first

professional experience in journalism came with the publication of an article on a boxer named Jose Torres. Despite these experiences, writing was still a side interest for Hamill, and he continued to work—and to prosper—as a designer.

Hamill had never lost his early love of newspapers, though, and continued to read several each day. When the *New York Post* editor Jimmy Wechsler published a book called *Reflections of an Angry Middle Aged Editor*, in the spring of 1960, Hamill wrote him a letter in response. "I worked hard on that letter, making three drafts," he recalled in *A Drinking Life*. "I didn't think of it as a job application. That's what it turned out to be." On June 1, 1960, Hamill spent a "tryout" day at the *Post*, and was hired. He immediately quit the graphic design business. A year later, when Ernest Hemingway committed suicide in Ketchum, Idaho, Hamill was one of two reporters who worked on a special series of articles about the writer for the *Post*. These were later expanded and published as the book *Ernest Hemingway: Life and Death of a Man*. In 1962 Hamill was honored with two awards: the Meyer Berger Award for Distinguished Journalism, given by the Columbia University Graduate School of Journalism, and a special award from the Newspaper Reporters Association. Hamill married Ramona Negron, a Puerto Rican woman nine years his junior, in February of that year.

Their first daughter, Adriene, was born the following winter, the winter the printers' union went on strike in New York City. Hamill was without regular work for 114 days, an experience that altered his perspective. "I thought I'd work at the newspaper forever," he wrote in *A Drinking Life*. "The strike made me understand that in the newspaper trade, there was no such thing as forever." In July 1963 Hamill took his family to Barcelona in a conscious attempt to live the romanticized lifestyle of an expatriate writer. "Thus began too many years of wandering, of arrivals and departures, sitting in airport waiting rooms, packing and unpacking books, smoking strange brands of cigarettes, speaking badly the languages of strangers, and drinking their beer and whiskey." In 1964 Ramona gave birth to a second daughter, Deirdre.

Hamill spent the remainder of the 1960s traveling, sometimes with his family, sometimes not, and writing various types of journalism. By the decade's end, he would achieve an unusual level of celebrity for a print journalist, as well as a reputation as a spokesperson for the left. He began in Barcelona as the self-described "Europe guy" for the *Saturday Evening Post*, then continued in Dublin, and then to Rome. Each trip ended with a return to New York, and a failed attempt to settle into the routines of work—again at the *Post* and family life. In his memoir he described the recurring, uprooting force during those years as his own quest for what he called "the Great Good Place." After Europe, he returned to his original Great Good Place, Mexico City, then spent some time in San Juan, Puerto Rico, then Laguna Beach, California, and finally in Washington, D.C., as a political columnist for *New York Newsday*.

In a press release entitled "Why Columnists Leave Home," Hamill described the moment in the 1960s when his political beliefs, specifically his opposition to the Vietnam War, became too overpowering for him to continue as a journalist. "I was writing politics in Washington, ordinarily a marvelous assignment for someone with a taste for the absurd, but my heart was not much in it; everywhere I looked that season I saw men in collusion with death. . . . I decided it was time to quit and write a novel. . . . I was sick of the way I saw the world: politically, abstractly: and I was sick of the way I let Johnson and Rusk and McNamara and the war foul my home. I wrote this novel, not to effect a cure, but to walk away from a consciousness of the sickness."

A Killing for Christ was published in 1968, and in it Hamill wove a complex tale of a plot to assassinate the Pope. Reviewers detected plenty of the anger he was feeling at the time, although it was usually focused on older, more familiar targets. "Hamill is set on ripping the lid off the rotten church, the rotten upper classes, the rotten rightists," wrote John Casey in the *New York Times Book Review* (November 10, 1968). He went on to note that "In a thriller it's not a great deficit to have an emotionally charged social and political bias."

Around the same time, Hamill was facing the failure of his marriage to Ramona. She had first brought up the possibility of a divorce in the mid-1960s, and, as Hamill has said, the marriage "ended officially in 1970, but it had been over for a couple of years then." In the 1970s, Hamill was romantically involved with the actor Shirley MacLaine and the former first lady Jacqueline Onassis.

In 1971 Hamill published a collection of his essays, *Irrational Ravings*. The title was a phrase used by Vice President Spiro Agnew to describe Hamill's analysis of the infamous student riots at Kent State University. Karl Meyer of the *Washington Post* (December 19, 1971) called Hamill "our laureate of outrage," and wrote that "Any working journalist would be proud to put his name on this selection," of 10 years' worth of Hamill's best newspaper columns, along with a few magazine articles. A *New Republic* (December 4, 1971) reviewer felt the book's ultimate achievement was a portrait of Hamill himself, as "a passionate, convincing man."

Hamill had his last drink on New Year's Eve, 1972. As he describes the kicking of his habit in *A Drinking Life*, he only set out to stay sober for the month of January 1973. However, once he realized how much clearer all his experiences, his memories, his thinking became, he set higher goals. "I sat down and wrote my novella, *The Gift* [1973], in one miraculous spurt, working day and night, removed from the world. . . . Another dry month went by, and now my mind was teeming with ideas and projects. I realized that for years I'd been squeezing my talent out of a toothpaste tube. I'd misused it and abused it and failed to replenish it."

The following year, Hamill stopped writing for the *Post*. His next work of fiction, *Flesh and Blood*, was published in 1977. Critics often derided some elements of the novel, about an Irish-American boxer, as clichéd, but nonetheless admitted, like Christopher Lehmann-Haupt of the *New York Times* (November 18, 1977), that Hamill's was "a powerful story. Mr. Hamill's boxing material seems unusually savvy and authentic." Barbara Zelenko wrote in the *Library Journal* (November 15, 1977) that "Hamill knows the world of boxing, and he makes us care."

Also in 1977, Hamill returned to regular column-writing, this time for a different New York tabloid, the *Daily News*, and continued until 1979, when his column was dropped. "I was fired," he told *New York Newsday* (November 28, 1979). "[Daily News Editor Michael] O'Neill called me in on November 14 and told me he was dropping the column. I was stunned and angry and asked why. He said that it was too far left for the *Daily News*." Most accounts agreed that it was Hamill's stance on two issues, the trial of the labor leader Anthony Scotto and U.S.–Iran relations, that led to the O'Neill's decision.

In 1978 and 1979 Hamill published two crime novels, beginning his series about an ex-newspaper reporter named Sam Briscoe. Hamill described Briscoe, a Brooklyn-born Irish Jew with a fondness for Mexico, as his "attempt to create a left-wing hero," in an interview with *Ellery Queen's Mystery Magazine* (December 1977). "It is handled like the left-wing thrillers of the late 1930s. . . . Briscoe's enemies are multinational corporations, the CIA, FBI, secret police forces." *Dirty Laundry* was a success as a paperback thriller, as was its follow-up, *The Deadly Piece*. After the 1980 publication of a book of nonfiction stories, *The Invisible City: A New York Sketchbook*, Hamill added a third "Briscoe book," called *The Guns of Heaven* (1983).

Throughout the 1980s Hamill wrote columns for the *Village Voice* and other New York newspapers, yet perhaps his greatest accomplishment was the broadening of his craft, specifically into magazine writing. He began as a frequent contributor to *New York* magazine and *American Film*. In the late 1980s—after a three-month stint in 1987 as editor of the *Mexico City News*—Hamill became a regular columnist for *Esquire*, a job he held for two years.

In 1990 Hamill published *Loving Women*, his seventh novel. Critics had strong praise for Hamill's story of Michael Devlin, a Brooklyn kid who joins the Navy in 1953 and is sent to Pensacola for training. "In the course of reading this novel," wrote Thomas Fleming in the *New York Times* (April 2, 1989), "we touch that ancient blend of pity and fear that takes us beyond windy rhetoric and disfiguring outrage. . . . Michael Devlin's scarred older self knows history's wounds don't go away. They go on aching for centuries."

In May 1987 Hamill married the Japanese journalist Fukiko Aoki. The couple had met in Tokyo, when she was interviewing him. His next book was a collection of short stories called *Tokyo Sketches*, published in 1993. A *Publisher's Weekly* (February 1, 1993) reviewer noted that "his simple themes of love, loss, longing, and deception are joined to powerful emotions, and reveal a psychological bond" between the United States and Japan.

Soon after *Tokyo Sketches* was published, Hamill got a summons from his past: *the New York Post*, the paper where he had begun his career more than 30 years earlier, was in deep trouble. Steven Hoffenberg, who owned the *Post* at that time, invited Hamill to take the reins as editor-in-chief. With a slew of fresh ideas and enthusiasm, Hamill looked to be the perfect choice to initiate the paper's rebirth. However, on March 12, 1993, Abraham Hirschfeld won the right in court to buy the *Post*, and fired Hamill, who had been on the job for a month. Then the staff of the *Post* mutinied. With their leader gone, and convinced that Hirschfeld was intent on destroying the paper, they assembled a special issue for March 16. Its cover featured a portrait of Alexander Hamilton, the paper's founder, shedding a tear, and it contained story after story of Anti-Hirschfeld sentiment. Hamill's name remained atop the masthead. "That man [Hirschfeld] hasn't shown his face on this floor yet," Hamill bragged to Howard Kurtz of the *Washington Post* (March 17, 1993), from his freshly-recaptured office. "I don't advise him to." After further shenanigans, including a court order (quickly repealed) that barred Hamill from entering the editor's office and a day of self-imposed exile from the same office by Hamill to protest another Hirschfeld decision, the entire drama came to a screeching halt. Rupert Murdoch bought the *Post*, installed his own editor, and Hamill declined an offer to stay on as a columnist.

In 1994 Hamill published *A Drinking Life*, his unsparing look at his own life and his romance with the hard-drinking image of the writer. It became a best seller. "In the literature of drinking," Hamill told Alex Witchel of the *New York Times* (February 24, 1994), "there are only drastic or extreme cases. One of the things I was determined to do was not to make it worse than it was." Hamill's second collection of essays, *Piecework* (1996), collected many of his best magazine and newspaper articles from the 1980s and early 1990s.

On January 1, 1997, Hamill became editor-in-chief of the ailing *New York Daily News*, which was under the ownership of the notoriously fickle Mort Zuckerman. However, no one expected a repeat of the farce that had happened at the *Post*. Hamill again brought in many new ideas, a strong vision for the tabloid, and a contagious enthusiasm. He attempted to cut down on celebrity gossip in the new *News*, and to refocus the paper on citywide events. He also made a deliberate and controversial move toward making the *News* the "literate tabloid" of the city by serializing *The Gospel According to the Son,* the latest work by his longtime friend Norman Mailer, in 19 parts. By the end of August 1997, Zuckerman had decided he did not like Hamill's methods, and after some "conversations," Hamill resigned from his post on the morning of September 4. "What does it mean that the *Daily News* can't keep someone like Pete Hamill?" one of its reporters asked Frank Bruni of the *New York Times* (September 5, 1997). "It's not a good sign."

Hamill's most recent novel is *Snow in August* (1997), which is set in postwar Brooklyn. In this novel, Hamill revives the character of Michael Devlin, the protagonist of *Loving Women*, as an 11-year-old boy. Michael's father was killed in the Battle of the Bulge and he lives with his widowed mother in a tenement. He spends his nights reading comic books and fantasizing about Captain Marvel and the magical powers he gains by saying the word "Shazam." On his way to Mass one morning, he encounters a rabbi who begs him to come in and turn on his light. Michael obeys and the rabbi, named Judah Hirsch, explains that it is not permitted to do any kind of work on the Sabbath. Michael is fascinated by this as well as many other Jewish customs. Soon the pair strike a bargain: Michael will become his "Shabbos goy," teach Rabbi Hirsch about American culture and help him improve his English, while he will teach Michael to speak Yiddish and about the culture of his native city, Prague. "To write disparagingly of *Snow in August* would be akin to telling a child there is no Santa Claus," Sean Callery noted in *Commonweal* (August 15, 1997), and added: "This book is a good read."

For the Library of Contemporary Thought, Hamill wrote *News is a Verb: Journalism at the End of the Twentieth Century* (1998). Using his vast experience as a newspaperman, Hamill urges editors of today's city journals to leave the instantaneous news coverage to the nightly television news, and instead focus on being accurate and in depth. He implores publishers and editors to follow the example he set as editor-in-chief of *the Daily News*— to write about issues that affect their local communities, to avoid gossip and to write only about things which are actually newsworthy. He also stresses the need for newspapers to reach out to new audiences, particularly new immigrants and women.

Late in 1998, the year of Frank Sinatra's death, Hamill published *Why Sinatra Matters*, a slim eulogy to the great entertainer. Hamill felt compelled to write the book after reviewing the extensive media coverage of Sinatra's life, which the author found lacking. In his own words, Hamill felt that many of the tributes "had a stale, even hollow quality, probably because most of the obituaries had been ready for too many months." In his assessment, Hamill found two major themes in Sinatra's life that account for his influence on—and make him a quintessential symbol of—American culture of the 20th century. The first of these is the fact that

Sinatra was an American success story, a son of Italian immigrants who went on to become one of the most widely recognized entertainers of the century. The other is that Sinatra put everything—his pain and joy alike—into his music. He thus created a new style of singing, the knowing "urban American voice." Brian McCombie, writing for *Booklist* (September 15, 1998), called this work "a heartfelt and intelligent tribute to Ol' Blue Eyes."

SUGGESTED READING: *Booklist* Sep. 15, 1998; *Commonweal* p 26, Aug. 15, 1997; *Ellery Queen's Mystery Magazine* Dec. 1977; *Library Journal* Nov. 15, 1977; *New Republic* Dec. 4, 1971; *New York* p 34 +, Jan. 22, 1996; p 24-31, May 12, 1997; *New York Newsday* p 9, Nov. 28, 1979; *New York Times* Nov. 10, 1968, Nov. 18, 1977, Apr. 2, 1989, C p 1 +, Feb. 24, 1994; May 1, 1997; B p 1, Sep. 5, 1997; November 23, 1998; *Publishers Weekly* Feb. 1, 1993; *Washington Post* Dec. 19, 1971, B p 1 +, Mar. 17, 1993; *Who's Who in America, 1998*

SELECTED BOOKS: Fiction—*A Killing For Christ*, 1968; *The Gift*, 1973; *Flesh and Blood*, 1977; *Dirty Laundry*, 1978; *The Deadly Piece*, 1979; *The Guns of Heaven*, 1983; *Loving Women*, 1990; *Tokyo Sketches*, 1993; *Snow in August*, 1997. Nonfiction—*Irrational Ravings*, 1971; *The Invisible City: A New York Sketchbook*, 1980; *A Drinking Life: A Memoir*, 1994; *Piecework*, 1996; *News is A Verb: Journalism at the End of the Twentieth Century*, 1998; *Why Sinatra Matters*, 1998

Mary Randlett/Courtesy of Copper Canyon Press

Hamill, Sam

1943– Poet

The American poet, essayist, and translator Sam Hamill, while leading a life of political activism and poetry writing, has brought to everything he has done the mindfulness of Zen practice, which he has embraced since his youth. Some critics have termed his poems political diatribes, while others have seen his romantic approach as Whitmanesque; still others have placed Hamill in the tradition of Ezra Pound and Gary Snyder. He has written more than a dozen volumes of poetry and translated poetry from Chinese, Japanese, and Estonian.

For *World Authors 1990–1995*, Sam Hamill, born in 1943, writes: "Orphaned during World War II, I was adopted by a Utah farm family shortly after the end of the war. My adoptive parents read the great writers of their generation: Steinbeck, Hemingway, Eudora Welty, Carson McCullers. They gave me children's versions of Homer and Greek and Roman mythology. And my father recited a lot of poetry by the English Romantic poets, especially Shelley. As a small child I was enchanted by the rhythms and imagery of poetry and wrote my first poems while still a pre-schooler at four or five years of age. But I was also a badly abused child, and the violence at home drove me away. I hit the streets at fourteen.

"By the time I was fifteen, I'd been in several jails and had a heroin habit. I wanted to be a 'beatnik' and write poetry and play jazz. The poet Kenneth Rexroth found me living on the streets in San Francisco in 1959 and took me to his house where I kicked the addiction and eventually made a deal with the courts to expunge my juvenile record in return for my enlistment in the U.S. Marine Corps. Following Marine boot camp, I sailed for Japan.

"I had become interested in Zen Buddhism through the Beat writers, especially Rexroth, Jack Kerouac, Gary Snyder, and Philip Whalen, so it was natural that I began Buddhist studies while in the Marine Corps stationed on the occupied island of Okinawa. Zen brought discipline to my writing and I eventually became a Conscientious Objector. The Marine Corps wasn't pleased. I simply decided that the best solution to the problem of murder is not more murder. I decided that for me, killing is wrong, violence produces nothing but more violence, and that I would try to adhere to the Zen path at any cost.

"Upon my return to the U.S., I gave shelter to a young woman I'd known years before who had married a man who beat her terribly. She had no education, but I was able to use my GI benefits to help her get training. We married and our daughter was born in 1965. In 1966, I returned to college on the GI Bill. In 1968, active in civil rights and anti-war movements, I ran for California state assembly on the Peace & Freedom Party ticket. I edited the Los Angeles Valley College literary magazine and the newspaper. And my marriage ended.

"In 1970 I moved on to the University of California in Santa Barbara where I also edited the literary journal, *Spectrum*, receiving the Coordinating Council of Literary Magazines Award for producing 'the best university literary magazine in the nation' for 1972. With the prize money, I brought a printing press and founded Copper Canyon Press in Denver in November 1972.

"In 1974, I was invited to move the press to Fort Worden State Park in Port Townsend to become 'press-in-residence' with the nonprofit arts organization Centrum. With my partner Tree Swenson, I settled here, eventually building a small cabin in the woods several miles from town. My daughter came to live with us and graduated from Port Townsend High School.

"This has been a life of poverty and study and work without the kinds of health benefits and retirement programs and such that most Americans require. I began studying and translating classical Chinese poetry while living without running water or electricity, and I began more and more to see the ancient Greek, Chinese and Japanese poets as models for the conduct of my own life.

"Over the past quarter century I have published more than thirty volumes of poetry, essays, and translations from ancient Chinese, Japanese, Greek, Latin and Estonian. I have been a Contributing Editor at *The American Poetry Review* and at *Tricycle: The Buddhist Review*. I have been honored with fellowships from the National Endowment for the Arts, the Guggenheim Foundation, the U.S.-Japan Friendship Commission, the Lila Wallace Readers Digest Foundation and the Mellon Foundation. It has been my privilege to serve as editor for some of the best poets writing today, from Nobel and Pulitzer prize winners to younger poets presenting their first books.

"I have often said that I believe poetry saved my life. As I grow older, I believe so even more fervently. My daily Zen practice and my daily poetry practice and my daily three hours of study have shaped my life. I have lived outside the economic mainstream all my life. I believe that poetry is a gift, especially to its author, but a gift that is often in some way 'earned' through generosity. I have been fortunate to have spent thirteen years teaching in American prisons and thirty years addressing the problem of domestic violence. My practice of poetry cannot be separated from my Zen practice; my political activism eventually led me to become America's first nationally published Buddhist political columnist (for *Tricycle*). In Buddhist practice as in poetic practice, the search for the path is the path."

Sam Hamill has put into practice the Zen philosophy that he espouses. In his preface to *The Erotic Spirit* (1995), he explained something of the way in which Zen enhances ordinary life:

> Buddhism teaches the importance of not being overcome with desire, of not clinging. In the Zen tradition that dominates the classical poetry of China and Japan, Buddhist practice is centered in silent solitary self-illumination, whereby one transcends possessiveness, ego-driven desire, and other destructive attitudes that contribute to a very large degree to domestic disharmony. Compassion and affection are stressed. But Zen mind is not an exclusively transcendental mind. Zen mind gets up in the morning to take a leak. Zen mind plants rice and beans, washes clothes, changes diapers, makes dinner, all within the framework of the sacred erotic spirit of love, loving the work and play with a familial devotion that does not exclude sexuality.

In Hamill's poetry, as well, the immanence of the sacred prevails in the ordinary. In "Another Duffer," published in the *American Poetry Review* (July/August 1994), Hamill observed Zen golf:

> . . . the clear smooth arc
> of the ball leaves no mark
> across the sky and the eye
> must lift too late to see—
> beginning to foregone conclusion—
> what the mind already perceives
> accurately, in perfect detail: poem:
> like the man and the club and the turf
> and the ball in golf,
> like your finger and the moon, like
> the water and the whale,
> like three or four brands of Zen, various music of singer and song,
> *is,—are,—will be,—has been,—*
> and, finally, *am.*

All of Hamill's poetry aspires to an understanding of nirvana—ultimate bliss—while cheerfully acknowledging samsara—the endless cycle of birth, misery, and death in which humans are trapped by their karma. In "Ten Thousand Sutras," from *The Erotic Spirit*, he wrote, "Adrift in Samsara / we dream of blissful Nirvana," but nevertheless he can exult that "our body is a temple, / not a refuge."

Hamill's large body of work has evoked varying responses. Reviewing *Fatal Pleasure* (1984), a volume of poetry, in *Library Journal* (February 1, 1984), Laurie Brown remarked on Hamill's "easy, flexible lines," terming them "well suited to . . . narrative meditations." She concluded, however, that the flexibility was really a lack of tension, making the poems "soft and unfocused, often self-indulgently sentimental." Of the same volume, the

Choice (July/August 1984) reviewer said, "Working within the broad sweep of romantic nature poetry that stretches from Wordsworth through Jeffers and Snyder, Hamill, when he hits home, does it with total rightness and mastery." The reviewer concluded that Hamill gets "inside the American landscape" and "wears it like a second skin."

Of Mandala (1991), containing Hamill's poetry and Galen Garland's monotype illustrations, Jill Lebihan noted in Canadian Literature (Spring 1993) that the "visual images connect only abstractly with the poems." She observed that for those unable to connect completely with the embrace of Zen philosophy that the book's "mind games" offer, "Hamill's occasional lapse into irreverent self-consciousness provides relief for those of us not quite ready to contemplate the desubjectivised void just yet." Judy Hogan in Library Journal (September 15, 1991), termed the "meditative poems strongly within the tradition of Ezra Pound's Cantos but more accessible." She found "fresh enlightenment about humanity's place in the universal."

Basho's Ghost (1989) tells in both prose and verse of a journey following the path that the 18th-century haiku poet took to northern Japan. The Choice (April 1990) reviewer, A. V. Heinrich, deemed the poetry more successful than the prose in the volume. He commented that Hamill's attempt to encompass the Japanese poetic tradition, however, "seems juxtaposed against, rather than integrated with, his inward searching." Larry Smith in Small Press (December 1990) praised Basho's Ghost as "essentially a revealing and heartfelt homage to the Japanese poets and their deeply human poetry."

A Poet's Work: The Other Side of Poetry (1990) is a volume of essays on the poet's role in society. Jeffrey Luttrell in Library Journal (September 15, 1990) called some of Hamill's comments "political diatribes," but he observed that Hamill "treats big issues, such as the pervasiveness of violence or the political and moral significance of words, with refreshing vigor and intensity." B. Almon, the Choice (July/August 1991) reviewer, disagreed: "Hamill is most convincing when he is enthusiastic about a literary subject, not when he is posing as a social prophet, musing on life in America, or quoting Oriental sages." Almon considered the best essays to be "The Poetry of Kenneth Rexroth" and "An Answering Music: American Poets and Chinese Poetry." Larry Smith in Small Press noted that the "essays unfold like a strong poem. Hamill's writing manages to unite person and poet as his consciousness confronts and enlarges Trident submarines, facts on child and wife abuse, planetary pollution, publishing and teaching sellouts, nature's rich and sustaining detail, a progressive sense of place—all of this is given body and context in his deep appreciation for the wisdom and art of poetry." Hamill's poetry collection Gratitude, published in 1998, draws, like his previous works, from traditions of both the Eastern and Western worlds.
—S. Y.

SUGGESTED READING: Canadian Literature p147 Spring 1993; Choice p1328 Apr. 1990, p 1779 July/Aug. 1991; Library Journal p 183 Feb. 1, 1984, p78 Sep. 15, 1990, p80 Sep. 15, 1991; Small Press p54 Dec. 1990

SELECTED BOOKS: Nonfiction—At Home in the World, 1980; Basho's Ghost, 1989; A Poet's Work: The Other Side of Poetry, 1990; Poetry—Heroes of the Teton Mythos, 1973; Petroglyphs, 1975; The Calling Across Forever, 1976; The Book of Elegiac Geography, 1978; Triada, 1978; animae, 1980; Fatal Pleasure, 1984; The Nootka Rose, 1987; Passport, 1988; A Dragon in the Clouds, 1989; Mandala, 1991; Destination Zero: Poems 1970-1995, 1995; Gratitude, 1998; As translator —(Chinese) Night Traveling, 1985; The Lotus Lovers, 1985; The Art of Writing, 1986; Banished Immortal, 1987; Facing the Snow, 1988; Endless River: Li Po and Tu Fu, 1993; Midnight Flute, 1994; (Estonian) The Same Sea in Us All, 1985; The Wandering Border, 1992; (Japanese) Only Companion, 1992; The Sound of Water: Haiku by Basho, Buson and Issa, 1995; Selected Poems of Yosano Akiko, 1996; My Spring, 1997; As editor—Selected Poems of Thomas McGrath, 1988; Collected Poems of Kay Boyle, 1991; Death Song, 1993; The Erotic Spirit, 1995; The Gift of Tongues: Twenty-Five Years of Poetry from Copper Canyon Press, 1996

Hansen, Ron

Dec. 8, 1947– Novelist; short-story writer

Ron Hansen, the American novelist, decided—after his first two novels went unpublished—that writing to fit a genre would be more profitable. Accordingly, his first two published novels, Desperadoes (1979) and The Assassination of Jesse James by the Coward Robert Ford (1983), are Westerns, the stories of famous gangsters of the American West. Nebraska, his 1989 story collection, contains stories set in the pioneer days of that state. Despite what Mary La Chapelle, reviewing Nebraska in the New York Times Book Review (February 19, 1989), termed "Hansen's . . . noticeably masculine vision . . . with a rugged guns-and-hardware flavor," he went on to tell the story of a nun's relationship with her savior in Mariette in Ecstasy (1991). Hansen returned to a male-dominated outlaw world in his 1996 novel, Atticus, a mystery with the relationship between a father and son at its heart. Most reviewers have found that Hansen has succeeded in writing prose that is "as clear and beautiful as possible" and that he has produced "symmetry and harmony out of chaos—like medieval carvers who were trying to imitate what angels would do on Earth," as the novelist expressed his goal to Amanda Smith in Publishers Weekly (February 5, 1996).

Miriam Berkley

Ron Hansen

Hansen's novel *Hitler's Niece* was scheduled for publication in the fall of 1999.

An identical twin, Ron Hansen was born on December 8, 1947 in Omaha, Nebraska, the son of Frank Hansen, an electrical engineer, and Marvyl Moore. He attended Catholic schools and received his B.A. from Creighton University, in Omaha, in 1970. He then went into the army, while the Vietnam War was in progress, and was in charge of the office that dealt with casualties at Fort Huachuca, in Arizona. After leaving the army Hansen entered the Writers' Workshop at the University of Iowa. He found a friend and mentor in the novelist John Irving and lived with the Irving family, taking care of Irving's two young sons. After receiving his M.F.A. in 1974, he sold college textbooks for Random House for a time before doing further graduate study at Stanford University and the University of Michigan. He taught at several universities, including the University of Iowa and Cornell University, and took a position at the University of California at Santa Cruz in 1989. Having started there at about the time of a major earthquake, he laughingly told Amanda Smith that having grown up in Nebraska, with its blizzards and tornadoes, he "was used to natural phenomena that would destroy your life." In 1996 he became the Gerard Manley Hopkins Professor of Writing at the Jesuit-run Santa Clara University in Santa Clara, California.

The protagonists of *Desperadoes* (1979) are the Dalton gang, a real outlaw clan that flourished at the end of the 19th century in Kansas and the Oklahoma Territory. The Dalton brothers started as peace officers but soon became the core of a gang of cattle rustlers and train robbers. The story is seen through the eyes of Emmett Dalton, the only one of the gang left alive after the Coffeyville raid. Emmett Dalton survived to become a Hollywood celebrity, a collaborator on films, and a real estate agent after 15 years in prison. Hansen told Amanda Smith that the real subject of *Desperadoes* was "moral evil . . . the abuses, the terrible aspects of ambition."

Many reviewers praised *Desperadoes*, including Jerome Charyn in the *New York Times Book Review* (June 3, 1979), who called the writing "so accomplished" and "authoritative" that it was "difficult to think of this as a first novel," and Geoffrey Wolff in *Esquire* (May 8, 1979), who remarked that Hansen "punches through the scrim of legend to make dead bones walk again" and found that the "Daltons and their sidekicks pulse with life." The *New Yorker* (June 25, 1979) reviewer thought that while Hansen tried "too hard to dazzle us with the vivid phrase ('Grat slouched around, smelling like green cheese and fish heads' and 'scoops of shovelled earth flopped black as Bibles on top of the coffins') . . . there is real merit here, and satisfaction and pleasure."

The Assassination of Jesse James by the Coward Robert Ford (1983) tells of Jesse James, the famous and, according to legend, Robin Hood–like outlaw of Missouri, and of how he met Robert Ford, the 19-year-old brother of one of the James gang members. Although Ford idolized James, he would later betray him and shoot him in the back.

Sam Cornish observed in the *Christian Science Monitor* (December 28, 1983) that Hansen's "characters exist both as ordinary people in history and as the figures of legend, and he achieves this duality without loss of authenticity." Cornish particularly praised the language in the novel, terming it "dense and textured." He observed that "the voices of Hansen's characters alternate between harshness and beauty," making the reader want to pause to savor the sound of a line. Peter Prescott, writing in *Newsweek* (November 14, 1983), saw wisdom in Hansen's decision to concentrate on Jesse James's last days: "The novel works not despite our knowledge of what will happen, but because of it—a sense of fatality hangs over every scene." David Freeman remarked in the *New York Times Book Review* (February 5, 1984) that the chapter in which Bob, Jesse, and the rest of the gang hide out together is the heart of the story, "as assassin and victim are locked in a danse macabre that finally destroys them both."

When the title character of *The Shadowmaker* (1987) says, "I must've been daydreaming in wizard school. I should've paid closer attention," he is not speaking for his creator, whose children's book "contains some of the elements children love best, namely, the hilarious, the magical and—best of all—the spooky," in the words of Alice Hoffman, who reviewed the book in the *New York Times Book Review* (May 17, 1987). Hoffman also much to appeal to adults found in the tale of a wizard who attempts to give the people of a town new shadows.

Hansen returned to adult fiction with his story collection, *Nebraska*, for which he won an Award in Literature from the American Academy and Institute of Arts and Letters. Many of the stories are set in Nebraska, and many deal with acceptance or resignation in the face of the harsh life of that implacable place. Sometimes it is a blizzard that brings death, and sometimes it is only old age. The characters summon their strengths to deal with their adversities with honor, however.

In the opinion of Mary La Chapelle, writing in the *New York Times Book Review* (February 19, 1989), "Hansen's stories are powered by inexorable currents of fate." She wrote of one story, "Hansen's focus is the blizzard itself, a force that is amoral in its indifference to foolishness or heroism," a feature she found to be consistent with the "persistent impression of lives being guided intractably by fate." La Chapelle deemed Hansen "most effective with more realistic stories ('Can I Just Sit Here for a While?') and less so in fabulistic tales that are told through buried symbols ('Playland')." She acknowledged that most of the stories transcend Hansen's weaknesses, including his "sense of the alien" and "bleak sense of estrangement" when "he is describing or referring to women." In a review of a later book, Michiko Kakutani in the *New York Times* (November 5, 1991) characterized *Nebraska* as "a beautifully written collection" in which "ghosts, demons, witches, and cannibals all put in unexpected appearances. An evil spirit takes possession of an amusement park; a couple discover that their jealous feelings have taken the physical form of a monster; a woman inherits someone else's bad dreams." These paranormal characters and happenings are not, according to Kakutani, "conjured up by . . . Hansen to shock or titillate, but to remind the reader that life is full of surprises, that the extraordinary dwells next door to the mundane." Hansen's fictional world is always filled with the "miraculous and the strange," Kakutani observed.

Hansen's novel *Mariette in Ecstasy* (1991) is, to a large extent, a nun's story. Hansen had read *The Autobiography of Saint Therese of Lisieux* and was inspired by the story of a woman who had an "incredibly ardent relationship with God," he told Smith. His novel starts in 1906, when a postulant named Mariette enters a convent where her older sister is the mother superior. After her sister's death from cancer, Mariette, who has already attracted attention because of her great piety and beauty, experiences stigmata, occasioning some jealousy on the part of the other sisters. After only about six months, Mariette is sent away from the convent, and the rest of the novel deals with the ensuing 30 years of "her noncloistered life in which 'Christ still sends . . . roses' and 'overwhelms Mariette with great love,'" as Elizabeth McDonough put it in *America* (February 1, 1992). Hansen told Smith that he invented the story of this nun because he wanted to deal with "the very real phenomena [of] what happens with human beings when that sort of privilege is visited on another. There are rivals who feel like they've been ignored when they are equally worthy, so there's jealousy and hatred, and there are those who hope to piggyback on her experience; they consider her a saint and hope to use her as an intercessor with God."

There was widespread agreement with Michiko Kakutani's assessment in the *New York Times* (November 5, 1991) that Hansen, in "limpid, crystalline prose," created in *Mariette in Ecstasy* "an astonishingly deft and provocative novel." Patricia Hampl in the *New York Times Book Review* (October 20, 1990) particularly commended Hansen's language: "The poetic voice is an inspired choice. . . . He . . . refreshes even the most mundane action: a nun in a gray sweater and galoshes is 'flirting up fresh snow with a broom'; winds 'flute through' a chimney; even window washing has a dynamic presence as the panes 'yelp with hard polish.' Such language serves absolutely the contemplative mind, absorbing the acuity of detail, the eloquent silence of its world. Indeed," Hampl concluded, "much of the novel is devoted to a deft re-creation of a way of life that is fascinating for its own sake, but that is never treated as freakish." She further observed that it "is a testament to . . . Hansen's art that it is possible to weep for Mariette's lost glory as if for the death of a great love." Peter Prescott, writing in *Newsweek* (October 21, 1991), concurred. He noted that *Mariette in Ecstasy* follows the course of Hansen's previous novels by "playing with myth" and presenting "a figure larger than life can conveniently deal with," exemplifying the theme that "the unexpected appearance of visible proof of the truth of Christianity is an unendurable burden to professing Christians."

In *Atticus* (1996) Hansen combined in one novel the spiritual concerns that were manifested in *Mariette in Ecstasy* with the theme of the prodigal son. Atticus, a widower, is a rich American oil man whose son, Scott, an artist, lives in Mexico. Scott drove the car in the accident in which his mother was killed. He arrives to spend one Christmas with his father and shortly afterward is reported to have committed suicide. When Atticus goes to Mexico to claim the body, he encounters an assortment of strange, decadent characters who have found Mexico tolerant of their lifestyles. Atticus comes to the conclusion that his son was murdered, an idea that he embraces as he would a revelation of religious faith, as many reviewers pointed out. As it turns out, Scott is neither a murder victim nor a suicide: he is alive.

Janet Burroway, reviewing *Atticus* for the *New York Times Book Review* (February 18, 1996), saw the novel experientially: "The reader is allowed to understand every nuance of the son's guilt, reasoning and regret, cannot quite absolve him, and is shamed by the spectacle of the father who can. It is a rich and disturbing experience." Burroway concluded that *Atticus* "is a didactic novel. . . . It names great virtues and then looks at them . . . finding them in unexpected forms. . . . Hansen writes vigorously, and like an angel—so much so that *Atticus* may end up giving didacticism a good name." Wesley Brown, writing in the *Nation* (April 15, 1996), agreed with Burroway that Hansen was successful in creating—as Hansen described the book to Smith—a novel "about forgiveness." Hansen added that what he was concerned with in his book was "the loyalty and relentlessness of the father's love," a love that "makes the world work . . . and that is what allows other people to be as scattered and rebellious and full of loss and wreckage as Scott is and yet have the world struggle on. It's visited on people in different ways, but we see it perfectly exampled within a loving parent." Brown observed that Hansen's great achievement in *Atticus* was "that the ambivalences between father and son resonate most strongly not through the conventional route. . . . It's risky, but Hansen never falters in keeping his two protagonists in emotional proximity to each other even though they are physically separated for most of the novel." Guy Davenport, in the *Sewanee Review* (Summer 1996), saw in *Atticus* a universal theme that represents one of the main currents of contemporary literature: "[T]he dark and evil underworld that can be mere backdrop in a sensationalistic crime novel is an important vehicle of meaning in *Atticus*: the hoard of expatriate Americans and Europeans . . . infesting Mexico with their physical and spiritual illness is a powerful contemporary embodiment of the colonial theme of Conrad, Forster, Greene, and others—a theme that has been a truly major part of the fiction representing our century." That universality and Hansen's spiritual dimension have led his writing to be held in high esteem. For *Atticus*, Hansen was nominted for a PEN/Faulkner Award for fiction.

Hansen's novel *Hitler's Niece*, scheduled for publication in the fall of 1999, concerns the relationship between Adolf Hitler and the young woman of the title, Geli Raubal, with whom he was in love. The *Publishers Weekly* (July 5, 1999) reviewer called the book "ambitious" and "provocative." —S.Y.

SUGGESTED READING: *America* p6 Feb. 1, 1992, p28 May 25, 1996; *Christian Science Monitor* p18 Dec. 28, 1983; *Nation* p31 Apr. 15, 1996; *New York Times* Nov. 5, 1991; *New York Times Book Review* p14 June 3, 1979, p18 Feb. 5, 1984, p31 May 17, 1987, p11 Oct. 20, 1990, p4 Feb. 18, 1996; *New Yorker* p105 June 25, 1979; *Newsweek* p112 Nov. 14, 1983; p66 Oct. 21, 1991; *Publishers Weekly* p65 Feb. 5, 1996; *Sewanee Review* p466 Summer 1996; *Washington Post* B p2 Mar. 15, 1996

SELECTED BOOKS: Fiction—*Desperadoes*, 1979; *The Assassination of Jesse James by the Coward Robert Ford*, 1983; *Nebraska*, 1989; *Mariette in Ecstasy* , 1991; *Atticus*, 1996; Juvenile—*The Shadowmaker*, 1987; As editor—*You've Got to Read This: Contemporary American Writers Introduce Stories That Held Them in Awe* (with J. Shepard), 1994

Hardy, James Earl

Dec. 14, 1966– Novelist

With his novel *B-Boy Blues* (1994), James Earl Hardy may be said to have created the "Africentric, gay, hip-hop love story" genre. The main characters in that book and its two successors, *2nd Time Around* (1996) and *If Only for One Nite* (1997), are Mitchell Crawford, a journalist, and Raheim Rivers, a bicycle messenger, who become romantically involved. Hardy is a journalist as well as a novelist; he has produced pieces on a variety of topics for such publications as the *Washington Post*, the *Village Voice*, *Newsweek*, and *Essence*. In addition, he has written biographical profiles of Spike Lee and Boyz II Men for the African-American Achievers series.

In a statement for *World Authors 1990–1995*, Hardy writes, "I was born [on December 14, 1966] in the Bedford-Stuyvesant section of Brooklyn, New York, notoriously known as 'Do or Die Bed-Stuy' (a ghetto to some—mainly those who have never been—but always home for me). As the only child of a single mother, Brenda Vernice Hannah, who entered City College in New York just one month after giving birth to me, I learned very early that because of my familial station, I was not expected to be as smart as, as sharp as, as successful as others. While I inherited my mother's determination and understated strength, I was a rather quiet and shy child growing up, but soon found that I expressed myself best with the written word (with singing in my church choir and around the family coming a close second). At the age of eight, I wrote my first poem; at nine, I started keeping a journal. More than anything, I saw my writing as an outlet, a means through which I could relate to others what I couldn't verbally. I never thought that it would play such an important role in my life in later years— or, rather, become my life.

"As a preteen, my life changed when I picked up an issue of the *Amsterdam News*, an African American weekly newspaper in New York, and came across the work of Nelson George, a music critic and entertainment writer. I realized that one could actually pursue writing as a career—and write about those things that gave them pleasure. I followed Nelson's career path—literally. Like him, I've also reviewed music and / or been a feature writer for the *Amsterdam News*, as well as the *Village Voice*, *Vibe*, *Emerge*, and *Essence*. And, af-

James Earl Hardy

Courtesy of James Hardy

ter attending Edward R. Murrow High School in Brooklyn, I, like George, did my undergraduate study at St. John's University in Jamaica, Queens (I earned a bachelor of science degree in communication arts in May 1988).

"It was at St. John's that I was introduced to another publication that lit another kind of writing fire. A friend gave me a copy of *New Youth Connections*, a newsmagazine written by and for New York youth. I was impressed—a publication about the joys and pains of being a teenager, written with the type of courage and honesty I often saw lacking in the 'adult' press—and decided to contribute some work of my own by entering their monthly contest. The issue was whether abortion should be legal and I took a rather interesting view: while I may not agree with it, it is nonetheless a woman's right to do with her body what she wishes. The editors loved the essay and not only chose me as that month's winner but invited me to join their staff. And, from September 1985 through August 1992 (well past my teen years), I wore many hats at NYC (as it is called by its alumni): reporter, cultural critic, mentor, and big brother. My writing life at NYC taught me that there was indeed power in the pen and that one shouldn't take that power—or their own voice—for granted.

"After internships and fellowships with *New York Newsday*, the *New York Daily News*, and the *Village Voice*, I got my first—and, so far, my only—9-to-5 (it was more like a 10-to-6) working as an editor on *Update*, a current events magazine known in some circles as 'the *Time* Magazine for teens,' as I continued to freelance for others. But, feeling that I wasn't getting the attention I needed to polish my skills and become more disciplined, I decided to

pursue a dream I'd always had: to attend the Columbia University School of Journalism. It was one of the best experiences of my life (something I haven't heard many J-school grads say!). The very intense, rigorous training I was put through reminded me just why I chose writing as a life goal (or did it choose me?). I graduated with honors in May 1993, with freelance gigs doing research for *Newsweek*'s arts department and feature writing for *Entertainment Weekly* and the *Washington Post*'s Style section.

"But, just three months out of graduate school, I answered what could be called a calling—I wrote my very first novel (in fact, it would be my very first time dabbling in fiction). That I was attempting such a project surprised some—particularly since I had just spent $30,000 on a journalism degree—but I had been carrying the story I was about to tell around with me for some time, eager to explore another side of myself through writing that I hadn't before. I had complained more than once, out loud, about not seeing on a bookshelf something that mirrored the world that I and many other same-gender loving men of African descent I knew lived in. So, I finally sat down and allowed it to come out—and *B-Boy Blues* was born.

"Dubbed the first Africentric, gay, hip-hop love story, it tells the tale of a Black gay journalist who falls in love with a 'homeboy' from Harlem who is a bike messenger. The novel's novelty of depicting an intimate relationship between two Black men of very different economic, political and cultural stripes made it a hit with gay and straight, Black and white audiences, and turned it into a bestseller. As a result, two additional titles in the series have been published: *2nd Time Around*, in which the 'Africentric homosexual' is, for the first time in fiction, given a chance to speak, and *If Only for One Nite*. More than anything I've created, the B-Boy Blues series has touched the lives of others in ways I never could have dreamed. To know that the stories have enriched—and in some cases helped save—the lives of men of African and Caribbean descent who, like myself, were brainwashed to hate themselves, is the greatest gift I could ever receive as a writer.

"Besides Nelson George, the writers who have influenced me, as both a journalist and novelist, are Leonard Pitts Jr., pop culture columnist and critic for the *Miami Herald*, and the late James T. Jones VI, Black music critic and feature writer for *USA Today*. I have patterned my writing style after theirs, making it my own—adapting the rhythm and bluesy flavor of Black music (from jazz and rock to rap and house), incorporating song titles and lyrics to help set the mood, shade a character, define a moment or event, signify a feeling or thought. And through their example, I have dedicated my life to telling those stories that need to be told, giving a voice to those who have been invisible, and exploring and interrogating, from an Africentric homosexual perspective, white supremacy/racism in gay America and heterosexism/homophobia in African-America. I have naturally received a lot of 'criticism' because of this (the majority of it not constructive), but I welcome it: it tells me that I've been successful in challenging the status quo(s) and forcing folks to analyze their preconceived ideas re the 'lesbian and gay community,' the 'Black community,' and who same gender loving men of African/Caribbean descent are.

"Some say they write to stay alive; I write to keep from dying. If I couldn't do it, I'd be alive but I wouldn't be living."

James Earl Hardy is the son of James Albert Lee and Brenda Vernice Hannah. He received his B.S. from St. John's University in Queens, New York, in 1988 and his M.S. from the Columbia University School of Journalism, in 1993.

Although Hardy's first novel, *B-Boy Blues* (1994), was published by a small gay and lesbian press, it sold more than 40,000 copies, and thus went a long way toward best-sellerdom. In it, a sober young journalist (rather like Hardy himself), Mitchell Crawford, falls in love with Raheim Rivers, a wild bike messenger. Max Padilla, writing in *Out* (November 1996), contrasted *B-Boy Blues* with the novels of E. Lynn Harris, whose books "are likely to be tucked into the handbags of African-American women." On the other hand, Padilla noted, "Mitchell and Raheim's ribald antics are unquestionably written for gay men." That has not, however, stopped *B-Boy Blues* from selling to all kinds of audiences attracted by humor, although Padilla maintained that Hardy received more acclaim from the "mainstream media than the gay press." Padilla described Hardy's white characters as veering on caricature, like the "leering Mapplethorpe-like photographer," but Hardy insisted that "the real problem is that some critics can't abide [his] depiction of same-gender loving men of African descent skirting the white gay world." "Naturally, I got tagged the angry young black man, which quite frankly for me is a compliment," Hardy told Padilla.

It was the *Publishers Weekly* (October 7, 1996) critic, reviewing *2nd Time Around* (1996), the sequel to *B-Boy Blues*, who called *B-Boy Blues* the first "'Africentric' gay hip-hop novel." In *2nd Time Around*, the point of view is that of Raheim Rivers, who returns to his lover, Little Bit, after a separation. Another important relationship in Raheim's life is also explored—that with his son, Little Brotha Man; and, of course, Mitchell is also present. The *Publishers Weekly* reviewer described Raheim as a "man with an enormous capacity for love and for learning from his mistakes" and the novel as "an upbeat tale which, while confronting issues of violence, racism and homophobia, is romantic, absolutely sensual and downright funny."

In the next novel in the series, *If Only for One Nite* (1997), Hardy again focuses on the life of Mitchell Crawford. When he attends his 10-year high-school reunion, Mitchell encounters Warren, a gymnastics coach with whom he has had an affair. First in memory and then in the present, the encounter with Warren enables Mitchell to forge a more adult self. Don Belton, writing in the *Advocate* (September 16, 1997), observed that "Hardy's voice calibrates a charged balance between spareness and extravagance." Belton concluded that although Hardy creates many "stock characters that are too stock," in *If Only for One Nite*, he has fashioned "a humorous, assaultive, and sexy song . . . about . . . coming in—to a richer sense of belonging and self acceptance."

Self-acceptance has been one of the lodestars of Hardy's life and writing. In his journalism, he has often written without reference to his sexual orientation. In 1998, in an interview with Lincoln Pettaway for *Gay People's Chronicle* (January 9, 1998), Hardy nevertheless said that he had to be more open about himself. Speaking of an essay he had published in *Source* (December 1997), he admitted, "Like I say in that essay, I spent much of my career trying to avoid writing the word *homosexual*." He then observed, "Wait a minute, hold up, we're avoiding *me*. And how can you truly say that you value yourself as a person if you're avoiding yourself." Accordingly, as he told Quohnos Mitchell in *HX Magazine* (January 16, 1998), "My goal is to highlight the Afrocentric homosexual. . . . I am signifying lives that, for the longest time, have gone undocumented."

In fact, Hardy had never ceased to "signify" undocumented lives. In 1994 he wrote a *Washington Post* (June 25, 1994) profile of Eva Isaac, who is well-known to attendees of the Apollo Theater amateur nights, though few of them know her name. When, right off the farm, she saw the show at the Apollo for the first time, she decided to make a career of promoting future stars and making it clear to others that they had no future in show business. Her description of the impact the theater had on her could apply to Hardy's discovery of writing: "It just set me free, let this other me inside come out. I was ready to party, you hear?"

Hardy has received grants and scholarships from the E. Y. Harburg Arts Foundation, the American Association of Sunday and Feature Editors, the Paul Rapoport Memorial Foundation, and the Association of Black Journalists. He has won awards from the Columbia University Press Association and the Educational Press Association.
—S. Y.

SUGGESTED READING: *Advocate* p59 Sep. 16, 1997; *Gay People's Chronicle* Jan. 9, 1998, with photo; *HX Magazine* p18 Jan. 16, 1998; *New York Times Magazine* p8 Dec. 22, 1991; *Out* p64+ Nov. 1996, with photo; *Publishers Weekly* p66 Oct. 7, 1996; *Washington Post* G p1 June 25, 1994

SELECTED BOOKS: Fiction—*B-Boy Blues*, 1994; *2nd Time Around*, 1996; *If Only for One Nite*, 1997; Nonfiction—*Boyz II Men*, 1996; *Spike Lee*, 1996

Allford/Trotman/Courtesy of Doubleday Books

Harris, E. Lynn

1955– Novelist

In the past few years, E. Lynn Harris, a former computer salesman who poured his savings into the marketing of his first, self-published novel, has seen his gamble pay off handsomely. *Invisible Life*, which was picked up by Consortium Press in 1991 and reissued by Doubleday in 1994, has found a vast readership, and its treatment of the problems faced by black gays and bisexuals has sparked vigorous public debate. His subsequent novels, *Just As I Am* (1994), *And This Too Shall Pass* (1996), and *Abide With Me* (1999) have, together with *Invisible Life*, sold hundreds of thousands of copies and confirmed Harris as a leading voice for a segment of the population heretofore underrepresented in literature. "I hope that the success of my books . . . will make it possible for more black men, gay and straight, to tell their stories," Harris has said.

E. Lynn Harris was born in 1955 in Flint, Michigan, and reared in Little Rock, Arkansas, the oldest child—and the only son—in a poor family of four siblings. His mother, who reared her children alone, worked in a factory owned by the communications giant AT&T and held down other jobs as well, which limited the amount of time she could spend with her son and daughters. "My family has never been a sit-down-at-the-table-and-discuss-our-lives type," Harris told Kennette Crockett for a profile in the *Chicago Tribune* (December 5, 1994). "But there has always been a lot of love there." Harris met his father for the first time at the age of 14; his father died a year later.

Harris enrolled at the University of Arkansas at Fayetteville and became, as a writer for *People* (May 15, 1995) reported, the school's first black yearbook editor as well as its first black male cheerleader. It was during his years as an undergraduate that he discovered his bisexuality. He also realized in that period that he was interested in writing, and he decided to make journalism his major. He kept the nature of his sexuality to himself and put his desire to write on hold, however, after the computer corporation IBM recruited him as a salesman upon his graduation in 1977. He proved to be adept at his job, working his way up to an annual salary of $90,000.

While he possessed many of the trappings of personal success, Harris was unhappy during the more than 10 years he spent working for IBM. "At some points . . . the life that I was leading I thought was true and was the life I was supposed to lead," he said to Kennette Crockett. "But [that life] was based more on what society thought than what I thought." The need he felt to deny his bisexuality for the sake of social acceptance caused him to feel intense loneliness. "I was miserable because I was living a lie," he explained to Felicia R. Lee, who interviewed him for the *New York Times* (March 17, 1996). "I was like one of those people in high school who wins class favorite but really has no close friends." The misery he experienced in those years led him to drink heavily. One bright spot connected with his occupation was his meeting the African-American poet Maya Angelou at a conference in 1983. "She told me that I should write something every day, even if it was just one word," the novelist recalled in an interview for the *People* article.

Perhaps spurred by Angelou's advice, in the late 1980s Harris left IBM to write a novel about the pain of being a black bisexual in a society abounding in homophobia as well as racism. Having completed the novel, he took on what turned out to be the Herculean task of getting it published. After his manuscript had been rejected by a dozen publishing houses, some of which specialized in books with gay themes, Harris decided to pay his own printing costs and market the novel himself. With $25,000—the last of his savings—he purchased 5,000 bound copies. At one point, when his costly venture had resulted in the sale of a mere 42 books, Harris asked himself, "What have I done?"

Rather than give up on his quest to be a successful writer, however, Harris increased his efforts. He began peddling his book in beauty salons and black-owned bookstores, the places where he expected to find the readers his work would most easily attract. In this way he eventually sold thousands of copies of the novel. The word-of-mouth publicity generated by his activities resulted in a newspaper article, which, in turn, caught the attention of a literary agent. After Consortium Press published Harris's book, which *Essence* magazine subsequently named one of the 10 best novels of 1991, Martha Levin of Anchor Press—an arm of the publishing giant Doubleday—agreed to issue a new edition of the work.

The narrator of *Invisible Life* is the Alabama-born Raymond Winston Tyler Jr., a New York City lawyer. Beginning with his days at an Alabama university, Raymond gives accounts of his romantic relationships with Sela, his high-school and college sweetheart; Kelvin, the man who, during Raymond's senior year, makes him aware of his bisexuality—at a time when he is still involved with Sela; Quinn, the married father of two who becomes Raymond's lover in New York; and Nicole, the Broadway performer of strong Christian faith whom Raymond dates and dreams of marrying, even as he spends time with Quinn. While Raymond's male sexual partners know of the women in his life, his female lovers are unaware of his bisexuality, which is, to the eyes of the heterosexual world, "invisible."

Raymond's secrecy is not so much duplicitous as it is a concession to the taboos, particularly in his predominantly white law firm and in the black community, against acting on the homosexual impulses that he would suppress if he had a choice. ("No black man in his right mind would choose to be gay," he states.) Through his descriptions of gay-club–hopping with his platonic friend, the gregarious and openly homosexual Kyle, Raymond introduces the reader to gay-culture lingo and he sheds light on the ways in which gay people are forced to meet one another in a homophobic society. Confronting the lack of tolerance for his lifestyle, feeling torn between his male and female lovers, and taking the risk of alienating his parents by informing them of his sexual orientation, Raymond observes, "Life in the black gay community was not for the weak or the weary. It was not for sissies."

Harris's novel struck a chord with heterosexual readers—who found that it provided a revealing picture of a world about which they had known little—as well as with black gay readers, who relished seeing many of their own experiences reflected in Raymond Tyler's story. "*Invisible Life* . . . is one of those books that you cannot put down," Harriette W. Richard declared in the *Journal of Black Psychology* (May 1995). Citing important works by two other African-American writers, she continued, "*Invisible Life* has been compared with James Baldwin's . . . *Another Country* as well as Ralph Ellison's . . . *Invisible Man.* The implications are clear: *Another Country* dealt with the issue of black male sexuality, and Ralph Ellison's Invisible Man felt rage and anger because most of the time he was not recognized as being a part of society. It is the latter point that may be most salient. When individuals tell of their homosexuality in the black community, they risk becoming invisible. By hiding their homosexuality, individuals are making a part of themselves invisible through self-choice rather than having someone else render them invisible. . . . *Invisible Life* offers an excellent starting point to dialogue about not only black male sexuality, but the intersection of sexuality with family, religion, AIDS, politics, and culture."

In Harris's second novel, *Just As I Am*, the first-person narrative is provided alternately by Raymond and Nicole, whose paths—having diverged by the end of *Invisible Life*—eventually cross again. Raymond has moved to Atlanta to practice law at a firm that represents professional athletes; he has also, in the wake of the romantic complications detailed in *Invisible Life*, entered a period of celibacy. He nonetheless contemplates risking scorn and rejection from Jared, a young political consultant whose sexuality and views on homosexuals he has not ascertained, by revealing his amorous feelings for his new friend. Meanwhile, Raymond's job brings him into contact with the football player Basil Henderson, the arrogant, physically attractive closet bisexual introduced in *Invisible Life*. In New York, Nicole struggles to sort out her conflicting feelings about her upcoming marriage to Pierce, the Jewish doctor who has furthered her acting and singing career. She has also developed a close friendship with Kyle, for whom disaster looms. In *Just As I Am*, Harris touched on the politics of gay life. For example, when Raymond acts as legal counsel to Basil, who has beaten up a man for propositioning him in a bar, Kyle objects, telling Raymond, "You're actually promoting gay bashing when you defend people like Basil"; and Raymond, for his part, ultimately becomes involved in a cause related to his sexuality.

The reviews for *Just As I Am* were mixed. A writer for *Publishers Weekly* (January 24, 1994) acknowledged that Harris had "managed to capture the material aspects of the good life and the East Coast black gay scene" but complained that the novelist had "propped up his labored prose on a well-intentioned scaffold of gay activist issues. The result is more checklist than novel: when a character is introduced, a demographic stereotype is quickly outlined to elicit the reader's mechanical response." On the other hand, a reviewer for *Library Journal* (February 1, 1994), while noting that the "execution" of events in the novel was "too pat," declared, "Superb character development and insight make this a powerful sequel to *Invisible Life*. . . . Many gay readers will identify with the story, which often seems more truth than fiction." The novel's ambivalent critical reception apparently did not dissuade Harris's fans from buying the book, since *Just As I Am* sold 50,000 copies within a year of its initial printing.

And This Too Shall Pass concerns the intersecting lives of four characters: the enigmatic Zurich Robinson, an NFL starting quarterback; Sean Elliott, a journalist who, given the job of profiling Zurich, forms a close friendship with the athlete; Tamela Coleman, a romance-weary attorney; and the television sports reporter Mia Miller. After Zurich rejects Mia's romantic advances, he finds himself accused by her of rape and assault, and he hires Tamela as his legal counsel. As the story develops, Sean tries to decide whether or not to disclose his own attraction to Zurich. The novel received generally good notices. "In Harris's entertaining new work, the issues of sexual orientation that dominated his first two novels . . . take a back seat to universal questions of justice, love, and career," a writer for *Publishers Weekly* (January 29, 1996) observed. "Despite some stilted dialogue, this novel should broaden the author's readership and reinforce his growing reputation as an accessible, younger voice in African-American literature." Rebecca Sturm Kelm, reviewing *And This Too Shall Pass* for *Library Journal* (February 1, 1996), found the plot to be "intriguing" and added, "In an enjoyable novel, Harris is able to introduce the idea of various prejudices operating both within and against the black community."

In 1997 Harris published *If This World Were Mine*, a novel that follows the story of four former classmates 20 years after their graduation from a prestigious African-American college. Basil Henderson returns as the love interest of media consultant Yolanda Williams, and Dwight Scott, a new character, struggles with resentment toward whites. The main characters spend the duration of the book struggling with sexuality, a failing marriage, stalled careers, blackmail, and AIDS. While the book was popular, reviews were mixed. A critic in *Booklist* (June 1, 1997) wrote that Harris spins the intricate story "effortlessly, if a trifle woodenly." A reviewer from *Kirkus Reviews* (June 15, 1997) remarked: "What starts off as an amiable enough soap opera quickly becomes mired in Byzantine subplots and friends-stick-by-each-other cliches."

Abide With Me (1999), the concluding volume in the trilogy which began with *Invisible Life* and continued in *Just As I Am*, picks up a few years after the latter book leaves off. The reader is reintroduced to Raymond Tyler and his partner, Trent, who are happily living in Seattle, Washington, until Raymond's nomination for a federal judgeship threatens to destroy the lives they have built for themselves. In desperation, Raymond flies to New York to seek the council of his closest friend, Jared, who is married to Raymond's old flame Nicole. Nicole is starring in a revival of *Dreamgirls*, the show she has wanted to do all her life. However, her understudy Yancey Harrington Braxton is determined to move in on the starring role. Other familiar characters return as well, most notably John Basil Henderson, sportscaster and ex-football player, who is attempting to come to terms with his bisexuality through therapy. Like its predecessors, *Abide With Me* has been a great commercial hit, cracking the top 10 on the *New York Times* bestseller list.

While his work has helped to elicit sympathy for the plight of homosexuals, Harris, as he made clear to Kennette Crockett, sees his race—rather than his sexual identity—as being central to his concept of himself. "Race is the first thing that people recognize about you," he explained. "My race is the one thing that I've always had pride in, even as a little kid. My sexuality is something that I'm becoming more comfortable with every day." The gay rights struggle, in his view, "is basically a white movement. Gay whites still have white status in this country. Sexuality is something people can change from the outward appearance. Unless [a white person] looks 'gay,' [he or she] can easily switch to their white status and not suffer any injustices." Discussing what many consider to be the high level of intolerance for gays in the black community, Harris expressed his opinion that "most blacks are homophobic because black gays and lesbians have been so closeted and invisible that black people really believe that this is not a part of their community." His attempts to understand the sources of homophobia notwithstanding, Harris told Crockett, "It's a shame that any group has to fight for its god-given rights. I'm a romantic. I think that the bottom line is that we all want to be loved."

Harris himself seems to have achieved that goal, judging by the enthusiasm with which he is greeted by fans. As Felicia R. Lee reported, readers of Harris's novels have gone to unusual lengths to show their appreciation for his work; many have sent him flowers, compact discs, and baked goods, and one claimed to have photocopied *Invisible Life* in its entirety to mail to friends around the country. Some readers have offered the writer advice on his plots and the development of his characters. Harris revels in the public's adoration, as he told Kennette Crockett: "The people lift me up. Even if I'm tired, when I get to a store and enthusiastic fans greet me, I get adrenalized."

Kennette Crockett described E. Lynn Harris as an "imposing, tall man," and Felicia R. Lee took note of the novelist's "soft southern accent." Like several of his characters, he is a devout member of the Christian faith. He also has in common with many of them a love of sports. He is currently working on a memoir, whose working title is "For Colored Boys Who Have Considered Suicide When Being Gay Was Too Tough" (an allusion to the African-American playwright Ntozake Shange's work *For Colored Girls Who Have Considered Suicide/When the Rainbow is Enuf*). Harris divides his time between Chicago and New York City.
—C.T./C.M.

SUGGESTED READING: *Booklist* June 1, 1997; *Chicago Tribune* V p1+ Dec. 5, 1994; *Journal of Black Psychology* May 1995; irkus Reviews June 15, 1997; *Library Journal* Feb. 1, 1994, Feb. 1, 1996; *New York Times* p43+ Mar. 17, 1996; *People* p115 May 15, 1995; *Publisher's Weekly* Jan. 24, 1994, Jan. 29, 1996

SELECTED BOOKS: *Invisible Life*, 1991; *Just As I Am*, 1994; *And This Too Shall Pass*, 1996; *If This World Were Mine*, 1997; *Abide With Me*, 1999

Miriam Berkley

Harris, Eddy L.

Jan. 26, 1956– Travel writer

Eddy L. Harris is a respected travel writer whose unique perspective has won him many admirers. As a black man exploring wilderness both natural and urban, he has sought to define himself by his encounters with a variety of people including African tribesman, American bigots, small town diner waitresses, and street-corner hoodlums. For his first book, *Mississippi Solo*, (1988), Harris took a canoe trip down the length of the Mississippi River and recorded the people and places he saw along the way. His second volume, *Native Stranger* (1992), sent the author on a year-long African trip on which he visited 23 different countries in an attempt to see how similar African-Americans were to their African cousins. His next book, *South of Haunted Dreams* (1993), concerned his experiences on a motorcycle trip through the American South. In it the author sets out to confront the South of his nightmares, full of lynchings, hatred, and Jim Crow laws, but discovers a very different place. His most recent work, *Still Life in Harlem*, (1996) brought Harris to the cultural capital of black America. In this book he writes of not only the urban decay he sees around him, but of the lives of the people who struggle to make that community a better place.

Eddy Louis Harris was born on January 26, 1956, in Indianapolis, Indiana, the son of Georgia Louise Harris and Samuel Eddy Harris. Until the age of 10 he lived in a St. Louis ghetto, before moving with his family to the suburbs. While growing up in St. Louis he had his first experiences in the great out doors, with his oldest brother, a capable hunter

and fisherman; the two traveled through the Missouri woods, rifles in hand, sometimes accompanied by their father. These experiences apparently planted in Harris the love of adventure described in his books.

Harris received a bachelor's degree from Stanford University in 1977. Subsequently he traveled to many parts of the world and lived in Europe for a time before deciding to become a writer. At the age of 30, Harris embarked on a canoe trip down the Mississippi River from its point of origin in Minnesota to its mouth in New Orleans. Though he enjoyed the outdoors, as the author remarked in *Outdoors* Magazine (December 1997), "It was an impetuous plan, and one for which I was quite ill-prepared. I'd scarcely been in a canoe before. I'd been camping perhaps twice in my life."

In the fall of 1985 Harris put away his fears about sleeping in the woods and began his long journey down the great river. Along the way some of his fears about the undertaking were realized—some of them not directly connected to the natural world. In Tennessee he set up camp in the middle of a downpour. Sometime later a pack of feral dogs gathered around his tent hoping to catch some warmth. Pinned down for quite some time, the author was so frightened that he lay in his bedroll holding his pistol all night. When he emerged from his tent the next morning, one of the dogs jumped at him. He fired at it, and the pack dispersed into the woods. At a campsite in Mississippi he ran into more trouble, this time in human form. While he was setting up camp, two white hunters came out of the woods and threatened Harris with their shotguns. In self-defense he fired his pistol in their general direction and they fled, but he still broke camp and got into his canoe in the middle of the night.

Harris recorded these and other tales in *Mississippi Solo: A River Quest*, published by Nick Lyons Books in 1988. He received generally favorable notices for his work. Thomas J. Davis, writing for *Library Journal* (October 15, 1988), cheered: "His book is a commentary on America the beautiful, on the water, on helping hands, and on some not so helping—like those two shotgun toting bigots." James Idema, reviewing for *Smithsonian* (April 1989), had some harsher criticism, though he generally approved of the volume. He wrote: "The story of a young black man's voyage in a canoe down the length of the Mississippi River is ultimately rewarding . . . However, like the river itself, the story takes some getting used to. . . . [Harris would] have been helped in telling the tale of his adventure by more perceptive and sympathetic editing. . . . [It] is not a graceful book but it's an engaging one."

In 1992 Harris produced his second travelogue, *Native Stranger: A Black American's Journey into the Heart of Africa*. In order to discover more about his ancestry and himself, the author traveled to 23 different African nations within the course of a year. At the outset, Harris made no claims of being African, often asserting his Western attitudes throughout the book, but he also discovered that he is more African than he had previously supposed. In many ways he behaved like an American tourist; traveling in various ways (by car, boat, and horse), he took in sights including the world's largest basilica, in the Ivory Coast, Victoria Falls, in southern Africa, and Goma, in Zaire, one of the few remaining homes to the gorilla on the planet. Yet, unlike most American travelers, he tended to stay close to the average African in every country he visited. In this way he saw the everyday life of the poor.

Native Stranger received mixed reviews. Many critics, like David H. Anthony III of the *Chicago Tribune* (March 15, 1992), found much to like about the book. He remarked: "*Native Stranger* is carefully, even meticulously, constructed, and parts of the book are idyllic in their splendor. On the other hand, the saga loses interest once Harris has passed from West to Central Africa, and the concluding sections on Zimbabwe and South Africa are anticlimactic, as were those visits. . . . [This book] has much to recommend . . . both as a window on Black America and as a key to African melancholia." Robert G. O'Meally, reviewing the work for *New York Newsday* (March 1, 1992), cheered: "This book has value as an antidote to simplistic Afro- centricity, as a pre-primer for a new traveler to the so-called Third World, as a record of one passionate man's first trip to Africa and, perhaps most tellingly, as a reflection on things back in the U.S. of A.—that place where the natives also can feel so strange." One particularly negative review came from K. Anthony Appiah, who wrote in the *New York Times Book Review* (March 22, 1992): "Mr. Harris, like many Europeans and Americans before him, has conflated a dazzling variety of cultures into a single homogenous thing called Africa. . . . Despite the interest of his surroundings and his own manifest virtues, Mr. Harris's tale-telling is oddly uncompelling."

Harris's next book, *South of Haunted Dreams: A Ride Through Slavery's Old Back Yard* (1993), detailed his travels through the American South. As he tours this part of the country on a big blue motorcycle, he shares with the reader his thoughts on racism and slavery, reflecting on the lives of his great-great-great-grandfather—a freed slave from Virginia—and his father, who was run out of Louisville, Kentucky, in the 1930s for falling for the wrong woman. Harris also wonders why slaves didn't rebel more than they did and what constitutes the South's legacy. He half-expects to run into prejudice wherever he goes, fearing lynchings, segregation, and mobs looking to beat up a lone black man on a motorcycle. Most of these things, he finds, belong to a time that no longer exists, although he does run into a man who calls him "nigger" to his face. Yet he also records many acts of kindness: from a white man who opens his home to him on their first encounter, to a waitress who calls him "Sugar" and claims she knows him, to locals who sit on small-town park benches trading wisdom. *South of Haunted Dreams* received excellent reviews in the press. A reviewer for *People* (May 31, 1993) remarked: "*Haunted Dreams* reads at times like a Southern Walden: Woods, tobacco fields, North Carolina's Outer Banks—all evoke a much needed mystic serenity that contrasts with Harris's probing thoughts on history, race, color and identity." A reviewer for *Essence* (September 1993) enthused: "With honesty and humor, Harris lets the reader in on the fears, disappointments and joys this journey home brings."

In order to continue his exploration of the various aspects of black life around the world, Harris moved to Harlem, arguably the capital of black America, to research and write his next book. The result was *Still Life in Harlem*, published in 1996. In it the author looks at what Harlem has become since the 1920s and 1930s, the years of its spiritual and intellectual Renaissance. Much of the book is a study of the neighborhood's decline, but a great deal of it is also the author's reflection on himself and on his place as a black man in an often prejudiced world. Since the author has spent much of his life outside the ghetto, he approaches his subject as an outsider, and as a result, feels quite alienated from his surroundings. Yet at the same time he feels a great deal of empathy for the natives he encounters. Though he came to Harlem by choice and knows he can leave at any time, he also realizes that his experiences there will always be a part of him. He encounters much that disturbs him: he overhears a man beating a woman almost nightly outside his apartment's window, and a young man pulls a gun on him in the street after Harris bumps into him. Still, he sees much to admire as well: a Harlem native, now a lawyer, returns to his old neighborhood in order to help the younger generation; a woman spends late nights caring for the neighborhood's children. Harris, in turn, becomes less of an outsider, inspired by these good deeds to offer a writing class in a local after-school program. Overall, the author received high praise for *Still Life in Harlem*. Writing for *Booklist* (October 15, 1996), Lillian Lewis lauded Harris's skill: "His emotional engagement to Harlem is stunning; the 'still life' of the title may well reflect the beautiful image of Harlem that is trapped in Harris' very being. This is a powerful memoir of Harlem life and those who live there. It will find a place among other great African American writings about Harlem." A reviewer for *Kirkus Reviews* (October 1, 1996) had some quibbles, but wrote a generally favorable review: "The narrative is engaging, well-written, and sometimes insightful, but it stops short of extraordinary because of Harris's own ambiguous role. . . . The book's title becomes something of an unintentional double entendre: As an artist Harris has successfully captured the 'still life' of Harlem, a portrait of hopelessness and urban decay. But by the end he has subtly convinced the reader that there is still, in fact, life in Harlem. His own small transformations become his most compelling witness to that stubborn life."

Eddy L. Harris is the writer-in-residence at Washington University. He lives in St. Louis and Paris.

—C.M.

SUGGESTED READING: *Booklist* Oct. 15, 1996; *Chicago Tribune* 14 p 3, Mar. 15, 1992; *Essence* p 56, Sep. 1993; *Kirkus Reviews* Oct. 1, 1996; *Library Journal* p 90, Oct. 15, 1988; *New York Newsday* p 36 +, Mar. 1, 1992; p 35 +, June 3, 1993; *New York Times Book Review* p 18, Mar. 22, 1992; *Newsweek* p 61 +, Mar. 9, 1992; *Outdoors Magazine* Dec. 1997; *People* p 23, May 31, 1993; *Smithsonian* p 166, Apr. 1989; *Who's Who Among African Americans*, 1998–99; *Salon Magazine* Jan. 6-10, 1997

SELECTED BOOKS: *Mississippi Solo*, 1988; *Native Stranger: A Black American's Journey into the Heart of Africa*, 1992; *South of Haunted Dreams: A Ride Through Slavery's Old Backyard*, 1993; *Still Life in Harlem*, 1996

Miriam Berkley

Harris, Robert

Mar. 7, 1957– Novelist; biographer; journalist

The last thing the English writer Robert Harris suspected was that he would be a world-famous, best-selling novelist. After studying journalism at Cambridge University, he won respect with his political column for the *Sunday Times*. He wrote well-received nonfiction titles for a decade as well, but he seemed to show little interest in writing fiction. Yet the idea for his novel *Fatherland* (1992), which

he has traced back to his holiday in Sicily in 1987, came to him fully formed. "There were a lot of German tourists on the beach," he told the *New York Times* (October 11, 1995), "and if you closed your eyes you could just imagine you were in the victorious German empire. Suddenly, everything came to me as a novel. . . . I went splashing around in the water, and by the time I came back onto the beach I had it written in my mind." Harris believes that the storytelling aspect of writing is what comes most naturally to him—and what helped to make him a good journalist. He has a common-sense approach to fiction, believing that a writer should know his or her characters and have a firm grasp of plot. In an interview with *Publishers Weekly* (October 30, 1995), he said: "What I like is to work with a complex story. Yet today, when a writer says 'I am a storyteller,' it is practically shorthand for saying 'it's crap.' Of course it is perfectly legitimate to write novels which are essentially prose poems, but in the end, I think, a novel is like a car, and if you buy a car and grow flowers in it, you're forgetting that the car is designed to take you somewhere else." His most recent effort is *Archangel* (1999), a literary thriller set in modern-day Russia and concerning the search for a diary Stalin kept in his final years.

Robert Dennis Harris was born in Nottingham, England on March 7, 1957 to Dennis Harris, a commercial printer for a large firm in Nottingham, and Audrey (Hardy) Harris. Though Harris's childhood was working-class, his father read continuously. Harris described his father to *Publishers Weekly*: "He is one of those self-educated men who left school at 14, but he would read the latest Graham Greene, H. G. Wells, that kind of thing. I just always wanted to be a writer, from eight years old." When he enrolled in Selwyn College, Cambridge, he decided to study not literature but journalism. At Cambridge he was president of the student union and editor of the student newspaper. As he told Michele Field for *Publisher's Weekly*, he never attempted to write fiction before the monstrous success of *Fatherland* because "when I went to Cambridge, I got involved in student journalism, and I needed to earn a living. Although I never wrote poetry, never wrote short stories, I was interested in storytelling, and the desire to tell stories was satisfied by working in television and writing nonfiction stories for newspapers. The storytelling quality may be the one knack I have—a fondness for arranging things into fountains of stories."

Harris graduated from Cambridge with a B.A. in journalism in 1978 and soon went on to become one of the leading reporters in Britain. At the age of 30, he conducted a one-on-one interview with President Ronald Reagan. He became the left-wing political columnist of Rupert Murdoch's *Sunday Times* in the era of Margaret Thatcher's Conservatives. Of the experience, Harris quipped to Field: "I think it is good journalism for a paper to have a columnist the readers hate."

Book writing soon grew out of his journalism. In 1982, at the age of only 25, he published the first of several nonfiction titles—*A Higher Form of Killing*. The book, coauthored by Jeremy Paxman, is a detailed "secret" history of chemical and biological warfare. In the next two years he published works on British politics: *Gotcha!: The Media, the Government, and the Falklands Crisis* (1983) and *The Making of Neil Kinnock* (1984). The first of his books to receive international attention was *Selling Hitler* (1986), which is about the discovery of the secret diaries of Adolf Hitler and the press's ready acceptance of them as authentic. The book is a portrait of modern journalistic practices and of the major figures who helped to create this "news" and then readily dismissed it. *Selling Hitler* was also published in the United States, where it was highly regarded. A critic for *Library Journal* (May 15, 1986) remarked: "Especially interesting are Harris's colorful profiles of the leading players, including Gerd Heidemann, the German reporter who 'found' the diaries, and Hugh Trevor-Roper, the Oxford don who, to his lasting regret, originally authenticated the documents." Noting the continuing morbid fascination in the West with Hitler and Nazi memorabilia, a critic for the *Columbia Journalism Review* (July/August 1986) praised Harris's handling of the hypocritical way in which the press both condemned Hitler and yet viewed these diaries as a major find. "It is the story that Harris . . . assembles and tells in all its wonderful detail. The result is probably the best book about contemporary journalism in more than a decade and certainly the most entertaining." In 1991 *Selling Hitler* was turned into a five-part miniseries for British television.

Good and Faithful Servant: The Unauthorized Biography of Bernard Ingham appeared in 1990. Ingham was a major behind-the-scenes figure in British politics for more than a decade and was probably best described in the *Economist* (December 15, 1990): "By day, Mr. Bernard Ingham was a cipher, a humble civil-service officer who worked for 11 years for Mrs. Margaret Thatcher at Downing Street. By night (metaphorically speaking), he haunted Whitehall as one of the chief heavies of the Thatcher government." A reviewer for the *Spectator* (January 5, 1991) praised Harris's work: "Mr. Harris . . . has now produced a very good book about [Ingham]. . . . It is also most readable, even when he is describing Mr. Ingham's takeover of the Government Information Services."

Though Harris was a well-respected journalist and commentator on British politics and his books were widely praised, he had yet to write a bestseller. So it is not surprising that in the summer of 1992 Robert Harris seemed to many to have burst upon the literary scene with the publication of his first novel, *Fatherland*, a documentary-style fantasy whose premise is that Hitler won World War II. The year is 1964, and the Greater German Reich (which includes most of Europe and satellite nations such as France and England) is preparing for Hitler's 75th birthday celebration. Everything is going according to plan for the festivities, including the visit of the United States president Joseph P. Kennedy (father of John F. Kennedy). The visit of Kennedy is especially important—the two powers have been in a nuclear stalemate since the end of the war. The Germans are quietly suppressing their domestic problems, including guerilla warfare in what was the Soviet Union; the last thing they want is more turmoil, especially from controversy surrounding war "legends," such as the extermination of the Jewish population in Europe. When the body of a former high-ranking Nazi washes up on the shore of the Rhine, S.S. investigator Xavier March must learn the secret of what really happened to the Jews during the war in order to solve the murder.

The book was hailed on both sides of the Atlantic as a triumph. A critic at the *Washington Post* (June 15, 1992) wrote: "Robert Harris has managed to deliver a thoroughly accomplished first novel." The *Maclean's* (June 22, 1992) reviewer called Harris "a cunning maker of plots" and his book's final chapters "extremely suspenseful," noting, "Most impressive, it has a convincing moral dimension. The point of March's struggle is to show that no society is better than the conscience and courage of individual men and women." *Fatherland* was eventually translated into two dozen languages and had sold more than four million copies as of 1995. The auction for the U.S. paperback rights fetched $1.8 million—a first-novel record. The filmmaker Mike Nichols bought the film rights to the book prior to publication, and *Fatherland* was eventually turned into a HBO picture.

Harris's sophomore effort, *Enigma*, was published in 1995 to favorable reviews. *Enigma* is set in Bletchley Park, the secret, remote World War II British code-breaking center. In February 1943 Thomas Jericho, a young, inexperienced mathematician who has just cracked the Nazi code known as Shark, has returned to Cambridge in order to recuperate from a nervous breakdown. Before he is able to recover completely, he is called back into service to help crack the newest Nazi code, Enigma, which is generated on new four-rotor encrypting machines. Back at Bletchley Park, Jericho encounters Claire Romilly, with whom he has had a brief affair; his short reunion with her makes him suspect that she is a spy. Meanwhile, three enormous American merchant marine convoys are heading for a pack of Nazi U-boats, and it is up to Jericho to crack Enigma so that the allies' men and cargoes will not be lost.

The *Chicago Tribune* (October 16, 1995) critic was amazed to find, given all the World War II novels already published, that Harris had come up with a strikingly original plot: "It is to Harris's credit that he makes cryptography as exciting as any action-filled mission behind enemy lines. And he does this by wrapping the riddle of Enigma inside another mystery, this one involving a missing woman and betrayals large and small." Noting the critical work that was done behind the scenes for the war effort, Anthony Quinn of the *Financial Times* (September 16, 1995) remarked: "From this group portrait of men and women under terrifying pressure—fighting a war by proxy—Harris has fashioned a story that is as humane, intelligent, and gripping as documentary fiction can get."

Enigma was the first novel in a lucrative three-book deal with Random House. It has been the subject of a BBC documentary on the making of a best-seller, and it skyrocketed to the top of the best-seller lists on both sides of the Atlantic. His next novel, *Archangel* (1999) about a scholar's search for Stalin's secret notebook, generated a more mixed reaction. While many readers on Amazon.com complained that the book utilized too many stereotypes, book critics like Michael Specter of the *New York Times Book Review* remarked: "Robert Harris . . . has given those of us who retain some literary nostalgia for the Evil Empire exactly what we have been waiting for." Christopher Lehmann-Haupt, writing for the *New York Times*, had mixed feelings about Archangel, noting that it "is so outlandish as to defy credibility. But Harris makes you believe it as it's happening."

With the financial success of his fiction, the author has given up newspaper work and now devotes all his time to his books. (He is currently in the process of writing a biography of the author John Le Carré.) Robert Harris currently resides in a Victorian mansion in Berkshire, 60 miles west of London, with his wife—Gillian Hornsby, a journalist—and their two children.
—C.M.

SUGGESTED READING: *Chicago Tribune* V p3 Oct. 16, 1995; *Columbia Journalism Review* p25 July/Aug. 1986; *Economist* p86 Dec. 15, 1990; *Entertainment Weekly* p106 June 26, 1992; *Financial Times* II p11 Sept. 16, 1995; *Library Journal* p111 May 15, 1986, p74 Mar. 1, 1992; *London Review of Books* p22 Aug. 6, 1992; *Maclean's* p35 June 22, 1992; *New York Times* C p17 June 3, 1992, C p17+ Oct. 11, 1995; *New York Times Book Review* p46 Oct. 22, 1995; *Publishers Weekly* p42+ Oct. 30, 1995, p 7 July 27, 1992; *Spectator* p24+ Jan. 5, 1991; *Washington Post* C p2 June 15, 1992; *Contemporary Authors* vol. 143, 1994

SELECTED WORKS: Fiction—*Fatherland*, 1992; *Enigma*, 1995; Archangel, 1999. Nonfiction—*A Higher Form of Killing*, 1982; *Gotcha!: The Media, The Government, and The Falklands Crisis*, 1983; *The Making of Neil Kinnock*, 1984; *Selling Hitler*, 1986; *Good and Faithful Servant: The Unauthorized Biography of Bernard Ingham*, 1990

Harvey, John (Hooper)

May 25, 1911– Nov. 18, 1997 Nonfiction writer; historian

The English writer John Harvey, a specialist in the Middle Ages, wrote several important books that trace the development of Gothic architecture in England, the phenomenon of cathedral-building in England and Spain, and the history of formal gardens and decorative horticulture, as well as a brief, opinionated survey of the Plantagenet kings. An unabashed royalist and traditionalist, Harvey fastidiously insists on the spelling "medaeval," to guard against what he calls "the slovenly pronunciations me-dee-vl and me-die-vl." Although faulted by some critics for his eccentricity and partisanship, he was credited with bringing much previously hidden information to light about the artisans and architects who collaborated to build England's great medieval cathedrals. Among his important works are *Gothic England: A Survey of National Culture 1300–1550* (1947); *The Gothic World, 1100–1600: A Survey of Architecture and Art* (1950); *The English Cathedrals* (1950); *The Cathedrals of Spain* (1957); *The Master Builders: Architecture in the Middle Ages* (1971); and *The Medaeval Architect* (1972). His more generalized historical survey, *The Plantagenets: 1154–1485* (1948), is a paean to the when-knighthood-was-in-flower era that Harvey credits with giving England "its form and character."

For *World Authors 1990–1995*, John Hooper Harvey, who died on November 18, 1997, wrote: "Born in London, England, in 1911—early enough to realize some of the horror of the First World War, I soon afterwards learned of the murder of the Russian Imperial Family, a crime that marked my whole life. My outlook has always been profoundly monarchist, and this gave rise to my books *The Plantagenets* (1948, etc.) and *The Black Prince and His Age* (1976), with other studies including 'The Wilton Diptych—A Re-examination' (Society of Antiquaries of London, 1961). Most of my other published work falls into two main categories, derived from my heredity and my early environment: the history of garden plants, and the Gothic architecture of the Middle Ages. My mother (born Alice Mabel Wilcox at Grafton, New South Wales, Australia) was a daughter of James Fowler Wilcox, from Somerset, a member of the 'H. M. S. Rattlesnake' expedition of 1846–1851, who settled in Australia as a naturalist. On the voyage he was profoundly impressed by the flora of Rio de Janeiro and, many years later, introduced the jacaranda tree to Grafton, where the Jacaranda Festival became an institution. Through my mother I met her Irish friends in Dublin and in Ulster, and have spent much time in Ireland from the age of two years onwards: this accounts for my *Dublin—A*

Study in Environment (1949; enlarged edition 1972).

"My father, William Harvey, was an architect: a Gold Medallist of the Royal Academy in 1907 and winner of the Owen Jones Studentship in 1913. His studies in colour decoration, in Palestine and in Spain, were an essential part of my environment during childhood, and his work on the restoration of ancient buildings was to lead on to my own career and to my writings on medieval architecture, building craftsmen, and conservation. By the time I was five, my father took me to see his work on the repair of Westminster Hall roof, and I became enthralled by the romance of the skilled carpentry and masonry of centuries ago. It was this that, by about 1930, led to my starting to compile bibliographical material for the lives of masters of the Middle Ages, eventually published as *English Medaeval Architects* (1954; revised and enlarged 1984, with a Supplement 1987).

"In the meantime, the course of my life had been changed by the impact of the Depression of the later 1920s and '30s. My earnest hope had been to become a naturalist and explore for insects and plants, but this was denied me by the refusal of my headmaster to countenance such a career. When I left school in 1928 we were faced by a total lack of prospects, and within a few months my father became seriously ill and nearly died. For three years we depended on help from relatives, but through the kindness of my father's professional associates I was taken on to train as an architect, though I had little enthusiasm for the job. On my father's recovery he was selected to carry out a structural survey of the Church of the Holy Sepulchre, Jerusalem, then under British Mandate, and took me with him as his assistant. This was followed by a similar survey of the Church of the Nativity, Bethlehem; between the two surveys I returned to England, got married, and lived in Bethlehem until the summer of 1935. Back in England, I was eventually able to get work in the Ancient Monuments Branch of H. M. Office of Works.

"Impatient with routine work, I began in my own time to do research into old records and produced articles, while proceeding with the biographical dictionary. During the Second War this could not be published, but Harry Batsford suggested that I concentrate on a single life out of several hundred—that resulted in *Henry Yevele, c. 1329 to 1400, The Life of an English Architect* (1944; revised edition 1946), and then *Gothic England—A Survey of National Culture 1300–1550* (1947; revised edition 1948). These led on to the wider study *The Gothic World, 1100–1600, A Survey of Architecture and Art* (1950, etc.; expanded into *Cathedrals of England and Wales*, 1974; revised paperback 1988).

"Revisiting Spain for the first time since childhood, on holidays in 1948 and 1951, I became deeply involved in Hispanic art, was engaged to carry out a complete revision of the Blue Guide (*Northern Spain*, 1958; *Southern Spain*, 1964) and

produced my own *The Cathedrals of Spain* (1957). For some years I was heavily committed to work for Winchester College, William of Wykeham's foundation of 1382, both as Consultant Architect (1947–1986) and as Archivist (1949–1964), but eventually brought out an edition with translation (from the Latin) of *William Worcestre: Itineraries 1478–1480* (1969). After a period of nearly seven years in the Royal Commission on Historical Monuments at York, I was able to return to books with *The Master Builders* (1971), *The Medaeval Architect* (1972) and *Medaeval Craftsmen* (1975), as well as *Conservation of Buildings* (1972) and *York* (1975; 2nd edition 1983). A detailed study of later Gothic in England: *The Perpendicular Style* (1978) followed.

"At long last I began to get into print some of the material I had been collecting over the years on the history of garden plants and their introduction from one country to another and from continent to continent. Much of the basic sources consisted of lists, from which I compiled *Early Gardening Catalogues* (1972) and then *Early Nurserymen* (1974). Soon after I was commissioned to produce a major work, based largely on fresh research, *Medaeval Gardens* (1981; revised edition 1990) and then a consideration of how to rehabilitate old gardens, *Restoring Period Gardens*, (1988, revised edition 1993). A keen member of the Garden History Society, I was elected their President for 1982–85."

When John Harvey began publishing his books, in the late 1940s, the sun was already beginning to set both on the global British Empire and the old feudal class system he so idolized. Whether his subject is architecture or regiculture, Harvey unequivocally comes down on the side of royalty and the unique way that northern European 'civilisation' has flourished in its English incarnation, in which "personal freedom and individuality have been most highly developed." His preface to *The Plantagenets* (1948) begins with the point-blank statement: "Kingship is at a discount," a reference to the rapid dissolution of all the old monarchies "south of Scandinavia," along with the "Asiatic empires" of China, Russia, and Turkey. Harvey bemoaned the fact that monarchs had been deposed and their reputations besmirched with unflattering regularity since the days of the French Revolution, and that the term "royalist" had become "far more effectively abusive than 'radical' or 'bolshevik' had ever been." He hoped that his book would help answer two basic questions: Why did these monarchies collapse on the continent but survive in Britain? Was this an accident of insularity or a proof of divine endurance? Harvey's temperament is conservative and traditional, and he fears that "we are living in an age of swift transition toward what may be a new Dark Age of utter chaos" unless we are propelled by medaeval values toward a "new epoch of creative energy."

The Plantagenets is hardly Harvey's most highly regarded book, but its style and content serve to illustrate the worldview that informs much of his subsequent scholarship on architectural history. Obviously a diehard fan of the Plantagenets, Harvey writes of them in an unflappable third-person superlative, as in: "The most nearly perfect realization of human aims took place during what are loosely termed the 'Middle Ages.'" In England, he wrote, this roughly covered the years from 500 to 1500, from the founding of the Wessex dynasty by Cerdoc (Caradoc) "up to the usurpation of the Plantagenet throne." He dismissed the "earlier and darker of these 10 centuries" in favor of the 300-year period from the reign of Henry II onward, when the Plantagenets were in flower, discussing the way in which these 13 kings (not counting the child king Edward V) had given "new form, a specific English guise, to the eternal values of Man's knowledge and Man's will." These monarchs, with the flourishing golden broom as their symbol, were, in Harvey's mind, remarkable for their "personal genius as artists and provokers of genius in others."

The Plantagenets was faulted by reviewers, even in England, for its royalist bias, but the work can be enjoyed for its charm and antique flavor. A writer for the *Times Literary Supplement* (October 23, 1948) stated: "Mr. Harvey is guided throughout by the faith of classic royalism, that the king is preeminently the father of his people, and their natural leader and defender against the self-interest of the great. . . . To maintain this as a consistent motif from 1154 to 1485 needs a certain amount of special pleading, or at any rate careful selection from the evidence; but although Mr. Harvey necessarily omits much that others would consider relevant, he uses only facts that are accepted by the best contemporary scholarship." Other, more serious historical scholars disagreed: Sidney Painter wrote in the *American Historical Review* (October 1948) that "the only feature of this book that is of real interest to historians is the illustrations. . . . For the rest, Mr. Harvey's work is not to be taken very seriously. He makes no pretense of having used original sources, and if his bibliography is to be taken as an indication of the secondary works consulted, he made no very thorough perusal of this type of material." Still, the book is characteristic of Harvey's dramatic, sometimes elegiac prose, as in its closing sentences, a description of the funeral procession of Richard III, whose "wounded and despoiled" body was taken "along the ancient highway, across the great rolling open fields. The loaded horse plodded on, while the long summer gloaming deepened into dark. Night fell."

It is as an architectural historian that Harvey is more respected. He worked closely with his father, an architect who assisted in the restoration of many historic English buildings, including Westminster Hall. Spurred by his "Chesterbellocian" interest in England's Middle Ages—a reference to the pro-medievalism of Hilaire Belloc and G. K. Chesterton—he produced a series of important books on the cathedral architecture of the period. In 1947 he published his *Gothic England: A Survey of National Culture 1300–1550*), his attempt to redress the "unjust neglect" of English art between the Black Death and the Reformation that had occurred because of the influence of John Ruskin and of classicists to whom the period was "contemptible." Harvey thought this analogous to the way that Shakespeare was allowed, in the words of G. K. Chesterton, to throw "a gigantic shadow back" upon all that went before. With much attention to detail, he discussed the "Perpendicular" as the "national style of England." A *Times Literary Supplement* (July 5, 1947), review of the book paid tribute to him as a "serious and learned writer, with a sense of style and a remarkable knowledge of Gothic architecture, and the men who created the English versions of it," and Lionel Brett saw fit to mention in his *Spectator* (July 18, 1947) review that "the strong-nerved reader, clinging tightly to the rigging, should be able to weather [the author's] Bellocian storms and will find much to reward him in this diffuse, enthusiastic, and eccentric book."

Harvey wrote the text for a comprehensive study titled *The English Cathedrals*, published in 1950, to accompany photographs by Herbert Felton. Again, Harvey insisted that he saw those cathedrals not just as brick-and-mortar structures but as remnants of a once-viable spiritual and aesthetic tradition: "It has not been common to regard them primarily as a series of related works of art: art consecrated to the service of God, truly, but still best to be apprehended as the creation of inspired human genius." It is clear where his sympathies lay when he wrote that in medieval England, "the cathedral was the ruling art form, as the symphony was in the Age of Taste." Post-medieval buildings, he wrote, cannot be said to come from "the soul and spirit of a people." One of the paradoxes examined in this book is how England, such a close-knit, insular country, could have produced such a broad diversity of architectural styles when uniformity would be expected from such a setting. On the contrary, Harvey asserted that "no country is so rich in variety of artistic invention." He explained this paradox by noting that the lack of competing styles and viewpoints such as existed on the continent gave the English the luxuries of time and energy to develop more particular embellishments and ornamentation. "Its enrichment provoked the finest flight of the decorative artists," he wrote.

Harvey's *English Medaeval Architects: A Biographical Dictionary Down to 1550* (1954) was the culmination of assiduous research through thousands of "dry documents" such as contracts, receipts, and other "nonliterary" sources. Arranged alphabetically, the book—a compilation inclusive of carpenters and tradesmen as well as architects and clerics—lists hundreds of names, both celebrated and obscure, connected with building in England. An example of an entry, chosen at random, shows that one Thomas Grene, a carpenter, "was paid 3s. 4d. in 1456–57 for making an oriel in the mansion house at Macclesfield, Chester." Other entries add interesting tidbits to the store of knowledge about prominent historical personages, as, for example, that Henry III borrowed "five casks of wine from his mason." The book is especially valuable for helping to dispel the mythology built around the notion that the medieval cathedrals were products of anonymous, self-abnegating craftsmen. Harvey's skill in giving a human face to the cathedral-builders was further developed in his later books *The Medaeval Architect* (1972) and *The Master Builders: Architecture in the Middle Ages* (1972). Intended for a lay, nonspecialized readership, *The Medaeval Architect* described its subjects as professionals, "not too different from the modern practitioner," who engaged in systematic study and apprenticeship and were members of professional organizations. "Particularly noteworthy," wrote a reviewer for *Choice* (November 1972,) "is Harvey's convincing argument against the fanciful interpretations which have tended in the past to diminish the architect's individuality and to emphasize anonymity in the building of the Gothic cathedrals."

Later in his career Harvey returned to the Plantagenet era for a study of *The Black Prince and His Age* (1976), an attempt not at full-scale biography but at putting the character of Edward in historical and cultural context. The book is regarded as a well-written if superficial treatment with a monarchical bias undiminished: H. T. Keenan wrote of its "essentially conservative, elitist interpretation" in the *Library Journal* (December 15, 1976). This time, the notice in the *American Historical Review* (April 1976) was only slightly more favorable, as Michael Altschul wrote: "The writing is engaging and zestful, and the plan of the book intriguing: but it does not provide a full or balanced account of the careers of the Black Prince and of Richard II, or of the connections between political values and artistic achievement in 14th-century England."

Harvey also served as an architectural consultant to several projects involving the repair of medieval buildings, lecturing on this topic at the University College, University of London. In addition, he served the Archdiocese of York as a member of its commission on redundant churches. Beginning in the early 1970s, he published several significant monographs on medieval horticulture and the evolution of the English garden, publishing, at the age of 79, his book *The Nursery Garden* (1990) and serving as president of the Garden History Society from 1982 through 1985. He received an honorary doctorate from the University of York in 1976.
—E. M.

SUGGESTED READING: *American Historical Review* p280 Oct. 1948, p341 Apr. 1977; *Choice* p1120 Nov. 1972; *Library Journal* p2571 Dec. 15, 1976; *Spectator* p86 July 18, 1947; *Times Literary Supplement* p335 July 5, 1947, p1350 Oct. 23, 1948

SELECTED BOOKS: *The Heritage of Britain: Our Historic Past Through 53 Centuries*, 1940; *Henry Yevele, c. 1329 to 1400: The Life of an English Architect*, 1944; *Gothic England: A Survey of National Culture 1300–1550*, 1947; *The Plantagenets: 1154–1485*, 1948; *An Introduction to Tudor Architecture*, 1949; *The English Cathedrals*, 1950; *The Gothic World, 1100–1600: A Survey of Architecture and Art*, 1950; *Slyfield Manor and Family of Great Bookham, Surrey*, 1953; *English Medaeval Architects: A Biographical Dictionary Down to 1550*, 1954; *The Cathedrals of Spain*, 1957; *Northern Spain*, 1958; *Dublin: A Study in Environment*, 1960; *The Wilton Diptych—A Re-examination*, 1961; *Southern Spain*, 1964; *The Master Builders: Architecture in the Middle Ages*, 1971; *The Medaeval Architect*, 1972; *Early Gardening Catalogues*, 1972; *Conservation of Buildings*, 1973; *Man, the Builder*, 1973; *Early Horticultural Catalogues: A Checklist*, 1973; *Sources for the History of Houses*, 1974; *Early Nurserymen*, 1974; *Cathedrals of England and Wales*, 1974; *Medaeval Craftsmen*, 1975; *York*, 1975; *The Black Prince and His Age*, 1976; *The Perpendicular Style*, 1978; *The Georgian Garden*, 1983; *English Medaeval Architects, Supplement*, 1987; *The Availability of Hardy Plants of the Late Eighteenth Century*, 1988; *Restoring Period Gardens*, 1988; As editor and translator— *Worcestre, Itineraries 1478–1480*, 1969

Harvey, John (Robert)

June 25, 1942– Novelist

Throughout his nearly 20 years as a professional writer, the Englishman John Harvey has repeatedly demonstrated his aptitude for both fiction and nonfiction. The author of the novels *The Plate Shop* (1979), *Coup d'Etat* (1985), and *The Legend of Captain Space* (1990) as well as the nonfiction works *Victorian Novelists and Their Illustrators* (1970) and *Men in Black* (1995), he has tackled a broad range of subject matter, producing, for example, a documentation of the history of the color black in men's clothing, a fictional account of two days in a dingy English factory, and an examination of life under a repressive dictatorship. Widely respected for his simple, rhythmical prose, which has elicited comparison to the work of Hemingway, Harvey has won praise from critics on both sides of the Atlantic.

In a statement submitted to *World Authors 1990–1995* discussing his life and works, the author—born John Robert Harvey on June 25, 1942— writes: "I was born in Bishops Stortford, Hertfordshire, a small country town twenty-five miles from the University city of Cambridge, where I have lived and worked for most of my adult life. I would not seem to have got very far, if it were not for my (first, and continuing) marriage to Julietta Papadopoulou Harvey, who, in the waterlogged flats of East Anglia, misses her own precipitous country greatly. As a result we spend as much of the summer as we can in Greece, most of that time living in our cottage in the village of Sotiros, on the shoulder of a mountain on the island of Thasos in the northern Aegean. So I now speak Greek fluently in a rustic accent, and keep reasonably fit repairing stone terraces, scything nettles and carrying bags of cement up a 30 degree slope. We have however accumulated several generations of word-processors there, which survive the winter under the beds, and in the summer enable us both to make progress with our novels and criticism.

"My most recent book is *Men in Black* (1995), a study of the use of the colour black in men's dress. What interested me is the way in which the colourless colour of black, which used to be the colour of death, of grief, of humility, of shame, has over the centuries, in men's dress especially, become the colour of religion, of rank, of responsibility and professionalism, of authority and possession—in a word, of power. I pay special attention to those Christian countries where the adoption by men of a smart but gloomy fashion for black coincided with that country's rise to its highest-ever position of financial and imperial dominion—Fifteenth Century Burgundy, Sixteenth Century Spain and Venice, Seventeenth Century Holland. Nineteenth Century England. Though black can be smart, dashing and sexy, a 'fun' colour, still it seems to me there is always some play with its more sombre meanings. In the Twentieth Century of course black is worn more by women than by men (who have retreated, often, to deep charcoal grey), but this goes I think precisely with the fact that in the Twentieth Century women have gained a better access to such things as responsibility, possession, professionalism, power.

"In part, *Men in Black* built on an earlier book of mine, *Victorian Novelists and their Illustrators* (1970) which was, I believe, the first full modern study of the intimate cooperation of novelists with artists, which was a regular part of the Nineteenth Century publishing scene. Novelists like Dickens and Thackeray needed to have good relations with artists, because their novels came out in monthly parts, four chapters a time, which relied on their illustrations, displayed in booksellers' windows, to advertise them and point their moral. But in any case Dickens and Thackeray had vivid visual imaginations; and the illustrators such figures as George Cruikshank, 'Phiz' (Hablot Knight Browne), John Leech had been raised not at art school but in the caricature tradition of Hogarth, Gillray, and Rowlandson. Their pictures speak, as the novelists' words 'see,' and novel and etching work together, in black and white, to capture the tumultuous voracious busy-ness, and the shadows and tears, of that triumphal but haunted century.

"I have published criticism on a number of authors and artists (for instance, Beckett, Blake, Tolstoy, Shakespeare), but still the work on which I have been most deeply engaged is my fiction. My first novel, *The Plate Shop* (1979), describes the last two days in the life of an engineering factory, bought up and scheduled for closure and asset-stripping. The novel is based on a factory where I had worked (the major factory in my home-town, where also my grandfather and other relatives had worked), and it is true that the destruction of that factory, and of the community that depended on it, made a profound impression on me: as also did the vigour of shop-floor life—something that, in English fiction anyway, has often been presented as greyly mechanical. But when men work closely with machines, the men do not become mechanical, rather the machines acquire an uncanny life: there is a kind of iron heart at the centre of a factory.

"*The Plate Shop* won the David Higham Prize, and started me as a novelist. My second novel, *Coup d'Etat* (1985), is a broader undertaking, which follows the course of the Colonels' Dictatorship in Greece from 1967–1974—something which my wife and I had seen at very close quarters, since we spent much time in Greece in those years, and some of our friends were interrogated, tortured and imprisoned. The novel is not all about prison and dictatorship—I hope it is rich with the life of my second country—but I do try in it to give an anatomy of the life-process of a dictatorship, and to trace the logic by which an army dictatorship builds its power, extends, corrupts, and collapses. It was interesting to me to see, in the years in which *Coup d'Etat* appeared, that the dictatorship in Argentina followed a very similar course (both dictatorships ending in the last-gasp fiasco of a failed invasion of a nearby island—Cyprus for the Greeks, the Falklands or Malvinas for the Argentinians).

"My third novel, *The Legend of Captain Space* (1990), is about a mother who runs away from her baby (and from her marriage as well). It is set in a world of long-distance road-haulage and motorcar-racing, and the offices and clubs of British business life, and I think it reflects the brokenness and harshness of much of English life now. But its central subject is family life, and especially it is concerned with how alien and terrifying the most intimate and precious things (like love and having babies) can be.

"A chapter of the novel I am currently completing has just been published (March 1997) in *New Writing 6*, edited by A. S. Byatt and Peter Porter, under the title *Europa*. The novel follows an intimate crisis in the life of a contemporary painter, but the theme is I hope broadened by the fact that this painter is obsessed with the earlier painter Rubens, and is engaged on a suite of prints that follow Rubens's attempt, in his visit to England in 1629–30, to play the diplomat and negotiate peace between Spain, England and the Netherlands. Rubens was very sincere in his efforts—for the reason

I think that a painter who loved the sensuous human body as deeply as Rubens did *would* hate war and mutilation and injury. But still there is violence and conflict behind the plump lovely surface of Rubens's paintings, and behind the stately success of his life, and I hope the novel will engage both at large and intimately with the war between Love and War. I try to make my moves between the centuries, and indeed to make most of my emotional moves, by visual means, and to suggest rich pictures, even though my present-day painter is himself heading towards broken pictures. I am in this novel very much concerned with the way we live through what we see, and with the eloquence, charge and treachery of things seen. The same is true of my critical writing, and in this sense my productions are of a piece."

Harvey's first novel, *The Plate Shop*, was published in 1979. "There have been factories in England for 200 years, but they haven't appeared much in fiction," he noted in one interview. "Even when a novel is supposed to be about industrial life, the factory is usually only a backdrop to, for instance, a worker's affair with the boss's wife. It seemed to me that fiction should not be so shy of the place where most people spend most of their lives. In *The Plate Shop* I have tried to give a direct picture of life *inside* the factory." After receiving excellent critical reviews, *The Plate Shop* was chosen by the *Observer* as one of the best books of 1979.

Harvey's most recent foray into nonfiction, his 1995 book *Men in Black*, was similarly well-received. This history of the use of the color black in menswear in Western cultures over the past 500 years was deemed "readable, imaginative, and not a bit obscure" by Eugen Weber in the *Times Literary Supplement* (January 26, 1996) and "arguably the best contribution to the growing body of literature on the meaning of clothes and colors" in *Library Journal* (January 1996). Further praise was added by Michiko Kakutani in the *New York Times* (November 7, 1995): "Harvey wisely grounds his theorizing in a lot of specific examples (drawn, among others, from the work of Shakespeare, Dickens, George Eliot, Caravaggio, Rembrandt, Whistler, and Courbet), using his knowledge of literature and art to trace subtle changes in the cultural Zeitgeist. The resulting book is a lively and informative history of the color that Castiglione once noted 'hath a better grace in garments than any other.'"

In addition to writing books, Harvey is a frequent contributor to magazines and literary journals including *Encounter* and *Cambridge Quarterly*. Additionally, he has reviewed more than 75 works of fiction, literary biography, and criticism for such publications as the *London Review of Books*, the *Sunday Telegraph*, and the *Sunday Times*.

—J. P.

SUGGESTED READING: *Booklist* p530 Nov. 15, 1995; *Library Journal* p96 Jan. 1996; *New York Times* p17 Nov. 7, 1995; *New York Times Book Review* p23 Dec. 17, 1995; *Times Literary Supplement* p36 Jan. 26, 1996; *Contemporary Authors* vol. 93–97, 1980

SELECTED BOOKS: Fiction—*The Plate Shop*, 1979; *Coup d'Etat*, 1985; *The Legend of Captain Space*, 1990; Nonfiction—*Victorian Novelists and Their Illustrators*, 1970; *Men in Black*, 1995

Dave Phillips

Hassler, Jon

Mar. 30, 1933– Novelist

Described by one reviewer as "Sinclair Lewis without an attitude problem" and by another as "Minnesota's most engaging cultural export," Jon Hassler has written nine novels and several books for younger readers that, in the terminology of an earlier era, would have classified him as a "regionalist" author. Hassler often uses the fictional towns of Staggerford or Rookery, Minnesota, as the setting for his novels, which include *Staggerford* (1977), *A Green Journey* (1985), *North of Hope* (1990), *Dear James* (1993), *Rookery Blues* (1995), and *The Dean's List* (1997). As the setting for his fiction, Hassler has carved out a recognizable niche in the American imaginative landscape: the far northern plains of Minnesota, where his characters—small-town eccentrics, country priests, and rural academics—live out lives of everyday longing far from the centers of power and glamour. Upon the publication of Hassler's eighth novel, *Rookery Blues* in

1995, Bruce Allen noted in the *New York Times Book Review* (October 1, 1995) how adeptly the writer's novels "have surveyed the small-town culture of the northern Midwest with a beguiling blend of mockery and affection." Hassler's probing of characters who are caught in moral dilemmas and who contemplate ultimate questions of hope and redemption prompted the sociologist-priest Andrew Greeley, himself a veteran novelist, to describe Hassler in the Jesuit periodical *America* (November 17, 1990) as "one of the leading lights of contemporary Catholic fiction." Asked to reminisce on his career for a *Minneapolis Star-Tribune* article (July 20, 1997), Hassler said, "I think a novelist needs a lot of life before he can start writing anyway. I didn't know any writers and didn't have a role model." He admitted, however, admiring such authors as John Cheever, Kingsley Amis, Philip Larkin and Richard Hugo. First Lady Hillary Clinton, who claims to have read all his books, invited Hassler to read at the White House in 1993, partly, she said, to seek reassurance from him that his works were not getting "darker in tone."

In March 1998 Jon Hassler sent the following autobiographical sketch to *World Authors 1990–1995*, noting that "I have lifted it from my memoirs, which I am just now completing, a book entitled *Days Like Smoke: Recollections of a Happy Boyhood*." He continued: "Unlike the rest of my several friends, I, as a boy, grew into a position of importance in the three-block business district of our town of 1,500 souls, for at the age of 11 I donned my first apron and trimmed my first head of lettuce, candled my first egg, and carried out my first sack of groceries to a customer's car, and over the next seven years I became, by my father's example, proficient at stocking shelves, freshening the produce and jollying the customers who patronized us in ever increasing numbers, but I never got the hang of bookkeeping. Having developed, under my mother's tutelage, a sharp eye for the odd personality—the more eccentric the better—I kept being distracted from the figures in the books we kept by the human figures populating the two aisles of our little grocery store. Also, it was from my mother the schoolteacher that I picked up what little facility of language I can claim for myself.

"Whenever I read 'Fern Hill' and come to the line where Dylan Thomas speaks of himself as 'prince of the apple towns,' I picture myself going about my father's business on Main Street and I remember the satisfaction of living in a community small enough to fit your mind around. By the time I graduated from high school and went off to college, I had come to know all our customers by name, where they lived, whom they were related to, and most important to a novelist-in-waiting, I had watched the events of their lives unfold year after year like chapters in a book: births and deaths, house fires and suicides, new cars and picnics, 50th wedding anniversaries attended by hundreds. Although I would put off writing for another 20 years, I've always thought of the Red Owl Grocery

Store in Plainview, Minnesota, as my training ground, for it was there that I acquired the latent qualities necessary to the novelist, namely, from my dear German father, endurance, patience, resilience and sound working habits, and, from my dear Irish mother, the fun of picking the individual out of a crowd and the joy of finding the precise words to describe him. I dare say nobody ever got more nourishment than I did out of a grocery store."

Jon Francis Hassler was born in Minneapolis, Minnesota, on March 30, 1933, the son of Leo Blaise and Ellen Frances Callinan Hassler. He received his bachelor of arts degree from St. John's University in Collegeville, Minnesota, in 1955, and his master's from the University of Notre Dame, in Indiana, in 1961. In 1965, after 10 years as a high-school teacher in various Minnesota districts, he joined the faculty of Bemidji State University, in Minnesota. He moved to Brainerd Community College in 1968, where he taught until 1980, the year he won a Guggenheim Fellowship. In 1981, he became writer-in-residence at his alma mater, St. John's, where he remained until he retired, in 1998, with the title of Regents' professor emeritus.

In 1977 Atheneum published Hassler's first novel, *Staggerford*, a poignantly comic narrative of the last week in the life of Miles Pruitt, a high-school English teacher. The novel doubled as a narrative of small-town manners and a satire of hayseed "ackcomedia," a malaprop coined by the mother of the school's spinster librarian. The novelist Joyce Carol Oates reviewing the book for the *New York Times* (July 24, 1977), declared "Jon Hassler's easygoing, understated prose expresses succinctly the arid state of Miles's soul; nothing much has happened in Staggerford in the past and nothing much will happen in the future. . . . Jon Hassler's characters are rather close to being two-dimensional . . . yet there is something likable about the novel itself." R. C. Anderson, writing in *Best Sellers* (September 1977), compared Hassler to one of his considerably more acerbic Minnesota forebears: "One cannot avoid comparing Hassler's novel to the famous *Main Street* by Sinclair Lewis. . . . Hassler's passive, unevaluative tone softens considerably the heavy-handed ridicule to which Lewis subjects his characters, and if his work is less vivid, it lacks also Lewis' cloying self-righteousness." *Staggerford* was named the 1978 novel of the year by the Friends of American Writers. The Staggerford locale and characters later reappeared in several of Hassler's later works, inspiring some reviewers to dub him the author of a "Staggerford cycle."

Hassler's second novel, *Jemmy*, a book for younger readers, appeared in 1980. It is a coming-of-age story of one year in the life of Jemmy Stott, an adolescent girl of mixed heritage—one parent is Native American—who is forced into the role of caretaker for her household by her mother's death and her father's alcoholism. Thanks to a chance meeting with an artist and his wife during a snowstorm, Jemmy eventually develops the stability and self-confidence she needs to fulfill her new obligations. A reviewer for *School Library Journal* (August 1980) called it "a touching story of a quiet girl who must struggle against poverty, ignorance, and prejudice in order to learn her own identity as an Indian, a woman and an artist."

When *The Love Hunter*, Hassler's third adult novel, was published by William Morrow in 1981, Randolph Hogan wrote in his *New York Times* (August 16, 1981) review, "Jon Hassler is a writer good enough to restore your faith in fiction. Unlike so many contemporary writers, he creates characters you come to care about and believe in. His subjects are life, love and death—what the best novels have always been about—and he writes with wisdom and grace." *The Love Hunter* is a first-person narration by Chris MacKensie, a 40-something college counselor on the rebound after a failed marriage. Chris is given a new lease on life when he begins helping his best friend, Larry Quinn, deal with his multiple sclerosis. While doing so, however, Chris falls in love with Larry's wife, Rachel, then concocts a plot to kill his disabled friend on a duck-hunting trip, at once removing him from pain and freeing Rachel to marry again.

Considered part of Hassler's "Staggerford cycle," *A Green Journey*, published in 1985, follows retired Catholic elementary-school teacher Agatha McGee on an impulsive love pilgrimage to Ireland to meet her pen-pal, James O'Hannon, with whom she had begun to correspond after reading one of his letters in a traditionalist Catholic periodical. The two seem destined for romantic involvement until Agatha discovers that O'Hannon had concealed from her his true identity—that of a parish priest in a Dublin suburb. Despite this temporary setback, Agatha resumes writing to him as an antidote to her loneliness in Staggerford, and she finally comes to understand the parallels between his battles with Irish village politics and her struggles at her small-town Catholic parish in Minnesota. These later letters form the substance of *Dear James*, a 1993 sequel to *A Green Journey*. In *Dear James*, Agatha and James resume their correspondence after a hiatus of three years, during which time Agatha's school—she is now its principal—closes its doors and cancer forces Father O'Hannon into retirement. The two eventually rendezvous in Rome and Assisi, two focal points of Catholic pilgrimage, where they deepen their relationship (but remain chaste). Reviewing *Dear James* for the *Washington Post* (May 23, 1993), Dennis Drabelle described how the friendship between Agatha McGee and James O'Hannon "slowly develops into love." "Watching that love grow is one of the novel's chief rewards," he wrote, and "Jon Hassler plausibly depicts a passionate friendship that will not culminate in bed. It's not, to paraphrase Marlene Dietrich, that they couldn't; but the great gifts of companionship and affection which they exchange are made possible only by their unspoken but well-understood agreement that breaking vows and commandments is out of the question." Drabelle, who admitted that he had become hooked on the Staggerford novels, concluded, "Anyone who reads these engrossing and mind-broadening novels is likely to think twice before condescending to people who live seemingly constrained lives. Such as pious old maids in the boondocks."

In an article she wrote for the *Minnesota Star-Tribune* (December 31, 1995), the novelist Faith Sullivan called Hassler's books "a moral compass." She continued, "People are reassured by Hassler's work by a set of values that is rather stringent when set beside what we find generally in American literature." John F. Hafner wrote in *America* (November 17, 1993) that "Hassler does for his Catholic, upper-Midwest world what John Cheever did for his WASP New England one, though Hassler seems to have more affection for his characters than Cheever had for his." The themes of love, hope, and redemption explored through the prism of midwestern Catholicism have led some critics to call Hassler a quintessentially "Catholic" author, a once-common label that fell into disuse in literary circles in the post–Vatican II era. Once indiscriminately applied to everything from banal devotional works to apologetics by G. K. Chesterton to the fiction of Graham Greene, Evelyn Waugh, Flannery O'Connor, Edwin O'Connor, Walker Percy, and J. F. Powers, the "Catholic author" label has reemerged in substantial reviews of Hassler's fiction in such periodicals as the *National Catholic Reporter* and the Jesuit periodical *America*. In his article "The Catholic Novels of Jon Hassler" for *America* "November 17, 1990), Andrew Greeley, described Hassler's *North of Hope* as a "Catholic classic in the making" and decried Hassler's lack of recognition in Catholic circles. "Three or four decades ago," Greeley wrote, "the subject of 'The Catholic Novel' fascinated *America* and similar Catholic publications . . . and courses in Catholic fiction were taught in Catholic high schools and colleges. . . . A marvelous Catholic writer like Jon Hassler is [now] considered unimportant because, in the curious neo-pragmatism of *fin de siécle* American Catholicism, Catholic writing is unimportant."

Hassler's ninth novel, *North of Hope* (1990), is a warm narrative of struggle and midlife crisis involving Frank Healy, a Roman Catholic priest who finds his calling ministering to a tiny community on an Indian reservation in the far north of Minnesota, and Libby Girard, his childhood sweetheart, who reappears in Healy's life during a marital crisis. These could be the ingredients for a cliché-ridden potboiler of flesh-vs.-spirit, but Hassler crafts a "novel of hope" in which Healy strives to stanch the "leak" that has opened up in his soul and that threatens to drain away his spirituality. The following passage is typical of the personal though unsentimental attitude Father Healy assumes in his dealings with the Almighty:

"They came to Sovereign Lake. Frank turned off the road and drove carefully down to the ice. Crossing the lake, he gave more thought to God's personality. Most of God's attributes were a mystery to Frank, but not God's ambivalence concerning his people. God was a loner, no doubt about it—thousands of years of scrutiny by prophets and theologians and he was still as evasive as ever. Yet, like Frank, he was apparently a loner who wanted it both ways. He was always urging you to follow him, always out there ahead of you, calling to you from over the next hill or from deep in the trees, promising to fulfill your hopes. And so you toiled on and on, searching him out."

Reviewing *North of Hope* for the *New York Times* (October 1, 1990), Christopher Lehmann-Haupt pointed out what he saw as its stylistic and character flaws, but he concluded: "Mr. Hassler . . . has apparently won himself an enthusiastic local following with his novels about small-town life and the dimensions of human charity. On the evidence of *North of Hope*, one can understand why. The temperature is way below zero in his pages. The jack pine–ridden landscape is bleak. But the heart of the book beats warmly."

The insular world of small, rural colleges is the setting for several of Hassler's later novels, including *Rookery Blues* (1995) and *The Dean's List* (1997). The books unwind, a generation apart, on a fictional remote campus near the Canadian border called Rookery State College, whose faculty is less interested in "publish-or-perish" than "struggle-and-survive" and whose unsophisticated students are often depicted as either glorified high-schoolers or aimless draft dodgers. *Rookery Blues* is set in the turbulent and idealistic 1960s, when the campus is astir over plans to set up a faculty union. Inspired by a muse in the form of spirited singer-saxophonist Peggy Benoit, several members of the administration and faculty organize a blues combo, the Icejam Quintet, only to find themselves quickly confronted with discord on the campus and the world beyond. *The Dean's List* revisits the same campus a quarter-century later, in the more cynical 1990s, when issues like sexual harassment and athletic endorsements have elbowed aside the issues of militarism and racism that had prevailed a generation earlier. Hassler aims his barbs at pomposity in the academy by introducing a white-haired New England poet named Richard Falcon, who, uninvited, regales the campus with parodies of Robert Frost at his worst, as in the following: "A sultry night in Tipton Town, / The moon climbing over High Street // Like a ballooning bag of sweat, // The stars Leo Gorcey and the Bowery Boys // Projected on the west side of the grain // Elevator, in 'Spooks Run Wild' . . ." In his review of *The Dean's List* for the *Minneapolis Star-Tribune* (June 1, 1997), Dave Goldsmith wrote, "If Lake Wobegon had a college, it would be Rookery State."

Hassler has adapted two of his novels for dramatization at Minnesota's Lyric Theatre: *Simon's Night,* in 1991, and *Grand Opening,* in 1996. Of the latter, he told the *Minneapolis Star-Tribune* (September 6, 1996): "I think of a play as a streamlined novel. You have to cut away everything that doesn't move it along. A play is like a poem. Every line counts. In a novel you have so much room to move around. You can add texture and use narration." His novel *A Green Journey* was adapted for the 1990 television movie *The Love She Sought,* starring Angela Lansbury.

In 1998, after being diagnosed with Parkinson's disease, Hassler resigned his writer-in-residence position at St. John's and was given the title of Regents' professor emeritus. Steadfastly maintaining that he is merely slowing down a bit, the author is planing for many new books. He took strong exception to the way in which the *Minneapolis Star-Tribune* (December 31, 1995) had disclosed his diagnosis, in a prominent article under the headline, "Minnesota Novelist Jon Hassler Faces His Own Ending." Responding in a letter to the editor published on February 4, 1996, he charged the newspaper with an alarmist attitude that was misleading the public about his condition through its "cute, clever, pun-filled headlines." After reminding the editors that he had written two novels, begun his memoirs, and not missed a day of teaching since his diagnosis, he wrote, "I'm facing my own ending, but what's newsworthy about that? Aren't we all?"

Since that time, Hassler has continued to write articles for the *Star-Tribune* to educate people about Parkinson's disease, including one (February 13, 1997) in which he voiced his concerns through the mouthpiece of Agatha McGee, a character from some of his early Staggerford novels. In the article, McGee talks impersonally about a "certain Minnesota novelist" and the motor dysfunctions he was experiencing. She imagines God saying, "Listen, Hassler, this affliction is bigger and stronger than you are, and there's nothing you can do about it, so just relax and leave everything to me." When Hassler tells her he refuses to believe that God could be a "nag," Agatha McGee has the last word: "Tetchiness—symptom No. 13."

Hassler lives in a Minneapolis townhouse with his wife, Gretchen. He has three grown children, Michael, Elizabeth, and David, from his previous marriage, to Marie Schmitt.

—E.M.

SUGGESTED READING: *America* p366+ Nov. 17, 1990, p20+ Sep. 25, 1993, p7+ May 14, 1994, with photo; *Christian Science Monitor* p11 July 2, 1993; *Commonweal* p28+ July 16, 1993; *Library Journal* p1524 July 1977; *Minneapolis Star-Tribune* A p1+ Dec. 31, 1995, with photo, A p20 Feb. 15, 1996, E p1+ Sep. 6, 1996, with photo, A p22 Feb. 13, 1997, June 1, 1997, F p1+ July 20, 1997, with photo, A p20 Feb. 4, 1998, Sep. 16, 1998; *National Catholic Reporter* p31+ Feb. 1, 1991, p35+ Nov. 22, 1991, p33 May 28, 1993, with photo; *New York Times* C p20 Oct. 1, 1990; *New York Times Book Review* p14 July 24,

1977, p19 Aug. 3, 1980, p9 Aug. 16, 1981, p30 June 7, 1987, p39 Oct. 21, 1990, p18 June 27, 1993, Oct. 1, 1995, p20 June 1, 1997; *Publishers Weekly* p28+ Oct. 19, 1990, with photo, p52+ May 17, 1993, with photo; *School Library Journal* p76 Aug. 1980; *Washington Post* X p7 May 23, 1993, A p21 June 12, 1993, X p11 Aug. 8, 1993; *Who's Who in the Midwest 1994–1995*; *Who's Who in Writers, Editors & Poets: United States & Canada 1995–1996*

SELECTED WORKS: Novels—*Staggerford*, 1977; *Simon's Night*, 1979; *The Love Hunter*, 1981; *A Green Journey*, 1985; *Grand Opening*, 1987; *North of Hope*, 1990; *Dear James*, 1993; *Rookery Blues*, 1995; *The Dean's List*, 1997; Juvenile— *Four Miles to Pinecone*, 1977; *Jemmy*, 1980

Tim Wydronek/Courtesy of Farrar, Straus and Giroux

Havazelet, Ehud

1955– Short-story writer

Ehud Havazelet is a short-story writer whose ability to employ the voices of characters from varying backgrounds has impressed readers and critics alike for over a decade. His two collections have received high praise for their solid writing, their empathy for the human condition, and the subtle way in which characters' motivations are revealed through the plot of the story. His first collection, *What Is It Then Between Us?*, was published in 1988. Havazelet was lauded for creating a strong sense of place and for spinning images that effectively conveyed the characters' mindsets. His second collection, *Like Never Before* (1998), was pub-

lished 10 years later, also to rave reviews. *Like Never Before* looked at three generations of a Jewish family and how tis members adapt and change through their immigration from Europe to America. It also captured the inability of the family's members to convey their feelings toward one another, and how, in the end, that failing brings about their downfall.

In an autobiographical statement expressly written for *World Authors 1990–1995*, Ehud Havazelet discusses his life and his work: "I was born in 1955 in Jerusalem, descending on both sides from distinguished rabbinical stock. My mother's is one of Israel's oldest Jewish families, first emigrating to Palestine in the early 1800s. Her great-grandfather was leader of the group that founded the 'new' city of Jerusalem, the first Jewish agricultural settlement outside Jerusalem (now Petakh Tikvah), as well as starting the country's first Hebrew newspaper. My father's lineage traces back to the Baal Shem Tov, the founder of the Hasidic movement. Both my grandfathers were well-known rabbis, though of entirely different stripes, the American a leading scholar in Judaic studies, the Israeli a figure of folk legend, written about by S. Y. Agnon in his stories. My father is a scholar and author, a professor at Yeshiva University in New York, and my mother recently retired as Director of the Patient Accounts Division of a major New York hospital. Scholarship, a love for reading, and our family's central role in Jewish culture were dominating presences in my childhood.

"We moved to New York in 1958, and many early prevailing memories are of realizing I was different from the unequivocally American kids I met. Perhaps here I first experienced the outsider sensation which seems a necessary ache to a writer, and my work has always returned to the issues of borders, of those on the outside gazing in at a—often illusory—refuge. As an immigrant boy in American New York; as a Jew in a predominantly Christian society; as a child of a religious caste growing up in the foment of possibilities in the 1960s; and as a secular soul among devout scholars, I seem, to myself, to have always seen the world from its perimeters.

"My education was in yeshivas, Jewish parochial schools, where the focus was on Jewish culture, history, ethics. What struck me most, however, were the narratives, Biblical, Talmudic, stories culled from centuries of folktelling. Books were everywhere in our house, and reading was what we all did together. From as early as I can remember I read whatever I could, supplementing religious reading with science fiction, adventure books, comics, anything I could find. I began to write early, but took a long time to develop the patience and thick skin necessary to engage the craft, longer to accept myself as a writer.

"My other love was music. I began playing guitar at 12 and in college discovered the Delta Blues guitarists, Reverend Gary Davis, Blind Blake, Willie McTell. I was drawn by the wonderful orchestral sound these musicians had created for the guitar, and to the blues itself, its narratives of loss and defiance. Until I began writing in earnest, I hoped for a career in music.

"My first collection of stories, *What Is It Then Between Us?*, was written in various voices and styles, and had as a central theme the misunderstandings that often thwart our best efforts at love. Looking back now this book seems to float in an anonymous, post-Sixties American landscape, and in my second book, *Like Never Before*, I returned to the society and landscape of my youth, a Jewish family in New York. Many of my thematic interests abide in this book, in which I focus mainly on the tensions between three generations of a family in its passage from insular pre-war Europe to the shifting, allurements and disappointments of American life.

"I am interested in the short-story form. Many of the writers most important to me are story writers, from the originators of the modern story, Chekhov, de Maupassant, Mansfield and Babel, to recent and contemporary masters, Malamud and O'Connor, Carver, Paley, and Munro. I remain intrigued by the dictates and possibilities of the story form, with its foreshortened scale and heightened tension, and the ways in which, in the best stories, everything—point-of-view, voice, theme, setting, character—all indicate and sustain the whole."

Havazelet published *What Is It Then Between Us?* in the spring of 1988. Though the running theme of his collection was how misunderstandings often break relationships, each of the stories was very different in terms of plot and narration. In "Glass," one of the outstanding tales from the collection, an elderly draftsman named Wright watches and listens as his welfare-hotel neighbors engage in such acts as tossing soda bottles—and even a small refrigerator—out of windows to watch them explode. Meanwhile, he desperately wants to communicate with his roommate, fearing something has gone wrong between them, but his words often fail him and he realizes that he is coming across as a lunatic. In "What Everybody Wants," the narrator has problems conveying to her boyfriend her feelings about her mother's recent suicide attempt. Her frustration is compounded by the fact that she is unable to explain to her father that she doesn't want a family of her own. Almost opposite to these feelings are those of the narrator in "The Only Thing You've Got," who believes the life he wants is in reach: he has married a wonderful woman and raised a daughter, only to discover that all he has loved and worked for is falling away, while he is left to contemplate how things went so wrong.

Michiko Kakutani, the notoriously hard-to-please critic for the *New York Times* (April 30, 1988), had nothing but praise for the author's achievement. She wrote that this collection "marks the debut of a gifted young writer. Mr. Havazelet is

an agile ventriloquist, practiced at throwing his voice and making it emerge convincingly from a wide variety of characters, from a drug addict to an adolescent boy to an embittered woman; and he is also the owner of that rarer gift of sympathy, an unsentimental compassion for bruised and disordered lives."

Like Never Before, the author's second collection of short fiction, was published 10 years later, in 1998. As with his earlier collection, the author weaves the theme of thwarted love into every story. However, in this collection, the focus is chiefly on two characters, Max and David Birnbaum, a father and son struggling with their generation gap. Max, a Holocaust survivor, is steeped in old Jewish ways and customs and is terribly disappointed in his bright son, who has left architectural school and married twice, each time against his father's wishes. The stories are not in chronological order; the earliest of them takes place in 1943, the most recent several decades later. In the story "Leah," Max and David play very small parts in the actual narrative, which is told by David's sister. The narrator tells of growing up with her brother and her cousin Leah, a devout Jew who prayed for the salvation of her bohemian cousin. Another story, "The Street You Live On," looks at the reaction David's wife Maura has to the news that a woman on their block has been murdered; the incident indirectly reveals tension in the couple's marriage. In "Pillar of Fire" the reader is shown an older version of David, shortly after his separation from his first wife.

As with his earlier collection, Havazelet received good reviews for *Like Never Before*. Craig Seligman, writing for the *New York Times Book Review* (November 1, 1998), proclaimed: "Plenty of short story writers have called their collections novels; Havazelet abstains very honorably from making this claim, yet he could have done it truthfully. From one angle, the book appears to be an intensely conventional collection of stories. From another, it looks like a reticent, fragmented, chronologically disarranged, thoroughly 20th-century novel, not post modern but high modern. I have no idea what Havazelet's intention was, and no doubt it tells more about me than about him that I should be worrying about the issue, because what matters is the writing, and the writing soars." —C.M.

SUGGESTED READING: *New England Review* p31+ Summer 1997; *Southern Review*, p376+ Spring 1997; *New York Times* p18 Apr. 30, 1988; *New York Times Book Review* p11+ Nov. 1, 1998

SELECTED BOOKS: *What Is It Then Between Us?*, 1988; *Like Never Before*, 1998

Miriam Berkley

Haynes, David

Aug. 30, 1955– Novelist

After 12 years spent teaching elementary school, David Haynes published his first novel, *Right By My Side*, in 1993. Since then he has become one of the preeminent chroniclers of middle-class African-American life. Much like Terry McMillan's *Waiting to Exhale*, Haynes's novels attempt to tell realistic stories about African-Americans without resorting to stereotypical inner city tales of crime and drugs. Haynes has also gained recognition as a writer of juvenile and young adult literature with his *West 7th Wildcats* series, which includes the titles *Business As Usual* (1997) and *The Gumma Wars* (1997).

In an autobiographical statement submitted to *World Authors 1990–1995*, David Haynes wrote: "The only creative artists I knew when I was growing up were performing artists, and I only knew them through television or recordings, or from the occasional musical plays we would attend at the Municipal Opera in Forest Park. I certainly didn't know any writers.

"My father did auto body repair work and my mother worked in the home. My older brother, (who died in a car accident in 1991) and my younger sister and I were encouraged to excel in school, which I often did, especially in the early grades. I found high school oppressive and unstimulating, and performed as a scholar only intermittently and only to the minimum level needed to get by. We lived in a working-class community, where, for the most part, young people were pushed in the direction of sound and stable vocations (if they were pushed at all.) The arts were something that you

pursued as a member of the church choir, or perhaps by taking up a hand craft or hobby.

"I fell in love with books young, and despite some discouragements—particularly from English teachers of the sort who insisted there was only one correct way to understand a text: theirs—that love of literature stayed with me. One of my ambitions at an early age was to be a 'bookkeeper.' I wanted to be the person who got to keep (own) all the books. The word *librarian* didn't get a lot of air time in our house.

"Needless to say, a kid such as I was, in a working class neighborhood, grew to be something of an outsider. I wrote about this in an autobiographical essay entitled 'Breckenridge Hills, 63114,' collected in the anthology *Imagining Home* [1995]. I believe that this outsider's perspective is critical for all writers, allowing me as I was growing up to listen and to observe and to try to make sense of everything I experienced.

"I wrote my first short story when I was 11 and in the sixth grade. It wasn't an assignment and I don't really know why I did it. In hindsight, the act feels like some kind of compulsion.

"I remember there was a John Wayne movie on TV that night and not much else. I typed the story on an ancient manual typewriter my mother had purchased sometime shortly after such machines were invented. The keys were clotted with ink to the point that any letter that has what a handwriting teacher once called a belly on it was filled and stamped on the paper a perfect black circle. The story was about two kids who go to a grocery store on an errand. After checking out, they stop and buy a Coke from one of those old fashioned machines—the kind that dispenses a cup and then fills it with syrup and fizzy water. They deposit their money and get syrup and fizzy water, but no cup. Worse, the syrup and fizzy water keep coming and keep coming, and there is a sticky flood all over the grocery store.

"I cribbed the plot for that story from a comedy album by Godfrey Cambridge. (Although the continuous flow of beverage was an invention all my own!) Such was my storytelling mentorship—sitting around one of those old console hi-fis with the family, listening to recorded comedy routines by Cosby and Redd Foxx and others.

"I took the story to school the next day, and the teacher read it out loud to the class. Everyone made a big fuss over me for a day or two. And though I never saw that particular manuscript again, I became hooked on the process and on the outcome. I knew that writing would always be a part of my life.

"I also wanted to be a teacher, a vocation I pursued at Macalester College. Though I'd received little encouragement on the writing front, my professors did see a potential teacher in me.

"Graduating from college, I worked for several years for a textbook publishing company [C.V. Mosby, 1978–1981], but spent most of the next 20 years teaching elementary school, a job I enjoyed tremendously. Once I settled into my career, I decided to figure out how to make the writing part of my life happen. I wrote a few stories and had some publication success, particularly in 1983, winning the first annual *City Pages* (a Twin Cities based weekly) fiction prize. Still, I knew that I couldn't do much creative work in the time after school each day, I knew the key to the puzzle was figuring out how to exploit the long summer vacations that were available to me.

"Beginning in 1985, I began spending my summers in art colonies and retreat centers. The concentrated time helped me hone my voice and find the material I have been given to tell. I found, for example, that despite my frequent attempts to write ponderously, my natural tendency is as a comic novelist.

"Over the next seven summers I generated an abundance of raw material, which I spent the school years editing and shaping into fiction. While there wasn't much time leftover for marketing the work, I did feel satisfied that I was generating decent material.

"In 1993, my first novel, *Right By My Side*, was selected for publication as part of New Rivers Press' Minnesota Voices series. As often happens, when one book breaks through, people come looking for others. In the next four years, seven more books appeared. My head still spins from the way this has changed my world.

"I write these notes on my life, again on retreat in Central Virginia. As always the writing flows and feels like the old friend that it is, and, I am also, as always, eager to see the directions it takes me. Somehow it is never quite what I expect."

David Haynes was born on August 30, 1955, in St. Louis, Missouri. He graduated with a B.A. degree from Macalester College in 1977, and began his teaching career in 1981 in St. Paul, Minnesota. In 1989 Haynes received his M.A. degree from Hamline University. After the publication of *Right By My Side* in 1993, he stopped teaching to devote more time to his writing.

Right By My Side focuses on a teenage boy trying to put his life in order after his mother abandons him. The American Library Association listed the novel among the best books of 1993 for young adults, despite Haynes's claim that he wrote it for mature adults.

Throughout the course of his second novel, *Somebody Else's Mama* (1995), the narrative point of view shifts among characters. "By far the most powerful of the book's voices is Miss Kezee's," wrote Jill McCorkle in a *New York Times* (June 18, 1995) review. "This cantankerous old woman is the book's great strength—and the source of its occasional weakness. She is so vibrant a character that she sometimes takes over the novel." The book won the Friends of American Writers Adult Literary Award.

In 1996 Haynes published two novels, *Live at Five* and *Heathens*. In *Live at Five*, Haynes addressed racial issues for the first time, in the story of an African-American television news anchor who improves his program's ratings by broadcasting on-location reports of "life in the ghetto." *Heathens*, in which Haynes presents a realistic look at African-American family life, has been described both as a novel and an anthology of interconnected stories.

Haynes was more active than ever in 1997, publishing three books within the year. *All-American Dream Dolls* follows 30-something Deneen Wilkerson as she runs home to her mother after her being dumped by her boyfriend. After wallowing in depression for days, she becomes aware of the outside world again thanks to her 12-year-old half-sister, who is trying to win a beauty pageant. Haynes also began his *West 7th Wildcats* series of children's novels with the books *Business As Usual* and *The Gumma Wars*, both of which were targeted at an upper-elementary school readership. Haynes is keenly aware of the stigma attached to writers of juvenile fiction. "People are dismissive of children's literature in this country," he commented to Nathalie Op de Beeck for *Publishers Weekly* (April 22, 1996). "Writers tend to ghettoize their colleagues who work on children's books, much more so I think than the public does." In an assessment of *Business As Usual*, a critic for *Kirkus Reviews* (June 15, 1997) criticized Haynes for bland storytelling and unbelievable characters.

Haynes struggles for a universality in his representation of African-American characters, and intentionally avoids the stereotypes and limits imposed by many race-oriented narratives. He prefers to write about relationships and the struggle for identity. As a result, he has, in the past, been encouraged by major publishing houses to include more seamy elements in his novels, in order to conform to the "norm" of "black fiction." "I don't tell the popular narratives, the commercial narratives, that one is supposed to tell as an African-American writer, and there is a price to be paid for that," Haynes told Op de Beeck. "There's an orthodoxy about that subject matter in this country, and I've been actively bucking it in my writing."

Haynes was selected by *Granta* magazine as one of the best young American novelists of 1996. He was a visiting scholar and writer at Morehead State University and Mankato State University in 1994, and has held faculty positions at Hamline University (1995) and Warren Wilson College (1996–1997). Two of his short stories have been dramatized and recorded on National Public Radio. In 1998 he coedited *Welcome to Your Life: Writing for the Heart of Young America*, an anthology of poetry and short fiction that includes stories from multiracial and multiethnic perspectives.—B.S.

SUGGESTED READING: *Kirkus Reviews* p950 June 15, 1997; *New York Times* VII p21 June 18, 1995; *Publishers Weekly* p40+ Apr. 22, 1996, with photo

SELECTED WORKS: *Right By My Side*, 1993; *Somebody Else's Mama*, 1995; *Live At Five*, 1996; *Heathens*, 1996; *All-American Dream Dolls*, 1997; *Business As Usual*, 1997; *The Gumma Wars*, 1997; *Welcome to Your Life: Writing for the Heart of Young America* (coeditor), 1998

Heat-Moon, William Least

Aug. 27, 1939– Essayist; travel writer

William Least Heat-Moon is the pen name of the American travel and nature writer William Lewis Trogdon. He became famous for his first book, *Blue Highways: A Journey into America* (1982). His second book, *PrairyErth (A Deep Map)* (1991), stands in direct contrast to his first, being, rather than a journey, a delving into one place—an in-depth look at Chase County, Kansas, in America's heartland. Heat-Moon's *River Horse*, scheduled for publication in October 1999, details his travels through America's waterways, from the Atlantic Ocean to the Pacific.

Heat-Moon was born on August 27, 1939 in Kansas City, Missouri, the son of Ralph G. Trogdon, a lawyer, and Maurine (Davis) Trogdon. He was educated at the University of Missouri, Columbia, where he earned a B.A. (1961), M.A. (1962), and a Ph.D. (1973) in literature and later obtained a B.A. (1978) in photojournalism. From 1964 to 1965 he served in the U.S. Navy, after which he taught English at Stephens College, in Columbia, Missouri. In early 1978 he lost his teaching job due to declining enrollments at the college. At the time, he had been separated from his wife for some nine months. (That first marriage eventually ended in divorce, and Heat-Moon later married Linda Keown, a teacher.) Disconsolate and agitated, he decided to "chuck routine" and "live the real jeopardy of circumstance." He converted his 1975 Ford van into a rudimentary camper, and on the first day of spring he set out to explore America's forgotten back roads and small towns, a voyage chronicled in his phenomenally successful first book, *Blue Highways: A Journey into America*. His financial assets were meager: four gasoline credit cards and less than $500 in cash (the remnants of his savings account). Along with the usual camping provisions—a portable gas cookstove, a sleeping bag, and a tool kit—he carried a satchel of notebooks and pens, a couple of cameras, a miniature cassette recorder, and two "vade mecums": J. G. Neihardt's *Black Elk Speaks* and Walt Whitman's *Leaves of Grass*. The influence of Whitman, whom he quoted frequently throughout the book, is evident in Heat-Moon's own work, and John Steinbeck's *Travels with Charley* was also an inspiration. In a 1985 interview, Heat-Moon acknowledged how much Steinbeck's book had influenced his but expressed

disappointment that "most of the people who appear in [*Travels with Charley*] are generalized—mere shadows. . . . I wanted a journey that would present people, specific people, with names and addresses almost, so that the reader could pick up a Rand-McNally and follow along and know almost mile by mile where this particular traveler was."

Blue Highway (blue, the author explained in a brief introductory note, was the color used to represent back roads on old highway maps) is divided into 10 sections, each corresponding to a segment of the journey and labeled simply with a compass direction. The first leg of his journey, covered in the sections "Eastward" and "East by Southeast," took him from Columbia, Missouri, to Roanoke Island, North Carolina, the site of Sir Walter Raleigh's ill-fated "lost colony," one of the earliest European settlements on the North American continent. "Out on Roanoke," one man told him, "you can *feel* the beginning," and Heat-Moon remarked that the natives there still speak "with the Old London accent of the Banks that some believe to be the speech of the Elizabethans." Beginnings of a more personal sort also occupied Heat-Moon during the first part of his journey. Near Franklinville, a remote hamlet in central North Carolina, he hiked deep into the pine forest in search of the grave of an ancestor, one William Trogdon (1715-83), a miller who, Heat-Moon noted, supplied the Carolina militia with "sundry items" during the Revolutionary War, was gunned down by Tory sympathizers, and "thereby got his name into volume four of *Makers of America*."

Although *Blue Highways* is narrated in the first person, the author provided only a few particulars about his own life and background. Near the beginning of the book he devoted a mere two-page chapter to himself, promising, "When done with it, I will shut up on *that* topic." Then, echoing Melville, he introduced the persona who will serve as narrator: "Call me Least Heat Moon. My father calls himself Heat Moon. My elder brother Little Heat Moon. I, coming last, am therefore least. It has been a long lesson of a name to learn." Heat Moon, we learn, is a Sioux term for the seventh month, "a time also known as the Blood Moon." He briefly discussed the significance of bloodlines, noting that all too often a "mixed blood" is viewed as "a contaminated man who will be trusted by neither red nor white." Yet the degree of Heat-Moon's own American Indian ancestry is left—almost certainly on purpose—maddeningly ambiguous. (The back cover of his second book, *PrairyErth*, states that Heat-Moon is "of mixed English-Irish-Osage ancestry," and that volume contains some further reflections on the origin of his Indian name and the "different inclinations" embodied in his dual identity as Trogdon/Heat-Moon.) He christened his converted camper Ghost Dancing, which he admitted was "a heavy-handed symbol alluding to ceremonies of the 1890s in which the Plains Indians . . . danced for the return of warriors, bison, and the fervor of the old life that would sweep away the new." Ghost dances, he observed, were "desperate resurrection rituals . . . the dying rattles of a people whose last defense was delusion." By renaming himself Heat-Moon, and by calling his ordinary, somewhat dilapidated vehicle Ghost Dancing, the author revealed much about how he envisioned the journey ahead. Describing his state of mind as the trip began, he wrote, "With a nearly desperate sense of isolation and a growing suspicion that I lived in an alien land, I took to the open road in search of places where change did not mean ruin and where time and men and deeds connected."

After leaving North Carolina, Heat-Moon traveled south and west, through Georgia, Alabama, Mississippi, and the Louisiana bayou. He meandered through Texas and the desert southwest, then cut north, through the mountains of Nevada, Utah, and northern California, reaching the Pacific Ocean at Depoe Bay, Oregon. His route east hewed through the northernmost tier of the continental United States, through Washington, Montana, and the northern plains states. He crossed Lake Michigan by ferry, passed briefly through Ontario, traversed rural upstate New York, and continued into Vermont, New Hampshire, and Maine. He then followed the eastern seaboard south to the pine barrens of New Jersey, and from there went westward again through Maryland, West Virginia, and Kentucky, arriving back in Missouri near the beginning of summer. In the course of circumnavigating the United States, he traveled some 13,000 miles—a distance, he noted, roughly equivalent to the circumference of Earth. With few exceptions, he steered clear of bigger towns and cities; his typical stopping places were remote burgs and country crossroads uncharitably referred to by many as backwaters, and he often went out of his way to visit those with intriguingly peculiar names—among them Brooklyn Bridge, Kentucky; Nameless, Tennessee; Dime Box, Texas; and Remote, Oregon. He sought out conversation in lunchrooms, bars, roadside cafes, college cafeterias, and parks, and in almost every place he visited he found at least one local resident willing to expatiate on the history and folkways of the town. Heat-Moon encountered a remarkably diverse array of American characters and always paid careful attention to the ways in which people's lives have been shaped and defined by their physical surroundings. He noted, for example, how specially designed farm equipment is used to cultivate the Palouse region of southwestern Washington, the steepest cropland in America, where the "treeless, rounded hills, shaped by ice and wind and water to a sensuous nudity, were sprouting an intensely green fuzz of winter wheat."

Blue Highways immediately found a broad and enthusiastic audience. Robert Penn Warren hailed it as "a masterpiece." Anatole Broyard, writing in the *New York Times* (January 13, 1983), noted, "On finishing the book one can be forgiven a little flush of national pride." The *New York Times Book Review* (February 6, 1983) contributor Noel Perrin commented, "There are at least a hundred memorable characters in *Blue Highways*. Taken together . . . they give a striking sense of what America was, is, and will be." *Blue Highways* was named a notable book of the year (1983) and one of the five best nonfiction books of the year by the *New York Times*. It also received the 1984 Christopher Award and the 1984 Books-Across-the-Sea Award.

Not every critic, however, offered such generous praise. John Updike, writing in the *New Yorker* (May 2, 1983), faulted Heat-Moon for being a "self-dramatizing but not self-revealing" narrator: "He does not tell us that, set adrift by spouse and employer, he has embarked on an odyssey determined to redeem his life with a literary feat, though this would appear, from the determined manner of his peregrinations and his prose . . . a plausible conjecture." Moreover, Updike found that "no inner curve of feeling tells us if this grandly invoked search reaches or fails to reach its objective. . . . No Moby-Dick of an envisioned thesis surfaces on the horizon to pull the worlds of detail toward some gravitational center." In the *Hudson Review* (Summer 1983) Robert McDowell examined the pitfalls inherent in writing a first-person, or confessional, narrative, which, he noted, "more than anything else must tell the truth." Heat-Moon, he decided, "is telling the truth perhaps 40 percent of the time." McDowell criticized Heat-Moon for implying that "only the highly visible have-nots and outcasts are capable of self-analysis, worthy of praise."

In many respects, *PrairyErth* (1991) is a radical departure from *Blue Highways*. In the first book, the accent is on movement and distance, and the author rarely stays in one spot for more than a few days. In *PrairyErth* the focus is on rootedness and depth, as Heat-Moon provides a massively detailed portrait of just one place—Chase County, Kansas, a sparsely populated, 774-square-mile plot that very nearly occupies the geographical center of the United States. Heat-Moon here delves into such diverse realms as philosophy, botany, natural history, ethnography, autobiography, and even etymology (he documents 140 variations on the spelling of Kansas). Interspersed throughout the text are selections entitled "From the Commonplace Book," a diverse lot of quotations from sources both celebrated and obscure, related (however tangentially) to the subject of Kansas. The name of the state derives from Kansa, the white man's rendering of the name of the native people and the Siouan dialect they spoke. "I suppose," Heat-Moon wrote, "over the last four centuries, that this place called Kansas has come, like a murky chunk of softened glass, to fill the mold of its name, and I believe that today we see it through that now hardened form descended from unlettered explorers, careless map printers, and travelers and settlers who deemed red people worth no name but heathen."

Critical reaction to *PrairyErth*—the title is an antique geological term for the soils of the central grasslands—was almost uniformly positive, but, perhaps because of its length, difficulty, or stubborn eccentricity, the book never achieved the popular success of *Blue Highways*. "In several important ways," Mary Warner Marien wrote in the *Christian Science Monitor* (October 16, 1991) "*PrairyErth* is not about Chase County, Kansas, but about reading, and the relationship between authors and readers." The *Times Literary Supplement* (December 6, 1991) critic John Sutherland viewed Heat-Moon as a latter-day American transcendentalist working in the tradition of Emerson and Thoreau. After praising Heat-Moon's "consistently sharp eye and ear for the quirky detail, or phrase," Sutherland concluded, "In the end, *PrairyErth* is less a book about an America that has been rediscovered than a lament for a landscape which will soon be gone forever." Although he found the numerous catalogs and digressions at times diverting and faulted Heat-Moon for making his book "almost entirely a celebration of Kansas," Paul Theroux deemed *PrairyErth* "a salutary book because it goes against the notion that America is all newcomers and flux. . . . By concentrating his scrutiny on this small area of rural America, . . . Heat-Moon has succeeded in recapturing a sense of the American grain that will give the book a permanent place in the literature of our country." —S. Y.

SUGGESTED READING: *Christian Science Monitor* p17 Oct. 16, 1991; *Hudson Review* p 420+ Summer 1983; *New Yorker* p121+ May 2, 1983; *New York Times* Jan. 13, 1983; *New York Times Book Review* p1+ Feb. 6., 1983, p25+ Oct. 27, 1991; *Science Books & Films* p366 Dec. 1991; *Washington Post Book World* Dec. 26, 1982; *World Literature Today* p385 Spring 1992; *Times Literary Supplement* p8 Dec. 6, 1991; *Contemporary Authors* vol. 19, 1987, nrs vol. 47, 1995

SELECTED BOOKS: *Blue Highways: A Journey into America*, 1982; *PrairyErth (A Deep Map)*, 1991; *River Horse*, 1999

Gordon Gagliamo

Hegi, Ursula

May 23, 1946– Novelist; short-story writer

Ursula Hegi, the American novelist and writer of short stories and nonfiction, attempted to wrench herself away from the Germany of her birth both culturally and geographically. After setting her first two books, *Intrusions* (1981), a novel, and *Unearned Pleasures* (1988), a collection of short stories, in America, she felt ready to deal in her fictional work with the truth of the German past. The results, *Floating in My Mother's Palm* (1990) and *Stones from the River* (1994), set in a German town like Hegi's birthplace, drew high praise from critics for being able to draw forth readers' compassion. Hegi's most recent work is the nonfiction book *Tearing the Silence: On Being German in America* (1997).

In an essay submitted to *World Authors* in 1996, Ursula Hegi writes: "I was born in a small German river town in 1946, a year after the war ended. I learned how to read when I was five, and by the time I was six, I had figured out that the only thing that could possibly be more exciting than reading would be writing. But I didn't know anyone else who wrote. It seemed a weird thing to do. I'd walk along the Rhein by myself, sit on the jetties, write poetry. I wrote stories. Began a novel. Finished half of it on lined paper.

"I was a greedy reader, a fast reader. I would read four or five hours a day. By the time I was twelve, I'd gone through nearly everything my parents had on the shelves in the living room—Kafka and tales of saints; Edgar Wallace mysteries and Goethe; Dostoyevsky and young girls' adventure sequels. What I looked for then—just as I do now— were books that sucked me into their pages, books that let me identify with their characters, books that made me forget my surroundings and even the fact that I was linking words and turning pages. I was a Christian martyr in Rome. A murderer in Russia. A grandmother in Norway. I gave birth a decade before I ever became pregnant. Rode a horse through the American West years before I arrived here as an 18-year-old immigrant.

"Some immigrants keep seeing their world through the lens of their birth country. I yanked out that lens when I came to America, wanting a life that was new and clear and separate. I tried to shed my German heritage, to make myself nationless. I wished I'd come from another culture. Since I came from a country that had a history of oppression and violence, I could neither trust that community nor identify with it. I found that Americans my age knew much more about the war years than I. Gradually I learned more about the Holocaust: I listened; I read; I ran from what I found out; I hid in the familiar silence of my childhood for years, surfaced again and again, feeling increasingly distant from Germany.

"My first two books, *Intrusions* and *Unearned Pleasures and Other Stories*, were set here in America. I waited many years—too many years, perhaps—to write about Germany, but once I began, my writing took on an extra layer, a deeper way of seeing. When I wrote my third book, *Floating in My Mother's Palm*, I felt no loyalty to preserve the secrets of my country of origin—only the loyalty to myself to tell the truth as I perceived it, regardless how flawed my vision might be. And to preserve the integrity of my vision, I had to risk not belonging to any community.

"During the year after I completed *Floating in My Mother's Palm*, one of its characters, the dwarf woman Trudi Montag, continued to develop on her own—independent of my conscious imagination—presenting me her story as a gift in *Stones from the River*. For a while the material came too fast—quite a change from my daily writing habits—and I would take notes while driving or sitting in restaurants. Finally, I bought a cassette recorder so that I could listen to Trudi and transcribe her words onto tape. Much of my research material was in German, and I was living more within the language than I had in 27 years. I moved deeper and deeper into diary entries of people in concentration camps, read interviews with Holocaust survivors.

"My fifth book, *Salt Dancers*, is set here in America again, and my sixth book is a work of nonfiction, interviews with Germans of my generation, born after the war or during the war years, who left Germany and now live in the United States. I'm still working on this book, exploring what we're doing with the silence that was such a numbing presence in our lives when we were growing up in postwar Germany.

"Another major focus in my work is what it means to be linked to two cultures. Since I cannot separate from Germany, I have to understand it, have to come to terms with it though—many times—I still wish I'd been born into another country. But the fact is that I come from Germany. My initial stage of that journey was far more than geographical—it was a wrenching away which I assumed would be forever. Each subsequent stage of that journey has changed me, and now I've begun

to reach across with my writing, to tear through the silence, to try and understand with all the compassion I can summon."

Clearly, Hegi's motivation for leaving Germany at the age of 18 had to do with her uneasiness at being in a country of people who not only repressed their own memories of the Nazi past but also discouraged the publication of that history and attempts to understand it. She had to live for a while in an atmosphere where the Holocaust could be openly discussed before she could allow her German past into her writing.

Hegi told Kitty Harmon in an interview in *Publishers Weekly* (March 14, 1994), "We knew a lot about those old Greeks and Romans." She was referring to her early education in Germany, in which history lessons began with the classical period and ended with World War I. In the United States, after working for a German accounting firm, she began her university education at the age of 28, completing her B.A. and M.A. at the University of New Hampshire. She was a lecturer there in the English department until her divorce, in 1984. Although she had written her first, unpublished novel—which she considered a failure—soon after arriving in the United States, it was at the University of New Hampshire that Hegi truly began to consider herself a writer among other writers. Her first published novel, *Intrusions*, appeared in 1981.

The breakthrough for Hegi, in terms of her ability to confront her childhood in Germany and transmute it into literature, came with her novel *Floating in My Mother's Palm*, which takes place in Burgdorf, a suburb of Dusseldorf. Its 18 chapters, telling the stories of the townspeople as seen through the eyes of a little girl, are contained in under 200 pages, and some reviewers, such as Edward Hoagland in the *New York Times Book Review* (March 18, 1990), complained of its being too short. Hoagland nevertheless called it a "substantial advance over" the story collection *Unearned Pleasures*. "As our pilot, Hegi's voice over the intercom during these new tales of grotesqueries is assured and reassuring," Hoagland commented. Joan Frank in the *San Francisco Review of Books* (Winter 1990–91) concurred, writing that each of the chapters is an "exquisite self-contained short story. . . . Hegi's acute details lace these tales together—restoring us repeatedly to the riotously sensuous present-tense of childhood." She concluded that the book is "a feast."

Hegi explained to Kitty Harmon that although she had told a National Public Radio interviewer that she would not return to the setting of Burgdorf, a character from *Floating in My Mother's Palm*, Trudi, a dwarf librarian, took possession of her. Trudi demanded "her own book," Hegi told Harmon. That book became *Stones from the River*, described by Suzanne Ruta in the *New York Times Book Review* (March 20, 1994) as a "complex, ambitious work." According to Ruta, "Trudi has the ornery courage to find both love and a calling as the town's gossip, storyteller, and informal historian, hoarding secrets that have driven others mad. . . . Like Oskar, the dwarf in Günter Grass's novel *The Tin Drum*, she incorporates the best and the worst of Germany. And in her progress from malicious gossip to serene artist, she hints at the ambiguous roots of the writer's vocation."

Trudi and her father survive World War II and help hide Jews. Trudi identifies with the Rhine, which has always embodied the spirit of Germany: ". . .Trudi would ride its turbulent waves, dart beneath them in her frog-swim, heart beating fast as she became the river, claiming what was hers. As the river, she washed through the houses of people without being seen, got into their beds, their souls, as she flushed out their stories and fed on their worries about what she knew and what she might tell."

The torments endured by a woman who must live as a dwarf echo to some extent the experiences of Jews in Nazi Germany. Several commentators have noted that Hegi's theme of childhood anguish also touches on the deformed childhoods of those who became Nazis. As Ruta observed, *Stones from the River* "explores the way private grief can break out as political madness." She concluded that this "moving, elegiac novel commands our compassion and respect for the wisdom and courage to be found in unlikely places, in unlikely times."

Although in *Salt Dancers* (1995) Hegi returned to an American setting, she continued to deal with the theme of coming to terms with the memories of an unhappy childhood. Beaten by her father, deserted by her mother, Julia, pregnant for the first time at 41, travels across the country, from east to west, to confront her father. The novel had a mixed reception. Margaret Flanagan in *Booklist* (August 1995) declared that in "achingly beautiful prose," Hegi "at once shatters and rebuilds the myth of the family unit." She deemed *Salt Dancers* a "tragic and triumphant tale of the death and resurrection of an indomitable human spirit." John Skow in *Time* (August 21, 1995) disagreed, stating that although the "scenes, as character grates on troubled character, are real and vivid," the plot "might have been designed by a committee to illustrate how bitter, unresolved childhood memories can be coped with." He termed the conclusion the stuff of soap opera. But Abby Frucht, writing in the *New York Times Book Review* (August 27,1995), found the book to have a freshness which she attributed to Hegi's "refusal to sentimentalize" and to the "adroitness with which the book shifts from the reality of daily life to the surreality of imagined or remembered moments."

For *Tearing the Silence*, Hegi interviewed a number of people who, like herself, were born in Germany but came to the United States early in their lives. In quoting these individuals, Hegi sought to humanize them and demonstrate their plight—their "collective shame of coming from a country that murdered millions." In the opinion of Amei Wallach, writing in the *Nation* (July 28August 4, 1997), this nonfiction book—for all its biographical documentation—failed to reflect the humanity evoked by Hegi's novels and stories. Wallach complained of a "cacophony of voices," finding that there was "no one there to extract the melody, and fact alone isn't up to the task." Wallach concluded, "Leave oral history to the sociologists; Hegi has other gifts at her disposal: for language and character and situation."

On October 21, 1967 Hegi married Ernest Hegi, a management consultant, from whom she was divorced in 1984. The union produced two sons, Eric and Adam.

—S. Y.

SUGGESTED READING: *Booklist* Aug. 1995; *New York Times Book Review* p5 Mar. 18, 1990; p2 Mar. 20, 1994; p12 Aug. 27, 1995; *Publishers Weekly* p52+ Mar. 14, 1994; *San Francisco Review of Books* p45 Winter 1990–1991; *Time* p68 Aug. 21, 1995

SELECTED BOOKS:Fiction: *Intrusions*, 1981; *Unearned Pleasures and Other Stories*, 1988; *Floating in My Mother's Palm*, 1990; *Stones from the River*, 1994; *Salt Dancers*, 1995; Nonfiction— *Tearing the Silence: On Being German in America*, 1997

Herrera, Juan Felipe

Dec. 27, 1948– Poet

Juan Felipe Herrera is a highly respected Chicano poet, noted for his practice of weaving together English and Spanish in verse enjoyed by children and adults alike. His first collection, *Rebozos of love we have woven sudor de pueblos on our back* (1974), was remarkable for the way in which the author connected longer verse with haiku "bridges" between poems. Many of his collections focus on life in the Latin American community, including volumes for mature readers, such as *Exiles of Desire* (1983) and *Akrílica* (1989), as well as *Calling the Doves/El canto de las palomas* (1995) and *Laughing Out Loud, I Fly* (1998), which are intended for children and young adults.

Juan Felipe Herrera was born in Fowler, California, on December 27, 1948, the only child of migrant workers from Mexico. His father, Felipe Emelio Herrera, was born in a small town in Chihuahua, Mexico; his mother, Maria de la Luz Quintana de Herrera, was one of nine children from a Mexico City family. The poet's father came to the United States at 15 and began working as a ranch and farm hand. In 1920 Maria's brothers joined the U.S. Army in order to move to America. They arrived in El Paso, Texas, and the rest of their family moved to the city a year and a half after their arrival. Once there, Maria wanted to join a local Mexican theater group, but her family did not allow her.

Herrera's parents met in El Paso, married, and subsequently moved to California, following the seasonal crop route. Up until the time he was eight years old, Herrera wandered across the United States with his family. His parents finally settled in San Diego in 1956, giving their son the stability he had long lacked. At first they lived in Barrio Logan, a long-time Latino district. As Herrera was about to attend junior high school, the family moved downtown. "All of a sudden I was a downtown boy," Herrera noted in an interview with Sesshu Foster for the *Americas Review* (Fall–Winter 1989). "I used to spend a lot of time downtown alone . . . in Market Street in La Placita, in the movie house, near the Cine Azteca, the Casino Theater, the Savoy Theatre, the Moon Cafe. . . . I used to spend day after day in the Greyhound bus depot, looking for things in the lockers, playing the pinball machines, taking photos for 25 cents. . . . It was a strange scene. I was more used to the Logan atmosphere, which was more festive, more of a family neighborhood."

Herrera attended Roosevelt Junior High School and San Diego High School, where he demonstrated interests in theater, art, and music. He was accepted at the University of California, Los Angeles, graduating in 1972 with a bachelor's degree in social anthropology. In 1968, while still an undergraduate, Herrera had seen El Teatro Campesino for the first time. Mesmerized by the company's performance, he formed his own theater group, Teatro Tolteco. In 1970 he submitted a proposal to the Mexican-American Center at UCLA to go to Mexico to study theater. It was accepted, and Herrera has claimed that the experience changed his life. In his interview with Sesshu Foster, the poet explained: "I didn't get anything out of school. What I got out of it was the moment, the political moment, the cultural artistic, theatrical moment; the moment of personal development, of artistic expression."

Herrera's first collection of poetry was *Rebozos of love we have woven sudor de pueblos on our back* (1974), written between 1971 and 1972. The book alternates between haiku style poems and longer verses; the author used a mingling of Spanish and English to create a new way to interpret the Latin American oral tradition.

Shortly after the book's publication, Herrera left San Diego for San Francisco. Between 1974 and 1976 he compiled two additional manuscripts, which extended the types of themes he had embraced in his first collection, but he destroyed them. In 1977 he was accepted into the anthropology program at Sanford University. For several years he worked on his master's degree while writing poetry. In 1984, as he worked on his doctoral thesis, he quit the anthropology program, having become frustrated with the department. He had more success with his poetry; a year earlier he had published his second collection, *Exiles of Desire* (1983).

The poems in *Exiles* were begun in 1980, while the author was traveling between Seattle and San Francisco. Many of them were written in English, a good many dealing with the alienation and anger created by a society more and more mechanized.

Herrera was quite productive in the next few years, releasing a book almost yearly. First came *Night in Tunisia* in 1985, which was co-authored by Margarita Luna Roble, then three more collections of poetry: *Facegames* in 1987, *Zenjosé: Scenarios* in 1988, and *Akrílica* in 1989. *Akrílica* was completed in 1981 and written before *Exiles of Desire*, but did not find a publisher until Alcatraz Editions brought out a bilingual edition almost eight years later. Herrera conceived of this book as something like a "verbal art gallery"; indeed, the first chapter is called "Galería" (Gallery), in which each poem is considered a painting. *Akrílica* was written almost entirely in Spanish.

Herrera published two books in 1994: *Night Train to Tuxtla* and *The Roots of a Thousand Embraces: Dialogues*. He followed these with *Calling the Doves/El canto de las palomas*, a children's book, in 1995. In it the author reflects on his youth as the son of farm workers in rural California. He discusses how he learned to love poetry from his mother and to respect the land from his father. Written for grades one through three, *Calling the Doves* is written in both English and Spanish and illustrated by Elly Simmons. Many critics, like Annie Ayres of *Booklist* (January 1–15, 1996) praised this work: "A poetic picture-book memoir that will add beauty to any literature, Latino culture, or biography collection." Roger Sutton of the *Bulletin for the Center of Children's Books* (December 1995) disagreed: "Aside from one brief fragment in which the boy's father tells him of the difficult lives and deaths of his own parents in Mexico there is little sense of hardship here. . . . While the prose-poem is not strong on narrative, its images are evocative of the warm bonds between people and between people and their work and landscape."

Love After the Riots appeared in 1996 and *Mayan Drifter: Chicano Poet in the Lowlands of America* in 1997. Like many of his early works, *Mayan Drifter* stretches the boundaries of poetry and storytelling by incorporating poetry, a number of narrative voices, and a play. In it the author details the Spanish invasion of Mayan lands and the modern-day goverment, which allows gigantic corporations to further pollute the lands. Though dwindling in numbers, the Mayan people continue to resist.

With Laughing Out Loud, I Fly (1998), Herrera produced another significant bilingual poetry collection for children. Each of the 22 poems in this collection are written from a child's perspective and are printed next to Karen Barbour's illustrations from Mexican folk art. A reviewer from *Kirkus Reviews* (May 15, 1998) noted: "This is poetry to read aloud, to read quickly, to understand more with the heart than with the head." Herrera's most recent publication is a new collection of poetry, *Border-Crosser with a Lamborghini Dream* (1999).

Juan Felipe Herrera has been the recipient of a number of important grants and awards, including two National Endowment of the Arts Awards (1980, 1985), as well as the 1985 University of Texas at El Paso Chicano Poetry Prize, and the 1987 American Book Award.—C.M.

SUGGESTED READING: *Americas Reviews* p 68–87, Fall–Winter 1989; *Booklist* p 823, Jan. 1–15, 1996; *Bulletin for the Center of Children's Books* p 129, Dec. 1995; *Kirkus Reviews* May 15, 1998

SELECTED WORKS: Poetry—*Rebos of love we have woven sudor de pueblos on our backs*, 1974; *Exiles of Desire*, 1983; *Night in Tunisia* (with Margarita Luna Robles), 1985; *Facegames*, 1987; *Zenjosé: Scenarios*, 1988; *Akrílica*, 1989; *Night Train to Tuxtla*, 1994; *The Roots of a Thousand Embraces*, 1994; *Calling the Doves/El Canto de las palomas*, 1995; *Love After the Riots*, 1996; *Mayan Drifter: Chicano Poet in the Lowlands of America*, 1997; *Laughing Out Loud, I Fly*, 1998; *Border-Crosser with a Lamborghini Dream*, 1999

Hank Seaman/New Bedford Standard-Times/Courtesy of Everett Hoagland

Hoagland, Everett

Dec. 18, 1942– Poet; professor; editor

Although not widely known, poet Everett Hoagland has for the past three decades been one of the most productive artists addressing black culture. Using a gentle turn of verse and a keen eye for the details of his surroundings, Hoagland has transcribed present-day social issues, such as violence and racism, into poetic symphonies. Many of his poems also reveal the positive side of the black American experience, and some explore traditional African rituals, such as tribal music and dance.

Everett Hoagland was born on December 18, 1942 in Philadelphia, Pennsylvania, to Everett Jr. and Estelle (Johnson) Hoagland. The future author remained in Philadelphia for much of his youth,

and with parents who were voracious readers, quickly learned to appreciate the literary masters. While he was still a young child, Hoagland became fascinated with poetry, and he developed a sense of lyrical fluidity, taking time to memorize particular poems in which he was interested. Soon he was composing his own poetry, creating odes to the simple things around him, such as his mother's cooking. Later, during his teen years, he made a habit out of reading a book each day, returning to the library every day after school to return a book and pick up another to read that night.

Hoagland decided to enroll at Lincoln University in Pennsylvania and, despite his obvious inclination toward the literary arts, decided to major in biology, gearing his career toward wildlife conservation. Completing the math formulas proved difficult for him, however, and as he excelled in English, he decided to switch directions and major in English literature. It was at this point that he began to take his poetry seriously, and presented some of his work for the noted poet Langston Hughes to critique. "It was immature and amateurish," Hoagland said of his early poetry to Mark Johnson of the *Providence Journal-Bulletin* (April 22, 1998). "He was kind and generous and constructive." Soon after adopting Hughes's suggestions, Hoagland managed to win a creative writing award from the university. The author has stated that his early influences also include Robert Hayden, Sterling Brown, Jayne Cortez, and Ntozake Shange.

After graduating, in 1964, Hoagland began teaching English in the public schools of Philadelphia, a position he maintained for the next three years. In 1967 he began a two-year stint as the assistant director of admissions at his alma mater, Lincoln University. During this time, Hoagland published his first book of poetry, *Ten Poems: A Collection* (1968). By 1969 he had begun a dual job as administrative assistant and teacher of black poetry at the Black Studies Center of Claremont College in California. The following year, he was the college's poet in residence, and it was during this period that his second collection of poetry, *Black Velvet* (1970), made its appearance. This book was highly significant, as it was one of the first published collections of erotic poetry ever authored by an African-American. In 1972 he went back east to work as a humanities instructor at Swarthmore College, in Pennsylvania. After a year at this institution, Hoagland received his master's degree from Brown University and joined University of Massachusetts-Dartmouth, where he is now associate professor of English.

During this time period, he released another collection of poetry, *Scrimshaw*, and for several years was a columnist for the *New Bedford Standard-Times*. Since 1976, when not teaching poetry writing and literature of the African diaspora, Hoagland has been busy composing poetry. His subjects have ranged in subject from historical figures, such as the Revolutionary War seaman Paul Cuffee, to victims of violence and racism, to simple reflections on urban life. However, regardless of the subject, one of the most prominent staples of Hoagland's poetry has always been African pride, and he has written extensively about the African roots of black Americans, exploring traditional African customs with a fascinated eye. The author has also delved into how these customs translate into American black culture, chronicling the experience, both culturally and socially, of being a minority in America. While his work has not received much critical review, according to the *Dictionary of Literary Biography* (1985), Hoagland's poetry "has grown through the years. Accompanying it is an outrage at all that has thwarted the development of human beauty. The result is a poetry which seeks to teach as well as to entertain. . . . his poetic style has become an eclectic fusion of agit-prop, historical narrative, and bebop." Writer Linda E. Scott also notes that Hoagland's many anthology contributions indicate a "reader appreciation for his work."

In 1994 Hoagland was made the poet laureate of the city of New Bedford, Massachusetts. For the next four years, the poet portrayed in his work the events, people, and special features of his adopted home. A city rich in history as a whaling center and abolitionist landmark, New Bedford is also a racially harmonious, culturally diverse city, a characteristic which, in addition to the area's small-town feel, has kept hold of Hoagland's poetic gaze. "I like the warmth and civility of the people in this post-industrial town of a city that has so many of the positive characteristics of village life . . ." he told Johnson. "What is here is the most cosmopolitan small city I have ever encountered." As he has done since his move there in 1973, Hoagland rises each morning just before sunrise, to sit at his kitchen table and watch as day breaks over the horizon of the city; he composes verse as the denizens of New Bedford begin their day. "The day is brand new as dawn comes," he said to Johnson. "It's pastel, nascent, fresh, clean. The day itself is a clean slate."

In 1997 Hoagland published another collection of poetry, *This City and Other Poems*, which also focuses on New Bedford, both from a historical and contemporary viewpoint. One poem contained in the volume is "Just Words: Frederick Douglass, 1838," a tribute to the escaped slave who fled to New Bedford and devoted his life to the abolitionist cause. That poem was the basis for a symphonic piece—*Symphony of Just Words*, composed by Andrew McWain for the New Bedford Symphony Orchestra. *Symphony of Just Words* had its premiere in front of a packed audience on May 17, 1998. "I think Douglass would have been delighted," Hoagland told the *Standard-Times* (April 4, 1997), adding that the former slave was also an amateur violinist.

One of his most recent works is a poem titled "At The Access," a meditative reflection and gentle glimpse at nature. "The view is always renewed," he wrote. "Today/as I descended the weathered steps of the lake/access, I paused to look at shadowed Champlain. . . . I sank/into deep, dark, cold silence; a sullen/city frame of reference made the mirroring/water more than forty stories deep. . . . "Dedicated to his father, a "nature lover," "At The Access" is, according to Hoagland, the "best meditative poem" he has written in 20 years.

In 1998 Hoagland decided to give up his post as New Bedford's Poet Laureate, stepping aside to open the door for another poet. "I think that the people and the arts and cultures of New Bedford deserve to be chronicled or focused upon with poetry," he told Johnson.

Hoagland's poetry has been published in numerous periodicals, including *Essence*, the *American Poetry Review*, the *Iowa Review*, the *Progressive*, the *Journal of Black Poetry*, *Communications Education*, *Caliban*, *Black World*, the *Massachusetts Review*, *World*, and *First World*. His work has also appeared in many anthologies, including *Patterns*, *The New Black Poetry*, *Significance: The Struggle We Share*, *New Black Voices*, *Beloit Poetry Journal*, *Giant Talk*, *The Jazz Poetry Anthology*, and an anthology edited by Clarence Major titled *The Garden Thieves: Twentieth Century African American Poetry*. Among his many honors and prizes, Hoagland won the Gwendolyn Brooks Fiction Award and has twice been a winner in the state-wide annual poetry competition for Massachusetts Artist Fellowships. In addition, since 1984 he has been a contributing editor for the *American Poetry Review*. The Author continues to travel around the United States, reading his work at colleges, political rallies, churches, museums, and community organizations. He is a divorced father of four children, Kamal, Nia, Ayan-Estelle, and Reza Eve.

—D.B.

SUGGESTED READING: *Providence Journal-Bulletin* Apr. 22, 1998; *Standard-Times* Apr. 4, 1997; *Contemporary Authors*, 1987; *Dictionary of Literary Biography*, 1985; *Who's Who Among African Americans*, 1998–99

SELECTED WORKS: *Ten Poems: A Collection*, 1968; *Black Velvet*, 1970; *Scrimshaw*, 1976; *This City and Other Poems*, 1997

Hobhouse, Janet

Mar. 27, 1948– Feb. 1, 1991 Novelist; biographer; journalist

"Janet Hobhouse . . . writes like a brilliant figure skater, carving long, looping, intricate patterns with her words, and dazzling the reader with her verbal spins and leaps," Michiko Kakutani wrote in a *New York Times* (January 1, 1993) review of Hobhouse's posthumously published novel, *The Furies* (1993). Such praise has been liberally heaped upon the American author of six books that include *Everybody Who Was Anybody: A Biography of Gertrude Stein* (1975) and the novels *Nellie Without Hugo* (1982) and *Dancing in the Dark* (1983). Hobhouse is probably best known for her deep examinations of human emotions— particularly the bond shared by mother and daughter. "We are all used to thinking of a woman obsessing over a male lover, or perhaps even over a child," Margaret Anne Doody wrote in the *London Review of Books* (March 11, 1993). "Few have tackled a daughter's love for her mother as a central fact of her existence. . . . Women readers, as well as men, are accustomed to assuming that a woman ought, as Freud advises, to find a 'mature' or 'adult' heterosexual male beloved. Directed toward the mother, adoration looks 'unnatural'. . . . Yet Hobhouse is . . . one of the best writers of recent times in describing female heterosexual love; indeed, in representing this passion, I think she has very few competitors."

Janet Hobhouse was born on March 27, 1948 in New York City, the daughter of an American mother and English father. Her parents separated when Hobhouse was two, and she was subsequently raised by her mentally unstable mother, Fran Liedloff, in a series of low-rent New York City apartments. Her temperament, even to close friends like Elisa Segrave, could be notoriously off-putting. "Being with her was like being on a roller-coaster, an exhilarating, intense, even frightening experience—a roller coaster you often wanted to get off," Segrave wrote in her essay "Remembering Janet Hobhouse," published in the *London Review of Books* (March 11, 1993). "Janet was affectionate and bullying, brutal yet tender, vulgar yet refined, tragic but with a tremendous life force," she added.

Educated at Lady Margaret Hall, Oxford University, Hobhouse received her bachelor's degree in English with honors in 1969. After graduation, she returned to New York, where she worked as an art reviewer for *Arts Magazine*. In 1972 she once again moved to the United Kingdom, where she worked as an art reviewer for *Studio International*. A year later she began working as an editor at Secker & Warburg Ltd. Publishers, in London. Despite the fact that she began her career as an art reviewer, Segrave wrote in the *London Review of Books* article, Hobhouse always "looked down on journalism and politics, considering those worlds inferior to the struggles of 'the artist.'"

According to Segrave, Hobhouse had a profound, almost unnatural attachment to her mother. "Janet's relationship with her mother was the most important thing in her life, unfortunately for her, as her mother was so unstable," Segrave wrote. "I remember her once asking me about the feelings I had had as a small child towards my own mother. She was puzzled that I had never experienced the same thing she had—the longing to be with her mother all the time and at the same time the conviction that she was the most important thing in her mother's life." The loss of her mother to suicide in the mid-1980s was a defining event in Hobhouse's life. "She once said that if a person you love commits suicide, as her mother did, you spend the rest of your life trying to find similar relationships and playing out the ending you never had with the person who died," Segrave wrote.

Also deeply troubled were Hobhouse's relationships with men. She had virtually no contact with her father until, at the age of 16, she arranged to go to England to meet him. Though by all accounts her father subsequently tried to include her in his life, his absence throughout her childhood had lasting ramifications. "The way she played friends off against each other, telling one person what another had done for her . . ., I now see as the neediness of a greedy child who didn't have enough childhood and who was longing for her own father to love her," Segrave wrote. Hobhouse was once married, to Nick Fraser, a man whom, according to Segrave, Hobhouse treated in "the dominating, patronizing, yet maternal way she treated most men—indeed most people." She frequently criticized Fraser, a British journalist, for his work for *Newsweek* and the *Sunday Times* and for coauthoring biographies. The couple's marriage ended in divorce.

Hobhouse's first book, *Everybody Who Was Anybody: A Biography of Gertrude Stein*, an examination of the life of the American art patron and author of such works as *Three Lives* (1909) and *The Autobiography of Alice B. Toklas* (1933), was published in 1975, when the author was only 27 years old. The book explored Stein's relationships with her brother Leo, Alice B. Toklas, and Picasso as well as her connection to the Cubists and Ernest Hemingway and other writers of the so-called Lost Generation. Hobhouse also examined the way in which these connections and various events in Stein's life corresponded to the development of Stein's writing. *Everybody Who Was Anybody*, which was the sixth Stein biography published in four years, received mixed reviews. Some critics praised the book's packaging, which included more than 100 illustrations, and Hobhouse's objectivity. "[The book] offers more objective substance than any except the still-standard Elizabeth Sprigge, *Gertrude Stein* [1957] and J. R. Mellow, *Charmed Circle* [1974]. . . . Her book is worth the price just for the richness of its illustrations," a reviewer wrote in *Choice* (February 1976). Others, like David Carter in the *Times Literary Supplement* (March 12, 1976), saw the book as somewhat lacking in depth. "As a superficial description of where she lived and what she did, it is readable, well illustrated, thorough, and well documented," he wrote. "As an attempt to understand another human being and a puzzling writer it is lamentable. The tone is one of condescension, irritation, and, occasionally, of slightly veiled envy or malice."

Seven years after penning *Everybody Who Was Anybody*, Hobhouse published her first novel, *Nellie Without Hugo* (1982). The book explores the romantic and familial relationships that Nellie, a 32-year-old woman who works at New York City's Metropolitan Museum of Art, develops when her husband leaves for a two-month period. Deemed an "introverted, psychological, boring novel" by Barbara Parker in the *Library Journal* (June 1, 1982), *Nellie Without Hugo* was not well received by most critics. "Theorizing unstoppably about relationships, [the book] is full of holes when it comes to portraying them," Peter Kemp wrote in the *Times Literary Supplement* (March 12, 1982). "Despite all its reference to coexistence, the book is imprisoned in its heroine's narcissism, rarely allowing us to escape from the self-hugging confines of her personality. . . . There are long teetering metaphors, extended until they collapse like a child's construction kit."

After the novel *Dancing in the Dark* (1983), an analysis of a marriage, Hobhouse published *November* (1986). That novel centers on Zachariah Quine, a man who has been deserted by his wife, suffered a series of failed relationships, and quit his job to pen an opera—a project he has recently abandoned. In an attempt to lift his spirts and break out of a daily routine that has deteriorated into a nonstop television watching and junk-food binges, he decides to visit his brother, Michael, in London. Once there, Zachariah meets and becomes enamored with Anne, a troubled partygoer with a past filled with loss and unsuccessful romances. "As she did in her last novel . . . Ms. Hobhouse demonstrates a keen eye for social detail, an ability to conjure up her characters' yuppie-bohemian world with visually precise description," Michiko Kakutani wrote in the *New York Times* (December 6, 1986). "The SoHo world of would-be New York artists and musicians . . . the London club scene of debutantes and punks . . . and the world of young British executives . . . all are sketched in with humor and knowing detail; and Ms. Hobhouse is often equally adept at conveying to the reader her characters' moods and nervous relationships." Kakutani noted, however, that *November* is not without its flaws. "In the end . . . what irritates the reader most about *November* is its characters'

relentless self-absorption—their endless arguing over definitions of happiness, their talk of living on 'the edge,' their attempts to turn hedonism and irresponsibility into some kind of noble quest". . . . As a result, the novel suffers from a certain brittleness of tone and a narrative that turns in on itself like a narrow Möbius strip, instead of opening out onto the world."

Hobhouse's final novel, *The Furies*, was published posthumously in 1993. The book draws heavily on the author's own life. "One cannot read a sentence of this book—a mesmerizing, hauntingly autobiographical work—without thinking of the author's death, without feeling that Hobhouse was searching for answers to consuming questions about her family, her choices, her life, trying to put at least some of her demons to rest before it was too late," Elizabeth Gleick wrote in the *New York Times* (January 10, 1993). *The Furies* is the story of Helen Lowell, the last in four generations of headstrong and demanding women descended from a German-Jewish family who settled on New York City's Upper West Side. An examination of Helen's relationships—particularly with her mother and her other female relatives— the book examines the tangled mix of despair, abandonment, love, hatred, and suicide that shapes her life. Though *The Furies* was, at the time of Hobhouse's death, a not-quite-finished manuscript, it garnered rave reviews from numerous critics. "*The Furies* is a work of passion and courage," Tess Lewis wrote in *New York Newsday* (January 6, 1993). "Even at her most willfully blind and exasperatingly self-destructive, Helen fully engages the reader's compassion and admiration. In her final work, Janet Hobhouse illuminates the complex, conflicting forces that underlie intimate relationships, especially those between mother and daughter." Further praise was offered by Michiko Kakutani in the *New York Times* (January 1, 1993): "Where her earlier novels elegantly, if somewhat tiresomely, delineated the self-indulgent anxieties of rich, stylish bohemians, *The Furies* moves outward from that self-conscious, circumscribed world. . . . Ms. Hobhouse understands the stealthy ways in which familial love can both nourish and undermine a child's self-confidence, the subtle ways in which hopes, fears, and yearnings can be passed down, generation to generation, mother to daughter, like pretty but dangerous heirlooms. She has written a dark, lyrical, and wonderfully luminous book."

On February 1, 1991, Janet Hobhouse, then living in New York City, died after a six-year battle with ovarian cancer. "As far as I know, Janet never admitted she was dying, either to herself or to her friends, but [her final novel] reads like a last testament in its nakedly confessional tone," Elisa Segrave wrote. "I was appalled by the terrible sorrow and loneliness it describes. . . . I admired her courage, not least in being able to describe the kind of grief that most people shy away from."
—J. P.

SUGGESTED READING: *Choice* p1571 Feb. 1976; *Library Journal* p2138 Nov. 15, 1975, p1112 June 1, 1982; *London Review of Books* p19+ Mar. 11 1993; *New York Newsday* p48+ Jan. 6, 1993; *New York Times* p16 Dec. 6, 1986, p10 Feb. 4, 1991, p25 Jan.1, 1993; *New York Times Book Review* p31+ Feb. 10 1991, p11+ Jan. 10, 1993; *Times Literary Supplement* p289 Mar. 12 1982; *Contemporary Authors* vol. 57-60, 1976, vol. 133 1991

SELECTED WORKS: Fiction—*Nellie Without Hugo*, 1982; *Dancing in the Dark*, 1983; *November*, 1986; *The Furies*, 1993; Nonfiction—*Everybody Who Was Anybody: A Biography of Gertrude Stein*, 1975; *The Bride Stripped Bare: The Artist and the Female Nude in the 20th Century*, 1988

Eliot Holtzman

Hochschild, Adam

Oct. 5, 1942– Nonfiction writer; journalist; memoirist

Adam Hochschild, an American writer of nonfiction and political commentary, is known for offering insightful analyses of societies that were forced to redefine themselves in the 1980s and 1990s. A product of the leftist journalism of the 1960s and 1970s, Hochschild was one of the founders of *Mother Jones* magazine and has written for other countercultural publications, such as *Ramparts* and *The Progressive*, as well as for mainstream ones including *Harper's* and the *New Yorker*. The son of a mining-company executive, he was radi-

calized by the realization that his own privilege depended on the deprivation of others. He has explored his ambivalence in a personal memoir, *Half the Way Home: a Memoir of Father and Son* (1986), and has also written books on the emergence of a new order in two closed societies: South Africa, in *The Mirror at Midnight: a South African Journey* (1990), and the former Soviet Union, in *The Unquiet Ghost: Russians Remember Stalin* (1994). In 1997 Syracuse University Press published *Finding the Trapdoor*, a collection of "essays, portraits, and travels" written over a quarter-century. His nonfiction work *King Leopold's Ghost: a Story of Greed, Terror and Heroism in Colonial Africa*, appeared in 1998.

For *World Authors 1990–1995*, Hochschild writes: "I was born in New York City in 1942. Soon after getting out of college I went to work as a newspaper reporter in San Francisco. Later came stints as a writer and editor at two magazines: *Ramparts* and *Mother Jones*, of which I was a co-founder, and for which I've written many articles. I still do occasional articles and book reviews for various periodicals, but for the last decade and a half I've been mainly writing books.

"My first, *Half the Way Home: a Memoir of Father and Son*, appeared in 1986. My father was a corporate executive who had some difficulties with his left-wing writer son. Curiously, however, the strain was far more personal than political. The book is the story of that relationship, and of the peace finally made between us.

"In 1990 came *The Mirror at Midnight: a South African Journey*. I had made a number of reporting visits to South Africa over the years, and went back there in 1988 at the time of the 150th anniversary of a pivotal event in South African history: the Battle of Blood River. This was the crucial showdown that decided whether the Boers or the Zulus were going to rule that part of Africa. The battle has always been celebrated by white Afrikaans-speaking South Africans with tremendous fervor, including pageant-like reenactments on the day itself. The book winds together two threads of narrative: one is the story of the events leading up to the battle in 1838, the other is my own journey around the country, visiting some of the same places 150 years later. I'd long known of the great pleasure of going to far-off places to write about them; with this book, I discovered the similar enjoyment of leaping backwards and forwards in time.

"Another time and place that has long fascinated me is Russia in its most repressive years. How could the country that gave the world Tolstoy and Chekhov also give us the *gulag*? In 1991, my family and I spent nearly six months living in Russia, and I traveled across the country talking with people who were using their new-found freedom of expression to do something impossible a few years earlier: to explore the Soviet Union's self-inflicted genocide under Stalin. I visited former prisoners, retired secret policemen, reform-minded historians, and people digging up mass graves. I traveled to some of those grave sites, and to some distant corners of Siberia where there were snow-covered ruins of prison camps, still surrounded by rusted barbed wire. Through sheer accident of being in the right place at the right time I was, I was told, the first American writer to see the inside of the KGB archives. The result of all this was *The Unquiet Ghost: Russians Remember Stalin*, published in 1994.

"Someone looking over my books might say: 'This guy can't decide what he's interested in; he writes on a completely different subject each time.' And this is true. But that's also what makes me love my work. If an explorer explored the same territory on each journey, he'd get bored. The only thing that limits me is that I stick to what really happened. Which makes me a nonfiction writer, I suppose. Although I sure wish someone would think of a better word: the first novelists did not call themselves nonpoets or nonplaywrights.

"When needed, I can tailor my writing to where it must fit—a newspaper's news columns, a magazine's book review section—but it's much more fun to float free of such constraints. There's nothing I like better than weaving together personal memories, interviews, travel, history and meditation in the same book, as I've tried to do in my books about South Africa and Russia. Our lives are a mixture of many such strands; why shouldn't our books be?

"I've recently finished two more books. One is a collection of shorter pieces—reportage, essays, reviews—published over the last two decades or so. Far more than I would have expected, I found it an enormous pleasure to revise and polish these articles. Why? I think because most of the time we look back at the past and think, 'Damn! If I had the chance to live that year or that part of my life over again, I sure would do it differently.' Now I was given a chance, in a literary sense, to live over a number of little parts of my life and to try to do it better this time.

"The other book, which I spent almost all my work time on for three years, is my first full-scale excursion into writing history. It is basically a nonfiction account of the time and place that Conrad wrote about in *Heart of Darkness*: the conquest of the Congo. This was by far the bloodiest part of the European scramble for Africa: the population of that territory was slashed by some 10 million people over several decades. I was first curious about why mass murder on such a vast scale has gotten almost totally forgotten. As I immersed myself in the period I also began to realize that I was being handed on a platter the greatest gift a writer can receive: an extraordinary cast of characters. They range from a villain of Shakespearean dimensions, King Leopold II of Belgium, to a remarkable and little-known quartet of heroes who blew the whistle on him, two of them black Americans. I felt as if I made new friends and enemies both, and I was sorry to leave them when the book was done."

"Unlike other mammals, writers are not born into the world knowing how to make their own particular noise," Adam Hochschild wrote in the prologue to his 1997 book *Finding the Trapdoor: Essays, Portraits, Travels* (the essay originally appeared in the Spring 1996 issue of the literary magazine *Zyzzya*). "Almost from the beginning, wolves howl; hogs grunt, bears growl. They need no MFA programs in growling, or summer workshops in discovering the grunt within. . . .But writers are different: all too easily they mistake someone else's sound for their own. For many years, that's what happened to me."

From childhood, Hochschild harbored dreams of being a writer. He has recalled being especially influenced by John Galsworthy's story "The Apple Tree," which presented him with the either-or choice of living out a conventional middle-class existence or of following a chancier dream—in his case the allure of writing.

Like that of many of his peers in the 1960s, Adam Hochschild's rebellion took the form of political activism and literary bohemianism. Hoping that journalism would be a stepping-stone to a career as a novelist, as it had been for Hemingway and Stephen Crane, he became a reporter for The *San Francisco Chronicle* in the late 1960s and also contributed to muckraking publications such as the "zany but exciting" *Ramparts*.

For a time in the late 1960s, Hochschild and his wife, Arlie, then a graduate student, shared a "pleasant but slightly dilapidated brown-shingle building in Berkeley", where they "lived, if not in Chekhovian poverty, at least in conspicuous simplicity. We drove a VW Beetle, and our threadbare furniture came from the Salvation Army store." He burned to write a novel, and "miraculously" a New York publisher gave him a $5,000 advance in 1969, leading him to become enamored of the romantic trappings of writing a novel, such as being interviewed for the *Paris Review*. To his horror, the publisher rejected his manuscript when it was finished, leaving him crushed and feeling "like a groom abandoned at the altar. . . . My editor, I was sure, had committed a felony against American literature." Finally, in a moment of candid self-analysis, he re-read the manuscript and concluded that "the characters were stiff and one-dimensional. The novel lacked the sound of a human voice."

In 1974 he returned to journalism, and, adding what he called the "ill-gotten gains" from a family inheritance to similar contributions from others, he joined some friends in starting *Mother Jones*, named for the Irish-born firebrand who took up the cause of oppressed miners in the United States during the struggle for unionization a century ago. Their timing was fortuitous, coming during the Watergate period, when antiestablishment, investigative journalism was highly regarded by the public. "Unexpectedly, I found myself learning something enormously valuable from this work," he wrote for a 1996 *Zyzzya* article, which became the title piece of his 1997 collection, *Finding the Trapdoor.* "The job demystifies words. It reminds you, as you look at letters to the editor and reader surveys and listen to what subscribers tell you, that readers are impatient and busy. You have to compete for their attention. . . . Whether it's an exposé, a piece of reportage, or a short story, you learn that no piece of writing is sacred. The reader, not the writer, comes first. And nothing has value just because *you* wrote it."

During this period, as he began to reevaluate the craft of writing, he discovered a crucial coincidence while reading the books of a writer he admired greatly: Victor Serge, the Belgian-born anarchist who had fought with the Bolsheviks in the Russian Civil War only to be banished by Stalin years later. Hochschild realized, ironically, that both Serge and his own beloved White Russian uncle by marriage, Boris Sergievsky, a swashbuckling pioneer who had married Hochschild's aunt, had fought in the same crucial battle of the Russian Civil War, only on opposite sides. With this in mind, Hochschild went to Russia in search of the battlefield and of the places where the two combatants had lived. Afterward, he discovered that "for the first time in my life, I had written something in my own voice," and that this voice was not one of fiction, but of nonfiction.

The death of Harold Hochschild as Adam was nearing his 40th birthday also helped the younger man find his writer's voice. He decided to explore his "quiet rebellion" against his father by exploring their complex relationship in a memoir. This decision "mysteriously opened a lock," he reported, and he finished a rough draft in two and a half months, while working on many other kinds of writing at the same time, including magazine articles, book reviews for *Mother Jones*, and commentary for National Public Radio. He wrote in his *Zyzzya* article: "By accident, I had learned that each of us does not have just one voice, but many, and that speaking in one of them can help bring the others to life."

The memoir was published to highly favorable reviews by Viking Penguin as *Half the Way Home: A Memoir of Father and Son* and was later reprinted in a 1996 softcover edition by Syracuse University Press. It was included on the Notable Books of the Year list of the *New York Times Book Review* and of the American Library Association, and it appeared on the Best Books of the Year List in *Library Journal.* Studs Terkel called it "an exquisite memoir of a boy growing up in a world of privilege and the one beyond. It is in coming to understand his powerful father that Adam Hochschild is able to understand both worlds." Hochschild soon realized that this memoir was really a later version of his first novel, which had been rejected nearly 20 years earlier. "The underlying feelings I was trying to evoke—clumsily and unsuccessfully the first time around—were the same," he wrote. Describing his relationship with his father, Hochschild wrote in his memoir: "There was always a stiffness

in the air between us, as if we were both guests at a party and the host had gone off somewhere before introducing us." He described in unsentimental detail the childhood terror he felt at being left alone with an older man perpetually anxious about his status as an American of Jewish heritage as well as the confusion and pain occasioned by his visits to South Africa, whose unjust society he linked to his father's complicity. "I think South Africa had come to represent for me in purest form the pattern of worldwide inequity from which I had benefitted so much," he wrote.

When Hochschild was 19, in 1962, he spent the summer in South Africa writing for an antiapartheid newspaper. He was in the country when Nelson Mandela was arrested and when some of the draconian laws were passed that brought the country's racial cauldron to a slow boil. It was his first exposure to a place where politics was a matter of life and death, he wrote. He returned several times over the years to write articles for *Mother Jones*, *Harper's*, and other journals, and spent a month there at the end of 1988. These experiences led him to write *The Mirror at Midnight: A South African Journey,* published by Viking in 1990. The book weaves together the histories of all players in South Africa, the Afrikaners who trace their hegemony to the 1838 Battle of Blood River, the Zulu warriors who clashed with them, and their contemporary descendants, who in 1988 were still locked in struggle. While his liberal worldview is apparent in the book, Hochschild takes pains not to portray the struggle as a simplistic "black-versus-white" polarity. He explores the nuanced subtexts of the situation, creating, as Mark Mathabane pointed out in his *Washington Post* (October 28, 1990) review, "an important addition to the debate about South Africa." *Publishers Weekly* (October 5, 1990) called the book "a stunning blend of reportage, travelogue, history, and meditation." Hochschild believes that the prospects for real democracy are stronger in South Africa, where the political landscape was altered by a grass-roots movement, than in the former Soviet Union, where the system collapsed from the top down.

Hochschild had been interested in the Soviet Union since his youthful fascination with the great Russian novelists and with the writings of Victor Serge. He visited the former Soviet Union several times on journalistic assignments and, in 1991, became the first American allowed to examine the archives of the KGB, the Soviet secret police. He was living in Russia at the time, researching a book on the *gulag*, visiting many of the victims of Stalin's purges and the places of their exile, such as Kolyma in northeastern Siberia, where children still use human skulls in gathering blueberries. "What was it like to live and work daily among such reminders of mass murder?" he wrote, struggling to comprehend how a revolution so idealistic could have resulted in the arrest of 19 million people and the execution of seven million. Hochschild concluded that "human beings have a longer memory for fear than they do for most other emotions." *Glasnost* and the unraveling of the Soviet system made it easier for him to move freely about the country, and he talked with both executioners and victims to write *The Unquiet Ghost: Russians Remember Stalin,* published by Viking in 1994. Of this book, a *Kirkus Reviews* (January 1, 1994) critic wrote: "As sensitive, subtle, and moving as Chekhov; journalism raised to the level of art."

Published in 1997, *Finding the Trapdoor* is a collection of 21 "essays, portraits, [and] travels" Hochschild wrote over the years during his travels in Africa, the former Soviet Union, Latin America, and Europe, plus commentaries on such topics as various as the legacy of John F. Kennedy, the civil-rights movement, his prep-school days, and sex manuals. *Finding the Trapdoor* won the PEN / Spielvogel-Diamonstein Award for the Art of the Essay, awarded to the year's best book of essays.

King Leopold's Ghost: A Story of Greed, Terror and Heroism in Colonial Africa was published in 1998. This nonfiction work details the Belgian King Leopold II's domination of the Congo in the late 19th and early 20th centuries, which resulted in the deaths of millions of Africans. *King Leopold's Ghost* won the Gold Medal of the California Book Awards as well as a J. Anthony Lukas Award, and was a finalist for the National Book Critics Circle Award.

In his *Zyzzya* article, reprinted in *Finding the Trapdoor,* Hochschild compared the situation of a writer looking for a voice to that of a singer trapped in a dark house, seeking for an opening to the stage. "Bumping about in the darkness, most of us tend to group toward the traditional grand aperture: those French windows of the novel. . . . There are other traditional openings, too: the smaller window of the short story, the doorway of the poem.

"But now, I am beginning to see, there are all sorts of other ways out of the darkened house as well, and all of them let the light in and your voice out: dormer windows, a little wicket for the meter-reader, skylights that swing open, chimneys you can stick your head up, the secret trap door hidden under the rug. Some day, perhaps, I'll stumble upon those French windows and write a novel. But if not, I won't be disappointed. Recently I have found myself writing very short stories for very small children. My kids have now grown up, and those stories simply need somewhere to go."
—E. M.

SUGGESTED READING: *Chicago Tribune* XIV p4 Dec. 23, 1990; *Library Journal* p50 Jan. 1995, with photo; *Los Angeles Times Book Review* p7 Jan. 10, 1999; *New York Newsday* p35+ Mar. 20, 1994; *New York Times Book Review* p8 Sep. 20, 1998; *Progressive* p31+ July 1994; *Publishers Weekly* p83 Oct. 5, 1990; *Washington Post* C p3 Apr. 10, 1994; Gordon, M. *Good Boys and Dead Girls and Other Essays,* 1991

SELECTED BOOKS: *Half the Way Home: A Memoir of Father and Son,* 1986; *The Mirror at Midnight: A South African Journey,* 1990; *The Unquiet Ghost: Russians Remember Stalin,* 1994; *Finding the Trapdoor: Essays, Portraits, Travels,* 1997; *King Leopold's Ghost: A Story of Greed, Terror and Heroism in Colonial Africa,* 1998

Jerry Bauer

Hoffman, Eva

July 1, 1945– Memoirist; historian; critic

The Polish-born American author Eva Hoffman is a noted book reviewer as well as a lauded memoirist and historian. For a decade Hoffman was an editor and book critic for the *New York Times.* Over the years she has also taught a number of classes in literature and creative writing at such institutions as Columbia University, the University of Minnesota, the Tavistock Institute in London, Tufts University, and Harvard University. Her first book, the autobiography *Lost in Translation* (1989), was praised for its touching portrayal of a young immigrant girl facing linguistic and social challenges as she begins the transition from her native Polish to English, and ultimately, from one way of thinking to another. Her second work, *Exit into History* (1993), explored the changing political and social experience of the people of Eastern Europe since the collapse of communism. Her most recent book is *Shtetl* (1997), a study of Polish-Jewish relations for the past several centuries. In it she questions the assumptions that all Poles are anti-Semitic and were willing participants in the Holocaust. Hoffman's works have been celebrated for their graceful language, honesty, and assessments grounded in painstaking research.

Eva Hoffman was born Ewa Wydra, the daughter of Boris and Maria (Burg) Wydra. After her immigration from Poland to Canada, her first name was changed by her school teacher. In January 1997 Eva Hoffman wrote the following autobiographical essay for *World Authors 1990–1995*: "I was born in Cracow, Poland, in July, 1945. We are, of course, born into families rather than into historical facts. And yet, these bare bits of data—Cracow, Poland, 1945—were packed with condensed personal implication. Poland after World War II was a country cruelly ravaged, impoverished, and in effect colonized by a foreign political system. In addition, my family was Jewish; and that fact as well carried a complex cargo of meaning. My parents lived through the war in a small shtetl near Lvov, in a region of the Ukraine where Jewish survival was statistically a near-impossibility. Their lives were saved by local peasants who hid them for nearly two years; but all other members of their families were murdered by the Nazis.

"The war seemed to be my true origin, the place from which I sprang; and its horrors shadowed my external and internal world from the beginning. And yet, I would not want to give the impression that I had a grim or unhappy childhood. On the contrary, I remember Cracow as a space of happiness, born perhaps of the interplay between shadows and light, between intuitions of pain and of beauty. The signs of suffering were everywhere—in the almost palpable presence of those who perished, in the illness and deprivation, and men with missing limbs—but so were signs of solidarity and strength. My parents started up their new lives with optimism and zest. In our tiny and extremely modest apartment, there was always traffic of friends, intimate gossip and rudimentary goods hard-won and freely exchanged. In the harsh postwar circumstances, people needed each other, and that brought them close.

"Then there was Cracow itself, which had been spared from ruin, and whose quiet parks and ancient streets, deep courtyards and Renaissance perspectives, brimmed, to my childish sensibility, with both mystery and the promise of knowledge. In the summer, there were long vacations in mountain villages with quicksilver rivers, where peasant dress, houses, customs, and ways of plowing the land remained unchanged for centuries. Time moved honey-slow during my childhood, in dreamy, contemplative rhythms. Later, I understood that it was, to some extent, pre-modern time. In the villages, there was no electricity, and people went round barefoot; in Cracow, I did not use a telephone until I was twelve, and never saw a television at all. But there were lots of books, animated conversations, outings with peers, and with adults. When I was seven, I started taking piano lessons, and was pronounced talented. Music was to be my career, and, as I felt it then, my Destiny; but it was also another key to human passions, and their alternation between light and dark. It was through music that I received my most powerful sentimental education; it was through the political and human atmosphere around me that I imbibed some of the Polish romanticism which produced Chopin, and which derived from a courtly ethos of honor, flair, and fiery resistance to oppression.

"But if my psyche was formed in Poland, my consciousness was forged through the vicissitudes of emigration and transculturation. In 1959, my family, along with most of the remaining Jewish population in Poland, took advantage of the lifting of the emigration ban, and left for Canada. My parents were driven by a double desire to escape the anti-Semitism still pervasive in Polish society, and to find better opportunities in more open and hopeful climes. Our destination was Vancouver, the far-flung city on the Pacific coast. My parents, younger sister, and later her family settled there; but after three and half years, during which I began and finished high school, I left for Houston, Texas, to attend Rice University. This was a period when the contrasts between Eastern Europe and the West were at their most extreme; and surely, there could have been no antipodes further removed from Cracow than the two brash, booming, technologically advanced and culturally raw towns to which I was so confusingly transported. My sense of dislocation was acute—but perhaps precisely for that reason, highly illuminating. The country of our childhood is often paradise to us, and I grieved the loss of mine. At the same time, I knew that I had a new world to decode, and set to this task with some energy. I was amazed and baffled by many features of high-school and college life: the dating rituals and the football rites, the social hierarchies and the sexual ones. But the experience of "culture shock" also held some deeper and more abiding lessons—skin and bone instruction in the fundamental, primary importance of culture and language. For a while, as I made the transition from Polish to English, I existed, in effect, outside language; and from my glimpses of black wordlessness, I learned that if we cannot name the world, the world loses its outlines and clarity; if we cannot articulate our subjectivity, then we are left in a terrifying, inchoate internal vacuum. As with language, so with culture: As I tried to understand what it meant to be "American," I came to understand that 'culture' is not something outside ourselves, but that it exists within, structuring and shaping us from the beginning. In order to become truly American, I needed not only to learn something about the Constitution or the Transcendentalists, but to transpose myself into a different mode of personality, a new system of perceptions, and even emotions. Paradoxically, as time went on, and I formed more intimate friendships and relationships with people, I became more aware of those minute rifts and gaps in which cultural difference expresses themselves. I saw how culture informs our most profound and seemingly most private assumptions, not only about food, clothing or politics, but about what counts as good, bad, aggressive or sensitive; about the distances we tolerate between ourselves and others, and how we like to adjust our own inner atmospheres.

"In the meantime, I graduated from Rice University [in 1967], and went on to receive a Ph. D. from Harvard University in English and American literature [in 1976]. While I was trying to decode 'the culture,' 'the counterculture' was born and got into full swing. I was fascinated by the dynamism of this self-confident, sometimes self-indulgent youth movement, and by its critiques of postwar America; but its desire for wholesale, highly self-conscious transformation, for dispensing with limits, history and reality-principles, was disorienting as well. Figuring out where I was located on the suddenly swirling American map; trying to hold on to an authentic 'I' as I became bicultural; attempting to make English truly mine—such elusive aims were my consuming and sometimes strenuous life-project, even as my studies and career outwardly followed along rather normal, fairly successful tracks. It took many years before English permeated my psychic cells sufficiently to enter my dreams; it took just as long before I felt I had 'assimilated' to America sufficiently to call it home, and assimilated America to some extent into myself.

"But other themes, other problems, came into the foreground at various times. I got married and, several years later, divorced, in the perhaps overly insouciant way of my generation; like so many of my peers, I had more appetite, sometimes to my own peril, for ever-renewing intensity, than for settled security. I moved to New York and worked, over a ten-year period [between 1979 and 1990], for The New York Times—an experience which I found, on the whole, bracingly stimulating and which provided invaluable glimpses into the workings of the world, and of a prominent American institution. But journalism, as many writers have found, can also be excellent training for more extended creative efforts. For me, it was particularly useful in overcoming the 'approach anxiety' in writing, the fear that, as I put pen to paper, nothing might come out at all. Under the pressure of an assignment and a deadline, one learns that something comes out every time.

"Eventually, the pressure of things I wanted to say from within began to build and simmer, and I left the newspaper to write my first book [Lost in Translation, published in 1989]. I went back for nearly three years after it was done; and then left again, first to travel in preparation for my second book [Exit into History, published in 1993], and then, more permanently, to take up the writing life. I was still susceptible enough to immigrant anxieties about sheer survival to find such decisions difficult; but I have come to value the luxury of free-lance time. I have done some teaching, journalism, radio and television work. I took up the study of psychoanalysis, which I see as a continuation of the philosophic tradition—our way of asking how 'human nature' is made, and what constitutes the good, full life.

"In 1992, I moved to London. I wanted, for a while at least, to update and perhaps develop the interrupted, 'European' parts of myself, and to disentangle my youthful fantasy of Europe from the current realities. As it happens, I have found London, along all kinds of dimensions, a satisfying midway point between Manhattan and Cracow. It is also a place where hybrid contradictions can be genially and tolerantly contained. I mean to live here for a while; but I am glad that my choices are no longer so stark or mutually exclusive as they were in my Cold War emigration. My writing has taken me to Eastern Europe more than I would have predicted; but America is by now deeply embedded in my psyche; it has become the point of reference from which I depart, and which gives the impetus to my real and mental travels. I want to turn to fiction next, and explore that imaginative space in which 'home' can be everywhere, and lives most truly in language itself."

In 1989 Hoffman published her memoir Lost in Translation: A Life in a New Language, which focuses on her adaptation to Western culture following her 1959 emigration to Canada. The author uses the theme of adjusting to the use of a new language (and by extension to a new way of thinking) to bring to life the immigrant experience. A critic for Library Journal (January 1989) noted how "Hoffman makes one feel intensely the pain of an abrupt rupture with one's culture and native language, as well as the difficulties of adjusting to a new idiom." The Nation (June 12, 1989) cheered: "Eva Hoffman's obsession with words has paid off handsomely: her language is crisp and precise when summing up essential experience, and richly evocative when lingering on detail."

Hoffman's next book detailed a journalistic trek she took through Eastern Europe just after the collapse of the Berlin Wall. Most of the book is dedicated to the time she spent in her native Poland, but it also covers her travels through the former Czechoslovakia, Hungary, Romania, and Bulgaria. In doing the research for this book, Hoffman made two trips to Eastern Europe, taken about a year apart. Published in 1993, Exit into History: A Journey Through the New Eastern Europe was highly praised by critics. Most lauded the author's finely crafted paragraphs describing both the shoddy postwar architecture and the older and more beautiful medieval buildings still preserved. Many also noted how skillfully she described the myriad social and political conditions she encountered. Robert D. Kaplan, reviewing the book for the New York Times (November 21, 1993), remarked: "While many journalists concentrate on what has happened in the former Yugoslavia, and what might happen in neighboring countries, Ms. Hoffman looks at what has not happened. The result is a travel document of subtle hues in which the author's perceptions provide the drama rather than any 'events' or situations." Manuela Hoelterhoff of the *Wall Street Journal* (January 3, 1994) wrote: "Ms. Hoffman['s] . . . memoir provides a refreshingly unpretentious contrast to the pile of dreary post-wall fall books whose numbers could probably rebuild a fair chunk of it. Observant, thoughtful, charming, the Polish-born writer . . . proves a wonderful listener, recording with sensitivity and wit how jolly censors, compromised dissidents, among others, seek to knit their complicated pasts to an uncertain future."

Hoffman's most recent work, *Shtetl: The Life and Death of a Small Town and the World of Polish Jews* (1997), focuses on Jewish-Polish relations through several centuries, concluding at the end of World War II. The town Hoffman centered on for this study was the village of Bransk, 100 miles east of Warsaw, near the prewar Soviet and Lithuanian boarders. Before 1939, the first year of the war, the small village had a population of 4,600, half of whom were Jewish. In November 1942 the entire Jewish population of Bransk was loaded onto train cars and shipped off to the concentration camp Treblinka, where they were gassed to death on the 10th of November. Only 76 Bransk Jews—most of whom went into hiding—survived the war. No Jews live in Bransk today.

In *Shtetl* ("Small town" in Yiddish), Hoffman offers documented facts to counter the argument (offered by numerous historians) that the majority of Poles were willing collaborators with the Nazis in the extermination of European Jews. Hoffman impresses upon the reader that the relationship between Poles and Jews has always been complicated. Throughout the centuries Jews were welcomed into Poland by nobles who often used the skills of Jews trained as merchants or artisans to their benefit. While Poles and Jews did not associate with each other socially, they knew one another from markets and shops and were neighbors. Though numerous Poles watched the roundup, and oftentimes the murder of Jews, many other Poles risked their lives by hiding Jewish families. Critics praised the insightfulness of Hoffman's work. Richard Bernstein of the *New York Times* (October 15, 1997) wrote: "Ms. Hoffman's project is certainly worthy, and the book she has produced amply proves her point, that the history of the Poles and the Jews is morally complicated." Eunice Lipton, writing for the *Nation* (November 3, 1997), remarked: "*Shtetl* is a daring and generous book, measured in style, passionate in intent. It was, I do believe, written for love. Not for the love of a person or a country, but for some configuration of home, for a laying bare of mysterious and destructive ancient mechanisms, that, once understood . . . may bring warring partners, even a divided heart or country, to actually *see* on the other side, allowing each to have a home, a place from which to understand and to desire."

In addition to her books and her work for the *New York Times*, Eva Hoffman has contributed articles to numerous publications, including the *Atlantic Monthly* and *Civilization*. For a number of years, Hoffman also taught literature and creative writing classes at Harvard University (1973–1976), the University of New Hampshire (1976–1977), and at Tufts University (1977–1978). In 1994 she returned to teaching, this time in London as an associate lecturer at Tavistock Institute. The next year she gave lectures and workshops as a visiting writer to the University of Minnesota. Most recently she taught a master's class in creative writing at Columbia University (1995) and worked in a program for creative writing at the University of East Anglia (1997).

Hoffman has received a number of fellowships and awards, including the Woodrow Wilson Fellowship (1967–1968), the Danforth Graduate Fellowship (1969–1974), the Carnegie-Mellon Post-Doctoral Fellowship (1977–1978), the American Council of Learned Societies Fellowship (1985–1986), the American Academy and Institute of Arts and Letters Award (1991), the Whitling Award for Writing (1992), and the Guggenheim Fellowship (1992–1993).

Eva Hoffman lives in London, England, and is currently working on a novel.—C.M.

SUGGESTED READING: *Library Journal* p91 Jan. 1989; *Nation* p248 June 12, 1989, p26 Nov. 3, 1997; *New York Times* C p15 Nov. 8, 1993, VII p3 Nov. 21, 1993, VII p8 Oct. 12, 1997, E p9 Oct. 15, 1997; *Wall Street Journal* p5 Jan. 3, 1994; *Contemporary Authors vol. 132*, 1991

SELECTED WORKS: *Lost in Translation: A Life in a New Language*, 1989; *Exit into History: A Journey Through the New Eastern Europe*, 1993; *Shtetl: The Life and Death of a Small Town and the World of Polish Jews*, 1997

---

hooks, bell

Sep. 25, 1952– Essayist; poet; educator

The African-American feminist writer bell hooks prefers to spell her name in lower-case as a statement "about ego: What's in a name? It is the substance in my books, not who is writing them, that is important." She has been referred to on separate occasions as "one of America's most indispensable and independent thinkers" and as "one of the foremost black intellectuals in America today." The author of 16 books and dozens of essays, hooks has focused attention on the myriad forms of racism, from subtle to blatant, in the United States. She has also criticized the way in which the plight of black women has either been ignored or worsened not only by what she has termed the "white suprema-

Courtesy of Donna Dietrich

bell hooks

cist capitalist patriarchy" but, in many instances, by the mainstream feminist movement and the black-liberation struggle. In addition, she has frequently cited the roles played by television, film, and advertising in perpetuating racism and sexism. Hooks is on the faculty of the English Department at the City College of New York.

The daughter of Veodis Watkins, a custodian employed by the postal service, and Rosa Bell Watkins, a homemaker, bell hooks was born Gloria Jean Watkins on September 25, 1952 in Hopkinsville, Kentucky. She has a brother, Kenneth, and five sisters: Sarah, Theresa, Valeria, Gwenda, and Angela. While she was growing up, one interest that her family shared was poetry. Hooks has recalled that when storms caused power outages in her neighborhood, her family would sit in their candlelit living room and stage impromptu talent shows, and during those events hooks would recite the works of such poets as William Wordsworth, Langston Hughes, Elizabeth Barrett Browning, and Gwendolyn Brooks. Her family's love of poetry inspired her to write verses of her own, some of which were published in a local Sunday school's magazine.

Hooks was exposed early on to the racism and sexism that she would make it her life's work to oppose. The southern community in which she grew up was segregated, and she has written that her father held rigid, traditional ideas regarding sex roles. Those influences were offset, however, by the actions of other people with whom she had regular contact. "Though I admired my father," hooks wrote in *Black Looks: Race and Representation* (1992), "I was more fascinated and charmed by black men who were not obsessed with being patri-

archs." Such figures included Felix, "a hobo who jumped trains, never worked a regular job, and had a missing thumb," and her maternal grandfather, Daddy Gus, who "spoke in hushed tones, sharing his sense of spiritual mysticism." As she wrote in *Sisters of the Yam: Black Women and Self-Recovery* (1993), Daddy Gus taught her that "everything in life was a dwelling place for spirits, that one only had to listen to hear their voices."

Hooks's environment was also replete with strong female role models. She wrote in *Sisters of the Yam* that life in her community involved "an ever-present and deep engagement with the mystical dimensions of Christian faith" and that, "despite the sexism of that segregated black world, the world of spirituality . . . was one where black women teachers, preachers, and healers worked with as much skill, power, and second sight as their black male comrades." The accomplishments of those women gave hooks faith in her own capabilities, and she decided as a young girl that she would be a writer.

After graduating from Crispus Attucks High School, in Hopkinsville, hooks enrolled at Stanford University, in Stanford, California, from which she obtained a B.A. degree in English in 1973. Three years later she earned her master's degree in the same subject at the University of Wisconsin at Madison. She then embarked on her teaching career, serving as an English instructor and as a senior lecturer in ethnic studies at the University of Southern California, in Los Angeles, where she remained until 1979. In the early 1980s she taught courses in creative writing, African-American literature, composition, and other subjects at various institutions, including the University of California at Santa Cruz and San Francisco State University. Concurrently, she worked toward her doctorate, which she received from the University of California at Santa Cruz in 1983, having written her dissertation on the works of the African-American novelist Toni Morrison.

In the meantime, she had published a chapbook of poems, *And There We Wept* (1978), and her first full-length work, *Ain't I a Woman: Black Women and Feminism* (1981), a book she had begun writing when she was 19 years old. For those projects the author had adopted the pseudonym bell hooks. She explained to Rebecca Carroll for *Elle* (December 1994) that one of her great-grandmothers, a Native American, was named Bell Hooks and that her own use of the name is "about celebrating female legacies."

Ain't I a Woman took its title from the refrain in a speech delivered in the 19th century by the black feminist Sojourner Truth. In her book, hooks challenged certain ideas regarding the place of black women in the feminist and black-liberation movements. With respect to the latter, hooks castigated the unabashedly sexist treatment of women on the part of male black leaders, but she also described such behavior as being indicative of the internalization, begun during the years of slavery, of

American patriarchal values. "Clearly," she wrote, "black men need to employ a feminist analysis that will address the issue of how to construct a life-sustaining black masculinity that does not have its roots in patriarchal phallocentrism." In addition, she found fault with the theory, put forth in studies by Daniel Patrick Moynihan and others, that black men have been psychologically castrated by a lack of economic opportunity, a situation that has in turn led to the predominance of matriarchs in the black community. That theory is unsound, hooks claimed, because the word "matriarch" suggests power that most black women—whether or not they are heads of their households—do not possess and because black males have never viewed their masculinity as being determined solely by their ability to act as breadwinners.

Hooks documented the way in which white advocates of women's rights in the late 19th and early 20th centuries not only excluded black women from their platforms but also convinced white supremacists that suffrage for white women would help strengthen institutionalized racism. She cited the contributions to freedom that were made, in spite of such exclusion, by black feminists, among them Truth, Mary Church Terrell, and Frances Ellen Watkins. She also attacked what she felt to be the arrogance of present-day white feminists, who have invited black women to join "their" struggle and thereby revealed their belief that "the word woman is synonymous with white woman, for women of other races are always perceived as Others, as dehumanized beings who do not fall under the heading woman." At the conclusion of *Ain't I a Woman*, hooks declared, "I have . . . heard black women express a belief in feminism and eloquently critique the women's movement, explaining their refusal to participate. . . . Only a few black women have rekindled the spirit of feminist struggle that stirred the hearts and minds of our 19th-century sisters. We, black women who advocate feminist ideology, are pioneers. We are clearing a path for ourselves and our sisters. We hope that as they see us reach our goal—no longer victimized, no longer unrecognized, no longer afraid—they will take courage and follow."

Reviewers' opinions of *Ain't I a Woman* were largely positive. "This exciting book reveals [hooks] to be a lucid, persuasive writer and an extraordinary penetrating and original thinker," Mary Biggs wrote in *Library Journal* (December 1, 1981). "Her wide-ranging analysis of sexist and racist oppression of black women in America . . . leaves no group uncriticized, no assumption unchallenged, no doctrine unravaged, no sacred cow ungored. . . . Her book should be widely read, thoughtfully considered, discussed, and finally acclaimed for the real enlightenment it offers for social change." A writer for *Choice* (April 1982) declared *Ain't I a Woman* to be "a provocative, readable, and worthwhile study" but found fault with hooks for "never carefully demonstrat[ing]" her "simplified assertion that 19th-century black

women were more feminist than their 20th-century counterparts."

Hooks expanded on many of the arguments put forth in *Ain't I a Woman* in her next book, *Feminist Theory: From Margin to Center* (1984). That work called for a new direction for the women's movement, toward a recognition of the diversity of women's backgrounds and experiences. Such recognition would be achieved, according to hooks, by an acknowledgement that race and class play as big a role as gender in the subordination of poor and nonwhite women. In *Ms.* (October 1985), Paula Giddings took exception to one of the conclusions in *Feminist Theory*: "[hooks] writes, 'Revolutionary ideology can be created only if the experiences of people on the margin who suffer sexist oppression . . . are understood, addressed, and incorporated.' Understood, addressed, incorporated by whom? By her terms of address, [h]ooks, perhaps unwittingly, has assigned proprietary rights to the same 'privileged' women she criticizes for their narrow perspective. . . . Hooks fails to make an important distinction: women on the margin of this society are not necessarily on the margin of feminist aspirations or activism." That criticism aside, Giddings found the premise of *Feminist Theory* to be "especially provocative."

In *Talking Back: Thinking Feminist, Thinking Black* (1989), hooks recounted some of her personal experiences as examples of ways that readers might overcome the psychological injuries inflicted by a racist and sexist culture and might apply to their daily lives informed thinking about race, sex, and sexual orientation. *Yearning: Race, Gender, and Cultural Politics* (1990) contains essays in which hooks analyzed, from a black and feminist perspective, films, rap songs, and advertisements. Evaluating *Yearning* for the *Women's Review of Books* (September 1991), P. Gabrielle Foreman noted the wide range of subjects covered as well as the unpredictable nature of the author's opinions. "Inevitably," Foreman wrote, "a reader will cheer through one essay and scowl through another." Writing in *New Statesman* (November 30, 1990), Barbara Burford pronounced *Yearning* to be "a formidable step forward on the way to creating a black cultural criticism."

Breaking Bread: Insurgent Black Intellectual Life (1991) is a collaboration between hooks and the African-American writer, educator, and activist Cornel West. *Breaking Bread* consists of five chapters penned alternately by hooks and West, two sections in which one writer interviews the other, and two "dialogues" between the authors. The book outlines the forces motivating and the challenges facing black intellectuals and addresses the connection between scholarship and social activism. "*Breaking Bread*'s fundamental contribution," Patricia Hill Collins wrote in *Signs: Journal of Women in Culture and Society* (Autumn 1994), is that "it not only theorizes about how a transformed intellectual power might fuse deep moral concern and political engagement—it actually does it."

The title of hooks's seventh book, *Black Looks: Race and Representation*, refers both to the way African-Americans are depicted in film, television, advertisements, and literature and to what hooks feels is the need for blacks and others to "see" the continuing hold of racism on the American imagination and thereby allow their minds to be "decolonized," to use her term. She was especially critical of what she called the "commodification" of blacks—the profit-driven use of black images to generate and satisfy a public hunger for "different" cultural experiences, a practice she saw as a modern version of colonization and a reflection of a desire simply to consume other cultures. In hooks's opinion, the appropriation of such images should be, but rarely is, accompanied by an openness toward the values—and not merely the symbols—of the peoples being represented. For example, she faulted Jennie Livingston's film *Paris Is Burning*, the videos of the pop-music icon Madonna, and the ads of the clothing manufacturer Benetton for reducing African-American culture to spectacle.

Black Looks met with qualified praise from most reviewers. "The 12 essays are uneven in their analytical complexity and originality of thought," D. Soyini Madison wrote in the *New York Times Book Review* (February 28, 1993), adding that many of the book's passages nevertheless "provide insight into race, representation, and dominance." Itibari M. Zulu observed in the *Multicultural Review* (March 1993), "At times [b]ell [h]ooks's essays are a bit preachy (or overly politically correct), but she redeems herself by revealing a witty personal experience related to the sermon that flows through [most of] her narrative." Evaluating the book for *Library Journal* (July 1992), Beverly Miller offered a favorable opinion: "[h]ooks continues to produce some of the most challenging, insightful, and provocative writing on race and gender in the United States today."

Sisters of the Yam: Black Women and Self-Recovery was the culmination of several projects undertaken by hooks. In the 1980s she had established a support group for black women after realizing that many of her female African-American students, regardless of their economic backgrounds, were suffering psychologically as a result of either physical abuse or "fear of being unmasked as the inferiors of their white peers." She had also begun writing a monthly column, addressed to black women, in *Zeta* magazine. Both the column and the support group were called Sisters of the Yam, after a passage in Toni Cade Bambara's novel *The Salt Eaters*. Hooks considered the yam to be "a life-sustaining symbol of black kinship and community," for "everywhere black women live in the world, [they] eat yam. It is a symbol of [their] diasporic connections. Yams provide nourishment for the body as food, yet they are also used medicinally—to heal the body."

The theme of healing runs through *Sisters of the Yam*. One crucial step in the healing process, hooks wrote, is to do away with "the myth of the 'strong' black woman, according to which every African-American female is "somehow an earthy mother goddess who has built-in capacities to deal with all manner of hardship without breaking down, physically or mentally." Adherence to that myth, she claimed, obscures and contributes to the fact that black women have often turned to drugs and alcohol rather than acknowledge their need for viable support systems. Hooks called for communication and bonding among black women, for the good of individuals but also for the political and social gains of the group as a whole. "When wounded individuals come together in groups to make change, our collective struggle is often undermined by all that has not been dealt with emotionally," she wrote. Finally, *Sisters of the Yam* was intended as a celebration of the bonding that had already taken place among black women.

Reviewing *Sisters of the Yam* for *Library Journal* (July 1993), Kathleen E. Bethel noted, "Readers trying to unlearn racism and sexism will respect hooks for politicizing the self-recovery movement. Highly recommended." In the *Women's Review of Books* (October 1993), Vanessa Northington Gamble granted that black women "know how to survive" and "how to struggle" but added that hooks "reminds us . . . that we must break out of 'struggle mode.' We have to develop habits of caring, loving, and flourishing."

The year 1994 saw the publication of two works by hooks, *Teaching to Transgress: Education as the Practice of Freedom* and *Outlaw Culture: Resisting Representations*. In *Teaching to Transgress*, hooks sought to apply to American society the philosophy of the progressive Brazilian educator Paulo Freire, who has advanced the idea that students must develop "critical consciousness" by becoming participants in, and not mere receivers of, their own educations. Like *Yearning* and *Black Looks*, *Outlaw Culture* is comprised of essays on a wide array of subjects, including the writings of Camille Paglia and Kate Roiphe, contemporary films, rap music, and perceptions of beauty. In his review of *Teaching to Transgress* and *Outlaw Culture* for the *New York Times Book Review* (December 18, 1994), Jerome Karabel expressed the opinion that the first-named book was "often marred by a disconcerting reliance on pop psychology." He noted, however, the "jarring character of [the book's] insights" and declared that both works force readers "to confront the political undercurrents of life in America."

Again, in 1995, two books by hooks were published in the same year. *Art on My Mind: Visual Politics* includes essays on contemporary art, focusing on the discord between the traditional Western aesthetic and the aims of black artists. *Killing Rage: Ending Racism* is also a collection of articles, which, while not setting forth "a comprehensive plan for achieving [the] subtitle's promise," display hooks's "sensitivity to the intersection of race, class, and gender," in the opinion of a reviewer for *Publishers Weekly* (July 17, 1995).

In 1996 the publishing company Henry Holt released *Bone Black: Memories of Girlhood*, a slim volume with brief, impressionistic essays about hooks's growing-up in the South. *Bone Black* does not claim to be a detailed rendering of childhood events; as hooks explained in the foreword, it is "not an ordinary tale. It is the story of girlhood rebellion, of my struggle to create self and identity distinct from and yet inclusive of the world around me." Assuming the voice of a distant narrator, she explored with respect and sensitivity the traditional rural life that surrounded her, paying homage to her female ancestors and discussing her nascent sexuality. She pointed out that even at an early age a boy's sexuality "can be celebrated, talked about with smiles of triumph and pleasure" while a girl's sexuality is "something done to them" that "pull[s] her into pain as well as childbirth and welfare." Hooks's *Reel to Real: Race, Sex, and Class at the Movies* (1996) was followed by the autobiographical *Wounds of Passion: A Writing Life* (1997), which discusses her early struggle to live the life of a writer while maintaining a romantic relationship based on progressive values. *Remembered Rapture: The Writer at Work* (1999), a collection of essays, deals with the process of writing.

In addition to her books, hooks has contributed dozens of essays to such publications as *Callaloo*, *Emerge*, *Essence*, the *Utne Reader*, and *Catalyst*. She also founded a literary magazine, *Hambone*, with the poet Nathaniel Mackey, whom she met while she was an undergraduate at Stanford and with whom she lived for more than 10 years. Her second poetry collection, *The Woman's Mourning Song*, was published in 1993. In 1985 hooks taught African and Afro-American studies and English at Yale University, in New Haven, Connecticut. In 1988 she was an associate professor of women's studies and American literature at Oberlin College, in Oberlin, Ohio, and in 1994 she accepted the post of distinguished professor of English at the City College of New York, where she currently teaches. Later in the same year, she received the Writer's Award from the Lila Wallace–Reader's Digest Fund, which brought with it a cash prize of $105,000.

The writer bell hooks stands five feet, three inches tall and has short black hair and brown eyes. She divides her time between an apartment in the Greenwich Village section of New York City and a house in Oberlin. She loves the color red, deep shades of which can be found in the furniture and art in her two homes. She has described herself as being "into" Buddhism and "the spiritual experience." In her interview with Rebecca Carroll for *Elle*, hooks said, "My idea of a delicious time is to read a book that is wonderful. And then I have the usual passions: romance, fashion—I am totally into shoes. People are constantly calling me Imelda Marcos 2d. . . . I'm a big fashion girl. And I'm really into art and deeply into culture. I am passionate about leading my life with a certain quality of elegance and grace. But the ruling passion of my life is being a seeker after truth and the divine. That tempers everything else."
—C.T. / E.M.

SUGGESTED READING: *Elle* p78+ Dec. 1994, with photo; *New York Times* F p1+ Nov. 13, 1997, with photos; *Essence* p187+ May 1995; *Interview* p122+ Oct. 1995; *Times Higher Education Supplement* p20 Oct. 13, 1995; Bell-Scott, Patricia, ed. *Life Notes: Personal Writings by Contemporary Black Women*, 1994; *Contemporary Authors* vol. 143, 1994; Gates, Henry Louis, ed. *Bearing Witness: Selections from African-American Autobiography in the Twentieth Century*, 1991; hooks, bell. *Bone Black: Memories of Girlhood*, 1996

SELECTED WORKS: Nonfiction— *Ain't I a Woman: Black Women and Feminism*, 1981; *Feminist Theory: From Margin to Center*, 1984; *Talking Back: Thinking Feminist, Thinking Black*, 1989; *Yearning: Race, Gender, and Cultural Politics*, 1990; *Breaking Bread: Insurgent Black Intellectual Life*, 1991; *Black Looks: Race and Representation*, 1992; *Sisters of the Yam: Black Women and Self-Recovery*, 1993; *Teaching to Transgress: Education as the Practice of Freedom*, 1994; *Outlaw Culture: Resisting Representations*, 1994; *Art on My Mind: Visual Politics*, 1995; *Killing Rage: Ending Racism*, 1995; *Bone Black: Memories of Girlhood*, 1996; *Reel to Real: Race, Sex, and Class at the Movies*, 1996; *Wounds of Passion: A Writing Life*, 1997; *Remembered Rapture: The Writer at Work*, 1999; Poetry—*And There We Wept*, 1978; *The Woman's Mourning Song*, 1993

Hospital, Janette Turner

Nov. 12, 1942– Novelist

"I am very conscious of being at ease in many countries but belonging nowhere," Janette Turner Hospital said in a 1995 interview. This feeling of nomadism (rightly earned, as for many years she has divided her time among Australia, the United States, Canada, and elsewhere) is ever-present not only in her life, but also in her works. The author of such novels as *The Ivory Swing* (1982), *Charades* (1988), *The Last Magician* (1992), and *Oyster* (1996), Hospital is known for fiction that conveys the intricacies of the lives of society's quintessential misfits—those who defy classification, who are in some way caught different between cultures, norms, or beliefs.

The novelist was born on November 12, 1942 in Melbourne, Australia, the daughter of Adrian C. and Elsie (Morgan) Turner. (She added the name Hospital in 1965, when she married Clifford G. Hospital, a professor.) She was educated at Univer-

Courtesy of Janette Turner Hospital

Janette Turner Hospital

sity of Queensland, in Australia, where she received her bachelor's degree in English literature in 1965, and Queen's University, in Canada, where she received her master's degree in 1973.

In a statement submitted to *World Authors 1990-1995*, describing her life and career thus far, she writes: "Even before I left Australia, before the first major geographical dislocation in my life (the 1000 mile move, at the age of 7, from chilly Melbourne, the city of my birth, to Brisbane, the steamy slatternly sub-tropical capital of the northern state of Queensland, which seemed to be a completely different country from southern Australia), I found it necessary to tell myself stories to explore the meaning of the bewildering contradictions I kept bumping into. From my first day in Grade 1, I felt like a space voyager, travelling daily between alien planets, home and school, two closed systems whose languages and customs were incomprehensible to each other. This turned out to be excellent training for the rest of my life.

"I grew up in a micro-culture radically different from the macro-culture I encountered at school. My home life existed within that particular pocket of lower working-class culture which, instead of finding meaning in pub, racetrack, violence, and sport (the usual sources of working-class cohesion), found consolation and validation for a marginalized existence in fundamentalist evangelical religious fervor. My home life was severely circumscribed (quaintly and richly, it seems to me now). I was, for example, 20 years old before I had seen a movie, watched television, been to a doctor, or tasted alcohol. But also—and this was what people on the other planet I visited could never comprehend—family life was warm, rollicking, rich in

love and hilarity. Indeed, my first experience of intolerance and the terrible cruelties which attend it came not from fundamentalists (the designated 'bigots' in the eyes of society at large, as I was not to realise until many years later), but from school: and not only from bullying kids both fearful and scornful of difference, but from teachers, those symbols of liberal enlightenment. This has given me a lifelong fascination with the nature of prejudice, with comparative dogmatisms, with parallel systems of 'absolutes', with the incipient fascisms of the 'radical' and the 'enlightened.'

"Though I've put a great deal of distance (in all senses) between me and my fundamentalist background, I am nevertheless constantly amazed by the unwarranted, unearned, and deeply uninformed glibness and bigotry of intellectuals toward non-intellectual sub-cultures (or, more accurately: toward non-standard-intellectual sub-cultures; for the appropriating and privileging of one small facet of the intelligence by western academics and by the anointed guardians of High Culture are in themselves acts of aggressive intolerance). The demonizing of the Other goes both ways; and the exploration of this phenomenon is part of my subject matter.

"My urgent childhood need to decode a bewildering sign system in order to make sense of and to function at school has made me an instinctive semiotician. Dislocation (of belief systems, of geography, of culture, of trauma) and the ways in which characters mediate for themselves massive disruptions and disturbances in their lives are my constant subject matter, but in exploring these issues, my attention is always focused at the edge of the stage, in the margins, on the 'bit players' and the extras. I am an avid listener to, and engager in conversation with, the people no one much listens to. Silences and absences haunt me. I am absorbed by the ways in which silence can be a form of protection, dignity, and survival. My writing, I suppose, is a kind of map making (always provisional) of the potent unseen and unheard.

"Since those early school days, I've crossed a number of other cultural divides. More by happenstance than design, I've lived for extended periods of time in the USA, Canada, India, England, and France. I can't remember when I last spent an entire year in only one country. I've become more or less constantly and culturally nomadic. Professionally, also, I keep crossing borders. I've been an academic and have taught at universities in a number of countries. I have also taught in a maximum-security prison. I have also, under the sharp spur of economic need and geographic dislocation, been a typist, a dressmaker, an insurance agent, and a businesswoman, and think it likely, given the vagaries of literary income, that I will make return forays into any or all of these subsidiary activities before I'm through.

"In consequence, I am always interested in the parallel universes of everyday life; by the ways in which so many sub-cultures, unknown to the macro-culture, exist invisibly within it, like a hand inside a glove. I am fascinated by those characters who must move back and forth between worlds, constantly negotiating borders both literal and metaphorical: the Westerner in Asia, the immigrant Asian in North America; the long-term prisoner re-entering the outside world; the shattered survivor of violence in the indifferent world of the safe, the refugee among the settled.

"Language also matters immensely to me: its images, cadences, rhythms. I have a sharp ear for regional idiom and for accents. (My own is often considered unplaceable, though it pleases me that I can still pass for a local in an outback Australian pub, and have been asked in Paris if I am French or French-Canadian.) My work is meant to be read aloud. I hear it aloud in my head. Having grown up in a family where the Bible was read aloud after dinner every evening, I am steeped in its rhythms, particularly those of the Psalms. I am therefore a slow and painstaking writer, since each sentence has to sound not only perfect in itself, but in relation to the sentences preceding and following. Language is, for me, the delectable stuff of music, and I bring its phrases into harmony and counterpoint with each other as a composer does. The novel, for me, is a kind of fugue (of sounds, rhythms, motifs, ideas, fluid characters, inter-dissolving worlds)."

Hospital's first novel, *The Ivory Swing*, was published in 1982. Winner of the Seal First Novel Award, the book tells the tale of a university professor's wife, who goes with her husband and children to India for a year—something Hospital actually did in 1977 and 1990—and begins to grapple with questions of the nature of love and marriage, differences in cultures, and freedom. Deemed "a disturbing meditation on the clash of cultures and the rebellion and feminine rage in each" by a *Washington Post Book World* (June 5, 1983) reviewer, the novel was extremely well received. In *Quill and Quire* (October 1992) Gail Pearce wrote that *The Ivory Swing* was "compelling and enjoyable reading" and noted that "the plot is well constructed [and] the characters are plausible and sympathetic."

In the years following the publication of *The Ivory Swing*, Hospital wrote two novels—*The Tiger in the Tiger Pit* (1983) and *Borderline* (1985)—and *Dislocations* (1986), a collection of short stories. Her fourth novel, *Charades*, appeared in 1988. That book revolves around a young Australian graduate student involved in an affair with a professor of cosmology; the student, a woman who has very few recollections of her early life, offers her lover nightly stories in which she speculates about her past. Eventually the details and incidents she fabricates come together to form a past that she then begins to accept as the truth. Critical reaction to *Charades* was extremely positive. Hospital "writes with luminous and ripe sensuality about the sublime and the wretched. . . . It is a measure

of [her] lush talent that none of this seems contrived," Valerie Miner wrote in the *Los Angeles Times Book Review* (April 23, 1989). "She takes the reader on an exuberant tour of quantum physics, Middle Eastern mythology, [and] the comparative cultural legacies of British Imperialism and still leaves you caring about her characters." Further praise was offered by Alan Cheuse in the *Chicago Tribune* (March 13, 1989), who noted that the novel possessed a "mixture of intelligence and sensuality, idea and deeply felt drama."

In 1990 Hospital, writing under the pseudonym Alex Juniper, temporarily abandoned her more serious literary endeavors to publish the crime thriller *A Very Proper Death*. That same year, Hospital, again writing under her real name, published *Isobars*, her second collection of short stories. The book received mixed reviews. Though he deemed Hospital's writing as "too feverish and preachy" at times and the book's irony "too heavy-handed," Richard Burgin, writing in the *New York Times Book Review* (September 29, 1991), conceded that "much more often [Hospital is] able to fuse her disparate talents and concerns to create an original, convincing vision of our struggles with ourselves and others, and with our memories and dreams."

Two years later, Hospital published *The Last Magician*, her first novel to be set entirely in her native Australia. An exploration of betrayal and the dark side of love, the book concerns four people who share a secret—one whose ugliness haunts them for years and eventually draws them into "the Quarry," a seedy maze of underground passageways populated by derelicts, prostitutes, and drug addicts. Lauded by critics, *The Last Magician* was listed among *Publishers Weekly*'s "Best 16 Novels of 1992" and the *New York Times*'s "Most Notable Books of 1992" and was a finalist for both the Miles Franklin Award (Australia) and the Trillium Award (Canada). "The real magic at work here is, of course, the writer's," Edward Hower wrote in the *New York Times Book Review* (September 13, 1992). "Janette Turner Hospital . . . knows how to cast a spell that makes us as eager as her narrator to uncover the truth. Much of the novel's appeal lies in the ingenious ways in which discordant elements are connected and shadows are elaborately illuminated, but [Hospital] can also tell a traditional story with great skill. She fills her novel with evocative settings, characters we care deeply about, and language that is entrancingly lyrical. *The Last Magician* is an ambitious, intense, and satisfying book."

Hospital's *Collected Stories 1970-1995* appeared in 1995. A year later she published her latest novel, *Oyster* (1996). The tale of Outer Maroo, a fictional small town in the Australian outback, *Oyster* intertwines two main plot lines: one involving two strangers who come to town searching for a missing family, the other explaining the bizarre and violent history of the community. "Followers of Turner Hospital will find some recognizable themes here: ramifying secrets that need to be unraveled, the abuses of theoretical knowledge, the telling coincidence," Markman Ellis wrote in the *Times Literary Supplement* (September 13, 1996). "But there is some new material here too. For a start, Oyster is simpler than earlier works like *Charades . . .* or *The Last Magician. . . .* Although hardly simplistic, it coheres in a less demanding and more likable way. Less ambitiously difficult, the novel gains in power and resonance. Janette Turner Hospital has the bravery of a consistent risk-taker, and *Oyster* is an engaging novel."

Throughout her career, Hospital has been active in academia. She has served as a lecturer or writer in residence at numerous universities, including Massachusetts Institute of Technology (1985-1986, 1987, 1989), Boston University (1991), and La Trobe University (1991-1993). Additionally, she was awarded an honorary doctorate from Griffith University in Queensland, Australia, in 1995.

—J. P.

SUGGESTED READING: *Library Journal* p94 Sep. 15, 1992; *Los Angeles Times Book Review* p3+ Apr. 23, 1989; *New York Times Book Review* p18 Sep. 29, 1991, p15 Sep. 13, 1992; *Quill and Quire* p31 Oct. 1982; *Times Literary Supplement* p22 Sep. 13, 1996; *Washington Post Book World* p10 June 5, 1983; Pearlman, M. *Listen to Their Voices: Twenty Interviews with Women Who Write*, 19 1994; *Contemporary Authors* vol. 48, 1995

SELECTED BOOKS: *The Ivory Swing*, 1982; *The Tiger in the Tiger Pit*, 1983; *Borderline*, 1985; *Dislocations*, 1986; *Charades*, 1988; *Isobars*, 1990; *The Last Magician*, 1992; *Collected Stories 1970-1995*, 1995; *Oyster*, 1996; As Alex Juniper—*A Very Proper Death*, 1990

Sigrid Estrada

Hustvedt, Siri

Feb. 15, 1955– Novelist; poet

Siri Hustvedt is an up-and-coming author who in her two novels, *The Blindfold* (1992) and *The Enchantment of Lily Dahl* (1996), has sought to introduce new elements to the coming-of-age tale. Her first book was a collection of poetry, *Reading to You* (1983), and though she no longer writes verse, a certain lyricism pervades her fiction. Discussing one of her books with an interviewer—and perhaps in the process summing up her philosophy as a writer—she noted that in *The Blindfold* "the place

between the narrator, Iris, and the other characters in the book is what determines both the events and identities. Iris is made through the eyes of others, as, I think, we all are. . . . I suppose the mystery of the novel is the omnipresent sense of not knowing: that both the self and others are ultimately enigmatic." Finding Hustvedt to be an enigma herself, critics have been unable to place her novels in a single genre—part autobiographical fiction, part mystery, her works force readers to abandon previously held notions of fiction. Her most recent book, *Yonder*, is a collection of essays published in 1998.

In an autobiographical essay written for *World Authors 1990–1995*, Hustvedt details aspects of her life and work: "I was born on February 19, 1955 in Northfield, Minnesota, a small town in the southern part of the state, to a Norwegian mother and a Norwegian-American father. I spent my entire early life in Northfield with the exception of three trips to Bergen, Norway, which, all in all, amounted to about two and a half years. Despite the fact that I have mostly lived in English, Norwegian was my first language and has remained with me. My father was a professor of Norwegian language and Scandinavian literature at St. Olaf College where I would get my B.A. in 1977. In short, my three younger sisters and I were surrounded from birth by people and things Norwegian, and that culture has had a strong influence on me.

"I grew up outside of town in a rural area, and my sisters and I played in the woods near Heath creek that ran right behind our house or on the broad lawn outside my grandparents' place on the outskirts of Cannon Falls, Minnesota. Before they lost half of their land during the Depression, it had been their farm, and what remained had the feeling of a lost immigrant world.

"The desire to write always came from the pleasure of reading. When I was 11, my mother gave me Blake's *Songs of Innocence and Experience* and

The Selected Poems of Emily Dickinson, and although I did not really understand these poems, their music and strangeness had a powerful effect on me. Two years later, she gave me *Jane Eyre* and *David Copperfield* to read, and those two books live inside me as markers of a change in my life. A door opened, and I walked through it.

"I read and wrote poetry through my adolescent doldrums, and by the time I got to college, I had long had an insatiable appetite for books. I wrote fitfully during that period, bad poems and some very short stories. I started a novel, but had no idea where to take it. I graduated in History, spent a year as a bartender in Northfield and then set off for New York City to attend graduate school in English at Columbia University. During those first years in New York, I read constantly—philosophy, theory, fiction, poetry. I read Freud again and Jacques Lacan's revision of Freud. I read the linguists Ferdinand de Saussure, Roman Jakobson and Emile Benveniste. I fell under the spell of M. M. Bahktin, the Russian critic. I discovered Wallace Stevens and the New York School poets, in particular Kenneth Koch, Frank O'Hara and John Ashbery, and although I had read a lot of Henry James, I read *The Turn of the Screw* for the first time, a work that I return to in my mind again and again as the quintessential psychological ghost story.

"This exposure to what for me were new ideas overturned my thoughts about language. I wrote more poems. They seemed to be getting better. I sent my first 'good' poem to *The Paris Review* in 1981, and to my delight it was accepted. I published a prose poem in *Pequod*. A 10 page work, it had been written in a one night stint to loosen writer's block. Then I spent three months editing it. The effect of writing prose was so liberating, I never returned to writing in lines. I published a small book of poems and prose poems called *Reading to You* with Station Hill Press in 1983.

"In late February of 1982, just after my 26th birthday, I met Paul Auster whom I married a year later. I read his poems, his essays and the first half of his memoir *The Invention of Solitude*, which he had then finished, and was deeply impressed by his work, a feeling which has only grown through the years of our marriage, during which he has produced nearly all of his prose fiction. On July 6, 1987, Paul and I had a daughter together: Sophie Hustvedt Auster.

"I defended my dissertation on language and identity in Charles Dickens in May of 1986 and received a Ph.D. Not long after that I began writing my first novel, *The Blindfold*, which grew out of an idea for a story. During my early days alone in New York, I answered an ad for a job and met a strange man. That encounter left me with an uncanny feeling, and the novel as a whole became an exploration of that ambiguous, unsettling emotion. It was published in America in 1992 and later in 13 foreign editions.

"My second novel, *The Enchantment of Lily Dahl*, is set in a mythical or dream version of Northfield, Minnesota. This book too was inspired by real events in my hometown: the public suicide of a young man whose brother I knew, the discovery of a woman's corpse that made it clear she had been buried alive, and two very dirty patrons of a real restaurant: The Ideal Cafe. But the magic of the book is somewhere else—in the borderland between art and the world. I am now finishing a book of essays and have started another novel."

Published in 1992, *The Blindfold* met with mixed reviews. The story of a young Columbia University graduate student, Iris Vegan, the book is far from being an average coming-of-age book—it is an exploration of the human character and a murder mystery rolled into one. Because of *The Blindfold*'s dual ambition, many reviewers, like Jenifer Levin in the *New York Times Book Review* (June 7, 1992), felt confused by the book: "It is difficult to know quite how to discuss Siri Hustvedt's first novel, *The Blindfold*, which, although the product of obvious talent, is in the end less likable and successful than one hopes for." Levin went on to note Hustvedt's obsession with the possible significance of inanimate objects, suggesting that such a penchant "raises bold and grand ideas. But the author fails to take us through the door she toys at opening. The rest of the novel rapidly loses the bizarre and evocative sense of direction implied by the intriguing first chapter's trail of ideas, traveling off into vague intellectual explorations of notions of identity, brutality, nothingness, and love, and does not hang together."

The *Washington Post* (September 10, 1992) reviewer Alexander Theroux had similar comments about Hustvedt's first novel. "Sections of *The Blindfold* are promising. Part 1, for example, has all the markings of a first-rate thriller. I found much of Siri Hustvedt's writing fine, but the entire novel is inconsequential, its drive not so much aimless as not there." Possibly the most mixed of reviews was from Michiko Kakutani of the *New York Times* (April 28, 1992), who called Hustvedt's book a "genuine achievement" but also remarked that "it leaves the reader curiously unsatisfied, hungry for at least a hint of emotional catharsis."

With her next novel, *The Enchantment of Lily Dahl*, published in 1996, Hustvedt received more encouraging notices. This novel, like her first, is a coming-of-age story, this time set in a small Minnesota town populated by eccentrics. Lily Dahl is a 19-year-old aspiring actress who works the morning shift in the Ideal Cafe and deals with more than her fair share of abnormal patrons. A writer for the *Independent* (February 1, 1996) raved: "With *The Enchantment of Lily Dahl* Hustvedt's themes are more fully integrated into the narrative, woven in with the skill of a natural born storyteller." This novel, like her previous one, seems to cover many gcnres, and some critics, put off by this, pointed to what they considered a lack of coherence. The *New York Times Book Review* (October 20, 1996) stated: "Part mystery, part ghost story, and part psychological thriller, this curious hybrid never quite settles into itself, reading at times like an entertaining potboiler, at others like an existential puzzler or an erotic adventure. And yet, despite the lurching tone, Ms. Hustvedt keeps things moving with a cast of eccentric characters, a plot that won't quit, and a creepy denouement."

Publishers Weekly (July 1, 1996) concurred: "The novel is much stronger as a coming-of-age tale than it is as an existential mystery . . . and Hustvedt has created a charming and scrappy heroine in Lily Dahl."

In 1998 Hustvedt published *Yonder*, a book of six essays on her life and work and on literature and culture in general. In particular she analyzes the role language played in her childhood, especially since she grew up with a mixed Norwegian and American heritage. A critic for *Kirkus Reviews* (March 1, 1998) called the book "a strong collection." A reviewer from *Booklist* (May 15, 1998), noting the skill with which Hustvedt crafts her novels, noted how "she brings this fruitful orientation to her essays with equal force, elegance, and originality."

Siri Hustvedt lives with her husband, the novelist Paul Auster, and their daughter in the Park Slope section of Brooklyn, New York, an area that in recent years has become the home of many writers and editors. In addition to her daughter, she has a stepson, Daniel.—C.M.

SUGGESTED READING: *Booklist* May 15, 1998; *Independent* p8 Feb. 1, 1996; *Kirkus Reviews* Mar. 1, 1998; *New York Times* C p18 Apr. 28, 1992; *New York Times Book Review* p33 June 7, 1992, p30 Oct. 20, 1996; *Publishers Weekly* p 41 July 1, 1996; *Times Literary Supplement* p 22 Nov. 22, 1996; *Washington Post* C p 4 Sep. 10, 1992; *Contemporary Authors* vol. 137, 1992

SELECTED BOOKS: Fiction—*The Blindfold*, 1992; *The Enchantment of Lily Dahl*, 1996; Poetry—*Reading to You*, 1983; As translator—*Fyodor Dostoyevsky: A Writer's Life*, 1987; Nonfiction—*Yonder*, 1998

Hyde, Lewis

Oct. 16, 1945– Literary critic; poet

A versatile author of poetry, nonfiction, and literary criticism, Lewis W. Hyde recently published his first book in 10 years, *Trickster Makes This World: Mischief, Myth, and Art* (1998). The work is an anthropological study of the "trickster" figure in world folklore, finding that it relates to the role of the artist in modern society. Among other accomplishments, Hyde is a former teacher of literature and writing, the author of a collection of poetry entitled *This Error Is the Sign of Love* (1988), and the editor of a volume of collected criticism on the influential Beat poet Allen Ginsberg.

In an autobiographical statement submitted to *World Authors 1990–1995*, Lewis W. Hyde writes in the third person: "Lewis Hyde was born in Boston in 1945 [October 16] and educated at the universities of Minnesota and Iowa. His much reprinted essay "Alcohol and Poetry: John Berryman and the Booze Talking" (1975) grew out of his experiences as an alcoholism counselor. He has also worked as an electrician and a carpenter to support himself while writing. His edition of the selected poems of the Nobel Prize–winning Spanish writer Vicente Aleixandre was published by Harper & Row in 1979. His 1983 book *The Gift: Imagination and the Erotic Life of Property* is an inquiry into the situation of creative artists in a commercial society. He has edited a volume of criticism in response to Allen Ginsberg's poetry [*On the Poetry of Allen Ginsberg* (1984)]. Milkweed Editions has pub-

lished a book of his poems, *This Error Is the Sign of Love*. His most recent book about art and culture, *Trickster Makes This World*, was published by Farrar, Straus & Giroux in January 1998.

"Hyde has received grants from the National Endowment for the Arts and the National Endowment for the Humanities. In 1991 he was made a MacArthur Fellow. His poetry and essays have appeared in numerous journals, including the

Kenyon Review, the American Poetry Review, the Paris Review, and the Nation.

"For six years Hyde taught creative writing at Harvard University where, in his last year, he was director of the creative writing faculty. Since 1989 he has been Henry Luce Professor of Art and Politics at Kenyon College. He and his wife divide their time between Gambier, Ohio, and Cambridge, Mass."

Both intellectuals, Hyde's parents were Walter Lewis Hyde, a physicist, and Elizabeth Lee Sanford Hyde, a librarian. Lewis Hyde was already writing poetry by the time he was in collage, and in 1966 he was awarded the Academy of American Poets Prize. He received a B.A. from the University of Minnesota in 1967, then moved on to the University of Iowa. He obtained his first teaching job as an instructor of literature at the University of Iowa in 1969. Hyde continued student teaching until 1971. In 1972 he earned an M.A. from the University of Iowa.

His stint as an alcoholism counselor, which would later inspire the aforementioned essay, took place at Cambridge Hospital in Cambridge, Massachusetts, from 1974 to 1976. After leaving the hospital, Hyde spent a short time in 1976 at Harvard University working as a researcher in the study of adult development. He continued pursuing his interest in writing throughout this time, and was granted National Endowment for the Arts (NEA) Creative Writing Fellowships in 1976 and 1977.

In his early years as a writer Hyde played an important part in making the poetry of Vicente Aleixandre accessible to an English-speaking readership. Prior to the more extensive A Longing for the Light: Selected Poems of Vicente Aleixandre (1979), Hyde, along with Robert Bly, edited and translated a smaller sampling of Aleixandre's work that was published in 1977 as Twenty Poems of Vicente Aleixandre. The following year he received the Columbia University Translation Center Award. Hyde's work continued to attract fellowships, including a National Endowment for the Humanities (NEH) Fellowship for Independent Study and Research in 1979 and a poetry fellowship from the Massachusetts Council on the Arts and Humanities in 1980.

In November of 1981 Hyde married Patricia Auster Vigderman, an editor. The following year, while working with David Unger on another translation of Aleixandre's poems, Hyde received another NEA Creative Writing Fellowship. The result of his collaboration with Unger, Vicente Aleixandre, World Alone, was published in 1982.

In The Gift: Imagination and the Erotic Life of Property (1983), Hyde delved into the problems of the artist in a commodity-based society and discussed what an artist's place might be in a gift-based society such as that of the Tobriand Islanders or of Ancient Greece. Among the individuals whose work is examined in Hyde's exploration of

the concept of art as gift are the American poets Walt Whitman and Ezra Pound.

Hyde returned to Harvard in 1983, accepting a position as a lecturer in expository writing. In 1984, while still lecturing at Harvard, he served as a writer-in-residence at the Centrum Foundation in Port Townsend, Washington. After two years as a lecturer at Harvard, he ascended to the rank assistant professor of English. He was awarded an NEA Nonfiction Fellowship (1986) one year later. Hyde held his assistant professorship at Harvard until 1989, when he moved to Kenyon College in Gambier, Ohio.

For the next several years, Hyde devoted his time to publishing poetry and works of criticism in journals, most notably the Kenyon Review. During this time Hyde received a MacArthur Fellowship (1991–1996) and a Getty Scholarship (1993–1994).

Hyde's most recent book, Trickster Makes This World, continued the exploration he began in The Gift, tracking the perception of art and the artist throughout history and into the present. In this work, however, he focused on the "trickster," a prevalent figure in folklore from around the world. These playful, mischievous, often wise characters violate the laws of nature and society and disrupt everyday life. Trickster Makes This World recounts many trickster tales from around the world and argues for the universality of the figure. The author suggests that artists—individuals who keep society in perpetual motion and establish new truths through the clever arrangement of fabrications—are the tricksters of today. Among the modern artists Hyde cites to support this argument are Pablo Picasso, Allen Ginsberg, Robert Mapplethorpe, and Maxine Hong Kingston.

In the New York Times Book Review (February 15, 1998) Paul Mattick expressed some dissatisfaction with the book's arguments. "Hyde seems not to have studied the scholarship of art as thoroughly as he has read his way through the trickster stories," he wrote. "Hyde . . . believes he is comparing individual realities with a cultural archetype, seeking the 'moments when the practice of art and this myth coincide." Hyde, Mattick added, does not sufficiently explain his selection of the individual artists included in his discussion, and fails to offer adequate supporting information to identify these men and women as tricksters. He also found many of Hyde's attitudes toward art to be remarkably conservative, pointing to his identification with the 19th-century concept of art as a substitute for religion.

In addition to his original works, Hyde has published translations in various periodicals such as the American Poetry Review, the New York Times, and the Paris Review, as well as anthologies such as Poetry from Spain 1900–1975. He is a member of the PEN American Center, the Authors Guild, and the National Writers Union. Hyde also belongs to the Lepidopterists Society, an organization of enthusiasts of the lepidopteran group of insects, which includes butterflies and moths. In 1985 he served as vice president of the Artists Federation. Hyde has one stepson. —B.S.

SUGGESTED READING: *The American Poetry Review* p45+ Jan./Feb. 1998; *New York Times Book Review* p18 Feb. 15, 1998; *Who's Who in Writers, Editors and Poets 1995–1996*

SELECTED WORKS: Nonfiction—*The Gift: Imagination and the Erotic Life of Property*, 1983; Alcohol and Poetry: John Berryman and the Booze Talking, 1986; *Trickster Makes this World: Mischief, Myth, and Art*, 1998; poetry—*This Error Is the Sign of Love*, 1988; as editor—*On the Poetry of Allen Ginsberg*, 1984; as translator—*Vicente Aleixandre, World Alone*, 1982 (with David Unger); as editor and translator—*Twenty Poems of Vicente Aleixandre*, 1977 (with Robert Bly); *A Longing for the Light: Selected Poems of Vicente Aleixandre*, 1979 (with others)

Irokawa, Daikichi

1925– Historian; nonfiction writer

Historian Daikichi Irokawa's own lifetime spans the era that is the subject of his most celebrated work, *The Age of Hirohito: In Search of Modern Japan* (1991). He was born in 1925, just one year before the accession of Hirohito, whose imperial reign from 1926 to 1989 is now known as the Shōwa period—hence the book's Japanese title, *Shōwa shi to Tennō*, reflecting the Japanese custom of referring to a past emperor by the name of his reign, in this case, "Enlightened Peace." In the book, Irokawa offers a frank and learned analysis of how that nation's ancient imperial traditions have been reinterpreted and adapted to the realities of 20th-century living. By focusing on this pivotal period in Japan's history, the author has traced the evolution of his homeland from the militaristic "dark valley" years of the 1930s and 1940s through the postwar occupation and modernization that have transformed it into a global economic power. Because personal anecdotes about his own life are interspersed through the text, *The Age of Hirohito* has been described as a "profoundly personal book" by American historian Carol Gluck, who wrote the book's foreword. Irokawa's earlier work, *The Culture of the Meiji Period* (1984), focused on the period from 1867 to 1912, which marked the restoration of imperial power and the development of Japan as a modern nation-state.

Of rural stock, Daikichi Irokawa was born in 1925. His formative years took place during a period when Japanese policy sanctioned military excursions in China and the Pacific to expand Japan's sphere of influence in the "Greater East Asia Co-Prosperity Scheme." He related many personal anecdotes of this period in *The Age of Hirohito*. When the teenage Irokawa enrolled in middle school, for example, his mother addressed him formally, telling him "Henceforth, you must do your best because you are entering a school where the object is to prepare you for your rise to the top of society as an outstanding person." Since his "country folk" parents had achieved only an elementary-school education, his entering middle school was a matter of great prestige. Irokawa entered Tokyo University in the fall of 1943, in the midst of World War II. At the time, as he related in the opening sentences of *The Age of Hirohito*, "contemporary history was not recognized as a subject for study," and "events after the Meiji Restoration of 1868 were 'not appropriate' for scholarly investigation." This was a reference to the restoration of the imperial power in the person of the Emperor Meiji after 250 years of rule by the shogunate, whose power had collapsed in the wake of modernization catalyzed by the "opening" of Japan to American and European commercial and cultural intercourse.

Life for Irokawa was difficult in the immediate postwar years, as it was for all Japanese. He recounted in his books the deprivations suffered during the Occupation, including his bout with tuberculosis, which caused him to have part of his right lung removed. "For the Japanese economy, Shōwa was a period of great turbulence," he wrote, "from the Great Depression and the wartime economy to Japan's defeat and the enormous damage and confusion that resulted." Irokawa reported that he and many others escaped starvation by eating food, supplied by the United States, that would ordinarily have been used as animal feed. "Rice was supposed to be supplied by the government," he added, "but distribution was delayed and often no rice ration was provided." After his discharge from the Army in 1946, Irokawa returned to Tokyo University, where, "in desperation, we dug up the university lawn and planted yams, which we divided among us and cooked—stems, roots, and all. On Sundays we searched for grasshoppers."

After graduating from college with a history degree, Irokawa accepted a post as a junior-high-school teacher in a remote mountain village, but he soon returned to Tokyo to work at the Democratic Chamber of Commerce (he had also studied tax law and accounting). In this capacity, he negotiated tax assessments on behalf of small businesses that were trying to rebuild the private sector under guidelines recommended by Carl S. Shoup, a Columbia University professor who worked as a financial adviser to the American Occupation. Irokawa believed that the Shoup plan was harmful to small entrepreneurs, and he joined in demonstrations that advocated its repeal. As he pointed out in *The Age of Hirohito*, the economic restructuring engineered by the Occupation "had many victims: numerous poorly managed small and medium-sized businesses went into bankruptcy and, as a result, many people committed suicide. But once these rough times had been weathered, inflation was controlled and the economy began to stabilize. However, Japan also benefited from the special procurements during the Korean War, referred to by some as a gift from heaven."

Irokawa's book, *Shōwa shi to Tennō* was published in Japan in 1990 and in English in 1995 as *The Age of Hirohito: In Search of Modern Japan*. It is divided into three sections: "War and Peace," to recognize how the Shōwa era spanned both the militarism of the 1930s and 1940s and the renunciation of military force in the postwar period; "The Lifestyle Revolution," which describes the shift from an agrarian nation to an urban and information society; and "The Emperor and the People," a study of the essential, sometimes mystical, characteristics of the imperial system that Westerners often find obscure but that affect national ideology, the constitution, and relations with other countries. By focusing on these three themes, Irokawa wrote at the conclusion of the book's introduction "The Limits of Contemporary History," he hoped "to present a basic understanding of the Shōwa period. I then close with a reflection on what Japan has achieved, what it has failed to achieve, and what remains for Japan in the 21st century."

Irokawa's book tries to acknowledge the burden that Japanese women suffered, especially during the 1930s and 1940s. "Women bore twice as much persecution as male advocates of ideological principles—simply because they were women," he declared in the "War and Peace" section, discussing the role of peace advocates and war resisters, many of them part of the illegal Japanese Communist Party. "Male intellectuals have labeled the period from 1931 to 1941 the 'dark valley.' But for activist women, this era was much worse than these men can imagine. . . . Unless the few remaining people who lived through this dark valley relate its history accurately, the stories of those who were victimized during this period will be forgotten." While Irokawa maintained that Japanese dissenters were treated much more mildly than in Nazi Germany and in Soviet Russia, he still faulted imperial Japan for its "relentless and ruthless" practices. "The thorough suppression of dissent, the witch-hunts directed against those who rejected the national policy (*kokutai*), and the unspeakable discrimination and oppression inflicted on the Korean and Chinese minorities in Japan cannot be erased from the pages of Japanese history," he wrote.

Only recently has a younger generation of Japanese begun to shed some of the taboos that once precluded any open discussion of imperial matters, especially in relation to the Shōwa emperor's role in World War II and Japan's policy toward other Asian peoples within its borders.. This prompted Janet Goff to write in her *Japan Quarterly* (October 1996) review how Irokawa's book "differs markedly" from an earlier, more sympathetic biography of Hirohito written by Kawahara Toshiaki in 1983. Irokawa, on the other hand, painted a more

critical portrait of the emperor, citing Hirohito's personal recollections ("perhaps the most important historical discovery, a first-rate historical document") that were published in 1990, a year after his death. "Though the emperor complains about those who wanted to continue the war, he did not take any action to save the nation," wrote Irokawa, adding later that "even 45 years after the end of the war, Japan had not formally apologized to these people or compensated them [victims of Japanese aggression in Asia, including Chinese, Koreans, Taiwanese, and others]. Can such a nation be said to have any moral principles?" he asked. Distancing himself from the apologetic stance taken by other Japanese writers, Irokawa wrote with candor about how contemporary Japanese people have changed their personal views toward the imperial system, prompted by the American-imposed postwar constitution that retained the Shōwa emperor as a figurative head of state while denying his divine origins. In researching this part of his book, "The Symbolic Emperor," Irokawa talked to many students and found their attitudes toward the emperor to be "surprisingly cool and indifferent" when compared with those of earlier generations. "A qualitative change has occurred in the relationship between the emperor and the people," he wrote. In his final chapter, "Facing the Twenty-First Century," Irokawa noted the strong hold that the Imperial Household Agency still has on the imperial family, whose comings and goings are still couched in ancient Shintō rituals. "But in the 21st century," he added, "Japan needs an emperor who can be a completely free person in society." Proposing that "the emperor should no longer be the symbol of the state and unity of the people, and succession to [the] throne should not be hereditary," Irokawa believes that the imperial family should leave its sequestered life in Tokyo and return to the traditional imperial capital of Kyoto where, stripped of constitutional obligations, they should devote themselves to the preservation of traditional arts and culture.

Among the other issues Japan needs to deal with as it enters the 21st century, Irokawa wrote, are the destruction of the environment, political corruption, and the inconsistency of Japanese foreign policy. "The 40-year rule of the Liberal Democratic Party produced systemic problems for Japanese democracy: corruption, political stagnation, irresponsible conduct, and loss of public confidence in politicians. To make a contribution to the world appropriate to its national strength," he wrote, "Japan first must institute political reforms by fundamentally restructuring the political parties." To Irokawa, the dominance of the United States in Asian affairs caused Japan to have "no genuine foreign policy. As a result, Japan was viewed in the international arena as an anonymous, faceless follower country—a country without an identity or a position." While Japan's Axis partner, Germany, engaged in "stringent self-criticism for its war crimes," Japan has tried to deny and whitewash its

role during the war. "This attempt to cover up war crimes reveals a dark underside to the mind set of those Japanese who have meekly, quietly followed the United States," Irokawa wrote. Japan, he believes, also needs to deal with issues of sexism and with its racism toward its Korean population and the outcaste *burakumin*, both of whom are treated as second-class citizens at home.
—E. M.

SUGGESTED READING: *Choice* p1001 Feb. 1996; *Japan Quarterly* p100+ Oct. 1996; *Journal of Asian Studies* p458+ May 1996; *Library Journal* p81 May 15, 1995; *New York Times Book Review* p36 Sep. 24, 1995; *Wilson Quarterly* p 87 Autumn 1995

SELECTED WORKS: *The Culture of the Meiji Period*, 1984; *The Age of Hirohito: In Search of Modern Japan*, 1995

Miriam Berkley

Isler, Alan

Sep. 12, 1934– Novelist; professor; short-story writer

Alan Isler began his writing career at the age of 60, and has since carved out a niche for himself as a successful author of fiction. He has written two novels, *The Prince of West End Avenue* (1994) and *Kraven Images* (1996), and a short-story collection, *The Bacon Fancier* (1997). Isler focuses mainly on Jewish life, particularly the day-to-day experiences of Jews in a Gentile environment. Before turning to fiction, Isler was an associate professor of English

at Queens College in New York for almost 30 years. He retired from teaching and returned to his native London in 1996.

Alan David Isler was born September 12, 1934, in London, England. At the age of 18, he left England for the United States, settling in Manhattan. He attended Hunter College of the City University of New York (CUNY), attaining his bachelor's degree in 1961. One year later, he received a master's degree from Columbia University. In 1965, just prior to turning 31, he began working at Huron College of the University of Western Ontario as an assistant professor of English. He continued his education at the graduate level, achieving a Ph.D. in 1966 from Columbia, specializing in 16th-century literature.

One year after finishing his Ph.D., Isler departed Huron College and settled into the institution where he would teach English as an associate professor for the next three decades, Queens College (a branch of CUNY, like his alma mater Hunter).

Isler did not begin publishing fiction until the age of 60, when *The Prince of West End Avenue* (1994) was published by the fledgling Bridge Works publishing house. A comic novel, *The Prince of West End Avenue* is set in a retirement home on Manhattan's Upper West Side. The story focuses on a production of *Hamlet* being put on by the residents of the home. The main character and narrator is Otto Korner, a Holocaust survivor who is forced to confront memories of his past brought to light by events surrounding the production. Many of the elderly characters were inspired by Isler's experiences in the immigrant cultures of New York and England. "They are a composite of many, many people whom I met over the years . . .," he told Mary Cummings in the *New York Times* (July 10, 1994). "There is a lot of Korner in me," said Isler to Cummings. "Like him, I love the old verities."

The Prince of West End Avenue was a project Isler had been toying with for 25 years. He had originally been inspired by a 1969 newspaper article that described a production of *Macbeth* staged by residents of a Brooklyn nursing home. "Something had to be done with the idea," Isler told Mary Cummings. However, Isler was at the time focusing on writing for scholarly journals, and he did not get around to writing the novel until 1984. Once he committed himself to the fictional work, it took him only 15 months to complete it. "I undertook it with the same kind of pleasure that a crossword puzzle addict undertakes a difficult crossword, but one that can be solved," the author told Lorraine Kreahling of the *New York Times* (April 21, 1996). "I was an amateur. I didn't do it with the intention of getting it published." Friends encouraged Isler to send his manuscript to publishers. Isler, however, could find no publisher willing to print it, and eventually gave up. Ten years later, he tried again, sending the manuscript to London publishers, who in turn recommended it to Bridge Works in the U.S., the company that finally picked it up.

"Reading this book is like eating paella if you are allergic to shellfish," Judith Dunford wrote in a *New York Newsday* (May 4, 1994) review of *The Prince of West End Avenue*. "A lot has to be picked out and pushed to the edge of your plate, but what remains is still savory." Dunford praised Isler's flair for comedy, but complained that he often took the gags too far. Although she criticized some of the novel's characterizations as one-dimensional, she found many of them engaging as well. Isler's crowning achievement, according to Dunford, was the realistic way he portrayed Otto Korner.

In the *New York Times* (May 29, 1994), Bette Pesetsky lauded the way Isler used "the mythic power of the theater" to his advantage in *The Prince of West End Avenue*. She complimented Isler's sharp wit and skillful characterizations, but she also noted that Isler did not give his female characters the kind of three-dimensionality he gave his male characters.

The Prince of West End Avenue earned Isler a National Jewish Book Award and a nomination for the National Book Critics Circle Award. It has been translated into seven languages and was a bestseller in numerous countries in addition to the United States. Miramax, an adult-oriented film subsidiary of Disney, optioned the motion picture rights in 1996 and hired British playwright Ronald Harwood to write the screenplay.

In 1996 Isler retired from teaching and returned to his native country of England. That same year he published his second novel, *Kraven Images*. Also a comic novel, *Kraven Images* is about Nick Kraven, an Englishman who takes up a teaching career in the United States while posing as his deceased cousin Marcus. "I think of it as a kind of Jeckyll and Hyde story in which Dr. Jeckyll puts on the mask of his wicked cousin," Isler explained to Lorraine Kreahling. In America Kraven fulfills all his dark, lustful fantasies, free from reproach under the shelter of his assumed identity.

Walter Goodman of the *New York Times* (July 14, 1996) described *Kraven Images* as a modern updating of Restoration comedies of manners. Once again, Isler's sense of humor was praised, but Goodman was quick to point out that the novel is one of great depth. While Goodman found some parts of the novel overdone and forced, he also praised the author's imagination, writing, "Mr. Isler is the first scholar I know to explain why Merlin must have been a Jew, or to compose a 20-line rhymed version of 'Paradise Lost.'"

Even before *Kraven Images* hit bookstores, Isler was at work on his next book, the short-story anthology *The Bacon Fancier* (1997). Each of the four stories in *The Bacon Fancier* takes place in a different century and deals with anti-Semitism in various ways. One story examines Shakespeare's *The Merchant of Venice* from the point of view of Shylock, the Jewish moneylender, while another, set in the present day, tells the story of a struggling Jewish actor who accepts a part in a musical despite its offensive material.

In a *New York Times* (July 22, 1997) review, Michiko Kakutani lauded Isler's storytelling abilities but found the devices used to link the stories to be contrived. Nevertheless, Kakutani wrote, "There is an assurance to his writing that enables him to fold digressions and speculative asides effortlessly into his tales, coupled with a wry affection for his characters that makes their stories poignant and funny and sad."

In a review for *Publishers Weekly* (May 5, 1997), a critic wrote, "Isler has an acute ear for dialogue, as well as dialects; the voices of his characters are distinctive and distinctly Jewish, though they emanate from different centuries, and brutally candid about their circumscribed lives." The reviewer also noted Isler's deft use of wordplay and—in direct contrast to Kakutani of the *Times*—his skill at connecting the four stories.

"I don't feel impelled to write," Isler told the *New York Times* (April 21, 1996). "I'm not a very disciplined person. I don't feel like I have to be at the computer at eight every morning. I work as the muse whispers, because that's all I need to do now, which is really nice and pleasant and I get quite a lot done."

Alan Isler spent the 1971–1972 academic year as a visiting lecturer at Tel Aviv University in Israel. He is a member of the Renaissance Society of America. Among the periodicals to which he has been a contributor is the *University of Toronto Quarterly*.—B.S.

SUGGESTED READING: *New York Newsday* p40 May 8, 1994, with photo; *New York Times* VII p9 May 29, 1994, XIII p14 July 10, 1994, with photo, XIII p10 Apr. 21, 1996, with photo, VII p9 July 14, 1996, C p14 July 22, 1997, with photo; *Publishers Weekly* p198 May 5, 1997

SELECTED WORKS: *The Prince of West End Avenue*, 1994; *Kraven Images*, 1996; *The Bacon Fancier*, 1997

Iyer, Pico

Feb. 11, 1957– Essayist; novelist; travel writer

The early years of Pico Iyer, an American essayist, travel writer, and novelist, prepared him well for what he does: travel the world and write about his impressions of what he sees. The son of two Indian philosophers, he was born in the United Kingdom and spent much of his childhood and adolescence commuting between his British boarding school and his parents' home in California. A contributing editor to *Time* since 1982, Iyer divides his time between homes in Kyoto, Japan, and Santa Barbara, California. His *Video Night in Kathmandu* (1988) and *Falling Off the Map* (1993) are collections of essays in which he explored such diverse places as

Mark Richards/Courtesy of Alfred A. Knopf

Pico Iyer

North Korea, Argentina, Bhutan, and Ethiopia. *The Lady and the Monk* (1991) is an account of a year he spent in Japan, and *Cuba and the Night* (1995) is a novel—set mainly in Cuba—about a photojournalist who becomes captivated by Havana and by a woman he meets there. *Tropical Classical* (1997) is a compendium that reflects of many of Iyer's interests; it includes literary criticism, humorous essays, and transcriptions of interviews with Norman Lewis, Peter Brook, the Dalai Lama, and Peter Matthiesen. Iyer's definition of "tropical classical" writers may be said to describe Iyer himself: Such writers come from the outposts of the former British Empire and write in English, "showing us a new way of forging identities. . . . Their most liberating assumption, in fact, is that identity is assumed and the self is what we make of it."

In an autobiographical statement submitted to *World Authors 1990–1995*, Pico Iyer writes: "I was born in Oxford, England, in 1957, the only son of two philosophers from Bombay who were teaching at the university there. England in those days was a protected, settled world just beginning to accept its loss of Empire. When I was seven, my family moved to Santa Barbara, California, in the early stages of its 'Consciousness Revolution,' and so, while still in elementary school, I was already used to seeing the world through the foreign eyes of double exile. Whether in England or America or India, I was always an alien, one of those lucky souls able to see even a trip to the local candy-store as a voyage through a foreign world in which nearly everything looked exotic and nearly nobody looked like me.

"When I returned to boarding-school in England at the age of nine, I got a further training in living on planes—and between cultures: a perfect training, some would say, for accommodation and detachment. The Dragon School in Oxford, a warm Dickensian nursery for the children of academics and diplomats, enabled me to win a scholarship to Eton, and that led in turn to scholarships to Oxford and Harvard. Formally, I studied English, English and more English for eight years (near-fatal for a writer), while, in my teenage summers, traveling around India, working as a bus-boy in the Pancho Villa Inn in Southern California, and going by bus, with a school friend, around Central and South America. Informally, I was being trained in Empire and the subjugation of the natives, only to find, upon graduation, that the Empire was dead and I was a native myself.

"After so many years of studying nothing but literature, I was qualified for nothing but gainful unemployment, and two weeks before I was to commit myself to this, *Time* magazine, quite out of the blue, signed me up as a writer, in 1982. Undeterred by the fact that I had no training in journalism more useful than writing *Let's Go* guidebooks to Europe during summer holidays, and moved by my undisguised claim that, studying and teaching English for so long, I knew no difference between Iran and Iraq, my famously generous employers set me to writing on World Affairs, a crash course in learning how to write simply, clearly and concisely, and in curing myself of some of the bad habits of the academy (principally by learning that the main goal of the writer is to communicate to the reader—and the reader is not always oneself). My new job also allowed me to learn, relatively quickly, some of the main features of the countries I was describing from afar as, each week, in my little cubicle in Rockefeller Center, I wrote vivid eyewitness accounts of civil war in the Philippines, the struggle against apartheid in South Africa, or the drug trade through the Americas.

"Deciding at last to visit some of the places I was writing about, I began, thanks again to the largesse of my bosses, taking long holidays in Burma, Thailand, Indonesia and Japan. Deciding to try to make these holidays permanent, and eager to spend more time in Asia, I took a seven-month leave of absence in 1985, and spent the first four months traveling everywhere from Brunei to Tibet, and the final three months writing the bulk of my first book, *Video Night in Kathmandu*. After such a heady taste of freedom, I could not easily return to incarceration in New York City, and so, partially sponsored by *Time*, I have lived ever since on my own, initially traveling around places like Cuba, Iceland, Paraguay, and North Korea, and then, increasingly, settling down with a loved family in Japan.

"For me, the life of writing lies in that natural, breathing rhythm of going out into the world to see what it looks like, and then returning to a solitude almost monastic to make sense of it; writing at its best offers a way of balancing contemplation and social action, and allows one, by taking in the details of the world, to make one's sense of paradise more plausible. Like traveling, it encourages one to pay attention to the world, and to see the issues that lie deepest in one through eyes very different from one's own; and when I came at last to see writing as a way of uncovering the hidden possibility in every moment, I stopped traveling much externally and embarked upon more inward adventures. In the books that followed, I have often alternated excursions into a world of which I am an increasingly typical reflection (mongrel, many-selved, itinerant) with more private discussions of faith in solitude and romance, all filtered through a voice wavering between the irony in which I was trained in Britain and a hopefulness that may be native to India and California. The beauty of writing for me is that it offers a way not to express but to cross-examine the self and, like meditation or self-questioning or dream, it offers up a pathway into the unexplored passageways within that one can share with the world at large.

"For this reason, the writers who are my heroes are Emerson and Thoreau, who rhyme cheerfulness with realism, and fashion a careful sunlit affirmation of unity that sings. And for that same gift—the ability to see the world clearly and without illusions, yet with love—I have found my greatest fictional inspiration in the books of Graham Greene. In him, as in the finest prose writers from Melville to Wilde, wisdom is always chastened—made human—by compassion."

From a life of internal and external travel, Pico Iyer has produced a multiplicity of essays and a novel that place him in a context he has created—the "tropical classical"—a group of authors in which he includes Derek Walcott, Michael Ondaatje, and Richard Rodriguez. "The revolution such individuals are enacting has gone largely unremarked, in part because they are so individual, and so various in their forms," Iyer noted in "Welcome to the Age of Tropical Classical," an essay in *Tropical Classical* (1997). He referred to writers of the postcolonial world who have "the ability to season high classical forms with a lyrical beauty drawn from the streets and beaches of their homes. To learn from the tradition of Homer and Herodotus and Augustine . . . and yet to enliven and elevate those dusty forms with the rhythms of Saint Lucia, the colors of Sri Lanka, the love songs of the Latin South."

The title of Iyer's first book, *Video Night in Kathmandu and Other Reports from the Not-So-Far East* (1988), explains the point of view Iyer took in examining the life of foreigners in Hong Kong, sexual customs in Thailand, life on the island of Bali, the film industry in India, and baseball in Japan. He analyzed the part that Western culture plays in the life of Asian countries, examining how "America's pop-cultural imperialism spread through the world's most ancient civilizations." Michiko Kakutani, reviewing the book for the *New York Times* (April 16, 1988), observed that "*Video Night in Kathmandu* surprises as it informs.*" She quoted Iyer: "The Westerner is drawn to the tradition of the Easterner, and almost covets his knowledge of suffering . . . but what attracts the Easterner to the West is exactly the opposite—his future, and his freedom from all hardship." When the New Yorker turns into a barefoot ascetic in Asia and the Nepali peasant turns out to be a traveling salesman, the "upshot is confusion," Iyer wrote. Kakutani praised Iyer's distinctions between the British and American impacts on Asia and termed *Video Night in Kathmandu* "a meticulously observed and reported book—a magical mystery tour through the brave new world of Asia." Jennifer Howard, writing in the *Nation* (June 18, 1988), was also impressed by Iyer's "surprising and clever book," maintaining that Iyer had discovered that "cultural crossover can be as stimulating and as psychically dangerous as a voyage up the Amazon, and very possibly more educational." Other reviewers, such as the *New Republic*'s (May 23, 1988) James Fallows, agreed that Iyer "has a good eye," but found his style too similar to that of a newsmagazine, because the author succumbed to a "strong temptation to wrap up ideas with a clever-sounding twist." Fallows thought Iyer's understanding of other cultures was shallow, as did Gail Pool, who, in the *Christian Science Monitor* (September 13, 1988), wrote that Iyer's "description of baseball in Japan—fascinating as description—seems unenlightened without an understanding of traditional Japanese concepts of work and play, perfectionism and the expression of emotion."

Iyer deepened and enlarged his knowledge of Japan even before *Video Night in Kathmandu* was published. *The Lady and the Monk* (1991) is Iyer's chronicle of his year (1987) in Kyoto, a city that is home to many famous Zen Buddhist temples. Iyer studied Japanese literature (in translation), weaving some of "the plaintive love poems and stories of Buddhist priests into his narrative," according to Susan Fifer Canby, the reviewer for *Library Journal* (September 1, 1991). He discovered the literature "to be a very feminine art form," in the words of Lesley Downer, who reviewed the book for the *New York Times* (September 29, 1991). Iyer did not speak Japanese, and so spent his time with "old Japan hands," Western students of Zen living in Kyoto, and women and children. He met Sachiko, a married woman with two children, and their friendship became a love affair. Downer added that "*The Lady and the Monk* is an idiosyncratic and lyrical account . . . , full of sharp and accurate insights into the country and the people. . . . But it is not merely a love story or even merely a book about Japan. As the title indicates, it is also a mediation on larger themes: What is the relationship between the life of religion and the life of the senses? Is it possible to redeem yourself through love? Is the lady only a temptress for the monk? Or can the experience of love itself be a path to enlightenment?" Ann Jansen, writing in *Quill & Quire* (September 1991), observed that "Iyer's careful chronicling" displays "sensitivity to the shifting and elusive underpinnings of the famed Japanese restraint," doing "justice to a complex society."

Iyer once again traveled the world for his next book, *Falling Off the Map: Some Lonely Places of the World* (1993). This time his itinerary included places in the Western hemisphere—Argentina, Cuba, and Peru—as well as Australia, Bhutan, North Korea, and Vietnam. These are, in Iyer's mind, "places that don't fit in, the places that have no seat at our international dinner table." In the *New York Times Book Review* (June 6, 1993), Peter Conrad remarked that "false paradises are . . . Iyer's specialty." His pleasure is in the paradoxical "lobotomized jollity of North Korea, the frigid austerity of Iceland, and the almost extraterrestrial remoteness of Bhutan." Although Brian Kelly, who reviewed the book for the *Washington Post* (June 13, 1993), felt that too much had already been written about Argentina, Australia, and Cuba, he judged the other countries worthy subjects. Like critics of *Video Night in Kathmandu*, however, Kelly and other reviewers felt that Iyer's "affinity for sights and sounds" is greater than his insights into people and politics. Mary C. Kalfatovic, writing in *Library Journal* (May 1, 1993), found that while Iyer's "cool, ironic style" may be similar to that of Bruce Chatwin, "Iyer is a bit too detached, too unruffled by what he experiences." She also maintained that Iyer "does not fully convey to us the strangeness of the strange places he has visited." Nevertheless, Kalfatovic found his impressions "interesting reading." Annette Kobak, a *Times Literary Supplement* (August 6, 1993) critic, felt that Iyer's "cosmopolitanism constantly yields unforced insights." Donna Seaman in *Booklist* (May 1, 1993) found *Falling Off the Map* "flawless" and "full of wistfulness and eccentricity."

In 1995 Iyer published his first novel, *Cuba and the Night*. The title comes from a line by José Martí: "*Dos patrias tengo yo: Cuba y la noche.*" ("I have two fatherlands: Cuba and the night.") The novel is about Richard, a freelance photojournalist who travels the world, much the way Iyer has. Richard is captivated by Havana, finding it "even easier to be in love with a place than a person." He also falls in love with Lourdes, a young woman who wants to escape the shortages and slogans that seem omnipresent in Cuba. Unfortunately, Richard's cynical nature prevents him from making a commitment to Lourdes. "This wearisome predictability of arrested emotional development and hip cynicism is balanced . . . not so much by the mechanics of plot as by the author's skillful, absolutely inerrant eye for setting and atmosphere . . . ," David Haward Bain wrote in the *New York Times Book Review* (April 30, 1995). "The major engine that drives suspense and reader interest is . . . curiosity about Richard's next emotional dodge and our dawning desire for his dramatic and irrevocable

comeuppance." Although Bain felt that Iyer's "scenic backdrops are more vivid and complex than his narrator's emotional life," he "deserves as much credit for building this suspense over his character's fate as he does for his atmospheric and haunting glimpses of life in the Cuban countryside." William Boyd, Iyer's colleague at *Time* (May 8, 1995), observed that "one of the subtle strengths of this novel" is that "it quietly subverts the note of tropical passion and romance that it initially seems to promise." Boyd, who described Iyer as "among the finest travel writers of his generation," declared that Iyer "provides the undercurrent of cool reality about people's lives, their impossible dreams and inevitable disappointments that makes *Cuba and the Night* the most promising and beguiling of fiction debuts."

Coco Fusco, who reviewed *Cuba and the Night* for the *Washington Post* (May 14, 1995), had a less favorable assessment of the novel. She felt that "real understanding of Cuba is lacking. Little of the culture's extraordinarily sardonic humor or of the ingenuity people demonstrate in their everyday rituals of survival appears in this story." She did find in the novel "a seemingly unself-conscious study of the manners and morals of the international press corps."

Iyer's next book, *Tropical Classical: Essays from Several Directions* (1997), touches on multiple places, people, books, and themes. Iyer presented his views on such authors as Barbara Pym, Don DeLillo, Anita Desai, Diane Johnson, Paul Theroux, and Anita Brookner. The places he covered include Ethiopia, Tibet, Bombay, and New York. He also offered interviews with Norman Lewis, Peter Brook, and Peter Matthiesen, among others. His themes include innocence and culture-crossing imagery. His squibs included "Confessions of a Frequent Flier," in which he admitted to being addicted to acquiring frequent-flier miles to such an extent that he entered programs by which "if I called Zaire every day for a week—for 17 straight weeks—I could get a free ticket to Detroit." He also wrote comically of pressures on writers; Bill, for example, is being nagged (by his wife, who is also his agent) to "touch all the bases" in his work; that is, to write about "a black guy; a high-society blonde whose old man's a senator. This Cassio guy, fooling around with a streetwalker. That stuff about Cyprus, Rhodes, the Middle East . . . ." In the *New York Times Book Review* (May 4, 1997), Elizabeth Hanson called Iyer "a gentle yet astute observer of a variety of foreign locales, a thoughtful, generous reader and a versatile writer happy to grace with his rich, witty prose topics like punctuation, the number nine, or book-cover blurbs." Richard Bernstein, writing in the *New York Times* (May 2, 1997), called Iyer "aloof and involved at the same time, understanding ways in which two colliding worlds fail to understand each other." He preferred Iyer's observations about exotic places to his essays on America. "It is as if he is trying to make them more special than they really are by dressing

them up with musical, perfectly balanced phrases applying for entry into *Bartlett's Familiar Quotations.*" Nevertheless, Bernstein deemed that, in a dozen or so essays in which Iyer "reflects back at us images from a post-colonial world that is gorgeously complex and stubbornly elusive, yet firmly within his grasp," he reaches his great potential as a writer.
—S. Y.

SUGGESTED READING: *Booklist* p1566 May 1, 1993; *Christian Science Monitor* p20 Sep. 13, 1988; *Library Journal* p105 May 1, 1993; *Nation* p28+ Oct. 6, 1997; *New York Times* May 2, 1997;

New York Times Book Review p13 Sep. 29, 1991, p11 June 6, 1993, p26 Apr. 30, 1995, p20 May 4, 1997; *Quill & Quire* p54 Sep. 1991; *Time* p90 May 8, 1995; *Times Literary Supplement* p11 Aug. 6, 1993; *Washington Post* X p8 June 13, 1993; X p5 May 14, 1995

SELECTED WORKS: Fiction—*Cuba and the Night*, 1995; Nonfiction—*Video Night in Kathmandu and Other Reports from the Not-So-Far East*, 1988; *The Lady and the Monk: Four Seasons in Kyoto*, 1991; *Falling Off the Map: Some Lonely Places of the World*, 1993; *Tropical Classical*, 1997

Marita S. Boullata

Jabra, Jabra Ibrahim

Aug. 28, 1920– Dec. 12, 1994 Novelist; short-story writer; poet; nonfiction writer

The Palestinian novelist, short-story writer, poet, literary and art critic, essayist, translator, and film-script writer Jabra Ibrahim Jabra, who wrote works in both Arabic and English, is best known for his novel *Hunters in a Narrow Street* (1960), written in English, and for his memoir, *The First Well* (1995). The latter volume, translated into English by Issa J. Boullata, was described in *Publishers Weekly* (October 9, 1995) as having "a Proustian attention to details" and as conveying "humor and tenderness" in its description of a Palestinian village boyhood.

Jabra was born on August 28, 1920 in Bethlehem, Palestine, the son of Ibrahim Jabra, a handyman, and Maryam Jabra, both of whom belonged to the Syriac Orthodox Church. He attended local schools in Bethlehem, then moved with his family in 1932 to Jerusalem, where he enrolled in the Rashidiyya Secondary School and then the Arab College, from which he graduated in 1937. He taught school in Jerusalem for a while, then won a four-year government scholarship to study English literature in England, spending the first year, 1939-1940, at Exeter University and the remaining three, 1940–1943, at Fitzwilliam House, Cambridge University, where he earned a B.A. degree in 1943 and an M.A. degree in 1948.

On his return to Palestine, which was to remain under British rule until 1948, he taught English literature at the Rashidiyya Secondary School (1943–1948) and began to write and be active on the cultural scene, heading the Arts Club at the Jerusalem YMCA, which sponsored regular public lectures, concerts, and art exhibits. He published some of his English verse in *Forum* in Jerusalem, and in 1946 he wrote his first English novel, "Screaming in a Long Night," which he later published in Arabic as *Surakh fi Layl Tawil* (1955).

In the military hostilities between Palestinian Arabs and Jews that followed the United Nations resolution of November 29, 1947 to partition Palestine upon the termination of the British mandate on May 15, 1948, Jabra lost his home in Jerusalem as well as his job. He and his family lived briefly as refugees in Bethlehem; he then left Palestine in the summer of 1948 to look for a job elsewhere. He was eventually appointed professor of English literature (1948–1952) at the College of Arts and at other colleges of what later became the University of Baghdad. Meanwhile, he became involved in that city's intellectual and artistic activities. As a painter and art critic, he founded with the Iraqi painter and sculptor Jawad Salim and other Iraqi artists the Baghdad Modern Art Group, which became, through its manifesto, exhibits, and art criticism, an influential movement in the development of modern Iraqi and Arab art. As a poet, rebelling against traditional Arabic poetry, Jabra participated in the newly growing Iraqi movement of Arabic free verse, soon to spread in the Arab world. As a short-story writer, he contributed to the enrichment of Iraqi and Arabic fiction by encouraging local color and social themes. He published his short stories in Arabic periodicals and later collected them in his *Araq wa Qisas Ukhra* (1956, Arak and Other Stories).

In 1952 Jabra married a colleague at the Teachers' Training College, Lamia Barqi al-Askari, with whom he had two sons. The daughter of a notable Iraqi family, Lamia had an M.A. in English literature from the University of Wisconsin at Madison. To marry her, Jabra converted to Islam, as required by Islamic law, because she was a Muslim. He then accepted a two-year Rockefeller Foundation Fellowship to do research in literary criticism at Harvard. When he returned to Iraq from the U.S., he was appointed head of publications at the Iraq Petroleum Company in Baghdad (1954–1977), then cultural consultant to the Iraqi Ministry of Culture and Information, a post he held until he retired in 1984.

While at Harvard Jabra wrote his English novel *Hunters in a Narrow Street*, later translated into Arabic by Muhammad Asfur as *Sayyadun fi Sharic Dayyiq* (1974). The narrator and one of the main characters in this novel, Jameel Farran, is a Palestinian Christian whose fiancée is killed in Jerusalem in the 1948 hostilities. He goes to Baghdad to become a university professor and falls in love with Sulafa, an Iraqi young woman he tutors, who is the daughter of a traditional Muslim notable from the rich landed gentry. Jameel meets with frustrating difficulties involving tradition.

In his writings, Jabra was trying to infuse a spirit of modernity and freedom in the Arab value system in order to propel Arab society from restrictive, age-old traditions into a modern and free life. The Arab city was the major arena of his literary interests as he saw it grow phenomenally and witnessed its people trying to deal with its power to crush individuals. The fact that he was a Palestinian, who felt his homeland was crushed by the interests of Great Powers, enlivened his vision of freedom and strengthened his call for rejuvenation and renewal.

In his novel *Al-Safina* (1970), later translated as *The Ship* (1985), Jabra placed several characters on a ship cruising the Mediterranean. They are all attempting to escape from the city but bring their problems—which largely concern love and relationships—on board with them. These characters discuss various topics, including Arab social problems, in a detached, rarefied atmosphere; by the end of the cruise, not much in Arab society has changed. The English translators, Adnan Haydar and Roger Allen, wrote in their introduction to *The Ship* that Jabra's novels are tragic in a way that is different from Shakespeare's notion of tragedy, in which life is restored to order at the end, and they added: "Jabra's novels are tragic because 'the center cannot hold,' because past is present and future salvation is a distant possibility."

Jabra's next work, *Al-Bahth can Waleed Mascood* (1978, Search for Waleed Mascood), is a more intriguing novel, in which Jabra tried to expose Arab bourgeois hypocrisy. Waleed Mascood, a Palestinian Christian of humble origins who has amassed a great fortune in exile after 1948, mystifies his friends in Baghdad when he suddenly disappears in 1972. In his car, abandoned on the Iraqi-Syrian border, he has left a rambling tape. Meeting to discuss the contents of the recording, his friends in Baghdad reveal their own bourgeois complexities on remembering their relations with him. Translated into English by Adnan Haydar and Roger Allen, this novel is awaiting the completion of an introduction by a well-known critic in the U.S.

Jabra coauthored a novel with Abdelrahman Munif entitled *Alam bila Khara'it* (1982, World Without Maps), a metafictional work with an unusual, seamless narrative telling the story of a project to write a novel. Jabra then wrote two Arabic novels which have not been translated: *Al-Ghuraf al-Ukhra* (1986, The Other Rooms) and *Yawmiyyat Sarab Affan* (1992, Journals of Sarab Affan). In the former, the protagonist is led into a labyrinthine building for a purpose he does not know; he is then accused of acts he believes he never committed and is made to feel that his very identity is in question. The mercurial persons he meets keep changing appearances and attitudes. In the end, he is smuggled out through a tunnel and taken to an airport; cordially met there by the first person—now going by another name—who received him in the building; and escorted to a surprise dinner in his honor, at which he is expected to autograph copies of a book, bearing his name, which he did not write. The absurd world of this novel and its black humor are meant to symbolize the modern world, but they also allude to Arab autocratic regimes, which crush individual identity and will by their repressive measures. In *Yawmiyyat Sarab Affan*, Jabra returned to a love theme, but this time with a postmodern twist. The narrator is a 26-year-old woman with a college degree she finds useless. She works as a typist in a commercial office, where, between tasks, she types the love story she has written about Randa Jouzy, her other self—whom she calls "my tragic mask, my comic mask." The novel blurs imagination and reality, which mirror each other in the course of life.

Jabra wrote four collections of Arabic poetry: *Tammuz fi al-Madina* (1959, Tammuz in the City); *Al-Madar al-Mughlaq* (1964, The Closed Circuit); *Lawcat al-Shams* (1978, The Anguish of the Sun); and *Al-Acmal al-Shicriyya al-Kamila* (1990, Complete Poetic Works), which contains the former three volumes as well as later poems. In all his poetry, Jabra discarded traditional Arab meters and rhyme schemes and created in free verse a new poetry with a qualitative harmony of its own. Some of it has been translated into English. In *Modern Arab Poets, 1950-1975*, Issa J. Boullata rendered Jabra's short poem, "The Trumpet," as follows:

If I carried a trumpet to my mouth
with which to electrify my shout,
even the mere clearing of my throat
would have been
akin to the roar of a lion.
But, like the people of our mountains,
I still prefer a shout
from the highest rock,
a shout of the throat,
to an instrument that can be bought
and sold.
The trumpet is hypocrisy
which submits to every deception.

Jabra's poetry is rebellious, intimate, and genuinely concerned with the need for freedom and modernity in the tradition-bound Arab world. Its language is anguished by a spiritual and emotional search for truth and self-discovery, and it succeeds in communicating "his experience of the particular by socializing it and laying it open to be shared by others as an instrument of change," as Issa J. Boullata wrote in *Edebiyât*.

Jabra also wrote two volumes of autobiography: *Al-Bi'r al-Ula* (1987, tr. *The First Well: A Bethlehem Boyhood*) and *Sharic al-Amirat* (1994, Princesses' Street). The former volume chronicles his boyhood in Bethlehem and Jerusalem up to the age of 12, describing the first sources of his literary and artistic sensibility. In it he described how he fell in love with the Arabic language, whose "words glowed in my mind; they glittered like gold and sparkled like jewels. I imagined myself walking on colored silk carpets spread over the waves of a wondrous sea of dreams." The latter volume offers a few episodes from his student days in England (1939–1943) but concentrates on the year 1951, which, in a personal communication to Issa J. Boullata, he called his annus mirabilis (it was the year during which he met his future wife). In both autobiographical works, Jabra wrote frankly and sensitively, trying to understand the world, and the factors that shaped his life.

Most of Jabra's literary and art criticism is in Arabic; but what he wrote in English is equally inspired, revealing his eagerness to discover and embrace new talent, encourage innovation and creativity, and prod Arab writers and artists toward modernity. As he said in an interview cited by Issa J. Boullata in *Edebiyât*, he wanted Arab writers to be an effective part of their age—to appreciate their past without repeating it. He added, "Some people imagine that by returning to tradition you will renew it. This is not true, for by returning to tradition you renew nothing. But by setting out from it and adding to it, you renew its power because only by addition can you prepare the future path for the living sap within it." Some of his best literary-critical writings in English are collected in *A Celebration of Life* (1988) along with other essays. His art criticism in English is mainly in his books: *Art in Iraq Today* (1961), *Contemporary Iraqi Art* (1972), and *The Grass Roots of Iraqi Art* (1983), all published in English in Baghdad.

Jabra translated into Arabic seven of Shakespeare's plays, *Hamlet, King Lear, Coriolanus, Othello, Macbeth, The Tempest*, and *Twelfth Night*, and introduced each with a scholarly essay. He also translated 40 of Shakespeare's sonnets and provided critical notes with the translations. Furthermore, he translated more than 30 other Western classics, including "Adonis," a part of James Frazer's *The Golden Bough*; William Faulkner's *The Sound and the Fury*; Samuel Beckett's *Waiting for Godot*; Edmund Wilson's *Myth and Symbol*; and Jan Kott's *Shakespeare, Our Contemporary*.

Beginning in the mid-1950s, Jabra was involved in writing commentaries and scenarios for documentary films. In 1978, when the Iraqi General Institute for Cinema and Theater asked him to write a scenario for a movie on Babylonian civilization, he chose to write on Nebuchadnezzar (630–562 B.C.). After a first sequence on this Chaldean king's early life, Jabra focused on the year 586, B.C. when Nebuchadnezzar besieged and destroyed Jerusalem after the rebellion there of his appointed vassal, Zedekiah, and carried the Jews in exile to Babylon. In 1986 Jabra published this screenplay in a book entitled *Al-Malik al-Shams* (The Sun King). In 1988 he published the screenplay of another movie, *Ayyam al-Uqab* (Days of the Eagle), dealing with the Arab general Khalid Ibn al-Waleed, who commanded the Islamic army against Byzantine Syria, took Damascus in 635 A.D., and won the decisive battle of Yarmook in 636 A.D.

A multitalented person, Jabra was mourned by Edward Said in *Al-Ahram* as "the last of the first-rate Arab writers who not only felt at home in all the main literary forms but also were not defensive about or alienated by the Western tradition, which I thought he cherished as much as his own."
—S. Y.

SUGGESTED READING: *Edebiyât* no. 3, 1978; *Gilgamesh* no. 1, 1988; *Jusoor: The Arab American Journal of Cultural Exchange, Present and Future* nos. 5/6, 1995, nos. 7/8, 1996; *Publishers Weekly* p81 Oct. 9, 1995; Allen, R. *The Arabic Novel: An Historical and Critical Introduction*, 1982; Barakat, H. *Visions of Social Reality in the Contemporary Arab Novel*, 1977; Jayyusi, S. K. *Trends and Movements in Modern Arabic Poetry*, 1977; *Contemporary World Writers*, 1993; *Encyclopedia of World Literature in the 20th Century*, 1993

SELECTED BOOKS: Fiction—*The Ship*, 1985; *Hunters in a Narrow Street*, 1960; Nonfiction—*Art in Iraq Today*, 1961; *Contemporary Iraqi Art*, 1972; *The Grass Roots of Iraqi Art, 1983*; *A Celebration of Life*, 1988; *The First Well: A Bethlehem Boyhood*, 1995

V. Tony Hauser, Toronto Canada

James, Kelvin Christopher

1945(?)– Novelist; short-story writer

Kelvin Christopher James is a critically praised author of short stories and novels. He is known for his lush descriptive prose and his use of unusual phrasing, which reflects the speech patterns of people in his native Trinidad. In the mid-1970s the future author traveled to New York City to persue his education in the sciences. By 1981 he was on his way to becoming a freelance author, with the publication of his first story in Columbia University's literary journal. In 1989 he received a fellowship from the New York Foundation for the Arts, which helped him to write *Jumping Ship and Other Stories* (1992). A year later he published his first novel, *Secrets* (1993), which explored the relationship of a father and daughter living on a Caribbean island. Most recently he has written *A Fling with a Demon Lover* (1996), an erotic horror novel about a woman seduced by a much younger man.

Kelvin Christopher James was born in about 1945 in Port of Spain, Trinidad. He received his bachelor of science degree in 1967 from the University of the West Indies and thereafter became a high school science teacher in Trinidad. In the mid-1970s he "jumped ship," as he explained it, and came to New York to study for his master's degree at Columbia University. In an interview with John Blades of the *Chicago Tribune* (June 1, 1992), James said that, although he had had an excellent teaching position in Trinidad at that time, he felt "bored by the routine and [was] getting into trouble. . . . America was the gold mountain, getting a further education the lure I had to follow." He talked his way into a lab technician's job at a hospi-

tal in New York City, even though he had no work visa. "Part of it was boldness," he told Blades. "That's how I operate. I go in and do it." James worked at the hospital as a clinical technologist between 1973 and 1979 while working on his graduate degrees. From Columbia, James received three degrees: his M.A. in 1975, his M.Sc. in 1976, and his doctorate in education in 1978.

After completing his doctoral degree, James decided he wanted to write fiction. "I knew I had the facility with words," he told Blades, especially since he had won the top three prizes in a story contest while in Trinidad. "Ties," the first story James completed in the United States, was published in *Quarto*, Columbia University's literary magazine, in 1981, but he published nothing else until 1989.

In that year James became a fellow of the New York Foundation of the Arts. With this fellowship, he began working on a number of stories, many of which would find their way into his collection *Jumping Ship and Other Stories* (1992). The stories follow a trajectory similar to that of James's own life, starting in the steaming tropics of Trinidad and moving to Harlem, the author's adopted home. A motif in the first stories in the collection is the ripeness of fruit or the richness of the Caribbean jungle: in "Littleness" two brothers fight over a ripe orange; in "Succulence" a 15-year-old boy discovers a garden of delicious-looking fruit—as well as a mysterious woman. Other stories, such as "Vagabond's Center" and "Jumping Ship," focus on the challenges faced by West Indians who leave the tropics for the borderlands. In the later tales, the author looks at life in New York City. "Guppies" is a story of drugs and murder in the inner city.

Jumping Ship and Other Stories received mixed reviews. In the *Washington Post* (May 7, 1992), Charles R. Larson wrote, "What succeeds most imaginatively in *Jumping Ship* . . . is the powerful balance between the best of Kelvin Christopher James's stories set in the West Indies and his most convincing tales of the Big Apple. Images of raw life, of vicious activity both in nature and in man intermix the two environments into one swirling vortex." *Kirkus Reviews* (January 15, 1992) called the work "an uneven debut," adding that it was "macho-flavored, visceral material too often undercut by verbal and structural convolutions." Tom Piazza in the *New York Times Book Review* (October 25, 1992) generally admired the work but had a few complaints. He wrote that "Mr. James is at his best when teasing narrative out of the appetites and impatience of children and adolescents, as in the opening story, 'Littleness,' in which two young brothers match wits. Many of the collection's other characters—including a conjure woman, an adolescent who's both a straight-A student and a drug dealer, and a bizarre forest recluse—are interesting, yet they can also be two-dimensional, like figures in folk tales. Mr. James's hothouse prose promises a greater depth and complexity than he delivers here; it makes one wonder if his natural métier might not be the novel."

Critics did not have long to wait for James to produce a novel. *Secrets* (1993) was set in the Caribbean and followed the life of Uxann, a teenage girl who keeps house for her father, Seyeh, an overseer of an estate and a respected man in his community. Though she lives to please her father by cooking and cleaning for him, she also attends the local Catholic school and does very well there. Seyeh, in turn, hopes to see his daughter get a fine education and rise above the station of her friends in the village. To this end, Seyeh hires Keah, Uxann's best friend, to do the housework so that his daughter will be able to study more. Though Keah cannot cook or clean very well, Seyeh enjoys having her around the house, and eventually sleeps with her. When Uxann discovers what has happened she gets very drunk and later discovers she is pregnant.

The novel received high praise from critics. *Booklist* (September 1, 1993) reviewer Donna Seaman proclaimed that "James has crafted a stunningly lush, intrepid, and indelible tale about the slow but deadly poison of secrets too well kept." *Kirkus Reviews* (July 15, 1993) called the book "a stunning tragedy of carefully calibrated horror and pulsating sensuality that is more a tropical murder of the innocents than a conventional rites-of-passage novel." Perhaps the highest praise of all came from Donald McCaig, who wrote in the *Washington Post Book World* (December 26, 1993), "*Secrets* is the finest novel to come out of the Caribbean experience since V. S. Naipaul's *A House for Mr. Biswas*. Of writers about the islands, only Naipaul and Derek Walcott are well-known to American readers. With his passions, boldness, and exactitude of language, I predict that James will join their company."

Only Michael E. Ross of the *New York Times Book Review* (January 2, 1994) disputed the general critical assessment of the novel. He remarked: "In his use of patois and poetical imagery, Mr. James has written not so much a novel as a dark fable. Uxann's most pivotal experience is telegraphed well before it happens, which diminishes its impact. Mr. James may be aiming to depict the agonies of hard-won growth in the manner of Alice Walker or Toni Morrison, but his story feels shallow and derivative, out of step with the powers he has so convincingly shown he can command."

A Fling with a Demon Lover, James's 1996 novel, follows the life of Sassela Jack, a Harlem schoolteacher approaching her 40th birthday. Tired of her job and her live-in boyfriend, she begins flirting with Ciam, a Caribbean man in his 20s. Sassela wins a two-week vacation to a Greek island, and Ciam unexpectedly appears on the plane. When they arrive, Sassela and Ciam begin an affair, while noticing that the native men are either extremely old or very young; after a number of people warn Ciam that harm may come to him if he stays, he is touched by a young girl, who the couple discover is a demon bent on draining him of his youth and vitality. Many critics were unimpressed by this outing. Nancy Pearl of *Booklist* (May 15, 1996) la-

mented that while "James' use of unusual speech patterns and sentence structures adds an aura of exoticism to the novel. . . . even a strong main character and an interesting writing style cannot quite overcome the thin and unbelievable plot." *Kirkus Reviews* (April 1, 1996) detected "some tantalizing moments that recall James's gift for lyricism and atmosphere, but not enough to give his tale the edge and snap it needs to make it a modern horror tale of eros and evil on the lam."
—C.M.

SUGGESTED READING: *Booklist* Sep. 1, 1993, May 15, 1996; *Chicago Tribune* V p3 June 1, 1992; *Kirkus Reviews* Jan. 15, 1992, July 15, 1993, Apr. 1, 1996; *New York Newsday* p70 Oct. 21, 1993; *New York Times Book Review* p20 Oct. 25, 1992, p14 Jan. 2, 1994; *Washington Post* D p4 May 7, 1992, D p2 May 31, 1996; *Washington Post Book World* p3 Dec. 26, 1993; *Contemporary Authors*, vol. 138, 1993

SELECTED BOOKS: *Jumping Ship and Other Stories*, 1992; *Secrets*, 1993; *A Fling with a Demon Lover*, 1996

Japrisot, Sébasatien

1931– Mystery writer

The French mystery novelist Sébastien Japrisot is an acknowledged master of his genre. Formerly best known as J. D. Salinger's French translator, he soon received recognition for his own literary achievements with *Les mal partis* (Awakening), his 1950 novel. *Piège pour Cendrillon* (Trap for Cinderella), his second novel, was published in 1962 to rave reviews and won the Grand Prix de la Littérature Policière, the highest crime novel award in France. For his 1966 mystery *La dame dans l'auto avec des lunettes et un fusil* (The Lady in a Car with Glasses and a Gun), Japrisot received the Prix d'Honneur. Some of the author's recent novels include *La passion des femmes* (The Passion of Women) in 1986 and *Un long dimanche de fiançailles* (A Very Long Engagement) in 1991. Japrisot has also written many of the screenplay adaptations for his novels.

Sébastien Japrisot was born Jean Baptiste Rossi in France in 1931. His pen name is an anagram of his given name. His first literary achievement came with the 1950 publication of his novel *Les mal partis* (Awakening); three years later he received greater recognition when he translated J. D. Salinger's *Nine Stories* into French. Both critical and popular acclaim came with the publication of his 1962 novel *Piège pour Cendrillon* (*Trap for Cinderella*). In that work, two women are burned beyond recognition in a fire. One of them survives, but she is so disfigured that no one knows if she is the heiress or the heiress's sister, who may have set the fire. Compounding this mystery, the burned woman wakes up with no memory of who she is. Questions abound—is she the murderer, or is the person who tried to kill her still alive? In the *New York Times Book Review*, Anthony Boucher (July 5, 1964) wrote: "This is a beautifully intricate essay in novel-writing and mystery-making. . . . *Trap* certainly maintains Japrisot's reputation as a highly original and professional writer of murder- suspense."

Compartiment tueurs, Japrisot's 1963 mystery, was published in the United States as *The 10:30 from Marseilles* that same year, and as *The Sleeping-Car Murders* in 1978. Essentially a police story involving Inspector Grazziano of the Police Judiciaire, the novel opens with the murder of a young woman on a train and focuses on Grazziano's investigation of the remaining five compartment passengers. During the course of the investigation, several of the passengers are murdered. The version of the novel translated by Francis Price was reviewed by Anthony Boucher in the *New York Times Book Review* (November 17, 1963): "[*The 10:30 from Marseilles*] clearly reveals the most welcome new talent in the detective story to reach us from France since . . . well, probably since the early Simenons almost three decades ago. . . . In all, a highly satisfactory import that makes one hungry for more." The author adapted *Compartiment tueurs* into a 1966 film with the help of Constantin Costa-Gavras, who also directed.

In 1966 Japrisot produced a new mystery, *La dame dans l'auto avec des lunettes et un fusil* (*The Lady in the Car with Glasses and a Gun*). This novel, which spent months on the best-seller list in France, is narrated by a near-sighted advertising secretary, who takes her boss's Thunderbird for a joy ride on a trip to the shore. As she travels through an area she has never seen before, more and more people identify her as a murderer. This novel received high praise from Howard Junker of *Newsweek* (December 18, 1967) who wrote: "Unlike most novels published this year, *The Lady in the Car* can be—and must be—read in one sitting. It cannot be put down, and that, mystery-lovers, is the ultimate test. . . . Japrisot is obviously a great talent, whom students of the popular novel and of the narrative form in general will want to analyze. . . . It is a chilling, baffling psychological fooler that sparkles with all the juicy terrors that can attack the heart and body." The author converted this novel, like its predecessor, into a screenplay for the 1970 film of the same name.

During much of the late 1960s and 1970s, Japrisot primarily focused on writing screenplays. The first of these was *Adieu, l'ami* (Goodbye, Friend) in 1968. This was followed by a pair of René Clément–directed films: *Le passager de la pluie* (Rider on a Train), co-authored by Lorenzo Ventavoli in 1969–70, and *La Course du lièvre à travers les champe* (And Hope To Die) in 1972. Japrisot was also the screenwriter for *Histoire d'O* (*The Story of O*) in 1975.

In 1979 Japrisot returned to the novel form with the publication of *L'été meurtrier* (One Deadly Summer). Told in first person by four of the main characters, the story involves a small village near the Combes Pass in the south of France, population 143, and a rash of lynchings and other violence that has taken place there. Though it is set mainly in the summer of 1976, the novel also flashes back to the winter of 1955. Reviewing the English translation in *Newsweek* (June 30, 1980), Jean Strouse noted: "Japrisot slices into these small-town European lives with all the precision of a fine surgeon. . . . By the end you feel more sympathy than horror at the ghastly truth." As with many of his earlier works, the author adapted this novel for the screen in 1983, this time with the help of director Jean Becker.

In 1986 Japrisot published his most erotic novel to date—*La passion des femmes* (*The Passion of Women*). As in some of his earlier work, the author used a variety of narrators to tell the story, about a young man who escapes from a military prison, where he was sent for a murder he didn't commit. Throughout the book the protagonist is known to a number of women by various names, but several aspects of his story remain constant through each tale: he is running from the law; he claims to be innocent of any crime; and he is a seducer of women. The reader first sees the hero through the eyes of Emma, a young bride he kidnaps on her wedding night. Next, he seduces Belinda, who hides him after he claims to have been shot by a bride he had kidnapped. Six other encounters with women are detailed throughout the remainder of the novel, in which each new discovery adds to the mystery. The book was greatly praised in the *West Coast Review of Books* (January 1991) by Christine Watson, who wrote in her review: "Just as we think we have a grip on who this man is and what is going on, Japrisot deftly changes focus again, and we realize we are no closer to understanding than we were at the beginning. With his smooth prose and his careful construction, he draws us into his story as surely as his mystery man draws these women into his life." The novel also received less enthusiastic reviews. *Kirkus Reviews* (August 1, 1990) noted: "The chapters are by turns steamy and touching, but they don't generate much momentum. . . . The solution to the mystery of who shot the hero is a letdown, but Japrisot's neatest puzzle—why are all these desirable women dreaming of romance in terms of such a narcissistic male fantasy?—is resolved by an ending that (though a bit of a cheat) is perfectly in keeping with the texture of the hero's insouciant adventures." Charles Mackey, writing for the *French Review* (May 1988), expressed qualms about the women's characterizations: "His women speak with a voice and a diction that carefully evoke their milieus, but at the bottom there is an exasperating dissonance in their conception, a jarring shallowness in their 'passions' and in the elusive truths that each of our mirrors tries to capture."

In 1991 Japrisot published *Un long demanche de fiançailles* (*A Very Long Engagement*), a novel that many have argued is his most fully realized work to date. The mystery begins in January 1917, during the First World War. Five French soldiers convicted of having mutilated themselves in order to get out of the war are marched to the front lines with their hands tied and left for dead. The next day, after the battle, five bodies are retrieved. Their families are told that the men died in the line of duty. Two and a half years later, Mathilde Donnay receives a letter from a dying ex-soldier who claims that he met her fiancé, one of the men who was killed, just before his death. As she goes over his story, she notices a number of discrepancies and discovers that at least one of the men may not have died. From that moment on, the wheelchair-bound Mathilde devotes herself to uncovering the truth about what happened to her beloved. Critics were generally pleased with this complex mystery and love story. A reviewer from *Kirkus Reviews* (July 1, 1993) found that novel was "as tricky as Japrisot's earlier bestsellers in his native France . . . but also precisely, surprisingly evocative of the lingering pain of mourning and the burdens of survival." Chard Eder, writing for *New York Newsday* (August 8, 1993), also appreciated the author's characterizations: "Japrisot . . . gives us not only the story but its characters in a series of successive passes, each of which uncovers a new layer of configuration. . . . As for Mathilde, her evolution and revelation is both similar and different. . . . there is a brilliant light on her from beginning to end, and

her only mystery is that of a life lived so completely as to entirely fulfill itself." In the *New York Times* (September 21, 1993), Michiko Kakutani wrote that Japrisot had written "a fierce, elliptical novel that's both a gripping philosophical thriller and a highly moving meditation on the emotional consequences of war."

Sébastien Japrisot is also the author of the screenplays for the films *Juillet en septembre* (1987) and *Enfants du Marais* (1999).—C.M.

SUGGESTED READING: *French Review* May 1988 *Kirkus Reviews* July 1, 1993; *Newsweek* Dec. 18, 1967, June 30, 1980; *New York Newsday* p 35, Aug. 8, 1993; *New York Times* C p 17, Sep. 21, 1993; *New York Times Book Review* Nov. 17, 1962, July 5, 1964, p 24, Sep. 12, 1993; *West Coast Review of Books* Jan. 1991; *World Literature Today* Winter 1979; Contemporary Literary Criticism, vol. 90, 1996

SELECTED WORKS: Fiction—*Awakenings*, 1950; *Trap for Cinderella*, 1962; *The 10:30 from Marseilles*, 1963 (published as *The Sleeping-Car Murders*, 1978); *The Lady in the Car with Glasses and a Gun*, 1966; *One Deadly Summer*, 1979; *The Passion of Women*, 1986; *A Very Long Engagement*, 1991; Screenplays *Goodbye, Friend*, 1968; *Rider on a Train* (with Lorenzo Ventavoli), 1969–1970; *And Hope to Die*, 1972; *The Story of O*, 1975; *Juillet en Septembre*, 1987; *Enfants du Marais*, 1999

Jencks, Christopher

Oct. 22, 1936– Nonfiction writer; sociologist

Over the past quarter-century, Christopher Jencks has earned a reputation as one of the nation's most incisive writers on public-policy issues. Through half a dozen books and numerous articles in serious journals, this author and sociology educator has contributed significantly to the national dialogue on poverty, homelessness, welfare reform, the underclass, and public education. He first emerged on the national scene in 1972, with the publication of his controversial book *Inequality*, which challenged Americans' "recurrent fantasy that schools can solve their problems" and called for a restructuring of institutions along socialistic lines as the only way to eliminate the inequities in the public-education system. He was also an early advocate of school vouchers that would offer a wider array of choices for children's education. But it would be a serious error to pigeonhole Jencks as a polemicist, for he has always insisted on the need to apply rigid qualitative and quantitative methodologies in any analysis of issues, which he sees as being far more nuanced and complex than

do many ideologues of either left or right. In the early 1980s, foreseeing the serious and far-ranging consequences of the "Reaganomic" restructuring of the domestic economy, he sought to initiate a dialogue in the *New York Review of Books* designed to forge a new vision of the role of the public sector as a guardian of the safety net and of equal opportunity—a goal toward which he continues to work to this day, as contributing editor of the liberal journal *New Prospect*. Jencks began his academic career at Harvard, his alma mater, taught for 20 years at Northwestern, and then returned to Harvard in 1996 as professor of public policy at the John F. Kennedy School of Government. His most significant books include *The Academic Revolution* (1968), written with *Lonely Crowd* sociologist David Riesman; *Inequality* (1972); *The Urban Underclass* (1991); *Rethinking Social Policy: Race, Poverty, and the Underclass* (1992); and *The Homeless* (1994).

Christopher Jencks, the son of Francis Haynes Jencks, an architect, and Elizabeth (Pleasants) Jencks, was born on October 22, 1936 into a Baltimore, Maryland home that was described as "vigorously intellectual" in *Time* (September 18, 1972). After graduating from Exeter Academy in

New Hampshire, he received his bachelor of arts in English from Harvard University in 1958 and his masters in education the following year, then did postgraduate work at the London School of Economics for two years. Returning to the United States at the beginning of the Kennedy administration's "New Frontier," he spent two years as associate editor of the *New Republic*. "When I arrived in Washington as a very junior editor at the *New Republic* in 1961," he wrote in his introduction to *Rethinking Social Policy*, "the term 'social policy' was not part of America's political vocabulary. . . . Except for the Social Security Act, the federal government had almost no policies or programs for solving social problems." He recalls the earnest national debate in the Kennedy and Johnson era over the government's plans to assume a larger role in social policy, initiatives that were routinely blocked by conservatives and Southern Democrats until the 1964 elections gave a mandate to Lyndon Johnson's "Great Society" programs. During this period, Jencks served on a number of private and public commissions, including the Congressional Seminar on Educational Policy (1964–65); the Citizen's Crusade Against Poverty (1965–66); and the President's Science Advisory Committee Panel on Educational Innovation (1966–67).

After his stint at the *New Republic*, Jencks began working for a "left-of-center Washington think tank called the Institute for Policy Studies, where hardly anyone paid much attention to quantitative research. I myself was a former English major, whose only training in such matters had been a one-semester undergraduate course in statistics," he wrote. Jencks had been strongly influenced by two reports that were among the first to use rigorous statistical surveys and computer analysis to describe social phenomena and analyze trends. The first was James Coleman's study, published in 1966, about the achievements of schoolchildren. The "Coleman Report" made a "strong impression" on the young Jencks, for it substantiated some of the anecdotal evidence he had gathered in his brief experience teaching high school: that children were far more influenced by their peers and home environments than by teachers. In his 1972 book, *Inequality: A Reassessment of the Effect of Family and Schooling in America*, Jencks would write: "The character of a school's output depends largely on a single input, namely the characteristics of the entering children. Everything else—the school's budget, its policies, the characteristics of the teachers—is either secondary or completely irrelevant." Jencks also found food for thought in by a report by Peter Blau and Otis Dudley Duncan, also published in 1966, which, to him, "raised serious questions about the widespread assumption that poverty was largely inherited" by clearly implying that, in our economic and social system, "many [people] were poor because they had slipped down the social ladder into poverty." Jencks credited these two reports with catalyzing

his own paradigm-shift on these issues: "My assumption that America was being more meritocratic—a notion implicit in almost everything I had read up to that point in my life—therefore appeared to be wrong," he wrote. "Reading these two studies changed my career," he added. "From 1961 to 1966 I saw myself as a journalist and political activist. By 1967 I had become convinced that the war on poverty would fail even if it got as much money as the war in Vietnam was getting. . . . I therefore decided to embark on what proved to be a lengthy and only partially successful effort to rethink the liberal approach to social policy" by "getting the facts more or less right" through the medium of quantitative social science.

Thus energized, he returned in the summer of 1967 to Harvard's Graduate School of Education, where he learned statistical analysis under the tutelage of Marshall Smith and taught from 1969 until 1973. Before that he had been, since 1959, working with David Riesman on a Carnegie Corporation–funded study of higher education. In 1968 their collaborative work was published as *The Academic Revolution*, a 580-page attempt at a "sociological and historical analysis of American higher education." Admitting that "as sociology it must be superficial at many points"—the authors visited only about 150 of some 2,000 colleges in the United States, in most cases spending less than a day on campus—the coauthors were able to talk or correspond with several thousand professors. *The Academic Revolution* includes chapters on the different types of colleges in the United States, such as those with Catholic, Protestant, or "Negro" roots. The book also charts the "Anti-University" movement and the fecund growth of community colleges in the 1960s as well as the student-protest movement that was beginning to gain headway at mid-decade. *The Academic Revolution* is not full of statistical and quantitative information, being rather a summary of conclusions based on empirical data. The book won that year's Borden Prize for Best Book on Higher Education from the American Council on Education.

In 1970 Jencks was asked by the Office of Educational Opportunity to draw up a prototype for a tuition-voucher program for financing elementary-school education, which had a pilot project in San Jose, California. This and other experiences led to the 1972 book *Inequality: A Reassessment of the Effect of Family and Schooling in America*, which touched off a firestorm of controversy with its claim that educational reform was impossible without a broader redistribution of wealth along socialistic lines. Jencks wrote, "Equalizing opportunity is almost impossible without greatly reducing the absolute level of inequality, and the same is true of eliminating deprivation," concluding, "we will have to establish political control over the economic institutions that shape our society. This is what other countries usually call socialism. Anything less will end in the same disappointment as the reforms of the 1960s." *Inequality* was translated into five languages and named the best book in sociology for that year by the American Sociological Association. The 399-page book challenged the long-held assumptions that education was a sure ticket to economic success, as articulated in such familiar slogans as "To get a good job, get a good education" or in Horace Mann's dictum "Education prevents being poor." Instead, it concluded, in the words of a critic for the *Saturday Review* (November 11, 1972), that "economic success depends primarily on competencies and chance factors that are almost unrelated to one's class or origin, genes, or schooling [and] . . . that 'school reform is never likely to have any significant effect on the degree of inequality among adults.'" And George Levine wrote in *The New York Times* (November 26, 1972): "Coolly and dispassionately, [Jencks] makes a revolutionary case for restructuring not education but society."

Among the few defending Jencks's thesis were Daniel Patrick Moynihan and Daniel Bell; among its chief detractors was Edward H. Levi, then president of the University of Chicago, who criticized the book's methodology and ideology in a speech to his faculty in January 1973. "The concepts are never developed," he argued. "A subject to which an intellectual tradition has given much thought and explication is lopped off by his methodology. . . . Mr. Jencks, perhaps unwittingly, sees the schools as places of therapeutic busyness, or existential pain or pleasure. But he gives them no mission."

Inequality was a controversial work that sent "shock waves throughout the academic community," wrote the editors of *Christopher Jencks in Perspective* (1973), a response to the book by 10 educators and researchers published by the American Association of School Administrators (AASA). In the book's foreword, Paul B. Salmon, executive secretary of the AASA, wrote, "Jencks presents a stunning as well as a sweeping conclusion. And it is sure to be hotly debated. . . . His chief recommendation—that the country turn to a vast socialistic overhaul of its economic institutions as the only way to guarantee equality—will get little support." While some respondents in *Perspective* paid tribute to Jencks's honesty and integrity and laid blame for much of the brouhaha on misinterpretation, others criticized both the methodology and assumptions of *Inequality*. Typical of the favorable reactions was one by Charles S. Benson, professor at the School of Education at Berkeley, who began his essay: "Taken together in large doses, dogmatism and social science can produce bad education policy. The present volume offers more than its share of examples."

With the coming of the Reagan era in 1981, Jencks was disturbed to see how "the conservative critique of egalitarian social policy began to dominate the mass media, and liberals were on the defense everywhere." He wrote that he was "less sanguine" than other liberals who saw this as a natural cycle and that "in time, the fever would pass." He

therefore resolved to do a series of long book review/essays for the *New York Review of Books*, which he considered "the best and the most widely read serious journal in the country." These, with some revisions, became the first three chapters of his 1992 book *Rethinking Social Policy*. This book calls for a serious liberal rethinking of some of the key and now-endangered New Deal and Great Society issues that came under scrutiny in the late 1980s and 1990s: affirmative action, strong federal initiatives in the social arena, and the creation of a "safety net" through such programs as aid to dependent children, welfare, and Medicaid.

The book is in keeping with Jencks's nonideological approach. In the book's introduction, Jencks admitted, "My distinctive combination of prejudices may also confuse readers who have learned to expect ideological consistency in what they read. Oversimplifying, I would say my prejudices favor cultural conservatism, economic egalitarianism, and incremental reform. . . . My cultural conservatism makes me favor traditional social norms about how people ought to behave until I am convinced that new norms really work better." He amplified this statement with a personal reference: "Having been divorced twice, for example, I am quite aware that marriage is an imperfect and fragile institution. Still I see no evidence that having children out of wedlock does a better job of ensuring that children get the economic, social, and moral support they need. So I cling to the old-fashioned view that couples who have children without marrying are putting their children's welfare in jeopardy. . . . This prejudice makes me willing to use morally loaded terms like 'illegitimacy' that many liberals regard as antiquated and intolerant."

By affirming values such as industry and the work ethic, Jencks appeared on the surface to be endorsing conservative principles, but he asserted with equal vigor, "I do not believe that a culture built on undiluted individualism can survive for very long." He expressed disdain for selfishness and irresponsibility from whatever quarter, whether they stem from the excesses of "ghetto culture" or from "yuppie culture."

Rethinking Social Policy does not so much offer a new "laundry list" of solutions as it tries to shed light on social-policy issues by means of clear-headed analysis based on objective facts instead of ideological biases or anecdotal evidence. "The book does not propose a coherent alternative to traditional liberalism or conservatism," Jencks wrote. "If it has a single consistent message, it is that all such ideologies lead to bad social policy." Instead, he proposed looking at his various topics not in a generalized way but in terms of how practical situations work out. On the subject of affirmative action, for example, he agreed with liberals that some system of numerical targets for minority employment is desirable, while admitting that such numbers are frequently manipulated for ideological purposes. "Both outcomes perpetuate racial conflict," he concluded. Jencks also wrote that "damaged lives are hard to make whole, regardless of whether the victim is black or white," and that employers who acts on this assumption are more "reasonable people than closet racists." He advocated a reappraisal of the entire issue, an admission that reverse discrimination is also bad social policy, and a case-by-case reevaluation of hiring goals in specific firms rather than a blanket national standard.

Two other books published in the early 1990s reflected Jencks's deepening concern with the persistence of homelessness and class stratification in the United States. He and Paul E. Peterson edited *The Urban Underclass* (1991), a Brookings Institution publication that brought together 19 essays by leading social scientists, together with an extensive array of statistics. The essays were originally presented in 1989 as part of a conference sponsored by the Social Science Research Council and Northwestern University. Again, Jencks tried to depoliticize a term that has been variously interpreted across the left-right spectrum. The editors' preface asserts that their aim is to "try to separate the truth about poverty, social dislocation, and changes in American family life from the myths that have become part of the contemporary folklore." In his own essay "Is the American Underclass Growing?", Jencks cautioned against the too-facile use of convenient class labels that serve to obfuscate a clear definition of the realities of the situation. "If the American class structure is changing . . . ," he wrote, "the change is not that a completely new class has come into existence but that the old lower class has grown larger and perhaps more isolated from mainstream society."

In his next book, *The Homeless* (1994), Jencks cautioned against anecdotal evidence and misuse of statistical information by "sidewalk sociologists," arguing, "We have no good national data on the number of people outside shelters before 1987." Furthermore, there is no agreed-upon definition of what it means to be "homeless"—whether this category should include "doubled-up" households, people in prison, people with roommates, and temporarily displaced people, for example. There is also the case of the "neat and clean" homeless, who might even go to work each day and "blend into the urban landscape unnoticed." Public perceptions also have an impact: "In the late 1980s," Jencks wrote, "most Americans assumed that everyone on the streets who looked unkempt or confused was homeless. In the late 1970s, we assumed such people had a home unless we saw clear evidence to the contrary, such as a grocery cart full of personal possessions. These assumptions play a big role in determining what we remember." But Jencks wrote that he defines the phenomenon more narrowly, focusing on the "visible homeless—people whose presence on the streets upsets the more prosperous classes." He rejects as unrealistic the claims of such homeless advocates as Mitch Snyder that there were as many as three million homeless Americans in the late 1980s.

But Jencks does not deny that there was a significant swelling in homelessness during this period and that it grew out of a confluence of several factors. He wrote, "As far as I can tell, the spread of homelessness among single adults was a byproduct of five related changes: the elimination of involuntary commitment, the eviction of mental hospital patients who had nowhere to go, the advent of crack, increases in long-term joblessness, and political restrictions on the creation of flophouses." Shifts in the relative valuation of needs-versus-wants played a role, too. "The arrival of crack in the mid-1980s changed this picture substantially," he wrote, noting that "a large fraction of the single adults in the New York shelters who test positive for cocaine presumably think that a crack high, however brief, is worth more than a scuzzy cubicle." In Jencks's view, the "long-term homeless are mostly people for whom almost everything imaginable has gone wrong for many years."

In addition to producing books on these themes, Jencks continues his public-policy analysis in the pages of the new liberal journal *New Prospect*, of which he is a contributing editor. In 1998 he co-edited, with Meredith Phillips, *The Black-White Test Score Gap*. He has also been deeply involved in the movement to criticize the conclusions of *The Bell Curve*, a book by two conservative researchers who asserted that blacks were genetically predisposed to score more poorly than whites in standardized IQ tests. Jencks was quoted as faulting *The Bell Curve* for "contribut[ing] to an atmosphere of polarization, animosity, and distrust." In his article "Can We Put a Time Limit on Welfare?" in *New Prospect* (Fall 1992), he suggested a program that would allow single mothers to work and make ends meet by guaranteeing child care and medical care for their offspring. He wrote, "In my judgment, a program of this kind would be worth the price, both because it would make children and single mothers better off and because it would do so in a way that is consistent with deeply held American values about work." But to achieve this system that rewards self-help, "liberals must join conservatives in trying to make sure that mothers who work do better than mothers who do not. If liberals fail at that, as they have over the past half-century, the public will continue to see welfare as a menace, and will continue to punish legislators who appear intent on making it more generous. If we create a system that rewards work, the politics of helping the poor would be completely transformed. Americans love to help people who are trying to help themselves."
—E. M.

SUGGESTED READING: *New Prospect* 32+ Fall 1992, p43+ Winter 1995; *New York Times* p3 Nov. 26, 1962; *New York Times Book Review* p1+ Apr. 24, 1994; *Saturday Review* p49+ Nov. 11, 1972; *Times Literary Supplement* p12 June 10, 1994; *Current Biography Yearbook 1973*; *Who's Who in America 1997*

SELECTED BOOKS: *The Academic Revolution* (with D. Riesman), 1968; *Inequality: A Reassessment of the Effect of Family and Schooling in America* (with others), 1972; *Who Gets Ahead?*, 1979; *Rethinking Social Policy: Race, Poverty, and the Underclass*, 1992; *The Homeless*, 1994; as editor—*The Urban Underclass* (with P. Peterson), 1991; *The Black-White Test Score Gap* (with M. Phillips), 1998

Jerry Bauer

Jen, Gish

Aug. 12, 1955– Novelist; nonfiction writer

The daughter of Chinese immigrants, the novelist Gish Jen has emerged as a forceful and sometimes controversial spokesperson of a generation of young Asian-American writers who are openly challenging narrow ethnic stereotypes in contemporary fiction. Her first novel, *Typical American* (1991), is squarely in the "immigrant saga" tradition in its sympathetic depiction of the vicissitudes of the Chang family in its 1950s passage from the "old country" to a promised land of opportunity. Its sequel, *Mona in the Promised Land* (1996), set in 1968, takes a lighthearted, satirical look at that experience through the voice of Mona, a hip, second-generation Chang who wants to "cross-dress" her ethnic identity by becoming the Jewish "Mona Changowitz" in her mythical New York suburb of "Scarshill." The story collection *Who's Irish?* appeared in 1999. Gish Jen has also written essays and critical commentaries exploring the changing dynamics of identity politics in the multicultural America of the 1990s. She told inter-

viewer Jesse Garon in 1996, "In this time of huge, public embracing of ethnic roots, I wanted to show how our lives are more complex than what we're born with. . . . We make ourselves in this country; even people who are racial and ethnic minorities transform themselves. The different groups have spent a lot of time rubbing elbows, rubbing off of each other, and while the melting pot model of assimilation was unhealthy, with its one-way melting of people into generic Barbies and Kens, the idea of assimilation is still with us in ways that we don't necessarily have to be afraid of."

For *World Authors 1990–1995*, she writes in the third person: "Gish Jen was born in 1955, the second of five children. Her parents were Chinese immigrants who had come to the United States in the forties; her mother was a school teacher, and her father a professor. She grew up in Queens, Yonkers, and Scarsdale, New York, and received her undergraduate degree in English from Harvard University in 1977. Upon graduation, she worked briefly in publishing; she also attended Stanford Business School and taught English to coal-mining engineers in China before receiving her MFA from the Iowa Writers' Workshop in 1983. She has taught Fiction Writing at Tufts University and the University of Massachusetts/Boston, and was a fellow at the Bunting Institute of Radcliffe College in 1985–86.

"She has subsequently received grants from the Michener/Copernicus Society, the Massachusetts Artists' Foundation, the National Endowment for the Arts, and the Guggenheim Foundation. Her short work has appeared in numerous magazines and journals, including *The Atlantic Monthly*, *The New York Times*, *The New Republic*, and the *New Yorker*, and has been reprinted in dozens of textbooks and anthologies, including *The Best American Short Stories 1988* and *1995*, *The Heath Anthology of American Literature*, and *The Bedford Introduction to Literature*. Her first novel, *Typical American* (Houghton Mifflin, 1991), was named a *New York Times* notable book of the year, and nominated for the National Book Critics' Circle Award; *Mona in the Promised Land* (Knopf, 1996) was also a *New York Times* notable book, and was named one of the ten best books of 1996 by *The Los Angeles Times*.

"Gish Jen lives in Massachusetts with her husband and 5-year-old son, Luke, and spends most of her non-writing time discussing orca whales and rockets."

When, as a teenager in Scarsdale, New York, Lillian C. Jen decided on a writing career, she adopted the "Gish" surname in homage to the silent-screen actress. "It was part of becoming a writer," she told an interviewer, "not becoming the person I was supposed to be." Years later, after she achieved some notoriety as a novelist, she described herself to interviewer Jesse Garon (*Beatrice* website, *www.beatrice.com*, July 1996) as a "literary type" who did not really start writing seriously until she took a college course in prosody with the poet and translator Robert Fitzgerald, who gave his class weekly assignments in verse. "But I'm the daughter of immigrants, and I'd completely internalized all their practical ideas, so I didn't even consider for a moment becoming a poet," she added. After trying to find a "practical career" in the mold of second-generation immigrants ("I was pre-med, pre-law, in business school, thought about being an architect, a contractor, an antiques dealer"), she finally realized that writing was to be her life's pursuit. Like many writers, she sits at the keyboard and "wait[s] for my books to write themselves; the conscious mind doesn't really know much about getting that to happen on a schedule."

Even though she is among the first generation of Asian-American writers to have "reinvented" ethnicity, she says: "I can't say that being a writer is an extension of my being an Asian-American. Quite the contrary. My life as a fiction writer is directly related to my assimilation, particularly to the Jewish community in Scarsdale where I grew up. That was a community that greatly esteemed fiction writing." Although she doesn't like this "pigeonholing" and prefers to be a "universal" writer, Jen also recognizes that "we live in a culture where if you're not labeled you disappear."

Gish Jen's family had arrived in the United States nearly two decades before the relaxation, in 1965, of Asian immigration restrictions, so the formative experiences from which she writes bear the imprint of that more distant time. Hers was the only Asian-American family in her Westchester County neighborhood in the 1960s, a family that, lacking easy access even to familiar foodstuffs, had to make do in an unfamiliar setting: "I was always suspicious of my mother's cooking," she told an interviewer. "I mean, I never ate the kind of Chinese food they serve in restaurants." (She now lives with her son, Luke, and husband, David O'Connor, in a Cambridge, Massachusetts home "with a freezerful of pork-stuffed glutinous rice wrapped in lotus leaves.")

Not surprisingly, the leitmotif that dominates Jen's fiction is identity—more precisely, the *fluidity* of identity, as explained by Jacqueline Carey in her review of *Mona in the Promised Land* in the *New York Times Book Review* (June 9, 1996): "For Ms. Jen tribal identity may be important—central, in fact—but it's also fluid. Each of her characters can stand for different types of people because over time each one actually becomes different types of people. There is a rich comic tradition of gender bending (from *Twelfth Night* to *Tootsie*); here ethnicity is bent instead." This sentiment was echoed by Achy Obejas, who wrote in the *Chicago Tribune Books* (September 8, 1996): "That's the book's coda. Are we fixed in our ethnicity? Are our personalities a matter of where and when we were born, with each ethnic group having assigned traits like astrological signs? Jen suggests that ethnicity, like the stars, compels but doesn't necessarily impel."

Jen once said that the characters in her fiction reflect "the ghosts of her family." Her first novel, *Typical American*, which echoes the saga of her own family's immigrant experiences, tells the story of the newly arrived Changs: Ralph, an engineer who becomes obsessed with "making it" through a fried-chicken emporium; his wife, Helen, who craves the suburban lifestyle as defined in the pages of glamor and fashion magazines; and Ralph's misfit sister, Theresa ("almost glad to be all wrong in some sphere"). To the Changs, "assimilation" has less to do with high culture and everything to do with playing their appointed roles as consumers in America's dollar-driven postwar society. For Ralph Chang, getting a driver's license and a convertible is as much an immigrant rite of passage as it is for a male teenager. This is as illustrated in the family's madcap maiden voyage around New York City in its new car, which gives them quick access to Chinatown, where they gorge on Chinatown street-vendor fare as a symbol of their newfound American consumerism ("More! More! Buy more! They urged Helen"), and equally quick access to the highways ("*Faster!*" Ralph answered. "*Faster and faster*") that lead them to their new home in suburban Connecticut ("*Beautiful, beautiful, beautiful. . . . It's almost as nice as China!*") But Ralph also drives alone, with the top down, prompting this paean to American rugged individualism: "Mister, it was great to be out and around! . . . So giant! So clangorous—such screeching, rumbling, blaring, banging! Such hiss! . . . So much ambition! No equation could begin to describe it all." Even seeing the stars is impossible without a car: "If you don't get out for a spin every now and then, you forget all about them. Anything is possible. A man is what he makes up his mind to be." The closing lines of *Typical American* place Ralph Chang squarely in the line of the American hero defined by his ability to reinvent himself: "What escape was possible? It seemed to him at that moment, as he stood waiting and waiting, trapped in his coat, that a man was as doomed here as he was in China. *Kan bu jian. Ting bu jian.* He could not always see, could not always hear. He was not what he made up his mind to be. A man was the sum of his limits; freedom only made him see how much so. America was no America. Ralph swallowed." Reviewing this novel for the *Washington Post Book World* (March 24, 1991), Wendy Law-Yone wrote: "*Typical American* is a rich addition to the ever-growing body of immigrant literature, a lovingly imagined, thoroughly satisfying account of one Chinese family picking its way through the hazards of the American dream."

Jen's second novel, *Mona in the Promised Land*, set in the turbulent year of 1968, upended the melting pot and its traditional notions of ethnic assimilation in narrating the exploits of Mona Chang. Introduced in the earlier novel, Mona is a teenage Chinese-American suburbanite who decides she wants to be Jewish and so renames herself Mona Changowitz. In an interview with Jesse Garon, Jen herself claimed that the two novels are "very different in tone and feeling. The characters from my first book do appear, but the emphasis [in the second] is on the younger generation. The first book is more tragic-comic, while *Mona in the Promised Land* is more purely comic."

The burlesquing of suburban pieties attracted reviewers' acclaim, who were willing to forgive some of the novel's flaws in order to enjoy its light-hearted tone. In *Harper's Bazaar* (May 1996), Martha McPhee wrote: "In contrast to the earnest tone of *Typical American*, *Mona* is fast and confident, broadly comic, filled with screenplayish dialogue and staccato descriptions. . . . The effect of this roundelay is a playful appreciation for the predicament of hyphenated Americans."

Under Jen's broad penstrokes, Mona Changowitz emerges as an outspoken, often irreverent protagonist whose experience is that of a lone Chinese-American in the largely Jewish-American suburb of "Scarshill," New York— a high schooler who has attended "so many bar and bas mitzvahs, she can almost say herself whether the kid chants like an angel or like a train conductor." She soon believes that "if you want to know how to be a minority, there's nobody better at it than the Jews. . . . American means being whatever you want, and I happened to pick being Jewish." After all, as she tells an interviewer, "It's not as much of a joke for a white person to try Buddhism as it is for a Chinese person to try Judaism." To Mona Changowitz, deft quick-change artistry is really a matter of conversion, as summed up in her advice to her Japanese boyfriend: "Everybody who's born here is American, and also some people who covert from what they were before. You could become American. . . . You only have to learn some rules and speeches." Many of the scenes in *Mona* poke fun at the liberal sacred cows of the idealistic 1960s, as when Mona and her Jewish boyfriend invite a group of Black Panthers, friends of the black cook at the Changs' pancake house, to move into the mansion occupied by Mona's best friend, Barbara Guglestein. Despite finding fault with the novel's structure and melodramatic tone, Valerie Miner, in the *Nation* (June 17, 1996), pronounced this "hilarious, episodic novel" a source of political and social insight: "Those of us who, like Mona and Callie, are first generation are brought up with a bifurcated identity and a weighty sense of privileged duty," she wrote, adding, "*Mona in the Promised Land* might be a fairy tale if it were not that in the epilogue Mona, now a mother herself, faces the next dangling question: How will Mona Changowitz, authentic Chinese-Jewish-American-progressive-feminist, cope 10 years from now when her daughter Io begins to take charge of shaping her own quite separate, yet inseparable identity?" When Julie Shiroishi reviewed *Mona* for the *San Francisco Bay-Guardian*, she described it in popular-culture terminology: "Imagine P. G. Wodehouse reincarnated as an American-born Chinese person writing the novelization of the screenplay for a movie codirected by Woody Allen and Wayne Wang."

Jen's *Who's Irish? And Other Stories* appeared in 1999. The eight tales concern Chinese-Americans who are still, after years spent in the United States, adjusting to American styles and mores. A writer for *Kirkus Reviews* (April 12, 1999) called the book "sharp-eyed."

Gish Jen's nonfiction, whether in the form of essays, magazine articles, or interviews, are much more serious in tone than her second novel, reading almost like status reports on the flux of American identity politics at end-of-century. In her article "Who's To Judge? Identity Politics v. Inner Lives," published in the *New Republic* (April 21, 1997), Jen wrote of an all-too-familiar dilemma: "Perhaps political mobilization always involves the extolling of social facts at the expense of the ever-wayward inner life. In any case, many minority writers like me, once marooned by prejudice, now find ourselves marooned again by identity politics. For the first allegiance of artists in general is to the very inner life that identity politics denies." Jen cannot identify with the writers who reject wholesale the notion that art and power never intersect ("these dinosaurs are the profoundly, irrevocably, un-p.c.," she has written), but, much to the discomfort of some of her peers, she also sympathizes with the dilemmas of those who appreciate the subtle nuances of these issues: "But many other majority and minority writers who do care about diversity in the public sphere . . . who perhaps even explore the effects of social injustice on the heart, have nevertheless found it necessary to brand themselves anti-p.c. Identity politicians have left them no middle ground: multiculturalism has become synonymous with political correctness."

Gish Jen caused no little controversy when she published her article "Challenging the Asian Illusion" in the *New York Times* (August 11, 1991). "Until recently, it did not occur to most of us that the absence of Asian and Asian-American images was symptomatic of a more profound invisibility," she wrote. "Over the years, Asians have been the form onto which white writers have freely projected their fears and desires. That this is a form of colonialism goes almost without saying; it can happen only when the people whose images are appropriated are in no position to object." She went on to criticize the stereotyped construction of "Oriental" images in popular culture— both malicious and benign—such as the "cunning" Fu Manchu and the "Asian whiz kid" detective Charlie Chan. Jen made the point that Asians were portrayed either as sinister figures or as a "model minority" with which other minorities could be negatively compared. When Miramax announced that it would release new Charlie Chan movies with Russell Wong in the title role, Gish Jen expressed her approval of a film that would "subvert" the old Charlie Chan image; she was quoted in the *New York Times* (January 5, 1997) as saying: "It would be a lot of fun to see Charlie Chan made in a way that's sensitive. It would be great to see an Asian-American in that role rather than someone in yellowface."

In her article "An Ethnic Trump" in the *New York Times Magazine* (July 7, 1996), Gen used the metaphor of the "trump card" to describe America's contemporary racial-ethnic pecking order. In the example she offered, that of her Irish-American husband and their then four-year-old son, Luke, she noted that her son is always perceived as Chinese, not Irish, even though he is of mixed ancestry. "For as we all know," she wrote, "it is not only certain ethnicities that trump others but certain colors: black trumps white, for example, always and forever; a mulatto is not a kind of white person, but a kind of black person. And so it is, too, that my son is considered a kind of Asian person whose manifest destiny is to embrace Asian things. The Chinese language. Chinese New Year. No one cares whether he speaks Gaelic or wears green on St. Patrick's Day. For though Luke's skin is fair, and his features mixed, people see his straight black hair and 'know' who he is."

As a solution to these conundrums, Jen returns to her fictional wellsprings with a suggestion to "spoof the stereotypes" in the manner of *Mona in the Promised Land* or the short-lived TV show *Shannon's Deal*, which poked good-natured fun at the foibles of a pony-tailed Korean immigrant. "Here were clear signs for hope," she wrote in "Challenging the Asian Illusion"; "the immigrant at first appeared to be an all-knowing Charlie Chan, but turned out to be at once less and more. At moments way ahead of the investigator Shannon, he proved to be way behind at others; he knew all the aphorisms but had trouble passing the bar exam, and discussed his own tendency to drop pronouns." Jen also looks hopefully to the new generation of Asian-American writers, which includes Wayne Wang and Philip Kan Gotanda, in whose works "Asian Americans are presented in far greater complexity than is typical of the mainstream media; the characters seem more captured than constructed, more like flesh-and-blood than cartoons. This is partly a matter of their status as protagonists rather than peripheral figures."

But challenging the Asian illusion may prove to be daunting. Jen recalled an incident in which she shared a dinner platform with former United States senator Warren Rudman, who offered a tear-jerking tribute to Japanese-American senator Daniel K. Inouye and the heroic 442nd Regiment, comprised of Japanese-Americans who volunteered for service while incarcerated in American [internment] camps during World War II. "For every time Rudman said the words 'Japanese' or 'Japanese Americans,' he turned clear around from the lectern to look, dramatically, at me. Never mind that I am Chinese-American. Never mind that no one related to me had been called on to prove his patriotism so vividly, seeing as how, in the war, China was a U.S. ally, remember? Rudman just wanted to let everyone know that he saw me and was aware of my kind; and that nowadays, goddamn it, I mattered. Whatever the hell I was."
—E. M.

SUGGESTED *READING: Chicago Tribune Books* p3 Sep. 8, 1996; *Harper's Bazaar* p94+ May 1996, with photo; *Nation* p35+ June 17, 1996; *New Republic* p18+ Apr. 21, 1997; *New York Times* II p1+ Aug. 11, 1991; *New York Times Book Review* p16 June 9, 1996; *New York Times Magazine* p50 July 7, 1996, p55+ Jan. 5, 1997; *San Francisco Bay-Guardian* May 29, 1996; *Washington Post Book World* p1 Mar. 24, 1991

SELECTED BOOKS: *Typical American*, 1991; *Mona in the Promised Land*, 1996; *Who's Irish? And Other Stories*, 1999

Jia Pingwa

1953– Novelist; short-story writer

During the 1980s Jia Pingwa emerged as a prominent writer in the group known as the "Westerns," or writers from China's Northwest region, who were trying to redefine Chinese literature in the post-Mao era. He is also included in the "root-seeking" school of fiction that flourished in the late 1980s and seeks the soul of China in closed, traditional rural communities untouched by modern materialism. Jia has since written 24 books, including three novels and several novellas and collections of short stories. His lengthy novel *Fuzao* (translated by Howard Goldblatt and published in English in 1991 as *Turbulence*), part epic and part love story, won the Pegasus Prize for distinguished works of fiction from countries whose literatures are rarely translated into English. Described as a "rustic" writer who still keeps a local accent and writes about the countryside, this prolific author continues to draw his inspiration from his native region, presenting a picture of his homeland as bleak and barbarous yet teeming with a native beauty and vitality that has nurtured generations of survival-bound peasants.

Jia Pingwa was born in 1953 of peasant stock in the Shangzhou area of Shaanxi province, near the ancient capital of Xi'an. After making his way to college through the national examinations, he graduated from the Chinese department of Northwest University in 1982 and took an editorial job with the Shaanxi People's Publishing House for a monthly salary of 39+ yuan, roughly equivalent to five U.S. dollars. Between work assignments, he wrote fiction and, after receiving more than a hundred rejection slips, finally succeeded in getting published. By the middle 1980s, his stories had attracted national attention.

JIA PINGWA

In his fiction, Jia Pingwa weaves a vast panorama of life in China's rural Northwest, chronicling the changes wrought by the nation's recent push toward a market economy. It was through this region that the Silk Road had passed a millennium earlier and where Xi'an, the old imperial capital, had been a thriving cosmopolitan center. When trade shifted to the sea route and the imperial capital moved eastward, the Northwest gradually deteriorated and became one of the most backward parts of the country. Entrenched in tradition and closed to the outside world, it often became a refuge for political exiles. It was in this isolated area that the Communist Party established its base in the 1930s, gradually taking over the entire mainland. Writers of the "Western" school, as they were dubbed, consisted of locals like Jia and sophisticated writers from more cosmopolitan regions who traveled to the area looking for material. Jia had the advantage of being a down-to-earth local with a solid education and literary sophistication.

Jia's fiction dispels the stereotypes of the "happy peasant" who has been rescued first by collectivization and then by privatization. With his deep understanding of, and compassion for, the rural classes, Jia describes the peasants as having been victimized from all sides by irrational regulations that are alien to their culture and destructive of their livelihood, whether under imperial rule or the Communist regime. In his story "Family Chronicle of a Wooden Bowl Maker," the old father exclaims, "What are we anyway, that our sons should make so much money in the twinkling of an eye! It is not right!" Here, the author notes with sad irony how, in the peasants' view, salvaging the wreckage of river floods becomes a heaven-sent chance for enrichment, while making money through business acumen is an act to be viewed with suspicion.

Like the works of his contemporary, Mo Yan, Jia Pingwa's stories are often written in the form of family chronicles or regional annals that take on an epic quality when viewed as a single entity. They are colorful and episodic, full of sound and fury, signifying the dizzying social and psychological changes going on in the vast Northwest. Faced with these new and complex realities, Jia wrote: "It is traditional virtue matched with modern beauty, as well as traditional evil matched with modern vice." The conflicts are numerous: between innovation and tradition, between sharp city men and simple country folk, or between clever, ambitious peasants and their more complacent counterparts. These innocence-versus-experience conflicts are reflected in differing attitudes to the soil, morals, marriage, sexual relationships, family, and community. Through unusual, even grotesque, situations, Jia creates characters who show innate decency, strength of character, and a sense of honor under painful trials and crises. In his story "Renji" (1988, The Extreme for Man, tr. "How Much Can a Man Bear?"), two friends live in a mythic friendship beyond the understanding of their worldly neighbors. In "Ji Wowo Renjia" (1991, tr. "The People of Chicken's Nest Hollow"), the social upheaval penetrates family relationships as two couples break up and exchange partners, while remaining on good terms with each other. "Tiangou" (1991, tr. "The Heavenly Hound") describes a strange ménage à trois wherein a young man makes up a "third" with his master and his wife in order to support the incapacitated husband; ironically, by refusing to exercise his conjugal rights over the woman they share, he drives his master to suicide.

Jia Pingwa won the Pegasus Prize in 1988 for his novel *Turbulence*, in which a drama of peasant life is interspersed with an exposé of the local Party organization as a seething vipers' nest of corruption and intrigue. The novel received this honor when an independent committee organized by the Chinese Writers' Association selected it from among the best novels written in Chinese in the past decade. *Turbulence* demonstrates how Party infighting and business rivalries can be viewed as continuations of old clan feuds, evidence of the deep feudal roots of present-day China.

With its alternating depictions of town and country, Jia's novel reveals a densely populated world of peasants, boatmen, and handicrafters toiling at the bottom of society, beneath a canopy of shameless business deals and political intrigues. It is even hinted that supernatural powers oversee the fates of humans in the generalized "turbulence" of this novel. Into such a chaotic world, Jia launched Golden Dog, a young high-spirited man whose origins are cloaked in superstition (is he the child of a water demon and a reincarnation of a bird with a canine snarl?). Rising from peasant to boatman to local newspaper reporter, Golden Dog moves from one adventure to another, suffering much disillusionment but achieving maturity, especially through the complex and various relationships he has with three women: his lover Water Girl, his fiancée Yingying, and his seductress, the married Shi Hua.

Critical reception to *Turbulence* in the United States has been mixed. "With its large scale and wealth of incident, the book feels like the work of a Chinese Dreiser," Michael Upchurch wrote in the *Washington Post Book World* (November 17, 1991), "except that its thoroughgoing social commentary comes at the expense of its character portraits rather than serving as a catalyst for them. . . . Without a *Sister Carrie* to give it psychological weight, *Turbulence* may fail as a work of the imagination. But as a pulse-taking piece of social commentary, it's still a valuable book to have on hand." Lauren Belfer's brief review in the *New York Times Book Review* (September 22, 1991) elicited a letter of rebuttal from China-watcher Harrison Salisbury (November 10, 1991). Belfer criticized the "stiff and cliched translation," the "formulaic and stylized" structure, and the many characters she saw as "merely two-dimensional figures voicing platitudes." Salisbury's retort paid tribute to Jia Pingwa's "picaresque, earthy epic of peasant life" unaffected by "alien doctrines of communism of which [the peasants] know little." *Turbulence*, he concluded, is a "documentary of China as it is, lusty and eternal."

In 1994 Jia achieved some notoriety with the publication of his sensational best-selling novel *Feidu* (Abandoned Capital), consciously modeled on *The Golden Lotus*, a classic novel of erotica from the Ming dynasty. The novel reflected a mood of cultural nihilism that was pervasive among younger Chinese writers in the 1990s. In *Feidu*, Jia again exposed the dark side of society by following in explicit detail the sexual adventures of a young rake and writer in the ancient city of Xi'an. The author explained to an interviewer that he was trying to portray Xi'an as the "abandoned capital of China," China as the "abandoned capital of the planet earth," and the planet earth as the "abandoned capital of the universe." When the book was offered in a Beijing bookstore, Jia had to be given a police escort through the mob of would-be buyers who showed up.

In a 1991 talk at Columbia University, Jia Pingwa claimed proficiency in astrology and palm-reading, perhaps tongue-in-cheek, for despite his "rustic" persona, he is well-grounded in formal classical learning, Buddhism and Taoism, and calligraphy and Chinese painting. A popular biography titled *Guicai Jia Pingwa* (The Uncanny Genius Jia Pingwa) has already been published in China.
—E. M.

SUGGESTED READING: *New York Times* C p15 Aug. 2, 1995, with photo; *New York Times Book Review* p52 Sep. 22, 1991, p67 Nov. 10, 1991; *Washington Post Book World* p7 Nov. 17, 1991, with illustration; Martin, H. and J. Kinkley, eds. *Modern Chinese Writers: Self-Portrayals*, 1991; Zha Jianying, *China Pop*, 1995

SELECTED BOOKS IN ENGLISH TRANSLATION: *Turbulence*, 1991

Courtesy of Ha Jin

Jin, Ha

Feb. 21, 1956– Poet; short-story writer

A former member of the People's Liberation Army of China, Ha Jin is now a poet and short-story writer living in the United States who is considered by literary critics to rank among today's most accomplished Chinese-American authors. Partly as a result of the Tiannanmen Square massacre in 1989, Jin has remained in the United States, writing ex-

clusively in English, his second language. He has achieved his greatest recognition for the short story collections *Ocean of Words* (1996) and *Under the Red Flag* (1997), which provide disturbing glimpses into the realities of Maoist China during the early years of the Cultural Revolution in the late 1960s and early 1970s; he is also the author of the novels *In the Pond* (1998) and *Waiting* (1999). Despite the success he has attained, Jin remains skeptical about the value of his work, still deeply affected by the anti-intellectual influences of his years in the Chinese military.

In an autobiographical profile submitted to *World Authors 1990-1995*, Jin wrote: "I was born in Jin County, Liaoning Province, in 1956. My father was an official and my mother a policewoman. They could not live together at that time because they worked in different towns; so at age one, I was put under the care of a local civilian couple, the Wangs, with whom I lived, on and off, for about 10 years. I have always felt attached more to them than to my parents. Before I attended elementary school, I was chosen for a larger, better school, run by the army, in Dalian City. For another two years I lived away from home, returning every other week. Because I had three siblings at the time and my parents couldn't continue to afford to let me stay at that elite school, I returned to the rural town where my parents and the Wangs lived. A year later the Cultural Revolution broke out; we had nothing to study in school, so we played on the streets or went into mountains to pick up peanuts and sweet potatoes left by the peasants in the fields.

"My family didn't live in the barracks because my father's unit was stationed on the fringe of the small town. So my brothers and I played with the peasants' children most of the time. We often fought with the army kids. But we were never accepted by the peasants' kids as their own. We lived in between the army and the peasants.

"From the age of 14 to 19 I volunteered to serve in the People's Liberation Army, staying at the northeastern border between China and the former Soviet Union. I wanted to defend the country, ready to die for it; but there may have been a psychological reason unclear to me at the time, namely that I wanted to escape from home. I was an artillery man and then an orderly in my first year; then I was trained to become a telegrapher. I served for five and a half years. Those years were the happiest time in my life; I was secure, relatively carefree, and idealistic, though the living condition was stark. In 1971, my second year in the army, my father visited me and advised me to study on my own. Soon I began teaching myself middle- and high-school courses, working on textbooks when my comrades were sleeping. I dreamed of going to college one day. Fortunately, my parents could find and mail me some textbooks, and I worked by myself in a telegraph room, which enabled me to study alone. But college remained closed because of the Cultural Revolution. There were very few good books available. I read a lot of propaganda stuff. One book, however, was very close to my heart, i.e. Gorky's *My Universities*.

"The army wanted to promote me to officer, but I was determined to go to college, so I was discharged in 1975. Still, colleges were closed. I worked as a telegrapher in a railroad company for three years in Jiamusi, a remote city in Heilongjing Province. In 1976 the city began to broadcast an English learners' program, from 5:00 to 5:30 A.M., Monday through Saturday. I could follow the radio because I slept in a small telegraph room alone. That was how I started to learn English. I knew Friedreich Engels had written a book in English, i.e. *The Condition of the Working Class in England.* I thought that someday I might be able to read that book in the original.

"In the winter of 1977 colleges reopened, and I passed the entrance exams and went to Heilongjiang University in Harbin to study English. I hadn't applied for the English major. Because I passed the written exam in English, I was assigned to learn it. I received a B.A. in 1981. Then I went to study American literature at Shandong University, where I received a M.A. in 1984. The next year I came to the U.S., doing graduate work at Brandeis University, from which I earned a Ph.D. in English in 1993. In the meantime, I studied fiction and poetry writing with Leslie Epstein and Frank Bidart. I wrote my first book of poems, *Between Silences* (1990), in a factory in Watertown, Mass., where I worked as a watchman.

"After the Tiananmen massacre, I decided to immigrate, unwilling to serve the brutal government. But I had always planned to return to China teaching American literature, so I was at a loss to know what to do with my life in the U.S. I hadn't intended to become a writer. I had written *Between Silences* only because I had felt I would burst if I didn't let the poems out. I used to imagine myself becoming a man, useful, well learned, well experienced, and significant to China, who in his old age would write a book that summarized his life, packed with wisdom—a memoir sort of thing.

"Since my dissertation was written mainly for the Chinese job market, it was hard for me to find employment in my field here, which was modern poetry. But I had already published a book of poems in English, which was well received; that meant I might find a job teaching creative writing eventually. After hesitating for two years, I decided to focus on creative writing. I told my wife, who had suffered a good deal from my uncertainty and anguish, that I might find a decent job after I published four or five books, but she might have to wait for a long time for that to happen, probably 10 years. She agreed to wait. Fortunately Emory University hired me to teach poetry writing in 1993. Since then I have held the same job and been writing devotedly. In addition to *Between Silences*, I have published another book of poems, *Facing Shadows* (1996), and two books of short fiction, *Ocean of Words* (1996, PEN/Hemingway Award) and *Under the Red Flag* (1997, the Flannery O'Connor Award for Short Fiction).

"In retrospect, I have lived a good part of my life in between different families, different groups of people, different languages, and different worlds. I consider myself a Chinese-American writer now, as I am an American citizen, writing exclusively in English. I like the hyphen, which indicates the condition of my existence—I was born an exile."

Ocean of Words: Army Stories (1996) was Jin's first short-story anthology. The stories—many of which are set in Communist China during the days of the Cultural Revolution—draw heavily on Jin's own experiences in the military at that time. The title story focuses on a soldier who works for social change through his writing yet, at the same time, doubts the value of his literary talents. Among the collection's other stories are "Too Late," about a soldier who deserts the army after his superiors forbid him to continue his relationship with the woman he loves; and "The Lecture," a sobering tale of a veteran of Mao's army who is asked to speak of the overthrow of Chiang Kai-shek as part of a nationalist propaganda rally but, instead of glorifying the war, speaks of its horrors.

Initially, Jin had trouble publishing *Ocean of Words*. He had finished the book by 1993, but publishers didn't see any commercial value in it. It took three years before he was able to find a company willing to take a chance on the anthology.

The collection received rave reviews upon publication. Andy Solomon, in the *New York Times* (June 2, 1996), referred to *Ocean of Words* as "a compelling collection of stories, powerful in their unity of theme and rich in their diversity of styles." Solomon praised Jin's ability to evoke the humanity of his characters and the way those figures formed a "group portrait" of an entire people fighting to preserve their individuality in the face of the Maoist regime.

The *Publisher's Weekly* (February 26, 1996) reviewer stated that in *Ocean of Words*, Ha Jin "quickly draws the reader into Chinese army life with all its rivalries, propaganda and poignancy." The critic commented that Jin's writing showed a striking sense of humor, particularly in stories such as "Miss Jee," which features a soldier who is ridiculed by his comrades. Jin is at his best, wrote the reviewer, when writing about characters "forced to choose between ideology and love." *Oceans of Words* will move "not just readers interested in China or the army life," but, as the reviewer added, "any reader vulnerable to good writing and simple human drama."

In *Under the Red Flag* (1997) Jin returned to the setting of China during the Cultural Revolution, focusing on the inhabitants of the rural town of Dismount Ford. This short story collection looks at such issues as marital and family difficulties, political unrest, and the clash between the traditional and the revolutionary in China. The effects of government on individual life are also explored. The first piece, "In Broad Daylight," details the humiliations suffered by a woman accused of prostitution, and how her plight is seen through the eyes of the townspeople.

A *Publishers Weekly* reviewer (October 13, 1997) declared that *Under the Red Flag* successfully captures the feel of a rural Chinese town circa 1970. "Jin uses these simple stories to explore larger themes about human relationships," the reviewer wrote. The reviewer, however, also pointed out that at times Jin's simple allegories are a bit *too* simple and lack color or feeling.

Likewise, Peter Bricklebank, in the *New York Times* (January 11, 1998), described Jin's narrative style as "as plain and stuffy as a Mao uniform." He also expressed disappointment in what he perceived as a lack of freshness in *Under the Red Flag*. "These sorts of political exigencies seem awfully familiar," he wrote, "especially when used in the service of well-worn themes." Bricklebank went on to criticize the book for lacking in psychological richness and expressive elegance.

Paul Gray of *Time* (December 1, 1997) stated that the strongest story in *Under the Red Flag* is "Winds and Clouds Over a Funeral," in which a communist official is forced to make a decision between his dying mother's wish to be buried and his party's insistence on cremation. He compared Jin's evocation of Dismount Fort to Isaac Bashevis Singer's recreation of rural Polish villages (*shtetls*) in his stories.

Under the instruction of Leslie Epstein at Boston University, Jin learned to develop his writing talents. "He taught me what good prose should be like," he said in an interview with Stephen Martin of the *Chronicle of Higher Education* (April 25, 1997). "Not too fancy; not vulgar, either." Epstein also exposed Jin to 19th- and early 20th-century

Russian literature, which has had a great influence on him. Among his inspirations, Jin has mentioned such masters as Anton Chekhov and Fyodor Dostoyevsky. His interest in these writers led him to see a similarity between the characters in their works and the people of contemporary China. Both, according to Jin, have been led by difficult landscapes and climate conditions to develop a deep emotionalism and fervent nationalism.

In his poetry Jin has drawn on the works of such ancient Chinese poets as Li Po, Tu Fu, and Po Chu-li. Meticulous in his approach to writing, Jin goes through numerous edits and revisions—sometimes producing up to 30 drafts—before he is satisfied with a piece. Jin has said that writing poetry is something he finds very demanding, requiring an even greater mastery of language than prose writing. In comparing the two, he said in the *Chronicle of Higher Education* interview: "Poetry is more risky, more challenging. Fiction is equally hard, but in different ways. . . . As long as you have a good story, the work will succeed."

Although Jin has rejected the propaganda he was exposed to as a young man, his attitude toward writing still shows some of the effects of the anti-intellectualism that was an integral part of the Cultural Revolution. "There are many other things more meaningful than writing," he told Martin, "Retreating to the pen and the page is not the only way to live."

The name Jin was given at birth is Xuefei (shoo-FAY). He adopted the pen name Ha once he began publishing because he felt that his birth name would be too difficult for Westerners to pronounce.

Jin married Lisah Bian on July 6, 1982. They have one child, Wen. Included among the numerous awards he has received throughout his writing career are three Pushcart Prizes for fiction, a fiction prize from the journal *Kenyon Review*, and the Agni Best Fiction Prize.

Ha Jin finished his first novel, *In the Pond*, in the fall of 1998. It tells the story of a worker in the Chinese countryside during the 1980s. His novel *Waiting*, set amid the changes occurring in China between the 1960s and the 1980s, concerns a doctor, Lin Kong, trapped in a loveless arranged marriage and unable—because of Communist Party doctrine—to act on his love for a nurse. "Though inaction is a risky subject and the thoughts of a cautious man make for a rather deliberate prose style (the first two sections describe the moments the characters choose *not* to act), the final chapters are moving and deeply ironic," a reviewer wrote in *Publishers Weekly* (August 23, 1999). —B.S.

SUGGESTED READING: *The Chronicle of Higher Education* pA8 Apr. 25, 1997; *Georgia Review* p601+ Fall 1996; *New York Times* VII p21 June 2, 1996; VII p14 Jan. 11, 1998; *Publishers Weekly* p98 Feb. 26, 1996, p58 Oct. 13, 1997; *Time* p 94+ Dec. 1, 1997

SELECTED WORKS: Fiction—*Ocean of Words: Army Stories*, 1996; *Under the Red Flag*, 1997; *In the Pond*, 1998; *Waiting*, 1999; Poetry—*Between Silences*, 1990; *Facing Shadows*, 1996

Jones, Gayl

Nov. 23, 1949– Novelist; short-story writer; poet

In a biographical note to her 1983 poetry collection, *The Hermit-Woman*, Gayl Jones is described as a writer "who sees herself as a story-teller rather than a novelist" and one who "is particularly interested in language as it is heard, not read, a preference which lifts both her stories and her poems to a rare vividness and sense of reality." Her early novels, *Corregidora* (1975) and *Eva's Man* (1976), focus on the struggles of abused black women. In the 1980s she published three poetry collections (*Song for Anninho*, 1981; *The Hermit-Woman*, and *Xarque and Other Poems*, 1985) that reflected her deepening interest in the African diaspora in Brazil during the period of Portuguese colonization, works in which she again focused on the lives of oppressed women. Her critical study *Liberating Voices: Oral Tradition in African American Literature* (1991) traces the contributions of oral folklore and traditional music to the literature of such 20th-century black literati as Paul Lawrence Dunbar, Langston Hughes, Zora Neale Hurston, Ralph Ellison, and Alice Walker. In February 1998, a month after the publication of *The Healing*, her third novel and her first in 20 years, Jones was briefly committed to a mental hospital after being involved in a bizarre incident at her home in Lexington, Kentucky, in which her fugitive husband killed himself in a dramatic standoff with local police. *The Healing* was subsequently nominated for a National Book Award. Her novel *Mosquito* was published in early 1999.

Gayl Jones was born in an impoverished section of Lexington, Kentucky, on November 23, 1949, the daughter of Franklin Jones, a restaurant cook, and Lucille Winston Jones, a homemaker with ambitions to be a writer herself. The couple also had a younger son, Franklin Jr. The siblings attended local segregated public schools and were among the first black children to enroll at the newly integrated Henry Clay High School, which had a good academic reputation. Gayl credits her early interest in writing to the oral storytelling tradition handed down by her mother and her grandmother, who lived nearby. She also acknowledges a fifth-grade teacher who encouraged her pupils to listen to music as a catalyst for their creative writing exercises and a high-school teacher, Anna Dodd, who regaled Jones and her fellow students with tales about expatriate writers in Paris in the 1920s. Another teacher, Ann Allen, was quoted in a *New York Times Magazine* (July 19, 1998) article as re-membering Gayl Jones's ambition to write like Henry James.

With the assistance of Elizabeth Hardwick, Robert Lowell's wife and a native of Lexington, Jones matriculated at an elite New England school, the then all-female Connecticut College, which provided a radically different environment for the budding author. There, she came under the influence of black scholar and poet Robert Hayden, a visiting professor from the University of Michigan. After she received her bachelor of arts degree in English from Connecticut College, in 1971, Jones enrolled in the creative writing program at Brown University, studying with poet Michael S. Harper and receiving her masters' degree in 1973. She received a doctorate in creative writing from Brown in 1975, the year she was awarded the *Mademoiselle* award for fiction, and joined the English faculty at the University of Michigan, in Ann Arbor, where she remained until 1983.

It was at Brown that Jones also encountered the writings of the Brazilian intellectual Gilberto Freyre, who had written considerably about the intersection of African and Brazilian culture, especially during the period of Portuguese colonization of Brazil in the 17th and 18th centuries. Fascinated with the communities of former slaves at Palmares and New Palmares that existed there, albeit tenuously, around 1700, Jones used this region of Brazil as the setting for her several books of poetry published in the 1980s and as the psychic landscape for her first novel, *Corregidora*. This novel, which a reviewer in *Time* (June 16, 1975) compared to Richard Wright's *Native Son*, has for its protagonist a contemporary Kentucky blues singer named Ursa Corregidora, descended from a line of women—all named Corregidora—who trace their ancestry to an incestuous relationship with an eponymous Portuguese slaveowner, the father of both Ursa's granmother and mother. Ursa is first portrayed as an enabling victim in a destructive relationship with her abusive husband, Mutt, whose physical brutality causes her to lose her child and undergo a hysterectomy. She finally leaves Mutt and marries Tadpole, the owner of her blues club, but retains an ambiguous affection for her tormentor. Jones wrote the novel as an indictment of the sexism and racism that have pervaded the New World since the colonial period and that still affect contemporary relationships. Novelist John Updike hailed the publication of *Corregidora* in a *New Yorker* (August 18, 1975) review in which he declared that the book "persuasively fuses black history, or the mythic consciousness that must do for black history, with the emotional nuances of contemporary black life"; he commended Jones for being willing "to explore exactly how our sexual and emotional behavior is warped within the matrix of family and race."

Jones soon began attracting the attention of a new generation of African-American literary scholars. Writing a lengthy article in *Signs: Journal of Women in Culture & Society* (Winter 1995),

Madhu Dubey pointed out that earlier writers including Alice Walker and Zora Neale Hurston had been credited with "recurrently us[ing] the metaphor of matrilineage to authorize their construction of a black feminine literary tradition," citing Virginia Woolf's dictum that "women writers 'think back through [their] mothers.'" Dubey's article, entitled "The Matrilineal Metaphor of Tradition," focused on *Corregidora* and Jones's 1981 poetry collection, *Song of Anninho*. According to Dubey's thesis, both works "rehearse the founding gesture of matrilineage theory in presenting the mother as the medium of the daughter's access to history. In both texts, the mother's oral discourse gains its oppositional value when positioned against the misrepresentations and absences of official historiography." Jones herself told Michael Harper, in an interview printed in his and Michael Stepto's 1979 book *Chants of Saints: A Gathering of Afro-American Literature*, "it's necessary [for African-American and Native American writers] to make connections between the oral traditions and written documentation . . . It's necessary to document the [oral] traditions—to counteract the effects of false documentations."

Jones was termed an "original presence" by Stelamaris Coser, who gave *Corregidora* a close reading in her 1995 book *Bridging the Americas: The Literature of Toni Morrison, Paule Marshall, and Gayl Jones*. Coser's fourth chapter, "The Dry Wombs of Black Women: Memories of Brazilian Slavery in *Corregidora* and *Song for Anninho*," compared Jones's writing with that of Latin American writers, especially Carlos Fuentes and Gabriel García Márquez. "Unlike classic accounts that privilege the Colombian saga and the European outlook," wrote Coser, "Jones's exploration of American history looks for the untold feelings of black people under the oppression of slavery and during its aftermath." On the surface, she added, "the story seems as thrilling and profound as any grocery-store rack romance," but she declared that Jones "adds to it an immense, almost insurmountable burden of hate and repression, centuries of dark memories passed on from generation to generation of black women . . . Jones connects them to the violence against black women perpetuated in the present, disrupting female identity and sexuality and undermining the possibility of love." By writing of a line of women who have maintained the name Corregidora down through the generations, Jones has created a lineage of resistance, argued Coser, who saw parallels between this novel and Gilberto Freyre's *The Masters and the Slaves*. Jones thus critiqued the nuances of a male patriarchal system, as influenced by colonialism, that has forced black men, themselves chattel, to treat women as their property.

Published by Beacon Press in 1976, Jones's second novel, *Eva's Man*, is a starkly naturalistic portrait of Eva Medina Canada, a woman caught in another vicious cycle of sexual abuse and pathology. Incarcerated for the mutilation and murder of a lover, Eva speaks in a graphic first-person narrative that includes flashbacks to childhood sexual abuse and testimonials to the horrors of living on the fringes of conventional society. Despite the harshness of her character's situation, Jones often invested Eva's language with a haunting poetry: "He did it while I was sleeping. I was bleeding but he went ahead and did it. His eyes were blood-colored like the eyes of those men who work in metal factories drilling holes in things with their visors to help protect their eyes;" or, "*An owl sucks my blood. I am bleeding underneath my nails. An old owl sucks my blood. He gives me fruit in my palms. We enter the river again . . . together. They are doing with this woman. See. They are doing with this woman. See what they are doing with this woman.*" The novel was praised by Darryl Pinckney in the *New Republic* (June 19, 1976) and by John Updike in the *New Yorker* (August 9, 1976). An anonymous reviewer of *Eva's Man* for *Choice* (October 1976) found the book "too lurid for younger readers" and acknowledged links with William Faulkner's work: "To some degree, the novel sounds like a tract against pursuing males; and to some degree it is of interest only for its investigation into abnormal psychology. Yet because there are various levels and because these are interwoven in something of the manner of Faulkner's middle prose—impressionistically linking by memory logic rather than narrative or rational logic—there is cumulative power in the book."

In 1977 Random House published *White Rat*, a collection of short stories in which Jones continued her exploration of themes such as miscegenation, lesbianism, violent sexuality, and the predatory male. Some reviewers found the collection disappointing, but Diane Johnson, writing in the *New York Review of Books* (November 10, 1977) saw the influence of Hemingway and Jean Rhys and pronounced Jones "a vernacular novelist with a marvelous ear, for whom black speech is the only medium." During the 1980s Lotus Press in Detroit published three collections of Jones's poetry, all of which were inspired by the culture created by African slaves in Brazil during the period of Portuguese colonization. These collections, *Song for Anninho*, *The Hermit-Woman*, and *Xarque and Other Poems*, established Jones as a chronicler of incidents and situations that had been overlooked by other writers. In *Song for Anninho*, Jones paid tribute to Palmares, one of seven *quilombos* (settlements) established by escaped African slaves in the Alagoas palm-forest region of northeastern Brazil during the latter part of the 17th century. After withstanding attack by Portuguese forces over a 20-year period, Palmares was finally destroyed, but a small group kept alive a determination to reestablish the settlement. *Song for Anninho* is narrated in a woman's voice, that of Almeyda, a wounded survivor of Palmares—her breasts were mutilated in the battle—who is recuperating under the care of Zibatra, a wizard-woman in the Barriga Mountains outback. Encouraged by Zibatra, Almeyda composes this poem as a love song to her warrior-lover, Anninho. The poem's opening lines express the anguish of its wounded narrator: "The trees are tall here. / The men are tall. / The men are the color / of the black bark. / But men are not trees. / Sap is not blood. / Bark is not the flesh of men. / I do not believe the trees / can hear me singing." After many long tales of dashed hopes, confrontations with the Portuguese, and stoic resistance, Almeyda declares the triumph of love and commitment, concluding, "You had made yourself a cigarette. You went away / and came back and sat near me. I watched you, / and found some deep place in you where I could go / any moment./ Now I make roads for you, Anninho. I make roads."

In *The Hermit-Woman*, time alternates between the 17th century and the present. All the poems in this second volume are narrated by women except "Ensinança," which is written in the voice of a "modern man, / in modern times, / an engineer in Rio,' / scientific, rational," who is all too conscious of the spiritual maladies that such rationality leaves in its wake. In the poems that followed, Jones deepened her exploration of woman as a healer and explorer—in short, a subversive figure vis-à-vis her colonial oppressors. In "Wild Figs and Secret Places," at 30 pages the longest poem in the book, Jones opened with the image of the mosquito: "Memory is a mosquito / pregnant again / and out for blood / . . . Who am I / Who needs to know? / I am merely a human woman / claiming one of the earth's places . . . " The narrator, a woman with "a map of the country / the whole territory / in the veins of my hands" offers "a way into the mountain," though "There are parts of the map / I will not show. / There are places I will / always keep secret." "The Machete Woman," another long passage in *The Hermit-Woman*, is narrated by a woman who lives "within the sword / within rage and outrage," who took refuge in a Christian convent in Brazil in 1637 and is drawn to new revelation by a sorcerer who reminds her of her ancestral roots.

Xarque and Other Poems, a sequel of sorts to *Song for Anninho*, is set in 1741, 20 years after the destruction of the settlement of New Palmares. The title poem is narrated by Euclida, the granddaughter of Almeyda, narrator of the earlier book. Euclida, who now works in a dried-meat factory, still harbors dreams of her warrior-grandmother and, transcending her own reticence, claims her position in the proud lineage of African-Brazilian slaves: "I am a shy woman / who fears change. / I dream of soft hammocks / of feathers and grass, / while my mother cuts turnips / and throws them in the master's soup. / I dream of wild figs / and my warrior grandmother. / But I am a shy woman." In recounting her stories of longing, Euclida shows herself to be more of a daydreaming contemplative than a woman of action.

The publication of *Xarque* marked the end of one phase of Jones's life and work. In 1983 Jones's husband, Bob Higgins, was arrested after brandishing a firearm at a gay-rights rally in Ann Arbor. The incident prompted Jones to abruptly resign from the faculty of the University of Michigan, and the couple moved to Europe, citing racism as their motivation for this self-exile. Both returned to her hometown of Lexington, Kentucky, in 1988, but Jones published no new fiction for another 10 years. In 1991 Harvard University Press published a book she had essentially completed before leaving Michigan: *Liberating Voices: Oral Tradition in African American Literature*, a study of how "modern African-American writers began to shape and modify their literature using models not only from European and European American traditions, but also from their own distinctive oral and aural forms." In this work, Jones argued that writers such as Langston Hughes, Paul Lawrence Dunbar, Zora Neale Hurston, and Alice Walker had "redefined Western literature and literary influence either by incorporating . . . folktales, spirituals, blues, within the traditional framework . . . or by drawing dramatic and lyrical counterpoints from a whole spectrum of oral referents." She argued that it was a mistake to dismiss oral stories as "crude" offerings of a preliterate culture, preferring to see them as "the continuing, complex, inventive heritage" of the cultures from which they emerged. In the postscript to the book, Jones acknowledged that she had completed the book in 1982, "at a time when nearly all African American literary criticism emphasized theme and content," as opposed to the close reading of texts that had become fashionable later in the 1980s.

In February 1998, fallout from the Ann Arbor incident of 1983 caught up with the Joneses when the police in Lexington tried to serve Bob Higgins's 15-year-old arrest warrant, leading to a three-hour standoff with police during which Higgins threatened to kill himself and his wife. As police stormed their cottage, Higgins killed himself by slitting his throat, and Gayl Jones was taken to a state mental hospital for fear that she would inflict harm on herself. Newspaper reports of the incident indicated that Jones had threatened to join her husband in suicide to protest society's racism. The incident became a life-imitates-art scenario revolving around a woman "tightly bound to destructive men," in the words of *New York Times* (March 2, 1998) reporter Richard Bragg, who concluded: "The question of whether Ms. Jones finally became something much like a character in her books will be pondered by people who love her writing, perhaps forever. In 1978, in a poem called 'Deep Song,' dedicated only to 'B.H.,' she wrote: "He is a dark man. / Sometimes he is a good dark man. / Sometimes he is a bad dark man. / I love him."

The incident profoundly saddened Jones's admirers, for it came just a month after Beacon Press had published *The Healing*, Jones's first novel to have appeared in 20 years; the book had led John Updike and other fans of her work to celebrate her re-emergence on the literary scene. *The Healing* is a first-person narration by Harlan Jane Eagleton, a woman who leaves her job as manager of a rock singer to embark on her new found calling as a faith healer: "If I ain't a faker, then I'm a crazy woman that just believes in her own fakery. . . . Maybe I'm a crazy woman, though, 'cause there's been plenty to say I'm crazy, but in the small tank town I'm going to they'll welcome me". Valerie Sayers, reviewing the novel for *The New York Times Book Review* (May 10, 1998), thought *The Healing* marked an important development in Jones's style: "In loosening the tight control she exercised over her earlier fiction, Jones risks all kinds of gaps in logic and development . . . [but] the illogic of Eagleton's story gathers its own authority and strength; illogic, in time, becomes connected to healing and faith. The paradoxically convincing quality of Jones's story is accomplished as much through the power of narrative as it is through realistic detail." Sayers concluded that *The Healing* marked out new territory for its embattled author, writing, "Both of Jones's earlier novels ended on muted notes of hope; this ending is full-throated . . . the delights of *The Healing*, along with the promise of new work—Jones has apparently written several novels in the past few years, and a new novel, according to the author's note, will be published next year—should be cause for hope, sustenance, and even celebration."

Jones's novel *Mosquito* appeared in early 1999. This is the story of the political and cultural education of a female African-American truck driver, Sojourner Nadine Jane Johnson (nicknamed "Mosquito"). While becoming involved in the "new underground railroad," through which she helps to bring Mexicans into the United States, Mosquito learns about the cultural history of her own people and that of other oppressed groups. "Nothing much more really happens" in *Mosquito*, according to the *Kirkus Reviews* (December 15, 1998) writer, who termed Jones's book a "fascinating" work that is "arguably both something more and something less than a novel" and is a "discursive, free-form dramatization of the raising of a consciousness."

According to Beacon, Jones "has a reading knowledge of six languages and is learning Japanese and Indonesian."

—E. M.

SUGGESTED READING: *African American Review* p393+ Fall 1995; *American Literature* p391 June 1993; *Callaloo* p132+ Winter 1993, p193+ Winter 1996; *Choice* p445 Nov. 1991; *College English* p787+ Nov. 1990; *Essence* p76 Feb. 1998; *Nation* p30+ May 25, 1998; *Newsweek* p68 Feb. 16, 1998, with photo; *New York Review of Books* p28 May 10, 1998; *New York Times* A p15 Feb. 24, 1998, A p11 Mar. 2, 1998; *New York Times Book Review* p28 May 10, 1998; *New York Times Magazine* p32+ July 19, 1998; *New Yorker* p74 Aug. 9, 1976; *Publishers Weekly* p18 Dec. 8, 1997; *Signs: Journal of Women in Culture & Society* p245+ Winter 1995; Braxton, J. and A. McLaughlin, eds. *Wild Women in the Whirlwind:*

Afra-American Culture and the Contemporary Literary Renaissance, 1990; Coser, S. *Bridging the Americas: The Literature of Toni Morrison, Paule Marshall, and Gayl Jones*, 1995; Harper, M. and Michael Stepto, eds. *Chants of Saints: A Gathering of Afro-American Literature*, 1979

SELECTED WORKS: Drama—*Chile Woman*, 1974; Fiction—*Corregidora*, 1975; *Eva's Man*, 1976; *White Rat*, 1977; *The Healing*, 1998; *Mosquito*, 1999; Nonfiction—*Liberating Voices: Oral Tradition in African American Literature*, 1991; Poetry—*Song for Anninho*, 1981; *The Hermit-Woman*, 1983; *Xarque and Other Poems*, 1985

Jones, Gwyneth A.

Feb. 14, 1952– Novelist

In 1992 Gwyneth A. Jones, the English critic and writer of science fiction and fantasy, shared the first annual James Tiptree Jr. Award for her science-fiction novel *White Queen*. The award is given annually to works in that genre that deal positively with gender issues by exploring and expanding the roles of both women and men. Originally a writer of children's fantasy, Jones has in recent years emerged as one of the leading advocates of a transgressive science fiction that emphasizes interpersonal relationships over purely technological imagination, and she maintains that science fiction is the "folklore of the 21st century." Other novels in which she explores these issues include *North Wind* (1995) and *Phoenix Café* (1998), sequels to *White Queen*; *Escape Plans* (1986), based on Judeo-Christian imagery; and *Divine Endurance* (1987), based on Hindu myths she encountered while living in the Far East.

For *World Authors 1990–1995*, she writes: "I was born in Blackley, Manchester, UK in 1952. I can't say I was an urban child. As long as I lived at home the city centre remained 'town,' psychologically if not physically distant. I grew up in a village; spent all the time I could in the woods and fields of the urban fringes—all vanished now. My father was a factory worker and a trade unionist. My mother, the oldest of seven children brought up in a two-bedroomed model labourer's cottage, was a teacher, and eventually headmistress of the Roman Catholic Infant's School. Family legend has it that they met on an anti-Franco march, when my mother was fourteen and my father twenty-four. They were (and still are) socialists of a reformist, liberal hue; Catholics, music lovers, public speakers, great readers.

"I wrote stories and poems when I was very young. More significantly I *told* stories to my younger sister and my brother. My father told us fairy tales, customised for our entertainment. My mother was passionately interested in the future. Through her, we were avid followers of the Space Race: both Russian and American programmes; we were not partisan. When I took over my father's role I used for copy the TV fantasy thrillers of the sixties: *The Avengers, The Man From U.N.C.L.E., The Prisoner.* In the final phase of my family storytelling I wrote out some of these epics. But I don't remember having a driving ambition to be a writer. To work for a living and write for pleasure seemed to me a fair bargain. What I wanted to be was a scientist. Since I could not overcome my weakness in Maths, I chose a University course almost at random, and by chance found myself studying the scientific revolution of seventeenth-century Europe. I can't remember working very hard. But those years reading, or trying to read, Kepler, Galileo, Descartes; Karl Mannheim's *Ideology and Utopia,* Tom Kuhn's *The Structure of Scientific Revolutions,* had a lasting effect.

"My first published book was a novel for children (*Water in the Air,* 1977). That came about by accident. I had written a series of modern fairy tales, customised fables that I gave to my friends as presents. A friend who was an editor at Macmillan, the publishers, showed them to the children's editor, Marni Hodgkin. This was before the fantasy genre explosion, and he could not imagine adults wanting to read stories about princesses, dragons, and witches, not even if they featured telexed news updates; and motorcycle escorts for the enchanted royals. She asked me to try and write a book.

"By the time [this] first children's novel was published . . . I had given up my job in the Civil Service, and moved with my husband to Singapore. In Singapore I continued to reprocess my memories of childhood and adolescence, and Macmillan continued to publish them. But one of my old 'modern fairy tales' began to take shape as a much bigger book: a romance, a tragic history of the far future. *Divine Endurance,* my first novel for adults, was strongly influenced by the culture of Java, Sumatra, Thailand and the Malaysian Peninsula: especially the borrowed themes of Hindu mythology that are beloved throughout South East Asia. It was also shaped by my feminism. I had always known that I was a complete human being: at least as much so, as much the model of the species, as any man. When I became a science fiction writer it was natural for me to express this truth. *Divine Endurance* was about human beings faced with the problem of the *dream machine,* the ultimate technology, that can satisfy every wish of the human heart. My characters were women, not to the exclusion of men but with a natural bias towards my own sex—just as, I had observed, the men wrote primarily about men. I wrote about women in power, bad women and good women, women as avatars of the divine, women as socialists, artists, practical Utopians. My next book, *Escape Plans,* 1986, asked the same question: *what happens if we attain our heart's desire?* This time the informing spirit was Judaeo-Christian. It

seemed appropriate to make the setting a Space-Race future, all slick *Star Trek* corridors and transparent jumpsuits. Again, most of the characters were women. I wrote a third book on this theme (*Kairos,* 1988), set in a bleak, near-future UK, that comes nearest to stripping the story bare, and decoding the allegory of my own background. I was born and bred a socialist, idealist, a child of the Utopian politics of postwar Britain. The perfect revolution, the achievement of the Good State, is not the subject in these fictions. Utopia is incidental. Utopia is not enough. The subject is the moment of utter change itself, the *kairos.*

"I still write for children, under the name Ann Halam. I'm not sure how to describe the difference between the two kinds of writing: I know that I wouldn't like to give up either. Ann Halam writes fantasy, horror stories, ghost stories; and notably a deep-ecology trilogy (*The Daymaker; Transformations; The Skybreaker*) about a mutated England, that transforms again, like those first Macmillan books, my remembered childhood. In my recent books for adults, *White Queen, North Wind,* and the forthcoming *Phoenix Café,* I have written about a future earth colonised by some merchant-adventurers, accidental empire builders; unwitting catalysts of the death of the native civilisation. What happens between my humans and my aliens reflects on the history of European colonial power in China, Africa, India, South America. It's equally a science fiction about the present and future relationship between women and men. The *White Queen* books are less engineered than the three that went before: less definite in their conclusions, more fuzzy at the edges. I feel I'm moving deliberately, as an artist, with the real world science that I still follow closely as I can, away from Theories of Everything: toward ideas of contingency, contiguity, evolution, and history. But it could be that I'm simply getting older, and more humble."

––––––––––

In a confessional moment, Gwyneth A. Jones discussed writing habits that partake of a not-quite-tidy domesticity: "I usually survive on bread and butter munched at the keys," she wrote, "shredding crumbs which play hell with my poor mouse's balls. But I find food prep is an excellent way to relax after a long hard week at the keyface." Never far from her fingertips, though, is "the untidiness of fantasy," which, "though it may fill some young readers with distaste, will become for others a way of restoring a lost continuity of experience." From children's fantasy in the 1970s to gender-transgressive science fiction in the 1990s, Jones has emerged as a serious practitioner of a genre that has often been spurned for its appeal to popular tastes.

"Every book I write is made of other books: it takes gold to make gold," declared Jones in enumerating her literary influences, a list that is catholic enough to embrace works by Marcel Proust, C. V. Wedgwood, and Flora Annie Steel as well as James

Bond thrillers and Flash Gordon comic books. In Proust's monumental *Remembrance of Things Past* ("my lifetime bedtime reading"), Jones finds enough magic among the *longueurs* to deem the multivolume work "one of the few justifications for the existence of the human race." Wedgwood's *The Thirty Years War* provided her with a "rational and passionate unraveling of this long-ago fiasco" and "taught me to understand that war is the opposite of civilization," an invaluable insight for Jones's self-affirmed calling as "a student of the future." Steel was the late-Victorian novelist who championed the rights of women when she lived in British India.

But Jones also draws her imagery from sources closer to home: her early works for children echo the Wordsworthian notion that literary gold is most precious when mined from the deep lode accessible only to children and those possessed of a childlike state of being. "The creation of fiction isn't something learned," she wrote. "It is something unlearned, by most of the population." From the vantage point of her mid-40s ("middle-age rave-up"), Jones is convinced that "the veil of adolescence between me and my childhood is beginning to thin out and break up at last," and that her adult novels were brought into being by her ability to tap into her own childhood fantasy and memory. Recalling how she used to lead her siblings in imaginative oral-storytelling sessions, she wrote: "The full flower of our wordsmithing came with a cast of plasticine characters who evolved when (I think) I was about eight years old: and their saga went on for years and years. . . . I never thought of it when I was writing the book, but now I see through the adult fictionising of *Divine Endurance* and I know that *Cho*, *Divine Endurance*, *Gress*, and their journey were foreshadowed long ago." The memory of these playful narratives led her to comment, "An artist works for God or self alone. Any trimmings added for commercial reasons are mere decoration, leaving the core and structure of the work unrepentantly angular and individual. I'm not an artist, I'm an entertainer. I learned my trade in front of a live audience." Another key factor in Jones's literary apprenticeship was her mother's naive interest in "futurology," described above: "I always tell people how my mother's love of the future started me off on sf [science fiction], how passionately excited we were at our house over the whole Space Race." Soon afterwards, she read Thomas Pynchon's *Gravity's Rainbow* and in it "recognised the informing myth of my times."

Jones's works have attracted much interest partly because of her unwillingness to dismiss science fiction as trivial, suited only for the pulp press. This stance has contributed to her reputation as a serious critic of the genre, thus further validating it for its significant contribution to contemporary letters. In a Language and Society conference paper, "Deconstructing the Starships" (June 11, 1988), Jones wrote, "At first it might seem there is an embarrassment of riches in terms of sf's penetration into popular culture: from a space shuttle called after a fictional starship to the Transformer cutouts on the back of your cereal packet. Something that passes by the name of science fiction has become the folklore of the 21st century." In that same paper she drew parallels between science fiction and more fashionable academic discourses by noting that the "icons of *la nouvelle critique* [such as "plurality of meaning, fluidity and process, an understanding of language as contingent"] are the familiar tools and usage of science fiction."

Her reviews of other writers confirm her own analytical and critical abilities. She calls Sarah Lefanu's *In the Chinks of the World Machine*, for example, "a study of the intersection between feminism and science fiction," invoking "the genre's power to deconstruct and inform, and its towering preoccupations; the fictional world that deals . . . with the problem of difference in all its aspects." Jones sees power in this transgressiveness, identifying as "the thoughtful centrepiece of this study" Lefanu's analysis of "the female man" as one who "was surviving . . . in the chinks of her male persona," a reference to pioneering science-fiction writer Alice B. Sheldon, who did not achieve validation until she began using the pseudonym James Tiptree Jr. In her review, Jones added that "there should be a stronger acknowledgment of the fact that it is exactly the essentialism of the inadequate and rightly dismissed role-reversal stories, however transformed, which defines the phenomenon of feminist sf." Likewise, in reviewing E. P. Thompson's 1988 work *The Sykaos Papers*, she wrote (September 2, 1995): "The purposes of satire and science fiction are closely linked: it would be hard to find any sf completely innocent of a secret agenda."

Gwyneth Jones has herself been admired by other critics for bringing a female-centered consciousness to the male-centered world of science fiction, especially in the trilogy begun with *White Queen*. However, her fiction is not merely polemical. Set in the year 2038, *White Queen* is considered to be unlike most other "alien" novels for the subtlety and complexity of its characters' emotional lives and the way in which it "avoids the cliché of vastly superior aliens swooping down to subjugate humanity and strip its resources," as C. Douglas Baker put it in a review for the *Linköping Science Fiction & Fantasy Archive* Web site. "Instead," he wrote, "Jones's aliens live among humans for awhile cloaking their existence, until a strange emotional relationship between Johnny Guglioli, a UFO chaser, and Agnes/Clevel, an alien residing in Africa, leads to their discovery." In her back-cover blurb, one of Jones's peers, author Suzy McKee Charnas, pointed out the book was "casually ruthless in its challenges to our usual assumptions about sex." And when *White Queen* won the James Tiptree Jr. Award in 1992, one of the judges reportedly wrote: "The real reason this book is so good is its moral complexity. You don't know whether to root for the heroes as they challenge the seemingly benevolent aliens or to pity the heroes for their xenophobia. Jones makes that decision as difficult for us as the decision to support the PLO or the IRA or the Mojahadeen (take your pick) is for people today. The book is infuriatingly and justifiably inconclusive; the characters are as confused as most of today's viewers are." Jones considers *North Wind* a sequel to *White Queen*. Published in 1995, it describes a race of hermaphroditic aliens called the Aleutians, who, in the words of a *Publishers Weekly* (December 18, 1995) review, "escape across lands ravaged by the Gender Wars—ongoing battles that pit Traditionalists (who believe in male superiority) against various Reformers. . . . Imbued with creative extrapolations on sex, politics, and immortality, this is sf at its ruminative best." Completing the trilogy begun with *White Queen* is *Phoenix Café* (1998), set on Earth in the 24th century, 300 years after an alien invasion that has permanently alterered human culture.

In assessing the future of the very future-oriented genre of science fiction, Gwyneth A. Jones rhetorically invoked two authors of the 19th century. "Did Balzac create sf? He was passionately interested in the cutting-edge of any kind of technology, and didn't mind wrecking his reader's concentration with pages and pages of technical-manual details. Did Dickens? His characters are caricatures, acting out minatory pantomimes of so-cial comment. I predict that in coming years, as a result of the 21st-century folklore effect—compounded by current literary theory—we will see a further blurring of the line between mainstream fiction and sf: to the extent that the fiction of the constructed world may even become as respectable as that other, always more favoured nonrealist genre, magical realism."
—E. M.

SUGGESTED READING: *Gwyneth Jones Gopher* (on-line); *Language and Society Paper*, "Deconstructing the Starships: Putting SF to Work," June 11, 1988; *Mirrorshades 94:19* Mar. 26, 1995; *Mirrorshades 94:24* Apr. 6, 1995; *Mirrorshades 94:36* Sept. 5, 1995; *New York Times Book Review* p36 Mar. 15, 1998; *Publishers Weekly* p44 Dec. 18, 1995

SELECTED BOOKS: Fiction—*Escape Plans*, 1986; *Divine Endurance*, 1987; *Kairos*, 1988; *White Queen*, 1992; *Identifying the Object: A Collection of Short Stories*, 1993; *Flowerdust*, 1995; *North Wind*, 1995; *Seven Tales and a Fable*, 1995; Young Adult and Juvenile—*Water in the Air*, 1977; *The Influence of Ironwood*, 1978; *The Exchange*, 1979; *Dear Hill*, 1980; As Ann Halam—*Ally Ally Aster*, 1981; *The Alder Tree*, 1982

Jones, Rodney

Feb. 11, 1950– Poet; professor

Considered by many to be among the foremost American poets of his generation, Rodney Jones has carved an impressive niche for himself during what is widely viewed as a less-than-stellar period in American verse. His work has gained attention for its vivid imagery, gritty language, and distinctive voice and as a result has won numerous awards, among them the 1989 National Book Critics Circle Award in poetry for *Transparent Gestures* (1989). Among his other collections are *The Story They Told Us of Light* (1980), *The Unborn* (1985), and most recently, *Elegy for the Southern Drawl* (1999). The chief subject in much of his poetry has been the culture of the American South.

Rodney Jones was born February 11, 1950, in Hartselle, Alabama, the son of E. L. Jones and Wilda (Owen) Jones. He grew up in a rural area, where his father was a farmer and factory worker. The environment in which he was raised was quite rustic and without many modern amenities, such as electricity. As in earlier times, a vital oral tradition flourished in his hometown, perhaps contributing to the love of the sounds of language that comes through in much of his poetry.

Gloria Jones/Courtesy of Houghton Mifflin

In the late 1960s, Jones enrolled in the University of Alabama, where he received his B.A. in 1971. He then pursued graduate studies at the University of North Carolina at Greensboro. In 1972 he married Virginia Kremza, while working toward his master's degree, which he received the following year.

Beginning in 1978, Jones was a writer-in-residence at Virginia Intermont College in Bristol, Virginia. He and Virginia Kremza divorced in 1979. The 1980s saw Jones emerge as a published poet. His first poetry anthology, *The Story They Told Us of Light*, was published in 1980 by the University of Alabama Press.

For the next several years Rodney Jones concentrated on his writing residency at Virginia Intermont College. He remarried, this time to artist Gloria Nixon de Zepeda, on June 21, 1981. His time at Intermont College concluded in 1984, and it wasn't until the following year that his second volume of poetry, *The Unborn* (1985), was published by Atlantic Monthly Press. The collection won him the Lavan Younger Poets Award from the Academy of American Poets in 1986.

Following *The Unborn*, Jones continued to publish a number of poems in journals and magazines. In 1986 the General Electric Foundation gave him their Young Writers Award for poetry that appeared in the journal *River Styx*.

The third poetry anthology published by Rodney Jones was *Transparent Gestures* (1989). It brought him greater acclaim than ever, garnering him the Jean Stein Prize from the American Academy and Institute of Arts and Letters, as well as the prestigious National Book Critics Circle Award in poetry for 1989. In their award citation, the Critics Circle declared Jones "a brand-new world-class poet." Amazon.com judged *Transparent Gestures* to be a work of great significance, warmly familiar yet at the same time refreshing and daring. "Not content with simply visual awareness," read the review, "Jones takes the reader to a place where intuition can flourish." *New York Times* (September 2, 1990) critic Stephen Dobyns praised the "robust energy" of the poems collected in *Transparent Gestures*, as well as the vital imagination.

The first volume of poetry Jones published in the 1990s was *Apocalyptic Narrative*, brought out by Houghton Mifflin in 1993. With Jones in his early 40s, the theme of the collection is coping with middle age. A review in Amazon.com described *Apocalyptic Narrative* as a work that "evokes the past and haunting memories while incisively portraying life in America today."

Rodney Jones's next poem anthology was *Things That Happen Once*, published in 1996. The collection contains more than 40 poems, among them "First Coca-Cola", which compares the first experience of drinking the aforementioned beverage with that of witnessing an execution, and "Beautiful Child," in which childhood attitudes toward parental affection are discussed. Jones's preoccupation with southern culture is uninterrupted, as are his fascinations with moral commitment and sexual desire. "His poetics are subtle," wrote Donna Seaman in a *Booklist* (May 15, 1996) review, "but his imagery, his stories, and his wry observations of the transcendent and the inexplicable reach your consciousness like lightning on a hot, dark night."

After the publication of *Things That Happen Once*, Rodney Jones continued to publish poetry in journals and magazines. His most recent published anthology is *Elegy for the Southern Drawl*, released by Houghton Mifflin in March of 1999. The majority of the poems in the collection focus on anecdotes from the lives of young southern white males, and many of them contain examples of the titular accent. A review from Amazon.com describes the book as "a bawdy, witty revelation by an award-winning poet who celebrates the soul of the South in jest and in elegy," and goes on to say that "[Jones's] poems burst with wit, robust experience, and earthy intelligence." Among the pieces in the collection is "Plea for Forgiveness", which takes as its subject the great American poet William Carlos Williams.

Rodney Jones has often been cited as one of America's leading poetic voices. Gerald Stern, winner of the 1998 National Book Award for Poetry, says on Amazon.com, "[Jones] is one of the two or, at most, three best poets of his generation. He is a true poet of his own culture. He is brilliant, wise, deeply sane, incredibly knowledgeable about the craft, tender, moving, honest, and pure. I love reading him. It gives me hope for poetry." The *New York Times* (September 2, 1990) described Jones as "a rowdy sort of poet who packs his language with noise."

As of the summer of 1999, Jones was a professor of creative writing and poetry at Southern Illinois University at Carbondale and a member of the Illinois Arts Council's advisory panel on literature. He is also a member of Associated Writing Programs and the Modern Language Association. He has been both a National Endowment for the Arts fellow and a Guggenheim fellow. He has two children, Alexis and Samuel.
—B.S.

SUGGESTED READING: Amazon.com (online); *Booklist* May 15, 1996; *New York Times* Sep. 2, 1990

SELECTED WORKS: *The Story They Told Us of Light*, 1980; *The Unborn*, 1985; *Transparent Gestures*, 1989; *Apocalyptic Narrative*, 1993; *Things That Happen Once*, 1996; *Elegy for the Southern Drawl*, 1999

Miriam Berkley

Kadohata, Cynthia

July 2, 1956– Novelist

The American novelist Cynthia Kadohata draws on her memories of growing up in a Japanese-American family to explore themes of coming-of-age, the search for intimacy, and rootedness in a diverse society. Although themes of ethnicity and cross-cultural interactions serve as backdrops for her works of fiction, which include the novels *The Floating World* (1989) and *In the Heart of the Valley of Love* (1992), she downplays more topical issues in her work, a strategy that has drawn criticism from other Asian-American writers who prefer a more radical stance concerning identity politics.

For *World Authors 1990–1995*, Kadohata, born on July 2, 1956, writes: "I was born in Chicago, but my earliest memories are of Georgia, where my family moved when I was two years old. My father sexed chickens—separated the male chicks from the female—for half a penny a chick. Previously my parents [Toshiro Kadohata and Jane Akiko Kaita] had owned a small grocery store, but the store lost money and my father decided to change professions when he saw a sexer driving a Cadillac. I don't know how that sexer could afford a Cadillac. My father, who worked as many as a hundred hours a week, owned the same red-and-white Oldsmobile for more than a dozen years. All I remember about Georgia is a set of twins named David and Daniel. Their father sexed chickens with my father, and died shortly after he turned 30. The hatchery my father worked for folded, and we moved to Arkansas—poultry country.

"In Arkansas my father continued to sex chickens. Often he worked all night, taking speed to stay awake as most of the sexers did. Sometimes at night my mother slept with my brother, my sister, and me in our backyard, where the magical constellations lit up the sky and light my memories still.

"My mother was a devout Christian, and every Sunday we attended a Presbyterian church where we were the only nonwhite members. I devoured the Sunday school storybooks, but I did not make any friends.

"The first time I ever saw my mother cry was when President Kennedy was shot. I was seven years old, and I did not enter the living room while my mother cried. Instead I peeked around the corner as the funeral procession marched across our television. I was to see my mother cry many times in the future.

"By now my mother had discovered books. My father says this discovery was the downfall of their marriage. Previously she was the prettiest of all the sexers' wives, and as shy and sweet as she was pretty. Now she renounced the church, and quoted Kierkegaard to her young children. She fought bitterly with her mother and with several people in the small local Japanese community. My father broke down doors and twisted her arms and sobbed as much as she did as their marriage dissolved. I think my father loved her and us children more than he has loved anyone before or since. His loneliness was intense. He lost his passion, except for drinking.

"When my parents divorced he stayed in Arkansas, to do the only work he knew, while my mother and siblings moved to Chicago. I loved Chicago and the Sixties! I loved Twiggy, the Beatles, the clothes. I loved Bobby Kennedy, and the night he died I slept on a concrete floor in our apartment and prayed and cried myself to sleep. Later I loved taking speed, and I loved secretly staying at the beach overnight with my friends.

"My mother worked full-time and went to school nights, taking the subway home and returning late to find us still awake. We were all three good students, and we were never punished, for anything.

"We moved to Los Angeles when I was sixteen, and the next year I dropped out of high school. My father says today that my dropping out was one of the darkest hours of his life. Previously I had been a straight-A student. But for some reason I could no longer understand what my teachers were talking about. I could not understand algebra, and I did not understand what 'theme' meant when applied to a novel. History was so boring I could not bear to open my book. I would sit for two hours at the table with my books in front of me, but I could not open them.

"Like my father I had lost my passion, and did not regain it for many years. When I was twenty-five and completely directionless, I took a Greyhound bus trip up the West Coast, and then down through the Southwest and South. On the bus I met people I never would have met otherwise, and fell in love with the landscape as I had fallen in love with the stars as a child. During my trip I met an old woman who said she was dying and taking her last journey away from her home in California. We traveled together for twenty hours. For some reason, I felt driven to bombard her with questions about her life, what it had been like, what or who had made her heart feel empty, and what had made it feel full. I wanted to know everything about her! Doctors had recently removed half her stomach in an operation; now she was taking the bus to where she'd been born in Texas. She wanted to visit a dying sister and also to clean off the grave of her first child, who'd died at the age of two. Almost everyone she'd loved had now passed away. She told me about all of these people and about how, in the 1930s, she had been displaced by drought and had moved to California to pick fruit. I told her she'd lived a fascinating life, and she was so surprised her head snapped back and hit the window. She said she'd lived a terrible life. She exuded generosity. When we parted in Amarillo, we hugged and she seemed to search her mind for words, but all she could come up with was 'Have a nice life!' I could not wish her the same, though I wanted to.

"It was during that bus trip, which lasted a month, that I felt as if I had rediscovered in the landscape the magic I'd known as a child. Though I'd never considered writing fiction before, the next year I decided to start. I sent one story out every month either to the *New Yorker* or to the *Atlantic Monthly*, and about forty-eight stories later the *New Yorker* took a story.

"I have been writing since."

Although Cynthia Kadohata can properly be described as a *sansei* (third-generation Japanese-American), she avoids such pigeonholing, telling one interviewer: "I get mad because they are always very dogmatic about it . . . Sometimes I want that identity, but not always . . . When I want to be an Asian writer, then I am one, but I don't like people saying you have to be an Asian writer, and if you do something different, then you're a banana or whatever. . . . To have to be a Japanese-American writer one day, a woman writer the next, etc. By being each of these things separately, rather than being all of them at once, you disempower yourself, which may be precisely the aim of the people who want you to be only one part of yourself at a time—rather than whole."

Still, the shared experience of the Japanese-American community was paramount in her growing up, and during the 1980s Kadohata emerged as one of a growing number of American writers who were coming to prominence through the new ways in which they were negotiating their Asian heritage in fiction and nonfiction. Asians in those years were becoming much more visible in American society due to new immigration patterns after 1965

and to the "mainstreaming" that the children and grandchildren of immigrant groups had undergone throughout American history. The work that catapulted her to prominence, *The Floating World*, is an episodic, semiautobiographical novel that drew heavily on the incidents she describes in the first-person sketch she contributed to *World Authors 1990–1995*. It won for its author the Mrs. Giles Whiting Foundation award for fiction and a National Endowment for the Arts grant. Its title is a reference to *ukiyo zoshi*, the central genre in 18th-century Japanese literature, translated as "stories of the floating world," a reference to the everyday and mundane as subject for literary scrutiny. The title may also express Kadohata's own experience during her 20s, when she moved frequently from place to place in search of her voice as a writer. She told interviewer Mickey Pearlman, for the book *Listen to Their Voices: Twenty Interviews with Women Who Write* (1993), how she decided on a career as a writer while living in Boston, then went to Pittsburgh for a writer's program but left it, disappointed, to enroll at Columbia University. "I went there and I still didn't feel I was getting better, faster," she stated, "so I said, 'Forget it. In the old days they used to say that a young writer has to live in New York to establish a career, but you don't have to anymore.' I had read that somewhere and I said, 'I'm leaving.'"

The Floating World is the story of how Olivia Osaka, its 12-year old narrator, "comes to belong in change, movement, and transition" as she comes of age in a community that has been shattered by the forcing of 110,000 Japanese-Americans into remote internment camps during World War II. But the novel is not a polemic, and many reviewers welcomed Kadohata's mellow voice and insight into character, especially of Olivia and her eccentric, cigar-smoking grandmother, Obasan, who gives Olivia this bit of ancestral wisdom: "Smile at them . . . *Hakujin* [white people] don't know when a smile is an insult." Diane O'Hehir wrote in *The New York Times Book Review* (July 23, 1989) that "*The Floating World* is about families, coming-of-age, guilt, memory and, especially . . . magic. Ultimately it is also about being Japanese-American in the United States of the 1950s, but this latter theme is so subtly presented that the readers tends to lose sight of it for long periods of time . . . Ms. Kadohata's narrative tone is straightforward and direct, and Olivia's personality emerges in similarly economical glimpses. Her aim and the book's seem to be one: to present the world affectionately and without embroidery. To notice what's there." Anne Paget agreed, writing in *School Library Journal* (January 1, 1990), "This story flows like a clear stream, revealing at every eddy unexpected depths and the startling beauty of examined lives. Those who seek exotica will not find it here. Instead, in the shifting light of truck-stops, small-town porches, and seedy Hollywood apartments, Kadohata depicts the struggles of three generations coming to terms with their history. Their search for grace illuminates our own pathways through the floating world."

Kadohata eventually settled in Los Angeles, where she feels the relaxed pace is more conducive to her writing than the frenetic energy of New York. "Southern California is a relief," she told an interviewer. "Maybe at some point I'll feel, My God, this is driving me crazy: Nobody reads books! But I haven't felt that yet." Los Angeles provided the setting for her second novel, *In the Heart of the Valley of Love*, in which Kadohata shifted gears from the nostalgic and apolitical style of *The Floating World* to a semisurreal, futuristic novel of love and racial conflict in the middle of the 21st century, a time in which "minorities" are the "majority" in Los Angeles and the rest of the country. Set in 2052, the novel describes how its central character, Rachel, age 17, seeks love and affirmation against the backdrop of a dystopia where the affluent live in "drichtowns" and the underclass fend for themselves in a nightmarish world of disorder. In *Listen to Their Voices*, Kadohata ex-

plained that her device of setting the novel in the future was chosen to afford readers a sense of fresh perspective. She is quoted as saying: "It's not like everybody has a particular idea, or everybody has the same idea, but everybody thinks about race and ethnicity, and if it's set in the future, maybe you won't look at in the same way."

—E. M.

SUGGESTED READING: *New York Times Book Review* p16 July 23, 1989; *Publishers Weekly* p48+ Aug. 3, 1992; *School Library Journal* p127 Jan. 1990; *Times Literary Supplement* p1447 Dec. 29, 1989; *Women's Review of Books* p5 Nov. 1989; Pearlman, M. *Listen to Their Voices: Twenty Interviews with Women Who Write*, 1993; Zhang, W. *Writers of Multicultural Fiction for Young Adults*, 1996; Zia, H. and S. Gall. *Notable Asian Americans*, 1995

SELECTED BOOKS: *The Floating World*, 1989; *In the Heart of the Valley of Love*, 1992

Keene, Donald

June 18, 1922– Nonfiction writer

By virtue of his voluminous and groundbreaking work as a translator, critic, historian, and teacher, Donald Keene is widely regarded as the Western world's foremost authority on Japanese literature. Although his reputation in the United States is confined primarily to the scholarly community, he is well known to the general public in Japan, where, in addition to his scholarly work, he has lectured widely and written regularly for a variety of popular journals, including the influential newspaper *Asahi Shimbun*. He was the first non-Japanese to win the prestigious Yomiuri Literary Prize, which he received in 1985 for *Hyakudai no Kakaku* (later published in English as *Travelers of a Hundred Ages*), a book on Japanese diarists based on a series of articles written for the *Asahi Shimbun*. He received the Grand Prize of Japanese Literature for the same book. The author of more than 30 books and scores of articles (he writes in Japanese as well as English, though he still prefers to compose in English), he has received a host of other honors, including the National Book Critics Circle Ivan Sandorf Award. Keene has been a central figure in the promotion of Japanese literature as an academic discipline in American universities. During his long tenure at Columbia University, from which he formally retired in 1992, he helped to train several generations of Japan specialists. Currently he is Shincho Professor of Japanese Literature and University Professor Emeritus at Columbia.

For *World Authors 1990-1995*, Donald Keene writes: "I was born in New York on June 18, 1922. My earliest memories are of the radio. Broadcasting had started only two years earlier, but had already spread to every middle-class home. My mother once told me that my first word was an imperfectly articulated sound which she interpreted as meaning 'music.' I hope she was right. Music has meant far more to me, throughout my life, than anyone would guess from reading my bibliography.

"I was educated in neighborhood schools. In recollection, they seem to have been extremely good. One experience (at the age of nine) gave my studies a focus not common to all pupils: my father, who travelled to Europe on business every year, took me with him one summer, and I realized from unsuccessful attempts to communicate with French and German children that it was important to learn foreign languages. Beginning in junior high school I studied French, always my favorite subject. I began studying Spanish in high school because my father expected to move the family to Spain in 1936, but the outbreak of the Spanish Civil War that year made this impossible. If that war had not broken out, my whole life would surely have followed a quite different course.

"I entered Columbia in 1938 on a Pulitzer Scholarship. Under the influence of a high school teacher I planned while at college to study four languages—Greek, Latin, French, and German—and if possible nothing else. Columbia was unusually liberal in its requirements, but there were some I could not avoid. This meant that my Latin and German suffered, but the required courses brought me in contact with great teachers who profoundly enriched my life, especially Mark van Doren, who communicated his love of literature. In his course, which I attended as a freshman, I sat next to a Chinese. We became friends, and it was because of this friendship that I eventually studied his language, at first with him as my teacher, later in class. The accident of seating in a classroom determined my future work.

"In my senior year I first began the study of Japanese, as a corollary to Chinese. When the war broke out three months later I volunteered for the Navy Japanese Language School and was accepted early in 1942. I had eleven months of intensive study of Japanese, and was then sent out to the Pacific to serve as a translator and interpreter. I was stationed in Hawaii, but took part in operations in the northern Pacific and on Okinawa. At the end of the war I was sent with the Marines to China.

"I was released from military duty early in 1946 with the rank of lieutenant. Most of my classmates at the language school had already decided on their future professions, but being one of the youngest, I had nothing special in mind and decided to stick with Japanese, though there were absolutely no jobs in that field at the time.

"I spent a year and a half as a graduate student at Columbia, where I had another teacher whose influence I cherish—Ryusaku Tsunoda. After a year at Harvard, in 1948 I received a fellowship to study at Cambridge University. I had planned to study Arabic and Persian, hoping to learn more about Asia, but I was discouraged, in view of the short time I was likely to remain in Cambridge. It was suggested that I teach Japanese instead, and that is how I found my first job.

"I remained in Cambridge for five years. My first three books were published in England, though interest in Japan was then minimal. I was inspired especially by Arthur Waley, the great translator of Chinese and Japanese literature, and hoped for a time to emulate him; but I found that Japanese literature alone was all I could handle.

"I expected to spend the rest of my life in Cambridge, but my plans changed as the result of obtaining a Ford Foundation fellowship in 1953 for study in Japan. The year flew by so quickly that I asked Cambridge permission to remain another year. This was refused; but just at this time I was offered a job at Columbia and assured I could remain an extra year in Japan. This settled matters. I left Cambridge with regret, but the second year in Japan was even more productive than the first. I met major Japanese writers, travelled widely, and began to publish in Japanese. I discovered that, although I had supposed I wanted nothing more than to be a typical Cambridge don, immersed in studies that might yield a brief but flawless article every ten years, I was more suited to writing for the general public.

"I returned to America in 1955, just in time for the Japan boom. After the remoteness from the public I had felt in England, it was exciting to be asked my opinion not only of Japanese books but of films and of Zen. The first printing of my *Anthology of Japanese Literature*, published in the autumn of 1955, sold out in two months, to the astonishment of the publishers, and has kept selling since. I followed this with the anthology *Modern Japanese Literature*, and then with translations of works by Mishima Yukio and Dazai Osamu.

"I wept when I left Japan in 1955, thinking I would never have enough money to return; but in fact, I have managed to get back every single year. This has been useful to my study of Japanese literature, and it has also enabled me to have a second life in Japan, as a critic. The alternation between the quiet life of a professor in New York and the life of a more-or-less public figure in Tokyo has given me much pleasure.

"Of my translations, my favorite is *Essays in Idleness*, by the fourteenth-century monk Kenko. Probably my most important achievement has been the writing of a four-volume history of Japanese literature. The volumes are known by separate titles: *Seeds in the Heart*, *World Within Walls*, and the two volumes of *Dawn to the West*."

After earning an M.A. from Cambridge University in 1949, Keene received his doctorate from Columbia University in 1951. His first book, *The Battles of Coxinga*, a scholarly analysis of a puppet play by the Japanese dramatist Chikamatsu, was published that same year. But many of Keene's subsequent works are designed to elucidate Japanese literature to the non-specialist Western reader. His early book *Anthology of Japanese Literature*, which he prepared during his first extended sojourn in Japan, from 1953 to 1955, contains translations (many of them by Keene himself) of works ranging from the eighth to the 19th century. *Library Journal* (November 1, 1955) reviewer Joseph Bram deemed it "a wonderful book," and a *New Yorker* (October 29, 1955) critic noted, "This . . . is the first comprehensive collection of the riches of Japanese writing ever offered in English, and it would be difficult to conceive of a more satisfactory one." Keene's brief book *Japanese Literature: An Introduction for Western Readers* was praised by a *Manchester Guardian* (April 28, 1953) reviewer as "a remarkable feat of virtuosity." In another of his early works, *Living Japan*, Keene turned to an examination of Japanese mores, attitudes, and everyday life. Reviewing the book in the *New Statesman* (June 4, 1960), G. S. Fraser compared it favorably with Basil Hall Chamberlain's 19th-century classic *Things Japanese*, and noted, "This is a beautifully produced book, and an invaluable aid to understanding a very ancient and very modern civilisation."

In 1964 Keene decided to write a comprehensive history of Japanese literature, a project that would occupy him for more than 25 years. At the time, there was only one such history in English, published in 1899 by W. G. Aston. One reason for his undertaking, then, was simply to revise Aston's material, and to correct what he considered to be

Aston's parochial literary judgments. More importantly, Keene hoped to offer readers some explanation of what it was about Japanese literature that moved him so deeply. He did not, however, anticipate that the entire project would take so long to complete. Thus, as Keene recounted in his autobiography, he was somewhat disheartened by critics' reactions—"lukewarm or worse"—to his first volume, *World Within Walls: Japanese Literature of the Pre-Modern Era, 1600-1867*, on which he worked for nearly 10 years.

However, the next installment of his history, the two-volume study *Dawn to the West: Japanese Literature in the Modern Era*, was greeted with widespread critical acclaim. *Dawn to the West* begins its account of Japanese literature in 1868, the first year of the Meiji Restoration, the period when feudalism in Japan was abolished and the country underwent enormous social and political changes, many of them effected by increased contact with Western cultures. According to Keene, the Meiji era sparked a literary renaissance in Japan, as Japanese writers in ever greater numbers were influenced by Western literature. The modern novel in Japan, he noted, began when Japanese writers "discovered" two hitherto unknown phenomena, romantic love and the individual. Hence, many Japanese novels of the late 19th century are either amorous adventures or examples of the so-called "I novel," in which the author explores his own mental attitudes or his various personal shortcomings. The first volume of *Dawn to the West* covers fiction writers, while the second is devoted to poets, dramatists, and critics.

Jay Rubin, writing in the *New York Times Book Review* (May 13, 1984), hailed the publication of *Dawn to the West* as an important event for modern Japanese literature, one which, he thought, would help "to establish [it] as one of the major literatures of the world." Praising the books' essays as "readable, yet thoroughly scholarly," Rubin noted, "These two volumes alone could stand as a respectable life's work for any scholar, but they make up only the second half of Mr. Keene's projected four-part history." *New Republic* (June 25, 1984) reviewer Donald Richie noted that, like most Japanese critics, Keene had a penchant for writing descriptive, nontheoretical literary history. Keene's approach to literary criticism, he observed, is "very Japanese" in that his work is "not at all opinionated" and eschews anything "maverick or heterodox." Although he detected certain "limitations" in this brand of purely descriptive literary criticism, Richie acknowledged that Keene's literary history "will long remain the authoritative account," and called his multivolume work "an impressive gathering of information, fully and impartially described."

Perhaps the harshest criticism of Keene's *Dawn to the West* came from Masao Miyoshi, a Japanese-born critic living in the United States. Writing in the *Washington Post Book World* (May 6, 1984), Miyoshi noted that Keene had "probably . . . read more Japanese authors and works than anybody else in world," and that the "basic facts" contained in his book "are simply staggering." Nonetheless, he saw the books' problems as stemming precisely from Keene's "author-oriented" approach and his tendency to be encyclopedic, which, he noted, "weakens any potential for interpretation." Moreover, Miyoshi felt that the title *Dawn to the West* was ambiguous and perhaps misleading, and that Keene's method of literary evaluation, although ostensibly objective, was steeped in assumptions that take "the Western model to be normative and universal." "The immense distention of *Dawn to the West*," Miyoshi concluded, "cannot ultimately compensate for the fragility at its core." *New York Times* (May 5, 1984) book critic Anatole Broyard, although he recognized the magnitude of the author's achievement, found the volumes "relentlessly specific," and noted, "In self-defense, the reader wishes that Mr. Keene were fonder of generalizations, or pauses for perspective, or breath."

The final volume of Keene's comprehensive history of Japanese literature, *Seeds in the Heart: Japanese Literature from Earliest Times to the Late Sixteenth Century*, appeared the year after his retirement from Columbia. Keene has remained active and prolific into the 1990s. In his warmly received autobiography, *On Familiar Terms: A Journey Across Cultures* (1994), Keene concentrated on his wartime activities, his life in Japan, and his friendships with Kobo Abe, Yukio Mishima, and other Japanese literary luminaries. *New York Times* (February 21, 1994) book reviewer Christopher Lehmann-Haupt praised the book for its wit and self-effacing charm, but wondered why Keene had not been more forthcoming about the reasons for his attraction to Japanese literature and culture. "What's important," Lehmann-Hallpt concluded, "is how much of Japan he has explained to America in the course of his career, and how much of America to Japan."

—Charles Wagner

SUGGESTED READING: *Library Journal* p2517 Nov. 1, 1955; *Manchester Guardian* p2 Apr. 28, 1953; *New Republic* p28+ June 25, 1984; *New York Times* p18 May 5, 1984, p22 Feb. 21, 1994; *New York Times Book Review* p11+ May 13, 1984; *New Statesman* p834 June 4, 1960; *New Yorker* p164 Oct. 29, 1955; *Washington Post Book World* p10+ May 6, 1984; *Contemporary Literary Criticism* vol. 34, 1985

SELECTED BOOKS IN ENGLISH: *Japanese Literature: An Introduction for Western Readers*, 1953; *Living Japan*, 1960; *Dawn to the West* (two volumes), 1984; *Seeds in the Heart: Japanese Literature from Earliest Times to the Late Sixteenth Century*, 1993; *On Familiar Terms: A Journey Across Cultures*, 1994; As editor— *Anthology of Japanese Literature*, 1955

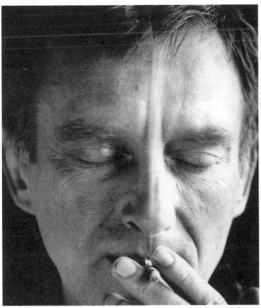

Murdo MacLeod/Courtesy of James Kelman

Kelman, James

1946– Novelist; short-story writer; essayist

The Scottish novelist, short-story writer, and playwright James Kelman has couched his work mainly in interior monologues spoken by the dregs of society, somewhat in the style of Samuel Beckett. His characters are so alienated that their making any human contact at all can be seen as a miracle; their persistence in merely living, where no life would seem to flourish, is their heroism. Kelman's first books were collections of short stories, the form at which most critics believe he excels. *An Old Pub Near the Angel* (1973), *Three Scottish Writers* (with Tom Leonard and A. Hamilton, 1975), *Short Tales from the Nightshift* (1978), and *Not Not While the Giro* (1983) were followed by the novels *The Busconductor Hines* (1984), *A Chancer* (1985), and *A Disaffection* (1989). He then produced the short-story collections *Lean Tales* (with Agnes Owens and Alasdair Gray, 1985) and *Greyhound for Breakfast* (1987); the plays *Hardie and Baird and Other Plays* (1991); another short-story collection, *The Burn* (1991); and a collection of essays, *Some Recent Attacks* (1992), before his novel *How Late It Was, How Late* (1994), the story of how a suddenly blind tatterdemalion makes his way home, won the Booker Prize. *Busted Scotch* (1997) is an anthology of various Kelman stories from his previous books, which drew the comment from Richard Burgin in the *New York Times Book Review* (May 18, 1997) that only the "unexpected feeling of connection with others introduces an element of hope . . . and helps to balance . . . the bitterness of . . . Kelman's brilliant fictive universe." Kelman's story collection *The Good Times* appeared in 1999.

For *World Authors 1990–1995*, James Kelman, born in 1946, writes: "I left school at the age of 15 and worked at a variety of labouring and semi-skilled jobs (these included bus conducting and stocking shelves in shops), emigrated to the U.S.A. with my family, and returned to Scotland with them in 1964 (one of my five brothers has remained there and lives in Long Island).

"When I was living in London in 1968–9 I wrote my first short stories; through the agency of the American writer Mary Gray Hughes, a small collection of them was published by Puckerbrush Press (Orono, Maine, 1973). . . . Some of my work has been translated. . . . But I accept that translation is difficult. I use the English language from my own cultural base, which is rooted in Glasgow . . . and as such subject to a great variety of linguistic influences."

James Kelman was born in Glasgow, the son of a frame-maker and picture restorer. Kelman was a voracious reader and eventually enrolled at the University of Strathclyde as a student of philosophy. But the niceties of this subject seemed irrelevant to him after the first two years, and during the third he quit. His voice began to be heeded in Scotland when he published the story collection *Not Not While the Giro;* but it was the novel *The Busconductor Hines*, based on his own experiences as a bus conductor, that first drew serious attention. Almost all of Kelman's stories and novels have the same sorts of characters and settings, described by Michiko Kakutani of the *New York Times* (January 16, 1988) in her review of *Greyhound for Breakfast*. The stories, according to Kakutani, "delineate lives circumscribed by poverty, class, and lowered expectations. It's a world of pubs and betting shops, rented rooms and small furnished flats, a world where people pass the time playing poker, making bets, and lingering over beers. Many of the characters appear to be out of work, and nearly all are perpetually 'skint' and forced to cadge cigarettes and free drinks. . . . Meals, for the most part, consist of eggs and chips; cold tinned meat and instant coffee or tea."

In his first published book, *An Old Pub Near the Angel* (1973), Kelman often used a dialect, characterized by Denis Donoghue in the *New York Times Book Review* (June 8, 1995)—and indeed by Kelman himself—as "demotic Glaswegian." He continued to employ this form of Scottish speech, in his later works, in which it became increasingly more comprehensible. In the story "Nice to Be Nice," from *An Old Pub*, a character referred to as "auld Erchie" hangs about (or "hings aboot") a certain spot in a pub when he's "skint" (broke), waiting for someone to ask him to get a drink from the bar so that he can cadge one for himself. The narrator says of another character, "A mean he disny let me doon, he's eywis goat it merr ir less whin he says ho wid bit—nice tae be nice—know what A mean? See A gave him a sperr key whin we wir daen up the kitchen in let him hang oan tae it efterwirds kis sometimes he's nae wherr tae sleep in A let him kip wi me." This translates as, "I mean he does not let me down, he's always got it more or less when he says he would—nice to be nice—know what I mean? See, I gave him a spare key when we were doing up the kitchen and let him hang on to it afterwards because sometimes he has nowhere to sleep and I let him sleep with me." All Kelman's people tend to survive in that cadging way, and it is the fact that some think it is "nice to be nice" that enables that survival, since Kelman's stated belief, according to Donoghue, is that "Nothing was ever given freely by the ruling class." The sponging and cadging are done without loss of pride, so that when someone gives to someone else, a tiny ray of common humanity breaks through the pall of loneliness that hangs over all Kelman's characters.

Kelman was one of three distinctively Scottish authors who contributed to *Lean Tales*. Reviewing the volume, D. W. Nichol noted in *Books in Canada* (October 1985) that Kelman "sings of the lowlifer passively witnessing his body's decay, the punter who loses his pay packet on the first wager, the rogue who scores a knapsack in the British Museum loo." Campbell found Kelman's sense of place predominant and thought he "conveys to the reader, as no other writer does, the feeling of Glasgow, the smell and sight and sound of pubs and betting shops, working-men's cafes, the texture of the streets."

Another characteristic feature of Kelman's writing, one sometimes severely criticized, sometimes praised, is his frequent use of scatological or obscene language. Michiko Kakutani noted that *Greyhound for Breakfast* was "liberally spiced with four-letter words (one of which is used in various forms, as an all-purpose verb, noun, adjective, and adverb throughout this volume)." Kakutani observed that most of Kelman's characters are in a downward spiral, like the man in the title story who buys a greyhound and thinks he can make some money racing it, only to realize that the dog is "a pathetic distraction from his own more intractable problems." Very little happens in most of the stories, apart from the rare intrusion of a bit of violence, which might be considered a justification for the paranoia that the characters exhibit. Kakutani found these tales and fragments of tales constricting: "Kelman's stories give us a picture of Glasgow as a city that suffocates dreams, snuffs out ambition. To live there is to resign oneself to 'the stench of poverty, violence, decay, death'. . . . By the time most readers have finished this volume they will never want to hear about another person bumming a cigarette, placing a bet, or drinking a beer. They will feel nearly as suffocated as . . . Kelman's characters do," Kakutani concluded.

Arnold Weinstein, reviewing *Greyhound for Breakfast* in the *New York Times Book Review* (March 20, 1988), disagreed. He found that although "Kelman's tenements and boarding houses are prison camps" and "their derelict inmates are losers of the battle for existence," like the man in "The Guy with the Crutch," who loses his prosthetic leg and has to use a broken crutch, Kelman's "prose poems echo like lost tragifarcical chords." Weinstein observed that "Kelman's . . . obscenities are defanged by obsessive frequency; the poverty of vocabulary is an economic analogy. His imagery may seem equally impoverished, featuring so many cigarettes . . . but cigarettes here stand for smoldering." He concluded, "Kelman's originality assimilates all into his own hilarious genius for detail, his casual social subtext, his unique refreshing burr that echoes the shivering slums, his and ours."

Kelman's 1989 novel, *A Disaffection*, was shortlisted for the Booker Prize. The hero, Patrick Doyle, is a teacher in Glasgow who regards the institution where he teaches as "the instrument of a repressive state." He pursues Alison—another teacher—romantically, but he has trouble connecting with her in a meaningful way. Karl Miller in the *London Review of Books* (February 24, 1989) noted that "*A Disaffection* is a problematical book," because of "the avoidance of developed perspectives on Doyle from those who surround him, those with whom he has his tender and abrasive dealings, with whom he airs his invectives and bitter ironies, with whom he conducts his antagonisms and ingratiations." He nevertheless found the "funny and depressing" volume "pretty terrific." Most reviewers agreed with Edward St. John in *Library Journal* (April 15, 1989) that "Kelman's linguistic virtuosity . . . can make the most depressing statements sound hilariously funny." Many concurred with Miller's view that *A Disaffection*, whether or not it is autobiographical, "is the portrait of an artist." Kelman was awarded the James Tait Black Memorial Prize in 1989 for the novel.

By the time *The Burn* (1991), Kelman's collection of 26 stories, was published, Jenny Turner was able to write in the *London Review of Books* (June 27, 1991) that while Kelman's "novels of course are great," it is "in the shorter form . . . he's most free, most at home." She felt that reading *The Burn* "is like studying philosophy, or like looking at paintings or like listening to music." Guy Mannes-Abbott agreed, noting in the *New Statesman & Society* (May 10, 1991) that the "short story is the perfect vehicle for Kelman's relentlessly bald prose and street-level screams." Mannes-Abbott noted that Kelman had hardened his tone with regard to the political situation "in response to the collapse of welfare provision." Angela McRobbie in the London *Times Literary Supplement* (April 26, 1991) observed that the "realist label is a misunderstanding of Kelman's work, which takes aspects of working-class life as its raw material but which quickly moves inwards to explore a kind of psychic pain and paralysis." She saw in these stories of Glasgow men a "stranded and strangulated masculinity," which she judged to be Kelman's real theme. His characters represent to McRobbie "the writer's collective alter ego." She concluded, "The triumph of the writing . . . is the way it simultaneously reflects and transcends their paralysis of will."

Sammy Samuels, the protagonist through whose consciousness *How Late It Was, How Late* (1994) is filtered, is another small-time crook who becomes a victim. He wakes after a drunken binge, gets beaten up by a group of soldiers, is arrested and brutalized by the police, and is finally thrown out on the street, blinded from the beatings, to make his way home. There he discovers that Helen, with whom he lives, has disappeared. He is arrested again and questioned about the activities of his friend, who is believed to be a political terrorist. Helen may have been harmed, for which the police will implicate him. When Sammy discovers that she is gone, he considers "parking the head in a gas oven." He decides, however, that there "wasnay much he could do, there wasnay really much he could do at all. No the now anyway." His motto is, "So, okay, batter on, just batter on." In a life like Sammy's, merely continuing to live is heroism.

Richard Bausch, praising the novel in the *New York Times Book Review* (February 5, 1995), considered that "Kelman's down-but-not-out pub-crawler charms us into rooting for him." Bausch observed that "while Sammy is a shoplifter, ex-con, chronic drinker, and ne'er-do-well, he happens also in his strange, almost surreal predicament to demonstrate most of the cardinal virtues. He's unfailingly industrious; he's loyal, self-reliant, oddly optimistic, courageous, generous, and dauntless. He accepts the blame for his mistakes; he refuses to whine or complain and he tries in every instance, even when he's being grossly mistreated, to give the benefit of the doubt."

Other critics, including the majority of Booker Prize judges, had agreed with Bausch, who remarked, "*How Late It Was, How Late* deserves every accolade it gets." The awarding of the Booker Prize to *How Late It Was*, however, aroused a great deal of controversy. Two of the five judges dissented, and one, Rabbi Julia Neuberger, "declared that the book was unreadably bad" and called honoring it a "disgrace," according to Sarah Lyall, writing in the *New York Times* (November 29, 1994). Lyall noted, however, that Janette Turner Hospital "called . . . Kelman a 'poet and magician' and said the book was a 'passionate, scintillating, brilliant song of a book.'" Many reviewers found Sammy's actions as chivalrous as those of a medieval knight. Benedict Pinckney, writing in the *Washington Post* (January 24, 1995) found "something antique about Sammy, something almost quaint, as though he had stepped from the limits of an ancient, tattered tapestry somewhere. . . . He possesses a kind of chivalry, a sense of simple honor that will not allow him to inform on friends who happily betray him to the police, that will not even allow him to file suit against the authorities when he goes blind after a brutal 'doing' while in police custody."

For Brian Morton in the *New Statesman & Society* (March 18, 1994), Sammy's loss of sight is a metaphor for "social invisibility, the gaps in the netting through which people fall, the jeopardies of casual self-definition." He considered Kelman successful in *How Late It Was* in championing "the dispossessed and the overlooked with unsentimental urgency." Andrew O'Hagan, writing in the *London Review of Books* (May 26, 1994), deemed Kelman's ability to slip in "perceptions and psychological tics" to be "astonishing": "It's the way people talk to themselves that he gets so brilliantly, so matchlessly," O'Hagan concluded. He observed that Kelman's "central characters have always had a wonderful way with words, with parts of words and myriad inflections of the same word, as they form themselves inside their own heads." Denis Donoghue, reviewing *How Late It Was* in the *New York Review of Books* (June 8, 1995), referred to Kelman's belief in his own independence from literary tradition and influence, although most critics, when discussing Kelman, do not fail to mention the name of Beckett. Donoghue wrote of Kelman that "for his purposes, it appears, literature might as well have been invented yesterday. When he started writing, he reports, 'there were no literary models I could look to from my own culture.' . . . He refers to the 'things I knew about: snooker halls and betting shops and pubs and DHSS offices and waiting in the queue at the council Housing office.' These or similar experiences turn up in *How Late It Was, How Late*, *A Disaffection*, and the short stories in Kelman's *An Old Pub Near the Angel* and *Greyhound for Breakfast*." Donoghue called Kelman's books, like those of other contemporary Scottish writers, his contemporaries and friends, "fictions of hard times in Glasgow."

Winning the Booker Prize, worth about $31,500 when Kelman received it and worth much more in increased book sales, enabled Kelman to move from an apartment to a house, to buy a new computer, and to have his spouse, a social worker among the homeless, work fewer hours. Kelman also felt, according to Sarah Lyall, that his winning the prize was a victory that encompassed all those from impoverished and discriminated-against communities. Another result of being a Booker Prize winner was that Kelman was able to publish, in 1997, a volume of selected stories that had appeared before but would now receive greater attention. Terming the stories in *Busted Scotch* "fiercely beautiful," Richard Burgin in the *New York Times Book Review* (May 18, 1997) observed that Kelman "has fashioned a vision of the world so tormented and despairing" that he has had to turn to "exquisitely precise . . . language and a humor that is by turns dry, fanciful, slapstick, and savage" and to develop "the masterly internal monologues of his characters" in order to make his work "not only palatable but entertaining." Barbara Love in *Library Journal* (May 1, 1997) declared that Kelman's characters, who "live in squats, caravans, and tenements, on the dole and on the edge," would be "working-class if they worked, but they're lay-abouts and idlers who prefer to sponge off their mates and neighbors." She concluded that readers "may not wish to know these characters well but will be grateful for the opportunity of this brief meeting."

Kelman's 1999 story collection, *The Good Times*, comprises 20 tales written in first-person. In contrast to most of his earlier work, some of the stories in *The Good Times* are told by middle-class characters. Kelman's "language sings as before," a reviewer for *Booklist* (June 1, 1999) wrote. ". . . . The stories are rich with layered meanings." "Bleak, almost surreal stuff, sure enough," observed a *Kirkus Reviews* writer, "but every fragmented encounter or stark monologue here contains a nugget of hard-earned, bitter truth."

Kelman explained to Lyall, defending himself against charges that his stories were "just oral tradition" and "debased," that when criticized thus, writers "have to be much more precise and bloody pedantic. You have to revise and revise and proof at every bloody stage to insure that everything's spot on, especially because you're working in what other people regard as inconsistent ways, so you have to be really sure." Above all, he concluded, "You have to trust the fact that you're a writer."

—S. Y.

SUGGESTED READING: *Books in Canada* p35 Oct. 1985; *Library Journal* p99 Apr. 15, 1989, p142 May 1, 1997; *London Review of Books* p191 Feb. 24, 1989, p20 June 27, 1991, p8 May 26, 1994; *New Statesman & Society* p39 May 10, 1991, p56 Mar. 18, 1994; *New York Review of Books* p45+ June 8, 1995; *New York Times* p16 Jan. 16, 1988, C p15 Nov. 29, 1994; *New York Times Book Review* p19 Mar. 20, 1988, p8 Feb. 5, 1995; (London) *Times Literary Supplement* p529 May 10, 1985, p191 Feb, 24, 1989, p18 Apr. 26, 1991; *Washington Post* E p1 Jan. 24, 1995

SELECTED BOOKS: Fiction—*An Old Pub Near the Angel*, 1973; *Three Scottish Writers* (with T. Leonard and A. Hamilton), 1975; *Short Tales from the Nightshift*, 1978; *Not Not While the Giro*, 1983; *The Busconductor Hines*, 1984; *A Chancer*, 1985; *Lean Tales* (with A. Owens and A. Gray), 1985; *Greyhound for Breakfast* (1987); *A Disaffection*, 1989; *The Burn*, 1991; *How Late It Was, How Late*, 1994; *Busted Scotch*, 1997; *The Good Times*, 1999; Drama—*Hardie and Baird and Other Plays*, 1991

Kenan, Randall

Mar. 12, 1963– Novelist; short-story writer; biographer

American author Randall Kenan has created his own world in Tims Creek, a mystical town in the swamps of North Carolina, founded by slaves who escaped their captivity. Kenan's various narrators describe their "real" lives and their folklore with equal force. Like William Faulkner, Kenan has mastered the ability to write from a tangle of perspectives and is able to move seamlessly between the present and the past, providing a strong sense of the town's history. The author's first novel, *A Visitation of Spirits* (1989), introduced readers to Tims Creek by following Horace Thomas Cross through one long night in 1984, during which he reflects on his life, his family's history, and the history of the town. Using varied points of view, Kenan further explored life in Tims Creek in *Let the Dead Bury Their Dead and Other Stories* (1992), an ambitious collection of stories about time, reality, imagination, and gender. In 1994 Kenan produced a biography, for children, of the author James Baldwin, and in 1999 he published a survey of African-American life in the 1990s, *Walking on Water: Black American Lives at the Turn of the Twenty-First Century*.

Randall Kenan was born on March 12, 1963, in Brooklyn, New York, but grew up in Chinquapin, North Carolina. His writing style reflects the rural

Miram Berkley

environment in which he was reared, one in which several generations sat around kitchen tables or on porches recalling events long past or stories that had been given mystical attributes as they were passed down. As the author told *New York* (August 14, 1989), "In the South, you're hit over the head with the oral tradition. And I was raised by a bunch of people in their sixties and seventies. They're a *very* loquacious lot. They can't move around, so they talk." In addition to the oral tradition, Kenan watched television and read comic books.

At age 17, Kenan left Chinquapin to attend the University of North Carolina at Chapel Hill. He went to the university under the impression that he would major in physics and someday own his own robotics company, but he became sidetracked by an interest in science fiction. By the winter of his sophomore year, he was writing constantly. In 1985 he received a degree in English and subsequently traveled to New York to find a job in publishing. While writing in his spare time, he took an entry-level position at Random House. By 1989 he was an assistant editor at Alfred A. Knopf.

That same year he published his first novel, *A Visitation of Spirits* (1989). The book follows Thomas Cross one night in 1984 as he is taken on a journey into the past by demons—whether real or imagined is never clear—and is confronted by the guilt and disgust he feels at his own homosexuality. The narration often shifts away from Thomas to his older cousin, who takes an aunt and uncle to visit a terminally ill relation. During this trip, the trio enlightens the reader on Thomas's and the town's history. The skillful narrative impressed reviewers. "Truth is," George Garrett wrote for *Chicago Tribune Books* (August 13, 1989) as cited in *Contemporary Authors*, "Kenan tries pretty much of everything and pretty much gets away with all of it, too."

As the novel won acclaim in literary circles, offers and awards began pouring in for the young author. At age 26 he was given a grant by the New York Foundation of the Arts; a year later he received a MacDowell Colony Fellowship. In 1989 he left his job at Knopf and began lecturing in creative writing at Sarah Lawrence College in Bronxville, New York, and at Vassar College in Poughkeepsie, New York. In 1990 Kenan began lecturing at Columbia University.

In 1992 Kenan published his next work of fiction, *Let the Dead Bury Their Dead and Other Stories*. The tales in this volume mix fact with fable as they track the residents of Tims Creek through the past and present. Many of the stories, such as "Run, Mourner, Run," feature Percy Terrell, a white businessman who enjoys ruining people's lives. Kenan also focused on female characters who lead troubled lives—such as Lena, the widowed nurse of "What Are the Days?," who regains her love of life through her encounter with a young man. Another story, entitled "This Far; or, a Body in Motion," looks at a historical figure—Booker T. Washington—who travels to Tims Creek in 1915 to visit a set of twins with whom he once studied. In the title novella, Horace Cross (the main character in *A Visitation of Spirits*) discovers that his family name is the same as that of the plantation owner whose slaves had run away to found Tims Creek in around 1854.

Howard Frank Mosher wrote in the *New York Times Book Review* (June 14, 1992) that "Randall Kenan's second work of fiction is nothing short of a wonder-book: one of those striking literary anomalies . . . that are nearly as difficult to classify as they are enjoyable to read and re-read." The *Nation* (July 6, 1992) reviewer noted that the author "explores the territories between the living and the dead, between the fantastic and the mundane in an energetic, inventive prose that never descends to contrivance or sentimentality. These sensual, humorous, eventful stories mark Randall Kenan as a writer of startling, imaginative compassion." A rare criticism came from Jean Hanff Korelitz of the *Washington Post Book World* (August 2, 1992), who suggested that the book "might well have been a stronger collection without two or three of its weakest stories." Regardless of such quibbles, the work was nominated for the National Book Critics Circle Award in 1993; a year later it won the $30,000 Whiting Award, given annually to writers of exceptional skill.

For his next project Kenan was hired to write a biography of James Baldwin, for students between 14 and 19 years of age. Chelsea House Publishers commissioned the book as the first installment in its Lives of Notable Gay Men and Lesbians series. Kenan's *James Baldwin* was published in 1994 to generally favorable reviews, though many in the educational community were up in arms at the idea of putting Baldwin's sexual orientation alongside his literary achievements in a book for children. However, a reviewer for *School Library Journal* (June 1994) found that "while the series title might suggest an exclusive focus on his sexual identity, this biography simply adds that perspective to the existing mosaic of his life with a candor that reflects Baldwin's own self-presentation. Previous studies written for young people make no mention of his sexual orientation. Kenan's book acts as a corrective . . . It introduces young people to this eloquent witness to an individual and collective American minority experience." Sally Echhoff of the *Voice Literary Supplement* (May 20, 1994) compared the work with David Leeming's biography of Baldwin and noted: "No less reverent and perhaps more touching is Randall Kenan's *James Baldwin*. . . . Unfortunately, what's missing from both is the sound—the actual pitch and timbre—of Baldwin's evangelical voice."

Kenan's most recent work is a sampler of more than 200 interviews he conducted with people of African ancestry living in North America. *Walking on Water: Black American Lives at the turn of the Twenty-First Century* (1999), is, according to *Kirkus Reviews* (February 1, 1999), the author's "personal history of the last five years." It also contains discussions of writing and the author's other reflections and observations. "For the most part [Kenan's personal musings merit reading and reflection. . . . Definitely worth reading," said a critic for *Kirkus Reviews*. Amazon.com (July 9,

1999) describes the book as "delicious and diverse."

—C.M.

SUGGESTED READING: Amazon.com (on-line) July 9, 1999; *Booklist* p1248 Mar. 1, 1994; *Chicago Tribune* IV p6 May 3, 1992; irkus Reviews Feb. 1, 1999; *Nation* p28 July 6, 1992; *New York* p24 Aug. 14, 1989; *New York Times* C p18 Jan. 19, 1993, C p13 Mar. 1, 1993, C p26 Oct. 28, 1994; *New York Times Book Review* p12 June 14, 1992; *School Library Journal* p155 June 1994; *Voice Literary Supplement* p20 May 20, 1994; *Washington Post* D p1 Oct. 27, 1995; *Washington Post Book World* p1 Aug. 2, 1992; *Contemporary Authors*, vol. 142, 1994

SELECTED WORKS: Fiction—*A Visitation of Spirits*, 1989; *Let the Dead Bury Their Dead and Other Stories*, 1992; *Walking on Water: Black American Lives at the Turn of the Twenty-First Century*, 1999; Nonfiction—*James Baldwin*, 1994

Miriam Berkley

Kerr, Philip

1956– Novelist; nonfiction writer

Named one of the "20 Best British Novelists" by the literary journal *Granta* (1993), Scottish author Philip Kerr is probably best known for his numerous cerebral thrillers—*Dead Meat* (1994) and *The Grid* (1995) among them—which have frequently been likened to those of American author Michael Crichton. A writer with a penchant for creating intricate plots, Kerr notes that the fact that none of his novels are character-driven is more than just coincidence. "I can't get really excited about 'the form of the novel' stories," he told Michele Field for a *Publishers Weekly* (April 8, 1996) interview. "I like stories." Often, the stories Kerr creates are filled with very dark elements. Episodes of graphic violence and an overall feeling of pessimism abound in many of his novels. Kerr, who has described himself as "a very morbid person," attributes this fact to his nationality. "We Scots are a gloomy lot," he told the *Publishers Weekly* interviewer Michele Field. "Scots are distrustful of the future, they are very cynical, very hard-headed."

Philip Kerr was born in Edinburgh, Scotland, in 1956. The details of his life from that point until 1989, when he published his first book, are scant. It is known that throughout his childhood and adolescence, Kerr's family, particularly his father, was very vocal in its desire for Kerr to study law. Writing aspirations of any kind were never encouraged. "I think the only thing that encouraged me was a sense—well, not even 'a sense of my own worth' but that very Scottish thing, the 'chippy' thing, the Scottish-Protestant work ethic, which gives you a sense that you want to prove something, maybe just to yourself," Kerr said to Michele Field. "I think it is the thing that matters most in your life—the thing you have to prove to yourself." According to Field, Kerr is "a lawyer by qualifications" and worked for seven years as a copywriter at a London advertising firm where the author Salman Rushdie was once employed. "I spent my lunchtimes—throughout my entire 30s—living a double life," Kerr told Field. "I was saying to someone yesterday that the Dr. Jekyll and Mr. Hyde duality is really about a writer: after the proper job in the day, at night you roam free in the world of your own making."

Kerr began his writing career with *March Violets*. A dark crime novel, *March Violets* introduced the public to the character Bernie Gunther, a German private investigator living in Nazi-era Berlin. During the next two years Kerr published two more Bernie Gunther novels: *The Pale Criminal* (1990) and *A German Requiem* (1991). In the United States, all three novels were published in one volume, *Berlin Noir* (1993).

During the same year that Kerr wrote the third Bernie Gunther novel, he also edited *The Penguin Book of Lies* (1991), a nonfiction book about lies and liars throughout history. Two years later he published his fourth novel, *A Philosophical Investigation* (1993). Set early in 21st-century London, the book was described by Scott Veale in the *New York Times Book Review* (June 13, 1993) as "part techno-thriller, part futuristic detective story, part diary of a serial killer." In it, the government regularly subjects its citizens to a host of tests, including brain scans and genetic fingerprinting, in order to identify those with criminal tendencies. When a man who is obsessed with philosophy and debating the nature of good and evil—and who has been labeled a potential killer—breaks into the government's central computer to erase his name, he finds the names of others who have been similarly labeled and embarks on a quest to kill them. Before he gets too far, however, a crack inspector (a woman named Jake) is called in to capture him. *A Philosophical Investigation*, despite grumblings from both Kerr and critics about its off-putting title, was extremely well-received. "Mr. Kerr clearly has more on his mind than standard slasher-fiction as he deftly weaves passages depicting the nitty-gritty of Jake's police work with chilling glimpses into the psycho's mind, then sets them against a bleak, nasty vision of a future world," Veal wrote in the *New York Times Book Review*. "This is a crime novel with a twist," Lawrence Rungren wrote in *Library Journal* (March 15, 1993). "The ideas of the real Wittgenstein play a key role in [Jake's] struggle to identify her sophisticated foe. Philosophy, literature, and abnormal psychology mix in this unusual and intellectually stimulating thriller."

In 1993 Kerr also edited *The Penguin Book of Fights, Feuds and Heartfelt Hatreds: An Anthology of Antipathy*, a nonfiction work whose detailed title straightforwardly sums up the book's content. A year later Kerr published *Dead Meat*, a thriller involving a Moscow investigator who is sent to St. Petersburg to study anti-Mafia operations and stumbles on a string of mysterious murders. Critical reaction to the book was mixed. "This is the closest Kerr has come to a straight detective novel (Russian accents aside)," Richard Sutherland wrote in *Eye Weekly* (March 16, 1995). "The problem is, Kerr isn't very good at writing normal detective fiction." A reviewer for *Booklist* (April 15, 1994), however, had quite a different opinion. "This novel works both as a gritty cop novel in a unique setting and as a lens on a troubled and tragic country," the reviewer wrote. "Kerr really did his homework; he secured the cooperation of the St. Petersburg militia's organized crime unit, rode with its officers, and took part in several operations against the Mafia. His research gives the book special weight, for example, in his explanations of the ethnic foundations of Russia's gangs. Equally important, however, Kerr lived with the incredible privations that nearly all Russians endure. His illumination of those hardships in the lives of his characters is almost painful at times, and the startling crime . . . has a terrible plausibility in grim contemporary Russia."

Kerr's subsequent novel, *The Grid* (1995; published in the United Kingdom as *Gridiron*), involves a completely automated Los Angeles skyscraper whose computer, capable of learning and spawning new generations of itself, goes awry and begins killing off the building's inhabitants. The book depicts numerous characters who show either disinterest in or downright hatred toward their jobs—an attitude with which Kerr sympathizes. "That was exactly my own experience of business," he said in the interview with Michele Field. "I spent many years in a high-rise building somewhere wishing I was somewhere else. I think

The Grid is in part an exorcism of my fear of being back in a 9-to-5 job, and being with people I didn't really know, and who didn't know each other." Deemed a "fairly exciting techno-thriller" by James Polk in the *New York Times Book Review* (July 14, 1996), the novel, whose film rights were promptly purchased in a $1 million-plus deal, received only tepid reviews from literary critics. "Mr. Kerr . . . has shown that he can do better, but *The Grid* still has its moments," Polk wrote.

In 1996 Kerr published *Esau*, his seventh novel. An adventure story mixed with elements of New Age mysticism and political intrigue, *Esau* tells the story of Jack Furness, an American rock climber who stumbles upon the skull of a yeti, or abominable snowman, on one of his climbs in the Himalayas. After returning to the United States with the skull, an expedition (one that includes an undercover government agent among its members) is soon sent back to Nepal—this time to trap a live yeti. Though several critics complained that the book's ending did not adhere to the spirit of the rest of the book, reviews of *Esau* were mostly favorable. "The daredevil feats of the mountaineers, the impossible cold, and the endless miles of glacier and snow in the little-visited Annapurna Sanctuary make this novel a marvelous armchair travelogue, but it's far more: a complicated yet visceral thriller in which monsters, human and otherwise, roam the earth and hunt each other," a reviewer wrote in *Publishers Weekly* (March 3, 1997). "Kerr manages his large cast of characters with a sure hand, while the plot gathers speed and power like a Himalayan avalanche."

In Kerr's *A Five-Year Plan* (1999), two characters chase the same criminals for very different reasons. Dave Delano, who has taught himself Russian while serving a five-year prison sentence for a crime he did not commit, plans to hijack a ferry smuggling drug money and put the cash in his bank account in the former Soviet Union. Kate Fury is an FBI agent following the trail of cocaine and money, in the hope of bringing off a career-making drug bust. A *Kirkus Reviews* (March 1, 1998) writer called the book "amusingly overplotted." Many reviewers also noted the novel's debt to the work of Elmore Leonard.
—J. P.

SUGGESTED READING: *Booklist* p1518 Apr. 15, 1994; *Electronic Telegraph* Oct. 5, 1996; *Library Journal* p107 Mar. 15, 1993, p162 Feb. 15, 1997; *New York Times Book Review* p20 June 13, 1993, p16 July 14, 1996; *Publishers Weekly* p43+ Apr. 8, 1996, p63+ Mar. 3, 1997

SELECTED BOOKS: Fiction— *March Violets*, 1989; *The Pale Criminal*, 1990; *A German Requiem*, 1991; *Berlin Noir*, 1993; *A Philosophical Investigation*, 1993; *Dead Meat*, 1994; *The Grid*, 1995; *Esau*, 1996; *A Five-Year Plan*, 1999; As editor— *The Penguin Book of Lies*, 1991; *The Penguin Book of Fights, Feuds, and*

Heartfelt Hatreds: An Anthology of Antipathy,
1993

August Kleinzahler

Kleinzahler, August

Dec. 10, 1949– Poet

The American poet August Kleinzahler has gained
the respect and admiration of Helen Vendler, one
of the major literary critics in the United States, for
his "astringent, terse, comic" personal style. His
collections of poetry, *Storm Over Hackensack*
(1985), *On Johnny's Time* (1988), *Earthquake
Weather* (1989), *Like Cities, Like Storms* (1992),
Red Sauce, Whiskey and Snow (1995), and *Green
Sees Things in Waves* (1998) have gained him a devoted following of readers who appreciate his wry,
illuminating insights. "Like all good poets," Daniel
Guillory wrote in *Library Journal* (May 1, 1995),
Kleinzahler makes "'what is dormant' in the reader
'become electric.'" "You learn something or register annoyance, but something's happening, the cir-
cuits are alive," Kleinzahler wrote in *Small Press*
(Spring 1994), reviewing another writer's collection of essays, in terms that apply to his own work.

For *World Authors 1990–1995,* August Kleinzahler writes: "I was born in Jersey City in 1949,
the youngest of three children, and raised in Fort
Lee, New Jersey, right across the George Washington Bridge from upper Manhattan. Palisades
Amusement Park was only three blocks away and
at the foot of the block was the home of Albert An-
astasia, the head of Murder Incorporated, who was
shot dead in a barber chair in Manhattan when I
was seven.

"My father's father was from a village in central
Hungary, Hidasnemeti. His mother, Augusta, was
born near Canal Street in New York and her antecedents were from East Prussia. My mother's parents were from the Ukraine. All Jews. Both of my
parents were born and raised in Jersey City, the
children of shop keepers. My mother attended and
graduated from the University of Maryland.

"My father dropped out of high school during
the Depression; however, he was always a keen
reader and autodidact. He wrote professionally as
a very young man, a humorous journalism somewhat in the manner of S. J. Perelman. From his
mother he inherited a great feeling for the visual
arts. Our house looked like the Collections room of
a museum, especially after we were grown. There
were oil paintings from the 17th, 18th and 19th
centuries, most by well-known painters and of no
small value, but most of what was up and about
consisted of etchings and assorted Buddhas and
bodhisattvas. My father was especially fond of
bronze. Almost all of these objects d'art were
picked up at flea markets and junk shops for a song.
He was very proud of this. Also, he loved museums
and auctions. No little boy from New Jersey in the
1950s logged more weekend hours at the Metropolitan Museum of Art, the Frick, the Whitney and the
Museum of Modern Art. Mostly I enjoyed his company and he would buy me a bag of chestnuts to
keep me quiet when necessary. But I do remember,
as do many children of that era, Rousseau's *Sleeping Gypsy* in the lobby of the Modern Art. I also remember a painting by Derain of a bridge across the
Seine or Thames that always delighted me. My father painted himself for a time in his 40s and 50s,
first in the manner of Vlaminck, then in a more abstract style, perhaps along the lines of Kandinsky
and Klee. This ended when my older brother took
his own life in December of 1971, a few days short
of my 22nd birthday.

"At that time I was studying at the University of
Victoria in British Columbia, and, most significantly, was studying with the poet Basil Bunting who
was the visiting writer. These two events, not to
mention their simultaneity, had the most telling effect on my determination to be a poet, to see it out,
to get it to a place where it lived a vigorous life of
its own and could provide pleasure to the alert,
disinterested reader, especially the one who seldom reads poetry.

"I have been writing since I was 15 or 16 years
of age. It has been the one constant in a somewhat
irregular life. My influences are too various to mention. Certainly Bunting. Oddly, perhaps not so
oddly, the translations I've been reading since a
youth are of Chinese and Japanese poetry. The former will explain to some extent my concern with
sound and rhythm; the latter interest may indicate
certain of my tendencies to set the emotional tone
through allusions to the weather. I regard the city
and life in the city as the central fact of contemporary existence, and I have chosen the city as my
most abiding landscape, though customarily with

'weather.' I have also for quite some time loved jazz, particularly the piano trio music of the '50s, and have attempted, with at best mixed success, to incorporate some of its thrust, dissonances, and irregular beats into my verse.

"As I write this in the winter of 1997 I am completing a seventh collection of poetry. I have been exploring the longer line, blank verse, hexameter, even 14ers, drifting in and out of meter. But my impulse is not to cleave to any regular pattern very long and to break from it when the time feels exactly right. I seldom deal in abstractions. I feel that only now am I coming into my strength."

August Kleinzahler is known for putting a great deal of distance between himself and his work, preferring that the distilled essence of poetry, rather than obfuscating elements of the poet's life, come through to the reader. Consequently his life in the New Jersey suburb of New York City where he grew up is a very private one, as had been his life in San Francisco, where he previously lived. Biographical data are very scarce.

Storm Over Hackensack, published in 1985, began Kleinzahler's string of books with unexpected poetic forms but consistently adhered-to poetic themes. He stuck closely to his chosen leitmotifs of the city landscape and the weather, but varied the rather startling imagery with which he described them.

He continued throughout the 1980s and the 1990s to produce volumes of poetry: *On Johnny's Time*, *Earthquake Weather*, and *Like Cities, Like Storms* followed *Storm Over Hackensack*. When *Red Sauce, Whiskey and Snow* was published in England (it was the first of his books to appear there), Lachlan Mackinnon, reviewing it in the *Times Literary Supplement* (September 15, 1995), called the book "very welcome." He gave a few of Kleinzahler's poems a close reading, observing that they are "[s]ketchy, elusive, compact." For example, he pointed out that the use of words like "but" and "keep" in the lines "but the docs keep pumping diuretics and Prednisone / into them, doing valve jobs, / so it's slow, terribly slow" in "Going," a poem about old age and death, have deep significance: "The 'but' and 'keep' seem to resent medical intervention, which would make the 'terribly' sympathetic to their condition. . . . " Mackinnon concluded that it "is helpful to think of [Kleinzahler] as a consciously urban poet steeped in the postmodern condition, but not a postmodernist."

"Two distinct landscapes" was what Daniel Guillory termed Kleinzahler's imagery, reviewing *Red Sauce, Whiskey and Snow* in the *Library Journal* (May 1, 1995). "The first is a jagged urban space inhabited by the likes of Jimmy the Lush, a place where 'tributaries of Amaretto and Schlitz meander through the broken glass,' a world where 'Eddie took a shiv in his gut' and old people fall apart like 'vintage Studebakers.' But set against this tragic cityscape of 'bummy' smells and anthrax is an utterly beautiful, 'insect-simple' world of nature where 'the pattern discloses itself' in the form of 'damselflies and the ganglia of dark branches'—a space always available 'if you just slowed down.'"

Helen Vendler, reviewing *Red Sauce, Whiskey and Snow* in the *New Yorker* (April 8, 1996), contrasted the "elegiac" poetic style of Mark Doty with Kleinzahler's "more lively" vision. She quoted the end of Kleinzahler's poem about a California earthquake: "But the earth continues to wobble, / and the cat keeps to his odd new perch / on top of the mantel, / that same fierce look in his eyes." She pointed out the renewal of the will "to fight back against nature, even if the wobbly earth holds all the cards" that Kleinzahler demonstrates. "If poetry is meant to delight and instruct, deft implications are Kleinzahler's means of instruction. His means of delight are his light-handedness with language, his willingness to strike up a dance or a tune, his offbeat structures, and his reveling in the comic grotesque," Vendler concluded.

The poems in Kleinzahler's 1998 collection, *Green Sees Things in Waves*, sketch subjects ranging from dreams to encounters with animals to the visions of the man in the title poem, who has a "flashback" several years after taking acid. A writer for *Booklist* (May 1, 1998) announced that the poems "snap like flags in a brisk wind" and that, "for all their smartness," they "have an aura of wistfulness."

—S. Y.

SUGGESTED READING: *Library Journal* p100 May 1, 1995; *New Yorker* p100+ Apr. 8, 1996; *Times Literary Supplement* p25 Sep. 15, 1995

SELECTED BOOKS: *Storm Over Hackensack*, 1985; *On Johnny's Time*, 1988; *Earthquake Weather*, 1989; *Like cities, Like Storms*, 1992; *Red Sauce, Whiskey and Snow*, 1995; *Green Sees Things in Waves*, 1998

Knox, Bernard

Nov. 24, 1914– Essayist; nonfiction writer

In recent years, Bernard Knox has added his voice to the growing number of those in favor of preserving classics studies in American schools and universities. In his recent published works, he has passionately promoted the merits of ancient Greek culture, and has recognized that society as the cornerstone of Western civilization. He disagrees with those who want to remove such studies in favor of an approach in which cultures are represented equally, regardless of influence or impact on the world as a whole. While he believes that many of these cultures should and must be added to the curriculum, in works like *The Oldest Dead White European Males* (1993) and *Backing into the Fu-*

ture (1994), he stresses the relevance of Greek culture in modern Western society by noting that, for instance, modern democracies are modeled on ancient Greek ideals. Knox is also a noted scholar of Greek tragedies, particularly the works of Sophocles, as demonstrated by his several studies on the subject: *Oedipus at Thebes* (1957), *The Heroic Temper* (1964), and *Word and Action* (1979). He also published *Essays Ancient and Modern* (1989), a collection of autobiographical pieces that focus on the influence of the ancient Greeks on warfare in the 20th century.

Bernard MacGregor Walker Knox was born in Bradford, Yorkshire, England, on November 24, 1914, the son of Bernard and Rowena (Walker) Knox. As an undergraduate at St. John's College at Cambridge, he studied classics but was more interested in left-wing politics. An ardent anti-fascist, Knox was convinced by John Cornford, a Cambridge friend, to fight in the Spanish Civil War. Knox received his degree from Cambridge in 1936, then hurried to Spain to fight with the Republicans, aided only by his familiarity with a Lewis gun from his time spent in cadet corps training at school. He fought and was wounded in the siege of Madrid in November 1936 and returned to England to recover.

On April 12, 1939, Knox married Betty Baur, an American girl he had met at Cambridge. They settled in the United States, partially because of Knox's dislike of the British government's appeasement of Adolf Hitler during that period. He soon gained an immigration visa, but his domestic bliss did not last long. When the United States declared war on Japan after the bombing of Pearl Harbor, Knox joined the American army. He received his naturalization papers while stationed in a U.S. camp in East Anglia, England. As a soldier in World War II, he fought in Brittany and later in Italy. During his tour of duty he was promoted to the rank of captain and received the Bronze Star with cluster and the French Croix de Guerre.

Oddly, it was in the heat of battle that Knox decided to return to the classics. While taking cover from machine gun fire in a ruined Italian villa, he stumbled across an elegantly bound edition of Virgil. As bullets were flying all around him, he dimly wondered if he could still read it. He opened the book to a random page and believed what he read there to be his fortune, following the medieval tradition of *Sortes Virgilianae*. The passage he read was the end of the first Georgic, a section that mourns the reversal of right and wrong in the world, while bitterly noting that fields had been left neglected because their workers had been conscripted to fight wars raging all over the world. In his book *Essays Ancient and Modern* (1989), Knox describes his feelings after reading that passage: "These lines, written some 30 years before the birth of Christ, expressed, more directly and passionately than any modern statement I knew of, the reality of the world I was living in: the shell-pocked, mine-infested fields, the shattered cities and the starving population of that Italy Virgil so loved, the misery of the whole world at war. . . . As we ran and crawled through the rubble I thought to myself: 'If I ever get out of this, I'm going back to the classics and study them seriously.'"

Knox returned to the United States when the war ended in 1945. He immediately set out to fulfill the promise he had made to himself in that ruined Italian house. By 1947 he was teaching at Yale University while working toward his Ph.D, which he received in 1948, in the classics. That same year he became an assistant professor and fellow of Branford College at the university; he was made an associate professor by 1954 and a full professor by 1959. In 1961 he left the university in order to become the director of the Center for Hellenic Studies (CHS) in Washington, D.C., a position he held until 1985, when he retired.

Although his long CHS directorship is testament enough to his devotion to the classics, his well-respected books give a clearer picture of Knox's influence as a thinker, as well as his opinions about the world of antiquity's influence on the modern age. His first book, *Oedipus at Thebes: Sophocles' Tragic Hero and His Time* (1957), is a discussion of Sophocles' *Oedipus Tyrannus* as well as a social history of life in ancient Athens. Specifically, Knox looks at the philosophy, science, and math of ancient Greece, as well as the medical, political, and religious aspects of Athenian life in the era. Critics admired the work, especially his reading of Sophocles' play. Moses Hadas, the reviewer for the *New York Times* (June 16, 1957), praised the "stimulating study of Sophocles' tragedy . . . In showing that arguments depending on word patterns and echoes can be made accessible and submitted to the judgement of Greekless readers, Mr. Knox has performed a real service." A reviewer for *The New Yorker* (September 14, 1957) wrote, "Professor Knox follows key words and images through the play and comes up with a superb analysis, demonstrating that when classical study is aware of Freud and the techniques of modern literary criticism, it can be as exciting nowadays as it must have been during the Renaissance." Knox followed this study of Sophocles with a new translation of his tragedy *Oedipus the King* in 1959.

In 1964 Knox published *The Heroic Temper: Studies in Sophoclean Tragedy*. This work focuses on the tragic heroes of Sophocles' works, with an intense focus on the characters' individuality. As he had done in his first volume on Sophocles, Knox divided his material into two sections: a look at the characters' heroism as it pertains to the author's ideas and language, and the place for these ideas in ancient Athens. As *Classical World* (May 1965) best summed it up: "Writers have recently looked especially to Sophocles' heroes for an understanding of the tragedies. Fierce, unyielding, unteachable, they refuse to accept the limitations of the human situation 'and in their failure achieve a strange success.' Knox's is the most convincing and most balanced presentation of this conception of the 'heroic temper.'" The *London Times Literary Supplement* (October 28, 1965) called the collection "valuable," but noted that "Professor Knox sees Sophocles as turning away from the Aeschylean adaptation of the heroic spirit to the conditions of the polis and going back to the irreconcilable Achilles of Homer, and he accounts for this regression by the suggestion that Sophocles's personal religion was hero cult. The likeness of any of the six heroes to the Homeric Achilles is not great, and 'his personal religion' is a large structure to build on the stories connecting Sophocles with Asklepios and Herakles."

In 1979 Knox published *Word and Action: Essays on the Ancient Theatre*, a collection of essays on Greek dramas with an emphasis on present-day performances and translations. Many of the essays had been previously published. The reviewer for *Choice* (June 1980) particularly enjoyed one entitled "Myth and Attic Tragedy," which focuses on certain points in the works of Aeschylus, Euripides, and Sophocles, and those essays that were "written with such great lucidity, fluency, and solid common sense that they can be recommended to readers of almost every level of sophistication." The reviewer added that "The work included in this volume . . . is a tribute to the range and perceptiveness of Knox's scholarship, and anyone interested in Greek drama will find instruction and illumination." J. P. Hershbell of *Library Journal* (January 15, 1980) wrote that "[In] very readable articles . . . the book brings together the informed insights of a foremost interpreter of Greek tragedy. Despite some specialized pieces, the book provides on the whole a surprisingly coherent and comprehensive introduction to the ancient theater."

Several years later, Knox was a contributor and editor for *The Cambridge History of Classical Literature* (1986). In 1989 he published *Essays Ancient and Modern*, a collection of autobiographical pieces that trace his intellectual development from his days as a soldier in the Spanish Civil War and in World War II. Knox also writes of how he wished to be a professional soldier as a young man, sometime before he discovered that copy of Virgil among the ruins of an Italian villa. Many of the essays focus on the author's feelings on warfare, and on his belief that it has not changed much since the ancient Greeks—except that it has become more destructive. In fact, he concluded that the fears, the tactics, the needed courage, the ultimate devastating ends have not changed very much at all. Jasper Griffin of the *New York Review of Books* (October 26, 1989) remarked that Knox's "own writing on war, apparently unemphatic in style, restrained but never suggesting self-consciousness, conveys with lucidity and power the courage, the companionship, and the horror of war in the 20th century. This collection of essays is the work of a man whom one would like to have as a friend." Peter Green of the *Washington Post Book World* (August 10, 1989) felt that "*Essays Ancient and Modern*

reaches out to a wider audience than his previous, more strictly classical, works, giving readers of all sorts the chance to enjoy his widespread wisdom and enthusiasms, his extraordinary life, and some of the best anecdotes I've read in years."

For *Essays Ancient and Modern* and earlier literary accomplishments, Knox received two major prizes in 1990. In March he became the first recipient of the PEN/Spielvogel-Diamonstein Award, which carried a stipend of $5,000, for *Essays Ancient and Modern*. In September he received the Charles Frankel Prize, another $5,000 award, presented by the National Endowment for the Humanities.

In March 1992 Knox was named the Jefferson Lecturer in the Humanities. He became the 21st person to be so honored; the award is presented every year by the National Endowment of the Humanities to a person of outstanding intellectual achievement. That year Knox's lecture was on the relevance of the Greek society to our modern age and was considered by many to be a response to the claims of ardent multiculturalists that schools should eliminate the overwhelming influence of the Greeks in their curricula. "There is sort of a general feeling among radicals that the whole of the Western tradition—and the Greeks are the heart of that tradition—is something that has to be repudiated," Knox explained in an interview with Joel Achenbach of the *Washington Post* (May 6, 1992). "I feel appalled. God only knows what the world would be like if we were all brought up on the stuff they'd like us to read."

This Jefferson Lecture was included in his next book, *The Oldest Dead White European Males* (1993), a collection of three lectures that attempts again to emphasize the importance of the Greeks to modern American culture. "I'm not exclusively, so to speak, for the Western tradition, but I still think it's the basic one for us, as a Western nation," Knox told Achenbach. Like many in the academic community, Knox believes that the canon should be expanded to include the literature of other cultures, but emphasizes "What I'm against is jettisoning the old one and putting in an entirely new one." Many critics had favorable opinions of the book; Nick Fisher, writing for the *Times Literary Supplement* (February 11, 1994), called the book "an enjoyable collection of three public lectures." Reviewing the book for *New York Newsday* (May 9, 1993), Mary Lefkowitz wrote that Knox "speaks about the ancient Greeks with great respect and clarity, but without apology for their shortcomings and cruel practices. He does not fail to observe that their treatment of women would not win the approval of modern feminists. He describes in some detail the bloody ritual of animal sacrifice that was a central feature of their worship of the gods. He points out how different they were from ourselves and from the blue-eyed, golden-haired Oxford undergraduates whom 19th-century writers imagined them to be. . . . Knox provides some brief but telling examples of why this seemingly remote people still deserve our attention. They valued leisure, not so much for self-indulgence, and they produced a literature that continually forces its audience to confront significant moral issues." Reviewing the book for the *New York Times Book Review* (April 25, 1993), Richard Jenkyns lamented, that although each lecture was given on an important occasion, "it has to be said, with reluctance, that they make a thin book in more than one sense. Mr. Knox has certainly earned his laurels, but here he is sitting on them, and leaving them a little bedraggled in the process."

The next year Knox published another collection of essays on the topic of reviving the classical tradition. *Backing into the Future: The Classical Tradition and Its Renewal* (1994) argues that these long-dead Greek authors must be reanimated for the modern generation's use, to enable it to see how ancient Athens is alive in modern society and literature. As explained by a *Publishers Weekly* (January 10, 1994) reviewer, "Knox gauges modern encounters with classical tradition, such as T. E. Lawrence's immersion in Greek literature and philosophy, refracted through his travels in Arabia, and Derek Walcott's epic poem *Omeros*, which appropriates Homeric tradition to tell the saga of villagers in his native Caribbean island of St. Lucia." A critic more in tune with modern literary criticism, Bruno Maddox of the *Washington Post Book World* (February 13, 1994) questioned if Knox's book truly cut to the heart of the debate. "Modern academe's problems with the classical tradition . . . run slightly deeper than a simple knee-jerk reaction against Dead White European Males. The reality is that in post-deconstruction literary criticism there is little room for a discipline that proceeds from the assumption of certain authors' Absolute Greatness—and it is here that Knox fails to break new ground. To a generation brought up to believe that no text is inherently important, Knox's essay on whether or not Homer's Achilles had chest hair is a laughable exercise, and rightly so."

Bernard Knox has been lauded by academia with a variety of awards and honors that include, among others, a 1956–1957 Guggenheim Fellowship, an honorary M.A. from Harvard University in 1962, a literature award from the National Institute and American Academy of Arts and Letters in 1967, and a George Jean Nathan Award for Dramatic Criticism from Manufacturers Hanover Trust in 1978.

Bernard Knox was the president of the American Philological Association in 1980 (from which he received a distinguished service medal in 1996) and the chairman of the American Academy of Arts and Sciences, Society for the Preservation of the Greek Heritage in 1977. He has also been a member of the American Association for the Advancement of Science, the British Academy, the Special Forces Club, and the Cosmos Club. He has recently published another book *The Black Hunter: Forms of Thought and Forms of Society in the Greek World*, 1998.

Bernard Knox and Betty Baur have one son, Bernard MacGregor Baur Knox.
—C. M.

SUGGESTED READING: *Choice* p534 June 1980; *Classical World* p284 May 1965; *Library Journal* p206 Jan. 15, 1980; *London Times Literary Supplement* p963 Oct. 28, 1965, Feb. 11, 1994; *New York Newsday* p35 May 9, 1993; *New York Review of Books* p39 Mar. 20, 1980, p46+ Oct. 26, 1989; *New York Times* p14 June 16, 1957, II p63 Sep. 2, 1980, B p6 Mar. 9, 1992; *New York Times Book Review* p3+ Apr. 25, 1993; *New Yorker* p179 Sep. 14, 1957; *Publishers Weekly* Mar. 15, 1993, Jan. 10, 1994; *Times Literary Supplement* Feb. 11, 1994; *Washington Post Book World* p1+ Aug. 6, 1989, p15 Mar. 11, 1980, C p1 May 6, 1992, p6 Feb. 13, 1994; *Contemporary Authors*, vol. 128, 1990; *Who's Who in America*, 1998

SELECTED BOOKS: Nonfiction—*Oedipus at Thebes: Sophocles' Tragic Hero and His Time*, 1957; *The Heroic Temper: Studies in Sophoclean Tragedy*, 1964; *Word and Action: Essays on the Ancient Theatre*, 1979; *Essays Ancient and Modern*, 1989; *The Oldest Dead White European Males*, 1993; *Backing into the Future: The Classical Tradition and Its Renewal*, 1994; As translator—*Oedipus the King*, 1959; As editor and contributor—*The Cambridge History of Classical Literature*, 1986; *The Black Hunter: Forms of Thought and Forms of Society in the Greek World*, 1998

Koontz, Dean

July 9, 1945– Novelist

"I don't want to sound like Shirley MacLaine," Dean Koontz said in an interview with *People* (April 13, 1987), "but it's almost as if story ideas are beamed to me. I can sit down for 15 minutes and come up with a dozen ideas. A lot of writers fall into this the-muse-has-left-me thinking and walk away from their work. I find that the muse never leaves me. I have to shove her out." Indeed, American writer Dean Koontz, who has published nearly 70 books since 1969, ranks among the most prolific writers of popular fiction alive today.

The author of such novels as *Darkfall* (1984), *Lightning* (1988), *Hideaway* (1992), and *Strange Highways* (1995), Koontz is a master of combining elements of suspense, science fiction, horror, and romance. Critics have often compared his work—which includes novels written under eight different pseudonyms—to that of Steven King. It is a comparison, however, that Koontz often tries to eschew. "He pretty much embraces the horror label, and I don't," he said in an interview with *News-*

week (February 11, 1991). If fact, a typical Koontz book, despite being crammed with evil deeds and a psychotic killer or two, is actually quite optimistic—good always wins out over evil. "I have no patience whatsoever for misanthropic fiction, of which there is too much these days," he said in one 1996 interview. "In fact, that is one reason why I do not wish to have the 'horror novel' label applied to my books even when it is sometimes accurate; too many current horror novels are misanthropic, senselessly bleak, and I do not wish to be lumped with them. . . . Very little if any great and long-lasting fiction has been misanthropic. I strongly believe that, in addition to entertaining, it is the function of fiction to explore the way we live, reinforce our noble traits, and suggest ways to improve the world where we can." Koontz's novel *Fear Nothing* was published in early 1998.

Born on July 9, 1945 in Everett, Pennsylvania, the son of Ray and Florence Koontz, Dean Ray Koontz had a childhood that was far from ideal. His father was an often unemployed, violent alcoholic (some sources say he was also schizophrenic) who brutalized young Koontz and his mother. "I was always in physical fear of my father," Koontz told *People* (April 13, 1987), "because he would get drunk, smash furniture, and carry on terribly. My childhood was almost unrelenting terror." Though he says he never loved his father ("How can you love someone who never showed you affection?"), Koontz stresses that his mother, who passed away in 1969, showered him with love and tried to protect him from his father's wrath. "If he came up the driveway really fast with gravel flying, and you'd hear bonk, bonk, bonk on the horn, that's when my mother would usher me into my room, close the door , and say, 'Don't come out,'" he told an *Entertainment Weekly* (March 22, 1996) reporter. "When my father tried to hit me, she would stand between us," he added. The violent, unstable atmosphere in his household led Koontz to seek a route of escape at a very early age. He found that escape in writing.

Koontz was educated at Shippensburg State College, in Pennsylvania, from which he graduated in 1966. While still a student, Koontz started selling his stories. When he was 20 he won an *Atlantic Monthly* contest with a story about a farm girl whose father drowns her kittens—and later tells her that the culprit was actually God. After earning his bachelor's degree, Koontz married his high-school sweetheart, Gerda Cerra, and accepted a $4,000-a-year position as a teacher in the Appalachian Poverty Program. A year later he took a position as a high-school English teacher. In 1969 his wife announced that if Koontz, who had continued to sell his stories throughout his teaching years, wished to devote all of his time to his writing, she would support him for five years—ample time, she believed, for him to establish a career. Indeed, it was, for by 1974 Koontz had published an astonishing 18 novels, including *Star Quest* (1968), *Fear That Man* (1969), *Beastchild* (1970), *The Dark*

Symphony (1970), *The Crimson Witch* (1971), *The Haunted Earth* (1973), and *Demon Seed* (1973). "This prolific production was both a boon and a curse," he has said. "Even the low advances from my early science-fiction novels were welcome, for my wife and I began married life with much less than $500 to our name. The curse lies in the fact that much of the early work is of lower quality than what came after, both because I was so young and unself-critical and because the low earnings of each book forced me to write a lot of them in order to keep financially afloat."

In 1976, with Koontz's career looking extremely bright (he had recently published several novels, including *Nightmare Journey* [1975], *The Long Sleep* [1975], and *Night Chills* [1976]), he and his wife, having endured one too many frigid Pennsylvania winters, decided to move to California. The couple did not go alone. In a decision that has perplexed many an outsider, the Koontzes also decided to relocate Ray Koontz so that they could watch over him. "What I did was a selfish thing," Koontz said about this decision in an interview with *Entertainment Weekly* (March 22, 1996). "From the time I was a kid I said, 'I'm never going to be like my father.' Never brought in any money, never spent time with me, humiliated me when he could. But if I abandon him, that's what he did to me as a child. So I took care of him instead." Caring for the elder Koontz was no easy task. A hypochondriac, Ray Koontz would frequently telephone his son in the middle of the night demanding to be rushed to the hospital. He also frequently threatened to kill his neighbors. In 1989, after attempting to kill his son with a knife, Ray Koontz was put on antipsychotic medication and moved to a nursing home, where he remained until his death in 1990.

Koontz's choice to care for his father is all the more interesting in light of some details he revealed in an *Entertainment Weekly* (March 22, 1996) interview. Growing up, Koontz said, he always wondered why he did not look at all like his father or any of his father's relatives. This, together with the memory of an overheard conversation between his mother and his uncle (his mother's sister's husband), in which the latter—whom Koontz strongly resembles—said, "We married the wrong people," sparked in Koontz a feeling that his uncle may have actually been his real father. Later in the interview Koontz noted that in 1969, when Florence Koontz was on her deathbed, she said to him, "There's a secret you should know about your father." At that very moment Ray Koontz walked in and the younger Koontz left the room. When he returned, his mother had died. In the years since, Koontz, still unsure of his true parentage, has resisted the idea of getting his blood matched to a sample left over from one of Ray Koontz's many stays in the hospital. "If I found out that he *was* my father, then the fantasy that he *wasn't* would be over," he said.

In 1980, several years after his move to California, Koontz published the book that would prove to be his first major commercial success. The novel, *Whispers*, is the story of Bruno Frye, a madman obsessed with a female screenwriter. In *Sudden Fear: The Horror and Dark Suspense Fiction of Dean R. Koontz* (1995), Michael A. Morrison wrote that, at first glance, *Whispers* appears to be " a simple genre novel of the psychopathic-madman-assaults-woman variety." But he noted that certain undeniable parallels between the two main characters add a greater depth to the novel. "Both are victims of parental abuse, and both carry deep-seated neuroses as a consequence. Indeed, all the main figures of Koontz's novel reflect the constricting influence of childhood on adult life—the sins of the fathers and mothers." Despite its popularity with fans, *Whispers* received mixed reviews from critics. One *Publishers Weekly* (April 4, 1980) reviewer praised the author's portrait of the psychotic Bruno Frye but complained that the author had made the mystery too easy to solve by giving away too many clues. That same reviewer, echoing the sentiments of many critics, also noted that readers will need "strong stomachs to tolerate the overheated scenes of rape and mayhem."

Koontz considers *Whispers*, along with his 1986 novel *Strangers*, to be among his best work. "*Strangers*. . . and *Whispers* are the exemplars to which I refer while working on future novels," he has said. "Both of these books rely heavily on character and background for their impact. Without doubt, both novels have strong, suspenseful plots, as well, and I intend that all my future novels will be what are called 'page turners'; however, the older I get the more I find that well-drawn characters and vivid backgrounds are just as important as plot to the success of a book."

The publication of such books as *Whispers* and *Strangers* ushered in a new era for Koontz—one in which each successive book, including *Watchers* (1987) and *The Bad Place* (1990), seemed to become more popular than the last. Koontz's tremendous popularity and widespread name recognition makes all the more baffling the fact that in 1991 he suddenly found himself the victim of plagiarism. Apparently oblivious to the fact that most plagiarists tend to borrow from relatively obscure sources, two sisters, Dawn Pauline Dunn and Susan Hertzell, writing together under the name Pauline Dunn, copied the plot, characters, and even entire paragraphs of Koontz's *Phantoms*, published in 1983, for their 1991 novel *The Crawling Dark*. This was the second time the authors had borrowed from the same Koontz novel: subsequent investigation found that the duo's 1990 novel, *Demonic Color*, also borrowed from *Phantoms*, albeit less extensively. It was not an editor or publisher who first noticed the books' undeniable similarities, but one of Koontz's fans. "When I started reading it, it was like déjà vu," Linda Kuzminczuk, the fan who spotted the plagiarized material, said in an interview with the *New York Times* (June 24,

1992). "It happens that Dean Koontz is one of my favorite authors and *Phantoms* is one of my favorite books. I knew what they had done as soon as I read the opening scene." Kuzminczuk promptly sent Koontz a letter outlining the material from *Phantoms* that had been incorporated into the other authors' book. "I was more than a little astonished," Koontz told the *New York Times* (June 24, 1992) reporter. "And it struck me as particularly odd since the book is not exactly obscure. It's in something like its 33rd paperback printing." To resolve the issue Dunn and Hertzell were ordered to return their advance to pay for Koontz's legal fees and to take out a half-page ad in *Publishers Weekly*, a trade magazine widely read by publishers, announcing that their book was no longer being distributed due to its many similarities to *Phantoms*.

In the years immediately following the plagiarism incident, Koontz published a slew of novels, including *Dragon Tears* (1992), *Mr. Murder* (1993), and *Winter Moon* (1993). He also packaged earlier works—some of which had originally been published under pseudonyms—and released them as *Dean R. Koontz: A New Collection* (1992), which contains *Watchers*, *Whispers*, and *Shattered*; *Three Complete Novels: Dean Koontz: Lightning; The Face of Fear; The Vision* (1993); and *Three Complete Novels: Dean Koontz: Strangers; The Voice of the Night; The Mask* (1994).

In late 1994 he published his hugely popular novel *Dark Rivers of the Heart*. A high-tech thriller, *Dark Rivers of the Heart* centers on Spencer Grant, an ex-policeman who falls in love with Valerie Keene, a waitress and computer hacker. After Keene suddenly disappears, Grant, who is searching for clues at her apartment, is nearly killed by a team of assassins. He soon discovers that he is the target of a secret government agency and is forced to go on the run. The book, Curt Suplee wrote in the *Washington Post Book World* (December 11, 1994), contains "so much novelty and so many asides, new characters and screwball subthemes that there's a fresh surprise on virtually every page." In *Entertainment Weekly* (November 18, 1994) Tom De Haven wrote, "*Dark Rivers of the Heart* (a lousy title for such a superb thriller) deserves to go to No. 1 on the best-seller list."

In the following year Koontz published *Intensity*, a novel about a game of cat-and-mouse between a serial killer who enjoys eating photographs of his victims and an extremely intelligent and resourceful female graduate student. In a review of the book in *Entertainment Weekly* (January 12, 1996), Mark Harris deemed *Intensity* "a work of lean, distilled terror that should enhance [Koontz's] status even more." Though he outlined certain plot similarities between *Intensity* and Thomas Harris's *The Silence of The Lambs*, Mark Harris stressed that Koontz's novel has abundant merits. "[Koontz] almost never resorts to moments of head-slapping illogic, he ends every chapter with a cliff-hanger, and he stays relentlessly focused on the practical, horrible, terrifying particulars of how to survive a day and night with someone who wants to kill you," he added.

Koontz's novel *Sole Survivor* was published in 1997. In it, Joe Carpenter, a former crime reporter for a Los Angeles newspaper, loses his wife and daughters in a mysterious plane crash. A string of eerie encounters, chases, and visits follows, convincing Carpenter that the doomed plane was also carrying a man who had discovered proof of life after death—and who was marked for death by a top-secret government agency. Critical reaction to *Sole Survivor* was mixed. A reviewer for *Library Journal* (February 15, 1997) deemed it "probably [Koontz's] best novel to date." In *Entertainment Weekly* (February 14, 1997), however, Tom De Haven argued that "the solution to the novel's mysteries depends on the kind of 'way cool but goofy' pseudoscience found in superhero comic books" and that the book is "strewn, maddeningly, with technophobic kvetching and New Age grousing." In the thriller *Fear Nothing* (1998), set in a California town, the protagonist—whose genetic disorder makes him sensitive to sunlight and able to go outside only at night—tries to untangle the mystery of why his dead father's body has been switched with that of a murdered hitchhiker.

—J. P.

SUGGESTED READING: *Entertainment Weekly* p97 Nov. 18, 1994, p50+ Jan. 12, 1996, p47+ Mar. 22, 1996, p54 Feb. 14, 1997; *Library Journal* p162 Feb. 15, 1997; *Newsweek* p62 Feb. 11, 1991; *New York Times* C p15+ June 24, 1992; *Publishers Weekly* p61 Apr. 4, 1980; *Washington Post Book World* p8 Dec. 11, 1994; Munster, B., ed. *Sudden Fear: The Horror and Dark Suspense Fiction of Dean R. Koontz*, 1995; *Contemporary Authors* new revision series vol. 52, 1996

SELECTED BOOKS: Fiction—*Star Quest*, 1968; *The Fall of the Dream Machine*, 1969; *Fear That Man*, 1969; *Anti-Man*, 1970; *Beastchild*, 1970; *Dark of the Woods*, 1970; *The Dark Symphony*, 1970; *Hell's Gate*, 1970; *Soft Come the Dragons*, 1970; *The Crimson Witch*, 1971; *A Darkness in My Soul*, 1972; *The Flesh in the Furnace*, 1972; *Starblood*, 1972; *Time Thieves*, 1972; *Warlock*, 1972; *A Werewolf Among Us*, 1973; *Hanging On*, 1973; *The Haunted Earth*, 1973; *Demon Seed*, 1973; *After the Last Race*, 1974; *Nightmare Journey*, 1975; *Night Chills*, 1976; *The Vision*, 1977; *Whispers*, 1980; *Phantoms*, 1983; *Darkfall*, 1984; *Twilight Eyes*, 1985; *Strangers*, 1986; *Watchers*, 1987; *Lightning*, 1988; *Midnight*, 1989; *The Bad Place*, 1990; *Cold Fire*, 1991; *Three Complete Novels: Dean R. Koontz: The Servants of Twilight; Darkfall; Phantoms*, 1991; *Hideaway*, 1992; *Dragon Tears*, 1992; *Dean R. Koontz: A New Collection*, 1992; *Mr. Murder*, 1993; *Winter Moon*, 1993; *Three Complete Novels: Lightning; The Face of Fear; The Vision*, 1993; *The Mask*, 1994; *Dark Rivers of the Heart*, 1994; *Strange Highways*, 1995; *Icebound*, 1995; *Intensity*, 1995;

Tick-Tock, 1996; *Sole Survivor*, 1997; *Fear Nothing*, 1998; As Brian Coffee—*Blood Risk*, 1973; *Surrounded*, 1974; *The Wall of Masks*, 1975; *The Face of Fear*, 1977; *The Voice of the Night*, 1981; As Deanna Dryer—*The Demon Child*, 1971; *Legacy of Terror*, 1971; *Children of the Storm*, 1972; *The Dark of Summer*, 1972; *Dance with the Devil*, 1973; As K. R. Dryer—*Chase*, 1972; *Shattered*, 1973; *Dragonfly*, 1975; As John Hill—*The Long Sleep*, 1975; As Leigh Nichols—*The Key to Midnight*, 1979; *The Eyes of Darkness*, 1981; *The House of Thunder*, 1982; *Twilight*, 1990; *Shadowfires*, 1987; As Anthony North—*Strike Deep*, 1974; As Richard Paige—*The Door to December*, 1985; As Owen West—*The Funhouse*, 1980; *The Mask*, 1981; Nonfiction—*The Pig Society* (with G. Koontz), 1970; *The Underground Lifestyles Handbook*, 1970; *Writing Popular Fiction*, 1973; *How to Write Best-Selling Fiction*, 1981

Kotzwinkle, William

Nov. 22, 1938– Novelist; short-story writer; poet

William Kotzwinkle, the American novelist, poet, short-story writer, and author of children's books, achieved bestsellerdom in an unusual way for a literary author—with a novelization requested by Steven Spielberg for his movie *E. T., The Extra-Terrestrial* (1982). Kotzwinkle had already published *The Fan Man* (1974), described by Dan Wakefield in the *Nation* (November 4, 1996) as "the hilarious saga of a consummate hippie." He first demonstrated his ability to enter the half-magic world of children with *The Fireman* (1969) and continued, aided often by the illustrations of Joe Servello, an old school friend, to produce such children's favorites as *Trouble in Bugland: A Collection of Inspector Mantis Mysteries* (1983), *The World Is Big and I'm So Small* (1986), and *The Empty Notebook* (1990). Kotzwinkle's adult books have ranged from the comical stories of his first collection, *Elephant Bangs Train* (1971), to science fiction in *Doctor Rat* (1976), to historical fantasy in *Fata Morgana* (1977), to satire in the novel *The Bear Went Over the Mountain* (1996), termed a "genuine parable for our time . . . as full of truth as it is of humor" by Dan Wakefield. Some critics have compared Kotzwinkle's whimsical lyricism to the writings of Richard Brautigan and Tom Robbins.

William Kotzwinkle was born on November 22, 1938 in Scranton, Pennsylvania. His father, William John Kotzwinkle, who managed a printing department, pointed out to him the beauties of the Lackawanna Valley, where Kotzwinkle grew up. He attended Rider College in Lawrenceville, New Jersey, and went on to Penn State back in Pennsylvania. After being dismissed from the latter school in 1957 for having a female in his room, he went to New York City and entered the world of Beat poets and writers. He maintained himself with a series of odd jobs—short-order cook, department store Santa Claus, copy editor, and scandal-sheet writer.

In 1970 Kotzwinkle married Elizabeth Gundy, also a writer, and they soon left New York for New Brunswick, Canada. Gundy later authored *Naked in a Public Place* (1975), *Bliss* (1977), *The Disappearance of Gregory Pluckrose* (1985), and other novels. The couple subsequently moved to the Maine coast.

Kotzwinkle began to publish children's books in the late 1960s, while also writing adult fiction. *Elephant Bangs Train* contained elements of the surreal and, of course, the comic, for which he was to become best known. *The Fan Man*, a novel with experimental syntax and punctuation, about one Horse Badorties, a beatnik of the East Village, became a cult classic. Most reviewers were enchanted with its nuttily compulsive but completely disorganized hero, a "filthy, hippie dope fiend and dealer," as William Kennedy wrote in the *New Republic* (March 2, 1974). Kennedy congratulated Kotzwinkle on his creation of a "heroic . . . splendid creep, a sublime prince of the holy trash pile." Horse Badorties attempts to organize a concert by the Love Chorus, a group of young girls, at St. Nancy's on the Bowery. He winds up wandering in Van Cortlandt Park, the wilds of New York, far from where the concert finally takes place. Martin Levin in the *New York Times Book Review* (February 10, 1974) called Horse Badorties "a human dada, full of one-line gags and comic perceptions." He concluded that *The Fan Man* is a "happy conception . . . with brightly opalescent hallucinations." Richard Todd, in the *Atlantic* (May 1974), however, viewed the novel as "cute" in an entirely pejorative sense.

The 1970s were very productive years for Kotzwinkle. His children's books included *The Ship That Came Down the Gutter* (1970), *Elephant Boy: A Story of the Stone Age* (1970), *The Day the Gang Got Rich* (1970), *The Oldest Man, and Other Timeless Stories* (1971), *The Return of Crazy Horse* (1971), *The Supreme, Superb, Exalted, and Delightful, One and Only Magic Building* (1973), *Up the Alley with Jack and Joe* (1974), *The Leopard's Tooth* (1976), *The Ants Who Took Away Time* (1978), *Dream of Dark Harbor* (1979), and *The Nap Master* (1979). *The Fan Man* was followed by *Night-Book* in 1974.

In 1976 Kotzwinkle's *Doctor Rat*, a science-fiction novel, created something of a sensation. The *Choice* (November 1976) reviewer called it "a strong, highly readable piece of social science fiction written in a controlled, coldly objective prose." *Choice* also termed *Doctor Rat* "the finest piece of antivivisectionist prose yet written. . . . It is a work that could change our perceptions." Doctor Rat, described by Knopf, Kotzwinkle's publishers, as a "respected and prolific author of technical papers," wants only to continue receiving enormous grants for such articles as "Average Lethal Doses for Rats." His fellow animals revolt, however, and Doctor Rat "dedicates himself to protecting mankind from the worldwide mobilization of the ungrateful animal kingdom."

Robert Stone, in *Harper's* (June 1976), although he judged *Doctor Rat* "an unashamed moral statement" with "a lot of humor," found it "aggressively ingratiating" and lacking in irony. The *New York Times Book Review* (May 30, 1976) critic R. P. Brickner thought *Doctor Rat* only "appears to be so feeling" and found it "disturbingly frivolous" while at the same time "technically sportive and sometimes successfully lyrical." Thomas LeClair, in the *Saturday Review* (May 29, 1976), agreed, terming *Doctor Rat* "a fictionalized antivivisectionist tract" and noting its lack of success: "[A]fter . . . the initial shocks of roasting rats and suffocating dogs, Kotzwinkle fills the narrative with an animal uprising and lyrical animal reveries. . . . Neither device works."

Fata Morgana, Kotzwinkle's 1977 novel, was deemed by some a fantasy, by others a historical crime novel. Set in Paris—and other parts of Europe—in the time of Louis Napoleon, it is the story of how a police detective, down on his luck, investigates the life of a conjurer accused of mesmerizing all of Paris with a machine that predicts the future. Inspector Picard pieces together "a kind of history of Ric Lazare, who may have been a toy maker, an acrobat, and a murderer in his numerous incarnations," according to Jerome Charyn in the *New York Times Book Review* (May 1, 1977). Moving from "the mundane to the grotesque, from magic to hard-nosed fact," as Charyn put it, Kotzwinkle created a suspenseful entertainment. The *Library Journal* (July 1977) reviewer praised Kotzwinkle's use of "fairy-tale props—toys and toy makers, magic and sorcerers, arch-criminals and enchanting women." Although these may make the novel "appear as insubstantial as the mirage from which it takes its name," it is "a good novel," Grove Koger concluded. Phoebe-Lou Adams in the *Atlantic* (July 1977) disagreed, noting, "Kotzwinkle has done the unforgivable: he has bailed out of a fantasy by turning it all into a dream." Kotzwinkle was further guilty in Adams's eyes of pilfering the "climactic scene" from "an old movie."

With the novelization of *E.T., The Extra-Terrestrial*, which followed his novella *Herr Nightingale and the Satin Woman* (1978) and the satirical, semiautobiographical coming-of-age novel of a boy under the spell of the Lone Ranger and Captain Marvel, *Jack in the Box* (1980), set in central Pennsylvania, Kotzwinkle entered the world of major films and became a best-selling author, as well. In *E. T.*, an alien, who is stranded briefly with an American family before being able to summon the starship that will return him to his own planet, becomes a mythic representation of the oneness of the universe and a possible healer. Christopher Lehmann-Haupt in the *New York Times* (July 2,

1982) felt that the novel was almost better than the film because it provided explanations of such phenomena as E. T. turning ashen: "The pressure that Earthlings are putting on his spirit" makes him collapse in upon himself and turns him into a "white dwarf." Kotzwinkle's characters also seemed more fully developed to Lehmann-Haupt. "Most dramatically of all, he succeeds in making E. T.'s sickness a threat not only to Elliott, his devoted friend, but also to the entire planet Earth," Lehmann-Haupt concluded. His counterpart on the *New York Times Book Review* (August 29, 1982), Gerald Jonas, on the other hand, deemed the book "much less appealing in every way than the movie. . . . In print this limited fairy tale (no real villains, no freshly alien point of view) is sadly out-of-date." The *Voice of Youth Advocates* (December 1982) reviewer, although she conceded that Kotzwinkle "exposes the thoughts and motives of the characters, especially E. T.," considered the novel a failure: the "emotional power of the movie is replaced by self-indulgent amusement wavering between sarcastic and pathetic." Susan L. Nickerson, in *Library Journal* (August 1982), thought the novel had "the same enchanted feeling, laced with some devilish humor and a few new dimensions that the movie couldn't convey."

Kotzwinkle wrote a sequel to *E. T., The Extra-Terrestrial*, *E. T.: The Story Book of the Green Planet*, published in 1985. In this novel, also calculated to appeal both to children and adults, "E. T. is home again and can't keep his mind off Earth," according to Jill Grossman, writing in the *New York Times Book Review* (May 5, 1985). He "designs a giant turnip propelled by 'Fusion Blooms'" to propel him back to Earth. "Kotzwinkle's strong suit here is his imagination and playfulness with language, be it the frisky slang of Earth that he and E. T. cherish, or the inventive people and plants of the Green Planet." Grossman concluded that fans of *E.T.* would find this story "funny and sweet."

Another of Kotzwinkle's delvings into the humorously crazy world of Manhattan characters was his *Christmas at Fontaine's* (1982), a Christmas fable. A store Santa Claus, a window decorator, a cafe waitress, and a security guard populate the pages, along with the bag lady Mad Aggie. Eve Ottenberg, in the *New York Times Book Review* (November 7, 1982), declared that wherever "Kotzwinkle looks, he manages to find something zany and, at the same time, touching."

Late 1983 saw the publication of *Trouble in Bugland: A Collection of Inspector Mantis Mysteries*, illustrated by Joe Servello. Set in a mock Victorian England populated by insects, the stories have the flavor of Sherlock Holmes tales. The book is now regarded as a classic of children's literature. The "excitement in the five mystery stories in *Trouble in Bugland* derives from the ingenious crimes and the use of Holmesian themes—stolen treasure, terrifying apparitions, exotic and deadly poisons," according to Ann Cameron in the *New York Times Book Review* (January 1, 1984). She felt that children would "appreciate the book's sly mock seriousness and flights of rhetoric and imagination."

With *Queen of Swords* (1983), Kotzwinkle maintained his "firm grip on the deed to fantasy land," according to Joanne Kaufman in the *New York Times Book Review* (May 20, 1984). Like *Jack in the Box*, the novel *Queen of Swords* has autobiographical elements. The story of Eric, "a famous unknown writer . . . given to philosophic inquiry," and his affair with a woman who has a black belt in karate, *Queen of Swords* satirizes such New Age fads as est and aromatherapy. Eric ultimately realizes that he must return to Janet, his wife. "But Eric's tardy epiphany that 'Janet had shattered the porcelain bowl of my mind and freed me to see instead—the stars,' bounces foolishly and unconvincingly off the page," Kaufman wrote.

Reviewing *Jewel of the Moon* (1985), a collection of tales for adults, Robert Cohen in the *New York Times Book Review* (December 29, 1985) evoked Horse Badorties, the hero of *The Fan Man*. He found that many of the tales in *Jewel of the Moon*—parables—were not successful, not yielding "much beyond a quality . . . Kotzwinkle has shown . . . to better advantage: a genuine flair for comic book fantasy inflected by the mystical." Cohen praised the better stories, however, as "lovely, brooding," and "delicate." "Everywhere," he noted, "we find . . . Kotzwinkle's love of the embattled marginal figure—seeker, artist, alien—all succumbing to chimeras and enchantments on their way to transcendence; trying, as old Horse once put it, to touch the cloud, man."

Herbert Gold, the novelist, writing in the *New York Times Book Review* (May 10, 1987), deemed Kotzwinkle's "stylish shadings of black humor, fantasy, and psychological conjecture" in *The Exile* (1987) successful, observing that "his achievement here in the line of bitter laughter and plain fun may earn him the reputation his quirky talents have long merited." In *The Exile*, Kotzwinkle's protagonist, David Caspian, a contemporary movie star, an "intelligent actor," finds his personality being taken over by that of the Nazi Felix Falkenhayn, a German black marketeer. "[T]ime curves in and around these two," Gold wrote, explaining the novel's simultaneous setting in Nazi Germany and contemporary Hollywood. He praised Kotzwinkle's satiric but compassionate grasp of moviemaking. "The story of the Nazis is energetic in the way of skillful melodrama, filled with intrigue, sex, torture, and Wagnerian brooding," he added. "Kotzwinkle's attractive ambition begins to offer lyrical returns, and the comedy, despair, horror, and technical storytelling delight make this an ambiguous, entertaining, unsettling performance."

Kotzwinkle's next novel, *The Midnight Examiner* (1989), is set in a world of sleazy tabloid newspapers and supermarket magazines. The central character is Howard Halliday, head of Chameleon Publications and editor in chief of the eponymous tabloid. "*The Midnight Examiner* reads as if it were written by the staff of *Mad* magazine, in consultation with the cartoonist Robert Crumb," Gloria Jacobs wrote in the *New York Times Book Review* (May 14, 1989). "It has a kind of pop brilliance to it—but one that is easily tarnished by passages of goofy humor, giving what is often a very funny book the one-dimensional tone of the Sunday comics. . . . It's just too difficult to parody a form that is a parody already," she concluded. The novel, in fact, had its roots in the real-life job that Kotzwinkle held on a *Midnight Examiner*–like tabloid in his beatnik days. While Jacobs found the novel too filled with slapstick, the *Village Voice* (August 8, 1989) critic Bill Marx termed Kotzwinkle a premier "mondo trasho master farceur."

Hot Jazz Trio, a collection of three stories, also appeared in 1989. In the longest story, "Django Reinhardt Played the Blues," such real denizens of the Paris of the 1920s as Jean Cocteau, Pablo Picasso, and André Breton make appearances. Diane Manuel, in the *New York Times Book Review* (February 25, 1990), praised the story as transporting readers "through enchanting adventures in which familiar characters glow with 'infinite possibilities' and inanimate objects are 'open to suggestion.'" The shorter stories in the book, "Blues on the Nile: A Fragment of Papyrus," about a selfish Pharaoh, and "Boxcar Blues," about circus artists, drew less praise.

Kotzwinkle's next book, *The Game of Thirty* (1994), a mystery novel, was the last book published by Seymour Lawrence before his death. To honor his publisher Kotzwinkle relinquished the pleasures of his cabin in the wilds of Maine, where his avocations are directing experimental theater, writing songs, and studying insects, to set off on a book tour, armed with "home-brewed Chinese herbal tinctures—ginseng and deer antler, to wake me up; licorice to drive out the toxins I'll acquire in cities; ho shu wu to calm my nerves while I'm reading to large crowds of strange people, and peony to help me sleep," as he told the *New York Times* (June 8, 1994).

The novel itself, a stylistic nod to Raymond Chandler and Dashiell Hammett, drew praise as light entertainment, but its story, similar to that of Hammett's *The Maltese Falcon* and set against a background of an ancient Egyptian game that, in a sense, pits the players against fate and death, was not taken seriously by reviewers. Michael Dirda in the *Washington Post* (June 27, 1994) observed that "many of the elements in *The Game of Thirty* are entertaining, including its throwaway sentences (out on the lake in Central Park, 'the water sparkled brightly around some teenagers trying to kill a duck with an oar'), but Kotzwinkle never seems able to decide whether he's writing Hammett/Chandler pastiche or a genuine suspense novel." Daniel Easterman in the *New York Times Book Review* (June 19, 1994) also noted the resemblances to Hammett and Chandler, but said that although his "world . . . is theirs in its broad dimensions . . . it is far from being as mean or as bruised at heart. Just pulling in child abuse and pedophilic

videos isn't enough. The taint of corruption never seems to seep through into the world of the central characters."

In a profile in the *Washington Post* (January 25, 1997), Kotzwinkle explained that he had once eaten a Christmas tree ornament to make an impression and had later fictionalized the incident in *Jack in the Box*. When the novel was filmed as *Book of Love,* he watched an actor recreate his feat with an edible ornament. The scene was cut from the film, however, because the director thought no one would believe that anyone could be so stupid. Another incident that Kotzwinkle transmuted into fiction had to do with the fire he and Elizabeth Gundy had in Canada, in which their manuscripts were burned. They subsequently began keeping their manuscripts in briefcases in the woods when they went away, so that the same misfortune would not befall them twice. On returning from one trip, they discovered that one of the briefcases was not in its hiding place. An old lumberjack told them that a bear had probably found it; indeed, when recovered, the briefcase had been clawed open. The manuscript was intact, perhaps because the bear had been looking for food and not literature. Kotzwinkle thought about what would have happened if the bear had read the manuscript and found merit in it, and he used that idea as the basis for *The Bear Went Over the Mountain* (1996).

In the novel a bear finds a novel in a briefcase, takes the name Hal Jam, gets an agent, and becomes a best-selling author. Christopher Lehmann-Haupt commented in the *New York Times* (October 17, 1996) that much of Kotzwinkle's "kidding of the book business will seem mild in the context of reality. . . . Luckily for the real humor of *The Bear Went Over the Mountain*, Mr. Kotzwinkle . . . indulges his comic sense of quirkiness, particularly in . . . the character of Hal Jam, the bear. Hal wants badly to become a person, especially when he discovers how effectively humans have hoarded the good things in life, like pies and honey."

Dan Wakefield, reviewing the novel in the *Nation* (November 4, 1996), made note of the fable's "telling subplot," in which we "last see the celebrity bear in a limo heading to New York City, munching on a bag of 'Cheesy Things,' while the former professor [the real author of the bear's manuscript] goes into the forest, finding true peace of mind as 'he fed on fish, wild plants, and berries.'"

David Streitfeld in the *Washington Post* (January 25, 1997) called *The Bear* "the funniest novel in years." He quoted from Kotzwinkle's description of the bear's attempt to become human by joining a health club, where "men and women were grunting and panting as they rowed and lifted and pedaled and climbed stairs that didn't go anywhere. Soon he'd be climbing stairs that didn't to anywhere either and then he'd be a full-fledged human." Humans may seem all too willing to express their animal nature, but Kotzwinkle's literary theory rests on the absurdity of their attempts to gain metahuman experiences. As he told Streitfeld, "In ancient Egypt, people walked around believing in crocodile-headed men. The fantastic was just part of daily life. We haven't lost that level of our psyche, just buried it. But it's down there running around, and it wants its daily news." Kotzwinkle has made a literary career of giving us that news. —S. Y.

SUGGESTED READING: *Atlantic* p128 May 1974, p87 July 1977; *Choice* p1134 Nov. 1976; *Harper's* p252 June 1976; *Library Journal* p1525 July 1977, p1487 Aug. 1982; *Nation* p31 Nov. 4, 1996; *New Republic* p32 Mar..2, 1974; *New York Times* C p20 July 2, 1982, C p19 Oct. 17, 1996; *New York Times Book Review* p8 Feb. 10, 1974, p8 May 30, 1976, p11 Aug. 29, 1982, p13 Nov. 7, 1982, p23 Jan. 1, 1984, p15 May 20, 1984, p24 May 5, 1985, p18 Dec. 29, 1985, p1 May 10, 1987, p27 May 14, 1989, p18 June 19, 1994; *Saturday Review* p38 May 29, 1976; *Village Voice* p49 Aug. 8, 1989; *Voice of Youth Advocates* p38 Dec. 1982; *Washington Post* D p2 June 27, 1994; B p1 Jan. 25, 1997; *Dictionary of Literary Biography* vol 173, 1996

SELECTED BOOKS: Fiction—*Elephant Bangs Train*, 1971; *Hermes 3000*, 1972; *The Fan Man*, 1974; *Night-Book*, 1974; *Swimmer in the Secret Sea*, 1975; *Doctor Rat*, 1976; *Fata Morgana*, 1977; *Herr Nightingale and the Satin Woman*, 1978; *Jack in the Box*, 1982; *Christmas at Fontaine's*, 1982; *E. T., The Extra-Terrestrial*, 1982; *Superman III*, 1983; *Queen of Swords* (ill. J. Servello), 1983; *Jewel of the Moon*, 1985; *The Exile*, 1987; *The Midnight Examiner*, 1989; *Hot Jazz Trio*, 1989; *The Game of Thirty*, 1994; *The Bear Went Over the Mountain*, 1996; Poetry—*Seduction in Berlin* (ill. J. Servello), 1985; Juvenile—*The Fireman*, 1969; *The Ship That Came Down the Gutter*, 1970; *Elephant Boy: A Story of the Stone Age*, 1970; *The Oldest Man, and Other Timeless Stories*, 1971; *The Return of Crazy Horse*, 1971; *The Supreme, Superb, Exalted, and Delightful, One and Only Magic Building*, 1973; *Up the Alley with Jack and Joe*, 1974; *The Leopard's Tooth*, 1976; *The Ants Who Took Away Time*, 1978; *Dream of Dark Harbor*, 1979; *The Nap Master*, 1979; *Trouble in Bugland: A Collection of Inspector Mantis Mysteries* (ill. J. Servello), 1983; *E. T.: The Story Book of the Green Planet* (ill. D. Wiesner), 1985; *The World Is Big and I'm So Small* (ill. J. Servello), 1986; *Hearts of Wood and Other Timeless Tales* (ill. J. Servello), 1986; *The Empty Notebook* (ill J. Servello), 1990

Kozol, Jonathan

Sep. 5, 1936– Nonfiction writer

Jonathan Kozol has remained one of the most prominent "scholar-activists" to have emerged from the counterculture of the 1960s. For more than 30 years, this durable critic and author has written works that view the crisis of the American underclass not as an aberrant pathology but as one systemically interwoven with the structure of private and public institutions. To Kozol's thinking, a response to social crises involving illiteracy, poverty, homelessness, crime, and addiction must involve the nation as a whole, which he faults for the way it complacently compartmentalizes these problems. In recent years he has emerged as a forceful advocate for the forgotten and despairing children of the nation's inner cities, writing of them not with the cold abstraction of the social scientist but in the warm narrative of a writer considering flesh-and-blood human beings. The evangelical fervor he sometimes brings to his writing comes not from a pious devotion but from an activist's concern for transcendent values in the context of social justice.

Jonathan Kozol was born on September 5, 1936 in Boston, Massachusetts, the son of Harry Leo Kozol, a physician, and Ruth (Massell) Kozol, a psychiatric social worker. Of his early years, Kozol told an interviewer in 1996 that he grew up in a Re-

Jonathan Kozol

form Jewish tradition with "very little reference to God or to good and evil. To some degree the community in which I grew up was more a cultural community than it was a religious community, which was characteristic of many Reform Jewish communities during the 1940s and 50s, and it may still be to some degree." Although the sermons he heard as a youngster were "more like book reviews," he recalled, "My mother read the Bible and she took it very seriously, and in a sense she and my grandmother on my father's side gave me my sense of religion. My mother quoted Isaiah and Jeremiah to me when I was a child." He remembers especially the Old Testament passages about welcoming the stranger in the midst of community, with their particular resonance to the memory of Jewish people as strangers in Egypt—memories that would help give a prophetic and theological resonance to some of his works half a century later.

Reared in what he called a "privileged and insulated" environment, he came in contact with those less fortunate than he only on those rare occasions when he accompanied his father as the latter drove their live-in maid to her home in Roxbury, Boston's black ghetto, on her one day off a week. "Not by the intention of my mother and father, but by the enormous distance that divided my suburban life from anything that happened on that distant street of darkened houses where we dropped her off on Wednesday nights, I was inoculated against the pangs of conscience," Kozol wrote in his introduction to his 1985 book, *Illiterate America.*

At first Kozol seemed destined for a traditional academic career. He graduated from the Noble and Greenough School, an elite prep school for boys in Dedham, Massachusetts, and received his bachelor's degree in English, summa cum laude, from Harvard University in 1958. He was named a Rhodes Scholar, studying for the 1958–59 academic year at Magdalen College of Oxford University. At about that time Houghton published his first novel, *The Fume of Poppies,* the story of a brief, idyllic love affair between two American college students vacationing in Europe. Although he was criticized by some reviewers for his sexual explicitness, Kozol was regarded as a promising novelist by others. Granville Hicks wrote in the *Saturday Review* (October 11, 1958): "Young as he is, Mr. Kozol has learned a good deal about the craft of writing, and the book has many excellent pages, but it stays close to the surface."

Eager to adopt a career as a writer, Kozol resigned his scholarship in 1959 and moved to Paris, where he rented a small room on the Left Bank and settled down to write a novel about his Russian émigré grandparents. His work showed promise, and in 1962 he received a Saxton Fellowship in creative writing from Harper and Row, but the following year, his novel still unfinished, he returned to Boston "tremulous with terror," as he recalled in an essay for the *New York Times Book Review* (March 3, 1985). "It had taken me all that time to realize that while I knew something about 'voice' and 'style' and 'the structure of the novel,' I knew very little about living."

Returning to the United States in 1963, Kozol thought about preparing for a career as a university professor of English. But this was a time when young people were engaging themselves in the struggles against poverty and racial discrimination, as such issues were rising to the top of the national agenda. In 1964, galvanized by the murders of three young civil-rights workers in Mississippi, Kozol volunteered as a tutor in a summer-school program in Roxbury, sponsored by the Congress of Racial Equality (CORE). That September, he left the academic milieu of Harvard Square to take a position as a fourth-grade "permanent substitute" teacher in the Boston public-school system, at the Christopher Gibson school in Roxbury. The decision was a fateful one: "I signed up to teach in the Boston public schools," he told Christopher Zimmerman for the *Plough* (Spring 1996), "and then very quickly I was drawn into civil disobedience. I also became a housing organizer in the civil rights movement. . . . So my first day as a housing organizer for CORE . . . I was running a rent strike, and by the end of the year I had been in demonstrations, and briefly jailed, and the year ended with my being fired from the Boston public schools for reading the poetry of Langston Hughes." From that point forward, Kozol devoted his life to advocacy for education and social justice, especially for American children disadvantaged by economic exploitation and racism.

Kozol described his first year as a teacher in his 1967 memoir *Death at an Early Age*, which received a National Book Award in 1968. Serialized in the *Boston Globe,* it was published in the midst of an acrimonious Boston mayoral campaign between Kevin H. White, a civil-rights liberal, and the Boston School Committee's antibusing champion, Louise Day Hicks. The book sold more than two million copies over the years and catapulted Kozol to prominence as a teacher-activist. Its subtitle, *The Destruction of the Hearts and Minds of Negro Children in the Boston Public Schools*, is an ironic commentary on the Vietnam war, blamed for the ultimate failure of Lyndon Johnson's ambitious war on poverty. (Supporters of the war, including President Johnson himself, had often justified military spending in order "to win the hearts and minds of the Vietnamese people.") Kozol's book documented the abuse heaped upon the black students by white teachers as well as by a built-in attitude of lowered expectations and systemic racism. Child psychiatrist Robert Coles, reviewing *Death at an Early Age* for the *New York Times* (October 1, 1967), found it "an honest and terrifying book" and recommended it to Congressmen who were investigating the causes of the unrest that was then plaguing America's inner cities, adding, "Mr. Kozol charges the Boston School Committee and the system they run with spiritual and psychological murder. Nothing in what they say, some of it supplied word for word in the books' notes, makes the accusation seem excessive." Social critic Nat Hentoff, reviewing the book in the *New Yorker* (March 16, 1968), wrote, "I expect that *Death at an Early Age* will be read in the future, as [Dickens's] *Nicholas Nickleby* is now, by those whose habit it is to look back in wonder at the barbarism of past civilizations." Kozol donated his $1,000 National Book Award prize to community leaders in the Boston ghetto, noting in his acceptance speech that too much attention had been paid to the author of the book and too little to the frightening and tragic conditions that he had described.

When he was dismissed from the Boston school system after his first year, Kozol taught for a while at a white elementary school in suburban Newton and served briefly as a consultant on curriculum development for the United States Department of Education, but soon threw himself into the nascent alternative-schools movement, helping set up the community-run New School for Children and then, in 1968, the Storefront Learning Center, which he codirected until 1971. A Guggenheim Fellowship in 1970 allowed him to travel around the country to study the growing free-school movement. He also served as an instructor in alternative education at the Center for Intercultural Documentation Institute in Cuernavaca, Mexico, and as a visiting lecturer in more than a score of American colleges and universities. Two books he wrote over the next few years chronicle these efforts: *Free Schools* (1972) and *The Night Is Dark and I Am Far From Home* (1975), its title taken from a line in Cardinal Newman's hymn "Lead, Kindly Light." *Free Schools* documents the "unforgettable energy and locomotion" Kozol and his colleagues devoted to establishing several more Learning Centers as experimental free schools outside the traditional public school system. It was in this endeavor that Kozol met his future wife, whom he described as "a shy and serious young woman" among a group of 40 college-student volunteers in 1968. "We became friends and learned to struggle together," he wrote. *Free Schools* was highly critical of the entrenched bureaucracy that Kozol believed was hampering the American public-school system. Kozol wrote of the "incredible building codes, obtuse bureaucracies and openly inconsistent supervisors [that] seem to be a number of the constants in the ritual of North American oppression," adding: "If municipal agencies wanted to set out to devise a strategy for turning gentle and utopian liberals into cynical and rage-minded radicals, they could not do a better job than by imposing upon the Free Schools both the out-of-date regulations in themselves and the out-of-date human beings who come in to enforce them. . . . In Boston, it is easier to start a whorehouse, a liquor store, a pornography shop or a bookie joint than it is to start a little place to work with children."

Kozol continued to maintain his belief that education was a national cause in which all should participate, decrying the huge inequities between poor and rich school districts that rely on the antiquated real-estate tax to finance public education. "It is still one nation . . . ," he wrote, "It is not one thing in Lebanon, New Hampshire, one thing in the heart of Harlem." In an article for the *New York Times* (April 1, 1971), he scolded young activists

for their retreat into self-centered smugness, writing, "In spite of the implications of much of the counterculture literature, rich white people in blue jeans and beads did not all at once discover sunshine, the smell of the warm earth in April, or the good taste of homemade bread in winter. It just that they alone have the inherited freedom and the lobotomized consciousness to build a whole lifestyle out of the possession and the monopolization of these luxuries. . . . The poor are still here and the people in the ghetto are still dying; but the children of the slumlords are too busy weaving baskets. Struggle is out, but balance-scales and macramé are in."

Such essays became part of *The Night Is Dark and I Am Far from Home*, an angry indictment of middle-class American society and its skewed value systems that tolerate and condone social inequities and human suffering. The book received generally mixed notices; many critics, among them Vivian Gornick, who reviewed it for the *New York Times Book Review* (November 2, 1975), agreed with Kozol's ideological viewpoint but objected to the "fever pitch" of his writing style. "It is all there in the writing, everything that is deeply wrong with this book," she wrote. "Page after page of exclamation points, screaming italics, redundant adjectives, sentimentalized usage, whole sentences printed in capital letters." In Gornick's view, the belligerence of Kozol's style wiped out the humaneness inherent in his view, "thereby defeating his own stated purpose: to make us all self-conscious allies in the social war against class-dictated greed and injustice." The book concludes with a chapter in which Kozol expresses his admiration for the work for the Brazilian scholar and educator Paulo Freire, whom he had met in Cuernavaca in 1969 and came to know better during the latter's tenure as a visiting lecturer at Harvard. It was Freire who inspired Kozol to undertake his next project, a study of literacy and education in Castro's Cuba.

Kozol visited Cuba in 1976 and again in 1977, documenting his findings in another book, *Children of the Revolution: A Yankee Teacher in the Cuban Schools* (1978). Greatly impressed with what he learned about the Cuban experience and with the enthusiasm of the young volunteer literacy teachers, who used methods initiated by his Brazilian mentor, Kozol began to think about the implications of these methods for attacking high-illiteracy rates among both adults and children in the United States. He was commissioned by the Cleveland Public Library to design a literacy plan for the nation's large cities, a plan that became the model for a major effort sparked by the State Library of California. Kozol's subsequent book, *Illiterate America*, became the centerpiece of a campaign to spur state, federal, and private action on adult literacy, despite scathing comments from some reviewers in the popular press. Andrew Hacker dismissed the book in his review for the *Nation* (May 25, 1985) as "tendentious" and "repetitious," and David Harman wrote in the *New Republic* (May 27, 1985) that the "tortuous haughtiness of Kozol's prose conceals neither his simplistic exposition of the troublesome dilemma of illiteracy nor the sophomoric nature of the solutions he offers." The book fared much better in specialized reviews for library and educational professionals, however. Harvey Frommer wrote in the *Library Journal* (March 1, 1985) that the book was "passionate and disturbing," and "both a consciousness raiser and a primer for action . . . The two-thirds of America that can read has an obligation to read *Illiterate America.*"

In the mid-1980s, Kozol turned his attention to another element in the complex, interrelated web of urban pathology, that of homelessness, which was then exciting media attention—but, as he pointed out, only because the homeless were now being noticed in the more "upscale" areas of the nation's cities. In 1996 he told Christopher Zimmerman, "In the early and mid-1980s, thousands of families became homeless in New York City, partly as a consequence of the policies of the Reagan era. Inevitably these people walked the streets and stood outside the restaurants and theaters, and their presence was abhorrent in the middle of Manhattan. The civic boosters of the city were alarmed. This would hurt tourism. The last thing theater owners wanted as to have a wealthy couple spend $200 to see *Les Misérables* and then come out from the theater and see the real thing! There was often bitter irony in that situation. I walked by that theater sometimes and would notice people who had been presumably weeping for the poor children in Paris a few minutes before in the theater; now, coming out on the street, they were miserably offended by the sight of people begging on the sidewalk." True to his practice of "hands-on" activism, Kozol began spending nights in a homeless shelter in New York City to have conversations with mothers and children whom he befriended there. From this experience emerged his book *Rachel and Her Children: Homeless Families in America*, a narrative portrayal of the day-to-day struggle of some of the poorest people living on the streets of America's wealthiest city. When *Rachel and Her Children* was published in 1988, *Newsweek* (February 1, 1988) called it "bitterly eloquent" and the *New York Times* (January 28, 1988) called it "a searing indictment of society." It won the Robert F. Kennedy Book Award and the Conscience in Media Award of the American Society of Journalists and Authors.

Still concerned about the inequities inherent in the American public-school system, Kozol set out in 1989 to revisit the issue that had first fueled his passion a quarter-century earlier. He visited rich and poor schools in more than 30 communities coast to coast, concluding that despite the struggles of the 1960s and judicial efforts at desegregation, America's schools still remained "separate and unequal." The book that followed, *Savage Inequalities: Children in America's Schools* (1991), was a serious indictment of a society's failure to address its touted ideal of free public education for all. Alex Haley, the author of *Roots*, wrote: "This book digs so deeply into the tragedy of the American system of public education that it wrenches the reader's psyche." *Savage Inequalities* was a finalist for the 1992 National Book Critics Circle Award and was awarded the New England Book Award in nonfiction.

By the early 1990s, Kozol began concentrating his research on New York City's South Bronx, a neighborhood that had become a national symbol for intractable social pathologies of poverty, illiteracy, crime, substandard housing, and addiction. It was also the neighborhood that had served as a dumping ground for the homeless people who had so alarmed the midtown "civic boosters" a decade earlier. He spent two years in conversations with children, parents, teachers, and religious leaders in the community in researching his 1995 book, *Amazing Grace: The Lives of Children and the Conscience of a Nation*. Despite the harsh reality of its subject matter, the book is a gently written narrative that acknowledges and gives voice to the reflections of the young children themselves and describes the ways in which they are spiritually transcending the pathology around them. The book became a national bestseller in three weeks. In a front-page review for the *Washington Post Book World* (October 22, 1995), Marie Arana-Ward found the book "devastating" but "as good as a blessing" in its tribute to the courage of its subjects.

Shortly after its publication, Kozol addressed a gathering of the nation's publishers, telling them: "I believe the questions that we should be asking about justice and injustice in America are not chiefly programmatic, technical, or scientific. They are theological. But I disagree with those who think we should be asking questions of theology primarily to those who live in poverty. I think we need to ask these questions of ourselves." Unlike most other writers who have attacked social problems, Kozol sees these issues in a spiritual context, as symbols of a deep fracturing of our relationship with transcendence. In the book, Kozol wrote: "If there are amazing graces on this weary earth, I believe that they are these good children sent to us by God and not yet soiled by the knowledge that their nation does not love them," and "If the ghetto were a mistake, we would have fixed it by now. Mistakes can be fixed quite easily. I think that the ghetto is a sinister creation that serves a function for the larger society. It provides us with a place to put our outcasts. It provides us with an opportunity to cleanse our own neighborhoods of people we may regard as less than human. . . . To this degree the South Bronx is not simply another ghetto; it is an artfully created piece of quarantine. And this was done with considerable ingenuity. Perhaps not with malice, but certainly with ample awareness. If that is not a sin, I don't know what the word 'sin' means."

Some of the world's leading advocates for justice and human rights have come to recognize Kozol's insights into the human condition. Nobel Prize–winner Elie Wiesel wrote: "Jonathan's struggle is noble. What he says must be heard. His outcry must shake our nation out of its guilty conscience." Marian Wright Edelman, director of the Children's Defense Fund, wrote that *"Amazing Grace* may turn out to be one of THE books of our times. . . . I encourage all Americans to buy it and read it."

In one sense, this theological interpretation represents a "coming-home" for Kozol. He told Christopher Zimmerman how some of his early, suppressed religious feelings "came back later, especially in these past two to three years, when I've been with so many deeply devout black and Hispanic people, particularly the mothers and grandmothers in the South Bronx. In some ways they reminded me of my mother and grandmother."

—E. M.

SUGGESTED READING: *America* p9 Oct. 7, 1995; *Booklist* p2075 Aug. 1991; *Christian Century* p216 Mar. 2, 1988; *Common Cause* p24+ Spring 1993; *Essence* p60+ Aug. 1992; *Nation* p616+ Nov. 20, 1995; *New York Times Book Review* p7 Jan. 31, 1988, p24+ Feb. 16, 1989, p7 Oct. 6, 1991, p26 Oct. 15, 1995; Publishers Weekly p40 Aug. 16, 1991; *School Library Journal* p226 Mar. 1988; *Time* p74 Feb. 8, 1988

SELECTED BOOKS: Fiction— *The Fume of Poppies*, 1958; Nonfiction— *Death At An Early Age*, 1967; *Free Schools*, 1972; *The Night Is Dark and I Am Far From Home*, 1975; *Children of the Revolution*, 1978; *On Being A Teacher*, 1981; *Illiterate America*, 1985; *Rachel and Her Children*, 1988; *Savage Inequalities*, 1991; *Amazing Grace*, 1995

Eric Kraft

Kraft, Eric

Oct. 29, 1944– Novelist

The American novelist Eric Kraft is a pioneer in the evolving genre of nonlinear hypertext fiction, in which modem-equipped readers can move cursorily through his elaborately interlinked works, *The Complete Peter Leroy (so far)*, or Web site, *Forever Babbingtonian Magazine*. Over a writing career spanning three decades, Kraft had spawned a continuing saga of episodic novels revolving around the character and narrator Peter Leroy in the fic-

tional town of Babbington, Long Island ("clam capital of America"). With the advent of new electronic media over the past decade, Kraft began translating his work into hypertext, earning himself a sizable cult following as one of contemporary literature's leading and most innovative cyberauthors. A review in *Newsweek* (July 17, 1995) called his work "the literary equivalent of Fred Astaire dancing: great art that looks like fun." Kraft's interactive fiction brings "point-and-click" technology to new heights, offering readers a dizzying entree into multilayered connections, creating a sense of being in a literary hall of mirrors with their unexpected reflections of the familiar.

For *World Authors 1990–1995*, Kraft, born on October 29, 1944, writes: "For more than thirty years, I've been working to construct a single large work of fiction composed of many smaller parts related in intricate ways, like the components of a complex machine, or the neighborhoods of a city, or the ingredients in a good clam chowder.

"My work began one cold afternoon in the winter of 1962, when I dreamed up the central character of this big work. *Created* would be far too grand a term, since I was dozing over a German lesson at the time. I was a sophomore at Harvard. I was sitting at a table in Lamont library, with my feet up and my chair tilted back. The room was warm, and I was tired. I dozed. When I woke up, I was lying on the floor, my books were scattered around me, people were laughing, and I was embarrassed. I gathered my things and rushed out of the library, and in the cold air, the memory of a dream returned to me: a snapshot of a nameless little boy, sitting on a dilapidated dock, in the sunny warmth of a summer day, dabbling his feet in the water.

"From time to time, after that moment in the library, the memory of the dream returned, and from time to time the dream itself returned. It wasn't an obsession—not yet. It was just a pleasant amusement, a diversion, a vacation from whatever I was working on, thinking about, or worrying about. I could drift into that dream and play with it, and in playing with it, exploring it, I began improving it. The boy got a name: Peter Leroy. I added a context for him—an island, where the old dock was—an abandoned building on the island—a grand house, perhaps, or an abandoned hotel—I wasn't sure which—a gray bay—the mainland, where the town of Babbington lay. I wrote none of this down. This was not writing—not yet. I had no intention or expectation of making a piece of writing out of this. It was daydreaming.

"Soon, however, like most people who read books, I began to want to write one of my own. Like most people who want to write books, I really wanted to write a book about myself."

Eric Kraft is an author sui generis: an experimental fiction writer who inhabits a metafictional universe to the extent that it is practically impossible to distinguish among his several voices: those of "real-life" author of, chief character in, omniscient narrator of, critical commentator on, and publicist for, his own fictive polylogues. By conflating these voices into a single, self-reflective narrative that is at once voice and echo—all while telling stories renowned for the ordinariness and near-banality of their settings—Kraft occupies a singular niche in contemporary American letters and in the emerging "Cyberia" of Web-driven writing, with clear echoes of earlier endeavors by such writers as Proust, Richardson, and Twain.

The "book about himself" Eric Kraft began writing consists of six print novels published since 1988, all of which are now linked in the hyperfictional *The Complete Peter Leroy (so far)*: *Herb 'n' Lorna*, *Reservations Recommended*, *Little Follies*, *Where Do You Stop?*, *What a Piece of Work I Am*, and *At Home with the Glynns*. But the road to authorship was a tortuous one. Of Kraft's conventional life in the third dimension among the page-turners, it is known that the Harvard graduate was born in Bay Shore, Long Island, and grew up in nearby Babylon. Kraft described himself in this fashion in his *"Who's Who and What's What"* concordance to his fiction: "He has taught school and written textbooks, and he was for a time part-owner and cocaptain of a clam boat, which sank. He has been the recipient of a fellowship from the National Endowment for the Arts, and he was for a time chairman of PEN New England. He is the father of two sons, Scott and Alexis, and lives with his wife, Madeline [whom he married at 18, in 1963], in East Hampton, New York."

For more than 20 years, Kraft devoted much of his creative energy to developing new pedagogical methods for the language arts. After graduating from Harvard's Graduate School of Education in 1966 with a master's degree (he had received a bachelor's degree, cum laude, in English from Har-

vard the year before), he taught English for two years in the public schools of Arlington and Winchester, Massachusetts, in classes that were, at his request, heavily populated with "'slow' or 'problem' students, reluctant readers, and potential dropouts." In 1968 he began a career in educational publishing, as an editor of language-arts textbooks with Ginn and Company and D. C. Heath. Laid off from his full-time job in 1975, he became an independent supplier of freelance editorial services. The shock of readjustment helped focus his literary goals. He wrote: "My editorial-services business grew, and as it did it put useful tools at my disposal—copying machines, electric typewriters, word processors, tax deductions for stationery supplies—all the things one needs to publish in samizdat," a reference to the clandestine system of publishing in the former Soviet Union. Since 1975 Kraft has been editorial director of his own Kraft & Kraft Editorial Services, overseeing the editing of textbooks, creating a series of programs for reading and vocabulary development, and, since the early 1990s, developing several CD-ROM writing-software programs for elementary and secondary schools for such publishers as Prentice-Hall and Houghton-Mifflin.

"In the next couple of years," he wrote on his *Forever Babbingtonian* Web page, "I self-published some of Peter Leroy's juvenilia—'Larry Peters Is Missing' and 'Larry Peters, Child No More'—and a manifesto or prospectus for the work I had in mind—'Large and Unsolicited Fiction,' which imitated the form of an article in a magazine much like *Scientific American*." Kraft's thesis statement underscores how this jargon-filled prospectus was meant to be a parody of the excesses of technical writing: "Size in fiction may be specified usefully according to Ng's volumetric analogy, and the insulating effect of smaller fictions may permit the construction of very large ones, but what then?"

For some years thereafter, he methodically sent fragments of his works to friends. He also continued to mail photocopied fragments of manuscripts to a growing mailing list of readers, which numbered about 200 by 1981. He was by then publishing a four-page leaflet "almost monthly" that provided a kind of serial account of Peter Leroy and of Larry Peters. "I thought I had found the ultimate form for the work," he wrote. Economic constraints forced him to curtail his newsletter feuilletonage, however, and he sought to have fragments published as a novel, but was dissuaded from so doing by a small literary publisher who convinced him that part of the appeal of the Leroy saga was its serendipitous appearance in fragmentary form. The editor suggested that Kraft continue publishing four novellas a year, with no anticipated end to the series.

Kraft wrote: "Well, I thought, why not? Here was a chance to start again, at the beginning. I took it." Thus began the creation of a saga in which, as Kraft-cum-Peter wrote, "The usual descriptions—author and character, ventriloquist and dummy, left brain and right brain—are inaccurate and inadequate. . . . Each of us has found himself liberated by the other, and each of us has found that to a certain degree he has become what he is through the agency of the other. . . . We are not the same person, though we share a mind."

Around 1980, Kraft invented an electromechanical game device he called "The Game of Forking Paths," later renamed "The Babbington Game", a primitive precursor to a hypertext model of nearly infinite linkages. The game device was a box with nine lights controlled by switches that controlled the others. "It seems to me that there are implications about hyperfiction in the design of this game," he wrote.

The publication of his novels by Crown after 1988 helped establish Kraft as a new voice in American fiction, one with a knack for exposing the underlying masks and artifice in the American psyche. When *Herb 'n' Lorna* (1988) appeared, Cathleen Schine wrote a front-page review in the *New York Times Book Review*, calling it "a historical farce, a comedy of four generations of happy errors. This very funny novel—as graceful, complicated, and exhilarating as a quadrille—is an appreciation of folly." His second book, *Reservations Recommended* (1990), is a Swiftian jab at the pretentiousness of big-city restaurants in the yuppie-dominated 1980s. Each chapter describes one of the eateries and includes a restaurant review by B. W. Beath, the pen name of the book's principal character, middle-aged toy designer Matthew Barber, a mediocre Walter Mitteyesque figure who disintegrates into self-absorbed madness—"from soup to nuts," as Malcolm Jones Jr. wrote in *Newsweek* (May 14, 1990). Richard Gehr, writing in *The Village Voice Literary Supplement* (June 1990), added that "Kraft writes honestly and sympathetically about Matthew's emotional vicissitudes and disentangling relationships. But, like all Kraft's work, *Reservations* rejoices in games, frames, masks, and artifice."

Published in 1992, *Little Follies* is a single-volume edition of the first nine installments of *The Personal History of Peter Leroy*. It is a comically nostalgic memoir of Peter Leroy's growing up in 1950s Long Island, told through the self-conscious narrative of the lost language of boyhood and the accumulation of layered allusions to literary classics, such as those by Proust, Thoreau, and Aesop. Anna Shapiro wrote in the *New Yorker* (July 6, 1992) that "at times, reading Kraft is like stumbling across memories of your own life, and yet the work is self-consciously—pointedly—literary . . . In effect, you're always reading two stories: the manifest one, which is clever, anecdotal, suspenseful, and funny, and a mystery, full of clues about the construction of the very book you are reading. . . . Everything seems to mean more than what you're told it means. Eliciting this sensation is the job of literary art—to catch life in its snares and, by the pattern and form of the snares, to accumulate meaning."

Kraft's next book in the Peter Leroy saga, *Where Do You Stop?* (1992), is a first-person narrative of Peter as a seventh-grader in Babbington trying to cope with his newly discovered worlds of quantum physics and quondam sexuality. Like the earlier books, it is full of wit and literary allusion. Walter Satterthwait, reviewing the book for the *New York Times Book Review*, praised Kraft's "elegant, supple, uncommonly precise prose that glides, silk-smooth, from pathos to parody, from slapstick to sentiment, from the mysteries of moonlight on Bolotomy Bay to the mysteries of particle physics." The book that followed, *What a Piece of Work I Am* (1994), adds a soupçon of adolescent sexuality to the (clam) chowder, with the introduction of Ariane Lodkochnikov, the older sister of Peter's imaginary boyhood chum Raskol. Karen Kabo, writing in *The New York Times Book Review* (April 17, 1994), wrote that Kraft, "a master at illuminating the shoals and shallows of a young person's heart," has created "a heroine as complex as his narrative." Peter soon develops a crush on the rebellious Ariane, who, as one of Babbington's "bad girls" in the 1950s, had taken a literal "back seat" to many of her male counterparts. But Ariane is a creation of Peter's own evolving imagination, a girl who had "really" died in a house fire but is willed back to existence by Peter himself. This conceit led Mark Ciabattari in the *Washington Post Book World* (April 24, 1994) to comment, "Novelist Eric Kraft's niche in contemporary literature might well be as a sunny, upbeat American version of the Argentine fabulist Jorge Louis Borges. Like the latter's magic realism, Kraft's writing focuses on personal identity as an ephemeral, ever-changing construct . . . " *At Home With the Glynns*, published in 1995, introduces Peter to an existential world peopled by eccentric characters, including Albertine Gaudet, who would eventually become his wife, and the precocious Glynn twins, Margot and Martha, whose idea of erotic foreplay is having Peter act out the plots of foreign films. *Leaving Small's Hotel* (1998) finds Peter and Albertine trying to sell their failing hotel as Peter continues his memoirs.

One of the pages in the *Forever Babbingtonian Magazine* Web site is bylined "Mark Dorset," who turns out to be another persona of Kraft's multimirrored ego, in which characters assume personae as "real people" and vice-versa, another indicator of how Kraft continues to straddle the limina of belief and stretch conventional notions of epistemology. Realizing that Kraft was trying to accommodate the material, as well as his thinking, to the medium of the printed book, Mark Dorset explains in the "Afterword: On HyperFiction" to *The Complete Peter Leroy (so far)*: "The heart of the electronic version is the books that already exist. They are a given, and their form as narratives is a given, which means that reading them is a page-turning, linear experience, but experiencing the total work, the whole universe of Peter Leroy, has its nonlinear aspects. There are hypertextual elements built into the books, links that take the reader from one book to another at various points, implanted allusions that link the one book to another at various points, implanted allusions that link the books in many ways and at many points."

And the saga continues. In describing the folding-upon-itself structure of his complex fiction, Kraft finds it useful to employ four wildly disparate metaphors: the old-fashioned American small town, an organic molecule, a Niels Bohr model of the atom, and "a good clam chowder." He likes to think of his readers-as-voyeurs wandering through streets and alleyways lined with shops and houses, lingering in the air of a summer evening to peek in windows. He also likens his work to the "ball-and-stick models of an organic molecule that high school biology teachers construct," in which "the molecule is truly more than the sum of its parts, with characteristics that the component atoms do not have alone or even in the aggregate." Next, Bohr's model of the atom as a "little solar system" can suggest Peter Leroy's personal history (the nucleus) surrounded by other books (the orbiting electrons) "that stand a bit apart from Peter's tale of himself but are bound to it invisibly, powerfully." Finally, in keeping with Babbington's heritage as the "clam capital of America," Kraft suggests his fiction is like a good clam chowder: "If you use good fresh clams," he writes, "you're going to get some dark, gritty bits at the bottom, too, some sand and bits of shell and—how shall I put this—artifacts of the clam's digestive process. Holding all these disparate bits together should be a rich broth. . . . The chunky bits in this chowder are the books. . . . The broth is the whole system of cross-reference and allusion that links and flavors and spices the chunky bits. Taken as a whole—that is, as a chowder rather than as a bowl of the components of a chowder—it is a metaphorical approximation of the mind of Peter Leroy."

Despite the lack of conventional linear sequence in his works, the mind of Eric Kraft has created a quirky but benevolent universe in which he himself is player, protagonist, and character, one rescued from solipsism by the endearing stories he weaves, by the nature of the new medium that he is mastering, and by the connectedness he has established with a growing coterie of loyal readers. —E. M.

SUGGESTED READING: *Booklist* p1552 May 1, 1995; *Library Journal* p131 Mar. 15, 1992; *Newsweek* p72 May 14, 1990, p56 July 17, 1995; *New Yorker* p76+ July 6, 1992, p109 May 16, 1994; *New York Times Book Review* p8 Sep. 6, 1992, p11 Apr. 17, 1994; *Time* p75 Sep. 28, 1992; *Voice Literary Supplement* p6 June 12, 1990, p29 Mar. 10, 1992; *Washington Post Book World* p4 Apr. 24, 1994

SELECTED BOOKS: Some of the work described below had earlier been self-published by the author in epistolatory form, photocopied, and distributed via mail in the 1970s and 1980s. Fiction in Book Format—*Life on the Bolotomy*, 1986; *The Static of the Spheres*, 1986; *My Mother Takes a Tumble*, 1986; *Herb 'n' Lorna*, 1988; *Reservations Recommended*, 1990; *Little Follies*, 1992; *Where Do You Stop?*, 1992; *What a Piece of Work I Am*, 1994; *At Home with the Glynns*, 1995; *Leaving Small's Hotel*, 1998; Fiction in Hypertext Format—*The Complete Peter Leroy (so far)*, 1997; *Immortal* Hilarity, 1997

Courtesy of Gary Krist

Krist, Gary

May 23, 1957– Novelist; short-story writer

The American short-story writer, travel writer, and novelist Gary Krist has taken as his major theme, in his story collections *The Garden State* (1988) and *Bone by Bone* (1994) and his novel, *Bad Chemistry* (1998), the dread—as Ron Carlson put it in the *New York Times Book Review* (May 29, 1994)—that lies at the heart of rites of passage. Describing one of Krist's narrators, an adolescent boy, in a comment that might apply to other of Krist's protagonists, Carlson wrote that the boy recognizes that "forces beyond his power are shaping all [the characters'] lives. And that understanding makes the stories ring true."

For *World Authors 1990–1995*, Gary Krist writes: "I was born in New Jersey in 1957 and enjoyed an untroubled suburban upbringing that was fairly typical of the time and place. My mother, a British war bride, came from a family of Cornish sea captains, while my father stemmed from earthier roots: immigrant workers from the Sudetenland.

Neither of my parents went to college, but it was expected that I and my siblings would. This was postwar America, and children were naturally expected to climb past their parents on the socio-economic ladder (an optimism that seems hard to believe nowadays).

"It's said that I take after my maternal grandfather more than anyone else in the family. He was a Devon-based civil engineer, the first male in the family to defy tradition by not going to sea. He died when I was very young, but the stories of his tall tales are numerous; I remember being firmly convinced that the man could see through walls. I also think I inherit something from my paternal grandfather, a worker in a New Jersey silk mill who was blacklisted for his union-organizing activities. He stopped speaking for the last years of his life—probably as a result of a stroke—which made him an object of intense interest to me during my childhood.

"I grew up during the Sixties, but I can't say that my involvement in the era went much beyond wearing a Nehru jacket and a pair of powder-blue bell-bottoms. I've always been a late developer, and didn't have my political consciousness raised until my last year of high school. I was too busy discovering books and classical music, both of which were relatively new phenomena to me. The thought occurred to me in high school that becoming a writer might be a romantic thing to do, and this thought persisted through college, though I wrote virtually nothing until my Fulbright year in West Germany, where I was supposed to be studying literary criticism but instead used the time to travel and write short stories. My work at this time was highly surrealistic/fantastical—callow and arty stuff that reflected the pretensions of a Jersey kid who came late to highbrow culture but then tried to make up for the delay at Princeton. In any case, I was writing.

"When I returned to the US, I moved in with and eventually married Elizabeth Cheng, my college flame, and found a position (with the imposing title 'Logic Coordinator') writing standardized test items in New York City. By this time the 1980s had begun, and I thought I'd better toss aside the fake magic-realism and get on with my real life's work. So I started to write stories about New Jersey—stories about the moral tribulations of ordinary people, written as simply and honestly as I could manage. The result was *The Garden State*, which was published in 1988. This first collection, unlike many, is not in the least autobiographical, though the settings may hint otherwise. The stories are fundamentally comic in that they represent generally good-humored attempts by decent people to understand and control a reality that refuses to be understood or controlled. But there's a deeper strangeness and darkness to some of the stories that seemed to elude all but a few reviewers.

"After *The Garden State* received an award and some other bits of good fortune, I briefly entertained the delusion that I might now be able to quit my day job and devote myself to writing. Unfortunately, though, the royalty checks did not begin to arrive with the regularity I had hoped for, and I found that I had to continue coordinating logic (though only part-time now). Meanwhile, I'd started working regularly as a book reviewer and travel writer, and while neither activity affected my fiction much, I did enjoy the free books and free trips. Because of all this extracurricular activity, however, it took me six years to produce my second collection, *Bone by Bone* (though I do have one and a half desk-drawer novels to show for the period). The stories in this bigger book are, I feel, the work of an older, less optimistic man; their strangeness and darkness is more overt, their outlook less sanguine. I've often speculated that fatherhood may have had something to do with the gloomier quality to my later stories, since having a daughter (Anna) has definitely sharpened my sense of the peril, both moral and physical, at large in the world. But why should I blame my daughter? One certainly needs no excuse in this world for an increasingly bleak outlook.

"In 1994, my wife landed her dream job at *National Geographic* magazine in Washington DC and so we left New York. I took the move as an excuse to quit my day job finally (although in the last few years it had turned into a fairly serious editorial position in educational book publishing). I decided that the time had come to write a novel addressed to a somewhat broader audience than that of my earlier work. I changed publishers (from Harcourt Brace to Random House) and began *Bad Chemistry*, a literary thriller that is, I hope, as much about marriage and the ambivalent hope of technology as it is about drugs, deception, and skullduggery on the Internet. Even in this more popular genre, though, I find that the same basic concerns keep worming their way into my work—in particular, my concern with the question of why it is so difficult for ordinary people to contrive happy, morally responsible lives in the relatively disaster-free atmosphere of contemporary middle-class America."

The fragility of human relationships, the shifting ground of truth and reality, and betrayal—intentional or inadvertent—are among Gary Krist's prominent themes. In *Bone By Bone*, for example, three stories, "Ghost Stories," "Giant Step," and "Numbers," deal with the Erikson family—mother Faye, father Cal, sister Elise, and Cliff, the narrator. The mother betrays the father by losing a pregnancy and attending a Catholic church; the daughter betrays the mother by revealing to her father that her mother has shown the children her fearfulness when he was away; the father betrays the mother by having an affair; the mother betrays her children by taking a job at Jungle Habitat and giving her love to the animals; the son betrays the mother by assuming she is having an affair with his older friend. At the conclusion of the Erikson stories, the

14-year-old Cliff ruminates, as he and his mother are concocting a story to explain his broken arm (the result of a fight with her purported lover): ". . . I thought of asking my mother again whether what I suspected about Hank was true. But I never did, not only because I felt she wouldn't answer me . . . but also because I knew that her answer would have been irrelevant. The damage was done, no matter what she told me. The actual truth was beside the point." Cliff and his mother agree to say that his arm was broken in a fall when he was alone. "It was a lie that said nothing, but that said everything. And it was ours. That lie, in fact, was the last thing my mother and I ever truly shared."

Ron Carlson, reviewing *Bone by Bone* in his *New York Times Book Review* article, noted that most of the stories feature "ordinary people learning to swim in hot water." Jessica Treadway, writing in *Ploughshares* (Fall 1994), observed that in *Bone by Bone*, "Krist gives us 13 compelling variations on the 'what if?' theme, pushing plot and character beyond conventional comfort zones and into the realm of discovery which comes only through risk." She cited the stories "Baggage," in which a man's friends help him make a move that would have no significance except that he is leaving behind a woman grown helpless with multiple sclerosis, and "Bludgeon," in which two men escape from a rehab facility and obtain liquor and a gun from a man in a wheelchair. "What happens then reminds us, with a shiver, of how compassion sometimes lies down with cowardice, and how a good intention can still come to a bad end," she concluded.

In *Bad Chemistry*, Krist's first novel, two characters—14-year-old Evan and a former police officer, Kate—are brought together after Evan discovers a dead body, minus its head and hands, and Kate's husband turns up missing. "Gary Krist . . . has written a first novel that walks and quacks like a skillfully carpentered mystery. But lying not far beneath its polished surface are the outlines of something that seems to interest him far more than the standard questions of 'Whodunit?' and 'Why?' . . . What makes *Bad Chemistry* more than another well-constructed genre novel are those dark shadows beneath the surface, those intimations of everyone's need for what [a character named Joel] calls an 'amazing secret' and what Evan describes as 'something really important. Finally.'"

Surveying travel books in an article in the *New York Times Book Review* (December 6, 1992), Gary Krist perhaps hinted at his own purpose as a writer. "Travel writing—as a result of several decades of institutionalized tourism—has become a subversive act. In all too many places nowadays the travel writer must be a kind of guerrilla, infiltrating the Disneyland facades built by a tourist establishment that is determined to make travel into something safe, predictable, and maximally profitable. Much of what the . . . tourism industry has created—the artificially restored 'historic districts,' the mass-produced 'traditional crafts,' the prefabricated 'cultural events'. . . actually stands in the way of a genuine travel experience, which requires overturning the prepared and marketed version of a place in order to find the real, the unprocessed and, in many cases, the actively suppressed." Krist has, in his own writing, been that guerrilla, taking the hard road to find "the real . . . and . . . the actively suppressed."
—S. Y.

SUGGESTED READING: *New York Times Book Review* p9+ Dec. 6, 1992, p7+ May 29, 1994; *Ploughshares* p245+ Fall 1994; *Contemporary Authors* vol. 132, 1991

SELECTED BOOKS: *The Garden State*, 1988; *Bone by Bone*, 1994; *Bad Chemistry*, 1998

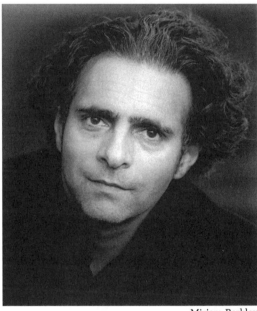

Miriam Berkley

Kureishi, Hanif

1954– Novelist; playwright; screenwriter

Of mixed Pakistani and English parentage, the British screenwriter, playwright, and novelist Hanif Kureishi first won international acclaim in 1985 with his screenplay for the hit movie *My Beautiful Laundrette*, which portrayed with honesty and humor the world of the Asian immigrant population in London. In a subsequent screenplay for the 1987 film *Sammy and Rosie Get Laid* and in short stories and novels like *The Buddha of Suburbia* (1990) and *The Black Album* (1995), Kureishi has continued to explore the life of an immigrant community that until then had not been investigated in literature or film. His directorial debut and third screenplay, *London Kills Me* (1991), deals with homeless youth and the drug scene in and around Notting Hill Gate and Portobello Road. A short-story collection, *Love in a Blue Time*, appeared in 1997, and his novel *Intimacy* in 1999. From the late 1980s Kureishi's essays, reviews, and cultural commentaries have regularly appeared in the pages of *New Statesman & Society*, and he co-edited, with Jon Savage, *The Faber Book of Pop* (1995). Kureishi's themes encompass racism, colonialism (particularly the problem of how comparatively recent immigrants of color can be assimilated into a centuries-old white culture), and all varieties of sexual relationships. He has been praised for the multidimensionality of his characters and the compassion with which he depicts them. His work has proved to be controversial, however, especially among members of the Pakistani and Indian communities in Great Britain, who have complained that Kureishi depicts them in too negative a light.

Hanif Kureishi was born in 1954 (some sources give his year of birth as 1956) in the London suburb of Bromley, in Kent, where he grew up. His Pakistani father, Rafiushan Kureishi, a clerk and part-time political journalist, came to England in 1947 to attend college; his mother is English. During the 1950s and 1960s, the first wave of Asian and black immigrants arrived in Great Britain, and their presence was resented by some members of the native population. As the only Asian in his school, Kureishi became an early victim of racial fear and prejudice. One teacher called him "Pakistani Pete," and as he told Glenn Collins of the *New York Times* (May 24, 1990), "Kids I'd known since the age of five began spitting at me and kicking me around." Although young Kureishi wanted to fit into British society, he found himself torn by a severe personal conflict. As he wrote in "The Rainbow Sign," an autobiographical essay that he published with his script for *My Beautiful Laundrette*: "From the start I tried to deny my Pakistani self. It was a curse and I wanted to be rid of it. I wanted to be like everyone else."

Although he majored in philosophy at London University, Kureishi was more interested in writing, which he had been doing since the age of 14, with the encouragement of his father. As a teenager he wrote four novels (none of which were published), because he found in writing an emotional outlet that was unavailable to him elsewhere. "When people insult you, when friends of yours become skinheads and go out Paki-bashing and you don't have anyone to talk to about your feelings and you're far too nervous to confront your friends directly, you have to express yourself somehow," he said during an interview with Ginny Dougary for the London *Observer* (April 1, 1990). Kureishi was also attracted to the theater, where a new wave of British dramatists, among them John Osborne, Joe Orton, and Harold Pinter, had been experimenting with innovative approaches to their craft. "In the middle sixties until the middle seventies the theater in Britain was re-

ally exciting," Kureishi told Marlaine Glicksman for *Rolling Stone* (November 19, 1987). "There was a lot of fringe stuff, there were a lot of companies around. A lot of good writers. That was where the energy was."

After leaving college Kureishi began an apprenticeship in London theaters. "They liked me because I was Indian, and lower middle class," he explained somewhat sardonically to Glenn Collins. "That was chic." Kureishi devoted part of the day to writing plays and, to support himself, spent the rest of his time contributing pornographic fiction to magazines under the pseudonym Antonia French. His first full-length play, *The Mother Country*, was staged in 1980 and won the Thames Television Playwrights Award. After working as an usher at the Royal Court Theater, one of the most progressive and innovative theaters in London, Kureishi became one of its writers in residence, and in 1981 the Royal Court produced his second play, *Borderline*, about the problems of Asians living in London, a subject about which he had first-hand knowledge. To augment that knowledge, he had spent several weeks interviewing Indians and Pakistanis in the heavily immigrant Southall area of London.

Birds of Passage, Kureishi's next play, was staged in 1983. Later in the same year, the Royal Shakespeare Company presented his play *Outskirts*, about a pair of adult friends who share the guilty secret of a childhood crime. *Outskirts* was accompanied by two shorter plays, *Tomorrow—Today!* and *The King and Me*, the second of which deals with a young woman's obsession with Elvis Presley. Reviewing the three dramas in *British Book News* (February 1984), Judy Meewezen wrote: "For readers who don't seek a hint of real optimism, these pictures of urban tragedy, of those who exist on the outskirts of social, moral, and material prosperity, are tense and fascinating." The Royal Shakespeare Company also commissioned Kureishi's adaptation of Bertolt Brecht's *Mother Courage and Her Children*, in 1984.

It was in the medium of film that Kureishi was soon to enjoy his first major success. The writer traces his inspiration for *My Beautiful Laundrette* to a conversation he had with a friend who suggested that he write about his own life and that of Asian immigrants in Britain. Kureishi realized immediately that he had found his ideal subject. "It came to me as a great illumination," he told Marlaine Glicksman. "It was an epiphany. I suddenly thought, 'Oh, this material is rich.'"

Kureishi wrote the screenplay for *My Beautiful Laundrette* while visiting his relatives in Karachi, Pakistan in 1985. It was only then, he later reported, that he developed a genuine understanding of Pakistani culture and began to acquire insight into the experiences of his father and other Pakistanis who had immigrated to England. Kureishi visited Pakistan at least partly to resolve questions within himself about where, given his mixed racial heritage, he truly belonged. "It helped to fill the gap;

by absorbing your past you can go forward," he told Ginny Dougary. "They thought I was a bit of a bum," Kureishi said of his relatives. "Living in a poor Third World country, they thought wanting to be a writer was dreamy and impractical. It was my first taste of living under a dictatorship. People would come to my uncle's house who had been rotting in jails with rats climbing over them because they were political dissidents. It was disturbing and made me think more carefully." It also made him realize that even though he was not fully accepted in England, that country was nevertheless his true home.

Directed by Stephen Frears, *My Beautiful Laundrette* is the story of a Pakistani family in South London and its struggle to move into the upper middle class. Originally made for British commercial television on a budget of just $900,000, it was subsequently picked up for theatrical release. "I wrote it as a recycling of material that I used before, because I wasn't very serious about screenwriting," Kureishi explained to Marlaine Glicksman. "I suddenly thought, 'Well, I'll have a go at it; I need the money. I'll just try it.'" He decided to make the story a comedy, he later said, because he "didn't want to write a film about a minority, a ghetto film about these strange people with their strange problems." After airing on British television, *My Beautiful Laundrette* was screened at film festivals in Toronto, London, and Edinburgh to considerable acclaim. It was voted the most popular film at the Rotterdam Festival and won the best film of the year award from the London *Evening Standard*.

Although the Pakistanis in *My Beautiful Laundrette* have to struggle to succeed in an alien land, Kureishi does not present them as victims. The film's central figure, Omar, is an ambitious Pakistani teenager who both understands and accepts the values of Prime Minister Margaret Thatcher's "enterprise" society and gives every indication of being able to prosper in it. Omar's mentor and role model is his uncle Nasser, who, having learned how to milk the system ("There is no such thing as race in a free-enterprise culture," he says), has become a successful businessman by operating parking garages and laundries and by profiteering from slum housing. The corruption of capitalism is represented by another of Omar's relatives, Salim, who saunters around in well-cut suits and has no qualms whatsoever about his racketeering and drug-dealing activities. Once a successful journalist in Pakistan, Omar's father now spends his days in bed drinking vodka. He wants his son to attend college, but Omar has other ideas and accepts an offer from Nasser to take over one of his businesses, an unprofitable self-service laundry in a seedy neighborhood. With money from the theft of a drug shipment, Omar renovates the Laundromat—or laundrette—and converts it into a neon-lighted fun house, complete with pinball machines and a stereo system.

The film's candid treatment of the family's sexual morality was among its most-discussed elements. Although he is married to a Pakistani woman, Nasser has an English mistress; Tania, one of Nasser's daughters, is promiscuous; and Omar is homosexual. A focal point of the movie is Omar's love affair with Johnny, a punk whom he hires to work at the Laundromat. Despite the protestations of his skinhead friends, who resent his involvement with a "Paki," Johnny stays loyal to Omar, and the film ends with a love scene between Omar and Johnny that emphasizes the purity of their feelings for each other.

When *My Beautiful Laundrette* was released in the United States, in February 1986, critical reaction was largely enthusiastic. Jack Kroll of *Newsweek* (February 24, 1986) called it "a delightful surprise in every way. . . . It's a sharp, sophisticated, funny, sexy, compassionate picture about . . . real . . . arresting characters. . . . Its politics are embedded in its humanity. The screenplay . . . grinds no ideological axes in its loving and ironic examination of Pakistanis caught between cultures." In his review for the *New York Times* (March 7, 1986), Vincent Canby declared that the film "puts its own truth above the fear of possibly offending someone. Without showing off, it has courage as well as artistry. . . . *My Beautiful Laundrette* is a fascinating, eccentric, very personal movie." Canby also praised Kureishi for creating characters "so complex they can't be easily categorized as good or bad," and he noted Kureishi's "comic paradox that his upper-class Pakistani immigrants have become the exploiters in a land that once exploited them."

Some reviewers, however, thought that *My Beautiful Laundrette* tried to tackle too many issues and that the mix did not work. But that minority opinion, even when expressed, was usually balanced by positive criticism as well, as in David Denby's review in *New York* (March 3, 1986): "[Kureishi] plunges right in, and his work is bracingly direct. But it's also the work of a playwright, not a screenwriter. He constructs dialectically, with balanced, warring forces; he's impatient with mere atmosphere (the lifeblood of the cinema), and he's much too explicit—his characters have the annoying habit of exactly representing themselves in every speech. Kureishi packs too much in; the plot forms itself too easily into contrasts and climaxes. . . . But still, in comparison with the chicken feed we usually get in movies, *My Beautiful Laundrette* is a work of substance."

One quarter in which the film was not well received was the Pakistani community in Britain, whose members resented such a warts-and-all depiction of their culture. Even more distressed by *My Beautiful Laundrette* were Pakistani immigrants living in New York City, who showed their displeasure by picketing the film. Kureishi was unrepentant, however. "People think you're supposed to show them exclusively as strong, truthful, and beautiful," he told Glenn Collins. "It's just exactly what Philip Roth went through," he said, alluding to the Jewish-American novelist, who has often been attacked for portraying Jews in what some consider an unfavorable light. *My Beautiful Laundrette* brought Kureishi an Oscar nomination for best original screenplay and the New York Film Critics Circle Award for best screenplay.

Kureishi continued his partnership with Stephen Frears in *Sammy and Rosie Get Laid*, a film that for marketing reasons was released first in the United States, in October 1987, before opening in England in January 1988. The movie's baldly explicit title led the Motion Picture Association of America to refuse to register it and the advertising departments of some newspapers to identify it with discreet simplicity as *Sammy and Rosie*. Made with a larger budget than *My Beautiful Laundrette* (although, at $2 million, the film still qualified as low-budget), *Sammy and Rosie Get Laid*, like its predecessor, focuses on immigrant life in London. Set against a backdrop of racial violence, the film includes frequent shots of white policemen battling black, stone-throwing rioters—scenes inspired by the race riots that occurred in the largely black Brixton area of South London during the mid-1980s. In the midst of that battle zone live Sammy and Rosie, a married couple. Sammy is an Asian accountant; Rosie, a white, feminist social worker. They live in a 1960s-style "open" marriage that permits Sammy to enjoy his lover, an American photographer named Anna, and Rosie to acquire a lover as well, a black man named Danny.

The emotional core of the movie lies not in the dispiriting lives of Sammy and Rosie, however, but in the story of Sammy's father, Rafi, a businessman-politician in his native Pakistan, who returns to London to be reunited with his son, whom he has not seen since the boy was five, and with Alice, a former lover, whom he had deserted thirty years before. Rafi is shocked to discover that England is not the civilized, tolerant place he remembers from the past. Stunned by the race riots, he is also taken aback by the new climate of sexual permissiveness, especially by an open display of lesbian love that he happens to witness. Rafi has considerable charm and is presented in a more sympathetic light than the other characters, until the devastating revelation that he had sanctioned the torture of political opponents in his homeland. Although he dismisses the charge as being of no importance, the film implies that Rafi cannot escape the consequences; he is followed by a curious, spectral figure (perhaps one of the torture victims), and his rekindled love affair with Alice fails to work out. The movie ends with his suicide and the shared grief of Sammy and Rosie.

In discussing *Sammy and Rosie Get Laid* with Marlaine Glicksman, Kureishi said, "It's about the kind of moral positions that people have to take around a very complicated issue [the Brixton riots]. So, like *Laundrette*, it's about public issues and private issues at the same time: the private lives of the people involved in it and the larger issues that are pressing on them, about which they have to make choices, have to take stands." In an interview granted to Helen Dudar during the filming of *Sammy and Rosie Get Laid*, Kureishi, only half-jokingly, said that the goal of each day's shoot was to turn out a film with maximum "filth and anarchy," and he expressed a strong desire to avoid making a genteel British film in the vein of *A Room with a View* and *A Passage to India*. "They have a kind of suburban—or bourgeois—quality that enrages me," he told Dudar, as quoted in the *New York Times* (November 8, 1987). "You want a movie to be wilder and dirtier and kind of rough and cheap—and defiant as well."

Sammy and Rosie Get Laid collected mixed reviews. Among the film's supporters was Jay Scott, who in his review for the Toronto *Globe and Mail* (October 30, 1987) called it "the best British film of the year" and "one of the best films of the year from any country." Equally enthusiastic was Patricia Hluchy of *Maclean's* (November 16, 1987): "A giddy tour through a fun house of satire and surrealism, *Sammy and Rosie Get Laid* ranks as one of the most exhilarating—and ambitious—comedies of the year." Disagreeing were Desson Howe of the *Washington Post* (December 25, 1987), who found *Sammy and Rosie Get Laid* even more "convoluted and pointless" than *My Beautiful Laundrette*, and Martin Sutton of *Films & Filming* (January 1988), who wrote, "If ambition were the only criterion, *Sammy and Rosie* would be a masterpiece. As it is, the film is too strained and confused, overreaching itself to the point where political and dramatic bewilderment sets in."

In spite of the success of his first two screenplays, Kureishi has insisted that he does not see himself exclusively as a screenwriter. In keeping with that view of his vocation, he became a regular contributor of reviews and cultural essays to the *New Statesman & Society*. Among his most incisive articles for that publication (July 21, 1989) was his "England, your England," in which the London-born Kureishi confronted the question of his own identity while visiting Karachi. "'My country' isn't a notion that comes easily," he wrote of his earlier struggles to maintain ties with his ancestral land (the nation-state Pakistan, of course, emerged as a postcolonial invention on the Indian subcontinent). "It is still difficult to answer the question, where do you come from? I have never wanted to identify with England. When Enoch Powell spoke for England, I turned away in final disgust." Yet, he continued, "despite all this, some kind of identification with England remains. It is strange to go away to the land of your ancestors, to find out how much you have in common with people there, yet at the same time to realize how British you are." The essay concludes with a plea for native Britons and new immigrants to decide about the future while affirming that their fates are inextricably intermixed. "This decision is not one about a small group of irrelevant people who can be contemptuously described as 'minorities,'" he concluded. "It is about the direction of British society. About its values and how humane it can be when experiencing real difficulty and possible breakdown. . . . The future is in our hands."

During this period Kureishi also began turning his talents to a different genre: fiction. His first published novel, the semiautobiographical *The Buddha of Suburbia* (1990), is a compendium and recapitulation of the themes with which he had dealt in his two screenplays. Much of the novel was loosely based on Kureishi's own experiences as an adolescent of mixed parentage coming to maturity in the England of the 1970s. The first-person narrator is Karim Amir, the son of an Indian father and an English mother who lives in the London suburb of Orpington before moving to the city itself, where he becomes involved in the punk scene of the 1970s, has a variety of sexual adventures with both men and women, and eventually becomes a highly successful actor. The "Buddha" of the title is Karim's father, a businessman who, in his spare time, cashes in on the vogue for Indian mysticism by posing as a spiritual guru to gullible suburban audiences.

The Buddha of Suburbia, which won the Whitbread Prize for the best British fiction debut of 1990 and which has been translated into 23 languages, met with a mixed critical reception. It was awarded high praise by Michiko Kakutani of the *New York Times* (May 15, 1990), who called it "a wickedly funny novel. . . . that's at once a traditional comedy of manners and a scathing satire on race relations in Britain. . . . [Kureishi] has a gift for locating the hypocrisies that inform relationships between the white and nonwhite worlds, and absolutely no misgivings about exposing those hypocrisies on both sides." Reviewing the novel for *Vogue* (May 1990), Quentin Crisp was equally positive, calling *The Buddha of Suburbia* "delightful—curious, perceptive, and funny." A book critic for *Publishers Weekly* (February 23, 1990) was also impressed: "Resembling a modern-day *Tom Jones*, this is an astonishing book, full of intelligence and élan."

A number of other critics, however, found the novel a promising achievement rather than an accomplished one, and a few pointed out that Kureishi had failed to go beyond what he had already done in his screenplays. For Lee Lescaze of the *Wall Street Journal* (May 8, 1990), this was a considerable flaw. "Like Mr. Kureishi's movies, *Buddha* has an array of interesting characters and subplots, but without the dramatic power of visual images, the novel seems rambling and inconsequential." Lescaze also criticized the first-person narration: "Karim is a naive teenager when the novel opens, and he seems awkward and adolescent to the end. He observes, but never becomes an emotionally engaging character." For Clark Blaise, writing in the *New York Times* (May 6, 1990), Kureishi had failed to fully master the transition "from screenwriting . . . in which competing subplots and quick cuts establish their own daring rhythm, to the conventional *bildungsroman*, in

which nothing exists without a textured, modulated, layered consciousness."

Returning to screenwriting with *London Kills Me*, which premiered at the London Film Festival in November 1991 and was released theatrically in the United States in August 1992, Kureishi assumed the role of director for the first time. "I was frightened, terrified. I never wanted to be a director; it wasn't something I wanted to do all my life," he told the London-based American critic Matt Wolf in a *New York Times* profile (July 14, 1991). Kureishi added that he had accepted the director's role at the behest of producer Tim Bevan, who had also financed *My Beautiful Laundrette*. "It would have been perverse to say no," he said, "if the only reason was that I was too frightened, which it was. Also, I'm not afraid of failure because writing's my main thing, anyway. If I don't direct again, it's no loss for the world—or for me." Like his other screenplays, *London Kills Me* treats with sympathy the aspirations of a group of young people on the cultural fringe, although race is no longer the focal point. Instead, Kureishi turned to the intertwined themes of drug abuse and homelessness, as he told J. B. Miller for the *New York Times* (August 2, 1992): "Drugs are high-risk capitalism. Ecstasy was the ultimate Thatcherite drug, because you could get blissed out on the weekend and still go to work Monday morning. Not like LSD. The kids around Portobello Road are into the sixties scene without the politics, just the culture. It's all about hedonism. The squatting scene is massive." Kureishi had earlier told Matt Wolf that *London Kills Me* was "less ideologically oriented" than his earlier films. "It's not about race; it's not about class. It's a story about these guys searching for these shoes and what happens to them." Trying to maintain a low profile in the face of death threats by Islamic fundamentalists, Kureishi's friend Salman Rushdie had to turn down an invitation to appear in this film—as he had earlier declined the opportunities to make cameo appearances in *My Beautiful Laundrette* and *Sammy and Rosie Get Laid*.

To some reviewers *London Kills Me* was as aimless as the lives of its characters. In his evaluation for the *New York Times* (August 7, 1992), for example, Vincent Canby lamented the absence of Stephen Frears's direction: "Frears . . . might have persuaded the writer to shape this very raw material to make some dramatic or even political point. *London Kills Me* now plays as if Mr. Kureishi had filmed his notebook. It's an accumulation of ideas for characters and scenes that remain undeveloped and without focus. . . . Of far more interest than the film is the new Penguin paperback *London Kills Me*. It contains Mr. Kureishi's three produced screenplays and four essays. . . . He's not yet a film director, but he's a first-rate writer."

In 1993 Kureishi went to New York to supervise an adaptation of *The Buddha of Suburbia* for a BBC mini-series, with music by David Bowie and under the direction of Roger Mitchell, who co-wrote the screenplay. Due to the squeamishness of American broadcasters, it failed to find an airing even on cable channels, but it was finally shown at the end of 1994 at the Public Theater in Manhattan. Discussing the controversy in *New York* (September 20, 1993), Jeannette Walls wrote that the show was "apparently too raunchy for American viewers" and that "American broadcasters are nervous . . . because there are 27 bare breasts in the first half-hour, which doesn't seem to bother the British too much." In his *New York Times* (December 29, 1994) commentary on the controversy, television critic John J. O'Connor defended *The Buddha of Suburbia* as "actually gentle and quite nonaggressive." Caryn James had earlier praised the Public Theater screening, writing in the same newspaper (December 9, 1994) that the film "affirms how rare it is to find a vision as perceptive and blunt as Mr. Kureishi's. It is a relief to find him in top, entertaining form."

Kureishi has since devoted himself to prose writing. In 1995 he co-edited, with Jon Savage, *The Faber Book of Pop*, an 813-page reference anthology of writings on postwar popular music designed, in Kureishi's words, "to give a sense of the range and variety of pop writing; perhaps to present—if sketchily—the alternative history of our time told from the standpoint of popular music." The book garnered generally favorable reviews, though Liz Thomson lambasted it as "a long ramble on a road without signposts" in a column in Kureishi's own *New Statesman & Society* (May 12, 1995) that criticized its length, unevenness, and "lack of intellectual rigor."

The Black Album, Kureishi's second novel, was also published in 1995 as a sequel of sorts to *The Buddha of Suburbia*. Set in the London of 1989, a time when the expatriate Muslim community was riven by the controversy over Salman Rushdie's *The Satanic Verses*, *The Black Album* focuses on the struggles of college student Shahid Hasan to negotiate the treacherous shoals of love, sex, identity, and politics that threaten to devour him. Politically, he oscillates between supporting the orthodox purity demanded by his neighbor, Riaz, and the more relaxed Western attitudes typified by his radical-feminist teacher Deedee Osgood; personally, he is buffeted between his hedonistic brother Chili and his wife, Zulma, a rich Indian feminist. These contradictions are deftly probed by Michelle Har Kim in her review of the novel in the *Nation* (September 11, 1995). Describing Shahid's "tragic collection and recollection of his identity" as he makes his home "on the boundary," she writes: "It's hard, but also thrilling, to be young in Hanif Kureishi's London." Kim continues: "Like *The Buddha of Suburbia*, *The Black Album* is a tumultuous exploration of identity, belonging and responsibility, and once again conclusions are elusive, with uncritical discussion of race and superficial interrogation of Muslim fundamentalism."

During the 1990s Kureishi's short stories began appearing with increasing frequency in such periodicals as the *New Yorker*, *Granta*, *Harper's*, the *London Review of Books*, and the *Atlantic*, all with a single theme: the struggles for identity and authenticity by his generation of East Asian immigrants in London. In 1997 ten of the stories were published in the collection *Love in a Blue Time* (1997). Among the stories are "My Son the Fanatic," in which a worldly father is puzzled over his son's embracing of Islamic fundamentalism, with violent results; "D'accord, Baby," about a man who reaches a new insight into life's meaning in the midst of cuckoldry; and "With Your Tongue Down My Throat," about the conflicts between traditional and contemporary sexual mores.

The year 1999 saw the publication of Kureishi's novel *Intimacy* and the London production of his play *Sleep with Me*. The former focuses on a writer who leaves his wife and two boys for a younger woman; the latter is about the neurosis-tinged interactions among a wealthy writer, his unloved wife, and his professional associates during a weekend at the writer's country house. In *Booklist* (January 1, 1999), Bonnie Johnson wrote that *Intimacy* "brilliantly explores love's dying throes." By contrast, Hal Jensen, assessing *Sleep with Me* for the *Times Literary Supplement* (May 21, 1999), found it to be a "laboured and unilluminating account of middle-class *crises nerveuses*."

The events in Udayan Prasad's 1999 film *My Son the Fanatic*, whose screenplay Kureishi based on one of his own short stories, revolve around Parvez, a Pakistani cabdriver living in the north of England. Among the factors contributing to Parvez's frustration with his life are his clientele, largely made up of prostitutes and their customers; his son, who has broken off his engagement with a policeman's daughter and embraces religious fundamentalism; the barbed comments from his wife; and the comparison of his childhood friend's success with his own situation. Janet Maslin of the *New York Times* (June 25, 1999) felt that the film, "written with delicacy and wry humor by Hanif Kureishi, ... remains essentially a character study, an open-ended short story rather than a full-fledged drama."

Kureishi, who lives in London, considers jazz and cricket his main avocational interests.
—E.M.

SUGGESTED READING: *Atlantic Monthly* p68+ Sep. 1996; *Economist* p67 July 15, 1995; *Film Comment* p70+ Sep. 1987, with photo; *Harper's* p22+ May 1986; *Interview* p139+ Apr. 1990, with photo; *Lambda Book Report* p48 May 1993; *Melody Maker* p15 May 20, 1995; *Nation* p245+ Sep. 11, 1995; *New Statesman & Society* p19+ Oct. 28, 1988, p41 Jan. 6, 1989, p27+ July 21, 1989, with photo, p29 Nov. 12, 1993, p37 May 12, 1995; *New York* p13+ Sep. 20, 1993; *New York Times* B p25+ Nov. 8, 1987, with photo, C p17+ May 24, 1990, with photo, H p12 July 14, 1991, with photos; *New York Times Book Review* p42 Sep. 17, 1995; *Rolling Stone* p33+ Nov. 19, 1987, with photo; *Spectator* p44+ May 13, 1995;

Times Educational Supplement pSS14 June 2, 1995; *Toronto Globe and Mail* C p4 Nov. 28, 1987, with photos; *Vogue* p366+ Sep. 1995; *Contemporary Literary Criticism* vol 64, 1991; *International Motion Picture Almanac*, 1991; *International Who's Who, 1997–98*

SELECTED WORKS: Fiction—*The Buddha of Suburbia*, 1990; *The Black Album*, 1995; *Love in a Blue Time*, 1997; *Intimacy*, 1999; Drama—*The Mother Country*, 1980; *Borderline*, 1981; *Birds of Passage*, 1983; *Outskirts*, 1983; *Tomorrow—Today!*, 1983; *The King and Me*, 1983; *Mother Courage and Her Children* (adaptation of work by B. Brecht), 1984; *Sleep with Me*, 1999; Screenplays—*My Beautiful Laundrette*, 1985; *Sammy and Rosie Get Laid*, 1987; *London Kills Me*, 1991; *The Buddha of Suburbia* (with R. Mitchell), 1992; *My Son the Fanatic*, 1999; As editor—*The Faber Book of Pop* (with J. Savage), 1995

Kwitny, Jonathan

Mar. 23, 1941– Nov. 26, 1998 Journalist

Jonathan Kwitny, the American investigative reporter, earned a reputation for exposing corrupt practices in American business and government. His first book, *The Fountain Pen Conspiracy* (1973), demonstrated how "entrepreneurs" set up financial empires on paper and defrauded thousands of innocent investors. *Vicious Circles: The Mafia in the Marketplace* (1979), an indictment of the cost to the public of Mafia involvement in business, particularly the meat industry, documented criminal activity virtually ignored by some branches of law enforcement. In *Endless Enemies: The Making of an Unfriendly World* (1984) and *The Crimes of Patriots: A True Tale of Dope, Dirty Money, and the CIA* (1987) Kwitny turned his attention to the makers of American foreign policy and the leaders of international banking. *Endless Enemies* was a runner-up for a Pulitzer Prize in 1985.

With *Acceptable Risks* (1992), Kwitny entered the controversy over American drug research that started with the AIDS epidemic. He returned to the world stage with his biography of Pope John Paul II, *Man of the Century* (1997).

Jonathan Kwitny was born on March 23, 1941 in Indianapolis, Indiana, the son of Julia Goldberger and Dr. I. J. Kwitny, the president of the medical staff at St. Vincent's Hospital in Indianapolis. Jonathan Kwitny received a bachelor's degree in journalism from the University of Missouri in 1962 and a master's degree from New York University in 1964. Meanwhile he joined the Perth Amboy, New Jersey, *News Tribune* as a reporter in 1963; he received a prize for distinguished public service from the New Jersey Press Corps the following

year. After a stint as a Peace Corps volunteer in Nigeria in 1965–66, he returned to the *News Tribune*, remaining with that paper until 1969. He was again awarded first prize for distinguished public service by the New Jersey Press Corps in 1967. When Kwitny became a reporter for the *Wall Street Journal* in 1971, his career as an investigative journalist took off. Covering the New York City beat for that newspaper led him to sniff out corruption in certain industries and unions.

Kwitny's first book, *The Fountain Pen Conspiracy*, dealt with fraudulent market manipulations in the pre-computer era—particularly, those engineered by shady businessmen who lured unsuspecting investors by setting up dummy companies with fictional but authentic-looking Dun and Bradstreet credit ratings. Robert Molyneux, the *Library Journal* (August 1973) reviewer, observed that "however interesting this book is," Kwitny's "impressive research job" made it "a serious work." *Best Sellers* (October 15, 1973) termed *The Fountain Pen Conspiracy* "a real treasury of protective information for investors."

Kwitny's next two books, *The Mullendore Murder Case* (1974) and *Shakedown* (1977), involved crime of a more personal nature. *The Mullendore Murder Case* provided a factual account of a murder in Oregon, and *Shakedown*, a novel, concerns fictional crime.

In *Vicious Circles: The Mafia in the Marketplace*, Kwitny returned to investigative reporting on a larger scale in an examination of the role of the Mafia in what is considered legitimate business. Kwitny argued that "when the Dons dominate the marketplace, they bring murder, arson, and violence with them," and he demonstrated how complacent public officials become co-conspirators through their acceptance of organized crime. Kwitny used recorded telephone conversations, trial transcripts, police records, and personal interviews to document Mafia involvement in the meat industry, the lunch-wagon business, cheese-processing plants, garment factories, banks, brokerage houses, and the Teamsters', butchers', and longshoremen's unions, mainly in New York. Reviewing *Vicious Circles* for *America* (May 5, 1979), Joseph P. Parkes felt that Kwitny "marshals a convincing body of evidence to demonstrate that the Mafia does indeed exist, and that it has penetrated the American business system. . . . Kwitny shows how easy it is for organized crime to beat raps, even when the evidence is overwhelming." Thomas Powers concurred in the *New York Times Book Review* (April 15, 1979) that "even the most jaded citizen is likely to come away from his meticulous book with an angry, helpless understanding of how the Mafia manages to shrug off the law and thrive."

Kwitny's next book, *Endless Enemies: The Making of an Unfriendly World*, roams the globe in search of a coherent rationale for American foreign intervention. Almost nowhere did the author find compelling reasons or unifying threads in the schemes, cabals, wars, and economic double-dealing in which the United States and its agents engaged in Africa, Asia, Central and South America, and the Middle East. "For destabilizing governments and economies and reckless arms sales and unsound bank loans, Mr. Kwitny indicts the malicious and the well-meaning with equal ferocity," Martin F. Nolan wrote for the *New York Times Book Review* (July 29, 1984). Kwitny indicted the Cold War mentality for providing a cover for the malign dealings of unscrupulous business and government officials. He regards the ordinary American citizen's mistrust of government policy statements as "one of the saddest results of the whole anti-communist crusade." Officials, Kwitny wrote, "who constantly lie for what they see as the greater good create more loss of life, through every war and covert action the country is sucked into."

In *The Crimes of Patriots: A True Tale of Dope, Dirty Money, and the CIA*, Kwitny probed the activities of an investment bank, the Nugan Hand Bank, which, the author alleged, acted as a transfer agent of billions of dollars, moved around the world in the service of the heroin trade and tax fraud. In addition, the bank's activities included arms dealing in Africa, intelligence-gathering on military capabilities and troop movements in Southeast Asia, and the manipulation of Australian politics. Although, Kwitny stated, "Nugan Hand had enough generals, admirals, and spooks to run to a small war," he documented its real activities as "a mammoth drug-financing, money-laundering, tax-evading investor-fraud operation." Many of the investors bilked were former American service personnel, who placed their trust in the panoply of admirals and generals, their former commanders, who were running the operation.

According to Howard Blum, writing in the *New York Times Book Review* (September 6, 1987), Kwitny "offers no firm resolution to this fools-or-knaves riddle. . . . In the end, he offers not proofs but theories. And that is part of the book's strength. . . . *The Crimes of Patriots* is a model of responsible investigative journalism because it avoids claiming to be more than it is. . . . The unanswered questions—and their implications about the conduct of this country's foreign policy—are as resonant as the ones he does answer." Reviewing the book for the *Christian Science Monitor* (September 18, 1987), Leonard Bushkoff found Kwitny too angry and "not always relevant" in his condemnation of the Central Intelligence Agency. He called the book "full-blooded muckraking" but felt Kwitny should have used "the rapier, not the bludgeon." The *Nation* (November 7, 1987) reviewer, Nick Tosches, gave full credit to Kwitny for "lucidity": "The book's complex story, with its dozens of international characters, never becomes confused or obscure." Richard Immerman wrote in the *Journal of American History* (September 1988) that although academics might cavil at Kwitny's "irregular citations" of some dubious source material, "one cannot help but be impressed by the re-

sourcefulness, perseverance, and attention to detail with which he conducted his research. . . . Subsequent analysts will benefit from what Kwitny has uncovered."

Kwitny next turned his attention to AIDS research, a field made controversial by the complaints of patients and activists that the Food and Drug Administration (FDA) blocked promising drugs from being investigated or made available with appropriate alacrity. The FDA's countering argument was that trials were necessary to demonstrate the safety and efficacy of drugs, and that such trials require a certain amount of time. In *Acceptable Risks* Kwitny focused on the efforts of Martin Delaney and Jim Corti to speed up the rate at which promising drugs could be administered to patients with AIDS who would otherwise soon die. The title of the book came from a speech given by Delaney, in which he said that only patients had the right to determine what risks were acceptable in the search for a cure for the devastating disease. Corti established a smuggling network that brought drugs mainly from Mexico to the United States. Delaney also started by smuggling drugs, but soon decided to concentrate on changing the system. He thus founded Project Inform, whose mission was to educate patients, doctors, and drug companies about possible new treatments and to establish "guerilla" trials, in which doctors would try to establish protocols for use of the compounds by testing them on volunteers. Many patients, knowing that their lives were on the line, wanted the compounds rather than the dummy drugs that would have been used on some patients in a regular trial.

Kwitny was "aware of the inherent conflicts of interest between the needs of individual patients and scientific documentations of results in clinical trials," according to Mary Chitty, who reviewed the book for *Library Journal* (October 15, 1992). Although he used reconstructed dialogue to convey the drama of the situations, he also conducted extensive interviews and provided meticulous footnotes, making *Acceptable Risks* "both absorbing and informative." Beryl Lieff Benderly of the *Washington Post* (October 4, 1992) felt that Kwitny's energetic "legwork and earnest digging" were not sufficient to "convey subtleties of character and motivation, limn a shifting social background, and plumb moral ambiguity" well enough to do justice to the story of Delaney and Corti. But David L. Kirp, writing for the *Nation* (April 5, 1993), felt that while "a reporter inclined to docudrama-type sensationalism . . . could produce a tale with greater best-seller potential but less reliability, . . . Kwitny shows how to avoid these traps and still write a compelling book."

Kwitny's 1997 biography, *Man of the Century*, depicts Pope John Paul II as a charismatic visionary who was almost single-handedly responsible for the collapse of communism in Eastern Europe and the end of the Cold War, and whose leadership was behind the Solidarity movement in Poland. In addition, in the author's view, the Pope's commitment to social justice led him to play an instrumental role in the downfall of Augusto Pinochet, the dictator of Chile. Kwitny described a 1987 open-air mass in Chile attended by hundreds of thousands of people: the crowds began demonstrating "as John Paul . . . gave . . . one of his great speeches, endorsing the work of Chilean priests for justice, condemning the terrorism, and assuring people that 'suffering for the sake of love, truth and justice is the sign of fidelity to God.' As he spoke, police lobbed tear gas canisters and fired buckshot and water cannons to drive back crowds, while the pope proclaimed loudly, 'Love is stronger, love is stronger.'" Within two or three years, Pinochet was no longer a major force in the Chilean government.

Critical responses to *Man of the Century* varied widely. George C. Higgins stated in *America* (November 22, 1997) that Kwitny "has written a biography of the Pope, not an ecclesiastical or theological tract for the times," which is "an informative, highly readable but less than . . . perfect interim journalistic study of a towering religious leader whom [Kwitny] greatly admires." On the other hand, for Ray Olson, writing in *Booklist* (August 1997), Kwitny "may be the perfect biographer of Pope John Paul II while that pontiff lives" because, as a journalist, "he has developed a grandness of perspective that academics, mostly specialists, seldom acquire."

Kwitny married Martha Kaplan, a lawyer with whom he had two children, in 1968. Kaplan died in 1978. Kwitny married Wendy Wood, a poet and writer, in 1993 in a Roman Catholic ceremony. Kwitny died of stomach cancer on November 26, 1998.
—S.Y.

SUGGESTED READING: *America* p377 May 5, 1979, p24 Nov. 22, 1997; *Best Sellers* p318 Oct. 15, 1973; *Booklist* p1844 Aug. 1997; *Christian Science Monitor* p20 Sep. 18, 1987; *Columbia Journalism Review* p57 Jan./Feb. 1993; *Journal of American History* p679 Sep. 1988; *Library Journal* p2276 Aug. 1973, p90 Oct. 15, 1992; *Nation* p528 Nov. 7, 1987, p458 Apr. 5, 1993; *New York Times* C p16 July 17, 1984, IX p11 Sep. 3, 1993; *New York Times Book Review* p9 Apr. 15, 1979, p8 July 29, 1984, p3 Sep. 6, 1987, p30 Nov. 22, 1992; *Washington Post Book World* p4 Oct. 4, 1992

SELECTED BOOKS: Fiction—*Shakedown*, 1977; Nonfiction—*The Fountain Pen Conspiracy*, 1973; *The Mullendore Murder Case*, 1974; *Vicious Circles: The Mafia in the Marketplace*, 1979; *Endless Enemies: The Making of an Unfriendly World*, 1984; *The Crimes of Patriots: A True Tale of Dope, Dirty Money, and the CIA*, 1987; *Acceptable Risks*, 1992; *Man of the Century: The Life and Times of Pope John Paul II*, 1997

Lane, Simon

May 19, 1957– Novelist; short-story writer

The English author Simon Lane writes lyrical, dreamlike fiction that conjures up images of the many places he has traveled—such as Australia, India, Mexico, Italy, New York, Berlin, and Paris. He is equally adept at creating vivid characters. Lane's first novel, *Le Veilleur*, was published in Europe in 1992, followed shortly thereafter by the trilogy comprising *May*, *In New York*, and *The Clipper Seaman's Bride*. More recently the author has seen his work published in the United States, starting in 1993 with *Still Life with Books*, the story of a would-be author named Leonard who reflects on his three-way relationship with his cousin and a woman named Azadina. In 1998 Lane applied his eclectic style to three interlocking narratives in the novel *Fear*, his second to be published in the United States.

In August 1998 Simon Lane submitted the following autobiographical statement for *World Authors 1990–1995*: "I am a twin, born on 19th May, 1957, in Birmingham, England. My brother preceded me by 20 minutes. For the poet, time is often illusory, although the mother of the poet may incline to differ.

Courtesy of Simon Lane

"My mother has suggested we fought during her pregnancy. If that was the case, we entered the world under a cease-fire and soon developed a language of our own. Time. Language. Twin themes suckled from infancy.

"Childhood was idyllic, a sequence of snap shots incorporating a smile made no less indelible through the weakening fixative of memory, a third theme, creating the first bibliographical entry, 'View From My Window,' a short story which would have been considerably shorter had my parents not restrained me. Yes, I could have fallen, apt metaphor for the work, the life in general. Curiosity, after all, is not something easily abandoned.

"My beloved parents engendered in me a spirit of generosity, a word often restricted in meaning but which, in its noblest sense, signifies an openness of mind and soul to the world, without which existence remains moribund, rather like a bank statement. Life was a celebration, as well as a gift, and I took to it gladly: a singularity of vision, hardly at odds with my twininity, along with an extroverted disposition, allowed me the luxury of pursuing it in my own fashion. Disinterested in convention and in the inane mechanics of success—the ultimate catastrophe—I can avow to the fact that, at the age of 41, the limited control I feel over my chosen art—or rather the art which chose me—is clear proof that that upbringing so dear to my heart was all that could have been desired, a fact for which I am eternally grateful.

"As for the work itself, writing was always a view through a window and my life opened in order to encompass it. I have always sought that wavy horizon first glimpsed through the haze of a summer evening, for I conducted my early years in the countryside on the fringes of that unwieldy city in England's heart, moving further into Warwickshire as time passed. Shakespeare's ghost accompanied my furtive ramblings through the landscape—I see an oak tree, a hedge, the shadow of a tin can holding sticklebacks, and, always, a pub—a bucolic chapter cut short by that first journey to a boarding school near Bath, Somerset.

"From the age of eleven to eighteen, I struggled and prospered, alternately, within the quaint ideals of empire and a rigorous pedagogy whose strictness enlarged that tenderest of muscles: the brain. When daunted, I was rescued by literature, in the guise of the English teacher, Mr. Vickery, whose encouragement provided a neat counterpoint to the corporal punishment meted out by others. Rules being designed to be broken, I was offered a limitless amount and became something of a rebel. The poet was born and through the enveloping cloud of adolescence, he subsisted on scribbles of dizzying naivety.

"I learned that writing is a matter of description, inward or outward, and that it is indeed a craft, if unlike any other. I chose to teach myself and have learned over the years to be my own worst editor. I was always interested in the beauty of surface, but not in superficiality, in the sometimes unwholesome cohabitation of form and content and, more generally, in the incorrigible doggedness of the lone scribbler at work in a world adopted, by force of circumstance, as his own. My preference is usually for dead writers rather than living ones, but for all that, I still view my contemporaries without bias, my only prejudice being that I prefer the sound of a well sharpened pencil to the grinding of an axe. I soon learned to agree with Oscar: 'Books are well written, or badly written. That is all.'

"On leaving school, I eschewed university and went to art school in London. I wrote, performed and drew, racing in the ever increasing circles of that golden age of youth in which the student becomes the insatiable prey of his own latent innocence. Many edges were subsequently worn by the practical realizations of life. Money and security, however, were always disposable, wholly subservient to the idea that art is a salvation: hardly sacred, hardly a storm in a teacup either, something which may or may not invite immortality but which, incontrovertibly, gives meaning through its open invitation to respond to all things as long as the subject is prepared to work at his dreams.

"The autodidact had much to learn. My first journey away from home to school one hundred miles away lent me a restlessness which has never left me. Early trips to what the English call Europe presented an exotic alternative to the splendid isolation of Albion. I had long ago caught *estranofilia*, and I still have it, along with another malady contracted this spring, which, but for love and science, might well have rendered this an obituary.

"I had only to quit England in order to jettison myself into a world of my own within the orbit of an ever widening constellation. This I did in 1979, taking up residence in Berlin, Italy, New York, Portugal and then Paris, writing short stories and novels, performing my work in public, and working as an illustrator, teacher or translator. Paris always seemed the eye of the storm and it was here that I met my first editor, Gérard-Georges Lemaire, who edited much of my work during the 1980s, as well as my first novel, *Le Veilleur*, which appeared in 1992. During this period, various novellas and lithographic editions—including the trilogy, *May, In New York* and *The Clipper Seaman's Bride*—also found the light of day.

"I actually settled—for want of a better word—in Paris, in 1988 and, apart from sojourns in India, Mexico, Australia and New York, it has remained a home of which I am inordinately fond, a fact clearly reflected in my two subsequent novels, *Still Life with Books* and *Fear*—both edited by Barbara Phillips at Bridge Works Publishing, New York. Writing apart— not that it ever is, except, of course, when one is not actually doing it—I have worked in film and television (that clumsy marriage of ego and equipment) and, more satisfyingly, radio: simpler, anonymous.

"The pen never runs dry, the window remains securely open. Identity being a game, I still play with it, as I did with my other half, switching narrators, alter egos, impostors. Thematic analysis I leave to the critic, keeping for myself a love of words and language, of the immediacy of an immemorial art and of the power of observation, witness to that human comedy which is life seen through the top, or the bottom, of the glass, always half-full.

"I am currently writing a new saga—*The Vinkristina Saga* (my first, *The Slapshield Saga*, was published by Gordon Lish in *The Quarterly* in 1993) a pseudo-mythological glance at something rather more real, a dose of cancer which, all things being equal, will soon—in its lean, pallid manifestation—join that ill-fixed photograph album somewhere within the storage facilities of memory."

Still Life With Books (1993), Lane's first novel published in the United States, is narrated by Leonard, an unpublished British writer living in Australia, who recollects a three-way affair—involving himself, his cousin Aldous, and an Egyptian woman named Azadina—which took place in Paris years earlier. Leonard mulls over everything from Van Gogh to X rays and dust while repeatedly denying his guilt over Aldous's death from a wasp sting. This unusually structured novel shifts with ease from a dream world to harsh reality, but the story itself received some mixed reviews from critics. In *Library Journal* (September 1, 1993), Donna L. Schulmann complained that Lane "has written a self-conscious rumination on love, obsession, and art that is long on sensual description and short on story and plot. Not recommended." On the other hand, *Publishers Weekly* (July 5, 1993) cheered that, "Like a prime *Seinfeld* episode, nothing really happens in this sometimes melancholy, often funny and always beautiful novel."

In his next novel, *Fear* (1998), Lane once again looked at the life of a writer, but this time he explored the contradictory goals of art and commercialism. *Fear* features three layers of narrative: The first-person, dream like reflections of an unnamed female writer upon finding a book of haiku; the third-person tale of a poor English poet named Fear reduced to writing an erotic novel to support himself; and Fear's novel itself, about an affair between an American airline pilot and a girl from Pigalle. "This book reveals the selling out of a writer," read the review in *Library Journal* (February 15, 1998), "but Lane's own elegantly crafted prose loses nothing in the undertaking. Even as Lane faithfully details the paranoia often experienced by those deep in debt, he inspires the same yearning for the beauty, romance, and creative energy of Paris that Ernest Hemingway expressed generations ago." —C. M.

SUGGESTED READING: *Booklist* p1428 Apr. 15, 1998; *Library Journal* p222 Sep. 1, 1993, p170, Feb. 15, 1998; *New York Times Book Review* p31 July 21, 1998; *Publishers Weekly* p61+ July 5, 1993

SELECTED WORKS: Novels—*May*, 1992; *In New York*, 1992; *The Clipper Seaman's Bride*, 1992; *Le Veilleur*, 1992; *Still Life with Books*, 1993; *Fear*, 1998

Langer, Lawrence L.

June 20, 1929– Professor; author

In a career that has spanned almost 40 years, author and professor Lawrence L. Langer has emerged as a prominent thinker on the subject of the Holocaust. After following the war crimes trials of World War II Nazis in Europe during the 1960s and touring former concentration camps, Langer became intrigued by the manner in which such a horrid event could be reflected in art and literature. He has since produced a series of extensively researched anthologies that explore the lasting effects of the Holocaust. In all of these collections, which include both fictional and nonfictional tales, artwork, poetry, and interviews with survivors, the author manages to look beyond the typical bravery-in-the-face-of-danger gloss that has sometimes characterized works on Holocaust victims. Instead, Langer moves into the area of "deep memory," where psychological wounds prove to be lasting and easy answers to the questions of how such a horrendous crime could have occurred, and how people live after that crime, are not quickly found.

In a statement submitted to *World Authors 1990–1995*, Lawrence L. Langer writes, "I was born on June 20, 1929, in the Bronx, New York City, son of Irving Langer and Esther (Strauss) Langer. I attended the Bronx High School of Science and received a B.A. in 1951 from the City College of New York (CCNY). I did my graduate work at Harvard University, obtaining an A.M. in 1952 and a Ph.D. in 1961. I taught for one year (1957–1958) at the University of Connecticut and spent the rest of my academic career at Simmons College in Boston, from which I retired early as Alumnae Chair Professor of English in 1992 in order to devote full time to writing and lecturing. I married Sondra Weinstein on February 21, 1951. We have a son and daughter and five grandchildren and live in West Newton, Massachusetts, summering at Wellfleet on Cape Cod.

"Initially, my main field of interest was American Studies, and I spent a year as Fulbright Professor of American Literature at the University of Graz in Graz, Austria (1963–1964). While there a lengthy war-crimes trial known as the Auschwitz

Office of Public Information, Simmons College
Lawrence L. Langer

Trial was in process in Frankfurt, and I read excerpts from the testimony almost daily in the Frankfurter Allgemeine. Then on Memorial Day in 1964 I drove through Czechoslovakia into Poland with a colleague to visit the Auschwitz and Birkenau concentration and death camps. A few months later, at a museum in Munich (the Alte Pinakoteke), I saw a large rural landscape painting from the eighteenth century whose title was "Dachau," and since I had visited the Dachau concentration camp outside of Munich only the day before, I was struck by the disjunction between the pre- and post-war images summoned up by that designation. A few days later, in Frankfurt, I attended the trial I had been reading about all year, and once again I was impressed by the contrast between the tranquility of the courtroom and the utter horror of the testimony I was hearing. This led me to wonder how artists, and writers in particular, might imagine the grotesque reality reported by the witnesses in the Auschwitz trial and what I saw in my visit to the site, and thus began my investigation into the field that for me originally was "Holocaust literature" and since has come to be know as Holocaust Studies.

"After I returned to Simmons College I started teaching (in 1965) one of the first courses in the country on Holocaust literature, called "The Literature of Atrocity." A few years later, on sabbatical in Munich, Germany (1968–1969), I began writing *The Holocaust and the Literary Imagination*, which I finished in 1970. It took four years to get the manuscript accepted for publication. It was rejected by nearly a dozen leading academic presses and at least a half dozen commercial publishers, until Yale University Press agreed (with enthusi-

asm, I should add) to publish it in 1975. The topic was simply too unfamiliar in those days. Holocaust Studies have come a long way since then.

"My main interest in the Holocaust has always been the question of how to represent experiences that have variously been called "unimaginable," "unspeakable," and "indescribable." At first I believed that only the literary imagination would be able to conjure up the ordeal of fending off death under the unsupportable conditions of ghettos and camps, so alien to the experience of modern consciousness. But gradually I expanded the possibilities to include written memoirs and oral testimonies, films, and more recently painting, especially the art of Vilna ghetto survivor Samuel Bak. Today I am convinced that any form of expression that sheds even a minimum of light on the dark human and inhuman ordeal we call the Holocaust deserves our attention. The topic is truly interdisciplinary.

"Much of my writing on this subject over the decades has been a reaction against the popular and occasionally scholarly assumption that to have survived the Holocaust deserves to be acclaimed as a triumph of the human spirit. This has always seemed to me an evasion of the nature of the atrocity we are challenged to confront, one in which no one's survival can be separated from the death—more precisely the murder—of someone else. My current research is concerned with the question raised by Buchenwald survivor and novelist Jorge Semprun: how to "make life with all that death." If the Holocaust led to a rebirth for those who survived it, there is much evidence to suggest that it also led to an accompanying "redeath," which available vocabulary and thought offer us few strategies to describe. I am persuaded that such a dilemma is not restricted to the Holocaust and is destined to afflict modern consciousness well into the future."

Langer's first book on the Holocaust, *The Holocaust and the Literary Imagination* (1975), is a detailed study of the various literature that emerged out of the horrors of World War II. Some of the authors included in this anthology are Elie Wiesel, Nellie Sachs, Paul Celan, Anthony Hecht, and Ilse Aichinger. Critical reception to the book was generally warm, with *Choice* (February 1976) calling it an "important book" and labeling Langer "an excellent comparativist," adding that his "range is wide, and he can be trusted to use impeccable literature scholarship." *Christian Century* (December 31, 1975) announced that "generous samples of literary expressions" make *The Holocaust and the Literary Imagination* a "stunner", while *Library Journal* (October 15, 1975) called it "an outstanding piece of scholarship" that "fills a need" while acknowledging that it is "terrifying, heart-breaking reading."

In an opposing critique, *America* (February 28, 1976) writer Peter Heinegg enthusiastically commented that Langer "brings to his terrible subject not just sympathy, but moral passion and analytic rigor." However, the tone of his review turned darker when he clarified, "Nevertheless, his book must be judged a failure—an ill-conceived, unconvincing, badly written critical essay." One of the central bones of contention for Heinegg was Langer's claim that the Holocaust was a unique event, a statement that rings false, he wrote, in the face of such past human tragedies as the Turkish massacre of Armenians. "This basic error, repeated throughout the book, leads to further absurdities . . ." the reviewer wrote, noting Langer's comparison of some of the more obscure authors in his book with those who have created masterpieces. Heinegg commented that, overall, the book "is strewn with solecisms, redundancies, mixed metaphors and unintentional jokes."

Again using the atrocities of the Holocaust as a base but broadening his topic, in *The Age of Atrocity: Death in Modern Literature* (1978), Langer examined senseless death as a general theme and how writers deal with this topic in their work. In addition to analyzing the works of renowned authors such as Thomas Mann and Albert Camus, Langer looked at first-person testimony from individuals who were about to face violent death.

Reviews for this second book were more mixed, with *Library Journal* (May 1, 1978) commenting that Langer "tends to mythologize the importance of his subject with abstractions about 'the modern imagination' of 'Western civilization.' " and that readers "would do well to read these writers themselves; Langer's citations from them stand in forceful contrast with his comments on them." *Critic* (April 1979) called the book "bone-dry" but conceded that Langer manages to make "some sense" out of humans' growing desensitivity toward death "along with some first rate literary explication, but only if you have the patience to slog through the linguistic swamps of academe. In other words, it's pretty heavy going." The *Virginia Quarterly Review* (Spring 1979) stated simply that "*The Age of Atrocity* is a brave and important book of exceptional erudition." *Commonweal* (February 16, 1979) meanwhile, praised Langer for possessing "an Edmund Wilson-esque gift for finding books so intriguing that you wish life could go on forever just to let you read them all . . ." The reviewer concluded that "generally the writing is felicitous, though overwriting mars a few passages. A kind of giddiness does ensue, not through any fault of Langers' but from trying to absorb so much on the subject of death."

Langer's next literary offering was 1982's *Versions of Survival: the Holocaust and the Human Spirit*, a book that explores Holocaust survivor stories and critiques various theories of survival that appear in Holocaust literature. In particular, Langer took issue with "metaphorical presentations" of the death camps, which he asserted have the effect of "trivializing—indeed of distorting—the essential qualities of life and death in the camps" (*Contemporary Authors*, 1994). Critical reviews of *Versions of Survival* were largely positive, with *Choice* (July/August 1982) stating that the book "is in many ways terrifying, but it is essential reading." *Comparative Literature* (Summer 1984) praised the author for sharpening "our perception of the ethical and philosophical issues that divide scholars who examine the literature of the ghettos and the camps."

The 1991 collection *Holocaust Testimonies: The Ruins of Memory* is perhaps Langer's most famous and critically acclaimed work. In addition to winning the 1991 National Book Critics Circle Award for Criticism and the 1991 Eugene M. Kayden Press Prize, it was chosen as one of the "ten best books" of 1991 by the editors of the *New York Times* and in the 100th Anniversary Issue of the *New York Times Book Review* (December 1996) was listed as one of 13 "books of particular permanent interest" that had been published in the past 100 years.

Holocaust Testimonies is an in-depth analysis of 300 of the thousands of videotaped Holocaust survivor interviews from the Fortunoff Video Archive at Yale University. Langer set out to address the various interpretations of these interviews and the issue of memory as revealed by the interviewees. Although sometimes these individuals speak from "common memory," Langer writes—meaning they relate their experiences during World War II in a mannered, chronological way—at other times, they tell their stories out of "deep memory," a reliving of past horrors. These two levels of memory, Langer asserts, "interact and intersect" throughout the interviews, with the survivors themselves completely unaware of the change, and subsequently confused by the erratic flow of their narratives. Langer examined the way in which these interviews reveal more about the lasting personal and social effects of an atrocity such as the Holocaust than the more commonplace romanticism of victims' "courage under fire."

A *Choice* (September 1991) reviewer wrote, "Refusing false comfort, Langer nevertheless will not accept the notion that those who have not experienced the Holocaust will never understand it." The critic concluded that it is a "difficult and painful book, but suitable for all levels of readers." *Library Journal* (February 1, 1991) wrote that *Holocaust Testimonies* "establishes new boundaries in our understanding and interpretation of the Holocaust experience. The oral testimonies are stark and direct, unadulterated by the literary devices of written memoirs." *New York Times Book Review* (April 21, 1991) critic David S. Wyman offered kudos to the author, calling his work "an unsparing attempt to address some critical problems . . ." The reviewer opined that "While still affirming the value of common memory, Mr. Langer emphasizes the great importance of the unrefined testimony from deep memory" and that this type of "demythologizing is useful, and Mr. Langer argues the case persuasively." Wyman also commented that a "minor problem" with the book is the absence of a conclusion. "Even a comparatively short closing summary would have been helpful in sorting out the many meanings and complexities Mr. Langer offers in his thoughtful essay," Wyman wrote.

The *Commentary* (November 1991) review was less complimentary, stating that "Langer's use of poetic language masks the controversial nature of his claims. To begin with, they fly in the face of common sense . . ." At issue for the reviewer was Langer's assertion that confrontation with the videotaped accounts "begins in separate narrative and ends in collective memory." Critic David G. Roskies counterpoints ". . . this cannot be. For if, as he claims, these solitary faces on an otherwise blank screen defy the moral vocabulary of Western civilizations and speak only as oracles of random victimization, then they are finally consumed by their own nihilism and cannot serve the purposes of 'collective memory.'" Roskies bitterly concluded, "The cumulative impact of all these 'former victims' baring their souls to the merciless camera is to rob their lives and stories of any larger significance, and to consign the Holocaust to a purgatory outside the course of human events."

Four years after releasing this controversial book, Langer produced two collections: *Admitting the Holocaust: Collected Essays* (1995) and *Art from the Ashes: A Holocaust Anthology* (1995). The former is a compilation of essays on the Holocaust, covering a wide assortment of topics, from memory of the event, to how it is perceived by our culture, to its portrayal in literature and the media. The latter is a collection of art, prose, drama, and poetry that emerged out of the Holocaust, including work done by both Jews and non-Jews, survivors and those who were not physically present, all of which combine into a vast portrait of the lasting effects of this atrocity. *Booklist* (November 1, 1994) labeled *Art from the Ashes* "an exceptional collection of Holocaust literature" and in another review (November 15, 1994) called *Admitting the Holocaust* "a horribly bleak, undeniably important book." The *Kirkus Reviews* (October 15, 1994) critic was appreciative of Langer's effort in *Admitting the Holocaust*, writing that the author provides "a highly sensitive but unsparing eye." As in previous critiques, however, the critic disputed Langer's assertion that the Holocaust was a unique event of horrendous proportions. "Langer's only questionable contention," the review stated, "is that 'Auschwitz introduced the realm of the unthinkable into the human drama.' What, one wonders, of the mass deaths of millions during WWI's trench warfare or Stalin's murder of as many as 30 million in the USSR during the purges?" The review goes on to note that "Generally, however, Langer writes superbly [and] applies his insightful, razor-sharp pen to others' works about an event that, he convincingly maintains, carries neither lesson nor moral but instead overpowers memory, mocks the pretensions of civilization, and leaves an absurd, irredeemable legacy."

Reviewer Walter Reich of the *New York Times* (January 29, 1995), noted that "It is important that Lawrence L. Langer has given us two books . . . to bring us back from the vacancy of words to the density of physical reality." Reich added, "These books provide a sense of how Europe's Jews experienced, on a daily basis, the pressure of the Holocaust's ever-tightening vise . . ." While calling three of the pieces in *Art from the Ashes* "utterly gripping," Reich devoted most of his review to *Admitting the Holocaust*, noting that in the essays "Mr. Langer illuminates the literature of the Holocaust." The fiction that Langer gathered for his anthology, the reviewer wrote, "much of it by survivors themselves, like Aharon Appelfeld, highlights the reality of the Holocaust with stunning intensity." Reich closed his critique of Langer's work by offering, "The essays in Mr. Langer's book constitute a collective and persuasive argument against distorting the Holocaust by attempting to derive some message of hope from it."

After providing an essay and commentaries for *Landscapes of Jewish Experience: Paintings by Samuel Bak* (1997), Langer released 1998's *Preempting the Holocaust*, which is a collection of his many essays about the literature and art that resulted from the Holocaust experience. The *New York Times Book Review* printed this comment about Langer and his work: "Always thoughtful and provocative, he writes about complex moral issues in a lucid and forceful style, although his terse eloquence masks an underlying outrage." *Kirkus Reviews* (September 1, 1998) agreed, calling Langer "one of our most eloquent Holocaust scholars" and his collection "an essential work on one of the central historical moments of this century." The critic went on to note that "At a time when the daily newspapers are filled with renewed versions of genocide and atrocity, but also a time in which the last of the perpetrators of the Holocaust and their victims are dying of old age, this volume is a useful corrective to the foolish sentimentalizing of these events or their application as a hideously inappropriate lesson on the 'triumph of the human spirit.'"

Although he is now retired, Lawrence L. Langer continues to try and provide information and gripping testimonial about the Holocaust to his readers, maintaining that such works should be as truthful as possible. "I don't believe it should be sweetened," Langer said in an interview with the *New York Times* (January 29, 1995). "If you are going to teach something, it must be taught truthfully. I'm convinced there is an audience out there eager to learn more, and they're being fed a lot of bad, sentimentalized material." Langer continues to devote his time to writing essays and articles for a variety of publications and anthologies, and in 1999 he provided commentary for another collection of Samuel Bak's art, *The Game Continues: Chess in the Art of Samuel Bak*. He and his wife make their home in Massachusetts.
—D.B.

SUGGESTED READING: *Amazon Books* (online); *America* Feb. 28, 1976; *Booklist* (online) Nov. 1, 1994, Nov. 15, 1994; *Choice* Feb. 1976, July/Aug. 1982, Sept. 1991; *Christian Century* Dec. 31, 1975; *Commentary* Nov. 1991; *Commonweal* Feb. 16, 1979, Sept. 27, 1991; *Comparative Literature* Summer 1984; *Critic* Apr. 1979; *Kirkus Reviews* Oct. 15, 1994, Sep. 1, 1998; *Library Journal* Oct. 15, 1975, May 1, 1978, Feb. 1, 1991; *New York Times* Jan. 18, 1976, Apr. 21, 1991, Jan. 29, 1995; *Virginia Quarterly Review* Spring 1979; *Book Review Digest* 1976, 1979, 1982, 1991; *Contemporary Authors*, 1994

SELECTED WORKS: *The Holocaust and the Literary Imagination*, 1975; *The Age of Atrocity: Death in Modern Literature*, 1978; *Versions of Survival: The Holocaust and the Human Spirit*, 1982; *Holocaust Testimonies: The Ruins of Memory*, 1991; *Admitting the Holocaust: Collected Essays*, 1995; *Art from the Ashes: A Holocaust Anthology*, 1995; *Landscapes of Jewish Experience: Paintings by Samuel Bak*, 1997; *Preempting the Holocaust*, 1998; *The Game Continues: Chess in the Act of Samuel Bak*, 1999

Courtesy of Joe Lansdale

Lansdale, Joe R.

Oct. 28, 1951– Novelist

Joe R. Lansdale dislikes labels. "What is a genre?" he asked in an interview with James Hynes for *Publishers Weekly* (September 29, 1997). "All of this is the American preoccupation with putting things in boxes. Am I a commercial writer? You bet. Is John Updike giving his books away? Did Hemingway cash his checks? I mean, come on, this is silly." Lansdale prefers to blend the components of several genres to produce works in his own unique style: In early novels, such as *Dead in the West* (1986) and *The Magic Wagon* (1986), the author interwove threads of horror and the grotesque with those of the traditional Western; to his horror novels, like *The Drive In* (1988) and *The Drive In 2* (1989), Lansdale added elements of fantasy and science fiction. Lansdale also writes novels based on comic

book characters, such as his *Batman: Captured by the Engines* (1991) and *Jonah Hex: Two-Gun Mojo* (1994), and pulp fiction, like the book *Tarzan: The Lost Adventure* (1996). His first novel, *Act of Love* (1981), was a crime novel, and he has recently returned to crime fiction with an ongoing series featuring Hap Collins and Leonard Pine, the Holmes and Watson of East Texas. The titles in the series include *Mucho Mojo* (1994), *The Two Bear Mambo* (1995), and *Bad Chili* (1997).

In an autobiographical statement for *World Authors 1990–1995*, Joe R. Lansdale writes: "I grew up rural and small town, and loved every minute of it. I suppose my family was poor, but we liked to think of ourselves as broke. Never saw a writer, never knew a writer until I had sold a number of articles on my own, but I was aware from the age of nine that I not only wanted to be a writer, but had to be one.

"Grew up reading both pulp and literary fiction. Edgar Rice Burroughs to Robert Bloch to Ray Bradbury to Jack London to Stephen Crane to Hemingway and on. But it was the Southern writers who most influenced me. Harper Lee, Carson McCullers, William Faulkner, and especially Flannery O'Conner.

"A short story in an Alfred Hitchcock anthology by Ardath Mayhar, also an East Texan, made me realize I could write about my own part of the country and in my own voice. Before reading that story, I was trying to write about places I didn't know, talk in voices that weren't mine. Although that seems obvious to me now, then, it was an important revelation.

"Although my father could not read or write (with time he did learn to read the newspaper, comics and write a few words), and my mother only had a tenth grade education, reading and writing were much cherished in our household. My mother loved to read and read to me when I was a child. She fostered in me the love of books and the respect for writers and writing, and my father, having suffered from lack of education, pushed me to pursue reading and writing.

"Still, like most parents, once they realized I was serious about being a writer, they encouraged me to have 'something to fall back on.' My fall back position was to consider being a full time martial arts instructor, but that's a harder profession than writing. I stayed with the martial arts (34 years and counting) but put the martial arts school on the back burner and began to pursue a college education while working a variety of jobs, everything from aluminum chair factory to janitor.

"I've always been fascinated with history, archeology and anthropology, and thought of a possible career in one of those subjects. I managed 60 hours of college over about a four year span while, and finally in 1981, shortly after selling my first novel, I went full time, and have managed to be a full time writer ever since, working not only in books and short stories, but also film (books optioned, scripts sold, but nothing actually on film yet) and comics, television cartoons, and non-fiction.

"The bulk of my work is cross pollinated by numerous genres, no one genre more important than the other, therefore creating a genre I call 'Lansdale.' I hope readers will come to my work to see what I'm doing next, instead of looking for the next mystery, horror, or western story.

"I have been honored many times for my writings, having won numerous awards and recognitions, but it's the writing that matters. Unlike many writers who say they enjoy having written, but not the act of writing itself, I not only love having written, I love the actual act of writing. I love everything about it except the business side. Worrying about money, sales, distribution, the whole nine yards. The joy of writing is the work itself, the rest is a headache.

"Currently I write three hours a day, own a martial arts school, and have a wonderful wife and two fine kids. Who says dreams don't come true, even if now and then you get a headache."

During the 1970s Lansdale attended a variety of colleges—Tyler Junior College (1970–71), the University of Texas at Austin (1971–1972), and Stephen F. Austin State University (1973, 1975, 1976). He married Cassie Ellis in 1970 (they divorced in 1972), and then his current wife, Karen Ann Morton, in 1973; they have two children, Keith Jordan and Kasey JoAnn. An occasional collaborator, Karen encouraged Lansdale to write full-time. "I was a house dad," he noted in an interview with *Texas Monthly* (March 1997). "Once, my wife was working as a dispatcher at the fire department, and I was staying home and writing while baby-sitting my son, who hardly ever slept. So I wrote in 20-minute patches. Some of that early stuff is just dreadful. I got a thousand rejects."

In 1981 Lansdale sold his first novel, *Act of Love*, a police mystery, and followed it with the western *Texas Night Riders* (1983), which he published under the name Ray Slater. Under his own name he produced two more Westerns, *Dead in the West* (1986), which brings to life the pioneer days of a fictionalized Texas town where the dead still walk the range, and *The Magic Wagon* (1986), which is also set in Texas, and follows a traveling medicine show of 1909 that showcases a chimpanzee who wrestles and the body of Wild Bill Hickok. In 1987 Lansdale published a second mystery, *The Nightrunners.*

Lansdale had been writing horror-esque material since the 1970s, and he decided in the 1980s that he wanted to concentrate on horror exclusively, since it had suddenly become a booming industry. "Stephen King's first few books had exploded in popularity," he remarked to Anne Dingus for *Texas Monthly*, "and suddenly there was an acknowledged horror genre. And it was a paying genre too." Lansdale wrote short stories, which he published in magazines and periodicals, and eventually attracted a cult following. This short fiction was later collected under the titles *By Bizarre Hands* (1989), *Stories by Mama Lansdale's Youngest Boy* (1991), and *Best Sellers Guaranteed* (1993).

Lansdale's first novel that could be classified as mostly horror was *The Drive In: A B-Movie with Blood and Popcorn, Made in Texas* (1988). In this tale, the customers of a Texas drive-in movie theater are transported to a world in which the horror films they have been watching are real and the drive-in itself forms the boundary of their reality. In the book's sequel, *The Drive In 2: Not Just One of Them Sequels* (1989), the customers escape the drive-in, only to discover that the outside world is inhabited by dinosaurs and vampires. Lansdale portrays rape and acts of necrophilia and cannibalism in such a way that, according to Richard Gehr of the *Village Voice* (February 6, 1990), the two books "turn the horror spectacle upon itself."

With his *Drive In* novels and his short-story collections, Lansdale attracted a large following, not only in Texas but beyond as well. He switched genres again, however, with the thriller *Cold in July* (1989), which he followed with *Savage Season* (1990), the first of the Hap Collins and Leonard Pine mysteries. The two main characters are longtime best friends: Hap is a straight white man, an occasional field hand, and a 1960s draft dodger; Leonard is a homosexual black man, a Vietnam veteran skilled in the martial arts. In *Savage Season*, Hap's ex-wife, Trudy, persuades him to help her locate some stolen money at the bottom of the Sabine River in East Texas. Hap, in turn, talks Leonard into helping him. Along the way they are forced into dealing with a dangerous gang with which Trudy has connections. Even though the novel was not the breakout book that Lansdale's agent, Barbara Puechner, was hoping for, the author decided to continue writing in the crime novel vein.

After hiring a new agent, Jimmy Vines, Lansdale broke out of cult status with his next Hap and Leonard mystery, *Mucho Mojo* (1994). In this mystery, Leonard inherits a house from an uncle who had been like a father to him before Leonard revealed his homosexuality. The house, which represents a posthumous reconciliatory gesture, is dilapidated. Leonard asks his friend Hap to help with the renovations, and during their repairs, they come across the skeleton of a small child under the floorboards. A few years earlier several small boys disappeared from the neighborhood, and this evidence suggests Leonard's uncle was the culprit. Leonard cannot believe his uncle committed these crimes, and he and Hap begin to investigate. Daniel Woodrell, in the *New York Times Book Review* (October 2, 1994), wrote that "Mr. Lansdale writes in a style that tends to be discounted by literary types, which is fine, but it would be a shame if the considerable literary intelligence at work in *Mucho Mojo* were to be overlooked. Mr. Lansdale portrays scenes of interracial dating and sex, squalid crack houses, exquisite neighborliness and mounting horror with a folklorist's eye for telling detail and a front-porch raconteur's sense of pace." *Mucho Mojo* became a *New York Times* Notable Book of 1994.

Buoyed by that success, Lansdale produced another Hap and Leonard adventure, *The Two-Bear Mambo* (1995), which also became a best-seller. In this, the third installment in the series, Hap and Leonard investigate the disappearance of Florida Grange, Leonard's lawyer and Hap's old girlfriend. They dicover that Florida, wanting to jumpstart her journalism career, went to Grovetown—a stronghold of the Ku Klux Klan—to investigate the alleged suicide of the imprisoned son of a legendary blues singer. Fearing that Florida has been killed, Hap and Leonard settle into town and continue to search for the truth. Instead they find uncooperative cops in league with the Klan, an exhumation in a voodoo graveyard, and a murder. Reviewing the work for *Booklist* (August 19, 1995), Wes Lukowsky wrote that Lansdale's "ability to generate sidesplitting laughter and gut-wrenching terror on the same page is unique in modern fiction. There's something special going on here, and it ought not be missed. Lansdale used to be a cult favorite, but he's outgrown that."

For his next project, Lansdale took a break from his mystery series to work on a Tarzan manuscript left unfinished by Edgar Rice Burroughs at the time of his death in 1950. *Tarzan: The Lost Adventure* was first released as a series of four pulp paperbacks in 1995 and then bound into a hardcover edition a year later. In this tale, Tarzan protects an American archeological party on their way to the Lost City of Ur. Along the way, he fights off all who attempt to plunder the jungle or molest the party under his protection, battles the inhabitants of Ur, and confronts a giant mantis creature from the center of the Earth. The reviewer for *Publisher's Weekly* (March 11, 1996) noted that this work was not for the faint-hearted nor for those admirers of the Tarzan movie series, since "this Tarzan is in the spirit of the Burroughs novels, and he's revived with pulpish glee by Lansdale, a smart choice whose own fiction . . . acknowledges the ferocity of life."

In 1997 Lansdale returned to the Hap and Leonard crime stories with *Bad Chili*, in which Hap and Leonard go after the biker who first stole and later murdered Leonard's boyfriend. When the friends realize that the police in LaBorde, Texas, have very little interest in investigating what they regard as merely a homosexual killing, Hap and Leonard tackle the case themselves and uncover gay bashing in the porn industry, police corruption, and a strange business scam run by the local chili king. A reviewer for *Booklist* (July 19, 1997) praised Lansdale's craft: "In his unique way, he reveals the human condition—our darkest secrets and our proudest moments, all within the unlikely confines of an East Texas adventure featuring the two scruffiest protagonists in modern crime fiction." Writing for the *New York Times Book Review* (September 21, 1997), Marilyn Stasio noted that "The mayhem is always flashy in these Texas Gothics, and the foulmouthed jokes would keep a crew of oil riggers in stitches. But there's more true art in the loopy bar conversations and front-porch anecdotes that Lansdale tosses back like peanuts."

In Lansdale's 1998 Hap and Leonard mystery, *Rumble Tumble*, the pair involve themselves in more mayhem when Hap agrees to help his girlfriend, Brett, retrieve her daughter, who has become a prostitute in Oklahoma City. During the road trip the trio find themselves in a shootout with a biker gang and Leonard fights hand-to-hand with one of the pimp's thugs. Through dialogue that is both hilarious and moving, Hap and Leonard debate the problems of the world and their roles in it. A critic for *Kirkus Reviews* (August 1, 1998) called this novel "a routine adventure," but "still enlivened by dollops of the most pungent dialogue this side of Quentin Tarrantino." Wes Lukowsky of *Booklist* (July 19, 1998) noted that "the fifth Collins-Pine adventure is a bit more dour than its predecessors but is still extraordinarily entertaining. Lansdale's dialogue is a magical mix of profanity and profundity, the action scenes are print versions of Sam Peckinpah's six-gun ballets, and the friendship between Hap and Leonard belongs in the Men's Hall of Fame." Lansdale published another novel, *Freezer Burn*, in 1999.

Joe R. Lansdale is also the author of two novels based on comic books: *Batman: Captured by the Engines* (1991) and *Jonah Hex: Two Gun Mojo* (1994). He has also served as editor on a number of anthologies, including *Best of the West* (1986), *The New Frontier: Best of the West 2* (1989), *Razored Saddles* (1989), with Pat Lo Brutto, and *Dark at Heart* (1992), with his wife, Karen Lansdale. He has contributed to many periodicals, including *Horror Show*, *Modern Stories*, *Espionage*, and *Mike Shayne*.

Lansdale is a member of the Horror Writers of America and the Western Writers of America, and has served as vice president of the former in 1987–1988 and as treasurer of the latter in 1987. He has been widely recognized for his work, garnering two Bram Stoker Awards for horror writing in 1988 and 1989, as well as an American Horror award in 1989, and a British Fantasy Award, also in 1989. —C.M.

SUGGESTED READING: *Booklist* Aug. 19, 1995, July 19, 1997, July 19, 1998; *Kirkus Reviews* Aug. 1, 1998; *New York Times Book Review* p37 Oct. 2, 1994, p 36 Sep. 21, 1997; *Publishers Weekly* p45 Mar. 11, 1996, p59+ Sep. 29, 1997; *Texas Monthly* p100+ Mar. 1997; *Village Voice* Feb. 10, 1990; *Contemporary Authors New Revised Series* vol. 50, 1996

SELECTED WORKS: Fiction—*Act of Love*, 1981; *Texas Night Riders*, 1983; *Dead in the West*, 1986; *The Magic Wagon*, 1986; *The Nightrunners*, 1987; *The Drive In: A B-Movie with Blood and Popcorn, Made in Texas*, 1988; *The Drive In 2: Not Just One of Them Sequels*, 1989; *Cold in July*, 1989; *By Bizarre Hands*, 1989; *Savage Seasons*, 1990; *Stories by Mama Lansdale's Youngest Boy*, 1991; *Batman: Captured by the Engines*, 1991; *Best Sellers Guaranteed*, 1993; *Mucho Mojo*, 1994; *Jonah Hex: Two-Gun Mojo*, 1994; *The Two Bear Mambo*, 1995; *Tarzan: The Lost Adventure*, 1996; *Bad Chili*, 1997; *Rumble Tumble*, 1998; *Freezer Burn*, 1999; As editor *Best of the West*, 1986; *The New Frontier: Best of the West 2*, 1989; *Dark at Heart* (with Karen Lansdale), 1992

Larsen, Jeanne

Aug. 9, 1950– Novelist; poet; translator

The American novelist, poet, and translator Jeanne Larsen has been widely praised for three historical novels—*Silk Road* (1989), *Bronze Mirror* (1991), and *Manchu Palaces* (1996)—set in the China of the imperial dynasties, in which she creates a "luminous, self-contained, fluid world," in the words of one critic. Although often involving brutality, her novels are laden with "the exquisite sensibilities of Chinese poetry, lush descriptions of nature, and quiet evocations of mood," according to the *Library Journal* (September 15, 1996) reviewer of *Manchu Palaces*. Her *James Cook in Search of Terra Incognita: A Book of Poems* (1979) won an award from the Associated Writing Programs, and she is the translator of *Brocade River Poems: Selected Works of the Tang Dynasty Courtesan Xue Tao* (1987).

For *World Authors 1990–1995*, Jeanne Larsen writes: "I was born in Walter Reed Army Hospital in the District of Columbia. My mother was forty, a former college teacher who had just—because of impending motherhood—ended her career as an officer in the Women's Army Corps. Two weeks later, we moved to Fort Leavenworth, Kansas, where my father entered the next stage of his own military career, much of which was spent as student or instructor within the Army's educational system.

T. H. Mesner

"Thanks to my parents, who spoiled me and pushed me and taught me to regard what were surely blessings, I gained more than I lost from the moves that followed: Fort Lee, Virginia, three homes/two schools in Pennsylvania, Arlington, and then three posts in Germany—'West Germany' it was, and every adult remembered World War II. I was ten the year my dad spent in Korea, close to the DMZ. He sent me lacquer chopsticks, an iron miniature of the Great Buddha in Kamakura, Japan.

"We lived, during those Cold War decades, in a far-flung small town, a rather Southern one, I think. Friends left or were left, but some—not the civilians—might turn up again on down the road. Parents had ranks. People connected by telling stories set where they once were stationed. Kids had rules, and one way or another, learned to deal with them. The community had its code, its cause. We were oddly closed-in, oddly close.

"The crucial five years in Europe—we traveled from Norway to Greece—sharpened my sense of needing to figure out how cultures work, and how to live within them. I was just twelve when we went, and going-on-seventeen when we returned to the States, days after my graduation from a Department of Defense–run high school in Frankfurt. The first year (in Idar-Oberstein and Giessen) I attended German schools: I wish I'd learned more of the language, but I know why I later found my zest for Chinese and Japanese, and for phrasebook glibness in any other tongue.

"After one year of college, I left a small duchy of political indifference and frat parties (the disdain was pretty much mutual) for Oberlin. Its counter-culture (or counter-culture manqué) of earnest intellectuality, co-op housing, demonstrations, and late-sixties' high jinks suited me exactly.

One course in East Asian religions, and I changed my major from Psych to Phenomenology of Religion. Every semester I took an English class—it seemed like breathing—and one fall day in upstate New York I realized what I had to do was not just keep writing poems, but be a writer.

"Still, I took the chance to finish college a few months early, and spent the next years moving. In Atlanta, I baked bread, lived cheap, and knew that for all the talk of the times I was inextricably a part of American society. My parents gave me a tough, wonderful summer of archaeology in Israel. The year I went through the M.A. program in writing at Hollins taught me about the power of a limber imagination and the beauty of southwestern Virginia; I've been learning from the mind and writing of R. H. W. Dillard ever since. Coming back in 1980 to teach at Hollins may have been the most fortunate move of all.

"But first, Taiwan (two years' teaching at Tunghai University), Ohio (back to Oberlin, the last phase of the fellowship that opened my pathway into Chinese culture), Iowa for Ph.D. work in Comp Lit, and nineteen months (dissertation research, mostly) in Japan. *James Cook in Search of Terra Incognita: A Book of Poems*, was published just before I left Nagasaki. Iowa City gave me my husband, Tom Mesner, and my two step-kids, Scot and Kili. I can't imagine a better gift.

"Or here's another way to tell the story. All that time, from before I can remember, I read. My mother wanted to raise a genius; she used to say I taught myself, although one day she added that she'd explained once how the same letter could stand for different sounds. Words, I learned, were tricksy but worth snaring; my father often had my younger brother Rod or me bring the dictionary to the dinner table, to settle an argument, explain a joke. Wherever the local library was that year, I started my most significant journeys there. My mother hoped I would become 'a lady doctor,' but early on I decided—though I forgot this till I started imagining *Silk Road*—that I'd write the kind of books I liked best, the ones about myths and magic, the fairy tales.

"Or I could tell about the importance of the living creek behind one house of ours at Carlisle Barracks, and the girl-centered world of Scouting, that offered summers deeper in the woods. Or describe the self-declared tomboy who made snug homes and small thrilling dramas—for her dolls. Or recount the autobiography of my body, or reel off a few grants and awards. I could name patient teachers, dear friends, beloveds, and gradeschool awkwardnesses like those most any writer grew up with. Somewhere in all these tales rests the reason I always say I don't much write about my own life.

"Instead, I like to say, I lie. Because the world is richer and more interesting. Because the game and craft of lying is the best truth we have. The Chinese poetry that means so much to me is traditionally read like this: to know the poem is to know the man, or woman—even when its persona, images,

words, clearly signal a long history of other poems behind it. I can't argue. I just think that every person we believe we know is made of poems, and other narratives.

"The stories of art, like the stories of religions and other histories, invent and save us. They are more true than this one."

Jeanne Larsen started her professional writing career as a poet. Her first book, *James Cook in Search of Terra Incognita: A Book of Poems* was published in 1979, four years before she received her Ph.D. in comparative literature.

Larsen's first novel, *Silk Road*, is subtitled *A Novel of Eighth-Century China*. In it a little girl named Parrot, sold to a courtesan, eventually rebels to go in search of her mother, who has been kidnapped by "a besotted river godling," according to Edna Stumpf in the *New York Times Book Review* (September 10, 1989). The novel verges, with its "myths and magic," to use Larsen's phrase, on being a fairy tale—one encompassing narrative conceits as well as bits of poetry and prose translated from old Chinese documents. The majority of reviewers were enchanted by *Silk Road*. A. M. B. Amantia, writing in *Library Journal* (May 1, 1989), found it to be a "gently humorous fantasy" with a clever blend of "feminism, Chinese history and myth, and beautiful language." Stumpf, in the *New York Times Book Review* article, observed that the "wonderfully mellow tone" of the novel "accommodates much merriment, and moments of sadness and joy. . . . *Silk Road*, in its prodigal layering of narratives, projects the theme of the artist as inventor of history; the heroine's story is told by goddesses and gods, and she prevails to retell it among them." Felicia Kornbluh, writing in the *San Francisco Review of Books* (Fall 1989), however, felt that *Silk Road* transgressed the strictures of political correctness laid down by Edward W. Said in *Orientalism*. She found it a "vision of the Orient, wrapped in the form of a 19th-century novel and suffocated by an embarrassment of writerly techniques from the 1980s."

Bronze Mirror, Larsen's next novel, also has a setting in Chinese antiquity. Like *Silk Road*, it became a Book of the Month Club selection. *Manchu Palaces*, her third historical novel set in China—this time in the 18th century—is, like her first novel, the story of a quest. Larsen won universal critical approval for *Manchu Palaces*, mitigated only by reviewers' cavils about interpolated sections of the book that purport to be the work of later scholars—a translator, a Portuguese adventurer, a British cartographer, a Presbyterian missionary, and one Hedda Svensdatter, whose letter is dated 1930. Complicating the story further is the fact that the main character, Lotus, a bond servant at the imperial court in the Forbidden City, is sometimes called by other names, as are other characters. Lotus, before she can attempt an advantageous liaison with a prince, as she is trained to do by her father's concubine, must lay her mother's ghost to rest. She must also accomplish a task for another ghost—an artist—by restoring Buddhist statues to a mandala in the Five Crest Mountains. Completing these tasks will enable her to achieve enlightenment. Terming Lotus's story "a gently intriguing, brilliantly detailed tale," the *Publishers Weekly* (September 16, 1996) reviewer felt that although the interpolated material weakened it somewhat, "Lotus's singular story of enlightenment . . . is the radiant center of these diversions."

Kathryn Smith, in the *Anderson (South Carolina) Independent-Mail* (February 9, 1997), adjured readers to "revel in the poetic language of the book, which adds brilliance to such everyday activities as watching ducklings swim in a pond and drinking a cup of scented tea." Larsen's use of "rich details about the customs of imperial China" is "always . . . a complement to the story," she concluded. "*Manchu Places* is sometimes challenging, but well worth the effort the reader puts forth."

As a translator, Larsen has produced a book, *Brocade River Poems: Selected Works of the Tang Dynasty Courtesan Xue Tao*, and has contributed translations of other Chinese female poets to such journals as the *Literary Review*.

—S.Y.

SUGGESTED READING: *Anderson (South Carolina) Independent-Mail* p40+ Feb. 9, 1997; *Kirkus Reviews* Aug. 15, 1996; *Library Journal* p99 May 1, 1989; *New York Times Book Review* p26 Sep. 10, 1989; *Publishers Weekly* p70 Sep. 16, 1996; *San Francisco Review of Books* p14 Fall 1989

SELECTED BOOKS: Novels—*Silk Road,* 1989; *Bronze Mirror,* 1991; *Manchu Palaces,* 1996; Poetry—*James Cook in Search of Terra Incognita: A Book of Poems,* 1979. As translator—*Brocade River Poems: Selected Works of the Tang Dynasty Courtesan Xue Tao,* 1987

Courtesy of Matthew O'Grady

Larson, Jonathan

Feb. 4, 1960– Jan. 25, 1996 Playwright; songwriter

"It's not how many years you live, but how you fulfill the time you spend here. That's sort of the point of the show," Jonathan Larson said of his musical *Rent* to Anthony Tommasini of the *New York Times* (February 11, 1996). Throughout his life, Larson lived by this maxim: he dedicated himself passionately to his goal of reinventing American

musical theater and to living life to the fullest. Larson's optimism in the face of economic hardship and the deaths of close friends made his own untimely death that much more of a tragedy. Larson passed away on January 25, 1996, at the age of 35, after suffering an aortic aneurysm. *Rent* is the legacy he left to the world, and he imbued it with his "seize the day" approach to life.

Larson had been working on his rock opera, for which he wrote the book, the music, and the lyrics, for seven years. He died during the night following the last dress rehearsal before the show's premiere, which took place at the New York Theater Workshop, a 150-seat theater in New York City's East Village. Had Larson lived to see *Rent*'s official opening three weeks later, he would have witnessed his creation's unbridled success. Twenty-four hours after the glowing reviews appeared, the entire five-week run of the show was sold out. A month-long extension sold out a week later, and then negotiations began for a move to Broadway, where *Rent* opened at the Nederlander Theater in April 1996. In addition to being a huge hit among audiences, *Rent* became, as of 1996, the most critically acclaimed and awarded musical of the decade. Larson posthumously received the Pulitzer Prize for drama for *Rent*, as well as the Tony Awards for best book of a musical and best score of a musical, and the show also won for best musical and best featured actor in a musical. One of the reasons for its appeal was that *Rent*, which tells the story of struggling young artists faced with the certainty that they would soon die, rang with authenticity for many of its fans, an authenticity that was underlined, tragically, by Larson's own death. "It seems like he knew whereof he spoke when he was talking about 'No day but today,' a lyric from the show," Anthony Rapp, the actor who portrays

Mark, a video artist, in *Rent*, said of Larson to Evelyn McDonnell of the *Village Voice* (April 30, 1996).

Jonathan Larson was born on February 4, 1960 to Allan and Nanette Larson, and he grew up in comfortable circumstances in White Plains, New York, a suburb of New York City. Before retiring, Larson's father was an executive with a marketing business; he and Larson's mother now live in New Mexico. As a youth, Larson studied the piano and played the tuba in his high school marching band. He also played the lead in a school production of *Fiddler on the Roof*, and in high school, he studied music theory and composition, the only formal training in those areas that he received. At Adelphi University, in Garden City, New York, Larson majored in acting, but he was already writing songs for cabaret-style musical revues produced at the school. Upon graduation, he moved to a dingy apartment in New York's Greenwich Village to pursue a career as an actor. His father commented on his living conditions to Anthony Tommasini of the *New York Times* (March 17, 1996): "It [Larson's apartment] looked like it hadn't been sanitized in 50 years. It was the kind of place my father, a Russian Jewish immigrant, probably lived in when he came here in 1900. But Jonathan loved his life. And he was not a dilettante, sitting there saying, 'Dad, send me money because I'm writing the great American opus.'" It was to this bohemian lifestyle that Larson paid tribute in *Rent*. The characters in the musical make a practice of throwing the keys to their apartment out the window to friends on the street to let them in, just as Larson had done, because the door buzzer on their old building is broken.

Larson supplemented the meager income he earned as an actor by waiting tables at the Moondance Diner, in the downtown New York neighborhood of SoHo. But before long, he shifted his focus from acting to composing. A catalyst for this shift was his association with the composer and lyricist Stephen Sondheim, who wrote such groundbreaking musicals as *Sweeney Todd* and *Sunday in the Park with George*. Larson had written a fan letter to Sondheim, who had responded by inviting Larson to his house for a drink, and encouraged him to pursue composing. "Don't be an actor," Sondheim advised, as recounted by John Istel of the *Village Voice* (July 4, 1995). "There's more dignity playing piano in a bar." Sondheim continued to act as a mentor to Larson, and in 1994, he helped him obtain a $45,000 Richard Rodgers Studio Production Award that funded a workshop presentation of *Rent*.

Meanwhile, in 1988, a workshop version of Larson's musical *Superbia*, which Istel described as a "satirical sci-fi black musical comedy," was produced at Playwrights Horizons in New York. While Larson won praise in the theater community for his music and lyrics, the show failed to generate interest among producers. In 1990, Larson debuted his rock monologue "Tick, Tick . . . Boom!" which he

eventually performed at Second Stage Theater, the Village Gate, and New York Theater Workshop. "In this intense, angry solo, a man wakes up on his 30th birthday, downs some junk food, and complains for 45 minutes about his frustrated ambitions, turning 30 in the tenuous 90s and much more," Tommasini wrote. "Toward the end, he sings of a friend who has just revealed he is HIV-positive." In fact, Larson had lost many friends to AIDS over the years, and this piece served as an outlet for his anger. Some of his friends feel this had an effect on *Rent*; in that by the time Larson began to work on the musical, he was ready to imbue it with a more positive message. Also during the 1990s, Larson composed the songs for a musical based on the life of the 19th-century investment banker J. P. Morgan, who famously bailed out the New York Stock Exchange when they ran short of cash in 1907. The musical, *J. P. Morgan Saves the Nation*, had a book and lyrics by Jeffrey M. Jones and was produced as a site-specific performance in front of the Federal Building at Wall and Broad Streets in New York City in 1995. While Larson received a number of grants, he still needed his job as a waiter, as well as a number of freelance gigs, to make ends meet. Among these were jobs writing songs for the popular public television children's show *Sesame Street*, as well as for children's book cassettes based on the Steven Spielberg films *An American Tail* and *The Land Before Time*. Larson also created musical soundtracks for the home movies of *Rolling Stone* founder Jann Wenner.

Throughout this period, Larson had been developing *Rent*. The idea originated with Larson's friend Billy Aronson, who had wanted to create a 1990s version of Puccini's classic opera *La Bohème*, which chronicles the lives of young artists in Paris around 1830. Larson had never seen the opera, but he remembered a puppet version of the tale he had seen as a child. He knew the story well enough to envision a new version that would capture the mood of America's disenfranchised youth—a "*Hair* for the 90s" that would "bring musical theater to the MTV generation," to quote Tommasini. Larson and Aronson began working together on the project, with Larson composing the score and Aronson writing the lyrics. They had created first drafts of three songs that remain in the show today when the duo decided they had different visions of the project, and Aronson agreed to let Larson take over.

Larson and Aronson's first discussion about the project took place in 1989; in 1992, Larson had finished a first draft of the entire show. Around that time, he was riding his bicycle through the East Village and noticed that construction was being done on the New York Theater Workshop. He wandered into the theater and realized it would be a perfect venue for *Rent*. Larson tracked down the artistic director of the space, James C. Nicola, and gave him a tape of the score and a copy of the script. Nicola was impressed by the material, although it still needed work; he offered to help Larson develop *Rent* at the New York Theater Workshop. He told Tommasini, "What drew Jonathan and me together in a philosophical place was the belief in how tragic it was that pop music and theater music had gotten a divorce. I felt he was the first composer I had run into who had the possibility of doing something about it." In the spring of 1993, a staged reading of the show was produced. The response to the music was positive, but the plot still needed some work. Michael Greif, the artistic director of the La Jolla Playhouse, in La Jolla, California, was brought in to direct Larson's musical, and together they worked through the problems. "Jonathan had firm ideas and he loved battling them out with us," Greif told Tommasini. "But there was give and take. Probably only a third to a half of the material that existed at that time remains in the play today." The 1994 workshop production was the final stage of development before the show was produced in the spring of 1996. With a budget of $200,000, it was the New York Theater Workshop's biggest production to date at that time.

Rent's characters are drawn from the community of aspiring artists among whom Larson lived in the East Village, and the central plot revolves around Roger, an HIV-positive punk-rock musician trying to write one perfect song before he dies. He is recovering from his girlfriend's suicide and is therefore wary of romantic entanglements, but when he meets Mimi, an AIDS-infected nightclub dancer and a heroin addict, he falls in love with her. The other characters include Roger's roommate, Mark, a video artist; Mark's former performance-artist girlfriend, Maureen; Maureen's new lover, Joanne, a lawyer and sound engineer; Tom Collins, a New York University professor and self-styled philosopher, who falls in love with Angel, a transvestite street musician who comes to Tom's aid after he is mugged; and Benjamin, Roger, and Mark's yuppie landlord, who embodies the sellout mentality that the show rails against. The characters are almost all directly based on those found in Puccini's opera, and some scenes in the musical are culled directly from the original as well. When updated for *Rent*, a Latin Quarter cafe scene peopled with children and street vendors in *La Bohème* becomes a Christmas Eve tableau set among the homeless along New York's St. Mark's Place.

Critics praised *Rent* for presenting three-dimensional and sympathetic characters, rather than resorting to stereotypes. *Rent* was also lauded for its music, which is played on stage by a five-piece band and incorporates an array of musical styles, including punk, reggae, gospel, rhythm and blues, and ballads. Ben Brantley wrote in the *New York Times* (February 14, 1996), "Sustained by a glittering, inventive score, the work finds a trans-fixing brightness in characters living in the shadow of AIDS. . . . Mr. Larson has proved that rock-era song styles can be integrated into a character-driven story for the stage with wildly affecting success." Patti O'Brien of *Rolling Stone* (May 16, 1996) wrote, "Rent confronts a number of sobering is-

sues—AIDS, drug addiction, romantic disillusionment, artistic struggle, death—but it's not overly moralistic. It's also not a downer. Sure, there are several tear-inducing scenes, but Larson places more emphasis on love, friendship, and survival."

The week before *Rent*'s first previews at the New York Theater Workshop, Larson visited emergency rooms twice after suffering from chest pains. One hospital diagnosed him with food poisoning, the other with a virus; both sent him home after a routine exam. He had quit his job waiting tables about two months earlier, and when he spoke with Tommasini after *Rent*'s last dress rehearsal, Larson was optimistic about his future. "I'm happy to say that other commissions are coming up, and I think I may have a life as a composer," he said. Later that night, Larson died in his apartment. The next day, instead of going ahead with the first scheduled performance, the cast invited Larson's friends and family to the theater to listen to them sing *Rent*'s songs. Adam Pascal, who portrayed Roger, said to O'Brien of the audience that night, "They were all crying, and we were all crying, and we were trying to sing these songs, which are really beautiful. It felt so wonderful because it was so cathartic. I'm not one to lose it, but you can't help it in a situation like that. It was probably one of the most moving experiences in my life." It is typical for important revisions to take place during the preview performances of a show, and Greif and the other artistic staff felt an immense responsibility to shepherd Larson's creation through the final stages. Of their discussions about changes to *Rent* during that period, Greif said to McDonnell, "Because Jonathan is not here to argue with, I need to include his argument in my argument." While it is tragic that Larson did not live to see the tremendous success of his musical, he did accomplish the goal his character Roger establishes for himself at the beginning of *Rent*: he created one great work for which he will be remembered. As the actor Anthony Rapp said to McDonnell, "We were left with this piece he created and we have only now to do it, because we're not going to get a chance to work with him again, we're not going to get a chance to hear his music again, we're not going to get a chance to know what else he might have created. We have to do this for as long as we can, and we have to do it as best we can."

—J. P.

SUGGESTED READING: *New York Times* B p9 Jan. 26, 1996, with photo, II p5+ Feb. 11, 1996, with photos, C p11 Feb. 14, 1996, with photo, II p7+ Mar. 17, 1996, with photos, C p13 Apr. 30, 1996, with photo; *People* p59 Apr. 22, 1996, with photos, p93+ Feb. 24, 1997, with photos; *Rolling Stone* p54+ May 16, 1996, with photos; *Time* p71 Mar. 4, 1996, with photos; *Village Voice* p73+ Jul. 4, 1996, with photo, p27+ Apr. 30, 1996, with photo

SELECTED PLAYS: As composer—*J. P. Morgan Saves the Nation*, 1995; As composer, librettist, and lyricist—*Superbia*, 1989; "Tick, Tick . . . Boom," 1990; *Rent*, 1996

Leavitt, Caroline

Jan. 9, 1952– Novelist

The novelist Caroline Leavitt has won praise for her honest portraits of everyday life and is often compared for her subject matter and style to Anne Tyler. Her first novel, *Meeting Rozzy Halfway* (1981), was published when she was 28 years old, not long after she won first prize in *Redbook*'s Young Writers Contest. Several novels followed in quick succession: *Lifelines* (1982), *Jealousies* (1983), and *Family* (1987). In 1993 she published *Into Thin Air*, the story of a man who attempts to pick up the pieces of his life after his wife disappears. It won a Fiction Award from the New York Foundation of the Arts. *Living Other Lives* (1995) was based in part on her own experiences dealing with the death of her fiancé two weeks before their wedding. An excerpt was printed in *Good Housekeeping* that same year.

In her autobiographical statement for *World Authors 1990–1995*, Caroline Leavitt writes: "I was born in Quincy, Massachusetts, in 1952 and as soon as I could hold a pencil, I was writing. I filled up dimestore notebooks with novels about a young girl and her adventures, and later, when I got to school, I began illustrating my 'books' as well. "I was never really encouraged. In fact, while at Brandeis, a writing professor suggested I give up writing altogether and think about teaching small children as a career! Needless to say, I didn't listen. It wasn't until I was out of college that I began to be really serious about my work. Richard Price had just published *The Wanderers* to rave reviews. He was just 24 years old, and I felt competitive, and every night, I began to write for several hours.

"My game plan was to be a short-story writer and then, maybe years later, to write a novel, but it didn't work out that way. For nearly a decade, I received enough rejection slips to paper my apartment, but finally I sold a short story about the skeptical daughter of a psychic to the *Michigan Quarterly Review*. They paid me all of fifty dollars, but I was thrilled. I was 28 years old, and it was my last year to enter *Redbook* magazine's Young Writers Contest. I didn't think they'd be interested in a dark story about two sisters growing up in Boston, one of them slowly turning mad, but I sent it anyway. I won First Prize.

"All of my novels deal with relationships and are probably rooted in autobiography—the tortured drive for family and the need to escape it. I am fascinated by obsessions, be it with knowing the future as the psychic did in my second novel

Lifelines, or the jealousy a second girlfriend harbors for a first with disastrous results in *Jealousies*. "I also find myself writing a lot about how the past intrudes on the future. In *Family*, I examined how early loss kept a man from truly loving his wife and daughter. In *Into Thin Air*, a young woman's disappearance on the eve she gives birth to her first child colors her young husband's life for years to come because he keeps expecting her to return. And in my latest novel, *Living Other Lives*, which is based on my own experiences, the death of a young woman's fiancé changes her life forever.

"I read everything I can get my hands on. I don't like minimalist fiction. I like books which have a deep sense of felt life to them. And hopefully, some humor. I also write scripts. "I've had good writing years where all I've had to do is stay at home and write, and I've had rougher years, where I've had to take on day jobs to help pay the rent. In my time, I've been a Job Corps counselor, a teacher, a typist, a book buyer, a cashier, a dog walker, a high fashion copywriter (which is amusing since I live in black tee shirts and blue jeans and sneakers) and a video magazine writer. All these jobs are fodder for writing.

"I've been married since 1993 to Jeff Tamarkin, the editor of *Goldmine Music Magazine*. We live in a 120-year-old-house we restored along with two cranky cats and a sardonic tortoise. My latest work in progress is a joint effort. We are expecting a baby boy in July 1996!"

In 1993 Leavitt published her fifth novel, *Into Thin Air*. The story of a young husband whose wife disappears not long after she gives birth to a baby girl, it won the Fiction Award from the New York Foundation of the Arts. Lee, the disappeared wife and mother, was a troubled teenager, whose mother died of cancer and whose father quickly married a woman Lee despised. Like many other teens, Lee rebelled in a number of ways, involving herself in troubling sexual relationships, drinking too much, and staying out too late. Then she met Jim Archer, an easygoing pharmacology student. They married, and Lee soon became pregnant, but she also started to become disenchanted with Jim and his all-enveloping love. After Lee gives birth to a girl, Joanna, she deserts her husband and daughter, feeling strangled by her responsibilities. The novel follows Jim and Lee's parallel lives: Jim spends years longing for his lost wife before remarrying, while Lee travels the lonely backroads of America before seeing a little girl who reminds her of her own daughter and the life she left nine years earlier. In the end, Lee returns to Jim and Joanna and shatters their lives, though it is suggested that healing may come. Though it was an award winner, critics had mixed feelings about *Into Thin Air*. Janet Boyarin Blundell, in *Library Journal* (January 1993), remarked: "While somewhat slow to start, this novel . . . ultimately involves the reader when it begins tracing Lee's growth." Critic David Hinckley, writing for *Kirkus Reviews* (November 15, 1992) disagreed with this assessment of the novel and of Lee's character: "As protagonist, Lee's a tough sell, and even though Leavitt does everything she can to explain why the girl does the rotten things she does, she doesn't capture her voice—which keeps the justification purely clinical. Some attractive prose, then, but beyond that the effect is anesthetizing."

In *Living Other Lives* (1995), Leavitt used her own tragic experience—the death of her fiancé just a couple of weeks before their wedding—in a novel which explores the grief of those left behind. The main character, Lilly, watches in horror when her fiancé Matt is killed in a freak diving accident. Lilly is so grief-stricken she isn't able to take care of Matt's daughter, Dinah, who is estranged from her own mother. Lilly subsequently begins a meandering trip across country, trying to escape her grief. When Matt's mother has a stroke and is no longer able to take care of Dinah, Lilly returns and, somewhat reluctantly, takes care of Dinah as if she were her own daughter. The plot of the novel explores the way in which the women Matt most loved in the world—his fiancé, his daughter, and his mother—deal with his death and how their own lives are changed. Many critics were impressed with *Living Other Lives*. Wendy Smith of the *New York Times* (July 30, 1995) noted: "Caroline Leavitt's sixth novel showcases her ability to create believable characters who can behave badly without forfeiting the reader's sympathy." Reviewing the work for *Library Journal* (June 1, 1995), Barbara E. Kemp wrote: "Leavitt . . . affectingly portrays the pain and confusion of loss and the difficulty of learning to live without a loved one. The fact that the women are not always likable makes them all the more real, and the reader cannot help but understand and sympathize." "Although the prose is occasionally overcharged," a critic for *Publishers Weekly* (April 24, 1995), "that won't prevent readers from surrendering to the heartfelt and beguiling story."

In 1996 Caroline Leavitt gave birth to a son, Max. The difficult pregnancy left her with a rare blood disease, Factor VIII, in which the blood stops clotting. After a number of operations, the author has fully recovered from her condition and has written about her ordeal in several magazines.
—C. M.

SUGGESTED READING: *Kirkus Reviews* Nov. 15, 1992; *Library Journal* p 166, Jan. 1993; p 200, Jan. 1994; p 160, June 1, 1995; *Mademoiselle* p 51, Nov. 1998; *New York Times* Sep. 7, p 14, July 30, 1995; *Publishers Weekly* p 61, Apr. 24, 1995; *Salon* (on-line) Dec. 1997; *Contemporary Authors* vol. 150, 1996

SELECTED WORKS: *Meeting Rozzy Halfway*, 1981; *Lifelines*, 1982; *Jealousies*, 1983; *Family*, 1987; *Into Thin Air*, 1993; *Living Other Lives*, 1995

LeClair, Tom

Mar. 25, 1944– Nonfiction writer; novelist

Tom LeClair began his literary career with interviews of such established writers as John Barth, Donald Barthelme, and Toni Morrison, which he published as *Anything Can Happen: Interviews with Contemporary American Novelists* (1983). That book, co-edited with Larry McCaffery, established LeClair as a leading academic supporter of modern American fiction. He added to his reputation with the publication of *In the Loop* (1987), a discussion of the novels of Don DeLillo. Two years later he published another work, *The Art of Excess: Mastery of Contemporary American Fiction* (1989), in which he presented his interpretations of works by such noted authors as Thomas Pynchon, Joseph Heller, and William Gaddis. In 1996 he joined the ranks of fiction authors with the publication of his first novel, *Passing Off*, the story of a man who poses as a Greek-American in order to play on an Athenian basketball team. The *Washington Post* called this first attempt at fiction "one of the most literate and entertaining sports novels of the decade."

Thomas LeClair was born in Rutland, Vermont, on March 25, 1944, the son of C. E. and Florence (Spaulding) LeClair. He studied English literature at Boston College, and received his bachelor's degree in the spring of 1965. From there he went to the University of Vermont and received his master's degree in 1967.

In 1970 LeClair became an English instructor at the University of Cincinnati, in Ohio. He received his Ph.D. from Duke University in 1972 and became an assistant professor at Cincinnati the next year. He went on to become an associate professor in 1976 and a full professor in 1980. For the 1981–82 school year he was a Fulbright lecturer at the University of Greece; his time spent in Greece would make up the background for his novel *Passing Off*.

LeClair's first notable work was "Avant-Garde Mystery," an essay on modern fiction, for which he received a 1983–84 Pushcart Prize from the Pushcart Press. In that same year he and Larry McCaffery edited *Anything Can Happen: Interviews with Contemporary American Novelists* (1983), a collection of conversations with 18 contemporary masters of fiction who came into the national spotlight in the 1970s. The authors included Rosellen Brown, Robert Coover, Don DeLillo, E. L. Doctorow, Stanley Elkin, Raymond Federman, Bill Gass, John Irving, Diane Johnson, Steve Katz, Toni Morrison, and Tim O'Brien. Each speaks about his or her life and work and the question of how real fiction should appear to a reader. The group was evenly divided among those who wished to create their own reality and those who wanted to reflect the reality of those around them. Critics generally approved of *Anything Can Happen* and compared it to George Plimpton's *Writers at Work* series. Paul

E. Hutchinson of *Library Journal* (February 15, 1983) called it "an excellent book that will be of interest to both the reader of fiction and the diligent practitioner." The reviewer for *Choice* (July/August 1983) noted: "The interviews are to the point—the interviewers' homework long since done—and the results should fuel any number of graduate papers for the next few years. In short, this is an enormously valuable volume for readers interested in the happily healthy state of the art of fiction-writing in our time." David Montrose of the *Times Literary Supplement* (September 23, 1983), however, did not believe it to be as noteworthy as Plimpton's celebrated series. "The editors have departed from their original goal of providing a valuable critical document, but not sufficiently to reproduce the peculiar appeal of the *Writers at Work* series. . . . LeClair and McCaffery should be complimented, though, for paying attention to some relatively new authors."

LeClair's next book was *In the Loop: Don DeLillo and the Systems Novel* (1987). LeClair attempted to demonstrate the influence of "systems theory," a modern scientific model that focuses on ecological systems' reciprocal communications, on DeLillo's fiction. In *Choice* (June 1988), C. G. Masinton noted that "LeClair persuasively argues that DeLillo, who has been largely ignored by academic critics, deserves to be acknowledged as one of the leading American novelists of our time. . . . LeClair also offers an excellent introduction to systems theory at the beginning of his book and a handy bibliography on the subject at the end." Wayne B. Stengel in *American Literature* (March 1989) remarked, "LeClair's contention that the systems novel, capable of both reconstructing and deconstructing its subject, is modernist and not postmodernist in heritage and provides welcome insight for scholars discontented with contemporary fiction's fascination with self-referentiality and despair."

LeClair's next publication was also an interpretive literary study. *The Art of Excess: Mastery in Contemporary American Fiction* (1989) interpreted a number of modern novelists' works, including Thomas Pynchon's *Gravity's Rainbow* (1973), Joseph Heller's *Something Happened*, Robert Coover's *The Public Burning*, Joseph McElroy's *Women and Men*, and Ursula LeGuin's *Always Coming Home*. LeClair's work essentially calls for a new medium through which to interpret fiction; his own interpretation mixes scientific observation, cultural criticism, and a great understanding of literature. Critics had mixed feelings about LeClair's theories. Observing that his deconstructionist approach aids in the appreciation of new American fiction, W. B. Warde of *Choice* (January 1990) also noted that "LeClair strains in explaining the 'seeming excess of the novels.' . . . This study and the seven 'systems' novels . . . suffer from an encompassing and unassimilable inundation of information." Martha Turner of *American Literature* (June 1990) remarked: "For those concerned about

the human and environmental toll exacted by our resource-abusing society . . . LeClair's courageous blend of literary scholarship, scientific theory, and cultural criticism will reveal new possibilities for a socially engaged study of literature."

Most recently LeClair has produced a novel, *Passing Off* (1996), about life in the Greek Basketball Association as seen through the eyes of Michael Keever, an American player who couldn't make the National Basketball Association in the United States. Keever's agent is able to procure him a spot on one of the four Greek teams—if he changes his last name to something more Greek-sounding. He does so, telling no one—including his wife—and endlessly complicating his life. Reviewing the book for the *Washington Post* (February 10, 1997), Frederick L. McKissack Jr. remarked: "What makes the book so enticing is LeClair's skillful depiction of the quality that all good point guards possess: the power to deceive. . . . Keever deceives on the court as well as off it, and his weaves, moves and fakes make *Passing Off* one of the most literate and entertaining sports novels of the decade."

Tom LeClair lives in Cincinnati, Ohio. He has three children: Thomas, Mary, and Casey. He reviews fiction for the *New York Times Book Review*, the *Washington Post*, the *New Republic*, and *USA Today*.—C. M.

SUGGESTED READING: *American Literature* p132 Mar. 1989, p360 June 1990; *Choice* p597 July/Aug. 1983, p1556 June 1988, p798 Jan. 1990; *Library Journal* p397 Feb. 15, 1983; *Times Literary Supplement* p1025 Sep. 23, 1983; *Washington Post* Feb. 10, 1997; *Contemporary Authors, New Revised Series*, vol. 43, 1994

SELECTED WORKS: Fiction—*Passing Off*, 1996; Nonfiction—*In the Loop: Don DeLillo and the Systems Novel*, 1987; *The Art of Excess: Mastery in Contemporary Fiction*, 1989; As editor (with Larry McCaffery)—*Anything Can Happen: Interviews with Contemporary American Novelists*, 1983

Lee, Li-Young

1957– Poet; memoirist

With the publication of two poetry collections, *Rose* (1986) and *The City in Which I Love You* (1990), and an autobiographical memoir, *The Winged Seed: A Remembrance* (1995), Li-Young Lee has secured his place as one of the significant new voices in American letters to have emerged from the Asian diaspora. Lee, whose childhood language was not English, was born in Djakarta, Indonesia to Chinese parents forced to wander about Asia as political refugees before finally entering the United States with their four surviving children in the early 1960s. In 1986 BOA Editions published Lee's first poetry collection, *Rose*, which included a foreword by Gerald Stern that compared its young author to John Keats, Rainer Maria Rilke, and Theodore Roethke. His second collection, also published by BOA, won the Lamont Prize from the Academy of American Poets in 1990. Simon & Schuster, which published his memoir, described it as "a literary event—a luminous, wise, and magical work of memory and myth." The authenticity of Lee's message has been acknowledged by his peers, including Japanese-American author and literary historian Garrett Hongo, who paid him this tribute in a jacket blurb: "This is the finest book I've read that testifies to the experiences of Asian refugees in America—their pride and hope, their cultural alienation and social pain, their faith in personal redemption. *The Winged Seed* is a memory palace of exile, diaspora, and retribution."

Despite these accolades, literary virtuosity did not come easily to Li-Young Lee. In *The Winged Seed*, he described the frustration he encountered in trying to master the English language as a schoolboy in East Liberty, Pennsylvania, where his family eventually settled: "My mouth was a shame to me, an indecent trench. A recurring dream of mine as a boy who'd just arrived on the continent with my parents was my mouth full of rotten teeth, hundreds of teeth in my mouth and all of them cavity-ridden, brown, chips of burnt bone embedded in my gums." His recollection of practicing Chinese calligraphy at his mother's table allows him to express perplexing questions of self-identity: "Here, as in childhood, it is the same solitude. Here as in childhood, I practice my Chinese, writing right to left, while my mother walks back and forth saying the words I write. My father's name was *Perfect Country*, which I write by drawing a spear enclosed in a heart and piercing the heart from within. My mother's name is *House of Courage*, and as she paces back and forth, uttering, as my grandmother's cane taps past the window, down the red-brick path, my head bends to the task. . . . I remember how the difficult wilderness gleamed beneath my hands, all that hard, dark, rosewood of my inheritance, polished to bright knock and no entrance."

Central to Lee's poetry and prose is his father, who looms as almost a semimythical figure in his son's consciousness even though he had been imprisoned for sedition by the Indonesian Sukarno regime when Li-Young was barely 18 months old. The elder Lee, affectionately called "Ba" in his son's writings, had been the personal physician to Mao Zedong but was forced to flee China to escape political turmoil in the early 1950s, together with his wife, Jiaying, the daughter of an old aristocratic family. They settled in Indonesia, where Li-Young was born in 1957. Lee wrote in *The Winged Seed*: "I remember I was born in the City of Victory [Djakarta] on a street called Jilan Industri, where each morning the man selling sticky rice cakes goes by

pushing his cart. . . . I remember I was named twice, once at my birth and once again after my father, in his prison cell, dreamed each night the same dream, in which the sun appeared to him as a blazing house, wherein dwelt a seed, black, new, dimly human." Writing about his father's arrest, Lee continued: "What does a seed enclose that might be considered dangerous to anyone?. . . What was it my father said. Did he say seed is good news, our waiting done? . . . . *Seed dies*, he thought, *but rice never sleeps, rice is unvanquished*."

Ironically, Lee's imprisoned father bore a striking resemblance to Sukarno, and his children often mistook a face depicted on pro-government posters with that of their father. "Ba" was rescued by a fellow Christian, who secured his passage to Hong Kong, where the elder man became a successful evangelist, the founder of the Ling Liang Assembly and the Ambassadors of Christ. The family emigrated to the United States in 1964 and Lee's father entered Pittsburgh Theological Seminary and became pastor to an all-white congregation in western Pennsylvania. Gerald Stern wrote in his foreword to *Rose*: "This is not a quaint and literary father-figure he is writing and thinking about. It is a real father—an extraordinary and heroic figure—at least as Lee sees him: personal physician to Mao, medical adviser to Sukarno, political prisoner in an Indonesian swamp, and, finally, Presbyterian minister in a tiny western Pennsylvania town. . . . If the father does become mythical, it is partly because of his dramatic, even tragic, life, and it is partly because Lee touches powerful emotional psychic layers in his search. . . . Maybe Lee—as a poet—is lucky to have had the father he had and the culture he had. Maybe they combine in such a way as to make his own poetry possible. Even unique."

The "winged seed" metaphor reappears in many guises over the course of Lee's discursive 205-page memoir: the handfuls of black seeds found in his father's pocket after his death; the biblical parable of the sower and the seed about which his father preached; the seeds of authenticity his father represented in the face of political turmoil; the seeds of awakening sexuality; the seeds fertilized in life's cycles of death and rebirth that fly "from unrest to unrest . . . from its birthplace . . . its flying . . . closing the desolate expanses ahead, its flying reveal[ing] ever greater expanses behind it."

Some of the most memorable passages in *The Winged Seed* are almost elegiac in their descriptions of the intricate bond that had developed between father and son, as when the teenage Li-Young accompanies his father to bring communion visits to shut-in parishioners or bathes his debilitated father as he lies near death. Others, also built around the "seed" imagery, show Lee's facility in absorbing details of his new environment, as from the vantage point of a ramshackle shed, where "I could witness hundreds of dandelion seeds float slowly over the valley, each carrying a spark of the late sun, each turned to gold by what it bore from one side of the river to the other."

When the *Rose* collection appeared in print in 1986, a reviewer for *Choice* welcomed "an important debut" in these words: "Rarely does one find a first book of poems as finished and as passionately charged with a sweeping range of emotion. . . . There is not a weak poem here. All are graceful and passionate, and although they are controlled, they seem effortlessly rendered." Lee opened the collection with a poem entitled "Epistle," a reference to the narrative force of words in letters as well as to their weight as biblical text:

> But there is wisdom
> in the hour in which a boy
> sits in his room listening
> to the sound of weeping
> coming from some other room
> of his father's house,
> and that boy was me, and he
> listened without understanding, and
> was soon frightened
> by how the monotonous sobs resem-
> bled laughter.

Throughout *Rose*, Lee revisits the harrowing scenes of exile in Indonesia before his family's flight to America, including remarkably autobiographical details, as in "Water." In this poem, Lee narrates how he washes his invalid father's water-bloated feet ("A respirator mask makes him look like a diver" and reminds him of the time, before Li-Young's birth, when his father suffered torture in China.

> I dry, then powder them
> with talc rising in clouds
> like dust lifting
> behind jeeps, a truck where he sat
> bleeding through his socks.
> 1949, he's 30 years old,
> his toenails pulled out,
> his toes beaten a beautiful
> violet that reminds him
> of Hunan, barely morning
> in the yard. . . .

The second poem in the collection, titled "The Gift," echoes this incident and clothes it with delicate nuances of both Christ's passion and the passion of connubial love in its description of Li's father pulling out a painful splinter from his son's palm:

> Had you entered that afternoon
> you would have thought you saw a
> planting something in a boy's palm,
> a silver tear, a tiny flame. . . . I bend
> over my wife's right hand.
> Look how I shave her thumbnail
> so carefully she feels no pain. . .
> . . . And I did not lift up my wound
> and cry
> *Death visited here!*
> I did what a child does
> when he's given something to keep.
> I kissed my father.

Other poems in *Rose* express the semicomic frustration of a young boy trying to adapt to an alien culture and language. In "Persimmon," he wrote about his sixth-grade teacher's punishing him for confusing the words "persimmon" and "precision." He resolved this situation by discussing the "precision" of choosing "persimmons," juxtaposing erotic images of his wife's body with a metaphysical linkage to his aged father's gathering despair. In a lighter vein, he wrote:

> Other words
> that got me into trouble were
> *fight* and *fright*, *wren* and *yarn.*
> Fight was what I did when I was
> fright was what I felt when I was
> Wrens are small, plain birds,
> yarn is what one knits with.
> Wrens are soft as yarn.
> My mother made soft birds out of
> yarn. . . .

Lee's mother, Jiaying (affectionately known as "Mu"), is sketched in greater detail in *The Winged Seed* than in the two books of poetry. The memoir reflects her role—somewhat more diminutive than the father's—in her son's interior life. She first emerges, as from the silken cocoon of old aristocratic China, from a household of courtesans, slaves, and her grandmother, the "Old President's wife" (in real life, the fifth wife of Chinese president Yuan Shih-k'ai, 1912–16). Or, as Lee puts it, his mother lived in a family compound in Tientsin in "a haunted mansion ruled by her father's mother, a woman as cruel as she is small and desiccated," who presided over a sewing hall full of countless cats, in which 30 seamstress-servants of the nine households toiled at stitching clothes for their privileged mistresses. But Lee did pay tribute to the "Westernized" literary tastes of his mother's family, as in this description of an outing: "On the trip up the narrow path, while one of her sisters reads aloud from Zola or Balzac, Jiaying nibbles on fresh lychees, which they carry up the mountain."

In *The City in Which I Love You*, more troubling and darksome images appear, as in the title poem, a love-seeking journey through a dissonant, alienating city where

> I mount the scabbed streets, the long
> shouts of avenues, and tunnel sunken
> night in search of you. . . .
> Past the guarded schoolyards, the
> boarded-up churches, swastikaed
> synagogues, defended houses of wor-
> ship, past
> newspapered windows of tenements,
> among the violated,
> the prosecuted citizenry, throughout
> this
> storied, buttressed, scavenged
> city I call home, in which I am a
> guest. . . .

Here, even Lee's father emerges in a more menacing light, as in "This Hour and What Is Dead," when the role of the seamstress is now assumed by the older man himself, who mends his son's pants "with various colors and too much thread / the stitching uneven." Lee continues:

> God, that old furnace, keeps talking
> with his mouth of teeth,
> a beard stained at feasts, and his
> of gasoline, airplane, human
> "Someone tell the Lord to leave me
> I've had enough of his love
> that feels like burning and flight and
> running away.

Reviewing Lee's second collection in the *New York Times Book Review* (January 27, 1991), Carol Muske wrote, "Like a pairing of Walt Whitman with the great Tang dynasty poet Tu Fu, Li-Young Lee emerges as an audacious and passionate poet-traveler. In the manner of Tang poetry, he speaks colloquially but metaphysically; he meditates, but always allows the noises of the world to enter." Muske described Lee's wrestling with self-definition when she wrote, "In his desire to find the immigrant soul and sense of identity (one of the recurring themes of this book), Mr. Lee ransacks many literary traditions. The result is an odd variety, an astonishing emotional virtuosity."

Li-Young Lee did not attempt a definitive explanation for his many references to seeds in *The Winged Seed*. Returning to one of his father's odd habits, he wrote: "I remember, as long as I knew him, my father carried at all times in his right suit-pocket a scarce handful of seeds. *Remembrance* was his sole answer when I asked him why. . . . I never asked my father in remembrance of what he kept those seeds. I knew better than to press him when I was a boy. Now I'm a man, and he is dead, and I feel a strange shame that I don't know what happened to those seeds." Later, he added: "When he died, his face was clothed to me forever. These days, his face has become a small glass pane at the end of the world, like one of those high windows in the ceiling of Union Station, each the size of my thumbnail. On the station floor are the human shadows, and in the air an anonymous voice is announcing departures and arrivals, and warning everyone *"Beware! Man trafficking in seeds!* The seed trade is a dark habit."

Lee studied at the University of Pittsburgh, the University of Arizona, and the State University of New York at Brockport, and has taught at Northwestern University and the University of Iowa. He has been the recipient of numerous awards, including the 1987 Delmore Schwartz Poetry Award from New York University, the 1988 Writer's Award from the Mrs. Giles Whiting Foundation, a 1989 Guggenheim Fellowship, and grants from the National Endowment of the Arts and from the state arts councils in Pennsylvania and Illinois. He lives in Chicago with his wife, Donna, and their children.

—E. M.

SUGGESTED READING: *American Poetry Review* p38 May 1990; *Christianity Today* p63 Sep. 2, 1988; *Nation* p416+ Oct. 7, 1991; *New York Times Book Review* p24 Oct. 4, 1987, p20 Jan. 27, 1991

SELECTED BOOKS: Poetry—*Rose*, 1986; *In the City in Which I Love You*, 1990; Nonfiction—*The Winged Seed*, 1995

Lethem, Jonathan

Feb. 19, 1964– Novelist; short-story writer

Jonathan Lethem, an author of novels and short stories, is celebrated for his ability to work unusual themes into unexpected genres. Lethem's first novel, *Gun, With Occasional Music* (1994), was hailed by critics for its unusual fusion of the detective novel with science fiction, complete with a kangaroo clad in a trench coat. *Amnesia Moon* (1995), his second book, combines elements of a road novel with Lethem's postapocalyptic vision of the future. *As She Climbed Across the Table* (1997) focuses on a man losing the love of his life—to an interdimensional void named Lack. *Girl in Landscape* (1998) is a coming-of-age story set on a distant world that is lorded over by "friendly" aliens who are fascinated by anything human. Lethem is also the author of a collection of science-fiction short stories, *The Wall of the Sky, The Wall of the Eye* (1996) and the recent novel *Motherless Brooklyn* (1999).

Jonathan Allen Lethem was born on February 19, 1964, in New York City, and grew up in the borough of Brooklyn. He is the son of the social activist Judith Frank Lethem and the artist Richard Brown Lethem, a painter who worked a second job to support his family. As a teenager Jonathan fully expected to follow in his father's footsteps and studied painting at the High School of Music and Art, a prestigious New York City public school. Yet on his long subway commute to and from school, Jonathan began reading novels by authors who would influence his own work—Thomas Pynchon, Kurt Vonnegut Jr., Philip K. Dick, and Jim Thompson, among others. Starting at the age of 15, he began working at a series of second-hand bookstores, where he read still more authors who inspired him.

After high school Lethem moved to Vermont to study at Bennington College. Future authors Bret Easton Ellis and Donna Tartt were contemporaries of Lethem's at Bennington, but Lethem didn't associate with them since he was a studio art major and kept his attempts at fiction under wraps. He stayed at the college for three semesters between 1982 and 1984 before dropping out to begin his first novel—a work that has never been published. "It was just the X number of bad pages I had to write," he told Elizabeth Gaffney of *Publishers Weekly* (March 30, 1998).

Mara Faye Lethem/Courtesy of Doubleday
Jonathan Lethem

Lethem then moved to Berkeley, California, and began working on short stories. He worked in used bookstores and wrote whenever he had a spare moment. "If you asked me then, I would have said I'd be working at bookstores until I was 45," he remarked to Gaffney. "You have to understand—all my heroes were dark horses. They all had embattled careers because of genre prejudice, something I've had the good fortune to be spared. It's like I'm standing on their shoulders. I sort of feel Philip K. Dick died for my sins." While in Berkeley Lethem also met and married Shelley Jackson, a graduate student there. The marriage was brief and intense, and later formed the autobiographical basis for Lethem's 1997 novel *As She Climbed Across the Table.*

In an autobiographical statement for *World Authors 1990–1995*, Jonathan Lethem writes: "I was born in New York City in 1964, and spent my childhood in Kansas City and Brooklyn. I went to the High School of Music and Art in New York, and was briefly a student at Bennington College, in Vermont, but left without a degree. As a teenager I'd been a painter, following my father's example, but I switched decisively to writing after my first year in college and dropped out, essentially, in order to work on a novel. The only job I've ever held besides authoring was as a clerk in a series of used and antiquarian bookstores, first in New York City, then in Berkeley, California, where I lived for ten years. The wide and eccentric reading habits characteristic of that work are traceable everywhere in my writing.

"That first, unsuccessful novel took three years to write. After finishing it I began *Gun, With Occasional Music*, which became my first published

novel (1994, Harcourt Brace). It's been translated into seven languages. My second novel, *Amnesia Moon*, was published in 1995, also by Harcourt Brace. My third novel is *As She Climbed Across the Table* (1997, Doubleday). My fourth is *Girl in Landscape* (1998, Doubleday). I've published over 50 short stories in a wide variety of periodicals and anthologies. My third book, *The Wall of the Sky, The Wall of the Eye*, was a collection of seven long stories.

"My work began in playfully critical exploration of literary genres, primarily detective and dystopian. Somewhere during the writing of *Amnesia Moon* I discovered the autobiographical element in my work, and I've pursued it increasingly in the past few years. It leads away from the formal and generic concerns of the earlier novels and stories—I know that much. Where it leads I suppose I'll discover.

"I've recently moved back to Brooklyn, partly in order to pursue this autobiographical urge in my work. I've just finished a draft of the first of two novels set in Boerum Hill. This first will be published by Doubleday in 1999, probably titled *Motherless Brooklyn*. Here in New York City I've also emerged from the relative literary isolation of California into some other activities—I'm the fiction editor for a journal called *Fence* and I'm editing an anthology for Vintage Books, on stories about amnesia."

———

In Berkeley Lethem wrote furiously and after about a year found a literary agent, Richard Parks. A year and a half later, Parks placed *Gun, With Occasional Music* with Harcourt Brace. The author had a stroke of luck when Malcolm Jones, a reviewer for *Newsweek*, discovered the book in a pile of review copies. "Novelists and moviemakers have fused sci-fi with detective stories for a long time . . . ," Jones wrote in *Newsweek* (April 18, 1994). "But nobody has ever done it this well. Lethem has conflated the two genres to fabricate a future that is frightening and funny and ultimately quite sad—a place where pleasure is had for the asking but happiness is hard to find . . . *Gun, With Occasional Music* is a dazzling debut."

Lethem's novel combines elements of the detective novels of Raymond Chandler with the sci-fi stylings of his hero Philip K. Dick. The story is set in the near future, in Oakland, California, in a world where children and animals speak and behave like adult human beings through "evolution therapy." The experiment proves to be a disaster and these "babyheads"—as the children are called in the novel—spend their days bitterly drinking and smoking in bars and speaking in a language only they know. The animals, in turn, gain nearly human status in order to replace the lost generation of children. The main character is detective Conrad Metcalf, who is hired by a doctor to investigate the murder of his wife. While tracking down the killer Metcalf runs into some shady characters, including a kangaroo named Joey Castle. The kangaroo eventually puts the gumshoe in cold freeze for six years. When he awakens from his imprisonment/hibernation, Metcalf scrambles to piece together the remaining clues in a society in which all memory has been outlawed. The reviewer for *Booklist* (February 15, 1994) agreed with Jones's assessment: "Lethem's first novel is a sparkling pastiche of Chandleresque detective fiction displaced to an almost comical postmodern landscape. . . . An outstanding debut for a welcome new voice in both [science fiction] and mysteries."

Amnesia Moon (1995), Lethem's second book, is a post-apocalyptic road novel. The story's central character is Chaos, who learns that the devastated landscape that he inhabits is merely a subjective reality, and so, with a furry mutant as a sidekick, he goes off to explore his world. The pair travel through a town whose populace was blinded when its air turned green. Another town is inhabited by people whose social status is determined by a governmental test that measures personal luck. They finally arrive in a San Francisco that may or may not be real. (The city's place-names are just slightly off: Ate Hashberry, the Submission District, the Callisto.) Many critics praised Lethem's overt nods to his predecessor Dick. "By deploying Dick's quirky and numinous sensibility to tell a story that is Dickian but ultimately Lethem's own," Gregory Feeley noted in the *Washington Post Book World* (November 26, 1995), "Lethem creates a postmodern pastiche that speaks in its own voice—and is incidently better written and more carefully structured than the revered Saint Phil's work usually managed to be."

In 1996 Lethem switched directions somewhat with *The Wall of the Sky, The Wall of the Eye*, a collection of seven straight science fiction stories. Two of the seven stories are original to the collection, while the rest had previously appeared in periodicals. Many of the tales have unusual subjects or twists, even for the realm of science fiction. In "The Happy Man" the dead return to life, the catch being that the souls of the resuscitated must journey back and forth between our world and hell. "Vanilla Dunk" tells the story of basketball players who take on the skills of former greats via computer. Two more notable stories are "Light and the Sufferer," which is about small feline creatures who feed off crack cocaine, and "The Hardened Criminals," in which the titular criminals are literally hardened and made a part of a prison's walls. Janice M. Eisen of the *Washington Post Book World* (September 29, 1996) was generally pleased with the collection: "Fortunately for those of us who love the [science fiction] genre, he is a writer of remarkable talent, who has the potential, if his development continues, of becoming one of the greats in the field."

Lethem's next novel, *As She Climbed Across the Table* (1997), was a departure of sorts due to its autobiographical nature: it was loosely based on his relationship with his former wife and is dedicated to her. In the story Philip Engstrand, a professor of anthropology, is in love with the particle physicist Alice Coombs. Alice's colleague, the Nobel Prize–winning Professor Soft, has conducted an experiment that has gone wrong: He has opened a void that could be a portal to an alternate reality. The void refuses to disappear and soon gains a name—Lack—and a personality. Lack accepts some things into its void (ice cream and a cat) and rejects others (a lovestruck Alice). Philip soon begins to wonder if Alice has fallen in love with Lack, especially since she spends most of her time in the chamber in which he/it exists. Eventually Alice leaves Philip for Lack and the mystery of the void. A writer for *Kirkus Reviews* (January 15, 1997) remarked that "the intriguing, if gimmicky, premise sometimes feels a bit thin, like a Donald Barthelme story stretched to novel length. But Lethem's clear-eyed prose and believably strange people ultimately make for a moving tale of narcissism and need."

In 1998 Lethem published the novel *Girl in Landscape*. Again using elements of science fiction, the author takes a girl's coming-of-age story and stands it on its head by placing the 14-year-old on a distant world. Young Pella Marsh and her family leave Brooklyn, New York, for the faraway planet to start their lives anew after the death of Pella's mother. Her father, a failed politician in Brooklyn, cannot adjust to his new surroundings and eventually deserts Pella and her two younger brothers. The children have little problem finding food—the Archbuilders, a mysterious group of aliens, have provided for that—though everything, human and alien, is infected with a seemingly benign virus. Pella soon becomes involved with an overly macho character, then stumbles across the secret of the virus, and in turn the dirty secrets of some of her fellow settlers. The novel received mostly positive reviews. *Booklist* (March 15, 1998) called it "a cool, quirky, and oddly compelling coming-of-age story that raises questions that linger long after the book is read." A critic for *Kirkus Reviews* (February 1, 1998) concurred: "Lethem's people are fully as real as the locale seems unreal. The protagonist Pella, a sturdy girl-woman altogether equal to the tests she undergoes, is especially memorable. Wonderful stuff. One waits eagerly to learn where Lethem will take us next." Not everyone agreed with such assessments; Gerald Jonas of the *New York Times Book Review* (May 24, 1998) lamented: "Pella's involvement with a macho character out of a John Wayne western seems strained, the product not of her own needs but of the author's determination to reinvent this backward-looking genre in a science fictional framework."

For his 1999 novel, *Motherless Brooklyn*, Lethem set aside science fiction for a tale of a detective, Lionel Essrog, who suffers from Tourette's syndrome. *Kirkus Reviews* called the book "a brilliantly imagined riff on the classic detective tale. the fifth high-energy novel in five years from the rapidly maturing prodigy."

Jonathan Lethem is fast becoming one of the most celebrated young authors in the United States and he seems delighted by his fame. In an interview with David Streitfeld of the *Washington Post Book World* (February 9, 1997), the author explained, "I meet people who are dumbstruck in my presence. I have to guide them through the moment because they're not sure how to talk to the author of *Gun, With Occasional Music*." When Streitfeld warned him to temper his ego, arguing that it was good for neither one's writing nor for maintaining one's friendships, the author responded, "It's a little too late. I was 11 or 12 when I just fell in love with myself, and the bloom is not off the rose."
—C. M.

SUGGESTED READING: *Booklist* Feb. 15, 1999, Mar. 15, 1998; *Kirkus Reviews* Jan. 15, 1997, Feb. 1, 1998; *Newsweek* Apr. 18, 1994; *New York Times* E p2 Feb. 2, 1998; *New York Times Book Review* May 14, 1995, May 24, 1998; *Publishers Weekly* p50 Mar. 30, 1998; *Washington Post Book World* p6 Nov. 26, 1995, p11 Sep. 29, 1996, p15 Feb. 9, 1997; *Contemporary Authors*, vol. 150, 1996

SELECTED WORKS: Fiction—*Gun, With Occasional Music*, 1994; *Amnesia Moon*, 1995; *The Wall of the Sky, The Wall of the Eye*, 1996; *As She Climbed Across the Table*, 1997; *Girl in Landscape*, 1998; *Motherless Brooklyn*, 1999

Fay Foto, Boston, Massachusetts

Lewis, Anthony

Mar. 27, 1927– Journalist

Anthony Lewis, the American journalist and author, is considered by many to be the dean of liberal columnists. An authority on the Supreme Court, having covered that beat for the *New York Times* from 1955 to 1964, he has authored two books on landmark decisions of the Court led by Earl Warren: *Gideon's Trumpet* (1964), about the case that established the principle that everyone—rich or poor—is entitled to representation by counsel when accused of a crime; and *Make No Law: The Sullivan Case and the First Amendment* (1991), about the case that made the burden of proof of libel fall more stringently on plaintiffs. Lewis's col-

umn in the *New York Times*, "Abroad at Home," can be counted on to anger conservative enemies of Palestinian rights; supporters of Serbian aggression against Croats, Albanians, and others; and those who would vitiate the Bill of Rights. He has twice won the Pulitzer Prize: in 1955, for his reporting on Senator Joseph McCarthy's role in getting innocent government employees dismissed as security risks; and in 1963, for his coverage of the Supreme Court.

Anthony Lewis was born in New York City on March 27, 1927, the son of Kassel Lewis, a textile executive, and Sylvia (Surut) Lewis. He was educated at the Horace Mann School in the New York City borough of the Bronx, where he showed an early bent for journalism, becoming editor of the school newspaper. Lewis served briefly in the U.S. Navy during World War II; he was discharged after three months because of an eye ailment. He completed his undergraduate studies at Harvard University, where he majored in English, in 1948—having served as executive editor and then managing editor of the daily *Harvard Crimson*. His first major newspaper job was at the *New York Times*, where for four years, from 1948 until 1952, he wrote for the "News of the Week in Review" section. After he wrote a story, "Harvard Goes Coed—But Incognito," for the *New York Times Magazine*, he was in effect fired—perhaps because his revelation of the fact that women could do the intellectual work required of Harvard students conflicted with the prevailing view of the time.

For a brief period, as a member of the Democratic National Committee, Lewis worked on Adlai Stevenson's first campaign for the presidency. He was soon back to work as a reporter, however, joining the staff of the *Washington Daily News* and continuing there until 1955, when he rejoined the *New York Times*. While working at the *News*, he became interested in the rights of people who had lost their jobs without due process—perhaps because, during what has come to be known as the McCarthy era, he covered the hearings while the senator led them. McCarthy had demanded that people be fired from government jobs because they were "security risks," either Communists or sympathizers of the Communist Party. One of Lewis's jobs was to keep track of the number of people fired and the number McCarthy claimed in his political speeches to have dismissed. (Frequently the two numbers did not match.)

Lewis began searching the records of federal employees who had actually been dismissed as security risks. He came upon the case of Abraham Chasanow, a civilian employee in the navy's Hydrographic Office, who had been suspended in July 1953 as a loyalty risk after more than 20 years' service, then cleared and finally discharged. According to an article about Lewis in the *New York World-Telegram and Sun* (May 3, 1955), "Chasanow wasn't a 'big name.' His firing had no political significance in the narrow sense. He was lost in a shuffle of suspicion and red tape, and now also had lost his job." After discovering that the charges against Chasanow were groundless, backed solely by malicious gossip, Lewis reported his finding in a series in the *News* and in an article in the *Reporter* (March 2, 1954). The articles persuaded the U.S. government to reconsider the case and ultimately to reinstate Chasanow. Chasanow's lawyer gave full credit to Lewis for his client's vindication.

Lewis continued to examine the overzealous efforts of the government to maintain national security at the expense of individual rights. In November 1954 he wrote an article for the *Reporter* in which he gave provided suggestions on how to reconcile security issues with the protection of individuals being charged with creating security risks. He advised the establishment of a division of personnel security within the Department of Justice to handle all reports on the security fitness of federal employees; the guarantee of a right to a hearing for those accused of security breaches or of being potential security risks; the granting of subpoena powers to hearing boards; and the establishment of a national review board. He demanded a return to the "basis of our justice, the American sense of fair play." Lewis further warned in a review in the *Reporter* (September 8, 1955) against "complacency that has arisen about the state of our security programs," pointing out that "a security proceeding is a damaging process, however it ends."

Lewis won the Heywood Broun Award of the American Newspaper Guild in 1955 for his exposure of the Chasanow case and was awarded the Pulitzer Prize for the best national reporting of the year. The news of the Pulitzer Prize came as Lewis was discussing an invitation to return to the *New York Times*. He did return to the *Times*, first as the Supreme Court and Department of Justice correspondent in the Washington bureau of the paper from 1957 until 1964. He prepared himself to be the pioneer full-time reporter on the Supreme Court by attending Harvard Law School for a year.

Lewis reported on the case of Clarence Earl Gideon, a poor man who had been sentenced to a five-year prison term for breaking into a poolroom. Gideon, unable to afford a lawyer to represent him, had written a letter to the Supreme Court asking if it was just that a poor man should be convicted without benefit of counsel. The Supreme Court had decided 20 years earlier that only in special cases or cases of capital crimes did state courts need to provide counsel for indigent defendants. Following Lewis's reportage, however, the justices agreed to hear Gideon's case and ultimately decided in his favor, thus allowing him a new trial, in which he was represented by a lawyer and won acquittal. Lewis's reporting gained him his second Pulitzer Prize, in 1963.

In the following year Lewis published *Gideon's Trumpet*, an account of the Gideon case and its ramifications. Because of the Supreme Court's ruling in the case, no poor person in the United States needs to go unrepresented by legal counsel. Alan Barth in *Book Week* (June 21, 1964) observed that Lewis had "the skills of a superb reporter—a shrewdly selective eye for livening and relevant detail and a reflective understanding of the great judicial institution." He termed Lewis's book a "patient, meticulous, and wonderfully illuminating account of the Supreme Court's processes" and "just about the best layman's handbook on the mysteries of legal procedure to be found anywhere." F. V. Roevekamp, writing in the *Christian Science Monitor* (June 25, 1964), concurred that "his passions, spelled out in the delicate, restrained language of the law, make the ideals of justice fresher, livelier, and more profound."

Lewis continued to defend freedom of speech and thought. In an article, "The Intimidated Press," in the *New York Review of Books* (January 19, 1989) he criticized two newspapers he felt had failed to live up to their reputation as beacons of truth: the *New York Times* and the *Washington Post*. In 1988 the *Post* had published an editorial criticizing Speaker of the House Jim Wright for "leaking" secret testimony about the role of the CIA in destabilizing Nicaragua. Lewis expressed outrage that the *Post* should have chided Wright rather than the CIA, writing that "a genuinely critical press would have taken a hard look at the facts before chastising a congressional leader for improper leaking or abuse of authority." What upset Lewis, in part, was the "reverential tone" of the editorial: "Its premise was that legitimacy rests in the executive branch of the United States government. . . . Congress, along with the rest of us, owes respect to the secrecy that the executive, with its special knowledge and expertise, deems necessary to the interest of national security." Lewis maintained that, on the contrary, "as a result of the Vietnam War [the *Times* and the *Post*] had come to realize that executive officials did not always have superior knowledge and expertise—and did not always tell the truth." He concluded that executive officials "were not entitled to reverence, from the press or Congress. The country would be better off—more wisely led—if policies were subject to unstinting scrutiny, including a good many . . . covered up by secrecy."

In 1965 Lewis became chief of the *New York Times* London bureau. He remained in that position until 1972. In 1969 he also became an editorial columnist for the *Times*. In 1972 he was granted a two-week visa to report from Hanoi, as United States involvement was winding down, but the civil war that was to end with the reunification of Vietnam was still raging. Lewis had been a stern critic of American participation in the war, writing columns of "moral outrage" in which he had called "the U.S. 'the most dangerous and destructive power on earth,'" according to an article in *Newsweek* (May 29, 1972). Once in Hanoi, Lewis sent back a dispatch to the *Times* maintaining that the North Vietnamese were clearing mines from Haiphong Harbor and moving ships in and out. That contradicted official Pentagon reports, which denied that shipping was continuing in the harbor. The *Times* ran the story on the front page as Lewis reported it, with the Pentagon denial sandwiched into it; the headline read "Communists Report Mines at Haiphong Swept, Ships Sailing." A spokesperson for the Nixon administration blasted the *Times* for becoming "a conduit of enemy propaganda to the American people." Lewis later said that the North Vietnamese claim could have been "mere bravado" and observed that "truth is difficult to establish in Vietnam." The administration, according to *Newsweek*, "could well ask itself whether its own record of miscalculation, lack of candor, and self-serving pronouncements on Vietnam had really earned uncritical acceptance of its statements." *Newsweek* maintained that the *Times* had permitted Lewis to go ahead more as a columnist than a reporter—without checking his sources too closely. Lewis continued to protest against U.S. involvement in the Vietnam War in his column.

An internationalist, Lewis later wrote in his "Abroad at Home" column trenchant criticisms of England's insularity and of its lack of a written constitution. A supporter of the European Community, he castigated the English for their foot-dragging in committing themselves to full participation in the Community. In his December 16, 1991 column, he wrote: "Suppose that 1 of the 13 original American states had at first stayed out of the constitutional union, then reluctantly joined but repeatedly dragged its feet on great national enterprises. . . .That analogy . . . gives an idea of Britain's attitude toward the European Community. Standing aloof at first, Britain finally joined— but continues to act as if membership were a burden, or even a menace, instead of an opportunity to share in one of the most promising ventures in contemporary history."

A column entitled "The King Can Do No Wrong" (December 30, 1996) contrasted the British ability to propose a new law, which "would give the police broad power to enter anyone's home or office without a warrant, rummage through papers and plant bugs," with the American Bill of Rights prohibition against unreasonable search and seizure. Lewis praised the more limited powers of the American government: "Fifty years ago Justice Hugo L. Black replied to an argument that the U.S. Supreme Court should follow English practice in a particular matter. Those who wrote our Constitution, he said, wanted Americans to have far greater protection against official abuse than the English had ever had." Lewis concluded that scrutiny of the new English bill alone would support his argument.

In a December 9, 1991 column, he contrasted American and British practices with regard to libel. The column focused on Robert Maxwell, head of a gigantic publishing and information conglomerate; shortly after his death, Maxwell's empire collapsed, having been constructed on lies and illegal transactions. "How could he get away with it for so long?" asked Lewis. He answered the question by pinpointing "Britain's stringent libel law, which makes it dangerous to write critically about a scoundrel like Mr. Maxwell." The libel laws in the United States, on the other hand, hold "that public officials must meet a difficult test when they sue, proving that a statement about them was published with knowledge of its falsity or in reckless disregard of the truth. The Court later extended the requirement to public figures like Mr. Maxwell." The law Lewis referred to had been established by the Supreme Court in the Sullivan case.

It was in 1991 that Lewis's second major book— *Make No Law: The Sullivan Case and the First Amendment*—was published. Like *Gideon's Trumpet*, *Make No Law* details the events surrounding a landmark decision made by the Supreme Court under Chief Justice Earl Warren. The title, *Make No Law*, refers to the First Amendment to the Constitution: "Congress shall make no law . . . abridging the freedom of speech or of the press." In this 1964 case, L. B. Sullivan, a city commissioner of Montgomery, Alabama, who was in charge of the Montgomery police, sued the *New York Times* for libel for publishing an advertisement soliciting support for Dr. Martin Luther King Jr. and the struggle for civil rights in the South. Sullivan accused the *Times* of allowing him to be defamed by associating him with illegal and terroristic denial of civil rights to black citizens. In a state court, he won a judgment of $500,000. The *Times* appealed the case to the United States Supreme Court, which reversed the Alabama verdict. The landmark decision resulted from the belief that "a profound national commitment to the principle that debate on public issues should be uninhibited, robust, and wide-open, and that it may well include vehement, caustic, and sometimes unpleasantly sharp attacks on government and public officials," as Justice William Brennan wrote.

The tremendous importance that Lewis gave to the verdict in the Sullivan case, as he explained in the *New York Times Magazine* (December 1, 1991), stemmed from the history of the First Amendment, which "did not make us free when it was ratified in 1791. Far from it. Not until 1927 did anyone claiming a constitutional right to freedom of speech or press win a case in the Supreme Court." It was only when the American public watched children being attacked as they tried to desegregate schools, and saw freedom marchers shocked with electric cattle prods, that a climate of opinion was produced that could prevent local officials from muzzling the press with threats of libel suits. The Sullivan decision was a sign of this shift. "Speaking truth to power is never going to be easy," Lewis concluded. "Indeed, the very idea of unregulated speech remains daring. 'The constitutional right of free expression is powerful medicine in a society as diverse and populous as ours,' Justice John Marshall Harlan wrote in 1971. But it is, as Holmes said, our great experiment." The outcome of that case prevented southern state courts from effectively hijacking the civil-rights movement by silencing the press about the brutal enforcement of segregation by granting huge libel awards to the enforcers based on flimsy errors of fact or unsubstantiated allegations in a report.

Make No Law was generally well received by reviewers. "Anthony Lewis ably intertwines multiple themes—free speech, racial justice, judicial compromise, and public-versus-private power, for example—in recounting the story of the most important libel ruling in United States history," Curtis J. Sitomer remarked in his review in the *Christian Science Monitor* (October 1, 1991). Alex Kozinski in the *Columbia Journalism Review* (December 1991) termed *Make No Law* "a brilliantly conceived and executed constitutional detective story." Martin Garbus in the *Nation* (October 28, 1991) praised the book by declaring he had "never read a livelier book of constitutional history." Garbus, a constitutional lawyer, concluded that the "political, social, racial, sexual and other prejudices of jurors must not be allowed to defeat the principles of the First Amendment. The right to prevent this from happening—to which Anthony Lewis makes an important contribution—honors both the Founding Fathers and the documents they drafted."

From the opposite, more conservative, side of the political spectrum, however, came a dissimilar opinion. Francis Flaherty, reviewing *Make No Law* for *Commonweal* (January 17, 1992), found that while "the case may make for high drama on the stage of history, it simply is not the stuff of a good tale." He was unable to avoid terming the volume "serviceable," however.

Lewis served as a lecturer on law at Harvard University from 1974 to 1989. In 1983 he became the first James Madison Visiting Professor in First Amendment Issues at Columbia University. In his address inaugurating a new Center for the Study of First Amendment Issues, Lewis spoke of attempts by the administration of President Ronald Reagan to suppress First Amendment rights. After detailing some of the Reagan administration's more blatant attacks on freedom of speech and of the press, Lewis concluded on an optimistic note that the nation would not give up "Madison's commitment to freely examining public characters and measures. And I do not believe we are going to let a government of zealots end the American experiment now and impose on our ebullient, productive democracy a mantle of silence."

Lewis has continued to expose any mantling of criticism, both of foreign and domestic policy, in his column in the *New York Times*, "Abroad at Home." In 1998 and 1999 he heaped scorn on what he saw as the unconstitutional behavior of Kenneth Starr, the independent counsel whose investigation led to the impeachment trial of President Bill Clinton.
—S. Y.

SUGGESTED READING: *Book Week* p1 June 21, 1964; *Christian Science Monitor* p7 June 25, 1964, p13 Oct. 1, 1991; *Columbia Journalism Review* p85 Dec. 1991; *Columbia Magazine* p27+ Nov. 1983; *Commonweal* p24 Jan. 17, 1992; *Nation* p522+ Oct. 28, 1991; *Newsweek* p79 May 29, 1972; *New York Review of Books* p26+ Jan. 19, 1989; *New York Times* A p17 Dec. 9, 1991, A p19 Dec. 16, 1991, A p15 Dec. 30, 1996; *New York Times Magazine* p72 Dec. 1, 1991

SELECTED BOOKS: *Gideon's Trumpet*, 1964; *Make No Law: The Sullivan Case and the First Amendment*, 1991; Young Adult—*The Supreme Court and How It Works*, 1966; As Contributor—*Portrait of a Decade: The Second American Revolution*, 1964

Lightman, Alan

Nov. 28, 1948– Nonfiction writer; scientist

The astrophysicist and author Alan Lightman's *Einstein's Dreams* (1993) propelled him to national fame and to the top of many best-seller lists. A romantic and speculative endeavor, the novel depicts dreams Einstein may have had while he was working on his special theory of relativity. The book, with its nearly psychedelic imagery, was followed by another novel, *Good Benito* (1995), the story of a young scientist's search for meaningful human relationships. Though Lightman has written several accessible nonfiction books on science in the past, it was only with the publication of his fiction that he received widespread acclaim. His most recent book, *Dance For Two* (1996), is a return to his roots as a nonfiction writer, the essays it comprises representing the best of his work from previous volumes. Still, the author maintains that he will continue to write fiction because it is the "best form for writing about emotions," as he told Amanda Smith for *Publishers Weekly* (January 9, 1995).

The oldest of four brothers, Alan Paige Lightman was born on November 28, 1948, in Memphis, Tennessee. His parents, Richard Louis and Jeanne (Garretson) Lightman, who were owners of movie theaters, indulged his creative endeavors, including rocket building and poetry writing. Amanda Smith quoted Lightman as saying: "By age seven, I had a chemistry set and burned a hole in the rug. I built something like a tesla coil. . . . When I turned it on, it knocked out every TV in the neighborhood. The neighbors became very wary of me. I used to fire off rockets that came down in their backyards or through their windows, so they gave me a wide berth." Lightman also watched many movies as a boy. "In retrospect, I think they made a big impression; images became very important to me," he told Amanda Smith. As for his poetry, Lightman continued writing it, even after he arrived at Princeton. Unsure as to what path to take in his undergraduate studies, the future author kept quiet about his literary endeavors. Eventually deciding on a degree in physics, he graduated from Princeton in 1970 and went on to receive his Ph.D. in physics at the California Institute of Technology in 1974. His reasoning was simple. As he told Smith of Publishers Weekly: "I knew of a few scientists who had become writers, but I didn't know of any writers who had become scientists, so I figured that I should start my career in science and then come back to the writing."

In 1974 he began his two years of postdoctoral work at Cornell University in Ithaca, New York. There he met Jean Greenblatt, whom he married on November 28, 1976. The year before they married, Lightman had published his first work, a textbook entitled Problem Solving in Relativity and Gravitation (1975), and soon followed it with Radioactive Processes in Astrophysics (1979). Lightman had by this time attained an assistant professorship at Harvard, where he studied such phenomena as black holes and distant galaxies, about which scientists can only hypothesize. In his interview with Smith, the author noted: "I think that I delighted in my theoretical work, concentrating on things that had a very flimsy connection to the data and observations. In retrospect, I can see that this was my poetic or literary side coming to the surface."

In 1979 Lightman left Harvard to become a staff scientist at the Smithsonian Astrophysics Observatory. During this period he began publishing scientific articles, written in layman's terms, as well as such full-length nonfiction titles as Time Travel and Papa Joe's Pipe: Essays on the Human Side of Science (1984) and A Modern Day Yankee in a Connecticut Court, and Other Essays of Science (1986). In the former, the author discussed topics such as astronomy, cosmology, and particle physics. In the latter, he considered subjects including darkness, space exploration, snowflakes, and even the ordinary and sometimes boring aspects of the life of a scientist.

In 1989 he left the observatory for the Massachusetts Institute of Technology, where he became a professor of both physics and writing. In 1990 Lightman coauthored a book with Roberta Brawer entitled Origins: The Lives and Worlds of Modern Cosmologists, containing interviews in which 27 modern cosmologists discuss their personal lives, their ideas, and recent developments in science. The book won the Most Outstanding Science Book in Physical Science Award from the Association of American Publishers. Lightman's other nonfiction works are Ancient Light: Our Changing View of the Universe (1991), Time for the Stars: Astronomy in the 1990s (1992), and Great Ideas in Physics (1992). Each of these titles is written so that the reader can easily comprehend the author's explanation of complicated scientific ideas. With each new publication, Lightman became more comfortable with his literary side.

Einstein's Dreams, a slim and powerful novel, details what the great scientist might have been dreaming about in the year 1905, just as he was about to publish his special theory of relativity. The novel is a fantastical trip involving an alternate form of time; Bern, Switzerland, where Einstein was living and working during that period, is the setting. Bern transforms itself with each chapter, adapting itself to the type of time Einstein may have imagined while working on his theory. A reviewer for the Washington Post (February 7, 1993) wrote: "This is not a short book for the lazy; indeed if you are a languid reader, you won't get past page five. What is most successful here is that without equations, without diagrams, without the usual trappings of profundity, Lightman has made himself into a Rod Serling of Physics and provided a Twilight Zone of the cuckoo clock." The New York Times Book Review (January 3, 1993) reviewer concurred and added: "Mr. Lightman spins these fantasies with spare poetic power, emotional intensity, and ironic wit, although he often veers towards sentimentality. If time is a burden, he implies—too often—the attempt to escape it is an even deadlier burden."

Lightman's next novel, Good Benito, follows the life of a scientist, Bennett, as he comes of age and learns to deal with his emotions. The book is based in part on the personal and professional development of Lightman himself, who told Publishers Weekly why he wanted to write this book: "I'm interested in the theme of the intuitive versus the rational, the struggle which the main character has throughout the book. And I think that fiction is the best form for writing about emotions." A writer for the Times Literary Supplement (June 23, 1995) did not believe that the author depicted that struggle well or even interestingly: "Lightman's prose is too neutral to sustain the reader's interest for long, and without much in the way of plot or character to keep the pages turning, the novel feels empty and even heartless." A critic for the Christian Science Monitor (January 31, 1995), noting that the author had said that the events of the novel were partially autobiographical and partially based on the lives of his students, remarked: "Unfortunately, Lightman sacrifices any hope of plausibility by making all of these tragedies happen to Bennett." By contrast, Michiko Kakutani of the *New York Times* (January 6, 1995) found *Good Benito* to be "considerably more conventional than *Einstein's Dreams* but also more moving and direct."

Lightman's most recent literary outing is *Dance For Two* (1996), a collection of two dozen essays published in earlier nonfiction works. Critics observed that some of the better pieces in the collection grew out of the author's notion of the sharp division between art and science. As a writer in the *New York Times* (April 4, 1996) noted: "The problem for Mr. Lightman is that science, being objective, 'offers little comfort to anyone who aches to leave behind a personal message in his work.' This presumably is why he set out to write fiction. You can see him taking his first steps in this collection in the way he plays with time travel, a favorite subject of his."

Alan Lightman remains a professor at MIT, where he continues to teach physics and writing. He lives in Massachusetts with his wife, the painter Jean Greenblatt, and their daughters, Elyse and Kara.

—C. M.

SUGGESTED READING: *Christian Science Monitor* p 12 Jan. 31, 1995; *New York Times* C p16 Jan. 5, 1993, A p17 Feb. 8, 1993, C p28 Jan. 6, 1995, C p16 Apr. 4, 1996; *New York Times Book Review* p22 Sep. 29, 1991, p15 Aug. 4, 1991, p10 Jan. 3, 1993, p18 Feb. 5, 1995; *Publishers Weekly* p47+ Jan. 9, 1995; *Times Literary Supplement* p 27 June 23, 1995; *Washington Post* D p1 June 9, 1993; *Washington Post Book World* p4 Feb. 7, 1993; *Contemporary Authors* vol. 141, 1993; *Who's Who in America 1997*

SELECTED WORKS: Fiction—*Einstein's Dreams*, 1993; *Good Benito*, 1995; Nonfiction—*Problem Solving in Relativity and Gravitation*, 1975; *Radioactive Processes in Astrophysics*, 1979; *Time Travel and Papa Joe's Pipe: Essays on the Human Side of Science*, 1984; *A Modern Day Yankee in a Connecticut Court, and Other Essays on Science*, 1986; *Origins: The Lives and Worlds of Modern Cosmologists* (with R. Brawer), 1990; *Ancient Light: Our Changing View of the Universe*, 1991; *Time for the Stars: Astronomy in the 1990s*, 1992; *Great Ideas in Physics*, 1992; *Dance For Two*, 1996

Lipset, Seymour Martin

Mar. 18, 1922– Social scientist; nonfiction writer

The American political sociologist Seymour Martin Lipset has made the varying aspects of American exceptionalism his specialty for nearly half a century. His fellow sociologist Todd Gitlin, reviewing Lipset's book *American Exceptionalism: A Double-Edged Sword* (1996) for the *Nation* (May 6, 1996), observed that for Lipset, "the history of ideas about America is a succession of footnotes to Tocqueville." In his two dozen books, Lipset has demonstrated that the American creed—liberty, egalitarianism, individualism, populism, and laissez-faire—has remained constant over the centuries and has produced the seemingly contradictory characteristics of American society: respect for law and high crime rates, a low level of support for the poor and a high level of support for education, and a belief in egalitarianism and great divergences in income, to name a few. As a social scientist, he is descriptive rather than prescriptive. Although he long ago placed himself in the liberal camp and has remained consistent in his ideas throughout his career, he has been praised by such conservatives as Francis Fukuyama, who, in the *New York Times Book Review* (February 2, 1997), called him "the most thoughtful contemporary authority on American exceptionalism, on the way in which our public policies are deeply rooted in basic American values."

Courtesy of Seymour Lipset

In a statement for *World Authors 1990–1995*, Lipset writes, "The basic facts of my life and career can be stated briefly. I was born in New York City, in Harlem, then partially a Jewish district, in 1922. My Russian-born printer father and seamstress mother moved to the Bronx six months later and I grew up there. My undergraduate education was at the City College of New York and my graduate study one mile away at Columbia University, where I received a Ph.D. in 1949. At City College I was politically active in socialist organizations. My first teaching position was at the University of Toronto. I have had a peripatetic job career, moving between the East and West Coasts, from Columbia to Berkeley, then to Harvard and Stanford. I am on the retirement roster of the last three. After retiring from Stanford in 1990, I accepted a position, which I still hold, as the Hazel Professor of Public Policy at George Mason University. I retain my affiliation with the Hoover Institution of Stanford, as a senior fellow.

"My main academic work from my Ph.D. dissertation to my current research has been in political sociology. What this means basically is applying a sociological analytic schema to the study of political phenomena and institutions. I have written about social movements, both left, *Agrarian Socialism*, and right, *The Politics of Unreason*. I have looked at stratification as the major existential factor affecting macroscopic political cleavage or consensus in *Social Mobility in Industrial Society, Political Man, Revolution and Counterrevolution, Conflict and Consensus*, and in two books I edited with Reinhard Bendix, *Class, Status and Power*, and with Stein Rokkan, *Party Systems and Voter Alignments*. I have been particularly concerned with the role of the inhabitants of universities, faculty and students, in intramural status and change in *The Divided Academy: Professors and Politics, Rebellion in the University*, and assorted articles and edited books.

"Specifying the conditions associated with democracy and authoritarianism, stability and instability in organizations and national polities, have been continuing interests from my second book *Union Democracy* (with Martin Trow and James S. Coleman), to *Political Man, The First New Nation: The United States in Historical and Comparative Perspective*, and a group of articles dealing with 'the Social Requisites of Democracy,' the first in 1959, the most recent in 1996. I have also edited and written about the subject for many books, some with Larry Diamond and Juan Linz, including a three-volume set dealing with *Democracy in Developing Countries*, another on *Politics in Developed Countries* and a four-volume *Encyclopedia of Democracy*, edited by me alone.

"During the 1990s, I published three books that involve my efforts to come to terms with American exceptionalism. The term was coined by Alexis de Tocqueville and has meant that this country is qualitatively different than other nations. The first one, *Continental Divide: The Institutions and Values of the United States and Canada*, continues themes first presented in *The First New Nation*. Both books reflect my conviction that it is only possible to understand a country by looking at it in comparative perspective. A person who knows only one country knows no country. I believe that the best comparative reference for the United States is Canada. As I have frequently emphasized, two nations came out of the American Revolution: Canada, the country of the counterrevolution, and the United States, the country of the revolution. The northern nation reflects Tory (noblesse oblige) values: communitarian, elitist, group-oriented, and deferential. The southern is Whig, classically liberal (libertarian): individualistic, antistatist, laissez-faire, populist, and less deferential. The two countries located on the same continent, with most of their people speaking the same language, vary considerably in outcomes, such as church attendance, crime rates, divorce statistics, legal structures, party systems, electoral participation, strength of labor organizations, welfare and health policies, and many others.

"The second book of the 1990s, *Jews and the New American Scene* (in collaboration with Earl Raab), seeks to analyze the American Jewish community as it is today. We note that American Jewry reflects the exceptional characteristics of the United States and differs in systematic ways from coreligionists in other countries, where the dominant Christian denominations are predominantly hierarchical and state-related. To understand the way Jews vary cross-nationally, it is necessary, as Heinrich Heine noted, to see how the gentiles differ. More recently, I have published *American Exceptionalism: a Double-Edged Sword*, which seeks to pull together much of my research and thinking about the ways in which the United States differs from other countries, basically how it works. America is still unique, though in some new as well as old ways. The reference in the title to a double-edged sword reflects the fact that American exceptionalism means that while America is better than other countries by some criteria, it is also worse by others. Thus, the United States has the lowest level of voting, the highest violent crime rate, and the most unequal distribution of income among developed countries, but it has the most open educational system, the greatest emphasis on equality of respect, and the strongest guarantees of personal rights. Compared to other developed nations, it has the smallest government, the lowest taxes, less welfare and health benefits, the weakest trade union movement, and is the only one which has never had a viable social democratic or labor party. Although *American Exceptionalism* is not a book about politics, it emphasizes that the nation's libertarian organizing principles, its ideological identity, go far to explain both the unique absence of a socialist party and the fact that the Republican party is the only major antistatist libertarian party in the industrialized world. The greatest incongruities that I seek to explain are that while America is the most meritocratic nation, more open to talent from all strata into elite positions, and the richest country in per capita purchasing power terms, it has the most unequal distribution of wealth and income in the developed world and is more stratified racially."

Seymour Martin Lipset was born in New York on March 18, 1922, the son of Lena Lippman and Max Lipset. As an undergraduate he was a member of the group at City College that came to be recognized as the theoreticians of liberal postwar intellectual life in the United States. When he developed his Ph.D. dissertation and the book, *Agrarian Socialism* (1950), that came out of it, the question that preoccupied him was why socialism had failed to take root in America. This question expanded into the concern about what was special about America—what was its "exceptionalism" based on? A steady stream of books followed to enlarge Lipset's investigation of political culture in an attempt to seek out social "laws" that govern public behavior.

Political Man: The Social Bases of Politics (1960) examines "the conditions necessary for democracy in societies and organizations: the factors which affect men's participation in politics, particularly their behavior as voters; and the sources of support for values and movements which sustain or threaten democratic institutions," as Lipset announced in the foreword to the book. The critical reception that greeted *Political Man* was similar to that given to many of his books: Lipset's marshaling of facts and statistics to shatter clichéd views of social behavior won praise from such critics as A. S. Kaufman of the *Nation* (June 4, 1960), while Lipset's broader philosophical principles, supposedly derived from his evidence, found less favor. "Lipset's failure to tear himself loose from the parochial moorings of so much of contemporary sociology . . . seriously impairs an otherwise provocatively brilliant assessment of the conventional wisdom about democracy," Kaufman concluded. Samuel J. Eldersveld, writing in the *American Political Science Review* (September 1960), agreed that Lipset's "synthesis of data" from surveys of political, social, and cultural phenomena filled a gap in knowledge. He found, however, some "empirical juggling . . . which mars the acceptability of interpretations." Nevertheless, he wrote, "while one must be cautious in applying the analytical findings and interpretations of this work, it is still a good book in social and political theory." D. H. Wrong, the reviewer for *Political Science Quarterly*, declared *Political Man* to be "the most important single volume on the sociology of voting yet to appear." "What really gives the book its unity and focus is less the kind of empirical data considered . . . or the comparative approach than the dominance of a common theme," he wrote. "The theme is the attenuation of class conflict in Western societies."

In *The First New Nation: The United States in Historical and Comparative Perspective* (1963), Lipset again looked at social institutions in the United States. George Whitbeck in *Library Journal* (December 1, 1963) called *The First New Nation* a "treatise analyzing the interplay between the conflicting values of equality and achievement in American society." Lipset showed how the value

Americans place on equality enabled the United States to have more equality of opportunity. The emphasis on achievement, however, tends to make the differences between individuals more prominent. Lipset this time contrasted social institutions with those in other democratic nations, particularly other English-speaking countries, and examined the conditions that make it possible for democracy to succeed. While Whitbeck termed *The First New Nation* brilliant sociology and the *Christian Century* (November 13, 1963) reviewer gave the same accolade to the chapter on religion, secularism and voluntarism, other critics, such as Paul Pickrel for *Harper's* (November 1963), found Lipset's prose turgid, hovering "in the neighborhood of pretentious truism" and lacking "the kind of energy, the architectonic imagination, that sweeps up a mass of facts and ideas and fuses them in one great span of argument." The reader, Pickrel concluded, "must work out for himself the place of these fragments in the whole conception." He admitted, however, that "probably the material . . . for a great book, perhaps for several" could be found in *The First New Nation*.

In 1967 and 1968, Lipset's name appeared on the title pages of at least seven books, which he wrote or edited alone or with others. As editor or co-editor, he produced *Class, Status and Power*, *Social Structure and Mobility in Economic Development*, *Student Politics*, *Party Systems and Voter Alignments: Cross-National Perspectives*, *Elites in Latin America*, and *Turner and the Sociology of the Frontier*, the titles of which reveal themes that have engaged him throughout his career.

Lipset's *Revolution and Counterrevolution: Change and Persistence in Social Structures* (1968) is an examination of the lingering effects of major historical events on political institutions and behaviors. As he explained in the preface, the "revolution which is referred to in the title is the American Revolution, and the counterrevolution is the preservation of British rule and monarchical and elitist institutions in Canada." The book contains portraits of three social scientists—Harriet Martineau, Moisei Ostrogorski, and Robert Michels—who inaugurated the method of "analyzing from a historical-structural perspective the character of changing societies and politics," in Lipset's words. Robert L. Heilbroner, reviewing the volume for the *New Republic* (July 13, 1968), noted that it "bristles with interesting findings, insightful comparisons, and unexpected similarities," but that the "barrage of statistics and research" vitiates the "core of principal contentions."

Lipset joined with Earl Raab to examine long-term attempts to deny one group or another legitimacy in *The Politics of Unreason: Right-wing Extremism in America* (1970). The publisher billed the volume as an "analysis of right-wing extremism throughout American history" that traced "efforts from 1790 on to preserve the values, interests, or status of various political, religious, ethnic, class, and status groups." In the *Christian Science*

Monitor (November 28, 1970), Arnold Beichman observed that "the Lipset-Raab findings can apply with a little effort to left-wing extremism as well." T. M. Gannon, writing in *America* (November 28, 1970), appreciated what he considered the focus on contemporary extremism, "rooted not in racism but in the economic discontent of the white lower-middle class and working class." The *Library Journal* (August 1970) reviewer labeled *The Politics of Unreason* "a work of the highest scholarship" and concluded that it satisfactorily explained the positions of working-class rightists who are against civil liberties and more affluent rightists who may be willing to allow civil liberties but are economically very conservative. The book won the Gunnar Myrdal Prize.

In *Passion and Politics: Student Activism in America* (1972), Lipset returned to the issue of student protest. He summoned his usual array of facts and statistics to examine the causes of student uprisings in the United States and abroad. Reviewers praised Lipset's lucidity in presenting "an overview of the historical and sociological dimensions of student activism . . . both interesting and helpful," in the words of P. G. Altbach in the *Christian Century* (February 23, 1972). R. S. Berman, writing in *American Scholar* (Spring 1972), singled out "discussions . . . that should be fundamental to future research on students, their politics and, indeed, their identity as a historical and social group." Berman judged the most important of Lipset's discussions to center on "student activism in the past and the strange alliance between students and their ideological models."

Lipset returned to a consideration of campus life in *Education and Politics at Harvard* (1975), a volume he wrote with David Riesman. Lipset's essay "Political Controversies at Harvard, 1636–1974" examines the battles at Harvard, both those involving students, faculty, and administration and those involving external religious and political forces. In his consideration of 20th-century politics, Lipset found that every radical movement, starting with those dating from the beginning of the century and continuing with such groups as Students for a Democratic Society (SDS) in the 1960s, had its largest chapter at Harvard. The *Choice* (November 1975) reviewer observed that Harvard, the nation's leading university, was the source of many trends in higher education and that Lipset's book demonstrates that the 20th century, particularly the 1960s, has "no monopoly on student activism." Robert McCaughey, reviewing *Education and Politics at Harvard* for the *Times Literary Supplement* (September 29, 1975), remarked that the "crucial difference" between Lipset's and Riesman's respective essays can be seen through Lipset's observation that the Puritan founders of Harvard were "people of the book." McCaughey pointed out that for Lipset, the crucial book was Ecclesiastes, while for Riesman, it was the Apocalypse. "Both [Lipset's and Reisman's respective] commentaries," McCaughey concluded, "leave the literature of American universities broadened and enriched."

Lipset returned to the larger polity in *The Confidence Gap: Business, Labor, and Government in the Public Mind* (1983), which he wrote with his former student William Schneider. In *The Confidence Gap*, Lipset and Schneider analyzed the eroding confidence of Americans in business and political leaders in the 1960s and 1970s. Dealing with the perceived "gap . . . between the promise and performance of major societal institutions" in the public eye, as John R. Sillito observed in *Library Journal* (May 15, 1983), they created "a valuable and significant work and a major reference tool for understanding American attitudes." Arnold Beichman, writing in the *National Review* (October 14, 1983), noted that the authors had "impeccable credentials and a rare ability to separate personal beliefs and ideologies from their science," resulting in "a masterly job of research and fascinating analytical insight." Other reviewers, however, were less sanguine about the usefulness of the authors' analyses. Theodore J. Lowi, writing in the *New York Times Book Review* (April 19, 1983), thought that although Lipset and Schneider had demonstrated that people were alienated from the institutions of big government, big business, and big labor, as well as from educational and religious institutions, the authors had failed to "develop a broader political context in which to interpret the data." Lowi maintained that the book was "an incredible piece of establishment writing . . . because the authors . . . blame the victim." The lack of confidence in the performance of institutions is not a malady but a sign of health, according to Lowi. "The reputed decline in public confidence or trust can be seen as the emergence of a mature, modern citizenry appropriate to a mature, modern state," he wrote.

In *Continental Divide: The Institutions and Values of the United States and Canada* (1990), Lipset returned to the theme of American exceptionalism by contrasting the two nations that emerged from the American Revolution. In the *New York Times Book Review* (May 13, 1990), the Canadian historian Michael Ignatieff suggested that the book was really addressed to people in the U.S. "Its message is that at a time when Americans are uncertain about their role in a changing world, their future as an economic power, even their ethnic and racial identity, they might regain a clearer sense of themselves if they took a long hard look in the Canadian mirror," he wrote. Ignatieff found a number of surprises amid the wealth of information, such as the fact that "despite [Canadians'] cherished image of themselves as being less dogmatic about government intervention in the economy than the Americans, in fact, American regulatory agencies are much more aggressive and effective in controlling business than Canadian ones are." Ignatieff declared that *Continental Divide* "is welcome because in its quiet, carefully documented way it chips away at self-flattering illusions on both sides of the border."

In *Jews and the New American Scene* (1995), Lipset continued to document American exceptionalism. Written with Earl Raab, the book describes how American Jews differ from other Jews in the world because of their Americanness. The fact that Jewish values seem compatible with the American entrepreneurial spirit has made Jews a very successful ethnic group in terms of education and income, but paradoxically, because there is no official discrimination and relatively little prejudice against Jews in the U.S., the number of Jews who claim membership in a synagogue has declined, because of a high intermarriage rate and a low birthrate. *Jews and the New American Scene* aroused controversy; some people, such as Jay P. Lefkowitz of the *Wall Street Journal* (May 10, 1995), saw it as a warning to Jews to do something to insure the survival of Jewish life in America. Lefkowitz called it "an important book" and observed that the authors' pessimism with regard to the American Jewish community was "well-founded." Philip Lopate, in the *New York Times* (March 26, 1995), gave *Jews and the New American Scene* short shrift. He found the authors' prediction that "the Jewish community as a whole will be severely reduced in numbers by the middle of the next century" not "particularly arguable," but not surprising. The sociologist Nathan Glazer was so incensed by Lopate's dismissive review that he wrote a letter to the *Times* (April 16, 1995) defending the book as "interesting and authoritative on the situation of American Jews today and on the particular dilemma of maintaining separateness in an open and welcoming society," and he declared that "no present book on American Jews can match" its "hardheadedness" and scholarship.

American Exceptionalism: A Double-Edged Sword (1996), dubbed Lipset's "masterpiece" by Martin Walker in the *Washington Post* (April 7, 1996), is a comprehensive explanation of Lipset's thesis that America's strengths and weaknesses stem from the same roots. For Lipset, a historical continuum links the founding principles of the nation with today's political and social institutions and behaviors. He reexplores his earlier work on the feeble position of socialism in the United States, Jews, unions, political parties, and voting patterns, adding a chapter on the African-American exceptions to American exceptionalism. Lipset makes it clear with a mass of data that he takes exception to "those who call for a fundamental change in our national values to stop a moral decline." What these naysayers do not realize, Lipset wrote in the chapter entitled "a Double-Edged Sword," is "that what they find fault with is the dark side of American exceptionalism; developments which, like many of the positive features, derive from the country's organizing principles. . . . The American creed . . . fosters a high sense of personal responsibility, independent initiative, and voluntarism even as it also encourages self-serving behavior, atomism, and a disregard for communal good." Although individualism can promote "a particularly virulent strain of greedy behavior," Lipset observed, "it represents a tremendous asset, encouraging the self-reflection necessary for responsible judgment, for fostering the strength of voluntary communal and civic bonds, for principled opposition to wars, and for patriotism." Lipset pointed out that many respondents to a poll in 1993 thought widespread floods were God's punishment for sin. He decried such an idea; the "readiness of Americans to cite a spiritual or moral explanation for a natural disaster is similar in many ways to ascribing the perceived dissolution of the social fabric to moral decline," he explained.

Critical responses to *American Exceptionalism* were largely admiring. James P. Pinkerton, in the *New York Times Book Review* (February 11, 1996), cited Lipset's "ability to sift vast evidence and pluck out apt conclusions." He complained, however, about Lipset's tendency to be all-inclusive, noting that the chapters on Japan, African-Americans, Jews, and intellectuals diverge from the main point of the book. Todd Gitlin, in the *Nation* (May 6, 1996), termed Lipset an "unregenerate anti-utopian whose doubts about radical departures have kept him rather consistent . . . across decades of shifting ideological fashion." Byron E. Shafer, who reviewed *American Exceptionalism* for the *Times Literary Supplement* (March 29, 1996), described the book as "a surprisingly coherent whole, informed by a dominant argument, repeatedly demonstrated." Lipset, according to Shafer, gave the reader a tour through the five elements of the American creed—liberty, egalitarianism, individualism, populism, and laissez faire. "It is the grand tour; evidence is rich, and consistently marshalled towards the overall argument," he concluded.

From his first marriage, in 1944, to Elsie Braun, Lipset has three children. His wife died in 1987. In 1990 he married Sydney Guyer. Now 77, Lipset has continued to do, with unabated vigor, what he has always done—write books and hold faculty positions, currently at George Mason University and the Hoover Institution of Stanford University.
—S. Y.

SUGGESTED READING: *American Political Science Review* p737 Sep. 1960; *American Scholar* p296 Spring 1972; *American Sociological Review* p753 Oct. 1960; *Choice* p1215 Nov. 1975; *Christian Century* p1405 Nov. 13, 1963; *Christian Science Monitor* p13 Nov. 28, 1970; *Harper's* p119 Nov. 1963; *Library Journal* p4657 Dec. 1, 1963, p1012 May 15, 1983; *Nation* p 496 June 4, 1960, p28+ May 6, 1996; *National Review* p1286 Oct. 14, 1983; *New Republic* p26 July 13, 1968; *New York Times Book Review* p 7 Apr. 10, 1983, p41 May 13, 1990, p20 Mar. 26, 1995, p31 Apr. 16, 1995, p7 Feb. 11, 1996, p24 Feb. 2, 1997; *Political Science Quarterly* p265 June 1960, *Society* p246 Jan. 1998; *Times Literary Supplement* p1047 Sep. 19, 1975, p7

Mar. 29, 1996, with photo; *Wall Street Journal* A p12 May 10, 1995; *Washington Post* X p4 Apr. 7, 1996; *Who's Who in America, 1998*

SELECTED BOOKS: *Agrarian Socialism*, 1950; *Political Man*, 1960; *The First New Nation*, 1963; *Revolution and Counterrevolution*, 1968; *Rebellion in the University*, 1972; *Professors, Unions and American Higher Education*, 1973; *The Divided Academy*, 1975; *Consensus and Conflict*, 1987; *Continental Divide: The Institutions and Values of the United States and Canada*, 1990; *The Educational Background of American Jews*, 1994; *American Exceptionalism: A Double-Edged Sword*, 1996; (with others) *Union Democracy*, 1956; with R. Bendix—*Social Mobility in Industrial Society*, 1959; with E. Raab—*The Politics of Unreason*, 1970, *Jews and the New American Scene*, 1995; with E. Ladd—

Academics and the 1972 Election, 1973; with D. Riesman—*Education and Politics* at Harvard, 1975; with I. L. Horowitz—*Dialogues on American Politics*, 1978; with W. Schneider—*The Confidence Gap*, 1983; as editor or co-editor: *Class, Status, and Power*, 1953; *Labor and Trade Unionism*, 1960; *Sociology: The Progress of a Decade*, 1961; *Culture and Social Character*, 1961; *The Berkeley Student Revolt*, 1965; *Class, Status, and Power in Comparative Perspective*, 1966; *Social Structure, Mobility, and Economic Development*, 1966; *Elites in Latin America*, 1967; *Party Systems and Voter Alignments*, 1967; *Students in Revolt*, 1969; *Issues in Politics and Government*, 1970; *Failure of a Dream? Essays in the History of American Socialism*, 1974; *Democracy in Developing Countries*, 1988–89; *Politics in Developing Countries*, 1990; *The Encyclopedia of Democracy* 1995

Christopher Arabadjis

Liu, Timothy

Oct. 2, 1965– Poet

Timothy Liu, born in California of immigrants from mainland China, started writing poetry at 14, a pastime that was fueled further by his discovery—as a college freshman—of Sylvia Plath's *Ariel*. Since then, he has published three books of poetry to much critical acclaim and approbation of his fellow poets. With images resonating from the unlikely symbiosis of his Mormon upbringing and an emergent gay sensibility, Liu fuses the spiritual with the sexual in such collections as *Vox Angelica*

(1992), *Burnt Offerings* (1995), and *Say Goodnight* (1998). He has been designated as editor of *Word of Mouth*, the Talisman anthology of gay male poets who wrote between 1950 and 1999, to be published in 2000. Liu is on the faculty of William Paterson University, in Wayne, New Jersey.

In a third-person, autobiographical essay for *World Authors 1990–1995*, Timothy Liu writes: "Timothy Liu (Liu Ti Mo) was born and raised in San Jose, California [October 2, 1965], by immigrant parents from Mainland China. His father, Chung Chuan Liu, is an electronic engineer; his mother, Lida Lin Lu, was a librarian. Their son was named after the Chinese poet Hsu Chi Mo (1896-1933), a leader of the Crescent School, who later died in a plane crash. Timothy started writing poetry at the age of fourteen, the same year he joined the Mormon church (against his father's wishes). He started reading poetry at the age of eighteen as a freshman at U.C.L.A. where he encountered Sylvia Plath's *Ariel*. Up until then, a diet of rock lyrics from the likes of Peter Gabriel, Rickie Lee Jones and Robert Plant sustained his early work. He returned to finish his B.A. in English at Brigham Young University after serving a two-year Mormon mission in Hong Kong where he learned to speak Cantonese, adding to the Mandarin dialect he was raised on. At Brigham Young, Liu studied with the Welsh poet Leslie Norris, and soon swept up all the poetry prizes the university had to offer. During his residency there, Dennis Clark (the poetry editor at *Sunstone*) published Liu's first chapbook, *A Zipper of Haze*, as part of the Liahona Chapbook Series.

"Upon graduating in 1989, Liu journeyed south to the University of Houston for graduate work. Living in a metropolitan area also helped Liu to come out of the closet, as did Richard Howard, who mentored him and published some of Liu's first poems in *Western Humanities Review* and *The*

New Republic. Another significant presence in Liu's writing life was the editor Gordon Lish, who subsequently published more than forty of Liu's poems in his notorious journal, *The Quarterly*. Liu received his M.A. in 1991. *Under Pressure*, his master's thesis juried by Richard Howard and Edward Albee, was accepted for publication by Alice James Books in the Fall of 1991 and renamed *Vox Angelica*, which would go on to win the 1992 Norma Farber First Book Award from the Poetry Society of America. Carolyn Forché, who served as the judge, remarked: 'This is a wounding poetry, corporeal, the body inhabited and awake, bearing the unbearable. I am astonished at Timothy Liu's poetic gifts, his spare and mystical lyricism. His work is unique, a rarity in its serious apprehension of love, mortality and redemption. With *Vox Angelica*, we welcome among us a poet, and I am honored to be one of the celebrants.'

"Liu relocated to New England in order to become an active member of the Alice James Books cooperative, a two-year commitment akin to his Mormon mission. He also fled Houston on the heels of a volatile affair with a violist in the Houston Symphony, much to the chagrin of William Davis Gunter Jr., Liu's companion, to whom *Vox Angelica* is dedicated. Liu was accepted into the PhD program at the University of Massachusetts and received a fellowship which enabled him to pursue research on Asian-American Poets. Liu also met his life companion there, Christopher James Arabadjis, a nuclear physicist turned painter and subsequent dedicatee of both *Burnt Offerings* and *Say Goodnight*. Although Liu completed the required doctoral coursework, an offer to serve as an Assistant Professor at Cornell College in Mt. Vernon, Iowa, brought an end to his formal studies. He elected to complete a second book of poems rather than his dissertation.

"Liu spent four years in Mt. Vernon, Iowa, a rural town twenty miles north of Iowa City. During summers, he would teach workshops for the Iowa Summer Writer's Festival at the University of Iowa. Frequent four-hour drives to Chicago during the school year would also keep things lively, the Lyric Opera of Chicago and the Art Institute being the chief pitstops. *Burnt Offerings* and *Say Goodnight* were both assembled in Iowa, particularly through retreats to a Trappist monastery just outside of Dubuque where Liu would take a vow of silence. While the Midwest afforded little worldly distraction for Liu's reading and writing routine, its land-locked cultural confinement grew intolerable as the years wore on, and Liu longed to free himself from the tyranny of small-town life. A brief respite was to be had on the West Coast when Robert Hass, then U.S. Poet Laureate, invited Liu to serve as the 1997 Holloway Lecturer at U.C. California, Berkeley, an invitation that came after Liu's poems and papers (1980-1995) had been acquired by the Berg Collection at the New York Public Library. There, he taught a graduate poetry workshop that focused on the dialectic between mainstream and vanguard poetics. Liu's real pardon came by way of a job offer from William Paterson University in Wayne, NJ, allowing him and his partner to pack up all that they owned (along with their cats Colette and Tosca) and move back East."

Timothy Liu's poems offer a reconciliation of contradictions: spirituality and gay sexuality, longing and fulfillment, observation and commentary, Asian heritage and American sensibility. The jacket copy of his first collection, *Vox Angelica*, says that he is "living a life full of contradiction and beauty," a reference to the unlikely juxtaposition of a carnal aesthetic and a Mormon sensibility. This reconciliation of opposites is suggested in the collection's opening piece, "Ariel Singing," whose title is a tribute to his Sylvia Plath epiphany. In "Ariel Singing" he wrote

In the glass I saw
one soul, not two colliding into one.
Nothing shattered. What is fragile came af-

"Ariel Singing" concludes with an invocation toward the world, not toward the gods who demand its denial, but one that is nuanced with biblical imagery:

The priests continue to hold out their fast
offerings to the weak. Amen. Teach me
how to sing in a grove of olive trees,
to fall as a sparrow. It is all I want.

Vox Angelica was published by Alice James Books, a publishing cooperative in Cambridge, Massachusetts, that has brought the work of significant gay and lesbian poets to a wide audience. In the book's foreword, an "awe-struck" Richard Howard welcomed the emergence of a newly emerging poet who writes "a consistent and therefore recoverable gist of experience—writes *poetry* rather than poems merely." Howard stresses Liu's mystic, religious sensibility, which he feels is akin to the "sorrowing Catholic poets" of the late 19th century, such as Coventry Patmore and Francis Thompson, but without their "high symbolist diction of inflammable gas." Instead, it is Liu's "transfiguring (though volatile) faith, and the victimage of erotic despair," Howard wrote, that help make this an "astonishing first book of poetry." Howard chose a passage from Liu's title poem as an illustration of how the poet subverts conventional pietistic language by audaciously claiming the language of spirituality as his own:

I think of how the mystics read
by the light of their own bodies.
What a world of darkness that must have
to read by the flaming hearts
that turn into heaps of ash on the altar,
how everything in the end is made
equal by the wind.

The 39 poems in *Vox Angelica* are presented in three sections. In the first, Liu presents himself "as is" to a world of quotidian events but also as one bedazzled with the white heat of the mystic, declaring himself open to rapture of soul and body.

In "Passion," for example, he is transported in his late-afternoon reverie ("By mid-afternoon, all is imprecision") to visions in which a gay-bashing on Christopher Street in New York City becomes a counterpoint to the last despairing words of Christ on the cross. The voice of the narrator in these first 14 poems is observational, even tentative, the voice of a man still discovering himself as a being set apart from the realm of everyday life. Even in "White Stone," in which a processional of sexual partners and the vividness of imagery from the Book of Revelation shape the poet's awakening to passion and self-transcendence, "He used the third person to avoid / intimacy, refusing to speak his name / in the presence of the elders, taking / the host into his mouth for sins he had / not yet committed." Here also, he offers an homage to Sylvia Plath, his muse, in an image redolent both of her isolation and of the intrusion of compulsive man-love in his own experience: "knelt down / to the grains of rice he had garnered / in a bell jar. The addiction became / unbearable, a death like many deaths / collecting holy relics left behind: / lipstick-stained statuettes, shattered vials / of olive oil." The title poem, "Vox Angelica," is placed as the final piece in this first section. It offers a reply to the poet's request, in "Ariel Singing," for a sparrow's due. Thus the opening lines of the final poem—"I sing to a breeze that runs through the rafters"—are possible to the poet because of what has transpired in the 12 poems between the first and the last, until, after all, he sees "how everything in the end is made / equal by the wind."

Liu's poem "Mama" opens the second section, a contemplative segment in which the poet meditates on the feminine aspect of life as exemplified by his own mother, who alternatively appears as healer and madwoman, in the guise of both the angelic and the daemonic. In this section, the poet contemplates his own journey from innocence to sexual awareness as his mother moves to a place beyond sanity. In "Canker," the final poem in section two, raw emotions are unleashed in a welter of resentment and pain over the unraveling of a parent's marriage and a mother's descent into madness Liu wrote: "The nurses cutting roses from the cards I sent have put them / in a tub of scalding water. The kisses have come undone." And later, "My mother entered me with a kiss. . . . I wanted her in the earth, her body contained." There is closure, however, in the poet's concluding lines: "*Mother, nothing heals completely as long as I stay alive.*"

Thus prefaced by invocation of muse and mother, the more frankly sexual poems of the third part emerge smoothly, almost organically, from what has preceded, as if the poet cannot make body-sense of his anonymous same-sex encounters without their benediction. In this part, the poet affirms his own power and autonomy as an erotic being in a two-spirit realm where sex can be a source of validation, not a wound of abuse and treachery. In the introductory "Eros Apteros," the poet revisits the bird imagery of the earlier sections with his para-

doxical self-discovery that he has indeed gotten his wings but that "The wings are no longer there to lift this god out of time." Sex has now become a life force, a tantra, as in his description of a steamy encounter:

No one could break our connection,
a spinal cord wrapped around my neck,
inches burning against my aching
wrist as I held on to the white
circumference of his perfect waist.

Burnt Offerings, Liu's second collection, was published by Copper Canyon Press in 1995. After a muse-invoking "Invocation," the book, like its predecessor, is divided into four sections, though Part II is composed of a single poem, the 13-page "With Chaos in Each Kiss." Parts one and three have nine and 21 poems, respectively. Here, the invocation rings with a darker, almost menacing voice, the voice of a great roar of an inner lamentation, a plunge into a *De Profundis* far deeper than the superficial wounds of ordinary life. Contemplating his growing older, and with an echo of Rilke in the *Duino Elegies*, Liu summons wilder, manic beasts to oversee and guard his fragile symbiosis of sex and the spirit, as with, "I call upon you, voice forbidden / from the beginning, a sibylline spell to summon / a god—that o-shaped flume descending / into breath's dark furnace. . . . It sounds like a great lamentation." This "voice forbidden" is a reference to homoeroticism that "drives many of the poems in this collection," in the words of Joel Brouwer in the *Harvard Review*. Brouwer singles out Liu's poem "Apostasy" as an example of the transgressive nature of the author's content modulated by lyric tension:

We open our mouths and the seasons
change, screech owls lifting mice
into the sky those starless hours
when schools of fish are darting
under windows made of ice. Oh Christ
in the chords of an old harmonica
held up to a child's mouth, a solemn
hymn whose words we dare not sing.

Other reviewers praised *Burnt Offerings* for Liu's sensibility and facility with language, as L. Winters of the College of Saint Elizabeth, who wrote in *Choice* (April 1996) of this "haunting and tender collection of poems [that] is reminiscent in voice and technique of the poetry of Donald Justice, Robert Creeley, and Mary Oliver. . . . Liu is particularly skilled in a postmodern, deadpan delivery of the toughest news about the interconnections between flesh and spirit, longing and desire." Timothy Donnelly wrote in the *Boston Review*: "What distinguishes this poetry is Liu's deft handling of the graphic material, his skillful and taut braiding of it with an artful imagery and transcendent lyricism. . . . We value the brutal insofar as it makes a book tender as this."

In 1998 Copper Canyon Press published Liu's third collection, *Say Goodnight*. In this volume Liu has found a more serene voice than before, though his subject matter has lost none of its graphic and visceral urgency, as in his deliberate portrayal of a world that juxtaposes fast-food restaurants, abattoirs, cross-burnings, and animal mutilation. This incarnational vision is most striking in such poems as "Easter 1996," with its opening lines: "Meat hardly resurrects these days, / dear abattoir," or in "Ripened Fruit Pulled Earthward to the Ground," another selection with the unexpected gravitas of Easter: "No bread in the house nor / birds in the yard, a pale stone / with my name on it rolled up / to the door. *Say Goodnight* is Liu's amplest collection to date, with 100 poems included in four sections, beginning with "That Room in which Disaster Played a Part" and ending with "Vespers," in which the poet writes, "So many want to be blessed / I only want to kneel in a quiet room / To love what we have or not exist / at all. . ." In *Say Goodnight*, Liu writes from the "morning after," from the perspective of a maturer life, one whose passions have been transmuted into a serenity but that has not shed the marks of mortal struggle, that still discloses a sexual / spiritual symbiosis at white-hot pitch. "Say Goodnight," the title poem, is a resurrected memory of a youthful, highly charged sexual encounter between the poet and an unnamed stranger, who submit to each other

> between the legs
> of my mother's piano where we had been
> rehearsing hymns that we knew by heart
> as twin shafts slid through valves of spit,
> pure grip rammed into bruised hips, the
> mere plinth to the masterpiece we were.

In "Herring Cove Beach," Liu fuses forbidden images of adult male arousal with the so-called "innocence" of childhood, as in the lines: "The curves of their sex gleaming / under spandex briefs—the way life / desires to unfold—a child / dismantling rosehips, spilling / a secret horde of seeds. . ." In this mute acceptance of things as they are, freed at last from moralistic prohibitions, there is something "like grace—something that would save us / when our bodies failed."

Again, reviewers called attention to Liu's lyrical craft, as in *Publishers Weekly*'s (March 30, 1998) judgment that "*Say Goodnight* . . . takes us from youthful quietude to ironic *eros*, while never quite lapsing into jaded nonchalance" or Jeff Galbraith's paean in the *Boston Book Review* (April 1998), which paid special attention to Liu's poem "Reading Cavafy." Galbraith wrote, "When Liu mediates his experiences through metaphor he creates powerful poems," and added, "Like Cavafy's subject, Liu pretends no 'ridiculous shame' concerning the form of his pleasure." Liu, in Galbraith's opinion, "seems most skillful in the realm of the love poem, where the two sides of his conflict unite."

With a sensibility that is able to embrace a Mormon worldview and an unabashed homoeroticism, Liu has ventured into realms beyond the comfortable circumferences of both those warring camps. Indeed, some reviewers think Liu is essentially a religious poet precisely because he so capably embraces the erotic within the spiritual, in the deeper

sense of religion-as-ligature, of religion as embodying the primeval forces of deep incarnational involvement with flesh and blood. Jeff Galbraith wrote in the *Boston Book Review* (April 1998): "If Timothy Liu is a religious poet, and I think Richard Howard accurately classifies him so, then I would further say that he is a Jacob figure in that he wrestles with God. Unlike the biblical archetype, however, Liu continues to wrestle after knocking down the received idea of God he contends with." Liu's wrestling toward reconciliation is perhaps best summed up in a statement by Marily Hacker that appears as a back-cover blurb for *Burnt Offerings*: "Timothy Liu is a poet of *eros* in all its guises, from acts performed defiantly, worshipfully, in public toilet stalls to the intricate dance of the senses and spirit that is two men's loving, or losing each other. His *eros* is *agape* also, a love-feast for his readers as it modulates through loss to a celebration of the numinous quotidian, the precisely graceful details through which memories and histories survive."

Timothy Liu is editor of *Word of Mouth: A Talisman Anthology of Gay American Poetry, 1950–1999*, scheduled for publication in 2000 by Talisman House. The anthology will include works by several dozen "gay male poets who identify themselves as such and who have published important works" in the second half of the 20th century. Describing this project to the editors of *World Authors*, Liu wrote in January 1999: "I'm interested in how one's sexuality informs one's textuality and to what extent identity politics impinges on one's poetics in poems that span traditional to radical forms. Most of the gay anthologies around merely mirror back 'gay experience' (which has certainly met an important need but remains something I'd like to go beyond)."

—E. M.

SUGGESTED READING: *Antioch Review* Fall 1991, Winter 1998; *Boston Book Review* Apr. 1998; *Harvard Review* Fall 1994, Fall 1995; *Kirkus Review* Apr. 1, 1998; *Library Journal* Mar. 15, 1998; *New York Times Book Review* p35 Jan. 28, 1996; *Ploughshares* Winter 1996 *Publishers Weekly* Mar. 30, 1998

SELECTED BOOKS: *Vox Angelica*, 1992; *Burnt Offerings*, 1995; *Say Goodnight*, 1998

Marion Ettlinger/Courtesy of Alfred A. Knopf

Livesey, Margot

Novelist

After spending her childhood in a remote village in the Scottish highlands, Margot Livesey studied at the University of York in England and then traveled around Europe and Canada before settling in the United States to write—and teach writing—in the early 1980s. She has since become a familiar face on the writers'-workshop circuit from coast to coast. Like many literary expatriates, Livesey writes from locales far removed from her own roots but continues to use her native land as the locus for her narratives. She is the author of two acclaimed novels, *Homework* (1990) and *Criminals* (1995), and a collection of short stories, *Learning by Heart* (1987), and the coauthor of a textbook, *Writing About Literature* (1986). Although criminals and pathological characters often appear in her fiction, she does not define herself as a crime or detective novelist. "Like most people," she told an interviewer, "I'm interested in bad behavior, but I'm also intrigued by the moral dilemmas that we bring upon ourselves by trying to do the right thing." Livesey draws much of her narrative power by approaching the world of children and childhood on its own terms, as she once stated: "One of the things I was always conscious of as a child, and I remain conscious of it as an adult who knows children, is that children occupy very much their own world, which in many ways is quite separate from the adult world: different preoccupations and different priorities."

Margot Livesey's novels about the fragile texture of human connection and the vital sustenance offered by friendship and community have their ori-

gins in the isolated childhood she spent in the village of Glenalmond in the desolate Scottish highlands, where her father had been a schoolteacher. "Our house was always orderly and quiet," she later recalled, remembering how her reclusive parents would not encourage their daughter to bring friends home. Painfully shy and self-conscious, young Margot was even driven to self-destructive acts to avoid encounters with troublesome classmates, once dropping a heavy radiator on her foot, "breaking a small bone which saved me for a fortnight." In a 1994 autobiographical essay entitled "The Valley of Lost Things," she wrote: "This period of desolation which lasted from the age of eight until the age of twelve seemed endless, and, in the midst of my loneliness, I turned to animals." She found companionship with a pet dog and the hens, ducks, and calves she tended on a neighbor's farm, naively expecting the fulfillment of a legend that animals acquired the power of human speech at midnight on Christmas Eve.

For a while, Margot was a day pupil at the Craigmount girl's boarding school, where she was a "miserable outcast," in her words. After the school failed, much to her glee, she was sent to live with the family of her friend Sally. She described this time as a "halcyon period" that enabled her to enjoy the warmth of family life apart from the cocoon her parents wove about themselves. It was around the dinner table in this adoptive family circle that she learned the skills of social interaction and adult conversation that were to serve her well later as a storyteller: "Details of a personal misfortune, like a flat tire, were acceptable, but only if converted into an amusing anecdote," she wrote, adding, "Sally's parents were both wonderful conversationalists who made these rules seem as natural as breathing. Nowadays, as I struggle with my taciturn characters, I often recall the skill with which they transformed the dullest sows ears into silken stories."

Margot Livesey echoed many similarly situated women in decrying the "lack of models for women's friendship in literature." She was able to find her own inspiration in weekly comics—her favorite was "The Four Marys"—and in the classics of children's literature that featured girls, such as *Anne of Green Gables* and *Little Women*. A graduation gift of *Robinson Crusoe*, Defoe's novel of a man marooned on a desert island, achieved particular resonance with young Margot, who, under its spell, "daydreamed about startling achievements and popularity."

After receiving her bachelor's degree in English and philosophy at the University of York, Livesey traveled around Europe and Canada for several years. Earlier, at 17, she had met a Canadian man whose "inspired imagination" had a profound influence on her own journey for her "missing self." She visited his homeland to stay close to him and soon began publishing some stories in Canadian magazines, taking on a managerial job at a Toronto restaurant at the same time. Livesey quickly became mesmerized by the "dazzling openness" of the lives of people in North America, who bared their souls in easy self-disclosure, in stark contrast to the introversion and self-concealment she had known in her native Scotland. Of this period, she later wrote: "One day in my late 20s I realized that I had made myself into an exile, that I was living between two countries and two cultures, and that I would be hard-pressed now to make my home entirely in either." Not long afterwards, she decided to leave Canada for the United States to develop a career of teaching writing on the university level.

During her time in the United States, Livesey has striven to reconcile the conflicting demands of a teaching and writing career. She has taught at Rutgers, the University of Washington, Tufts, Carnegie Mellon, Williams College, and Brandeis University, amassing a coterie of devoted students. While teaching she has written two novels, *Homework* and *Criminals*; published a collection of short stories, *Learning by Heart*; and coauthored, with Lynn Klamkin, a textbook entitled *Writing About Literature*.

"One of the ways I start writing," Livesey told an interviewer, "is by looking at newspapers, listening to people, looking for something to capture my interest. You'll probably catch me in the drugstore reading the *National Enquirer* and calling it research," she told Jesse Garon for a *Beatrice* (April 1996) interview. Her first novel, *Homework*, was provoked by a letter she had read in a newspaper about a malevolent girl who took perverse delight in terrorizing her own family. The novel describes the havoc visited upon a thirtysomething live-in couple, Stephen and Celia, when Jennie, Stephen's daughter by an earlier marriage, moves in with them. Despite Celia's support of the girl, Jennie responds with pranks, deception, and growing insolence, much to the discomfort of the two adults. In discussing this novel, Mickey Pearlman declared that "all of Livesey's fictional children are what might be called marvelous deviants, full of a kind of familiar evil that is both innocuous and powerful," and American novelist Francine Prose, an admirer of Livesey's work, compared *Homework* to Henry James's *The Turn of the Screw* in its "brave . . . willingness to illuminate the dark side of childhood and our own most closely guarded notions of innocence and evil." Livesey has acknowledged that she was "looking over her shoulder" at James's book while writing her own, but cautions that the character Jenny should not be interpreted as "evil" or as "a kind of Iago character acting malevolently for no motive." *Homework* invites the reader to consider the submerged psychological issues at work in the mind of a rootless child thrust into a world of unserene adults who are themselves seeking identity, stability, and emotional support. "I was interested in the ambiguity that James managed to create and maintain," she told Pearlman, "the sense that everything is always in question and that the nature and the spirit of children are most in question: how much they know and how deeply implicated they are."

Like *Homework*, Livesey's second novel, *Criminals*, is set in Scotland, but this time the locale moves from the Edinburgh of *Homework* to the rural regions near Perth that Livesey remembered from childhood, with side excursions to Italy and America. Isolation, lapses in self-confidence, and failed communication are its themes. The novel opens with the discovery of a baby in a bus station restroom by Ewan, a banker on his way to the highlands to visit Mollie, his mentally unstable sister, who lives in a farmhouse with the evocative name Mill of Fortune. In his state of blundering nonchalance, Ewan takes the baby along with him (the bus doors close before he has a chance to stammer out details about his find), and Mollie immediately welcomes the baby, whom she names Olivia—the baby's real name is Grace—as a way of living out her own fantasies of motherhood and belongingness. Meanwhile, Kevin and Joan, the parents of the abandoned child, track down Ewan and resort to extortion in their efforts to retrieve the infant; Kevin, who had left the infant in the lavatory, even follows Ewan to the highlands on the same bus, fearing to make a scene lest his embarrassment be revealed. On the surface, the plot seems incredible, but Livesey rescues the narrative from incredulity with her skilled evocation of characters who are complex and bumbling but basically affectionate and well-meaning, wounded yet redemptive. Her depiction of the characters' inner monologue and motivations makes *Criminals* a psychological thriller of the first order.

Candice Rodd, reviewing *Criminals* for the *Times Literary Supplement* (August 16, 1996), wrote of how this "catalogue of almost catastrophic crime, deception and cruelty" has been "perpetrated by characters who, if challenged, would vigorously insist that they had meant no harm." She concluded: "For all its apparent dependence on improbabilities, and its mischievous insistence of fate and portents, its most compelling achievement is in the rich and subtle detail, the quiet but unremitting exposure of little foibles and vanities that play as big a role as chance in constructing the disturbing drama." Similarly, Greg Johnson wrote in the *New York Times Book Review* (March 31, 1996) that, despite Livesey's "occasional use of metafictional gimmickry (especially the novel within a novel) [that] detracts somewhat from the fully textured conviction of her main narrative," *Criminals* "is a wonderful novel, impeccably written and thoroughly engrossing." He called attention to how the "wordlessness" of the central characters gives birth to "chilling but potentially redemptive insights. . . . The wordless infant, appropriately named Grace, becomes the impetus for the adults' lacerating articulations of one another's personal crimes," ranging from the stuttering Ewan's lapses of judgment to the semiliterate Kevin's self-serving scheming to the near-wordless Joan's "final and unexpectedly blunt judgment on them all."

Margot Livesey told an interviewer in 1994 that she was then in the midst of working on two other novels, each yet unpublished, based on the "orderly and quiet" life of her childhood, though she was struck during her research by how very little she really knew about her reclusive parents. The first of these, preliminarily titled "Eva Moves the Furniture," is loosely based on fragments of memories about her mother's ability to "see" poltergeists in their house. Livesey's explanation of why she chose the name "Ruth" for her own character (a two-year-old) in this novel evinces the deep feelings she associates with her own childhood: "I associate the name with sorrow and exile, and the word *rue*, and didn't [the Biblical] Ruth shed tears amid the alien corn?" The other unpublished work, tentatively titled "A Confirmed Bachelor," is a work-in-progress about her schoolteacher father, a man who left no letters or records upon his death in the 1950s. "It's astonishingly hard to find out about him, and it's a real lesson in how quickly people disappear," she told Mickey Pearlman. Frustrated at being unable to find much information from retired colleagues of her father's, Livesey decided to reconstruct his life at a distance by interviewing people of his age and social class—solicited through advertising and old-school networks—who might have "lived parallel lives to his." A stymied search for her own father's identity has thus impelled her to broaden the scope of her inquiry toward painting a portrait of his entire generation. She is using a Studs Terkel–like oral-history methodology with which she hopes to recapture a sense of the daily life of ordinary people from 1904 to 1945—interviewing elderly Britons,

born in the fading days of the Empire, who remember the First World War and the class struggles of the 1920s and 1930s, as well as the "finest hour" of World War II.

Margot Livesey herself sums up her writing career in these lines from her autobiographical essay "The Valley of Lost Things": "Sometimes, nowadays, people ask me why I write, and although I have practiced articulate answers, my replies are incoherent. No reason seems sufficient; all seem spurious. But part of the answer is that I yearn to escape the narrow confines of my own singular experience. When I try to create a character on the page, that attempt gives me a sense of what it is like to be someone else. Friends, too, offer me that greatest of luxuries in a more profound way—the possibility of a life beyond my own. Ariosto [in the classic Italian poem *Orlando Furioso*] went alone to the Valley of Lost Things on behalf of his friend. My friends go with me, take me with them, and together we bring back what we can."
—E. M.

SUGGESTED READING: *Library Journal* p172 Dec. 1989; *New York Times Book Review* p15 Mar. 31, 1996; *Publishers Weekly* p57 Dec. 11, 1995; *Times Literary Supplement* p 23 Aug. 16, 1996; Pearlman, M., ed. *Between Friends*, 1994; Pearlman, M. *Listen to Their Voices: Twenty Interviews with Women Who Write*, 1994

SELECTED BOOKS: Fiction—*Learning by Heart*, 1987; *Homework*, 1990; *Criminals*, 1995; As editor—*Writing About Literature* (with L. Klamkin), 1986

Lord, Bette Bao

Nov. 3, 1938– Writer

Bette Bao Lord has an unusual perspective on the changes that China has undergone in the 20th century. Chinese-born but American-bred, the author has been able to give Western readers a taste of what the Chinese people have endured since the rise of communism on the mainland in 1949. With empathy, alternately using fiction and memoir as her means, Bette Bao Lord has constructed a body of work that, though not extensive given the more than 30 years she has been writing, is richly evocative of the enduring spirit of the Chinese people. She first received literary acclaim with the publication of her sister's life story, *Eighth Moon* (1964), and has continued writing nonfiction titles such as *Legacies* (1990), a collection of eyewitnesses' accounts of brutality in China. She has also written a children's book, *In the Year of the Boar and Jackie Robinson* (1984), about her childhood in Brook-

lyn, and two novels, *Spring Moon* (1981) and *The Middle Heart* (1996).

Born in Shanghai, China, on November 3, 1938, Bette Bao Lord first came to the United States in 1946 with her father, Sandys, and her mother, Dora (Fang) Bao. Lord's father had accepted assignment to the United States an official of the Nationalist Chinese government. Expecting their time in the U.S. to be brief, the Baos left their younger daughter, Sansan, who at the time was an infant and too young to travel, in China. With the Communist victory in 1949, the Nationalists were driven to Taiwan and the Baos were forced to settle permanently in the U.S. The family lived first in Brooklyn and later moved to Teaneck, New Jersey. Talking about growing up in the United States, the author told Enid Nemy of the *Chicago Tribune* (September 6, 1981): "I had a very Chinese family life. It was not American in philosophy." Still, in terms of material comfort, the Baos maintained a very American lifestyle—owing to Sandys's status as an official of the Nationalist government. (The United States supported the Nationalists both before and after the Communist victory and did not officially rec-

Berle Cherney

Bette Bao Lord

ognize the government of mainland China until after President Richard Nixon went there in February 1972.)

The author was not a pampered child of diplomats. She worked from the age of 12 to help finance her education. One of her first jobs was typing envelopes for an insurance company. She made few errors in her typing, a skill that would prove useful to her when she was working on her novel, *Spring Moon* (1981), from midnight to 5 a.m. five days a week for six years. Initially, Lord did not want to be a novelist. "Becoming a novelist was not a girlhood dream," she explained in an interview, "but a middle-aged happenstance. Perhaps if I had known what I know now about the agony of the blank page, the imperative of endless revision, the rigors of technique, I would have never begun a first novel. Blissfully ignorant, I was driven by the idea that I had something to say about China to a Western audience." Lord had other interests growing up, chief among them dancing and photography.

Lord began attending Tufts University in 1955, graduating with a B.A. in 1959. She then went to the Fletcher School of Law and Diplomacy, in Somerville, Massachusetts, where she met her future husband, Winston Lord. At the time both she and Winston wanted to enter the foreign service. Winston did so, but Bette, who was not yet a U.S. citizen, could not. After completing her master's degree in 1959, she instead served as assistant director of the East-West Cultural Center at the University of Hawaii in Honolulu during 1960 and 1961 and then as program officer for the Fulbright Exchange Program in Washington, D.C., from 1961 to 1963. On May 4, 1963, the Lords married. (They now have two children, Elizabeth Pillsbury and Winston Bao.) Bette Bao Lord became a naturalized U.S. citizen in 1964, just after her family was reunited with her sister, Sansan, whom they had not seen in 16 years.

In explaining how she came to write her first book, *Eighth Moon*, Lord has said: "I stumbled into writing. I wrote *Eighth Moon*, my sister's story, because she only spoke Chinese and I knew of no writers who did. Ignorant of how difficult it was to get into print, I took up the task. When it was published, it did surprisingly well."

Eighth Moon began to take shape when the sisters, who had had no contact in all those years, started talking about Sansan's experiences growing up in China. At first Bette recorded Sansan's monologues on tape, interviewing with her only later. Lord had accumulated more than 250 pages of notes when she completed her interviews with her sister. (Comparing this book with her first novel, Lord noted that *Eighth Moon* took only nine months to write. "Fiction is immensely more difficult a form," she has said.)

The book sold well, spending weeks on the *New York Times* best-seller list. Decades after its original publication, it was still being used in high-school classrooms and had been translated into more than 15 languages. The story of Sansan living in modern-day China, struggling every day with manual labor and long food lines, moved even the most cynical of critics. A critic for *Best Sellers* (September 15, 1964) noted how "the simple, poignant events in the life of this young girl are more moving than any statistical cross-section can ever be! Here in microcosm is life under totalitarian rule. . . . [This] should be required reading for every high-school student and college freshman." The *New York Times Book Review* (September 27, 1964) read: "This book is not a propaganda piece; it indulges in no generalizations. . . . For an insight into real-life Communist China, *Eighth Moon* is highly recommended."

After the publication of her first book, Lord returned to her early love—modern dance. After studying under the legendary Martha Graham, Lord began teaching as well as performing modern dance in 1964, in both Geneva and Washington, D.C. She stopped dancing in 1973. During that time her husband was working in the White House and with the State Department; Winston Lord accompanied then-secretary of state Henry Kissinger on his missions to China, just after the United States had granted official recognition to the Communist government. On their sixth mission, Bette was able to accompany her husband to the land of her birth after an absence of 27 years. As she wrote in a piece for the *Washington Post* (April 7, 1974), she realized that "like all overseas Chinese, I continued to hold special ties and feelings for the land of my ancestors." One result of her visit was her first novel, *Spring Moon*, on which she worked obsessively for six years. Though she originally intended it to be a personal memoir, the book changed in its rewrites into a novel of unusual depth.

The novel follows the developments in the lives of a Mandarin Chinese family from 1892 to 1927, with an epilogue from 1972. The story comes to the reader through the eyes of the main character, Spring Moon, a daughter of the House of Chang, who submits to all the traditional Chinese rituals, including the painful foot-binding ceremony. Through her the reader sees the development of modern China. The critics were amazed by *Spring Moon* the reviewer for *Library Journal* (October 15, 1981) called it "a highly readable and fascinating account of an important period in Chinese history." A critic for *The Saturday Review* (October 1981) perhaps best summed up the purpose of the book: "This [is] one of the most remarkable novels ever to explain the East to the West. . . . Bette Bao Lord . . . writes in a low-key style that suggests the understatement of traditional Chinese poetry. . . . This beautifully written first novel manages to be both poignant and restrained." The novel was translated into 12 languages. *Spring Moon* introduced Lord to international fame, but that fame came with some unwelcome consequences. In Taiwan large portions of the book were rewritten or distorted, and Lord publicly condemned the translation. "This is a flagrant assault upon my artistic integrity and personal reputation," she stated in a telegram to the secretary general of the Kuomintang (Nationalist) Party. "I also think that the translator's actions impugn the honor of Taiwan."

Three years later Lord converted her memories of being a young Chinese girl growing up in Brooklyn into a children's book, *In the Year of the Boar and Jackie Robinson*, illustrated by Marc Simont. In the next year Lord returned to her homeland with her husband, who had been appointed ambassador to the People's Republic of China. As wife of the American ambassador, she was able to preside over dinner parties for Chinese writers, arrange showings of American movies for Chinese intellectuals, and send hundreds of Chinese artists and writers to study in the United States. This was a period of openness to American and Western ideas, something that would have been impossible earlier in Chinese history. As Lord told the *Washington Post* (September 2, 1987), explaining the motivation for her activities: "The Chinese are so proud of their Olympic gold medals. But where are the gold medals for writing, or for painting?"

The Lords were, in fact, ardent supporters Deng Xiaoping's China and of the cultural changes they observed during the years Winston Lord was ambassador. This all changed with the violent suppression of the student-led, pro-democracy protest in Tiananmen Square in June 1989. The Lords' time in China ended with that massacre, but they continued to protest the Bush administration's eagerness to overlook, for the sake of global politics, what had happened in Tiananmen Square.

Lord was a consultant for CBS News during that struggle for democracy in Tiananmen Square and stayed on until the Square was cleared. After she left China, she published a book, *Legacies*, which collected residents' accounts of daily life in modern China. The witnesses either spoke to her in person or gave her tape recordings. Describing a country where quiet endurance in desperate situations is commonplace, these stories resonated with American readers as both astounding and horrifying.

The critics agreed and generally praised the work. The writer for the *New York Times Book Review* (April 15, 1990) called *Legacies* "the work of an expert storyteller . . . an assemblage of indelible portraits that get at the essence of what it means to be Chinese in our times, of what the Chinese Communist Party has bequeathed its people." Noting how the people Lord interviewed trusted her, a reviewer for the *Wall Street Journal* (April 10, 1990) wrote: "She has rewarded that trust by making readers understand the forces that have caused so many Chinese to fall victim to the tyranny of their Communist rulers." The *New York Newsday* (March 25, 1990) article gave the book a favorable review generally but criticized the author's attempt to inspire "sympathy for Mao's victims by reducing them to types: the scholar, the peasant, the actress."

Lord's second novel, *The Middle Heart*, was published in 1996. It is similar to its predecessor, *Spring Moon*, in that it attempts to encompass a large portion of Chinese history through the eyes of a few main characters. The narrative begins in 1932, when three children, two boys and a girl, unite in their animosity for the conquering Japanese and begin a lifelong friendship. Over time, their loyalty to country and one another is tested by the changes that take place in China. *The Middle Heart* found no lack of compliments waiting for it. The *Library Journal* (February 1, 1996) review read: "Much like Pearl S. Buck, Lord has the ability to reveal the soul of China through her characters." While most critics agreed with his assessment, a *New York Newsday* (February 25, 1996) critic noted: "Conveniently—sometimes too much so—her three protagonists' occupations situate them at key events of these tumultuous times." However, Barbara Holliday, writing in the *Chicago Tribune* (March 18, 1996), felt that this feature of the novel helped to display an essential part of the Chinese character in violent and revolutionary times: "Despite the turmoil of politics, the national character shines though. Gentleness and civility to those we meet, loyalty to those we love, endurance in the face of hardship."
—C.M.

SUGGESTED READING: *Best Sellers* p229 Sep. 15, 1964; *Chicago Tribune* XII p6 Sep. 6, 1981, XIV p5 Apr. 1, 1990, V p3 Mar. 18, 1996; *Library Journal* p2049 Oct. 15, 1981, p98 Feb. 1, 1996; *New York Newsday* p20 Mar. 25, 1990, p 39 Feb. 25, 1996; *New York Times* p58 Aug. 30, 1981, C p18 Mar. 26, 1990; *New York Times Book Review*, Sep. 27, 1964; p15 Oct. 25, 1981, p9 Apr. 15, 1990, p34 Feb. 11, 1996; *Publishers*

Weekly p14 Oct. 8, 1982; *Saturday Review* p 75 Oct. 1981; *Wall Street Journal* p 26 Nov. 23, 1981, A p22 Apr. 10, 1990; *Washington Post* p17+ Apr. 7, 1974; D p1 + Sep. 2, 1987; *Contemporary Authors* vol. 107, 1983

SELECTED WORKS: Fiction—*Spring Moon*, 1981; *The Middle Heart*, 1996; Nonfiction— *Eighth Moon*, 1964; *Legacies*, 1990; Juvenile—*In the Year of the Boar and Jackie Robinson*, 1984

Dušan Totić

Lord, James

Nov. 27, 1922– Biographer; memoirist

The American expatriate memoirist and biographer James Lord has lived in France almost continuously since the end of the Second World War, and in the years following his arrival there, he got to know many of the notable figures who populate his writings, such as Picasso and Giacometti, Gertrude Stein and Alice B. Toklas, Jean Cocteau and Lord Acton. All of his books are based on personal, often intimate, reminiscences of these and other prominent figures in the haute monde of art, literature, cinema, and fashion in postwar France. His lengthier memoirs of Picasso and his mistress Dora Maar, and of Giacometti and his circle, offer expansive and controversial if not always impartial glimpses of these notable figures from the point of view of an "American in Paris" who continues to write as "observer/participant" in his mid-70s.

For *World Authors 1990–1995*, Lord writes: "In response to your request for autobiographical detail, I have little of interest to offer. But what there is follows.

"I was born on November 27, 1922 in Englewood, New Jersey, a middle-class suburb of New York City, where my father worked in Wall Street as a broker. The second of four sons, my childhood, insofar as I remember it, was happy. It was at a very early age, say twelve or thirteen, that I began to write poems and stories.

"I attended several schools, none of them of any distinction, nor was I a distinguished pupil. My studies at Wesleyan University were interrupted by World War II. I spent more than three years in the U. S. Army, a member of the Military Intelligence, serving principally in France, a country for which I felt, and have ever since retained, a profound affection. After the war I returned for a single year to Wesleyan but found my stay there profitless and left without taking a degree in order to return to France, where I devoted my entire time to writing. I have never had any other occupation and have spent most of my life in France, making my home in Paris. The produce of my writing career has not been of particular merit with the exception, perhaps, of a biography of Alberto Giacometti published in 1985 and three volumes of memoirs published since: *Picasso and Dora*, *Six Exceptional Women*, and *Some Remarkable Men*. I hope to finish a fourth, final volume of memoirs, and thereafter do not know quite what I might undertake."

The author's self-deflecting commentary above belies the fact that James Lord traveled in what would be a "charmed circle" to most readers: the Montparnassian coterie of world-class artists, aristocrats, and aesthetes who inhabited postwar Paris. Dubbed the "Boswell to the art stars of our century" by the writer Phyllis Rose, Lord writes in an opinionated but even-tempered voice about the artists and writers and those of their admirers he has befriended during his half-century in the French capital. As was the case with Dr. Johnson's amanuensis, James Lord's ruminations about his subjects are interwoven with many fascinating details of Lord's own persona and views.

A prime example of this "observer/participant" style is Lord's 1993 book, *Picasso and Dora: A Personal Memoir*, which, in a method reminiscent of biblical genealogical charts, does not yield details about Picasso and his mistress until the reader has first waded through many passages about Lord's own ancestral tree, from Protestant rebels of the 16th century through Revolutionary-era orator Patrick Henry, and finally to his own offshoot as one of four sons of Albert Lord and Louise Bennett. Lord grew up in Englewood, New Jersey, "a community in the twenties as yet unspoiled by the proliferations brought about by the convenience of the George Washington Bridge," he wrote. The family lived part of the time at a farmhouse in Paris, Maine, and Lord has recalled with nostalgia his discovery of his homosexuality in the course of an idyllic boyhood summer there. He has also reported almost with detachment how his parents were "unnerved" by financial setbacks in the Depression era. During World War II, Lord enlisted in the army and was stationed in France with the Military Intelligence Service. It was with the help of a three-day pass in Paris that he arranged a visit with Picasso, simply because he wanted to meet him. He later wrote that as "an industrious reader of biographies, I noted that the great had often been acquainted with one another, and perhaps it occurred to me that the proximity of greatness might have something to do with possession of it."

The decision was pivotal, and Lord soon became a familiar figure on the boulevards and in the cafes and ateliers of Paris. One of his first ventures in biography was *A Giacometti Portrait* (1980), based on Lord's 18 sittings for a portrait by the surrealist master. During these sessions, the author took surreptitious notes so as not to make the artist feel like "a specimen under observation." Lord committed other details to memory, and in the evenings he wrote long letters to a friend in New York based on his recollections. The memoir underscores the fact that the subject for a portrait is not passive, but an active and creative participant in the process. Only by the fifth sitting, Lord wrote, "did I begin to feel that both of us were really involved in the painting." By the 18th sitting he felt "elated and alarmed. If the work went badly that afternoon, there would be no changing it afterward. The picture would remain for ever as it was." He concluded: "I hope that others may see in it a small part of what makes him such a remarkable man and such a supreme artist. To see even so little will be to see very much." Years later, Lord recalled in a telephone interview with a *New York Times* writer that "striking up a conversation with Giacometti was the easiest thing in the world to do. He was a wonderful conversationalist. He loved to talk, and he loved to listen."

Thirty years after his portrait-sitting sessions, Lord completed a full-length biography of the artist, published as *Giacometti* in 1985. Dan Hofstadter, reviewing the book for the *New York Times* (September 22, 1985), called attention to the subjective tone of Lord's research when he wrote: "Mr. Lord also understands that the chief function of biography is to retail gossip. Clever people have known this ever since Goethe rediscovered the autobiography of Benvenuto Cellini, a book so preposterous in all its parts that we finish it convinced it is true. . . . Mr. Lord gossips perceptively. His tales have the breath of life. He has been conscientiously collecting them from all over Montparnasse and the rest of the Western world for a decade or more; some he passes on with a mischievous air, allowing you to make of them what you will." But, Hofstadter concludes, "It is not for nothing that James Lord has lived in Paris since 1946; he has mastered more than the cafe wit. He is a keen psychologist, given to the sort of convoluted probing one finds so often in old French diaries and letters." Not long after the book's publication, a dis-

pute over the artist's estate involved Lord, who was sued by Giacometti's widow over the provenance of some of the sculptures in his collection, but Lord emerged unscathed.

Lord's acquaintanceship with Picasso over the years led to his writing *Picasso and Dora: A Personal Memoir*, published 48 years after Lord's first encounter with the artist. This work is perhaps Lord's most unselfconscious "gossip piece." In its preface, he wrote, "My friends say I am secret and devious. They are right. That such an individual should undertake a work of autobiography, albeit one purposefully superficial and optimistically impersonal, must seem at least perverse and at best brazen. It is. But therein may dwell a certain stimulus to titillation, if not to honorable intellectual exertion." And, further, "An autobiographer is in the business of doing for himself what he wishes not to be done to him by anyone else. This is sometimes called self-abuse. Neither modest nor shy, I nevertheless recognize that words say more than a writer surmises."

As in his other books, Lord acts as both protagonist and chronicler—as in his recording of Picasso's reaction to the open letter, criticizing the artist for his left-wing sympathies, that Lord published in French newspapers after the Hungarian uprising in 1956. In that letter, Lord had written, "I ask you to today to repudiate the errors of your political sympathies. I ask you to make common cause once again with the sufferings and the hopes of the anonymous masses of whom you were able long ago to create such gripping and unforgettable images," a screed to which both Picasso and Dora Maar, his ex-mistress, reacted with understandable coolness. The memoir had earlier taken an even more intimate turn, for it is also about Lord's affair with Dora Maar, herself a painter, after her breakup with Picasso. Lord had always admitted a certain fondness for her ("When with her, one feels at an extraordinary altitude") and wrote that she "possessed an infallible capacity for representing me to myself as superficial and naive, which I resented and accepted and, in fact, appreciated as evidence of her esteem and affection."

Lord wrote several other books about notable men and women he had known, notably *Six Exceptional Women*, published in 1994, and *Some Remarkable Men*, published in 1996. Both books bore the subtitle "Further Memoirs." *Some Remarkable Men* included chapters on Harold Acton, Jean Cocteau, Balthus, and, again, Giacometti. Of his subjects, Michael Kimmelman wrote in the *New York Times* (September 9, 1996), "To Mr. Lord each one is an exotic European of serpentine and exquisite sensibility, a condition he seems to find both compelling and something of a liability, except in the case of Giacometti, who is for him (as he was for many other people), a near-saint." *Six Exceptional Women* (focusing on Gertrude Stein, Alice B. Toklas, the actress Arletty, the art patron Marie-Laure Bischoffsheim, the exiled Errieta Perdikidi, and the author's own mother, Louise Bennett Lord) led

Florence King to comment in the same publication (May 1, 1994), "Many centuries from now, the memoirist James Lord's exquisite gift for female friendships and the filial grace of his relationship with his mother may well earn him quasi-mythological status, like the Flying Dutchman and the Wandering Jew, as the Man Who Talked to Women. His new book, a collection of six essays on six women who were privileged to know him, transported me from today's hateful world of intersexual warfare and left me with a sense of civilization regained." In this book, as in his others, Lord remained averse to romanticizing his subjects. Recalling, for example, his brief meeting with Gertrude Stein not long before her death in 1946, he could remember only how this "figure in those shapeless tweed suits made me think of a burlap bag filled with cement and left to harden."

A Gift for Admiration: Further Memoirs appeared in 1998. This book, "really more a compilation of short biographical sketches than a memoir," as Ted Loos wrote in the *New York Times Book Review* (June 7, 1998), focuses on Peggy Guggenheim, Henry McIlhenny, and four other acquaintances of Lord's who were influential in the world of art in the 20th century.

In his review of *Some Remarkable Men*, titled "An American in Paris," for the *New York Times Book Review* (September 15, 1996), Edmund White offered a fit summary of James Lord's style and process: "Mr. Lord subscribes to the concept of genius, which, in true Romantic fashion, he sees as something thrust on the individual, who obeys it as he might serve a jealous, even malign, deity. The constant interplay between the usual human vices of vanity, pettiness, and greed and this single dominating and almost divine virtue is Mr. Lord's subject and method."
—E. M.

SUGGESTED READING: *Art & Antiques* p112 Dec. 96, with photos; *Art Review* p24+ Feb. 94, with photos; *New York Times Book Review* p1 July 18, 1993, p12 May 1, 1994, p23 June 7, 1998; *Publishers Weekly* p76 July 29, 1996

SELECTED BOOKS: *A Giacometti Portrait*, 1980; *Giacometti*, 1985; *Picasso and Dora: A Personal Memoir*, 1993; *Six Exceptional Women: Further Memoirs*, 1994 *Some Remarkable Men: Further Memoirs*, 1996; *A Gift for Admiration: Further Memoirs*, 1998

Lott, Bret

Oct. 8, 1958– Novelist; short-story writer

The American writer Brett Lott, in novels—*The Man Who Owned Vermont* (1987), *A Stranger's House* (1988), *Jewel* (1992), and *Reed's Beach* (1993)—and short-story collections—*A Dream of Old Leaves* (1989) and *How to Get Home* (1996)—details the lives of ordinary working people trying to maintain family stability in the face of such realities as the loss of a child, the mental retardation of a child, a miscarriage, and the death of a spouse. Reviewers have characterized Lott's prose as "spare" and "graceful" and his characterizations as "empathetic" and "attuned to the intricacies of the human drama." His memoir, *Fathers, Sons, and Brothers: The Men in My Family* (1997), explores the same concerns. His nominal thriller, *The Hunt Club*, appeared in 1998.

For *World Authors 1990–1995*, Bret Lott, born on October 8, 1958, writes: "I was born in Los Angeles, the second of four children: three brothers and a sister, the youngest. My father was a salesman for Royal Crown Cola at that time, and worked for the company throughout my childhood and adolescence and early adulthood, my mother over the years a baker, a bank teller, one of those women who gives out free samples of food at the grocery store. But my earliest memories involve RC Cola, my dad's sales route, we three boys brought along on Saturday mornings, so that it seems inevitable, finally, that my first novel, *The Man Who Owned*

Courtesy of Brett Lott

Vermont (Viking, 1987), is about an RC salesman, his route, what his life is like having to push product.

"In 1967, my dad was transferred to Phoenix, Arizona, where we lived until he was transferred back to Los Angeles in 1975. I graduated high school in 1976 with every intention of becoming a forest ranger, attending the School of Forestry at Northern Arizona University my freshman year. When Forestry turned out to be nothing more than matters of forest yield and management—I'd dreamt of riding a horse through a national park somewhere—I withdrew and enrolled at California State University, Long Beach, as a marine biology major for no clear reason except that I liked the ocean. A year later I failed a physics course I had to pass in order to proceed in the major.

"I quit school altogether, worked about a year as a cook in a restaurant, then decided that the job selling RC Cola my dad offered me every time I came home to leech a free meal or do laundry—I had moved out at age 19—was what I wanted to do. I was then given my own sales route, and worked in the same business as my father until I had had enough only a year later. I decided to re-enroll at Cal State, this time as an education major, again for no clear reason except that I thought I'd like to teach.

"Before starting up again at Cal State, I took a class at a local community college in order to get back in the groove of being a student. It could have been any course—history, science, anything—but the one that worked with my schedule was a class called Creative Writing, and I took it, showed up each Tuesday night in my RC uniform, fresh off the route.

"I enjoyed it, and when I went back to school full-time I took another creative writing class as an elective, started student teaching as part of the education major and hated it, and then, finally, declared an English major.

"This is to say, then, and in a most roundabout manner, that I never gave writing a thought, never grew up believing I would someday publish novels and stories, though I read my brains out from an early age, read and read and read, and simply lived my life in a way that led by process of elimination—salesman, cook, would-be teacher, wannabe scientist—to this, now: a writer.

"After graduation, I attended the University of Massachusetts, Amherst, where I studied under Jay Neugeboren and the late James Baldwin, and received my MFA in 1984. While there, I started publishing my first stories, most notably in the *Iowa Review* and the *Yale Review*, the latter of which got noticed by a prominent agent in New York, the former of which published the story "This Plumber," which was later included in an anthology, *20 Under 30*, which led, in the Byzantine manner the New York publishing world works, to the publication of *The Man Who Owned Vermont*.

"I am convinced that this never having thought to become a writer, coupled with the working-class family and life I have been given, has served to keep my work informed by what I believe are the important stories: people at work, trying to live their lives and hold on to who they love. Over the years it has come to me that I inevitably write about what I fear might happen to me were I not so blessed with a marriage intact, two children who love me and whom I love, a family: *The Man Who Owned Vermont* is about a marriage that breaks up over a miscarriage; *A Stranger's House* is about a couple who cannot have children; *Jewel*, based on the life of my grandmother, is about a woman who gives birth to her sixth child, a Down Syndrome baby, and the sacrifice of family she must make throughout her life in order to best take care of that single child; *Reed's Beach* is about a couple whose only child is killed in an accident, and how or if they can reconcile after the fact; and the story collections, *A Dream of Old Leaves* and *How to Get Home*, represent permutations on the same question it seems each novel poses: How shall we then live?

"And because at age 19—long before I ever took that creative writing class at the community college—I was born again, and accepted Jesus Christ as my Lord and Savior (these terms, however archaic, perhaps hayseed they may seem in these late days, are viable, have true meaning in my life), the answer I have found in the writing of each of these stories is, We must continue to live as best we can, accommodating our lives to what has been dealt us without forsaking one another. The dead child will never come back, a Down Syndrome child will always be a Down Syndrome child, a miscarriage cannot be forgotten; the only story left is that we love each other, thereby gaining our strength to go on."

In his works Brett Lott has dealt one by one, as he has noted, with his deepest fears of what would drive his family apart. In his first novel, *The Man Who Owned Vermont*, a man may or may not be the cause of his wife's miscarriage, but the couple is driven apart by guilt and blame. Lott's real theme, however, as Michiko Kakutani pointed out in the *New York Times*, is the "redemptive power of love."

A Dream of Old Leaves was termed a collection of "enjoyable stories with backbone" by the *Library Journal* (June 1, 1989) reviewer. Eils Lotozo in the *New York Times Book Review* (September 10,1989) deemed Lott's "spare, emotionally restrained fictions" the work of "a minimalist John Cheever." "Neighbors, brothers, husbands, and wives signal to one another across a gulf of disregard or misunderstanding until some disturbing event—an infidelity, a fire, a death, a spouse's exotic new friend—reveals secret dreams, sorrows, and resentments." Paul Stuewe in *Quill and Quire* (December 1989) noted how in the title story, a child's awakening in the night "seems to be the main issue at hand; but through a deft concluding twist, we realize it is his father's understanding of what it means to be a parent that is really being explored."

Lott has devoted a great deal of his fiction—and nonfiction, as well—to what it means to be a parent. In his novel *Jewel*, Lott apotheosizes parental love. Jewel, the eponymous mother, is not someone from a background calculated to produce parenting skills. She was orphaned early, raised by an abusive grandmother, and sent to an "industrial school" in the deep South. Yet, when her sixth child is born mentally retarded, Jewel engages first in an intensive effort to keep her alive and then in an odyssey to Los Angeles with her family that Judith Freeman in the *New York Times Book Review* (March 1, 1992) likened to the Joads' trip from Oklahoma in Steinbeck's *The Grapes of Wrath*. The retarded daughter emerges as a "wholly compelling character," according to Freeman, "enabling us to understand the contours of her special world." Freeman compared her as a character to Flaubert's Felicité in "A Simple Heart," the epitome of one "who endures, with a kind of quiet nobility, the hardships of her life."

In Lott's novel *Reed's Beach*, a couple tries to come to terms with each other and with the rest of their lives after the death of their only son in a traffic accident. They go to the New Jersey shore to spend time in a borrowed cottage. There, after befriending neighbors, a strange old couple who reverse traditional roles—he cooks, she builds—they begin to express their grief and restore their lives. As James Polk put it in the *New York Times Book Review* (February 13, 1994), "through a community of secret sufferers . . . they gradually learn a shared vocabulary of loss." The wife makes a decision not to renew her birth control prescription: "Nor would she tell him the secret, but would keep it, hold it tight, just as she would hold tight her memory of the taste of each pill and how on that taste she saw her son's face, the touch of their own blood in his looks, his gestures, his words. With her surrender to the next child they would find, she would make new room in her heart to hold close two snow angels, wings touching, flying together, and to hold close the troll of the forest and to hold close her son's figure receding into snow-filled woods, herself following him, calling his name, calling him."

Polk, although he conceded that criticizing a novel with such a theme might be comparable to "criticizing what the widow wore to the funeral," considered *Reed's Beach* a failure: "Lott has overwhelmed with interminable introspection a story that cries out for simplicity. He appears not to trust us to figure out for ourselves what motivates his characters and so tells us endlessly, using too may words to describe what no words really can."

In the 1996 collection of a novella and stories, *How to Get Home*, Lott returned to a spare style, with results that a *Publishers Weekly* (June 17, 1996) reviewer termed "breathtaking." "Thanks to incisive, empathetic characterization and graceful prose, these 16 stories and one novella of often difficult situations—adultery, job loss, the death of a spouse—exude energy and wisdom," the reviewer commented. The novella, "After Leston," has as its protagonist a newly widowed woman—Jewel, the title character of Lott's earlier novel—who must take care of her mentally retarded daughter. Barbara Quick in the *New York Times Book Review* (Au-

gust 4, 1996) called "After Leston" "a model of compression, spare writing, and poignancy . . . a simple story told by a plainspoken woman." Quick found that although the story is simple, "it speaks volumes about love and loss, about the competition between our own ideas about the world and those of the people nearest to us—about where a family ends and an individual begins." All the stories in the volume evoke "the yearning to find home . . . that is felt by the nomadic citizens of late-20th-century America."

Lott's memoir *Fathers, Sons, and Brothers: The Men in My Family* was described as "engrossing" by the *Publishers Weekly* (April 14, 1997) reviewer. Permeated by a vivid sense of the importance of connection, the book deals with "the similarities and differences in outlook between generations. . . . Lott sees how the humorous stories that his uncles and father tell about their adolescent adventures are reflected in what he and his brothers remember of their youthful days, and he wonders what stories his sons will pass on."

In *Booklist* (February 1, 1998), the reviewer, Joanne Wilkinson, cautioned readers not to be fooled by the billing of Lott's book *The Hunt Club* (1998) as a thriller—for "at the heart of this wonderfully well written novel is a haunting coming-of-age story." The event that sets the novel in motion is 15-year-old Huger Dillard's discovery of a headless corpse. "The thriller aspect of the tale, though suspenseful, is somewhat convoluted and suffers from erratic pacing," Wilkinson wrote. "However, Lott's lyrical descriptions of the landscape in the Low Country around Charleston and his delicate unveiling of the mystery of Huger's parentage are terrific. This may well give Lott and his layered, hypnotic prose the visibility they so richly deserve."

In an article in the *Gettysburg Review* (Autumn 1995) that reads like a short story, Lott described a walk taken with his younger son, Jacob, after an unusual snowfall in Charleston, South Carolina. From that jumping-off point he reflected back on Jacob's birth: "a baby wet with blood and fluids and howling . . . and he's warm, this thing is *warm*, and he's crying, and now I'm crying. . . ." He also moved forward in time to when Jacob, after a tonsillectomy, refuses to finish a popsicle; after Lott has chided the boy for having pestered him for the popsicle, it turns out that the child's throat is hemorrhaging and that he has to be rushed to the hospital, and Lott feels a terrible guilt for having yelled at him. Lott concluded the piece with a description of "what fatherhood is about," a passage that might sum up his recipe for a story: "stupidity, adventure, threats, silence, blood, fear. The immensity of a night sky. Love. . . . All this lies before us, and behind us. For now, though, there is only this moment, the two of us on a street glazed with ice, the world growing blue."

—S. Y.

SUGGESTED READING: *Booklist* p 899+ Feb. 1, 1998; *Gettysburg Review* p561+ Autumn 1995; *New York Times Book Review* p21 Mar. 1, 1992, p18 Feb. 13, 1994, p18 Aug. 4, 1996; *Publishers Weekly* p48 June 17, 1996, p61 Apr. 14, 1997

SELECTED BOOKS: Fiction—*The Man Who Owned Vermont*, 1987; *A Stranger's House*, 1988; *A Dream of Old Leaves*, 1989; *Jewel*, 1992; *Reed's Beach*, 1993; *How to Get Home*, 1996; *The Hunt Club*, 1998; Nonfiction—*Fathers, Sons, and Brothers: The Men in My Family*, 1997

Loury, Glenn C.

Sep. 3, 1948– Nonfiction writer; essayist; columnist; economist

Considered a "neoconservative" among African-American scholars for his advocacy of the self-help strategy of Booker T. Washington over the protest-oriented one of W. E. B. Du Bois, the economist and university professor Glenn C. Loury first came to national prominence during the Reagan administration, when issues like affirmative action, welfare reform, and the demonization of the black underclass were at the forefront of the national agenda. After strenuously advocating a new debate on racial matters that went beyond the DuBoisian civil-rights strategy of the 1950s and 1960s, Loury, a Harvard faculty member, was poised for appointment to a subcabinet position in the Reagan administration until his personal life came unraveled due to serious drug-abuse problems. Crediting a born-again Christian experience for catalyzing his recovery, Loury overcame his personal demons to return to life as an academician and writer. He joined the economics faculty of Boston University in 1991 and, in 1995, saw the publication of *One By One From the Inside Out*, a book-length collection of his essays and reviews. In 1996 he became a contributing editor for the *New Republic* magazine.

Glenn Cartman Loury was born on September 3, 1948 in a working-class African-American enclave on the South Side of Chicago known as Park Manor, where he lived with his mother, stepfather, and younger sister. Robert S. Boynton's profile of Loury in the *New Yorker* (May 1, 1995) offers many details of his upbringing. Loury's father was "a successful civil servant with the Internal Revenue Service who went to law school at night," and his uncle Adlert was an assistant state's attorney in Illinois. Describing other relatives involved in less savory occupations, Loury told Boynton: "My family spanned the entire continuum of engagement with conventional society. And although I was on the most conventional end of it, I was nevertheless intimately connected to the rest." As a youngster, he refused overtures from cousins who wanted to convert him to the Nation of Islam. He belonged to the "square and soft" group of neighborhood kids known as the Ivy Leaguers, though he admitted to fathering two children by a girlfriend, whom he eventually married. After five years, they separated, and he later married Linda Datcher, with whom he had two sons born in the 1990s, Glenn Jr. and Nehemiah.

Loury graduated with honors from Harlan High School and attended a technical college for a short time, but quit to work in a printery. When he was 18, Loury underwent a profound experience that was to inform his viewpoint on racial identity for the rest of his life. He related the incident in the prologue to his 1995 book, *One By One From the Inside Out* (an earlier version of the text had appeared in *Commentary* in October 1992, and it was reprinted in Gerald Early's 1994 anthology, *Lure and Loathing*). As he told it, Loury experienced shame after he pusillanimously refrained from vouching for a close childhood friend, Woody, a "very light-skinned" youth whose racial credentials were being questioned at a black-power rally they were both attending. "Upon reflection," he wrote in his prologue, "my refusal to stand up for Woody exposed the tenuous quality of my personal sense of racial authenticity. The fact is, I willingly betrayed someone I had known for a decade, a person whom I loved and who loved me, in order to avoid the risk of being rejected by strangers . . . I had feared that to proclaim before the black radicals in the audience that this 'white boy' at my side was in fact our 'brother' would have compromised my own chance of being received among them as a genuine colleague."

Awarded a scholarship to Northwestern University, Loury received a bachelor of arts degree in mathematics there in 1972; he was the outstanding graduate of the math department. He received his Ph.D. in economics in 1979 from the Massachusetts Institute of Technology, where he studied with Robert M. Solow and Paul Samuelson. Recalling his star pupil, Solow was quoted in Boynton's *New Yorker* profile as saying: "Glenn was an extraordinarily bright student, absolutely first class . . . There is no doubt in my mind that had he continued in economic theory he had the talent to win the Clark Medal"—described as "an award that is considered a prelude to a Nobel Prize in Economics." Loury returned to Northwestern in 1976 as an assistant professor of economics, and from 1980 to 1982, he was a professor at the University of Michigan, after which he became a professor of political economy at Harvard University's John F. Kennedy School of Government. Loury was candid in his explanation for the move, telling Boynton, "I choked. I was just too terrified that I would fail to make the grade in economics. Moving to the Kennedy School was a good cover story for my little crisis." Since 1991, after his recovery from serious personal problems involving substance abuse, he has been professor of economics at Boston University.

Loury first came to national prominence in the early 1980s, during the first Reagan administration, when he began publishing articles in scholarly journals and right-of-center political periodicals that showed that his philosophy had diverged from the ideology and strategy that the civil-rights movement had adopted since the desegregation and voting-rights struggles of the 1950s and 1960s. One of the first of these articles, his landmark "The Moral Quandary of the Black Community," appeared in *Public Interest* in Spring 1985 and was reprinted in *One By One From the Inside Out*. Declaring the emergence of "the post civil-rights era," Loury wrote that "the civil rights strategy—seeking black advancement through the use of the legal system to force America to live by its espoused creed—has reached the point of diminishing returns." The essay opened with these words: "The civil rights movement now confronts its greatest challenge—to redefine an agenda created during the turbulent 1950s and 1960s, so that it may conform with the sociopolitical realities of the 1990s and beyond. My argument here is that this redefinition should be centered around an effort to expand the range of activities that directly seek to mitigate the worst conditions of lower-class black life." In this essay, Loury reminded his readers of the long tradition of self-help that had characterized the black community since long before Emancipation, and concluded: "It is now beyond dispute that many of the problems of contemporary black American life lie outside the reach of effective government action, and require for their successful resolution actions that can be undertaken only by the black community itself." While he did not discount the pervasiveness of racism, Loury maintained that the pathologies of the black underclass will not be solved by ideas in the mold of the Great Society or other federally funded liberal-Democratic programs. He stopped short of arguing, however, that government should be absolved of all responsibility. "For blacks, the problem has always been not the existence of racism but its management," he wrote. Criticizing black-on-black violence and the failure of many blacks to achieve educational or economic success, Loury endorsed Senator Daniel Patrick Moynihan's classic analysis of the problems of the black underclass, which blamed single-parent families for black America's ills. He further rejected as specious the argument that the pathologies of the black underclass are merely the results of racist oppression. "Blacks' problems lie not in the heads of white people," he wrote, "but rather in the wasted and incompletely fulfilled lives of too many black people." "The pride and self-respect valued by aspiring peoples throughout the world cannot be the gift of outsiders," he wrote; "they must derive from the thoughts and deeds of the people themselves." Addressing a National Urban Coalition meeting in 1984, Loury reportedly reduced Coretta Scott King to tears with a blunt speech that included these words: "The real problem is the black poor. You've exhausted your moral capital with your whining. Legislative solutions won't do any good. In short, the civil-rights movement is over."

Despite his characteristic bluntness, Loury has always taken pains to situate his commentary squarely within the historical tradition framed by the two towering intellectuals of early 20th-century racialist thought: Booker T. Washington and W. E. B. DuBois. Indeed, Loury believes that he is simply reviving the old debate that confronted American Negroes in the early 1900s, when they were asked to choose between the gradualism of Washington and the more confrontational nationalism of DuBois. In the essay "Two Paths to Black Progress," written for a journal of the Institute of Religion and Public Life (*First Things*, October 1992) and reprinted in *One by One From the Inside Out*, Loury discussed these options in depth, while making clear his belief that the DuBois alternative had now exhausted itself. The late black Supreme Court Justice Thurgood Marshall represented the DuBois tradition, he thought, while newly installed Justice Clarence Thomas heralded a return to the Washington approach, as described in words with which Loury concluded his essay: "Advocates of a new public philosophy for black Americans, like Clarence Thomas, are drawing on an old wisdom that is well suited for our times. . . . [T]o take this line of departure from the orthodoxy of the day is to speak what, for many blacks, is a truth inherited from our ancestors: a truth we know as a result of our awareness of our history coming out of slavery, and a truth reflected in the ambiguous but great legacy of Booker T. Washington."

His advocacy of such positions during the 1980s had earned Loury the praise of such neoconservative thinkers as Irving Kristol, Norman Podhoretz, and others favored by the Reagan White House. Boynton offered this explanation for Loury's lionization: "In addition to a keen intelligence and a forceful style, Loury had an impressive Horatio Alger background. . . . His scholarship was rigorous and eloquent, he was personally charming, and, most important, he was black." In 1987 Loury was about to be named Deputy Secretary of Education, but he abruptly withdrew his nomination for "personal reasons." It was revealed that Loury had developed a serious substance-abuse problem, with a pattern of dysfunctional behavior; he was also being accused of assaulting a 23-year-old woman whom he had been supporting financially, maintaining her in a Boston apartment without the knowledge of his wife. Although the charges were later dropped, the incident marked the beginning of a downward spiral for Loury. Several months later, he was arrested for possessing marijuana and cocaine, and after a marathon session of freebasing cocaine, he entered a Boston hospital for rehabilitation, later moving to a halfway house.

Loury spent the next four years trying to mend his shattered life. During this period he underwent a born-again Christian experience that he credits for his eventual recovery. Soon afterward, he and his wife had a child, Glenn Jr., an act Loury interpreted as a symbol of his own rebirth, since earlier attempts at conception had failed. The couple had a second son, whom they named Nehemiah, after the Old Testament prophet who convinced the Jews to overcome their despair and rebuild the walls of Jerusalem. Loury connected his harrowing personal experiences with his own pronouncements on self-help, writing, "What does it really *mean* for a city not to have walls? It's a powerful metaphor, and closely related to black people's situation today. A city without walls has no integrity, or structure; it is subject to the vagaries of any fad or fancy. Without walls, you are lost, as opposed to having some kind of internally derived sense of who you are to help you decide what you will and won't do." In 1991, fortified with his newfound faith in God and himself, Loury joined the Boston University faculty and began concentrating on economic theory, which had been his original field of study. It seemed for a while that he was retreating from the commentary on racial and social issues that had earned him such notoriety during the 1980s. The controversial nomination of Clarence Thomas to the Supreme Court in 1991 galvanized Loury into action, however, and he soon reentered the cultural wars with further refinements of some of the positions he had taken earlier. To Loury, the Thomas affair proved his contention that not all black people shared a single, "politically correct" opinion. As he complained to Peter Applebome of the *New York Times* (July 13, 1991), "There's an expectation you're going to hear something from blacks, and when you don't hear it, you get defined as a conservative." Likewise, Loury tried to dispel the illusion that all blacks were overwhelmingly supportive of affirmative action. His "restoration to grace" was further assured with the reappearance of his byline in periodicals and academic publications. Loury's groundbreaking essay "Free At Last: A Personal Perspective on Race and Identity in America" appeared as the first selection in Gerald Early's 1994 book *Lure and Loathing: Essays on Race, Identity, and the Ambivalence of Assimilation*. Reviewing *Lure and Loathing* for the *Washington Post* (May 9, 1993), Matthew Rees described Loury's "contrarian view" as the "most insightful" of all the essays: "Loury concludes that it is detrimental for blacks to stake their personal identity entirely on their race, saying that to do so is to embrace 'too parochial a conception of what is possible and what is desirable.'" Boynton later wrote in his 1995 *New Yorker* profile: "Now that Loury's arguments about the importance of intact families and the role of behavior in the formation of the underclass don't sound quite so radical, he hopes that his diagnosis may receive a second hearing." Among Loury's most loyal defenders have been the iconoclastic black essayists Shelby Steele and Stanley Crouch, the latter quoted by Boynton as saying: "Look, a lot of people smoke crack and have kids out of wedlock and *don't* have anything important to say . . . For all his foibles, Glenn Loury does."

In 1995 the Free Press published Loury's only book to date, *One by One from the Inside Out*, a collection of about two dozen of his essays and book reviews, most of them dating from the period after his rehabilitation. In the book's final essay, an epilogue entitled "New Life: A Professor and *Veritas*," he alternated between the rhetoric of preachers and the reasoned cadences of the academy in describing the spiritual journey that led to his return to productive living. "For the fact is that I have been born again," he wrote. "I was dead and now I am alive, not because of my own recuperative powers, but due to the power of Christ to mend a broken life, to 'restore the years the locusts have eaten.'" Discussing the writings of Charles Colson, whom Loury describes as "the Christian apologist who is an infamous figure from the Watergate era," he confessed hubris to be "the sin in which I was entrapped . . . I suffered from a vastly inflated sense of my own self-importance. I thought of myself as the center of the universe . . . Nothing seemed beyond my grasp; the rules (whether moral or legal) were for others, not for me." The book was soundly criticized in the pages of *The New Republic* (May 21, 1995) by its senior editor, Michael Kaus, though the periodical invited Loury to join its stable of contributing editors less than a year later. Kaus wrote: "What is striking about this book is not how Mr. Loury's thinking has evolved, but how it hasn't. The collection's various pieces, written in wildly varying political climates over the course of a decade, add up to a coherent, cuttingly idiosyncratic position on the race issue and its attendant controversies (including affirmative action). It turns out that Mr. Loury is not now, nor has he ever been, a full-fledged conservative. But his vision is certainly not liberal, and it is not neoliberal. It is also not complete. What it offers is a good opener for the more candid national 'conversation' that Mr. Loury says is needed regarding America's great social problem." Still, Kaus thought the book was "valuable" and that its author wrote "with clarity and power, if not an excess of entertaining detail. . . . Mr. Loury recognizes that the way to resolve America's race problem is to find a solution for its underclass problem, and he is willing to make an enemy of anyone who stands in the way of that solution. He just doesn't know what it is." Richard Bernstein, who reviewed the book for the *New York Times* (August 11, 1995), was similarly disappointed. He faulted Loury for not giving a "full accounting" of his run-ins with the law during his personal crisis in the late 1980s, but credited him for at least confessing to his errors. "The main fault in Mr. Loury's collection," Bernstein wrote, "is that he dwells too much on the fault of others and not enough on the practical solutions to the black plight, as might be expected of a professor of economics. . . . Sadly, . . . Mr. Loury's reach is too limited."

Despite these disappointing reviews, Loury accelerated his appearances and statements on public issues. He and Robert L. Woodson announced they were severing their ties with the American Enterprise Institute because of their objections to Dinesh D'Souza's newly published book, *The End of Racism*, citing the fact that the conservative think tank had sponsored D'Souza as a research fellow. William Raspberry quoted Loury on the subject in the *Washington Post* (September 18, 1995): "'I don't disagree with everything D'Souza has to say,' [Loury] says, 'but the intemperate, irreverent, insulting way in which his book is written so offends me . . . to be silent in the face of this book, written by a conservative colleague, would make us Uncle Toms.'" Loury clarified his remarks in an interview with the same newspaper several days later (September 22, 1995): "I agree with many of [D'Souza's] policy positions. . . . but I'm very upset with Mr. D'Souza when he writes about civilization and barbarism when it's applied to a constituent part of the United States of America. These people living in ghetto America are no such thing. They didn't invent feminism, gay rights activism, Menendez brothers relativism. Why would he be projecting all the serious problems of American civilization onto these suffering few? It really is madness."

Loury also testified with other conservatives, William J. Bennett and the Reverend Dave Camp, before a House Ways and Means subcommittee in support of the Republicans' welfare-reform proposal, which would deny cash payments to unmarried teenage mothers. On the occasion of his elder son's admission to a public school in Boston, Loury wrote an essay for the *Washington Post Book World* (August 6, 1995) in which he urged African-American parents to adopt a self-help strategy in supporting their children with positive learning environments at home, emulating the practice he saw in many Asian-American communities. Speaking "as a middle class black American," he wrote: "We must now spare no effort to ensure that our children take their rightful place as fully equal participants in the national enterprise. Today the schools are the primary arena within which this 'race' is being run. We had better get busy." When Louis Farrakhan announced plans for his Million Man March in Washington, D.C., in the fall of 1995, Loury emerged as a firm and vocal critic. Appearing with Farrakhan on the television interview show *This Week With David Brinkley*, Loury was quoted in the next day's *Washington Post* (October 9, 1995) as saying: "Look, if I had a million black men together to do something, I wouldn't march them to Washington . . . I'd march them into these housing projects. I'd march them into these orphanages. I'd clean up the trash from these communities. I'd deal with drugs. I would march them to the boys who don't have fathers and try to reconstruct the civil life of the African American community." Responding to the "media-generated national theater" in the O. J. Simpson verdict, he wrote in an essay, also published in the *Washington Post* (October 15, 1995): "Notwithstanding the disparity of perception, the objective social reality

in America can be read to suggest that the circumstances of blacks and whites are not growing apart, but instead are converging." He told his readers: "It is worth remembering that the so-called 'black underclass' is a relatively small fraction of the total black population —perhaps 3 to 5 million out of 32 million persons. (Keep in mind too that not every poor person is a member of the underclass) . . . Yet just about every social problem of concern to Americans today occurs in far larger absolute numbers among whites than among blacks and derives from broad social and economic forces affecting all Americans."

Since 1996 Loury has been a contributing editor at the *New Republic*, where his commentary on social and economic issues is regularly printed in that magazine's "The Hard Questions" column. His first contribution to that publication came in the magazine's January 1, 1996 issue, entitled "White Lies, Black Lives: Rethinking Race and Crime." In a column called "Black Americans' Impossible Dilemma," Loury angered many of his racemates by reiterating his claim that urban violence was a predominantly black-on-black phenomenon. "Black criminals generally prey on their own," he declared, much to the discomfort of some. "Urban violence on such a scale, involving blacks as both perpetrators and victims, poses a profound dilemma for black leaders and intellectuals," who must "counter the demonization of young black men in which the majority culture is now feverishly engaged." According to Loury, the criminal activities whites have come to associate with inner-city youth has bred a contempt that "has in turn produced a truly remarkable degree of publicly expressed disrespect and disdain for blacks." He added, "Middle-class blacks must admit, and begin to overcome, their fear in the face of this carnage. We are afraid to go into these communities. We do not recognize these kids as us; the distance is great and difficult to bridge. We are also embarrassed by their behavior; we pick up the newspaper with trepidation, bracing ourselves for news that the latest crime has been committed by a black person. This silence cannot continue." Despite his earlier inveighing against the Million Man March, he admitted that its participants "seemed instinctively to understand this." Loury also took pains to praise such "tough-love" advocates as Brooklyn's Reverend Johnny Ray Youngblood and others who are preaching a new gospel of self-discipline and dignity.

In another "Hard Questions" essay (*New Republic*, May 19, 1997), Loury argued in favor of Afrocentric education, out of the need to "project positive racial images to . . . students," while he cautioned against its over-romanticized and even racist images ("there are racists among the black nationalists who trumpet a glorious African past," he wrote). He concluded his essay with the exhortation: "Forget about the influence of Africa on Egypt 2,500 years ago. It is the influence of Africa on America over the past 250 years that deserves our attention."

—E. M.

SUGGESTED READING: *American Enterprise* p29+ Nov. 1995, with photo, p92+ Mar. 1996; *Booklist* p1458 Apr. 15, 1995; *Christianity Today* p17+ Jan. 8, 1996, with photo; *Economist* p32 July 6, 1996; *Essence* p68 Nov. 1995; *Insight* p58+ Apr. 10, 1989; *Jet* p16 Oct. 9, 1995, with photo; *Mother Jones* p5+ Mar. 1993; *Nation* p567+ Apr. 24, 1995; *National Review* p56+ June 26, 1995; *New Republic* p21+ Jan. 1, 1996, p25 May 19, 1997, p25 June 30, 1997, p29 Oct. 13, 1997, p9+ Jan. 5–12, 1998, p16+ Feb. 23, 1998, p10+ Apr. 6, 1998, p10+ May 18, 1998, p14+ June 29, 1998; *New Yorker* p33+ May 1, 1995, with drawing; *New York Times* p1 July 13, 1991, with photo, C p29 Aug. 11, 1995, with photo, p24 Nov. 5, 1995, p26 Aug. 1, 1996, D p15 Nov. 24, 1996, with drawing, A p23 Apr. 23, 1997, with photo, A p10 Sep. 1, 1997, D p17 Sep. 7, 1997, D p9 Nov. 30, 1997, D p16 Dec. 7, 1997; *New York Times Book Review* p3 May 21, 1995, with drawing, p11 June 23, 1996, with drawing; *Public Interest* p125+ Winter 1996; *Publishers Weekly* p49 Mar. 20, 1995; *Reason* p60+ May 1995; *Washington Post* X p6 May 9, 1993, with photo, C p2 Feb. 13, 1994, A p6 Jan. 21, 1995, C p1 Apr. 2, 1995, A p19 Sep. 18, 1995, F p3 Sep. 20, 1995, D p1 Sep. 22, 1995, B p1 Oct. 8, 1995, A p12 Oct. 9, 1995, C p3 Oct. 15, 1995, C p1 Dec. 17, 1995, C p3 July 21, 1996, A p31 Nov. 22, 1996, A p27 Mar. 21, 1997; *Washington Post Book World* p1 Aug. 6, 1995; *Wilson Quarterly* p77+ Summer 1995

SELECTED BOOKS: *One By One From the Inside Out*, 1995

Barnaby Hall/Courtesy of Houghton Mifflin

Lux, Thomas

Dec. 10, 1946– Poet

The noted poet Thomas Lux has stressed the importance of poetry in American society for a number of years. The author of several collections of poetry, including *The Glassblower's Breath* (1976), *Sundays* (1979), *Half Promised Land* (1986), *The Drowned River* (1990), and *Split Horizon* (1994), Lux emphasizes the importance of accessible poetry in both his own work and in his lectures at Sarah Lawrence College, where he teaches English. A reviewer for Amazon.com, the Internet bookseller,

remarked on Lux's work: "His writing has escaped the confines of academia, bringing a ringing lyricism, raw humor, and a raging heart to the stuff of everyday life. More accessible than lofty his poems still retain a mysterious awe for language."

Thomas Lux was born on December 10, 1946, in Northampton, Massachusetts, the son of N. O. Lux and the former Eleanor Healey. The future poet was raised on a small dairy farm, run by his grandfather and uncle; his own father was the milkman. Many of the sounds and sights of farm life would remain with him all of his life and later become a part of his poetry. In 1966 he enrolled at Emerson College in Boston, where he became immersed in the college's fledgling writing program. In a profile of the poet for *Ploughshares* (Winter 1998–99), the poet's professor James Randall recalled: "In the late 1960s when Lux came to us, the writing program was new. He looked vaguely like a hobo in dress and manner, but he stayed on. There was a freshness and openness about him, and he spread his enthusiasms to others. Before we knew it, we had a serious poetry group at our college."

After Lux graduated from Emerson in 1970, he was asked to stay on as the school's poet-in-residence. He did so until the fall of 1971, when he enrolled at the famed Writers' Workshop at the University of Iowa. He stayed in Iowa until the spring of 1972, but left without graduating in order to return to Emerson. In 1975 he took a position at Sarah Lawrence College in Bronxville, New York, where he continues to teach English and writing. In his lectures and interviews, he advocates poetry that is original and comprehensible to the reader, not murky and obscure for the sake of being so. In an interview with Donna Greene of the *New York Times* (January 4, 1998), the poet noted how poetry was considerably more accessible in the 19th century, "but with modernism came this new notion that poetry is something that is not as direct or accessible, and poetry became something that needed to be deciphered, a kind of riddle. . . . And, of course, a lot of people are put off by this. A lot of people read poetry, and they don't understand it and it makes them feel resentful. They also tend to think if they don't understand it that means it's good poetry because you're not supposed to understand poetry. We've been conditioned in this century to believe this. And, of course, that makes a lot of people not want to read it."

In 1970 Lux published *The Land Sighted*, his first chapbook of poetry, under the imprint run by his professor James Randall. This collaboration between professor and student was renewed two years later with the release of *Memory's Handgrenade*, Lux's first full-length collection. At the same time, the young poet started his own small press, Barn Dream Press, with the aid of Joe Wilmott and Patrick Botacchi. They published several struggling young poets, including Marvin Bell, Paul Hannigan, Bill Knott, William Matthews, and Charles Wright.

In 1976 Lux published *The Glassblower's Breath*, a collection printed by Cleveland State University Press. Three years later he was well on his way to critical recognition on a national level with the publication of his collection *Sundays* (1979) by Houghton Mifflin. William Logan, reviewing the book for *Library Journal* (September 1, 1979), wrote: "Lux has mastered a surrealism that, unlike the giddiness of James Tate's or Bill Knott's, equates surprise with seriousness. . . . Despite some arbitrary details and slack exercises, Lux has moved, like Charles Simic, toward making the surreal an alternate vision of the world. Recommended." David Kalstone, writing for the *New York Times Book Review* (May 4, 1980), had mixed feelings on *Sundays*. He wrote: "Mr. Lux's poems are often good at identifying a lyric occasion, but don't structure the poem to catch his feelings on the move. Frequently a poem will seem undernourished. . . . It is odd to find a writer so well along in his career and so wasteful of his insights since on occasion he is more tautly focused, as in the haunting 'Graveyard by the Sea.'"

Four years later, Lux produced a new collection of poems for Houghton Mifflin, *Half Promised Land* (1986). In it, the author used his childhood memories of life on the dairy farm as metaphors for the struggle between his ideals and reality. A critic for *Choice* (November 1986) praised this outing highly: "Sometimes the poems falter, swinging away into urban scenes and attempts at social comment that show us little new. Sometimes the poems clearly exist as mere staging for tricky endings. Yet, when the poet stays close to his first love, he is effective, as when he convincingly presents wild watercress . . . Lux's forte is magic." Daniel L. Guillory, writing for *Library Journal* (May 15, 1986), cheered: "Lux is an entertaining and inventive poet, painfully aware of the 'half promised land' of death, which he opposes with a powerful imagination. . . . [This book] heightens the read-

er's sensory awareness of every page, evoking a whole range of imagery, not merely the visual but the auditory . . . and the olfactory. . . . Highly recommended for all collections."

In his next collection, *The Drowned River* (1990), Lux took on the daily struggle of everyday human beings, reminiscing about people throughout history over the course of 48 poems. He was widely praised for his efforts. Beatrix Gates in the *Nation* (January 21, 1991) wrote: "Lux describes us as 'drowned' in the full tilt of living, in the flood of history and in our own short breath relative to time's long view. . . . There are terrible songs in this book, terrible because their construction is so beautiful. . . . The clear-eyed detail in [the author's] poems stuns." Noting that Lux "chooses . . . to exploit the ironic, the harsh, the grotesque" in life, Fred Muratori remarked in *Library Journal* (February 15, 1990): "Though Lux's points may sometimes be less disturbing than they are obvious, his vision of the world is bleak and ornate at the same time, and his use of formal prosody actually enhances the weirdness."

Lux's collection of poetry *Split Horizon* was published in 1994 to very positive reviews. Remarking on the author's surreal and comic abilities as a poet, Fred Muratori of *Library Journal* (August 1994) noted "what saves all this from seeming too 1970s–frivolous is Lux's very astute ear, as in describing a storm: 'when your house bears/the branches' lash, big winds/life and slam the clapboards.' And it's the nick-of-time humor that rejuvenates and restores perspective in an otherwise overbearing atmosphere of ironic pessimism, just as it should—Lux seems to be telling us—in real life as well." In his *Antioch Review* (Summer 1995) article, Dan McGuinness enthused: "Let there be Lux. And here is Lux with another set of missives from the land of plain talk. We all want to get there but don't know the way. Lux could light us but we'd still get lost in our specific interioralities. But he tries, in a kind of poem that brims with joy and says 'Look what I just found.'" In 1995 Lux was presented with the Kingsley Tufts Poetry Award for *Split Horizon*, one of the most lucrative poetry prizes presented in the United States.

In recent years Lux has kept busy amassing collections of poetry by himself and others. In 1994, with the aid of Jane Cooper and Sylvia Winner, Lux edited *The Sanity of Earth and Grass: the Complete Poems of Robert Winner*. Winner—a quadriplegic since age 16 after a diving accident—died in 1986. Lux, Cooper, and Sylvia Winner gathered all of Winner's work from his two previously published collections, along with 31 unpublished poems. "In two very personal forewords, Thomas Lux and Jane Cooper remember Winner . . . as brave, honest, tender, and funny. All these adjectives apply to his poetry. Each poem shows his love for language and sincere emotion," wrote Elizabeth Gunderson in her review for *Booklist* (June 1–15, 1994).

In 1996 Lux gathered his own poems for *The Blind Swimmer: Selected Early Poems 1970–1975*. He followed this collection the next year with *New and Selected Poems 1975–1995*. Janet St. John, in a very favorable review for *Booklist* (July 19, 1997), believed that this collection proved that Lux "is a biographer of the ordinary, and perhaps because of that, a chronicler of our times."

Thomas Lux lives in upstate New York near Sarah Lawrence College, where he continues to teach. He is divorced; his daughter, Claudia, has often been a subject of his poetry. He has been the recipient of a number of awards, including a 1970 Bread Loaf scholarship and a MacDowell Colony fellowship for 1973. He continually promotes the importance of poetry in his interviews and articles for magazines and newspapers, and he frequently gives readings of his own poetry around the country. In addition to lecturing and writing, he has been the managing editor of the *Iowa Review* (1971–1992) and *Ploughshares* (1973).

C.M.

SUGGESTED READING: *Antioch Review* p 382, Summer 1995; *Atlantic* Oct. 1998; *Booklist* p 1763, June 1–15, 1994; July 19, 1997; *Choice* p 478, Nov. 1986; *Library Journal* p 1703, Sep. 1, 1979; p 189, Feb. 15, 1980; May 15, 1986; p 91, Aug. 1994; *Nation* p 64, Jan. 21, 1991; *New York Times* Sect. 14WC p 3, Jan. 4, 1998; *New York Times Book Review* p 15, May 4, 1980; p 20, Apr. 19, 1987; *Ploughshares* Winter 1998–99; *Washington Post Book World* p 2, Nov. 2, 1997

SELECTED WORKS: Poetry—*The Land Sighted*, 1970; *Memory's Handgrenade*, 1972; *The Glassblower's Breath*, 1976; *Sundays*, 1979; *Half-Promised Land*, 1986; *The Drowned River*, 1990; *Split Horizon*, 1994; *The Blind Swimmer: Selected Early Poems 1970–1975*; *New and Selected Poems: 1975–1995*; As co-editor—*The Sanity of Earth and Grass: Complete Poems of Robert Winner*, 1994

Maalouf, Amin

Feb. 25, 1949– Novelist; journalist

Amin Maalouf, a Lebanese expatriate novelist living in France, writes from a dual cultural perspective—that of an Arab Christian now in the West—and tries to include various cultural perspectives in his fictional narratives. He won the prestigious Prix Goncourt in 1993 for his novel *The Rock of Tanios*, which one reviewer described as "a vision of love in Lebanon in 1830 and a moving historical re-creation of the country's past." Faced with the crisis of the Lebanese civil war in the mid-1970s, he had given up a promising career in journalism to devote himself to "telling stories" about the human condition that are frequently drowned out by the rhetoric of nationalism and xenophobia.

For *World Authors 1990–1995*, Amin Maalouf writes (in French): "I was born in Beirut, Lebanon, on February 25, 1949. My parents were married in Egypt, where my mother was living. My father, Ruchdi Maalouf, was a writer, teacher, and journalist. As for myself, after studying sociology and economics, I began working as a journalist in 1971. During this period, I took numerous journeys, such as to Vietnam just after the fall of Saigon, and to India, Bangladesh, Ethiopia, Somalia, Kenya, Yemen, and Algeria.

"On April 13, 1975, something happened that changed the course of my life. I returned that morning from a long trip to Asia when a bomb exploded under the window of apartment. The first big violent incident of the Lebanese civil war had taken place under my very eyes. I could count about 20 dead bodies lying in my street. The country sank into horror, and my life with it. After 14 months of hesitation, during which time daily life had become more and more difficult for me and those close to me, I decided to emigrate. In the absence of any other mode of transport, I left on a ship bound for Cyprus, then flew on to Paris. My wife and my three children joined me there several weeks later. Ever since, we have been living in France.

"In Paris, I continued to work as a journalist. All I had to do was change my language: in Lebanon, I would use Arabic, my native tongue, and in France, I had to use French while working in the press. But it was the same work for me—and the same passion—keeping close tabs on world events.

"In going from one continent to another, from one cultural environment to another, and from one language to another, I was struck with the extensive lack of understanding that exists between East and West. Each event of past or present is perceived differently depending on which side of the cultural boundary one occupies. It is rare that someone takes the time to 'walk a mile in another's shoes' to see how things appear differently from the other side. This state of events led me to write my first book, *The Crusades Through Arab Eyes* (1983). It seemed to me that there was no one except me who had his foot on both sides of the Mediterranean, and that I had the duty to build in whatever way I could 'bridges' between different cultures, not necessarily to find a synthesis in them, but to reduce the risks of confrontation that have their origins in cultural differences and the resentments they engender: confrontations that often develop into bloody conflicts. I had the opportunity to observe this development in my own native country: in Lebanon, I was well aware of the period of coexistence between different communities, with interactions that were sometimes strained, but often creative and enriching, but I also experienced the opposite: the disrespect, the tearing-apart, the fanaticism, the impoverishment at once intellectual, moral, and material. A phenomenon that would soon be observed, alas, in many regions of the world in the years to come, notably in Africa and the former Communist-bloc countries.

"An idea began to haunt me, one that gave me a source of constant inspiration, an idea born out of my exile and also out of my refusal to submit to the mentality of exile. It was this: since my identity is made up of numerous parts, why should I reject certain parts that would limit me to one. Why couldn't I assume all my 'parts'? Wouldn't it impoverish me, mutilate me, if I were to cut off one of these parts of myself? I am—like so many other of my contemporaries—now at a crossroads of several cultures, several languages, several beliefs, several world views. My true homeland is all of these at once! My roots are the sum of all my parts.

"It is these convictions, and all the ruptures I have experienced in life, and all the turmoil that has beset my era, that gave birth to the six novels that I published between 1986 and 1996. The first, *Leo the African* (1986), recounts the life of a 16th-century traveler, born in Andalusia, who roamed Africa and the Mediterranean world; *Samarkand* (1988) was inspired by the life of the Persian poet Omar Khayyam, both hedonist and mystic, and enemy of bigotry and fanaticism; *The Gardens of Light* (1991) evoked Mani, reputed founder of Manichaeanism; *The First Century After Beatrice* (1992) treats, in parable form, the complex ways in which science and ethics reinforce each other in today's world, as well as the connections between the First and the Third worlds; my last two novels, *The Rock of Tanios* (1993) and *Les Echelles du Levant* (1996), deal with the recent past in the Middle East, the difficult relations between various communities, and men and women whose existence is troubled by world events.

"From the moment they were published, I have had a chance to see my books accepted by readers. They have been translated into more than 20 Eastern and Western languages, which allows me to devote all of my time to writing. For several years, I traveled little, spending most of my time in my apartment in Paris and in a little fisherman's house I acquired near the Atlantic coast. My files are full of projects for novels and essays, and I hope to have the time to complete some of them."

—tr. E. M.

When he won the Goncourt Prize in 1993, Maalouf told a reporter from *Time*, "I came to France from Lebanon with a suitcase in my hand, and now I've won the Goncourt, which I dreamed about as a child without even daring to expect it." This uncomplicated statement conceals the fact that his writings occupy a pivotal fault line in the contemporary literary world. As a Catholic Arab expatriate from Lebanon, Maalouf has attracted much critical attention for his demonstrated fluency in straddling Arabic and European cultures and for his having endowed fiction with a voice that strives to understand and accommodate both influences. He writes from a keen awareness that a shrinking world places obligations on the storyteller, especially one who tries to "re-tell" history from the point of view of the "other side." After the publication of his novel *Les Echelles du Levant*, he told an interviewer: "From the first, I saw history as an inexhaustible reserve of personalities, of events, of movements, and of eras to rediscover. . . . There is no 'objective' history in the real sense of the term. I think that each person has a memory that is all his or her own, which endows each event with a value that is not the same as for anyone else. When you tell a story, you are contributing [your share] to enriching the memory of others. . . . In truth, I've made it my profession to tell history as I see it: to transmit a certain degree of understanding, of values, of attitudes, of sensibilities. . . . And that, in my eyes, is the function of the novel."

Some 30 years after his graduation from Jesuit schools in Beirut, Maalouf wondered why he did not concentrate more in history, since that is the area that interests him most today. As a student, he felt the strong pull of journalism, following in the footsteps of his father and other members of his family: "I was interested in that since childhood," he said; "I lived in that milieu." As a reporter, in his early 20s, he traveled abroad extensively, gathering experiences of new people in faraway places that, he has said, would surface in his later work. "You accumulate lots of experience in these encounters with new countries, new cultures, diverse towns. You don't know exactly how that takes place, but these experiences always reappear in your writing, in the midst of places, personalities, and sensibilities. . . . Journalism is present in everything that I've done: sometimes by a certain way of telling a story, sometimes by the way that I address myself to my reading public, the way in which I pose a question. . . . "

After leaving war-torn Lebanon in 1976, he first made his living as a journalist in France and was part of the "Young African" press corps, writing for *Jeune Afrique* as well as several other periodicals, including *An-nahar Arabe et International*. He worked in this fashion until 1983, when he decided to devote himself to writing his first book, *Les croisades vues par les arabes* (translated into English and published in London as *The Crusades Through Arab Eyes*), summarizing his motivation for the book in these words: "Because I needed to reflect on my life, on my century."

Following this work came a series of novels, including *Léon l'Africain* (1986, tr. *Leo the African*), a romanticized biography of Hassan Al-Wazzan, also known as Jean Leon de Medicis, a Muslim who was born in Grenada, Spain, in 1488 and died in Tunisia around 1555. He had been baptized a Christian by Pope Leo X. Laurence Vidal, in the Parisian daily *Le Figaro* (November 9, 1993), wrote that this book depicted " a man who summarized in himself—and reconciled—all the contradictions, the cleavages, the conflicts of his epoch."

Maalouf's second novel, *Samarkand*, represented Maalouf's attempt to correct European misperceptions through imagining a new dialogue around Omar Khayyam's *Rubáiyat*, whose Victorian-era translation by Edward Fitzgerald introduced Arab culture to modern readers. *Samarkand* paints its own imaginative portraits of Khayyam, as well as of the despotic vizier Nizam al-Mulk and assassin leader Hassan, before fast-forwarding to the 20th century to trace the fate of Khayyam's original manuscript, discovered by a wealthy collector whose short-lived triumph ends when it—and he—are lost on the *Titanic*. Despite the impressiveness of the novel's scope and its fantastical settings, reviewers found fault with its dramatic structure. In his review for the *New York Times Book Review* (July 7, 1996), Philip Gambone wrote, for example, "Mr. Maalouf seems to want to make Samarkand—both the place and the novel—symbolize 'the inescapable meeting between man and his destiny.' . . . Paradoxically, Mr. Maalouf is a strong storyteller but not much of a dramatist, which is finally the chief disappointment of *Samarkand*. The enormous canvas on which the action is played out simply overwhelms the human dimension. In the end, one is left not so much with the satisfaction of participating in an intimate drama as with a sharpened and respectful admiration for what the narrator describes as 'the whole of the Orient.'" A reviewer for *Library Journal* (March 15, 1996) wrote in a similar vein: "Despite its exotic locales, this is a curiously dry historical novel from the author of the science fiction parable *The First Century After Beatrice*." That book, set in the 21st century, imagines the consequences of a new fertility drug that guarantees the birth of males, resulting in a scarcity of girls and women, who end up being sold and traded on the black market. It was described by a reviewer in the same publication in August 1995 as "a compelling novel" and "a thought-provoking and sometimes terrifying novel."

Maalouf explored the world of Manichaeanism in his 1995 novel *The Gardens of Light* by writing what Jon James in the *Times Literary Supplement* (December 13, 1996) called "a romantic and affectionate tale" about Mani, the founder of the religious faith that is "now little more than a crude metaphor for the conflict of good and evil." In this work, Maalouf brought his personal experience of sectarian warfare to bear on the fate of the third-century visionary reared in a community of Mesopotamian Christians called the "White-clad Brethren." James concluded: "The telling of Mani's life and of his message is one that is long overdue, yet one that—perhaps inevitably—suffers from the competing claims of history, fiction, and philosophy. In the end, however, the life of Mani, told by an author who is journalist by trade and storyteller

by nature, is the poignant story of a man born before his time."

Maalouf is not a polemical writer, but his works do resonate with emotion born out of clashing social and cultural viewpoints. In an interview with Rima Jureidini, posted on a World Wide Web site in 1997, Maalouf said of his Lebanese homeland: "I am for peace, and I think that the entire region has suffered entirely too much . . . Lebanon, in particular, has suffered, and it is time to stop the suffering and to envisage our future in a different manner. We can coexist only in an environment of liberty and of justice, where each human being is appreciated for his or her own value, not because of usefulness . . . I think that this belief is linked to my origins: when you have lived in Lebanon, the preeminent religion you have is the religion of coexistence."
—E. M.

SUGGESTED READING: *Library Journal* p96 Mar. 15, 1996, p118 Aug. 1996; *New York Times Book Review* p15 July 7, 1996; *Times Literary Supplement* p23 Dec. 13, 1996

SELECTED BOOKS IN ENGLISH TRANSLATION: *The Crusades Through Arab Eyes*, 1985; *Leo Africanus*, 1987; *Samarkand*, 1989; *The First Century After Beatrice*, 1989; *The Rock of Tanios*, 1994; *The Gardens of Light*, 1996

MacEoin, Denis

Jan. 25, 1949- Novelist

Daniel Easterman is the better known of the two pseudonyms used by prolific Irish thriller author Denis MacEoin. MacEoin, who also writes under the name Jonathan Aycliffe, is a Middle Eastern scholar whose literary fiction is enhanced by his vast knowledge of religion and politics. While his work is generally regarded as popular genre fiction, it also displays an intelligence and a deep regard for research rarely found in novels falling under the same classification. As Daniel Easterman, MacEoin writes richly detailed, exotic action-suspense novels. As Jonathan Aycliffe, he pens ghost stories that are almost old-fashioned in their sophistication. In an interview with *The Scotsman* (December 24, 1994), he remarked: "Much modern horror is relatively gross and tends to take place in an unreal world. Ghost stories, in order to work well, must be rooted in a strong sense of reality, with which the reader can identify, and relax. Into that world you introduce the ghost." The author of nine Easterman titles (translated into 10 languages) and five Aycliffe titles (translated into three languages), MacEoin has mastered the art of writing vivid, well-paced suspense novels that impress the reader with both their intelligence and their ability to inspire terror.

MacEoin, in a autobiographical sketch written for *World Authors 1990–1995*, describes his life and work: "I was born in Belfast in 1949, and grew up there until I was eighteen. My background was not propitious for a writer. Neither of my parents read more than newspapers and magazines, and I had no relatives of a literary bent. I was, however, not terribly healthy throughout my childhood. Asthma kept me at home a lot, and I managed to find enough to read to satisfy a growing appetite. *Rupert Bear* annuals (a staple of British children in the 40s and 50s, and still very popular) were my first real introduction to the world of the imagination. Later, I discovered the local library, and after that moved to one of the region's top schools.

"As a teenager, I not only read voraciously, but wrote a lot of stories and poems—all mercifully forgotten now. I also discovered a love of the theatre and studied part-time at a drama school attached to the Lyric Players Theatre, where I first learned a love of W. B. Yeats and Irish culture.

"Initially, I seemed set for some sort of career in literature. On leaving school I went to Trinity College, Dublin, where I studied English for four years. However, I'd already been converted to a religious movement known as Baha'ism, with which I remained until my early thirties. That led me in a very different direction. On leaving Dublin, I went to Edinburgh University to study Persian, Arabic, and Islamic Studies, and was transformed into a fully-fledged academic. From Edinburgh, I went to Cambridge, studying for a Ph.D. at King's College from 1975 to 1979. The thought of a career in fiction now seemed impossibly remote.

"In 1975 I married my wife Beth. We've been together now for twenty-two years, we're more in love than ever, and we spend as much time in one another's company as we can. She has degrees in English and Art History, but she later studied to be a homeopath. Now, she's not just a successful practitioner, but the author of several books on health, beauty, and related matters.

"In 1979 Beth and I moved briefly to Morocco, where we taught at the University of Fez. We had big problems there, the worst of which was that most of my salary remained unpaid. Since my academic books and papers were now either at sea or in boxes, I took the opportunity to write part of what became my first novel, *The Last Assassin*. With an Iranian setting and a plot drawing on political events after the Iranian Revolution, it seemed the right way for an academic with my training to move into fiction.

"On returning to Britain, we lived for nine months at Beth's old home in Wales, where I completed work on the novel. A post teaching Arabic and Islamic Studies came up in Newcastle Upon Tyne, and we moved there in 1981. After long efforts, I finally found an agent and sold *The Last Assassin* to my first publisher, Hodder and Stoughton.

"With my second book, *The Seventh Sanctuary*, which is set in Israel and the deserts of Saudi Arabia, I moved to Grafton Books, who became part of Collins, who became Harper Collins. I've been with them ever since, both in the U.K. and the U.S.

"My post at Newcastle University was not renewed in 1986. It had been funded by the Saudi government, who did not like the way I taught Islam, and who eventually replaced me with a Saudi teacher. By then, I was earning enough as a writer to decide not to stay in full-time academic life, and ever since I have kept my academic interests going as a side-line.

"I became aware from quite early on that it would be a mistake to set all my novels in the Middle East, since that would limit me in too many ways. Although Easterman stories are basically adventure yarns, they do have a more serious edge than most thrillers, and I wanted the opportunity to tackle wider issues. As a result, the settings I have used have ranged from Tibet and Mongolia to Egypt, Haiti, Ireland, Venice, Russia, Sardinia, Paris, Washington of the 1940s, and (still to come), India and North West China.

"I had always enjoyed well-written ghost stories, and in 1990, inspired by Susan Hill's *A Woman in Black*, decided I'd like to try my hand at a full-length story in this genre. The result was *Naomi's Room*, which I published under my second pen-name, Jonathan Aycliffe. Since then, there have been another four Aycliffes, with two more ready for publication, as well as a stage adaptation ready to open this year, and plans for other projects, including a collaboration with photographer Simon Marsden. Currently I write one Aycliffe and one Easterman a year, besides short stories and some academic pieces and the occasional book.

"Within all this, I try to keep up my interests in various fields, ranging from my ongoing academic concern with Islam and Iran to alternative medicine (I'm chairman of the U.K.'s main consumer charity in the area), to human rights issues such as censorship and the problem of human rights in Islam.

"As a genre writer, I try to avoid being too readily pigeonholed. I believe it is both possible and desirable in a culture that is rapidly selling out to the gimcrack and the banal, to write popular fiction in intelligent and literate prose. As a result, I receive letters from readers who range from college professors to poorly educated teenagers. I consider that a worthwhile achievement, since it means I have provided entertainment without dumbing down. It proves that readers with Ph.D.s also love action or terror, and that readers who might not tackle Tolstoy can tackle long words and complex constructions when set in a storyline that holds their attention."

Critics have been overwhelmingly impressed with MacEoin's work. After the publication of *The Last Assassin* (1985), which garnered favorable reviews, MacEoin (as Daniel Easterman) went on to publish *The Seventh Sanctuary* (1987), the story of a young American archaeologist's search for the Ark of the Covenant. A writer for *Kirkus Reviews* (January 1, 1987), while noting the book's "superficially silly and partly derivative (from the Indiana Jones cycle) premise," found that the author's "authoritative knowledge of the Mideast . . . and of the archeological arcane invests his painstaking description of David's decoding of [the lost Jewish city's] location, and his superbly realized settings . . . with a bedrock authenticity that grounds the fantastic plot." With *The Seventh Sanctuary*, MacEoin began producing an Easterman title a year, about a variety of places and subjects: *The Ninth Buddha* (1988) is an adventure set in India; *Brotherhood of the Tomb* (1989) concerns the discovery of Christ's remains, along with those of the Virgin Mary and St. James; and *Night of the Seventh Darkness* (1991) is a journey into voodoo in Haiti.

After the appearance of *Night*, MacEoin began publishing his horror titles under the pseudonym Aycliffe as well. The first of these ghost thrillers was *Naomi's Room* (1991), the story of a Cambridge don, his wife, and their daughter, Naomi, who is abducted and brutally murdered. Their lives become intertwined with—and taken over by—those of the family who lived in the same house during the Victorian era. A reviewer for *Publishing News* (October 11, 1991) noted: "There is a terrible and gripping inevitability about all that happens, compelling that the book be read in one sitting." MacEoin he soon published more Aycliffe titles: *Whispers in the Dark* (1992), *The Vanishment* (1993), and *The Matrix* (1994), a horror tale involving a grieving widower investigating popular occult practices in Edinburgh. Of the latter, a critic for *Time Out* (January 31, 1996) commented: "This is a genuinely frightening novel, the more so because of the mature characterisation and authentically dark, wintry Edinburgh setting. On another level, it's also a study of loss—loss of friendship, of love, and ultimately of innocence." MacEoin's most recent Aycliffe title is *The Lost* (1996).

MacEoin's later Easterman titles have been as successful as his Aycliffe titles of the same period. With *Name of the Beast* (1992), the author introduced a world at the end of the 20th century, in which fundamentalist Muslims conspire to take over Egypt and parts of Europe as well. In Egypt they dismantle all non-Islamic structures, including the Pyramids, using their stones to construct a massive wall across the Egyptian border. The *Chicago Tribune* reviewer (December 12, 1992) praised the work, recognizing how "the entire book is suffused with a dark, feverish poetry that's difficult to forget long after the final page has been reached." The *Denver Post* (January 1, 1993) praised it as well: "Easterman packs more excite-

ment into this tale than most thriller writers produce in five." With *The Judas Testament* (1994), MacEoin introduced his readers to an ancient scroll—a letter signed by Jesus—which reveals that Christ was nothing more than a fundamentalist Jew and a firm supporter of the law of Moses. Everyone, especially officials of the Roman Catholic Church, wants the scroll, and international intrigue follows. Of the novel the *Daily Telegraph* (September 24, 1994) commented: "Mr. Easterman writes excellently, enriching the clichés of his trade. The scenes in Moscow and Paris are especially vivid. . . . [The novel] is well in the front row of this year's thrillers." Since that time, two more Easterman titles have been published to triumphant reviews: *Night of the Apocalypse* (published in Britain as *Day of Wrath*) in 1995 and *The Final Judgement* in 1996.

Denis MacEoin's forthcoming titles are *K*, in his Daniel Easterman guise, and *A Shadow on the Wall* and *The Talisman*, as Jonathan Aycliffe.
—C.M.

SUGGESTED READING: *Chicago Tribune* Dec. 12, 1992; *Daily Telegraph* Sep. 24, 1994; *Denver Post* Jan. 1, 1993; *Interzone* p63 Feb. 1992; *Kirkus Reviews* p6 Jan. 1, 1987, p568 Apr. 15, 1989; *Publishing News* Oct. 11, 1991; *Publishers Weekly* p72 Sept. 16, 1996; *Scotsman* Dec. 24, 1994; *Time Out* Jan. 31, 1996; *Washington Post* B p2 Apr. 4, 1989; *Contemporary Authors* vol. 141, 1994

SELECTED BOOKS: As Daniel Easterman—*The Last Assassin*, 1985; *The Seventh Sanctuary*, 1987; *The Ninth Buddha*, 1988; *Brotherhood of the Tomb*, 1989; *Night of the Seventh Darkness*, 1991; *Name of the Beast*, 1992; *New Jerusalems: Reflections on Islam, Fundamentalism, and the Rushdie Affair*, 1993; *The Judas Testament*, 1994; *Night of the Apocalypse*, 1995; *The Final Judgement*, 1996; As Jonathan Aycliffe—*Naomi's Room*, 1991; *Whispers in the Dark*, 1992; *The Vanishment*, 1993; *The Matrix*, 1994; *The Lost*, 1996; As Denis MacEoin—*A People Apart: the Bhai Community of Iran in the Twentieth Century*, 1989; *The Sources for Early Babi Doctrine and History: A Survey*, 1992; As editor—*Islam in the Modern World* (with C. Thompson), 1983

MacLaverty, Bernard

Sep. 14, 1942– Novelist; children's writer; screenwriter; radio writer

Throughout the past two decades, Bernard Ma-cLaverty, an author of deftly crafted and emotionally charged fiction, has amassed a critically acclaimed body of work. The British writer has published three novels and four short-story collections, and has written for television, film, and radio. Two of his novels, *Lamb* (1980) and *Cal* (1983), have been adapted into motion pictures. He is known for his rhythmic, lyrical language, low-key plots, and rich characterization. In his most recent work, the novel *Grace Notes* (1997), MacLaverty explores the nature of human relationships while dealing with the question of the purpose of art.

In a personal statement submitted to *World Authors 1990–1995*, Bernard MacLaverty writes: "I was born in Belfast (14.9.42) and was educated there at Holy Family Primary School and St. Malachy's College. After leaving school in 1960, with A levels in Chemistry and English, I was employed by Queens University as a Medical Laboratory Technician in the Anatomy Department and later, in the Medical Biology Centre.

"I then enrolled at the University as a mature student and on qualifying became a teacher of English. In 1975 I moved to Scotland with my family to take up a teaching post at St. Augustine's High School in Edinburgh. Three years later I went to the island of Islay as Principal Teacher of English at the High School there. I gave up teaching in 1981 to write full time and since then have had no other visible means of support. In the mid-eighties, over a period of two years I was invited to be Writer-in-Residence at the University of Aberdeen. For short periods I have been a guest writer at the University of Augsburg and at Iowa State University. In Ireland I have been a member of Aosdana since the mid-eighties. I now live and write in Glasgow.

"I have published four collections of short stories and three novels. I have written versions of these fictions for other media—radio plays, television plays, screenplays.

"I began writing in my last year at school. Bad poetry. I didn't set out to write bad poetry, it's just the way it came out. I liked everything about words—their sound, the multiple meanings, their rhythms when strung together. I even liked reading *Roget's Thesaurus.* Twenty different ways to say the same thing.

"But it took a long time before I finished anything. I was always writing fragments of things. And copying other people's ways of writing (Kafka and Joyce and Gerard Manley Hopkins). Then I wrote a story, *The Exercise,* which was in my own voice about a place and people I knew. It was accepted by the BBC and that got me started.

"It is in the nature of every child to play and when I was young I used to like playing farms—setting out the toy animals, ducks on a round mir-

Miriam Berkley

ror pond, and the farmer and his wife, maybe one day face to face, the next day with their backs to each other. Making up a world, moving people within it. Writing is perhaps the grown up version of this activity—a way of trying to make sense of the world."

Bernard MacLaverty was born to commercial artist John MacLaverty and the former Molly Boyd. Shortly after graduating from high school, MacLaverty began reading the works of authors such as Dostoyevsky and Kafka, and was soon inspired to attempt to create some poems and stories of his own. He continued writing while working at the medical lab, and later, while pursuing a bachelor's degree at Queen's University, which he received in 1975.

He published his first book, a collection of short stories titled *Secrets and Other Stories*, (1977), two years later. The collection, filled with touching accounts of life in Ireland, brought MacLaverty his first taste of critical success. His follow-up project was *A Man in Search of a Pet* (1978), a book for children that started as a series of drawings MacLaverty had done for his own children.

A number of MacLaverty's works appeared in 1980. His first novel, *Lamb*, is the tale of an instructor in an Irish reformatory who forms a bond with an epileptic student. MacLaverty also composed a radio and television play called *My Dear Palestrina*. The radio version of *My Dear Palestrina* was honored with the Pharic McLaren Award for best radio play from the Radio Industries of Scotland, while the television version earned MacLaverty the Jacobs Award for best teleplay from Radio Telefis Eireann.

After completing *Secrets* (1981), a radio play based on the title story of his *Secrets and Other Stories*, MacLaverty returned to short stories with the publication of *A Time to Dance and Other Stories* (1982). That same year he wrote another television play, *Phonefun Unlimited*. In 1983 he completed *No Joke*, a radio play, and his second novel, *Cal*.

Cal, which deals with issues of guilt, represents MacLaverty's first effort to write about "the troubles" in Northern Ireland. The title character is a man who was involved in the murder of a police officer and who later falls in love with the officer's widow. After winning the woman's love, he is overwhelmed with feelings of guilt and self-loathing over his dark secret. In *Cal* (as in later works like *Grace Notes)* MacLaverty used the political upheaval in Northern Ireland as a metaphor for troubles in personal relationships.

In 1984 MacLaverty was called in to write the screenplay for a film version of *Cal* starring Helen Mirren. The following year the author wrote the screenplay for his novel *Lamb*. In 1987 *Lamb*, which starred Liam Neeson, was chosen as best film by the youth and ecumenical juries at the Lucarno Film Festival.

MacLaverty followed up his foray into motion picture screenwriting with a third television play, *The Daily Woman* (1986). The following year he published his third short-story anthology, *The Great Profundo and Other Stories*.

In 1988 MacLaverty published his second children's book, *Andrew McAndrew*. He also penned the radio plays *The Break* and *Some Surrender*. Shortly after the completion of those projects, he wrote the television play *Sometime in August* (1989), as well as the television adaptation of *The Real Charlotte* by Somerville and Ross.

MacLaverty has been extremely productive throughout the 1990s. A selection of his finest short stories from his previous three collections was anthologized in 1990. In 1992 he penned a radio play version of *Lamb*. He also wrote his first documentary, *Hostages*, which aired in the United States on the cable television channel HBO. His children's book *Andrew McAndrew* was released for the first time in the U.S. in 1993. In recent years he has devoted an increasing amount of time to writing fiction, publishing his fourth anthology, *Walking the Dog and Other Stories*, in 1994, and his latest novel, *Grace Notes*, in 1997.

MacLaverty's characters in *Walking the Dog and Other Stories* are people trying to survive a world of social ills and random violence with their dignity and integrity intact. The title story features a man who is kidnapped by the IRA while walking his dog. Another piece, "A Silent Retreat," deals with a Catholic schoolboy who develops a bond with a Protestant prison guard. "In these and other stories," Gabrielle Burton wrote in the *New York Times* (October 22, 1995), "Mr. MacLaverty catches individual people momentarily breaking out of formalized battles, creating their own personal armistices."

Grace Notes (1997) deals with the importance of art in coping with human suffering and political turmoil. The focus of the novel is Catherine McKenna, an Irish Catholic woman who becomes a renowned composer. The book opens with her returning to Ireland from Scotland for her father's funeral. Her somewhat overbearing father had taught her to hate Protestants—a prejudice she has questioned in her adult life. The conflict is symbolized by the fact that she incorporates the lambeg, an instrument used in Anglican rites, into one of her compositions. The first half of the book details Catherine's return to her homeland. The other half centers on her life on the Scottish island of Islay, where she lives with her alcoholic boyfriend, Dave, and her daughter, Anna. It is a "carefully written, elegantly unfolded story," Bernard O'Donoghue wrote in the *Times Literary Supplement* (July 4, 1997). O'Donoghue added that "much of the writing is unashamedly literary in its claims, partly maybe in parody of many of the most celebrated Irish novels of the past generation whose cosmopolitanism can be obtrusive." He compared MacLaverty's vivid use of language to that of Irish writer Seamus Heaney, winner of the 1995 Nobel Prize in literature. "*Grace Notes* ends on a note of achievement, but it is a pessimistic view of the world, founded on opposition and non-reconciliation. . . ." O'Donoghue concluded. "Eloquently as it is put in this impressively accomplished novel, it is hard to feel greatly comforted by it."

In the *London Review of Books* (October 2, 1997), Tobias Jones criticized what he described as MacLaverty's "emotional overload" in *Grace Notes*, claiming that the musical metaphor is overdone. "Instead of giving his novel form and frisson by opposing the ineptitude of words to the score, each sentence is bloated with 'musical' significance, full of import. . . . The result is a tasteless sandwich with, lurking between the white-slice prose, the spam of the ever-portentous piano. . . ." Jones asserted that in this setting, the character Catherine is nothing more than a mouthpiece for the themes of the novel. Jones also criticized the novel's interior monologue, which he saw as artificial. MacLaverty's close attention to detail, hailed by some critics, was deplored by Jones, who wrote that "it's as if the novelist had actually set out to describe the drying of paint."

One of the hallmarks of MacLaverty's work is a highly emotional, yet finely crafted style which, according to many critics, is most clearly exhibited in his short stories. Both his short stories and novels often deal with human relationships, alienation, and the difficulties people face in making contact with one another. He often focuses on minute details; the action in his stories is sometimes limited, with more emphasis placed on psychological character study.

MacLaverty has received several awards from the Northern Ireland and Scottish Arts Councils, including one in 1978 for *Secrets and Other Stories* and one in 1988 for *The Great Profundo and Other Stories*. He received the Irish *Sunday Independent* Award (1983) for *A Time to Dance and Other Stories*, and the London *Evening Standard* Award for his 1984 screen adaptation of *Cal*. In 1988 he was a co-winner of the Scottish Writer of the Year Award. He won the Irish Post Award in 1989.

Bernard MacLaverty married Madeline Mc-Guckin in 1967. They have four children: John, Ciara, Claire, and Judith.—B.S.

SUGGESTED READING: *London Review of Books* p32+ Oct. 2, 1997; *New York Times* VII p36 Oct. 22, 1995; *Times Literary Supplement* p22 July 4, 1997; *International Authors and Writers Who's Who*, 15th ed., 1991/98; *Larousse Dictionary of Writers*, 1994

SELECTED WORKS: Fiction—*Secrets and Other Stories*, 1977; *Lamb*, 1980; *A Time to Dance and Other Stories*, 1982; *Cal*, 1983; *The Great Profundo and Other Stories*, 1987; *Walking the Dog and Other Stories*, 1994; *Grace Notes*, 1997; Documentary *Hostages*, 1992; Drama—*My Dear Palestrina*, 1980; *Secrets*, 1981; *Phonefun Unlimited*, 1982; *No Joke*, 1983; *Cal*, 1984; *Lamb*, 1985; *The Daily Woman*, 1986; *The Break*, 1988; *Some Surrender*, 1988; *Sometime in August*, 1989, *Lamb*, 1992; Juvenile *A Man in Search of a Pet*, 1978; *Andrew McAndrew*, 1988

Maharidge, Dale

Oct. 24, 1956– Journalist

Dale Maharidge writes forthrightly and clearly about significant social issues facing America at century's end: multiculturalism, ethnic and racial conflict, homelessness, the legacy of poverty. He won a Pulitzer Prize in 1990 for *And Their Children After Them* (1989), in which he and photographer Michael Williamson retraced the steps taken by James Agee and Walker Evans in the Depression-era Alabama classic *Now Let Us Praise Famous Men*. Maharidge's book tracked down the descendants of the sharecroppers profiled in the Agee book to study the pervasiveness of a culture of deprivation. His and Williamson's first book, *Journey to Nowhere: The Saga of the New Underclass* (1985) was the fruit of a three-year journey through homeless encampments from coast to coast. It inspired Bruce Springsteen to write several songs for his album *The Ghost of Tom Joad*; the singer wrote an introduction for a reissue of the book in 1996. Other books by Maharidge include *The Last Great American Hobo* (also with Williamson, 1993), *Yosemite: A Landscape of Life* (with photographer Jay Mather, 1990), and *The Coming White Minority: California's Eruptions and the Nation's Future* (1996), a book that offered a hopeful solution in America's contentious battle over multiculturalism.

Dale Dimitro Maharidge was born in Cleveland, Ohio, on October 24, 1956, the son of Steve Maharidge, a toolmaker, and Joan Kopfstein Maharidge. One of his most memorable childhood experiences is recorded in the preface to his 1990 Pulitzer Prize–winning book *And Their Children After Them*: "My first trip to the South was made when I was a child, somewhere around 1967, when I traveled through the region with my parents. I remember seeing old black men selling watermelons from mule-drawn wagons. My mother told me they were sharecroppers. As we drove away, I stared—fascinated by the shacks they lived in. That was my first image of the South, and, like most first images, it dominated my perception for a long time to come." The day after he graduated from high school, in 1974, Maharidge set off with a friend in a cross-country odyssey in a well-worn Chevy from Cleveland to the Grand Canyon. Two years later, he hiked alone through the rugged landscape of Utah and Arizona. Both these formative experiences would be echoed in his itinerant cross-country journeys in the 1980s and 1990s, as he documented the plight of the homeless, the hobo, the migrant, and the sharecropper in his award-winning books.

From 1974 to 1976, Maharidge attended both Cleveland State University and Cuyahoga Community College. He worked as a reporter for the Medina *Gazette* for a year before moving to the Cleveland *Plain Dealer*, serving as a freelance reporter from 1977 to 1980. Maharidge next moved to California and joined the reporting staff of the *Sacramento Bee*, where he would remain until 1991. It was at the *Bee* that he met staff photographer Michael Williamson, with whom he would collaborate on the books that made both of them nationally known as chroniclers of the American underclass.

For his first book, *Journey to Nowhere: The Saga of the New Underclass*, Maharidge and Williamson took leaves of absence from the newspaper to examine hobo culture first hand, by riding the rails and living in encampments of unemployed, homeless people who had lost their jobs and residences as a result of the downsizing in American industry during the 1980s. They started their journey in Youngstown, Ohio, whose steel mills were then vanishing. The book was published in 1985 and republished in 1996 with an introduction by Bruce Springsteen, who credits the book with having awakened his interest in the problems of the American working class. The singer/songwriter said he was inspired by the book to include the songs "Youngstown" and the "New Timer" in his album *The Ghost of Tom Joad*. Maharidge was surprised but pleased with the attention. "What Springsteen is trying to do is something so incredible," he was quoted as saying in the *Chronicle of Higher Education* (January 19, 1996). "He's a musical Steinbeck, in that he is bringing popular approval to this thing. . . .What took me hundreds of words to say, Bruce said in 70 words. He captured it so tightly."

The book that won Maharidge a 1990 Pulitzer Prize for general nonfiction, *And Their Children After Them*, was a collaboration between him and Michael Williamson. The two retraced the steps of author James Agee and photographer Walker Evans, whose 1941 book *Let Us Now Praise Famous Men* had awakened Depression-era readers to the realities of poverty in rural Alabama. Maharidge and Williamson set off on their second odyssey, this time in search of the children and grandchildren of the sharecroppers whose lives had been chronicled in the Agee/Walker book. Their title, like that of Agee's book, was drawn from a verse in the apocryphal Old Testament book of Ecclesiasticus (also known as Sirach in some translations). As Maharidge explained in his preface: "For three years, Michael Williamson and I spent a considerable amount of time in the Deep South. We made many trips, the longest in July and August of 1986. By 1988, our work was finished. We were involved in an endeavor that seemed at the start odd, later foolish, but ultimately rewarding." When the two began their field trips, Maharidge expected to see some of the sharecroppers that had so fascinated him two decades earlier, they were not to be found, having fallen victim to agricultural mechanization and other socioeconomic forces. As he explained in an article he wrote for *Rolling Stone* (March 23, 1989): "Of the original 23 people, we found 11 still living, as well as 117 descendants." Maharidge followed Agee's practice of inventing pseudonyms for his subjects in order to protect their privacy. "A few didn't want to be part of history," Maharidge continued, "and they hate Agee and Evans (and us by extension) for exposing their families' misery to the world. Most were open, though; they almost seemed to be waiting for someone to return and write the next chapter in their families' lives."

Most of the subjects in the book are white, as were the subjects in *Let Us Now Praise Famous Men*. The editors of *Fortune* magazine, which had assigned the story to Agee—one of its staff writers—only to kill it later, "did not document the struggle of black sharecroppers, because the editors . . . did not think their readers would be shocked by scenes of black poverty," Maharidge wrote in his *Rolling Stone* article, explaining that he and Williamson had added the stories of some black sharecroppers to their book. *And Their Children After Them* revealed that some ex-sharecroppers have risen into the middle class, while millions of their descendants have become "first-generation casualties of the debilitating mind-set of that system." Some descendants have traded the hardships of sharecropping for other perils, as is the case with a young man who hauls

sacks of toxic chemicals in a factory. In the book's coda, Maharidge wrote: "It is obscene when you travel this nation in 1988 as a journalist and listen to people tell you they are going to vote for the party [the Republicans] on whose watch a nation of homeless were recruited because, as one man said with blunt honesty, 'I'm greedy.' Greed, once a pejorative, has become the national credo."

And Their Children After Them won praise from popular reviewers and academic critics alike. In his review for the *Journal of American History* (June 1990), Ralph F. Bogardus of the University of Alabama compared the book to Thoreau's *Walden* as well as to Agee's *Let Us Now Praise Famous Men* as an example of the "eccentric" American books that "have dotted the literary landscape and often outshone more conventional works in their rough-hewn genius." Of *And Their Children After Them*, Bogardus wrote: "Joining these works in its eccentricity if not its genius, the book reviewed also shares another thing with them. It closely examines lives as really lived. . . . Though not strictly a historical work, their study can teach historians much, for it not only reflects intelligently on a problem whose causes can only be understood in historical terms but also breathes human life into that problem and makes it impossible for us to blame the victims." And Herbert Mitgang described the book in his *New York Times* (June 17, 1989) review as one "that reaches into this country's heart of darkness. . . . A tragically human story more telling than a thousand polls."

Maharidge's next book, published in 1990, a collaboration with the photographer Jay Mather, was titled *Yosemite: A Landscape of Life*, a homage to the unspoiled wilderness preserved in America's national parks. In this and other venues, Maharidge has argued for the preservation of free access for hikers to trails in the national park system. In an op-ed piece for the *New York Times* (December 30, 1996), he protested the imposition of the Park Service's "recreation fee demonstration program" by warning that "allowing this fee-for-service mentality" would set an "alarming precedent" that would discourage young people from experiencing the beauty and grandeur of nature. "Reality used to be free," he wrote. "Something is amiss when our national treasures are compared to theme parks. . . . Charging for open space—especially space owned by all Americans—is immoral."

In 1991, after 11 years at the *Sacramento Bee*, Maharidge left to pursue other forms of writing and to teach, for a year, at Columbia University's Graduate School of Journalism, in New York City. A year later he became Chandler Chair lecturer at Stanford University, where he taught courses in magazine writing and journalism. Describing himself "a writer who happens to teach," he told Tom Schoenberg for the *Chronicle of Higher Education* (January 19, 1966), "I'm one of the only working journalists at the university. I feel like a bass living around a school of trout."

In 1993 Maharidge and Williamson collaborated on the book *The Last Great American Hobo*, about the century-old hobo subculture that had been a part of American life and folklore, especially during the Depression years. Defending himself against critics who think he writes from a bias—an editor once called him the "bum writer"—Maharidge wrote in the *Nieman Reports* (Spring 1997) that reporters definitely should start "talking about class. . . . It is important to have a point of view of looking at the larger picture. It's a mistake to write about the homeless, welfare clients, or the rich as separate and unrelated issues. And it's not biased to offer ways out. Too often, journalists merely tell what is broken. It's vital that we show how to fix things by highlighting people and programs and ideas that offer answers."

Since 1994 *Mother Jones* magazine has published several features by Maharidge on ethnic conflicts in California, a topic he analyzed in depth in his 1996 book, *The Coming White Minority: California's Eruptions and the Nation's Future*. Maharidge, who wrote that California is "America's multicultural tomorrow," believes strongly that the state offers a model of how American society will or will not handle pluralism in the 21st century. Maharidge decried efforts by a frightened white minority to erect physical and legal barricades against new immigrants from Mexico. In an article entitled "Walled Off," published in *Mother Jones* (November/December 1994), he described the beleaguered community of Dana Point in Orange County, where whites have created "gated communities" to protect their turf from what they perceive as a threat from Mexican immigrants and others. "But after two years spent researching the cultural changes behind California's 'Orange Curtain,'" he writes, "I've found that nothing is simple. I talk with Latinos, who think I'm on their side. Then I go to whites, who think I'm on *their* side. It makes for schizophrenic nights hacking out notes on my computer. Both groups, however, are correct. What do you do if you've worked all your life to buy a dream home, and suddenly the neighborhood becomes more dangerous. . . . And what do you do if you're a hardworking, law-abiding immigrant who just wants to make a buck and better your life, but other people want you to get the hell out?" Kate Kelly, who reviewed *The Coming White Minority* for *Library Journal* (September 15, 1996), wrote: "This book attempts to get beyond the hysteria often accompanying the immigration debate to the voices of ordinary people. . . . A highly readable book on an emotional and topical issue."

In *The Coming White Minority*, Maharidge suggested that Americans, right and left, refocus themselves outside of the limiting, theoretical frameworks of the past and argued that a newly "polyethnic" nation needs to move beyond the solutions of that past. In the "Walled Off" article, he had written, "As the nation grows more diverse, the center needs to hold. Even though racism still exists, it isn't the 1960s anymore. The left will lose

if it keeps fighting the old in-your-face battles; the right shouldn't keep driving race as a wedge issue." Instead, Maharidge advocated a model proposed by Kirk Knutsen, a policy analyst for the state of California, which rejects both the "melting pot" vision advocated by many whites and the "separate identity" vision advocated by many minorities in favor of a "polyethnic" model that allows all groups to maintain their own identities while remaining part of the collective culture of the United States. To give a more personalized slant to his ideas, Maharidge focused on four Californians of varying ethnic backgrounds who are trying to be part of the solution: Don Northcross, a black sheriff in Sacramento; Maria Ha, a Vietnamese-born Chinese student at Berkeley; Martha Escutia, a first-generation Mexican-American in the California state legislature; and Bill Shepherd, a white man living in a gated community in Dana Point. They were chosen because they represent the complex middle ground of the debate over cultural identity that has often proved to be fractious and divisive. For these four people, Maharidge writes, "California is a dream train of hopes and ideals at the end of the road. . . . In many ways, California and its residents exist on a frontier just as bold as the one present in 1849, only this time it is a cultural one."
—E. M.

SUGGESTED READING: *Booklist* Jan. 15, 1991, p190 Sep. 15, 1996; *Chronicle of Higher Education* A p7 Jan. 19, 1996; *Economist* R p9+ Feb. 15, 1997; *Hispanic* p70+ May 1997; *Historian: A Journal of History* p135+ Autumn 1990; *Journal of American History* p357+ June 1990; *Journal of Southern History* p134+ Feb. 1991; *Library Journal* p76+ May 1, 1989, p130 Nov. 1, 1993, p84 Sep. 15, 1996; *Mother Jones* p26+ Nov./Dec. 1994, p52+ Nov./Dec. 1995; p56+ Jan./Feb. 1998; *New York Times* IV p17 Dec. 8, 1991, I p30 Jan. 1, 1992, A p15 Dec. 30, 1996, A p26 Jan. 3, 1997, *Nieman Reports* p48+ Summer 1989, p47+ Winter 1989, p91+ Fall 1992, p7+ Spring 1997; *Oral History Review* p109+ Spring 1991; *Publishers Weekly* p421 Aug. 5, 1996; *Rolling Stone* p87+ Mar. 23, 1989; *School Library Journal* p118 July 1997; *Sewanee Review* plxii+ Summer 1991; *Tikkun* p88+ Nov. 1990; *Village Voice* p58+ Aug. 29, 1989

SELECTED *WORKS: Journey to Nowhere: The Saga of the New Underclass* (with M. Williamson, photographer), 1985 (reprinted with introduction by Bruce Springsteen, 1996); *And Their Children After Them* (with M. Williamson, photographer), 1989; *Yosemite: A Landscape of Life* (with Jay Mather, photographer), 1990; *The Last Great American Hobo* (with Michael Williamson, photographer), 1993; *The Coming White Minority: California's Eruptions and the Nation's Future*, 1996

Makine, Andrei

1957– Novelist

Emigrating to France from the Soviet Russia in 1987, Andrei Makine was initially unable to publish any of his work in his new country. In recent years, however, he has won acclaim with *Dreams of My Russian Summers* (*Le Testamente Français*) in 1995 and *Once Upon the River Love* in 1998, written originally in French. The former earned Makine the Goncourt and Medicis prizes—two of France's most prestigious literary awards; Makine holds the distinction of being the first foreigner to win the Goncourt Prize. Makine's ficiton is highly autobiographical in nature.

Andrei Makine was born in Russia in 1957. His grandmother Charlotte was French by birth, and his relationship with her helped him to become familiar with the French language from an early age. By the time he was five, he was composing poems in both French and his native Russian.

Makine continued writing as a young man. He moved to France in 1987, at the age of 30, to study, and soon made the decision to stay with the intention of making a career out of his writing. Although he began writing in French in order to appeal to the national readership, he was afraid that French publishers would not believe that a Russian immigrant could write so well in their language. Therefore, he marketed his work to publishers as if they were translations from Russian. He even invented the names of fictitious translators. The publishers of his second novel demanded to see the "original" Russian manuscript, leaving Makine no choice but to hurriedly translate the book into Russian. Despite his clever ploys, his first three novels sold poorly.

During those years Makine lived in poverty, renting an unheated, unfurnished attic apartment. His only source of warmth was an electric heater eventually provided for him by a generous benefactor. Makine later acquired a writing table from the same benefactor; he had previously had nothing but his lap on which to write. Prior to obtaining the apartment, circumstances had been even worse: Makine wrote his books while sitting on a park bench, and spent his nights in a cemetery crypt.

Publishers lacked faith in Makine, and it took him eight months to find one willing to take a chance on his fourth novel, *Le Testament Français*. During those months the publishers constantly eluded his questions and criticized him for his impatience. Finally, Simone Gallimard of the Gallimard subsidiary of the French publishing house Mercure de France contacted him. Gallimard agreed to publish the book, and offered Makine a $2,000 advance, as well as the guarantee of a 3,000-copy printing.

Once the novel was released to the French public, it became a best-seller. The story revolves around Charlotte Lemonnier (based on Makine's own grandmother), a Frenchwoman by birth and upbringing who lived most of her adult life in Soviet Russia. Witnessing World War II, the purges of Stalin, and the deterioration of communism, she has a lengthy and moving tale to tell her grandson and his sister. As a grown man the grandson narrates the book, vividly recalling his childhood summers spent listening to his grandmother's stories. Much like Makine, he escapes as an adult to France, where he pursues a career as a writer.

Le Testament Français won Makine France's coveted Goncourt Prize in 1995, making him the first foreigner to do so. This caused a furor among French literary critics and publishers. The Goncourt usually leads to high book sales, and many competing publishers resented the fact that it was going to an "outsider." In fact, it was later revealed that one competitor had tried to manipulate things so that Makine would win a different French award, the Medicis Prize, a week before the Goncourt Prize was to be decided. It was thought that the Goncourt judges would not give the prize to a book that had just won the Medicis, but the plot backfired and Makine wound up with both awards. The novel was eventually translated into English and published in the United States as *Dreams of My Russian Summers* in 1997.

In a review of *Dreams of my Russian Summers* for the *New York Times* (August 7, 1997), Victor Brombert praised the way in which Makine blended memory and imagination using a highly poetic voice, "merging the particular realities of Soviet life with a timeless evocation of a sensitive adolescence." Brombert called the novel "skillfully constructed and elegantly written," and noted that it refrains from becoming merely anecdotal nostalgia. Makine is at his most effective, Brombert remarked, "when he sketches moments so painful that there appear to be no words to describe them," such as when Charlotte's husband returns from the war, his body horribly scarred. "Andrei Makine has given us a major novel," Brombert concluded.

In the *New York Review of Books*, Tatyana Tolstaya drew the conclusion that Charlotte is a metaphor for Russia itself: "raped (by a criminal), loving (her husband), tormented by her adopted country and incapable of leaving it (and not wanting to), accepting both her children equally—the offspring of her beloved husband and her rapist—she refuses to die." Although Tolstoya felt that at times the prose was tedious or the action slow, she concluded that a determined reader would be rewarded by the depth of meaning contained in the book.

Makine's next book, *Once Upon the River Love*, was published in 1998. The novel focuses on a group of teenage boys living in a small Siberian village in the 1970s. The boys (one of whom is the narrator) become disenchanted with life in their small town and dream of something greater. Exemplifying the allure of the West for those behind the Iron Curtain, the book follows the three boys as they are inspired to seek out their dreams beyond the boundaries of their village after discovering the films of actor Jean-Paul Belmondo. They eventually escape Siberia, each following his own path.

"If *Dreams of My Russian Summers* marked Mr. Makine's arrival on the literary scene, *Once Upon the River Love* indicates that he will remain there," Richard Bernstein wrote for the *New York Times* (July 15, 1998). Bernstein praised the novel's effective prose and complex characters, and added that "Mr. Makine writes with just that touch of distance, that lightening element of self-mockery that the adult brings to the most piercing visions of boyhood."

However, in a *New York Times* (September 6, 1998) book review, William Boyd criticized Makine's use of "airy soliloquizing." According to Boyd, such soliloquizing prevented the novel from sustaining interest for any prolonged period of time. The work is saved, wrote Boyd, by the setting as well as the "mundane exoticism of eastern Siberian life." —R.S.

SUGGESTED READING: *New York Review of Books* p4+ Sep. 20, 1997; *New York Times* Aug. 7, 1997, E p1 Oct. 8, 1997, E July 15, 1998, VII p8 Sep. 6, 1998; *Publishers Weekly* p18 July 17, 1997

SELECTED WORKS: *Dreams of My Russian Summers*, 1997; *Once Upon the River Love*, 1998

Marion Ettlinger/Courtesy of Houghton Mifflin

Mallon, Thomas

Nov. 2, 1951– Novelist; nonfiction writer

To his successful career as an academic, the American author Thomas Mallon has added a sideline as a well-regarded novelist in the past 10 years. Mallon used his previous experience as a professor and writer of such widely praised nonfiction works as *A Book of One's Own: People and Their Diaries* (1984) and *Stolen Words: Forays into the Origins and Ravages of Plagiarism* (1989) to construct well researched, historically accurate settings for his fictional storylines. Mallon's historical novels include *Aurora 7* (1991), *Henry and Clara* (1994), and *Dewey Defeats Truman* (1997), and have won him acclaim from such luminaries

as the author John Updike, who has called Mallon "one of the most interesting novelists at work."

Thomas Mallon was born on November 2, 1951 in Glen Cove, New York to Arthur Vincent and Caroline (Moruzzi) Mallon. Thomas grew up in one of the many suburban developments built on Long Island in the years after World War II. In a statement submitted to *World Authors 1990–1995*, Mallon writes: "I once wrote about having had 'the kind of happy childhood that is so damaging to a writer,' and if the latter part of the statement was facetious, I think the first part is largely true. I grew up during the 1950s and 60s in the middle-class suburbs of Long Island, where our fathers were all World War II veterans and our mothers were always at home. When in my work I've looked back on this life, I've resisted the aesthetic and political scorn routinely showered on it. It was an earned and, in its way, exotic existence, and as things turned out, a rather brief moment in the culture. The principal shapers of my imagination were, I now feel sure, the Catholic church; the brink-of-apocalypse international situation; and the early space-age exploits of Project Mercury.

"The first in my family to go to college, I went all the way to a Ph.D. At Brown, where I was an undergraduate [B.A., 1973], I discovered the writings of Mary McCarthy, who eventually became an important influence and friend. But I lacked the confidence to pursue my own fiction-writing ambitions very hard. Academic life seemed a more attainable fulfillment, and I went on to five years of graduate study at Harvard [M.A., 1974; Ph.D., 1978]. My early, scholarly writing—*Edmund Blunden* (1983), a critical study of the English war poet, grew out of my dissertation—now seems very remote, and I have come to regard my long stretch of teaching at Vassar College throughout the 1980s [1979–1991] as an extended detour. I regret staying as long as I did, but I would trade away none of my long literary education, which made possible my books on diaries and plagiarism (as well as the one I'm slowly doing on letters) and enriched the novels I would come to write.

"That book on diaries (*A Book of One's Own*, 1984) was a turning point. Conceived as a rather academic study (the kind of book that gets one tenure), it evolved into a quirky, old-fashioned volume of belles-lettres with an unexpectedly personal voice. I was surprised by its strong sales and reviews. It opened up many opportunities for me in literary journalism (my ticket out of college teaching) and gave me the confidence to make a serious attempt at writing fiction.

"*Arts and Sciences* (1988) is in many respects a typical coming-of-age comedy, though it concentrates on a later period of time (my graduate-school days) than most such books—perhaps a reflection of my delayed adolescence. It doesn't much prefigure the rest of my fiction, which got off to its real start, I think, with *Aurora 7* (1991). This, too, is autobiographical, at least in its rendition of one day (May 24, 1962) in the childhood I describe above. But the novel's use of an historical event (Scott Carpenter's space flight) and its focus on the bystanders to that occasion, set the pattern for what followed: *Henry and Clara*, which deals with the real-life couple who shared Abraham Lincoln's box at Ford's Theater; *Dewey Defeats Truman*, set in the hometown of Thomas E. Dewey during his supposedly surefire run for the presidency in 1948; and the novel I'm now working on about some astronomers (both real and invented) at the old U. S. Naval Observatory during the discovery of Mars' two moons in the summer of 1877.

"These books are marked, I hope, by the kind of painstaking research I learned as a scholar. I try to give them an authentic and accurate 'feel,' even when, as in *Dewey*, the fictional action borders on the improbable and romantic. Narrative was the last and hardest thing I learned to write, and these books, for better and worse, are recognizably the novels of somebody who began his career as an essayist. I think their focus on 'minor characters' transformed by great events reflects the religious outlook of my childhood, with its sense that we are players in a great plan, susceptible to sudden exaltations and catastrophes beyond our own imagining and control.

"I left Vassar in 1991 to become the literary editor of *Gentlemen's Quarterly,* where for several years I bought short fiction from the best American writers producing it: Russell Banks. Robert Olen Butler, Alice Adams, and dozens of others. I still write the magazine's books column, and continue to do the kinds of reporting pieces that appeared in my 1993 book *Rockets and Rodeos* (articles on politics, spaceflight, and various American spectacles) for a number of publications, especially the *New York Times Magazine*. Non-fiction and journalism rarely feel like interruptions to me; in fact, I think my ability to write the kind of fiction I do would suffer if I didn't also engage real life present-day events as things to be evoked and explained and judged directly, without any fictional displacement.

"I never quite shake the sense of having got a late start doing what I truly want to do, and a feeling of pleasurable surprise over being able now to do it. I work more or less constantly, dividing my time between Connecticut and New York City, along with frequent trips to Washington. I am politically conservative; optimistic about the country's overall prospects; more pessimistic about its literary and cultural life."

A Book of One's Own: People and Their Diaries was a wide spectrum of autobiographical entries, ranging in scope from famous personal accounts, such as those by Virginia Woolf and Dostoyevsky, to the more obscure, but equally engaging narratives, like those written by female pioneers making their way across the Great Frontier. The book is divided into chapters, each dedicated to a different type of diarist—thus chapter names include "Chroniclers," "Creators," and "Confessors." To add further depth to his collection, Mallon included some of his own diary entries, which provide a brief look into how diaries, both his and others, have figured in his own literary life. *A Book of One's Own* was praised for its diverse subject matter as well as for the range of emotions it evoked in readers with its mix of poignant and lighthearted pieces. Brad Leithauser of the *New York Times Book Review* (March 31, 1985) called the book "winsome and ingratiating," and Naomi Bliven of the *New Yorker* (January 21, 1985) summarized Mallon's effort as "inclusive . . . but not a bit long-winded. It is learned but never pedantic. It is also charming, diverting, and exceptionally intelligent. The book is literary criticism, yet it is something more—a knowing, sympathetic, but not soppy commentary on humanity. . . . By bringing together so many diverse people at their most candid . . . Mallon offers us a glimpse of human possibility we could get no other way."

With his next work, Mallon struck out for uncharted territory—fiction. He drew on his own graduate school experiences to write *Arts and Sciences: A Seventies Seduction* (1988), the comedic coming-of-age story of Artie Dunne, a nervous, Keats-worshiping graduate student at Harvard University who pursues a heated relationship with an older, more sophisticated divorcée named Angela Downing. The novel explores the transformations both Artie and Angela undergo as their relationship develops over the course of the academic year. Angela tries to transform Artie, and the result, according to Georgia Jones-Davis of the *Los Angeles Times* (February 14, 1988), is that "Artie finds himself standing a little taller and Angela . . . is exhibiting signs of emotional wear and tear." The novel, which Jones-Davis called a "sweet, frothy story," was mostly well-received, although some critics labeled it "slight" and dismissed it as a simplistic comedy. According to *Contemporary Authors* (1997), *Newsday* writer Edward Guereschi called *Arts and Sciences* "a skillful fictional debut."

For his next literary venture, Mallon returned to nonfiction with *Stolen Words: Forays into the Origins and Ravages of Plagiarism* (1989). The book is a collection of examples throughout history of both perpetrator and victim in the crime of plagiarism. Mallon took pains to provide a full history of the act, looking at cases from the 16th century up to the 1980s, as well as the psychology behind plagiarism, which has occurred in the writing of respected scholarly journals as well as that of television series. "After the first chapter, *Stolen Words* abandons the social-historical approach in favor of a more or less chronological series of anecdotes, each illustrating one of plagiarism's paradoxes or dead ends," observed *New York Times Book Review* (October 29, 1989) contributor Walter Kendrick. "Overall, the effect is a bit scrappy, exacerbated by Mr. Mallon's tendency to digress. Sometimes . . . he piles up many more details than the point of the tale warrants. But he writes vivaciously, and is almost never dull. Along the way, he assembles a beguiling portrait of the plagiarist (at least the habitual one) as an oddly plaintive psychopath."

Mallon's next try at fiction was *Aurora 7* (1991), a novel that looks at the lives of a variety of people on the day in 1962 when astronaut Scott Carpenter orbited the earth three times. One of the central characters is a fifth-grade boy named Gregory Noonan, who is fascinated by the space mission and who mysteriously disappears from school that day. *Aurora 7* was well received by the public and critics alike; Marianne Gingher of the *Washington Post* (February 17, 1991) called it "vast with insight, charming and provocative" and "one of the most engaging and intelligently energetic books I've read in some time." In particular, she enjoyed "The mingling and meshing, the nearly calamitous interplay of characters created in this dazzling, spare book."

What followed was *Rockets and Rodeos and Other American Spectacles* (1993), a book of essays chronicling Mallon's cross-country adventures in search of diverse individuals and lifestyles. Whether at a rodeo or a political campaign event, Mallon made sure to stake out his subjects, as he wrote in the introduction to his book, "in an attitude of active passivity—not so much busy-bee reporter as fly on the wall." The result is a collection of vividly insightful snapshots that allow the reader to hear, to see, and—most importantly—to understand the people and phenomena Mallon witnessed. With such startling attention to minutiae, Mallon, according to a reviewer at *USA Today* (February 24, 1993), proved his "knack for noting the small but telling details, and for using them astutely so that his essays have what every writer must hope for—the ring of truth."

In 1994 Mallon published another work of fiction, *Henry and Clara,* a speculative account of the real-life couple who shared the theater box with President Lincoln on the night of his assassination. The novel follows the couple from the first embers of their love affair (as stepbrother and -sister, they were brought up together in the same house) to the events of the night Lincoln was killed, and finally to the downturn in their lives in the subsequent years of their marriage. The strength of *Henry and Clara* was, once again, Mallon's extensive research into his subject matter. "I'll probably never find another story like that," Mallon remarked to Francis X. Clines of the *International Herald Tribune* (February 1–2, 1997). Critics across the country applauded him for turning terse bits of documented text into a searing love story. Perhaps the highest acclaim for *Henry and Clara* came from John Updike, who in his review for the *New Yorker* (September 5, 1994), wrote that the author "hones a multitude of details to a gleaming, smoothly oiled fit." He summarized Mallon's book by admiring its "nice mezzotint evenness, a steel-engraving stiltedness to the overall picture. The period details are generously supplied, but they rarely, even in the thick of the heavily documented Civil War, detract from the central erotic and psychological drama of the loving couple." *Henry and Clara* was named one of the best books of 1994 by *Publishers Weekly*.

Mallon's most recent work, *Dewey Defeats Truman,* was published in 1997. This time Mallon set his novel in Owosso, Michigan, circa 1948, as the small, rural town's most notable son, Thomas E. Dewey, is making his run for the presidency of the United States. Drawing on the real-life hoopla which overran Owosso in the months just prior to the election, Mallon offered a peek at the lives of residents who became both directly and indirectly entangled in the political moment. Mallon's characters include a young novelist, Anne Macmurray, who is trying to decide whether she loves a conventional, Truman-supporting labor union organizer, or an arrogant Dewey enthusiast; Mrs. Herrick, a mother grieving for a son killed in World War II, who regularly attends the funerals of unknown soldiers brought home; a science teacher, Frank Sherwood, who befriends Mrs. Herrick and comes to terms with his sexuality; Margaret Feller, a young woman who becomes involved with two local teenagers; and Horace Sinclair, an elderly man who, for a secret reason, is one of the few non-Dewey supporters in the area. Although the Anne Macmurray love triangle is the central storyline, Mallon draws on all of the characters to paint a picture of small-town life just after World War II.

Dewey Defeats Truman received some positive reviews upon its publication, but many critics offered caveats. Michael Malone of the *Yale Review* (July 1997) called the book a "sharp, sweet, beautifully nuanced recreation of a time in America when small-town neighbors squabbled and gossiped and cared about each other's well-being." In the *New York Times Book Review* (February 2, 1997), Jay Parini called the book a "lovely meditation on the interplay between past and present." However, he criticized Mallon's lack of dramatization regarding Frank Sherwood's character, and felt that the story about Margaret and her boyfriends verged on caricature. Similarly, Dwight

Garner, book review editor for the on-line magazine *Salon,* wrote that the central love story was "corny" and that the reader is never given the opportunity to know Thomas Dewey in the novel. "The candidates are absent from the book, and while the townsfolk are constantly having brow-furrowing discussions about the election's 'issues' the discussion remains superficial—this is a novel that doesn't feel grounded by the force of ideas."

Despite some less-than-favorable comments on his latest work, both *Henry and Clara* and *Dewey Defeats Truman* are widely considered to be Mallon's best fiction. *Dewey Defeats Truman* was named one of the best books of 1997 by *Publishers Weekly* and one of the notable books of 1997 by the *New York Times Book Review.* Mallon continues to contribute articles to such publications as *American Spectator,* the *Washington Post,* and the *Wall Street Journal.* Among his many honors and awards, Mallon was named a Rockefeller Foundation Fellow (1986—87) and, in 1994, received the Ingram Merrill Award.—D.B.

SELECTED WORKS: Nonfiction—*Edmund Blunden,* 1983; *A Book of One's Own: People and Their Diaries,* 1984; *Stolen Words: Forays into the Origins and Ravages of Plagiarism,* 1989; *Rockets and Rodeos and Other American Spectacles,* 1993; Novels—*Arts and Sciences: A Seventies Seduction,* 1988; *Aurora 7,* 1991; *Henry and Clara,* 1994; *Dewey Defeats Truman,* 1997

SUGGESTED READING: *International Herald Tribune* Feb 1–2, 1997; *Los Angeles Times Book Review* p15 Feb. 14, 1988; *New York Times* Dec. 7, 1989, Feb. 2, 1997; *New York Times Book Review* Mar. 31, 1985, Oct. 29, 1989; *New Yorker* p92+ Jan. 21, 1985, p102+ Sep. 5, 1994; *Salon* (on-line) Jan. 7, 1997; *USA Today* p20 Feb. 24, 1993; *Washington Post* XXI Feb. 17, 1991; *Yale Review* p135+ July 1997; *Contemporary Authors,* Vol. 57, 1997

Mamonova, Tatyana

Dec. 10, 1943– Nonfiction writer; activist

Considered to be the founder of the modern Russian feminist movement, Tatyana Mamonova struggled for years behind the Iron Curtain, attempting to shed light on gender inequality in the former Soviet Union. She tried to publish the first underground Russian journal dedicated to women's writings and issues, but her efforts were thwarted at every turn by the KGB. Eventually forced to flee the USSR, the fiery activist took her cause to other parts of the world, continuing to publish her journal from outside her homeland. Along the way she has completed several volumes of essays, interviews, and speeches devoted to a wide variety of feminist topics, including pornography, workplace wages, sexual harassment, and spousal abuse. In addition, Mamonova is an accomplished artist, creating watercolor works that have been displayed around the world. Today she continues to write, and, bringing her cause into a new medium, has used advances in technology to produce video information sources and to provide material via the Web site for her organization, Women and Earth.

Tatyana Mamonova (Tatiana, according to some sources) was born on December 10, 1943, in Jarolaw (now Russia), USSR, to Arsenii Mamaonov, a lawyer, and Valentina (Panova) Mamonov, an accountant. The budding writer was not aware of feminism as a young woman, but she was well aware of the derogatory manner in which women were treated in Russia. As she told *Ms.* magazine (November 1980), women were treated as inferior beings by men who often used the word baba (equal to the American word "broad") to refer to them. Mamonova was similarly alarmed at the lack of opportunity afforded women in the workplace. Although the Soviet government preached a policy of equality, men held all of the upper management positions in the workforce. Consequently, women did not achieve the type of professional success that men did; the few women who did hold high positions, Mamonova thought, were there as a mere figureheads, installed to display a supposed egalitarian society but deprived of any real power. Mamonova attributed this uneven schism to traditional mores and attitudes rather than governmental decree.

Mamonova worked as an assistant in an antibiotics laboratory from 1961 to 1966 and then as a television writer in Leningrad from 1967 to 1968. The following year, wanting to focus her career more exclusively on writing, she took a position as a poetry reviewer and translator for a youth magazine called *Aurora.* Women's issues or, rather, the lack of focus on these issues in the Soviet Union, remained central to Mamonova's agenda, however, and she attempted to fill the dearth of Soviet feminism by writing essays devoted to the subject. Her efforts proved fruitless, though, as she was often censored. She persevered, though, and in addition to her writing, began painting in her spare time. In 1973 she married Gennady Shikarev (also transliterated as Schikarioff), a graphic artist, who, unlike many men in her native country, supported his wife's feminism—an attitude that earned him scorn among his fellow men.

Despite marriage and motherhood (a second full-time job for the majority of Russian women—at the time, it was reported that more than 80 percent of women in Russia worked outside the home), Mamonova continued her efforts to make public women's issues in Russia. After examining the lifestyles of working married women, Mamonova sought a way for these women to share their common experiences. She approached the feminist philosopher Tatiana Goricheva, the poet Yulia Voznesenskaya, and the novelist Natalya Malakhovskaya with a proposal for the founding of a literary forum where women could share their common experiences and express their own, personal stories. After several meetings and discussions about form and content, a journal was born.

Consisting of a diverse group of essays, poems, fictional stories, and articles, *Woman and Russia* explored a variety of women's issues, including spousal abuse, abortion, and alcoholism among Soviet men. In the first issue the central topic of discussion was birth control, or lack thereof, in the Soviet Union. Even in 1979 all forms of birth control were virtually nonexistent in Russia (a prophylactic pill was available in Bulgaria, but side effects were so severe, many women opted not to use any method), and as a result, the legal option of abortion became a highly popular choice of birth control. *Woman and Russia* looked at the health conditions in some of the major abortion clinics in Russia and found that many undertook unhygienic and even barbaric practices, such as performing the operation without anesthesia. Another article in the premiere issue of *Women and Russia* examined the oppression women faced due to a lingering patriarchal system. The essay was unique in its sympathetic look at the sacrifices that modern Soviet women had to endure in order to juggle career and family, and also exposed the frightening abuse (due to alcohol) that many of these women had to accept to keep their husbands content.

An uproar greeted the debut issue of *Women and Russia*. Women across the Soviet Union rejoiced in the exposure of their suffering, which allowed them to see and understand their own feminist feelings for the first time. The Soviet government, meanwhile, was alarmed at this new feminist ideology thrust into the hands of its constituents, and soon the KGB ordered the women to cease publication. Mamonova doggedly disobeyed: according to *Ms.* magazine, she declared, "We are not ashamed to openly state what we believe to whomever wants to listen, be that person a Russian, a foreigner, or an agent of the KGB."

Mamonova and her fellow editors were warned once again later that year, but the feminists paid them no heed. Soon afterward, the KGB issued Mamonova an ultimatum: Either she would stop publication of the second issue of *Woman and Russia*, or she would be arrested. The KGB had been keeping her under surveillance for months—intercepting her mail, listening to her phone conversations, and following her family and friends. Although she reported the KGB's activities to a higher authority, her pleas fell on deaf ears, and Mamonova was faced with a difficult decision of whether or not to leave the Soviet Union and publish her work from the outside. A burgeoning feud amongst the editors of *Woman and Russia* further complicated her decision. Malakhovskaya, Voznesenskaya, and Goricheva were all active members of the Orthodox church, and as such, wanted the journal to include a combination of social and spiritual women's issues. Mamonova, however, desired a more secular stance, and felt the religious beliefs of the other editors threatened the feminist ideology they hoped to present. Mamonova believed that the nonreligious women in Russia—who accounted for the majority of the female population—would become alienated by an Orthodox feminist movement. When the editors could not reach an agreement on how the journal should be politically and religiously situated, they ended their collaboration.

Mamonova wanted to continue her work on a journal in Russia, but pressure from the KGB increased, and in 1980 the Soviet Union exiled Mamonova and her family. The expulsion coincided with the opening day ceremonies for the Olympics in Moscow, and Mamonova has stated that she believes the "coincidence" was planned by the Soviet government, intent on discouraging the spread of information on Soviet feminist activity to the West. A copy of the original *Woman and Russia* journal had already reached the West, however, grabbing the attention of writers in Paris, and from there it was reprinted and distributed.

Mamonova was determined to continue her work after being forced out of Russia, and began to once again publish *Woman and Russia* while working both in the West and in Third World countries as a lecturer on feminist issues. In 1984 she edited *Women and Russia: Feminist Writings From the Soviet Union*, a book of essays translated by Rebecca Park and Catherine A. Fitzpatrick. Her first publication since her exile, *Women and Russia* received positive reviews from American critics, who celebrated the work as a significant step in altering the role of women in the Soviet Union. As the reviewer for *Choice* (October 1984) wrote, "These voices are simple, clear, passionate, anguished. Although not offering a sophisticated analysis of the situation of women, this book is an important first testimony about the possibilities for feminist thought and activity in the Soviet Union." Other reviewers were impressed with the book's thoroughness, even if some pieces were not as clearly focused as others. "'Feminist Writing' does not fully describe the book; the pieces include history and folklore, and some do not particularly concentrate on women. . . . some pieces are confused, minor, or obscure . . . the pluses are several clear-eyed analyses of Soviet women's position in the state," a reviewer for the *Library Journal* (March 15, 1984) wrote. Jodi Daynard wrote for the *New York Times Book Review* (May 27, 1984) that the volume of essays was "perhaps the most informative and diverse collection of Russian feminist writing to become available in English." Daynard mentioned, however, that the book serves to "offer rare views into little-known aspects of Soviet Life," but that "some issues American readers might expect to hear about—male chauvinism, sexual harassment and liberation—are barely touched on." Daynard concluded that the texts were "well-translated and poignant" essays that "bring us closer to an understanding of Soviet women than has previously been possible."

During this time Mamonova traveled throughout Europe and the U.S., speaking about her exile and the work that still needed to be accomplished for equality in Russia. In addition to her role as writer and editor, she was a Bunting Institute Fellow at Harvard University from 1984 to 1985. She was a scholar in residence at the University of Michigan the following year, and then at Hartford College for Women from 1987 to 1989.

Mamonova's next literary venture, a book titled *Russian Women's Studies: Essays on Sexism in Soviet Culture* (1989), was another collection of feminist writings, this time in speech form. J. Simmerman of *Choice* (September 1989) opined that while the speeches are diverse and intelligent, they lack a common goal or focus. Simmerman wrote, "This is a collection of pieces, indifferently translated by various hands, and it is difficult to determine the intended audience." Simmerman then added, "Mamonova turns a lively and committed mind to issues such as Soviet pornography, attitudes toward women among emigrants, the religiosity of emigrants, and homosexuality in the Soviet Union, among others." Florence A. Rudeman of *Society* (May/June 1990) concurred with this view, writing, "Most of the topics [in this book] are fascinating. But Mamonova's treatment of each is sketchy, disjointed, often without a clear focus or discernible train of thought . . . Mamonova does not examine relevant literature; nor does she develop any other form of evidence for her views . . . Mamonova seems lost." Marilyn French offered a mixed commentary for the *New York Times Book Review* (September 24, 1989), describing the book as "unpretentious prose," but adding that it "lacks the intellectual rigor, breadth, and authority we expect in cultural criticism. Impressionistic appreciation or disparagement may be an acceptable form in the Soviet Union, and perhaps should be here, for the volume of intelligent, passionate essays offers the general reader a portrait of the Soviet state, its cultural and its modern anguish by a woman who will not be silenced." Lesley A. Rimmel of the *Women's Review of Books* (May 1989) wrote, "Scholarly readers may be put off by the essays' declamatory tone and lack of evidence for some claims." She added, however, that "the importance for Western readers of this book, I think, is what it indirectly tells us about sexism in Soviet culture, about what is not known about women and feminism."

From 1990 to 1992 Mamonova was again a scholar in residence, this time at the Graduate Center of the City University of New York. Two years later she completed *Women's Glasnost vs. Naglost:*

Stopping Russian Backlash (1994), a collection of 17 interviews and five essays that further explore a range of issues concerning the women of Russia, including pornography and the rise of women's organizations in the post-Glasnost era. In writing about the book for *Choice* (May 1994), A. H. Koblitz noted, "Mamonova is provocative and entertaining as always, though perhaps more self-contradictory than usual. . . . The essays provide something of interest to everyone, from the specialist in Slavic or women's studies to the general reader." However, Koblitz added, "Somewhat disappointing . . . are the repetitious and tedious interviews that make up most of the volume. Contrary to statements in the forward, the interviews do not represent a 'wide cross section' of society." A reviewer for *Women's Review of Books* (June 1994) critiqued not the interviews contained in the volume, but the inferred, simplistic solution to the issue of inequality in Russia: "[The interviews] do convey the intractability of the problems faced by women in the Soviet successor states today," the reviewer wrote. "But overall, the formula for Stopping Russian Backlash that the subtitle promises is more than Mamonova or her interlocutors can deliver."

In the early 1990s Mamonova founded Woman and Earth Global Eco-Network, an organization devoted to providing information to the women of Russia and the former members of the USSR. The network is not affiliated with any government or religious group, and acts as an independent means by which women can express themselves artistically and verbally. Woman and Earth also produces the *Woman and Earth Almanac,* an international Russian/English eco-feminist publication for which Mamonova serves as editor. The almanac is a continuation of Mamonova's original *Woman and Russia* journal, and as such is distributed free to both individual women and women's groups in the U.S., Russia, and Eastern Europe. The group also produces a video series, *Woman and Earth Productions,* which consists of interviews with famous feminists, including Bella Abzug, Kate Millett, and Andrea Dworkin.

Over the years Mamonova has written articles for a variety of newspapers and magazines including *Ms.* and *Encounters.* She has also written poetry, which has been included in the *American Poetry Anthology,* among other publications. In addition she is an accomplished watercolor artist, contributing her work to two children's books, *Das Radieschen* (1981) and *I Remember* (1995). Her artwork has been exhibited in shows around the world, including Leningrad, Moscow, Vienna, Paris, Milan, London, and New York.

Among her many awards and honors, Tatyana Mamonova has received the Woman of the Year Award from *F Magazine* (1980), Prix litteraire des lectrices book of the year from *Elle* (1982), and the Sono Art Festival Award (1988). Mamonova recently completed a book of short stories and poems titled *Russia Renaissance 2000* (1997). She currently lives with her husband and son, Philip, in Hartford, Connecticut.—D.B.

SUGGESTED READING: *Amazon Books.*; *Ms.* Nov. 1980; *Choice* Oct. 1984, Sep. 1984, May 1994; *Library Journal* Mar. 15, 1984; *New York Times Book Review* May 27, 1984, Sep. 24, 1989; ociety May/June 1990; *Woman and Earth.* Nov. 16, 1998; *Women's Review of Books* May 1989, June 1994; *Book Review Digest* 1984, 1990, 1996; *Contemporary Authors* 1985; *Something About the Author*, 1997

SELECTED WORKS: *Women and Russia: Feminist Writings from the Soviet Union*, 1984; *Russian Women's Studies: Essays on Sexism in Soviet Culture*, 1989; *Women's Glasnost vs. Naglost: Stopping Russian Backlash*, 1994; *Russian Renaissance 2000*, 1997; as illustrator— *Das Radieschen*, 1981; *I Remember*, 1995

Manguel, Alberto

Mar. 13, 1948– Editor; translator; novelist; nonfiction writer; radio and television writer

In the 1990s the editor and translator Alberto Manguel has come into his own as an author. Although he received good notices for *The Dictionary of Imaginary Places*, co-written with Gianni Guadalupi and published in 1980, he has received even greater praise for his novel *News From a Foreign Country Came* (1991) and his nonfiction work *A History of Reading* (1996). He is also a widely respected anthologist, who has compiled a number of unique and fascinating collections which include: *Black Water* (1983), an assortment of science fiction and fantasy; *Dark Arrows* (1984), a group of stories about revenge; *Other Fires* (1986), a collection of fiction by Latin American women; *The Gates of Paradise* (1993), an anthology of erotic fiction; and *In Another Part of the Forest* (1994), a group of stories by prominent gay authors.

The son of Pablo Manguel, a diplomat, and the former Rosalia Finkelstein, Alberto Adrian Manguel was born on March 13, 1948, in Buenos Aires, Argentina. He was educated at the Universidad de Buenos Aires and graduated in 1968. He began his literary career in the late 1960s, as the editor of a pair of Spanish-language story collections for which he also wrote the introductions, *Variaciones sobre un tema de durero* (1968) and *Variaciones sobre un tema political: Cuentos* (1968). A few years later he compiled another collection: *Antologia de la literatura fantastica argentina* (1973). Manguel once claimed that he started compiling anthologies in order to get his friends to read stories he enjoyed. During this period he also wrote many tales of his own, including a number of short stories in Spanish as well as a radio play, *Faire un voyage*, for France Culture Radio in 1972.

In 1980 Manguel and Gianni Guadalupi co-authored *The Dictionary of Imaginary Places*, which was expanded in 1987. A reader's guide to 1,200 imaginary worlds created by authors from all ages, it includes detailed images and maps of such mystical places as Atlantis, Camelot, Dracula's Castle in Transylvania, Jonathan Swift's Brobdingnag, L. Frank Baum's Oz, and Franz Kafka's Penal Colony. Entries include a history of the area, a description of the natives, and a reading list in the form of a travel guide. In his review for *Newsweek* (February 19, 1981), Peter S. Prescott remarked: "Presented with mock solemnity and written with grace and wit, this book is a work of genuine scholarship that is also a pleasure to read." Paul Hornbeck wrote in *Quill and Quire* (January 1981) that "The real allure of the *Dictionary* is not the imaginary places one remembers, but the new ones still to be investigated. And the first-class index (with cross-references for author and book title) makes it reasonably simple to find your way around the more than 1,200 imaginary places." A reviewer for *Library Journal* (January 15, 1981) concurred: "The compilers seem to have done a great deal of research; the dictionary includes both familiar imaginary worlds created by Tolkien, Le Guin, and Lewis Carroll, and unfamiliar and surprising worlds by Gilbert and Sullivan, John Lennon, and Vincente Minelli."

Manguel then edited *Black Water: The Book of Fantastic Literature* (1983), a collection of 72 strange tales of dreams, time warps, hauntings, and bizarre creatures. The anthology featured works ranging from those by such past masters of fantasy as Edgar Allan Poe to those of such modern writers as like Ray Bradbury and Cyntha Ozick. The collection was widely praised. Gregory Maguire, writing in *Horn Book* (SeptemberOctober 1984), noted that "The fantastic never becomes commonplace . . . even in so large a dose—a high compliment to the editor's choices and arrangement." Jack Sullivan in the *New York Times Book Review* (April 26, 1984) called *Black Water* "an uncommonly satisfying collection," and remarked that "Mr. Manguel has introduced each of these 72 imaginative selections with informative, pungent commentary."

Two years later, Manguel put together another anthology, *Dark Arrows* (1985), a collection of stories by late 19th- and early 20th-century authors of various backgrounds, all on the topic of revenge. The variety of writers—Irish, German, British, American, Indian, Brazilian, and Argentine—was so wide it disturbed some critics, like Paul Wright of *Books in Canada* (AugustSeptember 1985), who felt that "At the end, as at the beginning, one is left with the question whether an assortment such as this, so various in tone and period, can effectively be unified, be given a significance and singularity, under such a category as revenge? For whom is the book intended? Will the admirer of Doctorow also sit still for Saki?" However, the reviewer for *Canadian Materials for Schools and Libraries* (November 1985) completely disagreed with Wright's assessment, calling the anthology "a highly recommendable selection of modern short story classics. . . . This collection makes excellent light reading for a very wide audience both lay and specialist." The reviewer added: "Here as elsewhere, we are greatly indebted to Manguel's exceptional skill as a translator and his enthusiasm for his chosen field."

Manguel's next anthology, *Other Fires* (1986), was an ambitious undertaking in which he collected 20 stories by 19 female Latin American authors. Manguel himself translated 13 of the tales into English, and also wrote prefaces for each story that consisted of a brief biography of the author and commentary on the work itself. At the end of the book, Manguel listed other works by the authors. Reviewing the collection for *Library Journal* (March 15, 1986), Marcia Tager called it "a remarkable collection," noting that although the writers "do not speak with a common voice, as they represent cultures and countries that evolved separately. . . . There is an overall aura of magic and surrealism that readers of recent Latin American novels will recognize." "*Other Fires* fills a serious gap in our knowledge of Latin American literature," Mary Morris noted in the *New York Times Book Review* (May 4, 1986). "Still," she added, "one cannot help but wish that the stories in this volume had represented a wider range of its writers' concerns and provided us with more diverse images of the Latin American woman."

In the years since, Manguel has compiled a number of highly regarded anthologies with diverse themes. Among others, they include *Evening Games: Chronicle of Parents and Children* (1986), *The Oxford Book of Canadian Ghost Stories* (1990), *Black Water II: More Fantastic Literature* (1990), an anthology of children's literature entitled *Seasons* (1990), *White Fire: Further Fantastic Literature* (1991), *Canadian Mystery Stories* (1991), a collection of erotic fiction entitled *The Gates of Paradise* (1991), and a collection of gay short fiction called *In Another Part of the Forest* (1994).

In 1991 Manguel published his first novel, *News From a Foreign Country Came*. It is the story of Captain Antoine Berence, a retired French army officer who served as a military adviser to oppressive governments in Argentina and Algiers. The novel covers 40 years of Berence's extraordinary life, and is told by present-day characters reflecting on the past. After the captain retires, he moves to the Labrador coast of Canada, near Quebec, in order to enjoy a quiet life with his wife, Marianne, and his daughter, Ana. When one of the pieces of his past is uncovered by his wife, it threatens to destroy his whole world. Ana is caught between her parents without completely understanding what has happened. Still, she is able to read the writing on the wall when two men come to Canada to hunt a former intelligence officer who had worked with the Argentine dictatorship. *News from a Foreign Country Came* received generally positive reviews. David Keymer of *Library Journal* (February 1, 1991)

remarked that "Manguel . . . has crafted an achingly intense novel, outstanding in its empathy." Amanda Hopkinson of the *New Statesman and Society* (April 19, 1991) concurred, arguing that Manguel's "voice is at once poetically associative and philosophically categorical, on such themes as cruelty, guilt and shame. . . . [A] highly original and striking new voice to listen for." Richard Ryan, critic for the *Washington Post Book World* (May 5, 1991), raved that "*News From a Foreign Country Came* is written with watercolors of melting poetry, but it's the substance that lingers after the style has echoed away. In his depiction of history collapsing into a tangle of guilt, Alberto Manguel has created a grim parable of considerable power. This impressive first novel suggests that Manguel has both the intellect and the voice to speak to his readers on the highest levels of fiction."

Five years later Manguel wrote a nonfiction book, *A History of Reading* (1996), a collection of related essays about the love of reading throughout the ages. Manguel skips back and forth in time, from discussions of reading in ancient Sumer and Greece to looks at the reading habits of relatively modern literary celebrities like Walt Whitman and Rainer Maria Rilke. Manguel also included autobiographical anecdotes, such as his experiences as the personal reader for Jorge Luis Borges after the author went blind. The book received mixed reviews. Michael Milburn of the *New York Times Book Review* (November 17, 1996) complained that "Its fascinating content notwithstanding, this book is often a chore to read. Mr. Manguel possesses a plain, occasionally plodding prose style, and his frequent lyrical and autobiographical passages prove far less lively than the historical sections," but concluded his review with the admission that, "Stylistic complaints aside, one feels . . . envious of [the author's] passion and grateful for this prodigious book." Gabriel Josipovici, reviewing the book for the English edition of *New Statesman and Society* (July 19, 1996), remarked on how "there are interesting things here, notably Manguel's account of what reading to the blind Borges was like, and his close examination of Rilke's German translations of the poems of the 16th-century French poet Louise Lab. . . . Too much of the rest of the book merely made me nod—often in agreement, but just as often as a prelude to falling asleep." Finally, Nancy Shires of *Library Journal* (July 1996) called it "a fascinating book to dip into or read cover to cover."

Manguel has also written a number of television and radio plays for Canadian broadcasting. They include the radio works "Death and the Compass" (1984), adapted from the story by Jorge Luis Borges; "Secret Ceremony" (1984), adapted from the story by Marco Denevi; "The Man Who Liked Dickens" (1986), adapted from the story by Evelyn Waugh; "The Word for World is Forest" (1988), adapted from the novel by Urusla K. LeGuin; "The Alley Cat" (1989), adapted from the novel by Yves Beaand uchemin. His television plays include "Reunion" (1989) and "Voodoo Taxi" (1991) for the Canadian series *Inside Stories*. He has been a contributor to such noted periodicals as *Commonweal*, the *New York Times*, *Saturday Night*, the *Village Voice*, and the *Washington Post*.

In addition, Manguel is a translator of books, from English and French into Spanish and from French, Spanish, Italian, and German into English. For his thorough work, he has been called a "literary outrider" by a reviewer at the Toronto *Globe and Mail* (November 26, 1994), one who is "bringing news of the world to those of us locked in the provinciality of our monolingualism."

In 1975 Alberto Manguel married Pauline Ann Brewer, a teacher, before traveling to the University of London a year later in order to continue his education. The couple divorced in 1986. Their marriage produced three children: Alice Emily, Rachel Claire, and Rupert Tobias. In 1982 Manguel immigrated to Canada and became a naturalized citizen six years later.—C.M.

SUGGESTED READING: *Books in Canada* p19 Aug.Sep. 1985; *CM* p255 Nov. 1985, p19 Jan. 1987; (Toronto) *Globe and Mail* pE 10 Nov. 26, 1994; *Horn Book* p631 Sep.Oct. 1984; *Library Journal* p136 Jan. 15, 1981, p79 Mar. 15, 1986, p106 Feb. 1, 1991, July 1996; *New Statesman and Society* p36 Apr. 19, 1991, p48 July 19, 1996; *New York Times Book Review* p16 Aug. 26, 1984, p35 May 4, 1986, p37 Nov. 17, 1996; *Newsweek* p86 Feb. 9, 1981; *Quill & Quire* p30 Jan. 1981, p70 July 1984, p67 Sep. 1996; *Washington Post* p6 May 5, 1991; *Contemporary Authors New Revision Series*, vol. 44, 1994

SELECTED WORKS: Fiction—*News From a Foreign Country Came*, 1991; Nonfiction—*The Dictionary of Imaginary Places* (with G. Guadalupi), 1980, expanded 1987; *A History of Reading*, 1996; As editor—*Varianciones sobre un tema de durero*, 1968; *Variaciones sobre un tema political: Cuentos*, 1968; *Black Water: The Book of Fantastic Literature*, 1983; *Dark Arrows*, 1984; *Other Fires*, 1986; *Evening Games: Chronicle of Parents and Children*, 1986; *The Oxford Book of Canadian Ghost Stories*, 1990; *Black Water II: More Fantastic Literature*, 1990; *Seasons*, 1990; *White Fire: Further Fantastic Literature*, 1991; *The Gates of Paradise*, 1991; *In Another Part of the Forest*, 1994; Drama adaptions—*Death and the Compass*, 1984; *Secret Company*, 1984; *The Man Who Liked Dickens*, 1986; *The Word for World is Forest*, 1988; *The Alley Cat*, 1989

Mantel, Hilary

1952– Writer

Hilary Mantel is the savagely funny author of such satirical works as *Every Day Is Mother's Day* (1985) and *Vacant Possession* (1986) as well as her most recent novel about growing up in the 1950s and 1960s, *An Experiment in Love* (1996). Though many of the ideas for her novels come from her youth—she grew up poor and Irish in an unsympathetic England—she has also traveled extensively and in doing so has broadened the scope of her writing. She has written about foreigners' experiences in such places as Saudi Arabia and Africa in works such as *Eight Months on Ghazzah Street* (1988) and *A Change of Climate* (1994), respectively. She has also written a surrealistic satire on the Catholic Church, *Fludd* (1989), which brought her critical praise and a wider readership, and in 1992 she published the book whose subject had drawn her to writing in the first place—*A Place of Greater Safety*, a massive historical novel set during the French Revolution. Discussing *Every Day Is Mother's Day* with one interviewer, the writer remarked: "All my characters had created prisons for themselves, and the more they tried to break out, the more securely they found themselves confined. The ultimate prison is the lack of imagination; the characters are so tightly sealed into their own worlds that they are oblivious to the dire events laying waste to everything around them." It is a description that applies to *Every Day Is Mother's Day* and to much of her writing as a whole.

In an autobiographical sketch written for *World Authors 1990-1995*, the author discusses how her life has influenced her work: "I was born in 1952 in a mill-village in Derbyshire, in the north-west of England. Most of my ancestors were poor, Irish and Catholic. My great-grandmother, who had 12 children, could not read. My grandmother left school at 12 to work in the mill. My mother left the school at 14 to work in the mill. She was an intelligent and beautiful woman who wanted better things for me, her first child. The village was a bleak place, dominated by gossip: harsh people in a harsh moorland landscape. I wrote about this village in my novel *Fludd*.

"I was a very timid and bookish child who lived in my own head. The dominant emotion of my childhood was terror. I was ill a great deal, fevers of unknown cause. I was afraid of ghosts, and also that my family would break up.

"When I was 11 my stepfather took us—my mother and myself, and my two younger brothers—to live in a new town a few miles away in Cheshire, and to make a new start. I went to a convent school called Harrytown Convent, where at first I felt a bit of an outsider because my accent was all wrong; the British class system has always been a great oppression to me. Within a year or two I had found my feet and realised that I was intellectually able, which I had not understood until this point. I became happy at school, but not at home.

Having grown up a Catholic, I lost my faith at 12. Through my teens I fed my imagination with novels and with left-wing ideology. At 18 I became head girl of my convent school and a member of the Young Communist League, a contradiction I felt quite able to embrace.

"At eighteen I went to the London School of Economics to read law. I wrote about this period of my life (and about childhood too) in *An Experiment in Love*, though my heroine Carmel grows up in a different town and has different parents. My rightward drift began—I joined the Labour Party. In my second year I transferred to Sheffield University and married Gerald McEwen, a geology student, whom I had known since I was 16. My health broke down, and I came out of university with no clear plans.

"Gerald got a teaching job, and I became a social work assistant in a geriatric hospital, drawn as I was to extremes of wretchedness. When I was 22 I decided I would make it my life's work to write a novel about the French Revolution. I left my job and took jobs as a saleswoman, because then my mind was free for much of the time. I gave my evenings and weekends to research.

"In 1977 Gerald got a job as a geologist in Botswana. We lived there for five years. By the end of 1979 I had completed two drafts of *A Place of Greater Safety*. As soon as I had finished it I became overwhelmed by illness. I was found to have severe endometriosis, which explained the pain I'd been in through my adult life. I had major surgery—it was a life-crisis—and decided I must continue be a writer—beyond the French Revolution book—because I would not be fit for anything else.

"I decided to write a novel which would be short, commercial but the best I could do. We went to live in Saudi Arabia and I completed *Every Day Is Mother's Day*. In 1985 it was published in England, and was very well reviewed. Gerald and I returned to England in 1986, just as my second novel *Vacant Possession* came out.

"I then wrote my Saudi Arabia novel, *Eight Months on Ghazzah Street*. (I have written about Africa in *A Change of Climate*). I began to pick up a bit of book reviewing, and entered and won the Shiva Naipaul Prize for travel writing, for a 4,000-word essay on Saudi Arabia. The *Spectator* wanted a new film critic and were prompted to try me out, and I stayed with them for four years. At one time or another I've written for almost every newspaper, above the level of the tabloids, and for most literary magazines. I've done a political comment column, and at the moment I preview TV for the *Observer*.

"My fourth novel, *Fludd*, won three literary prizes, and was a break-through for me as far as sales and public recognition are concerned. I started *A Change of Climate*, but a friend persuaded me to take my French Revolution book off the shelf. I did a third draft at enormous speed, and it was published in 1992, winning the £20,000 Sunday Express 'Book of the Year' award. My latest book, *An Experiment in Love*, won the Hawthornden

Prize. This prize, founded in 1919, is the one I always coveted. I wanted to win it so that I could walk in the footsteps of Evelyn Waugh, one of my favourite writers—whose son, Auberon, has been a most kind mentor to me.

"I live in a dormitory suburb in Surrey with Gerald, who now works for IBM, and my cats. I try to live as quiet a life as possible, outwardly, because of the constant seething turmoil in my head. I am a benevolent public presence, who sits on committees, judges prizes, advises young writers, corresponds with academics and potters through life with a serene smile. I do this to puzzle people, as I do not think it is wise for a writer to be too well-understood. I am really a sort of undercover terrorist, setting out to create frequent small explosions in the psyche of my readers. My writing is funny—I hope—but also savage, and my subject matter is not for the squeamish. I like to work at the interface between the personal and the political, and I write quite a lot about power and its abuse. Transformation is a major theme of my work, perhaps its chief preoccupation. Danton: 'We are trying, you see, to alter the nature of things.' Fludd: 'I have come to transform you, transformation is my business.'

"I am committed to fiction that is accessible but layered, and I try to escape categories and keep on the move. Shakespeare is my God, and Brecht my greatest influence."

———

Hilary Mantel's first book, *Every Day Is Mother's Day*, and its sequel, *Vacant Possession*, take aim at the welfare services in the north of England. As Mantel stated in one interview: "With those two books, I wanted to make people laugh; to make some points about social work theory and practice; and to give a picture of the state of England as I saw it."

The critics, including Auberon Waugh, writing in the *Daily Mail* (March 28, 1985), praised Mantel as a "major new talent," while noting that *Every Day Is Mother's Day* "starts as a black comedy and then slips into a savage satire on social services." Bill Greenwell, who reviewed *Vacant Possession* for *New Statesman & Society* (May 30, 1986), called the book an "exceptional novel" that was "filled with fiendish glee, all of it held in hysterical check by the writer's wry style. . . . It has a wittily nasty plot, but never gloats over its victims."

Through Mantel's work is not strictly autobiographical, elements of her life's experiences have pervaded her novels. She lived for three and a half years in Saudi Arabia, and that experience influenced her next work, *Eight Months on Ghazzah Street*. The novelist has said that the book "is based on my experiences in Jidda, Saudi Arabia, but it is certainly not a disguised autobiography. It is about Frances Shore, a young Englishwoman living in the city; her circle of British and American friends; and her involvement—which turns out to be a rather dangerous involvement—in the affairs of her Muslim neighbors."

For her next novel, *Fludd*, Mantel returned to England for her setting, but her new target for mockery was the Catholic Church. The plot revolves around the arrival of the bishop at the midland parish of Fetherhaughton, where disillusioned, alcoholic Father Angwin leads an ambivalent flock. To help the condition of the church, the bishop sends a curate—Fludd, who brings with him small miracles for every downtrodden character in the novel. Clare Plodden, reviewing the book for *The Spectator* (September 16, 1989), wrote: "The implausible plot . . . seems to have given fresh impetus to Hilary Mantel's comic genius, for this is a book which in its light touch and pointed wit, its rapid pace and deliberately mannered style, rivals Muriel Spark at her best." A critic for *New Statesman & Society* (September 15, 1989) noted: "Fludd . . . is a quaint and lovely novel, thick with images and angry jubilant characters who defy the authority of a finger-wagging God and his 'pork-butcher' bishop and choose mystery and unholy expectations. It doesn't only believe in miracles; it believes in happy endings."

In 1992 Mantel published the historical novel about the French Revolution she had been working on since 1979—*A Place of Greater Safety*, a sprawling epic at 749 pages. Though there were a few critics who complained about the book's length, most were impressed with Mantel's deft handling of her fictional characters against the backdrop of history. Some confusion resulted when Mantel presented fictional conversations between historical figures. The *New York Times Book Review* (May 9, 1993) critic wondered: "Are we reading history amplified by the empathy of the novelist or fiction dressed up in historical costume?" Yet a writer for *New York Newsday* (March 18, 1993) found: "Although it is a little long, Mantel's novel is subtle and ironic while keeping up a sweeping excitement." Michael Upchurch, reviewing the book for the *Washington Post Book World* (July 20, 1993), believed: "It almost goes without saying that this novel is a keen study of factional excess in a situation of total social breakdown. On a more sublime level, it rigorously explores the hazards of translating ideas—especially *ideals*—into reality, when reality can all too easily assume a life of its own, often inverting and perverting its very sources of inspiration."

With *A Change of Climate*, Mantel returned to the modern day and the realm of her own experiences. This time she explored Africa, where she and her husband lived for five years. The book follows the lives of Ralph and Anna Eldred, from the time they first become missionaries in South Africa in the 1950s to the period of their involvement in the anti-Apartheid struggle, which leads to their arrest and eventual deportation. It is after they are moved across the border to Bechuanaland that they encounter catastrophe. The reviews of the book were mixed. The *Financial Times* (March 19, 1994) reviewer J. D. F. Jones commented: "My only hesitation is that . . . Ralph and Anna both remain a fraction under-exposed. They remain always at a certain distance. We recognize them, but we do not enter their private lives, and so we are impressed where we should be moved." A critic for the *London Review of Books* (April 28, 1994) suggested: "Ultimately this is a morality tale without a moral. The heave of good and evil goes on (and in the South Africa chapters at a very great pace), but Mantel is a curiously invisible author, and doesn't make her affections and sympathies either clear-cut or clearly felt."

Mantel's most recent novel, *An Experiment in Love*, is considerably more conventional than her previous two, since it reflects on the moral and psychological growth of one little Irish girl, Carmel Bain. Carmel, who is also the narrator, is an anorectic. Through the course of the novel the reader sees Carmel change in response to the changes of those around her: Karina, the daughter of Polish immigrants who continually gains weight as Carmel loses it, and Julianne, the daughter of a dentist. Meeting in a northern English grammar school in the 1950s, the threesome eventually enroll at London University together. Though the action of the book revolves around the changes that take place in all the girls, the *New York Times Book Review* (June 2, 1996) observed: "This is Carmel's story, but it is that of her generation as well: girls at the end of the [1960s], caught between the two sets of values, who had the pill but still ironed their boyfriends' shirts." A reviewer for the *Globe and Mail* (July 1, 1995) found that the book "has an intellectual architecture that is decorated with wit and sagacity, and it's exceptional because it demands a thoughtful response from the reader."

—C.M.

SUGGESTED READING: *Daily Mail* Mar. 28, 1985; *Financial Times* II p17 Mar. 19, 1994; *Globe and Mail* C p6 July 1, 1995; *London Review of Books* p13 Apr. 28, 1994; *New Statesman & Society* May 30, 1986, p34 Sep. 15, 1989; *New York Newsday* Mar. 18, 1993; *New York Times Book Review* p21 May 9, 1993, p 11 June 2, 1996; *Spectator* p44 Sep. 16, 1989; *Washington Post* D p2 July 20, 1993; *Contemporary Authors* vol. 125, 1989

SELECTED WORKS: *Every Day Is Mother's Day*, 1985; *Vacant Possession*, 1986; *Eight Months on Ghazzah Street*, 1988; *Fludd*, 1989; *A Place of Greater Safety*, 1992; *A Change of Climate*, 1994; *An Experiment in Love*, 1996

Marable, Manning

May 13, 1950– Historian; journalist; college professor

Manning Marable, a prolific African-American historian and social critic, has placed himself on the firing line with his column, "Along the Color Line," published for more than 20 years in more than 100 African-American newspapers. In his column and in many books of essays, Marable has advocated "transformationist" politics for African-Americans. As opposed to integrationists, who want to become part of the already existing structure, and nationalists, who want to create separate institutions, transformationists seek to form alliances with other disadvantaged groups and transform society into a more democratic, egalitarian model. Marable has also written a biography of W. E. B. DuBois, widely praised for its author's skill in depicting the scholar and activist's life while maintaining a disinterested attitude toward DuBois as a social theorist.

Manning Marable was born on May 13, 1950 in Dayton, Ohio, where his mother, June Morehead Marable, was an educator and a minister in the AME church. Marable attended Earlham College, a Quaker institution in Indiana, receiving his A. B. degree in 1971. He began his graduate studies at the University of Wisconsin in Madison, where he obtained his master's degree, then completed work on his Ph.D. at the University of Maryland in 1976. His career as an educator began at Tuskegee Institute in 1969. By 1982 he had moved up the academic ladder to Luce Distinguished Professor at Williams College.

Marable later became a professor at Fisk University and director of its Race Relations Institute; at Colgate University he was director of the African and Hispanic Studies Program. In addition, he has served as director of the University of Colorado's Center for the Study of Race and Ethnicity, and at Columbia University he has served as professor of history and director of the Institute for Research in African-American Studies. He thus emerged as one of the most important spokespersons for the left in the African-American community. Between his graduating from college and his assuming the position at Columbia, he published unceasingly as a syndicated columnist in African-American newspapers (his column, appearing in more than 100 newspapers, is entitled "Along the Color Line") and as a writer of books.

For Marable, Christopher Columbus did not merely discover America. "Columbus's landfall set in motion an epoch in which a thing called 'race' was discovered and social dominance was based on it. . . . Columbus represents fundamentally the beginnings of modern white racism and the constructions of racial identities in America," Marable declared at a gathering sponsored by the National Congress of American Indians, according to Lynne Duke, writing in the *Washington Post* (October 11, 1992). "The only way we can end the patterns of prejudice," Manning had told Duke for another *Washington Post* (June 8, 1992) interview, "is to deconstruct the idea of race." He defined race as "an unequal relationship between social groups, rooted in power and privilege."

Americans identifying themselves as politically left of center should reexamine and revise "socialist politics," Marable observed in his prescription for "a new American socialism" in *Progressive* (February 1993). The left, according to Marable, would need to resolve the practical problems facing, for example, racial minorities and initiate political interventions that would empower the oppressed. The socialists should merge their struggle with "larger, stronger currents for social change," such as people of color, environmentalists, and other groups with pressing agendas. Marable had already declared in an article published in both the *Grand Rapids Times* (April 25, 1991) and the *Utne Reader* (September 1991) that the only true source of black empowerment would be the reinvestment in the community of the profits of entrepreneurship. Businesses run by whites, because they are generally larger than their black-owned counterparts, can sell their goods and services more cheaply, draining money from black communities; thus, self-empowerment for African-Americans would come only from the creation of jobs arising from investment capital in the black community.

Marable's position as a leader of the ongoing struggle against racism has scarcely changed over the years. It is the social reality that is different. "The historical circumstances have changed fundamentally from the days we sought an integrated cup of coffee," he said at the NAACP conference in Chicago in 1994, according to a report by Don Terry in the *New York Times* (July 10, 1994). The movement to desegregate the nation was successful, but "The terms of the debate are not about integration anymore," Marable maintained. "The issue now is black survival in an era when the number of black people who are in prison doubles every seven years. . . . The problems facing African-Americans today require a whole new set of political assumptions and skills." Applying that idea to black studies programs, he told Peter Applebome in a *New York Times* (November 3, 1996) interview, "Black studies . . . has to be socially responsible. . . . *It only has vibrancy and meaning if it illuminates problems in the daily life of black people and its historical roots.*"

Marable's overall philosophy of liberation is "neither nationalist nor integrationist but rather 'transformationist,'" as George M. Fredrickson commented, reviewing Marable's 1995 volume, *Beyond Black and White: Transforming African-American Politics*, in the *New York Review of Books* (April 18, 1996). Marable expressed the view in this book that only "symbolic representation" has been achieved by policies that have placed individuals in positions of prominence and responsibility but have failed to empower the disadvantaged group as a whole. Basic social and economic problems have not been addressed. Only by transforming the paradigm of race relations, which stem from a social construction and not from biological fact, can true equality be achieved. The transformationists, according to Marable, "seek the redistribution of resources and the democratization of state power along more egalitarian lines."

In his books, Marable has consistently maintained the need for a theoretical underpinning to societal transformation. While he was director of Fisk University's Race Relations Institute, he published *How Capitalism Underdeveloped Black America: Problems in Race, Political Economy, and Society* (1983). The book's thesis is that "American capitalism has always systematically underdeveloped, by constant expropriation of surplus value created by black labor," people of color. Marable presented accounts of the exploitation of black women, the poor, and prisoners by capitalism and described the systematic destruction of black educational and religious institutions. The *Choice* (July 1983) reviewer declared the book to be of little value because Marable replaced true Marxist analysis with "assertions." William Z. Schenck, writing in *Library Journal* (June 15, 1983), agreed that the book's "one-sidedness" detracted from its usefulness.

From Marable's Marxist viewpoint, establishing a sense of class consciousness is extremely important, but Americans in general have a "historic inability to link theory to practical political endeavors," which "contributes to the Black elite's failure to advance a systemic criticism of US capitalism," as Marable wrote in *Black American Politics: From the Washington Marches to Jesse Jackson* (1985). "The labor theory of value," he added, "is alien to the accommodationists and to most reformers."

Marxist historian Philip S. Foner, reviewing *Black American Politics* for *Choice* (February 1986), called it "a major contribution to the literature of black politics . . . that makes clear that race and class in America are closely interrelated." He complained, however, that Marable's attitude toward black struggles was less than positive, conveying "the impression of unavailing black protest against persistent exploitation." Cedric Herring, writing in *Contemporary Sociology*, felt that from a scholarly viewpoint Marable's attacks on "the sacred cows of Black Marxists, nationalists, integrationists, and accommodationists" could "provide a theoretical framework that makes sense of the various modes of expression that Black Americans and other oppressed groups historically have found to facilitate their political and economic interests."

In Marable's *African and Caribbean Politics: From Kwame Nkrumah to the Grenada Revolution* (1987), he examined the rise of authoritarianism in postcolonial Africa and the Caribbean. He cited as examples Kwame Nkrumah in Ghana, Forbes Burnham in Guyana, and Maurice Bishop in Grenada, men whose "political leadership is . . . orga-nized on charismatic personalism and a repressive institutionalism," according to Alvin Magid, the *Choice* (January 1988) reviewer. Magid felt that Marable's study was too narrow an analysis of "the roots of contemporary political authoritarianism in Africa and of the black diaspora." Paul Gilroy, writing in the *New Statesman* (June 19, 1987), disagreed, maintaining that Marable's "wide-ranging, activist scholarship is centrally concerned with how an authentically democratic socialism can be constructed in societies which lack the revolutionary agency of a fully-fledged, industrial proletariat." He praised Marable for an "attempt to develop the African diaspora as a unit of radical historical enquiry." However, Gilroy, too, felt that Marable's analysis was vitiated by appeals "to the sterile formulae of anachronistic Marxism."

In *Beyond Black and White: Transforming African-American Politics* (1995), a collection of essays from various periods, Marable attempted to create new definitions of race for an evolving culture. He observed in the preface that "'race' as it has been understood within American society is being rapidly redefined, along with the basic structure of the economy, with profound political consequences for all segments and classes." He called for new alliances to be formed between African-Americans and all other disadvantaged peoples. "By dismantling the narrow politics of racial identity and selective self-interest, by going beyond 'black' and 'white,' we may construct new values, new institutions, and new visions of an America beyond traditional racial categories and racial oppression," Marable wrote. Marable's call for new leadership, according to George M. Fredrickson, who discussed *Beyond Black and White* in the pages of the *New York Review of Books* (April 18, 1996), stems from his belief that only "symbolic representation" has been achieved by integration and that "successful blacks are not accountable to the black community and too readily become pawns of the white establishment." The appointment of Clarence Thomas to the Supreme Court is an example of "the bankruptcy of 'symbolic representation.'" In "Beyond Racial Identity Politics: Toward a Liberation Theory for Multicultural Democracy," Marable presented the "transformationist agenda": "Unlike the integrationists, who seek 'representation' within the system as it is, or the nationalists, who generally favor the construction of parallel racial institutions controlled by blacks, the transformationists basically seek the redistribution of resources and the democratization of state power along more egalitarian lines." Fredrickson found Marable's ideas to be utopian and complained that they were often couched in "rhetoric that seems tired and anachronistic," but he held out hope for Marable's transformationism, noting that visions "of a better society that seem utopian today may become feasible . . . in the future under conditions that we cannot yet foresee."

Fred McKissack, writing in the *Progressive* (February 1996), agreed that "Marable doesn't offer any great new insight into what we could do to attain his vision of a multiracial and truly democratic movement." He conceded, however, that Marable had "articulated the goal well." Herbert Shapiro, reviewing *Beyond Black and White* for *Choice* (May 1996), was also sympathetic with Marable's effort to avoid "a parochial, narrow nationalism" and found "a persuasive affirmation of the need to set black advancement in the context of struggles for basic social change." He termed the book "a valuable, informed analysis of the changing dimensions of the racial question in US society."

Another collection of Marable's essays, *Black Liberation in Conservative America* (1997), continued Marable's dissection of American and international society with a focus on race. He took on NAFTA, conservative politics and racism in the 1990s, and transnational perspectives on race and revolution; discussed such polarizing figures as Louis Farrakhan and O. J. Simpson; and analyzed from a progressive viewpoint "the ways race, class, and gender—our modern 'peculiar institutions'—disempower most Americans," according to Mary Carroll, who reviewed *Black Liberation in Conservative America* for *Booklist* (February 15, 1997). L. H. Grothaus in *Choice* (June 1997) commented favorably on Marable's explanation that "Americans who have been on the losing end of major economic changes" are also on the losing end politically in the "Richard Nixon/George Wallace, Ronald Reagan/George Bush, and the Newt Gingrich eras;" Grothaus supported Marable's call for "a new paradigm in which. . . . class unity" produces "a multicultural acceptance of differences and a recognition of common interests."

Marable has continued to oppose the concept of leadership based solely on charisma. "A radical democratic alternative ideology and politics would begin by popularizing the idea that the people, not charismatic leaders, have the capacity to challenge U.S. Government and corporate power," he wrote in an essay in the *Nation* (December 22, 1997). Marable endorsed the principles of the Black Radical Congress and its call for "the renaissance of a black antiracist, anticorporate movement that defines politics as the struggle for grassroots power." His book *Black Leadership*, a critique, was published in 1998. Also in 1998, Marable published in the *Nation* (December 14) an essay, "Beyond Color-Blindness," in which he issued a clarion call for integration—a term he defines as cooperation among all who struggle to protect reproductive rights, oppose the death penalty, and seek a living wage. Still, "new formations composed primarily if not exclusively of racialized ethnic minorities," he wrote, "have a special responsibility for crafting new strategies of political intervention and mobilization." In a new, more democratic social order, race would "disappear" as a "fundamental category for the distribution of power, material resources and privilege." Until that is fully achieved, however, white "progressives can help that process along by working closely with us, but not always in the same political movements and organizations."
—S.Y.

SUGGESTED READING: *Booklist* p999 Feb. 15, 1997; *Choice* p919 Feb. 1986, p835 Jan. 1988, p1545 May 1996, p1730 June 1997; *Contemporary Sociology* p639 July 1986; *Library Journal* p1261 June 15, 1983; *Nation* p21+ Dec. 22, 1997, p29+ Dec. 14, 1998; *New Statesman* p29 June 19, 1987; *New York Review of Books* p16+ Apr. 18, 1996; *New York Times* IV p6 Nov. 1, 1992, A p24 Nov. 3, 1996; *Progressive* p42+ Feb. 1996; *Washington Post* A p1 June 8, 1992, A p10 Oct. 11, 1992

SELECTED BOOKS: *Race, Reform, and Rebellion: The Second Reconstruction in Black America 1945–1982*, 1984; *Black American Politics: From the Washington Marches to Jesse Jackson*, 1985; *W. E. B. DuBois, Black Radical Democrat*, 1986; *African and Caribbean Politics: From Kwame Nkrumah to the Grenada Revolution*, 1987; *The Crisis of Color and Democracy: Essays on Race, Class, and Power*, 1992; *Blackwater: Historical Studies in Race, Class Consciousness, and Revolution*, 1993; *Beyond Black and White: Transforming African-American Politics*, 1995; *Speaking Truth to Power: Essays on Race, Resistance, and Radicalism*, 1996; *Black Liberation in Conservative America*, 1997; *Black Leadership*, 1998

Margolis, David

Jan. 31, 1943– Writer

David Margolis, the American-born fiction writer and journalist, emigrated to Israel in 1993 to accept a writer's residency in a program in the Negev region. The relocation was, for him, a culmination of sorts, for much of his writing immediately prior to the move had been a journalistic exploration of his own Jewish roots and of the changing face of the Jewish community in America, as seen in his role as an editor and writer for a number of ethnic periodicals. His decision to sink new roots in Israel brought a "burst of energy" to his literary life, as evidenced by the fact that all of his published books—the novels *The Stepman* (1996) and *Change of Partners* (1997), the short-story collection *The Time of Wandering* (1996), and a Holocaust memoir, *The Muselmann* (1994), which he cowrote—have emerged since 1993. In the 1960s and 1970s, Margolis had lived a somewhat itinerant life, moving through several communes and sustaining himself as a professor in small colleges

Courtesy of David Margolis

David Margolis

and as a Hollywood story analyst before immersing himself in writing about Jewish concerns.

For *World Authors 1990–1995*, he writes: "I was born in Brooklyn in 1943; all my grandparents were Yiddish-speaking immigrants, both my parents were native New Yorkers. I was 'educated' in public schools, where I became aware of myself as a writer in my junior year of high school. I didn't have much context for such a career choice, but I read a lot about the lives of artists.

"I began as a poet. In those years—the early Sixties—the world was beginning to catch on fire. I dropped out of college in my sophomore year and went adventuring—looking for love and, with the catch-all ambition of a writer, for 'experience.'

"I spent much of my 20s wandering with notebook in hand—to France, to Mexico, to that strange country called California—learning reality and taking notes on it in the form of poems. I believed then that the poet's careless drifting was likely in the end to have more focus than the ordinary man's careful plan, and I still think I was half right.

"The watershed experience of those years was an 18-month stay on a country commune in southern Oregon. There I learned the essential worldly lessons of my young manhood: how to use tools, how to work hard, how to live with people, how to love a piece of land.

"That time of communal living marked for me a transition between wandering and coming home, for I met my wife there. We left the commune, together with her two small children, to pursue a more private life. Soon after, I tumbled down (in Byron's phrase) to prose.

"Writing stories seemed to me then a brilliant gesture toward practicality. More practical still, I finished college, earned an MFA, taught writing in college and, as *pater familias*, increasingly came to understand that the kind of family I wanted—the only kind I understood, really—was a Jewish family.

"Much followed from this perception, combined with my continuing search for a reliable intellectual and spiritual path: immersion in Jewish sources and Jewish religious observance, labors of love translating Hebrew texts, deep involvement in Jewish communal life in the various places I lived, and a career as a journalist writing particularly about Jewish communal issues.

"As a journalist, too, I wrote 'stories'—true ones, as we journalists like to claim—and meanwhile discovered a lot of useful stories that can only be written as fiction. For seven years, I also contributed a wide-ranging opinion column, 'In the Neighborhood,' to the Los Angeles *Jewish Journal* and other weekly papers around the country.

"Another fruit of journalism was the book *The Muselmann: Diary of A Jewish Slave Laborer*, a Holocaust memoir which I composed from notes left behind after his death by Holocaust survivor David Matzner (published by KTAV, 1994). There are by now many memoirs of the Holocaust in print, all horrifying, each unique, and all in some ways grimly the same. But the concluding chapter of *The Muselmann* contains a narrative detail that, I think, ranks among the unforgettable grotesqueries of Holocaust literature; readers with limited time should start with Chapter 9.

"My interests as a fiction writer were partly determined by my having come of age in the Sixties: wandering, escape, ecstatic experience, the search for community, how men and women make each other crazy, disappointment. However, many of those same interests crop up again, reunderstood, as the literary and intellectual interests of a Jew reinvestigating his tradition. The vocation of poet is deeply mixed in, too, announcing itself in the insistence that language itself has a story to tell and that visionary truth may crouch hiding inside mundane events and objects. Most of these concerns, and the various voices that their expression demands, are explored in *The Time of Wandering*, a collection of my short stories published in 1996 (Bright Idea Books, Jerusalem).

"My first novel, *The Stepman* (Permanent Press, 1996), tells the story of a troubled marriage and stepfamily. Its deeper themes, however, are the awful inescapability of one's own personality and the task of truly becoming married to the life one has made for oneself.

"*Change of Partners* (Permanent Press, 1997), a love story set in a West Coast country commune in the early 1970s, tells the story of a young man's encounter with the pleasures and dangers of a life without conventional boundaries. The novel is ribald and wild, as befits a work about a time and place that seems now almost like another planet.

It is also, I think, the most accurate and yet loving account of the Sixties communal experience yet to appear in fiction.

"In 1993–94, I was awarded a writer's residency at the Arad Arts Project, in Israel's Negev region. Such residencies always offer a heady mix (alas, only temporary) of financial security and unfettered time to do one's work—they're heaven, in short. This one also allowed me to realize a long-time dream to live in Israel—to test the waters, so to speak. The waters being fine, the following year I returned to Israel as an immigrant—doing it again, like my grandparents. I currently live in Jerusalem with my wife, the artist Judith Margolis, and our teenage daughter.

"A Jewish writer in Israel, I am continually struck by how American I am—forever an American writer, writing in American. Though my subjects have shifted over the years, what matters to me most as a writer has not, I think, changed much. These are: the dreadful pleasure of inventing and shaping language until it teaches me what I want to say, and the private struggle between the poet's work of opening up any moment like a flower and the novelist's work of getting on with the story."

After returning to college in the late 1970s, this restless dropout from the countercultural 1960s earned his bachelor's degree from San Francisco State University in 1977 and went on a Danforth Fellowship to Cornell, where he won his master of fine arts degree in creative writing in 1980, with a minor in Hebrew translation. Armed with what he described as this "terminal degree," he taught creative writing for the next three years at Ithaca College and at Cornell, "coaching students to do exactly what I was trying to do in the hours I was apart from them; get to the point, tell the truth, be accurate, be clear, get the work out," he wrote. It was in Ithaca that he wrote his novel *Change of Partners*, though he had to wait 20 years for it to be published, with a new epilogue set at the 20th-anniversary reunion of the commune.

Margolis moved his family to Los Angeles in 1983 to permit him to work as a story analyst for several major motion-picture studios such as Columbia Pictures, ABC, Lorimar, Twentieth Century Fox, Disney, and Paramount.

It was during this time on the fringes of Hollywood that he wrote *The Stepman*, later remarking that "its deeper theme . . . is the awful inescapability of one's own personality." A thinly veiled account of Margolis's own communal past and his foundering marriage, *The Stepman* is a semiserious, semipicaresque novel about the adventures of Brooklyn-bred Abner Minsky. With "a name combining biblical warrior with burlesque king," Abner narrates the unraveling of his life during the Vietnam-Watergate era, a period that witnesses his poetic vocation ("a form of biblical burlesque," in his own words), his residence in a communal

house ("like a leftover stage-set from the Sixties . . . crowded with people, noisy and disorganized"), and, 10 years and 40 pounds later, his life as a college instructor and second husband in an angst-ridden marriage ("perfidy raised to the level of social principle"). A reviewer in *Publishers Weekly* (September 8, 1996) praised this "very funny" book that follows the relationship of Abner and Lora Sachsman from "hippie idyll in San Francisco" to "festering impasse." The "Stepman" in the title refers to Abner's role as the father in a newly blended family. Arlynn Nellhaus, in a review for *The Jerusalem Post Literary Supplement* (1996), described the fledgling novel as "a penetrating account of this imperfect contract known as marriage based on the inexplicable and undependable emotion called love."

During these years, Margolis felt a continued desire to explore his heritage, and he contributed to magazines and newspapers serving the American Jewish community. Of this experience he wrote, "I mean the word 'serve' here as more than a mealy synonym for 'get their subscribers from,' for it has been a special joy for me to write for a community I care about in the monitoring and mirroring role that good journalism can provide. . . . As a journalist, I have striven to contribute what I think is my unusual sensibility and viewpoint—serious about spiritual issues but open-minded, committed but irreverent, traditional while fully engaged in contemporary culture, and willing to amaze readers by acknowledging uncertainty or ambivalence about the great issues of the day." From 1988 to 1989, the Fund for Journalism on Jewish Life commissioned him to investigate two issues: the phenomenon of religious Jews who "leave the fold" and the experience of Jews in the prison system. From 1990 to 1991 he was the Los Angeles correspondent for the *Jerusalem Report*, an international magazine published in Israel. His article "Ellis Island Revisited" won the 1993 Rockower Award for feature writing from the American Jewish Press Association. During the early 1990s, he was also senior staff writer for the Los Angeles *Jewish Journal*, the largest Jewish weekly west of the Mississippi, and he remains connected to that paper as a contributing editor.

Around this time, Margolis accepted a commission to write a memoir based on notes that the Holocaust survivor David Matzner left after his death. The book was published in 1994 by KTAV as *The Muselmann: Diary of a Jewish Slave Laborer*.

Several of Margolis's short stories have attracted notice in both Jewish and secular circles; several of them were published under the title *The Time of Wandering* by Jerusalem's Bright Idea Books in 1996, though Nellhaus thought them "bottom-of-the-barrel," as he wrote in the *Jerusalem Post Literary Supplement* in the same year. One of the stories, "Gauguin," had, however, won honorable mention in the *Boston Review*'s national fiction contest in 1994, and soon afterwards, *Tikkun* magazine had published "Sex in Israel," which the author has described as "a tale of conflict between religious and secular worldviews configured as a romance" though he cautions that it "has no sex in it." This and other stories, such as "Walking Away," are, he says, "part of a developing collection of short stories that derive their inspiration, form or content from tales and issues of Jewish life as it has unfolded from biblical times to the present."

In his second novel, *Change of Partners*, which was published in August 1997, Margolis drew on his earlier experiences in communal living in telling of the lives and loves of Sam Shames, as he " tunes in, drops out," and joins a laid-back extended family at the fictional Pine Ridge Farm in southern Oregon.

While expressing his satisfaction that he has "acquired and developed my 'voice,' as writers like to say," Margolis craves one other elusive goal: "time to work." In the midst of his fictional endeavors, the author has also accepted the position of head writer at SuperStudio, an educational CD-ROM producer in Jerusalem that creates "literate and beautiful products" for the American market. "In addition to writing and editing scripts," he has written, "I am responsible for the accuracy and thoroughness of all content and supervise a staff of six writers and researchers. This socially useful job nonetheless impedes the work that I believe represents my best contribution to society."

At this stage in his career, Margolis turns for sustenance to the legacy of writers who have gone before him, writing: "The great thing, Kafka told his journal, is to reach the place where you can no longer turn back. I've reached that place. Now I need the time—the open space—to move forward from there."

—E. M.

SUGGESTED READING: *Jerusalem Post Literary Supplement* p6 1996; *Jerusalem Report* Dec. 26, 1996; *Publishers Weekly* p63 Sep. 9, 1996

SELECTED WORKS: Fiction—*The Stepman*, 1996; *The Time of Wandering*, 1996; *Change of Partners*, 1997; Nonfiction—*The Muselmann: Diary of a Jewish Slave Laborer* (with D. Matzner), 1994; CD-ROM recordings— *Artrageous! The Amazing World of Art* (with others), 1995

Margolis, Seth Jacob

1954– Novelist

By his own description, novelist Seth Jacob Margolis blends "real life" with "larger than life" in his stories. He writes about realistic, accessible characters, but places them in situations that go far beyond the everyday. For instance, while his first novel, *False Faces* (1991), takes place in a quiet summer community and has a Long Island police officer as its main character, the plot is that of a complex murder mystery. In fact, the majority of Margolis's works have been in the mystery genre— the notable exception being his most famous work, *Losing Isaiah* (1993), a novel about transracial adoption that was made into a film by Paramount Pictures in 1995.

In a personal statement submitted to *World Authors 1990–1995*, Seth Margolis writes: "I was born in 1954 and have led an exceptionally unexceptional life, which perhaps explains why my books tend to be about ordinary people facing extraordinary situations. I grew up in a suburb of New York City, graduated from the University of Rochester with a B.A. in English, then worked in publishing for a few years. In the late '70s I submitted a short story to the *New Yorker*. When this was rejected I promptly applied to business school, exhibiting a tendency to overreact that I still must work hard to suppress. After receiving an M.B.A. from New York University I worked in marketing for a few years. Still not completely cured of the writing bug, I wrote a mystery novel in my spare time, mostly evenings. It was published in 1991 as *False Faces*.

"I chose the mystery genre both because I enjoy reading mysteries and because a mystery novel imposes certain structural parameters that, as a new writer, I found reassuring. There must be a crime, an investigation, a solution—and of course a protagonist who figures it all out. (A lot of first novels are coming-of-age stories, which impose similar constraints.) The setting of *False Faces* was actually my inspiration. The novel takes place in the summer resort of Fire Island, New York, a narrow strip of land south of Long Island marked by several distinct communities and a lack of automobiles. I thought this would make an excellent setting for a murder mystery, particularly one of the communities populated by single Manhattanites sharing houses for the summer.

"The protagonist of *False Faces* is Joe DiGregorio, known as Joe D., a Long Island cop who masquerades as a yuppie to infiltrate the Fire Island singles community. He takes up with a woman he meets on the job, Alison Rosen; they soon develop a passionate but difficult relationship. Joe D. lives just a few miles from Fire Island, but he's truly an outsider in the tight-knit singles community; this gave me an opportunity to explore and comment on the mores of the New York dating scene from an alien perspective.

"I wrote a second mystery, *Vanishing Act* (1993), that included both Joe D. and Alison Rosen, who in this book are living together in Manhattan, where he's now a private investigator. *Vanishing*

Act begins when a retailing mogul asks Joe D. to fake his death; Joe D. refuses, but the mogul soon ends up dead for real. Joe D., once again, is an outsider; this time he's an alien in Manhattan, and his observations on city life were the most interesting parts to write.

"I had great plans for Joe D. and Alison, but never went beyond those first two novels. I feel a vague sense of guilt about this, as if I'd abandoned two people very close to me in a kind of fictional limbo. Perhaps I'll return to them one day. There's something very comforting about writing a mystery series with ongoing characters. A big part of the writer's job—creating convincing, three-dimensional characters—is already done.

"My next novel was *Losing Isaiah* (1993). This book concerns an interracial adoption and a custody battle pitting a poor African-American birth mother against a white, upper-middle-class adoptive couple. A movie based on the novel, starring Jessica Lange and Halle Berry, was released in 1995; the sale of movie rights enabled me to write full-time.

"*Losing Isaiah* has become something of a touchstone in the transracial adoption controversy. But when I wrote the book the issue of race was actually not my prime concern. In fact, in researching adoption issues I found just one case of a custody battle involving race. My wife and I were expecting our first child at the time I began *Losing Isaiah*, and I was intrigued with the question of what makes a good parent. You need a license to drive a car or fish for trout, but anyone past puberty can be a parent. What if you were forced to testify in court as to your fitness as a parent, or take a test? Who among us would be deemed acceptable? This is exactly what happens to the adoptive parents in *Losing Isaiah*. They're good people who've led imperfect lives—and must reveal every peccadillo in front of a judge in order to keep custody of the child they adopted.

"The adoption issue, in particular the interracial adoption issue, is what reviewers of the book and film have focused on, and I notice when surfing the Internet that *Losing Isaiah* is often included among adoption resources. This used to disturb me ("It's fiction!" I want to protest. "I made it up!"), but I now take some satisfaction in the fact that I managed to describe the adoption experience, and the prospect of losing a child, with sufficient accuracy for the book to serve the interests of parents undergoing real-life adoption dilemmas.

"My most recent book represents yet another change in direction. *Perfect Angel* (1997) is a suspense novel that turns on hypnosis. The protagonist, Julia Mallet, is an advertising executive and single parent living in Manhattan. One night she hypnotizes six of her oldest friends as a lark, but unleashes a murderous alter-ego in one of them. The killer leaves a signature that only Julia can read—she alone knows that one of her closest friends is a killer. This forces her to confront her notions about trust and intimacy—how well does she really know these six people who she's always considered her closest friends.

"*Perfect Angel* grew out of an actual college experience. A young woman I knew had taught herself hypnosis and used to gather a bunch of friends in a dorm room and hypnotize as many people as possible. Those of us not in a trance would then plant all sorts of silly post-hypnotic suggestions in the subjects. Innocent, sophomoric fun—until one kid went a little crazy under hypnosis and the hypnotist couldn't pull him out. That was our last time playing at hypnosis, but the event always struck me as a wonderful premise for a suspense novel, since the out-of-control subject revealed aspects of his personality under hypnosis that none of his friends had been aware of.

"A small-town cop who gets caught up in the world of fast-living yuppies. A well-meaning couple whose flaws may force them to lose the child they've raised for five years. A thirty-something advertising executive whose innocent party game leads to murder. Ordinary people facing extraordinary challenges. I seem incapable of, or perhaps just uninterested in, writing "bigger than life" characters. Even my villains are ordinary people just slightly off.

"On a personal level, I live in Manhattan with my wife and two children (Maggie, b. 1990, and Jack, b. 1992). I'm working on a new suspense novel while writing occasional nonfiction pieces."

In 1992, before *Losing Isaiah* had even been published, Paramount Pictures offered to purchase the book's film rights from Margolis. The film remained in development limbo for a couple of years, but in 1994 it went into production. Margolis was surprised that the novel was put into development, as it had not been an overwhelming commercial success in its initial publication. He had remained wary all through the development stage, aware of the fact that most novels-in-development never actually make it to production.

Sales of the novel received a boost from the publicity surrounding the motion picture adaptation, and the book was eventually translated into a total of seven languages. Additionally, as the date of the film's opening neared, Margolis found himself catapulted to minor celebrity status among his friends and acquaintances. "If I've learned one thing since Paramount Pictures bought the rights to *Losing Isaiah* more than three years ago," he wrote in the *New York Times* (April 2, 1995), "it's that nothing gets people excited like knowing someone connected, however remotely, to the movie industry."

Margolis screened the film at Paramount's New York headquarters before it was officially released. His overall reaction was positive, although he did note some significant changes from his original vision. "The basic story I'd written had survived more or less intact, and once in a while a bit of familiar dialogue surfaced like an old friend in a crowd of strangers," Margolis wrote in the *New*

York Times. "But the New York I'd so painstaking-ly described had become Chicago. A character named Selma was rechristened Kaila. Calvin was now Eddie. The white lawyer I'd given birth to had become Samuel L. Jackson." While unsettled by some of the changes, which he felt weakened the work, Margolis found it even harder to deal with the changes that actually improved it. "Why didn't I think of that? is one of the cruelest thoughts a writer can have," he wrote. The film earned only $2.7 million in its opening weekend and was not a hit at the box office, but as Margolis pointed out, the number of people who saw the film in its first two days of release (approximately 350,000) was far greater than the number of people who had pur-chased the novel in its first hardcover edition.

Margolis's latest novel, *Perfect Angel*, is a return to his murder mystery roots. The book is a study in human relationships that hinges on a complex, suspenseful plot. Julia Mallet and all her friends are successful, seemingly contented people; this changes after the innocent hypnosis incident de-scribed by Margolis in his statement. When the sit-uation suddenly gets out of control, Julia must bring her friends out of the hypnotic trance with-out removing the subconscious suggestions she had planted. One of these suggestions, employed by Julia to prove that she had actually hypnotized her subjects, involved the compete deletion of the letters D and H from each friend's memory.

A series of murders occurs, perpetrated by a kill-er known only as "The Wizard." Police discover the murderer's moniker scrawled at the scene of the crime, "T E WIZAR," and the evidence points to Julia and her circle of friends. As the characters learn more about each other's deepest secrets, they soon find many of their friendships are based on superficialities.

According to Margolis's *New York Times* article, *Perfect Angel* was optioned by Paramount Pictures prior to publication. No film adaptation has yet gone into production.—B.S.

SUGGESTED READING: *New York Times* II p12 Apr. 2, 1995

SELECTED WORKS: *False Faces*, 1991; *Vanishing Act*, 1993; *Losing Isaiah*, 1993; *Perfect Angel*, 1997

Marías, Javier

Sep. 20, 1951– Novelist; essayist

The Spanish novelist and essayist Javier Marías, the son of noted philosopher Julián Marías and the disciple of José Ortega y Gasset, has given his own works a philosophical cast. In his novels *Todas las almas* (1989, tr. *All Souls), Corazón tan blanco* (1992, tr. *A Heart So White*), and *Mañana en la batalla piensa en mí* (1994, tr. *Tomorrow in the Battle Think on Me*), he has been concerned as much with the properties of truth, the effects of language, and the nature of reality as he has with the movement of plot. Michael Kerrigan declared in the London *Times Literary Supplement* (November 15, 1996) that "it is the profound ontological uncertainty at the heart of his work which makes it at once so un-settling and so true."

Javier Marías, born on September 20, 1951, wrote (in Spanish) for the Rómulo Gallegos Prize Committee: "I was born in Madrid, in Chamberí, the classiest neighborhood, whose denizens used to be called 'moneybags,' an appellation now given to all Madrileños. Within a month of my birth, nev-ertheless, I was taken with my older siblings to the United States, and there I apparently spent the first year of my life while my father, the philosopher Ju-lián Marías, taught at Wellesley (Massachusetts), where at one time was one of my favorite teachers, Vladimir Nabokov. My mother, Dolores Franco, published a book a little after our Civil War, an an-thology about my country entitled *España como preocupación* (An Obsession with Spain). The mixture of this title with my mother's name did not please Franco's censors, so my aunt, Gloria Franco, whose name seemed more propitious, was going to sign it. [*Dolores* means 'sorrows' but *Gloria* means 'glory.'] "My mother died in 1977, and by then I had already published two novels and one pair of translations from English.

"I was 17 years old when I began to write my first novel, *Los dominios del lobo* (The Wolf's Do-minions); 18 when I finished it and 19 when it was published, in 1971, thanks to my teacher and friend Juan Benot, who was pleased enough by this juvenile work to recommend it to a publishing house. He had already been my teacher, but then he became my friend. Two years later came *Trave-sía del horizonte* (1973, Crossing the Horizon) and then I remained silent for six years. Those two first novels had been deliberately mimetic and had served me as an exercise. I did not, however, want to make more of the models than was due them. The truth is I was too young to have much to say. I then did translating work, and received my first award, the National Prize for Translation (1979), for the book that had been the most work, *Tristram Shandy*, by Laurence Sterne, which had given me my first contact with Alfonso's magnificent ver-sion, *Reyes de un viaje sentimental*. I also translat-ed the stories of Thomas Hardy, the poems of Ste-venson which in Spanish resemble those of Borges, a fiendish book by Joseph Conrad, the poetry of Ashbery, Wallace Stevens, Auden, Faulkner, my own Nabokov, Yeats's tales, and a neglected classic of the 17th century, Sir Thomas Browne, whom previously only Borges and Bioy Casares had both-ered to translate partially into Spanish.

"I am sure that translation is the best possible apprenticeship for a writer, if you will forgive me for saying so: it is an enterprise both scorned and ill-paid. Later came two novels that I now regard as transitional: *El monarca del tiempo* (1978, The King of Time) and *El siglo* (1983, The Century). They came about somewhat inadvertently, they were dense books, difficult, somewhat experimental, baroque, and overburdened. The first of these I will never reprint; the second was republished in Spain, and to my surprise, is already in its fourth edition. It makes me happy in retrospect, for I had put into it many of my illusory visions, which did not come to pass.

"In 1986 I won the Herralde Novel Prize with *El hombre sentimental* (Sentimental Man), also my first book to be translated into another language, French. In 1989 came *Todas las almas* (tr. *All Souls*), which was also awarded a prize, the Barcelona Prize, and brought me numerous 'real' satisfactions, thanks to a blurring of fiction and reality. A book of stories, *Mientras ellas duermen* (1990, While They Sleep), and a volume of essays and articles, *Passiones pasadas* (1991, Past Passions), preceded my novel *Corazón tan blanco* (1992, tr. *A Heart So White,*) which won the Crítica Prize in Spain.

"I should add that I did something else in life besides writing and translating. Between 1983 and 1985 I taught at Oxford University, and later, as fate would have it, I taught briefly at the same Wellesley College, an exclusively female university, that was witness to my first year. Finally, for four years I taught the theory of translation at Universidad Complutense de Madrid. Afterwards, I abandoned teaching, or perhaps it was teaching that abandoned me.

"A book of brief biographies of writers, *Vidas escritas* (1992, Written Lives), was curiously what, as I understand it, made my name somewhat known for the first time in Latin America, at least in Mexico. Much later I published a second collection of articles and essays, *Literatura y fantasmas* (1993, Literature and Ghosts). After that my novel *Mañana en la batalla piensa en mí* (1994, tr. *Tomorrow in the Battle Think on Me)* within two months was awarded the Royal Spanish Academy of Language's Fastenrath Prize, and the Rómulo Gallegos International Prize, I'm not sure deservedly, but it was a great honor and joy for me. Some months later I published a third collection of articles, *Vida del fantasma* (1995). In the prologue to this title I explain why I keep feeling more and more like my favorite literary image, the ghost. And now that I think of it, perhaps the generosity of the jury of the Rómulo Gallegos Prize might be excessive toward someone who, above all, hovers around."

—tr. S. Y.

Marías drew on his experience teaching at Oxford University for the novel *All Souls*, translated by Margaret Jull Costa. Taking place at All Souls College of Oxford, it describes, according to Michael Kerrigan in the *Times Literary Supplement* (November 15, 1996), "the charged hectic idleness" of college life. *A Heart So White*, also translated by Margaret Jull Costa, is an "ironic tale of love and betrayal," according to *Publishers Weekly* (January 8, 1996). Narrated by Juan, it is the story of the previous marriage of Ranz, his father, to his mother's sister, ultimately a suicide, as extracted by his own young bride. Like Marías himself, Juan is a translator, and on his travels, "Juan sees, overhears, and stumbles upon scenes that increasingly remind him of what he is slowly learning about his father's world," according to *Publishers Weekly* (January 8, 1996). Luisa, the young wife, "chivvies [Ranz] into revealing his ugly secret," the *New Yorker* reviewer wrote. "This novel of ideas proposes that language is inherently treacherous," that reviewer concluded, quoting from the novel: "The truth doesn't depend on things actually existing or happening, but on their remaining hidden or unknown or untold."

Tomorrow in the Battle Think on Me was also translated by Margaret Jull Costa. In it, Marta, a woman with whom a man named Víctor is about to have an affair, dies suddenly. Víctor then becomes fascinated to a fault by Marta's husband and younger sister. The *Publishers Weekly* (July 21, 1997) critic deemed the novel, "despite its . . . flashes of antic humor and its mournful awareness of mortality," somewhat unsuccessful because of Marías's attempt "to impose a philosophic pattern on material that resists it." On the other hand, Michael Kerrigan wrote in the *Times Literary Supplement*, "Javier Marías writes with elegance, with wit, and with masterful suspense."

Marías won the IMPAC Dublin literary award in 1997. The prize, which is quite remunerative, was given for *A Heart So White*.

—S. Y.

SUGGESTED READING: *Publishers Weekly* p59 Jan. 8, 1996, p180 July 21, 1997; (London) *Times Literary Supplement* p24 Nov. 15, 1996

SELECTED BOOKS IN ENGLISH TRANSLATION: *All Souls*, 1992; *A Heart So White*, 1995; *Tomorrow in the Battle Think on Me*, 1996

Johanna Markson

Markson, David

Dec. 20, 1927– Novelist; nonfiction writer

The American novelist and critic David Markson was an early exponent of the works of the expatriate English novelist Malcolm Lowry (1909–1957) and, like him, spent several years in the 1950s living and writing in Mexico. Returning to New York, Markson spent a lackluster period as an editor and writer of pulp detective novels before achieving his first commercial success in 1966, with *The Ballad of Dingus Magee*, a broad-humored spoof of Wild West fiction. Over the years, however, Markson himself saw his books "becoming less and less fictional," to the extent that he termed his own 1996 novel, *Reader's Block*, as "seminonfictional semifiction." Described as a "literary" and "erudite" novelist by one reviewer, Markson has written books, notably *Going Down* (1970), *Springer's Progress* (1977), and *Wittgenstein's Mistress* (1988), that are admired by critics for their rich literary allusions and non-narrative techniques. When, in 1990, the *Review of Contemporary Fiction* devoted half of its summer issue to a retrospective look at Markson's literary career, interviewer Joseph Tabbi paid tribute to Markson's place in contemporary American letters by writing: "In a decade increasingly characterized by 'minimalist' novels and academic assaults on the academic canon, Markson remains one of the most allusive of novelists, a writer who continues to demand from his readers a knowledge at least of the central modernist texts. He does this not out of any conservative desire for a return to classroom 'standards'— Markson is not an academic or political novelist— but rather from a belief in the sheer pleasurability of creative recognition in the reading of literature."

David Markson was born on December 20, 1927 in Albany, New York, the son of Samuel Markson, a newspaper editor, and Florence Stone Markson, a schoolteacher. He did his undergraduate work at the nearby Union College in Schenectady while working as a staff writer on the *Albany Times-Union*. In the 1990 *Review of Contemporary Fiction* issue described above, Burton Feldman, a fellow student, reminisced about their college days in Albany: "Dave and I spent evenings hitting the bars and wolfing the girls, broke and nursing each cheap glass of beer to the bitter end. And talked books nonstop. One night at a bar, I remember we solemnly agreed that *Finnegans Wake* would last a thousand years. I'm not sure either of us had finished reading it by then. No matter."

But it was young Markson's reading of Malcolm Lowry's *Under the Volcano* in his senior year at Union that "quite literally knocked me out of my chair," he told Joseph Tabbi. "Within a couple of years I'd read it probably half a dozen times. And then I finally sent him a letter. Saying God knows what—be my father, or something as asinine. But evidently it did strike the right chord, since one of the first letters I got back ran on for 20 or more pages."

After graduating, in 1950, Markson entered Columbia University in New York City, during which time he made the acquaintance of such contemporary writers as Dylan Thomas and Jack Kerouac and became a proselytizer of William Gaddis and, of course, Lowry. In 1952 Markson made a pilgrimage to western Canada to visit the older man in his squatter's shack near Vancouver, and two years later, with his wife, Elaine, he hosted Lowry during the latter's brief, gin-soaked visit to New York. Recalling the visit years later, Markson wrote how his mentor was then "like some great defective machine breaking apart." Around this time, Lionel Trilling rebuffed Markson's aspirations to write his thesis on Lowry with the words, "What is this drunkenness?" Despite Trilling's attitude, Markson was able to persuade his advisers at Columbia to approve his 20,000-word thesis, a chapter-by-chapter analysis of *Under the Volcano*, which he described as "the finest single novel in the English language in my lifetime" and a work squarely in the tradition of other modernist writing. In his 1978 critical study, *Malcolm Lowry's Volcano: Myth, Symbol, Meaning*, Markson claimed, for example, that Joyce and Lowry each had "an undeniable affinity of method, i.e., that constitutional insistence upon reference and allusion which calls forth archetypal equations; or of Eliot, also, with quotations from 25 different writers in the 400–500 lines of 'The Waste Land.' Lowry is not Joyce; nor Eliot. But he would have been a radically different Lowry had not both . . . infected the contemporary literary bloodstream before him."

For a few years during the 1950s, Markson worked as a freelance writer and as an editor with several New York publishing houses, including Dell and Lion Books, before moving to Mexico, where Lowry had written *Under the Volcano*. Returning to New York in the mid-1960s, he continued writing, also serving as an assistant professor of English at Long Island University in Brooklyn and as a part-time lecturer at Columbia University. After publishing several crime pulp novels for Dell in the 1960s, Markson attracted his first real attention in 1966, with the publication of *The Ballad of Dingus Magee*, a parody of the shoot-'em-up Wild West novel. In the interview with Joseph Tabbi, Markson discussed his late start in publishing serious fiction in these words: "My father would have called it sheer barnyard laziness and probably not have been far off the mark. In the beginning, there might have been an element of fear in it too, very likely there was. But even now when I do have a moderately acceptable body of work behind me I can still go months, sometimes even years, without writing a solitary word. And of course I'm just baffled, baffled by those people who seem to publish a new book every 19 days. There's a kind of compulsion there, or need, that I simply do not possess to any degree whatsoever." The full title of the 1966 novel belies Markson's comic, tongue-in-chaparral sensibility: *The Ballad of Dingus Magee: being the immortal true saga of the most notorious and desperate bad man of the olden days, his blood-shedding, his ruination of poor helpless females & cetera; also including the only reliable account ever offered to the public of his heroic gun battle with Sheriff C. L. Hoke Birdsill, Yerkey's Hole, New Mex., 1884, and with additional commentary on the fateful and mysterious bordello-burning of the same year; and furthermore interspersed with trustworthy and shamelessly interesting sketches of 'Big Blouse' Belle Nops, Anna Hot Water, 'Horseface' Agnes, and others, hardly any remaining upright at the end; composed in the finest modern English as taken diligently from the genuine archives.* In 1970 he sold the book to MGM "for a ton, the only time I've ever made money writing in my life," he told Alexander Laurence in a review for *QWERTY Arts* (1996). Describing the genesis of the book, Markson said, "An editor friend told me he'd take a straight Western if I did one, but after about three pages I called him back and told him not to count on me. I was writing a Western, but I realized by page two that I couldn't take it seriously. So I turned everything upside down, all the men cowards, all the women homely as sin, and played it for the humor." The book was adapted as the 1970 film *Dirty Dingus Magee* with Frank Sinatra and George Kennedy.

In 1970 Markson published his second "serious" novel, *Going Down*—generally considered his most "traditional" novel—which he had started writing, with the help of a grant in Mexico, even before he wrote *Dingus Magee*. Burton Feldman wrote: "He'd always had the language, extraordinary rhetorical power he could shake out of his wrists, and living down in Mexico had taken to things Spanish, dark, and violent. Both flowed through *Going Down*, making it (to use a phrase

from that book) 'something fabrific in the look, something driven, or wild.' But it was also a book under tether; its splintered narrative, roiling poetry, heavy climate (transposed from Mississippi to Mexico, one tropic to another) and even expository devices and syntax were very Faulknerian and Lowrian."

Years of hanging out in New York's drinking and writing saloons helped inspire the setting of Markson's 1977 novel, *Springer's Progress*, which takes place in Greenwich Village's only recently shuttered Lion's Head. "Back then—in the late sixties, the seventies—it was one of the few genuine writer's bars around. More so, and better, than the White Horse Tavern had been, which I'd known earlier. An awful lot of warmth and friendship, and an awful lot of drinking, but by writers who were really achieving good work." *Springer's Progress* foreshadowed the collage techniques Markson would use in his later works, as in this passage: "Dotes on such speculations, Springer does. Pretty much an intrinsic inflection of the saloon anyway. Joint's awash in authors, prime theme indisputably'd be *gelt*. Pussy and/or baseball running a tight second, however." But the novel is also an attempt at mythology in the fashion of Joyce and others, with such devices as catalogs of names and layers of historical and literary allusions, as in, "Ah, dear gobbly Jess, just keep right on and he'll float into space. Xanadu's soon . . . Leglocked and enswathed she's got him, he'll squander seed now until he's raving. Alluvial Mesopotamia, eternal Euphrates, anyone about to heed? Springer's just invented agriculture."

After 54 rejections, his novel *Wittgenstein's Mistress* was finally published in 1988, by Dalkey Archive, a "small press that wasn't going to be worried about recognition value in Downers Grove, Illinois, or among the knuckleheads at a sales conference," Markson said, decrying what he saw as the growing commercialism of American trade publishing. Originally conceived as a short story about "a woman essentially alone," *Wittgenstein's Mistress* was expanded by the author into a story whose only character, Kate, is also the only woman on Earth, making it a narrative on human angst as well as a wry commentary on the style and implications of Ludwig Wittgenstein's *Tractatus*, with its short paragraphs and the "frequent sequences of variants that go through Kate's mind on a single idea. So that if I wanted to be silly I could have borrowed Wittgenstein's textual numbering system, even," said Markson, adding that he was delighted to have Kate called "an intellectual bag lady" because "what's in that bag is what *I* chose to put there. Which incidentally almost means that you could call this one an autobiographical novel of a certain sort, too." Markson has hinted that the novel can also be read as a commentary on recent fashionable critical trends.

Published in 1996, the novel *Reader's Block* is arguably Markson's most untraditional novel, described in the text itself as "a novel of intellectual references and allusion, so to speak. . . . " The author described his methodology to interviewer Alexander Laurence: "I wrote it in a funny way, first sitting here for months, making random notes. I'd stare at the shelves and ask myself, hm, what sort of quirky piece of information do I remember about Freud, say? Or Piero di Cosimo? Or Aquinas? Eventually I had about a three-foot stack of file cards. Which eventually had to be shuffled and sorted and put into order—not to add worked into that framework of my character 'Reader' having it all get in his way while he thinks about writing a novel."

A brief, randomly chosen excerpt illustrates Markson's style:

> Someone nodded hello to Reader on the
> street yesterday.
> To me, or him?
> Someone nodded hello to Reader on the
> street yesterday.
> Church bells were already ringing, to announce the Armistice in November, 1918,
> word reached Wilfred Owen's family that he
> had been killed in battle one week before.
> Picasso made Gertrude Stein sit more than
> eighty times for
> her portrait.
> And then painted out the head and redid it
> three months later
> without having seen her again.
> Pablo Casals began each day for more than
> seventy years by
> playing Bach.
> I have come to this place because I had no
> life back there at
> all.
> I have, Reader, has?
> Reader has come to this place because he
> had no life back
> there at all.

And so on, through 193 pages of intricately woven historic and literary allusions. Reviewing this novel in *QWERTY Arts* (1996), Thomas Lecky wrote: "A beautifully crafted condensation of knowledge, *Reader's Block* is the poetic novel for century's end, recalling those great modernist novels at century's beginning. Concerning the struggles of a writer named Reader, who tries to write about a character named Protagonist, *Reader's Block* is Markson's most refined example of his telescopic and allusive style. The reader enjoys an indelible language, told in terse, paratactic sentences, and it is my opinion that Markson has always written an absolutely tactile prose."

Publishers Weekly (August 12, 1996) agreed, with an unsigned review that stated in part: "Now in his 60s, Markson continues to blossom as an experimental writer. . . . What Markson accomplishes, despite his doubts, is an utterly fascinating document that in itself is a small education in the history of Western literature, seen through the eyes of a gravely impassioned litterateur. The quotations from his reading that have become Markson's

signature are so remarkably sustaining that the book, despite its lack of narrative, is hard to put down: the fate of Auden's royalties (Chester Kallman's dentist father's second wife); the suicide of Adrienne Rich's husband; Conrad's version of *Moby-Dick* ('not a single sincere line'); the Sappho fragment, 'Raise high the roof beam, carpenters.'" And Michael Dirda, reviewing the book for *The Washington Post Book World* (November 3, 1996), called attention to the book's "stoic and rueful gaiety (as Gilbert Sorrentino dubs it). Or the soul-satisfying pleasure of testing one's own literary connoisseurship. . . . What truly matters is that David Markson's 'seminonfictional semifiction' is exhilarating, sorrowful, and amazing. Indeed, a minor masterpiece."

Markson has been the recipient of fellowships from the Centro Mexicano de Escritores in Mexico City and from the National Endowment for the Arts. In 1993 Dalkey Archives published his *Collected Poems*, but Markson himself downplayed the poems' importance, writing in the foreword that "some are only playful. Certain others are lyrics of a time generally deemed antiquated. I would also appear not to have been paying attention when they abolished iambics." The silence of dissenting critics perhaps confirms this self-judgment.
—E. M.

SUGGESTED READING: *Publishers Weekly* Aug. 12, 1996; *Review of Contemporary Fiction* p91+ Summer 1990; *Washington Post Book World* p3+ Nov. 3, 1996, with illustration

SELECTED BOOKS: Novels—*Epitaph for a Tramp*, 1959; *Epitaph for a Deadbeat*, 1961; *Miss Doll, Go Home*, 1965; *The Ballad of Dingus Magee*, 1966; *Going Down*, 1970; *Springer's Progress*, 1977; *Wittgenstein's Mistress*, 1988; *Reader's Block*, 1996; Nonfiction—*Malcolm Lowry's Volcano: Myth, Symbol, Meaning,* 1978. Poetry—*Collected Poems*, 1993; As editor—*Great Tales of Old Russia*, 1963

Matthews, Greg

May 21, 1949– Novelist

Greg Matthews, an Australian novelist living in the United States, has often written about the American Midwest and West in daring new ways. His first novel, *The Further Adventures of Huckleberry Finn* (1983), divided American critics, as some argued that the book was a mockery of Mark Twain's classic novel while others maintained that it was in keeping with the spirit of the original. His second novel, *Heart of the Country* (1986), challenged the stereotypes of the Wild West. Matthews's next two novels, *Little Red Rooster* (1987) and *The Gold Flake Hydrant* (1988), looked at the

Greg Matthews

Courtesy of Greg Matthews

unhappy life of a modern American adolescent living in the Midwest, while his ambitious *One True Thing* (1990) focused on the lives of three generations of a Kansas family in the years from World War II to the present. He has written one novel about Australia, *The Wisdom of Stones*, published in 1994. Recently the author has turned to mystery writing, producing a pair of novels, *Far From Heaven* (1997) and *Come to Dust* (1998), that follow the misadventures of 1940s screenwriter Keith Moody. Praised for his ability to create believable portrayals of downtrodden individuals who attempt to make something of their lives, Matthews has been compared to such authors as Sinclair Lewis and Thomas Hardy.

In his autobiographical statement for *World Authors 1990–1995*, Greg Matthews wrote: "My birthplace in 1949 was Melbourne, Australia. My father was a mechanic in a knitting mill, my mother a housewife. I decided early on to be a writer, and as a result fared badly in school (the school of life would give me the only real education I required). After a personal conflict with my parents I left home at 17, and worked for several years as a warehouseman and freight loader. I still wished to be a writer, but a lifelong fascination with the movies caused me to make the first professional mistake of my life; I decided to be a screenwriter.

"This decision led me to London in 1974 (Australia at that time had virtually no film industry, and colonials were welcome in England). I worked there as a warehouseman for nine years, submitting scripts that failed to elicit interest. Finally, in desperation, I did what I should have done a decade earlier, and wrote a novel. I picked as my first attempt an affectionate homage to the cornerstone

of modern American literature; the result was *The Further Adventures of Huckleberry Finn*, which, when published in the United States caused either appreciative laughter or howls of outrage. I followed this with another historical effort, an attempt to topple the widely accepted cliches of the West. *Heart of the Country* was praised and panned for doing exactly that.

"By then I was living in America, and my impressions formed the basis for my next two books, *Little Red Rooster* and *The Gold Flake Hydrant*, both narratives of Burris Weems, the ultimate alienated teen. I followed that with another contemporary novel, *One True Thing*, the bleak portrait of a fractured Midwestern family over several generations. Then came a fallow period of several years, after which I returned to the West for a theme, and wrote *Power in the Blood*, this time embracing all the Western cliches, yet at the same time standing them on their head. I followed this with my first Australian book, *The Wisdom of Stones*, about the clash of Aboriginal stone age culture with our own, under the shadow of a threatened Japanese invasion in 1942.

"I'm sometimes asked how it is that a writer who jumps from the past to the present in his work can have a unified theme to his body of work. I see no difficulty, since past or present, people are the same, psychologically, with only the slightest of differing social pressures to render the human of yesterday distinct from the human of today. My protagonists tend to be out of step with society in any case, in pursuit of their own moral agenda, usually with results far from those anticipated.

"My newest novel is *Far From Heaven*, a jaundiced look at Hollywood in the 1940s. The hero, unsurprisingly, is a successful screenwriter who considers himself a failure at his trade."

Matthews's first novel, *The Further Adventures of Huckleberry Finn* (1983), was intended as a direct continuation of Mark Twain's *The Adventures of Huckleberry Finn*, and was, like the original, narrated by Huck. After being falsely accused of Judge Thatcher's murder, Huck is freed from prison by Jim, and they subsequently head west to join the California Gold Rush of 1849. Along the way they meet a colorful cast of characters—including American Indians and Huck's father—before finally reaching California, striking gold, and later losing it all. Matthews's book caused quite a stir among American critics. Some thought it was presumptuous to continue the narrative of one of America's most treasured novels, while others lauded the author's ability to maintain the feel of the original throughout the new work.

Reviewing the novel for the *New York Times Book Review* (September 25, 1983), Tom LeClair complained, "Mr. Matthews's continuation of the teenage Huck is merely exploitation. Not even Twain, who was known to re-use material, kept Huck going." The reviewer for *Library Journal* (November 1, 1983), however, disagreed, believing that "first novelist Matthews has pulled off an audacious feat in this overlong but always entertaining sequel. . . . Matthews is an Australian, but his impersonation of American frontier boy Huck is word perfect." Perhaps the greatest praise came from David Kirby in the *Christian Science Monitor* (October 14, 1983), who wrote, "In *The Further Adventures*, the social issues are smaller, and consequently there is more of a focus on pure adventure. This book makes terrific reading, but it is something more as well: it reintroduces the original to old friends and perhaps to a new audience, as no purely scholarly book could. *The Adventures of Huckleberry Finn* is the closest thing we have to a Great American Novel, and Mr. Matthews' faithful, energetic continuation of the tale is an important reminder of that."

Matthews's second novel, like its predecessor, was set in the American Old West. *Heart of the Country* (1986), however, challenged the romanticized notions surrounding the era. The main story revolves around Joe Cobden, the illegitimate, half–American Indian son of the mayor of the Kansas settlement town Valley Forge, and his search for identity. A number of corrupt serve to illustrate the book's negative view of 19th-century Western life; the local preacher commits incest and the town mortician is a necrophiliac.

The critical reaction to *Heart of the Country* was generally positive. Sam Cornish of the *Christian Science Monitor* (June 9, 1986) found the book to be "a bittersweet portrait of long-suffering relationships between generations of men and women and children and their parents. . . . Matthews presents all his people and landscapes so as to extend the conventions of historical fiction, and *Heart of the Country* succeeds in a way in which few novels of the American West have done." The *New York Times Book Review* (May 4, 1986) critic cheered, "Mr. Matthews's dialogue is right on the mark, and he's done his research . . . The book is a page-turner that might be too grisly for some; but fortunately for the faint of heart, the author glosses over descriptions of sexual adventures in a euphemistic prose of almost Proustian delicacy."

For his 1987 novel, *Little Red Rooster*, Matthews moved forward in time to the modern era but maintained his preoccupation with the American West and Midwest. The novel is set in a small town in Indiana and focuses on 15-year-old Burris Weems, who narrates his story into a pocket tape recorder. Burris is by no means the teen idea of a hero: he has one leg two inches shorter than the other and brings home failing grades. The book recounts a number of bizarre adventures that lead to the boy's failed attempt at suicide. Part Huck Finn and part Holden Caulfield, Burris Weems is in many ways the quintessential American teenage boy. Reviewing the novel for *English Journal* (February 1988), Judith M. Beckman and Elizabeth A. Belden remarked, "Australian-born Greg Matthews views American adolescence with a clarity, wit, and

compassion many native writers lack. . . . Burris narrates . . . displaying verbal fluency, wit, intelligence, and a love of punning and rhyming. He may make readers cringe at his language, and flinch at his bluntness, but he will remain with them long after they have closed the book." Matthews followed his success with a second Burris Weems novel, *The Gold Flake Hydrant* (1987).

With *One True Thing* (1990), the author continued to examine the intricacies of American small town life, focusing on three generations of the Kootz family. While in the Pacific at the end of World War II, Lowell Kootz has a vision—to build the Thunderbird Motel, a collection of concrete tepees off the state highway. But after the motel is built and occupied by his family, Lowell cannot rid himself of the desolation he feels in his soul, desolation that matches the emptiness of the Kansas landscape or the largeness of the Pacific Ocean. Each subsequent generation of the family is similarly plagued by feelings of emptiness. Like Lowell, his descendants feel burdened by the toil of everyday life and by dreams that seem unreachable. Reviewing the novel for the *New York Times Book Review* (March 25, 1990), Richard Russo wrote, "Greg Matthews clearly owns in abundance the very things that his characters can only borrow in matchbook-size quantities—lively intelligence, a healthy dose of cynicism, a truly wicked sense of humor. There's also evidence of compassion for his bewildered creations, all of whom want urgently to find that 'one true thing' to hang their hopes on. Mr. Matthews seems to argue, as Twain was fond of doing, that the damned human race may not be responsible for its own damnation. If everyone in the novel succumbs to selfishness; it seems to be because they (and, by extension, we) are made that way."

In his next book, *Power in the Blood* (1993), Matthews returned to the 19th-century American West. The book's protagonists are three orphaned siblings (two brothers and a sister) who suffer a variety of hardships when they are sent to live with three separate families. Critics found them believable or enjoyable in their adventures. *Kirkus Reviews* (January 1, 1993) deemed the book "redolent with frontier flavors," and added that "the violence and menace, and even the supernatural effects, ultimately prove more gratuitous than gripping."

Matthews centered his seventh novel closer to home—Australia at the beginning of the Second World War. *The Wisdom of Stones* (1994) concerns Clive Bagnall, a former teacher in Britain who journeys to Australia to take over his recently deceased uncle's ranch, only to find that a female cousin, Val Lansdowne, also has a claim to it. Neither of them is particularly adept at running a farm until they meet a third character, Doug Farrands, who can make the farm productive again. Eventually Clive and Doug both go off to war, leaving Val behind to tend to the farm and her children as the Japanese begin their invasion of the continent. Elsa Pendleton in *Library Journal* (March 1, 1994) suggested that "there is something here for every reader: heroic action by prisoners of war, romance and heartbreak; and history made understandable as likeable characters learn to grow. Matthews . . . relies a bit too heavily on coincidences and stereotypical characters. But he makes up for it with luminous passages describing the effects of climate, geography, and culture on his people." The reviewer for the *New York Times Book Review* (May 29, 1994), Tobin Harshaw, wrote that the author "is at his best when bringing the reader into the minds of several well-conceived minor characters." Harshaw added, however, that "Doug, Clive, and Val never slow down long enough to be more than clichés. Perhaps they're just overwhelmed by their antagonists: a plot overloaded with implausibility, and the sublimely treacherous badlands of Mr. Matthews' native Australia."

In 1997 Matthews published *Far From Heaven*, the first of his two Keith Moody mysteries. In World War II–era Hollywood, Keith Moody is a B-movie screenwriter who has just gotten a big break: he's been promised the screenwriting credits for a major new war film about his cousin, a pilot named Russell Keys. When Keys disappears after a plane crash, problems begin to mount up, both for the film and for Moody—who, in his search for the truth, finds himself entangled in a web of blackmail and murder. Reviews of *Far From Heaven* were mixed. A reviewer for *Library Journal* (August 1997) proclaimed, "Matthews has the atmo-sphere down pat, including the studio bickering, wannabe actresses, and B-movie dialogue. A first mystery and a safe bet for larger collections." *Publishers Weekly*'s (June 16, 1997) reviewer, however, complained that "the convoluted plot is overcrowded with flat characters portrayed broadly and with only boilerplate humor. Matthews fails to breathe life into his 1940s Hollywood setting, racks up an unbelievable body count and, in the end, produces a story that resembles one of Moody's B-movie scripts." A second Moody mystery, *Come to Dust*, appeared in 1998.—C.M.

SUGGESTED READING: *Christian Science Monitor* p39 Oct. 14, 1983, p30 June 9, 1986; *English Journal* p82 Feb. 1988; *Kirkus Reviews* Jan. 1, 1993; *Library Journal* p108 Nov. 1, 1983, p119 Mar. 1, 1994, p139 Aug. 1997; *New York Times Book Review* p14 Sep. 25, 1983, p52 May 4, 1986, p27 Mar. 25, 1990, p14 May 29, 1994; *Publishers Weekly* p49 June 16, 1997; *Washington Post* D p2 June 2, 1994; *Contemporary Authors vol. 135*, 1992

SELECTED BOOKS: *The Further Adventures of Huckleberry Finn*, 1983; *Heart of the Country*, 1986; *Little Red Rooster*, 1987; *The Gold Flake Hydrant*, 1988; *One True Thing*, 1990; *Power in the Blood*, 1993; *The Wisdom of Stones*, 1994; *Far From Heaven*, 1997; *Come to Dust*, 1998

Maupin, Armistead

May 13, 1944– Novelist; journalist

"I think the trick to being a successful writer is to remain very close to universal themes while recording the minutia of the day," Armistead Maupin told *World Authors 1990–1995*. "Then, what you have years later, is something that's interesting in a historical sense but still remains true to human behavior." Throughout his 23-year career as a fiction writer, Maupin has kept his eye on both common human experience and the causes in which he strongly believes. An openly gay writer, Maupin portrays the gay community not as a separate, foreign entity but as an integrated, vital contributor to society. In the mold of writers such as Charles Dickens, the author revived an all but defunct tradition, serializing in the daily newspaper his San Francisco–based *Tales of the City* series, which eventually spawned six novels and two television miniseries. With its alternately poignant and biting prose, *Tales of the City* remains as popular today as it was in its infancy, more than two decades ago.

The son of a prominent southern lawyer, Armistead Jones Maupin, and an amateur actress, Diana Jane (Barton) Maupin, Armistead Maupin was born on May 13, 1944, in Washington, D.C. The oldest of three children, he was reared in North Carolina; he has described his conservative family as one who "worshiped its ancestors." Although he tried to an extent to break free of his father's reins, acting in local theatrical productions with his mother, the young Maupin was programmed with the notion that he was to eventually follow in his father's footsteps and become a lawyer. Despite these expectations, Maupin knew from a young age that he had the talent to be a good storyteller, and he felt drawn to artistic endeavors. An avid watcher of the *Twilight Zone* and Alfred Hitchcock suspense stories, Maupin also soaked up local North Carolina ghost stories and took pleasure in retelling them to his friends. Simultaneously, he took pains to please his father, and so, despite the encouragement of a high school English teacher, he did not initially pursue a career in writing. Looking back on his childhood, Maupin commented to *World Authors,* "I wasn't aiming myself towards a creative life even though all of my instincts lay in that direction."

Maupin also realized from an early age that he was "different" from the other boys on the block. Although it was not until his teenage years that he realized he was attracted to other males, and many more years afterward that he admitted to himself that he was gay, he says that the signs were always present. "I felt like a separate creature. I knew that I didn't like to play the war games that the other little boys were playing," he said. "In some ways, I'm glad that I developed that instinct because I think my creative instincts grew out of it."

Instead of pursuing that instinct, Maupin was set on pleasing his father, and after receiving a B.A. from the University of North Carolina at Chapel Hill in 1966, he began law school. Maupin soon realized that he was not cut out to be a lawyer, so he dropped out of school and took a job as a reporter for the WRAL television station in Raleigh, where archconservative, antigay senator Jesse Helms was an executive.

After his brief stint at the station, Maupin again attempted to win his father's approval by joining the U.S. Navy and then volunteering for duty in Vietnam, where he served as a lieutenant from 1967 to 1970. He did not see much combat in the war; perhaps for that reason, he has said he was glad to have been able to see that part of the world. After the war he returned to Vietnam to build houses for disabled Vietnamese and, as a result, received a Presidential Commendation from Richard Nixon. When he returned home, he took a position as a reporter for the *News and Courier* in Charleston, South Carolina, where he covered the military beat and wrote occasional feature pieces. He then accepted an offer from the Associated Press to join their San Francisco bureau. Thus in 1971 he packed up all of his belongings and, as he told *World Authors*, "moved out to Oz."

For Maupin, moving to San Francisco was akin to rebirth, a journey away from the restrictive, conservative atmosphere of his southern upbringing to an urban community of openly gay and lesbian transplants who lived in harmony with their accepting straight friends and neighbors. In essence, what he found there, he said, was "a city as compassionate as it was beautiful . . . it felt like heaven on earth."

Maupin soon realized, however, that his new job with the AP was a much tighter fit. After only five months of journalism, Maupin says, his creative instincts kicked in and he realized that he did not want to be a reporter. "I found that every new story just stimulated my imagination more and I was consistently filling in the blanks on my own," he told *World Authors*.

For the next three years, Maupin embarked on a quest—involving a wide variety of temporary jobs, from selling silk to writing for an Episcopal minister—to find a career that would satisfy his creative urges. It wasn't until 1974, while working for the *Pacific Sun* newspaper, that Maupin, almost by accident, finally realized his desire to write fiction. Sent to cover a local "phenomenon"—dubbed "Single's Night" by area residents—at a Safeway supermarket in the Marina district of the city, Maupin found that no one in the supermarket would admit they were there, not for grocery shopping, but to find a date. Frustrated, he went home and created a fictional character named Mary Ann Singleton, a naive 20-something from the Midwest who comes to San Francisco on a lark and decides to try her luck at the Safeway scene. The creation of this plotline led to a weekly fictional series in the *Pacific Sun*, and when Maupin left to pitch his series to the *San Francisco Chronicle* in 1976, he brought Mary Ann along with him.

Hired to write fiction for the newspaper, Maupin titled his series "Tales of the City" and created a cast of transplanted San Franciscans who come into contact with each other through ironic and elaborate plot twists. Many of these characters reside at the fictional tenement of 28 Barbary Lane in the Russian Hill section of the city, and their behavior—including promiscuous sex and casual drug use—is chronicled with the same "live and let live" attitude that Maupin has said permeated 1970s culture in San Francisco. Maupin's chief characters include Mrs. Anna Madrigal, an eccentric, marijuana-growing landlady with a secret past who runs 28 Barbary Lane and calls her tenants "family"; Michael "Mouse" Tolliver, a southern Romeo desperately searching for his "Mr. Right"; DeDe Day, a former debutante whose low self-esteem and philandering husband lead her to an affair with a Chinese delivery boy; Mona Ramsey, a free-spirited, bisexual advertising copywriter who searches for direction in her life; and Brian Hawkins, a promiscuous civil rights lawyer turned waiter who is not above picking up women in laundromats and diners.

Maupin's characters (all pieces of himself, he has said) and their behavior, which ranges from admirable to questionable to despicable within the course of any given storyline, are nothing, critics contend, if not true to life. But while they may be truthful embodiments of human nature itself, they also garnered criticism from those who scold the sex, drugs, and rock and roll anthem of the 1970s and point to the decade's "debauchery" as the gateway to, among other things, the rise of drug addiction and sexually transmitted diseases. For Maupin, however, the 1970s mean only treasured memories. "I think one of the misconceptions about that age that is now foisted on it is that people who lived through the 70s in San Francisco now deeply regret their behavior," he told the *Washington Post* (January 10, 1994). "I regret nothing. I had a wonderful time. I discovered more about myself and humanity at that time than I had ever learned before."

What Maupin discovered in San Francisco was that he wanted to be true to himself, and so he came out as gay to friends and acquaintances. The process, he says, helped him to find himself—and to then place himself in his writing. "My talent developed after I came out of the closet, because I was able to look into every corner of my heart and see what was there," he told Kim Hubbard for *People Weekly* (March 5, 1990). Maupin came out publicly to his family through the character of Michael, who, later in the series, outs himself in a letter to his parents after learning of their support of the "Save Our Children" antihomosexual campaign spearheaded by Anita Bryant in the late 1970s. Maupin's family, like Michael's, initially expressed shock and disappointment, but later grew to accept his orientation.

Maupin's series made a name for him on a global scale. "Tales of the City" was the first serialized fiction to appear in a daily newspaper in over 30 years, and with its exploration of gay issues, it broke new ground in the merging of fiction and journalism. Even before its popularity boom, Maupin was cognizant of the fact that his series was shattering previously long-held beliefs on what "belongs" in a newspaper. "I was well aware that I had just received the break of a lifetime," he told World Authors. "I knew with a certainty that I was in the right place at the right time with the right material."

For many of the San Francisco Chronicle's readers, "Tales of the City" struck a familiar, endearing chord, and the popularity of the column grew immensely in a short span of time. In fact, the series soon took on an almost cult-like status: "Tales" fans would send flowers when a character was ill, erupt in hysterics if they somehow missed one day's episode, and approach Maupin at book signings to introduce themselves by the characters' names. "Tales'" success even spilled over to other publications in cities across the country, as newspapers began to adapt their own fictional series. By 1979 Maupin had undertaken discussions to produce a film version of the series, although he would not actually see any of the deals come to fruition for another 15 years.

The series continued for several more years, the characters maturing and aging along with Maupin himself, and each time a set of 115 installments was produced, Maupin had them published in book form. The first book, Tales of the City (1978), was followed by More Tales of the City (1980), Further Tales of the City (1982), and then Babycakes (1984). More Tales follows Mary Ann, now fitting more comfortably into her San Francisco surroundings, as she embarks on a love affair with an amnesiac. Brian also engages in an affair, while Mona searches for her roots in a Nevada brothel. Mrs. Madrigal continues to keep peace at the house, while Michael and his favorite doctor, Jon, struggle with their relationship and a crippling disease that Michael has contracted. The impending birth of DeDe's twin Eurasians and a mysterious religious cult also play a part.

Further Tales of the City, taking place in the early 1980s, introduces a new character, Prue Girioux, a socialite/columnist who falls for a mysterious homeless man. Mary Ann, now dating Brian, builds a television career, while Michael attempts to find new love or possibly rekindle an old flame. DeDe, meanwhile, tries to protect her young children from a man who has escaped Guyana.

In Babycakes (1984) Michael, in mourning, swaps apartments with a Londoner named Simon who has deserted the Royal Navy upon visiting San Francisco with the Queen. Brian tries to fight old demons while playing househusband to ambitious TV reporter Mary Ann, who has her own agenda for the visiting English gentleman. Meanwhile, across the ocean, a former resident of Barbary Lane, Mona, makes an appearance and tries to repair a broken friendship with Michael.

Maupin has skillfully avoided the most common pitfall awaiting gay writers: writing solely about gay life. Maupin believes such exclusivity reduces the effectiveness of a novelist's work, so he tries to present an all-inclusive viewpoint in his own writing. "The books show gay people in context," he told Tom Spain of Publishers Weekly (March 20, 1997). "They give their relationships the blessing of heterosexual friends and make them more real, I hope." The line between gay activist and gay writer is a thin one for most, but Maupin asserts that he has no "political agenda," and that he is first and foremost a novelist.

Due to his decision to include homosexuals in his work, and because he is gay himself, Maupin has often been labeled a "gay writer." While the term does not offend him, he does think it is a circumscribing and clinical name for a genre that attempts to record the commonplace, rather than the anomalous. "The thing of calling something a 'black' or a 'gay' or a 'women's' novel: it sounds like some medicine that you've got to take," Maupin told Adam Block from Mother Jones (November 1989). "And that does a terrible disservice to those of us who are simply trying to tell stories about the real world, simply trying to include the people into the real world where they belong." The diversity of characters evident in his serial, he says, comes down to some of the most basic elements of society: love and understanding. As he told Spain, "I try to celebrate difference through the books, the way 19th-century writers did, to show all the classes, the richness of humankind."

In attempting to convey an accurate portrait of society, Maupin's fourth novel, Babycakes, was a departure from his previous books in that it took the series in a somber new direction, one that was dictated by the changing times in his beloved city. With the emergence of the AIDS epidemic, and its devastating effects on San Francisco's gay community, Maupin felt the impact personally, as he watched many of his friends die from the disease. He brought AIDS to Barbary Lane with the death of Michael's lover, Jon, who dies of the disease "off camera" sometime before 1984 (when the novel takes place). Public reaction to having Jon, an extremely popular character, die as a result of AIDS was severe. Many readers were outraged and sent critical, sometimes threatening letters regarding Maupin's decision. Maupin himself admits that the task of bringing a topic as serious as AIDS into an often humorous series was a daunting one, but that he was up to the challenge. After completing

Significant Others (1987), the fifth book in the series, and one that deals with AIDS on an even deeper level than did *Babycakes,* he told Stephanie Mansfield of the *Washington Post* (November 5, 1986) how the disease has changed his writing. "It has made it darker and more reflective in a lot of ways," he said. "Before I could go with pure humor, and now I have to show the way humor arises out of a tragedy and that's a tougher job to do. But it does arise."

Maupin left behind his title "Tales of the City" when he jumped in 1986 from the *San Francisco Chronicle* to the *San Francisco Examiner,* where he continued the series under the title "Significant Others." For the first time since starting "Tales," Maupin signed a book deal prior to the series' commencement, and this new sense of writing for what would ultimately become a novel affected Maupin's writing style. "This time, I'm deliberately lessening the number of twists and turns in the plot to give the reader a sense of character studies," Maupin told Spain. "Some readers object that there aren't as many cliff-hangers as there used to be. But when I have a novel in mind, I can't have that herky-jerky rhythm anymore." In turning his serial into novel form, Maupin was also able to add racier dialogue and sexual situations that daily newspapers would not allow in print.

Significant Others follows the characters Mary Ann, Brian, Michael, Mrs. Madrigal, and DeDe once again. This time, much of the action takes place in the redwood forest, where a women-only music festival leads to some soul searching by DeDe and her lover. Meanwhile, Brian reflects on his sexual history as he awaits word on an HIV test.

In his sixth book, *Sure of You* (1989), Maupin chose to bring closure to his "Tales of the City" serial, since he "wanted the story to remain vital" and feared becoming bored with the characters. For Maupin, who spent more than 10 years living with his characters, the decision to end the series was a weighty one. "Writing is a difficult process for me anyway," he told *World Authors,* "and I can't do it unless I remain stimulated at all times." The final entry in the series follows Michael, unsure about his future as a man living with HIV, and his life with partner, Thack, a gay activist. Mary Ann is back, more determined than ever to become successful in her field, which puts her at odds with her husband, Brian, and their daughter.

Sure of You explores the breakdown of relationships and friendships, and also examines the prospect of public figures contributing to public homophobia through their decision to stay in the closet. The latter issue is a topic that Maupin knows intimately, having tried to persuade a friend, the actor Rock Hudson, to "come out" for years before he died of complications from AIDS in 1985. "It focuses on what I see as the extraordinary hypocrisy of closeted celebrities," Maupin told Hubbard about *Sure of You.* "They've structured an elaborate network of lies to protect their careers and in doing so have cut themselves off from friends who are in life-or-death situations with AIDS."

In reviews of *Sure of You,* many critics took note of Maupin's decidedly darker tone, and the result was a mixed bag of commentary. A critic for *Newsweek* (October 30, 1989) wrote that the book is "likely to promote Maupin once and for all from underground humorist to mainstream satirist." David Feinberg of the *New York Times* (October 22, 1989) noted that the mood of the book is "rawer, tense, sadder than earlier books in the series, with an undercurrent of anger." However, he conceded that Maupin still managed to produce writing that is "light as a soufflé, whimsical, cozy, and charmingly innocent." Conversely, Harriet Waugh of the *Spectator* (February 10, 1990) felt that by the time *Sure of You* was written, "the action has slowed down somewhat." She continued, "A glum domesticity seems to reign, and the humour is overlaid with sentiment. What should be moving fails because the writing is not quite good enough, or possibly because Mr. Maupin has a strong sentimental streak in his make-up which over the years has come to dominate his humour."

Many critics believe this shift in Maupin's writing style was also due to his relationship with Terry Anderson, a fellow southerner whom Maupin met while on a book tour in 1985. The two fell in love and set up house together, at which point they discovered that Anderson was HIV positive. Living in such a "mixed" (Maupin has not tested positive for HIV) relationship for over 10 years presented an emotional rollercoaster, but Maupin told Tony Clifton of *Newsweek* (October 30, 1989) that the couple was not overwhelmed by their situation. "It's very hard to tell you how it feels to be in love with someone who might be dead in six months," Maupin said. "But the knowledge makes love infinitely more exquisite."

After retiring his long-running serial, Maupin began to concentrate on writing his first "non-Tales" novel. For inspiration he looked no further than his friend Tamara de Treaux, a 31-inch dwarf who inhabited the title alien's costume in the popular movie *E.T.* Tamara served as the model for the character Cadence Roth, also a dwarf, who works as a struggling actress in Maupin's 1992 novel, *Maybe the Moon.* Cadence fruitlessly tries to build her career, which peaked years ago with a turn in the spotlight as the person inside the costume in a popular *E.T.*-like movie, *Mr. Woods,* a role in which she was completely concealed for the duration of the film. *Maybe the Moon* examines how Cadence, forgotten by Hollywood, attempts to leave her mark on the entertainment world, amid a network of supportive gay and straight friends, as well as a blossoming romance with a "regular-sized" musician.

Reviews of *Maybe the Moon* were mixed. *Publishers Weekly* (September 7, 1992) offered one of the more enthusiastic notices, the reviewer writing that the lead character's "impact on the reader's emotions is enormous." The reviewer went on to comment that Maupin relates his story "with humor and compassion" while "telling a suspenseful story whose subtly foreshadowed ending delivers a dramatic clout." In the *Village Voice* (December 1, 1992), *Maybe the Moon* was lauded by David L. Ulln for a plot "that's pure Maupin, full of delicious ironies and ripe for the tweaking. As usual, the author's portrayals of his characters' tangled motivations, their longings and desires, are right on the mark." Ulln, however, acknowledged that "despite its inspirational flashes, *Maybe the Moon* doesn't take shape as successfully as *Tales of the City* did." Furthermore, according to the reviewer, "all the editorializing tends to trivialize his story, turning it into a snapshot rather than a reflection of the times." Similarly, a *New York* magazine (November 2, 1992) reviewer wrote that while the story begins "amiably enough," the pleasure one takes in the numerous wisecracks "dims when it becomes apparent that they are the extent of the characterization, and especially when they are overtaken by sentimentality."

After the publication of *Maybe the Moon*, Maupin saw one of his greatest dreams realized when a deal was finally put together to make a movie version of his *Tales of the City* book. Since its original publication, the *Tales* movie languished in various stages of development among an array of film companies, all of which were afraid to film the movie as written. Maupin would not concede to the sweeping changes that the studios asked for, which included reducing all of the gay characters to minor, "walk-on" roles in the film. Maupin's response: "Taking the gays out of Maupin is like taking the poor out of Dickens" (*New York Times* February 28, 1993). Other suggestions (such as turning the benign Jon into a serial killer) were met with equal indignation from Maupin, who strove to create a film as close to his original novel as possible. "The studios tried to cannibalize my exotic storylines but not remain faithful to the spirit of the books," Maupin told London's *Financial Times* (September 26, 1993). In the end, Britain's Channel 4 decided to take on Maupin's book, with Richard Kramer directing. Kramer did not shy away from the challenge of bringing Maupin's book to the screen fully intact. "What I wanted to capture was the stories' innocence, their sweetness, which to me counterbalances the outrageousness," he told *USA Today's* Matt Roush (January 10, 1994). He admired Maupin's book, he added, because it "filters experience through a satirical and sentimental eye, mixed with real storytelling bravado."

The *Tales of the City* film, a six-hour miniseries that aired on Channel 4 in Britain and on PBS in the U.S. in 1993 and 1994, was not without controversy. Several affiliate stations of PBS objected to the film's nudity, profanity, and drug use. One station received a bomb threat and subsequently refused to air it. Conservative groups also targeted the miniseries, compiling a 12-minute tape of all of the "bad" parts of the movie and distributing it to various outlets. Despite the controversy surrounding the movie, Maupin remained steadfast in his determination to tell his story his way. As he explained to Roush, *Tales* is a "moral work about tolerance, acceptance and honesty . . . [there's] value in truth. We can't really examine our behavior unless we depict ourselves honestly."

The miniseries, which featured Oscar-winner Olympia Dukakis as Mrs. Madrigal, scored ratings that were among the highest for a drama in PBS history at the time, and also won the prestigious Peabody Award. Critics wrote favorable reviews, and John J. O'Connor of the *New York Times* (January 10, 1994) called it "uncommonly fine television." Still, PBS, who had gone into the project in conjunction with Channel 4, bowed out of producing the sequel, *More Tales of the City*. While PBS maintained that its decision was based on financial issues, Maupin and other critics pointed to the surrounding controversy as the motivating factor in the station's sudden disinterest. The sequel remained in limbo for the next four years.

Eventually the cable movie channel Showtime offered relief when it stepped up with an offer to produce the movie. *More Tales of the City*, sporting a new director and minus a few of the original cast members, made its debut on Showtime in June 1998 as a five-hour miniseries, once again garnering favorable reviews from critics. John Carman of the *San Francisco Chronicle* (June 5, 1998) wrote that the production's lighting was a problem in the movie, but characterized both the original miniseries and its sequel as comprising "a viewing experience that feels apart from other television."

Maupin told *World Authors* that he hopes the success of *More Tales of the City* will mean that the remainder of his books will be adapted for the screen, and that plans are currently in the works to make *Further Tales of the City* into a movie. In addition, theatrical productions of *Babycakes* have been performed in the U.K., and Maupin hopes to see *Significant Others* emerge as a Broadway production in the future. The author has also adapted *Maybe the Moon* for the screen, but as of yet, there are no production deals in the works for that novel.

In the summer of 1998, the *More Tales of the City* miniseries was nominated for Emmys in five separate categories, while Maupin's *Tales* books continued to thrive, selling over 10 million copies and being translated into 10 different languages. In an article for the *New York Times* (June 7, 1998), novelist Stephen McCauley attempted to explain the mass appeal of Maupin's series, writing that "the explanation for the almost cult-like following of the stories lies deeper than their entertainment value." He concluded that "the warmth generated by the crazy-quilt clan that resides at 28 Barbary Lane is felt by readers across the entire spectrum of sexual preference, marital status and gender, and is, I believe, the single most important reason for the enormous popularity of Mr. Maupin's work."

The author himself is still in a state of bewilderment at the impact he has had on the literary world. "I still marvel at the fact that I'm still peddling the same story 22 years later," he told *World Authors,* adding that part of the reason behind his success is that his fiction "never attempted to be hip. It's fundamentally a very sentimental and human-based story, and while it recorded the trends of the time, it never deeply believed in them."

Maupin's novel *Night Listener* is due out in early 2000. The book is a psychological suspense story set in modern-day San Francisco and featuring a 53-year-old gay writer as its central character. As he did with *Maybe the Moon,* in this novel he will bring back a minor character from *Tales,* one of DeDe Day's children who came into being as a result of her affair in the first novel. For the author, the plot device serves as a poignant chapter in his own literary history. "It was very satisfying to me to be able to have a character who very closely resembles me, in conversation with a character who was conceived in the first novel I wrote," he told *World Authors.*

Armistead Maupin still lives in San Francisco, although he no longer shares a home with Terry Anderson, who remains his business partner. While no longer romantically involved, both men maintain that they will share a bond as "soul mates" for the rest of their lives. In an attempt to reach out to devotees old and new, Anderson recently launched a Web site dedicated to *Tales of the City* and its fans. The author's work has earned him the Exceptional Achievement Award ALA in 1990, the Best Dramatic Serial award, Royal TV Society in 1994, and the Outstanding Miniseries award, Gay and Lesbian Alliance Against Defamation in 1994.—D.B.

SUGGESTED READING: *Chicago Tribune* p17 Apr. 28, 1983; *Entertainment Weekly* p35+ Dec. 17, 1992; *Financial Times* p2 Sep. 26, 1993; *Guardian* p29 Apr. 22, 1988, p4 Sep. 22, 1993; *London Review of Books* p21+ Mar. 25, 1993; *Mother Jones* p54 Nov. 1989; *New Statesman & Society* p36+ Mar. 2, 1990; *Newsweek* p77 Oct. 30, 1989; *New York* p92 Nov. 2, 1992; *New York Newsday* p64+ Nov. 11, 1992; *New York Times* p26 Oct. 22, 1989, p24 Nov. 29, 1992, p27 Feb. 28, 1993, C p11 Jan. 10, 1994, June 7, 1998; *Out* p84+ May 1998; *People Weekly* p51+ Mar. 5, 1990; *Plays & Players* p24+ Oct. 1993; *Publishers Weekly* p53+ Mar. 20, 1987, p74 Sep. 7, 1992; *San Francisco Chronicle* E p1 Aug. 27, 1997, C p2 May 13, 1998, p38 May 31, 1998, C p1+ June 5, 1998; *Spectator* p32 Feb. 10, 1990, p34 Feb. 20, 1993; *Time* p83 Dec. 7, 1992; *Village Voice* p58 Dec. 1, 1992; *Washington Post* D p1 Nov. 5, 1986, B p1 Jan. 10, 1994; *USA Today* D p3 Jan. 10, 1994; *Contemporary Authors,* 1990, 1997

SELECTED WORKS: *Tales of the City,* 1978; *More Tales of the City,* 1980; *Further Tales of the City,* 1982; *Babycakes,* 1984; *Signifcant Others,* 1987; *Sure of You,* 1989; *28 Barbary Lane,* 1990; *Back to Barbary Lane,* 1991; *Maybe the Moon,* 1992

McCall, Nathan

1955– Journalist; memoirist

In his 1994 memoir, *Makes Me Wanna Holler,* the African-American journalist and essayist Nathan McCall traced his transition from a violent teenage criminal—resentful of white authority, steeped in a culture of machismo and "craziness"—to a *Washington Post* reporter and celebrated author. His collection of essays analyzing black American life, *What's Going On,* was published in 1997.

Nathan McCall was born in 1955. He grew up in Portsmouth, Virginia, in a neighborhood of spacious homes and well-kept lawns called Cavalier Manor. His hardworking mother and stepfather, although they had little education themselves, valued its benefits and desired it for their children. Nathan did well in school, which belied his rebellious nature; he thought of his parents and other adults he knew as patsies of the white man's system, and after he was bused to an integrated school where he endured the abuse of white students, his resentment of the white establishment hardened into hatred. He and his friends "could not bear to think about a future in which we were wholly subject to the whims of whites," McCall wrote in an article in the *Washington Post* (January 13, 1991). That article, "Dispatches from a Dying Generation; Revisiting My Violent Past—And the Friends Who Never Escaped—On the Mean Streets of Home," became the basis for his autobiography, *Makes Me Wanna Holler: A Young Black Man in America* (1994).

Unlike his friends, McCall did not drop out of high school; this decision had less to do with a love for education than with a desire to meet girls. He continued to feel outrage over the fact that his parents had to struggle for mere survival—and over their seeming acceptance of their situation. When he was among his friends, his rebelliousness took the form of theft, assault, and armed robbery, and he was jailed for each of these crimes. He went to prison for the last time at the age of 20, for robbing a McDonald's fast-food restaurant at gunpoint. Sentenced to 12 years, he was paroled after three. (He escaped being charged with gang rape and drug dealing, in which all of his friends were involved.)

While he was in prison, McCall's mind was extraordinarily active; he became the prison librarian and read as much as he could. One of the books that influenced him was *The Autobiography of Malcolm X*. In addition, he and other intellectually inclined inmates discussed philosophy and politics. However, as Paul Ruffins pointed out in his review of *Makes Me Wanna Holler* for the *Washington Post Book World* (February 6, 1994), McCall—unlike Malcolm X, Eldridge Cleaver, and George Jackson, all of whom "discovered religion or revolution" in prison—found "his salvation in smaller ideas like, 'Work hard,' and 'Think before you act.' Reading Malcolm X didn't convert McCall to Islam, but to thinking." McCall worked hard to improve his image of himself during this time. He wrote: "I walked around silently repeating to myself, 'You are an intelligent-thinking human being; you are an intelligent-thinking human being.'"

So well did this mantra work that upon his release from prison, McCall enrolled in Norfolk State University, in Virginia, and trained to be a reporter. He got a job at the *Virginia Pilot/Ledger Star* and then at the *Atlanta Constitution*, where he worked until 1989. That year, on his second try, he got a job as a reporter at the *Washington Post*.

McCall has specialized in reporting on the African-American community—and often on himself. In a *Washington Post* (November 14, 1993) article entitled "My Rap Against Rap," he traced his former code of machismo to the influence of a violent movie, *The Godfather*; having seen that film and adopted the values of its characters, McCall once shot a man who had insulted his girlfriend. The man lived, and McCall, given a light sentence, "discovered what I really was: a silly, scared teenager who was mixed up in the head." In the article, indicting gangsta rap as a force promoting violence, McCall pleaded for "black America" to "give our children something better than violence and abuse to fantasize about." He believed that his own violent acts had been fostered by outside influences: "Why wasn't I prepared to accept the consequences of my actions or concede to being branded a killer if I took someone's life? Because, on some level, I was certain that the person who shot that guy was not really me—it was some person I'd thought I wanted to be. I'd been fantasizing, and fantasies don't deal with consequences."

McCall's autobiography, *Makes Me Wanna Holler*, published in 1994, purported to explain the real reasons for his violent past and his conversion to a respectable life in which, as he wrote, "I had just as much right to be alive and happy as anybody else." Reviewers of *Makes Me Wanna Holler* found in McCall's story "a rare view of the hellish and racist underbelly of American society," as David Holmstrom observed in his notice in the *Christian Science Monitor* (March 28, 1994). McCall's book is a partly cautionary tale, in which he warned, "I have no pithy social formulas to end black-on-black violence. But I do know I see a younger, meaner generation out there now—more lost and alienated than we were, and placing even less value on life." Some critics, such as Adam Hochschild, in the *New York Times Book Review* (Febru-

ary 27, 1994), felt that "McCall's fury . . . becomes a substitute for any real analysis of why his early life turned out as it did, and of what can be done to save a generation of young black men from the same fate." Hochschild found fault with McCall's decision to write the book when he did: "If he had waited a bit longer to write *Makes Me Wanna Holler*," he might have been better able "to move beyond anger to empathy and healing." For Paul Ruffins, writing in *Washington Post Book World* (February 6, 1994), however, *Makes Me Wanna Holler* is in itself a kind of atonement for the author's past wrongdoing. McCall's "greatest guilt isn't over shooting men or assaulting women, but about living away from his children, as his own father did," Ruffins wrote. "But reading *Holler* should help [his son] and thousands of other young black men in America to avoid—or recover from—the self-destructive cycle by teaching them the value of thinking, and of voicing the emotions they may feel but can't express."

Makes Me Wanna Holler was optioned for a film to be directed by John Singleton, who made *Boyz 'n the Hood*. McCall published a book of his essays called *What's Going On* in 1997. *New York Times Book Review* (November 2, 1997) critic Michael E. Ross found *What's Going On* "almost an extension of *Makes Me Wanna Holler*." The essays "reinforce the moral authority McCall previously brought to the issue of America's racial schisms," opined Ross, who also found the book to have been written somewhat hurriedly.

—S.Y.

SUGGESTED READING: *Christian Science Monitor* p13 Mar. 28, 1994, with photo; *Entertainment Weekly* p56+ Mar. 4, 1994, with photo; *New York Times Book Review* p11 Feb. 1994; *Washington Post* C p1 Jan. 13, 1991, A p17 Feb. 15, 1994; *Washington Post Book World* p2 Feb. 6, 1994; *Washington Post Magazine* p21 Jan. 30, 1994

SELECTED BOOKS: *Makes Me Wanna Holler*, 1994; *What's Going On: Personal Essays*, 1997

McClatchy, J. D.

Aug. 12, 1945– Poet; nonfiction writer

The author of poetry collections including *Scenes from Another Life* (1981), *Stars Principal* (1986), *The Rest of the Way* (1990), and *Ten Commandments* (1998), J. D. McClatchy is well known for his intricate style, which often employs multiple layers of meaning. "[McClatchy's] poems hew to a standard of stylistic elegance not often seen nowadays except in some poets of the preceding generation—Hecht, Merrill, Hollander," Robert B. Shaw wrote in *Poetry* (December 1982) in a review of Mc-

Marion Ettlinger

J. D. McClatchy

Clatchy's first collection of original poems, *Scenes from Another Life*. Referring to the title poem of the book, Shaw continued, "Aesthetic and moral judgment are so closely meshed here they can scarcely be separated. This is not what is sometimes pejoratively called 'fine writing'—it is fine thinking and feeling." Similar comments have greeted McClatchy's other works.

In a statement submitted to *World Authors 1990–1995*, the poet—born Joseph Donald McClatchy Jr. on August 12, 1945—writes: "Any writer's 'life'—or any account of how he came to life—is a history of his reading. But let me first describe a sensibility. When I was growing up, after the war, the suburbs were not quite complete. The one I was raised in, outside Philadelphia, still had a couple of odd properties, and they became the poles of my imagination. One was a small working farm, always referred to as Toland's Farm. I loved spending time there: the smells of meadow grass and cow dung, the iridescent feathers on the rooster, the green slime of hen droppings, their warm eggs in the straw, the horse's drool, the cobblestone yard. And if I walked in the opposite direction, there was Gibson's Woods. This was—or seemed—an immense forest, complete with grotto, brookside stone hut, paths and log roads, all surrounding a castle. At least there were granite walls, high windows through which I could spy a chandeliered ballroom, a tower with a slate witch's-cap spire. When, years later, I read Alain-Fournier, I realized I'd had my own magical demesne. I would play here by the hour, imagining myself king or peasant, wizard or wanderer. These, then, were what drew out my imagination: nature and fantasy.

"A third element was religion. I was raised a Catholic, and schooled first by nuns and later by Jesuits. The religion left me with a suspicious enthrallment to guilt, ritual and pomp; the education (I started with Greek and Latin at age fourteen and kept at it until I graduated from college) shaped my literary style and piqued an inquiring, querulous disposition. The disciplines of a Catholic education probably just reinforced the preferences of my temperament. Whatever it has to do with— whether my zodiacal sign or overzealous toilet training—I am forever straightening piles of paper, filling fountain pens, weeding the garden, arranging files, washing dishes. It's the same temperament that from the start has preferred formal strategies for poems. Of course one counts on accidents . . . or plans for them. Without some sort of plan, a poem (or a life) can lose sight of itself, run out of steam or into whimsy.

"Finally, I grew up gay—a fact, like a drop of ink in a glass of water, nowhere overpowering but suffusing everything. From the beginning, I instinctively learned to disguise my feelings, repress or encode my desires. Disguise—not hiding things but making them difficult to see—is the whole point of art. Any adolescent has a lot to hide, and a gay teenager more than most. What first attracted me to certain writers—Oscar Wilde, say—was the need to slip behind what was being said in order to understand what was meant.

"Which brings me back to the beginning—to reading. I had a happy and privileged childhood, suburban, middle-class; I was encouraged to read, listen to music, excel in school. But as a child, I never read poetry and disdained fiction. My favorite reading was, oh, *The Lives of the Saints* or *The Lives of the Noble Greeks and Romans*, Paul De Kruif's *Microbe Hunters* or Clarence Darrow's autobiography. The elegant and compelling arrangement of facts, in other words, seemed to me from the start more exciting than the easy self-indulgence of make-believe. By the time I started to write, as they say, 'seriously,' I was out of college and in graduate school, in my twenties. I knew a lot about everything but myself. So I wrote about poetry's most obvious subject: language. Looking back now, of course, I'm embarrassed by the deliberate obscurity and mannered emptiness of most of those poems. They seem now to have all been written by someone with long fingernails and a raised eyebrow.

"I was 36 before that first book of poems appeared. And as I've said, the writing of it was complicated with studies. For most of my life I have taught, but I did graduate work in order to become a reader. I wanted to be a Renaissance scholar, but the war in Vietnam heated up. To avoid it, I had to drop out of school and set up as a teacher. During the three years before I could return to school, I read contemporary poets for the first time—and never looked back. But over the years I have kept at criticism, and respect the title 'poet-critic.' Since that first book I have tried to learn more and loosen up. Intelligence, I hope, is now used more as an instrument of analysis than as a screen of allusions. I've tried, in my recent books, to write more openly of my life, but I have felt free to lie in order to make the facts into a truth. I suppose that, in the end, any artist makes his own history into a myth. Part of mine concerns the trials of intelligence: how it helps make and unmake experience, its war with instinct, its dry-eyed consolations. But for the most part it's a matter of tone. Rather than the glamorously anonymous voice of the Lyric Ego, I will often try now for the gripped and groping voice of the muddled feelings; an individual—me (or rather, 'me')—and his discontents. It takes a good deal of intelligence, I've found, not to sound merely smart.

"My day-to-day life is haphazardly regimented. As editor of the *Yale Review*, a good deal of my time is spent reading manuscripts and assembling issues. My work in opera keeps me busy in the theater as well. I write on the run, during stolen hours. I live with the graphic designer Chip Kidd, and divide my time between a shoebox apartment in New York City and a small house in the coastal village of Stonington, Connecticut, where my study opens onto a garden—mimicking perhaps those two ways I would walk as a child."

Lantskip, Platan, Creatures Ramp'd (1983) was followed by *Stars Principal* (1986), another collection of McClatchy's original poems. Except for scattered complaints about his "rococo use of vocabulary" and "slippery" meanings, that book was extremely well-received by critics. In a *Times Literary Supplement* review of *Stars Principal*, Jay Parini wrote that "the poet appears to have found his subject—the labyrinth of self-deceit into which we are led by, among other things, language itself, by the difficult reformulation of one's own story." Parini added that McClatchy's writing in this volume was indicative of a "new urgency and honesty" and concluded that McClatchy is "an ironic self-portraitist, sketching himself against a background of family, religion, and school, against the imagined landscape of his literary forebears."

Also included among McClatchy's works are the poetry collections *Kilim* (1987) and *The Rest of the Way* (1990). Noted for its forthright presentation of such timely issues as terrorist violence and the AIDS epidemic, *The Rest of the Way* garnered rave reviews from critics. "A daring and unsettling collection, this book contains both 'Fog Tropes,' a subtle, moving poem about a dying friend and 'Kilim,' an improbably successful crown of sonnets about a Middle Eastern terrorist," Kathleen Norris wrote in *Library Journal* (October 1, 1990). "A richly textured and rewarding book by a remarkably accomplished poet."

The praise of McClatchy's writing also extends to his work as an opera librettist. His libretto for a 1994 opera based on Thomas Mann's story "Mario and the Magician" inspired a *New York Times* (March 14, 1994) reviewer to comment, "Mr. Mc-

Clatchy's pungent libretto was true to the architecture of the story, but it also had a dramatic logic and coherence of its own. It did not simplify or drain the story of ambiguity; it both condensed the tale and amplified its resonance." The reviewer further commented that the combination of McClatchy's libretto and the score, composed by Francis Thorne, was "so intelligent and coherent that the steadily accumulating evidence of the magician's abilities left me as uneasy as the members of his onstage audience."

Critics were somewhat more reserved with their compliments when commenting on McClatchy's 1989 essay collection, *White Paper: On Contemporary American Poetry*. In the book, McClatchy attacked certain methods of teaching and the writing that resulted from these methods. In a *Times Literary Supplement* (September 15, 1989) review, Mark Ford pointed out that McClatchy's professed distaste for both the gimmickry of certain avant-garde writers and the "new literalists" being produced by numerous writing schools was more than a bit ironic. "It is unsettling to learn from the dustjacket that [McClatchy] himself earns a living from the writing school system he denounces," Ford wrote. In the *New York Times Book Review* (July 9, 1989) Harold Beaver also commented on the apparent discrepancy between McClatchy's words and actions. Beaver wrote that McClatchy "himself writes in part from the very establishment he seems to be attacking, without realizing he may be its victim."

McClatchy's editorship of Yale University's *Yale Review* almost did not come to fruition because of the publication's declining circulation and faltering finances. In July 1990 Benno C. Schmidt Jr., president of Yale University, after citing budgeting difficulties and voicing a "concern that the review does not serve effectively as a vehicle for the writing of the Yale faculty," announced that the university was closing the 80-year-old review. The backlash against Schmidt's decision was immediate and fierce. "More was at stake than just a magazine," McClatchy, the quarterly's poetry editor for 10 years, said in an interview with the *New York Times* (August 5, 1991). "There was also the commitment on the part of universities, not just Yale, but others, to finance and support these kinds of intellectual vehicles." In an attempt to save the journal, 56 prominent literary figures signed a petition protesting the decision, and Pulitzer Prize–winning author John Hersey resigned his post on the University Council. In August 1991 Schmidt announced that the university had discovered sufficient funding for the *Yale Review*, and he named McClatchy as the new editor. "I think the protests against the closing uncovered a great deal of unsuspected support," McClatchy told *Yale* (October 1991), "and this enabled the president to find ways to revive and support the whole venture. At a time of shrinking resources, it is both a clear-sighted and noble decision."

Published almost simultaneously in 1998 were McClatchy's poetry collection *Ten Commandments* and a volume of essays, *Twenty Questions.* A writer for *Kirkus Reviews* (March 15, 1998) found that *Ten Commandments* was McClatchy's "most personal volume to date," one in which he "exploits his literary friendships in poems that are more relaxed and autobiographical than his previously arch and allusive books." The pieces in *Twenty Questions* examine the lives and work of poets and other artists; the figures under scrutiny range from W. H. Auden to Gertrude Stein to Stephen Sondheim.

McClatchy has received numerous awards, including the O. Henry Award (1972), the Chase Going Woodhouse Poetry Prize (1976), the Michener Award (1982), the Levinson Prize (1990), and the Poetry Society of America's Melville Cane Award (1991). Additionally, he has received grants from a variety of institutions, among them the Ingram Merrill Foundation (1979) and the John Simon Guggenheim Memorial Foundation (1988).
—J. P.

SUGGESTED READING: *New York Times* C p9 Aug. 5 1991, C p14 Mar. 14 1994; *New York Times Book Review* p35 July 13, 1986, p21 Feb. 15, 1987, p33 July 9, 1989; *Publishers Weekly* p52 June 24, 1996; *Times Literary Supplement* p41 Jan. 9, 1987, p557 May 22, 1987, p1001 Sep. 15, 1989; *Washington Post Book World* p4 Dec. 14, 1986, p6 Feb. 1, 1987; *Yale Review* p22 Oct. 1991; *Who's Who in America 1997*

SELECTED WORKS: Nonfiction—*Anne Sexton: The Artist and Her Critics*, 1978; *For James Merrill: A Birthday Tribute*, 1986; *Twenty Questions*, 1998; Poetry—*Scenes from Another Life*, 1981; *Lantskip, Platan, Creatures Ramp'd*, 1983; *Stars Principal*, 1986; *Kilim*, 1987; *The Rest of the Way*, 1990; *Ten Commandments*, 1998; As editor—*Recitative: Prose by James Merrill*, 1986; *Poets on Painters: Essays on the Art of Painting by Twentieth Century Poets*, 1988; *The Vintage Book of Contemporary American Poetry*, 1990; *Woman in White: Selected Poems of Emily Dickinson*, 1991; *The Vintage Book of Contemporary World Poetry*, 1996; Librettos—*A Question of Taste*, 1989; *Mario and the Magician*, 1994; *Orpheus Descending*, 1994; As translator—*The Art of Poetry*, 1993

McCracken, Elizabeth

1966– Novelist; short-story writer

The work of Elizabeth McCracken, who was named one of *Granta*'s best American novelists under the age of 40 in 1996, has been described by Ian Jack, the editor of that literary journal, as "delicate and witty and profound. Wise in a way that a lot of writing isn't." Indeed, consisting so far of only one collection of short stories, *Here's Your Hat, What's Your Hurry?* (1993), and one novel, *The Giant's House* (1996), McCracken's slim oeuvre (one whose brevity may be attributed to a decision to abandon writing to attend library science school and become a certified librarian before returning to writing) has already attracted more attention and praise than the work of many authors of substantially more material. Among the themes in McCracken's fiction is the way in which people's personalities develop because of, as well as in spite of, their physical characteristics. Despite her success as an author, McCracken still admits to missing her work as a librarian. "I really miss that sense of being paid to be nice to people all day," she said in an interview with *Library Journal* (July 1996). As a librarian, she noted, "you're right there at the front door. You see everybody who comes in. You get to know them."

In a statement submitted to *World Authors 1990–1995*, describing her life and career as a writer-turned-librarian-turned writer, McCracken writes: "Having to write anything autobiographical fills me with dread and boredom. This is why I write fiction, so I can talk about make believe people instead with more interesting lives than mine, and occasionally slip in disguised information about myself.

"Nevertheless, here are the bare facts: I was born in Brighton, MA, in 1966, and moved (with my parents, Samuel and Natalie, and older brother, Harry) to Portland, Oregon, when I was 9 months old. We lived in London for a year somewhere in there, and moved back to Boston when I was 7.

"I had a pleasant, uneventful childhood, with a lot of cats and dogs, and many trips to Des Moines, Iowa, where my father's parents and mother's mother lived. I was not a sickly child, nor badly behaved, nor lonely nor introspective nor possessed of any particular talents. No tragedies befell me, or anybody I knew. Perhaps this is the only kind of childhood that could lead to a fascination with Des Moines and West Des Moines, which are towns that shaped me, in an odd way. My grandmother owned Jacobson's Apparel, of West Des Moines; my McCracken grandparents lived in a large house that had once been owned by the editor of *Better Homes and Gardens*.

"Most of my important—or interesting—biographical details actually have to do with my relatives. My father's father was a classicist who translated *City of God* for the Loeb Library. His wife, Emily, was an amateur writer, and serious volunteer. My father's family is Presbyterian; my mother's is Reform Jewish. Both sides of the family were interested in telling stories about relatives: Aunt Mary George, who was a fearsome character; Rabbi Sharasefsky, the first ordained rabbi in Des Moines; the Jacobs children, in descending order of age, Annie Idy Fannie Mosey Rosie Hattie (Idy was my great-grandmother). Rabbi Sharasefsky, my mother's great-grandfather, briefly preached in Wilkes-Barre, PA, where my father's grandfather was the president of the bank. I don't know whether they ever met, but the pleasure I get when I think of this coincidence is what I'm aiming for when I write fiction.

"When I was a teenager in Newton, Massachusetts, I got my first job in a public library, shelving fiction A–SM (the library was an old, odd building, and fiction SM–Z were in another room). I worked there for seven years; eventually I was promoted to working behind the circulation desk. I'm not entirely sure I would ever have become a fiction writer if I hadn't worked at the Newton Free Library, which taught me two important lessons: books, finally, were objects that people took home, and humanity is more various than any psychology or sociology class would lead you to believe. I've never had a job that wasn't in some way connected to libraries or writing.

"I never graduated from high school, because I ended up a few credits short in the physical education department. I feel it's finally safe to admit to this; I can't say it had any real effect on my adult life.

"I went to Boston University (where my parents worked) as an undergraduate, where I was able to study with an impressive line-up of writing professors—Sue Miller, Derek Walcott, and George Starbuck, among others. From there I went to the University of Iowa, where I studied with Allan Gurganus, which was a little like thinking you might want to be a Christian and studying with Billy Sunday. In the years after graduate school, I was twice a fellow at the Fine Arts Work Center in Provincetown (a gift I can never repay), went to graduate library science school in Philadelphia, and finally became the Circulation Desk Chief at the Somerville Public Library.

"Right now, anyhow, I am not working as a librarian. I am unemployed, unmarried, childless, cheerful—not the stuff of riveting autobiography.

"My fiction isn't, strictly speaking, autobiographical, though things do slip in from time to time. Still, I don't know how to write without making up people, partly because any time I've ever attempted to base a fictional character on someone I know, I fail: real people are too slippery and complex and contradictory—for me, anyhow—to ever get on the page. Certainly some of my obsessions find their way into my work: physical difference of any kind, family myths, height, tattooing, the circus, the Empire State Building, cranky children, cranky pets, Elvis Presley, libraries, family caretakers, family bricabrac, Des Moines. In practically anything I've ever written, there appears a scene with one character lying down and another standing along-side. I don't know what this means, exactly, except that one of the things that interests me—in life as well as fiction—is how who we are physically shapes who we are spiritually: the ways we transcend our physical selves as well as the ways we never can."

McCracken's first book, *Here's Your Hat, What's Your Hurry?*, a collection of nine short stories she sold to a Random House shortly before entering library science school, was published in 1993. These tales, Patricia T. O'Connor wrote in the *New York Times Book Review* (July 4, 1993), "are about people who are taken in—in all senses of the word . . . [but the stories] are also about the way in which the world's misanthropes, with their odd shapes and ragged edges, knit themselves into the fabric of life." The title story describes the elderly "Aunt Helen," a woman who has come to stay with a family in rural Washington. Once she is settled in, the family discovers that "Aunt Helen" is actually a con woman—one who is completely unrelated to them and has spent most of her life traveling from "relative" to "relative." Another tale, "What We Know About the Lost Aztec Children," involves an armless woman from Cleveland who one day brings home an acquaintance from her days as a performer in a circus sideshow. "In the end, these nine elegantly written tales are more optimistic than cynical," O'Connor wrote. "For Ms. McCracken's protagonists, happiness may be out of reach but grace is not."

Three years after the publication of *Here's Your Hat, What's Your Hurry?*, McCracken published her first novel, *The Giant's House*. The book concerns the friendship and romance between a young New England librarian and an 11-year-old boy destined to become the world's tallest man. Though the boy becomes the sole passion of the otherwise withdrawn librarian, she keeps her love for him concealed, partly because of the unwelcome attention that could ensue if such an affair came to light but, more importantly, because she fears that her love may not be reciprocated. The novel was extremely well received by critics. "*The Giant's House* is the work of a writer who is as singular and astute as the characters she creates," Lavinia Greenlaw wrote in the *Times Literary Supplement* (November 29, 1996). "Her book is funny, ambitious, and precise. It is also a beautifully composed portrait of people struggling against themselves with the full force of their courage and desire." Similar praise was offered by Adam Mazmanian in *Library Journal* (July 1996): "This is a terrific first novel, and McCracken is definitely a writer to watch."

—J. P.

SUGGESTED READING: *Library Journal* p162+ July 1996; *New York Times Book Review* p17 July 4, 1993; *People* p31 Sep. 9, 1996; *Times Literary Supplement* p22 Nov. 29 1996

SELECTED BOOKS: *Here's Your Hat, What's Your Hurry?*, 1993; *The Giant's House*, 1996

Miriam Berkeley

McDermott, Alice

June 27, 1953– Novelist

Each of Alice McDermott's novels revolves around a key event and moves back and forth among the past, present, and future. Her first novel, *A Bigamist's Daughter* (1982), was warmly received by critics, and her second, *That Night* (1987), built on that promise and earned a National Book Award nomination. McDermott's third novel, *At Weddings and Wakes* (1992), chosen as a Book-of-the-Month Club selection, also received enthusiastic reviews. *Charming Billy*, published in 1998, was judged her "most challenging" by Rand Richards Cooper, writing in *Commonweal* (March 27, 1998). John Skow in *Time* (January 12, 1998) called it "a novel whose strong, shrewd opening pages should be taught in college writing classes." For *Charming Billy*, McDermott won the National Book Award in 1998.

McDermott's books are set in the New York City borough of Queens and on Long Island, New York, where McDermott came to maturity, in the 1960s. "The *idea* of the suburban life was really wonderful," McDermott told a reporter for the *Washington Post* (April 21, 1992). "The impulse behind it was a better place for your kids to grow up. . . .Maybe that's why suburbia is my subject. Not so much as a social place but as a manifestation of that impulse to do better for your children."

Alice McDermott was born on June 27, 1953 in Brooklyn, New York, the daughter of William J. McDermott, a business representative for Con Edison, the utility company, and Mildred (Lynch) McDermott. She grew up in Elmont, Long Island, where she attended Roman Catholic schools. Although she drew on her Irish background for *At Weddings and Wakes*, McDermott has admitted that it played only a minor role in her upbringing. "We did not have an Irish household at all," she told the *Washington Post* reporter. "My parents were first generation; their parents had all been born in Ireland but we didn't talk about Ireland; my parents had never been there. There was no yearning for it. We were *American*." While books were an important part of life in the McDermott household, and her father would sometimes quote favorite lines from Shakespeare and recite Tennyson, writing as a profession was not encouraged. As McDermott told Wendy Smith for *Publishers Weekly* (March 30, 1992), "I think my family, with completely good intentions, discouraged me [from becoming a writer] because it seemed so removed to them; they saw me starving in a garret and tried to steer me away from it the same way they tried to steer me away from cocaine: 'I know it sounds very appealing right now, but believe me, you'll regret it!'"

Following her graduation from high school, Alice McDermott entered the State University of New York at Oswego. After receiving her B.A. degree, in 1975, she struck a compromise between her parents' suggestion that she hone her secretarial skills and her own growing desire to write: she got work at a vanity press. (She later drew on her year's experience there for *A Bigamist's Daughter*). When she entered the graduate writing program at the University of New Hampshire, in 1976, she was still so unsure of her writing abilities that she decided that if she failed to get a short story published by the time she completed the two-year program, she would abandon her literary aspirations.

McDermott's involvement with the University of New Hampshire's graduate writing program proved an essential step in making her career as a writer, teaching her everything from establishing work habits to creating goals and taking on role models. In particular, McDermott credited Mark Smith, one of her instructors, with nudging her toward a professional writing career. "In my second year, he asked me what I had sent out," she recalled to Wendy Smith. "When I admitted I hadn't submitted anything, he said, 'Look, you've got the talent, but you've got to take yourself seriously. Is this a career, or just something that you're doing?' He treated me as a colleague, which was a wonderful confidence-builder; he helped me see myself as something other than apologetic about what I did."

McDermott began submitting short fiction to magazines, and she was pleasantly surprised when first *Ms.*, then *Redbook*, *Seventeen*, and *Mademoiselle* bought some of her stories. After receiving her M.A. degree from the University of New Hampshire, in 1978, she spent a year lecturing in the university's English department. In 1979 she became a fiction reader for *Esquire* and *Redbook* and summoned enough courage to submit a few short stories and 50 pages of an unfinished novel to Smith's literary agent, Harriet Wasserman. Smith had written to Wasserman, "You're going to kiss my feet in Macy's window for the writer I'm going to send you." Soon after that, McDermott received a call from Wasserman, asking for everything she had written up to that point and inquiring whether she would prefer a male or female editor. The fledgling writer was placed in the care of Jonathan Galassi, a young editor who was making a name for himself in publishing circles. When Galassi left Houghton Mifflin for Random House, in 1982, McDermott followed him, and later that year Random House published *A Bigamist's Daughter*.

A Bigamist's Daughter tells the story of 26-year-old Elizabeth Connelly, the cynical editor in chief of Vista Books, a Manhattan vanity press that publishes books with such titles as *Gouged of Womanhood: Poems of Two Mastectomies* and *Walk This Way*, by a legless Vietnam veteran who wants to appear on *The Gong Show* as a sit-down comic. Vista prints every manuscript submitted, at the author's expense, but since the books are vehicles for catharsis, not saleable commodities, they never get farther than the stockroom. Nevertheless, grateful authors confide their woes and dreams to Elizabeth, telling her, "Now I know why these things happened, why I was lonely, hurt, why my child died, my husband left me, why I lost, missed out, messed up: *So I could write about it*." Elizabeth's cynicism begins to peel away after she meets Tupper Daniels, a handsome southern writer who is seeking an ending to his novel about a bigamist. As she becomes romantically involved with Tupper, Elizabeth begins to question her father's frequent extended absences from home when she was a child and starts to wonder if perhaps he, too, was a bigamist.

A reviewer for *Publishers Weekly* (January 1, 1982) was unimpressed by *A Bigamist's Daughter*. "This is McDermott's first novel, and we are sorry to say, it is not a good one. It has an interesting conceit, but no soul." But most critics expressed more favorable opinions. In her review for the *New York Times* (February 1, 1982), LeAnne Schreiber called McDermott "a very tough-minded and talented young writer," adding that the novel "proceeds by unexpected turns, until, like the affair between Tupper and Elizabeth, it takes on a fun-house quality, full of thrills that frighten as well as amuse." Also impressed was Jean Strouse of *Newsweek* (March 22, 1982), who found *A Bigamist's Daughter* to be a "remarkably good first novel. . . . On the unlikely hook of bigamy, Alice McDermott has hung a wise, sad, witty novel about men and women, God, hope, love, illusion, and fiction itself." Rand Richards Cooper, writing in *Commonweal* (March 27, 1998), found little to like in the novel but saw in it signs of McDermott's great talent:

"Burdened with backstory, plot contrivances, and stilted dialogue . . . the novel was a classic case of a writer fighting her own strengths. . . . *A Bigamist's Daughter* was ostensibly a smart '80s novel about a woman finding her strength. But trapped inside it was a very different book, less breezy and ironic, more lyrical and backward-looking, and far less conventional."

Praise for her first novel did not quell Alice McDermott's doubts about her writing ability. In fact, she was so ambivalent that she announced to family and friends that she intended to give up writing and attend law school instead. "I said, 'Okay, I got a first novel, I got a few nice reviews, I got it out of my system. I'm going to go to law school,'" McDermott told a reporter for the *Washington Post* (April 21, 1992). "And then I started thinking, I don't want to spend the hours of my life reading *briefs* when I could be writing." Instead of taking up the law, she began work on another novel, but events in her personal life distracted her. Her father died, and she spent a year living with and taking care of her mother in a summer home on Long Island. With her husband, David Armstrong, she then moved to the West Coast, where she accepted a teaching position at the University of California at San Diego. With all of the upheaval in her personal life, McDermott found it difficult to concentrate on the novel she had begun, and eventually she decided to abandon that project in favor of the work that became *That Night*. "I knew that given the year I had had, I would have to write some of it out, and that was in many ways what I was trying to do," she explained to Mervyn Rothstein for the *New York Times* (May 9, 1987). "So in some ways it was a purging."

Published in 1987, *That Night* is set in a tract-house community on Long Island in the early 1960s and is based on an incident that Alice McDermott had heard about while growing up in Elmont. "It was something I had told to friends when they asked me what my childhood was like," she told Rothstein. *That Night*, narrated by a woman who was 10 years old at the time the story takes place, centers on a doomed love affair between two teenagers, Rick and Sheryl, the latter a neighbor of the narrator's. After Sheryl discovers that she is pregnant, her mother sends her to stay with relatives in Ohio until after the baby is born. When the mother refuses to disclose Sheryl's whereabouts to Rick, the frustrated lover rallies his friends in a desperate bid to find her. The band of teenagers circles the quiet suburb in their souped-up cars until their anger culminates in a confrontation on the lawn of Sheryl's house. The men in the neighborhood, including the narrator's father, arm themselves with gardening implements and makeshift weapons and successfully repel the toughs. The novel shuttles between the past and the present, linking the events of that night to the future lives of Sheryl, Rick, and the narrator.

As Alice McDermott explained to Kim Heron for the *New York Times* (April 19, 1987), her aim in *That Night* was "to take very simple emotions and redeem them, to show that they are still serious, or can be." She chose a story about love and the pain of separation, she said, because "despite what's lost and how many of your beliefs are confounded by reality, there's still that longing to try again, to believe that something will save you." While writing *That Night* she was worried that the brief clash around which the novel revolves might not prove a sturdy enough base. "My fear all along was that it wouldn't open up enough to become a novel," she told Heron. "[But] when you spend that much time on the implications of such a brief incident, you see things that, within a larger story, would never be that clear. And to me, the teller is as interesting as why the story is told—discovering why a person would be so haunted by a story to recall it with such detail and imagination."

In her review of *That Night* for the *New Republic* (May 25, 1987), Karen Ahlefelder Watkins noted the link between story and storyteller: "McDermott's first novel, *A Bigamist's Daughter*, explored the way people use fictions to hide or transform the defeats and banalities of their lives. . . . By the end of that novel, Elizabeth is more comfortable with unadorned reality. In *That Night*, McDermott goes one step further and introduces a narrator who is both a character within and the creator of the story she tells, and who, also, embellishes her story in an attempt to transform the ordinary into the mythical—thereby revealing the transforming powers of memory and of stories themselves."

Other reviewers lauded McDermott's ability to take an uncomplicated plot and weave it into a richly textured story. "What distinguishes this novel from the mass of literature that takes on the barely middle-class suburban experience is the almost baroque richness of Ms. McDermott's sentences, the intellectual complexity of her moral vision, and the explicit emotion of her voice," the novelist David Leavitt wrote in the *New York Times* (April 19, 1987). "*That Night* gloriously rejects the notion that this betrayed and bankrupt world can be rendered only in the spare, impersonal prose that has become the standard of so much contemporary fiction, and the result is a slim novel of almost 19th-century richness, a novel that celebrates the life of its suburban world at the same moment that it mourns that world's failures and disappointments."

Michael J. Bandler, who reviewed *That Night* for the *Chicago Tribune* (April 30, 1987), proclaimed, "McDermott is a spellbinder, adding a cachet of mystery and eloquence to common occurrences. . . . *That Night*, a dazzling mosaic of details and images, should etch her permanently onto the literary landscape." Literary critics were not alone in recognizing McDermott's talent. *That Night* was nominated for a National Book Award, and in October 1987 McDermott was among the 10 recipients of the annual Whiting Writers' Awards.

After the publication of *That Night*, McDermott and her husband made another cross-country move, this one to Bethesda, Maryland. Just before the move, she began preliminary work on a third novel, in which, as she informed Wendy Smith, she tried "to deal somehow with Irish Catholic things," but she abandoned the project because she "just wasn't settling into it right." One night her son implored her to sit with him until he fell asleep. While McDermott sat on his bed, her attention drifted to the poster on his bedroom wall, a reproduction of an illustration from Maurice Sendak's *In the Night Kitchen*. The print was a cityscape in which the buildings are actually kitchen utensils, boxes, and other objects. "I thought, that sort of dark Brooklyn street, that's it exactly," she told Wendy Smith. "Clearly it's not an accurate drawing of any real place, but I liked that sense of giving an almost impressionistic feel, just the darkness and the strangeness of it. That gave me the idea for the opening chapter of *At Weddings and Wakes*."

Published in 1992, *At Weddings and Wakes* deals with four middle-aged Irish Catholic sisters and their elderly stepmother, known simply as Momma. The sisters are May, an ex-nun and the subject of both the wedding and the wake of the title; Agnes, an emotionally cool executive secretary; Lucy, the only married sister; and Veronica, a reclusive alcoholic. As in *That Night*, the action takes place in the early 1960s, and again as in the earlier novel, McDermott tells the tale through the eyes of children, in this case Lucy's three youngsters, who are part of the story yet distanced from it. The trio accompany their mother on her twice-weekly trips from Long Island to the Brooklyn apartment where Momma and the three unmarried sisters live. May is courted by and marries Fred, a mail carrier, but the union is short-lived, since May dies just four days after the wedding. The exploration in *At Weddings and Wakes* of how memory comes into being and how it changes echoes *That Night* thematically. Stylistically, the two novels share a time structure that dispenses with chronology.

Critical reaction to *At Weddings and Wakes* was enthusiastic. A reviewer for *Publishers Weekly* (January 27, 1992) called the novel "delicately nuanced, elegiac, and emotionally charged" and lauded McDermott as "a formidably gifted prose stylist [who] can make each sentence a bell of sound, a prism of sight." Equally complimentary was a critic for the *Chicago Tribune*, who called *At Weddings and Wakes* "a brilliant, highly complex, extraordinary piece of fiction and a triumph for its author." Jill Smolowe of *Time* (April 20, 1992) declared that "with her third novel, McDermott secures her reputation as a mesmerizing and innovative storyteller." Laura Shapiro of *Newsweek* (April 13, 1992) wrote, "You'll find yourself reading every single word . . . not because it's complicated but because such wonderful things happen deep inside the sentences. . . . *At Weddings and Wakes* is as dense with activity as a green lawn at eye level."

McDermott's fourth novel, *Charming Billy*, is also set in Irish Catholic Long Island. Like its immediate predecessor, it has as its thematic center a death and the events surrounding it. The death is that of the title character, a man who succumbs in middle age to the alcoholism that has dogged him most of his life. He has spent much of that life mourning the death of Eva, a young Irish woman who visited a beach resort on Long Island when he was in his 20s and with whom he fell in love. He sent her the money to return to him from Ireland, where she claimed to have gone, but, unbeknownst to him, she used it to buy a gas station and marry her childhood sweetheart. Billy's cousin and best friend, Dennis, knew what had happened, but to protect Billy's honor and sense of self, he tells Billy that Eva is dead. After many years Billy visits Ireland, to see Eva's grave. To his astonishment, he finds Eva herself. The novel is narrated by Dennis's daughter, to whom Dennis tells the story of the deception on the day of Billy's funeral. The guests at the postfuneral lunch, talking amongst themselves at the table, wonder whether Billy's wife had known about Eva, and they speculate about the cause of Billy's alcoholism and decline.

"McDermott's fiction," Alida Becker wrote in the *New York Times Book Review* (January 11, 1998), "has always been preoccupied with the way that an individual's life can be distorted by the expectations of others—and with the way that romantic mythologizing can achieve the power of religious devotion." *Charming Billy*, Becker wrote, "works on our sympathies with an insistent sadness and an ingratiating charm"; McDermott, she observed, has used the shifting perspective of time to undercut "the whole pretense of authorial omniscience" in presenting the story of a man's life and the unresolved question of who is responsible for his death." As Becker put it, "Just below the surface is a much trickier question: whether it's possible for this kind of responsibility to be pinned down at all."

Rand Richards Cooper, writing in *Commonweal* (March 27, 1998), found a correspondence between McDermott's prose style and the thematic structure of *Charming Billy*: "There's something almost willful in the baroque extravagance of McDermott's style. It's as if she feels her previous books haven't gone far enough, that this time she's determined not merely to write *about* loss, but to take it down into the basic structure of the novel itself, fashioning a syntax of melancholy, a prose that gasps with sadness and doubles back on itself like the tangled contingencies of fate." For Cooper, McDermott's grand theme is that of immigrant assimilation into American mores; the freedom assimilation brings also results in the loss of roots. "To shrug off the burdens of group identity is also to shrug off ferocious attachments; and McDermott's novels express doubt about whether, as ties attenuate and the old neighborhood sinks further into the past,

anything as vivid and nourishing will take their place."

In discussing with Wendy Smith her affinity for unchronological structure, McDermott explained, "That seems to me to be true to our experience about life; it's all seen through time. You don't look at the past just once, and you look at it with the knowledge of the present, which was the future. I like that going over, seeing an event through other events that have occurred since, seeing it again and seeing it in a different way, from a different perspective as time goes on—to me that's very much what fiction does. I see so much of the process of fiction in memory, and I guess that appeals to me." Kurt Jensen, reviewing *Charming Billy* for the *Boston Book Review* (on-line), agreed; McDermott, he wrote, is "a writer who has tackled the problem of intimate coherence by disrupting the passage of time in her fiction and allowing themes and continuities, other than those revealed by the plod of the calendar, to emerge." Nevertheless, he felt that McDermott had not solved the problem successfully in *Charming Billy*. "The distortions of time require some grounding, perhaps an expansive narrative voice, or an event of great reverberating magnitude. *Charming Billy* has neither of these, and the result is a story whose appeal consists of a set of related, unremarkable observations about people and their stories."

The National Book Award jury awarded *Charming Billy* its 1998 prize for fiction. At the awards ceremony, the novelist Allegra Goodman "praised the book's 'beauty' and called it a favorite among the nominated works," according to the Associated Press (November 19, 1998). McDermott, who also spoke at the ceremony, recalled her grandmother's advice not to get a swelled head. "I will clutch onto my Irish humility with great vigor," McDermott declared.

Alice McDermott and her husband, David M. Armstrong, a medical researcher at Georgetown University, in Washington, D.C., have been married since June 16, 1979. The couple live with their children in Bethesda, Maryland. McDermott has taught writing workshops at American University in Washington, D.C.
—S. Y.

SUGGESTED READING: *Commonweal* p10+ Mar. 27, 1998; *Boston Book Review* (on-line); *New York Times* A p13 May 9, 1987, with photo, A p27 Dec. 25, 1997, Nov. 23, 1998; *New York Times Book Review* p8 Jan. 11, 1998; *Publishers Weekly* p85+ Mar. 30, 1992, with photo; *Time* p92 Jan. 12, 1998; *Washington Post* D p1+ Apr. 21, 1992, with photos

SELECTED WORKS: *A Bigamist's Daughter*, 1982; *That Night*, 1987; *At Weddings and Wakes*, 1992; *Charming Billy*, 1998

Courtesy of Eugene McEldowney

McEldowney, Eugene

June 27, 1943– Novelist

The Belfast-born journalist and novelist Eugene McEldowney sets his crime thrillers in an Ireland that is a "far cry from the mythic country of smiling colleens and fresh-faced children, happy greeting and church of a Sunday," as a writer for the *Sunday Times* (July 28, 1996) phrased it. McEldowney's tales are infused with criminality, corruption, and characters often plucked from the lowest strata of society. The Ireland of McEldowney's novels is a country "with serious drug problems, casual and meaningless sex, and the abuse of wealth and official power," in the words of the *Sunday Times* writer. Not surprisingly, his first two novels, *A Kind of Homecoming* (1994) and *A Stone of the Heart* (1995), both set in the tumultuous city of Belfast, touch upon the "Troubles" between Protestants and Catholics in contemporary Northern Ireland. The 1994 cease-fire (which ended in late 1996), however, left McEldowney in a position "somewhat akin to that of a Cold War spy novelist after the fall of the Soviet Bloc," as Keith Jeffery put it in the *Times Literary Supplement* (March 29, 1996.) He thus shifted the setting of his third novel, *The Sad Case of Harpo Higgins* (1996), to Dublin, where he has resided since 1972. In addition to his career as a novelist, McEldowney retains the position of night editor of the *Irish Times*, one of Ireland's national newspapers.

In a statement submitted to *World Authors 1990–1995* describing his career and life thus far, Eugene McEldowney—born on June 27, 1943—writes: "I was born in Belfast, Northern Ireland, the first of three children. My father was an electrical

welder in the shipyards but was often unemployed. Belfast in those days was a bitterly sectarian city and still is.

"We were Catholics who are in the minority in Northern Ireland. Catholics have an Irish identity whereas the majority, Protestant, population have a Unionist or British identity. When I was growing up, I quickly became aware of this division in our society. I also became aware that Catholics were being discriminated against in houses and voting rights, but particularly in jobs. Unemployment among Catholics has always been much heavier than among Protestants. I grew up resenting this.

"I left school at 17 and went to work in England, but I missed Ireland and wanted to go back. I realised that to do this I would need a better education so I studied at evening classes to get the necessary qualifications for access to university.

"I returned to Belfast in 1964 to study English Literature at Queens University. It was a very exciting time. Catholics were beginning to campaign for civil rights and I became involved in this. I was on the infamous Derry march in 1969 which was ambushed by Loyalists in collusion with the police. The situation in Northern Ireland quickly deteriorated after this and the IRA campaign of violence began. It has been continuing ever since.

"I got a job as a teacher but in 1972, I moved to Dublin and became a journalist with the *Irish Times* newspaper. I am currently night editor. In 1994, my first novel, *A Kind of Homecoming,* was published. This has been followed by two more novels, *A Stone of the Heart* and *The Sad Case of Harpo Higgins.*

"I believe my writing has been influenced by my upbringing and background and early education. My first two novels are placed in Belfast and deal with the Northern Ireland violence. Their central character is a Protestant RUC man, Cecil Megarry. I decided to create this character, because I felt it would be a challenge for me to make the imaginative leap across the religious divide and get inside the skin of someone coming from the opposite background to my own.

"I also wanted to make the point that there is good and bad in all people and what unites us is our common humanity.

"The novels deal with the Northern Ireland violence but they are not propaganda. I don't believe in pushing a heavy political message at the reader. If there are points made about the political situation in Ireland, I hope I have made them in a subtle way.

"The novels are written in the genre of crime or mystery fiction. This is a genre which I greatly enjoy for my own reading, though I have very catholic tastes in literature. The writers I most admire are Graham Greene, Thomas Hardy, Irvine Welsh, Elmore Leonard and Gore Vidal. I greatly admire the poetry of John Donne and W. B. Yeats.

"I believe that good crime writing can hold its place with the highest forms of literature. It lays particular demands on the writer—strong characters, plot, dialogue. Above all pace. Something MUST happen in a crime novel. Characters cannot be allowed to sit around engaged in navel-gazing. They must DO something.

"I am presently completing my fourth novel, and I have plans for a fifth. I have also been approached to adapt some of my work for television. However, I may decide to try other forms and genres.

"I began writing late in life (age 46) and now regret that I did not begin earlier. I continue to work as a journalist but most of my spare time is taken up with creative writing.

"I live in Howth, which is a fishing village on the outskirts of Dublin, with my wife and two children. I like to relax by walking and jogging and listening to folk music and song."

Introduced in his debut novel, *A Kind of Homecoming*, was Cecil Megarry—a character who has appeared in all of McEldowney's novels to date. A senior Special Branch detective in the Royal Ulster Constabulary, Megarry is a late-middle-aged man with marital problems, declining health, and a temper that is quick to ignite. Nonetheless, Megarry is a devoted officer with a flair for investigating—and solving—the most baffling of cases.

In McEldowney's second novel, *A Stone of the Heart*, Cecil Megarry has just returned to the police force after having been cleared of charges in the death of a senior intelligence officer. While investigating a bank robbery in which the thieves left behind a cache of valuable jewelry and took only a small amount of cash and some seemingly useless bank records, Megarry begins to think the heist was only a part of a much bigger—and vastly more evil—plot. McEldowney's narrative focus alternates between Megarry's quest to uncover the mysteries behind the robbery and happenings in the life of Sean Morgan, a crippled young man from one of Belfast's roughest neighborhoods. Eventually, as Megarry realizes that the bank robbery was conducted by terrorists with political motives, the stories of the two men begin to intertwine. *A Stone of the Heart* was generally well-received by critics. "Eugene McEldowney's *A Stone of the Heart* is a moody, tumultuous novel set in Belfast, Northern Ireland, that will appeal to any lover of first-class mysteries," a reviewer wrote in *Washington Post Book World* (December 24, 1995). Further praise was given by a reviewer in *Publishers Weekly* (August 28, 1995): "McEldowney untangles the lines that link Megarry and Morgan with admirable expertise. Most impressive is how he steers clear of atmospheric excesses as he hews to a somber tone and deft understatement."

McEldowney's third novel, *The Sad Case of Harpo Higgins*, published in 1996, begins with Megarry, now reunited with his wife, enjoying a doctor-ordered vacation in Dublin after suffering a mild heart attack. While there, he renews an old acquaintanceship with a Dublin police officer and is

swept into an investigation of the drug-related murder of "Harpo" Higgins. Described by Keith Jeffery in the *Times Literary Supplement* (March 29, 1996) as "much the best of the three [McEldowney novels released thus far]," *The Sad Case of Harpo Higgins* was applauded for its character development and complex plot. "The book has a more engrossing plot than hitherto, along with a genuinely sympathetic and realistic cast of characters," Jeffery added. "Megarry himself emerges as less unremittingly dyspeptic and one-dimensional; a handily complete creation who could serve McEldowney well in future narratives."
—J. P.

SUGGESTED READING: *Kirkus Reviews* Sep. 1, 1995; *Publishers Weekly* p105+ Aug. 28, 1995; *Times Literary Supplement* p23 Mar. 29, 1996; *Washington Post Book World* p4 Dec. 24, 1995

SELECTED BOOKS: *A Kind of Homecoming* (1994), *A Stone of the Heart* (1995), *The Sad Case of Harpo Higgins* (1996)

McIlvanney, William

Nov. 25, 1936– Novelist; poet

The Scottish fiction writer and poet William McIlvanney has devoted a large portion of his writing to the subject of class division. Specifically, as he did in his own life, McIlvanney's characters struggle to bridge the gap between working-class family life and middle-class education in an economically depressed Scotland. McIlvanney has won praise for his detective thrillers featuring Jack Laidlaw, a philosophical policeman whose learning does not interfere with his understanding of the underside of Glasgow—and who embodies the class struggle with which McIlvanney is concerned.

William McIlvanney was born on November 25, 1936 in Kilmarnock, Scotland, to William Angus McIlvanney, a coal miner, and Helen (Montgomery) McIlvanney. During the Great Depression of the 1930s, Kilmarnock withered with the decline of its primary industries of mining, shipbuilding, and engineering. Growing up, McIlvanney became aware of the divide separating his working-class upbringing and his middle-class-geared education, which included an M.A. from the University of Glasgow. In issues ranging from speech to career choices, he was torn between his native Scottish culture and his English influences at school. He would later comment on this period in his autobiographical essay "Growing Up in the West" in which he wrote, "Much is made of the bright student forging ahead into a new life, while his alienated relatives plod the old ways, bemused and often hurt. Indeed, I've seen so many examples that I've come to believe in a kind of intellectual nouveau riche, those who employ their new-found intellectualism to bolster the self-containment of their own lives and to cut their families off . . ."

This conflict is present in McIlvanney's first novel, *Remedy Is None* (1966), which received many comparisons to Shakespeare's *Hamlet*. Focusing on a college student, Charlie, who is the son of a coal miner, the novel delves into the themes of class struggle and revenge that preoccupy Charlie's mind after his father confesses his failures on his deathbed. Suddenly Charlie sees his upper-class education as a hindrance to the working-class values that his father taught him and that continue to bind him to his family and town. Charlie's once contented life is turned upside down by the revelations, and unable to cope, he takes revenge on his mother (who had left Charlie's father) by brutally killing her new husband.

The novel received high marks from critics. Irving Wardle from *The Observer* (May 29, 1966) wrote of *Remedy Is None*, "Where novels are concerned, powerful talent generally seems to have two accompanying factors: a firm outer shell withstanding great stress from within; and the presence of characters who kill the reader's superior detachment and make him feel that he might not put up much of a show in their company. On both counts William McIlvanney passes with honour." Wardle went on to comment that "Among other things, this is an extremely funny book . . . this amplitude is reflected in the style. It is highly correct, but flexible enough to accommodate remote images and ideas and make them relevant. . . . But it is the tension between emotional and intellectual passion that defines the book's quality . . . I have rarely seen it operating as powerfully as in this first novel."

The *Times Literary Supplement* (June 16, 1966) critic found that McIlvanney ". . . takes for his theme a human situation of primary importance and he explores it with a passion and perception." The writer added that "The skill with which ordinary life is evoked and commingled with Charlie's contemptuous and despairing vision of it is admirable" and closed by remarking that "In spite of a somewhat cursory ending, *Remedy Is None* is a memorable novel."

McIlvanney's next book, *A Gift From Nessus* (1968), takes the opposing side of the class struggle so vividly portrayed in *Remedy is None*, a side which McIlvanney himself occupied while he was a university tutor and teacher during the late 1960s and early 1970s. This time, the setting is the middle-class suburb of West Central Scotland, and the main character is Eddie Cameron, a salesman struggling to please both his wife and his mistress. The novel focuses on more than simple marital problems, however, using the rather commonplace plotline to examine class struggle and the growing contrast between old and new Glasgow. *A Gift From Nessus* was also well received by critics, even picking up the Scottish Arts Council Book

Award, although some expressed less enthusiasm than they had over his previous novel. *New Statesman* (August 2, 1968) gushed in its review that "To have written as strongly as he has a story with a plot which might just be considered as a television play, is not short of remarkable. The style is adroit yet latinate; he can savour more meaning and emphasis in words such as 'performance' and 'dilemma' than any writer I can recall . . ." In a similarly positive review, the *Times Literary Supplement* (September 19, 1968) wrote that ". . Cameron's interior monologue of soul-searchings is given in prose of great verve and sensitivity, the arid wastes of business Glasgow are sketched with energetic irony and authenticity, and Mr. McIlvanney's handling of a large group of minor characters is assured and skillful." The reviewer did offer one minor criticism however, commenting that "Only in his dialogue is Mr. McIlvanney still showing an uncertain touch: the gift of style, valuable in other respects, betrays him into excessive smartness in many passages of conversation." The review concludes that the book is overall a stylistic triumph and that McIlvanney, "in his treatment of the central dilemmas of his characters . . . shows himself already a writer of unnerving insight and substantial promise." Still, in a less positive review, *The Listener's* (August 8, 1968) Kenneth Graham offered the opinion that "The plot . . . is very secondhand" and "The events are so expected; the ideas, the values, the feelings so estimable, so banal. The Glasgow background is not overindulged . . . but some such solidity might have balanced so much inner anguish." Graham concludes his unfavorable review by noting that "Above all, the style . . . is clotted with forced similes and metaphors."

McIlvanney's next work, *The Longships in Harbour* (1970), is a collection of poetry. In *Poetry Review* (Winter 1970–1971), Leonard Clark wrote that "William McIlvanney's voice [in *The Longships in Harbour*] is a welcome one." Clark went on to note that the writer "chooses his language carefully, making good use of telling images. There is a tautness and toughness about his poems in direct contrast to much of the sprawling prose which passes for poetry today. Yet he always writes clearly and powerfully."

After completing another volume of poetry, *Landscapes and Figures* (1973), McIlvanney published the novel *Docherty* (1975), which looks at a working-class Scottish community before modern tensions set in and takes place during the period around World War II. The residents portrayed in the novel are replicas of McIlvanney's own family and friends from his childhood, and serves as a tribute to Scottish working-class life. The novel focuses on the Docherty family, whose head figure, Tam Docherty, is a hard-working miner. Tam possesses a deep consciousness and understanding which his limited education and dialect do not allow him to properly express. His three sons all represent different aspects of the struggle which younger generations of working-class residents must contend with as they face two very separate cultures. With his fine ear for local dialect, gestures and colloquialisms, McIlvanney's novel captures the essence of this struggle and the effects it has on multiple generations of family and community members.

The *Observer* (March 16, 1986) classified the novel as "defiant, painstaking, rumative," calling it "a memorial to a working-class generation at the turn of the century, whose experience is at once deceptively available to us, and temptingly alien, inviting myths." The review added however, that while "*Docherty* does manage a difficult honesty . . . it would have been even better if the author wasn't tempted to remind you of it so often." More harsh was the *Times Literary Supplement* (July 8, 1983) critic James Campbell, who commented that the novel doesn't have a plot and surmised the reason to be that "McIlvanney's purpose is too serious to admit an artificiality of which he proves himself quite capable in his thriller-writing. In *Docherty*, he means to speak not about his characters but for them." Campbell goes on to note ". . . there are few occasions when the story moves with its own momentum. William McIlvanney has smothered his characters with love, so that at times we have difficulty seeing them . . ." The reviewer also remarked of the author that "in poetry, journalism and fiction, he tends to write—and more to the point to overwrite—in the same dazzling fashion. There is an unwillingness in all he does to sacrifice his attention-seeking style to the subject it supposedly attends." Campbell concluded with the advice that "Perhaps its author should sacrifice the glitter which has become his trademark and put his talents to a new test."

Regardless, *Docherty* won McIlvanney both the Scottish Arts Council Award and the Whitbread Fiction Award. Leaving his teaching position to focus on writing full-time, McIlvanney was next put under contract to produce a series of thrillers, the first of which, *Laidlaw* (1977), has proved to be one of McIlvanney's most successful novels. Another multidimensional creation, Jack Laidlaw is a troubled police officer, a man who believes devotedly in justice and who waxes philosophical even as he tracks down murderers and robbers. The novel's plot—Laidlaw trying to balance his personal life with the investigation of a gruesome crime involving a sexually confused young man—goes beyond the genre's usual potboiler fare and provides the setting for Laidlaw's sophisticated handling of the city's seedy underside.*Laidlaw* was praised for its fully fleshed-out characters. The *Time* (June 27, 1977) review noted that "[McIlvanney's] novel goes down smoothly and with just the right amount of bite." The *New Republic* (September 24, 1977) went a step farther, proclaiming that in the book "Every figure is carefully realized. Every line serves the purpose of motion and explication at once, every scene rings true." The critic concluded with the enthusiastic declaration, "It has been a long time since in have read a first mystery as good

as this one." The *Washington Post Book World* (July 17, 1977) offered the opinion that "Sometimes McIlvanney doesn't shut the door soon enough on the brooding. And the novelist at times overreaches for an excessive, strained metaphor. But it is a small price to pay for a first mystery of such accomplishment and the promise of a superior new series."

In 1983 McIlvanney completed *The Papers of Tony Veitch,* a sequel to his 1977 novel *Laidlaw.* The detective is again working on a murder case in this novel, this time trying to crack a case that no one else appears to care about—that of a wino who was poisoned and left clutching two small pieces of paper with mysterious information on them. As in the original book of the series, Laidlaw delves deep into the underground crime scene of a gray and murky Glasgow, all the while trying to answer moral questions about his work. The response to *The Papers of Tony Veitch* was mixed. On the more positive side, the *New York Times Book Review* (June 5, 1983) notice read, "As in *Laidlaw*, the writing is unusually probing. Mr. McIlvanney shapes phrases like an artisan, with a lavish use of unhackneyed imagery . . . [the] book's characterizations are all three-dimensional." The review concluded that "As a stylist Mr. McIlvanney leaves most of the competition far behind." Offering an opposing view, the *Washington Post Book World* (October 16, 1983) stated, "This second Laidlaw novel doesn't have the stunning impact of the debut book. Then McIlvanney was in control of his material. In *The Papers of Tony Veitch*, the action is not as focused in a confusion of subplots . . ." Still, the writer conceded that despite these flaws, the book remains a "superior crime novel."

McIlvanney next completed a collection of poetry titled *These Words: Weddings and After* (1985), which includes both his characteristic poetry of the common people as well as a long essay, "The Sacred Wood Revisited," in which he takes writer T.S. Eliot to task for intellectual elitism. The *Times Literary Supplement* (April 26, 1984) was less impressed with this essay than with McIlvanney's poetry, concluding that "McIlvanney's long poem is admirable in its vigour and mystifying in its badness."

His next novel, *The Big Man,* takes the reader into the life of Dan Scoular, a strapping, well respected man among the citizens of the West Scotland village where he resides. He is asked to compete in a bare-knuckles bout, which will cement his status in the village, but in which he is reluctant to take part. Meanwhile, his marriage turns sour, and his wife heads to the arms of another man. The novel, though more low-key than McIlvanney's previous fiction, was fairly well received by critics. The *Observer* (September 1, 1985) called the novel "an absorbing study of a man and the small, economically depressed Scottish town that has formed him." However, the critic also added that the novel is "rather old-fashioned, solid and occasionally stolid" but "a little too carefully plotted, as if McIlvanney were hankering back to his successful thrillers." Still, according to the newspaper, "At his best, McIlvanney digs deep and fruitfully into a class unconscious . . ."

McIlvanney completed another collection of poetry in 1988, titled *In Through the Head*. His most recent novel, 1992's *Strange Loyalties*, brings back popular detective Jack Laidlaw for another murder mystery. This third novel in the series takes Laidlaw on his most personal case thus far, in which his brother is killed. In reviews of the novel, the overall opinion was one of enthusiasm, critics again reveling in McIlvanney's expert skill in creating multidimensional characters. The *New York Times Book Review* (May 24, 1992) critic wrote that *Strange Loyalties* is a "beautiful and wrenching novel" and added that the character of Laidlaw is "the kind of demon-driven hero most genre authors can only dream of creating."

William McIlvanney married Moira Watson in 1961; the couple have two children, Siobhan and Liam. He continues to reside in Scotland and has been a contributor to a number of publications and anthologies, including *Memoirs of a Modern Scotland* (1969), *Glasgow, 1956–1989: Shades of Grey . . . and Some Light Too* (1987), and *Walking Wounded* (1989).

—D.B.

SUGGESTED READING: *Amazon Books* (online); *The Listener's* Aug. 8, 1968; *London Magazine* Aug. 1966; *New Republic* Sep. 24, 1977; *New Statesman* Aug. 2, 1968; *New York Times Book Review* July 31, 1977, June 5, 1983, May 24, 1992; *The Observer* May 29, 1966, Sep. 1, 1985, Mar. 16, 1986; *Poetry Review* Winter 1970–1971; *Time* June 27, 1977; *Times Literary Supplement* June 16, 1966, Sep. 19, 1968, July 8, 1983, Apr. 26, 1985, Sep. 13, 1985, Aug. 16, 1991; *Washington Post Book World* July 17, 1977, Oct. 16, 1983; *Book Review Digest*, 1977, 1992; *Contemporary Authors*, 1991; *Contemporary Literary Criticism*, 1987; *Dictionary of Literary Biography*, 1977

SELECTED WORKS: Fiction—*Remedy Is None*, 1966; *A Gift From Nessus*, 1968; *Docherty*, 1975; *Laidlaw*, 1977; *The Papers of Tony Veitch*, 1983; *The Big Man*, 1985; *Strange Loyalties*, 1992; Poetry—*The Longships in Harbour*, 1970; *Landscapes and Figures*, 1973; *These Words: Weddings and After*, 1984; *In Through the Head*, 1988; contributions *Memoirs of a Modern Scotland*, 1969; *Glasgow, 1956–1989: Shades of Grey . . . and Some Light Too*, 1987; *Walking Wounded*, 1989

McInerney, Jay

Jan. 13, 1955– Novelist

The novelist Jay McInerney shot to fame with his stunning first book, *Bright Lights, Big City* (1984), the sadistically clever but sobering odyssey of an angst-ridden, cocaine-snorting preppie through the purgatory of Manhattan's downtown nightlife circa 1980. The first original title in Random House's Vintage Contemporaries quality paperback series, the novel quickly attracted a cult membership among young, upwardly mobile urbanites, sold more than 150,000 copies within a year, sparked a general trend to trade-paperback novels, and spawned a motion-picture adaptation starring Michael J. Fox. Since that early success, however, McInerney has faltered somewhat in the eyes of critics. Regarded by many as a gifted satirist, he has nonetheless, in the opinion of many others, failed to produce works that fulfill his early promise. Still, since the publication of his second novel, *Ransom* (1985)—which sold well but met with less critical success than his first book received—McInerney has challenged himself with ever more ambitious projects. In his third novel, *Story of My Life* (1988), McInerney covered, from a female narrator's perspective, the same drug-heavy club scene visited in *Bright Lights*. He moved on to an overview of the 1980s in *Brightness Falls* (1992),

Miriam Berkeley

his satirical look at corporate takeovers and moral corruption. Most recently he has moved away from shallow yuppies as subject matter, taking on the study of a friendship in the 1960s in *The Last of the Savages* (1996).

The son of an international sales executive with the Scott Paper Company, Jay McInerney was born on January 13, 1955, in Hartford, Connecticut. Because his father was transferred once a year or more, McInerney grew up in a series of North American and European cities, including London, England, Vancouver, Canada, and Pittsfield, Massachusetts, and he attended 18 elementary schools before entering high school in Pittsfield. From 1972 to 1976 he did his undergraduate work at Williams College, near Pittsfield, where he majored in philosophy and minored in English. After graduation, he and a fellow student at Williams, Gary Fisketjon, who would later become McInerney's editor at Random House, bought a second-hand car and traveled around the United States.

Aiming at a writing career but wanting to broaden his experience, McInerney worked for about a year at a wide variety of places, including a mink farm and the offices of the *Hunterdon County Democrat,* a New Jersey weekly newspaper. Going to Japan on a Princeton in Asia Fellowship in 1977, he took Japanese courses at the Institute for International Studies, outside Tokyo, taught English to aspiring future leaders of Japan at Kyoto University, and immersed himself for two years in samurai studies. After returning to the United States in 1979, he worked in New York City as a fact checker at the *New Yorker* magazine for a few months and then as a reader of unsolicited manuscripts at Random House. Gary Fisketjon, by then at Random House, introduced him to the short-story writer and poet Raymond Carver, who was at that time teaching at Syracuse University. Carver told McInerney that if he wanted to concentrate on writing fiction, he ought to leave the hubbub of New York City and take refuge in a Ph.D. program at Syracuse.

Leaving behind a failed marriage to a fashion model and the nightlife that would provide grist for *Bright Lights, Big City,* McInerney went to Syracuse University on a literary fellowship in 1981. At Syracuse, he met his second wife, Merry Reymond, then a Ph.D. candidate in philosophy, who became a strong stabilizing influence in his life. "All my serious writing dates from the time I met my wife," he told Joyce Wadler for a profile in the *Washington Post* (December 12, 1984).

McInerney's short story "It's Six A.M. Do You Know Where You Are?," first published in the Winter 1982 issue of the *Paris Review,* became the beginning of his first novel, *Bright Lights, Big City,* which Gary Fisketjon chose to publish as the first original entry in the new Vintage Contemporaries trade soft-cover series that he was editing for Random House. (All of the other books in the series had been reprints of hardcover titles.) Based loosely on McInerney's own experiences in New York City between 1979 and 1981, *Bright Lights, Big City* is, in his words, a picaresque story about an "almost suicidal" young man "coming to terms with failure." At the same time, it was intended to be "a satire about the mindless fashion-following of the 1980s," the "yuppie" trendiness in clothes, such drugs as "Bolivian marching powder," and "even nutrition" (sushi is *de rigueur* one week, "Tex-Mex" the next). McInerney also felt that he was writing "a modest critique of an age" in which glitter was more important than substance, "in which getting into a [chic] nightclub [was] seen as a significant achievement."

The story of the anonymous young protagonist of *Bright Lights, Big City* is narrated in the second person, an unusual, challenging fictional device that somehow works in the book. That protagonist, a would-be author, is seen in the midst of a severe identity crisis. His marriage has just broken up, he is losing his job in the research department of a highbrow New York magazine (an hilarious lampoon of the *New Yorker*), and, worse, he has for a year been suppressing his bereavement over the death of his mother. The crisis is compressed into one week of cocaine-fueled Manhattan rock club–crawling, a catharsis culminating in the decision that he "will have to learn everything all over again."

Although some reviewers regarded *Bright Lights, Big City* as "sophomoric," "snotty," and "elitist," the vast majority of notices were favorable, and many were glowing. Roz Kaveney, writing in the London *Times Literary Supplement* (May 24, 1985), described the book's hero as "amoral, sentimental, charming." "What saves [the novel] from sentimentality," she wrote, "is McInerney's very precise eye and ear and his sense of the comedy that comes from character. . . . A Chandleresque palette full of urban description convinces us that there is something to this self-wasting voice worthy of our consideration and our regard." In the same publication a year later (April 18, 1986), Galen Strawson noted that the book is "essentially plotless . . . a weakly coupled series of single scenes, stylish add-ons, and touching peripherals," but he considered it nonetheless "an impressive start: clever, fast, and emotionally plausible, an intense, witty concatenation of drug-propelled incident rapped out in short sentences."

Danny Karlin, writing in the *New York Review of Books* (June 5, 1986), described *Bright Lights, Big City* as "the story of a young man whose carefully constructed identity cracks up in the course of a few frenetic New York days and nights," and he saw in the book the theme of "a discontent that cannot be assuaged." That same theme was more fully explored in McInerney's second novel, *Ransom,* about Christopher Ransom, a young man from an affluent family who is in conflict with his father, a playwright who has turned to lucrative television work and thereby, in Christopher's view, prostituted his talent. Feeling that he has "lost his bearings spiritually" and wanting "to reclaim himself," Ransom goes to Japan and seeks to become "morally taut" through the discipline of martial arts, although he knows that he will not lose the sense of social alienation, of lack of community, that he carries with him. "In the scope of its ideas,"

Karlin wrote, "*Ransom* is definitely an advance on *Bright Lights, Big City,* but the first novel is much more adventurous in style and structure. . . . Nevertheless, though not as striking, *Ransom* is a stronger, and in the end a more disconcerting book. *Bright Lights, Big City* does not feel to have deserved the redemption, however tentative, with which it ends. Ransom's abrupt death, at the end of *Ransom,* is more convincingly the American destiny of a stranger in a strange land."

The reviewer for *Publishers Weekly* (July 19, 1985) also found "more substance" in *Ransom* than in *Bright Lights, Big City.* "This is a better novel," he wrote, "more complete, more complex and textured, with the same deft touches of wry humor and ironic insight that distinguished [the] first work." John Lownsbrough, however, writing in the Toronto *Globe and Mail* (November 16, 1985), thought that "what slight comic relief there is [in *Ransom*] tends to an over-reliance on phonetic bloopers and Japanese mangling of American colloquialisms." Galen Strawson, the reviewer for the *Times Literary Supplement,* saw *Ransom* as a bid for a stronger plot than that of *Bright Lights, Big City.* "Like so many of the best phrasemakers, McInerney is not a natural story-teller," Strawson wrote. "He is an accumulator of moments, small-scale set pieces, and he has to work hard to provide a narrative vehicle for them. He has worked hard [in *Ransom*]. He has tried to write a 'proper' novel. And in a rather stiff and formal way, he has succeeded. Unlike *Bright Lights, Big City,* which just came to a stop, *Ransom* comes to an end." Among the most scathing notices was that of David Remnick of the *Washington Post* (August 25, 1985), who dismissed both of McInerney's first two novels as "trivial" and judged *Ransom* to be the "less skilled, less felt" of the two. "Once more," Remnick wrote, "the few pleasures of McInerney's work can be found in its rather ordinary journalism, its witty feature writing."

Following such mixed reviews for *Ransom,* McInerney returned to a more familiar setting with *Story of My Life,* published by Atlantic Monthly Press in 1988. The narrator is the spoiled but suffering, 20-year-old Alison Poole, who tells of two months of wild living in Manhattan's Upper East Side. A talented aspiring actress, she is continually lured away from her aspirations by casual sex, cocaine, and rich men. Like its predecessor, *Story* was greeted with mixed reviews. The *New York Times Book Review* (September 25, 1988) noted: "The unrelieved use of slang, coupled with a general lack of structure, causes the novel to read, at times, like the random jottings of a diary kept by a zonked-out teenager. One can only hope that in his next novel Mr. McInerney moves on to a new theme and a new setting." Yet the reviewer for *New Statesman & Society* (September 2, 1988) could not have disagreed more, noting that "in creating Alison as his narrator, McInerney has taken an even greater gamble than he did in risking the 'you' technique in *Bright Lights, Big City.* . . . Alison never

comes across as the cute or peevish bimbo she could have so easily become, and her account is unerringly sharp and hard-edged."

As the 1980s drew to a close, McInerney's life underwent some adjustments. His second wife filed for divorce after only a few years of marriage; in 1991 he was married again, this time to Helen Bransford, a southern socialite and jewelry designer. Meanwhile, the boom of the 1980s had ended in 1987 with the crash of the stock market on Black Monday, and McInerney's work began to reflect the changing times. His next book, *Brightness Falls* (1992), one of his most ambitious novels to date, chronicled the end of the decade of excess and particularly the lives of Russell and Corrine Calloway, a yuppie couple. Russell is a book editor who made his mark years ago, when he published the collected stories of his best friend, Jeff Pierce; Corrine, who originally wanted to teach and raise a family, instead has taken a high-paying job as a stock analyst in order to provide for her and her husband's high living. When things go sour at work, Russell attempts to take over his company, with the help of a stereotypical New York City financier, Bernard Melman. Once again, reviews were mixed. The *Wall Street Journal* (June 12, 1992) notice read: "Mr. McInerney's writing is ironic, penetrating, and at times even lyrical. For all that the author has been criticized for leading a fast life in New York, at least he has observed his night clubs' habitues with the eye of an ornithologist watching an endangered species of bird." Noting that the book is actually a morality tale, in which love and friendship are seen to be more important than power and ambition, the *Maclean's* (July 13, 1992) reviewer wrote: "Russell learns that lesson the hard way. Evidently, a little humbling was just what McInerney needed, as well. With his latest novel, he proves . . . he belongs at the big table." As ever, McInerney had his detractors, such as Rhonda Koenig, wrote in *New York* (June 22, 1992): "Fiction should anticipate events, or cast some new light on the past, but all those articles on the caring nineties have got there ahead of McInerney. This isn't writing, it's marketing."

For *The Last Of the Savages,* McInerney abandoned the decade he had studied for so long in favor of what was arguably the most influential decade of the latter half of the 20th century—the 1960s. The book follows the 30-year friendship between two men: Patrick Keane, of Irish Catholic stock, and Will Savage, the last of an old southern family. By the time they meet in a New England prep school, they have already taken on the roles they have chosen for themselves—Patrick as a social climber, Will as a rebel prepared to do anything that will anger his conservative father, including marrying a black woman. Compared with those for several of McInerney's other books, the reviews for *The Last of the Savages* were highly favorable. The *Detroit News* (June 5, 1996) notice read: "With this book and his last, *Brightness Falls,* McInerney has matured as a stylist and expanded beyond his *Bright Lights, Big City* fame to become a social satirist in the tradition of Edith Warton, John P. Marquand, and Louis Auchincloss—and . . . of the late Peter Taylor." The *Economist* (June 15, 1996) concurred: "This book . . . is intelligently paced, consistently funny, and delightfully unpredictable. It is sensibly and believably anchored in historical fact, but the factual references never weigh too heavily on the reader's mind or interrupt the flow of the narrative." Finally, *Entertainment Weekly* (May 17, 1996) noted that McInerney "has always been an elegant and witty writer, but here, the fluidity and comic grace of his prose is all in the service of storytelling rather than of show-offiness, and the sorrow that courses through *Savages* has tempered his glibness with regret."

The author returned to the Manhattan scene with *Model Behavior* (1998), a novel and a collection of seven stories. Connor McKnight, the main character, is miserable in his life as a celebrity journalist and soon discovers that all the world's beautiful people are not really happy. Though many critics have compared the work to *Bright Lights, Big City*, it has received many positive reviews. Benjamin Svetkey of *Entertainment Weekly* wrote: "True, the terrain is not altogether unfamiliar, but so what? Frankly it's a kick having McInerney back in town."

Jay McInerney has also published numerous short stories and articles for such distinguished magazines as *Esquire, The Atlantic, Rolling Stone,* *The New York Times Magazine* and *Vogue.* With his wife, Helen Bransford, and their two children, McInerney divides his time between in New York City and Franklin, Tennessee.
—C.M.

SUGGESTED READING: *Detroit News* June 5, 1996; *Economist* p3 + June 15, 1996; *Entertainment Weekly* May 17, 1996; *Globe and Mail* Nov. 16, 1985; *Maclean's* p47 July 13, 1992; *New Statesman & Society* p38 Sept. 2, 1988; *New York* p62 June 22, 1992; *New York Newsday* p33 May 24, 1992, B p2 May 14, 1996; *New York Review of Books* June 5, 1986; *New York Times* C p13 June 1, 1992; *New York Times Book Review* p12 Sep. 25, 1988, p7 May 31, 1992, p11 May 26, 1996; *People* p95 + Sep. 19, 1988; *Publishers Weekly* July 19, 1985; *Times Literary Supplement* May 24, 1985, Apr. 18, 1986, p927 Aug. 26, 1988; *Wall Street Journal* A p1 June 12, 1992; *Washington Post* Dec. 12, 1984, Aug. 25, 1985; *Contemporary Authors* vol. 45, 1995; *Who's Who in America* 1997

SELECTED WORKS: *Bright Lights, Big City*, 1984; *Ransom*, 1985; *Story of My Life*, 1988; *Brightness Falls*, 1992; *The Last of the Savages*, 1996; *Model Behavior*, 1998

McIntyre, Vonda N.

Aug. 28, 1948– Science fiction novelist

The career of Vonda McIntyre has been marked by both critical and commercial success. One of the best-known science fiction writers to emerge in the past 25 years, she has won Nebula and Hugo Awards for such novels as *Dreamsnake* (1978) and *The Moon and the Sun* (1997). Much of her widespread fame among sci-fi readers can be attributed to her novels based on *Star Trek* and *Star Wars*, the two most recognizable film/television franchises in the genre. She is also the author of the well-regarded *Starfarers* series, which includes four novels published between 1989 and 1993.

Vonda Neel McIntyre was born August 28, 1948, in Louisville, Kentucky, the daughter of H. Neel, an electrical engineer, and Vonda Keith McIntyre, a volunteer worker. She attended the University of Washington at Seattle as a member of the honors program. While pursuing a bachelor of science degree, which she obtained in 1970, she began to write seriously. Upon graduation she moved on to graduate study in genetics, giving it up after a year in favor of freelance writing.

Miriam Berkeley

As is so often the case, McIntyre's early attempts at getting published proved frustrating. "I'd estimate that half the stories I've ever written have been bounced at least once with the comment, 'I really like this story, but it's too much for my readers,'" she told Gloria Glickstein Brame for the *Eclectic Literary Forum* (on-line). "An editor once apologized to me for turning down a story on these grounds, and [later] said he wished he'd published it. But that didn't stop him from turning down the next story I sent him!"

In 1974, McIntyre published the short story "Of Mist, and Grass, and Sand" in *Analog*, the most respected magazine for science fiction. The story introduced Snake, a mysterious healer who uses genetically altered venomous snakes to cure illness. The piece was a critical success, and when the Science Fiction Writers of America handed out their prestigious Nebula Awards, "Of Mist, and Grass, and Sand" won for Best Science Fiction Novelette, making the 26-year-old McIntyre one of the youngest Nebula-winners ever.

In 1975 McIntyre published her first novel, *The Exile Waiting*, which the Science Fiction and Fantasy Writers of America nominated for the Nebula Award for Best Science Fiction Novel of the year.

After her first novel appeared, McIntyre worked as co-editor, along with Susan Janice Anderson, on *Aurora: Beyond Equality*, a science fiction anthology. Among the authors whose works were included were Ursula K. Le Guin and James Tiptree.

McIntyre's second and perhaps most acclaimed novel, *Dreamsnake*, was published in 1978. A continuation of the story begun in "Of Mist, and Grass, and Sand", *Dreamsnake* follows Snake's search for a new snake to use in her healings. *Dreamsnake* won both the Nebula Award and the Hugo Award (presented by the World Science Fiction Convention) for Best Science Fiction Novel. It was also nominated for the American Book Award.

Following the success of *Dreamsnake*, in 1979 McIntyre published a collection of short stories entitled *Fireflood and Other Stories*. Some of the stories were previously published pieces, such as the Nebula-winning "Of Mist, and Grass, and Sand." A number of the other stories contained in the collection feature characters who have been biologically altered. Perhaps the most notable among these stories is "Aztecs", a tale of starship pilots whose hearts have been replaced with electronic pumps so that they can withstand the rigors of faster-than-light space travel. In addition to *Fireflood*, McIntyre also contributed some of her short stories to the 1980 anthology *Interfaces*, edited by fellow female science fiction writers Ursula K. Le Guin and Virginia Kidd.

Vonda McIntyre took her first step into the world of genre tie-ins, the work for which she is perhaps best known, in 1981 with the publication of *The Entropy Effect*, a novel set in the 23d-century universe of Gene Roddenberry's *Star Trek*. McIntyre's book has the U.S.S. Enterprise dispatched to transport a deranged, murderous scientist to a rehabilitation colony. In her interview with the *Eclectic Literary Forum* (ELF), McIntyre defended her work in movie and television-based novels: "Those of us who write *Trek* novels, and support our original fiction by doing so, are told we're betraying the field and should do the ethical thing and get a real job . . . Media tie-ins, we're told in mounting tones of hysteria, are ruining the field. . . . Personally, I don't believe it. One of the reasons for writing, say, a *Star Trek* novel . . . is that one hopes the readers will also read one's original fiction."

Paramount Pictures must have been impressed with McIntyre's handling of James T. Kirk and his spacefaring crew, because they selected her to write the novelization of the motion picture *Star Trek II: The Wrath of Khan* in 1982. The decision was made by the studio rather late in the production schedule, and McIntyre was left with only five weeks to adapt the screenplay; the final 10 pages of the script were not delivered to her until several days before the deadline. In describing her experience getting involved with the *Star Trek* media franchise, McIntyre told the *ELF*, "It didn't really make much difference in my life except that it was fun to do . . . and subsidized a number of my original novels. . . . Gene Roddenberry's universe was great fun to play in, and I thoroughly enjoyed the time I spent there. The optimism is a factor a lot of people mention. Spock as perennial outsider is an archetype that a lot of people respond to."

The author followed up her first *Star Trek* movie novelization with *Superluminal* (1983), her first original novel in five years. Just as *Dreamsnake* was a continuation of "Of Mist, and Grass, and Sand", *Superluminal* was a continuation of "Aztecs", the short story featured in *Fireflood*. In 1984, with the production of *Star Trek III: The Search for Spock*, McIntyre was again contacted to write the adaptation.

Remaining within the *Trek* milieu between films, McIntyre next published *Enterprise: The First Adventure* in 1986. The novel tells the story of the beginning of the "five year mission" chronicled on the 1960s *Star Trek* television series, recounting how Captain Kirk gained command of the U.S.S. Enterprise and showing his first encounters with Spock, Dr. McCoy, Scotty, and the rest. Later in the year, McIntyre was called upon to adapt yet another *Star Trek* film, *Star Trek IV: The Voyage Home*, which completed a three-part story cycle begun with McIntyre's first movie effort, *The Wrath of Khan*. An audio version of McIntyre's novel narrated by *Star Trek* actors Leonard Nimoy (Spock) and George Takei (Sulu) was nominated for a Grammy. McIntyre closed out 1986 with a fourth original novel, *Barbary*.

The Voyage Home was, as of this writing, Vonda McIntyre's last *Star Trek* novel. In 1989, Vonda McIntyre published her first book in three years, *Starfarers*. The novel was the beginning of something new for McIntyre but a tradition in science fiction literature: a multi-part series. Over the course of what would become a four-book saga, McIntyre chronicles the adventures of J.D. Sauvage, an alien contact specialist embroiled in an ongoing rebellion. Reader enthusiasm for the new series was so high that a Starfarers fan club had already sprung up before the first book was published.

In 1989, McIntyre's novella *Screwtop* was published by Tor Books in a combined edition with James Tiptree Jr.'s *The Girl Who Was Plugged In.* McIntyre continued the *Starfarers* series in 1991 with *Transition*, followed closely by *Metaphase* (1992), the third installment. Finally, 1993 saw the publication of the final *Starfarers* volume, *Nautilus*, in which J. D. Sauvage and her crew must make a critical decision regarding the future of Earth.

The Chesterfield Film Company gave McIntyre a screenwriting fellowship in 1994. For a year, she attended writing workshops in Los Angeles sponsored by Universal Studios and Amblin Entertainment, and worked on two scripts, *Illegal Alien* and *The Moon and the Sun.* She also adapted two of her previous novels, *Dreamsnake* and *Barbary*, into film scripts. However, her experience in the L.A. can best be summed with what she told *ELF*: "It mostly made me realize that I'm probably not cut out to be a screenwriter . . . I'm not good at the auxiliary requirements such as pitch meetings and deciphering what people in Hollywood mean when they're talking to you."

McIntyre's next project was a return to sci-fi tie-ins, only this time not *Star Trek*, but *Star Wars*. At the end of 1994, she published *The Crystal Star*, a novel which tells an all-new story featuring Luke Skywalker, Han Solo, Leia Organa, and the other characters who appeared in George Lucas's beloved film trilogy. As with many *Star Wars* novels, the story takes place after *Return of the Jedi*, the final film of the original trilogy. The children of Han and Leia are kidnapped, and in their search to recover them the heroes are led to a bizarre planet revolving around a star which is slowly crystallizing. *Booklist* (October 1, 1994) critic Carl Hays made mention of the hard-science approach McIntyre brought to the *Star Wars* universe, presumably stemming from her experience with the more science-oriented *Star Trek*. "McIntyre neatly weaves together gripping, edge-of-your-seat action with intriguing, original plot developments and characters," wrote Hays.

In an effort to prevent her script *The Moon and the Sun* from becoming too long, she also wrote it in the form of a novel, which was published in 1997. The story is set during the 17th-century reign of Louis XIV in France, where McIntyre traveled to research the work. Stretching the boundaries of science fiction, the novel centers on a mermaid-like creature brought to the king's court by seafaring naturalists. Louis superstitiously believes he can gain immortality by consuming the entrails of the creature, but one of the court maidens discovers the being's intelligence and seeks to protect her from the Sun King. Reviewers such as Roland Green of *Booklist* (July 19, 1997) praised McIntyre's meticulous attention to historical detail.

However, Green criticized the novel as well for a lack of convincing characterization. A critique in the *Kirkus Reviews* (July 1, 1997) described the book as "a dazzling and spirited evocation of the passions, intrigues, and preconceptions of the age . . . an enchanting slice of what-if historical speculation." *The Moon and the Sun* earned McIntyre her second Nebula Award for Best Novel.

Over the years, Vonda McIntyre has gained a reputation as a science fiction writer able to effectively portray the individual humanity in her characters. Particularly, her full realization of female characters has often been praised.

Vonda McIntyre is a member of the Authors Guild, the Authors League of America, Science Fiction Writers of America, and the Planetary Society. She also holds membership in Greenpeace and the National Organization for Women (NOW). She has been a featured writer at several writers workshops. She has spoken at Rutgers University and the Harbourfront International Author's Festival, and has been the guest of honor at national science fiction festivals in New Zealand and Finland. —B.S.

SUGGESTED READING: *Amazon.com*; *Booklist* Oct. 1, 1994, July 19, 1997; Brame, Gloria Glickstein. "An Interview with Vonda N. McIntyre." *Eclectic Literary Forum* (on-line); *Kirkus Reviews* July 1, 1997 (on-line)

SELECTED WORKS: *The Exile Waiting*, 1975; *Dreamsnake*, 1978; *Fireflood and Other Stories*, 1979; *The Entropy Effect*, 1981; *Star Trek II: The Wrath of Khan*, 1982; *Superluminal*, 1983; *Star Trek III: The Search for Spock*, 1984; *Enterprise: The First Adventure*, 1986; *Star Trek IV: The Voyage Home*, 1986; *Barbary*, 1986; *Starfarers*, 1989; *Transition*, 1991; *Metaphase*, 1992; *Nautilus*, 1993; *The Crystal Star*, 1994; *The Moon and the Sun*, 1997; As editor with Susan Janice Anderson *Aurora: Beyond Equality*, 1976

McKibben, Bill

Dec. 8, 1960– Nonfiction writer; critic

Bill McKibben has made a high-profile career out of writing books, giving lectures, and engaging in environmental activism, all in an effort to warn of the dangers facing the earth from untrammeled development. *The End of Nature* (1989) deals with global warming and the tearing of the ozone layer and their ramifications, which involve every aspect of the environment. *The Age of Missing Information* (1992) explores the role of television in cutting humanity off from nature and encouraging a purely consumerist lifestyle. In *The Comforting Whirlwind: God, Job, and the Scale of Creation* (1994), McKibben used the Book of Job as an exem-

Nancie Battaglia/Courtesy of Watkins/Loomis Agency
Bill McKibben

plar of the hubris of assuming that humans are at the heart of creation. His *Hope, Human and Wild: True Stories of Living Lightly on the Earth* (1995) extends the premise of *The End of Nature*, holding out hope by demonstrating that health and happiness abound in some societies in which people exploit the earth's resources to a comparatively low degree. *Maybe One: A Personal and Environmental Argument for Single-Child Families* appeared in 1998. McKibben "does us a service in raising the possibility of alternative concepts of the good life," Richard Bernstein remarked in the *New York Times* (October 11, 1995), but Bernstein and other reviewers have remained slightly skeptical about McKibben's proposed solutions.

For *World Authors 1990–1995*, Bill McKibben, born on December 8, 1960, writes: "My father was a newspaperman, and I assumed growing up that I would follow in that tradition. I worked for the local papers as a sportswriter as a boy, and then served as president of the *Harvard Crimson*, a daily newspaper, while I was in college. But William Shawn read some of my work there, and asked me to come to the *New Yorker* as a staff writer. (He was kind enough to ask twice; I hung up the first time he called, figuring it was a prank.) I spent five extremely happy years there, writing two or three 'Talk of the Town' stories most weeks, as well as a little bit of (very) light fiction, a few longer fact pieces, and short political essays that appeared in the 'Notes and Comment' section of the magazine.

"When Mr. Shawn was ousted as editor in 1987, I left the staff of the magazine and moved with my soon-to-be wife, the writer Sue Halpern, to the Adirondack mountains of upstate New York, about five hours drive north of the city. The Adirondacks

formed much of the basis for my later work—they are the one great wilderness left east of the Mississippi, a wild, cold, and sparsely populated chain of mountains that cover an area larger than Yosemite, Yellowstone, Grand Canyon, and Glacier Parks combined. Despite my suburban and urban upbringing, I quickly fell in love with these woods, and found in their protection a cause that reshaped my life.

"It was at this period that scientists were first starting to talk about phenomena like global warming, a problem that caught my attention in the extremely hot North American summer of 1988. A thought overwhelmed me: that this type of ecological damage was so quantitatively different from all that had gone before that it became qualitatively different too. Instead of simply changing the physical world in the small areas surrounding our homes, fields, and factories, we were now changing the temperature—and hence the flora and fauna, the windspeed and evaporation rate, the rainfall and snowmelt—of every inch of the planet's surface. Hence the title of my first book, *The End of Nature*, which combined the first long look for the general public at the physical aspects of these global problems with the metaphysical speculation described above.

"The book was successful, eventually translated into 15 foreign editions, and also controversial. The implications of these large problems of environmental change were and are unsettling. Among other things, there is no technical fix possible, as there is for troubles like smog. Only large changes in behavior, coupled with technical improvements, offer hope for addressing them. And it is those changes in behavior that have occupied much of my time since. For example, the next book I wrote, *The Age of Missing Information*, described a lunatic experiment I had undertaken in the effort to understand why we seem so paralyzed personally and politically. I found the largest cable television system on the planet, and taped everything that came across it for 24 hours. I took my 2,400 hours of videotape home and spent a year watching it, trying to figure out what the world would look like were that your main source of information. Among other things, I concluded, television helped anchor the consumer society by convincing each of us as individuals that we represented the absolute center of the world.

"In subsequent books, I have looked at the role religious faith might play in reshaping environmental attitudes and weaning us away from consumerism (*The Comforting Whirlwind: God, Job, and the Scale of Creation*) and searched the world for possible models to break out of our consumerist enchantment (*Hope, Human and Wild: True Stories of Living Lightly on the Earth*). I've also had the good fortune to write many essays about the out-of-doors, and to join others in the community of nature writers as they fight on many fronts to save the natural splendor that dims daily before our eyes. This is a field where work and passionate activism are hard to separate, and though I hope I retain the good judgment of a reporter, I also hope I will continue to play a small role in the epic story of our lifetimes."

———

Bill McKibben was born William Ernest McKibben in Palo Alto, California, the son of Gordon C. McKibben and Margaret (Hayes) McKibben. He grew up in the Boston, Massachusetts, area, where both of his parents worked for the *Boston Globe*. McKibben, as he told Michael Coffey in an interview for *Publishers Weekly* (November 13, 1995), always saw himself as "a newspaperman." He went to Harvard, where he became president of the student newspaper, the *Harvard Crimson*, and journalism consumed him. McKibben told Coffey that Harvard "became the end of my education; all I worked on was the *Crimson*." He graduated and moved to New York at the age of 21 to write for the *New Yorker*. During the five years he spent with the *New Yorker*, he wrote over 400 pieces for the "Talk of the Town" section, as well as longer essays and pieces of humorous fiction. In one piece, McKibben traced the origins of all the items that came into his apartment and the final whereabouts of everything that left it. As Coffey pointed out, the theme of all McKibben's books—"what do we consume, why do we consume it, and what are the consequences?"— can be seen in his work for the *New Yorker*.

When McKibben left the *New Yorker* in 1987, he went to a writers' colony in the Adirondack Mountains of New York State. The Adirondacks, among the oldest mountains in the world, became his permanent home and provided him with the passion for wilderness that inspired his first book, *The End of Nature*.

In the *New York Times* (September 20, 1989), Herbert Mitgang wrote of *The End of Nature*, "McKibben has pulled together a great deal of scientific, environmental, and government information, joined it with first-hand observations from several unspoiled areas of the country, and placed his material in a historical context." In the *New York Times Book Review* (October 8, 1989), Nicholas Wade explained that McKibben's thesis that nature is no longer a force independent of humanity has two striking examples: first, the global impact of pollution, seen especially in the greenhouse effect of global warming and the destruction of the ozone layer of the outer atmosphere; second, the management of climate and the use of such technologies as genetic engineering to "further erode the independence of nature." Wade noted that McKibben's concerns in the volume went beyond the scientific and economic, however. "McKibben contends there is something wrong with the terms of a debate in which the beauty and uniqueness of the rain forest count for nothing, and he is surely right," Wade concluded.

Verlyn Klinkenborg noted in *Audubon* (November/December 1995) that the work encompassed "a deeply depressing vision of the global annihilation of wilderness by man." The facts that McKibben cited, along with scientific predictions for the "greenhouse world" we live in and are continuing to promote, are far from hopeful. In the book McKibben argued that the pumping of carbon dioxide, methane, and other gases into the atmosphere is increasing at such an alarming rate that, for example, "in Massachusetts . . . between 3,000 and 10,000 acres of oceanfront land . . . might disappear by 2025." Higher temperatures and increased carbon dioxide levels, McKibben warned, will not only raise water levels but will also devastate crops and lower food yields around the globe.

The End of Nature sparked debate among many of its reviewers and readers. In describing the public reaction to the message put forth by *The End of Nature*, Scott Russell Sanders noted in *Orion* (Spring 1996) that "irate commentators seized his apocalyptic title and skipped his well-documented argument." One reviewer, Dennis Drabelle in the *Washington Post Book World* (October 8, 1989), wrote that McKibben, with his "lucid, closely argued" work, "may hold some guttering hope that we can stave off the worst disasters." Along with the scientific evidence that McKibben presented, there is also a call in *The End of Nature* for human action and change. What people must do, McKibben stated, is change their destructive habits, by making both "technological adjustments" and "mental adjustments"— making it a moral imperative to "never again put our good ahead of everything else's." Otherwise, he argued, humans are on a path to self-destruction. "The choice of doing nothing—of continuing to burn ever more oil and coal—is not a choice," he wrote. "It will lead us, if not straight to hell, then straight to a place with a similar temperature."

In his second book, *The Age of Missing Information*, McKibben examined television's role in our cultural attitude toward nature. According to Noel Perrin, writing in the *New York Times Book Review* (April 26, 1992), *The Age of Missing Information* shows that "McKibben has been wondering why so few people are moved to corrective action when the biosphere and we with it are in such mortal danger. Do they not know? Do they not care? If not, why not?" The reason, according to McKibben, is clearly related to the amount of time people spend watching television. The book is centered on the analysis of 2,400 hours' worth of television videotapes and compares what can be gained from watching television for a day with what McKibben has learned during 24-hour stretches spent outdoors, near his home in the Adirondacks. William C. French observed in the *Christian Century* (January 6, 1993) that "McKibben meditates on the distinctive ways that TV impoverishes our culture by cutting us off from . . . information . . . that earlier generations once received from the farm, the woodlot, or the starry night sky."

Due to television's influence on our lives, McKibben maintained, we are living "at a moment of deep ignorance, when vital knowledge that humans have always possessed about who we are and where we live seems beyond our reach." We must change the "habits of mind and body" that television encourages, he argued, by looking beyond television's message of consumption. As for positive models that provide other options, McKibben declared that religious communities are "potentially capable of elevating and celebrating sacrifice, or embracing some goal besides . . . human material progress."

McKibben took this theme further in *The Comforting Whirlwind: God, Job and the Scale of Creation*. Phyllis Tickle, in her review for *Publishers Weekly* (May 9, 1994), deemed the volume "a provocative reading" of the Book of Job. According to Carolyn Craft of *Library Journal* (June 1, 1994), "McKibben uses the biblical story of Job to articulate modern assumptions that hide us from the larger perspective of God's grand and glorious creation." The "more is better" attitude of our culture, which McKibben blames for the destruction of our environment, is given an alternative: a view of nature that is, in the words of Tickle, "grounded in celebration of its wonder and beauty as well as in a humbler perception of our place in it."

In his *Orion* article Scott Russell Sanders, comparing three of McKibben's books, including *Hope, Human and Wild: True Stories of Living Lightly on the Earth*, wrote: "If *The End of Nature* is the Inferno in his environmental trilogy, and *The Age of Missing Information, Hope, Human and Wild* might be the Paradiso." McKibben said, according to Coffey, that with *Hope, Human and Wild* he had aspired to "convince myself and others that it is not completely pie-in-the-sky to imagine there could be other ways to conduct ourselves." Randy Dykhuis in *Library Journal* (November 15, 1995) termed the work "tantalizing, infuriating, and intelligent." "Now [McKibben] argues that there is a reason for optimism," declared the *Publishers Weekly* reviewer.

"I'm done mourning," McKibben wrote in the book. "Innocence gone, we need to work wisely to build societies that allow natural recovery, that let the rest of Creation begin, however tentatively, to flourish once more."

The models that McKibben used to express his hope are three localities: Curitiba, a city in Brazil; Kerala, a region in the south of India; and the northeastern portion of the United States. High literacy and life-expectancy rates exist side by side with poverty in Kerala. "Demographically," McKibben wrote, "Kerala mirrors the United States on about one-seventieth the cash." Curitiba, Brazil, he declared, is a city "that actually meets people's desires," due to its careful design. Together, those areas are models for "learning to do with less . . .with buses instead of cars, with community instead of splendid suburban independence, with preventive health care instead of high tech medicine . . ." The regrowth of wilderness in the Adirondacks is the third example McKibben cited in pointing to hope for the environment. "This book," he wrote, "offers no utopias . . . what I have been seeking instead are models of some post-utopia."

Assessing McKibben's *Maybe One: A Personal and Environmental Argument for Single-Child Families* for the *New York Times Book Review* (June 14, 1998), Ann Hulbert wrote: "McKibben's real accomplishment in *Maybe One*, appropriately enough, is humbler than his sometimes sanctimonious tone suggests. . . . As he himself acknowledges, index-laden psychological studies of family health and success won't clinch the case for most people, unless, like McKibben, they've already made up their minds. . . . By reminding us that an only child is only and completely a child, not a freak or part of an unfinished family, he makes two children seem like a lucky luxury. A small revelation, it is all McKibben's own case for cutting back requires."

In his slim 1998 volume *Hundred Dollar Holiday: The Case for a Joyful Christmas*, McKibben advocated fighting the commercialization of Christmas—and returning the feeling of togetherness to the holiday season—by spending no more than $100 per family and by giving as gifts items that facilitate family interaction. A chapter is devoted to examples of such gifts.

"Does it make sense to have things the way we have them, that's what all my books are about," McKibben told Michael Coffey for *Publishers Weekly*. "Is it desirable? Is something else possible? What I have learned so far is that what is sound and elegant and civilized and respectful of community is also environmentally benign."

Bill McKibben is active at his local Methodist church, where he teaches Sunday school and is also the Sunday school superintendent. He was a Lyndhurst Fellow from 1988 to 1991 and a Guggenheim Fellow from 1993 to 1994 and has received honorary degrees from Lebanon Valley College and Green Mountain College. Since he became a freelance writer in 1987 he has written about the natural world in a variety of contexts; in addition to the books he has written on his own, he has coauthored two volumes and published many articles. With his wife, Sue Halpern, he has one daughter, Sophie.
—S. Y.

SUGGESTED READING: *Audubon* p 104+ Nov./Dec. 1995; *Christian Century* p22 Jan. 6–13, 1993; *Library Journal* p112 June 1, 1994, p95 Nov. 15, 1995; *New York Times* C p25 Sep. 20, 1989; *New York Times Book Review* p9 Oct. 8, 1989, p7 Apr. 26, 1992; *Orion* p 58+ Spring 1996; *Publishers Weekly* p40 May 9, 1994, p64 Aug. 14, 1995, p 43+ Nov. 13, 1995; *Contemporary Authors* vol. 130, 1990

SELECTED BOOKS: *The End of Nature*, 1989; *The Age of Missing Information*, 1992; *Look at the Land* (with A. MacLean), 1993; *Three Essays* (with T. T. Williams and W. L. Heat-Moon), 1993; *The Comforting Whirlwind: God, Job, and the Scale of Creation*, 1994; *Twenty Five Bike Tours in the Adirondacks* (with S. Halpern, B. Lemmel, and M. Hay), 1995; *Hope, Human and Wild: True Stories of Living Lightly on the Earth*, 1995; *Maybe One: A Personal and Environmental Argument for Single-Child Families*, 1998; *Hundred Dollar Holiday*, 1998; As editor—*Birch Browsings: A John Burroughs Reader*, 1992

Miriam Berkeley

McKnight, Reginald

1956– Short-story writer; novelist

The characters created by novelist and short-story writer Reginald McKnight are primarily African-Americans who, like McKnight himself, entered adulthood after the civil rights movement of the 1960s and are coming to terms with what it means to be black in the contemporary world. He first addressed such issues in his master's thesis, a work of fiction published under the title *Moustapha's Eclipse* in 1988. Two years later he published his first novel, *I Get on the Bus*, in which the main character, a young African-American male on a quest for his roots in Senegal, discovers he has little in common with the people of his ancestry. In McKnight's two subsequent short-story collections, *The Kind of Light That Shines In Texas* (1992) and *White Boys* (1998), the author explored how the black middle class in the United States

makes connections with co-workers and neighbors. He is also the editor of *Wisdom of the African World* (1996), a volume in the Classic Wisdom Collection.

Reginald McKnight was born in Fuerstentelbruek, Germany in 1956, to Frank McKnight, a contractor, and the former Pearl M. Anderson, a dietician. In his late teens, he served in the United States Marine Corps, receiving an honorable discharge in 1976. After his military service he continued his education at Pikes Peak Community College, from which he received his associate's degree in 1978. He completed his undergraduate education at Colorado College, earned his B.A. in English there in 1981.

McKnight taught English as a second language at the American Cultural Center in Dakar, Senegal, for a year after his graduation from Colorado College. He returned to the United States in 1982 to teach English at a language school in Colorado Springs. Around that time, he also began working toward his master's degree at the University of Denver. "*Moustapha's Eclipse* was my master's thesis," he told *Contemporary Authors* (1990), "so it was my desire to graduate with and M.A. that prompted me to write the book more than anything." In 1985 McKnight's writing career received a shot in the arm when he won a fellowship from the Thomas J. Watson Foundation and the Bernice M. Slote Award for Fiction from the University of Nebraska, both for the story "Uncle Moustapha's Eclipse." McKnight received his master's degree in 1987, and the following year *Moustapha's Eclipse* was published by the University of Pittsburgh Press. Almost immediately the collection of short stories began winning awards. The first of these was the Drue Heinze Literature Prize, perhaps the most prestigious prize in America for emerging writers of short fiction, from the University of Pittsburgh in 1988; a year later he received the Ernest Hemingway Foundation Award from the PEN American Center.

However, McKnight was still interested in his teaching as well as his writing. In 1987 he became a lecturer at Arapahoe Community College in Littelton, Colorado. The following year he became an English instructor at Metropolitan State University in Denver, Colorado. In 1989 he left both of those positions to join the staff at the University of Pittsburgh as an assistant professor of English.

Though he moved around a great deal in these years, McKnight continued to produce a steady flow of quality fiction. He published his first novel, *I Get on the Bus*, in 1990, a work he based in part on his experiences as a young man in Senegal. McKnight's protagonist, Evan Norris, is a descendant of slaves who has grown up in the affluent Denver suburbs. He joins the Peace Corps and journeys to Senegal in order to escape his domineering fiancée and life among the African-American bourgeoisie. Yet instead of the reclamation of his roots he had expected, Evan is bombarded by a culture he finds largely inscrutable. He suffers from disease and hallucinations, and attempts to lose himself in a haze of marijuana. Reviews of *I Get on the Bus* were, for the most part, positive. "As he metaphorically—and metaphysically—boards the bus, Evan has such lucid hallucinations that neither he nor the reader is ever certain whether they're real or surreal," Karen Brailsford noted in the *New York Times Book Review* (September 16, 1990). "But the haze that hovers above the novel . . . does not frustrate. Instead, it intensifies and propels our curiosity, as does the author's evocative prose." In *Library Journal* (May 1, 1990), David W. Henderson remarked that "this first novel is not easy reading. It unfolds slowly, perhaps a bit too slowly, but those who persevere will find it rewarding." And a reviewer for the *New Yorker* (July 16, 1990) wrote that "Mr. McKnight doesn't manage to sustain the novel's rush of images and introspection to the end, but there is an exhilarating breadth to the book's best passages, and his hero is a not unworthy successor to Ralph Ellison's invisible man."

McKnight's next book was another collection of stories, *The Kind of Light That Shines in Texas*, published by Little, Brown in 1992. The title story is about two young black boys: 12-year-old Clinton Oates, the narrator, and Marvin Pruitt, the bully who tortures Clinton. Clinton struggles to prove to his teacher (and, as he sees it, the white world) that all black people are not like Marvin Pruitt. Another story, "Roscoe In Hell," follows Roscoe, a 19-year-old drug-overdose victim, into an afterlife where everybody gets high all the time and women continually want to have sex with him. As the story's title indicates, Roscoe finds out that he has landed far from paradise. "Into Night" is seen through the eyes of a grandmother listening to her daughter beat her misbehaving young son. The older woman recalls that she herself had beaten her daughter just as severely, and that she had been beaten by her father—and suddenly realizes how the pattern of abuse can be traced all the way back to the days of slavery. Overall, the collection was joyfully received; Joyce Reiser Kornblatt, reviewing the work for the *New York Times Book Review* (March 8, 1992), wrote that "Reginald McKnight dazzles us again with his gift for capturing voices. This is a writer who hears the complex symphony of daily talk, who functions as a kind of medium for his varied narrators' manic confessions, lyric incantations, heartbroken appeals, and indictments. Each monologue in *The Kind of Light That Shines on Texas* is verbal music, music whose orchestration is so compelling that it threatens to overwhelm the events and characters meant to be served by the energy of the language." Writing for the *Washington Post Book World* (March 12, 1992), Beverly Lowry claimed that "the narrators of the stories . . . are always threatening to get out of hand. The short story form holds them back, barely. They bump against it, like a cat in a cage. But so what? In art, it's always better to be sorry than safe. Reginald McKnight knows and proves this in a major way. Congratulate him for letting his talent take him full-out

where it has to, and for allowing his people to *speak*." McKnight was awarded for his literary daring with a 1995 Whiting Writers' Award worth $30,000.

In 1998 McKnight published *White Boys*, another book of short stories. The collection looks at the connections that unite people across the racial divide. The clearest example comes in the title story, which is about two military families—one black, one white—who live near one another on an Air Force base in Louisiana in the late 1960s. The main character, Derrick Oates, is a shy, 12-year-old black boy bullied by schoolyard toughs and strict parents. He soon becomes friends with a white neighbor and classmate, Garrett Hooker, whose father, a sergeant, has an extreme animosity towards blacks. The story details the day-to-day racism on the base—from Mrs. Hooker's botched attempts to apologize to Mrs. Oates for Sergeant Hooker's behavior to a decision Garrett must make regarding a horrible joke his father wants him to play on Derrick. Other stories follow in a similar vein—in "The More I Like Flies" a black mess-hall attendant listens to his white coworker rant about how multiculturalism has ruined the United States Marine Corps; in "Palm-Wine" a group of Senegalese men confront a tipsy African-American doctoral student about his views on Africans. "To McKnight's credit, *White Boys* deals with race, America's most volatile four-letter word, without resorting to simplistic racial parables," William Jelani Cobb of *Emerge* (May 1998) remarked. Even greater praise came from Rand Richards Cooper, an author reviewing the book for the *New York Times Book Review* (February 1, 1998), who also commented on McKnight's style: "McKnight's favorite form is the monologue. These stories tend to hit the ground running, in midconversation. His style is digressive and colloquial, vesting minimal action in the present frame of the narrative. Indeed, his plots themselves often revolve around telling and listening."—C.M.

SUGGESTED READING: *Emerge* p76+ May 1998; *Library Journal* p115 May 1, 1990; *New York Newsday* p36 Feb. 23, 1982; *New York Times* C p15 Oct. 30, 1995; *New York Times Book Review* p22 Sep. 16, 1990, p8+ Mar. 8, 1992, p30 Feb. 1, 1998; *New Yorker* p85+ July 16, 1990; *Washington Post Book World* C p2 Mar. 12, 1992; *Contemporary Authors*, vol. 129, 1990

SELECTED BOOKS: Fiction—*Moustapha's Eclipse*, 1988; *I Get on the Bus*, 1990; *The Kind of Light That Shines in Texas*, 1992; *White Boys*, 1998; As editor—*Wisdom of the African World*, 1996

Jonathan Exley / Courtesy of Terry McMillan

McMillan, Terry

1951– Novelist

The novelist Terry McMillan has much in common with the four African-American women featured in her best-selling novel *Waiting to Exhale* (1992): like them, she is gutsy, bright, independent, and successful. And ever since she burst upon the scene in 1987, with the publication of her first novel, *Mama*, McMillan has drawn upon those strengths to chart her career, in the process transforming herself into a publishing phenomenon. The unexpected success of *Mama*, which sold out the initial press run of 5,000 copies—an unusual occurrence for a first novel—for instance, was due almost entirely to McMillan's efforts to publicize the book herself, for the publisher, Houghton Mifflin, had earmarked meager funds for its promotion. Taking matters into her own hands, McMillan sent out thousands of letters urging booksellers to stock her novel, scheduled readings, and arranged a promotional tour. She again demonstrated her strong-mindedness when her editors at Houghton Mifflin asked her to revise the manuscript that became her second book, *Disappearing Acts* (1989): she refused and sold it to Viking instead. The novel, a contemporary urban romance, went on to garner critical acclaim and to sell over 100,000 copies in paperback.

McMillan's rare combination of determination and inventiveness is just one of the factors contributing to her emergence as a literary celebrity. She is also a gifted writer who, in each of her novels, has offered a compelling portrait of life among contemporary African-Americans as they strive to live the proverbial American dream. One of her most

recent renderings of that struggle, *Waiting to Exhale* (1992), struck an especially responsive chord among readers. Indeed, during the 20-city book tour that she made in the summer of 1992 to promote the novel, she was regularly greeted by throngs of fans thanking her for giving voice to their everyday concerns. McMillan's heroines even won the heart of Oprah Winfrey, who invited the writer to appear on her television talk show. With the novel in her hand, Oprah declared to her 20 million viewers, "Don't you love it when you read a book and you're laughing out loud?" McMillan, who only a few years before had been licking envelopes as part of her campaign to hustle her first novel into bookstores, was so overwhelmed by the media attention that she likened it to an out-of-body experience. "It's wonderful, it's a writer's dream, but it doesn't really feel like it's happening to me," she told Wendy Smith, who profiled her for *Publishers Weekly* (May 11, 1992). "[It's like,] 'There's this chick I know named Terry McMillan and, gee, I can't wait to read this *Waiting to Exhale*—its sounds like a good book!'"

Terry McMillan was born in the factory town of Port Huron, Michigan, in 1951, the oldest of the five children of Madeline Tillman and Edward Lewis McMillan. She has described her mother, who supported the family by working in auto plants and, at one point, a pickle factory, as a survivor who taught her "how to be strong and resilient." Her father, a blue-collar worker, was an alcoholic who regularly beat his wife. Madeline divorced him in 1964; he died three years later. To help her mother make ends meet, at about this time Terry got a job shelving books at the local library for $1.25 an hour. The job proved to be fortuitous, for it introduced her to the world of books. But it was some time before she realized that not all authors were white. Her first encounter with a novel by a black writer—James Baldwin—was a revelation. "I remember feeling embarrassed and did not read his book because I was too afraid," she has written, as quoted in the *Washington Post* (November 17, 1990). "I couldn't imagine that he'd have anything better or different to say than Thomas Mann, Henry Thoreau, Ralph Waldo Emerson. . . . Needless to say, I was not just naive, but had not yet acquired an ounce of black pride."

While she may have lacked "black pride," McMillan had inherited a strong dose of her mother's feistiness, and at the age of 17, having concluded that there was no future for her in Michigan, she left home in search of a new life in Los Angeles. She soon found work as a secretary and signed up for a course on black literary classics at Los Angeles City College. Her interest in literature remained academic, however, and the notion that she would one day become a celebrated novelist in her own right never entered her mind. Her first writing, in fact, was a love poem. "I fell in love and wrote this poem because he broke my heart," she recalled to Jacqueline Trescott, who profiled her for the *Washington Post* (November 17, 1990). "That is how it started. It kept going and it started turning into this other stuff, started turning into sentences."

After reaching the "sentence stage," McMillan transferred to the University of California at Berkeley, where she majored in journalism. During her years there, she had the good fortune to meet Ishmael Reed, a novelist and the founder of the Before Columbus Foundation, which distributes the work of little-known ethnic writers. Her first short story, "The End," impressed him so much that he published it in 1976. Her work also won praise from the writer Quincy Troupe, who has since become a good friend of hers, and the poet and playwright Ntozake Shange.

Upon receiving her bachelor's degree from the University of California at Berkeley, McMillan once again felt it was time to move on. Her destination was New York City, and her arrival there marked the beginning of a troubled period in her life. Tired of subjecting her creative impulses to the rigorous requirements of journalism, she enrolled in a master's degree program at Columbia University to study screenwriting, but, on finding the school to be "very racist," as she has described it, she soon dropped out and took a job as a word processor in a law firm. Meanwhile, her personal life was in a shambles. Her boyfriend, Leonard Welch, with whom she lived, had lost his job and had turned to dealing cocaine to support himself, and she herself was drinking and using drugs. "I didn't drink every day, you didn't see me stumbling," she told Jacqueline Trescott. "But it was a problem and I couldn't handle it." In the early 1980s she recognized in herself the seeds of the alcoholism that had consumed her father and resolved to overcome her addiction. Since then, she has been drug-free and sober.

The one positive development during that period of her life came about as a result of her membership in the Harlem Writers Guild: It was there that she discovered her voice as a writer of fiction. During one of the group's sessions, McMillan read a short story to her fellow members. "After I finished reading, the room got real quiet . . . ," she told Audrey Edwards, who profiled her for *Essence* (October 1992). "Finally somebody said, 'That doesn't sound like a short story to me. It sounds like the beginning of a novel. You sure can write!'" Although she had scant time to devote to her writing, she became so involved in her story that, before long, she realized she had written the first chapter of a novel. During a two-week stay at the MacDowell Colony, in about 1983, she completed the first draft of what eventually became *Mama*. She put the finishing touches on her manuscript during her subway commute from her Brooklyn apartment to her word processing job in Manhattan.

A moving chronicle of the life of Mildred Peacock, a strong-willed woman modeled after McMillan's mother, and her family, *Mama* (1987) was greeted warmly by most of its reviewers, with one describing it as an "often hilarious and insightful exploration of a slice of black urban life that is rarely seen in contemporary black women's fiction." Like many first novels, however, *Mama* was not widely reviewed, and for a time, it seemed destined to fade into literary history. But McMillan was unlike most first novelists. "'I'm not just going to sit back,'" she remembered telling her publisher, whose efforts to promote the book were negligible, in her interview with Wendy Smith. "'I've never been passive, and I'm not going to start now!'" As a result of the publicity blitz that she subsequently launched, several thousand copies of the book were sold before its official publication date. "My editors called and said, 'Terry, we don't think this would have happened if you had not done all this,'" she told Smith.

Following the publication of *Mama*, McMillan headed west, where she had landed a teaching job at the University of Wyoming at Laramie. What she left behind in Brooklyn was a failed relationship with Leonard Welch. That relationship served as the inspiration for her second novel, *Disappearing Acts* (1989), which tells the story of an explosive love affair between an aspiring songwriter, Zora Banks (the character's name honors the African-American author Zora Neale Hurston, whose *Their Eyes Were Watching God* [1937] delineates a similarly volatile romance), and an often unemployed building contractor, Franklin Swift. Much of the strain in the relationship is the result of Franklin's frustration with his lot in life. A high school dropout with a drug problem, he has nonetheless set high goals for himself. The narrative shifts back and forth between two accounts of the affair, one offered by Zora and the other by Franklin.

According to many readers, the character of Franklin is a psychological tour de force, an opinion with which McMillan might be inclined to agree. "I don't think I've gone that far in any story I've told, and I don't know if I'll ever be able to go that far again," she told Quincy Troupe, who interviewed her for *Emerge* (October 1992). "I mean, . . . it was like it wasn't Terry McMillan. I was Franklin Swift, and I really understood." In fact, McMillan's editors at Houghton Mifflin considered her characterization of Franklin to be such a feat that they wanted her to write the entire book from his point of view. McMillan, however, was so offended by the suggestion that she abruptly broke off her working relationship with them and sold her manuscript to another publisher. "It was going to be this coup," McMillan recalled to Wendy Smith. "Black woman writes story from black man's point of view, it's never been done, blah, blah, blah, blah, blah. Well, I didn't write *Disappearing Acts* to prove anything; that was the way the story had to be told. When my editor told me Zora sounded kind of preppy, I said, 'Look, she's not barefoot and pregnant, living in the projects. . . . I cannot apologize because some of us have been to college, O.K.?'"

Once *Disappearing Acts* was published, the book generated yet another controversy: Leonard Welch filed suit against McMillan, alleging that he had been defamed by the character Franklin Swift. The case was decided in McMillan's favor in April 1992. Despite the problems associated with its publication, *Disappearing Acts* marked a turning point of sorts in McMillan's career. The book went on to sell several hundred thousand copies, making Terry McMillan a household name among African-Americans. The novel's success, in turn, piqued the interest of Hollywood. MGM has since bought the movie rights to the book and commissioned McMillan to write the screenplay.

Notwithstanding the popular appeal of her books, or perhaps because of it, McMillan has failed to win acceptance among many of her fellow black writers, especially women. The poet and novelist Thulani Davis, for instance, described McMillan's work as "more bup art"—that is, art for black yuppies—"than black art," and more established writers, such as Toni Morrison and Alice Walker, have scarcely acknowledged her contribution to the growing canon of modern black literature. In an interview with Esther B. Fein for the *New York Times* (July 1, 1992), McMillan expressed her disappointment in the apparent lack of support for her work among black intellectuals: "I've gone out of my way to show respect for other black female writers, but I've yet to be acknowledged by some of the more successful ones, and it hurts."

For her part, McMillan has done her best to be supportive of her fellow black artists. For instance, her interest in promoting the work of black writers has led her to compile and edit *Breaking Ice: An Anthology of Contemporary African-American Fiction* (1990). "There are a lot of writers in this anthology whose work is very good," she told Jacqueline Trescott. "There are people in this book who write circles around me."

Meanwhile, by 1989, McMillan and her son, Solomon, born to her and Leonard Welch in 1984, had moved to Arizona, where she had accepted a teaching position at the University of Arizona at Tucson. In an autobiographical essay that appeared in *WigWag* (November 1989), McMillan wrote about the difficulties she was having in cultivating a viable relationship with any of the men she met. "From the time I got to Tucson I've been trying to have a good time," she wrote, "but the most reliable form of entertainment seems to be taking my five-year-old son to the zoo." Her female friends, she knew, were trying to deal with similar problems: all in their mid-30s, she and her friends were accomplished, attractive, funny, smart, financially secure—but alone. McMillan knew there was a story there.

That story eventually became *Waiting to Exhale* (1992). Its four main characters are Savannah Jackson, a cool, confident, and successful television producer who, when among her friends, admits that she is tired of being alone; Robin Stokes, an insurance company executive who cannot bring herself to break up with Russell, even though she concedes that he is "a lying, sneaky, whorish Pisces";

Bernadine Harris, Savannah's college roommate who, after being married for 11 years to a shrewd and successful businessman, is faced with the news that he is leaving her for his blond, 24-year-old bookkeeper; and Gloria Matthews, the owner of a hair salon, who has a weight problem that is apparently rooted in her fear of entering into an intimate relationship with a man.

Although McMillan had, on the strength of her first two books, made a name for herself as an important contemporary novelist with a considerable following, the commercial success of *Waiting to Exhale* was astonishing by any measure. By the end of 1992, over 700,000 hardcover copies of the book had been sold and the paperback rights had been purchased for $2.64 million—a record figure for a novel by an African-American author and one of the highest sums ever paid to any writer. Moreover, at public readings around the country, during which she would read passages from her book, her fans could barely contain themselves, many of them shouting "Amen!" and "You can say that again, sister!" so loudly that McMillan herself could hardly be heard.

McMillan believes that the phenomenal success of *Waiting to Exhale* is due to its engaging narrative, and her admirers—both ordinary readers and literary critics—agree, with many saying that the dialogue is so true-to-life that they find themselves immediately drawn into the characters' lives. In her assessment of the novel for the *New York Times Book Review* (May 31, 1992), Susan Isaacs wrote, "McMillan's heroines are so well drawn that by the end of the novel, the reader is completely at home with the four of them. . . . Reading *Waiting to Exhale* is like being in the company of a great friend. It is thought-provoking, thoroughly entertaining and very, very comforting."

One feature of the novel, however, drew the fire of many reviewers: like *Disappearing Acts*, it contains extensive profanity. But McMillan met that criticism with characteristic directness. "So what?" she declared in response to the suggestion that much of the obscenity was gratuitous, as quoted in the *Publishers Weekly* article. "That's the way we talk. And I want to know why I've never read a review where they complain about the language that male writers use!"

McMillan had also expected to be accused of "black-male-bashing," in much the same way that other black female writers have been, because all of the men in her book turn out to be deceitful, faithless, self-absorbed, or dependent on drugs. She considers the charge, which had surfaced in reviews of *Disappearing Acts*, to be unjustified. "I have about had it with how negatively we supposedly portray black men in our work, because it gets on my nerves that people think of us as sociologists or anthropologists," she told Curtis Taylor, who interviewed her for *New York Newsday* (September 20, 1992). "I was trying to portray [Franklin] as realistically as I could to get the reader to understand what his frustration is, but at the same time not whip out the violins." With *Waiting to Exhale*, however, the anticipated attack never came.

McMillan sold the film rights to *Waiting to Exhale*, and as part of her contract with Twentieth Century Fox, had planned to write the script. However, she soon realized that she was too closely connected to the novel and enlisted a cowriter, Ron Bass, to help her make the necessary changes to the script. "When you've written the novel, it's hard to distance yourself from the work. Ron helped me connect the dots," she told *Quarterly Black Review* (November 1995) writer Veronica Chambers.

The movie version of *Waiting to Exhale* made its onscreen debut in 1995 to largely mixed reviews. Many critics and viewers alike were disappointed that the film, starring Angela Bassett, Whitney Houston, Loretta Devine and Lela Rochon, deviated from the original novel. The *San Francisco Examiner's* Barry Walters (December 22, 1995) wrote that while the movie "maintains the sense of frustration and friendship" that made the book so successful among women, it also condenses the plot into a "series of humiliation and battles scenes" with the end result being that the "pattern of disrespect and disengagement becomes more numbing than uplifting." Similarly, the reviewer from *USA Today* (Dec. 12, 1995) noted that screenplay writers McMillan and Bass managed to "retain much of the book's earthy language and bawdy bedroom humor" but felt that the movie, directed by Forest Whitaker, ultimately "runs out of breath." The critic for the *San Francisco Chronicle* (December 22, 1995) expressed disappointment with the screenplay adaptation, with staff critic Edward Guthmann writing that while the novel, which celebrated the "rich, ribald humor of black women, as well as their loneliness and angst" was exemplary material for a good movie, *Waiting to Exhale* is ultimately "hit-and-miss—not a stinker for the ages, but certainly not the gem that McMillan's work deserved." The movie, however, was a success at the box office.

In the years prior to *Waiting to Exhale*'s release, McMillan suffered some personal blows that would ultimately alter and shape her career. In October 1993 her mother, with whom she had been very close, died suddenly from an asthma attack. At the time McMillan had been working on a new novel titled *A Day Late and a Dollar Short*, but the story centered on a loving mother similar to her own, and she could not bring herself to finish it. A year later McMillan was dealt another blow when her best friend, a fellow novelist from New York City, died of liver cancer. In an effort to heal her pain, McMillan took an extended trip to Jamaica, where she met and fell in love with a young hotel worker. The 20-year-old man eventually moved to the U.S. with McMillan and moved into her California home, which they share with her teenage son.

In 1996 McMillan produced another work of fiction, *How Stella Got Her Groove Back*, a semi-autobiographical story of a 42-year-old woman, Stella, who, while in Jamaica, falls in love with Winston, a man half her age. The book was written in a stream of consciousness style, with many long, unpunctuated run-on sentences, indicative, McMillan has said, of the way in which her mind was working when she was writing it. The lengthy prose and unstructured style of the book drew criticism, with the reviewer for *Booklist* (April 15, 1996) admitting that the narration of the story was a "bit awkward at times." Other reviews were decidedly mixed. In *Time* (May 6, 1996), John Skow stated that the book "barely qualifies as beach literature" and in a comparison to McMillan's previous novel, wrote that the character of Winston "burbles along cheerfully but lacks the satirical bite of *Waiting to Exhale*." Richard Bernstein for the *New York Times* (May 15, 1996) wrote that as a whole, the book is not "deeper or more searching than the average sitcom, no more dramatically powerful than a backyard barbecue," but that it does contain "a cast of likeable, truculent characters, funny lines, smart repartee, and a warm and fuzzy ending." Despite its flaws, Bernstein concluded that *How Stella Got her Groove Back* is "an irreverent, mischievous, diverting novel that at times will make you laugh out loud." McMillan sold the movie rights for *Stella* for an undisclosed, seven-figure amount in 1996. The movie version, another collaborative writing effort by McMillan and Bass, stars Angela Bassett, Whoopi Goldberg, and Taye Diggs, and debuted in theaters in August 1998.

In addition to writing novels, McMillan has reviewed books for the *New York Times Book Review*, the *Atlanta Constitution*, and the *Philadelphia Inquirer*, and she has contributed pieces to the *New York Times Magazine*'s "Hers" column. The recipient of many awards, including a New York Foundation for the Arts Fellowship (1986), a Doubleday/Columbia University Literary Fellowship, and a National Endowment for the Arts Fellowship in literature (1988), she has also won fellowships to the Yaddo Artist Colony. In 1993 she won an NAACP Image Award in the literary category for *Waiting to Exhale*.

In the years since she wrote *Mama*, McMillan's circumstances have changed dramatically. Among other things, she has added to her collections of art and designer clothing, and she herself has metamorphosed from an attractive though somewhat inconspicuous "girl next door" into a striking woman with a distinctive sense of style. As Wendy Smith observed, "She fills the room with personality even before she begins to speak."
—D.B.

SUGGESTED READING: *Booklist* Apr. 15, 1996; *Chicago Tribune* VI p10 June 13, 1993, with photo; *Ebony* p23+ May 1993, with photos; *Emerge* p47+ Oct. 1992, with photos; *Essence* p77+ Oct. 1992, with photos; *Los Angeles Times* B p10+ June 19, 1992, with photos; *New York Daily News* p10+ July 26, 1992, with photos; *New York Newsday* June 7, 1992, with photo,

Sep. 20, 1992; *New York Times* May 31, 1992, C
p1+ July 1, 1992, with photos, C p17 May 15,
1996; *New York Times Magazine* p20+ Aug. 9,
1992, with photo; *Publishers Weekly* p50+ May
11, 1992, with photo; *Quarterly Black Review*
Nov. 1995; *San Francisco Chronicle* Dec. 22,
1995; *San Francisco Examiner* Dec. 22, 1995;
San Francisco Focus p62 May 1992, with photo;
Time p47 May 6, 1996, with photo; *USA Today*
D p1+ July 7, 1992, with photos, Dec. 12, 1995,
with photo; *Washington Post* D p1+ Nov. 17,
1990, with photo; *WigWag* p37+ Nov. 1989;
Contemporary Authors, 1998; *Contemporary
Literary Criticism* vol. 50, 1988, vol. 61, 1990

SELECTED WORKS: Fiction—*Mama*, 1987;
Disappearing Acts, 1989; *Waiting to Exhale*,
1992; *How Stella Got Her Groove Back*, 1996; As
editor—*Breaking Ice: An Anthology of
Contemporary African-American Fiction*, 1990

Jerry Bauer/Courtesy of Rob Weisbach Books

Meltzer, Brad

1970– Novelist; lawyer

Brad Meltzer began writing fiction while he attended Columbia Law School. He earned his degree in
1996 at the age of 26, and his first novel, *The Tenth
Justice*, was published the following year. Drawing
from personal experience, Meltzer's novel is a legal
thriller focusing on a young aide to the Supreme
Court who accidentally leaks the results of an upcoming judicial decision. While the legal thriller
genre has been an area dominated in the past by the
likes of John Grisham, Meltzer has insisted that his

work stands out in that its perspective is distinctly
that of a young person. His second novel, *Dead
Even*, was published in 1998 and tells the story of
two married lawyers forced to oppose each other
on a case that neither of them can afford to lose:
each one has been separately informed that if
he/she loses the case, his/her spouse will be killed.

A biographical profile submitted to *World Authors 1990–1995* by Meltzer's publicist reads as follows: "Brad Meltzer grew up in Brooklyn, New
York, and later moved with his family to Miami.
While in high school, he served as student government president and was featured in *Parade* magazine after he started a school protest by wearing a
skirt (the air conditioning had broken down and
the dress code dictated that boys couldn't wear
shorts.) *Parade* crowned him one of the 'Worst
Fashion Statements of 1988.'

"Brad was the first in his family to attend college, graduating with High Distinction from the
University of Michigan in 1992. He majored in History and minored in English. His senior paper was
entitled, 'Comic Books as Propaganda in World
War II.'

"After receiving his undergraduate degree, Brad
was recruited by Eli Segal, publisher of *Games*
magazine, to become the head of the magazine's
marketing department. Shortly after Brad arrived
at *Games*, Eli Segal left to become Bill Clinton's
Chief of Staff for the 1992 Presidential campaign.
Brad stayed at *Games* until the fall of 1994 when
he moved to New York City to study law at Columbia University. In the summer of 1994, Segal once
again recruited Brad, and brought him to Washington, D.C. to work for President Clinton. In Washington, he served as a speech writer for AmeriCorps, Clinton's National Service program. He co-
wrote the oath of service, which was delivered by
President Clinton to new AmeriCorps members.

"It was that same year that Brad developed the
idea for his debut novel, *The Tenth Justice*. While
visiting the Supreme Court, he interviewed former
Supreme Court clerks and was encouraged to hear
that his storyline was plausible, especially when
one former clerk declared, 'The scariest thing is
that it could really happen.'

"Brad completed writing *The Tenth Justice*
while at Columbia Law School, where he convinced one of his professors to give him academic
credit for the novel. He also taught law to eighth
graders in Harlem, served as Senior Editor of the
Columbia Law Review, and was a Harlem Fiske
Stone Scholar.

"After graduation in May 1996, Brad Meltzer
moved to Washington, D.C. with his high school
sweetheart-turned-wife, Cori Flam, who is also a
lawyer.

"When *The Tenth Justice* was published in May
1997, it became an instant *New York Times Best-
seller*, and hit virtually every other major national
bestseller list.

"*Dead Even*, Brad Meltzer's second novel, [was]
published by Rob Weisbach Books on May 13,
1998."

Brad Meltzer was born in 1970 in the Sheepshead Bay section of Brooklyn, New York. At the age of 22, he resolved to write novels in his spare time. His decision to study law did not work against his literary goals, as he had decided to write a novel based on the legal world. The AmeriCorps facility where he worked over the summers proved valuable for off-hours research while Meltzer continued to work on the novel.

The first novel he attempted came to a total of 800 pages, which he later edited down to 500. He did no further work on it, choosing instead to begin another novel, which eventually became *The Tenth Justice*. That work is the story of a young Supreme Court clerk who accidentally reveals the results of an upcoming judicial decision to a dangerous criminal faction that, in turn, translates the information into a stock market jackpot. The young clerk's roommates aid him in his attempts to correct his mistake but eventually begin to distrust one another.

The completed manuscript for the novel was accepted for publication in 1996, just as Meltzer attained his law degree from Columbia University. He used the advance given to him by the publishing company to help pay off his student loans. The novel was published in 1997. It immediately entered the *Publishers Weekly* best-seller list at number seven, and was termed "Page-Turner of the Week" in *People* magazine (May 19, 1997). It also made the recommended summer reading lists of such publications as *Time* and *Cosmopolitan*. Most notably of all, *The Tenth Justice* spent eight weeks on the *New York Times* best-seller list.

In a *New York Times* (August 24, 1997) review, Erik Burns praised the novel's "snappy" dialogue, but found the plot implausible. According to Burns the book's unlikely "mix of intrigue, romance and legal trivia" severely weighed down the story.

Meltzer gained a great deal of attention for publishing his first novel at such a young age and early stage in his career. The *New York Times* ran a profile of him on May 18, 1996, in which his rise to fame was discussed. Meltzer's agent, Jill Kneerim, assured James Barron, the author of the article, that Meltzer was "on the same course he was two years ago, three years ago, four years ago. It's like a photograph that's developing. He knew it was going to be this picture, and here it comes." In the same profile, some of Meltzer's professors at Columbia compared him to legal fiction writers John Grisham and Scott Turow. One professor even went so far as to compare Meltzer to early 20th-century author F. Scott Fitzgerald, "in terms of being able to write about the young elite and how they are responding to their situation."

Before *The Tenth Justice* was even finished, Jill Kneerim was already pushing her client's work, showing the incomplete manuscript to numerous Hollywood executives in the hopes of a motion picture deal. The option was picked up by Dick Clark Productions and Wind Dancer Films, and a film version of *The Tenth Justice* was put into production by the Fox 2000 studio. "Brad writes very filmically," explained Kneerim in *Publishers Weekly* (January 13, 1997). "He's terrific on dialogue. It made sense to shop the film rights first."

Meltzer's second novel, entitled *Dead Even*, was published in 1998. The novel mines the same legal territory dealt with in *The Tenth Justice*, but also explores issues of loyalty within marriage. The two main characters are married Manhattan lawyers who find themselves on opposing sides of the same case. Each is approached by extortionists, who threaten to kill their lawyer's spouse if their side does not win the case. Neither the husband nor the wife discusses the threats, not wanting to upset the other.

Dana Kennedy of *Entertainment Weekly* (May 29, 1998) described *Dead Even* as "uneven but mostly smart." Kennedy found the novel's dialogue "crisp and dead-on," but judged the plot to be heavy and formulaic, not to mention overly long. There was also, according to the reviewer, an overabundance of weak subplots that detracted from the main storyline. Nevertheless, Kennedy wrote, "Meltzer is so good at tapping into the yuppie psyches of [his main characters], their psychological game of cat and mouse, and the chilling office politics, that the book still manages to race along like a great beach read."

In addition to his efforts as a novelist, Brad Meltzer has also written for *Details* magazine. He is married to his former high-school girlfriend, Cori Flam, who accepted a proposal from her future husband at the top of the Eiffel Tower.—B.S.

SUGGESTED READING: *Entertainment Weekly* p68+ May 29, 1998, with photo; *New York Times* I p21 May 18, 1996, with photo, VII p19 Aug. 24, 1997; *People* May 19, 1997; *Publishers Weekly* p48 Jan. 13, 1997, p22 May 26, 1997

SELECTED WORKS: *The Tenth Justice*, 1997; *Dead Even*, 1998

Menaker, Daniel

Sep. 17, 1941– Novelist; short-story writer

The American writer Daniel Menaker has created in his story collections *Friends and Relations* (1976) and *The Old Left* (1987) and in his novel *The Treatment* (1998) characters who return to human connectedness. His young male protagonists are teachers who manifest a true concern for the welfare of their students and for humanity in general. Menaker has attempted to memorialize two endangered species—old leftists and true Freudians—in characters who, although they may be comic, are also deeply moral, as demonstrated particularly by Dr. Ernesto Morales, the Cuban psychi-

Sara Barrett

Daniel Menaker

atrist in *The Treatment* who attempts to save souls as well as minds.

Daniel Menaker writes the following for *World Authors 1990–1995*: "I was born in 1941 in New York City. I lived in Greenwich Village and went to the Little Red Schoolhouse in elementary school. My father was an exporter, my mother a proofreader and later an editor at *Fortune*. Both were involved in the leftism of the Village of that era. I went to junior high school and high school in Nyack, New York, which at the time was less a suburb than a small, wonderful Hudson-River town. I attended Swarthmore College and graduated with high honors in 1963, and then went on to get an M.A. in English, in 1965, from the Johns Hopkins University. I taught English at the George School, a Quaker boarding school in Bucks County, Pennsylvania, for one year, and then at the Collegiate School in New York City for two years. In 1969 I joined the staff of the *New Yorker* as a fact-checker, and then, after holding several other editorial positions, I became a senior editor, in 1976, dealing primarily with fiction. Some of the writers I worked with were Mavis Gallant, Alice Munro, Richard Dooling, Alan Sillitoe, Pauline Kael, Elmore Leonard, and Isaac Bashevis Singer. In 1972, my own writing—short fiction and humor—began appearing in the *New Yorker* and other magazines and newspapers. William Maxwell was my editor at the *New Yorker* and it was he who taught me directly about editing and finished my education as a writer, and who helped me to become a senior editor. In 1976, I had a book of stories published by Doubleday—*Friends and Relations*. It had some good things in it but was mostly callow and a little too arch. In 1987 I had another book of stories pub-

lished by Alfred A. Knopf called *The Old Left*, based on my own life and my brother's death and my relationship with a complex and charismatic and ultimately wonderful uncle. Many of the stories involved his house in New Marlborough, Massachusetts, which he bequeathed to me, and where I am writing this autobiographical sketch. In 1998, Knopf published my first novel, *The Treatment*, based on some *New Yorker* short stories.

"In 1980 I married Katherine Bouton, a friend and colleague at the *New Yorker*. She went on to be a free-lance writer and then began working for the *New York Times*. Eventually she became Deputy Editor of the *Times Book Review* and is now Deputy Editor of the *Times Magazine*. We have two excellent children, William, 15, and Elizabeth, 11.

"Influences on my writing include all the dead and alive white males and females in the literary pantheon and some dead and alive black writers and some dead and alive Indian writers (from India). Specifically, I would cite Maxwell, who taught me about clarity; Pauline Kael, who taught me about voice; and Katinka Loeser, who taught me about how moving and funny ordinary life and death are and who never ended a sentence for the sake of ending it. Throw Updike and Roth and Jane Austen into the specific pile—and Dickens. Oh, Joseph Heller and Fitzgerald and Kingsley Amis, too. And definitely Alice Munro.

"Writing fiction is an effort to dramatize in an intelligent and entertaining way insights into human character and behavior—behavior in isolation and in society. People and events are made up, out of the author's life, experiences, and perceptions, in order to arrive at and demonstrate truths about our actions and our condition. A writer's style is his or her habitual ways of saying things, and those ways demonstrate their styles of thinking and feeling, too. My own style seems to me classical (often long-winded and qualified, as in this parenthesis), ironic, and prosaic, with flashes of directness and the logic and the vernacular tossed in. Like this. I believe that writing and speaking stories are attempts to share what is common and interesting in life in a distinctive and enlightening way, attempts to make sense of what is essentially our nonsensical situation, which consists of the means to wonder why we are here and what our lives signify— that means being the cerebral cortex and the intellect it gives rise to—without hope of ever finding any real answers. Writing and other narrative and even non-narrative art forms take us to the edge of the great dark sea of what we don't know (nearly everything, it seems to me) and ultimately make us aware of—and amused, affected, and dismayed by—our existential impasse. I have to say, however grandiosely, that that's what I try to do. On the way to that dark shore I'd like my readers to enjoy and get caught up in the stories I try to tell."

The body of work that Daniel Menaker has created in the short-story collections *Friends and Relations* (1976) and *The Old Left* (1987) and the novel *The Treatment* (1998) can be considered a seamless whole. The world of these stories is New York City and the Berkshires, and the characters are, for the most part, the heirs and descendants of the Old Left. Characters move from one story to another and appear in Menaker's novel, *The Treatment*. The *Choice* (April 1977) reviewer of *Friends and Relations* termed the characters "self-absorbed and isolated protagonists" and observed that the "pompous and bumbling young male characters will be all too familiar to the contemporary reader." Most of the stories have a youngish male character who is a teacher, as Menaker was earlier in his career. Frederick Engels Menaker, Daniel's father's brother, appears in all his books. Menaker told Jonathan Bing in an interview for *Publishers Weekly* (June 1, 1998) that his uncle was "a central character" in his life, "in some ways more important than my father and mother."

Assessing *The Old Left* for the *New York Times Book Review* (May 3, 1987), Daniel Stern observed that it had "the connections if not the scale and heft of a novel." Most of the stories involve David Leonard, a young teacher; his uncle Sol; and his girlfriend, Elizabeth. A prototypical member of the Old Left, Sol has lived through all of the struggles of the 20th century, from World War I to the Spanish Civil War and on. Sol's death will mark the end of an era and the descent into darkness of the history he represented. Stern remarked that the question raised in Menaker's book is, "What are we to do with the history that [the Old Leftists]—deceived and self-deceived—embody, their vitality powered by an idea about human existence as a sort of shared enterprise?" Menaker, according to Stern, "sings a tender song"; some of "the lyrics may have been forgotten, but the melody lingers on."

Menaker allowed some of the melody of Uncle Sol and David Leonard to sound briefly in *The Treatment*, but the loudest tune that emerges from that book is the one sung by Dr. Ernesto Morales, the psychiatrist who is treating Jake Singer, a prep-school teacher in his early 30s, who serves as Menaker's alter ego. Singer lost his mother at an early age and his girlfriend at a later one, and although he has a trust fund, a job, and an apartment in New York, he is discontented with his life. Morales, a Cuban Catholic, is "the last Freudian," as he declares at the end of the novel. "I am the last of a line that stretches from Moses to Aristotle through Cicero to our good Lord Jesus Christ and Aquinas and Maimonides and Shakespeare and Montaigne and finally to Freud and then to me. A line of fascination with and respect for the dignity, the very concept, of the human soul." He tells Jake that by ending his treatment he has denied himself "even secular maturity." Jake, Christopher Lehmann-Haupt wrote in the *New York Times* (May 28, 1998), is "satisfied with an incomplete under-standing of his soul's mystery. He'll settle for magic and illusion and the sort of comedy of happenstance so entertainingly realized here."
—S.Y.

SUGGESTED READING: *Choice* p201 Apr. 1977; *New York Times* E p7 May 28, 1998; *New York Times Book Review* p12+ June7, 1998; *Publishers Weekly* p41+ June 1, 1998, with photo

SELECTED BOOKS: Fiction—*Friends and Relations*, 1976; *The Old Left*, 1987; *The Treatment*, 1998

Osmund Geier/Courtesy of Barbara Mertz

Mertz, Barbara

Sep . 29, 1927– Novelist; Egyptologist

The romance and suspense novelist Barbara Michaels and the mystery writer Elizabeth Peters are both personas of Barbara Mertz, who began writing nonfiction books in her area of expertise—the ancient world—before starting a career as a fiction writer in the 1960s.

Barbara Mertz was born Barbara Gross on September 29, 1927, in Canton, Illinois, to Earl D. Gross, a printeer, and Grace (Tregellas) Gross, a teacher. At the University of Chicago she pursued a career in education, following in the tradition of the women in her family. However, an infatuation with history beckoned, and Mertz heeded the call, sneaking over to the Oriental Institute at the university and managing to talk her way into the program. In an interview with *Publishers Weekly* (October 23, 1987), Mertz attempted to explain to Dulcy Brainard her attraction to Egyptology, saying, "It combines the appeal of the mystery story—scholarly interpretations are similar to an investigation—and the instinct for treasure hunting."

After receiving her Ph.D., in 1952, Mertz and her husband (Richard R. Mertz, whom she married in June 1950 and later divorced) moved to Washington D.C. The academic arena was still dominated by males, and even with a Ph.D, Mertz could not land a job. To acquire a secretarial job, she was forced to leave mention of her degrees off her applications out of fear of being thought "overqualified." She loved to write fiction, and during this period she and her husband began composing spy stories. It was a popular genre at the time, but one that did not yield much success for the couple. Still, Mertz persisted with her writing, acquiring an agent who suggested that she try another angle. With her interest in archeology, she began producing nonfiction, and thus her writing career started with the academic books *Temples, Tombs and Hieroglyphs: The Story of Egyptology* (1964); *Red Land, Black Land: the World of the Ancient Egyptians* (1966); and *Two Thousand Years in Rome* (with Richard R. Mertz, 1968).

By the mid-1960s, another literary movement began to take shape, this one driven by the Gothic novels of Victoria Holt and Mary Stewart. "I was still doggedly writing mystery stories," she told Brainard. "and I thought, 'Aha, this is what I'd like to write.'" Her first attempt, *The Master of Black Tower*, was met with rejection after rejection before finding a publisher in 1966. "From that point I never looked back," she continued. "A matter of being on the right spot at the right time with the right product."

The Master of Black Tower, which leans heavily on the Gothic staples of ghosts, castles, and romance, tells the story of a woman, Damasis Gordon, who comes to work at the Scottish estate of a wealthy but disfigured and bitter man named Gavin Hamilton. Damasis is intrigued by the seemingly cruel man, and attempts to find out the truth surrounding his wife's mysterious death and the "accidents" which have plagued his family. Even as she fears that he may have been involved in his wife's demise, Damasis finds herself falling in love with Gavin. The book met with favorable reviews, and Mertz's career began to gain momentum.

While she was breaking into the mystery genre, her agent suggested that she begin publishing under three separate names, to correspond with her three different types of books. For the nonfiction, she would continue to write as Barbara Mertz; for her romance/suspense novels, the name Barbara Michaels was adopted, and for her straightforward mystery novels, which she began writing in 1968 with *The Jackal's Head*, she used the name Elizabeth Peters, an amalgamation of her two children's names. According to an interview with the *Washington Post*'s Sarah Booth Conroy (June 11, 1989), the author was so relieved to have her books reach the shelves of stores, that she "would've accepted the pen name 'Jack the Ripper.'"

Mertz soon began to produce novels regularly, often writing a book under each pen name in the same year. To date she has authored more than 30 novels with popular Gothic elements. (Still, the author refuses to identify her work as "Gothic." As she told Brainard, "Gothic is a term I hate," "the only things those novels and some of the things I've done have in common is setting—ruined castles off in the mists.")

For the most part, the novels published under the name Elizabeth Peters feature one of three characters: Amelia Peabody, Jacqueline Kirby, and Vicky Bliss. In an interview with *USA Today* (July 27, 1989) Mertz stated that she views the Michaels books as "more mainstream and somewhat more difficult to write," while the Peters books "involve more humor." All of Mertz' books, regardless of the nom de plume attached to them, share heroines who are strong, intelligent, and witty, as well as completely independent. Mertz, who has long followed the feminist movement, has often stated that she takes pride in having been one of the first writers, particularly in the mystery and detective genres, to create such strong-minded female characters. Despite literature's progress in this area since her female protagonists first emerged, Mertz still finds there is a prejudice against romantic suspense novels. As she told Brainard, "People say women write cozy, damsel-in-distress, had-I-but-known stories, while men, on the other hand, write tough, realistic novels about the streets." On the contrary, Mertz argues, suspense novels written from a female perspective are no less a part of the genre. Adding to this thought in her interview with Conroy, Mertz said, "I can't see why it's worse to coddle rather than addle the reader. Our mysteries are as realistic and well written as the sub-genre called 'mean streets' mysteries. I sell well enough, writing about the domestic scene, and I'm not acquainted with the mean streets. Why should critics take more seriously the nitty gritty books about those who murder people they don't know well enough to hate."

After *The Master of Blacktower*, the Barbara Michaels books continued with *Sons of the Wolf* (1967), *Ammie, Come Home* (1968), and *Prince of Darkness* (1969). In 1970 Mertz wrote *The Dark on the Other Side*, a novel that relied heavily on topics of supernatural forces. The story line revolved around a woman named Linda Randolf, who begins to hear her house, and all the objects contained within, talking to her. Her husband tells her she is going insane, and she begins to wonder if that is in fact the case, but soon starts to suspect that her husband may be dealing with darker forces than she could have ever imagined. *Crying Child*, the novel which followed in 1971, also hinges on the supernatural, this time taking a look at a woman who, after losing her baby during childbirth, begins to hear a baby's crying around her house. Like Linda, she also thinks she is losing her mind, and her sister, who comes to visit, begins to have similar thoughts. However, soon even the sister is hearing the child's cries, and suddenly new pathways of intrigue and hidden family history must be explored.

Subsequent Michaels mysteries include *Grey-gallows* (1972), *Witch* (1973), *House of Many Shadows* (1974), *The Sea King's Daughter* (1975), *Patriot's Dream* (1976) and *Wings of the Falcon* (1977). The latter book takes the reader on a journey to Italy, where a woman named Francesca, recovering from the pain of the death of her father, seeks the solace of her mother's family. Once there, however, she meets The Falcon, a mysterious horseman who is attempting to ignite a rebellion against the aristocracy. Francesca finds herself falling in love with The Falcon, even as his identity remains a mystery.

After this novel came *Wait for What Will Come* (1978), *The Walker in the Shadows* (1979), *The Wizard's Daughter* (1980), *Someone in the House* (1981), and *Black Rainbow* (1982). The following year, Mertz published *Here I Stay*, a story with another old, spooky residence, this time a country mansion that Andrea Torgesen tries to turn into an inn along with her brother Jim, who is recovering from an auto accident. It seems to be a perfect fit, until the siblings realize that the haunting voices and noises indicate the presence of a powerful and evil force.

As the 1980s progressed, Mertz continued to produce, on average, one Michaels book per year. In 1983 she also published *Dark Duet*, followed by *The Grey Beginning* in 1984. The ensuing years saw *Be Buried in the Rain* (1985), *Shattered Silk* (1986), and *Search the Shadows* (1987). Two years later, Mertz wrote *Smoke and Mirrors*, this time mixing a smattering of politics into her Gothic tale. The story involves a woman, Erin Hartsock, who joins the campaign staff of a congresswoman from Virginia whose campaign headquarters are housed in her creepy, old Victorian mansion. At first Erin sails along at her new job, and even acquires a new boyfriend as well. But when a series of fires begin to break out and a supposedly accidental death appears anything but, Erin starts to suspect that there is more to the campaign staff than meets the eye. Reviews for *Smoke and Mirrors* were largely favorable, with *New Woman* magazine (February 1989) complimenting the author for capturing "the old-fashioned tone of a Nancy Drew mystery."

During the next five years, Mertz published *Into the Darkness* (1990), *Vanish with the Rose* (1992), and *Houses of Stone* (1993). This last novel, which tells the story of a female professor seeking out a writer's lost manuscript and encountering intrigue along the way, was well-received by critics. *Booklist* (October 15, 1993) hailed it as one of Michael's best novels to date, calling it a mystery that is "brimming with suspense yet revolves around authorial research rather than money and multiple murders." *Kirkus Reviews* (September 1, 1993) offered tempered praise for *Houses of Stone*. "It never gets the heart pounding," the critic wrote. "But it's diverting—with a refreshingly intelligent and unstereotypical heroine."

Stitches in Time (1995) was the next Michaels novel. The book's main plot surrounds a woman's quest to learn more about women's folk art in preparation for her master's thesis on the subject. She goes to work in her friend's vintage clothing shop and is soon wrapped up with mysterious robbers—all while attempting to deal with a long-standing crush on her friend's husband. *The Literary Times* was impressed with the intensity of the mystery and wrote, "When Barbara Michaels turns up the suspense, watch out! A word to the wise; don't read this in bed alone! Fascinating detail and hair-raising suspense!" *Booklist* (May 1, 1995) also put forth a favorable review: "The unraveling of the mystery proves fascinating, and any stitcher or mystery lover will fall under this novel's spell."

After completing *The Game of Troy* in 1997, Mertz wrote *The Dancing Floor* (1997), a tale that moves from tragedy to mystery, against the backdrop of historic Britain. In the novel, Heather Tradescant is still trying to recover from the death of her parents in an auto accident when she decides to quit her job and take the British vacation she and her father had been planning prior to his death. The trip is more depressing than she had originally anticipated, and she is about to return home when she decides to visit the gardens of Trayton. Here she encounters Trayton House, as well as a diverse group of enigmatic and wealthy inhabitants, and is asked to stay and assist with the restoration of the gardens. But soon she is forced to solve a series of puzzles, involving a missing child, a cryptic clay figure, and a mysterious legend of local witchcraft. *Booklist* (January 1, 1997) called the book a "well-crafted mystery of place and time." *Publishers Weekly* (January 13, 1997) stated that the character Heather as well as "other well-delineated characters" make this story "everything a romance reader could ask for." A *Kirkus Reviews* (December 15, 1996) critic, meanwhile, admitted that the tale "will not knock your socks off" but that "the intrigue just won't quit. . . . The supernatural stuff never gets silly or overblown, while Michael's own subtle touch lends an effective air of spookiness to an intriguing study of a woman's coming into her own."

In 1999 Mertz released *Other Worlds*, a book consisting of two novellas exploring traditional detective work as well as the supernatural. The action begins on a foggy evening in a smoke-filled club, where a disparate group of crime "specialists" (including Harry Houdini) discuss two unsolved cases.

Up until the early 1980s, the novels that Mertz wrote as Elizabeth Peters, including *The Jackal's Head* (1968), *The Camelot Caper* (1969), *The Dead Sea Cipher* (1970), *The Night of 400 Rabbits* (1971), *Legend in Green Velvet* (1976), *Devil-May-Care* (1977), *Summer of the Dragon* (1979), *The Love Talker* (1980), and *The Copenhagen Connection* (1982), featured an array of protagonists. The novels have since focused mainly on either Jacqueline Kirby, Vicky Bliss, or Amelia Peabody. Jacqueline is the librarian turned writer, Vicky the blonde art historian, and Amelia the Victorian Egyptologist. Each of these women is brave, charming, and intelligent and finds herself involved in all manner of mystery and intrigue. Mertz has said that creating those characters affected her own growth as a woman. " I used to be the most timid woman you'd ever want to meet, but I write about women who won't admit limitations, and there's a way your characters influence you. I think Amelia Peabody is one of the reasons I've become so outspoken. She would totally despise me if I sat by and kept quiet. How could I not live up to her?"

The Seventh Sinner (1972) was the first novel in the Jacqueline Kirby series, although it is done from the perspective of a character named Jean Suttman who travels to Rome on a fellowship and begins an expedition to an ancient temple. Soon she and her group of fellow students become entangled in a murder mystery. As the plot unfolds, it is not Jean who emerges as the central figure but Jacqueline Kirby, who accompanies the group on the expedition.

Subsequent novels in the series include *The Murders of Richard III* (1974), *Die For Love* (1984), and *Naked Once More* (1989). This last novel tells of an offer Jacqueline Kirby receives to write the sequel to a best-seller from many years ago. The author of the original book, which became a cult classic, never wrote another novel, and after disappearing for several years, was declared legally dead. Jacqueline decides to try and write the sequel to "Naked in the Ice" out of boredom with her regular writing. Encouraged by her new agent, who was also the agent for the missing author, Kathleen Darcy, Jacqueline heads off the Appalachian hometown of the author. Here she encounters a highly dysfunctional group of Darcy relations. *Naked Once More* is the last novel thus far in the series, which remains popular among readers. *The Washington Post* (October 10, 1989) called it "an expertly made fun read," and the novel was reviewed by Florence King for the *New York Times* (October 15, 1989), who presented a fairly positive critique, although she wrote that the book seemed to sufferer from an "overabundance of clues and events."

The first novel in the Vicky Bliss series was *Borrower of the Night*, a mystery published in 1973, which has Vicky and her paramour Tony travel to Schloss Drachenstein in Germany, on a mission to find lost artwork. In the process, the duo meet murder and mayhem. The next novels in the series include *Street of the Five Moons* (1978), *Silhouette in Scarlet* (1983), *Trojan Gold* (1987), and *Night Train to Memphis* (1994), the last book in this series thus far. *Night Train to Memphis* has Vicki Bliss still working as a curator in a German museum, and still attempting to understand the relationship she has with sometime-paramour and international thief Sir John Smythe. When she is asked by the police to pose as an expert on Egyptian art in order to stop a gang of thieves in Egypt, she embarks on a cruise down the Nile. Here she encounters shad-

owy characters and a mysterious art connoisseur, along with Sir John himself, who is onboard with a new wife. As she struggles to help the police, she finds herself in danger as well, in a romantic mystery which was not as favorably received as past novels. The *Houston Chronicle*'s Ronald Scott (January 8, 1995) wrote that few of Peterson's characters are "drawn in anything but superficial strokes" and opined that not only are they "lightweight" but "the situations seem unbelievable, and the author keeps intruding in the story to plug earlier books through footnotes and asides to the reader." Scott concluded with the advice that "If you want realistic fiction or a heroine who controls her own destiny, look elsewhere."

The Crocodile on the Sandbank (1975) serves as the introduction to the heroine Amelia Peabody, the most popular and mainstream character of all of the Peters books. The novel follows Egyptologist Peabody in Victorian times as she travels from Rome to Egypt, where she meets a woman who has been left by her lover with no means of support. After Amelia takes the woman under her care, strange incidents begin to occur, and Amelia sets out to uncover exactly who is out to get her new friend. The novel, which has proven a classic among Peters fans, introduces the character Radcliff Emerson. Ensuing novels in this series include *The Curse of the Pharaohs* (1981), *The Mummy Case* (1985), *Lion in the Valley* (1986), *Deeds of the Disturber* (1988), *The Last Camel Died at Noon* (1991), *The Snake, the Crocodile, and the Dog* (1992), *The Hippopotamus Pool* (1996), *Seeing a Large Cat* (1997), *The Ape Who Guards the Balance* (1998), and *Falcon at the Portal* (1999).

In *The Last Camel Died at Noon*, Amelia Peabody is headed down the Nile with her husband and precocious son Ramses in tow, as the trio try to solve a complex mystery involving an inheritance, a mysterious map, and a lost desert world. The *New York Times*'s (October 20, 1991) Peter Theroux observed that "Egyptian verisimilitude is one of the Elizabeth Peter's strong points," adding, "It is [this] mixture of the beautiful and unsettling that sustains *The Last Camel Died at Noon.* . . . Ms. Peters has a knack for a light, even mock-trashy style . . . Her wonderfully witty voice and her penchant for history lessons of the Nile both ancient and modern keep this high adventure moving for even the highest brows." He concluded by writing that "If the reader is tempted to draw another obvious comparison between Amelia Peabody Emerson and Indiana Jones, it's Amelia—in wit and even daring—by a landslide."

The following year's *The Snake, the Crocodile and the Dog* was another hit. Mertz this time took Amelia Peabody back to Egypt, where a series of kidnappings occurs during a search for Nefertiti's tomb. Four years later, *The Hippopotamus Pool* appeared. In that novel, thievery and conniving abound as Amelia and her brood return to Egypt for a dig at a Royal tomb. The novel received many negative reviews.

The following year, Mertz brought back Amelia Peabody and for *Seeing a Large Cat*, a novel that involves mummies as well as issues of family, friends and affairs of the heart—including those involving her now-teenage son. *Booklist* (May 1, 1997) was enthusiastic in its review, which stated that "As usual, Peters's zesty characters . . . are marvelous, and there's plenty of lively repartee to push the story along. The comedy is great, as well, with Peters knowing precisely how to balance starchy Amelia's officious social responsibility with her penchant for meddling in other people's affairs." *Kirkus Reviews* (May 15, 1997) was slightly less appreciative of the novel, noting that "Peters compensates for ordinary prose and fussy plotting with humor and nicely calibrated domestic psychology. Fans will follow her, if only to learn how Amelia copes with Ramses's love life."

In 1998 Mertz published the 10th book in the Amelia Peabody series, *The Ape Who Guards the Balance*. The novel takes Amelia from England to Egypt as she attempts to uncover a new tomb; meanwhile, a murder investigation inconveniences her entire family. In this installment, in which Mertz experimented with different narrative perspectives, the new millennium and the emergence of Amelia's son into manhood are themes that are explored. *Kirkus Reviews* (August 1, 1998) was not impressed with this newest effort, calling it a "long-running, long-winded series" and complaining that "By the time the major source of evil is uncovered, it's just one more unconvincing twist in the tangled plot." The book, according to the review, is "a fun trip for readers with an interest in Egyptology; for others, a confusing, fussily written, long, long trek." *Publishers Weekly* (June 8, 1998), by contrast, stated, "The plot is complicated and involving, but the maturing of Ramses, Nefret and David offers particular pleasure and gives the book depth and poignancy. Rich in characterization, incident and humor, this latest adventure of Amelia Peabody is a grand, galloping adventure with a heart as big as the Great Pyramid itself."

The Peabody storyline continued in 1999 with *Falcon at the Portal*. In this mystery, a new family member is suspected of dealing in forgeries. The reviewer for *Booklist* (April 15, 1999) was pleased, writing "Peters pulls it off with the aplomb of, well . . . Amelia Peabody."

Mertz remains a highly successful author under all of her pen names, and her books have been translated into more than 20 languages around the world. She produces a new novel on an average of once every nine months, and each novel is rewritten three times before it is published.

In 1997, Barbara Mertz received one of the most prestigious awards for her genre when she was crowned the Grand Master of mystery writers by the Mystery Writers of America. She continues to make her home in Frederick, Maryland, in an old stone house with several cats and dogs named after assorted mystery writers, Washington Redskins players, and ancient pharaohs.

—D.B.

SUGGESTED READING: *Booklist* Oct. 15, 1993; May 1, 1995; Dec. 15, 1995; Jan. 1, 1997; May 1, 1997; Apr. 15, 1999; *Houston Chronicle* Jan. 8, 1995; *Kirkus Reviews* Sep. 1, 1993; Feb. 15, 1996; Dec. 15, 1996; May 15, 1997; Aug. 1, 1998; *New Woman* Feb. 1989; *New York Times* Oct. 15, 1909; Oct. 20, 1991; Oct. 18, 1992; *Publishers Weekly* Oct. 23, 1987; July 27, 1992; Feb. 12, 1996; Jan. 13, 1997; June 8, 1998; *USA Today* July 27, 1989; *Washington Post* June 11, 1989; Oct. 10, 1989

SELECTED WORKS: As Barbara Mertz—*Temples, Tombs and Hieroglyphs: The Story of Egyptology,*1964; *Red Land, Black Land: The World of the Ancient Egyptians,*1966; with Richard R. Mertz—*Two Thousand Years in Rome,*1968; As Barbara Michaels—*The Master of Blacktower,* 1966; *Sons of the Wolf,* 1967; *Ammie, Come Home,* 1968: *Prince of Darkness,* 1969; *The Dark on the Other Side,* 1970; *Crying Child,* 1971; *Greygallows,* 1972; *Witch,* 1973; *House of Many Shadows,* 1974; *The Sea King's Daughter,* 1975; *Patriot's Dream,* 1976; *Wings of the Falcon,* 1977; *Wait for What Will Come,* 1978; *The Walker in the Shadows,* 1979; *The Wizard's Daughter,* 1980; *Someone in the House,* 1981; *Black Rainbow,* 1982; *Here I Stay,* 1983; *Dark Duet,* 1983; *The Grey Beginning,* 1984; *Be Buried in the Rain,* 1985; *Shattered Silk,* 1986; *Search the Shadows,* 1987; *Smoke and Mirrors,* 1989; *Into the Darkness,* 1990; *Vanish with the Rose,* 1992; *Houses of Stone,* 1993; *Stitches in Time,* 1995; *The Game of Troy,* 1997; *The Dancing Floor,* 1997; *Other Worlds,* 1999; As Elizabeth Peters—*The Jackal's Head,* 1968; *The Camelot Caper,* 1969; *The Dead Sea Cipher,* 1970; *The Night of 400 Rabbits,* 1971; *The Seventh Sinner,* 1972; *Borrower of the Night,* 1973 *The Murders of Richard III,* 1974; *The Crocodile on the Sandbank,* 1975; *Legend in Green Velvet,* 1976; *Devil-May-Care,* 1977; *Street of the Five Moons,* 1978; *Summer of the Dragon,* 1979; *The Love Talker,* 1980; *The Curse of the Pharaohs,* 1981; *The Copenhagen Connection,* 1982; *Silhouette in Scarlet,* 1983; *Die For Love,* 1984; *The Mummy Case,* 1985; *Lion in the Valley,* 1986; *Trojan Gold,* 1987; *Deeds of the Disturber,* 1988; *Naked Once More,* 1989; *The Last Camel Died at Noon,* 1991; *The Snake, the Crocodile, and the Dog,* 1992; *Night Train to Memphis,* 1994; *The Hippopotamus Pool,* 1996; *Seeing a Large Cat,* 1997; *The Ape Who Guards the Balance,* 1998; *Falcon at the Portal,* 1999

Courtesy of Paul Metcalf

Metcalf, Paul

Nov. 7, 1917– Jan. 21, 1999 Novelist

The American novelist Paul Metcalf, who authored more than 20 books, described as a "thinking man's writer" by one reviewer, wrote mostly for small presses during a variegated career that included an adolescent friendship with the young Charles Olson, a period of "studying and drinking" with Conrad Aiken, and a succession of odd jobs that included selling storm windows, insurance, and real estate. The great-grandson of Herman Melville, Metcalf was associated with the Black Mountain school in the 1950s and came to be regarded as a formidable prose stylist by an admiring cadre of writers and critics including Guy Davenport, Robert Creeley, and William Gass and small-press publishers such as Allan Kornblum of Coffee House Press, which late in 1997 issued the third and final volume in the series of his complete works. Upon the publication of the first volume, Kornblum wrote, "Paul is a major American writer who didn't get the credit he deserved. I regard [Metcalf's] books as the most important I've published. His work is unclassifiable. It's about merging of genres, an amalgam of history, poetry, fiction, ethnography, geology, anthropology, ecology." News of the first volume's publication prompted the poet Robert Creeley to write: "Much like his great-grandfather, Herman Melville, Paul Metcalf brings an extraordinary diversity of materials into the complex pattens of analogy and metaphor, to effect a common term altogether brilliant in its imagination." On May 20, 1987, the American Academy of Arts and Letters paid tribute to Metcalf's inventiveness with a formal citation giving him credit for

"originat[ing] a genre of fiction which included a montage of historic New World documentation mixed with poetry, an original mode of imaginative composition."

For *World Authors 1990-1995*, Paul Metcalf, who died of heart failure on January 21, 1999, wrote: "I was born November 7, 1917, in East Milton, Massachusetts. (This is the same birthdate that was celebrated by the late Union of Soviet Socialist Republics.) My father, Henry K. Metcalf, was in the insurance business in Boston. He came from an old Rhode Island family, and was a direct descendant of Roger Williams. My mother, Eleanor M. Metcalf, was the oldest granddaughter of Herman Melville, and she became his literary executrix. I have one brother, David, in theater most of his life, now retired.

"I was raised in Cambridge, in a very Melvillean household—and all this Melville business turned me off, until I was well into my twenties.

"I attended private, progressive schools—until they got so progressive I got myself kicked out. I finally graduated from a formal Connecticut prep school. Entering Harvard in the fall of 1936, I lasted until Christmas, when I dropped out. I had not been attending classes. (I note here that I, and Bill Gates, CEO of Microsoft, are Harvard dropouts; the alleged Unabomber graduated from Harvard with honors. Make of that what you will.)

"I joined Hedgerow Theater, a small, high-quality repertory group near Philadelphia, where I learned a good deal about stagecraft, and trained as an actor. Here, I became exposed to playwrights, and determined that writing would be my field. I left Hedgerow after two years, and began several years of writing bad plays, bad poems, and bad novels. As the saying goes, I had not yet found my 'voice.'

"Disappointed in 'an affair of the heart,' I blew out of Philadelphia in my $20 '31 Ford Roadster, and wound up in Charleston, South Carolina. I took a job as publicity director for the Dock Street Theater, and joined a playwrights group under Dubose Hayward—and met and subsequently married Nancy Blackford, of South Carolina and West Virginia background.

"Around 1940 or so I spent a summer living and studying (and drinking) with the poet Conrad Aiken. Nancy and I then moved to New York, where I held a series of dull business jobs, writing on the side. In 1945, I came down with a mild case of tuberculosis; our first daughter, Anne, was born by then, and Nancy, Anne, and I moved back to Cambridge, and eventually to the mountains of north Georgia, where I convalesced for a year—and did a voluminous amount of reading, all the reading I would have done in college, and more. . . .

"When my health came back, we moved to western North Carolina, and there was again a series of dumb jobs—clerk, salesman, whatever. My first published book, *Will West*, came out of these years. We began visiting Black Mountain College, nearby, and renewed an association that had begun when

I was 14, with Charles Olson. Through Olson I met Jonathan Williams [of the Jargon Society], who became my first and for many years my only publisher.

"Somewhere in here I broke through the Melville barrier. I sat down and engorged him, and produced the book *Genoa*. Instrumental in this process of liberation, or breaking of the dam, was a short but intense interest in the popular 'science,' Dianetics.

"In 1954, our second daughter, Adrienne, was born.

"Somewhere in here, my parents treated me to a trip to South America, out of which emerged the book *Patagoni*.

"For a number of good reasons we left North Carolina, for the Berkshires, in Massachusetts—this was in 1963—and we are still living in the house we purchased then. Although I had published three books, I needed an income, and there was no public reputation to 'interfere.' I started a real estate business, which eventually became quite successful—and I stayed away from writing for a time. In the late sixties, both my parents died, leaving enough of an inheritance to ease the pressures. At the same time I got the urge to write again, and I began to get some public consideration—invitations to teach, to give readings, etc. So I sold the real estate business, and have been, for the first time, professionally, a 'writer,' ever since.

"Beginning in the fall of 1996, Coffee House Press in Minneapolis is now publishing a three-volume edition of my *Collected Works*."

When the first volume of these *Collected Works* appeared, Coffee House Press called Metcalf "one of America's great undiscovered writers," a sentiment echoed in reviews such as the unsigned one in *Publishers Weekly* (September 9, 1996) that exclaimed, "At last, [Metcalf's work] is open to the general public." In his introduction to Volume One, Guy Davenport wrote of how Metcalf "has notoriously and scandalously been at the periphery. This is partly due to his modesty and reticence, and to the fate of his books with publishers."

Despite their familial connections with Herman Melville, few in Metcalf's household regarded their literary ancestor with high esteem, most considering the author a failure and trying to discourage visiting scholars from seeing his papers. One of the scholars, however, made a lasting impression on the young Paul. His name was Charles Olson. Years later, Metcalf recalled the meeting in an article he wrote for the *North Carolina Literary Review*: "When I was 14 years old, Charles Olson, who was 20 at the time, showed up at our house in Cambridge to talk to my mother, Eleanor Melville Metcalf. Later to become known as a poet, he was in his role then as Melville scholar, and more than any of the other Melvilleans who flocked to our house, Charles treated me as a human being. We kept up a casual friendship over the years, seeing

each other whenever we happened to be living in the same area. Then, some time in the 1950s, Charles showed up at Black Mountain." Olson became rector of the innovative Black Mountain College, which attracted some of America's leading experimental poets. In his introduction, Davenport concluded: "Olson's *Call Me Ishmael*, the most imaginative of books about Melville, gave Paul the purchase he needed to look great-granddad in the eye."

Metcalf lived in North Carolina from 1946 until 1963, settling first in Skyland, near Asheville, where he did his first writing in a log house while "scraping a living together hawking storm windows, driving oil rigs, and crawling around in neighbors' basements with a flashlight in one hand and a termite insurance contract in the other," wrote interviewer Josie Rawson. Metcalf later recounted his days as a young writer: "With more aspiration than experience, I read eclectically, without discipline or pattern (I was blessedly relieved of formal education after three months at Harvard). I found myself drawn to the passion of D. H. Lawrence, the quirkiness of Hart Crane, and particularly, to the poets Ezra Pound and William Carlos Williams. I admire the way they could incorporate history and other documentary matter 'in the poem.'" Believing that the vital tradition of American literature was being betrayed by commercial novelists, he began publishing his own work, mostly in chapbooks or in small literary presses, and began to attract the notice of serious poets and prose experimenters.

A self-proclaimed "juxtaposer," Metcalf mines a rich lode of sources, ranging from the journals of early explorers written in Elizabethan English and commentaries on the slave trade of the Middle Passage to logs of whaling voyages, Civil War narratives, and contemporary newspaper accounts of crime and cupidity. By "paralleling" events from different historical periods, told in disparate voices, Metcalf creates, through simultaneity of narrative, a multilayered mosaic in which his subjects reveal themselves without the intrusive intervention of an omniscient narrator.

His first book, *Will West* (1956), about a Cherokee baseball pitcher who goes on the lam after murdering a young white woman, was constructed as a parallel narrative that explores the nature of racial memory, of otherness, of alienation in an anomic society, and of the way in which such "constants" as geographic place are interpreted by different cultural perspectives, presaging the contemporary discussion of competitive hegemonies. Will West's flight westward to Mississippi is juxtaposed, for example, with Hernando DeSoto's explorations, with the 1830s forced "Trail of Tears" migration, and with General Grant's siege of Vicksburg, making his tale not just the story of a single body but of the body politic, equally beleaguered. In a later retrospective of Metcalf's literary career, William Corbett gave special note to the "lineaments of story and narrative" in this first of Metcalf's books, as he wrote: "I concern myself with the form of *Will West* because it is Metcalf's growing knowledge of how to handle his materials that gives the book its tension and acts to illuminate the effect of *Genoa* and *Patagoni*. The heaps that these books are, the clutch of fact and fiction, the coherence Metcalf manages in setting one thing beside another—all this is prefigured in *Will West*."

Metcalf himself wrote that *Will West* was "a novella, really . . . in which I began to tinker with the form, integrating historical and cultural matter in the flow of fiction." He added: "*Will West* was a formal experiment—mixing document and fiction." On the subject of his earlier reading of Williams and Pound, he explained, "I admired and envied the way they could incorporate all sorts of material, from many periods, in the form of a long poem."

After writing his first book, Metcalf became interested in L. Ron Hubbard's Scientology movement and took a six-week crash course at headquarters in Wichita, which certified him as the only Dianetic auditor in the southeastern United States, though he later concluded that Hubbard was a con man. Of his stint as an "auditor," Metcalf wrote: "Results were spotty. . . . Some results were weird: one woman, who had always made her own clothes and had accommodated for the fact that one arm was shorter than another, reported that, after her sessions with me, the arm grew to its proper length. Another guy, the best I could do for him was cure his hangover. And he stiffed me for part of his fee." Still, Metcalf gleaned two valuable lessons from the Dianetics experience that he was able to apply to his writing: that "all memory is theoretically recoverable" and "that a physical injury is remembered not only in the memory cells of the brain but in the actual cells in the injured part of the body." Metcalf extrapolated this insight, derived from the experience of an individual human being, to comment on the whole of human history, holding that the latter might be marked with "signal incidents or events" that might be closely related. "Until I had worked my way through to this, via the Dianetic experience," he wrote, "*Genoa* would not have been possible. And the method works, and continues to work, in many if not most of my subsequent books."

Genoa, published in 1965, represented Metcalf's coming to terms with his suppressed Melvillean patrimony. "Free of the shackles of fiction," he created this book, complete with a bibliography of 75 entries, as a literary and historical collage, interspersing his own narratives with passages from novels by his illustrious great-grandfather. He recalled how he began writing it at the same time that his mentor Charles Olson was writing *The Maximus Poems*. Subtitled "A Telling of Wonders," *Genoa* juxtaposes narratives of the fictional Mills family with Christopher Columbus's search for the New World and Herman Melville's story of the equally relentless hunt for the great whale. Shifting between historical scenes and contemporary events, such as a notorious 1950s Midwestern kidnapping, the book's narrator, clubfooted Michael Mills, draws a portrait of his own relationship with a hydrocephalic brother, Carl, who emerges as a spiritual sea-brother to Columbus and Captain Ahab. Paul Davenport wrote that *Genoa* "is built: it is an architecture of analogies, similitudes, and Melvillean metaphors. It proceeds with a whale's vision, eyes at right angles to each other and with a ton of forehead to obviate a stereotypical view."

Genoa was published at a time when many readers were unfamiliar with this still-experimental genre of fiction writing, but literary colleagues were quick to declare the prescience of the still-obscure author. In a review of *Genoa* entitled "Parallel Patterns," author William H. Gass wrote in the *New York Times Book Review* (June 19, 1966): "Literature has for some time been moving gently in *Genoa*'s direction. We love our documents and trust them more than we trust ourselves. We edit beautifully, anthologizing everything. Why not, since we lead such symbol-stimulated lives? Even Eliot larded 'The Waste Land' with fat from his reading, and Pound has succeeded, sometimes, in giving interest to his cranky snippets from economic history by surrounding them with masterly poetry. *Moby-Dick* itself begins in a noisy gaggle of quotations. . . . *Genoa* invites us to pass our minds down a new but ancient track, to become, ourselves, both fact and fiction, and to discover something true about the geography of time."

Patagoni, published in 1971, is probably Metcalf's most intricately collaged work, almost linking Melville and Columbus as fraternal twins, in a book descrying the Western Hemisphere as a body to be explored and exploited, at once physically and psychically, by purveyors of a purely commercial culture. Metcalf weaves together a narrative involving his own sojourns to Henry Ford's Detroit and to ancient Inca sites in Peru, where the "RE-INCA(R)-NATION" of that culture testifies to the impact of industrial and commercial values where the great pre-Columbian empires had once been. Reincarnation itself is a motif in this work, a theme harking back to Metcalf's earlier work with Dianetics and his breakthroughs concerning the persistence of memory. Guy Davenport linked the structure of this book with Ezra Pound's *Cantos*, "where images in a field of force make a complex sign, just as the radicals in a Chinese character add up in a kind of poetic arithmetic to a meaning. . . . Each of Metcalf's books is an ideogram." Richard Grossinger, reviewing *Patagoni* for *The Phoenix* (January 19, 1972), wrote: "The simultaneity of absolutely incommensurable worlds is one of the wonders of our being; North and South America are worlds at entirely different stages of incarnation; thus, Metcalf traces single objects, like Coca-Cola, or Ford Motor Cars, through them, and describes the nature of the distortion."

The Middle Passage (1976), subtitled "a triptych of commodities," is a short but persuasive screed (45 pages, with bibliography, in the Coffee House anthology) on the linkages Metcalf sees between factory slavery, plantation slavery, and whaling. By juxtaposing documents about the Luddite and the abolitionist movements with logs of whaling expeditions, the author indicts the commodification and brutalization of humans and animals. Hayden Carruth in *Bookletter* (January 31, 1997) called it "a triptych of commodities indeed! There is no doubt in each case what the commodity is: death. This is a book about the buying and selling of life for profit, a 'dark' book, as a note on the dust jacket says, for it leads into the deepest recesses of human history and psychology. Yet it is all done objectively, by documentation and suggestion. . . . [Metcalf's] method so closely combines documentary with art that they are inseparable; their structure is one."

Another of Metcalf's major works, and the fourth work in the first volume, *Apalache*, concerns itself with colonial-era confrontations between European settlers and the Native American population, with homage to Metcalf's real-life ancestor Roger Williams, banished from Massachusetts for being an "incendiary." In this book, Metcalf pays extraordinary attention to the euphonious resonance of Native American place names set against Elizabethan English, having the effect of the King James Bible and an aboriginal gazetteer being read as a responsive litany, as in "and what else we know not yet, because our daies are young/*accokeek acquack/up the susquehanna and juniata, across the mountains at kithanne. . . .*" *Apalache* further explores the hidden underbelly of the American tradition of alternating violence with liberty, as in the comparison of Roger Williams's fate with that of "Telemaque" (Denmark Vesey), a black man who instigated a slaves' insurrection in the early 1800s, and Robert F. Williams, a civil-rights activist of the 1950s and 1960s. Again, Metcalf revealed an ironic fascination with little-known, often suppressed, facts and events in American history, told in tandem with contemporary newspaper clippings and references to the Telemachus of Homeric legend.

In December 1995—after Metcalf had written nearly 20 additional works—Robert Creeley paid tribute to Metcalf in a letter responding to the news of the Coffee House edition: "All his life as a writer he has undertaken formal and contentual sorties that have taken him well away from the sources of commercial backing and interest." And, in the words of Guy Davenport, "Every page of Paul Metcalf is a score for the voice. Or, as the truth is, for the imagination. For each page is a careful construct of voices, written voices for the most part, found in other texts by a searcher with eyes far sharper than ours, and infinitely more diligent in their search." Davenport likens Metcalf's technique to those of such classical writers as Plutarch, Montaigne, or Richard Burton, "all of whose books are new contexts for other voices."

Metcalf's recurring theme of journeys is carried forth in Volume Two of his *Collected Works*, dealing with the period from 1976 to 1986. The volume opens with "I-57," which derives its title from the Interstate Highway that serves as metaphor and locale for "a journey . . . on several levels. From madness to sanity, from inside the skull . . . to outside . . . from me to you." The work, wrote Metcalf, is "not a poem, not a novel, not a history, not a journal . . .an idiosyncratic approach to a place, a region, and to an interior and exterior life." "I-57" is followed by the fanciful "Zip Ode," another testimony to Metcalf's fascination with Americana, which is composed entirely of the names of towns and cities through the 50 states as found in the official zip-code directory from the U.S. Postal Service. Other significant works by Metcalf include *Willie's Throw*, a detail-rich meditation on a 1951 New York Giants baseball game, *Waters of Potowmack*, a geographical and historical survey of Washington, D.C., from colonial times through the Civil War to the civil unrest of the 1960s, and *The Wonderful White Whale of Kansas*, a juxtaposition of Melville's *Moby-Dick* with L. Frank Baum's *The Wonderful Wizard of Oz* that exposes both Captain Ahab and the Wizard as "con men," in Metcalf's phrase. Volume Three of the *Collected Works* include materials published between 1987 and 1997, plus some original pieces. Metcalf reported in the fall of 1997 that he and another author were collaborating in a work of "industrial archeology and anthropology," documenting the fate of an abandoned mill near his home in the Berkshires of western Massachusetts.

Metcalf won a Ford Foundation grant for 1970 and 1971 to prepare a stage adaptation of *Genoa* for the National Theater of the Deaf. He has been a visiting lecturer at several universities, including the University of California at San Diego and the State University of New York at Albany. In 1978 he won the Morton Dauwen Zabel award from the American Institute of Arts and Letters.
—E. M.

SUGGESTED READING: *Bookletter* Jan. 31, 1977; *Booklist* Nov. 15, 1996; *Credences* Mar. 1980; Lillabulero 12, Winter-Spring, 1973; *New York Times Book Review* June 19, 1966; *Phoenix* Jan. 19, 1972; *Publishers Weekly* p67 Sep. 9, 1996; *Review of Contemporary Fiction* Summer 1981; *Scrawl* Winter 1996; *Village Voice* Aug. 2, 1976

SELECTED BOOKS: Fiction—*Will West*, 1956; *Genoa*, 1965; *Patagoni*, 1975; *Apalache*, 1976; *The Middle Passage*, 1976; *Willie's Throw*, 1979; *Zip Odes*, 1982; *U. S. Dept. of the Interior*, 1980; *The Island*, 1982; *Both*, 1982; *Waters of Potowmack*, 1982; *Louis the Torch*, 1983; *Golden Delicious*, 1985; *Where Do You Put the Horse?*, 1986; *Firebird*, 1987; *I-57*, 1988; *Headlands: The Mabin Coast at the Golden Gate*, 1989; *Winslow Homer at the Addison*, 1990; *Mountaineers are Always Free*, 1991; *Enter Isabel: The Melville*

Correspondence of Paul Spark and Paul Metcalf, 1991; *Araminta and the Coyotes*, 1991; *Paul Metcalf: The Collected Works, Volume One*, 1996; *Paul Metcalf: The Collected Works, Volume Two*, 1997; Drama—*An American Chronicle*, 1980; As editor—*October Mountain: An Anthology of Berkshire Writers*, 1991

Millhauser, Steven

Aug. 3, 1943– Novelist; short-story writer

The *New York Times* (January 11, 1988) book critic Michiko Kakutani wrote of the American novelist and short-story writer Steven Millhauser that he has "an ability to catch his perceptions in a bright butterfly net of prose," which lends his fiction "a lovely afterlife, colorful and lively, in the reader's mind." Millhauser has demonstrated that gift in works increasingly given to elements of fantasy: his first novel, *Edwin Mullhouse: The Life and Death of an American Writer 1943–1954 by Jeffrey Cartwright* (1972), a parody of a literary biography, which tells the story of a boy novelist who dies at 11; *Portrait of a Romantic* (1977), by a young man recounting his life from the ages of 12 to 15; *In the Penny Arcade* (1986), a collection of short stories and a novella; *From the Realm of Morpheus* (1986), in which a man enters the realm of Morpheus, in much the same way that Alice enters Wonderland; *The Barnum Museum* (1990), another story collection; the three novellas comprising *Little Kingdoms* (1993); the novel *Martin Dressler: The Tale of an American Dreamer* (1996), the story of "an entrepreneur whose career is a metaphor for the construction of the modern city," as Dinitia Smith phrased it in the *New York Times* (April 9, 1997); and the story collection *The Knife Thrower* (1998). *Martin Dressler* garnered for Millhauser the 1997 Pulitzer Prize for fiction.

Steven Millhauser was born on August 3, 1943 in New York City, where his father was a professor at City College of New York. The family was living in Brooklyn when his father was appointed a professor of English at the University of Bridgeport, in Connecticut. Millhauser attended high school in Fairfield, Connecticut, and then graduated from Columbia University, in New York. He went on to study medieval and Renaissance literature at Brown University—in Providence, Rhode Island—from 1968 to 1971. During his time at Brown, he was "secretly writing at night," completing *Edwin Mullhouse: The Life and Death of an American Writer 1943–1954 by Jeffrey Cartwright*, as he told Dinitia Smith in an interview in the *New York Times*.

Edwin Mullhouse purports to be a biography, by one Jeffrey Cartwright, of the 11-year-old boy who was his best friend. Edwin is the genius who wrote *Cartoons*, in Jeffrey's opinion the world's greatest novel, and only with his biography can Jeffrey out-

do his friend. The biography is written in the solemn, almost Victorian tone of one great man writing about another. By his 11th birthday, Edwin has decided to commit suicide—an aesthetic decision to enable him to see his last days with the clarity with which he envisions the ending of a piece of fiction he is writing: "Yes, it was the idea of design that led him on; it was as if he wished to imprison in the glass globe of Art, the dancing and unpredictable waters of Life. None of which, incidentally, kept him from doing his homework faithfully each afternoon right through the end of June." Coincidentally, Jeffrey has concluded his biography. Edwin may not mean to carry out his suicide, but his dear friend and biographer Jeffrey is with him to press his finger on the trigger of the gun.

"Jeffrey is no oleaginous and self-pitying Charlie Brown; the novel has no Christian Message. Jeffrey is a Nabokovian child: witty, literate, perceptive, and disturbingly complex. Edwin is different, an artist of the Beckettian sort," the *New Republic* (September 16, 1972) reviewer wrote, calling *Edwin Mullhouse* "Millhauser's beautifully shaped and polished description of the pleasures, sorrows, and evils of childhood, of art and of life. . . . a mature, skillful, intelligent and often very funny novel." While other reviewers agreed that Millhauser displayed virtuosic skills in his first novel, not all were persuaded that he had gone in the right direction in making *Edwin Mullhouse* a satire. "This novel has some of the most beautiful pointless prose in recent fiction. Moreover, the other level. . .—that of commentary on, and remembrance of, childhood—is licked . . . by the distance a satirical style imposes," Joseph Kanon commented in *Newsweek* (October 9, 1972).

Millhauser spent the years from 1972 to 1977 "dimly earning a living," he told Smith. He wrote in his parents' attic in the evenings and published *Portrait of a Romantic* in 1977. Another story of childhood ending in a death, *Portrait of a Romantic* is the autobiography of an adolescent who, with his friends, flirts with suicide. "Despite secret ceremonies, locked rooms, feigned illnesses, yearnings for death, and late-night meetings, Arthur's world persistently returns to beaches, potato salad, glasses of milk, homework, . . . games of canasta, and endless, unromantic sunlit days," the *Choice* (January 1978) reviewer observed. Len Gougeon, writing in *Best Sellers* (December 1977), found "perfidy here. Truth has been supplanted—reality annihilated." He thought that Millhauser's replication of adolescent boredom lacked vitality; Millhauser's concept—that it is in some sense ennui that drives acts of romantic desperation—left him cold. The *Choice* reviewer, on the other hand, found *Portrait of a Romantic* to be "a beautifully constructed story" by a writer "of obvious and abundant talent."

The *Choice* (July/August 1986) reviewer termed Millhauser's next book, *In the Penny Arcade* (1986), a collection of stories and a novella, "a fair cross-section of the contemporary fabulist tradition." In the opening novella, "August Eschenburg," a boy in Germany at the end of the 19th century learns to make automated models of people. He creates a magical theater with his figures, but its commercial appeal declines when a rival automaton theater with pornographic shows opens. The next section of the book is devoted to stories of the awakening of young women's sensibilities—the awareness of sexuality, the dawning of love, and the acknowledgment of loneliness. In the last section, magic and artifice are dominant in stories set amid abounding snow figures, a penny arcade, and a fabulous city called Cathay.

Michiko Kakutani of the *New York Times* (January 11, 1986) noted that "pretty, frightening, and amazing things" like the images in a penny arcade grace these stories, in which "magicians bring statues to life with a flick of the wrist, men change themselves into automatons, snowmen—along with snow maidens, snow birds, and snow unicorns—suddenly materialize in a town." Although given events can be explained as "a sleight of hand trick, a case of mistaken identity, the work of children playing in the snow," Kakutani felt that "Millhauser and his characters, however varied, all seem blessed with a child's easy access to the world of imagination and dreams . . . open to the transformations worked on nature by time and art, and . . . transfixed by the beauty in, say, the tiny gears of an antique clock, in the changing silhouette of the moon, in the unexpected appearance of a silver blimp in the sky. . . . all hold . . . the possibility of wonder . . . the perception of the marvelous."

While David Gates, the *Newsweek* (March 17, 1986) reviewer, remarked that Millhauser's "otherworldly imagination is both his great gift and his besetting sin," Robert Dunn in the *New York Times Book Review* (January 19, 1986) agreed with Kakutani that "Millhauser continues to pursue fiction as a mysterious, magical, enlightening experience." He quoted Millhauser in saying that "his fiction leads us 'away from the torpor of the familiar into a dark realm of strangeness and wonder.'" Dunn concluded: "As the narrator of *Penny Arcade* realizes, 'I recognized that I myself had become a part of the conspiracy of dullness. . . . I saw that I was in danger of becoming ordinary, and I understood that from now on I would have to be vigilant.' . . . Millhauser is more than vigilant; he creates for us this splendid arcade. And he asks us also to be vigilant as we venture with him into the common corners of our ragged world, where the marvelous glows and true meanings breathe life."

A man in *From the Realm of Morpheus*, during a baseball game, chases a foul ball into a thicket and winds up going down a hole and descending a stone staircase to the antechamber to the kingdom of dreams. This *Alice in Wonderland*–like beginning to the plot is the first of a series of sly references to such literary classics as *The Odyssey*, *Gulliver's Travels*, *The Divine Comedy*, *The Picture of Dorian Gray*, and works by Jorge Luis Borges. In the *New York Times* (September 17, 1986), Michiko Kakutani judged *From the Realm of Morpheus* to be a "manipulation of old myths, Freudian theories, and literary allusions . . . clever embroidery, worked on themes and ideas patented by the masters." According to John Crowley, writing in the *New York Times Book Review* (October 12, 1986), Morpheus "is jolly and self-indulgent, but his realm is not in fact ease, indulgence or sloth; the stories are largely about dissatisfaction, insufficiency, thwarted desire, and love gone bad." Crowley, too, judged Millhauser in danger of being taken over by his "own skill at pastiche, enjoying for its own sake the re-creation of bypassed modes."

Millhauser continued to create imaginary worlds and to experiment with varied literary techniques in his next book, *The Barnum Museum*, a collection of stories. The museum of the title story "represents the imagination," Millhauser told Smith. The museum, as described by Jay Cantor in the *New York Times Book Review* (June 24, 1990), is "filled with seemingly magical displays, flying carpets, half-glimpsed mermaids that disappear into a haze, and invisible beings that 'brush lightly against our arms.'" The museum's air of trickery . . . only calms the patron as she wanders through its maze of halls, allowing her more easily to fall into the museum's dreams." Michiko Kakutani in the *New York Times* (June 12, 1990) observed that Millhauser had included a sinister element in the "subterranean levels," leading visitors who are overly enmeshed in what the museum offers to get lost, "and those who completely succumb to its seductive charms often lose touch with their real lives, abandoning everything they know and love to wander its many towers and halls."

Although Cantor wished "that . . . Millhauser's stories had had more of the bluster and intrusion of history, those unhappy collective imaginings," he concluded that Millhauser's "elegantly told, charming stories about the nature and muscle of storytelling often provided . . . delight." Mary Soete in *Library Journal* (June 1, 1990), reviewing *The Barnum Museum*, observed that with a "funhouse gallery of fictive techniques and ideas," Millhauser created stories "about crossing the boundaries between art and life, appearance and reality" with a "mix of stylistic dazzle and erudite wonder."

Millhauser's next book, *Little Kingdoms* (1993), is a gathering of three stories, all of which embody meditations on the nature and value of art. The first, "The Little Kingdom of J. Franklin Payne," is set in New York after World War I and tells the story of a pioneer in animated cartoons who is so absorbed in his art that he loses his wife and sacrifices the happiness of his home. The second, "The Princess, the Dwarf, and the Dungeon," has a medieval setting, a fairy-tale atmosphere, and a narrator who questions the new, realistic art: "Is there not a risk that our art lacks mystery?" In the third story, "Catalogue of the Exhibition: The Art of Edmund Moorash 1810–1846," the catalogue of an art exhibition is the vehicle used to tell a story in which two pairs of brothers and sisters become sexually and artistically entangled, resulting in tragedy.

Little Kingdoms drew critical responses similar to those inspired by Millhauser's previous books. Reviewers did not resist the temptation to reexamine his whole body of work, as did Michael Dirda in the *Washington Post Book World* (September 5, 1993) and Frederic Tuten in the *New York Times Book Review* (October 3, 1993). Dirda compared Millhauser to Jorge Luis Borges and Italo Calvino, found each of his "spellbinding literary fantasies" to compose "a little world made as cunningly, and as exquisitely, as a Faberge egg," and observed that Millhauser's great strength lies in his "fanatical particularization." "Grouped together the three novellas of *Little Kingdoms* subtly question each other about the imagination and its power. An artist's perhaps unhealthy bliss, the blessings and terrors of art, the blasted lives of those who love an artistic genius—each sounds a variation on this single rather somber theme," Dirda concluded.

"Millhauser's stories are . . . evidence of his often-realized and obvious wish to create works of beauty that while rooted in the real world are yet out of time and out of place—and outside the restraints of the diction of contemporary life," Frederic Tuten observed. He termed the stories in *Little Kingdoms* "beautiful" and noted that Millhauser "circles back from the border of parody to plunge us into the very heartland of human complexity and folly."

With his next novel, *Martin Dressler: The Tale of an American Dreamer* (1996), Millhauser took a different tack, which reviewers, nevertheless, considered a variation on his themes of fantasy art and artistic obsession. Martin Dressler, an American dreamer on the scale of Walt Disney, aspires to create an alternative world that, although it is composed of artifice, can replace the real world. He starts his career in the late 19th century as an assistant in his father's cigar store, and goes on to become a bellboy, then desk clerk, then manager in a hotel, which he later owns. He starts a chain of restaurants, with each being the same as the others, prefiguring McDonald's. The ultimate fulfillment of his dream is the building of a gigantic hotel, which extends 30 stories up and 12 stories down and contains such fantasy worlds as an Arab bazaar, in which the salespersons are dressed in Arab costumes and trained to bargain, and a wax museum in which the wax figures are actually live actors. Millhauser encapsulates Martin's trajectory in the first paragraph of the novel:

> There once lived a man named Martin Dressler, a shopkeeper's son, who rose from modest beginnings to a height of dreamlike good fortune. This was toward the end of the 19th century, when on any streetcorner in America you might see some ordinary-looking citizen who was destined to invent a new kind of bottle-

cap or tin can, start a chain of five-cent stores, sell a faster and better elevator, or open a fabulous new department store with big display windows made possible by an improved process for manufacturing sheets of glass. Although Martin Dressler was a shopkeeper's son, he too dreamed his dream, and at last he was lucky enough to do what few people even dare to imagine: he satisfied his heart's desire. But this is a perilous privilege, which the gods watch jealously, waiting for the flaw, the little flaw, that brings everything to ruin, in the end.

Robert McLaughlin, writing in the *Review of Contemporary Fiction* (Fall 1996), pointed out that Martin Dressler, thinking of renovating an old hotel, "argues, 'people liked telephones and the new electric elevators and private toilets and incandescent lights, but at the same time they liked old-world architecture, period furniture, dim suggestions of the very world that was being annihilated by American efficiency and know-how.' This argument for the up-to-date hidden in the form of the familiar serves as a metaphor for the novel itself: its conventional fictional form houses contemporary ontological and epistemological concerns." McLaughlin considered Millhauser's real concerns to be "the hollowness of the American Dream and the cultural legacy of Manifest Destiny . . . the uncontrollable world and the unknowable self."

Jonathan Yardley in the *Washington Post Book World* (April 28, 1996) compared *Martin Dressler* and *Edwin Mullhouse*, finding that in the intervening collections of stories, "Millhauser was steering himself toward *Martin Dressler*, a book quite different from *Edwin Mullhouse* but similarly accomplished. In those books Millhauser was experimenting with ways of treating American mythology, of intermingling the realistic and the fantastic into a unique fabric that might help us see ourselves in a clearer and more revealing light." Yardley saw "the American longing for illusion and escape, but also the pitfalls of great ambition and the rise and fall of the modern city" as the themes of *Martin Dressler*, and considered the novel successful in embodying those themes. Diana Postlethwaite in a *Nation* (May 6, 1996) review also compared *Martin Dressler* to *Edwin Mullhouse*, observing that although the novels "appear radically different in subject and scope," both "Edwin Mullhouse's biography and Martin Dressler's hotel are really cities of the mind, archeologies of the imagination."

Martin Dressler: The Tale of an American Dreamer was awarded the Pulitzer Prize for fiction in 1997. Millhauser was handed a note to that effect while teaching his fiction workshop at Skidmore College in Saratoga Springs, New York. "I told my students that a grotesque error had been committed, and that I had to straighten it out,"

Dinitia Smith reported the shy Millhauser as saying. *Martin Dressler* was also a finalist for the National Book Award in 1997.

Millhauser's follow-up book was *The Knife Thrower and Other Stories* (1998). In the *New York Times Book Review* (May 10, 1998), Patrick McGrath, while complaining that this book seemed simply to revisit themes Millhauser had covered earlier, had praise for two stories: "The Dream of the Consortium," a satire on American consumerism, and "Kaspar Hauser Speaks," about a real-life 19th-century teenager barely able to walk or talk.

"The art of creation is the art of instilling in yourself a waking dream and learning to convey it on paper," Millhauser said in an interview in the *New York Times Book Review* (January 19, 1986). "It is sometimes hard for a writer to know what deeply compels his imagination," he continued, mentioning such "noble" things as the death of a friend and the "less obvious, like little toys." He concluded, "The point is to rid oneself of distinctions like that and to face what catches your imagination."

Millhauser was a 1987 finalist for the American Academy and Institute of Arts and Letters Award and a runner-up for the PEN/Faulkner Award in 1991. He lives in Saratoga Springs; he is married and has two children.
—S. Y.

SUGGESTED READING: *Best Sellers* p258 Dec. 1977; *Choice* p1677 July/Aug. 1986; *Library Journal* p182 June 1, 1990; *Nation* p68 May 6, 1996; *New Republic* p30 Sep. 16, 1972; *Newsweek* p106 Oct. 9, 1972, p74 Mar. 17, 1986; *New York Times* p12 Jan. 11, 1986, C p24 Sep. 17, 1986, C p17 June 12, 1990; *New York Times Book Review* p9 Jan. 19, 1986, p9 Oct. 12, 1986, p16 June 24, 1990, p9 Oct. 3, 1993, p8 May 12, 1996; *Review of Contemporary Fiction* p185+ Fall 1996; *Washington Post Book World* p5 Sep. 5, 1993, p3 Apr. 28, 1996

SELECTED BOOKS: *Edwin Mullhouse: The Life and Death of an American Writer 1943–1954 by Jeffrey Cartwright*, 1972; *Portrait of a Romantic*, 1977; *In the Penny Arcade*, 1986; *From the Realm of Morpheus*, 1986; *The Barnum Museum*, 1990; *Little Kingdoms*, 1993; *Martin Dressler: The Tale of an American Dreamer*, 1996; *The Knife Thrower*, 1998

Mitgutsch, Anna

1948– Novelist

Austrian author Anna Mitgutsch's first novel, *Three Daughters* (1987), looks at three generations of women in an Austrian family and the patterns of child abuse that have been passed from mother to daughter. *Jakob* (1991) told the story of Marta and her autistic son and the abuse inflicted on them by unfeeling friends, family, neighbors, and the medical institutions that are supposed to help. Her most recent work of fiction, *Lover, Traitor: A Jerusalem Story* (1997), is about a young woman who travels to Jerusalem intending to explore her family's Jewish heritage, but instead falls in love with a young Palestinian terrorist. Also a professor of English and German literature, Mitgutsch is an author who portrays the lives of modern women—and their individual searches for identity.

Waltraud Anna Mitgutsch was born in Austria in 1948. She first studied English and German literature in Salzburg before continuing her education at the Institute for American Studies in Innsbruck. She subsequently spent a great deal of time traveling throughout Europe and, later, Great Britain, North America, and Asia. In 1987, around the time her first novel was published in the United States, the author was living in Boston and teaching German literature.

Three Daughters was published in German in 1985 and translated into English in 1987. Mitgutsch's novel of inherited abuse begins with Ma-

Margit Hahn/Courtesy of Anna Mitgutsch

rie, the matriarch and a very stern woman, frustrated by her marriage and somewhat remote from her daughter Vera. When Vera fails to meet the high goals Marie sets for her, Marie beats Vera—as Marie herself had been beaten as a young girl on her family's farm. After Vera becomes a mother, she makes a conscious effort not to hit her own daughter but ends up failing the child in other ways. The author sees child abuse as a delayed role reversal— the abused seem destined to become abusers. *Three Daughters* also examines the experiences of Austrians in the 20th century, from village peasants to inhabitants of modern small towns, and from the era of Nazi oppression to that of Austria's recent affluence. By the time the book had reached America, it had already received two distinguished awards—the Goldene Claassen Rose and the Brüder-Grimm-Preis.

Jakob, Mitgutsch's second novel, was published in German in 1989 and in English in 1991. Similar in its theme to *Three Daughters*, it focuses on a mother and child in distress. Marta, the only child of working-class parents, has used her intelligence to get ahead in life; she has a doctorate and a job she loves. She believes her next step is marriage to Felix, a wealthy young man, even though she's not sure that she loves him. Around the time Marta becomes pregnant, she realizes that Felix is cold and inconsiderate. She gives birth to a son, Jakob, who is autistic. Felix accuses Marta of having had an affair with Jan, who he claims is the real father of Jakob. Marta begins to understand that raising her child is not nearly as difficult as dealing with the people in her life: Her husband is cruel, her family and friends are callous, and her neighbors are downright malicious. Worst of all is the medical community, the doctors and nurses who are unwilling to help at all with young Jakob, let alone show any small amount of sympathy for Marta's situation. She also refuses to have Jakob institutionalized, until she is forced by her own illness to do so. Yet even in her darkest hour, Marta refuses to believe that she is to blame for Jakob's condition or that he is merely retarded, believing instead that he has a unique beauty. Robert Schwarz of *World Literature Today* (Winter 1991) wrote that the novel is "a harsh indictment of the mental-health profession, the medical technocrats lacking in human warmth and finding their wisdom exclusively in their seminar notes." Later in the review, he added, "It will take the reader some time to get over the indolence, sadism, and intolerance of fellow citizens when confronted with sharply deviant behavior. A cursed disease and a pitiless society cannot kill Marta's spirit, which is love. Closing the book, one recalls a line from Ortega y Gasset: 'There is but one salvation for the tired soul: love for another person.'" The reviewer for *Kirkus Reviews* (August 1, 1991) disagreed with this assessment, noting: "Yes, mothers are sometimes blamed unfairly; fathers can be selfish; and people are often cruel; and, yes, Mitgutsch . . . has written a searing portrait of a mother's fierce love for her child. But it is a portrait without shading, and this ultimately vitiates the themes."

Lover, Traitor: A Jerusalem Story, published in English in 1997, is about Devorah, a young woman on a quest to rediscover her family's history. Austrian-born, she was raised a Catholic in the United States, and was told her family had emigrated from Vienna in 1941 because her grandmother opposed the Nazi regime. Yet, Devorah learns from old official Austrian records that her grandmother was actually a Jew, and had decided to hide her ethnicity in order to protect herself and her family. Thus Devorah goes to Jerusalem, where she looks up old family friends in hopes of assembling an accurate picture of her family's past, and discovering the reasons the family had wandered for so many years. In this city of ancient Jewish custom, Devorah loses more and more of herself to her family's heritage. At the same time, she begins an affair with a young Arab named Sivan, who claims he is an Armenian Christian but who is in all likelihood a Palestinian terrorist. Sivan disappears at odd times, and dozens of people die when a bus is blown up in the Old Town, but Devorah cannot fully accept who she is and who Sivan very well might be, because doing so would make them enemies.

Lover, Traitor: A Jerusalem Story received high praise in the press. "Within the private drama of Devorah's own uncertainty about herself and her real identity, Sivan provides a vivid and excruciating reminder that she's straddling a fence between two very different and hostile worlds . . . ," remarked a critic from *Kirkus Reviews* (August 1, 1997). "Powerful, moving, and deft: Mitgutsch makes good use of the private meanings reflected in public events, and understands that the distinctions between them are as arbitrary and tenuous as any boundary drawn in the desert." Judith E. Chettle of *The World & I* (January 1998) suggested that "what gives this deceptively small novel so much resonance is Mitgutsch's ability to explore scrupulously all the contradictions and conflicts that Devorah experiences. And equally admirably, never flinching from the unpalatable, she limns these paradoxes in glowing, luminous prose." Writing for *World Literature Today* (Autumn 1996), Maria Luise Caputo-Mayr proclaimed, "Mitgutsch powerfully conveys the eternal attraction between cultural, religious, and ethnic opposites and effectively portrays Jerusalem as a locus of revelation, insight, and despair, but also of maturation and some measure of happiness for her new heroine."

Anna Mitgutsch lives in the United States and Austria. She is also the author of *In Foreign Cities: Studies in Austrian Literature, Culture, and Thought* (1995).—C. M.

SUGGESTED READING: *Kirkus Reviews* Aug. 1, 1991, Aug. 1, 1997; *New York Times* p12 Dec. 28, 1997; *The World & I* p278 Jan. 1998; *World Literature Today* p105 Winter 1991, p949 Autumn 1996

SELECTED WORKS: Fiction—*Three Daughters*, 1985 (tr. 1987); *Jakob*, 1991 (*Ausgrenzung*, 1989); *Lover, Traitor: A Jerusalem Story*, 1997 (*Abschied von Jerusalem*, 1995); Nonfiction—*In Foreign Cities: Studies in Austrian Literature, Culture, and Thought*, 1995

Mo Yan

1956– Novelist; short-story writer

Somewhat of a "romantic idealist," the Chinese novelist Mo Yan endorses a personal quest for the heroic in China's new age of increasing consumerism, which he sees as eroding both revolutionary ardor and a sense of traditional culture. Born Guan Moye in Gaomi county of Shandong province, Mo Yan first achieved recognition in the West through Zhang Yimou's film adaptation of his novel, *Hong Gaoliang jiazu* (The Red Sorghum Clan, tr. *Red Sorghum*, 1993), originally written in the form of five novellas. His later novel, *Tiantang Suantai zhi Ge* (The Song of Paradise Garlic, tr. *The Garlic Ballads*, 1995), banned in China after the Tiananmen Square uprising, exposes official corruption and bureaucratic stupidity in the countryside. Mo Yan is deeply influenced by Latin American writers, notably Gabriel García Márquez, and is regarded as the representative of "magical realism" in contemporary China, especially due to his use of the surreal in such well-known short stories as "Baozha" ("Explosions") and "Touming de Hulopo" ("The Transparent Carrot"). He is also associated with the authors known as "root-seekers," who sought in the mid-1980s to create a more realistic, non-polemical fiction. His native Shandong province, the birthplace of Confucius, also linked with the bandit-heroes of Chinese history and legend, is the landscape upon which Mo Yan drew heavily in creating his own characters of heroic men and passionate women. By writing fiction that celebrates larger-than-life heroes in the primitivist milieu of a mythical past, Mo Yan strives to challenge what he perceives as the spiritual vacuum in post-Mao China. Japanese Nobelist Kenzaburo Oe asserts, "If I were to choose a Nobel laureate, it would be Mo Yan."

Mo Yan was born in 1956. In his native Gaomi he dropped out of school to work in a factory during the Cultural Revolution. At the age of 20, he joined the army. It was while in military service that he first began writing. In 1984, while a student at the army's art and literature institute, he published his first short story, based on life in the rural region he called home. This was the first of a series of novels, novellas, and short stories that he set around Gaomi, which he now calls his "literary republic."

Mo Yan's writing is often loosely labeled as part of the "root-seeking" fiction of the middle 1980s. The "root-seekers" comprised a varied lot of writers, some chronicling the stark poverty and barbaric backwardness of northwestern China, some seeking exotic stories from among the national minorities, others exploring human degradation in the more cosmopolitan south. Mo Yan expresses a quest for the heroic in writing fiction that relies heavily on the device of the family myth. The words "My father . . ." open *Red Sorghum* and many other of his stories. This book was written in the form of five novellas that were translated by Howard Goldblatt and published in the United States in 1993. From its beginnings on an autumn day in 1939, during the war against Japan, the story portrays three generations of a Chinese family trying to survive amidst the prevailing anarchy. Here the "yang" element of masculine activity predominates, with graphic narratives of male valor being tested among scenes of sheer brutality. In *Red Sorghum* bands of peasant guerillas both kill and give up their lives with the same passion, fighting each other as savagely as they fight the Japanese, with much rape, pillage, and banditry. Mo Yan argues that today's patriots must draw their fervor from ancient historical traditions and fight for "the land of their fathers."

Reviewing *Red Sorghum* for the *New York Times Book Review* (April 18, 1993), Wilborn Hampton praised Goldblatt's "vibrant translation" in writing: "The canvas of history rarely stretches comfortably over the frame of fiction. But when it succeeds, the result can illuminate a time and place as it excites the imagination." Hampton was firm in his belief that *Red Sorghum* "brilliantly and fondly re-creates this life with visceral writing that reeks of gunpowder, blood, and death."

The heroes in *Red Sorghum* are portrayed as participants in a primitive vitality symbolized by the blood-red sorghum. "I didn't realize until I'd grown up that Northeast Gaomi Township is easily the most beautiful and most repulsive, most unusual and most common, most sacred and most corrupt, most heroic and most bastardly, hardest-drinking and hardest-loving place in the world," says Douguan, the "regressed" descendant of former heroes, mythical men who ate sorghum gruel and drank sorghum wine, made love and planted their seed in the sorghum fields, and ambushed the invading Japanese under the cover of tall sorghum plants. The book ends with a rhapsody to sorghum: the last descendant is admonished to "wield it high as you re-enter a world of dense brambles and wild predators. It is your talisman, as well as our family's glorious totem and a symbol of the heroic spirit of Northeast Gaomi Township."

This theme of lineage is carried out in Mo Yan's short stories, many of which rely on the device of a child telling the story of elders and recent ancestors. In this fiction, history is in effect reinvented through family sagas of peasants whose innate goodness and raw ability for survival enable them to overcome the tradition of violence in which they have been raised. In "Autumn Waters," for instance, a young narrator recounts the story of how his grandfather, a common laborer, had eloped with the young daughter of the gentrified family for whom he worked. The couple lived together in a wilderness, witnessing murders just as their child, the narrator's father, was being born. This and other stories are also notable for their strong female characters: besides the heroine in "Autumn Waters," there is in *Red Sorghum* a female brewery owner who throws in her lot with a bandit. Predictably, critics have detected influences of William Faulkner and Gabriel García Márquez in these sagas, and Mo Yan freely acknowledges his indebtedness to these and other masters of Western fiction, including James Joyce. But above all Mo Yan is inspired by the wild beauty of his native land and the enduring valor of its people reared in their own tradition of honor and courage.

Mo Yan has been successful in introducing contemporary issues into his fiction, as in the story "Baozha" (tr. "Explosions"), whose main conflict revolves around a woman's abortion, a highly politicized issue in China as elsewhere. The story contrasts the conflicting motivations of the various characters: the woman herself wants the baby in order to hold on to her marriage; the grandfather, who has only a granddaughter, wants the baby to continue the family line; the husband, a Communist and an army officer, firmly insists on the abortion to keep himself in good standing with the Party. Another political story, "Ling Yao" ("Effective Medicine", tr. "The Cure"), contrasts two kinds of killing: the first the double execution of a so-called landlord and a so-called village chief during the land reform movement of the 1950s, and the second by a superstitious peasant who seeks to harvest his victim's organs for their curative powers. Mo Yan frames the first story as an abhorrent and highly calculated act of political violence designed to mobilize a village's support of the Communists, but presents the "killing" in the second story as an act of filial piety by an ignorant peasant who believes that live liver and kidney tissue can cure his mother's eye disease.

These themes are further developed in Mo Yan's novel *The Garlic Ballads*. In this long and complex story of peasants set in mythical Paradise County in the new era of the 1980s, nothing has changed much from the bad old days: officials still prey on peasants, destitute peasants still sell their daughters—their only assets—and are reduced to near bestiality. Finally, after the government encourages the peasants to grow mountains of garlic that they cannot sell, the farmers riot against the county government. *The Garlic Ballads* uses the narrative device of ballads sung by a blind minstrel—a modern Homer—who links contemporary events to ancient dynasties, reinforcing the general mood of regress and despair. Mo Yan's lush, descriptive prose richly evokes an atmosphere of rural life, while cryptic half-sentences bring out the hard-boiled atmosphere that surrounds his macho heroes. The "positive hero" Gao Ma is a social outcast who has only contempt for a system into which he cannot fit either as predator or prey. He prefers to die rather than defend himself against trumped-up charges. As in his other writings, Mo Yan underscores his central theme that the human spirit has been shackled and debased by social and cultural forces.

The Garlic Ballads was banned in China following the Tiananmen Square uprising in 1989. With the official crackdown on dissidents in the late 1980s, Mo Yan found his work being criticized for bordering on the lewd and pornographic. Steven Mufson noted in the *Washington Post* (February 3, 1996), "A newspaper in Shenzen criticized a novel called *Plump Breasts and Portly Buttocks* by Mo Yan. . . . The article suggested Mo was seeking commercial success through base appeal. 'Sensuality is fine, as long as it's not pornography and obscenity,' the article said." But reaction to *The Garlic Ballads* in the West has been favorable. Richard Bernstein wrote in the *New York Times* (June 12, 1995) of "this raw, brilliant, eventful new novel by one of China's best writers," adding that "Mr. Mo . . . has emerged as a major writer, a kind of Chinese magical realist whose stories, grounded in gritty naturalism, in the smells and fluids of real life, are nonetheless full of hallucination, demonic possession, and the grotesquery of dreams."

A number of Mo Yan's short stories have been translated and appear in English in various anthologies and magazines, including Howard Goldblatt's survey of contemporary Chinese writing, *Chairman Mao Would Not be Amused*.
—E. M.

SUGGESTED READING: *New York Times* C p13 July 12, 1995; *New York Times Book Review* p28 Apr. 18, 1993; *Washington Post* A p14 Feb. 3, 1996, with photo; Leung, L., ed. *Morning Sun: Interviews with Chinese Writers of the Lost Generation*, 1994; Liu, K., and X. Tang, eds. *Politics, Ideology and Literary Discourse in Modern China*, 1993; Lu, T., ed. *Gender and Sexuality in 20th Century Chinese Literature*, 1993

SELECTED BOOKS: *Red Sorghum*, 1993; *The Garlic Ballads*, 1995

Moody, Bill

Sep. 27, 1941– Mystery writer

An expert on the history of jazz, Bill Moody has chosen to share his erudition with others in a unique manner. Moody has been a jazz drummer with a number of bands, and he began his professional writing career with a nonfiction volume about American jazz musicians in Europe. In 1994 he published the first work in his ongoing series of mystery novels starring Evan Horne, a fictitious jazz pianist who is forced to take a break from his career due to an injured hand. While not performing, Horne tends to stumble onto bizarre mysteries, all of which are tied to jazz musicians—the famous and the not-so—of the past. Moody's Evan Horne series, now three books along, has proven highly successful with critics, who admire Moody's ability to construct a page-turning thriller around the lives of legendary jazz musicians.

Bill Moody was born to Hugh and Helen (Shaw) Moody in Webb City, Missouri, on September 27, 1941—a date that, as Moody wrote in his autobiographical essay for *World Authors 1990–1995*, is "the same [birth] date as trumpeter Red Rodney and pianist Bud Powell, so I guess I was destined for a life in jazz. My mother was a pianist and a writer, so growing up in southern California, I was surrounded by books and music. I studied piano and drums, and sometimes I feel like my career in music was all training for writing about jazz.

"I was first published in the Santa Monica high school paper with a weekly column. During the years I spent on the road with a number of different bands, I wrote the occasional piece for music magazines, but didn't really concentrate on writing until I went back to school for a masters degree at the University of Nevada, Las Vegas. I began to experiment by fictionalizing some of my music experiences, and mixing fictional characters with real life musicians. I soon realized that writing about music had not been done well or often, but I was inspired by the work of James Baldwin's short story, "Sonny's Blues," and John Clellon Holmes, whose novel *The Horn*, is arguably still the best novel about jazz.

"Three years in Europe triggered the nonfiction work, *The Jazz Exiles: American Musicians Abroad* [1993]. I came across so many American jazz musicians living and working in foreign countries, writing about them from a fellow musician's perspective seemed natural. By then I was also formulating a plan to write more lengthy fiction.

"I was very interested in the mystery framework. I find many parallels in jazz, where a soloist begins with the framework of a tune and improvises. Crime fiction can be approached the same way, at least for me. I wanted to write about jazz but also attempt to take the mystery to another level. In creating the character, pianist Evan Horne, I was able to deal with jazz, the mystery, and his coming to terms with suddenly not being able to do what he does best—play the piano.

"*Solo Hand* [1994] introduces Evan. His promising career is sidelined by an automobile accident that damages his right (solo) hand. We see him undergoing therapy and coming to terms with his plight while getting involved with unsolved mysteries in the jazz world that allowed me to write about long forgotten jazz musicians."

In *Solo Hand*, Evan Horne is residing in Los Angeles when he becomes entangled in a blackmail plot involving his estranged friend, a singer named Lonnie Cole. As a way of proving to Lonnie that he was not part of the extortion plot, Horne begins to investigate the case on his own. Though only an amateur sleuth, Horne manages to solve the case in an adventure filled with characters from and references to the world of jazz. Reviews for *Solo Hand* were mixed. "Matching the novice detective who is learning to detect with an open, unpretentious voice, the author creates a likable, memorable sleuth," wrote Gail Pool in *Wilson Library Bulletin* (May 1994). A *Kirkus Reviews* (December 1, 1993) contributor, whose assessment was reprinted on the Amazon.com Web site, was far less impressed: "This first novel peoples its savory music-industry background with such forgettable characters that it actually gets less interesting as it goes along."

For his next novel, Moody continued with his Evan Horne character, and cooked up another mysterious incident involving a jazz musician. In *Death of a Tenor Man* (1995), Horne is slowly recovering from his accident in Las Vegas when he begins to research the questionable demise of tenor saxophonist Wardell Gray in 1955. Officially, Gray died of a drug overdose, but Horne begins to believe otherwise, and as he investigates he is threatened by an assortment of organized crime figures who warn him to quit his inquiry. Nevertheless, he perseveres, and along the way learns about the atmosphere of the racial tension that loomed over Las Vegas in the 1950s. The Gray case is a true story, and Moody incorporated many other true anecdotes of jazz figures in *Death of a Tenor Man*.

Moody's second Evan Horne novel was well received by critics, including Marilyn Stasio in the *New York Times Book Review* (January 7, 1996), who called Horne an "immensely likeable hero." Stasio went on to write that although Moody does not seem "entirely comfortable writing about the 'Godfather dudes' who figure in his sad, bluesy story," his other characters "have life and soul." *Booklist* (October 15, 1995) also provided a largely positive assessment of *Death of a Tenor Man*; despite calling the book "formulaic mystery fare," the reviewer wrote that the "Vegas setting is nicely realized and the use of the real-life Gray case proves fascinating."

The Sound of the Trumpet (1997), the third installment in the Evan Horne mystery series, takes the protagonist into yet another case involving a great jazzman's death. This time, Horne's friend Ace draws him into a mystery regarding the lost tapes of dead trumpet player Clifford Brown. When a collector is killed over the tapes, Horne tries to find out the truth about the tapes and the murderer through his own investigation. The inquiry also leads to a history of the jazz scene itself, and Horne encounters various real-life musicians.

Bill Ott's review of *The Sound of the Trumpet* for *Booklist* (February 15, 1997) was favorable, although he demonstrated a thinning patience for the book's familiar plot-line. Ott wrote: "One can't help but wonder how long Moody can continue this pattern without straining credibility, but the ungainly premise does permit him to mix historical and fictional plot lines, which he accomplishes effectively, and to provide fascinating insider information on various aspects of the jazz world. A must for jazz fans, who will appreciate Moody's grasp of the music." Rex E. Klett of *Library Journal* (January 1997) recommended the book and deemed it "Well written, plausible, and down to earth."

In Moody's next book, *Bird Lives!* (1999), a series of jazz musicians are murdered and small feathers symbolic of alto sax great Charlie Parker are left on the bodies. The reviewer for *Booklist* (April 15, 1999) had mixed feelings, noting: "[There is] too much first-person agonizing and some clunky dialogue. But the witty premise and all the jazz talk will more than satisfy series fans."

Moody's books have brought him wide acclaim, as both a mystery author and an authority on jazz history. In his statement for *World Authors 1990–1995*, Moody commented on his success: "The books have been well received, by mystery and jazz fans alike. It's been very gratifying to have people tell me they've been introduced to jazz through my books. My favorite critical response was from the *New York Times* (February 16, 1997), which said, 'When Bill Moody writes about dead jazz musicians, you can hear the blue notes bouncing off the walls.' Another reviewer said, 'Moody has come up with one of the most unlikely premises in crime fiction.' That remark tells me I'm still on the right track."

Bill Moody is a member of the Mystery Writers of America and the International Crime Writers Association. He resides in Las Vegas, where he works as a jazz deejay on a local radio station, as well as a writing instructor at the Nevada campus of the University of Phoenix. He also continues to play music, and has toured and recorded songs with such notables as Lou Rawls, Maynard Ferguson, Earl "Fatha" Hines, and Jon Hendricks.
—D.B.

SUGGESTED READING: *Amazon.com*; *Booklist* Oct.15, 1995, Feb. 15, 1997; *Kirkus Reviews* Dec. 1, 1993; *Library Journal* p152 Jan. 1997, Apr. 15, 1999; *New York Times* p24 Jan. 7, 1996, p28 Feb. 16, 1997; *New York Times Book Review* p28 Feb. 16, 1997; *Contemporary Authors*, 1997

SELECTED WORKS: Fiction—*Solo Hand*, 1994; *Death of a Tenor Man: An Evan Horne Mystery*, 1995; *Sound of the Trumpet: An Evan Horne Mystery*, 1997; *Bird Lives!: An Evan Horne Mystery*, 1999; Nonfiction—*The Jazz Exiles: American Musicians Abroad*, 1993

Moody, Rick

Oct. 18, 1961– Novelist; short-story writer

Often described, much to his chagrin, as the successor of the "suburban school" of fiction as practiced by John Cheever and John Updike, Rick Moody emerged in the 1990s as a representative of a new generation of American authors who are probing beneath middle-class respectability to explore the dark underbelly of the American bourgeoisie. His first three books could be called his "tristate trilogy," for each was set in a different part of the New York metropolitan area: New Jersey (the novel *Garden State*, 1991), Connecticut (another novel, *The Ice Storm*, 1992), and New York City itself (a collection of short stories and a novella, *The Ring of Brightest Angels Around Heaven*, 1995). For his fourth book, *Purple America* (1997), he returned to suburbia to tell a story, with admittedly autobiographical nuances, of a son and his invalid mother. Moody and Darcey Steinke also collaborated on *Joyful Noise: The New Testament Revisited* (1997), a collection of essays on the Christian Scriptures, which they had commissioned 19 other contemporary authors to write. Moody told an interviewer for *Time Warner Electronic Publishing* that he keeps writing about the suburbs because "American civilization comes from the middle class" and because he needs to "penetrate" and "explicate" when faced with "that impulse to get under the skin and see what's there."

Rick Moody was born in New York City on October 18, 1961. "Childhood pretty uneventful. We moved to the suburbs. I always read a lot," Moody wrote in his experimental-format autobiographical story, "Primary Sources," the final selection in *The Ring of Brightest Angels Around Heaven*. The budding writer was "raised in the privileged realm of Fairfield and Westchester Counties," in the words of Constance L. Hays, who interviewed him for the *New York Times* (October 23, 1994) after the publication of *The Ice Storm*. Interested in writing since childhood, Moody attempted a novel at age 11 but did not begin taking his talent seriously until after the favorable reception of a story he wrote during his senior year at the prestigious St. Paul's School in New Hampshire. During his time at St. Paul's, he encountered the short stories of John Cheever, who would become a sort of on-again-off-again source of inspiration to the young author. On a graduation trip to Europe, Moody recalled, he "did nothing in London and Paris but read the Cheever stories." Like many of his peers, Moody experimented with drugs and alcohol in boarding school. He wrote in a passage in "Primary Sources:" "In 1978, back at SPS, I took six hits of 'blotter' acid and had a pretty wrenching bad trip. Eternal damnation, shame, humiliation, and an endless line of men in clown costumes chanting my name and laughing." Believing then that "the church seemed like the only thing that would get me through adolescence," Moody received baptism at the age of 15 from a friend-of-the-family minister who couldn't remember his name; he hoped to get confirmed, "but instead I started drinking." He continued such indulgences during a period of rebelliousness against the middle-class values he found in the Cheever stories and in his own family. Describing his flirtation with punk rock in his essay "John

Cheever and Indirection," he wrote: "I began to ridicule the very archipelago of suburbs that had spawned me. I ripped holes in my T-shirts and jeans. I had my ear pierced by a friend."

At Brown University, in Providence, Rhode Island, he played in a band called Forty-five Houses, whose name was derived from an early surrealist manifesto. While in the school's creative writing program, in which he studied with Angela Carter and John Hawkes, Moody began to scorn writers like Cheever and Updike, now "suddenly included on the list of enemies of my new state." He wrote: "From freshman year forward . . . the mention of Cheever and any of his ilk was enough to provoke in me tirades about conformism and hypocrisy and oppression, about the schoolyard and country club cruelties I'd known back home." By 1986, however, Moody had experienced a sea-change in his attitudes toward the writings of John Cheever, the author who had once obsessed him, and of John Updike. He began to appreciate their richness and ambiguities, and the "oblique ambitions . . . that I had been too rigid to notice earlier." Moody waxed lyrical in describing his epiphany: "Here, in the twilight of the Cheever oeuvre, yearning and disgrace, generosity and cruelty, love and contempt are all equally near."

After graduating from Brown, Moody entered the master's program in creative writing at Columbia University in New York, where he maintained a precarious, alcohol-soaked existence between a series of short-term, low-paying jobs. "I was a clerk at Shakespeare [book sellers]," he later recalled, "and I got fired after one month. They said, 'We really like you and we respect you as a writer, but this cash register thing is just not working out.'" He told Hays, "I keep hoping they'll ask me to read there, so I can turn it down, out of revenge." He later worked as an editorial assistant for Simon & Schuster and as a managing editor at Farrar, Straus & Giroux. Evicted from his Columbia housing for non payment of rent, Moody found a cheaper apartment across the river from Manhattan in Hoboken, New Jersey, an old industrial town that was in the 1980s beginning to reinvent itself as a "yuppie suburb" with inexpensive housing. In Hoboken he began, in 1987, to write his first novel, Garden State, an effort that took several years to complete. Despite rejections from many publishers, he began a second novel, The Ice Storm, and accepted a summer position at Bennington College, in Vermont, where he taught fiction writing. He later joined the writing faculty of the State University of New York at Purchase.

Meanwhile, Garden State won the 1991 Editors' Book Award given by Pushcart Press for manuscripts that had been overlooked by mainstream publishers. It went on to sell about 4,000 copies in both hardback and paperback. Describing its emergence, Bill Henderson of Pushcart was quoted as saying, "Rick's manuscript turned up in the pile and I found it unforgettable."

Described by one critic as "stunningly depressing," Garden State is set in the mythical Haledon, New Jersey, a postindustrial site of disaffection and disillusionment that often serves as the backdrop for Moody's narratives. The novel, with inflections of the songs of Bruce Springsteen, describes two months in the lives of a gaggle of rootless 20-somethings who occupy, in the words of Leslie Brenner's review in the New York Times (May 24, 1992), "a bleak landscape of hydroelectric plants, dilapidated factories, industrial waste, fiery smokestacks, and disintegrated families." Brenner concluded that the book was an "auspicious debut for a writer who, unlike his characters, can surely look forward to a rosy future."

Fortified with his Pushcart credential for Garden State, and with a new agent, Moody found that editors were more receptive to his work, and his second novel, The Ice Storm, was published by Little, Brown just a year after Garden State appeared in print. Narrated from several points of view, The Ice Storm depicts the lives of several suburban Connecticut families who are stranded at home during a fierce winter storm and whose unsettling narrative unfolds point-counterpoint to the mayhem outside. Set in the "Cheever country" landscape of New Canaan, Connecticut, in 1973—Moody and his family had moved there from Darien in 1969—the novel exposes the outwardly respectable bedroom communities as a kind of wife-swapping, pill-popping "dysburbia." Michael Pietsch, who was Moody's editor at Little, Brown, was quoted in the New York Times (October 23, 1994) as saying: "It was territory previously written about by Updike and Cheever, though [Moody] was grasping that territory with an extraordinary level of inventiveness. Even though the territory was familiar, the writer was warping it in a very exciting way." Reviews were enthusiastic. Dani Shapiro described it in People Weekly (August 22, 1994) as "a gripping roller-coaster ride through the dark side of the American Dream." Claire Messud wrote in the Village Voice (October 17, 1995) that Moody had been established as "his generation's foremost chronicler of middle-class malaise in tri-state exurbia." In the New York Times (August 20, 1995), The Ice Storm was described by Michael Gorra of Smith College as "a parodically heightened and bitterly shrewd suburban comedy—a kind of Pulp Fiction of Cheever country." Later, Ang Lee directed a film version of the novel, with the same title, much to the discomfiture of some vocal New Canaanites who found fault with its theme as well as the inconveniences they suffered during its on-site filming. Quoted in a New York Times (May 19, 1996) article about the making of the movie, longtime resident Paul Killiam said, "The book portrays New Canaan as another Peyton Place," adding that the filmmakers "exploited our town and did us a disservice."

Moody's third book, The Ring of Brightest Angels Around Heaven, a collection of 10 short stories and the title piece, a novella, was published by Little, Brown in 1995, and Moody dedicated it to John Hawkes, one of his mentors at the publishing house. The book drew much critical acclaim, including a jacket comment by George Plimpton, who called it "a remarkable work, full of wit and drama . . . a powerful indication that the art of the novel is in the best of hands with the younger generation." Some of the pieces had previously appeared in Plimpton's *Paris Review* and in *Esquire*, *Harper's*, and *Mississippi Mud*. For the setting of the title novella, a naturalistic narrative that was one of the *Paris Review* pieces, Moody shifted his focus away from his familiar suburban communities and into New York City of the late 1980s,— "the old New York, the quarreling New York." Moody wrote of New Yorkers who inevitably "figure out after a while how the people around you, in New York City, are like so much *dark matter*. You don't know who they are, you never meet them, but they shadow you. Your movements implicate one another; your good stretches and disconsolate moments are one and the same." Yet the menace that pervades Moody's city in its disconsolate moments, epitomized by a louche, anything-goes sex club known as the Ruin, is nonetheless softened by the likeability of its leading character, a sometime drifter and peep-show habitué named Jorge Ruiz, whose obsession with the erotic and the exotic is charged with an appealing innocence.

"*The Ring of Brightest Angels Around Heaven* [the novella] is a spectacular tribute to the banality of degradation," Claire Messud wrote in her review for the *Village Voice* (October 17, 1995), which concludes with these words: "This is a fine but unsettling work, not least because Moody's relation to his material remains unclear. Voyeur and participant, sage and celebrant, he wants to be the man with all the tricks. He captures with piercing clarity the vacuity of his characters' lives but seems, at the same time, to pay tribute to their desperate extremity, in a gesture more social than literary."

Other selections in this collection, many of them experimental, include "The Preliminary Notes," a narrative of marital infidelity told in the form of meticulous annotations made by a man while secretly taping his wife's telephone calls; "Treatment," a single, syntax-defying sentence stretching 12 pages in which life imitates film and vice-versa; and "The Apocalypse Commentary of Bob Paisner," in which an imaginative college student uses the biblical book of Revelation as a framework for his own proclamations about life and love. The collection closes with "Primary Sources," which is told in the form of bibliographic footnotes.

For *Purple America* (1997), his third novel, Moody returned to suburbia, rekindling the critical notion that he was reclaiming his connections to the Cheever and Updike traditions. According to Matthew Debord in *Publishers Weekly* (March 31, 1997), the circumstances surrounding the publication of this work proved how far Moody had come in a few years: "[the book] was backed by a $75,000 marketing campaign and a first serial sale to the *New Yorker*." *Purple America*, with its twin themes of nuclear power and terminal disease, tells the story of young man taking care of his invalid mother, who has been abandoned by her second husband, a nuclear-reactor employee ("a family slouching toward meltdown," wrote Debord). The story had its origins in the author's own life; Moody told Lois Blinkhorn of the *Milwaukee Journal-Sentinel* (May 11, 1997, on-line) that his own mother had cared for his grandmother for 10 years before her death from Alzheimer's disease, in 1988. "It took a while for me to internalize the damage to the family," Moody told Blinkhorn. "Time to process it emotionally and then come up with the words to describe it." He further explained his motivations for this book when he told an interviewer for *Time-Warner Electronic Publishing*: "In *Purple America*, my presumption is that my readers want to see me stretch and tackle broader issues than what I've produced in my previous work. *Ice Storm* proved to be a domestic narrative, and I know that I can do that. I wanted to try something bigger. To challenge a novel and find a big enough canvas—to find a broad narrative and setting and tackle big, big things. I am most supportive of ambition. Perhaps I will return to the one thing really well (*Ice Storm*), but I wanted to try something more."

Predictably, *Purple America* again drew comparisons to the work of John Cheever. Janet Burroway wrote in the *New York Times Book Review* (April 27, 1997) of how Moody and Cheever shared "the same knockabout whimsy careering into keen lament. But Mr. Moody's work has a distinctive rawness," she continued; "it's more steeped in rage. He's also funnier, and to that degree less reconciled to the world as he finds it. Cheever had less to forgive; the waterfall of language here is full of toxic sludge. Perhaps this is only to say that John Cheever belonged to midcentury, while Rick Moody is a chronicler of the middle class for the millennium." When Moody was asked how he felt about the Cheever comparisons, he replied, as recorded by Blinkhorn: "Well, he's my hero. I think we're similar topologically, but not stylistically. I think there's a tendency to try to lump all WASPy writers together."

Christian spirituality has been important in Moody's life as far back as his prep-school days, when he found refuge from the vicissitudes of adolescence in baptism. During a mid-1990s dinner-party conversation about the pernicious influences of the religious right, Moody and author Darcey Steinke decided to ask a group of their contemporaries to contribute writings that would be gathered into an anthology of reflections on the New Testament. Published by Little, Brown in 1997 as *Joyful Noise: The New Testament Revisited*, it included Moody's introductory essay, "The Parable of the Hidden Treasure," and Steinke's afterward, "The Baby," subtitled with a passage from the apocryphal Gospel of Thomas. Sandwiched between these are contributions by 19 other writers, including Madison Smartt Bell, Benjamin Cheever (John's son), bell hooks, Ann Powers, and Stephen Westfall. Moody explained in his introduction that he has been "a sort of armchair hermeneuticist for some years" and that "[his] generation often abdicates its responsibilities when faced with the chance to articulate what it believes, whether these beliefs are Christian or of any other stripe." He hoped that *Joyful Noise* would mark the reclamation of spiritual territory too often ceded to "more conservative voices." For *Joyful Noise*, he and Steinke vowed to avoid dogmatic exegesis or theological speculation, and instead encouraged their contributors to "deal, in some way, with the *text* of the New Testament, whether directly or intuitively." Moody himself chose the parable of the hidden treasure (Matthew 13:44) as his own textual starting-point to underscore the fact that he, a "dubious miscreant," and his contemporaries "come here— to the realm of spiritual investigation—to claim the treasure for ourselves, to steal it, if necessary, from those who have repressively guarded the field in which this treasure has lain hidden for so long." As Moody wrote in his introduction, he envisioned *Joyful Noise* as a "*de facto* reopening of the biblical canon"; indeed, "*a whole new set of Gospels*, with free and liberal interpretations of Jesus' ministry ringing out like really good jazz from the mid-sixties, ringing out with the kind of sublime poetry that we find in the King James Version of the Bible. With this in mind, we might see that the great ethical remarks of the late 20th century emerge not only from the church, but also from where they are least likely to be. In John Coltrane's solos, in Mark Rothko's paintings, in doodlings of preschoolers . . . even in the writings of outspoken atheists like say, Michel Foucault: 'Do not think that one has to be sad in order to be militant, even though the thing one is fighting is abominable.'"

Moody lives in Brooklyn Heights, New York, where he writes while listening to minimalist music of Arvo Pärt and Philip Glass. In his spare time, he also enjoys creating his own music, admitting to playing "a lot of things badly," including the guitar and the keyboard. As he told Constance L. Hays: "Music creates some kind of improvisatory rapture, for want of a better word, where I go and I make these long run-on sentences. I have fits where I can write 5 or 10 pages in an hour, first-draft stuff, where I don't even blink." In the same interview, he announced his intention of continuing to write fiction and of resisting the temptation to write screenplays. Screenplay-writing, he told Hays, is "kind of a hired-gun way of life. And it's not an interior medium, it's resolutely exterior. So I feel no pressure in that direction at all. Although it would be nice to have the recognition of the paycheck."

"Writing novels is so incredibly tedious and time-consuming," he continued, "that you have to have conviction. Books that have no conviction are just transparent immediately—you wouldn't want to read them. If I wanted to write like Stephen King, I would write like Stephen King. But that's not where my interest lies. That's not where my heart is inclined." Ever aware of the precariousness of the author's lot, Moody told Hays: "Last week I went to Barnes & Noble, on 22nd Street, and looked and they actually had both of my books. And you think that would cheer me up. But the vast, vast majority of what is published is doomed to obscurity," he added, quoting Graham Greene's admonition that "success is an interval between failures."

—E.M.

SUGGESTED READING: *Booklist* p1424 Apr. 1, 1994; *Economist* p98 June 18, 1994; *Library Journal* p125 July 1995; *Milwaukee Journal Sentinel* (on-line) May 11, 1997; *New York Times* XIII p1+ Oct. 23, 1994, with photo, II p54 Sep. 10, 1995, XIII p1 May 19, 1996, with photo, IX p6 Nov. 23, 1997; *New York Times Book Review* p7 Aug. 20, 1995, p7 Apr. 27, 1997; *People Weekly* p24 Aug. 22, 1994; *Publishers Weekly* p46 June 12, 1995, p46+ Mar. 31, 1997, with photo; *Time* p65 May 30, 1994, with photo; *Time Warner Electronic Publishing* (on-line); *Times Educational Supplement* p19 Aug. 12, 1994; *Times Literary Supplement* p18 Aug. 5, 1994; *Vanity Fair* p76 Aug. 1995, with photo; *Village Voice* p75+ Oct. 17, 1995, with photo; *Vogue* p82 July 1994; *Washington Post* X p12 Jan. 12, 1997, with photo; Morrow, B., ed. *Tributes: American Writers on American Writers*, 1997

SELECTED BOOKS: Fiction—*Garden State*, 1991; *The Ice Storm*, 1992; *The Ring of Brightest Angels Around Heaven*, 1995; *Purple America*, 1997; As editor—with D. Steinke *Joyful Noise The New Testament Revisited*, 1997

Moore, Lorrie

Jan. 13, 1957– Novelist; short-story writer

The American short-story writer and novelist Lorrie Moore has chronicled the situation of contemporary women ranging in age from adolescence to middle age, showing "how the everyday hides terrors like boredom, lovelessness, aging," as Caryn James wrote in the *New York Times Book Review* (October 9, 1994). Moore's first books— *Self-Help* (1985), a short-story collection, and *Anagrams* (1986), a novel—won praise for their humor but were also faulted for the self-conscious wit that sometimes seemed to distance the author from passionate involvement with her characters. The story collections *Like Life* (1990) and *Birds of America* (1998) and her second novel, *Who Will Run the Frog Hospital?* (1994), were generally considered more successful and solidified Moore's growing reputation for limning with witty insight "men and women struggling with displacement, disappointment, the breakdown of both the earth's environment and their own sense of emotional stability," as Stephen McCauley observed in the *New York Times Book Review* (May 20, 1990). One of the most highly regarded American fiction writers of her generation, Moore began publishing while still in her teens, winning first prize in *Seventeen* magazine's annual short-story competition in 1976. She has since garnered a host of awards and honors, including fellowships from the National Endowment for the Arts and the John Simon Guggenheim Memorial Foundation. Her short fiction has appeared in the *New Yorker*, *Granta*, *American Short Stories 1990*, and *Prize Stories, The 0. Henry Awards*. Moore is also a frequent contributor to the *New York Times Book Review*.

Lorrie Moore was born Marie Lorena Moore on January 13, 1957 in Glens Falls, New York, the daughter of Harry T. Moore Jr., an insurance company executive, and Jeanne (Day) Moore. She graduated summa cum laude from Lawrence University in 1978 and earned an M.F.A. from Cornell in 1983. After lecturing for several years at Cornell, she began teaching English at the University of Wisconsin at Madison in 1984 and became a full professor there in 1991.

Moore had meanwhile gained widespread attention with the publication of her first, critically acclaimed short-story collection, *Self-Help*. Six of the nine stories in that collection employ narrative techniques associated with popular self-help manuals, such as the present tense and the second person, in which readers are addressed directly. In "How to Be an Other Woman," for example, Moore wrote: "After four movies, three concerts, and two-and-a-half museums, you sleep with him. It seems the right number of cultural events."

Most of Moore's protagonists, in both this first collection and in her later work, are intelligent, educated, witty women, readily able to dissect their own problems and discern the source of their anxieties but unable, ultimately, to escape them, except perhaps through coruscating humor and frantic wordplay. The *Ms.* (June 1985) reviewer Jennifer Crichton considered Moore's use of the self-help format appropriate to the circumstances her characters encounter: "Every emotional landmark we and her characters reach—being the other woman, being cheated on, falling out of love—is clichéd; we've already read about it or seen it on television, but that doesn't stop us from actually being there, clumsy emotion skimmed over by glib awareness." The novelist Jay McInerney, roughly Moore's contemporary, noted in the *New York Times Book Review* (March 24, 1985), "In *Self-Help*. . . . Lorrie Moore examines the idea that lives can be improved like golf swings and in so doing finds a distinctive, scalpel-sharp fictional voice that probes, beneath the ad hoc psychic fixit programs we devise for ourselves, the depths of our fears and yearnings."

Like McInerney, the *New York Review of Books* (August 15, 1985) critic Robert Towers compared the ironic, language-obsessed landscape of Moore's stories to that of tales by Grace Paley. While he found the "emotional range" of Moore's stories to be "narrow" and complained that the 'how-to' device became, "after two or more examples, something of a gimmick," Towers concluded, "Lorrie Moore's wit, her psychological acuity, and the deadly accuracy of her social observations are such that one looks forward to what she will write next." Indeed, a number of critics, Towers among them, found Moore's comic gift to be the collection's saving grace. As the London *Times Literary Supplement* (November 8, 1985) reviewer David Montrose noted, "Written differently—all tangled prose and anguish, say—Moore's stories would make bleak reading. Her prose, however, is clean and sharp. . . . She also deploys a deadpan wit to admirable black-comic effect: her characters joke even as they hurt, because they hurt." The *Kirkus Reviews* (January 15, 1985) critic provided one of the few thoroughly negative assessments of *Self-Help*, terming it a "flimsy, strained collection . . . variations on a single gimmick."

In her first novel, *Anagrams*, Moore fully unloosed her penchant for narrative experimentation and pun-drenched black humor, although the result, according to most critics, had only occasional flashes of brilliance. Divided into five independently titled chapters, *Anagrams* focuses primarily on the travails of a young woman named Benna Carpenter, who appears, at different points in the book, in a variety of guises—an aerobics instructor, a nightclub singer, a poet, and a writing instructor at a local community college. Gerard Maines, Benna's next-door neighbor, is (among other things) a cocktail lounge piano player with operatic aspirations; he is presented sometimes as Benna's lover and at other times as her close friend. The other two principal characters are Georgianne, Benna's adorably perfect daughter, and Eleanor, Benna's compulsively wisecracking best friend. In the course of the novel's five chapters—each of which is virtually a self-contained story—these four characters are presented in a series of transforming roles and relationships; Georgianne and Eleanor, we eventually learn, are creations of Benna's imagination. The novel itself is an elaborate, if imperfectly constructed, anagram.

Anagrams received, for the most part, mixed reviews. The *New York Times* (October 18, 1986) critic Michiko Kakutani praised Moore's "capacity for tenderness and felt emotion" but noted, "The bulk of *Anagrams* is so glib and self-consciously witty that the reader is kept at arm's length from Benna and her problems." Similarly, *Boston Review* (December 1986) critic Matthew Gilbert derided the novel as "witty, witty, witty," and noted, "The danger is that the fiction itself will seem finally to be as unsatisfying as its characters' dependency on their own jokes." Even *Los Angeles Times Book Review* (September 14, 1986) critic

Laura Furman, whose overall opinion of the novel was more favorable than most, "missed the sense of a continuing, dramatic present," noting that because of its episodic structure, *Anagrams* read "like a series of one-liners or illustrations of contemporary middle-class social problems, a kind of novelized 'Hers' column."

Whether or not she was consciously responding to her critics, Moore headed into new fictional territory with the publication of her second short-story collection, *Like Life*. As Stephen McCauley noted in the *New York Times Book Review* (May 20, 1990), "The stories are traditionally told, less capricious and far more capacious [than her earlier work]. There's a stronger sense of place, a unity of time and a new richness and variety of characters." Mary Warner Marien of the *Christian Science Monitor* (August 2, 1990) also had praise for Moore's new direction, noting that she "included fewer droll moments here than in her previous novel and stories, giving full throttle to the formidable engine of her plot skills." In *Like Life*, Moore continued, nonetheless, to explore many of her usual themes—the perpetual conflict between duty to self and commitment to another, the pain of love gone bad, and the stinging awareness of one's own mortality. Also, her trademark black humor and acerbic wit remained very much intact. The protagonist of "Joy" is an assistant manager in a cheese shop in the "deep Midwest," where "meat sections in the grocery stores read: BEEF, PORK, and FISH STICKS." Harry, the main character in "Vissi d'Arte," is a playwright living alone—after his girlfriend abandons him—in a ratty apartment near Times Square. Sinking into poverty and desolation, unable to complete the play he has been working on for years, Harry swallows his artistic integrity and meets with a slick Hollywood agent about a possible television writing job. Hoping to impress the agent, Harry regales him with witty dialogue from his unpublished play, pretending all the while that he is speaking extemporaneously. Harry is later horrified to learn that the agent has used his words and ideas in a television sitcom, offering him neither acknowledgment nor a job. The quietly apocalyptic title story, "Like Life," based on the opera *La Bohème*, has a quasi–science fiction flavor and is set in New York City at some unspecified time in the near future. The main characters—Mamie, a freelance illustrator, and Rudy, a talented but commercially unsuccessful painter—live in a run-down apartment in a marginal neighborhood. Told by a doctor that a mole removed from her back is "precancer," Mamie responds, "Precancer? . . . Isn't that . . . like life?" "Moore has learned to slow down her short fiction and register the subtler notes," Ralph Sassone wrote in a *Voice Literary Supplement* (June 1990) review of *Like Life*. "The new collection is her most conventionally structured book, but it may also be her boldest." The *Listener* (September 6, 1990) reviewer Nick Hornby feared that perhaps Moore had "been listening to advice from grown-ups: 'Rein

yourself in! . . . Don't feel you have to be witty all the time!'" Hornby thought Moore did her best work, in *Like Life* and elsewhere, when she gave free rein to her unconventional tendencies—when, in effect, "she sticks her tongue out at the grownups." "[M]ost of all," Hornby wrote, "Lorrie Moore is funny, funnier than just about anyone operating in this territory."

Berie Carr, the narrator of Moore's second novel, *Who Will Run the Frog Hospital?*, is, like most of her previous protagonists, a near contemporary of the author herself—in this case, nearing the age of 40. The novel opens in Paris, where Berie has come with her husband, a medical researcher attending a conference; most of the novel, however, takes the form of an extended reminiscence, as Berie focuses on events more than 20 years in the past, during the summer of 1972, when Berie and her best friend, Sils, both of them 15, worked at Storyland, a theme park near their upstate New York hometown of Horsehearts. At Storyland, where employees dress as characters from children's fables and nursery rhymes, the precociously beautiful Sils wears the Cinderella costume, while the plainer, less physically developed Berie is a pinafore-clad ticket seller. Because Berie is largely estranged from her parents and siblings (most of whom remain shadowy figures throughout the narrative), she spends hours sequestered with Sils in the latter's bedroom, smoking marijuana, listening to rock music, and sharing a semi-private patois. Berie and Sils seem to occupy a world unto themselves until, inevitably, Sils acquires a boyfriend. When Sils becomes pregnant, Berie takes it upon herself to pay for an abortion—a newly legalized option in 1972—by stealing money from the ticket booth at Storyland. Sils gets the abortion, although Berie's theft is eventually uncovered, leading to a series of painful and embarrassing confrontations with her family. The poignancy of Berie's tale is heightened by glimpses we receive of her current, unhappy life with her husband and her account of a visit to Sils and Horsehearts on the occasion of Berie's 10-year high-school reunion.

Like Moore's other books, *Who Will Run the Frog Hospital?* is a slender volume. Most critics agreed that it represented a significant artistic advance over her previous work. As Tom Shones noted in a *Times Literary Supplement* (November 4, 1994) review of the novel, "Here . . . she has found a subject which gives her smart-aleck tone more room for manoeuvre, and also more rationale: it is a story about where that tone comes from, and what first caused the smart-aleck to smart." Observing that Moore "seems to have relaxed," Shone wrote, "The opportunities for humour in the book are taken up gently, on the wing, rather than en route to a punchline, and she has invented a wonderful tone for her ugly duckling narrator: braced by embarrassment, but never loitering for picturesque gawky effect." According to *New York Times Book Review* (October 9, 1994) contributor Caryn James, "Lorrie Moore has never been the glitziest writer of her generation, but she may be the most astute and lasting. Trendier novelists . . . blazed into stardom with tales of clubs and drugs, works that seem like period pieces a decade later. Meanwhile, Ms. Moore has been steadily chronicling the more mundane lives of her contemporaries."

Less mundane are some of the situations portrayed in *Birds of America* (1998). The stories in this collection include "Beautiful Grade," in which a 24-year-old man, romantically involved with a middle-aged woman, falls in love with another, married woman—who, he discovers, is having an affair with his best friend. In "Real Estate," a woman with cancer and a philandering husband is spurred to drastic action. "Though these stories might sound in summary like movie-of-the-week scenarios," Michiko Kakutani wrote in the *New York Times* (September 11, 1998), "Ms. Moore writes with such psychological precision, such sharp, unsentimental knowledge of her characters' hopes and fears that she is able to invest these melodramatic situations with a heartfelt understanding of the precariousness of everyday life, its unexpected losses and terrors."
—S. Y.

SUGGESTED READING: *Boston Review* p30 Dec. 1986; *Christian Science Monitor* p12 Aug. 2, 1990; *Commentary* p57+ Feb. 1987; *Kirkus Reviews* p58 Jan. 15, 1985; *Listener* p27 Sep. 6, 1990; *Los Angeles Times Book Review* p8 Sep. 14, 1986; *Ms.* p68 June 1985; *Nation* p525+ Nov. 15, 1986; *New York Review of Books* p26+ Aug. 15, 1985; *New York Times* p13 Oct. 18, 1986, p46 Sep. 11, 1998; *New York Times Book Review* p32 Mar. 24, 1985, p7 May 20, 1990, p7 Oct. 9, 1994; (London) *Times Literary Supplement* p1267 Nov. 8, 1985; *Voice Literary Supplement* p15 June 1990; *Contemporary Authors* vol. 116, 1986, new revision series vol. 39, 1992; *Contemporary Literary Criticism* vol. 39, 1986, vol. 45, 1987, vol. 68, 1991

SELECTED BOOKS: Fiction—*Self-Help*, 1985; *Anagrams*, 1986; *Like Life*, 1990; *Who Will Run the Frog Hospital?*, 1994; *Birds of America*, 1998; Juvenile—*The Forgotten Helper*, 1987; As editor—*I Know Some Things: Stories About Childhood by Contemporary Writers*, 1992

Morris, Jan

Oct. 2, 1926– Journalist; author

Jan Morris, who in the person of James Morris established a reputation as a leading British journalist at 27, is one of the most prolific and admired travel writers in the world today. In the years that followed his exclusive account for the London *Times*, in 1953, of the British conquest of Mount Everest, James Morris had traveled throughout the world as a foreign correspondent. After becoming a freelance writer in 1961, he settled down to the production of books that he considered "of varying quality, subject, and success." In 1972 Morris underwent the transsexual surgery so eloquently described in the book *Conundrum*. Now, as Jan Morris, the writer continues to demonstrate skill as a prose stylist specializing in books about travel created in a "light-hearted, romantic vein," and especially concerned with "the wonder of cities."

Jan Morris was born James Humphry Morris on October 2, 1926 in Clevedon, Somerset, England, the son of W. H. Morris. As James Morris, the writer was first educated at the choir school of Christ Church, Oxford, and later at Lancing College, a noted public school near Shoreham, in Sussex. After leaving Lancing in 1944, Morris joined the editorial staff of the *Western Daily Press,* a newspaper published in Bristol. In 1944 Morris enlisted in the elite Ninth Queen's Lancers, serving as an intelligence officer in Italy and Palestine until 1947, when he left the army with the rank of lieutenant. After his military discharge, Morris remained in the Middle East on the editorial staff of the British-run Arab News Agency in Cairo, Egypt. In 1948 he returned to England, and in the following year resumed his interrupted education at Christ Church, Oxford University, where he studied English literature and edited *Cherwell,* the undergraduate newspaper. Morris left Oxford with a B.A. degree with second-class honors in 1951, and 10 years later he found time to complete the requirements for his master's degree.

Joining the London *Times* in 1951, James Morris became the paper's special correspondent in Egypt, Scandinavia, the Netherlands, India, and the United States. When the *Times* bought exclusive rights to reportage on the Hunt-Hillary assault on Mount Everest in 1953, Morris was assigned to cover it. His evocative dispatches, describing the ascent and announcing the mountain's conquest just before the coronation of Queen Elizabeth II, made his reputation. Later that year Morris took a year's sabbatical from the London *Times* as a Commonwealth Fund Fellow for the United States. That sojourn resulted in his first book, *As I Saw the U.S.A.,* which did not appear in print until 1956, when Morris became free of the London *Times*'s prohibition of staff writers publishing books on their own. Published by Pantheon in the United States, it appeared in England in the same year under the imprint of Faber & Faber, with the title *Coast to Coast.*

Leaving the London *Times* in 1956, Morris joined the *Manchester Guardian* (now the *Guardian*) as a "wandering correspondent" who reported on the Suez affair, the Algerian coup that brought

General de Gaulle to power, and the celebrated trials of Francis Gary Powers in Moscow and of Adolf Eichmann in Jerusalem. It was at the *Guardian* that Morris began writing the travel essays that were to become his specialty. In *Conundrum* Jan Morris looked back upon the *Guardian* years as follows: "I was least comfortable with the *Guardian* . . . [it] was kind to nearly everyone, and kindest of all to me, for it let me go more or less where I liked, and seldom cut a word or changed an adjective. Yet I was never at ease with it. There was, I thought, something pallid or drab about its corporate image, something which made me feel exhibitionist and escapist, romantically gallivanting around the world while better men than I were slaving over progressive editorials at home."

After the publication of *As I Saw the U.S.A.*, which won the Café Royal Literary Prize in England, Morris produced book after book with amazing speed. In 1957 alone he published two books, both about the Middle East: *Sultan in Oman* (Faber; Pantheon) and *Islam Inflamed* (Pantheon), which was published in England by Faber & Faber as *The Market of Seleukia*. The reviewers of his early books identified certain qualities in his writing that critics have admired to this day. Phoebe-Lou Adams' encomium for *Islam Inflamed* in the *Atlantic* (September 1957) is typical: "[He] writes with such verve that he can make even statistics about oil barrels entertaining. Mr. Morris has the qualities of a good travel writer, an eye for landscape and an irrepressible curiosity about people. His descriptions of cities and countrysides are equally vivid, and he conveys the emotional tone of a place as sharply as its shape and color."

In 1958, five years after the heroic Himalayan expedition that it commemorated, *Coronation Everest* (Faber; Dutton) appeared. It was followed by *South African Winter* (Faber; Pantheon, 1959) the next year, and by *The Hashemite Kings* (Faber; Pantheon, 1960) the year after that. A prolonged stay in Venice resulted in the publication of *The World of Venice* (Pantheon, 1960); entitled simply *Venice,* it was published in the same year by Faber & Faber in England, where it won the prestigious Heinemann Award for Literature. A collection of folktales from various parts of the world, *The Upstairs Donkey and Other Stories* (Faber, 1962; Pantheon, 1961), represents Morris' only attempt at writing for children so far.

Having been commissioned in 1960 to write an account of the work of the International Bank for Reconstruction and Development, Morris traveled for 18 months to Colombia, Thailand, Pakistan, India, Italy, and the United States. The result was *The Road to Huddersfield* (Pantheon, 1963), which had as its British title *The World Bank* when it was published by Faber & Faber in the same year. A Book-of-the-Month Club selection in the United States, it was described in *Newsweek* (August 5, 1963) as "not merely an objective account of the bank's efforts to raise living standards around the world, but a study in the ironic disparities of modern civilization." Morris used the Yorkshire mill town of Huddersfield as a grim example of what happens to those benighted individuals "who pine to exchange their pastorals for the blast of foundries. "

A steady flow of political and geographical studies resulted from Morris' travels over the next five years. Two were not published in the United States: *South America* (Manchester Guardian and Evening News Ltd., 1961) and *The Outriders: A Liberal View of Britain* (Faber, 1963). *Cities* (Faber, 1963; Harcourt, 1964,) is a cornucopia of essays about 74 cities, ranging alphabetically from Accra in Ghana, West Africa to Wellington, New Zealand, compiled from Morris' previous books and magazine articles. *The Presence of Spain* (Harcourt, 1964), embellished with photographs by Evelyn Hofer, does not merely evoke the "grandeur and magnetism" of Spain but also attempts to capture the "Spanish character." It was published in 1970 by Faber & Faber in England. Morris's next book, *Oxford* (Harcourt, 1965; Oxford University Press, 1965), was described by a reviewer in the *Times Literary Supplement* (November 18, 1965) as an escorted tour "into almost every church, chapel, library, museum and college" of the fabled university town where Morris lived for several years.

Heaven's Command (Faber, 1973; Harcourt, 1973), the first segment of Morris's trilogy about the Victorian British empire, was published five years after its central volume, *Pax Britannica* (Faber, 1968; Harcourt, 1968), appeared. *Heaven's Command* not only recounts the story of Queen Victoria's reign from 1837 up to her Diamond Jubilee in 1897 but also "revives, with grace, the spirit of a past as much deserted as lost," according to a reviewer for the *New Statesman,* November 30, 1973. A critic for *The Times Literary Supplement* (November 7, 1968) hailed *Pax Britannica* as "a tour de force, offering a vast amount of information and description, with a style full of sensuality and perfumes. . . . [The author] carries us on his grand tour of Empire inviting us to see its splendours . . . with his own wide eyes." *Farewell the Trumpets* (Faber, 1978; Harcourt, 1978), the final volume of the trilogy, is a chronicle of the British Empire from 1897 up to the time of Winston Churchill's funeral in 1965. (Although the second and third volumes appeared after the metamorphosis of James Morris into Jan Morris, the former name was retained for the authorship of the two books for the sake of uniformity.) While reviewers indicated that the trilogy was not so much a traditional history as a subjective portrait of what the Victorian Empire felt like to James Morris, they acclaimed his ability to revitalize familiar material.

By 1968 James Morris had become so widely known for his ability to make the "complex personality of cities" come alive for his readers that he was commissioned by the director of the Port of New York Authority to write a book about New York as a point of entry that can be approached by land, by water, and by air. Using the resources of the Port Authority, Morris explored not only its facilities but every nook and corner of the metropolis, recording its "vital energy" . . . its "insatiable passion for movement" . . . as the place where "the pace of material progress is set: the progress of perpetual change." His exploration of New York resulted in *The Great Port* (Harcourt, 1969; Oxford Univ. Press, 1985), a book packed with so fantastic an amount of detail that A.B.C. Whipple of the *New York Times Book Review* (October 19, 1969) was prompted to observe that "Morris discovered more about the port and the city than most of the natives have ever learned." *Places* (Faber, 1972; Harcourt, 1973), a second collection of travel essays about various cities, was the last book that was written by James Morris before he was transformed into Jan Morris.

Soon after her final surgery, Jan Morris wrote *Conundrum* (Faber, 1974; Harcourt, 1974), the opening line of which succinctly sets forth the central dilemma of James Morris's life: "I was three or four years old when I realized that I had been born into the wrong body, and should really be a girl." But it was not until 1964, at the age of 38, that James Morris began to make the strange and painful journey that bridged the physical transition from male to female. Over the next eight years, according to Jan Morris's own estimate, she took at least 12,000 female hormone pills. In *Conundrum* she recalled that eventually "those thousands of pills . . . transformed my physique: if I was not a woman, I was certainly a strange sort of man." In 1972 she traveled to Casablanca for the surgery that constituted the final step in her transformation. During an interview with John F. Baker for *Publishers Weekly* (April 29, 1974) she told him that *Conundrum* was "by far the best thing" that she had ever done, and she informed Sally Quinn in the *Washington Post* (October 13, 1974) that she "would rather be remembered as a great woman writer than a great male writer."

The critical response, both in Great Britain and the United States, ranged from tasteless commentary to sympathetic approval of a courageous enterprise, and from puzzled attempts to understand James Morris's dilemma to voyeuristic curiosity about his momentous decision to change his sex. Some reviewers expressed their dismay or utter disbelief. Among them was Rebecca West, who wrote in the *New York Times Book Review* (April 14, 1974) that she could not "accept *Conundrum* as the story of a true change of sex, viewing it as "rather a record of a strange self-treatment for a neurotic condition." On the other hand, Bernard Levin, writing in the *London Observer* (April 28, 1974), noted that "as a communication of the incommunicable, *Conundrum* is very good indeed; but it is even more than that. It is also, in many ways, a straightforward autobiography rippling with humor."

Perhaps inevitably, a certain amount of controversy and unwanted notoriety followed in the wake of the publication of Jan Morris's autobiography. Sally Quinn in the *Washington Post* interview reported that it had "aroused the British public as no book had in years," while John F. Baker in *Publishers Weekly* revealed that enough annoying crank mail had arrived at the office of the author's publisher to make her stay, during a promotional visit to New York, at the home of her literary agent rather than in a hotel. Morris nevertheless told Sally Quinn somewhat defensively: "I'm an innocent sort of person. . . . I was a bit frightened about coming to America for the first time after the operation. I thought Candid Camera would be following me about the streets. But nothing bothers me. . . . I have such a marvelous time, on balance."

Following *Conundrum* Jan Morris published *Travels* (Harcourt, 1976), another collection of essays. She also edited two anthologies, *The Oxford Book of Oxford* (Oxford University Press, 1978) and *My Favorite Stories of Wales* (Lutterworth Press, 1980). She wrote another book about Venice: *The Venetian Empire* (Faber, 1980; Harcourt, 1980), a history of the Adriatic republic's overseas empire, and collected, in *Destinations* (Oxford University Press, 1980), travel essays originally written for *Rolling Stone* magazine. Of these essays, the *Christian Science Monitor* (June 9, 1980) wrote that Morris proves "charming, funny, courageous, and very human. And perhaps her presence is the element that makes her writing more than travelogue." A reviewer for the *New York Times Book Review* (April 27, 1980) was even more enthusiastic about the collection, calling the essays "erudite, thoughtful and thoroughly literate" pieces which contain " impressions and moods which are finely drawn from Morris' deep sense of history." The reviewer concludes that "ballasted with experience and bright with astonishment, *Destinations* is a marvelous book." The next year, Morris also edited, with an introductory essay, *The Stones of Venice* (Little, Brown, 1981), in which she tried to show how John Ruskin's personal life had influenced the writing of that classic guide to Venetian architecture.

The year 1982 witnessed the publication of a variety of other books that reveal the breadth of Jan Morris's many-sided interests: *The Spectacle of Empire* (Faber; Doubleday), which a reviewer for *Publishers Weekly* called "an overblown picture album" but a critic for *Quill Quire* (February 1983) called "a worthwhile amalgam of artistic and literary pleasures"; *Wales, the First Place,* in collaboration with Paul Wakefield (Potter); *The Small Oxford Book of Wales* (Oxford Univ. Press); and *The Venetian Bestiary* (Thames and Hudson), about the real animals within the city and the imaginary ones featured in its art and architecture.

Perhaps Jan Morris's most personal work since *Conundrum* was *The Matter of Wales: Epic Views of a Small Country* (Oxford University Press, 1984). Morris once described herself as a "Welsh patriot . . . dedicated to the peaceful separation of Wales . . . from the United Kingdom," and has come to consider herself in recent years as being more Welsh than British. That book on her homeland was even more subjective than usual. Part history, part description of the culture, landscape, climate, flora and fauna of Wales, and part meditation upon the life of Owen Glendower, the 15th-century Welsh patriot (*New York Times,* March 1, 1985), *The Matter of Wales* received generally enthusiastic reviews. Her first work of fiction, *Last Letters from Hav* (Viking, 1985) is a "mildly playful exercise in cultural pastiche," according to Adam Mars-Jones, who reviewed it for the *Times Literary Supplement* (October 18, 1985), in which historical figures including Sigmund Freud, Princess Grace, and Nikolai Rimsky-Korsakov find their way to the imaginary city of Hav. Comparisons with the fiction of Jorge Luis Borges were inevitable. The *Economist* (October 26, 1985) however, called it a "depressing and unsatisfactory little book" in which Morris ". . . brings a terrible banality of vision to what promised to be as marvellous an imaginative creation as Italo Calvino's 'Invisible Cities'" Equally negative was *Library Journal* (May 1, 1985) which summarized that in the book, "Individuals are introduced as types, or stereotypes, and they are not fleshed out. There is no conventional plot . . . The reader never finds out what happens, or why." The review concludes that "While stylistically excellent and in some ways very clever, this book is not likely to have wide appeal." Later that year, Miss Morris returned to nonfiction with *The Matter of Wales* and *Among Cities* (both published by Oxford in 1985) and with *Scotland* (Crown, 1986).

In 1987 Morris published *Manhattan '45*, a look at the New York City borough as it was transformed in the 1940s and 1950s. A reviewer for *Library Journal* (April 1, 1987) wrote that the "Vivid descriptions and diverting anecdotes of life make for a fascinating and enjoyable tour. Morris conveys the excitment of being in New York City as it awakens to a new age in a book that will absorb all lovers of Manhattan." A critic for *Time* (April 20, 1987) however, was dissatisfied with what it viewed as an over-enthusiastic tone. "[This portrait of New York is a] little too wonderful perhaps," the revierer wrote. "[The author] stages an uncritical celebration . . . Morris, whose customary voice is that of cool detachment, allows a geewhiz tone to mar the text." Her next book, *Hong Kong* (1988), offers alternating chapters of history and social analysis of the city. A *Christian Science Monitor* (March 30, 1989) critic noted that the book is "written with the affection of a lover of cities and peoples, and with a cleareyed appreciation of the triumphs and horrors of the British Empire." The review goes on to state that the book "may be one of the most useful studies of the place before the great change of governmental control takes place in 1997." A *Wall Street Journal* (February 13, 1989) reviewer was less impressed with the effort, calling it a "vivid

and compelling" book, but noting that while Morris "is especially good at describing [British] lives and manners," she is "less astute about the rest of Hong Kong's 5.6 million inhabitants." The reviewer goes on to explain that while the author's "impressions of the British seem formed from the vantage point of a civil servant's veranda or the deck of a tainpan's junk, she appears to have gleaned her knowledge of the Chinese more from observing them in cafes or on the Star Ferry." The critique concludes that "By no measure does *Hong Kong* fall into the 'aren't-the-natives-cute' school of travel writing, but Ms. Morris could have done more to move beyond the stereotype of Hong Kong Chinese as virtuoso money-makers."

The next year, Morris returned to autobiographical writing with *Pleasures of a Tangled Life* (1989), a book which serves as a "companion volume" to her earlier memoir, *Conundrum*. With this book, written in an unstructured, relaxed style, Morris intended to discuss the happier moments in her life, and how they relate to her specific gender at different points in her life. "The more I thought about the things that gave me pleasure, the more it dawned upon me how specific they must be to my particular sensibility," she told the *Globe & Mail's* William French (November 25, 1989). French wrote that while "some of the essays are more interesting than others . . . all bear evidence of her usual jaunty self-assurance." A critic for *Library Journal* (October 15, 1989) prescribed the book only for those who are already familiar with Morris's writings, advising that *Pleasures* "has little to offer the uninitiated." The reviewer also concedes that "The memories here are in random order, but the style and vivid imagery that have won Morris acclaim as a travel writer and journalist are evident."

As she entered the 1990s, Morris completed *City To City* (1990, later reissued as *O Canada*), a collection of travel essays spanning 10 Canadian cities from St. John's to Toronto to Vancouver. Toronto's *Globe & Mail* (October 6, 1990) offered one of the harsher reviews of the book, writing that Morris' work is "sometimes usefully provocative, but in the main annoying." Reviewer David Olive added that he was not "fooled by her faint praise" and that overall, "More crusty than benign, Morris is fond of the sucker punch" in her assessment of Canada's major cities. A critic for the *Christian Science Monitor* (May 20, 1992) was more congenial, saying that while "some readers will find her comments brusque and irreverent . . . Still, amid the sentiment and the sentiousness, Morris evokes a version of Canada worth attending." Similarly, a reviewer for *Library Journal* (February 15, 1992) offered that although "in some essays Morris attempts to cover too much in too little space, the overall content is informative, varied, and interesting."

Morris published a social and historical look at Sydney, Australia, in 1992 titled *Sydney*, and the book earned a host of mixed commentary, including a review from the *Guardian* (May 14, 1992) in which it was noted that "Historically, her portraits of the city's Hogarthian past contain sketches of wit, sweep and accuracy" and that "In her descriptions, particularly of the suburbs, there are flashes of urban lyric." The critic then poses the question, "So why the flavorless advertorial style elsewhere, laden with prim generalisations and brochures?" and concludes that "for all Jan's professed affections, Sydney ends up at arm's length, in a relationship cool and remote, and a book that is sadly less a declaration of passion than a travel book crossed with a tourist board memorandum." A reviewer for *Library Journal* (April 15, 1992), however, wrote that Morris presented a "clear and accessible" book which reveals that she "has come to delight in the city and its people, yet is not afraid to expose the prejudice and excess which are also present."

After completing *Locations* (1993) and *A Machynlleth Triad* (1994), Morris took her writing into a more personal arena with the completion of *Fisher's Face* (1995). The book is largely a biography of British Admiral John Fisher, a man who was instrumental in implementing sweeping changes for the British Navy during the late 1800s and early 1900s. An ardent admirer of Fisher throughout her life, Morris presents the many sides of this complex man, only occasionally overstepping these precincts to place herself within her narrative. A critic for the *New York Times Book Review* (June 11, 1995) wrote that although she moves beyond the boundaries of biography, "the rest of the book is convincing and enormously entertaining." The reviewer adds that Morris " . . . has shown us that for all of his shortcomings Fisher was a great and, in his own peculiar way, a noble man. Hers is a most worthy biography." Similarly, a critic of *Booklist* (May 1, 1995) called *Fisher's Face* a "remarkably insightful, gorgeously presented book," and *Library Journal* (May 15, 1995) announced that Morris "combines personal imagination and actual description in a unique and enjoyable writing style."

Morris finished *The Princeship of Wales* and the *World of Venice* in 1995 and then wrote *Fifty Years of Europe: An Album* (1997). This book examines the many, deeply felt changes which Europe has undergone since World War II, changes which Morris herself was a first-hand witness to, as both a man and a woman. A critic for the *New York Times Book Review* classified the historical compilation as "an unusual book, almost easier to define by what it is not: it is not a travel or a history or a geography book, although it has elements of all three; it also lacks a narrative flow since it ignores chronology and comprises hundreds of loosely connected anecdotes, portraits, recollections, history lessons and quotations." *Kirkus Reviews* (September 15, 1997) noted the duality of Morris's writing, stating, that "Morris's is truly a unique voice." *Kirkus* went on to write that "For every nation, for every region or town, from Finland to Greece, Morris delivers a precise, moving, and eloquent reflection. *Fifty Years of Europe* is a delight."

Jan Morris, who is a fellow of the Royal Society of Literature, received the George Polk Memorial Award for journalism in 1961.
—D.B.

SUGGESTED READING: *New York Times* p19+ Mar. 17 1974; *Newsweek* p43 Aug. 5 1963; *Washington Post* pG1+ Oct. 13, 1974, pC1+ July 3, 1980; *Contemporary Authors*, 1981; *International Who's Who*, 1985; *World Authors 1950-1970*

SELECTED WORKS: *As I Saw the U.S.A.* (also published as *Coast to Coast*), 1956; *Sultan in Oman*, 1957; *Islam Inflamed* (also published as *The Market of Seleukia*), 1957; *Coronation Everest*, 1958; *South African Winter*, 1959; *The World of Venice*, (also published as *Venice*), 1960; *The Upstairs Donkey and Other Stories*, 1961; *The Presence of Spain*, 1964; *Oxford*, 1965; *Pax Britannica*, 1968; *Heaven's Command*, 1973; *Conundrum*, 1978; *Farewell the Trumpets*, 1978; *My Favorite Stories of Wales*, 1980; *The Venetian Empire*, 1980; *The Spectacle of Empire*, 1983; *The Matter of Wales: Epic Views of a Small Country*, 1984; *Manhattan '45*; 1987; *Hong Kong*, 1988; *Pleasures of a Tangled Life*, 1989; *City to City*, 1990; *Sydney*, 1992; *Fisher's Face*, 1995; *Fifty Years of Europe: An Album*, 1997

Mosley, Walter

1952– Mystery writer; novelist

In 1992 Bill Clinton, then a candidate for the presidency, did for the mystery writer Walter Mosley what President John F. Kennedy had done for Ian Fleming, the creator of the fictional master spy James Bond, three decades earlier: pronouncing Mosley his favorite writer of thrillers, Clinton helped to increase sales of the novelist's works almost overnight. While Mosley welcomed the future president's endorsement, it could be argued that he did not need it, since his novels—*Devil in a Blue Dress*, *A Red Death*, and *White Butterfly*, which were published in successive years beginning in 1990—had already received wide acclaim. *Black Betty*, *RL's Dream*, *A Little Yellow Dog*, *Always Outnumbered, Always Outgunned*, and *Walkin' the Dog* followed in 1994, 1995, 1996, 1997, and 1999, respectively. *Gone Fishin'* (1997), written earlier than Mosley's other books, depicts the beginning of the character Easy Rawlins's career. With *Blue Light* (1998) Mosley produced a twilight world set in San Francisco.

The hero of most of Mosley's novels is the black detective Easy Rawlins. Tough, principled, and affable, Easy frequently encounters people who do not share the latter two traits, and he has a way of landing in situations that are all the more danger-

Miriam Berkley

Walter Mosley

ous for their ambiguity. For him, detective work is neither a steady job nor a hobby but a method of survival, one that exposes him to amorality and racism on both sides of the law. Just as Easy does not pursue sleuthing for its own sake, Mosley does not view the mystery story as an end in itself. "I don't really concentrate on plot," he told Paul Engleman of the *Chicago Tribune* (August 24, 1992). "The stories are about character. And the mysteries are internal, not external. Most people don't care who did it. They're interested in Easy and how he's doing . . . how he makes decisions." Easy's friend and sometime rescuer is Raymond Alexander, better known as Mouse, whose unthreatening size is offset by a trigger-happy nature.

The protagonist of *Always Outnumbered, Always Outgunned* is Socrates Fortlow, a man who has spent 27 years in prison for murder and seeks to improve his life after his release. Socrates is not a detective per se, but "a middle-aged ex-con striving to redeem a life that for most of his years was a ruin," according to Richard Bernstein, writing in the *New York Times* (December 29, 1997). Socrates's story continues in *Walkin' the Dog*. The protagonist of *Blue Light* is Orde, a hippie who becomes a New Age prophet.

Walter Mosley was born in 1952 in the Watts section of Los Angeles, California, the only child of Leroy Mosley, a black school custodian, and Ella Mosley, a woman of Russian Jewish descent who worked as a personnel clerk for the Los Angeles Board of Education. As a boy Walter Mosley listened to the stories told by relatives on both sides of his family. He explained to Elizabeth Gleick for *People* (September 7, 1992) that members of his mother's family regaled him with "old Jewish sto-

ries about the czars and living in Russia" and that his father's relatives, who, like Easy Rawlins, hailed from the South, spun yarns about "violence and partying and eating and drinking." Many of the characters in Mosley's novels were inspired by the latter tales. "[The characters] are all composites but real," Mosley revealed to D. J. R. Bruckner in an interview for the *New York Times* (September 4, 1990), adding that Easy Rawlins "has some of my father in him, some of other people I knew and heard about, and some of me." (Like Easy Rawlins, Leroy Mosley earned a second income by purchasing and maintaining rental properties.)

Mosley graduated from high school in 1970. Eager to leave Watts, which had erupted in riots in the late 1960s and had remained a focal point of racial tension, he enrolled at Goddard College, a small, progressive institution in Plainfield, Vermont. A lackadaisical student, Mosley spent much of his time "hitchhiking around the country while he was supposed to be attending class," as Paul Engleman reported in the *Chicago Tribune* article. After being expelled from Goddard, Mosley remained in Vermont, supporting himself with a number of different jobs. He eventually began taking courses at Johnson State College, in Johnson, Vermont, which awarded him a bachelor's degree in political science in 1977. Continuing his education, he studied the same subject in graduate school at the University of Minnesota for a short time, then moved to Boston to be with Joy Kellman, a dancer and choreographer, whom he had met in 1979. There, he tried his hand at a variety of different occupations, including making and selling pottery and operating a catering business. In 1982 he and Kellman moved to New York City, where Mosley found employment as a computer programmer.

As a youngster, Mosley had been interested in writing but had later given up the idea. While working as a computer programmer for Mobil Oil in New York, however, his desire to write was rekindled, at least partly by his reading *The Color Purple* (1982), Alice Walker's Pulitzer Prize–winning novel about a black woman in the South. "I'd read a lot of the French—Camus and all that—and I love their writing," he recalled to Elizabeth Gleick. "But that voice, that narrative—I couldn't write like that. Then when I read Walker, I thought, 'Oh, I could do this.'" One day in about 1985, Mosley wrote a sentence "about people on a back porch in Louisiana," as he described it to D. J. R. Bruckner. "I don't know where it came from. I liked it. It spoke to me." He was so taken with his new pastime that he signed up for creative-writing classes at the City College of New York. Among his instructors were Frederic Tuten, the head of the college's writing program, and the writers Edna O'Brien and William Matthews, who gave Mosley advice on his work.

During the time Mosley was taking courses at City College, he produced a novella, "Gone Fishin'," that featured the characters Easy Rawlins and Mouse but was not a mystery story; the work was turned down by more than a dozen literary agents. In the wake of those rejections, Mosley came across Graham Greene's screenplay for the atmospheric thriller *The Third Man*, and, as he told Bruckner, it "made some things so clear" to him. Through revisions, the novella about Easy and Mouse evolved into the novel *Devil in a Blue Dress*. In 1989 Mosley showed the finished work to Frederic Tuten, who, without informing the writer, gave the manuscript to an agent. Soon after that, the book was sold.

Devil in a Blue Dress (1990) is set in Los Angeles in 1948; Easy (his given name is Ezekiel) Rawlins, a native of Texas and a World War II veteran, has just been laid off from his job at a defense plant. Strapped for cash, he accepts an assignment from a mysterious white man who wants him to locate Daphne Monet, described to Easy as a white woman who frequently associates with blacks. Easy soon discovers that Daphne has absconded with $30,000 belonging to her rich, powerful lover, and the people he encounters in the course of his investigation keep turning up dead. To ensure his own survival, Easy enlists the aid of the sociopathic Mouse, who only contributes to the body count.

In writing *Devil in a Blue Dress*, Mosley sought to depict "the migration of blacks to Los Angeles after World War II," as he told Paul Engleman. The book evokes the texture of black southern/rural life as transplanted to the West Coast. Easy, who narrates the novel, offers insights into the relationships between blacks and whites and into the misunderstandings, willful and otherwise, that occur on both sides. For example, when a group of racist white men threaten Easy after misinterpreting his conversation with a white woman, the text reads: "'Leave him alone!' Barbara shouted. 'He was just saying where he was from.' I guess she was trying to help me, like a mother hugging her child when he's just broken his ribs."

Although some reviewers found the plot of *Devil in a Blue Dress* to be too complicated, nearly all expressed admiration for Mosley's writing. "The notion of a fictional black detective in forties Los Angeles sounds gimmicky, but on the first page of his first novel, Walter Mosley proves he has the talent to make this idea work," Malcolm Jones Jr. wrote in *Newsweek* (July 9, 1990). "Here, the cynicism that pervades most detective fiction looks less like a literary conceit and more like the lot of the average black citizen familiar with the lies of the powerful and the casual brutality of cops. . . . Best of all is Mosley's main creation, Easy Rawlins, a man as hard-nosed as he needs to be yet still capable of relishing decency when he finds it." *Devil in a Blue Dress* won the Shamus Award from the Private Eye Writers of America, and it was nominated for an Edgar Award from the Mystery Writers of America.

The action in *A Red Death* (1991), the second entry in Mosley's Easy Rawlins series, takes place in about 1953, during the era of political witch-hunting generally associated with Senator Joseph R. McCarthy. Easy Rawlins, having acquired a large sum of money as a result of the events in *Devil in a Blue Dress*, is now the owner of several apartment buildings. Wanting to keep a low profile, he pretends to be the janitor while his underling, the obese, cigar-chomping Mofass, poses as the landlord. The ruse fools everyone but an IRS agent, who promises not to arrest Easy for tax evasion—provided Easy helps the government investigate a Jewish union organizer, a decent man who has been performing charity work in the black community. Meanwhile, Easy further courts danger through his romantic involvement with Mouse's ex-wife.

Assessing *A Red Death* for the *San Francisco Review of Books* (Fall 1991), Joseph Ferrandino observed: "Beneath the conventional and trite mystery plot lies a subtext in which the author exhibits the sinewy moral intellect of [the black writer] James Baldwin at his best. Mosley is a social critic posing as a mystery writer, much as his character, Easy, is a landlord posing as a maintenance man. Mystery fans may find *A Red Death* to be a bit disappointing; students of the human condition will find it an absorbing read." Katherine Dieckmann echoed that sentiment, declaring in the *Voice Literary Supplement* (October 1992), "In Mosley's noirlike 1950s Los Angeles, the necessity of work, any work, and the insidious intersection of politics and race run fierce and familiar. . . . This narrative shoves pulp tropes through a scrim of color and prejudice, resuscitating a weary form in the process."

Easy Rawlins is one of few fictional detectives who age and develop significantly from book to book. *White Butterfly*, Mosley's third novel, finds Easy about a decade older than he was in *Devil in a Blue Dress* and married, with a biological daughter, Edna, as well as an adopted son, a seemingly mute boy named Jesus. Easy's marriage is imperfect; he does not tell his wife, Regina, about, among other things, the apartment buildings he owns, and she begins to resent his secretiveness. The main storyline in *White Butterfly* concerns the apparently connected murders of three black bar girls in Los Angeles; after the third woman's death, the police ask Easy, who has sworn off detective work, for help. "I was worth a precinct full of detectives when the cops needed the word in the ghetto," Easy muses. He refuses to cooperate, but when a fourth victim—a white college student who moonlights as a stripper—turns up dead, the police demand that Easy get involved, telling him that their lead suspect, Mouse, will otherwise go to prison.

Like its two predecessors, *White Butterfly* came in for considerable praise. "Mr. Mosley grows deeper and richer in his third Easy Rawlins story," Herbert Mitgang wrote in the *New York Times* (August 7, 1992). "The hard-boiled California school of [the mystery novelists] Raymond Chandler and Dashiell Hammett is worth emulating; why not walk in the footsteps of the masters? He does, but he continues to reveal the inside of the black-and-white encounter in his own voice." Making a different literary comparison, Dick Adler noted in the *Chicago Tribune* (June 28, 1992), "*White Butterfly* grabs you by the elbow from the get-go, letting you know that you're in for some rough but very interesting times. And not since Chester Himes began to shake up the literary world with his Harlem-based crime novels has a black writer used the mystery genre to expose the kind of racism that has always lurked behind the benign, smoggy grin of Los Angeles."

Black Betty (1994) is set in the early 1960s, during the Kennedy administration and the burgeoning of the civil-rights movement under the leadership of Martin Luther King Jr. Easy's wife has left him, taking their daughter with her, and Easy is struggling to raise Jesus and Feather, a mixed-race orphan he has rescued, on his own. Having made some unsound business deals, he has seen his real-estate properties all but disappear. He is therefore in no position to refuse when he is offered $400 to find a rich family's missing housekeeper. The housekeeper is Elizabeth Eady, better known to Easy as Black Betty, whom he remembers from his childhood as the most desirable woman in his hometown (she was "a great shark of a woman," Easy recalls. "Men died in her wake"). Meanwhile, Mouse, who has just been released after spending several years in jail for killing a man outside a bar, is hot on the trail of whoever informed on him—and, as the novel progresses, he grows more and more suspicious of his friend Easy.

Gene Lyons, evaluating the novel in *Entertainment Weekly* (Summer double issue, 1994), was less than impressed. "What really lies behind a Beverly Hills family's willingness to pay Easy . . . to locate a missing housemaid? Alas, readers familiar with Mosley's earlier novels can all too easily guess," Lyons complained. Still, the novel drew praise from others. A reviewer for *Publishers Weekly* (April 25, 1994), for example, found that it contained "quietly emotive prose" and that its resolution "fully satisfies." The novelist Barry Gifford, who appraised *Black Betty* for the *New York Times Book Review* (June 5, 1994), was especially taken with what he called Mosley's "sweet ear" for language: "There are echoes of *Farewell, My Lovely* in *Black Betty*, but that doesn't make Walter Mosley the black Raymond Chandler, any more than echoes of *The Real Cool Killers* make him the heir to Chester Himes. Every modern fighter who can hook off the jab and circle south owes a debt to Sugar Ray Robinson, but that doesn't mean much if he hasn't got the heart to go with it—and nobody will ever accuse Walter Mosley of lacking heart. This man comes at you kind of herky-jerky; his words prowl around the page before they pounce, knocking you not so much upside the head as around the body, where you feel them the longest." As an example, Gifford quotes Easy, who says at one point, "Poor men are always ready to die. We always expect that there's somebody out there who wants to kill us. That's why I never questioned that a white man would pull out his gun when he saw a Negro coming. That's just the way it is in America."

In his review of *Black Betty*, Gene Lyons had advised Mosley to "lose Mouse," whom he described as a "one-dimensional psychopathic bore." During an interview for the May 26, 1994 edition of the National Public Radio program *Fresh Air*, Mosley explained Mouse's significance to Terry Gross. "I see Mouse as the hero of the world that Easy is talking about," he said. "He's a sociopath—he's very violent, he's willing to kill people, and it doesn't affect him. Easy is the hero of these books because these books are about him. But [in] the world he lives in, Mouse is really the hero, the man who's willing to stand up and fight and not be pushed down for any reason—not for a political motive, [but] because he's crazy, he's been driven crazy by the world he lives in." In *A Little Yellow Dog* (1996) Mosley does "lose" Mouse—maybe. R. W. B. Lewis, calling Mouse "a genuinely vibrant invention," described in the *New York Times Book Review* (June 16, 1996) how Mouse dies. "The nurse in the intensive care unit assures Easy, in words that break his heart, that Mouse is dead. And yet," Lewis concluded, "given the circumstances, and perhaps recalling the report of the death of Sherlock Holmes in *The Final Problem*, one may allow oneself to hope."

In *Gone Fishin'* (1997) Easy remembers how Mouse has saved him from a severe beating and possible death by sticking a stiletto into the man doing the beating and then threatening to "stir the soup." "I din't save you," Mouse tells Easy. "I just wanted to cut that boy 'cause he think he so bad. . . . See what he think now." *Gone Fishin'* takes place in 1939, when Easy, 19 years old, hooks up with Mouse and takes to the road—from Houston to Los Angeles, with a stop in Pariah, Texas, home of Mouse's detested stepfather, Reese Corn. *Gone Fishin'* is a coming-of-age and male-bonding novel rather than a true mystery, although Easy and Mouse find themselves involved with an escaped killer, witchcraft, and other assorted elements of the thriller. The extraordinary significance of this novel is that Mosley, forgoing his usual six-figure advance, published the book with Black Classic Press, a small publisher based in Baltimore, rather than with Norton, his usual publisher. Explaining his decision, Mosley told Michael Rogers for *Library Journal* (December 1996) that when he and Max Rodriguez, the editor and publisher of the *Quarterly Black Review*, were on a panel together, Rodriguez suggested that it might be a good idea for black writers to approach black presses with their books. "I thought that was a good idea," Mosley recalled. The Black Classic publisher, Paul Coates, was happy to get the book. Reviewers were largely happy with it as well; in *Library Journal* (December 1996), Michael Rogers, for example, declared *Gone Fishin'* a "more spiritual" novel than the previous Easy Rawlins books, and one "that reaches into the characters' pasts to reveal their souls." In the *New York Times* (January

26, 1997), Bill Kent warned that readers would be disappointed with the novel's "plodding Southern Gothic" aspect, but he found the final armed confrontation between Mouse and Reese significant—"a confrontation that curses our hero with a morally ambiguous vision of fathers and sons, and the sins that bind them together."

RL's Dream (1995) is Mosley's first venture outside the crime novel. It is a tribute to Robert Johnson, the blues legend who is said to have inspired modern rock-'n'-roll. Set in New York rather than Los Angeles, it is the story of an aged Mississippi Delta blues musician, Soupspoon Wise, who, on his quest to find the secret of Johnson's music, is made homeless and is taken in by a young woman who provides him with illegal health insurance to treat his cancer. Paula L. Woods, writing in the *San Francisco Review of Books* (October 1995), found *RL's Dream* to be "a masterful extension of the themes of communal connection, memory, and the meaning of friendship explored in the Easy Rawlins mystery novels." She maintained, however, that "*RL's Dream* clearly stands on its own merits as a mesmerizing and redemptive tale of friendship, love, and forgiveness. . . . [It is] the author's finest achievement to date."

Bob McCullough, who interviewed Mosley for *Publishers Weekly* (May 23, 1994), reported that the novelist writes for about three hours every morning before paying visits to friends and colleagues. Mosley told McCullough that he learns more about writing with each new novel, including what not to put in a book: "If you're writing a scene, you're writing about one particular thing that's going on. . . . But to write that scene, there may be ninety-nine other things going on at that time that are assumed, and you have to know about every one of them. I find that when I'm unhappy with what I've done, most of the time what's happened is that one or two of those things that need to be assumed has crept into the writing." Mosley also told McCullough, "I'd like to be remembered in the canon of genre writers in this field. I'd like my name to be mentioned with Raymond Chandler, Hammett, Ross McDonald, people like that. If people mention my race, I won't be unhappy."

In *Always Outnumbered, Always Outgunned* (1997), Mosley created another new protagonist, one who sets out "to explore the implications of moral action in a society that has lost all purchase on the spirit of the law," Sven Birkirts wrote in the *New York Times Book Review* (November 9, 1997). Socrates Fortlow is a man who has killed. But he is on a quest to try to "find the springs of his own honor and decency, even as he knows that there are old wrongs that cannot be righted," Birkerts observed. "His quest is that of the Christian as well as that of the moral philosopher, but one would have to theorize a good deal to establish this. For *Always Outnumbered, Always Outgunned* is a book of rough talk and strong gesture." Socrates administers comfort to the dying and tough love to Darryl, a boy he tries to guide. He also helps rid the

community of crime, always remembering what prison does to people. "Once you go to prison you belong there," he says. In the *New York Times* (December 29, 1997), Richard Bernstein wrote, "Socrates has new rules now, and as we see them realized on the hard ground where he lives, we gain a sustained and compelling view of a struggle for redemption we won't soon forget." Mosley wrote about Socrates again in *Walkin' the Dog*.

In *Blue Light* (1998), Mosley chose to draw from a genre—science fiction—through which he felt he could best express a spiritual message. Set in the San Francisco area in the 1960s, it is the story of what happens after a mysterious blue light called "God's tears" has touched certain people, killing them, driving them crazy, or infusing them with preternatural abilities. One of the people who has survived the experience is Orde, who becomes a prophet and guru to the other "blues," 16 in number. The narrator, Chance, not a blue but an obedient disciple of Orde's, was a Ph.D. candidate driven to suicidal despair: "I spoke the white man's language. I dreamed his dreams. But when I woke up, no one recognized me." Another of the blues is Horace LaFontaine, a black man who has been resurrected a second after his death by the blue light and whose body is possessed by Gray Man. "Until the novel's final clash, LaFontaine remains a tortured, wretched shell, whose spirit is imprisoned in the 'Attica cell' of Gray Man's mind," Mel Watkins wrote in the *New York Times Book Review* (November 15, 1998). It is "the internal war for dominion between Gray Man (death) and Horace (life) and the blues' struggle to escape Gray Man's relentless attempt to annihilate them, that inform and adumbrate this allegorical tale." Watkins concluded that Mosley may be saying that we missed our chance for "atonement and reconciliation" during the 1960s.

McCullough described Walter Mosley as being "affable" and "thoughtful" with "an almost jovial nature," and he noted that it was "easy to imagine the amiable author as a more intellectual version of his fictional alter ego." Mosley is a member of the Executive Board of the PEN American Center, and he is on the board of directors of the National Book Awards. A film version of *Devil in a Blue Dress*, starring Denzel Washington as Easy Rawlins, was made by Jonathan Demme.
—C.T. / S.Y.

SUGGESTED READING: *Chicago Tribune* V p1+ Aug. 24, 1992, with photo; *Library Journal* p144 Dec. 1996; *New York Times* C p13+ Sep. 4, 1990, with photo; *New York Times Book Review* p18 June 16, 1996, with photo; *People* p105+ Sep. 7, 1992, with photos; *Publishers Weekly* p67+ May 23, 1994, with photo; *San Francisco Review of Books* p12 Oct. 1995; *Vanity Fair* p46+ Feb. 1993, with photo

SELECTED BOOKS: *Devil in a Blue Dress*, 1990; *A Red Death*, 1991; *A White Butterfly*, 1992; *Black Betty*, 1994; *RL's Dream*, 1995; *A Little Yellow Dog*, 1996; *Always Outnumbered, Always Outgunned,* 1997; *Gone Fishin'*, 1997; *Blue Light*, 1998; *Walkin' the Dog 1999*

Mura, David

June 17, 1952– Nonfiction writer

Born near Chicago, David Mura, a sansei (third-generation) Japanese-American essayist, has written two important books exploring his Asian-American identity through the focal points of cultural memory and sexuality. The first of these, *Turning Japanese: Memoirs of a Sansei* (1991), is an account of the observations he made while spending a year in Tokyo in the 1980s with his wife, a white woman he had met while a student at Grinnell College. The second, *Where the Body Meets Memory: An Odyssey of Race, Sexuality, and Identity* (1996), combines reflections on his upbringing with personal confessions about his sexual obsessiveness during the 1970s and 1980s, interpreting this behavior in the light of cultural constructions of sexuality. *Turning Japanese* was chosen by the *New York Times* as one of the outstanding books of 1991. Mura has also published several collections of poetry and has written performance pieces in collaboration with the African-American writer Alexs Pate. In 1994 he was one of 10 writers to have received the $105,000 Writers Award from the Lila Wallace–Reader's Digest Fund.

David Mura was born in Great Lakes, Illinois, on June 17, 1952, the son of Tom K. and Tesuko Mura, a nisei (second-generation Japanese-American) couple who, during World War II, had been incarcerated in U.S. government internment camps—Ichiro in Arkansas and Wyoming and Tesuko in Idaho. The family's original name, Uyemura, had been shortened to Mura "for better bylines" by David's father, who worked his way up from a job as a nurseryman/gardener to a position as a writer for the International News Service. The elder Mura had also served as editor of the *Nisei Vue*, a short-lived magazine chronicling the experience of his generation in the United States after World War II. After their release from the internment camps, the Muras moved to Chicago, where David grew up in a close-knit community. As he wrote in his book *Where the Body Meets Memory: An Odyssey of Race, Sexuality and Identity*, during his childhood in Chicago he lived "surrounded by relatives and other Japanese Americans, going to the Japanese American Congregationalist Church, marching as a bugler in the Nisei Drum and Bugle Corps, which practiced at the Uptown Buddhist Church. I lived in our little ethnic enclave cozily unconscious of race." When David was eight, the Muras moved to

suburban Morton Grove, upon Tom's having secured a position in the communications division of the American Medical Association. As David matured, he experienced an unsettling suspicion that his parents had erected an intimidating zone of secrecy around matters involving both sexuality and their internment-camp experiences, topics that helped shape the tone of his later writings about the body and the concept of otherness. Awareness of this secrecy is crystallized in a poem he dedicated to his mother, "An Argument: On 1942," in which he wrote:

> Yes, Mother hid tins of *tsukemono* [Japanese pickles] and eel
> beneath the bed. And when the last was clamped tight her lips, growing thinner and thinner.
> But cancer not the camps made her throat

Mura reversed this allusion to color in a passage he wrote for *Where the Body Meets Memory*, in which he reflected on the allure of the forbidden—specifically, on discovering his father's cache of *Playboy* magazines in his parents' bedroom closet: "The images there, the beautiful white bodies, are not too far away for me to dream of, though they seem beyond my touching. By coming back to them again and again, perhaps I am completing a path of desire that my father started, driving further into the psyche of America, piercing beyond his sense of sexual possibility."

The typical growing pains of adolescence were complicated in Mura's case as he grappled with conflicting claims of Asian versus American identity, especially as implied in images of women as class- and race-codified commodities of erotic desire. "It's difficult to underestimate how much as a teenager I wanted to fit in, how deeply I assumed a basically white middle-class identity," he continued, adding later, "I was aware of racial differences in standards of beauty, that my sexual desires were crossing racial lines. Yet I had no one to talk with about this, nor any language to describe it, even to myself. Since I was so desperate to deny my racial identity, I never sought to break out of this zone of silence, to become more conscious of how race or ethnicity affected my life and my desires."

As a high-school student, Mura became drawn to language and literature, though he remembers being baffled by an assignment to read Henry James's *Portrait of a Lady*, a book whose locales and "prolix, August prose" he found foreign. He abandoned the assignment in favor of James Joyce's *Portrait of the Artist as a Young Man*, which more nearly mirrored the emotional and spiritual upheavals surrounding his nascent sexuality, leading him to identify with the prurient interests of Stephen Daedalus. "I was an upstart, and no one, really, likes an upstart, including perhaps the upstart himself," declared Mura, who recalled that he grew more self-conscious during this period, adopting the attitude of "the loner, someone drifting away from the hubbub of the crowd, alluding vaguely to a wider world, attuned to a quieter, more meditative mode." It was in this arena of conflicting demands between doing the right thing and indulging in sexual-obsessive fantasy that he began to develop the introspective habits of a writer. At first, Mura was especially drawn toward writing poetry, though he also entertained the idea of being an attorney who specialized in poverty law.

Mura began writing poetry seriously during the 1970s, and in 1977 he won the Fanny Fay Wood Memorial Prize from the American Academy of Poets. In 1985 he won a National Endowment for the Arts Literature Fellowship. Two years later he was one of the winners of the 1987 new poets' competition sponsored by the *Nation* magazine (April 25, 1987). His poetry collection *After We Lost Our Way* (1989) was a National Poetry Series winner. His most recent book of poetry, *The Colors of Desire* (1995), won the Carl Sandburg Literary Award from the Friends of the Chicago Library. In the meantime he received his bachelor's degree, with honors, from Grinnell College in 1974, took graduate courses in English at the University of Minnesota–Twin Cities from 1974 to 1979, and received his master's of fine arts degree from Vermont College in 1991. His first professional position was as a creative writing instructor in the COMPAS artists-in-residence program in the Minneapolis area; he eventually became the associate director of its literature program. In 1982 he joined The Loft, an alternative school, as a faculty member, later becoming president of its board of directors. In 1990 he became a member of the faculty of St. Olaf College, in Northfield, Minnesota.

Describing the origins of his poetic sensibility, Mura told Daniel Kane in a "Poets On Poetry" interview for the on-line *Teachers & Writers Poets Chat* (November 1999): "I feel I'm very much an American poet. I write a lot about the experiences of my family in America, and what it feels like to become American. In that way you might say I come out of the tradition of Whitman and W[illiam] C[arlos] Williams. But my influences aren't so neatly divided. I look at Eliot's *Wasteland* [*sic*], and I read it as one of the original performance poems of the twentieth century. . . . On one level I've been a proponent of modernist and postmodernist techniques, but my own poetic imagination tends to run much more toward traditional formal devices." Mura credits Wallace Stevens's blank verse, the poetry of Seamus Heaney, and even various translations of Dante as offering inspiration for his own poetry.

While Mura believes that injecting identity politics into literature can truncate the understanding of a poem for both reader and writer, he also finds such an experience useful on some levels. As he told Daniel Kane in his "Poets on Poetry" interview: "There are many ways to read a poem. If someone reads my work with the consciousness of 'I am reading a Japanese-American writer,' I feel that such a reading is useful and valid; it reveals certain aspects of the work and helps them to understand it. At the same time this lens doesn't limit the number of interpretive opportunities. It's not the only way to approach the work." Mura added: "Poetry is also giving voice to all different sides of an issue. For me, political poetry is not so much about espousing a view point. It's really about trying to write about the human experience of going through a political/social event, which is a different phenomena than proclaiming an opinion."

In 1991 Atlantic Monthly Press published Mura's first major book, *Turning Japanese: Memoirs of a Sansei*, in which he elucidated his struggles with identity, sexual compulsion, and history. Grants from the National Endowment for the Arts, the U.S. / Japan Friendship Commission, and the Bush Foundation had enabled him to spend a year in Japan, from which his grandparents had emigrated in 1908. Like many second- and third-generation Americans, Mura initially had no particular desire to visit his ancestral homeland, especially since the tribulations of the internment and war years had been so instrumental in Americanizing (more correctly, "de-Japanizing" his parents). But eventually, he came to feel differently, and the voyage was one of discovery for Mura. *Turning Japanese* emerged as the first such memoir from the sansei generation. Mura explained the reasons for his book: "I didn't want to be a mere tourist. . . . Certainly, I didn't want to go to Japan simply as a sightseer or an information gatherer, making the humanist assumption that human beings are all alike beneath the skin, all desire the same things, all think in the same basic ways. Because of my background, I saw myself as someone with an ability to look at Japan without the blinders of prejudice and ideology that hampered many of the accounts I had read. I did not realize that my sense of being able to write without the blinders of prejudice and ideology was chimerical. Instead, Japan was to help me understand more fully my own blinders." The trip would also allow Mura to achieve a stricter literary purpose, too. While reading such "voices of power" as T. S. Eliot and John Donne, Mura was struck by the realization that he, a Japanese-American, was an "unlikely candidate for a poet of the English language" and began to identify with another person of color in similar circumstances, the Caribbean poet Derek Walcott. Mura concluded that his time in Japan would give him the opportunity to "learn to write out of my sense of duality, or rather plurality, to write not in slavish imitation of the European tradition but to use it and combine it with other elements of my background, trying to achieve a difficult balance. In order to understand who I was and who I would become, I would have to listen to voices that my father, or T. S. Eliot or Robert Lowell, did not dream of. Voices of my family, of Japan, of my own wayward and unassimilated past. In the world of the tradition, I was unimagined. I would have to imagine myself."

In *Turning Japanese*, Mura recorded in meticulous detail his observations about the year he and his wife, Susie, spent in Japan. They lived in a small flat in Tokyo but made numerous side trips to such places as Hiroshima and even the Philippines. Most memorable was his visit to Shingu, his grandparents' ancestral home, "and the vision of them waving outside a temple, underneath a cedar, beside a pop machine glowing in the dark." Even for readers not particularly interested in his glosses on ethnic identity, the book offers a colorful portrait of daily life in Japan during the 1980s, a period of enormous economic growth and paradigm shift. As Mura wrote: "Japan allowed me to see myself, America, and the world from a perspective that was not white American. I do not feel as bound now by my national identity, do not feel that being an American somehow separates me from the rest of the world. He added, "In Japan, I saw how much I am not reflected in American culture, how much it is not my culture." The experience also helped Mura come to a greater appreciation of the position of his nisei parents, a "deeper understanding of how far they had to travel in their childhood, from the mainly Japanese world of their *Issei* parents to the America of their schools, the streets of L.A. and Seattle."

Critical response to the book was positive, and *Turning Japanese* was named by the *New York Times* as one of the notable books of 1991. It had been earlier reviewed in that publication (March 31, 1991) by novelist Jay McInerney, who pronounced to be an author "quite good on the sexual politics of race" and one whose "general observations on the landscape and customs can be fresh and revealing." Reviewer Kunio Francis Tanabe wrote in the *Washington Post* (April 21, 1991) that "*Turning Japanese* is an honest, thought-provoking portrait of a young man who happens to be a very interesting fellow" and who describes his ancestral land "with a poet's sensibility and an unfailing eye for irony." He noted how the author's initial euphoria soon gave way to "a realization—more an epiphany or *satori*—of how American he is, 'how deeply rock and roll and football and Whitman and Huck Finn' reside in him."

In 1996 Anchor Books / Doubleday published Mura's second nonfiction book, *Where the Body Meets Memory: An Odyssey of Race, Sexuality, and Identity*. Asian-American playwright David Henry Hwang offered a supportive blurb: "With the passion of a revolutionary, the insight of an empath, and the redemptive touch of a poet, David Mura transforms the secret lives of Asian American men into a fiery and compassionate work of art." In this memoir, Mura interrupted his own autobiographical musings—a section called "All American Boy"—to meditate on the world of exclusion his father had faced a generation earlier; this section is called "A Nisei Father." Drawing his inspiration from personal conversations and from letters his father had written to and from his parents in the internment camps, Mura tries to imagine his father before his marriage, as an 18-year-old bound for Chicago in 1945, wondering whether fellow passengers viewed him as they did the Japanese with whom the country was at war. Driving his father to his 50th high-school reunion, at the Disneyland Hyatt in Anaheim, David Mura steers the conversation to the internment camps and begins to learn some of the details denied him for so many years by the family's shame and reticence. The younger man realizes a kinship with the older man in realizing how the two of them were possessed of similar ambitions when faced with the responsibilities of supporting a family. "My father laughs, a moment of mutual recognition about fatherhood and what it means," he wrote. He also learns that his father had also made some effort at writing poetry around the age of 20 and that he had "lived with two beings inside of him": the American striving for respectability, studying Shakespeare and attending the Episcopal church, and the other self of the internment camps and of the "old-world" culture of soy sauce and rice, of issues of loyalty and traditional music. "All those years in Kalamazoo," Mura wrote, "my father's Japanese self seemed to be gasping for breath, its being gradually forgotten. This self believed in the quickness of spirits, the unspoken messages both of the silence that rests in the Japanese language, in the messages of gestures and hovering implications, in the visions that reside in dreams. This self, like his mother, was becoming a ghost." He is amazed to see the "freshness and exuberance" of *Nisei Vue*, the magazine his father edited immediately after World War II, and at finding stories stashed away much as he had found the stashed-away *Playboy* magazines years earlier.

The third section of *Where the Body Meets Memory* is entitled "The Descent." With an introductory passage from Joyce's *Portrait of the Artist as a Young Man*, about Stephen Daedalus, who "wandered up and down the dark slimy streets peering into the gloom of lanes and doorways . . . [and who] wanted to sin with another of his kind," Mura details his own "descent" into sexual obsession and craving, from his early days as a Grinnell student in 1970 and his junior-year meeting with Susie, the woman who would become his wife. The passages express Mura's literary evolution, his finding the reading of Yeats and Rilke superior to the "hollow boredom" of the commuters while accompanying his father on a Chicago commuter train. Mura detailed his graduate work at the University of Minneapolis in 1974, and the discovery of new literary heroes in the persons of John Berryman, Robert Lowell, and Delmore Schwartz, "all manic-depressives, brilliant talkers, hard drinkers, poets who left wrecks and wives in their wake, the hard shimmering detritus of genius." This was a period of sexual experimentation, too, with partner-swapping and visits to a gay bathhouse with his wife and a gay male friend. "We were busy bursting past boundaries, experimenting, abandoning our sense of propriety, the morals of our parents. I told myself this was part of my investigations as a poet, part of some romantic credo imitating Byron, taking inspiration from the legends of

Dylan Thomas or John Berryman, poetic and sexual mentors. The truth was, I could not stop." Another section of *Where the Body Meets Memory* is called "Jinnosuke's Biwa," in which Mura meditates on his grandfather, who eventually returned to Japan—another "relocation." Mura recalled listening to traditional songs and trying to absorb them into his being: "Like my grandmother, like my grandfather, I'm blessed and cursed with images of the future and the past. I hear the camps in these lines. . . . I am part of the Tara clan that vanished, defeated by treachery and folly and pride, and the force of fate, our earthly presence reduced to syllables in an old man's mouth. I learn the lessons I need to go out into the world, to take this poetry to the ear of strangers." Ironically, Mura came to a conclusion that seems to justify the very "zone of silence" that he had found so unpalatable as an adolescent. Reflecting on how he would transmit important information to his own daughter, he wrote, "Should I tell her of my own desires for a 'hallucinatory whiteness,' of how such a desire fueled in my twenties a rampant promiscuity and addiction to pornography, to the 'beautiful' bodies of white women? These elements of my story are all too much to expect her to take in. They should not even be written down. They should be kept hidden, unspoken. . . . In the end, what I want to give to my daughter are not *my* answers, but the courage to ask her own questions and to keep asking them, no matter how confusing, frightening, or threatening they may be."

Where the Body Meets Memory did not impress some reviewers as favorably as had his earlier book. An anonymous *Publishers Weekly* reviewer was uncomfortable with the disjointed confessional style in what purported to be a more serious critique, writing, "Although this frank account of his difficulties gives circumstantial evidence of the effects of racial discrimination on Japanese families and individuals, the link is somewhat weakened by the fact that many of the very problems he attributes to it—e.g., rebellion against parents, infidelity—are common in all groups; and the disordered nature of Mura's discourse lacks the impressive style of his acclaimed earlier work, *Turning Japanese: Memoirs of a Sansei*."

In 1994 Mura was one of 10 writers who each received $105,000 as Writers Awards from the Lila Wallace–Reader's Digest Fund. Among the other writers so honored were Christopher Durang, Ian Frazier, Jessica Hagedorn, bell hooks, and W. S. Merwin. The grants enabled the winners to work with nonprofit cultural and community organizations trying to foster a greater appreciation of contemporary literature. Mura has also been a vocal participant in the Asian-American community's own dialogue about identity and its place in the larger society, serving since 1991 as artistic director of the Asian American Renaissance Conference and in 1991 and 1992 as president of the Center for Arts Criticism. In 1992, during a wave of xenophobia perhaps fueled in part by books like Michael

Crichton's *Rising Sun* and George Friedman and Meredith Lebard's *The Coming War With Japan*, he wrote an op-ed piece for the *New York Times* (April 29, 1992) entitled "Bashed in the U.S.A." In it, he railed against the "Orientalism" that hauled out ancient stereotypes of the Japanese as being "duplicitous and cruel." "Often, when white Americans tells me they are not racist," he wrote, "I reply that I grew up thinking of myself as less than 100 percent American. In certain ways I hated the way I looked and felt ashamed of my heritage. If I took racist values from society, I ask them, how is it they did not?" In another *Times* essay (August 22, 1996), entitled "How America Unsexes the Asian Male," he complained about the popular image of Asian men as eunuchs and of Asian women as "exotic, submissive, and sensual." A discussion of this state of affairs with the African-American novelist Alexis Pate—who replied, "And black men are the sexual demons"—led to the two collaborating on "Slowly, This," a performance piece broadcast on public television, in which the two men talked about their lives as men of color and as writers in a society still guided by white male hegemony.

—E. M.

SUGGESTED READING: *American Poetry Review* p36 Sep. 1989; *Booklist* p732 Dec. 15, 1994; *Far Eastern Economic Review* p45 Aug. 1, 1991; *Library Journal* p107 Jan.1995; *New York Times* A p25 Apr. 29, 1992, A p22 May 20, 1992, C p9 Dec. 22, 1994, C p9 Aug. 22, 1996, C p9 Sep. 19, 1996, C p7 Sep. 26, 1996, II p20 Jan. 5, 1997; *Nation* p544+ Apr. 25, 1987; *New York Times Book Review* p10 Mar. 31, 1991, with photo, p18 July 28, 1996; *New Yorker* p104 Apr. 15, 1991; *Partisan Review* p186+ Winter 1994; *Publishers Weekly* p49 Mar. 11, 1996; *Washington Post Book World* X p6 Apr. 21, 1991, with photo, X p12 May 31, 1992, X p11 July 28, 1996; *Who's Who Among Asian Americans*, 1994-95; *Woodhouse Library* (Aquinas College, on-line)

SELECTED WORKS: Nonfiction—*A Male Grief: Notes on Pornography and Addiction*, 1987; *Turning Japanese: Memories of a Sansei*, 1991; *Where the Body Meets Memory: An Odyssey of Race, Sexuality, and Identity*, 1996; Performance Pieces—*Slowly This* (with Alexs Pate), 1996; Poetry—*After We Lost Our Way*, 1989; *The Colors of Desire*, 1995

Murray, Albert

May 12, 1916– Novelist; nonfiction writer

"Albert Murray may well be African America's undiscovered national treasure," Warren Carson wrote in the *African American Review* in 1993, speaking for the fans of the man Sanford Pinsker called "the black intellectuals' maverick patriarch" in the *Virginia Quarterly Review* some three years later. A novelist, essayist, music historian, and public intellectual, Murray has produced three novels, four essay collections, a memoir, and dozens of articles, none of them published before his 54th birthday. He also collaborated with Count Basie on the latter's autobiography, published in 1986. As a social critic, Murray has leveled spirited attacks against social scientists and others who promote what he feels are misperceptions about the black community based on academic theory rather than experience. In all of his work, Murray has celebrated African-American tradition and achievement, phenomena that he regards as integral to the American experience as a whole. Murray's sensibility is firmly grounded in jazz and the blues, and the rhythms of those musical idioms have informed his books, including *The Omni-Americans* (1970), which "may be the most important book on black-white relations in the United States, indeed on American culture, published in this generation," according to the novelist Walker Percy, and *Stomping the Blues*, which the critic Stanley Crouch has called "the most eloquent book ever written about African-American music." More recently, his 1996 collection, *The Blue Devils of Nada* (1996), included essays on seminal figures in 20th-century American culture, including Duke Ellington, Louis Armstrong, Romare Bearden, and Ernest Hemingway. The following year marked the publication of *The Seven League Boots*, the third novel in Murray's so-called "Scooter trilogy"—the earlier ones were *Train Whistle Guitar* (1974) and *The Spyglass Tree* (1991). Also in 1997, Murray was inducted into the American Academy of Arts and Letters.

Albert Lee Murray was born on May 12, 1916 in Nokomis, Alabama, and adopted soon after birth by Hugh Murray, by turns a sharecropper, railroad crosstie cutter, dockworker, and sawmill hand, and Mattie (James) Murray, a homemaker. As Henry Louis Gates pointed out in "King of Cats," his essay on Murray published in the *New Yorker* (April 8, 1998): "Murray's birth parents were, as he slowly learned, well educated and securely middle class—people who belonged to an entirely different social stratum from that of his adoptive parents. His natural father, John Young, came from a well-established family in town. His natural mother [a 'Miss Graham'] had been attending Tuskegee as a boarding student. . . . When she learned that a close encounter with John Young had left her pregnant, she had to leave town—'because of the disgrace,' Murray explains." Following the death

of their mother (Mattie Murray's sister), three additional children, who were older than Albert, joined the Murray family.

Albert Murray grew up on the outskirts of Mobile in a neighborhood called Magazine Point, where, as Mark Feeney reported in his profile of Murray for the *Boston Globe Magazine* (August 1, 1993), he "knew a world that was at once intensely parochial . . . and surprisingly cosmopolitan." "From Pullman porters and black World War I veterans, there were tales of cities far away," Feeney continued. "Murray and his friends took pride in such heroes as the young Satchel Paige (who often pitched in Mobile) and the blues singers who would appear at local juke joints." Murray's love of storytelling was a natural outgrowth of his environment, for he, like the protagonist of his novel *Train Whistle Guitar*, spent time "sitting around the fireplace just listening to people talk," as Murray told *Current Biography* in 1994.

Murray attended the Mobile County Training School, whose principal, Benjamin Francis Baker, had a strong influence on the boy, impressing upon him and the other students that their obligation to past and future generations of African-Americans required them to succeed in their endeavors. At school, Murray was as interested in athletics as he was in classroom work. He was active in track and field events and football, and he was captain of the basketball team as well as a pitcher for the local baseball team during the summer months. He also performed so well in his studies that he was voted best all-around student at the Mobile County Training School and was awarded a tuition scholarship to college. After graduating from the school, he enrolled at the Tuskegee Institute, in Tuskegee, Alabama, in the fall of 1935. As a college student, Murray immersed himself in the works of Ernest Hemingway, William Faulkner, and Thomas Mann, the literary giants of the day. He also nurtured what he has called his "consuming passion" for the music of the jazz pioneers Duke Ellington and Count Basie. Ahead of Murray at Tuskegee was Ralph Ellison, who would later write the groundbreaking novel *Invisible Man*. (Ellison and Murray were to become friends years later, in New York City.) Murray received his B.S. degree from Tuskegee in 1939.

After doing graduate work at the University of Michigan, in 1940 Murray returned to Tuskegee, where he taught literature and composition and directed student theatrical productions. In 1943 he enlisted in the United States Army air force for the duration of World War II. In 1951 he was again assigned to active duty, which included a four-year tour as air force ROTC associate professor of air science and tactics, a two-and-a-half-year tour in Morocco, and station assignments in California and Massachusetts. ("You want Colin Powell? I've done that too," he jovially remarked to a *Publishers Weekly* [February 26, 1996] interviewer just before his 80th birthday.) Murray took advantage of the opportunity, afforded him by his airman's status, to travel both domestically and abroad. "I could go to Rome. I went to Istanbul," he told Mark Feeney. Having aircraft at his disposal proved beneficial in other ways as well. "We used to have a group of guys who were real collectors of Ellington records and all the other good stuff that was [around] then," Murray's friend and protégé Stanley Crouch quoted him as saying in his book *Notes of a Hanging Judge* (1990). "We would take one of those planes, which you could do in those days, and fly a long ways as part of your training or keeping up your skill, and get the latest Ellington, say, and fly right back."

Between periods of active military service, Murray found time both to teach at Tuskegee and to continue his formal education, receiving his M.A. degree from New York University, in New York City, in 1948. While living in New York, he made, in his words, "regular weekly rounds to hear [the jazz greats] Dizzy Gillespie, Charlie Parker, and young Miles Davis on Fifty-second Street." He also studied at Northwestern University, the University of Chicago, Ohio State University, and the University of Paris, among other institutions. Following his retirement from the air force, in 1962, with the rank of major, Murray adopted New York City as his home base and held a series of visiting professorships at institutions that include Colgate University, in Hamilton, New York, where he was O'Connor Professor of Literature and also received an honorary doctorate of letters; Columbia University and Barnard College, in New York City; Emory University, in Atlanta; and the University of Massachusetts at Boston. He also committed himself to writing, publishing essays in a variety of journals.

Some of those essays appeared in Murray's first book, *The Omni-Americans: New Perspectives on Black Experience and American Culture*, which also featured new material and which was published when Murray was 54 years old. He asserted in the book that many fashionable sociological theories about black Americans, whether sympathetic to blacks or not, are inaccurate, based on little actual experience, and overly concerned with portraying blacks as a people rendered pathological by their experience in the United States. He further argued that blacks who internalize and espouse those theories are as guilty as the (usually white) social scientists who concoct them; that African-American culture, a historically resilient entity, is a much more nurturing and positive force than it is often given credit for being; and that blacks, linked to other Americans by bloodlines and culture alike, have both shaped and been shaped by American society, which Murray calls "incontestably mulatto." Among those whose works are singled out for criticism in the book are the novelists Richard Wright and William Styron and the statesman Daniel Patrick Moynihan, whose 1965 Labor Department study, *The Negro Family: A Case for National Action*, presented what Murray considered to be a distorted picture in showing the black family as an institution ruined by centuries of racial discrimination.

The Omni-Americans received generally favorable reviews. According to Robert A. Gross of *Newsweek* (March 23, 1970), Murray "writes with a fine combination of iconoclasm, polemic, and wit" and his "approach merges common sense, historical understanding, and cultural criticism." Expressing a different view, the black scholar J. Saunders Redding wrote in the *New York Times Book Review* (May 3, 1970), "The pieces [that make up *The Omni-Americans*] never should have been brought together in a book. They bear no logical relationship either to each other or to an intellectual point of view. Read all at once, they leave the reader wondering what the author really thinks, what his convictions are. . . . The subtitle of *The Omni-Americans* is a put-on. Perhaps the book itself is too." But the conclusion drawn by Robert Coles in the *New Yorker* (October 17, 1970) was more typical: "Every American reporter and critic and social scientist could profit from this book."

South to a Very Old Place appeared in 1971. Written in the second person, the book recounts a trip through the South taken by Murray as part of an assignment for *Harper's* magazine; the narrative intersperses conversations with childhood acquaintances and noted southern writers with bits of autobiography, observations about modern fiction, and condemnations of what he considers fallacious thinking about race, on the part of everyone from Afrocentric militants to ostensibly well-meaning white liberals. Two of his assertions are that American blacks will find their true heritage not in Africa but in the accomplishments of their ancestors in the United States, and that "your compassion-oriented white liberal . . . seems entirely unaware of the possibility that when he writes off outstanding Negroes . . . as tokens he could well be creating an effect on young people's horizons of aspiration that may be even more restrictive than segregation. After all, brutal exclusion often inspires determination, whereas the downgrading of achievement could easily lead to exasperation and cynicism."

The book is, above all else, a homage to black southern values and traditions. In what might be considered vintage Murray, the author reconstructed a discussion about race, held by several of his Alabama "homefolks," and compared the interplay of voices to a jazz performance, thereby tracing the rhythms of jazz to the people who produced it: "'Hey, man, me, man (*One trumpetlike statement begins*), you know how come I don't be paying no mind to none of that old talk?' . . . 'Hey!' (*this could be another trumpet, say with a parenthetical mute, or it could be an alto, or a getaway tenor*), 'Hey, but you know something else some of this old stuff put me in the mind of?' . . . 'You and me both' (*you remember this as a baritone statement, barbershop Amen-corner baritone*)." Murray then called on the black leaders of the time to draw inspiration from jazz and blues, which he terms "music for good times earned in adversity" and "a sound track for an affirmative lifestyle," when seeking advances for their people—to bring to their struggles the grit, resourcefulness, and capacity for improvisation that go into the creation of those musical forms.

The critical response to *South to a Very Old Place* was similar to that accorded *The Omni-Americans*. "[Murray] charms, provokes, amuses, and spreads wisdom at every stop," Robert A. Gross wrote in the *Saturday Review* (January 22, 1972). "And from this potpourri he creates a disciplined piece of art: a reflective and elegant rendering of a man's coming to terms with his roots." Toni Morrison declared in the *New York Times Book Review* (January 2, 1972), "It is black music no less than literary criticism and historical analysis that gives [Murray's] work its authenticity, its emotional vigor, and its tenacious hold on the intellect." *South to a Very Old Place* was nominated for a National Book Award.

In 1972 Murray delivered the ninth Paul Anthony Brick lecture series at the University of Missouri, giving three lectures: "The Social Function of the Storyteller," in which he compared the writer to the fictional hero, declaring that each must be capable of improvisation (as must the jazz / blues performer) in recognizing and overcoming conflict; "The Dynamics of Heroic Action," in which he derided naturalism and protest fiction for viewing circumstance as all-important and thus making the actions of the hero irrelevant; and "The Blues and the Fable in the Flesh," a discussion of characters, such as Homer's Odysseus and certain Hemingway protagonists, who meet Murray's definition of a "blues hero." The lectures were published in 1973 in the collection *The Hero and the Blues*, which, according to Stanley Crouch, advanced "a fine literary theory." James Alan McPherson, in the *Atlantic Monthly* (December 1974), praised Murray for "[taking] to task those writers who abandon to the social sciences the storyteller's role as myth-maker and value-maker."

Elizabeth Schultz, writing in the *Dictionary of Literary Biography* (1985), speculated that Murray, "perhaps conscious of the irony that he included neither black heroes nor heroines, neither black writers nor women writers among his examples of storytellers and their heroes [in *The Hero and the Blues*], . . . decided to tell his own story, to create his own fictional hero." The result was *Train Whistle Guitar* (1974), Murray's first novel. An autobiographical work, the book tells the story of Scooter, a black boy coming of age in the 1920s in Gasoline Point, Alabama. In relating Scooter's adventures and the details of life in Gasoline Point, Murray celebrated, as he had in his nonfiction, the nurturing quality of the black southern community. According to James Alan McPherson, Murray also succeeded in creating characters who conform to his own definition of the blues hero: "[Murray's] characters] confront, acknowledge, and proceed, in spite of as well as in terms of 'the ugliness and meanness inherent in the human condition.' What is more, they do it with style. . . . For those who

seek an uncluttered understanding of the quality of life among black Americans, *Train Whistle Guitar* offers valuable insights." The novel received the Lillian Smith Award for Southern Fiction in 1974.

Since most of Murray's books use black musical idioms as a frame of reference for discussing other subjects, his editor at the McGraw-Hill company suggested that Murray—who had planned to follow *Train Whistle Guitar* with a sequel to the novel—instead write a book on the blues aesthetic. Murray took the suggestion and wrote *Stomping the Blues* (1976). A history as well as an explanation of the blues, containing scores of photographs complete with lengthy captions, the book won the American Society of Composers, Authors, and Publishers Award in 1977. In *Down Beat* (October 20, 1977), John McDonough criticized the book, complaining that Murray, in placing more emphasis on the instrumentation in blues than on vocalization, "never seems to realize that he is leaving blues behind him and proceeding into the larger world of jazz, of which the blues is only a small part." Numerous others, however, lauded Murray for arguing that the blues is a life-affirming, not defeatist, art form that requires skill and training and not merely unbridled emotion. Robert G. O'Meally, in a complimentary echo of John McDonough's observation, referred to *Stomping the Blues* in the *Washington Post* (October 17, 1993) as "one of the best teaching tools jazz has ever had."

The composer Alec Wilder recommended Murray as a co-writer for Count Basie's memoirs. In gathering material for the project, Murray spent the years following the publication of *Stomping the Blues* "hanging out with Basie," as he told *Current Biography*: "He didn't have time to pick out six months or something like that to work on his book. So . . . every time he came to New York, he would find time to work, and if he was going to be in certain other places long enough, and was not going to be inundated with local people, he would send for me. We went to Kansas City, so we could go and look at each landmark that was involved in that part of the story, in that part of his development. So I went there, and then I would go down to the Bahamas, where he lived. Well, that took about five years. Time just got away. . . . I didn't know how long it would take to edit these *tapes* that I [had]." As it turned out, the organization, writing, and editing of the book proved to be such a mammoth undertaking that Basie, who died in 1984, did not live to see his memoirs published.

Good Morning Blues: The Autobiography of Count Basie as Told to Albert Murray (1986) won considerable praise from critics. "Albert Murray . . . has assisted with research that puts Basie's more than half a century of music-making into a more accurate framework than could be expected from memory alone," a reviewer for *Choice* (July/August 1986) observed. "Murray's most valuable contribution, however, is the preservation of Basie's personality and character on the printed page." Amy Duncan, who evaluated the book for the *Christian Science Monitor* (February 7, 1986), declared, "Unquestionably, this is, and will continue to be, the definitive Basie book."

Murray's second novel, *The Spyglass Tree* (1991), focuses on Scooter—the protagonist of *Train Whistle Guitar*—as he attends college and grows to manhood in the 1930s. "Is Albert Murray America's best black writer?" Charles Monaghan asked in the *Washington Post Book World* (November 3, 1991). "There is certainly a case to be made for it, and his second novel . . . only makes the case stronger." In the *New York Times* (November 22, 1991), Michiko Kakutani gave the novel more qualified praise: "Although portions of *The Spyglass Tree* are mannered and forced . . . the book, as a whole, works beautifully to conjure up a vanished place and time. Like all good bildungsroman, it leaves the reader with a vivid portrait of a young man and his struggles to come to terms with his receding past and his beckoning future."

In February 1996, just three months shy of his 80th birthday, Murray saw three more of his books roll off the presses, two new releases and a reprint: Pantheon published both *The Seven League Boots*, the third novel in the "Scooter" series, and *The Blue Devils of Nada: A Contemporary American Approach to Aesthetic Statement*, a new collection of essays, while Vintage reprinted *The Hero and the Blues*, originally published in 1973.

The Blue Devils of Nada included essays about several artists Murray considers to have been important contributors to 20th-century aesthetics: Duke Ellington, Count Basie (who shares an affinity with Matisse, he claims), Louis Armstrong, Ernest Hemingway, and the painter Romare Bearden, who up until his death in 1988 was a close friend of Murray's. Reflecting on his own fiction in an early passage of that book, Murray writes: "I am not primarily concerned with recording what it is like or what it means to be a Southerner or even a down-home grandson of slaves. My concerns are more fundamentally existential, which is perhaps to say epical, if by epic we mean to suggest an account of a hero involved with elemental problems of survival rather than with social issues as such. In any case, my stories are really about what it means to be human. . . . [R]egional particulars— the idiomatic details, the down-home conventions, the provincial customs and folkways—must be *processed* into artistic statement, *stylized* into significance." An interpretation of Hemingway the storyteller as a "blues singer," though an unconventional approach, is justified by Murray, who wrote that Hemingway (who saw himself as an "honorary Negro") "wrote fiction that always expresses essentially the same fundamental sense of life as that which underlies the spirit of the blues. . . . Hemingway. . .did not write in terms of the blues, but what he wrote was the literary equivalent of blues music." Reviewing both new books for the *New York Times Book Review* (March 10, 1996), Charles Johnson noted Murray's intellectual continuity with Ralph Ellison's "blues es-

thetic" and praised *The Blue Devils of Nada* as a group of "wise and authoritative essays" that surpass Ellison's insights—and Murray's own, in *The Hero and the Blues*. "I hope," wrote Johnson, "that the publication [of these books] will be cause for widespread celebration. Like . . . Ralph Ellison, Mr. Murray . . . has always managed to navigate stylishly around what he calls 'the folklore of white supremacy' and the 'fakelore of black pathology.'" Murray has long been impatient with readers, liberal and otherwise, who seem to expect black writers to pontificate over their own problems; in a prologue to *The Blue Devils of Nada*, he lashed out at critics who feel that "unless brownskin U.S. writers are pissing and moaning about injustice they have nothing to say."

Johnson was less enthusiastic about Murray's novel, *The Seven League Boots*, acknowledging its elegant diction but dismissing it as a "novel without tension" that offered no conflict for its protagonist, Scooter, nor a sense of plot for readers to navigate. Likewise, Gene Seymour complained in the *Nation* (March 25, 1996) of a didactic prose "weighed down" with the need to convey an "imperious orthodoxy," in a "hermetically sealed novel of values whose sole purpose is to Uplift and Improve." Seymour added that "the elegiac fairy-tale wistfulness of *Train Whistle Guitar* has by *Boots* given way to a narrative approach best characterized as Horatio Alger with a swing beat." Despite their lack of enthusiasm for his fiction, neither Johnson nor Seymour deny Murray his stature in American letters. Johnson believes that Murray and his colleague Ellison, "a pair of Depression-era schoolmates from Tuskegee," have given us "some of the most original works of literary theory and practice in American letters since World War II."

In March 1997 the National Book Critics Circle gave Murray its Ivan Sandrof Award for lifetime achievement. In May he was inducted into the American Academy of Arts and Letters, and that November he was honored with the Langston Hughes Award of the City College of the City University of New York. Also that year, Murray appeared, with James Baldwin, Louis Farrakhan, O. J. Simpson, and others, as one of the subjects in *Thirteen Ways of Looking at a Black Man*, a book by Henry Louis Gates Jr. Here, Gates delivered an in-depth analysis of the intellectual symbiosis between Murray and Ralph Ellison and commented on their estrangement and eventual reconciliation. In "King of Cats," the essay that had earlier appeared in the *New Yorker*, Gates described Murray as "the most outrageous theorist of American culture," a polymath who "likes to elaborate on his points and elaborate on his elaborations, until you find that you have circumnavigated the globe and raced through the whole of post-Homeric literary history—and this is what he calls 'vamping till ready.'" As Gates added, "Every literary culture has its superego and its id; Albert Murray has the odd distinction of being both." Murray was also acknowledged by Stanley Crouch as the "intellectual hero" of Crouch's 1998 book *Always in Pursuit: Fresh American Perspectives*, in which Murray is praised for avoiding "the kind of social protest that we associate with Southern Negroes who feel it absolutely necessary to make sure that the shadows of hanging trees forever darken their pages, obscuring any recognition of family, religious ritual, adolescent whimsy, romance, the passing on of transcendent wisdom, and so on."

Albert Murray married Mozelle Menefee Murray, whom he met at Tuskegee, in 1941. The couple live in a book-filled apartment in Harlem. Although Murray's various physical ailments have turned the act of writing into "hard labor," as he has phrased it, he still works diligently. In a brief commentary on the medical problems of older adults, published in the *New York Times* (November 1, 1998), an 82-year-old Murray wrote, "I'm doing more than ever, but it's harder now. I'm in constant pain." He added that a "steady stream of visitors" offered compensation for his ills. "Contact with young people keeps me young." With Stanley Crouch, Rob Gibson, and the trumpeter Wynton Marsalis, Murray helps direct Jazz at Lincoln Center, in New York City, and he was a visiting professor at Washington and Lee University, in Virginia, in the fall of 1993.

Murray's daughter, Michele, has performed with the Alvin Ailey dance troupe; Albert Murray himself wrote program notes for Ailey—"such good ones, in fact," Stanley Crouch wrote, "that the master choreographer joked, 'Now I understand better what I've been trying to do all these years!'" In a similar vein, Duke Ellington once described his friend Murray as "an authority on soul from the days of old." "He doesn't have to look it up," Ellington wrote. "He already knows. If you want to know, look him up. He is the unsquarest person I know."

—C.T./E.M.

SUGGESTED READING: *Boston Globe Magazine* p15+ Aug. 1, 1993, with photos; *Nation* p25+ Mar. 25, 1996; *New Yorker* p70+ Apr. 8, 1996; *New York Times* C p15 Dec. 11, 1995, C p22 Apr. 3, 1996, with photo; *New York Times Book Review* p4 Mar. 10, 1996; *Publishers Weekly* p78+ Feb. 26, 1996, with photo; *Voice Literary Supplement* p17+ Feb. 1996, with photos; *Contemporary Literary Criticism* vol 73, 1993; Crouch, Stanley. *Notes of a Hanging Judge*, 1990; *Dictionary of Literary Biography* vol 38, 1985; *Who's Who Among Black Americans*, 1994-95; Maguire, Robert S., ed. *Conversations with Albert Murray*, 1997

SELECTED BOOKS: Fiction—*Train Whistle Guitar*, 1974; *The Spyglass Tree*, 1991; *The Seven League Boots*, 1997; Nonfiction—*The Omni-Americans: New Perspectives on Black Experience and American Culture*, 1970; *South to a Very Old Place*, 1971; *The Hero and the Blues*, 1973; *Stomping the Blues*, 1976; *Good Morning Blues: The Autobiography of Count Basie as Told to Albert Murray*, 1986; *The Blue Devils of Nada: A Contemporary American Approach to Aesthetic Statement*, 1996

Nagy, Gloria

1945– Novelist

"You remember the movie *Moonstruck* where Cher slaps Nicolas Cage and says 'Snap out of it!'?" the American author Gloria Nagy asked *New York Times* (August 5, 1990) reporter Denise Mourges. "What I like to do is give that little slap." Indeed, Nagy, the author of seven novels, including *A House in the Hamptons: One Summer Near the End of the Lie* (1990), *Looking for Leo* (1992), and *Marriage* (1995), is known for using fiction to skewer certain population segments, particularly yuppies and the nouveau riche. "Moral crossroads are what I write about," Nagy told Mourges. "I've always used social satire as my vehicle, because I think we now live in a society that if someone isn't making us pay attention, laugh at it, and see through it, if people take it any more seriously than they have for the last 10 years, we're going to have a bunch of monsters on our hands." Nagy says her books offer readers a much-needed dose of reality to counteract the glitz and flamboyance—both in literature and society—of the 1980s. "Many commercially successful novels of the last decade were novels of excess," Nagy said in an interview. "People have always been fascinated by the rich and famous, but during the eighties, even what that meant got very distorted—you couldn't be beautiful, you had to be gorgeous; you couldn't be rich, you had to be a billionaire; you couldn't have one mansion, you had to have five. If you had values, you were compromising all the time. . . . I want my books to have a certain social immediacy. We're navigating our way through a pretty hazy, rudderless decade. I'm trying to extend a comforting hand in the dark."

Born in about 1945 and reared in the "fantasy world" of Beverly Hills, Nagy grew up surrounded by the trappings of wealth and fame. "[Beverly Hills] was not like any other place you could live, especially in the fifties and sixties," Nagy said in an interview. "When I was a child it was still a village—a wealthy village—but basically families with first-generation money who had all moved there from somewhere else. It was very traditional in its odd sort of way. We just accepted that Dean Martin lived next door and that his kids were chauffeured to school." After attending Beverly

Reven T. C. Wurman/Courtesy of Delacorte Press
Gloria Nagy

Hills High School, Nagy went on to study at San Francisco State University, the University of Southern California, and the University of California at Los Angeles. By this time, however, she was beginning to become disenchanted with her hometown, a city she would later describe in an interview with *Newport This Week* (September 7, 1995) as "a truly horrifying place to live."

By the late 1970s, Nagy began channeling her contempt for the superficiality and materialism of the Beverly Hills lifestyle into writing. Her first two published novels, *Virgin Kisses* (1978), the story of a Beverly Hills psychiatrist who leads a female patient to suicide, and *Unapparent Wounds* (1981), a tale set largely at Beverly Hills High, both savagely attack Los Angeles's moneyed elite. *Virgin Kisses* was optioned twice for movie production by the actor Michael Douglas, who, according to Nagy, has said in an interview that without *Virgin Kisses* there might not have been *Fatal Attraction*, the hit film starring Douglas and Glenn Close. The novels *Natural Selections* and *Radio Blues* followed in 1985 and 1988, respectively.

In the meantime Nagy and her husband, writer and editor Richard Saul Wurman, had moved to New York City. "I'd always felt like I was in one of those dumb vice-versa movies—a New York writer thrust into a California locale," she said in an interview with *Los Angeles* (July 1990) magazine. In addition to their downtown Manhattan apartment, the couple purchased a Victorian summer home in the Hamptons—a group of villages on the east end of Long Island. Before long, however, the couple realized that the Hamptons were not exactly the picturesque, sleepy towns they had envisioned. "What attracted me was the sense of history and

tradition," Nagy told Denise Mourges for the *New York Times* article. "The towns have been settled and developed for hundreds of years, and not by rich people who said, 'We'll go out and make a lawn.' There were fishermen and farmers who came to the end of this island to forge an existence. This wasn't just a glitz community like Malibu or Palm Springs. But, they're here!" Nagy's experiences in the Hamptons, which would eventually inspire her to write *A House in the Hamptons*, were both eye-opening and disheartening. "The need to flaunt wealth is overwhelming, but the moneyed crowd can't do it in the city—they'd get their throats slit," she said in the interview with *Los Angeles* magazine. "So they head to the Hamptons, where they can show off for one another. The resulting mix of Maseratis, cellular phones, and 17th-century graveyards is very unsettling."

A House in the Hamptons, released in 1990, is Nagy's most critically acclaimed novel to date. In it, members of two wealthy families, the Harts and the Jamiesons, best friends for more than 20 years, meet for an annual summer retreat in the Hamptons. The tranquility of their sabbatical is suddenly broken by the appearance of a beautiful woman with whom both Mr. Hart and Mr. Jamieson were smitten in high school. The book describes the Hamptonites' often hilarious struggles to preserve their marriages and their never-ending efforts to climb the social ladder. A *Publishers Weekly* (May 18, 1990) reviewer deemed *A House in the Hamptons* "as much an astute sociological study of yuppies in late '80s New York as it is amusing, hip, highly readable fiction." Further praise was issued by Georgia Jones-Davies of the *Los Angeles Times Book Review* (June 17, 1990). "Nagy's talents are journalistic. . . . Her understanding of the Old Money–New Money battle out in the Hamptons could have been the backbone for a dandy piece of *Vanity Fair* reportage."

Nagy's subsequent novel, *Looking for Leo*, follows the three ex-wives of Leo Lampi on their around-the-world search for their elusive former husband. Lindy and Willa, wives number two and one, respectively, grew up as best friends in Beverly Hills, and team up to find Leo when Lindy's daughter becomes ill. While on their adventure-filled quest, the two encounter a third ex-wife, who joins them in their pursuit. *Looking for Leo*, Nagy said in an interview, was the result of a rather difficult decision to once again use Beverly Hills as a backdrop for a book. "When I started *Looking For Leo*, I thought, 'Oh no, Beverly Hills again!' I was propelled back," she said. "Maybe it's because [I'd] been away long enough. I realized that I had a lot of unfinished business there, as well as material that I hadn't even begun to mine." The book was generally well received by critics. "Leo's rugged charm and seductiveness are adroitly played, as are the warm friendships that develop among his abandoned lovers," Sybil Steinberg wrote in *Publishers Weekly* (May 18, 1992).

In 1995 Nagy published *Marriage*, a tale of modern middle-aged love between Mickey and Annie Wilder, childhood sweethearts now married with grown children. "I was fascinated," Nagy said in the interview with *Newport This Week*, "to see what happens to those people who find their soulmates as children and then encounter serious middle age, not just ordinary losses but real challenges. Do they make it?" Mickey and Annie's happy world begins to fall apart when Mickey's TV series is canceled, Annie decides she no longer enjoys her job as a travel writer, the couple experience a huge financial crisis, and both partners embark on extramarital affairs. Critics praised Nagy for *Marriage*'s humor and emotional realism. "There's recognition aplenty here as the reader hangs on through all the deliciously funny, sadly poignant, strange and familiar twists of plot which one minute is pure soap opera and the next is life lived in your own kitchen," Eileen Warburton wrote in the *Newport This Week* piece. "Nagy's snappy humor

satirizes contemporary pastimes while making this novel quite readable," wrote a *Library Journal* reviewer (June 15, 1995).

Nagy and her husband now live in Newport, Rhode Island. She has two children from a previous marriage.

—J. P.

SUGGESTED READING: *Library Journal* p96 June 15, 1995; *Los Angeles Times Book Review* p8 June 17, 1990; *Newport This Week* p18+ Sept. 7, 1995; *New York Newsday* p35+ July 30, 1995; *Publishers Weekly* p69 May 18, 1990, p58 May 18, 1992; *Contemporary Authors* vol. 148, 1996

SELECTED BOOKS: *Virgin Kisses*, 1978; *Unapparent Wounds*, 1981; *Natural Selections*, 1985; *Radio Blues*, 1988; *A House in the Hamptons: One Summer Near the End of the Lie*, 1990; *Looking for Leo*, 1992; *Marriage*, 1995

Naumoff, Lawrence

July 23, 1946– Novelist

After showing great promise as a student, Lawrence Naumoff didn't write anything for nearly 15 years. Then, in 1988, he published his first novel, *The Night of the Weeping Women*. In the years since, he has gained a reputation as a novelist who champions women, even though he claims he does not consciously do so. On the other hand, since Naumoff's strong and independent female characters are not necessarily heroes so much as survivors, some reviewers have questioned what they perceive as an underlying hostility toward women. Either way, many critics agree that Naumoff's novels feature female characters developed to a degree achieved by few male novelists. His most recent book, *A Plan for Women*, was published in 1997.

In a personal statement submitted by Naumoff to *World Authors 1990–1995*, the author wrote: "In late 1945, my father [Philip Naumoff], who was in the Army Medical Corp during World War II and stationed in Italy and North Africa, returned home. He had not seen my mother [Esther (Zuckerman) Naumoff], his wife, for two and a half years.

"Presumably, when a man hasn't been with his wife for that long, there are some memorably passionate moments, and out of one of those, I was bred.

"Nine months later, July 23, 1946, I was born in Charlotte. My mother says it was a long hot labor on sweat-soaked, rubber sheets.

"I had two older sisters already, and by 1957, two more younger ones. It has always been said by reviewers and critics that my particularly acute and compassionate understanding of my female characters comes from having been the only son in

Carolyn Vaughn, Imageworks/Courtesy of Harcourt Brace & Company

the middle of four daughters. I don't think so. It's more complicated than that.

"Find other men who grew up in the middle of four sisters. Are they writers? I doubt it. If so, do they write like me, with my vision and style? Likely not.

"Not knowing I wanted to write, I entered UNC, in Chapel Hill, and was quickly 'discovered' by a teaching assistant in my freshman English course. She said to me, 'You're a natural writer and you should be in the Writing Program.'

"Taken to Jessie Rehder, the old-time bohemian head of the department, I was accepted, and for the first time in my life, I felt as if I were home, had a home, knew what it was like to 'be home,' and did not want to leave it.

"Leave it, though, I did, after writing three novels and 60 short stories, and publishing and winning prizes under the name of Peter Nesovich [between 1967 and 1970], I stopped, completely.

"Russell Banks once told a sister of mine that, 'of course Lawrence stopped. He had to. The University pounced on him like they'd finally found their next Thomas Wolfe, and he had to get away from it.'

"Miserable, difficult years followed, and I lived with my first wife, Julie [Horner; married March 18, 1967], in Mexico, in the wilds of Maine, and finally in an unheated, waterless, even outhouseless, cabin on the Haw River in Chatham County, about twenty miles from Chapel Hill.

"The cabin was old. It's previous occupants had been such pitiful trash they'd not only never had the money or clarity of mind to drill a well, but they'd never even dug an outhouse hole and put a building around it. They'd used the woods around the house, for their entire life.

"Two years later, I assumed a Federal Land Bank loan on a farm in Silk Hope, near Chapel Hill, as well, and was asked to come to work with a group of Quaker carpenters, who built, from the foundation up, most of the better houses for the farmers in the area. It was an honor to be a counter-culture outsider, and be asked to work with them. They'd noticed I was industrious, they told me.

"I stayed with them for about five years, then people began to ask me to build their houses for them, and eventually I was talked into going on my own. I asked my first wife to leave in 1977, 10 years after we'd married, and, being kind-hearted, she did. I was an absolute jerk during my marriage to her, and she deserved, from day one, someone better than me. Young men are usually a lower lifeform than young women, and I was unworthy of her.

"Soon after she left, my farm house burned to the ground, and my three unpublished novels, all my letters, book, heirlooms from my czarist Russian ancestors, everything burned.

"That life, exaggerated and clarified and altered, is part of *The Night of the Weeping Women*.

"Soon after that, I married my second wife [Marolyn Summers, on March 7, 1978]. For comments on that, see the novel *Rootie Kazootie*. Dramatized, of course. The characters do not resemble anyone, living or dead.

"My son was born to number two. She was a zealous Christian Scientist. She thought keeping a fixed smile on her face and thinking non 'erroneous' thoughts would cause life to be perfect.

"She was wrong.

"I was at work one day when she called at 2:45 to say she was ready to have the baby. I picked her up at 3. We went to the hospital birthing room and at 3:15 she gave birth, under the supervision of a nurse-midwife, to Michael. By 5:30 we were all back home and she was cooking me supper.

"Michael was born with mild Down's Syndrome. I raised him, and he and I are closer than I would ever be with anyone else. He has had a wonderful life, and reads, does simple math, is absolutely competent in almost all ways, and has a clearer memory than me. He is also a better human being than anyone I know, and has taught me humility and patience.

"Leaving wife number two was far from easy, but I got away and with Michael, and we've been together even since.

"Never married again, but have been with Marianne Gingher for seven years as of this month, (Jan. 1998). We live in separate houses. She's the best thing in the adult world, that ever happened to me.

"Writing life:

"After not writing for at least 10 years, I started again, got an agent in 1987, finished *The Night of the Weeping Women*, and sent it up to NY to that agency, Barbara Lowenstein Associates, where I am still.

"Three houses wanted it immediately, and we went with Morgan Entrekin, who had just moved to Atlantic Monthly Press, along with Gary Fiskajon.

"I left there with my next book and moved to Farrar Straus & Giroux, where I had a good editor in Linda Healey, and an excellent assistant editor in Amy Peck.

"After they published *Rootie Kazootie*, I left when no one there would buy my most visionary, to that date, book, *Taller Women*.

"I took it to Harcourt Brace Jovanovich, and have been there for my other books, as well, *Silk Hope, NC*, and, *A Plan For Women*, which came out in Aug. of 1997.

"Here are some comments people have made about my books:

"In 1988, Reynolds Price said: 'Lawrence Naumoff violates one of the last great American taboos—he looks at marriage honestly. What he sees is outrageously—hilariously, tragically—undeniable, and he sets it all down with effortless looking brilliance.'

"In 1990, *Time Out*, the British magazine, said this about *Rootie Kazootie*: 'A painful but compelling tale of anger, desire and need, with an insight and sensitivity that borders on genius.'

"And Michael Dorris, who, by the way, I still believe in and consider having been a good human being and I hope that history will prove me right, said this about *Rootie*: 'Funny, original and sprinkled throughout with beautiful writing. We believe every word.'

"And then, after FSG wouldn't publish *Taller Women*, Fay Weldon, the British novelist, read it and said: 'Naumoff creates a new genre—call it if you like the new male fiction of feeling (fin-de-siecle division). He is so funny, so clever, so disturbing, so unputdownable about men and women he seems to be summing up the fictional achievements of the last thirty years.'

"I like what those people said. My books have a powerful effect on some people; conversely, some readers, and especially, reviewers, many of them, in fact, hate what I write enough to wish my demise or at least that I would never write again.

"In the tradition of respectable and well-raised (I do not use the term, reared, since I am not gay) Southern men, I have let other people speak for me, and presented myself as simply as possible, which is the way I am, actually, except on the page.

"The wonder of writing is that one can go beyond oneself, finding a voice and expressing a vision and creating lives that are so complex, deep, moving and enlightening that the final work, the book, transcends what passes for everyday life and thought.

"There is a thrill to hearing a reader tell me about the depth to which a book affected her, or him, and there is a thrill to going out on the edge of solid ground, jumping off, and seeing if I can fly. Having flown, then, I try for more.

"Having been initially radicalized in the '60s when an unmarried friend of mine became pregnant, and was denied maternity benefits by Blue Cross/Blue Shield because, they said, 'we don't offer help to women who get pregnant out of wedlock,' I find my books celebrating women, and equating their lives to the acts of injustice in the culture, at large.

"Women, then, as a symbol of goodness and innocence, and of that goodness and spiritedness denied, remain the central characters in my books, and the focus of my writing."

Early on, Naumoff's desire to write was influenced by a perception of himself as an outsider. Brought up Jewish in the midst of the predominantly Christian South, he was drawn to authors who saw themselves as "marginal," such as Paul Bowles and William Burroughs.

Naumoff graduated with a B.A. degree from the University of North Carolina at Chapel Hill in 1969, the year he won two prizes for his writing: a Discovery Award from the *Carolina Quarterly* for the short story "Escape Artist With Trick Knee" and the Thomas Wolfe Memorial Award. The following year he was presented with a grant from the National Endowment for the Arts (NEA), but he soon stopped writing altogether.

In 1971 he began a career as a carpenter and licensed general contractor. Naumoff claims his time among the Quaker carpenters in North Carolina influenced his later writing endeavors. "I learned to work in a relaxed and thoughtful way," he told Margaret Langstaff for *Publishers Weekly* (June 13, 1994). "I learned to build novels the way they built houses."

Naumoff did not return to writing until 1985, when he started working on *The Night of the Weeping Women*, which was published in 1988. The

Night of the Weeping Women met with a positive reception.

Naumoff followed his first novel with *Rootie Kazootie*, published in 1990. The main characters, Richard and Caroline, have drifted apart after 10 years of marriage; Caroline talks constantly, while Richard remains broodingly silent. Richard conducts an affair with Cynthia, a wealthy divorcée who has hired him to install kitchen cabinets, because she appears to be a peaceful alternative to his wife. Eventually Richard tells Caroline of the affair, which sets her off on a rampage: She punches Cynthia out and drives a tractor through a wall of the other woman's home. The surprising result is that Richard and Caroline's marriage warms up again.

Rosemary Daniell of the *New York Times* (March 11, 1990) enjoyed the resolution to the novel, but felt that the story dragged a bit in the middle. She also took issue with the novel's omniscient narration, which she felt distanced the reader from the characters. She maintained, however, that the story possessed an engaging energy. "Mr. Naumoff," she wrote, "has fun with us, making the two women in one man's life interchangeable. Because of his ability to evoke the nuances of relationships, we end up believing that Caroline, Cynthia, and Richard are real people out there somewhere, struggling to live and love as we are."

In *New York Newsday* (February 4, 1990), Dan Cryer praised Naumoff's narrative control in *Rootie Kazootie*. He pointed out the author's skill at handling tempestuous emotion without losing his perspective and also drew attention to Naumoff's "rare ability to compose scenes almost entirely of dialogue." Cryer complained, however, about the opaqueness of Richard's character, which he felt was never sufficiently exposed to the reader. He found Caroline, on the other hand, to be a "memorable heroine" whose scenes of over-the-top revenge are among the most compelling in the novel.

The writer Marianne Gingher, who reviewed *Rootie Kazootie* for the *Washington Post* (February 27, 1990), claimed to have "read *Rootie Kazootie* . . . so obsessively that my copy's still hot to the touch," and particularly admired Naumoff's fluid prose style and quirky characters. Naumoff and Gingher came to know each other as a result of the review, and soon became romantically involved.

In 1990 Naumoff was one of 10 writers to receive the Whiting Foundation Writers Award, which brought with it the sum of $30,000 and was given in recognition of each writer's achievement and potential in writing.

Naumoff's third novel, *Taller Women: A Cautionary Tale*, was published in 1992. The book, more shocking in its imagery and social commentary then its two predecessors, displeased some critics. The novel focuses on the extremes in tumultuous relationships between men and women, including domestic abuse and rape. In one particularly controversial scene, a woman who has been raped by a group of ex-convicts is described as having been penalized. "The book is about wantonness in women," Naumoff explained to Langstaff, "and how it is always, in the end, punished, whether they're just doing what the men are asking them to do or following their own impulses, however bighearted and well-intentioned they may be."

"Feminism doesn't appear to have made Gargantuan gains in the nameless Southern town that serves as the setting of . . . *Taller Women: A Cautionary Tale*," Lisa Zeidner commented in the *New York Times* (September 20, 1992). "In this queasy account of the battle of the sexes, the men are winning decisively." Zeidner discussed Naumoff's spare storytelling style, and opined that his narrative voice was at its strongest in his descriptions of characters' encounters with the bizarre. Unlike some other critics, Zeidner suggested that Naumoff did not maintain sufficient narrative control. "*Taller Women* inhabits its own kinky ZIP code, an outpost between realism and fairy tale," she wrote. "It's a tricky tone to sustain, and Mr. Naumoff doesn't always manage to do so." The "quirky, omniscient [narrative] viewpoint," she concluded, is decidedly male, and "can sometimes be annoying."

Dan Cryer of *New York Newsday* (September 21, 1992) adopted a more positive view, and hailed *Taller Women* as "a fascinating, powerful hybrid" and "dark domestic fiction of an unconventional kind." He felt that the novel's strangely deadpan narrative voice effectively underscores the oddities, horrors, and frustrations the novel brings to light. Cryer specifically praised the intricate blending of narrative techniques.

In 1994 Naumoff published *Silk Hope, NC*. More optimistic than much of his previous work, the novel deals with two sisters, one reckless and one conservative, and their efforts to succeed as independent women. Once their mother dies, they quarrel over whether to sell the family farm. The title of the work, in which Naumoff seemed to demonstrate a new sympathy for his heroines missing from his earlier efforts, refers to the town in which the story takes place, which is also the town in which Naumoff lived during the 1970s. James Marcus of *New York Newsday* (June 26, 1994) noted that "Episodes that would seem wacky and helium-light are anchored by the novel's elegiac core. . . . And hope, the novel's namesake, does just what it's supposed to, keeping despair successfully (but just barely) at bay."

Lawrence Naumoff published his latest novel, *A Plan for Women*, in 1997. Once again he explored the theme of women attempting to assert their identities while also trying to escape the shadow of overbearing men. The novel features Walter, the director of a North Carolina charity devoted to the betterment of blacks in the community. He falls in love with and marries the young and innocent Louise. Later a jealous ex-boyfriend threatens to send Walter a video he had secretly made of himself and Louise together. Walter confiscates the tape and

changes his opinion of Louise after watching it. Their relationship suffers as Louise for the first time beholds the more controlling side of her new husband.

A *Kirkus Reviews* (June 15, 1997) critic generally praised *A Plan for Women*, noting the presence of "Some odd bits—including a male amnesia victim formally adopted by [Walter's sister] Mary and used as her sex toy—but a thoughtful story in spite of its quirks, written in a style both crisp and clever."

Naumoff's novels all feature strong female characters who find themselves in conflict with society. Often, society takes the form of the sentimental or self-centered men in their lives. The women are often made to suffer for their innocence or their aggressive natures, but they generally prove themselves to be survivors, if not always heroines. Naumoff's work is also known for its strong sense of humor.

Discussing why he is drawn to female characters in his writing, Naumoff told Langstaff, "I like the company of women. I like the way they think, I like the potential women have to offer the world. But it's very hard today to know what's the right thing to do. In the past there were universally accepted constraints and codes of behavior. I do feel there are right ways to live involving duty and honor and virtue. It's the way I try to live and it's what I write about."—B.S.

SUGGESTED READING: *Kirkus Reviews* p903 June 15, 1997; *New York Newsday* p24+ Feb. 4, 1990, p44 Sep. 21, 1992, with photo, p39 June 26, 1994, with photo; *New York Times* VII p28 Mar. 11, 1990, VII p15 Sep. 20, 1992; *Publishers Weekly* p45+ June 13, 1994, with photo; *Washington Post* Feb. 27, 1990; *International Authors and Writers Who's Who 1997/98*

SELECTED WORKS: *The Night of the Weeping Women*, 1988; *Rootie Kazootie*, 1990; *Taller Women: A Cautionary Tale*, 1992; *Silk Hope, NC*, 1994; *A Plan for Women*, 1997

Neugeboren, Jay

May 30, 1938– Novelist; professor

Since the publication of his fifth novel, *The Stolen Jew*, in 1981, Jay Neugeboren has maintained a reputation as a fiction writer adept at portraying conflicts involving religion. He is also willing to take on other difficult subjects, as he did in *Imagining Robert: My Brother, Madness, and Survival—A Memoir*, an account of his brother's mental illness. Still, much of his fiction, such as his story collection *Don't Worry About the Kids* (1997), evokes the drama that attends everyday situations.

Stephen Long/Courtesy of William Morrow and Company
Jay Neugeboren

In an autobiographical statement submitted to *World Authors 1990–1995*, Neugeboren writes: "I was born in Brooklyn, New York, on May 30, 1938, the first child of first-generation Americans. My four grandparents and most of my older uncles and aunts (my father was next-to-the-youngest of nine children, and my mother was third-from-the youngest of eight, two of whom died as infants) were born in Europe, in the Pale of Settlement—then Galicia, now the Ukraine. I was named for my father's father, who had died before my parents met, and for the first three days of my life my American name was Jacob Mordecai Neugeboren (Ah that it were now!). But my parents fought over this name—my (nonreligious) mother wanting me to have a Jewish name, my (religious) father wanting me to have an American name. Three days after I was born, the name Jacob Mordecai was crossed out on my birth certificate and the name Jay Michael written in above it.

"For the first five years of my life, I was taught to believe that the Memorial Day parades (in one, on Linden Boulevard, around the corner from our house on Martense Street, a victorious General Eisenhower rode by) were for me. My mother was a Registered Nurse, and my father, who was, at the time of my birth, in what was called the Installment business, started various printing and stationery businesses throughout my growing up, but failed at all of them, and eventually went bankrupt; my mother, often by working double and triple shifts as a private duty nurse, supported the family.

"My brother Robert, my only sibling, was born on April 17, 1943 (two days before the Warsaw Ghetto uprising). I attended Crown Heights Yeshiva for one term, and then transferred to my neigh-

borhood elementary school, P. S. 246. When P. S. 246 became J. H. S. 246 (Walt Whitman Junior High School) in 1950, I became its first President. As a young boy I loved sports, put on magic shows for friends and relatives, and read voraciously, sometimes finishing three or four books between the end of school one day, and the start of school the next morning. When I was eight years old, I wrote a 70-to 80-page novel that I read to my fourth grade class, a chapter at a time, on Monday mornings.

"I attended Erasmus Hall High School for four years, and graduated in 1955. I was a good, but not exceptional student, much more interested in sports and girls than in things literary or intellectual. While in high school I was selected for the All-City Radio Workshop, and for a year-and-a-half I was an actor in radio programs produced by the Board of Education for WNYE-FM. I was accepted to Columbia College and began my studies there in 1955, in which year I listed as my possible vocations: acting, TV directing and producing, advertising, and architectural engineering.

"I commuted to Columbia for my first three years, and lived near campus during my senior year. I graduated, Phi Beta Kappa, in 1959. Near the end of my sophomore year, in the spring of 1957, I was operated on and radiated for cancer (Hodgkin's Disease). Believing (in part) that I had only a year to live, I decided to do what I had always wanted to do, and had not thought of doing since I was eight years old: to write a novel. I completed it, and gave it to Charles Van Doren, who tried, unsuccessfully, to help me get it published. In my senior year, under the direction of Richard Chase, I wrote my second novel.

"After graduating from Columbia, I went to Indiana University on a fellowship, but dropped out within my first year to complete a third novel. I worked for the General Motors Corporation, as an Executive Trainee in Indianapolis, for six months, then returned home for half-a-year to complete a fourth (unpublished) novel. The following year I taught at the Saddle River Country Day School, in New Jersey, and completed two more books. During that year, my brother Robert, with whom I was very close, had the first of what would, alas, prove to be a life-long series of mental and emotional breakdowns. I have, through most of these years, been his primary caretaker.

"In 1963, I returned to Indiana and completed my Master's Degree, after which I returned to New York, where I taught at Columbia for two years. I was married in 1964. By this time I had completed eight unpublished books. My first published novel, *Big Man*, appeared in 1966. The year after that I was a Visiting Writer at Stanford University (whose writing program had rejected me seven years earlier), and for two-and-a-half of the next three years, I lived in Europe, mostly in Spéracèdes, a small village in the south of France. I have written of these years in my first essay in my autobiography, *Parentheses: An Autobiographical Journey* (1970).

"My second novel, *Listen Ruben Fontanez*, was published in 1968, and my first collection of stories, *Corky's Brother*, in 1969. Between 1970 and 1997 I published eight other books, two of which won prizes: *The Stolen Jew* (American Jewish Committee Award for Best Novel of 1981), and *Before My Life Began* (Edward Lewis Wallant Prize for Best Novel of 1985). I guest edited a special fiction issue of *Ploughshares* (1980), a volume of Martha Foley's *Memoirs* (1980), and had one of my screenplays produced (*The Hollow Boy*, on American Playhouse, in 1991; it won top prize at the 1992 Houston International Festival).

"*Imagining Robert: My Brother, Madness, and Survival—a Memoir*, a *New York Times* Notable Book of the Year, was published (after 41 rejections) in 1997, and in it I tell the story of my brother's life, in and out of mental hospitals for the past 35 years, and of our relationship through these years, and through the years of our growing up together. Since 1971, I have been Writer-in-Residence at the University of Massachusetts in Amherst. I have three children—Miriam (28), Aaron (25), and Eli (23)—for whom, for most of their lives, I have been the sole parent."

During his time at General Motors, Neugeboren became increasingly dismayed by the racial injustices in Indianapolis as well as the dehumanizing policies implemented at the plant. He began reading political essays and eventually became involved in the burgeoning antiwar and antinuclear weapons movements of the era. He became a fierce crusader for leftist causes, and wrote articles on his favorite issues for a variety of popular magazines. As he explained in *Parentheses*, "The feeling was obsessive, ferocious: if I didn't do something to fight the evil (the people) around me, nobody would." Neugeboren relocated to France in the late 1960s. "I had come to Spéracèdes in order, for the first time in my life, to have nothing to do for a full year except write fiction," he wrote in *Parentheses*. "Once in Spéracèdes, however, I found that certain events (from America) were with me continuously—unless I dealt with them directly, I felt, they would continue to haunt, they would invade my fiction in ways I would, I knew, be unable to control." According to Neugeboren, *Parentheses* was his attempt to find out "who I am and where I've been."

Meanwhile, Neugeboren had published his first novel, *Big Man*, in 1966. The book drew on Neugeboren's memories of high school, when he immersed himself in a variety of sports and girlfriends in an effort to smother his interest in writing, a hobby that went unsupported at home. The narrator, a black basketball player named Mack Davis, is banned from playing professionally because he was involved in a betting scam during his college ball days. In his critique for the *New York Times Book Review* (March 19, 1968), Lex Lardner wrote that the "descriptions of the joys of schoolyard basketball are superb" in *Big Man*, and added that "the author's great triumph is his poignant characterization of Davis."

Neugeboren's second novel, *Listen Ruben Fontanez*, was published in 1968, and his first collection of stories, *Corky's Brother*, in 1969. *Listen Ruben Fontanez*, which depicts the conflict between an older Jewish teacher and his Puerto Rican student, earned Neugeboren high praise from critics, as did *Corky's Brother*, which won an award from the *Transatlantic Review*.

The baseball story *Sam's Legacy* (1974), Neugeboren's third novel, did not fare well with critics, nor was it a commercial success. The novel that followed, *An Orphan's Tale* (1976), was narrated from the point of view of orphan Danny Ginsberg. In the *New York Times Book Review* (August 15, 1976), Peter Spackman lauded *An Orphan's Tale* as a "marvel of compact and intricate imagination far more searching in its exploration of contemporary writing than anything our 'experimental' writers have produced to date, as well as being more accessible to the general reader."

Neugeboren's next novel, *The Stolen Jew*, was turned down by 16 publishers before making its way into print. Neugeboren rewrote the manuscript as a series of short stories, which he then sold individually to literary and special-interest publications. Eventually, the stories gained enough notice that an editor who had originally rejected the novel agreed to publish the manuscript in its entirety. In an article for *Coda* magazine (November/December 1982, on-line), the precursor to *Poets and Writers Magazine*, Neugeboren spoke of his struggle to get *The Stolen Jew* published. "The editors who considered buying *The Stolen Jew* said they admired my previous works and that this book was clearly my most ambitious, perhaps even my best. . . . But they weren't looking for a big, complex novel by a writer with a mediocre track record . . . My last few books have had hard times finding publishers, and that wasn't easy on me. . . . Having your novel go begging is a distinctly unpleasant experience, and there were many years when I was angry and bitter and unhappy."

The Stolen Jew is about Nathan Malkin, who has written a complex, psychologically probing novel (titled "The Stolen Jew"). Malkin and his nephew begin a scheme to aid Russian Jews, and in the process, Malkin's nephew trades places with an imprisoned Jew so that the prisoner may escape with Malkin to America. The scenario eerily echoes that of Malkin's own novel, in which a young kidnapped boy takes the place of a wealthy Jew's son. In an article for *America*, as cited in *Contemporary Authors* (1987), Vincent D. Balitas wrote, "In *The Stolen Jew* we get a tapestry into which is woven, in a Proustian way, not only the theme of man's responsibility to self and others, but also a consideration of fictionmaking."

Reviews of *The Stolen Jew* were mixed; some critics seemed unable to get past the novel's religious aspects, which, combined with the Jewish setting of *An Orphan's Tale*, earned Neugeboren a reputation as a literary champion of Jewish nationalism. In a review for the *New Republic* (September 16, 1981), Tova Reich wrote, "*The Stolen Jew* is composed with ardor and has a strong propulsive force that keeps it aloft." Acknowledging that the novel is "hard on the nerves," Reich also admitted that "what it lacks in particulars, it makes up for in passion." The critic concluded that the novel is "earnest and high-minded; it is rich in information, in meditations on the nature of God and the universe, and in stories." Vivian Gornick commended Neugeboren in the *New York Times*, calling him "an experienced novelist. He writes well, he is deeply familiar with the tradition in which he is writing, and, what's more, he longs for the world that gave rise to that tradition." Yet, Gornick wrote, "not one of his characters has a single arresting thing to say or is submitted to an interesting circumstance or arrives in a psychologically surprising place." Gornick continued: "the conversations are predictable, the memories are set pieces, what occurs seems like the events in a television drama."

In his sixth novel, *Before My Life Began* (1985), Neugeboren created two personalities for his protagonist. David, the wealthy son of a Jewish family with mob ties, murders an assailant from a rival family, and subsequently must begin a new life as "Aaron," a Freedom School teacher in Mississippi. In the course of the novel, David is once again forced into violent confrontations. Reviews of the book were again mixed, although generally upbeat and lacking the "Jewish expressionist" label that had appeared in previous reviews of his work. In *Columbia* magazine, as cited by *Contemporary Authors* (1987), Rex Roberts wrote that Neugeboren "luxuriates in his versatility . . . he can give us an artist at his sketch pad, a lynching, or the final minute of a heated basketball game with equal ease."

After writing his next novel, *Poli: A Mexican Boy in Early Texas* (1989), Neugeboren wrote *The Hollow Boy* for PBS's *American Playhouse*, an endeavor which would later earn him the Special Juror's Prize for Best Screenplay at the Houston Film Festival (1991).

In 1997 Neugeboren produced one of his most personal books, drawn primarily from his relationship with his brother Robert, called *Imagining Robert: My Brother, Madness, and Survival—A Memoir*. Robert was diagnosed with mental illness in his late teens, and has been on and off various treatments ever since. Once a normal-seeming, personable young man, Robert has spent the past 30 years in a state of almost constant mental confusion, subjected to dangerous, often humiliating treatment at the hands of unskilled mental health practitioners who prescribed one drug after another, each time giving Neugeboren another false hope. *Imagining Robert* chronicles Robert's history of mental illness

and Jay's struggle to get his brother the proper care. Neugeboren wrote of his brother as two people—one an institutionalized schizophrenic, the other a bright, active member of society. "Mr. Neugeboren finds his brother's noble moments, his triumphs of wit, the true Robert locked behind the trembling hands, the speeding talk, the frightening outbursts," Frederick Busch wrote for the *New York Times* (February 9, 1997). "Jay finds Robert by using his art: he imagines him for us, he makes his incoherent journey into a narrative that is organized and useful." Neugeboren also explored his family history of instability, including his mother's descent into Alzheimer's disease, his children's problems, and his doubts about his own mental health.

Reviews of *Imagining Robert* were overwhelmingly positive; many critics praised Neugeboren's sensitive treatment of his brother's journey through the world of psychosis. "Neugeboren has written a detailed, exquisitely painful and always thoughtful account of his younger brother's struggle with mental illness," wrote a reviewer for *Publishers Weekly* (December 30, 1996). *Kirkus Reviews* (December 15, 1996) called the memoir an "uncommon tale of brotherly love" that is "rich, textured, and deeply sad." Equally lauded in many reviews was the chastisement of the mental health system, particularly in New York, where Robert has spent most of his time. Writing for the *Washington Post* (March 2, 1997) Peter D. Kramer expressed amazement that "this indictment of the mental health system is embedded in a narrative that is mostly pleasurable to read." Calling Neugeboren "engaging company and a trustworthy host," Cramer continued: "As details of the brothers' interactions accumulate, what emerges is a meditation on identity and epistemology."

Neugeboren next published a collection of 15 short pieces, *Don't Worry About the Kids* (1997). Except for a spy story set in France, the tales are gentle glimpses into everyday domestic situations. For instance, "Tolstoy in Maine" portrays a successful filmmaker, recently divorced, who is visiting a seacoast town. There he unexpectedly and briefly finds love in the form of a fellow divorcée, whose own past is then also recounted. Other stories in the collection are about city life, mental illness, and a boy grieving over the death of his father. A reviewer for *Kirkus Reviews* (August 15, 1997) wrote of *Don't Worry*, "Neugeboren's sensibilities are exclusively northeastern and upper-middle class, which probably describes his readers as well. This time, he gives them their money's worth, and then some."

Most recently Neugeboren published *Transforming Madness: New Lives for People Living with Mental Illness* (1999), a survey of mental health care. The author presents his case that certain social structures can be used to restore the mentally ill to productive and happy lives. Brian McCombe wrote for *Booklist* that the volume is "a compassionate overview of an issue the U.S. is just beginning to look at squarely." The book also received a positive review from a critic at *Kirkus Reviews*, who noted that the author's "story and others related here drive home the message that not only is our biological understanding of mental illness grossly incomplete, but that progress in improving care has been distressingly slight."

Jay Neugeboren continues to work as professor and writer-in-residence at the University of Massachusetts in Amherst, and resides in Northampton, Massachusetts.—D.B.

SUGGESTED READING: *Booklist* Dec. 1, 1996; *Coda* Nov./Dec. 1982; *Kirkus Reviews* Dec. 15, 1996, Aug.15, 1997; *New Republic*, Sep. 16, 1981; *New York Times Book Review* Mar. 19, 1968; p10 Feb. 9, 1997, p16 Jan. 4, 1998; *Publishers Weekly* Dec. 30, 1996; *Washington Post* p6 Mar. 2, 1997; *Book Review Digest* 1967, 1968, 1969, 1970, 1974, 1981; *Contemporary Authors* , 1987

SELECTED WORKS: Fiction—*Big Man*, 1966; *Listen Ruben Fontanez*, 1968; *Corky's Brother*, 1969; *Sam's Legacy*, 1974; *An Orphan's Tale*, 1976; *The Stolen Jew*, 1981; *Before My Life Began*, 1985; *Poli: A Mexican Boy in Early Texas*, 1989; *Don't Worry About the Kids: Stories*, 1997; Nonfiction—*Parentheses: An Autobiographical Journey*, 1970; *The Story of Story Magazine: A Memoir*, 1980; *Imagining Robert: My Brother, Madness, and Survival A Memoir*, 1996; *Transforming Madness: New Lives for People Living with Mental Illness*, 1999; Screenplays—*A Hollow Boy*, 1991

Courtesy of Geoff Nicholson

Nicholson, Geoff

Apr. 3, 1953– Novelist

Described by a *New York Newsday* (July 23, 1995) reviewer as "a master of controlled lunacy, of turning the seemingly ordinary into the bizarre," British author Geoff Nicholson is celebrated for his ability to fashion fantastic, often hilarious happenings out of the mundane occurrences of everyday life. "In his books," said the *Newsday* reviewer, "everyday places like car repair shops, department stores, and restaurants become the scenes of extravagantly twisted plot developments. The members of a tony private club turn out to be cannibals. A cable TV weathercaster lands in the middle of a plot by neo-Nazis to gain control of Hitler's greatest treasure. A trailer park finds itself hosting a Volkswagen-lovers' convention and a New Age hippie gathering on the same weekend—which wouldn't have been so bad, perhaps, except that the combination offers those same neo-Nazis the perfect site to unleash their energies."

Now the author of nine full-length works of fiction, including *Hunters and Gatherers* (1994), *Still Life with Volkswagens* (1995), *Footsucker* (1996), and *Bleeding London* (1997), Nicholson has become popular with critics and readers on both sides of the Atlantic. His works have been variously labeled "wickedly funny" (*Library Journal*), "sharp, hyper-aware, and comically fatalistic" (*New Yorker*), and "delightful" (*New York Times*).

In a statement submitted to *World Authors 1990–1995*, Nicholson, born on April 3, 1953 in Sheffield, England, writes: "It is always interesting, and sometimes alarming, for an author to see who critics and reviewers are comparing him to. When my first novels appeared in England I was compared to Tom Sharpe and George and Weedon Grossmith. With my later novels the comparisons were more literary and I was said to be writing black comedies in the manner of Evelyn Waugh. The most recent reviews of my books, especially those from America, have tended to remark on similarities to Pynchon, Perec, even Kafka.

"Of course I'm not foolish enough to trust what reviewers say about me and my books, but I think this list of comparisons suggests that as time has gone by either they or I have discovered a high seriousness in my work. All I can say, is that I was pretty serious from the beginning.

"This, of course, is the problem that besets almost everyone who is involved with any form of comedy, and I'm aware that nothing is more pathetic than the former entertainer or comedian who now wants to be taken seriously. However, I have never consciously 'tried to be funny' in my novels, never consciously written and inserted jokes. They just come out that way. The comedy is intrinsic. Of course I'm aware that I'm not writing high tragedy or melodrama but that's a categorization that comes after the fact.

"I find myself dealing with modern obsessions, or at least with characters who have such obsessions. On the other hand I have never consciously written about an 'issue.' I try to be to be current without being journalistic, to be on the ball without being a victim of literary or other fashion. So I write about cars, food, Volkswagens, cities, the electric guitar, Errol Flynn, sexual fetishism; which is perhaps only to say that I'm interested in the quirkier manifestations of human experience.

"It seems absurd to claim to be 'influenced' by the likes of Laurence Stern, Beckett, Nabokov or Borges, but these were the authors I discovered for myself comparatively early in life. They've stayed with me, and I m sure I've stolen from them all. If readers can find positive echoes of their work (as well as of Tom Sharpe, Evelyn Waugh et al) in my own writing, then I am both pleased and flattered."

Despite the outrageous bent of his books, by all appearances, Nicholson's own life has been comparatively sedate. Born in Sheffield, England, the son of Geoffrey Howell Nicholson, a carpenter, and Violet Theresa Moore, a bookkeeper, he was educated at Gonville and Caius College, Cambridge University, where he received his bachelor's degree in 1975. According to one source, Nicholson received master's degrees from both Cambridge University and the University of Essex in 1978. Before becoming a full-time writer, he worked as a gardener, chef, dustman, furniture salesman, and driving instructor. Nicholson's first two full-length works of fiction were *Street Sleeper* (1987), a road novel set in contemporary England, and *The Knot Garden* (1989), a book that utilizes various devices of a detective novel to mediate on such subjects as death and nature. Nicholson's *Hunters and Gatherers* tells the tale of Steve Geddes, a bartender turned writer who decides to pen a book about collectors and their collections. "I planned to find a series of dubious but entertaining eccentrics who had unlikely, bizarre, or exceptionally useless collections," Geddes explains. "I was looking for the oddball and the kitsch. I wanted to interview the collectors, ask a few gentle, ironic questions, let them talk and hope they made endearing fools of themselves." He quickly finds a bounty of wacky collectors—Edwin Rivers, England's foremost collector of beer cans; Victoria Havergal, a woman who accumulates sexual experiences; Eve Leviticus, a woman who collects noises and sounds on a tape recorder; and Ted Langley, a stand-up comedian who is said to own one of the world's largest collection of jokes. After a variety of complicated plot twists, including a trip to Scotland to visit novelist Thornton McCain, the development of a romantic interest between Havergal and Geddes, and another character's receipt of a mysterious encyclopedia, *The Books of Power*, that tempts him to leave his job at a used car lot to become a game show contestant, Geddes gradually learns the motivations behind the characters' obsessive collecting. "We gather to us what seems urgent and necessary," Geddes says in the book. "It might be objects or it might be money or it might be people. That's our personal collection. That's what we have to show. When you die the collection gets broken up."

Critical reviews for *Hunters and Gatherers* were generally enthusiastic. "[The novel] is a clever, entertaining, and intriguing British import, literate and rich with references to culture high and low, and it's enlivened by a ripe cynicism," Eric Kraft wrote in the *New York Times Book Review* (February 5, 1995). Other critics, like Michiko Kakutani of the *New York Times* (December 20, 1994), disliked Nicholson's tendency to philosophize, but raved about his ability to string together multiple plot lines coherently. "Although Mr. Nicholson is heavy-handed, at times, in his use of such developments to score philosophical points, his orchestration of the novel's many jangling plot lines is so fluent, his understanding of his hapless characters so sure, that the reader barely notices," Kakutani wrote. "Indeed, his own novel stands as a charming little testament to the ordering impulses of art."

In 1995 Nicholson released *Still Life with Volkswagens*. In it, several stories unfold about a group of disparate people connected by one thing—Volkswagens. Characters include Charles Lederer, a once prominent and respected man whose life took a dramatic downturn after "a man in a Volkswagen stole his daughter, slept with his wife, invaded his house, turned the media against him and caused his incarceration." Now in a mental hospital, Lederer, having compiled a scrapbook of world disasters in which a Volkswagen can be seen in every photograph, is convinced that Volkswagens are "quite clearly the car of the devil." Also featured in the book is Barry Osgathorpe, the very man whom Lederer accused of ruining his life, who is eventually kidnapped by a neo-Nazi, and Fat Les, "the Veedub King," a Volkswagen customizer. The book is also filled with tidbits of Volkswagen trivia and chapters titled with cultural allusions—for example, "Gentlemen Prefer Volkswagens" and "I Beg Your Pardon, I Never Promised You a Volkswagen"—altered to follow the book's theme.

In *Library Journal* (August 1995), David Sowd hailed *Still Life with Volkswagens* as a "hilarious tale of obsession, in which everyone from Adolf Hitler to Charles Manson makes a cameo appearance. . . It's a wickedly funny read from beginning to end that invites comparison with the best of Robbins and both Amises." It was equally well received by Anna Shapiro of the *New Yorker* (March 18, 1996). "By the end of the book, the title has also accumulated meaning beyond the frivolity of its allusion, and enough emotional velocity to become subtly moving," Shapiro wrote. "Yet Nicholson's jokey premise never loses its wit—and for this reader exploding Volkswagens and rampaging skinheads have to be handled *very* cleverly to be funny." Also released in 1995, *Everything and More* revolves around Haden Brothers, a huge London department store, where, as the title suggests, one can buy just about anything imaginable. The tangled cast of odd characters includes Arnold Haden, the last surviving Haden brother, a rather bizarre, withdrawn man who lives above the store in a stark, all-white apartment and dresses only in that color; Vita Carlisle, a woman who aspires to work at Haden Brothers because she loves to shop there; and Charlie Mayhew, a recent college graduate who harbors aspirations of being an artist and who works as a furniture porter at the store. The extremely complicated plot includes incidents of shoplifting, bomb threats, a hostage crisis, and a love triangle involving Vita, Charlie, and Arnold. "Influenced by the literary extravagances of Huysman and Georges Perec, *Everything and More* might, in comparison, be lightweight, but it is subversive enough to parody its voyeuristic tendencies," a reviewer wrote in the *Financial Times* (September 17, 1994). "Combining speculation and accusation, Nicholson . . . delights in defying categories."

Perhaps the most bizarre of Nicholson's book to date is *Footsucker*, published in the United Kingdom in 1995 and in the United States in 1996. *Footsucker* is the story of an unnamed man who has a foot fetish. The man's obsession runs so deep that he often takes to the street posing as a public relations consultant to ask passing women intimate questions about their feet. When the man meets Catherine, an American woman whose feet are "a wonder of nature" that just happen to fit a pair of specially designed shoes ("made of black and white snakeskin . . . each shoe had at its apex the head of a real snake, the eyes glassily black, the mouths wide open, fangs visible"), the pair begin a torrid affair. The relationship, however, comes to an abrupt end when Catherine decides that things have gone too far. "Just think of me as a stupid, scared woman who simply got cold feet," Catherine announces. Truly bizarre happenings then ensue, including a visit to a "professional" ("Love me love my feet," the woman's business card announces), a murder, and the disappearance of Catherine. Additionally, woven throughout *Footsucker* are massive doses of foot trivia and detailed accounts of the narrator's foot- and shoe-related obsessions. "The book is outrageous, but author Geoff Nicholson pulls it off," Carolyn Banks wrote in the *Washington Post* (December 29, 1996). "We walk more than a mile in *Footsucker*'s shoes, laughing much of the way. We even chuckle at an ending, that might have, earlier on, made us gag. To put it simply, the book is a kick."

Bleeding London (1997), Nicholson's most recent book, focuses on two characters: Stuart London, who decides to walk down every street of the city of the title and record his observations in a diary, and Mick Walton, a yokel who has come to London to avenge the rape of his stripper girlfriend. "Local color and Nicholson's delightfully cynical sense of humor don't quite justify the length of time it takes Mick and Stuart to cross paths," declared a *Publishers Weekly* (August 4, 1997) reviewer. "Even so, getting there's most of the fun." —J. P.

SUGGESTED READING: *Grand Street* p181+ Summer 1995; *Library Journal* p119 Aug. 1995; *New Yorker* p106+ Mar. 18, 1996; *New York Newsday* Q p32 July 23, 1995; *New York Times* C p21 Dec. 20, 1994; *New York Times Book Review* p12 Feb. 5, 1995; *Publishers Weekly* p63 Aug. 12, 1996; *Washington Post Book World* p9 Dec. 29, 1996; *Contemporary Authors* vol. 130, 1990

SELECTED BOOKS: *Street Sleeper*, 1987; *The Knot Garden*, 1989; *What We Did On Our Holidays*,1990, *The Food Chain*, 1993; *Hunters And Gatherers*, 1994; *Everything and More*, 1995; *Still Life with Volkswagens*, 1995; *Footsucker*, 1996; *Bleeding London*, 1997

Courtesy of Stewart O'Nan

O'Nan, Stewart

1961– Novelist; short-story writer

Because he is known as an author whose stories offer an intriguing combination of "dead-on diction, an eye for detail, sinewy syntax, [and] a sense of drama," as Ron Tanner put it in *Studies in Short Fiction* (Winter 1995), it may come as a surprise to many that Stewart O'Nan originally planned to have a career in a decidedly nonliterary field. He studied aerospace engineering at Boston University and worked for five years as a test engineer at Grumman Aerospace in Long Island, New York. Fortunately for his numerous readers and fans, O'Nan subsequently decided to earn a master's degree in fiction from Cornell University and try his luck at being a writer. "It's the only thing I'm really good at," he said in an interview with the *New York Times* (June 9, 1996). "I was always a mediocre engineer."

The author of the novels *Snow Angels* (1994), *The Names of the Dead* (1996), *The Speed Queen* (1997), *A World Away* (1998), and *A Prayer for the Dying* (1999) as well as the short-story collection *In the Walled City*, (1993), O'Nan has achieved a solid literary reputation in a very short time. *In the Walled City* received the Drue Heinz Literature Prize, and in 1996 the British literary magazine *Granta* selected O'Nan as one of the "Best of Young American Novelists." O'Nan's stories and novels are often tales of failed love, involving imperfect, sometimes very cruel characters trapped in dismal lives. "I'm trying to give someone a voice who would not otherwise have one," he has said. Critics contend that O'Nan's willingness to expose the flaws of his protagonists and their surroundings is balanced by his ability to add complexity to characters readers might otherwise dismiss as evil or unsympathetic. "[By] creating a spare, often bleak world, he has exceeded the limitations of minimalism by illuminating the vulnerability of his people, making them sympathetic, if not likable," Tanner wrote in *Studies in Short Fiction*.

In a statement submitted to *World Authors 1990–1995*, Stewart O'Nan, born in 1961 in Pittsburgh, writes: "My own life isn't terribly interesting, even to myself, and that may be why I write about people and places—even times—so different from the ones I know. I get interested in people. Acquaintances, people in the street. When I can't understand why certain people do things, I try to figure them out. Mysteries, like, why do you kill your own child, which is a very common thing, or, how do you recover from loss? I try to put myself in other people's shoes and say, realistically, what would happen next? I can't really do it, simply because I'm not them. I'm not that smart, not that sensitive, but I think if I try to be generous with them and honest about how they live their lives, I might come up with something. It's naive, finally, my way of working, but it's the only way I know. So, no, I've never lived in the country, I'm not a Vietnam vet, I don't have Alzheimer's or race pigeons, I'm not born-again or Chinese or divorced.

"But I do care for everyone I write about, and many of those people are what editors and critics call unsympathetic characters. People do terrible things to each other. I try not to lay blame, though some of the things they feel they have to do are hard, even shocking. One critic remarked that my characters are too real to be sympathetic; typically, I didn't know whether to be flattered or angry. I see my characters as truly voiceless people, and voiceless not merely by choice, but by personality. They're not quirky and quotable, they don't carry the political history of any one group on their shoulders. Their lives are quiet, routine, like most of ours. If you asked them what they have to say to the world, they'd just shrug like you must be kidding and turn away. They have trouble just coming up with conversation. They're private, they live inside.

"I write tragedies, which aren't in fashion right now. Even *The Speed Queen*, for all its zaniness, turns around death and loss, broken dreams, love come to grief, difficult memories. Is my imagination Gothic? Do I have a grim view of the world and the human heart? It's a coin flip. I think most people try to be good, that their desires are for the most part noble, yet, sadly, even that can lead to tragedy. Faith doesn't always save us, just as despair can sometimes keep us alive. As a reader, I grew up on Camus and Stephen King, William Maxwell and Sylvia Plath. When I sit down to write I don't know how I'm going to address the big questions, let alone answer them. While there may be an underpinning of grandiose, even dire religious and philosophical ideas to my novels, at heart I'm interested in characters—or, more correctly, people. The apocalyptic vision is surely from Faulkner by way of Flannery O'Connor, while the taste for personal salvation must come from Tolstoy. And yet, in my unwillingness to judge one character guilty and the other innocent, I hope I lean toward Woolf and Chekhov.

"I'm hopeful. I'm rooting for my characters, for things to turn out well. But I'm not going to lie to you—a lot of times they don't.

"The other thing I should mention is the metafictional angle, that is, how *Snow Angels*, *The Names of the Dead*, and *The Speed Queen* all debate the healing power of memory or storytelling, both explicitly, in dialogue between characters, and implicitly, through structure and plot elements. I suspect this is a hangover from the experiments of the French *nouveau roman* and the more formally ambitious American literary fiction of the '60s and '70s, but it could be more. I've only been writing for ten years now, and often I'm just trying things out to see if they'll work."

In 1994 O'Nan released *Snow Angels*, his first novel. The book, a tale of a murder in a poverty-stricken town in western Pennsylvania, met with great critical praise. "Moving, beautifully constructed, morally complex . . . a fine first novel," a reviewer wrote in the *Washington Post Book World* (January 29, 1995). The *New York Times* (January 8, 1995) reviewer described it as a "stunning first novel." In the story, half of the chapters are narrated by Arthur, a teenage boy faced with the constant fighting and eventual separation of his parents. Other chapters use an omniscient voice that shifts among the perspectives of various townspeople and details the events leading up to the murder of Annie Marchand, Arthur's former babysitter. "These glimpses into the soul of Annie herself, her estranged husband, her mother, her boyfriend, and a number of supporting characters, allow the novel to flow in unexpected ways," Andrea Barrett wrote in the *Washington Post* review. "In other hands this could have been a mundane story of a boy victimized by his parents' divorce or yet another squalid tale of domestic violence. But the braiding of the two stories, and the combination of first-person and omniscient voice, make a whole person that's much more than the sum of its parts."

In O'Nan's second novel, *The Names of the Dead*, Larry Markham, a baked-goods deliveryman and decorated Vietnam veteran, begins to have flashbacks of the war. Larry's life, to say the least, is not going as planned—his wife has recently left him, taking with her the couple's learning-disabled son; he despises his job; his father is showing signs of Alzheimer's disease; and Larry himself is being stalked by an ex-CIA assassin. In *The Names of the Dead*, O'Nan exhibited what a *Library Journal* (March 1, 1996) reviewer referred to as an "encyclopedic knowledge of the period and a poet's feel for army slang," despite being far too young to have served in Vietnam. His novel offers nightmarish images of the realities of war. O'Nan wrote of pieces of dead bodies hanging from tree branches "like drying laundry" and described a fatal head wound as "a bloody custard spilled in the dirt." Though his use of vivid detail was applauded, some critics remarked that detail alone cannot carry an entire novel. "O'Nan's method seems to be to let the sad and horrifying details accrue and to trust that, by the force of their own gravity, they will somehow coalesce into a meaningful story," A. O. Scott wrote in the *Nation* (April 22, 1996).

Perhaps the most criticized aspect of *The Names of the Dead* is the inclusion of Creeley, the character who stalks Larry. "It's boilerplate stalker stuff," Rand Richards Cooper wrote in the *New York Times Book Review* (April 7, 1996): "a remorseless killer, trained as a CIA assassin; confessions tumbling from the lips of a woman in a nursing home; ominous phone messages; sexual blackmail; and even that sine qua non of cyberdrama, a computer chase." Scott noted in the *Nation* that "Creeley is at bottom a purely literary confection, inserted into the novel to heighten its narrative effects and thematic resonances. But no themes resonate." Critics were, however, quick to point out that *The Names of the Dead* was not without its merits. The novel "offers a confident, gripping narrative, as well as some of the most searing wartime storytelling in recent memory," a reviewer wrote in *Publishers Weekly* (January 22, 1996). Rand Richards Cooper declared in the *New York Times Book Review* that the book was generally good but had one complaint: "It's as if Mr. O'Nan has studied admiringly at the feet of eminent predecessors, absorbing certain hallmarks of each—Robert Stone's conspirato-

rial and existential darkness, Michael Herr's harsh absurdity, Tim O'Brien's haunted directness—and then tied everything up with a high-concept Hollywood scenario. . . . Hear the hiss of air rushing out? That's the sound of a good novel collapsing into a movie."

Even before its publication, O'Nan's 1997 novel, *The Speed Queen,* was embroiled in controversy. The book's original title, *Dear Stephen King* (a nod to Gordon Lish's *Dear Mr. Capote*), had to be changed after King's lawyers threatened to file a lawsuit. In it, an unnamed writer, described as the author of *Misery* and *The Shining* (actual books by King), has bought the rights to the life story of convicted murderer Marjorie Standiford, also known as the Speed Queen, one of the infamous Sonic Killers. Standiford recounts the events of her life— her amphetamine habit, various arrests, a lesbian love affair, and her murderous rampages—to the author just hours before her execution. *The Speed Queen* received highly favorable reviews. "O'Nan has created a remarkably vivid and original storyteller in Marjorie, whose hilarious and tragic tale enthralls," Adam Mazmanian wrote in *Library Journal* (February 1, 1997).

Comparing *The Speed Queen* and O'Nan's next book, *A World Away* (1998), Matthew DeBord wrote in *Publishers Weekly* (May 25, 1998), "Two more divergent novels would be hard to imagine." Set during World War II, *A World Away* focuses on the troubled Langer family, both in the United States and on the battlefront. DeBord called the novel "alternately melancholy and profane." Discussing the painstakingly written work in his conversation with DeBord, O'Nan predicted, "Most of the people who read *The Speed Queen* read it in one sitting. Many of the people who start *A World Away* aren't going to finish it."

Also concerned with war—in this case, with its indelible scars— is O'Nan's fifth novel, *A Prayer for the Dying* (1999). The narrator, who refers to himself in the second person, is Jacob Hansen, who is haunted by the memories of his actions in the Civil War and who must contend with a no-win situation: in the town of Friendship, Wisconsin, where he is preacher, sheriff, and undertaker, the citizens are quarantined because of a diphtheria epidemic, at the same time that brush fires threaten the town, making everyone want to flee. Assessing *A Prayer for the Dying* in the *New York Times Book Review* (May 2, 1999), Patrick McGrath called it "a fine, terse novel about the circumstantial nature of evil and the terrible fragility of man."

In addition to his very active writing career, O'Nan has taught creative writing at Trinity College in Hartford, Connecticut, since 1990. He currently resides in Avon, Connecticut, with his wife and two children.

—J. P.

SUGGESTED READING: *Library Journal* p106 Mar. 1, 1996, p107 Feb. 1, 1997; *Nation* p34+ Apr. 22, 1996; *New York Times* CT13 June 9,

1996; *New York Times Book Review* p26 Mar. 27, 1994, p29 Jan. 8, 1995, p10 Apr. 7, 1996; *Publishers Weekly* p58+ Jan. 22, 1996, p391+ Jan. 20, 1997; *Studies in Short Fiction* p101+ Winter 1995; *Washington Post Book World* p8 Jan. 29, 1995

SELECTED BOOKS: *In the Walled City* (1993); *Snow Angels* (1994); *The Names of the Dead* (1996); *Speed Queen* (1997)

J. P. Ostriker

Ostriker, Alicia

Nov. 11, 1937– Poet; nonfiction writer

The American wordsmith Alicia Ostriker has made a name for herself as a poet by engaging the themes of illness and loss and as a critic by challenging assumptions of patriarchal society and positing a feminist revolution in cultural expression. In her volumes of poetry and prose poems *Songs* (1969), *Once More Out of Darkness* (1971), *A Dream of Springtime* (1979), *A Woman Under the Surface* (1982), *The Imaginary Lover* (1986), *The Mother/Child Papers* (1986), *Green Age* (1989), *The Crack in Everything* (1996), and *The Little Space* (1998), she has moved from formal expression to a more dramatic and individual voice, in which she has continued to expose her own identity, both personal and—in spite of the resulting criticism— political. Robert Phillips, reviewing *The Crack in Everything* in the *Hudson Review* (Winter 1997), called Ostriker "one of our finest poets" and noted particularly her "range, not only of subject matter . . . but tone." Her books of criticism, *Vision and*

Verse in William Blake (1965), *Writing Like a Woman* (1983), *Stealing the Language* (1986), *Feminist Revision and the Bible* (1993), and *The Nakedness of the Fathers: Biblical Visions and Revisions* (1994), have also been widely praised. Maeera Shreiber, reviewing *The Nakedness of the Fathers* in *Tikkun* (January/February 1996), called Ostriker "an important voice in American letters."

For *World Authors 1990–1995*, Alicia Ostriker, born in Brooklyn, New York on November 11, 1937, writes: "I had always written formal poetry. My mother was an English major and a poet, and she read me Shakespeare, Tennyson, Browning, along with her own poetry on birds and daisies. My first masters were Keats, Hopkins, Auden. Oh yes, I was a romantic—although Professor J. V. Cunningham tried to shame me in the one creative writing class I took as an undergraduate, he failed. In graduate school I fell in love with William Blake, rule-breaker and revolutionary, and wrote my dissertation on him in a year. I was also pregnant that year. What was I thinking of? Our first daughter was born a week after I submitted the dissertation, in August 1963; she was a week late. *Vision and Verse in William Blake* was published eighteen months later, and has become the standard text on Blakean metrics. Blake would remain my guru in matters spiritual, psychological and political for ten years. Meanwhile in my own poetry I was gingerly stepping into open form. A foot in the water, a knee, a plunge.

"After the dissertation, a year playing with the baby while my husband finished his Ph.D. in Astrophysics. Then a postdoctoral year in Cambridge, England, where our second daughter was born (this is called family planning) on Valentine's Day of 1965 in a nursing home run by starched nuns, and I worked on my first long poem, *Once More Out of Darkness*, which a friend later called 'a poem in nine parts and a post-partum.' *Once More* gave me my first conscious taste of rule-breaking. At that time I had never read anything written by a woman about pregnancy and birth, for the subject was, in mixed company, taboo.

"When I began teaching at Rutgers University in 1965, my models for a living art almost immediately became Whitman, Williams, Ginsberg. We were in Vietnam time; if you paid your taxes, you were burning South Vietnamese babies alive. Everyone I knew marched and sang in antiwar demonstrations. It was also an era of sex and drugs and rock and roll. People younger than myself inventing utopia and smashing themselves against the stone heart of what Ginsberg calls Moloch. To sustain an American poetics of inclusion and hope you needed open form, a language able to ride the elevator from vernacular basement to Latinate penthouse, and a refusal to divide the sacred from the profane. Between 1970 and 1980 I worked on the book I later called *The Mother/Child Papers*, begun a few days after my son was born in May, 1970, and a few days after some students demonstrating against the American invasion of Cambodia were killed by

State troopers. To write that book I needed to confront violence, within and without, and to imagine a love that could grapple and win. Almost impossible. By the mid-70's, as I lifted my head after editing Blake's complete poems for Penguin and writing two hundred pages of notes to those poems, I began reading women poets. Reading? No, rather devouring. Two books of poetry emerged from that gluttonous time: *A Woman Under the Surface* (1982) and *The Imaginary Lover* (1986), which thrilled me by winning the William Carlos Williams Award. That period also produced a book of criticism, *Stealing the Language: the Emergence of Women's Poetry in America* (1986), which tries to say what the collective voices of women were doing, that had never been done before in the history of literature.

"Since the mid-seventies I have written as a woman poet, and since the mid-eighties as a woman poet and critic obsessed with the Bible. What did I want with that patriarchal document, with its father God and its string of male patriarchs, warriors, judges, kings, and prophets? Like Blake, I have turned out to be a heterodox visionary—female variety—determined to rewrite scripture, turn it inside out if necessary, and wrestle a blessing from it. I had used the term 'revisionist mythmaking' in *Stealing the Language*, to describe what happens when women rewrite traditional stories. Of course it is one thing when you write about Odysseus from Penelope's point of view and Orpheus from Euridice's. It is quite another when you make the claim that God the Father swallowed God the Mother in prehistory. That's a little more unsettling—as is the reimagining of that demoted Mother-goddess Eve, or those trickster characters Rebecca and Rachel, or those erotic figures, the Shulamite in the Song of Songs, and the Magdalen in the Gospels. In *The Nakedness of the Fathers*, I combined Biblical commentary, fantasy, autobiography and poetry, in the effort to discover what those compelling stories mean to me, what I love and what I hate in them. In *Feminist Revision and the Bible*, I tried to describe what other women poets, from Emily Dickinson to Lucille Clifton, did with that material: how they spun it.

"Meanwhile I stayed miraculously married to my astrophysicist husband, raised three children into excellent human beings, taught literature and creative writing at Rutgers University, travelled to various parts of the world, spent time in California, hiked mountains, rode my bicycle, drove my car, and wrote about all these things. Of late I seem to have more politics in my poems. But I also keep writing about sex, love, the family, the body. Car poems. Art poems. God poems. I remain Whitmanic in intention, hoping to include whatever I can grasp of human experience within my art—the good and beautiful, the evil and chaotic. I tell my students that they must write what they are afraid to write; and I attempt to do so myself. My most recent book of poems, *The Crack in Everything*, was a National Book Award finalist, to my intense delight. The title comes from a Leonard Cohen song of which the refrain is 'There is a crack, a crack in everything, / That's how the light gets in.' There's metaphysics for you. It could be a teacup, or the mad mortal mind, or a broken wall, or the shards of vessels which according to Kabbala shattered because they could not hold the sparks of divine light at the beginning of the universe. When a friend sent me that Cohen tape, I knew I had my title. The poems touch on war, famine, brutality, illness, aging, death, and I hope a certain degree of light shines through them."

Reviewing Alicia Ostriker's first book, *Vision and Verse in William Blake*, Elizabeth Nelson remarked in *Library Journal* (November 15, 1965) that Ostriker's comments on Blake's prosodic "innovations and 'renovations' provide insight not only into Blake's poetry specifically, but to poetry in general." The *Choice* (March 1966) reviewer found that Ostriker illuminated the "poetic ideals of obscurity, complexity, freedom, and harshness" embodied by Blake's revolutionary prosody. Ostriker's first volume of poetry, *Songs* (1969), which contains poems influenced by Auden and Blake, has an almost academic flavor, which led one reviewer to note a "clinical coldness" in the poems.

Marriage to Jeremiah Ostriker, an astrophysicist, in 1958 and the birth of Rebecca, the first of her three children, in 1963, had a transforming effect on Ostriker's writing. She made a concerted effort in *Once More Out of Darkness* and *A Dream of Springtime* to incorporate the meaning of motherhood and other concerns of women into her work. In *The Mother/Child Papers,* she made a direct connection "between personal history and public fact," according to Mary Kinzie in the *American Poetry Review* (July/August 1981). The poems in the book are concerned with personal and family events that are overshadowed by the Vietnam War.

In *A Woman Under the Surface*, Ostriker's poems "illuminate the places where myth and daily life converge," in the words of Suzanne Juhasz in *Library Journal* (September 1, 1982). Ostriker chose for her subjects the interaction between a father and son, motherhood, craziness on the New York subway, politics, and authors of classic works—the topics of her daily life. Juhasz pointed out that Ostriker's uses of myth extend from reworkings of classical myths to recounting "contemporary primarily political experience as if it were chapters in a mythology." She commended Ostriker for writing "with much intelligence, in a language characterized by the clarity of its images and the precision of its rhythms." X. J. Kennedy, writing in *Poetry* (March 1983), remarked that "acerbic wit, verve, and energy insure that no page of Ostriker's collection is a bore." D. S. Earnshaw in *World Literature Today* (Winter 1983) placed Ostriker "among the finest American poets," deeming her one who "knows how to create out of plain English speech lines whose rhythm and imagery glow from within."

The Imaginary Lover, Ostriker's 1986 collection, an exploration of several aspects of love—male-female, mother-daughter, the "form in the mind"— drew a varied but mostly favorable response from critics. Patricia Hampl in the *New York Times Book Review* (June 7, 1987) found "some clunky lines" but thought "the candor and thoughtfulness of the poems . . . winning." She praised "Ostriker's tendency to locate a sustaining force for the rest of life—a force that is both passionate and honorable." Clair Wills in the *Times Literary Supplement* (July 10, 1987) thought Ostriker "at her best when most urbane and ironic," and added, "Her satirical descriptions (of intellectuals, businessmen, occasionally even herself) reveal a relaxed and witty facility with the language." Wills concluded that Ostriker should "concentrate on the side of women which meshes with culture rather than nature." For M. P. White, writing in *Choice* (July/August 1987), the poems in *The Imaginary Lover* "bring into focus some very complex and difficult situations: the process of spiritual decline, the nature of mourning, the acceptance of accidents and signs of aging that are rehearsals for death, and the intricate workings in a marriage of long standing."

With *Green Age*, Ostriker came into her own as a poet. Her voice is often filled with anger as she explores her own life, the world around her, and the spirit world. "The turning point in this collection," M. P. White wrote in *Choice* (March 1990), "is a sequence of four death ghazals. Ostriker uses the ancient Persian form to convey contemporary versions of death: the extinction of species, the spiritual decay of committeemen and businessmen, and the death of Vietnam soldiers, boys 'clad in ironic olive, on both sides.' The ghazals are echoed again in . . . a sequence of love poems written in emulation of Rumi's poems about erotic and spiritual longing. In another astonishing . . . sequence, Ostriker meditates on the traces of the ancient goddesses 'buried for 80 generations' in the Jewish tradition." For Cristanne Miller, writing in *Library Journal* (September 15, 1989), these "are poems of quiet passion, lyric movement, and of thought . . . forceful, provocative, persuasive."

In the mature poems of *The Crack in Everything*, Ostriker dealt in a "fresh, brave, and unself-pitying" way, according to Robert Phillips, with her bout with breast cancer and "psychological recovery." Ostriker, Phillips noted in his *Hudson Review* piece, "is as comfortable writing about Babi Yar (if comfortable could be the word!) as she is cracking Jewish jokes." For Patricia Monaghan in *Booklist* (May 1, 1996), Ostriker writes in *The Crack in Everything* "with calm authority and almost rocklike solidity." She felt that in "The Mastectomy Poems," Ostriker's "impressive craft rises to meet a demanding subject so fully that these poems stand among the classics of the poem-sequence genre."

In "After Illness," Ostriker makes an ironic comparison of illness to a voyage on a ship:

Through a starless moonless night,
You hear the engine thud, the hiss of water,
You limp through the humid black
To a railing: there,
You can see lights flowing
From a lower deck
Dimly illuminating the
Dizzy white foam, and
You're so alone, but you hear music too,
So you bravely resolve to explore the ship,
And after all, what choice do you
And after a few years
You discover they are all
On the same ship, oh yes,
All your friends, your cohorts,
Everyone from before, in their new
Flesh and bones, you agree it's won-
No cause now to be melancholy.
Reading? Dancing?
Get up, stand up, thumb some folly
Without which there's no wisdom,
you have to
Trust that, you have to take a chance.

Ostriker's critical study *Stealing the Language: The Emergence of Women's Poetry in America* was published after *Writing Like a Woman*. By 1986 Ostriker had become a "woman poet" analyzing other woman poets. The first chapter of *Stealing the Language* surveys poetry by women in America from 1650 to 1960. The rest of the book deals with poetry by women from 1960 to the mid-1980s. Reviewing the volume in the *New York Times Book Review* (July 20, 1986), Liz Rosenberg, who could also claim the status of "woman poet," was frank in agreeing with Diane Wakoski, quoted by Ostriker as saying, "I hate being thought of as a Woman Poet." Rosenberg, calling the book "a hodgepodge of pop scholarship, by turns insightful and myopic, elegant and sophomoric," claimed that the poems Ostriker cited "were selected in light of their relation to her argument and to feminist doctrine rather than for their virtues as poetry." She nevertheless expressed herself as "grateful for the essentially humanitarian stance of this book and its remarkable insights into certain issues and poems."

Feminist Revision and the Bible, a volume of essays, was followed by *The Nakedness of the Fathers: Biblical Visions and Revisions*, a book of essays and poems. *The Nakedness of the Fathers* "represents Ostriker's most sustained effort to interrogate the Hebrew Bible from a feminist perspective," according to Maeera Shreiber, writing in *Tikkun*. The first section, "Entering the Tents," deals with Ostriker's own relationship to the Bible, presenting the divided loyalties that she, as a Jew but also a woman excluded from much of Jewish ritual, experiences. Creation, exile and loss, and a contemporary examination of patriarchy— sometimes viewed from a comic perspective—are the themes of the middle sections. Shreiber observed that the book "concludes on a prophetic note with a section titled 'The Return of the Mothers.' This section is based on the work of feminist theorists "who seek to recover a long-repressed history of feminine representations of the godhead." In the book, Ostriker "gives voice to quasi-historical female figures who have been largely silent. . . . Ostriker adopts a heretical approach to culturally revered stories, using colloquial (and often comic) language to counter any charges of sentimentality to which she might be vulnerable," Shreiber observed.

In the poem "A Meditation in Seven Days" in *Green Age*, Ostriker adumbrated a position that she has succeeded in fulfilling:

Fearful, I see my hand is on the latch.
I am the woman, and about to enter

In her poem "Krishna Speaks to the Summer Carpenter," published in *TriQuarterly* (Winter 1995-1996), she showed her sense of humor about shifting gender roles. Speaking as the Hindu deity Krishna addressing a young man, she wrote, "I'm not particular. When / Next fall your pretty wife. . . / Throws a final fit and walks out, / I'm her too."

A writer for the *Village Voice*, reviewing Ostriker's *The Little Space: Poems Selected and New, 1968–1998*, found that Ostriker "explores the eroticism implicit in all relationships. . . . her poems read like passionate letters to a familiar you, utterly specific, yet tantalizingly mysterious."

Alicia Suskin Ostriker became a full professor of English at Rutgers University in New Brunswick, New Jersey, in 1972. She has been the recipient of Guggenheim and Rockefeller Foundation grants.
—S. Y.

SUGGESTED READING: *Booklist* p1485 May 1, 1996; *Choice* p1695 July/Aug. 1987, p1146 Mar. 1990; *Hudson Review* p663 Winter 1997; *Library Journal* p1663 Sep. 1, 1982, p114 Sep. 15, 1989; *New York Times Book Review* p21 July 20, 1986, p15 June 7, 1987; *Poetry* p349 Mar. 1983; *Tikkun* p 94 Jan./Feb. 1996; *Times Literary Supplement* p748 July 10, 1987; *World Literature Today* p115 Winter 1983; *Dictionary of Literary Biography*, 1992

SELECTED BOOKS: Poetry—*Songs*,1969; *Once More Out of Darkness*, 1971; *A Dream of Springtime*, 1979; *A Woman Under the Surface*, 1982; *The Imaginary Lover*, 1986; *The Mother/Child Papers*, 1986; *Green Age*, 1989; *The Crack in Everything*, 1996; *The Little Space*, 1998; Nonfiction—*Vision and Verse in William Blake*, 1965; *Writing Like a Woman*, 1983; *Stealing the Language*, 1986; *Feminist Revision and the Bible*, 1993; *The Nakedness of the Fathers: Biblical Visions and Revisions*, 1994

Paglia, Camille

Apr. 2, 1947– Nonfiction writer

Celebrated by some, reviled by others, Camille Paglia is the controversial author of the best-selling scholarly book *Sexual Personae: Art and Decadence from Nefertiti to Emily Dickinson* (1990). A feminist who deplores what politically correct feminism has become, she embodies contradiction without ambiguity and often offends everyone with her rapier-sharp tongue. She is at once radical and conservative, though only in the strictest sense of both terms, and votes the Democratic ticket while railing against the liberal academic establishment. Paglia upholds the erstwhile "boy-toy" Madonna as "the true feminist."Although Paglia had set out to intimidate men with her book, she was surprised to find she was usually alienating women instead.

After 20 years of teaching English in relative obscurity, Paglia has reveled in her sudden status as one of America's most charismatic scholars, and has shared her ideas on a wide range of subjects, from educational reform to date rape. At the heart of her universe is an Apollonian–Dionysian dualism that permeates everything from great works of art to the eternal state of war between the sexes. Like Freud, she believes that the supreme accom-

plishments of Western civilization are the result of the male drive to set himself against nature, and therefore against the Dionysian, or, as she prefers to call it, chthonian element of humanity, represented by woman and the mother. "If civilization had been left in female hands, we would still be living in grass huts," she has written. She explained her ideas to Lesley White in an interview for the London *Sunday Times* (June 7, 1992): "There is no female Mozart because there is no female Jack the Ripper. Great art and great crime are similar deviations from the norm that require a megalomania, an utter obsession. . . . Most women have too much empathy to want to be involved in anything like that."

Claiming to be "the greatest woman scholar since Jane Harrison [an early 20th-century British scholar]," Paglia has described herself as a "Joan of Arc willing to burn others at the stake," as one born with the "killer instinct" necessary for achieving greatness. Others' assessments of her confrontational, controversial style tend to be extreme: People seem either to love her or to hate her, to extol her as brilliant or to denounce her as a lunatic. She has been called everything from "America's premier intellectual renegade" to "a crassly egocentric, raving twit" by her fellow academics and writers. Paglia herself is an intriguing and inconsonant figure whose theories and public image often appear at odds with her actual life. She states that she is a feminist, but attacks the modern feminist movement. Some, like Naomi Wolf, author of *The Beauty Myth*, have accused Paglia of intellectual dishonesty for her (mis)representations of feminism as prudish and women's studies as an attempt to assert the sameness of men and women. Paglia supports pornography, prostitution, abortion, and the legalization of drugs, and her conception of radical feminism touts prostitutes and drag queens as primary role models and figures of female empowerment. Her critics have called her "Phyllis Schlafly in black leather." She maintains that she is a former Catholic who left the faith 25 years ago, but still regularly attends mass on holidays. An out lesbian, Paglia has criticized gay activists and the politics of the gay movement. She claims to be one of the most insightful American academics, but displays an utter disgust for theoretical debate on an academic level. Despite so much discord—or more likely because of it—Camille Paglia remains one of the most talked-about social theorists of the 1990s, and her writings are the focus of intense debate among all segments of the population.

Born in Endicott, New York, on April 2, 1947, Camille Paglia has one sister, Lenora, who was born when Camille was 14 and who is now an art conservator. Their mother, Lydia Paglia, was born in Ceccano, Italy, and came to the United States at the age of six. Their American-born Italian father, Pasquale Paglia, was a professor of Romance languages at Le Moyne College, a Jesuit institution in Syracuse, New York. Camille grew up in Syracuse, where she attended public schools, and her father encouraged her to pursue her unconventional and creative tendencies. As a child, for instance, Camille's Halloween costumes often reflected her interest in history and literature: Escamillo (the toreador from *Carmen*), a Roman soldier, Napoleon, and Hamlet. Camille was soon defying even her father's advice. "He realized he had created a monster," she admitted to Lesley White. "I rebelled against everything, I had a violent outlaw quality, . . . and I think it makes me a better role model for women today than all these sex-phobic feminists."

In a wide-ranging, in-depth interview with Francesca Stanfill for *New York* magazine (March 4, 1991), Paglia said her Catholic upbringing implanted in her an early fascination with the forbidden and erotic elements of art. The images of Saint Sebastian "voluptuously pierced with arrows" and of Saint Michael the Archangel "trampling the dragon" were particularly affecting because of the dualism of "the angel and the demonic. I don't identify with humans." Another longstanding preoccupation manifest itself early on was her seemingly paradoxical high regard both for contemporary film and for the history and literature of the ancient and classical periods. "Egypt and Hollywood were equivalent phenomena to me, equally rich and fabulous," she recalled in an interview with Martha Duffy for *Time* (January 13, 1992).

Paglia's strong personality derives, she believes, from the attention she received as an only child (until the age of 14) and, especially, from her grandmothers, who took care of her when her mother went to work in banking after having stayed home during Camille's infancy. "I got my intellectuality, studiousness, and severity from my father," she told Francesca Stanfill. "And I got my energy, optimism, and practicality from my mother. And from both I got the Italian capacity for hard work and the ancient Roman genius for organization."

If Camille Paglia had anything in common with other young girls, it would have been her search for someone to admire. Her selection of heroines, however, and the lengths to which she would go in pursuing their legacies was uncommon. So enamored was she of Amelia Earhart, for instance, that she spent three years researching the life of the aviation pioneer, and she collected 599 photos of Elizabeth Taylor. When she read *The Second Sex*, by Simone de Beauvoir, whom Paglia has called "one of the most learned women who ever lived, the last major thinker in sex," the 16-year-old Camille determined "to do something massive for women." Another object of her enthusiasm, Susan Sontag, turned out to be a major disappointment when Paglia met her in 1973, because Sontag failed to fill the role of mentor. "If she'd taken an interest in my mind I would have gotten published, you know," she asserted in an interview with Henry Allen for the *Washington Post* (April 15, 1991). As it turned out, Paglia became disillusioned with Sontag for "backtracking" from writing about popular culture when she was criticized in academic circles for having begun to do so. "I was stunned because I thought she was going to be this major intellectual," she told Francesca Stanfill.

At that time, Camille Paglia was well on the road to fitting that description herself. She had graduated summa cum laude, with highest honors in English, in 1968 from Harpur College of the State University of New York at Binghamton, where she had been an editor of the college literary magazine. She obtained her Ph.D. degree in English in 1974 from Yale University, in New Haven, Connecticut, which she attended from 1968 to 1972. At Yale, which she had entered as a Woodrow Wilson Fellowship Designate, she finally found a mentor in the iconoclastic literary critic Harold Bloom, who supervised her dissertation, *Sexual Personae* in its embryonic form. From 1972 to 1980 she taught at Bennington College, in Vermont, where she became notorious for getting into fist fights with students. In her conversation with Francesca Stanfill, she described that time in her life as "a series of psychodramas, all grand opera and El Greco storm clouds. My Amazon-feminist period."

An even more difficult period followed. Since she lacked an academic specialty, Paglia found it hard to penetrate the job market. "I believed that when you're looking for a candidate for a job, you want the best candidate, the strongest candidate," she said to Francesca Stanfill. "Right? *No!* That was one of my biggest illusions about life, O.K. Colleges and universities do *not* want the strongest. They want a colleague who will fit into the already existing power structure." She taught for one year at Wesleyan University in Middletown, Connecticut, and for three years part-time at Yale and the University of New Haven. At the last-named school, her night classes included on-site instruction for workers at the Sikorsky Aircraft Factory in nearby Stratford. In 1984 she joined the faculty of the Philadelphia College of Performing Arts, a school for dancers, actors, and visual artists that later merged with its next-door neighbor, the Philadelphia College of Art, to form the present University of the Arts.

Throughout the 1970s Paglia tried unsuccessfully to publish completed sections of her manuscript. During those years of rejection by magazines and journals, she has said, she rewrote the manuscript to make it even "ruder" and "nastier." Finally, in 1985, the first of two volumes (both of which she had completed in 1981) was accepted by Yale University Press after having been rejected by seven major New York publishers.

The first volume, *Sexual Personae*, was published in February 1990 with a clever dust-jacket cover of a face that is half Nefertiti, half Emily Dickinson. The book, which was nominated for a National Book Critics Circle Award and has since been optioned for television, became a bestseller shortly after it was published in paperback by Vintage in September 1991. Delineating the pornographic, voyeuristic, and sadistic elements in the art and literature of ancient Egypt and Greece, the Renaissance, and the Romantic period, Paglia aimed to demonstrate that "Judeo-Christianity never did defeat paganism, which still flourishes in art, eroticism, astrology, and pop culture," as she wrote in the preface. "My stress on the truth in sexual stereotypes and on the biologic basis of sex differences is sure to cause controversy," she continued. "I reaffirm and celebrate woman's ancient mystery and glamour. I see the mother as an overwhelming force who condemns men to lifelong sexual anxiety, from which they escape through rationalism and physical achievement."

Many critics interpreted such passages as a reactionary backlash against the relatively recent gains of the women's movement, but Paglia contended that her brand of feminism predates the current movement and that, while she wanted to recognize the immense power of nature; she never suggested that women surrender to that power. "The more woman aims for personal identity and autonomy, the more she develops her imagination, the fiercer will be her struggle with nature—that is, with the intractable physical laws of her own body," Paglia wrote. She also asserted that it takes a strong woman to admire the strength of men, and acknowledged her own debt to men, noting in her book that "the Apollonian line of Western rationality has produced the modern aggressive woman who can think like a man and write obnoxious books."

Unsurprisingly *Sexual Personae* incurred a great deal of negative criticism. Much of the flak Paglia received came from reviewers who lamented that her views might be or had been thoroughly embraced by some group or other, be it the literati or the neoconservatives, but oddly enough none of those groups has stepped forward in print to claim her as one of its number. Molly Ivins, for instance, wrote: "That this woman is actually taken seriously as a thinker in New York intellectual circles is a clear sign of decadence, decay, and hopeless pinheadedness." Some of Paglia's readers, on the other hand, have been quick to praise her. The actress and model Lauren Hutton has called her "the greatest living American philosopher," and, of course, Harold Bloom extolled her "remarkable book" in the article by Francesca Stanfill for *New York*: "It is provocative, it is stimulating, it is brilliant, it is original, and it compels one to rethink the entire question of the literary representation of human sexuality."

Paglia's theories also demanded a rethinking of American educational priorities. She laid the blame for the liberal rejection of the literary canon squarely at the feet of Jean-Jacques Rousseau, who saw nature as benign and civilization as corrupting. Paglia, like her hero the Marquis de Sade, believes the converse: that nature is brutal and violent and that society protects us from our own potential excesses rather than oppresses us, as the liberals and feminists, both "heir[s] to Rousseau," would have us believe.

Liberals and orthodox feminists are not only wrong, in Paglia's view, but are also unable to "think their way out of a wet paper bag," as she put it in a discussion about television with Neil Postman that was published in *Harper's* (March 1991). "They have absolutely no training in logic, philosophy, or intellectual history." Having become members of the establishment, she contended, they have grown mushy in their thinking. "Today's academic leftists are strutting wannabes, timorous nerds who missed the 1960s while they were grade-grubbing in the library and brown-nosing the senior faculty," Paglia wrote in the Boston University–based *Arion: A Journal of Humanities and the Classics* (Spring 1991). The true radicals, whom she considers the best of her generation, either destroyed themselves with drugs or lost their way along the career path. The liberals in charge, lacking a firm foundation for their beliefs, have too easily succumbed to the winds of political correctness in their willingness to dilute the canon with what she considers mediocre works by various marginalized groups.

"To me, the ideal education should be rigorous and word-based—logocentric," Paglia said in her conversation with Neil Postman. "The student must learn the logical, hierarchical system. . . . All parents should read to their children. Education is, by definition, repressive. . . . There is nothing pleasant about learning to read or to think." In an interview with Jim Bencivenga for the

Christian Science Monitor (October 8, 1991), in which she spelled out her agenda for educational reform, she added that students of the humanities should be taught by generalists in small classrooms. Professors should not be forced to choose between publishing and perishing—their teaching should come first—and "the concentration of essay writing at the heart of the humanities curriculum is discriminatory against people of other cultures and classes and must share respectability with the visual image and musical performance." In addition to a knowledge of the classics, students should be required to study black jazz and blues and the major religions, Paglia said.

As for women's studies, which she would abolish or overhaul completely, Paglia wrote in *New York Newsday* (January 27, 1991) that "academic feminism is lost in a fog of social constructionism. It believes we are totally the product of our environment. . . . [Academic feminists'] view of sex is naïve and prudish. Leaving sex to the feminists is like letting your dog vacation at the taxidermist's." The women's movement, to which Paglia might have belonged had she not found it so narrowminded and fanatical, turned her off from the start. One graduate school incident in particular remains engrained in her memory. She had declared the Rolling Stones to be a great rock band and was sharply reprimanded by some feminist New Haven townies, who "screamed at" her that the group's sexist lyrics meant that they could not possibly be great musicians. During the ensuing tumult, Paglia shouted back that the one had nothing to do with the other. In the same spirit, she told Francesca Stanfill that Picasso's derogation of women was not related to the caliber of his art: "My attitude is that if Picasso took a machine gun and cut down a line of grandmothers, O.K., it would not affect my opinion of his art." "From the moment the feminist movement was born, it descended into dogma," she has insisted. Critics of Paglia have suggested that it may be an equivalent crime for her to dismiss all the varied strains of feminism as one monolithic, Stalinist orthodoxy.

One issue on which most feminists agree has been the importance of stemming the tide of date rapes on college campuses by disseminating guidelines of proper behavior and forming committees to deal with infractions. With her emphasis on personal responsibility and individualism, Paglia departs radically from that approach. She believes that rape is an outrage, a serious crime that should be reported to the police and not to campus grievance committees, a practice that seems to her to be "an outrageous infringement of civil liberties" that emasculates men and "is unworthy of strong women." In her extremely controversial *New York Newsday* piece, she averred that "the only solution to date rape is female self-awareness and self-control. A woman's number-one line of defense against rape is herself." A strong woman, she believes, is capable of determining on a case-by-case basis whether she wants to be seduced and take her

chances or whether she should sacrifice some measure of freedom in the interest of personal safety. "When she makes a mistake," Paglia wrote in *New York Newsday*, "she must accept the consequences and, through self-criticism, resolve never to make that mistake again."

Exciting, sexually charged encounters with new acquaintances necessarily and inevitably carry with them the threat of being raped, according to Paglia. "Modern feminism's most naïve formulation," she wrote in *Sexual Personae*, "is its assertion that rape is a crime of violence but not of sex, that it is merely power masquerading as sex. But sex *is* power, and all power is inherently aggressive. Rape is male power fighting female power. It is no more to be excused than is murder or any other assault on another's civil rights. Society is woman's protection against rape, not, as some feminists absurdly maintain, the cause of rape. Rape is the sexual expression of the [Nietzschean] will-to-power, which nature plants in all of us and which civilization rose to contain. Therefore the rapist is a man with too little socialization rather than too much." Paglia's detractors charge her with blaming the victim by placing the responsibility for avoiding date rape on women's ability to negotiate their way out of a potentially threatening situation, but Paglia calls her approach commonsensical and respectful of women's "right to freely choose and to say yes or no." "Everyone should be personally responsible for what happens in life," she added in a *Playboy* (October 1991) interview.

In September 1992, Paglia published *Sex, Art, and American Culture*, a collection of her past articles, essays, interviews, and lectures. As an appendix, she provided space for reproductions of cartoons satirizing her and a bibliography of magazine and newspaper articles concerning her work. Included within the book are some of her most controversial works, including her essays on date rape, the legalization of drugs and prostitution and, one of her favorite icons, the pop star Madonna. In addition to being "the true feminist" in the Paglian pantheon, Madonna is "the latest atavistic discoverer of the pagan heart of Catholicism," according to her most vocal admirer. "Madonna is the closest we've ever come to that combination of a full female sensuality with a masculine political astuteness," Paglia said in the *Playboy* interview.

Like her articles themselves, Paglia's compilation drew a sharp blend of potent criticism and virulent praise. A critic for *New Statesmen and Society* (January 8, 1993), while giving the book a largely negative review, offered one of the more positive reflections on *Sex, Art, and American Culture*, calling it "more coherent" than *Sexual Personae* and arguing that the book showcases Paglia as "an ace polemicist." The reviewer went on to note that "Paglia uses an arresting prose style to present complex ideas in accessible ways. In these essays, she writes about art and politics with passion and knowledge, if still with too much adjectival overkill." Ultimately, the *New Statesman* critic derided

Paglia for using a lot of energy on "throwing bile at her predecessors. What a pity most of it's just catty girl's stuff."

Christopher Thomas wrote in *Commonweal* (June 4, 1993) that while he did not always agree with her point of view, he admired her fluidity as a writer. "Beneath her bluster Paglia is a woman of staggering learning and a fine writer, one who takes the craft seriously," Thomas wrote. He lauded her stark style of writing for a "heat and directness" not often found in the writing of humanities analysts today. The reviewer went on to recommend the book as an important guide for those just being introduced to Paglia's work. He wrote: "Her style of presentation, more or less that of a stormtrooper in jackboots, has not always made it easy to hear her, and this book makes a valuable introduction to her ideas and opinions." However, Thomas did take exception to Paglia's "obsession" with sexuality, particularly darker forms of sadomasochism, and her stereotyping of men as "primitive, macho denizens of forest and sports bars." He concluded that while "enjoying Paglia's chutzpah and being challenged by her daring," readers should remain conscious of Paglia's seduction. "She asks good questions, and her answers are often refreshingly liberating," he wrote. "Her bias against theory is a valuable corrective, but we all operate from theories, and hers must be seen as theories too, not gospel."

Michiko Kakutani offered a harsher critique in the *New York Times Book Review* (September 15, 1992). Taking a bemused look at some of the phrases which Paglia uses to describe herself (such as "a woman born ahead of my time" and an "anti-establishment maverick" who represents a "classically American story, the loner riding out of the desert to shoot up the saloon and run the rats out of town"), Kakutani noted that to the descriptions Paglia provided, "one might add, egotistical, arrogant, and boastful." Kakutani felt that "although there are lots of ideas in this volume—some of them astute, some of them embarrassingly lamebrained—all of them are overshadowed by Ms. Paglia's loud, irritating persona." While she acknowledged the significance of some of Paglia's work (such as her attack on the French philosophers Jacques Derrida and Michel Foucault), the reviewer concluded that "unfortunately, such useful and interesting ideas are undermined, in this volume, by Ms. Paglia's crackpot opinions on other matters."

Two years later, while the world was still digesting *Sex, Art, and American Culture*, Paglia unleashed yet another challenge to society in the form of *Vamps & Tramps*, a collection of her essays. It included some of her longer, more controversial pieces, such as "No Law in the Arena" (which explores, among other topics, pornography, sexual harassment, rape, and abortion), as well as less abrasive works, such as a gentle reflection on several gay friends who were instrumental in shaping her perspective. As with her previous collection,

reaction to *Vamps & Tramps* was predictably extreme, with critics either praising or slamming Paglia. Michiko Kakutani of the *New York Times* (November 15, 1994) was one of the few to offer a mixed assessment: while she commented that the book is "seasoned with silly, sophomoric statements," she also admitted that Paglia is "most convincing in this volume when she abandons all the demagoguery, turns down the volume on her prose, and simply lays out her arguments in a straightforward fashion." Kakutani further commented that Paglia's "writings on education and the absurdity of curriculums based on trendy, politically correct agendas are highly persuasive, just as some of her essays on the perils of regulating pornography and the puritanical excesses of the women's movement radiate a fierce common sense." The reviewer also found the "Memoirs and Adventures" section of *Vamps & Tramps*—though marred, as usual, by Paglia's "exaggerated" sense of self—"highly moving" in its "earnest" look at the influence of Paglia's friends and relatives.

Richard Corliss offered a similar review in *Time* (December 12, 1994), noting that the book's generally "huffy" reception from the press suggests Paglia is in her "16th minute of fame," which he thought a "shame, since it discounts Paglia's roguish intelligence and genius for mischiefmaking." Francine Prose of *New York Newsday* (November 6, 1994) found that in *Vamps & Tramps*, "Assaultive and repetitive, occasionally refreshing and more often dangerously irresponsible, Paglia once again vaults onto her frothing, snorting high horse to tilt at familiar windmills." However, Prose stepped back from her attack to note that the book "does have its rewards; offhand statements and throwaway asides provide telling insights into this admirably inexhaustible gadfly and self-mythologizer." Steve Sailer of the *National Review* (December 31, 1994) called the volume "never dull . . . [but] repetitive." Although Sailer seemed to include himself among her frustrated "admirers who wish she'd get back to scholarship," he found her thoughts on contemporary American culture to be nonetheless incisive. "By focusing on the enduring allure of sexual archetypes, Miss Paglia explains the appeal of our tabloid divinities more successfully than normal news pundits, who can recognize only their supposed novelty," Sailer wrote. "The crazier the world seems, the saner Camille Paglia sounds."

In 1998 Paglia published *The Birds*, a collection of essays , writings, and quotations about the 1963 film of the same name, directed by Alfred Hitchcock. Raphael Shargel, writing for Amazon.com, quoted Paglia on her reasons for publishing such a work: "Overwhelmed by the film when I saw it as an impressionable teenage, I view it as a perverse ode to women's sexual glamour, which Hitchcock shows in all its seductive phases, from brittle artifice to melting vulnerability. . . . In this film, as in so many others, Hitchcock finds woman captivating but dangerous. She allures by nature, but she is the chief artificer in civilization, a magic fabricator of persona whose very smile is an arc of deception."

Paglia has claimed that her sharp, aphoristic prose style comes from the "percussiveness" and "muscular" beat of rock-'n'-roll, likening herself to "the first great [rock guitar] player who is a woman"; it may also derive partly from having labored under the belief that her work would only be read posthumously. "My best sentences are written as if this is going to be the only thing left, *just one sentence*," she told Francesca Stanfill. "Two thousand years from now, . . . someone will find this one sentence, and in that one sentence you should be able to re-create it all." For her rapid-fire oratory, she has been compared to "Joan Rivers on double-dose amphetamines," and her teaching style is consciously that of a stand-up comic. This fiery presentation, as much as her ideas, has made her a sought-after—if not beloved—guest speaker. "I never read prepared texts when I lecture on the road," she told Lesley White. "I'm just there shouting and the students are shouting back and hissing at me and I'm shaking my fist at them—it's, like, interacting, right?"

Some students disagree, and in recent years, Paglia has developed a notorious reputation for shouting down students who dare to question her reasoning. In 1994, *Rolling Stone* (October 20, 1994) published an article on Paglia's nationwide campus visits, calling her public speaking tactics a "baiting and bullying of students." The magazine also published a list of her offenses, including a 1992 visit to Princeton University where she yelled at a student, "You are an idiot . . . You are in the presence of one of the great women scholars of your time, and you behave like an ass, and you're gonna know about it when you're 50 years old. Eat my socks!"

In an effort to resist the corrupting influence of her recent celebrity, Paglia has refused to give up her privacy or freedom of movement, despite having been pursued by admirers since her first book came out. She has stated that she was a lesbian until the late 1980s, but that she now also dates men. She was more oblique in her reply to Stanfill's query about her sexuality. "My experience has been dual," she said. "I've gone through various phases of sexual identity during my adult life. I consider myself neither gay nor straight, neither male nor female, and neither human nor animal."

Standing five feet, three inches tall (not including the military-style black boots in which she is often photographed), Paglia is "small and not uncurvaceous," according to Stanfill, "with a memorable head: high cheekbones, a hint of the Etruscan about the eyes and mouth, and long pearly teeth. Her clothes are studiously sedate, . . . as if to offset the stream of verbal coloratura." Paglia is seldom pictured smiling, with the exception of the deep-décolletage-and-red-nails photo by James Hamilton in *Vanity Fair* (September 1992), but she does seem fond of creating dramatic images of herself:

she has posed with a knife á la *West Side Story*, with a sword, and in her office with her poster of her "kindred spirit" Madonna.

Camille Paglia teaches and lives in Pennsylvania.—D.B.

SUGGESTED READING: *America* p10+ Nov. 12, 1994; *Arion: A Journal of Humanities and the Classics* Spring 1991; *Christian Science Monitor* Oct. 8, 1993; *Commonweal* p25+ June 4, 1993; *Harper's* Mar. 1991; *London Sunday Times* p5 June 7, 1992; *The Nation* p615+ Nov. 21, 1994; *National Review* p58+ Dec. 31, 1994; *New Republic* p32+ Jan. 25, 1993; *New Statesman and Society* p40 Jan. 8, 1993; *New York* p22+ Mar. 4, 1991; *New York Newsday* Jan. 27, 1991, p34 Nov. 6, 1994; *New York Times Book Review* Sep. 15, 1992, Nov. 15, 1994, Nov. 20, 1994; *Playboy* Oct. 1991; *Rolling Stone* p87+ Oct. 20, 1994; *The Spectator* p26+ Jan. 16, 1993; *Time* p62+ Jan. 13, 1992, Dec. 12, 1994; *Vanity Fair* p238+ Sep. 1992; *Washington Post* B p1+ Apr. 15, 1991; *Contemporary Authors*, 1993

SELECTED WORKS: *Sexual Personae: Art and Decadence from Nefertiti to Emily Dickinson*, 1990; *Sex, Art, and American Culture: Essays*, 1992; *Vamps and Tramps*, 1994; As editor *The Birds*, 1998

Palliser, Charles

Dec. 11, 1947– Novelist

Despite numerous attempts by critics and fans alike, the American-born, British-educated novelist Charles Palliser continues to evade all efforts to circumscribe his work. His three novels, all well-received by critics, have displayed wildly different styles of writing—from comedy to minimalism to a form concerned with the minutiae of everyday life. His ability to reinvent himself as a writer has become the hallmark of his work.

Palliser's debut effort, *The Quincunx* (1989), described by Sally Emerson in the *Washington Post Book World* (June 16, 1991) as "a mammoth 788-page pastiche of a Dickensian novel," bombarded readers with scores of characters and in-depth examinations of literally thousands of facets—everything from 19th-century dishwashing techniques to turnpike-tollbooth architecture—of Victorian English society. He followed *The Quincunx* with the 1991 release of *The Sensationist*, a 153-page novelette "so spare, so compressed, and so late-20th-century in mood," wrote Tim Gooderham in the *Times Literary Supplement* (February 22, 1991), that, when compared with *The Quincunx*, "it seems a deliberate swing to the other extreme." With *Betrayals* (1994), Palliser proved himself to be a comic writer of considerable

Miriam Berkley

Charles Palliser

talent, capable of, as Robert Grudin wrote in the *New York Times Book Review* (March 5, 1995), "sometimes exploding into hilarity."

Palliser's tendency to adopt new styles parallels a nomadic upbringing in which the author often had to adapt to new surroundings and cultures. In an autobiographical statement submitted for inclusion in *World Authors 1990–1995*, Charles Palliser writes: "I was born in Holyoke, Massachusetts, New England, on 11th December 1947. My American father and my mother, who was Irish but had spent most of her life in the UK, had met during the War when my father was stationed in England with the American air Force. Their backgrounds were different in every way and since they were temperamentally ill-matched as well, it's not surprising that the marriage failed very soon. My mother, my two brothers, and I returned to the UK when I was two. We lived first in North Wales, then in Bath, and then for a memorable period in Switzerland in a little village high up in the mountains. When I was nine we returned to the US because my parents made an attempt to live together again. When this failed my mother, my younger brother, and I moved out. After a difficult period we eventually returned to England and lived in Bath again before moving to Cornwall.

"By now I was very confused culturally and educationally, having attended at least eleven schools in three different countries. From the age of twelve, however, I was educated at a fee-paying, single-sex school in Cornwall. It was Philistine, anti-intellectual, militaristic, and hostile to anyone who did not conform. Not surprisingly, I was bullied a great deal both physically and psychologically. Almost in spite of the teachers, however, I

began to do well academically and found that I enjoyed learning. It was now, at about twelve, that I decided I wanted to become a writer. I had always been a passionate reader and I think the world of the imagination represented both an escape and the promise of a better reality. In my imagination I could create something that could not be bullied or jeered at or forced to compromise because nobody even knew that it existed. (I still haven't resolved the paradox that writing fiction is an intimate and secret process which is then made public.)

"At about 16 the idea of going to Oxford became my dream, though it was very hard to do this from a small and academically undistinguished school. After a first humiliating rejection, I succeeded in scraping into Exeter College, where I started in October 1967.

"Although Oxford was in many respects a disappointing experience educationally, I enjoyed many things about it. I read English language and literature and gained a First in June 1970. I stayed on to obtain a second degree because I had decided that a career teaching in a university would combine well with writing novels. From 1972 until 1990 I taught English literature—first in Yorkshire, then in Glasgow, with a brief spell at Rutgers, New Jersey.

"From my early teens I was always writing something. The problem was that my novels always became too long and too complicated and by about 1977 I had several abandoned projects behind me. I decided to write something relatively short and simple. The same process occurred, however, and the novel spiraled almost out of control. But this time I was determined to finish the book and so, half a million words and twelve years later, *The Quincunx* was published. Its success enabled me to give up my university post and became a full-time writer in 1990. (Though I still teach creative writing when I have the opportunity.)

"Why I write is one of the hardest questions to answer. Unlike many writers, I think I'm motivated by curiosity more than by the urge to communicate something that I already understand and believe. Writing a novel is a way of finding out something that I don't yet know. That has two aspects, one of which is the appeal of encountering something which is 'other' and strange like a different personality or a different historical epoch. For example, I've always been fascinated by the past and one reason for writing *The Quincunx* was that I found myself wondering what it was really like to be poor in London in the early 19th-century and whether Dickens and other novelists of that era were describing things as they really were or presenting an ideologically distorted version of reality. And in my second novel, *The Sensationist*, I attempted to get inside the mind of someone very different from me—unintrospective and easily bored. In my current novel I'm trying to imagine what it would be like to be a young woman of 24 whose closest friend has been murdered.

"The second aspect of discovering something through fiction is that writing a novel forces me to work out what I 'really' believe about something by requiring me to think hard about difficult issues, to try to go beyond the evasions and half-truths that I might be satisfied with in my own life but which are ruthlessly exposed within a novel."

The publication of Palliser's *The Quincunx* set off a frenzy of media praise. The book, which details a complex mystery involving a young man in Victorian England who appears to be the victim of a conspiracy—possibly two—to rob him of his inheritance, and possibly his life, was quickly deemed superb. "It is robust and hugely enjoyable, filled with forebodings and complex plotting," Emerson wrote in the *Washington Post Book World* review. In April 1991 the book received the Sue Kaufman Prize for First Fiction from the American Academy and Institute of Arts and Letters.

Palliser's follow-up novel, *The Sensationist*, is a stark tale of alienation set in an unnamed Scottish city. The main character, David—whose last name is not mentioned—moves to this grim town to take a high-powered job in financial markets. Once there he has a series of casual sexual affairs. David eventually meets Lucy, an aspiring artist whose secretiveness and apparent indifference to his advances causes him to become fascinated with her. As soon as Lucy begins to truly need David, he loses all interest in her, leading to a dramatic and tragic conclusion. The novel is a study of various themes, including "the self-destructiveness of modern life, the agony of the artist lacking confidence, [and] the consequences of an inability to show affection," Gooderham wrote in the *Times Literary Supplement*. Noting that Palliser did not attempt to impose his own moral views on the characters or their actions, Emerson wrote in the *Washington Post Book World*, "The Sensationist is fragmentary and elliptical and leaves the reader interestingly dissatisfied, as it intends."

In sharp contrast to the relatively simple plot machinations of *The Sensationist*, Palliser's third novel, *Betrayals*, is a work of dizzying complexity. The book, which has no main character and proceeds in a nonlinear fashion, begins with an obituary and concludes with a 13-page index of names with more than 175 entries. "In between, there are, among other things," Daniel McMahon wrote in the *Washington Post Book World* (March 5, 1995), "stories within stories; a homicidal maniac's diary that includes a redaction of two television shows and oblique references to his pastime; a series of letters from only one correspondent; an academic's one-sided explanation of a scandal in which he was involved; a short story, 'The Trap,' purportedly translated from the Arabic; a bad book review; and a hilarious, horribly written apologia by a popular novelist-turned-murderer who uses product placements in his potboilers and plagiarizes another man's work." Linking all of these apparently disparate elements is the recurring motif of betrayal. "[Palliser] takes betrayal beyond its legal and moral context and into underlying areas of perception, identity, and communication," Grudin wrote in the *New York Times Book Review*. "In these realms he suggests that a person's betrayal of others is simultaneously self-betrayal, and that a person's deception of others is simultaneously a form of confession." The novel's extreme complexity, McMahon wrote in the *Washington Post Book World*, is one of its greatest assets. "A great deal of the fun in reading this novel is cumulative and derives from the intellectual pleasure one gets from reading carefully and recognizing the elements from earlier stories and from trying to piece together the 'truth' about the various episodes."

Notable among Palliser's other literary accomplishments are *The Journal of Simon Owen*, a 90-minute radio play commissioned by the BBC in 1982, and *Obsessions: Writing*, a short television film broadcast by the BBC in 1992.
—J. P.

SUGGESTED READING: *New York Times* C p17 June 27 1991; *New York Times Book Review* p11 July 14 1991, p17 Mar. 5 1995; *Tech* p8 Apr. 13, 1990; *Times Literary Supplement* p19 Feb. 22, 1991; *Washington Post Book World* p9 June 16 1991, p8 Mar. 5, 1995

SELECTED BOOKS: Fiction—*The Quincunx*, 1989; *The Sensationist*, 1991; *Betrayals*, 1994; Television—*Obsessions: Writing*, 1992; Radio—*The Journal of Simon Owen*, 1982

Parks, Tim

Dec. 19, 1954– Novelist; translator

"I don't believe there is any moral virtue in anything I do, or any 'meaning' in what I do, but I do have a sense that this is what I do," British-born novelist and translator Tim Parks once told *Publishers Weekly* (July 6, 1992). What Tim Parks has done over the past 15 years is write critically acclaimed novels, many dealing with families struggling to care for their ailing members or with children rebelling against their parents' religiosity.

Tim Parks was born on December 19, 1954, in Manchester, England, to Harold James and Joan (McDowell) Parks. His father was a clergyman, and both of his parents were highly religious or, as Parks once put it, "traditional but very evangelical" Anglicans "from the left wing of the Church" (*Publishers Weekly*, (July 6, 1992). His parents, he told *Publishers Weekly*'s Michele Field, were "dangerously close to the pushy, 'progressive' side of religion." His upbringing as the youngest child of three was a difficult one, marked by the extremes of his siblings, whom he described to Field as "an elder sister who was very 'pro' my parents, and an elder brother whose rebellion was very unpleasant."

Parks grew up in various parts of England, including Liverpool and London, and attended Cambridge University. When he received his degree, in 1977, he decided to go to the U.S., where he earned an M.A. degree from Harvard University. It was during this period that Parks began to write fiction regularly. (He also wrote for a public radio station in Boston, WGBH.) While he was in Massachusetts, Parks met his future wife, Rita Baldassarre, who worked as an Italian tutor at Harvard. The two were married on December 15, 1979, and moved to London when Parks received his degree. Shortly afterward, they moved to Italy, where they remained, in a small village outside the city of Verona, for more than a decade.

While writing fiction, Parks began working as a language teacher and translator in Italy. Having received numerous rejections of his own work, he had all but despaired of being published when his *Tongues of Flame* made an impression on the judges of the Sinclair-Heinemann prize for unpublished fiction. The novel was runner-up for the prize in 1982 and was published in 1985 by Heinemann, one of the companies that had originally rejected it. The following year, *Tongues of Flame* was bought by Grove Press and published in England, where it picked up further accolades, including the prestigious Somerset Maugham Prize for writers under 35, and the Betty Trask Award, given to debut novels by authors who display a promise in the genres of romantic or traditional fiction.

Set in late 1960s London, *Tongues of Flame* tells the story of a guilt-ridden teen, Richard, who lives in the suburbs with his devoutly religious family. Richard, the narrator, details the pressure building in the family as a result of the tension between his traditionalist father and his older brother, Adrian, who defies authority by—among other things— smoking marijuana and having sex in the family's home. Richard is torn between his father's brand of moralistic propriety and his awakening sexual desires, while both detesting and admiring his brother's audacious actions. The *New York Times* (January 4, 1987) reviewer called *Tongues of Flame* a "hilarious and original portrait of a young boy grappling with good and evil," noting that Parks possesses "a good eye for period detail." Reviewer Meg Wolitzer also wrote that Parks' characters are "well drawn and interact convincingly" and that the novel proves to be a "compelling family drama."

Parks has translated some very successful novels, the first of which was Alberto Moravia's *Erotic Tales* (1985), which the *New York Times Book Review* (January 5, 1986) critic said provides a "lighter gait" to Moravia's thick prose. *The Voyeur* (1986), also by Moravia, was "competently translated from the Italian" by Parks, according to the *New York Times Book Review* (March 29, 1987). These translations were followed by those of Anto-

nio Tabucchi's *Indian Nocturne* (1988) and, two years later, his *The Edge of the Horizon* (1990). The year 1993 saw two more translations by Parks, *The Marriage of Cadmus and Harmony* by Roberto Calasso and *Sweet Days of Discipline* by Fleur Jaeggy.

Parks's next work in translation came with Italo Calvino's *The Road to San Giovanni* (1993), a collection of five "memory exercises" by the Italian author, which received mixed reviews. The *Booklist* (September 1, 1993) reviewer wrote that Parks "renders what must be demanding Italian into English of the utmost clarity and precision." Meanwhile the critic for *Kirkus Reviews* (July 1, 1993) took an opposing stance, declaring that "none of the quintet is especially well brought into English by Tim Parks." Two years later, Parks returned to Calvino's work with the release of *Numbers in the Dark: And Other Stories* (1995), a translation which, the *New York Times Book Review* (November 26, 1995) reviewer wrote, was "perfectly in tune with the various dialects and discourses that Calvino assimilated during his career." Parks, the reviewer stated, uses many "inspired choices" in his work which make it "more than accurate and readable" but "inventive" as well.

In 1998 Parks offered two more translations, *Last Vanities* by Fleur Jaeggy and *Ka* by Roberto Calasso. The latter book received high praise from critics, with a reviewer for bookseller Amazon.com writing that Parks's translation "preserves Calasso's sensitivity to the visionary power of language, presenting the reader with a pathway that leads through dizzying awe to gradual recognition of a more familiar world." The *Booklist* (October 1, 1998) reviewer was also impressed, commenting that the book was "rendered beautifully into English by Tim Parks."

Parks's own second novel, *Loving Roger* (1986), begins with the title character already lying dead after having been stabbed by his girlfriend, Anna. The tale of their rocky relationship is explored, revealing how this mismatched pair—he an ambitious, egotistical playwright and sales executive and she a doting, mousy typist—came together in the first place. Reviews of the novel differed widely, with many praising Parks's prose while criticizing the story's development. The *New York Times* (January 10, 1988) reviewer noted that Parks "is very good at describing Roger's caddish creepiness and Anna's passive goodness—too good as it turns out . . . Roger's behavior . . . becomes too intolerable for the reader, let alone Anna, and even her passitivity becomes tiresome in the end, so we can hardly blame Roger for wanting to flee her endlessly repeated declarations of love." The reviewer concludes that "*Loving Roger*, as poignant as it is, has the feel of an inflated short story, and by the time it comes around full circle to the initial stabbing, we can't help feeling that murder is too kind a fate for Roger Cruikshank and too simple a one for us."

Parks followed *Loving Roger* with *Home Thoughts*, a tale of British expatriates living in Italy and pursuing relationships both platonic and sexual. At the center of the story is Julia Helen Delaforce, a single woman in her 30s who arrives in Italy full of hope and aspiration but soon, after getting involved in dead-end jobs and affairs, descends into a cloud of depression. The *New York Times* (October 23, 1988) critic wrote that for such a short book (less than 250 pages), the novel contains "an impressive number of characters in full dress." The reviewer went on to note that by having almost all of the characters write letters, commenting on their writing style and state of mind, the author "is not only exhibiting a forceful, authorial self-consciousness, but is putting on an amusing sideshow for himself, not unlike those Italian Renaissance paintings in which the painter has put himself in the scene and is looking out boldly at the viewer." The review concluded by stating that although "there are moments in this book when Tim Parks becomes a little too entranced with his own cleverness, *Home Thoughts* is a startlingly sharp and impressive piece of work."

Family Planning is the title of Park's fourth novel. Its story line revolves around a family that is slowly succumbing to the pressure of caring for a schizophrenic adult. Raymond is the 32-year-old burden with whom the Baldwin family must contend, a man who can be paranoid and delusional as well as cunningly intelligent and perceptive. Raymond's father abandons the family and moves to another country, while his older sister, Lorna, leaves her husband to move back in with her mother and help take care of Raymond. The family struggles with both the physical demands of caring for Raymond and the guilt that often accompanies such situations. The *St. Louis Post-Dispatch* (March 4, 1990) reviewer wrote "The author's ability to get inside each character—to BE the character—so that the reader sees them all in a sympathetic light, makes each turn of events inevitable, anguished, and yet, in the end, understandable."

For the creation of a suspense thriller that served a departure from his other novels, Parks decided to write under the pseudonym John MacDowell for his fifth novel, published as *Cara Massimina* in England and as *Juggling the Stars* in the U.S. *Goodness* (1991) was Parks's next novel; in it he once again explored the concept of having a family struggle with a disabled child. In *Goodness*, George Crawley is a successful, happily married computer software designer who believes he has escaped his troubled youth, which he spent with his missionary father, pious mother, abusive grandfather, and mentally retarded aunt. But his contented life in London is shattered when his wife gives birth to a severely retarded daughter. Response to *Goodness* was overwhelmingly positive.

Italian Neighbors (1992), the book that Parks published the following year, is perhaps the author's most personal work to date. The book looks at Parks's initial experiences in Italy, as he and his pregnant wife tried to adjust to new rules, customs, and mores. His characters, though fictionalized in the book, are based on his own neighbors in the small village outside Verona where he lives. The *Kirkus Reviews* (May 15, 1992) critic characterized *Italian Neighbors* as "Always zestful" and "sometimes gripping." The *New York Times Book Review* (July 26, 1992) critic called it a "delightful" book and wrote that it "Splendidly characterizes his Italian neighbors and their hang-ups."

Using his background as a translator for the Italian quarrying industry, Parks created *Shear* (1993), a geological thriller. After completing a sequel to his highly lauded *Juggling the Stars*, a novel called *Mimi's Ghost* (which London's *Financial Times* (January 7, 1995), reviewer called "Hilarious"), Parks wrote another sequel of sorts, *An Italian Education* (1995). For this largely autobiographical book, Parks recalled events from his life in Italy that took place after the appearance of his previous work on the subject, *Italian Neighbors*. However, whereas the first book focused on the quirks, pleasures, and annoyances of Italian society in his small village, *An Italian Education* takes on the subject of children, specifically the task of raising children in a culture different from one's own.

Parks's novel *Europa* (1997) probes the inner turmoil of middle-aged Jerry Marlow, a professor at the University of Milan, who joins a caravan of colleagues and students as they head toward Strasbourg and the European Parliament to protest new Italian laws against hiring foreigners. Although Marlow isn't even supportive of this action, he goes along to be with his ex-lover. Marlow had left a wife and 18-year-old daughter for the foreign lecturer, a woman whom he never speaks of by name, only referring to her as "she" and "her" until the last sentence in the novel. The woman left Marlow after a rocky relationship that often left her beaten as a result of his jealous rages. The novel finds Marlow analysing the motives of the disparate group of which he has become a part while reflecting on the course of his own life.

Although the novel was generally well received, one lone voice of disappointment emerged from the reviewer for the *New York Times Book Review* (November 15, 1998), who wrote that as readers, "we keep waiting for some sign that [Parks] doesn't take his narrator, Jerry Marlow, as seriously as Marlow takes himself" but that "as page after page goes by and Parks still hasn't slapped him down, it becomes dishearteningly clear that Marlow's feisty heterodoxy is supposed to make him a significant figure." The reviewer was also critical of the literary device Parks used of having the ex-lover's name unmentioned until the end of the novel, writing that "This device seems intended to set her apart, but the effect is to render her even more distant." The review concluded by commenting that "Parks may be an old pro, but this is amateur stuff." The *Booklist* (October 1, 1998) critic was more congenial, calling the book a "tale of gripping psychological complexity that reflects the paradoxes of the world at large" and noting that "every exchange, from the most erotic to the most formal, is charged with anguish and wit and refracts the depth of the divides between men and women, nations and faiths."

Tim Parks published *Adultery and Other Diversions* in 1999. He continues to make his home in Italy with his wife, Rita, son, Michele, and daughter, Stefania.

SELECTED WORKS: *Tongues of Flame*, 1985; *Loving Roger*, 1986; *Home Thoughts*, 1987; *Family Planning*, 1989; *Goodness*, 1991; *Italian Neighbors*, 1992; *Shear*, 1993; *Mimi's Ghost*, 1994; *An Italian Education*, 1995; *Europa*, 1997; *Adultery and Other Diversions*, 1999; As translator—*Erotic Tales*, Alberto Moravia, 1985; *The Voyeur*, Alberto Moravia, 1986; *Indian Nocturne*, Antonio Tabucchi, 1988; *The Edge of the Horizon*, Antonio Tabucchi, 1990; *Journey to Rome*, Alberto Moravia, 1990; *The Marriage of Cadmus and Harmony*, Roberto Calasso, 1993; *Sweet Days of Discipline*, Fleur Jaeggy, 1993; *The Road to San Giovanni*, Italo Calvino, 1993; *Numbers in the Dark*, Italo Calvino, 1995; *Last Vanities*, Fleur Jaeggy, 1998; *Ka*, Roberto Calasso, 1998; as John MacDowell—*Cara Massimina* (*Juggling the Stars*), 1990 REF=SUGGESTED

READING: *Amazon Books* (online); *Booklist* (online) May 1, 1993, Sep. 1, 1993, July 1995, July 19, 1995, Oct. 1, 1998; *Book Sellers* p38 July 2, 1993; *Christian Science Monitor* p11 Apr. 6, 1993; *Denver Post* (online) Oct. 11, 1998; *Financial Times* p18 Sep. 18, 1993, p12 Jan. 8, 1995; *Kirkus Reviews* (online) Aug. 1, 1991, May 15, 1992, July. 1, 1993, Mar. 15, 1993, May 1, 1994; *Library Journal* Sep. 15, 1991; *London Review of Books* p21 Nov. 4, 1993; *Observer* p54 Sep. 1, 1991; *New Statesman & Society* p30 Sep. 6, 1985; *New York Newsday* p50 Mar. 23, 1993, pB19 July 11, 1994; *New York Times Book Review* p6 Jan. 5, 1986; p9 Jan. 4, 1987, p15 Mar. 29, 1987, p10 Jan. 10, 1988, p15 Oct. 23, 1988, p22 Mar. 8, 1992, p15 July 26, 1992, p21 Mar. 14, 1993, p20 July 18, 1993, p8 July 31, 1994, p7 Aug. 6, 1995, p22 Nov. 26, 1995, p8 Nov. 8, 1998, p12 Nov. 15, 1998; *Publishers Weekly* p32 Nov. 14, 1986, p35+ July 6, 1992; *Salon Magazine* (online) Dec. 11, 1998; *St. Louis Post-Dispatch* (online) Mar. 4, 1990; *Times Literary Supplement* p1001 Sep. 13, 1985, p19 Aug. 30, 1991; *Wall Street Journal* p26 Apr. 26, 1993; *Washington Post* pD2 Nov. 20, 1991, pB2 Dec. 13, 1993; *Book Review Digest*, 1987, 1993; *Contemporary Authors*, 1991

Paton Walsh, Jill

Apr. 29, 1937– Novelist

Jill Paton Walsh gained her literary reputation as an author of books for children and young adults. In novels such as *Fireweed* (1969), *Goldengrove* (1972) and its sequel, *Unleaving* (1976), *A Parcel of Patterns* (1983), *Torch* (1987), and *Grace* (1992), she explored the spiritual and ethical patterns that emerge between the formative years and adulthood. Particularly famed for her sense of place (many reviewers term the settings of her books the major protagonists), she has written about the past and the future, as well as the present, in such places as Greece, Cornwall, and Derbyshire. Her adult novels, particularly *Knowledge of Angels* (1994) and *The Serpentine Cave* (1997), have a metaphysical quality; characters in Paton Walsh's novels exhibit a questing for the spiritual even as they come to terms with the world's betrayals and imperfections. Paton Walsh has entered the realm of the mystery with her own detective series, featuring Imogen Quy, who appears in *The Wyndham Case* (1993) and *A Piece of Justice* (1995), as well as with *Thrones, Dominations* (1998), a completion of the last book in the Lord Peter Wimsey series, left unfinished by Dorothy L. Sayers.

In an autobiographical statement submitted to *World Authors 1990–1995*, Jill Paton writes: "I was born a Londoner, just before WWII, and was shut-

tled between the Blitz and my grandmother's home in Cornwall as family crisis dictated. Added to these changes of scene, and the accompanying separation and reunion with my younger brothers and sister, was the arrival in our home of a stream of my mother's relatives, needing shelter. My mother's family lived in Burma, and had walked out through the jungle as refugees from the Japanese. They brought with them ideas and attitudes which were highly abrasive; they had been rich and privileged, we were commonplace and hard up. Above all they detested cleverness in little girls, finding it pushy and ridiculous. Little girls should aim to please. This childhood taught me early to define myself as a rebel, rejecting the ethos of most of those around me, and to centre my sense of rebellion around a habit of voracious reading.

"My young adult life was conventional. I won a scholarship to Oxford, making a higher education possible, met and married a fellow undergraduate, trained as a teacher and taught until the birth of my first child. Then, confined in the house caring for a baby, I began to write fiction. My fiction was intended for young readers like those I had been teaching. The difficulties of my childhood had made me very interested in the situations children find themselves in, and had also made me believe that what people read in childhood has very considerable importance in influencing their view of life. While my own children grew up I wrote over 20 books for children, ranging from picture books to teen-age novels. I always thought that something which was not good enough for adult readers was not good enough for children; I was trying to write in a way which self-respecting children and adults could share and enjoy alike.

"Eventually however, as my children grew up, and as grandchildren were seemingly indefinitely postponed, I became an adult novelist. The writing and reading of novels seems to me the most subtle and compelling way of truth telling about the nature of our moral lives, and the nature of the world we live in. The source of its potency is its power to disguise both writer and reader temporarily as other than themselves.

"The masked narrator and the masked reader are engaged in a ritual transaction, an ancient dance of feeling and meaning with very unpredictable effects. Children love dressing up, trying on roles, pretending, and once they get the hang of it they love wearing one after another the masks for readers implicit in the books they read. The mask wearers are disguised, and disguises liberate people. Being in their unmasked lives remarkably powerless, and at the disposal of other people, children are more in need of this escapism, this empowerment, than most readers. Those who prefer their children meek, obedient and pliable would do well to fear literature.

"But this strange process, which puts us out of ourselves and gives us a perspective which is not our own, is good for adults too!

"The high point of my career as an adult writer so far looked at first like a disaster, when a book I had written with particularly intense feeling, *Knowledge of Angels*, failed to find a publisher in Britain, though it was published and doing very well in the United States. Luckily John Rowe Townsend and I were running a tiny imprint of our own, 'Green Bay Publications,' for publishing criticism of children's literature, and such noncommercial titles. We decided to publish *Knowledge of Angels* ourselves, and it sold wonderfully, and was short-listed for the Booker Prize. This made me very famous for a while, especially among the many writers who feel aggrieved at the commercialism of publishers. But I had as much cause to be grateful to the American publisher as to be angry with the British ones.

"Like many writers I have not lived an outwardly eventful life. I used to live on the edge of London and now live in Cambridge, where there are wonderful bookshops and libraries. I live companionably with another writer, John Rowe Townsend, and we work, read, walk, and see our friends. The happenings are all in our heads."

Jill Paton Walsh was born on April 29, 1937 in Finchley, a suburb of London. Her parents were John Llewellyn and Patricia Dubern Bliss, the daughter of John Llewellyn, an engineer, and Patricia Dubern Bliss. She had a younger sister and two younger brothers. Until the advent of World War II,

the family lived in happiness and harmony. She noted in an autobiographical sketch for *Fourth Book of Junior Authors and Illustrators* that although her home was in Finchley, "the general nastiness of the blitz persuaded my stepgrandfather to take the family to St. Ives in Cornwall for a while; when my mother went home to London with the other children I was already at school, and so I stayed behind, blissfully happy in that lovely place, which is the setting for *Goldengrove*, my own favorite among my books." She completed her early education in a strict Catholic school.

Paton Walsh went on to university studies at St. Anne's College of Oxford University, where she attended lectures by such notables as J. R. R. Tolkien and C. S. Lewis, both scholars and authors, as well, of fantasies widely read by children. during this time she met Anthony Edmund Paton Walsh, who became her husband in 1961. After she got her degree, she taught in a secondary girls' school until the birth of her first child. Having disliked teaching, and also finding that she disliked being a full-time homemaker, she turned to writing; after the second of her three children was born, her book *Hengest's Tale* (1966)—inspired by a fragmentary narrative in *Beowulf*—was published. Having convinced herself that she was a writer, Paton Walsh became extraordinarily prolific, producing more than 26 children's books and more than 12 adult books.

Her novel *Fireweed* (1969) garnered many accolades and was chosen as a prize work in the *Book World* Children's Spring Book Festival in 1970. A story for young adults that can be enjoyed by adults as well, *Fireweed* takes place during the blitz in London, when people spent nights in Underground train stations to avoid the bombs that might be destroying their houses. The *Times Literary Supplement* (October 16, 1969) reviewer praised both the development of a relationship between two teenagers, "a touchingly real and beautifully understated picture of a growth of feeling," and the setting, a "picture given without squeamishness or apparent overemphasis of London in the blitz—the humour, the fear, the misery, the sometimes uncanny normality."

Goldengrove (1972), the story of an adolescent named Madge, who discovers that her cousin is really her brother and feels betrayed by her father as a result, was on the *New York Times* list of outstanding books of the year. Barbara Wersba, reviewing *Goldengrove* for the *New York Times Book Review* (November 5, 1972), termed the novel "brilliant," especially for its technique. "Set in the present tense, the story weaves in and out of the thoughts of its characters, all the while holding a steady narrative line and creating vivid atmosphere," she wrote, expressing regret that such "beautiful and highly original work" might be missed by adults. The *Times Literary Supplement* (November 3, 1972) critic agreed that the technique served the first part of the novel well: "As the story gathers momentum, the deeply understood characters, the golden atmosphere, the small changes of everyday pleasures and the ageless tragedies of the sea are all put over with such newly-seen immediacy and such controlled mastery that the reader is carried along like a surf rider on the crest of a wave." The *Times Literary Supplement* deemed that the wave broke, however, and "the very force of the author's style topples her over into histrionics."

Paton Walsh's *Unleaving* won the *Boston Globe-Horn Book* Award for 1976. A sequel to *Goldengrove*, its main character is again Madge, this time seen both as a 17-year-old, sharing her newly inherited beach house with a group of philosophy students and teachers, and as Gran, who shares that same house with her grandchildren and other relatives. Elaine Moss, in her notice of the book for the *Times Literary Supplement* (April 2, 1976), felt that it was only on a second reading that "the intricacies of its construction, the full force of its intellectual argument and the comfort of its spiritual message—that feeling, experiencing, reacting emotionally to life is what matters—stand boldly forth, as challenging and beckoning as the symbolic Godrevy light."

A Parcel of Patterns (1983), the story of how a package of dress patterns spreads a plague in the 1660s, was lauded by most reviewers. Margery Fisher wrote in *Growing Point* (January 1984) that the book was "a fine example of the way imagination and craftsmanship can work on fact without distortion, without partiality, without romanticization" to "bring the past within our view."

Gaffer Samson's Luck (1985), an illustrated book for children from ages nine to 11, is set in the English Fens, a marshy area, where a boy's search for his aged and dying neighbor's "luck"(a leaf-shaped stone) is complicated by the flooding that plagues the area. "Most admirable," Phyllis Theroux wrote in the *New York Times Book Review* (June 16, 1985), "is the language. *Gaffer Samson's Luck* fairly drips and shines with the 'grounded radiance' of the flat, boggy, Fens marshland." Theroux termed it "a slightly dreamy, otherworldly book that nevertheless manages to convey the reality of death, friendships, travails, and dislocation very nicely."

Paton Walsh's young-adult novels encompass a wide variety of settings in time and place. *Torch* (1988), for example, takes place in the future on a Greek island. The people live a more primitive life than do moderns, as technology has been lost, along with knowledge of the past; two young people go on a quest for the meaning of the Olympic Games. Carolyn Polese, writing in the *Christian Science Monitor* (May 6, 1988), commented, "Skillfully, Walsh weaves elements of our own and past cultures into the ageless patterns of mythology to explore themes of freedom and faith."

Paton Walsh returned to the past for her young adult novel *Grace* (1991). Based on the life story of Grace Darling, who helped her father to rescue nine survivors of a shipwreck in 1838, the novel is a tale of the results of unwanted fame. Grace, who had "acted out of pure Christian charity, without thought of a reward," according to P. J. Kleeb, the *Times Literary Supplement* (November 21, 1991) reviewer, is showered with gifts and money, leading her to doubt her own motivations. "Probably it is a universal human instinct to set a price on all-too-rare goodness, and thus to diminish its value in the eyes of its possessor," Kleeb wrote. " The novel is . . . modest in aims, limited in vision, simple and traditional. . . .And it deserves, like Grace, a small place of its own among works of merit." *Knowledge of Angels* (1994), set in the 15th century on an island off the coast of Spain, is a philosophical novel about the problem of proving God's existence. Two strangers enter the domain of Severo, the cardinal-prince. One is Amara, thought to be a 13-year-old girl raised by wolves, and the other is Palinor, a shipwrecked engineer, who comes from a land of atheists. Seeing an opportunity to prove the existence of God, Severo has the wolf-girl trained by nuns who will not mention God to her. He believes she will spontaneously acknowledge a higher power when she acquires speech, as he believes that arguments will lead Palinor to acknowledge the existence of God. Palinor, however, persuades one of his interlocutors to relinquish his Christian belief. Palinor, consequently, is scheduled for execution.

Responses to *Knowledge of Angels* varied widely. Some reviewers, such as Ruth Pavey for the *New Statesman and Society* (August 19, 1994) found that this novel "about questions of faith and intolerance . . . is never boring." She found its interest to lie in the "compelling nature of its various stories: of Amara, the wolf child, of the novice nun who cares for her, of Palinor's arrival, his fisherman rescuers, his villa servants." She found further fascination in Paton Walsh's "beautiful, spare language." Ilene Cooper, writing in *Booklist* (February 15, 1994), thought that Walsh looked at "faith through a kaleidoscope. Is it innate, ingrained, instinctive, necessary?" Although Cooper found the book to be "a tangle of disconnected fragments" in places, she observed that "Walsh is always able to twist the kaleidoscope's lens just a bit, allowing a new pattern to emerge." Albert Manguel in the *Globe and Mail* (October 8, 1994) had high praise for the novel. It is, he wrote, "a delight to read, and its intertwined plots have the quality of a necessary fable. . . .Walsh has managed to create complex breathing creatures who will not be reduced to a single adjective." He observed that "*Knowledge of Angels* has a disturbing and fascinating quality"and that "the story of the cardinal's quest for an answer is, in Walsh's telling, as gripping as a thriller. The moral, brilliantly turned on its head in the last pages . . . is thoroughly compelling, and, as in all the best fables, the story transcends the moral and becomes its own justification."

One of the negative opinions about *Knowledge of Angels* came from John Sutherland in the *London Review of Books* (October 6, 1994). He thought that the book "commits the unforgivable sin of fable, in that its meanings are too accessible and determinate," so as to grate "condescendingly on the adult ear." Jill P. Baumgaertner, on the other hand, who reviewed the novel for the *Christian Century* (October 12, 1994), felt that when, as he was about to be executed, Palinor "wondered ruefully why it is those who believe most passionately in a merciful deity are themselves most murderous and cruel," he was not asking a trivial question—but that "the way it is presented in *Knowledge of Angels* is trite and predictable." She also criticized Paton Walsh's lack of knowledge of language acquisition theory, asking if "the author cannot get her basic facts straight, can the reader trust her to tell the truth about human motivation, about the church, about God and the knowledge of angels?"

In an article in the *Bookseller* (June 9, 1995), Paton Walsh took on her critics, maintaining that they were prejudiced against her because she was known as a children's-book author. She observed that if children were not encouraged to read, the market for adult books would soon "crash." "Those who write and publish rewarding books for children, and the loving and enthusiastic people who put the books into children's hands at the right moment, are more, not less, crucial to the prosperity of literature than the hugely prestigious writers working at the top of the ivory tower," she wrote.

Paton Walsh's 1997 adult novel *The Serpentine Cave* garnered less praise than had *Knowledge of Angels*. Returning to St. Ives in Cornwall for part of her setting, Paton Walsh based this novel partly on a 1939 event in which many people lost their lives in a lifeboat disaster. The protagonist, Marian, a middle-aged woman, goes to her mother's home when the old woman—an artist—is dying after a stroke that has taken away her speech. The mother cannot answer Marian's questions about the past, involving the identity of Marian's father and the location of a serpentine cave where Marian remembers being trapped as a girl—both details that relate to the lifeboat tragedy.

The reviewer for *Booklist* (October 1, 1997), Nancy Pearl, termed *The Serpentine Cave* a "potentially poignant novel" and predicted that it would prove disappointing for seekers of more complex literature. Nevertheless, she called it "a superior 'gentle read.'" For Barbara Love, writing in *Library Journal* (November 1, 1997) the book was "quick, engrossing reading." Rob Kinsman for *Pure Fiction* (1998) thought that the characters, locations, and emotions were "expertly conveyed" but that the "lack of anything really happening" made it "extremely slow."

Paton Walsh's 1998 entry into the adult-fiction market was a completion of Dorothy Sayers's *Thrones, Dominations*. It features Sayers's famous detective, Lord Peter Wimsey, and his wife, Harriot, returned from their honeymoon and living in London. Rex E. Klett, writing in *Library Journal* (January 1998), found *Thrones, Dominations* "perhaps not vintage Sayers" but thought it possessed "all the requisite stock characters, witty dialog, social satire, and red herrings of a classic Sayers." Michael Tropman, writing for the *New Statesman* (February 20, 1998), found that the "pace picks up" when Paton Walsh takes over, presumably after the first six chapters. "The dialogue gets crisper and there are twists on every other page. What we lose, though, is the subtle texture of Sayers's work." For Gary Krist, writing in the *Hudson Review* (Autumn 1998), *Thrones, Dominations* was "a disappointment. . . .The mystery itself. . . is extremely modest, with certain elements of the crime requiring more than the usual suspension of disbelief." He, too, however, found the pace quicker after Paton Walsh took over. "People begin to talk to each other in a way that doesn't suggest that they are all overbred mannequins. The novel begins to breathe." Paton Walsh had earlier created her own series detective, Imogen Quy, a nurse for St. Agatha's College of Cambridge University. After Imogen Quy's solution of a mystery in *The Wyndham Case*, Paton Walsh brought her back in *A Piece of Justice*. In the latter novel, Quy's tenant is assigned to write a biography of a dead mathematician and discovers that the three previous biographers have either died or disappeared mysteriously. Stuart Miller in *Booklist* (August 19, 1995) remarked that a "clever plot and the likable Imogen are the main features here, along with Walsh's rather good send-up of academicians and their pretensions." He concluded that the novel was an "excellent mystery in the very English tradition."

—S. Y.

SUGGESTED READING: *Booklist* p1062 Feb. 15, 1994, Aug. 19, 1995, p309 Oct. 1, 1997; *Bookseller* p28+ June 9, 1995; *Christian Century* p927+ Oct. 12, 1994; *Christian Science Monitor* B p6 May 7, 1970, B p1 May 6, 1988; *Globe and Mail* C p11 Oct. 8, 1994; *Growing Point* p4179 Jan. 1984; *Hudson Review* p623+ Autumn 1998; *Library Journal* p118 Nov. 1, 1997, p147 Jan. 1998; *London Review of Books* p15 Oct. 6, 1994; *New Statesman* p47 Feb. 20, 1998; *New Statesman and Society* p39 Aug. 19, 1994; *New York Times* C p18 Sep. 14, 1994; *New York Times Book Review* p6 Nov. 5, 1972, p30 June 16, 1985; *Times Literary Supplement* p1187 Oct. 16, 1969, p1319 Nov. 3, 1972, p375 Apr. 2, 1976, p24 Nov. 22, 1991; *Fourth Book of Junior Authors and Illustrators*, 1978

SELECTED BOOKS: Fiction—*Farewell, Great King*, 1972; *Five Tides*, 1986; *Lapsing*, 1986; *A School for Lovers*, 1989; *The Wyndham Case*, 1993; *Knowledge of Angels*, 1994; *A Piece of Justice*, 1995; *The Serpentine Cave*, 1997; *Thrones, Dominations*, 1998; Nonfiction—*The Island Sunrise: Prehistoric Britain*, 1975; Juvenile—*Hengest's Tale* (ill. J. Margrie), 1966;

The Dolphin Crossing, 1967; *Fireweed*, 1969;
Wordhoard: Anglo-Saxon Stories (with K.
Crossley), 1969; *Goldengrove*, 1972; *Toolmaker*
(ill. J. Roy), 1973; *The Dawnstone* (ill. M.
Dinsdale), 1973; *The Emperor's Winding Sheet*,
1974; *The Huffler* (ill. J. Palmer), 1975;
Unleaving, 1976; *Crossing to Salamis*, 1977; *The
Walls of Athens*, 1977; *Persian Gold*, 1978;
Children of the Fox (trilogy comprising *Crossing
to Salamis, The Walls of Athens*, and *Persian
Gold*, ill. D. Smee), 1978; *A Chance Child*, 1978;
The Green Book (ill. J. Stubbs), 1981; *Babylon*
(ill. J. Northway), 1982; *A Parcel of Patterns*,
1983; *Lost and Found* (ill. M. Rayner), 1984
Gaffer Samson's Luck (ill. B. Cole), 1984; *Torch*,
1988; *Birdy and the Ghosties* (ill. A. Marks),
1989; *Grace*, 1991; *When Grandma Came* (ill. S.
Williams), 1992; *Matthew and the Sea Singer*,
1993; *Connie Came to Play*, 1995; *Pepi and the
Secret Names*, 1995; *When I Was Little Like You*,
1997

Courtesy of Wendy Barrows

Patterson, James

*Mar. 22, 1947– Advertising executive; nonfiction
writer; novelist*

In addition to being a best-selling author, James
Patterson is the CEO and chairman of J. Walter
Thompson North America, a billion-dollar advertising company. As a writer he has achieved his
greatest success with mystery novels and thrillers.
Most notable among these is the series featuring
Patterson's psychologist/detective character Alex
Cross, including *Along Came a Spider* (1993), *Kiss
the Girls* (1995), *Jack & Jill* (1996), and *Cat & Mouse*
(1997). His newest novel, *When the Wind Blows*,
was published in 1998. The film version of *Kiss the
Girls*, starring Morgan Freeman as Alex Cross, premiered in 1997 and as of late 1998, *Along Came a
Spider* was in production, with Freeman reprising
the lead role.

James Patterson was born on March 22, 1947, in
Newburgh, New York. His father, Charles Patterson, was an insurance broker, and his mother, Isa-
belle (Morris) Patterson, was a grammar-school
teacher. James grew up with three younger sisters,
Mary Ellen, Teresa, and Carole. He attended St.
Patrick's Catholic school, where he got "incredibly
disciplined, to the point where work, compared to
high school, is nothing," he told *New York* (February 8, 1993). He graduated from the high-school division of St. Patrick's in 1965, the valedictorian of
his class.

Patterson attended Manhattan College, in the
New York City borough of the Bronx, and majored
in English literature. On a school break he worked
part-time as an aide at the McLean Hospital, a psychiatric facility in Belmont, Massachusetts. His experiences there would later prove to be a great influence in his writing. One of the patients at the

hospital was the renowned poet Robert Lowell,
who befriended Patterson. "When he was not depressed, he would talk about his poems and why
he wrote them," Patterson recalled to *People*
(March 20, 1995).

After earning a B.A. degree from Manhattan College, in 1969, Patterson enrolled at Vanderbilt University in Nashville, Tennessee. In place of a master's thesis, he wrote an unpublished literary novel
entitled *Father Wrote a Hemingway Novel*. While
at Vanderbilt he also made an aborted attempt—
not for the first time—at composing a novel called
"A Choirboy's Tale". At some point he abandoned
his plan to become a professor of literature, and he
left Vanderbilt after receiving an M.A. degree, in
1970.

Patterson then moved to New York City, taking
up residence in the Hell's Kitchen section of Manhattan. He became determined to make a living at
writing—specifically, writing suspense fiction—in
1971, after reading Frederick Forsyth's *The Day of
the Jackal* and William Peter Blatty's *The Exorcist*.
However, his writing career did not progress as he
had hoped, and he finally took a job as a junior
copywriter at the advertising firm J. Walter
Thompson to support himself. He continued to
write on the side, and also began a relationship
with Jane Blanchard, an account representative at
another advertising agency.

In 1976, after receiving 30 rejections, Patterson
published his first novel, *The Thomas Berryman
Number*. The book, which remains his most critically acclaimed work to date, earned him the Mystery Writers of America Edgar Award for best first
mystery novel. That same year, Patterson became
a vice president at J. Walter Thompson.

Patterson next wrote *The Season of the Machete* (1977) and *The Jericho Commandment* (1979). The most commercially successful of his early efforts was *Virgin* (1980); an offbeat novel about Christ's Second Coming in the 1980s, it sold more than 600,000 copies and was at one point optioned by a motion-picture studio.

In 1981 Jane Blanchard developed a brain tumor, and three years later she died. Following her death, Patterson pursued his advertising career with greater vigor than ever before, throwing himself into his work in an attempt to keep his mind off his great loss. "Jane's death was so devastating to me that I didn't want to have free time," he admitted to *Biography* (May 1998). During the next few years, he coined such ad slogans as "I'm a Toys 'R' Us Kid," "Have You Driven a Ford Lately," and "Aren't You Hungry for Burger King Now." In 1988 Thompson named him chief executive officer, and in 1990 he became chairman of the company.

In 1986, after a six-year hiatus in his writing career, Patterson published *Black Market*, a story of terrorist activity on Wall Street. The novel was a great success in the foreign market, but considerably less so domestically. "It didn't quite work," Patterson told *Business Month* (May 1990). "It was a ridiculous premise."

With *The Midnight Club* (1989), Patterson hit on the formula that would eventually bring him broad-based commercial success: he focused on the attempts of a heroic detective to track down a ruthless criminal. For *The Midnight Club* he created John Stephanovitch, a New York City police officer searching for the crime boss who had killed his wife and injured him so severely that he had to use a wheelchair. *The Midnight Club* was not a runaway hit—perhaps, its publisher speculated, because readers might have had difficulty accepting a handicapped protagonist. The film producer Joe Wizan considered making the novel into a movie, and Sylvester Stallone expressed interest in the lead role, but no film has yet materialized.

In 1991 Patterson teamed up with Peter Kim, another J. Walter Thompson executive, to write *The Day America Told the Truth*, a nonfiction compendium analyzing the results of surveys in which they had queried nearly 6,000 Americans on various moral issues. The book, which presents a shockingly amoral American public, was a national best-seller and led to an appearance by Patterson and Kim on *Oprah*.

Along Came a Spider, published in 1993, established Patterson as a major writer of crime fiction. Eager for more than just the moderate success his previous works had achieved, Patterson took an active role in the marketing of the novel. Instead of sending the manuscript directly to publishers, he sent it to Hollywood agents, who in turn recommended it to publishers in New York. Patterson also had a great deal of input in the physical appearance of the book; in particular, he made changes to the proposed artwork for the dustjacket. The novel debuted in the top 10 of the *New York Times* best-seller list.

Along Came a Spider was the first novel to feature the character Alex Cross, a psychologist and deputy chief of detectives in Washington, D.C. The story follows Cross's efforts to save the children of two Washington luminaries, who have been kidnaped by a psychopathic killer. "There's no pretensions about it; this is a page-turner," Patterson told *New York* magazine (February 8, 1993). In an interview for *Publishers Weekly* (October 19, 1992), he explained how *Along Came a Spider* differed from his previous efforts. "My purpose for writing in the past was as a hobby. This time, I wanted to come up with an incredibly commercial book, something to knock the socks of people who like to read this kind of fiction."

Patterson's eighth novel, *Kiss the Girls*, brought back Alex Cross in another suspense-filled thriller; this time he faced the combined menace of not one but two sadistic serial killers. The book made the best-seller list one week after publication. Paramount Pictures paid a reported $1 million for the movie rights, and a film adaptation of it came out in 1997, starring Ashley Judd and Morgan Freeman.

The adventures of Alex Cross were continued in Patterson's books *Jack & Jill* (1996) and *Cat & Mouse* (1997). The former deals with two simultaneous murder sprees that Cross must stop, one targeting upscale victims, and the other, lower-class ones. In *Cat & Mouse*, Cross is once again confronted with the killer he apprehended in *Along Came a Spider*, as well as an even more dangerous murderer on the loose in Europe. "The Cross books . . . are about nightmares that I have," Patterson told *Publishers Weekly* (October 21, 1996), "not literal nightmares but nightmares that I have about the world. And one of those is of domineering men."

Critical reviews of Patterson's Cross novels have often been mixed. The most positive to date have been for *Along Came a Spider*. In the *Washington Post* (January 25, 1993), George P. Pelecanos praised the novel's uniqueness, as well as the richness and depth of the character of Alex Cross. Patterson's portrait of a local cop in a real-life neighborhood is remarkably plausible, according to Pelecanos. Lorenzo Carcaterra of *People* (February 15, 1993) also praised the strength of both the novel's characters and of the plot.

Several other of the Cross novels have not fared as well. "An absurd concoction" was how reviewer Gene Lyons described *Kiss the Girls* in *Entertainment Weekly* (January 20, 1995). Lyons pointed out Patterson's overly maudlin prose style and all-too-perfect characters. "If author Patterson had half the zeal for criminal psychology and police investigative techniques as he has for describing grisly scenes of sexual torture," Lyons wrote, "he might sustain the reader's interest."

In a review of *Jack & Jill* for *Entertainment Weekly* (September 6, 1996), Tom De Haven described Alex Cross as having "the nuanced realism of Sam Catchem." While he admitted that the book's premise has potential, he was highly critical of the way Patterson had fleshed out the story. "Chapters are clotted with stiff dialogue and strewn with hackneyed plot twists," he wrote. "Brand names masquerade as description and single-ply cardboard substitutes for characterization. The clichéd derring-do . . . is juicelessly dramatized."

Marilyn Stasio praised Patterson's imaginative powers in a *New York Times* (November 23, 1997) review of *Cat & Mouse*, but felt that his writing style left something to be desired. She was critical, for example, of what she labeled the "absurd grandiosity" of the characterizations of the novel's two killers. This made them boring instead of menacing, Stasio argued.

In 1999, two new Patterson books were released, *Miracle on the 17th Green*, coauthored with Peter Dejonge, and *Pop Goes the Weasel*, another Alex Cross mystery. *Miracle on the 17th Green* is, according to a reviewer from Booklist, "It's a Wonderful Life, golf version" and a "silly, blatantly commercial attempt to sell sentiment and golf."

Patterson wakes at 5:30 a.m. and writes for a while before going to his office at Thompson. "It's a matter of getting something down every day. I always force something to happen," he explained to *Business Month* (May 1990). His first drafts are usually extremely rough, and he revises them, by hand, several times before he is satisfied. His authorial pursuits provide a break from the pressures of his job. "Writing is very restful," he told Barbara Hetzer for *Business Month* (May 1990). "It's like dreaming or floating, being totally free." Patterson has also stated that his day job has affected his writing style. "Aspects of it probably have had some influence," he explained to *Publishers Weekly* (October 21, 1996). "One is that you become very aware of an audience that is responding or not responding to what you do. It helps if you can project, if you can think of the audience a bit."

Despite his tremendous financial success as a novelist, Patterson has maintained that he has no intention of leaving the advertising field. "I always thought that if I made a lot of money writing, I'd leave advertising," he said in *Fortune* (January 30, 1989). "But when my second book was successful, I was depressed. I didn't want to retire. A dual career is exciting. The books removed the urge I felt to compete with my advertising colleagues." Patterson told Barbara Hetzer that he has "a certain fear of the loneliness of writing." Furthermore, he explained to Maria Speidel for *People* (March 20, 1995), "I like to go inside myself, but I also need to go outside and meet other people, and I like the ad work."

In 1997 Patterson married Sue Solie, J. Walter Thompson's art director. The couple has a son named Jack.—B.S.

SUGGESTED READING: *Biography* p28 May 1998, with photo; *Business Month* p81+ May 1990, with photo; *Entertainment Weekly* p46+ Jan. 20, 1995, p68 Sep. 6, 1996; *Fortune* p192 Jan. 30, 1989, with photo; *New York* p46+ Feb. 8, 1993, with photo; *New York Times* VII p44 Nov. 23, 1997; *People* p28 Feb. 15, 1993, with photo, p83+ Mar. 20, 1995, with photo; *Publishers Weekly* p22+ Oct. 19, 1992, with photo, p58+ Oct. 21, 1996, with photo; *Washington Post* B p2 Jan. 25, 1993

SELECTED BOOKS: Fiction—*The Thomas Berryman Number*, 1976; *The Season of the Machete*, 1977; *The Jericho Commandment*, 1979; *Virgin*, 1980; *Black Market*, 1986; *The Midnight Club*, 1989; *Along Came a Spider*, 1993; *Kiss the Girls*, 1995; *Hide and Seek*, 1996; *Jack & Jill*, 1996; *Cat & Mouse*, 1997; *See How They Run*, 1997; *When the Wind Blows*, 1998; Miracle on the 17th Green, 1999 (coauthored with Peter Dejonge); Pop Goes the Weasel, 1999; Nonfiction—with Peter Kim: *The Day America Told the Truth*, 1991; *The Second American Revolution*, 1994

Pears, Tim

Nov. 15, 1956– Novelist

"I think human beings are preoccupied by the same things they've always been preoccupied with: Where do we come from, why are we here, where are we going?" British author Tim Pears said in an interview with *Contemporary Authors* (1994). "How should we live our lives? What are our hopes, responsibilities, dreams? How can we love and be loved? The things that spring us from sleep at night in a state of misery or joy. I just want to create characters I love and explore their lives." The author of *In the Place of Fallen Leaves* (1993) and more recently *In a Land of Plenty* (1997), Pears's work has been compared by some critics to that of Thomas Hardy. Extremely skilled at interweaving country lore with modern rural life, Pears, with his debut novel, earned nearly universal praise from critics on both sides of the Atlantic.

In an autobiographical statement submitted to *World Authors 1990–1995*, Pears wrote, "I was born in Tunbridge Wells, England, Great Britain in 1956 (the Suez Canal and my mother's birth canal are thus forever entwined in a personal take on my country's history; two troubled and troublesome passageways.) The month of my birth was November [the date was the 15th.] Zodiac-wise, I am a Scorpio, with Scorpio ascendant. Actually, between you and me, I don't believe in star signs. But such skeptical nonsense is typical of Scorpios.

"My father [W. S. Pears] was an Anglican priest, which was a good decision on his part: being a Roman Catholic would have been more controversial. My sisters and I grew up in the industrial grime of Crewe, its steel foundries and stockyards at the centre of British Railways. We played football [soccer] in the street and went to the cinema on Saturday morning. *Taras Bulba*, *The Vikings*, *Cheyenne Autumn*, *Helen of Troy*: these epics inspired in my unformed soul a lifelong love of Hollywood movies (which I fortunately grew out of later.)

"When I was eight or nine, and, I now realize, past my prime, the family moved at our mother's request to bucolic Devon, down in the southwest peninsula of England. The freedom of the city streets was replaced by the freedom of the woods and the fields, which seemed like a fair swap. England won the World Cup. The Sixties blossomed far away. Our Dad preached intellectual sermons to a deaf congregation. He introduced marijuana to his prayer group, tried to set up a commune, became a school teacher and a driving instructor in his spare time.

"When I was twelve (one sister older, the other younger) our mother [Jill Charles-Edwards Scurfield Pears] ran off with a local farm labourer. They sprinted down the drive. He really couldn't have been more local: he and his young wife rented rooms at the end of our huge nineteenth-century rectory. Having made her contribution to the dismantling of barriers in our class-ridden country, our mother left us to be looked after by our father. He cheerfully called the four of us his little Soviet, and having fought in the Second World War alongside Tito's Yugoslav Communist partisans he knew what he was talking about. At the end of the war, while being debriefed by British Military Intelligence, my father had found himself alone in an office and stole the opportunity to look up his own file. In it he found himself earmarked as a Fellow Traveller. He put the file in his bag, took it home and burned it.

"(Many years later he would teach a course in Communism for the sixth form of Exeter's most upstanding grammar school for girls, but that's another story.)

"By this time I was trundling through school, eleven years of stultifying boredom, some of which I spent dreaming of growing up and forgetting; of having children myself and sending them to school. How the hell would they like it? I wondered. At sixteen, I left, with no qualifications, expertise or talent, to my father's despair. Unfortunately, having given each of his children sovereignty over their lives as they attained the age of reason, it was too late to take it back. Still, he kept open the door of his study and I proceeded to read his extensive collection of nineteenth-century Russian novels.

"I soon discovered that the boredom of school is nothing as compared to the drudgery of unskilled labor, but at this time I resolved not to throw in the towel after a mere eleven years but to stick at it. I worked at thirty or forty different things. Farm laborer (Oedipal or not?), nurse in a mental hospital, pianist's bodyguard, painter and decorator, video maker, college night porter, art gallery manager, etc. etc. One of the best was an early one, while still in Devon, I worked in a public library that was closing down but kept a couple of sections open so that someone had to be on the front desk for the two or three borrowers who came in each day. The basement, meanwhile, was stacked full of fiction. I'd choose a different author for the week, and read one of their books a day. Nabokov, Steinbeck, Conrad. A plum bunk-off job for young people of a sort that seems to be in short supply these days.

"Winter's the worst for working outside. Unclogging blocked drains with your hands deep in icy filth. Glazing a new house with fingers not quite numb, unworkable, nicking them so you have to go back afterwards and wipe the blood off the glass panes. I was writing poetry all the time, such bad poetry I can't believe anyone published it. Come to think of it, nobody did. They weren't so stupid, those magazine editors. Except that none of their magazines ever lasted for very long. They were too busy sending bums like me rejection slips. With which I once covered an entire wall in the cottage in Wales I was then living in: they reminded me what a dunce I was and also kept out the drafts.

"In 1979 I moved into Oxford and Mrs. Thatcher moved into Downing Street. She's gone now, of course, and I'm still here in the same street, but that means nothing. She and her ilk beat down my generation, because we spent her tenure dreaming of the end of ideology, and when the dark days were over it wasn't values that had taken ideology's place, but bureaucracy. Better management. Better image.

"Me, I sought refuge in the personal, and married a belly dancer. She is expecting twins. I expect nothing, but hope for everything. It's a Devon saying: Walk in hope and you walk backwards."

In 1993 Pears graduated from Britain's National Film and Television School in London. That same year he published his debut novel, *In the Place of Fallen Leaves*. Interestingly, the book might never have come about had it not been for some experimentation Pears conducted with one of his poems. "One day I transposed a poem into a short story and set it in the tiny Devon village in which I had grown up," he said in an interview with *Contemporary Authors* (1994). "It was a moment of liberation: Writing was no longer simply an intellectual process; it became physical, the world of my adolescence vividly recalled—I could smell the lanes after the rain, hear a mother calling her children in for tea, touch the sharp blades of grass we blew notes from through our fingers." The birth of Pears the fiction writer was also the death of Pears the poet. He told *Contemporary Authors* (1994) that after that day he wrote "no more poems but many stories." All of these stories were set in the same village of his youth. "I found that there was nothing that interested me that couldn't be adapted to fit into this place," he added.

In the *Place of Fallen Leaves* tells the story of Allison Freemantle, a 13-year-old British girl living in a small farming community with her family, including her amnesiac father and her eccentric grandmother. Set during the scorching summer of 1984, the novel centers around Allison's friendship with Jonathan, the son of an impoverished aristocrat. *In the Place of Fallen Leaves*, for which Pears was awarded the 1993 Ruth Haden Memorial Award, received widespread critical acclaim from the British press. A reviewer for the London *Telegraph* (March 27, 1993) deemed the book "comic, and wry, and elegiac, and shrewd and thoughtful all at once." Writing for the *Oxford Times* (April 23, 1993), Martyn Bedford hailed Pears's novel as "an utterly convincing portrayal of the life and times of the Devon countryside, deeply evocative and rich with sensuous imagery—sad and funny . . . but never mawkish."

Two years later, when the novel was first published in the United States, it met with similar praise. "Tim Pears's first novel is too subtle to be sentimental, too well written to be obvious," Peter Finn wrote in the *New York Times Book Review* (February 5, 1995), "but it is shot through with an affecting melancholy as Mr. Pears collapses the history of one farm family to the breaking point— and with it, a way of life."

In a Land of Plenty, Tim Pears's second novel to date, was published in 1997. Its plot encompasses the entire marriage of one Charles Freeman and Mary Wyndham, beginning with their wedding in 1952 and concluding four decades later. A wide array of supporting characters appears along the way, and the vast scope of British history over the second half of the twentieth century acts as a backdrop.

Reviews for *In a Land of Plenty* were generally positive, but not quite as enthusiastic as they had been for the author's first effort. Jonathan Yardley of the *Washington Post* (Mar. 1, 1998) praised Pears's ambition in undertaking a novel of such scale, and characterized it as "a modern tale in a traditional setting." Yardley also had kind words for Pears's incisive portrayal of relationships between men and women. His only major criticism was that the work tries too hard to be like an old-fashioned Victorian epic novel, thereby arguably reaching beyond its grasp. In *Publishers Weekly* (Jan. 5, 1998), the reviewer acknowledged that there are moments in *In a Land of Plenty* that are equal to *In the Place of Falling Leaves*, but conceded that "this big novel lacks the binding gravity required to unify its satellite plots and characters." The reviewer did, however, applaud Pears's compelling depiction of James, the son of the two main characters. A review by Lucy Hughes-Hallett of the *Spectator* (Apr. 5, 1997) criticized the novel for what she felt was its lack of drama and stereotyped characters. "*In a Land of Plenty*," she concluded, "takes its place in a distinct subgenre of modern fiction . . . which consists of novels which are both compelling, in the way that eavesdropping is compelling, and a little dull."

—J.P./B.S.

SUGGESTED READING: *Contemporary Authors* vol. 143 1994; *Daily Mail* April 22, 1993; *New York Times Book Review* p14 Feb. 5, 1995; *Oxford Times* Apr. 23, 1993; *Publishers Weekly* p56 Jan. 5, 1998; *Spectator* p34 Apr. 5, 1997; *Telegraph* March 27, 1993; *Washington Post* X p1 Mar. 1, 1998

SELECTED WORKS: *In the Place of Fallen Leaves*, 1993; *In a Land of Plenty*, 1997

Peck, Dale

July 13, 1967– Novelist

Dale Peck, an American novelist, achieved a towering reputation before he reached the age of 30. His novels *Martin and John* (1993) and *The Law of Enclosures* (1996) are innovative in their narrative structure, embodying the fragmentation and alienation of the times with their shifts in chronology and point of view and with their examination of similar narratives from several different vantages. Peck's experiments in narrative continued in *Now It's Time to Say Goodbye* (1998), in which there were fewer autobiographical elements than in his previous works. Craig Seligman, writing in the *New Yorker* in 1996, summed up Peck's career to that time: "The author's technical sophistication, his age (under 30), and his sexuality . . . make *The Law of Enclosures* an even greater feat of virtuosity than its virtuoso predecessor. He is as piercing on old age as on youth, as comfortable writing about women's bodies as about men's. . . . Peck . . . reminds us that novelists . . . are blessed, because, unlike the rest of us, they can put their rotten memories to use." And Michiko Kakutani in the *New York Times* (May 19, 1998) called *Now It's Time to Say Goodbye* the fulfillment of the promise of Peck's first two novels, "the capstone, thus far, of his impressive career."

The American novelist and AIDS activist Dale Peck was born on Long Island, New York, on July 13, 1967 to Eileen Staplin and Dale Peck. His father was a plumber. After his mother's death, he and his father moved to Kansas, where the boy spent most of his childhood. Peck received a B.A. degree from Drew University, in New Jersey, in 1989. By then he had joined the militant protest group ACT-UP, which carried on demonstrations to demand more funding for AIDS research and better use of available resources. One tactic required Peck to disrupt a news broadcast.

At the age of 25, Peck published his first book, *Martin and John*, an autobiographical work emblematic of the life of a gay man in the age of AIDS. Peck created a literary sensation with his revolutionary approach to the genre: stories weave in and out of the narrative, and the characters John, the narrator, and Martin, who might be termed the object of desire, change significantly in age and role in different sections. John's parents, Hank and Bea, too, have various roles, relationships, and ages. Sometimes it is the father in John's dysfunctional family who dies; sometimes it is the mother. The father is usually a tough character who behaves violently toward both his wife and his son. Martin, the lover, dies of AIDS. Sometimes the lover is rich, and sometimes it is the father who has money. In many of his guises, John has a deformed hand, which was mutilated by his father's abuse. Martin plays the piano, sometimes professionally.

Catherine Texier, in her notice in the *New York Times Book Review* (February 28, 1993), wrote that the "lyrical power" of Peck's writing obviated any confusion these fluid identities and shifting stories might induce. She found a fugue-like effect, "creating a flow of narration seething with life. By breaking the story line and blurring the identity of his characters and the hard boundaries between the stories, Dale Peck succeeds in exploring the experience of being gay with a remarkable complexity and depth of feeling," she concluded. Mona Simpson, the *Chicago Tribune* (March 28, 1993) reviewer, agreed, calling *Martin and John* "a book to be read . . . for its own stark and violent beauties." Michiko Kakutani, after she had given the book a glowing review in the *New York Times* (February 9, 1993), later observed in the *Times* (March 12, 1993), in an overview of the effect of AIDS on literature, that Peck's "innovative narrative technique" serves both to tell "the story of a young man's attempts to cope with his lover's death from AIDS" and also to show "his imaginative efforts to reinvent that tragedy and lend it a meaning and a shape."

In *The Law of Enclosures*, two couples—one being a young Beatrice and Henry and the other an older Bea and Hank—exist in alternate chapters but at the same time, the year of the Persian Gulf War. Clearly, although they are in a time warp, they are the same people at different stages of their lives. The young Beatrice and Henry are poor and in love. Henry has a brain tumor. Obviously, he survives, and although they are more prosperous, the older Bea and Hank have descended into misery and hostility. The central section of the novel is an autobiographical narration by "Dale Peck," describing his mother's death when he was three and his father's three later marriages. His relationship with his violent, alcoholic father is important to him, but his father seems to embody the principle that "desire and contempt are manifestations of the same impulse."

For Stephen Henighan, writing in the *Times Literary Supplement* (February 16, 1996), Peck "demolishes chronological time" in *The Law of Enclosures* to demonstrate the "contradictions of feeling encountered over the course of a long marriage." The father's violence, he found, "demands a more detailed treatment," and his life "still beckons to be transformed into fiction." John Brenkman, the *Nation* (January 29, 1996) reviewer, observed that Peck "has defied the boundaries of autobiography and novel. . . . There is an extraordinary sense of the risk and adventure of writing in . . . this novel, a daring that would surely dissipate if 'Dale Peck' were merely a fictional narrator, ensconced in the comforting shelter of a persona."

Peck reveals the writer's raw material, much as the back of a transparent watch shows the workings, in the novel's autobiographical sections. Michiko Kakutani, writing in the *New York Times* (January 23, 1996), described this "complicated narrative machinery" as being "meant to call attention to the fiction-making process, to remind the reader of the magical acts performed by the writer in alchemizing life into art." She deemed the novel, if "imperfect," nevertheless "an astonishing work of emotional wisdom" with which Peck "has galvanized his reputation as one of the most eloquent voices of his generation."

Now It's Time to Say Goodbye, Peck's third novel, marked a departure from the autobiographical vein that had gained him so much favorable recognition. It is set in a fictional small town in Kansas, much like the one where Peck was raised. The racially segregated town is observed partly from the point of view of a rich novelist from New York, who has arrived seeking a kind of refuge from the AIDS epidemic, which is killing off his friends. He and his young lover are threatened, robbed, and beaten. An albino black man, wrongly accused of raping a young white girl, has been lynched, and his accuser is raped, abducted, and tortured. Various townspeople take turns narrating the sometimes gruesome story.

The book drew mixed notices. Michiko Kakutani, reviewing the novel in the *New York Times* (May 19, 1998), called *Now It's Time to Say Goodbye* "an utterly gripping thriller—crammed full of suspense, Gothic horror, and often startling violence—and a highly sophisticated piece of literary legerdemain." She concluded that the violence and melodrama in the novel are "ultimately employed in the service of a deeply humane vision," and she termed *Now It's Time to Say Goodbye* "a novel commensurate with [Peck's] ambitions . . . a big galvanic novel."

Craig Seligman disagreed, complaining in the *New York Times Book Review* (June 21, 1998), "The book feels like one of those low-budget horror movies in which a place is being stalked by a lunatic. . . . At roughly 450 pages, though, it's something like a 27-hour movie." He found Peck's dialogue lacking in humor and in verisimilitude. "The somber decency of Peck's earlier work has given way to an obscene yet at the same time pious jokiness that doesn't hit a single true note," he wrote. According to Seligman, Peck had not lost his talent and was neither "irresponsible or crazy." He is simply "a restless experimental writer," all in all a good thing. Peck "isn't the first brilliant artist to have created a monster," Seligman concluded.

Peck's overriding theme, according to Penelope Mesic, who reviewed *The Law of Enclosures* for the *Chicago Tribune* (February 18, 1996), is "the terror and obscenity of this precarious union between pleasure and death." She was reminded of D. H. Lawrence, observing that Peck was engaged in the same "desperate gamble to reveal by means of language that the body is eternal, holy, and transcendent despite the corruption and decay that say it is not."
—S. Y.

SUGGESTED READING: *Chicago Tribune* XIV p5 Mar. 28, 1993, XIV p5 Feb. 18, 1996; *Nation* p31+ Jan. 29, 1996; *New Yorker* p73 Jan. 15, 1996; *New York Times* C p15 Feb. 9, 1993, with photo; *New York Times Book Review* p12 Feb. 28, 1993, p22 Jan. 14, 1996; *Times Literary Supplement* p23 Feb. 16, 1996

SELECTED BOOKS: *Martin and John*, 1993; *The Law of Enclosures*, 1996; *Now It's Time to Say Goodbye*, 1998

Courtesy of Farrar, Straus and Giroux

Pelevin, Victor

Nov. 22, 1962– Novelist

Only recently exposed to English-speaking critics and media, Victor Pelevin, who has been described as "the leading Russian novelist of the post-glasnost era," has already garnered comparisons to some of the most respected writers—Vladimir Voinovich, Mikhail Bulgakov, Ernest Hemingway—of both the East and West. The author of four novels that have been translated into English, *Omon Ra* (1996), *The Yellow Arrow* (1996), *The Life of Insects* (1997), and *The Clay Machine-Gun* (1999), as well as two collections of stories, *The Blue Lantern* (1997) and *A Werewolf Problem in Central Russia* (1998), Pelevin has repeatedly demonstrated his talent as an "unusual and strange writer, one with the kind of mordant, astringent turn of mind that in the pre-glasnost era landed writers in psychiatric hospitals or exile," as Richard Bernstein phrased it in the *New York Times* (June 12, 1996).

Born in Moscow on November 22, 1962, the son of Oleg and Zina (Efremova) Pelevin, Victor Pelevin was educated at the Moscow Institute of Power Engineering and the Moscow Institute of Literature. Few details of his life prior to his emergence on the American and western European literary scenes have been made public. Even on the rare occasions that Pelevin has responded to questions regarding his personal life and beliefs, his answers have often been extremely enigmatic. For instance, in one 1997 interview, Pelevin commented that his political beliefs lie somewhere "left of rights centrists" and that his religion is "Tantric agnosticism."

Though he has been an acclaimed writer for several years in Russia, none of Pelevin's works had been translated into English until 1996. That year saw the appearance of the English-language versions of the novels *Omon Ra* and *The Yellow Arrow*, published in Russia in 1992 and 1993, respectively. *Omon Ra*, a spoof of the Soviet space program, revolves around Omon Krivomazov, a man who has long dreamed of becoming a cosmonaut. "Everything I remember from childhood is linked in one way or another with a dream of the sky," Omon, the story's narrator, says. Eventually Omon is selected to be a cosmonaut and adopts the code name Omon Ra (Ra being the name of the ancient Egyptian sun god). Upon entering training, he quickly discovers that the glorious history of the Soviet space program has been completely fabricated. "Nothing in history is like it is in the textbooks," Omon is told by Colonel Urchagin, the Assistant Political Instructor of the Special Cosmonauts Detachment. ". . .We just didn't have time to defeat the West technologically. But in the battle of ideas, you can't stop for a second. The paradox . . . is that we support the truth with falsehood, because Marxism carries within itself an all-conquering truth." The falsified voyages and deeds of Soviet cosmonauts, as Omon learns upon being recruited for a special mission, are not just a thing of the past. He is assigned the task of manning a supposedly unmanned spacecraft to the moon (the technology for unmanned flight doesn't exist in *Omon Ra*'s Russia), setting up an exploratory vehicle that will broadcast Communist messages, and, when out of view of the camera, killing himself. Oman Ra's adventures in space do not go exactly as planned, and the story culminates in what one *Library Journal* (June 1, 1996) reviewer described as "a bizarre surprise ending that fittingly tops off this cynical send-up of the Soviet space program." Upon the publication of its English version, *Omon Ra* met with a great deal of critical acclaim. In the *New York Times Book Review* (June 30, 1996), reviewer Tom Ferrell deemed the book "a plot-driven astonishing-discovery rich adventure novel." Further praise was offered by the *New Yorker* (July 15, 1996): "Omon's adventure is like a rocket firing off its various stages—each incident is more jolting and propulsively absurd than the one before."

Also published in 1996 was the English translation of Pelevin's *The Yellow Arrow*, a surreal story of a Russian train, the Yellow Arrow, speeding toward a wrecked bridge. Life on the train appears to be a metaphor for life in contemporary Russia—the conductors operate shady moneymaking schemes involving silverware, the passengers abide by a strict code of segregation by social class, and those who die while en route are simply heaved out a window and forgotten. "Pelevin's signature elements—deadpan wryness, the flotsam of American culture in his brain, a slight preference for today over yesterday—surface throughout," Carlin Romano wrote in the *News-Times* (June 19, 1996, online). "Enterprising passengers try to turn their cars into joint ventures. [The narrator] sees his face in the mirror and thinks it's going out of style, 'along with flared trousers, transcendental meditation and Fleetwood Mac.' Still, Andrei prefers his present situation and train crew: 'At least this lot don't throw people out of windows while they are still alive.'" Despite its abundance of gloomy subject matter, this "spare, Kafkaesque satire on post-glasnost Russia," as Romano deemed it, is not without a hint of optimism. For in the end, the train stops short of its destination, allowing the passengers to disembark.

Pelevin's most recent novel, *The Life of Insects*, was published in 1997. The book tells the story of Sam Sacker, an American mosquito in Russia. While detailing his interactions with the local insects and his love affair with a beautiful and promiscuous fly who meets an untimely end after getting stuck to a piece of flypaper, the novel simultaneously delves into a myriad of issues and practices relating to post-Communist Russia. "Obsolete party slogans, bureaucratic institutions, and authoritarian bullying have been transformed into capitalist initiatives and Mafia power struggles, in an atmosphere of grubbiness and cynicism," Zinovy Zinik wrote in the *Times Literary Supplement* (March 14, 1997). "But Victor Pelevin is not interested in the social implication of the change. He is fascinated by the mechanics of it. He registers the incongruity of the disparate and grotesque manifestations of life as they collide in front of our eyes, an incongruity of images which is visual as well as ideological." Indeed, the book is replete with images—all involving insects—that demonstrate odd combinations of the old and new and East and West. One such scene involves an aging

fruit fly forced to find food among the rotting garbage at a fruit stand that sits across from a new video shop where one can rent French postmodernist films. The book details a world without many distinctions; it is not only the political and geographic borders that are nonexistent—but also the boundary between human and insect. "Creatures easily mutate and become transformed into each other," Zinik explained in his review of the book in the *Times Literary Supplement* article. "There is an insect in every human being which sometimes just shows itself and takes over. Time and space are warped and transmuted here, too. The bluebottle prostitute, Natasha, who entraps and lays Sam Sacker at the beginning, will have been hatched as an egg in the later part of the novel." This decidedly nonlinear style drew raves from some critics. "Pelevin, one of the new generation of Russian writers, has not only created a world of his own, he has also written a parody of the stultified tradition of Russian prose," Zinik wrote. "Such acts of stylistic conjuring and philosophical insight could have been achieved only by a writer who, in the Russian world of linear narratives, was gifted with multifaceted vision like that of an insect."

Similar praise was given to *The Blue Lantern and Other Stories*. "Nearly every story in this collection contains an ongoing dialogue about the nature of reality—between two Moscow prostitutes, between two cocaine-snorting soldiers in revolutionary Petrograd, and, in a story called 'Hermit and Six-Toes,' between two truth seekers who, in the end, turn out to be chickens plotting their escape from the Lunacharsky Broiler Combine," Ken Kalfus observed in the *New York Times Book Review* (December 7, 1997). Kalfus pronounced Pelevin's "existential inquiry" to be "fresh and relevant." Pelevin's second collection, *A Werewolf Problem in Central Russia: And Other Stories* appeared in 1998. A reviewer for *Publishers Weekly* (September 28, 1998) complained that Pelevin "sometimes gets lost in the telling of tales, leading to poorly developed characters and satires that fall flat"—but nonetheless singled out for praise two of the stories: the title piece and "The Ontology of Childhood," a story of prison life that the reviewer found to be "reminiscent of *The Blue Lantern*."

Pelevin's novel *The Clay Machine-Gun*, translated by Andrew Bromfield for publication in England in 1999, concerns Pyotr Voyd—a patient in a mental hospital whose hallucinations frequently take him, and the reader, back in time to the Russian Civil War.

—J. P.

SUGGESTED READING: *Library Journal* p150 June 1, 1996; *New York Times* p16 June 12, 1996; *New York Times Book Review* p26 June 30, 1996; *New Yorker* p79 July 15, 1996; *Times Literary Supplement* p21 Mar. 14, 1997; *Contemporary Authors* vol. 154, 1997

BOOKS IN ENGLISH TRANSLATION: *The Yellow Arrow*, 1996; *Omon Ra*, 1996; *The Life of Insects*, 1997; *The Blue Lantern*, 1997; *A Werewolf Problem in Central Russia*, 1998; *The Clay Machine-Gun*, 1999

Courtesy of Arturo Perez-Reverte

Pérez-Reverte, Arturo

1951– Novelist; essayist; screenwriter

The Spanish novelist, essayist, and screenwriter Arturo Pérez-Reverte emerged as an internationally best-selling author almost immediately after he gave up journalism for creative writing. His ingeniously plotted mystery novels published in English translation—*The Flanders Panel* (1994), *The Club Dumas* (1997), *The Seville Communion* (1998), and *The Fencing Master* (1999)—won critical praise for being "reminiscent of Umberto Eco's" works, in the words of Michael Eade, reviewing *The Flanders Panel* in the *Times Literary Supplement* (August 12, 1994).

Arturo Pérez-Reverte, born in 1951, sent the following (in Spanish) to *World Authors 1990–1995*: "Arturo Pérez-Reverte, born in Cartagena, Spain, has devoted himself exclusively to literature for the last few years, after having supported himself as a newspaper, radio, and television reporter, covering international conflicts for 21 years from 1973 to 1994.

"A graduate in political science and journalism, he spent 12 years as a reporter on the daily *Pueblo* and 9 in the information service of Spanish Television (TVE), specializing in terrorism, illegal trafficking, and armed conflict. He won the Asturias

prize in journalism for his TVE coverage of the war in the former Yugoslavia and the Ondas prize in 1993 for the program *La ley de la calle* (Street Law) on Spanish National Radio (a successful program that stayed on the air for five years). Arturo Pérez-Reverte has covered, among other conflicts, the war in Cyprus, various phases of the war in Lebanon, the war in Eritrea, the 1975 campaign in the Sahara, the Sahara war, the Falklands war, the war in El Salvador, the war in Nicaragua, the war in Chad, the Libyan crisis, the guerrilla war in the Sudan, the war in Mozambique, the war in Angola, the coup in Tunisia, etc. The last armed struggles that he experienced were in Romania (1989-1990), the war in Mozambique (1990), the Gulf war (1990-1991), the war in Croatia (1991) and the war in Bosnia (1992, 1993, 1994). In May 1994, he left Spanish Television to dedicate himself to work as a novelist. A well-known essayist, he also published a weekly opinion column in *El Semanal*, a Sunday supplement published simultaneously in about 20 Spanish newspapers (circulation 1,500,000).

"As a novelist, Arturo Pérez-Reverte sold more than two million copies all over the world in 1996. In France he was named by the magazine *Lire* as one of the 10 best foreign novelists for *La tabla de Flandes* (1990, tr. *The Flanders Panel*, 1994; 250,000 copies sold between the regular and paperback editions). In 1994 that novel received the Swedish Academy's detective novel prize for the best foreign translation and was cited by the *New York Times Book Review* as one of the five best foreign novels published in the United States. *El club Dumas* (1993, tr. *The Club Dumas*, 1997), published in France in April 1994, also made the French best-seller list (200,000 copies sold) and the same thing happened in Germany, where at the time of its publication in April 1995 it had already gone through two editions. It has just come out (1997) in the United States, Great Britain, and Australia. In Denmark in 1995 this novel won the Pelle Rosenkratz prize. In Mexico, Colombia, and Argentina, his novels are automatically placed near the cashier's stations. In Spain, *The Club Dumas* sold 170,000 copies during its first year. *Territorio comanche* (1994; Comanche Territory) passed 180,000, and the separate editions of *El maestro de esgrima* (1988, *The Fencing Master*) and *The Flanders Panel* have already exceed 300,000 copies. Since *La piel del tambor* (The Drumskin) appeared in December 1995, with a first edition of 150,000 copies, it has exceeded 350,000 copies, being the only Spanish novel of recent times that has lasted longer than 11 months on the best-seller lists.

"Pérez-Reverte has been translated into 16 languages (English, French, German, Portuguese, Hebrew, Russian, Chinese, Japanese, Swedish, Norwegian, Polish, Danish, Dutch, Italian, Greek, and Hungarian) and published in more than 30 countries. Two of his works have been filmed: *El maestro de esgrima*, which won the Goya prize for the best screenplay adapted from a novel and a prize in the French Cognac festival and was a finalist for an Oscar in 1992, and *The Flanders Panel*, directed by Jim McBride. *Un asunto de honor* (An Affair of Honor) was also filmed under the title *Cachito*. Three of Pérez-Reverte's other novels are in the process of being filmed: *The Club Dumas* with a screenplay by Anthony Shaffer, *La piel del tambor* and *Territorio comanche*, which, with a screenplay by Pérez-Reverte himself and produced by Gerardo Herrero, will be directed by Gerardo Herrero in a French, German, and Argentine coproduction. Its wheels were set in motion in October 1996 in Sarajevo.

"In Spain, his novels *El husar* (1986), *El maestro de esgrima*, *The Flanders Panel*, *The Club Dumas*, the tales of *La sombra del águila* (1993, The Eagle's Shadow), *Cachito (Un asunto de honor)* and *Territorio comanche*, and his *Obra breve* (1995) continue to be displayed in the best-seller sections of bookstores. The success of his novels makes him dedicate more and more of his time to literature and to his other delight, the sea and sailing."

—tr. S. Y.

When *La tabla de flandes,* translated as *The Flanders Panel,* appeared in 1994, Marilyn Stasio in the *New York Times Book Review* (June 12, 1994) termed it a "sleek and sophisticated chamber mystery about art, life, and chess." Michael Eade in the *Times Literary Supplement* (August 12, 1994) deemed "Pérez-Reverte's plotting . . . much tighter and his narrative . . . more exciting" than Umberto Eco's. In the novel, when an art restorer uncovers an inscription under a 15th-century Flemish painting—"Quis Necavit Equitem?" ("Who killed the knight?")—she starts a chain of events that include the chess game depicted in the painting and the murder of her former lover. Because knowledge of chess is vital in solving the mystery, she calls on "a nerdy clerk who happens to be a brilliant theoretician of the game and a connoisseur of its infinite and exquisite enigmas," in Marilyn Stasio's words. Michael Eade, although he called the characters "crass stereotypes," thought that the chess game as a plot element was "ingeniously used" and that the "number of sudden shocking twists" in the plot more than made up for the "undistinguished" prose style, the "pedestrian" descriptions, and the "no more than expository" dialogue. The *Booklist* (May 15, 1994) reviewer, however, thought the characters "fascinatingly complex" and the "incorporation of art, literature, and music" innovative. All reviewers praised Margaret Jull Costa's translation. Marilyn Stasio referred to its "elegant style."

Margot Livesey complained, in reviewing *The Club Dumas* for the *New York Times Book Review* (March 23, 1997), that "Pérez-Reverte's work seems to be very slow in making its way across the Atlantic." *The Club Dumas*, which was, in her words, "eloquently translated" by Sonia Soto, appeared in the U.S. four years after its Spanish publication. Livesey hoped that Pérez-Reverte's next novel would not be so slow in appearing.

Lucas Corso, the hero of *The Club Dumas*, variously described as "frequently churlish" and "misanthropic," is an authority on antiquarian books. He is involved in authenticating a manuscript of Chapter 42 of Dumas's *The Three Musketeers*, the previous owner of which may or may not be hanged, and at the same time he is engaged in a search for the three extant copies of an old necromantic volume (Pérez-Reverte's invention) containing instructions for summoning the Devil. The book, which was banned in the 17th century, got its original publisher burned at the stake. Only one copy is believed to be authentic, and clues as to which one lie in the nine woodcuts that illustrate the book. The owners of two of the copies are murdered, and Corso is trailed to Paris by a beautiful woman named Irene Adler. The novel's various plot strands are woven together and resolved at a secret meeting of the eponymous Club Dumas.

Pérez-Reverte used the woodcuts as illustrations for *The Club Dumas* itself, so that readers can make their own analyses of the differences between the necromantic volumes. All three may be authentic. The *Times Literary Supplement* (September 6, 1996) reviewer considered this device rather unsuccessful: "Introducing new matter at the explication" automatically causes readers' guesses to be wrong.

Barbara Hoffert in *Library Journal* (September 1, 1996) described *The Club Dumas* as a "literate mystery." She found the "learned detail about early printing, the occult, and Dumas" to be "stimulating." Margot Livesey, although she had some cavils about "the farfetched antics of the clandestine society that lies at the heart of his plot," considered *The Club Dumas* an "intelligent and delightful novel."

The hero of *The Seville Communion*, published in 1998 and translated by Sonia Soto, is Lorenzo Quart, a combination priest and secret agent in the employ of the Vatican's Institute for External Affairs. The story involves an ultimately deadly struggle between those who wish to demolish a 300-year-old church in Seville and sell the property and those who resist closing the church. "Almost all of Pérez-Reverte's characters are plausible, but usually as types," Paul Baumann wrote in his assessment of the novel for the *New York Times Book Review* (May 3, 1998). But he acknowledged that the "vivid descriptions of the city . . . are more resonant. . . . You'd have to be a remarkably faithless reader not to want to visit Seville after finishing this flavorful confection." *The Fencing Master* was published in Spain in 1988 and in English—with a translation by Margaret Jull Costa—in 1999. The protagonist, Jaime Astarloa, teaches fencing in Madrid in 1868, just before the overthrow of Isabel II. "*The Fencing Master* is an intelligent novel about trying to maintain old-fashioned notions of loyalty and decency against a degenerate tide," Michael Eade wrote in the *Times Literary Supplement* (April 9, 1999). Eade judged the novel to be "a much more rounded, if less complex, work than [*The Flanders Panel*]; perhaps his best."

—S. Y.

SUGGESTED READING: *Booklist* p1667 May 15, 1994; *Library Journal* p211 Sep. 1, 1996; *New York Times Book Review* p42 June 12, 1994, p10 Mar. 23, 1997, p33 May 3, 1998; *Times Literary Supplement* p23 Aug. 12, 1994, p23 Sep. 6, 1996, p27 Apr. 9, 1999

SELECTED BOOKS IN ENGLISH TRANSLATION: *The Flanders Panel*, 1994; *The Club Dumas*, 1997; *The Seville Communion*, 1998; *The Fencing Master*, 1999

Courtesy of Graham Petrie

Petrie, Graham

Dec. 10, 1939– Novelist; nonfiction writer

The Canadian author Graham Petrie has repeatedly demonstrated his considerable talent for both fiction and nonfiction writing. For much of his early career, he concentrated on books that analyzed various aspects of movies and the film industry, among them *History Must Answer to Man: The Contemporary Hungarian Cinema* (1979), *Hollywood Destinies: European Directors in America 1922–31* (1985), and *Before the Wall Came Down: Soviet and East European Filmmakers Working in the West* (1990). In recent years, Petrie has developed a reputation as a novelist of "oddly entertaining little works of sustained strangeness, deadpan horror, and sudden violence," as James Hynes wrote in the *Village Voice* (April 2, 1996). To date he has produced two novels, *Seahorse* (1980) and *The Siege* (1996), both of which were well received

by critics and readers alike. Multiple critics have suggested that these novels were heavily influenced by the author's interest in film. "Petrie has written books on Truffaut and Tarkovsky, and perhaps not coincidentally, his novels seem to fall about halfway in between: more brooding and mystical than Truffaut, but more rueful and a lot funnier than Tarkovsky," Hynes wrote.

In a statement written for *World Authors 1990–1995* discussing his life and writing career, Petrie, born on December 10, 1939, writes: "I was born of Scottish parents on the island of Penang, in what is now Malaysia. My father worked for the local civil service and my mother, who had attended Glasgow University, was a teacher. They had moved to Penang shortly after they were married, in 1938, and enjoyed the kind of life style there that was still possible for people of moderate financial means in the fading days of the British Empire. In 1941 they were on leave in Australia when the Japanese army invaded Malaya; my father, who was a member of the local volunteer defense force, returned to help defend the country and was almost immediately taken prisoner when Singapore surrendered. He spent the remainder of the War in a prisoner of war camp, and worked on the notorious Burma railroad—an experience that he would never talk about in any detail, even to his wife. My mother remained in Australia with me until late 1943, when she was given the opportunity to undertake the still very dangerous sea journey back to Scotland. After my father's release the family returned to Penang in 1947, where my brother Ian was born in 1948. I spent two years at a boarding school at Cameron Highlands on the Malayan mainland until the school was forced to close as a result of the activities of the Communist guerrillas operating in the area. After a year at school in Penang, I returned to Scotland and to Dollar Academy, first as a boarder and then, after my father's retirement, as a day pupil. Although my mother would reminisce frequently about her early days in Malaya in particular, I never learned much about my father's time as a prisoner and it was only much later, after his death, that I began to investigate more fully the circumstances of my parents' life and to use that, and my own memories, in my recently completed novel, *Mysterious Friends*.

"Although my earliest, and continuing, interest has been in literature, I began to take a serious interest in film in my final years at school, and at university at St. Andrews in Scotland and Brasenose College, Oxford, in the late 1950s and early 1960s. This was the heyday of the French New Wave and of the work of Bergman, Fellini, Antonioni and others and, at Oxford in particular, I spent as much time in the cinema as in the library working on my thesis (on Sterne's *Tristram Shandy*, which I particularly admired for its use of the kind of 'cinematic' effects which I saw being developed in the work of such directors as Alain Resnais). Friendship at college with students from Canada led me to apply for a teaching position there and in 1964, recently married to Anne Baillie, I began to work at McMaster University in Hamilton, Ontario, first of all teaching literature and then introducing courses in film, which soon became my primary, though not exclusive, area.

"From my childhood on, I had always been interested in writing and, in the mid-1960s, I began to publish poems in American and Canadian journals. After a time, however, I began to concentrate on fiction instead and, shortly after the publication of my first book of film criticism in 1970, on the films of François Truffaut (whose *The 400 Blows* had so dazzled me on my first viewing that I sat through it twice, unable to leave the cinema), my first short stories appeared, in *Playboy* and *Encounter*. I had just completed a year's sabbatical leave spent partly in London and partly in Italy, with Anne and our adopted daughter Alison, and aspects of the Italian experience appeared, in somewhat transmuted form, some years later in my first novel, *Seahorse*.

"In 1973 a fortuitous series of circumstances led me to spend some time in Budapest, studying Hungarian film. I returned there frequently over the next 15 years, publishing a book on Hungarian cinema in 1979, and also visiting other countries of the then–Soviet bloc, such as Poland, Czechoslovakia, and Bulgaria. Once again, much transformed, some of these experiences provided settings and incidents for my second novel, *The Siege*. In the late 1980s, research on another film book, this time on the work of Andrei Tarkovsky, that I cowrote with Vida T. Johnson, took me several times to Moscow during the death-throes of the Soviet Union.

"In 1974, while we were on our way to stay at a house in Provence belonging to the friends through whom we had met, Anne, who had suffered from kidney disease as a child, fell suddenly ill and died in hospital in Marseille. The next few years, with two children to care for (we had adopted a second daughter, Janet, in 1973) were difficult, though I had much help from friends and especially from Catherine Gibbon, a painter whose presence can be felt in *The Siege*, who became a second mother to my children and with whom I now live. I was thus able to continue publishing stories and film criticism on a fairly regular basis. During the 1980s we spent a good deal of time in England, renting a cottage in Somerset on a regular basis until quite recently. Though I am now a Canadian citizen, I retain a strong emotional attachment to Britain, and to Scotland in particular, and return there—and also to favourite European cities such as Paris and Budapest—for visits as often as I can.

"My writing in the 1970s and 1980s was strongly influenced—not always for the good—by the then-fashionable techniques of magic realism. I have always, however, been keenly attracted to non-realistic styles of fiction—Kafka, Calvino, Russell Hoban, and major writers of science fiction, children's fiction, and other types of what is loosely called '"fantasy."' Among classic writers, I am particularly fond of Dickens, Dostoyevsky, Faulkner, and Conrad (whose "Youth" made an indelible impact on me when I read it at the age of around 10 in the appropriate setting of Malaya). Although I now write, on the whole, in a more 'realistic' mode, I believe that literature—and film—should transform, rather than merely reflect, our understanding of reality; Tarkovsky achieved that magnificently in film and I would be happy if I could approximate at least something of this in fiction."

———

Petrie's first novel, *Seahorse*, was published in the United Kingdom in 1980 and in the United States in 1996. The book is an eerie, surreal tale that unfolds in a fishing village where the inhabitants believe that their souls migrate each night to a deserted island to mingle with other souls and recharge for the coming day. The unnamed narrator, whose purpose for visiting the island is never disclosed, is clearly perplexed by both the natives' strange beliefs and the bizarre happenings in the village. "I have been among them long enough to know that sometimes, unpredictably, or perhaps following some pattern to which I have not yet seized the key, they reverse the order of information: cause follows effect, answer precedes question, time is jumbled, fragmented, deconstructed," he says near the beginning of the novel. Events turn stranger still—some of the village children demonstrate their ability to walk on water, the narrator's landlord teaches him a card game designed to foretell the future, and the narrator learns of the villagers' fear that Dr. Damon Daniels, a scientist at a forbidding research facility known as "The Institute," may somehow be tampering with their nightly pilgrimage. *Seahorse* garnered extremely warm reviews. "Petrie . . . precisely evokes a world permeated with ancient folkways, myths, and beliefs, and fraught with irrational actions, temporal dislocations, Oedipal yearnings, and bizarre incidents," one reviewer wrote in *Publishers Weekly* (October 23, 1995). "Petrie's universe here is disquieting, but true to its own inner logic."

In *The Siege*, London lawyer Roger Everest accompanies his wife, Dorothy, an art historian, to an unnamed, war-torn country bearing strong similarities to the former Yugoslavia. Dorothy is there to study several recently discovered medieval frescoes reputedly painted by one Sister Margaret. The story combines present and past by interweaving excerpts—including accounts of an affair with a married duke and the death of her infant daughter—from Sister Margaret's diary. Roger, meanwhile, becomes obsessed with the country's civil war and witnesses the torture and murder of an acquaintance. "Petrie juxtaposes past and present in a comic and grotesque dance of infinite possibilities," W. B. Warde Jr. wrote in *Choice* (June 1996). "The novel becomes a social, civil, political, religious, and artistic satire revealing the horrors that lie just below the thin veneer of civilization—from

sexism, sadism, and prejudice to torture, war, and death. This retrospective and associational novel answers no questions, but it provides an intriguing mock philosophy." Further praise was offered by a reviewer in *Publishers Weekly* (October 25, 1996): "Petrie, a sterling storyteller, here exchanges the surrealities of his first novel for harsher truths, excavating the roots of violence and inhumanity."
—J. P.

SUGGESTED READING: *Choice* p942 Feb. 1991; *New York Times Book Review* p37 June 8, 1986; *Publishers Weekly* p59 Oct. 23, 1995

SELECTED BOOKS: Fiction—*Seahorse*, 1996; *The Siege*, 1996; Nonfiction—*History Must Answer to Man: the Contemporary Hungarian Cinema*, 1979; *Hollywood Destinies: European Directors in America, 1922–1931*, 1985; *Before the Wall Came Down: Soviet and East European Filmmakers Working in the West* (with R. Dwyer), 1990; *The Films of Andrei Tarkovsky: A Visual Fugue* (with V. T. Johnson), 1994

Petroski, Henry

Feb. 6, 1942– Essayist; historian

"Pencil head" is a nickname given in the academic world to engineers. It is doubly appropriate in the case of the American civil engineering professor Henry Petroski, who like Henry David Thoreau—an engineer who worked in the pencil manufacturing business—has also made his name as a writer, with works that include *The Pencil: A History of Design and Circumstance* (1990). In that and other books, among them *To Engineer Is Human: The Role of Failure in Successful Design* (1985), *Beyond Engineering: Essays and Other Attempts to Figure Without Equations* (1986), and *Invention By Design: How Engineers Get from Thought to Thing* (1996), Petroski has detailed the evolution in design that is necessary to produce objects that are truly useful. He has scrutinized objects that range from the humble pencil and paper clip to such massive structures as the Brooklyn Bridge and the Golden Gate Bridge. Both engineering and writing, as he told Jennifer Howard in a *Publishers Weekly* (September 4, 1995) interview, "rely on structure, whether it's mechanical or grammatical." His most recent book is *Remaking the World: Adventures in Engineering* (1997).

Henry Petroski was born on February 6, 1942 in New York and grew up in Brooklyn and Queens. Entering college at about the time that the Soviet Union sent up Sputnik, the first space satellite, and the United States mobilized to create more scientists and engineers in order to remain competitive in the space race, Petroski majored in engineering at Manhattan College, where he got an B.M.E. degree in 1963. He did graduate work at the University of Illinois at Urbana-Champaign, receiving his Ph.D. in 1968. He taught at the University of Texas, Austin, from 1968 to 1974, moving on to become a mechanical engineer in the Reactor Analysis and Safety Division of the Argonne National Laboratory of the University of Chicago. In 1980 he joined the faculty of Duke University, in Durham, North Carolina, where he eventually chaired the Department of Civil and Environmental Engineering and became a professor of history as well.

Petroski had a solid background in fracture mechanics, or, as he termed it in *Publishers Weekly*, "failure analysis," before he wrote his first book, *To Engineer Is Human: The Role of Failure in Successful Design*. In that work he put forth the thesis that honest mistakes lead to corrections that improve design. The book was generally praised, particularly for Petroski's discussion of the collapse of elevated walkways in a Kansas City hotel in 1981. Daniel LaRossa in *Library Journal* (September 1, 1985) termed *To Engineer Is Human* "a gem of a book" that "in marvelously clear prose . . . gives valuable insight into the limits of engineering and its practitioners." Michael Markow complained in the *New York Times Book Review* (December 1, 1985), however, that Petroski failed to provide "a complete sense of the challenges and constraints that engineers face in designing and building a project, the roles of research, development, and testing in advancing knowledge less painfully than through failure, or what characterizes engineering creativity and genius."

Petroski's next book, *Beyond Engineering* (1986), is a collection of essays on the same topic covered in *To Engineer Is Human*. Andrew Sage, reviewing the volume for *Science Books and Films* (January/February 1987) called it an "often witty, entertaining, and perceptive book." He was particularly taken with the first essay, "which details the need for engineers to be familiar with the literary as well as the technical culture." Daniel LaRossa, the *Library Journal* (August 1986) reviewer, was less impressed, deeming that "the ideas are too often obvious."

The Pencil struck a chord with reviewers, winning kudos almost universally. As its title suggests, *The Pencil* tells everything anyone could possibly want to know about the history, design, manufacture, and significance of the pencil, which started as an invention when graphite was discovered in England in the mid-16th century, gained in usefulness when clay was added in the late 18th century (pure graphite had become unavailable in France,) and, came into universal use in the 19th century, when the supply of graphite was replenished from mines in eastern Siberia and modern industrial techniques improved the pencil's manufacture. Jonathan Rosen in the *Voice Literary Supplement* (February 1990) remarked that Petroski's study "is the kind of book a pencil might write if a pencil could write what it wanted. . . . The overall effect of his scholarship is impressive, even poetic." Christopher Lehmann-Haupt in the *New York Times* (January 22, 1990) quoted as the rationale for writing the book Petroski's observation, "Even the most able and articulate of ancient engineers, whether they were known then as artisans, craftsmen, architects, or master builders, might have had no more time or inclination or reason to articulate what it is they did and how they did it than do some of the most able of today's engineers."

Petroski continued to articulate what engineers do and how they do it in *The Evolution of Useful Things* (1992), another book based on his maxim "Form follows failure." He detailed the progression in design that produced the latest advances in knives, forks, spoons, fasteners, aluminum cans, and telephones and gave the specifics of the workings of such seemingly simple conveniences as paper clips, zippers, windshield wipers, and Post-It notes. John Updike speculated in the *New Yorker* (January 18, 1993) about Petroski that "perhaps he does belong with the poets, extending, in the manner of a celebrant as well as that of a naturalist, the Romantic embrace of nature to the invented, manufactured world that has become man's second nature." Updike did have a mild cavil—that the saying "Form follows function" is something of a "straw dictum," which Petroski knocks down repeatedly in an "attempt to give 'perceived failure' something like the central position that 'natural selection' occupies in Darwinism." Jan Adkins noted in the *Washington Post* (January 28, 1993) that "Henry Petroski is a valuable resource—an engineer who examines the simplest, most ubiquitous tools in our lives with an appraising eye." Adkins, nevertheless, faulted *The Evolution of Useful Things* for "its failure to communicate design" and its "preachy, pedantic, and . . . almost impenetrable prose." The *Library Journal* (December 1992) reviewer, Carol Binkowski, maintained, on the contrary, that the book "offers hours of delight" with "an intricate look . . . at the technology and basic rationale behind a number of items we often take for granted . . . told with warm regard" and "illuminating thoughts on the theoretical, historical, and cultural frameworks that influenced these creations."

When Petroski turned his attention in *Engineers of Dreams: Great Bridge Builders and the Spanning of America* (1995) from the small to the gigantic, the *Library Journal* (October 15, 1995) reviewer termed it his best book. "By focusing on a half-dozen bridge engineers who did epochal work, he manages to capture something of what it is about bridge building that inspires passion and dedication from the engineers who design, build, and study them," Mark Shelton wrote. Calling the book a "fascinating and lively account," Witold Rybczynski observed in the *New York Review of Books* (November 16, 1995), "Petroski writes lucidly and at length about the various technical issues that affected the design of bridges, but he does not neglect aesthetics. The chief question is whether a bridge should merely reflect its structural function, or whether adornment should not also be a part of bridge design." Michael Wise in the *Washington Post* (November 7, 1995) called *Engineers of Dreams* "a paean to the delicate balance of art and science that the best bridges represent," which "heightens our appreciation of these most utilitarian of monuments." Adding to the paean of praise for the book, M. R. Montgomery in the *New York Times Book Review* (October 15, 1995) wrote that "Petroski's unique achievement . . . is to place civil engineering precisely in the practical world that dreamers must inhabit." Montgomery did fault Petroski, however, for not including "a clearer explanation of just how difficult, taxing, and tedious was the art of engineering in the days of pencils, slide rules, and calculus."

In *Invention by Design: How Engineers Get from Thought to Thing*, Petroski returned to "the invention of devices and their refinement over time by others," according to Mark L. Shelton, writing in Library *Journal* (September 1, 1996).The book is another expansion of his thesis that useful inventions derive from competition to improve on failure of previous designs. Delving into "the philosophy and cultural study of the process of invention," Shelton wrote, Petroski presented studies of the refinement of such items as the paper clip, the zipper, the fax machine, and the Boeing 777 airplane. A *Washington Post Book World* (December 29, 1996) reviewer, Curt Suplee, felt that Petroski had proven his point "that 'the simplest of things can hold as much mystery and provide as many lessons about the nature of engineering as the most complex.'"

Petroski's *Remaking the World: Adventures in Engineering* (1997) is a collection of essays, previously published in *American Scientist*, that discuss the creative process—from conception to finished product—behind such structures as the Golden Gate Bridge, the Hoover Dam, and the Panama Canal. In this work Petroski "exhibits the graceful style and flair for storytelling that he brought to *The Pencil* and *Engineers of Dreams*," in the opinion of a *Publishers Weekly* (November 10, 1997) reviewer.

Henry Petroski is married to Catherine Petroski, a writer of young-adult fiction. As of 1995 his daughter was working on a Ph.D. in English, and his son has studied mechanical engineering.

Ultimately, Petroski is seeking the philosopher's stone of a universal principle, as he told his *Publishers Weekly* interviewer, Jennifer Howard. "I see the process of creativity in synthesizing ideas or objects or things as being very similar. . . . We tend to segregate things—engineering, architecture, legislation—but there are a lot of common features. We're all human beings, just focusing on different aspects of what effectively is a single big problem."

—S. Y.

SUGGESTED READING: *Library Journal* p20 Sep. 1, 1985, p164 Aug. 1986, p117 Dec. 1992, p85 Oct. 15, 1995, p206 Sep. 1, 1996; *New York Review of Books* p12 Nov. 16, 1995; *New York Times* C p16 Jan. 22, 1990; *New York Times Book Review* p25 Dec. 1, 1985, p22 Oct. 15, 1995; *New Yorker* p104 Jan. 18, 1993; *Publishers Weekly* p41 Sep. 4, 1995, p69 Sep. 30, 1996; *Voice Literary Supplement* p5 Feb. 1990; *Washington Post* C p2 Jan. 28, 1993, E p2 Nov. 7, 1995; *Washington Post Book World* p8 Dec. 29, 1996

SELECTED BOOKS: *To Engineer Is Human: The Role of Failure in Successful Design*, 1985; *Beyond Engineering: Essays and Other Attempts to Figure Without Equations*, 1986; *The Pencil: A History of Design and Circumstance*, 1990; *The Evolution of Useful Things*, 1992; *Design Paradigms: Case Histories of Error and Judgment in Engineering*, 1994; *Engineers of Dreams: Great Bridge Builders and the Spanning of America*, 1995; *Invention By Design: How Engineers Get from Thought to Thing*, 1996; *Remaking the World*, 1997

Sigrid Estrada

Pileggi, Nicholas

Feb. 22, 1933– Nonfiction writer

Nicholas Pileggi, a journalist and longtime chronicler of the Mafia, has earned a reputation for revealing the realities beneath glossy popularized images of the mob. "I'm not interested in how the Rigatoni family took over the Spumoni family," Pileggi told Tim Appelo and Meredith Berkman for *Entertainment Weekly* (October 12, 1990), using the names of a pasta and a kind of ice cream to comment on the many highly fictionalized and, he feels, romanticized tales of the Mafia. "I'm fascinated by the true story. It speaks to the dark side of American life." Pileggi has authored two bestselling nonfiction books that detail the inner workings of organized crime, both drawn largely from his interviews with key players. *Wiseguy: Life in a Mafia Family* (1985) is based on Pileggi's extensive

conversations with Henry Hill, an average mob criminal who worked the streets but nonetheless had extensive knowledge of those higher up the ladder. (In Mafia slang, a "wiseguy" is a low-level mobster.) *Casino: Love and Honor in Las Vegas* (1995) recounts the diminishment of the mob's involvement in Las Vegas casinos as related primarily by Frank "Lefty" Rosenthal, one of the linchpins in the Mafia's operations there in the 1970s and 1980s. Both books have been made into successful films, *Goodfellas* (1990) and *Casino* (1995) respectively, directed by Martin Scorsese, with whom Pileggi co-wrote the screenplays.

Nicholas Pileggi was born on February 22, 1933 and grew up in Brooklyn, New York, the son of Nick and Susan (Defaslo) Pileggi, immigrants from Calabria, the southern Italian province closest to Sicily. His father owned a shoestore. Some of Pileggi's neighbors in the Bensonhurst and Bedford-Stuyvesant sections of Brooklyn were involved with the Mafia, and Pileggi was acutely aware of their presence during his youth, even though no one spoke openly about them. When he was a child, a relative of his was found dead in a trash can; dressed as a priest, he was riddled with bullets. "They wouldn't explain it to me," Pileggi recalled, as quoted by Appelo and Berkman. "Nobody would talk, but I knew."

Pileggi attended Long Island University, where he majored in English and intended to pursue a career teaching literature. After he got a job as a copyboy at the Associated Press (AP) during his last two years of college, however, he was drawn to journalism. He told Joseph Barbato for *Publishers Weekly* (February 7, 1986), "Once I saw what being a reporter was like, I was hooked. You were always where everyone wanted to be. You were always seeing what was happening—crossing the police lines, seeing the bodies or the fire. You were the messenger. You would go back and tell everybody what it was like. I found that fascinating as a kid. I loved the idea of doing it." After graduation Pileggi was offered a job as a reporter for the Associated Press in New York City, where he worked from 1956 to 1968, covering police, labor, and political activities. Pileggi actually did very little writing as an AP employee; rather, he gathered information, all the while developing a strong background in subjects that he would later write about. "The city was broken into police districts then," he told Barbato. "And reporters actually covered the cops. You didn't write a story; you gave in notes." Gradually, Pileggi began writing articles, which were published in magazines such as *Esquire*, during his off-hours. In 1968 he left the AP to become a contributing editor of the newly formed *New York* magazine, where he specialized in reporting on New York City crime and politics. For that magazine, he has written dozens of articles on such topics as the activities of the mob boss Paul Castellano, rumors that former New York governor Mario Cuomo harbored Mafia connections, and corruption among rank-and-file city employees. "The magazine has been a terrific base, because the stories I do are not global in any sense," Pileggi told Barbato. "They're New York stories about politics, crime, and corruption."

Pileggi's first book, *Blye, Private Eye* (1976), is an account of the day-to-day work of Irwin Blye, a real-life private detective whom Pileggi spent a year observing with the intention of writing the book. In stark contrast to his fictional counterparts, Blye spent most of his time obtaining legal forms and poring over old tax returns and telephone bills. While Pileggi's objective was to document the mundanities of the private detective's job and thus give the lie to fictional images of intrigue and glamour, many critics found *Blye, Private Eye* a fascinating read.

In 1981 Pileggi became acquainted with Henry Hill, a career criminal who, confronted with a life sentence on a narcotics charge, had decided to testify against his associates and begin a new life in the government's Witness Protection Program. Hill's lawyer contacted the publisher Simon and Schuster about the possibility of creating a book based on Hill's experiences with the mob, and the publisher in turn contacted Pileggi's agent. The idea of writing a book about the Mafia's version of an average workingman—as opposed to a *Godfather*-type crime boss—appealed to Pileggi. As he told Barbato, Hill "was a worker. And I thought by taking a look at the worker ant, so to speak, you had a better opportunity to tell how the whole colony works." After he had settled on this approach, Pileggi told Selwyn Raab for the *New York Times Book Review* (January 26, 1986), a single conversation with Hill convinced him he had found the perfect subject. "Once I realized I was not judgmental about his life, he was unbelievably open and full of details," Pileggi told Raab. "I checked him out with the FBI and prosecutors and they all agreed he was a moneymaker, not a shooter or a muscle man." Pileggi spoke with Hill by telephone almost every day for two years. As Pileggi told Raab, they also met in person at prosecutors' offices in New York and in cars, parks, hotels, and restaurants in cities in the Midwest. Because of Hill's participation in the Witness Protection Program, he had received a new identity, and Pileggi does not know Hill's new name and address.

Half Sicilian and half Irish, Hill grew up in Brooklyn, where he began working for the mob as an errand boy at age 11, in 1955. By the time he was a teenager, Hill was committing arson, using fake credit cards, working at crap games, and using counterfeit $20 bills to make small purchases and then pass the change to his superiors. He also collected loan-shark payments for Paul Vario, a boss in the Lucchese crime family, eventually becoming recognized as one of Vario's regular crew. Later Hill was involved with bribing the Boston College basketball team to participate in a point-shaving scam, and most notoriously, he credits himself with obtaining the information that allowed his friend James Burke—also known as Jimmy the Gent—to organize the largest cash robbery in history. That heist—which included over $6 million in cash and jewels stolen from Lufthansa Airlines at Kennedy Airport, in New York City, in 1978—resulted in 12 murders after Burke refused to share the take with the others who had helped with the job. One of those Burke threatened to kill was Hill himself.

To relate the stories of Hill's life as a criminal, the author interspersed his subject's first-person accounts with those of Hill's wife and Pileggi's own straightforward retelling. Pileggi won praise from critics for keeping his writing simple and allowing the events Hill described to speak for themselves. In the *New York Times Book Review* (January 26, 1986), Vincent Patrick wrote, "*Wiseguy* evoked for me the quality of the best documentary films." This impression was in keeping with Pileggi's intentions. He told Barbato, "I never thought of this as a cops-and-robbers book. It's more like an anthropological study—watching wiseguys in Samoa, in a sense." After reading *Wiseguy*, Martin Scorsese called Pileggi to express his interest in collaborating on a screen version of the book. "I told him I had been waiting for that phone call all my life," Pileggi recalled to Patrizia DiLucchio for *People Online*. *Goodfellas* (1990), which starred Ray Liotta as Hill and featured performances by Robert De Niro and Joe Pesci, is widely considered to be one of Scorsese's best films.

The three main players in Pileggi's third book, *Casino*, are the gambling genius Frank "Lefty" Rosenthal, who moved from Chicago to Las Vegas in 1967 to look after the mob's interests in its casinos; the woman he married there, Geri McGee, formerly a high-class call girl; and Tony "the Ant" Spilotro, a mob heavy and sometime friend of Rosenthal's who came to Las Vegas to pursue his own criminal interests. *Casino* shows how the personality of each of the three and the clashes among them contributed to the curtailment of the Mafia's involvement in the Las Vegas casino industry. The narrative was culled primarily from Pileggi's conversations with Rosenthal, with supporting material drawn from court and FBI records and other sources. Pileggi told DiLucchio, "I did try something new with *Casino*: I had the cooperation of real people who had actually been there and I felt the story told by the real people in their own [words] was so compelling to me that I decided to get out of the way and let these people tell their own story. There is not one blind quote in the book. You have a man telling you what it is like to be blown up in a car, and you have a hit man complaining about how hard it is to kill one of his victims. I didn't feel I wanted to get between the reader and the original material. I guess it worked for some people and didn't work for others, but I didn't feel there was any other way for me to deal with the material I had." As with *Wiseguy*, critics were impressed by the way Pileggi created a gripping narrative from his material without reducing the impact of the raw testimony of his subjects. Robert Lacey, writing for the *New York Times* (October 8, 1995), commented that Pileggi "polishes [his raw material] with the narrative skills of a novelist or screenwriter." Lacey added that one of the book's strengths lay in "Pileggi's ability to convey that satisfying unease that is the essence of gangster drama. Something nasty, we feel certain, is waiting for us around the corner—and each character is so vivid that we are willing to follow wherever he leads."

In the case of *Casino*, Pileggi's collaboration with Scorsese began before the book was published; in fact, the film was released in 1995, about one month after the book became available to the general public. Although the names of the people in the book were changed for the film, Robert De Niro's character was based on Rosenthal; Joe Pesci played the character based on Spilotro; and in what was widely thought to be the performance of her career, Sharon Stone portrayed the character based on McGee.

Pileggi has commented that like many other Americans, he had associated Mafia life to some degree with the romanticized images disseminated by films such as *The Godfather* (a movie he much admires), until he discovered that the real lives of gangsters are "grubbier" than he had expected. He told Barbato, "There are occasional pay days, but there are far more empty days. The romantic notion of that world is so far from the truth. I can't imagine anyone in his right mind reading [*Wiseguy*] and saying, 'Oh, that's what I want to be. I want to be a gangster.' It's a career filled with pain, much of it inflicted on others. . . . They're not those characters in movies. There's nothing noble about them. They're quite loathsome."

Pileggi is married to the writer and film director Nora Ephron, who has two sons from a previous marriage. When asked by DiLucchio how they manage to juggle their marriage and their creative projects, Pileggi responded, "We cope blissfully. Nora reads everything I write and may be the best editor I've ever come across in my life. And she shows me just about everything she's working on and I try to help." In 1986 Pileggi received the Peter Kihss Award for excellence in reporting on New York City government.

—Olivia Jane Smith

SUGGESTED READING: *Chicago Tribune* XIV p10 Oct. 29, 1995, with photos; *Entertainment Weekly* p39 Oct. 12, 1990, with photo, p54+ Oct. 6, 1995, with photo; *New York Times* C p21 Jan. 16, 1986, with photo, B p10 Dec. 15, 1986, C p17 Sep. 28, 1995, with photo; *New York Times Book Review* p7 Jan. 26, 1986, with photo, p28 Oct. 8, 1995; *People Online*; *Publishers Weekly* p56+ Feb. 7, 1986; *Contemporary Authors* new revision series vol. 52, 1996

SELECTED WORKS: Nonfiction—*Blye, Private Eye*, 1976; *Wiseguy: Life in a Mafia Family*, 1985; *Casino: Love and Honor in Las Vegas*, 1995; Screenplays—*Goodfellas* (with Martin Scorsese), 1990; *Casino* (with Martin Scorsese), 1995

Jan Press / Courtesy of Delacorte Press

Plain, Belva

Oct. 9, 1919– Novelist; short-story writer

Though not a favorite among most critics, Belva Plain has been a best-selling author for more than 20 years. In the early 1960s, after having published numerous short stories in magazines, she took time off to devote herself to her family. She did not return to writing until she was in her 50s, at which point she began a successful career as a novelist. Starting with *Evergreen* (1978) and continuing in such novels as *Random Winds* (1980), *The Golden Cup* (1986), *Tapestry* (1988), *Treasures* (1992), and *The Carousel* (1995), Plain's work has focused on families—particularly women—experiencing dramatic difficulties. Her novels typically feature melodramatic plot twists and, in part for this reason, have been criticized as little more than soap operas, a label Plain adamantly rejects. Her novels *Legacy of Silence* and *Fortune's Hand* were published in 1998 and 1999, respectively.

The writer was born Belva Offenberg on October 9, 1919 in New York City, the only child of a contractor, Oscar Offenberg, and his wife, Eleanor. Her interest in writing manifested itself early on, when she edited her high-school literary magazine. While attending Barnard College, in New York City, she submitted several pieces to the campus literary journal. Shortly after graduating from Barnard, in 1941, she married Irving Plain, an ophthalmologist, with whom she would eventually have three children. The Plains lived in Philadelphia for six years while Irving completed his residency, and then, in 1947, moved to South Orange, New Jersey, where they lived for many years.

Starting in the 1940s Plain published short fiction in such women's magazines as *Cosmopolitan* and *Good Housekeeping*, at the suggestion of a friend who provided illustrations for some of those periodicals. The stories were formulaic, focusing on women's romantic problems. Plain continued writing for magazines until the early 1960s, when she devoted herself full-time to her responsibilities as a homemaker. "It became difficult to do two things at once," she told Carol Horner for the *Chicago Tribune* (September 17, 1980). During her years away from writing, Plain also served as president of the local parent-teacher association and sat on the boards of various charitable organizations. All the while, she jotted down notes and fragments of fiction, which she intended to use when she resumed her career as an author. She got back into writing in the 1970s.

Plain, who is Jewish, was troubled by the representations of Jews in much of the fiction she was reading. "I was tired of the stereotyped Jewish mother whose chicken soup renders her son impotent," she told *People* (August 7, 1978). "I thought it was time to write about the kind of people I know." The result was her first novel, *Evergreen*, published when Plain was 58 years old. The book, which opens in about 1900, tells the story of a Jewish immigrant who works as a maid and falls in love with the son of her employers. *Evergreen* was a major departure from Plain's material for women's magazines, in that it recorded the trials and triumphs of three generations of a Jewish family, following them from the ghettos of Warsaw to the suburbs of America. An immediate success, the novel spent 41 weeks on the best-seller list and sold 3.5 million copies. (According to *Contemporary Authors* [1997], 11 million copies are in print, in a dozen languages.) With the novel's brisk sales, Belva Plain became, at age 59, a major name in the world of popular fiction. "I'm a younger Grandma Moses," she mused, as quoted in the *New York Times* (July 30, 1978). In 1985 NBC produced a miniseries based on *Evergreen*.

Two years after the publication of *Evergreen*, Plain's second novel, *Random Winds* (1980), appeared. The novel features a doctor married to a woman suffering from curvature of the spine. The idea for the story came to Plain after she observed a couple in which the woman suffered from the same malady.

Plain continued to publish prolifically into the 1980s. In 1982 she released *Eden Burning*, a story set on a Caribbean Island, about the fall from grace of a wealthy planter's daughter. Two years later she published the ambitious *Crescent City*, a tale of an American Jewish family during the Civil War. *The Golden Cup*'s plot unfolds in New York City at the beginning of the 20th century; its protagonist is one of *Evergreen*'s secondary characters, who is much more idealistic than the rest of her well-to-do family and seeks to help the poor. At the same time she must deal with her husband's womanizing.

In *Newsday* (October 12, 1986), Frances A. Koestler expressed her disappointment in *The Golden Cup*, a book she thought was weakened by the reappearance of the two main characters from *Evergreen*. Koestler suggested, however, that this less-than-satisfying effort should not permanently turn readers away from Plain, whom the reviewer described as an "indisputable talent."

The third novel in the trilogy begun in *Evergreen* and continued in *The Golden Cup* is *Tapestry*. Here, Plain examined the generations that followed her original characters. The book spans the years from 1920 to just before World War II; with the power of the Nazis ever growing, the characters must reassess their identities as Jews. Writing for the *New York Times Book Review* (June 19, 1988), Karen Ray expressed the view that the novel was a step down from the trilogy's previous two installments. "Despite her ambitious plotting," Ray wrote, "Belva Plain has produced a serviceable saga that lives, if at all, only in the shadow of her earlier books." Plain's first published effort of the 1990s was *Harvest* (1990). Continuing the exploits of the characters first introduced in *Evergreen*, *Harvest* takes place in the 1960s, a generation after the previous installment in the series, and centers on the illegitimate daughter of *Tapestry*'s main character. Joanne Kaufman of *People* (August 27, 1990) proved even less kind to *Harvest* than Karen Ray had been to *Tapestry*. "Nothing a reviewer can say will stay Belva Plain from her appointed rounds—spinning twaddle," Kaufman wrote. The reviewer singled out the novel's "pat, platitudinous writing" for particular criticism.

With *Treasures*, Plain departed at last from the family saga begun in *Evergreen*. The novel deals with the conflict between family values and worldly values, tracing the aspirations of three siblings who make different decisions when faced with the choice between maintaining an old-fashioned lifestyle and seeking glamour and fortune in the big city. In the end, Plain suggests that life's true "treasures" come from within. While the review in *Publishers Weekly* (January 27, 1992) described this message as somewhat trite, it noted that Plain's "warm narrative nevertheless endears itself to the reader and provides a rewarding reading experience." In the *New York Times Book Review* (May 17, 1992), Katherine Ramsland found fascinating the novel's perspective on Manhattan's upper class but criticized the lack of tension and the predictable plot.

Continuing to explore the myriad relationships and emotional interconnections of the extended family, Plain published *Whispers* in 1993. The family presented in the novel maintains an elaborate façade, hiding such problems as physical abuse behind a veneer of success and comfort. The novel's main female character is in the end made to face her family's numerous difficulties. The book received many negative reviews, but a writer for *Publishers Weekly* (March 22, 1993) praised the author's effective characterizations and avoidance of melodrama.

Daybreak (1994), the story of two babies switched at birth, takes up issues of Jewish life explored in Plain's earlier novels, as one of the infants grows into an anti-Semitic adult, unaware that he is Jewish. Jean Hanff Korelitz remarked in the *New York Times Book Review* (May 8, 1994) that the novel's imagery derives from clichéd language and that the dialogue "suggests background music." Nevertheless, Korelitz felt that the book's "plot device . . . is meaty enough to compensate for these shortcomings."

Plain has continued to write prolifically, publishing novels throughout the 1990s. *Daybreak* was followed by *The Carousel* (1995), *Promises* (1996), *Homecoming* (1997), and *Secrecy* (1997). In the last-named book, Plain followed a young rape victim's struggle to overcome her fear of intimacy. The plot of Plain's novel *Legacy of Silence* begins in Germany at the brink of World War II and concludes in present-day America, as it follows the fates of two daughters of a rich Berlin family. *Fortune's Hand* traces the peaks and valleys—both material and moral—in the life of Robb MacDaniel, a schoolteacher turned lawyer.

To fight what she perceives as the stereotype of the "Jewish mother" that exists in much of popular American culture, Plain fills her works with female characters of exceptional strength and dignity. They deal courageously with problems that often stem from their heritage as well as their family lives. The author's tremendous success over the years has proven that her stories have a wide appeal that extends beyond a Jewish readership. "I think I show real people and a real understanding of human nature, how people function and react to their environment," Plain told the *Chicago Tribune* (October 12, 1984).

One of the overriding themes of Plain's work is forbidden love. In this respect her novels bear a resemblance to the stories she published in the earlier portion of her career. Many of her female protagonists are faced with difficult decisions regarding matters of the heart. Yet despite the frequency of love affairs in her novels, Plain has made it a point not to include gratuitous sex scenes. "I think they're vulgar," she told the *Chicago Tribune* (October 12, 1984). "People [have written] love stories, the greatest in the world, and didn't feel it necessary to include those scenes." In this regard, Plain has always considered her work to be far above the often lurid novels that make up a good deal of the romance genre.

The author has also made it clear that her material comes purely from observation and imagination, not from experience. "I had one love affair in my life and that was . . . Irving," she told the *Chicago Tribune*. Her happy and somewhat traditional family life contrasts sharply with the tumultuous events of her characters' lives.

Many book critics have labeled Plain's novels soap operas, charging that they substitute sensationalism and sap for believable plot structure and character development. During a *Chicago Tribune* (September 17, 1980) interview, Plain asked rhetorically, "What is a soap opera? An attractive young woman is married to a stodgy man. She takes a lover . . . and goes away with him. He tires of her, and she is terribly jealous. She commits suicide, and he is overcome with guilt. . . . Is that a soap opera? It's the plot of *Anna Karenina*." She went on to accuse her critics of "intellectual snobbery."

Plain's daily regimen involves writing for five hours each morning, then recording her material on tape for a secretary to type. Her husband, Irving, died in 1982.

—B.S.

SUGGESTED READING: *Chicago Tribune* p13+ Sep. 17, 1980, with photo, p2+ Oct. 12, 1984, with photo; *New York Times Book Review* p30 July 30, 1978, with photo, p20 June 19, 1988, p35 Sep. 30, 1990, with photo, p35 May 17, 1992, p18 May 8, 1994; *Newsday* p22 Oct. 12, 1986, with photo; *People* p85 Aug. 7, 1978, with photo, p32+ Aug. 1, 1988, p30 Aug. 27, 1990, with photo; *Publishers Weekly* p89 Jan. 27, 1992; *International Authors and Writers Who's Who 1997/98*

SELECTED BOOKS: *Evergreen*, 1978; *Random Winds*, 1980; *Eden Burning*, 1982; *Crescent City*, 1984; *The Golden Cup*, 1986; *Tapestry*, 1988; *Blessings*, 1989; *Harvest*, 1990; *Treasures*, 1992; *Whispers*, 1993; *Daybreak*, 1994; *The Carousel*, 1995; *Promises*, 1996; *The Homecoming*, 1997; *Secrecy*, 1997; *Legacy of Silence*, 1998; *Fortune's Hand*, 1999

Posner, Gerald

May 20, 1954– Nonfiction writer; lawyer

Gerald L. Posner has married his past training as an attorney to his considerable writing skills to become a widely respected investigative author. His tenacious approach to his subjects reflects a deep-seated desire to inform and educate the public on many contemporary issues. Posner's books—on topics ranging from fugitive Nazis to Chinese Mafia members to a 1996 third-party presidential candidate—are often labeled "compelling" by reviewers and scholars. He relies not on sensationalism but on a mixture of well-crafted prose and hard facts to tell his stories. His two "assassination books"— about John F. Kennedy and Martin Luther King Jr.—have brought new light to hotly debated subjects and earned critical acclaim. In addition to his nonfiction, Posner has ventured into fiction writing, while continuing to act as a consultant to the law firm he founded more than a decade ago.

Gerald L. Posner was born on May 20, 1954, in San Francisco, California, to Gerald G. and Gloria Posner. Posner's father worked as a shipping executive and his mother as a homemaker. The younger Posner was interested in writing, but did not initially pursue it when he enrolled at the University of California at Berkeley, deciding instead to heed the advice of his father and major in political science. "My father dealt with a lot of lawyers," Posner told Paul Galloway for the *Chicago Tribune* (October 3, 1993). "He said, 'Son, these fellows charge fees you can't believe.'"

After graduating with a bachelor's degree in 1975, Posner headed to Hastings College of Law, where he graduated summa cum laude with a J.D. degree in 1978. It was not long before he landed a job as litigation associate for the prestigious Wall Street law firm of Cravath, Swaine, and Moore. The youngest attorney ever hired by the firm, Posner was handed a daunting first assignment: an anti-trust suit against IBM that had originally been filed in 1968. The case involved an enormous amount of paperwork—more than one million pages of exhibits and over 100,000 pages of trial transcript—and Posner quickly acquired the skills he needed to wade through large amounts of data in an efficient manner. "It was a blessing in disguise," he told John F. Baker of *Publishers Weekly* (April 13, 1997). "It made me completely unafraid of paperwork, unlike some journalists."

In 1980, Posner decided to leave Cravath, Swaine, and Moore and start his own firm, Posner and Ferrara, in New York City. In 1981, Posner took on a very different type of case from those he had tackled at his Wall Street firm. This one involved a Jewish survivor of the Auschwitz concentration camp who had been a victim of Nazi Josef Mengele's pseudo-scientific "experiments" during World War II. The man wished to receive monetary compensation for the health problems he continued to encounter as a result of Mengele's brutality.

Working pro bono, Posner sued both the Mengele family and the German government. As he had expected, the suits were not successful, but in the process of performing research, Posner uncovered a huge amount of information on Mengele's postwar years, when the Nazi lived a comfortably anonymous life in Argentina. The lawyer became fascinated with the subject and even made a trip to Buenos Aires, where he tried in vain to gain access to the federal police file on Mengele, a file to which even U.S. government officials had been unable to gain access for years. Then, nearly two months later, two police officers suddenly appeared at Posner's hotel and told him the new president of Argentina had given him permission to peruse the Mengele files. The incident was just one of many in which Posner says he was merely in the right place at the right time. "They were going through a spasm of democracy," he told Eric Parkurar for the Random House magazine *At Random* (February 1998), "and I benefitted from it."

The files turned out to be a treasure trove of information, and while it was too late to aid Posner's lawsuit, after five years of collecting thousands of documents, he decided to write a book on the subject. Working in collaboration with John Ware, Posner published *Mengele: The Complete Story* in 1986. Using the information he obtained in Argentina, as well as hitherto unpublished excerpts from Mengele's diaries, which Mengele's son provided, Posner created an in-depth portrait of one of the most notorious modern war criminals. In the process, Posner also managed to debunk many rumors that surrounded Mengele after his disappearance from Germany.

The book sold well, and Posner donated 20 percent of the proceeds to a group of Auschwitz survivors led by the man who had originally retained him for the lawsuit. Book reviewers were largely pleased with *Mengele: The Complete Story*; many called it a superior effort compared to previous Mengele biographies. *Library Journal* (June 1, 1986) commented that the book's greatest strength comes from the wealth of personal materials. The *New York Review of Books* (May 28, 1987) praised the book as "well researched and wonderfully free of all of the customary fantasy and exaggeration." The *Times Literary Supplement* (June 12, 1987) reviewer, however, felt that the book did not live up to its subtitle of being "the complete story." The reviewer called it "misleading" and remarked that little "is offered in the way of analysis."

The success of his first book prompted Posner to concentrate on his writing full-time, although he remained a counsel for his law firm. In 1988 he published *Warlords of Crime: Chinese Secret Societies—The New Mafia*, another thoroughly researched nonfiction work on a largely unexplored subject. *Warlords of Crime* examines the history of secret Chinese societies that were originally formed in the 17th century as political organizations. These groups, or "triads," have evolved over the years, first into a society of trained assassins and, most recently, into controllers of the global heroin trade. As he did with his first book, in *Warlords of Crime* Posner delved deeply into his subject, providing his readers with both historical and current information and peppering the narative with chilling facts. The book involved months of research, including extensive travels in Southeast Asia, and received critical accolades.

The following year, Posner decided to take his writing in a new direction, and released his first work of fiction, *The Bio-Assassins* (1989). The book is an espionage thriller about secret CIA research into biological warfare. As the story evolves, a deadly virus, eerily similar to the one which causes AIDS, is obtained by the KGB, who plan to use it against the United States. The tightly constructed plot takes the reader along on a wild ride through politics and murder. Posner's first novel was commercially successful.

Posner returned to nonfiction with another look at the legacy of Nazism. In *Hitler's Children: Sons and Daughters of Leaders of the Third Reich Talk about Themselves and Their Fathers* (1991), Posner used interviews he conducted with the children of some of the most notorious figures of World War II, including Rudolf Hess, Karl Saur, Claus von Stauffenberg, and Josef Mengele, to create an insightful, thought-provoking book. *Library Journal* (February 15, 1991) noted that the memories and reactions of these sons and daughters "have much to teach us about history and family psychology" and called the book "absolutely essential for most public and academic libraries." Similarly impressed was Cathy Chauvette, who wrote in *School Library Journal* (April 1992), "Confusion over the gulf between public and private personae, horror at the discovery of their fathers' deeds, and denial, all are made vivid." The reviewer went on to observe, "While the author does not remain completely objective, this is nevertheless a valuable primary-source view of the war from a unique perspective."

One critic however, was less than enthusiastic about Posner's style and method of telling the story. "A certain tedium intrudes on the experience of reading Mr. Posner's case histories," wrote Christopher Lehmann-Haupt for the *New York Times* (June 24, 1991), "which follow a set pattern of first narrating the parent's early career objectively and then, where possible, telling the latter part of it from the child's point of view." The reviewer continues with the suggestion, "Perhaps it would have been more enlightening had Mr. Posner studied fewer cases more intensely, or even a single case from the most intimate point of view. But as it is, most of what Hitler's children have to say is not especially interesting." While admitting that the book's various stories do make for a fair share of "fascinations," Lehmann-Haupt was left searching for a more complete explanation as to how these fathers, and the society they created, were allowed to carry out such atrocities. "The explanation for such a society . . . lies deeper in history," he

wrote, "and is scarcely touched upon in *Hitler's Children*."

Posner's next work was based on an issue that had consumed him for several years—the conspiracy theories surrounding the murder of President John F. Kennedy in 1963. Ever since the shooting, the arrest of Lee Harvey Oswald, Oswald's subsequent murder, and the hastily released report on the assassination by the Warren Commission, conspiracy buffs have produced innumerable movies, books, papers, articles, and Web sites devoted to the notion that Oswald was not the lone shooter. Using statistical analogy, a detailed examination of all 26 volumes of the Warren Commission Report, a computer-assisted analysis of the famed Zapruder film, and more than 200 new interviews with various officials and witnesses to events surrounding the crime, as well as with associates and family of the accused and the implicated, Posner finally concluded that there had been one and only one shooter—Lee Harvey Oswald.

The publication in 1993 of *Case Closed: Lee Harvey Oswald and the Assassination of JFK* drew attention not only for its controversial conclusion, which contradicted a persistent theory—that of a governmental cover-up of JFK's death—but for the book's thoroughness in exploring and then debunking many views of the case. Reviewers of *Case Closed* were overwhelmingly impressed with Posner's detailed analysis of the assassination, and many praised the author for his investigative reporting techniques and solidly drawn conclusion. Several critics even suggested that Posner's book be used in the future as the ultimate reference source for information regarding the assassination."This is the book on the JFK assassination, the definitive work that cuts through all the confusion and misinformation," wrote the *National Review* (October 18, 1993). Speaking for many critics, Jeffrey Toobin wrote in the *Chicago Tribune* (September 12, 1993) that he began reading *Case Closed* "as a skeptic" but found the book "utterly convincing in its thesis." He added that in the end, "this fascinating and important book won me over. Case closed, indeed."

Guy Halverson of the *Christian Science Monitor* (September 28, 1993) offered the opinion that Posner "has produced the most authoritative work to date on the Kennedy assassination" and added that "his gripping and convincing depiction seems likely to stand as the starting point for any future examination of Kennedy's death." However, Halverson did write that Posner's conclusion is a little too neat for his taste. "Posner attributes the crime to Oswald's troubled past and malevolence," he wrote. "but that explanation is almost as tidy as many of the conspiracy theories."

For his next endeavor, Posner chose a much different project, this time focusing his attention on the rise of 1992 presidential candidate Ross Perot. In his attempt to chronicle Perot's life, Posner employed the same vigorous research and interview method he had used for his earlier books. One of the few books to broach the subject of Perot's failed presidential bid and the road that led to it, *Citizen Perot: His Life and Times* (1996) earned largely favorable attention from the critics.

The following year, Posner tackled the assassination of Martin Luther King Jr., another case that has been muddled by conspiracy theory for three decades. In this instance, the supposed killer, James Earl Ray, lived to tell his story—and maintained his innocence. Again, the U.S. government was named in the cover-up, and as with the JFK assassination, the public had trouble accepting the notion that such an inept, petty criminal could have taken the life of such an important figure. However, in this case, Ray was so persuasive in his defense, that he managed to convince the King family of his innocence. Posner was moved to call the case "the most complicated political assassination I've ever come across."

After his intense period of research for *Killing the Dream: James Earl Ray and the Assassination of Martin Luther King, Jr.* (1998) was completed, Posner was himself stunned at his findings. He drilled holes in many of Ray's claims and did not conclusively rule out the possibility that Ray acted alone. Posner left room in his tightly constructed investigation to surmise that Ray may have been motivated to kill King in order to land a hefty bounty that had been placed on the leader's head by racist southerners—a monetary reward he was to share with his brothers. Still, Posner also noted that King had many other enemies who could have been involved. "In the end, this book is really not about King," he told Parkurar. "The book turns out to be about who killed him and why. It turns out to be the unraveling of a mystery story, and I get to take the reader on the hunt for the real assassin."

Killing the Dream was hailed as "first-rate" by the *Washington Post* (April 12, 1998) and called a "heavily researched and well-written examination" of the assassination by *CNN Interactive Book Reviews* (April 27, 1998). *USA Today* (April 9, 1998) concluded that Posner does for the King murder what he had previously done for the JFK assassination through "combining fresh reporting with a careful review of investigations, and using the common sense that is a scarce commodity in this field." The *New York Times Book Review* (April 26, 1998) praised *Killing the Dream* as a "superb book: a model of investigation, meticulous in its discovery and presentation of evidence, unbiased in its exploration of every claim," adding that it is also "a wonderfully readable book, as gripping as a first-class detective story."

Gerald L. Posner has been described as a "compactly built man with a stylishly cut cap of dark hair, an impish grin" and a quick mind. In 1981, on a blind date, Posner met Trisha, a former fashion model from Britain. The two were married three years later, with Trisha soon giving up her career to assist her husband in his research. The couple are currently set to embark on a new literary adventure, this time a study of Motown and the role possibly played by the Mafia in the business. "I think of it as a popular piece of social history, offering commentary on a lot that was going on in America in the 1960s," he told Baker. "I'm not sure how it fits in with the rest of my work, though—perhaps I'm on a sort of sabbatical."

Among Gerald L. Posner's many awards and commendations, he received the Kennedy Medal and the Miklejohn Award in 1975 and was a finalist for the Pulitzer Prize in the history category for *Case Closed* in 1993. He lives and works in New York City.

—D.B.

SUGGESTED READING: *At Random* (online) Feb. 1998; *Chicago Tribune* p1 Oct. 3, 1993, p3+ Sep. 12, 1993; *Christian Science Monitor* p13 Sep. 28, 1993, p15 Oct. 7, 1996; *CNN Interactive Book Reviews* Apr. 27, 1998; *Dallas Morning News* (online) May 3, 1998; *Library Journal* June 1, 1986, Feb. 15, 1991; *National Review* p72 Oct. 18, 1993; *New York Review of Books* May 28, 1987; *New York Times* C p18 Sep. 9, 1993, p15+ Nov. 21, 1993, Apr. 22, 1998; *New York Times Book Review* C p15 June 24, 1991, Apr. 26, 1998; *New York Newsday* p52+ Sep. 1, 1993; *The Posner Files* (online); *Publishers Weekly* p44+ Apr. 13, 1997; *School Library Journal* Apr. 1992; *Times Literary Supplement* p625 June 12, 1987; USA Today Apr. 9, 1998; *Virginia Quarterly Review* p18 Winter 1997; *Wall Street Journal* A p7 Sep. 3, 1993; *Washington Monthly* p54+ Oct. 1993; *Washington Post* Apr. 12, 1998; *Book Review Digest* 1987, 1992, 1997; *Contemporary Authors*, 1994

SELECTED WORKS: with John Ware—*Mengele: The Complete Story*, 1986; *Warlords of Crime: Chinese Secret Societies—The New Mafia*, 1988; *Hitler's Children: Sons and Daughters of Leaders of the Third Reich Talk about Themselves and Their Fathers*, 1991; *Case Closed: Lee Harvey Oswald and the Assassination of JFK*, 1993; *Citizen Perot: His Life and Times*, 1996; *Killing the Dream: James Earl Ray and the Assassination of Martin Luther King, Jr.*, 1998; Fiction—*The Bio-Assassins*, 1989

Powell, Padgett

Apr. 25, 1952– Novelist; essayist

"Bad luck at fishing and worse with women made me what little writer I am," the American author Padgett Powell said in an interview. "Had things turned out a bit differently, I'd be Doug Flutie." While any claims of prowess on the football field will probably forever remain unchallenged and unproven, Powell's writing—which has been compared to that of J. D. Salinger, Mark Twain, Tennes-

Marion Ettlinger/Courtesy of Henry Holt and Company
Padgett Powell

see Williams, and a host of others—stands as testament to a talent that is undeniable. Described in a *Time* (April 2, 1984) review of his first novel, *Edisto* (1984), as an author who had "all the literary equipment for a new career: a peeled eye, a tuning fork ear, and an innovative way with local color," Powell has gone on to carve out his literary niche with more books, including *A Woman Named Drown* (1987); *Edisto Revisited* (1996), about the people and customs from the area with which he is best acquainted—the American South; and the short-story collection *Aliens of Affection* (1998).

Born in Gainesville, Florida, on April 25, 1952, Padgett Powell is the son of Albine Batts Powell, a supervisor in a brewery, and Bettyre (Palmer) Powell, a teacher. He was educated at the College of Charleston, in Charleston, South Carolina, where he received a bachelor's degree in chemistry in 1975. He then moved west to Houston, Texas, where he worked as a day laborer and later as a roofer. An avid reader with a particular interest in the work of William Faulkner ("I've read a third of Faulkner," he has said; "The third I've read was more important than the totality of any other writer"), Powell eventually enrolled in the University of Houston's graduate creative writing program, from which he received his master's degree in 1982. After being a full-time writer for a little more than a year, in 1984 Powell accepted a position teaching creative writing at the University of Florida, in his hometown of Gainesville—a post he continues to hold today.

The year 1984 would prove to be particularly eventful for Powell. In addition to moving back to Florida and beginning his teaching career, he also married poet Sidney Wade and published his first book. Originally written as his master's thesis, *Edisto*, Powell's highly successful first novel, took its title from the name of a rural, predominantly African-American section of the South Carolina coastline near the resort area of Hilton Head. The book tells of the coming-of-age of Simons (pronounced "Simmons") Manigault, the 12-year-old narrator. A child of separated parents, Simons lives with his college-professor mother, whom the local townspeople refer to as "the Duchess" who, after deciding that Simons should become a writer, begins a campaign of immersing him in classic literature and writing assignments. In exchange for his cooperation in these literary endeavors, Simons is given permission to do virtually anything he pleases—including frequenting the Baby Grand, a local nightclub and bar. Described by R. Z. Sheppard in *Time* (April 2, 1984) as "one of the most engaging fictional small fry ever to cry thief: sly, pungent, lyric, funny, and unlikely to be forgotten," Powell's Simons has been likened to several extremely high-profile fictional American adolescents, including Holden Caulfield and Huck Finn. An American Book Award nominee for first fiction and one of *Time's* five best books of 1984, *Edisto* received excellent critical reviews. "I found myself increasingly charmed by the book's wit and impressed by its originality," Robert Towers wrote in the *New York Review of Books* (May 31, 1984). "Some turn of phrase, some flash of humor, some freshly observed detail, some accurately rendered perception of a child's pain or a child's amazement transfigures nearly every page." Further praise was offered by *Publishers Weekly* (February 10, 1984). "A born writer makes his debut here," the reviewer wrote. "With his ability to render an inspired spectrum of richly cadenced southern voices and patterns of behavior, his acute, insider's view of the subtleties of race relations and his flair for eccentric, memorable characters, Powell may evoke comparisons with Flannery O'Connor, but he has his own distinctive voice, an antic imagination, and a highly original way of looking at the world. Moreover, the book is a treasury of stunning images that create an almost palpable atmosphere."

In 1987 Powell published his second novel, *A Woman Named Drown*. In it, Al, a Ph.D. candidate in inorganic chemistry, moves in with an aging actress—whose last role was in a play entitled *A Woman Named Drown*—after his girlfriend of six years suddenly ends their relationship. The couple then travels around Florida, until the actress leaves Al. Like *Edisto*, *A Woman Named Drown* was well received by critics. The novel recreates "the distinctive, understated humor that is Mr. Powell's signature," T. Coraghessan Boyle wrote in the *New York Times Book Review* (June 7, 1987). "He presents a terrific, hyper-real dialogue in quick, bludgeoned pieces, and his narrator's phrasing and dialect are always surprising and inventive."

In the same year that he published *A Woman Named Drown*, Powell also contributed an essay to *A World Unsuspected: Portraits of Southern Child-*

hood (1987), a book of memoirs edited by Alex Harris. Four years later, Powell published *Typical* (1991), a collection of 23 stories on subjects as diverse as accidental decapitation ("Wayne's Fate") and paranoid delusions ("The Modern Italian"). Reactions to the book were decidedly mixed. "It is exciting to see Mr. Powell move from novels to this shorter form, where distillation and timing and bull's eye observation are required, and to see him succeed as well at the one as he has at the other," Amy Hempel wrote in the *New York Times* (July 21, 1991.) Other critics, like the *New York Times* (August 16, 1991) reviewer Michiko Kakutani, conceded that the book includes "some wonderfully demented monologues" and "plenty of strange images that reverberate with poetic power," but argued that parts of the book have a rushed and unpolished feeling. "While half the stories in this volume are finely crafted word portraits of individuals in extremis—angry, fed up or insane—the others are windy, stream-of-consciousness improvisations that read like outtakes from a late-night jam session," Kakutani wrote.

For his most recent novel, Powell chose to return to very familiar ground—Edisto. In *Edisto Revisited* (1996) Simons Manigault, now a recent graduate of Clemson University, returns to Edisto to meet up with his mother—who arrives accompanied by Simon's cousin, Patricia Hod. After having an affair with Patricia, Simons leaves Edisto to embark on a series of adventures in America's Deep South. Throughout his journey Simons contemplates accepting the various responsibilities of adulthood. "*Edisto Revisited* is a puzzling work of high style, a rendering of haplessness that seems to poeticize passivity," Scott Spencer wrote in the *New York Times Book Review* (March 31, 1996). "While his novel may make you wonder if it has much of what is called meaning, Mr. Powell finally overpowers such doubts with his countless quotable passages, his humor, and his seductive evocation of the romance of giving up."

In an advance review of *Aliens of Affection* for *Library Journal* (October 1, 1997), Christine DeZelar-Tiedman stated that Powell "has written a sometimes baffling, often fascinating, and always unique collection of short stories" featuring "drinkers, strippers, the mentally ill, and others you may not want to meet in real life. . . . [Powell's] style is at times excessive, and his verbs have a tendency to get lost from their subjects amid extended modifying clauses, but the author's willingness to take risks is admirable."

—J. P.

SUGGESTED READING: *Library Journal* p119+ Apr. 1, 1996; *New York Review of Books* p35+ May 31, 1984; *New York Times* p6 July 21, 1991; *New York Times Book Review* p9 June 7, 1987, p21 Aug. 16, 1991, p14 Mar. 31, 1996; *Publishers Weekly* p187 Feb. 10, 1984; *Time* p82+ Apr. 2, 1984; Harris, A., ed. *A World Unsuspected: Portraits of Southern Childhood*, 1987; *Contemporary Authors* vol.126, 1989; *Contemporary Literary Criticism* vol. 34, 1985

SELECTED BOOKS: Fiction—*Edisto*, 1984; *A Woman Named Drown*, 1987; *Typical*, 1991; *Edisto Revisited*, 1996; *Aliens of Affection*, 1998; Screenplays—*Edisto*, 1985

Powers, Richard

1957– Novelist

Richard Powers is an American novelist celebrated for works that take on such subjects as politics, history, and science to probe the complexities of modern living. His six novels, among them *Three Farmers on Their Way to a Dance* (1985), *The Gold Bug Variations* (1991), and *Gain* (1998), have been variously deemed "overtly intellectual," "ambitious and dazzling," and "brilliantly imaginative." Powers himself was described in the *Nation* (July 10, 1995) as "one of the few younger American writers . . . who can stake a claim to the cerebral legacy of Pynchon, Gaddis, and DeLillo."

More than a decade after the publication of his first novel, Powers, thanks to his fierce desire for anonymity and to his having chosen to live abroad for much of the late 1980s and early 1990s, remains one of the most enigmatic figures in contemporary literature. He has frequently declined to answer questions about his personal life. "I really don't see what connection all that has with the work . . . ," he has said. "All that sort of thing just creates confusion about the nature of the book, deflects attention from what you've done. That's what always seems to happen in this culture: you grab hold of a personality and ignore the work."

Powers's reticence notwithstanding, throughout the years various journalists have been able to piece together a very hazy picture of his life. It is known that he was born in 1957 and reared in the American Midwest and that he worked for some time in the computer field. Powers himself admits to having acquired "a quasi-preprofessional knowledge of music, as a studious cellist for many years." Additionally, one source indicates that Powers trained as a physicist prior to his literary career.

While critical reaction to Powers's novels has generally been very positive, some critics have stated that the audience for his novels may be somewhat limited by the scientific and intellectual subject matter of his works. "To read [Powers's] work is to be wowed by his verbal muscularity and by his ability to stitch seemingly disparate elements into a larger metaphorical fabric," Meg Wolitzer wrote in the *New York Times Book Review* (July 18, 1993). "But sometimes we don't want to be wowed. Sometimes we just want quiet." The vast majority of reviewers, however, have described Powers's writing—particularly because of the complexity of his narrative structures and themes and the inventiveness of his prose—as consistently excellent, often making comparisons to the work of writers as diverse as John Updike and Thomas Mann. "In a few short years—in literary terms overnight—Richard Powers has vaulted from promise to attainment. . . . Powers must now be seen as our most energetic and gifted novelist under 40," Sven Birkerts wrote in the *Chicago Tribune* (May 23, 1993).

Powers's debut novel, *Three Farmers on Their Way to a Dance*, appeared in 1985. The novel takes its title from August Sander's 1914 photograph of three well-dressed young men walking outside Cologne, Germany, just before the outbreak of World War I. Interwoven with stories of the three young men are those of two other characters—both living in contemporary America—who stumble upon copies of Sander's photograph. The book examines the significance of the photo for the two modern characters and, ultimately, the interconnectedness of all events and people. "His writing engages, and his recreation of the characters' thoughts captures postmodern, fragmented 1980s consciousness well," Marco Portales wrote in the *New York Times Book Review* (September 1, 1985). *Three Farmers on Their Way to a Dance* was further praised by Gregory L. Morris in *Prairie Schooner* (Spring 1996): "This is a remarkably accomplished first novel," he wrote. "As a technical, structural experiment, the book generally succeeds, despite the occasional staginess of some of the narrative. More exciting and more satisfying, though, is the intellectual stamina of the book; both story and idea engage the reader, lure him into the web of time and mystery and connection that is the real fabric of this very fine book."

In 1988 Powers released his follow-up novel, *Prisoner's Dilemma,* the story of a highly dysfunctional family learning to come to terms with death and with their own emotions. Dominating the family is 52-year-old Eddie Hobson, an ex-history teacher who is now suffering from a mysterious malady, possibly caused by the time he spent stationed near Alamogordo, New Mexico, the testing site for the atomic bomb. Each of Hobson's four grown children contributes to the narration of the story. Hobson offers additional commentary in the form of multiple audiotapes he has made over the years describing Hobstown, an imaginary village. When one of his children secretly begins to listen to the Hobstown tapes, he gains new insight into his father's various peculiarities. Critics applauded Powers's ability to deftly interweave the family's plight with historic events and political changes. "Powers is the most accomplished practitioner of what I call the 'systems novel,' a fiction

that uses postmodern techniques to model the dense and tangled relations of modern history, politics, and science," Tom LeClair wrote in *The New Republic* (April 25, 1988). Powers was also commended for his innovative use of narrative techniques. "Powers has great novelistic gifts—an ear for speech that expresses character, an intense command of significant realistic details that can easily be assimilated to a larger symbolic pattern, a stylistic range and control that can cope with Alan Turing, Kraitchik's paradox, a Ouija board, a grocery list, and Walt Disney's magic kingdom—and still sound like one narrator," Richard Locke wrote in the *Washington Post Book World* (April 10, 1988).

The Gold Bug Variations, Powers's third novel, was published in 1991. Its story shifts back and forth between the 1950s and the 1980s, following the career and life of Stuart Ressler, a biologist who was once involved with DNA research and now works at a database corporation. A complex web of computer technology, science, and romance, *The Gold Bug Variations* also follows two of Ressler's present coworkers, who attempt to uncover why he discontinued his scientific work. The coworkers eventually become romantically linked, but their romance is quickly threatened by another inquiry. Louis B. Jones wrote in the *New York Times Book Review* (August 25, 1991) that the novel is "a dense, symmetrical symphony in which no note goes unsounded." He added, "Just seeing so much sheer cleverness packed into 639 pages is a remarkable experience."

Powers's fourth novel, *Operation Wandering Soul*, was published in 1993. The novel, set in the near future, focuses on Richard Kraft, a brilliant surgical resident assigned to the pediatric ward of a public hospital in Angel City. Already scarred by a traumatic and nomadic childhood, Kraft teeters on the brink of emotional devastation in the face of his patients' suffering. Eventually he becomes romantically involved with Linda Espera, an optimistic child therapist who attempts to bring Kraft out of his despair. *Operation Wandering Soul* received mixed reviews from critics. Powers was applauded for his prose style and abundant historical and cultural references. His plot and character development, however, were widely criticized. "[The novel] is, despite its considerable length, a one-note book with so little plot development that its style is its only interest . . . ," a reviewer wrote in the *Wall Street Journal* (July 13, 1993). "It is hard to think of another novel in which such sophisticated presentation wraps such a simple core."

In 1995 Powers published *Galatea 2.2*, a novel that examines the processes, perils, and ethics of artificial intelligence. The main character, a man who happens to be named Richard Powers, returns to an American university after living in the Netherlands for several years. Powers falls under the guidance of Professor Philip Lentz, who persuades him to participate in an experiment that involves teaching a computer to pass the master's comprehension exam in English literature. During the experiment, Powers is forced to rethink the ramifications of such advanced technology for humanity. *Galatea 2.2* may be Powers's most well-received novel to date. "Powers's exposition of the linguistic and perceptual intricacies underlying consciousness is nothing less than brilliant," John Updike wrote in the *New Yorker* (August 21–28, 1995).

Powers's 1998 novel, *Gain,* is made up of two narratives; one involves the Clare Company, a maker of agricultural and chemical products, while the other concerns Laura Bodey, whose ovarian cancer seems to be connected with chemical wastes from Clare's factories. The novel is a comment on the dangers of unchecked corporate activity in contemporary society. Writing in the *New York Times* (August 11, 1998), Michiko Kakutani found that *Gain* dispensed with the "cerebral razzle-dazzle" of Powers's earlier works in favor of an approach and message whose simplicity she found disappointing. On the other hand, in the *New York Times Book Review* (June 21, 1998), Bruce Bawer commented on what he felt to be the "remarkable artistry and authority with which Powers, in this dazzling book, continues to impart his singular vision of our life and times."

During his career Powers has received numerous citations and awards, among them a PEN/Hemingway Foundation special citation for *Three Farmers on Their Way to a Dance,* an award from the American Academy and Institute of Arts and Letters, and two nominations for the National Book Critics Circle Award for *Three Farmers on Their Way to a Dance* and *The Gold Bug Variations*). Additionally, he received a so-called "genius" grant from the MacArthur Foundation in 1989.

—J. P.

SUGGESTED READING: *Chicago Tribune* p1+ May 23, 1993; *Gentleman's Quarterly* p86+ June 1995; *Hudson Review* p122+ Spring 1986; *Nation* p64+ July 10, 1995; *New Republic* p40+ Apr. 25, 1988; *New Yorker* p105+ Aug. 21 & 28, 1995; *New York Times Book Review* p14 Sep. 1, 1985, p9+Aug. 25, 1991, p19 July 18, 1993; *Prairie Schooner* p108 Spring 1986; *Time* p72 June 12, 1995; *Wall Street Journal* A p14 July 13, 1993; *Washington Post Book World* p5 Apr. 10, 1988; *Contemporary Authors* vol. 148, 1996; *Contemporary Literary Criticism* vol. 93, 1996

SELECTED BOOKS: *Three Farmers on Their Way to a Dance,* 1985; *Prisoner's Dilemma,* 1988; *The Gold Bug Variations,* 1991; *Operation Wandering Soul,* 1993; *Galatea 2.2,* 1995; *Gain,* 1998

Proulx, E. Annie

Aug. 22, 1935– Novelist; nonfiction writer

E. Annie Proulx (who has lately gone by simply Annie Proulx) emerged from obscurity to win, between April 1993 and April 1994, four major literary awards—one for *Postcards* and the remaining three for *The Shipping News*. While the settings of the two novels are different, each is concerned with both its characters' relationships to the land on which they live and with such universal themes as death and failed love. The careful depiction of place is crucial in the opinion of Proulx, who has said that if the setting of a story is handled well, "the characters will step out of it, and they'll be in the right place. The story will come from the landscape." Critics have also taken special note of Proulx's economical, poetic prose, of her beautiful, haunting imagery, and of the extraordinary amount of violence in her works, particularly in her 1996 novel *Accordion Crimes*. In the *New York Times Book Review* (June 23, 1996), Walter Kendrick referred to "the abattoir without walls that is Ms. Proulx's America."

Only a few years before she became the toast of the international literary community, Proulx was virtually unknown. She did not publish her first book of fiction, *Heart Songs and Other Stories,* un-

Jim McHugh

til she was in her early 50s. Fiction writing is only the most recent full-time pursuit for Proulx, who has also been a freelance journalist and a postal worker, among other things. "I certainly don't regret [becoming a writer] later because I know a lot more about life than I did twenty years ago, ten years ago," she told Sara Rimer in an interview for the *New York Times* (June 23, 1994). "And I think that's important, to know how the water's gone over the dam before you start to describe it. It helps to have been over the dam yourself." She elaborated on her philosophy of writing in an interview with Sybil Steinberg for *Publishers Weekly* (June 3, 1996), referring to "this very unpleasant trend that one should only write about one's personal experience. . . . If only people would write about what intrigues them, what they don't know, would do a little research, would become questioning as well as observant. That's the pleasure in writing."

The daughter of George Napoleon Proulx, the vice president of a textile company, and Lois Nelly (Gill) Proulx, a painter, Edna Annie Proulx was born on August 22, 1935 in Norwich, Connecticut. Her mother's family had lived in Connecticut for 300 years, and most of her maternal ancestors had earned their living as farmers or mill workers. While she was growing up, her family moved frequently, and she lived in various towns throughout New England and in North Carolina. Proulx has credited her mother with helping her to develop the powers of observation she would later put to use in her fiction. "From the time I was extremely small, I was told, 'Look at that'," she recalled to Sara Rimer for the *New York Times* profile. She was taught to see "everything—from the wale of the corduroy to the broken button to the loose thread to the disheveled mustache to the clouded eye." When she was 10 years old, Proulx wrote her first story. (She cannot remember its plot.)

In the 1950s Proulx enrolled at Colby College, in Waterville, Maine, but she left without graduating. It was not until 1969 that she obtained a bachelor's degree in history, cum laude, from the University of Vermont. In the meantime, she had supported herself by working variously as a waitress and a postal employee, among other jobs. In 1973, while she was living in St. Albans, Vermont, Proulx received a master's degree in history from Sir George Williams University (now Concordia University), in nearby Montreal. At the same institution, she began working toward a Ph.D. degree in history, but after passing her oral examination in 1975, she abandoned work on her dissertation in favor of a career as a freelance journalist, which she pursued from an isolated shack in the insular town of Canaan, Vermont. While living there, she fished, hunted, and foraged for her food, a practice that apparently suited what she has called her "fondness for harshness." Moreover, such a lifestyle "makes you very alert and aware of everything around you, from tree branches and wild mushrooms to animal tracks," as she explained to John Skow in a *Time* (November 29, 1993) interview. "It's an excellent training for the eye. Most of us stagger around deaf and blind."

For the next dozen or so years, Proulx churned out "tedious nonfiction," to use her term, including such books as *Sweet and Hard Cider* (1980) and *The Complete Dairy Foods Cookbook* (1982) and magazine articles on topics ranging from architecture to horticulture. After moving to Vershire—one of the 13 Vermont towns in which she has lived—she founded a newspaper, the *Vershire Behind the Times*. In her spare time, she wrote short stories. "I yearned to write fiction, but there wasn't any money in it," she told David Streitfeld in an interview for the *Washington Post* (April 21, 1993). "I could only write one or two short stories a year. It was my pleasure, my indulgence, when I wanted to do something that wasn't fishing or canoeing." Although her output was small, she was able to sell most of her stories, to such periodicals as *Blair & Ketchums Country Journal* and the very different *Esquire*.

The nine tales collected in Proulx's first book, *Heart Songs and Other Stories* (1988), are set in rural towns in New England and concern the lives of working-class people, most of them men. In "On the Antler," for example, the two main characters, a storekeeper and a quiet, book-loving hunter, hatch plots against each other that exceed the bounds of practical jokes; in "Bedrock" the devious central figure arranges a marriage between his sister and a widower for the purpose of gaining control of the widower's farm. Evaluating *Heart Songs* for the *Chicago Tribune* (December 11, 1988), Kerry Luft applauded Proulx's "lyrical" and "vivid" style and pronounced the book to be "such a dazzling debut" that the reader was made to "wonder where [Proulx had] been hiding." Kenneth Rosen observed in the *New York Times Book Review* (January 29, 1989) that Proulx's stories were "most compelling when they're rooted in a coarse rural sexuality" and that, at such times, her "sometimes enigmatic, often lyrical images seem to complement New England's lavish but barren beauty."

The contract that Proulx had signed with her publisher called for her to produce, in addition to *Heart Songs*, a novel. Having written only short fiction up to that time, she "had not a clue about writing a novel, or even the faintest desire," as she admitted to Sara Rimer. "I thought of myself as a short-story writer. Period, period, period." After *Heart Songs* was published, however, and she was forced to confront the prospect of writing the novel, Proulx found her attention drawn to some old postcards she had been given years earlier. Dating from the 1930s and 1940s, the postcards featured reproductions of mug shots of escaped convicts. She was especially intrigued by one photograph, of a "really handsome guy" with "incredibly wavy hair," and, as she recounted to Rimer, "within a half-hour" of her sitting down to write, "the whole of *Postcards* was in [her] head."

The "handsome guy" who had piqued Proulx's interest became Loyal Blood, the central character in *Postcards* (1992). Early in the story, having killed and buried his lover, Loyal flees westward, leaving his parents and siblings with the seemingly impossible task of operating their Vermont farm without him. As the story progresses from World War II to the 1970s, the chapters alternate between those chronicling Loyal's meanderings across America and those depicting the Blood family's struggle for survival. Each chapter begins with a facsimile of a postcard, complete with address and cancellation stamp, written by a character familiar or unknown to the reader. The postcards, ambiguous in terms of the information they present, evoke, through their language and contents, the flavor of different time periods and geographical regions and thus provide a context for the narrative action. The technique, Proulx explained to one interviewer, lets the reader use his or her imagination in "filling in the blanks" in the book. "The reader writes most of the story," she said.

In the eyes of a majority of critics, *Postcards* represented a successful attempt to capture the essence of a particular people, place, and time. Declaring in the *New York Times Book Review* (March 22, 1992) that Proulx had "come close" to "writing a Great American Novel," the novelist David Bradley concluded his highly favorable appraisal by saying, "Story makes this novel compelling; technique makes it beautiful." Frederick Busch, evaluating *Postcards* for the *Chicago Tribune* (January 12, 1992), concurred. "This powerful novel is about powerful matters. It is made with a language that demands to be lingered over—for the pungent bite of its effect and for the pleasure of learning how good, and even gorgeous, sentences are written. . . .What makes this rich, dark, and brilliant feast of a book is its furious action, its searing contemplations, its language born of the fury and the searching and the author's powerful sense of the gothic soul of New England."

In a conversation with Esther B. Fein for the *New York Times* (April 21, 1993), Proulx reflected on the experience of creating *Postcards*. "It was astonishing how easy writing a novel was compared to writing a short story. I was so used to cramping thoughts and situations and cutting, and suddenly I had room to expand. It was like getting into a warm bathtub." Not surprisingly, her next fiction project was another novel, *The Shipping News* (1993). She had first visited its setting, Newfoundland, during a fishing trip in about 1987. As she related to John Blades for the *Chicago Tribune* (March 29, 1993), she "just fell quite madly in love with" the island. She described Newfoundland's coast as "rugged" and "immensely interesting" and its people as the "warmest, kindest, most interesting anywhere."

The protagonist of *The Shipping News* is Quoyle, a third-rate, small-town newspaper reporter and innocent soul described by the novel's narrator as having "a great damp loaf of a body," a "head shaped like a Crenshaw, no neck, . . . features as bunched as kissed fingertips," and a "monstrous chin, a freakish shelf jutting from the lower face."

Widowed when his aggressively unfaithful wife, Petal Bear, is killed in an auto accident, after having attempted to sell their two young daughters to a pornographer, Quoyle is left "swimming with grief and thwarted love" until his indomitable Aunt Agnis comes to stay with him and his daughters and helps them rebuild their lives. Taking his aunt's advice, Quoyle attempts to make a fresh start by moving his family from upstate New York to Newfoundland, the land of his ancestors. There, he gradually finds a sense of belonging among his eccentric neighbors and his co-workers at the local weekly newspaper, the lurid and gossipy *Gammy Bird*, whose reporters invariably end up covering stories that exploit their "private inner fears," as one of Quoyle's colleagues points out. Quoyle, for example, is asked to photograph car wrecks "while the upholstery is still on fire and the blood still hot."

The Shipping News is ironic, and sometimes comic, in tone, and is written in spare language that includes incomplete sentences, such as "Then, at a meeting. Petal Bear. Thin, moist, hot. Winked at him." The novel inspired wide and largely unreserved praise. "As a stylist, Proulx is earthy and intelligent, never overwrought, grounding her lyric flights in extraordinarily vivid description," Dan Cryer wrote in *New York Newsday* (March 22, 1993). "If I have any complaint, it is that at times she carries her own brand of poetic compression too far," Howard Norman declared in the *New York Times Book Review* (April 4, 1993). Still, he complimented the novelist for her "surreal humor and . . . zest for the strange foibles of humanity" as well as for her "inventive language."

Literary enthusiasts who were not already aware of Proulx's work were soon alerted to her talents by the number of major awards she received in seemingly rapid succession over the 13 months immediately following the publication of *The Shipping News*. In April 1993 she was given the PEN/Faulkner Award for fiction, for *Postcards*, becoming the first woman to be so honored; *Postcards* was selected over 284 other works for the prize. Four months later the *Chicago Tribune* chose Proulx as the recipient of its Heartland Award for fiction, for *The Shipping News*. In the following month that novel won the *Irish Times* International Fiction Prize, and, in November, in the U.S., it took the National Book Award. Early in 1994 *The Shipping News* was nominated for a National Book Critics Circle Award, and then, in the spring of that year, the novel won the Pulitzer Prize. "I've run out of being stunned," Proulx told David Streitfeld for the *Washington Post* (April 13, 1994), after learning of the last-named award. "Except I am stunned. Each time this happens, I can't believe it."

In *Accordion Crimes* (1996), Proulx used the device of tracing the history of an accordion from the time it leaves Sicily in its maker's hands in around 1890 to Florida in the 1990s, when it falls under a truck. The accordion, which goes from owner to owner in the novel, was—as Proulx told Ellen Kanner in an interview for *BookPage*—"the immigrants' instrument." It "stood for the old folk and their old ways, their peasant hands and stooped backs, their limited language skills. Younger generations could funnel their feelings into hatred of the accordion, a joke instrument." Thus, the device provides a way of penetrating various cultures—African, Basque, German, Norwegian, Mexican, Polish, Irish-Scotch, French Canadian, and Italian—as they enter the American melting pot. Judging from Proulx's attitude toward her dominant symbol, she did not view the immigrant experience in America as particularly positive. She explained to Steinberg, "I wanted to get a sense of that looming overculture that demands of newcomers that they give up their language, their music, their food, their names. I began to wonder: where did our taste for changing our identity come from? Was it the immigrant experience where the rite of passage was to redefine yourself as an American?"

Accordion Crimes does not employ a straightforward narrative. As Proulx explained to Steinberg, instead of one story, there are four interlinking parts, within which there are nine stories with a different immigrant group as the focus of each. "Within that, there is an increasing multiplicity of shorter stories of intersecting lives," including those of several generations of the families in each group. The novel also contains "tiny flashforwards, fiction bites." Proulx was quite specific about her intentions: "Instead of the river of time, you get a lawn sprinkler effect, a kind of jittery, jammed, off-balance feeling. . . . I wanted the mosaic of apparently random violence to exist within the sense of continuity," Proulx told Steinberg. She also wanted to portray the dark side of the American dream. Almost all of the characters live in poverty and die horribly, often by random violence; one young woman's arms, for example, are sheared off by a piece of metal that falls from a truck. Only one person gets rich, doing so in the junk business.

Accordion Crimes drew critical responses that ranged from the horrified to the awestruck. Walter Kendrick, in the *New York Times Book Review* (June 23, 1996), was impressed by the language in which Proulx described monstrous events, such as the scene in which Vela Gasmann loses her arms: "Birds, building materials, and human body parts are equal grist to Ms. Proulx's language mill, which grinds brilliant prose out of them all." Kendrick was ultimately unable to find value, however, in the beautiful prose: "Proulx wrings glorious language from her characters' agony, yet in the end the spectacle is both repellent and trivial." In the *New York Times* (June 17, 1996), Christopher Lehmann-Haupt wrote that Proulx had produced an "epic drama that estranges you from the characters in a manner reminiscent of what Brecht promoted as his so-called alienation effect, a device to distract the audience from individual stories and concentrate their attention on the larger social picture." Proulx, he wrote, "seems to be concentrating the reader's attention on the failure of her immigrants' search 'for the golden America they had imagined, a place they believed existed somewhere.'" The immigrants are "squashed together in ways they don't fit," Lehmann-Haupt observed. "Everyone crushed to unhappiness by accordion crimes." Michael Dirda, on the other hand, writing in the *Washington Post* (June 16, 1996), was struck by the exuberance and accuracy Proulx brought to her descriptions of ethnic food and music. "*Accordion Crimes* is by no means a depressing book. Instead it seems properly clear-eyed, even shrewd with peasant wisdom, about how the future is 'crouching at a dark side road on the path of events' and seldom has any good in store for us. We must, it seems, find pleasure where we can, while we can—in food and drink, love, music, stories. All these, of course, *Accordion Crimes* supplies with the exuberant and loving excess of a good Polish wedding."

Close Range: Wyoming Stories, Proulx's first collection of short fiction, appeared in 1999. Richard Eder, who wrote about *Close Range* in the *New York Times Book Review* (May 23, 1999), found that "Geography, splendid and terrible, is a tutelary deity to the characters," who include "hardpan ranchers, battered cowpokes and bull riders, bar girls and bar brawlers. . . . The strength of this collection is Proulx's feeling for place and the shape into which it twists her characters." Assessing Proulx's success at crafting stories as opposed to novels, Eder continued, "The difficulty with several of the pieces is the opposite of what short-story writers often encounter when they attempt a novel. It is the problem not of sustaining the story but of compressing it. [Proulx's] material is as richly worked as brocade: like brocade it is hard to trim into too small a swatch. Her solution in several of the stories is to impose a labored climactic rhythm or a gotcha ending." Still, Eder singled out for praise two of the stories, "Brokeback Mountain" and the tale he felt to be the best in the book, "The Mud Below."

While Proulx has said that writing novels is "easy" compared with crafting short fiction, several reporters have noted the extensive research that went into *Postcards*, *The Shipping News*, and *Accordion Crimes*. For *The Shipping News*, which Howard Norman described as "almost an encyclopedia of slang and lore," she not only made several trips to Newfoundland but also pored over the *Dictionary of Newfoundland English* in order to capture the dialect of that island's inhabitants. "I literally slept with that book for two years, in the bed," she told Sara Rimer. "I'd fall asleep while I was reading it. This is the point in work. You get it right, or you don't do it. Everything depends on your getting it right." In *Accordion Crimes* Proulx's "linguistic range is enormous . . . ," Walter Kendrick wrote in the *New York Times Book Review* (June 23, 1996). "Proulx also loves gear and tackle and trim. . . . She revels in the arcana of things made by hand or repaired; her characters are forever tinkering, carving . . . or baking bread, and she always lets her reader know exactly how they go about it."

E. Annie Proulx has been married and divorced three times. From her last marriage, to James Hamilton Lang, she has three grown sons: Jonathan Edward Lang, Gillis Crowell Lang, and Morgan Hamilton Lang. Proulx has also acknowledged a daughter, Muffie Clarkson, about whom she told Sybil Steinberg in 1996, "I recently rediscovered her. I love her dearly. It seems a good time to include her with her brothers." She has hinted in interviews at what she labels the "reckless" nature of her past. In a letter to David Streitfeld of the *Washington Post*, she provided a list of her adventures (and misadventures) to illustrate her self-described recklessness: "Leaping a barbed-wire fence and not making it; being grabbed on a lonely back lane by a strange older guy but biting and escaping; running away through the rain on the eve of a wedding and finding self three-quarters across wet ties over railroad bridge over river when the train appeared at the far end of the bridge; getting caught in a thunderstorm on third flying lesson; throwing a knife at (and thank God missing) someone I thought I hated; driving north in the south-bound lane; hanging out with a wide variety of rough dudes in a wide variety of situations; swimming across a lake when eight months pregnant; speeding and rolling a car late one night on the way north and coming to in a hospital considerably messed up; using old shotgun that misfired; doing a 360 on icy street in Montreal morning rush hour; falling off ladder; ladder falling on me; etc., etc."

Proulx counts fly-fishing, canoeing, and playing the fiddle among her hobbies. According to David Streitfeld, she is also active in the fight against illiteracy—a cause she took up after learning that her great-grandmother, who left behind no letters or diaries upon her death, could not read or write. Proulx's passion, however, is clearly writing fiction. "I'm desperate to write. I'm crazy to write. I want to write," she told Sara Rimer. "I have . . . three novels sitting in my head, waiting to get on paper, and I know exactly how each one is going to go. Each one is like a wrapped package." At the time Rimer interviewed her in 1994, the novelist was living in Vershire, Vermont, in a house that was "tall, strong, and unadorned, like her" and "cozy and welcoming" on the inside, "full of books and rocks and colors." By 1996, however, Proulx had relinquished her attachment to New England but not to the rugged countryside. She actually wrote *The Shipping News* and *Postcards* in Wyoming. After her mother's death in New Hampshire in 1995, she took up permanent residence in Wyoming in a pine-log cabin in a town with a population of 100, telling Sybil Steinberg in her *Publishers Weekly* interview, "what an enormous help the sight lines were, and the room to walk. There's something about being able to shoot your eyes very far ahead."

—C.T. / S.Y.

SUGGESTED READING: *Bookpage* (on-line); *Chicago Tribune* V p3 Mar. 29, 1993, with photo; *Maclean's* p57 Apr. 25, 1994, with photo; *New York Times* C p1+ June 23, 1994, with photo, C p14 June 17, 1996; *New York Times Book Review* p7 Mar. 22, 1992, with photo, p12 June 23, 1996; *Publishers Weekly* p57+ June 3, 1996, with photo; *Time* p83 Nov. 29, 1993, with photo; *Washington Post* B p1 Apr. 21, 1993, with photo, B p1+ Nov. 16, 1993, with photo, X p1 June 16, 1996; *Who's Who in America, 1995*

SELECTED WORKS: Fiction—*Heart Songs and Other Stories*, 1988; *The Shipping News*, 1992; *Postcards*, 1993; *Accordion Crimes*, 1996; *Close Range: Wyoming Stories*, 1999; Nonfiction—*Sweet and Hard Cider* (with L. Nichols), 1980; *What'll You Take for It?*, 1981; *The Complete Dairy Foods Cookbook* (with L. Nichols), 1982; *The Gardener's Journal and Record Book*, 1983; *Plan and Make Your Own Fences and Gates, Walkways, Walls and Drives*, 1983; *The Fine Art of Salad Gardening*, 1985; *The Gourmet Gardener*, 1987

Quammen, David

Feb. 24, 1948– Novelist, short story writer, nonfiction writer

Though David Quammen began his career as a writer of fiction, he has, in recent years, become widely recognized as an essayist whose layman's treatises on the natural world have been hailed as some of the best nature writing in print today. An *Outside* magazine columnist for nearly 15 years, Quammen has collected many of his nature articles into nonfiction collections, including *Natural Acts* (1985), *The Flight of the Iguana* (1988), and *Wild Thoughts from Wild Places* (1998). He is the author of *The Song of the Dodo* (1996), a work in which he reflects on the fragility of life on earth and the near-extinction of many species. In addition to these works of nonfiction, he is also the author of three novels—*To Walk the Line* (1970), *The Zolta Configuration* (1983), and *The Soul of Viktor Tronko* (1987), as well as a collection of short stories, *Blood Line: Stories of Fathers and Sons* (1988).

In an autobiographical statement submitted to *World Authors 1990–1995*, David Quammen discusses his life and work: "I was born in 1948, near the outskirts of Cincinnati, Ohio, and spent much of my boyhood in an eastern deciduous forest there. My interest in the natural world—hiking through woods, grubbing in creeks, collecting insects, taking reptiles hostage and calling them pets—was so all-consuming that I would eventual-

David Quammen

ly need remedial training in basketball. At an early age I learned the word *herpetologist* and decided I might like to be one. But I had always been interested, too, in writing; and at age 17 I met a life-changing teacher, a Jesuit priest, who fostered my literary ambitions and prospects, partly by suggesting that I go to college at Yale. Why Yale? I asked. Because they have a superb English department, including people such as Penn Warren, said the priest. Who's Penn Warren? I asked. The priest explained that Robert Penn Warren, novelist and poet and critic, was one of America's great literary figures. Fool's luck was smiling upon me, as were generous and trusting parents, and three years later I found myself studying Faulkner at the elbow of Mr. Warren, who became not just my second life-changing teacher but also my mentor and friend. The Jesuit was pleased.

"The Jesuit, a vast-hearted curmudgeon named Thomas G. Savage, died young in 1975. *The Song of the Dodo*, my 1996 nonfiction book about evolution and extinction in a world of fragmented landscapes, is dedicated to him.

"In 1970, just out of college, I published *To Walk the Line*, a novel about friendship across the racial fault lines of late-1960s Chicago. The book had been steered toward daylight by Mr. Warren. Also that year, I began a two-year fellowship at Oxford University, England, where I continued studying Faulkner, loathed the climate, loathed the food, loathed the vestiges of class snobbery, met a few wonderful people, and spent much of my time playing basketball (the remedial training had helped, though I was still far more avid than adept) for one of the university teams. Promptly after Oxford I moved to Montana, carrying all my possessions in a Volkswagen bus to this state in which I

had never before set foot. The attractions of Montana were 1) trout fishing, 2) wild landscape, 3) solitude, and 4) its dissimilarity to Yale and Oxford. The winters are too cold for ivy.

"Moving to Montana, and staying for what now equals half my lifetime, has been one of the two wisest things I've ever done. However, please note: A wondrous place in its way, Montana is not for everybody. Endless winters, ice, fallow wheat fields to the horizon, an anemic economy, loneliness. Not recommended.

"Until 1979, I made my living as a bartender, waiter, ghost writer, and fly-fishing guide. Since then, having discovered I can support myself from nonfiction while only occasionally reverting to fiction, I've written full time. In 1982 I married Kris Ellingsen, a fierce and beautiful Montana woman even more devoted to solitude than I am. This was my second wise act.

"I've published eight books and a few hundred magazine pieces, of a disorderly variousness in genre and subject. Besides *Dodo* and *To Walk the Line* there have been two spy novels (of which the second, *The Soul of Viktor Tronko*, is a fictional meditation on the real-world case of a Soviet defector named Yuri Nosenko, whose dubious tale-telling nearly paralyzed the counterintelligence wing of the CIA throughout the 1960s); a collection of short stories about father-son relationships (*Blood Line*); and several collections of essays on science and nature (*Natural Acts*, *The Flight of the Iguana*). From 1981 through 1995, I was natural-science columnist for *Outside* magazine, and in 1987 I received the National Magazine Award in Essays and Criticism for work that appeared in the column. That year also I was granted a Guggenheim fellowship to begin work on *Dodo*. In 1994 I was co-winner of another National Magazine Award. In 1996 I received an Academy Award in literature from the American Academy of Arts and Letters, and in 1997 a Lannan Literary Award for nonfiction. *The Song of the Dodo* too was generously blessed with awards: the John Burroughs Medal for nature writing, the Helen Bernstein Award for a book of journalism, the BP/Natural World Book Prize in Britain. My most recent book is *Wild Thoughts from Wild Places* (Scribner, 1998), a collection of essays about science, nature, travel, and sport, drawn mainly from my later work in *Outside*.

"After 25 years, I remain a Montana resident, despite the arrival of cappuccino. But I don't do horses or cows, and my land holdings (with Ms. Ellingsen) amount to a quarter acre."

Quammen's first novel, *To Walk the Line* (1970), was based on his experience working in a ghetto in Chicago. The plot follows the misadventures of John Scully, a white Yale dropout, who joins a group of radicals who intend to fight real estate abuses in the inner city. Scully becomes friends with Tyrone Williams, a young black man who is committed to violent revolution. As they become closer, they begin to think alike, despite having divergent ideas initially. Eventually Tyrone's revolutionary ideology is put to the test. The novel received mixed reviews. On the one hand, Elizabeth Storey, writing for *Library Journal* (February 15, 1971) remarked: "This is no cut-and-dried, simplistic story about race relations. The characters and their interactions are subtly drawn (and sometimes humorous)." On the other hand, Martin Levin of the *New York Times Book Review* (November 15, 1970) bemoaned: "It is unfortunate that the characters who flesh out such intriguing social paradoxes are thin-blooded creations, low in the vital juices."

Quammen did not publish a second book until 1983. Starting in 1981, however, he began a 15-year stint at *Outside* magazine, writing a monthly natural science column entitled "Natural Acts." (Many of these articles were collected and published in book form, but not for some time.) His next publication was a political thriller, *The Zolta Configuration* (1983). In it, he detailed the development of the first hydrogen bomb, using real-life figures and facts to bolster his plot. In the *New York Times Book Review* (July 3, 1983), Stanley Ellin remarked that, though the book makes use of historical detail, "never for an instant does it give off the musty whiff of scientific treatise. Mr. Quammen's portrayal of actual people involved in making the bomb brings each to life at a touch, so we have a profound emotional stake in them and in their experience." T. J. Binyon of the *Times Literary Supplement* (February 15, 1985) agreed with Ellin's appraisal, noting how Quammen "has put in a good deal of research on this book."

The author followed this thriller with *Natural Acts: A Sidelong View of Science and Nature* (1985), a collection of his essays originally published in *Outside* magazine. Over the course of 31 essays, Quammen looked at nature not as a scientist but as a layman interested in the natural world. Among his topics are the more than 300,000 species of beetles known to exist in the world; the disemboweling of sea cucumbers; hatcher fish; and other intriguing natural phenomena. With such a straightforward nature study, Quammen appeared to have found his niche, if the generally positive reviews were any indication. Michael D. Kramer, writing for *Library Journal* (March 15, 1985), observed, "Although not a scientist but a self-described follower of science, he writes in the vein of Gould and Thomas. Quammen's nontechnical discussion incorporates wit and fascination. Readers of all ages will absorb the knowledge he offers, and one hopes, his respect for our natural world." Noting that some readers with scientific backgrounds might enjoy this book more, Pam Spencer of the *School Library Journal* (September 1985) nevertheless agreed "all that is really needed in order to enjoy this book is an interest in and a curiosity about science. Quammen writes so well that these essays offer role models for writing experi-

ences in science classes." In the *New York Times Book Review* (April 21, 1985), Tom Ferrell wrote: "David Quammen does the hard work for us. . . . Hard and soft at once, like teeth and tongue, is Mr. Quammen's mind; both qualities are required for these nifty articulations on all those beings that aren't us."

Quammen released another thriller, *The Soul of Viktor Tronko* (1987), two years after this first nature collection appeared. This book deals with the C.I.A.'s search for a possible Soviet agent in their ranks. It received mostly good reviews. Writing for the *Washington Post* (August 4, 1987), Daniel Drabelle found the work somewhat confusing: "the novel proceeds via long conversation with retired agents, each of whom insists on depositing an arabesque background and only then going on to answer [the investigator's] questions." But Drabelle still thought the novel had "a freshness that old hands might emulate." Alan Cheuse, in a review for *Tribune Books* (July 5, 1987), was even kinder in his assessment of this thriller, believing that the author "has leaped to the head of the pack of American thriller writers" with this publication. He followed *The Soul of Viktor Tronko* with a collection of short fiction *Blood Line: Stories of Fathers and Sons* (1987).

Quammen returned to nature writing the next year and has remained with it ever since. *The Flight of the Iguana: A Sidelong View of Science and Nature* (1988) is a collection of 29 essays on natural history, again taken from *Outside*. Like his earlier nature collection, this received excellent reviews. Katharine Galloway Garstka applauded the author's latest endeavor in *Library Journal* (June 15, 1988), remarking that his "widely varied and thought-provoking essays range over humans and their interactions with ecology, including both desert and swamp." Writing for the *New York Times Book Review* (June 26, 1988), Harry Middleton favorably reviewed the work, believing that Quammen "is a rarity among those with never enough to write about nature. Not only does he have an exceptional eye for detail and a highly original mind, he is absolutely unafraid to voice misgivings, uncertainties and incredulity about the outdoors and the natural sciences. The result is a prose loaded with ideas and emotions that is as thrilling and upsetting as a wild ride on a slightly unsettled roller coaster."

The Song of the Dodo, Quammen's next book, was not published until 1996. In this nonfiction book, the author explored endangered ecosystems on islands across the globe. The result is one of his most ambitious books to date. "Everything you might want to know about life and death on islands here, there, and everywhere on the globe can be found in Quammen's study of island biogeography," noted a critic from *Kirkus Reviews* (January 15, 1996). "Quammen provides abundant examples of the variables that can foster or doom populations . . . The book's virtues include Quammen's vivid account of his treks to the world's wild places and interviews with the experts he finds there. The downside is too much of a muchness; Quammen's zeal to spill all his notes and a breezy style that grows wearying. Taken in small bites, however. There is much to glean here about the wonders, and also the fragility, of life on earth."

Quammen's most recent foray into nature writing, *Wild Thoughts from Wild Places*, was published in 1998. As with his earlier collections, this book's essays were gathered from magazine articles, especially from his "Nature Acts" column for *Outside*. In them he informs the reader about the merits of natural places that are often overlooked on the road of progress. Much of what Quammen wrote resonated with critics. Writing for the *New York Times Book Review* (March 1, 1998), James Gorman noted: "Except for my ungrateful wish for less weight and less meaning [in the metaphors of this work] . . . about the only complaint I can make about this book is that there are four reports on kayaking, at least two too many for me. That said, David Quammen easily passes the acid test of any essayist: he is a good companion. He has been to far places and done unusual things. He has tales to tell and things to say, and he does that well."

In addition to writing for *Outside*, David Quammen has contributed to *Audubon, Esquire, Rolling Stone, Harper's*, and the *New York Times Book Review*. He has been the recipient of a number of notable awards, including two National Magazine Awards (1987 and 1994), a 1985 Pacific Northwest Booksellers Award, a 1988 Guggenheim Fellowship, and a Genesis Award from Art Trust (1991). He has been presented with the Academy Award for literature from the American Academy of Arts and Letters (1996), the BP Natural World Book Prize from Great Britain (1996), a 1997 John Burroughs Medal for nature writing, and a Lannan Literary Award for Nonfiction (1997), among other honors.— C.M.

SELECTED WORKS: Fiction—*To Walk the Line*, 1970; *The Zolta Configuration*, 1983; *The Soul of Viktor Tronko*, 1987; *Blood Line: Stories of Fathers and Sons*, 1988; Nonfiction—*Natural Acts: A Sidelong View of Science and Nature*, 1985; *The Flight of the Iguana: A Sidelong View of Science and Nature*, 1988; *The Song of the Wild Dodo: Island Biogeography in an Age of Extinction*, 1996; *Wild Thoughts from Wild Places*, 1998.

SUGGESTED READING: *Audubon*, p 64+, July 1997; p 52+, Jan. 1998; *Harper's* p 57+, Oct. 1998; *Kirkus Reviews*, Jan. 15, 1996; *Library Journal* p 748, Feb. 15, 1971; p 66, Mar. 15, 1985; p 63, June 16, 1988; *New York Times Book Review*, p 68, Nov. 15, 1970; July 3, 1983; p 39, Apr. 21, 1985; p 39, June 26, 1988; p 10, Mar. 1, 1998; *School Library Journal*, p 157, Sep. 1985; *Times Literary Supplement*, Feb. 15, 1985; *Tribune Books*, July 5, 1987; *Washington Post*, Aug. 4, 1987

Raban, Jonathan

June 14, 1942– Travel writer, novelist; critic

The travel Jonathan Raban does much more than use flowery adjectives to describe tourist stops. He is an explorer, one who gets to the heart of a region by immersing himself in its daily life. In *Soft City* (1974), the first of his critically acclaimed nonfiction titles, he described life in major cities such as New York and London, weighng the problems and the benefits of big-city living. A few years later he traveled through the Persian Gulf to see how the lives of people in oil-rich nations differed from those of their oil-poor neighbors. His observations and conclusions were recorded in *Arabia: A Journey Through the Labyrinth* (1979). In 1981 he published *Old Glory: An American Voyage*, which details a trip he made two years earlier down the Mississippi River. The book became a best-seller and made Raban a literary celebrity. Since then he has produced two more titles on American life. The first, *Hunting Mr. Heartbreak: A Discovery of America* (1991), relates his travels from the biggest of American cities (New York) to the smallest of its towns (Guntersville, Alabama) and details his impressions of the people he met along the way. The second, *Bad Land: An American Romance* (1996), discusses the lives of people in the plains states, from the first homesteaders of the early 1900s to the present. Raban is also the author of *Coasting* (1987), the story of his one-man trip around his native Great Britain by boat; *For Love and Money* (1987), in which he talked about his lifelong obsession with writing; and *Foreign Land* (1985), a novel.

Jonathan Raban was born on June 14, 1942, in the village of Fakenham, in Norfolk, England. The son of Peter Raban and the former Monica Sandison, he is descended from minor English gentry and grew up in a house decorated with portraits of the family's ancestors. Peter Raban was a strict Anglican parson who forbade his son to play with the children in the village, since he considered them beneath their station. This prohibition left young Jonathan somewhat lonely, with books his only companions. He particularly liked American books, especially Mark Twain's *The Adventures of Huckleberry Finn*. At the end of his street was a small stream about four feet across, and as a boy he would often pretend that the stream had been transformed into the mighty Mississippi River. Since his childhood he has dreamed of Huck and Jim on their raft as they floated down the river. "I have loved America ever since I could read its literature," Raban told an interviewer for *People* (November 16, 1981). "I'm obsessed with it."

At 18 Raban enrolled in the University of Hull, in Yorkshire, where he met the poet Philip Larkin, Hull's librarian. Raban intended to become an actor after graduation, in 1963, but after a few weeks, he realized that he was not cut out for it. A year of postgraduate work followed, and soon Raban qual-

Jean Lenihan/Courtesy of Pantheon Books
Jonathan Raban

ified to teach. He began working on his doctoral thesis—a study of Jewish-American novelists of the previous 100 years—but stopped shortly after completing the second chapter, because he had received an appointment to lecture at the University College of Wales. He stayed in that post for two years, then went on to teach English and American literature at the University of East Anglia, in Norwich, from 1965 to 1969. He diversified his activities by writing short stories, reviews for the *New Statesman*, and television plays. He also wrote three academic books during this period: *The Technique of Modern Fiction: Essays in Practical Criticism* (1968), *Mark Twain: Huckleberry Finn* (1968), and *The Society of the Poem* (1971).

In late 1969 to early 1970, Raban decided to try to make a living as a freelance writer. "In retrospect, a lot of my motive for becoming a full-time writer was the prospect of living in London," he told *Publishers Weekly* (February 13, 1987). Around the same time, Raban reviewed the poet Robert Lowell's collection *Notebook* for BBC Radio, and Lowell invited him to lunch. The two became fast friends and fishing companions. They also became housemates when Raban moved into the basement and ground floor of Lowell's Redcliffe Square house. The move proved to be greatly beneficial to the aspiring author. He edited *Robert Lowell's Poems: A Selection*, which came out in 1974.

In the same year Raban completed what he has since called his first "real" book: *Soft City* (1974). In it, the author offered his impressions of what it was like to live in London, New York, and Cambridge, Massachusetts. Robin Wright of the *Christian Science Monitor* (October 16, 1974) praised

Raban's study, noting, "From the somewhat limited perspective of [three cities] the author . . . effectively documents through human encounters and essay [sic] what sociologists, urban planners, and local politicians have been trying to explain in formal language and one-sided fragments for years. The common message essentially is that image and atmosphere are as important as architecture." Anthony Thwaite of the *Economist* (March 16, 1974) concurred; *Soft Cities*, he wrote, "has easily discernible . . . nuggets of solid base metal that deserve being struck into the coinage of planners, politicians, and all urban dwellers." In the *New York Times Book Review* (November 10, 1974), Richard Sennett cheered: "This is one of a handful of nonfiction books about the quality of life in a city which is more than a catalogue of horrors."

Raban's next book, *Arabia: A Journey Through the Labyrinth*, was published in 1979. In researching this book he spent 14 weeks in the Middle East studying the people and cultures of the oil-exporting nations (Qatar, Bahrain, and Abu Dhabi) and the oil-poor countries (North Yemen, Egypt, and Jordan). Aside from taking 12 lessons in Arabic from an Egyptian girl, the author made no preparations for his trip. He learned about each nation's culture by immersing himself in the everyday lives of ordinary people. His in-depth observations impressed reviewers of *Arabia*. "While no conclusions are offered, the reader is left with the impression that there may be no winners in this headlong clash of cultures, technologies, and wealth—only survivors. This is an important and provocative book for these times," H. M. Otness wrote for *Library Journal* (October 15, 1979). In the *New York Times Book Review* (October 14, 1979), Benny Green wrote, "The virtue of Jonathan Raban's book is that in addition to being delightful journalism, it serves as useful corrective to the idea that every Arab is rolling in [oil]." Edward Hoagland, reviewing the work for the *New Republic* (October 20, 1979), wrote, "No writer alive could be better company than Raban, as he tiptoes around in tiny satellite states bordering the great Arabian peninsula (Saudi Arabia didn't admit him). . . . Raban has a sharp tongue, on occasion . . . and, at his brilliant best, he is the most valuable traveler Britain or America has sent to the Persian Gulf in the last 30 years."

Old Glory: An American Voyage, Raban's most heralded work, appeared in 1981. Two years earlier the author had flown to St. Paul, Minnesota, and bought a very small outboard boat, to start the 1,400-mile trip down the Mississippi River to New Orleans. On the way he met a number of locals in the towns he visited, everyone from local drunks to members of the Knights of Columbus. While this trip was, in many ways, his childhood dream realized, in that he was traveling down the same river Huck and Jim had traversed, he was not quite the outdoorsman they were. Huck and Jim ate catfish from the river and slept on their raft; Raban stayed in hotels. Still, the author's interactions with people along the river proved rewarding, and *Old Glory* garnered him some of the best reviews of his career. R. R. Harris of the *Saturday Review* (September 1981), proclaimed, "Raban has a novelist's eye for the telling detail that surprises and provides perspective. . . . [He] excels at writing about the river and the towns on its banks. He takes to these places—some dull, some run-down, others thriving. . . . [He] ate, drank, fished, talked politics . . . and went to church with these people. He deftly describes them all." In *Library Journal* (September 15, 1981), Kathleen Farago declared, "The uniqueness and charm of this book is in Raban's description of his encounters with people, especially with those in the smaller towns. Raban also tells of the dangers and fascinations of the river. This is a well-written book for both the armchair traveler and anyone interested in American life." Noel Perrin, in the *New York Times Book Review* (September 6, 1981), called the book a "stunning success," with "two modest reservations." As with *Huckleberry Finn*, he wrote, "the book falls off a bit at the end. The other fault is that Mr. Raban cannot do an extended scene. He is a master of the quick sketch. . . . [However, the book] remains more successful than 99 percent of the books about America since de Tocqueville's *Democracy in America*."

Foreign Land (1985) is a fictional tale about George Grey, an Englishman returning to the United Kingdom after working abroad for many years, first in the navy, then as a ship hand, and finally in Bom Portor, Montedor, a small, imaginary West African state. While away from England, George has remained an Englishman in every way, at least in the ways he remembered Englishmen to be. When he returns home he discovers that England has become a place he does not like. He doesn't understand the popular television programs; his quaint boyhood village has been replaced by a modern suburb with a mini-market, video store, and hastily built modern houses. He is shocked by the rudeness of his taxi driver as he whisks through a London filled with garbage. Having nowhere else to go, he settles in his parents' retirement home in the coastal village of Cornwall, only to discover that the only thing he can do there is grow old and die. So, instead of settling into his life, George buys a boat and plans a trip to London by sea. But on reaching Rye, he reloads the boat with new charts and fresh supplies and sets course for Biscay and then the open sea.

Raban's first novel received mostly positive reviews. The critic for *Publishers Weekly* (August 23, 1985) wrote, "Rich in sailing lore, in African color and custom, in sex, sport, and the making of relationships, this novel . . . sets the senses flying." The *London Review of Books* (July 4, 1985) concurred, adding that the well-sketched character of George drives the plot: "Raban has managed to breathe individual life into a character who is recognizably a general type. The models for George's inadequacy and loneliness are pedigree English.

His consistent failure to communicate with those near to him, to correct misunderstandings before they become irremediable, to seize the fateful moment—in short, his failure to get the hang of life—is the failure of a certain common sort of Englishness, muted, passive, buttoned-up and sad." Paul Gray, writing for *Time* (November 11, 1985), grumbled that "Raban garnishes Grey's odyssey with plenty of details. . . . Such raw information will probably baffle most landlubbers. Worse, it increasingly obscures the hero's reasons for being on the water in the first place . . . a fascinating portrait of a body and mind adrift gradually yaws into a manual of navigation."

Foreign Land and Raban's next nonfiction work, *Coasting* (1987), both derived from his experience circumnavigating the British Isles. On April 1, 1982, the author set sail from Fowey Estuary in a 30-foot ketch, beginning a six-month voyage in which he would sail for a while and then anchor at a port town and see what was going on. He varied his land-bound activities throughout the trip: in Douglas he gambled, in Plymouth Sound he studied the docked warships that had been used in England's Falklands Islands War, in Georgie and Ken he went crabbing, and in Lymington he visited his parents. He also met the writer Paul Theroux, who was then traveling around England by train and on foot.

Reviewers were for the most part impressed with Raban's observations. "*Coasting* is half travel book, half autobiography, half novel (never mind the arithmetic) marvelously written and superbly constructed," Beryl Bainbridge wrote in the *Spectator* (September 27, 1986). "The author's intention was surely to sail through time and place, to chart the coast-line of his own past, to take soundings of his future while bobbing round the edges of Britain. . . . It's the sort of book you put among those favorite books you keep on your desk or your table, the ones you pick up over and over again to re-read with undiminished pleasure, the sort you wish you had written yourself." Christopher Lehmann-Haupt of the *New York Times* (January 26, 1987) noted that the author "builds with minutely observed details and his narrative is always alive with crosscurrents of amusing ambiguity." A notable dissenting voice was that of Denis Donoghue, who, in the *London Review of Books* (December 18, 1986) complained, "The most interesting parts about *Coasting* are the technical bits about winds, tides, what to do with the *Gosfield Maid* when things get choppy. Any business on board is better than having Raban go on yet again about Mrs. Thatcher and the Falklands. Or indeed about the state of Britain in our time."

Also in 1987 Raban released *For Love and Money: Writing, Reading, Travelling 1969–1987.* (It was published two years later in the United States as *For Love and Money: A Writing Life 1969–1989.*) This overview of Raban's writing amused critics. In the *Christian Science Monitor* (November 20, 1987), Thomas D'Everlyn wrote, "*For Love and*

Money is an invitation to travel through a world of wonderful books, ideas, places, and people." Janette Turner Hospital, writing in the *New York Times Book Review* (October 1, 1989), noted, "There is something both reckless and vulnerable, both exhibitionistic and self-effacing, about this revealing non-autobiography." In 1989 Chatto & Windus published Raban's *God, Man, and Mrs. Thatcher.*

Hunting Mister Heartbreak (1991) describes Raban's travels from one coast of the United States to the other between 1988 and 1990. This book got excellent reviews. The *Publishers Weekly* (March 15, 1991) critic, for example, wrote, "Wonderfully observant, often hilarious, the book is written in almost sensual prose with the astonished integrity of a visitor who dropped in from another planet."

In *Bad Land: An American Romance* (1996), Raban discussed the anger many people in the modern American West feel toward the federal government and examined the reasons for their hostility. Many of the people he talked with were descendants of the original homesteaders, who accepted the federal government's offer of free land in the plains of Montana and the Dakotas in 1909. People came from the East and from Europe to farm land that Raban referred to as "the Great American Desert"; it "looked suspiciously like the surface of the moon," he wrote. According to the author, the homesteaders were duped by a corrupt federal government and the growing railroad companies into thinking that this area was able to support crops. In 1917 a drought hit, and many homesteaders gave up, moving further west. Many of those who stayed were ruined during the Great Depression and the dust storms of the 1930s. By the mid-1990s, few farms remained on the Montana plains, but a great deal of animosity toward the federal government persisted. In the *New York Times* (November 14, 1996), Christopher Lehmann-Haupt called *Bad Land* "entertaining and instructive." The *Washington Post Book World* (December 1, 1996) proclaimed, "Raban's genius gives those who might have been no more than characters in a cautionary tale the triumphant credibility of real human beings—some betrayed by their own greed and shortsightedness, others done in by circumstances they could not control, but all forced to deal with the consequences of one more American dream gone terribly wrong."

Jonathan Raban is the author of several plays, including the teleplays *Square* (1971), *Snooker* (1975), and *The Water Baby* (1975). In 1977 his play *The Square Touch* debuted at the Old Vic Theatre in Bristol, England. He is also the author of *Mother*, produced for BBC-TV, as well as *A Game of Tombola* (1972), *The Anomaly* (1973), and *The Daytrip* (1976) for BBC Radio 3. He is the editor of the *Oxford Book of the Sea* (1992).

Jonathan Raban is a fellow of the Royal Society of Literature, the Society of Authors, and the Royal Geographical Society. For his book *Old Glory*, he has received the Thomas Cook Award (1981) and the Heinemann Award from the Royal Society of

Literature (1982). In 1997 he received the National Book Critics Circle Award for nonfiction for *Bad Land.*—C.M.

SUGGESTED READING: *Christian Science Monitor* p13 Oct. 16, 1974, p13 Nov. 20, 1987; *Economist* p116 Mar. 16, 1974; *Entertainment Weekly* p50+ May 31, 1991; *Financial Times* p26 Mar. 25, 1995; *Guardian* p10 July 19, 1979; *Library Journal* Oct. 15, 1979, Sep. 15, 1981; *London Review of Books* p11 July 4, 1985, p10 Dec. 18, 1986; *New York Times* C p33 Jan. 26, 1987, C p20 Nov. 14, 1996; *New York Times Book Review* p7 Nov. 10, 1974, p7 Oct. 14, 1979, p1 Sep. 6, 1981, p20 Oct. 1, 1989, p7 May 12, 1991; *New Republic* p34 Oct. 20, 1979; *People* p85+ Nov. 16, 1987; *Publishers Weekly* p62 Aug. 23, 1985, p76+ Feb. 13, 1987, p61 Aug. 7, 1981, p46 Aug. 18, 1989, p49 Mar. 15, 1991; *Saturday Review* p57 Sep. 1981; *Time* p92+ Nov. 11, 1985, p19 May 13, 1991; *Spectator* p42+ Sep. 27, 1986; *Washington Post* D p1 Jan. 3, 1997; *Washington Post Book World* p1 Dec. 1, 1996; *Contemporary Authors New Revision Series*, vol. 65, 1998

SELECTED BOOKS: Fiction—*Foreign Land*, 1985; Nonfiction *The Technique of Modern Fiction: Essays in Practical Criticism*, 1968; *Mark Twain: Huckleberry Finn*, 1968; *The Society of the Poem*, 1971; *Soft City*, 1974; *Arabia: A Journey Through the Labyrinth*, 1979; *Old Glory: An American Voyage*, 1981; *Coasting*, 1987; *For Love and Money*, 1987; *God, Man, and Mrs. Thatcher*, 1989; *Hunting Mister Heartbreak: A Discovery of America*, 1991; *Bad Land: An American Romance*, 1996; As editor *Oxford Book of the Sea*, 1992; Drama *Square*, 1971; *A Game of Tombola*, 1972; *The Anomaly*, 1973; *Snooker*, 1975; *The Water Baby*, 1975; *The Daytrip*, 1976; *The Square Touch*, 1977

Redonnet, Marie

Oct. 19, 1948– Novelist; poet; playwright

The French novelist, poet, and playwright Marie Redonnet has won a reputation as a postwar, postmodernist successor to Nathalie Sarraute, Marguerite Duras, and the other New Novelists. Her "triptychs"of novels (rather than "trilogies" because the characters and settings of each work are different)—*Splendid Hôtel* (tr. *Hôtel Splendid*, 1994), *Forever Valley* (tr. 1994), and *Rose Mélie Rose* (tr. *Rose Mellie Rose*, 1994)—and plays, *Tir & Lir*, *Moby-Diq*, and *Seaside*, are concerned, as she says, with heritage and with memory in the sense of Dali's *The Persistence of Memory*: fluid, unconventional, dreamlike. Between 1985 and 1992, Redonnet produced a large body of work, including her first book, the poetry volume *La Mort & Cie* (Death

Marie Redonnet

John Foley Photography

and Company); *Doublures* (1986), a collection of short stories; the two "triptychs"; *Silsie* (1990), a novella; and *Candy Story*, (1992), a novel. *Nevermore*, another novel, was published in English in 1996.

Calling hers "an astonishing imagination" and a "voice that has few equivalents in contemporary literature," Redonnet's principal translator, Jordan Stump, declared that she "remains very much outside the mainstream of French literature, even of 'progressive' French literature, a fascinating and often troubling voice that stubbornly refuses categorization." The characters in her novels are aspects of one character—stages of female life, "a going-back in time, a crossing-over of death, a resurgence of submerged life and sex," in Redonnet's words, according to Stump. Redonnet described the male characters in her triptych as "either decrepit and suicidal . . . or completely assimilated into their social function" in an interview with Stump appended to *Forever Valley*.

The sense of life (even vegetable life) as change and decay emerging into new life is paramount in Redonnet's work, as is the sense of isolation, of otherness. Her style could be called blatantly minimalist. "But," Redonnet remarked in the interview with Stump, "isn't any style, when it carries a world inside itself, in a state of rupture or scandalous otherness in relation to what tradition calls style?"

For *World Authors 1990–1995*, Marie Redonnet, born on October 19, 1948, writes (in French): "I was born in the 13th arrondissement in Paris. My father was then 38 years old, a bus conductor. My mother was 37, a seamstress in a haute couture establishment. I am their only daughter. My father's

people had working-class roots: my grandfather started as a miner in the Auvergne, and my grandmother delivered bread. In my maternal line I have found exile, uprooting: Spanish émigrés came to establish themselves in the last century in a village of the Val d'Aran at the Spanish border. They quickly left their village of exile, which had no future. My great-grandfather worked in Paris as a police agent in the prefecture, and my grandfather in his turn worked for the police as an inspector.

"I lived until I was 20 in Kremlin Bicetre, a working-class suburb close to Paris. I have no souvenir of Kremlin Bicetre. I was a good student in elementary school which allowed me to pursue my secondary education in Paris, at the Lycee Claude Monet. I discovered literature in adolescence—along with sexuality and revolution.

"I was 20 in 1968. While waiting for the revolution, which I believed imminent, I got married, and I passed the examination in modern literature to become a secondary school teacher. I left to teach in Sfax, in Tunisia, as an exchange teacher and then returned to France where I taught in a technical high school in the north of Paris. It was then that I realized that the revolution was not coming and that I was ill suited for my job as teacher in a high school in a northern suburb of Paris. And for what was I not ill suited? My father died in 1974. I began a psychoanalysis, with a follower of Lacan. I did not know who I was and I was not who I was.

"In the middle of my psychoanalysis at the age of about 30, I began to write a few fragments of poetry that I didn't know how to use. I had then no vocation to be a writer nor any gift for writing. Jacques Géraud, my husband of that time, had also begun a psychoanalysis. A little while later, at the same time as I began to write my little fragments, he had, while reading Proust, the revelation that he had to become a writer. A few days later, I decided to follow him.

"From that day on, every day for hours, I sat at my desk with my notebook open. The words did not come. I did not give up. Months passed. At last some little characters appeared: the dwarf, the smaller dwarf, the madman. Their interlocutors were God, Death, the king, the ruler of the kingdom. My language was basic, as though in beginning to write I had lost the great language of French literature. I wrote as if I had lost the memory of literature. I called my first book *La Mort & Cie* (Death and Company) after my analyst, who had played dead throughout my analysis. I took a pen name for that book. I took my mother's name, Redonnet, and abandoned my father's, L'hospitalier. I took two letters off my first name to make Marie. At the end of my psychoanalysis I had written *Doublures* (Doubles), 12 short stories, 12 little marionette characters who tried to get rid of repetition and doubles.

"Within three years after my psychoanalysis I had written a double trilogy: novels—*Splendid Hôtel*, *Forever Valley*, and *Rose Mélie Rose*—and plays—*Tir & Lir*, *Mobie-Diq*, and *Seaside*—focused on the question of heritage and memory. How to emerge alive from mourning a heritage of which the memory is lost, how to begin a new history? The years that followed the double trilogy were years of crisis, a tentative search for a path between two times and two histories: *Silsie, Candy Story,* and *Nevermore.* There again the novel was echoed in drama: *Le Cirque Pandor, Fort Gambo.* During those years of crisis my mother died, I was divorced, and I quit teaching.

"I am presently writing my doctoral thesis on Jean Genet. I must live (to write perhaps, but differently) a new history."

—tr. S. Y.

Marie Redonnet's writing style consists of "deceptively simple syntax, odd transitions, and obsessive imagery," according to John Taylor in the *Times Literary Supplement* (June 2, 1995). The setting of *Hôtel Splendid* is a decaying hotel on the edge of an encroaching toxic swamp. The hotel was built by the narrator's grandmother, and the narrator lives there with her two aged and dying sisters, who may be only aspects of herself. Redonnet, strongly influenced by Samuel Beckett, can produce a kind of hope out of despair and decay. Jordan Stump, her translator, on the other hand, found a contrast between Beckett's characters' slide "toward extinction, resignation, and silence" and Redonnet's characters' "force for life and creation that borders on the triumphant." At the end of *Hôtel Splendid,* when the encroaching swamp has been halted by frost, and the narrator has buried her two sisters, she stands, with the hotel, as a symbol of endurance:

> The signs are working again, but only halfway. I only turn them on at night. When night falls and I turn them on, only one word is lit up, the second one, Splendid. That word stands out against the sky. Travelers cannot help but see it. But since the word Hôtel isn't lit up, the travelers cannot know that the Splendid is a hotel. That explains why there are fewer and fewer guests. I still have the boarder. He has no desire to leave. In the evening, I stand at the window. The Splendid with its half-lit signs is reflected in the snow. The letters are leaning, like the hotel. You might think you were on a boat. From far away, the Splendid must look like a boat that has run aground there on the snow, with its wooden hull half rotted away. There is no chance of it sinking, since it has run aground. The embankment was swallowed up. Grandmother and my sisters belong to the swamp. The Splendid is open day and night. Guests are always welcome.

As Stump wrote in his translator's introduction, Redonnet's narrators "retain even in the darkest situations a remarkable persistence, openness, and above all hope, a hope that may well be, however unspectacularly, repaid in the end."

Although *Forever Valley,* the next book in what Redonnet calls her triptych, is narrated by a 16-year-old girl, she is part of the same feminine continuum as the narrator of *Hôtel Splendid.* She lives, like the narrator of *Hôtel Splendid,* in isolation, in a hamlet, taking care of a priest who is old and paralyzed. She refers to him as "the father": "I was raised by the father. The father is much too old to move to another parish. He was happy to be able to keep the rectory. . . . The father must have raised me so I can look after him in his old age. . . . He is very disappointed that he never managed to teach me to read. . . . I do not want to leave Forever Valley." The narrator is forced to leave Forever Valley, however, after it is flooded by a dam. "I am not 16 anymore," she says at the end, "But I am still not developed." She does not like her new life, with its new-fangled electricity. She refuses to visit the cemetery: "I don't like the dead or the graves. I don't like the valley below either or the Forever Valley dam with the mountains reflected in the water and the pass that you see just at the bottom, where the former hamlet of Forever Valley is hidden." For Redonnet, mere mechanical modernity adds nothing to life.

In the last book of the triptych, *Rose Mellie Rose,* the isolated narrator is a 12-year-old girl, Mellie, a foundling raised by an old woman, Rose, in a hermitage. The old woman dies soon after the opening of the novel: "I buried her in the grotto, where she found me twelve years ago. It makes a good shelter. I carved her name into the wall, and mine too. And then I drew a line between them. It says Rose and Mellie on the wall of the grotto."

Mellie does develop: she gives birth to a new Rose in that same grotto and then dies herself in an old Buick on the beach: "The wind picks up the sand on the beach. There are no footprints on the sand because of the wind that erases them all. The seagulls flew off all together with one great flurry. They abandoned the Buick." She has left a child, however—a new life, a new Rose— and 12 photographs that tell the story of her life, interleaved with the elder Rose's book of legends. Redonnet thus posits the continuity of both life and art.

In the interview with Jordan Stump included at the end of *Forever Valley,* Redonnet explained the reasons for the minimalist style that, according to Stump, evokes visual images despite a complete lack of description. Redonnet said that her style perhaps has "a poetic power to make visible that which has been neither described nor expressed by metaphor, but rather only evoked. . . . What my writing tries to do is to appropriate the power of the photographic image and especially the cinematic image. This allows the writing to capture the real, to make it visible. But the fact that the image is born of the power of language alone means that it is not only an image, but also a thought that creates meaning."

In that interview Redonnet explained also her relation to "the great period of feminist struggle and the writings that illustrated it." In the triptych, it is the women who fight, who seek, who create. Declaring that her triptych could have come about only after that period of struggle, since it "tells of a violent cultural crisis between men and women, at a time when women, through their emancipation, were forging a history," Redonnet observed that she sees "literature as an act with a political dimension" in which humor plays an important part: "Humor is play, freedom, insolence, and intelligence, against the crushing weight of evil, pain, and stupidity. . . . But to humor I add poetry, which is love, dreams, and songs."

In "The Story of the Triptych," appended to *Rose Mellie Rose*, Redonnet pointed out that she was trying to recapture voices "that recount the lost history of women. . . . women who live in madness and death, or in an alienating identification with a conquering modernity. The narrators alone are figures of the emancipation of women: they are the ones who fight, who build, who seek, who pass down a work." Redonnet again mentioned her feminist purpose: "Historically linked to the moment at which women gained their emancipation and at which the old utopias died, the triptych seeks both to say farewell to an entire history and to save the part of that history that must not die, but which must be rewritten in another way: poetry, myth, utopia, love."

Susan Ireland in *Review of Contemporary Fiction* (Summer 1995) deemed Redonnet successful in the triptych: "The narrators . . . display remarkable persistence. In a small yet heroic way, each affirms the survival of the human spirit in the face of adversity and struggles to pass on a legacy—however small—to those who come after her." Ireland pointed out the "eternal return" in Redonnet's work: "Echoes of familiar tales recur . . . and events are governed by atemporal cyclical rhythms. The characters—like Redonnet herself in her search for a new style of writing—strive to break out of these repetitive cycles, to bury the dead in their family, and to move on. In this sense, the novels convey a quiet optimism, a belief in the possibility of renewal after decay."

Silsie, a novella, which Redonnet told Stump she considered an epilogue to the three novels of the triptych, is, like the novels, pervaded by water imagery. In *Hôtel Splendid* "the devouring swamp . . . carries violence and death," according to Redonnet. In *Forever Valley*, the water brought by the new technology drowns the hamlet. In *Rose Mellie Rose*, although there is a stagnant and dying lagoon, Redonnet has introduced "living" water. The sea, Redonnet remarked, is the "place of poetic and mythic quests." Although the sea is a life force, Redonnet believes one must "resist its deadly fusional appeal," in a symbolic sense. Thus Redonnet has expressed the urge toward creativity, which involves a separation, an expulsion, from a womblike existence. In *Silsie*, therefore, a mere channel "is replaced by the center of the ocean, toward which the lifeboat moves. A myth of death gives way to a myth of rebirth."

The double is another of Redonnet's symbols, representing, she told Stump, "the Uncanny that Freud talks about." It, too, is a necessary point of departure, starting "from that strangeness in order to leave it and to enter into another one, that of otherness from the world and from the other. . . . Leaving behind the double means trying to leave behind—after having told the story—the psychosis of which the literature of modernity was, with Beckett, to die."

In *Candy Story*, a writer, Mia, is the protagonist. In the novel, "nothing happens as planned. We meet characters who die off a few pages later. The places Mia visits are all in disrepair. Yet from these ashes Mia finds a story to tell," according to the *Library Journal* (November 1, 1995) reviewer. "In *Candy Story*, as in her first three novels, Redonnet addresses the broad questions of time, memory, love, and death, and she now focuses more explicitly on the subject of writing and its relationship to these broader themes. . . . The variations on the theme of writing convey a sense of Mia's precarious balance between the opposing poles of life and death, decay and reconstruction," Susan Ireland wrote in the *Review of Contemporary Fiction*.

Many reviewers found the setting of *Nevermore* "vaguely American." Redonnet wrote about a circus and a run-down nightclub in a "border town" on the "west coast." Despite the American milieu, the evil overtones lead back to the Nazi Holocaust. The town is "haunted by nearby sinister 'camps' where the prodigal deputy, Willy Bost, lost both parents. The Babylon and the Fuch Circus are sites for murders, intrigues, and secrets revealed," according to the *Publishers Weekly* (July 8, 1996) reviewer. Reviewers were favorable to the novel, which *Publishers Weekly* found to be "like a good French noir film." John Taylor in the *Times Literary Supplement* (June 2, 1995) termed *Nevermore* a "frenetic erotic thriller." He concluded that the "over-the-top plot, the inconclusive ending, the allusions to the Holocaust, and the ominous yet ironic title in the end provide a chilling portrait of mankind's vulgarity and duplicity."

Redonnet's plays explore the same themes as her fiction. For example, Elizabeth Mazza-Anthony in *Studies in 20th Century Literature* (Summer 1996) declared that "the ebb and flow of references, characters and situations between *Splendid Hôtel* and *Seaside* seems unending." Redonnet declared that the doubling in *Doublures* is at the heart of a "story that returns in the murderous family of *Tir & Lir*, locked inside a heinous and deadly twinning." John Taylor observed that "Redonnet's plays make use of . . . settings and stories" similar to those in her novels and that "*Fort Gambo* recalls the author's fascination with mining, mysterious 'frontiers' and landscapes reminiscent of the Old West." *Le Cirque Pandor* returns to the world of the circus and its performers that was the focus of like *Nevermore*. *Moby-Diq*, part of Redonnet's first dramatic triptych, was translated into English in 1995 by Dan McGillicuddy.
—S. Y.

SUGGESTED READING: *Library Journal* p107 Nov. 1, 1995, p114 Aug. 1996; *Publishers Weekly* p79+ July 8, 1996; *Review of Contemporary Fiction* p206+ Summer 1995; *Studies in 20th Century Literature* p491+ Summer 1996; *Times Literary Supplement* p22 June 2, 1995

SELECTED BOOKS IN ENGLISH TRANSLATION: Fiction—*Hôtel Splendid*, 1994; *Forever Valley*, 1994; *Rose Mellie Rose*, 1994; *Candy Story*, 1995; *Nevermore*, 1996; Drama—*Moby-Diq*, 1995

Reed, Adolph L.

Jan.14, 1947– Essayist; critic; journalist

Adolph L. Reed Jr., a gadfly among African-American intellectuals, has criticized his fellow thinkers and writers for their "quietism" and has inveighed against popular ideas of famous black leaders in his books *The Jesse Jackson Phenomenon: The Crisis of Purpose in Afro-American Politics* (1986) and *W. E. B. DuBois and American Political Thought: Fabianism and the Color Line* (1997). He has decried the tendency to cling to an old style of politics in which charismatic leaders acted as spokespersons for the black masses. This approach is outdated not only because of "a diversity of opinion," as Reed told Don Terry of the *New York Times* (July 10, 1994). There is also "a diversity of interests. There used to be a least common denominator. There isn't any more." Reed stands with those who demand "a living wage."

Adolph L. Reed Jr., the African-American historian, political analyst, and journalist, was born on January 14, 1947 in New York City. He obtained his bachelor's degree from the University of North Carolina at Chapel Hill in 1971, and he received his master's and Ph.D., both in political science, from the University of Atlanta in 1974 and 1981, respectively. He taught at Yale University from 1981 until 1991, then at Northwestern University, in Evanston, Illinois, until 1997, when he joined the African-American studies department at the University of Illinois at Chicago.

Reed's first book, *The Jesse Jackson Phenomenon: The Crisis of Purpose in Afro-American Politics*, started, according to his preface, as an "irate letter to the editor of the *Nation*" about a "panegyric" the magazine had published in response to Jesse Jackson's announcement that he would run for president in 1984. The letter did not get written; instead, Reed decided to compose a "conference paper on the Jackson campaign and its significance in the present state of Afro-American politics." The projected 20-page paper expanded into a book, exhaustively detailing the impact of the campaign and what Reed believed to be the true story behind the media hype allocated to it. Reed wrote that the Jackson phenomenon was a key exemplar of "important conditions and tendencies driving Afro-American politics" in the 1970s and 1980s and, in addition, provided "a window onto the larger dynamics that have structured post-civil rights era black political activity." These conditions, tendencies, and dynamics include, according to Reed, "(1) the development of competing criteria for legitimation of claims to black political leadership; (2) the sharpening of lines of socioeconomic stratification within the Afro-American population; and (3) the growth of centrifugal pressures within and external attacks on the national policy consensus represented in the Democratic coalition, . . . the main context for articulation of black political agendas. . . ." In simpler language, R. W. Coan wrote in *Choice* (September 1986) that Reed "asserts the campaign was a step back to a charismatic, 'protest' style of leadership which, he feels, can no longer represent a diverse and increasingly complex black community."

Reed accomplished his purposes in what was to become his typical gadfly manner, beginning with a first chapter, "The Context of Elite Competition,"—in which he seized on the manner in which Jackson became the predominant spokesperson for the African-American masses in the eyes of the media as well as the white liberal establishment. Contending that his leadership was more symbolic than real, Reed pointed out that Jackson had never held elective office when he ran for president, and in fact had only just registered to vote for the first time. Jackson, Reed maintained, claimed to be an "organic" leader, a person who led through a network of churches and other black organizations. Reed characterized this approach in "The Jackson Phenomenon and Leadership Ratification" as ignorant of the post–civil rights gains that enabled the rise of an elected, "institutional," black leadership elite. The problem with Jackson's style, Reed wrote, "is that—while ostensibly popular and immediately representative—it is fundamentally antidemocratic." It "leaves acclamation as the sole principle of popular validation" because "without palpable mechanisms of ratification, no evidentiary base exists from which to determine veracity of leadership claims."

In "Mythology of the Church in Afro-American Politics," Reed challenged the supposed monolithic hold of the church on black politics, specifically questioning Jackson's claim—based largely on his being a minister—to leadership. Reed maintained that although from 1956 to 1959, "church-based leadership . . . was pivotal in originating direct protest activity," both before and after that period the business and professional world dominated the leadership of black politics.

In "Blacks and Jews in the Democratic Coalition," Reed presented the argument that Jewish elites tended to view affirmative-action "strategies" as "infringements on norms for allocation of privilege from which they benefit and which they interpret as rights" and that this "is the substantive basis of black/Jewish conflict in the current period." He condemned Jackson's stance, however, in the conflict as "simple-minded anti-Semitic discourse," which "reflects his opportunistic appropriation of an upwardly mobile but harried stratum in the black community, a stratum which—like Kafka's burrowing animal—is consumed by fearful visions of antagonists pressing from all sides. This outlook yields a meanness of spirit and small-mindedness that historically have opened to proto-fascistic articulations," he concluded. The real damage done by Jackson's anti-Semitic rhetoric, Reed pointed out, was to his own position on the Middle East: "In one stroke Jackson sacrificed the moral authority on which he might have stood to demand a Middle Eastern policy that acknowledges the legitimacy of interests other than Israel's."

Reed charged that the media anointed Jackson as the paramount black leader, "despite lack of enthusiasm from the 'black leadership family.'" As a result, the Democratic Party abandoned any attempt to obtain greater African-American representation or to debate real black concerns. Instead, before the nominating convention, the party was preoccupied with "negotiation of a package of practical and symbolic payoffs that could secure Jackson's support for a Mondale-led ticket."

Clarence Page of the *Chicago Tribune* (June 22, 1986) agreed with Reed's suggestions that Jackson had hoodwinked the media and the public—by maintaining "the old protest elite" in the face of newer professionalism on the part of African-American politicians, and by holding rallies designed to make his candidacy look like a mass movement. Page criticized Reed's style, however, observing that "much of what this book has to offer gets lost in its verbiage. Most of its statements seem designed less to attract readers than scare them away." C. Vann Woodward, writing in the *New Republic* (June 2, 1986), concurred that Reed's "political-science prose" might be opaque but stated that "persistent efforts in translation are rewarded by some illuminating analysis and original findings." In the *Nation* (November 28, 1987), Mary Summers lauded *The Jesse Jackson Phenomenon* as "a major contribution toward the democratic debate as to what sort of political agenda is necessary to change the conditions of life in our nation's ghettos and what sort of political strategy might help to achieve this."

In his 1997 volume, *W. E. B. DuBois and American Political Thought: Fabianism and the Color Line*, Reed analyzed the work of the black activist and scholar, in turn using DuBois's achievements as a standard by which to critique today's racial politics. Ironically, Reed decried the use of the works of past writers to justify one's own position, or "vindicationism." He also criticized "presentism," or the belief that history is a continuum in which past events evolve into the present. Although W. E. B. DuBois, who was born in 1868 and died in 1963, changed his political position several times in his life, Reed maintained that there was an underlying consistency in his views. DuBois started as a revolutionary elitist, believing that a "talented tenth" of the black population should lead the rest. Although he was a member of the Communist Party at the end of his life, he maintained his belief in the leadership of a few. For Reed, DuBois was, however, all his life a "collectivist," someone who believed that the condition of the masses could be ameliorated by an administrative "social-engineering" approach—the essential quality of Fabian socialism. DuBois, he wrote, "remained committed throughout his life to the realization of a fundamentally elite-driven organizational model for the black population . . . notwithstanding his various changes of political affiliation and program."

Reed used his interpretation of the scholar to criticize black intellectuals who have a different view of DuBois. Among his targets were Houston A. Baker Jr., an English professor at the University of Pennsylvania, who in seeking a distinctive black aesthetic also wrote about Booker T. Washington; and Henry Louis Gates, who embraced a literary—rather than political—view of DuBois.

"The oddest aspect" of Reed's book, according to Alan Wolfe for the *New York Times Book Review* (September 14, 1997), "is that he enthusiastically commits the mistakes he attributes to his adversaries. . . . 'Who died and left Houston Baker in charge of designating black authenticity?' Reed asks. But it is Reed who justifies a theory of interpretation on the subjective grounds that he himself finds it 'the most reasonable substantive view of how the social world works.' Canon formation as practiced by Gates is viewed as an exercise in presentism—that is, in reading the past as a prelude to the present. But so is Reed's insistence that his DuBois is a more appropriate guide to today's controversies than Gates's DuBois." Concluding that the book is a "prosecutorial polemic," Wolfe wondered if Reed's belief that "intellectuals. . . . held the keys to history" might better be exercised with "openness to the imagination."

Railing against the general lack of attention paid to *W. E. B. DuBois and American Political Thought*—as well as against Wolfe, whom he characterized as a "neoconservative academic,"— Adam Shatz pronounced Reed "one of the nation's most refreshing and radical pundits" in his review of the book in the *Nation* (January 19, 1998). Reed's polemics, according to Shatz, have been wrongfully dismissed by the media, and Reed himself "discussed as if he were an exotic bird," outside the "Ebony Tower" in which other black intellectuals are placed. Despite "his love of a good insult, Reed's intentions are serious, even courageous," Shatz wrote. "In Reed's view, middle-class black intellectuals have abandoned questions of political strategy on their way to the literary salon, while dressing up their quietism in the radical drag of 'cultural politics.'" Shatz placed Reed under the "mantle of black intellectuals like E. Franklin Fra-

zier and Harold Cruse, who likewise wrote causti-
cally of peers grown complacent."

Shatz concluded that "Reed is especially enraged at Du Bois scholars for 'substituting literary
history for the history of political thought.'" On
this point, Shatz felt Reed had been too harsh. "The
literary turn in black studies may be 'petit bourgeois' and politically moderate," Shatz wrote. "But
it has also brought the black American experience
a level of visibility and a sensitivity of attention
that DuBois and his contemporaries could scarcely
have envisaged."

Reed has also had a thriving career as a journalist, unleashing his tirades in such publications as
the *Nation*, the *Progressive*, and the *Village Voice*.
In the *Progressive* (April 1997) he wrote that President Bill Clinton's "penchant for staging photo-ops
at black churches to add credibility to his nasty social policies has always struck me as particularly
offensive." In the October 1997 issue of the *Progressive*, Reed confronted such black conservatives
as Shelby Steele, Clarence Thomas, Thomas So-
well, Glenn Loury, and Jeff Brown. His attacks
stem from more than simple antagonism; for example, Reed is outraged at Clinton's dismissal of pro-
posals for a "living wage," one of Reed's basic demands, and he feels that white racists can justify
themselves by citing the black conservative viewpoint. Reed points to a need for governmental in-

tervention rather than calls for "attitude changes."
Referring to President Lyndon Johnson's policy
during the height of the civil rights struggle, he
wrote in the *Progressive* (December 1997): "Johnson understood that assertive government action
can define acceptable practices and behavior, and
ultimately change the world in which attitudes are
formed." "The problem," he declared, "isn't racial
division or a need for healing. It is racial inequality
and injustice." As Reed sees it, the solution is
still—as it was in the South of the 1960s—legal
change, not more discussion.
—S. Y.

SUGGESTED READING: *Choice* p216 Sep. 1986;
Nation p621+ Nov. 28, 1987, p25+ Jan. 19, 1998;
New Republic p32 June 2, 1986; *New York Times*
p6 July 10, 1994; *New York Times Book Review*
p34 Sep. 14, 1997; *Progressive* p16+ Apr. 1997,
p18+ Oct. 1997, p18+ Dec. 1997

SELECTED BOOKS: *The Jesse Jackson
Phenomenon: The Crisis of Purpose in Afro-
American Politics*, 1986; *W. E. B. DuBois and
American Political Thought: Fabianism and the
Color Line*, 1997; As editor—*Race, Politics, and
Culture: Critical Essays on the Radicalism of the
1960s*, 1986

Revell, Donald

June 12, 1954– Professor; poet; translator

The literary critic Susan M. Schultz has compared
Donald Revell to the poet John Ashberry. Revell,
whose work was first published in *From the Abandoned Cities* (1983), has become known for his unusual manipulation of language, often within traditional poetic structures. Many of his poems, in
such collections as *The Gaza of Winter* (1988), and
Beautiful Shirt (1994), deal with personal suffering. Revell has written numerous book reviews for
the *Ohio Review*, and in 1995 he published an English translation of the French poet Guillaume
Apollinaire's 1914 anthology *Alcools*. Revell's
most recent poetry collection is *There Are Three*
(1998).

Donald Revell was born on June 12, 1954, in the
Bronx, New York. His father, Donald George Revell, was a mechanic, and his mother, Doris (Len-
hard) Revell, was a secretary. As a child, Donald
Revell was deeply immersed in the Episcopal faith.
Through exposure to religious hymns and the Protestant Book of Common Prayer, he began to nurture
a love for language and a keen awareness of word
order, which would manifest themselves in his poetry.

He attended the State University of New York
(SUNY) at Binghamton, receiving his B.A. degree
in 1975. Two years later, he earned his M.A. degree, also from Binghamton. He then switched
from Binghamton to SUNY's Buffalo campus to
work toward a Ph.D., which he received in 1980.

Revell began his professional career as an instructor of English at the University of Tennessee
at Knoxville in 1980. He taught at Knoxville until
1982, when he moved to Ripon College and a position as assistant professor in Wisconsin.

In 1983, Donald Revell published his first volume of poetry, *From the Abandoned Cities*. It was
a critical success, winning the National Poetry Series Open Competition for that year. A theme that
recurs in many of the poems in the collection is the
relationship between opposites. In a review for *Library Journal* (April 1, 1983), Robert Hudzik
praised Revell's ability to dramatize such relationships. In contrast, Alan Williamson in the *New
York Times Book Review* (November 13, 1983)
found some of the anthology's poems "ambitious
but somehow uninviting." He felt many of the
pieces lacked "fire and grace," explaining that Revell is at his best in the collection's simpler
poems: "Pruning seems to give eloquence both to
the pentameter and to the dogged, depressed tone."

Two years after the publication of *From the
Abandoned Cities*, Revell moved from Ripon College to the University of Denver, where he contin-

ued to work as an assistant professor, specializing in English and creative writing. In 1988 he was promoted to associate professor; also in 1988, he received a fellowship from the National Endowment for the Arts and published his second volume of poetry, *The Gaza of Winter*. The poems contained in this work focus on the emotional suffering of the narrator, whose personal turmoil (inspired by the breakup of the poet's own marriage) is paralleled by the political turmoil in the Middle East, from which the title is derived. Among the devices Revell used in *The Gaza of Winter* are unusual takes on traditional poetic forms such as the villanelle and sestina.

His third volume of poetry was *New Dark Ages*, published in 1990. Following *New Dark Ages*, Revell went to work on two volumes of poetry simultaneously. The first was *Erasures*; published in 1992, it was influenced by some of the political changes going on in the world at the time. Next was *Beautiful Shirt*, released in 1994. It was praised by *Booklist* (December 15, 1994), whose critic Elizabeth Gunderson was impressed by Revell's unexpected juxtaposition of common words. Still, she felt that some of the poems suffer from the presence of their first-person narrator. "When the narrator doesn't appear," she stated, "and the poem is allowed to stand on its own, Revell's language becomes richer and definitely more delectable."

Revell's next project was an English translation of French avant-garde writer Guillaume Apollinaire's 1914 poetry anthology *Alcools*. The edition was published in 1995, and was generally hailed as a definitive English translation of the work. Revell's sixth and most recent original poetry collection, *There Are Three*, was published in 1998.

For the most part, critical response to Revell's work has been positive. One aspect of his poetry that has intrigued critics has been the way he contrasts traditional poetic forms and nontraditional content. A common criticism, however, has been that his poems are sometimes overly cryptic.

In the *Virginia Quarterly Review* (Spring 1991), the influence on Revell of the prominent American poet John Ashberry was examined by critic and Ashberry scholar Susan M. Schultz. She described Revell as taking Ashberry's vision and revising it "to fit a more social context." Scultz also traced Revell's innovative use of language to Ashberry.

In addition to the awards previously mentioned, Donald Revell was also the recipient of the Pushcart Prize in 1985, an Ingram Merrill fellowship in 1990, and the PEN West Medal in Poetry and the Shestack Prize (both in 1991). He has contributed poems to such periodicals as *New England Review*, *Antaeus*, *American Poetry Review*, *Paris Review*, and *Antioch Review*, and has written poetry criticism for such journals as *Western Humanities Review*.

—B.S.

SUGGESTED READING: *Amazon.com*; *Booklist* Dec. 15, 1994; *Library Journal* Apr. 1, 1983; *New York Times Book Review* Nov. 13, 1983; *Virginia Quarterly Review* p295+ Spring 1991; *Book Review Digest* 1984

SELECTED WORKS: Poetry—*From the Abandoned Cities*, 1983; *The Gaza of Winter*, 1988; *New Dark Ages*, 1990; *Erasures*, 1992; *Beautiful Shirt*, 1994; *There Are Three*, 1998; As translator—*Alcools*, Guillaume Apollinaire, 1995

Rios, Alberto

Sep. 18, 1952– Poet; professor; short-story writer

An acclaimed writer of poetry and short fiction for the past 20 years, Alberto Rios has incorporated much of his personal and cultural background into a compelling body of work. His Mexican American heritage has provided him with a rich spectrum of traditions and folklore, as have his childhood experiences in southern Arizona. He published his first volume of poetry, *Elk Head on the Wall*, in 1979, and has since produced such poetry collections as *Whispering to Fool the Wind* (1982) and *Five Indiscretions* (1985). He has also published several short-story collections, among them *The Iguana Killer* (1984) and *Pig Cookies* (1995).

Alberto Alvaro Rios was born on September 18, 1952, in Nogales, Arizona. His father, Alberto Alvaro, was a justice of the peace; his mother, Agnes (Fogg) Rios, a nurse, was of English descent. Alberto Rios attended the University of Arizona, from which he graduated in 1974 with a B.A. degree in English literature and creative writing. Continuing his education at the University of Arizona, Alberto received a B.A. degree in psychology in 1975 and a B.F.A. (bachelor of fine arts) degree in 1979. In addition to these studies, Alberto enrolled at the University of Arizona's law school during the 1975–76 academic year.

Rios first earned public recognition for his writing in 1977, when he won an Academy of American Arts poetry contest with his poem "A Man Then Suddenly Stops Moving." In 1978 he entered the Arts-in-Education Program of the Arizona Commission on the Arts, and in 1979 the commission awarded him a fellowship in poetry. That same year he published his small poetry volume *Elk Heads on the Wall*.

In 1980 Rios received another fellowship grant, this time from the National Endowment for the Arts. He also began working as a writer-in-residence at Central Arizona College, a position he would retain for the next two years. A second chapbook, *Sleeping on Fists*, was published in 1981. Rios's first full-length poetry collection, *Whispering to Fool the Wind*, was published in 1982. The book was awarded the Walt Whitman

Award from the National Academy of American Poets.

Rios began his teaching career in 1982, when he accepted an assistant professorship at Arizona State University in Tempe. In 1984, Rios's first work of prose, *The Iguana Killer: Twelve Stories of the Heart*, earning Rios the Western States Book Award for fiction. The following year, Arizona State University promoted him to associate professor.

Rios's fourth book of poetry, *Five Indiscretions*, was published in 1985. In a review of the book for *Library Journal* (May 1, 1985), Rochelle Ratner noted that the poems revealed Rios's "deep social commitment and rare ability to identify with others." Ratner also wrote that Rios's writing on the lives of women contained insights not commonly found in the works of male authors. In a review of *Five Indiscretions* for the *New York Times Book Review* (February 9, 1986), Carol Muske focused on the connection between Rios's Mexican-American background and his rich, textured language and commented on the poet's combination of English and Spanish syntax and unusual use of common words. "[Rios's] concerns are historical and cultural," Muske wrote, "and he seems to be without the ironic detachment and self-preoccupation that mark so much contemporary American poetry."

Rios directed Arizona State's creative writing program from 1986 to 1989, when he accepted a promotion to full professor of English, a position he continues to hold (he has been Regents Professor of English since 1994). He also continued writing; he published *The Lime Orchard Woman*, a novel, in 1988 and *The Warrington Poems* in 1989.

Rios's first published work of the 1990s was another poetry collection, *Teodoro Luna's Two Kisses* (1990). Most of the poems were inspired by fables, parables, and the poet's remembrances of childhood. Leslie Ullman of the *Kenyon Review* (Spring 1991) described the collection as "boldly playful" and "gymnastic and surreal in its reach." Its "benevolent magic," Ullman wrote, enabled Rios to create "presences out of absences, or new presences out of old presences." In a negative review of *Teodoro Luna's Two Kisses* for *Library Journal* (September 15, 1990) Ivan Argüelles wrote, "There is nothing marvelous in the flat, minimalist lines" in the poems. "These poems offer no enigmas, no magic, no insights, no depth, no tension, and only a marginal sense of human drama," the reviewer complained. He felt that the poems, with their dearth of innovation and subtlety, might as well have been prose.

Rios's published the short-story anthology *Pig Cookies* in 1995. The 13 stories focus on a small village in northern Mexico at the turn of the 20th century. Each piece offers a different slice of life in the tiny hamlet, such as the tale of a coffin maker shocked by a not-quite inanimate corpse, or the title story (named for gingerbread cookies shaped like pigs, a local delicacy), in which a young man becomes a baker in order to get closer to the woman

of his dreams. Sandra Scofield, writing in the *New York Times Book Review* (September 17, 1995), admired the "gentle pathos" with which Rios invested each story. Scofield pointed out the debts many of the stories owe to traditional folklore, and lauded the author's ability to breathe life into many ancient customs. "Part of the delight of [Rios's] stories comes from their lyricism and part from their wisdom," the reviewer wrote. "Mr. Rios has a poet's eye and a storyteller's voice."

In addition to his writing and teaching, Alberto Rios has been the co-chair of the Hispanic Research and Development Committee at Arizona State University since 1983 and a member of the board of directors of both the Arizona Center for the Book and of Associated Writing Programs since 1988. He is a member of the National Endowment for the Arts Poetry Panel and a judge in the New York City High School Poetry Contest.

Rios's awards include the *New York Times* Fiction Award, bestowed in 1983, and the Pushcart Prize for both fiction (1986) and poetry (1988 and 1989). He has contributed fiction and poetry to various anthologies, including *Hispanics in the United States* (1980) and *The Norton Anthology of Modern Poetry* (1988), as well as such periodicals as *American Poetry Review, Bloomsbury Review,* and *Paris Review.* His latest short-story collection, *The Curtain of Trees,* was published in 1999.

Alberto Rios married Maria Guadalupe Barron, a librarian, on September 8, 1979. They have one son, Joaquin Alvaro Jesus.—B.S.

SELECTED READING: *Kenyon Review* p179 Spring 1991; *Library Journal* p64 May 1, 1985, p81 Sep. 15, 1990; *New York Times Book Review* p28 Feb. 9, 1986, p25 Sep. 17, 1995

SELECTED WORKS: Fiction—*The Iguana Killer: Twelve Stories of the Heart,* 1984; *The Lime Orchard Woman,* 1988; *Pig Cookies,* 1995; *The Curtain of Trees,* 1999; Poetry—*Elk Head on the Wall,* 1979; *Sleeping on Fists,* 1981; *Whispering to Fool the Wind,* 1982; *Five Indiscretions,* 1985; *The Warrington Poems,* 1989; *Teodoro Luna's Two Kisses,* 1990; Nonfiction *Capriotada: A Nogales Memoir,* 1999

Ríos, Julián

Mar. 11, 1941– Novelist; composer

Turning his back on straightforward narrative and plot, Julián Ríos has written novels that are truly novel, and in so doing has established himself as one of the most celebrated Spanish writers of his generation. His books are distinguished by intricate twists and turns and multilingual wordplay, in a way that not only entertains and diverts but also challenges the reader. Commenting on his

Miriam Berkley/Courtesy of Alfred A. Knopf

Julián Ríos

love affair with language, Ríos told David Streitfeld for the *Washington Post* (July 26, 1998), "If I were a movie director or a photographer, I could count on the collaboration of actors and models, people of flesh and blood. But characters in a literary work are made of words, no more and no less . . . People tend to think that words are abstract. Writers often envy painters for their ability to use plastic materials and dip their fingers into the paint. But for me, words are also tactile and plastic; they have an inherent sensuality. As a writer, I attempt to show the sensual, physical, material aspects of words."

Julián Ríos was born on March 11, 1941, in Galicia, Spain, to Fernando and Regina F. (Taboas) Ríos. His father was a surgeon. Early on he loved words and wordplay, and he started writing stories as a youngster. He told David Streitfeld that learning different languages in childhood influenced his approach to storytelling. "Each tale in my childhood was a forked tale. People usually mixed Galician and Spanish. A sort of cocktail," he said.

He attended Madrid University from 1958 to 1962. Beginning in the 1970s, Ríos worked as an editor in Spain. While working for the Editorial Fundamentos publishing firm in 1974, he founded both the *Espiral* magazine and the *Espiral* literary series.

Ríos's first contribution to literature was *Solo a dos voces* (1973), a collaborative effort with the Mexican writer Octavio Paz, who later (in 1990) won the Nobel Prize in literature. The entire book records a conversation between Ríos and Paz. It was followed by another joint effort, *Teatro de signos* (1974).

Larva: A Midsummer Night's Babel, Ríos's most successful and well-known book to date, was published in 1983 (translated into English in 1990). Intended as the first of a series of five books, *Larva* tells the story of two lovers, Milalias and Babelle, who attend a masquerade party in London, costumed as Don Juan and Sleeping Beauty, respectively. Sexual overtones and bawdiness prevail, and multilingual puns and wordplay spice the text. The *Philadelphia Inquirer* (December 23, 1990) described *Larva* as "the adventures of a language-crazed Don Juan in a wordscape composed of Joycean puns and Lewis Carroll-like portmanteau words." The book consists of five separate parts: the central narrative on the odd numbered pages; annotations on the even pages; an index of names; a section called "Pillow Notes," written by Milalias and Babelle; and 32 pages of glossy photos, taken by Ríos, of the London locales where the action takes place, as well as a foldout map of the city.

Described by the *Encyclopedia Britannica* as "an instant postmodern classic: without doubt the most disturbingly original Spanish prose of the century," *Larva* was immediately hailed a literary masterpiece in Spain, where it was first published. Reviewers compared the work's multilayered, word-twisting linguistic style to that of James Joyce's *Finnegans Wake*. But in an interview with Tom McGonigle for the *Guardian* (February 1, 1991), Ríos dismissed such comparisons. "*Larva* is a novel that can only represent itself, and just barely, but I do agree that the aim of all great books is to stand for all works," he told McGonigle. "My highest ambition would be to write a book that would permit all of literature to be rewritten if they burned down every library in the world. This is impossible, of course, but authors write to seek the impossible and they have to remain impassible about doing so."

Although *Larva* was a smashing success throughout Europe, Asia, and Latin America, the novel caused barely a ripple when it debuted, in translation, in the United States, in 1990. Many critics complained that the novel would confuse rather than inspire American readers. In the *Nation* (March 11, 1991), Earl Shorris wrote, "While the interplay we are treated to over the course of 585 pages is often funny, it does not always succeed. . . . Very little happens . . . And that is, finally, the insurmountable problem of the book. The conclusion to every action is a phonic joke." He conceded, however, that although the novel "is complex . . . [it is] never deliberately arcane; any well-read person with a dogged sense of play and a willingness to engage the language will find that Ríos has gone to great pains to make his work available." Ríos, he continued, "whose sense of structure and of the intricacy of the relationship between language and that which is described by language is masterful, has not . . . integrated his ideas into life, as the subjects of his investigations always did." A *San Francisco Chronicle* (January 13,

1991) critic, by contrast, loved *Larva*, calling it "one of the most splendidly, cleverly innovative books since Leopold Bloom [of James Joyce's novel *Ulysses*] wandered the streets of Dublin with a potato in his pocket. . . . *Larva* is a garden of earthly delights."

Ríos's next novel in his five-book series was *Poundemonium* (published in the U.S. in 1997), an homage to the American poet Ezra Pound. The book centers on a group of young Spanish Bohemians (including the *Larva* characters Milalias and Babelle) who set off to explore Pound's London haunts after they hear of his death. Like *Larva*, the book is a sort of collage, with Milalias serving as the voice for much of the book, Babelle providing maps and photographs as accompaniment to the storyline, and a third character breaking in with puns, footnotes, and other comments on the pages facing the main text. Critics' reaction to *Poundemonium* was strongly divided, very likely because, as a reviewer for *Booklist* (December 15, 1996) noted, the novel is "both astoundingly confusing and tremendously funny" and even "less accessible" than *Larva*. In a similar vein, Dwight Garner wrote in the *New York Times Book Review* (February 16, 1997) that the book "walks a fine line between being a sly meditation on an unconventional poetic talent and being an inchoate word-goop." Garner concluded, "The reader finishes the novel feeling both charmed and slightly exasperated, and very much in awe of the skills of the translator." The translators of Ríos's work into English have received high praise in reviews. The *Library Journal* (November 1, 1996), for example, called Richard A. Francis's translation of *Poundemonium* "beautiful," while *Kirkus Reviews* (January 1, 1997) declared that Francis had "performed quite brilliantly."

Ríos's next book, *Loves That Bind* (1997), is about a painter, Emil, whose girlfriend, Babelle, has left him. He composes a series of letters to her, each one describing a different lover from his past—26 in all, one for each letter of the alphabet. Each of these women resembles a female character from world literature, and the reader's job is to guess the identities of the characters and the writers who created them. Among the women included are Proust's Albertine, Fitzgerald's Daisy, Nabokov's Lolita, and Queneau's Zazie.

Ríos has said that he doesn't want readers of *Loves That Bind* to focus on solving his literary puzzles. As he told Streitfeld, "If you concentrate on that element too hard, you lose the pleasure of the narrative . . . Inside any good literary novel is some mystery. Maybe you'll pass through *Loves* quickly and not get everything, but another time you will."

Some critics questioned Ríos's A to Z selections. Among them was Michiko Kakutani of the *New York Times* (June 9, 1998), who wrote that Ríos "tends to focus on the same unsavory aspects of womankind in letter after letter. A rich gallery of literary heroines, consequently, is reduced to a surprisingly narrow spectrum of stereotypes: women

as faithless sluts, women as scheming man-killers, women as self-pitying doormats." Kakutani went on to attack Ríos's simulations of literary creations, categorizing many of them as possessing "dubious quality." "Some of his chapters read like little more than flat-footed pastiches of the original author's work," she charged. "Others read like misconceived—or very poorly executed—parodies." Kakutani acknowledged that Ríos's work may have lost something through translation, but concluded that regardless, "Ríos quite plainly has a tin ear for language and locution—a fatal flaw, it turns out, for a book constructed around the idea of literary mimicry and improvisation." While calling the premise of the book one that "promises the reader a post-modern send-up of the gaps and overlaps of literature and life, as well as some entertaining literary high jinks," she declared that "Ríos does not deliver on the enormous potential of his idea. Though *Loves that Bind* has moments of real cleverness and sleight of hand, it is largely a paint-by-numbers performance, lacking the sort of sustained literary ardor that might have turned it from an experimental cuRíosity into a tour de force."

In the *New York Times Book Review* (June 14, 1998), Abigail Lee Six wrote that for all of the novel's "stylistic innovativeness, it narrates what is ultimately a rather old-fashioned man's attitude toward women." However, Six did allow that Ríos's "virtuoso use of language: multilingual puns, neologisms galore, dazzling networks of extended metaphor . . . elevate what might otherwise have been a rather shabby and even objectionable narrative."

Kirkus Reviews was more forgiving in its critique of *Loves That Bind*, calling it "a hoot, and perfectly accessible to anybody who's ever read a book or been, even fleetingly, a fool for love." Similarly, *Booklist* (May 15, 1998) characterized it as an "inventive yet sweet novel by one of Europe's most imaginative and playful novelists" that "engages first the mind and eventually the heart." The *Washington Post* (May 24, 1998) offered one of the most enthusiastic reviews of the lot, warning readers that they would become "fascinated by this gallery of women and the ways they pursue their sense of the erotic." The reviewer described *Loves That Bind* as "charming, clever, often profound, and frequently moving," and added "I live for novels like this one."

Ríos has also published nonfiction books on various topics, among them an appraisal of the artist Ronald B. Kitaj, titled *Impresiones de Kitaj: La Novela Pintada* (1989). Among his other books are *La Vida Sexual de las Palabras* (1991), *Las Tentaciones de Antonio Saura* (1991), and *Retrato de Antonio Saura* (1991). In addition, Ríos has served as co-illustrator, with Eduardo Arroyo, of the books *Ulises Ilustrado* (1991) and *Hats Off to Alice!* (1993). Julián Ríos is currently at work on a new novel titled *Monstruary*.

Little information is available about Ríos's personal life. It is known that he was once married, has two adult children, and divides his time between homes in France and Spain.—D.B.

SUGGESTED READING: *Booklist* Dec. 15, 1996, May 15, 1998; *Guardian* Feb. 1, 1991; *Kirkus Reviews* Jan. 1, 1997; *Library Journal* p108 Nov. 1, 1996; *Nation* p312+ Mar. 11, 1991; *New York Times Book Review* p18 Feb. 16, 1997, p7 June 9, 1998, p8 June 14, 1998; *Philadelphia Inquirer* Dec. 23, 1990; *Publishers Weekly* p69 Nov. 25, 1996; *San Francisco Chronicle* Jan. 13, 1991, May 10, 1998; *Times Literary Supplement* p18 May 3, 1991; *Washington Post* p3 May 24, 1998, p15 July 26, 1998; *Book Review Digest* 1991, 1997; *Contemporary Authors*, 1994

SELECTED WORKS: with Octavio Paz: *Solo a dos voces*, 1973; *Teatro de signos*, 1974; *Larva: A Midsummer Night's Babel*, 1983 (translated 1990; *Poundemonium*, 1986 (translated 1997); *Impresiones de Kitaj: La Novela Pintada*, 1989; *La Vida Sexual de las Palabras*, 1991; *Las Tentaciones de Antonio Saura*, 1991; *Retrato de Antonio Saura 1991; Loves That Bind*, 1997; as illustrator—with Eduardo Arroyo: *Ulises Ilustrado*, 1991; *Hats Off to Alice!*, 1993

Courtesy of University of Massachusetts Press

Roazen, Paul

Aug. 14, 1936– Nonfiction writer

The American writer Paul Roazen, who describes himself as a "political theorist," is one of the world's foremost chroniclers of Freudian studies, having devoted a career spanning some 30 years to a methodical and often controversial study of the movement and its followers. Roazen sees psychoanalysis as being both a core belief system of 20th-century Western culture and as a movement growing out of a kind of "extended household" with its roots in bourgeois Vienna. By personally interviewing many in Freud's circle, ranging from loyal relatives and admiring colleagues to stoic patients and truculent detractors, Roazen adds a human dimension to narratives that other intellectual historians generally suppress in favor of a more clinical style. In writing such books as *Freud: Political and Social Thought* (1968), *Freud and His Followers* (1975), *Meeting Freud's Family* (1993), and *How Freud Worked: First-Hand Accounts of Patients* (1995), Roazen came to realize "that even the most elaborate doctrines do not exist in some abstract space, apart from the human actors who conceived them. The creative acts of individuals take place in a special social and cultural setting, which can require considerable effort to recapture." Roazen is today credited for having helped break the strong grip—intimidating, by some accounts—that Anna Freud and others exercised as inheritors of the Freud mantle. The Roazen corpus describes the evolution of Freudianism from a seemingly impregnable orthodox system to one under challenge for its bourgeois patriarchal bias, one whose very viability is now subject to potential obsolescence in the wake of psychopharmacology and other therapeutic models.

For *World Authors 1990–1995*, Paul Roazen, born on August 14, 1936, writes: "I was born in Boston, Massachusetts, and grew up from the age of five in the town of Brookline, where I attended public schools. From 1954 until 1958 I was an undergraduate at Harvard College, and my field of concentration was Government; I wrote my honors thesis on the ideas of Walter Lippmann, and graduated *magna cum laude*, having been elected to Phi Beta Kappa. The next year I studied, on a Woodrow Wilson Fellowship, in the Department of Political Science at the University of Chicago, and in 1959–60 I was enrolled in the B.Phil program in Politics at Oxford where I was a member of Magdalen College. I then returned to the States and the Government Department at Harvard; I was a Teaching-Fellow in 1961–62 and 1963–65.

"It was as a graduate student at Chicago that I first developed a working acquaintance with Freud's ideas and began to consider the significance of unconscious motives in human behavior for political philosophy. Since that time I have tried to work out some of the ways of using psychodynamic concepts in political theory. Political scientists have continued to be highly suspicious about imputing any motives to people other than those of rationally calculated self-interest. Even social philosophers have been reluctant to try to take on Freud as the great figure in the history of ideas that I believe him to have been.

"My 1965 Ph.D. dissertation was on Freud and Political Theory, which I thoroughly revised for the sake of my first book, *Freud: Political and Social Thought*, which came out in 1968. While that text had been immediately hailed among orthodox psychoanalysts, my next book, *Brother Animal: The Story of Freud and Tausk* (1969), shocked the traditional analytic community. Anna Freud, from her home in London, England, helped lead an organized assault on my reputation, and more than one book was written to contest the proposition, which I had never dreamt of advancing, that Freud was personally responsible for having driven Tausk to commit suicide. I had thought of myself as rather identified with Freud in the struggle against Tausk, but in an era when it was still taboo to talk about Freud as a human being it looked like I had suddenly become one of his detractors. My aim in writing about Tausk had been to reinstate him within intellectual history, just as with Freud I had been trying to ensure his standing within political philosophy.

"In the mid-1960s I interviewed some seventy people still alive who had either known Freud or been professionally concerned with the history of analysis, and I have subsequently sought to use this material in order to put Freud's work in cultural and human context. In 1973 I edited *Sigmund Freud* for a series on the makers of modern social science, and then in 1975 I published my longest book, *Freud and His Followers*. The next year my *Erik H. Erikson: The Power and Limits of a Vision* came out, since I thought a critical examination of his ideas, and their relevance for social thought, was worth undertaking.

"One of my key sources had been Helene Deutsch, herself a pioneering analyst who happened to live in Cambridge, Massachusetts. (I continued to teach at Harvard as an Instructor and Assistant Professor from 1965 until 1971.) In 1985 my biography of Helene Deutsch, which had been initially undertaken with her cooperation, finally appeared. Later I edited her first book, *Psychoanalysis of the Sexual Functions of Women* (1991), and also a collection of her essays, *The Therapeutic Process, the Self, and Female Psychology* (1992). I also edited a collection of Tausk's papers, *Sexuality, War, and Schizophrenia* (1991). My more traditional concerns with political theory found expression in my editions of Lippmann's *The Public Philosophy* (1989) and his *Liberty and the News* (1995). I tried to pay tribute to my Ph.D. supervisor, Louis Hartz, by editing and transcribing lectures of his on nineteenth-century political thought, which appeared as *The Necessity of Choice* (1990).

"*Encountering Freud: The Politics and Histories of Psychoanalysis* (1990) was a re-worked collection of previously published essays and reviews. *Meeting Freud's Family* (1993) grew out of my interviewing in the mid-1960s, as did my *How Freud Worked: First-Hand Accounts of Patients* (1995). I also collaborated on *Heresy: Sandor Rado and the Psychoanalytic Movement* (1995).

"Over the years I have attempted to keep up with the literature by reviewing hundreds of books, all concerned with the intersection of politics and social thought. And I have published numerous essays which have remained uncollected since my *Encountering Freud*. Although psychoanalysis is no longer as fashionable in the States as it was in the 1960s, Freud's ideas abroad have retained their vitality, and analysis is, for example in France and Argentina, being taught within a university context for students who have no intention of becoming analysts themselves. My books have been translated into French, Spanish, Italian, German, Portuguese, Japanese, and Serbo-Croatian.

"From 1971 until 1995 I taught as Professor of Social and Political Science at York University in Toronto, Ontario, and was elected a Fellow of the Royal Society of Canada in 1993. I am also on the editorial boards of *Psychohistory Review*, *The Journal of the American Academy of Psychoanalysis*, *The American Journal of Psychoanalysis*, and *Psicoterapia e Scienze Umane*. I took early retirement from York in the summer of 1995, and then moved to my house in Menemsha, Massachusetts on Martha's Vineyard. I am divorced and the father of two grown sons."

Paul Roazen has focused his entire professional career on a detailed examination of the role of psychoanalysis in society and on the impact of Freudianism as a linchpin of modern Western thought (Roazen had early on been fascinated, for example, with the influences of Nietzsche and Dostoyevsky on Freud's thinking). In so doing, he prefers to emphasize the cultural over the clinical aspects of his material. Recalling his early interest in these issues, he wrote in *Meeting Freud's Family*: "My central concern in 1965 was not child therapy but the history of ideas. The import of my inquiry did not ride on the success of psychoanalysis as a treatment process; in my view Freud primarily mattered as a notable aspect of Western culture." He added: "When I taught psychoanalysis to university students it was always in the broad context of intellectual history." But Roazen has also devoted much of his work to focusing attention on the all-too-human characters who created and maintained the Freud "mystique" in the 20th century, not surprisingly attracting the animosity of those whose foibles and intrigues he had exposed.

Roazen's self-identification as a "political theorist" derives from his early admiration for the work of Walter Lippmann, whom he described as having been "absorbed by the implications of psychoanalytic theory for viable democratic convictions." Yet Roazen found scant support from professional colleagues, recalling, "My interest in psychoanalysis, indeed in any form of psychology, was . . . viewed as an aberration in my field of political science. Political scientists like to think of themselves as tough-mindedly concerned with the successful pursuit of power." Despite his frustration at how "political science continues to treat psychoanalytic thinking as an annoying stepchild" (a reference to Harold Lasswell's 1930 book *Psychopathology and Politics*, which had "relied on clinical evidence in developing its argument"), Roazen adheres firmly to a belief in the "interdisciplinary nature of all the social sciences and to the specific relevance of psychology for social thought."

Such conclusions did not emerge from ivory-tower speculation: in 1964, while completing his doctoral work at Harvard, Roazen participated in a year-long series of clinical psychiatric conferences at the Massachusetts Mental Health Center. He began his investigations in an era when Freudian hegemony prevailed: "So in 1964, whether one ambitiously sought to reconstruct one's childhood in an analysis in the hope of overcoming adult difficulties, or instead went for brief counseling assistance, the teachings of Freud were paramount in the climate of opinion then prevalent," he wrote. As the years passed, he made personal and not uncontroversial contact with many of the figures in the psychoanalytic "movement," including Freud's relatives, notably daughters Anna Freud and Mathilda Hollitscher, and disciples such as Helene Deutsch and Eric H. Erikson. In his books, Roazen refused to shrink from recording his personal though never sensational commentary about those he interviewed, a style that added human dimension to his intellectual narrative. Even these early encounters were fraught with tension. Describing his meeting with Hollitscher in 1966, he wrote, "I was a bit concerned that what I had unearthed would have already rendered me unacceptable to the family." In his first meetings with Anna, he detected the anti-American attitude she and her father had shared, possibly a result of the impact Woodrow Wilson's policies had on the vanished world they had once inhabited in Vienna. The time of their meeting coincided with the publication of *Thomas Woodrow Wilson, Twenty-Eighth President of the United States: A Psychological Study*, a controversial book by Freud and William C. Bullitt, one of the American diplomats at the Versailles conference, who died in 1967. Based on discussions between Freud and Bullitt over the years, the book cast an unfavorable light on Wilson's psychological makeup. The authors agreed not to allow its publication until after the death of the second Mrs. Woodrow Wilson, which occurred in 1961. Roazen recounted that the work was known within the profession as the "Bullitt-Freud" book, helping "downplay Freud's co-responsibility."

In the introduction to his first book, *Freud: Political and Social Thought*, Roazen expressed his belief that "by using psychoanalytic concepts to understand the origin of Freud's ideas, it may prove possible not only to give depth to our knowledge of Freud's thought, but also to establish more securely the relevance of psychoanalysis to political and social thought." The book was the first of many that Roazen would write over the next 30 years, all of which illuminated various aspects of the armored world psychoanalysis had come to represent for many.

As Roazen continued his systematic interviews with the Freud circle, he found it easy to compare the "movement" to a kind of extended, codependent family trying to preserve secrets by conspiring to oppose those who might intrude too closely on the charmed circle. Roazen always remained aware of the innate tension between historians and family members who want to preserve a reputation. In *Meeting Freud's Family* he wrote: "I understood that there exists a principle in biography-writing to the effect that historians and the families of their subjects almost inevitably have an adversarial relationship. This palpable tension between a biographer and the surviving heirs of his subject is difficult to bear. . . . But there is no way a biographer can hope to accomplish his or her objective if the biographer remains completely under the family's control."

As expected, Roazen's research proved discomforting to the Freud inner circle. He revealed that Anna had herself undergone analysis by her father and charged her with exercising an arbitrarily censorial role over the publication of Freud's correspondence, unchallenged by a timid therapeutic community afraid of the consequences of crossing her. Of the former revelation, Roazen wrote: "My willingness to put such a sensitive subject into print was an autonomic historiographic reflex on my part, since it was telling about so many hypocritical aspects of the history of psychoanalytic technique. Yet, for those who wanted to defend the status quo, my impiety was unforgivable." When he raised the censorship issue in his first book, in 1968, his protest was met with silence: "No reviewer, even in professional journals, took notice of what I had said." But the complicity was short-lived. His 1969 book, *Brother Animal: The Story of Freud and Tausk*, "gave an appalling example of an excision from a Freud letter in connection with the suicide of Victor Tausk." Tausk, one of Freud's most brilliant pupils, committed suicide after the two men became bitter rivals. Roazen's book explores this dynamic through "an examination of [Tausk's] life in relation to psychoanalysis." Peter Lomas, reviewing it for the *New York Times Book Review* (October 12, 1969), pointed out flaws in the book's organization and style but asserted that it is "refreshingly easy to read and convincingly presents aspects of Freud and Tausk that the more respectful biographies omit." Roazen credits his book with finally putting an end to the "hanky-panky with Freud's correspondence"—he wrote approvingly of the publication of the uncensored Freud-Jung correspondence in 1974—even as it spelled an end to his own standing in the Freud "movement": "By then," he wrote, "I was on the outs with the powers-that-be in psychoanalysis for having exposed all the dubious editorial practices connected with Freud's correspondences."

Roazen's 1993 book, *Meeting Freud's Family*, describes the author's decades-long study to penetrate the secrecy and obscurity that surrounded the Freud Archives. He recounted here that he had first met Anna Freud in 1965, describing her as "oddly old-fashioned" in her hand-sewn clothes, while noting that "the analytic couch in [her] consulting room seemed to me extraordinarily prominent." A year later, he met and interviewed Anna's sister, Mathilda Hollitscher, Freud's first-born child, who, at 11, had been described by her famous father as "a complete human being and of course altogether feminine." From their first meeting, Roazen realized that Anna was considered "a kind of modern saint, beyond rational criticism" but was unsaintly enough to "take . . . sharp offense at my publications." Undaunted by Dr. Michael Balint's warning that "Anna Freud will destroy you!," Roazen was determined to present an accurate and undistorted picture of Freud and his circle, a picture he thought had been muddied by the "immense distortions" of Dr. Ernest Jones's authorized biography. Soon after Anna had written witheringly to Eva Rosenfeld, "All I can say is that Roazen is a menace whatever he writes," Roazen replied: "Any independent writer, should, I believe, be proud of such a tribute."

Roazen did not find every colleague of Freud to be so intractable. He found Helene Deutsch especially amenable to sharing information about her life and thinking. She trusted him even with the keys to her house, where Roazen discovered a cache of letters, which she had thought to be lost, from her Polish lover. "The failure to obliterate historical evidence is a sign of security," Roazen wrote, "in that she more than half-consciously felt able to withstand the closest scrutiny." (She did, however, destroy the originals before her death at 97, knowing that Roazen had made copies.) In 1985, after seven years of research and interviews, Roazen published the authorized biography *Helene Deutsch: A Psychoanalyst's Life*, which he called "an intimate record of the life of this outstanding woman, a giant in the history of psychoanalysis." In it, he credited Deutsch with helping advance the role of women in modern psychoanalysis beyond the strict, patriarchal world from which it had sprung, observing how "unlike Freud's views on women were her own." He also tried to clarify some of the misinterpretations that he believes have clouded her reputation over the years: "The outrage that Freud aroused still surrounds Helene Deutsch's name," Roazen wrote in the book's introduction. "To some feminists she is infamous, a traitor to her sex; they have focused their attack against sexism on some of her theories," he noted, cautioning that Deutsch "wrote, of course, in a society radically unlike ours, and it is unfair to extract her ideas from their proper cultural context . . . despite all that her detractors say today, she *was* trying to use psychological theory for the sake of female emancipation."

For his 1990 book, *Encountering Freud: The Politics and Histories of Psychoanalysis*, Roazen assembled a formidable armoire of essays and book reviews arranged according to their subject matter. While some critics faulted him for his breezy, un-

substantial style—Edith Kurzwell in *The American Historical Review* (October 1991) sniffed that "in a scholarly book we expect more substantive and structural analyses than in media publications"—others, like Roberta Satow in *Contemporary Sociology* (January 1991) concluded that "Roazen's views on each of the books are interesting and lively. Scholars interested in the history and politics of psychoanalysis will find this critical summary of the literature a useful tool."

Roazen's later books probed his chosen subjects by examining Freudian practices from the point of view of the analysand. His 1995 study, *How Freud Worked: First-Hand Accounts of Patients*, is a culmination of a project begun in the mid-1960s, when Roazen began interviewing 25 people who had undergone analysis with Freud himself. Some reviewers found it informative, but Sarah Boxer called attention to Roazen's "shady" methodology and "addled" arguments in a *New York Times Book Review* (December 17, 1995) article that announced, "These are Paul Roazen's recollections of the conversations he had 30 years ago with 10 people who Freud analyzed when his health was fading."

Despite these charges directed against his scholarship, Paul Roazen remains a prolific commentator on the Freud "movement" in the 20th century, with dozens of book reviews and scholarly publications to his credit. He himself agrees that there are "humanly attractive aspects to Freud which are easy to miss." Attempting to summarize his outlook in the afterword to *Meeting Freud's Family*, he wrote: "I think that the study of history should lead us to question the present. Unlike those who think that family life is getting progressively better, I want seriously to question whether our own time can be said to have evolved in any way superior to the Freud family circumstances. It is too easy to be dismissively patronizing about Freud's kind of patriarchalism. . . . Psychoanalytic psychology represents a tradition of thought that should enrich us. By examining past theorists, from Freud to the present day, we can enlarge our imaginative capacities. The early Freudians had an attractive kind of idealism, and if their sectarianism can be put aside, and all the old shibboleths about heretics or deviations are ignored, past theorists can be examined on their own merits and limitations."
—E. M.

SUGGESTED READING: *American Historical Review* p1152 Oct. 1991; *American Journal of Psychiatry* p975 June 1993; *American Scholar* p135+ Winter 1989, p455+ Summer 1996; *Choice* p1506 May 1994, p1394 Apr. 1996; *Contemporary Sociology* p118 Jan. 1991; *New York Times Book Review* p49 Oct. 13, 1969, p38 Dec. 17, 1995; *Psychology Today* p73 Aug. 1985; *Society* p77+ May 1989; *Virginia Quarterly Review* p749+ Autumn 1989

SELECTED BOOKS: *Freud: Political and Social Thought*, 1968; *Brother Animal: The Story of Freud and Tausk*, 1969; *Freud and His Followers*, 1975; *Erik H. Erikson: The Power and Limits of a Vision*, 1976; *Helene Deutsch: A Psychoanalyst's Life*, 1985; *Encountering Freud: The Politics and Histories of Psychoanalysis*, 1990; *Meeting Freud's Family*, 1993; *How Freud Worked: First-Hand Accounts of Patients*, 1995; *Heresy: Sandor Rado and the Psychoanalytic Movement* (with B. Swerdloff), 1995; As editor— *The Public Philosophy*, 1989; *The Necessity of Choice*, 1990; *Psychoanalysis of the Sexual Functions of Women*, 1991; *Sexuality, War, and Schizophrenia*, 1991; The *Therapeutic Process, the Self, and Female Psychology* 1992; *Liberty and the News*, 1995

Gillman and Soame/Courtesy of W. W. Norton

Robb, Graham

1958– Biographer

Graham Robb, an expert on 19th-century French literature, came to prominence in the 1990s as the author of three important studies, each of which focused on one of the giants in French literature during his era of specialization: *Balzac: A Life* (1994), *Unlocking Mallarmé* (1996), and *Victor Hugo: A Biography* (1997). Each of the books won important scholarly awards, confirming the eminence of its author, who was educated at Oxford and Vanderbilt Universities. Robb was a fellow in French at Exeter College, Oxford, until the publication of the Hugo biography, when he resigned to devote himself full-time to writing. Critics and reviewers have

praised him for his engaging prose style and for his ability to write interesting and reliable narrative that can be appreciated by a scholarly audience while remaining accessible to the educated lay reader.

For *World Authors 1990-1995*, Graham Robb writes: "I was born in Manchester in 1958. My mother was a hospital almoner (medical social worker), my father a probation officer (later Chief Probation Officer of Hereford and Worcester). My first schools were in Wolverhampton, Stafford and Powick, near the Malvern Hills. From 1969 to 1976, I attended Worcester Royal Grammar School.

"In 1975, I discovered Baudelaire's urban poems and Paris at the same time. Returning to Paris after A-levels in 1976, I eventually found work washing trucks and lived in mock poverty on the Boulevard Barbès for six months. At Exeter College, Oxford (First Class Honors, 1981), I studied under Jim Hiddleston and taught for a year at Flaubert's old school, the Lycée Corneille in Rouen. Thus far, my only literary efforts were strictly personal, unless lyrics for a school rock-band can be called 'literary.' Periodic liquidations have left no material or mental traces to speak of, though I do remember some Mallarmean poems written in an artificial language which, theoretically, could be read either as English or as French. I felt that I could hardly expect anyone to take an interest in my own lucubrations when there was already so much to read.

"Having some practical and anecdotal knowledge of social work, I was attracted to a profession which gives an exact measure of success and an impression of doing good. But I also wanted to pursue academic interests. Schoolteaching seemed to offer a worthy compromise and in any case a chance to live in London again. (I had spent a summer working in a fiercely indolent department of Lambeth Council in the luxurious Brixton Town Hall, a short time before the Brixton riots.) In 1982, I qualified as a secondary school teacher at Goldsmiths' College in the University of London (P.G.C.E., Distinction).

"Teaching practice (in the East End) consisted of keeping a semblance of order and imparting token bits of French language to severely frustrated children, some of whom had yet to learn English. In smoky staff-rooms full of heroic but weary educators and cynical barbiturate addicts, graduate study suddenly seemed a good idea. I left for Vanderbilt University to study at the W. T. Bandy Center for Baudelaire Studies. I taught French to undergraduates and published an edition of satirical articles on Baudelaire's first newspaper (*Le Corsaire-Satan en Silhouette*, 1985). My Ph.D. thesis, published in Paris as *Baudelaire lecteur de Balzac* (1986), was directed by Claude Pichois.

"After an indecisive year in Paris, Provence and Brittany, during which I worked on an edition of Henry Murger's *Scènes de la Vie de Bohème* (Gallimard, 1988), I took up a British Academy Post-Doctoral Fellowship at Exeter College, Oxford (1987-90). A light teaching load enabled me to complete *La Poésie de Baudelaire et la poésie Française,1838-1852* (1993). By reading as many of Baudelaire's obscure contemporaries as possible, I hoped to reveal the compost-heap of mediocrity on which he grew his *Fleurs du Mal*. It was intended as an antidote to the generalizations which pass from critic to critic and which are usually based on a highly selective knowledge of the period. This kind of exhaustive study is a luxury which is very hard to give up. It satisfies the collecting instinct and then supplies a cure since the finished work demands the sacrifice of at least half the material amassed.

"My translation and adaptation of Claude Pichois and Jean Ziegler's biography of Baudelaire was published in 1989. It was the first book I had written in English. I decided then to burn my academic bridges and write a biography of my own.

"The choice of biography was dictated in part by impatience with academic habits and their interference in the presentation of facts and ideas. Even now, comments are made in a ritual fashion about the shortcomings of biography as a genre. These comments are usually dictated by current academic prejudice or by the pedagogical imperatives of institutions, though the rules that govern academic genres are far more restrictive and rarely mentioned or even noticed.

"I thought it should be possible to find a middle path between the 'popular', Romantic biography and the 'scholarly' biography in which the reader is often presented with a half-digested wad of file-cards. Could an exciting narrative be constructed without simplification or distortion? I continued to give occasional tutorials until 1994, more out of pleasure than a sense of duty, but biography proved to be a full-time job and a pedagogical enterprise in its own right.

"*Balzac: A Biography* (a *New York Times* "Book of the Year" in 1994) and *Victor Hugo* (Whitbread Biography Award, 1997; Royal Society of Literature Award, 1997) each took about four years to write. *Unlocking Mallarmé* (MLA Prize for Independent Scholars, 1996), which overlapped with *Balzac*, is the explanation and illustration of an idea which is suddenly revealed to me the guiding principle of Mallarmé's verse poetry.

"I live in Oxford where my wife, Margaret, whom I met at Vanderbilt, is the Social Studies Librarian in the University of Oxford. I publish occasional articles on nineteenth-century French literature and review regularly for *The Times Literary Supplement*."

Robb's first book was his biography of Honoré de Balzac, published in 1994 as *Balzac: A Life*, the first major biography in English of that author in half a century. Reviewers welcomed the new life of Balzac. Dennis Drabelle described it in the *Washington Post Book World* (August 28, 1994) as "witty and admirably succinct," and declared that "to have crammed the life of this seams-bursting figure

into just over 400 [sic] pages of text is a feat. And the prose consistently sparkles with epigrammatic polish." Eugene Weber, himself a social historian of France, paid tribute especially to Robb's engaging style, writing in the *New York Times Book Review* (September 11, 1994) that *Balzac* "unfolds like a detective story from incident to incident and from clue to clue. Chatty and urbane, the author, like the subject, tends to use three sentences where two might do. But he also shares Balzac's love of anecdote, of color, and of human interest. Thoughtful and informed, Mr. Robb proves, as Balzac did, that literature can be even better when it chatters than when it is concise." One of the innovations of this biography was Robb's frank exploration of Balzac's ambisexuality, an aspect of his life that was ignored by earlier scholars. Eugene Weber, himself a social historian of France, was doubtful of Robb's conclusions, however, as when he wrote in the *New York Times Book Review* (September 11, 1994), "Mr. Robb brings out what he calls Balzac's feminine aspects, 'traditionally ignored,' which come down to some kind of latent or so not latent homosexuality. I do not find this argument convincing. . . . Balzac's interest in homosexuality, so appreciated by Oscar Wilde, was part of his interest in everything, and of his ambition to incorporate all human experience in his work. We do not cite his interest in criminals or in manufacturers of hair tonics to argue for his inclination in either direction."

In his review of *Balzac* for the *Spectator* (June 18, 1994), Jonathan Keates praised the author for objectivity and clarity, writing that the biography "is admirably precise, investigative, and sharply detailed on this as on every other aspect of the self-driven epic. The definitive character of his book encourages him to probe several areas glossed over by earlier Balzacians, too deferential or else too prudish toward a man who would have wanted them to be neither." Keates added, "Few recent literary chronicles have measured themselves so successfully against the heroic proportions suggested by their subject." Keates predicted that Robb's book would generate a "spate of new translations" of Balzac. *Balzac: A Life* was one of the finalists for the Whitbread Biography Prize and was selected by the *New York Times* as one of the best books of 1994.

As he explained in the book's Foreword, Robb wrote *Unlocking Mallarmé* "to provide the reader of Mallarmé's verse poetry with a key. Not, of course, a key which gives access to some essential treasure-trove of definitive meanings; rather, a guiding principle which makes it possible to pass from one part of the labyrinth to the next without losing the thread or uprooting the hedges." Robb claims that he was inspired to write the book after he read Jacques Heugel's *Dictionnaire de rimes Françaises* (1941) and observed that Mallarmé frequently used words that rhymed with no or few other words. "Why would a poet who so obviously enjoys producing rich rhymes use so many unrhymable words?" Robb asked. He concluded that for Mallarmé's writings, especially after 1868, "the very process of producing rhyming verse constitutes . . . an allegorical drama." *Unlocking Mallarmé* won the Modern Language Association's Prize for Independent Scholars in 1996.

The genesis of Graham Robb's biography of Victor Hugo was, as he put it, partly "in the bowels of the ferry that mysteriously stops its engines in mid-Channel and sits in total darkness for several hours before sailing for Guernsey with the first light of dawn." On one of those crossings, Robb began reading Hugo's *L'Homme Qui Rit*, cognizant of the fact that it had been written in Hauteville House, not far from his destination. But that "magnificent delusion" of a work, as Robb described it, was only the spark: "[The biography] is an attempt to explore Victor Hugo in his entirety by using the work on which he lavished the greatest amount of love and ingenuity: his life." Robb spent four years working on the book, but, as quoted in Martin Arnold's *New York Times* (March 12, 1998) review, he had "a head start" because of his teaching French literature at Oxford. Robb continued: "Teaching, I had come across a lot of different Hugos. I couldn't grasp the whole subject. This gave me a chance to come to grips with it." He added, "I wanted to write something between a popular biography and a scholarly biography, readable, accurate and dependable, scholarly enough but something intelligent people like to read."

Robb wrote in his introduction to *Victor Hugo: A Biography* that he intended the work "primarily to provide its author with an excuse to spend four years reading the works of Victor Hugo. It contains new letters, verses, anecdotes, facts and sources. Some mysteries have been solved, others created. . . . Many of the quotations from Hugo's works and letters have never before appeared out of French—not necessarily a sign of progress in Hugo's view: 'How does one recognize intelligence in a nation? By its ability to speak French.'" Robb maintains that the concept of an "exhaustive, 'definitive' biography" is in principle unattainable, a myth except "in the case of a plant or a worm—unless, that is, one accepted Hugo's view that even stones have souls."

Robb has also commented in interviews on the process of writing a biography, as he did for Martin Arnold's *New York Times* (March 12, 1998) article: "When you start, there's some distance between you and your subject. You are objective. By the end, you are so imbued it's impossible to think of yourself as objective. You delude yourself into an intimate relationship with the subject, and you have to rid yourself of that." Reviewers, again, responded positively to Robb's new biography. Peter France, the editor of the *New Oxford Companion to Literature in French*, wrote in the *New York Times Book Review* (February 15, 1998) that *Victor Hugo* "is both necessary and highly readable, and easily outclasses all existing Hugo biographies in English. It is very fully documented and makes use

of the latest research, but is never ponderous." Paul Berman wrote a somewhat more mixed review for the *New Yorker* (January 26, 1998), in which he called the book "solid, thick (almost 700 pages), factually reliable, genially knowledgeable about French literature, and cleverly written" but added the caveat that "Robb's enthusiasm for the monumental novels and some of his other literary judgments leave me unpersuaded, however, and his indignation at Hugo's personal life and self-promotional habits goes a bit far. But the principal failing of this book—a terrible failing, characteristic of too many literary biographies—is that it quotes only a few snippets of the poetry." This latter point was echoed in Douglas Johnson's review in the *Spectator* (December 20–27, 1997), in which Johnson faulted Robb for minimizing the importance of some of Hugo's profoundest poems and for offering a "clumsy translation" of his famous "Demain dès l'aube. . ." written as a memorial to Hugo's daughter. And David A. Bell, professor of French history at Johns Hopkins, wrote in the *New Republic* (April 6, 1998) that Robb gave short shrift to Hugo's oeuvres, especially the poetry, and that he mistakenly gave the impression of modernism and avant-garde tendencies in Hugo's writings.

Upon completion of the Hugo biography, Robb set to work on writing a biography of French symbolist Arthur Rimbaud.

—E. M.

SUGGESTED READING: *Atlantic Monthly* p101+ Feb. 1995; *New Republic* p38+ Apr. 6, 1998; *New Statesman & Society* p37 Aug. 1995; *New York Review of Books* p22+ Jan. 12, 1995; *New York Times* E p3 Mar. 12, 1998, E p2 May 11, 1998, II p14 June 7, 1998; *New York Times Book Review* p14 Sep. 11, 1994, p3 Dec. 4, 1994, p7 Feb. 15, 1998; *New Yorker* p76+ Jan. 26, 1998; *Spectator* p31+ June 18, 1994, p71+ Dec. 20–27, 1997; *Voice Literary Supplement* p18 Oct. 1994; *Washington Post Book World* X p1 Aug. 28, 1994

SELECTED BOOKS: Nonfiction (untranslated from the French)—*Baudelaire lecteur de Balzac*, 1988; *La Poésie de Baudelaire et la poésie Français, 1838-1852*, 1993; Nonfiction (written in English)—*Balzac: A Life*, 1994; *Unlocking Mallarmé*, 1996; *Victor Hugo: A Biography*, 1997; as translator—Pichois, C. and J. Ziegler. *Baudelaire*, 1989

Robbins, Tom

July 22, 1936– Novelist

With the appearance of the hardcover edition of his first novel, *Another Roadside Attraction*, in 1971, Tom Robbins quietly entered the literary world. The edition was not a commercial success, and, at first, the mass-market paperback printing, which came out a year later, seemed destined to fare no better. By the late 1970s, however, *Roadside* had gained a cult following numbering in the hundreds of thousands, and Robbins's second novel, *Even Cowgirls Get the Blues* (1974), proved even more popular among the college-age readers responsible for the impressive sales of the first book. Together, the two novels have earned Robbins a reputation as both "the Prince of the Paperback Literati" and the quintessential counterculture novelist.

According to many readers, the immense appeal of *Roadside* and *Cowgirls* derived from their anti-establishment and feminist themes and the flamboyant, wildly inventive prose in which they are written—features that are prevalent in each of Robbins's four subsequent novels. All of Robbins's novels, moreover, reflect his penchant for chronicling the bizarre events that take place in a surreal world of his own imagining—a world populated with suitably eccentric characters (some of which are inanimate objects). Although his work at first glance appears lighthearted, his underlying goals have always been, by his own account, "deadly serious." "I write playfully, but I write to change people's lives," he explained to Mitchell S. Ross in an interview for the *New York Times Magazine* (February 12, 1976). "I can come to no other conclusion but that playfulness is a form of wisdom and not frivolity."

The oldest of the three children of a utility company executive, Thomas Eugene Robbins was born on July 22, 1936, in Blowing Rock, North Carolina. His mother, Katherine (Robinson) Robbins, wrote children's stories for religious magazines. Tom developed a passion for reading at an early age. "I was always reading as a kid," he told Larry McCaffery and Sinda Gregory, who interviewed him for *Alive and Writing: Interviews with American Authors of the 1980s* (1987). "I taught myself to read when I was five years old because I couldn't wait to get into books." At about the same time, he began "writing" stories of his own by dictating them to his mother. One such story involved a pilot who, after crashing on a deserted island, discovers a brown cow with yellow spots. "I wouldn't find that story out of place in what I'm doing now, and so I guess I haven't changed all that much," Robbins told Michael Rogers in an interview for *Rolling Stone* (November 17, 1977). "I had a very rich fantasy life as a child. And I still do as an adult."

Robbins's imagination was fueled by the transformation that Blowing Rock, which he once described as "a Dogpatch town whose economic backbone was picking up empty beer bottles for returns," would undergo each summer, when it would become a luxurious resort village. Businessmen who spent the rest of the year in Palm Beach, Florida, and Paris would flock to Blowing Rock to open their exclusive boutiques, while tourists drove through the streets in their expensive automobiles. "The dichotomy between the rich, sophisticated scene and the hillbilly scene affected me very much," he told McCaffery and Gregory. "It showed me how the ordinary suddenly could be changed into the extraordinary . . . , instilling in me the romantic idea of another life."

In the mid-1940s Robbins's family moved to Virginia. There Tom visited a circus for the first time and became fascinated with magic, a subject that would have an enormous influence on his writing. "I think maybe the carnival—the kind they had in the rural South—and the circuses were really the last vestiges of pagan celebrations. A dull, boring, vacant lot would suddenly fill with these strange people, and tents and banners and flags, and that night it would light up with neon," Robbins recalled to Michael Rogers. "It was a magical transformation, and I loved it." While working for the circus one summer, Robbins became infatuated with an exotic, blond coworker, who wore black patent-leather riding boots and breeches. "She had this pet black snake and scars on her arm where it had bitten her," Robbins told Peter Whitmer in an interview for *Saturday Review* (January/February 1985). "I have always been a romantic—one of those people who believes that a woman in pink circus tights contains all the secrets of the universe."

While attending high school in Warsaw, Virginia, Robbins played basketball, dated cheerleaders, and gained a reputation as an outgoing and generally rebellious youth. He also read voraciously, though he felt compelled to conceal his intellectual bent from his peers because, as he told Mitchell Ross, in the rural South "to read at all was to be a laughingstock." Eventually, his mischievous behavior led his parents to place him in Hargrave Military Academy. After graduating from high school, Robbins entered Washington and Lee University, also known as "the Princeton of the South," in Lexington, Virginia, where he was expected to mature into a more serious person. Two years later, however, Robbins withdrew from the university after he was kicked out of his fraternity for "lobbing biscuits at the housemother," he recalled to McCaffery and Gregory. As he explained to Michael Rogers, "It finally became apparent that I didn't have the makings of a southern gentleman."

Once freed from the constraints of a conventional university life, Robbins embarked on an existence as a peripatetic hippie, thumbing his way across the United States. "Hitching was a revelation," he recalled to Mari Edlin, who profiled him for *Publishers Weekly* (May 25, 1990). "I had always dreamed of travel, but I came from a family with no sense of mobility." His wandering lasted a decade, during which he crisscrossed the nation; at the same time, he also developed the literary voice that would later find expression in his fiction.

Robbins's first destination was Greenwich Village, in New York City, to which he moved in 1956 with hopes of becoming a poet. However, unable to support himself with his writing, he eventually decided to join the United States Air Force. The rigors of military life did little to reform his wayward tendencies. Robbins was stationed in South Korea, where he taught meteorology to the South Korean air force, but by his own account, he spent much of his time operating a black-market ring that dealt in cigarettes, soap, and toothpaste. "Later I found out that most of it was going into Red China," he told Mari Edlin, "so I figure that for about 13 months I was supplying Mao Tse-tung with all his Colgate."

On his return to the United States, Robbins enrolled at the Richmond Professional Institute, an art, drama, and music school that later expanded to become Virginia Commonwealth University. After graduating from the school, with academic honors and a grade-point average of 3.7, in 1960, Robbins took a job as a copy editor for the conservative *Richmond Times-Dispatch*, but he fit in no better there than he had in the military or at school. He first discovered that his journalistic instincts were out of sync with those of the paper's editors when, after illustrating Earl Wilson's syndicated music column with a photograph of the legendary black trumpeter Louis Armstrong, he was reprimanded by his boss. He was determined not to cater to the paper's racist editorial policies, however, and a few months later he defied the ban on featuring black musicians by running a photograph of Sammy Davis Jr. and his Scandinavian wife, May Britt.

He also resolved to move as far away from Virginia as he could without leaving the United States.

In 1962 Robbins moved to Seattle, Washington, the city that had been the home of the painters Morris Graves and Mark Tobey. "I was intrigued about what kind of landscape could produce a school of mystic painters," Robbins told Michael Rogers. Robbins's interest in mysticism led him to take courses in Eastern philosophy at the University of Washington's Far East Institute. During that period he also began to experiment with LSD and other psychedelic drugs, his first such experience taking place on July 16, 1963, which he has since described as his most "rewarding day ever." By then, he was working at the *Seattle Times* as a features editor and arts and entertainment critic. Over the coming years, and prior to the publication of his first novel, Robbins would contribute art criticism to *Seattle* magazine, *Artforum, Art in America,* and *Art International* as well as to the *Seattle Times,* and for this work he would be honored in 1997 with Seattle's Golden Umbrella award for lifetime contribution to the arts.

One day early in his career at the *Seattle Times,* Robbins called in "well," explaining to his manager that he had been ill since beginning work at the paper, but now that he was well he would be staying at home. During his interview with McCaffery and Gregory, Robbins talked about the effect that his experimentation with drugs had on him: "Mainly, psychedelics left me less rigid, intellectually and emotionally. . . . The borderlines between so-called reality and so-called fantasy, between dream and wakefulness, animate and inanimate were no longer as distinct, and I made some use of this newfound mobility in my writing."

In 1963 Robbins moved back to New York City, where he met Timothy Leary, the psychologist who had become famous for his experiments with mind-altering substances. "We were both at a vegetable stand and I was buying brussels sprouts," Robbins recalled to Peter Whitmer. "[Leary] said 'How can you tell the good ones?' I told him 'You pick the ones that are smiling.'" Leary and Robbins remained friends until Leary's death in 1996.

Within a year Robbins had returned to Seattle, where he took a job writing an art column for *Seattle* magazine and worked as a disc jockey for a rock music radio station. For some years, Robbins had been wondering about the impact on Western civilization if Christ's body were to be discovered in the Roman catacombs. Thinking that the idea might form the basis of a novel, Robbins began to research the history of early Christianity, and before long he became a "walking encyclopedia" on the period. Meanwhile, in about 1968, an editor from Doubleday had expressed his admiration for Robbins's *Seattle* art columns and asked him if he were interested in writing a book of creative criticism. Robbins used the opportunity to pitch his idea for his novel about Christ, even though the novel did not yet exist. "Robbins told him [the manuscript] was still a little rough," Michael Rogers reported, "and promptly went home and started writing."

While writing the book, Robbins attempted to evoke the spirit of the psychedelic revolution, a goal that he achieved by conceiving a nonlinear story line that "radiates" simultaneously, as he has put it, in many different directions. He also strove to promote the notion that Christianity, and organized religion in general, have prevented their practitioners from living truly spiritual lives. "You know, religion is organized spirituality," he told McCaffery and Gregory. "But there's an inherent contradiction there, because the moment you try to organize spirituality, you destroy its essence. So religion is spirituality in which the spiritual has been killed."

The completed novel, *Another Roadside Attraction*, centers on Plucky Purcell, a somewhat shady character who steals the mummy of Jesus Christ from the Vatican catacombs and transports it back to the state of Washington, where Purcell and his friends live at a roadside zoo and hot dog stand. Robbins's self-consciously extravagant prose enhances the novel's bizarre plot and unifies its underlying theme—which, according to the author, is the notion that meaning in life can be found simply by choosing "joy in spite of everything." "My characters suffer, they die, they look the beast of totalitarianism straight in the chops and still opt for joy," he told Ross. "I think this is what is appealing to people."

Sam Vaughan was one of the many Doubleday executives who were impressed by the manuscript. "I've read lots of loose-limbed manuscripts, full of all the freedom and license and nonsense of the moment," Vaughan said, according to the *New York Times Magazine* article. "But the difference between Robbins's stuff and the others, published and unpublished, is how well he writes, how right he often is, and the precision of his language. . . . I think he is a more intelligible but still funnier Brautigan, a Swiftian Shulman for our times, a witty and talented man." Doubleday promptly agreed to publish Robbins's novel, and the hardcover edition of *Another Roadside Attraction* appeared in 1971.

Sales of the hardcover edition were modest, apparently because the book's target audience, the so-called youth market, found the price of the book too high. However, after Ballantine reissued the book as a much less expensive paperback in 1972, sales picked up, albeit slowly, and by the late 1970s some 700,000 copies had been sold. "There was no hype, no hard sell; the book just took off by word of mouth," Robbins recalled to Mari Edlin. "I made more in royalties in six months than during the previous seven years combined." Female readers in particular have identified with Robbins's characters; one of his fans was so moved by his work that she traveled from her home in Arkansas to Washington to visit him. "A lot of women come by here," Robbins told Mitchell Ross. "It's one of the great fringe benefits of my life."

Meanwhile, Robbins had started to write his second novel, *Even Cowgirls Get the Blues*, and had acquired an agent, Phoebe Larmore, who in 1974 sold his novel-in-progress to Bantam for $50,000—20 times what he received for his first book. At that time, however, Bantam did not publish hardcover books, so in an unorthodox move, Bantam sold Houghton Mifflin the rights to publish both hardcover and trade paperback editions of the book, which came out in March and April 1976, respectively. Bantam published the mass-market paperback edition one year later. Getting the mass-market edition out so quickly proved to be a winning strategy, and *Cowgirls* became even more of a success than Robbins's first effort had been, selling some 1.3 million copies by 1980.

Even Cowgirls Get the Blues chronicles the adventures of Sissy Hankshaw, a beautiful, southern-born woman who, because she has abnormally large thumbs, is regarded as a freak by nearly everyone she meets. However, Sissy is wise enough to realize that her strength lies in what makes her unique, and she goes on to become the country's greatest hitchhiker. Among other places, she visits Rubber Rose Ranch, a health spa in North Dakota that has been taken over by a clan of feminist cowgirls who hope to turn the spa into the first female-run ranch. For many readers, and for the author as well, the book is first and foremost "a celebration of the feminine principle," Robbins told Mitchell Ross.

Because of the enormous commercial success of Robbins's first two books, Bantam more than tripled his previous advance when its editors decided to publish his third novel. Following its release, *Still Life with Woodpecker: A Sort of a Love Story* (1980) was an immediate hit among his readers. The novel tells of a love affair between a modern environmentalist princess and a good-hearted terrorist whose alias is The Woodpecker, and one of its messages is that to find meaning in life, an individual must realize that love and personal gratification are more important than collective happiness or the common good.

Robbins's fourth novel, *Jitterbug Perfume* (1984), was also a popular success; it quickly climbed the *New York Times* bestseller list, on which it remained for several months. In this book, as in the others, Robbins weaves the mystical with the poetic, combines seriousness and silliness, and often finds meaning in the absurd. At the center of the novel is a concern with scents, their ability to arouse desire and call forth memory, and their connection to spirituality and the supernatural. One plot line involves Priscilla, a waitress in Seattle who stumbles upon the coveted formula for a powerfully sensual perfume; another focuses on a deposed medieval king and his lover as they confront violence, disease, and starvation on their way to gaining immortality. At the novel's end, all the characters meet at a Mardi Gras celebration.

In the *Washington Post* (November 25, 1984), Rudy Rucker discussed the merits of *Jitterbug Perfume* in the context of Robbins's artistic evolution over the previous dozen years. "*Another Roadside Attraction* and *Even Cowgirls Get the Blues* were sixties novels—filled with mushrooms and visions, radicals and police," Rucker observed. "*Still Life with Woodpecker* is about the seventies viewed as aftermath of the sixties. How does *Jitterbug Perfume* fit in? Has Tom Robbins moved into the eighties? Yes and no. Robbins is still very much his Pan-worshipping self, yet his new book is lovingly plotted, with every conceivable loose end nailed down tight. . . . The ideas are the same as ever, [but] the form is contemporary, neorealistic craftsmanship."

In Robbins's next novel, *Skinny Legs and All* (1990), the author once again expressed his skepticism regarding organized religion and his reverence for the mysterious power of female sexuality. The book tells the story of Ellen Cherry Charles, a struggling painter, and her husband, Boomer Petway, a redneck welder-turned-sculptor who, despite his lack of talent, achieves artistic stardom. Robbins also introduced his readers to a band of inanimate objects that make a pilgrimage to Jerusalem. Yet another of the many threads of the narrative concerns Salome, an exotic dancer whose performance of the Dance of the Seven Veils in a restaurant where Ellen works as a waitress constitutes the novel's climax. As she takes off the veils in which she is clothed, each of which represents an illusory aspect of life, she challenges both the audience and the reader to choose truth and life over deception and death.

In 1994 the director Gus Van Sant made a movie version of *Even Cowgirls Get the Blues*, starring Uma Thurman and Keanu Reeves. Expectations were high, but the movie was a disappointment for both critics and fans. "Much of the liveliness of Mr. Robbins's novel comes from the way it scatters all over the place," the *New York Times* (May 20, 1994) noted. "Mr. Van Sant's movie is all over the place, too, but that strategy makes the film scattershot instead of vibrant."

In late 1994 Robbins published the novel *Half Asleep in Frog Pajamas*, in which another array of unique characters undertake a fanciful adventure. The story depicts four days in the life of a young woman named Gwen, a stockbroker in Seattle, who meets Larry Diamond, a former broker now suffering from rectal cancer. While Larry seeks a cure from an unconventional doctor, Gwen searches for a friend, a 300-pound psychic, who has disappeared.

"My theory on Tom Robbins is that unless his work was imprinted on you when you were 19 and stoned, you'll find him forever unreadable," Karen Karbo wrote in the *New York Times* (October 30, 1994). "A sober 21-year-old is already too steely-eyed and seasoned to frolic in Mr. Robbins's trademark cuckoo plots, woo-woo philosophizing, overwrought metaphors and cheerful misogyny." She concluded that, while she did not enjoy *Half Asleep in Frog Pajamas*, the novel is "vintage Robbins, a recommendation for those of you who can stand it." *Booklist* (August 19, 1994), however, was more enthusiastic, claiming that while the novel may seem "gimmicky" at first glance, it possesses a "genuineness, a warmth, a humor, and an incredibly compelling plot, which hold our attention to the end."

Throughout his life, Robbins has worked to cultivate a positive outlook. "You can change the world by how you look at it," he told Edlin. "It will become primarily what you are looking for." Despite his carefree nature, Robbins is extremely self-disciplined. Because he writes only one draft of each novel and never uses an outline, he has been known to spend as much as an hour on a sentence, and he rarely completes more than two pages a day. "I'm probably more interested in sentences than anything else in life," Robbins told Deirdre Donahue in an interview for *USA Today* (April 18, 1990). After completing a book, he usually takes a year-long holiday, during which he travels as far away from Western civilization as possible, to such places as eastern and southern Africa. Traveling, Robbins has explained, helps him appreciate the mystical, erotic, and romantic parts of life.

According to many of those who have met him, Tom Robbins is a soft-spoken man who cherishes his privacy. He lives in the fishing village of La Conner, Washington, 65 miles north of Seattle. "Being alone is one of the most difficult things to learn, but you can't succeed if you can't spend time by yourself," he told Mari Edlin. "It does, however, tend to make you abnormal." He no longer rides motorcycles, though he collects miniature replicas of motorcycles along with other toys and rubber stamps. His home is decorated with Andy Warhol silkscreens and lush plants. With his second wife, Terrie, he has one grown son, Fleetwood Star, whom he has called "the apple, the pineapple, the mango, the orchard of my eye." (The marriage ended in divorce in 1974.) Robbins's free spirit and love for life and women has not gone unnoticed by those close to him. As he recalled to Michael Rogers, one woman with whom he had a romantic relationship once told him, "The trouble with you, Tom, is that you have too much fun."

Robbins's seventh novel, *Fierce Invalids Home from Hot Climates,* is scheduled to be published by Bantam Books in May 2000.—D.B.

SUGGESTED READING: *Booklist* Aug. 19, 1994; *Kirkus Reviews* Aug. 15, 1994; *New York Times* p10 May 20, 1994, p27 Oct. 30, 1994; *New York Times Magazine* p17 Feb. 12, 1976; *People* p123+ Apr. 1, 1985; *Publishers Weekly* p41+ May 25, 1990; *Rolling Stone* p66+ Nov. 17, 1977; *Saturday Review* p50+ Jan./Feb. 1985, with photos; *USA Today* Apr. 18, 1990; *Washington Post* Nov. 27, 1984; *Alive and Writing: Interviews with American Authors of the 1980s*, 1987; *Book Review Digest*, 1995; *Contemporary Authors* vol.

81–84, 1979; *Contemporary Authors New Revision Series* vol. 29, 1990, vol. 59, 1998; *Contemporary Literary Criticism*, 1985, 1991; *Dictionary of Literary Biography Yearbook*, 1980

SELECTED WORKS: *Another Roadside Attraction*, 1971; *Even Cowgirls Get the Blues*, 1974; *Still Life with Woodpecker: A Sort of a Love Story*, 1980; *Jitterbug Perfume*, 1984; *Skinny Legs and All*, 1990; *Half Asleep in Frog's Pajamas*, 1994

Paddy Cook

Roberts, Michèle

May 20, 1949– Novelist; poet

The novelist and poet Michèle Roberts is known for her powerful portrayals of women and her use of religious and mythical symbolism in her fiction. Particularly notable for these attributes are the novels *The Wild Girl* (1984), a reinterpretation of the Gospels through the eyes of Mary Magdalene; *The Book of Mrs. Noah* (1987), which follows the journey of six women as they explore the history of women while traveling in an imaginary ark; and, most recently, *Impossible Saints* (1997), in which a woman who loosely resembles Saint Teresa leaves her convent on a quest to become a writer and to found a colony for feminists. Roberts is also a popular poet, and has published four collections: *Licking the Bed Clean* (1978), *Smile, Smile, Smile, Smile* (1980), *The Mirror of the Mother: Selected Poems 1975–1985* (1985), and *All the Selves I Was: New and Selected Poems* (1995).

Michèle B. Roberts was born in Bushey, Hertfordshire, England, on May 20, 1949, to an English father and a French mother. Her father, Reginald George Roberts, worked as a businessman; her mother, the former Monique Pauline Joseph Caulle, taught school. In an autobiographical statement written for *World Authors 1990–1995*, Roberts claimed that her background was intrinsically important to her development as an author: "Being half-French and half-English helped make me a writer, since from the start I loved language and had to wrestle with belonging to two cultures and feeling most at ease on the boat crossing the sea between England and France. Being brought up a Catholic also inspired me: the misogyny of Catholic theology contradicted by the richness of image and legend." Her interest in language was also stimulated by her cockney-accented English grandmother, who amused her grandchildren by making up comedic rhymes. "We kids were convinced that 'brimming chamber pot' was the funniest phrase in the language. My grandmother's tales made me long to be a story-teller, too," the author noted in an interview with Brenda Polan of the *Guardian* (May 27, 1987).

Roberts was educated at Oxford University and graduated with honors in 1970. Two years later she received a library associate degree from the University of London with the intention of becoming a librarian. During the years she spent finding her particular writer's "voice," she worked as a cook, a librarian, a teacher, a cleaner, a researcher, and a counselor. Only after many years in a women's writing group—and after accepting the tenets of feminism as her own creed—did she find the strength to write honestly and in her own voice. As she explained to Polan: "There was a problem, in the earlier years of the women's movement, of being excluded from the mainstream, of being treated as a literary ghetto, a bizarre genre called 'the hysterical feminist movement.' Yet when you get a man writing about the world, you get a male perspective on the world and it's called the human perspective; why shouldn't men read about the world from a female perspective?"

In 1978 the Women's Press published Roberts's first novel, *A Piece of the Night*. The novel described a young woman's development from school girl to wife and mother to, ultimately, lesbian and feminist. As Roberts may have expected, the book was treated as a cornerstone of the "hysterical feminist movement." In the *Times Literary Supplement* (December 1, 1978), Blake Morrison complained that a great deal of the novel "gives the same impression of a book written under the stern eye of a women's workshop group, and not much interested in winning the hearts of those outside the charmed circle." Valentine Cunningham of the *New Statesman* (November 3, 1978) found the work to be "a runaway chaos of inchoate bits, an incoherence that slumps well short of the better novel it might with more toil have become." After weathering the bad press, Roberts won the *Gay*

News Literary Award of 1978 for *A Piece of the Night.*

The harsh criticism did not prevent the young author from publishing again. That same year, Roberts, along with a number of other notable female authors, including Alison Fell, printed short stories in the collection *Tales I Tell My Mother.* She also released her first collection of her own poetry, entitled *Licking the Bed Clean,* and in 1980 she released her second, *Smile, Smile, Smile, Smile.* Roberts's poetry appeared with that of Judith Karantris and Micheken Wandor in *Touch Papers: Three Women Poets,* in 1982.

The Visitation, Roberts's second novel, was published in 1983. The story follows a woman named Helen, both in the present day, as she contacts female archetypes in her dreams, and in her childhood, as a way to explain her present views on religion and the Catholic Church. In a review for the *Times Literary Supplement* (October 26, 1984), Laura Marcus found that the novel clouded "the distinctions between reality and fantasy in a prose which is full, resonant, and at times overcharged."

Roberts's next novel, *The Wild Girl* (1984), was also one of her most controversial. The novel professes to be the fifth gospel, told by Mary Magdalene, the prostitute who repented and became a follower of Jesus. While the Mary of *The Wild Girl* is, in many ways, similar to the figure in the Gospels, she is also Roberts's creation, and over the course of the novel she becomes a full messenger of the Word as well as the mother of Jesus's daughter. Needless to say, the book sparked a major controversy in England. While many people accused Roberts of blasphemy, others, like the reviewer for *Time Out* (December 1984), found the book to be "a powerful attack on the law of the Father and a timely reminder that old myths do not just fade away." Many critics, however, debated the effectiveness of Roberts's feminist argument. Kate Fullbrook of *British Book News* (January 1985) found that "the sentiments that animate this novel are fine, even noble. But the fiction itself never comes alive. Mary Magdalene remains nothing but a committed feminist of the 1980s; Jesus becomes nothing but a simple archetype for the non-sexist male."

In 1987 Roberts published her next novel, *The Book of Mrs. Noah.* Once again challenging religious folklore, the author presented Mrs. Noah, a librarian who imagines that a group of disenchanted women from various time periods and of many ages have gathered together on an ark. While on board the ship, a symbolic womb containing the dreams of all the women, Mrs Noah hopes that they will collaborate on the great history of womankind. The book received mixed notices. Reviewing the novel in the *Listener* (September 10, 1987), Jennifer McKay wrote that "The trouble is that as a novel of ideas Mrs. Noah's ideas are not especially novel and they form too heavy a load for the fragile narrative." Helen Birch disagreed with this assessment in her review for the *New Statesman and Society*

(May 22, 1987) calling it the author's "most ambitious and carefully conceived novel to date." Brenda Polan found the book to be "a slow, rich read of pleasurable complexity which taps a whole library of mythologies and mingles them with wonderfully immediate accounts of the lives of her Sybils, a bunch of modern-day writers who meet up in a Creative Writing Group in the chapel on board Mrs. Noah's Ark."

In the Red Kitchen (1990), Roberts's next novel, follows the lives of four main characters through three eras—ancient Egypt, Victorian England, and present-day London—as Roberts explores the idea of female bonding by women in different eras. As the novel's present-day heroine, Hattie, is restoring a run-down Victorian house, she awakens the ghost of a former inhabitant—Flora Milk. Flora, based on the 19th-century spiritual medium Florence Cook, guides readers through the maze of characters and eras. In an interview with Pamela Johnson for the *Guardian* (March 22, 1990), Roberts explained how she developed the concept for the novel: "I was investigating an idea of femininity which has to do with getting your house in shape. Women have taken on men's evaluation of housework—dirty work which no one wants to do. . . . To cherish a home is to make reparation to a damaged, female maternal body."

Roberts produced her next two novels in quick succession: *Psyche and the Hurricane* appeared in 1991 and *Daughters of the House* in 1992. Of the two, *Daughters of the House* is the more notable. In it, Roberts recounted the lives of two cousins, Thérèse and Léonie, who were raised in a small Norman town in France. They help each other through puberty and the death of Thérèse's mother but are later separated when Léonie marries and Thérèse enters a convent. When Thérèse returns after a 20-year absence, having permanently left the convent, she discovers that their relationship has changed for the worse. Although the novel garnered Roberts some of her most glowing notices, it also attracted some mixed reviews. In *New Statesman and Society* (October 9, 1992), Judy Cooke remarked: "This author allows her characters their full complexity. . . . An unhappy, intelligent pair, their rivalry for maternal affection is to prove longer-lasting than any subsequent emotion. This is a fascinating story, full of psychological insight. Its necessary obscurities and slow unravellings are balanced by rich descriptive writing." In the *Times Literary Supplement* (September 18, 1992) Roz Kaveney wrote that "*Daughters of the House* derives nourishment from Gothic and detective novels, yet its direction proves profoundly subversive of those genres. When, towards its end, decisions are made and mysteries provided with an explanation, we feel this is a closing down of fertile possibilities, rather than as resolution or enlightenment. . . . This is a book in which choices have consequences, and stories morals, but Michèle Roberts has the wisdom not to make any of these overwhelming." Patricia Craig of the *London Review of*

Books (December 3, 1992), however, bemoaned, "Michèle Roberts, it seems, is one of those writers who equates obscurity with depth. . . . The novel itself gives the impression of something buried in the cellar."

Roberts's most recent novel, *Impossible Saints* (1997), explores the history of women's writing through the experiences of three generations of women: Josephine, her mother Beatrice, and Josephine's niece Isabel. The novel concentrates on Josephine, who leaves a convent to write "more hasty, more honest" stories than ever before— particularly about the 11 female saints whose lives are chronicled in Jacobus de Voragine's medieval text, *The Golden Legend*—and who founds a colony for women writers. A representative of the earliest generation of female writers, Beatrice is unable to reveal her love of writing and books to the world, and instead keeps her work locked away in a chest. After she dies, Josephine reads her mother's books and writings, but her angry father burns everything just after she discovers it, and then sends her to a convent. When Josephine herself dies, Isabel takes up her aunt's story, and begins the process of editing the saints' tales. Reviewing the work in the *London Review of Books* (October 2, 1997), Elaine Showalter remarked: "While in some respects Roberts is writing what is by now a familiar, even classic narrative of the saving power of sisterhood to resist women's cultural silencing, her work has a violent subtext that tells another story. Along with conventional post-Freudian images of female selfhood as treasure chest, secret chamber, or dream house, are images of mutilation, dismemberment, chopping, wounding, and biting. Roberts writes lovingly about food, but almost all her 'saints' are hunger artists who slice into vegetables as if they were animals, and salivate over books."

Michèle Roberts's other works also include the books *During Mother's Absence* (1993) and *Flesh and Blood* (1994), as well as *All the Selves I Was: New and Selected Poems* (1995). She is a contributor of nonfiction to *City Limits* and of poetry to other well-established periodicals. She was also a poetry editor at *Spare Rib* between 1975 and 1977, and at *City Limits* between 1981 and 1983.—C.M.

SUGGESTED READING: *British Book News* p49+ Jan. 1985; *Guardian* p10 May 27, 1987, p19 Mar. 22, 1990; *Listener*, Sep. 10, 1987; *London Review of Books* p28 Dec. 3, 1992, p 34 Oct. 2, 1997; *New Statesman and Society* p590 Nov. 3, 1978, p 27+ May 22, 1987, p 34 Oct. 9, 1992; *Time Out* Dec. 1984; *Times Literary Supplement* p1404 Dec. 1, 1978, p 1224, Oct. 26, 1984, p 23, Sep. 18, 1992; *Contemporary Authors New Revision Series* vol. 58, 1997

SELECTED BOOKS: Novels—*A Piece of the Night*, 1978; *The Visitation*, 1983; *The Wild Girl*, 1984; *The Book of Mrs. Noah*, 1987; *In the Red Kitchen*, 1990; *Psyche and the Hurricane*, 1991; *Daughters of the House*, 1992; *During Mother's Absence*, 1993; *Flesh and Blood*, 1994; *Impossible Saints*, 1997; Poetry—*Licking the Bed Clean*, 1978; *Smile, Smile, Smile, Smile*, 1980; *The Mirror of the Mother: Selected Poems: 1975–1985*, 1985; *All the Selves I Was: New and Selected Poems*, 1995

Robinson, Kim Stanley

Mar. 23, 1952– Science-fiction writer.

The award-winning science-fiction writer Kim Stanley Robinson takes great pains to ensure that nothing in his stories contradicts the laws that govern the physical universe, and according to most aficionados of science fiction, he has succeeded to a remarkable degree, even though he has no background in science. While working on his famous *Mars Trilogy*, Robinson amassed a library of books about cold-weather engineering and the biology of aging. "I was working at the edge of my understanding," he told Elisabeth Sherwin for the *Davis Virtual Market* (January 21, 1996, on-line). "If I had a technical editor, I would be greatly helped."

The lack of a technical editor notwithstanding, the *Mars Trilogy* established Robinson as "the preeminent contemporary practitioner of science fiction," Edward James wrote in the *Times Literary Supplement* (May 3, 1996), in a review of *Blue Mars*, the final novel in the trilogy. "He has earned that position by taking the central tenet of science fiction—the extrapolation of current trends and beliefs into the construction of a future history—to greater lengths than any of his predecessors, and the *Mars* books are likely to be the touchstone of what is possible in the genre for a long time to come." Robinson is the first science-fiction writer to win one of the grants awarded through the National Science Foundation's Antarctic Artists and Writers Program.

In an autobiographical statement submitted to *World Authors 1990-1995*, the author had this to say: "More and more, I think of myself as a California writer. I grew up in California, and now I am living here again, and for good, and I feel that I am in my own country, in a way that being 'in America' never makes me feel. California is country enough for anyone.

"Even my choice of genre, science fiction, follows from this love for California. I grew up in Orange County, when it was still mostly orange groves, and being an intense reader as a child, I often imagined I was in a community much like Tom Sawyer's and Huck Finn's. The land supported this illusion, and I grew up in a kind of Hannibal,

Miriam Berkley

Kim Stanley Robinson

approaching an ecological crisis, brought on by the human population reaching the planet's carrying capacity; civilization has to change to meet this challenge, or disaster will result. So utopia is not just a theoretical exercise, but necessary planning or modeling. And California, being quickly inundated by people is at the forefront of the problem. At the same time it remains a landscape of tremendous beauty and variety. It seems possible here to invent a sustainable way of life, a permaculture, that will not be a giant world- city (an impossible old sf dream) but rather some kind of supremely sophisticated reintegration with nature, as yet unimagined.

"So science fiction and wilderness could perhaps be reconciled, in this attempt at a California utopia. From a distance I wrote 'A Short, Sharp Shock,' which is a kind of fantasia or love letter to the California landscapes; then I moved back home, and began work on my Mars trilogy. Virginia Woolf once said that the usefulness of a book for the writer is how much it allows the writer to say what he or she wants to say anyway. By that criterion the Mars books were the best experience of my career. In them the terraformed Mars comes more and more to resemble California's Sierra Nevada; meanwhile, by expanding the form of the novel to include great masses of expository material (I am by no means the first novelist to do this) I was able to discuss at length human character, utopian social structures, our relationship to technology and to landscape, and the processes of history. Mars served not only as a fascinating and real place in its own right, but a good metaphor for our current situation.

"My Antarctic novel came about as a by-product of my research on Mars. It was a relief to write again about a place I had really seen. I had great fun with it, and believe it expresses the joy of the people in that place, much as my book *Escape from Kathmandu* did for the Himalayas. I hope other books like that, celebrating places I have visited, come to me. Meanwhile I am embarked on another long science fiction novel with utopian aspects. I plan to stay in Davis, California, and learn more about the land and the people here, and do what I can to help make California a good place for the long haul, by writing science fiction novels."

Missouri, of the mind. But in reality it was the beginning of the 1960s, and in that tumultuous decade I grew up, and the orange groves were cut down, to be replaced by the horrible freeway-mall-and-condominium sprawl one sees there now. It was a rapid transformation, and I think now that I experienced very powerfully what people call 'future shock.'

"I went to the University of California, San Diego, and there discovered science fiction, at the height of [science fiction's] New Wave, perhaps the artistic peak of the genre, and immediately I felt that this was the literature for me—it spoke most clearly to me, and expressed my experience best—it was what life felt like. I began writing stories at that time, and they were science fiction from the start.

"I also began spending a lot of time backpacking in California's Sierra Nevada. I loved science fiction and I loved the mountains; for a long time I experienced this as a kind of contradiction or paradox, an oddity. Sometimes I tried to force the two interests together, but mostly they were separate spheres.

"I wrote three science fiction novels set in Orange County, each describing a radically different future: an after-the-fall novel, a dystopia, and a utopia. The utopian novel, *Pacific Edge*, was by far the most difficult to write. I felt the burden of having to plausibly solve all the world's problems, and the form of the novel as I had been pursuing it up until then was not adequate to the task of describing large-scale social change. But the revealing of the problem was the beginning of coming to grips with it. I saw that utopia was the concept that brought all my interests together. We live in a world that is

Kim Stanley Robinson was born on March 23, 1952, in Waukegan, Illinois. While he was still quite young, his family moved to Orange County, California, an area that is the setting of three of Robinson's novels—*The Wild Shore*, *The Gold Coast*, and *Pacific Edge*. Robinson earned a B.A. degree at the University of California (UC) at San Diego. He then attended Boston University, in Massachusetts, where he received a master's degree in English. While working toward a doctorate at his undergraduate alma mater, he wrote short stories, many of which were published in magazines. In 1982, UC San Diego awarded him a Ph.D.

in English and American literature. Afterward, with his wife, Lisa Howland Nowell, he moved to Zurich, Switzerland, where his wife completed a postdoctoral dissertation in environmental toxicology. During the two years that the couple lived abroad, Robinson continued to write short fictional pieces.

Robinson's first novel, *The Wild Shore*, came out in 1984. It was published by Ace Books, a firm that is well-known for discovering excellent but as-yet-unknown authors. *The Wild Shore* is an account of the aftermath of a nuclear holocaust in the United States. For reasons that are never made clear, the United Nations has strictly prohibited the reconstruction of the nation, and its technology and infrastructure remain woefully primitive. The story is told by a 17-year-old boy named Henry who lives in what had been Orange County. Intrigued by tales describing the nation as it used to be, Henry joins a new group of American resistors who refuse to accept the UN's sanctions.

The Wild Shore was applauded not only for its appeal as science fiction, but also as a work of literature: In the *Magazine of Fantasy and Science Fiction* (May 1984), Algis Budrys, who has been called "the premier book reviewer" of science fiction, wrote, "Robinson's approach to storytelling is the traditional literary one, in its best sense, rather than the unique tone science fiction has developed in years of trying to translate commercial values into literature. . . . What he has here is a Class A science-fiction idea, in that he has proposed a future which is both clearly possible and yet has not hitherto been notably proposed. Taken purely as a proposition in the futurology of political science, this milieu demands serious attention." In *The Washington Post* (April 22, 1984), the critic Stephen P. Brown wrote, "Robinson, in his quiet low-key way, has avoided [the] trap [of becoming trite] by relying on one of the most powerful weapons in any writer's arsenal—rich, eccentric characterization." *Locus* magazine awarded *The Wild Shore* its 1985 Locus Award for best first novel.

Robinson's next works included the novels *Icehenge* (1984), in which a Stonehenge-like structure is found on the planet Pluto in the 23d century, and *The Memory of Whiteness* (1985), in which the solar system is fully colonized by cultures that have only orchestral music in common. In 1986, a collection of Robinson's previously published short stories appeared, under the title *The Planet on the Table*.

In *The Gold Coast* (1988), which takes place in the 21st century, Orange County is grotesquely overdeveloped. "People are as frantic as the landscape is dense, and there's a deadness in the soul[s] of most," T. Jefferson Parker wrote in the *Los Angeles Times Book Review* (March 13, 1988). The hero of *The Gold Coast* is Jim McPherson, a young poet who joins an extremist group bent on destroying the national defense system. He feels ambivalent about their mission, though, because his father works for a defense contractor. "Robinson has suc-

ceeded at a novelist's toughest challenge," Parker concluded: "He's made us look at the world around us. This isn't escapist stuff—it sends you straight into a confrontation with yourself." *Pacific Edge* (1990), the third novel that Robinson set in a futuristic Orange County, records the struggle to preserve the county's last piece of wilderness.

The Mars Trilogy is the series for which Robinson remains best known. The first of the three books, *Red Mars* (1993), describes how humans go about "terraforming" the unarable planet; simultaneously, it poses questions about the moral and political ramifications of such an undertaking. While *Red Mars* was indisputably one of the most successful science-fiction works of that year—it won the 1993 Nebula Award from the Science Fiction and Fantasy Writers of America—it received mixed reviews. In an enthusiastic assessment for the journal *New Science* (January 30, 1993), David V. Barrett wrote, "Readers may learn more about the reality of Mars . . . than [they would] from most textbooks—and with far more enjoyment. . . . [The story] is believable; there is not a single tentacled monster in sight. . . . There is, however, a lot of narrative tension and even the odd bit of swashbuckling." And in the *New York Times Book Review* (January 13, 1993), Gerald Jonas described *Red Mars* as "an absorbing novel of ideas, notable for the opportunity it provides to watch a scientifically informed imagination of rare ambition at work." John Gribbin, by contrast, who also critiqued *Red Mars* for *New Science* (March 13, 1993), complained that the book "could be described as all science and no fiction." "It was difficult to care [about] what happened to any of the characters, and the failure to be good fiction is even more serious than the failure of others to get the science right. . . . I would sooner read . . . NASA manuals."

Green Mars (1994), the second book in the trilogy, earned the World Science Fiction Society's 1994 Hugo Award. In *Green Mars*, the terraformed planet bears a strong resemblance to Earth. A diverse group of rebels—sons, daughters, and grandchildren of the planet's original settlers—want to liberate Mars from Earth. Many of the pioneers who appeared in *Red Mars* have become the populace's wisest mentors. According to Roland Green, writing for *Booklist* (February 1, 1994), *Green Mars* was "Robinson's best book and possibly the best of the many and various our-future-on-Mars novels to date." In the *New Statesman* (October 29, 1993), however, David Barrett wrote, "The diversity of political morality is excellent, the planetary setting utterly credible, and the science impeccable. So why is this . . . novel such heavy going? Robinson has labored so hard to make it real that he's forgotten that a novel . . . should entertain as well as educate."

The final book of the *Mars Trilogy*, *Blue Mars* (1996), won the 1997 Hugo Award and is one of the best-selling science-fiction novels of all time. This book deals with the completion of the terraforming of Mars, the settlers' fight for independence from Earth, and the threat of an approaching ice age. In *New Science* (June 1, 1996), Elizabeth Sourbut wrote that *Blue Mars* "combines Big Science and real people. Robinson is a master of characterization, and he . . . succeeds in keeping his characters from being swamped by the huge Martian landscape he evokes. . . . [He] tackles the difficult questions that most writers gloss over [and] comes up with difficult questions that most writers gloss over." "Robinson's research into Mars and its areography threatens, occasionally, to overwhelm the reader," Edward James acknowledged in the *Times Literary supplement* (May 3, 1996), but, he added, "it also adds to his authority, and to the paradoxical realism of this very impressive work of the imagination." Writing for the *New York Times Book Review* (June 30, 1996), Gerald Jonas contended that *Blue Mars* "represents a breakthrough even from [Robinson's] own consistently high level of achievement. . . . With *Blue Mars*, it becomes clear that this trilogy is not a loosely connected series of variations on a Martian theme, but a tightly constructed novel on an epic scale that must be read in chronological order to appreciate fully." Shortly after completing the trilogy, Robinson published a companion volume called *The Martians* (1999), a collection of fiction and nonfiction about Mars written by others and also some of his reminiscences of experiences writing the *Mars* series.

As Robinson explained in his autobiographical statement, he chose the setting and the theme of *Antarctica* (1997), his most recent novel, while doing research for his *Mars Trilogy* in the early 1990s. "I kept running across references to Antarctica," he wrote in a piece for his publisher's web site. "It was the part of Earth most like Mars, and scientists studying Mars often went to Antarctica to do research. I had read about the classic Antarctic explorers when I was young, and now, reading about it again, my interest was rekindled." In the acknowledgments in a book he had read, he had noticed a reference made to the National Science Foundation's Antarctic Artists and Writers Program, and he subsequently learned that those chosen to participate in the program "had to be doing art or literature that was specifically about Antarctica. They would not, for instance, send me down there to do research for a book about Mars. So, I thought, I'm going to have to write a book about Antarctica."

Robinson spent six weeks in Antarctica in 1995. Because of the extremely harsh weather, his plans to meet with scientists who were working out of McMurdo, the American base camp at Antarctica, often fell through. "Only at the moment of a flight could you be sure it was really going to happen," Robinson explained on the web site. "At first this was disorienting, even maddening. But when I became used to it, I realized what it was; it was freedom. . . . I got outrageously cold, and ate huge meals, and laughed a lot, and listened to a million stories. And of course all the time I was thinking, 'What about my story? What story will I tell?' I wanted Antarctica to be more than just an exotic backdrop for a story that could have happened anywhere. I wanted to do more than just retell the classic stories in an updated form. I wanted to tell Antarctica's true story."

In light of the vast amount of oil that lies beneath the massive ice cap that covers Antarctica—Earth's fifth-largest continent—the international dispute that occurs in Robinson's *Antarctica* could all too easily happen in reality, in spite of the Antarctica Treaty, which at present governs the activities of all nations on the continent. "In the next century, things will get interesting," Robinson said to Elisabeth Sherwin. "I think we're headed for an environmental crisis, and it has to do with massive overpopulation. I'm not cheerful about the future. Historically, the world has not responded well to crises, but I want to remain hopeful. We have the spiritual and technical abilities to pull through. . . . We could get in balance with the environment and manage the population."

Kim Stanley Robinson has won Hugo, Nebula, and World Fantasy Awards for various short stories. The writer lives in West Davis, California, with his wife, Lisa Howland Nowell, and their two sons. A passionate lover of the natural world, he enjoys swimming and mountain trekking, and, he told Sherwin, "I try to fit wilderness writing into science fiction as much as I can."
—B.S.

SUGGESTED READING: *Bantam Doubleday Dell* (on-line); *Davis Virtual Market*, Jan. 21, 1996 (on-line); *More About the Author* (on-line); *Los Angeles Times Book Review* Mar. 13, 1988; *Magazine of Fantasy and Science Fiction* May 1984; *New Science* Jan. 30, 1993, Mar. 13, 1993, June 1, 1996; *New Statesman* Oct. 29, 1993; *New York Times Book Review* Jan. 13, 1993, June 30, 1996; *Times Literary Supplement* May 3, 1996; *Washington Post* Apr. 22, 1984; *Contemporary Authors* vol. 126, 1989; *Contemporary Literary Criticism* vol. 34, 1984

SELECTED BOOKS: Fiction—*The Wild Shore*, 1984; *Icehenge*, 1984; *The Memory of Whiteness*, 1985; *The Planet on the Table*, 1986; *The Gold Coast*, 1988; *Pacific Edge*, 1990; *Red Mars*, 1993; *Green Mars*, 1994; *Blue Mars* 1996; *Antarctica*, 1997; As editor *The Martians*, 1999

Robinson, Roxana

1947– Biographer; novelist; short-story writer

Due to the label's connotation of a "morally deficient" privileged class, Roxana Robinson is wary of being branded a "WASP writer." Yet she has indeed chosen to write about wealthy white Anglo-Saxon Protestants residing in such places as Manhattan's Upper East Side and Greenwich, Connecticut. Rather than exploring issues of money and power, Robinson instead probes the relationships of marriage and family. The results—the short-story collections *A Glimpse of Scarlet and Other Stories* (1991) and *Asking for Love and Other Stories* (1996), and the novels *Summer Light* (1987) and *This Is My Daughter* (1998)—are works of fiction containing characters often described by critics as rich in depth and emotion, despite their stereotypically shallow and passionless lifestyles. Robinson is also the author of *Georgia O'Keeffe: A Life* (1989), a landmark biography of the great American artist.

Robinson submitted the following autobiographical profile to *World Authors 1990–1995*: "I was born in Pine Mountain, Kentucky, where my father, Stuyvesant Barry, had gone to teach at a settlement school in Harlan County. Our family lived there for three years before moving back to the Northeast. My father was from New York, where he had been a lawyer, like his father, before he left the law and the Episcopal Church to become a teacher and a Quaker.

"I grew up in Bucks County, Pennsylvania, which was at that time farm country, quite rural and beautiful. Horses were my childhood passion, and at the age of twelve I was given an unschooled three-year-old mare, which I rode bareback and haphazardly across the countryside. I spent much of my time outside, in that open gentle landscape. I was the fourth of five children. We all attended the Buckingham Friends' School, of which our father became the principal. Because my father stayed late every day, I spent long solitary afternoons in the school library, where I read every book on horses that they had. I went on to boarding school at The Shipley School, in Bryn Mawr, (where I received the Prize for Fiction). After graduation I went to Bennington College [in 1964], where I studied with Howard Nemerov, Stanley Edgar Hyman, and Bernard Malamud; Malamud was my counselor. After my sophomore year I left and went to New York where I worked for a year at Dodd, Mead Publishers, reading unsolicited manuscripts. I then married [David Alger, in 1967] and finished my degree at the University of Michigan [in 1969]. I returned to New York (where I actually took my last half-year at the New School).

"I worked for several years at Sotheby's [from 1970 to 1974], in the American Paintings department. It was a wonderful place to learn, and it was there that I became interested in American art. I was then writing fiction, but not publishing it, and

I began to write about American art. After Sotheby's, I worked briefly at another gallery [the Terry Dintenfass Gallery, from 1974 to 1975], then I moved to the country outside New York and began writing full time.

"Writing was a habit in my family. Harriet Beecher Stowe and Catherine Beecher were great-great-great aunts, and many other family members—less famous—were also writers. I grew up with books, read everything I could find, and began to write as soon as I could read. My parents read out loud to us—Thurber was a family favorite. The arrival of the *New Yorker* was a great event, and my mother still has those issues with J. D. Salinger's Franny and Zooey stories.

"It took me a long time to get published, but I was fortunate in having the encouragement of two supportive editors, Mary D. Kierstead at the *New Yorker* and Michael Curtis at the *Atlantic*, both of whom came later to publish my work. My first published story was "Daughter," which came out in *McCall's* in 1980.

"When I started writing, fiction was what I found most compelling. John Updike, with his incomparable style and boundless sense of humanity, was certainly the writer who influenced me the most, but some others whom I devoured while I was starting out were Elizabeth Bowen, Elizabeth Taylor, and Henry Green, as well as—of course—Virginia Woolf.

"When Georgia O'Keeffe died in 1986, I was asked by Harper & Row to write her biography. She was a wonderful subject, and in some ways that book was like a novel. I was given the plot and the characters, and my task was to find the material and the understanding that would make it all come alive for the reader.

"What interests me most as a fiction writer is the theme of the family. I find it endlessly fruitful, remarkably complex, and breathtakingly rich. The family is where the heat is, it's the center of all our lives. Love, rage, resentment, jealousy, forgiveness, tenderness—this is where it all begins. The family is the place that starts us, that nourishes or starves us, the place from which all our secret feelings derive. It has formed us, no matter what we think or wish.

"This is my subject. What I hope to do is to treat it with compassion and clarity. I want to render the characters whole and their motivations clear, I want them to be understood and so forgiven."

As a child, Roxana was encouraged to write by teachers who recognized her potential. "Since I was ambivalent about teachers, it made me ambivalent about writing," Robinson told Wendy Smith of *Publishers Weekly* (June 15, 1998). "I was slightly rebellious, didn't see myself as doing whatever I was told, so the fact that I was told early on that I should write put me off." The novelist Bernard Malamud, her college counselor, proved to be one of the greatest influences in her life. "He never suggested that I change the way I wrote," she remarked to Wendy Smith. "He gave me that sense of meticulousness that is so crucial . . . He told us that you had to sit down and write every day—no waiting for inspiration. . . . His calm, focused attentiveness to craft was what stayed with me."

Robinson and Alger divorced in 1975, and on February 20, 1976, she married the investor Hamilton Robinson Jr. The experience she had gained working at art galleries allowed her a career as a writer of art-history books, beginning in the mid-1970s—work she did, she has admitted, mainly because she could not get her fiction into print.

In the 1980s Robinson began publishing short stories in various magazines both in the United States and Great Britain. After a story of hers appeared in the British publication *Fiction Magazine*, she received a letter from an English editor soliciting a novel from her; the result was her first published novel, *Summer Light*. The protagonist of the book is a young photographer who has separated from her husband but is unable to dedicate herself to her lover or her job because she devotes all her energy to her son. Her estranged husband confronts her at her summer home in Maine and forces her to reevaluate her priorities. This first book on issues of family and their impact on the well-to-do set the stage for Robinson's future fiction endeavors.

When Edward Burlingame of Harper & Row asked Robinson to write a biography of Georgia O'Keeffe, she found the offer too extraordinary to pass up despite her new dedication to fiction. "O'Keeffe was a towering figure with a hugely powerful grasp on people's imaginations, and there was very little published about her," Robinson told Smith. "It was just irresistible." She received total cooperation from the late artist's family, including access to O'Keeffe's personal letters. *Georgia O'Keeffe: A Life* was published in 1989. Nominated for a National Book Critics Circle Award and selected for the *New York Times* list of recommended books of the year, the book received a great deal of critical attention, most of it positive. Stefan Kramer of *Time* (November 20, 1989) described the work as a "romantic but insightful biography." In *New York Newsday* (October 22, 1989), Jennifer Krauss praised the effective way in which Robinson examined O'Keeffe's relationship with her husband Alfred Stieglitz and the way it affected her art. "Her comprehensive biography is a major achievement in both art history and women's studies," Krauss wrote, but she found fault with what she considered to be Robinson's overzealous defense of the artist in the face of an exaggerated patriarchal establishment.

Robinson's first short-story anthology, *A Glimpse of Scarlet and Other Stories*, continued to investigate the marital and family concerns taken up in *Summer Light*; the majority of the pieces focus on such issues as infidelity and parents' relationships with their stepchildren. Reviewing the collection in the *New York Times Book Review*

(June 30, 1991), Bret Lott was most impressed with the title story, in which a happily married woman witnesses two presumably adulterous lovers take their afternoon leave of one another. Lott was less enthusiastic about some of the anthology's other selections, including "Second Chances," a tale of parental acceptance, and "Snowfall"—"a politically correct apology for the stories of the landed gentry that will follow." Nevertheless, Lott concluded that "Roxana Robinson's first collection of stories is at once poignant and brutal, a book of New York stories filled with the bitter joys and tender sorrows of marriage and parenthood."

Robinson published a second anthology in 1996, entitled *Asking For Love and Other Stories*. In the *New York Times Book Review* (March 24, 1996), Brooke Allen declared "Breaking the Rules" to be "perhaps the most moving story in the collection." In it, a woman is still upset about the death of her father, which occurred a year earlier, when the two were not on speaking terms because of a petty disagreement. Allen felt that Robinson's "outlook is somewhat limited in that it is an exclusively feminine one. Ms. Robinson's sole concern is with human relations, particularly those between family members or lovers. She gives no consideration to the themes that have traditionally been considered masculine, like the bleak and solitary battles with worldly ambition and failure . . . . Within her chosen boundaries, however, she can be an effective artist, and occasionally a powerful one."

Robinson's most recent novel, *This Is My Daughter*, was published in 1998. The book chronicles the efforts of white-collar newlyweds to establish a family despite the hesitance of their children from previous marriages. She told Wendy Smith that she found the adjustments and mixed loyalties involved in second marriages to be "a very interesting dynamic that has a very broad resonance right now."

Since she is from an upper-class background herself, Robinson has sought to portray her characters as complex and sympathetic individuals instead of mere stereotypes of a portion of American upper class. "It was hard for me to write about people who were affluent and privileged without a kind of conspiratorial aside to the reader that I understood that they were in some way morally deficient," she admitted to Smith. Despite their comfortable lives, Robinson's characters are realistic people with realistic problems. But sometimes, as the she explained to Cynthia Magriel Wetzler of the *New York Times* (January 5, 1997), "Using real people is a difficult issue for fiction writers. There are moments when friends do get wary or upset. What I say to them is that I am trying to record a part of the emotional history of the late twentieth century. That's my task, so I must include parts of reality."

In 1987, Robinson was made a fellow of the National Endowment for the Arts. Her work has been included in several anthologies, including *Best*

American Short Stories of 1994. She has one daughter, Roxana Scoville Alger, from her previous marriage.—B.S.

SUGGESTED READING: *New York Newsday* p24+ Oct. 22, 1989, with photo; *New York Times* XIIIWC p4 Jan. 5, 1997, with photo; *New York Times Book Review* p9 June 30, 1991, p9 Mar. 24, 1996 *Publishers Weekly* p37+ June 15, 1998, with photo; *Time* p104+ Nov. 20, 1989

SELECTED WORKS: Fiction—*Summer Light*, 1987; *A Glimpse of Scarlet and Other Stories*, 1991; *Asking for Love and Other Stories*, 1996; *This Is My Daughter*, 1998; Nonfiction—*Georgia O'Keeffe: A Life*, 1989

Nancy Crampton

Rudman, Mark

Dec. 11, 1948– Poet; nonfiction writer

The American poet, literary critic, and translator Mark Rudman has achieved renown for his epic-length poetic autobiography, published in three volumes, *Rider* (1994), *The Millennium Hotel* (1996), and *Provoked in Venice* (1998). Rudman has also shown his poetic mettle with collections that include the highly praised *The Ruin Revived* (1986), *By Contraries* (1988), and *The Nowhere Steps* (1990) and his broad learning and philosophical range in the essay collection *Realm of Unknowing: Meditations on Art, Suicide, and Other Transformations* (1995), but it was his autobiography-in-poetry that David R. Slavitt, a fellow poet and literary critic, referred to in the *New England*

Review (Summer 1995) as "rich, complicated, thoroughly satisfying . . . evidence . . . of Rudman's interest in exploring that territory between verse and prose."

For *World Authors 1990–1995*, Mark Rudman writes: "I was born in Manhattan on December 11, 1948. My mother's mother's family came from Alsace-Lorraine, her father's family from Russia. My father's family were Russian Jews. There were terrific (and destructive) class tensions between my mother and father. My parents lived on the Upper West Side during the year and a half they stayed together. After that, while my father was off having fun in Havana, my mother whisked me away with her to southern California, where many of her relatives either lived or, like her father, spent part of the year. These frequent journeys, some by air, some by train (on The Big Chief) set up an enduring dialectic of east and west. One of my earliest memories is of Indian children hawking cactus dolls while the train paused in Albuquerque station.

"My mother, though intelligent, lovely, and talented, was inhibited (I did not say prevented) by her father from attending college, or pursuing a career as an artist, but she did paint throughout her life. My father aspired to be a composer, and studied at NYU, but was soon tempted by the fast line of, to use a favorite phrase of his, 'the world of advertising,' and went to work at Grey (Advertising) where he met people like the legend who invented the phrase 'the five-o-clock-shadow.' He ended up in the psychological aptitude testing business, of which his brother-in-law, Jack Klein, was one of the founders.

"I attended L'Ecole Francaise for pre-k and kindergarten. And while I picked up a smattering of French (and a liking and affinity for French culture through the scattered artifacts, like the intriguing Toulouse-Lautrec posters), I also incurred the wrath of the headmistress for not speaking French all the time, as was required. When I was five, my mother began dating a Rabbi, and she married him in Bermuda in February of 1954 while my father took me to see *Peter Pan* in New York. I stress these details now because they had an intense impact upon me then (and reappear in my more autobiographical poems), engendering a certain curiosity and suspicion: why on that day we were headed to a Broadway musical instead of the usual movie? The Rabbi had been working at the Village Synagogue in collaboration with a Presbyterian minister and now saw fit to leave this job which, though congenial, 'didn't pay enough,' and the three of us headed for Illinois where I began a massive and interminable period of adjustment. I went under my own name in the public schools I attended but was known as 'Strome' in the Rabbi's temple world. Around this time, I developed acute asthma for which there was no real relief when it was bad. Meanwhile the Rabbi had grown dissatisfied with his vocation, and we moved to Chicago so he could 'go into Public Relations.' Though we lived in Hyde Park, I was sent to an elementary school on the south side that was predominantly black and entirely a war zone. Until I somehow arrived in graduate school at Columbia, I didn't think about much in school other than physical survival. Luckily, I was a precocious reader so I could educate myself as I saw fit once outside the school environments.

"I had encounters with books filtered through a complex system of signs. My mother claims she read to me all the time, but from the *Book of Knowledge*, not fairy tales, *Winnie the Pooh*, or fiction. There were the books my Rabbi stepfather had on his shelves, the Everyman editions of *Minor Seventeenth-Century Poets* (Crashaw, Donne, but even then that 'minor' seemed presumptuous and condescending) and Spinoza with the rough-faded green covers, books I grazed in at a very young age, fascinated by the stanzaic designs, the numbered sentences on the page and the absence of any story. There were the books I obtained, never in the abridged edition if I could help it, after I read the Classic Comics. In third and fourth grade I read the first eighty or so pages of *The Count of Monte Cristo* and *The Man in the Iron Mask*. I think I read all of *The Three Musketeers* and while I 'identified' with D'Artagnan I was obsessed with the darker figures, exiled from themselves, burdened with disturbing secrets. I held myself responsible for not being able to read every word of these books even though the type was small and the stories themselves top-heavy and overwrought. I made up for this in fantasizing endlessly about their fates. Something must have stuck or this would not have resonated for me while composing a poem called 'Chrome' about riding motorcycles in the Sonoran desert:

> Once I rode toward it (the cliff's edge)
> hearing only the hush of the tires,
> the pure elation of it taking my head
> off as I took
> a horseshoe curve at 50 and ap-
> an even sharper one—the slender cy-
> cle shaking apart—;
> and I wondered what to do, like
> going back to the bomb he'd planted
> to make sure
> he'd lit the fuse . . . when—
> BOOM!—;

"I was thankful to discover Poe and his exquisite (I can hear Fortunato's bells jangling as I write this sentence) 'The Cask of Amontillado,' 'The Purloined Letter,' and other more atmospheric and always blessedly brief tales. (Rereading is still the greatest pleasure.) When things were turning out too badly in stories, I wanted to intervene, as Buster Keaton's projectionist in *Sherlock Jr.* does when he dreams himself into the film he's showing.

"The next move broke my heart. I had worked hard to be accepted in the small town of Kankakee, Illinois, which was a wonderful place for an American childhood. After the seventh grade I was part of a community for the first time in my life (and last until I entered—and I mean this without presumption—the community of poets).

"My father had contempt for what he called these 'nothing towns' and believed that my only chance of survival was 'psychiatric help.' On the weekends when I longed to play with my friends, I took the train some fifty miles into Chicago to see an esteemed child psychiatrist who smoked a pipe, played whatever games I wanted, and rarely said a word. I watched him watching me. His compliance to my every wish had to be some kind of trick.

"I came east every summer between five and twelve to go to sleepaway camp, which I liked a lot. I noticed that the kids seemed to like me more at this camp than they did at home. Not long ago I was telling a friend about this camp and she said 'Oh, I've heard of Camp Wayne, it's a famous Jewish camp.' I had thought about these kids coming mainly from posh suburbs and having lots of stuff my friends in Illinois and I didn't have—but not that they were Jewish. I realized that I had still repressed the degree to which a lot of my early fights (wars, battles) with other kids in a plethora of schools had to do with this religious issue.

"Aged twelve, I was lying on my bunk in camp when I was informed that my stepfather had taken a pulpit in Salt Lake City. I lay with my head in my pillow, envisioning immense boulders and felt sick inside for the next three years (and only mildly better until I was out of school entirely). The one saving grace of Salt Lake City was the availability of public golf courses. My grandfather's stories of having won the French Amateur in the thirties and of having played with legends like Tommy Armour and Walter Hagen whetted my appetite for one game at which I eventually came to excel.

"The first book I read whose majesty and solemnity and mystery overpowered me (the way hallucinogenic drugs did so many of my generation) was *Great Expectations*. It was an assignment sophomore year at Highland High School in Salt Lake City and when my teacher handed back my paper she said, 'I've given you a B+ because it's so much better than anything else you've done in this class I'm not convinced you wrote it. Otherwise, you deserved an A.' By the middle of my sophomore year, I had essentially dropped out, (as the 'Dropouts' section of *Rider* implies) in part because you couldn't graduate high school without passing ROTC and after one Monday morning's drill I had been caught by an 'officer' taking off my woolen uniform, under which I wore jeans and a tee shirt, in the bathroom. I refused to take ROTC the next year and now I begged to be sent away to school, and instead of attending one of the Eastern private schools where my father was convinced I would finally begin to 'blossom,' schools that, as I saw it, would condescend to admit me if I repeated my sophomore year, I chose to go to Judson, a school outside of Scottsdale, Arizona, where total credits counted as much as grades and the focus was more on riding than reading, and the kids were wild.

"I probably would have skipped college entirely if a BA hadn't already become the equivalent of an old high school diploma. The trick was to find a school where I could concentrate solely on my obsessions and that meant Bard, Godard, or the Seminar College at the New School in its early stages. The latter also allowed me to be in close proximity to my (just happily remarried) father for the first time. Almost all the classes I took mixed works from many disciplines (ancient and modern theoretical texts, plays, novels, lyric poems, films, etc.), and this along with Hart Crane's *The Bridge* and the films of Jean-Luc Godard may have been a seed toward my future explorations with the mosaic forms in both poems and essays. I didn't write any poems when I was still officially working toward a BA, but the moment I graduated and didn't feel I had to report to anyone I began to experiment wildly. After reading Kenneth Koch's essay in the *New York Review of Books* on teaching children to write poetry I decided that this was the perfect way to reconcile avocation and vocation, so I made a brazen, reckless gesture and called Kenneth to ask how I might find some work in the field. He told me who to call and within the week I was earning money as a poet. After a year of writing, teaching, and working as an office temp, I applied to Columbia's School of the Arts because I respected the faculty (though only a fraction of the listed names appeared for more than an afternoon!).

"That summer I met a woman on the beach in the Hamptons, the (future) mathematician Madelaine Bates. Like many people of our generation we waited as long as possible to get married and then to have a child. (Our son, Samuel, was born in 1985.)

"I had never taken a poetry workshop or shown my work to anyone who would look at it seriously, so the critical response I received from Stanley Kunitz and Mark Strand, and fellow students like Mei-Mei Bersenbrugge, Gregory Orr and Paul Nemser, had a tremendous impact on me. It also added to my confidence when national journals like *The Atlantic Monthly* and *Harper's* accepted my first submissions, and the critic Philip Rahv published an essay for his second *Modern Occasions Anthology* (along with work by such heroes of my youth as Saul Bellow and Alberto Moravia etc.).

"I saw translation as part of a poet's apprenticeship and began translating Apollinaire, Char, and Reverdy. Through Stanley Kunitz, I met Bohdan Boychuck, with whom I first translated several Ukrainian poets and then cajoled into helping me with the elusive, mysterious early poems of Boris Pasternak, the book *My Sister—Life*, which he wrote in the revolutionary summer of 1017. Translation was my formal training ground. And in the past several years have I have been working on 'palimpsests' of Horace and Ovid.

"In 1976 I was asked to become the poetry editor of *Pequod* and in 1985 became Editor in Chief. From 1985 to the present I have taught . . . creative writing, literature, and translation, specializing in courses that attend to the borderline between poetry and prose, to graduates and undergraduates at NYU and Columbia (both the School of the Arts and General Studies)."

With *By Contraries* (1988), Rudman found his voice. "A sentient self emerges clearly in Mark Rudman's work—complex, despairing, seeking to confront the contradictions offered up by contemporary urban life, and to achieve reconciliation with them," Leslie Ullman wrote in the *New York Times Book Review* (October 16, 1988). Rudman's complex relationship with New York City, "a sunless and purgatorial place," where "twilights fix the city in a moment of magic followed by a moment of terrifying darkness before the lights go on," in Ullman's words, is "fuel" for his "quirky energy." Still, some of the poems are set in Italy, with its landscapes and Roman ruins, and others on the Maine seacoast from which Rudman derived the title of his collection: "If we proceed by contraries we keep pace with the waves / breaking on the way in, whispering on the way out." His form in this volume, which contains the title poem, "In the Neighboring Cell," from an earlier collection, is varied, with prose passages alternating with what Ullman called "poems-within-a-poem." Ullman concluded, "*By Contraries* beautifully balances personal history with a strong social consciousness, inner landscape with outer. . . . Rudman allows us . . . to borrow his sensibility as it evolves from articulate despair to an easing, a willingness to live with the burden of vision."

"Rudman has found a way of writing from the everyday with all its 'unpoetic' contingencies and does good work toward making it intelligible," Steven Ellis commented in *Library Journal* (November 15, 1996), reviewing *The Millennium Hotel*. "Livelier and more interesting than *Paterson* [by William Carlos Williams] and almost as large in its concerns as the *Cantos* [by Ezra Pound], this series of reports from Rudman's mental and psychic frontier has the associative structure and, more important, the scale of those modernist works," David Slavitt said of *The Millennium Hotel* and its predecessor *Rider*, as quoted in the *Dictionary of Literary Biography* (1996).

Rudman apparently struck a vein of poetic gold when he decided to write "a memoir in verse, the equivalent of a prose piece with all the boring parts left out," as Slavitts called it in the *New England Review*. *Rider* won the 1994 National Book Critics Circle (NBCC) Award for poetry, and both it and *The Millennium Hotel* were universally praised.

"Writing," Rudman said in his acceptance speech for the NBCC Award, "more than arts mediated by technology, is particularly good at charting the mind's growth. . . . I've tried to give myself a certain license, the license to digress, to mix tonalities, but at the same time to maintain lyric intensity." Later, he remarked that he was "looking to bring back to poetry that bitter jousting spirit that Shakespeare's fools embody in their dialogues with their sober masters. . . ."

In a self-interview published in the *Denver Quarterly* (Spring 1997), Rudman noted that living "in transition may have alerted me to the symbolic potential of the real." The interlocutor—who is Rudman himself—asked, "Did translating Pasternak's *My Sister—Life* with its neo-Kantian emphasis on the thing influence you here?" Rudman replied that he "was searching for a way to render emotion, and character, obliquely" and that Pasternak helped him "trust in objectification" as a "way of making a statement without generalizing. Poetry," he added, "makes life bearable insofar as it allows us to be elliptical, abjuring narrative while retaining the skeleton of a story."

In "Flying Into Rome," published in the *New England Review* (Spring 1997), Rudman described himself and his young son, unable to sleep, flying in the morning into the city of the title. His imagination sweeps him over the city, now that "Everything is open that is not under reconstruction." The Eternal City exerts its fascination, joining him with his son in "some mysterious communion five miles above the earth," as he said in the self-interview.

> Yet there must be more than this uneasy turbulence
> that will not let us sleep in the starless dark.
> Why have they always portrayed heaven as being
> bound up with cumulus, and heights
> . . .
> When the morning light still lights on the cold porphyry and the steps leading down
> to the brackish Tiber, hale—despite its sluggish, exhausted stride.

This passage exemplifies what Ullman referred to as the evolution from "articulate despair" to "a willingness to live with the burden of vision."

In the preface to *Realm of Unknowing*, Rudman explained why he wrote the essays in the book. "Each essay," he declared, "is a 'raid on the inarticulate,' a series of forays—sparked by a certain disturbance. . . . " The essays explore subjects that include the life of his uncle, an obscure film director who committed suicide at the age of 44, leaving a "black hole . . . in what was once a close-knit, colorful, and supportive family." Other topics are the films of Michelangelo Antonioni and Rudman's own life—the latter discussed in "My Best Friend," described by Rudman as "a memoir as much concerned with intimacy and eros, as experienced by prepubescent children, as with class and race." The essays mirror "each other at oblique angles . . . organically connected, almost as if spores floated between them," Rudman wrote. They deal with "failure, ruin, suicide," a "hydra-headed trio" that "shadows our lives" and are imbued with a sense of regret for lost opportunities. Rudman said of his uncle: "This is what the suicide relinquishes: the chance to see the morning light caress a leaf one more time. . . . "

The final volume in Rudman's trilogy, *Provoked in Venice*, was published in 1998. In it, a visit to Venice serves as the occasion for the narrator to reflect on the past and the present of a city rich in history—and to reveal things about himself. In *Publishers Weekly* (December 21, 1998) Mark Rotella called the book "fast-paced" and "confident," and added, "[Rudman's] own experience allows a broader perspective on the city—perhaps the next best thing to being there."

Rudman's translations from the Russian, his criticism, and his teaching form the matrix of his life, and they, rather than "readings to try to sell books," have provided him with a living, as he told *World Authors*. His credo was perhaps expressed in his translation of a passage from "Conversation about Dante," by Osip Mandelstam, published in the essay "M." in *Raritan Review* (Spring 1996): "The quality of poetry is determined by the speed and decisiveness with which it embodies its plan of action. . . . One must run across the full width of a river, crammed with Chinese junks moving simultaneously in various directions—this is how the meaning of poetic discourse is created. The meaning, its route, cannot be reconstructed by interrogating the boatmen: they will not tell how and why we were leaping from junk to junk."
—S. Y.

SUGGESTED READING: *Denver Quarterly* Spring 1997; *Library Journal* p65 Nov. 15, 1996; *NBCC Journal* p3+ July 1995; *New England Review* p187+ Summer 1995, p62+ Spring 1997; *New York Times Book Review* p42+ Oct. 16, 1988; *Raritan Review* p17+ Spring 1996; *Dictionary of Literary Biography*, 1996

SELECTED BOOKS: Poetry—*In the Neighboring Cell*, 1982; *The Mystery in the Garden*, 1985; *The Ruin Revived*, 1986; *By Contraries*, 1988; *The Nowhere Steps*, 1990; *Rider* 1994; *The Millennium Hotel* 1996; *Provoked in Venice*, 1998; Nonfiction—*Robert Lowell: An Introduction to the Poetry*, 1983; *Diverse Voices: Essays on Poets and Poetry*, 1993; *Realm of Unknowing: Meditations on Art, Suicide, and Other Transformations*, 1995; As translator—*My Sister—Life* (with B. Boychuck), 1983; *Memories of Love* (with D. Ignatow and B. Boychuck), 1989

Rush, Norman

Oct. 24, 1933– Novelist; short-story writer

In 1983, after he and his wife, Elsa Scheidt, had completed a five-year stint as country codirectors of the Peace Corps in Botswana, American novelist and short story writer Norman Rush returned to the United States bringing with him not only a newfound love and appreciation of Africa, but also three cartons of notes—the basis of his two major works, the story collection *Whites* (1986) and the novel *Mating* (1991). "I was astonished by Africa,"

Courtesy of Norman Rush

Norman Rush

Rush said in an interview with the *New York Times*. Rush's time in Botswana familiarized him with the racial and political difficulties of a nation bordering South Africa during the waning years of apartheid. "Everybody was there," he said in an interview with the *New York Times Book Review* (September 22, 1991), "and everybody was intriguing and trying to get a stake in southern Africa's future. Apartheid was falling apart, and nobody knew how the pieces would be put back together." Botswana, in those years, was the prime destination for those fleeing the oppression of apartheid. "Before the border was electrified," Rush explained, "they came across the Limpopo River. The South Africans would come in helicopters and surround a house they thought was filled with ANC people and shoot it up, usually killing the wrong people."

Whites and *Mating*, both critically acclaimed, deal with the role of Westerners amid this tumultuous backdrop. "The white embrace of Africa keeps changing," Rush told another interviewer. Speaking of *Whites*, he said, in a comment that might apply to *Mating* as well: "In these stories I concentrate on whites, especially American whites, as they define themselves against the contours of African life and encounter the limits and contradictions of the Western undertaking in that part of the world."

Norman Rush was born on October 24, 1933 in San Francisco, California, the son of Roger Rush, a trainer of salesmen, and Leslie (Chesse) Rush, a teacher and weaver. He was briefly educated at what he described in a statement for *World Authors 1990–1995* as "an experimental college" in Los Angeles. A refusal to register for the Korean

War draft, however, soon landed Rush in a federal prison in Tucson, Arizona. Following his release on parole, after serving nine months of a two-year sentence, Rush decided to continue his education at Swarthmore College, from which he graduated in 1956.

After graduation, Rush was self-employed as an antiquarian book dealer for nearly 15 years. This decision had a distinct logic behind it. "I had always wanted to write, but decided not to pursue an academic career," Rush has been quoted as saying. "My aim was to devise a particular kind of life for myself that would give me more freedom." Eventually, however, Rush did pursue an academic career. In 1972 he became an instructor of English and history and codirector of College A at Rockland Community College in Suffern, New York. Six years later, he decided to send an unsolicited story to the *New Yorker*. His story, "After the Life Class," a chronicle of his experiences as a teacher, was accepted and ran in the magazine in 1978.

That same year, Rush and his wife, whom he had met and married while at Swarthmore, were approached by the talent search department of the Peace Corps about the possibility of being the codirectors of a country's Peace Corps program. Initially skeptical, the couple nonetheless decided to undergo the rigorous interviewing and screening process. After deciding to pursue the opportunity, Rush and Scheidt, who both had backgrounds in French, decided to interview for the positions of codirectors for the African nation of Benin. While they were in the final screening process, a bureaucratic mix-up, confusing African countries beginning with the letter "B," caused them to interview for the positions of country codirectors of Botswana rather than Benin. The couple were smitten and soon accepted the posts in Botswana. "Botswana is a democratic country with a free press and elections," Rush said in an interview with the *New York Times* (April 19, 1986). "That's one of the reasons why my wife and I decided to go there instead of to one of the authoritarian countries in Africa."

Upon returning to the United States in 1983, Rush began organizing the hundreds of pages of notes he had amassed during his stay in Africa. ("I was too busy to write there," he has noted.) The result was *Whites*, a six-story collection that deals with whites—Canadian, British, Dutch, and American—living and working in Africa. The book was a finalist for the Pulitzer Prize and the National Book Award in 1987. Critics were quick to hail *Whites* as "powerful and original," as Christopher Lehmann-Haupt wrote in the *New York Times* (February 27, 1986), and to praise Rush's "subtle ear for the local nuances of bureaucracy, prejudice, and cultural conflict," in the words of a critic for *Booklist* (February 15, 1986). Some critics were even more complimentary. "*Whites* is a terrific book, important for our understanding of white people in the world, particularly of the roles of whites in Botswana," Steve Katz wrote in the

American Book Review (March/April 1987). "Everyone should read it. . . . I wish there were more books in print by Norman Rush. I would read them now."

One of the stories in *Whites*, "Instruments of Seduction," received the Aga Khan Fiction Prize after its original publication in the *Paris Review*. The story depicts Ione, an American dentist's wife with a penchant for seducing men, who is surprisingly fascinated by her brush with revolutionary politics. Ione is one of the few characters, wrote Leslie Marmon Silko in the *New York Times Book Review* (March 23, 1986), who manage "to grasp the possibilities for personal salvation Africa offers them despite all its contradictions and ugly colonial legacies. . . . She not only fashions a sense of self and identity that keeps her humanity intact, she also manages to realize how the terrifying atmosphere of Botswana can actually be used to deliver her from isolation and loneliness."

In 1991 Rush published his first novel, *Mating*. The book follows an unnamed female Ph.D. candidate from Stanford (the same character also appeared in "Bruns," one of the stories in *Whites*) who comes to Botswana to complete her dissertation in nutritional anthropology. Frustrated by her inability to complete her project, the woman decides she needs a "companion." She eventually meets Nelson Denoon, a man who has built an entirely self-sustaining community in the Kalahari Desert, run for and by abused African women. Denoon is, as Jim Shepard wrote in the *New York Times Book Review* (September 22, 1991), the "kind of Serious Man the narrator thought extinct: utterly committed to his world-saving work as well as supernaturally savvy and erudite, able devastatingly to criticize all previous human plans for coexistence and yet, no nihilist, to offer one of his own, a plan of disarming simplicity and appeal." To impress Denoon, the woman travels across the desert to visit his utopian community. After reaching her destination, the woman, an ardent feminist, is bothered by her seeming reliance on a man for personal happiness and by a difficulty in reconciling her pursuit of Denoon with her highly valued independence. She fears that even in "the most enlightened and beautifully launched unions" she can recognize "the master-slave relationship moving its slow thighs somewhere in the vicinity." The woman realizes that she must make a decision that will have far-reaching ramifications for her. *Mating* received the National Book Award for fiction in 1991 and the Irish Times and Aer Lingus International Fiction Prize in 1992. Critics commended the book's sensitive exploration of modern relationships. "His novel illuminates why we yield when we don't have to," Jim Shepard wrote. "It seeks to illuminate the nature of true intimacy— how to define it, how to know one has achieved it." Critics further lauded Rush's use of narration. "The voice of Rush's narrator is immediate, instructive, and endearing in ways that may encourage comparison to Walt Whitman's or Huck Finn's. In his first novel Norman Rush commanded my attention as few other contemporary writers do," Thomas R. Edwards wrote in the *New York Review of Books* (October 10, 1991).

Rush has been the recipient of several fellowships, from organizations including the National Endowment for the Arts (1986), the Guggenheim Foundation (1987), and the Rockefeller Foundation (1990).
—J. P.

SUGGESTED READING: *American Book Review* p12+ Mar./Apr. 1987; *Booklist* p850 Feb. 15, 1986; *New York Review of Books* p33+ Oct. 10, 1991; *New York Times Book Review* p7 Mar. 23, 1986, p3 Sep. 22, 1991; *Contemporary Authors* vol. 126, 1989; *Contemporary Literary Criticism* vol. 44, 1987; *Who's Who in America 1997*

SELECTED BOOKS: *Whites*, 1986; *Mating*, 1991

Spielman

Sallis, James

Dec. 21, 1944– Novelist; short-story writer; poet; nonfiction writer

The American novelist, poet, and critic James Sallis is the creator of Lew Griffin, the detective of *The Long-Legged Fly* (1992), *Moth* (1993), *Black Hornet* (1994), *Eye of the Cricket* (1997), and *Bluebottle* (1998). In a review in the *Washington Post* (January 27, 1994), Sallis expressed his desire for "a syncretism, some fundamental reintegration of our literature: that poets and short-story writers start getting together over lunch, that academic and commercial writers acknowledge how much they stand to learn from one another. Then perhaps 'literary' fiction wouldn't forfeit the astonishing energy and symbolic potential of genre writing, and 'popular' fiction' need not withdraw defensively behind its sales figures." Sallis has attempted to achieve for himself the syncretism of which he wrote, producing, concurrently with the Lew Griffin series, the avant-garde novel *Renderings* (1995) and the spy novel *Death Will Have Your Eyes* (1997). Also a musicologist, Sallis has written the biographical study *The Guitar Players: One Instrument and Its Masters in American Music* (1982). In addition, he is the author of *Difficult Lives: Jim Thompson, David Goodis, Chester Himes* (1993).

In a statement for *World Authors 1990–1995*, James Sallis writes: "I was born on the banks of the Mississippi, about an hour south of Memphis across from Oxford, in a river town that had been, in the Thirties and Forties, a major center of blues activity. I always insist that I had no childhood; that I spent it hiding away in books. My older brother, philosopher John Sallis, proved a major and continuing influence in my life. I was deeply honored by his dedicating his most recent book, on painting, to me.

"Age 17, already writing seriously, I went off to Tulane on scholarship, then after a couple of years (I still have no degree) settled briefly in Iowa before heading off to London to edit the landmark science-fiction magazine *New Worlds*, at that time a major outlet for work by such as J. G. Ballard, D. M. Thomas, Brian Aldiss, and Tom Disch. By this time I'd sold perhaps a dozen stories.

"In London I developed my love of American crime fiction and of French literature. By 1970 I was publishing poems, short stories, translations, reviews, and criticism in a wide array of literary and commercial magazines, everything from *Galaxy* and *The Magazine of Fantasy & Science Fiction* to *transatlantic review* and *Alfred Hitchcock's Mystery Magazine*.

"Over the following years I lived in Boston, New York City, New Orleans, and Texas. Looking for a way to make my living writing—this having been always my intention—I turned to writing about music, publishing dozens of articles, hundreds of reviews, and two books, while also teaching stringed instruments and theory.

"The music books were recently reissued by University of Nebraska Press. Others include a collection of essays on original paperback novelists of the Fifties, a critical anthology on Samuel R. Delany's writing, a translation of Raymond Queneau's novel *Saint Glinglin*, two short-story collections, the novels *Renderings* and *Death Will Have Your Eyes*, and five novels about a black New Orleans detective.

"I'm currently at work on a biography of African-American, expatriate writer Chester Himes to be published [in 1999]; a collection of essays, *Gently into the Land of the Meateaters*, is also scheduled for 1999. I spent last fall in Paris writing an original filmscript for a major French producer. Recent shorter work appears in *Poetry East*, *High Plains Literary Review*, *The Chariton Review*, *Oasis*, *Negative Capability* and many others.

"As a writer, I inhabit something of an odd space here in the U.S., poised on a poorly traveled borderland between the commercial and the literary, at once an advocate of avant-garde European literature and an authority on science fiction and the mystery, neither novelist, poet, translator, essayist, nor critic, but all these in turn: an old-style man of letters.

"The most popular of my books by far have been those dealing with New Orleans detective Lew Griffin: *The Long-Legged Fly*, *Moth*, *Black Hornet*, *Eye of the Cricket*, and *Bluebottle*. With these novels I've consciously set out to combine the unrelenting energy of genre fiction with the penetration and substance of 'literary' fiction: to bring together two aspects of my own taste and thereby create a kind of book that, as reader, I am always seeking and too seldom find.

"As a general credo of what I'm about in my work—and I don't differentiate my work as poet from that of mysteries or of more avant-garde work such as the novel *Renderings*—I'd take a line from my poem 'For a Russian Friend,' its expression of what we are to do with our lives: 'Find beauty, try to understand, survive.'"

James Sallis was born on December 21, 1944 in Helena, Arkansas. He attended Tulane University, in New Orleans, for a time. Although he left the South for the Midwest and then for England in his early manhood, he continued to draw on it for his writing. His fictional detective, Lew Griffin, is an African-American resident of New Orleans. Sallis's first novel, *The Long-Legged Fly* (1992), in which Lew Griffin makes his debut, was reviewed by crime-novel critics, such as Marilyn Stasio of the *New York Times* (September 6, 1992); nevertheless, it has been described as being less a detective story than a series of stories about a person who happens to make his living as a detective. Richard Lipez, in the *Washington Post* (September 20, 1992), termed *The Long-Legged Fly* "a series of nightmarish sketches" in a "disjointed narrative." The novel comprises four episodes that take place, respectively, in 1964, 1970, 1984, and the present. Griffin investigates the disappearance of three women, including a civil-rights activist. In one sketch, he searches for his own son.

In the opinion of Richard Lipez, Griffin, an alcoholic who ignores his dying father and is indifferent to the fate of his ex-wife, is "emotionally stunted." Stasio observed that although Griffin is given a lot of racial pride and cultural awareness by his author, Sallis "uses blackness as a metaphor for the alienation of his lone-wolf hero," whose "sensitivity . . . too often comes across as morbid self-absorption." Lipez observed that "Sallis is awfully good at recognizing strong people's inner demons and showing what can happen when they suddenly take over." Both reviewers agreed that *The Long-Legged Fly* was a genre-transcending and auspicious beginning for an unusual novelist. Ralph Lees, a reviewer for *Tangled Web* (on-line), observed, "With his concern to tackle the big moral questions and his liberal use of literary allusions Sallis is firmly based in the PI tradition." Lees deemed Sallis "easily good enough" to live in the company of the African-American mystery novelists Walter Mosley and Chester Himes.

Sallis continued to defy the limitations of genre with his next Lew Griffin book, *Moth* (1993). Ruth Bayard Smith, reviewing the novel in the *New York Times Book Review* (October 17, 1993), referred to Griffin as "a private detective turned professor of literature." In this novel Sallis's propensity for literary allusions is indulged when Griffin turns his hand to teaching. He is dragged back to detecting, however, when asked to find the children of two people from his past. Smith found *Moth* "engrossing and at times disturbing."

Black Hornet (1994), Sallis's next Lew Griffin book, looks back to the 1960s. It tells of how Griffin, a literary alcoholic who freelances for a collection agency, becomes a detective. A white female journalist, while in Griffin's company, is shot by a sniper—believed to be black—who has been terrorizing the city. After he is arrested, Griffin is forced to find out what is really happening. "They knew I wasn't involved in the shooting. But black man/white woman was a formula they just couldn't leave alone. That people were getting shot like paper targets out there in the streets was nothing compared to THIS danger. Eternal Vigilance," Griffin thinks. He forms an alliance with a white police officer, and "the subsequent plot involves the Black Panthers and a number of black activists of the time, the Caribbean religion Yoruba and several black mercenaries," as Catherine Texier wrote in the *New York Times Book Review* (November 20, 1994). She deemed the book "a powerful evocation of New Orleans in a time of great racial tension," in which the best part "is its rich tapestry of social unrest and vividly evoked characters and settings." Although Texier felt that the book lacked suspense and suffered from moralizing, she observed that "it still manages to work as a novel of character and atmosphere, leaving the reader with indelible images of New Orleans." "Lew Griffin," Bill Ott declared in *Booklist* (October 15, 1994), "is the real thing, a cynic out of Celine or the Hemingway of *In Our Time*. . . . This is powerful stuff, not for those to whom 'hard-boiled' is just a matter of style." For Pat Dobell, writing in the *Washington Post Book World* (October 16, 1994), "Sallis depicts his romantic hard-boiled hero with . . . mellow ease in this slender, haunting book."

By the time the fourth Lew Griffin book, *Eye of the Cricket* (1997), was published, Griffin had become not only a detective and a teacher but a writer as well. When a down-and-outer appears in a New Orleans hospital with a copy of one of Griffin's

novels and claims to be him, Griffin must investigate his own past. He is also seeking three missing young men, one of whom happens to be his estranged son. As the *Tangled Web* critic observed, "There are answers and more questions; there are threats and the promise of salvation; and there is a dangerous descent into . . . alcoholic haze. . . . Lew Griffin's investigation is the hero's journey, mythic and strengthening and thoroughly satisfying."

In his next book, *Death Will Have Your Eyes* (1997), Sallis put aside the Griffin series to write about a spy who goes back into the cold. The ex-spy, now a sculptor, is sent on a mission to track down the only other surviving member of his elite unit, now gone rogue. He leaves his girlfriend, telling her, "Everything you know about me, everything you think you know, is false." *Kirkus Reviews* (June 15, 1997) expressed the view that the "flip, absurdist tone—part Thomas Berger, part Richard Brautigan . . . subverts the conventions of the spy novel even more profoundly than Sallis's earlier novels . . . deconstructed the detective story. . . . The reward for patient readers is a finely poetic quality to every understated scene—despite a cargo of allusions to Voznesensky, Cendrars, Pavese, Cavafy, MacLeish, Apollinaire, and Homer."

Sallis returned to Lew Griffin in *Bluebottle* (1998), the fifth in his series. In this novel Griffin recovers from being shot by an unknown assailant while leaving a bar with a white woman. The woman had told him, untruthfully, that she was a reporter. His job is to find out whether he was set up by the woman as well as who shot him and why. In the course of his investigation, he tangles with the Mafia and white supremacists. "Lew confronts both sets of no-goods with his customary panache, generating in the process his usual spate of literary references and allusions . . . ," *Kirkus Reviews* (November 15, 1998) commented; Sallis, the reviewer complained, is "the poster boy for inconclusiveness." The *Publishers Weekly* (November 16, 1998) reviewer, on the other hand, in a starred review, termed the novel "unforgettable": "Griffin's first-person narrative abounds with literary quotes and allusions as readers are transported on a tide of evocative language into an impressionistic story of the year that Griffin spent recovering from wounds."

In addition to his careers as a novelist and poet, James Sallis has had a career as an editor, not only of magazines but of collections of writings on topics dear to his heart. *The Guitar in Jazz: An Anthology* (1996), an edition of a volume first issued in 1984, is an exhaustive exploration of the jazz guitar. Aaron Cohen in *Booklist* (May 15, 1996) referred to the dearth of literature on the instrument compared with that devoted to the saxophone and observed, "Sallis strives to set that situation aright with a collection of concise essays championing the instrument and its great innovators." Tom Graves wrote in the *Washington Post* (June 23,

1996), however, that while the book had some excellent articles, the scholarly apparatus caused it to bog down in detail. Sallis is also the author of *The Guitar Players: One Instrument and Its Masters in American Music* (1982), which was reissued in 1994.

Difficult Lives: Jim Thompson, David Goodis, Chester Himes (1993) explores the lives of writers who perhaps had something in common with Sallis, in that all wrote of hard-boiled yet tenderhearted detectives who are among the underdogs of society. *Ash of Stars: On the Writings of Samuel R. Delany* (1996) is a collection of essays explicating the works of the science-fiction writer Delany, whom Sallis calls "this most individual of America's individualist writers" and whom he compares to Gabriel García Márquez, Thomas Pynchon, and Günter Grass, among others. He cites Lionel Trilling's statement that literature has a "clear purpose of detaching the reader from the habits and thoughts and feelings that the larger culture imposes" as being in accordance with Delany's "basic adversary intention." Trilling's statement might apply equally to the writings of James Sallis.

—S. Y.

SUGGESTED READING: *Booklist* p404 Oct. 15, 1994, p1569 May 15, 1996; *Kirkus Reviews* June 15, 1997, Nov. 15, 1998; *New York Times Book Review* p17 Sep. 6, 1992, p42 Oct. 17, 1993, p36 Nov. 20, 1994; *Publishers Weekly* p58 Nov. 16, 1998; *Tangled Web Books* (on-line) May 21, 1998; *Washington Post Book World* p4 Sep. 20, 1992, p2 Jan. 27, 1994, p10 Oct. 16, 1994, p6 June 23, 1996

SELECTED WORKS: Nonfiction—*The Guitar Players: One Instrument and Its Masters in American Music*, 1982; *Jazz Guitars: An Anthology*, 1984, reissued as *The Guitar in Jazz: An Anthology*, 1996; *Difficult Lives: Jim Thompson, David Goodis, Chester Himes*, 1993; Fiction—*The Long-Legged Fly*, 1992; *Moth*, 1993; *Black Hornet*, 1994; *Renderings*, 1995; *Death Will Have Your Eyes*, 1997; *Eye of the Cricket*, 1997; *Bluebottle*, 1998; As editor—*The Guitar in Jazz: An Anthology*, 1996; *Ash of Stars: On the Writings of Samuel R. Delany*, 1996

Salzman, Mark

Dec. 3, 1959– Novelist; memoirist

Mark Salzman, an American writer, dedicated his life to Chinese culture in his early teens. Although he has described himself as having been a "quitter" in his youth, he hung on to his early enthusiasms to the point of getting a degree in Chinese language and literature from Yale University. His first book, *Iron & Silk* (1986), an account of two years spent teaching English at a medical college in China, was dubbed a "quiet classic" by the *Library Journal* (February 1, 1987) reviewer, and "quiet" became a term often applied to Salzman's writing. Salzman's first novel, *The Laughing Sutra* (1991), is a picaresque tale of a young Chinese man and his 2,000-year-old guru's adventures hunting for an ancient manuscript in America. The hero of his next novel, *The Soloist* (1994), belongs to another world in which Salzman has immersed himself: like Salzman, he is a cellist. In *Lost in Place: Growing Up Absurd in Suburbia* (1995), a comedic memoir of Salzman's teen years in Connecticut, he described how he came to be who he is—a writer dedicated to Chinese philosophy, culture, and language; a cellist of moderate achievement; and a seeker after eternal verities.

Mark Salzman was born on December 3, 1959 in Greenwich, Connecticut, and raised in Ridgefield. His father, Joseph Salzman, a painter, worked as a social worker, a job he hated, to support his family. His mother, Martha Zepp Salzman, postponed a career as a concert harpsichordist to raise her three children and gave piano and oboe lessons.

As a child Salzman devoted himself to pursuing a variety of ambitions. Under the influence of his artistic parents, he began playing the cello at age seven and participated in his father's hobby, astronomy, "as soon as . . . I . . . was old enough to stay awake past eight o'clock," he noted in *Lost in Place*. Salzman discovered Chinese philosophy and martial arts when he was 13 years old. In *Lost in Place*, Salzman wrote that he "decided that the life of a wandering Zen monk was the life for me. I announced my willingness to leave East Ridge Junior High School immediately and give up all material things, but my parents did not share my enthusiasm. They made it clear that I was not to become a wandering Zen monk until I had finished high school." In the meantime, he lived and meditated in the family basement dressed in dyed pajamas, looking "like an eggplant wrapped for Christmas," and wearing a Surprise Bald Head Wig, because, although his father disapproved of his long hair, he disapproved even more of a shaven head.

When Salzman reached high school, he was encouraged by an unusually inspiring teacher to begin to learn to speak, read, and write Chinese, and the experience broadened his interest in Chinese philosophy. While he gave up martial arts studies when he realized that his teacher, Sensei O'Keefe, was self-destructive and dangerous to others, he did find a master to teach him Chinese landscape painting. After graduating from high school, he took a year off from his studies to play jazz cello before entering Yale University as a music student. He so thoroughly enjoyed learning Chinese, however, that he ended up receiving his B.A. in Chinese language and literature, in the process becoming a disciple of a Chinese "poet / scholar / philosopher," who taught him calligraphy.

While he was a student at Yale, Salzman received word that Michael, his best friend and a fellow student of Sensei O'Keefe, had been killed while driving under the influence of drugs. After Salzman had departed from Sensei's school, Michael had gone on to earn his black belt in kung fu, and the two friends had drifted apart. Michael's death, however, precipitated Salzman into a depression, in which everything seemed pointless. He went home and declaimed dramatically to his father, complaining that in effect his dreams and ambitions were "just a smoke screen I throw up to distract myself. Now that I don't even have that anymore, all I can see is fifty or sixty years of drudgery, after which I'll probably drop dead in a retirement home. That's what it's all about, isn't it?" Joseph Salzman restored his son's calm with one word: "Welcome."

After graduating from Yale University, summa cum laude, in 1982, Salzman obtained a position teaching English at Hunan Medical College in Changsha, China. He remained in China until 1984 and then returned to the United States to teach martial arts in New Haven. During this time a friend suggested that he turn one of his many stories about China into a written narrative. Thus was born *Iron & Silk* (1986), a chronicle of his two years spent teaching English and studying martial arts and calligraphy in China. He explained that "in the West, Chinese martial arts are called 'kung fu' or 'gong fu', but the word *gong fu* actually means 'skill that transcends mere surface beauty.'" This term can be applied to prowess in calligraphy as well as in the martial arts. Donald Morrison, reviewing the book in *Time* (March 2, 1987), noted that one of the central stories in *Iron & Silk* concerns Pan Qingfu, "the country's foremost master of . . . the Chinese martial art," who acknowledged that Salzman had finally acquired gong fu. Morrison concluded, "No other term is as apt for a book that describes the land and its people with such deftness and delight."

Charles W. Hayford noted in *Library Journal* (February 1, 1987) that *Iron & Silk* is "a bouquet of sketches which distill a range of Chinese people into essences and scenes we immediately understand and feel." Richard Selzer remarked in the *New York Times Book Review* (February 1, 1987) that each anecdote in the book is "intended to give a glimpse of a circumstance of life in China or a trait of the Chinese." He observed that it was "all written in a jerry-built teenage prose that is oddly appealing for all its habit of bumping into itself."

Salzman wrote the screenplay for *Iron & Silk*, a movie version of his book directed and produced by Shirley Sun. He played the lead role, and Pan Qingfu, the master of *wushu*, as the Chinese call the martial art, played himself. The film, released in 1991, was slightly fictionalized, with the addition of a romance between "Mark Franklin" and a young woman named Ming. Janet Maslin in the

New York Times (February 15, 1991) noted that the film "has an essential guilelessness that makes up for its initial false notes." The film drew the comment from Richard Bernstein in the *New York Times* (March 17, 1991) that despite its "sweet and gentle tone, authoritarian politics and China's continuing struggle to adapt to the challenge of the modern world are never far away."

The action in Salzman's first novel, *The Laughing Sutra* (1991), also starts in China. A boy, Hsun-ching, is raised by a Buddhist monk after the death of his mother and imbued with Buddhist ideals. Young Red Guards appear, however, during the Cultural Revolution to abuse the old monk and force Hsun-ching to join them. Hsun-ching escapes to America to recover a legendary sacred text (the Laughing Sutra) so that the monk, his foster father, who has been searching for it his whole life, can die happy. He is accompanied on this venture by Colonel Sun, a man who claims to be a centuries-old warrior. Once in the United States, Hsun-ching must choose between returning to China to fulfill his promise to the monk or remaining to enjoy a better life. The encounter of Hsun-ching and the colonel—two embodiments of China—with American culture is the substance of the book.

Salzman told Suzanne Mantell in an interview in *Publishers Weekly* (January 17, 1994), "The book explores the question of the boundary between loyalty to yourself and loyalty to those you love. . . . Anyone with parents knows you find yourself in situations when you do have to make these decisions. And often the sides are so evenly balanced."

In the *New York Times Book Review* (January 27, 1991), Penelope Lively called *The Laughing Sutra* "an odd and beguiling novel." She considered its subject to be "no less than the apposition of Communist China and the United States" and noted that Salzman, "awed by the enormity of the topic and writing within the late-20th-century tradition of flight into fantasy in the presence of social and political circumstances that seem to defy description," has created an "allegory of innocence and adventure." Martha Duffy, writing in *Time* (February 4, 1991), called Salzman's decision to opt "for the picaresque" a "tough act to bring off because ordinary headlines make tall tales look tame." Salzman, she observed, "is skilled at using his meandering tale to comment on such varied matters as the Cultural Revolution, the Hong Kong drug trade, American amusement parks, and the idiocies of slob art in West Coast galleries." She felt, nevertheless, that the relationship between "earnest seeker and his wizardly mentor" and the contrast between "an old dormant civilization and a young bombastic one" were overly familiar subjects.

Salzman's second novel, *The Soloist* (1994), features a former musical prodigy—Renne Sundheimer—whose cello career ended in his late teens when his gift deserted him. It is difficult for him to give up his prodigy status, and he becomes a socially graceless and reclusive college professor dreaming of a musical comeback. Sundheimer, now in his mid-30s, undergoes several rejuvenating changes. When he is called for jury duty in the trial of a disturbed young man who has killed a Zen master, he becomes involved with a fellow juror and is shaken out of his emotional constriction. At around the same time he accepts a nine-year-old Korean cello prodigy as his student. Through these experiences he eventually is able to come to terms with himself and his own talent. Salzman told Suzanne Mantell, "I wanted to create a character who had a hard time with his dreams. . . . So many people I deeply admire feel they didn't live up to their own ideals, and what I admire is that they can live with that in a dignified way. Both my parents have dealt with that situation. I think my fear is that I won't be able to."

Keddy Ann Outlaw in *Library Journal* (October 15, 1993) wrote of *The Soloist*, "The mesmerizing first-person narration reveals Renne's self-tortured character, keen intelligence, and troubled heart as he ponders classical music, human nature, astronomy, and sanity/insanity. A spiritual journey not to be missed." In the *New York Times Book Review* (February 6, 1994), Diane Cole remarked, "Salzman's portrait of Renne as a wounded artist recalled to life is both absorbing and touching." She found some of the dialogue "stilted" but found Salzman's comparisons between "the disciplines of meditation and music" to be "engaging," as is the knowledge of Eastern philosophy he displayed in the novel. Wilfrid Mellers, writing in the *Times Literary Supplement* (October 14, 1994), also found Salzman's theme in *The Soloist* ambitious: "the relationship of God to man, as exemplified in the musical genius of two child prodigies." He termed the book "brilliant journalism," however, and felt it did "not make 'incarnate' its grand themes."

Lost in Place: Growing Up Absurd in Suburbia chronicles Salzman's growing up under the care of unusually tolerant and loving parents, who, although they both held "day" jobs—his father as a social worker, his mother as a music teacher—were artists: his father a painter and his mother a concert harpsichordist. At age 13 Salzman discovered Asian mysticism and martial arts. His ironic self-regard, however, did not let him describe himself as a true seeker after enlightenment:

The Buddha . . . made himself homeless and destitute first and then sought nirvana because he figured that it was worth seeking only if it was available to even the poorest person on earth. I, on the other hand, wanted to become a Zen master because I hoped perfect enlightenment would make me more popular—specifically more datable. . . . I hoped that if I became a living Buddha, I would never again have to hear the words 'You're just like a little brother to me' when I asked someone

on a date. . . . I wanted to become a Zen master because I thought it would impress my father. Like most boys, I wanted to prove myself by doing something my father couldn't do, but also like most boys, I thought my dad could do anything. He could drive, paint, name the constellations, set up a tent and had been in the air force—what else was there? The answer came the first night I saw David Carradine [the star of the television drama *Kung Fu*], about to be ambushed by a gang of murderous cowboys, sit cross-legged on the ground and play his bamboo flute.

Salzman decided to become an "unflappable sage" to make his father both proud and envious. In his bouts with existential questions, one conclusion he drew was that "the possibility of our being forever unable to know everything all at once may be the best design feature of this whole human experiment."

Joanne Wilkinson observed in a review of *Lost in Place* for *Booklist* (September 1, 1995) that the book is "a gentle memoir of [Salzman's] teenage years that is also a loving tribute to his gloomy father." She considered Salzman's conversations with his father the "highlights" of the book. Blake Morrison, on the other hand, writing in the *New York Times Book Review* (August 13, 1995), found that while Salzman's accounts of his youth, although "beautifully observed," were somewhat "predictable," it is "Mark Salzman's strange but wonderful addiction to kung fu that makes *Lost in Place* come alive."

Salzman has used events from his own life to exemplify the human quest for "something more." He explained in *Publisher's Weekly*, "In my writing I love to take real-life situations and say: What if they were much worse? I use fiction as a form of problem-solving."
—S. Y.

SUGGESTED READING: *Booklist* p37 Sep. 1, 1995; *Library Journal* p70 Feb. 1, 1987, p127 Nov. 1, 1990, p90 Oct. 15, 1993; *New York Times* C p12 Feb. 15, 1991, II p13 Mar. 17, 1991; *New York Times Book Review* p9 Feb. 1, 1987, p11 Jan. 27, 1991, p22 Feb. 6, 1994, p11 Aug. 13, 1995; *Publishers Weekly* p357+ Jan. 17, 1994; *Time* p76 Mar. 2, 1987, p66 Feb. 4, 1991; *Times Literary Supplement* p25 Oct. 14, 1994

SELECTED BOOKS: Fiction—*The Laughing Sutra*, 1991; *The Soloist*, 1994; Nonfiction—*Iron & Silk*, 1986; *Lost in Place*, 1995

Eva Sanders

Sanders, Scott R.

Oct. 26, 1945– Novelist; short-story writer; essayist

Guided by his aphoristic "Only by understanding where I live can I learn how to live," the Midwestern author Scott Russell Sanders is deeply devoted to "place" in his writing, the notion that it is essential for people to expand their awareness of the multifarious links—ancestral, physical, psychological, and social—that tie them to whatever local environment they call "home." In a series of well-regarded children's books as well as collections of philosophical essays, he has written of the durability of folk memory and the fragility and the wonder of life while unabashedly celebrating the sustaining values of community, nonviolence, work, and family. Although Sanders has systematically studied and written about America's pioneering era, he refuses to "hark back to some idyllic past, like the one embalmed in the *Saturday Evening Post* covers by Norman Rockwell or the prints of Currier & Ives," thus escaping easy categorization as either a "nature" writer or a "rural regionalist." With a commitment to communitarian American values tempered by his youthful revulsion against war and environmental exploitation, he pleads for a science divorced from militarism and challenges readers to consider the consequences of the traditional American "cult of the individual." In "essays of substance and beauty" in such books as *The Paradise of Bombs* (1987), *Staying Put*, (1993), *Writing from the Center* (1995), and *Hunting for Hope* (1998), Sanders echoes Henry David Thoreau, John James Audubon, Annie Dillard, and Wendell Berry in their forthright celebration of the specific and the preciously unique. He won the Lannan Literary Award for nonfiction in 1995.

For *World Authors 1990–1995*, Scott Russell Sanders, born October 26, 1945, writes: "In one of my earliest memories, I am toddling beside a railroad track and singing 'Chattanooga Choo-Choo,' imagining that if I sing hard enough a train will come chugging along. In another early memory, I look up from the barn doorway to see a sky full of green tickets fluttering down from an airplane; I rush out to snatch one and discover that the green paper is covered with neat black marks—a wonderful gift, if only I could read.

"The place would have been our farm outside of Memphis, my first home, and I would have been two or three years old. Learning new words every day, hearing the music in speech, I already felt the power of language. When I was four, my sister taught me to read on the screened-in porch of that Tennessee farmhouse, and suddenly those ink marks on paper set whole worlds moving inside me. Before I was able to print block letters with a fat pencil, that same patient sister wrote down the wild, rambling tales I dictated to her.

"Just before I started school, my father's work carried us to Ohio, where we lived first on a military base and then on a nearby farm. In both places I spent much time out of doors, prowling through munitions dumps or rambling through woods, spying on soldiers playing war games or on beavers building dams, walking the fields on the lookout for shell casings or arrowheads. The green world seemed exuberant, indestructible; the human world seemed violent and vulnerable.

"In fear and fascination, I wanted to know how the planes flew, how atomic bombs exploded, how rockets lifted satellites into orbit. In the month I turned twelve, Sputnik was launched, confirming my desire to study physics and astronomy, to discover the secrets of the universe. I figured maybe we could start over on a new planet and do things right. During my sophomore year in high school, President Kennedy promised that America would land astronauts on the moon before the end of the decade. During my junior year, Ohio's own John Glenn became the first American to orbit the earth.

"Then in October of my senior year, satellite photos showed that the Soviets were placing missiles in Cuba, within easy reach of the United States. One night after basketball practice, during a break in the dress rehearsal for a play, about a dozen of us huddled around a transistor radio in the school cafeteria and listened to President Kennedy warn the Soviet Union to remove those missiles or face grave consequences. My friends and I, sitting there in our costumes and greasepaint, knew that within a few hours everything we cared about could be erased. Bombers sliced the air constantly, and submarines cruised the sea. From one heartbeat to the next, the turning of keys could set warheads flying. Not just the senior class play, but our entire lives seemed like a flimsy skit that could be blown away at any moment.

"Wildness, by contrast, was reassuring. Every spring without fail, green shoots broke the ground. Geese honked by overhead. I was intrigued by the dirt under my feet, by the fields and forests nearby, by the Ohio Valley and the great fertile interior of America. I wanted to know how the land had been shaped. I wanted to know how people had lived here, from the early hunters and gatherers to the French and English explorers, from the settlers who came on horseback over the mountains, right up to the recent immigrants who arrived by airplane or car. It seemed to me, even in my school years, that we had abused the land. Oil slicks glistened on the surfaces of ponds. Rivers ran brown with eroded topsoil. Bulldozers and chainsaws gnawed away at the woods. The highways were spattered with the carcases of animals.

"I went off to college uncertain whether to study the vast and impersonal universe revealed by science, or the intimate landscape revealed by my senses. Had Brown University offered a degree in natural history, that's probably what I would have chosen. Instead, I began with physics, switched to religious studies, and wound up in literature. I learned as much outside of class as I learned inside, especially from joining the movement for civil rights and women's rights, and the struggle against the war in Vietnam.

"In the summer after graduation, I married the woman whom I had met as a girl at a science camp five years earlier. We enjoyed a four-year honeymoon in England, while I studied for a Ph.D. at Cambridge University. During those years, faced with a choice between jail, exile or Vietnam, I declared myself a conscientious objector, but my draft board dismissed my case without rendering a verdict. Traveling around Britain and Europe, I discovered that the human world is much older and sturdier than I had ever suspected. I also discovered that many other people shared my dismay over our misuse of the earth. Talking and marching, reading and writing, I began trying to figure out how our relations with the rest of nature had gone wrong, and how they might be set right.

"After finishing my degree at Cambridge, I returned home to teach at Indiana University, in Bloomington, where my wife and I have lived now for over twenty-five years. For the first decade or so, I wrote nothing but fiction, stories and novels mostly about the midwestern past and the global future. The coming of our two children, Eva and Jesse, set me thinking more urgently about what sort of creatures we are, how we dwell together in families and communities, and how we might live more wisely on the land. Such thinking led me increasingly to the writing of personal essays, book-length narratives and meditations.

"The challenge for any writer is to be faithful at once to your vision and your place, to the truth you have laboriously found and the people whom this truth might serve. In order to work, I must withdraw into solitude, must close my door against the world, close my mind against the day's news. But unless the writing returns me to the life of family, friends, and neighbors with renewed energy and insight, then it has failed. My writing is an invitation to community, an exploration of what connects us to one another and to the earth.

"Insofar as my writing is important, it gains that importance from what it witnesses to. I have written from the outset with a pressing awareness of the world's barbarities—the bombing of cities, oppression of the poor, extinction of species, exhaustion of soil, pollution of water and air, murder, genocide, racism, war. If I stubbornly believe that nature is resilient, that love is potent, that humankind may be truly kind, I do so in the face of this cruelty and waste. Without denying evil, literature ought to reduce the amount of suffering, in however small a degree, and not only human suffering but that of all creatures.

"The desire to articulate a shared world is the root impulse of literature as it is of science. Individual scientists, like writers, may be cutthroat competitors, out for their own glory; but science itself, the great cathedral of ideas slowly rising, is a common enterprise. Perhaps the symbol for literature should be a rambling library, to which each of us adds a line, a page, a few books. Whether one is a scientist or a writer, the universe outshines those of us who glimpse a bit of it and report what we see. Right now we urgently need to rethink our place on earth, to discover ways of living that do not devour the planet, and this need is far more important than the accomplishments of all writers put together. The health of our land and our fellow creatures is the ultimate measure of the worth and sanity of our lives.

"Whether writing fiction or nonfiction, at some level, I suppose, I'm still hoping to summon up a train with a song, still trying to call something desirable into existence with the power of words."

Scott Russell Sanders was born in Memphis, Tennessee. His father came from a family of Mississippi cotton farmers and his mother from an immigrant doctor's family in Chicago. The military base where he spent part of his Ohio boyhood was the Ravenna Arsenal, whose stark contrasts of "place" stimulated his budding literary imagination. "Surrounded by fences, the Arsenal was a wild sanctuary, with deer and fox, coyote and beaver," he wrote; "and at the same time it was a storage depot and testing ground for tanks, fighter jets, and explosives. This place, which I have written about in *The Paradise of Bombs*, set the pattern for my later preoccupation with nature, science, and community." The hardscrabble environment around the military base also made an indelible impression on the young Sanders. "Outside the Arsenal," he wrote, "our neighbors were mostly poor, living in trailers or tar-paper shacks, often out of work, forever on the shady side of luck. Several of these aching people, their lives twisted by fanaticism or loss, would show up in my first book of stories, *Fetching the Dead*."

Studying physics on scholarship at Brown University, Sanders recalls that "the other students seemed to me dauntingly clever and sophisticated, so I worked hard to prove that a backwoods boy from the Midwest belonged there." But these were the turbulent 1960s, and he came to feel "grave misgivings about the militarization of science," so he changed his major to English. In the meantime, he had fallen in love with Ruth Ann McClure of Indianapolis, and they were married soon after graduation. They had two children, Eva Rachel and Jesse Solomon.

During the couple's four-year residence in Cambridge, Sanders started writing essays and fiction, and his early work appeared in British magazines. "Ruth and I considered staying overseas," he recalled, "in the end, however, we could not bear to become expatriates, and so we returned to the United States." Since 1971 he has been on the faculty at Indiana University, where he is now Distinguished Professor of English.

"In all of my writing I have been concerned with our ways of inhabiting the earth, our relations within families and communities, and the search for a spiritual center," he wrote. For his doctoral thesis and first book, he chose to study D. H. Lawrence, "who dwelt upon these same themes." But he soon turned his attention to more familiar territory. With roots in Ohio and Indiana, the northwest region that was the first to be heavily settled outside of the original 13 colonies, Sanders began to scrutinize this American experience of expansiveness and Manifest Destiny and asked how otherwise idealistic pioneers had succeeded in rendering their natural and psychic environments so desolate. To this end, he undertook a study of the history of exploration and settlement of America's "wild interior." Five books resulted from this study: *Wilderness Plots* (1983), a collection of tales; an anthology; *Wonders Hidden* (1984), a novella about the early years of John James Audubon; *Hear the Wind Blow* (1985), stories inspired by American folk songs; *The Audubon Reader* (1986), and *Bad Man Ballad* (1986), a novel based on an 1813 murder in Ohio.

Sanders described these books as "meditations on the past," an attempt to find durable value in a rapidly changing world. The voice that emerges in them is a vibrant and homespun one, reminiscent of Carl Sandburg in its celebration of American folk traditions. *Hear the Wind Blow* is subtitled "American Folk Songs Retold." It is a collection of 20 tales based on familiar American folk songs, such as "Yankee Doodle," "John Henry," and "The Blue-Tail Fly." Jean Fritz, in the *New York Times Book Review* (January 26, 1986), wrote of Sanders: "He can take a sentence and swivel it around his head like a lasso, then bring it curling down in a circle around his feet as if it were no trick at all. His language sits up and begs to be read aloud, and at the end of every story there is nothing to do but sing, so it's a pity there is no music to go with the songs." In her review of *Bad Man Ballad* for The

Horn Book (March/April 1987), Ethel R. Twichell paid tribute to Sanders's "gift for brilliant metaphors, happy sense of the ludicrous, and spellbinding zest for storytelling" in writing for children.

Sanders's work is as future-oriented as it is concerned with the past. He has described three of his works—*Terrarium* (1985), *The Engineer of Beasts* (1988), and *The Invisible Company* (1989)— as "ecological novels that consider where our fear of wilderness and our infatuation with technology might lead us." Commenting on *Terrarium*, a speculative tale of a 21st-century dystopia in which humanity has abandoned Earth for a numbing, artificial "Enclosure," Ursula K. Le Guin, another master of this genre, acknowledged Sanders's "keen eye . . . sensuous and exact imagination, and . . . buoyant spirit." Written for young adults, *The Engineer of Beasts*, about the proprietor of a mechanical zoo called a "disney," is based on another dystopic vision, that of a frightening zoo that mirrors society's obsession with the artificial, devoid of any ties with nature.

Another series of books stem from Sanders's "attempt to fashion a life that is firmly grounded—in household and community, in knowledge of place, in awareness of nature, and in contact with that source from which all things rise." These collections of essays represent the author's declaration of hope in the face of nuclear weaponry, impending ecological disaster, social pathology, and individual dysfunction.

For *The Paradise of Bombs*, Sanders drew upon his boyhood reminiscences of living at the Ravenna Arsenal and memories of his 1960s student protests against militarism. This collection of essays concerns "the truth about our condition" on a fragile planet whose physical and communitarian ecology is endangered by a war economy that disdains values such as family ties, self-reliance, and simplicity. The book won the Associated Writing Programs Award for Creative Nonfiction in 1986, prompting Kim R. Stafford to write in the *New York Times Book Review* (May 24, 1987) that readers are "hungry . . . for what some are calling a 'literature of fact,' a blending of information and vision. We share this hunger, because like the author we know we are living in a good world under siege."

In *Secrets of the Universe: Scenes from the Journey Home* (1991), Sanders explored, in a collection of 15 essays, his moral evolution as a writer deeply engaged with the world. Some of the essays reveal difficult personal struggles, as the first, "Under the Influence," which deals with the guilt and responsibility he felt as a child over his father's alcoholism. George Cone, reviewing the collection in *The Sewanee Review* (Summer 1992), called attention to the author's ability to be "artful in being artless while pursuing his apparent aw-shucks simplicity (which is not cornpone in the least). . . . Sanders, in redefining the commonplace, enables us to look afresh at the mundane world in which we are stuck."

Writing from the Center (1995) was described in *Choice* (Febuary 1996) as "part memoir, part poetic rumination, part academic discourse," the product of "a literate, lyrical, self-conscious journey to find what is discrete and distinctive about life in the nation's middle border." The book is a collection of 12 essays in which Sanders explored "centeredness" from perspectives such as ancestral history, landscape, work, faith, community, and livelihood. But "centeredness" also refers to Sanders's own spiritual roots in the Midwest, which has always supplied fertile soil for his literary harvest. He explained his purpose in these words: "I want to know how my region has been inhabited and how it has been imagined, because I am convinced that we need to live in our places more conservingly and more lovingly, and that we can only do so if we see our places more truly. . . . The earth needs fewer tourists and more inhabitants, it seems to me—fewer people who float about in bubbles of money and more people committed to knowing and tending their home ground."

Sanders was spurred to write *Hunting for Hope: A Father's Journeys* (1998) by a conversation he had with his son while the two were backpacking in the Colorado Rockies. "You make me feel the planet's dying, and people are to blame, and nothing can be done about it," his son told him. "Maybe you can get by without hope, but I can't. I've got a lot of living still to do. I have to believe there's a way out of this mess. Otherwise what's the point? Why study, why work—why do anything if it's all going to hell?" The essays that Sanders wrote in response argue, in part, that cause for hope can be found in family relationships and in the beauty of nature. Writing in *Booklist* (September 1, 1998), GraceAnne A. DeCandido called *Hunting for Hope* "a small, bright arrowhead of a book: carefully hewn, piercing, balanced; betraying in its form its very substance."

In an essay entitled "The Web of Life," published in the spring 1994 issue of *The Georgia Review*, Sanders explored the contradictory nature of the American experience: "We have a Bill of Rights, which protects each of us from a bullying society, but no Bill of Responsibilities, which would oblige us to answer the needs of others," he wrote in describing a national spirit that, from the pioneer era, celebrated the rugged individualism of Mike Fink and Daniel Boone while participating wholeheartedly in voluntary associations and community-minded enterprises, much to the admiration of Alexis de Tocqueville. "This history of local care hardly ever makes it into our literature," he complained, "for it is less glamorous than rebellion, yet it is a crucial part of our heritage," one that Scott Russell Sanders acknowledges and celebrates.

—E. M.

SUGGESTED READING: *Choice* p953 Feb. 1996; *Georgia Review* Spring 1994; *Kenyon Review* p206+ Summer 1996; *New York Times* C p18

Sep. 20, 1995; *New York Times Book Review* p13 May 24, 1987, p67 Nov. 10, 1991; *School Library Journal* p134+ Feb. 1996; *The Sewanee Review* p56 Summer 1992

SELECTED BOOKS: Fiction—*Wilderness Plots: Tales About the Settlement of the American Land*, 1983; *Fetching the Dead: Stories*, 1984; *Wonders Hidden: Audubon's Early Years*, 1984; *Terrarium*, 1985; *Hear the Wind Blow*, 1985; *Bad Man Ballad*, 1986; *The Engineer of Beasts*, 1988; *Aurora Means Dawn*, 1989; *The Invisible Company*, 1989; Nonfiction—*D. H. Lawrence: The World of the Major Novels*, 1974; *In Limestone Country*, 1985; *The Paradise of Bombs*, 1987; *Secrets of the Universe: Scenes from the Journey Home*, 1991; *Staying Put: Making a Home in a Restless World*, 1993; *Writing from the Center*, 1995; *Hunting for Hope*, 1998; As editor—*The Audubon Reader: The Best Writings of John James Audubon*, 1986

Sigrid Estrada/Courtesy of Farrar, Straus and Giroux

Sante, Luc

1954- Nonfiction writer

Luc Sante, the Belgian-born American nonfiction writer and critic, has had a fascination with the past—his own and that of his adopted home, New York City—for quite some time. As an author he attempts to reconstruct the lives of unknown people and a forgotten past he's discovered in old, yellowing photographs. "I'm fascinated by the notion of lost history," he explained to the *New York Times* in 1993. "What is history, anyway? History is what happened to big powerful people, and I'm really interested in what happened to obscure people about whom nothing is known. The more obscure and buried it is, the more it fascinates me." He has published two books, *Low Life* (1991) and *Evidence* (1992), about the seedier side of New York, particularly the area known as Bowery, in the period between 1840 and 1919, just before the beginning of Prohibition. What Sante uncovered was a society, which in many ways, was worse than our own: crooked cops and politicians on the take from gamblers, madams, and prostitutes; gangs for hire, willing to break an arm or worse for the right price; and illegal bars that served their customers spiked drinks called "Mickey Finns," which made it easier for them to be robbed and possibly murdered. His most recent book *The Factory of Facts* (1998) is a memoir concerning his return to Belgium, the country of his birth.

In an autobiographical sketch written in early 1996 for *World Authors 1990-1995*, Luc Sante discusses his life and work: "I was born in Verviers, Belgium, in 1954. My parents, both from working-class backgrounds, were then just beginning to get a toehold in the middle class. My father had ascended from the labor ranks to a junior management position at an iron foundry that made wool-carding machines. Unfortunately, the textile industry that had sustained the region for centuries was in its last stages of life. In 1958, less than two years after my parents finally bought their own house, my father's employer went bankrupt; there were no other employment options. At the urging of a war-bride friend living in the United States, my parents decided to emigrate. We arrived in 1959, and the dream immediately fell apart. My father could only find work mowing lawns at $50 a week. Plans were made for our return. But things were no better in Belgium, and we re-emigrated in 1960. A pattern was taking shape; for four years my family, or elements thereof, ping-ponged across the Atlantic. I attended Catholic schools in installments, in Belgium and in New Jersey. In 1964, after the last of my grandparents had died, my parents finally and grudgingly decided to stay in America. That same year I learned to dance, fell in love, and decided to become a writer.

"As a child I made stabs at historical fiction, satire, light verse. I read everything, indiscriminately. When I was 13 I attended Expo 67 in Montreal, and in a bookstore there discovered French poetry, specifically Rimbaud and Apollinaire; my idea of literature changed dramatically. Within the next few years I stumbled on the works of, among others, Andre Breton, Alfred Jarry, William Burroughs, Thomas Pynchon, Raymond Chandler, and Nathanael West. Through my teens I wrote primarily poetry, under the sway of all this reading as well as movies (everyone from D. W. Griffith to Jean-Luc Godard) and rock-n-roll (Bob Dylan, the Rolling Stones, Captain Beefheart, the Velvet Underground).

"I attended Regis High School in New York City, an all-scholarship institution run by the Jesuits, to which I commuted, but intoxicated by life, art, and New York City I soon lost interest in my classes and was expelled in the middle of junior year. The pattern repeated itself at Columbia University, which I also attended on a scholarship; I made it through four years, but left with nine incompletes and no degree. I did, however, pursue a self-directed course of study in literature and art, switched to prose and wrote prolifically. I wanted to marry the high and the low, make abstract slang lyricism and write underworld philosophy in words of one syllable.

"I held various menial jobs while for six years or so living the traditional bohemian life downtown, loitering in clubs and bars, ingesting many drugs, hanging out with friends who primarily made movies and music. I wrote sporadically, with no clear direction, publishing seldom. Finally, after working in the mailroom of the *New York Review of Books* for a couple of years, I decided to try writing a piece for it. To my surprise it was published, then other publications followed, and somehow I began cobbling together a career as a critic and cultural journalist. In 1984 I quit the *Review* to become a full-time writer, a move made possible only by the fact that the rent on my small dark apartment was less than $200 a month. I reviewed books and movies and crime as a fine art, wrote profiles and local-color pieces. Along the way I wrote two bad novels, never submitted for publication, both concerning the mysteries of New York City.

"When two editors approached me to ask what kind of non-fiction book I would like to write, I blurted out that I wanted to write a history of the New York slums. The result, five years later, was *Low Life*. In retrospect I can see that it is a work of sublimated autobiography. It carries all the mingled feelings of hope and despair and delight and disgust I had for the city, with an urgency supplied by my realization that the place had changed, irrevocably. I had come to the city in the last interval when New York was both the capital of the world and the refuse-heap of Western civilization, a final moment when the poor were mostly ignored by power and could thus jerry-rig an environment for themselves. The change came with the Reagan administration, which blew the whistle for a land-rush by speculators and profiteers. Not coincidentally, my youth was ending at the same time, my circle was breaking up, my friends were getting into bad trouble, mostly drug-related. The great flaw of *Low Life* is that it omits this whole side of the story.

"My second book, *Evidence*, came about fortuitously, as a result of my picture research for *Low Life*. I first saw those New York Police Department evidence photographs, from 1914-1918, as extraordinary documents of the period, but they haunted me and drew me into thinking more about photography and its relationship to time and death. I have since written a great deal more about photography, an art I think has been too little considered, for all its obvious importance.

"I am now completing *The Factory of Facts*, which I can best summarize as an enquiry into my own background. I wonder about how I was shaped by a culture, that of Walloon, Belgium, that has been at once emotionally crucial and physically far removed for most of my life. I am curious about bonds and ties—to family and nation—about how one can have an affiliation to time as much as to place, about languages and their particular effects, about migration and dispersal and how they are changing the face of the world. I am not interested in these things statistically or in the abstract; they are personal and specific. I want to identify the reciprocal relationship between history and my life.

"I live in Brooklyn with my wife, Melissa Holbrook Pierson."

Between 1976 and 1979, Luc Sante worked as a clerk in the paperback department of the Strand Book Store, where his job was to receive and sort through boxes of old books the store had purchased from estates. In these packages were not just paperbacks but lifetimes' worth of mementos—photographs, postcards, and letters. Sante became fascinated with uncovering ordinary people's lives. As he told the *New York Times*: "It became almost an obsession with me. It was great to sort through all this documentation and try and imagine what the lives behind all this junk had been. I'd find myself feeling rather intimate toward people I had never met and whom I could only speculate on, based on these assorted impedimenta and artifacts. I had a feeling like that with these photographs of people surrounded by their familiars. It was also that the pictures themselves were so beautiful as photographs, and that they really spooked me. It goes into some territory that's more metaphysical than anything."

Such thoughts led Sante to begin thinking about old New York, particularly the neighborhood in which he was then living, the Bowery. The Bowery had always been a tough neighborhood, filled with immigrants and pock-marked by crime, and seemed an ideal central theme for his book. What he discovered through his five-year odyssey in researching and writing *Low Life* was that New York had always had its bad neighborhoods, crime, corruption, and scandal. He also realized that there really is no "good old days" when referring to New York. *Low Life* received both good and mixed reviews. It was praised by critics for the author's passion and for the thoroughness of his research, but some reviewers, such as Sally S. Eckhoff of the *Village Voice* (October 15, 1991), were concerned that Sante "caters to a public taste that may be too delicate to deal with the graphic evidence that could strip the sepia-toned quaintness from his characters. . . . Sante's Bowery garbage does not stink. Those trouble boys with their vendettas, parlor

house ladies, crooked cops, and hopheads add an element of 'realness' to Sante's book that seems almost stagy." A reviewer for The *New York Times* (September 29, 1991) wrote: "*Low Life* captures the rollicking atmosphere of city life during the period. . . . Mr. Sante reclaims an essential piece of the city's past, one that should reassure contemporary New Yorkers. This is far from the worst of times."

His research for *Low Life* had brought him to the Municipal Archives, where he was presented with a library cart filled with what remained of the police department's photographic records. When workmen were cleaning out the old police headquarters on Centre Street in the early 1980s, they dumped thousands of crime-scene and evidence photos from the 19th century into the East River, just as workmen some years earlier had dumped all the 19th century mug shots into New York Bay. The pictures left at the Municipal Archives were those that had been left in a small room under a staircase which had been overlooked by the workers. From these 1,400 photographs Sante collected 55 pictures relating to violent crimes and suicides, and coupled them with his commentary and the original news articles regarding the events depicted in the photos. The result was *Evidence* (1992), his second nonfiction work. *Library Journal* (November 1, 1992) called *Evidence* "a striking and highly original piece of social history." Thomas Boyle, reviewing the book for the *New York Times Book Review* (January 10, 1993), stated: "Mr. Sante has decided to rely on his strong suits: a talent for the striking, impressionistic insight and the ability to write transcendental prose."

Sante's most recent book is *The Factory of Facts*, a memoir published in 1998. In it he traces his own "lost history" and that of his family's home town in Belgium. Sante received noteworthy reviews for this work, including the following from a reviewer at *Kirkus Reviews* (December 1, 1997): "The elegance, originality, and humor of Sante's new book provide a deeply satisfying reading experience. . . . He retains an ironic distance from the past that enables him to maintain a self-conscious affection for less dispiriting times than the present. Beyond its Belgian grayness and fascinating specificity, Sante's shrewd and lyrical treatise on the past speaks to us all."

Luc Sante's freelance writing has appeared in the *New York Times* and the *New Republic*, among other publication. Sante won the Whiting Writer's Award of the Mrs. Giles Whiting Foundation in 1989 for literary and film criticism and nonfiction. He was also the winner of a Guggenheim Fellowship in 1992–1993 for work on the idea of nationality. Since 1994 he has been an adjunct assistant professor of writing for Columbia University's School of the Arts.

—C.M.

SAPPHIRE

SUGGESTED READING: irkus Reviews Dec. 1, 1999; *Library Journal* p163 June 1, 1991, p104 Nov. 1, 1992; *New York Times* IX p8 Feb. 21, 1993, A p31 Dec. 9, 1993, IV p15 June 4, 1995; *New York Times Book Review* p14 Sep. 29, 1991, p31 Jan. 10, 1993; *New York Times Magazine* p31+ May 12, 1995; *Village Voice* p79 Oct. 15, 1991; *Contemporary Authors* vol. 147, 1995

SELECTED BOOKS: *Low Life*, 1991; *Evidence*, 1992; *The Factory of Facts*, 1998

Sapphire

1950– Poet; performance artist; novelist

"I'm often not seen as a writer," the African-American poet and novelist Sapphire once told Patricia Bell-Scott for *Ms.* (March/April 1997). "I'm seen as the homosexual, the ex-prostitute, the incest survivor—the thing as opposed to the artist." The author and former reading teacher first made a name for herself as a poetic commentator on society, composing her free verse on such hot-button topics as the 1989 rape of a jogger in New York City's Central Park and the 1991 shooting of a young black girl by the Korean owner of a store in Los Angeles. Her controversial poetry landed her at the center of a national debate on federal funding for the arts. Rising to the occasion, Sapphire defended her work, and garnered an even larger audience for her public poetry performances. She next wrote a novel that drew on her experiences as a teacher of underprivileged teens. Told in the initially fragmented speech of an illiterate incest victim, *Push* was lauded for its gritty, realistic look at a wide spectrum of contemporary issues.

The second of four children, Sapphire was born Ramona Lofton in 1950 in Fort Ord, California. Her father was a noncommissioned officer in the army, so Ramona grew up on army bases in various states—California, Pennsylvania, Texas—and in other countries. Her family, she would later comment to Dinitia Smith for the *New York Times* (July 2, 1996), was church-going and highly disciplined. "My father was very much into being a father on the surface," she told Smith. "My mother was a housewife, wanted us to have nice clothes, do well in school. They had a deep need to appear normal."

When Ramona was barely 13, her father decided that the family should settle in Los Angeles. Her mother refused, and essentially abandoned the family; she also became an alcoholic in the process. Soon after the departure of her mother, Ramona dropped out of high school. She became involved in the emerging Black Power movement, and participated in protests. She also began traveling and experimenting with drugs.

Ramona Lofton became Sapphire in the mid-1970s, when she was living in the Tenderloin section of San Francisco. She read the work of black and Hispanic poets such as Sonia Sanchez and Jayne Cortez, and studied at San Francisco City College, where she entertained thoughts of becoming a doctor, but became fascinated with dance instead. According to the author, many of her friends in the San Francisco post-hippie scene were changing their names, and she chose Sapphire in part because it is an old slang term in African-American culture for an evil woman. Sapphire confessed, however, to D. T. Max of *Harper's Bazaar* (July 1996) that her choice was also "a New Age thing. I had read somewhere that the rays emitted by sapphires can change the molecular structure of other gemstones—and that was exactly what I wanted to do with my life."

Sapphire's talent for writing slowly emerged during this period. She kept a journal of her thoughts and experiences as a way, she has said, of finding validation that her life was important. As she told Bell-Scott, "For me, writing is always a creative process, and everything I write is not beautiful or publishable. But everything starts in my journal. And most things do not start as themselves. I just write, and then within the writing a poem or story will appear."

In 1977, Sapphire arrived in New York City with no more than $20 in her pocket. She intended to get an education and begin her writing career, but instead found herself working as an exotic dancer in Times Square. However, she continued to write on her own; she published some poems in feminist journals and read her work aloud in Greenwich Village cafés. She also began to explore her sexuality, declaring herself a lesbian (she now says she is bisexual) and joining New York's lesbian scene. With the money she made dancing topless, Sapphire took dance classes at the City College of New York, and finally earned her bachelor's degree with honors in 1983. She then took a position teaching reading and writing to high schoolers in Harlem and the Bronx, a job she held for more than seven years. The experience had a profound impact on her life, as it brought her into contact with many young girls who were trying to become literate despite dire situations at home. As she told Nicolas A. Basbanes of *George Jr.* magazine (November 1996), "I saw a generation of kids who were six and seven when I got there have babies, go off to jail, get killed. I'm in the neighborhood seeing all that, and at the same time I'm teaching, and it's devastating to me."

At this juncture in her life, Sapphire also began to piece together the story behind some disturbing feelings she had experienced since her childhood. From the depths of her psyche, she recovered a memory of being sexually abused by her father, and suddenly she felt she understood her lifelong feelings of intense isolation. Although she confronted her father with this accusation, he denied ever having abused her. However, Sapphire's sister also remembered being sexually abused by their father.

During this time, Sapphire also had to contend with the deaths of both her mother and brother. Her brother's death in particular was difficult for her—a schizophrenic, he had lived a transient existence, and was murdered in a Los Angeles park in 1986. The attendant emotional stress led Sapphire to attempt to write again. "I mean, I was dealing with my [expletive] life being robbed," she told Max. "A shade opened up, and suddenly my life was rescued for me. I [expletive] got to work."

The first works Sapphire produced were poems she read as performance pieces, which dealt with such extreme family issues as violence and incest. She was influenced, she told Bell-Scott, by performers such as Ntozake Shange, who experimented in choreography and poetry. Sapphire's readings, at clubs and bookstores in New York City, were similar hybrids of literature and dance.

At the age of 40, experiencing something of a midlife crisis, Sapphire decided to take her career in a new direction. Perhaps because she had been trying to perform and to write simultaneously, her success at both art forms had been somewhat limited. When her business manager pushed her to write a book, Sapphire accepted the challenge. "I felt that I had not really done much with my life, when I compared myself to my mentors like Ntozake, who had five to six books," she told Bell-Scott. "Then I looked at some of the reasons I hadn't tried. A lack of confidence—a belief that maybe I couldn't do it or that I wasn't good or smart enough. I also realized that I had never committed myself to any one thing. I had always tried to dance, act, and write at the same time."

With a new perspective and drive, Sapphire enrolled in 1993 in the graduate writing school at Brooklyn College, from which she earned an M.F.A. degree in 1996. She started collecting her work for publication. What emerged, *American Dreams* (1994), was a volume of poetry and prose packed with deeply personal and harshly honest musings on a wide variety of contemporary issues, including racism, incest, disease, and death. In her interview with Bell-Scott, Sapphire said that her writing "has always been about erasing a certain kind of invisibility, about saying that someone like me exists. . . . There were no first-person poems by a black woman like me—someone who had been involved in the sex industry, someone who was expressing ambivalence about sexuality."

"Wild Thing," one of the most controversial poems in the book, was written from the point of view of one of the young men who raped a jogger in Central Park in 1989. An attempt to show how poverty and racism breed violence, the poem garnered a great deal of attention—mostly negative. Some women's groups took offense at what they saw as a sympathetic look at rape. Federal funding for arts programs was at the time coming under heavy fire from religious leaders and government officials who took issue with the "obscenity" they saw in some government-sponsored work. The Reverend Donald Wildmon, who endorsed a "family values" group called the American Family Association, discovered "Wild Thing" in a publication that received funding from the National Endowment for the Arts (NEA); while giving a speech in front of Congress, he cited the poem as an example of such an obscenity, focusing on a particular homoerotic passage involving Jesus Christ and a clergyman. After Wildmon circulated copies of the journal to Congress as part of his campaign, the chairman of the NEA was forced to resign.

The controversy helped push Sapphire and her book into the limelight. Critical response to *American Dreams* was largely favorable, although some reviewers took issue with its style. Yet even those critics who found Sapphire's writing to be flawed applauded the strength of her ideas and their straightforward presentation. A *Booklist* (January 15, 1994) writer opined that "these harsh but sometimes beautiful pieces may be seen as a barbaric yawp howled Ginsberg-like into the wind, but their words and the images they evoke are hard to dismiss." Katherine Dieckmann of the *Voice Literary Supplement* (April 1994) also commented on the poems' intensity: "Most have the effect of a sudden punch to the gut. They insist upon deliberation, a strong measure of receptivity and empathy to match her own act of laying herself bare."

On the style of *American Dreams*, Margaret Randall wrote in the *American Book Review* (March-May 1995) that Sapphire is "less successful when she combines prose and the poetic line; some narrative pieces dwindle into several pages of lines rambling to no purpose I could discern." However, the reviewer conceded, "I have a feeling hearing Sapphire read might help to resolve some of my questions about why she has chosen this particular style. On the page it doesn't work." Terese Svoboda wrote in the *Kenyon Review* (Spring 1995) that while Sapphire is successful in presenting a picture of the American dream both shattered and idealized, "sometimes the imagery weaves too far from its frighteningly concrete base, as in 'Rabbit Man,' and sometimes the prose is not urgent enough, as in 'A New Day for Willa Mae.'" However, Svoboda's final assessment was that "the breadth of the poet's sympathy overwhelms any flaws."

Ellen Kaufman of *Library Journal* (February 15, 1994) also praised Sapphire's realistic, hard-hitting verse: "In spite of a tendency toward cliché, the confessional pieces included here are painful and affecting; their explicit, sordid detail is utterly convincing, and the author's intelligence allows her to generalize beyond personal anger and pain." Kaufman objected to Sapphire's poems about well-known events like the Central Park rape, calling them "merely descriptive and sensational." The reviewer was quick to add however, that the poems in general are "volatile stuff, and not all of it works, but the pieces that do, go over with a bang."

Sapphire's next literary venture was born of her experiences teaching reading and writing to underprivileged students. While studying under the novelist Susan Fromberg Schaffer, Sapphire brought her the rough draft of a novel, and Schaffer encouraged her to take it to a publisher. The end result was *Push* (1996), a harrowing tale of sexual abuse, illiteracy, and isolation as seen through the eyes of Precious Jones, an overweight 16-year-old African-American girl who lives in Harlem. Precious is degraded by her classmates, dismissed by the system, and abused both emotionally and sexually by her parents. Pregnant with her second child by her father (her first child, Mongo, short for Mongoloid, was born when Precious was 12 and suffers from Downs Syndrome), Precious is kicked out of her high school, but dreams of one day learning to read and gaining independence from her mother, a malicious, abusive woman who blames her for "stealing" the affections of her boyfriend—that is, Precious's own father. Precious gains admittance into an alternative school where she meets Blue Rain, a reading teacher who encourages her still preliterate students to keep a written journal of their feelings and experiences. For the first time in her life, Precious begins to explore the world of literature. She begins to find a sense of self-worth and hope for her future, despite her dreary environment. However, she soon becomes homeless, and then discovers that her father is dying of AIDS and that she has been infected with the HIV virus. Still, Precious perseveres, drawing strength from the novels she reads that depict situations similar to her own (such as Alice Walker's *The Color Purple*) and, at the encouragement of her teacher, joining an incest survivors' group. The novel ends with a lengthy postscript that reveals the writings of some of Precious's fellow classmates, who divulge stories of their own impoverished lives.

Like *American Dreams*, *Push* is characterized by a straightforward, no-holds-barred style. The book, which in large part is composed of Precious's journal entries, begins with a very primitive fragment of a sentence: "li Mg o mi m" or "Little Mongo on my mind." Sapphire's use of a voice that defies all conventional rules of spelling and grammar made for a trying read but also a strong statement about the power of education. As the novel progresses, so does Precious's writing ability and her sense of self, and by its end she is contemplating going to college. *Push*'s title reflects the underlying message Sapphire wanted to communicate in her work. "Precious pushes when she gives birth, but she also pushes for herself, pushes forward," the author told Max. "To push is the opposite of being passive." Reviews for *Push* were generally favorable, although, as with her previous book, the author's topic and writing style were both controversial. Sapphire herself did not shy away from the attention, confronting the issue head-on before any comments had even been cast her way. "I expect a lot of people who read *Push* to be hostile to me," she told Max. "People will say I'm riding the incest

train. The HIV community, some lesbians, they won't like it either. Black people will say it's bad for the community, bad to air our dirty laundry in public. . . . But what if that dirty laundry is deadly? Do you keep silent? There was a hole where this book now is."

"I see *Push* as a healing novel and a story of triumph," she told Bell-Scott. "The writing, however, wasn't particularly healing for me. In contrast to my autobiographical writing, which is cathartic, here I created homelessness, HIV, and this horrible mother and father. I lived with tension and pain. I tried to show that a profound alteration in this child's consciousness could allow her to love herself and her son. If there is anything to learn from this novel, it's that Precious is a valuable human being."

Overall, critics were impressed by Sapphire's brave, realistic look at a number of contemporary social issues, but were divided on both her underlying mission and her inconsistent use of broken English. Michiko Kakutani of the *New York Times* (June 14, 1996) described *Push* as a novel "that manages to be disturbing, affecting, and manipulative all at the same time. . . . Although the reader comes to feel enormous sympathy for Precious, one is constantly aware of the author standing behind the scenes, orchestrating her heroine's terrifying plummet into the abyss and her equally dramatic rescue." Kakutani concluded that "In trying to open out her heroine's story and turn it into a more general comment on society, Sapphire has made the tale of Precious decidedly less moving than it might have been."

Rosemary Mahoney of the *New York Times Book Review* (July 7, 1996) found Sapphire's use of broken English an "occasionally uneven stylistic device [that] threatens to obstruct the narrative, but the intensity of Precious' persona swiftly overrides whatever irritation the reader may feel at having to puzzle through her not always convincingly misshapen words." Mahoney also saw "no apparent reason" for Sapphire's temporary switch early in the book from Precious's semiliterate, first-person accounts to an eloquently written third-person voice. Another flaw, the critic asserted, was the reading teacher, whose entrance "[turns] the social commentary . . . somewhat proselytizing. Ms. Rain is an inexplicably underdeveloped character with some surprisingly wooden dialogue." Nonetheless, Mahoney raved about the characterization of Precious: "Her sardonic voice is blunt and unadorned, sorrowful as a foghorn and so wholly engulfing that despite its broken words it generates single-handedly the moving power of this novel. . . . Without benefit of intricate plot or beautiful language, masterly structure or terribly complex characters, Sapphire has created in *Push* an affecting and impassioned work that sails on the strength of pure, stirring feeling."

Sapphire's work has appeared in a number of anthologies, including *High Risk 2: Writings on Sex, Death & Subversion* (1994), *Critical Condi-*

tion: *Women on the Edge of Violence* (1993), and *Women on Women: An Anthology of American Lesbian Short Fiction* (1990). In 1994 she won a MacArthur Foundation Scholarship in Poetry and later that year *Downtown Magazine*'s Year of the Poet III Award. The author continues to write and work in New York City.

"The more I live, the more I understand that people are brought into the world for different reasons," Sapphire told Bell-Scott. "Some are brought to have the perfect child, some to have the perfect relationship, or for other reasons. I know that this writing is what I was brought here to do. And my purpose is to get out the word, to witness, and to give testimony. So I'm on a mission—definitely on a mission." —D.B.

SUGGESTED READING: *American Book Review* p26 Mar.–May 1995; *Booklist* Jan. 15, 1994; *Dia Center for the Arts* (on-line); *George Jr.* (on-line)

Nov. 1996; *Harper's Bazaar* p109+ July 1996; *Kenyon Review* p157+ Spring 1995; *Kirkus Reviews* Apr. 15, 1996; *Library Journal* p160 Feb. 15, 1994, p152 June 1, 1996; *London Review of Books* p25 Feb. 6, 1997; *Los Angeles Times Book Review* p1+ July 7, 1996; *Ms.* p82 July/Aug. 1996, p78+ Mar./Apr. 1997; *New York Times* B p8 June 14, 1996, B p1+ July 2, 1996; *New York Times Book Review* p26 Feb. 27, 1994, p9 July 7, 1996; *Publishers Weekly* p61 Apr. 22, 1996; *Village Voice* p70 June 25, 1996; *Voice Literary Supplement* p28 Apr. 1994; *Book Review Digest*, 1994, 1997; *Contemporary Literary Criticism*, 1997

SELECTED BOOKS: *American Dreams*, 1994; *Push*, 1996

Saro-Wiwa, Ken

Oct. 10, 1941– Nov. 10, 1995 Novelist; short-story writer; journalist

On November 10, 1995, Ken Saro-Wiwa, a Nigerian author, journalist, and television writer, was hanged in Port Harcourt, Nigeria, for his outspokenness in protesting the "genocide" perpetrated against that country's Ogoni minority by petroleum interests, especially Royal Dutch/Shell. Over a 20-year period, Saro-Wiwa, himself an Ogoni, had published several acclaimed novels and short stories and written the scripts for *Basi & Company*, a popular Nigerian television sitcom. His highly acclaimed novel, *Sozaboy* (1986), about a young Biafran soldier boy, was written in "New Englishes," a term Saro-Wiwa used to describe a mixture of Nigerian pidgin and idiomatic English. He published two collections of short stories, *A Forest of Flowers* (1986) and *Adaku and Other Stories* (1989). Saro-Wiwa began writing political commentary as a journalist during the period of the Biafran civil war and then resumed, especially after 1990, his forceful criticism of the collusion he saw between the nation's military regime and foreign petroleum interests. His books *Nigeria, The Brink of Disaster* (1991) and *Genocide in Nigeria: The Ogoni Tragedy* (1992) established his reputation as that nation's most prominent dissident writer and did much to focus world attention on the situation there. His work earned him the respect of human-rights activists and garnered him a Nobel Peace Prize nomination. Published posthumously from computer diskettes that had been smuggled out of Nigeria, and with an introduction by his friend William Boyd, *A Month and a Day: A Detention Diary* (1995) was a first-person account of Saro-Wiwa's 1993 detention and of the history of the resistance movement.

Ken Saro-Wiwa was born in the Khana region of Nigeria, in the Rivers State town of Bori, the son of J. B. Saro-Wiwa, a businessman, and Widu, a farmer. He attended mission schools and won a scholarship to the University of Ibadan, near Lagos, the nation's capital. As a schoolboy, he made it a practice of commenting on local political happenings by writing anonymous letters to the editor of local newspapers. Saro-Wiwa taught for several years at a government college in Umuahia, at Stella Maris College in Port Harcourt, and at the University of Lagos. In 1967 and 1968, during the Biafran civil war, he was the administrator for the oil depot at Bonny Island, after which he served for five years in the Rivers State cabinet as a regional commissioner for education. He was removed from this position after he began to express strong opinions about autonomy for the Ogoni people. During this period he established several retail and real estate ventures as well as the Saros publishing company, which brought most of his books into print.

Saro-Wiwa first came to the attention of the literary world with a television play, *Transistor Radio*, which won the BBC African Theater Award in 1972. Soon afterwards, his first journalistic works began appearing in newspapers and other periodicals published by Sam Amuka-Pemu ("Sad Sam"), the editor of several Nigerian newspapers and magazines, who was killed in 1977 after founding *The Punch* magazine. Several pieces of short fiction first published in Amuka-Pemu's periodicals grew into the novels that brought growing acclaim to the young Saro-Wiwa. During this period Saro-Wiwa also wrote political columns for Amuka-Pemu's daily newspaper, the *Vanguard*, and, from 1989, wrote the "Similla" column for a local Sunday newspaper. A prolific writer of children's and adult fiction, he was also known throughout West Africa as the writer and producer of more than 150 episodes of Nigeria's leading television soap opera, *Basi & Company*, which poked fun at the antics of a crew of Lagotians as they hatch one get-rich-quick scheme after another. The series was immensely popular in a period when Nigeria was rapidly industrializing and when Lagos was emerging as a crowded, sprawling capital city. Several of the Basi stories were adapted in children's books, such as *Mr. B Again* (1989), *Mr. B Is Dead* (1991), and *Mr. B's Mattress* (1992).

Sozaboy (1986) remains Saro-Wiwa's most highly acclaimed work. The title of this novel, derived from the "rotten English" word for "soldier boy," is both an antiwar polemic and a coming-of-age tale of a young village boy who is pressured by recruiters with the words "all your friends are making *soza*" to serve in the Biafran army during the civil war in the late 1960s. Derived from Saro-Wiwa's personal memories of that period, the novel foreshadows his later political activity in that the secessionist state of Biafra contained most of Nigeria's oil reserves, whose disposition would continue to dominate national politics and, of course, Saro-Wiwa's own fate. It is written in what he calls "New Englishes," a mixture of West African pidgin English (called "rotten English" by its author), idiomatic English, and the formal received standard English. "This language is disordered and disorderly," Saro-Wiwa wrote in his preface to the book, because he used it to mirror the discordant society that Nigeria has become. An excerpt from *Sozaboy* is illustrative of this style:

> However, you know as Lagos girl concern, she must want plenty money and other good things because, after all said and done, no be fine that woman will chop. As they used to sing for gramophone, 'no money, woman no go follow you, even if you fine fine pass everybody.'

Two weeks after his execution, the *New Yorker* published an "in memoriam" piece entitled "Death of a Writer," in which William Boyd told of his long friendship with Saro-Wiwa. "*Sozaboy* is not simply a great African novel but also a great antiwar novel—among the very best of the twentieth century," he concluded.

A collection of stories, *A Forest of Flowers*, was published in 1986 and reprinted in 1995, the year of his execution. These stories reflect Saro-Wiwa's growing political disillusionment, of people thwarted by corrupt officials, superstitious villagers, envious relatives, and petty shopkeepers, but they retain a nostalgic intimacy with everyday life and African ancestral heritage, as in the lead story, "Home, Sweet Home," which concludes:

> And out of the bowels of the night came the rhythm of drums in the distance, the hooting of owls, the swooping and beeping of bats, the burping of toads, the humming of night birds and the words of a mournful song welcoming me to the embrace of the spirits of my home, my sweet home.

In another story in this collection, "The Stars Below," Saro-Wiwa deepened his search for spiritual meaning in narrating a tale about Ezi, an educated villager who is mocked for his erudite habits of ostentatiously consulting the *Oxford English Dictionary* or *Roget's Thesaurus*. Isolated, he goes to the seaside and remembers an old folk tale of the sky visiting the earth, enabling him to experience a spiritual rebirth in "dancing with the stars."

Saro-Wiwa's *Adaku and Other Stories* (1989), dedicated to his sisters, is a collection of 18 short stories, 12 of which deal with "the condition of women." In many of them, innuendo and gentle humor are used to comment on the quickly changing social mores in Nigeria, as in "Cross Pollination," about a Lutheran church that tries to enforce moral rectitude and increase its coffers by requiring parishioners to pay fines after publicly confessing their sins. (Saro-Wiwa remarked that some of the letters on the sign on the front of the church had been obliterated by the rain, causing it to appear as "Lut an"—the missing letters being "her".) One day, a couple "living in sin" pay the price of their transgression, but not before the boyfriend delivers spellbinding and side-splitting testimony to the "beauty of the multiplication table" as inspired by the biblical admonition to "increase and multiply."

Lemona's Tale, published posthumously in 1996, explores the changing moral landscape of Nigeria as it moves rapidly from a tradition-bound, agricultural society to the largest industrialized economy in western Africa. In this novel, a woman, awaiting execution for a murder she committed in a love triangle some 25 years earlier, confesses her life's story to the adult child of her victims. It is a story of innocence gone awry, of a girl seduced by a monstrous woman, Maybel, who assembles around her a stable of young women like Lemona to barter for business contacts.

In his fiction, television scripts, and newspaper columns, Saro-Wiwa had, from the beginning, taken a critical view of government corruption, tempering it with humor and satire, but it was not until the early 1990s that his writing became more of a crusade, in response to his growing anguish over the depredation of the Ogoni people that he saw victimized both by the Nigerian military regime and by the Royal/Dutch Shell petroleum interests. Boyd suggested that Saro-Wiwa's "awful grief" over the sudden death from heart failure of his 14-year-old son, an Eton student, during a rugby game "gave a new force to his fight for his people's rights." In 1990 Saro-Wiwa founded the Movement for the Survival of the Ogoni People (MOSOP) and also founded a more radical youth movement that reputedly engaged in increasing sabotage and harassment against Shell, which finally decided to cease operations in Ogoniland in January 1993. The decision resulted in the loss of only three percent of Nigeria's total oil output, but MOSOP's success made it a threat to the military government, which responded by replacing Ogoni police officers with personnel from other ethnic groups, resulting in violent confrontations. Despite deep rifts in MOSOP, Saro-Wiwa urged the Ogoni people to boycott the presidential elections and to resist the authority of traditional tribal chiefs and regional officials, whom he viewed as "vultures" and "collaborators." David Owens Wiwa, his younger brother, told Joshua Hammer for *Harper's* (June 1996) that this militancy contributed to his younger brother's downfall: "MOSOP was changing the traditional structure. Those who benefitted from the old establishment, from government contracts, were seen as depriving the people of their due." The director of the Ministry of Education in Port Harcourt recounted how young Ogoni militants had burned down her house and those of six other tribal chiefs for not moving quickly enough for MOSOP.

At around this time, Saro-Wiwa published *Nigeria, The Brink of Disaster* (1991), dedicated to his old mentor, Sam Amuka-Pemu. The essays recount Saro-Wiwa's frustration at seeing Nigeria and its minority peoples victimized by official corruption and chicanery. He concluded, "I am unfortunate to be a Nigerian—I would rather not be, but I am doing my level best to be one, and a good one at that." In the following year, he published a slim volume, *Genocide in Nigeria: The Ogoni Tragedy*, that infuriated officials who began to see Saro-Wiwa as a threat to their hegemony. This 103-page book summarized all of the grievances that Saro-Wiwa wanted to raise on behalf of this minority people. Condemning Shell and British Petroleum for years of systematic exploitation, he wrote that they displayed "the ugliest possible face of international capitalism" in behaving "cruelly, stupidly, and in a racist manner" against "a peasant population. The book presents detailed petitions that describe in detail the economic, ecological, and social disruptions that Shell-BP had brought to a formerly agricultural economy. Saro-Wiwa's prose alternates between reportage and pithy personal commentary, as in his statement, "This Company's antics make me sick."

Early in May 1994 the Nigerian government circulated an internal memo that declared a crackdown on MOSOP. Hammer described Saro-Wiwa telling Greenpeace, an international organization of environmental activists, "This is it. They are going to arrest us all and execute us. All for Shell." On May 21, his premonition became reality: Saro-Wiwa was arrested on his way to a political rally, and a number of his relatives and supporters in MOSOP were slain in the palace of the village chief at Giokoo, where a meeting of Ogoni chiefs was underway. The following day, government troops moved into Ogoniland and arrested other activists, allegedly raping and murdering hundreds of civilians.

A year after his arrest, Saro-Wiwa and 14 other Ogoni activists were charged with murder for their role in instigating the massacres at Giokoo. Saro-Wiwa, who had been in prison all this time, was tried before a panel of two civilians and one military judge, called a kangaroo court by many human-rights activists, which found him and eight other defendants guilty and sentenced them to the gallows. By this time, human-rights activists around the world were pleading for his release, but to no avail. After he was hanged on November 10, 1995, several nations, including the United States and Canada, withdrew their ambassadors from Lagos, and Nigeria's membership in the British Commonwealth of Nations was suspended. The South African president Nelson Mandela himself attended the biennial Commonwealth conference in Auckland, New Zealand, that suspended Nigeria's membership in the British Commonwealth of Nations. Human-rights groups such as PEN, Amnesty International, and Greenpeace lent their support and publicized the circumstances surrounding Saro-Wiwa's activities on behalf of the Ogoni people. A letter written by Saro-Wiwa from prison, published in the *Mail & Guardian* (May 1995) around the time of his trial, blames the British government for supplying arms to the Nigerian military leaders, but also attests to his belief in the rightness of his struggle and his solidarity with other dissident African writers: "Fearful odds. Hardly. The men who ordain and supervise this show of shame, this tragic charade, are frightened by the word, the power of ideas, the power of the pen; by the demands of social justice and the rights of man. Nor do they have a sense of history. They are so scared of the power of the word that they do not read. And that is their funeral."

William Boyd's *New Yorker* article, reprinted as the introduction to *A Month and a Day: A Detention Diary*, concluded with another of Saro-Wiwa's last letters, this one smuggled out of prison just before his death: "There's no doubt that my idea will succeed in time, but I'll have to bear the pain of the moment. . . . The most important thing for me is that I've used my talents as a writer to enable the Ogoni people to confront their tormentors. I was not able to do it as a politician or a businessman. My writing did it. And it sure makes me feel good! I'm mentally prepared for the worst, but hopeful for the best. I think I have the moral victory."

Saro-Wiwa did not live to fulfill the hope he expressed in the final sentences of *A Month and a Day: A Detention Diary*: "The genocide of the Ogoni had taken on a new dimension. The manner of it I will narrate in my next book, if I live to tell the tale."

—E. M.

SUGGESTED READING: *Christian Science Monitor* p14 Jan. 22, 1996; *Harper's* p58+ June 1996; *Los Angeles Times* p11 Sep. 15, 1996; *New Yorker* p56+ Nov. 27, 1995; *New York Times* A p8 Dec. 7, 1994, C p18 Nov. 29, 1995; (London)*Times Literary Supplement* p857 Aug. 5, 1988

SELECTED WORKS: Fiction—*Sozaboy*, 1986; *Adaku and Other Stories*, 1989; *A Forest of Flowers: Short Stories*, 1986; *Lemona's Tale*, 1996; Nonfiction—*A Month and a Day: A Detention Diary*, 1995; Television—*Basi & Company: Four Television Plays*, 1988

Sayers, Valerie

Aug. 8, 1952– Novelist

The American novelist Valerie Sayers has made a corner of the South her domain, setting her novels in the small, fictional town of Due East (a thinly disguised Beaufort, South Carolina) and creating a world in which characters from one book reappear in others. Not exactly autobiographical, *Due East* (1987), *How I Got Him Back* (1989), *Who Do You Love?* (1991), *The Distance Between Us* (1994), and *Brain Fever* (1996) capture the details of place, while their characters live out some of Sayers's fantasies and grapple with her spiritual concerns as a Catholic. Elizabeth Benedict in the *New York Times Book Review* (March 17, 1996) noted that, in her novels, Sayers grapples with the themes of "fidelity, apostasy, and salvation." Her characters struggle with misfortune and loss but always retain a saving grace.

In a statement for *World Authors 1990–1995*, Sayers writes, "I was born [on August 8, 1952] in Beaufort, South Carolina, into a large Irish-American Catholic family. The combination of that place and that family may go a long way toward explaining how I came to be a novelist. My family used to sit in the Ocean View Café—it was really on the bay, not the ocean—where old men gathered every morning to drink coffee and tell each other stories as exaggerated as the name of the restaurant. My parents listened with fascination, horror, and delight: everything about Southerners was foreign to them (they were transplanted Yankees), but they loved the stories. I got the idea early on that telling a good story was a good thing. My parents loved language, especially jokes, puns, and any aphorism that sounded better in French; my father went around saying *Nul est prophet dans son pays*, and he was absolutely right.

"I was crazy about Beaufort—it's a pretty little town perched on a sea island, and its landscape is lush and watery—but because my family were latterday carpetbaggers, I felt myself an outsider there. Beaufort's defined by its strong sense of history; it was occupied early in the Civil War and so its antebellum architecture and surrounding plantations still stand, reminders of the slave economy that fueled its past. I was coming of writing age as the struggle for civil rights was heating up and firing my own imagination. When I left the South, I had plenty to write about, beginning with my own ambiguous position and working through the turmoil and growth that faced my hometown.

"I resisted thinking of myself as a writer. My parents had pegged me, early on, as the designated writer in the family and my teachers egged me on, too. I knew from my earliest writing days that it was easy for me to dash off a page of prose or poetry, hard to claim any of my work as true or earned or finished. I guessed, that is, that being an honest writer (or a good writer, anyway), is a rough business. I wanted no part of the loneliness. I wanted glitz, and I went off to New York City when I was 17, thinking that I'd be an actress. I was disabused of that notion after about two weeks, but I did act a little in college and found it frustrating. I didn't like reading someone else's lines. Meanwhile, as an undergraduate at Fordham [University], I was working with Robert Nettleton, an unknown poet and former engineer who taught me in Hemingway and Faulkner seminars and in a poetry workshop. He convinced me that I was a writer. His own approach to language was gleeful and anarchic. I was reminded of those old gents in the Ocean View Café.

"Homesick, I went back to Beaufort after I graduated to see if I could keep up a serious writing pace. I stayed a year. I taught in a local technical college and wrote some pretty bad stories at night (it would take me a few more years to figure out that if I did have a gift, it was probably for a longer form). That one year back in the South, where I began to confront the themes that would consume me, was crucial. I began to think of my fictional town of Due East (suspiciously like Beaufort) as a moral landscape where I could explore my characters' relationship to an evolving culture, to religious faith, to racial tension, to their own sexual passion. I went on to get an M.F.A. at Columbia, but I wilted fast in that hothouse, and it took me a while to get my writing courage back. I have been teaching and raising my two magnificent sons as I have written my novels to date, and though I am always desperate for time, my children have forced me to live in the everyday present in a way that has been extremely useful for my fiction.

"All my novels thus far—*Due East* (1987), *How I Got Him Back* (1989), *Who Do You Love?* (1991), *The Distance Between Us* (1994), and *Brain Fever* (1996)—take place at least partially in Due East; the last three are also set in New York City (where I lived for 20-odd years). I am still working the same themes, and working to find new narrative forms to contain them. *The Distance Between Us* has a screenplay in its middle, *How I Got Him Back* is a pastiche that includes one character's bad poetry and phone conversations; the novel I'm writing now, 'Cab Ride to Dixie,' makes use of e-mail as the new epistolary form. My work cannot help but be affected by my Catholicism and by my upbringing in the South, but since I think of myself as a dubious Southerner and a cantankerous Catholic, the novels are naturally full of characters ambivalent about those two ways of being. I am a lefty in my politics and so are many of my characters. I am now professor of English at the University of Notre

Dame (a natural spot for a writer with my concerns), and I find that teaching is a good complement to the isolation of writing. My husband has put up with a lot. I was right, as a child, when I thought that writing was unglamorous, hard work. I find it harder as the years go by."

Valerie Sayers is the fourth of the seven children of Paul and Janet Hogan Sayers. Her father, a psychologist employed at the Parris Island marine base, died when Sayers was a sophomore at Fordham University, his alma mater. Sayers has recycled her youth in Beaufort many times, leading interviewers to ask her if she had an unhappy childhood. She told David Streitfeld, however, in an interview for the *Washington Post* (April 21, 1991), that she had had "a swell time," but got for herself a "cheap psychoanalysis to be able to write about this place over and over." Nevertheless, she told Streitfeld, the people of Beaufort have been "just nice" about Sayers's reconstruction of their town. Their main comment has been, "I'm so happy for you." Moreover, many of them continually confess—falsely—to being the characters in her novels.

Many of her characters do not relive her life, but live her fantasies instead. In her first published novel, *Due East*, a pregnant 15-year-old, Mary Faith, is the main character; Sayers told Streitfeld that when she was 15 she herself had a fantasy of becoming pregnant and showing her high school how stoic she could be. As Streitfeld reported, "She didn't attempt to make it a reality." Mary Faith, by contrast, dreams of seducing one of "the shy, slow boys"—and does. The father of the child subsequently kills himself, and Mary Faith assures everyone that hers has been an immaculate conception. Her father, in trying to find out who fathered his daughter's child, seduces the mother of the boy he suspects and impregnates her. Carl Mitcham, a reviewer for *Commonweal* (May 22, 1987), saw a religious lesson in the novel. "This novel is not only a good story and good literature; it is also good spiritual reading. It is a fictive study of our rejection of God, the motherhood of faith, and how both depend on and transcend our relationships with others." Jack Butler, writing in the *New York Times Book Review* (March 8, 1987), on the other hand, observed that "Mary Faith is so shrewdly perceptive and the people who frustrate her are so unrelievedly small-minded and mean that the story nearly degenerates into the familiar tale of the good and sensitive teen-ager against the cruel and insensitive world." Butler found *Due East* "a bitter wafer, an antistory parallel to that other virgin birth, . . . a hard-eyed if not hard-hearted tale," and observed that the one moment at the end "that suggests . . . that its characters are able to conceive warmth, peace, and affection in the midst of unrelenting woe" is a "true miracle." Sayers told Brewster M. Robertson, who interviewed her for *Publishers Weekly* (February 7,

1994), that *Due East* "is about faith and the hope of redemption."

In her 1989 novel, *How I Got Him Back; Or, Under the Cold Moon's Shine*, also set in Due East, Sayers experimented with narrative technique to tell the stories of women attempting the act denoted by the title. The characters in *How I Got Him Back* are mainly members of the Roman Catholic parish of Our Lady of Perpetual Help. Mary Faith, the protagonist of *Due East*, reappears as the love interest of a married man whose wife is trying to win back her husband; Becky's husband threatens to leave her for a redhead named Judi; and Tim Rooney, described by Alfred Corn in the *New York Times Book Review* (January 29, 1989) as "a sort of Berriganish avant-garde Catholic," makes his first appearance in Sayers's fictional town, having an affair with Eileen, whom Corn called a "plain dish of ordinary sex improved by the salsa of exhibitionism and bondage." Moral guidance comes from Father Berkeley, a "whisky priest." Corn observed that the "characters are memorable and believable, however much they startle with excursions into the abnormal," and he commented on the "Christian-symbolic substructure" of the novel. The story is narrated in the first and third person, through stream-of-consciousness monologues, letters, and crude verse, producing what Corn termed a "mixture of soap-opera plot, sacred story, sitcom humor, sex and analysis." He deemed that Sayers would go far with her "gift for voice and . . . honest gritty commentary about human behavior in stressful circumstances."

In her third novel, *Who Do You Love?*, Sayers captured a moment in American history. The action unfolds mainly in the course of one day, November 21–22, 1963, when President John F. Kennedy was assassinated. Dolores, who is pregnant with her fifth child, feels guilty about her earlier affair with a cousin who then became a priest and another brief affair after her marriage. Suddenly, a young reporter arrives in town, to cover a court martial at Parris Island. Although Dolores and the reporter are attracted to each other, what Howard Frank Mosher in the *New York Times Book Review* (April 7, 1991) described as a "wonderfully affirmative ending" takes place. Dolores achieves "a remarkably wise insight into herself and her relationship with her big, squabbling, funny, smart, problem-ridden and immensely likable family." Sayers "invests the situation with emotional complexity and historical resonance by setting the story during the evening before, and in the morning of, November 22, 1963," Brewster M. Robertson wrote in *Publishers Weekly* (February 7, 1994).

"There are writers one reads for wisdom, and writers, like Sayers, to whom one turns for something more like a re-creation of life's actual chaos," Liz Rosenberg wrote in the *Chicago Tribune* (March 20, 1994). Rosenberg was reviewing *The Distance Between Us*, Sayers's 1994 novel, a story of the coming-of-age and beyond of flirtatious Franny and rich, detached Steward, who have grown up on opposite sides of the tracks in Due East. The third main character, Michael, whom Franny marries, takes her away to Brooklyn, where she ends up as an unknown artist and mother. Michael has written the screenplay for the movie Franny has urged Steward to make; the screenplay, which appears in the middle of the novel, includes a twisted account of Michael and Franny's honeymoon. Some reviewers deplored the addition of the screenplay. Rosenberg, despite her admiration for Sayers's re-creation of "life's actual chaos," observed that both "the usually drunk or drugged-out" Michael and his "awful" screenplay are nearly "too unlikeable to bear." Brewster W. Robertson, in *Publishers Weekly* (February 7, 1994), however, called the screenplay "one of the most effective parts of the narrative." Reviewers generally found *The Distance Between Us* spiritually rewarding.

After noting in the *Washington Post* (January 23, 1994) that the "small-town South" is Sayers's subject, Jonathan Yardley wrote, "She brings an unusual and interesting approach to it; her principal characters are Catholics, who . . . are . . . set apart by religion from the rest of white middle-class society. This . . . gives Sayers's novels their own distinct perspective." Yardley, however, did not see an underlying spiritual theme in *The Distance Between Us*, and he judged the book to be strongly autobiographical. "The novel's deficiency in narrative energy," he complained, "is distinctly characteristic of autobiographical fiction as now practiced in literary America."

Mary Faith, the protagonist of Due East, returns in *Brain Fever*, as does Tim from *How I Got Him Back*. Mary Faith—an unmarried mother who is both a Baptist and an atheist— and the tormented Catholic Tim have become engaged. Tim, who has had several breakdowns and has stopped taking his antidepression medication, descends again into madness. He runs away to New York, deserting Mary Faith, her son, whom he has planned to adopt, and his faith. Father Berkeley, named after the 18th-century bishop who believed that matter has no existence outside of perception and the mind of God, tries to persuade Mary Faith that Tim has not lost his faith; rather, he's lost his mind. The old priest explains to her, "You cannot call it walking out on you when he's having a breakdown," and tells her that she cannot "hold him to the behavior you'd expect of an ordinary man," leading her to think, "Suddenly it was wrong of me to ask Tim not to leave us. Suddenly it was wrong of me to resent his asking me to leave him be."

Elizabeth Benedict, writing in the *New York Times Book Review* (March 17, 1996), described the chapter in which the priest pleads with Mary Faith as the "most moving in the novel," which, as a whole, she termed one of "large ambition, compassion, and psychological depth, not to mention the pleasures of Valerie Sayers's graceful prose." Michael Parker, who reviewed *Brain Fever* for the *Washington Post* (February 25, 1996), deemed it suitable for Sayers to choose New York as the place

to which Tim would go to have a breakdown because New York "seems another planet from Due East." He concluded that for a "writer as brash and supple as Sayers, whose previous novels have shown her to be strongest in creating a world at once mysterious and credible, another planet would not seem to pose a problem." He cited her underlying "theological" idea of humanity: "Sayers may have moved her characters northward, but her conception of our freakishness remains rooted in the Christ-haunted South. In *Brain Fever*, she is able to conceive not only the whole man but the society that forms him, and even though this tale of maladjustment is too well-adjusted in the telling, it is graced by a tenacious and generous vision."

Sayers was awarded a creative writing fellowship by the National Endowment for the Arts in 1992. She served on the NEA Creative Writing Fellowships panel in 1997. She reviews books frequently for the *New York Times Book Review* and the *Washington Post Book World*.
—S. Y.

SUGGESTED READING: *Chicago Tribune* XIV p6 Mar. 20, 1994; *Commonweal* p329 May 22, 1987; *New York Newsday* p62 Feb.3, 1994, with photo; *New York Times Book Review* p9 Mar. 8, 1987, p7 Jan. 29, 1989, p23 Apr. 7, 1991, Feb. 20, 1994, p8 Mar. 17, 1996; *Publishers Weekly* p66+ Feb. 7, 1994, with photo; *Washington Post Book World* p15 Apr. 21, 1991, with photo, p3 Jan. 23, 1994, p7 Feb. 25, 1996

SELECTED BOOKS: *Due East*, 1987; *How I Got Him Back: Or, Under the Cold Moon's Shine*, 1989; *Who Do You Love*, 1991; *The Distance Between Us*, 1994; *Brain Fever*, 1996

Schulman, Grace

Apr. 23, 1935– Poet; nonfiction writer

The American poet and editor Grace Schulman has published three collections of poetry—*Burn Down the Icons* (1976), *Hemispheres* (1984), and *For That Day Only* (1994)—in addition to her substantial contributions to many leading literary periodicals. Schulman's voice was nurtured by a variety of sources: ancestral memories captured from her family's middle-European heritage, the poetry of John Donne and Gerard Manley Hopkins, and the interest taken in her work by the poet Marianne Moore, to whom she was introduced by a mutual friend. For 10 years she directed the prestigious Poetry Center at the 92nd Street YM / YWCA in Manhattan, New York City, and has served, since 1972, as the poetry editor of the *Nation* magazine.

For *World Authors 1990–1995*, Grace Schulman, born on April 23, 1935, writes: "I was born in New York City, the daughter of Bernard and Mar-

Grace Schulman

Jerome L. Schulman

cella Waldman. My father came to New York from Poland, and became, in succession, an actor, a lawyer, and finally, an advertising executive. My mother's maternal great-grandfather, Schmuel, came from Rumania with the Homestead Act of 1862 to Garden City, Kansas, where he wore a Star of David and a sheriff's badge, and sideburns and a beard, and carried guns. Her paternal grandfather was a cantor whose son, my grandfather Dave, was a lawyer who so loved music that to listen conveniently he accepted walk-on roles at the Metropolitan Opera.

"My poetry arose from my family's devotion to music and the law—which became for me the music of language and the mysteries of God's sacred law. I studied the piano, but thrilled to another sound—the human voice. My earliest memories are of my grandfather intoning the poetry of Whittier and my father declaiming, in Polish, the poetry of Adam Mickiewicz. Even after falling under the influence of Donne and Hopkins, I have never forgotten those early song-like recitations.

"I grew up during World War II. My American family were safe from the Holocaust, but haunted by rumors of death camps in a pre-TV age when scant facts gave rise to fantasies of horror. One of my earliest poems, 'Letter to Helen,' was written to my father's sister, who had chosen to remain in Poland and was missing throughout the war. After the Allied victory, we learned that in the Warsaw ghetto she had climbed the tower of a municipal building, pulled down the Polish flag from its staff and held it in the air before she was shot down by a Nazi guard. A surviving eyewitness wrote: 'Hers was a gesture of anger at the Poles for having given her away. Her death gave me the courage to survive.'

"After the war, I began reading in earnest and writing out of an instinct to thank writers who moved me. Those were, apart from Hopkins and Donne, Herbert, Shakespeare and the bible. Through my parents' friend, E. McKnight Kauffer, an artist, we met Marianne Moore, and she remained close to us for many years. From the beginning, she taught me the value of sheer persistence. Once she wrote to me: 'There is nothing like "coming through" something difficult.' When my first poems appeared in print, she wrote: 'This is splendid, Grace, and I think you will have more such encouragements, on and on, in later months. (Writing is tenacity, no matter how many hits you achieve. But if it were automatic it would be no fun—would it?)' I was struck by her kindness and impish humor. Once, when I wrote to her without mentioning my poems, she replied, 'How is your work?' Then, asking to see new poems, she said wryly, 'Send them to me—I have a pile of manuscripts in the next room,' and then commented on my 'flawless typing.' Her poems taught me to look at objects carefully and from all sides in a journey to find 'the rock crystal thing to see.'

"I believe my most meaningful achievement is my latest book of poems, *For That Day Only*. The writing of it delighted me, for it called upon my predilection for opposites: the clear image of the poem's dark road; ironies; paradoxes; speech rhythms that contend with received forms. While my first book, *Burn Down the Icons*, contrasts fixed images with life's laws of change, the current poems turn on that moment when the sacred becomes secular, liturgy turns into story and song, and language rings like 'bits of praise/fallen out of prayer.'

"In writing *For That Day Only*, I feel I traveled far to see its landscapes, whether they are in modern Italy, 14th century England, or the next block. Things I've looked at for themselves turned me outward to other cultures, and inward, to my past. Many of the poems in *For That Day Only* are set in New York, now and in history. In [one] poem, a young woman wakes to the streets of a 19th century immigrant neighborhood. Another . . . is seen from the eyes of three people—mine, Whitman's, and Grandfather Dave's. 'New Netherland, 1654' is spoken by a settler who came to New York from Brazil aboard a ship bound for Amsterdam. There are poems about painting ('El Greco's St. James, the Less'); marriage ('The Present Perfect'); statues in the Luxembourg Gardens; the rescue of a sculptor in Italy by a statue of Christ that washes up on a shore; Auden on the IRT. The poems I am working on now are in a voice released by *For That Day Only*. They take up my early interest in the Creation ('God Speaks' is my most recent), and the relation between ritual and art.

"I live near Washington Square Park with my husband, Jerome Schulman, a scientist. From the roof of our apartment building, we see two rivers and four bridges, the World Trade Center, steeples and cupolas and towers. We never tire of the Metropolitan Museum, the Frick, and the Cloisters. We have a small house in East Hampton near a bay inhabited by oyster catchers, piping plovers, egrets, and blue herons. These scenes are familiar to me and yet the closer I look at them, the stranger they become. I see them—as I see many objects that become my images—for what they are, and at the same time, for what they reveal about other cultures, history, my inner self. I'm thankful to be living and writing in this time and place, and want to go on in this terrifying and utterly joyful way for as long as I can."

When *For That Day Only*, Schulman's latest book, appeared, the following comment appeared in the *New Yorker*: "Schulman's beautiful poems are deft and intimate without ever becoming confessional. There are poems of marital bliss and woe, poems about works of art, poems on ancestral or historical themes—the raw poignancy of 'Grandfather Dave, an immigrant, a Jew.' along with the Washington Square of Henry James. The sacred realm of god and myth and the mundane one of error and expulsion unite and resound in both classical and contemporary ways. In these 'tales of Creation,' the emotional or dramatic import is typically set between the 'altering light' of an earthly fragmentation and the heavenly pursuit of the 'world in one glance'—the recognition of an ultimate coherence, the belief that 'as things fade to live . . . loss/makes trees grow green.' Clarity of idea and clarity of sound, rhythms equally at home in formal and in blank verse meet in an idiom that is perfected to a chiseled resonance.' Reviewing *For That Day Only* in the *New York Times Book Review*, Robert Richman, calling Schulman "one of the finest poets of the city," wrote: "In 'Site,' the 'absence of a house' encourages the poet to reconstruct what once took place. She thinks that

> things survive in their sites, in the
> ghosts of houses,
> linger in the incandescent images
> of what we imagine has occurred; the
> parlor
> after the guests have gone, the broken
> phrase
> somebody whistled once; the the-
> ater's curtain
> that holds the mark of the dancer's
> perilous leap
> skyward—the flexed plié, the twist
> and spin
> so high it seemed he would never de-
> scend.

Writing of her latest book in *Poetry* (May 1995), Robert B. Shaw said: "Urban pastoral, a form put to celebrated use by Whitman, Crane, and Williams, offers Grace Schulman many of her best opportunities to display her skill in this . . . She links her grandfather, a cantor's son, to Whitman's visit to 'a synagogue on Crosby Street':

> 'The heart within
> felt awed,' he said, and his speech fell
> under minor chords that enchanted
> when you were there, an immigrant,
> a Jew
> who read the Law and knew the ritu-
> al.

"As she notes, much of the once-Jewish neighborhood is now Chinese:

> Winter-melon bins
> replace old pushcarts filled with
> knives and buttons;
> on shop windows, brush-strokes read
> high-to-low,
> not right-left, as your letters did, and
> now
> graffiti on metal doors are calligraph-

"The poem's own letters may run left to right, but an informing presence of other eras and alphabets glints between the lines, making it like the history it confronts, an intriguing palimpsest.

"Schulman applies the same level and humane scrutiny to the times, seasons, and surroundings of her own life as she does to those of her ancestors and poetic precursors. In 'The Present Perfect' she delicately balances the satisfactions and regrets of a loving but childless marriage, having attained 'that have-been state where past and future merge':

> We have been married thirty-four
> I see the kids we were frisk on this
> In the late afternoon's unnameable
> Too late for them, and for their un-
> born kids,
> but not too late for us, here among ce-
> to praise the fires in rose petals on
> white rhododendrons, a fountain's
> rainbow.

"Similarly, in 'Crossing the Square,' the hub of her neighborhood, Washington Square Park, serves as a mirror for the endurance of a relationship, offering an epiphany in the bleakest depth of winter":

> faces upturned to test the whirling
> in new masks, we whistle to make
> breath-clouds form
> and disappear, and form again, and
> my love, there's sun in the crook of
> your arm.

Schulman's poems of marriage have engaged other critics as well. Mary Ann Caws wrote in *North Carolina Humanities* (Fall 1992): "One of the most effective of present-day poems about . . . regenerative grace is Grace Schulman's 'After the Division.' This brief epic statement acknowledges separation shattering, knows how to speak of cracking apart and up, of separation and then of convergence, like the two Platonic halves of man and woman joined; it is about holding fast to being as it wakes in unity, starting over. What the poet's invention wants to find is where you may start again, after the fall into discord:

I wake with you and feel the sun
invent one shadow that starts out
from us,
and know the time has come to begin
our lives.

Of *Hemispheres*, her second book, Liz Rosenberg wrote in *The New York Times Book Review*: "Grace Schulman's *Hemispheres* is full of beautiful, clear writing, and it has that first requisite of poetry—the world comes alive in her work. It opens with a blessing, a poem that leaps into the flames:

Blessed is the light that turns to fire,
and blessed the
flames that fire makes of what it
Blessed the inexhaustible sun, for it
feeds the moon that
shines but does not burn.
Praised be hot vapors in earth's crust,
for they force up
mountains that explode as molten
rock and cool, like
love remembered.
Holy is the sun that strikes sea, for
surely as water burns
life and death are one.

Schulman's fellow poets have, from the beginning, acknowledged the importance of her work to that infrastructure of contemporary poetry in which their own work is fashioned. William Stafford wrote of her first book, *Burn Down the Icons*: "So steady in vision, so congenial in human associations, so fluent and inventive in language, Grace Schulman renews our faith in ourselves and in the language we use for finding each other." May Swenson commented: "Shown in the poems is a person every reader will recognize as his or her inner self—that self which is significant and, at the same time, so elusive to express or explain. She probes our most secret marrow at times, while expressing her own." And early on, writing of Schulman's first book for the *New York Times Book Review*, Alfred Corn said: "When feelings flare up, when speech burns with a Pentecostal flame, Schulman is in her element. *Burn Down the Icons* is written by a poet posted in a firetower, who dreads and waits for the next change, and 'change is holy.' As a memorial of change, a brand subsists, an icon. Throughout the book runs the curious word 'veronica'—and the figure of Saint Veronica, who mopped Jesus's brow before the crucifixion, the image of His face imprinted thereafter on her handkerchief. Her name means 'true icons.' Schulman explores these resonances, discovering the paradox that 'Iconoclasts impress indelible / Veronicas on living things'."

In a 1997 interview with *World Authors*, Grace Schulman recalled her quarter-century post as poetry editor at the *Nation*, which has published poetry continuously since its founding in 1865. Buoyed by Marianne Moore's admonition that young writers should cultivate the virtue of "tenacity," Schulman had sent some of her poems to 50 magazines before they were finally accepted by the *Nation*, which published three of them on a half page. "I was so thrilled," said Schulman, who was asked to take over the poetry editorship of the periodical in 1972. "I am a liberal and agree with the *Nation*'s principles," she said, "though the poetry is selected not for its political content. I do not direct writers toward a particular point of view, for our policy is simply to care about excellence. I don't believe, however, there could be good poems in the world that omit the framework of human decency and the wideness of human sensibility." Speaking admiringly of the *Nation*'s archives, with their articles and reviews by and about Henry James, Emily Dickinson, Marianne Moore, W. B. Yeats, and others, Schulman credits the publication for its important contribution to what she calls the "print record of poetry."

Grace Schulman attended Bard College, where she studied literature with Theodore Weiss, and Johns Hopkins University. She later received her master's and doctoral degrees from New York University, where she worked with M. L. Rosenthal. From 1972 to 1984, she was director of the Poetry Center at the 92nd Street YM/YWCA in New York City, which continues to bring the world's leading poets to audiences through its famous Monday-night poetry readings. Also since 1972, she has been poetry editor of the *Nation*. She is professor of English at Baruch College of the City University of New York and has taught the writing of poetry at Princeton, Wesleyan, Columbia, Hofstra, Bennington, and Warren Wilson College. In 1996 she received the Delmore Schwartz Memorial Award for Poetry from New York University.

—E. M.

SUGGESTED READING: *New Yorker* p78 Sep. 5, 1994; *New York Times Book Review* p21 Feb. 1, 1987, p12 Oct. 30, 1994; Rosenberg, T., ed. *Testimony: Contemporary Writers Make the Holocaust Personal*, 1989; *Best American Poetry 1995*; *Oxford Companion to 20th Century Poetry*, 1993

SELECTED BOOKS: Nonfiction—*Marianne Moore: The Poetry of Engagement*, 1986; Poetry—*Burn Down the Icons*, 1976; *Hemispheres*, 1984; *For That Day Only*, 1994; As editor— *Two Decades of New Poets*, 1983; *Ezra Pound*, 1974; As translator—*At the Stone of Losses*, 1983

Scofield, Sandra Jean

Aug. 5, 1943– Novelist

The American novelist Sandra Jean Scofield has chosen for her theme the fragile anchoring of rootless lives. Because she got a late start as a writer, her sense that she hasn't "got any time to waste" has propelled her into writing eight novels in less than a decade, between 1989 and 1997. Although she describes herself as not being adventurous, Scofield did set her first novel, *Gringa* (1989), about her heroine's sexual and political adventures, in the wild Mexico where Scofield spent part of her own "aimless" youth. Next came *Beyond Deserving* (1991), "one woman's view of the 'Iron John' phenomenon" and other bizarre aspects of "our therapeutic society," according to Rand Richards Cooper in the *New York Times Book Review* (October 13, 1991). *Walking Dunes* (1992) is a story of a young man's initiation into society in a community as lacking in foundation as the tumbleweed surrounding it. In *More Than Allies* (1993), Scofield turned from examining what makes a man to looking at the women's movement and the lives of women without men. *Opal on Dry Ground* (1994) deals with ambivalent feelings toward men on the part of a woman and her daughters. In *A Chance to See Egypt* (1996), a man mourns the death of his wife in Mexico and then is able to find new love. All of these novels have won critical acclaim. *Plain Seeing* (1997) is a different kind of probe into lives in crisis, creating, as Scofield says, a mythopoetic aura around family relationships.

For *World Authors 1990–1995*, Sandra Jean Scofield, born on August 5, 1943, writes: "I was born into a working-class family in Texas; my grandmother Frieda's job packing flour had saved them from poverty. I was born to unmarried, beautiful Edith, still living with her mother and sister, my Aunt Mae. These three women were my whole childhood, although my mother married R. D. Hupp in 1946 and bore another daughter, my sister Karen. He adopted me, but after my mother's death in 1959, he faded out of my life. Although my mother was always sick, my childhood wasn't unhappy. I was much-loved and coddled in my bookishness. I was well-taught in Catholic school. I lived with the nuns (Sisters of St. Mary, in Wichita Falls and Ft. Worth) four years, until shortly before my mother died. The switch to a large public school threw me. My sullenness and moodiness turned to melancholy and a lack of self-guardedness. My young adulthood was a blur of aimlessness; I'd left college at 19 for New York and then Mexico. Later I went to Chicago, California, and ultimately Oregon. Although I eventually went into education, I never held any job more than one year (from bar waitress to college professor). I had a short stormy marriage to a Vietnam veteran, Allen Scofield, who died in 1975. The birth of my daughter in 1973, and my second marriage, to Bill Ferguson, in 1975, finally gave me stability. When I lost a teaching position at 40, I began writing seriously at last.

"It took me three years to shape *Gringa*, originally a 1300 page tome that took Abilene Painter through the turbulent sixties, and two more to find a small publisher. Meanwhile I was writing *Beyond Deserving*. I had always written, in dabs, usually poems or spurts of autobiography. I didn't think 'being a writer' was possible. 'Other people' did that. Especially men. (I loved the fiction of war and the exotic, such as Graham Greene, D. H. Lawrence, Lawrence Durrell, Albert Camus; later, Robert Stone and V. S. Naipaul. The intellectualism of Flannery O'Connor. The affections of Eudora Welty.) In the 70's, though, the back pages of *Redbook* had introduced me to women writers like Toni Morrison, Margaret Atwood, and Marge Piercy, and I saw that there were other themes, ones I might tackle. Since I myself had always been a loner (not entirely by choice), beset by depression, low-grade, steady anger (everything always so unfair) and plain old shyness, it's not surprising my heroines have tended to be less than heroic. At first it hurt that I was criticized for it, but over time I've decided that all I can write about—or want to—is what interests me, including passivity in the face of fate. (The favorite author of my adolescence was Thomas Hardy.)

"I don't think I'm driven by any thematic obsessions, although I note, looking back, that the majority of my characters seem to be people who need to grow up. I've always liked to put them in positions where they have to make choices about who they are going to be for the rest of their lives. I've never been as interested in feminist issues as in class. I don't write to preach, though. I simply like to tell stories about people who interest me, about questions that come up and won't go away. I don't see myself as 'giving voice' to anyone but myself, though I hope my stories touch people in some deep core where they are capable of empathy. I've never felt I had to write only about women. Fish, in *Beyond Deserving*, is a Vietnam vet who can't come into the mainstream. David Puckett, in *Walking Dunes*, is a charismatic high school boy who faces big moral choices too soon. And Tom Riley, in *A Chance to See Egypt*, is a middle-aged pet store owner. Not surprisingly, mother-daughter relationships intrigue me. In *Opal on Dry Ground* I mined some family story; in *Plain Seeing* I turned family story into a myth of my own making.

"Foreign settings still intrigue me, and I plan to return to Mexico for more novels. I mind that I haven't had the experience I might have as a more adventuresome person, but I have a fat notebook of ideas, and I've learned I can write out of research and imagination. I am intrigued by form as well as story. Because I was lucky enough to get a little critical attention early on, I've been spared some of the anguish of the literary writer in this culture—I stress some—so I can look to the work without the wolf at the door. I feel a deep rightness in what I do. My lack of social skills and political awareness doesn't matter. I can work all night, and get up and start back in, still wearing pajamas. Writing, in many ways, has 'saved my life,' by giving me a focus. I don't write to give meaning to the world, nothing so grand, but it does give meaning to my solitariness. And I love the work of writing, finding connections, discovering layers of character and story, entering worlds of my own making. It's really all I do, except for clerking part-time at a bookstore (my 'social life!'). Because my daughter is an artist, I do love to travel to see art, and read about it.

"I'm constantly challenged and disturbed and sometimes exhilarated by the sense that I am called to write about things I don't fully understand; consequently, my ambition (for the work) gets larger. The result is a sort of equilibrium of frustration and stubborn determination to push on through. I'm afraid I'll die before I do the really good work. I haven't got any time to waste."

Sandra Jean Hupp, as she was styled after being adopted by her stepfather, attended Odessa Junior College, in Texas. She continued her education later at the University of Texas in Austin, where she received her B.A., and she obtained her Ph.D. at the University of Oregon in 1978. She also attended Northern Illinois University and Cornell University, where she studied acting. She was always driven to writing, however, as she says: she held no other job for very long. She began writing shortly after the birth of her daughter, Jessica, but continued working day jobs until she had the confidence to write full-time.

Gringa is the story of Abilene, a woman from Texas, who becomes the mistress of a Mexican bullfighter, a man who spends his money freely on the many women in his life, including his "gringa" mistress. While she is separated from him, she becomes involved with leftist students and journalists who are eventually slaughtered for demonstrating at Tlatelolco Plaza in 1968. Not a true political animal herself, she considers the left "the kind of reality she hungers for: a mirror that may give her some clue as to her own true nature," according to Michael Upchurch, who reviewed the paperback edition of the book in the *San Francisco Examiner & Chronicle Book Review* (January 22, 1995). Scofield observed the historical events described in the novel during her stay in Mexico in 1968. *Gringa*, which Scofield called "my ignored first (and my favorite) novel," was termed by Upchurch "no apprentice work" but a "powerhouse of a book." He added that with "its sensual conjuring of place, its dour wit, and its keen eye for culture clash," the novel "satisfies on every level." Michele Wolf, writing in the *New York Times Book Review* (April 23, 1989), had also been taken with its "richly sensory portrait of a world of exile."

"Like . . . *Gringa*, *Beyond Deserving* sets forth a fascination for strong men and the women who love them," according to Rand Richards Cooper.

The novel tells the story of the compromises that must be made by a woman married to a hard-drinking Vietnam veteran just released from prison—compromises with her husband; with her lover, a biologist; with her husband's unhappy, middle-class twin brother; and with her father-in-law. "The notion that men, in becoming sensitive, have abdicated some essential maleness makes *Beyond Deserving* a timely novel," Cooper declared. He described a moment in the novel when the protagonist and her friend are watching a grossly fat woman shake all over as she blubbers on *Donahue*. "There's simple wicked fun in this; but the moment is also part of a consistent animus in the novel against the notion that all unhappiness can be, should be, worked out." One character in the novel says, "There's good reason to be sad once in a while." Cooper concluded that the lesson that Scofield is trying to get across in her "intelligent and observant novel" is that "the man who's truly in touch with his feelings is the one who has feelings in the first place." *Beyond Deserving* received an American Book Award and was a finalist for a National Book Award.

In *Walking Dunes*, the main character is David Puckett, a in high-school senior, self-involved and ambitious to escape from the west Texas oil-boom town where he lives. "This is a place where folks are so lightly planted in such shallow soil that one fears all vestiges of civilization there may blow away," Jane Vandenburgh wrote in the *New York Times Book Review* (September 13, 1992). She considered the main character "a center that cannot hold," believing that if "the writer had focused on David's struggles with his difficult father . . . he might have won our sympathy." The *Library Journal* (September 15, 1992) reviewer disagreed, maintaining that good "character development combined with a strong sense of place add to this carefully constructed novel's overall strengths."

One of the main characters in *More Than Allies*, Maggie, a single mother, thinks that "children are like great huge sacks of flour to be lugged and handled and lifted and kept" and "would like to close her eyes and think there was nobody out there who needed her." Nevertheless, Scofield has placed at the "core of this novel . . . a deep-rooted belief in the nurturing ethos," according to Wendy Martin in the *New York Times Book Review* (November 28, 1993). Maggie has refused to leave Oregon to follow her husband to his job in Texas; also remaining in Oregon with her children is Dulce, whose husband wants her to return to him in Mexico. "Ultimately, though, *More Than Allies* retreats from self-sufficiency as an ideal. Even though romantic love, marriage, and motherhood are tested, they are finally embraced, however tentatively," Martin wrote.

In *Opal on Dry Ground*, the 57-year-old title character must nurture her two divorced daughters, who have moved in with her and her third husband. "Opal, who doesn't know when to stop mothering, must learn to fly out of her nest, too, and become her own person," Elizabeth Levitan Spaid remarked in the *Christian Science Monitor* (July 14, 1994). Spaid and Vicki Cecil, the *Library Journal* (April 1, 1994) reviewer, agreed that Scofield demonstrated in *Opal on Dry Ground* "a real talent for diving past surface descriptions and getting inside the lives of her characters," in Spaid's words. "Love, for Opal, remains an unidentified flying object, darting in secret from plate to table, from heart to mouth," Abby Frucht wrote in the *New York Times Book Review* (July 24, 1994). Frucht found that Opal's husband's "sweet, simple notion of what makes a home" provides a "wise lesson." She observed that that "lesson is revealed in a novel whose plot, like a vast open sky, is enlivened with a fireworks display of colorful, twisting, brilliantly rendered emotions."

Reviewers also found that in *A Chance to See Egypt*, Scofield's gift for creating characters and allowing them to make choices was apparent. In the novel an American man returns to the town in Mexico where he spent his honeymoon to mourn his wife, with whom he was supposed to visit Egypt to celebrate their 10th anniversary. In this familiar territory, he tells his sister, "I can cry in some warmer place, at least." As Janet Kaye wrote in the *New York Times Book Review* (June 2, 1996), "Tom's journey is a metaphor: without Eva, he thinks he cannot cover new ground." This "absorbing story," as Kaye termed it, "allows us to delight in . . . the unexpected gift of a life renewed."

In addition to receiving the American Book Award and a nomination for the National Book Award, Scofield has won fellowships from the National Endowment for the Arts and the Oregon Arts Commission and Oregon Institute of Arts. She is a member of the Texas Institute of Letters.
—S.Y.

SUGGESTED READING: *Christian Science Monitor* p 5 July 14, 1994; *Library Journal* p134 Apr. 1, 1994, p152 Aug. 1992; *New York Times Book Review* p14 Oct. 13, 1991, p27 Sep. 13, 1992, p10 Nov. 28, 1993, p9 July 24, 1994

SELECTED BOOKS: *Gringa*, 1989; *Beyond Deserving*, 1991; *Walking Dunes*, 1992; *More Than Allies*, 1993; *Opal on Dry Ground*, 1994; *A Chance to See Egypt*, 1996; *Plain Seeing*, 1997

Searle, Elizabeth

1962– Novelist; short-story writer

Although still a relative newcomer to the literary scene, Elizabeth Searle has already made a name for herself among her peers. Winner of the 1992 Iowa Short Fiction Prize for her first collection of short stories, *My Body to You* (1993), Searle has captured the attention and praise of critics around the country. The stories in her debut collection are thoughtful examinations of the inner turmoil of young girls and women. Her powers as a fiction writer were confirmed with the appearance of her first novel, *A Four-Sided Bed*, in 1998.

Elizabeth Searle was born in Pennsylvania in 1962 and spent her childhood there, as well as in South Carolina, Kentucky, and Arizona. In an autobiographical statement submitted to *World Authors 1990–1995*, Searle writes: "With all my family's moves, a stable center of my childhood was the elaborate imaginary world I formed with my sister. Isolated in the South Carolina countryside, we played pretend games until I was well into my teens. We wrote our own 'movie' and 'soap opera' scripts. Acting in high school plays enabled me to make a belated transition into 'real life.'

"My parents encouraged my writing and my reading. My father had run for Congress twice in Pennsylvania, the valiant 'underdog' Democrat in heavily Republican districts. He followed the news avidly and held dinner-table debates with his children. My mother was a lifelong student and reader who taught biology and later became a librarian.

Mikki Ansin

With her encouragement, I dipped into adult authors such as John Updike and Joyce Carol Oates.

"At Arizona State University, I took my first creative writing class. Instantly hooked, I whipped out a 100-plus page novel about two sisters. From it, I salvaged my first short story—published in *Redbook Magazine* when I was 19. At Oberlin College, where I majored in creative writing, I met my husband, John Hodgkinson, nine years my senior. His rich and varied past is a constant inspiration to me. We married after I graduated, age 22.

"Helping put my husband through graduate school in computer science at Yale, I worked as a special education teacher. I found that I could relate to the autistic, with their intense inner worlds. The raw and uninhibited passions of these people fascinated me. At the New Haven Regional Center, a state institution, I was exposed to a variety of emotionally and mentally disabled adults. I learned to change adult diapers. I was attacked by violent patients. And I began working on a series of stories taking place in the world of special education, centering around female characters.

"In the graduate writing program at Brown, I studied fiction writing with inspiring and adventuresome teachers—especially my mentor, John Hawkes. His erotic and deeply unsettling fiction inspired me to focus my writing even more intently on my characters' sensual selves, their bodies.

"In my first collection, *My Body to You*—written at Brown and in the years following my 1988 graduation—I wrote intimate portraits of girls and women. They pilot their bodies through a shifting universe of lovers old and young, parents devoted or destructive, sisters of different sexes and children and adults living in the mysterious world of autism. My characters included a young woman drawn into the emotional and sexual life of an autistic boy obsessed with the number eight, an old woman who has a physical breakdown and spiritual breakthrough in a supermarket's vegetable department and, in the title story, a girl in love with a gay man she calls Sister Kin."

Critical response to *My Body to You* was overwhelmingly enthusiastic. In a review for the *Boston Globe* (April 9, 1993), Matthew Gilbert noted Searle's ability to make her characters' "consciousness both hypnotic and sensible." Calling her writing style "sensual," Gilbert also wrote that *My Body to You* is refreshingly frank in dealing with obsessions normally filtered out of short stories, raising the "gnawing questions of life, death, and the hunger in between." The book, he wrote, "has its rough edges, its overindulgences, but they are the symptoms of Searle's bold risk-taking."

In 1992 *My Body to You* was awarded the Iowa Short Fiction Prize, a momentous occasion for Searle, as she told *World Authors*: "[The contest] was judged that year by one of my own favorite writers, James Salter. Like the other writers who mean the most to me—Virginia Woolf, Joyce Carol Oates, Vladimir Nabokov, David Foster Wallace, Marilynne Robinson, Don DeLillo, Alice Munro, Maria Flook—his writing is characterized by intensity, intelligence, and sensuality. My favorite writers fully and vividly convey their characters' experiences: thoughts, feelings, sensual perceptions; what one of Woolf's biographers called the 'texture' of her characters' minds."

Searle's next literary offering, *A Four-Sided Bed* (1998), expands the title story from *My Body to You* into a bittersweet tale of love and passion within the context of unconventional relationships. In the book, a couple who met in college, JJ and Alice, are married and living a comfortable life in New Haven when past lovers come back to haunt them. For several years Alice has known about JJ's stay in a mental health facility, and about Kin, the lover he had while he was there. When a mysterious woman named Bird attempts to make contact with JJ, however, Alice learns not only that Bird is another of JJ's former lovers, but that Kin is a man. While Bird and her new husband, Kin, who is dying of AIDS, try to rekindle the relationship they had with JJ, Alice tries to sort out her own feelings about marriage, monogamy, and sexuality in general. Presenting the point of view of Alice, as well as that of Bird (via her letters to JJ, which Alice intercepts), Searle's debut novel proved to be an intense exploration of sexuality and love, written in a rich, lyrical style.

In her autobiographical statement, Searle wrote of the book: "*A Four-Sided Bed* began with my fascination for a couple I've known since high school and wrote about first in my story 'My Body to You': a gay man and a sexually confused woman who—for love and for free flights on an airline employee-and-spouse pass—married. I wanted to follow their round-the-world travels. I wanted to take on a love story unique to our gender-bending times. And I wanted to create a mix of characters who could truly do what a *Los Angeles Times* critic said my short-story characters do: 'test the limits' of the 'sexually possible.'

"For the novel I added a third party to my friends' story: a man whom they could both love. In exploring a ménage à trois plus one 'outsider', I found I could explore, too, some favorite fascinations of mine: gender identity, mind/body splits, creative variations on 'marriage', obsessive loves.

"Moving to Boston with my husband after we'd finished graduate school, I taught at Emerson College. I wrote the first draft of my novel in three months, the summer of 1993; then I rewrote the manuscript for three years. I was inspired by the singer k.d. lang, who said that she sets out to 'seduce' her whole audience: men and women, gay and straight alike. I tried to make the three-person love scenes in my book 'work' for readers from across the sexual spectrum. A three-way love story has a unique potential to 'hook' or provide a 'way in' to readers of all orientations. Ideally, I wish readers of my novel could be 'seduced' into experiencing, fictionally, a sexuality different from what they think of as their own.

"While *A Four-Sided Bed* features a trip around the world, the main 'trip' I want my reader, like myself, to take is an internal one. In the novel as well as in my stories, I want to explore the different ways people can intimately connect; the infinite variety of things they can do-as my character Bird puts it-'with, to, for each other.'"

A Four-Sided Bed was published to great acclaim. *Booklist* (January 1–15, 1998) lauded it as a "bold, beautiful book" that offers an "intense, moving portrait of the different ways people can connect." *Kirkus Reviews* (December 1, 1997) deemed it a "powerful, unsettling" novel as well as a "bright, distinctive, haunting debut." The review further stated that Searle "captures, in a terse prose having the rhythm and vigor of real speech, four painfully convincing figures struggling to find a way in which to preserve love." Brigid Hughes of the *Chicago Tribune* (March 15, 1998) also gave a favorable review, saying that the novel as a whole is a "remarkable accomplishment" for Searle. Hughes, however, offered one small complaint about *A Four-Sided Bed*, arguing that Searle adequately addressed all of the desires and needs of the ménage à trois, but did not sufficiently deal with Alice's feelings. "The implication that [Alice's] needs and desires don't deserve the same attention (and certainly aren't granted the allowances) given to the other characters' unbalances the otherwise carefully considered narrative," Hughs wrote. She tempered this criticism, however, by pointing out that the lack of a fully developed character in Alice is "more than compensated for in the marvelously rendered portrait of Bird and Kin."

In addition to winning the 1992 Iowa Short Fiction Prize, Elizabeth Searle was given the Chelsea Fiction Prize in 1991 for her short story "What to Do in an Emergency," and several of her short stories have been awarded the Best American Short Stories honor. Her stories have appeared in the fiction anthologies *Lovers* (1992), *The Time of Our Lives* (1993), *Breaking Up is Hard to Do* (1994) and *American Fiction* (1995). In recent years, Searle has taught at Suffolk University and the University of Massachusetts. She continues to teach at Emerson College and resides with her husband, John, in Arlington, Massachusetts.—D.B.

SUGGESTED READING: *Booklist* p779 Jan.1–15, 1998; *Boston Globe* Apr. 9, 1993; *Chicago Tribune* p15 Mar. 15, 1998; *Kirkus Reviews* Dec. 1, 1997; *Los Angeles Times* Mar. 14, 1993; *Philadelphia Inquirer* May 16, 1993; *Publishers Weekly* Dec. 1997

SELECTED BOOKS: *My Body to You*, 1993; *A Four-Sided Bed*, 1998

See, Carolyn

Jan. 13, 1934– Novelist; memoirist

The American novelist and memoirist Carolyn See came, according to her memoir *Dreaming: Hard Luck and Good Times in America* (1995), from a family in which the American dream had become a shambles, ruined by "the three Ds"—divorce, drink, and drugs. She proclaims below, however, that she is not one to believe in the redemptive power of suffering. As Susan Fromberg Schaeffer observed, reviewing See's novel *Making History* (1991) in the *New York Times Book Review* (September 15, 1991), "See sets out to catch the sound of our world singing its way into the future." In her more recent novels, *Golden Days* (1986), which deals with the American nightmare of nuclear war; *Making History* (1991), in which a man tries to create an ideal world; *The Handyman*, whose narrator is a budding painter; and earlier novels, *The Rest Is Done with Mirrors* (1970), *Mothers, Daughters* (1977), and *Rhine Maidens* (1981), See has attempted an unsentimental yet life-affirming portrait of America, especially from the vantage point of California: "We've been dead before, plenty of times. But we always get over it," See said of the southern California dream in an interview with the *New York Times* (August 14, 1992). She has even, in *Blue Money* (1973), been able to cast a sprightly eye on pornography and find that it does not clash with her feminist slant.

Marilyn Sanders/Courtesy of Random House

For *World Authors 1990n1995*, Carolyn See, born on January 13, 1934, writes: "Some . . . quotidian details [are] my tough-as-nails mother, my engaging, if irresponsible, father, two ex-husbands, different as can be in lifestyle, but remarkably similar in their charm and goofiness. I should say I have two grown daughters—both married. Lisa See, I believe, will be the Tony Hillerman of the 21st Century. She's at work on her second book—a beautifully structured thriller set in contemporary China. Clara Sturak, my younger, works now for Random House, but her real calling is changing the world. She raises money for DayBreak, a center for homeless mentally ill women. She says the business shingle for our family should be: WE CHANGE LIVES. And the distinguished professor and writer whom I've lived with for the past 22 years, John Espey, has been a shining example of this: I can't go anywhere with him without some stranger plucking his sleeve: 'Mr. Espey, you don't know me, but you changed my life.'

"All this is not as self-congratulatory as it sounds. Those who've read my later novels, *Rhine Maidens*, *Golden Days*, *Making History*, and my recent memoir, *Dreaming*, know that my family history and my early life were constructed as a series of tragedies and disasters. Somehow the emotional wiring that goes with these kinds of events translates out to: 'I suffer, therefore I must be smart.' Most of my adult life has gone to figuring out strategies to reject that line of thinking. It seems to me that—even in twentieth-century America—there ought to be a way to make the equation read: 'I see life clear and love it anyway. Some days I'm even happy.'

"This isn't a very popular position. Maybe it is for the general reader or the intelligent reviewer, but where I teach it's seen as bordering on the moronic. I've been called shallow and superficial and caring only about the surface of things. Because I postulate happy endings, some of my colleagues have questioned my ability to think. I'm grateful to have this opportunity to answer them.

"Perhaps I am shallow. In *Golden Days* I suggest that even if the Bomb does finally drop, some people will be left, and they might possibly reinvent society in a form kinder to human beings. (The real terror and horror is the scenario that we concoct for ourselves before the disaster.) In *Making History* I suggest that even if the worst, worst thing happens to us— if our child dies—there might be another world, and a satisfactory way of negotiating a transition from this life to the next. And in *Rhine Maidens* I postulate that even the meanest human on earth has the capacity to change for the better if she finds the life she was made for. I personally don't think this is moronic and superficial, but I do think it breaks from Euro-American tradition, Christian tradition. It is, for instance, in direct opposition to Dostoyevsky's position, that the more you suffer and make everybody else's life a living hell, the more 'profound' you are. He wrote some great novels, but there must be another way to produce significant art. (Let's not even think about the bad drunks in the last hundred years who passed themselves off as great artists and never wrote a word.)

"I've been thinking a lot lately about externals and 'the surface of things.' I've been forced to notice that a lot of 'profound' thinkers have thought themselves on to Prozac, and they still don't feel that wonderful. I love the journalistic side of writing because journalists get ideas and then go chasing out of the office to see if their ideas pan out. They're involved in action, and action doesn't preclude thinking. The two should enhance each other. (Not a new idea, but I'm surprised at certain literary theorists who sit pat in their fluorescent-lit cubicles and grow the moss of depression and life-long funk on their north side.)

"WE CHANGE LIVES! I guess I can say that my daughters and I changed our lives—from dismal to pleasing—and I'm all for it. If that's shallow, then so be it. I'll still go on writing about the atomic bomb and shattering car crashes and vindictive parents and how we can transform all that, if we want to, into something more useful, more humane.

"My next novel takes another 'superficial' plot. A young man, about 30, has hit the existential wall. He has his education, he has his ambition (but he's going nowhere); he's cute enough to get all the sex he wants (but he's not in love). He can't even get a decent job. He's, obviously, like 80% of 30 year old American guys. In my novel, he's brave, even through his hopelessness. He does a good deed, and because of that, he finds love and work. And happiness!

"Happiness. It isn't that we're happier than anyone else. Far from it, some days. But I believe we value it, and that's the difference. It's the exact same game we used to play, just turned on its head. With my first and second husbands, I often used to think, how can I drive this guy nuts in the most efficient way? Now, thanks to my daughters and to John Espey, my beloved companion and mentor, I sometimes think: How can I get my students a job? What if I give away a bunch of books? What if I go with a girlfriend to Paris, just for fun?

"Someone told me last week, 'If there's anyone society hates more than a woman, it's a happy woman.' At my age, I have to think of the consequences of that statement. But maybe 20 years from now, some curmudgeonly academic will end up saying: 'She was as thin as K Mart tissue paper! She lived for giggling and dancing and drinking and talking on the phone! But she wrote *Making History* and *Golden Days*. By God, I *like* that in a woman!'"

See's first novels were autobiographical. She was a graduate student when she met her first husband, and *The Rest Is Done with Mirrors* is a story of a young couple who are graduate students. *Mothers, Daughters* involves the reasons for a divorce. *Rhine Maidens* was inspired by See's relationship with her mother. Although these novels were critically well-received, they did not enjoy tremendous commercial success.

After See, her daughter Lisa, and her companion, John Espey, collectively adopted the pseudonym Monica Highland for the purpose of creating the commercially successful romance adventure novels *Lotus Land* (1983) and *110 Shanghai Road* (1986), See's "literary" works took a less personal tone. With *Golden Days* she entered the realm of speculative fiction. Her characters, southern Californians, survive a nuclear attack. Reviewers regarded the novel as a commentary on California New Age mores but expressed varied opinions about its success. The *Christian Science Monitor* (January 22, 1991) commentator Merle Rubin found *Golden Days* to be a "distressing novel . . . a trivializing and, finally, intensely dispiriting treatment of a subject you'd think would be sufficiently dispiriting in and of itself." Carol Sternhell, writing in the *New York Times Book Review* (November 30, 1986), on the other hand, judged it See's best book. She found one character's "opportunistic concoction of pop psychology and Eastern mysticism" to be "life-affirming," in that it causes survivors of the nuclear holocaust to declare it "good to be alive." Sternhell liked the fact that See "burns her world to ashes and sings with joy." Reviewer R. Z. Sheppard in *Time* (September 24, 1986) took a position on *Golden Days* between those two: "Much of the novel reads like a catchall of California behaviors and the confessional sociology that passed for journalism in the '70s." Sheppard found that sometimes "See is right on the money. . . . But there is not enough . . . to pass for serious fiction in the '80s."

With *Making History*, See took on the subject of the utopia that is the goal of Jerry Bridges, the novel's protagonist. Blind to the inevitability of chaos, destruction, and accident in human life, he sets out to create an earthly paradise in New Guinea. In Los Angeles, where he lives, however, automobile accidents are the vehicle that the goddess of destruction, Kali, uses to wreak vengeance on Jerry for ignoring her principle. "How Jerry comes to accept the contradiction inherent in his hunger for perfection—which, in this novel, is equated with lifelessness—and his hunger for passion (which embraces and perhaps induces chaos) is at the heart of the novel," Susan Fromberg Schaeffer wrote in the *New York Times Book Review* (September 15, 1991). "Nothing in . . . See's teeming world is silent. Everything has its own song and story. . . . The miracle is how well she has succeeded [in telling it]," Schaeffer concluded.

Marilynne Robinson in the *Yale Review* (April 1992) observed that "the wit and also the tenderness of the novel comes from the respect with which it treats everything it touches." She noted that *Making History* "claims a larger moral and temporal space for its action than realism would grant it, yet it does not distance itself from the fetishes and mythologies that structure and clutter contemporary life." Michiko Kakutani in the *New York Times* (September 20, 1991) also remarked on the millennial overtones of the novel, but she felt that the use of a ghost and a psychic to give a California flavor and a "vaguely mythic undertow" to the narrative lend a false note to "what is otherwise a fiercely observed and deeply affecting parable

about the precariousness of contemporary life." She commented favorably on See's shifting point of view, which, she felt, enables the reader to "see the complex web of emotions" that both separate and bind the various characters.

See wrote *Making History* after her younger daughter was involved in two automobile accidents. She told Laurel Graeber for the *New York Times Book Review* (September 15, 1991) that her daughter healed by beginning to accept that there might be a God, even though the universe still seemed random. *Making History* might be considered See's attempt to explain how the universe might work. She told Laurel Graeber that although Eastern philosophy was part of the novel's spiritual background, Einstein's theories were also "the thought behind it."

See returned to autobiography in *Dreaming*, a memoir that includes "a wicked, bittersweet account of the chronically dysfunctional Laws family, a Scottish and Irish clan caught in a web of fighting, hard times, drugs and alcohol," according to the *New York Times* (August 17, 1995), with "accounts of [See's] grandmother's bathroom suicide, her mother's abuse of her half-sister and her own drinking, drug use and failed marriages." Not a chronicle of despair, however, *Dreaming* drew the comment from Linda Gray Sexton in the *New York Times Book Review* (March 5, 1995) that the narrative offers "the opportunity to perceive, along with all the domestic tragedy, the other side of . . . See's troubled family: the liberation and lack of restraint that can bring with it laughter and freedom and a zany lust for living." In See's words, "There's something to be said for free fall, the wild life. . . . It's given us our stories; and made us who we are. It has to do with dreaming, inventing, imagining, yearning. . . ." After See wrote *Dreaming*, but before it was published, she survived the Los Angeles earthquake of 1994 and wrote an op-ed piece about it for the *New York Times* (January 20, 1994). The hard-nosed realism and capacity for humor that characterize her, no matter what the circumstances, were manifest when she declared: "A lot of people here are saying that the quake was ennobling. I think it's the sourest of disasters. Nature shakes you cruelly, meanly; it makes it clear that you count for nothing. And then it makes you clean up your room."

The 28-year-old protagonist and narrator of See's 1999 novel, *The Handyman*, is Bob Hampton, an aspiring painter who travels to California to attend art school. The summer before classes begin, Bob advertises his services as a handman, thereby making the acquaintance of a number of lonely and amorous housewives and widows. David Willis McCullough, assessing the novel for the *New York Times Book Review* (March 21, 1999), detected a note—intended or otherwise—of sexism: "Does Carolyn See really mean to be saying these things? . . . Most of *The Handyman* is taken up with examples of how pathetic and inept women can be unless there's a good man around to keep them whipped into shape." He did feel, however, that See had "breathed genuine life into her narrator," who is "a likable guy, assuming you are looking for someone who combines the qualities of Mary Poppins, Mr. Clean, and Lady Chatterley's lover."

See, who earned a Ph.D. at UCLA in 1963, has been a professor of English there and at Loyola University in Los Angeles. She has often reviewed books for the *Los Angeles Times*. She was the recipient of a grant from the National Endowment for the Arts in 1974 and won the Bread and Roses Award of the National Women's Political Caucus in 1988, among many other honors and awards, both for her writing and for her political activism. A longtime liberal, she has expressed a belief that some illegal drugs are tacitly approved by the government as a substitute for the failure of the American dream.

—S. Y.

SUGGESTED READING: *Christian Science Monitor* p22 Jan. 22, 1987; *New York Times* C p19 Sep. 20, 1991, A p25 Aug. 14, 1992, A p21 Jan. 20, 1994, C p13 Aug. 17, 1995; *New York Times Book Review* p9 Nov. 30, 1986, p8 Mar. 5, 1995; *Time* p94 Nov. 24, 1986; *Contemporary Authors* nrs vol. 52, 1989

SELECTED BOOKS: Fiction—*The Rest Is Done with Mirrors*, 1970; *Mothers, Daughters*, 1977; *Rhine Maidens*, 1981; *Golden Days*, 1986; *Making History*, 1991; *The Handyman*, 1999; As Monica Highland (with J. Espey and L. See)— *Lotus Land*, 1983; *110 Shanghai Road*, 1986; Nonfiction—*Blue Money*, 1973; *Dreaming: Hard Luck and Good times in America*, 1995

Miriam Berkley

See, Lisa

Feb. 18, 1955– Novelist; nonfiction writer

Despite having an established writer—Carolyn See—for a mother, throughout her youth Lisa See was never inclined to pursue the profession herself. It was See's love of travel that inspired her to test her talents as a writer. Taking up the life of a traveling writer/reporter, in turn, led her to explore her Chinese-American ancestry. The resulting books, the nonfiction work *On Gold Mountain* (1995) and the novels *Flower Net* (1997) and *The Interior* (1999), draw on See's childhood experiences in Los Angeles's Chinatown as well as her later travels to Beijing.

In an autobiographical statement submitted to *World Authors 1990–1995*, See writes, "I was born in Paris, France, on February 18, 1955. My parents (my father had just gotten out of the Army) had been bumming around Europe as students. Six weeks after my birth—having already traveled in Italy and Yugoslavia—I returned home to Los Angeles. A couple of years later, my parents divorced. I went to live with my mother and her new husband, Tom Sturak. Nevertheless, throughout my childhood I spent a lot of time with my grandparents and great-aunts and uncles in Los Angeles's Chinatown. That time would eventually prove to be very important to my writing, but that was still a long way off.

"I never wanted to be a writer. My mother, Carolyn See, started writing when I was a kid. She did a lot of magazine work in those days and I saw how often she was at the mercy of feckless and often pretty dumb or obtuse editors. But in 1976, I was living on the island of Patmos in Greece. I knew I didn't want to get married or have kids. All I wanted to do was travel, live out of a suitcase, have no ties. But how could I afford to do that? That's when I realized I should become a writer. After I returned to Los Angeles, I enrolled at Loyola Marymount College, broke up with my boyfriend and moved home with my mother and John Espey, a writer and my mother's significant other for the last couple of decades. My mother helped me get my first two magazine assignments—one was about my former stepfather's new wife who held the world's record in the woman's marathon for *Sporting Times*, the other was about birth control on the college campus for *Forum*. Not long after, I got my first assignment from *TV Guide*. Since those early days, I have written for numerous magazines and newspapers, as well as book reviews for the *New York Times*, *L.A. Times*, and *Washington Post*.

"One night my mother, John, and I were watching a miniseries called "Wheels," in which Lee Remick turned to Rock Hudson and said, "You're looking at a truly desperate woman!" We looked at each other and said, "We could do better than that!" Although we started out thinking we'd write a miniseries, we ended up writing three books together under the pseudonym of Monica Highland: *Lotus Land,* published by Coward-McCann in 1983; *110 Shanghai Road*, published by McGraw-Hill in 1986; and *Greeting from Southern California*, published by Graphic Arts Center Publishing in 1988.

"In 1983, I was hired by *Publishers Weekly* as west coast correspondent, which meant that I covered everything that was happening in the publishing world west of the Mississippi. I wrote about the struggles of independent booksellers, the growth of the superstores, interesting marketing gimmicks that independent publishers came up with, trends in publishing (crystals, juicing, meditation, yoga), and author profiles. The thirteen years I worked for *Publishers Weekly* are very important to me. I learned how to meet deadlines for a weekly publication, how the business works, how not to be afraid of a blank page, how to pick up the phone and keep calling until my questions were answered. Most important, I learned how other very successful writers work—how they did their research, how they organized their family lives, how they operated in the larger world. All this became increasingly important to me since, despite my earlier wishes in Greece, I had gotten married to Richard Kendall in 1981 and we had two sons. Alexander was born in 1982, and Christopher was born in 1985.

"In the fall of 1988, my career took a very different turn. My great-aunt asked me to come and listen to her stories about the Chinese side of the family. At first I thought I might write one of those Christmas card letters that I'd send out to the family, then I wanted to write an article. But five years later—after interviewing about 70 relatives, friends, and scholars, after traveling to my great-grandfather's home village in China, and after doing hours and hours of research in dusty archives—I finished *On Gold Mountain*, which was published by St. Martin's Press and became a *New York Times* Notable Book for 1995."

On Gold Mountain tells the story of four generations of See's Chinese-American heritage, beginning with her great-grandfather, Fong See, one of many immigrant workers who helped build the first transcontinental railroads. Fong See was one of the few Chinese laborers who was officially sponsored by the railroad project. He was also a trusted herbalist among his fellow laborers, who had little faith in Western medicine. The historical account, which includes such dramatic and harrowing tales as secret weddings and child kidnappings, follows Fong See's long (he lived to be 100)

and prosperous life on "Gold Mountain," which is a Chinese slang expression for North America. *On Gold Mountain* also explores the lives of Lisa See's great-grandmother, a white woman who was one of Fong's four wives, and her Aunt Sissee, who was rejected by her husband's Chinese family for being half-Caucasian.

Indeed, the theme of Chinese and Caucasian cultures mixing and clashing is prominent in the book, as well as in See's own life. In the foreword to *On Gold Mountain*, See wrote that her Chinese sources for the book referred to Caucasians as "lo fan" and "fan gway," which can be translated as "white ghosts." Although she possesses features that are more traditionally European than Asian, Lisa See was always aware of her father's family's culture growing up. As a child she often turned to her grandparents and their store in Los Angeles's Chinatown for comfort during her parents' turbulent divorce years. As she told the *New York Times* (August 17, 1995), "the weekends with my grandparents became the real center for me. . . . It was the side of my family I identified more with. It was fun, romantic, solid." However, while Lisa identified strongly with her Chinese heritage, others, even in her own family, had difficulty accepting her red hair and fair features. Many years later, when interviewing her family members for *On Gold Mountain*, she noted that "often, someone would say, by way of explanation, 'You know, she was a Caucasian like you'. . . . They never knew how startling it was for me to hear that, because all those years in the store and going to those wedding banquets, I thought I was Chinese."

On Gold Mountain was enthusiastically received. In the *New York Times Book Review* (August 27, 1995), Elizabeth Tallent praised See for doing a "gallant and fair-minded job of fashioning anecdote, fable, and fact into an engaging account." Many reviewers complemented See for her extensive research into her subject, and the detailed and intricate genealogy she produced. However, Denise Chong of the *Washington Post* (August 20, 1995) criticized See for being "too charmed by her material" and added that she "sometimes dallies over ordinary details and meanders into the lives of incidental characters." Chong, however, acknowledged that by documenting such an extensive family history See had created an "enviable, lasting achievement." In her statement for *World Authors*, See remarked that *On Gold Mountain* "is the most gratifying work I've ever done and I think it's because it combines so many of my interests and loves—travel, my family, history, and old-fashioned storytelling."

After completing *On Gold Mountain*, See continued to explore Chinese culture and traveled extensively throughout China. She had met a wide variety of individuals on her many trips there with her husband, who works as a lawyer representing the Chinese government in the United States. At home, she investigated relevant stories such as that of the *Golden Venture* (a ship full of illegal Chinese immigrants that ran aground in New York harbor in 1993) and tagged along with an undercover agent from the U.S. Fish and Wildlife Agency. The result of all this research was a new writing adventure, this time in the form of the fictional *Flower Net*. In her statement, See wrote, "While I was working on *On Gold Mountain*, I came up with the idea for *Flower Net* (HarperCollins, 1997), which is an international thriller set in contemporary Beijing. While there's plenty of murder and mayhem, what really interests me about the book is that it offered me a way to continue to talk about China and family dynamics. In the U.S., we tend to think of China in terms of politics. We know very little about how people in China actually live. I wanted to put a face to those people."

Flower Net, which takes place in both Beijing and Los Angeles, begins with the discovery of a murder victim underneath an icy pond; he is later revealed to be the son of a United States ambassador to China. See next takes the reader to the U.S., where a hurricane off the coast of California has pushed a Chinese freighter into American territory, and authorities have discovered the remains of a young Chinese "red prince," or son of a powerful man in China. In China, Liu Hulan, a female detective for the Chinese Ministry of Public Security, begins to investigate the murder of the American, while David Stark, an assistant district attorney, simultaneously begins to work on the case of the "red prince." The two, who had been lovers years earlier, discover that their cases are connected and team up to solve them. As a result the novel's action moves back and forth not only between the U.S. and China, but also between the two vastly different investigative tactics of the pair. *Flower Net* combines the culture and atmosphere of two distinctive cities, Los Angeles and Beijing, and explores the mingling of Chinese and American traditions.

See's first work of fiction brought mixed reviews. *Library Journal* (August 1997) was one of the many publications that applauded See's research and vivid descriptions of Beijing, but expressed disappointment in other aspects of her storytelling. "See offers readers many interesting insights into Chinese culture and recent history, but the writing is marked by cardboard characters, wooden dialogue, and an unfortunate tendency to tell what's happening rather than showing it." In the *New York Times Book Review* (October 26, 1997), Gary Krist also criticized See for her plot devices and character dialogue: "when it comes to plotting, See unfortunately adopts the old policy of letting a hundred improbabilities bloom . . . a nagging aura of inauthenticity hangs over the novel's investigative mechanics." However, Krist also praised See for her accurate and vibrant portrait of Beijing, and called *Flower Net* a "colorful first novel." Similarly, a *Booklist* (August 19, 1997) critic wrote, "This formidable portrayal of China's culture and the country's harsh system of justice constitutes a striking backdrop for See's compelling

tale." *Flower Net* went on to become a *New York Times* Notable Book for 1997, and the publication rights were bought in 14 countries.

See writes in her statement, "When I came to the end of *Flower Net*, I couldn't get the characters of David and Hulan out of my mind. Also, as I was traveling and talking to people about this book, I began to take my thoughts about American ignorance of China one step further. How odd that people don't 'think' about China when so many of our clothes, toys, and Christmas ornaments are made there. Not only are they made in China, but they're also manufactured under very difficult circumstances. So, *The Interior*, which I'm working on now and will be published in 1999 by HarperCollins, follows David and Hulan as they go deeper into the country of China to try and solve a series of murders in an American-owned factory."

In *The Interior*, whose action takes place several months after the events depicted in *Flower Net*, Hulan and Stark investigate related deaths—those of a former associate of Stark's and a childhood friend of Hulan's. "The mechanics of the international thriller clank noisily in the novel's conclusion," Jon Garelick wrote in the *New York Times Book Review* (October 17, 1999), "but See's China is as vivid as Upton Sinclair's Chicago."

"As I look ahead," See writes, "I know that I'll continue to write about the intersection of family and history. So often we think of history in terms of wars and dates, or how momentous events have affected racial, ethnic or gender groups. I think we need to remember that history is something that happens to individual people. It's through those individual stories that we can not only understand the great moments in history but also see into the depths of the human soul."

Lisa See resides in Los Angeles with her husband and their two sons.—D.B.

SUGGESTED READING: *Booklist* Aug. 19, 1997; *Denver Post Online* Aug. 24, 1997; *Library Journal* p135 Aug. 1997; *New York Times* C p13 Aug. 17, 1995, with photo; *New York Times Book Review* p20 Aug. 27, 1995, p14 Oct. 26, 1997; *People* p20 Aug. 28, 1995, with photo; *Publishers Weekly* p259 Aug. 11, 1997, with photo; *Washington Post* X p1 Aug. 20, 1995, X p5 Sept. 21, 1997

SELECTED BOOKS: Nonfiction—*On Gold Mountain*, 1995; Fiction—*Flower Net*, 1997; *The Interior*, 1999; As Monica Highland (with J. Espey and C. See)—*Lotus Land*, 1983; *110 Shanghai Road*, 1986; *Greeting from Southern California*, 1988

Jerry Bauer

Shacochis, Bob

Sep. 9, 1951– Novelist; short-story writer; journalist

Although his "shelf" is still minimal—one novel, one book of nonfiction, and two short-story collections—Bob Shacochis has been called one of the most gifted American writers to emerge in recent years. He was awarded one of the nation's most prestigious literary awards, the National Book Award, for *Easy in the Islands* (1985), a collection of short stories about coastal Florida and the Caribbean. Filled with gritty details and native dialect, Shacochis's first book is a compelling, engaging effort that captures the disparities in a tropical paradise. His next book, another collection of short stories called *The Next New World* (1989), moved beyond the island lifestyle to reflect a diverse array of settings and eras, from the South in the 1920s to England in the time of Shakespeare. Shacochis then published his first novel, *Swimming in the Volcano* (1993), a complex thriller set on a fictitious Caribbean island on the brink of natural and political disaster. In 1994 Shacochis compiled a collection of his "Dining In" columns from *GQ* in the nonfiction work *Domesticity: A Gastronomic Interpretation of Love*. Shacochis, who has been hailed by critics for his gentle mix of scholarly and pop-entertainment references, is working on a new book, and continues to contribute to a variety of publications.

Bob Shacochis was born Robert G. Shacochis on September 9, 1951, in West Pittston, Pennsylvania, to John Shacochis, a civil servant, and the former Helen Levonoski, a medical secretary. Bob Shacochis left his home state to attend the University of Missouri at Columbia, from which he received his bachelor's degree in 1973 and his master's degree in 1979. He received his M.F.A. degree from the University of Iowa in 1982.

Shacochis spent the beginning of his career as a journalist. He made this decision partly out of distaste for the fiction of the day, preferring instead the writing of such "New Journalists" as Tom Wolfe and Gay Talese. From 1975 to 1976 Shacochis served as an agricultural journalist for the Peace Corps in St. Vincent, Barbados, and St. Kitts in the West Indies. In 1980, he worked as a reporter for the Palm Beach (Florida) *Evening Times*.

His experiences in the Caribbean and Florida inspired the stories in *Easy in the Islands*. Consisting of nine tales, some of which had originated as part of the master's thesis Shacochis turned in at the University of Iowa, *Easy in the Islands* explored the maritime lifestyle of southern Florida and the Caribbean, confronting head-on the dual nature of some of the world's most extravagant tourist meccas, where the contrast of lifestyles—rich, sunny, and glamorous for some; poor, dark, and seedy for others—is stark. Many of the stories were drawn directly from incidents that occurred during Shacochis's days in the Peace Corps, when he was required to keep a log of activity for the Ministry of Agriculture. One such story is "The Pelican," a tale of a young anthropologist named Bowen who happens to meet a group of pelican hunters carrying a load of dead and dying birds. As Bowen unsuccessfully tries to put the dying birds out of their misery with a dull pocketknife, the hardened locals watch him in amusement, and mock his naïvete.

Other stories in the collection include "Easy in the Islands," "Dead Reckoning," "Hot Day on the Gold Coast," "Lord Short Shoe Wants the Monkey," and "Mundo's Sign." All provide poignant and humorous glimpses at the underbelly of the seeming paradise of the Caribbean and Florida. To make his stories even more authentic, Shacochis used native dialect, a task that drew some criticism from reviewers who felt he was "condescending." In response, Shacochis has pointed out that Mark Twain and Charles Dickens both depended on dialect to address class in their writing.

Most reviewers, however, had only high praise for the first-time author. Stephen Goodwin of the *Washington Post* (March 18, 1985) was so impressed with the effort that he labeled *Easy in the Islands* a "stunning first book." "[Shacochis] evokes the islands, the flora and fauna, the rhythm of the language, the feel of the air and the presence of the sea," he added. "In the best stories, the details transport the readers to a foreign place and an even more foreign way of life." *Time* (February 18, 1985) contributor Paul Gray was similarly impressed with Shacochis's "keen awareness of lush disparities" and his ability to combine scholarly writing with entertaining plots. "Shacochis has had the commercial prudence to learn and write about an uncommonly fascinating part of the hemisphere," Gray wrote. "Better still, his talent seems much more than a match for the subjects at his hand."

Although his original plan was to attempt a novel after *Easy in the Islands*, Shacochis's second literary work evolved into another collection of stories, most of which had been previously published in magazines and other periodicals. *The Next New World* (1989) contains eight short stories, each with a different theme and setting; as Richard Bausch wrote in the *New York Times Book Review* (February 19, 1989), "each story . . . *is* a next new world" for the reader to experience. One of the more unusual and charming stories in the book is "The Trapdoor," which takes place in London during the Elizabethan era. A theater company is staging a production of *Hamlet*, in which Shakespeare himself will play the ghost. The reader is then given a glimpse into the minds of some of the audience members as they watch the performance, and each person's thoughts, touching on the significance of the play in relation to their own lives, are explored. At the same time, a drama begins to unfold beneath the stage's trapdoor, where one of the actresses reveals to the Bard that she has become pregnant by another member of the cast. "The story turns, and then turns again," wrote Bausch, "like a jewel showing its light at different angles."

Other stories in the collection draw on Shacochis's experiences in the South, namely "Where Pelham Fell," which takes place in Virginia, where an elderly man who is "recuperating from the shingles and a number of years of spiritual fatigue" finds rejuvenation in the form of ancient bones discovered in a former Civil War battlefield. The tales range in tone from the comical "I Ate Her Heart," told by a blues harmonica player, to the touching "Celebrations of the New World," which examines the issue of Alzheimer's disease amid a hectic family gathering. The latter story was highlighted by Paul Gray in his *Time* (January 16, 1989) review as indicative of Shacochis's "ability uncommon among younger writers to treat sensitively, without condescension, the perils of middle and old age." V.R. Peterson of *People* (February 13, 1989) called Shacochis "a remarkable storyteller, willing to take risks and grace difficult topics with a sensitive vitality."

Shacochis finally published a first novel in 1993, and its immediate success cemented his reputation. *Swimming in the Volcano* is a complex story centered on a fictional Caribbean island, St. Catherine, which, as the novel opens in 1977, has just gained independence from Britain. Mitchell Wilson is a young economist who comes to the island to work for the Ministry of Agriculture and who soon becomes wrapped up in the turbulent political climate. He also becomes entangled with an ex-lover named Johnnie, a cocaine-fueled woman who has returned to the island after a five-year absence. All the while, St. Catherine's previously dormant volcano is showing signs of life, which serves as a metaphor for the awakening island itself.

Swimming in the Volcano—part thriller, part political commentary—was greeted with largely positive reviews, although many critics took exception to Shacochis's wordy prose. Peter S. Prescott, writing for the *New York Times Book Review* (May 2, 1993), felt that "Lacking a compelling narrative, or even compelling characters, the novel shouldn't work at all, but to a large degree it does— at least for a reader blessed with time and tolerance." Despite his objection to the "encyclopediast" way in which Shacochis tells his story, Prescott concluded that each of the scenes in the novel "is expertly wrought, and the sum of the parts is greater than the whole."

Douglas Kennedy, reviewer for *New Statesman & Society* (January 7, 1994), offered similar criticisms of Shacochis's novel. "Be warned: Shacochis revels in hyper-imagery. He is in love with the musicality of his metaphors and doesn't know how to prune his dense-thickety prose." Kennedy advised: "Simplify, simplify, Mr. Shacochis (and buy yourself a red editing pencil while you're at it)," and emphasized that the author must "learn how to cut to the 'heart of the matter' at half the length." But Kennedy also commended Shacochis on his politically astute novel and his "eye for telling detail and atmospheric complexity." Similarly, *America* (December 11, 1993) reviewer Edward J. Dupuy wrote glowingly about *Swimming in the Volcano*, saying Shacochis "fills this first novel with prose as redolent as Styron's and a narrative as textured and complicated as any by Faulkner or Melville."

In February 1994, Shacochis published *Domesticity: A Gastronomic Interpretation of Love*, a collection of his "Dining In" columns, which he regularly writes for *GQ* magazine. The pieces are ostensibly about cooking but they also concern Shacochis's common-law marriage to Barbara Petersen, whom he simply calls "Miss F." *Domesticity* explores cooking for another person as a medium of love; as a result, the dinners profiled are pampering, seductive, or healing, depending on what events take place in the couple's house that particular day. Shacochis also uses his columns (and therefore the book) as a method of venting whatever grievances he has on any given day, with subjects ranging in scope from foreign policy to "being nice." "About being nice," Shacochis wrote, "I'll say this: I'm against it, both as a gastronomic standard and as an overall policy of behavior."

But while Shacochis does not mince words regarding "niceness" or even vegetarianism (which he's also against), *Domesticity* is not easily dismissed as simply the aggrieved rantings of a temperamental chef. It contains reflections on love and relationships as well as such offbeat topics as aphrodisiacs and the history of breakfast. "*Domesticity* nourishes the senses and the soul," wrote *New York Times* (April 3, 1994) reviewer Eils Lotozo. Charlie Haas of the *Washington Post* (February 13, 1994) concurred, writing in his review, "At its best, *Domesticity* is a love letter, and even for a reader whose limited skill makes quick-fried catfish heroes a tour de force, its celebration of the cook's greatest need-the significant eater-rings sweetly true."

Shacochis's most recent book is *The Immaculate Invasion*, which was published in 1999. A consideration of the 1994 American incursion into Haiti, the book received resoundingly positive reviews. A *Booklist* (January 1, 1999) reviewer called it a "brilliant" account which "captures fine, novelistic details that reveal an entire culture." Similarly, Amy Wilentz, writing in the *New York Times Book Review* (March 21, 1999), praised Shacochis as "a writer of rare grace and intuition."

Bob Shacochis spent one year as a visiting lecturer in English at the University of Missouri at Columbia (1984–1985) and worked in a similar position at the University of Iowa in Iowa City the following year. He has won numerous awards for his work, including the prestigious National Book Award in 1985 for *Easy in the Islands* and the Prix de Rome for *The Next New World*. He is a regular contributor to a wide variety of publications, among them *Harper's*, *GQ*, *Outside*, *Playboy*, and *Esquire*.—D.B.

SELECTED WORKS: Fiction—*Easy in the Islands*, 1985; *The Next New World*, 1989; *Swimming in the Volcano*, 1993; Nonfiction—*Domesticity: A Gastronomic Interpretation of Love*, 1994; *The Immaculate Invasion*, 1999

SUGGESTED READING: *America* p19+ Dec. 11, 1993; *Booklist* Jan. 1, 1999; *New Statesman & Society* p42 Jan. 7, 1994; *New York Times Book Review* p10 Feb. 19, 1989, p15 May 2, 1993, p16 Apr. 3, 1994, Mar. 21, 1999; *People Weekly* p35 Feb. 13, 1989; *Time* Feb. 18, 1985, p72 Jan. 16, 1989; *Washington Post* Mar. 18, 1995, pX2 Feb. 13, 1994; *Contemporary Authors*, 1988

Sheehan, Neil

Oct. 27, 1936– Journalist

Widely acclaimed for his controversial—and truthful—coverage of the Vietnam War during his years in Saigon as the bureau chief for United Press International and, later, as a correspondent for the *New York Times*, the journalist Neil Sheehan has remained obsessed with the paradoxes of the United States' involvement in that war. Sheehan played a major role in the 1971 publication by the *New York Times* of the Pentagon Papers, since he was the reporter to whom Daniel Ellsberg entrusted the top-secret documents revealing how successive administrations had purposely misled the public about America's involvement in the Vietnam War.

In 1972 Sheehan attended the funeral, in Washington, D.C., of John Vann, a lieutenant colonel who had left the army after becoming disillusioned with American policy in Vietnam only to return there as a civilian adviser wielding the powers of a general. Sheehan was struck by the number of political and military figures with pivotal roles in influencing American policy in Vietnam who were at the funeral to pay their last respects. "I had the very strong feeling that day that we were burying more than John Vann; we were burying what Henry Luce so boastfully called the American century. We were interring the mind-set that had led us into Vietnam," Sheehan told an interviewer in 1988. Intrigued, Sheehan set out to investigate and explain the factors behind Vann's behavior in Vietnam—an endeavor that took 16 years. The result, *A Bright Shining Lie: John Paul Vann and America in Vietnam* (1988), has been called the most important book ever written about the Vietnam War, winning the 1988 Pulitzer Prize for nonfiction and the 1988 National Book Award, among other honors. Sheehan's 1992 book *After the War Was Over: Hanoi and Saigon* details his 1989 visit to Vietnam, during which he interviewed many Vietnamese survivors of the war, discovering that the Vietnamese triumph of gaining independence and its people's remarkable ability to forgive old enemies ameliorated, but did not obliterate, the deep scars left on the nation by the war. He found Vietnam still, in 1989, a wounded nation.

Cornelius Mahoney Sheehan was born in Holyoke, Massachusetts, on October 27, 1936 to Cornelius Joseph and Mary (O'Shea) Sheehan. "My father was a hardscrabble dairy farmer, my mother an Irish immigrant who had worked as a housekeeper until her marriage, and yet I had been taken into Harvard on a scholarship," Sheehan wrote in *After the War Was Over*. He majored in Middle Eastern history and graduated cum laude in 1958. During summer vacations, he worked on a highway construction crew. Sheehan was active in the Republican Club during his Harvard years, although he did not affiliate with any political party after that.

After his graduation from Harvard, Sheehan served in the United States Army for three years, from 1959 to 1962, working as a journalist in Korea and Tokyo. During his assignment in Tokyo, where he edited the *Bayonet*, the weekly newspaper of the Seventh Infantry Division, he was able to moonlight for UPI on the condition that he did not receive a byline.

In 1962 Sheehan left the army and took a full-time job with UPI as its Saigon bureau chief, becoming the third full-time American correspondent stationed in Vietnam. The other two were Malcolm W. Browne of the Associated Press and Homer Bigart, the legendary *New York Times* war correspondent, whom Sheehan esteemed deeply and followed on his assignments. Sheehan learned the hard way that "hot tips" could be erroneous. One such tip—that 200 Viet Cong had died in a skirmish near the town of My Tho—led to Sheehan's filing a story that had to be retracted after it turned out that only 12 guerrillas had been killed there. The story also took precedence over one that Bigart filed on the battle. "I was mortified and certain I would be canned," Sheehan recalled to William Prochnau in an interview for the *Washington Post Magazine* (October 9, 1988). Although Bigart was angry at first, after Sheehan filed an amended version of his story, Bigart told him: "Don't feel so bad about it, kid. Just don't let it happen again while I am here." When Bigart left Vietnam several months later, he left a note for his successor, David Halberstam, about Sheehan, which read, "The kid from UPI is going to be very good." Sheehan and Halberstam, who became close friends, learned to develop their own sources rather than take official statements at face value, and they often accompanied troops into battle to gain firsthand information.

When Sheehan started covering the war from Saigon, he at first shared the American military leaders' optimism that the United States would prevail. As he told William Prochnau: "I thought the war was a glorious adventure. First of all, we believed in the American cause. We believed totally in the American cause. When I went out on my first operation and there were bullets, I was thrilled. Some people got killed around me. Small arms fire. The South Vietnamese got scared. I looked at them and said, 'Look how fearful they are!' I wasn't afraid. We were winners; we were invulnerable; we were right."

"I was convinced that this was the right war in the right place," he wrote in *After the War Was Over.* "There was an international Communist conspiracy. . . . To me, the domino theory was not just a theory; if South Vietnam fell, the 'Sino-Soviet bloc,' as the Army security clearance forms referred to our opponents, would seize the rest of Southeast Asia and then move on toward Japan."

Lieutenant Colonel John Paul Vann, the American military adviser who was headquartered in My Tho, became a valuable source of information to the news correspondents covering the war, for he offered outspoken views about the established military policy. Vann thought the war should be fought with knife and rifle rather than with indiscriminate bombings, and he revealed the ineffectiveness of having the South Vietnamese lead their men into exchanges without American strategic know-how. Vann wanted the United States to take over the corrupt South Vietnamese government and carry out social reforms that would win the allegiance of the peasants.

Patriotic optimism gave way to disillusionment after the battle of Ap Bac, on January 2, 1963, which the South Vietnamese Army lost disastrously to a much smaller Viet Cong force, though the top military brass reported a victory to Washington, D.C. The next day, Sheehan drove to the battlefield, where he saw some 80 bodies sprawled in the rice paddies. While he was there, the village was attacked again by the South Vietnamese—who were shelling their own people. "I never saw any glory in war again," Sheehan told Prochnau, "and I never again went into a battle unafraid." Vann took early retirement from the army that July (although he was to return as a civilian adviser in 1965), and Sheehan's articles became increasingly pessimistic about American efforts. By October 1963 UPI had begun killing Sheehan's stories, insisting that he was acting too emotionally. One story that got the ax connected the United States ambassador, Henry Cabot Lodge, with a plot to overthrow the South Vietnamese leader, Ngo Dinh Diem. UPI sent Sheehan on a one-week vacation to Tokyo, during which time the anticipated coup took place.

The Nieman fellows of Harvard University, however, recognized the importance of the American correspondents' controversial and aggressive coverage of the Vietnam War, and in 1964 they presented the first Louis M. Lyons Award to Sheehan, Halberstam, and Browne for conscience and integrity in journalism and for documenting "the truth as they saw it . . . without yielding to unrelenting pressures."

In June 1964 Sheehan moved to the *New York Times,* where he worked on the city staff until he was assigned to Jakarta, Indonesia, in January 1965. Six months later he returned to Saigon, after Charles Mohr, the *New York Times*'s Saigon bureau chief, asked him to cover the escalating war with him. Transferred to Washington in 1966, Sheehan served as Pentagon correspondent for two years before becoming White House correspondent during the final six months of President Lyndon B. Johnson's administration. He subsequently worked as an investigative reporter, covering political and military issues. Neil Sheehan received some media coverage of his own in January 1971, after he wrote a review, at the request of the editor of the *New York Times Book Review,* of Mark Lane's *Conversations with Americans,* a collection of tape-recorded interviews with 32 American servicemen who claimed to have firsthand knowledge about atrocities committed by American soldiers in Vietnam. In his December 27, 1970 review, Sheehan called the book irresponsible. From the routine investigation that he conducted on the interviewees' backgrounds, he had discovered that their professed records and some of their allegations did not check out. "Mr. Lane did not bother to cross-check any of the stories his interviewers told him with army or Marine Corps records," Sheehan wrote. "I asked him why in a telephone conversation. 'Because I believe the most unreliable source regarding the verification of atrocities is the Defense Department,' he said."

It was after Sheehan wrote another, very different, review for the *New York Times* (March 28, 1971), on 33 books dealing with American war crimes in Indochina, that Daniel Ellsberg, a former

Defense Department analyst who had known Sheehan in Vietnam, decided to release to the *New York Times* reporter the 47-volume history of American involvement in Vietnam from 1945 to 1967, which Ellsberg had helped compile for Secretary of Defense Robert S. McNamara in the late 1960s. In conducting his research for that project, Ellsberg had become convinced that the Vietnam War was essentially an act of aggression by the United States and not a civil war, as it was officially described. When his attempts to change American policy failed, Ellsberg decided to leak the Pentagon study to the press and contacted Sheehan.

Once the Pentagon Papers were in his hands, Sheehan traveled to New York City, where he placed the papers on the desk of the *New York Times*'s managing editor, A. M. Rosenthal. "The decision to publish was made almost the moment it came into our hands," Rosenthal told a reporter for *Time* (June 28, 1971) magazine. Sheehan and Gerald Gold, the assistant foreign editor at the *New York Times*, encamped in a hotel room in Washington to organize the information, but they soon realized that more than two people were needed for the job, and on April 22 they moved to the New York Hilton. There, they were joined by eight or nine other reporters, who became known as the "Project X" team. Working seven days a week for seven weeks, virtually sequestered in their hotel suite, the team read, analyzed, and condensed the papers. The first installment appeared on the front page of the *New York Times* on June 13, 1971.

After the third installment was published, on June 15, the government obtained an injunction preventing further publication of the series, but the *Washington Post*, the *Boston Globe*, and other newspapers continued to publish excerpts and articles. On June 30, based on the First Amendment protection against prior restraint, the United States Supreme Court decided in favor of the *New York Times* and the *Washington Post*. According to David Halberstam, in his article "Portrait of an Outsider," Sheehan's life was "totally disrupted" for months as he coped with a grand jury investigation, long sessions with his lawyers, and reports that his friends had been visited by the FBI.

Although the *New York Times* received the Pulitzer Prize in the public service category in 1972 for its publication of the Pentagon Papers, Sheehan did not receive any personal recognition for his role. It was the second time he had been passed over for the prize. (In 1964 he had been nominated for his articles on corruption in South Vietnam.) "I took a lesson from that experience," Sheehan told a reporter for *Newsweek* (May 15, 1972). "The people on the advisory board act for institutional considerations that have nothing to do with your work." In the same *Newsweek* article, it was reported that the Pulitzer Prize jury had recommended that Sheehan be cited along with the *New York Times*, but that the idea had been overruled by the advisory board, which claimed that the Pentagon Papers had "dropped in Sheehan's lap." "This is

really Neil Sheehan's award," A. M. Rosenthal told the *Newsweek* reporter. "It's his, whether it has his name on it or not." In December 1971 Sheehan received the first annual Drew Pearson Prize for excellence in investigative reporting, from the Drew Pearson Foundation.

In *The Arnheiter Affair* (1972), his first book, Sheehan explored the reasons behind the removal of Lieutenant Commander Marcus Aurelius Arnheiter from his post on the USS *Vance* off the coast of South Vietnam, after only 99 days, in early 1966. During that command, as Sheehan demonstrated, Arnheiter exhibited increasingly peculiar behavior, such as requiring his officers to give speeches on the proper etiquette of the finger bowl, among other topics. Writing in the *New York Times Book Review* (February 6, 1972), Gaddis Smith described *The Arnheiter Affair* as "an entertaining account of a hilarious and yet deeply disturbing episode of the Vietnam War." In January 1974 Arnheiter sued Sheehan for libel. The author spent 10 months writing a defense, which ended up being longer than his original manuscript and detailed his sources for documents and interviews. Arnheiter's suit failed.

Although the war was winding down, Sheehan remained preoccupied with the Vietnam experience. "Something was unfinished in me," he explained to Prochnau. "It was eating at me. I had to get this thing out of my system. I needed to leave something behind." After attending the funeral of John Paul Vann in Washington, D.C., in June 1972—a funeral that was heavily attended by government officials who had been involved in the Vietnam War, including Major General William C. Westmoreland and William E. Colby, the head of the CIA, who were pallbearers—Sheehan hit upon a way to deal with his obsession. He would write a biography of the man whom he saw as personifying America's irrational optimism about the war. "Vann epitomized the way we like to think of ourselves in his drive to succeed, his unwillingness to admit defeat, his personal fearlessness," Sheehan told Walter Gelles in an interview for *Publishers Weekly* (September 2, 1988). "He was full of good intentions, many of them misguided. In the end, he was driven by illusions, just as our war in Vietnam was fueled by illusions."

Taking a leave of absence from the *New York Times* to work on his book, Sheehan expected to complete the project within two or three years. His research was aided by several fellowships, including a Guggenheim fellowship in 1973–74, an Adlai Stevenson fellowship, from 1973 to 1975, a Lehrman Institute fellowship in 1975–76, and a Rockefeller Foundation fellowship in the humanities in 1979–80. During this period, Sheehan made two trips back to Vietnam to interview various people, but his schedule was disrupted in November 1974, when he was seriously injured in a head-on collision. Sheehan suffered 11 fractures and was hospitalized for two months. His recovery took over a year and a half, during which time he suspended work on the book.

According to William Prochnau, who described Sheehan's ordeal in *Once Upon a Distant War* (1995), the anguish Sheehan suffered as a result of the accident evoked his painful memories of Vietnam as well. His body broken, his finances in disarray, unable to sleep or to socialize normally, Sheehan could only plod on, trying desperately to complete his book: "The pain, the anxiety, the fear—the same deadly fear he felt in combat—set in later, and tried to take over again. He had to beat it down. Beat it down every day. . . . For sixteen years he did what he had learned to do in Vietnam: He fought his demons." Sheehan told Prochnau, "I would get so overwrought I would get this godawful insomnia, and you have to sleep to work, and I had to work."

Sheehan had resigned from the *New York Times* to devote all his time and energy to his project. He completed his basic research by 1976 but did not find the right organizing structure until 1977. In 1979, when his funds were exhausted, a one-year fellowship from the Woodrow Wilson International Center for Scholars, in Washington, D.C., provided him with $30,000 and the use of an office, so that by the fall of 1981 he had completed two-thirds of the manuscript. Random House gave him a second advance of $200,000 in 1981. When that ran out, William Shawn, then the editor of the *New Yorker*, advanced him $40,000 for the rights to excerpt the book. By August 1986 the manuscript was completed, but it ran to 470,000 words. Sheehan agreed to trim his book down to about 350,000 words. He bought a personal computer, learned word processing, and spent another year editing the text.

Over the 16 years he worked on the book, Sheehan became a virtual recluse in his Washington, D.C., home. He worked six nights a week, reserving Sundays for walks in the countryside, and appeared in the daytime only for neighborhood walks and brief breaks in his garden. His work proceeded slowly, as he painstakingly checked facts and conducted some 385 interviews. For documentation, he relied on Vann's papers and classified documents, including the 7,000-page Pentagon Papers. He went through some 640 tape cassettes and 186 notepads. "I concentrate on one thing at a time to get it right—journalism taught me that," Sheehan told a reporter for *Publishers Weekly* (January 6, 1989). Over the years, he lost 15 pounds and, as he told Prochnau, "I got this overwhelming anxiety, the anxiety would just be enormous, and it went on for years and years and I had to find a way to control it."

Both Sheehan and Vann had changed their opinions about the war, but in opposite directions. "John Paul Vann at his death was not the John Paul Vann Sheehan thought he knew in those days of youth and innocence in the delta," Prochnau wrote in *Once Upon a Distant War.* "Like his country, Vann had been drawn in by the delusion. Like his country, he had escalated from the naiveté of the beginning to the insanity of the end. . . ." As

Sheehan revealed in *A Bright Shining Lie*, John Paul Vann's personal life paralleled his behavior in Vietnam. A painful childhood (an illegitimate child, he had been abandoned by his mother) created rage and insecurities, manifested in part by sexual promiscuity, that "made him constantly try to prove that he was braver and tougher than anyone else." Although Vann was at first outraged by the indiscriminate killing of civilians, by the end he had given in to the temptation to subject the countryside to bombings and artillery raids. "[Vann] ended up prolonging the war, but he didn't know that," Sheehan told Alvin P. Sarnoff in an interview for *U.S. News & World Report* (October 24, 1988). For Sheehan, Vann symbolized many of the contradictions in the American character: "We like to think of ourselves as a simple country with simple motives, when that's not the case. The insecurities that drive us can produce a very unrealistic view of a particular situation, as they did in Vietnam."

Critics were effusive in their praise of *A Bright Shining Lie: John Paul Vann and America in Vietnam,* citing its immense power and describing it as the best book ever written about the Vietnam War. Reviewing *A Bright Shining Lie* for the *New York Times* (October 10, 1988), David K. Shipler described the work as "one of the few brilliant histories of the American entanglement in Vietnam. . . . Skillful weaving of anecdote and history, of personal memoir and psychological profile give the book the sense of having been written by a novelist, journalist, and scholar all rolled into one." Joseph Nocura of *Newsweek* (October 10, 1988) stated unequivocally, "Thus . . . 16 years after he began, Neil Sheehan has written not only the best book ever about Vietnam, but the timeliest," and Ronald Steel remarked in the *New York Times Book Review* (September 25, 1988) that the book was "vividly written and deeply felt, with a power that comes from long reflection and strong emotions." In his review for the *Washington Monthly* (October 1988), Taylor Branch wrote: "Sheehan leaves many of the war's most difficult issues exposed but unresolved. This is a book of scalding reportage, not interpretation. By capturing within the life of one small obsessive daredevil the essence of something so vast and benumbing as Vietnam, Sheehan has written by far the best single account of the war."

In 1988 *A Bright Shining Lie* won the Pulitzer Prize, the National Book Award in nonfiction, and the Robert F. Kennedy Book Award. It was a main selection of the Book of the Month Club and was excerpted in four installments in the *New Yorker.* Terry George directed a 1998 television film version of the book.

Although he saw the Vietnam War as a tragic mistake, Sheehan believed that America's involvement might have prevented a greater tragedy later on. Unlike earlier American soldiers, "the Vietnam veteran brought home a different kind of wisdom," Sheehan told Sarnoff. "He learned that you can fight a bad war, that you can get killed for nothing, that it's a complicated world. This wisdom is necessary to a country over the long run. In that sense, Vietnam can be a very good experience for Americans, and to some extent it already has been."

Sheehan received emotional support in his effort from his wife, Susan Sheehan, an accomplished writer in her own right, whom he married in 1965, and from their two children, Maria Gregory and Catherine Fair. Wrestling with Vann's biography was itself a kind of combat, and, as he told Prochnau, he applied a lesson he had learned in the army: "It may be raining, it may be snowing, the sun may be shining, but you get up and YOU MARCH."

Sheehan credited his wife not only with support but with collaboration on the reporting that went into *After the War Was Over: Hanoi and Saigon* (1992). Not exactly a nostalgic tourist, Sheehan described the aftermath of war and of Communist rule on Vietnam as he saw it in 1989. A deeper and, in many ways, sadder understanding of Vietnam was a result of that trip for Sheehan. In Hanoi, for instance, he investigated hospitals, finding them filthy, lacking in modern equipment and drugs, and overcrowded. Widespread poverty and destruction of the infrastructure prevailed in the North, the aftereffects of the disastrous Communist rigidity. Although the regime had relaxed into a more modern approach to free enterprise, Vietnam was still being boycotted by the United States and remained a poor country. The chief difference between the North and the South was the element of corruption that, although reduced from the time of the war, still prevailed in the South.

In general, *After the War Was Over* is a tribute to the spirit of the Vietnamese people, who had struggled for centuries to preserve and recapture their independence. Sheehan found a climate of forgiveness toward the United States, although maimed victims of land mines and old grenades were prevalent. Although a former general in the ARVN (the South Vietnamese army), who was a friend of Sheehan's, had been forced to spend 12 years in re-education camps, he had expected worse—to be executed immediately by the Communist victors. Only the Chinese—the ancient enemies of the Vietnamese—were the targets of revenge after the Vietnamese gained their independence.

"After the riveting, up-close combat descriptions and profiles of *A Bright Shining Lie*," David Gelman wrote in his review of *After the War Was Over* for *New York Newsday* (July 12, 1992), "the present volume seems strangely detached and impersonal, its prose merely workmanlike. But as a kind of postscript, it may be sufficient to its modest purposes." Christopher Lehmann-Haupt, writing in the *New York Times* (July 27, 1992), on the other hand, found it a "luminously clear" report. And Kenneth W. Berger in *Library Journal* (July 1992) found the volume filled with "insightful and informed observations," which should help in "un-derstanding the past and breaking down the emotional and cultural barriers of the present."

Sheehan received a doctorate in literature from Columbia College in Chicago in 1972; the Columbia Journalism Award in 1972; the Sidney Hillman Foundation Award in 1972; the Page One Award from the Newspaper Guild of New York in 1972; the Distinguished Service Award and Bronze Medallion from Sigma Delta Chi in 1972; and the citation of excellence from the Overseas Press Club of America, for the Pentagon Papers series, in 1972. —S. Y.

SUGGESTED READING: *Chicago Tribune* V p1+ Oct. 9, 1988, with photo; *Esquire* p49+ July 1984, with photo; *Library Journal* p107 July 1992; *Publishers Weekly* p83+ Sep. 2, 1988, with photo; *New York Newsday* p33 July 12, 1992; *New York Times* C p18 July 27, 1992; *Rolling Stone* p117+ May 18, 1989; *US News and World Report* p73 Oct. 24, 1988, with photo; *Washington Post Magazine* p23+ Oct. 9, 1988, with photo; Prochnau, William. *Once Upon a Distant War: David Halberstam, Neil Sheehan, Peter Arnett—Young War Correspondents and Their Early Vietnam Battles*, 1995

SELECTED BOOKS: *The Arnheiter Affair*, 1972; *A Bright Shining Lie: John Paul Vann and America in Vietnam*, 1988; *After the War Was Over: Hanoi and Saigon*, 1992

Simmons, Dan

1948– Novelist; short-story writer

The four-part Hyperion/Endymion science fiction saga by Dan Simmons has been compared to such monumental achievements in the genre as Frank Herbert's *Dune* chronicles and Isaac Asimov's Foundation series. Certainly Simmons's long list of accolades bears out such comparisons: he won a Hugo Award for the initial Hyperion novel, and has won numerous other prizes such as the World Fantasy Award and the Bram Stoker Award, both notable honors in the fantasy/horror field. Although best known for the four books in the Hyperion/Endymion tetralogy, Simmons is also the author of horror novels such as *Carrion Comfort* (1989) and *Children of the Night* (1992). His most recent publication was *The Rise of Endymion* (1998), the final episode in his epic set in the distant future.

Dan Simmons was born in 1948 in Peoria, Illinois. His parents raised him in the Catholic faith, but he has said that he "became a nonbeliever at an early age" (*Event Horizon* on-line chat, February 25, 1999.) It was also at an early age, specifically the third grade, that he gained an interest in writing. He attended Wabash College in Indiana, where he majored in liberal arts.

In the late 1960s, Simmons began working as an elementary-school teacher. He spent much of his spare time writing, but did not at first aspire to publication. In 1977, Simmons was the recipient of a Fulbright scholarship. Shortly thereafter, at the beginning of the 1980s, he began writing seriously with the goal of seeing his work in print.

Simmons's first published fiction was a short story entitled "The River Styx Runs Upstream," which appeared in *Twilight Zone* magazine in 1982 (it was published on the same day Simmons's only child, Jane, was born). The story earned Simmons *Twilight Zone*'s award for best short story of the year. At that time, he had begun attending science fiction writing workshops, where he received encouragement from such prominent writers of the genre as Harlan Ellison and Edward Bryant. Soon, Simmons began pursuing publication more seriously. More and more of his stories began to appear in science fiction and fantasy magazines.

Simmons's first novel, *Song of Kali*, was published in 1985. Although it was categorized as a horror novel, several critics have noted that it uses violence to make a statement about non-violence; in fact, the story's serious moral message initially made publishers hesitant to publish it. The book is set in Calcutta, where the daughter of an American journalist is kidnapped by members of a cult of the Hindu death goddess Kali. Simmons has stated that the story was inspired in part by the year he spent studying in Calcutta on his Fulbright scholarship. The novel received tremendous critical acclaim, and was given the World Fantasy Award for best first novel. According to many critics, Simmons was on the cutting edge of horror fiction, adroitly meshing scenes of gory violence with a genuinely chilling, suspenseful plot. "This rich, bizarre novel practically reeks with atmosphere," stated Fiona Webster of *Amazon.com*.

Simmons decided in 1987 to leave the teaching profession and write full-time. "I loved being in the classroom, but I got sick of the egalitarian ignorance of school districts," he said of his decision in his *Omni* chat (August 14, 1997). He contributed a short story to the anthology *Night Visions V* (1988), edited by Stephen King. Simmons's next novel after *Song of Kali* was *Hyperion*, published in 1989. The novel represented the first in what would become a tetralogy of books set centuries in the future, featuring a human civilization known as the Hegemony that is spread across the cosmos. The Hegemony is a society in decay as a result of the conflict between religion, in the form of a futuristic Roman Catholic Church, and science, in the form of an artificial intelligence called Technocore. The book won the Hugo Award for best novel, as well as the best novel award presented by *Locus*, a well-regarded science fiction magazine. The idea for the Hyperion books started while Simmons was teaching elementary school in Missouri. He would tell the story to his students during their storytelling hour (this experience became fictionalized as the subject of "Death of a Centaur," included in Simmons's anthology *Prayers to Broken Stones*, 1990).

Both *Hyperion* and its sequel *The Fall of Hyperion* follow one continuing storyline, which borrows its structure from Chaucer's *The Canterbury Tales*. Seven pilgrims travel to the planet from which the novel takes its title, each one recounting a personal experience explaining why they have embarked on the voyage. In each story, Simmons experiments with various science fiction styles and devices.

Further literary inspiration for Simmons's writing can be found in the titles of the two books, which come from poems by John Keats. Simmons addressed this aspect of the series in an interview with *Bookpage* (online): "I think the readers who know that literature can enjoy pursuing those references, and that can deepen their Hyperion experience—it certainly did for me. . . . In fact, when I first started writing *Hyperion*, I knew I'd have to deal with Keats's long poems, *Hyperion* and *The Fall of Hyperion*. I really appreciated his theme of life evolving from one race of gods to another, with one power having to give rise to another."

Hyperion was followed quickly in 1989 by *Phases of Gravity* and *Carrion Comfort*. The latter won the horror fiction genre's highest accolade, the Bram Stoker Award for best novel. Focusing on the tried-and-true horror subgenre of vampires, the novel is about a group of influential, upper-class bloodsuckers with powerful telepathic abilities who are challenged by a band of humans led by a survivor of the Holocaust. *Phases of Gravity* is notable for possibly being the first historical novel written about the space program; its main character is a former astronaut who once walked on the moon.

In 1990, Simmons continued his four-part science fiction saga with *The Fall of Hyperion*. The adventure begun in *Hyperion* is here continued, this time revolving around mysterious structures known as the Time Tombs. The novel represents the end of the first portion of the series, which Simmons would not resume for six years. *Locus* magazine again awarded Simmons their best science fiction novel prize, and he also received the best novel award from the Science Fiction Chronicle.

Additionally, Simmons published three short-story anthologies in 1990: *Banished Dreams, Entropy's Bed at Midnight*, and *Prayers to Broken Stones*. The first two were released in limited edition only. The third, *Prayers to Broken Stones*, was a return to the horror genre, and garnered Simmons his second Bram Stoker Award, this time for best short- story collection.

By now publishing at a rapid pace, Simmons released *Summer of Night* in 1991. Set in 1960, *Summer of Night* features an enigmatic creature that preys on the children of a small Midwestern town. Simmons borrowed some of the details in the novel, such as the character and place names, from his own childhood. The novel earned Simmons his third Locus award.

In 1992 Simmons published *The Hollow Man*, another science fiction novel with a title taken from literature (this time the source was a poem by

T. S. Eliot called "The Hollow Men.") Simmons's novel concerns a psychic who goes on a bizarre metaphysical journey after the death of his wife. The novel was an expansion of a short story entitled "Eyes I Dare Not Meet in Dreams" which originally appeared in *Omni*. Its structure partially resembles Dante's *Inferno*.

Next followed Simmons's second vampire novel, *Children of the Night*, also published in 1992. The central figure of the book is a young boy born with a rare blood condition which allows him to assimilate and purify any blood transfused into his body. His adopted mother, a hematologist, believes her son's condition could help produce a cure for AIDS, but she soon discovers that the boy is being hunted by none other than Dracula himself, who wishes to indoctrinate him as his successor. The *Kirkus Reviews* (May 1, 1992) termed the novel Simmons's greatest ever. At the time of this writing, Simmons was working on a screen adaptation.

Lovedeath (1993) is Simmons's fourth short-story anthology. "This collection of Simmons's novellas demonstrates the full range of one of the most gifted writers in the psychological horror field," wrote Elliott Swanson of *Booklist* (Oct. 15, 1993). Swanson particularly praised "The Great Lover," a re-creation in diary form of the experiences of a soldier in World War I. "Simmons has never been more stylish than here," read the *Kirkus Reviews* (September 1, 1993) discussion of the book, "with the short novel form compressing his effects and squeezing a lurid glow from each page." The reviewer also noted how each story stands out distinctly from the others, "with writing of an unhackneyed freshness seldom found among the kings and queens of gore." Another of the stories included was "Death in Bangkok," about a vampire prostitute. The piece was awarded the Bram Stoker Award for best novelette.

After *Lovedeath*, Simmons returned to the novel, with *Fires of Eden* (1994). A surreal fantasy, the work concerns a wealthy real estate tycoon who angers Hawaiian volcano gods by building property on their holy ground. The novel also contains a flashback subplot involving Mark Twain. It won the *Locus* award for best horror novel.

Simmons returned to the far-future civilization he had explored in the Hyperion novels with *Endymion*, published in 1996. Set nearly 300 years after the Hyperion books, *Endymion* introduces the reader to Raul Endymion, a character who plays a vital role in the fate of a "techno-religious" society that spans the galaxy. In *Endymion* he becomes the protector of Aenea, a messianic cyborg woman being hunted down by the religious orthodoxy, who consider her a threat because her blood is poisonous to the parasitic life forms which grant them immortality. An *Amazon.com* review praised Simmons's prose style in *Endymion*, and stated the novel has "something for everyone."

Before concluding his vast Hyperion/Endymion tetralogy, Simmons briefly departed the sci-fi genre to write *The Crook Factory*, a work of historical fiction that was published at the end of 1997. The title is taken from Ernest Hemingway's name for the makeshift espionage group to which he belonged during World War II. The novel's main character, FBI agent Joe Lucas, must infiltrate this group. The book includes other real-life figures, such as Ingrid Bergman, Ian Fleming, and Marlene Dietrich.

With the 1998 publication of *The Rise of Endymion*, Simmons's chronicles of humankind's distant future were brought to an end. In a final bid for control of humanity, the Catholic Church, now united with former enemy Technocore, continues its pursuit of the messiah Aenea, still under the protection of Raul Endymion. Separated from his charge, Endymion travels across several fantastic worlds with the help of time portals. This final book in the series clears up many of the mysteries running through the previous three, such as the identity of the enigmatic Shrike, a robotic creature integral to the overall plot. John Mort of *Booklist* (Aug. 19, 1997) gave the novel a positive review, and was particularly impressed with Simmons's imaginative rendering of the bizarre worlds encountered by Endymion. A writer for the *Kirkus Reviews* (June 15, 1997) complained of too much filler, but remained in awe of the grand scope and inventiveness of the work.

Among readers and critics, Simmons is known for the complex, challenging themes in his novels, which many feel refute the prevailing stereotype which exists among mainstream literary critics, of horror and science fiction as the print equivalent of junk food. Simmons is also known for his spirit of experimentation, which often leads him to expand the boundaries of what is too— often thought of as merely "genre fiction." Discussing this issue in an online chat for *Omni* (Aug. 14, 1997), Simmons commented, "SF and horror bring the energy, the human element, and respect for large ideas that have been sorely missing in [literary] fiction for some time. I think our genres are revitalizing fiction to become the serious literature of the next century."

In addition to his contributing to *Twilight Zone*, Simmons has contributed fiction to such periodicals as *Omni* and *Galaxy*, and he wrote screenplays for two episodes of the 1980s horror TV series "Monsters." The author is currently working on several projects, including a novel entitled *Darwin's Blade*, about the Russian mob and insurance fraud in California; another book tentatively named *The Great Oven*, said to be a historical novel featuring Charles Dickens; and finally a novel called *The Hounds of Winter*, a sequel to *Summer of Night*. Simmons and his wife Karen have one daughter, Jane.

—B.S.

SUGGESTED READING: *Amazon.com*; *Booklist* (online) Oct. 15, 1993; Aug. 19, 1997; *BookPage* (online) Aug. 1997; *Event Horizon* (online) Feb. 25, 1999; *Kirkus Reviews* (online) May 1, 1992;

July 15, 1992; Sep. 1, 1993; Aug. 15, 1994; June 15, 1997; *Locus* (online) May 1997; *Omni* (online)

SELECTED WORKS: Fiction—*Song of Kali*, 1985; *Hyperion*, 1989; *Phases of Gravity*, 1989; *Carrion Comfort*, 1989; *Banished Dreams*, 1990; *Entropy's Bed at Night*, 1990; *Prayers to Broken Stones*, 1990; *The Fall of Hyperion*, 1990; *Summer of Night*, 1991; *Children of the Night*, 1992; *The Hollow Man*, 1992; *Lovedeath*, 1993; *Fires of Eden*, 1994; *Endymion*, 1996; *The Crook Factory*, 1997; *The Rise of Endymion*, 1998

Ruven Afanador/Courtesy of Knopf

Simpson, Mona

June 14, 1957– Novelist

Mona Simpson's highly acclaimed first novel, *Anywhere but Here* (1986), a moving portrait of the complex relationship between a mother and daughter, "earned [her] a place beside domestic pioneers like Anne Tyler and Alice Munro," Sven Birkerts wrote for the *Chicago Tribune* (January 11, 1987). Simpson's auspicious debut, which seemed to some observers to have occurred virtually overnight, was actually the result of years of hard work and careful preparation. According to Paula Span, who profiled the author for the *Washington Post* (January 27, 1987), Simpson "had been groomed for success for close to a decade, a series of teachers, mentors, and grant givers bringing her along, waiting for the day she would prove them prescient." With *The Lost Father* (1992), a sequel to *Anywhere but Here* and her second novel, Simpson

solidified her reputation as one of the brightest novelists of her generation. *A Regular Guy*, Simpson's 1996 novel, had the extraordinary cachet of being a roman à clef about her half-brother Steve Jobs, the founder of Apple Computers. Simpson converted her narrative voice to the third person for *A Regular Guy*, which, like its predecessors, deals with a daughter abandoned by her father.

Mona Elizabeth Simpson was born on June 14, 1957 in Green Bay, Wisconsin. Her ancestors had settled in Sheboygan, Wisconsin, in the late 19th century, when her maternal great-great-grandparents, the Horns, emigrated from Germany. Her great-grandmother Hattie Horn Ziegler also made her home in Sheboygan. A generation later, her grandmother Irene moved to Green Bay, where she and her husband made a living by raising mink and running a photoengraving business and two small gas stations.

Simpson's parents were less satisfied than their forebears with small-town life. Her father, a college professor who was originally from the Middle East, abandoned his family when Mona was 13 years old. At that point, her mother, a speech therapist, moved with her two children, Mona and an older son, to Beverly Hills, California, where Mona experienced what she has called "total culture shock." In an interview with a reporter for *People* (March 16, 1987), she recalled, "I didn't do anything terribly wild. I got scholarships and stuff to college and knew I couldn't screw up that much or I might not be able to go." She excelled in school, and wrote poetry and made pottery in her spare time. Reflecting on her early creative impulses, Simpson told Paula Span, "I wanted to make things that explained the world to me. I wanted to write my own Bible; I heard Robert Stone say that once."

Following her graduation from high school, Simpson enrolled at the University of California at Berkeley, from which she graduated with a B.A. degree in 1979. While she was a student, she had submitted short stories to various magazines but without much success. Encouragement came in the form of a prestigious writing prize from the university, but after graduating from college she decided to try her hand as a reporter; as she explained to Mickey Pearlman for the book *Inter/View: Talks with America's Writing Women* (1990), she had always "loved journalism." For the next two years, she worked as a general-assignment reporter for local newspapers in the San Francisco area. "I interviewed circus performers, a carillon genius, . . . Buddhist bakers, . . . my local *dim sum* chef, a woman leading an incest victims' group, performance artists, city attorneys, merchant marines," she told Pearlman. "But I'm too slow, really, for daily newspapers, and also I'm not always interested in the 'news' of news."

In 1981 Simpson won a scholarship to the graduate program in writing at Columbia University, in New York City. She moved to the city with $3,000 that had been left to her following the death of her grandmother. Among Simpson's classmates at Columbia were Susan Minot, Nancy Lemann, and Patty Dann, all of whom later became published novelists; her teachers included the novelists Elizabeth Hardwick and Edmund White. On the suggestion of the writer Richard Price, she applied to Yaddo, the writers' colony in Saratoga Springs, New York, where she found the peace she needed to begin writing in earnest. "It was really nice and pretty there," she recalled in her conversation with Paula Span, "and I'd had this hard year in New York in this awful Columbia apartment with no kitchen. And in eight weeks I wrote the whole first draft [of *Anywhere but Here*]. . . . I'd written it so fast it was sort of incoherent."

Simpson had written the "core" of the novel's opening scene at the age of 23. In that scene, Adele August and her 12-year-old daughter, Ann, are escaping Adele's bad second marriage. With Adele at the wheel of a stolen car, they are on their way from the fictional Bay City, Wisconsin, to Beverly Hills, where Adele hopes to marry a rich man and to help Ann become a child star. At one point, Adele forces Ann, the narrator for much of the story, to get out of the car, then drives away, leaving her daughter alone on the road. "I got out," Ann recalls. "It was always a shock the first minute because nothing outside was bad. The fields were bright. . . . The scenery went all strange, like a picture on a high billboard. The fields, the clouds, the sky; none of it helped because it had nothing to do with me."

In her interview with Mickey Pearlman, Simpson explained that she had written that scene without a plot in mind and without any idea of what the mother and daughter were running from or toward. "I just wrote this little patch about the impervious quality of physical landscape, even of beauty, how the great open monumental forms of the American West become drained for us without the infusion of love. So right from the beginning this novel was about deracination, about a kind of immigration. I hope the book holds not only the blankness of loss but the exhilaration of possibility in the new, the immigrant's greed, the American hope of self-transformation."

In addition to Ann's narration, Ann's Aunt Carol and her grandmother Lillian provide some historical perspective. The reliance on female narrators "was the most unforced, intuitive decision of the book," Simpson told Kim Heron for the *New York Times Book Review* (January 11, 1987). "I tried some of the men's voices, but it seemed too fractured. And in a certain way, their side of the story isn't the point. The book is about the people who stayed in their hometowns and put down their roots and the people who went west and tried to get more from life, because that seems to me the story of life in America."

Likening the writing process to a piling on of layers, Simpson revealed to Pearlman that, in her case, "a chapter or a story doesn't really find its shape and emphasis, its color, until the fifth or sixth draft," and that she revises many more times

"just to polish the stones." In her conversation with Pearlman, she cited Raymond Carver as her inspiration for doing so. "He revised twenty to thirty times, and his stories live on now as hard, perfect, compact monuments. He is truly our [generation's] Chekhov." Simpson has also expressed admiration for the work of the novelists Marcel Proust, Gustave Flaubert, Jane Austen, George Eliot, Leo Tolstoy, and Joseph Conrad and the poets Rainer Maria Rilke and Emily Dickinson. "[Reading] Proust and Tolstoy, I look for a specific paragraph, find it, read it over ten times, and then I keep going until I make myself stop a hundred pages later," she explained to Pearlman. "I think you need a certain voice at a certain time, the way a pregnant woman craves food which contains a particular necessary mineral."

The manuscript that would become *Anywhere but Here* went through four years of revision. Among those who commented on various drafts were Elizabeth Hardwick, Louise Erdrich, and George Plimpton, the editor of the *Paris Review*, where Simpson worked as a part-time editor and for which she once interviewed Raymond Carver. Impressed by her, Carver later included one of her stories in the 1986 edition of *Best American Short Stories*, which he edited. By then she had published short stories in *Ploughshares*, the *Iowa Review*, the *North American Review*, and the *Paris Review*, among other literary journals. Meanwhile, she had earned an M.F.A. degree from Columbia University in 1983. She supported herself by working as an acupuncturist's assistant and as an usher at the Bleecker Street Cinema. Simpson occasionally supplemented her income with grants, including a $20,000 fellowship from the National Endowment for the Arts and a $25,000 award from the Whiting Foundation, both of which she received in 1986.

When Simpson decided that she had revised her manuscript as much as she could, she submitted it to the publisher Alfred A. Knopf through the influential literary agent Amanda Urban, to whom Simpson had been recommended by the critic James Atlas. "There *is* a kind of network that's involved," her writer friend Allan Gurganus told Paula Span. "She has a genius for friendship and I think that's one of the reasons things have worked out so fabulously for her." Knopf accepted Simpson's novel almost immediately, and *Anywhere but Here* was published in December 1986. When asked how she felt about that long-anticipated event, Simpson admitted to Paula Span that she was merely "kind of excited." "It was like, well that's nice. Now what? . . . I think emotions run away from spotlights. One can't feel on cue the way one is supposed to."

Calling *Anywhere but Here* "stunning," Michiko Kakutani of the *New York Times* (December 24, 1986) felt that, in relating the mother-daughter story, Simpson "takes on—and reinvents—many of America's essential myths, from our faith in the ever-receding frontier to our uneasy mediation between small-town pieties and big-time dreams. . . . Simpson also succeeds in creating a wholly original work—a work stamped with the insignia of a distinctive voice and animated by two idiosyncratic and memorable heroines." Noting in her interview with Mickey Pearlman that "American literature gives us a long tradition of men going west, of trying to change their lives materially, of obliterating their origins," Simpson explained that she wanted "to write about a woman's way in this same attempt, with these driving desires." She added that "many of the institutions that shaped the assumptions, the premises beneath the 19th-century novel, have irrevocably changed. . . . But families are still the basic element of any community life. Moral choices and virtues start, as they always did, at home. Even if that family is led by a single mother."

Simpson's background in poetry was evident, according to many reviewers, in her striking imagery as well as in her starkly detailed descriptions of her characters' experiences. "Mona Simpson's rare and welcome achievement in *Anywhere but Here* is to fuse the minimalist style of an Ann Beattie with the shrewd family insights of an Anne Tyler," Dan Cryer declared in his review for *New York Newsday* (January 15, 1987). "The flat, seemingly emotionless tone furnishes the smoothest and cleanest of surfaces under which the deepest longings rumble. This is real life, genuine feeling, the prose proclaims in sentence after sentence. This is real heartbreak, this is America crashing and, in spite of everything, going on."

Ann survives the love/hate relationship with her mother during the six years covered in *Anywhere but Here* only to face another trial in its sequel, *The Lost Father*, in which Ann, who is in her late 20s and has taken an Egyptian name, Mayan, embarks on a search for her father, who had abandoned her when she was a child. Mayan's obsessive quest takes her across the United States and even to Egypt on an enervating journey that depletes her life savings, ruins her academic standing, and jeopardizes her physical and mental well-being. Perhaps even more threatening than her mission, however, is the all-consuming void that her father's long absence has left her with; she feels she will have no control over her destiny until she finds out what happened to him.

The Lost Father received overwhelmingly positive reviews. Calling the novel "brilliant, astonishing, and wholly original" in her evaluation for *Newsweek* (February 3, 1992), Laura Shapiro contended that "Simpson is a master of discretion, pacing, and psychological drama, and she's created a marvel." In his assessment of the novel for *Mirabella* (February 1993), Vince Passaro observed, "Simpson's prose is languid and intense; it includes the reader and draws him in so that Mayan's sense of loss expands to touch on something larger, what you might call the essential fatherlessness and longing of our age." And Michiko Kakutani of the *New York Times* (January 21, 1992)

wrote, "*The Lost Father* ratifies the achievement of *Anywhere but Here*, attesting to its author's possession of both a dazzling literary gift and uncommon emotional wisdom."

Much of Simpson's writing has drawn on her family history. When Susannah Hunnewell, during an interview for the *New York Times Book Review* (February 9, 1992), asked Simpson about the extent to which she would consider her novels autobiographical, she replied, "I'm not sure what autobiography is. If you're talking about—strictly speaking—events, then no. It's definitely not a memoir; it's definitely not nonfiction. If autobiography includes our imagination, then, of course, everything that we write is autobiographical. I think, for people who write fiction or poetry, our wager is that what we imagine is truer or as true to us as the mess of life and the mess that happens." "I think all your characters are part of yourself," she said to Kim Heron, "and you're most attached to those who risk the most and lose the most."

Simpson had worked on the manuscript for "A Regular Guy" for two years before turning to *The Lost Father*. Her third novel, *A Regular Guy*, was finally published in 1996. Filled with minor characters, it describes 10 years in the life of Tom Owens from the point of view of Jane, a daughter born to his high-school girlfriend Mary. When Jane is 10, Mary teaches her to drive and sends her, alone, to find her father, who has never acknowledged her. Her father, meanwhile, has achieved fabulous success in a genetic-engineering company. Despite his extraordinary wealth and fame, he has no idea how to conduct his private life and lives only for his work. He is contrasted with Noah, a disabled but fulfilled scientist who has the emotional strength to reject Tom's blandishments. Many reviewers have seen similarities between Tom Owens and Steve Jobs, the founder of Apple Computer and Simpson's half-brother. Simpson has admitted only that the character is a "composite," as she told Jonathan Bing, who interviewed her for *Publishers Weekly* (November 4, 1996). For example, she shares Owens's vegetarian habits, though not to the same degree. "I'm a vegetarian but I'm not as good as Owens. I would like to be that rigorous but I'm not," she told Bing.

Although *Granta* named Simpson one of the best young American writers in 1996, reportedly on the basis of the first chapter of *A Regular Guy*, most reviewers found the novel disappointing. In the *Times Literary Supplement* (February 21, 1997), Wendy Brandmark wrote of Owens, "Nothing he says is remarkable, and his obsessions with diet and education seem indulgent rather than original, his love-life typical of a man afraid to commit himself to one woman. We have to wade through a rather cumbersome narrative to see Owens transformed into 'a regular guy,' yet we never believed even for a moment that he was a mythological figure. . . . His personality is not large enough to compensate for the flatness, the odd complacency of the writing." Michiko Kakutani, the reviewer for the *New York Times* (October 15, 1996), also found the character of Owens somewhat incomplete: although Simpson had tried to emphasize Owens's "charm and charisma," he "comes across as a rich egomaniac about whom it's impossible to care." Kakutani thought "Simpson . . . somewhat more adept at creating the rich emotional chiaroscuro that distinguished her earlier novels" when she turned to Jane's efforts to come to terms with her father. Nevertheless, Kakutani found all the other characters "satellites around Owens . . . a man, in the end, who is not 'a regular guy' . . . but an emotional black hole."

In an article for the *Writer* (May 1992), Simpson dispensed advice to would-be writers. "No one should have the power to tell you what you can and cannot do," she reminded them, because samples of current work do not indicate "what your imagination will be capable of in a year." Urging those who really want to write to have faith in themselves, invest time in their endeavors, and develop a solid and regular discipline, Simpson cautioned them not to try to be perfect and to avoid worrying about whether their work would be published. Instead, she wrote, they should revise extensively, explore all forms and methods of writing until they discover those that suit them best, "practice reading aloud," "read great books" for inspiration, and develop a trusted group of readers who will provide constructive criticism.

Mona Simpson is married to Richard Appel, a former attorney and prosecutor who became a television writer. She has one son. Simpson has done most of her writing in rented spaces or in restaurants and cafés. Among the close friends who have attested to her dedication is Allan Gurganus, who told Paula Span that Simpson was "the most concentrated and serious writer [he knew], of any age." Cherishing her solitude, Simpson has sacrificed vacations and has avoided going out to lunch, all in the name of reserving more time for writing. She prefers to work late at night or just before dawn, when no one else is awake. "I always use the same pen," she told Mickey Pearlman, "an old fountain pen I bought once in Boston, and I fill it up with blue or brown ink and write on yellow legal pads. Silence helps. Sometimes I sit at the desk at night with a candle." Claiming that all writers have "their drug, whether it's liquor or dope or coffee," Simpson described her "drug": "Mine is a certain kind of Swiss coffee that takes a half hour to brew, but I would try anything once for work. Anything."

Simpson's fiction has been anthologized in several collections, among them *The Pushcart Prize: Best of the Small Presses XI, Twenty Under Thirty* (1985), and *Louder than Words* (1990). She has taught a writing workshop in the graduate program at New York University, and she was a Bard Center fellow and a senior editor at the *Paris Review*.
—S. Y.

SUGGESTED READING: *Life* Apr. 1992; *New York Times* C p13 Jan. 24, 1987; *People* p62+ Mar. 16, 1987, with photo; *Publishers Weekly* p50+ Nov. 4, 1996, with photo; *Times Literary Supplement* p21 Feb. 21, 1997; *Washington Post* D p1+ Jan. 27, 1987, with photo; *Contemporary Authors* vol. 135, 1992; *Contemporary Literary Criticism* vol. 44, 1987; Henderson, Katherine Usher, ed. *Inter/View: Talks with America's Writing Women*, 1990

SELECTED WORKS: *Anywhere but Here*, 1986; *The Lost Father*, 1992; *A Regular Guy*, 1996

Sloan, James Park

Sep. 22, 1944– Novelist; biographer

"The question of form—the overall structure of a novel—is for me the most exciting and underdeveloped area of modern fiction," the American novelist and biographer James Park Sloan said in one interview. "Innovative form is far rarer than splashy language or even action. Modern readers, in fact, are a bit deadened to language and action." Whether formulating the serpentine twists and turns of an intellectual thriller told through diary excepts and computer printouts or finding inventive ways to bring forth the story of another author's controversial life, James Park Sloan, the author of such works as *War Games* (1971), *The Case History of Comrade V.* (1972), and *Jerzy Kosinski: a Biography* (1996), is constantly experimenting with—and indeed, evolving—the concept of form.

Sloan's flouting of tradition extends far beyond the idea of form. The independent thinking evident in his writing parallels a childhood and adolescence in which he often stood in defiance of conventional and accepted ideas. In an autobiographical statement for *World Authors 1990–1995*, James Park Sloan writes: "I was born in Greenwood, South Carolina, in 1944, the sixth American generation in a family whose members had been small farmers, tradesmen, and craftsmen—people of some virtue but no particular distinction. An important part of the heritage was that each male family member had served honorably and willingly in any American war which took place while he was of appropriate age. My great-great-great grandfather had, in fact, served as a private in the line in the American Revolution, being wounded by a musket ball at the battle of Musgrove Mill when already in his sixties, and my great-grandfather, for whom I am named, had served as an elected Confederate officer, being wounded three times, the last time at Gettysburg, where he was left on the field to survive the war in a Yank prison. My father and his two brothers enlisted on the day after Pearl Harbor and figured honorably as Navy and Army Air Force officers in World War II, my uncle John, a bomber pilot, becoming something of a hero while being shot down twice over Nazi-occupied Europe. The unassuming valor of these forebears and their devotion to duty as they saw it played a role in my volunteering for service in the dubious Vietnam conflict, and their innocent patriotism and devotion to tribal values has assumed increasing weight in my thoughts about the world as I have grown older.

"Growing up in South Carolina was in many respects horrific. The political and religious views which prevailed in Clinton, the town where I grew up, seemed neither lofty nor well thought out. The racism was appalling to me, even as a child. I fought against every effort of the community to inculcate its values in me, a major struggle being my refusal to memorize and recite the Westminster Shorter Catechism, a requirement of all children in the Presbyterian Seceder church to which my family had belonged for a century. I felt that I knew very well that nothing like the God my community believed in could possibly exist, and I saw nothing in the behavior around me to suggest that their belief served any humane purpose or gave meaningful inner strength in their lives. The net result of being an odd duck in a small Southern town was that I had to rethink most assumptions, from zero. It also made me tough. What doesn't kill, as Nietzsche said, makes you strong.

"You are given one life: what are you going to do with it? I try to consider this question every day, and it is the constant underpinning of my work as a writer. I try not to take anything for granted, and particularly not the commonplace pieties. Teachers ministers, rabbis, and your mother will all give you answers, of a sort, but in turning to any of them you have already reframed your question and decided on a narrow and inadequate answer. I always held this view, and even as a teenager I wasn't bashful about expressing it or very patient with people who seemed to think in slow motion. As a result, I was a pretty unpopular kid. While it is painful to be unpopular at age 15, it is a state I commend highly to anyone who wants to grow up to be a writer.

"I graduated first in my high school class, went to Harvard, left in the middle of my junior year to serve in the Army in Vietnam, returned to finish Harvard, and did a year of doctoral work at Harvard Business School. During my senior year at Harvard, I wrote a draft of my Vietnam novel, *War Games*, and when it was accepted I bagged business and became a writer. (I continue to follow the financial markets daily however; it is one of the great neglected sources telling you what folks have on their minds.) On the strength of the reception of *War Games* and *The Case History of Comrade V.* (which probed the plight of an individual at odds with society in a dystopist state), I was hired in 1972 to teach in the creative writing program at the University of Illinois at Chicago, and I have taught there ever since. Two extra-literary things have been important to me over the years: being a very

directive and present father to my two children, Eugene and Anna, now adults; and playing and teaching tennis. Physical fitness and athletics seem to me an important part of a complete life. Raising children may be the most important part of life, far too important to sub-contract out to society. Teaching is a very nearly sacred vocation, but needs, I think, to be approached with lightness and humor.

"I undertook my most recent book, *Jerzy Kosinski: a Biography* because Kosinski's life seemed to provide such an interesting opening into the important question: what should one do with a single life? My current work in progress, a story of the 200 years of ups and downs of my family, asks the same question in a different way. I believe it will remain my central question as long as I have life left to work with."

Sloan's debut novel, *War Games*, for which he received the Lakes Colleges Association New Writer's Award, was published in 1971. Its protagonist, a man who desires to write the quintessential Vietnam War novel, leaves Harvard to enter the military. Rather than going to Vietnam, however, he is sent to Korea. Eventually he receives a transfer to Vietnam, where he volunteers to go on a combat mission. Appalled by the actions of his fellow soldiers in the field, he kills the entire patrol. Completely misconstruing his actions, the military applauds his bravery and decorates him for valor. The protagonist then suffers from a series of illnesses and is eventually sent back to the United States. *War Games* was generally well-received by critics. "In the adventures of the would-be novelist, the reader is confronted with the gut issues not only of the war in Vietnam, but of war and militarism in general, from ancient Greece to the Pentagon," C. R. Andrews wrote in *Library Journal* (November 15, 1970). "The saving grace of wit and understatement keeps *War Games* from becoming a shrill manifesto on how the fertilizer of war can nurture the seeds of brutality, stupid malice, and destructive cunning that blessedly lie dormant in almost all of us. This small, tautly constructed first novel may become the *Catch-22* of the 1970s."

In 1972 Sloan published his second novel, *The Case History of Comrade V.* Described by a *New York Times* (April 13, 1972) reviewer as a "cerebral thriller," the novel revolves around the imprisoned Comrade V., who each day is forced to read a computer printout of his own case history. From the printout, which varies from day to day, the reader slowly learns that Comrade V., a former mathematician, has been jailed for voicing unpopular political views. Interwoven into the story are excerpts from Comrade V.'s diaries, which explain and correct the various inaccuracies in the printout and hint at a conspirator on the outside formulating a plot to help him escape. "We join Comrade V., his analyst, and the system in an agile puzzle which questions the foundations of sanity, the premises of sanity, and even perhaps the advantages of sanity, since it demonstrates, to my mind at least, that there are many advantages to madness," a *Book World* (April 23, 1972) reviewer wrote. "[This book] is intriguing . . . from start to finish." Further praise for *The Case History of Comrade V.* was offered by a *New York Times* (April 13, 1972) reviewer: "The stimulation . . . lies in the way Mr. Sloan keeps collapsing reality around us; and that despite its somewhat hyperintellectual quality and the overtrickiness of the ending, I lay awake after finishing it, trying to figure out who is sane, and who is crazy; what is sanity, what is madness."

Jerzy Kosinski: a Biography, Sloan's nonfiction account of the life of the troubled and enigmatic author of *The Painted Bird*, *Steps*, and *Being There*, was published in 1996. In the book Sloan stated that "few creative figures have left a more problematic oeuvre, and almost any categorical statement about it is subject to challenge." Indeed, prior to his suicide, in 1991, Kosinski came under fire for allegedly using ghostwriters to pen his books, possibly trafficking with the CIA, and lying about the supposedly autobiographical nature of *The Painted Bird*. In response to the third accusation, Sloan wrote, "Throughout his writing career, Kosinski would feel the need to appropriate an episode first as an autobiographical 'fact' before rendering it in the form of fiction." Sloan paraphrased a high-school friend of his subject in describing Kosinski's peculiar method of storytelling: "First, something happened," Sloan wrote. "Second, something happened and Kosinski was involved with it. Third, Kosinski was the chief character in what happened." Sloan presented Kosinski as be-

ing ultimately neither a literary genius nor a complete charlatan. "As a writer, he was clearly not the stylist he was initially credited as being—the surfaces of his books owed much to others—but neither was he the pure fraud that facile and incompletely informed criticism made him out to be," Sloan wrote. "He was, if nothing else, a great storyteller, whose stories at their best seemed to have mythic resonances." *Jerzy Kosinski: a Biography* was applauded by numerous critics. "Sloan's compelling and definitive biography justifies its subject and resolves the paradoxes of a haunted, self-promoting, but powerful storyteller," a reviewer wrote in *Library Journal* (February 1, 1996). "Sloan . . . has done a monumental job of research, including interviewing Kosinski's friends and family, to fill in the doomed psychological itinerary of a man who was schooled by his experiences of the Holocaust to hide and dissemble."

—J. P.

SUGGESTED READING: *Book World* p3 Apr. 23, 1972; *Library Journal* p3926 Nov. 15, 1970, p83 Feb. 1, 1996; *Nation* p28+ Mar. 11, 1996; *New York Times* C p18 Feb. 29, 1996; *New York Times Book Review* p6 June 18, 1972, p16 Apr. 21, 1996; *Contemporary Authors* vol. 29-32, 1978

SELECTED BOOKS: Fiction—*War Games*, 1971; *The Case History of Comrade V.*, 1972; *The Last Cold-War Cowboy*, 1987; Nonfiction—*Jerzy Kosinski: a Biography*, 1996

Smith, Hedrick

July 9, 1933– Journalist; nonfiction writer

The Pulitzer Prize–winning journalist Hedrick Smith, a *New York Times* correspondent from 1962 to 1988, is the author of two international best sellers whose graphic descriptions of daily life in the former Soviet Union have enhanced the general reader's understanding of Soviet society. After spending three years in Moscow as the *New York Times* bureau chief during the stagnant Leonid I. Brezhnev era, Smith wrote *The Russians* (1976), which introduced Westerners to the multifaceted richness of Soviet life, which had previously been obscured by official dogma and headline news. When Smith left Moscow in 1974, he was convinced that "fundamental change was impossible" and that economic privatization and political democratization were destined to remain beyond the pale for Soviet citizens. Returning to Moscow 14 years later, he was astonished by the "seismic transformation" that had begun under Mikhail Gorbachev and that would "carry on regardless of his individual fate," according to Smith's accurate

prediction in *The New Russians* (1990), an anecdotal survey of Gorbachev's twin policies of *perestroika* (restructuring) and *glasnost* (openness).

In his introduction to *The New Russians*, Smith characterized the Soviet transformation-in-progress as "a modern enactment of one of the archetypal stories of human existence, that of the struggle from darkness to light, from poverty toward prosperity, from dictatorship toward democracy. It represents an affirmation of the relentless human struggle to break free from the bonds of hierarchy and dogma, to strive for a better life, for stronger, richer values. It is an affirmation of the human capacity for change, growth, and renewal."

Smith has also brought his powers of illumination to bear on the United States capital, where he was the *New York Times* bureau chief from 1976 to 1979 and its chief Washington correspondent from 1979 to 1985. His best-selling book *The Power Game: How Washington Works* (1988), a dissection of the political process that focuses on Congress and the executive branch, with special emphasis on the presidency of Ronald Reagan, became the subject of a critically acclaimed documentary for public television in 1989. In addition to producing three wide-ranging, meticulously researched books that total more than 1,800 pages of text, Smith has contributed to four other books, served as the host of many public-television documentaries, and appeared as a regular panelist on the PBS current-affairs television show *Washington Week in Review*. His most recent book, published in 1995, is *Rethinking America*, which concerns the national economic picture.

Hedrick Laurence Smith was born on July 9, 1933, in Kilmacolm, Scotland, to American parents: Sterling L. Smith, a management consultant, and Phebe (Hedrick) Smith, an artist. Known to his friends as "Rick," Hedrick Smith spent his early childhood, before the outbreak of World War II, shuttling between Great Britain, Germany, and Spain. The family eventually settled in Greenville, South Carolina, where Sterling L. Smith became controller of the textile concern Deering-Milliken (now Milliken and Company). Following his graduation from the Choate School in Wallingford, Connecticut, Hedrick Smith enrolled at Williams College in Williamstown, Massachusetts, where he studied American history, literature, art, music, architecture, and philosophy and was voted most likely to succeed by his classmates. After graduating summa cum laude with election to Phi Beta Kappa in 1955, he attended Balliol College of Oxford University on a Fulbright scholarship during the 1955–56 academic year, and then spent three years in the United States Air Force as an intelligence officer.

Smith began his journalistic career, in 1959, with United Press International, covering the civil rights movement in Tennessee and Georgia and the space program in Cape Canaveral, Florida. Hired by the *New York Times* in 1962 on the recommendation of David Halberstam, whom Smith had met when Halberstam was on the staff of the Nashville *Tennesseean*, Smith spent his first year reporting from the South and from Washington, D.C. From 1963 to 1964 he covered the war in Vietnam. He then spent two years in Cairo, Egypt, before returning to Washington for a two-year stint as diplomatic correspondent, including service as a special correspondent at the Paris peace talks in 1968. He took the 1969–70 academic year off to study Russian at Harvard University on a Nieman fellowship in preparation for a three-year stint as the *New York Times* bureau chief in Moscow, which would begin in 1971. In the meantime he returned to Washington as a diplomatic correspondent, from 1970 to 1971.

While in Washington Smith incurred the wrath of the Richard Nixon administration on two occasions. After the *New York Times* published an article under Smith's byline in May 1969 that described the administration's negotiation strategy concerning the return of Okinawa to Japanese control, the administration tapped Smith's home telephone, from June 1969 through August 1969. In 1973 disclosure of the tap came to light, and in 1976 Smith sued Nixon and four prominent officials in his administration. In 1987 a federal district judge ordered the logs of 138 conversations that were monitored during the wiretap to be expunged from government files and returned to Smith.

Although the second incident took considerably less time to resolve, it carried much greater significance for the nation. As a diplomatic correspondent, Smith had written a number of stories about the Vietnam War with his *New York Times* counterpart at the Pentagon, Neil Sheehan, which lead to his inclusion among the eight or nine reporters and editors who were summoned to the New York Hilton for seven weeks in the spring of 1971 to help Sheehan analyze and interpret the politically explosive Pentagon Papers. The 47 top-secret volumes of the Pentagon Papers had been acquired from Daniel Ellsberg, who had compiled them for Secretary of Defense Robert S. McNamara. A history of American involvement in South Vietnam from 1945 to 1967, they were published in installments, beginning on June 13, 1971, in the *New York Times*. After the third installment appeared, the Nixon administration secured a court order, on grounds of national security, that restrained the *New York Times* from publishing the politically damaging material. The newspaper took the case to the United States Supreme Court, which ruled on June 30, 1971 that prior restraint on publishing the Pentagon documents was unjustified and unconstitutional. In 1972 the *New York Times* won a Pulitzer Prize in the public-service category for its perseverance in publishing the Pentagon Papers, which had appeared as a book with that title in 1971.

In August 1971 Hedrick Smith went to Moscow as the *New York Times* bureau chief with the intention of reporting "something that had real flesh and blood to it," as he told Peter Young during an interview for the *Book-of-the-Month Club News* (February 1976). "What struck me as fresh and new to convey to readers," he wrote in his foreword to *The Russians*, "was the human quotient, the texture and fabric of the personal lives of the Russians as people." Reserving his analyses of politics and other newsworthy topics for his work as a *New York Times* correspondent—which won him a Pulitzer Prize for international reporting in 1974—Smith conducted his research by seeking out interviews with ordinary Russians, ranging "as widely as time and the Soviet authorities would permit." At first his contact was limited to "official Russians," such as tourist guides, translators, and others whose jobs entailed dealing with foreigners, but after two years he sensed a breakthrough, as he told Peter Young: "I began to acquire what seemed to me to be friendships that would be friendships anywhere in the world. And that's the point when you say to yourself 'Aha!', for now you are beginning to talk man-to-man and they're asking things of you that are not the standard 'How much does a pair of shoes cost in America' kind of question. They want to know about the fabric of life in America, and you're asking the same thing of them. You begin to see it the way they see it."

The success of *The Russians* undoubtedly owed something to Smith's open-mindedness, not to mention his habit of working 16-hour days and taking notes assiduously after (and sometimes during) each interview. "Knowing what the established clichés and images of Russia were," he told Peter Young, "I was ready to set them aside when life suggested that they didn't fit." He enumerated several of the exploded myths in his introduction to *The Russians*. The "myth of the classless society," for instance, was shunted aside by his newly acquired knowledge of "millionaire" Communists. His initial efforts to compare prices of consumer items in the Soviet Union with their values in the West were complicated by the realization that *blat* ("the influence or connections to gain the access you need") was a better way to measure the Soviet standard of living. And, most surprising of all to Smith, "the propaganda vision of shockworkers tirelessly building socialism was quickly dispelled . . . by the undisguised goldbricking" of workers in a country where pink slips were illegal.

Fascinated by "the irrepressible unruliness of human beings in a system of rules," Smith disseminated his recently gleaned information "vividly and with a greater feel for the texture of everyday life" than other observers, according to Paul D. Zimmerman's review for *Newsweek* (January 19, 1976). Concurring in an article for the *Saturday Review* (February 7, 1976), Adam B. Ulam wrote, "It has hardly been a secret that the allegedly classless society has in fact a very elaborate system of social stratification. In [this book] Smith brings more evidence on this count and presents the facts more vividly than I have seen done anywhere else. He has an unerring reporter's eye and ear for small but significant nuances of social and political behavior." Some reviewers, such as Gennady Shmakov and John Malmstad in the *New York Review of Books* (April 1, 1976), were of the opinion that Smith's nonacademic tone rendered his analysis somewhat diffuse: "The personal and anecdotal method provides much information, but the frightening implications of the experiences . . . often remain obscure." And George Feifer, though he noted in *Harper's* (March 1976) that Smith "ranges wide but not deep enough," nevertheless conceded that the reporter's "major achievement" was "to have de-enigmatized Russia, vividly, sensibly, and comprehensively." In 1976 Hedrick Smith was given an Overseas Press Club Award for *The Russians*.

After serving briefly as deputy national editor of the *New York Times* in New York City from 1975 to 1976, Smith spent three years in the nation's capital as Washington bureau chief, administering a Washington staff larger than that of any other newspaper in the United States. In 1980 he relinquished his administrative chores to become the *Times*'s chief Washington correspondent, a post he held until 1985. He took a leave of absence from the newspaper in 1985 to write *The Power Game: How*

Washington Works, which he began while he was a visiting journalist at the American Enterprise Institute from 1985 to 1986. Smith returned to the staff of the *New York Times Magazine* in 1987 as its Washington correspondent until 1988, when he ended his 26-year career with the newspaper.

In *The Power Game* Smith explored such diverse issues as the role of television in political campaigns, the power of lobbyists and the congressional staff, and "the politics of confrontation [as practiced by Senator Jesse A. Helms]: stalling, filibustering with marathon speeches, tying the Senate up in knots, frustrating others to achieve his own ends." He chose to investigate the political scene of Washington in terms of a power game in order to follow "the action amidst the babel," as he wrote in his introduction. "The game metaphor helps to explain the patterns and precepts that skilled politicians live by," Smith wrote, "regardless of party or administration, as well as the consequences in all of this game playing, for all of us. Actually the Washington power game is not one game, but an olympiad of games, going on simultaneously, all over town. My aim is to take that olympiad apart, play by play, game by game, player by player, so that the overall game of governing is revealed."

Whether or not Smith succeeded with *The Power Game* was a matter of contention among reviewers. Larry K. Smith, for example, writing in the *Atlantic* (March 1988), acknowledged that "Smith can be a first-rate reporter" but commented that his "accounts of the events of the Reagan years lack the full flavor his reporting could give them, because he uses them mostly as illustrations of general propositions about Washington behavior." In contrast, Guy Halverson wrote for the *Christian Science Monitor* (March 4, 1988) that "there can be no faulting Smith's prodigious analytical and investigative skills." Alan Brinkley, who in the *New York Times Book Review* (March 27, 1988) admired Smith's powers of illustration, nonetheless criticized his ability "to lay out a set of general rules of the game by which power is gained and lost. . . . Too often, the rules he proposes are merely truisms. . . . At other times, what he presents as rules are simply descriptions of what worked at a particular moment. Mr. Smith is a much better reporter than he is a political scientist. In trying to be both, he brings an unnecessary didacticism (and at times an annoying redundancy) to much of this otherwise lively book."

In 1989 *The Power Game* was condensed into a four-part series for public television, the fourth such program presided over by Smith in as many years. Harry F. Waters, in describing the televised version of *The Power Game* for *Newsweek* (January 2, 1989), wrote that it "offers everything we always wanted to know about high-level Washington but were afraid to ask, lest someone actually tell us." Smith's first public-television documentary, *Shielding America: Can "Star Wars" Make Us Safe?* (1985), was judged "a first-rate piece of work" by John Corry in the *New York Times* (November 12, 1985). His other television credits include *Jews of Moscow: An Inside Story Special Edition* (1986); *Chernobyl and Three Mile Island: A Spacebridge* (1987); *Transition '88* (1989); *Inside Gorbachev's USSR with Hedrick Smith* (1990), which earned him a Gold Baton, the highest Alfred I. Dupont–Columbia University award for broadcast journalism, and a George Polk Award, an honor also bestowed on *Soviets* (1991); "Guns, Tanks, and Gorbachev"(1991), a segment of the PBS series *Frontline*; the four-part PBS series *Challenge to America* (1994), a documentary that sought the reasons why German and Japanese companies have surpassed American firms; *Across the River* (1995), about Washington, D.C.'s attempts to take back its neighborhoods from drugs and crime; and, most recently, *The People and the Power Game* (1996). That PBS program, for which Smith won a Hillman Award, investigated the impact of print and broadcast journalism and of lobbyists on the American political scene.

While he was making *Inside Gorbachev's USSR*—whose four installments encompassed the conflict between reformers and old-line officials, *glasnost* in the media and education, bureaucratic obstruction of economic reform, and ethnic tensions in five Soviet republics—Smith gathered material for his book *The New Russians* (1990), which remained on the *New York Times* nonfiction bestseller list for 11 weeks. Between 1988 and 1990 he visited 25 major cities and nine republics, traveling more than 40,000 miles and interviewing everyone from agricultural workers and factory managers to local politicians, high school students, and high-ranking members of the Politburo. The result was a panoramic view of a nation in the throes of what he called "the most extraordinary peaceful revolution of the 20th century."

Ever fascinated by "the human story," Hedrick Smith set out in *The New Russians* to convey "the story of personal transformations: how people cope with reform, some promoting it, others resisting it or mouthing its slogans but secretly sabotaging it, still others floating in uncertainty, voicing hope for change but unwilling to take risks to make it happen." The story unfolds as the book progresses through its five sections from the roots of reform—its earliest manifestations as well as its first serious obstacles—to "the empire tearing apart" and "the taste of democracy." In his conclusion, Smith cautiously noted that "the old order has been dismantled, even if the new order has not yet taken shape."

Most reviewers of *The New Russians* praised Hedrick Smith's thoroughness but questioned his political judgment. Xan Smiley, in what would later prove to be a prescient article for the *New York Review of Books* (March 14, 1991), noted that Smith seemed "too sanguine about Gorbachev's chances of survival" and had underestimated the forces of non-Russian nationalism. The historian S. Frederick Starr, in assessing *The New Russians* for

the *New York Times Book Review* (December 9, 1990), commented: "Mr. Smith exaggerates the danger from the right wing of the party and minimizes the dynamism of the radical and independent left. Hence he fails to come to grips with Boris Yeltsin, the politician who understands better than anyone else the potential might of the democratic forces arising from below." Starr commended Smith, however, for being "as much a realist as an enthusiast; he never lets either side of his outlook dominate. With rare respect for his readers' intelligence, he sets forth his own contradictory views but at the same time provides masses of evidence from which the reader can draw his own conclusions. . . . This is, in short, a lively, rich, and provocative book."

In some critics' views, such as Sally Laird's, as expressed in the London *Observer* (November 25, 1990), Smith's thorough reporting and exhaustive research only made his limited conclusions seem all the more narrow. Citing his assertion that "the Russian character is made up of both coldness and warmth," she wrote of such conclusions, "It is not just their stunning banality that offends me. Scratch a page of 'objective reporting,' and what you tend to find is the pure American psyche, entirely unexamined and, as far as one can see, entirely untouched by the experience of Russia." But for most Americans, *The New Russians* was generally considered "an invaluable tool for those struggling to understand the Soviet Union," as Rose Bardy wrote for *Business Week* (January 21, 1991).

In the book *Across the River* (1995), Smith explored Washington, D.C.'s quest to take back its neighborhoods from drugs and crime. In another 1995 volume, *Rethinking America*, Smith brought his sharp insights to the economic home front, concerning himself with topics along the lines of his *Challenge to America* documentary of the previous year. In this book, Smith wrestled with the country's lagging economic competitiveness and made many comparisons between U.S. industries and those of Japan and Germany. The veteran journalist argued that American companies such as General Motors have inclined toward short-sightedness in their views, seeking to increase profits in the short-term by downsizing, instead of exercising the creative teamwork necessary to do better for the long haul in the new global market. Smith advocated reform, not only in the industries but in education and in the way Washington deals with trade barriers overseas. David P. Calleo, writing in the *New York Times Book Review* (June 4, 1995), had one complaint about the book: "Mr. Smith ignores the macroeconomic dimension of competitiveness, in particular the role of fiscal and monetary policies and their consequences for the dollar exchange rate." Still, Calleo noted that Smith's work "reads easily, with chapters like bushels of sound bites, and is well illustrated with numerous stories about American and foreign corporations."

Hedrick Smith contributed to *Fodor's Soviet Union, 1974–1975* and *Counterattack: The U.S. Response to Japan* (1983). He collaborated with Adam Clymer, Richard Burt, Leonard Silk, and Robert Lindsey on *Reagan: The Man, the Myth, the President* (1980) and with Paul Duke, Haynes Johnson, Jack Nelson, Charles Corddry, Charles McDowell, and Georgie Ann Geyer on *Beyond Reagan: The Politics of Upheaval* (1986). In 1975 his alma mater, Williams College, bestowed an honorary doctorate on him. His television company, Hedrick Smith Productions, Inc., was formed in 1990.
—C.M.

SUGGESTED READING: *Atlantic* Mar. 1988; *Book- of-the-Month Club News* Feb. 1976; *Business Week* Jan. 21, 1991; *Christian Science Monitor* Mar. 4, 1988; *Harper's* Mar. 1976; *Newsweek* Jan. 19, 1976, Jan. 2, 1989; *New York Review of Books* Apr. 1, 1976, Mar. 14, 1991; *New York Times* Nov. 12, 1985, C p14 Sep. 3, 1986, Mar. 27, 1988, B p18 Jan.3, 1994, D p20 Nov. 24,1995 *New York Times Book Review* Mar. 27, 1988, Dec. 9, 1990, p7 June 4, 1995; *Observer* Nov. 25, 1990; *Saturday Review* Feb. 7, 1976; *Contemporary Authors* new revision series vol. 41, 1994; *Who's Who in America*, 1997

SELECTED WORKS: Nonfiction—*The Pentagon Papers* (with F. Butterfield et al) , 1971; *The Russians*, 1976; *Reagan: the Man, the Myth, the President* (with L. Silk et al), 1981; *Beyond Reagan: The Politics of Upheaval* (with Paul Duke et al), 1986; *The Power Game: How Washington Works*, 1988; *The New Russians*, 1990; *Rethinking America*, 1995, *Across the River*, 1995; Documentaries—*Shielding America: Can "Star Wars" Make Us Safe?*, 1985; *Jews of Moscow: An Inside Story Special Edition*, 1986; *Chernobyl and Three Mile Island: A Spacebridge*, 1987; *Transition '88*, 1989; *The Power Game*, 1989; *Inside Gorbachev's USSR with Hedrick Smith*, 1990; oviets, 1991; *Challenge to America*, 1994; *Across the River*, 1995; *The People and the Power Game*, 1996

Courtesy of Pantheon Books

Spiegelman, Art

Feb. 15, 1948– Cartoonist; writer

Art Spiegelman, a seminal figure in the world of underground comics, was known primarily to aficionados of that fringe genre and to his fellow cartoonists until 1986, when he saw his fame grow exponentially with the publication of *Maus: A Survivor's Tale I: My Father Bleeds History*. An autobio-graphical work, *Maus* explores Spiegelman's difficult relationship with his father, who, over the course of the book, describes to his son his experiences as a Jew in Nazi-occupied Poland. Written in the form of a comic strip, *Maus* shows the nationality or ethnicity of each character by portraying the character as a certain animal; for example, Jews are represented as mice, Germans as cats, and Poles as pigs. Initially rejected by many book companies as unpublishable, *Maus* went on to become both a critical and a commercial success, selling more than 150,000 copies in its first edition. It was eventually translated into 16 languages, and its bemused author found himself being compared in the international press to such literary giants as Franz Kafka. In 1991 Spiegelman continued the story in *Maus: A Survivor's Tale II: And Here My Troubles Began*, which depicts the horrors of life in the concentration camps and is thought by some to be superior to its predecessor. Together, the two books earned Spiegelman a special Pulitzer Prize in 1992.

Art Spiegelman was born on February 15, 1948 in Stockholm to Vladek and Anja (Zylberberg) Spiegelman. Three years later the family immigrated to the United States, settling in the Rego Park section of the New York City borough of Queens. Vladek Spiegelman, who had been a wealthy textile salesman and manufacturer in Poland before World War II, worked in the garment trade and later in the diamond business. Spiegelman's parents had survived confinement to the Jewish ghettos and imprisonment in the infamous Nazi concentration camp in Auschwitz, Poland, and both bore the emotional scars of that experience. Anja Spiegelman suffered from periodic depression, and her husband, perhaps acting on instincts that had once been necessary for survival, was obsessively frugal. The traumas they had suffered were manifested in other ways as well: "It's only when I left home," Spiegelman revealed to David H. Van Biema of *People* (October 27, 1986), "that I got some sense that not everybody had parents who woke up screaming in the night." Art was his parents' second child; on the wall in their bedroom was a photograph of their firstborn son, Richieu, who had been poisoned by an aunt who also killed two of his cousins and herself just before the Nazis came to take them away.

As a boy, Spiegelman found an escape from the oppressive atmosphere at home in the world of comics. In an interview with Claudia Dreifus for the *Progressive* (November 1989), he described the genesis of his interest in drawing: "What probably started it all off was spending time with a doodling game my mother developed. She had very rudimentary drawing skills, and she would play this game when there wasn't anything else to do. She would make a scribble and ask me to turn it into something. That usually led to cartoon drawings....That made me realize I could do something with a pencil and paper." He added that he had thought of published comics as "a fact of the world," until he realized that they were drawn by people. "At that point, I stopped wanting to be a fireman, a policeman, or a cowboy—and opted for cartoonist." One day when he was about 10, Art, having already spent his allowance, asked his mother to buy him a book on cartoon-drawing. Deciding to indulge her son but mindful of her husband's frugality, Anja Spiegelman made a deal with the boy: if he could prove that he had benefited from the book, its cost would not be deducted from a future allowance. As it turned out, Anja paid for the book.

Spiegelman soon began filling notebooks with his drawings, copying the styles of his favorite artists, such as those who drew for the satirical magazine *Mad*, which he has called "a terrific influence." In the early 1960s he produced his own magazine, *Blasé*, an imitation of *Mad*, and he drew cartoons for the school newspaper at Russell Sage Junior High, where he was an honors student. By the age of 14, he was selling cartoons and illustrations to the *Long Island Post*. Intent on becoming a professional cartoonist despite the objections of his parents, Spiegelman set his sights on attending the High School of Art and Design, which offered commercial art courses. "They wanted me to become a dentist," Spiegelman told Lawrence Weschler for *Rolling Stone* (November 20, 1986). "For them, dentist was halfway to doctor, I guess....They'd point out how if I became a dentist, I could always do the drawing on the side, whereas if I became a cartoonist, I couldn't very well pull people's teeth during my off hours. Their logic was impeccable, just irrelevant. I was hooked."

While Spiegelman was still in high school, a representative from United Features Syndicate, impressed by several of the teenager's cartoon characters, such as the Ink Blot and the Termite, offered to help the young cartoonist develop his work into a syndicated comic strip. Realizing that he would be bored by the daily grind of turning out conventional cartoon panels, Spiegelman declined. He found a subsequent job offer, from the Topps chewing gum company, more appealing, and in 1966 he began to design Bazooka comics and baseball cards and to contribute his own ideas for other novelty items produced by the company. His relationship with Topps turned out to be a long and happy one. Until the late 1980s he designed various Topps items, including "Wacky Packages" (stickers, such as the one for "Rice-a-Phony," that spoofed widely advertised products) and "Garbage Pail Kids" (bubble-gum card takeoffs on the popular Cabbage Patch Kids dolls, with names like Acne Annie and Wrinkled Rita).

Meanwhile, in 1965 or 1966 (sources differ as to the exact year), Spiegelman enrolled at Harpur College (now the State University of New York) in Binghamton, where he studied art and philosophy. It was during that time that he began to develop a reputation as an "underground" cartoonist—one whose work appears in limited-circulation journals and does not conform to traditional standards of humor, narrative coherence, or, in the opinion of some, good taste. In addition to drawing for the college newspaper, he published comics in such magazines as the *East Village Other*, an outlet for cartoonists whose work defied the conventions of nationally syndicated comic strips.

As his career began to take flight, however, his emotional state became more and more precarious. Perhaps overwhelmed by the comparative freedom of college life, he took that freedom to extremes. As he recalled to Lawrence Weschler, "I was just kind of holding court, people were coming out to visit, and I found that if I just said whatever came into my mind, the atmosphere would get incredibly charged—and if I kept it up, within half an hour, either my guests would run out, screaming, or else we'd approach this druglike high....And this was going on for days on end. I wasn't eating...I was beginning to suffer from acute sleep deprivation. I was starting to experience these rampant delusions of grandeur. I was sure I was onto something, and sure enough, I was—a psychotic breakdown."

In 1968, on the advice of a college administrator, the 20-year-old Spiegelman entered a mental hospital in upstate New York. During the time that he spent there, he collected what he has since referred to as "a little pile of trash." Years later he realized that he had been imitating the behavior of his father, who, since his days in the concentration camp, had obsessively saved all manner of useless scraps, thinking he might need them later. "If you read psychological portraits of survivors' children, it is not uncommon that they try to re-create their parents' experience in the camps," Spiegelman explained to David Van Biema. After a month in the hospital, he was released into the care of his parents. Not long after his return home, his mother, who had been increasingly depressed after the death of her only remaining brother, committed suicide.

Spiegelman's way of coping with his mother's death seems to have been to immerse himself in his work. Moving to San Francisco, he became part of the burgeoning underground comics movement that included, among other cartoonists, the legendary R. Crumb. In the years that followed, he contributed cartoons to such periodicals as *Real Pulp* (under the pseudonym Skeeter Grant) and *Bizarre Sex* (as Joe Cutrate) and edited a free magazine for Douglas Communications. He also produced several books of comics, including *The Complete Mr. Infinity* (1970), *The Viper Vicar of Vice, Villainy, and Vickedness* (1972), *Zip-a-Tune and More Melodies* (1972), *Ace Hole, Midget Detective* (1974), *Every Day Has Its Dog* (1979), *Word and Turn* (1979), and *Two-Fisted Painters Action Adventure* (1980). He supplemented his income from those books with assignments for illustrations and book covers and with his work for Topps.

In 1972 Spiegelman was invited to contribute a cartoon to *Funny Aminals*, which he has described as an "anthology of warped, revisionist animal comics." Having learned in film class in college that in early animated cartoons rodent characters often represented black people, he thought of using mice to tell a story of blacks in America. As he told Lawrence Weschler, the idea lasted "for about 45 minutes. Because what did I know about the black experience in America? And then suddenly the idea of Jews as mice just hit me full force, full-blown. Almost as soon as it hit me, I began to recognize the obvious historical antecedents—how Nazis had spoken of Jews as 'vermin,' for example, and plotted their 'extermination.'" Inspired, he produced for the anthology a three-page cartoon in which a father, who is a mouse, tells his son a bedtime story about the Holocaust that ends with mice being taken to a concentration camp called "Mauschwitz."

On the heels of that strip came one about his mother's suicide. As Spiegelman recalled to Lawrence Weschler, he had until that time buried his feelings about her death: "And then one day, four years later, it all suddenly came flooding back, all the memories resurging. I threw myself into seclusion for a month, and in the end I emerged with 'Prisoner on the Hell Planet.'" Published in *Short Order Comix* in 1972, the four-page strip was narrated in the first person by a character in striped prison garb who relates the details of his mother's suicide as well as his own feelings of guilt, anger, and grief. The strip ends with the narrator, locked in a vast cell block, screaming, "You murdered me, Mommy, and you left me here to take the rap!!!" ("Hell Planet" later appeared in its entirety in the first volume of *Maus*.)

It was in 1978, when Spiegelman was 30 years old and ready for, in his words, "something serious," that he decided to employ elements from the "Hell Planet" and "Mauschwitz" cartoons—the cartoonist as a character within an autobiographical strip and mice as protagonists—in a longer work. In researching the project, Spiegelman, who had by then moved back to New York City, talked at length with his father about his Holocaust experiences. "Part of the motivation for taking [the project] on was that I was looking for some way to be with him. I was looking for a relationship," the cartoonist explained to Esther B. Fein for the *New York Times* (December 10, 1991). "We were always bickering, but I realized we got along during our...hours of interview. He didn't quite get what I was about, what I was doing. But he cooperated. Our relationship consisted of interviewer-interviewee." By the time Spiegelman had finished, he had taped more than 30 hours of material. He also made two trips to Poland, in 1978 and 1986, to do further research.

The first installments of "Maus" appeared in December 1980, in the second issue of *Raw*, a semiannual magazine that Spiegelman and his wife, Françoise Mouly, a French editor and graphic designer, had founded as a showcase for the work of an international group of cartoonists dedicated to exploring the possibilities of their medium. By the mid-1980s Spiegelman had drawn enough material to fill a book, but his proposal was turned down by one publisher after another. "Many of the rejections were quite loving," Spiegelman told Esther Fein, "but the bottom line was they all said, 'How on Earth! It's just not publishable.'" Spiegelman's plans to publish a book version of the "Maus" strips were further complicated when he heard that the filmmaker Steven Spielberg was preparing to produce an animated movie, titled *An American Tail*, about the persecution of a family of Jewish mice in Russia during the 19th century. As it turned out, the release of *An American Tail* was postponed, and in the interim Pantheon, whose editors had been sufficiently impressed by Spiegelman's book to take the risk of publishing it, shipped the first copies of *Maus: A Survivor's Tale* (1986) to bookstores.

The frame narrator in *Maus* is a cartoonist-mouse named Art Spiegelman, but much of the story is told in what one writer called "a curiously endearing...immigrant's English" by the cartoonist's father, Vladek, who, in flashbacks, relates the details of his life in Poland before and during World War II. The book is both a heart-wrenching tale of the victims of Nazism and a testament to the efforts of Art Spiegelman—as character and author—to establish a relationship with his complex, difficult father. The flashbacks end with Vladek and Anja Spiegelman being taken by the Nazis to Auschwitz; the book itself closes with Art's outrage over the discovery that his father, in a fit of grief years ago, destroyed the diaries that Anja had kept during the Holocaust and had wanted her son to read someday.

Maus was published to almost universal critical acclaim. In a representative assessment, Robert Grossman wrote in the *Nation* (January 10, 1987), "In addition to being whatever else it is—history or bedtime story, autobiography or allegory—*Maus* also happens to be a beautiful book. Its layout and style welcome the eye, and soon one is marveling at the amount of fear, hope, love, and pathos that can emerge from a sketch of a mouse's head scarcely a half-inch high." Many of the critics singled out for special praise Spiegelman's portrait of his father, who had died four years before the book's publication. Spiegelman has said that in creating *Maus* he was spurred partly by his pent-up anger at his father and his desire to take revenge by exposing the older man's negative qualities. Most readers, however, including the author himself, have generally found the portrayal of Vladek Spiegelman to be oddly sympathetic.

Some critics argued that by portraying Holocaust victims as mice instead of humans, Spiegelman gave his readers the emotional distance necessary to handle the story's disturbing content. Lawrence Weschler had a different view: "There have been hundreds of Holocaust memoirs—horribly, we've become inured to the horror. People being gassed in showers and shoveled into ovens—it's a story we've already heard. But mice? The Mickey Mice of our childhood reveries? Having the story thus retold, with animals as the principals, freshly recaptures its terrible immediacy, its palpable urgency." While they disagreed about the book's perspective, reviewers were virtually unanimous in applauding Spiegelman for having created an unusually moving work of startling originality.

A surprise bestseller (the book defied classification, appearing on both fiction and nonfiction lists), *Maus* transformed Spiegelman from an obscure underground cartoonist into a sought-after intellectual-at-large. In great demand as a speaker on college campuses and before various Jewish groups, he was even the subject of a documentary for European television. But despite his newfound status as a media celebrity, Spiegelman remained true to his avant-garde roots. In 1987 he and Françoise Mouly published *Read Yourself Raw*, a compilation of comics from the magazine. Since the appearance of its first issue, which had had a printing of five thousand copies, *Raw* had grown in popularity and was selling out printings of 20 thousand copies annually. In the years following the publication of *Maus: A Survivor's Tale*, Spiegelman continued to publish "Maus" comic strips in *Raw*.

The second volume of *Maus* appeared in 1991. *Maus: A Survivor's Tale II: And Here My Troubles Began* picked up where the first volume left off—at the gates of Auschwitz—and chronicled Vladek Spiegelman's experiences in the concentration camp as well as Art Spiegelman's introspection over whether the Holocaust could, or should, be depicted in a comic-book format. *Maus II* came in for as much praise as its predecessor. Discussing both books in the *New Yorker* (April 6, 1992),

Ethan Mordden observed, "In *Maus*, certainly, Spiegelman seems to have produced the first masterpiece in comic-book history," and Michiko Kakutani of the *New York Times* (October 29, 1991) declared that Spiegelman had "created one of the most powerful and original memoirs to come along in recent years." Like the first volume, *Maus II* was nominated for a National Book Critics Circle Award.

Spiegelman's most recent endeavor is a children's book, *Open Me . . . I'm a Dog!* (1997). An interesting take on story-telling, the book argues that it is not actually a book, but a dog magically transformed into a book by a wizard. It also seeks to prove itself a dog, offering all sorts of evidence, everything from an actual collar and leash to fuzzy orange endpaper. *Kirkus Reviews* (June 1, 1997) noted: "It's a winning conceit, with ingenuous tongue-in-cheek illustrations, though . . . some will wind that much of the humor is pitches over the heads of its target audience." Anita Gates wrote in the *New York Times Book Review* (December 21, 1997): "It's nice to see Spiegelman, the author of *Maus*, in this playful yet very direct mood."

Art Spiegelman has a slight build and dark, receding hair. Avis Berman, writing in *ART News* (May 1993), called him "an intense, dark-eyed man who is never far from a cigarette." When he interviewed the cartoonist for *People*, David Van Biema noted that Spiegelman's "penchant for black vests over plain white shirts [made] him look a bit like a 19th-century clerk" and that his smile was "one of those quick, flashing things typical of the very bright yet shy." Spiegelman and Françoise Mouly, who have been married since July 12, 1977, have a daughter, Nadja, and a son, Dashiell. Spiegelman has won, in addition to the Pulitzer Prize, a *Playboy* editorial award, a Yellow Kid Award for best comic strip author, and a Guggenheim Fellowship. His work has been showcased in two New York art exhibitions, at the Museum of Modern Art in 1991 and the Galerie St. Etienne in 1992. The shows featured the original sketches, storyboards, and photographs that had gone into the making of the *Maus* books. In 1979 Spiegelman began teaching classes in the history and aesthetics of comics at the School of Visual Arts in New York City, and in 1992 he accepted a post as artist and contributing editor at the *New Yorker*.

Spiegelman has expressed some bewilderment over people's surprise that a comic strip could deal adequately with the horrors of the Holocaust—or, for that matter, with any serious subject. "There's a presumption that if there is something good in the [comic-book] form that it is an exception," he explained to Esther Fein for the *New York Times* profile. "There is a real prejudice there....In reality, comics are far more flexible than theatre, deeper than cinema. It's more efficient and intimate. In fact, it has many properties of what has come to be a respectable medium, but wasn't always: the novel."

—C.T./C.M.

SUGGESTED READING: *Economist* p86 Nov. 30, 1991; *Entertainment Weekly* p98 Nov. 18, 1994; *Fish Rap Live* (on-line), 1992; *Kirkus Reviews* p880 June 1, 1997; *Library Journal* p160 Dec. 1991; *Nation* Jan. 10, 1987; *New York Times Book Review* p71 Dec. 7, 1986, p17 Nov. 3, 1991, p18 Dec. 21, 1997; *Newsday* A p4 Apr. 8, 1992; *Newsweek* p79 Sep. 22, 1986; *Publishers Weekly* p26+ Jan. 31, 1994; *Contemporary Authors* New Revision Series, Vol. 55, 1997; *Who's Who in America, 1998*

SELECTED WORKS: *The Complete Mr. Infinity*, 1970; *The Viper Vicar of Vice, Villainy, and Vickedness*, 1972; *Ace Hole, Midget Detective*, 1974; *The Language of Comics*, 1974; *Breakdowns: From Maus to Now: An Anthology of Strips*, 1977; *Work and Turn*, 1979; *Every Day Has Its Dog*, 1979; *Two-Fisted Painters Action Adventure*, 1980; *Maus: A Survivor's Tale*, 1986; *Maus II: A Survivor's Tale*, 1991; *The Wild Party*, 1994; *Open Me . . . I'm a Dog!*, 1997

Rob Kneller Photography

Spong, John Shelby

June 16, 1931– Nonfiction writer; clergyman

"I would rather die in a confrontation than die running away from it," Bishop John Shelby Spong once told the Episcopalian magazine *The Voice* (September 1997). "When I become convinced of something, I have to hit it head on; I cannot be diplomatic." Confrontation and controversy have been the two words most often associated with the noted author and social commentator, in a career

that has often defied all conventional notions of religious leaders. An outspoken man of determination and resolve, Spong has spent the better part of the past 40 years advocating, through his actions and many books and writings, ways to improve the Christian Church. In the early part of his career, he challenged religious fundamentalism and boldly stood by the belief that blacks should be treated equally, two convictions that were not only unpopular in the South, where he worked, but were often dangerous to those who held them. When he moved to the North and was ordained a bishop in Newark, New Jersey, he continued to push into the dialogue of the church the issues he most cared about—the ordination of women and openly gay men as priests, the end of literal Biblical interpretation, and a call for church reformation. His liberal views on sexual matters in particular have proved to be a sore point with many of his conservative critics, yet the bishop remains one of the most recognized and popular religious leaders in America.

In an autobiographical statement submitted to *World Authors 1990–1995*, Bishop John Shelby Spong writes: "I grew up as a conservative fundamentalist Christian in Charlotte, North Carolina. We lived about a half mile from the Graham Brother's dairy farm where a young man known as Billy Graham was emerging as an itinerant preacher. He reflects much of the Protestant evangelical religious mentality of my childhood. The Bible was God's word, ethical issues were solved with biblical quotations, only Christians could be saved, the term Christian might not even include Roman Catholics. We entertained no doubt but that our view of God was correct.

"I was educated in the public schools of Charlotte but by the time I got to high school my level of knowledge had increased to the place where I knew that the Bible was wrong on the time of creation, wrong on the centrality of the earth in the universe, wrong in the suggestion that women were not made in God's image and could therefore be treated as male property, wrong when it considered slavery to be legitimate, and wrong in its assumption that one can ascend into heaven by rising into the sky of a three tiered universe. So I simply de-emphasized my earlier religious training and became a devotee of the Catholic tradition of the Episcopal Church. Episcopalians did not worship the Bible, I concluded. We rather respected the teaching of the authoritative Church. I stopped saying 'The Bible says' and began saying 'The Church teaches.' It was an easy transition.

"At the University of North Carolina I majored in Philosophy and minored in Zoology and Greek. In this academic setting the whole framework of my religious tradition began to totter visibly. Certainty disappeared. The sense that I had answers faded. But I could never shake my sense of God and my conviction that I was destined not just to be a priest, but a questioning seeking ever journeying into the unknown priest.

"Getting my Master of Divinity degree at The Episcopal Seminary in Virginia I began a career in which the frontier thinkers of my tradition captured my attention: Dietrich Bonhoeffer, John A. T. Robinson, James A. Pike, Hans Kung, Edward Schillebeeckx, Michael Goulder, and many others.

"In a parish in Lynchburg I began an adult Bible class on Sunday mornings, quite deliberately designed to call people out of biblical fundamentalism. As such I became the counterpoint in that city to a young independent fundamentalist preacher named Jerry Falwell. Later while serving a church in Richmond, Virginia, lectures from a similar Bible class began to draw up to 300 people, were broadcast on a local radio station, and created the context out of which my writing career would someday emerge.

"I published my first book *Honest Prayer* in 1973. It was named the Seabury Book for Lent in the Episcopal Church that year. In 1974 I followed it with a book entitled *This Hebrew Lord*, my first attempt to portray Jesus outside the supernatural context of creedal Christianity. That book brought me into public dialogue with a Reformed Rabbi which produced another book, *Dialogue in Search of Jewish Christian Understanding* and made both the Rabbi and me household words in Richmond.

"I was elected Bishop of Newark in 1976. My election was challenged by conservative Episcopalians who said I was not an orthodox Christian. One who is a heretic cannot be allowed to be a bishop, they asserted. The challenge failed and I began my career as a bishop that was to last 24 years.

"In 1988 I published a book which challenged the Christian Church's position on matters of human sexuality. *Living in Sin?* suggested that the church must bless committed gay and lesbian relationships, establish a service of betrothal for young people who wished to live together short of marriage, and develop a service for divorcing people to enable them to separate with the Church's blessing. It raised a fire storm in religious circles and many a right wing preacher quoted the Bible to condemn this book. So I wrote a book entitled *Rescuing the Bible from Fundamentalism* to claim the Bible for a non-literalist religious public. Those two books established me as a major religious voice for liberal Christianity.

"Other books flowed in succession every two years. *Born of a Woman* examined both the birth stories of Jesus and the role played by "The Blessed Virgin Mary" in the oppression of women through the ages. *Resurrection: Myth or Reality?* and *Liberating the Gospels: Reading the Bible with Jewish Eyes* returned to the theme begun in *This Hebrew Lord* and sought to illumine the Christian story by seeing its Jewish antecedents.

"In 1998 I put all of the developing themes of my professional life into a volume entitled, *Why Christianity Must Change or Die*, which was designed to be my magnus opus. In this book I issued a call for a Reformation of Christianity that would be so total that it would dwarf the Reformation of the 16th century. I defined my audience in that book as 'believers in exile.' They were those who, like me, still experienced a God presence, even a God presence in Jesus of Nazareth, but felt themselves exiled from the literal creeds and dogmatic doctrines of Christian history that have sought to define and limit the Christian Experience.

"I have recently completed the first draft of an autobiography to be published early in 2000 to tell the story of how a southern fundamentalist grew to be the primary internal challenger of orthodox Christianity in the United States during the last quarter of the final century in the Second Millennium.

"I am married to Christine and we have five children ranging in ages from 27 to 43. I will retire in 2000."

Almost all of Bishop Spong's books have stirred up controversy among his fellow parishioners and fellow clergy. Some of his earlier publications include: *Christpower* (1975), *Life Approaches Death: A Dialogue on Ethics in Medicine* (1976), *The Easter Moment* (1980), *Into the Whirlwind, the Future of the Church* (1983), *Beyond Moralism, a Contemporary View of the Ten Commandments* (1986) and *Consciousness and Survival, an Interdisciplinary Inquiry into the Possibility of Life Beyond Biological Death* (edited and introduced by Spong, 1987). His 1988 book, *Living in Sin?: A Bishop Rethinks Human Sexuality*, however, sparked an intense national debate amongst religious leaders and their constituents.

According to Richard N. Ostling of *Time* (June 13, 1988), the situation of a lonely parishioner, who had taken up with a widow but did not want to divorce his paralyzed wife, forced the bishop to reconsider sexual morality. "For the first time," Spong said, "I faced the fact that it might be more loving and life-giving to have a relationship outside marriage than to be moralistic. It seemed to me nobody was hurt." *Living in Sin?*, Bishop Spong's examination of the church's conviction that celibacy is the only alternative to heterosexual marriage, grew out of this experience. In the book, he explored various types of sexual relationships, including homosexual relationships, and concluded that people, regardless of sexual orientation, who choose to live together in a committed, monogamous union should be blessed by the church. Such progressive thinking met with cheers from the gay community and others who had felt alienated by the strict sexual rules of the church but was simultaneously deemed radical, even blasphemous, by others. Indeed, the media reacted to the book with shock; as Richard N. Ostling proclaimed, "*Living in Sin?* is probably the most radical pronouncement on sex ever issued by a bishop."

The controversy ignited by the book *Living in Sin?* comprised only the beginning of the uproar that would surround Spong throughout the early 1990s. His views on homosexuals have often spiked a raw nerve among the more conservative factions of the church. He advocates that gay members of his church (along with women) be treated equally as parishioners and as priests. In an interview with Walter Schwarz of the *Guardian* (May 28, 1991), Spong related how his feelings shifted from outright homophobia to understanding as he began working with gay people in the New York region. He changed his stance on the morality of homosexuality, which many evangelists name as a sin denounced in the Bible, "because a, the scientific data has completely changed our interpretation; b, there are many, many more gays around than evangelicals ever admit; and c, it's absurd to accept biblical pronouncements uncritically."

In 1991 the controversy came to a head as Spong's name appeared in national headlines due to his decision to ordain Robert Williams, a noncelibate, openly gay man, as a priest in the Episcopal Church. Widely criticized for his actions, Bishop Spong sought to ease the uproar with a 19-page report, titled *Why I Ordained a Non-Celibate Gay Male to the Priesthood*, that he sent to 300 fellow bishops around the country. In the report Spong defended his decision to ordain Williams and supported a more progressive stance on homosexuality in the church. Spong wrote, as reprinted in a *New York Times* (February 12, 1990) article by Ari L. Goldman, "There was no question but that Robert had the gifts and talents that we look for in a priest. . . . He is a man gifted and called to a priestly ministry." He went on to write that although Williams was involved in a sexual relationship, it was a committed one based on a deep love and that ordaining such a man would only serve to strengthen the church. "With the ordination to the priesthood of Robert Williams, the Episcopal Church has taken a step into honesty and integrity," the bishop wrote.

The furor over this precarious issue was reignited when the newly ordained priest spoke out against monogamy during a presentation in a Detroit church. Claiming that monogamy was not essential for a Christian relationship, be it heterosexual or homosexual, Williams called celibacy an "inherently negative phenomenon" and suggested that, for example, Mother Teresa would have had a better life if she had been involved in a sexual relationship. When word of Williams's comments reached Spong, the bishop immediately disassociated himself from the speech, and demanded Williams's resignation. In addition, the bishop ordered Williams to cease working as a priest or speaking as one in public until an investigation could be performed to determine whether Williams had committed fraud during his interview process. For his part, Williams claimed that Spong had always known Williams's views on sexual issues and that the bishop had acted in response not to Williams's

comments on monogamy but to increasing pressure from the church. Williams told Goldman (February 12, 1990) that Spong wanted to use him as a figure of "this perfect gay priest, a cardboard cutout." Bishop Spong told Goldman that the ordination of Williams was a "terrible mistake" and that, with a popular perception of homosexuals as sexually promiscuous, the entire situation turned out to be ironic. "The tragedy is that we hurt the very people we were trying to help," he said. Still, even in the face of growing dissatisfaction with his handling of the gay issue within his congregation, the bishop did not express remorse over his attempt to effect change in the church. "I've always been a bishop who felt that in order to make the church speak to the world, you've got to take risks," he said. In retrospect, after the uproar had quieted to a low rumble, Spong told Paula Chin and Sue Carswell of *People* (July 1, 1991) that he had been upset with the criticism he had received. "The reaction was hypocritical. We have gay bishops; I know who they are. When I ordained Robert, all I did was to be honest. The church has been doing this for 2,000 years."

The use of Biblical passages to support attacks on Spong motivated the Bishop to write *Rescuing the Bible from Fundamentalism: A Bishop Rethinks the Meaning of Scripture* (1991). The book delves into some of the most oft-quoted passages and stories in the Bible and offers some unconventional new takes on them. Perhaps most controversially, Spong suggested that the apostle Paul was more than likely a closet homosexual—a claim, he wrote, that is substantiated in the Bible, although it is an interpretation that few Biblical scholars have acknowledged. "Nothing else, in my opinion, could account for Paul's self-judging rhetoric, his negative feeling toward his own body and his sense of being controlled by something he had no power to change," Spong said during an interview for the *Washington Post* (February 9, 1991). He did not, he said, bring such unpopular interpretations of the Bible to light to inflame conservative church groups but to illustrate that in God's eyes, love is unconditional: "To say to every human being, we all have a shadowy side. The message is not that Paul was sexually active, for I have no reason to believe he was. The message is that God can love all that is our humanity," he said.

Spong's next religious text, *Born of a Woman: A Bishop Rethinks the Birth of Jesus* (1992), sparked another round of heated debate. This time Spong put forth the notion that the Virgin Mary was not really a virgin at the time of Jesus's birth. In addition, he proposed that the traditional belief of Mary as an immaculate virgin, which he claims has kept women subservient in the church, be abandoned. "Someone known as the Virgin Mother cannot be presented with credibility to contemporary men or women as an ideal woman," Spong wrote in his book, as quoted by Ari L. Goldman of the *New York Times* (October 17, 1992). In a move that drew kudos from liberal factions and further ire from his conservative detractors, the bishop also called for an end to all dialogue with the Vatican. Citing the traditional Roman Catholic policies of male-only ordination and the exclusion of sexually active homosexuals from its ranks, Spong declared the church's policies repressive and prejudiced and stated that Catholicism was "in danger of losing its soul." "I am not willing to sacrifice women, divorced people, gay and lesbian people, or theological debate and the eternal search for God's truth upon the altar of seeking institutional or ecumenical unity inside the Christian Church," Spong wrote for the *Virginia Quarterly Review*, as it was reprinted in an article by Ari L. Goldman for the *New York Times* (April 1, 1992).

Spong published *Resurrection: Myth or Reality? A Bishop's Search for the Origins of Christianity* in 1994, followed two years later by *Liberating the Gospels: Reading the Bible with Jewish Eyes* in 1996. The latter book attempts to remind Christians that the Bible was written by Jewish authors for a Jewish audience, and it puts forth the argument that the Gospels are not historical stories but exercises in midrash, a "Jewish genre of biblical exegesis." Intended as a bridge to bring together those who interpret the Bible literally and those who dismiss it as superstitious fabrication, the book drew drastically varied reviews among readers in all religious sects. *Kirkus Reviews* (August 1, 1996) stated that it was "well written and scholarly, but unlikely to fill anyone's spiritual void," while the *Calgary Herald*'s (October 11, 1996) David Neale painted a more unflattering portrait. The problem with the book, he wrote, "is that Spong shows all the signs of a neophyte who wanders into a specialized field and is suddenly impressed and converted by everything he sees. . . . But this is not what makes Spong's book so annoying. It is his unrelenting skepticism of any historically reliable information in the gospels." Neale dismissed Spong's intentions, writing that "few thoughtful Christians practice the literalism Spong decries in the reading of these wonderful faith-filled reports of Jesus' life," and finally concluded, "Spong seems unaware of the interpretive advances the last 50 years of study of these documents have produced. We've come a long way away from simplistic fundamentalist interpretations, so please Bishop Spong, next time you deliver us—please do your homework."

Spong's most recent work, *Why Christianity Must Change or Die: A Bishop Speaks to Believers in Exile*, was published in 1998. In it Spong carefully examined the elements of Christianity, breaking them apart and revealing their weaknesses in relation to the Bible and to traditional church beliefs. He also proposed directions in which Christianity needs to move for it to prosper in the next century. "All Bibles, creeds, doctrines, prayers, hymns are nothing but religious artifacts created to allow us to speak of our God experience at an earlier point in our history," Spong wroted for the book, as reprinted in Dan Lattin's article for the *San Francisco Chronicle* (May 31, 1988). "But history

has moved us to a place where the literal content of these artifacts is all but meaningless. The God of Theism not only is dying but is also probably not revivable."

Reviews of the book were highly contentious. *Salon Magazine*'s (April 10, 1998) Michael Joseph Gross classified the title as "false advertising, and maybe even false witness, because the presumption of this book is that Christianity is already dead." As evidence that this is not the case, Gross pointed out that "church attendance is thriving (especially in conservative and fundamentalist congregations), and the political clout of the Christian Right is still strong enough to drain some plausibility from Spong's argument that Christianity is dead, at least as a spiritual or social force. . . . Spong's book engages conservative Christians only to dismiss the validity of their faith." He continued later, "abolishing so much of the imagery, stories, and devotional practices of Christian tradition, as Spong proposes, would not liberate preachers to deliver the self-actualizing new message that Jesus is a 'spirit person.' Instead, it would banish believers to a spiritually and imaginatively impoverished place, where we would have fewer resources for understanding how the God of the Bible is revealed in contemporary life." Gross concluded his assault on the book by stating that in place of Spong's notion that Christianity will die, "Reformation . . . would be more than good enough for most of us," but the book "doesn't offer much help for Christians who believe our religion needs reform."

Bishop John Shelby Spong continues to write for a multitude of magazines and newspapers and to make public appearances in a wide variety of media, including talk shows, and news programs. As he told Paula Chin and Sue Carswell, "I don't write because I'm convinced I have the final word. I do write because there are issues we've got to face openly and honestly. I think I've succeeded, and I'm awfully proud." Spong has received honorary Doctor of Divinity degrees from the Protestant Episcopal Theological Seminary, St. Paul's College, and Muhlenberg College. He enjoys an active interest in sports and was once a play-by-play announcer for several radio stations in the South, as well as the sports editor for *The Daily Southerner*, in Tarboro, North Carolina. Spong has three daughters (Ellen Elizabeth, Mary Katharine, and Jaquelin Ketner) from his 36-year marriage to Joan Lydia Ketner, who died of cancer in 1988. He continues to work and live in New Jersey with his second wife, Christine.

—D.B.

SUGGESTED READING: *Calgary Herald* Oct. 11, 1996; *Guardian* p17 May 28, 1991, p2+ Oct. 28, 1992; irkus Reviews Aug. 1, 1996; *New York Times* B p7 Feb 12, 1990, B p6 Apr.1, 1992, p32 Oct. 17, 1992; *People* p73+ July 1, 1991; *Salon Magazine* (online) Apr. 10, 1998; *San Francisco Chronicle* May 31, 1998; *Time* p56 June 13, 1988, p62 Feb. 18, 1991; *The Voice* Sep. 1997, Oct.

1997; *Washington Post* G p11 Feb. 9, 1991; *Contemporary Authors*, 1983

SELECTED WORKS: *Honest Prayer*, 1973; *This Hebrew Lord*, 1974; *Christpower*, 1975; *Dialogue: In Search of Jewish Christian Understanding* (with Rabbi Jack D. Spiro), 1975; *Life Approaches Death: A Dialogue on Ethics in Medicine* (with Daniel H. Gregory, M.D.), 1976; *The Easter Moment*, 1980; *Into the Whirlwind, the Future of the Church*, 1983; *Beyond Moralism, A Contemporary View of the Ten Commandments* (with Denise G. Haines,

Archdeacon), 1986; *Living in Sin?: A Bishop Rethinks Human Sexuality*, 1988; *Rescuing the Bible from Fundamentalism: A Bishop Rethinks the Meaning of Scripture*, 1991; *Born of a Woman: A Bishop Rethinks the Birth of Jesus*, 1992; *Resurrection: Myth or Reality? A Bishop's Search for the Origins of Christianity*, 1994; *Liberating the Gospels: Reading the Bible with Jewish Eyes*, 1996; *Why Christianity Must Change or Die: A Bishop Speaks to Believers in Exile*, 1998; As editor—*Consciousness and Survival, an Interdisciplinary Inquiry into the Possibility of Life Beyond Biological Death*, 1987

Layle Silbert/Courtesy of Random House

Stavans, Ilan

Apr. 7, 1961– Novelist; short-story writer; essayist

The Mexican essayist, literary critic, novelist, and short-story writer Ilan Stavans, born in Mexico of Jewish descent, came to the United States when he was 25 and decided to become American, adopting the English language. Much concerned with questions of Jewish-Latino identity, he has produced *Imagining Columbus: The Literary Voyage* (1993), *The Hispanic Condition: Reflections on Culture and Identity in America* (1995), *Bandido: Oscar "Zeta" Acosta and the Chicano Experience* (1995), and *Art and Anger: Essays on Politics and the Imagination* (1995)—volumes that are part of "an ongoing autobiography, a record of my metamorphosis and acknowledgment of the many masks I wear in English," as he said in the preface to *Art*

and Anger. Stavans's fiction, *The One-Handed Pianist and Other Stories* (1996), which includes his novel *Talia in Heaven*, first published in 1979 and revised in 1989, is concerned also with the flow of history and the Jews' place in it with respect to Latin America. Stavans has edited *Tropical Synagogues: Short Stories by Jewish-Latin American Writers* (1994) and *New World: Young Latino Writers* (1997); his nonfiction volume *The Riddle of Cantinflas* appeared in 1998. Marjorie Agosín in *Americas* (July/August 1996) called Stavans "unquestionably one of the most prolific writers in Latin America and perhaps in the United States."

The son of an actor, Stavans was born Ilan Stavchansky Slomianski on April 7, 1961 in Mexico City. Although he was educated in Jewish schools where the languages taught were Yiddish and Hebrew, he always knew Spanish as well and studied English. Stavans described his childhood world as a very peculiar one in "Lost in Translation," the epilogue to *The One-Handed Pianist*: "A secure, self-imposed Jewish ghetto (a treasure island) . . . We lived in an oasis completely uninvolved with things Mexican. In fact, when it came to knowledge of the outside world, students were far better talking about U.S. products (Hollywood, TV, junk food, technology) than about matters native—an artificial capsule, our ghetto, much like the magical sphere imagined by Blaise Pascal: its diameter everywhere and its center nowhere."

Stavans was perhaps a little disingenuous when he described his life in the Jewish "bubble," because, in the same essay, he depicted Sunday afternoons spent watching his father, an actor, perform on the stage. Amazed by his father's ability to assume other identities, he began to create his own: "I also wondered if I, Ilan Stavans (aka, Ilan Stavchansky Slomianski), was free to stop being his son?; could I also become other people—like Shakespeare, be one and many? To answer these many questions, I became a novelist. To write is to make sense of confusion in and around. (It was me who said that.)"

Stavans, unlike his richer friends who were sent to study abroad, had to complete his education at a Mexican university where he was forced, he has said, "to face Mexico *tête á tête.*" When he recognized "the artificiality of our oasis," the culture shock was tremendous. His solution was first to become a Communist, but he felt as alienated as a Jew in the party as he had felt in Mexico as a whole. He went on "to investigate my ethnic and religious past obsessively," delving into the works of Moses Maimonides, Judah Halevi, Walter Benjamin, Gershom Scholem, and Martin Buber.

At the age of 25, offered a scholarship to study at the Jewish Theological Seminary, Stavans moved to New York. He had been studying English for most of his life, but once in the United States he experienced a defining moment involving language. Assigned by a Spanish magazine to interview Isaac Goldemberg, a Jew from Peru and the author of *The Fragmented Life of Don Jacobo Lerner*, Stavans met him in a little Hungarian pastry shop near Columbia University. There, when Goldemberg told Stavans that he didn't want to perfect his English because he was afraid of losing his Spanish, Stavans had the revelation that he wanted the opposite—to perfect his English—"and thus become a New York Jew, an intellectual animal in the proud tradition celebrated by Alfred Kazin."

Within little more than a decade, Stavans had produced numerous reviews, largely of Hispanic literature, for publications such as the *Nation* and *Commonweal*, as well as a number of books. His Mexican publisher issued *Talia in Heaven* in 1989. It was included in *The One-Handed Pianist* and described as "a tale of love and guerrilla warfare set in a surreal 'city of rain' that plays against Gabriel García Márquez's mythic realm," by Bill Christophersen in the *New York Times Book Review* (May 5, 1996). "Paranagua is a nasty Macondo whose inhabitants . . . Stavans writes, suck tourists dry and 'leave them wriggling on their backs.'" Christophersen concluded, however, that Stavans used too many of Jorge Luis Borges's motifs: "labyrinths, mirrors, even an aleph." He observed that to "dress one's characters in borrowed robes . . . is to risk making them mannequins." The *Publishers Weekly* (January 1, 1996) reviewer described *Talia in Heaven* as a "tale that melds Jewish mysticism, thriller fiction, and soaring meditations on sexuality, love, God, and the roots of anti-Semitism."

Long fascinated by the significance of Columbus for both North and South Americans, Stavans published *Imagining Columbus: The Literary Voyage*, his first book written in English, in 1993. He examined the different representations of Columbus "in our collective literary imagination," the *Library Journal* (February 15, 1993) reviewer noted, dealing with "the various literary identities of Columbus and . . . biographies," going on in the second part of the book to focus on "19th- and 20th-century European and American literature." Stavans described in *Imagining Columbus* conversations he had as a child with his grandmother, who was obsessed with Columbus. In his grandmother's eyes, he wrote, "the Genoese . . . was a man like no other. This aura of excellence, this unique, magnanimous, poetic quality, was one reason for my fascination. I soon understood that the admiral she fantasized about was nothing but an invention she would joyfully create to make Columbus concrete, to feel close to him, to make him part of herself. . . . " To Stavans's grandmother, Columbus was both a savior and a traitor. Wondering why she could not make up her mind which of these Columbus had been, Stavans found that he was "ultimately forced to understand the profound subjectivity and contingency with which history has approached this gigantic figure." The *Choice* (March 1993) reviewer described the book as a survey of works about or in some way touching on Columbus, "always seeking to identify whatever hidden agenda may be operating in each author's case."

Stavans's 1994 collection *Tropical Synagogues: Short Stories by Jewish-Latin American Writers* joins stories by Jewish writers from Latin America with stories about Jews by Jorge Luis Borges. "The introduction alone," Marjorie Agosín noted in the *Americas* article, "is undoubtedly one of the most significant documents of Jewish experience in Latin America." In Latin America, according to Stavans, the "particular is continually being devoured by the monstrous whole." He considers Jews "part of that particular." Although, according to Stavans, Jews have been used as a scapegoat, the "political and economic turmoil has stimulated them to create a literature that bears witness to their deep historical transformation in that environment." The *Booklist* (October 15, 1993) reviewer considered the volume successful in representing Stavans's aims: "Themes steeped in allegory and metaphysics abound in this uncommon anthology."

In *The Hispanic Condition: Reflections on Culture and Identity in America*, Stavans took on the influence of Hispanic (he chose the term *Hispanic* because he believes strongly in the overall primacy of language in forming culture) mores on attitudes of Hispanic people toward sexuality and race, among other cultural determinants. This controversial topic elicited a variety of attitudes among reviewers. *Booklist's* (March 15, 1995) Mary Carroll found the book to be a "thoughtful, probing, often lyrical analysis" of the "centuries-long, hemispheric encounter between Anglos and Hispanics." In the *New York Times Book Review* (May 21, 1995), Peter Temes called the book "much more than autobiography." He maintained that it is "an argument for accepting social identity broadly, in the most cosmopolitan terms." He noted that Stavans's "impulse is to broaden, not to narrow; he finds understanding through the complications of identity, not through the easy gestures of ethnic politics." Jose Luis Sanchez in *MultiCultural Review* (December 1995), however, found that *The Hispanic Condition* was "insightful" and that it touched on "some interesting themes," but on the whole he found it "confused, unfocused, and unsuccessful."

Stavans's second book published in 1995 was *Bandido: Oscar "Zeta" Acosta and the Chicano Experience*. This is the story of Acosta, one of the more colorful characters in the Chicano movement of the late 1960s and early 1970s and the model for Hunter S. Thompson's Dr. Gonzo in *Fear and Loathing in Las Vegas*. Acosta ran for sheriff of Los Angeles in 1970. By 1974 he had disappeared in Mexico. "Stavans . . . offers an appreciation, not a biography, of Zeta Acosta as force of nature and a deeply troubled human being," Mary Carroll wrote in *Booklist* (September 1, 1995). David Unger, in the *New York Times Book Review* (March 10, 1996), noted that "after his awakening to Chicano identity" Acosta "mastered his inner confusions and found an articulate voice." He deemed *Bandido* to share "some of Acosta's virtues and faults. . . . Stavans does not let empathy blind him to his subject's literary and personal shortcomings" but he "appears to have rushed his writing, much as Acosta did."

Stavans's third 1995 book was *Art and Anger: Essays on Politics and the Imagination*, a collection of writings originally published in the *Nation*, the *Michigan Quarterly Review*, and other intellectual periodicals. Essays on the writings of Gabriel García Márquez, Mario Vargas Llosa, Alvaro Mutis, Fernando Pessoa, and Octavio Paz predominate. The opening essay, "Letter to a German Friend," however, is a more intimate piece. Addressed to a young German man, it describes Stavans's honeymoon trip to Czechoslovakia and Poland to visit the ancestral homes of his Polish and his wife's Czech forebears, all Jews, many of whom were murdered by the Nazis. "Our civilized life," he tells the young man, "is a precarious and insecure state of mind. It's a pendulum that alternates progress with barbarism, light with darkness."

The One-Handed Pianist, a collection of stories that appeared in 1996, was described by Marjorie Agosín as an attempt by Stavans "to pay tribute to the theater as art and as a mirror of the mind." She found the prevailing mood of *The One-Handed Pianist* to be "ambiguity, with magic and dread as its themes. The protagonists challenge the concept of God and of ambiguity itself. Religion and doubt are the bases for Stavans's continuing leitmotif." The *Publishers Weekly* (January 1, 1996) reviewer remarked on the "intense explorations of Jewish life and identity in the Hispanic world," featuring "individualists who relentlessly investigate spirituality beyond the realm of orthodox religion."

In *The Riddle of Cantinflas: Essays on Hispanic Popular Culture* (1998), Stavans examined the making of celebrities into idols, turning his eye, for example, to the singer Selena and the writers Carlos Fuentes and Sandra Cisneros.

Stavans won the Latino Literature Prize in 1992. He received a grant from the National Endowment for the Humanities and in 1994 was a finalist for the National Book Critics' Circle Excellence in Reviewing Award. He taught Latin American literature at Baruch College of the City University of New York in 1991 and later became a professor of Hispanic Literature at Amherst College. He was married in 1988.

Ilan Stavans wrote in the preface to *Art and Anger*, "I have come to realize that much of what I wrote in the last decade is about creativity and fury, the pen and the sword. . . . I can see how my views on writing are linked to messianic religion: the written word as a passport to the future, as a bridge toward one's deeper realms and the divide, literature as an attempt to decipher our human inadequacies. There is no art without anger, but anger alone does not make good art."
—S. Y.

SUGGESTED READING: *Americas* p44+ July/Aug. 1996; *New York Times Book Review* p32 May 21, 1995; p16 Mar. 10, 1996; p22 May 5, 1996; *Publishers Weekly* p59 Jan. 1, 1996

SELECTED BOOKS: Fiction—*The One-Handed Pianist and Other Stories*, 1996; Nonfiction—*Imagining Columbus: The Literary Voyage*, 1993; *Bandido: Oscar "Zeta" Acosta and the Chicano Experience*, 1995; *The Hispanic Condition: Reflections on Culture and Identity in America*, 1995; *Art and Anger: Essays on Politics and the Imagination*, 1995; *The Riddle of Cantinflas: Essays on Hispanic Popular Culture*, 1998; As editor—*Growing Up Latino: Memoirs and Stories* (with H. Augenbraum), 1993; *Tropical Synagogues: Short Stories by Jewish-Latin American Writers*, 1994; *New World: Young Latino Writers*, 1997; As translator—*Sentimental Songs*, 1993

Steele, Shelby

Jan. 1, 1946– Nonfiction writer

In the early 1990s Shelby Steele metamorphosed from a little-known professor of English at San Jose State University into something of a celebrity whose thoughts on race problems in America have sparked a national debate. Steele owes his status as an intellectual provocateur to the publication of his highly controversial book *The Content of Our Character: A New Vision of Race in America* (1990), which went on to win a National Book Critics Circle Award. In each of the essays included in the book, the author maintained that the poverty, chronic unemployment, and other societal ills confronting many African-Americans should not be ascribed solely to racism, as many black leaders have insisted. Instead, Steele contended, the crises facing much of black America can be traced to the black community's collective self-doubt and its belief that racism is the principal impediment to advancement. "We all know that there is racism, and that racism can be an excuse for not developing," he wrote in an article for *Emerge* (February 1991). "When we meet it, we must fight it like a pit bull, but we must never lose sight of the fact that our own struggle is more important than the racism we encounter. Otherwise our lives are contained and defined by the racism more than by our own dreams and ambitions." Steele published a second collection of essays, *A Dream Deferred: The Second Betrayal of Black Freedom in America*, in 1998, in which he extended his discussion to include affirmative action and other preferential practices set in motion by the U.S. government and supported by the black establishment. He argued that such programs are not interested in bettering the lives of everyday African-Americans, but instead exist to help alleviate white guilt for past wrongs against blacks.

As might be expected, Steele has been extolled by some white conservatives and black intellectuals for daring to speak the truth, as he sees it, about racism. Equally predictably, he has drawn the ire of some black cultural and political leaders, who have accused him of being dangerously out of touch with both the concerns of other black Americans and the effects of racism today. While Steele has been the first to admit that he does not "have all the answers" needed to solve the crisis facing much of black America, he believes that he has made a valuable contribution to the ongoing debate about how to check the persistent growth of the so-called black underclass. "I try to write what I know," he told Peter Applebome, who profiled him for the *New York Times* (May 30, 1990). "Some people say I shine a harsh light on difficult problems. But I never shine a light on anything I haven't experienced or write about fears I don't see in myself first. I'm my own first target. I spill my own blood first."

The son of Shelby Steele Sr., a black truck driver, and Ruth Steele, a white social worker, Shelby Steele was born on New Year's Day, 1946, in Chicago, Illinois. He grew up mainly in Phoenix, a working-class suburb of Chicago, where the family moved when he was two. Although Shelby Steele Sr. never completed elementary school, he and Ruth believed that blacks could succeed if they worked hard and obtained a good education, and they did their best to raise their four children (Shelby, his twin brother, and his two sisters) according to those values. Steele has also credited his parents, who had been involved in the civil rights movement since the 1940s, with helping him to understand the causes of racial discrimination. Being born into an interracial family also proved invaluable. "It was an absolute gift, the greatest source of insight and understanding . . . " he told Wayne Edwards, who interviewed him for *People* (September 2, 1991). "I could be rocked on the knee of my white grandfather one week and rocked on the knee of my black uncle the next week. So race was demystified for me."

Although his family was a model of racial harmony, Shelby did encounter racism as a child. In 1956, he recalled in *The Content of Our Character*, he was traumatized by the unusually cruel treatment he received from his sixth-grade teacher, a white ex-Marine. At the time, the two elementary schools in Phoenix were segregated—one was for whites and the other for blacks. Shelby attended the latter, which he described as "a dumping ground for teachers with too little competence or mental stability to teach in the white school in [their] district." The white ex-Marine, according to Steele, was just such an inferior teacher. On the first day of school, Shelby read a sentence incorrectly, and the teacher, instead of gently correcting him, encouraged the other children to laugh at him.

The humiliation Shelby experienced rendered him unable to do his homework, which, in turn, apparently made his teacher feel justified in meting out increasingly harsh punishment to the boy. The abuse climaxed on the day the teacher ordered Shelby to pick up, with his bare hands, the countless pieces of broken glass that littered the playground. There was so much glass, Steele recalled in *The Content of Our Character*, that "there were sections . . . that glared like a mirror in the sunlight." When, after half an hour, he abandoned the project—"more out of despair than rebellion," he recalled—the teacher told another boy to get on a bicycle and chase Shelby around the school grounds with a baseball bat.

On learning of the incident, Shelby's parents drew on their backgrounds as civil rights advocates and organized a boycott of the school, with the result that several of the teachers—including the ex-Marine—were fired. Thanks to their support, Shelby eventually regained both his self-confidence and his desire to excel in school. Indeed, he went on to become a highly visible member of his class at Thornton Township High, an integrated school in Harvey, Illinois, where he led student rallies and, in his senior year, became student council president.

After graduating from high school in 1964, Steele enrolled at Coe College, in Cedar Rapids, Iowa, where he underwent a transformation of sorts. In the early years of his college career, he told *Current Biography*, he led a student civil rights group called SCOPE, which was affiliated with the Reverend Dr. Martin Luther King Jr.'s Southern Christian Leadership Conference. By the late 1960s, however, Steele, like many of his friends, had become excited by the nationalistic rhetoric of the black power movement, whose leaders had begun to share the stage with the somewhat less militant leaders of the mainstream civil rights movement. Under their influence, Steele, who by then had acquired a penchant for wearing African-style clothing, led protests against the college administration on behalf of black students. Steele has cited Malcolm X as an especially strong influence.

In line with the nationalists' call to all blacks to unite and to demand redress from the "white establishment" for the wrongs that had been perpetrated against them over the centuries, Steele and his friends found themselves identifying with the most severely victimized black Americans. One of their favorite pastimes, in fact, was holding "nap-matching" sessions—contests in which they would try to top each other's tales of ill treatment at the hands of racist America. Steele has recalled that the horror stories, though sometimes less than horrific, did nonetheless confer upon Steele and his friends an identity as members of the larger black society.

Notwithstanding his attraction to the black power movement, Steele went on to pursue a traditional career in academia. On graduating from Coe College in 1968, he enrolled in a master's degree program in sociology at Southern Illinois University, in Edwardsville. In addition to his studies, he taught African-American literature in East St. Louis, an impoverished black community not far from the university, in an experimental program that provided poor blacks with the equivalent of two years of college. After receiving his degree in 1971, Steele entered the University of Utah, from which he earned a Ph.D. in English literature three years later. Soon afterward, he joined the faculty of San Jose State University as an instructor of freshman composition, and was eventually made a full professor of English literature. In recent years he has taught courses in African and African-American literature, his main area of interest. He has also taught courses in 20th-century fiction, Greek mythology, American drama, and 19th-century Russian fiction.

Steele's rise to a respected position within his profession coincided with his becoming a family man and a father. A year before graduating from college, he had married Rita Steele, a white woman and a fellow undergraduate who has since become a clinical psychologist. In 1974 their son, Eli, was born, and a year later his wife gave birth to their daughter, Loni. As it turned out, Steele's identity as a husband, father, and successful teacher led him to question the validity of his "black identity" as conceived by the leaders of the black power movement. "It was the space I cleared for myself by loosely subscribing to this identity that ultimately put me in conflict with it . . . " he wrote in *The Content of Our Character*. "By simply living as an individual in America—with my racial identity struggle suspended by my subscription to the black power identity—I discovered that American society offered me and blacks in general a remarkable range of opportunity if we were willing to pursue it."

That epiphany led Steele to begin to question what, in fact, lay at the heart of the problems facing many blacks in the United States. He came to believe that, while racial discrimination remained a potent force that compounded the struggle of many black Americans to become part of mainstream America, one of the greatest obstacles to their attaining a measure of prosperity was their failure to believe in their potential as individual human beings. According to Steele, lack of self-esteem was a natural condition for a people with a history of being oppressed and victimized by the powers that be; he knew from personal experience, however, that that condition could be overcome. These thoughts led him to conclude that many blacks were not only indulging in self-doubt but were using racism as an excuse for not even trying to become members of mainstream American society. "The exhilaration of new freedom is always followed by a shock of accountability . . . " he wrote in *The Content of Our Character*. "Freedom always carries a burden of proof, always throws us back on ourselves. And freedom, even imperfect freedom, makes blacks a brutal proposition: if you're not inferior, prove it."

In the years that followed, Steele grew increasingly frustrated by what he considered the tendency of black leaders to perpetuate half-truths about racism. As Steele saw it, civil rights advocates, to the detriment of black America, preferred to cast racism as the greatest barrier to black progress. Worse still, they tended to portray black people "primarily as racial victims," he pointed out in *The Content of Our Character*. Whites, on the other hand, "had to show both concern and a measure of befuddlement at how other whites could still be racist," Steele wrote. Steele's frustration became acute in 1986, on Martin Luther King Jr.'s birthday, when he found himself listening to a radio broadcast that featured a local black leader talking with an interviewer about problems facing black Americans. "I cannot say that the two men I listened to that afternoon were lying to each other, or that much of what they said wasn't true," he wrote in *The Content of Our Character*. "I can say, however, with much empathy, that they were boring. . . . The source of their boringness, I believe, was that each man had left his full self at home. . . . Each race has its politics and its party line that impose a certain totalitarianism over the maverick thoughts of the individual. Because of this we become a bit afraid of what we really think about race."

Steele was determined not to be afraid of expressing his views on race. After the radio program was over, he wrote an article expressing some of his thoughts on the subject; it later became the second chapter of *The Content of Our Character*. Over the next few years, he wrote several more pieces that were published in such prestigious magazines as *Harper's*, *Commonweal*, and the *American Scholar* and were later republished in his book. In each of the essays, Steele drew heavily on his personal experiences, thinking that, as he later wrote in *The Content of Our Character*, his reflections on his "private self" might be properly applied to the "public reality."

In "Being Black and Feeling Blue," which appeared in the January 1988 issue of *Commentary*, for instance, Steele reflected on, among other things, the effects of his maltreatment at the hands of his sixth-grade teacher, who, he realized in retrospect, was "[probably not] even particularly racist." What struck Steele as an adult was the extent to which his self-esteem had been wounded by the teacher's cruelty. Steele's self-image had been further damaged by the well-intentioned efforts of some of the black adults in the community, who told him, "Don't worry. They treat all blacks this way." Their words of intended consolation only compounded Steele's sense of inferiority and helplessness. Based on his analysis of this incident, Steele concluded that black Americans were plagued by a far more insidious evil than the racism of some white Americans; they were haunted by "the racist within." "This internal racist is not restricted by law, morality, or social decorum," he wrote. "It cares nothing about civil rights and equal opportunity. It is the self-doubt born of the original wound of racial oppression, and its mission is to establish the justice of that wound and shackle us with doubt."

The magazine essays, in turn, captured the attention of the filmmaker Thomas Lennon, who approached Steele about doing a documentary on race in the United States. In August 1989, at about the time the two men were trying to come up with the best approach for such a film, an event occurred that divided New York City—and much of the nation—along racial lines: A black youth named Yusuf K. Hawkins was murdered by a gang of white teenagers in Bensonhurst, a largely Italian-American section of Brooklyn, New York. Two of the youths were arrested and charged with the killing. Local black leaders, most notably the Reverend Al Sharpton, led other blacks on marches into Bensonhurst, where they were greeted by hostile residents shouting racial slurs. The killing and the events surrounding it made the national news, which triggered an increase in racial tension in many parts of the country.

Steele and Lennon considered the Bensonhurst incident a good subject for their documentary. The result was an installment of *Frontline*, a weekly program on public television, entitled "Seven Days in Bensonhurst," which aired on May 15, 1990, and was narrated by Steele. In addition to expressing his anger over the killing, Steele made the point that the incident had provoked an unusually high degree of racial enmity among New York City residents, and suggested that the hostility was caused not so much by the incident itself but by the exhibitionism and posturing of activists, politicians, and media personalities. The reaction to Steele's commentary on the incident was sharply divided. On the one hand, a writer for the *New York Times* (May 15, 1990) hailed the film for offering viewers "an uncommonly sophisticated look at how racial animosities, political calculation, and the press and television worked on one another in the week following the killing." But a *Village Voice* writer castigated Steele for making "enfeebled and handwringing apologias for the state of American racial discourse."

If "Seven Days in Bensonhurst" brought on a shower of controversy, *The Content of Our Character: A New Vision of Race in America*, which was published in the fall of 1990, generated a torrent. Black liberal politicians and intellectuals were especially outraged not only by the content of Steele's ideas but by the media's apparent infatuation with him. "I do not say black people are without fault or that there is not a lot of effort required on our part to move us out of our predicaments," Roger Wilkins, a widely respected civil rights activist, told Gene Seymour of *New York Newsday* (October 10, 1990). "But our fundamental problem is not in our fears or uncertainties or defensiveness. Our fundamental problem is that we live in a racist society that's tilted against us." Steele's detractors were equally critical of his methodology. Adolph Reed, a professor of political science at Yale University, for instance, wrote in the *Nation* (March 4, 1991), "This is an abominably thin, simpleminded book. . . . [It] is unburdened with facts outside a particularly limited compass of personal experience, and its analysis is innocent of social or political complexity. . . . I am outraged at having to confront once again, as if they were innovations, arguments that amount to claims that black Americans are a genetically defective human subspecies." But the book also had many defenders. Diana Schaub, for instance, wrote in *Commentary* (February 1991), "Although portions of Steele's argument echo the conservative critique of the politics of racial preference, *The Content of Our Character* is more than a litany of misguidance and betrayals of liberal leadership, black and white alike. Its uniqueness . . . is Steele's insightful analysis of the racial self . . . . Although it is generating disputes, [the book] is not really a disputatious work; instead, in conception and execution, it is introspective."

Steele offered Seymour his thoughts as to why his book had generated such a heated debate among black civil rights activists: "Any time you talk about hidden human motivation, that's very threatening to everyone. Some of those pieces were very painful for me to write inasmuch as I was looking at my own life and seeing where there might have been psychological blockages due to my own racial thinking. So it cuts deeply, it cuts sharply."

Whatever anxiety the controversy may have produced in Steele, it has not stopped him from continuing to voice his concerns about the plight of black Americans; since 1990, he has contributed articles to *New Republic*, *Utne Reader*, and *Harper's*, among other magazines. In 1998 he published a collection of four essays, *A Dream Deferred: The Second Betrayal of Black Freedom in America*, in which he set forth his controversial views on affirmative action, which he sees as a gesture of self-consolation by and for white Americans. As the reviewer for *Booklist* (September 1, 1998) noted: "The enormous irony of this situation, as Steele sees it, is that it defers to white sensibilities, just as, with much more destructive consequences, the systems of slavery and Jim Crow did. The only blacks who benefit from redemptive liberalism are the leaders of what Steele calls grievance groups, and they are, ultimately, utterly dependent on white indulgence. In his last and best written essay, Steele generalizes much of his critique to other minorities and to women when they are perceived as an oppressed group. . . . Despite some awkward writing, this is a deeply engaging public-policy criticism."

When he is not writing about racial issues, Steele continues to teach in San Jose, where he lives with his wife and children.
—C.M.

SUGGESTED READING: *Booklist* Sep. 1, 1998; *Commentary* Jan. 1988, Feb. 1991; *Current Biography* Feb. 1993; *Emerge* Feb, 1991; *Nation* Mar. 4, 1991; *New York Newsday* Oct. 10, 1990; *New York Times* A p18 May 15, 1990, May 30, 1990; *People* p79+ Sep. 2, 1991; *Time* p45 Aug. 13, 1990, p6+ Aug. 12, 1991

SELECTED WORKS: *The Content of Our Character: A New Vision of Race in America*, 1990; *A Dream Deferred: The Second Betrayal of Black Freedom in America*, 1998

Courtesy of Alfred A. Knopf

Steinhart, Peter

Aug. 17, 1943– Essayist; conservation writer

Peter Steinhart is a widely recognized conservation author whose books and articles have amassed critical praise for their uncompromising honesty, their deft rendering of ecological history, and their spare but powerful statistical observations. As a small boy, Steinhart lived in California's Santa Clara Valley before it became industrialized, and he spent his summers in the deep backcountry of the Sierra Nevada, where it was possible for a person to travel for days without seeing another living soul. While those experiences contributed to his ecological concerns, the author believes that his in-

terest in activism and in writing is also a result of the positive influences of various figures in his life—prominent among them are his father, an attorney, who devoted his efforts to Jewish charities and who was a member of the United States Civil Rights Commission, and one of Steinhart's college professors, the writer Wallace Stegner, who was an active voice for the protection of American wilderness. Thus inspired, Steinhart has gone on to publish numerous essays and four books: *Tracks in the Sky* (1987), *California's Wild Heritage* (1990), *Two Eagles/Dos Aguilas* (1994), and *The Company of Wolves* (1995). The naturalist suggested in one interview that writing has many purposes: "Much of my writing has been about what we do to our own character and outlook when we change the setting in which we live. I am convinced that the more we remove ourselves from the complexity and diversity of nature, the more we resign ourselves to selfishness, stupidity, and small-mindedness."

In an autobiographical sketch written expressly for *World Authors 1990–1995*, Peter Steinhart discusses his life and work: "I was born in San Francisco, August 17, 1943. Mother: Jean Nichols Steinhart (housewife and omnivorous reader). Father: John Henry Steinhart (attorney). I grew up in the Santa Clara Valley and watched its plum orchards and wheat fields become the freeways and industrial parks of Silicon Valley, and watched the small town congeniality and trust vanish with the rural landscape. I've been convinced ever since that what we do to our setting changes the human heart in profound ways. I grew up looking at things in nature and learning to give them proper names but also to see them in more confiding ways. I think seeing is the greatest pleasure, and is also something complicated and inconstant. I suppose today I write, more than anything else, to go on seeing. I was fortunate to have—right in my own neighborhood—some extraordinary guides to seeing and interpreting nature. At the age of eight, I saw Ansel Adams pushing a camera-laden burro through the high Sierra backcountry; I knew who he was—his images already hung in my imagination. In college (Stanford University, BA in History, 1965), I lucked into a writing program headed by Wallace Stegner and into an unexpectedly provocative course in evolution taught by Paul Ehrlich, who later attained fame as a critic of population growth. Konrad Lorenz, Niko Tinbergen and George Schaller were all at Stanford while I was there, and while I never met any of them, their views trickled down, and I soon read their books. David Brower was (and still is) the most eloquent and compelling voice for conservation in the neighborhood.

"I got a Masters degree in history at U.C.L.A., and began in a graduate seminar there to think about the ways we think in symbols and act in symbolic ways. That led me to see that wolves, mountains, rivers, soil—everything in nature, had meanings on deeper psychological and cultural levels. I joined the Peace Corps and went to Kenya, expecting to spend two years marveling at the wildlife, and finding an even greater pleasure in the richness of its humanity. The two years taught me a lot about the relationships between culture and setting and the universality of human fears and hopes. Probably more important, the intensity and color of life, the constant novelty, were delights that clamored to be written about. At night, in the light of candles and pressure lanterns, I wrote a lot of letters home.

"When I came back from Africa and couldn't find a job teaching, I began in a sort of desperation to write about Africa. It was stilted, awkward, academic prose, lacking the life of the letters I had been writing. I had the good luck to discover that I needed to learn really how to write, and then had the even better fortune to guess that I ought to write about what I most cared about—which was the relationship between humans and the natural setting. It was by then the era of the first Earth Day, a time when the National Environmental Policy Act was just being implemented and the Endangered Species Act just being given teeth. Some of my college friends had become attorneys for environmental law firms. Drawing on their files, I began writing op-ed pieces about environmental issues for the *Los Angeles Times*. Publication and syndication of those pieces taught me some of the basics—including the idea that seems to most organize my writing, that good writing is usually good argument. I wrote for magazines, too, and in 1979 began writing an essay column for *Audubon* magazine, largely on the theme that what we do to nature we do also to ourselves, but with forays into the nature of perception and essays on our feelings for mountains or frogs or campfires or other things we found in nature. I think these essays were the most joyful writing I have done, and the column lasted uninterrupted for twelve years. During that time, I made my living writing for *Audubon* and other conservation magazines (*National Wildlife*, *Defenders of Wildlife*, *Wildlife Conservation*, *Sierra*) and for such general interest magazines as *Har-*

per's, *The New York Times Magazine* and *Reader's Digest*. For two of those years I wrote a column on environmental affairs for *California Magazine*.

"My first three books were visual format books and undertaken partly because they were good causes, partly because they offered a chance to get out to see the wider world. *Tracks in the Sky*, a collaboration with photographer Tupper Ansel Blake, explored the values and meanings of wetlands and took me out to see the finer remaining wetlands along the Pacific Flyway, from Alaska's Yukon-Kuskokwim Delta to Ecuador's Guayaquil Bay. *California's Wild Heritage*, a guide to threatened and endangered species in the Golden State, was purely an educational effort published jointly by the California Department of Fish and Game, the California Academy of Sciences and the Sierra Club. *Two Eagles/Dos Aguilas*, also a collaboration with Tupper Ansel Blake, was an exploration of the rich biological and cultural diversity of the United States–Mexico borderlands. My fourth book, *The Company of Wolves*, sought to explore the natural history and human meaning of wolves at a time when wolves were a clamorous political issue."

Like his columns and articles, Steinhart's books have received a good deal of attention. *Tracks in the Sky* explores the Pacific flyway—the migratory routes of birds in the mainland northern United States, Canada, and Alaska—and depicts in words and photographs what is currently happening to it. *Natural History* (November 1987), in its review, noted that the author "writes to communicate, not to dazzle. His style is expressive without being showy . . . [making] it clear that wetlands constitute the irreplaceable thread of the migratory journey." A writer for *Science Books and Films* (May/June 1988) believed: "The general reader and professional alike will enjoy this . . . volume."

Two Eagles/Dos Aguilas (1994), Steinhart's second collaboration with the photographer Tupper Ansel Blake, discusses the natural history of a single 100-mile area straddling the U.S.–Mexican border. In the text Steinhart described efforts to conserve the very diverse ecosystem that exists there as developers attempt to exploit it. Critics praised this collaboration as much as they had the first. *Library Journal* (December 1994) stated: "The concise, insightful text is well integrated with spectacular photos of wildlife and landscape, elevating the work from mere 'coffee-table book' status. . . . Essential for regional and subject collections and highly recommended for all others." *Science Books and Films* (November 1994) noted: "Blake and Steinhart do an excellent job of enlightening readers about the region's real value. . . . The impressive prints and text will likely encourage observers to connect with the natural world by stimulating a concern for conservation and a desire for visiting border wildlife habitats."

In 1995 Steinhart published another book, *The Company of Wolves*, which evaluates the relationship between human beings and wolves over the centuries and helps to debunk myths about wolves just as they are being reintroduced into certain areas of the wild, such as Yellowstone National Park, where they were hunted to extinction a century ago. As they had his other works, critics applauded Steinhart's thorough, well-researched book: "As Steinhart familiarizes us with wolf life, he also examines the conflicting motivations behind our attempts to destroy them, on the one hand, and reintroduce them into certain regions, on the other," a writer for *Booklist* (April 15, 1995) observed. The *Economist* (July 15, 1995) review read: "When he restrains his own mythologizing, Mr. Steinhart is able to assess and explain the emotional as well as the scientific debates over a complex piece of wilderness engineering. It is a rare talent."

Peter Steinhart married Judith Holland, a teacher, on his 25th birthday, August 17, 1968. The couple has two children, Jonah and Caitlin.—C.M.

SUGGESTED READING: *Audubon* p8+ Jan. 1987; *Booklist* p1461 Apr. 15, 1995; *Economist* p73 July 15, 1995; *Library Journal* p122 Dec. 1994; *Natural History* p96 Nov. 1987; *Science Books and Films* p284 May/June 1988, p234 Nov. 1994; *Contemporary Authors* vol. 148, 1996

SELECTED WORKS: *Tracks in the Sky*, 1987; *California's Wild Heritage*, 1990; *Two Eagles/Dos Aguilas*, 1994; *The Company of Wolves*, 1995

Sarah Bird/Courtesy of Bantam Books

Sterling, Bruce

Apr. 14, 1954– Science-fiction writer

Bruce Sterling has built a reputation as one of the foremost figures in the "cyberpunk" literary movement. His novels, which combine science fiction with slices of pop culture and a sense of technology-fueled alienation, look beneath the surface of contemporary scientific "solutions" to pose questions about the future of science and its relationship to mankind. He has also written nonfiction works, such as *The Hacker Crackdown: Law and Disorder on the Electronic Frontier* (1992), which chronicles the underground hacker culture and its run-ins with the U.S. government. His subsequent novels have examined such topics as ecological disasters and the search for self-fulfillment.

Bruce Sterling was born on April 14, 1954, in Brownsville, Texas, to M. B. and Gloria (Vela) Sterling. His father worked as an engineer, while his mother was employed as a registered nurse. Sterling attended the University of Texas at Austin from 1972 to 1976.

From 1977 to 1983 Sterling was employed by the Texas Legislative Council as a proofreader. During this time, he completed his first novel, *Involution Ocean* (1977), a science-fiction story set in a desolate world on which the only habitable region is a single crater. He also wrote *The Artificial Kid* (1980), which tells the story of the futuristic planet Reverie. Founded as a controlled, "equal" society, Reverie instead develops into a world ruled by the entertainment industry. Hovering over the surface of the planet are the wealthy, who watch the surface residents for entertainment.

Published during the late 1970s, when punk rock—itself a manifestation of youthful alienation—was invading the music scene, these two books, along with writings by William Gibson, served as the foundation of a movement that came to be known as "cyberpunk," an offshoot of science fiction concerned with the blurring of the line between human and machine. As the subculture evolved in the 1990s, computer hackers and "cypherpunks" (cryptography specialists) emerged as its heroes. Sterling's subsequent novels on the near future of technology (particularly *Islands in the Net* [1988]) made him one of the movement's most visible representatives.

Mirrorshades (1986), which Sterling edited, consists of 12 stories written by such noted authors as William Gibson, Rudy Rucker, and John Shirley. Reviews were mixed: The *Village Voice* critic Richard Gehr commented that Sterling's introduction to the book is a "dazzling, eye-opening ride through the modern world" but warned potential readers that "the remainder of the book barely justifies its claims"; Gerald Jonas wrote in the *New York Times Book Review* (January 18, 1987), "What we find . . . is a science fiction that takes the runaway power of science and technology for granted, that plays paranoia straight and finds comic relief in anarchy, and gives center stage to characters who ask of the future not, 'What's new under the sun?' but 'What's in it for me?'"

Sterling's thriller *Islands in the Net*, published in 1988, features Laura Webster, a resort manager who becomes tangled in a web of conspiracy when she accidentally uncovers a scheme involving her corporate bosses and their information-pirate cohorts. Set in the near future, *Islands in the Net* is essentially a story of the burgeoning information age, and of the Internet's vital role in connecting or isolating the "islands" that it surrounds. Noted author Tom Easton explained his take on the novel's meaning in *Analog Science Fiction/Science Fact* (December 1988): "The world is growing ever more tightly linked by computerized data exchanges, summing up to the 'Net' of the title, but there are a few places—islands—that parasitize the Net [by acting] as data pirates (e.g. Grenada, Singapore). There is also Africa, so beset by ecological and political disaster that it is a metaphorical island totally surrounded by the Net, but not part of it."

Reviews of *Islands in the Net* were overwhelmingly enthusiastic, and the book served to cement Sterling's reputation as one of the premier "cyberpunk" writers of the day. Indeed, the novel is widely considered to be *the* premier cyberpunk thriller. In a review for the *Washington Post Book World* (June 26, 1988), Roz Kaveney wrote, "Sterling has a real gift for turning ideas from the science pages of newspapers into entertaining science fictional conceits." A *New York Times Book Review* (October 2, 1988) reviewer felt that Sterling "reveals himself in his new novel to be a serious and insightful futurist . . . the always surprising plot jumps around the world from the Caribbean to Southeast Asia to Africa, but Mr. Sterling remains in firm control throughout."

Sterling's next book, *Crystal Express* (1989), was a collection of 12 of his stories, including the Nebula and Hugo award nominees "Swarm," "Spider Rose," and "Cicada Queen." In a review for the *Washington Post Book World* (February 26, 1989), Gregory Feeley wrote that the stories in *Crystal Express* are "characterized by intellectual playfulness, a careful, almost mannered style, and a flamboyant virtuosity in matters of formal invention."

Next came a collaborative effort, *The Difference Engine* (1990), co-written with noted cyberpunk author William Gibson. The book starts with Charles Babbage's idea for the Difference Engine, a steam-powered mechanical computer that was never built, a historical event—or non-event—in the history of analytical thought. In the book, the Difference Engine is actually built, which causes the industrial revolution to arrive ahead of schedule, which in turn wreaks changes great and small on the Victorian era. In the new world order, the

renowned poet Lord Byron becomes a tyrant in the technological society that emerges in England; his daughter Ada (who actually developed algorithms with Babbage) becomes a prostitute; and the United States is split into separate republics. At the novel's center, Sterling and Gibson create an intricate thriller concerning Ada and a mysterious box of punch cards.

Sterling and Gibson, who had teamed up previously on a short story in 1983, split their tasks for *The Difference Engine*: Sterling researched every aspect of Victorian culture, from food to slang terms; Gibson pored over the resulting information, writing most of the actual text. The end result combines history with science-fiction fantasy. "The best science fiction has always worked by the power of suggestion," Thomas M. Disch wrote for the *New York Times Book Review* (March 10, 1991), "and seldom has that power source operated so effectively as in *The Difference Engine*. Working together, Mr. Gibson and Mr. Sterling have written a book that is even better than their earlier and considerable solo efforts. Grateful readers can only hope that this represents the beginning of a long and fruitful collaboration." *Reason* (November 1991) was slightly less enthusiastic about *The Difference Engine*. While praising the technological aspects of the book, reviewer Greg Costikyan also made the observation that "it is strikingly odd that an ostensibly political work chooses to ignore the political developments of the time." Citing the lack of references to monumental British progressions such as the evolution of the Whig Party into the Liberal Party, Costikyan also commented that "Gibson and Sterling are excellent on the texture of life and the scientific controversies of the day; yet by ignoring Victorian liberalism, they have again missed a way to drive their point home." The writer concluded that "On the whole, *The Difference Engine* is an ambitious undertaking and an imaginative and compelling work—but doesn't quite hit its mark."

Sterling's next offering was *Globalhead* (1992), a collection of 13 satirical stories he had written over a period of seven years. The unique collection includes such diverse characters as a rock singer who is deemed the voice of the people, and "two lost souls who drive off the edge of the world and find each other." One of the more noted stories in the collection is "Our Neural Chernobyl," which is ostensibly a review of a fictional book about the history of DNA manipulation. Some of the stories, such as those focusing on Islamic culture, were declared duds by critics, and the *New York Times Book Review* (December 27, 1992) reviewer felt Sterling's attempts at topical humor were "uneven." However, the wide range of content in *Globalhead* earned the book high marks from reviewers. The *New York Times* review concluded, "as this collection shows, there is a lot more to Mr. Sterling than cyberpunk."

Sterling's first nonfiction book was a foray into the world of civil liberties as they pertain to cyberspace. *The Hacker Crackdown: Law and Disorder on the Electronic Frontier* (1992) tells the history of cyberspace and of the cluster of computer hackers that began to form as the gateways of opportunity opened up alongside the advances in technology. Specifically, Sterling examined the 1990 breakdown of AT&T's long-distance phone system, an incident that was initially blamed on malicious outside computer hackers but was ultimately found to be a result of a glitch in the company's software. The ensuing investigation conducted by the authorities, which led to the seizing of computer equipment and files from "innocent" teenage hackers across the nation, culminated in a trial and the creation of the Electronic Frontier Foundation, a group of civil libertarians funded by Lotus inventor/millionaire Mitch Kapor and former Grateful Dead lyricist John Perry Barlow. Although he acknowledged the sinister nature of acts by some hackers, Sterling used his book as a forum for pointing out what he deemed First Amendment infractions against benign computer enthusiasts. Along the way, as a means of providing context, he also included some background history on government organizations such as the Secret Service, as well as a look at the past of the telephone company.

Reviews for *The Hacker Crackdown* were mixed, with much of the criticism aimed at missing or inaccurate dates and information in the book. *Christian Science Monitor* (December 16, 1992) writer Simson L. Garfinkel commented, "Sadly, Sterling's work lacks accuracy on many details . . . he also fails to criticize his heroes, the civil libertarians, although finding such criticism in the law-enforcement community isn't difficult. *The Hacker Crackdown* is a good read, but a bad starting point for setting public policy." The *Financial Times* (March 16, 1993) echoed Garfinkel's statement, saying "This is an interesting but uneven book, in which fascinating facts are sometimes padded out with generalizations and a bit too much discussion of issues."

Another common criticism was that Sterling used computer jargon and hacker slang to the point of overwhelming his prose. As John Naughton wrote for the *Observer* (1993), "his only problem is that deep immersion in this sub-culture has done irreparable damage to his prose style, which has congealed into a sort of jargon-ised treacle." In countering this opinion, Chris Petrakos from the *Chicago Tribune* (November 6, 1992) wrote that the jargon only enhances the book and that Sterling "does an excellent job of explaining the wild and reckless subculture of the hackers," or "techno-cowboys." The end result of Sterling's thorough immersion into the society of hackers and their pursuers, according to Petrakos, is that the book gives its readers "an insider's feel," making it "a valuable addition to that literature [cyberpunk]."

Even Naughton admitted that *The Hacker Crackdown* was a "contentious and reasonably impartial account of the problems posited by 'cyberspace'" and other reviewers, such as Gregory Feeley of *New York Newsday* (December 8, 1992), called the book an "entertaining social history." While admitting that Sterling's vague mention of dates and fuzzy history of the movement's early history would likely "annoy social historians," he concluded that *The Hacker Crackdown* "remains the best account of the beginning of computer crime yet written." Further praise came from *Library Journal* (September 1, 1992), which highly recommended the book as a "well balanced look at this new group of civil libertarians . . . written with humor and intelligence."

The next book Sterling published was *Heavy Weather* (1994), a fictional tale of futuristic "Storm Chasers" set in the year 2031. By this time the buildup of "greenhouse" gases, such as carbon dioxide, in the atmosphere has resulted in severely distorted weather patterns and extreme weather. One result is that a string of deadly tornados rips through Texas and its neighboring states, killing thousands of people every year. The protagonists in Sterling's story, a group of zealous weather researchers who call themselves "Storm Troupers" and who chase the storms through the plains, document the tornados in hopes of coming across the Moby Dick of twisters, a classified "F-6" tornado. At the center of the drama are Jerry Mulcahey, a man eager to be the first to record an F-6 tornado, and Alex Unger, a wealthy, cynical young man who, although dying, is dragged along with the Storm Troupers by his sister.

Reviews for *Heavy Weather* were, for the most part, upbeat and warm. In the *New York Times Book Review* (October 16, 1994), Gerald Jonas wrote, "Mr. Sterling makes obsession seem not only believable, but attractive, and that is sufficient for his purposes. He creates an air of verisimilitude with a seamless blending of current and futuristic weather science." *Library Journal* (August 1994) announced that "Sterling . . . creates a drama of real world and virtual adventure set against the stark landscape of postgreenhouse America. . . . this high-tech disaster novel should appeal to a wide readership." Along the same lines, *Kirkus Reviews* (July 15, 1994) noted, "Sterling shows once more his skills in storytelling and technospeak. A cyberpunk winner." Writing about *Heavy Weather* for *New York Newsday*, (December 25, 1994) Gregory Feeley stated that "Sterling's narrative exuberance and characteristic zest are most immediately shown in his characters, who are invariably colorful, gratingly flamboyant, and passionately involved in the exotic particulars of their world." Feeley also commented on Sterling's characteristic style of writing, which he described as "outlandish, deadpan, mannered, and highly figurative." However, Feeley also noted that a common element of Sterling's novels, the subplot, was conspicuously absent from *Heavy Weather*. "Surprisingly, *Heavy Weather* is narrower in scope than Sterling's previous novels," Feeley wrote. "It contains almost all of the author's strengths, save for the heady sense of pushing the envelope. I hope he's feeling pushier in his next book."

In 1996 Sterling became involved in a project that grew out of his and fellow science-fiction writer Richard Kadrey's interest in extinct forms of human communication. As Sterling told a *New York Times* (March 11, 1996) interviewer, he and Kadrey "got mighty tired of all these eager, glossy, yelping books about the Internet, multimedia, and virtual reality." The pair came to the conclusion that they wanted to read a book that would "confront the postmodern Information Society with the topic it least likes to acknowledge: abject technological failure."

Accordingly, Sterling wrote an article titled "The Dead Media Project: A Modest Proposal and a Public Appeal," which was later published in the Winter 1996 issue of the underground publication *bOING bOING*. In the article Sterling proposed that someone write a book about failed types of media throughout history, which would serve as "a naturalist's field guide for the communications paleontologist." To get the ball rolling, Sterling and Kadrey provided a working title—"The Handbook of Dead Media"—and began an Internet newsgroup devoted to the topic. What resulted was an account of occasions in history when new ideas related to communication proved less than fruitful, one involving the short-lived 1959 experiment in which the U.S. Postal Service arranged for delivery of mail using guided missiles. Such instances of failed media are exactly what Sterling had hoped to uncover in his original manifesto. "There's a peculiar thrill whenever you unearth a particularly outlandish looking specimen," Bruce Sterling told the *Chicago Tribune* (July 7, 1997). "Someday we'll understand what the human race is actually doing to itself with 'media' and I intend to be one of the guys who helps figure this out."

While his "dead media" project continued to move along, Sterling continued to produce science fiction. In 1996 he published *Holy Fire*, a journey set in the 2090s involving Mia Ziemann, a 94-year-old woman who decides to undergo a radical new procedure that makes her young again. With the body of a 20-year-old, Mia makes her way to Europe, where she begins to associate with a group of "vivids," a clan of artists, philosophers, and other social outcasts. While her journey of self-fulfillment leads her toward photography, her newfound group of friends try to uncover the secret of the "holy fire," a type of spiritual epiphany. As Mia struggles to find her own, inner "holy fire" (the creativity and love that were present during her previous youth), readers follow her into the technological playground of the future, where psychedelic drugs and talking dogs are the norm.

This textured mix of the spiritual and the technical led *New York Times Book Review* (December 29, 1996) contributor Gerald Jonas to comment that

"Mr. Sterling understands that salvation in a posthuman world can only be a process, not a prize. He has written a book in praise of ambiguity that manages to find consoling moments of joy in the most unlikely places." Further compliments for the author came from *Spin* (October 1996) reviewer Richard Gehr, who wrote, "a perennial optimist, Sterling strains to dignify and replenish the absence at the heart of existence." Gehr added that, in all, "*Holy Fire* is hardly a page turner. . . . But the books's first and last thirds, consisting mainly of speculative chit chat about age, art, and what actually defines us as human beings, are as gripping as any pulp I've read this year." The critique in *Kirkus Reviews* (August 1, 1996) was less enthusiastic; it acknowledged "some flashes of wit and some good ideas here and there," but criticized *Holy Fire* as reminiscent of concepts Sterling had already explored in past novels. Of the plot, the *Kirkus* reviewer wrote, "We're watching people we don't care about do unsurprising and unedifying things amid interminable pages of chat." Still, a *Booklist* (October 15, 1996) critic found the novel to be right on target, and concluded that "Sterling imagines a totally plausible and often scary future, full of posthumans, wonderful and bizarre new technologies, and strange drugs."

Sterling's most recent novel, *Distraction* (1998), came about as a result of Sterling's coverage for *Wired* magazine of the meltdown the Soviet Union. "I was watching a huge 20th century superpower fall apart at the seams," he told Michael Krantz for *Time* (December 21, 1998). Transferring the situation to the United States in the year 2044, Sterling created Oscar Valparaiso, a political spin doctor, who attempts to change the decrepit American way of life. The book was extremely well-received. Jackie Cassada wrote in *Library Journal* (December 1998), "Sterling's gift for creating sympathetic yet fallible characters adds a vital personal dimension to this cautionary parable of the fall of the American way of life," while *Kirkus Reviews* (November 1, 1998) hailed, "Sterling, our former cyberpunk Svengali, is back with a bang with this uproarious, provocative, thoughtful, often hilarious, sometimes inspired medium-future deconstruction of politics, science, economics, and the American Dream."

Bruce Sterling currently lives in Austin, Texas, with his wife, Nancy Adell Baxter, whom he married in 1979, and their two children. He has recently published a new collection of short stories, *A Good Old-Fashioned Future* (1999).

—D.B.

SUGGESTED READING: *Analog Science Fiction/Science Fact* Dec. 1988; *Booklist* Oct. 15, 1996; *Chicago Tribune* p3 Nov. 6, 1992, p1 July 7, 1997; *Christian Science Monitor* p15 Dec. 16, 1992; *Financial Times* p16 Mar. 16, 1993, Nov. 1, 1998; *Kirkus Reviews* July 15, 1994, Aug. 1, 1996; *Library Journal* Sep. 1, 1992, Aug. 1994, Dec. 1998; *Maclean's* p63 Apr. 29, 1991; *The*

Nation p636+ May 8, 1989, p598+ May 6, 1991; *New York Newsday* p54+ Dec. 8, 1992, p43 Dec. 25, 1994; *New York Times Book Review* Jan. 18, 1987, p30 Oct. 2, 1988, p5 Mar. 10, 1991, p22 Dec. 27, 1992, p40 Oct. 16, 1994, D p5 Mar. 11, 1996, Dec 29, 1996; *The Observer* p57 1993; *Reason* p61+ Nov. 1991; *Spin* p144+ Oct. 1996; *Time* Dec. 21, 1998; *Wall Street Journal* A p7 Nov. 27, 1992; *Washington Post Book World* June 26, 1988, Feb. 26, 1989; *Book Review Digest* 1987, 1989, 1991, 1993, 1995; *Contemporary Authors*, 1994

SELECTED WORKS: Fiction—*Involution Ocean*, 1977; *The Artificial Kid*, 1980; *Schismatrix*, 1985; *Islands in the Net*, 1988; *Crystal Express*, 1989; *The Difference Engine* (with William Gibson), 1990; *Globalhead*, 1992; *Heavy Weather*, 1994; *Holy Fire*, 1996; *Distraction*, 1998; *A Good Old-Fashioned Future*, 1999; Nonfiction—*The Hacker Crackdown: Law and Disorder on the Electronic Frontier*, 1992; As editor—*Mirroshades: The Cyberpunk Anthology*, 1986

Martin J. Desht/Courtesy of Gerald Stern

Stern, Gerald

Feb. 22, 1925– Poet

The American poet Gerald Stern did not publish his first book, *The Pineys* (1971), until he was in his 40s. His first collection of poetry, *Rejoicings* (1972), had only a limited printing, and fame as a poet eluded Stern until his *Lucky Life* (1977) came out. The latter work expressed Stern's confidence

in his own powers, and *The Red Coal* (1981), *Paradise Poems* (1984), *Lovesick* (1987), *Leaving Another Kingdom* (1990), *Bread Without Sugar* (1992), *Odd Mercy* (1995), and *This Time: New and Selected Poems* (1998) bore him out, receiving glowing notices from his fellow poets and critics. *This Time* won a National Book Award. Able to find solace after grief, Stern is a poet of renewal who identifies, often in images of nature, sources of joy. In "Odd Mercy," for example, the source is the ticking of a clock: "a second heart for the cat and after a day / of odd mercy another one for me."

In an autobiographical statement submitted to *World Authors 1990-1995*, Gerald Stern writes: "I was born in Pittsburgh, Pennsylvania in 1925, the second child of Eastern European immigrant parents, Litvak and Ukrainian. They each were the youngest in their respective families, really small children when they came over, and though they were Yiddish speaking they were American to the core, with a passionate commitment to material comfort, new ideas, progressivism, gadgetry, and the future. They were struck a blow in their early 30s by the sudden death of their daughter, Sylvia, my only sibling and barely a year older than I, and never truly recovered. Sylvia's death, and their response, had a lasting effect on me, and only exacerbated my own sense of isolation and loneliness, something caused I'm sure partly by my own sensibility and partly by the fact that I was the only Jew in my elementary school during a time of ugly Jew-baiting, at least where I lived. There were no books, literally, in my house, save a couple of prayer books in Hebrew, and no records or paintings. And no photos. Yet there was a vague respect for reading and thought, given the nature of the religious practices and the fact that my mother's father, a Hebrew teacher and chicken killer, was 'learned.'

"I drew and painted at first but by the time I went to college I was writing poems and stories, though I was majoring in philosophy and economics. However, by the time I was 20, and in the army, I had made a commitment, and after that, in one way or another, I considered myself a writer. I was writing—and publishing—in small magazines in my early 20s, and moreover I had a strong sense of myself as a poet, but I didn't publish my first book until I was well into my 40s, something I can't really explain except to say I was too harsh a critic of my own work, and I couldn't focus my thoughts and feelings in a way that would satisfy me. In a way, I was too self-confident, too complacent, even too lazy, but in my late 30s I 'discovered,' after a terrible bout of depression, everything at once—voice, style, approach, and have been practically besieged by poems from that time on.

"When I first started reading, writing, and practicing the craft with a certain seriousness, in the late 40s and early 50s, there were no writing programs, at least not in Pittsburgh, and no poets or even English teachers to turn to. Nor would there be for years. Moreover, I was on the wrong side of the Allegheny mountains and the 'news' came quite belatedly. What I discovered I did alone, though luckily in the company, a few years later, of two others, Jack Gilbert and Richard Hazley. We were reading Auden, Cummings, Pound, Eliot, Frost, MacLeish, Moore, Jeffers, Thomas, Yeats, Crane. Stevens and Williams a little later. In general we recited or read poems to each other rather than exchanging our poems for criticism. Most of my 20s I spent between New York and Paris, pursuing degrees and buying time, and took my first full-time teaching job in the English department of Temple University in Philadelphia where I stayed for seven years before embarking on a series of other teaching positions at various universities, including Sarah Lawrence College, NYU, Columbia University, the University of Pittsburgh, Rutgers, and, for the last 15 years prior to my retirement in 1995, the Writers' Workshop at the University of Iowa.

"By the mid-'50s I had reduced the poets of the generation before mine I was still interested in to only two, Roethke and Lowell, and, after awhile, I lost interest in Lowell—because of the subject matter, I think, though the music was no longer enticing me. Berryman had not fully surfaced yet, and Bishop hadn't yet published her great poems. In the battle between the formalists and the anti-formalists of the late 50s and early 60s, I was more sympathetic to the anti-formalists and I admired such poets as Creeley, Duncan, Oppen, and Ginsberg, even as I was moving in my own direction, and I felt close to Wright, Bly, Kinnell, Rich, Merwin, as they moved into their new poetry in the early 60s. In the spring of 1966 I was writing short lyrics which I would collect in *Rejoicings: Selected Poems 1966-1972*. These poems marked a radical break from the loose iambics and the ironies of *The Pineys* (1971), the long political poem I started to write in 1958, and the poems which preceded it. With *Lucky Life*, published in 1977, I began to receive wider attention, and my poetry since then—since 1966 really—collected into 11 books, has been 'identifiable,' even as it has changed and developed with time.

"It is difficult to speak of influence. The connection with Whitman is obvious—the long line, *anaphora*, a certain rhetoric, exuberance, first person. But there is also, if I may say so, a profound difference in language, attitude, content, viewpoint, form, tone, vision, *tam*, as we say in Yiddish (taste in the mouth), and in the role of the speaker. I think of Coleridge and Blake and Donne and Marlowe and late Shakespeare and Cavafy and Rimbaud and late Ovid. And, of the moderns, Pound, Yeats, Williams, Crane, Roethke. And Amos and Hosea, Rabelais, Twain, Joyce, Cervantes. After a while, you are only yourself. You become the influence.

"I have, since the beginning, pursued the long poem—*Father Guzman, Bread Without Sugar, Hot Dog*. I am able, in such poems, to allow a more comprehensive consideration for my political and philosophical views, and to allow full rein to dramatic interconnections, and to combine, under one theme, diverse personal and cultural viewpoints. In both *Guzman* and *Hot Dog*, one a poem about a crazed New York Jew obsessed with justice and lost love, who presents himself as a Catholic priest in poverty-ridden central America, the other a poem about a mentally unbalanced African-American street-person, lost in the East Village, I am able to move freely from theme to theme and situation to situation in the manner I love best. My recent short poems, when they are successful, do the same thing, only, perforce, more economically. I am grateful that I was able to do the work I wanted to in this life, as teacher, administrator, and protester against injustice at the same time I was writing poetry; and I am grateful that, as I approach my 74th year, I have three new books in tow, and that I am still besieged."

Gerald Stern, born on February 22, 1925 (the month and day of George Washington's birth), has won renown as a bard in the tradition of Walt Whitman. In 1984, in an interview with Mark Hillringhouse for *American Poetry Review* (April 1984), Stern described the ultimately positive effects of a personal crisis that had involved aging and a sense of failure. Quoting from his essay, "Some Secrets," he told Hillringhouse that "it was my own loss and my own failure that were my subject matter. As if I could only start building in the ruins. Or that loss and failure were a critical first issue in my finding a new subject matter, that they showed me the way. Or that my subject was the victory over loss and failure, or coming to grips with them." In the aftermath of this crisis, Stern recouped his forces and found his poetry coming "easily and simply."

Stern's *Lucky Life* was the Lamont Poetry Selection of the Academy of American Poets and was nominated for the 1978 National Book Critics Circle Award. The title poem is, as Grace Schulman observed, reviewing *This Time: New and Selected Poems* in the *Nation* (May 11, 1998), "a hymn to renewal: 'Lucky you can be purified over and over again.'" Schulman pointed out that whether grim or joyful, "Stern is exuberant in lines whose recurrent images are of dance, song, and light."

Although Stern often writes of unbearably sad and horrific events—the Holocaust for one—using images that evoke anguish, overall he is a poet of recovery, of cleansing. The *Choice* (February 1970) reviewer of *Lucky Life* wrote, "In the centrally placed, representative title poem, Stern muses on 'moments of peace and pleasure, as I lie in between the blows.'. . . And his own catharsis is partially a remembrance of things past, the salvaging of a personality from decaying places and disappointing relationships, and the recognition of current attitudes toward the formative influences of Nietzsche and Van Gogh."

Jane Somerville was to point out in an essay in *American Poetry Review* (September/October 1989), later included in *Making the Light Come:*

The Poetry of Gerald Stern (1990), that Stern himself observed, "Maybe the subject of the poem [that is, all poems] is always nostalgia." Stern distinguished between "conventional nostalgia fits" and "the essential memory." The "vibrance" of a poem, Somerville added, "rests on a synergy of opposed yet simultaneous emotions: the pain of separation and the sweetness of remembered—or imagined—union."

The poet Hayden Carruth, reviewing *Lucky Life* in *Harper's* (June 1978), characterized Stern's poems as "doomsday among the tricycles and kittens." He remarked that while most poets who attempt Stern's approach to poetry succeed only in creating "trite magazine verse," Stern himself succeeds. The tone, according to Carruth, "of every poem—well, almost every—is . . . genuine, clear, compelling, right for its occasion."

The Red Coal, Stern's 1981 collection, drew one of the few negative comments Stern has received. Joseph Garrison wrote in *Library Journal* (March 15, 1981), "An early poem in *The Red Coal* contains these lines: 'I understand a delicacy and a mournfulness / that neither Nietzsche my one love / nor Van Gogh my other / could help me with, for all their knowledge and purity.' The rest of the book preens a similar solipsism." Other critics, such as Vernon Shetley in the *New York Times Book Review* (May 10, 1981), disagreed. "Alternating between conversational speech and slightly surreal outbursts, Stern's work achieves its effects through accumulations of rhetorical weight or sudden flashes of disjunctive imagery. . . . In poem after poem," Shetley continued, Stern "sets out for himself some temptation to despair over which he wins a lyrical triumph." The volume won the Melville Caine Award of the Poetry Society of America.

Robert Hudzik in *Library Journal* (August 1984), reviewing *Paradise Poems*, remarked that Stern's lyrics "are characterized by a ritualistic unfolding of voice, through lists, repetition, litany, creating songs of praise for the everyday. . . . Stern is one of our most musical poets, and in this volume he is able 'to convert / death and sadness into beautiful singing.'" Edward Hirsh, writing in the *Nation* (January 19, 1985), termed Stern "a romantic with a sense of humor, an orphic voice living inside history, a sometimes comic, sometimes tragic visionary crying out against imprisonment and shame, singing of loneliness and rejuvenation, dreaming of a social justice and community. . . an ecstatic Maimonides writing his own idiosyncratic guide for the perplexed."

In Stern's collection of (mainly) love poems, *Lovesick*, "the emphasis is on the poet himself in the role of Everyman; and there is a cosmopolitan, Jewish sensibility evident in the point of view that is at once sad, passionate, and ultimately positive," according to L. Berk, the *Choice* (January 1988) reviewer. Louis McKee in *Library Journal* (September 1, 1987) termed the entries in *Lovesick* "loving poems, gentle but not the least bit fragile." Stern

"long ago secured his place as one of our finest poets," he asserted.

Leaving Another Kingdom: Selected Poems elicited the comment from Bettina Drew in *Library Journal* (February 15, 1990) that Stern's was "an unending quest to understand the kaleidoscopic mystery of individual experience." Preoccupied in this volume with the American experience, Stern looked at an America "populated less by cultural landmarks than by grief and loss," according to Drew. For Steven Cramer, writing in *Poetry* (November 1990), Stern presented himself as "the dancing rabbi" and drew "on Hasidic tradition to eulogize Jewish historical sadness." He termed Stern "one of our most clear-eyed celebrants of the epiphanic occasion."

"Stern's eighth volume of poems would be memorable even if it included only the long, elegiac title poem and 'The Bull Roarer,'" L. Berk wrote of *Bread Without Sugar* in *Choice* (October 1992). "Like Whitman, Stern includes a large, raw, vanishing world in his poems and there is an honesty here that is at once adventuresome and profound," Berk concluded. David Baker in *Poetry* (November 1992) compared Stern to Robert Bly in his "rhetorical purity" and "unabashed ecstasy." He observed that "Stern brings a kind of shamelessness, an Old World elan and directness, to contemporary poetry. He's a seer and a singer during a time of carefulness and timidity."

Odd Mercy is divided into two parts. The first is a collection of shorter poems, many about Stern's mother and father and others elegies for lost friends. The second part of the volume consists of the long poem "Hot Dog," named for a homeless, mentally disturbed African-American woman Stern has seen on the streets of the East Village in New York. Hot Dog herself is the peg on which he hung his meditations on his own life in the neighborhood and his past: "I / who wanted to tell her how sorry I was, who longed / to know where she came from and know her true name and talk / about school with her and how it was she broke / away—and when—I tried to talk but we / couldn't reach each other—not that way."

Frank Allen in *Library Journal* (November 15, 1995), reviewing *Odd Mercies*, intimated that "Hot Dog" was one of Stern's "long difficult poems that defy reason but stir the imagination. With bizarre tension they end up where they start, craving mercy, illuminating 'dreary mysteries' of memory." He concluded, "Afraid of displacement, Stern takes delight in old, sad wisdom. For over two decades, no one has equaled his compassionate, surreal parables about the burden of and the exaltation at being alive."

"'The greatest joy is rising,' Gerald Stern wrote recently of stumbling into a manhole, and that dark rapture characterizes his art," Grace Schulman began her *Nation* (May 11, 1998) review of *This Time: New and Selected Poems*. "Stern's achievement is immense," she continued. "The poem quoted at the beginning of this review, 'Saving My Skin From

Burning,' is one of many (I count six of my favorites) that do not appear in this still splendid collection. . . . Following Whitman's example, Gerald Stern invites others to assume his joys and sorrows, his hard thanksgiving for the day's gifts: 'Now I brood, I grimace, how quickly the day goes, / how full it is of sunshine, and wind, how many / smells there are, how gorgeous is the distant / sound of dogs, and engines. . . .'"

Deborah Garrison concluded her review of *This Time* in the *New Yorker* (November 16, 1998) by observing that Stern's "desire to be pierced through by some arrow—be it poetry, love, or what he calls 'another insane devotion'—gives his verse an amplitude that is too often missing from contemporary poetry. 'I will have to tell you what it is like," he says about sleeping under the stars:

since I was the one lying on my back
with my arms in the air
. . . trying to make up my mind
whether it was a early heaven just being
or whether it was another bitter vertigo.

"Stern's encompassing embrace allows us to step into his delirium and experience both," Garrison wrote. *This Time* won a National Book Award for poetry in 1998.

Stern, in an essay entitled "Notes from the River," published in *American Poetry Review* (June 1987) referred to his dwelling places, reminiscing about them as "caves," and explains that "it may be just that caves are perfect locations— metaphors—for our instinctive, and extreme, philosophical and poetic states." After his meditations on the past, he described a search for "a leaf to read my future by." "I will follow the leaf's contour," he concludes. "I mean to say that I will begin again with empty pockets, as I always do. I mean to say that in the archways and the moss-grown tufa rocks, on the railroad tracks and the rusted cars, in the wall-hangings and the torn rugs and the multi-colored books, I will look again for wisdom."
—S. Y.

SUGGESTED READING: *American Poetry Review* p19+ Apr. 1984, with photo, p41+ June 1987, p39+ Oct. 1989; *Choice* p1649 Feb. 1978, p770 Jan. 1988, p302 Oct. 1992; *Harper's* p86 June 1978; *Library Journal* p664 Mar. 15, 1984, p1453 Aug. 1984, p186 Sep. 1, 1987, p189 Feb. 15, 1990, p79 Nov. 15, 1995; *Nation* p55 Jan. 19, 1985, p49+ May 11, 1998; *New Yorker* p103+ Nov. 16, 1998 with illustration; *New York Times Book Review* p12 May 10, 1981; *Poetry* p110 Nov. 1990, p99 Nov. 1992

SELECTED BOOKS: *The Pineys* , 1971; *Rejoicings*, 1972; *Lucky Life*, 1977; *The Red Coal*, 1981; *Paradise Poems*, 1984; *Lovesick*, 1987; *Leaving Another Kingdom*, 1990; *Bread Without Sugar*, 1992; *Odd Mercy*, 1995; *This Time : New and Selected Poems*, 1998

Suarez, Virgil

Jan. 29, 1962– Novelist; short-story writer; poet

The Cuban-born American author Virgil Suarez writes, he has said, to answer the question of who he is. His novels *Latin Jazz* (1989), *The Cutter* (1991), *Havana Thursdays* (1995), and *Going Under* (1996), his short-story collection, *Welcome to the Oasis* (1992), and his book of poems, prose poems, essays, stories, and photographs, *Spared Angola: Memories from a Cuban-American Childhood, 1962–1996*, which constitutes a memoir, deal with the experience of life in the United States from the point of view of Cuban immigrants—as well as with universal, eternal questions of human existence. Suarez has also compiled a number of anthologies. With his wife, Delia Poey, he edited *Iguana Dreams: New Latino Fiction* (1993) and *Little Havana Blues: A Cuban-American Literature Anthology* (1996), and with Victor Hernandez Cruz and Leroy Quintana he compiled *Paper Dance: 55 Latino Poets* (1995). His books have won increasing praise from reviewers.

For *World Authors 1990-1995*, Virgil Suarez, born on January 29, 1962, writes: "The question I am often asked is why do I write only about Cubans and more precisely about Cuban-Americans, and

Courtesy of Virgil Suarez

the answer is always the same: I can't write about anything else. I am consumed by the voices of my culture and heritage. I was born in Havana, Cuba in 1962. In 1970 my parents took me out of the country and we traveled to Madrid, Spain. Those eight years I spent in Havana left such a mark on me that I always feel that I could never exhaust the rich memories of those years—everlasting material to write about, I feel, for the rest of my life. I don't remember all that much about Madrid, other than the fact that my parents as well as all their friends and relatives abroad knew they would be living in exile indefinitely. It's been almost twenty-five years of exile for my parents. We moved to Los Angeles, California, in the fall of 1974, and there I would spend the next decade. Formative years without a doubt, but I still continued reaching back to my infancy and early childhood of the late sixties in Cuba.

"I came to writing about the Cuban-American condition because some crucial part of me felt singled out. Upon the advice of several of my teachers in college and later at the universities I attended, I started to write about my cultural heritage and background. I was constantly being asked where I was from. I felt I needed to answer as clearly as possible, so I wrote novels, short stories, poems as answers. My first novel written, second published, *The Cutter*, was such an attempt at answering. This book is quite autobiographical, except that most of what Julian Campos, the main character in the book, goes through is what my father went through. I think there's quite a bit of me in this book as well. The images and sounds come from the same personal well, only thinly disguised as fiction.

"I wrote *The Cutter* while I worked and went to school in California. I sold shoes on the weekends, went to California State University at Long Beach on weekdays. I wrote feverishly, as if possessed by some crazy notion that something terrible was going to happen to me—thank heavens I am still around to write this. After I graduated in 1984, I was accepted to do graduate studies at the University of Arizona. There I finished the work on *The Cutter* and started many of the short stories later collected in my only book of stories to date: *Welcome to the Oasis*. I also started work on *Latin Jazz*, a novel triggered by the Peruvian Embassy break-in in Havana on April 6th, 1980, when a bus commandeered by some desperate Cubans stormed into the embassy to seek asylum. I followed that incident blow by blow, part of me knowing that I was going to do something with what turned out to be the Mariel Exodus from Cuba. *Latin Jazz* came to me quickly and I wrote it, I think, within the time span of a year. It and *The Cutter* I feel were my learning books. I had a great deal of fun writing them, but I also remember all the long hours, sometimes entire weekends passed and I wouldn't go out of my room. Again, I wrote under the same crazy urgency—that I wouldn't live past 30.

"By 1987, I had graduated with an M.F.A. from Louisiana State University where I had studied and befriended Vance Bourjaily, one of my most important creative father figures. I couldn't find a teaching job right away, so I moved to Miami where my parents had moved to in 1985. Also, my father had had a disabling accident, and I felt I needed to be home with my mother to help out.

"I started teaching at a high-school in South Florida where I met my wife of almost a decade now. Delia Poey, I have to say, saved me from the self-destructive course I had charted for myself in Miami. She brought (and still does) meaning to my life. She's a wonderful human being, friend, and editor. She got me back on track with the writing, so we married, had children, and I've entered one of the most productive periods of my life. I have written two novels since we met, *Havana Thursdays* and *Going Under*, a collection of poems titled *Spared Angola*, and jointly we have edited two anthologies: *Iguana Dreams: New Latino Fiction* and *Little Havana Blues: A Cuban-American Literature Anthology*.

"All my work relates back to the Cuban-American experience. Life on the hyphen, as my friend and fellow writer Gustavo Pérez Firmat calls it. I am fortunate to have such a good life as a writer, surrounded by the nourishments of family, friends, and fellow Cuban-American writers who are producing some of the most exciting literature written this decade.

"Cubans and Cuban-Americans have made some lasting contributions not only to South Florida but to the entire United States. I feel the work so many of us are producing is a splendid record. My work deals mainly with the preservation of self and family in the United States.

"Politics and history, of course, are always in the background, and they do help inform my narratives and my work, but I am mainly in the business of telling stories. That's all I care to do, and believe me the time passes quickly, and in the wake of its passing, what joys, what pleasures, what a lucky and charmed life!"

Virgil Suarez's first published novel, *Latin Jazz*, traces a family's odyssey from Cuba to Los Angeles. The family is desperate to escape from the clutches of Fidel Castro, who has just come to power, but the overwhelming task of Americanization comes to dominate their lives. In this novel Suarez was concerned with bringing the plight of the Mariel refugees to the consciousness of the people of the United States, as well.

The Cutter, the first novel Suarez wrote and the second he published, also explores the particularities of Cuban-American life, this time with a protagonist who works as a cutter in the garment industry—Suarez's father's trade. This book, too, it is an expression of Suarez's search for his roots.

By the time of the publication of *Welcome to the Oasis and Other Stories*, Suarez had found a publishing home with Arte Publico, dedicated by its founder and publisher, Nicolas Kanellos, to the publication of Chicano literature and run under the auspices of the University of Houston. These stories, too, explore intimately the undersurface of Cuban-American life. In each, a young man is at a turning point in his life. A Cuban painter from the Mariel boat lift becomes embroiled in the affairs of an apartment complex he is painting and winds up in the clutches of the violent boss; a teenager is forced to sell ice cream for his father and breaks psychologically with the old man; another young man recalls a trip to New Orleans with three friends—an adventure in which they took drugs, met a young woman, and tried unsuccessfully to get her away from her alcoholic boyfriend. *Kirkus Reviews* (April 1, 1992) called the book "a tightly controlled but affecting exploration of fundamental tensions in a community for whom Suarez is becoming an eloquent and promising voice." James Polk in the *Philadelphia Inquirer* (June 28, 1992) saw *Welcome to the Oasis* as a chronicle of failure: "The horizons of life, which in their Latin American homelands were wide despite all hardship, become for Suarez's characters dim and shriveled in the land of opportunity. Where formerly people struggled to transcend their suffering, here in Gringoland they struggle to get through the day."

In *Havana Thursdays* the voices are mainly those of women: " a garland, a necklace of voices . . . beautiful and lasting," as Suarez told the press he wanted to create. The women are the wife, mother, daughters, daughter-in-law, sister-in-law, and niece of an agricultural expert, a Cuban emigré to Florida, who has died on a trip to Brazil. The family gathers to mourn him and gather their own strength as well. Sydney Trent in the Miami *Herald* (November 21, 1995) found the voices of the characters lovely indeed. "With a seductive style that combines simplicity with fine descriptive detail, [Suarez] invites us to care about his characters." Overall, however, Trent felt that something was missing: "Though the Torres women come together for the funeral, their distinct voices never mesh meaningfully." Mariela Meléndez in *Hispanic* (October 1995) observed that *Havana Thursdays* "effectively presents two important aspects of Latino culture: the family union and the role of the woman as its keeper." "You can feel the author rooting for his women characters as they attempt to break the double binds they're caught in and struggle to balance the need for privacy and independence— American values—with Cuban traditions of family solidarity," Suzanne Ruta wrote in *Newsday* (October 1, 1995).

Going Under is the story of a man's failure. Xavier Cuevas, an insurance salesman in Miami, pushes himself endlessly to fulfill the demands of "the American dream." He has a lovely wife, two children, a dog, a comfortable house, and all the other accoutrements of middle-class American life. He sees his partner, Wilfredo, as maintaining closer ties to the Cuban roots Xavier has discarded. Wilfredo, to Xavier's exasperation, persists in speaking English with an accent and pursuing women with more energy than he pursues new business.

When Xavier (he prefers Xavier to the Spanish-sounding Javier) breaks down in depression, Wilfredo sets in motion a chain of events that leads Xavier to a practitioner of Cuban *santería*. Xavier undergoes a ceremony of *limpieza y llamada*, "cleansing and summons," which involves going "back to the beginning," in order to "come in contact" with his old self. The narrator explains:

> At school no one ever made fun of him because he didn't look like an outsider. An immigrant. A wetback. He fit in and so the children left him alone. That was the beginning of the transition in the unbalance of identity. More American, less Cuban. He was second generation. For all practical purposes, he got by, and that was the problem.

Xavier's partner has advised him to stop analyzing himself, to "go with the flow." His final act is to go to the southernmost point of the United States, from which he can see Cuba, and start swimming toward his homeland. Lawrence Olszewski termed the novel in *Library Journal* (September 15, 1996) a "more successful attempt at dealing with the Cuban-American experience than Suarez's earlier *Latin Jazz*."

As a poet, Suarez occupies himself with the same themes that inform his novels and stories. His poem "The Wood Sculptor," which appeared in the *Massachusetts Review* (Winter 1995-96), is a portrait of an old wood carver:

> Oh the wood, wood like his worn
> hands, blistered, cracked & scarred.
> His eyes focus hard on the work
> as he knows the way to make the
> talk, come alive. He won't give up
> until he's done with everything.

For Suarez, this amounts to a statement of purpose for his own life's work. In addition to writing, Suarez teaches creative writing at Florida State University. His companions, in addition to Delia Poey and their children, include 100 canaries and a dog named Mongo, after Mongo Santamaria, the Cuban percussionist. Suarez's well-received, 90-page poetry volume *You Come Singing* was published in 1998.
—S. Y.

SUGGESTED READING: *Library Journal* p98 Sep. 15, 1996; *Herald* p2 Nov. 21, 1995; *Hispanic* p80 Oct. 1995; *Philadelphia Inquirer* M p3 June 28, 1992; *Contemporary Authors* vol. 131, 1989

SELECTED BOOKS: Fiction—*Latin Jazz*, 1989; *The Cutter*, 1991; *Welcome to the Oasis and Other Stories*, 1992; *Havana Thursdays*, 1995; *Going Under*, 1996; Nonfiction—*Spared Angola: Memories from a Cuban-American Childhood, 1962-1996;* Poetry—*You Come Singing*, 1998; As editor—*Iguana Dreams: New Latino Fiction* (with D. Poey), 1993; *Paper Dance: 55 Latino Poets* (with V. Hernandez Cruz and L.V. Quintana),

SU TONG

1995; *Little Havana Blues A Contemporary Cuban-American Literature Anthology* (with D. Poey), 1996

Su Tong

1963– Novelist

The Chinese writer Su Tong belongs to the post-Mao generation of young "New Wave" writers that came to prominence in China in the 1980s, producing experimental and avant-garde fiction. He has published 10 novels and collections of novellas and short stories, many of which have been translated into English and European languages. Notable among his works are the three novellas included in *Qi-qie Chengqun*, published in English in 1993 as *Raise the Red Lantern* (one of the novellas was adapted for film by Zhang Limou); the novel *Mi* (*Rice*, 1995); and the story "The Brothers Shu," published in 1993 and again, two years later, in a collection of new works from China, *Chairman Mao Would Not Be Amused*. Li Shaohong's 1996 film, *Blush*, is based on Su's earlier, untranslated novella, *Hong Fen* (1991, Ladies of Pleasure). Many of these works draw on pre-revolutionary China to create strange worlds of myth and legend, decadence and perversion, sex, violence, and alienated youth.

Born Tong Zhonggui on in 1963, in Suzhou, the southern city of gardens and canals known as the "Venice of the East," Su Tong began his schooling in his hometown and in 1980 enrolled in the Chinese department of Beijing Normal University. Upon graduation he chose to work in Nanjing, the old "southern" capital of China, where he still lives with his wife and daughter. After a brief stint as a teacher, he started writing professionally and joined the editorial staff of *Zhongshan*, one of the major literary magazines known for fostering new talent.

Su Tong had started writing at an early age and had won a composition prize in junior high school. After a series of rejection slips from editors, Su Tong got his first break in 1983, during his last year in college, when he published a short story. Taking advantage of the relative freedom of the post-Mao era, he became known as one of a new group of younger Chinese writers—apolitical, amoral, detached, cynical, and cool—who no longer felt compelled to appeal to society or address sociopolitical issues. Drawing from tradition and from the West, they consciously engaged themselves in creating a new kind of writing to express their individual senses of beauty and meaning. Su Tong soon emerged as one of the most outstanding writers in this group, which includes Mo Yan, Yu Hua, Can Xue, Liu Heng, and many others who are increasingly recognized outside China through film and translations. In 1987 a special literary seminar to discuss Su Tong's works was convened in Beijing.

Among these contemporary avant-garde writers, Su Tong is conspicuous for his skill at spinning stories that mesmerize with their anguished moods and richly evocative images. He is constantly preoccupied with mystery, irrationality, obscenity, decadence, doom, and death, and his characters present a disturbing panorama of beastly greed, demonic villainy, hunger for power, or doom through sexual obsession, though even his villains can be pitifully vulnerable under the caprices of fate.

Some of Su Tong's stories are grouped around certain localities whose bucolic names mask the human turmoil played out there, such as a Maple Village or a Cedar Street in a seedy little southern China town whose character is symbolized by a dirty river where condoms and dead babies regularly turn up. These interconnected stories of death and decay in imaginary locales have prompted comparisons with Faulkner, a writer Su Tong admires.

In "The Brothers Shu," translated by Howard Goldblatt in 1995 for the collection *Chairman Mao Would Not be Amused*, some of Su Tong's favorite topics are woven together: alienated youth; the returned native; and perverted sexuality. In this story, the narrator has come back to his old town after 15 years and pieces together from hearsay the story of his former classmate Shu Nong, a young criminal genius and bedwetter. Within the confines of an ordinary working-class environment, the story is full of sadistic cruelty, animal instincts, perverted behavior, and incest. Family life is dysfunctional, with mother and daughter, father and son, and husband and wife locked in deadly hatreds. The story takes place in 1974, during the Cultural Revolution, yet there is nothing political in the destructiveness that occurs. *Chengbei Didai* (The North Part of Town), a novel set in the same small town, continued the theme of rootless and self-destructive youth against the background of the post-Mao period.

The theme of escape figures prominently in many of Su Tong's works. In the short story "Escape," a half-witted peasant named Sanmai is driven by an existential compulsion to escape his circumstances: "Except for figuring out how to run away, you'd never know what else Sanmai wanted to do," wrote Su Tong. Sanmai escapes his wife to be a soldier; he runs away from the front and escapes to the northeastern forests to work as a forester, but dies under a felled tree just as his wife catches up with him. Sanmai's only interest was making kites, a symbol of escape. But even in death he barely escapes, for the kites he makes are like pennants that summon his soul back to life.

In his longer fiction, Su Tong is best known for his family sagas, which he handles with great skill to explore some of his favorite themes. In one of the novellas in *Raise the Red Lantern*, *Yijiu Sanjiu Nian de Taowang* (*Nineteen Thirty-four Escapes*), he ties together the themes of escape and the rise and fall of family clans. The story is set in Maple Village, where most of the inhabitants share the same family name. There, the sinister landlord Chen Wenzhi, always nursing a precious jade jar in his hands, oversees his estate from a tall black brick mansion while the peasants are bent over his rice paddies. The peasant Chen Baonian, grandfather of the narrator, leaves his wife, Jiang, and goes to town, making a fortune from bamboo products, while their eldest son, Gouzai, collects dog manure for fertilizer. In this multiplotted story, many symbols compete for attention: the jade jar containing extracted semen that later spills and causes a pestilence; the dusty road luring the men into town; the pestilential bog in which the dead lie rotting; the mysterious fire that destroys Chen Wenzhi's mansion; and the special bamboo-cutting knife that was to be Gouzai's patrimony. As the story progresses, Jiang is accused of bringing a curse on the family, and Chen Baonian's blind assistant masterminds his master's death and takes over his bamboo business. The ultimate "escape" is engineered by one Huanzi, Chen Baonian's mistress in town, who kidnaps and rears Jiang's last baby, the boy who was to carry on the family line, taking him far away from the Maple Village.

Another of Su Tong's family sagas, also set in Maple Village, is the novella *Yingsu zhi Jia* (Poppy Family, translated as *Opium Family*), also included in *Raise the Red Lantern*. This story of the accursed Liu clan, like that of the Chens in *Nineteen Thirty-four Escapes*, is also steeped in crime and perversity. In it, the patriarch Old Liu sells his daughter Suzi (from his first marriage) to an impotent old man for land and cheats his half-witted brother of his burial plot. Old Liu had also appropriated his father's former concubine Phoenix, who gives birth to a son, Chencao, who is actually fathered by a field hand, Chen Mao. Old Liu shuts an eye to the boy's true origin and brings him up as his heir. A crisis looms when bandits besiege Old Liu's mansion and demand either Chencao or Suzi. Caught between his blood daughter and his bastard heir, Old Liu gives up his own daughter. The second crisis occurs later when Chen Mao becomes the Communist leader and rapes Suzi as one of his first spontaneous acts of revolution, thus putting Chencao in the position of avenging his half-sister and vindicating the family honor by killing Chen Mao, his biological father. *Opium Family* thus personalizes the Communist revolution of the 1940s by portraying it as an overthrow of all familial, patriarchal ties.

Raise the Red Lantern is Su Tong's best-known work in the West. This is a tale of sexual intrigue played out during a time of social ferment—the story of a wife and three concubines competing for one man's favors. But it has an economic subtext, for behind the obvious competition for desirability is another desperate competition: for productivity. In the patriarchal society of this fiction, the women can insure their future only by begetting sons, perpetuating a system described by the patriarch Chen as he speaks of his third concubine: "She wants to lord it over me, but women will never lord it over

men." Ironically, his dominance brings about his impotence; in his approaching old age, women, once his playthings, have become threats to his safety. According to Su Tong, men dominating women in the social world is counterbalanced by women destroying men in a sexual context. Chen's only son and heir, the homosexual Feipu, is portrayed as being afraid of women, an expression of the disproportion of yin and yang in the house of Chen and a predictor of its inevitable doom. In this world, harmony can be restored only by the killing off of the women.

Although permeated by a general air of decay, Su Tong's fictional world never pursues decadence as an aesthetic end in itself. Exploration and revelation is at the core of this author's often disturbing fiction as he uses descriptions of decadence as a metaphor for the decay of the world in general or to explore the mystery of the human condition and the fearful retributions of fate. Su Tong is very skillful at using symbols. In his explorations of human perversion, for instance, one of Su Tong's favorite devices is to identify his characters with animals, especially cats. The cat image thus becomes an archetype for the perverted human, such as the "all-seeing" Shu Nong, the "catty" third concubine Meishan, or the "sinister" daughter Suzi.

The novel *Rice* centers on the demonic figure Five Dragons, who begs his way into town, marries the boss's daughter, and takes over the family's rice business while heading the local underworld. From a starving peasant, Five Dragons evolves into a monster, defined only by his obsession with rice and hellbent on revenge for his past poverty and humiliations. His family life is filled with loathsome violence as his business falls apart in the lawless world of the 1930s, but he is finally defeated when the bastard of his first wife—by now a Japanese collaborator—tortures him to death.

In his review of *Rice* for the *New York Times* (November 13, 1995), Richard Bernstein wrote that Su Tong was among a group of Chinese writers who were rejecting the Communist party's "good-news-only literature" in favor of a past tradition, which exposed and criticized the corruption of an earlier China with its "obedience to superstition, its blind patriarchal authority, and the meanness, spitefulness, and self-deceit of a people rubbed raw by hardship and backwardness." In lauding Su Tong as the author of "this powerful, irritating, bawdy, profane, and utterly bleak history of a Chinese family," Bernstein placed him squarely in the tradition of such earlier realists as Ba Jin and Lu Xun, writing that "in the case of Su Tong's *Rice*, the vision that has resulted is grimmer and more grotesque, weighed down by a pessimism that exceeds even that of his literary forebears."
—E. M.

SUGGESTED READING: *Booklist* p1945 July 1993; *Library Journal* p98+ June 15, 1993; *New York Times* A p25 Nov. 13, 1995; *New York Times Book Review* p12 July 25, 1993, p37 Oct.

22, 1995; *Washington Post Book World* p3 July 9, 1995, p10 Jan. 28, 1996; *World Literature Today* p389+ Summer 1991, p634 Summer 1994, p869+ Autumn 1995; *Columbia Anthology of Modern Chinese Literature*, 1995; Tonglin, L. *Femininity and Masculinity in Su Tong's Trilogy*, 1995

SELECTED BOOKS IN ENGLISH TRANSLATION: *Raise the Red Lantern*, 1993; *Chairman Mao Would Not Be Amused*, 1995; *Rice*, 1995

Svoboda, Terese

Sep. 5, 1990– Poet; film director; playwright; translator; novelist

Courtesy of Terese Svoboda

Although her literary work thus far has been largely in the genre of poetry, Terese Svoboda is best known for her breakthrough first novel, *Cannibal* (1994). A stark, realistic journey through Africa's Sudan desert region, *Cannibal*, based on Svoboda's own experiences, probes such issues as the role of the female in Third World nations. In addition to being a poet and novelist, Svoboda is a successful writer and producer of videos.

In an autobiographical statement submitted to *World Authors 1990–1995*, Svoboda writes, "I was born in Ogallala, Nebraska [on September 5,] 1950, eldest of nine children. My mother was an excellent painter, my father an attorney/gentleman rancher. My father drove to work; we did not live on a farm. An uncle, a professor of English, wrote poetry. After graduating from Ogallala High School, I attended Manhattanville College just outside of New York City for two years, majoring in philosophy. I spent a term at Oxford, Montreal Museum of Fine Arts, Stanford University and University of Colorado and finally graduated with a double B.F.A. in creative writing/studio arts with honors in both from University of British Columbia. Having worked my way through college, I spent a year in Boston selling pretzels, working as a magician's assistant, and making ceramic sculpture. In 1975, I was accepted in the Columbia University master's program for writing.

"I left graduate school for a year to travel around the world with a film crew, spending six months in the Cook Islands waiting for a boat that never came and a year in the Sudan, translating from the Nuer and making a documentary on Nuer women. Before leaving New York, I had received a PEN/Columbia grant to learn the Nuer language on the grounds that a poet could better translate literary works than a linguist. My experiences in Africa were akin to being reborn, having to rethink everything from basic survival to etiquette in the Third World.

"I obtained my master's degree from Columbia in 1978, winning the John Golden Award in playwriting that year which resulted in having my play produced off-Broadway. My education in British Columbia had suggested that writing in any genre was allowed, a European concept that often did not meet with American approval. When I found that my experiences abroad could not be contained in the poetry I was writing, I began working on a novel. I was trying to make sense of a woman's place in the world while experiencing both the sexual upheaval in my own country and the clearly defined roles of women in countries with different socio-economic perspectives. Everywhere I went in the Third World I had no position because I had no child. In the U.S., after I had a child, I had no position.

"At the time I was also translating the songs I had collected from the Nuer and working full-time at Columbia's Translation Center developing a 5-part film series on oral poetry around the world. By 1980 I had written and produced the pilot for *Voices & Visions*, a 12-part PBS series on American poetry. After my child died tragically in 1982, I left the series and returned to what I felt most strongly about—telling my own stories.

"In 1985, *All Aberration*, my first book of poetry was published, containing poems on my Nebraska childhood but also many poems on sorrow. That year also saw the publication of *Cleaned The Crocodile's Teeth*, the translations from the Nuer language I'd gathered in the Sudan. Rosellen Brown selected it for the "Writer's Choice" column in the *New York Times Book Review*.

"I continued to write for music videos, taught writing of any kind, curated a cable series for artists, and co-wrote scripts with my husband. After five years of struggling with my novel, I abandoned it and converted the material into the title poem of my second book of poems, *Laughing Africa*, which won the Iowa Prize in 1990. Most of that book explores finding one's place in a world of Thirds and Firsts and the actual people who live in New Zealand and Papua New Guinea and Africa. I had worked hard to reject the narcissistic voice brooding on lost love and event in order to take responsibility for what could be done. This book also contained "The Ranchhand's Daughter," a long Jeffers-like poem on incest between father and daughter.

"Out of my frustrations with making fiction, I began to experiment with video. At the time, most videomakers were fascinated solely with image or satire, few told stories. After seeing Chris Marker's short films, *Le Soleil* and *La Jetté*, I knew at least the essay form was possible. After writing and producing ten experimental videos which were exhibited and awarded prizes worldwide, I co-curated *Between Word and Image* at the Museum of Modern Art to highlight how the two can work together to create metaphor beyond illustration.

"In 1990, Gordon Lish, an editor at Knopf and former fiction editor of *Esquire*, accepted a story of mine and asked me to join his fiction class. His method of brutal insistence on the primacy of the word over its transparency within a work of fiction allowed me to completely rewrite my African novel. In 1994, *Cannibal* won several prizes and publication by New York University Press—only fifteen years after I'd first begun writing it. In the novel, a voice guides the reader through the terrors of Africa and a nightmarish partnership. It received a full page review in *Vogue* which opened up a new avenue of revenue—writing for magazines. Along with publishing many short stories in the following years, I also published a good deal of nonfiction, including a piece on my sister who had been permanently brain-damaged by the air in her EPA office which I turned into a video, later part of the "New Directions" series at the Museum of Modern Art.

"In 1995 *Mere Mortals* was published, my third book of poetry. It contained my 38-page version of Marlowe's "Faust" and a 40-part poem on a high school reunion, both dealing with how we try to trick death. Derek Walcott, one of my favorite contemporary poets at the time, often worked long and I had hoped to catch his breath.

"After twenty-five years of living in NYC, we are now moving to California where my husband will be working as a high-tech inventor. We have two children."

Reviews of Svoboda's poetry and fiction have been positive. About her second collection of poetry, *Laughing Africa*, the *Publishers Weekly* (March 30, 1990) reviewer wrote: "This urgent, spirited collection ranges in tone and subject matter from the vehemently political to the deeply personal. . . . Svoboda's vision is not entirely bleak . . .

and she pursues a recovered, Whitmanesque innocence as symbolized by the fertile, primitive landscape 'where we began': Africa." The favorable review of *Laughing Africa* concluded, "In deftly crafted poems alternately hard-edged, sensual, and tender, Svoboda delicately balances a harsh, yet convincing, indictment of Western culture with an equally ardent belief in the possibility of human compassion and responsibility."

Svoboda's third book of poetry, *Mere Mortals*, also garnered her high praise from critics. A *Library Journal* (August 1995) reviewer wrote glowingly of Svoboda's range in subject matter—the poems delve into everything from divorce to nature and religion—and concluded by writing that "In all, Svoboda's outlandish wit . . . stuns the face of culture's illusions like lightning. Negotiating a 'wacked-out' path to rueful wisdom, she casts a cold eye at love beyond innocence at the end of the 20th century." Similarly, *The Boston Review* (1996) carried a positive assessment of the work. "Few young poets today write with an imagination, ambition, and breadth of interest comparable to those of Svoboda. A resident of two of America's farthest reaches [New York City and Hawaii], no aspect of the cultural tarpaulin stretched out in between escapes her scrutiny." Referring to *Mere Mortals* as "keenly incisive, slightly hysterical reading," the critic lauded the writer for her skillfully unconventional manipulation of language: "Svoboda writes in defiance of expectation; her poems skew and contort, often masterfully, but not without running occasional risks. . . . Her long, deconstructive 'Faust' is a bit unmanageable, and there seem to be certain, softer emotions that she has steeled herself against." *The Boston Review* concluded that Svoboda "favors the shrill. But for the most part, she triumphs, wriggling out of her own verbal knots with the energy and wit of a sideshow star."

Svoboda's first novel, *Cannibal*, received impressive write-ups as well. *Vogue* (January 1995) writer Mark Richard was impressed with the breadth of Svoboda's first-person narrative, which he called "an obsessive monologue told in a measured whisper, desperate, chilling, seductive." He went on to comment that this type of narration "alters the novel's clock in much the same way terror slows the working of the mind, the mind suspending each bit of information one piece at a time to exhaust its possible meaning, trying to seek meaning." *Library Journal* (December 1994) found the narration similarly impressive, if somewhat difficult: "Many readers will find the narrator's interior monologue daunting as they try to keep up with who's who. But Svoboda deserves praise for this work." Babette Fraser Hale of the *Houston Chronicle* (February 26, 1995) frankly advised that "this novel is [not] what anyone would call an easy read. The uninflected prose style, in fact, seems designed to prevent quick or thoughtless consumption." She also acknowledged, however, that the difficulty of the prose reinforced the authenticity of Svoboda's first-hand experiences in Africa. Hale wrote that "the realism of the setting grounds the story and releases its power. And *Cannibal* is very powerful. It depicts a mortal struggle with both psychological and physical dimensions in one of the planet's more hostile environments."

In the quarterly publication *Rain Taxi Review of Books* (Fall 1994), Jessica Roeder admitted that the book is stark in its language, but agreed that a sense of gritty realism makes the story gripping. The reviewer bluntly stated that "*Cannibal* is not prettified. In fact, Svoboda offsets more than a century of white travel writing . . . that has in one way or another romanticized Africa, even when Africa is just a backdrop for the writer's solipsism." Roeder added that "the narrator's understated voice—working with her low-decibel, almost subliminal humor—keeps us alert to the story as language. The words and sentences are beautiful, even tactile, objects." Commenting that Svoboda "has achieved complexity and substance," Roeder concluded with the assessment that "*Cannibal* is a clever book, a well-crafted and somewhat crafty book. As such, it is also refreshingly resonant with emotion . . . it deserves, and rewards, multiple readings. With re-reading, her prose becomes—like the poems in her recent book *Mere Mortals*—more darkly humorous and more tragic." A *Kirkus Reviews* (October 15, 1994) critic, one of the few who found *Cannibal*'s distinctive qualities off-putting, called the book a "moving, albeit flawed, debut."

Svoboda's second novel, *A Drink Called Paradise*, recounts the story of a woman on a sojourn on a remote Pacific island following the accidental death of her child. While living with the natives, the woman must come to terms with her new habitat and its culture and with the discovery that the island may have been exposed to radiation. *Publishers Weekly* (March 15, 1999) called the book a "demanding, worthy novel," while *Kirkus Reviews* (February 15, 1999) found it "wonderfully written, though bafflingly obscure. Svoboda writes in a meditative style that seems incapable of containing a narrative, much less relating it."

In addition to her Iowa Prize for *Laughing Africa*, Terese Svoboda was awarded the Bobst Prize for *Cannibal*. She has also been a National Endowment for the Humanities translation fellow and a Jerome fellow for video.
—D.B.

SUGGESTED READING: *The Boston Review* 1996; *Houston Chronicle* p23+ Feb. 26, 1995; *Kirkus Reviews* Oct. 15, 1994, Feb. 15, 1999; *Library Journal* Dec. 1994, Aug. 1995; *Publishers Weekly* Mar. 30, 1990, Mar. 15, 1999; *Rain Taxi Review of Books* p38+ Fall 1994; *Vogue* p84 Jan. 1995; *Contemporary Authors*, 1995

SELECTED WORKS: Fiction—*Cannibal*, 1994; *A Drink Called Paradise*, 1999; Poetry—*All Aberration*, 1985; *Laughing Africa*, 1990; *Mere Mortals*, 1995; as translator—*Cleaned the Crocodile's Teeth*, 1985

Ray Ronci

Swick, Marly

Nov. 26, 1949– Novelist; short-story writer

Despite a relatively small body of published work, Marly Swick has developed a reputation as a polished writer of emotionally rich fiction. Her work often deals with characters who are living in the wake of tragedy. She first gained recognition as a writer of short stories, which have been collected in two anthologies, *A Hole in the Language* (1990) and *The Summer Before the Summer of Love* (1995). Her first novel, *Paper Wings*, was published in 1996, and her second novel, *Evening News*, in 1999.

In an autobiographical essay submitted to *World Authors 1990–1995*, Swick writes: "I was born in Indianapolis, Indiana, [on November 26,] 1949, and lived there about two weeks. Then we moved to Missouri, Georgia, Massachusetts, Delaware, California, and Michigan. My father worked for General Motors and was transferred every four or five years. My parents would bribe me with a canopy bed or a puppy because they felt bad about making my younger sister and me start over at new schools. I went to college in California—Mills College and Stanford University—where I majored in Creative Writing. After college, I stayed in the Bay Area and worked as a salesgirl at India Imports in Palo Alto (until I was robbed at gunpoint), a book store in San Francisco, a toy store, and so on until I couldn't stand it any more and went back to school to get a Ph.D. in American Literature at The American University in Washington, D.C. After getting my doctorate [in 1979], I couldn't find a job teaching literature and wanted to migrate back to California, so I ended up teaching Legal Writing at

Southwestern School of Law in L.A. (whose graduates include Marcia Clark and Christopher Darden). My fourth summer at the law school I went on a trip to Thailand and Bali. I came back in time for the fall semester but realized I couldn't stand another year there and quit my job instead. I started writing fiction again and, for the first time, actually sent out a couple of short stories. A year later, in 1984, my first story was published in *Redbook* the same week I arrived in Iowa City to start the Writers' Workshop, which a friend of a friend had suggested that I apply to.

"For the next couple of years, I continued to write and publish stories in a variety of magazines: *Redbook*, *The North American Review*, *Iowa Review*, *McCall's*, *Playgirl*, *Gettysburg Review*, *Indiana Review*, *The Atlantic Monthly*, *Colorado Review*, *O'Henry Prize Stories*, and others. Every time I was desperate for money and circling the Want Ads, I was lucky enough to be rescued by a grant that gave me another year to write—a James Michener Award [1986], a University of Wisconsin Creative Writing Institute Fellowship [1987], an NEA grant [1987]—which kept me afloat until I got hired by the University of Nebraska in 1988 to teach fiction writing. In 1990, my story collection entitled *A Hole in the Language* won the Iowa Short Fiction prize and was later published by HarperCollins in paperback under the title *Monogamy*. A second collection, *The Summer Before the Summer of Love*, was published in 1995, followed by *Paper Wings*, a novel, in 1996. I have now lived in Lincoln, Nebraska, twice as long as I've ever lived anywhere else and am still not acclimated to winter. I live with Ray Ronci, a poet/musician/painter, and am a part-time stepmother to his nine-year-old son, Robert."

Marly Swick was born to David Edward Swick and Margaret Catherine (Hailey) Swick. She received her B.A. from Stanford in 1971. In addition to her Ph.D. from American University, Swick also earned a Master of Fine Arts degree from the University of Iowa in 1986. Since 1987 she has been an assistant professor at the University of Nebraska.

Her first book of stories, *A Hole in the Language* (1990), met with positive reviews. Mark Dery of the *New York Times* (January 20, 1991) described the stories in *A Hole in the Language* as "cunningly wrought" and "deliciously bitter." He praised the way in which Swick's writing travels between two extremes, passing "between life's almost unbearable barrenness and it's sorrowful, sensual fullness."

Her second short-story anthology, *The Summer Before the Summer of Love* (1995), like *A Hole in the Language*, looked at the plights of upscale and sophisticated characters trying to achieve emotional well-being. One of the stories, "Heart," features a 10-year-old whose mother hallucinates that her estranged husband has returned to her. In "Elba," a middle-aged woman cares for her obstinate mother, who is dying of cancer.

In a *New York Times* (December 12, 1995) review of *The Summer Before the Summer of Love*, Michiko Kakutani lauded the stories as allegories for the general fragility and precariousness of life. "Writing in strong, unsentimental prose, Ms. Swick . . . ushers the reader into her character's well-lighted, pleasantly upholstered lives," Kakutani wrote, "then slowly and methodically reveals the fears, resentments, and sadnesses hidden there in the corners and the shadows." She praised the author's psychological insights into her characters, and declared that Swick "firmly establishes herself as a gifted practitioner of the art of the short story." Michael Gorra, who reviewed the collection for the *New York Times Book Review* (October 15, 1995), lauded the realism of Swick's stories, which he felt was often due to her willingness to leave elements of the plots unresolved. "What's startling . . . is the precision with which Ms. Swick's clear and unobtrusive prose defines an intricate emotional landscape," Gorra commented, "a precision that in itself produces a kind of thrill."

Swick continued to explore the emotional results of tragedy and loss in her first novel, *Paper Wings* (1996). The book focuses on a suburban housewife in the 1960s ominously named Helen Keller. Her depressing life is given new purpose during John F. Kennedy's presidential campaign, in which she takes an active part. With the assassination of the president, Helen slips into a deeper depression than ever before, and her entire family begins to fall apart. In an attempt to regroup, she takes a sabbatical with her 12-year-old daughter, Suzanne, to her hometown of Troy, Nebraska, where Suzanne gains a profound understanding of her mother.

As with her story collections, Swick's first novel was generally well-received by critics. A review in *Publishers Weekly* (May 27, 1996) applauded Swick's effective portrayal of family dynamics, particularly the relationship between mother and daughter. The novel is described as "beautifully composed and controlled, and steeped in the small details that produce emotional veracity." Lauren Picker of *New York Newsday* (July 14, 1996) cited the mother-daughter trip to Nebraska as the novel's most powerful section.

Swick's most recent book, the novel *Evening News* (1999), follows the suffering of a family after its youngest member is accidentally shot by her nine-year-old half-brother, Teddy, who narrates the book along with his mother, Giselle. Fearing that the sensational nature of the plot would have a detrimental effect on the writing in the novel, the reviewer for *Booklist* (October 1, 1998) happily noted that "[Swick] has avoided all the pitfalls of commercialization and written a powerful and dignified family tragedy." Most other reviews of *Evening News* were favorable. The critic for *Kirkus Reviews* (December 15, 1998), for example, thought it was "overlong, and its insights into the psychology of grief and guilt are unexceptional," but nevertheless deemed it "an engrossing domestic melodrama," and Michiko Kakutani of the *New York Times* (February 23, 1999) wrote, "[Swick's] account of Giselle and her family . . . remains so moving that the reader doesn't really care if the book's ending is a little too shapely, a little too pat, more the 'Lassie' version of real life, than the evening news." —B.S.

SUGGESTED READING: Booklist Oct. 1, 1998; *Library Journal* p164 July 1996; *New York Newsday* C p27 July 14, 1996; *New York Times* VII p26 Jan. 20, 1991, VII p38 Oct. 15, 1995, C p22 Dec. 12, 1995, with photo; *Publishers Weekly* p65 May 27, 1996

SELECTED WORKS: *A Hole in the Language*, 1990; *The Summer Before the Summer of Love*, 1995; *Paper Wings*, 1996; *Evening News*, 1999

Courtesy of Arthur Sze

Sze, Arthur

Dec. 1, 1950– Poet

Arthur Sze, an American poet of Chinese descent, has been termed an artist of Zen by various reviewers, because of the focus on mindfulness—a main tenet of Zen—in his work. Sze's collections *The Willow Wind* (1972), *Dazzled* (1982), *Two Ravens* (1984), *River River* (1987), and *Archipelago* (1995) contain poems that resemble ancient Chinese poetry in that the natural world is linked with a state of mind. In all of his poems he is concerned, as he says of "Archipelago," with the "one and the many." Rochelle Ratner stated in *Library Journal* (July 1995) that Sze's "vivid imagery proves we can

indeed achieve unity through diversity." As Sze wrote in "The Leaves of a Dream Are the Leaves of an Onion," published in *River River*, "No single method can describe the world: / therein is the pleasure / of chaos, of leaps in the mind." Sze won a Lannan Literary Award for poetry in 1995.

For *World Authors 1990–1995*, Arthur Sze, born on December 1, 1950, writes: "I was born in New York City. Like many Asian-Americans, I grew up with a high priority placed on math and science. I attended a private high school, Lawrenceville, and did extremely well in those subjects. In 1968 I enrolled at MIT, and it was there that, one day, bored in class, I began to write. A few days later I found myself writing again. Soon I was writing all of the time and knew I had discovered a deeper and more exciting challenge. In the fall of 1969, Denise Levertov came to MIT. I submitted a group of poems and was accepted into her writing class.

"In 1970, I decided to transfer to the University of California at Berkeley. In May, I hitchhiked three thousand miles west to California. I enrolled at UC Berkeley and, in the fall, took a writing class with Josephine Miles. I developed an independent studies major in poetry, and Josephine became my advisor. I often met with her on Saturday afternoons at her house and was fortunate to receive a rigorous and inspired response to my early writing. From 1970-72, I also studied conversational Chinese and classical Chinese poetry. I began to read character by character through many of the great Chinese poems by Li Po, Tu Fu, and Wang Wei. As a deliberate poetic apprenticeship, I decided to make a series of translations of classical Chinese poems.

"I published my first book, *The Willow Wind*, privately, in 1972. It included a section of poems as well as a section of translations from the Chinese. After graduating from the University of California at Berkeley (B.A., Phi Beta Kappa, 1972), I knew that I did not want to go to graduate school. I felt that I needed to earn my own voice and that I needed to travel, work, and write. I left California and traveled during the summer in Mexico and Guatemala. I walked across the bridge from Ciudad Juárez into El Paso and hitchhiked up to Santa Fe in one day. I was amazed by New Mexico: it felt like it was still outside of the rest of the United States.

"So, I have lived in New Mexico since 1972. I have made a number of journeys that have influenced my writing (Europe: 1969, 1971, 1976; China: 1985; Japan 1990) but Santa Fe has become my home. For ten years, 1973-83, sponsored by the New Mexico Arts Division, I worked as a poet in the schools. It was a wonderful way to experience the richness and diversity of New Mexico. I conducted residencies at Jemez Pueblo, Santo Domingo Pueblo, Las Vegas, Ojo Caliente, Española, Bernalillo, Los Alamos, Santa Fe. Sponsored by the Santa Fe Council for the Arts, I also conducted residencies at the New Mexico School for the Deaf and the Penitentiary of New Mexico. In later years, sponsored by the Alaska Arts Council, I conducted residencies at Edna Bay (1985) and Anchorage (1989). During the early years, I also worked in restaurants and did construction work. I remember going hungry: at one point I had only lemonade and bologna sandwiches in the refrigerator.

"From 1978 to 1995, I was married to Ramona Sakiestewa, a Hopi weaver. Our son, Micah, is now sixteen. Since 1984, I have taught at the Institute of American Indian Arts and in 1989 became Director of the Creative Writing Program. The Institute currently has 168 students who represent over sixty tribes across the United States. Native American culture—particularly Pueblo culture—has thus been a strong influence on my writing.

"In looking at the evolution of my work--*The Willow Wind*, *Two Ravens*, *Dazzled*, *River River*, *Archipelago*—I believe there has been a significant leap from book to book. My first two books—*The Willow Wind* and *Two Ravens*—each contain a section of classical Chinese translations as well as my own poems. The translations include work by T'ao Ch'ien, Li Po, Tu Fu, Wang Wei, Li Ho, Li Shang-yin, Ma Chih-yuan, Li Ch'ing-chao, and Wen I-to. It is a poetic lineage I draw heavily on. *Dazzled* is the first book that consists entirely of my own original work. Organized in four sections, I had in mind the intuitive structure of a string quartet. *River River* has to do with synchronicity and is arranged in one continuous motion.

"In 1990, I traveled in Japan and was amazed by the Zen garden at Ryoanji. There fifteen stones are set in a sea of raked gravel. The stones are arranged in clusters and are set in the gravel at varying depths. One of the startling features of the garden is that you can never see all fifteen stones at the same time. I used this fact as a metaphor for experience and created the title poem "Archipelago," as a meditation on existence. The book *Archipelago* resembles a series of islands. Its epistemology incorporates the one and the many: each poem and each sequence of poems has its unique configuration, but they are part of a larger whole."

Arthur Sze has pursued the dream of being an independent poet, free to wander and to write what he wants, partly by teaching poetry workshops in prisons. Such contradictions and contrasts have dominated his life and his poetry. In "Viewing Photographs of China," from *Dazzled*, the first book Sze published that consisted only of his original poetry, he set forth the poetic ideal from which he has never deviated:

And, in perusing
the photographs in the mind's eye,
we discern bamboo, factories,
pearls; and consider African wars,
the Russian Revolution, the
Tierra Amarilla Courthouse Raid,
And instead of insisting
that the world have an essence, we
juxtapose, as in a collage,

facts, ideas, images:
The arctic
tern, the pearl farm, considerations
of the two World Wars, Peruvian
horses, executions, concentration
camps; and find, as in a sapphire,
a clear light, a clear emerging
view of the world.

Sze continued to shed the clear light of his gaze on a collage-like variety of subjects in *River River*, but this time admiring what he calls the "synchronicity" of the universe. In the second stanza of "The Leaves of a Dream Are the Leaves of an Onion," he observes a separation between disparate parts of creation in a series of comparisons: "A Galapagos turtle has nothing to do / with the world of the neutrino. . . . / The invention of the telescope / has nothing to do with a red jaguar." But he corrects himself: "No, the invention of the scissors / has everything to do with the invention of the telescope. . . . / The man who sacrifices himself and throws a Molotov / cocktail at a tank has everything to do / with a sunflower that looks to the light." He concludes the poem with an ironic echo of William Butler Yeats: "The pattern of interference in a hologram / replicates the apple, knife, horsetails on the table, / but misses the sense of chaos, distorts / in its singular view. Then / touch, shine, dance, sing, be, becoming, be."

The widely praised volume *Archipelago* garnered the Lannan Prize for Poetry. Again, Sze employed recurring images. In the first stanza of "Archipelago," for example, Sze presented ". . . a line of Pueblo women dancing / with black-on-black jars on their heads; they lift / the jars high then start to throw them to the ground." In the fourth stanza a woman ". . . puts jars in a pit, covers them with sawdust, / adds a layer of shards and covers them, / . . . . She will not know/ for a few hours if the jars have turned completely / black and did not break cooling. . . . " And in the fifth stanza the dancers appear again: "They raise the jars with macaw and lightning patterns / to the six directions then form a circle / and throw them down on the center-marking stones." These images, like the others in the poem, are evoked by the stones in the Zen garden of the Ryoanji monastery in Kyoto, Japan. M. Bugeja, reviewing the book for *Choice* (February 1996), observed that those who had a knowledge of Zen and ancient Chinese poetry might get more from it than others. "But an existential fool for the absurd will do nicely," Bugeja admitted. "Sze's poems juxtapose nature images with state of mind in the classic Asian style. . . . and suggest, by juxtaposition, that all works lose meaning in translation," Bugeja added, implying that all poetry is a form of translation.

Rochelle Ratner in *Library Journal* (July 1995) observed that Sze "translates the poet's spiritual quest into memorable imagery." She found his form reminiscent of the Persian ghazal used by Adrienne Rich and Mark Strand. She noted further that Sze's poems are "meditative and philosophical" and "avoid rhetoric by cutting off their imagery midair."

Arthur Sze has been a contributing editor for *Tyuonyi* since 1985. He has served as editor of *Cuentos III*, an anthology of writing by inhabitants of nursing homes and members of senior centers in northern New Mexico. He has read his poetry at such venues as the Naropa Institute in Boulder, Colorado; the Poetry Project at St. Mark's Church in New York City; and various universities throughout the United States.

Sze's *The Redshifting Web: Poems 1970–1998* appeared in 1998.

—S. Y.

SUGGESTED READING: *Choice* p953 Feb. 1996; *Library Journal* p 85 July 1995

SELECTED BOOKS: *The Willow Wind*, 1972, rev. ed. 1981; *Two Ravens*, 1976, rev. ed. 1984; *Dazzled*, 1982; *River River*, 1987; *Archipelago*, 1995; *The Redshifting Web: Poems 1970–1998*, 1998

Tapahonso, Luci

1953– Poet; short-story writer; professor

Luci Tapahonso, a celebrated Native American poet and children's author, uses images from her childhood in her poetry, depicting modern Navajo life with realism and lyricism and mixing Navajo and English words while remaining true to the foundation of her writing—the storytelling tradition of her ancestors. Her first two collections of poems, *One More Shiprock Night* (1981) and *Seasonal Woman* (1982), were published while she was studying for her master's degree. She has since authored, among other works, two additional collections of stories and poems—*Saanii Dahataal: The Women Are Singing* (1993) and *Blue Horses Rush In* (1997)—and an alphabet book for children, *Navajo ABC* (1995), illustrated by Eleanor Schick.

Luci Tapahonso was born in Shiprock, New Mexico, in 1953, the daughter of Eugene and Lucille (Descheene) Tapahonso. The fifth of nine children, she grew up on a farm in a family of Navajo ancestry. Her first language was Navajo; she learned English when she began attending school at the Navajo Methodist Mission in Farmington. In an interview with the *Chicago Tribune* (September 5, 1993), she admitted that she is unable to write Navajo, though she can still speak it and uses it in her poetry and fiction. She began writing poetry at the age of nine.

Tapahonso served on the board of directors of the Phoenix Indian Center in 1974. By the late 1970s she was participating in a training program for investigative journalism at the National Indian Youth Council, but she switched to creative writing when, as a college student at the University of New Mexico, in Albuquerque, she became acquainted with Leslie Marmon Silko, a noted Native American author, who encouraged Tapahonso. With her background as the middle child of a large Navajo family, the young author realized that she had many wonderful stories from her own experiences to write about. "All I was doing really was rewriting stories I had heard, stories I had known," she told Steve Paul of the *Chicago Tribune* (September 5, 1993). "The more I learned about poetics and theory, and the more I read what are considered the classics in poetry . . . I realized there was a really strong connection between literary forms and the oral Navajo tradition." In 1980 Tapahonso received her bachelor's degree; three years later she earned an M.A. in English, also at the University of New Mexico.

While working toward her master's degree, Tapahonso published her first collection of poetry, *One More Shiprock Night* (1981), which was illustrated by her first husband, Earl P. Ortiz. She quickly followed this collection with *Seasonal Woman* (1982), illustrated by R. C. Gorman. This latter collection received an honorable mention from the American Book Awards in 1983.

From 1984 to 1986 Tapahonso served as a member of the New Mexico Arts Commission Literature Panel and taught at the University of New Mexico. In 1985 she received the excellent instructor award from the university and in 1986 was named one of the Top Ten Women of the Navajo Nation by *Maazo* magazine. From 1987 to 1989 she taught as an assistant professor of English at the University of New Mexico. During this period, she published an additional collection of poetry, *A Breeze Swept Through* (1987), and received a New Mexico Eminent Scholar Award from the New Mexico Commission of Higher Education in 1989.

In 1990 Tapahonso relocated to Lawrence, Kansas, where she joined the staff of the University of Kansas as an assistant professor of English. Three years later she published her long-awaited follow-up to *A Breeze Swept Through*—*Saanii Dahataal: The Women Are Singing* (1993), a cycle of stories and poems that describe the author's memories of Shiprock and the people she knew while growing up. This collection was widely and favorably reviewed. "Imagine yourself in a Navajo home near sacred Shiprock, listening to tales that both define and transmit the ancient ways told casually as people go about the business of living. Now you can imagine Tapahonso's work . . ." Pat Monaghan wrote in *Booklist* (March 1, 1993). "Tapahonso provides us with a true bridge to her culture and its spiritual insights." Lisa A. Mitten of *Library Journal* (March 15, 1993) concurred: "Tapahonso here celebrates the importance of conversation and the spoken word among her people. . . . this gifted writer recalls snatches of family memories and tribal songs through the intermingled forms of poetry, songs, prayers, and anecdotes. Ranging across Navajo history, this collection in English and Navajo is warm and witty." Despite some minor criticisms, B. Almon, writing in *Choice* (September 1993), also found the book generally appealing: "The writing occasionally lets nostalgia do the work of craft, especially in the prose pieces, but this is a book in which the whole is greater than the sum of its parts." In the *New York Times Book Review* (October 31, 1993), David Biespiel praised: "Ms. Tapahonso speaks the observed and spiritual world into existence." Tapahonso received a Southwest Book Award from the Boarder Library Association in 1994 for this work.

In 1995 Tapahonso published *Navajo ABC: A Diné Alphabet Book*, her first children's book, with illustrations by Eleanor Schick. In this straightforward alphabet book aimed at ages four to eight, Tapahonso included a glossary that gives the English translations for the Diné words. The book received positive notices. In her review for *Booklist* (December 15, 1995), as reprinted on the *Amazon.com* Web site, Karen Hutt opined that "the contemporary focus on a specific tribe is a welcome change from works that clump all Indians together in a historical context without mentioning individual languages." Reviewing the book for *Student Library Journal* (December 1995), Lisa Mitten remarked, "Tapahonso has created a wonderful introduction to her people and their language, and Schick's pastel pencil drawings are a perfect complement."

Tapahonso's most recent publication, *Blue Horses Rush In* (1997), is a collection of poems. Like its predecessors, the book takes its inspiration from the author's life, particularly from her experiences as a Navajo woman at the end of the 20th century. However, it was the author's intense focus on the spirituality of her people that drew some criticism from reviewers. Blake de Pastino from *Weekly Wired* (September 2, 1997) wrote that "the emphasis is placed so squarely on tradition, so heavily on spirituality, that Tapahonso seems to lose her narrative footing. For every well-wrought character or truly insightful story, there are two more pieces of sentimental excess." The reviewer went on to note, however, that Tapahonso "is an ongoing metamorphosis. Although this latest project lacks the best of what we know her for, there's still no telling where she will take us next."

Luci Tapahonso has been married twice. With her first husband, Earl Ortiz, an artist, she had two children: Lori Tazbah and Misty Dawn. She has three stepchildren—Robert Derek, Jonathan Allan, and Amber Kristine—from her marriage to Bob G. Martin, whom she married in 1989. Tapahonso continues to teach, now as an associate professor of English, at the University of Kansas and has received numerous awards for her writing, including a 1992 Hall Creative Work fellowship from the University of Kansas, the 1995 Frost Place Poet-in-Residence Award, and the 1998 Regional Book Award from the Mountains and Plains Booksellers Association. She has worked for a large number of associations, among them the Modern Language Association, the Association of American Indian and Alaska Native Professors, Habitat for Humanity (board of directors 1990–94), the Telluride Institute Writers Forum Advisory Board (since 1992), and the Kansas Arts Commission (as commissioner 1992–96).

—C.M.

SUGGESTED READING: *Booklist* p1150 Mar. 1, 1993, Dec. 15, 1995; *Chicago Tribune* VI p2 Sep. 5, 1993; *Choice* p125 Sep. 1993; *Hanksville* (on-line) Mar. 6, 1999; *Internet Public Library* (on-line) Mar. 6, 1999; *Library Journal* p81, Mar. 15, 1993; *Luci Tapahonso by Frances A. Scott* (on-line), Mar. 4, 1999; *New York Times Book Review* Oct. 31, 1993; *Student Library Journal* p100 Dec. 1995; *Weekly Wired* (on-line) Sep. 2, 1997

SELECTED WORKS: Poetry—*One More Shiprock Night*, 1981; *Seasonal Woman*, 1982; *A Breeze Swept Through*, 1987; *Saanii Dahataal: The Women Are Singing*, 1993; *Blue Horses Rush In*, 1997; Nonfiction—*Navajo ABC: A Diné Alphabet Book*, 1995

Terkel, Studs

May 16, 1912– Nonfiction writer

Studs Terkel, the radio and television personality and author of several best-selling oral histories, has had a variegated career. The gifted interviewer has been a radio and stage actor, sports columnist, disc jockey, playwright, journalist, lecturer, and host of music festivals. In the 1940s Terkel launched the first of his many talk shows, managing to attract a mass audience without making concessions to commercialism. He has since carried on his quest to record history as seen through the eyes of the "common people," noncelebrities who have experienced life fully. It is from these people, Terkel believes, that we can learn the most valuable lessons about ourselves and our society.

Like the late social anthropologist Oscar Lewis, Terkel has shown that the tape recorder can be an enormous asset to social research, dramatizing the thoughts and emotions of those anonymous and faceless Americans who might otherwise be known only as mere statistics. He has used that instrument with consummate skill to compile several penetrating studies of American life that were commissioned by the publishing house of Pantheon Books, in New York City. The first, *Division Street: America* (1967), tapped the sources of conflict that savaged urban America in the 1960s. It was followed in 1970 by *Hard Times: An Oral History of the Great Depression*, which consisted of personal memories of the 1930s and enriched our understanding of that era. One of Terkel's most revered contributions to what he calls "guerrilla journalism," *Working: People Talk About What They Do All Day and How They Feel About What They Do* (1974), transcribes with immediacy and power the frustrations that trouble contemporary attitudes toward work in the United States. His other works include *The Good War: An Oral History of World War Two* (1984), *Race: How Blacks and Whites Think and Feel About the American Obsession* (1992), and *Coming of Age: The Story of Our Century by Those Who've Lived It* (1995).

The third son of working-class parents, Studs Terkel was born Louis Terkel in the Bronx borough of New York City, on May 16, 1912. When he was about 11, he moved with his family to Chicago, where he has lived most of his life. Like Nelson Algren, Terkel developed indissoluble ties with that city and with its vast industrial population, whose problems impinged on his consciousness even when he was a boy. His father, Samuel Terkel, a tailor and superb craftsman, was eventually invalided by a heart ailment, but his mother, Anna (Finkel) Terkel, whom he remembers as a "tough little sparrow" of a woman whose pince-nez glasses were always slipping down her nose, helped to support the family by taking over the Wells-Grand Hotel for blue-collar workers, skilled mechanics, and craftsmen on the North Side near Chicago's Loop, in 1926. He has affectionate memories of that establishment and of his talks with the roistering workers who got drunk there on Saturday nights until the Great Depression transformed their paychecks into welfare checks. From 1925 through 1928, when he attended McKinley High School on Chicago's West Side, he became acquainted with another aspect of the city—its gangster element, which flourished in the Prohibition era.

Until 1934 Terkel's parents were not too badly hit by the Depression. By then they had managed to put him through two years at Crane Junior College, another two at the University of Chicago, where he received a Ph.B. in 1932, and three "traumatic" years at the University of Chicago Law School, which, he says, he entered "dreaming of Clarence Darrow—and woke up to see Julius Hoffman." Disenchanted with law when he obtained his J.D. degree in 1934, and having failed his first bar examination, Terkel accepted a $94-a-month job with the government, doing statistical research on unemployment in Omaha, Nebraska. After that he moved on to Washington, D.C., where he literally "counted" the baby bonds that veterans of World War I received as bonuses. To relieve the tedium, he acted in the Washington Civic Theatre and earned rave reviews for his performance as Shad Larue, the villain in a dramatized version of Sinclair Lewis's novel about American fascism, *It Can't Happen Here.*

In 1935 Terkel returned to Chicago, where he joined the Federal Writers Project and, along with such associates as Richard Wright and Nelson Algren, turned out weekly radio shows on WGN, Colonel Robert R. McCormick's station. Those led to assignments as an actor in such radio soap operas of that era as *Ma Perkins* and *Road of Life*, in which he usually played a gangster who came to a sudden and violent end. "With script in hand, I read lines of stunning banality," Terkel recalled in his preface to *Working.* During the late 1930s he returned to the stage with the Chicago Repertory Theater, and around that time rechristened himself "Studs," after Studs Lonigan, the protagonist of James T. Farrell's lumbering and elephantine novels about the Chicago proletarian Irish in the years before and during the Depression era.

In the early 1940s Terkel became an established voice on Chicago radio, first as a news commentator and sportscaster, then as a disc jockey who, in addition to knowing his way around folk music, jazz, and opera, promoted new talents such as the great gospel singer Mahalia Jackson. In 1945 he established *Wax Museum*, the first of the diversified radio programs he has since conducted on station WFMT, Chicago. In that, as in *Studs Terkel Almanac*, launched in 1958, he exhibited an uncanny flair for engaging people in spontaneous interviews, thanks to his warmth, curiosity, and empathy. Those same traits marked his first venture into television, a program called *Studs Place*, which, using a fictitious barbecue joint as its setting, featured banter between the bartending Terkel, his waitress, his house jazz pianist or folk singer, and any distinguished guest who might drop in. The basic idea behind *Studs Place*, which lasted from 1949 to 1953, was that "honest human relationships can make for good televiewing." The same conviction accounts for the success of his radio programs.

The 1950s and the 1960s were kaleidoscopic decades for Terkel. He wrote a jazz column for the *Chicago Sun-Times* and managed to find time to continue his stage career, with appearances both in Chicago and in summer stock in *Detective Story* (1950); *Of Mice and Men* and *Time of Your Life* (1952); *A View from the Bridge* (1958); *Light Up the Sky* (1959); and *The Cave Dwellers* (1960). His introduction to American jazz for young fans and neophytes, *Giants of Jazz* (1957), contained brief biographies of such titans as Bessie Smith and Louis Armstrong. He moderated panel discussions, lectured, narrated documentary films, and hosted the 1959 and 1960 Newport Folk Festivals, the 1959 Ravinia (Illinois) Music Festival, and the 1961 University of Chicago Folk Festival. Terkel's work in the mass media brought him several coveted awards during this period, including first award from Ohio State University in 1959 for *Wax Museum*, which was rated the finest cultural program in the regional radio category; the UNESCO East-West Values award in 1962 for best radio program; the Prix Italiana; and the Communicator of the Year award from the University of Chicago Alumni Association in 1969.

Intent on exploring new genres, in 1959 Terkel wrote a play entitled *Amazing Grace*, about a troubled family operating a sleazy urban hotel. It was not performed, however, until 1967, when the University of Michigan's Professional Theatre selected it for production out of one hundred plays by new playwrights that had been submitted to it. But Terkel's debut as a playwright was none too promising. Despite a generous budget, skilled directing, and an able cast headed by Cathleen Nesbitt and Victor Buono, *Amazing Grace* drew sharply divided reviews. Although the critics of the *Detroit Daily Express* and the *Toledo Blade* acclaimed it as a sterling drama, reviewers for *Variety* and the *New York Times* found it a "tasteless work" whose "earnest message" failed to deliver.

Given his extraordinary ability to strike up a rapport with "the man of inchoate thought" and his exceptional talent for in-depth interviews, it is not surprising that the literary form to which Terkel ultimately gravitated was oral history. In 1967 he published the first of his triptych of best-selling, tape-recorded works, *Division Street: America*, consisting of transcripts of 70 conversations he had had with people living in or near Chicago, including racketeers, landladies, steelworkers, bar owners, John Birchers, window washers, slum dwellers, executives, religious leaders, and social workers. He set out not with a thesis but with a desire to listen, to elicit the spontaneous feelings and opinions of representative Americans.

"The portable tape recorder . . . is for better or for worse," Terkel wrote in his introduction to *Working*. "It can be . . . a means of blackmail, an instrument of the police state or, as is most often the case, a transmitter of the banal. Yet a tape recorder, with microphone in hand, on the table or the arm of the chair or on the grass, can transform both the visitor and the host. . . . It can be used to capture the voice of a celebrity, whose answers are ever ready and flow through all the expected straits. I have yet to be astonished by one. It can be used to capture the thoughts of the non-celebrated—on the steps of a public housing project, in a frame bungalow, in a furnished apartment, in a parked car—and these 'statistics' become persons, each one unique. I am constantly astonished."

To Terkel, *Division Street* in Chicago was merely a metaphor for the divisiveness that he thought typified every major American city in the 1960s. The interviews themselves seemed to confirm that, since they not only revealed character in a remarkable way but also dramatized the antipathies of rich and poor, old and young, black and white, along with their common despair at the dehumanization of city life. In his long review of *Division Street: America* in the *New York Times* (February 5, 1967), Peter Lyon observed that it resembled "a modern morality play, a drama with as many conflicts as life itself, and as many remorseless, kindless villains." Many critics concurred, although a few detected a sentimental and populist bias in Terkel—a tendency to bypass some of the more ruthless Chicago inhabitants and focus on essentially decent people whose flaws can be attributed to corruption by society.

As if to refute that minority of critics, Terkel's next book, *Hard Times: An Oral History of the Great Depression* (1970), adopted a broader range of inquiry and a wider perspective. From interviews with 100 Americans, both famous and unknown, who had lived through the Great Depression or its peripheral years, he put together a "memory book" that, he said, has less to do with "hard facts" than the "small triumphs" of those who weathered that protracted ordeal. Thus the present generation of students and workers could rediscover a past they knew only in general terms, through academic history books. Terkel concentrated exclusively on personal memories and, in so doing, discovered a significant aspect of the Depression that no historian had observed before—a prevailing sense of guilt and failure on the part of those who had survived it. Among those interviewed were millionaires and prominent New Dealers along with the down-and-out.

Hard Times also revealed that the fear of loss fostered one of two reactions: either an obsession with money and property or a contempt for the entire system and its values. Those insights, coupled with the recollections of such disadvantaged groups as the blue-collar workers and blacks who were hit by hard times long before the stock market crash of 1929, resulted in a history of the Great Depression unlike any other. In the *New York Review of Books* (August 13, 1970), Murray Kempton joined in the chorus of praise for Terkel by noting that his book revises our notion of "Who-Deserves-To-Be-Taken-Seriously" because he found "our instructors in the most unexpected places." *Hard Times* was a best-seller for five months and, like *Division Street: America*, was translated into every major Western language as well as into Hungarian and Japanese.

One of Terkel's most ambitious contributions to guerrilla journalism was his next book, *Working: People Talk About What They Do All Day and How They Feel About What They Do* (1974). It is, according to Terkel, about "a search . . . for daily meaning as well as daily bread, for recognition as well as cash, for astonishment rather than torpor; in short, for a sort of life rather than a Monday through Friday sort of dying." For three years he used his trusty cassette tape recorder to interview 133 Americans from almost as many occupations, omitting professionals (the movie critic Pauline Kael and the actress Geraldine Page are among the few exceptions) and concentrating on the inarticulate workers whose attitudes towards their jobs have seldom been studied except by the social scientist.

The result is a book as profound in its revelation of personal longings and fears as it is in its insights into the collective American attitude toward work today. Most workers Terkel interviewed, whether white collar or blue, assembly line or executive, ventilated their dissatisfaction with the narrow monotony of jobs that offer scant chance for personal fulfillment and for what Freud called a "secure place in the human community." They see themselves as robots, machines, and objects, the inevitable consequence of a runaway technology that is rendering workers and their products more and more obsolete.

Although Terkel discovered that a few workers are still valued for their skills and can take delight in a job well done, an overwhelming number are more often singled out for censure than for praise. Those findings help to explain the disturbing American trends of absenteeism, shoddy work, and a disdain for craftsmanship. The longings that "ordinary people" harbor for work that affords some measure of dignity and individuality suggest, according to Terkel, that it is high time that we redefine the old work ethic and concentrate on "human matters."

A best-seller for 17 weeks, *Working* was almost unanimously hailed as a documentary that abounds in provocative and arresting insights into the troubled texture of contemporary American life. After reading it, Lewis Mumford went on record as saying: "No one can pretend to know our countrymen and the things that beautify or bedevil their workdays who has not taken in all that Terkel's collaborators say." The majority of critics agreed with Mumford. Only a dissenting minority felt that he had skewed his sample; that he had defined problems without proposing solutions; that it was difficult to generalize from his findings; and that his tendency to sentimentalize and mythicize the common man had resulted in a range of opinion that did not accurately represent the country as a whole. But Loren Baritz argued in the *New Republic* (April 6, 1974) that whatever Terkel's bias may have been, his taste, intuition, and involvement are such that "most available statistics, reified as they are, will not contradict the many voices of working."

Terkel explored new territory in his next two books. A year after publishing *Working*, he was one of the contributors to *Envelopes of Sound* (1975), a discussion among Terkel, fellow historians, anthropologists, and others, about the theoretical issues involved in the making of oral history. Edited by Ronald J. Grele, the book was well received, particularly in academic circles, and a reviewer for *Choice* (June 1976) called it "an important addition to the developing literature in oral history. . . . This book should be . . . in all academic libraries." Turning his focus inward for his next work, *Talking to Myself: A Memoir of My Times* (1977), Terkel reflected on the more interesting people and phenomena he had encountered in his life. Carey Horowitz of the *Library Journal* (April 1, 1977) wrote that "Terkel gives us a fascinating view of what goes on within him while he's interviewing" and that "he presents a timeless tableau that is much more evocative than the sum of its parts." Other reviewers were less impressed with the autobiography than with the author himself. In *Newsweek* (April 18, 1977), for example, Margo Jefferson commented that "*Talking to Myself* is not his best book;

but its best moments prove again that he is, in his own way, a master."And the reviewer for the *New Yorker* (May 2, 1977) wrote that Terkel was "an amusing, thoughtful, endlessly observant, and sometimes very funny fellow," but added that Terkel "apparently sees no need for any sort of editing. The reader, however, would be grateful for a little something along that line." R. J. Walton of the *Nation* (June 4, 1977) offered one of the most enthusiastic reviews, declaring that "This is not a book review but a celebration of a man, for this is one of those times when the writer and his book are one and the same. I'm not saying that Studs has not been artful. He has. But his life is so marvelously of a piece that he might have carved out quite different chunks of it and presented them in a different fashion with the same result: a triumph of commonality."

American Dreams; Lost and Found (1980), Terkel's next book, gathers autobiographical recollections by various individuals whom Terkel had met on his travels across the country during the previous several decades. The stories showcase the individuals' hopes, fears, aspirations, and disappointments regarding their country. Terkel himself contributed only an introduction, allowing the voices of the people to dominate the collection. T. M. Gannon of *America* (October 18, 1980) admired this feat, claiming that the book's "readability flows directly from the remarkable power of articulation (even though sometimes ungrammatical) possessed by Terkel's interviewees." Robert Sherrill of the *New York Times Book Review* (September 14, 1980) called the volume "a dark-hued book of frustrations and disillusionment, but it also is a stirringly hopeful book." While Stefan Kanfer of *Time* (September 29, 1980) offered the opinion that "in an age of faceless polls, sociological tracts, and psychobabble, politicians and historians would do well to discard ten pounds of printouts for every page of the author's impressive oral histories."

Terkel's book *The Good War: An Oral History of World War Two* (1984) contains more than 100 firsthand accounts from individuals from all walks of life who experienced World War II, from the Japanese and Germans to POWs to U.S. government officials. Widely hailed as a powerful oral history of the war, the book garnered high praise from reviewers, and won Terkel the Pulitzer Prize in 1985. James Kaufmann of the *Christian Science Monitor* (November 8, 1984) enthused that "like his earlier oral histories, *The Good War* is alive with the *feeling* of history rather than fact." Kaufmann concluded that "Terkel deserves considerable praise for his ability to elicit from person after person such fascinating reminiscences. The difference between regular history and Terkel's oral history is like the difference between reading a box score and actually seeing the game. There is life here, not statistics." In an equally positive review, Loudon Wainwright wrote in the *New York Times Book Review* (October 7, 1984), "Homely recall is common in the book, and there is an amazingly visual quality to much of the detail. . . . This sort of thing is tremendously compelling, somehow dramatic and intimate at the same time." However, Wainwright also noted that "occasionally the voices have a sameness and one sometimes feels that Mr. Terkel has never interviewed a man he didn't like." Wainwright overlooked this one flaw and concluded that "Still, Mr. Terkel's book gives the American experience in World War II great immediacy."

Terkel's next book, *The Great Divide: Second Thoughts on the American Dream* (1988), collects oral commentary on issues related to the 1980s, and specifically, how ideals and dreams have changed for Americans since the 1960s. Greeted with less enthusiastic responses than his last venture, Terkel's book was characterized by Paul Baumann of *Commonweal* (December 16, 1988) as depressing but truthful in its stories. "[This book] will depress you, and bore you, and may even wear you out. But it's no lie," he wrote. A particularly negative review came from Mel Elfin in the *New York Times Book Review* (October 9, 1988), who stated that "It's too bad that Studs Terkel . . . could not have understood more of what he was being told. Maybe the problem was that it is hard to understand what people are really telling you when you're listening from inside a time warp. Next time, perhaps, Mr. Terkel will step outside for some fresh air—and produce a better book."

In 1992 Terkel published *Race: How Blacks and Whites Think and Feel About the American Obsession* (1992), a book that, among other approaches, compares the attitudes that characterized the civil rights era of the 1960s with contemporary views on race equality. Michael A. Lutes wrote in *Library Journal* (March 15, 1992), "Terkel demonstrates how very skilled he is at drawing out interviewees' intrinsic feelings on race." Less enthusiastic was Alan Wolfe of the *New Republic* (April 13, 1992) who concluded that Terkel "specializes in finding 'types'" and that "these people have interesting stories to tell, but very few conclusions may confidently be drawn from them."

Terkel's next offering was *Coming of Age: The Story of Our Century by Those Who've Lived It* (1995), a look at American citizens aged 70 and older. The book offers their personal histories, stories that reflect both social ethics and work trends throughout the better part of the past century. The reviewer for the on-line version of the *Detroit News* (September 27, 1995), while generally complimentary about the collection, did offer one criticism, writing that "this marvelous book has one inherent flaw: The speakers tend to be somewhat repetitive, not so much in experience as in attitudes. . . . One would like to observe the speaker's body language, especially when they become passionate." Still, the reviewer went on to note that "to his credit, Terkel gives a strong hint of it by allowing his interviewees to speak without inane interruptions, so that they come off as fascinating essayists instead of mere talking heads." Rebecca Pepper Sinkler stated in the *New York Times Book Review* (Sep-

tember 24, 1995) that the people interviewed, "though diverse in their life histories, are an inordinately like-minded crowd, and the language spoken here is pure Terkel: the voice of the embattled old liberal shaking his stick at the 20th century." Sinkler went on to note that although the oral historian "may aim high, Mr. Terkel's interviews don't soar. . . . Maybe because the questions are so relentlessly pedestrian, they elicit banal answers." Even this unenthusiastic reviewer, however, admitted that "there are notable exceptions." In contrast to the general tone of Sinkler's review, Mary Carroll of *Booklist* (July 19, 1995) called the book a "superb oral history."

On July 2, 1939 Terkel married Ida Goldberg, a social worker from Ashland, Wisconsin, whom he met when they were both members of the Chicago Repertory Theatre. The marriage produced one son, Paul. As for his acknowledged ease with total strangers, Terkel insists that he has no conscious technique but simply engages them in conversation with much the same kinds of questions he might ask over a drink. His empathy, sensitivity, and the impression he radiates of his own vulnerability to time and circumstance are so compelling that most interviewees are eager to confide in him. Once they have, his real job begins—that of carefully editing the tapes to see that "the person is retained, the essence of the man, with nothing of me in it."

In 1997 Terkel published *My American Century*, an omnibus of his most memorable interviews from all eight of his books.
—D.B.

SUGGESTED READING: *Booklist* July 19, 1995; *Choice* June 1976; *Commonweal* Dec. 16, 1988; *Detroit News* (on-line) Sep. 27, 1995; *Grand Times* (online); *Kirkus Reviews* Feb. 1, 1992; *Library Journal* Mar. 15, 1992; *Manchester Guardian* Sep. 26, 1970; *Nation* June 4, 1977; *New Republic* Apr. 6, 1974, Apr. 13, 1992; *Newsweek* Apr. 18, 1977; New Yorker May 2, 1977; *New York Review of Books* Aug. 13, 1970; New York Times Feb. 5, 1967; *New York Times Book Review* Sep. 4, 1980, Oct. 7, 1984, Oct. 9, 1988, Sep. 24, 1995; *Time* Sep. 29, 1980; *Book Review Digest*, 1976, 1977, 1980, 1985, 1989, 1992, 1996; *Contemporary Authors*, 1996; *Who's Who in America*, 1974–1975; *Who's Who in the Midwest*, 1974–1975

SELECTED WORKS: *Giants of Jazz*, 1957; *Division Street: America*, 1967; *Hard Times: An Oral History of the Great Depression*, 1970; *Working: People Talk About What They Do All Day and How They Feel About What They Do*, 1974; *Envelopes of Sound* (with Richard J. Grele), 1975; *Talking to Myself: A Memoir of My Times*, 1977; *American Dreams: Lost and Found*, 1980; *The Good War: An Oral History of World War II*, 1984; *The Neon Wilderness* (with Nelson Algren), 1986; *Chicago*, 1986; *The Great Divide:*

Second Thoughts on the American Dream, 1988; *Race: How Blacks and Whites Think and Feel About the American Obsession*, 1992; *Coming of Age: the Story of Our Century by Those Who've Lived It*, 1995; *My American Century*, 1997

Theroux, Alexander

1939– essayist; poet; biographer

Alexander Theroux, satirist, novelist, essayist and erstwhile university professor, writes "highly literary" novels and essays recognized for their sophisticated wit, opulent vocabulary, and allusions to classical literature. The targets of his sometimes acerbic satire have ranged from self-righteous moralizers and pedantic academicians to shrewish women and the purveyors of (to him) a pusillanimous culture of political correctness. His first novel, *Three Wogs* (1972), was nominated for a National Book Award; his second, the semiautobiographical and encyclopedic *Darconville's Cat* (1981), was judged in the *National Review* as "the strongest work of fiction published in the United States since *Gravity's Rainbow* [1972]." More recent books include *The Lollipop Trollops* (1994), a collection of verse, the biography *The Enigma of Al Capp* (1999), and two essay collections, *The Primary Colors* (1994) and *The Secondary Colors* (1996), each of which contains discursive and arcana-rich ramblings on the multispectral nuances of meaning that colors have assumed in literature, history, mythology, and popular culture. Theroux's works defy easy categorization: Interviewer Paul West wrote in the spring 1991 issue of the *Review of Contemporary Fiction* that Theroux "has been grouped with postmodernists like Barth and Sorrentino, but the underlying conservatism in his work and his preference for linear storytelling make this an awkward grouping. . . . Instead, Theroux belongs to the line of literary outsiders, writers like Frederick Rolfe ("Baron Corvo"), Ronald Firbank, and Djuna Barnes whose work has little in common with that of their contemporaries and which instead amalgamates curious byways of literary tradition and eccentric genius onto something unique." Some of Theroux's writings and interviews evince an acerbic, even combative, style that has occasionally embroiled him in controversy, as when another writer accused him of plagiarism when she discovered a similarities between passages in *The Primary Colors* and passages from a novel published some 30 years earlier. Earlier, he had been, in his words, "rusticated" from Yale University when comments he made about a highly publicized violent crime in New York City were interpreted as racist in some circles.

Alexander Theroux was born into a "prolific family of writers" in the Boston suburb of Medford, Massachusetts, the second of seven children of Albert Eugene Theroux, a shoe salesman, and Anne Dittami Theroux, an elementary-school teacher and amateur painter. Describing the "drab working-class neighborhood" in which the Therouxs grew up, brother Paul, himself an accomplished author, concluded: "It's the uncongenial place that provides material for one's art." The Therouxs were raised in an environment where literature was highly esteemed, and household members were "eager collaborators in one another's lives," James Atlas wrote in a *New York Times Magazine* profile of the family (April 30, 1978). Still, Alexander Theroux wrote in a 1991 essay, "I never consciously decided to become a writer. I was one, in the way a person is tall or short or has a cowlick or a pink birthmark on the knee." His first opus was attempted in junior high school: a breezy 40-page novel tapped out on a friend's typewriter only to be ripped up soon afterwards by the friend's brother, "thus confirming an eradicable suspicion I had very early that literature, if it's really great, is always subject to outside threat."

Two factors that whetted young Theroux's literary sensibilities were the influence of his parents and the classical-based culture of his Roman Catholic upbringing. His mother encouraged all seven of her children to keep journals and compose essays about family trips and events, and his father was remembered by Alexander as "a born actor" who read to him and his brothers, by candlelight, dramatic bedtime stories from *The Arabian Nights* or such macabre tales as Poe's "The Tell-Tale Heart." Theroux later recalled how his father "held the candle high, and as the book shook, phantom shadows rose above his head on the ceiling, and I heard a voice so full of fright and choked with such delicious wickedness that my throat closed."

These pyrotechnics left a deep impression on Theroux. "In childhood, so little suffices to create a mystery. . . ," he continued. "In any case the hand that raised that candle bred a fever. It fired my imagination, especially for the written word, and later made me passionately curious about all sorts of things." Among these passions were reading stories of authors' lives as portrayed in an old encyclopedia at home, "people like Hawthorne and Irving and James Fenimore Cooper, whose names alone reemphasized from an unexpected direction all that I thought was magic and momentous and most important in life. These men were different. They were dreamers. They inflamed my imagination, as did my father."

Theroux also later recalled his fascination with the rhythm and sound of language in the work of poets as diverse as John Milton, Gerard Manley Hopkins, Emily Dickinson, and Wallace Stevens, as well as "ancient intonations from the liturgy of the Church" that he heard as an altar boy in Medford. For a time, he thought he wanted to be a monk, and he spent a brief novitiate in the Trappist monastery at Gethsemani, Kentucky, under the guidance of novice master Thomas Merton, himself a prominent author. Although Theroux soon left in pursuit of a more secular vision, he never quite lost a sense of the high calling of the literary vocation. Referring to James Joyce's alter-ego, Stephen Dedalus, he told an interviewer that "both [the priesthood and writing] are vocations. I was always a dreamer, an 'introspective voyager,' as Wallace Stevens put it. I never supposed divine things might not look divine. The Church sedulously encourages the imagination. . . . The Church gave me an interest in miracle, mystery, and ritual. . . . It also shaped my nightmare. I believe in grace, and I share Dedalus's interest in taxonomies. Catholic children, at least years ago, used to have to memorize many lists." Juxtaposed with linear narrative, such lists—together with litanies, bibliographies, extended syllogisms, and other elaborate compendia—have become integral components of a number of Theroux's books.

Leaving Gethsemani, Theroux resumed his literary pilgrimage in academe and received his bachelor's degree in 1964 from St. Francis College in Biddeford, Maine. He took his master's degree from the University of Virginia in 1965 and his Ph.D. from the same institution in 1968, then went abroad to Oxford as a Fulbright scholar. At Virginia he had found an outlet in amateur dramatics and penned many play scripts as vehicles for actor-friends. His semiautobiographical novel *Darconville's Cat* draws much on his graduate-school experiences in its satirical portrayal of "Quinsy College, est. 1839, ... a quaint old respectable school for girls . . . in the seminary tradition of the female academy: a chaste academic retreat, moral as peppermint, built in semi-colonial red brick and set back in a deep green delling where, alone—at least so felt the Board of Visitors (ten FFVs with swimming eyes, three names, and hands with liverspots)—one's daughter could be lessoned in character and virtue without the indecent distractions that elsewhere, everywhere else, wherever led to vicious intemperance, Bolshevism, and free thought."

But Theroux's first published book, *Three Wogs*, drew on his then-recent experiences in England. It is composed of three novellas, focusing in turn on three "wogs" ("Westernized [or Worthy] Oriental gentlemen") from the colonies as they confront the class stratification of the mother country, sometimes at their peril. Here, Theroux mocked the hypocrisies and pretensions of colonial-power England by exposing a frightening world of racism and violence beneath its veiled serenity, as in the tale of a matron, Mrs. Proby—who is slain by a Chinese shopkeeper she is conditioned to despise after decades of having been exposed to Sax Rohmer's portrayals of Asians as sinister Fu Manchu caricatures. Another of the stories, "The Wife of God," hints at sexual ambivalence in its implication of a homosexual liaison between a clergyman and his protégé, a male singer from Africa.

When *Three Wogs* was published, Theroux was hailed as "a certified, grade A, major, new talent" by D. K. Mano in the *New York Times* (April 16, 1972). A review published in the *Virginia Quarter-ly* faulted his somewhat overwritten, bombastic style but admired his grasp of the essential differences between American and British cultures. Nearly 10 years later, Benjamin DeMott, then a professor of humanities at Amherst, wrote in the *New York Times Book Review* (May 3, 1981) how "the volume was remarkable for its breadth of imaginative sympathy. Impoverished widows clinging to tea-table respectability, wretched adolescent drifters drunk on racist fantasy, graduate students up from Bombay struggling to replace the Victorian politesse, dutifully learned back home, with manners better suited to a late 20th-century metropolis—all came under intense, committed scrutiny."

Theroux's second novel, *Darconville's Cat*, appeared in 1981, to continued critical acclaim. Anthony Burgess included it in his 1984 compilation, *99 Novels: The Best in English Since 1939*, in which he found Theroux's "fictional gifts" much in evidence, even while commenting on the novel's "strong reek of the dictionary, which may be no bad thing in an age when much fiction has a painfully pared vocabulary." J. O. Tate declared in the *National Review* (May 29, 1981) that "*Darconville's Cat* may be the strongest work of fiction published in the United States since [Thomas Pynchon's] *Gravity's Rainbow*" some nine years earlier. Theroux later recalled that he had conceived of the novel on a plane in a low emotional state in 1973, while "pondering the binaries of love and hate" and how both emotions can be held simultaneously. The 704-page novel, rife with allusions to his childhood, religious influences, and schooling as well as to classical literature and to the political radicalism and sexual revolution of the 1960s, was to be his sweeping "encyclopedic novel, the so-called novel of learning" in the tradition of Sterne, Rabelais, or Cervantes. Among the targets of its barbed satire are academic pretensions, village morality, and sexual malaise in which Darconville (the name is derived from a martyred Elizabethan cleric), a contemporary schoolmaster who "always wore black," accepts a position at Quinsy College, "one of those dame schools in the south, usually called something like Montfaucon." Jilted by a student with whom he has a lengthy and comic-ridden affair, Darconville flees to Harvard, settling into a life of comfortable misogyny. But the complex Darconville is more than a pedagogue; he is also a writer, one who, armed with "a great fat pen he called 'The Black Disaster,'" "quite happily chose to live within his own world, within his own writing, within himself." In 1991 Theroux told interviewer Alexander Laurence that *Darconville's Cat* "in its compete[n]diousness takes language as its province. I use rich but not always general words to clarify not obfuscate." He added "satirists have always depended on language for their wit. Readers who are neither curious nor inculturated to the tradition of the 'encyclopedic' novel will find it all confusing." Theroux, for example, filled a chapter, entitled "The Unholy Litany" ("the queerest litany ever heard"), with 20 pages of imprecation against real and imagined women who plague the misogynistic Darconville, including "Frédégunde, the Frankish frisgig and assassin" and "the Red Queen and her scarlet queynt," as well as the very student who is the object of his dalliance at Quinsy, "Isabel Rawsthorne, than whom none here is more loathsome."

Theroux's most recent novel, *An Adultery* (1987), shifts the venue of his disaffections to Harvard, where its narrator, Christian Ford, struggles to come to terms with various infidelities as well as the pervasiveness of ambiguity in human relationships. This novel of betrayal is described as a "cautionary tale" by fellow author Ron Hansen, who wrote in the *New York Times Book Review* (October 18, 1987): "Nothing is simply put in Alexander Theroux's maximalist prose. His language is courageously archaic, acroamatic, archilochian, full of his own coinages from the Greek and Latin and some brawny, warty Anglo-Saxon words that have not been regularly used since the Middle Ages." Theroux himself later expressed his emphasis of character over plot in his fiction, describing his technique in these words: "Start delineating a figure—merely describe a person—and he or she will begin to act, do things, go in a particular direction. I set [*An Adultery*] up as a syllogism and purposely wrote balancing rhythmic and arrhythmic sentences." Still, the novel was regarded by some as yet another misogynistic missive from an author not known for his endearing female characters, with reviewer Hansen pointing out how Farol Colorado, the object of Christian Ford's affections, is "cruelly and continually appraised, psychoanalyzed, harped on, vetted, vitiated, and finally villainized." The publication of this novel further reinforced Theroux's almost religious belief that he stood outside the mainstream of commercial publishing: "Nothing there for the Leon Uris crowd—beach readers, military minds, people who flip pages to pass time. I wanted this book to be what it was, no self-promotion, no book for a publishing scheme. There's a mystical passivity in refusing the entrepreneurial."

Since the appearance of *An Adultery*, Theroux has published a collection of verse, *The Lollipop Trollops* (1994), and two collections of essays that describe in minute detail the associative nuances of the six basic colors in the visible spectrum: *The Primary Colors* (1994) and *The Secondary Colors* (1996). Theroux hopes to complement the series in a third book, to be titled *Black & White*. In his 1991 essay "The Detours of Art," Theroux also promised that an "eventual collection of essays will represent 20 years of non-fiction writing."

Taken together, the two *Colors* books represent an encyclopedic compendium of the history, usage, and symbolism of red, yellow, blue, orange, purple, and green. Theroux mined huge databases of literature, music, art, food, science, poetry, and popular culture in search of the arcana that he refined into six witty and nuanced narratives, one for each color, that are each about 100 pages long. Typ-

ical of the style and tone of these works is the introduction to the dissertation on "Green": "Green is power, nature's fuse, the color of more force and guises than are countable, a messenger announcing itself, paradoxically, as the hue of both renewal and reproduction or infirmity and illness. It is at once the preternaturally ambiguous color of life and death, the vernal sign of vitality, and the livid tinge of corruption, a 'dialectical lyric' (to borrow a term from Kierkegaard), responding with the kind of answers that perhaps depend less on itself than on the questions we ask of it." The books won the admiration of some of America's leading prose stylists: Author Guy Davenport wrote in a cover blurb how *The Secondary Colors* was "entertainment at its most civilized, a nonstop flow of information and interpretation" in its "dazzling essays on color [which] carry on a tradition in which Sir Thomas Browne, Montaigne, and Plutarch have shone"; and John Updike, in *QWERTY Arts* (1997), called the book "an amazing display of omnidirectional erudition and an omnivorous poetic instinct."

Theroux himself admitted that his choice of subject matter was less important than his approach and methodology, telling Alexander Laurence in *QWERTY Arts* that "*The Primary Colors* is a celebration not only of the colors red, yellow, and blue but the possibility of giving exuberant cross-cultural commentary on anything. I could have done the same thing about Morocco, Fatty Arbuckle, or the shapes of mouths." Commenting on his uneasiness about the intersection of art and popular culture in 1990s America, he said: "Novels are often not written as books qua books, dense products to be picked up and put down, compendia of wit and wisdom . . . like *Gravity's Rainbow* or *Middlemarch* or *One Hundred Years of Solitude*. Films seem to be on writers' minds. Hollywood. I'm not sure anymore that knowledge is important to writers. I know it is to me. To Nicholson Baker. To Updike."

In the 1990s Theroux became embroiled in several controversial situations. A charge of plagiarism surrounded the publication of *The Primary Colors* when Cynthia Martin Kiss, a technical editor, reported to the *New York Times* that she had discovered several passages in Theroux's book that seemed to have been lifted almost verbatim from Guy Murchie's 1954 book *Song of the Sky*. Theroux blamed "stupidity and bad note taking" for the situation, claiming that he had neglected to credit Murchie after he had gotten his notes for *The Primary Colors* mixed up with notes for another book he was writing. Holt promised to rectify the situation in future editions. In 1991 he was not rehired as a faculty member at Yale University after civil-rights activists, prodded by Harvard psychologist Alvin Poussaint and *Boston Globe* journalist Derrick Jackson, complained that Theroux had made racially offensive remarks about several sensational crimes then occupying public attention, notably against the black youths who assaulted a white female jogger in New York's Central Park. Commenting on this case in his introduction to *The Lollipop Trollops*, Theroux vented his spleen by characterizing Yale as "an effete nest of weak and charmless indefinites, sexless males, and literary and political termagants, many of whom, educated beyond their intelligence, are more interested in doing what's safe or politically advantageous than what is right." He further defended his *Three Wogs* and *Darconville's Cat* as "wholesale vilifications of prejudice, bigotry, and racism. But that involved reading, and this was a college, and who had the time?" The "rustication" he experienced, however, permitted him to enjoy more time for writing and confirmed his resolve "never to teach again if I can avoid it." Theroux's reputation for corrosiveness was further established by the scathing review he gave to his own brother's work (and life). Reviewing Paul Theroux's *My Other Life* for *Boston Magazine* (October 1996), Alexander wrote, "Paul Theroux's new book is venal, vengeful, spiteful, cowardly, lying, pretentious, self-promoting crap. Or so says his brother."

In 1994, the Dalkey Archive Press published Theroux's *The Lollipop Trollops*, a collection of verse consisting largely of intellectual greeting-card verse in the form of clever conceits and wordplay that its author had placed in alphabetical rather than chronological or thematic order. "A Boston Marriage" is typical of the tone of these works: "Miss Amy Lowell was butch / Miss Ada Russell was femme / Lowell was mostly apple / Russell was basically stem." So too is "Ars Poetica": "Poems are hammered and distinct / Of what once of course was molten / Precious and fluid and sweetly gold / As sesame oil in Szechuan." Some of the verse is more splenetic, as in a poem dedicated to a real-life priest-uncle who had often chided young Alexander for his habitual bedwetting. In that poem the cleric is relegated to a parched circle of hell situated immediately downstream from his loose-sphinctered nephew.

Despite Theroux's introductory essay, in which he admitted, "I've written my poems without coyness and made it a point of saying anything I wanted to of what I've felt," his rhymes met with rejection from most mainstream periodicals, provoking his frustrated comment that "Many editors can't tell a good poem from a proctoscope exam."

Nor does Theroux tolerate what he sees as the pretentiousness of fashionable academic trends, as when he told Laurence, "I know nothing about 'post-modernism' except that when I taught at Yale it was a name given to (a) poorly organized short stories handed in and (b) a spate of crapulous and egotistical criticism." He had earlier written in his introduction to *The Lollipop Trollops* that "deconstruction, after all, is not only self-congratulatory but more often than not the moon-desperate attempt on the part of literary critics with all their bilge and bile and obfuscation to claim that they themselves are also creative."

In this selfsame introduction, which doubled as a retrospective of his own literary career, Theroux concluded, "A writer's life, devoted, ideally to coming to terms with it . . . might be seen as a sort of staircase of which poems are not merely steps, or even parts of steps, but simply nails or reinforcements or kickboards. There is so much more above, beside, and underneath a poem. . . . There is always a poem not printed on paper, coincident with the secret disposition to respond to that which feeds it."

Theroux has been on the faculties of the University of Virginia, Harvard University, Phillips Academy, the Massachusetts Institute of Technology, the American School in London, and Yale University. He was a Guggenheim Fellow in 1974. His book *The Enigma of Al Capp*, about the life of the creator of the comic strip "Li'l Abner," appeared in 1999.
—E. M.

SUGGESTED READING: *National Review* p 620, May 29, 1981; *New York Times Book Review* p4 Apr. 16, 1972; p9 May 3, 1981; Apr. 30, 1987; Oct. 18, 1987; *QWERTY Arts* (1997, on-line); *Virginia Quarterly* Summer 1972; Burgess, A. *99 Novels: The Best in English Since 1939*, 1984

SELECTED BOOKS: Fiction—*Three Wogs*, 1972; *Darconville's Cat*, 1981; *An Adultery*, 1987; Nonfiction—*The Primary Colors*, 1994; *The Secondary Colors*, 1996; *The Enigma of Al Capp*, 1999; Poetry—*The Lollipop Trollops*, 1994; Children's Books—*The Schinocephalic Waif*, 1975; *The Great Wheadle Tragedy*, 1975; *Master Snickup's Cloak*, 1979

Timm, Uwe

Mar. 30, 1940– Novelist

The German novelist Uwe Timm grew up in Hamburg during and after World War II, and scenes from postwar Hamburg permeate his fiction. His novels published in English translation, *The Snake Tree* (1988), *Headhunter* (1994), *The Invention of Curried Sausage* (1995), and *Midsummer Night* (1998), have as their protagonists men with backgrounds similar to Timm's. His characters have varying professions, and some travel extensively, but they remain tied to their childhood memories of Hamburg. In his novels, Timm propagates a worldview in which modern society is being destroyed by unfettered capitalism, and communism is simply a ludicrously failed system. Like the Uruguayan writer Eduardo Galeano, Timm weaves the strands of his stories together to give his novels a braid-like structure.

Uwe Timm was born in Hamburg on March 30, 1940, during World War II. He apprenticed as a furrier before going on to study philosophy and philology, and received a D.Phil. degree from the University of Munich. After studying at the Sorbonne in Paris, he embarked on a career as a writer—of screenplays, philosophical essays, poetry, and novels.

The first of Timm's novels to be published in English, *The Snake Tree* (*Der Schlangenbaum*, 1986), appeared in England in 1988 and in the United States in 1990, translated by Peter Tegel. *The Snake Tree* is the story of a German, Wagner, who is offered the job of overseeing the building of three paper factories in South America, in the area where the bloody Chaco war took place. Although he has a wife and child, he immediately accepts the offer, which would involve a year away from his family. He ponders how to explain his decision to his wife: "He couldn't even explain it to himself. And yet not a single doubt arose in him over his decision. That day and the next . . . he kept trying every possible answer. The duty to work for a change in an underdeveloped country, to put his knowledge and experience to use there. She would only laugh. . . . And it wasn't the money either. . . . But then, he said to himself, even as a child he wanted to travel to the jungles of South America, and he had told Susan that, but as an explanation for his quick decision it was a childish excuse." Wagner is left with the feeling that he has been drawn to his fate by unknown forces. His friend warns him, "It's a suicide mission. Conditions being what they are, it could hardly be worse: a military dictatorship, guerillas, corruption, incompetence, and then the heat." The first misstep on Wagner's part when he arrives at the site is to run over an emerald green snake. According to local belief, killing a snake of that kind brings death.

Wagner almost immediately finds himself enmeshed in the disasters his friend had predicted; he has entered a "heart of darkness," where ex-SS men mingle with Jewish refugees at posh parties, while the wretched workers on the project are left to die alone when injured or shot. The project cannot be built because everyone involved is either incompetent, corrupt, or drunk; the building materials—those not stolen—are too shoddy to hold up. Wagner, a decent man, has tried, to no avail, to prevent some of the destruction, but despite his efforts for good, everything he does results in the opposite of what he intends. As a flood approaches, the military dictatorship unleashes its forces against a supposed uprising. At the end, Wagner is left alone in his house in a power outage with the troops and the flood waters creeping up:

"And Wagner thinks if the lights were to go back on again on the hill everything would continue as before, a power cut, but let it stay dark, he hopes for an abiding darkness in which the cockroaches will force their way into every house and every bungalow and the rats too, here on the hill but in Hamburg as well, there too, to feed on the refuse, on the accumulated wealth built on misfortune and suffering. No, the others would come, from the forest, from the huts, from the hovels of the city, and among them would be the labourer with the chopped-off finger and the man with the destroyed face. He could hold out his hand to them. He could help them over the wall."

The reviewer for the (London) *Sunday Times* termed *The Snake Tree* "a fug of tension that drips with jungle damp and cakes with soil . . . a book of subtle, evocative power." In the (London) *Observer,* a critic called it a "powerful evocation of clashing cultures and impotent endeavours," according to New Directions, the American publisher. Peter Tegel, the translator, won the 1989 Schlegel-Tieck Prize for his work on *The Snake Tree.*

Headhunter (*Kopfjäger*, 1991) was published in the United States in 1994, also with a translation by Peter Tegel. A dense and complex novel, it is the story of one Peter Walter, who has grown up in postwar Hamburg and, after numerous jobs—in one of which, as a window decorator, he got too creative and was fired for "pornography"—he winds up selling commodities futures and bilking investors with a partner, Dembrowski. The novel moves back and forth between Walter's various lives: his childhood in Hamburg, his married life in several apartments, his time on remand in prison awaiting trial for fraud, his exile in Spain, his flight to Brazil, and his final escape to Easter Island, where he is recaptured. These episodes are not presented chronologically, but interwoven and braided into what the publisher termed "a multilayered, multi-faceted book that addresses the times we live in and, most particularly, the role of money and the financial cannibalism of recent years."

The action in Timm's novel *The Invention of Curried Sausage*, which was published in Germany in 1993 as *Die Entdeckung der Currywurst* and translated by Leila Vennewitz for a 1995 English-language edition, takes place mainly in flashback to the last days of World War II in Hamburg. The unnamed narrator of the story, who seems to be a stand-in for the author, goes back to his hometown—Hamburg—to find the woman, Mrs. Brücker, who he believes invented curried sausage, a popular street food in Germany. He has often returned to Hamburg to savor the sausages at the stand she has operated since just after the war, but when, after many years, he finds her gone from her post, he decides to find her and interview her about her invention. After locating Mrs. Brücker, who is now blind and living in an old-age home, he has a series of conversations with her over a period of weeks. Slowly, as she spins her tale of life during and after the war, Mrs. Brücker comes to represent all that is good in the German people—creativity, resourcefulness, endurance, and an abiding hatred of war and senseless killing.

Declaring *The Invention of Curried Sausage* to be "as delectable as its subject," Paul E. Hutchinson wrote in *Library Journal* (May 15, 1995), that the novel "tells one remarkable woman's story and through her portrays the survival of a nation." Francine Prose, writing in the *New York Times Book Review* (June 11, 1995), felt the novel's structure was "programmatic." "Still," she concluded, "even if Mr. Timm stops short of portraying life in all its chaotic richness, *The Invention of Curried Sausage* reaches farther and deeper" than most modern fiction. "It's a wise and beguiling reminder to pay close attention to the world, and to study the history lessons that are sizzling away in our skillets."

Midsummer Night (1998), a translation by Peter Tegel of Timm's *Johannisnacht* (1996), is similar to *The Invention of Curried Sausage* in that it consists of a number of interlocking, chronological tales, hinging on an article of food—the potato. In this story, the narrator, a writer, investigates his uncle's amazing ability to determine the variety of any given potato, and to deduce where the spud in question was grown, as a wine connoisseur can taste a wine and name the vineyard and vintage. According to the novel's publisher, a critic from the German newspaper *Die Zeit* wrote that, "Timm sets all your senses to red alert, he sends your head spinning and then saves the day with the artistry of his storytelling."

Timm was influenced by Eduardo Galeano's *Memory of Fire* trilogy, and acknowledges that a story in *The Snake Tree* was inspired by that series' first volume, *Origins*. His methods of interweaving reality and fiction, of coming back to the same event from a slightly different perspective, and of inserting analyses of grand concepts of war and peace, communism and capitalism into seemingly trivial personal stories evoke Galeano's storytelling. In addition, Timm uses what seems to be autobiography as the background of his protagonists' lives: Reading his novels allows one to partake of his weltanschauung (Mrs. Brücker of *The Invention of Curried Sausage*, for instance, was first mentioned in *The Snake Tree*), which has a certain anarchic skepticism, along with a deep compassion. As he wrote in *Headhunter*, "the patterns can be infinite although the area of the thread is finite (oh beautiful chaos)."
—S. Y.

SUGGESTED READING: *Library Journal* p98 May 15, 1995; *New York Times Book Review* p31 June 11, 1995

SELECTED BOOKS: In English translation: *The Snake Tree*, tr. P. Tegel, 1988; *Headhunter*, tr. L. Vennewitz, 1994; *The Invention of Curried Sausage*, tr. P. Tegel, 1995; *Midsummer Night*, tr. P. Tegel, 1998

Tuten, Frederic

Dec. 2, 1936– Novelist; professor; translator

Despite long lapses between novels, the work of Frederic Tuten has been consistently inventive, experimental, and thought-provoking. His first novel, *The Adventures of Mao on the Long March* (1971), was followed by a 17-year hiatus during which the author devoted himself to teaching and writing articles for art magazines. He returned to writing novels in 1988 with *Tallien: A Brief Romance*, a fictionalized account of a historical figure. Five years later Tuten published *Tintin in the New World* (1993), in which he dropped the popular French comic-strip character Tintin into the "real" world. Tuten's most recent novel, *Van Gogh's Bad Cafe*, was published in 1997; in it the author follows the exploits of a time-traveling, morphine-addicted teenager from her 19th-century affair with the famous painter to her life as a punk rocker in the modern-day East Village of New York City.

Frederic Tuten was born on December 2, 1936, in the New York City borough of the Bronx, the son of Rex Tuten, a labor activist, and Madelyn (Scelfo) Tuten. His father left home when Frederic was 10 years old, and Frederic never saw Rex Tuten again until just before his death. "He was a romantic figure to me, an unhappy figure," Frederic Tuten told Wendy Smith for *Publishers Weekly* (March 3, 1997). "He believed in a better life for people, but in everyday life, he was a betrayer."

The author has attributed his love of books to his mother. "Her pleasure was to read, and she read everything; I got that habit from her," he told Smith. A new love, however, soon rivaled his affinity for reading—the love of art. In the early 1950s Tuten left high school to study painting at the Art Students League. Feeling outclassed by many fellow students whose work he considered vastly superior to his own, Tuten eventually departed from the Art Students League and enrolled in City College. He received his B.A. in 1959. On September 9, 1962, he married Simona Morini, a writer, and he earned his M.A. from New York University in 1964.

Tuten began writing for various art magazines in the 1960s, and in the process he met and befriended some of the most influential artists of the time, including Roy Lichtenstein, Eric Fischl, and David Salle. He considers artists, rather than his fellow writers, to be his kindred spirits. "They were talking and thinking about art," he told Wendy Smith. "I rarely hear writers talk about writing outside of who's publishing their book, what kind of an advance they got, where it's been reviewed—which I find tedious."

Tuten and his wife worked together as translators on two published works, *The House of Farnese* (1968), by G. R. Solari, and the collection *Charles Baudelaire: Letters from His Youth* (1970). Tuten received a Ph.D in 19th-century American literature from New York University, in 1971.

Soon after obtaining his doctorate, Tuten began teaching at City College as an associate professor of American literature, and in the same year published his first novel, *The Adventures of Mao on the Long March*. Tuten was initially unable to get the experimental, nonlinear work published. When his friend Roy Lichtenstein offered to illustrate the cover, however, publishing companies suddenly became interested in the book. Once published, the novel enjoyed critical if not commercial success.

In 1972 Tuten and Morini divorced. Two years later, he became director of City College's graduate program in literature and creative writing. Focusing on writing magazine articles and teaching, Tuten published no new books for 14 years, abandoning two novels before they were completed. Also during this time, Tuten received a Guggenheim fellowship, and wrote a film adaptation in Germany.

In 1988 he published *Tallien: A Brief Romance*. The novel is framed by a semiautobiographical, modern-day story of a son's attempts to come to terms with his dying father. Through most of the book, however, the son recounts the fictionalized life of Jean Lambert Tallien, an obscure real-life French revolutionary. In an assessment of *Tallien* that appeared in the *New York Times Book Review* (May 29, 1988), James A. Snead described the novel as "an exceptionally erudite and often witty meditation on political and erotic betrayal." However, Snead took issue with the insertion of 18th-century France into the contemporary father/son storyline. The novel, he wrote, would have been more coherent had Tuten confined its narrative to the modern setting. "The parallel drawn between the tales seems emotionally unconvincing," Snead wrote. "Mr Tuten's final chapter attempts, by the shock of anachronism, to graft the two together. Alas, it does not succeed."

Another five years passed before Tuten published his third novel, *Tintin in the New World*. Once again Tuten chose a pre-existing figure as a main character—this time, the protagonist of the hugely popular and long-running *Tintin* comic book series, by the French cartoonist Hergé. Tuten added depth to the innocent, two-dimensional character Tintin by turning him into a living, breathing being who discovers his sexuality, engages in philosophical debate, and commits murder. Hergé, who died in 1983, had given Tuten permission to use his character, at a meeting in France in the early 1970s. "Tintin was a ready-made boy hero I could invest lots of fantasy in," Tuten told Wendy Smith. "I didn't have to create an unknown youth who was innocent and valiant; he was already there for me. And I could build on that to create the kind of ennobled and mystical reacher

for truth I wanted to have." Like *The Adventures of Mao*, *Tintin in the New World* featured a Lichtenstein cover. The novel was Tuten's most commercially successful to date. "Hard for me to confess: I actually made some money!" he commented to Smith.

Tintin in the New World garnered more attention from reviewers than any of Tuten's previous works. Edmund White's assessment in the *New York Times Book Review* (June 6, 1993) was positive: "What seemed at first glance a pastiche of a comic strip . . . quickly [becomes] a sadder but more expansive meditation on the dubious perfectibility of human nature, the dreary devolution of love, and the randomness of individual luck." White praised the novel's inventiveness, noting that it overshadowed any minor flaws, and concluded that the work makes a statement "more personal than autobiography."

In a mixed review for *New York Newsday* (June 6, 1993), Richard Eder described *Tintin in the New World* as "an intriguing though awkward effort to contrast myth and story, and to show something of the properties of each." Eder made note of Tuten's attempt to preserve the comic-strip feel by retaining Tintin's melodramatic diction, but lamented that this device eventually works against the book. In the end Eder called the novel simply "a cartoon of a cartoon," which was in its own way just as implausible as its source material.

In 1995 Tuten retired from his position as director of City College's graduate literature and writing program. He continues to work there on a part-time basis, teaching one class per semester. "I would feel very deprived if I wasn't teaching," he told Wendy Smith.

Van Gogh's Bad Cafe, Tuten's fourth novel, was published in 1997. A surreal time-travel saga spanning the 19th and 20th centuries, the novel concerns a teenage morphine addict who becomes romantically involved with Vincent van Gogh, only to find herself suddenly transported to Manhattan's East Village in the present day. Inevitably, the author draws a parallel between the two settings. In his interview with Wendy Smith, Tuten claimed that he wanted *Van Gogh's Bad Cafe* to contain more of his own personality and emotions than his previous novels. "I'm giving myself permission to burn on the page . . .," he commented. "I think that fundamentally, I'm a lonely person. . . . I feel the loneliness of my characters very deeply; that's what I see when I read van Gogh's letters and in his intense activity not to be lonely by making art." Another of Tuten's artist friends, Eric Fischl, provided the cover illustration for the novel.

In the interview for *Publishers Weekly*, Tuten told Smith about a bizarre experience that inspired him to write *Van Gogh's Bad Cafe*. While bicycling to a friend's house on Long Island, he passed by a twilit field that bore a stunning resemblance to a van Gogh painting. Tuten read up on the painter at the library the following day, and was startled to discover that the previous day had been the anniversary of van Gogh's suicide.

The novel generated a positive reaction among critics. Scott Veale of the *New York Times Book Review* (March 30, 1997) cited Tuten's skill in weaving the novel's parallel timelines. In his depiction of van Gogh's final days, Tuten successfully avoided tired "artist" clichés, according to Veale. The reviewer described Tuten's work as "charged throughout with strange, sad magic." Donna Seaman of *Booklist* (March 1, 1997) described *Van Gogh's Bad Cafe* as "clever in concept, superb in execution."

Tuten married his second wife, Elke Krajewska, in November 1996. As of 1999, he was at work on a fifth novel.
—B.S.

SUGGESTED READING: *Booklist* p1676 May 15, 1993, p1112 Mar. 1, 1997; *New York Newsday* p37 June 6, 1993; *New York Times Book Review* p15 May 29, 1988, p9 June 6, 1993, p16 Mar. 30, 1997; *Publishers Weekly* p50+ Mar. 3, 1997, with photo

SELECTED WORKS: Fiction—*The Adventures of Mao on the Long March*, 1971; *Tallien: A Brief Romance*, 1988; *Tintin in the New World*, 1993; *Van Gogh's Bad Cafe*, 1997; Translations—*The House of Farnese* (with Simona Morini), 1968; *Charles Baudelaire: Letters from His Youth* (with Simona Morini), 1970

Courtesy of Douglas Unger

Unger, Douglas

June 27, 1952– Novelist

Douglas Unger is a critically acclaimed author of fiction who strives to make a point about injustice. Delving heavily into his own life experiences, this American novelist writes about the problems related to farming in the United States and the political turmoil in Argentina with eloquent and brutal realism. His first novel, *Leaving the Land* (1984), depicts one family's journey through the changes in farming since World War II. The sequel to that work, *The Turkey War* (1988), describes a town's takeover by the Safebuy Company and the corruption of one man's soul by corporate America. For his other two novels, *El Yunqul* (1986) and *Voices from Silence* (1995), Unger drew liberally from his observations as an exchange student in Argentina, where drastic and often disturbing political changes have occurred since the late 1960s. Often compared to John Steinbeck, Unger is currently at work on *Last Blade of Grass*, which completes his farm trilogy. *Leaving the Land* was a finalist for the Pulitzer Prize and the Robert F. Kennedy Award.

Douglas Unger was born in Moscow, Idaho, on June 27, 1952. His father, Maurice Albert Unger, and mother, Ruth Stoecker Mann, were born on Long Island, New York. Though Maurice Unger had been a practicing lawyer, after World War II he followed his dream out West to become a rancher. By the time Douglas was born, Maurice was teaching at the University of Idaho and was deeply immersed in the culture of the western United States. In his lifetime the elder Unger owned three ranches: the first in Steamboat Springs, Colorado, which he sold after the town became a ski resort; the second in Craig, Colorado; and the last in Newell, South Dakota. The family, which consisted of Douglas and two other sons, relocated frequently, owing to the fact that land values were part of the incentive to buy bigger and better farms in those days. When Douglas was 12, his parents divorced, his mother moving back to Long Island and his father staying out West. In an interview with Gregory L. Morris for the book *Talking Up a Storm: Voices of the New West* (1994), Unger recalled: "I kind of had a dual childhood. . . . I spent some school years [on Long Island] and some with my father in Colorado, so I went back and forth." His father married again, to a woman who had grown up in Gillette, Wyoming. Her stories of growing up and raising turkeys in the 1930s were the basis of the character Marge Hogan in Unger's first novel, *Leaving the Land*. The author described his stepmother to Morris as "a very tough Western woman. . . . I would listen to her talking with neighbor women a lot, and that generated much of the story. She also taught us how to ride, and how to deal with horses; she could cold-cock a horse, literally. She just had no fear."

When Unger was 16 he won an American Field Service scholarship to study in Argentina. At the time, Unger was involved in the counterculture and used drugs, including marijuana and LSD. The scholarship required that he live with an Argentine family who, as it turned out, were quite wealthy. Unger told Rahel Musleah of the *New York Times* (January 28, 1996): "My Argentine family . . . had a barber who made house calls. My purple T-shirts and tie-dyed sneakers disappeared into the rag bin. They set me up in tailored jackets and suits and even a tuxedo. I started living a prep school life and became a real student."

Argentina, during this period, was embroiled in civil unrest—the comparatively gentle military dictatorship was being challenged by leftists, paving the way for the return of Juan Perón in 1973. Just as students in the United States were protesting the actions of their government, so too were their counterparts in Argentina. Unger was right in the middle of it—dodging tear gas during student demonstrations and gaining exposure to Argentine politics. The author told Musleah: "I was educated intellectually and politically that year. I learned I wasn't the center of the world, and I learned how to observe things from the outside."

When Unger returned to the United States in 1970, he enrolled at the University of Chicago—at the time a hotbed of political activity. The university had just had a student strike (the students having taken over the administration building) and the antiwar movement had been in progress for a number of years. Unger himself became involved with the antiwar movement, helped the Black Panthers with their breakfast program (which provided hot breakfasts to schoolchildren before classes), and raised money for Jesse Jackson's Operation PUSH programs. Even while Unger was attempting to change society, he was interested in learning in the traditional sense, having finally had a taste of disciplined education in Argentina, and he read constantly.

As managing editor of the *Chicago Review*, he had a hand in getting William S. Burroughs, Allen Ginsberg, and Lawrence Ferlinghetti to read from their work on campus, and he persuaded the *Review* to have Anaïs Nin give a lecture. Unger recalled in his essay "Trying to Break Away," written for the collection *An Unsentimental Education: Writers and Chicago* (1995), that he had an argument with Nin in the car coming back from the airport. Nin maintained that there were some works written by and about women that men could never understand. "She was proposing a gender-divided way of reading. And I argued with her, just as a University of Chicago student would, aggressively coming back at her with *on the other hand.* . . . Maybe I was wrong then and am dead wrong now, but I still believe that writing and reading are not necessarily gender-divided experiences."

He also met a great many writers who influenced him—including Wayne C. Booth, Norman Maclean, Saul Bellow, and Unger's mentor, Richard Stern. Though Unger graduated from the University of Chicago with a B.A. in General Studies in the Humanities (a program which combined the studies of English, Spanish, and German literatures), his first passion remained writing. His reading had been done partially for the purpose of improving his own work. For his bachelor's thesis, Unger wrote a novel entitled "Fevertree," parts of which were eventually rewritten for inclusion in his second published novel, *El Yanqui*. Unger cited Stern, who repeatedly rejected the work until it became good enough to serve as a thesis, as being quite influential in the progress of "Fevertree." As Unger explained in "Trying to Break Away": "I made it turn, and [Stern] helped me make it turn, by encouraging me to keep doing it—by simply writing a lot, by writing and writing and writing. . . . He was patient. He read everything closely, carefully. I finally just wanted so much to write something he liked. So I pushed through, got honest, and started writing something more real. That was when he let me know that he approved, that writing was what I should be doing, and he really pushed me along." "Fevertree" was actually optioned by Jason Epstein of Random House, who suggested that Unger move to New York to work on the rewrites. Unger abandoned his scholarships and his graduate studies at the University of Chicago and went to New York, thinking that he had "made it" as a writer. From January to July 1974, he earned his living by ghost-writing and occasionally driving his roommate's cab at night. He rewrote his book three times during this period. Even after Unger thought the novel was ready for publication, Epstein kept suggesting further refinements. Following a huge argument, Unger left Random House and New York. With the help of Richard Stern, Unger got into the University of Iowa Writers Workshop, where he became a teaching-writing fellow.

At Iowa Unger learned a great deal, especially from working with Leonard Michaels and John Irving. Unger believes that Irving in particular was a good teacher for him. Irving found that the young author's strongest material was about rural places and suggested that he make those his focus. At the time, Unger was working on all sorts of stories that reflected his past travels—stories set in urban areas, in farm areas, and in South America. Unger believes that the rural stories were his most polished work of that period, during which he was still going back to his father's sheep ranch for summers and vacations. While in Iowa, Unger met Amy Burk, an actress and director, whom he would marry in 1980. (From that union Unger gained a stepdaughter, Erin.)

After graduating with an M.F.A. in English/Fiction in 1977, Unger moved with Amy to California, where, according to his interview with Morris, he spent "probably the drunkest, craziest time in [his] life." At this time he was working on the first drafts of *Leaving the Land*, which he described in that interview as having "this metafictional baggage behind it"—complete with an account of a Japanese firm showing up in South Dakota to raise turkeys on automobile tires and with the appearance of Karl Marx's reincarnation. The book was widely rejected by publishers because, according to Unger, he was "doing crazy things, ripping off a lot of effects, and writing the wrong way."

The couple then moved to New York, where Unger managed the East Side Bookstore for a year. They then moved to Iowa City before settling in Washington state. During these two years (1978–80), Unger claims he wrote no fiction at all. Believing that he had lost his creative abilities, Unger concluded that the book he had been working on all this time would never be published. Partly for that reason, he became a commercial fisherman in Washington. According to his interview with Norris, he considered it "an ideal life, really: you'd start work on a boat around June 1 and fish all summer and on through the middle of November, and then you'd get to collect unemployment the rest of the year." During his first year in his new occupation, Unger worked on a purse-seine boat. By the next season he had done so well he bought his own boat and ran his own operation. In his last season, however, his luck ran out. At around this time he became reinvolved with *Leaving the Land* and sent it to Ted Solotaroff at Harper & Row, who published the book in 1984. In the meantime, Unger had sold his boat and invested the money into Amy's family's farm, which had been abandoned for nearly 20 years, putting in a new well and a drain field.

That farm had an influence on the writing of his first novel. During the 1970s there was a major drought in the farmlands of the United States; it was during this period that Unger's father had abandoned his ranch. The second half of *Leaving the Land* was colored by the disrepair of his wife's farm, and as Unger was rewriting the book, the situation surrounding the farm described in it became darker. *Leaving the Land* is a harrowing portrait of how farming in America has changed since the 1930s. Through the eyes of Marge Hogan and her son Kurt Vogel, Unger offered a detailed account of the owner-occupied farms of the 1930s, which produced a variety of crops and animals before World War II. During the war all this changed when the government provided subsidies to farmers, asking them to raise only turkeys and to sell them to a single food wholesaler—Nowell-Safebuy. After the war, Safebuy raked in enormous profits and sold these turkeys at high prices in their own chain of supermarkets. From these profits Safebuy began acquiring land, displacing the farmers who had owned the land and hiring them as employees and managers. However, since employees do not put in 12-hour days as owners of farms did, production fell and the turkey plant closed, bringing the town down along with it.

The *New York Times Book Review* (February 5, 1984) critic believed that the book "shows family farming giving way to corporate farming and agribusiness. . . . One wonders why that had to be and whether, after all, it is good for the land, our nation, and the world at large." Anne Tyler, writing for the *Washington Post Book World* (March 25, 1984), remarked: "Some books are beautiful, and some books are purposeful; but you don't often find a book that is both. Douglas Unger's first novel is the exception." The majority of the novel's reviews, in fact, were favorable, with *Newsweek* (December 17, 1984) stating that Unger had "made a powerful debut" and *Time* (February 20, 1984) commenting, "A lot of true grit sifts through these pages."

Unger's next novel was based on his experiences in Argentina. The author had remained in contact with the family he had stayed with there, until 1975—the year they vanished like so many other people under the country's military dictatorship after the death of Juan Perón. After years in which he had no contact with the family, Unger received a censored letter from them in 1983. His novel, *El Yanqui* (1986), was published by Harper & Row three years later. It is the story of James, a young American student who wins a scholarship to study in Argentina for a year. James is like many American students of the late 1960s and early 1970s—dabbling in drugs and counterculture, wearing ratty clothes and long hair. In Argentina he lives with a wealthy family, the Beneventos, who treat him to all the pleasures of upper-class living. Renaming him Diego and treating him like one of their own sons, the family quickly converts James to the ways of wealthy Argentine society, cutting his hair, buying him fine clothes, and enrolling him in a Catholic prep school. James also becomes deeply involved with the growing leftist movement in Argentina at the time, led by Juan Perón, a leader and reformer from a bygone era of Argentine prosperity. During a leftist student demonstration, James is arrested but is later freed because of his *yanqui* (Yankee) looks. He then travels to the home of an uncle of the Benevento family, who is a rancher. When he returns to city life with the Beneventos, even their position cannot keep him safe from the oppressive military regime. James is arrested again, this time because of his *yanqui* looks, for dancing with a minor after midnight. Homesick, upon his release he takes his final exams and returns to his natural family in America, only to find that it has disintegrated—his older brother has lost his mind to drugs and the Vietnam War, and his parents have disowned their children. The brothers go their separate ways. Unger concluded his novel with a censored letter, dated 1983, from Diego's adopted mother, who begs him to return. She also describes her own suffering over the imprisonment, torture, and murder of her own sons by the military regime.

Reviews of Unger's second novel were mixed. While the *Orlando Sentinel* (December 14, 1986) praised the book and declared Unger to be "an agile storyteller who has spun here . . . a masterful coming-of-age tale," other reviewers believed that he had tried to cover too much ground in a single novel, offering political statement in place of character. Unger, the *Washington Post Book World* (October 15, 1986) suggested, "like most other novelists whose motivations are primarily political . . . [Unger] cares more about the politics than the people. . . . [The characters] all disappear into the political landscape." In the *New York Times Book Review* (November 30, 1986), Robert Cox, who had lived in Argentina for 20 years, found that Unger's understanding of the political situation there was slight. "Mr. Unger, whose acquaintance with Argentina seems to have been fleeting, does not have the knowledge to record its realities and lacks the imagination to reinvent its myths."

In 1988 Unger published *The Turkey War*, the second book in his projected three-volume farm series. The novel revolves around the life of Nowell-Safebuy chief yardman Mose Johnson, a deeply religious, middle-aged man who has lived alone since his wife, Adelle, ran off with a traveling salesman. In 1943 German prisoners of war start pouring into South Dakota to work in Mose's turkey-production line to replace the American men who are off fighting the war. Mose, who would rather breed his own turkeys than package someone else's, finds himself promoted to production manager over the hundreds of German POWs. The Germans, who are mostly either resistant or indifferent to Nazi politics and ideals, are very proud and work hard, eventually increasing production from 800 turkeys a day to an astounding 5,000. But as their level of productivity mounts, so does the pressure to maintain it, and because of this breakneck pace, quality declines and the number of accidents on the job increases, fueling resentment among the POWs. Mose's problems intensify when his boss orders him to quash a rebellion among the German prisoners. Their strong-willed leader, who cannot forget that he is still at war, takes the fight to American soil when he sabotages Nowell-Safebuy's factory. Mose kills this man, who is already wounded and suffering from hepatitis. Racked with guilt and unable to accept what has happened, Mose turns to drinking and to an affair with one of the farmer's wives.

Some critics, such as William O'Rourke of the *Chicago Tribune* (November 13, 1988), charged that the novel "suffers from the fact that Unger hasn't witnessed what he is writing about." *Publishers Weekly* (August 19, 1988) stated that the aim of Unger's novel seemed to be to show that German POWs were not all Nazis at heart—but claimed that "we never get to know these men well enough as individuals to feel much sympathy for them." Still, *The Turkey War* received many favorable reviews. The *Chicago Sun-Times* (October 16, 1988) critic remarked that Unger "makes us care

what happens to human beings caught in the tides of history." *Inside Books* (January 1989) gave the novel four stars and noted: "This is a taut tale of tragedy mixed with history and small-town life. *The Turkey War* moves at a brisk pace, packed with charm and reminding us of John Steinbeck."

Unger published the sequel to *El Yanqui* in 1995. *Voices from Silence* takes place 15 years after James, or Diego, left Argentina. At the request of his Argentine mother figure, Diego returns to witness the newly elected government's prosecution of the deposed generals who conducted the so-called "dirty war" between 1976 and 1983, in which thousands of Argentines disappeared, including two of the Beneventos' three sons. (The third son has recently returned from Paris after years of exile.) Diego's Argentine parents have suffered greatly during this period, having lost not only two of their sons but their wealth and status. The change in the character of the mother is particularly striking—once the dignified, upper-class lady of the manor, she has now fallen into common habits and is obsessed with sending newspaper accounts of recent developments to her expatriate friends. The story is told through Diego's interview of a once-prosperous prep-school friend, Jorge Gallo, who has in recent years been traveling around the world. Through Gallo, the reader learns much about Argentina's troubled recent history.

The book was generally praised, both for being a beautifully written novel and for containing an important message—thought by many to be a rare achievement in modern fiction. *Publishers Weekly* (June 3, 1995) called the book "a moving experience." The *New York Times Book Review* (September 17, 1995) critic wrote: "Mr. Unger does a fine job reproducing the texture of this era, from the hyperinflation to its still-true-believing Perónists." Still, there were other critics who "gave it the knife," as Unger told the *Las Vegas Review Journal* (September 7, 1995). Having received the greatest praise for his work as well as some scathing reviews, Unger tries to keep a positive attitude about such matters, remarking: "I always remember [Ralph Waldo] Emerson's line, '"If you don't offend somebody, you're not doing your job.'"

—C.M.

SUGGESTED READING: *Chicago Sun-Times* Oct. 16, 1988; *Chicago Tribune* XIV p5 Nov. 13, 1988; *Inside Books* Jan. 1989: *Kirkus Reviews* Aug. 18, 1988; *Las Vegas Review Journal* C p1+ Sep. 7, 1995; *Newsweek* p95 Dec. 17, 1984; *New York Times* p8 Jan. 28, 1996; *New York Times Book Review* p7+ Feb. 5, 1984, p26 Nov. 23, 1986, Nov. 30, 1986, p34 Sep. 17, 1995; *Orlando Sentinel* Dec. 14, 1986; *Publishers Weekly* p5 Aug. 19, 1988, p50 June 3, 1995; *Time* Feb. 20, 1984; *Washington Post* D p2 Oct. 15, 1986; *Washington Post Book World* p3+ Mar. 25, 1984; McQuade, M., ed. *An Unsentimental Education: Writers and Chicago*, 1995; Morris, G. L., ed. *Talking Up a Storm: Voices of the New West*, 1994; *Contemporary Authors* vol. 130, 1990

SELECTED BOOKS: *Leaving the Land*, 1984; *El Yanqui*, 1986; *The Turkey War*, 1988; *Voices from Silence*, 1995

Thomas King/Courtesy of Gerald Vizenor

Vizenor, Gerald

Oct. 22, 1934– Novelist; critic

"Like Coyote and the other great trickster figures of the Native American nations, Gerald Vizenor likes to stir things up," *Utne Magazine* declared in 1995, in naming Vizenor an "Utne Visionary" for that year, along with four other "people who could change your life." *Utne* continued, "What he likes best to stir up are the hoary notion that the Indian stands for something single and simple—savagery, tragedy, or tribal wisdom—and the idea that life can be lived without amazing, painful (and funny) contradictions every step of the way." As one of the most prominent intellectuals among contemporary Native Americans, Vizenor has written more than two dozen books and is represented in dozens of scholarly journals and popular anthologies. He serves as series editor of *American Indian Literature and Critical Studies*, published by the University of Oklahoma Press, which has published 25 titles under his direction. He is also a member of the editorial board of the *American Indian Lives* autobiography series at the University of Nebraska Press and a member of the editorial board of The Smithsonian Series of Studies in Native American Literature.

Among Vizenor's most significant works are the novels *Bearheart: The Heirship Chronicles* (1990), originally published in 1979 as *Darkness in Saint*

Louis Bearheart; *Griever: An American Monkey King in China* (1987); and *The Heirs of Columbus* (1991), which won a National Book Award. He has also written several critical studies of Native American literature and culture and its interaction with the dominant white culture, including *Wordarrows: Indians and Whites in the New Fur Trade* (1992) and *Manifest Manners: Postindian Warriors of Survivance* (1994). Author Ishmael Reed once described Vizenor as one who combined "ancient American storytelling with space-age techniques." "I don't know of anybody else who is doing this," Reed observed.

In a statement for *World Authors 1990–1995*, Gerald Vizenor writes: "George Raft moved my mother and, in that sense, he was the chance of my conception. She saw the thirties screen star, a dark social hero with moral courage, in the spirited manner of my father, a newcomer to the city from the White Earth Reservation in Minnesota.

"I was conceived on a cold night in a kerosene heated tenement near downtown Minneapolis. My father was a storier, my mother was lonesome, and they found each other in the agonies of the Great Depression. President Franklin Delano Roosevelt told the nation, 'The only thing we have to fear is fear itself.' My mother took some comfort in the words of the new president, but she was roused more by the romance of the movies.

"Clement William Vizenor, my father, was murdered three years later, one of many unsolved crimes that year in the city. I was two years old and would learn much later, as a college student, about the homicide in newspaper stories. My mother, who was nineteen years old at the time, never mentioned the death of my father, not to me, not to anyone.

"The *Minneapolis Tribune* reported that the arrest of a 'Negro in Chicago promised to give Minneapolis police a valuable clue to the murder of Clement Vizenor, 26-year-old half-breed Indian, who was stabbed to death in an alley near Washington avenue and Fourth street early June 27 [1936]. Vizenor's slaying was unsolved.'

"The racialist newspaper accounts of his death caused my family needless heartache. Later, that experience motivated me to be a more sensitive writer. Many of my stories as a journalist were about the courage and survivance of native people. My life, in a sense, is heard in others, in the creative presence of others in my stories. Curiously, my first personal association with a newspaper, other than my duties as a delivery boy, was not a daily in the city, but an iconoclastic newspaper on the reservation. At the turn of the last century my relatives published *The Progress*, and later *The Tomahawk*, the first newspapers on the White Earth Reservation.

"Theodore Hudon Beaulieu, editor of *The Progress*, announced in the first issue, March 25, 1886, that the 'novelty of a newspaper published upon this reservation may cause many to be wary in their support, and this from a fear that it may be revolutionary in character. . . . We shall aim to advocate and withhold reserve, what in our view, and in the view of the leading minds upon this reservation, is the best for the interests of its residents.' Theodore was my grandmother's uncle. His courage and dedication is an inspiration to me as a writer.

The *Minneapolis Tribune* hired me as a general assignment staff writer following my investigative report on Thomas James White Hawk who had been sentenced to death for the murder of a white man in South Dakota. I was the only journalist, at that time, who had once delivered the same newspaper that would bear his name and date line as staff writer. Frank Premack, the city editor, assigned me a desk and typewriter on June 3, 1968. He told me that the second coming of Jesus Christ was worth no more than a page and half, 'so, let that be your guide in writing news stories.'

"Robert Kennedy died of gunshot wounds in Los Angeles on June 6, 1968. Sirhan Sirhan was indicted the next day for murder. Premack ordered me to write a feature news story that the nation was not, in essence, violent. My assignment, three days into my career as journalist, was an extreme view at the time. My first story was published on front page of the feature news section. Every journalist must remember some stories more than others. I consider the first one, of course, and my front page story about the funeral of Dane White, a thirteen year old boy who took his own life in jail. He was awaiting a juvenile court hearing for nothing more than truancy from school. 'Kin, Friends Attend Rites for Young Indian' was published on the front page, November 21, 1968.

"Fifteen years earlier the United States Steamship Sturgis, with more than three thousand soldiers on board, was bound for the port at Inchon, South Korea. I was a private in the Army, worried about the peace negotiations. There were no indications that the war would end before we docked. The Sturgis, however, anchored in Tokyo Bay. I was saved from the war because a hospital ship held the last berth at Inchon. I was assigned, with two hundred other soldiers, to serve in the Seventieth Tank Battalion, First Cavalry Division, on Hokkaido, the northern island of Japan.

"I was honorably discharged on August 31, 1955. I bought a used car, a new suit, three shirts, and drove east to visit friends from the military two weeks [later]. I became a college student by chance as my friends persuaded me to join them at New York University.

"*Look Homeward, Angel*, and other novels by Thomas Wolfe, encouraged me as a writer. His stories were traces of an unnameable presence. I first read *A Stone, A Leaf, A Door*, at a military library, a 'stone, a leaf, an unfound door; of a stone, a leaf, a door.' His former faculty office, coincidentally, was occupied at the time by Eda Lou Walton, my first teacher of writing.

"I have published more than twenty books since then, including narrative histories, an autobiography, and six novels. My first books were collec-

tions of haiku poems, and my most memorable haiku teacher was Edward Copeland at the University of Minnesota. He started a literature course that summer with haiku in translation. That sense of impermanence is in the seasons, in the weather, he said, and in the images of haiku; at the same time, we must be aware of culture and tradition. Copeland translated, in class, a haiku poem by Basho: *furuike ya*, the ancient pond; *kawazu tobikomu*, frog leaps, or jumps; *mizu no oto*, sound of water, or splash. He invited us to consider the direct tease of the season, the subtleties of tradition, motion, and impermanence in my own haiku: 'march moon / shimmers down the sidewalk / snail crossing'; 'bold nasturtiums / dress the barbed wire fences / down to the wild sea'; 'fat green flies / square dance across the grapefruit / honor your partner.'

"My haiku images ascribe the seasons with shadow words, that tease of nature and creation. These traces of an unnameable sense of presence seem so natural to me in the translations of native stories and songs. The sky loves to hear me sing, and, as my eyes look across the prairie, I feel the summer in the spring, heartened invitation to the dreams songs of Anishinaabe or Chippewa, translated at the turn of the last century by Frances Densmore."

Gerald Vizenor navigates a treacherous path, one that strives to insert the narrative of American Indians, with its oral tradition and shamanistic imagery, into the literary tradition of a dominant culture that, armed with language and technology, exterminated much of the indigenous populations of the New World. Wishing neither to romanticize the "noble savage" nor to advance a politically correct agenda, Vizenor is a person of nuance who writes with the aim of combating "terminal creeds" that stifle imagination and authenticity. To Vizenor, "terminal creeds" are the impotent beliefs of stereotypical "invented Indians" created by a dominant society that, at best, relegates Native Americans to stock images in popular culture. As Vizenor told an interviewer in *Melus* (1981), "I'm still educating an audience. For example, about Indian identity I have a revolutionary fervor. . . . What I'm pursuing now in much of my writing is the idea of the invented Indian. . . . We're invented from traditional static standards and we are stuck in coins and words like artifacts. So we take up a belief and settle with it, stuck, static. Some upsetting is necessary."

The primal upset in Vizenor's personal life was the suppressed narrative surrounding the violent death of his father, a house painter. During his childhood, Vizenor lived with relatives and in various foster homes, and seemed headed down a road of delinquency until, at 14, he resolved never to have "cops in his life ever again." During this period he was sustained by the storytelling that was part of his culture, and he began to daydream about the characters that would later find their way into his fiction. Kimberley Blaeser, in her monograph *Gerald Vizenor: Writing in the Oral Tradition*, quotes him as saying, "The thing I remember mostly about stories—whoever was telling them: my grandmother, my uncles, the kids, even my mother—the thing that I remember most vividly is the idea of being set free." He told Blaeser: "To me there is no more profound gesture in communication, or I want to use the word *discourse* . . . than to set someone free in talk." Years later, he discussed his troubled childhood with Laura Coltelli for her anthology *Winged Words: American Indian Writers Speak*, telling her, "There's a darkness in me and there's light in me. I think I have a blazing light, at times. I think I have a blazing wit, at times. And sometimes it shows in spontaneous stories and sometimes on the printed page. . . . I internalized a lot of pain and suffering."

After publishing several small-press editions of haiku and other attempts at poetry, Vizenor's first novel, *Darkness In Saint Louis Bearheart*, was published in 1978 by Truck Press. It was reissued in 1990 with an afterword by Louis Owens, by the University of Minneapolis Press as *Bearheart: The Heirship Chronicles*. As he told Coltelli for *Winged Words*, "probably the darkest visions" are in this work, considered the first of his mature output. Set in a dystopian near-future time of oil shortages, the book traces the forced migration of Proud Cedarfair and his wife, Rosina, from reservations coveted for the energy potential of their scarce cedar trees. Owens quotes Vizenor's explanation: "I conceived of it as an episodic journey obliquely opposed to Western manifest destiny, a kind of parallel contradiction, of Indians moving south and southwest rather than west. What they're traveling through is the ruins of Western civilization, which has exhausted its petroleum, its soul." As he would do in many of his subsequent works, Vizenor here assumed a trickster role, in this case that of a bear narrator, a shamanistic device introduced by a Pawnee song "I am like a bear, I hold up my hands waiting for the sun to rise." Bear, as narrator, holds forth that the book is about "travels through terminal creeds and social deeds escaping from evil into the fourth world where bears speak the secret language of saints."

It was in *Bearheart* that Vizenor first posited his concept of "terminal creeds" and "terminal believers" to describe the perils of closed and static world-views, as in the chapter "Terminal Creeds at Orion," where Belladona says: "Listen to this shit, terminal creeds are terminal diseases. . . . The mind is the perfect hunter." After playful wordplay with a bishop ("sheep are terminal followers"; "your wall is more terminal than the church"; "what is your answer to that terminal phrase?"), a hunter replies "The perfect hunter leaves himself and becomes the animal or bird he is hunting. . . He lives on the edge of his own meaning and humor." Owens concluded that "To read *Bearheart* is to take risks, for no preconceived notion of identity is safe, no dearly held belief inviolable. To teach

Bearheart is even more dangerous, as I discovered several years ago when I learned that three students in my American Indian fiction course had reported me to a dean. My sin was including *Bearheart* in my syllabus. The three students, all mixed blood women raised in southern California, had known how to respond to the familiar tragedies of Indians—mixed blood or full—played out in novels by other Native American writers. But *Bearheart*, with its wild humor, upset them." For Owens, *Bearheart* represented a novel that dealt frankly with sexual violence, transsexualism, and multidimensional Indians "capable of cowardice as well as courage, of greed and lust as well as generosity and stoicism." Rather than being cowed by their criticism, Owens decided to insure this novel in every Native American literature course he teaches. "It is a brilliant, evocative, essential corrective to all false and externally imposed definitions of 'Indian.' It challenges all of us, and, like all trickster tales, it wakes us up." As Owens concluded, "*Bearheart* is a liberation, an attempt by the most radically intellectual of American Indian authors to free us from romantic entrapments, to liberate the imagination." Pulitzer laureate N. Scott Momaday, a fellow American Indian author, wrote in a jacket blurb that Vizenor "is at once a brilliant and evasive trickster figure. . . . He is perhaps the supreme ironist among American Indian writers of the twentieth century."

The notion of the trickster is central to much of Vizenor's mature work. But he takes pains to rescue that concept from the popular, first-world notion of the "con-man." As he told Laura Coltelli in *Winged Words*, "A trickster doesn't seize power; he doesn't control power in tribal cultures; it's a compassionate act; he disrupts, makes people very uncomfortable, unhappy, may even threaten them, but he never maintains the army, he never has established a university, he holds credentials which others must study in order to maintain their power in the field of academe. . . . [The trickster is] a survivor in the sense of comedy and comic worldview. He's not trying to establish a nation or a state or an automobile agency or an anthropology department. What the trickster wants to do in creating the new world is just get along, and he's not a tragic hero, he's a comic survivor."

Vizenor takes pains to distinguish the words "survival" and "survivance." The latter term was coined by Vizenor to describe the Native American experience, and it is crucial to understanding the author's cultural perspective. He defines it as "not just survival . . . but a quality and condition of remaining imaginative under domination and getting on with things." The notion of "survivance" is explored especially in his 1994 book *Manifest Manners: Postindian Warriors of Survivance*, published by Wesleyan University Press. Drawing on the theoretical work of Roland Barthes, Jean Baudrillard, and Susan Sontag, Vizenor sees "survivance" as a matter of prevailing in the "word wars" against what he calls "kitschyman" "museum specimen" fakery of "Indian simulations" in which native peoples can authenticate themselves only in the system of "reservation capitalism" where they can offer only the familiar "terminal creeds" for consumption by the dominant culture, which he sees as being co-dependently implicated in the Indian's situation. Even the "radical" identity politics and Wounded Knee imagery comes under Vizenor's deconstructive scrutiny: the cover illustration for *Manifest Manners* is Andy Warhol's portrait of Russell Means, subverted by Vizenor's repetitive comment "This portrait is not an Indian." Kimberly Glaeser finds this a particular feature of Vizenor's autobiographical method, which "becomes more than a literary exercise in subversion; it becomes a mode of tribal survivance, a way in which Native peoples can assert and create a new identity, one not contained by tragic or romantic visions of a vanishing race nor threatened by 'literary annihilation.'

Oral tradition and attention to mythology are also important signifiers in Vizenor's fiction. "When I was seeking some meaning in literature for myself, some identity for myself as a writer," he told a MELUS interviewer in 1981, "I found it easy in the mythic connections." But Vizenor looks at myths as dynamic, not static, as seen in this cautionary passage from Vizenor's preface to *Earthdivers*, also quoted by Owens: "Creation myths are not time bound, the creation takes place in the telling, in present-tense metaphors." In other interviews, Vizenor decries the fact that, as stories get written down by anthropologists and then translated, they lose the variation that is their natural habitat. In oral tradition, as he told Coltelli, "there's a lot of variation, a lot of room. But here comes an anthropologist, records one version, an anthropologist-linguist translates it, and these translations unfortunately become objects, material objects. And then they become kind of scripture, as if it's a litany, that you have to subscribe to and repeat and memorize. And that's not my idea. That's an idea of death—that's not an idea of imagination and life." This aspect of Vizenor's writing was the subject of Kimberly M. Blaeser's exhaustive study, *Gerald Vizenor: Writing in the Oral Tradition* (1996), in which she examined how the author had linked the traditional oral aesthetic with theories of modern literature. "Gerald Vizenor, mixed blood Anishinaabe, comes from a story-telling people," she begins. "Of the crane clan, he descends from the orators of that people. Stories form the foundation of his being, words the foundation of his career. In the worst moments of his life, he has survived by the power of these. 'You can't understand the world without telling a story,' he claims. 'There isn't any center to the world but story.'"

In 1981, two years after the original publication of *Bearheart*, several of Vizenor's Anishinaabe works from the early 1960s were revised and reprinted in the collection *Summer in the Spring: Ojibwe Lyric Poems and Tribal Stories.* That book was itself reprinted as *Summer in the Spring: An-*

ishinaabe Lyric Poems and Stories in 1993. The year 1981 also saw the publication of his *Earthdivers: Tribal Narratives on Mixed Descent*, a semi-autobiographical, semi-mythological work in which he identifies himself as a "mixed blood trickster" who "dive into unknown urban places now. . .to create a new consciousness." Except for *Matsushima: Pine Islands* and *The People Named The Chippewa: Narrative Histories* (both 1984), Vizenor published little after *Earthdivers* until 1987, when he achieved a psychic breakthrough of sorts with his novel *Griever: An American Monkey King in China.* Dedicated to "mixedbloods and compassionate tricksters," this book, which won the 1986 Illinois State University/Fiction Collective Award and a 1990 National Book Award, ushered in a prolific and creative period that has continued unabated for more than ten years. As Vizenor explained in the novel's epilogue, the book had its genesis during a period when he and his wife, Laura Hall, were teaching at Tianjin University for several months in 1983, when he was "overwhelmed" by the Monkey King trickster they saw in a Chinese opera production. Vizenor immediately recognized parallels with his Native American tradition, writing how "this Monkey King has survived the most incredible radical changes a nation could have ever imagined to go through . . . and here he is, and he is still loved, this wonderful wacky Monkey King . . . [who] was doing exactly the things that the woodland trickster was doing—upsetting, distracting, refocusing people who have power, challenging power, seeking ways to be immortal because he was bored being a mortal-just wonderful things." As he told Laura Coltelli, "*Griever*'s the first book I've done that I didn't intend to write . . . I'm not going to China to write a book, that's crazy. Every other dingbat's going over there to tell the world about their experience." Instead of writing a predicable travelogue about China, "I just wrote about me as a trickster." His trickster stance allowed him to write about a "homosexual clown" who "seemed to love the whole wide world," a "mind monkey" who "loved women, heart gossip, stones, trees, and he collected lost shoes and broken wheels."

Vizenor's continued to play with the possibilities of the trickster identity in his next book, *The Trickster of Liberty: Tribal Heirs to a Wild Baronage* (1988), in which, Blaeser points out, he "first pictures the inverted Indian memorialized on a coin and then appropriates, subverts, and radically transforms that static invention when he likens the trickster to 'a warrior on a coin that never lands twice on the same side.' He thus symbolically vivifies the Indian identity, picturing it in an endless process of transformation, engaged in a trickster dynamic. The world keeps on turning, trickster keeps on shifting, Vizenor keeps on writing. The mixed blood trickster earthdiver survives, 'a metaphor in a timeless tribal drama.'" In Vizenor's search for authenticity, he attempts to transcend the narrow limitations of identity in favor of a perpetually shifting persona that "liberates the mind in comic discourse."

Published a year before the Columbian quincentenary, *The Heirs of Columbus* (1991) is Vizenor's magical-realistic attempt to subvert and transgress the Eurocentric myth of Christopher Columbus by reclaiming him as a contemporary "crossblood trickster" descended from early Mayan explorers. One net result of this subversion is the consciousness that the world is indeed "round" though from the point of view more of cultural irony than of geography. As Vizenor wrote in his epilogue, " Christopher Columbus landed in the New World with a striven western gaze that would be overturned in five centuries by the tribal people he saw as naked servants with no religion. . . . Columbus arises in tribal stories that heal with humor the world he wounded; he is loathed, but he is not a separator in tribal consciousness. The Admiral of the Ocean Sea is a trickster overturned in his own stories five centuries later" as he voyages to the New World. In the first chapter, Vizenor writes, "The Admiral of the Ocean Sea, confirmed in the name of the curia and the crown, was an obscure crossblood who bore the tribal signature of survivance and ascended the culture of death in the Old World," traveling in the "*Santa María Casino,* the decorated bingo flagship," with "the *Niña,* a restaurant, and the *Pinta,* a tax-free market" being "simulated caravels." Vizenor weaves his new myth through the ancient voice of his own people, the Anishinaaabe, gathered at their traditional "stone taverns" to be in touch with the ancient "stone brothers" of the trickster-creator. He further comments in the Epilogue that his novelistic standard is derived from Milan Kundera, who wrote in *The Art of the Novel*: "The novel is born not of the theoretical spirit, but of the spirit of humor. . . A character is not a simulation of a living being. It is an imaginary being. . . . The novel is the imaginary paradise of individuals. It is the territory where no one possesses the truth."

Conscious of the obvious postmodern theoretical implications in *The Heirs of Columbus,* Arnold Krupat devoted two full chapters to Vizenor in his 1996 study, *The Turn to the Native: Studies in Criticism and Culture.* Michael Kramer in the *Boston Book Review* (on-line), called attention to Krupat's fascination with Vizenor's "wry, satiric writing" and commented, "In Krupat's opinion, Vizenor envisions a kind of universal tribalism . . . where all individuals are united by common tribal values. . . . Taking advantage of postcolonial theory's sensitivity to the ways in which irony operates, Krupat suggests that Vizenor's satire is meant to be taken seriously as a positive and constructive perspective on Native American identity."

In 1992 the University of Oklahoma Press published Vizenor's *Dead Voices: Natural Agonies in the New World,* a novel that gave voice to the myriad creatures that populate Native American narrative mythology: bears, crows, beavers, fleas, praying mantises, and others. The book is the second volume in the University of Oklahoma Press's American Indian Literature and Critical Studies Series, of which Vizenor is general editor. The book is narrated by Bagese, an elderly shaman whom the narrator observes talking to the birds on a street in Oakland, California. Structured around an Indian tarot-like card game called *wanaki,* in which players briefly assume the identity of the animals on the cards, each chapter describes a different animal and uses a variety of literary forms—narrative, jokes, and puns, with digs at the "wordies" and their literal-mindedness. Describing that book in the *New York Times Book Review* (November 8, 1992), Robert Crum said that Vizenor "appears to be wearing the trickster spirit on his sleeve." Crum added, "The attempt to rescue traditional myths and set them loose in the modern world is a creditable one. . . . Unfortunately, the characters in this book are less animals than puppets. We cannot believe in them; we can only remark on the artfulness of Mr. Vizenor's presentation." In extending his analysis of Vizenor's work to *Dead Voices,* Arnold Krupat speculated, in the words of Kramer, "whether contemporary Native American writers can faithfully carry on their oral tradition." "Vizenor's conclusion, according to Krupat, is that they cannot—too much of the magical fluidity and subtle symbolism of the oral tradition gets lost when written. . . . Krupat believes that the protagonist's choice [to publish stories anyway] signifies the need for Native American authors to struggle onward, to try to find new ways of incorporating storytelling into written works despite the difficulty of this project."

Fugitive Poses: Native American Indian Scenes of Absence and Presence was published in 1999. In the book, which comprises five essays, Vizenor came out in support of a fluid, inclusive concept of Native American identity, one that reflects the extent to which Native Americans have intermarried with other groups. Given the fact that "in the field of Native American literature, the question of identity is a vexed one," Susan Castillo wrote in the *Times Literary Supplement* (June 11, 1999), Vizenor's book "will have the impact of a large firecracker lobbed into the middle of a Sunday School picnic."

Vizenor, who says he prefers to write in the morning when he can more easily avoid distractions, was long accustomed to using a manual typewriter, shifting occasionally to longhand for making corrections. Finding electric typewriters "too noisy," he told Laura Coltelli that he wrote exclusively by hand until shifting to a word processor. "But sometimes I just keep going in writing," he confesses. "I just can't get out of handwriting. Than I'll transcribe it to a word processor." Vizenor added, "I'd like to do two things in storytelling: one, I'd like to discover myself in the story as imaginative, I'd like to feel good about it, at least about the trickster idea in stories. I'd like to imagine myself moving through certain contradictions and conflicts with good humor and maybe a lesson here and there and slipping past it without being damaged by it." In an essay published in Jane B. Katz's *This Song Remembers: Self-Portraits of Native Americans in the Arts*, he wrote, "I am still discovering who I am, the myth in me. . . . I am part crow, part dragonfly, part squirrel, part bear. I kick the sides of boxes out. I will not be pinned down. I am flying home in words and myths." In 1959 he married Judith Horns, with whom he has a son, Robert. He and Horns were divorced in 1969. In 1981 he married the British-born Laura Hall. His book *Postindian Conversations* is scheduled to appear in late 1999.

—E. M.

SUGGESTED READING: *Chicago Review* p50+ 1993; *Chronicle of Higher Education* A p8+ July 13, 1994, with photo; *Melus* 1981; *New York Times Book Review* p1+ May 3, 1992, p18 Nov. 8, 1992; *World Literature Today* p274+ Spring 1992; Blaeser, K. *Gerald Vizenor: Writing in the Oral Tradition*, 1996; Coltelli, L. *Winged Words: American Indian Writers Speak*, 1990; Katz, J. *This Song Remembers: Self-Portraits of Native Americans in the Arts*, 1980; Krupat, A. *The Turn to the Native: Studies in Criticism and Culture*, 1996

SELECTED WORKS: Nonfiction—*Thomas James White Hawk*, 1968; *Tribal Scenes and Ceremonies*, 1976, 1990; *Escorts to White Earth, 1868-1968: 100 Years on a Reservation*, 1968; *Beaulieu and Vizenor Families*, 1983; *The People Named the Chippewa: Narrative Histories*, 1984; *Crossbloods: Bone Courts, Bingo, and Other Reports*, 1990; *Wordarrows: Indians and Whites in the New Fur Trade*, 1992; *Manifest Manners: Postindian Warriors of Survivance*, 1994; *Shadow Distance: A Gerald Vizenor Reader*, 1994; *Fugitive Poses: Native American Indian Scenes of Absence and Presence*, 1999; Poetry—*Two Wings the Butterfly Haiku Poems in English*, 1962; *Raising the Moon Vines: Original Haiku in English*, 1964; *Seventeen Chirps: Haiku in English*, 1964; *Slight Abrasions: A Dialogue in Haiku*, 1966; *anishinabe nagamon: Songs of the People*, 1965; *Empty Swings: Haiku in English*, 1967; *Summer in the Spring: Ojibwe Lyric Poems and Tribal Stories*, 1981, 1993; *Matsushima: Pine Islands*, 1984; Fiction—*anishinabe adisokan: Tales of the People*, 1970; *The Everlasting Sky: New Voices from the People Named the Chippewa*, 1972; *Darkness in Saint Louis Bearheart*, 1978 (reprinted as *Bearheart: The Heirship Chronicles*, 1990); *Earthdivers: Tribal Narratives on Mixed Descent*, 1981 (reprinted from several earlier collections); *Griever: An American Monkey King in China*, 1987; *The Trickster of Liberty: Tribal Heirs to a Wild Baronage*, 1988; *Interior Landscapes: Autobiographical Myths & Metaphors*, 1990; *Bearheart: The Heirship Chronicles* (reprint of *Darkness in Saint Louis Bearheart*), 1990; *The*

Heirs of Columbus, 1991; *Landfill Meditations: Crossblood Stories*, 1991; *Dead Voices: Natural Agonies in the New World*, 1992; *Summer in the Spring: Anishinaabe Lyric Poems and Stories*, 1993; *Hotline Healers: An Almost Browne Novel*, 1997; As editor—*Touchwood: A Collection of Ojibway Prose*, 1987; *Narrative Chance: Postmodern Discourse on Native American Indian Literatures*, 1989, 1993; *Native American Literature: A Brief Introduction and Anthology*, 1995; Screenplays—*Harold of Orange*, 1983

Ken Miller/Courtesy of Viking

Vollmann, William T.

July 28, 1959– Novelist; journalist

It is said that the American fiction writer and journalist William T. Vollmann, a true wild man of the literary world, has given readings dressed in a SWAT uniform decorated with painted iceberg and prostitute motifs and brandishing a gun he shoots to indicate punctuation—"three shots, three dots: an ellipsis," he explained to a reporter from the *San Francisco Bay Guardian* (May 22, 1996). This extreme behavior seems to be more than a show. Known as a writer whose dedication to meticulous research knows no bounds, he has risked his life innumerable times, all for the sake of the story, in such acts as reporting on the war in Bosnia, abducting a child from a Thai brothel to free her from forced prostitution, and spending two weeks alone at the North Pole. Vollmann has written numerous magazine articles, particularly for *Spin*, for which he is a regular contributor, and 10 books (with some five more in production), including the novel *You Bright and Risen Angels: A Cartoon* (1987); the nonfiction work *An Afghanistan Picture Show; or, How I Saved the World* (1992); and *The Atlas* (1996), a partly fictional travelogue.

Born on July 28, 1959 in Santa Monica, California, the son of Thomas E. Vollmann, a professor, and Tanis Vollmann, a homemaker, William T. Vollmann is the oldest of four siblings. His early life appears to have been marred by feelings of guilt stemming from the tragic drowning death of his sister. The incident occurred when Vollmann, nine, was put in charge of watching his six-year-old sister while she played in a pond in New Hampshire. "It had sort of a shallow bottom, and then the bottom dropped off abruptly," he said in an interview with the *New York Times Magazine* (February 6, 1994). "She couldn't swim—I knew she couldn't swim. I just stopped paying attention at one point. I was lost in some kind of daydream." Feeling responsible for her death, Vollmann suffered through years of psychological trauma. "I had nightmares practically every night of her skeleton chasing me and punishing me, pretty much through high school," he said in the same interview. "I felt very uncomfortable at home. I felt that I wasn't exactly wanted there."

Deciding that he needed to leave home as soon as possible, in 1977 he enrolled in Deep Springs College, a small school in eastern California that each year accepts only a dozen male students with outstanding academic records. (The school sends brochures only to those boys who score in the top one-half of one percent on the SAT.) The college has a second, unusual function—it doubles as a cattle ranch. Academic studies are supplemented by such ranch-related activities as roping, riding, and caring for animals. Additionally, Vollmann noted in his interview with the *New York Times Magazine*, "They're real focused on trying to be of service to other people, which has always been something I kind of wanted to do. It's very hard to do—I'm just starting to learn how to do it." After leaving Deep Springs in 1979, he transferred to Cornell University, where he received a B.A. in comparative literature, summa cum laude, in 1981.

Vollmann's postgraduation activities were decidedly unusual. In 1982, when he was only 22, he went to Pakistan with the intention of crossing the border into Afghanistan (entry into Soviet-held Afghanistan was illegal for American citizens) to help the Mujahedeen, the Afghan rebels, fight the Soviets. "I was lured there by the thought of this unknown exotic experience—or by a whole bunch of exotic experiences," he said in an interview with Larry McCaffery published in the *Review of Contemporary Fiction* (Summer 1993). "I guess what I wanted to confront was this foreign 'other.'" Vollmann later immortalized this journey in his 1992 memoir *An Afghanistan Picture Show; or, How I Saved the World*.

Once safely back in the United States, Vollmann began graduate studies at the University of California at Berkeley, where he was a Regent's fellow but remained only until 1983. Details about his life from that point until 1987, when he published his first book, are scarce. Several sources indicate that for some, or perhaps all, of this time he worked as a computer programmer.

Vollmann's debut novel, *You Bright and Risen Angels: A Cartoon*, satirizes war and the information age via a story that involves the creation of a host of computer-generated characters (the "bright and risen angels" of the title) by the narrator, a computer programmer who goes by the name "the author." Once created, the characters quickly become embroiled in a power struggle, carried out much like an elaborate computer game, that pits the characters against the author and one another. Though some reviewers argued that the book included too many extraneous elements, among them a surreal account of the history of electricity, critical reaction to *You Bright and Risen Angels: A Cartoon* was generally favorable. "To the 27-year-old Mr. Vollmann, who appears in print for the first time with this novel, we can give credit for the ingenious creation of a universe whose bizarre characters and events illuminate our own," Gail Pool wrote in the *New York Times Book Review* (June 21, 1987). In 1988 the book earned Vollmann the prestigious Whiting Writer's Award.

The Rainbow Stories, published in 1989, is a collection of short stories based on Vollmann's experiences hanging out with prostitutes, pimps, skinheads, and homeless people in San Francisco's Tenderloin district. The research he conducted for the book, which Vollmann claims included smoking crack cocaine more than 100 times and having unprotected sex with prostitutes, gave rise to his reputation as a maverick with a general disregard for his own personal safety. Oddly, Vollmann considers this reputation unwarranted. "Nothing I do is *that* dangerous," he said in his interview with Larry McCaffery. "Others have built a mystique around my activities."

Critics had mixed opinions of *The Rainbow Stories*. Typical of the book's reviews was the one written by John Clute for the *Washington Post Book World* (July 30, 1989). "There is not much that William T. Vollmann does not ask of his readers, and not much that he is unprepared to give. Whether these gifts will be accepted is another matter," Clute wrote. "They include passion, amplitude, a deep love and knowledge of the underside of urban life in San Francisco, a muscular grasp of large issues of the imagination, and a dark and gruesome humor; but they are packaged in a text that is hugely overwritten, callow, logorrheic, unkempt and undeft, and incontinent. *The Rainbow Stories* is not an easy read."

In 1990 Vollmann published *The Ice Shirt*, the first volume in *Seven Dreams: A Book of North American Landscapes*, his seven-novel project (to date, three of the seven novels have been published) devoted to providing a fictionalized account of American history by focusing on several key events. Described by Noah Richler in *New*

Statesman & Society (June 8, 1990) as a "strange fusion of Norse myth and legend dealing with the arrival of the first colonists and their encounters with the native Indian and Inuit peoples," *The Ice Shirt* is a massive (1,524-page) work complete with sketches and maps penned by Vollmann. Drawing on such diverse sources as the Icelandic and Greenlandic sagas, the chronicles of explorers, tourism brochures, and conversations with drunks, this unusual mix of fact and fiction can be summed up, according to Vollmann, as "an account of origins and metamorphoses which is often untrue, based on the literal facts as we know them, but whose untruths further a deeper sense of truth." Though well received overall, *The Ice Shirt* drew some criticism for its overly complicated plot and lack of character development.

Vollmann followed *The Ice Shirt* with his 1991 short-story collection *Thirteen Stories and Thirteen Epitaphs.* That same year he published *Whores for Gloria; or, Everything Was Beautiful Until the Girls Got Anxious,* a novel in which the protagonist, Jimmy, goes around collecting stories from prostitutes in order to piece together a portrait of his imaginary girlfriend, Gloria. Described by Edward B. St. John in *Library Journal* (January 1992) as "a minor work by an important author," *Whores for Gloria,* unlike most of Vollmann's previous works, received only tepid reviews.

In 1992 Vollmann published *An Afghanistan Picture Show; or, How I Saved the World,* his account of his 1982 attempt to help the Afghan rebels fend off the invading Soviets. In the book, Vollmann's first straight nonfiction work, he revealed the reasoning behind his journey. "I just wanted to comprehend what had happened there," he wrote. "Then I would put myself at someone's service. I meant to be good, and was prepared to do good." As he admitted in the book, however, he was not able to provide many useful services. After Vollmann had failed to achieve the level of physical fitness necessary to fight a war and suffered the effects of chronic dysentery, his appearance and abilities elicited such comments as, "Why . . . like this? You not strong," from the Afghan soldiers. Indeed, when he finally did get to go along on a raid, he was more of a hindrance than a help. "The Young Man," Vollmann wrote, using a phrase he employed throughout the book to refer to himself, "was exhausted and terrified. He stumbled along, leaning on their shoulders. What a burden he was! As I recall this, you cannot imagine a tenth of the shame I still feel." Some critics faulted the book, which featured geographic and historical details, interviews with Afghan rebels, and recollections from Vollmann's childhood, for trying to combine too many disparate elements. "As for the form of the book, it is just possible that the jumble of ill-digested fragments—childhood reminiscences, interviews, moral self-flagellation, lists, dates, titles . . . is calculated in a post-modern way, to create a more active reader," Annette Koback wrote in the *New York Times Book Review* (July 26, 1992). "On the other hand, it may be laziness, an unwillingness to process thoroughly the material he's gathered. Certainly I felt more rather than less confused about the issues at stake by the end of the book, and believe that the author hadn't earned the right to ask me the closing questions: 'I ask the reader: What would your list of important issues be? Have I addressed them? How can *you* help?'" Other critics, however, lauded Vollmann's coverage of the complex issues and attitudes surrounding the conflict. "The aggregate portrait he paints of refugee existence in Peshawar is vivid and complex. Vollmann has come to bear witness to the plight of the Afghanis, but he does not sentimentalize them," William McGowan wrote in the *Los Angeles Times Book Review* (July 19, 1992). "He writes honestly, for instance, about the pervasive corruption in relief operations; the wildly exaggerated expectations of refugees who think America is a land of girlfriends, apartments, and Cadillacs just waiting for them; and cultural attitudes he finds unsettling."

In the years following the publication of *An Afghanistan Picture Show,* Vollmann published volume two of the *Seven Dreams* series, *Fathers and Crows* (1992), an examination of the clashes between North American Indians and the French Jesuit priests who sought to convert them to Christianity; *The Butterfly Stories* (1993), a novel (not, as the title would suggest, a collection of stories) about a journalist who travels to Southeast Asia to investigate prostitution; and the third installment (actually labeled volume 6) of the *Seven Dreams* series, *The Rifles,* an account of Sir John Franklin's disastrous expedition to the North Pole and the effects of Western society and various relocation policies on the indigenous people of North America. (Vollmann, trying to get a feel for Franklin's experience by spending two weeks alone at an abandoned weather station at the North Pole, nearly lost his life when much of his gear proved to be inadequate for the extreme temperatures he experienced.)

Vollmann's most recent book, *The Atlas* (1996), is, in the words of David Schau of *Library Journal* (March 1, 1996), "a highly personal look at the world through his unconventional prose." With essays on places as diverse Canada's Yukon Territory, Goa in India, Madagascar, and Bosnia-Herzegovina, the book offers another unusual blend of fact and fiction. Critical reaction to *The Atlas* was generally unfavorable. "Unfortunately, for all the traveling, Vollmann never manages to escape his own obsessions," a reviewer wrote in *Publishers Weekly* (January 15, 1996). "Whether he is discoursing on drinking beer or shooting heroin or smoking crack or chewing khat in San Francisco, Bangkok or Kenya, the reader is treated to the same lovelorn teddy-bear pining after a devastated whoredom, as if the world can be reduced to a rainy afternoon in a bug-infested hotel room. . . . Despite a structure that Vollmann says, in his preface, is a thematic palindrome, intrepid readers may find it a thematic monotone."

Vollmann is an obsessive writer whose regular 16-hour sessions on the computer resulted in a case of carpal tunnel syndrome that forced him to switch to notebooks. In addition to being a fiction writer and journalist, Vollmann is also an entrepreneur. He is the cofounder of CoTangent Press, a publishing company that specializes in highly unusual limited-edition books by Vollmann and other authors. Included among their offerings in 1991 was a hand-printed artist's edition of "The Happy Girls" (a story from *Thirteen Stories and Thirteen Epitaphs* about the seedy world of massage parlors), each copy of which was packaged with photographs, underwear, buzzer, bra straps, mirror glass, a peephole, and an electric red light. The book was priced at $4,000.

—J. P.

SUGGESTED READING: *Library Journal* p95+ Mar. 1, 1996; *Los Angeles Times Book Review* p3+ July 19, 1992; *New Statesman & Society* p38 June 8, 1990; *New York Times Book Review* p10 June 21, 1987, p10+ July 26, 1992; *New York Times Magazine* p18+ Feb. 6, 1994; *Publishers Weekly* p441+ Jan. 15, 1996; *Review of Contemporary Fiction* p9+ Summer 1993; *San Francisco Bay Guardian* May 22, 1996; *Washington Post Book World* p5 July 30, 1989, p1+ Aug. 2, 1992; *Contemporary Authors* vol.134, 1992

SELECTED BOOKS: Fiction—*You Bright and Risen Angels: A Cartoon*, 1987; *The Rainbow Stories*, 1989; *The Ice Shirt*, 1990; *Whores for Gloria; or, Everything Was Beautiful Until the Girls Got Anxious*, 1991; *Thirteen Stories and Thirteen Epitaphs*, 1991; *Fathers and Crows*, 1992; *The Butterfly Stories*, 1993; *The Rifles*, 1994; *The Atlas*, 1996; Nonfiction—*An Afghanistan Picture Show; or, How I Saved the World*, 1992

Kai Sibley/Courtesy of Anne Waldman

Waldman, Anne

Apr. 2, 1945– Poet

The American poet, translator, and performance artist Anne Waldman has, throughout her career, been associated with the Beat movement led by Allen Ginsberg and Jack Kerouac. Born in New Jersey, she grew up and attended elementary and secondary schools in the artistic, bohemian milieu of Greenwich Village in New York City. As a young woman she followed the New Age path of the times, working in Greece as an archeologist's assistant, attending the Berkeley poetry conference in 1965, meeting a prominent Buddhist lama, and traveling to India, Egypt, and Bali. She became a director of the St. Mark's Poetry Project and a founder with Allen Ginsberg of the Jack Kerouac School of Disembodied Poetics at the Naropa Institute in Boulder, Colorado. The emotional power of oral poetry gripped her, and she became a well-known performance artist. Waldman has published numerous books of poetry, including *Baby Breakdown* (1970), *Life Notes* (1973), *Fast Speaking Woman and Other Chants* (1975), *Journals and Dreams* (1976), *Helping the Dreamer* (1989), *Iovis* (1993), and *Kill or Cure* (1994); issued many recordings; and given countless readings and dance performances with poetry.

Following are excerpts from a work titled "Feminafesto," provided by Anne Waldman (born on April 2, 1945) for use in *World Authors 1990-1995*: "How different are times now for women writers, you ask. Woman anything. Woman scientists! Woman Buddhists! My mother suffered her creativity a scant generation ahead of me. She didn't have a 'room of her own.' Her children were her work. Only in her sixties did she have the confidence—with the support of a daughter and other women and poet-publisher Leandro Katz, to publish her translations from the French of Cesar Moro and Greek of Angelos Sikelianos. She died a decade later playing the 'spirit of heroin' in an off-Broadway production of Burroughs' *Naked Lunch*. By then she was an embodiment for me of the 'hag' who had thrown off shackles of mean expectation, could finally manifest beyond 'girl,' 'wife,' 'mother.' To some extent she'd stopped measuring herself against a heterosexist world. . . . She said when I first married 'I swear if I see you pushing a baby carriage a few months from now, I swear I'll come and shoot you.' She had a tall ambition for me and she was right to worry. For I was and still am, as they say—an incurable romantic. But little that has to do with having a family. 'A man needs a maid?' I never promised domestic bliss.

"And yet my father was a kind of heroic figure, survived the war, returned home from Germany sobered by his experience bringing spoils—Nazi bayonets, medals, haunting images. He was sensitive, literate, former bohemian 'piano player,' a frustrated novelist. As a couple—both had been married previously and my mother with one son—they were optimistic about building on some kind of ashes, shards of war, Depression, Prohibition. Things must have looked brighter. And he went to school on the G.I. Bill—all the way through a doctorate at Columbia University. My mother had been a college freshman-year dropout wanting to study painting, went to Provincetown, a distinctly alternative artistic community, then married age 19 the son of the famous Greek poet Sikelianos and sailed off to Greece the next day for a decade. She was close to her mother-in-law, Eva Palmer, Maine stock, libertarian who donned the garments she herself wove in classical Greek style and kept her red hair long. She had been close to Nathalie Barney in Paris and was part of that exotic cluster of lesbian and bi-sexual artists and poets who were dissatisfied with expectations back home and lived in a self-imposed ritualized exile. Gertrude Stein was another. My mother met Isadora Duncan in Greece. After a little more than a decade that chapter of her life was 'closed.' Divorce, the war, back to Provincetown, matured, met my father at an Isumu Noguchi party. He was living next door to John Dos Passos. They fell in love. A second marriage. Not that he held her back exactly. It was a condition to be in of the times. And you merge with the man in an imitation of enlightenment. Joining the 'other,' joining the 'light.' How close can you get?

"All my teachers in the formative years were male. I especially remember Mr. Grief at P.S. 8, our poetry teacher, who would hold female students by the scruff of their necks and bend them out the window. 'Mr. Grief brings us Grief' was the common chant like 'Rose is a rose is a rose.' He was clearly disdainful of the 'girls'; they were lesser beings. High school teacher Jon Beck Shank was gay, a blessing, whose recitations of classic and modern poetry I will never forget, nor his sympathy with 'the girls.' Because we were soft on poetry too? My male teachers in college thought us dilettantes. Always that persistent need to prove oneself. Get serious. Cut class. Write a poem. One of my mentors Howard Nemerov said to me 'You are both a peasant and a queen.' What did that mean? More categories of definition in a heterosexist world. And when I went to meet my first Buddhist teacher, Mongolian lama Geshe Wangyal, age 18, my boyfriend pleaded 'take off your lipstick, please; it's disrespectful!' And a husband could say with accusation, 'You are just like all the male poets. Just

like Robert Creeley! Traveling the globe leaving hearth and home, abandoning child, jawing with other poets til the wee hours, god knows, how can I trust you?' And how could he? For I wanted this other path, *desperately*; Poet, outrider, free woman. I could hold my own with the boys, I could 'drink like a man!' I could 'talk like a man!' Of course I'd always identified with the male protagonists in the novels I voraciously read as a kid. I was the constant reader. And I was hungry for their adventure. I wanted to be right inside Balzac's *monde*, hang out with actresses & dandies, twist in fatal political & love intrigues. I would follow, I would 'live' Siddharta's journey through the words of Herman Hesse. I had a box of exotic costumes. Favored disguise: Robin Hood, Prince Charming, Annie Oakley, priest. I played a character called Tom Boy Joe, and Shakespeare's 'merry wanderer of the night,' Puck, in grade school before I grew tender breasts. A later age I would yearn to play first Hamlet, then King Lear. And I saw myself as Puer, picaresque adventurer, traveler in boy garb, entering the Hindu temple in Puri strictly forbidden to women, or making the long Haj, the pilgrimage to Mecca. . . .

"When I came into power as a writer and I think also this had to do with becoming a mother as well, I could say outrageous things, could proclaim my 'endometrium shedding.' Could manifest the 'crack in the world.' I shouted 'You men who came out of my belly, out of my world, BACK OFF!' I could literally stomp & 'walk on the periphery of the world.' I could—as Sumerian Inanna did—get the male poets (my fathers) intoxicated on alcohol, methedrine, ecstasy, charm them with my wit, my piety, then steal their secrets. I could name all the various women who have been, to be. Cast a discerning eye at the progressive anthologies of poetry. . . . Do you agree, you'd almost have to, dear scholarly sisters, that the experiences of women in and with literature are different from those of men? Much feminist criticism has centered on the misogyny of literary practice—women as angels or monsters, mothers or nuns, daughters or whores— harassment of women in classic & popular male literature and text. You know it: Kerouac, Mailer, Henry Miller, Homer, the Bible, the Koran, the Vinaya etcetera. But I'd like here to declare an enlightened poetics, an androgynous poetics, a poetics defined by your primal energy not by a heterosexist world that must measure every word, act against itself. . . . I propose a utopian creative field where we are defined by our *energy*, not by gender. I propose a transsexual literature, a hermaphroditic literature, a transvestite literature, and finally a poetics of transformation beyond gender. That just sings its wisdom. That masculine and feminine energies be perhaps comprehended in the Buddhist sense of *Prajna* and *Upaya*, wisdom and skillful means, which exist in *all* sentient beings. That these energies coexist and are essential one to the other. That poetry is perceived as a kind of *siddhi* or magical accomplishment that understands these fundamental energies. . . . "

Anne Waldman has said, "I think of myself as a kinetic writer, thinker: amazed at the places writing originates from." Those "places" exist not only in the figurative sense that she intended but in a literal sense as well. After graduating from the Friends Seminary in New York City, where she already considered herself a poet, Waldman attended Bennington College, in Vermont, a place she thought of as a bucolic refuge from the city, and one where she was surrounded by sensitive, bright, mainly female students with artistic aspirations. Among her teachers there were Howard Nemerov, Bernard Malamud, and Stanley Edgar Hyman. Because one of the college's requirements was that students work off-campus for a time, Waldman worked in theater in Stratford, Connecticut, and in New York City. She then went to the American School of Classical Studies in Athens as a volunteer archaeologist. From there she was able to travel to Egypt, a land redolent of the ancient wisdom that was to fuel the emerging era of New Age beliefs. And during this period, in the early 1960s, she met a Buddhist lama who came from the Tibetan tradition. Thus began her continuing involvement with Buddhism.

In 1965 Waldman went to Berkeley, California, where she attended a poetry conference and heard many important modern poets read. That experience inspired her to commit herself not only to the writing of poetry but to the community of poets. She met her first husband, Lewis Warsh, also a writer, at that time. Waldman and Warsh were the guiding influences behind *Angel Hair*, a magazine and the name of a publishing venture for poetry. Waldman went back to Bennington, graduating in 1966, then returned to New York City, where she become a friend of the poet and artist Frank O'Hara, worked briefly at the Museum of Modern Art as a volunteer, and then went to work as an assistant in the St. Mark's Poetry Project, of which she ultimately became director. The St. Mark's Poetry Project became one of the most important venues in the country for the reading and celebration of poetry by such poets as Robert Bly, Denise Levertov, and, of course, Allen Ginsberg.

In addition to her work at St. Mark's, Waldman spent the years from 1971 to 1973 in intensive travel, which included visits to Central America (where she supported the Sandinistas in Nicaragua), South America, and, finally, India. She was deeply involved with Buddhism when, in 1974, she was invited to attend the first summer session at the Naropa Institute, founded by Chogyam Trungpa Rinpoche. There she and Allen Ginsberg created the Jack Kerouac School of Disembodied Poetics, their affectionate name for a school and gathering place for poets, where she and Ginsberg and other poets such as John Ashbery, Diane di Prima, and Gregory Corso continued to teach.

Waldman also continued her poetic practice, which consisted of writing long poems and performing them in a chantlike fashion and with

movement that could be considered dance. Critics spoke of her as an "oral poet." Gerald Malanga, reviewing her 1973 volume *Life Notes* in *Poetry* (January 1974), found her to be following in the footsteps of Jackson MacLow, Allen Ginsberg, Michael McClure, Gary Snyder, and Robert Bly in breaking away from the printed page. "She moves through language with a simplicity and grace and respect for language that gives her poems power, not only in the way they are written, but in what they have to say," Malanga wrote. The *Library Journal* (May 15, 1976) reviewer, on the other hand, termed Waldman's poetry "verbal doodles."

Her 1976 volume *Journals and Dreams* was reviewed in the *New York Times Book Review* (April 25, 1976) by Aram Saroyan, who called the poems "a kind of high-energy shorthand, elliptical brain-movies of her life and times." The *Library Journal* (May 15, 1976) reviewer, Norman Stock, remarked that Waldman maintained a childlike quality, while having mastered poetic technique. "The result is an engaging combination of quirky free associations and highly literary formal control," Stock wrote. The *Choice* (October 1976) reviewer, however, felt that the childlike quality predominated, to the point of triviality.

In 1980 Waldman married Reed Bye, with whom she had a son. Motherhood was a transforming experience for her, although she had always had a drive to nurture. Her son's asthma was one of the main reasons that she began spending more time in Colorado. She and Bye collaborated on *Rocky Ledge*, a magazine and also the name of a publishing house. They published interviews with Diane di Prima, Peter Orlovsky, and Edwin Denby, the dance critic who was a close friend of Waldman's.

Various reviewers and critics have consistently found Waldman's longer poems more satisfying than her shorter lyrics. The *Choice* (April 1, 1984) reviewer of *Makeup on Empty Space*, her 1984 collection, found Waldman's "shorthand" to be "private and remote" in the shorter poems but found "Matriarchy," one of the longer poems, haunting in its "chantlike refrains, the echoing of words and images within the poem, and the listing, in staccato fashion, of a hurricane of imagery and ideas." The *Library Journal* (April 1, 1984) reviewer also praised the chantlike quality of the poems, singling out the lines "I bind the massive rock / I bind the hanging night, the drifting night the / moaning night, daughter of troubled sleep."

Waldman's collection *Helping the Dreamer: New and Selected Poems 1966–1988* drew qualified praise for "stream-of-consciousness depictions of a modern urban mind, of a 'fast-speaking woman' who celebrates her awareness of the many roles a woman plays with incantations of contemporary flux," in the words of Frank Allen in *Library Journal* (July 1989). Robyn Selman in the *Voice Literary Supplement* (October 1989) remarked that although some of the poems "feel dated," Waldman can "be funny, brave, and care very deeply about all of our futures."

Perhaps inevitably, Waldman—a poet praised for her longer poems—turned to the epic form. Waldman created *Iovis* in an attempt "to fuse numerous leitmotifs: dreams and out-of-body experiences; fathers and sons (Waldman's father fought in World War II, and she studies religion with her son in Bali); gurus (John Cage, Jack Kerouac, and the Dalai Lama); men, or 'seed syllables'. . . ; women; . . . political concerns (arms control and human rights); shape-shifting and voices; . . . and opaque occult and heavy-metal imagery (she once 'nibbled' psychotropic drugs)," according to Frank Allen in *Library Journal* (March 1, 1993). Ken Tucker in the *New York Times Book Review* (September 5, 1993) termed the volume "one of the most open-minded and audacious of latter-day dialogues between the sexes." He observed that Waldman "challenges the 'many patriarchs at the top of the mountain,'" including William Carlos Williams and Ezra Pound, the "epic masters" who preceded her. Brooke Bergan, writing in *Small Press* (Summer 1993), praised Waldman's writing in "this traditionally male genre." She noted , too, Waldman's sly undercutting of the genre, as in the declaration, "the poet must be a warrior on the battlefield of Mars, o give me a break, thank you very much."

Between the dates of publication of the two parts of *Iovis*, in 1993 and 1997, some reviewers changed their minds on how to view epic poetry. In *Publishers Weekly* (January 25, 1993) the reviewer remarked that Waldman's "collage lacks the charm and happy accidents of true randomness, and the language falls short of the purity that makes minimalism interesting." A writer for the December 30, 1996 issue of the same publication declared that *Iovis, Book II* "retains a firm hold on relevance with its accrual of talon-sharp details."

In addition to acting as den mother to New Age poets, performing, and writing, Waldman has also become known as a translator and editor. She compiled *Nice to See You* (1991), an homage to Ted Berrigan; *Out of This World* (1991), an anthology of the St. Mark's Poetry Project, covering the years 1966–1991; *Disembodied Poetics* (1994), annals of the Jack Kerouac School, coedited by Andrew Schelling; and *The Beat Book* (1996), poems and fiction of the Beat generation with a foreword by Allen Ginsberg, termed "a fine volume . . . of . . . high quality" by Donna Seaman in *Booklist* (February 15, 1996).

Waldman and Andrew Schelling, with whom she fell in love at Naropa and who became her companion, translated *Songs of the Sons and Daughters of Buddha* (1996). The opening poem by Dhammapala, the original compiler of these songs by Buddha's first followers, forms a kind of credo: "listen / to the songs of these / disciplined ones / telling their names, their lives, / how they hungered for Dharma / how they struggled to / freedom. . ./ and so they touched the ageless unborn Way / so they lived / and so they set to song / the brave details / of their search."

Waldman's own poetic style is exemplified by "Nerves," published in the *American Poetry Review* (July/August 1995). The poem rhythmically echoes its title and displays many of Waldman's concerns, especially in its political leftism and the flavor of Buddhism. With satiric riffs on the merits of modern scholarship, it begins: "Nerves, blind attraction to, / scholar says / the margins are safe, / but deeper inside the book / we'll go, where nerves retreat and / study balances the mind / It was night. He was right." She brings up images of books with pages cut out and continues: "Pages of great ones being excised / for a greater purpose because they are / severe or salient manifestos / to be put up on all the lampposts. . . . " She concludes with a question: "Will intellectual rigor respond & / save all our miserable days / Pass the word around? / What sense of opulence did / a friendlier human score under, / An earlier benign time was it?"

Waldman received the Dylan Thomas Memorial Award in 1967 and the Bennington College Alumni Award for Achievement in the Field of Poetry in 1981. In 1985–86, Waldman was a consultant with the Festival of India Program in Poetry. In 1996 she left the United States. She told *World Authors* that she was going to Indonesia for an extended stay.
—S. Y.

SUGGESTED READING: *American Poetry Review* p8 July/Aug. 1995; *Booklist* p978 Feb. 15, 1996; *Choice* p829 Oct. 1976; *Library Journal* p1215 May 15, 1976, p724 Apr. 1, 1984, p83 July 1989, p82 Mar. 1, 1993; *New York Times Book Review* p18 Apr. 25, 1976, p21 Sep. 5, 1993; *Poetry* p236 Jan. 1974; *Publishers Weekly* p 60 Dec. 30, 1996; *Small Press* p82 Summer 1993; *Voice Literary Supplement* p5 Oct. 1989; *Contemporary Authors* nrs vol. 34, 1991

SELECTED BOOKS: Poetry—*On the Wing*, 1968; *O My Life!*, 1969; *Baby Breakdown*, 1970; *Giant Night: Selected Poems*, 1970; *Up Through the Years*, 1970; *Goodies from AW*, 1971; *Holy City*, 1971; *Icy Rose*, 1971; *Memorial Day* (with T. Berrigan), 1971; *No Hassles*, 1971; *Light and Shadow*, 1972; *Spin Off*, 1972; *The West Indies Poems*, 1972; *Life Notes: Selected Poems*, 1973; *Self Portrait* (with J. Brainard), 1973; *Fast Speaking Woman*, 1974; *Fast Speaking Woman and Other Chants*, 1975, rev. ed. 1978; *Sun the Blond Out*, 1975; *Hotel Room*, 1976; *Journals and Dreams*, 1976; *Shaman*, 1977; Four Travels (with R. Bye), 1979; *Polar Ode* (with E. Myles), 1979; *To a Young Poet*, 1979; *Countries*, 1980; *Cabin*, 1981; *First Baby Poems*, 1982, rev. ed. 1983; *Makeup on Empty Space*, 1984; *Invention* (ill. S. Hall), 1985; *Sink Meat Bones*, 1985; *Blue Mosque*, 1987; *The Romance Thing*, 1987; *Helping the Dreamer: New and Selected Poems, 1966-1988*, 1989; *Not a Male Pseudonym*, 1990; *Lokapala*, 1991; *Fait Accompli*, 1992; *Iovis: All Is Full of Jove*, 1993 *Iovis Book II*, 1997; *Troubairitz*, 1993; *Kill or Cure*, 1994; As editor—

Nice to See You, 1991; *Out of This World: An Anthology of the St. Mark's Poetry Project, 1966-1991*, 1991; *Disembodied Poetics* (with A. Schelling), 1994; *The Beat Book*, 1996; As translator—*Songs of the Sons and Daughters of Buddha* (with A. Schelling), 1996

Wallace, David Foster

Feb. 21, 1962– Novelist; short-story writer; essayist

With his first novel, *The Broom of the System* (1987), the American author David Foster Wallace struck reviewers as possessing "a wealth of talents," in the words of Michiko Kakutani of the *New York Times* (December 27, 1986). Jenifer Levin, in the *New York Times Book Review* (November 5, 1989), said of Foster's next book, the collection of short stories *Girl with Curious Hair* (1989), that the successful stories have "the quality of a dream: powerful, fixating, explosive, and mysterious." With *Infinite Jest* (1996), a novel of more than a thousand pages, Wallace carried on "the Pynchonian celebration of the renegade spirit in a world gone flat as a circuit board," according to Sven Birkerts in the *Atlantic Monthly* (February 1996). Kakutani, reviewing *A Supposedly Fun Thing I'll Never Do Again: Essays and Arguments* in the *New York Times* (February 4, 1997), declared that that volume "attests to his virtuosity, an aptitude for the essay, profile, and travelogue, equal to the gifts he has . . . begun to demonstrate in the realm of fiction." Wallace's story collection *Brief Interviews with Hideous Men* was published in 1999.

David Foster Wallace was born on February 21, 1962 in Ithaca, New York and grew up in Urbana, Illinois, where his father, James Donald, taught philosophy at the University of Illinois at Urbana-Champaign and his mother, Sally, taught English at a local community college. Wallace was a competitive tennis player in tournaments in the Midwest throughout his boyhood. He graduated from Amherst College, in Amherst, Massachusetts, and began his writing career immediately thereafter. His decision to write fiction was taken in spite of the fact that professors at Amherst had pegged him to become "an important philosopher," according to Frank Bruni's profile of Wallace, published in the *New York Times Magazine* (March 24, 1996). He received a master of fine arts degree in creative writing from the University of Arizona in 1987 and has also done graduate studies in philosophy at Harvard.

With the publication of his first novel, *The Broom of the System*, written when he was in his early 20s, Wallace began to enjoy a kind of cult status. He won the Whiting Writers' Award for the book, which concerns Lenore Stonecipher Beadsman, her friend Candy Mandible, her boss Rick Vigorous, and assorted other characters from whose point of view the story is sometimes told. The minimal plot lines emerge from a matrix of telephone messages, transcripts of psychotherapy sessions, corporatespeak memos, and submissions to a literary magazine. The philosopher Wittgenstein's notion that language is the tool with which we construct reality is the novel's dominant idea. "At book's end, Lenore remains a cipher. . . . Clearly, that's what Wallace intends—she hasn't found the words to put her self together," Dan Cryer wrote in *New York Newsday* (January 29, 1987).

For Michiko Kakutani, writing in the *New York Times* (December 27, 1986), *The Broom of the System* marked the debut of an important literary talent that might or might not fulfill its promise: "Wallace possesses a wealth of talents—a finely tuned ear for contemporary idioms; an old-fashioned story-telling gift (as evidenced, in particular, by the stories within stories contained in this novel); a seemingly endless capacity for invention and an energetic refusal to compromise. . . . *Broom* is no mean achievement—and yet only a shadow of what the author might accomplish given the application of some narrative discipline and the exchange of other writers' voices for a more original vision."

Caryn James, in the *New York Times Book Review* (March 1, 1987), remarked that Wallace's attempt "to create his own language game, a fictional system in which 'something's meaning is nothing more or less than its function'" has too-weak "philosophical underpinnings." She nevertheless declared that "*The Broom of the System* succeeds as a manic, human, flawed extravaganza."

With Wallace's second book, *Girl with Curious Hair*, a story collection, most reviewers deemed him well on the way, not only to becoming the next Jay McInerney or Bret Easton Ellis and a fitting heir to the metafictional novelists John Barth, Robert Coover, and Thomas Pynchon, but also to achieving his own voice. Douglas Seibold, for example, writing in the *Chicago Tribune* (January 21, 1990), remarked that while "Everything Is Green" is laden with the clichés of minimalist writing, "the story, a gem of a thousand words at most, is one of the best. . . . Wallace demonstrates that those minimalist conventions have become clichés only through their repeated abuse at the hands of less imaginative and less passionate writers."

Many of the characters have the names of actual historical figures or characters from television shows, running "the gamut from banal to psychotic," as Jenifer Levin noted in the *New York Times Book Review* (November 5, 1989). "If . . .Wallace's characters include the transcendent as well as the maimed, his style is similarly varied, running from prosaic to lyrical," she added. Levin commented on one particularly outstanding story in *Girl with Curious Hair*: "'John Billy,' a luminous explosion into the realm of myth in which a bandylegged Oklahoman is transformed by a near-fatal brush with death (and evil) into a creature of both darkness and light, one whose damaged eyes extend like the waving ends of antennae from his head, capable of finally seeing things. Those eyes . . . show him the wasted and bleeding countryside, linking him (like the Fisher King of myth) to the death of the land. . . . In this daring exploration of the mythological and metaphysical context of fiction—and thus of life itself . . . Wallace demonstrates his remarkable talent."

The following year, Wallace published with Mark Costello *Signifying Rappers: Rap and Race in the Urban Present* (1990), a nonfiction study of rap music. In this book, the two white men "use a mixture of street language and esoteric words to comment self-consciously on the violence, misogyny, vulgarity, anger, and braggadocio inherent in this music largely by and for black inner-city youths," the *Choice* (March 1991) reviewer noted. Gregory Stephens in the *San Francisco Review of Books* (Fall 1991) termed the volume "lively and far more humorous than the subtitle would indicate. This is one of the voices of rap's audience."

Wallace won a 1996 Lannan Literary Award for fiction for *Infinite Jest*, his eagerly awaited "big" novel. Set in the near future (how near is not exactly clear, because the calendar has been sold to commercial interests and it is mainly the Year of the Depend Adult Undergarment), the novel takes place "in parallel worlds of substance abuse and sports training" and "helixes the inhabitants of the suburban Boston rehab center Ennett House and its tonier, yet no less troubled, neighbor, the Enfield Tennis Academy," according to Richard Gehr in *Spin* (March 1996). What has been termed the "MacGuffin" of the novel, the central object like the white whale in *Moby-Dick*, is a missing film, *Infinite Jest*, supposedly made by the founder of the Enfield Academy, James O. Incandenza, who has committed suicide by sticking his head in a microwave oven. The film is also a weapon because it causes people to entertain themselves to death like cocaine- addicted rats who will seek the drug rather than food. (Wallace thus comments on the American public's addiction to mindless entertainment.) The chief characters in the novel are the tennis star Hal Incandenza; Don Gately, an addict from the rehab center; and a group of wheelchair-bound terrorists, Quebec separatists, angered that much of New England has been turned into a toxic waste dump and fobbed off on Canada. These latter characters want to use the film as a weapon.

Jay McInerney, in the *New York Times Book Review* (March 3, 1996), declared *Infinite Jest* alternately "tedious and effulgent." But, McInerney added, "What makes all this almost plausible, and often pleasurable, is . . .Wallace's talent—as a stylist, a satirist, and a mimic—as well as his erudition, which ranges from the world of street crime to higher mathematics. . . . And there are dozens of set pieces that double as dazzling mini-entertainments. . . . Equally lively is . . .Wallace's rendition of a New Age 12-step men's group in which bearded hulks sit in a circle clutching teddy bears that represent their inner infants. 'Can you share what you're feeling, Kevin?' asks the group leader. 'I'm feeling my Inner Infant's abandonment and deep-deprivation issues, Harv,' answers a weeping, bearded bear-clutcher." In the end, however, according to McInerney, "it is the dogged attempt of the recovering addict Don Gately to reclaim the simple pleasures of everyday life that overshadows the . . . pyrotechnics of the Incandenzas—and makes this novel something more than an interminable joke."

For Bharat Tandon, writing in the *Times Literary Supplement* (June 28, 1996), the success of *Infinite Jest* lies "not so much in its formal experiments as in its portrayals of the blurry hinterland where recreation meets slavery. . . . Aside from the obvious chemical and alcoholic fixes, Wallace has assembled any number of strange and malign 'virtual realities'. . . . It is the collapse of . . .crucial distinctions' that Wallace renders so well, conveying the sadness and confusion of an America where 'prosthetic man' has gone mad and people clamour for the simulations of experience over experience itself, all these images meeting in the elusive movie."

Michiko Kakutani in the *New York Times* (February 13, 1996), declaring that "perfect . . . *Infinite Jest* is not" (she compared Wallace to "Thomas Wolfe without Maxwell Perkins"), found the novel's "big psychedelic jumble of characters, anecdotes, jokes, soliloquies, reminiscences, and footnotes uproarious and mind-boggling, but also arbitrary and self-indulgent." She did note that the characters "tossed out" by Wallace's "word machine" have their "grotesque, willfully bizarre lives somehow rendered palpable, funny, and affecting."

Infinite Jest clearly contains many elements from Wallace's own life. The disquisitions on tennis playing come from personal knowledge, as does some of the drug lore. After writing *The Broom of the System*, Wallace had gone into a downward spiral. He drank heavily, took drugs, engaged in a series of short-lived affairs, and made one or more suicide attempts (he admitted to one, but Frank Bruni mentioned that Wallace's friends spoke of more). Wallace pulled himself together, however, and moved back to Illinois. There he got a job teaching at Illinois State University in Normal and moved to a house amid cornfields. Although Wallace has given many readings around the country to promote *Infinite Jest* and has gotten some mild enjoyment from the limelight, he remains a very private person.

Wallace's first book of essays, *A Supposedly Fun Thing I'll Never Do Again*, was published in 1997. Michiko Kakutani in the *New York Times* (February 4, 1997) thought the volume all of a piece with *Infinite Jest*: "Like *Infinite Jest*, *A Supposedly Fun Thing I'll Never Do Again* is animated by . . .Wallace's wonderfully exuberant prose, a zingy, elastic gift for metaphor and imaginative sleight of hand, combined with a taste for amphetaminelike stream-of-consciousness riffs." Kakutani also commented on Wallace's "old-fashioned love of character." He has, she noted, an "intimate sense of his characters' emotional and spiritual lives." This sense carries over to his essays, in which "those impulses are actually articulated, in what amounts to a kind of aesthetic manifesto." Rather than being driven solely by irony, a strong sense of which is necessary to expose the hypocrisy of modern life, Wallace is also engaged with "the deep moral issues that animated the work of the great 19th-century novelists." Laura Miller in the *New York Times Book Review* (March 16, 1997) agreed with Kakutani that *A Supposedly Fun Thing I'll Never Do Again* "reveals Mr. Wallace in ways that his fiction has of yet managed to dodge: as a writer struggling mightily to understand and capture his times, as a critic who cares deeply about 'serious' art, and as a mensch." She added: "Wallace wears his heart on his sleeve. And it turns out that he harbors high ideals for art in general and fiction in particular. . . . 'The new rebels,' he speculates, 'might be artists willing to risk the yawn, the rolled eyes, the cool smile, the nudged ribs, the parody of gifted ironists, the "Oh, how *banal*." To risk accusations of sentimentality, melodrama. Of overcredulity. Of softness.'"

Wallace's risks were well rewarded when he received a MacArthur Fellowship in 1997 for $230,000. The award was given to him as a "novelist noted for his inventive wordplay, intellectual rigor, and what has been called postmodern absurdism," according to the *New York Times* (June 17, 1997).

"Sex in its more disturbing modes is the . . . underlying theme" of Wallace's 1999 story collection, *Brief Interviews with Hideous Men*, as a writer for *Booklist* (May 1, 1999) put it. In its starred review of the book, *Publishers Weekly* (March 29, 1999) announced, "Some of the 23 stories in Wallace's bold, uneven, bitterly satirical second collection seem bound for best-of-the-year anthologies; a few others will leave even devoted Wallace fans befuddled. The rest of the stories fall between perplexing and brilliant, but what is most striking about this volume as a whole are the gloomy moral obsessions at the heart of Wallace's new work."
—S. Y.

SUGGESTED READING: *Atlantic* p106 Feb. 1996; *Chicago Tribune* XIV p7 Jan. 21, 1990; *Choice* p1145 Mar. 1991; *New York Newsday* p11 Jan. 29, 1987; *New York Times* C p15 Feb. 4, 1997, A p16, June 17, 1997; *New York Times Book Review* p22 Mar. 1, 1987, p31Nov. 5, 1989, p8 Mar. 3, 1996, p11 Mar. 16, 1997; *New York Times Magazine* p38+ Mar. 24, 1996, p189 Sep. 29, 1996; *San Francisco Review of Books* p51 Fall 1991; *Spin* p120 Mar. 1996; *Times Literary Supplement* p 22 June 28, 1996

SELECTED BOOKS: Fiction—*The Broom of the System*, 1987; *Girl with Curious Hair* 1989; *Infinite Jest*, 1996; *Brief Interviews with Hideous Men*, 1999; Nonfiction—*Signifying Rappers* (with M. Costello), 1990; *A Supposedly Fun Thing I'll Never Do Again*, 1997

Wallace, Michele

Jan. 4, 1952– Nonfiction writer; journalist

The impassioned black feminist Michele Wallace caused a stir in 1979 with the publication of *Black Macho and the Myth of the Superwoman*. In it Wallace argued that when the civil rights movement of the 1960s developed into the black power movement, black men abandoned the broader struggle for human rights and focused instead on instilling pride in black manhood. This shift, in Wallace's view, further marginalized black women, who were traditionally denied a voice in the affairs of African-American politics and who also appeared to be victims of a sexist ideology created by the white majority and affirmed by black men. While many supported Wallace, who was viewed as a spokeswoman for the black feminist movement, others claimed that she was fanning the flames of a controversy that didn't exist. Her most recent work, *Invisibility Blues: From Pop to Theory* (1991), looks at the seeming voicelessness of black women in American culture.

Michele Faith Wallace was born on January 4, 1952, in New York City, the daughter of Robert Earl Wallace, a musician, and the writer and artist Faith Elizabeth Ringgold. Although Michele was a young girl in the 1960s, when the civil rights movement was at its height, the importance of standing up for one's rights was not lost on her. In fact, some of the most radical movements of the 1960s—including the feminist movement and the black power movement (as personified by the Black Panthers)—greatly influenced her thinking, as did her mother, an ardent feminist. "My family specialized in superwomen of various sorts and women who just couldn't cope on almost any level," Wallace wrote in an autobiographical article for the *Village Voice* (February 13, 1996). "From an early age, you were expected to declare what you would be. I always thought Faith and I came to feminism at the same time, but I now suspect that I was following her lead in the way that a child sometimes can without being aware of it, especially since I was an inveterate mama's girl right through my early 20s." In the early 1970s, while Wallace was studying English literature as an undergraduate at City College of

New York, she aided her mother in a variety of causes, most notably the antiwar movement; with her mother's help, the future author also established the Women Students and Artists for Black Art Liberation, an advocacy group that sought to end the exclusion of black artists from certain museums.

Activism provided the context for her writing, which Wallace began in earnest during her college years. As a student she received the opportunity to read her feminist poetry to noted authors such as Audre Lorde, and in 1971 her essay "Black Women and White Women" was published in *Woman's World*. Theresa Schwartz of *The New York Element* sent Wallace to Washington, D.C., to cover the Black Panthers convention, where Huey Newton and the actress and activist Jane Fonda appeared. By the time she graduated from college, in 1974, Wallace had already gained experience as an activist and writer.

During this time she suffered from bouts of depression, drifting unenthusiastically through a collaboration with her mother, providing the texts for Ringgold's "Political Landscapes" art series. In the fall of 1974, things began to look a bit brighter when her friend Margo Jefferson, later a writer for the *New York Times*, helped to secure her a job as a book-review researcher at *Newsweek*. The job brought her new opportunities for intellectual stimulation, from the Newport Jazz Festival to the Public Theater to New York literary parties, where she hoped, as she noted in the *Voice* article, that "I would meet Norman Mailer, whose anti-feminist rants I secretly found hugely entertaining." While at *Newsweek*, she also worked on cover stories about such figures as Erica Jong and Toni Morrison.

Wallace, along with her mother, became a founding member of the National Black Feminist Organization. In 1974 she also became president of Art Without Walls, and two years later, along with Jefferson and the poet Pat Jones, she organized the Sojourner Truth Festival of the Arts at the Women's Interarts Center. While there, she met the playwright Ntozake Shange, who performed a piece from her play *For Colored Girls* at the festival, and Wallace subsequently interviewed her for the *Village Voice*. Wallace's visibility as a reporter helped her to establish ties with such black women writers as Alice Walker, Toni Morrison, Judith Wilson, and June Jordan. The group soon began meeting at Alice Walker's house in Brooklyn to discuss the role they should play in the feminist movement.

With new exposure to literary figures, Wallace's drive to become a well-known writer grew stronger. Although she had been a contributor to *Ms.* and had begun writing for the *Village Voice* in 1974, she remained unsatisfied until she wrote two pieces for the *Voice*: one was titled "Anger in Isolation: A Black Feminist's Search for Sisterhood," and the second focused on her growing up as a "black American princess" in the Harlem of the 1950s and 1960s. Together with the Shange inter-

view, the pieces solidified her identity as a black feminist and gained her considerable public notice—as well as a book editor (Joyce Johnson) and a literary agent (Maxine Groffsky).

With a book proposal drawn up with the help of Groffsky, and an advance from Johnson, Wallace quit her *Newsweek* job, moved from her mother's home to an apartment on Greene Street in the Soho section of New York City, and began working on her book. "Within a few months," she remarked in her *Voice* article, "I had whipped up the core of what I thought would be a single chapter on black men. But Joyce argued that it should be the centerpiece of the book and that I needed only another large section on black women. We then began the laborious two-year process of editing 'Black Macho' and constructing the much more difficult section of the book that would be called 'The Myth of the Superwoman.'" In the meantime, however, the struggling young author was running low on money, so she took a job teaching journalism at New York University.

An uproar ensued when *Black Macho and the Myth of the Superwoman* finally appeared, in early 1979. At the age of 26 Wallace was suddenly the most widely recognized black feminist in the country. In the book she argued that when the civil rights movement developed into the black power and black consciousness movements of the late 1960s and early 1970s, the struggle for basic human rights—which was essential to the civil rights movement—disappeared. What replaced it, Wallace contended, put black manhood at the center of black politics, and did little to discourage sexism in black men.

In the first section of the book, *Black Macho*, Wallace argued that black men began to equate black political power with masculinity, and thereby shut black women out of political affairs. Without a voice, the author suggested, the average black woman was no better off than in the days of slavery, when she did all the menial labor in her household and received no credit. In addition, according to Wallace, black men—motivated by revenge for the sexual abuse of black women by white men—began to pursue sexual relationships with white women, effectively abandoning black women. The author concluded that black men seemed to have assumed that black women were strong enough without them, an assumption based on the myth of the black woman as "super matriarch."

In the second part of the book, "The Myth of the Superwoman," Wallace contended that black women were denied equal rights because of widespread acceptance of the concepts of "black macho" and the "super matriarch" in the United States. Wallace argued that the only reason black women had not, to that point, embraced feminism was because they believed that being black was a greater burden than being female. The burden of blackness, along with black women's own beliefs that they were "super matriarchs," prevented them from developing their own identities.

The public wasted little time in expressing their confusion and outrage over the book. According to Wallace, many black people approached her, book in hand, questioning a number of the things she had written. The critical community was divided as well. *Library Journal* (March 1, 1979) called the book "A clear and original political argument against racism and sexism," one that was "unquestionably significant." Writing for *Newsweek* (February 5, 1979), Walter Clemons asserted, "Occasionally a book appears that can be criticized in several ways, and yet the work is so important that criticism slides off it like rain down a window. [This book] is like that, a powerful though flawed work which speaks to an essential and previously unrecognized need." Perhaps the most scathing criticism came from June Jordan, who wrote in the *New York Times* (March 15, 1978) that "[alternating with] fierce and freehand generalities are other pronouncements that reveal an astonishing ignorance at best. . . . You do have to concede champion qualities to Miss Wallace's capacity for the unsubstantiated, self-demeaning, ahistorical pronouncement. And from her total account of things, it is really hard to tell who is supposed to be the more contemptible: the black man or the black woman. Nor can I ever guess what she is for: what she loves, what she respects. . . . [This book] is nothing more nor less than a divisive, fractious tract devoid of hope and dream, devoid of even a competent scholarship that would signify respect for the subject so glibly undertaken."

Wallace soon found herself defending her book. She appeared on the cover of *Ms.* but was challenged in the same magazine with the question of whether or not she was up to the challenge of being a spokeswoman for black feminists. At every public appearance detractors questioned her ideas, her looks, and her manner of dress. Her mother felt snubbed by the book—even though Wallace had dedicated it to her—because she didn't feel she had received enough credit for her hand in molding her daughter's feminist beliefs. In an interview with Lisa Jones of the *Village Voice* (July 11, 1995), Wallace recalled that "for me, the experience of being criticized and being dumped on as a young woman was very painful. At the time, I was not really fully available to the criticism. And the baggage my critics were hitting me with wasn't as remotely painful as what I was laying on myself. The period is still wrapped in a haze of drugs, alcohol, cigarette smoke, and denial."

Around 1981, while still teaching at New York University, Wallace suffered a nervous breakdown. After some time she emerged, according to *Essence* (February 1991), "feeling lucky to be alive, born again." She returned to teaching, eventually at City College as an assistant professor of English, and she contributed short stories, articles, essays, and poetry to a number of magazines and newspapers, including the *Village Voice*, *Esquire*, and *Ms.*

In 1991 Wallace published 24 of these essays in the collection *Invisibility Blues: From Pop to Theory*. The essays, written between 1972 and 1990, ranged from pieces on Michael Jackson and Spike Lee to feminist takes on black culture, community, and family life. Although she recanted some of her early views, she remained committed to the idea that sexism is an extremely divisive force in the black community, and she sought to discover why black women are highly visible in American society but have almost no say in the political workings of the country. Critics were generally pleased with the collection. Barbara Burford of *New Statesman and Society* (November 30, 1990) remarked that "With this new collection of essays, Michele Wallace has returned like a prophet from the wilderness, her perception sharpened and rigour honed, to claim her voice and the right to speak as a black feminist." Janice Braun, writing for the *Library Journal* (December 1990), noted that "Wallace combines the techniques of autobiography and literary criticism with allusions to pop culture and the women of her acquaintance . . . to create a rich, impassioned social commentary. A valuable work for both public and academic collections."
—C.M.

SUGGESTED READING: *Essence* p36 Feb. 1991; *Library Journal* p616 Mar. 1, 1979, p146 Dec. 1990; *Nation* p181 Feb. 18, 1979; *New Statesman and Society* p39 Nov. 30, 1990; *New York Times Book Review* p15 Mar. 18, 1979; *Newsweek* p78 Feb. 5, 1979; *Village Voice* July 11, 1995, p 35+ Feb. 13, 1996; *Contemporary Authors New Revision Series* vol. 58, 1997

SELECTED WORKS: *Black Macho and the Myth of the Superwoman*, 1979; *Invisibility Blues: From Pop to Theory*, 1991

Waller, Robert James

Aug. 1, 1939– Novelist; educator

Robert James Waller was a little-known professor of business management at the University of Northern Iowa who dabbled in photography, music, and essay writing, when, during a two-week burst of creative energy in 1991, he wrote his first novel, *The Bridges of Madison County*. The novel, about a brief but intense love affair between an itinerant photographer and the wife of an Iowa farmer, was published with little fanfare in April 1992, but soon became one of the most talked-about books of the year, thanks in large measure to word-of-mouth promotion. *The Bridges of Madison County* first appeared on the *New York Times* and *Publishers Weekly* best-seller lists in August 1992, and within five months it had climbed to the number-one spot on both lists, where it remained for nearly a year.

Over four million copies of the novel had been sold when it was finally dislodged, to second place, by Waller's second novel, *Slow Waltz in Cedar Bend.* Waller's work has not been taken too seriously by the literary establishment (one reviewer dubbed *Bridges* "yuppie women's porno"), but it has won him a legion of ardent fans, some of whom have even made pilgrimages to the covered Iowa bridges of his first novel's title. Waller has recorded an album, *Ballads of Madison County*, and produced a music video. In 1995 a film version of *The Bridges of Madison County* was made, starring Clint Eastwood and Meryl Streep.

Robert James Waller was born on August 1, 1939, the only son of Robert Waller Sr. and Ruth Waller. (One source gives July 30, 1939 as the date of his birth.) He grew up in Rockford, Iowa, a rural community where his father worked as a chicken wholesaler, buying the birds from nearby farms and selling them to outlets in Milwaukee. As a boy, the young Waller helped his father with the business; he started out "at the bottom," as his father would joke, with the unpleasant task of scraping and shoveling chicken droppings into trucks. One of his earliest ambitions was to become a professional musician, like his uncle, but his father, a practical man, "didn't want [him] to have anything to do with music," Waller has recalled. "I dreamed as a child of making a living in the arts," he told Bill Shaw, who profiled him for *People* (November 8, 1993). "But [where I came from] you either worked in the tire or the tractor plant."

As a youth Waller was a talented basketball player, and, because his father loved the sport, he tried for a time to develop that talent. In 1957 he entered the University of Iowa on a basketball scholarship, but within a year he tired of athletic competition and transferred to the University of Northern Iowa. Again he followed his father's advice and studied math and economics and, after completing his undergraduate education, he studied business management at Indiana University, from which he took his Ph.D. degree in 1968. "I spent my life trying to please my father," he told Bill Shaw, "but I never knew him."

When he was not studying, Waller could often be found playing guitar, banjo, and ukelele. He would sometimes play and sing on weekends at the local Holiday Inn, and one night, in 1968, Charles Kuralt filmed one of his performances for a segment of *CBS Evening News*'s occasional series "On the Road." Among those who enjoyed the piece was Senator Robert F. Kennedy, who then invited Waller to sing on his campaign train in Indiana before the state's Democratic presidential primary.

After completing his doctoral program, Waller took a job as a professor of management at the University of Northern Iowa, in Cedar Falls. He continued to pursue his avocation as a singer and guitarist, and in the early 1970s, after briefly testing the waters as a country music songwriter, he returned to teaching. In 1979, the year his father died, he was promoted to the position of dean of the university's business school, and in the following years he lectured and wrote on such topics as business problem solving and decision making. Outside of the classroom, he served as a consultant to corporations and governmental bodies both in the United States and around the world. According to his colleagues and students, Waller was a maverick—"a hippie stuck in the sixties," in the words of one student—who wore blue jeans and cowboy boots. In addition to teaching, writing, and playing his guitar, he pursued his passion for foreign travel and his interest in photography.

In 1983 Waller met James Flansburg, then an editor of the *Des Moines* (Iowa) *Register*, who told Waller he was looking for new contributors to the newspaper. In the foreword to Waller's second collection of essays, *One Good Road Is Enough*, Flansburg recalled doubting that Waller would submit anything worthy of publication. But within a few months, Waller submitted an essay about his experience playing the guitar during Robert Kennedy's campaign tour in Indiana; other articles, on a wide variety of topics, followed.

Waller eventually decided to publish some of his pieces in a single volume. The result was *Just Beyond the Firelight: Stories and Essays by Robert James Waller* (1988), the title of which was drawn from an unfinished song Waller had written. The topics covered in the collection range from the personal ("Excavating Rachael's Room" is a meditation on cleaning his grown daughter's room after she left home, and "A Canticle for Roadcat" is about a stray cat who became "a friend and colleague") to the philosophical ("Going Soft Upon the Land and Down Along the Rivers" is, according to Waller, "a complex piece of writing and thinking . . . [on] such ideas as economic development, the preservation and enhancement of the natural environment, the future of Iowa, justice, beauty, and how these ideas all fit together").

Following the publication of *Just Beyond the Firelight*, Waller began receiving letters from readers throughout the country praising the book. One man wrote to say that the book was "an act of courage." In *English Journal* (April 1990), a high-school teacher who had used the book in one of his classes observed, "The collection introduces complex characters and situations about whom [late adolescents] can care and feel deeply. . . . Waller's gift for language weaves a spell that lures readers to the skilled storyteller's firelight." In 1990 Waller produced a second collection of essays, *One Good Road Is Enough*, which he described in the preface as "a continuation" of his effort "to run down and collar a slippery and shifting universe." Like its predecessor, *One Good Road Is Enough* includes pieces on intensely personal subjects, such as relationships; Waller's own life; and his love of nature, photography, and travel; as well as essays on politics and ecology. *Old Songs in a New Café*, his third collection of essays and stories, was published in 1994.

Meanwhile, Waller's job as university dean was becoming increasingly stressful. In 1985 he had an anxiety attack so severe that he was taken to a hospital emergency room for treatment. Following this incident, he resigned as dean and returned to a regular teaching schedule, only to find himself unable to tolerate the narrow-mindedness of his students. "I looked at them once and shouted, 'Didn't anyone here ever want to be an Amazon river captain?'" he recalled to Bill Shaw. "They looked at me like I was crazy." Finally, in 1991, he arranged to take an unpaid leave of absence from the university.

One day in the autumn of that year, Waller decided to visit Iowa's Madison County to take pictures of the old covered bridges that are among the area's main attractions. (One source maintains that he was photographing the bridges for a state-funded project.) The next day he started writing a story inspired by his visit to Madison County. He continued writing for fourteen days, during which time he slept just three or four hours a night. By the end of the fortnight, Waller had written his first novel, *The Bridges of Madison County*. "It all just came pouring out," Waller told Patricia O'Haire. "Practically wrote itself. I just typed it. Almost couldn't keep up with the words. I don't know where they came from."

The protagonist of the slim novel is Robert Kincaid, a middle-aged freelance photographer who in 1965 visits Iowa on an assignment for *National Geographic* to take photographs of Madison County's covered bridges. In need of directions, he stops at the home of Francesca Johnson, a passionate but lovelorn woman from Italy who buried her childhood dreams when, following World War II, she agreed to marry Richard, an American serviceman, and to settle down with him in Iowa's farm country. Robert Kincaid and Francesca Johnson are immediately attracted to one another and have an intense, four-day affair (Francesca's husband and two children are away at a state fair), at the conclusion of which Robert asks her to forsake all and spend the rest of her life with him. Out of a sense of duty to her husband and children, she refuses. The two never see each other again, though both yearn for each other for the rest of their lives.

After completing the manuscript, Waller showed it to several friends, one of whom passed it on to the New York literary agent Aaron Priest. "I thought it had potential because it was about a 20-hankie read," Priest told *Current Biography*. "I thought it would either fall like a stone or sell half a million copies." Several publishers rejected the novel before Maureen Mahon Egen of Warner Books offered Waller a $32,000 advance and agreed to publish it, with an initial printing of twenty-nine thousand copies. (According to some sources, the first printing was fifteen thousand copies.) "I believed in [the book] from day one," Egen was quoted as saying in *Advertising Age* (July 5, 1993), citing the novel's setting and "midwestern values" as its strongest points. To promote sales, Egen sent 4,000 free copies to booksellers, most of them proprietors of independent bookstores, across the country; she also enclosed a letter in which she praised the novel for its simplicity and universality and urged the store owners to read *Bridges* for themselves.

This focused, personalized marketing strategy proved to be successful. Many of the targeted bookstore owners loved the novel and began to recommend it to their customers, who in turn recommended it to their friends. Four months after its publication, *The Bridges of Madison County* leapt onto the best-seller charts, and before long, the novel was prominently displayed at bookstore chain outlets. Sales were also spurred by an interview that Waller gave on National Public Radio in January 1993, the publication of an excerpt of the novel in the February 1993 issue of *Cosmopolitan*, a Valentine's Day 1993 bookstore promotion launched by Warner Books, and Oprah Winfrey's declaration on her television talk show that *Bridges* was her "favorite book of the year" and "a gift to the country." By November 1993 more than 4.1 million copies had been sold.

Despite the novel's immense popular appeal, *Bridges* was at first virtually ignored by national mainstream magazines and newspapers, which did not consider it serious enough to merit critical attention. One exception was the *Washington Post Book World* (April 5, 1992). The reviewer, Susan Dooley, nevertheless shared the view of the literary establishment that the novel was flawed. She was especially critical of the characters, who, according to her, were "symbols" that had little in common with real people, and of the dialogue, which she found trite and pretentious. (Favorable notices appeared in a number of regional newspapers, including the *Indianapolis News*, the *Kansas City Star*, the *Miami Herald*, and the *Los Angeles Daily News*.)

Nearly a year later the book was finally reviewed in the *New York Times Book Review* (March 28, 1993), by Eils Lotozo. Echoing the sentiments expressed by Dooley, Lotozo lamented that instead of believable characters, "we get a lot of quasi-mystical business about the shamanlike photographer who overwhelms the shy, bookish Francesca with 'his sheer emotional and physical power.' Their love belongs more to the world of fantasy than reality." In the months that followed, other newspapers and national periodicals, including the *Los Angeles Times*, *U.S. News & World Report*, and the *New York Times Magazine*, provided similar assessments of the novel.

Meanwhile, satirists were having a field day with the book's plot and prose. The cartoonist Garry Trudeau ran a *Doonesbury* series entitled "The Washed-Out Bridges of Madison County," and Billy Frolick, an entertainment writer, wrote a parody of the novel, *The Ditches of Edison County*, under the pen name Ronald Richard Roberts. None of this fazed either Waller's fans or Waller himself. As he told Lynn Van Matre, who profiled him for the *Chicago Tribune* (August 5, 1993), "I can deal with criticism real well, as long as the reviewer doesn't intend to be mean just for the sake of meanness. . . . If you step out and do things, you have to expect some punishment. . . . It's only a bunch of cynics out there who scoff at romantic stuff."

In July 1993 Waller recorded an album for the Atlantic label, *The Ballads of Madison County*. Of the ten songs on the recording, four were written by Waller, including "The Madison County Waltz," which tells the story of Robert and Francesca and which was later made into a music video. Meanwhile, Waller had taken ten days out of his schedule to write his second novel, *Slow Waltz in Cedar Bend*, which was published in October with an initial printing of 1.5 million copies. Within one week of its release, the book shot to number two on the *Publishers Weekly* best-seller list. That autumn Waller embarked on an extensive book tour, paying special visits to the independent shops that had helped *The Bridges of Madison County* achieve its unprecedented success. Twentieth Century Fox immediately optioned the movie rights to *Waltz*.

Slow Waltz in Cedar Bend bears a striking resemblance to *Bridges* in terms of its story line, setting, and characters. The hero of the novel is Michael Tillman, an iconoclastic professor of economics who does not quite fit in at the university where he teaches, and the heroine is Jellie Braden, an intelligent and beautiful woman who is married to one of Michael's dull and conventional colleagues. When they finally consummate their adulterous passion, their lives are changed forever; she runs off to India to confront a secret from her past, and Tillman pursues her there.

Some reviewers found *Waltz* to be somewhat better written than its predecessor. Frank J. Prial, who assessed the novel for the *New York Times Book Review* (October 31, 1993), wrote that "[Waller's] self-conscious preachiness and gaseous prose . . . have been toned down. Some." That opinion was shared by critics for *New York Newsday* (November 9, 1993) and the *Chicago Tribune* (November 7, 1993), although not by Christopher Lehmann-Haupt of the *New York Times* (November 25, 1993), who argued that "all of Mr. Waller's more egregious qualities as a writer" were magnified in *Slow Waltz in Cedar Bend*. "If one could like these characters a little, their contortions would not seem so annoying," he continued. "But the more you learn about them, the shallower they seem." These and other criticisms had little impact on sales: In late 1993 *Waltz* topped the best-seller lists and was outselling *Bridges* by about two to one.

Border Music (1995), Waller's third novel, tells the story of Texas Jack Carmine, a drifter who takes up with an exotic dancer, Linda Lobo. Their relationship is threatened by the recurrence of post-traumatic stress suffered by Jack due to his experiences in the Vietnam War. "I empathize greatly with Jack Carmine," said Waller in *USA Weekend* (March 31, 1995). "He is exactly what I would have been without my father and my wife."

As with Waller's previous novels, *Border Music* was the target of an onslaught of negative reviews from literary critics. "High awfulness is Waller's specialty, and *Border Music* is by far his most loftily awful book of all," wrote Walter Kirn of *New York* (January 23, 1995). "Waller conquers whole new realms of wrongheaded lyricism and off-key poetry." Judith Dunford predicted in *New York Newsday* (January 29, 1995) that even those who liked *The Bridges of Madison County* would be disappointed with *Border Music*. "Written by anyone but the author of a phenomenon, *Border Music* would be a pleasant enough read at the dentist's," she wrote. In a *New York Times* (January 27, 1995) review, Michiko Kakutani criticized Waller for drawing on a stock supply of country music clichés, and described his prose style as "spectacularly awful." Kakutani summed up the feelings of many critics by stating that "*Border Song* must surely rank as one of the most dreadful novels to come along in a long time." Regardless of atrocious reviews, *Border Music* followed Waller's previous works to a lengthy run on the best-seller list.

Waller's next novel, *Puerto Vallarta Squeeze*, followed soon after *Border Music*, at the end of 1995. Its main character is Clayton Price, a middle-aged sniper on the run from the Mexican police. Price enlists the help of writer Danny Pastor and his girlfriend, uses his marksmanship to kill those blocking his path to freedom, and steals Pastor's girlfriend along the way. Bruno Maddox wrote for the *New York Times* (December 17, 1995) that the novel's narrative is burdened with overwrought and hackneyed characterizations. Maddox also expressed uneasiness about the protagonist's uncanny resemblance to Waller himself.

Waller, who, like his male protagonists, is tall and lean, has said that intellectually and emotionally he is "100 percent Robert Kincaid." He was married for 36 years to the former Georgia Ann Wiedemeier, a potter; they divorced in 1997. Waller and Wiedemeier have a grown daughter, Rachel.

—B.S.

SUGGESTED READING: *Chicago Tribune* V pl+ Aug. 5, 1993, with photo; *English Journal* Apr. 1990; *New York* p56+ Jan. 23, 1995, with photo; *New York Daily News* p35+ July 27, 1993; *New York Newsday* Nov. 9, 1993, p37 Jan. 29, 1995, with photo; *New York Times* Nov. 25, 1993, C p27 Jan. 27, 1995, with photo, VII p22 Dec. 17, 1995; *New York Times Book Review* Mar. 28, 1993, Oct. 31, 1993; *People* p109 Nov. 16, 1992, with photo, p50+ Nov. 8, 1993, with photos, p67+ Oct. 13, 1997, with photos; *USA Weekend* p4+ Mar. 31, 1995, with photos; *Washington Post Book World* Apr. 5, 1992

SELECTED BOOKS: Fiction—*The Bridges of Madison County*, 1992; *Slow Waltz in Cedar Bend*, 1993; *Border Music*, 1995; *Puerto Vallarta Squeeze*, 1995 Nonfiction—*Just Beyond the*

Firelight: Stories and Essays by Robert James Waller, 1988; *One Good Road Is Enough*, 1990; *Old Songs In a New Café*, 1994

John Isaac/Courtesy of Geoffrey C. Ward

Ward, Geoffrey C.

Nov. 30, 1940– Biographer; historian; nonfiction writer; television writer

A biographer and historian, Geoffrey C. Ward is best known for his work with the documentary film director Ken Burns. Together they scripted both *The Civil War* (1990) and *Baseball* (1994), two documentaries that set the standard for much of what has followed in that genre. As a solo scripter Ward has written such PBS documentaries as *The West* (1996) and *Thomas Jefferson* (1997), both produced by Burns. Geoffrey Ward has also either authored or edited several biographical/historical works, most notable among them a series of three volumes on Franklin Delano Roosevelt: *Before the Trumpet* (1985), *A First-Class Temperament* (1989), and *Closest Companion* (1995).

Geoffrey Champion Ward was born on November 30, 1940 in Newark, Ohio, the son of Frederick Champion and Duira Rachel (Baldinger) Ward. In his youth he spent some time in India, attending high school there. He later enrolled at Oberlin College, in Ohio, where he developed an interest in art and photography, and obtained a separate degree in studio art in addition to his B.A. degree, which he obtained in 1962. He also founded *Contemporary Photography* magazine while still a student at Oberlin.

After college Ward began working for *Encyclopedia Brittanica*, in Chicago. By 1964 he was senior picture editor of the encyclopedia, a position he held for four years. He then worked for a year as an art director and writer in the General Books division of *Reader's Digest*, located in Pleasantville, New York. In 1969 he returned to *Britannica*, this time in their New York offices, to take charge of picture-gathering, but he only stayed for a year. While working for *Brittanica*, Ward had begun to write photographic essays for various periodicals, and in 1970 he helped to found a new magazine titled *Audience*, for which he acted as editor for the next three years.

From 1973 to 1975 Ward wrote freelance articles for *Reader's Digest*. Shortly afterward he accepted a position as managing editor of *American Heritage*, a New York–based magazine for which he instituted many changes, including switching from hardcover to softcover and printing original pieces by noted writers such as Maxine Hong Kingston. After a year, he was promoted to editor in chief. His work in reference and historically oriented publications had strengthened his affinity for biographical history, and in 1978 he published his first book, *Lincoln's Thought and the Present*.

In 1982 Ward relinquished his editorial responsibilities at *American Heritage* but remained as a columnist from 1983 on. He again turned to freelance writing and committed himself to writing books. In 1983 Ward published *Treasures of the Maharajahs*, an installment in the "Treasures of the World" series put out by the Stonehenge firm.

Ward's long-running professional interest in Franklin D. Roosevelt (FDR) first found expression in *Before the Trumpet: Young Franklin Roosevelt, 1882–1905*. The book covers Roosevelt's early life, from his birth to his marriage. According to Joseph G. Harrison of the *Christian Science Monitor* (June 12, 1985), *Before the Trumpet* effectively portrayed the early experiences that helped form the public figure. "Particularly interesting are the book's chapters on the courtship of Franklin and Eleanor," Harrison added.

In that same year Ward made his first foray into the genre that would bring him his greatest fame—historical television documentaries. *The Statue of Liberty*, co-written by Ward and documentary film director Ken Burns, aired on PBS in 1985 and earned Ward, in 1987, the first of his two prestigious Christopher Awards. Ward again teamed with Burns for the television project *Huey Long*, which aired on PBS in 1986. Three years later Ward's first solo documentary script, *Thomas Hart Benton*, aired on PBS.

Ward continued his examination of FDR's early years with the publication, in 1989, of *A First-Class Temperament: The Emergence of Franklin Roosevelt*. Continuing where *Before the Trumpet* left off, this second volume traces Roosevelt's life from his honeymoon, in 1905, to his election as governor of New York, in 1928. The book, perhaps Ward's greatest critical success to date, earned him the National Book Critics Circle Award in the biography/autobiography category, the Francis Parkman Prize, and the *Los Angeles Times* Book Prize for biography. Stephen R. Graubard of the *New York Times Book Review* (August 20, 1988) called the book "an incomparable study of the young and middle-aged Roosevelt, immensely informative about his meteoric public career but also refreshingly honest about a private life that was both spacious and constricted." Graubard also admired the fact that Ward refused to defame his subject, as many other biographers choose to do. Of particular note, according to the reviewer, is the way in which Ward depicted the future president's life-defining struggle with polio. Garry Wills of the *New York Review of Books* (November 23, 1989) was also impressed with Ward's handling of Roosevelt's disease. "Ward's thorough book is always fascinating, despite its crowd of details," Wills added.

In 1990 Ward participated in a writing team that produced the script for the PBS documentary *Nixon*, which earned Ward and his colleagues a Writers Guild Award. That year also saw the PBS production of Ward's third solo script, *Lindbergh*.

Geoffrey Ward reunited with Ken Burns, in collaboration with Burns's brother Ric, to write the script for the groundbreaking 1990 documentary *The Civil War*. "Initially I told Ken he shouldn't do the movie," Ward explained to Robert Dahlin for *Publishers Weekly* (July 20, 1990). "It would be impossible to do [a documentary] based on a period with no film footage. But Ken said he'd just have to think of other things." The nine-part series, filmed by the Burnses, continues to influence the way documentary motion pictures are made. The "other things" incorporated by Ward and his co-writers included diary entries, rare photographs, and modern-day images of the locations of some of the Civil War's historic battles. Ratings for the television event were among the highest ever received in the history of public broadcasting. The film earned Ward an Emmy, in 1991, for outstanding individual achievement, as well as his second Christopher Award.

As a companion piece to the PBS series, Ward wrote *The Civil War: An Illustrated History*, a "coffee-table" book published in 1990. Ward's narrative text accompanied scores of photographs, many of which were not shown in the film version. "I took the script [of the documentary] and made it into the narrative spine of the book," Ward told Robert Dahlin. In the *National Review*, critic Paul Hubbard gave the volume a highly positive review, deeming it superior to the film version: "Powerful and haunting as the TV series was," he wrote, "it cannot fully substitute for the book version." David Howard Bain of the *New York Times* (September 9, 1990) described the book as "thoroughly researched" and "vividly written," and praised Ward's use of participants' testimony. Concurring with Hubbard, Bain declared, "this superbly designed book easily stands on its own."

The documentary projects on which Ward worked shortly after *The Civil War* include *Duke Ellington: Reminiscing in Tempo* (1991), which he scripted along with Robert Levi, and *The Kennedys* (1992), which he co-scripted with several others and which won him his second Emmy. Additionally, *Coney Island* (1991) and *The Donner Party* (1992) both featured Ward as senior creative consultant. In 1992 he co-wrote his third script with Ken Burns, *Empire of the Air: The Men Who Made Radio*.

Ward also continued writing his own books in the wake of the highly successful *Civil War* project. In 1991 he published *American Originals: The Private Worlds of Some Singular Men and Women*. Many of the articles included were book reviews Ward had written for various magazines, including *American Heritage*. Among the 40 notable men and women discussed are Jack Dempsey, Josephine Baker, Abraham Lincoln, and Charlie Parker. In a review of *American Originals* that appeared in the *Christian Science Monitor* (January 8, 1992), Ruth Walker wrote that while much of the information is fascinating, it works better if read in select portions instead of straight through. "The book sometimes makes one feel that one is looking . . . through binoculars that are focused too closely on too narrow a field," she commented. While praising Ward's effort, Walker recommended further reading into American history for a more complete picture. Jane Lii of the *New York Times* (February 9, 1992) found *American Originals* "lucid and engaging" and was particularly fascinated by the more personal anecdotes included by Ward.

Ward's seventh book, co-authored with Diane Raines Ward, was published in 1993. Entitled *Tiger Wallahs: Encounters with the Men Who Tried to Save the Greatest of the Great Cats*, the book points out the declining number of tigers in the wild—a result of forest depletion and excessive hunting over the course of the past few centuries—and recounts the efforts of groups such as Project Tiger to reverse the damage. In his *New York Times* (December 13, 1993) review, Gerald Durrell admired the Wards' beautiful, evocative writing, and the way it eloquently portrays both the Indian landscape and the work of those trying to save a dying species.

In 1994 Geoffrey Ward engaged in his second major collaboration with Ken Burns, the PBS documentary miniseries *Baseball*. Divided into nine two-hour episodes, the series chronicles the history of the American pastime from the 1840s to the 1990s. Many of the same techniques and devices used in the *Civil War* documentary were again employed, including excerpts from newspapers of the day and voiceovers from numerous celebrities.

As he had done with *The Civil War*, Ward followed *Baseball* with a companion book, *Baseball: An Illustrated History*. The narrative, according to Christopher Lehmann-Haupt of the *New York Times* (September 12, 1994), is engrossing and well-crafted, and David E. Jones of the *Chicago Tri-*

bunc (September 18, 1994) found the book an excellent accompaniment to the series, as well as a work that can stand on its own. *New York Newsday*'s Michael Seidel singled out the book's in-depth analysis of the African-American experience in baseball.

Ward's third book concerning the life of FDR was published in 1995. Entitled *Closest Companion: The Unknown Story of the Intimate Friendship Between Franklin Roosevelt and Margaret Suckley*, the book came about as a result of the discovery, after her death in 1991 at the age of 99, of the letters and memoirs of Margaret Suckley. Through the careful editing and arrangement of this material, Ward presented the story of Roosevelt and his very close, though platonic, relationship with Suckley. Ward's editing, according to Christopher Lehmann-Haupt of the *New York Times* (April 3, 1995), was not as thorough as it should have been, leaving the reader to sort through mundane material.

Over the next two years, Ward took part in two documentary projects, *The West* (1996) and *Thomas Jefferson* (1997), produced by his frequent coscripter Ken Burns. For *The West*, Ward once again followed the pattern of *The Civil War* and *Baseball* by publishing a companion volume, *The West: An Illustrated History* (1996). Ward's most recent co-writing collaboration with Ken Burns was the PBS documentary *Frank Lloyd Wright*, which aired in 1998.

Geoffrey Ward has contributed to numerous historical anthologies, including *A Tribute to John F. Kennedy*, *Illustrated History of World War II*, *The Negro in American History*, and *Great Events of the Twentieth Century*. He has also contributed articles to such periodicals as *National Geographic*, the *New York Review of Books*, and *Smithsonian* magazine. In 1995 he was the recipient of an honorary degree from Wilkes University.

Ward has two children, Nathan and Kelly.
—B.S.

SUGGESTED READING: *Chicago Tribune* XIV p3 Sep. 18, 1994; *Christian Science Monitor* p23+ June 12, 1985, p13 Jan. 8, 1992; *National Review* p51+ Dec. 17, 1990; *New York Newsday* p43 Sep. 11, 1994; *New York Review of Books* p3+ Nov. 23, 1989; *New York Times* p26 Sep. 9, 1990, p18 Feb. 9, 1992, p18 Dec. 13, 1993, p16 Sep. 12, 1994, with photo; C p17 Apr. 3, 1995, with photo; *New York Times Book Review* VII p13 Aug. 20, 1993; *New Yorker* p123 Sep. 11, 1989; *Publishers Weekly* p35 July 20, 1990; *Who's Who*, 1998

SELECTED WORKS: *Lincoln's Thought and the Present*, 1978; *Treasures of the Maharajahs*, 1983; *Before the Trumpet: Young Franklin Roosevelt 1882–1905*, 1985; *A First-Class Temperament: The Emergence of Franklin Roosevelt*, 1989; *The Civil War: An Illustrated History* (with Ken Burns and Ric Burns), 1990;

American Originals: The Private Worlds of Some Singular Men and Women, 1991; *Tiger Wallahs: Encounters with the Men Who Tried to Save the Greatest of the Great Cats* (with Diana Raines Ward), 1993; *Baseball: An Illustrated History* (with Ken Burns), 1994; *The West: An Illustrated History*, 1996; As editor—*Closest Companion: The Unknown Story of the Intimate Friendship Between Franklin Roosevelt and Margaret Suckley*, 1995; *The Best American Essays of 1996*, 1997

Robert Clifford/Courtesy of W. W. Norton

Welsh, Irvine

1958– Novelist; short-story writer; screenwriter

In a well-known passage from *Trainspotting*, the first novel by the Scottish writer Irvine Welsh, one of the protagonists, Mark Renton, considers the sort of life that his culture seems to be encouraging him to embrace: "Choose mortgage payments; choose washing machines; choose cars; choose sitting oan a couch watching mind-numbing and spirit-crushing game shows, stuffing . . .junk food intae yir mooth. Choose rotting away. . . .Choose life. Well, ah choose not tae choose life."

These words could be taken as the philosophy of life espoused by many characters in the world Welsh has created in his fiction; in *Trainspotting*, the characters, unwilling to choose a lifestyle that to them lacks meaning, choose heroin addiction instead. Yet, as Welsh has emphasized, while he was not passing judgment on his characters, neither was he interested in glamorizing their lives. "I didn't want to present the junkie as isolated and cut off," he explained to Elizabeth Young of the *Guardian* (August 14, 1993). "I wanted to focus on the relationships and cultural pressures surrounding these characters. Obviously, there are extremes of behavior people can get into, extremes of anti-social . . . behavior, and I didn't want to spare that."

Perhaps it isn't strange that a book by a member of the original punk-rock generation that is full of the lurid details of drug addiction and petty crime was very popular among readers in their teens and 20s. But it may seem surprising that many established literary critics have recognized Welsh's first book, and his later books, too, as more than trash pulp. James Lasdun of the *Village Voice* (July 23, 1996), for example, raved, "What distinguishes [*Trainspotting*] from other novels of low life is partly the sheer brilliance of the writing—beautifully individuated dialogue that snaps characters instantly into life, effortless realization of locale, unflagging dramatic invention—and partly also an unusually volatile intelligence that continually startles you with its sudden swerves between wit, rage, cynicism, and unexpected tenderness." Similarly, the *Bookseller* (May 12, 1995) announced that Welsh's "skills are those of all fine writers. The flexibility of his language, the pitiless compassion of his gaze, the truthfulness of his modulation between black comedy, anger, farce and tragedy: these qualities betray great literary talent, possibly genius."

Published in Great Britain in 1993 and in the United States in 1996, and unsparing in its depiction of the extreme, *Trainspotting* became one of the hottest novels Britain has ever seen; it enjoyed great success among critics and other presumed fans of literature. For his part, Welsh claims not to measure himself by their standards. "Middle-class critics, whether they like the book or don't, always write the same review," he told the *Bookseller*, "a string of adjectives like 'disgusting,' 'foul-mouthed,' 'violent,' and then either 'What a brilliant book' or 'What a horrible book.'"

Welsh's antipathy for mainstream literary criticism is consistent with his claim that he never intended to write a novel that might be regarded as traditional. "When I first started writing," he explained to Dennis Romero of the *Los Angeles Times* (June 26, 1996), "I thought it wouldn't really appeal to anyone because the audience I was writing to didn't really read books." That audience was members of the drug, rave, and slacker culture of working-class Scotland, and, though he didn't intend it to, his readership has grown to include a wide range of youths in England and elsewhere. "I think what you can't make up is that cultural context," he told Romero. "I like to feel as if I'm kind of immersed in the culture." This may be the second reason Welsh does not worry about critics: He can afford not to. He is a hero to his audience, which runs the gamut from real-life junkies to voyeuristic graduate students, many of whom devour everything he publishes.

Welsh gave John Mulholland of the *Guardian* (March 30, 1995) his take on the meaning of "rave" or "house" culture: "The whole point of the house thing is to be as apart from mainstream society as possible, not to be a part of it." For this reason, the predominantly European youth phenomenon held together by techno dance music and its various mutations (acid house, drum-'n'-bass, electronica, jungle, etc.) since the late 1980s has been remarkably devoid of "rock star"-sized personalities—until Welsh, that is. Welsh's attitude toward his writing reflects the ravers' affinity for fluidity and change. "I don't see myself as a writer," he told Young. "I'm just somebody who's written something and might write something else if I've got anything to say."

Many have pointed out that the nearly plotless *Trainspotting*, which presents the stories of Renton, Spud, Sick Boy, Begbie, Diane, and Tommy in a string of episodes, takes place in the mid-1980s, before rave culture came into existence, and, in terms of music, is obsessed with the proto–punk rock of Iggy Pop. Welsh, who at 39 is a lot older than most of the people who most appreciate his books, believes that the "rave kids" are newer, smarter versions of the youths who embraced punk, and that the defining characteristics of class and situation remain the same. He also believes that the style of his writing is influenced by fast-paced dance music. "I wanted to capture on paper the whole rave atmosphere of being taken on a kind of journey," he told L. C. Smith of *Spin* (August 1996). "To keep the pages turning, to keep the action moving, just like a DJ." He told Young that "music, television, magazines, and comic books have always influenced me more than books."

Most of Welsh's first novel is written in a phonetic approximation of a working-class Scottish brogue. "The language in *Trainspotting* is alienating at first," Jane Mendelsohn wrote in the *New Republic* (September 2, 1996), "exhilarating once you get the hang of it, and finally poetic in its complications." Many critics noticed a freshness and even-handedness in Welsh's treatment of drugs and the working class—something Welsh himself has often mentioned in interviews. "[The characters'] exuberance and humor, their apathy and pain, are the only story here. There's no lofty judgment-calling," Charlotte Innes observed in the *Los Angeles Times* (August 18, 1996), adding that "this is surely what struck a chord with British youth. . . . If Welsh has a message, it's simply this: Drugs can give you pleasure, . . . but then you have to pay the price." "What impresses me most about the story . . .is its fierce, uncompromising morality," Jonathan Coe wrote in the *Sunday Times*, as quoted by Dennis Romero. "Nothing his characters do is ever without its consequence."

Welsh's second book is *The Acid House* (1994; 1995 in the U.S.), a collection of 21 short stories and one novella. "From *Trainspotting* to *Acid House* I moved from urban realism into fantasy," Welsh explained to Mark Fisher of the *Observer*

(October 9, 1994). *The Acid House* was embraced by the young British audience—then still occasionally referred to as a "cult following"—that had made his first book a success. The subject matter, with its hallucinogenic overtones, brought Welsh closer, in substance as well as style, to his intended audience of "rave kids." Critics, too, had kind words for *The Acid House*. One criticism that did crop up frequently was a predictable one—that *The Acid House* was not *Trainspotting*. Nicholas Clee, however, writing in the *Times Literary Supplement* (March 18, 1994), declared that "the collection should not be described as a disappointment. The same talents are in evidence; only they are operating under lower pressure, serving miscellaneous effects." Others, like Shawn Whiteside of *New Statesman & Society* (April 1, 1994), were even more generous than Clee. "Aside from the vigor of the language, what is immediately striking is Welsh's narrative skill. The openers, 'The Shooter,' a tale of gangland revenge, and 'Eurotrash,' a reminiscence of junkies in Amsterdam, consistently second-guess the reader. Just when you think you've worked out not just what's going on, but what sort of story you're dealing with, Welsh pulls off a fine narrative trick. All the clues were staring you right in the face, but odds on you walked straight past them."

One trick for which Welsh was often praised was the comic—often "cosmic"—reversal that occurred in characters' lives. As Sarah Ferguson explained in the *New York Times Book Review* (April 16, 1995), "Even the most brutish and unrepentant are eligible for the occasional epiphany. One man gets a sex change, another is turned into a fly. Go figure." In one frequently mentioned story, Welsh brings the real-life celebrities Madonna, Kylie Minogue, Kim Basinger, and Victoria Principal together at a pool in Santa Monica, California, for a bawdy discussion—in working-class Scottish dialect—of suggestive pictures of Scottish furniture movers. At one point, Minogue says, "Ah widnae kick it oot ay bed." "What I'm trying to do is to undermine prejudices by shaking things up, by putting people into different situations that they would not usually be in," Welsh told John Mulholland. "With that kind of vignette you can say all kinds of things about the star system, about sexism, about class."

Welsh followed *The Acid House* with his second full-length novel, *Marabou Stork Nightmares* (1995; 1996 in the U.S.), the protagonist of which is Roy Strang, a football (soccer) hooligan with violent tendencies who has participated in a gang rape, has tried to commit suicide, and has been in a coma for the last two years. The book details Strang's efforts to remain in the coma while he sorts through the various violent episodes of his life that have made him the monster he is. At the same time, he fantasizes about an expedition to Africa to hunt the marabou stork, and it becomes clear that Strang's hope of killing the stork is really his hope of killing his own dark side. In contrast to Welsh's first novel, which is a loose collection of anecdotes, *Marabou Stork Nightmares* is a highly structured narrative in which conflict is always identifiable.

"What is remarkable about Welsh's writing," Guy Mannies-Abbott wrote in the *New Statesman & Society*, "is that it is good at almost everything it attempts, and it attempts a lot. There is something at stake in his work, which is firmly located, uncompromising, and formally inventive. *Marabou Stork Nightmares* embodies all these qualities—rare indeed in British writing—and is itself a bold development. [The book] is a wonderful success: a funny, cleverly composed, genuinely exciting and assured leap of a novel." James Lasdun, who found the narrative to be "flawed . . . by the fantasy passages," nevertheless declared the story to be "surprisingly touching," and praised it as "a sustained display of contemporary prose at its most supple and expressive."

Welsh gained a break from glowing, generous praise after the publication of his novel *Ecstasy: Three Tales of Chemical Romance* (1996). Reportedly, it, too, was a commercial success in the United Kingdom, but critics felt that "Welsh's literary rushes are beginning to wear off," to quote Pat Kane of *New Statesman & Society* (June 7, 1996). Charlotte Innes declared that "what might have been flaws in *Trainspotting* that were somehow transformed by that work's stylish presentation—an inability to portray women, puerile observations about life, naive politics—are in *Ecstasy* an embarrassment." Tobias Jones of the *Spectator* (May 28, 1996), however, had a different reaction: "The reader is dragged, breath held, through the dregs, but is finally brought to the surface holding a pearl; [Welsh's] romance is convincing because he shows how rare and precious it is."

The main problem with *Ecstasy*, according to Ian Parker, writing in the *New Yorker* (July 15, 1996), may be that Welsh had drifted too far from the aimlessness of both structure and characters in *Trainspotting*. "He began to write stories in which the point was that something, rather than nothing, had happened. His characters now aimed to have influence beyond their own bodies, and this did not seem to suit Welsh's voice." Welsh seemed to agree with Parker when he said, "I want to get back just to getting some bastards together and letting them [screw] each other over and generate a story. . . . Rather than trying to stage things for them."

Welsh seemed to follow that approach, at least in part, with *Filth*. That novel follows the activities—personal and professional—of Scottish Detective Sergeant Bruce Robertson, a man seemingly devoid of morals. Courtney Weaver, writing in the *New York Times Book Review* (September 27, 1998), found that the book "cranks . . . up a notch" the concentration on lowlifes and the "graphic fixations with bodily fluids, excrement, and abasement" that characterize *Trainspotting*. Weaver predicted that the novel would be best appreciated by those who "put a high value on shock content."

How Irvine Welsh came to write fiction is itself a somewhat mysterious story. The *Bookseller* called Welsh "a literary Kaspar Hauser" and "a one-man rebuttal" to Harold Bloom's theory of the anxiety of influence, and concluded that "he appears to have come, in literary terms, out of nowhere." Biographical details are not altogether absent, as Welsh's stardom has been amply covered by the media, but some are vague, or even conflict. He was born in Leith, the port section of Edinburgh, in 1958. Of this he is quite sure, and he showed Parker his passport to prove it—and thus rebut published reports in the *Observer* and elsewhere that he was born seven years earlier.

When he was a young boy, Welsh's family moved further out of town, to a housing project (or housing "scheme"—thus the characters in *Trainspotting* are "schemies") in Muirhouse. "I remember growing up in Muirhouse and there was always this thing about going camping but there was never anywhere to . . . go camping," Welsh told Mulholland. "You lived in this massive concrete scheme and you'd get a couple of bars of chocolate and go down to a desolate beach and try to build a treehouse. We were trying to live out all these Famous Five [the children's adventure book series by Enid Blyton] fantasies, but we had no material to hand to actually operate in that environment—we had no aunt in Cornwall or in Wales. Our aunts just stayed around the corner in the next street. . . .There was a massive gap between your own experience and the literature you read." Roy Strang's imaginary hunt for the titular marabou stork parodies the literature Welsh grew up reading. Similarly, the crew in *Trainspotting* is obsessed with James Bond. "If you look at kids growing up reading James Bond or Enid Blyton, you are confronted with these [literary] figures who never have anything bad happening to them and they're always upper- or middle-class figures."

Football, specifically the Edinburgh club the Hibernians, provided Welsh with his other childhood heroes. He began experimenting with alcohol in his mid-teens, then moved on to drugs, such as speed. After dropping out of school, when he was 16, he worked as an apprentice television repairman and then held odd jobs. In the late 1970s, he decided to move to London, to join the then-burgeoning punk scene. "The two things I really wanted to do," Welsh told the *Bookseller*, "were play football and be a musician: I was always much more interested in them than in writing. Unfortunately, I wasn't good enough at either of them." He told Young that "Iggy Pop was always my main man. And the Sex Pistols. . . . I used to write songs about five pages long—like a story." During that time in London, Welsh is reported to have been a member of a few unsuccessful punk bands, to have used large amounts of drugs, and to have been frequently arrested.

Then he wrote *Trainspotting*, according to early biographical pieces. However, these accounts omitted, perhaps intentionally, an entire decade of Welsh's life. According to other reports, Welsh got married and moved to Croydon, a town south of London, where he is said to have profited in real estate during the 1980s. However, acquaintances of Welsh have called this part of his story into doubt. The evidence is fairly strong that by 1988 he was back in Edinburgh, working for the local government. He has said, perhaps ironically, that he learned his craft by writing reports for the housing department. Welsh also attended Heriot-Watt University, where he earned an M.B.A. degree, and he has some experience as a computer-software consultant.

Welsh told Lesley Downer of the *New York Times Magazine* (March 31, 1996) that he began writing "because I was bored on this long bus ride between New York and Los Angeles." Downer did not report when this bus ride took place. Welsh was inspired to write *Trainspotting*, he said, after his 1988 homecoming, when he discovered that Muirhouse had become saturated with heroin, and that many of his old friends had contracted AIDS through the use of unsterilized needles. Mulholland cited 1988 as the year of the "acid house explosion," and reported Welsh's "total immersion in rave culture" from that year on. "I had become very anti-drug, so at first I was down on the whole Ecstasy scene," Welsh told L. C. Smith. "But then I got into it, and it really energized my life—it's the only place where people's collective personas are realized."

Irvine Welsh and his wife moved to Amsterdam, the Netherlands, after the success of *Trainspotting*. Stories from *The Acid House* have been produced for the BBC, and both the stage and film version adaptations of *Trainspotting* have been hugely successful. Welsh has tried his hand at writing plays and screenplays; he told the *Bookseller* that writing has been "a way of getting the characters and the culture across; but I'll do that in any way I can. I'd like to do things in different media. I don't have any particular reverence for books."
—Josh Robertson

SUGGESTED READING: *Bookseller* p28+ May 12, 1995, with photo; *Guardian* p8 Aug. 14, 1993, with photo, p8 Mar. 30, 1995; *London Observer* p6 Oct. 9, 1994, p17 Nov. 19, 1995; *Los Angeles Times* E p1 June 26, 1996, with photo; *New York Times Magazine* p42+ Mar. 31, 1996, with photos; *New Yorker* p25 July 15, 1996; *Spin* p22 Aug. 1996, with photo

SELECTED BOOKS: *Trainspotting*, 1993; *The Acid House*, 1994; *Marabou Stork Nightmares*, 1995; *Ecstasy: Three Chemical Romances*, 1996; *Filth*, 1998

Weschler, Lawrence

Feb. 13, 1952– Nonfiction writer

Lawrence Weschler, an American nonfiction writer and reporter with a knack for crafting a poetic phrase, has covered a number of different subjects in his professional career. Since the *New Yorker* accepted his two-part report, "And Then There Was Light," on the Solidarity movement in Poland in 1981, he has gone on to become a respected author of both serious political pieces and light social humor as a staff writer (and since 1992, a consulting editor) for that publication. He has also written articles for a variety of other magazines—*Artnews*, *Columbia Journalism Review*, *Harper's*, and *Interview*. Those pieces have ranged widely, from comparisons of U.S. media coverage of Eastern Europe and Latin America, to reflections on Poland, to art and opera reviews, to conversations with the chess champion Jeff Miller. Weschler has written several books on a variety of topics, many of which are based on his pieces for the *New Yorker* and other magazines.

For *World Authors 1990–1995*, Lawrence Weschler, born on February 13, 1952, writes: "After the *New Yorker* had accepted a couple of my pieces, early in the 1980s, I was called in for a meeting with William Shawn, the magazine's hugely esteemed editor of, at that point, well over 30 years. He indicated that my writing was all fine and good and that they were intending to offer me a more permanent arrangement, but there was one problem: my vitae indicated that I lived in California, but where, Mr. Shawn begged to inquire, had I been born? In Van Nuys, I replied, in the middle of the San Fernando Valley, outside Los Angeles. Okay, fine, Mr. Shawn shrugged indulgently, but where had I grown up? Right there in Van Nuys. He frowned, somewhat flummoxed, but persisted— And gone to college? At the University of California campus at Santa Cruz. For Shawn, the quintessential New Yorker, none of this computed, but he was as good a reporter as he was an editor, and he continued to burrow doggedly until he was finally able to get me to confess that all of my grandparents, on both sides, had been Viennese Jews, a category ('Aaah, I see') he could at least comprehend, so that all right, everything was okay, he was able to emerge from the interview with his prior estimations of California entirely unscathed.

"Actually, of course, by the 1950s and 1960s, it was possible to garner a cultural upbringing in California every bit as rich as (and in some respects more free and open-ended than) any one might receive on the East Coast. In particular my college education during the early glory years of Cowell College at UCSC (where my professors included Norman O. Brown, Page Smith, Sheldon Wolin, Maurice Natanson, and Harry Berger, and my classmates included future writers William Finnegan, Laurie Garrett, and Noelle Oxenhandler) was especially formful.

"But as I think back on my formation as a writer, it's indeed to those Viennese Jews that I tap back, and particularly to my mother's father, the modernist composer Ernst Toch (an enormously successful luminary, back in the Berlin of the late Weimar period, who never quite attained the same resonance during the American exile of the last half of his life). Although I inherited none of my grandfather's musical aptitude (an especially galling circumstance in that my grandmother on the other side, my father's mother, Angela Weschler, had been the head of the Vienna Conservatory of Music's Piano Department as well), I did inherit an intensely musical sense of the activity of writing itself, both in the sense of composition (the considered, formful revelation of thematic material across time) and voice (issues of modulation, timbre, resonance, etc.).

"Following my graduation from UCSC, where I majored in philosophy and cultural history, I initially took a job as an editor and interviewer at the UCLA Oral History Program, where my first task, actually, was to edit the nine-hundred-page manuscript of an interview sequence my grandmother, the composer's widow, Alice Toch, had only just completed a few weeks prior to her own death. (My father, Irving, incidentally, had been a professor at UCLA, a psychologist affiliated with the School of Industrial Relations and one of the early pioneers in 'sensitivity training'; he died in a car crash when I was ten and the oldest of four children whose upbringing thereafter fell entirely to our remarkable mother, Franzi.) Across my five years there at the Oral History Program I began to understand how an interview was only partly a way of gathering information; more importantly, it was a way of honing the question—figuring out, across a vast arc of interaction, just what the question was that would open up all this material. It was a lesson which, of course, would reverberate throughout my later career as a reporter.

"At UCLA, though I had to be able to interview on any subject with just a few weeks research notice, I tended to specialize in two areas: the legacy of Southern California's wartime emigre scene (the days of Mann, Brecht, Schoenberg, etc., as memorialized most notably, perhaps, through the optic of a more than 50-session, four-volume interview with novelist Lion Feuchtwanger's widow Marta) and the trajectory of the postwar L.A. art scene. In the latter capacity, I was editing an interview one morning that someone else had done with the light-and-space perceptual artist Robert Irwin, when, inspired and intrigued, I dropped him a note asking if he'd ever read Merleau-Ponty's *The Primacy of Perception*. An utterly untaught and naïve phenomenologist, Irwin was at the office door the next day. Even a few years earlier, he assured me, he'd have tossed a note such as mine into the trash, but he was just beginning to realize how traditional philosophy might indeed have some bearing on his avant-garde aesthetic concerns. We ended up, in effect, having lunch together for the next three years: he planted himself under a tree by the university's research library, where he proceeded to slog through the classics of the Western tradition. I shared with him what I knew of philosophy; he shared with me what he knew of art. Some years later these conversations formed the basis for my first manuscript, *Seeing Is Forgetting the Name of the Thing One Sees*, a biography of Irwin and his evolving artistic practice and ideas.

"By the late 1970s I'd quit the Oral History program to test my chances as a freelance writer, initially as a stringer for some of the newly founded local alternative weeklies. At a certain point I sent my *Seeing* manuscript, more or less over the transom, to the *New Yorker*, and I got incredibly lucky: they took it. I was invited to pursue a piece I'd been wanting to do about a wonderful museum in Denmark, and while there, more or less on a lark, I ventured over to Poland: it was May 1981, at the very height of the Solidarity period, and I returned completely enthralled; I drafted a preliminary manuscript entitled "Ninety-Four Visions of Poland," and it was after I turned in that piece, unbidden, that Mr. Shawn and I had our little talk.

"But he sent me back—my first two-part piece on Poland appeared in November 1981, just before the declaration of martial law—and then he sent me back again to cover the devastations of the state of siege (indeed, over the next fifteen years I made repeated return visits on reporting assignments, and in the process met and wooed and married a veteran of the Solidarity movement, Joanna, who in the meantime has become one of the leading international monitors at Human Rights Watch in New York). I also covered the aftermaths of torture regimes in Uruguay, Brazil, South Africa, and Czechoslovakia, among other places, all the while flitting back and forth, as I sometimes parsed matters, between such political tragedies and the cultural comedies which formed the other half of my *New Yorker* beat (an artist who drew money and spent his drawings; a rocket scientist who became an investment banker who then gave it all up to pursue his life's one true ambition, to become a clown; a teacher of rudimentary English from Bengalore, India, whose improbable fate it was to discover and promote a completely unknown and unrecognized first-generation abstract expressionist painter, etc.). Indeed, my *Seeing* book became the first of a series which I've taken to calling "Passions and Wonders" (the most recent of which was my book on the vertiginously marvelous Museum of Jurassic Technology, *Mr. Wilson's Cabinet of Wonder*, a work of magic-realist nonfiction which brought me full-circle back to Los Angeles)."

For his two volumes on Poland, Weschler received high marks. His first book on the topic, *Solidarity: Poland in the Season of Its Passion* (1982), was written after the author made three short trips to that country to report on the Solidarity movement for the *New Yorker* and was greatly expanded

from those pieces for its publication by Simon & Schuster. A reviewer for the *Library Journal* (May 15, 1982) remarked: "Weschler's comments on the causes of Poland's current economic distress, on the rulers' search for legitimacy, and on the legal versus moral authority of conflicting forces are unusually thoughtful." A writer for the *New York Times Book Review* (April 25, 1982), suggested: "To read this very personal account is, above all, very much like going to Poland. Mr. Weschler brings out the enormous difference between the Polish national character and that of almost any other European nation."

His second book on Poland, *The Passion of Poland*, published by Pantheon in 1984, was greeted by similar endorsements. Calling the book a "remarkable work" in the *New Republic* (September 10, 1984), Abraham Brumberg believed that Weschler "manage[d] to capture both the excitement and the pathos of a people defying its past, and for the first time since World War II bravely attempting to write its own history." *Newsweek* (May 14, 1984) observed that the "amount and diversity of the firsthand material" that Weschler gathered in Poland gave the book "an almost novelistic flow."

Since the early 1980s Weschler has continued to work for the *New Yorker*, while occasionally writing for other periodicals and publishing full-length works that expand on his *New Yorker* pieces. One of the more recent books, *A Miracle, A Universe: Settling Accounts with Torturers*, has been celebrated for its systematic discussion of torture methods used by the governments of Brazil and Uruguay and of how these neighboring nations came to terms in the 1980s with their sadistic former practices. The *New York Times Book Review* (April 15, 1990) stated that Weschler's "research is provocative and thorough; it leads him to conclude that adjudicating the crimes of ex-thugs is not easy to accomplish. It involves unsatisfactory compromises, where there are no clear winners or losers." A writer for *Newsweek* (April 30, 1990) remarked on how Weschler, in what the reviewer regarded as one of the book's most profound ideas, "shows how two nations rediscovered 'the capacity for acting as the subject rather than the object of history,' not by squaring accounts with their tormentors but by setting the record straight."

Mr. Wilson's Cabinet of Wonder, about the Museum of Jurassic Technology, was initially published by *Harper's* in a greatly abridged version. A finalist for both the Pulitzer Prize and the National Book Critics Circle Award, this book received laurels in the press similar to those bestowed on Weschler's other works. Many critics noted that one of the greatest enjoyments in the book is discovering which of the museum's pieces are real and which are false. "In the wake of its moment of climactic exposure, [the book] turns into an expedition in which Lawrence Weschler tracks down the overlaps, correspondences, and occasionally tenuous connections between historical and scientific reality on the one hand and the Museum of Jurassic Technology on the other," Wendy Lesser wrote in the *New York Times Book Review* (October 29,1995), calling the author "a nonfiction writer with a poet's ear."

Weschler carried over his skill at ferreting out the whole story to his next book, *Calamities in Exile: Three Nonfiction Novellas* (1998), an examination of the lives of three political exiles whose motives and actions may have been less than straightforward. As Lance Gould observed for the *New York Times Book Review* (June 28, 1998), "[Weschler's] thorough accounting of the men's covert operations, assumed identities, and strained relationships with fathers, wives, and colleagues creates a disturbing triptych of the perils of totalitarianism." Ron Hogan, a reviewer for Amazon.com wrote, "Given that his three subjects have each fought against oppressive regimes, it would be easy to portray them as simplistic heroes, but Weschler takes great pains to show the full complexities of their characters, even when it casts them in a less than flattering light."

Weschler's most recent publications consist of *A Wanderer in the Perfect City: Selected Passion Pieces* (1998) and *Boggs: A Comedy of Values* (1999). The first is a reprinting, with updates and some new essays, of many of the entries in his 1988 book, *Shapinsky's Karma, Boggs's Bills, and Other True-Life Tales*, with the exception of the essay on James Stephen George Boggs, which Weschler expanded into its own book. Reviewers once again praised Weschler's work, finding *A Wanderer in the City* to be an "absorbing new collection," whose pieces "are unpredictable in the way that only the best nonfiction can be," according to M. G. Lord of the *New York Times Book Review* (April 25, 1999), and deeming *Boggs* "an intelligent, ironic, and entertaining text . . . from an accomplished reporter, according to *Kirkus Reviews* (April 28, 1999).

Lawrence Weschler has received many awards during his years as a professional writer. They include the Mary Hemingway Prize for the year's best magazine reporting from abroad (1981) for his coverage of the Polish Solidarity movement for the *New Yorker*. In September 1983 Yale University presented him with a Poynter Fellowship; in April 1986 he was granted a Guggenheim Fellowship. Two years later he won the George Polk Award for cultural reporting for his work *Shapinsky's Karma, Boggs's Bills, and Other True-Life Tales*. In 1990 he received the Sidney Hillman Foundation Award for his 1989 reporting from Poland for the *New Yorker*. That same year he received honorable mention in the balloting for the James Aronson Award for Public Conscience Journalism, for his reporting on Latin America. In 1992 he was presented with the George Polk Award for magazine reporting for his work on Czechoslovakia.

—C.M.

SUGGESTED READING: *Kirkus Reviews* Apr. 28, 1999; *Library Journal* p980 May 15, 1982; *New Republic* Sep. 10, 1984; *Newsweek* p78 May 14, 1984, p72 Apr. 30, 1990; *New York Times* C p33 Nov. 10, 1995; *New York Times Book Review* p11 Apr. 25, 1982, p9 Apr. 29, 1984, p10 Apr. 15, 1990, p13 Oct. 29, 1995, June 28, 1998, Apr. 25, 1999; *Publishers Weekly* p55 Aug. 21, 1995; *Washington Post* B p3 Oct. 24, 1995

SELECTED BOOKS: *Seeing Is Forgetting the Name of the Thing One Sees: A Life of Contemporary Artist Robert Irwin*, 1982; *Solidarity: Poland in the Season of Its Passion*, 1982; *The Passion of Poland*, 1984; *David Hockney's Cameraworks*, 1984; *Shapinsky's Karma, Boggs's Bills, and Other True-Life Tales*, 1988; *A Miracle, A Universe: Settling Accounts with Torturers*, 1990; *Mr. Wilson's Cabinet of Wonder*, 1995; *Calamities of Exile: Three Nonfiction Novellas*, 1998; *A Wanderer in the Perfect City: Selected Passion Pieces*, 1998; *Boggs: A Comedy of Values*, 1999

Benno Friedman/Courtesy of Beacon Press

West, Cornel

June 2, 1953– Nonfiction writer; social activist

The author of books on subjects ranging from Christianity to Marxism, Cornel West is best known for his writings on race, and especially for his book *Race Matters* (1993). The book comprises eight essays in which West eloquently wrote about the crisis that has erupted in black America—a crisis manifest in events such as the 1992 Los Angeles riots. In little more than 100 pages, West called on black leaders to come up with solutions grounded in moral—rather than political—principles that would transcend what he viewed as the short-sighted, failed approaches of both liberals and conservatives. A man possessing tremendous energy and a restless intellect, Cornel West has been hailed by the black scholar Henry Louis Gates Jr. as "the preeminent African-American intellectual of our generation."

Cornel Ronald West was born on June 2, 1953, in Tulsa, Oklahoma; he has an older brother and two sisters. Their father, a civilian air force administrator, and mother, an elementary school teacher who went on to become a principal, moved around a great deal during their childhood, and eventually settled in a middle-class neighborhood in Sacramento, California. In his *New York Times Magazine* (September 15, 1991) profile of Cornel West, Robert S. Boynton wrote that Cornel had been "troubled" as a child, citing as an example an incident in which West "attack[ed] a pregnant teacher who forced him to salute the flag (he refused in order to protest black Americans' second-class citizenship)" and was "suspended for six months and eventually transferred to an accelerated school across town."

Cornel drew solace and inspiration from sources as diverse as the subjects he would write about in later life. At the nearby Baptist church, he listened raptly to members of the congregation who, themselves only two generations removed from slavery, shared stories about the challenges faced and met by their ancestors. Near the church were the offices of the Black Panthers, who taught him about the effectiveness of activism and introduced him to the writings of Karl Marx. Cornel's earliest role model, though, was Theodore Roosevelt, whose biography he discovered at the age of eight in a local bookmobile. As he recalled to Robert Boynton, "Teddy was very close to me because we both had asthma and would stay awake at night with our backs propped up by a pillow. But he overcame it, went to Harvard, and became a great speaker. So I decided I had to go to Harvard, too, although at eight I didn't know exactly what it was."

He eventually found out, and at the age of 17—having never been to the East Coast—West arrived as a freshman on the campus of Harvard University, in Cambridge, Massachusetts. West has recalled his father's words on that occasion: "When we got there, he said to me, 'Corn, we're so proud you got here, but we know it will be hard, so all you need to stay is three C's and a D,' which I appreciated because I was pretty scared." Scared or not, by the end of his first semester West had earned three A's and an A minus. Martil Kilson, a Harvard government professor, described West as "the most intellectually aggressive and highly cerebral student [he had] taught in [his] 30 years" at the university. For West, intellectual activity was apparently less a means toward obtaining good grades than an obsession from which he knew little respite: As a student he had "violent dreams in which philosophical concepts would take form and battle each other," and he once so agonized over the differences between two philosophers' ideas about God that he felt compelled to write an unassigned, 50-page paper to synthesize their points of view.

In 1973 West graduated magna cum laude—and one year early—from Harvard with an A.B. degree in Near Eastern languages and literature. He received an M.A. degree from Princeton University, in Princeton, New Jersey, two years later. While at Princeton, he was influenced by Richard Rorty, who was then writing his book *Philosophy and the Mirror of Nature*. According to Robert Boynton, West was taken with Rorty's "belief in the importance of literature and history for philosophy." After obtaining his master's degree, West returned to Harvard, this time as a Du Bois fellow, and, partly as a result of Rorty's influence, put off writing his doctoral dissertation in order to work on a novel (which remains unpublished).

West eventually resumed work on his doctoral dissertation and received his Ph.D. degree from Princeton in 1980. Since then he has delivered lectures at more than 100 colleges and universities and has been a visiting professor of religion at several institutions, including Yale University Divinity School, in New Haven, Connecticut (1979–80); Barnard College, in New York City (1981); Williams College, in Williamstown, Massachusetts (1982); Haverford College, in Haverford, Pennsylvania (1983); and the University of Paris (1987). From 1977 until 1984 he was an assistant professor of the philosophy of religion at Union Theological Seminary, in New York City, where he became an associate professor in 1984; from 1984 to 1987 he was an associate professor of philosophy of religion at Yale. He was then approached by Princeton University to revive, and direct, its Afro-American Studies department.

The year 1982 saw the publication of West's first book, *Prophecy Deliverance!: An Afro-American Revolutionary Christianity*. The book contained within its pages what has since become recognized as vintage West: the fusing of disparate, even contradictory, doctrines into a coherent system of thought that transcends ideology. In *Prophecy Deliverance!* West combined elements of Marxism, ideas found in the works of such black writers as W. E. B. Du Bois and Toni Morrison, the traditions of African-American Christianity, and the writings of such philosophers as Descartes. His aim, according to Robert Boynton, was "to supply [African-American] thought with a critical framework." *Prophecy Deliverance!* drew praise from several reviewers, although West himself has been quoted as saying that the book "didn't work."

With John Rajchman, West edited *Post-Analytic Philosophy* (1985), a book of essays that includes West's "The Politics of American Neo-Pragmatism." In 1988 he published a collection of his own writings, *Prophetic Fragments*, which further established his reputation for touching upon a variety of subjects in a single work. As Robert Boynton observed, "An essay expounding a socialist theory of racism is followed by a piece in which black rap is described as 'the last form of transcendence available to young black ghetto dwellers.'" The broad scope of West's writings has inspired some skepticism. The political scientist Adolph Reed, for example, has said that West's work "tends to be 1000 miles wide and about two inches deep." West has responded to such criticism by saying, as he did to Jill Nelson for *Essence* (March 1993), "There are intellectuals who grapple with one idea for years, but that's not my style. I want to be a provocative intellectual who writes about many unsettling issues."

The American Evasion of Philosophy: A Genealogy of Pragmatism (1989), West's fourth book, was West's attempt to invoke the populist spirit of such American philosophers as Ralph Waldo Emerson and apply it to a modern movement "that takes race, class, and gender seriously." Reviewing the book for the *Nation* (April 9, 1990), K. Anthony Appiah wrote, "West's earlier books . . . have ranged widely. Rooted in a sense of the continuing relevance of Christianity and socialism, his work displays an inexhaustible appetite for ideas and a compelling moral vision. But *The American Evasion of Philosophy* is the most ambitious and original project that he has undertaken. . . . West's deployment of intellectual history . . . is impressive and compelling." Robert Boynton called West's fifth book, *The Ethical Dimensions of Marxist Thought* (1991), "an innovative reading of Marx that tries to rescue him from the rubble of totalitarianism." Also published in 1991, *Breaking Bread: Insurgent Black Intellectual Life* is a dialogue between West and the black writer and critic bell hooks. The year 1993 saw the publication of *Prophetic Thought in Postmodern Times* and *Prophetic Reflection: Notes on Race and Power in America*, books containing West's speeches and interviews.

While those books—and a multitude of articles appearing in such periodicals as *Social Text* and *Monthly Review*—have been widely read and analyzed in academic circles, West's next book brought him to the attention of the mainstream media. *Race Matters* was published on April 29, 1993, the first anniversary of the 1992 Los Angeles riots, which were precipitated by the acquittal of four white police officers accused of beating Rodney King, a black motorist. Composed of previously published essays, the book covers subjects of relevance to the African-American community, including black-Jewish relations, what West calls "the crisis of black leadership," the resurgence of the popularity of the slain black activist Malcolm X, and the Los Angeles riots themselves. Pointing out that "of those arrested [in the riots], only 36 percent were black," West referred to the incident as "a multiracial, trans-class, and largely male display of justified social rage [that,] for all its ugly xenophobic resentment . . . and its downright barbaric behavior, [demonstrated] the sense of powerlessness in American society."

Reviews of *Race Matters* were generally favorable. In *New York Newsday* (April 25, 1993), Robert Boynton observed that "West's thinking consistently challenges the conventional wisdom. . . . Although politically a progressive, West isn't a cheerleader for any cause—every reader will find some sacred belief questioned. . . . West takes his place alongside such figures as Bayard Rustin and A. Philip Randolph in a tradition of principled black self-criticism." Boynton went on to call *Race Matters* "necessary reading." Michiko Kakutani announced in the *New York Times* (April 27, 1993) that West's book "should introduce him—and his anomalous and often compelling blend of philosophy, sociology, and political commentary—to the public at large."

Yet despite the book's wealth of intelligent commentary, Kakutani and some other reviewers felt that, "When it comes to proposing concrete solutions to the many problems afflicting black America today, Mr. West is less persuasive. Many of his suggestions are vague and sentimentally utopian. Sentences like 'our ideals of freedom, democracy, and equality must be invoked to invigorate all of us, especially the landless, propertyless, and luckless' may sound very nice, but they are the sort of platitudes lip-synched daily by the ineffectual politicians Mr. West says he disdains." Still, Kakutani conceded, "It's unrealistic to expect that real solutions to . . . problems that have defied the efforts of a generation of thinkers and government officials . . . could be articulated in a slim volume like this. One hopes Mr. West will amplify the ideas explored in *Race Matters* at greater length in a more commodious book. In the meantime, one can only applaud the ferocious moral vision and astute intellect on display in these pages."

West's next book, *Keeping Faith: Philosophy and Race in America*, was published in late 1993. A collection of previously published essays on various philosophical, political, and cultural issues, *Keeping Faith* demonstrated the eclectic range of West's intellectual interests. Among the many issues discussed are the damaging influences of both racism and capitalism. Donald E. Messer of *Christian Century* (September 21, 1994) believed that the book lacked focus. Michael J. Quirk of *Cross Currents* (Winter 1994–95) had the opposite opinion, stating that the book "can be read as a successful attempt to flesh out and focus in on the idea of prophetic pragmatism."

West left his position at Princeton University in 1994 and moved to Harvard, where he was appointed professor of Afro-American Studies and the Philosophy of Religion.

One of the causes for which West has fought has been the improvement of relations between blacks and Jews in America. Along with Jewish publisher Michael Lerner, he has co-authored two books on the subject: *Jews & Blacks: Let the Healing Begin* (1995) and *Jews & Blacks: A Dialogue on Race, Religion and Culture in America* (1996). Beginning in the fall of 1995, West and Lerner made a nationwide tour of religious institutions and college campuses to promote unity between the two communities.

West took part in the compilation of the *Encyclopedia of African-American Culture and History* in 1996, along with Jack Salzman and David Lionel Smith. The single-volume reference book contains more than 2,000 entries on a wide array of aspects of African-American life, culture, and history. In a review for the *Journal of American History* (March 1998), V. P. Franklin wrote that the work does not contain much information that cannot be found elsewhere. Franklin also criticized discrepancies in citations and references, but praised the wealth of statistical tables and charts included in the encyclopedia's appendices.

In 1996 West joined Henry Louis Gates Jr. in producing his most talked-about book since *Race Matters*. Entitled *The Future of the Race*, the ambitious volume addressed matters pertaining to the black community, using as a jumping-off point the writings of W.E.B. DuBois. The study arose in part from conversations between West and Gates, who are colleagues at Harvard University.

Eric J. Sundquist described *The Future of the Race* for *Commentary* (July 1996) as "a perplexingly fruitless book." Sundquist criticized the ways in which West and Gates made use of the writings of DuBois, often making his work seem inconsequential by choosing some of his lesser writings and not properly elucidating them. The essays contributed by West and Gates, respectively, did not deal effectively with their subject matter, according to Sundquist.

West collaborated with Sylvia Ann Hewlett on his next book, *The War Against Parents: What We Can Do for America's Beleaguered Moms and Dads*, published in 1998. The work takes a look at the difficult position in which parents are placed as they try to raise their children in a media-soaked modern-day environment. "It's like trying to write poetry after Shakespeare," West told a *People* (May 4, 1998) writer. "You do the best you can."

West's *The Future of American Progressivism: An Initiative for Political and Economic Reform* (1998) is another collaboration, this time with fellow Harvard professor Roberto Mangabeira Unger. A political tract calling for a return to America's philosophical foundation, the "religion of possibility", the book was well received; *Kirkus Reviews* (September 15, 1998) called it "a welcome breath of fresh air. Whether or not you agree with them, at least they don't mince words." The reviewer concluded that the book is "a bold political analysis that should inspire public life but, alas, probably will not." *The Cornel West Reader*, a compendium of some of West's previous writings along with some new material, appeared in 1999.

Cornel West lives in Princeton with his wife, Elleni, an Ethiopian-born social worker; two earlier marriages ended in divorce. From his first marriage, he has a grown son, Clifton Louis West.

Cornel West has made numerous television appearances on such programs as the *MacNeil/Lehrer Newshour* and *Firing Line*. He is a member of many organizations, including the American Academy of Religion, the American Philosophical Association, the Ecumenical Association of Third World Theologians, the Society for the Study of Black Religion, and the Afro-American Commission of Democratic Socialists of America, which he chairs. From 1980 to 1982 he was the executive director of the Black Theology Project of Theology in the Americas. He is a member of the editorial board of *Social Text* and of the journal of the New York Society of Black Philosophers, and he is on the advisory board of *Cultural Critique*. He is also associate editor of *Boundary 2: A Journal of Postmodern Literature*.

—C.T. / B.S.

SUGGESTED READING: *Christian Century* p864+ Sep. 21, 1994, p953+ Oct. 18, 1995; *Commentary* p60+ July 1996; *Cross Currents* p535+ Winter 1994–95; *Essence* Mar. 1993, with photo; *Journal of American History* p1471+ Mar. 1998; *Kirkus Reviews* Sep. 15, 1998; *Nation* Apr. 9, 1990; *New York Newsday* Apr. 25, 1993; *New York Times* Apr. 27, 1993; *New York Times Magazine* p39+ Sep. 15, 1991; *People* p45 May 4, 1998, with photo; *Time* p60+ June 7, 1993, with photo; *Washington Post Magazine* p14+ Aug 8, 1993, with photos

SELECTED WORKS: Nonfiction—*Prophesy Deliverance!: An Afro-American Revolutionary Christianity*, 1982; *Prophetic Fragments*, 1988; *The American Evasion of Philosophy: A Genealogy of Pragmatism*, 1989; *The Ethical Dimensions of Marxist Thought*, 1991; *Breaking Bread: Insurgent Black Intellectual Life* (with Bell Hooks), 1991; *Beyond Eurocentrism and Multiculturalism*, 1993; *Race Matters*, 1993; *Keeping Faith: Philosophy and Race in America*, 1993; *I Tell My Heart: The Art of Horace Pippin*, 1994; *Jews & Blacks: Let the Healing Begin*, (with Michael Lerner), 1995; *The Future of the Race* (with Henry Louis Gates Jr.), 1996; *Jews & Blacks: A Dialogue on Race, Religion and Culture in America* (with Michael Lerner), 1996; *Restoring Hope: Conversations on the Future of Black America*, 1997; *The War Against Parents: What We Can Do for America's Beleagured Moms and Dads* (with Sylvia Ann Hewlett), 1998; *The Future of American Progressivism: An Initiative for Political and Economic Reform* (with Roberto Mangabeira Unger), 1998; As editor—*Theology in the Americas: Detroit II Conference Papers* (with Caridad Guidote and Margaret Coakley), 1982; *Post-Analytic Philosophy* (with John Rajchman), 1985; *White Screens, Black Images: Hollywood from the Dark Side* (with Colin MacCabe), 1994; *Encyclopedia of African-American Culture and History* (with Jack Salzman and David Lionel Smith), 1996;

Struggles in the Promised Land: Toward a History of Black-Jewish Relations in the United States (with Jack Salzman), 1997

Alison Shaw/Courtesy of Doubleday

West, Dorothy

June 2, 1907– Aug. 16, 1998 Novelist

When Dorothy West published her second novel, *The Wedding*, in 1995, she brought to an end almost a half-century of literary hibernation and reminded the world of her status as the last living member of the Harlem Renaissance, the famed black literary and artistic movement. She had been close to such well-known writers as Langston Hughes, Countee Cullen, and Zora Neale Hurston in the heyday of the movement, which came to an abrupt end with the onset of the Great Depression. By the time she published her first novel, *The Living Is Easy*, in 1948, she had left New York for Martha's Vineyard, off the coast of Massachusetts, where she lived for the rest of her life.

Like *The Living Is Easy*, *The Wedding* examines the lives of prosperous blacks. It received a more favorable critical response than its predecessor, which had garnered mixed reviews, and it went through 10 printings within the first six months following its publication. West followed up *The Wedding* with *The Richer, The Poorer*, a collection of short fiction and nonfiction, in which she both demonstrates her skill as a storyteller and sheds new light on some of her fellow Renaissance writers.

West mentioned one reason for the long delay between publications to Alexis De Veaux of *Ms.* (May 1995): "I'm an old Bostonian; I always wrote about the class of people I know." The class she knew was "Negro society," or the black upper-middle class of the 1930s and 1940s, an elite group. Their preoccupations, such as the difficulty of finding reliable domestic servants, were out of sync with the overtly political concerns of her contemporaries, among them Ralph Ellison, the author of *Invisible Man.* "*The Living Is Easy* came out at the wrong time," West told De Veaux. "Nobody understood it." To prevent the same thing from happening to *The Wedding*, which the novelist apparently began within a decade of the publication of *The Living is Easy*, she decided to wait for a more favorable climate. However, with the rise of such leaders as Malcolm X and H. Rap Brown and militant groups like the Black Panthers, by the 1960s she had essentially given up hope that her book would find an appreciative audience. Although the novel was finished in 1994, it is essentially the same book that West began writing all those years ago, about a prosperous African-American family preparing for the wedding of one of their daughters at their summer home on Martha's Vineyard in 1953.

Dorothy West's family was one of the first among the black bourgeoisie to buy a summer home in the Oak Bluffs section of the Vineyard, a secluded locale that grew into a vacation community for affluent African-Americans like the ones portrayed in *The Wedding*. Her father, Isaac Christopher West, had made his fortune as a fruit wholesaler, and was known as the "black banana king" of Boston. The story of his success is truly inspiring. He was born a slave on a Virginia plantation; was freed at age seven, after which he helped his mother, a cook, by buying produce at the Boston market; and went into business for himself at age 10. "By the time I was born he was in Dun & Bradstreet," Dorothy West told Lynn Karpen for the *New York Times Book Review* (February 12, 1995). His example made a strong impression on his daughter, who has earned the criticism of some fellow African-Americans for dismissing accusations of race-based inequalities. "I get so tired of these young black people saying, 'I can't be anything because I'm black,'" she told David Streitfeld of the *Washington Post* (July 6, 1995). "They drive me crazy. They wouldn't be here if they didn't have strong ancestors."

West's mother, born Rachel Pease Benson, was one of 22 children. She was much younger than Isaac West, and had moved to Boston from Camden, South Carolina. The writer praised her mother for her beauty and her wisdom, and forgave her harshness. "My mother was a hellion and a tomboy who got two spankings a day," Dorothy West told Gerald Peary of the Toronto *Globe and Mail* (July 21, 1982). "Yet, as one of so many children, she had to be manipulative to get her way. She was put on earth to bring her family from the South, and that's just what she did." Apparently, Rachel West's primary method of settling her family in the North was to move them into the large house she and Isaac shared, which may have contributed to the unhappiness of their marriage.

Dorothy West sometimes appeared reluctant to reveal her age. Sources variously give 1907, 1909, and 1910 as the year of her birth, and when Peary inquired about the subject, she replied, "I'll give you the answer my mother always gave. I'm 102." She had no siblings, but the abundance of aunts and cousins living in her parents' house meant that she did not grow up like an only child, and her strong sense of family has always been a part of her work. "All my stories are about women and children," she told Peary. Like the family in *The Wedding*, West and her cousins were of varying hues, some light-skinned and others, like herself, dark. She said that she began to spend more time indoors as a child because she did not want to stigmatize her lighter-skinned cousins. She does not regret this self-confinement, which was a reason she took up writing at a young age.

When she was 10, she was admitted to the Girls' Latin School in Boston, and she published her first story, "Promise and Fulfillment," in the *Boston Post* at the age of 14. Having read in *Crisis*, a publication of the National Association for the Advancement of Colored People (NAACP), about the "Negro Arts Movement" that was occurring in New York City, she visited Harlem in 1926 with her cousin, the poet Helene Johnson, who was also in her teens. The two attended an awards ceremony, where West received an award for her second-place tie in a short story competition sponsored by the magazine *Opportunity: A Journal of Negro Life*. Her story was entitled "The Typewriter," and the writer she had tied with, for "Muttsy," was Zora Neale Hurston, then a student at Barnard College. After returning to Boston, West attended Boston University, but not for long: There was a renaissance happening in Harlem.

"It took her a long time to like me," West said of Hurston to Dorothy A. Clark for *American Visions* (April 1993). Other members of the community of literati later known as the Harlem Renaissance had no such problem. Countee Cullen and Langston Hughes welcomed her as the youngest of their group, Hughes calling her "the kid." In time she got to know all the big names of the movement: Jean Toomer, Wallace Thurman, Claude McKay, Arna Bontemps, James Weldon Johnson, and Nella Larsen. The Harlem Renaissance was at its height, and as the most junior member, West knew her place among the other writers. As Streitfeld pointed out, "she remembers sitting on the floor with her mouth shut, listening." Before she left New York in 1932, she received a marriage proposal from Cullen. "If I had married him," West told Karpen, "I would have had to go South, where he was going to teach. I didn't want to be one of those women who sat around and drank tea. I was not that person at all."

Indeed, West had places to go, and in 1932 she set sail with Langston Hughes and 20 other African-Americans for the Soviet Union. There the group was to film "Black and White," a portrait of race relations in the United States, sponsored by the Soviet government. For political and artistic reasons, the film was never made, but West and Hughes remained in the Soviet Union for another year. In a 1933 letter to Hughes, West proposed marriage. Hughes's exact response is not known, but the two never married. West avoided commenting on the exact nature of their relationship in the Soviet Union and the preceding years in Harlem.

By the time the death of her father brought West back to the United States in 1933, the Harlem Renaissance had clearly ended, and its many major figures were no longer living in New York. After taking stock of her career (she was then in her mid-20s), she concluded she had not realized her potential. In 1934 she founded a literary magazine, *Challenge*, of which she was editor, and put up her own money to get it started. The quarterly publication included only the very best examples of black writing—West's connections with such authors such as Hughes, McKay, Bontemps, Hurston, and Helene Johnson ensured she got just that. But the favoritism she showed for established authors was discouraging to younger African-American writers. Moreover, her editorial policy earned *Challenge* a reputation for being reserved at a time when innovation was in vogue, a perception that may have contributed to its demise, for financial reasons, in 1937. Within a year West launched another journal, *New Challenge*, which was edited by Richard Wright, who later wrote the novel *Native Son*. *New Challenge* folded after its first issue; money had been an issue again, and West had problems with Wright's leftist ideology. Along with Wright himself, Margaret Walker and Ralph Ellison were notable contributors to the issue.

West next worked with the Federal Writers' Project, a division of the New Deal's Work Project Administration, but did not publish much of what she wrote. The project ended in the mid-1940s, after West had left New York City for good, in 1943, to live in a modest cottage in Oak Bluffs, on Martha's Vineyard. From there, she continued to contribute stories to the *New York Daily News*, as she had been doing since 1940, and finished *The Living Is Easy*.

West's first novel is a semiautobiographical portrait of the Judsons, a prosperous African-American family in Boston: the rich father, Bart; the beautiful, conniving mother, Cleo; and the daughter, Judy, are based on Isaac, Rachel, and Dorothy West. Three of Cleo Judson's sisters and their families also live in the home. Sybil Steinberg of *Publisher's Weekly* (July 3, 1995) described the novel as "the story of a tempestuous marriage between fair-skinned Cleo Judson, who is obsessed with moving up in the world, and her dark-complexioned husband, an unassuming businessman."

The true critical response to *The Living Is Easy* is difficult to gauge. Many of those who reviewed 1995's *The Wedding* were quick to call the 1948 novel a success, as were articles written around the time of its mini-revival among feminists in the 1980s. But other sources suggest that the reaction had been mixed. For example, in a review for *Commonweal* (June 25, 1948), Florence Codman praised the characterization of Cleo Judson, calling her "the predatory female on the loose, a wholly plausible, tantalizing creature," although she also noted that "there are some loose places in the framework of the book." Similarly, Seymour Krim, writing in the *New Yorker* (May 15, 1948), found that "some of the writing as writing is loose—but the important thing about the book is its abundant and special woman's energy and beat. The beat is a deep one, and it often makes a man's seem puny."

West began working on another novel after the publication of *The Living is Easy*, but the samples she sent to publishers were not well received. "People say, 'You didn't write another book,'" she told Streitfeld. "Yes, I wrote another book, but no one would buy it. It's not peculiar to black writers. There are many white writers, I'm sure, who went through the same sort of thing." She kept thinking about her next novel, as well as writing her stories for the *Daily News*, and eventually came up with the plot for *The Wedding*. She believed she had a strong story this time, and was willing to wait a few years for it to receive its proper credit.

She waited out the 1950s. In the 1960s she stopped writing for the *Daily News* and took a job as a billing clerk for the *Vineyard Gazette*. With the rise of the Black Panthers, who "scorned the upper-middle class," she began to lose hope of publishing her novel. "I wanted to write about people like my father, who were ambitious. But people like him were anathema to the Black Panthers, who said that all black people are victims," she told Steinberg. "It was a discouraging time." She went on to say that she did not even feel that the book would get a fair shake from white readers. "I had a suspicion that the reviewers, who were white, would not know how to judge my work in that prevailing climate. In fact, if I had brought the book out then, white people would not have accepted it." By 1969 she had started writing a column in the *Gazette*, taken a seasonal job as a cashier at a seafood restaurant, and given up hope of ever seeing *The Wedding* in print.

West resurfaced in 1982, when the Feminist Press reissued *The Living Is Easy*, which had long since been out of print. She was honored in Boston during Black History Month of that year, and had numerous speaking engagements and book signings. The world had finally found a place for Cleo Judson. "Back in 1948 a leading women's magazine refused to publish chapters from my first book . . . because they feared losing subscribers," West told Karpen. "You see, no one knew what to make of my heroine, because the word 'feminist' had hardly been invented yet. *I* didn't know she was a

feminist until years later." At a luncheon at Radcliffe in July, perhaps as a result of the public's demonstration of its readiness, she said she intended to finish *The Wedding*.

Although she had regained a measure of her former celebrity status (even in 1982 journalists could call her the "last living member of the Harlem Renaissance") and gave the occasional lecture or interview, she did not progress toward finishing her novel until Jacqueline Kennedy Onassis, an editor at Doubleday, sought her out. The most famous resident of Martha's Vineyard, Onassis had read West's column in the *Gazette* and learned that she was sitting on a long-unfinished novel. Onassis secured a contract for West with Doubleday, and reportedly visited the writer every Monday during the summers of 1992 and 1993 to encourage West to finish it. Onassis did not live to see the publication of the novel, but West made sure their friendship was commemorated by dedicating the book to "the memory of my editor, Jacqueline Kennedy Onassis. Though there was never such a mismatched pair in appearance, we were perfect partners."

According to Streitfeld, a strange controversy surrounds the final events leading to the publication of *The Wedding*. During the fall of 1994, Henry Louis Gates Jr., the noted scholar of African-American studies at Harvard University, visited West, bringing with him one of many advance copies of the novel that Doubleday had already sent to reviewers. West, however, was still writing the ending of the book. It did not take the two long to realize that the publishers had put together their own ending—one that West apparently had no knowledge of. "Here is the oldest living person in the tradition I teach, telling me she has lost control of her text," Gates told Streitfeld. "It was a nightmare come alive." Gates called Doubleday, and was told that West had given her consent to their ghost-writing the ending from her notes, and that she must have forgotten. Gates flew into action, enlisting a professor from Harvard Law School, in the event that the matter were to go to court. With Gates threatening to go public, Doubleday agreed to wait one more month for West to finish her already four-decade-old novel. A spokesperson for Doubleday later asserted that the final chapter received by Gates and hundreds of other reviewers in the mail was pieced together from West's original outline and many hours of tape-recorded instructions, an explanation that Gates flatly denied. "That's a lie," he told Streitfeld. "That's slimy."

Because of uncertainty over which version of the novel reviewers received, the critical reaction is difficult to assess. For instance, a review by Valerie Smith that appeared in *Emerge* (January 1995) concludes, "Unfortunately, the end of the novel, melodramatic and abrupt, clashes with the subtlety of the rest of *The Wedding*." Not only does Smith note a sudden difference in style, but the review predates the publication of the novel itself by a month, so it seems likely that this piece was written about the "unauthorized" version. Further-more, in a review in *Publisher's Weekly*, dated November 21, 1994, the length of the novel is listed as 208 pages; the novel's length, as published the following February, was 240 pages.

Critics in general approved of the authorized version of *The Wedding*. "You have only to read the first page to know that you are in the hands of a writer, pure and simple," Susan Kenney wrote in the *New York Times Book Review* (February 12, 1995). "At the end, it's as though we've been invited not so much to a wedding as to a full-scale opera, only to find out that one great artist is belting out all the parts. She brings down the house." Merle Rubin of the *Christian Science Monitor* (February 2, 1995) expressed similar praise: "West draws the many strands of her story together in an ending that is genuinely cathartic, mingling elements of tragedy, loss, reconciliation, and hope." Although she appeared to like the book, Margo Jefferson voiced generic concerns in her *New York Times* (February 1, 1995) piece: "Ms. West has the mind of a historian and the sensibility of a memoirist. *The Wedding* falters as a novel; it takes its stand and holds its own as social history." A television version of *The Wedding* aired in early 1998.

West followed the success of her second novel with a well-received collection called *The Richer, The Poorer*, in July 1995. The book consists of 17 short stories and 13 reminiscences, including her prize-winning teenage effort "The Typewriter" and others written during that period. Although some of the stories were mildly criticized as too simple or formulaic, the nonfiction pieces about her youth and her fellow writers consistently delighted reviewers. "Her account of the life of the Writer Wallace Thurman . . . makes a major contribution to the history of the Harlem Renaissance," Judith Paterson wrote in the *Washington Post* (July 6, 1995). In *Time* (July 24, 1995), John Skow remarked, "West's strength is as a witness to a long-gone world."

The diminutive Dorothy West was a Vineyard institution, affectionately known as "Dot" or "Dottie" to its residents. In her last years, she expressed excitement that the stories she had to tell had finally found a welcoming audience. "I'm a creative writer," she told Clark. "I'm not a black with a chip on my shoulder." She died at the age of 91 on August 16, 1998, in a hospital in Boston.

SUGGESTED READING: *American Visions* p46+ Apr. 1993, with photo; *Chicago Tribune* XIII p22+ Apr. 2, 1995, with photo; *Commonweal* June 25, 1948; *Christian Science Monitor* Feb. 2, 1995; *Emerge* Jan. 1995; *Ms.* p73 May 1995, with photo; *New Yorker* May 15, 1948; *New York Times Book Review* p11 Feb. 12, 1995, with photo; *Publishers Weekly* Nov. 21, 1994, p34+ July 3, 1995, with photo; *Time* p67 July 24, 1995, with photo; *Toronto Globe and Mail* p9 July 21, 1982, with photo; *Washington Post* C p1 July 6, 1995, with photos

SELECTED BOOKS: *The Living Is Easy*, 1948; *The Wedding*, 1995; *The Richer, The Poorer*, 1995

Wilhelm, Kate

June 8, 1928– Novelist; short-story writer; playwright

In dozens of works of fiction, Kate Wilhelm, the American author, has presented in the guise of mysteries, science-fiction stories, and combined genres characters and plots that deal with "the impact of scientific discovery on people and their social structures," according to Gerald Jonas, the science fiction reviewer for the *New York Times*. Critiquing *Welcome Chaos*, Wilhelm's 1984 novel, in the *New York Times Book Review* (June 3, 1984), Jonas observed that Wilhelm had written "serious science fiction skillfully blended with elements of the suspense novel," which asked the question, "Are the dangers of unlocking nature's secrets so great that limits should be imposed on the inquiring mind?" Wilhelm's answer has been a resounding no, in her speculative fiction; in her mystery series, featuring Constance Leidl and Charlie Meiklejohn; and in her courtroom dramas, "starring" Barbara Holloway.

Kate Wilhelm sent the following autobiographical statement to *World Authors 1990-1995*: "I was the fourth child in a family of six children, a working class family, my father a millwright, my mother a farm girl transported to a big city. Although I was born in Toledo, Ohio, we had moved to Cleveland by the time I was two. My earliest memories are of Cleveland. I had a speech impediment when I was very young that persisted until I had therapy in kindergarten. It turned out that I spoke so rapidly that everywordrantogether. It didn't take long to make me pronounce every syllable separately and be understood, but what it meant to me was that for many years I couldn't communicate. I learned to read instead.

"Growing up, I read my father's Zane Grey collection, all of them: I read whatever my mother brought from the library—Pearl Buck, Agatha Christie, Mary Roberts Rinehart; I read my oldest brother's pulp magazines—*Doc Savage*, *The Shadow*, *The Saint*, and his Thorne Smith novels. My sister's romance magazines. Every fairy tale book in the library. *National Geographic* magazines, *Blue Book*, *Reader's Digest*. . . . Everything that came into the house. I read the daily newspaper,

Richard Wilhelm

Kate Wilhelm

the *Cleveland Plain Dealer*. This was in the early '30s, and the newspapers were full of stories of the Japanese air strikes against China. When we had an air show in Cleveland in the mid-'30s, I was terror stricken by the sight of all the aircraft that flew over our house, and I was at once a Chinese peasant working in a field and a child watching in horror. I became an instant pacifist. And I still am one.

"In high school I was chided by my English teacher who caught me reading Robert Benchley; there were so many great things to read, I was wasting my time. I didn't tell her that I was also reading *Crime and Punishment* and Gogol and Thomas Mann. My teacher, an Anglophile, what would she say about foreign writers? I read Nietzsche and Plato, Camus and Sartre, Dos Passos and Philip Wylie. I read novels, plays, short stories, anthropology and travel books, astronomy and philosophy, psychology and astrology. I read everything from the day I can remember hiding behind a chair to read my first real book when I was about four. I went to Africa, I discovered radium with Madam Curie, I explored the bottom of the ocean with Verne, spotted the rings of Saturn and the moons of Jupiter, and went to Mars with Wells. I learned the secrets of Machu Picchu, Patagonia, and Tibet. I helped build the pyramids and Stonehenge, toiled on the Great Wall of China, and painted bison and antelopes on cave walls.

"And I told stories. We lived in an ethnically mixed neighborhood where Norwegian friends of my oldest brother told stories of Nordic adventure, superheros doing superheroic deeds. By the time I was 11 or 12 I was telling stories to my two younger brothers, and today I tell stories to my grandchildren. Their parents are allowed to read real books

to them, but they insist that I tell stories, often they even choose the subject, and off we go. They are as entranced by the oral story as I was as a child 65 years ago.

"In high school I wrote stories, wrote everything in the school newspaper most of the time. Then during my senior year, the counselor asked me what I intended to pursue as a profession, a career. I wanted to be a chemist. I loved trying to unravel the secret of rocks, what was hidden inside lumps of stone. She advised me that I would end up teaching, or become a lab assistant somewhere, and further, she said I should become a writer. I didn't believe a word of it. Writers were magical, they could give me the entire world, uncover mysteries, reveal the secret selves of people hiding behind masks, weave spells. Besides, they were all dead. The library was jammed with the work of dead writers. The writers we studied in literature classes were all dead. I couldn't imagine why she would lie to me, but there it was. I graduated from high school and got married.

"Ten years later, married, the mother of two young children, still reading avidly, in the middle of a rather bad short story in an anthology, I put the book down and said to myself, 'I can do that.' I had given myself permission to write a bad story, I realized much later. That same night I started to write a story in longhand. I rented a typewriter, copied it, mailed it to an editor, and he bought it. I used that first check to buy the typewriter. That was in 1956, and I have not stopped writing since that day."

Kate Wilhelm was born on June 8, 1928 in Toledo, Ohio, to Ann McDowell and Jesse Thomas Meredith. She attended high school in Louisville, Kentucky. Her first book, the mystery novel *More Bitter than Death*, was published in 1962. It is a mystery novel, rather than a science fiction opus. Wilhelm has divided her writing career mainly among mysteries, science fiction, and what is called speculative fiction. Several of her novels and stories, however, display psychological acuity and feminist sympathies without having the plot structure or appurtenances of the above-mentioned genres. She has become famed for leading writing workshops, such as the Milford Science Fiction Writers Conference, of which she was co-director from 1963 to 1976, and the annual Clarion Fantasy Workshop, at Michigan State University, beginning in 1968. She has often collaborated with her second husband, Damon Knight, in workshops.

Wilhelm published her first book of science fiction, a short-story collection, *The Mile-Long Spaceship*, in 1963. In the volume are gathered stories from as early as 1959 and stories that were published here for the first time. The themes of womanly strength, intelligent machines or androids, "mad" scientists, and the psychology of fear were to become hers for the life of her career.

"The Planners," a short story, won Wilhelm her first Nebula Award in 1968. Collected in *The Downstairs Room* (1968), "The Planners" is a story of a male psychologist develops a female alter ego, who in turn questions the value of his experiments on primates. In the story, "Wilhelm reverses traditional moral polarities through canny management of point of view to give us a scientist who is perhaps mad, perhaps evil, and yet sympathetic. . . . She succeeds in subtly linking two seeming opposites, the post-Gothic . . . and hard sf," according to David G. Hartwell and Kathryn Cramer in *The Ascent of Wonder* (1994).

Wilhelm's first science fiction novel, *The Clone* (1965), was co-authored with Theodore Thomas. Not suggestive of the later, more complex attitudes she developed in her fiction toward clones and cloning, *The Clone* is a straightforward tale—that of a blob that eats every living thing in its path. Wilhelm's first solo effort in the science-fiction genre was *The Nevermore Affair* (1966), a story of a scientist, Stella Thayer, who discovers that another scientist, Alton Parnell, and two military men have taken control of an immortality drug and kidnapped the entire research team that has developed it. After Stella's husband, whom she has married for the money he provided to enable her to become a scientist, is able to rescue the researchers, she develops a new maturity—which allows her to appreciate her husband's qualities.

The subject of *The Killer Thing* (1967) is a robot designed to kill people on a distant planet. The novel, an antiwar statement, was published at the height of the Vietnam War. *Abyss: Two Novellas* (1971) consists of "The Plastic Abyss," first published in 1971, and "Stranger in the House," which dates from 1967. In "The Plastic Abyss" a woman's husband is involved in a deal over a substance that can create the illusion of invisibility. In fact, Wilhelm, seems to be saying, many things are invisible to those who refuse to see them. In "Stranger in the House" an alien creature inhabits a woman's mind so that she can help it return to the world from which it came. The woman's husband, like the husband in "The Plastic Abyss," refuses to see anything that does not fit in with his view of the right order of things. *Margaret and I*, Wilhelm's 1971 novel, has been considered by many a feminist statement. The protagonist is Margaret; the "I" of the title is her unconscious, narrating the story and referring to Margaret in the third person. Sex and psychology predominate as the themes, and the story is one of a woman's entering a number of liaisons before coming to see herself as a whole, emotional and sexual person.

By the mid-1970s Wilhelm's books were being regularly reviewed and highly praised by critics who thought she had largely transcended the limits of the genre. Her novel *Where Late the Sweet Birds Sang* (1976) is a post–nuclear holocaust story of cloning. In the book, one surviving family has the scientific knowledge to begin cloning human beings so that humanity will live on. The clones, however, who consider themselves a superior species, plot to take over the world and establish a utopian society. One female escapes to breed naturally and has a son, raised in secret, whose human nature troubles the smooth conformity of the clones when he is discovered. The clones eventually need his individualism, and he becomes the human savior of the species. Gerald Jonas in the *New York Times Book Review* (January 18, 1976) praised Wilhelm's emphasis on human creativity. He termed her "cautionary message" to be "loud and clear": "Giving up our humanity to save our skins is a bad bargain." *Where Late the Sweet Birds Sang* won a Hugo Award as well as a Nebula Award.

The Clewiston Test (1976) is another novel of science gone awry. Instead of a mad scientist, the protagonist is a brilliant woman whose scientific talents are superior to those of her husband. Anne Clewiston, who works for a pharmaceutical research company, has discovered a painkiller in blood serum, but is physically shattered by an automobile accident before it has been proven safe. The chimpanzees on whom it has been tested become murderously violent and then withdrawn. Anne's husband, suspecting that she has used the substance on herself, assumes control of her research. The company is eager to begin testing on humans and get the drug on the market. "The novel focuses on Anne," Jerome Charyn wrote in his *New York Times Book Review* (February 22, 1976) notice. "Confined to a wheelchair, she feels as if her life has shrunk to the dimensions of a terrarium. . . . *The Clewiston Test* is a horror story that avoids the usual trappings of its genre. Kate Wilhelm isn't interested in futuristic nightmares: it doesn't take much isolation, or grief, for any of us to fit under Anne's terrarium." Margo Jefferson, the *Newsweek* (February 9, 1976) reviewer, termed the novel a "taut drama of suspense," in which the power balance of a marriage is at stake. *Fault Lines* (1977) is another novel with a feminist theme rather than a science-fiction plot. In it, the protagonist directs a literary magazine and serves as a mentor to authors and artists. The fault lines of the title refer to the San Andreas Fault in California, the cause of a major earthquake.

Wilhelm returned to science fiction with *Juniper Time* (1979). Like her *Let the Fire Fall* (1969), *Juniper Time* examines the relationship between faith and hope, between true religion and those who manipulate the human need to believe in salvation from without. The main character is a linguist who lives in Oregon to escape governmental control of a population half-starved by massive drought and herded into refugee camps. She is dragged back into government machinations after scientists discover in space a golden capsule with a message that only she can decipher and authenticate. The message may be from aliens who possess the secret of ending the drought that plagues Earth. *Juniper Time* was nominated in 1980 for the American Book Award.

In the 1980s and 1990s Wilhelm continued to write novels and short stories (as well as some theater pieces) "mixing contemporary fiction, fantasy, science fiction and horror, with utter disregard for genre categories," according to Michael Swanwick, reviewing Wilhelm's 1992 collection of short stories, *And the Angels Sing*. In her genre-defying novel *Huysman's Pets* (1986), a genetic experiment has resulted in an orphans' home run by Dohemy, the former assistant of a late Nobel Prize–winning geneticist. The adults connected to the home are involved in counterfeiting and gambling, among other activities. The events of the novel are set in motion when the widow of the geneticist commissions his biography. The biographer recruits his ex-wife, the widow, and a group of young people who had escaped from the experiment for an investigative group to set a trap for Dohemy. Gerald Jonas, the science-fiction critic of the *New York Times Book Review* (March 9, 1986), found that the book left him with a sense of "dissatisfaction," although the dialogue was "clever and breezy" and Wilhelm produced "some imaginative speculation linking quantum mechanics and molecular biology." Jonas's complaint was that the characters were "too busy being mad or clever or cranky or sexy to think in any depth." Reviewers of books for young people, on the other hand, found *Huysman's Pets* "top-notch" (*School Library Journal*, August 1986). Dorothy M. Broderick, writing in *Voice of Youth Advocates* (April 1986), observed that the "combination of the SF theme of genetic manipulation of humans with the political intrigue of government officials willing to do anything to obtain and retain power makes for non-stop reading."

Wilhelm's forays into new genres have produced the eagerly awaited Barbara Holloway books. Holloway is an attorney who, in *Death Qualified: A Mystery of Chaos*, while defending a woman accused of killing her husband, comes upon computer disks that relate to chaos theory. "Wilhelm obviously agrees with one of her characters . . . that chaos theory is a major scientific revolution: 'Science has done a complete flip-flop. Reductionism is dead, holism lives. It's a brand-new game we're into," Charles Nicol wrote in the *Washington Post Book World* (July 7, 1991). He praised Wilhelm's combination of science fiction with mystery and judged that the satisfaction to be found in the ending of *Death Qualified* "comes from its science-fiction aspect." The reason for that, according to Nicol, is that chaos theory may turn the world upside down, and "the job of science fiction is to offer metaphors and extrapolations that dramatize such brave new worlds."

In *The Best Defense* (1994), Barbara Holloway, grieving over the deaths of her mother and her fiancé, has given up on the great legal career her father and partner had in mind for her. She reenters the vortex of the courtroom to handle a case of a woman, Paula, accused of murdering her own child. "The more Barbara investigates, the more certain she becomes that Paula is the innocent victim both of a right-wing fundamentalist with an ax to grind and of a legal system that has turned its back on an innocant woman," the *Booklist* (June 15, 1994) reviewer, Emily Melton, wrote. Melton concluded that *The Best Defense* "reaffirms veteran sf and mystery author Wilhelm's mastery of yet another genre—the courtroom drama."

Wilhelm's series starring fictional detectives—psychologist Constance Leidl and her husband, Charlie Meiklejohn—have also won great favor with readers. Emily Melton in *Booklist* (May 15, 1995) characterized *A Flush of Shadows: Five Short Novels Featuring Constance Leidl and Charlie Meiklejohn* (1995) as "provocative and riveting." Robin Wilson wrote in the introduction that the Constance and Charlie series "is a tilt . . . toward the verisimilitude and immediacy of the best contemporary novels of crime and detection." A touch of fantasy characterizes the Constance and Charlie stories as well. In the opening tale, "With Thimbles, With Forks, and Hope," a woman is inexplicably able to control others with her mind; she wants to experience their deaths without dying herself.

Wilhelm's 1998 novel, *The Good Children*, finds elements of the gothic infusing a psychological thriller. In it, four children who have lost their father and then their mother pretend to the neighbors that their mother is still alive.

Although reviewers have sometimes expressed disappointment with Wilhelm's ability to develop rounded characters, her plots have always won approval. *Kirkus Reviews* (January 15, 1999) observed that in *Defense for the Devil* (1999), a Barbara Holloway novel, "Wilhelm's skill in spinning out endless complications while keeping every subplot perfectly clear makes this legal thriller her best in years."
—S. Y.

SUGGESTED READING: *Booklist* p1780 June 15, 1994; *Magazine of Fantasy and Science Fiction* p19+ Nov. 1971; *Newsweek* p79 Feb. 9, 1976; *New York Times Book Review* p21 Jan. 18, 1976, p36 Feb. 22, 1976, p50 June 3, 1984, p23 Mar. 9, 1986, p31 Sep. 1, 1991, p33 Feb. 9, 1992; *School Library Journal* p113 Aug. 1986; *Voice of Youth Advocates* p43 Apr. 1986; *Washington Post* B p2 Mar. 9, 1992; *Washington Post Book World* p6 July 7, 1991; Hartwell, D. G., and K. Cramer. *The Ascent of Wonder*, 1994

SELECTED BOOKS: *More Bitter Than Death*, 1962; *The Nevermore Affair*, 1966; *The Killer Thing*, 1967; *The Downstairs Room, and Other Speculative Fiction*, 1968; *Let the Fire Fall*, 1969; *Margaret and I*, 1971; *City of Cain*, 1973; *The Clewiston Test*, 1976; *The Infinity Box: A Collection of Speculative Fiction*, 1976; *Where Late the Sweet Birds Sang*, 1976; *Fault Lines*, 1976; *Somerset Dreams and Other Fictions*, 1978; *Juniper Time*, 1979; *A Sense of Shadow*, 1981; *Listen, Listen*, 1981; *Oh Susannah!*, 1982;

Welcome Chaos, 1983; Huysman's Pets, 1986; The Hamlet Trap, 1987; Crazy Time, 1988; The Dark Door, 1988; Children of the Wind: Five Novellas, 1989; Smart House, 1989; Cambio Bay, 1990; Sweet, Sweet Poison, 1990; Death Qualified: A Mystery of Chaos, 1991; And the Angels Sing: Stories, 1992; Seven Kinds of Death, 1992; Justice for Some, 1993; The Best Defense, 1994; A Flush of Shadows: Five Short Novels Featuring Constance Leidl and Charlie Meiklejohn, 1995; Malice Prepense, 1996; The Good Children, 1998; Defense for the Devil, 1999

Courtesy of Joy Williams

Williams, Joy

Feb. 11, 1944– Novelist; short-story writer; essayist; travel writer

Joy Williams, an American novelist, short-story, and travel writer, gained recognition with her highly praised novel *State of Grace* (1973), set during a woman's pregnancy. Since then, in the short-story collections *Taking Care* (1982) and *Escapes* (1990) and the novel *Breaking and Entering* (1988), she has continued to examine modern life without sentimentality. Michiko Kakutani commented in the *New York Times* (January 5, 1990) that Williams's characters "do not really suffer from the nameless anomie and rootlessness" of Raymond Carver's or Ann Beattie's characters. Instead, "Williams's people are up against something more specific and more frightening. They are up against the fact of their own mortality—and the realization that nothing, neither love nor youth nor hope, can possibly last."

Joy Williams was born on February 11, 1944 in Chelmsford, Massachusetts, the only child of William Lloyd Williams, a Congregational minister, and Elizabeth Thomas. She grew up in Maine and spent her summers on Chappaquiddick Island, Massachusetts. As a child she read a great deal, and starting at an early age she kept a notebook in which she listed and evaluated stories she had read.

Williams was educated at Marietta College, in Ohio, graduating with honors in 1963. She went on to attend the Writers Workshop at the University of Iowa, where she received a master of fine arts degree in 1965. Her mentor there, the novelist R. V. Cassill, "made the idea of the writing life exciting and important," she told Molly McQuade for *Publishers Weekly* (January 26, 1990). Williams's goal then was to write stories that "would go on into some future."

After she completed the Iowa workshop, Williams, declaring herself tired of the Midwest, moved to Florida, where she lived in a trailer amid "snake farms and alligators." It was there that she wrote her first novel, *State of Grace*, which was published in 1973. That very well-received novel focuses on a young woman's pregnancy and delivery and explores her childhood and early adulthood in flashbacks.

In *The Changeling* (1978), Williams attempted to push further into "the borderland between psychosis and reality," as the writer Alice Adams put it in the *New York Times Book Review* (July 2, 1978). The novel tells the story of Pearl, who, with her child, runs away from an island commune where the residents believe in the occult. After the child's father persuades Pearl to return, she descends into alcoholism and, it is suggested, madness. A *Library Journal* (August 1978) reviewer observed, "Williams' precise yet poetic style works savagely well in the first half of the novel"; the second half of the book, according to the reviewer, was not successful. Alice Adams wrote that if a reader does not "know quite enough about a central character to be moved by his or her possible madness, or quite enough about the external events of the story to be sure what is actually going on," then the novel is rendered "unsatisfactory"; that is the case with *The Changeling*, she declared.

The novelist D. Keith Mano, who reviewed *The Changeling* for the *National Review* (August 4, 1978), had a different perspective—that of someone who believes that a writer's willingness to take on challenges is all-important for his or her growth as an artist. Mano called *The Changeling* "a book of risks: primeval myth, enchantment, animal metamorphosis, strange island symbolism, insanity: more Gothic architecture than Chartres has." He pronounced Williams's attempt to push beyond the traditional limits of the Gothic genre a necessary experiment: "Fine writers attempt more: they hazard—and learn." The overall response to *The Changeling* was negative, however. "The reviews of that book were such that you felt they wanted you to *die*—or if you refused to die, then you could at least stop writing," Williams told McQuade. "I . . . went back to writing stories, thinking, 'The novel is clearly not for me. I don't know how to do it, and I *won't* do it.'"

Williams's next book was *Taking Care* (1982), a collection of short stories. Years later, in an interview with Peter Catapano for the *New York Times Book Review* (January 21, 1990), Williams said that a short story "should break your heart and make you feel ill at ease. It should be swift and damaging." Several critics have described the style of Williams's stories as "hard-edged." Williams deals with the alienation and despair of modern life in short, sharp sentences. Fear, emotional betrayal, and death—the death of love and of marriages and other relationships—are the themes of many of her stories. Nevertheless, David Quammen observed in his assessment of *Taking Care* for the *New York Times Book Review* (February 14, 1982), "In even her dreariest pieces, . . . Williams is consistently percipient and witty. But she ends the collection triumphantly with a pair of stories, very different from each other, that are both masterly creations and also—pleasant surprise—moving affirmations." Brina Caplan, reviewing *Taking Care* for the *Nation* (April 24, 1982), disagreed, finding that Williams "uses her narrative skill . . . to make all sources of suffering appear equally mysterious and all sources of reparation equally futile."

Breaking and Entering (1988), Williams's next full-length fictional work and her first novel in a decade, has as its central characters Liberty and Willie, an alienated couple in their 20s, who, with their dog (dogs are prominent in Williams's writings), roam Florida beaches, breaking into and occupying empty houses. In this book Williams abandoned the poetic extravagances of her first two novels for "cool and elliptical" language that "reflects the characters' lack of emotion," as the novelist Bret Easton Ellis wrote for the *New York Times Book Review* (June 5, 1988). Although Ellis found "the motif of wounded, mutilated birds" to be "heavyhanded," he concluded that Williams "has never written as well." He added that at a time "when so many writers have a tendency toward a forced and grating optimism, this deadly serious novel is shot through with a healthy dose of cynicism about the age we live in." Williams, he noted, "proves that pessimism when written about with enough grace and precision can be effective and bracing."

In "The Skater," one of the stories in *Escapes*, Williams's 1990 collection, a family—Tom and Annie and their daughter Molly—have come from California to New England to inspect boarding schools for Molly. Molly's sister, Martha, one year older, accidentally choked to death the year before. Having Molly go far away to attend boarding school is the mother's idea: "She wants Molly to be free. She doesn't want her to be afraid. She fears that she is making her afraid, as she is afraid." Molly, for her part, "wants to ask [her parents] if they

are sending her so far away so that they can imagine Martha is just far away too. But she knows she will never ask such questions. There are secrets now. The dead have their secrets and the living have their secrets with the dead. This is the way it must be." As for Tom, "The sadness in him has become his blood, his life flowing in him. There's no room for him." The story finds the family at a moment of crisis, when they must come to grips with their grief. Reviewing the collection for *New Statesman & Society* (June 22, 1990), Mary Flanagan noted that Williams's stories "pose questions rather than supply answers. They are gravid with ominous import." She added that "Williams's way of snapping the reader out of the time continuum and into the frightening immediacy of the moment is not unlike Zen techniques for awakening initiates."

Reviewers have frequently praised Williams's ability to evoke the look and atmosphere of different settings in her novels and stories. Williams has written a series of travel pieces for *Esquire*, where many of her short stories have appeared (her husband, Rust Hills, is *Esquire*'s fiction editor). Her travel book *The Florida Keys: A History & Guide* (1986) is, according to McQuade, stuffed "in a leisurely way with tall tales . . . as well as the facts."

As a nonfiction writer, Williams is especially passionate on the subject of animals. "The Inhumanity of the Animal People," for example, which appeared in *Harper's Magazine* (August 1997), is a polemic against the mistreatment and slaughtering of animals. "The fact that animals are voiceless is a relief to us, it frees us from feeling much empathy or sorrow. If animals did have voices, . . . it is unlikely that they could save themselves from mankind. Their mysterious otherness has not saved them, nor have their beautiful songs and coats and skins and shells, nor have their strengths, their skills, their swiftness, the beauty of their flights," she lamented. Williams has also expressed in published works her fears for the world's ecology. In an essay for *Granta*'s special issue on children (Autumn 1996), she decried the world's alarmingly high birth rate, concluding that it is indicative of our species' selfishness, sentimentality, and global death wish.

Joy Williams has taught at the University of Houston (1982), the University of Florida (1983), the University of California, Irvine (1984), the University of Iowa (1984), and the University of Arizona (1987–92). Her honors include a National Endowment for the Arts grant (1973), a Guggenheim fellowship (1974), and an American Academy of Arts and Letters Strauss Living Award (1993–97), which provides $50,000 a year for five years. In 1992 Williams was one of a panel of judges who chose the winner of the PEN/Faulkner Award for fiction. Her stories, as well as being widely anthologized in such volumes as *Best American Short Stories* and *Matters of Life and Death*, edited by Tobias Wolff, have been published in the *Paris Review* as well as *Esquire* and other periodicals.

When *Publishers Weekly* interviewed Williams, she lived part of the year in Florida and the rest in Tucson, where she taught one semester every year at the University of Arizona.
—S. Y.

SUGGESTED READING: *Library Journal* p534 Aug. 1978; *Nation* p500 Apr. 24, 1982; *National Review* p969 Aug. 4, 1978; *New Statesman & Society* p51 June 22, 1990; *New York Times* C p28 Jan. 5, 1990, C p21 Mar. 4, 1992, C p15 May 22, 1997; *New York Times Book Review* p6 July 2, 1978, p39 Jan. 10, 1982, p11 Feb. 14, 1982, p26 June 5, 1988, p9 Jan. 21, 1990; *Publishers Weekly* p400+ Jan. 26, 1990, with photo

SELECTED BOOKS: Fiction—*State of Grace*, 1973; *The Changeling*, 1978; *Taking Care*, 1982; *Breaking and Entering*, 1988; *Escapes*, 1990; Nonfiction—*The Florida Keys: A History and Guide*, 1986

Williams, Patricia J.

1951– Nonfiction writer; columnist; law professor

Patricia J. Williams, the African-American law professor and essayist, is a proponent of "critical race theory," as espoused in her regular column for the *Nation* and in her books *The Alchemy of Race and Rights: Diary of a Law Professor* (1991), *The Rooster's Egg: On the Persistence of Prejudice* (1995), and *Seeing a Color-Blind Future: The Paradox of Race* (1998). In her essays, Williams combines amusingly written personal anecdotes with trenchant legal analyses of the state of race relations in the United States and elsewhere. A feminist to her core, she uses her experiences in rearing an adopted child alone as the basis for many of her comments. In addition to her *Nation* column, "Diary of a Mad Law Professor," she has written many op-ed pieces for newspapers including the *New York Times*.

Patricia J. Williams was born in 1951 in Boston, Massachusetts, and raised and educated in that area, receiving her bachelor's degree from Wellesley College in 1972 and her J.D. degree from Harvard Law School in 1975. Her legal career was to be an academic one. Williams expounded commercial and contract law to students at Golden Gate University, City University of New York, the University of Wisconsin, and Columbia University law schools. She was appointed professor of law at Columbia Law School, in New York City, in 1991. Meanwhile, she emerged in the classroom, in her books, and in the media, where she has been characterized as an "African-American public intellectual," as an eloquent spokesperson for what has come to be known as "critical race theory."

The title of Williams's first book of essays, *The Alchemy of Race and Rights: Diary of a Law Professor*, is emblematic of her writing, containing the word "alchemy," with its implications of a magical conjunction of ideas. Dealing with such topics as the Tawana Brawley case, in which a black teenager accused a group of white men, one of them a state prosecutor, of raping and defiling her; and the story of her own great-great-grandmother, a slave owned by a lawyer who impregnated her when she was not yet 13 years old, Williams's writing is, in the words of Melissa Benn in *New Statesman & Society* (August 9, 1991), part "essay, part autobiography, part poem / novel" in "fragmented passages of soaring prose." Williams "eludes the usual polarities of legal theory and politics," according to Henry Louis Gates, writing in the *Nation* (June 10, 1991), and "eschews up-against-the-wall style rhetoric in favor of dialogue and diagnosis." Williams treated the Tawana Brawley case as an example of the oppression of black women, despite the fact that Brawley is widely believed to have lied about what happened to her; whatever transpired, Brawley's "condition was clearly the expression of some crime against her, some tremendous violence," Williams maintained.

What Benn termed Williams's "combination of self-exposure and political assertion," which "acts as a paradigm for the trauma of all those women whom straight white male lawmakers would have us believe are incorporated, accepted and on their way," did not meet with as much approval from another lawyer-author, Wendy Kaminer, who critiqued the book for the *New York Times Book Review* (May 26, 1991). Because Williams believes that legal rules are mere "rhetorical gestures," according to Kaminer, real justice—in Williams's view—depends on being able to recognize the "hidden subjectivities" of written law. Thus, rather than couching her arguments and illuminations in academic rhetoric, Williams "advances," Kaminer wrote, a "nascent tradition of self-consciously self-referential, 'expressive' intellectualizing." *The Alchemy of Race and Rights*, in which Williams "darts from conversation to discourse," is described by Kaminer as "an alternately engaging and tedious book with valuable insights, weighed down by the baroque, encoded language of poststructural legal and literary theory." Her conclusion was that the "value of *The Alchemy of Race and Rights* can be found in its range—the connections it makes between seemingly disparate events—and the energy that drives the jargon."

In *The Rooster's Egg: On the Persistence of Prejudice*, Williams continued to put herself forth as an exemplar of "how cultural discursive practices generate, reflect, and reinforce the persistence of class, race, and gender prejudice," according to Paula M. Cooey, who reviewed the book for *Cross Currents* (Spring 1997). In the essay "Clarence X," Williams used the case of Supreme Court Justice Clarence Thomas as a springboard from which to examine the "achingly postmodern transformativity of the singular imagination." Thomas, who seemed to embody the opposite values of his hero, expressed admiration for Malcolm X—a contradiction Williams sees as "the American predilection for image over interest that crosses class, gender, racial, and ethnic boundaries," in Cooey's words. Williams called Thomas "the perfect cooptive successor—an heir transparent, a product with real producers; the new improved apparition of Malcolm, the cleaned-up version of what he could have been with a good strong grandfather figure to set him right."

For Elayne Rapping, writing on *The Rooster's Egg* in the *Women's Review of Books* (February 1996), Williams is "a literary essayist in the grand tradition of Thoreau and Montaigne and Swift." Despite her place in the grand tradition, however, she "offers a vision that transcends the dead-end of so much contemporary 'high' theory and narrow identity politics" to put forth a universal concept "where difference is respected but not worshiped, and human values triumph over those of the marketplace."

In 1997 Williams was chosen to give the Reith lectures in England. The Reith lectures, named for the founder of the British Broadcasting Corporation, call on distinguished lecturers—including, in the past, Bertrand Russell and Edward Said—to discuss topics of current interest. The year 1997 was the European Year Against Racism, and Williams spoke on the subject of unadmitted racial prejudice; her lectures were collected in her third book, *Seeing a Color-Blind Future: The Paradox of Race*. With her usual ability to slice through cant and received opinion, Williams dissected, for example, color-blindness as a concept taught improperly in the classroom. When, for instance, Williams was told by her young son's teachers that the boy was literally color-blind, Williams took him to an ophthalmologist, who found no trace of the condition; Williams discovered that the problem was that her son had been taught to say "I don't know" or "it doesn't matter," when asked about color. Meanwhile, racial stereotyping continued unabated in her son's school. As Richard H. King and Sharon Monteith observed in *Critical Survey* (1998, Vol. 9, No. 2), Williams "addresses social inequality in the post Civil Rights era. . . . She has 'smoked out that form of liberal racism that denies that racism exists.'" Williams herself commented that "the idea of vision" relates to "images and to one of the most powerful parts of being an African-American. . . .Your image is what strikes people first and foremost in the most literal sense of vision. It is interesting to note how many black people speak of encountering blind people and of sensing the difference in how they might be treated in the world at large if suddenly race didn't matter."

Williams has engaged in numerous public forums, symposia, and debates as a "black public intellectual." In 1996 she teamed with Christopher Hitchens, also of the *Nation*, to debate Dinesh D'Souza and Kate Walsh O'Beirne, who appeared on behalf of the conservative *National Review*. The debate was moderated by Edward I. Koch, the former mayor of New York. Williams sounded a passionate note in pleading for the continuation of affirmative action, according to the *New York Times* (May 16 1996), where the debate was summed up as "less an antidote to the absence of public discourse than an illustration of part of the problem— that each side talks mostly to itself and no one's mind gets changed." Williams was troubled by the perceptions dividing the audience and commented on that debate to King and Monteith: "I usually consider myself fairly mainstream. I'm surprised to find myself shifted further and further to the Left. It troubles me that if I'm perceived as the black radical, things are very out of step."

Williams has attempted to entertain and beguile readers into accepting her brand of feminism and social responsibility with her regularly appearing column, "Diary of a Mad Law Professor," in the *Nation*, her numerous op-ed pieces in the *New York Times*, and articles in such publications as the *New Yorker*. In the latter (March 4, 1996), in a piece titled "My Best White Friend," Williams wrote that her friend had asked if she had ever considered therapy. Williams replied that she had, because "we black women have bigger, better problems than any other women alive. We bear the burden of being seen as pretenders to the thrones of both femininity and masculinity, endlessly mocked by the ambiguously gendered crown-of-thorns imagery of 'queen'. . . .We black women are figured more as stand-ins for men, sort of like reverse drag queens: women pretending to be women but more male than men—sweat-glistened, plow-pulling, sole supporters of their families."

The entertaining quality of her writing and speaking has worried Williams a bit, she admitted to King and Monteith, because her output could be construed as "a little bit of a performance that makes people feel a little better than they ought . . . against a . . . backdrop of what is happening in urban America and in global economic terms." Nevertheless, Williams has not tired of demanding that her issues be brought to the fore. She told King and Monteith that she wants the media to "open up to discuss the many issues that are facing American citizens, not just blacks but whites, of how we can live with one another and break down the edges of segregation in our lives." After her adoption of a son, about which she has written in her columns and books, the urgency of maintaining the civil rights movement's gains in "labor policies, health protections, local efforts on behalf of human rights" is even more apparent to her. "I'm tired," she told King and Monteith, "of talking about what's wrong about race, about the worst fears and nightmare subtexts." Vowing her intention of continuing to expose "issues of equality," she concluded that there "is no vast number of conservatives oppressed by what people like me say."

In the *New York Times* (December 29, 1996), Williams evaluated "The Hidden Meanings of Black English" after the Oakland, California, school board voted to call "ebonics," or black English, a separate language. If the controversy "boils down to the old familiar ingredients of struggle for respect, resources, opportunity, and jobs," Williams wrote, "then we are really faced with just one more clarion call for commitment to public education as standard. This, in turn, depends on a more generous evaluation of the standards by which we judge each others' humanity," she concluded. Those standards continue to be Williams's theme.
—S. Y.

SUGGESTED READING: *Critical Survey* vol. 9, No. 2, 1998; *Cross Currents* p108+ Spring 1997; *Nation* p766 June 10, 1991; *New Statesman & Society* p36 Aug. 9, 1991; *New York Times* A p23 July 17, 1992, IV p9 Dec. 29, 1996; *New York Times Book Review* p10 May 26, 1991, p31 May 10, 1998; *New York Times Magazine* p53 Apr. 5, 1998; *Philosophy Today* Supplement p110+ 1997; *Women's Review of Books* p1 June 1991, p6 Feb. 1996; *Contemporary Authors* vol. 154, 1997

SELECTED BOOKS: *The Alchemy of Race and Rights: Diary of a Law Professor*, 1991; *The Rooster's Egg: On the Persistence of Prejudice*, 1995; *Seeing a Color-Blind Future: The Paradox of Race*, 1998

Susan D. Lippman/Courtesy of Pantheon Books

Williams, Terry Tempest

Sep. 8, 1955– Nature writer

Terry Tempest Williams, a highly regarded nature writer and naturalist, started writing books for children and young adults in the 1980s. *The Secret Language of Snow* (1984), co-authored with Ted Major, focuses on snow's relationship with the ecosystem of the Arctic; *Pieces of White Shell: A Journey to Navajoland* (1984) looks at life on a Navajo reservation; and *Between Cattails* (1985) is a free-verse poem about marsh life. Three major works for adults followed in the 1990s. The first, *Refuge: An Unnatural History of Family and Place* (1991), which ties together the death of the author's

mother and the rising waterline of the Great Salt Lake, was her first book to attract a significant amount of attention. In 1994 she published a collection of essays entitled *An Unspoken Hunger: Stories from the Field*, which tackles a variety of subjects, including women's studies, anti-nuclear protests, and discussions on Africa. Most recently she has written another prose poem, a four-movement reflection on a person's interaction with the land, entitled *Desert Quartet: An Erotic Landscape* (1995). The author is also an ardent environmentalist, and often contributes articles to such periodicals as the *New Yorker*, the *Denver Post*, the *Nation*, and the *New York Times*.

Terry Tempest Williams was born on September 8, 1955, in Salt Lake City, Utah, and, according to a brief publicity profile, she "grew up within sight of the Great Salt Lake." Raised in the Mormon faith by her mother Diane (Dixon) Tempest, young Terry had a profound spiritual appreciation for the land, especially the area in which she was raised. "I do . . . believe the culture I come from, which is Mormon, is in many ways a magical religion. Magic has been part of the theology's evolution . . . " the author noted in an interview with the *Iowa Review* (Spring 1997). "Add to this notion my family's love affair with the land where most of our time together was spent outside, and I became a prolific daydreamer. To imagine over a landscape came quite naturally. The natural world was the spiritual world. There were many times when I'd pretend to be sick just so I could stay at home and watch the birds in our back yard. I knew that there was something there and I knew that my grandmother—you talk about guides, she was always there with the field guide in her hand, always there with binoculars—understood those yearnings."

In the 1950s and early 1960s, the Tempest family was exposed to radioactive fallout when the United States performed atomic tests in the Nevada desert. This testing had an immense effect on Williams and her family; as of 1994 nine female family members had had mastectomies and seven had died of cancer, including her mother and grandmothers. Williams believes that the atomic testing was the direct cause of their ailments. Furthermore, she has suggested that the tests will claim yet another victim—herself. As a child she watched a mushroom cloud bloom over the desert. Doctors have advised her that it is not a question of *if* she will develop cancer, but *when*.

The illnesses and deaths in her family have tied Williams's love of the land to her desire to protect it and keep it safe. Because she also believed the government's blatant disregard for the people of the Western states is an outgrowth of its disregard for the Western lands, she soon began working toward an environmental career. At the University of Utah, she received a bachelor of science degree, in 1978, and a master of science in environmental education, in 1984.

Williams's first book, *The Secret Language of Snow*, co-authored with Ted Major and illustrated by Jennifer Dewey, had come out in 1984. The book examines over a dozen different types of snow, which is described in the various terms used by the Inuit people of Alaska. The work looks at the physical make-up of the snow and how it interacts with the Arctic environment. The book was generally praised by reviewers. In *School Library Journal* (August 1984), Jonathan Betz-Zall wrote that Williams's writing was "clear and concise." *Scientific American* (December 1984) asserted that "Any good reader close enough to snow and skis to sometimes dream of them will find this work a fine introduction, attractive for the proverbial age span, from 8 to 80." Still, not everyone had a high opinion of the book; Tony K. Meunier of *Science Books and Films* (January/February 1985) proclaimed, "This superbly illustrated book's fractured methodology and repetition of information makes reading it a struggle even for adults, although it is intended for junior and senior high-school students. . . . Overall, the information is accurate, but the purpose is not clear and the material not well organized."

After graduation Williams worked as a teacher at the Navajo Reservation in Montezuma Creek, in Utah. Teaching Navajo children aided in the development of her second book, *Pieces of White Shell: A Journey to Navajo Land* (1984). As she explained in the *Iowa Review* interview, the children taught her more than she taught them: "I thought I was going to create an environmental education curriculum for Navajo children. I was on the Reservation all of 30 seconds before I said, No, I don't think so, and threw the curriculum out the window." In a last-minute, desperate move, as she and the children sat silently in the classroom, Williams took a number of common objects from her pouch—a rock, some sage, some feathers—and the children began to share their stories with her, and she, through them, was able to find her own tale. "Somewhere in that cultural exchange we met on the shared grounds of our humanity, the trust once again, of our own relations."

Williams's next book, *Between Cattails* (1985), was also intended for children. Written in free verse about the lives of herons, muskrats, grebes, weasels, and various ducks, Williams described the animals' food supply and the wetland vegetation in order to give the reader an overview of their habitat. Like her previous book, *Between Cattails* received many good reviews along with a few more critical ones. Joreen Hendry of *Appraisal* (Spring 1986) wrote that "This book had some wonderful sections but ultimately is a disappointment. It attempts to blend poetic imagery with biological fact and left this reader wondering what the author wanted to accomplish. . . . The poetry-like pattern is lyrical; what she tells us often isn't. It is disconcerting to read species lists in what is visually a poem. It just doesn't work." In contrast, *The Bulletin of the Center for Children's Books* (February 1986) found *Between Cattails* to be "A fine balance of content and form . . . [that] describes a marsh habitat without compromise of either poetry or natural history." Karen Wehner of *School Library Journal* (December 1985) also liked the book. "Parents and teachers who want to instill a love of nature in children will probably find this book of value," she wrote.

In 1989 Williams published her next work, *Coyote's Canyon*, an account of the American Southwest. Two years later, with the publication of *Refuge: An Unnatural History of Family and Place* (1991), the author began to receive significant amounts of attention. In the book, Williams took two seemingly incompatible subjects—the death of her mother from cancer and the rising water level of the Great Salt Lake—and portrayed them as mirror images of each other. First, she detailed how the lake's slow rise was threatening a nearby bird sanctuary—and in turn the area's entire ecosystem—then she moved into a discussion of her mother's slow battle against cancer, which claimed her life in 1987. "To her credit," Grace Lichtenstein wrote in the *Washington Post Book World* (September 29, 1991), "Williams is able to help non-believing readers see her connection between mother and Mother Earth. Yet in the end it is the family saga that grips us. . . . There have been many books about tragedy in dysfunctional families; this is a heroic book about tragic events as handled by a functional one."

Williams also attacked the Mormon church in *Refuge*, for its part in covering up the effects of the fallout on "downwinders"—people who, like the Tempest family, lived downwind of the nuclear test sites in Utah. In her review for the *New York Times* (January 19, 1992), Margaret B. Guthrie remarked that she believed the author "deserves the highest marks for her description of her mother's death. Ms. Williams has been less than well served by her editor, however. Her questioning of her Mormon faith is not smoothly interwoven with the other two themes of *Refuge*, and interrupts the narrative flow. Most disruptive of all is the discussion of the atmospheric nuclear weapons testing in Nevada in the 1950s. . . . Coming without any foreshadowing, this material makes for a contrived ending."

An Unspoken Hunger: Stories from the Field, a collection of essays, was published in 1994. In it Williams looked at such subjects as women's earliest mythical connections to the earth, and her account of a recent protest against nuclear testing, which she had attended with her conservative, gun-toting uncle, a state senator, who had only come along in case he needed to bail his niece out of jail. Although she covered a wide range of topics in the essays, the author still managed to project one central theme: that women are intermediaries between human actions and the earth. Alice Joyce praised the author's talents in her review for Booklist (April 15, 1994). "She wastes no time in linking the natural world with spiritual realms, whether reflecting on memories of her disabled uncle or facing a history of cancer among family members. Hers is an expressive voice that brings a passionate reasoning to contemplative observations." In the New York Times Book Review (September 4, 1994), John Hanson Mitchell wrote that "Ms. Williams has a knack for integrating topical issues and detailed observation of nature into her narratives."

Most recently Williams completed Desert Quartet: An Erotic Landscape (1995), a prose poem broken into four sections: Earth, Fire, Water, and Air. The author explored the idea of broadening the term "erotic" to refer to any close relationship between a person and something else—another human being, an animal, the land. As a relationship develops, the author told the Iowa Review, "I think there is an exchange of the erotic impulse." When asked to classify Desert Quartet, Williams remarked: "It doesn't fit a particular genre. Is it fiction? Is it nonfiction? Poetry? Memoir? I wanted the book to be like a landscape one must enter on its own terms."

Terry Tempest Williams has also edited a number of books, including Great and Peculiar Beauty: A Utah Reader (1995), in collaboration with Thomas J. Lyon; Testimony: Writers of the West Speak on Behalf of Utah Wilderness (1996), with Stephen Trimble; and the anthology The New Genesis: Mormons Writing on Environment (1998). She has contributed essays and articles to a variety of journals, including Audubon, Backpacker, Common Boundary, the Denver Post, the Nation, Utne Reader, the New Yorker, Yellow Silk, and the New York Times. She is the recipient of the Lannan Literary Award (1994), the Susa Young Gates Award (1995), and the Rachel Carson Honor (1995).

Terry Tempest Williams is the naturalist in residence at the Utah Museum of Natural History. She lives in Salt Lake City with her husband Brooke Williams.

—C.M.

SUGGESTED READING: Appraisal p44 Spring 1986; Booklist p1487 Apr. 15, 1994; Bulletin of the Center for Children's Books p119 Feb. 1986; Iowa Review p1+ Spring 1997; New York Times Book Review p6 Sep. 4, 1994; Scientific American p27 Dec. 1984; Science Books and Films Jan./Feb. 1985; School Library Journal p88 Aug. 1984, p84 Dec. 1985; Washington Post C p1 Apr. 18, 1994; Washington Post Book World p6 Sep. 29, 1991, p18 Jan. 19, 1992; Women's Review of Books p10 Mar. 1992; Contemporary Authors vol. 153, 1997

SELECTED WORKS: The Secret Language of Snow, 1984; Pieces of a White Shell: A Journey to Navajoland, 1984; Between Cattails, 1985; Coyote's Canyon, 1989; Refuge: An Unnatural History of Family and Place, 1991; An Unspoken Hunger: Stories from the Field, 1994; Desert Quartet: An Erotic Landscape, 1995 As editor— Great and Peculiar Beauty: A Utah Reader (with Thomas J. Lyon), 1995; Testimony: Writers of the West Speak on Behalf of Utah Wilderness (with Stephen Trimble), 1996; The New Genesis: Mormons Writing on Environment, 1998

Martha Stewart/Courtesy of Professor William Julius Wilson

Wilson, William Julius

Dec. 20, 1935– Sociologist; educator; nonfiction writer

William Julius Wilson is considered by many to be the preeminent authority on the subject of America's urban poor, one who is consulted by such politicians as Chicago mayor Richard M. Daley and President Bill Clinton. The credentials that have made Wilson one of the most sought-after authorities on the subject include three sociological works—*The Declining Significance of Race* (1978), *The Truly Disadvantaged* (1987), and *When Work Disappears* (1996)—as well as a 25-year career at the University of Chicago. In 1996 he was named a professor at Harvard University's John F. Kennedy School of Government. In all of his efforts, Wilson has aimed to understand the root causes of crime, poverty, substance abuse, and the litany of other social ills (or "pathologies," as academics call them) associated with inner-city life. Wilson's *Bridge Over the Racial Divide: Rising Inequality and Coalition Politics* is scheduled to appear in 1999.

One of Wilson's best-known—and most controversial—theses, first discussed in *The Declining Significance of Race*, is that class, rather than race, has in the wake of the civil-rights movement come to constitute the principal impediment to social and economic advancement among the primarily black urban poor. Perhaps not surprisingly, that notion has rankled many veterans of the civil rights movement and scholars of the era as well as liberal policy makers—some of whom have gone so far as to label him a neoconservative. ("They have *severely* misinterpreted me," he once replied to a woman who had asked him about the accuracy of that statement.) He has also been attacked from the right, for his insistence on increased social spending for inner-city populations. But Wilson himself insists, as noted in the *Chronicle of Higher Education* (October 4, 1996), that he remains on the left wing of the Democratic Party. Whether he is lauded or criticized, his often provocative views have drawn considerable attention from all ends of the political spectrum, at least partly because they are rooted in first-hand observation: For more than two decades, the bespectacled, suit-and-tie sociologist was a familiar sight on Chicago's impoverished South Side, surveying (along with his team of researchers) the people who live and work there. In 1991 Wilson was elected to the National Academy of Sciences, one of the highest honors granted to American academics—and one usually bestowed upon natural scientists. He was listed in *Time* as one of the 25 most influential Americans of 1996. He has become a social thinker few elect to ignore. As Herbert J. Gans, a Columbia University sociologist, told David Remnick in the *New Yorker* (April 29-May 6, 1996), "Wilson's work is the work everyone has to answer to, one way or another."

William Julius Wilson was born on December 20, 1935 in Derry Township, Pennsylvania, the eldest of the six children of Esco and Pauline Wilson. As a boy he shared a bedroom with his five siblings in the family's house in Blairsville, Pennsylvania, a working-class community east of Pittsburgh where his father was employed as a coal miner. After Esco Wilson died of lung disease, when William was 12, the family's fortunes declined markedly. "We were struggling all the time," the sociologist recalled to David Remnick. "For a family of

seven, we had one quart of milk a week." But as he has been quick to point out—particularly to conservatives who have attempted to cite his personal history as proof that anyone who works hard can prosper—the fundamental differences between his childhood and those of the inner-city youths about whom he writes are that his own parents worked and that his family and community (despite occasional incidents of racism in a mostly white area) provided him with a sense of hope for the future. As he noted, "We were poor, but we didn't feel *trapped* in poverty. . . . Even though my parents didn't go past the ninth or 10th grades, it never occurred to me that I wasn't going to college." In fact, all six of the Wilson children obtained higher-education degrees.

As a child Wilson spent summers with his aunt, Janice Wardlaw, a psychiatric social worker in New York City. He has said that she exercised a great influence on his intellectual development, by encouraging him to read, introducing him to the city's cultural life, and instilling in him a sense of the importance of hard work. Wardlaw also gave her young nephew financial support when he attended Wilberforce University, a predominantly black school in Wilberforce, Ohio.

While at Wilberforce, under the guidance of sociologist Maxwell Brooks, Wilson became fascinated by urban sociology and the politics of race. Digesting the writings of Robert Park (one of the founders of the "Chicago School" of sociology, the leadership of which Wilson would later inherit) and the African-American educator W. E. B. Du Bois, Wilson began to envision for himself an academic career in the social sciences. After receiving his B.A. degree from Wilberforce, in 1958, and spending several years in the army, Wilson earned a master's degree in sociology from Ohio's Bowling Green State University, in 1961. While working toward his Ph.D., which he received in 1966, at Washington State University, he accepted an assistant professorship at the University of Massachusetts. In 1971, after six years of distinguished teaching there, during which he was named teacher of the year in 1970, he relocated to the University of Chicago's renowned sociology department. There, Wilson advanced rapidly, rising from associate professor to full professor by 1975. In 1978 he became the department chair. Honored as the Lucy Flower Chair in Urban Sociology in 1980, he became a distinguished service professor in 1984 and a university professor—the highest level of American professorship—in 1990.

Early in his academic career, Wilson became disillusioned by what he viewed as partisanship in much of the urban sociology that was being produced during the 1960s and 1970s. In response, he quickly developed a fact-based approach, and presented writings laden with graphs, charts, and statistics to bolster his claims. After publishing his first book, *Power, Racism, and Privilege: Race Relations in Theoretical and Sociohistorical Perspectives* (1973), a comparative study of race relations in the United States and South Africa, he focused his research on the significance of class in the African-American community.

At the time, many sociologists writing on urban America regarded racism as the root of ghetto poverty. Wilson, however, was troubled by what he saw as the failure of these writers to confront the increasing economic stratification of the African-American community and the isolation of those still living in the inner city as factors in urban decline. In his second book, *The Declining Significance of Race: Blacks and Changing American Institutions*, he articulated these concerns and argued that the civil-rights movement that had brought about increased opportunities (both in employment and housing) for some blacks had also resulted in an exodus of middle-class minorities from the inner city. As the chasm widened between middle-class, and increasingly suburban-dwelling, blacks and their poor, urban counterparts—who had also seen a sharp downturn in the availability of manufacturing jobs, many factories having moved out of cities—class had come to outstrip racial discrimination as the central obstacle to advancement among the urban poor.

The revisionist thesis of Wilson's provocatively titled book sparked a flurry of controversy in public-policy circles. Although the work was hailed by the American Sociological Association, which honored it with the prestigious Sydney Spivack Award in 1978, it was fervently criticized by others as an attack on some of the venerated tenets of modern liberal urban policy. According to many of his detractors, Wilson was giving credence to the "culture of poverty" argument, a notion, popular among conservatives, that dysfunctional patterns of living had become so thoroughly integrated into urban "culture" that inner-city residents were beyond the help of the government. *The Declining Significance of Race*, these critics charged, provided ammunition to those who sought to lay blame for the persistence of poverty on the poor. As the sociologist Charles Willie, as quoted in Remnick's *New Yorker* article, explained it, "By identifying the poor as cut off—as an underclass with no relation to anyone else—[the book] absolved the rest of society of responsibility." The Association of Black Sociologists went so far as to say that the book completely misrepresented the black experience. Most disturbing to Wilson, however, were accusations from the left that he was part of the burgeoning neoconservative movement, and congratulations from the right. He even received an invitation (which he turned down) for a personal audience with Ronald Reagan, who had been elected president in 1980 and was eager to meet with black conservatives.

During the 1980s, the tide of urban policy began to turn rightward. The culture of poverty theory was being replaced as the favored conservative doctrine by the "culture of dependency" model; right-leaning social scientists, such as Charles Murray, argued that aid to the urban poor was not merely useless but in fact damaging to them. Proponents of this new school of thought viewed programs such as welfare not as a safety net but as an instrument of dependence and maintained that such dependence could be broken only by cutting off aid programs. Only then, these specialists argued, would the inner city's destitute residents be forced to pull themselves together, get jobs, and rebuild their communities.

Wilson was incensed by such arguments, for, in his view, they failed to take into account how the exigencies of ghetto life worked against anyone trying to break the cycle of poverty. He offered his rebuttal to the neoconservatives in his landmark 1987 book, *The Truly Disadvantaged: The Inner City, the Underclass, and Public Policy*. Countering the conservative notion that core values like hard work and honesty had become irrelevent in the culture of poverty, Wilson argued that the loss of manufacturing jobs in the inner city, along with the flight of increasing numbers of middle-class blacks (and the businesses and community institutions they supported) to suburbia, had led to the creation of an increasingly isolated population in the inner city, one crippled by joblessness, crime, and an absence of positive role models. Although he acknowledged the existence of social pathologies in ghettos, such as violent crime, substance abuse, chronic unemployment, and single-parent households, he pointed out that the type of behavior learned by young people raised in such an environment made it all but impossible for them to compete successfully in the larger society. He showed, for instance, how the use of street lingo, arguably an effective survival tool in the inner city, made for poor performances in job interviews.

More than Wilson's previous works, *The Truly Disadvantaged* went beyond explanations of the problem to suggest solutions, and it became a favorite in left-of-center circles. One argument that many moderate-to-liberal readers found particularly enlightening was that affirmative-action programs, though they had been enormously successful among the black middle-class, had done little to help those at the bottom of the socioeconomic ladder. Expanding on his earlier theory regarding class, Wilson suggested that such programs should be tied to class more than race, since it was poor members of minority groups—and not minorities as a whole—who continued to have difficulty obtaining meaningful employment. He pointed out that a non–race-specific policy on fighting unemployment would be able to win broad political support and would ultimately benefit the most needy.

Some liberal critics, such as Adolph Reed of the *Nation* (February 6, 1988), argued that *The Truly Disadvantaged* was an example of Wilson's protracted failure "to break with the premises of Reagan-era discourse on the poor." In concurrence with other left-wing critiques, Reed wrote that "Wilson's entire interpretation springs from the conjunction of two disturbing and retrograde emphases"—namely, the focus on "pathology" or "deviance" as patterns set against objective moral ideals, and "a deeply patriarchal vision of 'mainstream' life." But many others believed the book "far surpass[ed] other attempts to explore these complex issues," as Robert Greenstein wrote in the *New York Times Book Review* (October 25, 1987), and was likely to "spur critical rethinking in many quarters about the causes and potential remedies for inner-city poverty." Indeed, many reviewers predicted that the book would become a focal point of urban-policy debate. Eight years after the publication of *The Truly Disadvantaged*, Dinesh D'Souza offered a critique of Wilson in his own controversial book, *The End of Racism: Principles for a Multiracial Society*. As philosopher Richard Rorty wrote in his *New York Times* (September 24, 1995) review of D'Souza's book, "People like William Julius Wilson, who in *The Truly Disadvantaged* traces the ghettos back to black unemployment, are, Mr. D'Souza believes, pretty well unredeemable. 'In Wilson's view,' Mr. D'Souza says sardonically, 'blacks just happened to arrive in the cities around the time that unskilled jobs were leaving'; Mr. Wilson cannot admit that the shortage of jobs is caused by the civilization gap, rather than vice versa."

Today, with his recommendations for increased social spending on the table, Wilson is no longer the darling of the neoconservative movement. And although he is still out of favor among some liberal thinkers because of his conviction that racial discrimination alone does not account for the plight of the urban poor, and that certain pathologies are in large measure to blame, Wilson has in recent years aroused the interest of many leading Democrats. Among others, he has been consulted by Mayor Richard M. Daley of Chicago; the recently retired senators Bill Bradley, of New Jersey, and Paul Simon, of Illinois; Mario Cuomo, a former governor of New York; and, since the early 1990s, Bill Clinton, who recruited him as an adviser during his 1992 presidential campaign. Clinton, according to David Remnick, "told all who would listen" that reading *The Truly Disadvantaged* made him "see the problems of race and poverty and the inner city in a different light." As president, Clinton has continued to consult Wilson regularly, but has not followed his advice on policy as much as Wilson had hoped: When the president signed a comprehensive welfare bill in 1996 that set strict time limits on eligibility and abolished Aid to Families with Dependent Children—the program at the center of the nation's welfare system—in favor of state-based aid programs, the renowned sociologist professed to be profoundly disappointed.

Around the time Wilson was completing work on *The Truly Disadvantaged*, he was also organizing a project known as the Urban Poverty and Family Life Study, which would grow into one of the most extensive ethnographic surveys of the urban poor in history. Rather than relying only on demographic data, he sought to incorporate the voices of real people into his study. Along with a squadron of graduate students, he organized interviews with nearly 2,500 poor Chicago residents and approximately 190 area employers, who were asked about their attitudes toward hiring minority workers. Presented in a symposium at the University of Chicago in 1991, the 21 papers that emerged from the project shifted even Wilson's opinion on the issue of race. The study showed, for instance, that employers were more likely to hire Hispanic men than African-American men. Overall, the project produced a wealth of information on cultural differences (emphasizing in particular the more cohesive structural organization of certain other minority communities) that helped to explain why many recent immigrant groups had gotten ahead of blacks economically.

Encouraged by the success of his poverty study, Wilson secured grant money to create a permanent organization for poverty research, inaugurated at the University of Chicago in 1993 as the Center for the Study of Urban Inequality. More than simply a research foundation, the center also makes specific policy recommendations and implements them in metropolitan Chicago. Among its goals are the creation of a databank of job-training programs, as well as the marshaling of support for car pools, job-referral services, and scattered-site housing. With Wilson at the helm, the center has rapidly become an integral part of the University of Chicago's public-policy network.

Wilson's most recent book, *When Work Disappears: The World of the New Urban Poor*, created great interest even before its fall 1996 release. (Rumor had it that Clinton's policy advisers were requesting review copies months before it was due in bookstores.) In this volume, Wilson detailed the central importance of regular employment in structuring adults' lives and setting examples for their children, and sought to show how the overwhelming absence of jobs among inner-city residents is one of the main causes of social pathologies. "High neighborhood joblessness," he argued, "has a far more devastating effect than high neighborhood poverty." The book paints a bleak picture of urban America: Streets that only several decades ago bustled during normal working hours are now empty, one of the results of unemployment in areas where not just a handful but most of the adult residents are unemployed. As a palliative, *When Work Disappears* recommends government employment initiatives, similar to those enacted by President Franklin Delano Roosevelt during the 1930s, that would guarantee a job to any American over 18 who wanted one.

According to reviewers like Sean Wilentz in the *New York Times Book Review* (September 29, 1996), this proposed solution, "without stipulating how such an ambitious program might be paid for," opened Wilson to "the risk of being dismissed as quixotic." But Wilentz conceded that Wilson "remain[ed] persuasive" on his major point about the devastating effect of the decline of urban manufacturing jobs on those on the bottom economic rungs of American society. David Remnick, in his *New Yorker* profile of Wilson, lauded the book for "provid[ing] an unflinching view of unemployment and its symptoms. Unlike some on the left, he does not look away from the behavioral problems of the ghetto . . . but, unlike many conservatives who focus on what they see as an inbred and irredeemable 'culture of poverty,' he emphasizes the structural obstacles to bringing about mainstream behavior and social mobility." But Robert J. Samuelson concluded in his *Washington Post* (September 11, 1996) review that Wilson's theory was "wrong." "The jobs are there," Samuelson wrote, citing statistical evidence, and he argued that a lack of "skills, discipline or desire" is the most serious barriers to full employment. "It's also hard to argue, as Wilson once did, that the declining economic status o black men caused family breakdown. . .The flaw is that, over time, the economic status of black men has risen. . . .[Wilson's] book can be read as part of a civil war raging in the black community, as it is in the larger society. . . . His theory aims to justify a radical jobs agenda to advance conservative goals." Another severe critic of Wilson has been the pundit Joe Klein, once-anonymous author of the political novel *Primary Colors*, whose cover article in the the *New Republic* (October 28, 1996) was entitled "Money Isn't Everything: What William Julius Wilson and Other Liberals Don't Understand about the Underclass." Klein's article, described as a "screed" and a "five-page racial slur" by Adolph Reed Jr. in the *Progressive* (December 1996), argues that lack of discipline, inertia, and the general social pathology of ghetto-dwellers are responsible for their plight.

In 1996, the year after he was awarded an honorary degree by Columbia University, Wilson left the University of Chicago to join Harvard University's esteemed John F. Kennedy School of Government as the Malcolm Wiener Professor of Social Policy. At the same time, he also joined the board of directors of Harvard's W. E. B. Du Bois Institute for Afro-American Research. His move to the East Coast was headline news in the academic community, and it was characterized as a profound loss to the University of Chicago's sociology department and as a notable addition to Harvard's burgeoning "dream team" of African-American intellectuals, which also includes Henry Louis Gates Jr. and Cornel West. In addition to his professorship in social policy, Wilson has joined Gates and West, who were instrumental in recruiting him, as a member of Harvard's growing program in Afro-American studies. Commenting on this move, Peter Applebome, who specializes in education, wrote in the *New York Times* (November 3, 1996), "If Mr. West is both scholar and showman, William Julius Wilson is so staid, serious, and somber, you figure he's the grown-up who's been brought in to maintain some semblance of order." He quotes Wilson as saying, "I didn't make the move because I was trying to enhance my academic career. . . . I made the move because I wanted to be around a community of scholars who are public intellectuals, people who are doing very, very careful work but are concerned about reaching a wide audience, people who are concerned about the direction of the country and are trying to influence public perception, public policy." Wilson added that he hoped to devote more energy to studying "the growing convergence between Europe and the United States with respect to the concentration of poverty and race and the ways countries deal with those issues."

Like his writings, William Julius Wilson's personal style tends to be quite formal. He prefers the time-honored garb of the professor: tweed jackets, white shirts, simple-patterned neckties, and flannel slacks, complemented by horn-rimmed glasses and, until fairly recently, a pipe. From his 1957 marriage to Mildred Marie Hood, which ended in divorce, Wilson has two daughters, Colleen and Lisa. In 1970, Wilson married a manuscript editor, Beverly Ann Huebner, who is white, with whom he has a son, Carter, and a daughter, Paula. Long-time residents of Chicago's South Side—the site of both the affluent University of Chicago campus and the dwellings of some of the city's poorest residents—the Wilson family relocated to Massachusetts in 1996.

—E. M.

SUGGESTED READING: *British Journal of Sociology* p377+ June 1996; *Business Week* p20+ Oct. 7, 1996; *Chicago* p80+ Dec. 1992, with photos; *Chronicle of Higher Education* A p12+ Oct. 4, 1996; *Ebony* p60+ Aug. 1989, with photo; *Meet the Press* p1+ Feb. 19, 1995; *Michigan Quarterly Review* p289+ Spring 1994; *Mother Jones* p20+ Sep. 1996; *Nation* p167+ Feb. 6, 1988, p196+ Feb. 13, 1988; *New Republic* p32+ Oct. 28, 1996; *Newsweek* p33 Apr. 3, 1995, with photo, p64 Feb. 19, 1996; *New York Review of Books* p8+ Nov. 28, 1996; *New York Times* IV p7 July 19, 1992, with photo, A p1 Mar. 15, 1995, B p3 May 18, 1995, p23 Aug. 19, 1995, A p16 Feb. 8, 1996, D p12 Aug. 25, 1996, A p17 Sep. 30, 1996, IV A p24 Nov. 3, 1996, with photo, p27 Aug. 17, 1997, D p9 Aug. 31, 1997, with drawing, A p27 Oct. 23, 1997; *New York Times Book Review* p9 Sep. 24, 1995, p11 July 14, 1996, with drawing, p7 Sep. 29, 1996, with drawing, p36 Nov. 17, 1996; *New York Times Magazine* p74 Dec. 4, 1994, p27 Aug. 18, 1996, p12 Sep. 8, 1996; *New Yorker* p96+ Apr. 29-May 6, 1996; *People* p81+ Jan. 17, 1994, with photo; *Progressive* p20+ Dec. 1996; *Time* p56+ June 17, 1996; *US News & World Report* p21+ Mar. 3, 1986, with photo; *Washington Post* C p1 Jan. 1, 1979, with photo, C p12 June 18, 1996, C p7 Aug. 25, 1996, A p23 Sep. 11, 1996; *Washington Post Book World* X p4 Aug. 25, 1996, with photo; *Who's Who in America, 1997*

SELECTED WORKS: Nonfiction—Greenberg, S. J. (ed.) *The New Majority: Toward a Popular Progressive Politics*, 1997; Wilson, W. J. *Power,*

Racism, and Privilege: Race Relations in Theoretical and Sociohistorical Perspectives, 1973; The Declining Significance of Race: Blacks and Changing American Institutions, 1978; The Truly Disadvantaged: The Inner City, the Underclass, and Public Policy, 1987; Sociology and the Public Agenda (American Sociological Association Presidential Series), 1993; When Work Disappears: The World of the New Urban Poor, 1996

Courtesy of David Wiltse

Wiltse, David

June 6, 1940– Novelist; playwright; screenwriter

"A major source of pride for me in my writing is my versatility," the American author David Wiltse said in an interview. "I have worked successfully on plays, television, films, novels, and magazines and in the full range of genre from farcical situation comedies through melodramatic adventure to drama. Some of this I do for love and some for money, and I am striving to reach the day when the two are the same." The variety of his writing credits is indeed striking. In 1973 he penned the screenplay *Hurry Up or I'll Be Thirty*. He has written numerous teleplays, most notably "Revenge of the Stepford Wives" (1980), which earned him the Mystery Writers of America's 1981 Edgar Allan Poe Award. His plays include *Suggs* (1972), *Doubles* (1985), and *A Grand Romance* (1986), and he has served as a contributing editor for *Tennis* magazine. Wiltse, however, is probably best known for his numerous novels, among them *The Wedding 3Guest* (1982), *Prayer for the Dead* (1991), *The*

Edge of Sleep (1993), and *Blown Away* (1996). The majority of his novels are thrillers, many chronicling the bizarre cases of FBI agent John Becker.

In a statement submitted to *World Authors 1990–1995* describing his early life and the evolution of his career, Wiltse writes: "I was born in Nebraska on June 6, 1940 and grew up in the small agricultural town of Falls City, the second son of an attorney and former FBI agent father and a bright, articulate, and ultimately frustrated mother whose feelings of superiority to the small town doubtless contributed to my immediate and lasting departure after graduation from the University of Nebraska.

"Following a tour with the U.S. Army in Germany, I settled in New York City and began to write plays and then screenplays.

"In essence, my career began after an apprenticeship of six directionless and scantily productive New York City years in which I was assured of my talent by various professionals and authority figures, but paid precious little for my skimpy output. In 1972 I moved to Connecticut—to a more sophisticated version of the small town America where I grew up—and in the same year my first play to be produced in New York, *Suggs*, was performed at Lincoln Center. A month later I wrote and sold my first screenplay and began a lopsidedly beneficial relationship with Hollywood that has continued ever since.

"Since the age of eight, when I was applauded by a teacher for my use of alliteration in a description of my pet, I have wanted to be, then assumed I would be, then desperately had to be a professional writer. The operative word is professional because through a combination of naivete and a lack of preparation for, or sufficient interest in, anything else, I have always taken it for granted that I would make my living exclusively by writing.

"My aversion to regular hours, steady employment, neckties, and the necessary social compromises required in an ordinary job grew to the dimensions of a phobia. This decision to write for pay has greatly influenced the nature and quality of my work, often to its detriment. I have plundered Hollywood on an annual basis for a quarter of a century, writing films and television shows for which I have eventually come to hold not the slightest expectation of production. For the most part my expectations have been met. It is tawdry work for the most part but I don't care to burnish the legend of the abused writer in Hollywood. The work is ludicrously easy and undemanding of quality and the pay is fine. It feels a bit like stealing, but that's how the game is played, and a sense of the meretricious is one of the prices a professional must pay in return for his relative freedom.

"In 1980, in order to be able eventually to show my children what I did with the time spent in my office, I wrote the first of my ten novels and simultaneously returned to my pursuit of the theater.

"My father died in a senseless accident when I was 21 and although I did not realize it for years, his absence and my subsequent reinvention of the man greatly influenced not only my novelistic imagination but provided me with a moral avatar against whose unwavering virtues I could judge my own, often wayward, progress in the world. With the shameless expedience of the writer, I used him—or is it wreaked revenge?—by employing his memory, or the hint of a suggestion of a recollection of the man's spirit, in many of my works. A very quiet, patient, forgiving man with recorded acts of genuine heroism in his past with the FBI, I recreated him in very rough approximation in my novel *Home Again*; but in a way he is the template for the heroes in all of my novels—with added filigrees of literary excess and flair which he would probably not recognize. He and my mother and myself and the smallest nugget of autobiographical truth also appear in the play *A Dance Lesson*. A bit of my mother's history is dramatized in *A Grand Romance*, a paean of sorts to my grandmother.

"The novels have been formed by the demands of the market place and to date have been in the thriller genre, a mode in which I have no particular interest but a certain functional skill. I hope to write better and on broader themes in the future but have already discovered that publishers want a marketable commodity to stay easily marketable. A tendency towards the protean is strongly discouraged.

"Oddly, the theater, that most compromised of art forms, has proven to be the best outlet for my versatility. I have written drama, melodrama, comedy, and lyrical history in eight plays with a fairly uniform lack of financial success save for one Broadway production but with the rich reward of a sense of accomplishment. Sadly the theater and its rapidly shrinking openings for most of the standard forms has also proven to be my greatest frustration. Productions of new American plays not documenting the AIDS plague in some way have become very thin upon the ground."

In 1991 Wiltse published *Prayer for the Dead*, a crime thriller that finds FBI agents John Becker and Karen Crist on the trail of a psychopath whose abusive childhood has him bent on making living corpses of men who remind him of his deceased father. Marilyn Stasio's *New York Times* (August 11, 1991) review of the book gave Wiltse the peculiar distinction of being dubbed "a writer of macabre suspense stories who discovered the serial killer before much of the literary competition knew how to spell I-c-e p-I-c-k." *Prayer for the Dead* was praised for its originality, some of it involving blood-curdlingly graphic details of the killer's methods. "Besides putting some spit and polish on the conventions, Mr. Wiltse also expands the genre to fields where no psycho has grazed before—and where some readers may not care to follow," Stasio wrote.

Agents Becker and Crist make a return appearance in Wiltse's 1993 novel *The Edge of Sleep*. This time, the pair are on the trail of a psychopathic

duo: Ash, a mildly retarded man who is controlled by Dee, an intelligent, violent woman. In a sort of twisted take on parenthood, Dee and Ash abduct young boys and then kill them when they refuse to accept Dee as a surrogate mother. Complicating the agents' search for Dee and Ash is the fact that the killers, believing that they are actually acting out of love, often behave in a manner inconsistent with their police profiles. "*The Edge of Sleep* stays on the ragged edge of suspense throughout," Mike Cuthbert wrote in the *Washington Post* (October 3, 1993). "Wiltse advances the story relentlessly, his characters fated to a desperate and bloody conclusion by their own inadequacies."

The year 1996 saw the appearance of *Blown Away*, another novel in the John Becker series. In it, Jason Cole, a highly unstable former professor has crippled New York City by blowing up routes into and out of Manhattan. Agent Becker, enlisting the help of such unlikely aides as Defone Lee, a drug-addicted thug from the Bronx, and gay hitman Donny "The Snake" Sabella, sets out to stop Cole. Before the case is solved, however, seemingly everyone in New York—street gangs, the Mafia, garbagemen, even the IRA and Cole's high-school chemistry teacher—gets in on the action. "These engaging folk will hold readers in thrall through a fast-paced, cleverly plotted tale that features plenty of action, on the street and off, and that will leave readers just as the title says," a reviewer wrote in *Publishers Weekly* (August 12, 1996).
—J. P.

SUGGESTED READING: *New York Times Book Review* p25 Aug. 11, 1991; *Publishers Weekly* p63 Aug. 12, 1996; *Washington Post Book World* p11 Oct. 3, 1993, p12 Aug. 7, 1994; *Contemporary Authors* nrs vol. 22, 1988

SELECTED BOOKS: Fiction—*The Wedding Guest*, 1982; *The Serpent*, 1983, *The Fifth Angel*, 1985; *Home Again*, 1986; *Prayer for the Dead*, 1991; *Close to the Bone*, 1992; *The Edge of Sleep*, 1993; *Into the Fire*, 1994; *Bone Deep*, 1995; *Blown Away*, 1996; Drama—*Suggs* , 1972; *Doubles,* 1985; *A Grand Romance*, 1986; *Crazy Horse and Three Stars*, 1991

Winton, Tim

1960– Novelist; short-story writer

Tim Winton, an Australian novelist and short-story writer, has inspired adults and children with his tales, almost all of which involve the sea or a river. His novels *An Open Swimmer* (1982), *Shallows* (1984), *That Eye, The Sky* (1987), *In the Winter Dark*, (1988), *Cloudstreet* (1992), *The Riders* (1995), and *Blueback* (1998) are imbued with a reverence for the environment and a message of redemption and hope that follows upon the disasters that prey on humankind. Like those works, his short-story collections *Scission* (1985), *Minimum of Two* (1988), and *Blood and Water* (1993) and his children's books have also been widely praised. During an interview with Winton for *Publishers Weekly* (May 29, 1995), Michele Field observed that "often the landscape in Winton's books . . . comes across as the really strong and reassuring element in the characters' lives." Winton responded, "Humans are pretty small beer—here for a short time and really of no particular consequence. . . . I've spent a lot of time in the landscape. It is where I feel the pattern of things. . . . After the fires of youth wear off, you are capable of listening."

Tim Winton was born in 1960 in the state of Western Australia and grew up in Perth. His father served with the police for 20 years, and his mother, he told Michelle Field, took in washing. Winton and his parents and his three siblings lived in housing subsidized by the government, where "everyone had a little boxy house and a sniff of the Australian dream," he said. Winton has indicated that his family life was happy. He was the first to have a university education, enrolling at Curtin University, in Perth and studying creative writing with Elizabeth Jolley.

Already a writer when he entered the university, Winton, by the time he graduated, was earning more money from writing fiction than his teachers. Believing himself "unemployable," he worked very hard as a writer, explaining to Field that pushing himself was "part of my Protestant working-class background: if it doesn't feel strenuous, it is probably not worth doing." Having started a family at a comparatively early age, he told Field, on the subject of being a full-time writer while supporting children: "I was up against a wall and a blow-torch was applied to me—it felt good. It is in times you *have to* write to live that you get to know yourself as a writer."

The first novel Winton published was *An Open Swimmer*. The book was joint winner of the 1981 *Australian* / Vogel Award. His next novel, *Shallows*, won the Miles Franklin Award and was published internationally, including in the United States, where it was acclaimed. Carolyn See, in the *Los Angeles Times Book Review* (July 7, 1986), judged it the work of a "great" novelist who "reminds us of what it is to be human, and reminds us to be proud of our humanity."

Shallows is a story of whaling, capturing the blood and guts of landing whales, and capturing, as well, the meaning of the end of the industry for an Australian town that had structured its economy around it. the book is set in the late 20th century, when whaling is not only economically unviable but is considered environmentally vile as well; eventually, a group of environmentalists comes to the town to shut down the industry. In the *New York Times Book Review* (August 3, 1986), Steve Erickson had mixed praise for the novel, complaining that Winton's "metaphors are relent-lessly literary, from the symbolism of the whales to the sexual sterility of ruthless and decadent tycoons; and the narrative sometimes lingers over pastoral moments while cascading across crucial ones." Elizabeth Ward, writing in the *Washington Post Book World* (April 5, 1992), remarked that *Shallows* "deserved to find a permanent place as a major work of Australian literature."

That Eye, The Sky is a novel in which Winton's Christian faith comes into play. The narrator is a boy called Ort. His family is plagued by a series of misfortunes: his father is disabled from a car accident; his family must take care of his bedridden grandmother; and even the trees around their house seem to be dying, as a strangely luminous cloud hovers above. Ort's parents are people of the 1960s, former hippies, and another ex-hippie, a preacher, comes to live with them. Although the preacher is a hypocrite—he sleeps with Ort's teenage sister—he is the catalyst for the transforming events of the novel, "the visionary and miraculous elements that in the end redeem the family's suffering," according to Elizabeth Ward, writing in the *Washington Post* (April 3, 1987). *That Eye, The Sky* was made into a 1994 film directed by John Ruane and starring Peter Coyote as Warburton, the preacher.

Winton's novel *Cloudstreet* is again set in Western Australia, in the city of Perth. It tells the story of two ill-starred families who share one house from the 1940s to the 1960s. One family owns the haunted house, and the other, more industrious one rents half of it and opens a grocery store in their front room. Sam Pickles, the landlord, has lost the fingers of one hand in a mining accident; his slatternly wife drinks; and Fish Lamb, a son of the other family has been brain-damaged in a near-drowning incident, for which his father and brother, Quick, feel responsible. The *New York Times Book Review* (August 23, 1992) critic, Joseph Olshan, found in *Cloudstreet* not only a story with a complex narrative structure—in which points of view switch sometimes confusingly, as all the characters are "under the shifty shadow of God"—but an insight into Australia's development. "By showing how the sins of the fathers are visited upon the children in these working-class multigenerational households in postwar Australia, Mr. Winton is offering a kind of microcosmic social history," Olshan wrote. "Winton captures social and commercial aspects of Western Australia's recent past: shrimping, phosphate mining, kangaroo hunting in the wheat fields." He concluded that although the novel "may begin unsteadily, like a dinghy drifting among the huge familiar barges of established literature," it slowly "edges past the danger of collision to make its way into the mainstream realm of elegies for working-class life."

In the *Washington Post Book World* (April 5, 1992), Elizabeth Ward, comparing *Cloudstreet* with *Shallows*, found that while *Shallows* is an outstanding work, "the distance, the jump, between *Shallows* and *Cloudstreet* is so great that the achievement brings out goosebumps. . . .Winton has perfected a colloquial Australian English of bulls-eye accuracy. . . . *Cloudstreet* gets you inside the very skin of post-war working-class Australians the way Joyce makes you feel like a turn-of-the-century Dubliner." Ward concluded that because "most of the novel is either so grim or so funny, Winton gets away with the few solemn and lyrical passages in which he openly broaches the idea of Christian redemption." She judged Winton to have "learned the lesson that timing and context are all when it comes to delivering visionary thunderbolts."

The *Voice Literary Supplement* (April 1992) reviewer, Joy Press, found the house described in the novel to be "packed to the rafters," a condition she judged "as frustrating for the reader as for the inhabitants." Nevertheless, she found that in *Cloudstreet*, "the strange becomes quotidian, and the daily grind coexists with giddy, unfettered insight." The narrative, she concluded, is "both epic and mundane, ethereal and earthy, with characters who are lovable, funny, and full of holes." The reviewer for *Library Journal* (March 1, 1992) observed that "Biblical imagery, a talking pig, a house that cracks its knuckles, a son who glows in the dark, and a mysterious black 'guardian angel' add spice to a book whose language resonates and charms." *Cloudstreet* won the 1991 Deo Gloria Prize for religious writing and the 1992 Miles Franklin Award.

In Winton's 1995 novel, *The Riders*, he continued to mine the vein of magical realism that had served him successfully in the past. This time he switched the setting from Western Australia to Europe, although the chief character, Fred Scully, and his family are Australian. Scully and his wife and young daughter have been traveling around Europe and decide to settle down in an old house in Ireland. While Scully fixes up the house, his wife takes the daughter back to Australia to conclude their affairs there. The night before they are to return to Ireland, Scully meets a band of apparitional, cloaked horsemen, the eponymous riders—an ominous sign. When he meets the plane, only his seven-year-old daughter, Billie, is on it, and she has been so traumatized by her mother's absence that she is mute. Scully, in love with his wife, drags the child around Europe frantically searching for her in the press, descending into a mire of alcohol and depression. Scully is ultimately redeemed by his daughter's love and by her need for him. Jonathan Coe, writing for the *London Review of Books* (May 11, 1995), saw the novel as embodying the "conflation of emotional expressiveness with a robust and candid feeling for the physical world," a "bruising, exultant novel which gives you that big church feeling." George Needham in *Booklist* (March 1, 1995) called *The Riders* a "powerful, sad, but finally hopeful novel." Some reviewers, on the other hand, thought the novel misogynistic. Robert Brain, writing in the *Times Literary Supplement* (February 17, 1995), reported that "a high moral tone, based on the old-fashioned values of patriarchy, Christianity, procreative sex, the nuclear family" were "hard-headed fundamentalist values" that "force everything into rigid categories." He considered all the women in *The Riders* "bad or mad or at least sadomasochists." The redeeming character for Brain was Billie, "the real hero of this book," who being "neither man nor woman . . . can step in between these hard-and-fast categories and create a more human order."

David Coad, who reviewed *The Riders* for *World Literature Today* (Spring 1995), found a "total lack of distance and irony on the part of the author." He felt that the "novel perversely demands a sympathy with . . . a bully and a boor. . . . However, with such a morally reprehensible, simpleminded, hollow character at its center, Winton's quest of Australian manhood at loose on the continent only serves to painfully expose its author's peculiar notions of masculinity and human dignity." *The Riders* was shortlisted for the 1995 Booker Prize. Winton won the Commonwealth Writers Prize for the best novel, South East Asia and South Pacific section, in 1995.

In addition to his fame as a novelist and short-story writer, Winton became known, particularly in Australia and Britain, as a writer of children's books. His *Lockie Leonard, Human Torpedo* (1991) is the story of a 14-year-old surfer who wins the girl of everyone's dreams with his skill at riding the waves. Although he is awkward on land, Lockie survives the challenges of puberty and learns to manage the new pressures on him. Some reviewers objected to Winton's use of Australian slang, feeling that it made the book difficult to understand for Americans, but Maeve Visser in the *Horn Book* (April 1992) termed the novel "full of life and humor" and the writing "fast paced."Although it "contains local references and Australian expressions," she concluded, "they add flavor rather than confusion to the text. Winton has created a loveable, vulnerable adolescent who manages his coming-of-age with humor if not grace." Lockie reappeared in Winton's 1993 book *Lockie Leonard, Scumbuster*.

In the Winter Dark, a film based on a story by Winton came out in 1998. The popular Australian movie was directed by James Bogle.

Again in *Blueback*, subtitled "A Contemporary Fable," Winton returned to water, this time the sea, for his leitmotif. In an interview with Murray Waldren, first published in the *Weekend Australian* in 1997 and posted later on the Internet, Winton observed that despite his suburban upbringing, he felt in retrospect "as if I spent all my time on, around or under the water. I felt surrounded by nature." *Blueback* is the story of a boy, Abel, who lives on the Australian coast with his mother. When they go diving for abalone, they encounter a giant grouper. Abel names the friendly fish, which becomes a presence in their lives, Blueback. Patrick Giles, reviewing the book in the *New York Times Book Review* (May 17, 1998), noted that "in a watery world endangered by pollution, coastal development, greedy fishermen, and increasingly unstable weather," tremendous dedication is required on the part of Abel, his mother, and, later, his wife, to protect their environment and the grouper's home. Although Giles found "an ecological message . . . being pitched here," he was grateful for the author's determination "to convince us of the preciousness of our oceans not through lectures but through his characters' steady wonder."

In his interview with Waldren, Winton discussed the "accumulated losses . . . suffered in Australia over the past few decades." He spoke of action to prevent further deterioration of the environment: "People are waking up, but it's a question of whether it's fast enough to maintain the historic contract we have between ourselves and the future. We have an obligation of stewardship, which requires sacrifice. . . . I don't know whether books like *Blueback* make a difference, but in an innocent way, it's discussing these things—we have been taking from the sea and the land for so long, it's time for us to give something back. I feel very specifically that I benefited from growing up . . . where so much revolved around the sea—in a way, it was a gift and I owe it something. If the sea is ultimately where we come from, and it seems we did, then it's our source, our ancestral life and we are obliged to nourish it," Winton concluded. He expressed thankfulness that he was able to give his three children something of the life that he had enjoyed, but lamented that his grandchildren might "have to experience nature in a virtual sense." —S. Y.

SUGGESTED READING: *Booklist* p1181 Mar. 1, 1995; *Horn Book* p212 Apr. 1992; *Kirkus Reviews* Feb. 1, 1992; *Library Journal* p121 Mar. 1, 1992; *London Review of Books* p21 May 11, 1995; *New York Times Book Review* p18 Aug. 3, 1986, p15 Aug. 23, 1992; *Publishers Weekly* p62+ May 29, 1995, Apr. 1992; *Washington Post Book World* p4 Apr. 5, 1992, with photo, p12 Nov. 21, 1993, p5 July 16, 1995; *Weekend Australian*, 1997; *World Literature Today* p430 Spring 1995

SELECTED BOOKS: Fiction— *An Open Swimmer*, 1982; *Shallows*, 1984; *Scission*, 1985; *That Eye, The Sky*, 1987; *In the Winter Dark*, 1988; *Minimum of Two*, 1988; *Cloudstreet*, 1992; *Blood and Water*, 1993; *The Riders*, 1995; *Blueback*, 1998; Nonfiction—*Land's Edge* (with T. Ainslie and R. Garwood), 1993; *Local Color: Travels in the Other Australia* (with B. Bachman), 1994; Children's Books—*Jessie*, 1988; *The Bugalugs Bum Thief*, 1991; *Lockie Leonard, Human Torpedo*, 1991; *Lockie Leonard, Scumbuster*, 1993

Wolff, Tobias

June 19, 1945– Memoirist; short-story writer; novelist

Tobias Wolff is a celebrated memoirist as well as one of the acknowledged American masters of short fiction. His first autobiographical work, *This Boy's Life* (1989), provided a humorous, melancholy portrait of his boyhood in the 1950s, and he followed it up with *In Pharaoh's Army: Memories of the Lost War* (1994), about his stint as an army officer in Vietnam. Prior to the publication of those works, Wolff had earned a solid reputation as the author of two short-story collections—*In the Garden of the North American Martyrs* (1981) and *Back in the World* (1985)—and the novella *The Barracks Thief* (1984). Whether writing fiction or nonfiction, Wolff has combined an eye for surface detail with an appreciation for his subjects' inner lives—their views of themselves as distinct from their standings in the world. His latest book is the story collection *The Night in Question* (1996).

Tobias Jonathan Ansell Wolff was born on June 19, 1945, in Birmingham, Alabama, the younger of the two sons of Arthur Samuels Wolff, an aeronautical engineer who went on to become an aviation industry executive, and Rosemary (Loftus) Wolff. His brother, Geoffrey Wolff, is a successful fiction and nonfiction writer whose books include *The*

Courtesy of Alfred A. Knopf, Inc.

Duke of Deception, a memoir about his complex relationship with his father—a charismatic and habitual liar who manufactured a distinguished past for himself and won high-level jobs by faking his credentials. Arthur and Rosemary Wolff divorced when Tobias and Geoffrey were about 4 and 11 years old, respectively. "The family was split right down the middle," as Wolff put it in a conversation with John Blades for the *Chicago Tribune* (December 8, 1985). While his brother moved with their father to Washington State and then to Connecticut, Tobias Wolff stayed with his mother in Florida.

There, Rosemary Wolff began to exhibit what Tobias has referred to as her "strange docility, almost paralysis, with men of the tyrant breed," and she became involved with an abusive man named Roy. In 1955, after spending five years in Florida, the mother and son set out by car for Utah, both to escape Roy and to take advantage of the reported uranium-mining boom there. Discovering upon reaching Salt Lake City that the mining prospects had dried up, Rosemary Wolff took a secretarial job—which she quit when Roy showed up in search of her. She fled again with her son, this time to Seattle, where she met Dwight, a widowed mechanic with three children, who lived in the town of Chinook, three hours to the north. During his mother's brief marriage to Dwight, Tobias's life was characterized by loneliness, delinquency, and psychological abuse, as well as the continual threat of its physical counterpart, from his stepfather.

When Wolff was a teenager, he reestablished contact with his brother, who was then a student at Princeton University, in New Jersey, and the two began trading letters and short stories they had written. During one summer their father arranged for Tobias and Geoffrey to visit La Jolla, California, where he was then living. Although the reunion was marred by Arthur Wolff's hospitalization, following a nervous breakdown, his sons nevertheless spent the summer together. Geoffrey acted as a tutor of sorts for Tobias, assigning him essays to write on various subjects. That summer proved to be one of the turning points in Tobias Wolff's life. He recalled to Francine Prose for the *New York Times Magazine* (February 5, 1989), "Geoffrey was the first person I'd ever met for whom books were the only way in which you could in good conscience spend your life. I already had the notion that I wanted to be a writer, but I'd never been with people to whom books mattered, people who had a sense that this was something a sane person would want to be."

At his brother's urging Wolff sought to escape his home environment by applying to prestigious boarding schools. Because he had been a lackluster student in high school, he felt that his only chance of being accepted at any of the institutions he favored lay in falsifying his transcripts and forging letters of recommendation from his teachers. The plan worked: he won a scholarship to the Hill School, in Pottstown, Pennsylvania. Once there, however, he found that the shoddy education he had theretofore received had not prepared him for his new course load. "I knew nothing," was the way he put it in *This Boy's Life*. "My ignorance was so profound that entire class periods would pass

without my understanding anything that was said." The school's officials eventually asked him to leave.

Following a number of odd jobs, in 1964 Wolff joined the United States Army. "It's part of the way the men I knew grew up," he explained to Francine Prose. "It's seen as a natural progression. It seemed the most natural thing in the world for me to go into the army." In *This Boy's Life*, he wrote that the army was an institution in which he "might still redeem" himself. Wolff underwent training as a member of the Special Forces. Having enlisted during the early stages of the Vietnam War, he learned Vietnamese before being sent to Southeast Asia, in 1967, as an adviser to the South Vietnamese military.

Discharged a year later with the rank of first lieutenant, "confused by the antiwar movement, and wanting to put [his] mind on something else," as he told Prose, he traveled with a friend to England. There, he became so enamored of Oxford University that he studied assiduously in order to pass the school's entrance exams. Within a year he had enrolled at Oxford, where he earned First Class Honors, receiving a B.A. degree in 1972. He then moved to Washington, D.C., and became a "terrible" reporter, as he described himself, for the *Washington Post*. Apparently not alone in that assessment, he lost his reporting job and went next to California. He wrote fiction while supporting himself through a variety of jobs, producing a body of work impressive enough to win him a Wallace Stegner Fellowship in creative writing to Stanford University, in Palo Alto, California. He received a master's degree from there in 1976 and went on to teach at, in succession, Goddard College, in Plainfield, Vermont; Arizona State University, in Tempe; and Syracuse University, in Syracuse, New York.

Meanwhile, in 1976 the high-profile *Atlantic Monthly* had accepted "Smokers," the first story Wolff had ever submitted for publication. The narrator of "Smokers," in his first year at the exclusive boarding school Choate, spurns the friendship of a poor, unpretentious fellow scholarship student and seeks that of a sullen blue blood, explaining his decision thusly: "I too was a scholarship boy, and I didn't want to finish myself off before I even got started by rooming with another, the way fat girls hung out together back home. I knew the world Eugene came from. I came from that world myself, and I wanted to leave it behind." In the next few years, Wolff published stories in such magazines as *Antaeus*, *TriQuarterly*, and *Vogue*.

"Smokers" was among the dozen tales collected in Wolff's first book, *In the Garden of the North American Martyrs* (1981). Several of the other pieces in that volume also focus on characters who either attempt, or futilely wish, to escape what they have been. The title story concerns a woman who, having survived as a professor at second- and third-tier schools by making herself as inoffensive as possible, mistakenly believes she has a chance at a position at a prestigious college. The central character in "Maiden Voyage" is a vaguely discontented man on a cruise with his wife to celebrate their fiftieth wedding anniversary. The narrator of "The Liar," to the chagrin of his upright, widowed mother, habitually spins morbid tales about his family. The collection of stories was published to generous praise from critics and won the St. Lawrence Award for Fiction in 1982.

Through shifting tenses and points of view, Wolff's novella *The Barracks Thief* (1984) relates the story of three men, stationed at a Georgia army base during the Vietnam War, who are drawn together after they survive a dangerous incident. A rash of petty thefts subsequently creates an air of distrust among the men, and the rest of their unit, as they wait to be shipped overseas. Several reviewers of the work complimented Wolff for the succinctness with which he created vivid characters; one praised the writer's "boundless tolerance for the stupid sorrow of ordinary human entanglements"; and Andre Dubus, in *America*, wrote, "If words on paper could make sounds, you would hear me shouting now, urging you to read this book." The novella won the PEN/Faulkner Award for fiction. In 1986 Bantam reissued *The Barracks Thief*, which had been published originally by Ecco Press, together with six stories from *In the Garden of the North American Martyrs*.

In a conversation with John Blades about fiction-writing, Wolff discussed both his preference for short stories over novels and his approach to crafting the former. He cited an epiphany in the life of the celebrated short-story writer Grace Paley, who, pressured by her publisher to produce a novel, "wasted four years working on something that had no life in it at all, and then . . . finally said, 'The hell with this. I used to enjoy writing.' . . . and began writing the stories that became *Later the Same Day*." Of the moral he drew from Paley's experience, Wolff said, "You're only here once, so you'd be crazy not to do what you like doing. What I like doing is writing short stories." Describing the slow, painstaking way in which he works, Wolff professed a kinship with another famous writer: "I don't mean to compare myself with James Joyce, but I did feel a great sympathy for him when I read how a friend had asked him if he'd gotten any writing done that day. 'Yeah,' he said. 'I had a good day. I wrote four words.' Then he said, 'Actually, I didn't write four words, but I changed their order so they're the way I want them now.' And I thought, 'Here's my man.'"

Another collection of Wolff's stories, *Back in the World*, appeared in 1985. The ten pieces in that book include "Desert Breakdown, 1968," about a self-involved young man who abandons his pregnant wife and young son at a filling station on a California highway; "Our Story Begins," in which a man in a coffee shop overhears a momentous exchange among three people at a nearby table; and "The Rich Brother," which concerns the relationship of the worldly, well-off title character with his younger, naïve, irresponsible brother. *Back in the World* received mixed reviews. While Michiko Kakutani of the *New York Times* (October 2, 1985) thought that the volume "abundantly demonstrate-[d]" that Wolff was "a masterful storyteller," Russell Banks, writing in the *New York Times Book Review* (October 20, 1985), took a different view: "This book is a considerable falling off for Mr. Wolff. . . . Whereas the [stories in his earlier collections] used digression to build a dialectic, to make something *happen*, these seem instead to meander into narrative cul-de-sacs." Banks did find, however, that two pieces in *Back in the World*—"The Rich Brother" and "Leviathan," about a group of friends reaching their thirties— kept the book "from disappointing one altogether." "If anything," he concluded, "one awaits Mr. Wolff's next book with all the more eagerness."

In contrast to *Back in the World*, Wolff's first memoir, *This Boy's Life*, received nearly unanimous praise. The book's title is an ironic reference to the magazine *Boy's Life*, whose wholesomeness finds a counterpoint in Wolff's picaresque account of his childhood and adolescence. Warning at the outset, "This is a book of memory, and memory has its own story to tell," Wolff provided an unsparing portrait of his lying, troublemaking younger self and of his stepfather, who was a dark and dominant figure in Wolff's boyhood. The writer once again embraced the theme of self-reinvention, relating the way in which, as a boy, he saw himself not as others saw him, or even necessarily as he really was, but as he believed he would be were his true, better self to come to the fore. He revealed that upon moving to the West with his mother, he renamed himself Jack, after the writer Jack London, in the belief that "having his name would charge me with some of the strength and competence inherent in my idea of him" and that the name-change was an important part of his resolve not to be in Utah "the same boy I'd been before." When he faked letters of recommendation from his teachers to the Hill School, he used "the words my teachers would have used if they had known me as I knew myself. These were their letters. And on the boy who lived in their letters, the splendid phantom who carried all my hopes, it seemed to me I saw, at last, my own face."

In the *New York Times Book Review* (January 15, 1989), Joel Conarroe pronounced *This Boy's Life* to be "literate and consistently entertaining— and richer, darker, and funnier than anything else Tobias Wolff has written." With reference to Wolff's statement about the unreliability of memory, Conarroe wrote, "It is possible, to be sure, that *This Boy's Life* is simply another of [Wolff's] fabrications. If that's the case, so be it—the book won me over. And that's the truth." Wolff won a Whiting Writers' Award, which carries with it a cash prize of $25,000, for the book. Michael Caton-Jones's film version of *This Boy's Life*, starring Leonardo DiCaprio, Robert De Niro, and Ellen Barkin, was released in 1993.

In *Pharaoh's Army*, Wolff's next book, offers an account of Wolff's wartime experiences. As Wolff revealed in this episodic memoir, he was initially enthusiastic about army life, due to his fondness for the physical challenge and to his desire to have the military experience so integral to the careers of his favorite writers, among them Ernest Hemingway and Norman Mailer. Gradually, however, that outlook gave way to cynicism and despair, with his discovery of the futility of the war effort and with his exposure to the mortal danger that was impervious to competence or caution. As with *This Boy's Life*, a vast majority of critics praised *In Pharaoh's Army*, with Michael O. Garvey, in *Commonweal* (May 19, 1995), pronouncing Wolff to be "a far better writer than anyone else who has yet tried to describe what happened in Vietnam."

The Night in Question contains 15 tales. The narrator of "Mortals," a newspaper reporter fired for neglecting to confirm facts in the course of writing obituaries, shares lunch with the subject of his latest death notice. "Two Boys and a Girl" concerns a potential love triangle among three graduating high-school seniors, and "Bullet in the Brain" is about a man who, in the instant of dying from a gunshot wound, recalls a single, theretofore forgotten moment from his childhood. Christopher Lehmann-Haupt of the *New York Times* (October 3, 1996), observing that "the most significant conflict in these stories" may be "that between the moralists and the ironists," pronounced the book "wonderful."

Tobias Wolff, a balding, bespectacled man with a thick moustache, married Catherine Dolores Spohn, who is currently a social worker, in 1975. The couple live in Syracuse with their sons, Michael and Patrick, and their daughter, Mary Elizabeth. In addition to his other books, which have been translated into more than 15 languages, Wolff has edited *Matters of Life and Death: New American Stories* (1982); *A Doctor's Visit: The Short Stories of Anton Chekhov* (1987); *The Vintage Book of Contemporary American Stories* (1994); and *Best American Short Stories 1994*. Wolff has been the recipient of numerous grants, including a Guggenheim fellowship and two such awards from the National Endowment for the Arts. In 1989 he received the Rea Award for the Short Story, for his "significant contribution to the short story as an art form."
—C.T.

SUGGESTED READING: Commonweal May 19, 1995; New York Times Oct. 2, 1985, Oct. 3, 1996; New York Times Book Review Oct. 20, 1985, Jan. 15, 1989; *New York Times Magazine* p23+ Feb. 5 1989, with photos; *Contemporary Authors* vol 117, 1986; *Contemporary Literary Criticism* vol 64, 1991; *Who's Who in America*, 1996

SELECTED WORKS: *In the Garden of the North American Martyrs*, 1981; *Back in the World*, 1985; *The Barracks Thief and Selected Stories*, 1986; *This Boy's Life*, 1989; *In Pharaoh's Army: Memories of the Lost War*, 1994; *The Night in Question*, 1996

Woodward, Bob

Mar. 26, 1943– Investigative reporter; nonfiction writer

After working for only nine months on the *Washington Post*'s metropolitan staff, Bob Woodward, an inexperienced but hard-driving and aggressive investigative reporter, fortuitously landed the journalistic assignment of the 1970s. Teamed with Carl Bernstein, he pursued the mushrooming Watergate affair from the break-in of the Democratic National Committee's headquarters in 1972 to the resignation of President Richard M. Nixon in 1974. For their reportage, the pair earned a number of journalism awards and won for the *Washington Post* the 1973 Pulitzer Prize for meritorious public service. "People say it's a victory for journalism," Woodward said shortly after the Pulitzer Prize was announced. "Actually, we've merely demonstrated what journalism can do, and has failed so badly to do, in the past." Their reporting gave birth to two books on the Watergate affair: *All the President's Men* (1974) and *The Final Days* (1976). Since that time, Woodward has pressed on as a investigative

journalist for the *Washington Post* and as a celebrated author whose books have detailed a variety of abuses within government. With Scott Armstrong he co-authored *The Brethren: Inside the Supreme Court* (1979), a look at the Supreme Court that handed down major decisions regarding abortion and school busing. He is also the author of *Veil: The Secret Wars of the CIA 1981–1987* (1987) and *The Commanders* (1991), which focus on the political and military strategists during the Persian Gulf War. Recently he has written two books about President Bill Clinton: *The Agenda: Inside the Clinton White House* (1994) and *The Choice* (1996), an account of the 1996 presidential campaign. His work might be said to have come full circle with the publication of *Shadow: Five Presidents and the Legacy of Watergate 1974–1999*.

The oldest of the six children of Alfred E. Woodward, the chief judge of the DuPage County (Illinois) Circuit Court in west suburban Chicago, and Jane (Upshur) Woodward, Robert Upshur Woodward was born on March 26, 1943, in Geneva, Illinois. Raised in nearby Wheaton, he attended the local public schools and, following his graduation from high school in 1961, enrolled at Yale University on a naval ROTC scholarship. "I had signed up for Navy ROTC at the end of my senior year in high school both for the scholarship and because my father had been in the Navy," Woodward explained to Leonard Downie in an interview for the latter's book, *The New Muckrakers* (1976). "I had always seen his Navy uniform in the closet. Military service seemed the inevitable and honorable thing to do. I had a crisis at Yale when it became clear what the Vietnam war was really all about, but I never considered going to Canada or anything like that."

At Yale Woodward majored in history and English literature and served as the chairman of the Banner Publications, which encompassed all campus publications except the daily newspaper. A few weeks after receiving his B.A. degree in 1965, he entered the United States Navy for a four-year tour of duty. He had spent two years as a communications officer aboard a Presidential flagship when he received orders for a Vietnam jungle command center. To avoid that "death trap," as he has put it, he asked for and received a transfer to a guided missile ship. In 1969 the Navy extended his tour for one year and reassigned him to Washington, D.C., where he was a communications liaison officer between the Pentagon and the White House, a job he has since described as "awful and boring." Before he was mustered out of the service in 1970, Woodward was awarded the Navy Commendation Medal.

Although he had been accepted by Harvard Law School for the 1970 fall term, Woodward applied for a job at the *Washington Post.* "I wanted to do something right away," he told Diane K. Shah in an interview for the *National Observer* (May 19, 1973), and "journalism seemed like honest work." After some negotiating Woodward eventually talked the skeptical Harry Rosenfeld, then the assistant managing editor of the *Post's* metropolitan news staff, into taking him on for a two-week tryout without pay. None of the 17 stories he wrote during those two weeks was printed. "They told me I was just awful," Woodward has said of that phase of his apprenticeship. "They told me to get some experience and return in a year."

With the help of some sympathetic *Post* editors, Woodward got a job as a $115-a-week cub reporter at the *Montgomery County Sentinel*, a Maryland weekly. For a few weeks he dutifully covered civic association meetings and rewrote press releases, but he hungered for a more substantial assignment and often argued with the *Sentinel's* editor about the tiresome "scut work." "I thought it was a waste," he told Downie. "So eventually I started assigning myself to better stories. I'd go out and get them on my own, and they turned out to be good stories so he published them. . . . I was not a good writer," he admitted. "But I was a good, fast reporter and I did more stories than anyone else on the *Sentinel.*" His persistent digging excavated a number of scandals in the county government, and, on several embarrassing occasions, the *Washington Post* was forced to follow Woodward's lead. Every

few weeks the reporter mailed a fresh batch of his clippings to Rosenfeld and asked for another chance at the *Post.* Rosenfeld hired him in September 1971.

Assigned to the 7:00 P.M.-to-3:00 A.M. police beat, the *Post's* baptismal assignment, Woodward cultivated the friendship of several veteran officers and, in return, got accurate tips for his investigative series on drug traffic and police corruption. Always on the lookout for a good story, in his free time he made the rounds of the municipal agencies and pumped low-level civil servants. His persistence paid off in bylined, front-page stories on Medicaid abuses, consumer frauds, and health code violations in the capital's most exclusive restaurants. In his first nine months on the job, Woodward accumulated more front-page bylines than any other reporter on the 60-man metropolitan staff. "If he had a single shortcoming," Barry Sussman, the *Post's* city editor, wrote in his book *The Great Coverup: Nixon and the Scandal of Watergate* (1974), "it was that his writing was sometimes awkward. He could do everything else by virtue of hard work and an incomparable nose for news."

Early one Saturday morning, on June 17, 1972, Woodward was awakened by a telephone call from Sussman. Five well-dressed men, wearing surgical gloves and carrying photographic equipment and electronic gear, had been arrested for breaking into the Democratic National Committee's headquarters in the Watergate complex. At the quintet's arraignment later that day, the astonished reporter heard James W. McCord Jr. admit that he was a former security consultant for the CIA. Woodward and seven other reporters put together an 83-column-inch, front-page story on the break-in, published under the byline of veteran reporter Alfred E. Lewis. Intrigued by the unusual circumstances of the case, Woodward readily agreed when Sussman asked him to follow up on the A. P.'s wire item identifying McCord as the security coordinator for the Committee to Reelect the President (CREEP). Within two days the reporter had linked the burglars to E. Howard Hunt, a White House consultant and one-time CIA operative.

Recognizing the potential implications of the case, the *Post* editors permanently assigned Woodward and Carl Bernstein to the Watergate story. Initially suspicious, the two reporters grew to admire each other's special talents. Bernstein, who had six more years of experience, was the better writer; Woodward was a smooth, subtle interrogator with a "physician's practiced bedside manner," according to a colleague. Both were indefatigable researchers.

Using the so-called "circle technique" of interviewing, the reporters hounded CREEP staffers, FBI and Justice Department employees, and White House aides, compiling a thick folder of leads. Perhaps the most valuable source was "Deep Throat," so nicknamed because he was always interviewed on "deep background," and could not be identified or quoted directly or indirectly. Deep Throat, a friend of Woodward's with an "extremely sensitive" job in the executive branch, seldom volunteered information but regularly corroborated the reporters' stories before publication. Guessing the identity of Woodward's mysterious, anonymous source (he never revealed Deep Throat's identity to his editors and only recently told Bernstein) became a popular Washington parlor game. Most informed speculators settled on J. Fred Buzhardt, Leonard Garment, and Charles W. Colson—all White House counsels—and on General Alexander M. Haig Jr., the White House chief of staff at the time of Nixon's resignation, although there were a few votes for Nixon's private secretary, Rosemary Woods, and even for Patricia R. Nixon, the President's wife. Others were convinced that Deep Throat was a composite figure. Political reporter Richard Reeves suggested that Woodward, using an "old newspaper tactic," had simply invented his secret source.

For the first few months, Woodward and Bernstein pursued the labyrinthine Watergate scandal virtually alone. Publicly denounced by Ron Ziegler, the president's press secretary, and other White House spokesmen, the reporters, in their eagerness to vindicate themselves and the *Post*, occasionally overstepped the bounds of ethical journalism. For example, after they had incorrectly reported that Hugh W. Sloan Jr., in testifying before a grand jury, had named H. R. "Bob" Haldeman, then Nixon's chief of staff, as one of the controllers of the secret slush fund that financed illegal campaign operations, they tentatively approached some of the grand jurors for confirmation of their story, and were severely reprimanded by Judge John J. Sirica. On another occasion they decided to publish the telephone records of Jeb Stuart Magruder, CREEP's deputy campaign director. "We didn't steal, we wouldn't, we didn't break the law," Woodward told John N. Berry 3d in an interview for *Library Journal* (May 1, 1976). "It's the problem of balancing rights in the society. . . . If I were investigating the local dog catcher, I wouldn't try to get phone records, but we had a story alleging that the President of the United States was involved in a conspiracy."

In just under four months Woodward and Bernstein, despite experiencing occasional setbacks, had connected the slush fund directly to John N. Mitchell, the campaign director of CREEP at the time of the break-in, and had implicated key White House aides in the sabotage of the Democrats' national campaign. By mid-1973 the team had acquired a staggering list of scoops: the participation of the FBI and the CIA in the Watergate coverup; laundered, illegal corporate campaign contributions; the planned character assassination of Senator Edward M. Kennedy; and the harassment of Nixon's "enemies" by the Internal Revenue Service. When Nixon resigned on August 9, 1974, the reporters "felt no triumph." "If anything, we felt our role had been blown out of proportion," Woodward said, as quoted in *A Portrait of All the Presi-*

dent's Men (1976). "I suppose we were a contributing factor, but we didn't bring down the President. I think there must be an adversary situation in any case of investigative reporting. They kept saying we were liars. We had to prove them wrong. The only way we could do it was with solid facts."

Woodward credits Robert Redford, the actor and producer, with inspiring the narrative style of *All the President's Men* (1974), the two journalists' best-selling re-creation of their coverage of Watergate. Written in the third person to afford a more detached perspective, *All the President's Men* was widely praised for its objectivity and attention to detail. "To appreciate [it] properly, one will have to wait until the storm of Watergate has subsided," Christopher Lehmann-Haupt wrote in his review for the *New York Times* (May 14, 1974). "Then, and only then, will one enjoy it for the classic in the art of political reportage it will unquestionably turn out to be." Released by Warner Brothers in the spring of 1976, the film version of *All the President's Men*, which was critically acclaimed as "an American Z," was an immediate popular success. Robert Redford and Dustin Hoffman starred as Woodward and Bernstein respectively.

Woodward and Bernstein followed *All the President's Men* with *The Final Days* (1976), a detailed, almost hour-by-hour account of Richard Nixon's last months in office, from the resignation of some of his most trusted aides in May 1973 to his own resignation the following year. A few days after Nixon's resignation, the reporters took a year's leave of absence from the *Post* and began six months of intensive interviewing. Of the 394 persons interviewed, all but 15 were interrogated by only one member of the team. To encourage candor, each person contacted, from a White House clerk to Secretary of State Henry A. Kissinger, was interviewed "on background." Using those interviews, government documents, court records, logbooks, diaries, tapes, and other information, Woodward and Bernstein reconstructed the "final days" of President Nixon. "This is no laundered version of history," Woodward said, as quoted in *Newsweek* magazine (April 12, 1976). "It includes material that is normally locked up for 50 years before being made public. It is an accurate account and will stand the test of time."

A torrent of adverse criticism, much of it based on the two titillating and gossipy 15,000-word excerpts printed in *Newsweek*, greeted *The Final Days* upon its publication in April 1976. Outraged by the inclusion of intimate, "backstairs" details of Nixon's personal and family life, some critics deplored the "purported omniscience" of the authors. Others questioned their methodology. One reviewer grumbled that because the reporters relied on anonymous sources, the reader of *The Final Days* had to deal with "394 Deep Throats." Even a few colleagues in the press corps condemned the book as "irresponsible" journalism. Veteran Nixon watcher John Osborne of the *New Republic* called it "the worst job of nationally noted reporting that [he'd] observed during 49 years in the business." Defending his work in an interview for *Newsday* (April 2, 1976), Woodward told Thomas Collins: "This is not psychohistory. . . . Reportorially, we did everything we could to make sure we had an accurate account." The majority of journalists and literary critics agreed with him and praised *The Final Days* as "a model of exhaustive reportage" and "an important contribution to contemporary history."

In 1979 Woodward co-authored *The Brethren: Inside the Supreme Court* with Scott Armstrong. As the title suggests, Woodward and Armstrong presented an insider's look at the functioning of the United States Supreme Court, choosing the period between 1969 and 1976, a time in which the Court made a number of landmark decisions on abortion, school busing, and the publication of the Pentagon Papers in the *New York Times*. The authors interviewed a number of the Justices, a few dozen employees, and 170 former law clerks in order to give a complete portrait of the workings of America's highest court. The book received mixed reviews. In the *New York Review of Books* (February 7, 1980), Anthony Lewis typified such a mixed opinion: "About the enterprise and ingenuity of Woodward and Armstrong there is no doubt. They have done what no one else, journalist or scholar, has attempted in the nearly 200 years of the Supreme Court's existence: shown, however partially, its process at work. . . . [The] question is whether the accounts of what went on in particular cases can be believed. . . . Reading this book, one senses a desire to bring a lofty institution down to the unheroic level of all others in these unglorious times—to show that Supreme Court justices are human in their faults and ambitions." In the *New York Times Book Review* (January 21, 1980), Renata Adler grimly advised, "One has to read every one of [the authors'] assertions from the most trivial to the most momentous, with the caveat 'if true' . . . There arises, then, the question of 'The Brethren' and the law—which the authors treat confidently, seriously, and at length. In small things and in large, with surprising frequency, they get it wrong. . . . Why is it an important book at all? . . . The relationship between the press and the courts, in our society, is rarely devoid of interest."

With the publication of *Wired: The Short Life and Fast Times of John Belushi* (1984), Woodward moved from the world of politics to the world of entertainment. At the request of Belushi's widow, Judy Jacklin, Woodward wrote a biography of the comedian, who had died of a drug overdose. Even though Woodward had had access to Jacklin's diaries and had conducted extensive interviews with Belushi's friends and family, Jacklin claimed that Woodward's book does an injustice to her late husband. Many critics agreed. "Unfortunately," Rosellen Brewer of *Library Journal* (August 1984) wrote, "[Woodward] left out the why—the soul of the man. All the reader gets is a portrait of a pathetic,

drug-crazed maniac; yes, Belushi was that man, but there had to be more or he wouldn't have had so many friends and the devotion of his wife. The reader yearns to understand what happened to this likable, successful guy." Writing for the *New York Times Book Review* (June 10, 1984), Joe McGinniss opined, "Perhaps a writer with a different sensibility could have imbued this story with tragic dimension or at least he might have aroused empathy in us. Mr. Woodward, however . . . for the most part confines himself to a level of insight appropriate to a style section profile in a newspaper. . . . What one feels at the end of this book is the desire to step outside and take a long, deep sniff—of fresh air."

In 1987 Woodward set off a heated debate with the publication of *Veil: The Secret Wars of the CIA 1981–1987*. The controversy did not stem so much from what Woodward had reported but from the methods by which he got his information. Three years earlier he had sought to do a behind-the-scenes book on then-CIA director William Casey, who went on record as saying that he would not cooperate. Over the next two years, Woodward wrote stories about Casey and the CIA, suggesting that they and the Reagan administration had ordered assassinations in Lebanon, along with several other illegal activities. When Woodward began to write an exposé on the Iran-Contra Affair (the secret selling of weaponry to the Iranian government and funding of counterrevolutionary activity in Nicaragua), Casey said he would cooperate. In late 1985, after discovering that he had brain cancer, the CIA director became more willing to give Woodward his account of certain CIA operations, excluding what he knew about the Iran-Contra Affair. At the climax of *Veil*, Woodward described a visit he had made to Casey while Casey was in the hospital. The journalist claimed that during this conversation, Casey acknowledged that he had known all about the Iran-Contra affair. Many critics were outraged by Woodward's claims, the way in which he gathered information, and the way in which the journalist accepted Casey's word at face value. In the *Nation* (November 14, 1987), Jefferson Morley bemoaned Woodward's lack of probing: "Woodward doesn't even try. He never speculates about why Casey and other top officials were talking to him. He doesn't attempt to take into account why various 'subterranean interests' within the Reagan Administration were doling out juicy tidbits to him. Unwilling to understand why he was receiving information, Woodward is unable to understand fully what he was learning." Reviewing the book for the *Wall Street Journal* (October 8, 1987), John Ranelagh groaned, "The cult of the journalist-as-star has overwhelmed the subject, and discussion now is of the author, his claims and methods, and not of the agency, Mr. Casey or Mr. Reagan. Tellingly, the discussion is far more interesting than anything in the book itself."

In 1991, shortly after the Persian Gulf War, Woodward published *The Commanders*, which looks at the political and military leaders of the war, including President George Bush, General Colin Powell, and General Norman Schwarzkopf. As he had for many of his other books, Woodward spoke to a variety of unnamed sources, including, as it was rumored at the time, General Powell. The book's most profound revelation is that Powell had advocated not taking military action against Iraq, instead suggesting to the president economic and political methods to drive the invading Iraqi army out of Kuwait. As with many of his other books, Woodward's methods and citations of hundreds of confidential sources irked many reviewers and journalists. "Woodward is the quintessential Washington insider and power-broker," wrote Leonard Bushkoff in the *Christian Science Monitor* (May 22, 1991). "This book, *The Commanders*, demonstrates how he squeezes that position dry, but it also hints at how an insider's view can be limited, unimaginative, and even self-serving." Sydney Blumenthal of the *New York Times Book Review* (May 26, 1991) had a similar impression: "The problem with Mr. Woodward's fabled access is that he cannot fully exploit it. Because his work is concept-free, he fails to excavate many of the most telling facts, such as those that might explain the role of politics in Mr. Bush's thinking. Equal weight is assigned to the meaningless and the meaningful. . . . Dot by dot he paints facts on his canvas, but, when one steps back to see the whole, they are just series of unconnected dots."

Woodward's next project was a series of articles on Vice President Dan Quayle, then considered to be a front runner for the Republican nomination for President in 1996. Co-authored with David S. Broder, this series was collected and put into book form under the title *The Man Who Would Be President—Dan Quayle* (1992).

Woodward's *The Agenda: Inside the Clinton White House* (1994) is the reporter's inside look at President Bill Clinton's economic policies during his first year in office. The book suggests that the Clinton White House during this period was essentially a scene of chaos, a place where policies were adopted and thrown away with every shift in the polls. Comparing this work to *Veil*, Frank Gannon of the *National Review* (August 1, 1994) wrote, "This time out, Bob Woodward does not strain our credulity quite as hard, and does manage to create a fairly credible picture of President Clinton at work. It's not a pretty picture. . . . Things are so chaotic in the Clinton White House that it is rather remarkable they get anything done at all." Although impressed that Woodward had gone to such lengths to recreate events during Clinton's first year in office, Marshall Ingwerson of the *Christian Science Monitor* (June 30, 1994) also noted, "The details [in this book] have gone unchallenged even by White House officials who dispute the unflattering light Woodward casts them in. . . . This book is unlikely to bolster anyone's confidence in Clinton's administration. But if *The Agenda* indicates anything, it shows that the Clinton White House is ever capable of learning."

Two years later Woodward produced *The Choice*, an account of the 1996 presidential race, between the Republican candidate, Senator Bob Dole, and President Clinton. In order to research *The Choice*, Woodward was granted a great deal of access to Dole, and he revisited the Clinton sources he had gained while writing *The Agenda*. Most reviewers commended his reporting but wanted more analysis of what he had witnessed. "Woodward has an eye for the telling detail, for journalism as anecdote . . . " Martin Walker observed in *New York Newsday* (July 4, 1996). "But this is a book that gets so close to the action that it neglects to analyze the deeper political process." In the *New York Review of Books* (September 19, 1996), Joan Didion remarked, "What seems most remarkable in this new Woodward book is exactly what seemed remarkable in the previous Woodward books, each of which was presented as the insiders' inside story and each of which went on to become a number-one bestseller: these are books in which measurable cerebral activity is virtually absent."

Shadow: Five Presidents and the Legacy of Watergate 1974–1999 examined the effects that the scandal of the title has had on presidential activity and decision making, as evidenced by the administrations of Gerald Ford, Jimmy Carter, Ronald Reagan, George Bush, and Bill Clinton.

Bob Woodward married Francie Barnard, a Washington correspondent for the *Ft. Worth Star-Telegram*, on November 29, 1974. As had an earlier marriage, that union ended in divorce. On November 25, 1989 Woodward married fellow *Washington Post* journalist Elsa Walsh. Woodward has a daughter, Mary Taliesin.

—C.M.

SUGGESTED READING: *Business Week* p12+ Oct. 19, 1987; *Chicago Tribune* p3 May 12, 1991; *Christian Science Monitor* p13 May 22, 1991, p14 June 30, 1994, p15 July 31, 1996; *Library Journal* May 1, 1976, p1442 Aug. 1984; *Nation* p562 Nov. 14, 1987; *National Observer* p6 May 19, 1973; *National Review* p60 Aug. 1, 1994; *New York Review of Books* p3 Feb. 7, 1980, p15 Sep. 31, 1996; *New York Sunday News* p74+ Apr. 25, 1976; *New York Times* May 14, 1974; *New York Times Book Review* p1 Dec. 16, 1979, Jan. 21, 1980, p16 June 10, 1984, p2 May 26, 1991, p5+ May 24, 1992; *Newsday* p49 May 14, 1973, Apr. 2, 1976, B p2+ June 15, 1994, B p7 July 4, 1996; *Newsweek* Apr. 12, 1976, p71 Dec. 4, 1989; *Publishers Weekly* p47 Apr. 20, 1992; *Wall Street Journal* p28 Oct. 8, 1987; *Washington Post Parade* p9+ Apr. 18, 1976; Downie, Leonard. *The New Muckrakers* (1976); *Who's Who in America*, 1998

SELECTED WORKS: *All the President's Men* (with Carl Bernstein), 1974; *The Final Days* (with Carl Bernstein), 1976; *The Brethren: Inside the Supreme Court* (with Scott Armstrong), 1979; *Wired: the Short Life and Fast Times of John*

Belushi, 1984; *Veil: The Secret Wars of the CIA 1981–1987*, 1987; *The Commanders*, 1991; *The Man Who Would Be President—Dan Quayle* (with David S. Broder), 1992; *The Agenda: Inside the Clinton White House*, 1994; *The Choice*, 1996; *Shadow: Five Presidents and the Legacy of Watergate 1974–1999*, 1999

Jerry Bauer

Youngblood, Shay

Oct. 16, 1959– Novelist; short-story writer; playwright

The inspiration for the works of the African-American short-story writer, novelist, and playwright Shay Youngblood has come largely from what she remembers hearing from the women who raised her. "I realized that I had a wealth of unfinished stories from my family and that I could use my imagination to complete the good parts," she said in a statement sent to *World Authors 1990–1995*. Many of those tales were published as *The Big Mama Stories* in 1989; others were adapted and used in *Shakin' the Mess Outta Misery*, a play that premiered in 1988 and was published in 1993. Youngblood's first novel, *Soul Kiss* (1997), was greeted with enthusiasm by reviewers. Her plays *Talking Bones* and *Amazing Grace* were published in 1998.

Shay Youngblood sent the following "Artistic Statement" to *World Authors 1990–1995*: "I was born in Columbus, Georgia in 1959. I was an only child, raised in a house of women who were in their 40's and 50's during my childhood. I made up stories to entertain myself when I wasn't listening

in on grown folks' talk. Their generation truly believed that children were to be seen and not heard, so questions from a curious child like myself were often answered with a question: 'Girl, why you talk so much foolishness?' or 'What do you think?' They often stopped telling a story right at the good part when I was in the room. I read everything I could get my hands on, including the Bible on more than a few rainy days when I couldn't get to the public library. I read books about foreign countries, outer space and books about cooking and interior decorating. When I discovered that black people wrote books I allowed myself to believe that one day so would I. In junior high school math classes I wrote serial drama stories to keep myself awake and entertain my friends. I failed math class but I learned what held a reader's attention. They were sort of black teenage soap operas where the characters led much more exciting lives wearing much more glamorous clothes than the ones we did growing up in housing projects between the railroad tracks and the cemetery. One of my high school English teachers gave me a creative writing assignment and suggested that I write about what I knew best. It was good advice for me. I realized that I had a wealth of unfinished stories from my family and that I could use my imagination to complete the good parts.

"My birth mother died when I was two years old and I was raised by great-grandmothers, great-aunts and -uncles, neighbors, the entire community really took on the responsibility for bringing me up. I called the women Big Mamas. When I began to want to write their stories and asked them to tell me what it was like for them growing up they said 'Those old stories not important, nobody wants to hear all that.' I came to realize that remembering their history was painful but important especially for me. I began writing seriously out of a desire to give the community who raised me a voice. When I sat down to write I created characters based on my Big Mamas, gave them names, histories. I put them in situations, then gave them obstacles to overcome or not. I gave them words to speak and I gave them hope.

"After graduating with a B.A. in communications from Clark College in Atlanta (where I changed my major at least five times) I joined the Peace Corps as an agriculture information officer. I kept writing. After the Peace Corps I worked as a house painter, delivering telephone books, as a librarian, an archivist and museum tour guide, as an intern photographer for the mayor of Atlanta, at a public television station (where I once wore a furry red Krystal Kritter costume to entertain children) and as an artist's model, au pair and poet's helper in Paris. I've left the South many times but it has never left me. My first collection of short stories, *The Big Mama Stories*, were written for and about women most of whom did not read or write but they told stories and sang songs that continue to find their way into the language, rhythm and lives of my characters. . . .

YOUNGBLOOD

"When I finished *The Big Mama Stories* I was living in the South of France at an artists' colony, alone in the middle of winter. James Baldwin's farmhouse was just over the hill and that alone made me feel like a real writer by association. We were breathing the same air, almost. I had been working on the stories for a few years and I was sad to have to leave all these women I had created and come to know deeper like a real family. I remembered that a local theater company director in Atlanta had said he liked my stories and thought that I'd write interesting plays. I decided to adapt the short stories into a play. The theater company in Atlanta saw the potential in the piece I had cut and pasted together and paired me with a director who worked with me on developing the piece for the stage. I learned about the communal nature of playwriting. First of all everybody wanted to rewrite the play, from the actors, to the director and producers. Some of their suggestions I took, others I did not. I did have to make changes. For example there were originally 20 characters in the first version I wrote. I hadn't really thought about the fact that each character had to get paid whether they had two lines of dialog or 20 pages. After quite a bit of reshaping my play *Shakin' the Mess Out of Misery* has continued to be produced all across the country for the last 10 years. It's been playing for three months in Chicago and [will] possibly be produced in London next year [1999]. The last story in the collection was written while we were working on the play to give the stories a context. The narrator is a young girl who when she gets her period is told stories by her big mamas to prepare her for being a woman. They even perform a ritual with song and dance to symbolically bring her into the circle of womanhood. . . .

"After my play was produced I became known as a playwright but I still felt there was a lot I wanted to learn about the craft of playwriting, so I went to graduate school. At Brown University I had the good fortune to work with Paula Vogel, who just won this year's Pulitzer Prize for Drama for her play *How I Learned to Drive*. In her workshops I wrote several plays but was frustrated with the form. After I graduated I decided that I wanted to challenge myself to write a novel. I felt that I needed a bigger canvas for the story that had been simmering in my head for a while. I wrote *Soul Kiss* in two years. One of the issues I wanted to explore was the ways in which parents and children eroticize each other, how they fall in love with each other a little bit. And I feel I need to say that this is not a book about incest but about early intimacy that everyone experiences but no one wants to talk about. . . .

"I like to experiment with language. . . . The novel I'm working on now ["My Body Is Bread"] mixes poetry and prose, the reality of a young girl who wakes up one morning to find that her body is changing and neither she nor her parents are prepared."

The Big Mama Stories, published in 1989, left no doubt that Youngblood was a real writer, not one "by association." The book is a series of interconnected stories that originated with, and are about, the various "big mamas" who raise her. Some of the mamas are male, but the world that the narrator inhabits is mostly female. When the narrator experiences menarche, the women hold a ritual initiation for her, lighting candles, burning incense, and offering gifts. The book concludes with the ceremony: "Standing in that circle of light behind the Eighth Street Baptist Church on a clear September night I was given my name and invited into the circle of women, no longer a girl. I was a woman now. All the stories they had told me were gifts, all the love more precious than gold. They tell me . . . now I know."

Writing about *The Big Mama Stories* in her volume *500 Great Books by Women* (1994), Erica Bauermeister particularly liked Williams's description of such incidents: "On occasion all the mothers come together, to heal an illness or to celebrate a rite of passage, and during these events the narrative soars," she declared. Bauermeister drew attention to such vibrant characters as Miss Corine, a hairdresser, who tells the narrator, "if you got to dance or dream or anything at all, take it a step at a time and don't let nothing and nobody get in your way when you doing right." For Bauermeister, *The Big Mama Stories* were invigorating: "Whether quiet or jubilant, sad or defiant or thoughtful, each story has power and pride, given freely to the narrator, and through her to us."

The *Publishers Weekly* (1982) reviewer hailed Youngblood's debut, noting that the stories "capture the dialect and climate of the black south of the 60s" and praising Youngblood's ability to maintain "a near-flawless cadence and a consistent tone with subtlety and grace." On the other hand, the reviewer observed a "flatness" in Youngblood's characters and "predictability in their actions."

Youngblood's play *Shakin' the Mess Outta Misery* was first performed in 1988. The central figure and narrator in the play, Daughter, absorbs the stories of, and is otherwise influenced by, several generations of female elders. The characters, among them the salty Aunt Mae, the beautician Miss Corine, and the lesbian carpenter Miss Tom, are evoked through dramatic dialogue, comedy, or a form of stylized dance. In an interview for the *Washington Post* (December 11, 1992), Jennifer Nelson, the director of a production at the Source Theatre, in Washington, D.C., told Jeanne Cooper that "one of the things that works so well about the play is that there's something that almost everybody, but especially black women, is going to identify personally with." Pamela Sommers, a reviewer for the *Washington Post* (November 24, 1992), entered the theater expecting that the play would turn out to be "just another heartfelt-but-hackneyed memory play"; she was pleasantly surprised: "*Shakin' the Mess*, a vivid portrait of the members of a tightknit community of African-

American women living in a small Southern town, is certainly heartfelt, and definitely a memory play, but it goes about its business in unpredictable and emotionally satisfying ways," she wrote. "First . . . is Youngblood's evocative language, which blends the poetic and the everyday into a potent stew of exclamations and descriptions, oaths and jive." *Shakin' the Mess Outta Misery* was published in 1993.

Soul Kiss, Youngblood's first novel, was published in 1997. A coming-of-age story set in Georgia and California, it centers on young Mariah Santos, whose mother leaves her with two elderly aunts when Mariah is seven. Mariah awaits the day of her mother's return, but it never comes, and her Aunt Faith slowly reveals that Mariah's mother is a drug addict who goes from one rehabilitation program to another. Mariah never loses the hope of recapturing the sweetness and bliss of the parental love she had known as a small child, and she decides to seek the father she has never seen—an artist nicknamed Matisse.

Responses to *Soul Kiss* were positive. In a starred review, a *Publishers Weekly* (April 14, 1997) critic concluded, "Saturating her writing with haunting eroticism, lyrical description, and complex characterization, Youngblood gets inside the soul of an acutely isolated girl and takes the pulse of her desire to break out of that solitude." Emily Barton wrote in the *New York Times Book Review* (February 22, 1998), "Though susceptible to awkward flights of poetic language, Mariah is an honestly drawn character who never evades complicated questions with simple answers. It is this quality that gives *Soul Kiss* its convincing air of human contradiction, of intelligent introspection." *The Women's Press* (on-line) called *Soul Kiss* "a sensuously written, haunting novel, infused with longing, about sexual awakening, the pull of memory and the need for relationship."

Youngblood has had a number of plays produced in addition to *Shakin' the Mess Outta Misery*. Among them is *Talking Bones*, which involves three generations of women and is set at a burial ground. The play, which Alvin Klein in the *New York Times* (May 9, 1993) termed "part real, part fantastical, part ritualistic," won the Kennedy Center's Lorraine Hansberry Playwriting Award in 1993. It had a staged reading at the Genesis Festival: A Celebration of New Voices in African-American Theater in New Brunswick, New Jersey, in 1995, and was published along with *Amazing Grace*, another of Youngblood's plays, in 1998.

Youngblood's play *Black Power Barbie* was performed at the Washington Theatre Festival in 1995. In the following year *Square Blues* had a production in Providence, Rhode Island. The main character in that play is Blue, who is opening a new café. In it he plans to place on a "wall of resistance" images of those who have inspired him, including Malcolm X and Angela Davis. His daughter is a lesbian activist with another slant on how to resist oppression. According to Beth Buschman-Kelly in

the *Brown Daily Herald* (March 7, 1996), Youngblood has called the play an "African-American drama about protest and resistance [in which] art activists, everyday revolutionaries, and interracial lovers are inspired by art, ritual, and the blues to effect change in the world they live in." In 1995 *Square Blues* won a Paul Green Foundation National Theatre Award and was a 21st Century Playwrights Festival Edward Albee honoree.

Fiction by Shay Youngblood is included in *Children of the Night: The Best Short Stories by Black Writers 1967 to the Present* (1997), edited and with an introduction by Gloria Naylor. The *Washington Post Book World* (February 9, 1997) cited Youngblood as one of the "emerging voices" among the "exemplary talents" represented in the collection.

In 1998 Youngblood began teaching creative writing at the New School University (formerly called the New School for Social Research) in New York City.
—S. Y.

SUGGESTED READING: *New York Times* XIII p7 May 9, 1993; *New York Times Book Review* p21 Feb. 22, 1998; *Publishers Weekly* p54 Apr. 14, 1997; *Washington Post* E p2 Nov. 24, 1992, N p43 Dec. 11, 1992, D p2 July 15, 1995; *Washington Post Book World* p12 Feb. 9, 1997; *Women's Press* (on-line); Bauermeister, E., with J. Larsen and H. Smith. *500 Great Books by Women*, 1994

SELECTED WORKS: Drama—*Shakin' the Mess Outta Misery*, 1993; *Talking Bones*, 1998; *Amazing Grace*, 1998; Fiction—*The Big Mama Stories*, 1989; *Soul Kiss*, 1997; Poetry—*One Red Shoe*, 1990

Zencey, Eric

Sep. 24, 1953– Novelist; essayist

Eric Zencey, a professor of history and social inquiry, was noted for his scholarly articles on entropy as metaphor and the philosophy of ecology before achieving commercial recognition in 1995 with the publication of *Panama*, a novel of crime and intrigue set in fin-de-siècle Paris. The novel, a fictionalized account of the political machinations surrounding plans by a French company to build a canal in Central America, has as its central character a real-life personage, the American intellectual Henry Adams (1838–1918), a prominent subject of Zencey's historical inquiry and a 19th-century editor of the *North American Review*, of which Zencey serves as a contributing editor. Zencey is also the author of *Virgin Forest: Meditations on History, Ecology, and Culture* (1998). Since 1982 he has been on the faculty of Goddard College in Plainfield, Vermont. His wife, Kathryn Davis, is also an author.

Sigrid Estrada

Eric Zencey

The son of Charles and Ruth Mills Zencey, Eric Zencey was born on September 24, 1953 in Delaware and grew up in St. Georges (population 400), itself a canal town on the Chesapeake and Delaware canal, built in the 19th century. His father was a photographer for the DuPont company and columnist for a weekly newspaper. His mother, Zencey told an interviewer for the *Burlington Free Press* (September 11, 1995), was "a great writer, and one of the projects I have in mind is editing the letters between my mother and her brother. I got my love of reading and language from both parents." Describing his growing-up years in St. Georges in his reflective essay "Cartography" in the *North American Review* (Summer 1989), Zencey charted a psychic landscape of exploration and discovery shared with his brother Carl, a journey stimulated by pictures of Christopher and Bartholomew Columbus in the boys' geography books. He described how their imaginations took flight toward a semireal "island of lost bicycles" that existed just beyond their kitchen window with its "bottle-bottom lens" serving as a makeshift telescope for their boyhood musings. "We had, then," he wrote, "the child's awe for the power of material things."

Eric Zencey received his bachelor's degree in economics and political science from the University of Delaware in 1976 and his master's degree in political theory and international relations from the same institution two years later. In 1985 he received a Ph.D. in philosophy, international relations, and the history of science from Claremont Graduate School in California, with his dissertation, "Entropy as Root Metaphor," an inquiry that has continued to serve as a source for his writing.

At Claremont he further developed his interest in the philosophy of John Dewey and in the dichotomy between "wilderness" or "nature" and "culture" in the American experience, an enterprise he discussed at length in his essay "The Hand That Wounds" in the *North American Review* (Summer 1990). "Even our wilderness is a human construct," he wrote, in support of his belief that our perceptions of nature have always been culture-bound.

The concept of "entropy as root metaphor" was popularized by Jeremy Rifkin in *Entropy*, the 1980 book he coauthored with Ted Howard. While Zencey admits the scholarly shortcomings of the Rifkin/Howard work, he nonetheless finds "entropy" a useful metaphor for organizing knowledge about historical and social phenomena and for providing a philosophical justification for certain aspects of the ecology and resource-conservation movements.

In 1991 the journal *Metaphor and Symbolic Activity* published Zencey's essay "Some Brief Speculations on the Popularity of Entropy as Metaphor." After describing entropy as having been used by formulators of the laws of thermodynamics in the 19th-century, Zencey makes significant references to Henry Adams, the American intellect who figures prominently in his novel *Panama*, and to Henry's brother, Brooks Adams (1848–1927), the author of *The Law of Civilization and Decay*. Zencey wrote: "Antitechnocrats Rifkin and Howard (1980) and Henderson (1978), for instance, all found in the idea of entropy the ultimate justification for a new-age politics of grass-roots decentralization and a new-age economics that values the handmade, homegrown, and durable over the store-bought, plastic, and disposable. . . . Rifkin and Henderson can be seen as constituting a contemporary reprise of B[rooks] Adams; all three were led by the organizing power of the idea of entropy to speak of cultural and political energy (and its dissipation in 'entropic' processes) in their efforts to establish a continuity of explanation between culture and its material basis in nature. H[enry] Adams, too, has his contemporary parallel, in the person of Thomas Pynchon—who explicitly modeled a character after [him] in his short story 'Entropy' (1959/1984)."

Zencey hypothesizes that "the idea of entropy serves the same function within the work of some recent and modern thinkers that Newtonian mechanism served in the 18th and 19th centuries," specifically in the writings of the Adams brothers. Zencey finds the metaphor useful in describing humanity's domination of nature since the Industrial Revolution. He wrote: "We once knew nature as chaos, a threatening realm of infinite danger, and we walled our cities against it. Now the roles are reversed: Culture instead threatens the planet, and the wilderness that is left is found in the tiny pockets surrounded by fence and farm." Citing a quote from Henry Adams ("Chaos is the law of nature. Order is the dream of man"), Zencey concluded:

"Entropy as root metaphor recaptures something of the psychic economy of the walled city, for it tells us that the elements of culture are statistically improbable and temporally parochial pockets of order in a world that marches toward maximum chaos."

The dichotomy of "nature" versus "culture" remains one of Zencey's key puzzlements. The essay "In Search of Virgin Forest" in the *North American Review* (September/October 1993) describes the author's attempts to follow Aldo Leopold's recommendation "to read a landscape for its history." Recalling his student days as an "unreconstructed romantic," when he wanted to participate, "pace Muir, in wilderness as the salvation of the world," he half-jokingly asserted that "ecology breeds misanthropy." To Zencey, a virgin forest is "not untrammeled forest" that is "innocent of human passage"; rather, it should be defined as one that has not undergone any "cutting activity." Thus, ironically, remnants of the great North American virgin forest can best be identified by octagonal brass numberplates affixed by forest inventory-takers. Zencey focused his observations on "Lord's Hill" in New Hampshire, designated in 1844 by the Millerite sect as the locus of apocalypse, concluding that "the most certain way to know you are in virgin forest on Lord's Hill is to look for the glint of brass."

Some years earlier, Zencey had decided that he wanted to "write things without footnotes for a while" and turned his attention to the personal and psychological drama that was playing itself out in Paris in the 1890s. This was the genesis of his historical novel, *Panama*. Someone had told Zencey, "'You want historians interested in entropy? Henry Adams would be the man to look at.'" Zencey's inspiration was also a reaction against the publication, in 1986, of one of the Blackford Oakes books by William F. Buckley Jr. Dismissing Buckley's "simple, us-good, them-bad" approach, Zencey thought it important to write "a novel that's a work of political intrigue—this is how you most directly write about politics." The concept of the historical novel had long exerted an appeal on Zencey's thinking. He discussed this in his review of Sarah Smith's *The Knowledge of Water* in the *Washington Post* (September 17, 1996): "One of the more subtle attractions of the historical novel is the reassurance that human nature is constant. Characters from long ago will (if the author has taken due care) dress differently, talk differently, and face different possibilities than we, but their interior lives are likely to be familiar. No matter that we, in the present, enjoy technologies that endanger the very existence of history; the historical novel soothes because it demonstrates history as unbroken continuity, a continuity that resides intimately within our lives. Despite the discomfiting changes that progress brings, it tells us, human nature endures, unchanging."

Panama appeared to much marketing hype in 1995. Zencey's publisher, Farrar, Straus and Giroux, ordered a first printing of 100,000 copies after Caleb Carr's *The Alienist*—like *Panama*, a detective thriller set in Paris of the 1890s—became a "surprise hit," in the words of *New Yorker* critic Stephen Schiff. Schiff added that Farrar, Straus was giving Zencey's book "the sort of big-time push generally reserved for books by departed O.J. jurors: the bidding for paperback rights starts at $300,000." *Panama* was a selection of both the Book-of-the-Month Club and the Quality Paperback Book Club.

Zencey had long been fascinated with Henry Adams's role as one of the keenest American observers of the mass culture that was emerging at the end of the 19th century. His 1991 essay "The Relevant Henry Adams," published in the *North American Review* (October/November 1991), is a reverential paean to the man Zencey called "the great heresiarch, a mocker contradicting the lockstep of progress and the dogma of national power, a modern Luther not so much posting theses as loitering near the doorway, sardonically surveying those who sought communion in the most popular church of the era." Adams has long been admired by one school of American historians for his essay "The Virgin and the Dynamo," which linked the spiritual energies of the 13th century with the optimism of his contemporary mechanical age. Zencey explained his interest in Adams to the *New Yorker* in these words: "I was drawn to the 1890s out of the truth of something that I learned from Geoffrey Barraclough in his *Introduction to Contemporary History*. . . . He says over and over again that if you look for the roots of the modern world, you return to the last decade of the 19th century. The world changed then in ways that made it completely unfamiliar."

Reviewers were nearly unanimous in their praise of *Panama*. Jonathan Yardley wrote in the *Washington Post Book World* (September 17, 1995) that "this novel by a little-known writer is a genuine rarity in contemporary American fiction: a serious entertainment. . . .The suspense he creates is entirely genuine." And John Skow, in *Time* (October 9, 1995), wrote: "The notion of placing such a figure [Henry Adams] at the center of a murder story in the Paris of 1892 must have seemed both absurd and superb when writer Eric Zencey hatched it, and in his novel *Panama*, that's exactly the way it turns out."

In the essays collected in *Virgin Forest: Meditations on History, Ecology, and Culture* (1998), Zencey described a variety of natural settings and their histories in order to make a case for environmentalism.

Summing up his self-definition as a writer, Zencey was quoted by Schiff in the *New Yorker* in these words: "It was a long time before I would let myself claim that title, having hung out in college with people who said they were writers but didn't actually write a whole lot," he explains. "So it

seemed to me that the world said that you're a writer—you don't say that for yourself."
—E. M.

SUGGESTED READING: *Atlantic* p129+ Oct. 1995; *Burlington Free Press* A p7+ Sep. 11, 1995, with photos; *Library Journal* p95 Sep. 15, 1995; *Metaphor and Symbolic Activity* p47+ 1991; *New York Times* C p18 Sep. 14, 1995; *New Yorker* p120+ Aug. 21 & 28, 1995; *North American Review* p58+ June 1989, p44+ June 1990, p58+ Sep. 1991, p50+ Sep. 1993; *Time* p85+ Oct. 9, 1995; *Washington Post* B p2 Sep. 17, 1996; *Washington Post Book World*, p3 Sep. 17, 1995; Slade, J. and J. Y. Lee, eds. *Beyond the Two Cultures: Essays on Science, Literature, and Technology*, 1990

SELECTED BOOKS: Fiction—*Panama*, 1995; Nonfiction—*Virgin Forest: Meditations on History, Ecology, and Culture*, 1998

Acknowledgments

The passage from *Lost in Place*, copyright © 1995 by Mark Salzman, is reprinted here by permission of Random House, Inc.

The poem "Flying Into Rome" by Mark Rudman, lines from which are reprinted here, first appeared in the Spring 1997 issue of the *New England Review*.

A portion of the poem "Ariel Singing" from *Vox Angelica* by Timothy Liu (Alice James Book, 1992) is printed here by permission of the publisher.

The poem "Another Duffer" by Sam Hamill, lines from which are reprinted here, first appeared in the July/August 1994 issue of *American Poetry Review*.

Mark Doty's essay "Horsehair Sofas of the Antarctic: Diane Ackerman's Natural Histories," a portion of which is reprinted here, first appeared in *Parnassus* in 1995.

Portions of the poems "Apostasy" from *Burnt Offerings* (1995) and "Say Goodnight" from *Say Goodnight* (1998), both by Timothy Liu, are printed here by permission of the publisher, Copper Canyon Press, Post Office Box 271, Port Townsend, WA 98368.

The passage from *Hôtel Splendid* by Marie Redonnet, translated by Jordan Stump (The University of Nebraska Press, 1994), is reprinted here by permission of the publisher.

Excerpts from "Epistle," "Water," "The Gift," and "Persimmons" from *Rose*, copyright © 1986 by Li-Young Lee, are reprinted by permission of BOA Editions, Ltd.

Excerpts from "The City in Which I Love You" and "This Hour and What Is Dead" from *The City in Which I Love You*, copyright © 1990 by Li-Young Lee, are reprinted by permission of BOA Editions, Ltd.

Portions of the poems "After Illness" from *The Crack in Everything*, copyright © 1996, and "A Meditation in Seven Days" from *Green Age*, copyright © 1989, both by Alicia Suskin Ostriker, are reprinted here by permission of the University of Pittsburgh Press.

The passage from *Reader's Block* by David Markson (Dalkey Archive Press, 1996) is reprinted here by permission of the publisher.

Lines from "Akhmatova" in *Rough Music* (1995), copyright © by Deborah Digges, are reprinted here by permission of Alfred A. Knopf, a division of Random House, Inc.

The passage from *Heaven's Coast*, copyright © 1996 by Mark Doty, is reprinted here by permission of HarperCollins Publishers.

The passage from *Daisy Bates in the Desert* by Julia Blackburn (Pantheon Books, 1994) is reprinted here by permission of the publisher.

The passage from *Martin Dressler* by Steven Millhauser (Crown Publishers, 1996) is reprinted here by permission of the publisher.

The passage from *The Erotic Spirit* by Sam Hamill, copyright © 1996, is reprinted here by arrangement with Shambhala Publications, Inc., P.O. Box 308, Boston, MA 02117.

The passage from *Divina Trace* by Robert Antoni (The Overlook Press, 1992) is reprinted here by permission of the publisher.